PIERS PLOWMAN

The Malvern Hills and River Teme from Bransford. Photograph by Bill Meadows.

Medieval Institute Publications is a program of
The Medieval Institute, College of Arts and Sciences

 WESTERN MICHIGAN UNIVERSITY

WILLIAM LANGLAND

Piers Plowman

A Parallel-Text Edition
of the A, B, C and Z Versions

VOLUME II:
INTRODUCTION, TEXTUAL NOTES,
COMMENTARY, BIBLIOGRAPHY and INDEXICAL GLOSSARY

By

A. V. C. SCHMIDT

MEDIEVAL INSTITUTE PUBLICATIONS
Western Michigan University
Kalamazoo

ALTERVM·HOC·VOLVMEN·IAM·AD·LVCEM

IN·IMPERFECTIS·VLTIME·PERFECTVM

DECEM·POST·ANNOS·AMICE·PRAETENDO

In memory of Colin Macleod (1943–1981)

Where shal man fynde swich a frend with so fre an herte?

CONTENTS

EDITORIAL PREFACE

The present work completes a two-volume edition of *Piers Plowman* begun some twenty years ago, of which Volume I (the Text) was published by Longman in 1995 and is now out of print. It is the plan of the publisher, Medieval Institute Publications of Western Michigan University at Kalamazoo, first to issue Volume II (the Introduction, etc) in a similar format, and at a later date to reprint it as a set, together with a corrected edition of Volume I, in paper covers at a reasonably affordable price. This was always my hope with the original Longman project, and I am therefore grateful to Medieval Institute Publications and especially to its Director of Publications for exploring the feasibility of the book and saving from interment in permafrost what one reviewer called a 'mammoth' enterprise. It gives me great satisfaction that my edition should appear under its imprint, and I am much obliged to Andrew Galloway for suggesting this to me at a time when commercial pressures had made the work too costly for its original British publisher. Nonetheless, I wish to express my thanks to Andrew MacLennan, Longman's Director of Publishing in 1985, for sharing my sincere (if ingenuous) belief that, with the appropriate single-mindedness and energy on my part, the two volumes might appear together within a decade. In fact they have taken as long to complete as Skeat spent on his EETS and Oxford editions together, and nearly as long as Langland did on writing *Piers Plowman*. As the manuscript was delivered in 2005, I have not been able to take account of scholarship since that date, except for citing a handful of important recent publications, which are recorded in the Bibliography. Langland's poem continues to find enthusiastic students in countries its author had never even heard of; the present edition is intended to help those who have got beyond a first acquaintance to probe more deeply into this endlessly fascinating masterpiece. I hope that the reader will find most of what he needs between these covers and conclude that 'A bouhte such a bargayn he was the bet evere'. For myself, I am content to make the poet's words my own: 'And yf Y be laboure sholde lyven, and lyflode deserven, / That laboure that Y lerned beste, therwith lyven Y sholde'.

AVCS

Oxford
2008

ACKNOWLEDGEMENTS

I am much indebted to Balliol College and Oxford University for four terms of leave from teaching that enabled me to work on this project, and for help with the cost of books, computing equipment and travel to libraries. I am grateful to Patricia Hollahan of Medieval Institute Publications at Kalamazoo for her faith in this project, and to the Institute for undertaking to publish it in the present form.

I wish to thank Helen Barr for her comments on part V of the *Introduction*; she of course bears no responsibility for the opinions expressed or the errors that remain. I am also grateful for help on particular points from John Burrow, Miriam Griffin, Jeremy Griffiths, Stuart Lee, Seamus Perry and Lawrence Warner. The friendly support and interest of Andrew McNeillie, Charlotte Brewer, Chacotta Bunting, Andrew Galloway, Anne Hudson, Tomonori Matsushita, Sarah Ogilvie-Thomson and Tim Wilson has been a heartening experience. I am immensely grateful to Gwen Appleby and Bill Meadows for providing the photograph that forms the frontispiece of this volume. My indebtedness to the previous editors of *Piers Plowman*, especially Walter Skeat, George Kane and E. T. Donaldson is writ large on every page of this edition. Indispensable for preparing the *Commentary* and *Glossary* have been the edition of the C Version by Derek Pearsall, of which a new edition has now been published by Exeter University Press (2008), the Glossaries of John Alford, *The Yearbook of Langland Studies* (*vade-mecum* of every wanderer in the wilderness of books and articles on *Piers Plowman*) and that *merveille* of twentieth-century collaborative learning, the *Middle English Dictionary*. A more general debt I wish to record is to the inspiration and example of two great Langland scholars whom it was my misfortune to know too little and too late, Jack Bennett and Elizabeth Salter: *Of hir wordes thei wissen us for wisest in hir tyme.*

To Judith Schmidt, finally, my obligations in respect of this entire work are beyond reckoning. Her lesser contributions included typing and pasting up the Apparatus of Vol I, producing the Concordance for the *Glossary*, printing the copy of Volume II and reading *forceres* of proofs of the first volume; her greatest has been patient submersion in *Piers Plowman* at sometimes unsociable hours, without (too often) *slomberyng into a slepyng*. Had I lacked the serene certainty of her support, the enterprise would never have been begun, let alone (after some twenty years) completed.

The second volume of this edition is dedicated to the memory of the brilliant scholar and poet, *Animae dimidium meae*, who first proved to me that *Treuthe is tresor trieste on erthe.*

ABBREVIATIONS

AC	*Analecta Cartusiana*
AM	*Annuale Medievale*
Archiv	*Archiv für das Studium der neueren Sprachen und Literaturen*
BJRL	*Bulletin of the John Rylands Library*
CHMEL	*The Cambridge History of Medieval English Literature,* ed. Wallace
CCSL	*Corpus Christianorum, series Latina* (Turnhout, 1954ff)
CCCM	*Corpus Christianorum, Continuatio Medievalis* (Turnhout, 1967ff)
ChR	*Chaucer Review*
EETS	*Early English Text Society*
EHR	*English Historical Review*
ELH	*English Literary History*
E&S	*Essays and Studies*
ELN	*English Language Notes*
e.s	*extra series* (EETS)
ESt.	*English Studies*
HLQ	*Huntington Library Quarterly*
IMEV	*Index of Middle English Verse*
JEGP	*Journal of English and Germanic Philology*
JLH	*Jahrtausend Lateinischer Hymnendichtung,* ed. Dreves-Blume
JWCI	*Journal of the Warburg and Courtauld Institutes*
LSE	*Leeds Studies in English*
MÆ	*Medium Ævum*
MED	*Middle English Dictionary*
MLN	*Modern Language Notes*
MLQ	*Modern Language Quarterly*
MLR	*Modern Language Review*
MP	*Modern Philology*
MS	*Medieval Studies*
NM	*Neuphilologische Mitteilungen*
NML	*New Medieval Literatures*
NQ	*Notes and Queries*
OCL	*Oxford Companion to Law*
OED	*Oxford English Dictionary*
o.s.	*ordinary series* (EETS)
PBA	*Publications of the British Academy*
PBSA	*Papers of the Bibliographical Society of America*
PG	*Patrologia Graeca*
PL	*Patrologia Latina*
PMLA	*Publications of the Modern Language Association of America*
PQ	*Philological Quarterly*
RES	*Review of English Studies*

SAC	*Studies in the Age of Chaucer*
SB	*Studies in Bibliography*
SP	*Studies in Philology*
Spec	*Speculum*
s.s.	*special series* (EETS)
YES	*Yearbook of English Studies*
YLS	*The Yearbook of Langland Studies*
AF	Anglo-French
Alf*C*	Alford, ed. *Companion to PP*
Alf*G*	Alford, *PP: Glossary of Legal Diction*
Alf*Q*	Alford, *PP: A Guide to the Quotations*.
AN	Anglo-Norman
AMA	*Alliterative Morte Arthure*
AP	Alan of Lille, *De Arte Praedicatoria*
AW	*Ancrene Wisse*
B&T-P	Burrow and Turville-Petre
Bn	Bennett, *PP: Pr & Passus I–VII*
CA	Gower's *Confessio Amantis*
CH	Alan of Lille, *Contra Haereticos*
CT	Chaucer's *Canterbury Tales*
DC	*Distichs of Cato*
DPN	Alan of Lille, *De Planctu Naturae*
E	Eastern
FM	*Fasciculus Morum*
GO	*Glossa Ordinaria*
HME	Mossé, *Handbook of Middle English*
IG	Indexical Glossary
IPN	Index of Proper Names
Ka	Kane, *PP:* A *Version*
K–D	Kane & Donaldson, *PP:* B *Version*
K–F	Knott & Fowler, *PP: A-Text*
L	Langland
M	Midland
MES	Mustanoja, *Middle English Syntax*
MS	*Mum and the Sothsegger*
N	Northern
NT	New Testament
OE	Old English
OF	Old French
OT	Old Testament
Pe	Pearsall, *C-text*
PP	*Piers Plowman*
PPCr	*Pierce the Ploughman's Crede*
PTA	*Parlement of the Thre Ages*

R–H	Robertson and Huppé, *PP & Scriptural Tradition*
R–K	Russell & Kane, *PP: C Version*
RRe	*Richard the Redeless*
RR; Rom	*Roman de la Rose*; Chaucerian translation (*Romaunt*)
S	South(ern)
SC	Bernard, *Sermones in Cantica Canticorum*
Sch¹	Schmidt, *B Text, 1st edn*
Sch²	Schmidt, *B Text, 2nd edn*
SEL	*South English Legendary*
SGGK	*Sir Gawain and the Green Knight*
Sk	Skeat
SS	*Summer Sunday*
SW	South-Western
SW	*Sawles Warde*
TC	Chaucer's *Troilus and Criseyde*
TL	Usk's *Testament of Love*
TN	Textual Notes
Vg	Vulgate Bible
VA	*Verbum abbreviatum*
VL	*Vetus Latina*
W	Western
WPal	*William of Palerne*
Wr	*Wright*
WSEW	*Select English Works of Wyclif*
WW	*Wynnere and Wastoure*

FOREWORD

The second volume of this PARALLEL-TEXT edition of *Piers Plowman* is divided into six parts: A, an *Introduction*; B, *Textual Notes*; C, a *Commentary*; D, a *Bibliography*; E, an *Indexical Glossary* to the four versions; and F, Four *Appendices* dealing with the Language and Metre of the poem, the Rubrics, the poet's 'Repertory', and corrections to errors in Volume I. Although a preferred status is not implied for the C-Text, all references in parts B, C and E follow the practice of Skeat's parallel-text edition in referring for convenience to this, the final version of the poem.

The *Introduction* consists of *five* sections: an analytical list of the manuscript sources; a critical survey of the editorial tradition, placing the present work in relation to its predecessors; an examination of the textual evidence for the four versions printed in volume I; an explanation of editorial principles and methods; and a concise account of the poem's authorship, audience and date, the order of the versions and *Piers Plowman*'s reception and influence. The *second* section of the Introduction requires no specialised textual knowledge and may be consulted in conjunction with the *fifth* by readers wanting a general perspective on the texts in volume I but not a detailed study of the manuscript sources and the problems of transmission. Familiarity with the first two sections is, however, presupposed by the more technical account in the *third* and *fourth*. The Notes to the *Introduction* will be found separately at the end of each of its five sections.

The *Textual Notes* contain a detailed sequential account of all major problems, justifying the readings adopted and, where space allows, discussing rejected emendations of other editors. The *Commentary* aims principally to elucidate the verbal and historical meaning of the text; but while it includes some critical discussion, there is no attempt to offer a conspectus of past or current debate on the wider interpretative issues touched on in parts of section V of the *Introduction*. The *Bibliography* lists the works cited and a selection of those consulted but not specifically mentioned. The *Glossary* offers a comprehensive and indexed explanation of all words appearing in the edited texts of the four versions. Finally, the *Appendices* cover in detail particular topics referred to only briefly in the *Introduction*, *Notes* and *Commentary*. Together, these six sections aim to provide the necessary material for advanced study of the poem's text and context.

A. INTRODUCTION

I. THE MANUSCRIPTS OF *PIERS PLOWMAN*

§§ 1–3 The Manuscripts. § 4 Single-Version
Manuscripts (nos. 1–41). § 5 Conjoint Manuscripts
(nos. 42–52). § 6 Conflated **ABC** Text (no. 53).
§ 7 Fragments (nos. i–iv).

§ 1. In his edition of *Piers Plowman* for the Early English Text Society (1867–88), W. W. Skeat (*Sk* hereafter) recognised five 'shapes' of the text. Three of these are authorial, the 'single' versions **A**, **B** and **C** (manuscripts nos. 1–41 listed below). The present edition also accepts as authentic a fourth version known as **Z**, a text of Prologue–VIII 92 surviving only in a 'conjoint' form with a text of **C** added later (no. 52 in the list below). Skeat also recognised two scribally-produced 'conjoint' forms combining portions of **A** and **C**, or of **B** and **C** (*Sk* II i, III ix, IV 832).[1] Of the conjoint texts (nos. 42–52) six are of **A** and **C** (46–51), of which one (no. 49) conflates parts of its **A** portion from **C**, and three are of **B** and **C** linked by a passage of **A** (nos. 43–5). Additionally there is one of **B** and **A** (no. 42) and one (no. 53) that conflates its text of **B** throughout with material from **A** and **C**. The fact that of the fifty-three manuscripts eleven (including the early copies nos. 43–5 and 52) are of the conjoint type suggests that non-authentic shapes of the poem were known, perhaps widely, in the generation after Langland's death. The following list acknowledges as much in the way it divides the witnesses (into 'single-version' and 'conjoint'). The manuscripts are through-numbered from 1–53; but for convenience in relating this section to the Textual Apparatus, the order *within* each division is that of the sigils after classification of the manuscripts, as printed in Vol. I, x–xii. Crowley's *editio princeps* of the poem (no. 13) has been accorded manuscript status, since it apparently derives from a source that is not among the manuscripts now extant (*Sk* II xxxvi–vii; see III, *B Version*, §§ 13–16).

§ 2. Detailed accounts of the *Piers Plowman* codices have appeared in Skeat's EETS editions, in the three volumes of the Athlone edition (1960–97) edited by Kane (*Ka*), Kane and Donaldson (*K–D*) and Russell and Kane (*R–K*), in that of the Z-Text (1983) by Rigg and Brewer (*R–B*), and in a number of special studies. The early manuscript copies in which the texts are preserved continue to attract much scholarly interest for the light they throw on the work's 'reception' and cultural context and hence potentially on its contemporary meaning. The manuscripts of **A** are described in *Sk* I, xii–xxvii and *Ka* 1–18; those of **B** in *Sk* II, vi–xxxix and *K–D* 1–15, adding no. 14 (unknown to Skeat), but most fully now in Benson and Blanchfield (*B–B* hereafter), who also reproduce marginal and other scribal additions; those of **C** in *Sk* III, xix–l and *R–K* 1–18, adding seven important copies not in *Sk*; that of **Z** in *R–B* and also in Brewer and Rigg's facsimile of Bodley 851 (1994). There are lists of the manuscripts of all versions in Brewer, *Editing 'PP'* (1996) 448–51 and (with notes) in Hanna, *Langland* (1993) 37–42, and valuable discussion by Doyle of many individual copies in Kratzmann & Simpson (1986) 33–48. Published facsimiles include a plain reproduction of Crowley's print (**B**) and full facsimile editions with detailed introductions of Bodley 851 (**Z**), of the Vernon ms (**A**), and of Hm 143 and the illustrated Douce 104 (both **C**), while full-page half-tone plates illustrating all the **B** copies appear in *B–B*. Full-colour facsimiles of the highest quality are becoming available through the *Piers Plowman Electronic Archive* (ed. Duggan *et al.*), in which hypertext editions of nos. 11, 17, 20, 21 and 23 of the B-Text have already appeared on CD-Rom.

§ 3. The following account, which is much indebted to the works mentioned above, provides for the *Piers Plowman* content of each copy concise information on the material, script, date, language, number of lines per page, and corrections; it also notes points relating to ownership and companion texts (if any). Since textually important material on the rubrics appears in the critical apparatus to the text in Vol. I, deviant varieties of the presumed sub-archetypal forms are noticed here only in cases of exceptional interest (for further details and discussion see Appendix Two). Occasional comments are included on the textual value of the copy, an asterisk before a sigil signifying that the manuscript has proved indispensable for establishing the text of the version in question. The list is complete except for the sixteenth- and seventeenth-century transcriptions and excerpts in Bodleian mss James 2, Wood donat. 7, the BL ms Sloane 2578 and the Caius College Cambridge ms 201 (a transcript of Owen Rogers' 1561 print), which have no textual value.

§ 4. Single-Version Manuscripts

A-TEXT

1 **D** *Oxford, Bodleian Library ms Douce 323*
Paper; a semi-cursive hand of late C15. 28–34 ll. per p. Mixed EW dialect. Contains Pr–XI. A member of group d of the sub-family r^1.

2 ****R** *Oxford, Bodleian Library ms Rawlinson Poetry 137*
Vellum; bastard anglicana of mid-C15; scribe signs *Tilot* at end. 30–4 ll. per p. SW Sussex dialect. The sole copy to have *prologus* as first heading. Contains entire text, the only one with Passus XII complete; VII 70–213a misplaced after I 179. A member of the sub-family r^1; substantively the most important **A** ms, but less suitable than T as copy-text (cf. L of **B**, no. 20 below). See further S. Horobin, 'The Scribe of Rawlinson Poetry 137 and the Copying and Circulation of *Piers Plowman'* in *YLS* 19 (2005) 3–26.

3 **U** *Oxford, University College ms 45*
Vellum, anglicana formata of $C15^1$; paper, bastard anglicana of $C15^2$. 30–8 ll. per p. (vellum); about 28 (paper). S. Cambs. dialect. Lacks I 33–99, X 211–XI 47, XII 20–117 through loss of leaves and (like R) misplaces VII 70–213a after II 23.

4 **V** *Oxford, Bodleian Library ms English Poetry a.1 (the Vernon ms)*
Vellum; anglicana of *c.*1400. 160 ll. per p. in two cols. N.Worcs. dialect. Lacks XI 184–313 and perhaps an original XII through loss of final leaf. No title or rubrics except at IX. *PP* followed by *Joseph of Arimathea*. Used by *Sk* as base-text but (though early) only moderately good member of sub-family r^2. Facsimile ed. Doyle 1987.

5 **H** *London, British Library ms Harley 875*
Vellum; two anglicana hands of $C15^{2-3}$. 36–41 ll. per p. N-W. Warws. dialect. Lacks VI 48–VII 2 through loss of leaf. Rubrics for only II–VI, VIII. The genetic twin of V.

6 *J *New York, Pierpont Morgan Library ms 18* (*the Ingilby ms*)
Paper; anglicana hand of *c.* 1450. 29–38 ll. per p. Lincs. dialect. *PP* text preceded by *Pistill of Susan* and Rolle's *Form of Perfect Living*. The major representative of the *r²* sub-family (see III, *A Version,* § 19) and the only one with any of XII (this last printed entire *Sk* IV ii 857–59).

7 L *London, Lincoln's Inn Library ms 150*
Vellum; anglicana hand of C15¹. Tall narrow 'holster' book; 50–55 ll. per p. Two leaves probably lost which could have contained VIII 157–end. *PP* preceded by two metrical romances and *Seege of Troye.*

8 E *Dublin, Trinity College ms 213* (*D.4.12*)
Paper; scrivener's hand; from watermarks C15³⁻⁴. 27–34 ll. per p. Durham or Northumberland with a more southerly element. Contains Pr–VII 44, with VII 70–213a misplaced after I 182 (cf. R and U). *PP* text followed by alliterative *Wars of Alexander.*

9 A *Oxford, Bodleian Library ms Ashmole 1468*
Paper; bastard anglicana hand of C15³⁻⁴. 22–30 ll. per p. W Norfolk dialect. Pr–I 141 lacking through loss of leaves.

10 *M *London, Library of the Society of Antiquaries no. 687*
Paper; free hand tending to cursive, of *c.* 1425. 28–35 ll. per p. NW Suffolk dialect. Unusual division at IX treating it as *prologus* to Dowel etc. Important as the only complete representative of the **m** family (see III, *A Version,* §§ 24–47 below). Facsimile by Matsushita (2007).

B-TEXT

11 *W *Cambridge, Trinity College ms B. 15. 17*
Vellum, 147 leaves (*PP* on ff.1r–130v); anglicana formata hand of *c.* 1400 resembling that of the scribe of Ellesmere ms of *Canterbury Tales* and a Staffordshire scribe of the same period [Doyle 1986:39]; display script bastard anglicana with Latin boxed in red. Carefully paragraphed with blue and red parasigns and blank line between paragraphs (cf. L, M, Y and R below). 33–5 ll. per p. Punctuated with raised points at caesuras and raised hooks or points at many line-ends. Possibly the product of a London or Westminster workshop. Dialect of Middlesex or London type. See further *Sk* II xiii–xiv; *K–D* 13–14; *B–B* 56–9, with facsimile pl. of f. 19v. *PP* text followed by Rolle's *Form of Living* and a devotional lyric *Crist made to man a fair present* (see *IMEV* 611). Substantively less good than **L** but has unusually consistent spelling and systematic grammar, close to that of the Hengwrt and Ellesmere mss of *The Canterbury Tales* (see Horobin and Mooney 2004). Printed by Wright (1842) and used as copy-text by Kane-Donaldson (1975), Schmidt (1978) and in the present edition. Now Vol 2 in the *PP Electronic Archive*, ed. Turville-Petre & Duggan (2000), reviewed by J. Sebastian in *YLS* 15 (2001).

12 Hm; Hm² *San Marino, Huntington Library ms 128*
Vellum; six anglicana hands with occasional secretary features, those of the *PP* texts anglicana formata of early C15. About 40 ll. per p. The product more probably of a clerical group than of a commercial workshop. S. Warws. dialect. Hm² preceded by *The Prick of Conscience,* Hm by *Siege of Jerusalem* and *How the Good Wife Taught her Daughter.* Pastedown has inscription 'Robert or William Langland made pers plow[man]', possibly by William Sparke, and John Bale's inscription 'Robertus langlande natus in comitatu salopie in villa Mortymers Clybery in the claylande, within viij myles of Malborne hylles, scripsit peers ploughman, li 1', followed by first line of *PP*. See Turville-Petre 2002:43–51.

13 Cr *Robert Crowley's* Three Printed Texts *of 1550*

   a Cr¹ *British Library C. 71. c. 29*
   Title *The Vision of Pierce Plowman, now fyrste imprynted by Roberte Crowley, dwellyng in Ely rentes in Holburne. Anno Domini, 1505* [error for 1550; Colophon has *M.D.L*].
The *editio princeps*, based on a lost ms of β type. Facsimile ed. by Bennett 1976.

b Cr^2 *British Library C. 71. c. 28*

Title-page *The vision...nowe the seconde time imprinted...Whereunto are added certayne notes and cotations in the mergyne, geuynge light to the Reader. And in the begynning is set a briefe summe of all the principall maters spoken of in the boke.* A reset reprint of *a* based on another lost ms compared throughout with it.

c Cr^3 *British Library C. 122. d. 9*

A reprint of Cr^2 with readings from yet another one or more mss. Cr is not included in *B–B* but Crowley's address to the reader is given in full in *Sk* II xxxii–iv. On *Cr* see Crawford 1957, King 1973, Thorne and Uhart 1986, Brewer 1996:7–19, Hailey 2007.

14 S *Tokyo, collection of Toshiyuki Takamiya ms 23* (formerly *London, Sion College Ms Arc. L. 40 2/E. 76*)^2

Paper; secretary hand of mid-16C (?George Hewlet). About 42 ll. per p. The ms was discovered in 1966; described in *K–D* and fully in *B–B* 112–15, with pl. A β-family text of w-type, very inaccurate and heavily modernised. Rejected for editing by K–D and likewise here.

15 G *Cambridge, University Library ms Gg. 4. 31*

Paper; secretary hand of C16^1. 33–45 ll. per p. Spelling somewhat modernised; passus-headings only as explicits, one out throughout, with Pr treated as Passus I. Table of contents by original scribe (*B–B* 133–36).

16 Y *Cambridge, Newnham College ms 4* (*Yates-Thompson ms*)

Vellum; anglicana formata of *c.*1430. About 40 ll. per p. Paragraphs separated by blank line; caesurae marked with various pointings. Dialect London with diluted W forms (possibly N Oxon). *PP* text followed by *Lay Folk's Mass Book,* in another hand.

17 O *Oxford, Oriel College ms 79, pt. 1*

Vellum; anglicana formata, of C15^1. About 39 ll. per p. Dialect N. Herts. Lacks XVII 97–342, XIX 283–362 through loss of leaves. Title *Pers plowman*. Marginal glosses and corrections by main scribe; further corrections by another C15 hand. Electronic edition ed. Heinrichs (2005).

18 C^2 *Cambridge, University Library ms Ll. 4. 14*

Paper; small anglicana, of C15^2. About 35 ll. per p. Dialect Cambs. (?Ely). *PP* followed by *Richard the Redeless,* English educational texts and a glossary of *PP* in secretary hand of mid-C16, possibly Robert Crowley (printed *Sk* II 421–6, with comments; *B–B* 148–9). Interlinear and marginal corrections by both scribe and glossator.

19 C *Cambridge, University Library ms Dd. 1. 17*

Vellum; anglicana formata, with headings and quotations in bastard anglicana, of *c.*1400. 61 ll. per p. (two cols.). Dialect mixed with N and SWM forms. A large folio of historical and religious works with *PP* in pt. 3 followed by English texts *On Visiting the Sick,* Mandeville's *Travels, Seven Sages of Rome,* and a Latin Gospel Concordance.

20 *L *Oxford, Bodleian Library ms Laud Misc. 581*

Vellum; anglicana formata, of *c.* 1400. Paragraphed and punctuated with mid-point caesurae. Possibly the product of a commercial London workshop (cf. Y, M, R). Dialect S Worcs. overlaid with some N and E forms from intermediate London copying. Corrections and notes by main scribe, including some interlinear glosses; many cross-shaped marginal marks, apparently for intended corrections, some actually made. Annotations in later hands, one of mid-C16 on f.1: 'Robart Langelande borne by malborne hilles.' Printed by Sk and Bn; substantively the best member of the β family, but less suitable as copy-text than W (no. 11 above). Electronic edition ed. Duggan and Hanna (2005).

21 M *London, British Library ms Additional 35287*

Vellum; varying anglicana, of early C15^1, resembling hand of Hengwrt-Ellesmere scribe (cf. 11). Paragraphed with blank lines but no parasigns. Heavily altered through erasure and overwriting by at least two correctors. About 40–1 ll. per p. Dialect mixed with relict Herefordshire forms. See Turville-Petre 2002:51–64. Electronic edition ed. Eliason, Turville-Petre and Duggan (2005).

22 *R *London, British Library ms Lansdowne 398*
Oxford, Bodleian Library ms Rawlinson Poetry 38

Vellum, the Lansdowne portion (ff. 77–80) being leaves 3–6 of the first quire, with 1–2, 7–8 lost, as also are leaves between ff. 95–6 of Rawl. (orig. quire 14); anglicana formata, with incipits and Latin in bastard anglicana, of *c.* 1400. Paragraphs separated with blank lines; frequent parasigns (cf. L, M, Y). 36–8 ll. per p. No title, and in place of final explicit *Passus ii^{us} de dobest*; passus-numbering one out from XI to XVIII (= X–XVII). Dialect basically S Worcs. with overlay of N and Suffolk from London copying. Ownership names include 'William Butte(s)' of early C16 (f. 101r). Imperfect representative of the α family, but the only sound one; unique portions first printed by Sk, subsequently by K–D, Sch; regarded as preserving a later recension of B-Text by Hanna (1996:215–29) and Taylor (1997), and see also Taylor, Dissertation 1995; but cf. III, *B Version*, §§ 52–5 below.

23 *F *Oxford, Corpus Christi College ms 201*

Vellum; current anglicana with Latin in 'fere-textura' (Doyle 1986:40), of *c.* 1400. Historiated opening initial of dreamer [Schmidt 1991, cover]. About 42 ll. per p. Dialect Essex. Title *Incipit pers þe plowman*; idiosyncratic passus-divisions (counting Pr as I and XX as XVI); see Adams 1985:228–9, Weldon 1993, *B–B* 207, and *Sk* II xxvii–xxx (entire). Corrupt and sophisticated but still important as the only α witness for the portions missing from R (Taylor 1996:530–48 maintains dependence of F on R). A facsimile hypertext edition is Vol. I of the *Piers Plowman Electronic Archive*, ed. R. Adams *et al.* (1999); reviewed by S. Shepherd in *YLS* 14 (2000).

C-TEXT

24 *X *San Marino, Huntington Library ms 143*

Vellum, occupying the whole (ff. 1–106v), preceded by three leaves of Chaucer's *Troilus*. Current anglicana formata, of *c.* 1400. Corrected a.h., the name 'Piers (Plouhman)' almost everywhere erased. Paragraphed with red and blue parasigns; foreign words and some keywords underlined, mostly in red. 36 ll. per p. Dialect SW Worcs. with signs of London copying. No incipit or final explicit; standard **x**-family passus divisions and '.W.' after 'Willielmi' in explicit to IX. Photostatic facsimile by Chambers *et al.* (1936); opening as frontispiece in Alford 1988; discussion in Chambers 1935:1–27, Russell 1984:275–300, Bowers 1992:24–6, 2005:137–68, Calabrese 2005:169–99, Horobin 2005:248–69. Unknown to Sk but selected by Chambers as base for **C** on grounds of completeness, language and early date; printed first by Pe, then used as copy-text by Sch and R–K.

25 *Y *Oxford, Bodleian Library ms Digby 102*

Vellum; two or three anglicana hands, of C15^{1}; on ff. 97v, 139v a *Dispute between the Body and the Soul*. Belonged to Kenelm Digby in C17 (cf. nos. 40, 49). But for want of Pr–II 156 (probably through loss of leaves) would be the best substantive witness of this version. See Schaap 2001 on marginalia.

26 I (J) *London, University of London Library ms S.L.V. 88 (the Ilchester ms)*

Vellum; anglicana formata with secretary features, of *c.* 1400–10, ascribed to London 'Scribe D' [Doyle & Parkes 1973]. About 31 ll. per p. Severely damaged with text missing through loss of leaves at XI 276–XII 19, XV 296–XVII 59*a*, XVIII 102–161, XXI 79–XXII 81; XXII 82–end only partly legible. Dialect S Worcs. (See Horobin & Mosser 2006). Not a conjoint text but Prologue the product of a compiler, setting passages from C IX in a frame-text of A Pr with C Pr 91–157 inset in second of three A-Text passages (printed entire R–K 186–94; 105–24 in Vol. I, App.; see Pearsall 1981). Highly valued as a **C** witness by earlier editors but of limited textual worth.

27 P^{2} *London, British Library ms Additional 34779*

Vellum; anglicana formata of *c.* 1400–10 (that of scribe of Rylands ms Eng. 90). Corrections by several later hands. About 39 ll. per p. Much damaged, esp. ff. 1, 5, 92. Dialect SE Shropshire.

28 U *London, British Library MS Additional 35157*

Vellum; anglicana formata, of *c.* 1400. About 32 ll. per p. Mostly unparagraphed with red underlining of foreign and some keywords. Corrections by main scribe (signed 'Preston' f. 124v). Dialect NW Worcs. from a SW Worcs. exemplar. Important as **x** witness where Y is defective. See Grindley 1996.

29 D *Oxford, Bodleian Library ms Douce 104*

Vellum; anglicana formata of $C15^1$; much erased and altered, partly by another anglicana hand. About 34–5 ll. per p. Stained with loss of text at ff. 49v, 50v and esp. 1r, 60v, 61r–3. After final *Explicit liber de Petro ploughman* the date of completion in m. h. [1427]. Dialect Hiberno-English. The only copy with illustrations; facsimile with colour pls. of these by Pearsall & Scott 1992, and study by Kerby-Fulton & Depres 1999.

30 *P *San Marino, Huntington Library ms 137*

Vellum; anglicana formata, of *c.* 1400; scribe signed Thomas Lancastre (or Dancastre) at end. Rubrics, foreign words, names and some keywords in red textura. 43 ll. per p. Dialect of Gloucester-Monmouthshire border. Important as complete early representative of p^1 branch of **p** family. The former Phillipps 8231, and the first **C** copy to be printed, by Whitaker 1813 (on which see *Sk* III li–lxvi, Brewer 1996:37–45) and then by Sk; see *Intro.* II, § 30.

31 E *Oxford, Bodleian Library ms Laud Misc. 656*

Vellum; anglicana, of *c.* 1400 (frontispiece to *Sk* III). About 40 ll. per p. *PP* text preceded by *Siege of Jerusalem* and followed by three religious works. Dialect N Oxon. Final *Explicit passus secundus de dobest. incipit passus tercius.*

32 A *London, University of London Library ms S.L.V. 17*

Vellum; anglicana formata, of *c.* 1400–10. About 37 ll. per p. Dialect W Worcs. *PP* lacks VII 236–83, XXII 88–end (cf. next). Originally the last portion of larger volume containing *Handlyng Synne* and Mandeville's *Travels* Text D.

33 V *Dublin, Trinity College ms 212 (D.4.1)*

Vellum; anglicana formata, of *c.* 1390–1400 (ff. 88v, 89r as pl. II in Kane 1965). Some corrections m.h. and l.h. About 41 ll. per p. Lacks VII 236–83, XXII 88–end (cf. *A.*). Dialect NW Gloucs. On f. 90v the important memorandum about Langland's paternity (pl. I in Kane 1965; *Intro.* V, § 4). See further Brooks 1951:141–53; Kane 1965^1:26–33.

34 R *London, British Library ms Royal 18 B xviii*

Vellum; bastard secretary hand, of $C16^1$; corrections and alterations on early ff. in three hands. 31–45 ll. per p. *PP* text preceded by *Piers the Plowman's Creed.* Sole witness to the p^1 sub-group <RM> where M is defective (see next).

35 M *London, British Library MS Cotton Vespasian B xvi*

Vellum; bastard anglicana, of *c.* 1400; some correction by erasure. About 41 ll. per p. Dialect W Warws. *PP* text preceded by four short pieces, including on ff. 2v–3v a poem against the Lollards [Robbins 1959:187], and followed by a Latin account of the Holy Blood of Hailes.

36 Q *Cambridge, University Library ms Additional 4325*

Vellum; anglicana formata, *c.* 1410; alterations m. h. and some corrections in another early hand. About 47 ll. per p. Dialect NW Gloucs. Damaged with some loss of text between V 131 and VII 96.

37 F *Cambridge, University Library ms Ff. 5. 35*

Vellum; textura quadrata of $C15^{1-2}$. 37 ll. per p. Dialect mid-Oxon. Imperfect through loss of leaves at VII 264–IX 181, XIII 93–XV 179. *PP* preceded by Mandeville's *Travels,* A-Text.

38 S *Cambridge, Corpus Christi College ms 293*

Vellum; anglicana formata with some secretary features, of $C15^{2-3}$. To p. 78. about 35 ll. per p., thereafter about 42. Dialect S Herefs. Imperfect (probably from defective exemplar) at VIII 267–X 95, XV 82–157, XXI 8–323.

39 G *Cambridge, University Library ms Dd. 3. 13*
Vellum; anglicana, of *c*. 1390–1400; heavily corrected m. h. 30–40 ll. per p. Dialect SE Herefs. and NW Gloucs. borders. Imperfect through loss of leaves at Pr 1–153, XIII 225*a*–XIV 40, XV 288–XVI 40, XXII 40–end; also lacks numerous other lines singly or in groups.

40 K *Oxford, Bodleian Library ms Digby 171*
Vellum; anglicana formata of *c*. 1400. About 33 ll. per p. Dialect SE Herefs. Imperfect from loss of leaves at beginnning and through defective exemplar at end, lacking Pr–II 216, XV 66–end. Belonged to Kenelm Digby in C17 (cf. nos. 25, 49).

41 *N *London, British Library ms Harley 2376*
Vellum; anglicana formata, of C15[1]. Dialect SE Herefs. The only complete representative of the group *p*[2] (III, *C Version*, §§ 54–6). For a study see Black in *MAE* 67: 257–90.

§ 5. Conjoint Manuscripts

B *and* **A**

42 H[3] *of* A-Text; ***H** *of* B-Text *London, British Library ms Harley 3954.*
Vellum, anglicana formata, of 1425–50, written by Heron (cf. no. 25). About 40 ll. per p. Dialect S Norfolk. Title *Perys Plowman*; final *Explicit tractatus de perys plowman*. Rubrics from I to VII and at end of X. Contains B Pr–V 125 foll. by A V 105–XI. H is much contaminated but important as perhaps representing an independent line of descent within the β tradition of the B-Text.

C, A *and* **B**

43–5 B *of* B-Text; **b** *of* C-Text

43 Bm *of* B-Text; **L** *of* C-Text *London, British Library ms Additional 10574*
Vellum; anglicana formata, of *c*. 1400–10. Missing XX 356–87 added by C19 owner Dr Adam Clarke.

44 Bo *of* B-Text; **B** *of* C-Text *Oxford, Bodleian Library ms Bodley 814*
Vellum; anglicana formata, two alternating hands, both of *c*. 1400–10.

45 Cot *of* B-Text; **O** *of* C-Text *London, British Library ms Cotton Caligula A xi*
Vellum; anglicana with secretary features, of C15[1]. Corrections m. h. and others.

All three members contain C Pr–II 128, then an expanded version of A II 86–198 followed by B II–XX, the transitions being carefully patched; have about 40 ll. per p.; and are in a dialect with N Gloucs forms residual from the common exemplar. (On the relations of the three mss see *Sk* II xxv–xxvii, 391–2; *K–D* 40–2; Davis 1997)

A *and* **C**

46–8 t *of* A-Text *and* C-Text

46 *T *Cambridge, Trinity College ms R. 3. 14*
Vellum; anglicana formata of *c*. 1400. 74 leaves; illustration on f. iii verso, with arms of Thomas Nevile, Master of Trinity 1593–1614 (frontispiece to Vol. I). 41–46 ll. per p. Dialect mixed, mainly EM with some relict W forms. Idiosyncratic

passus-divisions: continuous from I throughout **A** and **C** portions. At end of XI *Passus tercius de dowel. Breuis oracio penetrat celum*, then C XI 301ff; [XII] *Passus secundus de dobet;* [XVI] *P. sextus de dowel*; [XVII] *P. septimus de dowel & explicit*; [XVIII, XIX, XX] *P. pr., sec., ter. de dobet*; [XXI] *Expl. de dobet Et inc. de dobest*; [XXII] *secundus passus de dobest.* Final Explicit. The A-Text has no major omissions, lacking only 13 ll. of its *r¹* ancestor. Collated *Sk* I and adopted for its completeness and good spelling as copy-text in *K–F, Ka* and the present edition.

47 **H²** *London, British Library ms Harley 6041*
Paper; anglicana formata, of *c.* 1425. 31 ll. per p. One leaf missing and five as fragments. The **A** portion lacks some 200 whole and 70 part ll; **C** portion some 350 ll.[3]

48 **Ch** *Liverpool, University Library ms F. 4. 8 (Chaderton ms)*
Vellum; anglicana formata, of *c.* 1420. 30–6 ll. per p.

All three members of **t** contain A Pr–XI completed by C XI 301–end, with C XI 300*a* forming the conjuncture, and are in EM dialect with some W relict forms, esp. *heo, hy* in T.

49 **K** *of* A-Text; **D²** *of* C-Text *Oxford, Bodleian Library ms Digby 145*
Paper; free cursive hand, written 1531 by Sir Adrian Fortescue (see Turville-Petre 2000). 24–8 ll. per p. Contains A Pr–XI 313 [K], with rubric *Finis de dowell*, followed by C XI 301–end [D²], but omitting 300*a* (cf. **t** above). Standard **A** rubrics as in **t**; for **C**, standard **x**-type rubrics except that XII–XVII are *quartus-nonus de dowell*.

50 **W** *of* A-Text and C-Text *formerly Duke of Westminster's ms, Eaton Hall; now York, University Library, Borthwick Add. ms 196*[4]
Vellum; court hand of C15³. Contains A Pr–XI followed by C XII–end. Rubrics [I–VIII] *Passus primus-octauus de visione*; [IX] *prologus de dowel dobett & dobest*, [X, XI]; *primus, secundus de dowel*, [after XI 166] *Tercius passus de dowel*, [after XI 313] rubricator's guide *passus iiij de dowel*; [XIII–XVI] are *vᵘˢ~viiijᵘˢ de dowel*, [XVII–XXII] as in standard **p**-type rubrics.

51 **N** *of* A-Text; **N²** *of* C-Text *Aberystwyth, National Library of Wales ms 733B*
Vellum; anglicana hand of C15¹. 29–35 ll. per p. Contains A I 76 (legible only from 104)–VIII 185 [N], followed by C X–XXI 428 [N²]. **A** portion strongly contaminated from **C** in Pr, VI; **C** portion of mixed **x** and **p** character with sporadic contamination from a **B** source of β-type.

Z *and* C

52 *Z (the **Z** Version); **Z** of* A- *and* C-Texts *Oxford, Bodleian Library ms Bodley 851*
Vellum; 209 leaves, bound and foliated after 1439. Contains (ff. 124r–39v) *1:* the **Z** Version of *PP* [= ms Z of **A** for *Sk, Ka*]; small anglicana formata hand of late C14 ('Hand X' [Rigg-Brewer]), perhaps that of John Wells, monk of Ramsey, owner of the book. 50 ll. per p. *2:* A VIII 89–185, followed by a rhyming conclusion and *Explicit Vita et Visio Petri Plowman* (here treated as sigil Z of **A** Version), in anglicana hand with secretary features of C15¹⁻² ('Hand Q' [Rigg-Brewer]). *3:* C X–XXII in same hand (sigil Z of **C**). Dialect of SW Worcs. The *PP* text preceded by well-known Latin pieces incl. Map, *De nugis curialium*, Bridlington's *Prophecies* and *Apocalypsis Goliae*. See the edition by Rigg-Brewer 1983 and their *Facsimile* of the Z-Text 1994, also Matsushita, *Facsimile* (with diplomatic transcript) 2008; Schmidt 1984; Kane 1985; Duggan 1987¹; Green 1987; Hanna 1993. The sole representative of what is here taken as the '**Z**' Version of *Piers Plowman.*

§ 6. Conflated **ABC** Text

53 **Ht** *San Marino, Huntington Library ms 114*
Paper; anglicana formata, of C15². 26–36 ll. per p. Dialect SE Essex. A-Text of **B** type heavily conflated from **C** and to a less extent from **A**, with re-arrangements, substitutions and introduction of spurious matter. Title *Piers plogman* before Prologue, final *Explicit pers ploughman.* See *Sk* III xix–xx; Russell & Nathan 1963; *K–D* 114–15; Scase 1987; Hanna 1989.

§ 7. Fragments

i **P** *Cambridge, Pembroke College ms 312 C/6*
Vellum bifolium, C15. Dialect E Anglian. Contains most of A IV 106–V 29, VII 84–93, 212*a*–41, 242–82. See *Ka* 13.

ii **Hm²**
See no. 12 above.

iii **H** *Oslo, Shøyen Collection ms 1953 (formerly the 'Holloway' fragment)*
Vellum bifolium; anglicana formata, of *c.* 1400. Dialect SW Worcs. Contains C I 199–II 44, III 123–174, with 149–58 mostly lost through damage. Substantively and linguistically identical with **X** (no. 24 above); its readings added in Corrections to Apparatus.⁵ Described in Hanna 1993²:1–14.

iv **Ca** *Cambridge, Gonville and Caius College ms 669* / 646*
Vellum; bastard anglicana (scribe John Cok) of C15¹; p. 210 in a ms of religious works by Rolle and others. Contains C XVI 180–199*a*.

THE MANUSCRIPTS: NOTES

1 Skeat further specifies in IV xvii–xviii an early **A** form ending at Passus VIII (as in Harley 875), an **A** form without XII (Douce 323), an uncompleted revision to **B** (ms Harley 3954), a version intermediate between **B** and **C** (Rawlinson Poetry 38), and an early version of **C** (Ilchester). But none of these 'shapes' identified as authorial affected his treatment of the three edited versions, which represent the complete non-conjoint forms of the poem now known as **A**, **B** and **C**.

2 Discovered 1966.

3 In Vol. I, p. xi delete erroneous 'XXII 287–end defective'.

4 Sold to an anonymous purchaser at Sotheby's, July 1966; now on loan to University Library, York. A microfilm of the ms kindly provided by the Liverpool University Library was used for this edition.

5 After collation of a photocopy of H in the Cambridge University Library, the original was made available for examination through the kindness of the late Jeremy Griffiths, who was holding it for purchase by the Shøyen Collection.

II. THE EDITORIAL TRADITION OF *PIERS PLOWMAN*

The Present Edition and Previous Editions

i. *Towards a Parallel-Text Edition of* Piers Plowman

§ 1. *Piers Plowman* has received a great deal of attention from interpretative critics in the second half of the last century. The time now seems to be ripe for a fully-annotated and glossed critical edition of the poem in all its versions, to provide for our age what the Oxford Edition of W. W. Skeat did so well for his.[1] A partial example of a major single-version commentary is the excellent Clarendon Press edition by J. A. W. Bennett of the B-Text *Visio*.[2] But despite a five-page table of variants including some select readings from the **A** and **C** versions, the edited text of **B** to which Bennett's notes are geared, based on Bodleian Library manuscript Laud Misc. 581, differs little from that of Skeat's 1869 Student Edition of B Prologue–Passus VII. Bennett's work appeared only three years before the pioneering Athlone Press Edition of **B** by George Kane and E. Talbot Donaldson.[3] But any modern *Commentary* answering to Skeat's in fullness will have to take proper account of the important twentieth-century developments in our understanding of the poem's textual history most challengingly represented in the successive Athlone editions of **A**, **B** and **C**.[4] And these developments have such far-reaching implications for understanding of the poem as to require that a new interpretative Commentary should also be based on a freshly-edited text of *Piers Plowman* in all its versions. The multi-volume Athlone enterprise by many hands[5] will correspond when finished to the five-volume Early English Text Society edition produced single-handedly by Skeat between 1867 and 1885.[6] What it will not provide is an equivalent to his two-volume Oxford Parallel-Text of 1886. This provided the basis of most critical studies until the last quarter of the twentieth century. The edition now completed by this second volume is intended in part as a modern successor to it.

§ 2. The present edition, however, differs from Skeat's in five main features. The first is its inclusion, as a *fourth version*, of the unique **Z-Text** in manuscript Bodley 851. The second is its provision in Vol. I of a substantial *Critical Apparatus* to all the texts printed (Skeat's Oxford edition cited only a few of the variants given in his EETS volumes). In Vol. II a third feature is the long *Introduction*, including an extended account of the editorial issues, followed by a briefer treatment of non-textual matters such as authorship and background. The fourth is the body of *Textual Notes*, which are of the kind provided briefly in the EETS edition but in technical detail corresponding to parts of the Athlone Introductions. Finally, the *Indexical Glossary* resembles that in the EETS Vol. IV ii rather than the condensed form of it in Skeat's Oxford edition. The four Texts have been printed in parallel in one volume and the *Textual Notes, Commentary* and *Glossary* in a second so as to make it possible to study the texts and the relevant editorial material together. The choice of a *parallel* rather than a sequential format has been made only after consulting potential users of the edition. For though the reasons for adopting it may be evident, this way of printing *Piers Plowman* is not wholly free of drawbacks. Skeat's ingenious layout, which also recorded the poet's structural transpositions by a double presentation in smaller type of deferred or anticipated 'parallel' material, can distract if not confuse a reader wishing to read one version through. It is visually unappealing; it is quite unlike any text of the poem a medieval reader might have encountered; and its advantages for comparative study of the revision-process are probably now outweighed by the need to give each version its proper due. Though the last consideration most obviously affects the uncouth newcomer on the scene, **Z**, which can only suffer by being juxtaposed with its comelier successors, it applies as much to the mature but neglected **C** Version, the mere existence of which signifies Langland's reluctance to rest content with **B**. In the end, however, choice of a parallel format has been dictated by the nature of the texts themselves.

§ 3. Skeat, in producing his EETS volumes, did not systematically compare the readings of the **A**, **B** and **C** Versions, each of which he edited and published successively, though he did consult the **B** manuscripts when editing **A**.[7] And since the Oxford Edition reprinted his EETS texts with virtually no alteration, it is evident that he did not re-edit the poem in a 'parallel' or comparative way. This was understandable, given the pioneering nature of Skeat's enterprise, his initial lack of access to all the known copies of any one (let alone every) version, and his wish to complete the Oxford project rapidly after nearly twenty years spent on the EETS volumes. But as an editor, Skeat very seldom identified textual problems in **A**, **B** or **C** that could be solved, or best solved, only by recourse to one or both of the other versions. It seems that he made limited use of the numerous manuscript copies of each version he published. And, in fact, his main shortcoming as an editor was excessive trust in the readings of his chosen base-manuscripts, the *Vernon, Laud* and *Phillipps* copies of **A**, **B** and **C** respectively.

§ 4. For Skeat's successors, the solution to particular textual difficulties has not lain simply in choosing a better base-manuscript or making wider use of the diverse witnesses to the three versions. To take the case of **B**, what Elsie Blackman acutely perceived in 1918 and George Kane and E. Talbot Donaldson demonstrated at length some sixty years later, was that the archetype of the extant manuscript copies was itself very corrupt.[8] Many of its errors, they argued, could be corrected only by turning to the superior text of **C** and, in the half of the poem where it was present, that of **A**. Although open to dispute, this part of the Athlone editors' procedure proved indispensable to the present editor in preparing an annotated student's text of **B** twenty-five years ago.[9] When, a few years after this appeared in 1978, the opportunity arose to replace Skeat's Oxford Edition, it became quickly clear that **A**, **B** and **C** would have to be systematically edited in parallel. That is, every reading in each version would have to be established in the light of all variants not only in that version but also, where they existed, in the corresponding parts of the other versions. To some extent, Kane and Donaldson ('K–D' hereafter) had already done this for **B**; but the degree to which they had embraced the 'parallelist principle' only became explicit in 1988 when, in a 'Retrospect' to the second edition of his A-Text, Kane revealed that he now would have taken 'full account' of both **B** and **C** when emending corruptions in the archetypal text of **A**.[10]

George Russell and Kane, the editors of the third Athlone volume (1997), showed no hesitation in taking such 'account' of the implications of **A** and **B** for their edition of **C**. The present editor had reached the same position shortly before, when beginning work on the text of **C**, but unlike Russell and Kane ('R–K' hereafter) has made much less use of **B**, and none of **A**, for emending apparent archetypal errors in **C**.

§ 5. Less obvious than the need for 'parallel editing' was the requirement to print Langland's texts in parallel. Its advantage lay in complementing rather than duplicating the Athlone multi-volume format, and also in highlighting the manner in which the texts had been edited. Further, the familiar Skeatian layout would serve to focus attention on the readings of the **Z** Version even more effectively than would placing it as the first of four successive texts, let alone in the ambiguous isolation of an Appendix. But while choice of this format was more pragmatic than polemical, some reply is owed to the objection made by a reviewer of Vol. I[11] that a 'standard edition' was an inappropriate place for special pleading on behalf of **Z**. Firstly, then: a parallel-text edition provides an immediate stimulus to debate about the authenticity of **Z**. Secondly, printing **Z** alongside **A** is arguably not much more alarming than the Athlone editors' extensive use of **A** and **C** to emend the text of **B** or, more particularly, of **A** and **B** to emend that of **C**. Finally, given the peculiar difficulties posed by a multi-version work preserved in some fifty divergent copies, it may not even in principle be possible to produce a 'standard' edition that at once obeys the imperatives of parallel-editing and acknowledges current disagreements over the nature of the Z-Text. Thus, despite outwardly recalling the Oxford Edition accepted as 'standard' for nearly a century, this edition cannot take for granted what Skeat did when he digested his EETS volumes into parallel format. In relation to the Athlone texts, a growing divergence in approach on the part of the present editor has combined with differences of formal presentation to make of the present edition less of the supplement it was originally envisaged as and more of an alternative.

§ 6. Since the former aspect is explored fully below (§§ 55–134), it is enough here to illustrate the latter from a single major difference. Thus, while the Athlone Critical Apparatus provides a complete corpus of variants, the present edition prints variant readings only where the given version's archetypal text is in doubt. This economy is imposed by the parallel-text format, which rules out lavish citation of variants. But there is no need in any case to duplicate materials assembled with skill and thoroughness by the Athlone editors (and used with gratitude by the present editor in preparing the apparatus for **A** and **B**). This edition concentrates instead on foregrounding the parallelistic editorial process by the use of group sigils to bring out with maximum clarity the dual textual traditions attested in the **A**, **B** and **C** Versions. Its Apparatus therefore separates in an Appendix such information as the rejected unique readings of each version's base-manuscript. The purpose of this is to avoid distracting attention from the variants given, which are those relevant to establishing the key pairs of contrasted family readings. The rationale of the Apparatus is thus selection rather than comprehensive inclusion; it interprets, instead of simply recording, the mass of substantive manuscript data. Accordingly, textual information with no bearing on the establishment of the adopted text is usually not included.

ii. *Varieties of Editorial Experience*: *the* EETS, Knott-Fowler, Athlone *and* Longman *Editions*

§ 7. Despite this one notable difference, comparison will reveal some features that bring the present edition closer to Athlone than to Skeat. The first feature (as noted at § 4 above) is its use of the evidence of all versions to establish the text of any one. The second, sometimes operating in conjunction with it, is a willingness to use what is known as the 'direct method' of textual criticism, which seeks to identify among two or more manuscript variants the one that is most likely to have generated the other(s). This method proves its worth best in distinguishing which family variant more probably preserves the archetypal reading that both descend from, and also in evaluating group or individual variants when a family reading is itself in doubt. However, major decisions made in this way obviously need to be justified by an adequate account of the reasoning behind them. That is one of the main purposes of the *Textual Notes*, which follow the procedure employed in Skeat's EETS editions and Kane's Athlone edition of **A**.

§ 8. The decision to provide such notes in a 'traditional' form was partly due to dissatisfaction with the later Athlone texts of **B** and **C**, which abandon the use of critical end-notes and systematically describe the rationale of textual judgements in their *Introductions*. For while there are advantages, especially for illustrating an editorial theory, in categorising editorial decisions by the type of textual situation they exemplify, this procedure has two drawbacks. Firstly, the task of relating each discussion to the lines of text in question would prove inconvenient for the reader even with a system of internal cross-reference, something the Athlone editions fail to provide.[12] Secondly, major instances find themselves unhelpfully lumped together with minor ones where the 'harder' reading cannot be convincingly distinguished from an 'easier' reading and the 'direction' of variation reliably determined. But the 'direct method' has a significant impact mainly on major readings, so it is these that are given most attention in the *Notes*; for the numerous minor cases, the reader is left to infer why one has been found preferable to another. Although one reason for this selective approach is simply practical, another is the theoretical conviction that successful division of witnesses into 'groups' and 'families' must in any case be made chiefly on the basis of the major variant readings (see *Introduction* IV, §§ 25–36). This is because, over the course of copying *Piers Plowman*, it was in the myriad *minor* readings that scribes of manuscripts in different lines of descent tended to converge. The most important point of similarity, however, between the Athlone and the present edition, and one in which both differ fundamentally from Skeat's, is that each examines the readings of its base-text 'critically', in the light of all the available evidence.

§ 9. The EETS edition, it may be fairly said, managed to be 'critical' only in the minimal sense of citing from a few selected witnesses whatever variants Skeat thought worthwhile. For he rejected the remainder as textually useless and only occasionally emended the base-text from one or more of his collated copies. Skeat was thus an eclectic editor, who printed what seemed the best reading to his taste and judgement (which were considerable). But since he believed his chosen base-manuscripts to approximate pretty faithfully to what Langland wrote, Skeat was in practice also a positivist editor, regarding the manuscript readings as 'facts' that if possible should not be tampered with. However, he did not practise the 'strong' form of textual positivism that countenances emendation only of mechanical errors, those that occur even in a carefully written manuscript. An editor of this stripe aims to produce the sort of text a medieval reader would have found (if lucky) in a copy corrected by a responsible scribe after re-reading his exemplar. Skeat's chosen **B** ms *Laud Misc. 581*[13] is such a text; but he nonetheless emends it from other witnesses, and not only where Laud omits lines but where he judges its reading substantively wrong. As a result, Skeat's edited text resembles somewhat that of another **B** copy he consulted, *BL Additional 35287*, which reveals erasures and corrections by a second scribe using a different exemplar, and gives a text fairly close to that of an 'eclectic positivist' editor. Quite how far Skeat the positivist could carry his eclecticism is seen in his readiness to include in the B-Text longer passages lacking from Laud but preserved (as he thought, uniquely) in ms *Rawlinson Poetry 38*.[14] On the face of it, his attitude to this copy moves beyond the positivist towards the opposite 'rationalist' editorial position (see § 13 below). However, it seems that what Skeat mainly wanted was to incorporate material he believed was authentic but belonged to a **B** recension intermediate between his base-text and the **C** Version. He did not regard Rawlinson as an independent witness to a single archetype from which both it and Laud derived, with the editorial implications which that view (shared by the Athlone and the present editors) entails. He therefore made little use of its variants to correct what the latter both identify as family errors in the text of Laud.[15]

§ 10. A neo-positivism more thoroughgoing than Skeat's has recently arisen, perhaps less as a method of editing than as a substitute for one. In part a reaction against textual rationalism, it hankers after the fact (that is, the letter) of the text in the most material sense. But it also reflects a current interest in the medieval reception of *Piers Plowman* that is fuelled by converging developments in codicology and literary theory.[16] One manifestation is the recent facsimile editions of *Bodley 851*, which contains the unique text of **Z**,[17] and of *Douce 104*,[18] the only illustrated copy of the poem. Another is a descriptive catalogue of the B-Text codices that records in detail both scribes' and readers' underlinings and marginalia.[19] The third and most formidable expression of neo-positivism is the *Piers Plowman Electronic Archive*,[20] planned to make available on computer disc facsimile-texts of each manuscript that are, in some ways, superior in quality to the originals themselves. This project will furnish all necessary means of access to the information they contain on the work's material history, early reception and cultural significance. Meanwhile, for the more conservative who think an 'authentic' *Piers Plowman* should rather resemble a text the poet's contemporaries might have known, one with the limited editorial intervention of Skeat's may still provide the most satisfactory form in which to read the poem (though few scholars now use it). The present edition, however, is intended for readers who consider that respect for textual facts can combine fruitfully with textual reasoning controlled by empirical criteria to recover a form nearer the original than Langland's first public could have acquired, and certainly nearer than any that the extant manuscripts preserve.

§ 11. During the half-century after Skeat's edition, much scholarly energy was directed to the study of the *Piers Plowman* manuscripts. Particularly important was the work of R. W. Chambers and J. G. Grattan, whose pioneering efforts never bore fruit in the textually improved EETS edition they projected.[21] Of the successor to Skeat's Oxford Edition (with the commentary providing the special feature) planned by Bennett, the only part published was the B-Text *Visio* mentioned at § 1 above. The mantle of Chambers and Grattan fell to Kane, under whose general editorship appeared the three editions representing the approach here called 'rationalist' (in a sense to be defined more fully at §§ 65–79).[22] Between 1886 and 1960 the only full edition was that of the

A Version by T. A. Knott and D. C. Fowler (1952),[23] a worthwhile undertaking that suffered an (undeserved) eclipse thanks to Kane's critique of it in his edition of **A**.[24]

§ 12. The procedure adopted by Knott-Fowler ('K–F' hereafter) is not that of simply printing their base-manuscript, *Trinity College Cambridge R. 3. 14*, 'with occasional readings from other mss' (a close enough description of Skeat's eclectic positivism). Instead K–F follow, at least in theory, the alternative method of editing known as 'recension'. This aims to establish, by critical or comparative analysis of the variants, the text of the source or archetype from which they derive. But K–F make a point of allowing that their 'critical readings' are established 'by the weight of evidence, genealogical *and other*' (p.28; italics mine), an important rider that tacitly recognises a twofold problem. Just as the 'direct' method (described at § 8 above) is effective mainly with major readings, recension works only when the dependence of one extant witness (or convincingly inferrable lost source) upon another can be shown from the cumulative weight of their agreements in error. But since K–F's stemma acknowledges that none of the **A** manuscripts is a direct copy of any other,[25] no manuscript can be eliminated as a potential bearer of an original reading by direct descent. On the other hand, as both branches of their stemma derive independently from their postulated common original, neither branch can be proved secondary, and so neither can be eliminated. A third line of transmission, that of the **A** readings preserved in the **B** Version, though also perhaps independent, is judged by K–F to be merely ancillary. Their genealogy, therefore, since it cannot determine the choice of readings, is in effect otiose, and is in practice not relied on by K–F to any noticeable degree.

§ 13. Now, if the manuscripts in a textual tradition *can* be shown to descend vertically from a single archetype, even where lost group-ancestors or sub-archetypes must be posited, editing by recension reveals itself on examination to be a variety of positivism. But it is a more *logical* variety than the ordinary kind, and so nearer to rationalism, since its ultimate interest is less the facts *per se* than the causes that explain them. In other words, the main quarry that the 'logical positivist' editor has in view is the *archetype*, and nothing that may lie beyond it. However, in the *Piers Plowman* traditions, application of the recensional method is impeded by extensive convergent variation that confuses the relations between the witnesses forming the postulated genetic groups. K–F consequently end in the same eclecticism as Skeat, because their 'other' evidence (§ 12) acquires as much weight as the 'genealogical.' But the fact that this evidence is little else except the intrinsic value of the readings effectually opens the door to the 'direct method', the method associated with Kane and his colleagues. And it is replacement of the (at least in theory) near-mechanical operation of the stemma by critical *reasoning,* at all stages up to and beyond the archetype, that constitutes 'textual rationalism'.

§ 14. The Athlone *Piers Plowman*, when completed with its five-volume Commentary by Stephen Barney and others (the 'Penn Commentary') will form an even more massive work than the EETS edition produced single-handedly by Skeat. As the **A** Version was edited by Kane, **B** by Kane and Donaldson, and **C** by Russell and Kane, the three volumes perhaps inevitably show certain differences of handling. The first was based on the **A** manuscripts only, while the collaborative editions take the witness of the other two versions into account (see § 4 above). In other words, Kane's original approach to **A** has been abandoned, and **B** and **C** edited more or less 'parallelistically'. But while the three volumes embody a common attitude to the problems of

Langland's text,[26] it is nevertheless Athlone **A** that has exerted a far-reaching, even a constraining influence upon that of **B** and, to a less extent, **C**.[27] This is because the basic editorial principles of the later volumes remain those established by Kane in his edition of **A**.

§ 15. The Athlone project's continuity is reflected in its uniform layout. Each critical apparatus provides a complete corpus of variants, while the discussion of the text, from the classification of the manuscripts to the emendation of corruptions, forms a systematic introductory treatise. With the abandonment of end-notes in **B** and **C** has gone any residual resemblance to Skeat's EETS editions.[28] The Athlone Introductions' vast body of carefully organised and analysed primary material offers an enormously valuable resource for any subsequent editor. But it is perhaps less in their meticulous examination of the variational groups than in their wider view of the history of the texts, the character of the archetypes and the editorial obligation to restore (where possible) the originals, that the Athlone editions have proved so innovative and controversial. The attempt to recover the authorial text has been prosecuted most energetically in the edition of **B**. The edition of **A** was much more cautious about emending the archetype and that of **C** stops short of 'restoring' what its editors profess to believe was a work in progress and opts instead for the 'pre-archetypal' form as 'edited' by the poet's 'literary executor'. But allowing for these differences, which will be examined more fully below, the whole project can be fairly described as in essence 'rationalist'.

§ 16. The Athlone editors believe that the text of *Piers Plowman* was corrupted by the copyists from the earliest stages of its transmission. Not only was the archetype of the **A** manuscripts corrupt, so was the **A** copy used by the poet for revision to **B**. The text of **B** underwent massive deformation when the archetype of the extant witnesses was generated. As before, the scribal **B** manuscript used by the poet in composing **C** contained many errors, some of which provoked him to particular acts of revision. This latest (unfinished) version was in certain respects further damaged by the medieval 'editor' of the material from which the archetype of the **C** manuscripts was copied, as finally was that archetype itself. Editors who aim to recover what Langland wrote thus cannot avoid fashioning for themselves, as an instrument of guidance, something like an 'ideal' conception of the poet's *usus scribendi*. The latter term denotes the specific features of metre, style and expression that are criterial for authenticating the variants examined in the quest for each archetypal text and for assaying the 'originality' of that text where its readings are not in doubt. It is fundamental to this conception that scribal and authorial characteristics can be distinguished in most contested cases. In consequence, where the surviving evidence suffices, even one version's identifiably inauthentic archetypal readings may be drawn upon for reconstructing the hypothetical original in the light of one or both of the other versions. Moreover, in editing the 'middle' version, the most corrupt of the three, agreed **AC** readings can reliably guide correction of archetypal errors. In particular cases, even individual **A**, **B** or **C** copies may be judged to preserve their originals by 'good correction' from superior lost manuscripts of these versions. Finally, in the absence of direct textual evidence, an experienced understanding of the poet's *usus* and of the scribes' customary tendencies to vary from it may authorise conjectural emendation even of unanimously attested readings. For in the end, all the witnesses to a version, being descended from a bad archetype, may prove to be as untrustworthy as the chosen copytext itself.

§ 17. It should be clear from this summary account how far editorial 'rationalism' differs from Skeat's 'eclectic' and Knott-Fowler's 'logical' kinds of positivism. In principle, it allows greater freedom in the choice of readings; most important, though, it does not stop at the archetypes, but aims to recover their lost originals through inferential reasoning from the known character of scribal variation. Texts produced by such editing are bound to differ substantially from those available to Langland's contemporaries, in proportion to the rigour with which the direct method is followed through. Any 'ideal' conception of the poet's mind and art in general, and of his syntax, lexis and versification in particular, must of course be based on the witness of the extant copies. But this consideration does not inhibit the Athlone editors, where they believe the scribes have consciously or unconsciously substituted their own words for the poet's, from exerting to the full the force of their editorial 'reason' (which excludes neither imagination nor intuition) in order to recover or restore the 'original' poem. Rationalist editing may begin with the manuscripts, but it does not end with them.

§ 18. A judiciously mild form of 'rational' editing was Derek Pearsall's aim in his 1978 edition of **C** for the York Medieval Texts. This was the second of the three complete single-version editions to appear between the Athlone B-Text and Volume I of the present edition, published by Longman in 1995. It was dedicated to Skeat's memory and it follows his eclectic positivism, eschewing Knott-Fowler's claim to be 'critical'. But Pearsall's edition ('*Pe*' hereafter), admirably as it brings up to date its predecessor's notes in the light of a century's work on the sources and background, does more besides. Skeat had printed manuscript *Phillipps 8231* (now *Huntington 137*), as had Thomas Whitaker, who published the first edition of **C** in 1813 (see § 30 below). But Pearsall based his text on ms *Huntington 143*, the one also selected for the Athlone and the present edition. This copy, which represents a much better **C** tradition, was unknown to Skeat, as was the one (*BL Additional 35157*) that Pearsall used to correct errors in Hm 143. He further consulted two other manuscripts of the same family, the *Ilchester* and the *Trinity College Cambridge* copies, which Skeat had collated throughout and drawn on sporadically; but he also turned to Hm 137 to supply lines missing from all members of the family of Hm 143. Very occasionally, too, Pearsall resorted to **B** (in its edited Athlone form) to emend presumed archetypal errors in **C**, notably in the last two passūs, where both versions are almost identical. Use of Hm 143 as copy-text, as has already been noted, had been recommended by Chambers, who published a facsimile of it in 1936; and in 1967 Pearsall and Elizabeth Salter had co-edited for the York Medieval Texts *Selections* from **C** based on Hm 143 corrected from Add. 35157.[29] The York complete edition demonstrated what the *Selections* had adumbrated: that **C**'s poetic excellence, too often concealed by the 'prosiness, pedantry and fussiness' (*Pe*, p. 21) of Skeat's 'standard' text of the inferior Phillipps copy, deserved recognition in its own right. The high esteem **C** now enjoys (attested by a recent verse translation),[30] is due mainly to its first modern editor's advocacy. And it was in fact a detailed examination of Pearsall's text that convinced the present editor that the **C** version would offer an immensely interesting editorial challenge.

§ 19. A major stimulus to produce the annotated edition of **B** that appeared in the same year as Pearsall's **C** came from a similar scrutiny of the Athlone text of **B** a few years earlier. The remainder of Bennett's Clarendon B-Text (see § 1 above) then lay some distance ahead; and, even if completed, it seemed as though this would possess a 'pre-Athlonean' or at best a 'post-Skeatian' character. Although a new edition of **B** could obviously not be *based* on Kane-Donaldson, it seemed inevitable that its text would have to draw deeply on their material and take significant account of their methods. Thus, by contrast with the York C-Text, the present editor's 'Everyman' text (though designed for students) carried a *Critical Apparatus* and *Textual Notes* of equal length to its interpretative *Commentary*. The first of these features it shared with Knott-Fowler's **A** version, which had been re-printed in 1964. The Everyman edition did not, however, dispense with the use of square brackets around emended readings (as did *K–F* and *Pe*), and it printed the apparatus on the text-page (where *K–F* placed it at the end). But because it was setting out, like the Parson in the *General Prologue*, 'to winne folk...by fairnesse' to the poetry of Chaucer's great contemporary, it provided marginal glosses of difficult words and treated the work's textual problems only summarily (as had *K–F*). In modernising obsolete Middle English letter-forms, it was following Knott-Fowler and, before them, Wright (*Wr*; see § 31 below). But in its focus on structure, meaning and literary qualities, the Everyman Introduction's model was the Salter-Pearsall *C-Text Selections*. It was this inspired little work that prepared a way in the editorial wilderness for seeing Langland as a great religious poet rather than as the colourful chronicler of medieval society familiar since the days of Skeat.

§ 20. The provision of a Glossary in the 1982 reprint of the Everyman edition brought it into line with those of Knott-Fowler, Bennett and Pearsall. But in its handling of the text, its indebtedness to Kane and Donaldson was obvious (even if, while adopting their methods, it sometimes reached very different conclusions). Thus, despite greater caution in rejecting archetypal readings, the Everyman showed its 'rationalist' leanings in two ways. One was its citation of 'K–D' after a number of readings and emendations; the other was its use of the 'versional' sigils **A**, **C** or **AC** to support a variant or indicate the source of a reading not found in any **B** witness. Here, moreoever, the referent of '**A**' was the Athlone A-Text of Kane, that of '**C**' the Hm 143 text that would form the basis of the forthcoming Russell-Kane C-Text and had been cited by K–D in the Introduction to their recently published B-Text. These 'Athlonean' sigils contained the germ of a fully 'visible' parallel-edited text. Though no longer required in volume I of the present edition, which prints all the texts on facing pages, in the Everyman Second Edition (1995) they still serve their original purpose. However, since the latter has been extensively altered to accord with the Longman B-Text, what they now denote is the **A** and **C** Versions as printed in that text. But in the *Visio* section of the revised Everyman they are sometimes joined by a new versional sigil, **Z**.

§ 21. The addition of the sigil **Z** is explained by the publication of a third single-version edition some five years after the Everyman first appeared. Consisting of the first part of the *Piers Plowman* text in manuscript Bodley 851, it was designated by Skeat's sigil '**Z**', though Skeat (like Knott-Fowler and Kane after him) made no use of it when preparing his A-Text. However, George Rigg and Charlotte Brewer, the editors of this neglected text, saw it not as an eccentric abbreviation of **A** with spurious interpolations and lengthy omissions but as a substantive version anterior to **A**. And **Z**, they maintained, was not only unfinished, like **A**, but in a draft state, although they identified Bodley 851 as an early scribal copy, not a holograph.[31] Their argument is based on the '**Z**'-Text's formal coherence, linguistic integrity, stylistic consistency and unique textual relationship to **A**. But Rigg and Brewer ('R–B' hereafter) judge it independent in possessing some authentic readings that show the archetypal A-Text to be in error.

§ 22. The case for **Z** made by R–B was antecedently unlikely to receive a disinterested appraisal from the Athlone editor of **A**, who had dismissed it without consideration, and its wider reception was also somewhat muted. However, though the present project was still only a gleam in its editor's eye, what Bodley 851 suggested *prima facie* to that eye (still as sceptical about **Z** as any) was something more remarkable than an **A** copy re-written by an inventive scribe (like the singular B-Text in manuscript Corpus 201).[32] Its unique passages, in particular, appeared not simply expansions of an oddly truncated source but (at their best) novel and arresting. Its 'author' was evidently no mere follower of Langland, like the poets of *Pierce the Ploughmans Crede* and *Mum and the Sothsegger*. Strikingly, too, **Z**'s equivalent of **A**'s *Visio* differed not just in degree but in kind from other scribal 'versions,' despite revealing (like certain of them) what looked like contamination from **B** and **C**. Despite all these features, however, **Z** seemed initially interpretable as a remarkably 'creative' response by one reader-author-scribe who had encountered *Piers Plowman* in its earliest and probably in its later forms as well. If this was the case, then it properly belonged to the history of the poem's reception, not to that of its text. But for a prospective editor of a parallel-text there appeared no Gowerian *middel weie* between rejecting **Z** as spurious and accepting it as authentic. Manuscript Bodley 851 should either prove classifiable or have to be rejected as an irretrievably aberrant witness to the **A** tradition. To place **Z** apart in an Appendix as simply too interesting for total oblivion while unusable in editing would only defer judgement instead of making it. And if 'the business of textual criticism' was 'to produce a text as close as possible to the original,'[33] then an editor prepared to identify 'original' readings in any individual manuscript of an accepted version should not quail from doing as much in a text proposed but not yet accepted as a 'version.' To hypothesise **Z**'s authenticity during the process of systematic parallel-editing would, it seemed, facilitate discovery of its true nature through a minute comparison with the divergent manuscript texts of **A**, **B** and **C**, which could each, for the purpose of this exercise, be regarded as a scribal 'version'.

§ 23. The result (somewhat surprising in the event) was a conviction that, despite certain residual problems, R–B's case appeared sound. There was thus no alternative, after editing **Z** in parallel, but to print it as **A**, **B** and **C** were to be printed, in parallel. A cautionary example, however, lay ominously at hand: Skeat's bold attribution of *Richard the Redeless* to Langland, which is now universally rejected. Nonetheless, it was plain to see that the two cases differed in essence. For Skeat, the question of printing *Richard* in parallel with *Piers Plowman* obviously never arose; but one positive effect of his mistaken attribution was to bring *Richard the Redeless* an attention it would not otherwise have received. The editors of Bodley 851 had shown it to have at the least major textual implications for the **A** Version. These would be more vividly (though more provocatively) highlighted if **Z** did not figure as a mere sigil following its (at times perforce extended) variant readings in the critical apparatus to **A**.[34] Arguments in support of this decision have been offered below that it is hoped may prove convincing (see III, *Z Version*). But whatever doubts may persist in the minds of readers, **Z**'s inclusion here is not intended to assume its claims established once for all so much as to arouse rigorous debate on the proper criteria for recognising authenticity in the *Piers Plowman* tradition (there has been very little such as yet). The same may be said for citing **Z** in the revised Everyman Apparatus, which encourages its users to assess **Z**'s evidence and not (like Skeat and Kane) to ignore it.

§ 24. The preceding paragraphs have described what may be called, despite ruptures and changes in theory, a true editorial 'tradition', extending from the mid-nineteenth century to the present time. It is also one to which many notable contributions have been made by scholars who did not themselves succeed in producing editions. Amongst these, Chambers stands out as the second father of *Piers Plowman* editing, without whose pioneering studies the Athlone project might never have come into being.[35] Skeat's edition, which this section began with, was not the first, and the present one will doubtless not be the last. But while acknowledging its place in the tradition, this edition is intended as more than a continuation of earlier undertakings, if less than a total substitute for them. Drawing extensively on the efforts of the nine editors discussed, its aim is to offer an equivalent to what the earliest of them accomplished (like the present editor) with no collaborators, and also (unlike him) no true predecessors: a *Piers Plowman* for our time.

iii. *Earlier Editions: from* Crowley *to* Wright

§ 25. Both the distinctiveness of the present edition and its place in the tradition should emerge from the following examination of the strengths and limitations of those predecessors. Its purpose is to bring out through an extended historical critique the dimensions of and the most effective way of handling the textual problem. But it starts by considering the earlier editorial undertakings (now largely of historical interest) that kept knowledge of *Piers Plowman* alive between the manuscript period and the age of Skeat, with whom the scholarly tradition began. The *editio princeps* of the poem was the **B** Version published at Holborn in 1550 by Robert Crowley, who reprinted it twice in the same year.[36] Crowley the Protestant controversialist has the credit of rescuing Langland from the neglect into which most medieval writers except Chaucer fell under the combined impact of the Renaissance and the Reformation. His lost manuscript source, which was distinct from any of the extant manuscripts and which he seems to have reproduced rather inaccurately, contained few unique variants of real value (see *Introduction* III, *B Version*, §§ 13–16, esp. § 16, below). But a couple of major readings in Crowley's first print (Cr^1) will illustrate two positive features of his editorial work. The first shows him apparently consulting other versions to correct an unsatisfactory reading, initiating a procedure used by his successors from Wright onwards. In the famous description of divine love at B I 152 *And also þe plante of pees, moost precious of vertues*, Crowley's *plant* (as in parallel **A** and **C**) is both intrinsically 'harder' than the archetypal **B** reading *plente* and (*pace* Skeat) one that is unlikely to be a spelling-variant of the latter. Unless *plante*, a reading accepted as authentic by all modern editors, had entered his source from a lost **B** manuscript superior to the archetypal text, it must derive from one of the other 'auncient copies' (of other versions) mentioned in his prefatory Address to the Reader.[37] By contrast, *provided* at B V 165 is not too hard to be his own conjecture, though more probably a modernisation of an original **purveiede* introduced in his manuscript source to correct the unmetrical archetypal reading *ordeinede*. Crowley's second impression (Cr^2), re-set from another lost manuscript and collated throughout with Cr^1, lacks unique right readings. But Cr^3, mainly a reprint of Cr^2, provides in *wishen vs* a basis for reconstructing the original at B XII 270 from the corrupt archetypal reading *wissen*. Further, as Crowley's reading here could have been a correction prompted by the verb *wenen* at corresponding C XIV 195, his text may even reveal the rudimentary beginnings of a 'parallel' approach to editing the poem.

§ 26. These corrections, however, mark the limits of Crowley's achievement; for in other respects his own practice does not bear out his exhortation 'to walke in the waye of truthe'.[37] In the summary added in Cr² his confusion of Piers with the dreamer in Passus VIII helped mislead generations of readers, and it no doubt underlies the further error in William Webbe's 'commendation' (1586) of the 'auncient poet...*Pierce Ploughman*' as 'the first that...obserued the quantity of our verse without the curiosity of Ryme.'[38] More culpably still, to further his polemical aims Crowley (in Skeat's words) 'falsifies his text of set purpose'.[39] Thus for *And Marie his moder be oure meene bitwene* at B VII 197 he substitutes *And make Christe our meane, that hath made emends,* which preserves Langland's metre while reforming his theology. At B XII 85, instead of *For Goddes body myȝte noȝt ben of breed wiþouten clergie,* he has *For bread of gods body myght not be without cleargy,* another change designed 'to make this line...more suitable for his Protestant readers,'[40] though at the cost of barely making sense. In XIII 259 for *Ne mannes masse make pees* Crowley prints *There may no man make peace.* Here Langland's later replacement of *masse* by *prayere* at C XV 230 doubtless implies his own dissatisfaction with the original. But the poet's revision, so far from being 'Wycliffite,' may show rather an awareness that **B**'s phrase 'man's' mass' expresses a less than fully orthodox sense of the priestly minister as performing his ritual act *in persona Christi*. Finally, at XV 181 *He kan portreye the Paternoster and peynte it with Aues,* for *Aues* Crowley (as Skeat notes) 'ingeniously substitutes *Pitie*, thus adding a fourth initial *p*, contrary to Langland's usual custom.'[41] Here (as in VII 197) Crowley's 'ingeniousness' resides only in his *following* the poet's use of a fourth alliterating stave (by no means unusual, as Prologue 1 should have reminded Skeat). More serious is his deletion of Langland's emphasis on saying the Rosary as a penitential exercise similar to the Psalms and the Lord's Prayer (XV 179–81).

§ 27. Of a piece with Crowley's corruptions of the poet's Marian and Eucharistic emphases are the 'notes and cotations in the mergyne,' with what Brewer calls their 'clear polemical orientation',[42] offered for the reader's assistance on the title-page of Cr². One concerns confession, the importance of which in the **B** Version is shown by its threefold treatment in Passūs V, XIII and XX. Crowley's note against III 51ff ('The fruites of Popishe penaunce'), as J. N. King showed, elicited from a seventeenth-century Catholic reader Andrew Bostock a rejoinder ('Not the fruits but abuse of Penaunce') indicating a much better comprehension of the poet's purpose. The same reader (on f. xxxix^r of Douce L 205) answers Crowley's comment on B VII 172–73 ('Note howe he scorneth the auctority of Popes Math.vi') by succinctly stating the orthodox doctrine of indulgences, which Langland understood and (at 174–81) apparently endorsed.[43] These (fairly typical) examples suggest that Charlotte Brewer understates in finding 'perhaps a little strong' King's assertion that Crowley 'kidnapped' the poem in an attempt to 'interpret it as reformist propaganda.'[44] Kidnapping is a serious crime, even if the victim is one's spiritual rather than bodily offspring; but it fits the bill. Crowley's 'notes and cotations', far from 'geuynge light to the Reader,' belong with 'the worckes of darcknes' that he believed the poet, like Wycliffe, 'crye[d] oute agaynste.'

§ 28. Crowley is not, however, directly responsible for the 'faultiness and imperfection' that Thomas Tyrwhitt attributed to his lost manuscript source.[45] Being of the 'β' type, this source (necessarily) lacked the many lines and passages unique to the 'α' tradition (see *B Version*, §§ 7, 58 below); and his other 'auncient copies' presumably did not include any that, like the Rawlinson and Corpus manuscripts, preserve this tradition. Again, Crowley is not to blame that as late as Wright's edition (1842) his was the only form of **B** to have been published (as noted at § 31, Wright was much influenced by his print). Nor, finally, is it Crowley's fault that Owen Rogers, by including the Lollard-related *Pierce the Ploughman's Crede* in his 1561 re-issue of Cr[3], initiated the unhappy coupling of these texts that was repeated three centuries later by Wright. But Rogers's suggestion that the *Crede* was by the author of *Piers Plowman* could only lend colour to his predecessor's strong implication that the poet was a sympathiser with, if not a supporter of, John Wycliffe. All this adds up to a major failure of Crowley's in his editorial duty to print what the author wrote and explain what he meant, not what he thought Langland should have written or meant. His edition's contribution to the understanding of *Piers Plowman* is thus almost entirely negative, and its place is in the history of the poem's reception rather than of its editing. All the same, insofar as the text derives from a lost manuscript copy, 'Crowley' should have found a place in Benson and Blanchfield's volume describing the manuscripts of the B-Text.[46]

§ 29. Although it was never re-published entire until our time (see *Intro.* I, no. 13 above), parts of Crowley's text were reprinted in the eighteenth century. First Thomas Warton the younger included some 500 lines of extracts from Cr[2] in Vol. I of his *History of English Poetry* (3 vols., 1774–81), with glossarial and historical annotations foreshadowing Skeat's and, unlike Crowley's, genuinely 'geuing light to the reader.' Next, the antiquary Joseph Ritson in Vol. I of his *English Anthology* (3 vols., 1793–94) gave Passus V 1–441 from Cr[1] with some variants from Cr[2] and emendations of his own, but without annotation. It was, however, not until 1824 that Richard Price, a librarian at the British Museum, in a new edition of Warton's *History*, replaced his extracts with a text based on the early fifteenth-century manuscript *Cotton Caligula A xi*,[47] recording Crowley's readings in a critical apparatus. He also gave in an Appendix to Vol. II parallel passages from the antiquary Richard Heber's **C** manuscript (subsequently Phillips 8231 and now Huntington 137), corrected from two other British Museum C-Text copies, *Cotton Vespasian B xvi* and *Harley 2376*.[48] Price probably contributed more to the understanding of the textual situation than anyone before Skeat. He printed a selection of critical texts based on the manuscripts and recognised the value of comparing parallel passages in the different versions. More important still, he identified in manuscripts *Harley 875* and *6041*[49] a third version of *Piers Plowman*, known since Skeat as **A**, which he surmised was perhaps 'the first draught of the poem' (Vol. II, 482–83). Skeat, without naming Price, acknowledged his acuity, which has at last received due recognition from Brewer.[50]

§ 30. Price, however, was not the first to make available for comparison a version other than the one that Skeat, as late as 1869, still called 'the "Crowley" type, or Type B' (*Sk* II, p. i). That was the achievement of the Lancashire topographer Dr Thomas Whitaker, who in 1813 published an elaborate black-letter folio edition entitled the *Visio Willi de Petro Plouhman*. Based on his friend Richard Heber's manuscript (later Phillipps 8231, now Hm 137), this first complete Langland edition since Crowley was the *editio princeps* of the version Skeat named **C**. As well as an Introductory Discourse, Whitaker provided a glossary, a 'perpetual commentary' or continuous paraphrase on the page, brief notes and a detailed summary of the poem's content. He anticipated Price in illustrating the description of Wrath with parallel extracts from Crowley, the B-Text *Oriel College* manuscript[51] and another manuscript of Heber's now recognised as a conflated copy of **A**, **B** and **C**.[52] His edition, which has been recently examined by Brewer, was extensively cited by Skeat.[53] The latter recognised Whitaker's ignorance of Middle English as a disabling deficiency in his text and glossary, but offered what are comfortable words for any editor of the poem: 'if there are numerous inaccuracies, the desire to be accurate is none the less clear'.[54] Concerning Langland's supposed heterodoxy, Whitaker correctly observes that the poet's belief in 'almost all the fundamental doctrines of Christianity has no tendency to prove him a Wickliffite or Lollard' (p. xviii), proving that the 'historical' nineteenth century had early achieved a more balanced perspective on the turbulent fourteenth century than was possible for the sanguinary sixteenth. Whitaker's notion of Crowley's text as representing a later revision of the Phillipps version, which he calls 'the first but vigorous effort of a young poet' (p. xxxi), now seems hard to credit. But given Whitaker's ignorance of **A**, it seems only a degree more eccentric than Jill Mann's proposal that **A** may have been written after both **B** and **C**.[55] The worst to be said of his view is that it overlooks what internal evidence exists for dating the longer versions, e.g. **C**'s removal of **B**'s allusion to the coronation of the young heir and its bold new reference to popular disaffection with the king for encouraging 'custumes of coueytise.'[56]

§ 31. The title of *The Vision and the Creed of Piers Plowman*, which Thomas Wright published in 1842 and reprinted with a few extra notes in 1856, echoes Crowley's, while his inclusion of the *Crede* follows Owen Rogers's reprint. Familiar with medieval historical works, Latin satirical writings and over half the extant manuscript copies of the poem, Wright was much better equipped for his task than was his immediate predecessor. Yet he arguably advanced understanding of the poem less than Whitaker (whom he treated more unkindly than did Skeat after him) and certainly less than Price. As Wright admits, his edition 'differs very little' from Crowley's (*Vision*, p. xliv), perhaps unsurprisingly since its base-text *Trinity Cambridge B. 15. 17* belongs to the same sub-group of 'β' copies as did the Tudor printer's lost manuscript source.[57] Wright helpfully modernises its obsolete Middle English letter-forms; but his printing of the poem in half-lines misrepresents its metrical structure, wastes space and produces a line-numbering incompatible with any other edition. His transcription is generally accurate and his glossary greatly improves on Whitaker's. But a fault in the former can lead to error in the latter, as when for *bonched* he reads *bouched* in Pr 74 and glosses it 'to stop people's mouths.' The non-existent word *bouched* perhaps seemed real to Wright, as Crowley has it too, and his conjectured sense is historically plausible. This particular mistake, moreover, may be *lightly forȝyuen*; for in this manuscript *n* is often indistinguishable from *u*, as at XVI 20 where, again following Crowley, he has for a probably original *loue dreem* the reverse error of *lone dreem* (the manuscript could read either). Wright's attractive emendation *giltles* for *synneles* in Pr 34 (rejected by Skeat but adopted by K–D and the first Everyman edition) illustrates his adventurous acceptance of an other-version reading (here from **A**) solely for what he understands to be its superior metre.[58] His textual comments are few, his frequent citations of Whitaker highlighting the differences between the latter's version and his own, and his explanatory annotation, if sporadic and unsystematic, is not without interest. But Wright's edition made little difference to later understanding of the text or its meaning. Skeat's observations on it (*Sk* II xxxvi–xxxix) may seem neutral compared with his warm appreciation of Whitaker's more defective work; but it is hard to see how he could have learnt much from Wright.

iv. Skeat's *Editions*

§ 32. Walter Skeat brought to his editing of Langland far more philological and historical learning than any of his predecessors. But any comparison of his B-Text with Wright's had to wait until two years after the appearance of his A-Text, which initiated a twenty-year project for the Early English Text Society.[59] Begun in 1866 and published in 1867, this first volume pre-empted misapprehension with its lengthy admonitory title *The Vision of William concerning Piers Plowman, together with Vita de Dowel, Dobet, et Dobest, Secundum Wit et Resoun* and its subtitle 'The "Vernon" Text; or Text A.' Its limitations, such as excessive confidence in the base-manuscript[60] and inadequate use of the other collated manuscripts to correct its errors, persisted throughout the later editions. These defects might be largely discounted had Skeat used his 1886 Parallel-Text as an occasion for revision and improvement (he did not). But given that he had to make his own way, some of his A-Text's weaknesses may be due to his having no predecessor, as Wright had in Crowley. When compared with Whitaker's edition of **C**, which offered a negative model, its superiority is quickly evident. However, Skeat's naming of the **B** and **C** Versions the 'Crowley' and 'Whitaker' types respectively reveals his early awareness of working in an editorial 'tradition.'

§ 33. Skeat published before his edition a pamphlet that made available for comparison an eleven-line passage (= B III 76–86 //) drawn from manuscripts of all three versions.[61] Seven are from **A**, eleven from **B** (including Rogers's valueless reprint of Crowley) and eleven from **C**. Its main purpose was to elicit information about as yet unidentified copies of the poem. Among those that came to light was *Ashmole 1468*, which Skeat used in Passus XI together with *Harley 3954* to correct errors in *Trinity R. 3. 14* (his base here after the cessation of his main copy-text).[62] These two manuscripts, with one from Dublin (*TCD 213*) that he heard of too late to use and another not known till 1922 (*Society of Antiquaries 687*),[63] belong to a distinct family of the **A** tradition.[64] But it is very doubtful whether Skeat would have identified them as such, even had all four been ready to hand. For his declared method at this stage was to print the single manuscript he judged 'the oldest and best written' as having 'readings...on the whole better than those of any other' and to correct it from the copies collated only 'where it seemed to need it.'[65] Vernon (V) is indeed the earliest **A** copy and coaeval with most of the oldest **B** and **C** manuscripts (*c.* 1400),[66] though not as early as Skeat's 1370–80 (p. xv), which would have brought it to within a few years of **A**'s probable date of composition.[67] Unfortunately, however, Vernon lacks Passus XI's last 130 lines through loss of a final leaf; but Skeat's attraction to this imposing manuscript and mistaken belief that the 'conjoint' **AC** Trinity ms (T) was much later in date led him to discountenance T as his base-text, and this despite resorting to it in XI 184–313 and also for earlier corrections, including the supply of whole lines.[68] It is harder to understand why he included from *Harley 875* (H) some 27 lines absent from V and all other copies 'for completing the sense, in passages that seem incomplete', while acknowledging that a few were spurious (later editors unanimously reject all of them).[69] The last point indicates Skeat's initial inability to detect scribal interpolations by applying rigorous metrical and stylistic criteria.

§ 34. In the matter of A Passus XII, however, Skeat gave an admirably judicious treatment of the one text he had, the opening eighteen lines found in *University College ms 45*, which he printed with comments.[70] The full form with John But's ending, uniquely preserved in ms *Rawlinson Poetry 137* (R), came to light only after publication. This material he issued with his B-Text in 1869, numbering the pages *137–44 for binding-up with his A-Text. Skeat's identification of Passus XII as substantially authentic is supported in the present edition but for his acceptance of lines 99–105 (which is nonetheless defensible).[71] The third copy containing Passus XII, the *Ingilby ms* (J),[72] became known to Skeat only after the publication of **C**. This he duly printed in 1885 with emendations and notes in the second part of Vol. IV.[73] In his parallel-text edition five years later Skeat placed Passus XII in the main text and not in an Appendix as did Knott-Fowler and Kane later, and he was right to do so. This portion of his final edition, with its use of all extant authorities, its apparatus and its shrewd emendations, is as 'critical' a piece of editing as could be asked for. The inadequacies of Skeat's *A-Text* elsewhere are partly due to his incomplete access to the manuscripts, but more to his editorial inexperience at this stage. However, Skeat's early awareness of the relevance of **B** to the editing of **A** is implicit in his brief comparison of the two versions on pp. 156–58; and it is well illustrated by his inclusion (after V 201) of manuscript U's lines about Clement the Cobbler on the grounds that 'they appear in all later versions...and are certainly genuine.'[74] This greatly improves on his editorial treatment of the Harley 875 lines mentioned above. Skeat may overlook possible cross-version contamination in U; but the example is a delicate one, because the lines' appearance in the **A** family called **m** below (III, *A Version*, §§ 24ff) allows that they might also have been present in the original text of **A**.[75]

§ 35. More open to criticism is Skeat's neglect of another conjoint text, the **C** portion of which he was to designate 'Z'. As he observed in his *C-Text* Preface, Bodley 851 was completely overlooked because it lacks the lines B III 76–86 // chosen as the 'test-passage' for identifying *Piers Plowman* manuscripts, and so Skeat received no notice of it. His later judgement of its first part as 'an extremely corrupt text, mere rubbish...written out from imperfect recollection'[76] suggests that his notion of the poem's organisation and development had by then become fixed. As already noted, Skeat could have corrected his earlier oversight in the Parallel-Text edition; and, given the peculiar textual problems of a multi-version poem surviving in multiple copies, the necessity to do so was matched by a singular opportunity. But he was never to re-consider **A** in the light of Bodley 851's unique text. Skeat's EETS volume, the *editio princeps* of the **A** Version, with its original spelling, paragraphing, side-notes and introduction, nonetheless represents a great advance on its predecessors. Over thirty of his emendations to the base-text (whether Vernon, Trinity or Rawlinson) have stood the test of time and witness to his taste and understanding.[77] But the edition is now of mainly historical interest, and a measure of its inadequacy is that the first two twentieth-century Langland texts undertaken for editing should both have been of **A**.

§ 36. Skeat's B-Text of two years later is much superior, and it may still be regarded as a usable 'conservative' edition of the poem's only completed version. His base-manuscript Laud Misc 581 (L) has not been favoured by most recent twentieth-century editors.[78] But by contrast with the drawbacks he laboured under with both **A** and **C**, Skeat had access from the start to nearly all extant **B** witnesses. The exception is the *Sion College* manuscript, which was found as recently as 1966, but is a corrupt modernised copy of no use for editing.[79] However, Skeat managed to omit from his list of manuscripts, which is numbered consecutively through the versions, the **B** portion of the conjoint Harley 3954, which he had described and dismissed in his *A-Text*[80] and completely ignored in editing **B**. This copy, though contaminated from **A**, is now acknowledged to contain some readings with a good claim to be original, and has at least the value of a collateral authority.[81] But more than compensating for this omission is Skeat's effective recognition of the existence of two **B** traditions, one represented by Laud and the remaining copies except Corpus 201, and one by Rawlinson Poetry 38, of which copy he happily discovered some missing leaves in *BL Lansdowne 398* (joint sigil R).[82] Skeat did not attempt a genealogical classification of the **B** manuscripts, any more than he had done for **A**. But he recognised the affinity between both Wright's manuscript (W) and Crowley and that between the eight copies with the current sigils G, Y, O, C², C, Bm, Bo (= *Sk* B) and Cot (= *Sk* B.M.).[83] And of the relations between the last three, which K–D assign the joint sigil B, he gave a basically correct preliminary account.[84]

§ 37. Though Skeat had ignored ms Bodley 851 (Z) as relevant to establishing the text of **A**, he observed the 'peculiarities' of ms *Corpus 201* (F), a **B** copy in some ways comparable to Z, and he recorded in detail its eccentric passus-divisions (pp. xxviii–xxx). But though Skeat did not perceive that F is descended from the same common original as R, he did note (*pace* Brewer)[85] how F agrees with R at XIV 189 in the important right reading *pouke* against *pope* in L and the rest. It is nonetheless unfortunately true that, while he found F 'worth consulting in a case of difficulty' (p. xxx), Skeat gave no thought to the source of its good readings. But as these are many more than he realised, the oversight had adverse consequences, given that R remains incomplete even after the addition of the separated Lansdowne leaves. The main losses in L occur at XIX 56–9, 237a–38b and 337, where Skeat's omission of some evidently original lines preserved only in F leaves his B-Text defective. However, his bold step of incorporating Rawlinson's distinctive material in its entirety was wholly justifiable, even though his judgement of R as a **B** Version '*with later improvements and after-thoughts*' (p. xii), recently revived by Taylor and others, is rejected in the present edition.[86] Skeat's view of R can become tortuous, as in relation to X 291–303, lines present in both R and **A** but missing from all other **B** manuscripts except F. These, he maintains (pp. 406–07), were 'first cut out' but 'on second thoughts' retained, whence they reappeared in the C-Text in a different part of the poem [i. e. at V 146–55]. Skeat's is a much more complicated explanation than that of K–D, who argue that the lines were lost from the RF ('α') tradition by mechanical error.[87] His notion of Langland's compositional methods is nonetheless one that for Brewer (if not for the present editor) has 'a good deal to recommend it.'[88] Whatever the case, it seems clear that Skeat's interpretation of Rawlinson inhibited him from comparing it closely with Laud (L) and thus from acquiring manuscript authority to correct many errors that L shares with the other members of its family 'β' (see *Introduction* III, *B Version* §§ 41–3). It is evident, too, that while he recorded R's variants and compared the readings of his chosen **B** witnesses with those of the other versions, he did not see the significance of the frequent agreement of **A** and **C** with R against L and the remaining β copies. Thus at IV 94 *Thanne gan Mede to* meken *hire, and* mercy she bisou3te, L's *mengen* is challenged on intrinsic grounds by R's *meken* supported by all other versions, including Z (which of course Skeat ignored). His notion of R as a 'transition stage' between **B** and **C** (p. xii) would here require Langland's supposed 'afterthought' to have been either a restoration of **A** or an anticipation of **C**, a possible explanation but not the most economical available (cf. *Introduction* IV, *Editing the Text*, § 2). Though at times he corrected the text from other versions where his base-manuscript was hopelessly corrupt, Skeat did not systematically weigh L's readings against R's in the light of **A** and **C**. So when he draws on R to emend a reading attested by the other **B** copies, as at X 429a (*Sunt* for *Siue*), his emendation is on grounds of common sense and does not appeal to **C**'s authority for additional support.

§ 38. Skeat included as an appendix a sixteenth-century glossary found in manuscript *CUL Ll. 4. 14* and written in a hand that he suggests may be Crowley's.[89] As in his *A-Text*, he gives side-notes with helpful page-references to parallel passages and also the sources of Langland's abundant Latin quotations. His Critical Notes contain interesting comparisons with **C**, as at XIII 152–56 (on Patience's riddle) and 293–99, in relation to R as 'a copy of the B-Text with all the latest additions' (p. 411). But most notable is his very full record of the variants of *Cr¹* and many of its annotations, while his detailed account of it on pp. xxxi–xxxvi of the Preface usefully reprints Crowley's Address to the Reader entire. Skeat's textual notes often display shrewd insight, as at X 366 (*Sk* 368) where he supports his judgement of *non mecaberis* (*slee noȝt*) as 'the author's own mistake' by apt reference to A XI 254 = *Sk* 247. At XIX 434 = *Sk* 428 likewise, his restoration of L's deleted *pur* in *pursueth*, though made primarily on the basis of the five **B** witnesses collated, takes proper account of parallel **C**.

§ 39. Judged as a whole, Skeat's edition of **B** has lasting value as an accurate print of Laud Misc 581 supplemented by the distinctive portions of the almost equally important Rawlinson copy. Its success is due partly to his having had access to all the manuscripts, but much more to his skill in producing a text that is intelligently 'conservative' without being rigidly positivistic. Its impact was considerable, particularly through the annotated *editio minor* of Prologue–Passus VII (the '*Visio*') based on it, which provided the first taste of Skeat's remarkable abilities as a commentator.[90] Continuously in print until replaced by Bennett's Clarendon edition of 1972, the latter made *Piers Plowman* accessible to a far wider audience than the subscribers who read the parent work. The complete *B-Text* was incorporated without change into the Oxford edition and became the basis of nearly all interpretative studies for a century.[91] In his Preface, Skeat maintained that 'of the three forms of the poem in its integrity, the B-Text is the best' (p. xl). This view became universal and was to be repeated over a century later by the present editor,[92] though it can no longer be maintained without qualification in many respects. Whatever the case, as the next four paragraphs will bear out, the best of Skeat's three EETS editions is undoubtedly his text of **B**.

§ 40. The EETS edition of the C-Text appeared in 1873, accompanied by *Richard the Redeless,* which Skeat ascribed to Langland, and *The Crowned King*, which he regarded as an imitation[93] (only the latter judgement finds support today).[94] The unique text of *Richard* survives along with the glossed **B** copy (C²) in manuscript CUL Ll. 4. 14 (see § 38 above).[95] Skeat's arguments for this poem's Langlandian authorship are weak, his point about the *f / v* alliteration it shares with *Piers* probably confusing metrical idiolect with dialect.[96] But as noted at § 23, the attention attracted to *Richard* by its inclusion with *Piers* perhaps offsets Skeat's unfortunate following of Crowley in treating as Langland's a piece of accomplished imitation. Both works have been omitted since the 1959 re-issue of the *C-Text*, which contains corrections by J. A. W. Bennett of its mistranscriptions and the original Critical Notes, but not Skeat's one-hundred pages of prefatory material. As Bennett rightly states,[97] much of the latter remains in concise form in the Parallel-Text Introduction; but omitting its valuable 30-page description of the manuscripts (*C-Text* xix–li) rendered the reprint much less useful than that of the (unchanged) EETS B-Text. Also removed in 1959 was Skeat's pioneering comparative account of the versions (pp. lxxvi–xciv) and his critique of Whitaker's edition (li–lxiii), as lengthy as the treatment of Crowley in his edition of **B**. All references to his *C-Text* here are accordingly to the first edition of 1873.

§ 41. By this time, Skeat understood the poem's text far better than when he embarked on **A**; but he regrettably did not have access to all the important **C** manuscripts as when working on **B**. The C Version is now recognised as surviving in two main recoverable lines of transmission, described below as 'x' and 'p', of which the **x** tradition is much the better (see *Introduction* III, *C Version* §§ 62–4). Skeat knew several examples of both, and as many as ten of the twenty-two copies he described were of the **x** type. They are *Ilchester* (I), *Digby 102* (Y), *Additional 34779,* formerly Phillipps 9056 (P^2), *Douce 104* (D), *Bodley 814* (B), *Cotton Caligula A xi* (O), *Additional 10574* (L), *Trinity Cambridge R. 3. 14* (T), *Harley 6041* (H^2) and *Digby 145* (D^2).[98] But of these the last six are conjoint copies and the first four variously imperfect or damaged. Moreover, of the three extant **x**-type copies complete enough for consideration as a base-text, Skeat knew only Douce 104, which he judged (p. xlvi) an inferior member of 'the same sub-class as I and T' [i. e. the **x** family]. Of the other two that might have impressed him more favourably, *Additional 35157* (U) was acquired by the British Museum more than twenty years after Skeat's text appeared, and *Huntington 143* (X) came to light only as late as 1924.[99] Not surprisingly, therefore, Skeat based his text on a **p** manuscript, of which he knew thirteen of the sixteen surviving copies, over half of them complete. The eleven Skeat described were *Phillipps 8231*, now *Hm 137* (P), *Laud 656* (E), *Trinity Dublin D. 4. 1* (V), *Royal 18 B xvii* (R), *Cotton Vespasian B xvi* (M), *CUL Ff. 5. 35* (F), *Corpus Cambridge 293* (S), *CUL Dd. 3. 13* (G), *Digby 171* (K), *Harley 2376* (N) and the conjoint *Bodley 851* (Z). A second conjoint text, the *Westminster* manuscript (W, now York, University Library, Borthwick Add. MS 196) was to be described only in an Index of Additions in Part IV of the completed work (1885).[100] Having chosen P as his base-text, Skeat collated four other **p** manuscripts E, M, F and G, resorting also to S where G was defective. But while appreciating the **p** copy Z's **C** portion 'as furnishing collateral evidence' (p. xxxiii) for emendations to P made 'after collation with other MSS' (p. xxxii), he declined to cite Z in his apparatus (see further § 44). Of the **x** manuscripts, Skeat collated I and T throughout; but again, though noting that Digby 102 (Y) belonged to the 'IT sub-class' (p. xlvii), he passed it over. This was unfortunate, since this manuscript descends from a superior branch of the family now best represented by the complete copies X and U (*Intro.* III, *C Version* § 17).

§ 42. Skeat's *C-Text*, with an apparatus, summarising side-notes, and versional cross-references, now to both earlier texts, gives some sense of being 'parallelistic' in spirit if not in form. But his comparisons with **A** and **B** had no consistent critical impact on his editorial practice. Thus at Prologue [= *Sk* Passus I] line 41 Skeat replaces *tho gomes* PS by *god wot* from MF with no indication that this is also the **AB** reading, a fact which might be thought to have prompted scribal contamination. But *tho gomus* is certainly the archetypal reading, of which *wrecches* E and *gromes* N are scribal replacements of a neutral by a more hostile term. Skeat might have avoided emendation had he checked an accessible **p** copy such as R or an **x** copy like D. This he should have done, since both I and T are useless here, one being a jumbled **AC** composite in the opening, the other an A-Text, while Y does not begin until II 157. Skeat also ignored manuscript B at this point, citing few readings from it on the grounds that it 'cannot be much depended on' (p. xxxix). Quite possibly, it was instinctive distrust of B as a conjoint text that deterred him from ascertaining the quality of its **C** portion through comparison with other copies. But in this case he would have found B to agree not only with the 'IT type' manuscript D but also with the **p**-type manuscript R. Skeat thus adopts *god wot* simply because he prefers it, neither recording the weight of support for his base-text's reading nor suspecting that M and F could be contaminated from **B**, as they very probably are.

§ 43. Skeat's 'eclectic positivism' is illustrated at Pr 72, where for PE *bulles* (again the probable archetypal reading) he substitutes *breuet* from I and M,[101] a reading shared also by B (in this case arguably through contamination from the **B** Version). But he gives no reason for preferring *breuet*, whether for its superior sense, or because supported by **B**, or for both reasons. Earlier in the same line, by contrast, Skeat accepts **p**'s *blessed* where **x** has *bounchede* (known to him through I), a reading which seems more likely to be original than to be a sub-archetypal contamination from **B**.[102] But he would probably not have adopted *bounchede* even had he been aware that X and U here agree with I, since that reading is in fact attested by the other **x** copies P[2], D and B, which he knew. For Skeat generally seems to have relied not on 'critical' comparison but on personal taste and the privileged witness of his base-manuscript, as is illustrated by his unwise retention of **p**'s *vnwyse* at l. 49. At this point, manuscript I is unavailable to endorse M's superior alternative *wyse*; but had Skeat observed how M is supported by R, a **p** copy not suspect of contamination, comparison with the **x** witnesses B, P[2] and D might have made him recognise in *vnwyse* a scribal flattening of an original identical with **A** and **B**.[103] The number of such 'flat-tened' readings in P and its frequent padding-out of the text[104] have helped to form the still current opinion of **C** as poetically inferior to **B**. So it is ironic that Skeat should have been the first to reach that conclusion and his 'standard' edition be responsible for others' coming to share it.

§ 44. Skeat's edition of **C** is thus of limited value by comparison with his **B** (though, unlike his **A**, it does not contain any plainly spurious lines). This is mainly because he took insufficient account of the **x** family witnesses available to him and rarely corrected errors in P from G, K and N, which he was unaware belong to a better branch of **p** than EVRMFSZ (to name just those he used).[105] Skeat's suggestion that P and Z were both made 'from an early copy of the poet's own autograph copy' (p. xxiv; cf. pp. xxx) has no real basis. All the same, Brewer has no cause to wonder why Skeat, given his belief that Z was 'even more correct in its readings than P' (p. li), 'did not take [Z] as his copy-text in preference to P;'[106] for since its **C** portion begins only at Passus X, this manuscript is intrinsically unsuitable. But as with his view of the **B** copy R's 'intermedi-ate' status, which still has supporters (see § 37 above), there is little to be said for Skeat's opinion of Ilchester as 'clearly an earlier draught of the C-Text' (p. xxxvii).[107] Nor is there for Brewer's recent commendation of Skeat's view that ms I represents a separate branch of the **C** tradition as 'confirmed by later scholarship'; it is not.[108]

§ 45. The final part of Skeat's edition appeared in two sections.[109] Of these the first (1877) contained Notes to the three versions, Indexes to the notes and a Bibliography. The second (1884) had a Glossary, General Preface, Proper-Name Index and chronologically-arranged List of His-torical References to the poem, together with a revised form of the initial Parallel Extracts, which now brought the project full circle. Though these nearly thousand pages have dated in many respects, their positive qualities far outweigh the shortcomings of the earlier volumes. Skeat's explanations show a profound grasp of the poem's historical meaning and an even more impres-sive understanding of its copious and idiosyncratic language. The Glossary alone, produced without the aid of modern historical dictionaries or concordances, but clearly organised, comprehensive, etymological and indexed, makes the fourth part an invaluable resource. It shows Skeat as by natural leaning more of a lexicographer than a textual critic. This fourth part has been mined by later editors without the leisure or capacity to replicate his painstaking researches. Only Bennett has surpassed Skeat in the range and depth of his first-hand enquiries into the poem's sources and background; but his commentary unfortunately covers only B Prologue–Passus VII. Skeat's notes and glossary, though geared to the C-Text, refer to parallel passages in the other versions and annotate matter unique to them. This arrangement helped greatly to shorten the time he was to spend on the final work that rounded off his twenty-year stint as an editor of *Piers Plowman*.

§ 46. The two-volume Oxford Parallel-Text of 1886 made the poem available in the format of a classic 'standard edition' rather than one for Middle English specialists.[110] Skilfully condensing the material in the earlier six volumes, it contained little that was new. The Notes kept the essence of the EETS fourth part, while dispensing with illustrative material that was occasionally super-fluous even in the original setting. The Glossary omitted all but a few select etymologies and the abundant orthographic variants, but still occupies nearly thirty per cent of the second volume. By contrast, textual discussion was drastically limited to a brief description of the manuscripts and the editions of Crowley and Wright. The ten pages Skeat gave to *Richard the Redeless* could have been better spent bringing to bear on the text of *Piers Plowman* the comprehensive knowledge of all three versions he had lacked at the start of the project. His failure to do so may have been due to a wish to complete the work with a minimum of delay; but it is perhaps not surprising that he felt no need to re-think the C-Text, as he might have done if manuscripts X and U had already come to his attention.

§ 47. With the **B** and **C** Versions on facing pages and **A** running across the upper portions of both, the layout of the Clarendon Press text-volume is a triumph of simplicity and clarity. Skeat also had the inspired idea of printing again, in smaller type, material in **B** and **A** that was trans-posed in **C**, as well as **C** passages moved a significant distance from their previous positions, par-ticularly in Passūs XI and XIII of **B**. His treatment of the accidentals is ambivalent, using a raised medial point for the manuscripts' variously-shaped metrical markers, and only half-heartedly modernising letter-forms, replacing *þ* with *th* but retaining *ȝ*. Skeat's textual apparatus records the rejected reading of the base-manuscript and the source of the variant adopted; but the absence of even an abbreviated equivalent to the EETS Critical Notes is a lack. The result (doubtless unin-tended) is to make the text appear more certain than, by this stage, he knew it both was and would have seemed with fuller apparatus and textual annotation. These reservations aside, the edition fully deserved its warm reception. What it did above all was to make clear to a wider audience that Langland's work was not marginal, but belonged with Chaucer's at the centre of medieval English literature. No later editor of *Piers Plowman* has achieved as much.

v. *Towards a Critical Edition*

§ 48. Skeat's edition was nonetheless found wanting within a generation of its completion, as a result of major advances in the understanding of the textual traditions. In 1909 R. W. Cham-bers accordingly embarked on a new EETS edition of **A**, the obvious starting-point, as this was the least satisfactory of Skeat's three texts. It was never achieved, but the editorial principles put forward in an important article of that year with J. G. Grattan, a sort of equivalent to Skeat's 1867 pamphlet on the manuscripts, had far-reaching effects.[111] Chambers and Grattan initially con-ceived their text along expanded Skeatian lines, aiming to use as its base either *Rawlinson Poetry 137* (R) or *Trinity Cambridge R. 3. 14* (T), 'with collations of all the other MSS.'[112] But their arti-cle recognised, as Skeat had not, the observed fact of scribal 'improvement' and the consequential obligation for an editor to prefer the better of two available variants instead of adhering to the base-manuscript's reading except where it was plainly mistaken or nonsensical. What they really desiderated was a 'critical' edition, arrived at through comparing the readings of all witnesses so as to establish a family tree of their textual relationships.[113] Such was also the aim of T. A. Knott, the American scholar whose important article of 1915 criticised both the 'older' (Skeatian) eclecticism guided by personal taste and the new approach of Chambers and Grattan, who applied their analysis of the internal and external evidence of readings only to some manuscripts and not to others.[114] Knott also wished to use the Trinity manuscript, but as what is more accurately called a copy-text, being 'little more than the basis for spelling and dialect.'[115] The main difference between Chambers and Knott seems to lie in their views of how the genealogical method would operate in relation to the *Piers Plowman* manuscripts. Knott believed that persistent agreement in significant errors indicated their clear presence in the copy from which the manuscripts agreeing derived. Chambers wished to accord due importance to contamination, coincidence and change of exemplar as causes of the convergent variation in the witnesses that obscures vertical transmission and thereby hinders the construction of a stemma.

§ 49. Neither side brought out an A-Text, and their disputes can seem after nearly a century exaggerated in their espousal of supposedly antithetical standpoints. But the differences in theory have had a real bearing on subsequent editorial practice, even though, if Chambers' observation is limited mainly to minor variants, it will be seen to complement rather than contradict Knott's, which holds of major readings. The Chambers-Grattan approach was taken up and developed by George Kane as editor of the Athlone Press A-Text; and an edition of Knott's A Pr–VIII was published by D. C. Fowler, who completed the work by editing Passūs IX–XII himself. The competing views of editing now seem after a century in some ways matters of emphasis more than of irreconcilable principles. Chambers-Grattan and Knott-Fowler were each partially right about the text of Langland. Thus it now seems uncontroversial first, that selecting even the variants on which to classify manuscripts necessitates a measure of editorial 'judgement' and second, that extension of this judgement towards the making of 'critical' decisions cannot be dismissed as the mere exercise of 'personal taste', when its grounds are explicitly stated and rationally defended. For it is obvious that textual arguments to support the preferred readings in a poetic text cannot attain the impersonality possible in the case of legal or theological writings; nor should they be expected to. At the same time, the gradual emergence of variational groupings will affect assessment of the stemmatic weight of variants judged 'significant' on intrinsic grounds. But however hard a 'critical' editor may aim at theoretical consistency, the value of the text achieved will depend to a great degree on the strength of the argument for each specific choice of reading; and with major readings it is usually possible to make a genuine case. This case cannot exclude 'personal taste', but can recognise it openly in order to control it by reference to more objective criteria (on what these criteria might be, see further IV, *Editing the Text* §§ 14–22 below). Editorial decisions should ideally be neither mechanical nor arbitrary; but the reasoning behind them, however convincing, will often fall short of demonstration. This said, the true test of an editorial method's worth is not the absolute consistency of the theory it exemplifies but the credibility of the text it produces. It is not the text that is validated by the theory but the theory that is vindicated by the text. There may be a real, if limited, analogy here between critical editing and experimental science; but the crucial question with both is, does it work? The theory underpinning an editorial method should be as rigorous and lucidly expounded as the nature of its object allows, and that has at least been the present editor's aim. But if what has just been said is true, the determining 'test' of the arguments in part IV of this *Introduction* and in the *Textual Notes* must be the edited text presented in Volume I. In the end, a good edition will meet the needs of a specific readership; a better will serve several classes of reader; the best will be one that most nearly satisfies the largest number of different kinds of reader.

vi. *The* Knott-Fowler *Edition of the* A-Text

§ 50. To meet the needs particularly of the student rather than the specialist was the clear aim of the first modern Langland edition, although its critical apparatus (called 'Textual Notes') will interest primarily the latter. The Knott-Fowler A-Text (*K–F*) has the advantage of being based on all the extant **A** manuscripts, of which it gives a concise account. The three copies that remained unknown to Knott as to Skeat became available for Fowler to use in completing Knott's work: *National Library of Wales 733B* (N), *Society of Antiquaries 687* (M) and *Liverpool University F. 4. 8*, the 'Chaderton' manuscript (Ch).[116] Additionally at hand from the outset was the Ingilby ms (J), which ranks with M and Rawlinson Poetry 137 (R) as one of the three most important **A** copies. The *K–F* Textual Notes are printed at the end, an arrangement that has drawbacks but allows a full and clear presentation. So, for example, at I 127, II 83, IV 24, 61 (the last a major crux) the variants may be inspected even more conveniently than if the manuscripts were directly before the reader; produced half a century before electronic technology, K–F's textual data remain useable and useful. They include a valuable list of lines absent from each copy, and all variant rubrics (a feature omitted by Athlone **B** and **C**). Their main presentational defect, which they share with Athlone, is to provide sigils only for the variants and not for the manuscripts supporting the lemma. Requiring the reader to work out the strength of manuscript support for the reading preferred, this was a needless economy, given the generous layout adopted. But while the variants recorded are 'only a selection', the criteria for inclusion are (sensibly enough) 'wherever the critical reading is not readily apparent' or 'deviates from the reading of T' (p. 171). However, the want of 'critical notes' like Skeat's (and Kane's) is felt, since K–F's Introduction gives under ten pages to textual questions (their editorial principles, having been sketched at §§ 12–13 above, will not be described again). Textual information is therefore largely located in the genealogical trees on pp. 26 and 27, two being provided because three copies (H, E, L) fail, while one (N) ceases as an **A** witness before Passus IX, and because K–F see the *Visio* and *Vita* as distinct parts of the poem, though not as different works that circulated separately.[117]

§ 51. Knott-Fowler's section on Historical Background, seven times the length of that on the poem, belongs in spirit to the age of Skeat, in effect ignoring the important recent studies of its thematic content and literary character[118] (it was to be a generation before the fruits of twentieth-century literary criticism enriched the introduction and annotation of editions aimed at the non-specialist).[119] Their text is more attractive than Skeat's with its border of side-notes or Kane's later with its austere lack of paragraphing. The replacement of obsolete letter-forms and avoidance of square brackets around readings that depart from the copy-text combine to render the work as accessible as Chaucer's in a modern standard edition. Of these two economies (one followed by the Everyman, the other by the York edition), the second is linked to the editors' refusal of conjectural emendation. But while this decision lessens the need for 'critical notes,' the absence of any sign of intervention by the editors unintentionally conceals their avoidance rather than solution of textual difficulties. As will emerge,[120] K–F's classification of the manuscripts is also unsatisfactory. They find three lines of descent from the 'original' (either archetype or holograph): *x*, from which descend V (Skeat's base-text) and its genetic twin H; *y*, ancestor of all the other **A** manuscripts; and *z*, source of the **A** material preserved in the **B** Version (whether or not revised). However, as will be shown (III, *A Version* § 14ff), K–F's 'x' has the same common ancestor (to be designated r^2) as five of their 'y' copies, I [J], L, Di [K], W and N; the manuscripts T, H^2, Ch, D, R and U possess an exclusive common ancestor (r^1); and both r^1 and r^2 derive independently from one sub-archetypal source (to be designated **r**). Secondly, **r**'s line of descent is wholly distinct from that of K–F's 'minor' group EAMH^3 (called **m** at §§ 24ff below, and there argued to be far from minor). Thirdly, both **r** and **m** stand in immediate independent descent from a single archetype (Ax). Finally, Ax's errors show that it cannot be the author's original. This last point implies that some conjectural emendation may be inescapable in a genuinely 'critical' edition once the archetype has been arrived at. But in K–F's text the dagger of corruption is no more in sight than the bracket of correction. Their basic grouping of the manuscripts needs no significant modifications; but to judge from the edited text, it matters little that their identification of the sub-archetypes is faulty or that, given the lack of direct dependence of any extant copy upon another, neither diagram looks like a true stemma. For K–F evidently do not pay much heed to the constraints of the genealogy; and so if their text reveals a 'y' rather than an 'x' character, it is not because they have shown x to be secondary (derived from y), but because they have preferred the y readings on intrinsic grounds. The stemma has little to do with K–F's frequent rejection of r^1 readings, either where r^2 or where r^2**m** retain presumed archetypal readings from which r^1 diverges. But as they do not recognise **m**'s independent descent, they not surprisingly dismiss readings found *only* in **m**, whether or not x and y here agree, although comparison with the other versions shows these readings as very likely to be archetypal (see III, *A Version* § 48).

§ 52. To illustrate this last point more fully: in about 160 instances (nearly seventy of them major) where the present edition follows *K–F*,[121] 33 are r^2 readings, and in 20 of these r^2 is accompanied by **m**.[122] In some cases, however, the stemma has only partly influenced the choice of variant, and does not explain the variant rejected. Thus at II 83 *of mendis engendrit*, r^2 is supported by **B** but has been wholly corrupted in x, which has *a Mayden of goode* (the reading accepted by Skeat). This example would appear to confirm K–F's view of M as belonging to y, since its variant *for monnys engendryng* looks like a further smoothing of N's nonsensical *of mennis engendrid*, a misreading of *mendes*. However, the postulate of a y-family reading distinguishable from x is contradicted by *fendis* r^1, of which E's *frendis* is a corresponding smoothing. This, of course, is one case where dependence of both r^1 and M upon r^2 could plausibly be maintained, and the beginnings of a true stemma discerned. But since both r^1 and **m** are later found to be right against r^2, e. g. at (*a*) X 214 *same*] *schrewe*, with support from **B** (= K–F's source z), neither can be inferred to derive from r^2. Secondly, since r^1 is uniquely right at (*b*) XI 19 *construe* against both r^2 *conterfeteth* and **m** (*om*), r^1 cannot derive from either. Lastly, since **m** (supported by **B**) is uniquely right at (*c*) I 106 *mene*] *om* **r**, group **m** cannot be descended from r^1 or r^2. The r^2 variant (*a*) *schrewe*, which K–F properly reject, tells against their x / y division, since it is attested by both V and two of their y copies J and K. So they must be presumed to prefer *same* on 'other' (non-genealogical) grounds such as intrinsic character, majority support and the witness of **B**. In example (*b*), where K–F read *conterfeten*, their sole criterion must be intrinsic quality, since the majority have *construe* (the r^1 reading) and *contreuen* appears in only one **A** witness, K [Di], which they no doubt diagnose as contaminated from **B** or **C**. Here K–F's procedure is not easily distinguishable from either Kane's 'direct method' or Skeat's 'eclecticism'; and this is unfortunately a case where none of the editors explain their choice in a note.

§ 53. The last instance discussed illustrates K–F's inadequate notion of the poet's metre, which adversely affects their text in several places. For in following the majority reading here and ignoring the evidence of **m**, they are led to include among their acceptable 'variations' on Langland's 'basic pattern' [of *aa / ax*] the demonstrably inauthentic *aa / bb* (p. 16), despite the fact that the reading of **m** [= their T^2M] is here supported by **B** [= their source z]. It is partly owing to this defective understanding that K–F have no incentive to emend archetypal readings on metrical grounds. A notable such example is at V 200 *þrumblide*, where the reading of V *þrompelde* would actually support their view of x as a family directly derived from the archetype. But in choosing *stumblide* they seem unhappily misled by the presence of this unmetrical substitution-error in most **B** copies and in Skeat's C-Text, though the probable **C** and the possible archetypal **B** reading supports Vernon (and may be its source). K–F's unawareness of **m**'s critical significance[123] allows them not only to print an unmetrical form of VII 270 (and to accept another spurious pattern *aa / xa* at p. 16) but even to omit the AMH^3 variant from their textual notes (p. 231). If they thus overlook **m**, it comes as no surprise that, following Skeat and anticipating Kane, they make neither use nor mention of **Z**, a text which, as Rigg-Brewer were to show, cannot be ignored by an editor of the **A** Version. Neglect at I 110 of both **Z** and M (here the sole **m** witness) accordingly leaves their line with a metrical pattern of the form *ax / xa* found nowhere on their list.

§ 54. Many of these incoherences arise out of K–F's failure (like that of Kane after them) to edit the A-Text in the light of the other versions. This prevents them from formulating an empirically based theory of Langland's metre powerful enough to enable them to discriminate and correct scribal errors decisively. In part, the refusal to edit parallelistically may be due to K–F's belief that **B** was not written by the same author as **A**, although the Introduction remains uncommitted on this question. Where their text convinces, this is often due simply to the same good sense and feeling for style on which Skeat relied, but which Knott himself had called in question. Thus in so straightforward a case as Pr 44 *þo Robertis knaues* K–F presumably adopt the minority variant *þo* of H^2LM against that of their copy-text and the majority not because it appears archetypal (VH *þese* arising from *þo* and not from *as*) but simply because it gives sharper sense in the context. A similar instance is *Fayteden* Pr 42 as against *Flite þan* of the copy-text T and the whole r^1 subfamily supported by E and the r^2 manuscript K. Here such factors as the **BC** reading might have played a part in their decision; but without significant support from the variants, the genealogy itself cannot have been criterial. For since V's *feyneden hem* is likely to derive homœographically from *fayteden*, K–F can have adopted the latter only on grounds of 'intrinsic' superiority.[124] In conclusion, when they are right or wrong, it is owing to a successful or unsuccessful act of 'personal judgement.' Their reasons are not given, but on evidence like that examined, the genealogical imperative cannot have been the strongest. If K–F's text is better than Skeat's, it is in part because they have tested many readings 'critically'; but if it is often preferable to that of Kane, whose method is more rigorous and consistent, this is in spite of their theory, not because of it. In that paradox lies a lesson any editor of Langland would do well to ponder.

vii. *The Athlone Editions:* Kane's *Edition of the* A-Text

§ 55. The Athlone edition of the A-Text edited by George Kane (1960), based once again on the Trinity Cambridge copy, is aimed at scholars. Its focus is so exclusively textual that it dispenses with the literary and historical discussion and the supplementary material on date and authorship found in Knott-Fowler and Skeat. Five years later, Kane showed in a magisterial monograph that all three versions were written by William Langland,[125] a conclusion accepted from the outset as fundamental to the idea of the present edition (see further Part V, §§ 1–6). But the 'parallel' principle played no direct part in Kane's editing, and had he offered a stemma it would presumably not have contained the source *z* postulated (and to some extent used) by K–F (see § 51). Thus, in defining **A**'s distinctive character, while Kane takes account of text absent from, echoed in or revised by **B** and **C** (p. 21), he ignores text present in **B** and / or **C** with no or with minimal alteration. By strict definition, material in this last category is not 'distinctive'; but that K–F were right to think it relevant to editing **A** is a conclusion that Kane, after working on **B**, was tacitly to acknowledge in his 1988 'Retrospect'.[126] Like K–F, Kane uses all the witnesses except Bodley 851; but his implied view of the latter as a corrupt scribal **A** copy does not save him in his initial sentence from misdescribing the 'first version' as preserved in seventeen manuscripts and one fragment; for counting Z, the number is eighteen. This is a rare error in a work that sets the standard of accuracy for subsequent editors (a point to remember when reading the criticism of it below).

§ 56. Kane's *A Version* is printed with an *apparatus criticus* at the foot of the page, critical end-notes and a long *Introduction* on the problems of editing the text. Even without this last, the Apparatus alone, which is lucidly explained and justified on pp. 170–72, is invaluable to any subsequent editor. It improves in intelligibility on K–F's in always placing after a lemma the source of a reading selected in preference to that of the Trinity manuscript. Unlike theirs, it is also a comprehensive corpus of variants (a luxury that a parallel-text format precludes). And while its dense columns crowd the page-space in a ratio of 2:1 with the text, the arrangement has such obvious advantages that it has been followed in the present edition. The overflowing fullness of the Athlone Apparatus is partly due to its including non-substantive variants that could have been omitted without loss: e.g. at I 26, after the lemma *shuldist* come the immediate source-reading *schuldest* and five variants, all non-significant and two purely orthographic (*scholdist; scholdest*). Despite its historical-linguistic interest, which shows the residual influence of Skeat, such material is unnecessary for understanding the basis of the edited text, except in a few ambiguous cases. Kane's omission of the **A** rubrics from his apparatus is not a problem here, since they are recorded for each copy in the section on the manuscripts. Moreover, they could arguably be regarded not as authorial but as part of the scribal layout (though no argument to this effect is offered). Nonetheless, since the rubrics can be examined to reveal how the poem's divisions were understood as far back as the archetypal stage, their absence from later volumes becomes a fault, and the present editor has judged it necessary to include and analyse them (Appendix II). The want of any cross-references to discussions of particular readings in the *Introduction* is made good in the *Critical Notes*, which comment on conjectural emendations and problematic cases of discrimination among variants. But the omission of such notes in subsequent Athlone editions becomes a source of frustration. Like the latter, **A** makes no reference in the apparatus to the scholars who first printed the readings adopted, a courtesy surely obligatory for a 'critical' editor using earlier solutions to a difficult text's many problems. Thus (except for Skeat's emendations in Passus XII) some fifteen readings adopted after the **A** Version's first editor receive no acknowledgement, while some fifty of Knott-Fowler's major readings (about two-thirds of those accepted in the present edition) have no sigil to compensate for the strictures to which K–F's edition is subjected in the Introduction (esp. pp. 90–114). The unhappily Olympian suggestion of owing nothing to any predecessor is one that an editor should be strenuously at pains to avoid.

§ 57. Kane's text outwardly resembles Skeat's rather than K–F's in keeping the original spelling while introducing modern punctuation (with some reluctance, as Kane notes on p. 170). But inconsistently it eschews paragraphing, an unhelpful practice repeated in later Athlone volumes even where the copy-text is paragraphed (T itself has none). This makes Kane's edition (*Ka* hereafter) harder to use than K–F's, which employs modern paragraphing, or Skeat's, which preserves that of the Vernon manuscript. Following traditional practice, square brackets enclose any reading that diverges from Trinity's. Although not a difficulty in **A**, this procedure becomes one in **B** and **C**, which have many more conjectural readings not derived from an extant source, but no cross-references or critical notes to provide any help. Since the Athlone editors treat each base manuscript as a copy-text chosen for completeness, linguistic consistency and orthographic regularity rather than for substantive superiority, there is little gain even for the specialist in signalling every departure from it indifferently. Brackets that constantly remind of the 'edited' character of the text may be salutary in discouraging undue confidence in the uniformity of the witnesses. But as used here, they obscure a textually important distinction between readings rejected as non-archetypal and archetypal readings judged unoriginal. The present edition has accordingly followed a *middel weie* between the 'cleared' Knott-Fowler and the 'cluttered' Athlone layout, using brackets only around readings unattested in *any* manuscript of the version in question (see IV § 51). There are aesthetic arguments for reducing visible signs of editorial intervention, but they rank after the need for an open (if discriminating) recognition of the copy-text's 'instrumental' character.

§ 58. Kane's *Critical Notes* throughout display more penetrating textual insight than can be found in Skeat's *A-Text*. Where dealing with recurrent minor features like *ful* for *wel*, they helpfully cross-refer (as on Pr 26) to discussion in his *Introduction* of a whole category of scribal substitutions. The notes on lexical variants sometimes do the same, as at X 136 where *mynchons* Ch is preferred to *martires* *r²***mBC** and the *r¹* reading *nonnes* is judged a scribal substitution for the former (on these sigla see *Introduction* III, *A Version*, §§ 1–5). Kane is certainly right (pp. 161–62) to say that this and the other Chaderton variants he favours 'stand or fall as a group', and thus to consider them together (for the argument that his assessment here is mistaken see here *Intro*. IV §§ 32–3 below and the relevant *Textual Notes*). But his treatment of major lexical variants can be unsatisfactory, as at Pr 34 where he adopts the Trinity / Chaderton reading *giltles* as 'the only possible original of all the variants' and as 'also metrically superior.' The first statement is demonstrably untrue and is formally rebutted in the present edition's note to this line. For the second, Kane gives no reason; and this proves a revealing weakness of the enterprise, since a later discussion in the Kane-Donaldson *B-Text*[127] will accept as authentic the metrical pattern *aaa / xx*, which is that of the majority (and probably archetypal) reading here in **A**. Finally, in adopting the variant *giltles*, Kane omits to mention that Wright used it to emend B Pr 36 on the assumption that three staves confined to the a-half are impermissible. Although K–D convincingly refute this notion, they nonetheless retain Kane's emendation in their text of **B**, again without acknowledging its first proponent. Such is the confusion besetting the editor who does not consistently tread the 'parallel' way which, though winding *by many a wente*, alone offers egress from the *wilde wildernesse* of scribal variants. For this example graphically displays the later Athlone theory as at once in conflict with the earlier Athlone practice and, paradoxically, as determined by it. Similar inconsistencies persist into Athlone **C** and are neither few nor negligible.

§ 59. The smooth functioning of Kane's introductory discussions, apparatus and critical endnotes indicates that this procedure should have been retained in Athlone **B** and **C**. The present edition therefore retains separate critical notes in this second volume so as to facilitate consultation alongside the parallel text, discussing problems of a particular version and others shared by more than one version together as they arise rather than subsuming them under general categories of scribal error. For a wider danger of the Athlone approach adumbrated in **A** becomes clear from considering a particular case mentioned above. It is partly his judging Chaderton's *mynchons* original that leads Kane to interpret the majority variant *martires* as evidence that Langland used a corrupt scribal copy of **A** in revising to **B**, which has the latter reading. Despite this troubling (and significant) implication, *martires* is nonetheless printed in the a-half of parallel B IX 112 [= *K–D* 114], possibly under influence from *martres* in the b-half of parallel C X 206 [= *R–K* 205]. Here, K–D's acceptance in **B** of an **A** variant that Kane diagnosed as scribal fails to cohere with their earlier retention of *giltles* in B Pr 34 against *synnelees* in the **B** archetype (Bx). It must therefore raise a doubt whether the poet's supposed use of a 'scribal' **A** manuscript (an *a priori* possibility) can satisfy the critical canon of economy of explanation (IV, §§ 19–21 below), as it ought. For if *synnelees* supported by **B** and *martires* supported by **BC** are both retained, the need to postulate a 'scribal revision copy' disappears. Now, in itself, a particular inconsistency may not invalidate use of this latter postulate in relation to the revision of **B** to **C**.[128] But it suggests a need for caution in invoking it; for consistency here would entail adopting the 'harder' *mynchons* not only in **A** but also in **B** and **C**, a step too radical even for the Athlone editors. What becomes evident is that, while each decision purports to depend on what they judge original for any one version by intrinsic criteria, such judgement verges on the arbitrary when exercised without disinterested examination of the parallel evidence *throughout*. The inadequacy of such an examination in the second and third Athlone volumes indicates the constraining, even constricting effect of the first of them.

§ 60. For any later editor, Kane's specific failures when editing **A** without regard to **B** and **C** obviously carry a warning, with an implied imperative. But other deficiencies were remediable from the outset on the basis of the **A** tradition alone. Most notably, the Athlone A-Text retains inferior **r** readings in the face of better ones in the family **m**, readings later adopted in the second edition of 1988 (Ka^2). Thus at V 256 [254] *seke*] **r**; *go to* **m** and VIII 100 *to helle shalt þu wende*] **r**; *þe deuel shal haue þi soule* **m** Kane prints lines with the metrical pattern *ax / ax* that he and his collaborators (unlike K–F and the present editor) consider inauthentic; but at VII 233 *Actif lif oper contemplatif*] **r**; *transposed* **m** (where **B** is at hand supporting **m**), Ka^2 abandons **r** for **m** to adopt a line with this same 'inauthentic' scansion. At VII 270 *cole plantis*] **r**; *trs* **m**, Ka^2 will reject **r**'s unmetrical *aa / xa* line for *plaunte coles* in accordance with K–D's emendation of the (possibly) archetypal text at B VI 285 [286]; yet support for the ultimately accepted reading was already available in an 'A' source independent of **m**, manuscript Z (at VII 290). However, since Kane had earlier overlooked this copy as a possible **A** witness (see § 54), it should hardly cause surprise that his 'Retrospect' ignores **Z**'s attestation of the reading he now considers correct (Ka^2 p. 461).

§ 61. These four cases do more than betray only the inconsistency that any editor would be wise to admit may be at times unavoidable. They reflect a deep incoherence in the Athlone approach to Langland's text that persists from Kane's **A** through the collaborative editions of **B** and **C**. Thus Ka^1's statement that corrections of such Ka^1 readings as VII 270 are based not only on other-version evidence but on better understanding of the poet's 'metrical practice and of the quality of archetypal manuscripts' is only partly true. For the witness of **m** at VII 290 implies that the *archetype* of **A** (Ax) was correct, and was accurately preserved in this one family. The presence of the presumed scribal reading *cole plantis* in both the **A** family **r** and in the **B** family β may, initially, suggest that Langland revised from a scribal copy of **A** and overlooked the unmetrical line. But this particular error, as argued in the *Textual Notes* on C VIII 309, is of a type that could easily have recurred independently in the archetype of **B** (Bx), which is in any case strictly indeterminable here in the absence of the α family witness. What is clear is that there lay to hand from the outset a reading superior in metre and 'harder' in sense that Kane could not recognise as such. This might have been because, like Knott-Fowler, he failed to discern in **m** a line of descent from Ax independent of **r**. But even Ka^1 not only prefers three major **m** readings supported by **B** (I 37, V 87, 243 [241]), it adopts two important ones (XI 195, 245) with no parallel in **B**. Kane's explicit response to the challenge of these lines in the original Critical Notes stops short, however, at opining that the **m** copies 'were at some stage corrected' or that their right readings are 'due to restoration' and that it was 'the archetype of the surviving manuscripts' that was corrupt (*A-Text*, pp. 434, 441). This problematic notion of 'good correction' from a lost source superior to the archetype is one that the Athlone editors will invoke again in relation to both the **B** ms Corpus 201 (F) and the **C** ms NLW 233B (N^2). But as will be seen later, logically simpler explanations of these copies' right readings, such as contamination from the **A** and **B** traditions, are available without multiplying hypothetical entities beyond necessity. So here likewise in **A**, the postulate (III, *A Version* §§ 52–4) of **r** and **m**'s independent descent from a single archetype both explains the data economically and provides a firm basis for editing **A**. And it does this even before taking into account the witness of the other versions (including **Z**), which is confirmatory even where not indispensable.

§ 62. Three weaknesses are thus responsible for the edition's main lapses in congruity with the subsequent Athlone volumes. The first is Kane's failure to acknowledge **m** as a primary sub-archetypal branch of the **A** tradition, which contrasts markedly with the Athlone editors' later recognition of two independent lines of transmission in the longer versions.[129] There is of course no reason why the textual situation in **B** and **C** should have been reproduced in **A**, nor why 'good correction' of **m** should be ruled out in principle; for such correction is perceptible in the **A** tradition below the sub-archetypal level, e.g. in the group <TH^2Ch>. But since **m** consistently displays the same positive and negative characteristics of excluded, included, correct and incorrect material as later enable the Athlone editors to identify the sub-archetypal traditions of **BC**, there is little to favour a hypothesis that is intrinsically weaker by the canon of explanatory economy (see IV, §§ 19–21). More important, even Ka^2 apparently fails to grasp the significance of **m**. This is revealed by the *ad hoc* quality of Kane's comparison of the **m** readings that he adopts with those of **r** (pp. 461–62), as consultation of the present text will disclose.[130]

§ 63. The second weakness of Kane's editing lies in his unsatisfactory understanding of Langland's metre. This results in unmetrical archetypal lines printed without comment in 1960 being judged in 1988 to indicate that the poet 'once or even twice missed or did nothing about them' (Ka^2, p. 463), with the consequence that the editor need do nothing about them either. But if the ten lines Kane lists[131] are examined in the present edition together with the textual notes discussing them, their value as evidence that Langland used a scribal **A** manuscript for his **B** revision virtually disappears. Only three contain assured archetypal errors, and that two of these might have recurred coincidentally in archetypal **B** will hardly strain belief.[132] Nor are these the only incongruities; for lines left metrically defective in Ka persist unnoticed in Ka^2, though all may be corrected on the evidence of **m** and / or (an)other version(s), and still others may be emended by unadventurous conjecture.[133]

§ 64. The third defect in Kane's edition relates to the witness of manuscript Bodley 851, where Ka^2's support of Ka's silent dismissal of Z as 'useless for editing, if not actually misleading' (p. 459) proves a serious misjudgement. For at I 110, when Ka^2 diagnoses archetypal 'misreading of *l* as long *s*' and corrects *siȝt* to *liȝt* in the phrase *louelokest of liȝt*, Kane (whether in ignorance or defiance) overlooks that this is what Z reads. Now, even if Z were judged only an eccentric **A** copy, that would hardly make it more 'useless for editing' **A** than is, say, Corpus 201 for editing **B** or NLW 733B for editing **C**. For notwithstanding their gross corruptions, both those manuscripts win respect from the Athlone editors for their occasional 'superior' readings. So, if it registers a 'good correction' here, Z should merit similar recognition. But it could be, on the other hand, that Z is right because it preserves an authorial form of the poem *independent* of Ax, and of **A** itself, as Rigg-Brewer argue (and as will be maintained in *Intro*. III, *Z Version* §§ 1–12). Further significant information in **Z**'s version of line I 110 is also neglected by Kane; for the agreement of its b-half with the probable **m** form *Oure Lord seluen* obviates the need for his 'hard' scansion with two staves in *lóuelókest* by yielding a perfect line of standard metre. Loss of the last lift *seluen* in **r** is, moreover, mechanically ascribable to homoteleuton, since line 111 ends *hym*seluen. This example serves both to challenge Kane's understanding of **m** and his negative valuation of **Z**; but it has further implications for the Athlone text of **B**. For though K–D regard this line as archetypally lost from **B** (p. 205n154), they fail to observe that the form they conjecture is that of an extant manuscript. The distinction between ignorance and defiance now begins to look as fine as that between John Donne's 'air and angels'.

§ 65. Kane's *Introduction* is, nevertheless, outstandingly important for providing the most thorough account of the editorial process given to any Middle English text since *The Canterbury Tales* in the edition of Manly and Rickert.[135] Its description of the manuscripts, though more concise than Kane would have wished, is deficient only in omitting Bodley 851.[136] Equally exemplary in clarity and comprehensiveness is its discrimination of the poem's seven scribally-produced manuscript 'shapes' with **C** endings and interpolated **B** or **C** material from an authentic one characterised by 'some 400 lines not found in the other two versions' (p. 42). The scribal shapes are attested in seven copies, the authentic one in ten copies consisting of a prologue and eleven passūs (preserved in whole or part), and three containing some or all of a twelfth (Kane's conclusion, following K–F, that the latter passus was probably not in the archetype is accepted here). The 'literary examination' of XII deferred to another occasion remains unprovided in Ka^2. This lack is made good in the present edition, which finds XII authentic but for its last nineteen lines, and so differs from Ka and K–F in not treating it as an 'appendix' (III, *A Version*, §§ 65–71).

§ 66. In his classification of the **A** manuscripts, Kane rejects simple recourse to either the 'striking' or the 'commonplace' category of variants, respectively those designated 'major' and 'minor' readings in the present work (see IV §§ 25–36). This is because the first could be the product of 'correction' or conflation and the second of coincident variation. Abandoning classification with reference to selected variants, Kane also renounces editing on the basis of the resulting genealogy as proposed by Knott-Fowler. Instead, he treats major and minor variants alike at the classification stage and establishes his text after scrutinising all the variants so as to uncover 'the scribal tendencies of substitution' and thus determine the direction of variation from the authorial text. This way of identifying inauthentic readings depends on W. W. Greg's two-pronged criterion for recognising originality, according to which the preferred reading 'is itself satisfactory, and...explains the origin of the erroneous alternative' (p. 62).[137] A preliminary text obtained by applying this 'direct' method forms the required point of reference for Kane's subsequent analysis of the variational groups. Some groups are found very persistent, several less persistent and mutually conflicting, and over a thousand random, indicating conflation and / or coincident variation. Concluding that in these circumstances a stemma cannot be established, Kane proceeds to a summary and critique of K–F. He accepts some of their smaller variational groups as probably genetic but finds many more to conflict with the presumed genetic groups, and expresses scepticism about both the anomalous and the smaller, less stable groups they recognise. He ends by showing that, since K–F's division of their groups into two families x and y (see § 51) cannot be sustained, and the genetic relations between their constituents are qualified by 'an enormous amount of convergent variation...the use of recension for determining this text is unauthorised' (p. 68).

§ 67. Most of this section convincingly applies Greg's foundational editorial principle; but while Kane's judgement of many, perhaps most minor readings as coincidentally generated is plausible, few of the major ones can be convincingly shown to arise from conflation or 'correction' (sound or mistaken). Accordingly, there are no real grounds for rejecting a classification on the basis of some degree of selection, nor for assuming that, if K–F's stemma is unsustainable, no better one may be found on that basis (see *Intro.* III, *A Version*, § 5). For since the two categories of variants are qualitatively different, there are grounds for asking whether the major type generally may indicate genetic relationship, while the minor type may be in various instances (not always determinable) *either* genetic in origin *or* produced by random scribal substitution according to recognisable processes. But while in principle a classification by major readings alone might be expected to produce different groupings from one based on *all* readings taken together, in practice the differences turn out to be slight. This is because it is in minor readings, many or most of which are (as allowed) ascribable to coincidental variation, that numerically telling 'challenges' to postulated genetic groupings tend to occur. But where such challenges are major and conflation or 'correction' may or must be invoked, neither the number nor the proportion is ever significant enough to undermine the antecedent likelihood of a genetic relationship.[138] Kane's reasonable insistence (p. 68) that 'all conclusions about genetic relations' must be necessarily qualified, together with the fact (already recognised in K–F's stemma) that no **A** group or family ancestor derives from any other, effectively rule out recension as a sufficient means of 'fixing' the text. And these considerations also compel recognition of genetic evidence as 'only one of a number of available indications of originality' (p. 63). But such a conclusion does not entail that a recensional hypothesis is without indicative value, especially if based upon the evidence of *all major readings* taken as a distinct and comprehensive category. Nor, it need hardly be said, is it wholly at odds with K–F's opinion that the 'critical readings' are those 'attested in every case by the weight of evidence, genealogical and other.'[139] Kane's chief difference from his predecessors lies rather in his decision that those 'critical readings' are attainable 'without using recension' (p. 63), and in his attaching much less weight to the genealogical than to the 'other' evidence accumulated through discerning the 'direction' of scribal variation. Nonetheless, however skilfully this is applied, it remains doubtful to the present editor that such a 'direction' can be anywhere near as reliably ascertained for minor as for major readings as Kane appears to think (see *Intro.* IV, §§ 27 ff).

§ 68. Of enduring value in Kane's *Introduction* is his painstaking examination of variational groups made up of two to five witnesses. Since Kane's lemma is adopted after evaluating in the light of the genealogical evidence the readings initially produced by the 'direct method', it is obvious that different lemmata would generate a different number of readings within any group classed as 'variational.' This consideration, however, does not in itself render use of the method misleading, since the absolute number of agreements between any two or more manuscripts obviously cannot change. And while a lemma in itself contains no genetic information, and does not rigidly determine the composition of the groups, it is a valuable heuristic device for identifying, and a point of reference for classifying and displaying, readings relativistically designated 'variants'. It should moreover be observed that when, as it often does, the adopted text has (near)-unanimous manuscript support, it is antecedently likely to represent the archetypal reading.[140] Although Kane's agreements are sometimes miscounted to a not insignificant degree,[141] this section's accuracy and clarity make it indispensable. (The same holds good of the later Athlone editions, which follow the pattern laid down in **A**).

§ 69. Kane's most original contribution to the theory of editing is found in the account of his methods and resources. He begins uncontroversially enough by discussing the mechanical errors to which all scribes were prone through inattention, distraction and visual confusion from difficult copy. Under this category come larger errors of omission caused by similarity or identity of line-endings and beginnings (hom(œ)oteleuton; hom(œ)oarchy). But some are traceable to grammatical or semantic features of the authorial text that provoked copyists to shorten or simplify; and others are the scribes' deliberate substitution of their own words and phrases for those of the copy, through desire for what they considered greater correctness, intelligibility, emphasis or elegance (p. 128). Although an element of 'subjectivity' now starts to show through, Kane in practice vindicates his procedure by opening it to critical assessment at every stage. This is well shown in his analysis of the 'homœograph', the substitution of a word of similar shape for one the scribes found difficult for some reason. Two examples (p. 133) reveal Kane's general conviction that their main motive for altering the text was a wish to make it 'easier.' The likelier original will therefore be the *lectio difficilior*, the 'harder' reading that both gives satisfactory sense and explains the easier variant(s). This notion is central to the direct method of editing.

§ 70. In one example, for *kete* at XI 56, found only in manuscripts VKW, Kane recognises three variants as homœographic, *ked* DRU, *kid* TH[2]Ch and *cowrte* JA. A fourth he does not record here, though arguably *grete* MH[3] is no less a homœograph than *cowrte* (as acknowledged in his critical note, which conflicts with the list on p. 133) or else, like *cowrte*, a semantically-motivated replacement of *kete*, which looks unlikely to be a substitution for any of the others. This is a case where r^1 and the common original of MH^3 err disjunctively while Skeat's base-text Vernon (presumably following its immediate source) seems to preserve the original by direct descent: < v < r^2 < **r** < Ax < **A**. But the convergence of the genetically distinct **m** copy A with the r^2 copy J would seem to bear out Kane's belief that stemmatic relations based on major readings are distorted through scribal interventions in response to difficult sense. Here the context (*Clerkes and kete men*) indeed seems to have prompted copyists in two separate traditions to interpose a social group (nobles) conventionally associated with clerks, while another plausible category (the famous) has been introduced coincidentally by the scribes of D, <RU> and <TH^{2}Ch> or, more probably (given these copies' persistent affiliation), that of their exclusive common ancestor r^1. Such a complex situation invites more than one 'genetic' interpretation. Thus MH^3 may preserve **m**, and A may have replaced its reading with a term alliterating more exactly. Alternatively, **m** read *kete* and the MH^3 ancestor introduced one easier term, A another one that coincided with J's substitution for r^2's presumed correct reading *kete*. Where genealogical evidence is so ambiguous, it may indeed appear that only the direct method can suffice both to discriminate one reading as archetypal and to assess its originality.

§ 71. As it happens, in the above case of *kete clerkes* all four editors of **A** happily agree; but another of Kane's homœographs proves that significantly divergent conclusions may be reached even when applying the same method. It occurs at X 47, where for the majority reading *help* the group TH^{2}Ch have *halle*. Unlike the variants at XI 56, this must be considered only doubtfully a homœograph, since Kane's postulated original *allie* is not an extant variant but a conjecture (as is discoverable from a critical note cross-referring to the *Introduction*). Here, however, despite his acute analysis, Kane's emendation does not undermine Skeat's and K–F's belief that *help* is what the author wrote. The *Textual Notes* in the present edition should be consulted with a view to seeing if the variant *halle* can indeed be, as Kane insists, 'fairly accounted for'. But his judgement of *help* as a 'guess-gloss...very probably directed by [*help* in] line 49 below' (pp. 164–65) suffers from two weaknesses. Firstly, for *help* not to have been the archetypal reading (as Kane's explanation entails) assumes its fourfold coincidental substitution in the ancestors of D, RU and the unrelated r^2 and **m** (something theoretically possible). Secondly, however, if *halle* TH^{2}Ch is a homœograph, it must uniquely reflect the postulated archetypal reading *allie*. And that (unless 'superior correction' is invoked) could only have occurred via **r**, the exclusive ancestor this group shares with RU, D and r^2. The last three must therefore have coincidentally substituted a variant both distinct from the postulated archetype and further in form from it than that of TH^{2}Ch. This explanation, though historically possible, is much less economical than to see **r** as at once faithfully transmitted by RUDr^2 and as identical with **m**, and both traditions as here preserving Ax. That *help* should be both archetypal and original, far from being excluded, is arguably confirmed by its repetition at 49. What cannot be doubted is that, instead of its presence distracting from the effective operation of the direct method, as Kane holds, the lack of parallel evidence here measurably *lessens* the method's cogency. For while *allie* may in an absolute sense be 'harder' than *help,* it remains only a possibility, given that the majority reading is unexceptionable on grounds of sense and metre. This example illustrates what difficulties attend textual rationalism in the absence of other-version evidence, without which it is more or less hazardous to resort to reconstruction. (The wider aspects of the conflict between 'historical' and 'logical' approaches to textual problems will be touched on in IV § 36 below.)

§ 72. No less problematic are those substitutions that Kane traces to active scribal involvement in the content of *Piers Plowman* as 'a living text' (p. 136). He argues very convincingly that, since copyists who censored or toned down readings often needed to 'smooth' syntactical or metrical damage caused by their own interference, studying recurrent instances of this enables the editor 'to deduce the existence of several general tendencies of scribal substitution' (p. 143). That some manuscript readings may actually be 'author's variants,' however, Kane judges an undemonstrable hypothesis. Agreeing with this, the present editor would find it also an *unnecessary* one to account for what is more economically explained in terms of securely identifiable scribal variation alone. Pursuing the important question of the authority of the archetypal text, Kane argues (again very plausibly) that, while majority or even unanimous agreement does not in itself prove, it is a presumption of originality '*in the absence of all other considerations.*' Here he concedes that even the 'limited' results of genetic analysis 'may help to estimate the strength of the majority support' (p. 148). But Kane remains convinced that identifying scribal tendencies of substitution is the editor's 'final means of determining originality,' though he rightly sees his decisions as 'provisional only, subject to modification or rejection if further manuscript evidence should come to light' (p. 149). The laudably 'scientific' character of this conclusion should be acknowledged as a real advance in the theory of editing (see further IV, §§ 16–17 below).

§ 73. The foregoing account of the 'direct method' immediately raises an issue of principle that it is convenient to consider here, although Kane does not address it explicitly. Reliable identification of scribal 'tendencies' may be a major tool for discriminating the archetypal reading among conflicting variants; and archetypal readings may be capable of authentication by the same criteria. But the approach retains an *a priori* element in its presumption that 'authorial' characteristics *can* be securely recognised in being essentially different from those of 'scribal' variants. Thus several features of the poet's *usus scribendi* (his style, lexis and metre) are appealed to as criterial for authenticating the archetypal text of **A**, although the basis for identifying these features remains the versional archetype itself. The sole solution to this dilemma, one which Kane ignores, would seem to be reference to the other versions of *Piers Plowman*; for only when two or more versions agree in a line or reading can a valid claim be made for judging the text securely 'authorial.' This is because, on the basis of such 'common' readings, an analytical use of the term 'authorial text' becomes available which is also empirically sound; for what it denotes is the agreed text of the poem in its several versions. Now, that text appears, with varying degrees of ratification, only in these 'core-lines' of the poem (see IV, §§ 1–12). Consequently, what should emerge as properly criterial for Langland's practice is 'all and only those features found in these (doubly or trebly attested) lines and readings'. Other features found in lines archetypally attested in only one version, in order to avoid being classed as authentic only *a priori*, must satisfy stylistic and other 'norms' derived from the 'core-text'. Such 'universional' lines may (and in principle must be allowed to) contain some features absent from the core-text; but not being empirically validated, they obviously cannot furnish a sufficient standard for authenticity. Kane's claim that 'identification of the scribal tendencies of substitution equips the editor with his final means of determining originality' therefore strikes the present editor as mistaken. It is, at the least, very misleading; for the only 'final' means of establishing Langland's text is to use criteria derived from an analysis of the poem's core-lines. Kane's failure to reach this conclusion in his edition of **A** has adverse consequences, notwithstanding the penetration that enables him to achieve convincing results where his predecessors failed or to provide reasons for a textual choice where they were right but omitted to do so.

§ 74. Some at least of the divergences between the Athlone and the present text will therefore be traceable to differences in applying what is in effect the same method, e.g. in order to establish the 'harder' of two readings. A good example is at VIII 30 *And bete brugges aboute þat to-broke were* in which, out of the seven variants attested, *bete* (preferred by all other editors) is rejected by Kane for *bynde* 'on lexicographical grounds'. As this reading is discussed in the *Textual Notes*, it need only be said here that *bete* is also found in **Z** and that **B** paraphrases it as *do boote to*, for which *amende* at parallel C IX 33 is transparently an elucidatory synonym. The **C** reading is anticipated in the **A** copy M, where the word it appears as a scribal gloss on must be *bete*, the reading of H³ and most probably of the family original **m**. This example shows the risk involved when the 'direct' method is used without taking due account of the other versions or, in this case, of the genealogical evidence provided by the **m** witness H³'s agreement in reading *bete* with the *r²* copies VKN. Here, it may however be affirmed, it is not the method but Kane's application of the method that is at fault. For it is not disputed that in itself the d group variant *bynde* is lexically a 'difficult original' (see MED s.v. *binden* v.3 (d)). But the *sense* presumed for the adopted reading *bete brugges aboute* 'do repairs to bridges in the vicinity' cannot convincingly be called 'easier' than the sense 'reenforce by attaching lateral beams' of Kane's preferred *bynde*. The conclusion that emerges, paradoxical as it may seem, is that two competing readings, one of them perforce to be identified as scribal, may both be 'difficult,' one lexically and the other semantically, and the greater 'hardness' of either be indemonstrable. Unless, therefore, the remote assumption of laterally introduced 'author's variants' at the sub-archetypal stage is countenanced, the *lectio difficilior*, while usually a necessary, can never be a sufficient condition for determining originality in the text. (On the wider limitations that attend the concept, see further IV, §§ 15, 28).

§ 75. No less vexatious than the cases where one reading is to be identified as the harder or hardest of the available variants are five Kane himself distinguishes in which 'readings are of equivalent value and the support of the manuscripts is fairly divided' (p. 153), of which two may be examined here. At VII 20 *Chesiblis for chapelleynis chirches to honoure* Kane prefers *chapellis* as in the base-manuscript, while dismissing the support for *chapelleynis* from *r²*, **m** and one of the *r¹* copies Ch as well as from **B** and **C** (to which may be added **Z**). Before genetic evidence of such weight, *chapellis* could be preferred only for its 'hardness' and superior sense; but if it is not archetypal, its originality would have to be due to correction of T from a hypothetical superior lost manuscript (an entity about which scepticism is never amiss). This example highlights the weaknesses of the direct method as Kane himself sometimes practises it. The only explanation for his (to the present editor erroneous) decision is that, failing to make adequate 'application of genetic information' (p. 152) and to take into account the evidence of the parallel versions, he has mistakenly judged the competing readings as 'of equivalent value.' At X 86 *And þerof seiþ þe sauter, þi seluen þou miȝt rede* Kane prefers the *r¹* variant *þe salme* to *þi seluen*, the *r²* **m** reading accepted by Skeat, K–F and the present editor. With no parallel evidence and the decision to be made wholly on intrinsic grounds, Kane finds *þi seluen* 'the more emphatic expression, and therefore somewhat likelier to be of scribal origin' (p. 153). But even if this were granted, *þe salme* displays the greater 'explicitness' Kane likewise sees as 'scribal'. Now in this instance, genetic evidence in the form of support by two independent groups indicates that *þi seluen* and not *r¹*'s variant is more likely to be archetypal. So Kane's adherence to a base-manuscript reading he recognises as that of a 'probably genetic group' cannot be justified as it might be if the disagreement cut randomly across all three groups, or if the contested reading were of slight semantic import, like those to be considered next.

§ 76. Reservations about Kane's practice of the direct method in relation to major variants affecting the sense and metre of a line apply *a fortiori* to minor ones involving grammatical words or relatively insignificant differences in word-order and phrasing. The issue is candidly recognised in his conclusion that 'where...readings see[m] of equal value' and genetic information does not help, if neither meaning nor style is affected 'there is no choice but to let the text of the basic manuscript stand' (p. 152).[142] But from the twenty-five examples Kane gives, the following four, illustrating variations in tense, number and word-order, may be selected as controverting his claim that 'determination of originality is impossible because of the balance of representation and the equivalence of the readings' (ibid). What they show, on the contrary, is a near or absolute consensus of the other branches of the A tradition with some or all of the other versions. Firstly in III 3 Kane's preferred present-tense *calliþ*, where the r^1 group d is accompanied by two r^2 copies, should be rejected for past-tense *callid*, the reading of r^2, **m** and **ZBC**. Next at IV 38 singular *harm* tvE has the plural against it in the majority of **A** copies and **ZB**, just as in V 130 the singular *spynstere* of r^1 and K is opposed by the plural of r^2, **m** and **BC**. Finally in XI 4, against r^1's *sterneliche staringe Dame Studie* the preferred word-order *staringe Dame Studie sterneliche* is directly upheld by r^2 and **BC** and indirectly by **m** (whose substantively erroneous *scornynge* appears a corrupt reflex of the correct *staringe* in the same position). What these examples demonstrate is, firstly, that for minor readings the direct method proves a frail support without help from genetic and other-version evidence; secondly, that the expedient of relying on the copy-text is not the sole alternative, and is indeed a failure of the rationalism Kane's method embodies. In all these cases the truth is directly opposite to the Dreamer's assertion in B XVII 37–8 that *The gome þat gooþ wiþ o staf - he semeþ in gretter heele / Than he þat [teeþ] wiþ two staues, to sighte of vs alle.*[143]

§ 77. Conjectural emendation is, after the direct analysis of variation, the second main resort of a rationalist editor. Kane uses it only sparingly to correct archetypal corruptions, retaining lines 'of doubtful originality' (p. 156) if he finds the evidence too uncertain to justify intervention. A somewhat surprising case is XI 67 where Kane, though suspecting an original verb with *w* for archetypal *begiled*, does not print his conjecture *(be)wiled* (any more than does *Ka²*), despite the persuasive 'lexicographical grounds'[144] by which he sometimes sets such store (see on *bynde* at § 74). This decision sits uneasily with adoption elsewhere of (closely similar) dialectal variants on metrical grounds. Examples are the convincing *heo* for *she* at X 141 or *ȝerne* for *renne* at II 201, which he calls 'an obsolescent form of restricted currency' discernible for that reason as 'the harder reading' (p. 161). Kane explicitly disavows K–F's recognition of the **B** Version as attesting 'another branch of the **A** genealogy' (p. 157), no doubt understandably, given that in principle revision cannot be excluded at points where a **(B)C** reading might look superior to a suspect archetypal reading in **A**. But in only a few cases does he let the later versions even serve as 'guides to conjecture' (ibid.). One such is in VI 92 *And weue vp þe wyket þat þe wy shette*, where Kane argues for emending *wy* to *wif* (pp. 445–46) but cites in support only the Latin quoted at B V 603*a* and not the obviously relevant *womman* at parallel B V 602.[145] (This emendation deserves serious consideration, though it has not been accepted in the present edition).[146] A second instance is *comsiþ* for *beginneþ* at V 59, on which Kane's critical note (pp. 440–41) again makes no reference to parallel **B** or to the pertinent situation of I 139, where the **B** archetype at parallel I 165 reads the unmetrical *bigynneþ* for an original **comseþ* conjectured in the light of agreed **AC** (and again **Z**). Bracingly ascetic as is Kane's self-restriction to direct **A** evidence, his editorial stringency here verges on suffocation. Again, though logically justified in not using agreed **BC** readings to emend Ax errors, he overlooks the implication of **AC** agreement here against **B**. For the case of *comsiþ* and *beginneþ* indicates that identical errors could arise in the **A** and **B** archetypal traditions, and for the same reasons. This said, Kane's balance and sobriety command respect, and to the present editor far from prove his early 'ideal of conservative editing' the 'delusion' he came to judge it after editing **B**.[147]

§ 78. The supplement ('Retrospect') to Kane's Second Edition of **A**, which appeared midway between the Athlone **B** and **C**, makes good several deficencies of the first, particularly in drawing on **m** to emend errors in his mainly *r¹* text. But it does not openly acknowledge the wider import of these changes; and a few remaining inconsistencies display something rather less than the 'better' metrical understanding Kane now professes (cf. p. 460). This understanding is endorsed at III 21, where his convincing preference of *coppis* to *pecis* takes 'full account' of **B** and **C** (p. 460) and cites W (but not **Z**, which also has it), though without identifying W's variant as an 'enlightened correction' (p. 463) or a contamination from **C** (a frequent feature of this copy noted at III, *A Version* § 17). But an emendation of this type should for clearness be distinguished from one like that of **r**'s *seke* at V 256 [254] to *go to,* a variant cited from EAMH³ and K (and one supported by both **Z** and **C**). For while K's reading, like W's in the previous case, may well come from **C** (III, *A Version* § 21), **m**'s is almost certainly genetic. Further, since the **m** group shows no contamination from **C** and cannot derive from Bx (which is here corrupt), it is almost as certainly archetypal. The lack of perspicuity in the 1988 'Retrospect' contrasts with the lucidity of Kane's original critical notes, such as that on V 200 [198] *He [þr]umblide on þe þreshhewold and þrew to þe erþe,* which describes *þrumblide* in his text as 'taken from the corresponding line of the **C** Version...rather than on the authority of V' (the **A** copy in question presumably being judged contaminated from **C**). Similarly confusing is *Ka²*'s non-acceptance of Kane-Donaldson's emendation of *olde* to *yolde* at parallel B IX 163 [166], which leaves A X 187 unmetrical. Kane's tortuous notion that the poet's having overlooked these defective lines once or even twice 'gives them a kind of sanction' (p. 463) scarcely strengthens his rationale of emendation; for the direct method assumes that scribal and authorial readings are demonstrably different. And as it happens, such a case offers slender evidence that the revising poet *did* 'overlook' mistakes in his postulated scribal copy, given that so easy a substitution-error in the **A** archetype could have recurred in the archetype of **B**. Another line that Kane leaves unmetrical is VIII 136 [135], where a 'guide to conjecture' lay to hand in **BC**'s *book bible,* if not in ms M's *book of þe bible,* which may be an intelligent scribal guess. A third such line, XI 161, could have been emended by simple inversion of *nigromancie* and *perimansie* to scan *ax / ax.* This 'minimal' pattern Kane does not acknowledge as authentic, though he accepts an 'enriched' variant of it (*ab / ab*) at VII 233 *Contemplatif lif oþer actif lif Crist wolde it alse* on the evidence of **m** and **B**.[148] The last example highlights both Kane's inconsistency in applying his own criteria and the defectiveness of a metrical theory not founded on the evidence of the core-text.[149] The emendation of VII 233 in *Ka²* is also incongruous with the inclusion (p. 463) of V 14 among 'scribally corrupted' lines that 'would not be hard to emend conjecturally' (the sign of its 'corruption' presumably being again the *ax / ax* scansion). For by empirical criteria, V 14 is one of the securest lines in the poem, unvaryingly attested in the **ABC** tradition (and in **Z**). This instance points to an underlying incoherence in Kane's rationale of metrical emendation that will disable Kane-Donaldson's treatment of the archetypal text of **B** (see § 101 below).

46

§ 79. The preceding critique of Kane's A-Text has been in places severe; but it is this work that introduces into the editing of *Piers Plowman* principles that were to be applied, often with 'challengeable' outcomes, in the Athlone editions of the longer versions. Comparison with the present text will show how far it differs from Kane's, especially in its handling of minor variants, where archetypal readings with solid other-version support have seldom been rejected for those of the base-manuscript. By way of summary and conclusion, it may be said that the 1960 Athlone edition (and to some extent that of 1988) suffers from three main defects. Kane overestimates the value of r^1, fails to acknowledge the genetic significance of the r^2**m** agreements, even after accepting the continuous relevance of the parallel-text evidence, and relies on a demonstrably faulty metrical theory. In consequence he prints a text that, though little emended, is measurably further (to the present editor's judgement) than Knott-Fowler's from what Langland probably wrote. These defects, apart from the one concerning metre, differ somewhat from those of the collaboratively-edited B-Text, where speculative emendation is rife but the sub-archetypal traditions are clearly distinguished and fruitfully exploited. However, in some eighty cases, nearly sixty of them major, counting those added in Ka^2, Kane's discriminated readings and emendations (many established independently by the present editor before the appearance of Ka^2)[150] are endorsed in the parallel text of the **A** Version. Most impressive in Kane's edition are its rigorous presentation, full documentation and candid exposition, which establish a standard of accuracy and thoroughness no editor is likely to surpass. Kane's Introduction spells out exhaustively what textual rationalism may accomplish; if it also contains a warning, its combination of theoretical boldness with practical judiciousness sets a noble example.

viii. *The Athlone Editions:* Kane and Donaldson's *Edition of the* B-Text

§ 80. The *B Version* edited by George Kane and E. T. Donaldson (hereafter K–D for the editors, *K–D* for the work) appeared in 1975.[151] But although **B** is thrice the length of **A**, the volume is only half as long again as *Ka*. This is a measure of how far Kane's editorial theories are taken by K–D as largely settled.[152] A proportionately sized section of Critical Notes like those in **A** might have added a hundred pages, but now all textual problems are treated in an Introduction only a fifth longer than Kane's. As the presentation of Text and Apparatus follows *Ka* closely, the commendations and minor criticisms made above again apply. In the second volume, the exact number of agreements between pairs of manuscripts is stated (pp. 20–1), but those between three or more usually not. This caution may reflect a realistic sense of how easy it is to miscount: thus 250 agreements of CBmBoCot (p. 46) should be 263, while those of GYOC²CB (the group called 'g' at §§ 17–21 below) are some 230, as against K–D's stated 'more than 190' (p. 52). More significant are some omissions (pp. 67–9) from the list of lines found in WHmCrGYOC²CBLMH but absent from RF.[153] As most of these occur in Passus XIX, where R is defective, they could in principle have been present in the common source of RF and should have been listed here as having been lost for the same probably mechanical reasons invoked to account for the others.[154] This section has recently attracted intense critical scrutiny from proponents of a different explanation of the relationship between the two **B** families.[155]

§ 81. The Kane-Donaldson edition of **B** has proved both influential and controversial, its rigour and radicalism impressing even readers who question its use of **A** and **C** to correct archetypal errors and of bold conjecture where other-version evidence for reconstruction is lacking.[156] The

Athlone editors follow Kane's model in their lucid and thorough classification of the witnesses, from which the diagrammatic representation of manuscript relationships in the present edition substantially derives (see *B Version* § 10). However, like Russell and Kane later for **C**, but unlike Kane for **A**, they recognise for **B** a dual line of descent. As with the groups of witnesses in the **A** tradition, those in **B** do not allow the construction of a stemma that could decisively establish the archetype; for with one exception, no extant copy derives from another, nor does any group derive from a postulated ancestor of another group. The exception is the trio of manuscripts *BL Additional 10574* (Bm), *Bodley 814* (Bo, = Skeat's B) and *BL Cotton Caligula A XI* (Cot), to which K–D give the joint sigil B (adopted in the present edition). The close relationships within this genetic group recognised by Skeat (*B-Text*, xxv–xxvii) are analysed with notable economy and clarity (*K–D* pp. 40–2).

§ 82. In Athlone **B** the powerful techniques of Kane's direct method (cf. §§ 66–7 above) are concentrated on identifying some 750 readings as scribal errors in the archetypal text (called 'Bx' hereafter). An assumption fundamental to K–D's analysis is the traditional **A** > **B** > **C** sequence, supported from literary features and not from the external and internal evidence for dating, which may be insufficient to settle the issue finally (see *Intro.* V iii below). A definitive future case for re-ordering the versions would therefore gravely compromise their rationale of emendation, which appeals to the readings of **A** and **C** (severally or agreeing) for correcting presumed errors in Bx. No such case has been made, and in the present editor's view is unlikely to be made.[157] But this consideration brings out how Athlone **B** (and the present edition so far as it shares its presuppositions) resembles a 'scientific' hypothesis open to the test of 'falsification' by new discoveries. Whether the hypothesis is also able to *predict* specific data will be explored further below in relation to **Z**, a text that the Athlone editors ignore. This explicitly 'hypothetical' character differentiates *K–D* from *Ka,* which remained 'logically positivist' to the extent that it adhered to the readings of Ax, r^1 or even, in minor cases, the copy-text T. For *Ka* was 'rationalist' chiefly for its preferring editorial reasoning to genetic evidence in determining the direction of variation, not for its readiness to correct archetypal errors from other-version evidence or by conjecture. *Ka'*s residual 'conservatism' (to the present editor a virtue) is something that K–D declare 'mistaken' (cf. § 77).

§ 83. In its place K–D propound, in perhaps their most significant sentence, the fundamental editorial conviction that

> determination of originality in any version must include consideration in the first instance of *all* differences between versions and in the second particularly of those differences not evidently or probably resulting from authorial revision (p.75).

The Athlone editors here openly embrace the 'parallelistic principle,' though in respect of **A** they must perforce apply it retrospectively. This is because only with Ka^2 can the Athlone text adopt the **A** readings that K–D conclude are original after comparing it with **B** and **C** (see p. 75 n. 15). For recognising and correcting errors in the archetypal text of **B**, K–D rely on two central editorial pillars, the joint witness of **A** and **C** and that of either **A** or **C** alone. Recognising in the former 'the determinant circumstance in the editing of the **B** Version' (p. 76), K–D declare reasonably enough that unless the agreed text of **AC** is here 'itself unoriginal,' disagreement of **B** indicates either that the poet changed his mind in **C** and revised back to **A** or that the **B** archetype is corrupt. Given the character of the **B** readings and the number of **AC** agreements against **B**, they comprehensively prefer the latter interpretation. Two interconnected assumptions here bring out the character of their edition as a massive textual 'hypothesis'. One is that revision was linear and never reverted to an earlier form. Antecedently probable or not, this assumption may count as 'scientific' in being challengeable by specific examples and 'falsifiable' by the future discovery of dated holograph texts (such a discovery's improbability ensures the continuing viability of their hypothesis). The second is that the direct method, together with appeal to **AC** agreement, permits a 'compelling assessment of the quality of th[e] archetypal text' (p. 76). Both assumptions have survived the present 'parallelistic' analysis of all the versions undertaken in preparing this edition. But the possibility that the poet sometimes returned to an earlier reading must be countenanced.[158] For though the mere existence of **B** implies dissatisfaction with **A**, in principle Langland could at any point have restored in **C** what he first wrote in **A**: in response to readers' comments on **B**, for instance, he might have decided to say something again in the way he *first* said it (see further IV § 22 below).

§ 84. The second 'pillar' of K–D's edition, the witness of **A** or **C** alone for the discernment of archetypal error in **B**, is, however, less stable. Here, relying on a text of **A** established *without* consulting other-version evidence, they yet hold that 'if the possibility of revision were absent' some 300 readings (listed on pp. 84–9) would be less readily ascribable to ill-judged re-writing or to Langland's own 'scribal' error (p. 83) than to unconscious or deliberate 'scribal tendencies of variation.' Such readings they characterise as 'easier', 'more explicit' or 'more emphatic'; as arising from the copyist's conscious stylistic 'improvement' or censorship; or as evincing 'inferior' verse-technique. None of these categories is unproblematic, though in principle the third should be rigorously testable by reference to criteria founded on the poem's core-lines. In fact, most of the last group's 23 examples do display patterns that fail to meet such criteria. But as IX 32, 121 [123] and X 186 [189] scan *ax / ax*, emendation of these to read with **A** fails to convince; for the two-stave 'minimal' pattern (classed as 'Type IIIa' at IV §§ 39–43 below) is amply instanced in the core-lines and must therefore be accepted as authenticated empirically.[159] K–D's note on IX 32 *For þoru3 þe word þat he spak woxen forþ beestes* identifies a scribal 'unconscious substitution of the prose term [*spak*] or stylistic preference' (the latter presumably *not* unconscious) and invites comparison with an earlier use of *warp*. But the fact that the Bx scribe had no difficulty with *warp* at V 363 weakens K–D's case, as does their overlooking in parallel A V 206 the 'prose term' *spak* diagnosed later as scribal. It may be therefore that in IX 32 the author simply wished to avoid over-using a somewhat 'poetic' locution that appears only once elsewhere in **A** and **B** (in different places) and nowhere in **C**.[160] In relation to the second example *Conceyued ben in yuel tyme* K–D observe that *yuel* is 'more explicit' than *cursed*. But while *yuel* is more general, the two terms are virtually synonyms in the period, and any stylistic preference could have been the poet's, since he also replaces *cursid* at IX 123 when revising A X 155. Finally, in *A ful leþi þyng it were* at X 186, Bx *leþi* can scarcely be 'easier' as well as 'more emphatic' than K–D's preferred *lewed*, since by ordinary lexical criteria it is much the rarer word.[161] Whether or not a sense of the doubtful contextual suitability of *lewed* in **A** prompted the revising poet to prefer *leþi*, a scribe cannot plausibly be credited with substituting a uniquely-occurring word for one that Langland used over sixty times.[162] The 'intuitional' subjectivity of K–D's remarks, underpinned by a defective metrical theory, weakens confidence in such far-reaching changes to the archetypal text of **B**. It should not be surprising, therefore, that for their 'more than 300' (actually about 275) emendations of Bx on the basis of **A** alone, the present text has only about a dozen.[163]

§ 85. Although some of these criticisms have involved metrical issues, much of K–D's account of Langland's versification (pp. 131–40) is confirmed by the present editor's analysis of each line's metrical structure.[164] This account forms an important support for their rationale of emendation, since it is certain that 'establishment of the poet's verse technique is inseparable from the process of editing.' But K–D's conclusion contains a warning for the unwary; for to presume a line 'not to be evidence for that technique because for...discrete editorial reasons it appears to be scribal' and to treat 'the verse pattern it exemplifies...in other lines...as evidence of scribal corruption' is not only, as they concede, 'precarious,' it risks becoming circular. Nor is this presumption's *a priori* character sufficiently guarded against 'by the existence of controlled situations where the effects of unmistakable scribal corruption on the versification can be observed' (pp. 140–41). For much depends on 'observing' without mistake, and the only 'controlled situation' that can truly test K–D's contention is one where the verse must satisfy empirical criteria derived from the poem's core-text. But as has already been re-iterated, lines scanning *ax / ax* do occur in this core-text; and some are even admitted by *Ka²* as 'sanctioned' by the poet's 'overlooking' them.[165] The chief reason why the Athlone editors' 'observation' sometimes misidentifies corruptions is that their notion of a 'controlled situation' is flawed.

§ 86. Against K–D's use of **C** alone to emend Bx may be brought similar objections to those against their use of **A** alone. As in the comparison of **A** with **B**, the direction of variation can in principle be established almost as if both texts were witnessing to a single unknown hypothesised original. But an editor must be prepared to recognise (as Russell-Kane later do) that a revision may incorporate features of the text judged corrupt. Such recognition is logically less hazardous here to the extent that K–D are not antecedently committed to a text of **B** as they are to Kane's text of **A** (subject to the qualification noted at § 83). For during the course of analysis, the text of **B** is itself in process of being established, partly (and from Passus XI solely) in the light of **C**. Nonetheless, K–D detect 'similar differences with similar effects' (p. 91) and their 230 **C**-based emendations to Bx add up to about twice as many as in the present edition.[166] It is not necessary here to re-state the categories under which these are grouped (see § 69 above). Though some of their emendations immediately convince, many more than in **A** arouse scepticism by their subjectivity or ambiguity. Some measure of this is that the emendations from **C** in the present edition amount to about two-thirds of those in K–D's *final category alone*, which corresponds to the one discussed in connexion with **A** at § 84 above. This disproportion, much smaller than in relation to **A**, reflects the fact that many of the present editor's overlap with K–D's final group in diagnosing the presence of a corruption, if not always in adopting **C** to emend it. But K–D sometimes 'correct' a minimally-staved line[167] even where the reading they believe corrupt may be strongly defended. In two instances they in any case misanalyse the verse-structure; for XVII 80 [82] will readily scan if the stress is shifted from the first to the second syllable in *Ierúsalemward,* as will XIV 270 *Moore for coueitise of good þan kynde loue of boþe* after registering the existence of 'cognative' alliteration[168] on voiced and unvoiced palatal stops (k / g), a licence abandoned here in the **C** revision.[169] Of K–D's sixteen examples, the only two accepted here are V 497 *þerafter*] *after* and XX 54 *it tid*] *it*, the first on grounds of **C**'s superior sense rather than its metre, the second also because of the mechanical ease of the error (haplography).[170]

§ 87. Even more controversial than K–D's assessment, following Blackman (note 8 above), of Bx as corrupt is their conclusion that the poet's revision-manuscript of **B**, though better than

Bx, was significantly defective. The first evidence adduced is some hundred readings 'not manifestly created by authorial revision' but differing from the 'original preserved in the **A** tradition' and revealing 'a scribal reflex' of it in the reading of **BC** (pp. 98–9). It may not be solely the out-and-out positivist who will find their position questionable; for to common sense, a Bx reading retained in **C** has been confirmed by **C** and so, even if from *some* standpoint it may appear 'unsatisfactory', it should be accepted. The principle involved here is the 'canon of ratification,' which is fully discussed later (IV, *Editing the Text* § 22 below). This canon does admit of a handful of exceptions where the reading demonstrably fails to meet the core-text criteria.[171] But because alteration of ratified readings is also generally incongruous with the postulate of linearity that antecedently favours agreed **AC** against suspect Bx, it must always and only be done for compelling reasons. K–D's painstaking argument nonetheless demands careful examination, and their general view of Langland's revision-copy seems to the present editor to deserve assent, even if it prompts them to some unconvincing emendations. But it is the pre-eminent status accorded to **A** that has the least acceptable editorial implications, as late even as the Athlone edition of **C**.

§ 88. As evidence that Langland used a corrupt revision-copy of **B** in composing **C**, K–D adduce a hundred **BC** readings which they find on comparison with **A** have originated in mechanical errors, are more explicit, emphatic or easy, or exhibit other acknowledged 'scribal' features. These could in principle be revisions, the poet's own transcriptional errors or coincidentally-produced **BC** archetypal substitutions for an original identical with **A**. But the explanation K–D prefer is that these readings reflect corruptions present in a manuscript from a pre-archetypal stage in **B** that Langland allowed to stand 'for whatever reason' (p. 103). Support for their case lies in a type of situation where **A** appears original, the **B** archetype on comparison scribal, **C** a revision to a reading of such a kind that Bx cannot derive from it but must derive from **A**, and **C** finally a reflection of Bx and not of the putative **AB** original (p.104). K–D's carefully-analysed examples, though invariably of great interest, may often fail to persuade; but no diffidence qualifies their robust editorial rationalism. Now, when they refer to the '**A** tradition' both as 'presumably' original and as the 'putative original' shared with **B**, K–D necessarily mean Kane's A-Text. But they make no distinction between this text, established *without* consulting the parallel-version evidence, and its form as revised after a 'more rigorously logical editing' (*Ka²* p. 159, n. 78). This is, of course, because that 'editing' was subsequent to and consequent upon the outcome of editing the **B** Version, not simultaneous and co-dependent with it. The serious implications of these facts make themselves felt at IV 14 in K–D's replacement of *ryt ryȝt* (echoed in *rood forth* **C**) by *riȝt renneþ*, a *Ka* reading retained in *Ka²* though supported only by the *r¹* sub-family and not by the sub-family *r²* and the other family **m**, which are identical with **B**. But there is also a wider theoretical difficulty to be faced here. If, by the linear postulate (which the present editor accepts), **AC** agreement against Bx implies lack of revision in the middle version, **BC** agreements against **A** correspondingly *indicate* revision. This K–D apparently do not accept, though such is the basis on which they propose for credence the complex 'situation' described at the beginning of this paragraph. But contrary to what they suppose, agreed **BC** readings do not require proof (whatever form that might take) of being 'manifestly created by authorial revision' (cf. § 87). For, being empirically secure, they must be treated as authentic unless they breach the core-text criteria. This 'canon of ratification' K–D ignore because they are convinced that on intrinsic grounds, and even in minor readings, they can reliably tell scribal from authorial characteristics. Intuitional certitude may be necessary at times if a readable text is to be produced at all; but no editor should invoke it without apprehension.

§ 89. There is space here for only a few examples to bring out the full dimensions of K–D's approach. They are at their strongest when **C** keeps the **A** reading they prefer, if only as part of a revision echoing a suspect Bx reading, because this case comes nearer to the criterially firmer category of an **AC** agreement against the archetypal text of **B**. Thus at I 191 parallel *hardere* found in A I 165 appears at C I 186 and Bx *Auarouser* is reflected in C 187, which begins with *Auerous*.[172] Also persuasive is their argument on grounds of superior sense for re-ordering I 98–103 to accord with **A** rather than **C**, though not that in favour of rejecting **BC** *siluer* 103/100 for **A**'s *ȝeftis*, since the lines' dislocation and the (possibly authorial) lexical substitution are not necessarily connected. Similarly at X 458, although *clerkes most knowyng in konnyng* in parallel C XI 295 echoes Bx's *konnynge clerkes þat knowe manye bokes*, the word *konnynge* in the latter need not be questioned as a revision of **A**'s *kete*, a term absent from the later versions perhaps because it had been found difficult (cf. § 70 above). Here K–D virtually constrain the poet to restore an earlier expression that they prefer, something imaginable in an early reader but out of place in a modern editor.

§ 90. Various objections to specific unconvincing readings arouse wider unease about the Athlone procedure. In one instance (pp. 108–9) K–D reject Bx VI 223 *That nedy ben and noȝty help hem wiþ þi goodes*, which scans *aa / xx*, for the two-line **A** form, finding in **C**'s revised VIII 233 *In meschief or in mal-ese and thow mowe hem helpe* evidence that even the revision-copy of **B** had unmetrical *help* in its b-half. While possible, this is insufficient grounds for believing that the **B** original was identical with **A**. For it is hardly more improbable that the Bx scribe substituted *help* for some harder word[173] the poet finally replaced with a more familiar one than that *help* stood in his revision-manuscript, which like Bx was based on the first scribal copy of the holograph (as will be shown at III, *B Version* §§ 2–4). The comparative **BC** evidence here is too weak for specification either of the revision-manuscript's reading or of the 'putative' **AB** reading. While perhaps justified therefore in conjecturing that the undoubted damage to metre was caused by Bx's alteration of a single 'harder reading,' an editor cannot ignore the wider signs of revision in the environs of B VI 224–27. These indicate that the author deliberately reduced A VII 209–10 to **B**'s single line 223; and in doing so, he replaced **A**'s circumstantial account of the object and means of the recommended charity with an affirmation that the moral problem of undeserving recipients is a matter for God, man's business being to obey God, not judge other men. Rejecting K–D's text here amounts to seeing it as an 'editorial interpolation' of **A** lines which, while (obviously) 'authentic', need never have formed part of **B**. In the second example, at X 19 *Whoso can contreue deceites*, K–D substitute from A XI 19 *construe* 'construct' for Bx *contreue* 'devise'[174] and observe that **C**'s *Ho can caste and contreue* 'reflects a line with the archetypal **B** reading' (p. 110). Here there is little to choose between their conclusion and acceptance that the poet revised a word open to misconstruction. In absolute terms *construe* is 'harder'; but as the senses of both words are very close, an editor should refrain from finding in **C**'s *contreue* a 'reflection' of a (possibly) scribal reading that it does not at the same time ratify. For even if Langland did not originally write *contreue* in **B**, the revised **C** line implies his final acceptance of it. In here abandoning a satisfactory archetypal reading for that of **A**, K–D (without quite dictating what Langland should have written) ignore the 'custodial' dimension of editorial responsibility. In their remaining examples the present editor, who does not, is similarly unable to follow them.

§ 91. For the belief, however, that in revising **B** the poet did not use his own holograph copy there is solid evidence in the last two passūs, where the near-identical archetypal texts severally contain some disjunctive errors. This situation is most economically explained if **C**'s text substantially represents that of Langland's revision-copy (though K–D's view of this text as wholly unrevised is disputed at III, *B Version* §§ 71–4). But a major, much-discussed instance from earlier in the poem where revision has certainly occurred does, in the present editor's view, support their general case, and it has important implications for the emendation of Bx. The passage XV 53–68 has the same order in **C** and Bx, but this, as K–D argue on grounds of sense, is because it was dislocated mechanically at a pre-archetypal stage. In the terms of the hypothetical history of the text outlined in part III below, this took place in Bx's source, the second scribal copy 'B-Øa'.[175] But K–D's judgement that C XXI–XXII ('B^2') share with Bx an exclusive common ancestor (p. 116) is unacceptable; for B^2's *immediate* source ('B^1') can be shown to be based directly on the *first* scribal copy B-Ø (see III, *B Version* §§ 1–6, especially § 5). This divergence apart, the present editor accepts with K–D that in several other cases the archetypal texts of **B** and **C** indeed share a corrupt reading inherited from their *ultimate* common source, B-Ø. One is at I 160/155 *And a meene as þe mair is betwene þe kyng and þe commune.* Either scansion of this line, *aa / bb* or *aa / xa* (K–D), is inauthentic, and the Athlone editors plausibly reconstruct by transposing the b-half nouns to give the stress-pattern *commúne*.[176] Unlike the large-scale transposition in XV for which they provide a detailed explanation (pp. 176–78), I 160 does not definitively indicate corruption at this point, as such an error could have been coincidentally introduced by the scribe of the archetypal C-manuscript (Cx).[177] Likewise, of the twenty-five supposedly unmetrical lines listed on pp. 112–13, some at least must be discounted as scanning acceptably by the empirical 'core-line' criteria, which contradict the 'ideal' metrical norms K–D invoke.[178] But while most of the others are convincingly diagnosed as sharing a scribal error, the emendation adopted here does not always follow K–D.[179]

§ 92. Kane-Donaldson end their searching analysis with the important question of why the poet retained 'so many of the unoriginal readings present in the scribal manuscript' (p. 124). They suggest by way of answer that the apparent lack of revision in the last two passūs, and its nonsystematic and non-consecutive nature earlier, indicate a process 'almost certainly never completed' (p. 126). Thus, while allowing that Langland might have eventually managed to remove these residual errors, they conclude that the draft **C** Version was 'seen through the scriptorium by a literary executor' (p. 127), a hypothesis elaborated in the third Athlone volume (see ix below). But one might favour this explanation without necessarily sharing K–D's estimate of the number of scribal readings 'let stand,' the degree of **C**'s incompleteness, or the likely manner of its composition. While K–D are surely right that in textual criticism 'assessments of probability' depend not on 'numerical criteria' but on 'an editorial sense developed through experience,' their own 'demonstration' cannot be accepted as 'almost wholly empirical' (p. 123). On the contrary, it is seriously *un*-empirical in relation to their use of metrical criteria, into which the 'numerical' component they disparage must of necessity enter; in their rejection of **BC** agreement as tacit ratification of a reading; and in their judgement of some revisions as responses to corruption Langland perceived in his copy.[180] Although there is undeniably a place in textual criticism for such speculation, K–D's 'almost' needs heavy emphasis. For the impossibility of knowing why supposed scribal errors were 'allowed to stand' severely limits identification of **BC** agreements as containing or reflecting errors introduced in the archetype or the poet's revision manuscript. The present editor's own understanding, after editing **C**, is that this text is less a revision of **B** than a fresh 'version' of the poem that began at the beginning, where the writer immediately introduced striking new material. If **C** was never submitted complete for professional copying, it could well retain some readings that Langland might ultimately have corrected. But that is an argument for, not against, a fairly conservative approach to editing the text. Except in the last two passūs, therefore, it seems safer to emend **C** only sparingly on the basis of **B**, and scarcely at all on the sole basis of **A**.

§ 93. Kane and Donaldson's magisterial chapter on the text recognises three main stages in the work of editing. These are the recovery of the archetype, comparison of it with those of **A** and **C**, and an 'absolute' scrutiny of all the versions. The archetypal text of **B**, they maintain, is subject to scrutiny and control on comparison not only with **A**, **C**, **AC** and revised **C** but also in itself 'in terms of the results of the first four comparisons.' There is little here to dissent from except their rejection of 'conservative presentation of a reconstructed archetype' as inimical to recovery of 'the historical truth of the poem' and their full-blooded preference of 'foolhardiness to caution' when emending textual corruptions from extant textual evidence, or by conjecture. K–D unobjectionably describe their methods as 'a more extended application of the reasoning set out in Vol I,' principally in 'the use of evidence from the other versions.' But there is a price for 'extending' the application of 'reasoning' as a primary analytical tool. This is a subordination of the editor's custodial responsibility to the textual critic's speculative prerogative that permits a hypothesis about the lost original, as it crystallises into an edited text, to dissolve the substance of the archetype. K–D, notwithstanding, salute another tradition in laying claim to the textual criteria developed by nineteenth and early twentieth-century editors of the classics, the New Testament and Dante, and describing themselves as 'radical only in the greater degree to which they allow the logical force' of these criteria. Unconstrained by the consensus of witnesses or of previous editors, to whom they hardly refer, they consider *their* practice to exemplify a 'traditional' method. In a sense this is true, though it has been more generally thought of as a decisive break with the positivist approach previously dominant in the editing of medieval vernacular texts. K–D however believe that *Piers Plowman* has more in common with the works they mention, because it survives in abundant manuscripts subjected to active scribal intervention. They accordingly judge irrelevant to their task similar situations in other Middle English poems of comparable scope and find that 'the *Piers Plowman* problem is evidently *sui generis*' (p. 123).

§ 94. Kane and Donaldson's fundamental editorial assumption is the clear difference between the typical *usus scribendi* of scribes and that of the poet (p. 130), which they distinguish as 'vigorous, nervous, flexible and relatively compressed.' One may assent to each element here without being certain whether in any particular line it is always or evidently thus. For such a description might apply equally well to Wordsworth's *Prelude* or Eliot's *Four Quartets*, but not to all passages or at every point in any particular passage (and these are texts free from all scribal interference). Langland's 'sense' the editors not unreasonably claim to make out on the basis of their general familiarity with the poem's content and historical meaning. His metre they establish from their analysis of thousands of lines that 'presumably illustrate the alliterative principles the poet set himself and observed' because their 'originality is not in question or is confidently determinable' (p. 132). Such lines, they claim, may be contrasted with those that are identifiable as corrupt 'for discrete reasons' and reveal a scribal character in metrical deviance from these principles. An important feature of their argument, however, is that failures in style and sense usually co-occur with defects in alliteration, so that emendation *sola metri causa* tends to be relatively rare.

§ 95. K–D's acute analysis (pp. 133–40), recognising a wider range of metrical practices than Skeat's (though narrower than Knott-Fowler's),[181] forms the basis of their rationale for the discrimination of authentic lines, and it is accepted here, with certain important modifications. But K–D do not make sufficiently clear whether their 'thousands' of lines are adopted because they conform with an *idea* of the poet's style as 'vigorous, nervous etc' and his sense as 'a component of the whole meaning of the poem' (p. 131). If so, authentically 'Langlandian' lines will simply be those that meet the Athlone editors' requirements for being 'Langlandian'. There is thus an *a priori* feel to the features of sense, style and versification supposed to distinguish 'original' from scribal work. A truly empirical rationale is certainly implied by their appeal to 'evidence from other versions' (p. 129). But their notion of *usus scribendi* may be criticised for failing to meet three conditions imposed by criteria such as those on which the present edition is based. Firstly, there must be a body of irrefragable textual evidence (such as the core-text provides). Secondly, the 'confidence' this evidence gives in determining authenticity remains proportional to the degree of extrinsic support available (from four > three > two versions). Thirdly, such confidence is subject to the joint constraints of the 'linear postulate' and the canon of ratification (so that, save exceptionally, agreement of **AB** or of **BC** earns a reading authorial status). K–D contend in concluding that their case is not open to 'theoretical' objection and their text must be assessed 'in its detail' and 'by the quality of the arguments' supporting that detail and the appropriateness of their readings. This is because 'an edited text is essentially a hypothesis...' and 'its individual readings...elements of the hypothesis' (140, n. 48). True as this is, K–D's case *is* open to theoretical objection, specifically to the way in which its notion of metre defies falsification by empirical evidence. The Athlone editors may well have examined 'thousands of lines'; but the lines that are criterial for such an examination are those uniformly attested by two or more versions of the poem. There is indeed an editorial alternative to aprioristic rationalism: appeal to norms derived inductively from the core-text data. These, moreover, have applicability over a wider range than that of metrical practice; for while obviously not as strongly diagnostic in other areas, they do provide reliable guidelines concerning all aspects of the poet's sense and style (see IV §§ 1–13).

§ 96. The editorial criteria that K–D, for their part, consider as determined 'empirically' they apply through the three main processes of discrimination, reconstruction and conjecture. The discrimination of original variants where only **B** is present provides the textual situation that they call the 'simplest' (p. 141). But this is not (it should be stressed) necessarily the easiest, for in the absence of what they call 'distracting considerations' [*sc.* without any control from a parallel-version source], ascertaining the direction of variation may become a very subjective business indeed. After describing the process in detail, K–D consider cases where the texts 'lineally correspond' (p. 149), the comparison also uncovering errors in the archetypes of **A** and **C** (p. 159). Among their most striking 'extensions' of the principles pioneered in **A** is the importance they attach to convergent variation in undermining manuscript attestation as an indicator of authenticity. In consequence, K–D are ready to recognise that original readings may be preserved in one particular copy[182] (the copy in question being the 'formerly scorned' Corpus 201 [F]), even at points where it is otherwise corrupt or sophisticated. They isolate for consideration a group of cases (pp. 169–72) other than those where F may simply preserve the reading of its ancestral source ['α'] and where Rawlinson (R), the only other α copy, coincides in error with the other family ['β']. These readings K–D ascribe (pp. 171–72) to correction 'in the immediate tradition of F' [i.e. between the copying of α and that of manuscript F] from a manuscript superior at points to

Langland's revision-copy and 'intrinsically more authoritative' at those points where **B** is unique and cannot be compared with **A** or **C** (in terms of the present edition's stemma this would be the copy 'B-Øa' mentioned at § 91 above). But all of these readings unattributable to α can, it will be shown, be explained as due to contamination from **A**; and some that K–D judge 'intrinsically more authoritative' are in any case unconvincing.[183] The present edition makes occasional, and indeed unavoidable use of manuscript F. But it rejects the Athlone editors' high valuation of it and their account of F's good readings as due to correction from a superior lost **B** source, which fails to meet the principle of economy of explanation.[184]

§ 97. K–D's second main editorial process, the reconstruction of readings not instanced in any extant witness, is in essence speculative; but in using positive manuscript evidence it is distinguishable from pure conjecture. With impressive clarity and decisiveness, they arrange their reconstructions according to the types of situation exemplified, using in particular the evidence of **A** and **C**. This last procedure seems to the present editor indispensable for preparing a critical edition of **B**, and Skeat's failure to use it left his text marred by many easily remediable corruptions.[185] Nonetheless, K–D for their part sometimes reject adequate archetypal readings because of a particular interpretation of their sense, style and form, severally or in combination, which may be challenged. Thus in VII 30 they reconstruct Bx *Pouere peple and prisons, fynden hem hir foode* as *Pouere peple [bedredene] and prisons [in stokkes] / Fynden [swiche] hir foode [for oure lordes loue of heuene]* (pp. 173–74). Now, that K–D's lines sound 'Langlandian' is unsurprising, since they conflate C IX 34 with A VIII 34. But despite the Athlone editors' thoughtful argument, it is hard to see how, by their own criteria, they find the Bx line unacceptable. For in the absence of other metrical or stylistic faults, the survival of elements from **A** into the **C** Version does not in itself indicate the corruptness of the **B** archetype. What is observed here may instead be a (rare) case of 'non-linear' revision in **C**. But even if it is, the 'linear postulate' does not forfeit its status as generally trustworthy because of the occasional exception. There is, of course, no *a priori* reason why the poet should not have had access to **A** or have simply remembered what he first wrote (cf. *Intro.* V §§ 29–32). The **C** form already 'reconstructs,' using two lines, returning to the word-order of **A** at the beginning of IX 35 and 36, and echoing A VIII 34b in the second lift of its line 35. But along with **C**'s remoulding of earlier material goes its telescoping of the thought in **AB** 34/31 into a single half-line and its retention of **B**'s distinctive *prisons* in 34b. Most telling of all in the sequence of revisions are the prior survival of A 33a into B 30b and the rarity of the metrical pattern of B VII 30 (*aaa / bb*), virtually restricted to Langland and never found in an archetypal line suspect on other grounds. These points not only form a powerful objection to K–D's emendation, they encourage wider scepticism towards the textual rationalism it exemplifies. For the same arguments that identify an unusual metrical structure (*aaa / bb*) as authentic cannot be inverted or ignored to prove a line scribal, when on grounds of sense the case is fragile and on grounds of style non-existent.

§ 98. Despite these reservations, a number of K–D's 'simple' reconstructions of the archetype are convincing.[186] One example is the 'lexical re-interpretation' at V 440 *yarn*] *ran* in the light of // C VII 53. Here, though, it must be said in qualification that the **C** line, while 'evidently a revision of a corrupt **B** line' (p. 183), cannot strictly illustrate reconstruction from '**B** evidence alone', since the initial |j| of *yarn* is collaterally confirmed by **C**'s new verb *yede*. The Athlone editors can be triumphantly right in their corrections of palæographic error, as in their salvage of Bx *juel* from R's *euel* at XI 184, a variant that provoked a scandalised '(!)' from Skeat but is greatly superior to the flavourless β *heele* that he accepted. (One of several, however, that do not seem justified, since the archetype's sense is satisfactory, is XII 74 *were she*] *wher* K–D). A more controversial emendation that does have an identical **C** parallel is of *pisseris longe knyues* at XX 219, the 'extreme lexical difficulty' of which (p. 184) draws from K–D an emendation [*purses and*] *longe knyues* that is both metrically clumsy and semantically easier.[187] Of these supposedly 'simple' instances, many that have far-reaching implications are, in the present editor's view, too readily adopted. Thus K–D's notion that their reconstruction of *yet* V 400 as *so þe I* on the basis of F's *soþly* could be 'automatic' reveals insouciance towards the editorial obligation to justify major emendation. A similar change, *ynome* for *name* at XVI 161, which obliterates a significant emphasis on the name of Jesus with 'Crowleyan' assurance (cf. § 26), is rebutted in the *Textual Notes*. Among K–D's most radical suggestions (p. 186) is *a bouste* for *aboute* at XIII 153, the product of failing to read the allegory properly, which the present editor unwisely adopted in the first Everyman edition but now rejects (*Textual Notes ad loc*; *Sch²*, p. 391). Another such is *here-beyng* XIV 141, misanalysed as a 'random type-variant' that supposedly points to a 'polysyllabic original' *herberwyng* (p. 186). This emendation offends both against the rationalist editor's key criterion of *durior lectio*, since archetypal *here-beyng* (possibly Langland's coinage) is lexically much harder, and against the canon of ratification, since it is also the reading of // C XVI 9.[188] While this section of K–D's Introduction contains several instances of shrewd common sense[189] such as *Haukyns wil* at XIV 28 (where the oddity of Bx *Haukyns wif* escaped Skeat), it also illustrates their method at its most seductive, as one who has succumbed to it is bound to record.

§ 99. K–D's third and most controversial editorial process is the proposal of a hypothetical reading as the source of an archetypal reading diagnosed as unoriginal. Conjectural emendation, which they distinguish perhaps too sharply from reconstruction, is explicitly acknowledged as the most unsure, though an 'obligatory' part of the editorial process. One valuable control on conjecture is offered indirectly in the revised or pre-revised texts of **C** and **A** respectively. But the poem's very length, K–D believe, provides enough material to enable confident discrimination between scribal and authorial *usus scribendi*, and often deduction from the scribal reading of 'the authorial reading likely to have generated it' (p. 191).[190] This phase may be thought of as corresponding to that in which a scientific hypothesis predicts a particular outcome that is open to empirical falsification, until which point the account 'deduced' from the known data may function as a provisional theory of the text. (The empirical 'test' here would have to be the discovery of new manuscript evidence of an authoritative kind). The procedure's claim to acceptance, as K–D grant, necessarily varies in strength from case to case, and their success in identifying archetypal corruption must be gauged not only from the validity of their editorial criteria but also from their skill in applying them. Grounds for hesitation have been indicated; but no critical editor can deny the need for such a procedure, if aiding the reader's understanding is the aim of the enterprise. Proposing lost original readings, however, remains a speculative act, and their acceptability must depend largely, as K–D state, on 'the accuracy of the affective data and the informed reasoning applied to them' (p. 192).

§ 100. Like reconstruction, conjecture operates in relation to style, sense and verse-technique. K–D's exclusions of certain whole lines as spurious on the basis of style are endorsed here, except for V 233, 277, 282, XIV 34 and XIX 254. Emendations on grounds of sense, as K–D rightly aver, test total editorial understanding of the work's 'historical truth and meaning' and not just con-textual grasp of the poet's local intentions. An example is at VII 121, where their reading *werche* for *slepe* appears 'plausible' enough, though it does not impose itself in place of a Bx reading convincingly shown to be corrupt. Also questionable is their substitution of *Grekes* for *Iewes* at XV 389 and 500 notwithstanding the witness of // C XVII 156 and 252, a case where 'informed reasoning' upon the 'affective data' induces a strained (and *im*plausible) defiance of the canon of ratification. Most of K–D's diagnoses of defective alliteration prove acceptable where the metri-cal pattern instanced is (by reliable core-text criteria) recognisably deviant, such as *aa / xa*; and a further few are attractive if not inevitable, e.g. *barm* for *lappe* at XVII 71 and (less attractively) *maugree* for *ayein* at XVIII 351. Among these, moreover, some of the boldest accord felicitously with the poem's prevailing texture and tone, illustrating how for an editor of Langland there is in this phase no necessary correlation between cautiousness and persuasiveness. Examples are *bigg-yng*] *dwellyng* at V 128 [130]; *Tynynge*] *Lesynge* at IX 99 [101]; and *preynte*] *wynked* at XIII 86 (the last without acknowledging its proposer, Skeat). But others fall foul of the core-text norms,[191] e.g. *vndignely*] *vnworþily* XV 243 and *diuyse*] *discryue* XVI 66 where, even if the archetypal lex-emes are granted to be 'contextually easier' than those conjectured, both lines scan acceptably as *ax / ax*. In a number of cases that introduce a wholly new idea (though a satisfactory line is achiev-able by less radical means like simple transposition), conjecture 'involving actual addition...must seem… especially adventurous' (p. 197), as at IX 91 [93] where they read *luged wiþ* for *wors*. But that they feel no pressure to avoid conjecture is a measure of the Athlone editors' confidence in their grasp of the poet's *usus scribendi,* despite the apparent demurral. For K–D are not as anxious to save the archetypal text from their own 'adventurousness' as from that of the scribes.

§ 101. Where **B** is not open to comparison with other versions, and the main indicator of unoriginality is therefore Bx's defective metre, K–D admit to less assurance in their conjectures. In this situation, though they often pinpoint error with impressive accuracy, as at V 165 [167] and X 279 [285], their diagnosis of its causation can be less compelling and their emendation needlessly drastic. Thus at Pr 159 they read *salue* for *help* although the b-verse can be easily reconstructed from the 'split' variants preserved in β and α, and it is arguable that the archetype was not corrupt at all.[192] Similarly extreme is *purchace* for *haue* at IX 77 [79], where K–D do not recognise the 'cognative' alliteration on *p / b*, proved authentic by the core-text criteria (IV § 46), which obviates any need for emendation. (Of many such instances, most of those not mentioned in the *Textual Notes* have been considered in the Everyman editions of **B**). Among emendations that K–D judge neither certain nor likely but only possible come those in which 'the element of subjectivity is largest'. A major example is at X 242 [248], where they propose *man and his make* instead of *mankynde* as 'the least violent emendation' of an original 'also liable to be corrupted for emphasis to the archetypal reading.' But it may be objected that if *mankynde* is 'emphatic' (which is doubtful), *man and his make* is more explicit (which is not doubtful); so the emendation *is* more 'violent' than needful, adding a new idea (*make*) for which no textual evidence exists. By contrast, the emendation *animales*] *bestes* here preferred at least keeps the a-half intact, while offering in the b-half a difficult and rare synonym of the type more than once corrupted by the Bx scribe.[193]

§ 102. How far towards wholesale re-writing K–D's suspicion of the archetypal text can carry them is illustrated by a line scanning *ax / ax*, XV 313 *For we ben Goddes foweles and abiden alwey* for which they substitute *For we [by] goddes [behestes] abiden alwey.* Their justification of this emendation (p. 202) is a palmary instance of 'informed reasoning' upon 'affective data,' though with its appeal to 'two stages of substitution,' 'associational links,' 'homœography' and 'smoothing,' perhaps not of logical economy. Now, complex textual situations could have arisen for which complicated textual explanations might well be fitting. But this example reveals what can happen when rationalism gratuitously ousts a reading satisfactory in sense, style and metre so as to obscure a major thematic point, and the meddling editorial intellect wantonly misshapes a beauteous form. Into K–D's final category of 'complex textual restoration' falls another dire alteration at XII 288 [291] // C XIV 213, where for *And wher it worþ or worþ noȝt, þe bileue is gret of truþe* they read *And wheiþer it worþ [of truþe] or noȝt, þe] worþ [of] bileue is gret*. This fails by the canons of acceptability and of ratification, substituting for a line of good if not obvious meaning (and verbally identical with its **C** parallel) one that is doctrinally dubious and metrically inferior (in its having the masculine line-ending never found in Langland). Such 'prosthetic' emendation lops off a healthy limb and replaces it with a new one screwed in at the wrong angle. This particular intrusion (answered earlier and again here in the textual note *ad loc*) is wisely not adopted by Russell-Kane into their text of **C**; but it holds its place in *K–D²*, a re-issued volume virtually unmarked by a 'retrospective' ripple. This last example illustrates the confusion that afflicts textual rationalism when its sight-lines dip over the horizon of common sense.

§ 103. The above discussion has dealt with the main structure of Kane-Donaldson's theoretical argument and with some specific effects of their editorial approach on the text itself. But the full extent of their active intervention, signalised usually by the presence of square brackets, is not immediately obvious to the extent that it affects minor readings, as where comparison with **A** and **C** induces them to omit small words or phrases. Here, only a minute collation of their text, first with *Ka* and then with Russell and Kane's C-Text, would suffice to bring out how far K–D depart from the readings of the archetype. If, then, their *Piers Plowman* (which so little resembles any text available to medieval readers outside the poet's immediate circle) may nonetheless be thought to do honour (if not justice) to the poet, this is not because it closely approaches the original at all points, but because it takes the quest for that original with unprecedented seriousness. Many of K–D's discriminations, however, some of their reconstructions, and a few of their conjectures have been gratefully adopted here, even if more have been rejected and some rebutted (occasionally at length). In spite of these strictures, the text of **B** in the present edition, like its Everyman predecessor, recognises a sizeable debt to the methods pioneered by Kane and whole-heartedly applied by K–D. If it often arrives at different conclusions, this comes less from reluctance to pursue 'informed reasoning' to its limit than from a refusal to treat the archetype as corrupt when it cannot be shown as overwhelmingly likely to be so. With reconstructions, probability regarding the error diagnosed and the solution adopted often suffices; but conjectures demand a stricter standard of demonstration. Archetypal readings are, therefore, to be presumed authentic if they conform to the 'core-text' criteria. But it should be remembered that those criteria are applied in the present edition with an understanding of Langland's mind and art in many ways unlike that of the Athlone editors. The present B-Text is therefore, perhaps expectedly, even more different from *K–D* than the present A-Text is from *Ka*.

§ 104. In spite of these major qualifications, Athlone **B** must be saluted as a remarkable achievement. Numerous corruptions in the archetypal text are, as has been said, securely identified and successfully corrected. K–D's editing cuts much deeper than Skeat's into the substance of Langland's poetry, because their readings have been established with such expenditure of critical labour. A solid corpus of indispensable scholarly material, comprehensive and accurate, is contained in its apparatus and the less speculative portions of its Introduction. And the latter provides an enlightening initiation into textual criticism for the reader unintimidated by its lofty tone and hieratic manner. The edition as a whole, which for intellectual power stands out amongst the editorial enterprises of our time, has greatly stimulated thought about the nature of *Piers Plowman* and other texts over the last quarter of the twentieth century, and will doubtless continue to do so.[194] The main unhappy effect of its use as the normal citation-text during this period is one for which K–D themselves are not to blame. But spiriting away the multitudinous brackets around their emendations, as is regularly done by critics who do not fully grasp their implications (cf. § 57 above), is an irresponsible practice at odds with the tenor of what the Athlone editors call

> a theoretical structure...a complex hypothesis designed to account for a body of
> phenomena...governed by a presumption of the quality of Langland's art and...
> information about the effects of manuscript copying on...texts (p. 212).

K–D themselves disclaim absolute authority for their edition; but a complementary (and not unseemly) assurance marks their admonitory challenge (p. 220) to would-be future editors: 'Whether we have carried out our task efficiently must be assessed by reenacting it' (a labour that, perhaps unsurprisingly, has been carried out only once). K–D's term 'efficiency' does not adequately acknowledge their imaginative editorial boldness; but it is all the same a quality in which they stand unequalled.

ix. *The Athlone Editions:* Russell and Kane's *Edition of the* C-Text

§ 105. Appearing in 1997, and the longest in making of the three, the Athlone Edition of the C-Text edited by Russell and Kane ('R–K' hereafter) closely resembles its immediate predecessor. A full and clear description of the manuscripts is followed by their classification, and an examination of this is instructive. R–K begin with pairs having not less than 40 agreements, and of these five emerge as especially persistent: VA with 443, followed by RM and PE with around 270, and then by TH^2 with just under 200 and UD at about 130 (on these sigla see *Intro*. III, *C Version* §§ 5–13). As in the earlier editions, no distinction is made between major and minor readings; so while the sheer bulk of agreements at the upper end strongly suggests genetic relationship, the true significance of the twenty-one variational groups clustering at 45 to 100 agreements (p. 21) is not easy to grasp. To illustrate: though totalling about the same, PE has only 70 *major* agreements (26%) to RM's 120 (43%), some 17% less. Thus, despite the quantitative impressiveness of PE's total, the Athlone editors' refusal of any qualitative distinction at the initial stage can be potentially misleading. That is because, as they acknowledge, many minor agreements could arise by coincidence, and the main indication that these are genetic is their co-presence with a substantial body of major ones (a recognition tacitly conceding the latter's criterial character). This comes out clearly from a comparison of PE with AV; for of AV's 443 only 100 (22%) are major, a figure lower than that of PE's major agreements, although absolutely AV contains 38% more shared readings than PE. To estimate the true *weight* of shared readings it is therefore essential to distinguish major from minor agreements. Now it is an insufficient objection that this introduces a subjective element into the classification process, for a degree of 'subjectivity' is involved in identifying *all* agreements, and careful criteria for separating the two categories can be formulated and followed (cf. *Intro*. IV, § 28). This said, the results of R–K's classification, which prove uncontroversial, need not be further pursued here. With two main qualifications, it corresponds to that given in the analytical account at III, *C Version* §§ 5–13, the basis of the C-Text printed in Volume I.

§ 106. The first qualification concerns the position of **t**, the ancestor of the three conjoint copies TH^{2}Ch, which in their **A** portion also form a genetic group.[195] R–K see t as a member of **x** and express its relationship horizontally as $\{<[XYJP^2(UD)]D^2> <(TH^2)Ch>\}$. The prior part of this sequence accords with the one at III, *C Version* § 13 below except for the position of D^2, which is there placed with y (though the manuscript's restricted attestation makes this grouping only probable, not certain). R–K's analysis of **p** as expressed in the sequence $\{<[(PE)(VA)RM]$ $[Q(SF)ZW]> <K(GN)>\}$ is also broadly compatible with the diagram of manuscript relationships given there.[196] But they take no account of the tp agreements in error, ascribed at III, *C Version* § 38 to descent from a common ancestor x^2 and giving (when horizontally expressed) the relation $\{<x^1> <x^2[\mathbf{p}][t]>\}$'. As it happens, the effect of this difference upon R–K's concrete textual decisions is relatively small, since to editors relying on the direct method, tp agreements in error merely imply that the harder **x** reading was in those cases preserved only by the branch of that family here designated x^1. A second, more significant qualification concerns R–K's interpretation of manuscript NLW 733B (N^2) as containing corrections from a source superior to the archetypal C-Text (Cx hereafter). This judgement, which is rejected at III, *C Version* §§ 39–40 below, highlights the persisting influence of the textual rationalism challenged in the critique of Athlone **B** at §§ 93–102 above. For as with the lost source hypothesised for K–D's preferred readings from the **B** ms Corpus 201, N^2's superior variants, save a handful attributable to scribal inventiveness, can be shown to be due to other-version contamination, specifically from the β family of **B**.

§ 107. R–K speak habitually of 'the *revisions* of the **C** Version' rather than 'the **C** revision' and while they acknowledge the C-Text as 'a marvellous event of the creative imagination' (p. 64), they apparently regard it as a vigorously corrected form of **B** rather than (as it seems to the present editor) a work conceived afresh, though incorporating much of its 'source' with only small alterations. More significantly, they believe that errors in the poet's **B** copy were what provoked specific changes to the text. They also recognise in the unfinished nature of the work a major factor affecting both their treatment of Bx corruptions surviving into Cx and their identification of 'a number of **C** passages as uncompleted revisions' (p. 63). R–K are thus constantly on the watch for differences between Bx and Cx that may be due to **C**'s archetypal scribe 'or, in the unfinished state of the revision, editorial' (p. 63). This possibility 'derives initially from accumulated impressions' (influenced by the editors' prior experiences and general critical judgement) 'of distinctive shape and detail' (though evidently not so gross as to have made Skeat think of **C** as unfinished). R–K are further convinced that they can uncover the 'physical aspect of the revision and its editorial implications.' The 'physical processes of revision' that they discern are relocations of old text; supplemental insertions of new text with or without larger modification where Bx was corrupt; exclusion of (un)corrupted **B** material; re-writing of **B** where Bx was (un)corrupt; and contextual accommodation of **B** material following a major transposition.

§ 108. Now these 'eight broad classes of change' seem to the present editor undeniable, despite any disagreements as to just where they occur. More arguable is the precise sense of 'physical', as is most obvious in regard to a significant transference of material like that from B XIII to C V–VII. Since R–K acknowledge that Langland's exact motives for revision are a matter of speculation (p. 66) and that the circumstances of each alteration are 'largely unrecoverable,' these changes can be confidently judged 'physical' only in the trivial sense that 'matter' is now located at a different place in the text. But just how this was accomplished depends on the nature of the revision-copy, about which only informed guesswork is possible. If it was made up of bound manuscript leaves written on both sides, changes could have been effected *in situ* as R–K suppose, the poet indicating where they should be re-sited and inserting fresh material on separate sheets. But in the absence of any visible witness to such interventions (like that in the unique codex of *Beowulf*),[197] R–K's 'physical' is a misnomer, and the whole conception risks misleading if made too definite. For it is at best only probable (and to the present editor, no more than possible) that the revision proceeded as R–K envisage. Langland could just as well have planned his structural and verbal alterations in rough working papers and then re-drafted the new text one or more times as he progressed towards a fair copy. Alternatively, the text could have been written out afresh and a fair copy made by an amanuensis who might understand the poet's intentions. Indeed, it may be that the whole poem was produced in this way, with only rare passages such as the Ophni-Phineas lines in Pr 95–124 (and not necessarily even these) remaining in enough of a draft state to lend credence to the Athlone editors' postulated 'physical processes of revision.'

§ 109. None of this implies that R–K's account lacks foundation in the available evidence; but it is, all the same, largely inferential. To the present editor, impartial examination of their forty-odd cases of 'relocation' (pp. 65–6) as readily favours the alternative hypothesis outlined above. And, although the matter cannot be spelled out in detail here, the same holds broadly true of their seven other (sub)-classes and carries similar 'editorial implications'. R–K's disarming observation that 'literary speculation about particular instances does not belong in this edition' (p. 67) therefore fails to re-assure, since their whole notion of Langlandian 'revision' involves such speculation. This is clear from their claim that the poet's failure to check his **B** manuscript systematically 'must appear from the number of scribal errors that survived his revision' (p. 67). Such a statement can escape circularity only if those errors can be shown to exist in some abundance. Yet by the canon of ratification, Bx readings that 'survive' into **C** should not be suspected as scribal at all, unless they demonstrably breach the core-text criteria on which a valid test of authenticity depends (and to which the Athlone editors are oblivious). To regard as unoriginal any reading confirmed by **C** is nothing if not 'literary speculation,' as may be illustrated by one example from the supposedly corrupt Bx readings altered with 'additions of one to three lines.' Thus archetypal C Pr 37–8 now reads *Fyndeth out foule fantasyes and foles hem maketh, / And hath wytt at wille to worche yf þei wolde*, the new verb *Fyndeth out* having the tense of Bx *Feynen hem* but being lexically identical with // **A** *Fonden hem*. Such *prima facie* evidence may justify K–D's emendation of **B** to read with **A** and thus lend colour to the 'physical' hypothesis of the revision process, since the poet could easily 'so to speak pen in hand' (p. 67) have deleted the first *e* of *Feynen* and inserted a *d* before the second, struck out *hem* and added *out foule*. But closer inspection raises doubts; for the new phrasal verb *fynden out* means 'discover by mental effort' while **A**'s verb with reflexive pronoun means 'devise (a means of doing),' of which Bx *feynen* is virtually a synonym.[198] In other words, **C** here neither simply restores **A** nor ratifies **B**; what it does is to re-compose **B**'s a-half afresh, and then only after introducing a new line 36 *Wolleth neyther swynke ne swete, bote sweren grete othes*, from which *foule* develops naturally (in part perhaps to link annominatively with *foles* in the b-half). This example is thus far neutral as between the two competing notions of the revision process described at § 108; but the balance tips against the

Athlone editors' interpretation by 38b, which retains Bx, except for replacing *sholde* with *wolde* to make the line closer in texture to 37, with its four full staves.[199] Although the foregoing account has itself involved two examples of 'literary speculation,' it is not the superiority of these but the logical force of the canon of ratification that here renders emendation otiose.

§ 110. In this instance, judging that the poet let a corrupt reading stand has had no effect on R–K, who leave Pr 37–8 alone. But the 'editorial implications' of believing that Langland read his text 'with variable degree of critical attention' (p. 67) are more pressing in II 11 *And crouned with a croune*, where R–K find evidence against Bx in both **C** families and read *in* for *with* as in Athlone **A** and **B** (which follows **A**). This decision may not obviously infringe the canon of ratification, but it leaves unclear whether they regard *with* as a Bx corruption overlooked by the poet through lack of 'critical attention' or one that Cx introduced (like Bx) as supposedly easier than the common original attested in **A**. A further difficulty here is that the Athlone **A** reading, found in only five **r**-family copies, is not securely archetypal like that at Pr 37–8, though evidently judged so by Kane for its intrinsic hardness. In a sense, this last consideration is irrelevant, since the 'rationalism' seen in R–K's choice for **A** is still more obvious in the case of **C**. For while support for *in* and *with* divides significantly across both families (*in* p^1 + IP^2; *with* p^2 + XUD), *with* is the only variant to ratify the archetypal reading of a preceding version. Such instances of 'rationalism' conflicting with an 'empiricist' approach to the text fairly illustrate the continuity of R–K's practice with that of K–D; so the objections made to the earlier Athlone editions hold good.

§ 111. This remains true notwithstanding that R–K, in this unlike the editors of **B**, disclaim authority to correct Bx errors 'that survived into the fair copy of C Pr–XX' (p. 90). Their statement is important for its distinction between the pre-archetypal ('editorial') text they posit as having been prepared from Langland's working papers, which could be called, in line with earlier terminology, 'C-Ø' (see § 91 above), and the archetypal text recoverable from the manuscript tradition (Cx). The distinction usefully allows scope for emendation where the Cx tradition appears corrupt but remediable, and R–K's extensive and radical alterations indicate a very qualified regard for that tradition. An example is I 112 (*R–K* 113) *Luppen alofte in þe north syde* where they offer the imaginative 'literary speculation' *in lateribus Aquilonis* for the unmetrical b-half. Here, though they attribute the origin of the Cx reading to 'an intruded marginal or interlinear gloss' (p. 169), R–K do not make clear that, if the posited gloss *north* stood in the text itself, it must have been introduced in C-Ø. This might be plausible as an explanation; but the process of error-generation diagnosed is complicated, and its correction extreme. For the simpler, one-word emendation *lefte* proposed in the present edition also explains the error in the archetype, but on a more economical assumption: that its scribe, working from the author's fair copy, substituted a non-alliterating 'synonym' for an expression he found contextually difficult through failure to grasp Langland's 'directional' symbolism.[200] This example shows that, far from reverting to **A**'s relatively positivist procedure, the rationalism of Athlone **C** is well on the way towards radical intuitionism.

§ 112. R–K's definition of their editorial objective (p. 90) as 'to recover or restore' the readings of the pre-archetype leaves them ample room both 'to diagnose what went wrong' in its making and 'to guess plausibly what the poet had in mind' (p. 90). To call Cx's source (whether proximate or ultimate) the 'pre-archetype' for short doubtless oversimplifies their position. But there is actually little solid evidence for the 'indeterminate number of stages' R–K postulate between the early 'clean copy' of the poet's revision (call it 'C-Ø') and 'the exclusive common ancestor of the surviving **C** manuscripts' (Cx), though the notion releases heady possibilities for correcting 'scribal corruption' in the latter (p. 94). What mainly acts as a brake on such correction is R–K's decidedly non-rationalist decision to let stand 'archetypal **B** errors which the poet did not correct' (p. 90). Yet 'radical' is nonetheless how R–K describe their 'deliberate retention of confidently identifiable scribal readings' (p. 94) such as those K–D often emended by reference to individual **B** copies like manuscripts F and G. Their explanation of this paradoxical stance is that the presumed 'scribal substitution[s]...occurred in the first phase of transmission of the **B** Version' (p. 93), from which derived the copy Langland used in revising to **C**.[201] One example is the important line I 39 (= B I 40, A I 39) *And þat seeth þe* [*þi* R–K] *soule and sayth hit the in herte*, which in K–D's elaborate reconstruction from archetypal **A** and the **B** copy G reads *And þat* [*shendeþ*] *þi soule*; [*set*] *it in þin herte*. Now it is hard to see how Langland overlooked an early scribal alteration of his posited original **B** line, both because agreed BxCx differ substantially in sense from Ax and K–D's conjectured form, and because C I 40 completely revises a **B** line very probably identical with its source in **A**. Such an authorial oversight in 39 must, it seems, be logically presupposed, since anything else implies tacit approval. But while in principle possible, it strains belief to the limit; for **C**'s ratification of Bx more realistically suggests that Ax was in this case corrupt.[202] There is no want of candour or consistency in R–K's position here, as a parallel-text presentation of the three Athlone texts would bear out. But the persuasiveness of their account assumes prior endorsement of the **A** reading with which their emended **B** is made to accord. And even if Ax were original, the canon of ratification provides antecedent grounds for thinking **B** a revision, since in sense, style and metre the text is unexceptionable. But even if Ax is rejected as scribal, Bx, whether a revision or a restoration of original **A**, could not be questioned as inauthentic.

§ 113. In their discussion of the last two passūs, R–K recognise four possible interpretations, all four treating XXI–XXII as unrevised. The one they favour sees in this section a B-Text descended, like Bx, from a single source (designated 'B-Ø' at III, *B Version* § 2), but also containing some thirty errors introduced by the scribe of Cx. R–K accordingly incorporate K–D's emendations of Bx to present a text of these passūs that is substantively identical with the Athlone text of **B**. Although they allow as 'not inconceivable' (p. 91) that XXI–XXII were revised but unavailable to the copyist of 'C-Ø' (§ 111 above), they exclude a fifth possibility, that Langland's revision here was light but has left some traces in the extant archetypal text. This is because R–K identify all the 100-odd differences between Cx and Bx as scribal, whereas to the present editor enough appear likely to be authorial for a total harmonisation of the texts to be unjustified. In consequence of R–K's comparative examination of the two archetypes, the Athlone edition of **C** thus emerges as in effect an editorial 'conjoint text', though by their reckoning there neither can nor need be any critically-edited parallel text of the final passūs. However, while antecedent probability may not favour either account over the other, the extensive revision in XX, displaying Langland's art in unabated vigour, contrasts so strongly with the minimal changes in XXI–XXII as to lend *prima facie* support to R–K's understanding of the revision-process as terminated at XX by the poet's illness or death. Recognition in these final passūs of authentic changes, if minor and even perhaps preliminary, is of course not incompatible with such an interpretation. Yet it neither presupposes it nor rules out Langland's having been more or less satisfied here with what he had written, as he evidently was with other (if less extended) passages earlier in the poem.[203] From one point of view, the present edition's treatment is in this instance less 'economical' than the Athlone's; but its product is not a new conjoint text. The Cx form of these passūs is here several times emended from Bx, and *e converso*; but not all its right readings are assumed to be merely preservations of B-Ø necessarily to be adopted into **B**. The critically-edited parallel texts of XXI–XXII are therefore at once near-identical for the most part and recognisably independent versions.

§ 114. In total contrast, R–K's handling of the text up to XX postulates extensive, but sporadic and incomplete acts of revision. Their numerous emendations of the archetypal C-Text are accordingly based on identifying specific readings as scribal on comparison with their parallels in **B** or **AB**. Very few such find an echo in the present text; for although in these cases R–K do not breach the canon of ratification, they often ignore what seems to this editor a strong antecedent probability of revision. (In practice, therefore, R–K's diagnoses of presumed error are seldom shared; where space permits, they are refuted, inevitably by recourse to the same direct method, if to reach a contrary conclusion). However, it should be stressed that in this edition the Cx text is retained not on 'positivistic' but on 'critically empirical' grounds, and is found acceptable always and only if it conforms with the core-line criteria (a concept fully explained at IV §§ 1–13 below). As before, the Athlone editors divide their suspect archetypal readings 'according to the grounds for identifying them as scribal' (p. 95). Some of these may be briefly considered to illustrate how the present edition differs from theirs.[204] They fall into six categories: mechanical errors; misreadings, whether visual errors or 'miscomprehension' (p. 97); (un)conscious easier readings; deliberate variations (such as smoothings or lexical substitutions); and accidental omissions. Major and minor instances are not separated by R–K, though the distinction seems crucial to the present editor, so it is mainly in major ones that the *Textual Notes* deal with their objections, and then only if it seems there is a case to answer.

§ 115. In a few instances of the first type, the analysis is wholly convincing, as at VI 223–24, where Cx misdivides and omits *owene* in 224. The likelihood of both errors being mechanical is reinforced by the recurrence of the first in the **m** family of **A** and of the second in members of **m** and r^2, although the family originals in the latter case were presumably both correct. This example serves to illustrate the critical value of the 'parallel' approach to editing Langland's text. Firstly, the agreed **AB** reading *tests* the 'linear postulate' against the canon of acceptability based on the core-text criteria: while in itself obviously not an argument against revision, it here persuasively proposes an original **C** reading from which Cx's unmetrical a-verse will have been generated, and it further confirms the line-division after *quarter*.[205] But secondly, **AC** agreement in *when Y* at 224b // against Bx *whoso* also *endorses* the postulate's value for assaying the authenticity of Cx readings not suspect as scribal by core-text criteria. Of these two 'Athlone' readings, the first was initially discriminated by Kane in preference to K–F's and Skeat's unmetrical Vernon manuscript reading, while the second is a K–D conjecture questioning a Bx reading printed by Skeat. Another possibly mechanical error also rightly corrected is Cx's omission (through eyeskip) of *dum scit mens est* from the Isidorean list of Liberum Arbitrium's names at XVI 199a. But in most of the 90-odd cases of this type (pp. 95–6), the Athlone editors are rather less persuasive in judging the Cx reading a scribal reflex rather than a revision. An example is I 70, where for *wente* R–K read *yede* of // **ZAB**, tracing the supposed error to alliterative inducement from the following line. However, as the line is one of four (68–71) with running alliteration on *w* and the second in this sequence to alliterate translinearly,[206] authorial substitution of a commoner advancing synonym for stylistic reasons cannot be ruled out. The editor, bound by the linear postulate to the canon of acceptability, should here firmly resist the siren-song of *durior lectio*. The case for recognising revision is further strengthened by the replacement of **ZAB** *faire* with a new fourth stave *and tauhte* in 71, a Cx reading R–K also emend (though the reasoning behind their second intervention will be hard to locate for assessment).[207]

§ 116. When introducing the next class of suspect Cx readings, R–K specify as an 'easier' reading 'the one that differs less from a grammatically or an otherwise contextually postulable norm, or requires less attention or thought, than another' (p. 97). However, since Langland could sometimes have wished to accord with such a norm, R–K must be defining 'easy' not *simpliciter* but *secundum quid,* that is, by testing two or more variants in relation to one another. But once again, after allowing room for disagreement over particular cases, a more general problem arises in R–K's list of Cx readings judged 'easier' than their parallels in **B** (p. 98): its insufficient regard for the linear postulate. For while the direct method may often operate straightforwardly as between competing family variants in one archetypal tradition (or at a lower level in the stemma), matters are less simple when comparing successive versions. This is because the revising poet must be allowed to express himself at times in a manner *closer* to the 'postulable norm' than to his *usus scribendi* as specified by K–D in their edition of **B**.[208] Desire for greater clarity of statement, a recognised feature of the **C** Version, could even have been a main motive for revision. This reservation obviously applies to the 'minor' type of reading; but it holds particularly for major instances, where Langland may have consciously aimed to avoid obscurity or ambiguity if those qualities served no artistic purpose in the context.

§ 117. Three examples may illustrate this last point. At XX 78 *For he was knyht and kynges sone, Kynde forȝaf þat tyme* Cx substitutes *tyme* for Bx *prowe* in the otherwise unchanged line. A special feature here is that the indication of probability by the linear postulate is somewhat weakened by the fact of an earlier occurrence of *tyme* in the **B** family β. There can be little question that the α variant *prowe* is the harder, and so likelier to be authentic in **B**, or that the same judgement would obtain were these variants directly competing within the archetypal **C** tradition. Since they are not, however, a conflict arises between 'rationalist' regard for *durior lectio* and 'empiricist' acceptance of Cx readings that (whether or not they agree with a particular **B** variant) do not breach the canon of acceptability. But Cx *tyme* must be either a revision for the sake of clarity or a scribal substitution of a more for a lexically less common original. And lateral support for deciding against emendation is found in the immediately following line *That hadde no boie hardynesse hym to touche in deynge* which R–K, it should be noted, accept as revised. The b-half is totally re-written and the a-half substitutes *boie* (already used at 77) for **B**'s *harlot*. Here Langland's careful retention of the source-line's vowel-alliteration is balanced by the repetition of *boie*, no longer in stave-position but present perhaps for the *lexical* purpose of clarification, the point being the social status rather than the moral character of the person.[209] A few lines later, at XX 86 // B XVIII 84, where Cx's *To touchen hym or to trinen hym or to taken hym down and grauen hym* replaces **B**'s second verb *tasten* and the whole of its last lift *of roode*, R–K once more 'restore' both. But here Langland might have had a stylistic as well as a lexical motive for revision: to eliminate this particular end-rhyme and to avoid the unseemly ambiguity of *tasten*.[210] The latter verb is used elsewhere, at XIX 124 = B XVII 148 and earlier at VI 179 = B XIII 346, the survival unchanged of both **B** lines implying that neither occasioned the Cx scribe particular difficulty. But perhaps a more significant argument against R–K is that *trinen* is lexically much the harder, being virtually confined to Langland in this period.[211] Given these considerations, there seems little reason for thinking the new last lift unoriginal, since neither sense nor metre is objectionable. Finally, **B**'s *modicum* is replaced in Cx by *moreyne* at XX 224 *For til moreyne mete with vs*. If this were a straight comparison of stave-words within the Cx tradition, *modicum* would surely count as harder; but that is not what is at issue here. One reason for revising could be the relative obscurity of **B**'s macaronic stave; another, a wish to stress the religious significance of plague or (if *moreyne*'s contextual sense is 'mortality') of the *deth of kynde* mentioned at 219 (an idea explicitly linked with the plague among Kynde's *forageres* at B XX 85). Not one of these three cases plausibly indicates that the Cx readings are 'scribal substitutions for an original like that in the archetypal **B** text because they are easier' (p. 98). Emendations of this kind that use the direct method without regard for the linear postulate and the acceptability canon bring out vividly the limitations of the procedure they exemplify.

§ 118. While R–K's discussion of their cases of more emphatic scribal readings or smoothing cannot be examined here in detail, it should be noted that their account of **B** lines they believe were accidentally left out of Cx at least acknowledges that these might have been excluded in revision. In some like B XIV 105, already adopted in the present edition (= C XV 285), both the mechanical ease of omission and the case for inclusion on grounds of sense seem unarguable.[212] But instances like B Pr 115 *For to counseillen þe Kyng and þe Commune saue* are more problematic. R–K may be right to suspect its mechanical loss through visual attraction from *Kynde Wytt* 141 to the same phrase at the same line-position in C Pr 142. But omission of **B**'s point about the political rôle of the clergy could have been deliberate, given that 140 has been radically revised to make the knightly order and not the commons the source of the king's executive authority. Here the Athlone editors risk misrepresenting the poet's latest thought on a topic presumably at the forefront of his mind when revising. Rather less is at stake in their inclusion of *Si ius nudatur, nudo de iure metatur* from the Angel's speech at B Pr 137, a case which recalls *dum scit mens est* at XVI 199a (§ 115 above). This verse has, however, an undeniably minatory tone, and a further motive for omitting it might have been to join the last line of the speech with B Pr 136 so as to extend the sowing metaphor across two lines. Conceivably, this change was accompanied by a visual direction to place B Pr 137 after 135 (= C Pr 155), a speculation at all events consonant with R–K's 'physical' notion of the revision process and its material product. However, they place the line not after 155 but as in **B**, overlooking the evidence for its possible excision in the immediately following passage, which drops a Latin couplet and a single line originally found in **B**.

§ 119. Where R–K consider the text of Cx scribal on comparison with a Bx reading also found in one or more **C** witnessses, they rightly admit (p. 102) the possibility of coincident variation or of 'correction,' whether memorial or by consultation of another copy ('contamination', qualified as 'benign' where appropriate, would perhaps better cover both forms of the latter process). Particularly is this so with respect to manuscript N^2 in which, heavily sophisticated as it is, R–K profess to discern authoritative corrections from a lost source independent of the archetype (p. 102, n. 23). On a superficial view, one editor's 'correction' may look like another's 'contamination'; but the matter admits of more exact formulation. For as will be shown below (III, *C Version* § 40), apart from about five instances the N^2 variants should be ascribed to a **B** source, since some are peculiar to β where this family is in error and the presumptive Bx reading is that of α agreeing with Cx. In a wide range of instances R–K find the archetype unoriginal in its defective alliteration, omissions, and easier or more emphatic readings. But it must suffice here to single out two examples of lexical substitution and two of imperfect metre, both to vindicate the doubt already voiced concerning their judgements in these areas and also to affirm a measure of agreement with them. To begin with two of the latter, R–K, like the present editor, insert *leode* as the first lift in X 7. Here, the word's mechanical loss before *longed* is plausible, it is needed for sense as well as metre and, as the assured reading of **AB**, its insertion counts as a 'restoration'.[213] The linear postulate may therefore be set aside in this instance as there is little likelihood that the Cx reading, clearly defective by the core-text criteria, represents what the poet intended.[214] Similarly acceptable is R–K's adoption of $N^{2'}$s *grettore* for *wyddore* at XX 400, whether the Cx error be due to anticipation of copy, as they suppose (p. 104), or unconsciously induced by a common collocation. In this case, though both editions formally cite N^2 as source, the true authority for the emendation is the **B** Version, from which that **C** copy derives it (cf. the case of *þrumblide* in the Vernon copy of **A** discussed at § 78 above).

§ 120. Altogether different in character, however, is X 70 '*What art thow,*' quod Y, '*þat thow my name knowest?*' where R–K add the presumed **AC** reading *þo* after Y from one **C** copy, F. But the intruded adverb is not strictly needed for the sense and, more important, is unlikely to have been in Ax, as it is attested only by group t and manuscript J but not by **m** or the remaining members of both **r** sub-families. That Bx had *þo* is itself doubtful because, though present in β and ms F, its absence from R suggests that it was not in α. The metrical objection to Cx also falls once the line is seen to conform with the Type IIIa variant-pattern *ax / ax* illustrated by the core-text.[215] A case where R–K do detect contamination, but assign it differently from the present editor, is Pr 1[89] *And yf hym wratheth, ben war and his way roume.* Here they judge Cx *roume* a memorial contamination from 18[1][216] and 'correct' from the **x** family group b, a source demonstrably contaminated from the **B** Version.[217] But the 'stylistic' answer to R–K's stylistic objection is to recognise deliberate *repetitio* in Cx's second use of this verb (there are no grounds of sense for rejecting it). The same rhetorical device, much favoured in Langland's late phase, is evident at XV 10[3] *And take wittenesse at a trinite, and take his felowe to witnesse.* Here in the a-half R–K substitute *And þanne shal he testifie of a trinite* from **B**; but what they fail to observe in Cx is a real sense-difference between the two occurrences of *witnesse*,[218] the phrasal constructions being semantically distinct while lexically unified in their doubling of both verb and noun.

§ 121. The Athlone editors' rejections of several Cx readings as more explicit, easier or more emphatic than those of corresponding **B** include some where the present or an earlier edition anticipates them. At XX 226 *Forthy God, of his goednesse, þe furste gome Adam,* they are probably right in their implied judgement of t's alliterating synonym which, whether felicitous guess or memorial contamination, is most probably a scribal improvement of non-alliterating Cx *man,* not the preservation of an authentic reading by pure descent. Another example is VII 106 *And fithele the, withoute flaterynge, of God Friday þe geste,* where manuscript F has *geste,* a presumptively original reading answering in sense to **B**'s *storye,* for archetypal *feste.* This particular Cx substitution R–K class as that of an 'easier' reading, though it is one probably due to unconscious suggestion from the context of *festes* (97 above).[219] In a third case, at XVII 268 *And baptisede and bissheinede with þe bloed of his herte,* they rightly view the second verb in the corresponding (not strictly parallel) B XV 516 as harder than *bisshopid.* But they misidentify the latter as archetypal, though the Cx reading may be more credibly discerned as that of all x^1 witnesses but one and *bisshopid* better interpreted stemmatically as a criterial x^2 reading preserved in **pt** and inserted in P^2 by contamination from **p**.[220] The manuscript P^2 is also the sole **C** copy to read **B**'s *foulest* at XX 156 *For of alle fretynge venymes the vilest is the scorpioun.* But in this fourth case, where R–K identify Cx *vilest* as 'easier,' they ignore the antecedent likelihood of a change in a context that shows signs of extensive revision. For between 154–62 only three lines (157 and 159–60) escape some alteration, and **C** strengthens 156 by replacing its non-lexical first stave *For* with *fretynge*. It is in any case less than clear that *vilest* is easier than *foulest*; for the two lexemes overlapped semantically, as is indicated by the overt play on their aural affinity earlier at VI 432.[221] Most of the other readings in this section are minor, and in them R–K's grounds for preferring **B** to Cx become proportionately more subjective and more tenuous.

§ 122. The strengths and limitations of the Athlone editors' use of the parallel method appear in their account of the type of situation where one competing variant within the Cx tradition (usually **p** against **x**) is confirmed by a secure Bx reading. These include uncontroversial instances of palæographic errors and inadvertent omissions (pp. 106–7); but among twenty rejected as unmetrical, two misclassifications of probable Cx readings as of 'X and its associates' deserve attention for their wider implications. In XVI 279 (281) most manuscripts have *churche*, a formal substitution common at all levels of the tradition (including the archetypal),[222] but YDChN² attest *kirke*, giving a normative Type I line. As R–K plausibly find this form original, but without stating whether they consider it archetypal, they apparently rule out memorial contamination from **B**, though it would seem better to leave the issue open (the alternative explanation being correction, independently or from a lost source). But *kirke* seems unlikely, from the manuscript evidence, to have been archetypal, and *churche* is not emended in the present text as this is metrically unnecessary. In another example, at IX 23 *Ac* [*no* a] *pena et a culpa Treuthe nolde hem graunte,* it is obscure why R–K consider the **x** variant they reject to have 'anormative alliteration' since satisfactory scansion is obtainable by reading *no treuthe* or *nolde* in the b-half[223] (the present edition prefers *nolde,* but R–K adopt neither). Here they both misclassify the line (p. 106) and print a form of it with no staves at all, failing to see the revision process as a whole or to note that while **A** and **B** scan on *p* (as does **Z**), **C**'s replacement of *pope* with *treuthe* requires a new key-stave on *n* (*nolde*).

§ 123. Among many cases diagnosed of inadvertent substitutions by **x**, few provoke dissent, though a couple deserve closer study for the light they throw on the Athlone procedure. At X 71 '*That wost þou, Wille,*' *quod he,* '*and no wyht bettre*', R–K find *Wille* induced by *name* at 70 and accordingly emend to *wel* as in one **x** copy D, five **p** copies EQZKN and parallel **B**. But this is a bold change, given the manuscript indication that *Wille* is archetypal and so, since not deficient by the canon of acceptability, presumptively original (by the linear postulate). R–K's judgement is in any case dubious, since at 60 Thought has called the dreamer by his *kynde name* (so that the reader half expects to hear what this is) and the narrator has already been addressed as *Wille* by Holy Church after use of a similar phrase *calde me by name* (I 5). This earlier reading they do not emend, though the **B** parallel *sone* is attested within the **C** tradition by both manuscript I and group b, on which they rely at Pr 189 (see § 16 above). The two cases are hardly identical, since the earlier is not even partly diagnosable as mechanical; but this should not rule out the possibility that on each occasion the name may have been deliberately inserted as a kind of signature.[224] In both cases, the copies that read with **B** are suspect of contamination from the one earlier version likely to have been familiar.

§ 124. Of the numerous 'variants in this situation, attested by X and other copies' (p. 110) that R–K find scribal because more explicit or more emphatic, *Hit were to tore for to telle of the tenþe dole*; but a few notable major examples from the 'easier' category may be selected. In XIX 253 it is admittedly puzzling why Langland eliminated **B**'s *þe contrarie*; but since there is no mechanical reason for the loss, Cx is not clearly easier than **B** (though it is less explicit), and the line meets the acceptability canon, R–K are not justified in emending it. Less problematic is Pr 72 *bulles,* where again the **AB** reading *breuet* that R–K favour is attested by I and group b, now accompanied by M (and by P² marginally after deletion of its exemplar's *bulles*). But this appears another case of rhetorical *repetitio,* like that at Pr 189 discussed at § 120 above. Again, at XVI 185 the Cx reading *mens thouhte* (also that of the **B** family α) may seem 'easier' if read as a translation 'man's thought', but not if analysed as a Latin name followed by an 'internal' gloss. Scribal failure to grasp this might sufficiently account for the loss of *thouhte* from the **C** group u (as it would in β), though in the case of N², contamination from a β-type **B** copy seems more likely. But however the relative 'easiness' of the two variants is assessed, terminal *mens* would be ruled out by core-text metrical standards as producing the excluded masculine line-ending. Another type of case, where the rejected reading scarcely seems easier by normal lexical criteria, is instanced at XIX 143 *For þe paume hath power to pulte out þe ioyntes,* in which support for *pulte* and *putte* divides across, not just between, the families. Here R–K are unwise to assume that Bx read *putte,* since R's *pult* may preserve the reading of α (and hence of Bx), and as support is split in both archetypal traditions, the likelier original must be sought by establishing the direction of variation on intrinsic grounds. But the lexical evidence overwhelmingly supports *pulte* as harder in the context;[225] and R–K's argument may be refuted by applying their own method, here again so as to reach a different conclusion.

§ 125. In a still more complex situation, a range of readings appears in two or even all three canonical traditions, but none of the archetypes is certainly authentic (p. 112), so that the direct method is placed under the greatest pressure in seeking to isolate 'one variant...as the likely original of all the others.' An important instance is at XX 199 *Yf that thei touched þat [a QF] tre and of þe fruyt eten,* where R–K adopt *a* QF**B** and follow K–D's insertion (from Huntington 128) of *trees* before *fruyt*. The identification of Hm's variant as 'the likely original' of both versions rather than as the intelligent guess of a scribe aiming to improve the metre is bold, but its likelihood must be remote. There is a case for *a* instead of *þat,* as it effectively signalises the uniqueness of the tree of the Fall by stressing a non-lexical word in a line to be understood as scanning on vowels rather than on *t*. But *þat* can as plausibly be attributed to the author's wishing to clarify this point by eliminating the ambiguity of *a,* which (taken as the numeral) denotes 'one particular tree' but (taken as the indefinite article) may misleadingly signify 'any tree.' The Cx reading could arguably have been occasioned by scribal objection to repeated *tree*; but the closeness of the two archetypal texts suggests, in this context of ongoing changes (e.g. at 196b), revision by **C** as the likelier explanation. R–K's retention of the Athlone **B** emendation is therefore unjustifiable on grounds of sense. In fact they class the case as one of 'anormative alliteration' (p. 112); but while this is strictly correct, it is not equivalent to 'unoriginal', as becomes clear once Langland's metrical variant-types are properly recognised. As it stands in Cx, this line is classifiable as the 'reduced' Type IIIb with an extended a-half, a supplemental vowel-stave in final position, and counterpoint on *t*, giving the authentic scansion *abb / aa*.[226]

§ 126. The cases where readings of the base-ms X, more often than not presumed archetypal, are attested in other **A** and **B** copies include a number of varying interest and significance that R–K correct, as does the present edition. But at VII 131 they do not make clear that, since G, the single **C** copy with *siht* for *liht,* is unlikely to have substituted a harder reading independently, this is better interpreted as a 'benign' contamination from parallel B V 492. Here, the likeliest causes of the error in Cx and in six **B** copies will have been the visual similarity of the letter-forms *l* and long *s* and the presence of *liht* in the next line. Superficially similar but more problematic is a reading in a single **C** copy which is not that of archetypal **B**. This is Chaderton's *mery* at XX 181, which R–K (p. 115) prefer to Cx *mercy,* objecting to its sense on grounds external to the text. But here they make too little of the fact that Bx is identical with Cx, that the metre is correct and the meaning adequate, and that Ch's reading could be a visual error or a contextually induced aberration (of a kind not uncommon in this manuscript). R–K's analysis here is unsatisfactory and omits any reference to the acute discussion in *K–D* pp. 208–9. Somewhat enigmatic, too, is their inclusion (p. 115) among 'less interesting' variants of *reik* at Pr 201, a notable crux discussed at length in the present edition.[227] Among this group, moreover, the mere listing of **B** or **AB** parallels does not help the reader find where in the earlier Athlone editions the grounds for discriminating the variant preferred are set out. With a case like *close* for Cx *clanse* at VIII 65, by contrast, previous discussion can be easily located in *Ka*'s Critical Notes, a valuable feature unhappily abandoned in subsequent volumes.

§ 127. The significant distinction to be drawn between *close*] *clanse* and *mery*] *mercy* does not emerge with sufficient sharpness from the data as presented by R–K. Both their emendations are rejected here because they conflict with the canon of ratification, which prohibits alteration of an assured Bx reading retained in **C** unless it demonstrably infringes the core-text criteria, and both are decided simply on grounds of sense. But R–K do not make clear that whereas *mery* is found in only one copy of either version, *close* (attested in **C** solely in the group RM), as the reading of the r^1 sub-family of **A**, has some claim to be archetypal (neither case is in fact treated as archetypal in the present edition).[229] The point here is that the textual weight of the competing variants is hard to measure when they are lumped together to illustrate 'variation of X supported by other copies which appears easier than an alternative' (p.114). The problem with Athlone's way of systematically grouping readings for discussion is that it discourages a comparison of them in the context of their relative strength of attestation in the several versions. For without any cross-referencing, the stronger arguments for a particular textual choice (where these exist) cannot easily be found: vexatious fatigue for the reader trying to assess the editors' decisions is the cost exacted by their use of a 'categorial' rather than a 'sequential' format. The most helpful parts of R–K's Introduction are accordingly those examining individual readings in a detailed manner that combines the benefits of Athlone **A**'s Critical Notes with the fullness allowed by a discursive presentation. The concluding portion (pp. 118–136) on problems in XXI–XXII, where the text of **B** is comprehensively relevant as 'a factor in its determination,' is particularly forthcoming in its willingness to engage with contrary arguments in the Everyman first edition of the B-Text. The appearance of Athlone **C** between that of the present edition's volumes I and II has conversely made it possible to take full account here of R–K's replies to those arguments. Between them, therefore, these pages and the corresponding sections of the present *Textual Notes* provide a fairly full study of the main difficulties in the text of **C**. Though restrictions of space here rule out answering every one of the Athlone editors' points, the reader who wishes to compare the textual approaches of the two editions could do worse than turn to these sections of the respective volumes.

§ 128. R–K's textual arguments are nearly always penetrating and provocative; but two recurring sources of dissatisfaction are their treatment of Langland's metre and their negative attitude to the Z-Text. The first, by now familiar, may be illustrated from their rejection of Cx XXII 155 *And to forȝete ȝowthe and ȝeue nat of synne* and adoption instead of their emended parallel **B** reading *And [so] forȝete [sorwe] and [of synne ȝeue nouht]*, which has *sorwe* for *ȝowthe* but in Bx the two-stave metrical pattern *ab / ab* (p. 132). Their elaborate explanation finds in Cx a memorial contamination from XII 12 or 'metrical repair on that model.' But the change could more plausibly evince the deliberate re-writing of a **B** line that contained the seed of the new idea in **C**, since the referent of **B**'s *sorwe* is clearly 'sorrow for sins past' and that of *ȝowthe* is (metonymically) '(the sins of) one's youthful life.' R–K's alteration not only flouts the acceptability canon, but their dual-purpose emendation, replacing *to* with *so* and retaining the (now metrically normative) **B** line for **C**, does not afford superior sense. For while it is clear how forgetting contrition for sin might result from banishing fear of death and age, **C** makes the subtler point that Life's behaving like a stereotypical Youth is a way of 'forgetting' his own misspent youth. R–K's metrical argument is inconsistent with their acceptance elsewhere of Type III core-lines like V 116; but graver faults are their consigning to oblivion of an acceptable archetypal line in each version, alteration of Langland's meaning, and concealment of an interesting revision. The second point, concerning **Z**, is now of mainly historical interest, since the Everyman first edition's emendation of *alle kynne* to *alleskynnes* in XX 373 so as to provide an internal *s* stave proves otiose in the light of the present editor's improved understanding of the poet's metre.[230] However, it is worth commenting on R–K's objection (p. 130, n. 49) to this conjectured form as unlikely to be Langlandian because found 'in only one *Piers* manuscript, as a morphological variant in H³ at A X 27.' This sounds definitive in its assured use of the Apparatus evidence but, like an earlier observation of the Athlone **A** editor (noted at § 61 above), is wrong. The form in question occurs at Z III 172; and whatever else Bodley 851 may be, it is 'a *Piers* manuscript.'

§ 129. In dealing with new or revised matter in the text where no particular reference is made to **B**, R–K distinguish comparison of the two main family traditions so as to discern the original reading, and diagnosis, which involves 'an absolute comparison between actual readings and abstractions.' These important 'abstractions' could be thought of as the ideal forms from which archetypal lines found defective in metre or in 'the understood grammar of the poet's style' may be hypothesised to derive. And in this crucial (but potentially controversial) stage of the editorial process, while R–K acknowledge the risk of being 'arbitrarily subjective,' they take comfort from the 'handsome third' of such lines where they identify, in one or a few manuscripts, a variant of which they judge Cx a corruption (p. 138). That privileged reading, when it shows itself, they take to have come in by correction from 'a superior **C** copy' (ibid. n. 3); but they nonetheless recognise that scribes might have gone in for 'independent editorial adventurism' like that discoverable in the Corpus 201 copy of **B**. It has already been noted that the handy notion of 'a lost manuscript of superior quality to the archetype' infringes the canon of economy. It should now be emphasised that there is almost nothing in the **C** copies yielding the few readings admittedly superior to Cx's that cannot be ascribed to intelligent scribal guesswork or felicitous chance. In the 'unhandsome' remaining two-thirds, R–K must naturally have 'recourse to conjecture in full understanding of its implications.'

§ 130. Given how far-reaching these implications are, it is not surprising that Athlone **C** also becomes (in K–D's words cited at § 104 above) 'a theoretical structure...a complex hypothesis designed to account for a body of phenomena.' But its radical character is not evident at once from R–K's opening account of 'the more elementary unconscious errors' in X and its family ancestor, such as omissions and the usual easier and more emphatic readings that they confidently distinguish. Their observations are often plausible, as at XIX 100 *And Hope afturward of o God more me toelde,* where they offer both mechanical and interpretative reasons for preferring the x^2 reading *god* to x^1's *o god* (p. 149), and this section (pp. 143–75) contains some of R–K's most rewarding as well as most controversial arguments. But these need no further specification here, as they may be compared almost point for point with those in the *Textual Notes.*[231] At the other end of the scale, an example of invasive editing that induces deeper misgivings about the Athlone procedure is R–K's gratuitously elaborate 're-arrangement' of III 139–44 from the divergent texts attested in **x** and **p** 'which, if original, would account for the shape of both' (p. 159):

> godes forb[o]de eny more
> Thow tene me and treuthe: and thow mowe be atake
> In the Castel of Corf y shal do close the,
> Or in a wel wors, wo[ne ther as an ancre,
> And marre þe with myschef], be seynte mary my lady.
> That alle [women, wantowen], shal [be] war [by] þe one.

Apart from the archetypal inversion to prose order in the second line that R–K 'radically' leave with the inauthentic pattern *aa / xa* (cf. § 112 above), there is little in the **p** variants they favour that cannot be ascribed to this family's well-established tendency to pad out the terse original convincingly preserved by **x**, as noted by Carnegy (1934:12–13) and printed in the present text. But given the drastic treatment, it is hard to see why they also leave their third line with a masculine ending, unless they imagine that Langland wrote such lines (the core-text confirms the massive evidence of the separate archetypes that he did not).

§ 131. R–K finally discuss metrical and stylistic corruptions and claim to discern in one or a few individual copies original harder readings, some of which raise important issues of principle. One such is IX 26[2] *The tarre is vntydy þat to þe shep bylongeth,* where they prefer manuscript F's *tripe* to Cx *shep* (p. 164). The Athlone editors are doubtless right about the general unlikelihood of a scribe's substituting what would appear an 'intrinsically' harder word; but they here overestimate the power of the direct method's central editorial criterion. For if *tripe* is not a piece of 'scribal adventurism', it must be a correction from a lost superior source. Yet the Cx line possesses in the grammatical word *to* the mute key-stave that is almost a hallmark of this poet's practice (see Appendix I § 4). Now, where the *durior lectio* criterion clashes with the canons of economy and acceptability, the case for avoiding emendation should, on logical grounds, be held the stronger (see IV, §§ 27ff, esp. § 29 below). A wider implication of this analysis that should be highlighted is that, in some circumstances, a reading that is lexically harder in itself may nonetheless be judged scribal if the context provides a likely motive for substitution. Here such a motive is at hand in the failure of an otherwise intelligent scribe[232] to grasp a peculiar feature of Langland's versification, his consequent perception of the line as metrically defective, and his subsequent 'adventurous' emendation.

§ 132. The final textual situation R–K consider is one where no extant copy has a variant from which the Cx reading identified as scribal can have derived, so that emendation must rely on conjecture. One typical example of a conjecture that is not unreasonable in itself but is based on tortuous reasoning occurs among some seven cases where simple re-arrangement of word-order would render normative a line with the inauthentic alliterative pattern *aa / xa*. At VIII 30 R–K observe (p. 168, n. 26) that the **B** source-line in an archetypally corrupt form was what Langland 'received' in his revision copy: that is, a reading presumed identically corrupt in Bx and B[1] must already have been corrupt in B-Ø, the common source of both. B VI 31 *And go affaite þi faucons wilde foweles to kille* is emended in *K–D* to read as **A**; yet its sense, metre and style are unexceptionable and the reading is fully acceptable as a revision of A VII 33. What makes R–K's decision unsatisfactory is not its final product (identical in the present edition) but the faulty reasoning that underlies it. For if they believe that **B** originally read like **A**, then this line must be one of those 'overlooked' by the poet because of the conditions of his revision. From one point of view, therefore, their approach to the text is deeply conservative, despite what they appear to regard as the conjectural character of their emendation (cf. § 112 above). For the reading they print is not one uninstanced elsewhere but, if it is accepted that this underwent in Cx a simple transposition to prose order in the b-half, one that will require no more than a straightforward 'restoration' (III, *B Version* § 61) to the archetypal form of the preceding version. Yet its adoption in Athlone **C** is at odds with its rejection in Athlone **B**. From this, it emerges that any approach to editing *Piers Plowman* that is not 'parallelist' from the beginning risks ending in contradiction.

§ 133. It is, however, in the area of conjectural emendations on grounds of sense that the Athlone C-Text (like its predecessor) arouses most disquiet. For since metrical and stylistic objections are now absent, R–K must show by 'absolute comparison' why their 'abstraction' is preferable to the 'actual' reading. Here the stakes are high, since they risk destroying the author's sense and substituting their own. A striking example occurs at XVIII 236 *So is God Godes Sone, in three persones the Trinite,* which the Athlone editors find 'very strange theology' (p. 175). But the strangeness disappears if *sone* is seen as the subject and the b-half read as an ellipsis, with *and* and *is* to be understood respectively before *in* and *the*. In R–K's *So i[n] god [and] godes sone i[s] three persones, the trinite,* introducing the same two words understood in the proposed ellipsis, it is hard to connect the credal formula *qui procedit ab utroque* that they invoke in relation to 231 with the precise form of their emended line, which is strained in phrasing and disconcerting in sense. This is one instance where the archetypal text, however odd its conjunction of ideas, is not nonsense and may well be what Langland wrote, so that intervention is inadvisable. Again, at XVII 126 R–K alter the archetype's definition of Charity as *Lief and loue and leutee, in o byleue a lawe* to read *[Lif in] loue and leutee in o byleue [and] lawe.* Unfortunately, as cited on p. 174 the line they find 'hard to make sense of' reads *a leutee* for *and leutee*, making no sense at all. But assuming only a misprint here, the actual Cx reading may be defended as meaningful and, with its closeness in phrasal structure to the previous example, as redolent of authentic Langlandian idiom. Charity is being defined by two phrases in apposition, the first giving its components, the second a parallel statement about moral unanimity on the basis of unity in faith. R–K, whether as part of or independently of their larger emendation, alter the spelling of X's *Lief* to *Lif* as in **p** and the **x**-group u; but they are perhaps mistaken to do so, since Langland may intend a pun on 'life' and 'faith,' while group y's unusual spelling is indirectly confirmed by *leue* in the unrelated t. All this suggests the triad 'faith, love, hope' as the constituents of the comprehensive *charite* informing a distinctively 'mystical' late-Langlandian conception of 'the Church.' The passage, which shows the poet thinking at high pressure, may not be wholly lucid, but its drift is not in doubt. R–K's interference with an archetypal text that makes good sense is thus imprudent, even if it is not their quoted form that underlies their interpretation. But in XVII 131 *God lereth no lyf to louye withouten lele cause* their alteration of *louye* to *leue* for supposedly lacking contextual sense borders on *rechelesnesse*, as consultation of the following lines 136–139 on wrong or lawless 'loves' will bear out. For it is only 'love' that makes contextual sense, Langland's point being that what God wants from man is a rational or 'right' love based on orthodox belief and the morality that should arise from it. This notion, very close to that of XVII 126, again illustrates the unbreakable theological triad so prominent in the later Langland's thought. The received text is clear, sound and arresting, but as re-written by R–K nearly unintelligible. In all these instances, loss of an archetypal reading is not outweighed by the gain of any vivid new possibility. It is otherwise with R–K's 'adventurous' emendation *in lateribus Aquilonis* for *in þe north syde* at I 11[3]. This does not persuade the present editor to forsake the simpler and more economical *in þe [lefte] syde* but is, if not what Langland wrote, worthy of him.

§ 134. R–K's view of the history of the **C** Version and their treatment of its text are in most ways as radical as those of K–D. Particularly challenging are their high valuation of the sub-archetypal **p** tradition, consonant with their refusal to judge it secondary (as it is argued to be at III, *C Version* § 10), and their relatively low esteem for the archetypal text, in which they detect a host of 'errors' that baffle the present editor's most earnest scrutiny. R–K's arguments nonetheless expand and sharpen the reader's attentiveness to the details of Langland's art and meaning. If their Introduction lacks the urgency of Kane's and the penetration of Kane-Donaldson's, its 'theoretical structure' is built upon as solid and accurate a 'body of phenomena' as its predecessors'. The three Athlone volumes carry the rationalist understanding of Langland's text to its limits, and a good deal further than the present editor would be prepared to go; but they constitute, by any standards, a formidable achievement.

x. Rigg and Brewer's *Edition of the* Z-Text

§ 135. Fifteen years earlier, the edition of the Z-Text by George Rigg and Charlotte Brewer (*R–B* hereafter)[233] was published, halfway between the Everyman and York editions of **B** and **C** (1978) and the second edition of the Athlone text of **A** (1988). Kane in his 'Retrospect' was therefore obliged to take cognisance of Bodley 851, but merely dismissed it as 'useless for editing, if not actually misleading' (*Ka²* p. 459) with a reference to the footnote discussion in the Athlone **B** Version and his long review of R–B's edition.[234] Since the Athlone editors nowhere envisage **Z** as a substantive version of *Piers Plowman*, their verdict presumably relates to the manuscript only as evidence for the text of **A**. This verdict has already been shown to be mistaken (see § 64 above), even if Bodley 851 is taken as no more than a wayward **A** copy similar to F of the **B** Version and N^2 of **C**. R–B, however, argue for **Z** not simply as an independent **A** witness but as an authentic version anterior to **A**. Their claim, if substantiated, has important implications, immediately for the text of **A** and more generally for the work as a whole. Like the other versions, **Z** is considered fully in Part III of this *Introduction*; but here *R–B* will be examined as a pioneering contribution to the editorial tradition.

§ 136. In appearance, the edition resembles those of the EETS, but as there is only one copy of this 'version' its footnote 'apparatus' has no variant readings. Instead, at one level it records the **A** lines to which the **Z** lines correspond and supplements this with a useful ten-page Concordance

Table to the three other versions. A second level gives Critical Notes like those of the EETS and Athlone **A** editions on textual points, parallels, linguistic matters and problems of local meaning. Like Skeat, R–B mark expansions and keep the manuscript's idiosyncratic spellings, though not its word-divisions, record its (intermittent) paraph marks, and employ modern punctuation. Additionally, they place vertical lines in the margin to indicate **Z**'s differences in word-order from **A** and at a few points obeli to mark 'corrupt, unemended passages' (p. 34).[235] Otherwise their text's peculiar feature is the use of bold type for **Z**'s unique readings, which vary in length from single words to a 30-line passage at the end of Passus III.[236] (This feature, despite its obvious utility, has no place in the present edition; for as a putative 'version', **Z** is not treated differently from **A**, **B** and **C**, each of which contains distinctive material). Emendations, 'positivist' in scale, are limited to correction of mechanical errors and potentially misleading spelling mistakes, supply of missing letters, and provision of words deemed necessary for the sense.[237] R–B's final analytical section identifies the manuscript's archaic and South West Midland linguistic features as original and its non-Western forms as scribal, concluding that 'the linguistic appearance of **Z** suggests that it was copied from a text exactly answering to our suppositions about Langland's origins' (p. 127). Such 'traditional' philological interest is of a piece with their judgement that 'a unique copy of a unique version of the poem' (ibid.) should receive a conservative treatment of its text and accidentals alike. This judgement is accepted in the present edition which, however, goes beyond correcting a few more mechanical errors[238] to venture some reconstructions and conjectural emendations.[239]

§ 137. The physical features of MS Bodley 851 have proved a focus for disagreements with R–B's claims on behalf of its text. But that the codicological and textual issues can be disentangled is clear from the separate introductions to the same editors' subsequent *Facsimile* of **Z**.[240] Here the structure of the codex is analysed by Rigg at greater length and the text by Brewer, who takes account of the reception of their edition and more recent work on **Z** and its relations to **A**.[241] But the editors' two basic claims remain: first, that the *Piers Plowman* text up to VIII 92 (**Z**), forming Part III (a) of the manuscript, is by a single scribe, Hand X, who also wrote three of the Latin pieces in Part I (*Facsimile*, p. 25); second, that this scribe was John Wells, the Benedictine of Ramsey Abbey whose beautifully-drawn book-plate appears on fol. 6v. Rigg ascribes the book-plate inscription *Iste liber constat Fratri Iohanni de Wellis Monacho Rameseye* to Hand X and identifies the owner with the noted anti-Wycliffite monk who had been a student at Gloucester College, the Benedictine house at Oxford, before 1376, was *prior studentium* there in 1381, and died at Perugia in 1388. On the evidence of the handwriting and the Oxford associations of the manuscript, R–B accordingly date the Z-Text between 1376 (or earlier) and 1388, and locate its copying in Oxford (*R–B*, p. 5; *Facs.*, pp. 29–30). The manuscript's **C** portion of *Piers* (= C-ms Z) and nearly a hundred **A** lines linking **Z** to **C** they assign to a single scribe (Q) of the early fifteenth century. This account has been criticised by Ralph Hanna, who doubts that the book-plate inscription is by the scribe of **Z** and claims that the latter cannot be shown to be the Ramsey monk in the absence of any surviving autograph by Wells.[242] Hanna supports his preference for a date *c.* 1400 by noting that what he considers echoes of **C**, e.g. VI 309 and V 23–5 in Z V 124 and 142–4 (p. 18), rule out Wells as the scribe of **Z**, if C V is not earlier than 1388.

§ 138. The dating of **C** will be discussed below (see III, *C Version* § 1; V § 11); but with no independent external testimony about the latter, **Z**'s position in the sequence must depend on interpretation of the literary evidence, which necessarily lacks finality. This being so, Wells's death in 1388 cannot decisively exclude him as the copyist of Bodley 851, since **C** 'echoes' in **Z** could in principle reflect his acquaintance with the late version as a work in progress (something also possible in the case of Thomas Usk, who died a year before Wells in 1387).[243] Conversely, while certainty that **Z** was copied in the 1370s would confirm that its supposed **C(B)** 'echoes' were actually 'pre-echoes' or anticipations, this could not by itself prove **Z** 'a coherent and self-sufficient version' (*R–B*, p. 12) *anterior* to **A** that probably belongs between 1365 and 1370. Establishing an early date for the surviving copy of **Z** is therefore not crucial for settling either its nature or the period of composition of its text. Similarly, the internal consistency of the language and its recognised nearness to the author's likely dialect cannot demonstrate, though it may support, the text's originality.[244] **Z**'s claim to 'versional' status, in other words, must be tested in the same way as competing traditions of the canonical versions such as the α and β texts of **B**, the authenticity of which has never been in doubt. R–B's textual hypothesis should therefore be disengaged from too close a connection with the particularities of Bodley 851 and its scribes. For the text's credibility, as its first editors recognise, depends on critical assessment of its intrinsic character. They therefore begin by arguing that material believed by Kane to be evidence of **BC** conflation or contamination was instead 'integral to the original draft of the poem' but was 'omitted by manuscripts of the **A** tradition' (p. 10). Apart from three obelised passages where they associate the error in question with the text's draft form in the manuscript (I 101, V 124, VII 6), R–B judge all other corruptions to be 'of a simple mechanical kind.' But while they convincingly deny conflation, they do not consider whether the suspected echoes of **BC** may have been introduced by scribe X or the copyist of his exemplar. This suggestion would complicate matters; it is also incompatible with R–B's main hypothesis that such readings were original to **Z** and, after **Z** had been altered by **A**, were restored in **B** or **C**. But it perhaps merits fuller treatment than they provide; for these readings are not just 'clearly germane to the textual status of **Z**' (p. 36), they constitute a potential objection to its authenticity (III, *Z Version* §§ 26–7).

§ 139. R–B's literary argument, which may appear the more subjective, is nonetheless of equal importance, since the Bodley 851 text could hardly challenge consideration as a 'version' for its unique 'shape' without containing writing worthy of the poet of **A**, **B** and **C**. Their case that **Z** lacks signs of 'cobbling' and that its peculiar passages are beyond the capacity of a literate scribe 'able to write tolerable long lines' (*K–D*, p. 15, n. 95) does not seem overstated to the present writer. For the best **Z** lines contain thoughts and images at once suggesting the poet of the other versions and not obviously derived from these. They include Robert the Robber's macaronic couplet at V 142–3, which both 'integrates the Latin into the alliterative pattern' (p. 15) and employs the *f* / *v* alliteration of such characteristic lines as B XV 60 (see Appendix I, § 2 ii) and its revised **C** form; the 'word-wind' passage at V 34–40; and the lines on Truth's powers at VI 68–78. None would look spurious if found in **A** at these points, though reasons for their removal in revision are not far to seek.[245] R–B sensitively examine **Z**'s distinctive material (pp. 15–17); but in concluding that its Langlandian authorship 'cannot be proved one way or the other' (p. 15) they if anything understate their case. It is true that without substantial new external evidence there can be no 'proof' in such a matter; but what must and can be ascertained is whether or not these passages evince characteristics recognised as 'scribal' in the **ABC** traditions from the archetypal level downwards. One way of doing this is to compare **Z**'s unique material with known spurious passages such as those from Harley 875 (H) printed in Skeat's edition of **A**. Another way is to undertake R–K's 'absolute comparison,' not, however, with the Athlone editors' 'abstractions' but with the empirically-established core-text. There is no objection in principle to the latter exercise, since much of **Z**'s special material has no real parallel in **A**. But both comparisons would serve to counteract the subjectivity of the 'impression' on which an *initial* hypothesis of the text's originality is inevitably based. **Z**'s inclusion in the present edition is due to its having survived such comparative scrutiny; for its unique passages satisfy the core-text criteria and even illustrate metrical features exclusive to Langland.[246]

§ 140. R–B attribute **Z**'s 'few inconsistencies' to its being a draft or 'a partial revision of the earliest version of the poem' (p. 13) and see **A** as 'an authorial expansion of the shorter [**Z**]' rather than **Z** as 'an authorial (or scribal) abridgement of the longer [**A**].' The four or five local inconsistencies they examine do not, in their view, tell against the text's overall coherence. That its passus-divisions are 'quite acceptable' (though less satisfactory than **A**'s) and that no sophisticating scribe would have altered **A**'s to **Z**'s are claims that gain strength from a comparison with what such a scribe actually did in the case of the **B** manuscript Corpus 201.[247] R–B's conclusion, that the **A** passages Kane believed **Z** omitted had not yet been composed, is supported by the absence of inconsequentiality at points where these omissions supposedly took place. Finally, Kane's contention that 'some of the groups of "new" lines occur where approximate multiples of 20 or 40 lines are wanting (i.e. the presumptive contents of sides or leaves)' (*K–D*, p. 14, n. 95) has, as Brewer later remarks, 'been authoritatively demolished by Green.'[248]

§ 141. In considering the stylistic and metrical evidence for the text's draft status, R–B confine their comparison to **A**, though concisely noting both the relative inferiority of particular **Z** lines and the 'progressive elimination of a theme from one version to another' (p. 16). The 'draft' part of their hypothesis should perhaps not be invoked too readily to account for weaker lines explicable on the assumption of scribal carelessness, unless the larger context convincingly suggests incompleteness. But R–B (somewhat confusingly) resort to it even in the section of A-Text by Hand Q that links **Z** proper to Passus X of **C**, finding it 'arguable' that VIII 113–14 *And but yf Luk lye, he lernit vs anothir be foulys, þat we ne scholde / To besy be aboute to make the wombe joye* 'preserves Langland's original draft' (p. 111, note). But here (as shown in the *Textual Notes* on these lines) the substantive error of scribes in the sub-archetypal traditions of both **A** and **B** was to misidentify the referent of the noun *folis* in line 113 ('fools'), which was correctly preserved in the **m** and α traditions but misunderstood in both **r** and β as *foulys* 'birds', with subsequent smoothing and mislineation. It should also be acknowledged that features like defective metre, which are ambiguously interpretable as either scribal or draft work, cannot by themselves (dis)prove the authenticity of **Z**. To some extent, however, the impression of **Z** as a work in progress, which arises partly from specific 'oral' features that will be examined later (III, *Z Version* §§ 8–9), can be tested by comparing it with other Langlandian material that may also have come down in a draft state, C Pr 95–124 and Passus XII of **A**.[249]

§ 142. In many lines, however, the 'draft' thesis is not needed to account for what R–B call 'mere padding', which may be authorial in origin. For if the authenticity of these lines cannot be demonstrated, doubts about them may nonetheless be reduced by showing their conformity with uncontested lines in the other versions. For example, at II 177 *For eny mercy of Mede, by Marye of heuene*, it is not obvious that (taken in context) the a-verse *is* otiose, while supposed 'padding' like the b-half oath is instanced at C IV 139 *Ne thorw mede do mercy, by Marie of heuene*. If anything, comparison of these two lines might more immediately suggest **C** contamination in **Z**; but as they are not identical, no reason appears why scribe X (or his exemplar) should have interpolated a variant of the **C** line at this point. It is easier to suppose that the poet might have *removed* the line in **A** because a phrase recalling II 177a occurs at Z IV 140 (to which C IV 139 corresponds), a line unchanged in both **A** and parallel **B**. In this situation, some **ZC** correspondences may be better interpreted not as scribal contaminations but as instancing late authorial re-use of very early material. For though evidence exists that Langland lacked his original fair copy of **B** when composing **C**, there is no reason to think that he did not have access to other *Piers Plowman* materials, such as his working draft of **Z** (see V, *The Poem in Time*, §§ 29–30 below). Such a manuscript, moreover, is *ex hypothesi* unlikely to have been available to a *scribe* until after the poet's death, when renewed demand for *Piers Plowman* texts led to the production of the unique conjunction of the earliest and latest versions now to be found in Bodley 851 (see V §§ 14–15).

§ 143. Among a handful of possible 'pre-echoes' of **C** and **B** listed below,[250] perhaps the most notable suggesting scribal contamination from **C** is at V 124, where R–B print †*Quod ye nan* † *yelde ayeyn yf Y so myche haue*. Their astute note suggests that the meaningless obelised phrase may conceal either **Qwat I nam*, the apparent α and possible **m** reading, or **Quodque mnam*, a conjecture that is tentatively adopted in the present edition.[251] Kane's interpretation (1985:919–20) of the manuscript reading as *yeuan* (not *ye nan*) leads him to identify the line as a direct echo of C VI 309, which introduces the Welshman Evan. But although his conclusion is not accepted here, the problem hardly admits of a straightforward solution, and it is not an easy matter to eschew the positivism of R–B, who adopt neither solution that they recognise. The example deserves mention here as one of a very few where the present edition has preferred a reconstructed *durior lectio*, 'abstraction' though it may be, against the probable joint witness of two sub-archetypal variants (α and **m**), each of which may preserve the archetype of its respective version.[252] The main (if not the sole) justification for such privileging of conjectural reasoning is the exceptional ambiguity of the stemmatic indications in these cases (see the *Textual Notes* and cf. I 86).

§ 144. In relation to its immediate successor, **Z** is found unsurprisingly by R–B (p. 18) to have 'a bearing on several major cruces of the A-Text (sometimes affecting **B** and **C** also).' Thus at Pr 129, where *And that seuth thy soule* provides a basis for correcting the archetypal **A** line, although this could indicate **B** or **C** contamination, a more economical explanation is that Ax was here corrupt. The reason for thinking so is less the **ZBC** agreement in itself than the ease with which the inferior Ax reading may be derived from the posited original. Here the direct method and the weight of manuscript evidence happily lead to the same outcome. At I 86, by contrast, despite impressive support from the **m** family and Bx, R–B's wider claim for **Z**'s *plente of pes* as being also the true **AB** reading does not carry conviction. For since (as they recognise) *o* could have easily been misread as *e* if those versions had *plonte* (as **C** does), their preference of *plente* must both presume **C** a late revision introducing the 'plant' idea for the first time and ignore the context of **B**, where *plonte* fits better with the image elaborated in B 152–58. Here however it is better to retain the manuscript reading for **Z**, because it makes adequate sense, while not judging **m**'s *plente* intrinsically harder than **r**'s *plante* for **A**, a version in which the metaphor as yet lacks the development it is to receive in **B**. For *plante* (in contention as the reading of Ax) seems to contain the whole figure *in parvo* and would thus represent an evolving state transitional between

Z and **B**. In II 94, on the other hand, **ZB** *Dignus est operarius hys huyre to haue* can rightly be defended 'as the earlier, if not the superior reading' (*R–B*, p. 19). It is both, but also, more importantly, the near-certain reading of **m** (and thus, like **r**'s *plante* earlier, potentially that of Ax), while the longer form, with its unmetrical second line, looks like **r**'s corruption of a terse macaronic original. Given that R–B make these points in a note to the line (pp. 55–6), their Introduction clouds the issue by allowing that **Z** may here be contaminated from **B** (a point that would otherwise be of interest).

§ 145. The last example is another where Kane's 1988 Retrospect overlooks the confirmatory significance of **Z** in its suspecting parallel A II 87 as a place 'where revision in **B** indicates the corruption of an unmetrical **A** line' (p. 463); for the 'corruption' need only be that found in the family original of **r**.[253] This is something that *Ka²* correctly recognises (p. 461) in a parallel case at A VI 71, where **ZBC**'s a-half is attested against **r** by family **m**. At VII 5 **Z** is again associated with **m** in possessing the a-verse found in parallel **BC** but omitted from **r** (and replaced in sub-group t by a filler-phrase *so me god helpe*). In this third instance, however, *Ka²* retains **r**'s Ø-reading, although on grounds of sense it is **m**'s variant that looks original. For R–B, by contrast (p. 19), '**Z**'s support indicates that the line is genuine and that the loss of the second half must have taken place in the ancestor of the other **A** manuscripts' [i. e. in **r**]. This seems plausible enough; but though authenticity and archetypal character are usually related, they are in principle distinct. So while, by the canon of ratification, the presence of VII 5b in **B** and **C** may imply its genuineness, certainty that the **mZ** reading was in Ax and not borrowed from **B** would require definitively excluding contamination by a later version; and that is impossible. For to prove **Z** uncontaminated it is not *sufficient* that it should have a superior reading where one sub-archetype of Ax errs, as here; it is *necessary* that both sub-archetypes err and the favoured reading be unattested by **B** and **C**. In other words, since to be judged original against its Ax equivalent, a **Z** reading must be unique, demonstration of originality can proceed *only* from direct assessment of its intrinsic character. And this can go little beyond probability, though it may approach moral certainty if the readings in question meet the core-text criteria.

§ 146. An example of a hypothetical lost **A** reading (R–K's 'abstraction') occurs at VII 60 *Shal haue leue, by Oure Lord, to lese here in heruest*, where **Z**'s agreement with **B** is confirmed by the synonym *glene* in revised **C** but Ax's sub-archetypes are severally wrong. The probability of **to lesyn* as the original of **A** is recognised in *Ka²* (p. 447) but not adopted; yet the **m** variant *to leuyn* is barely interpretable as other than a corrupt reflex of Ax, which is likely therefore to have read like **B**. The contribution of **Z** here is only to corroborate, not to prove, a point that R–B may not highlight clearly enough. But the evidence for **Z**'s primary character that their hypothesis requires is at hand in a line such as I 58 *Ant was the louelokest of lyght after Oure Lord syluen*. Here, since M has the metrically necessary word *syluen*, this **Z** reading could descend from **m** and thence from Ax; but **Z**'s unique *lyght*, superior on grounds both of metre and harder sense, cannot. So if Bodley 851 is regarded as just an eccentric **A** witness, *lyght* must descend from **A** independently of the Ax tradition. If it derives from the **B** Version, this can only be *via* a lost **B** copy superior to the Bx tradition, from which the entire line appears to have been mechanically omitted.[254] But if, as it is more economical to suppose, **B** is not the source, **Z** will indeed be the earliest version as claimed by R–B and its unique right reading will therefore have been present in **A** but corrupted in Ax (though to prefer the second alternative obviously requires explaining satisfactorily all other readings that suggest contamination from within the Bx tradition).[255] A similar example is *tyleth* at VI 66, which both gives better metre than the (admittedly acceptable) Ax reading *to* and instances a lexically unfamiliar verb vulnerable to scribal substitution of *is*. No more than at I 58 is *tylith* likely to be a scribal 'improvement', even if its being what **A** read is a little less likely than for *lyght*. This second variant is ignored by *Ka²* which, though adopting the first (p. 462), also ignores its presence in **Z**. While the implications of these readings are understandably (if not excusably) lost on Kane, they also (surprisingly) pass unnoticed by R–B. Yet such examples are the strongest counter-evidence to the objection that **Z** readings superior to Ax must be due to contamination from one or other later version.

§ 147. The latter objection, which the **Z** editors do not answer, they nonetheless deny. But they also countenance an unnecessarily complicated theory of the well-attested agreements between **Z**, the **A** family **m** and **B**: that there may have been *two* authorial redactions of the **A** Version. In the first of these, represented by family **m**, some of **Z**'s readings will have been preserved, but in the second, **r**, eliminated, though afterwards reinstated in **B** (p. 25, n. 73). This explanation is sufficient to account for the presence in **r** (and **B**) of readings and passages not in **m**, since it posits **r** as subsequent to **m**; but it is not *necessary* in order to explain their *absence* from **m** (and **Z**). For no more than in the case of the α and β traditions of **B** or the x^1 and x^2 branches of **C** is the postulate of a two-stage tradition logically indispensable. This is because **r** and **m** (as similarly argued below in relation to the two longer versions) are more economically to be explained as severally defective descendants of a single archetypal text of **A**. Despite this last reservation about R–B's wider view of the early phases of the poem's composition, their work would be valuable were Bodley 851 only an **A** witness comparable to the **B** manuscript F. But if **Z** is accepted as an independent version, it becomes the most important addition to our knowledge of Langland since Price's discovery of the version now called **A**.

Conclusion

§ 148. Our analytical survey of the editorial tradition of *Piers Plowman* is now complete. It has shown that, whether or not printing in parallel is the best format in which to read the poem, parallel *editing* is the most satisfactory way to produce a truly critical text. In order not to pine for what is not, the editor of Langland must look before and after, even when the poet did not do so. For as most of Skeat's successors have recognised, each version contains some securely identifiable errors that can be emended only by recourse to securely identified right readings in the others (including sometimes **Z**). And as will be later argued (IV, *Editing the Text*, § 3), the most secure readings in any one version are those shared by one or more other versions. The usefulness and limitations of both the recensional and the direct methods of treating the versions of a major medieval work attested in multiple copies have been frankly but, it is hoped, fairly scrutinised, and the need for a correspondingly restrained (if not wholly non-interventionist) handling of the unique copy **Z** acknowledged. In the course of this account, support has been given at various points to three main 'conservative' editorial principles and one 'liberal' procedure. But it has been implied throughout that a 'critical' form of empiricism need not be equated with positivism, whether in its simpler or its subtler guises.[256] Instead, to arrest the tendency of editorial rationalism to slide towards a radical intuitionism, three fundamental canons of conformity, acceptability and ratification have been proposed. If the arguments used at IV § 3 below are valid, the 'custodial' force of these in relation to the text should be recognised even by the rationalists' most 'positive' opponents. For the methodological rules arising from these principles (all based on a more general principle of economy) favour textual explanations that make the fewest assumptions; and (save in exceptional circumstances) *their* tendency is to confirm, not to question archetypal readings found in one or more successive versions. At the same time, in acknowledgement of the force of the linear postulate, Kane and Donaldson's appeal to the agreed witness of **AC** for correcting Bx has been found a valuable editorial resort, though one not without some problematic aspects.[257] So against the varyingly rigid non-intervention of Skeat and Knott-Fowler, the Athlone editors' boldness and candour in emending archetypal errors has been welcomed as a valuable (indeed inevitable) part of the editorial process. For an edition of *Piers Plowman* to be 'truly critical', the textual evidence must be weighed, not only measured: as well as looking before and after, an editor needs to open windows on all sides, including occasionally the roof, to let in light from every possible quarter.

§ 149. Of the three editorial canons mentioned, the most important and fundamental is the first, which both expects the final text to conform with metrical and stylistic criteria derived from analysis of the poem's core-text and allows all lines that do so to be adopted in the text as authentic. Though implied to differing degrees in the practice of most editors since Skeat, this principle has not been explicitly formulated by any. Yet it is the most powerful of the three, because it sets a condition for 'originality' that is both sufficient and necessary, and because the empirically established core-lines supporting it are unchallengeable. The core-text criterion (based on attestation of the text by two or more witnesses) stands out as uniquely significant for determining authenticity at every level of transmission, and so for validating emendations. It accordingly forms the foundation of the editorial theory and practice that will be fully explained in Part IV of this *Introduction*. The above pages have shown that previous editors did not succeed in developing a coherent theory of the text; but any pretension to have done so here is bound to appear hazardous. The present editor leaves the matter to the reader and prefers to stress what he owes to a study of the strengths and weaknesses of so many dedicated predecessors, without whose efforts the synthesis attempted here would have been impossible. So whatever its shortcomings, the present enterprise should be seen not as an attempt to abandon the earlier tradition but to fulfil its promises. Reflection on this tradition suggests that an approach that *did* break with it in pursuing radically novel solutions to the problems of Langland's text would be destined to miscarry.[258]

§ 150. The third part of this *Introduction* will set out in detail the evidence for the text of *Piers Plowman*, beginning with the three accepted versions in the traditional order and ending with the most recently identified, **Z**, which is here recognised as the earliest, though as yet not widely acknowledged as authentic. The treatment of **A**, **B** and **C** follows a closely similar pattern; but in order to avoid repetition, the rationale of emendation applicable in each version is described only once (*A Version*, section vii, § 56). The discussion in part III is intended mainly for the specialist; so although the argument forms a whole, a reader less interested in the textual minutiae could omit sections iii and iv on each version and go on to section v, or proceed directly to parts IV and V. These cover the editorial treatment of the text, the wider issues of the poem's date, authorship and audience, the order of the versions, and the poem's reception and influence from the manuscript period to the first printed edition.

THE EDITORIAL TRADITION: NOTES

1 Walter W. Skeat, ed., *Piers the Plowman in Three Parallel Texts* (2 Vols., Oxford 1886).

2 J. A .W. Bennett, ed., *Piers Plowman: the Prologue and Passus I–VII of the B-Text* (Oxford, 1972).

3 George Kane and E. Talbot Donaldson, eds., *Will's Visions of Piers Plowman, Do-Well, Do-Better and Do-Best* (London, 1975; 2nd edn. 1988).

4 The first of these, by George Kane, was of the **A** Version (London, 1960; 2nd edn. 1988); the latest is the **C** version by George Russell and George Kane (London and Berkeley, 1997).

5 A foretaste of what may be expected is provided by Hanna in 'Annotating *PP*,' (1994), to which Fowler provides a response (1997) in the same journal. The enterprise is now being published by the University of Pennsylvania Press under the title of *The Penn Commentary on* Piers Plowman. At the time of writing, volumes 1and 5, edited by Andrew Galloway and Stephen Barney respectively, have appeared.

6 W. W. Skeat, ed., *The Vision of William concerning Piers Plowman. In Four Parts.* Early English Text Society (London, 1869–85) (hereafter *Sk*).

7 *Sk* I, 138.

8 Elsie Blackman, 'Notes on the B-Text MSS of *PP*', 503–4.

9 *The Vision of Piers Plowman: A Complete Edition of the B-Text* (Dent, Everyman: London, 1978; 2nd edn. 1995) (hereafter 'Everyman edition').

10 Kane, *A Version*, 2nd edn. 1988, p. 460.

11 Derek Pearsall in *Speculum* 72:517.

12 The lack has been made good through the industry of Peter Barney (*YLS* 7:97–114 [**A** and **B**], 12:159–73 [**C**]).

13 No. 20 in *Introduction* I, *The Manuscripts*; see further *Sk* II vi–x on this ms.

14 Most of them are also in the Oxford MS Corpus Christi 201 (no. 23 below), which Skeat examined without apparently noticing this fact.

15 See *Sk* II xi–xiii.

16 See B. A. Windeatt, 'The Scribes as Chaucer's Early Critics', *SAC* I:119–41; idem, ed., *Troilus and Criseyde* (London, 1984), Intro., 'The Scribal Medium' pp. 25–35; David Benson and Lynne S. Blanchfield, *The Manuscripts of PP: the B Version*, pp. 9–13; reviewed *Medium Ævum* 68:322–33.

17 Charlotte Brewer and A. G. Rigg, eds., *A Facsimile of the Z-Text* (Cambridge, 1994); and see the review in *Medium Aevum* 64: 314–15.

18 Derek Pearsall and Kathleen Scott, eds., *PP:A Facsimile of Bodleian Library, Oxford, MS Douce 104* (Cambridge, 1992); reviewed *Medium Ævum* 63:128–30.

19 Benson and Blanchfield, pp. 9–11.

20 Hoyt N. Duggan et al., *The PP Electronic Archive*, Mosaic (World Wide Web) 1994.

21 The story is told in detail by Charlotte Brewer, *Editing 'Piers Plowman': The evolution of the text* (Cambridge, 1996), pp. 181–342, a study to which this *Introduction* is much indebted.

22 See note 4 above.

23 Thomas A. Knott and David C. Fowler, *PP: A Critical Edition of the A Version* (Baltimore, 1952). See further §§ 50–4 below.

24 Kane, *A Version*, pp. 53–61.

25 Knott-Fowler, *A Version*, pp 26–7.

26 A contrast between the Athlone and the present editions is that whereas Kane later recognised the need to use **B** and **C** in editing **A** in an *appendix* of altered readings to his second edition of **A**, study of the four versions necessitated a *complete revision* of Everyman **B** as a central part of editing all the versions 'in parallel.' For although working from the outset with an eye on **A** and **C**, the present writer had neither edited them nor had any acquaintance with the **Z** Version.

27 See Russell-Kane, *C Version*, pp. 112 ff.

28 Here too the present volume returns to something like the practice of Skeat.

29 Elizabeth Salter and Derek Pearsall, eds., *Piers Plowman* (London, 1967).

30 G. Economou, *The C Version. A Verse Translation* (Philadelphia, 1996).

31 *Piers Plowman: the Z Version,* edited by A. G. Rigg and C. Brewer (Toronto, 1983). The Z-Text will be considered again below and the case for its authenticity as a separate version fully in *Intro*. III, *Z Version*, §§ 1–12.

32 See *Introduction* III, *B Version*, §§ 46 below.

33 Paul Maas, *Textual Criticism* (Oxford, 1956), p. 1.

34 Considerations of sheer economy might favour such a procedure in a single-volume reader's edition that printed **A, B** and **C** in succession, not in parallel.

35 See Brewer, *Editing 'PP'*, pp. 219–302.

36 Crowley's three impressions are briefly discussed by Skeat, *B-Text* pp. xxxi–xxxvi, Kane-Donaldson pp. 6–7, and more fully by Crawford (1957), King (1976) and Brewer (1996). They are currently being surveyed by Carter Hailey as part of the *PP* Electronic Project (ed. Duggan).

37 Printed in full by Skeat, *B-Text* pp. xxxii–xxxiv.

38 *A Discourse of English Poetrie* (1586), in Smith, ed., *Elizabethan Critical Essays* (Oxford, 1904) I, p. 242.

39 *B-Text*, p. xxxvii, n. 2.

40 *B-Text*, p. 409.

41 *B-Text*, p. 415.

42 Brewer, *Editing 'PP'*, p. 18.

43 King, 'Crowley's Editions of *PP*', pp. 351–2.

44 Brewer, *Editing 'PP'*, p. 18, citing King, *English Reformation Literature* (Princeton, 1982), pp. 22, 332.

45 *The Canterbury Tales of Chaucer* (1775–8), pp. 74–5, n. 57.

46 Benson & Blanchfield, *The Manuscripts of PP: the B Version*, Preface.

47 No. 45 in Introduction, I, *Manuscripts*, sigil Cot.

48 Intro. I, *Manuscripts*, respectively nos. 30 (P), 35 (M) and 41 (N).

49 These are respectively manuscripts nos. 5 and 47, sigils H and H^2.

50 Skeat, *Text A*, pp. xiii–xiv; Brewer, *Editing 'PP'*, p. 49.

51 Oriel College, Oxford MS 79; no. 17 in the list of mss, sigil O.

52 Subsequently Phillips 8252, now Huntington 114; *Manuscripts*, no. 53, sigil Ht.

53 *Sk*, III, pp. li–lxiii; Brewer, *Editing 'PP'* pp. 37–45.

54 *Sk* III, pp. lxii–lxiii.

55 See *Introduction*, V, *The Poem in Time*, §§ 13–22 below on the order of the texts.

56 See B Pr 125–31 and C III 206.

57 See III, *B Version*, §§ 13–16.

58 The reading is actually that of only two **A** manuscripts, T and Ch, and is quite unlikely to be archetypal in the **A** Version; see the *Textual Notes* on the line.

59 Described in detail by Brewer, *Editing 'PP'*, pp. 91–178.

60 I, *Manuscripts*, no. 4, Bodleian MS English Poetry a. 1 (V).

61 *Parallel Extracts from 29 MSS of 'Piers Plowman'* (1866).

62 I, *Manuscripts* nos. 9 (A), 42 (H^3) and 46 (T).

63 I, *Manuscripts* nos 8 (E) and 10 (M).

64 Called **m** at III, *A Version*, § 24f below.

65 *A-Text*, pp. xvi, xvii. They are Harley 875 (H), Trinity College Cambridge R.3.14 (T) and University College Oxford 45 (U) throughout; Bodleian, Douce 323 and BL Harley 6041 (in part); Bodl. Ashmole 1468 in Passus XI; see I, *Manuscripts* nos. 5, 46, 3, 1 and 47 respectively.

66 These are Oxford, Bodleian Laud Misc. 581, Trinity, Cambridge B.15.17 and Bodl. Rawlinson Poetry 38 for **B**; Huntington 143 and 137, Trinity, Dublin 212, C.U.L. Dd. 3.13 and Bodl. Digby 171 for **C**.

67 This could be so with one **C** copy, Dd. 3. 13, possibly as early as the 1390s.

68 Examples are Pr 14 *triʒely*] *wonderliche* VH; the whole of 34, 50–1, 109 (*om* V).

69 See Sk *A-Text* I 176–77, II 34, 182, III 98, 234, VI 1 (all unmetrical); II 31, 118, 135–43 (rambling expansion); III 19–20, 66, 91–4; VI 2; VII 26.

70 I, *Manuscripts*, no. 3; see *A-Text*, Critical Notes, pp. 154–55.

71 See *Textual Notes* on A XII 98 and *Intro.*, III, *A Version* §§ 67–8.

72 Now Pierpont Morgan MS 18 (J); I, *Manuscripts* no. 6.

73 In a section (Index VII) revising and supplementing the original pamphlet of Parallel Extracts, with J now numbered as XLV (*Sk* IV. ii. 856–59).

74 *A-Text*, p. 145.

75 A possibility rejected in this edition; see *Textual Notes* on C VI 408–13, where the lines are seen as a case of 'farcing' from **B**.

76 *C-Text*, p. xxx.

77 See I 4, 103; VI 70; VII 23; VIII 101, 108, 124*a*; X 157, 159, 179; XI 148, 197, 212, 254, 260, 291, 292; XII 9,

12, 14, 22*a*, 41, 46, 49, 50, 52, 65, 67, 72, 86, 91, 92, 93. Of these VIII 125*a* and X 157, where the archetype is in error, are the only conjectural emendations; both are commonsense corrections.

78 The main exception has been Bennett (see § 1f. above), and Laud has now appeared, with emendations from Kane and Donaldson's edition of B, in the Norton Critical Edition by Robertson and Shepherd (New York, 2006). *K–D* and *Sch* have preferred Trinity Cambridge B.15.17 (I, *Manuscripts*, no. 11) for its good grammar and regular spelling.

79 I, *Manuscripts*, no. 14; now Takamiya 23 (S).

80 *A-Text*, p. xxiii, where it is no. IX; see I, *Manuscripts*, no. 42.

81 See *Introduction* III, *B Version*, §§ 30–2.

82 I, *Manuscripts*, no. 22.

83 I, *Manuscripts*, nos. 15, 16, 17, 18, 19, 43–5.

84 Now superseded by Davis, 'Rationale for a Copy'.

85 Brewer, *Editing 'PP'*, p. 147; see Sk, *B-Text*, p. 213.

86 See Taylor, 'Lost Revision of *PP* B', answered in III, *B Version* §§ 52–4.

87 *B Version*, p. 66; a view questioned by Hanna 'Studies in the MSS of *PP*' and less radically by Adams in 'The R/F MSS of *PP*', who argues however that the scribes of both the α and β traditions incorporated authorial corrections made to the archetypal B-Text. Skeat's account is hardly more tortuous than that of Warner in his essay on 'The *Ur*-B *Piers Plowman*'; but see further Warner's extensively argued 'Ending, and End, of *PP* B', which appeared too late to be taken into account in the above discussion.

88 Brewer, *Editing 'PP'*, p. 143.

89 An opinion supported by Thorne and Uhart, 'Robert Crowley's *PP*', pp. 248–54.

90 *The Vision of William Concerning Piers the Plowman* (Oxford, 1869).

91 Exceptional is T. P. Dunning's *'PP': An Interpretation of the A-Text* (1937; 2nd edn Oxford, 1980).

92 Everyman first edition (1978), p. xi.

93 *The Vision of William*...Part III (1873), pp. cvii ff, p. cxxiv.

94 See H. Barr, *The Piers Plowman Tradition* (London, 1993), pp. 14ff.

95 I, *Manuscripts*, no. 18; see §§ 36, 38 above.

96 *C-Text*, pp. cxiii–xv. See Appendix I § 2.

97 *C-Text* (1959), Note on the 1959 Reprint.

98 I, *Manuscripts*, nos. 26, 25, 27, 29, 44, 45, 43, 46, 47, 49. They are given their current sigils, which occasionally differ from Skeat's.

99 I, *Manuscripts*, nos. 24 and 28.

100 I, *Manuscripts*, nos. 30, 31, 33, 34, 35, 37, 38, 39, 40, 41, 52, 50.

101 Followed (without acknowledgement) by Russell-Kane, *C Version*, Pr 72.

102 See § 9 above.

103 Analysis shows there to have been no perceptible contamination from **B** at the sub-archetypal level (i.e. in the recoverable text of either **x** or **p**).

104 As, e.g., at III 140–41 (where Russell and Kane choose to follow Skeat), 304; V 115; VII 204; and X 217.

105 One exception is his emendation *wyrdes* for *wordes* at XIV 32 (from KS).

106 Brewer, *Editing 'PP'*, p. 165. Skeat's *C-Text* is examined on pp. 159–78.

107 Russell, 'Some Aspects of...Revision', pp. 28–9, judged it a superior text to that found in the received version, and 'not a merely editorial attempt at repair', but abandoned this view (cf. Russell-Kane, *C Version*, p. 87. n. 36).

108 Brewer, ibid., p. 166. See III, *C Version* §§ 20–2 and *Textual Notes* on C IX 71–161.

109 *The Vision of William*..., Part IV, section I: Notes to Texts A, B and C (1877); Section II: Prefaces and Glossary (London, 1884).

110 *The Vision of William...in Three parallel Texts together with Richard the Redeless,* Vol. I: Text; Vol. II: Introduction, Notes and Glossary (Oxford, 1886).

111 'The Text of *PP*', *MLR* 4 (1908), pp. 359–89. Though published under their joint names, its argument is mainly Chambers's (Brewer, *Editing 'PP'*, p. 197, n. 38)

112 Art. cit., p. 384.

113 Brewer observes (*Editing 'PP'*, p. 203), that Chambers was indebted, as he later acknowledged, to the theory and practice of B. F. Westcott and F. J. Hort in their edition of *The New Testament* (2 vols, Cambridge, 1881 and 1882).

114 'An Essay Toward the Critical Text of the A Version of "PP",' *MP* 12 (1915) pp. 129–61.

115 Art. cit., p. 131.

116 I, *Manuscripts*, nos. 51, 48 and 10. N became known in 1915, M in 1922 and Ch only as late as 1943.

117 *A Version*, pp. 5–6.

118 E. T. Donaldson, *PP: the C-Text and its Poet* (New Haven, 1949) or D. W. Robertson Jr and B. F. Huppé, *PP and Scriptural Tradition* (Princeton, 1951).

119 In the York C-Text and the Everyman B-Text (§§ 18–19).

120 *A Version*, pp. 1–5.

121 As well as those listed in the next note the major ones occur at Pr 63, 100; I 47, 135; II 96, 161; III 193, 208, 237; IV 53, 119; V 113, 158, 252; VI 1, 68$^{1, 2}$, 92, 98; VII 57, 95, 178, 210, 238; VIII 74; IX 57; X 199; XI 177, 201, 232, 246, 263, 291, 301.

122 They are (*with* **m**): III 13, 122, 260; IV 24; V 55; VI 28; VII 128, 183, 201 (+ U); 210; X 189, 208; XI 5, 121, 211, 243–44, 250, 251, 268, 293; (*alone*): II 83; III 95; IV 19, 47, 141; V 16, 17; VI 6; 67 (+ D); VII 187 (from **B** after V), 238 (+ U); VIII 112 (+ Ch); X 193 (+ H^3).

123 They nonetheless print its reading at XI 244/45 [= *K–F* 238/9].

124 Reasons for preferring *fayteden* are given in the *Textual Notes*.

125 *PP: the Evidence for Authorship* (London, 1965).

126 *A Version*, 2nd edn (London, 1988), p. 460. The fullest discussion of Kane is in Brewer's *Editing 'PP'*, pp. 343–79 and her two articles 'Textual Principles' and 'Processes of Revision'.

127 Kane and Donaldson, *B Version*, pp. 137–39.

128 See below, III *B Version* §§ 72–5, *C Version* §§ 4–5.

129 On α and β see III, *B Version* §§ 7–10 and on **x** and **p** *C Version* §§ 62–4 below.

130 See III, *A Version*, § 47 below.

131 They are Pr 11; II 91; III 164; IV 12; V 14, 171 [169], 239 [237]; X 187; XI 67. Only Pr 11, X 187 and XI 67 need emending; but see the note also on V 239. At X 187 and XI 67 *Ka^2* incongruously forgoes *K–D*'s emendations at // B IX 163 [166], X 108 [109], the second a convincing dialectal conjecture accepted here.

132 These are X 187 and XI 67. On the special features of Pr 11 (also in **Z** and **B**) see the *Textual Notes*.

133 See VIII 61, 136, XI 1 and at XI 161, 191, 197 (see the *Textual Notes*). Other **m** readings superior to Kane's are at I 46 and II 154, both supported by **B** (and **Z**).

134 An apt parallel to this example is the conjecture *prescit* at C XI 208 (Schmidt 1980:107), later found to be the reading of Douce 104 and adopted (as by the Athlone editors) as unquestionably original. The case presumably would not support a judgement of ms D as 'useless for editing.'

135 This edition has come in for severe and in part justified criticism from Kane in *Editing Chaucer: the Great Tradition*, ed. Ruggiers (Norman, Okl.), pp. 207–30.

136 Kane and Donaldson's *B Version* does not make this mistake, since the two rejected mss (Huntington 114 and Sion) are both described and taken into account in the section on classification.

137 Kane's quotation is from Greg, *The Calculus of Variants* (Oxford, 1929), p. 20, n. 1.

138 See e.g. III, *A Version* § 12 (on T's agreements with Ch) and § 20 (on J's agreements with M). Both show about the same proportion of major agreements judged coincidental (25–27%); but while this qualifies the certainty of the postulated genetic groups <TH^2>Ch and <EA(MH^3)>, it is not enough to undermine it.

139 *K–F*, p. 28.

140 See III, *A Version*, § 54 below.

141 For example, those of H^3 with M should be 73 not 60, those of A with E 35 not 30, and those of E with M 90 not 80; see also III, *A Version*, Notes 8 and 9.

142 In this he cites the support of Greg, 'The Rationale of Copy-Text', p. 31.

143 Or, one might add, *three* staves, a number not strictly necessary for scanning Langland's lines but indispensable for editing his text.

144 See MED s.v. *biwilen* v., aptly illustrated from Laȝamon and the *Gawain*-poet; later adopted by Kane and Donaldson at parallel B X 108 as a 'conjecture', though its difference from 'reconstructions' like *liȝt* at A I 110 is not clear (*K–D* p. 205 and n. 154; cf. *Ka^2* p. 463).

145 Or, if it needs saying, the unique *wenche* at Z VI 88.

146 Among reasons given in the *Textual Notes* is the possibility that *wy* is being used with a rare feminine referent (see OED s.v. *Wye^1*, 3; MED s.v. *wie* n. (a) lacks an example).

147 Introduction to the Athlone *B Version* (p. 205, n. 154).

148 Similar unmetrical lines left without comment are X 68, 154 and XI 191, 197.

149 See *Intro*. IV §§ 39–42 and Schmidt, *The Clerkly Maker* (Cambridge, 1987), p. 33.

150 The major ones occur at Pr 73, 107; I 1, 37, 48, 122, 165; II 51; III 20, 62, 65, 201, 209, 258, 259, 269; V 1, 35, 59, 85, 87, 90, 132, 142, 243; VI 2; VII 29, 83, 128; VIII 102–03, 105, 136–37, 172; X 53, 89, 141, 215; XI 67, 75, 192, 195, 245, 308; XII 4, 12, 47, 74–6. *Ka²* adds I 110; III 21, 234; V 256; VI 71; VII 233, 270; VIII 179; IX 55; XI 266.

151 *Piers Plowman: the B Version* (London, 1975).

152 The discussion of **B** likewise assumes that the Athlone principles need not be rehearsed again and eschews detail, as the Everyman first edition's textual commentary offers something like an extended critique of *K–D*.

153 They are called respectively β and α at III, *B Version* §§ 7–9 below.

154 An example is at XIX 205–07, omitted from F through eyeskip occasioned by homoteleuton (*hem alle* 203... *hem alle* 207), a feature K–D note at Pr 171–2 and XVI 27b, 28b. As with **A**, all line-references are to the present edition; the *K–D* numbering is given in brackets if discrepancies of more than two lines occur.

155 See below at III, *B Version* §§ 51–6 for discussion and references.

156 See the reviews by David Fowler and Eric Stanley.

157 See Jill Mann, 'Reassessment of the Relation between A and B' and Lawler 'Reply', Kane, 'Letter'; also below at *Introduction* V, §§ 16–17.

158 See the *Textual Notes* on C IX 34–5 and *Intro.* V §§ 31–2.

159 See *Intro.* IV *Editing the Text*, §§ 1–14. It is also found in lines peculiar to **A**, e. g. at XI 117, 178 and to **C**, e.g. at III 342, XII 66, XIII 63.

160 See B V 86 and A IV 142.

161 K–D in fact replace not just the word but the whole line with A XI 141, whereas the reconstruction in the present edition is restricted to the b-half. See the *Textual Notes ad loc* and IV, *Editing the Text* § 26ff.

162 See the *Indexical Glossary* s.v. *lewed* and *leþi*, and MED s.v. *lethi* adj., (c)

163 See *Intro.* III, *B Version*, § 60 (I 98–9, 100–03; III 223/4; V 338) and § 62 (I 191; III 71, 224; V 591. VI 272; VIII 44, 100).

164 See *The Clerkly Maker*, ch. 2 and *Appendix I* on Language and Metre.

165 See *Ka²*, p. 463, on lines like A V 14, one of the most securely attested in the poem.

166 See *Intro.* III, *B Version*, §§ 62–2.

167 Described as Type IIIa in *Intro.* IV, §§ 39, 41–2.

168 On 'cognative alliteration' see *The Clerkly Maker*, pp. 40–1.

169 Another example of such a change is C VI 218.

170 The other twelve are III 296, 341; V 183 [185], 194 [196], 275 [276], 509 [508]; X 472 [478]; XI 355, 373 [374]; XV 237; XVIII 308 [309]; XX 163.

171 Such examples would be Pr 11, IV 91 (**ZAB**); III 260 (**AB**); and V 171 (**BC**), which all fail to meet the core-text metrical criteria and are conjecturally emended against the successive witness of two or three versions. See IV § 18.

172 For discussion of this emendation (accepted in the present edition) with what is hoped is appropriate diffidence, see *Introduction* IV § 30.

173 Such as *norisse, conjectured at B VI 223; see *Textual Notes* on C VIII 234.

174 See the *Textual Notes* on C XI 15–16 for lexical details.

175 For detailed examination of this question see below, III, *B Version* §§ 71–4.

176 The emendation is unaccountably not adopted by *R–K* for **C**.

177 For another analysis and solution of the problem see the *Textual Notes ad loc.*

178 See IX 182 [185] / X 289; IX 200 / X 205; X 313 / V 165; XI 14 / 173; XII 101, 162 / XIV 46, 106; XVII 31 [33] / XIX 34.

179 Examples appear at V 441 / VII 54; X 301 [307] / V 154.

180 It can be shown to occur in **B** specifically in the line's b-half, where (presumably unconscious) transposition to prose order is common.

181 *Vision of...PP*, IV, ii, pp. xlviii–li; Knott-Fowler, *A Version*, pp. 15–17. Both, however, accept the existence of occasional lines without alliteration in the b-half.

182 Something not evidenced in Kane's edition of **A** but repeated in Russell-Kane's **C** in relation to the manuscript N² (NLW 733B).

183 See *B Version* §§ 44–6 below and the *Textual Notes* at these points.

184 As will Russell and Kane's similar assumption for N² in their edition of **C**.

185 See e.g. V 330 (*Sk* B 336) and XVIII 159–61.

186 Strictly they should exclude those from 'split variation' where α and β have 'complementary corruptions,' since these are not *of* but *to* Bx, which is unknowable and may not have been corrupt. See § 101 below.

187 R–K (p. 135) subsequently defend it against these objections, which are elaborated and sustained in the *Textual Notes ad loc.*

188 R–K nonetheless retain this unjustified change in their edition of **C**.

189 Most of these are recorded below in III, *B Version* §§ 63, 64. See the *Textual Notes* for discussion of objections to this emendation.

190 A main reservation here is that it is not either of these considerations in isolation but their co-presence in a body of hierarchically-arranged core-text that must provide the required empirical 'control.'

191 These are the empirically-based norms with power to predict that all and only lines of this type are authentic.

192 See the *Textual Notes ad loc* and cf. n. 186 above.

193 For some possible examples cf. VI 138, X 246, XI 438, XVII 38 and XIX 90.

194 See for discussions Patterson, 'Logic of Textual Criticism' in *Negotiating the Past* (Madison, 1987), pp. 77–113 and Brewer, *Editing 'PP'* pp. 380–408.

195 See III, *A Version* §§ 11–13 below.

196 Their arrangement of q is to be preferred; but that of p^2 is contested at III, *C Version* §§ 52 and 56 respectively below.

197 K. Kiernan, *'Beowulf' and the Beowulf Manuscript* (Ann Arbor, 1996).

198 See MED s.v. *finden* 18 (a), *finden out*; ibid. s.v. 22 (a); ibid. s.v. I (a).

199 It is metrically an 'enriched' Type Ib; see IV §§ 41–2 below.

200 See the *Textual Notes ad loc.*

201 This is called 'B^{1}' at III, *B Version* § 2 below.

202 Bx is here, as it happens, supported by **Z**.

203 See, e.g., XIV 155–312 // C XVI 10–147 and most of B XVII // C XIX 204.

204 It hardly needs saying that as Volume One of this edition appeared two years before the Athlone, its disagreements with their decisions did not evolve in response to these, as did the texts of **B** and to a less extent **A**. However, it may not be immediately obvious to the reader that all *R–K* and *Sch* agreements in discriminated **C** readings are coincidental. For while R–K (pp. 119–21) answer some arguments concerning points in the last two passūs made in the Everyman first edition, they appear unaware that, for example, their conjecture *prescit* at XI 20[8] (p. 151) was proposed in Schmidt 1980 p. 107.

205 Loss of *owene* would be better ascribed to initial haplography than to a desire to shorten the line after misdivision; see *Textual Notes ad loc.*

206 On these stylistic devices see Appendix I §§ 7 and 8, *Clerkly Maker* pp. 52–9.

207 It is given on p. 95 of the edition.

208 Cf. II, § 94 above.

209 See MED s.v. *boie* n. (1), 2 (a); *harlot* n.

210 See MED s.v. *tasten* v. 2 (b) and 3 (a).

211 See MED s.v. *trinen* v. (1).

212 So also XIII 126b (= B XI 313b) but not XVI 92 (// B XIV 252–3), where metre and sense are satisfactory.

213 For a definition of these terms see below at III, *B Version* § 61.

214 Amongst R–K's seven other examples this is likewise true of XIX 28 (for the different conjecture *lich* preferred here, see *Textual Notes ad loc*), XX 22[6], 400 and, with slightly less certainty, of XI 9[2] (*man*).

215 This is Type IIIa, the 'minimal' type; see the evidence in IV, §§ 41–2.

216 This is R–K's 183, which they incorrectly refer to as 180 (p. 103).

217 See III, *C Version* § 27 below.

218 See *Indexical Glossary* and cf. OED s.v. *Witness* sb., 2a and 4a, MED s.v. 2 (a), 4 (a).

219 R–K typically fail to note that Skeat had already made the emendation.

220 As shown in detail below at III, *C Version* §§ 24–5. On x^2 see § 2 above and III, *C Version* § 35.

221 See *Glossary* and MED s.vv. *foul* adj. Id, (b) and (c); *vile* adj. I (c), 2 (c).

222 See e.g. XXI 445, XXII 120 and cf. III, *C Version* § 65 below on x^2.

223 Both editions reconstruct Cx's a-half from the split variants in **x** and **p**.

224 Cf. Chaucer's use of 'Geffrey' in *The House of Fame*, l. 729.

225 See MED s.v. *pilten* v., esp. under 1 (c), citation from *Southern Legendary, Inf. Chr.* 725.

226 See IV § 38 below and *The Clerkly Maker*, p. 63.

227 See the *Textual Notes ad loc.*

228 See Kane, *A Version*, p. 447.

229 An important instance where RM are argued in the *Textual Notes* to preserve such a reading uniquely is XVII 116, a line that R–K reject.

230 The line is an extended Type III with double counterpoint (*abb / ab*).

231 Similar examples at III 15[3] *maide*] *mede*, VIII 216 *fial*] *filial*, IX 2[59] *wriþen*] *wroken* (pp. 150–1); III 381 *londes*] *lordes* (p. 153); XIX 23[6] *hymsulue*] *on hymsulue* (p. 157); *manliche*] *nameliche* VIII 51 (pp. 169–70) are all cases where the present editor could adopt the Athlone reading without too much hesitation.

232 That the scribe of F was intelligent is shown by his substitution of *geste* for Cx *feste* at VII 106, though this may have been prompted by recollection of *storye* in B XIII 447. The criticism of R–K here is not contradicted by the present editor's own rejection of *to* for *tyliþ* at A VI 79, since the latter verb is the reading of **Z**, which is here understood as a version, not a single witness in a sub-family group. See further IV §§ 35–6.

233 *PP: The Z Version* (Toronto, 1983).

234 See *Ka²*, p. 459; *B Version* pp. 14–5 (n. 95); for Kane's review, *Speculum* 60 (1985) pp. 910–30.

235 I 101, V 124 (an important crux) and VII 6 are all conjecturally emended in the present edition. Empty square brackets used at IV 63 are not needed.

236 Omissions include I 91 *myleliche*, 114 *Ant eke, other*; II 49 *montayne heye*. Mistaken inclusions are VI 76, 79, 80 (but for the last lift).

237 See *woman* at I 14 (*women*); *bought vs* at II 6 (*boughtes*); *kyn* I 114; *gyue* II 117; *man that* IV 88 and *the* V 135 (haplographic omissions supplied for the sense). The **BC** emendation *none* at V 155 (*om* **Z**) is less simple than *nas* for *was*.

238 R–B's conservatism is seen in their retention of **Z**'s reading at V 18, whereas *we* is introduced in the present text after **AB**; at 127 *Than* (though the sense is forced), and several where they do not actually adopt the reading they favour: VI 56 *no*; VI 99 *yclecated* for the obviously wrong *yclecaked*; VII 22 *wyghtliche* for *wytliche*; *to dyne a-day* for *today* VII 312; VIII 23 *ant* for *ac*, 91 *a* for *at*. For other restorations in the present edition see I 29, 71, 79–80, 101/2, 113, 129, 131; II 141, 163, 171, 192, 199; III 163; IV 34, 54, 63, 117; V 27, 89, 147; VI 35, 87/8; VII 6, 50, 113; VIII 33.

239 For restorations see Pr 67, 129; for reconstructions, II 165/6; V 25, 155; for conjectures, Pr 12, V 124 (after *R–B*), 152; VI 15; VII 162. On the distinctions between the three types of emendation see III, *A Version* § 55 below.

240 *PP: A Facsimile of the Z-Text*, introduced by Charlotte Brewer and A. G. Rigg.

241 They include Kane's *Speculum* review but do not mention Brewer's important article on 'Z and the A-, B- and C-Texts of *PP*' in *Medium Aevum* 53.

242 Hanna, 'Manuscripts of *PP*', p. 17.

243 See III, *C Version* § 1 below and note 8.

244 Cf. Samuels, 'Langland's Dialect', p. 247, n.77.

245 See III, *Z Version* § 12 below and Schmidt, 'Visions and Revisions,' p. 17.

246 These include the 'T-type' lines at II 118, III 158, VII 38, 245 (*Intro.* IV §§ 40–4; Schmidt, 'Authenticity of Z-Text', pp. 297–8) and 'homolexical' translineation at IV 125/6 (*Intro.* IV § 48 and Appendix I, 8. v).

247 See *B Version* § 46, n. 28 below.

248 *Facsimile*, p. 19, n. 37. R. F. Green, 'Lost Exemplar,' adequately answers Kane's argument that the absent **A** lines were on folios lost from **Z**'s exemplar.

249 A XII's authenticity is considered at *Introduction* III, *A Version* §§ 67–71, **Z**'s possible draft status at III, *Z Version* § 6 below.

250 See III, *Z*, § 24 below. They include C Pr 5, 35, III 19 (= B III 18), 32–33 and B Pr 223, II 12, all of which are discussed in the *Textual Notes*.

251 The problem is considered at length in the *Textual Notes* on C VI 308–12.

252 Another is at Z Pr 12, where all three archetypes are emended identically.

253 Kane's note referring to the latter as the reading of the archetype (p. 436) ignores the true significance of M, which may be safely presumed to preserve **m**.

254 R–B's note to I 58 mistakenly records *lyght* as supported by 'some **B** MSS', but the line is absent from all **B** copies.

255 See the discussion at III, *Z Version* §§ 26–7 below.

256 As it is by Patterson, 'Logic', pp. 112–13. The previous argument has made clear that the present writer's idea of 'empirical' support for a textual argument differs from that of Kane and Donaldson, which Patterson shares. A different misunderstanding of the term 'empiricism' is shown by Benson (*Public PP* [Pennsylvania, 2004] p. 8), who seems to think it means 'common sense judgement without need for evidence'.

257 See III, *Z* § 26 below.

258   The possibility of a critical edition is precluded by two seemingly opposed approaches to the problem of L's texts. One is the type of radical scepticism about distinguishing the authorial from the scribal revealed in Brewer, 'Authorial vs Scribal Re-writing' and, in less moderate form, in Machan, 'Late ME Texts'. The other is the type of radical historicising found in Hanna 'MS Bodley 851', Adams 'The R/F MSS of *PP*' and Warner 'The *Ur*-B *PP*', which in varying degrees cuts up the textual tradition into a bevy of wriggling worms. But perhaps the true positive 'antithesis' to the rational 'thesis' represented by the work of Chambers and Grattan a century ago is to be found in the initial stage of the Electronic *Piers Plowman* project, in which the modern reader denied Langland's text in editorial dress is invited to put on medieval undress to read it. At a later stage, it is promised, a 'critical' ghost will emerge from the technological machine.

III. THE TEXT OF THE A, B, C AND Z VERSIONS

The A Version

i §§ 1–2 The Manuscript Tradition. ii §§ 3–5 The two families of **A**
manuscripts. iii §§ 6–23 The **r** family. iv §§ 24–48 The **m** family.
v §§ 49–54 Towards the Archetype: the agreed readings of *r²* and **m**.
vi § 55 The Archetypal Text of the **A** Version. vii §§ 56–60 Emendation
of Errors in the Archetypal A-Text. viii §§ 61–2 Readings of Indeterminable
Origin. ix §§ 63–6 Possible Contamination in the **A** Version.
x §§ 67–74 Passus XII. § 75 Conclusion

i. *The Manuscript Tradition*

§ 1. The A-Text is the earliest version of *Piers Plowman* to survive in multiple copies; but
most of the manuscripts date from 1420–50, and its tradition was probably the last of the three
to be generated.[1] Interest in the poem is likely to have been aroused by the success of the B- and
C-Texts, which were already receiving the tribute of imitation by the late 1390s.[2] A growing
desire to read the 'whole' work in any available form may be inferred from the number of 'con-
joint' copies extant (one-third of all **A** manuscripts), a sign that the A-Text's incompleteness was
recognised by early fifteenth-century compilers aware that longer versions existed. It remains
uncertain whether Langland himself 'published' the **A** Version, in the sense of releasing it for
copying by professional scribes at the request of potential purchasers. But it seems reasonable to
suppose that he showed a copy of the poem (here designated 'A-Ø') in its Pr–XI shape to personal
acquaintances who formed his immediate 'circle' of readers. Either this or, most probably, a sec-
ond copy made from it, was the archetypal text from which the surviving **A** manuscripts derive
(**Ax** hereafter). From Ax two further copies, here called **r** and **m**, were produced. Passus XII, by
contrast, which is incomplete and probably in draft form, descends from another exemplar. Its
restricted attestation suggests that it never passed beyond the poet's 'circle' and may have been
copied from his working papers after his death, in a manner similar to that later to be proposed for
the Z-Text (see § 74 below, and *Z Version* § 6). For although the three extant Passus XII witnesses
(RU; J) preserve in Pr–XI two distinct lines of transmission from Ax, both lines stem from copies
belonging to only one family original, **r**, and the other **A** family, **m**, is not represented at all.

§ 2. The lost archetypal manuscript of the **A** Version was, it seems likely, not the poet's holo-
graph. For as reconstructed, it can be shown to have contained about 80 substantive errors, some
35 of which are major ones that affect meaning or metre or both (see §§ 55–9). However, for a
poem of some 2447 lines, Ax was not particularly corrupt, as emerges clearly when it is compared
with the archetypal text of the **B** Version (**Bx** hereafter). For where **A** and **B** overlap, Bx has about
three times as many major errors as Ax. However Ax (like Bx) can be directly or inferentially
established in at most about 75% of the poem; for the remainder, the text of **A** is only of variable
certainty. Thus in about 7%, it has to be constituted from either **r** or **m**, and where even this is not
possible, from a number of readings that cut across both families. For it is a feature of the **A** tradi-
tion, one presumably connected with its lateness, that scribal corruption is not only widespread

but wayward. And this is true both in the groups comprising each family and in the manuscripts constituting these groups. It is thus often necessary, in order to discriminate amongst competing variants within and across families and groups, to consult the witness of the other versions, and especially **B**. In other words, to be edited 'critically', **A** must be edited in parallel.

ii. *The two families of* **A** *manuscripts*

§ 3. The two independent copies made from Ax, **r** and **m**, both in turn introduced a number of errors; but where they can be satisfactorily compared, **r** preserves the archetypal reading about two-and-a-half times as often as **m**. In the case of major readings specifically, it does so three times as often (see §§ 23 and 45 below). Additionally, since eight complete **r** mss of Pr–XI survive but only one complete copy of an **m** witness, an edition of **A** must inevitably be based on a manuscript of family **r**.[3] The hypothetical family original **m**, though not derived from **r**, was copied later, and after the B-Text had been composed, as is indicated by its greater lexical modernisation and by its occasional inclusion from **B** of Bx readings that seem inauthentic. A few **B** readings also occur in individual **r** mss, whether by collation with an **m** source or by contamination from **B**, but none were present in **r** itself.[4]

§ 4. At least two, but possibly three further copies of **m** seem to have been made (here called *e*, *m*, and *y*). From these descend respectively two pairs and a single further manuscript that attest the readings of this family (EA; MH[3]; W). Two early copies are likewise presumed to have been made of **r**, which are here called r^1 and r^2. Another two were made of r^1 (*u* and *d*) and at least six of r^2 (*v, j, l, k, w, z*), and from one or other of the latter all the extant **r** manuscripts descend. Neither r^1 nor r^2 is derived from the other or influenced by **m**; but a comparison of these two *sub-families* of **r** shows r^1 to have introduced about four times more major errors than r^2. The independent value of r^1 is therefore limited, though it cannot be eliminated from consideration in establishing the text, as it uniquely preserves at least nine major correct readings. Moreover, only in a manuscript belonging to this family throughout Pr–XI, *Rawlinson 137* (R), does Passus XII survive entire. Lastly, the most complete r^2 copy, *Morgan 818* (J), is half a century later in date than the earliest r^1 copy, *Trinity, Cambridge R. 3. 14* (T), and so is linguistically less suitable than T as a basis for the **A** Version. The present text, therefore, is substantively of r^2 type, corrected for the most part from **m** when its witness to Ax errs. But it is presented in the language of its base-manuscript, the r^1 copy T, and for Passus XII in that of R. This is not wholly satisfactory, since R (like J) was copied half a century later than T and its language is correspondingly further from the author's. But if XII descends from a separate archetype (§ 1 above), there is little justification for altering its accidentals to conform with T's. The present edition accordingly resembles those of Knott-Fowler and Kane, which also use T as copy-text, and more particularly *Ka*[2] in correcting **r**'s family errors from **m**. But it differs from both in occasionally drawing on the other versions, including **Z**, when Ax is in need of emendation.

§ 5. The relationships between the extant **A** manuscripts and their postulated ancestors in Pr–XI may be diagrammatically represented as follows:[5]

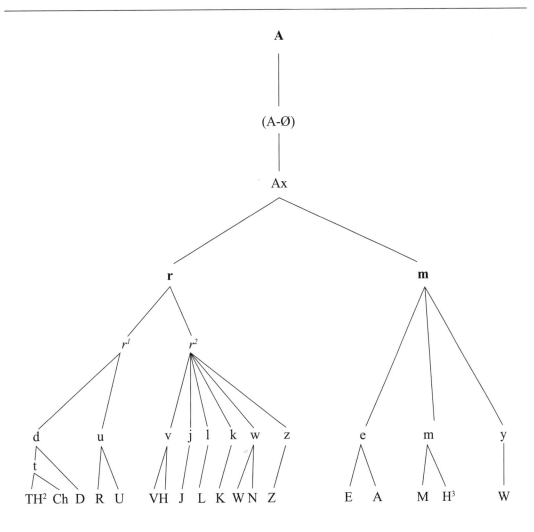

iii. *The **r** family of **A** manuscripts*

(a) *sub-family **r***^{1}

§ 6. The two **r** sub-families consist respectively of manuscripts **TH²ChDRU** and **VHJLKWN**. Although preserved in about the same number of copies, *r*^{1} and *r*^{2} differ greatly in weight of attested readings, since only three members of *r*^{2} (JKW) survive complete. But to counterbalance the disproportion, TH²ChD and RU each have an exclusive common ancestor (here called respectively 'd' and 'u'). This means that from *r*^{1} there are only two independent lines of transmission. By contrast, *r*^{2} with two pairs VH (< v) and WN (< w), plus the unrelated J, L, K (and Z), yields six lines of descent. However, not only do H and L give out before the end of Passus VIII (while Z is the mere 73 lines of VIII 93–185), *r*^{2}'s individual members exhibit the capriciousness characteristic of all extant **A** copies. Thus their combined attestation of the sub-family ancestor's readings remains uncertain as well as imperfect.

§ 7. The distinctive variants of the *sub-family* r^1 are constituted firstly by the 41 major agreements in error of both its component groups. In the following list of these, a minus sign before a sigil denotes a manuscript that diverges from r^1 in containing the reading judged correct (for reasons of space, only line-references are given).

I 153 -U. II 83, 163 -D. III 243 -R. 253 -U. 268 -D. 269. IV 4, 19 -D, 71 -H^2, 113, 127, 54. V 16, 17, 34, 91–2, 109, 114, 178, 244. VI 39 -H^2. VII 18, 20 -Ch, 25, 183, 227 -U. VIII 2 -U, 13 -R, 101 -U, 119. IX 6, 14, 17, 36. X 48, 86, 168 -U. XI 47, 250, 251.

Secondly, in another 17 instances, r^1 has a major error which is shared by one member of r^2 or of **m**:

V: XI 121. *K*: IV 29. V 159. X 103. XI 239. *L*: V 244. VII 306. *E*: V 161, VII 211. *A*: X 154, XI 268. *M*: III 132. V 131. X 104, 161. H^3: XI 211. *W*: X 34.

The sub-family is characterised, thirdly, by at least 24 minor errors where all members present agree:

III 139. IV 42, 48, 89. V 110, 143, 219. VI 94. VII 31, 185, 212*a*/213, 217/218. IX 44, 76. X 40, 198. XI 4, 78, 134, 159, 194/196, 236, 243/244, 244.

Half a dozen unique major right readings are, however, severally preserved in u, d and t (TH^2Ch). These may derive from r^1 rather than another **r** source (see §§ 8, 9, 13 below). In addition, r^1 certainly contained six such readings:

Major: XI 19 construe] conterfeteþ. 67 wy] man r^2**m**. 245 suche] seyth / syke J / K; *om* **m**. **Minor**: VII 282 poret] *pl.* r^2**m**. VIII 33 oure] þe / Ø r^2**m**. XI 241 cristene] cr. men / þei r^2 **m**.

It therefore cannot be eliminated.

§ 8. The *two groups* into which r^1 divides consist of four and two manuscripts respectively, **d** (TH^2ChD) and **u** (RU). Neither member of u can derive from the other, U because it is a generation earlier in date and R because it lacks U's distinctive major errors, such as the extra lines after V 200. The group **u** is a genetic pair defined by 219 agreements, about half of them major.[6] Most are not recorded in the apparatus, but the following 30 appear where the variants are diverse enough to merit complete listing:

Pr 102. I 1. II 42, 58, 168. III 13, 171, 234, 262, 268. IV 24, 47, 60. V 93, 102, 113, 114, 179, 216. VI 67, 92, 123. VIII 21. X 40, 199. XI 134, 156, 209, 281, 291.

Group u cannot be eliminated, as it contains three major variants (I 103, III 29–30, IX 57) that appear in the light of parallel (**Z**)**BC** to preserve original readings by direct descent (< r^1 < **r** < Ax). Additionally, in Passus XII its two members jointly attest lines 1–19, and from 89–end R is the unique witness to the text. R is a relatively late copy, but its completeness qualifies it to serve as the *citation-source* for correcting individual errors of the copy-text T (as later will L for the B-Text; see *B Version* § 39, and IV § 56 below).

§ 9. The other r^1 group, **d**, consists of two *sub-groups*, **D** and **<TH^2Ch>**. The second of these (here called **t**) is further differentiated into TH^2 and *Ch*. Neither D nor t derives from the other, because t's oldest member T is three generations earlier than D, while D lacks t's roughly 50 distinctive errors. But on the basis of their 94 agreements, 54 major and 40 minor (all recorded in the Apparatus), D and t may be regarded as a single genetic group. In the list of these, bracketed references indicate minor divergences from one recognisable substantive error:

Major I 171. II 51, 123. III 83, 102, 118, 171, 241, 257. IV 24, 114, 126, 148. V 16, 56, 93, 113, [119], 238, 253. VI 85, 92, 109, 125. VII 75, 95, 116, 164, 175, 178, 196, 222, 282, 304. VIII 26, 30, [70], 117, 141, 153, 154, 171, 172. IX 17, 30. X 64. XI 44, 124, 145, 192, 232, 235, 263, 298. **Minor** II 82, 86, 166. III 165, 206. IV 47, 58, 106, 135, 143, 145. V 114/115, 157, 193, 253. VI 69. VII 144, 172, 189, 277, 306. VIII 36, 46, 126, 164, 176. IX 15, 75, 84. X 84, 88, 181, 202. XI 3, 46, 129, 134/135, 195, 227, 280.

In two further major and five minor instances, one member of the group, Ch, has the right reading. In two minor ones another, H^2, is right where d appears to err:

Major *Ch*: III 208. XI 60. **Minor** II 95. IV 60, 95. X 201. XI 67. H^2: VIII 157. IX 54.

In the major cases particularly Ch may show correction from another source, probably of **r** type. Finally, in five major cases d shares an error with another **r** manuscript (of r^2 type) and in one with the **m** copy E:

V 161 and X 53 +V. II 94 +L. XI 186 +K. VIII 44 +W. VII 71 +E.

But seven instances (five accompanied by a single and one by two other copies), where t does not err, may represent d readings corrupted in manuscript D. Group d further attests four unique right readings and three more with the support of one other manuscript:

Major: III 27. X 30. **Minor**: VII 296 +N. XI 5 +J, 122, 195, 277 +J.

It therefore cannot be eliminated.

§ 10. The group's *singleton*, **D**, has individual major errors at I 159, III 268, IV 23, V 119, VI 29, VIII 134, 159, 170, IX 85, X 17, 208, 212, XI 80 and 246. But it also lacks a number of minor r^1 errors, perhaps as a result of correction from an r^2 source (though coincidental variation might account for them). They are Pr 75, II 88, VI 64, IX 56, 98, 111, X 172 and XI 264. However, as D contains *no* unique right readings, it could in principle be eliminated.

§ 11. The other *sub-group*, **t**, is attested by all its members **TH²Ch** in some 48 major and as many minor agreements that indicate an exclusive common ancestor:

Major I 110, 159. III 72, 95, 268. IV 23, 61, 119. V 17, 119, 198, 234, 252. VI 29, 53, 68, 107. VII 5, 30, 210. VIII 32 (1,2), 45, 129, 134, 159, 160 (1,2), 170. IX 85. X 4, 12, 17, 47, 78, 176, 208, 210, 212. XI 2, 55, 56, 80, 183, 211, 246, 260, 301. **Minor** I 59, 78, 101, 135. II 59, 131, 142. III 79, 109, 139, 251, 259. IV 61, 73, 112, 129. V 25, 57, 60, 81, 93, 98, 132, 179. VI 22, 37, 48, 52. VII 32, 196. VIII 7, 8, 61, 73, 100, 122. IX 7, 74, 109, 113. X 178, 180. XI 19, 71, 77, 81, 82, 110.

About another 50, 19 of them major, show agreement of T and H^2 where Ch has a different error or is right, presumably by faithful retention of d, as in these 15 cases:

Major III 92, 258. V 7, 29. VI 6. IX 39, 70, 79. X 191 (? *by intelligent guess*). XI 293. **Minor** VIII 21. X 39, 190. XI 229, 266.

§ 12. The consequently implied relationship <TH²>Ch is, however, challenged by some 25 readings, six of them major, where TCh agree but H^2 has a different error or, as in the following six major cases, is correct:

Pr 86 poundes] poynteþ. I 4 clyf] kiþ. II 96 a maiden of goode] of maides engendrit. III 193 *L. om.* IV 71–2 *Ll. om.* V 10 *L. om.*

Except for V 10 (where the ease of loss by homoteleuton is shown by agreement of the unrelated r^2 copies HN), these TCh errors seem too striking to be coincidental. It therefore seems likely that what H^2 shows is correction of the t readings of its exemplar rather than retention of d readings preserved in t but lost by TCh (as proposed for Ch at § 11 above). But this can only have come from an r^2 or **m** copy since, of the other r^1 witnesses, both D and u omit IV 72a and the whole of line IV 71.[7] With allowance, then, for a phase of correction, H^2 may be accepted as forming a genetic pair with T. The latter manuscript has no readings by correction, a feature it shares with the key **m** witness M.

§ 13. The sub-group t also agrees in a dozen almost certainly random errors with seven manuscripts from both families, and in one major instance with the other family disjunctively:

Major I 82 +J. VII 280 + **m**. X 193 +H^3 (*synonym-substitution*). VIII 75 +K (*censorship*). **Minor** VII 236. VIII 89 +R. III 271 +H. IX 19, 63 +J. IV 88 +W. V 46 +E. IX 13 +A.

But it also provides seven right readings, one unique, five shared with one other manuscript, and one shared with two other manuscripts from both families.

Major V 36 +M. VII 210 +VE. **Minor** I 25 (*partly*) +U. III 242 +A. IV 77 +L. X 100, 205 +V.

All of these right readings in t, like those in u considered at § 9 above, may be presumed to be present by direct descent ($< d < r^1 < r < $ Ax). This sub-group, therefore, could not be eliminated even if a manuscript other than T were chosen as copy-text.

§ 14. In conclusion, the sub-family r^1 remains essential for editing the **A** Version because some fifteen of its actual or probable variants, nine of them major, uniquely preserve from **r** an Ax reading lost by r^2 and **m**.

(b) *The sub-family r^2*

§ 15. This branch consists of **VHJLKWN**, which attest **r**-type readings distinguishing it from **m**, while it lacks the 65 clear agreements in error that establish r^1 (see § 7). The manuscripts divide into the genetic pairs **VH** and **WN**, and the individual copies **J, L** and **K**. Because three of its members H, L, N are incomplete and its representatives dwindle to only three in Passus X–XI (where W becomes an **m** witness), r^2 is much more sparsely attested than r^1, so the case for an exclusive common ancestor is largely inferential. The sigil r^2 is therefore used here mainly for convenience in differentiating the seven manuscripts' readings from those of r^1 on the one hand and **m** on the other (despite frequent agreement with **m** where r^1 errs). As the account of the individual r^2 copies below will indicate, none derives from any other. And though at least two genetic pairs appear, neither depends upon or is the source of any other member of r^2. In the list that follows, a minus before a sigil indicates that the r^2 member does not share the postulated sub-family variant, whether it has the right or a different wrong reading.

Major V 71 ouhte] miȝte -J [*right with r^1*] and -W [*wrong with* **m**]. VII 12 elles] ony -W [*right with* **m**]. VII 178 *Line-division and expansion* -LKW. X 214 schrewe] same. XI 19 conterfeteþ] can construe -K. 134 conterfetyd] contreuide -K [*right with* d**m**]. *Accompanied by one other MS:* VII 128 crowen] cowes -W, +M. 282 -W, +M. wolden] þouȝte +A. **Minor** XI 217 þo] þese. *With one or two other MSS:* VII 160 + MH^3 *Word-order*. IX 18 as me] me -J+M.

§ 16. The first of the r^2 pairs is **v**, made up of V and H, with V its sole representative after VIII 143. These have some 245 agreements in error,[8] the most important being the missing lines Pr 50–1, 99–100, 109, II 28–9 and IV 119. About a fifth of the other major errors are recorded where the lemma has a set of complex variants:

I 4, 39, 93, 135, 137, 139; II 9, 51, 87; III 14, 146, 193, 197, 208; IV 19, 24, 53, 61; V 129, 160; VI 6; VII 95, 183.

V cannot derive from H because it is half a century earlier, nor H from V because it lacks such errors as V's missing lines at Pr 34, I 149b–150a, 176–83, II 106–21, 129. The group v (or V alone, inferentially representing it) contains four unique right readings and another three accompanied by one r^2 copy. In the list of these, other-version support is indicated.

Major +**BC** V 159 warinar] weuer/ waffrer/ bereward. (V *only*, +**C**) V 200 þrompelde] stumblide. (V *only*, +**BC**) VII 187 hurde] erþe / ȝerd / hous / lond. **Minor** +**BC** Ac] And / *om.*

Group v therefore cannot be eliminated.

§ 17. The second r^2 pair, **w**, consists of the conjoint **A/C** copies W and N (*Manuscripts*, nos. 12 and 13), which are both present from I 76 to the end of VIII. After this w's sole representative in the **A** portion is W, but only as far as Passus IX; for at this point W ceases to be an r^2 witness and becomes a member of **m** in X–XI, apparently following a change of exemplar. The group is defined by 140 agreements in error,[9] about 35 major, the most important being:

(a) 4 *omitted lines*: I 131. III 206 +U, 208, 257. (b) 33–5 *added lines from* **C** *between* I *and* III: *after* I 129, 132, 152, 161; II 20, 45 (5 *added in* W, 7 *in* N), 56, 65 (12 *lines*), 131 (4 *lines in its place*), 194 (6 *lines*); III 33 (2 *lines*), 141 (*Latin*).

N adds a further 110 lines and two Latin lines taken from **C**, W another 59 and one of Latin from **B**, mainly in IV. After K (see § 21 below), these manuscripts are the most heavily conflated from the C-Text. Of the pair, **W** had the more complex history. Thus it lacks two key indicative errors of r^2 at VII 12 and at VII 128, where it agrees with r^1EH³ but has those at VII 160, 282 and at IX 18, where r^2 is accompanied by one **m** copy. Though generally grouping with **m** in X–XI, W could conceivably reflect collation with an **r** copy at XI 19; but this explanation is rejected at § 28 below. The five *earlier* major agreements with **m**, however, more plausibly suggest sporadic consultation of an **m** manuscript after W's initial copying from w. W reveals extensive recourse to **C**, the version it continues with, and also to **B**.

§ 18. Each member of group w uniquely preserves major right readings, W having four and N two:

W: I 48 +**ZB** ylik] lik. III 21 +**ZBC** coppis] pecis / other gyfteȝ. VI 2 +**ZC** baches. 52 he (*basis of emended* *hy). XI 308 + K; (*cf.* **BC**) kete] grete. *N*: V 189 +J vm] sum. 142 so þike] soþly / so mote I the / (*basis of the emendation*).

All but one of these apparent corrections to Ax errors seem likely to result from collation with copies of **B** and **C**. The exception is XI 308 (where K alone might have preserved r^2) and W, which is of **m** character in these passūs, could have consulted such a copy. At any rate, both *baches* (which is in **C**) and *kete* (which is not) seem too difficult to be scribal substitutions for the easier readings in their presumed exemplar. Group w therefore cannot be eliminated.

§ 19. The three remaining manuscripts, **J, L** and **K**, derive from r^2 through at most one intermediate source not shared substantially with any other. Of these **J** has, however, some 40 agreements in error with the r^1 copy U. The four major ones are:

I 122 troniþ hem] tryeste of. III 213 go] metyn. VIII 130 metelis] mater m. (matere U). VIII 132 Peris loue þe Plouȝman ful pensif] P. lyf pl. petusly.

The last is a noteworthy complex variant that differs in four particulars from the Ax reading and cannot be coincidental. It may be due to the U scribe's consulting the r^2 copy that was J's postulated intermediate source (**j**). U's five other major agreements with r^2, at I 153, VII 201, VIII 2, 101 and the Latin at XI 296, are compatible with this explanation. A sixth major agreement of U and r^2 at V 196, where J (like K and r^1) has lost 196b, could be accounted for as a mechanical error rather than as a faithful reflex of j. J groups, secondly, with the **m** copy A in three major readings:

III 19 merciede] myrthed. V 143 chaffare] crafte. XI 56 kete] cowrte.

These striking agreements are hard to explain as coincidental, for though each is a substitution for a more difficult word, none is the obvious one (as *thankede* for *merciede* might have been). If they are readings of source j, it is possible that A consulted J or that A's source consulted j; for on grounds of date J cannot have got them from A, which is at least a generation younger. Finally, J has 26 agreements with another **m** copy, M. Though seven are major, all are of such a kind as possibly to be coincidental substitutions:

III 141 barnes] childeryn. V 96 wiȝt] man [*more modern synonyms*]. IV 13 þe frek] consciens. VII 9 shedyng] spyllyng [*contextually more familiar term*]. VII 245 ete] ȝit [*visual mis-resolution of* *y-ete *prompted by misunderstanding of context; AH³ ȝet suggests that this was in fact the reading of* **m**]. XI 170 þe gode wyf] stody [*more explicit referent*]. XI 282 hadde he saluacioun] was [he] sauyd [*simpler expression*].

In conclusion, J's only significant relations with another manuscript are with U and possibly with the source of A, but these appear not to be genetic. Although it is the most complete representative of r^2, J is never the sole witness of a right reading in Pr–XI. But as one of the two surviving sources of lines 20–88 in XII, where it alone preserves the right reading in 22 out of 44 contested instances, J ranks with R and M among the three most important **A** copies to survive.

§ 20. The manuscript **L** is present in only four of the lines containing indicative sub-family readings (VII 12, 128, 160, 282), but it has all of these. It also shares some 16 errors with one member of the v group, H, two of which appear major, and two major ones with the **m** copy E:

H: I 1 merke] deope. III 164 gret] most [*adopted by* K–D *for* // III 177 *in* **B** *but not by* Ka² *for* **A**]. *E*: I 25 driȝeþ] thyrstes. VI 8 ampollis] saumples.

All of these, however, may be explained as easy coincidental errors. The first with H is both conventionally motivated and an unconscious echo of the actual phrase instanced in Pr 15. The second, an obvious use of a close synonym to 'regularise' alliteration, yields its claim to be the original in face of **ZBC** agreement with Ax. The first agreement with E is in a more explicit expression and the second is probably a visual error part-induced by the *s*-alliteration of the fourth lift with that of the next line. In the absence of any real evidence of relation with another **A** copy, L may therefore be taken as descending from r^2 through at most one intermediate source (*l*), postulated to account for some of its individual errors. Such a conclusion is not contradicted by L's two unique right readings (supported by **ZBC**), at VII 189 and 253. These are minor but rule out its elimination.

§ 21. The manuscript **K** is potentially important as one of three in the sub-family that is complete in Pr–XI. But its value is reduced by its extensive conflation with **C** (and in one instance **B**), exceeding that of WN (see § 17) and extending to over 400 lines:

C *lines introduced after* Pr 4, 12 (4 *ll.*), 14, 102 (140 *ll.*); I 31; III 45 (5 *ll.*); V 42, 219 (C VI 422–VII 61 *with omissions*), 252 (C VII 69–153 *with omissions*); VI 109 (2 *ll.*), 126 (C VII 291–305 *with additions*); *for* VI 20–95 *the passage* C VII 176–259; *after* V 39 *four lines* B V 50–1, 48–9).

All but one of these form no part of **A**. But after V 42, where Ax may have smoothed an original *hem* to *ȝow*, the reading from C V 200 (paralleled in **Z** and **B** in different forms) fills a sense-gap, and there may be a case for adopting it.[10] Also in Pr–IX **K** agrees with the w member W[11] in some 45 readings, 17 of them major:

Pr 44 knaues] hewyn (hyne W). V 126 Brochide] Prycked; 129 made] worched (wroght W) [*synonym-substitutes*]. VII 168 defendite] fett [*a misunderstanding, paralleled in* **Z**; *see* Textual Note]. II 80 bokes] chekes; VIII 55 bigge] sell; 155 lettres] seles W [(*canc. for* letturs K) *attempts to strengthen the sense*]. IX 27 stande] stomble [*the same, with possible contamination from* C X 35]. Pr 63 hy] charite; V 146 shrifte] chirche [*more explicit readings prompted by* Pr 61 *and* V 147 *respectively*]. VII 114 cunne] done; 196 ȝif þou wistest] of the [*substitutions of easier and smoother readings (as in* **B**, *here possibly an archetypal error*)]. IX 26 watir] wawes [*conventional association or attempt to avoid repeating* 25]. Pr 34 synneles] gylefully K; gylously W [*rejection of favourable original epithet and attempt to normalise alliterative pattern*]. VII 224 L. om. [*perhaps by eyeskip from* nam 223 > nam 225]. X 159 sed] seth [*visual error induced by preceding* seth].

All these agreements, however, reveal types of motivation that weaken the likelihood of a genetic link between K and W. That they derive from collation of K's medieval ancestor with W or a lost copy of w is therefore not very probable, as K has no disjunctive agreements with w or even with N. It is therefore better placed as separately descended from r^2, with one intermediary stage, its source, at which contamination might have occurred. But K uniquely preserves three major readings that seem original and shares a fourth such with W:

II 144 +**B**(**ZC**) fobbars] *five variants*. VI 1 +**B**(**C**)**Z** wight none] nane / fewe men. XI 80 +**B** whyys] *four variants*. XI 308 +W kete] grete Ax.

It therefore cannot be eliminated.

§ 22. From the above it emerges that 15 major readings judged authentic are severally preserved in six extant copies or in postulated group-ancestors of the manuscripts comprising r^2. The only individual copy that could in principle be eliminated is H, which has no unique right readings. The group r^2 exclusively attests 34 right readings (14 of them major), totalling over three times as many as r^1 (cf. § 14 above). In the following list of these, dissident members are denoted by a minus sign.

Major X -KW 159 sed] *om*. XI -J 56 kete] grete. +**ZBC**: I 127 kennyn me bettur] me bet k. / better to lere. II -vW 83 mendis] frendis. III -v 135 sixe] seue. VII 174 potful] potel. +**Z**(**B**)**C**: -vJw 17 segges] seyþ god / I say. +**BC**: IV -Vw 47 for hym vneth] vnn. on hym for / for hym to wynke ne. V -v 16 puffyd] put / passchet. VIII 142 diuinede] demide. +**B**: IV -H 154 leete] loue. X 202 vn-] no / my. XI -VJ 80 whyys] weyes / werkes / priuytes. +**C**: III B†; -vK 209 kenne clerkes] ben cl. / techyn chyldryn. IV -Vw 47 for hym vneth] vnn. on hym for / for hym to wynke ne.
Minor +**C** V 109–10 (*l. div.*). +**ZB** V 143. +**BC**-WK VI 95. +**ZBC** VI 101. +**BC** -L VI 115, 120. +**ZC** (*cf.* **B**) VII 171. +**ZBC**-LK VIII 38 (1). +**BC** VIII 168. +**BC** IX 56, 67, 74. +**B** IX 96. -K X 123–25 (*l. div.*). +**BC** X 172. +**B** X 188 (1,2). +**BC** 1X 193. XI 4; +**B** XI 9; 75–6, 163 (*l. div.*).

If the 15 readings of its individual members are taken as also preserving r^2, this sub-family will stand as the sole source of about 50 right readings, some 30 of them major. As most have other-version support, they may be inferred to preserve readings lost from Ax directly by **m** and indirectly by r^1 from **r**. Thus r^2 cannot be eliminated.

(c) The **r** *family: conclusions*

§ 23. The evidence for **r** as the exclusive common ancestor of the two sub-families is the 108 agreements in error (some 50 major) of r^1 and r^2. That these *are* errors may be established by comparing them both with the variants of the **m** family of **A** and with the parallel text of **Z**, **B** and **C** where present. The following list therefore divides readings not only into *major* and *minor* but also according to the *other-version support* for those adopted. The lemmata from the edited text are the readings of **m** unless otherwise specified; the variants are those of **r**, given in full for major instances, by reference only for minor ones. A plus sign accompanies **m** or **r** manuscripts having the rejected **r** or the adopted **m** reading in question.

Readings with other-version support

Major

+**Z**: I 110 seluyn] *om* +E. II 94 feytles] feythles / feyntles / faylere *&c.* VII 128 +KN Cacche] Chase +E. cowes] A; crowen r'**m**; gees r'EH[3]. 270 plante colis] *trs.* VIII 54 þe Sautir witnessiþ] seiþ þe s. 61 leiȝe I ouȝt trowe ȝe] ȝe wyten ȝif I leiȝe. +**ZB**: I 106 mene] *om.* 112 felawshipe] felawis. II 87 *as two ll.* +E. VII 15 comaundiþ] wille. VII 60 (*emendation*). +**ZC**: V 249 coupe] gilt +MH[3]. +**ZBC**: II 124 bad hem] *om.* 146 þise men] þe men. 154 cacche miȝte] *trs.* III 146 hym þe gate] hem ofte / hem euere / þe treuþe / so faste. V 243 *reddere*] red non. 256 +K go to] seke. VI 9 Sise] Synay. 13 first] H[3] (*om* E; fast AMW); faire **r**. 71 In no manere ellis] Loke þat þou leiȝe. 82–4 *Ll. om.* VII 5 and sowen it aftir] *om.* 60 leue] *om.* 86 masse] mynde +E. 230 +Ch hym bereuen] be hym bereuid (H[3]). 233 Contemplatif; actif] *trs.* [*Comparable with* **ZBC**: VII 59 hewe wiþ þe hatchet] any þing swynke. 294 +W or ybake] or rostid **m**; *om* **r**. + **B**: 87 +W *L. om.* VIII 54a] *om* +**Z**. 100 þe deuil shal haue þi soule] to helle shalt þou wende. 101 +W atweyne] assondir. 111 +wZ *Line-div.*; be folis] anoþer. X 32 shafte] shap. + **BC**: V 116 wayte] loke. 126 bat] pakke. 163; 167 +vN *Ll. om.* VII 61 þermyd maugree] wiþ þe corn. 68 hoten] holden. VIII 136 book bible] b. of þe b. M; bible **r**+AH[3]. X 22 +Ch fyue] sixe **r**+A.

Minor

+**ZBC**: I 49, 161. II 75, +W 177. III 5, 67, 129. IV 21, 106. V +W 40. VI 57 +wL, 86, +v 91–2, 103. VII 145] **r**+EAH[3], +UV 158, 275. VIII 27] **r**+AH[3], 84. +**ZB**: I 46, 69. IV 31, 33. VI 33 +N] **r** +EM; +w 73. VII 19. +**ZC**: II 1. +**Z**: II 137. VII 12, 16. + **B**: II 86 +HWH[2]] *om* (+Z). III 230. V +KW 80, +KW 90. VI 47. VIII 109, 111, 112. X 200. XI +J 162, 171, +J 205, 264. +**BC**: I 149. VI +LN 110, +VW 112, +VK 116. VII 73, 97 +E, 106 +EZ. VIII +v 87, 127, +v 132, +H[2]1 36–7, 175, +KZ 185. XI +K 5] **r**+AW; +R 305.

Readings with no other-version parallel

Major

V 79 (+J; *cf.* **B**) men] hym. VIII 105 (*cf.* **B**) belyue] liflode +A. XI 154 shewide] seide. 182 (+Ch; *cf.* **B**) he] she. 194–6 *Line-div.* 194 Dredles] God wot; wot þe soþe] *om;* 195 ben in office] benefices. 245 shewiþ..aftir] *om.*

iv. *The* **m** *family of* **A** *manuscripts*

§ 24. The second family, **m**, consists of five manuscripts. But of these only four at most appear at any one time together, **EAMH³** and **AMH³W**, because E ceases at VII 213 and W (following a presumed change of exemplar) does not decisively become an **m** copy until Passus X. They constitute a *family* because their postulated source, like **r**, descends independently from the archetype. This judgement is based first on **m**'s possession, with other-version support, of about 100 right readings (some 35 of them major) where **r** is in error. Even more important, in that it cannot be due to contamination from **B** or **C**, is **m**'s unique preservation of eight major readings with *no* other-version parallel which, if accepted as authentic on intrinsic grounds, can only be part of the original A-Text (see § 23, end). As collateral (or negatively 'criterial') readings, they will be mentioned again when the two families are compared at § 47 below. But it must first be shown that the two overlapping sets of four manuscripts form a genetic group deriving from a single exclusive ancestor, **m**.

§ 25. Of the five members of **m** only M is both complete and free of contamination from the other family (like T of r' at § 12 above). While a solid link between the two sets of four is provided by **AMH³** as their common core, difficulty arises even here on account of incomplete attestation and contamination in all three. Thus *A* has large omissions in Pr–II and briefly in VII and VIII. *H³*, more significantly, becomes an **A** copy only after V 104, before which it is the **B** manuscript H. *E* has had about a fifth of its **m** readings altered by reference to an **r** copy of identifiable type. Conversely, *W* has adopted a few sporadic **m** readings earlier in the text than Passus X. Finally, both *A* and *H³* show what look like corrections from an **r** copy rather than retentions of presumed **m** readings lost by the other members. In the account that follows, therefore, the certainty of the **m** readings lessens to mere possibility where the number of witnesses falls below three, breaking the unanimity of the 'core-group' AMH³.

(a) *The manuscript-group* **EAMH³**

§ 26. This group exhibits 44 isolative agreements (32 major) between V 109–VI 103 and VII 115–186. In the following list of them, the lemma is the reading of **r** unless noted otherwise. A minus sign before a sigil denotes an **m** manuscript with the correct reading; a plus sign, an **r** copy sharing the rejected reading of **m**.

Major V 109 *as* 2 *ll.* eiȝen] eyn as a blynde hagge (*so* Bx). 110 lollide] lokyd (likerd wer E). *Hereafter* B V 191–92 *added* MH³, 192 *added* E, *subst. for* 111 A. 115 Symme...Noke] synne it þouth me mery. 117 Ferst] -E; *l. om* A. 132 dede] *om*; -E, *corrupt* H³. 142 so þe Ik] so mote I the. 146 for to go to shrifte] to go on his wey. 147 hym to *kirkeward*] to chirche. 153 he] herry -E. 172 hitte] caste +ChH-E. 179 acorden] a. welle *trs* M; -H³; *l. om* A. 190 *After this* B V 341 *added*. 229 And...I²] Qwat euer I namm; And euerche man M; *l. om* A; -E. VI 20 callen] clepyn -E. 31 sewide] folwde +H. 37 oþerwhile] sumtyme -E. 44 swere] s. fast +L. 65 half] hand -M. 81 þing] *om*. VII 35 conseyuede] rehersede -E; *def.* A. 40 presauntis and] *om*. 139 to wraþen hym] *om*; -E. 142 pilide] pyned -E. 157 houpide] wyschid / clepid / wepyd AMH³;-E. 171 Faitours...fer] For ferd þese f. 176 ditte] holdyn +W; driuen EChu. 187 erde] lond; ȝerd EJu. 193 blody] *om*; bodely E. 222 mouþiþ] mevith. 235 here] *om*; +H. 280 ete] hente +t.
Minor V 117 -E; *l. om* A. 143 -E. 228 +H. 242 +J. VI 26 -M+Ch. 28 -E+DR. 39 -A+VJ. 42. 48. VII 122 -E. 190 -E.

EAMH³ also attest some 25 unique right readings. These, which presumably here preserve **m**, have been given in full among the lemmata at § 23 above; the major ones are V 116 (*l. om* E), 126, 243, [256 +K]; VI 9 (†H³), 71, 82–4, 91/2. The group therefore cannot be eliminated.

(b) *The manuscript-group* **AMH³W**

§ 27. This group is instanced mainly in Passūs X–XI, where there are 27 isolative errors, 24 of them major, and also in V–VII, where there are nine, one major.

Major VII 176 ditte] holdyn. X 53 going] good dede. 69 owyng] holde (+ChK; -H³). helpe] kepe. 70 folies] falsnesse & f.(-nesse) -ed A). 88 self] soule. 168 hem] hem brymme. 186 vncomely] vnkende*ly*. 215 *L. om*. XI 5 staring] scorn*yng*. 13 werkis] wordis. 18–19 *mis-division*. as...deseites] *om* (and deseaytes W). 21 conne] can do (*trs* AW). 22 seruid] sewit (folweþ;-A). 100 *As* 2 *ll*. expanded. 145 scole] lore. 146 I...Catoun] in c. þu may rede. 151 enemys] fomen. 164 Foundid...formest] formest Hem f. in feth. 228 lordis] londis. 239 any man] a *man* þat is. 245 suche] *om*. 284 *L. om*. 311 Souteris] Saweris.
Minor V 116 And] I (+N; *l. om* E). VI 74 -E. 109 -E. 125. VII 115. 143 +L. 157 þat] he -E. 213 wolde not] nolde (n. nouth H³W). XI 61. 144 Leue] L. now (*trs* A). 153. 213.

AMH³W uniquely attest six right readings, four major (XI 154, 194, 195, 245), that are accepted as preserving Ax through **m** and, like the right readings of EAMH³, listed in full at § 23. This group likewise cannot be eliminated.

§ 28. The most economical account of these two four-member groups with their shared 'core' of three manuscripts is that they are one in origin, E ceasing late in Passus VII and W joining AMH^3 in X after change of its r^2-type exemplar for one of **m**-type. W's eight minor **m** readings before Passus X may all be accounted for as coincidental. The one significant case (VII 176 *ditte out*] *holdyn out*) is of a type where convergent substitution may be invoked without seriously contradicting the general presumption that major shared errors are likely to be genetic in origin. For in this instance the phrasal verb in question is rare and the scribal variant an evident gloss.[12]

(c) **AMH^3** *and the other four groups of three*

§ 29. Between Passus V and XI, the three manuscripts forming the 'common core' of the two sets have 22 isolative agreements in error, 15 of them major:

Major (a) V 153 he] her*r*y. 159 warinar] bereward. VI 3 longe] to l. 37 oþerwhile] sumtyme. VII 139 to wraþen] *om.* 142 pilide] pyned. 187 erd] lond. 193 blody] *om.* **(b)** 235 here] *om* +H. 237 *pur*...konne] þat þu kenne me woldyst (k. me] me techin MH^3). VIII 18 passe] partyn. **(c)** X 19 hende] thride [*inadvertently omitted from Apparatus*]. 101 comsist] gynnyst. XI 19a] *om.* 94 mele] spekyn.
Minor (a) VII 122 and] *om.* 171 Faitours...fer] For ferd þese f. 190 I wot; wel] *trs.* **(b)** VIII 20 hadde] han. **(c)** X 18 haþ] hadde. XI 170. *With an r MS*: V 116 And] I + w. IX 102 ac] and + u.

The category (a) and (c) variants given here have already been included with those of EAMH^3 and AMH^{3}W respectively at § 23 above as representing the presumed readings of **m**. In (a) the E variants at V 159 and VI 3 seem to derive from AMH^3 (= **m**); at VII 139 E agrees in error decisively with **r** and in 187 with an **r** group-variant. Together, these features indicate that E's remaining three divergences, which are agreements with **r** in right readings, are due to its correction from **r** rather than to its faithful retention of **m** where the others have erred. The **r** copy used by E or its exemplar was specifically of u type, as may be deduced from the parallel presence in E of 49 errors, some 20 of them major, shared exclusively with RU (listed in *Ka* pp. 86–7).[13] In category (c), on the other hand, while W too may have been corrected from **r**, it could equally retain **m** from *y* where A, M and H^3 have lost it severally. Thus X 101 and XI 94 (where the Apparatus should record 'rW' for 'r') are of a type explicable as randomly convergent substitutions in each of the three copies and need not presuppose a common source. The same could also be true at X 19 (where W again reads with **r**), if **m** read **ende* (for *hende*) and each found it seemingly nonsensical. Likewise at XI 19, the survival in W of the single word *deseites* from 19a is better explained as a reflex of its **m**-type exemplar than as due to collation with an **r** copy. For whereas an attempted correction would presumably have been more complete, the subsequential smoothing with intruded *and* is plausibly attributable to W itself. On that supposition AMH^3 may correspondingly be held to have smoothed, but here by deletion of **m**'s postulated *deseites*. These last two examples might favour an immediate common ancestor between AMH^3 and the source they share with W and E; but as independent substitution / smoothing by each member here is not improbable, the evidence for a relation (E[<AMH^3>W]) remains slight.

§ 30. The core-group is not therefore proposed as disjunctive so much as representing **m** 'reduced' by the late and early absence of E and W respectively. As such, however, it appears challenged by three further sets of three manuscripts. Thus **AMW** has nine agreements:

Major II 161 tresour] þing. 168 preyour] thyng. VI 117 ingang] in. XI 33 neuere] neþer. 257 make] lette. 277 wende to] wynne me. **Minor** V 45 hire] *om.* XI 47 Is] Is þer. 61 &] ȝif þat.

In the first two, H³ is absent and could have read with AMW. In XI 277 H³'s *wonyn in* looks a possible visual error for the AMW variant. In VI 117 *ingate* H³, shared with uEK, may be an attempted correction of an **m** reading *in*, and *neuere* XI 33 a similar (and successful) attempt. Only XI 257 is problematic; but if *lette*, shared by the B-Text, is *right* (as it may be), H³'s agreement with **r** could be explained as an alliteratively-induced synonym-substitution. In the first minor variant, H³ is absent; the other two are trivial and could easily be coincidental (as may W's agreement with AM in an isolated right reading at V 40).

§ 31. The next group **AH³W** contains ten minor readings:

VI 3 þat] *om.* 74. VII 229 And] *om.* VIII 21 non] *om.* X 119. XI 82 to] *om.* 86. 120 Til] Whan. 136. 291.

The only comment required here is on the last two, both of which may be safely presumed to preserve **m** where now M has introduced an individual error; 136 is especially clear.

§ 32. The third set **MH³W** is identified by seven major and eight minor readings:

Major X 202 vntyme] no tyme. 204 also] lyuende. XI 21 yclepid] called. 22 serue] sewit (folweþ) W). 126 bible] bille. 132 garte] made. 149 techiþ] tellit. **Minor** V 245. VII 29 þat] *om.* 285 to] *on.* XI 87 And] But. 119. 175. 193 singe] and s. 217.

In the first two, A is absent and could have read the same. XI 22 and 126 look like visual errors in **m** that were noticed and independently corrected in A. XI 21, 119 and 149 could be coincidental substitutions, the last two obviously so. XI 87 and 175 are both absent in A and 193 is an easy case of addition in **m** (under influence from the Latin) and of omission in A (through alliterative attraction). Taken together, these three sub-groupings do not seriously question AMH³ as effectively representative of **m**. The core-group's status is collaterally confirmed by the 67 major agreements evidenced in its persistence throughout EAMH³ and AMH³W.

§ 33. By way of conclusion, there is a fourth set of three, **EAM**, which qualifies as deriving from a single ancestor distinct from **r** or either of its sub-families. But this does not decisively challenge AMH³ either, for it is instanced only before the conjoint H³ appears as an A-Text at V 105. Where all three witnesses agree in Pr–V, EAM may therefore be taken to represent, if with diminished certainty, the same postulated source **m** as do AMH³.[14] This identification is logically economical and (at least negatively) empirical. Since there are no other members of the complete family in this section, it would seem justified to employ the sigil **m** also to signify EAM (and EM, when A is defective). This group has about 45 agreements in error, some 30 major. A minus sign before a sigil indicates that the copy here has the correct reading, usually that of **r**:

Major I 143 -E pyne] tene. 145 pite] *om (added* E). 151 mete...ellis] to oþer (men) metyn. 152 ʒe; þerwiþ] *om*; vnto you. 157 in...houres] of heuenriche blys. 160 fet] fewte. 180 siʒte of] *om.* II 5 Loke...&] *om.* 6 -E hise...many] here f. many vnfeythful*ly* to knowe. 16 haþ...me] *at* me hase grevyd. III 11 merþe &] **r**; moche; good W. 21 coppis of siluer] other gyfteʒ mony. 22 -A *L. om.* 23 -A. *L. om.* 33 *L. om.* 74 -A on] *om.* 99 -A beʒonde] b. see. 273 leute] luve. IV 50–1 *L. div.* 50 -A manye] *om.* 67 euere] *om.* 82 pees...pur] pennys *for pes* & pecys of. 84 wile¹] *om.* 96 more] better. 129 wedde] gyff þe. 146 be...it] *to me* to bryng *þaim* togeder. 147 ledis] landes. 157 -E he faille] elles. V 39 ʒe...betere] þai be storyd wele E; ʒoure stor better; *l. om* A. 46 lord] *om.* 64 -A leyn] ben. 69 Venym] Weriues *or* Wermes (And seyde w. M). 70 Walewiþ] walkes. 74–5 -E *Ll. om.* 78 gode happis] godnes. 90 Awey] (And) also. 95 werse] (wel) w. *be dom of my selfe.* **Minor** I 164 ac...is] & ch. II 156 wolde] shuld. 158 +H neuere] no. 161 To] For to. 193 him] he. 197 fere] ferde. III 61 -E in] in ʒoure. 76 heo] hase. 78 Or] A*ls.* 105 -A Conscience...kyng] before *þe* kyng con. 265 +H *hem*; ʒou A. V 48 +N þere] þer*in.*

§ 34. The instances, four major and one minor, where E has the right reading may derive from the **r** copy it appears to have been collated with throughout its length. Nevertheless, E's retention of **m** family errors both here and after V 105, when H^3 joins the group, tends to confirm its proposed descent from **m**. Similarly, the six readings (five major and one minor) where A is right may be attributed to correction. The most striking of these, III 22 and 23, are unlikely to have been lost coincidentally from **m** by E and M, since no obvious mechanical reason appears. Throughout V 105–VII 213, where EAM constitute part of EAMH^3, there is almost no sign (in the shape of divergences by H^3) of a distinct genetic sub-group <EAM>. For only twice with other-version support (VII 80 and 186, both minor) does H^3 have the right reading against E(A)M, and both may be coincidental.

§ 35. The relation between **AMH^3** and its new partner W in Passus X–XI is, however, somewhat different. For while W's ultimate descent from **m** seems established by its 46 agreements in error (over half major) with the other three members of the set, it departs from the core-group AMH^3 in sharing six right readings with **r** (major: XI 52, 56, 94; minor: XI 70, 231, 255). However the minor readings here could be coincidental and in XI 52 the diverging M and H^3 variants might have simple causes (motivated and mechanical respectively), the agreement of each with another **r** witness tending to indicate their non-genetic character. In XI 56 W preserves a difficult **m** reading, here presumed archetypal, for which M, H^3 and A all have recognisably easier substitutions. The sole instance, therefore, which could seriously suggest an exclusive group-original for AMH^3 is 94 (where W should be recorded in the apparatus as agreeing with **r**). But as noted at § 29 above, coincidental substitution of a modernising synonym is here very likely. With so little support, the case for a relation <AMH^3>W, like that for <EAM>H^3, may be safely dismissed.

§ 36. From the evidence so far, it would seem reasonable to assume, firstly, that two sets of four manuscripts, EAMH^3 and AMH^{3}W, qualify as potentially genetic groups. Secondly, the persistence of AMH^3 as the common core of both groups is congruent with the descent of both from a single source, **m**. For despite the absence of E in VIII–XI and W's membership of **r** in Pr–IX, the groups reveal themselves *prima facie* not as two but as one, though only intermittently attested as a result of these absences and other losses in its constituent members. Thus, although AMH^3 does not have an exclusive common ancestor, it remains recognisably the core of what proves on analysis to be a manuscript family (cf. § 25 above). Its integrity survives challenge from the three sets of three manuscripts judged non-genetic above and is unaffected by the existence of the one other which appears genetic. For the latter, EAM, may without further argument be taken as standing for **m** before the point in Passus V where H^3 begins, just as AMH^3 stands for **m** after E ceases and before the group is joined in Passus X by W.

(d) *Six groups of paired manuscripts*

§ 37. Some further subdivisions are discernible within the postulated groups of four (in their full) and three (in their reduced) forms, EAM(H^3) and AMH^3(W). There are *five conflicting pairs* within EAM and EAMH^3 (denoted below by (a) and (b) respectively). Among these, **EA** has some 30 agreements in error (about 18 major), of which 22 appear in the apparatus among complex sets of variants:

Major (a) I 179. II 9 Ip.] Puryd. III 91 as s.] *om.* ?262. IV 23. 24. 38 gade-] gos-. V 17. 77 tunge] talys. 95. 102 +H^2. **(b)**

164 dykere] Drynkere. 166 *L. om.* 190. VI 2. ?68. VII 15. 99 Dik-] Digg-. **Minor (a)** I 165 ben au.] *trs.* II 15. III 51 wr.] þerin wr. IV 21. 98. V 94 wepe] wepyd. **(b)** VI 66 And] *om.* 94 þe²] þat. VII 31. 103 to pl.] pleasyd.

It should be noted that M has the right reading in about half the major cases where EA err, doubt-less because it preserves **m** faithfully. In the remainder it has either a different individual error or, after V 105, the same error as H³ (at VI 2). On this evidence, EA could be a genetic group; but it cannot be eliminated, as it preserves one right reading (minor) at III 230.

§ 38. The status of EA is challenged by disjunctive agreements of both its members with M. The first of these pairs, **EM**, presents an initially impressive agreement in some 85 (over 50 of them major), which is nearly three times as many as EA. In the following list of them, brackets denote cases of only approximate agreement:

Major (a) Pr 81. 84. 95 cuntre] peple. 96–7 *misplaced after* 89. I (35 þat lef is] lesse M; no blysse E). 39. 44. 69 wyt] hert. 86. (93). 98. 99 fyue score] fyftene. 118¹·². 119. 123. (127). 133. 138. 139. 141. II 23 forgid] *fangid*. 24 begon...so] ben for*th*ganger. 32. 38. 46. 47. 48 +U. 51¹·² (1 + v). 52. 53. (56) 65. 81. 103 his] *om.* 117 þi...wyf] weddyt (wendyd M). 118 +U. 121. III 146. 147. 158. 170 +Ch. 174. 206¹·². 211. 212 Alle kyn] *om.* (214). V 39 ȝe...betere] þai be storyd wele E; ȝoure stor b. M. **(b)** III 22 *L. om.* 35. 74. IV 50. V 64 leyn] ben. VI 106 aȝen] *om. With one or two* **r** *MSS:* **(a)** I 119² +RL. 137 +RK. II 48 +U. 51¹ +v. 118 +U. **(b)** III 129 +JK. 170 +Ch. 23 +v. **Minor (a)** I 37. 41. 57. 94. 102. 127 haue I] *trs.* II 29. 36. 101. 131. III 99. 105. 144 Barouns...br.] Offt sho br. b. & b. 159. 178. 201. 209. 216. IV 155. **(b)** IV 124 me God] *trs.* V 179. VI 83. VII 101 þer w.] *trs* (†H³). 195 hem²] þai (†A).

Most of these agreements appear where E and M are the only **m** witnesses; but no more than six major errors (or eight, if two where U agrees are counted in) occur in division (b) where A / AH³ are also available. Of these, the important omission of III 22–3, which are in A, could result from visual confusion caused by *gold* (at the caesura in 21 and the end of 23) and by *manye* at the end of 22 and *mayne* after the caesura in 23 (the latter the probable cause of loss of 23 in v). A's reading in 35 arguably reflects its scribe's judgement of ***m** *mylde-* as repeating *softely* 36. In 74 E and M may have coincidentally deleted *on* through mistaking it as a (contextually illogical) privative prefix. In IV 50 misdivision could have led to convergent omission by E and M of a word judged metrically superfluous. V 64 looks like a simple visual error and in VI 106 coincidental loss through allitera-tive attraction (*geten* > *grace*) and homoteleuton (*-en,-en*) would account for the EM agreement. In three major cases other-family concurrence with the agreements tends to confirm the likelihood of coincidental error (in 129 through alliterative inducement and echo of 128a). The minor cases all appear trivial. This suggests that, in the absence of A and H³, it is not more likely that EM are a genetic pair than that they simply preserve what the former two manuscripts would have read had they not proved defective. An argument from silence has little force, but here the positive case for <EM> appears on analysis too weak to rule out that for <EA>. EM, however, uniquely preserves fifteen right readings (five of them major) between I 46 and II 137 (see § 24 above), all presump-tively those of their ancestor **m**. The group therefore cannot be eliminated.

§ 39. The possibility that three other pairs involving A could be genetic will be considered after examination of **MH³**, which appears in both of the sets of four. This pair have some 75 agreements (33 of them recorded in the apparatus), but only 46 major and 22 minor readings unquestionably classifiable as errors are listed below. Here '(a)' signifies that all members of EAMH³ are present (but for one omission of 25 lines by E and two of 50 lines by A, in VII and VIII respectively); '(b)' that E is absent and only AMH³ can represent **m**; '(c)' that AMH³W are all present. An * signifies a noteworthy disjunctive error; a minus, that the copy has the right reading; brackets, only approximate agreement.

Major (a) V 108 (A *a corrupt version of* MH³; *E). 117 -E; *l. om* A. 147. (229)(*l. om* A). VI 2. 20 (*so* A, *different word-order*; -E). 28 -A; *om* E. 47 wilneþ] þenk*yn*. 120 Wyte] I vowe to. VII 35 -E; *def.* A. 60. 61. 99 balkis] Rotes -EA. 142 (A *a version of* MH³;-E). 171 (A *a version of* MH³; -E). **(b)** 223 vsen] wis(s)e -A. 235 of...hondis] *om*; -A. 237. 275 *l. om* A. 285 gart] get*yn* *A. VIII 38 *L. om* (A *def.*). 41 (A *def.*). 575 Þise...ben] For þe tresouris ben oure aldiris (a.] thralles þat is H³; A *def.*). 80 +**Z**. 110 lelly] truely. **(c)** IX 118 -A. X 13 -AW. 17 -AW. 25 calle] clepe -AW. 89 neuere] al woie *AW. 93 gynn*est*] *AW. 122 fruyt] frend -AW. 139-AW. 146. 175 Out-] but -AW. 205 -W; *l.om* A. XI 48 *AW. 56 -W; *A). 57 mene] fewe. 77 lelly] treuliche *W; *l. om* A. 130. 173. 182. 213. 238. 268. **Minor (a)** V 127 hem²] hym -EA. 179 -E; *l. om* A. 235 þe] *om*;-A; of E. VII 19. 26 -EA. 61² (EA *def.*). 89 my²] here -EA. **(b)** 233 Crist] (as) cr. himself (cr. oure lord A). VIII 23 God; m. hem] *trs*; -A. 32 w. not be; w.] *trs* (A *def.*). 73 (A *def.*). 110 Þat] (For) he þ. **(c)** IX 111 ne] no -AW. X 68. 104. XI 32 More] & m. 47 ne] & -A; *om* W. 100 whanne] wh. þat. 111 -A; *om* W. 115 Boþe; and] b. in; & in -AW. 151 And] He -AW. 252 To] Neiþer to -AW.

§ 40. This body of variants, even allowing that four major ones may be faithful reflexes of wrong **m** readings where A varies slightly, indicates that MH³ is likely to be a genetic group. It is attested with uniform persistency throughout the text and the fourfold recurrence of *treu(liche)* for *lel(liche)* is striking. The group, however, uniquely preserves six major right readings and one constituent member, M, has one uniquely:

Major VII 15 comaundiþ. 59 hewe with þe hatchet. 61 þermyd maugree. VIII 54 þe sauter witnessit (M). 54a. 61 leiȝe I out trowe ȝe (M). X 32 shafte.
Minor I 49 (M). VIII 84 in here.

All of these, like those attested by EM (§ 39 above), are likely to preserve **m** where the other family members are absent or err, and they are similarly judged archetypal and adopted. In addition one member, H³, contains half of a reading reconstructed at V 229. The group therefore cannot be eliminated.

§ 41. A fourth challenge to both EA and MH³, the two pairs so far judged likely to be genetic, comes from **AM**. This is attested in 47 readings (some 30 of them major), of which 24 are recorded in the apparatus as part of a lemma's complex variants. In the list below '(a)' denotes the section with EAM(H³) present, '(b)' that with only AMH³ and '(c)' that with AMH³W. A minus sign, asterisk and brackets signify as at § 39 above:

Major (a) I 143 -E. I 147 -ful] -i -E. II 6 -E. 193 likiþ] wolde (list EH). III (50 -E). 56 *E. 235 -E. 264 -E. IV 82 *E. 157 -E. V 24 *E. 49 affaiten] afeyntyn (*frete E). 74–5 -E. 95 *E. dryue] drawe -E. VII 95 pote] staf (-H³; *om* E +u). **(b)** VIII 3 & a] *om*;-H³. IX 28. 36. 60². 64 (H³ *def.* 28–64). **(c)** X 35 -H³W. (52-. 73 -H³W. 91 -H³W. XI 12 -H³W. 247 heiȝly] hol(l)y(che) -H³W. **Minor (a)** III 6 þat] *om*;-E. 61. 244 þe] to þe -E. 260. IV 129 þou] *om*; -E. V 30 He] And (*And als he E). 203 he] hym -E. VI 33 and] *om*;-E. VII 213 wolde not] nolde. **(b)** IX 3. 7 þis] þat. 20 alwey; at hom] *trs*. 47 wile suffre] sufferith. 50 þe] þe to. 82 haþ] *om*. 85 (H³ *def.* 3–85). **(c)** X 58 -H³W. XI 14 erþe] erde -H³W. 18, 257 if] ȝif it -H³W. 53 þe] here -H³; *om* W. 280 wiþ] in -H³W.

§ 42. It would appear likely that E's divergences, which create the impression of a possible sub-group <AM>, are due to its 'correction' from an **r** source in some 13 cases (it has individual errors in another six). That E's right readings do not simply preserve **m** against AM is shown by its omission at VII 95 of the group-variant presumed as that of AM (accurately corrected in H³). This is one of nearly 50 wrong readings throughout Pr–VII that E shares with the **r** manuscript U, its probable source for 'correction'. In the case of H³, since this copy is defective in IX, all the eleven readings in question could in principle have been identical with those of AM. Again, this is an argument from silence, but if the supposition is correct, as constituting further readings of the core-group AMH³, they could have there preserved the text of **m**. The matter would seem incapable of demonstration either way; but there are five important test cases in X and XI that might suggest a genetic group <AM>. Of these, however, X 35 could be a coincidental substitution suggested by *man...lik* in 32; *clense* 73 the replacement of a harder word, perhaps following visual confusion; *acordith* 91 the result of misidentification as an imperative through inducement from *wilneþ* 89 and *loke* 92; XI 12 an obviously easier synonym-substitution; and 247 (in any case not certainly identical in A and M) a possible visual error suggested by the contextual sense and the form of preceding *holde*. Of the two instances where H^3 is right against AM, its correction need not be inferred; for VIII 3 is a simple case of haplography (pen*a & a*), while at XI 53, W's zero-reading may be a true reflex of **m**, with AM convergently inserting *here* and H^3 independently *þe*. The six examples in (c) are all trivial, 18 and 257 illustrating the at times strikingly non-indicative character of this type of variant. All in all, a relation E<AM>H^3 would therefore seem unlikely, and so the earlier established groups EA and MH^3 may stand. AM cannot be eliminated, however, because it uniquely preserves (with other-version support) three readings that may be taken as transmitting **m** and, through it, Ax.

Major IV 136 mekenes. **Minor** VIII 127 I þoru3 here wordis. 175 And how.

§ 43. The fifth pair **AH^3** is attested by 33 agreements in error, about a dozen of them major, between V and XI. In the list of these '(a)' denotes the section where E is present and **m** therefore = EAMH^3, '(b)' that where E has ended but before W joins, and '(c)' that after W has joined the core-group, so that AMH^{3}W now = **m**. Unless specially noted, the other copies are right where AH^3 err.

Major (a) V 137. 153 he] herry (Heruy M; -E). VI 21 wy] wyte. 77–8 *L. div.* (no...lou3nesse *om* M). 92 weue] weyn (wynne M; out E). VII 121 sone] *om*. 178. 187. 243 wilnest] woldis hauen. **(b)** VIII 97. **(c)** XI 153 hotiþ] biddyth. 159 many] *om*. **Minor (a)** V 106 ne...me] may not. 200 He] And. VI 11 for] þat. 113 is] be. VII 11 it] *om*. 112 And] *om*. 187 him] *om* (+Z). **(b)** 300 (*M). VIII 20 hadde] han (þey han M). 92 al] *om*. **(c)** X 74 for] and. it] *om*. XI 15 rentis] *sg*. 89 to] *om*. 91 wile] schal. 93 þat] *om*. 157. 183 it is] *trs*. 190 hem^2] *om*. 207 þe^1] *om*. 304 for] in +**BC**.

Of the above variants, six could simply retain the family reading: V 137 (where E and M have each an individual error), 153; VI 77–8 (where M's error is a clear consequence of a misdivision ascribable to **m**), 92; VII 187 and VIII 97 (where M is lacking). The same may be true of VIII 20 and XI 190 (where M has only *h*). Convergent agreement is again possible in VI 21. In VII 178 *bedrede* has come in from 177 to replace the repeat-word *blynde*. XI 153 appears an easy synonym-substitution and 159 the result of haplography. VII 243 on its own seems an explicit expansion that could be coincidental. The minor variants, where not trivial, admit of easy mechanical explanations, e.g. at VII 161 (repeating *so* from 160) and XI 207 (eyeskip from *f* > *f*). Two readings have other-version support. VII 187 is a coincidence with the same error or with an original lacking the reflexive. The other, XI 304, is a substitution probably motivated by understanding *sermoun* as 'sermon-address' or 'discourse' rather than 'sermon-text' (a sense evidently preferred in the revision to **B**). Taken together, these variants have little weight and the group's claim to be genetic may be dismissed. AH^3, however, cannot be eliminated as they alone preserve one harder reading at VIII 109, which in the light of **B** may be judged that of **m** and thence of Ax.

§ 44. The sixth and final pair to question the status of EA and MH^3 as the only genetic groups within **m** is **AW**, which has 42 agreements, some 20 of them major. About half occur in X and XI, where the second set of four (AMH^{3}W) is strongly attested. The density here is probably best ascribed to W's change from its r^2 exemplar to one derived from **m** but distinct from the exclusive common ancestors of <EA>, <MH³>, called 'y" in the diagram at § 5. It is in these passūs that W joins AMH³ as a fourth witness to **m**, with some 32 agreements in error, although some signs of W's collation with an **m** copy have appeared earlier in the text (see § 18 above on W). In the following list '(a)' denotes the section where two or more of EAMH³ are present, '(b)' that after E ceases and AMH³W becomes theoretically possible, a minus and * as at § 41 above. Unless otherwise noted, EM / MH³ have the right reading where AW err.

Major (a) II 168 Er he be put] Put hym (Set hem M; Bot sett E). IV 2 sauȝte] acorde -EM. 111 robberis] robbyng -EM. V 88 Crist] god -EM. VI 66 heiȝ] holly *E*M. 75 kirnelis] corneris -EM. **(b)** VIII 107 L. *om.* IX 105 þre] *om.* X 88 clene] *om* -MH³. 89 Wilne...neuere] Whil...wonyst / art (*M*H³). 97 counseilliþ] techiþ -MH³. 117 porcioun] possessioun -MH³. 218 þat is] his. XI 21 conne] do can (can do MH³). 48 hunsen] hold (*MH³). 85 þou] he. 181 siþen] *om.* 191 and... oþere] *om* (*M*H³). 270 wrouȝte] wretyn -H³;*M. 272 werkis] clerkis -MH³. **Minor (a)** III 271 robe] *pl.* VI 94 For] *om.* 103 þe] ȝou. VII 91 to bedde; ȝede] *trs.* 131 me God] *trs.* 181 to kepe] and kepte. 183 Al] *om.* **(b)** 235 hondis] *sg.* 298 curse] Thay c. VIII 23 for] *om.* 144. how] of (þat M). IX 33 here on] of þis. 117 in] in þis. X 20 a] *om.* 30 of(2)] *om.* 94 so] *om.* XI 6 wittis] *sg.* 38 lewid] l. men. 158 þat] þis (*om* M). 200 and] in. 264, 275 And] *om.*

Of the major readings here, II 168 and XI 21 may be accurate reflexes of **m**, as may VI 66, from which E and M diversely vary (*it is þe way; fro morew*) in evident response to finding *heiȝ* difficult. VI 75 and X 117 could be coincidental visual errors leading to misexpansions. At XI 191 major divergent corruptions in M and H³ suggest that the b-half was lacking in **m**. The readings at IV 2, V 88, X 97 and XI 272 could all be coincidental substitutions, that at XI 272 dittography before *-ere* twice, the omissions mechanical, and such transpositions as VII 91 and 231 induced by the force of common usage. Finally, the singular / plural alternations should be treated as non-indicative of genetic origin since they are largely unconscious and can move in both directions, as at III 271 contrasted with VII 235 and XI 6. Perhaps most telling are the lexical variant at XI 48 (by no means an obvious substitution) and the phrasal one at X 89 (which is not, however, exact). Taken together, these readings fall short of establishing a genetic group, but in principle W's postulated **m**-type exemplar in X–XI could have been the same immediate source used by A. This is because most of the agreements occur after E has ceased and there is no grouping H³W to conflict with MH³, the firmest genetic pair.[15] Lastly, the three major readings IV 2, 111 and V 88 do not seriously question the other likely genetic pair EA, while the minor readings within the limits of E's presence do not question it at all. A and W cannot be eliminated, however, since both include at V 95 the substantive basis for reconstruction, while W uniquely preserves four right readings (see § 18).

(e) *The* **m** *family: conclusions*

§ 45. It emerges, then, that within the first set of four **m** manuscripts a relation (<EA> <MH³>) is probable and within the second a relation (<AW> <MH³>) possible. The pair <AW> however does not seem sure enough to warrant either accommodation in the diagram of hypothetical descent or, within the list of sigils, any disruption of the well-established core-group AMH³. W is thus perhaps best regarded as a belated addition to the family in X and XI and its immediate exemplar as directly derived from **m**. The most economical explanation of the two sets of four is, as already indicated (§ 28 above), that they are a single intermittently attested genetic group and constitute, on comparison with **r**, an independent family. Collateral support for this conclusion is found in the body of right readings **m** provides where **r** is unquestionably in error. These have already been listed with their other-version support at § 23 above but will be referred to again at § 47 below when the two families are briefly compared.

§ 46. It remains to list in full the substantive agreements in error which provide evidence for the family in eleven combinations of its five component copies. The preceding discussion has brought out that, while **m** is minimally attested throughout the poem almost without break, even its one complete member M is too corrupt to function as a 'representative' copy, as do R for **r** or L for the **B** family β. The main virtue of M is therefore a negative one: like the **r** manuscript T it is the sole **m** copy free of contamination from the other family. Nevertheless, despite the gaps in transmission that have made such detailed specification necessary, the 260 errors recorded below may be ascribed with fair certainty to the postulated family-original. The arrangement follows that adopted for **r** at § 23 but takes due account of the often reduced attestation of **m** and therefore sub-divides the variants according to the presence or absence of individual members. However, so as not to obscure the true order in which the variable groupings of **m** witnesses appear, these sub-divisions are denoted as follows: (a) = EM; (b) = EAM; (c) = EAMH³; (d) = AMH³; (e) = AM; (f) = MH³; (g) = AMH³W. In the case of (g), agreements of AW with **r** against MH³ are taken to indicate that AW here probably = **m** and the <MH³> variant is therefore an exclusive group error. Readings are categorised as major or minor to highlight the qualitative differences that are crucial in determining manuscript relations. The sequence, as for **r**, records other-version support available for the accepted reading, so as to facilitate comparative evaluation of the two families.[16] A minus sign indicates that the **m** copy specified has the reading adopted in the text, a plus sign that a member of the other family (or, rarely, another version) shares the rejected variant, an * an important corruption. The lemma is usually from **r**, but where **r** is wrong, its reading is given as a second variant after that of **m**.

§ 47. Readings with other-version support

(i) Major

+**Z**: **(a)** I 119 word] werke. 138 yedde] syng. II 32 coueitise] þing. 38 hous] bour. 46 þe writ] þai write. 48 fastnid] feffyd +U. 51 at his bode] *om* +v. 53 And...wille] In witnes of Simony & siuille his brother. 56 gredeþ wel heiʒe] crye (þe chartre). 58 feffe] fastne -E. **(b)** IV 67 euere] *om*. 96 more] better. 142 warpen] carpe +ChL. **(c)** VI 81 þing] *om*. VII 176 ditte] holdyn *E; +W. **(d)** VIII 18 passe] partyn. 38 *L. om*. **(f)** 41 graiþ] heye. 57 Þise...ben] For þe tresour*is* ben oure aldiris / thralles þat is. 60 resceyueþ] reseruit (*l. om* H³). +**ZB**: **(a)** I 86 telliþ] trow þou. 99 fyue score] fiftene. 119 writ] kirke +RL. 123 siʒte...textis] þe text. 128 compsiþ] coueitid (*l. om* E). III 154 þat...men] maynteners of hir. **(b)** IV 46 he...liþ] bad me thare to lye / had myn wyf badde me gon (*l. om* A). 50 manye] *om* (-A). 58 mede] I. 157 he faille] elles (-E). V 23 cumside] bygan (for) +HJ. **(c)** VII 171 Faitours...fer] For ferd þese f. -E. **(d)** 222 mouþiþ] mevith. +**ZC**: **(b)** III 130 harmede] h. hire M; harm dide E +HB. V 39 ʒe...betere] þai be storyd wele E; ʒoure stor better (*l. om* A). +**ZBC**: **(a)** Pr 81 parissh] kirkes. I 35 þat...is] no blysse E; lesse M. 39 and...herte] be war with þair wyles. 69 wyt] herte. 117 wenden...shuln] shal aftir hym wend / w. sh. after. 118 After...day] To þat Pyne endles; dwelle] won. 127 kenne me bettre] better to lere / lerne bettre. 133 I...treuþe] is trouth for soþe. 139 a miʒte] al myrth +R. 141 wiþ loue] kyndely. **(b)** 145 pite] *om* (*added* E). 151 mete...ellis] to oþer (men) metyn. 152 ʒe; þerwiþ] *om*; vnto you. 157 in...houres] of heuenriche blys. 160 fet] fewte. 180 siʒte...tixtes] þe text (*pl.* A). II 5 Loke...and] *om*. 6 manye] m. vnfeythfully to knowe. 16 haþ...me] at me hase grevyd. **(a)** II 81 weddyng] werkis. 117 þi...wyf] weddytt (wendyd M). 118 mery] faire +U. 125 wiþ hem] *om* +w; al E. **(b)** 147 tom] tong +ChU. III 11 merþe and] moche ?+W (good W). 21 coppis of siluer] other gyfteʒ mony; pecis of s. r. 22–3 *Ll. om* (-A). 33 *L. om*. 99 beʒonde] b. see -A. **(a)** 146 leiþ] alegges. 147 floreynes go] gold goys. 158 *L. om*. 170 þe] me +Ch. 174 kilde] gylyde. IV 82 Pees] pennys for p./ in (to) presen*s*. 146 be...it] (to me) to bryng (þaim) togeder. 147 ledis] lordis. V 46 lord] *om*; -E. **(c)** VI callen] clepyn -E. 31 sewide] folwde +H. 37 oþerwhile] sumtyme. VII 40 presauntis and] *om* (*def.* A). to wraþen hym] arise rE; *om* **m**. 193 blody] *om*; ?-E. **(d)** 280 ete] hente +t. +**B**: **(b)** I 143 pyne] tene -E. V 64 leyn] ben -A. **(a)** II 121 for euere] togeder. III 206 here bidding] mede. 210–11 *L. div. wrong*. **(c)** V 95 werse] w. *be* dom of my selfe. 115 symme...nok] synne it þouth me mery. 142 so þe Ik] so mote I the. **(g)** X 186 vncomely] vnkendely. 202 vn-] no (*l. om* A). XI 21 conne] can do (*trs* AW). yclepid] called -A. 29 lessoun] sermoun. 100 *As 2 ll.* knele] gon and knelid to ground. 119 half] hande -A. 146 I...Catoun] in c. þou may rede. 149 techiþ] tellit -A. 151 enemys] fomen. 162 þerewith] with hem +V. 163–64 *misdivided*. 164 Founded...formest] f. Hem fou. in feth. 228

lordis] londis. 311 Souteris] Saweris. +**BC**: **(a)** Pr 84 houuis of silke] silkyn h. +L. I 98 apertly] *om*; +**Z**. III 129 teiȝeþ]
fetteres +JK. 212 Alle kyn] *om*. **(b)** III 74 on] *om*; -A. **(c)** V 146 for...shrifte] to go on his wey. 147 hym to kirkeward]
to kirke. 172 hitte] caste ?-E+ChH. VI 44 swere] s. fast +L. **(f)** 60 resceyueþ] reseruit (*l. om* H[3]). lyuen] leden **(d)** VIII
97 no...fynde] non oþer pardoun. **(e)** IX 16 as a clerk] þo -A. 28 stif] fast. 57 liþen] lystyn +K. 64 wiȝt] man. 71 mylde]
meke. **(g)** X 19 hende] thride -W. XI 18b–19a] *om*. 284 *L. om*. +**C**: **(a)** I 137 plante] plente +RK. **(c)** V 109 eiȝen] e. as a
blynd hagge +Bx. VII 35 conseyuede] rehersede -E; *def.* A. *Cf.* **C**: III 211 alse] at þe male tyme +Bx.

Extra lines added in **m**: B V 341 after V 190; B V 352–7 after V 200 +U.

(ii) Minor

+**Z**: **(a)** II 33. 36. 60. **(b)** 161. III 112. 145 -E. 187 +w. VI 74 +W. **(c)** VII 115. 143 (+**BC**). +**ZB**: **(a)** I 57. 183. II 29.
101[1,2]. 116. III 143. **(b)** V 23 How] when. **(c)** VI 39 -A+VJ. **(d)** VII 254 +H. +**ZC**: **(b)** 65 +**B**. **(f)** VIII 73. +**ZBC**: **(a)** I
81. 94 taken] t. alle. 164 ac; is] & (+N); *om* -A. II 103 his] *om*. 106. 156. **(b)** 158. 193. 197[1,2] (1 -E). III 105. **(a)** 150. 157
+H[2]W. 159 Þe king] And (he). **(b)** IV 60 +w. 84. 92. 130. V 48. **(c)** VI 3. 28 +DR. 42. 48. 55 +uW. VII 80 (-H[3]; *def.* A).
157 þat] he (-E+W. **(d)** VII 286. 300 +H[2]. VIII 20 hadde] han. +**B**: **(b)** III 61 -E. 178 +LZ. 180 +UHKZ. V 79. 90[1,2]. **(c)**
116 (*l. om* E, +w). 131 (+L). 152 -M+N. 186 +uV. **(e)** IX 47 wile suffre] sufferith. 85. **(g)** XI 15. 86 -M. 105 +u. 111 -A.
153. 167 -H[3]. 170 -W. 175 (*l. om* A). 213. 217 -A. 255 W+J. +**BC**: **(a)** III 201. **(b)** V 24 +**Z**; *om* E. 36 +HWZ. **(c)** (228
+H. VI 109[1]+U;[2]+W. 123 +t. 125 +W. VII 62 (*def.* EA). 122 -E. **(e)** IX 3. 64 +D. **(d)** 102[1] +U;[2] -iþ] -id. 107. **(g)** X 11 +R.
18 haþ] had -W. +**C**: **(b)** III 76 (+**B**). 265 *A;+Bx. **(g)** XI 134 (+**B**. 138 (+**B**).

Readings with no other-version parallel

(i) Major (a) Pr 95 cuntre] peple. II 47 feffid] sesyd (+**Z**). 51 boun] buxoum +uJ; at his bode] *om*; +v. fulfille] do. 65
delites] likyng. III 35 meke-] mylde-. **(b)** III 56 ?*om*. 62 gyue] dele +J. 273 leute] loue. **(c)** VII 142 pilide] pyned -E. **(d)**
VII 235 here] *oM*; +H. **(g)** IX 36 watris] wawis. X 53 going] good dede. 69 helpe] kepe. 70 folies]; falsed & f. 80 douten]
dredyn +V. 88 self] soule. 89 wy] *om*; +DV. 101 comsist] gynny*st* -W. 168 hem] hem brymme. 204 also] lyuende (*l. om*
A). XI 22 serue] sewit -A. deuil] deuylis lore. 94 mele] spekyn -W. 145 scole] lore. suche] *om*. 257 -H+**B**. 277 wende
to] wynne me.

(ii) Minor (b) II 197. **(e)** VIII 152 +W. IX 95 +U. **(g)** X 88. 103 +J. 160. 163 +U. XI 23 -M;+V. 24. 82 -H[3];+u. 184 +K.
193 singe] and s. -A. 217 -A. 231 -W+u.

§ 48. These 260 separative errors in **m**, about 155 of them major, add up to more than twice
the total and more than three times the major errors in **r**. The number could well have been larger
but for imperfect attestation in, and further individual variation between, the extant **m** manuscripts,
two factors that require excluding several further probable **m** errors (e.g. those at III 214 and X 48).
There can therefore be little question that a text of **A** should be based on an **r** copy, as all previous
editors have agreed. But even so, the analysis given above indicates how far neglect of **m** by Skeat
and Knott-Fowler serves to weaken the usefulness of their editions. Kane's belated recognition of
m's value greatly improves the text of his second edition. But he ignores its serious implications
for his classification of the variants, and the form his recognition takes, an appended list of cor-
rected readings, conceals rather than signals the **m** family's full textual significance. For, as Brewer
was the first to realise,[17] **m** is an independent tradition essential for reconstituting the archetype, not
merely a subsidiary resource for solving occasional local difficulties. This emerges with particu-
lar clarity when **A** is edited in parallel with **Z**, **B** and **C**; for the other-version testimony compels
recognition of the probable authenticity of numerous **m** readings on comparison with those of **r**.
Moreover, as well as the 100-odd variants discriminated as original on the showing of **Z**, **B** and **C**
(though never on their sole basis), **m** uniquely preserves seven major right readings where *no* par-
allel material exists. These, not strictly criterial for **m** as a family, afford collateral support for its
existence. They appear at § 23 above as the lemmata in the final section of the list. As already said,
r has three times as many sole-version readings that are correct (§ 46 above); but the significance
of **m**'s contribution to the text of **A** is further substantiated by the material in the next section.

v. *Towards the Archetype*: *the agreed readings of* r^2 *and* **m**.

§ 49. A transition from analysis of the two **A** families to that of the archetypal text is provided by first considering the agreed readings of **m** with the r^2 branch of family **r**. In about 135 instances (some 55 of them major), **m** and r^2 together preserve against r^1 what is likely to be the text of the archetypal manuscript (Ax). These 'collateral' right readings are presented here in the framework employed earlier for categorising the erroneous ('criterial') readings of both families. The adopted readings are categorised according to their other-version support; where other versions attest the rejected variant, this is recorded after the latter. Lower-case bracketed letters denote the same variations in the attestation of **m** as in the list of **m** errors given above. The lemma is here the reading of r^2**m** and is taken from the first r^2 copy to attest it, in the sequence VHJLKWN; the variant in each case is the reading of r^1. A plus sign denotes agreement of an r^2**m** copy with the rejected variant, a minus, agreement of an r^1 copy with the lemma.

Readings of r^2m with other-version support

(i) Major

+**Z**: **(b)** IV 29 myle] myle wey +K;*E. 63 nomen] tok +JWE**BC**. **(c)** VII 123 holde] olde +WH³**B**. 183 cacche] chase. +**ZB**: **(b)** IV 57 þi-] my +KNA. 154 lee*te* þe I nulle] loue þe I wile +E. **(d)** VII 227 herde] hadde -U. +**ZBC**: **(a)** Pr 42 Fayteden] Flite þan +E. **(b)** I 153 For þei3 3e] For þi -U. **(a)** II 105 besitte] besette (†E). soure] sore +vE. 163 gurdeþ] gederiþ -D. **(b)** III 132 cotiþ] cloþiþ +M. 171 menske] mylde / auaunce. IV 71–2 *Ll. om*; -H². V 43 ran Repentaunce and] Rep. 55 his soule] hym +HJ. **(c)** 216 þe veil] (þer) while / wille +E. 241 worþe] werche +EA. VI 39 with-] ne -H². 100 forþ]] (þe) for. VII 18 longe] louely. 20 chapelleynis] chapellis -Ch. 201 benes] bones -U+vK. **(d)** 306 faille] falle -R+L. VIII 2 tilien þe erþe] his erþe tilien. +**B**: **(b)** V 127 pyned] pynned +VwC. **(c)** VII 96 clense] close +vwEH³. **(d)** VIII 101 pure] *om*; -U. **(e)** IX 6 wente] wene. 14 menours] maistris. 57 foulis] briddes. **(g)** X 48 þe...In.] In. is þe grettest. 161 suche wordis; seide] *trs*. 186 me þinkeþ] I wene. 189 barne bere] bere child. XI 47 noye] anguyssh. 121 liþer] li3eris. 211 romere] rennere +H³. 251 hethyn] hem. +**BC**: **(a)** I 1 myrk] derke +VKN. **(b)** III 260 I] In +K. wit] it +KE. 268 to trouþe] trewely. a3eyn his wille] a. ry3th / ony þyng / to þe wrong. 269 Leaute] His wykkide l. IV 4 Crist] god. **(c)** V 109 betil-] bittir-. 114–15. *Line-div. wrong*. 114 ben...caitif] ylouid coueitise q. he al my lif tyme. 161 Hugh] hogge / hobbe. nedelere] +E. 177 aparte] apertly -D. 196–97 *Line-div. wrong*. 196 like...bicche] *om*; -U+JK. 200 þreuh] fel +AMH³. VI 111 peple] folk +JL. **(e)** VIII 137 Daniel] Dauid -H²Ch+J. IX 17 synneþ] falliþ. 36 walwen] wawen. X 136 martires] nonnes. XI 296 *reges et*] *om*; -U.

(ii) Minor

+**Z**: **(d)** VII 227 -U+HLW. 240 -U+W. **(f)** VIII 54 -U+K. +**ZB**: **(b)** IV 91. **(c)** VII 37 +VJ. +**ZC**: VII 185. +**ZBC**: **(a)** Pr 44. I 25 -H². II 88 -D. III 139. **(b)** III 15. IV 42. 84. 89. 147. 35 +VJLNE. **(c)** V 219. VI 13 -U+JNM. 46 +W. 64 -D+W. 69 -Ch. 94. 100 +MW. VII 29–30. 31². 76¹ -U+E;² +W. 84 +E. 114 +WE. 141 +LKA. 143 +H. 190 +JLK. **(d)** 254 -U+K. 280 -U+KM. VIII 3 +M. 6¹,²-U. 36 +L. +**B**: **(b)** I 169 -Ch+HZ. **(a)** III 208 -U+LW. **(b)** V 66 -Ch. 78. 91. 104 +LW. 209 -Ch+Z. **(c)** VI 28 +E. **(e)** VIII 141 -Ch+JLW. IX 44 -D+M. 86 +A. **(g)** X 40. 151 +A. 185 -U. 188¹ -Ch+KH³;² +KAH³. 189 +JM. 198. XI 71 +V. 75–6 +K. 78. 108. 143 -Ch+AW. 173 -ChR+MH³. 205 +W. 226 +AH³. 229 -ChD+AM. 236. +**BC**: **(c)** V 110. 130. 178–9 VII 31. **(e)** VIII 154 -UZ. IX 67 +K. **(g)** X 168 -D+M. XI 5. 13 +JM. 129 +KMH³. 134, 134/5. 277 +M. +**C**: IX 100.

Readings with no other-version parallel

(i) Major (b) III 243] *L. om*; -R. **(c)** VII 210 be þe betere] *om* / at ese. 211] *L. om*; +E. **(e)** IX 98 here] his -D+H³. **(g)** X 86 þi seluen] þe salme. 154 kynde] kyn +A. 208 werche þat werk] do þat w./ wirche (208a *om* M). XI 293 ferþer] for (soþe) / Ø +M.
(ii) Minor (b) III 57] +D-N. **(c)** VII 212 Make] lat / And m. 212a–13] *Line-div. wrong*. **(g)** XI 159.

§ 50. Some comment is required here, particularly on the contribution of individual **r** and **m** copies to the postulated archetypal consensus signified by 'r^2**m**.'[18] It is noteworthy, first, that the accuracy of six of the seven r^2 copies in their presumptive preservation of **r** (and thence of Ax) is closely similar, despite the variable amounts of text attested. None exceeds 12% in defections from the sub-family reading where this can be firmly established. Thus major-reading divergencies are (in descending order): J:9; K:8; W:6; V, L:4; H:3; N:2. From this, even allowing for its lack of about four passūs, it is obvious how much greater N's textual value would have been, had its **A** portion been complete.

§ 51. All the r^1 copies except for T occasionally depart from their ancestral reading to join r^2**m**. The most frequent is U, with six major readings out of a total of fourteen. These point to a likely phase of correction in the course of U's descent from its group-original u. And that this was by reference not to an r^2 but to an **m**-type copy is suggested by U's lack of r^2's isolative errors (except at IV 129, VIII 151, IV 129 and VIII 38, the last two trivial) and by its possession of the lines on Glutton (= B V 352–7) found in **m** after V 200.[19] Of the major r^2**m** right readings found in other r^1 witnesses, Ch has three (out of a total of 14), H^2 and D two each (out of totals of four and ten respectively) and R one (out of a total of six). From among the 14 major r^2**m** readings in these five r^1 copies, one (*Daniel*] *Dauid* VIII 137) shared by H^{2}ChU, is of a kind that could be due to independent scribal intervention, as R's correction here by another hand graphically suggests. Two other important borrowings from r^2**m** occur at IV 71–2 (added by H^2 to its defective source) and III 243 (added by R to its defective u exemplar). In contrast to these, the major variants in Ch and D do not suggest correction from another copy. Two probably identifiable as commonsense scribal conjectures are *chapelleynis* VII 20 (Ch) and *gurdeþ* II 163 (D). The three right readings Ch shares only with r^2 are explicable in the same way: *3our*] *his* VIII 38; *3e*] *þou* VIII 68; *wel þe*] *wele* X 188. So also are D's *at*] *om* at X 172, *it be*] *on* XI 264 and Pr 75, VI 64 and IX 56. One D agreement at IX 92 is so significant politically as to suggest deliberate correction, but it could be just a scribal response to perceived incoherence in the syntax. On balance, then, the case for seeing correction of U, R and H^2 from an r^2 (or, in the case of U, an **m**) source would seem strong, that for Ch and D weak. The remaining r^1 copy T, as already remarked, is uninfluenced by r^2 or **m**.[20]

§ 52. The **m** witnesses display about the same proportional fidelity to their family ancestor as do the r^2 copies discussed above. Manuscript A fails in two out of fifteen major readings, a low figure, given its relative completeness, E in three out of six (over eight passūs), H^3 in four out of eleven (over seven passūs) and W in one out of seven (over its two passūs as an **m** copy). The average level of defections from the postulated **m** reading is thus about 8%. But this, which is somewhat less than for r^2, is probably attributable to the defective character of E, H^3 and W. For the one complete **m** copy M lacks some 12% of the family readings and this is the exact figure for the r^2 sub-family taken as a whole (see § 50).

§ 53. It goes without saying that the substantial agreements of r^2 and **m** in right readings do not indicate derivation from an exclusive common ancestor lower than the archetype. All they imply, on the most economical assumption, is faithful preservation of Ax at these points: by r^2 through **r** (where r^1 has gone astray) and by **m** directly.[21] However, r^2's agreement with **m** in major *error* would clearly question its linear descent from **r** and would point to a shared source intermediate between r^2**m** and Ax. It is therefore significant that only in six instances where r^1 has the right reading do r^2**m** in fact err jointly:

Major (a) r^1 *entire*: XI 67 wy] man + U, Bx. **(b)** r^1 = d *and* u *is wrong*: X 30 +C?**B** lisse] blysse + u. **(c)** r^1 = t: X 100 isent þe] *trs*; + u; sente D.
Minor (a) VII 282. XI 241. **(b)** VII 277.

Here the minor errors are trivial and X 100 looks like a felicitous t (or perhaps d) variant of what would have been an easy archetypal transposition. In X 30, although the **C** reading should help to discriminate the **AB** original, it is precluded by the linear postulate from being decisive. For not only is *blysse* acceptable in sense and metre, coincidental substitution in r^2 and **m** (through contextual suggestion) would have been easy, a possibility underlined by the fact that the r^1 manuscript U shares the variant. Finally, the word involved in XI 67 is one notoriously subject to synonym-substitution, as shown by the witness both of one r^1 member and of Bx.[22] Taken as a whole, the evidence for an r^2m source appears nugatory and so the relationships in the diagram at § 5 may be accepted as likely to be close to the historical situation.

§ 54. Added to some 250 readings preserved by **r** and some 100 by **m** (with or without other-version support), these 135 readings of r^2m produce nearly 500 that are very likely to be archetypal. The supporting testimony of the assured **Z**, **B** and **C** readings severally or combined is significant here, as in the many instances left out of the above categories where cross-family conflict of witnesses makes even the constituent groups hard to establish. The most important readings are examined in the *Textual Notes*, but limitations of space rule out particular consideration here. However, nothing like a majority of **A** lines should be regarded as seriously uncertain, despite difficulties at many points, especially where no other-version evidence is available. This will become clear from the next section, which shows how, in at least 60% of the poem, an archetypal text is attested with near-unanimity and in most doubtful cases the 'parallel' evidence proves virtually decisive between alternative readings otherwise of equal weight on intrinsic grounds. Ax itself is not free of corruptions; but the same comparative analysis that exposes them usually suffices for emending them.

vi. *The Archetypal Text of the* **A** *Version*

§ 55. The above sections complete the examination of the respective claims of **r**, **m** and r^2m to represent Ax. These have been set out in full with their other-version support where this exists. It remains to consider the body of presumed archetypal text preserved with little uncertainty in all the manuscripts, in a majority of them or, where there is random variation across families, in a few individual witnesses supported by one or more other version(s). The following list therefore contains lines judged to preserve the archetype (*a*) where there is (near)-unanimous support from both **r** and **m**; (*b*) where the text is attested by at least two manuscripts of both families; and (*c*) where direct analysis finds in not fewer than two unrelated copies a harder reading identifiable as the one from which the other variants are likely to have been generated (these are given in square brackets). On the basis of their intrinsic quality and in the light of the parallel **Z/B/C** text (where available), all lines listed are judged to preserve the original text, except that wrong line-division producing no substantive error has been ignored. Other-version support is recorded here only for the 47 category (*b*) and (*c*) readings. For the rest it may be easily found by consulting the text in Vol. I, where the location of lines not immediately parallel is noted in small type at the relevant points. Excluded from the list are lines with readings correctly attested (*a*) solely by one family, even when they appear original (and so presumptively archetypal) on intrinsic grounds, and have clear other-version support; (*b*) by r^2m (those given at § 49 above); and (*c*) all particular right readings judged after analysis as likely to have entered individual manuscripts by felicitous conjecture, coincidence or contamination. These last, as in effect 'editorially' introduced by a scribe, are noted instead amongst the emended readings, and many are discussed at §§ 60–6. Cases where the Ax reading itself appears undecidable are in brackets. Those that are certain but have been judged corrupt and corrected in the text by restoration, reconstruction or conjecture, are listed (according to the category of emendation) in §§ 55–9 and are discussed in the *Textual Notes*.

Pr 1. 3. 5–6. 8–10. 12–21. 23–6. 28–30. 32–3. 35–41. 43. 45–55. 57–62. 64–8. 70–2. 74–9. 82. 85. 87–8. 90–5. 97–9. 101. 103–6. +**BC** 107. 108–9.

I 2–3. 5–10. 13–24. 26–30. 32–6. (37). 38. 40–3. 45. 47. 50–6. 59–62. 64–8. (69). 70–3. 75–6. 80. 82–5. 88–9. 91–2. (93). 95–6. +**Z** 97. 99–101. 107–9. 111. 113. 115. 117. 120. 124–5. 129. 131–2. 134–6. 140. 142. 144. 147. 150. 154. 156. 158. 160–3. 165–8. (169). 170–3. 175–8. 181.

II 2. 4. 10–13. 17. 19–20. 22. 24–8. 30–1. 34. 39–42. 45. 50. 54–5. *59. (63). 64. 66–7. 69. 71–4. 76. 78–80. 82. +**B** 84. 85. 89–93. 95. +**BC** 96. 97–100. 102–3. 108–9. 111–14. 117. 119. +**B** 120. 123. 126. [+**ZBC** 128].129. 132–4. 136. 139. 141. 143. 145. +**ZBC** 149. 150. 153. 157. 160. 162. 164–7. +**B** 169. 170–3. 175–8. [+**BC** 180]. 183–4. (185). 186. 188. (189). 190–2. 194–6.

III 1–4. 6–7. 9–10. 14. 16–17. +**ZBC** 18. 20. (21). 24–6. (28). 30. 32. 34. +**B** 36. 38–46. +**BC** 48. 49. 51. 54. 58–60. 63–4. (65). 66. 68. 70. 72–3. (74). 75. 77. 79. 80–2. 84–5. 87. 90. 92. +**B** 93. (95). 98. +**ZBC** 99. 100–01. 103–4. 107–11. +**ZBC** 113–16. +**ZBC** 119–20. 123. [+**ZBC** 124]. +**BC** 126. +**ZBC** 127–8. 131. 133. 136–7. [+**ZBC** 138]. 140–42. +**Z** 148. 149. 152–3. 156. 160–64. 168. 172–3. 175–7.179. 181–4. (185). 188–9. 191. 193–4. [+**ZB** 195]. 197. (198). 199–200. +**B** 203. 204–5. 207. 212–13. 215. 217–18. 220–1. 221a. 224–5. 227–8. 231–3a. (234). 236–8. 240–2. 244–52. 254–5. 257. 261. 263. 267. 270–2. 275–6.

IV 2–3. 6–9. 15. 17–18. 20. 22. 25–8. 30. 32. (33). 34–9. 41. 45. 48–9. 51–4. 56. 59. 62. 64. 68–70. 73–6. 79–80. 86–8. 90. 101–5. +**Z** 107. 108–10. 112. 115–23. 135. 137–40. 144–5. +**ZBC** 148. 151. 153. (155). 157–8.

V 1–4. 6–9. 11–15. 18–20. +**ZBC** 21. 22. 25–7. 29–30. 32–3. +**ZBC** 35. 37–8. 41. 44–7. 49–54. 56–8. *59. 60–5. 68–9. 72–3. 76–7. 81–6. 88–9. (90). 92. (93). 94. (95). 96–100. 102. 105. 107. 111. 118–25. 128. 133–4. +**BC** 135. 136. 138–40. [+**C** 141]. 144–5. 149–50. 154. 157. (160). 162. 164–6. (168). 169–71. 173–5. 180–2. 184–5. 187–8. *189. 191–5. 197–9. 204–6. 210–15. 220. 223. 225. 227. (229). 230–2. 234. (237). 238–40. 247. 251–5.

VI 4–5. 8. 10–12. 14–19. 22–5. 27. 29–30. 34. (35). 36. 38. 40. 43. 49–51. 53–4. 56. 58–61. 66. [+**ZBC** 67]. (68). 70. 75–8. 80. 85. 87. 89–90. 93. [+**BC** 95]. (96). 97. 99. 102. 104–8. 114. 118–19. 121. (122). 124. 126.

VII 1. 3–4. 6–9. 11. 16–17. 21. 23–4. *(25). 26–8. 30. 32–4. 36. 38–9. 41–2. 44–55. 57–8. 63–7. 70–72. +**B** 73. 75. 77–8. (85). 87–8. 90–4. 102–5. 107–13. 116–21. 124–7. 129. 132–8. 140. 144–54. *155. 156. 159–62. 164. 167. 169–70. 172–3. 175. 177. 180–2. 184. 186. 191–2. 196–200. 202–6. 208–9. 213–21. 223–5. 228–9. 232. 234. 238–9. 241–4. 246. (247). 248–51. 255–7. 260–5. 267–8. 269. 271–4. 276–9. 281. 287–90. 292–3. 296–9. 302–5. 307.

VIII 1. 4–5. 7–12. 14–17. 20–7. 29. 34–5. 37. 39–40. 42–43. 46–53. 55–6. 58–9. 62–71. (72). 74–9. 81–3. +**ZB** 85. 86. 89–96. 98–9. 102–3. 106. [+**B** 108]. 113–18. 120–25. 126. 128–31. 133–4. 138–40. 143. 145–50. 153. 155–60. 162–71. 173–4. (177). 178. 180–4.

IX 1–2. 4–5. 8–13. 15–16. 19–27. 29–35. 37–43. 45–6. 48–9. 51–4. *55. 56. 58–9. 61. +**BC** 62. 63. 65–6. 68–70. 72. 75. 77–8. 80–3. 87–91. 94. 97. 99. 101. 103. 105. 108–18.

X 1–5. 8–9. [+**BC** 10]. 12–21. 24. 26–9. 31. 33. 35–8. 41–7. 49–52. 54–67. 70–9. 81–3. 85. 87. 91–2. 96. 98–9. (100). 102. 105–6. 108–9. (110). 111–14. 116–20. 122–29. 131–2. 134–5. 137–40. (141). 142–50. 152–3. 155. 158. 162. 164–7. 169–71. 173–5. 177–8. 180–1. 183–4. 190–92. +**BC** 193. 197. 199. 201. 203. 206–7. 209. 211. 213–4. 216–18.

XI 1–3. 6–8. 12. 14. 16–17. 20. (24). 25–8. 31–3. 35. 37–40. +**BC** 41. 42–6. 49–51. 54–5. 57–60. 62–6. 69–70. 72–4. *(75). 76–7. 79. (80). 81. 83. 85. 87–93. 95–9. 101–4. 106–7. 109–11. 113–18. 120. 122–31. 133. +**BC** 135. 137–9. 142. 147–8. 150. 152. 155–7. +**B** 159. 160. 165–6. 168–70. 172. 174. 176. (177). 178–9. 183. 185–90. 192–3. 196. 198. 200–04. 206–10. 213–16. 218–19. 221–24 +**B** 225. 229–30. 232–5. 238. 243. 246–7. 252–6. 259–63. 265. 267–71. 273–6. 278–83. 285–6. 288–90. 292. 294–304. +**BC** 305. 306–7. 309–10. 312–13.

vii. *Emendation of Errors in the Archetypal A-Text*

§ 56. On direct examination and, in most cases, comparison with one or more other version(s), Ax reveals some 53 errors of sense, style or metre. As will be found later with the archetypal texts of **B** and **C**, these errors are capable of being emended by three procedures that are broadly distinguishable from each other, the first more sharply than the second and third. They are (i) restoration, whereby a superior other-version reading is adopted as the probable original of which Ax is judged to be a corrupted form; (ii) reconstruction, using other-version evidence to produce a reading not actually attested elsewhere; (iii) conjecture, a further stage of reconstruction where little or no direct evidence exists. About half the emendations are introduced wholly or partly on metrical grounds and all simple cases of metre damaged by transposition are placed under (ii). Non-archetypal readings in one or more **A** manuscripts that are considered likely to be original on intrinsic grounds are recorded with those in (i) if they appear due to coincidence or contamination, but with those in (iii) if reasonably attributable to scribal guesswork. Only one example of (iii) is listed here, but single- or two-copy variants judged original are listed at § 59 below and will be found above in the sections on each sub-family and its groups. Emendations on metrical grounds are marked ^. Instances where, because of conflict between families or absence of one family, the Ax reading is undecidable and so not classifiable as certainly corrupt, are in brackets.

§ 57 (*i*) *Restored readings*

Some 34 archetypal errors, all but one certain, are corrected by restoration. Ten of these emendations are taken from **B** and **C**, and as they could in principle be products of revision, they are necessarily less secure than the rest (in no case does serious doubt arise).

ZBC: I 94 II 59, 142. III 167. V 28 +J. VI 21. VII 22 +VM.; ^29 +NE; 89; 130 +KL; (^139); 163; 189, 253 +L. **ZB**: I ^48 +W. 116. VII 100–01 +W. **ZC**: VI 52. **BC**: VI ^1 +K. VIII ^136 (+M). IX ^55. XI ^266. **Z**: I ^110. III 155. VI ^79. VII ^25. VIII 13. **B**: V ^59. 148. 189 +N. VIII 125*a*. XI 75. **C**:III 30.

(*ii*) *Reconstructed readings*

Seven certain and one probable Ax error are emended by reconstruction:

VII ^155, XI ^161 *trs.* IX (^106), XI ^191, ^197, ^248 [*word-form*]. X 157 [*proper name*]. XI (239) [*synonym-substitution*].

(*iii*) *Conjectural readings*

Twelve errors are emended by conjecture, seven being adopted also for the parallel line(s). The last example could be a scribal guess but since it occurs in one r^2 and one **m** copy, it might in theory be archetypal:

Pr ^11. ^III 239. ^IV 78. VII ^165, ^266. X 187. XI 67 [*parallel conjectures*]. VII ^236. X ^23, ^68, ^154. ? XI 308 (KW).

§ 58. Among the above, several illustrate mechanical errors of the kind common both in the sub-archetypes and the groups. They include haplography, as at III 239, IV 78, VII 236 (where Ax is uncertain); omission of a prefix, as at IV 157 (Ax uncertain); loss of a small stave-word (VII 266, XI 191) or of a letter needed for the metre (X 187); and substitution of a non-alliterating dialectal variant, as at IV 63, XI 67, 197 and 248. Some errors may be due to misreading the exemplar, as at I 110; II 59; V 142; VI 21; VII 165; VIII 13 (followed by smoothing) and 125*a*; or to mistaking the word-order, as at III 185 (Ax uncertain), VII 155, IX 55 (inversion to prose order) and XI 161 (promotion of a more familiar term). Errors likely to be deliberate are the substitution of a commoner non-alliterating synonym at X 23 and 154, an Anglicised equivalent of a Latin stave-word at I 94 and II 142, a more familiar proper name at V 160 (Ax uncertain), or a contextually easier term at VII 89. Cases of words that the archetypal scribe found 'hard' are III 167, VI 79, X 23, 68 and VII 60^2 (where Ax may have read as emended).

§ 59. In some twenty further instances the suggested editorial emendation of a major Ax error has been happily anticipated in a single manuscript. These are *V* at V 200 and VII 187; *J* at V 28; *K* at II 144 and XI 80; *W* at I 48, III 21, VI 2 and VII 100–01; *N* at III 95 and V 31, 131; *E* at II 137; *A* at VII 128; and *M* at II 94, 107, 124, 181 and VII 145. In some the reading could come by pure descent from Ax (as at VII 128) or as a result of consultation with another version (as at III 21 or VII 100–01). In a few other cases *two* copies, related or unrelated, contain the correct reading against a probable Ax error, e.g. RD at II 180, <RU> at IX 57, KL at VII 130 and KW at XI 308.

§ 60. Errors traceable to split variation are emended on the basis of available **A** manuscript evidence. Examples are at III 234 and VII 139, 294 or, less straightforwardly, V 112, 229 and XI 67 (the latter two receiving 'parallel' reconstruction in **Z** and **B**). More complex, and involving a greater degree of speculation, are IV 61 and VII 236, where Ax remains uncertain. Emendations of individual words start with near-certain examples where a parallel version furnishes the lexical item, as at II 59, III 167 and VII 89 (**ZBC**); VII 60 (**ZB**); V 142 (**B**, which N may echo); I 110; and VI 79 (**Z**). They go on to cases where a mechanical cause may explain the error, as at XI 191 and at III 239, IV 78, VII 165 and X 187 (the last four 'parallel' emendations). Finally come cruces resolved by pure conjecture, as at X 23, 68 and 154, which involve a current word presumed to have been supplanted by a commoner non-metrical synonym.

viii. *Readings of Indeterminable Origin*

§ 61. The text identified as certainly or inferentially archetypal adds up to nearly four-fifths of the whole. The remaining readings (not separately listed here) cut across families and display the characteristic random variation due to unconscious error or to deliberate intervention by individual copyists. This tendency appears mostly amongst minor readings and has no effect on metre and little on style or sense. Instanced at the very outset of the Prologue, it can only be addressed, as in the case of the major ones, through identifying the likely direction of variation as that from a harder (more probably original) to an easier (more probably scribal) reading. The direct method is not only necessary when the alternatives in **r** and **m** are being compared, it proves indispensable at every stage of the editorial process, including the final one where the versional archetypes are critically evaluated. This is evident from the first four entries in the apparatus to the **A** Prologue, which show how the method works most effectively where the other versions are present to serve as a control on editorial reasoning. The first, *shroudes* in line 2, attested in only four out of fourteen manuscripts, is initially recommended on grounds of sense and the support of **ZB** and the **x** family of **C**. On comparison, the singular *shroud* attested by *r¹* and **m** copies alike looks suspect as a scribal attempt (perhaps under inducement from singular *abite* in line 3) to insist on *one* garment for the dreamer. The JK variant shows the same misunderstanding of the verb *shop* that accounts for *shrobbis* in the **p** family of **C**. On purely lexical grounds, the hardest reading here might appear *shregges* (see MED s.v. *shragge* n.); but this must be simply one of the Chaderton scribe's typical aberrations, as the sense 'rag' is over-emphatic and contextually inappropriate. Secondly, in line 4 the reading with the subject-pronoun could be archetypal; but its recurrence in family **p** of **C** (accompanied by the **x**-family manuscripts U and D) points to it as syntactically the easier alternative, with *Wente* being confirmed by **ZB** and the y group in **C** family **x**. In line 7 the minority variant *ofwandrit* is favoured by **ZC** agreement and the uniqueness of the form. It is moreover quite probably what Ax read, as a scribe would not have replaced *for-* with the little-used intensive prefix *of-*. In line 8, which has no **C** parallel, *bourne* is preferable to *bournis* since the uninflected possessive is arguably harder, and it is confirmed by **Z**. This judgement recognises the modernising revision in **B** (or possibly in Bx) shared by three *r¹* copies and one **m** copy (all later in date than **B**). But that Ax was uninflected seems indicated by J, despite its variant being substantively wrong.[23]

§ 62. The fifth example on this same page of text, [*me*] *mete* 11, differs radically, since here the joint witness of two other versions **ZB** is *rejected* in favour of an emendation made on metrical grounds and the indirect evidence of the revised **C** line. As it is fully discussed in the *Textual Notes* (and see IV, § 18 below), further detail may be omitted here. But this case marks the extreme limit of the direct method of editing; for the reading judged likeliest to have generated an identical error in two archetypes and a unique copy with archetypal status is an editorial conjecture, not a variant found in a copy of any version. Such a judgement may be subjective, but it cannot be called arbitrary, as could the decision over the relatively indifferent *bournes*. And while hard cases are rightly thought to make bad law, it is also true that the exception proves the rule; so the fact that line 11 is one of only two instances (the other is at A IV 78 //) where the testimony of three versions is set aside may support a plea in mitigation. Not every reader will find *me meten* justified, but to the present editor it has seemed better to conjecture what the poet might have written than to retain a reading that appears inauthentic when examined in the light of the core-text criteria. This early archetypal crux deserves attention because it illustrates the essential difference between major and minor readings that is stressed throughout this edition, and highlights the importance of focussing editorial effort upon the former.

ix. *Possible* **B** *Contamination in the* **A** *Version*

§ 63. It was mentioned above (§ 59) that a few individual **A** copies contain corrections apparently taken from other versions ('benign contamination'). It is now necessary to consider the problem (also to be encountered in **Z**, **B** and **C**) of *lines* from another version having been present by inference in one of the sub-archetypes, in this case **m**. Thus at V 87 **m**, here joined by one *r²* copy W, has a line seemingly lost from **r** (as a result of repetition of the phrase *for þe peple* 86a at 87b). Also in this passus **m**, this time accompanied by the three *r²* copies VHN, completes the roster of tavern rogues with two lines, 163 and 167, that could have been borrowed by **m** from a **B** copy. As this supposition is strengthened by **m**'s earlier evidencing a *corrupt* archetypal **B** reading at V 109,[24] it might be further inferred that v and N have them by lateral transmission from a copy of **m**. However, those manuscripts do not share **m**'s error at 109, so it is at least possible that both lines were originally also in **r** but were omitted from its other constituent groups, 163 through deliberate censorship and 167 through visual error (*chepe...rop-...hep...chiere*).[25] Later in the description of Glutton there occurs after V 190 a line corresponding to B V 341; and after line 200 appear six lines corresponding to B V 352–7, the latter shared by the *r¹* copy U. The single line could have been lost by eyeskip from *gille* to *while*; but the six dealing with Clement the Cobbler look like a **B** addition borrowed by **m** because of its obvious liveliness and humour. U may have added the line from either **m** or **B** (as at 196, where it corrects an *r¹* error retained by its genetic twin R). Both the single line and the set of six are excluded from the text, though there is a case for seeing at least the first as part of **A** (see the *Textual Notes*).

§ 64. More problematic are the two pairs of lines found in **m** after IV 17 (= BC IV 18–19) and V 31 (= B V 32–3), which are shared respectively by the r^2 copies W and J. The presence of these lines in **Z** might, if that version is regarded as authentic, argue for their acceptance. But there are reasons for believing that they were first set aside in the revision to **A** and only later restored in **B**, from whence **m** could have derived them. In the first pair, the reason is the form of **Z**, in which the lines correspond effectively to A IV 17 after the verb *cald*, suggesting that *Catoun* replaced *Tomme Trewe-tonge* in the initial revision. In the second pair, the lines on Bette and his wife could have seemed to repeat too closely those on Thom Stowe and Felis (even if one wife is being chastised for shrewishness and the other for sloth). Given no obvious breach in sense after either IV 17 or V 31, the case for including both pairs is thus not compelling. In strong contrast are the three lines at VI 82–4. Here **m** has the **ZC** wording in 83; but 82 is not in the later versions at all and **m** gives a different final lift from **Z**. In 84, where the b-half is that of **Z** not **BC**, **m** again has a distinctive reading in the last lift. But the omission of Z 77–8 may be taken to illustrate **A**'s typical pruning of **Z**'s circumstantial detail (*Z Version* § 14 below, *passim*). As 82–4 can hardly derive from **Z**, they may therefore be accepted as part of the **A** Version. Nothing in the lines' sense suggests a motive for deliberate omission, so it could be that their loss in **r** was through a mechanical cause, the similar endings of 81/82 and 85/86.

§ 65. Of the seventeen lines shared by **m** with one or more other versions, six are retained. Only three have been included in previous editions, V 87 in Kane and V 163 and 167 in Knott-Fowler. In two other cases, **B** lines are attested by some but not all **m** copies present, one supported by two members of **r**. The more significant appears after V 42, where EM (but not A) and the r^2 copies KW have B V 59. As it stands in **r**A, line 42 reads more abruptly than either **Z**'s four-line parallel, with its evident translation-expansion of the Latin formula, or the terser **BC** reading, which simply provides an object for the verb *byfalle*. The text adopted is interpreted as representing **A**'s attempt to abbreviate **Z**, and **B** is understood as having ultimately restored (from the earliest version) the phrase now composing 59a (cf. *Z Version* § 25 below). Thus the expanded form of Reason's last sentence as found in EMKW, while deserving careful consideration, is here tentatively rejected as a **B** reading borrowed by the scribes of these copies severally to fill what was perceived as a gap in the thought. In the second and less important instance, after V 110, the ancestor of MH[3] (copies accepted at § 39 as a genetic pair) inserts the lines on Coueitise's chin and beard, E adds also that on his beard, while A omits them, here perhaps following the original reading of **m**. As this material has no parallel in **Z**, its claim as a possible part of the **A** Version is correspondingly weakened. Finally, after VIII 54 MH[3] (here the only **m** witnesses, as A is defective) include a Latin quotation absent from both the **r** family and **Z**. In principle, this citation-line could be a borrowing from B VII 51a, similar to those in H[3] after VII 74 [B XI 90], XI 152 [C V 58a] and 229 [B XIV 212a]. But in practice this would seem unlikely; for whereas the latter three illustrate memorial contamination from unrelated parts of the text, the quotation at VIII 54a correctly rounds off the sense of 54, which reads as incomplete in **r** and **Z**.

§ 66. In conclusion, it appears that one sub-archetype, **m** (in this respect quite unlike **r**), is likely to have been contaminated at points from a post-archetypal copy of a later version. But at least some of its **B**-type lines were arguably present in Ax, and by inference in its source, and so are included in this edition.

x. *Passus XII*

§ 67. The above completes our examination of the archetypal text of Pr–XI as attested, to varying degrees of completeness, in eighteen manuscripts. The continuation of **A** here called 'Passus XII' is entitled 'Passus Third of Dowel' in the only three copies that contain it. This designation acknowledges the inner sequential numbering of Dowel recorded in the colophon of VIII, which is a kind of Prologue to the *Dowel* section. The archetypal rubrics before XII are as likely as not authorial (see Appendix Two) but that of XII looks like a scribal attempt to integrate it with the preceding body of text. For as Fowler maintained, Passus XII, whether or not original, almost certainly did not form part of Ax. There is no trace of it in the r^1 group d nor in K and W, the only other members of r^2 which survive to the end of Passus XI. And while in the case of the conjoint copies, XII 'might have been suppressed by someone engaged in grafting the C-continuation to the A-Text,'[26] this could not be true for D, one of the four **r** copies with no C-Text following. More significantly, XII is not in M, the one complete descendant of **m**, the family original which there is no reason to doubt was directly copied from Ax. Thus, although Passus XII happens to survive in manuscripts that in Pr–XI are members respectively of r^1 (RU) and r^2 (J), it probably descends from a manuscript distinct from the source of Ax. This manuscript is unlikely to have been Langland's draft, though the coda by the writer who names himself John But in line 106 could no doubt have been added to a holograph obtained after the poet's death.

§ 68. At first sight Passus XII appears to have two distinct sources, since R and U (as earlier) share an exclusive ancestor (u) neither based on nor used by j, the presumed exemplar of J. Unfortunately, only in the first nineteen lines are all three copies available for comparison, as U lacks the rest of XII through loss of a leaf. In this portion, however, RU have five agreements in error, whereas J has none with either R or U; and each of these also has five individual errors, but J none. The implied superiority of j to u here continues in 20–88, where only R and J remain. For while both copies have about the same total of errors, J omits only one line (55) to R's five (65, 74–6, 78). This proportion is unlike that displayed in Pr–XI,[27] where r^2 (the sub-family to which J belongs) is right about four times more often than r^1. It seems unlikely therefore that in Passus XII u and j derived from sources forming parts of r^1 and r^2 respectively, these in turn from **r**, and **r** from Ax. Against the hypothesis of two sources (u and j), however, it must be noted that of the four cases where R and J have wrong readings (32, 34, 48, 88), one (32) shows what appears to be the same error. This could admittedly be a coincidental substitution, and it may not even be a scribal error if the exemplar was an authorial draft (cf. § 74 below). But slight as this evidence is, it may be just enough to suggest a common original for u and j. For the main counter-argument, that either witness omits *differing* sets of lines, fails if these lines can be shown to have been lost for mechanical reasons. R could easily have omitted 65 by eyeskip from *weye* 64 to *dayes* 66, and 74–6 by eyeskip from *For* 73 to *For* 76. The absence of 55 from J is harder to account for, but eyeskip from *I* 54 to *I* as initial word in 56 is a possible explanation. The most economical explanation of the origin of Passus XII may therefore be that a copy of the poet's manuscript became available to the scribes of u and j well after the archetypal copy of Pr–XI had been made and after the generation both of **r** and its immediate descendants r^1 and r^2. There is little difficulty in presuming that this copy came complete with John But's Appendix (ll. 99–117), written after Langland's death but before that of Richard II (who is referred to in l. 113 as still king); for both R and J were copied not less than fifty years later.

§ 69. The authenticity of Passus XII logically needs examining in relation to metre, style and thought before the question of emending any of its apparently corrupt readings can be addressed, though the two issues are unavoidably connected. John But's addition has here been taken as starting at line 99 and only from that point to the end has the text been treated as an 'Appendix'. This heading Knott-Fowler and Kane apply to the whole of XII. Skeat, by contrast, sees Langland's work as extending to line 105 (100), and it is certainly not beyond belief that the poet 'killed himself off, by way of finishing his poem.'[28] However, while Langland did indeed 'live to re-write it' (ibid.), he did not resort to killing himself off as a way of ending either **B** or **C**. Moreover, a reference by the *author* to 'other works...of Piers the Plowman' in 101–02 would have meant little to readers at this stage in the poem's likely evolution. Lines 99–105 are therefore better seen as part of John But's attempt to honour the dead poet's achievement (which would now have included the **B** and **C** Versions), in addition to wishing well to his soul.

§ 70. Examination of the authenticity of XII 1–98 may begin with the metre, which often appears defective by the norms derived from the poem's primary core-text.[29] Examples are lines 32, which scans *aa / xx*; 36, with a masculine ending; and 62, which is excessively long or, if divided before *welcome*, lacks a lift in the new a-half. But of these, the first admits of easy emendation, while 62 would scan vocalically with the first stave in *on* and the third in *whom* or, if divided, with a conjectural second stave **wye*. The awkward quality of lines such as 17 or 63, moreover, lessens once they are seen as examples of authentic metrical modifications. Others, with 'cognative' alliteration on voiced and unvoiced consonants, like 88 on *k / g* or 50 on *p / b*, present no problem in the light of such **B** lines as Pr 143 or V 208. Finally, features typical of Langland but seldom found in other alliterative poets are the rare line-types IIa at 38 and IIIa at 78, 90; the macaronic at 28; the mute staves at 24 and 56; and the liaisonal staves at 45 and 85 (for explanation of all these terms, see *Intro*. IV §§ 39, 43, 45).

§ 71. Weaknesses of style and expression also appear; yet the rhythm and phrasing of line 5, for instance, are very like those of I 180 and its b-half is not much flatter than those of C XIX 5 or B XVI 60. Among the poet's stylistic idiosyncrasies, the most striking evidenced in XII is the formally-scanning macaronic line with Latin staves composed of scriptural phrases. Examples occur at 28, which is reminiscent of C X 258 // and at 50–2, which splits the Pauline injunction in a manner suggesting B III 339–43. Another such device is wordplay, as at line 30 or in the macaronic 28, where it operates translinguistically across the caesura. A third is the compound name of an allegorical character, as at 82, which resembles that of Piers's wife at VII 70 (and is paralleled outside the canonical versions in Z VII 64–8).[30] A fourth is the citation of a Latin proof-text followed by its translation-paraphrase, as at 19*a*–21 and 22*a*–24, a feature illustrated notably at VIII 95–100. Finally, the passus has several examples of Langland's best manner, like the tersely epigrammatic line 6, the sardonic 85 or the lyrical 96, which anticipates B XVIII 327b in its pararhyming a-half. Throughout, there occur echoes of words and phrases found elsewhere in **A**, or 'pre-echoes' of the later versions. One such is 61, which evokes both IV 143 of **A** and its **Z** parallel. While these could in principle be attributed to an accomplished imitator, they exceed in quality anything found outside the *Piers Plowman* tradition and are more economically explained as authorial.

§ 72. The thought in Passus XII is generally Langlandian in character, though at times not coherent with that found elsewhere in **A**. Two examples are the notions of Wit as a cardinal (15) and of Kynde Wit as a confessor and Scripture's cousin (43). However, the latter character has little to do in **A**, and this Passus XII appearance may have been intended to create a rôle for him. In retrospect, it looks like a transitional step towards **B**, where Kynde Wit is closely associated with Conscience (as at III 284 and XIX 364) but remains a somewhat shadowy figure. Similarly anticipatory of later developments are the handling of the *Omnia-probate* text at 50–2 and the conception of Death and Life at 63–6 as hostile antitypes who prefigure the personages in Passus XX of **B**. But probably the strongest hint of a new direction occurs in the speech of Fever, Death's 'messenger' (as he will later become Kynde's 'forager' in B XX 81), which expands the thought further in lines 81–7.

§ 73. The broader autobiographical situation in Passus XII (which accords with Ymaginatif's allusion to *angres* at B XII 11), unless it is only a dramatic fiction, could reflect circumstances in the author's life that account for both cessation of work on **A** and this first effort to re-commence the poem. The latter was to prove abortive, but it would seem typical of Langland that he should try to conclude Passus XII in a way that deliberately echoes A I 119–21 as well as X 218 and XI 275–8, with a pregnant reference to 'working the word.' While, therefore, lines 99–105 remain arguably of a quality to be what Skeat thought them, 104 is probably better seen as John But's happy compression of B XX 100–05. These lines do not provide as satisfying an end to the passus as do 96–8; but given the uncertainty, they should perhaps be allowed an 'indeterminate' status somewhere between the authorial and the scribal, the authentic and the imitative. They seem good enough to be Langland's, but not too distinctive to be beyond the capacity of But's 'meddling' hand.

§ 74. There remains the further possibility that XII, even if it is the beginning of a formal continuation, might be only a draft and not a 'finished fragment'.[31] Such a presumption would help to explain why it formed no part of Ax's exemplar. For it may be that a copy of XII was preserved by one of the poet's associates after he himself, having shown it to them in its present form, abandoned the continuation in order to start afresh on what became the **B** Version. This is not to deny that, as a piece of authentic Langland, the lines deserve to be published, and under no obviously better heading than that of the final passus of **A**. But a reader unburdened by editorial concerns might reasonably judge the uncompromising last lines of Passus XI effective enough to 'make a good ende' to the version known as **A**: abrupt, but not much more so than those of **B** and **C**.[32]

Conclusion

§ 75. The above account of the text of **A** has begun to demonstrate the extent to which any one version cannot be edited adequately without reference to the others. These versions prove important both for discriminating between competing readings below the archetypal level and for diagnosing and correcting errors in the archetype. And they properly include not only the earlier **Z** (on which see *Z Version* §§ 13–19 below) but also the later **B** and **C**. This is because it is possible that the archetypal traditions of **B** and perhaps even of **C** preceded the generation of Ax and its sub-archetypes, among which **m** at least shows traces of influence from **B**. This possibility will be strengthened at the end of the next section, which deals with the only version of the poem that has for the last half-century been generally regarded as complete.

THE A VERSION: NOTES

1 The view of **A**'s publication taken here, developed in Adams 'Editing *PP* B', pp. 59–63, is adumbrated in Chambers and Grattan 'The Text of *PP*', p. 10.

2 Notably in *Pierce the Ploughman's Crede* (late 1390s), *Richard the Redeless* (*c.* 1400) and *Mum and the Sothsegger* (*c.* 1410); cf. *Intro* V § 14 below. One copy of *Pierce* precedes the poem in ms R of **C**, another is appended to ms T of **A**. See Helen Barr, *The Piers Plowman Tradition* for annotated texts and discussion of all three.

3 Skeat's is based on the Vernon ms, those of Knott-Fowler, Kane and the present editor on the Trinity College, Cambridge copy.

4 See § 61 below.

5 Passus XII is discussed separately in §§ 67–74 below.

6 Kane, *A Version*, p. 78; he lists only 210 agreements.

7 Cf. the discussion at § 7 above.

8 Not 230 as in Kane, p. 73.

9 Not 130 as in Kane, p. 77.

10 See *Textual Notes* to C 199–200 for full discussion of the arguments.

11 This supports K–F's recognition (p.26) of a relation (WN)K.

12 See MED s.v. *ditten* v. 3(b)

13 Of these the Apparatus records only Pr 42, III 260 and VII 177, 195 as parts of sets of complex variants.

14 This situation recurs yet more strongly where A fails, and only E and M represent **m**.

15 A conclusion not invalidated by instances *before* Passus X of W agreeing in error with **m**, since none contradict the hypothetical 'inner' grouping AW.

16 This method will be adopted below in discussing the **B** and the **C** traditions.

17 The present editor is much indebted to Charlotte Brewer for pointing out the importance of the **m** group in her unpublished D. Phil thesis 'Some Implications of the Z-Text' and for arguing it with force and acumen in 'Processes of Revision', pp. 71–92.

18 To simplify matters, in what follows reference is made only to major readings.

19 See Appendix, where the numbering should read not '204^a–209^a' but '200^a–205^a'.

20 However d, the postulated group ancestor of TH^{2}ChD, shares eleven errors (five major) with six r^2 mss. Of these notably X 53 (V), II 94 (L), XI 186 (K) and VIII 44 (W) may suggest consultation of one or more r^2 copies, though none is the likely reading of r^2 itself.

21 The relation of r^2 and **m** is thus quite unlike that between the **C** traditions **p** and **t**, which each preserve exclusive right readings but also share a body of separative agreements in error; see *C Version* §§ 37–8.

22 For the difficulty scribes found with *wy*, see the variants at X 89.

23 This is also the form of the **B** mss CrGHF and should doubtless have been recorded in the Apparatus; but the matter is in principle almost undecidable and in practice of no consequence.

24 Though it should be observed that at VIII 61 **m**, represented only by M, has what seems (on the showing of **Z**) the *right* reading, against the unmetrical reading in **r** and the totally corrupt one of Bx.

25 Mechanical explanation would also readily account for the similar loss of VII 211 from r^1 (*make....þe...Make...þe*).

26 Knott-Fowler, *A Version*, p. 149.

27 Cf. § 4 above.

28 *A-Text*, p. 141*.

29 See *Introduction* IV i below and *Appendix I* on the Language and Metre.

30 See III, *Z Version* § 21 below.

31 This is a question to be raised again in connection with **Z** as a whole, and with Pr 95–124 of **C**, which in different ways look like texts awaiting further work.

32 For a balanced discussion see Vaughan 'The Ending(s) of *PP* A', pp. 211–41.

The B Version

i. *The Manuscript Tradition*

§ 1. The **B** Version of *Piers Plowman*, the only one that can be confidently regarded as 'published' by the poet, does not merely continue from where the **A** Version ceased at the end of Passus XI. Langland attempted this in Passus XII of **A** but broke off, for whatever reason (*A Version* §§ 67–74). When he resumed at some time after 1370 it was to write the poem afresh, beginning from line 87 of the Prologue, if not earlier.[1] What the conclusion of B X achieves is to integrate the last lines of A XI by adding a dozen admonitory lines comparing clerks to reeves and then to embark on a new passus (B XI) beginning with the first of **B**'s two 'inner dreams'. This takes up some material from A XII, notably the 'scornful' Scripture whose rebuke precipitates the inner dream. But the formal structure is so novel as to suggest that A XII was put aside in draft (see *A Version* §§ 73–4 above). It is unknown whether Langland took up here rather than at the beginning, but there are two indications that he did so. One is that the revised Prologue preserves nearly every line of **A** with few changes, the other that it doubles **A**'s length not by expanding the text but by adding the wholly new 'Coronation' Scene and the Rat Fable. This latter circumstance makes it at least possible that B Pr 112–210, which must date from after 1376,[2] were inserted later; so there is no need to suppose as many as five years to have elapsed between Langland's abandoning A XII and commencing the **B** Version. On the other hand, there are structural reasons for regarding the new Prologue, which now appears a seamless whole, as planned in its entirety and executed according to plan. For its cautious opening treatment of kingly responsibility, within what appears an allegorised presentation of Richard II's coronation, is to be ironically recalled many passūs later in the sober handling of the theme of royal power at the end of Passus XIX. Any 'naturalistic' discrepancy due to **B**'s King in II–IV being still identifiable as Edward III (as in **A** and **Z**) evidently caused the poet little concern.

§ 2. Given the equally probable allusions to the Papal Wars of 1379 in XIX 431–32 and 445–51, **B** must have been completed no later than about 1380 (see *Intro.* V §§ 7–10, 15). For unless **A** was formally 'released' in an unfinished state, it is likely to be the longer version that the peasant rebel leaders alluded to in 1381, earning the poem a unique place in the political history of the age.[3] And unless Langland was himself one of John Ball's acquaintances, *Piers Plowman* must be supposed to have been made available to a readership wider than the poet's immediate circle. But for such 'publication' to occur, a copy would have had to be made from his corrected holograph as a basis for further such copies. It was this first scribal product (here called '**B-Ø**'), or an early descendant of it ('**B¹**'), and not the holograph, that Langland later used when composing the **C** Version (for supporting evidence see § 5 below). Passūs XXI–XXII of the **C** archetype

('**Cx**') are in fact regarded by the Athlone editors as a pure text of B XIX–XX. If they are right, this portion could have been independently added to the completed revision of C Pr–XX by an 'editor' who prepared the authorial manuscript of **C** for copying after the poet's death. On the other hand (as preferred by the present editor), its divergences from the main B-Text tradition may reflect preliminary touching-up of minor details in B^1. If so, there is no reason why Langland himself should not have positioned these two passūs after the fully-reworked C XX, where they now stand. Either way, they may be taken as in effect the last portion of the **B** manuscript he had worked from throughout his final revision. On this supposition, the second scribal copy, B^1, may be most economically identified as the direct basis of C XXI–XXII, into which some further corruptions will have been introduced by the scribe of Cx. Notwithstanding these, the concluding section is a unique dual source for the end of the **B** and the **C** Versions. To help keep this special feature in mind, the *substantive content* of the text in the last two passūs of the **C** tradition may be designated 'B^2.'

§ 3. The third early scribal copy that must be posited was the manuscript from which all the extant copies of **B** ultimately descend. This archetypal text, referred to hereafter as **Bx**, is derived, like B^1, at one or at most two removes from the holograph. The reality of all three copies so far postulated is not open to serious doubt, as will be briefly argued here (and more fully in §§ 70ff below) from a comparison of Bx in the final two passūs with the C-Text form of them, B^2. To begin with, the existence of the first scribal copy, B-Ø, is proved by the twelve major and three minor errors shared by Bx and B^2, which must both descend from it, B^2 immediately from B^1. Secondly, that Bx was not derived from B^1 is shown by its freedom from B^2's six major and three minor errors. Finally, that B^2 was not derived from Bx is clear from its lacking the latter's twenty-two certain errors (all major). On the evidence of these two passūs alone, it seems that Langland's revision-manuscript B^1 will have been about twice as accurate as Bx. In principle, most of the disjunctive errors here ascribed to B^1 (as already recognised at §2) could have been introduced by the copyist of Cx; for B^1's character can only be inferred from what the **C** tradition preserves as B^2. But the wrong readings shared by Bx and B^2 support the simpler (and the only logically necessary) explanation: that when Langland was working on **C**, he had access neither to his holograph of **B** nor to B-Ø but only to a copy containing at least the recognised B^1 errors.[4]

§ 4. A brief comparative analysis of C XXI–XXII and B XIX–XX (given in more detail at §§ 72–4 below) reveals that the postulated first scribal copy B-Ø, assuming it lacked the individual errors of B^1 and Bx, will have possessed only about one wrong reading in every 58 lines. It must therefore have been produced by a more accurate scribe than those who made either of the other early copies of *Piers Plowman* that are directly or indirectly accessible. For B^1 appears to have made about one error in every 35 lines and Bx one in roughly every 20. Even taking into account the shared B^1Bx errors that must derive from B-Ø, this last figure, confirmed by the general showing of the preceding Pr–XVIII, indicates how badly the text was corrupted during its initial stages of transmission (Bx's average error-rate over the whole poem is about one in twelve lines). This is important, because Bx is the only text to which analysis of a 'logically positive' type (see II, §§ 12–13) can attain. For the editor prepared to rely on the linear postulate, it becomes possible to recover some 60 of B^1's probable readings in the passūs up to // C XI (if only partially, because of revision) through examining the joint witness of **C** and **A** in this section. But in the approximately 3200 lines of **B** from where **A** ends to where the B^2 witness begins (B XIX / C XXI), correction of Bx's errors must take the form either of simple preference for a **C** reading unsupported by **A**, or of emendation, mild or drastic. If it is quite possible that B[1], and even perhaps B-Ø, was not thoroughly checked by Langland against his holograph, it seems overwhelmingly likely that Bx did not receive systematic authorial checking,[5] with or without reference to either of these.

§ 5. That the immediate exemplar of the archetype may not have been B-Ø is suggested by the high incidence of corruption in Bx by comparison with that in Ax and Cx, which points to a stage of copying between it and B-Ø. This presumption is not invalidated by two unusual facts about Bx's production. Firstly, while in Pr–X the error-rate is about one in every eight or nine lines, in XI–XX (and omitting for the moment Passus XVI) it falls to about one in seventeen. This discrepancy suggests *prima facie* that two scribes were responsible for copying the text, the later being nearly twice as accurate as the earlier. Secondly, the excepted passus, XVI, has only two certain archetypal errors in the entire course of its 275 lines, a figure representing an eightfold superiority to the work of the better of the two postulated scribes. Two explanations of this latter feature come to mind. One is that XVI was produced by a third archetypal copyist, something that seems antecedently improbable because of the level of accuracy it evinces. A second is that the passus was corrected by the poet, though why he checked a specimen of the scribe's work from so late a stage in the poem or why the 'better' Bx scribe did not take its lesson to heart remain unclear. However, if the latter was identical with the scribe of Pr–X, and he *did*, the relative superiority of XI–XX would be a measure of his improved accuracy. For it is notable that nearly all Bx's spurious lines occur in the section by the less accurate first scribe (whether the same man or not), although one more (exactly similar) such line appears in the postulated second scribe's portion, at XIX 373. It is therefore possible that the originator of the spurious lines was not the 'careless' first copyist but the scribe of another, earlier manuscript intermediate between Bx and B-Ø, which may be called **B-Øa**. If this explanation is right, the authorial corrections to Passus XVI would have been made in B-Øa and incorporated from it into Bx by the second scribe. In any event, the spurious lines, including the pair at XIX 373, are unparalleled in Cx; so none of them can have been present in B-Ø (the logically inferred common source of Bx and B[1]), unless they were all afterwards removed in **C**.

§ 6. From circumstances like these arise the major textual problems of the **B** Version, and some of those found in **C** as well. Langland's holograph must have passed out of his hands for copying; and when he began work on **C**, neither it nor B-Ø was available to him for revision, or to scribes in the archetypal and sub-archetypal traditions for correction of their copies. Access by some scribes to just such a superior lost source as B-Ø is, however, posited by the Athlone editors to account for individual readings in manuscripts like F and G that they and (in some cases) the present editor judge superior on comparison with Bx. But as argued below (§§ 28 and 46), such readings are better explained as due to contamination from one or more of the other versions of the poem that had become available by the time these copies' ancestors were produced. At any rate, nothing superior to B[1], a manuscript more accurate than Bx but still disfigured by probably not fewer than sixty errors,[6] seems to have been to hand when Langland began revising the poem for the last time. But whatever its exact pre-history, for Pr–XVIII Bx alone is directly accessible, through the agreed readings of its eighteen surviving descendants, or indirectly through critical reconstruction from them. And it is the high rate of error in Bx that forms the main challenge for the editor of the **B** Version.

ii. *The two families of* **B** *manuscripts*

§ 7. The Bx readings are (near)-unanimously preserved in some 70% of the poem (= 5126 out of 7276 lines).[7] In another 1700 lines (about 23% of the whole) two strongly contrasted traditions emerge, here called α and β, which descend independently from the archetypal manuscript, as Kane and Donaldson have argued.[8] In these lines, the Bx reading may usually be discriminated with tolerable certainty in either α or β, often with guidance from the parallel text of **A**, **C** and **Z**, severally or in agreement. In the remaining 450 lines, about 7% of the total work, where individual manuscript readings cut across both families, Bx may still be recoverable, though with lessened certainty, in the light of the parallel texts or, where these are not available, by tracing the probable direction of scribal variation.

§ 8. As with the **A** Version, the two families of **B** are very disproportionately represented. Only two witnesses to the α tradition survive, R and F, and while neither derives from the other, both in their different ways are seriously wanting. R is physically defective for about 10% of the whole poem, while F is sophisticated throughout and shows contamination from **A** and possibly also **C** (see § 46 below). Thus, though its internal structure is simpler than that of **m** in the **A** tradition, α offers a special problem in being the *sole* witness to about 187 lines of **B**, some of which have no other-version parallel. Similarly, β preserves some 200 lines lacking from the other family; but by contrast with α it has, like the **r** family of **A**, a complex internal structure. Thus at least four independent copies of β were made; these are represented by the sub-family here called γ (consisting of the twelve manuscripts WHmCrGYOC²CBmBoCotS) and by three unrelated copies L, M and H. Of the former, the mid-sixteenth century witness S, which is substantively very corrupt and modernised throughout, has not been collated and will not be further referred to in the main text. The remaining eleven γ manuscripts, with BmBoCot denoted by the sigil B for their exclusive common ancestor, fall into two groups, neither of which derives from the other. These are WHmCr and GYOC²CB, signified respectively by the group sigils w and g. There is solid evidence that one member of the latter group, G, derives directly from g by a separate line of descent and the remaining five from an intermediary copy of g, here called y (§§ 11–39 below).

§ 9. Owing to their independent character, none of the four main lines of transmission from the β family-original can be eliminated, as each contains some readings which may represent β and thence Bx. The source γ is likely to have been copied directly from β, but in the case of L, M and H an intermediary stage, here denoted by the lower-case form of each manuscript's sigil (*l, m, h*), may be posited (§§ 30–39 below). Of these individual copies, L is both complete and substantively the best, as Skeat recognised; but its relative lack of grammatical regularity and linguistic consistency renders it unsuitable as a basis for the text. Superior in these respects is W, the soundest γ representative, which was used by Wright and K–D and is adopted here. The present edition of **B** thus resembles that of **A** in taking as its base a copy from the larger manuscript family (β). Its errors are corrected by reference to the smaller (α) where this seems to preserve Bx, by restoration from the parallel texts in the other versions, and by reconstruction and conjecture when more direct evidence is lacking. The text is thus presented in the language of the earliest 'complete' B-Text copy to survive. As in the Athlone edition, the α and β traditions are understood as forming two partial and imperfect witnesses to a unitary **B** Version of *Piers Plowman* intermediate between **A** and **C**.[9] The present edition does not revert to Skeat's minimal interventionism; but while acknowledging its indebtedness to the methods and conclusions of Chambers, Blackman and Kane-Donaldson, often differs from them in its approach both to identifying originality and to emending archetypal corruptions.

§ 10. In the light of the above discussion, the inferential relationships between the collated **B** manuscripts and their hypothetical lost originals may be expressed in the form of the following diagram, which slightly modifies the one given on p. lvii of *Sch²* (an early, significantly different stemma is offered by Blackman, and a recent, closely similar one by Adams).[10]

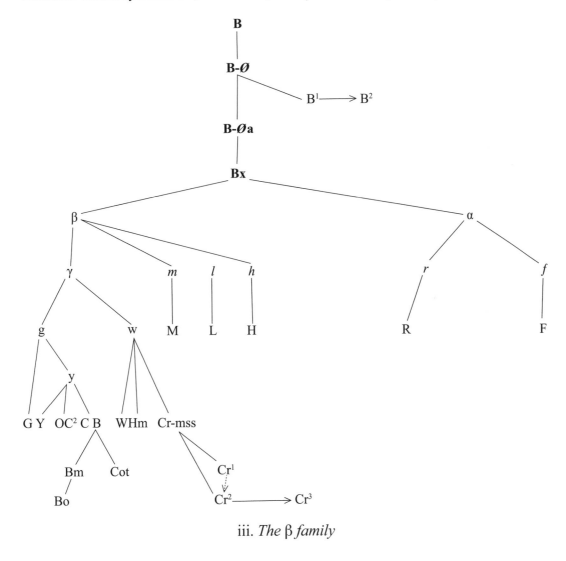

iii. *The β family*

(a) *sub-family γ*

§ 11. The two divisions of β are γ and the three manuscripts L, M and H, which do not share an exclusive common ancestor. The eleven collated members of γ may be thought of as a 'sub-family' rather than a 'group' because, first, they divide in turn into two distinct groups, **w** and **g**; and second, within g may be identified a further five-member group, *y*, itself containing at least two sub-groups, OC^2 and CB. The members of γ are virtually complete except for O, which lacks a quarter of Passus XVII, and B, the three constituents of which attest in Pr–II a C-Text linked by 110 lines of A-Text to the B-Text that follows from III 1. The sub-family γ is thus even more firmly attested than r^l of **A**, although, unlike u and d of **A**, its two major constituent groups w and g begin to be decisively differentiated only about a third of the way into Passus V.

§ 12. The distinctive variants of γ are made up first of the agreed readings of its component groups in some 38 instances, fourteen of them major, and two important (marked *). A further 25, of which 12 are major, are also found in one other β witness M,[11] the main exemplar of which was not a γ copy. In the following list of readings, a minus sign before a sigil indicates that a member manuscript diverges from γ in possessing the presumed β reading, which is judged correct unless otherwise noted.

Major II 162. V 203, 501, 542. VI 227, 326. VII 114. XV 63. XVI 8. *XVII 184b–85a, *286 *om*;-Cr, 304. XVIII 349. XX 8 -Cr; β in *error. With* M: V 351 (*over erasure*). VI 326 (*alt. to read with* L). IX 98a. XII 245 (*over eras.*). *XIII 283b–84a *om*. XIV 1, 239. XV 398, 506. XVI 50. XVIII 198. XX 287. **Minor** IV 54. V 210, 228, 446, 596, 631, 635 -Cr. VI 77, 145 -Cr, 248 -Y. VII 16, 71, 73a, 101. VIII 21, 28, 90. XI 48. XII 144. XIII 223, 374 -C. XV 91, 452. XVIII 354. *With* M: VIII 127 (*by erasure*). IX 190. XIV 146. XV 36, 396, 494. XVI 27, 60, 214 -W. XVII 15, 104 -Cr, 166 -Hm. XVIII 354.

On the assumption that the non-exclusive readings have entered M through collation with a w-type source (§§ 33–5 below), γ may thus be considered established by a total of 63 agreements in error, 26 of them major. It also has a major right reading at V 261 (in M added over erasure) and five minor right readings at V 446 (-B), ?VI 8 (*om* CB), XII 148, XIII 191 (-CB+F) and XIV 106 (added in M). Additionally, several such others appear, whether preserved by pure descent from γ or by correction, in one or other of its constituent groups w and g. A few appear in only some of their members, and in the case of G, OC^2, C and B this is almost certainly by correction from another version. The sub-family therefore cannot be eliminated.

Group **w**

§ 13. The first of the γ groups, **w**, contains the base-manuscript of this edition and (as earlier with group t of the **A** Version) accordingly receives an extended treatment here. The original of w cannot have derived from any member of the other γ group g, since W is older than all of these; or from g itself, since it is free of the latter's modernisations. Although half a dozen disjunctive variants appear before Passus VII, w's agreement with g in all major readings indicates that it preserved γ pretty faithfully up to that point. This may suggest that a second scribe was responsible for the text from there on (a situation similar to that posited for Bx at § 5 above). The group w is established by some 90 exclusive agreements in error, about 35 of them major and three important. This total includes twelve shared by M, which may nonetheless also be accepted as criterial for w since most of them have visibly entered this copy by alteration, addition or erasure, from a source very like the lost w-type manuscript used by Crowley.

Major VII 97. X 210, *246a *om*, 415, 437. XI 20, 130, 257, 339. XII 21, 47, *103 *om*, 209, 252. XIII 36, 49, 81, 96, 134, 352. XIV 23. XV 96, 152, 330, *373 *om*. XIX 78. XX 260. *With* M: VI 200 +?G. X 61. XI 398 -Cr+Bm. XIII 411. XIV 179, 300. XV 200, 224, 502. XVI 125 +F. XVIII 85, 109, 299.

Minor Pr 21. I 124. II 40. IV 29, 131, 189. V 81. VII 189. VIII 100, 128. IX 155. X 52, 205, 251, 252, 264*a*, 395, 433, 443. XI 80, 87, 150, 184, 219, 253, 298, 315, 332. XII 78, 204, 239. XIII 39, 73, 156, 205, 355, 395, 429. XIV 123, 226, 319. XV 549. XVI 43. XVII 229. XIX 276. XX 260. *With* M: I 6 +G. X 177. XV 8, 157, 455. XVIII 347.[12]

It is very probable also that in eight readings convergence of group w with the α manuscript F is coincidental: X 261, XIII 94, XVI 125 (major), X 450, XV 67, XVI 213, 255, XIX 391 (minor). The same holds of two readings shared respectively with Y (V 631) and with Cot (XI 323).

§ 14. Within w a further relation (WHm)Cr may be discerned on the basis of 55 exclusive agreements of W and Hm, some 18 of them major:[13]

Major III 36. XI 412. XV 223, 424 (*over erasure* Hm), 604 (Grekes] Iewis). XVII 20, 133, 167, 176, *210 (*l. om*), 231. XVIII 158, 224, 425. XIX 216. XX 114, 191, 235. **Minor** I 70. V 17, 31. VI 124. VII 97. X 260*a*, 268. XI 181. XII 132, 191, 239. XIII 93, 328. XV 82. XVI 78, 209. XVII 25, 120. XVIII 105, 172, 203, 208, 216, 331, 332. XIX 117, 124, 146, 169, 186, 187, 212, 292, 379, 383, 471. XX 234.

This group is not seriously questioned by the 20 agreements of *HmCr* (listed in *K–D*, p. 39). All are trivial save two, VIII 63 *wilde*] *wyde* (possibly a visual error) and XVI 22 *top*] *crop* (a synonym-substitute unconsciously suggested by 42 below), both probably coincidental.

§ 15. More challenging to WHm is the group *WCr* based on some 50 agreements, 15 of them major:[14]

Major V 195. IX 118 +M, *corr.*, 144. X 27. XIV 171, 267–8. XV 15, 107, 156, 410, 552 +M *added*. XVI 87, 204. XVIII 258. XIX 186. **Minor** Pr 77. I 126. III 222. IV 175. V 9, 248 +M *over* erasure, F, 560, 598. VI 65. IX 79. XI 82, 246, 348. XII 187. XIII 179 +M *over erasure*, 230, 241 +M *added*, 283, 284. XIV 288 +M, 308, 309, 317 +M *added*. XV 133, 139, 209, 396/7, 413, 601. XVI 159, 211. XVII 167, 241[1,2]. XVIII 74, 85 +M, 266, 312. XX 255 +F.

Of the minor agreements here, several illustrate common coincidental errors. These include spelling in XVI 159, XVII 167 and the substitution of a synonym (*mid* XV 139, XVII 241, both possible w readings from which Hm has varied) or of a contextually commoner expression (XVIII 74, 312), and all could be coincidental. Amongst the major examples IX 144 illustrates haplographic loss of *fore-* by *for* > *fer-* attraction, XVI 87 dittography and 204 unconscious syntactical variation occasioned by failure to grasp the metrical structure, while XVIII 258 is a visual error (a misexpanded contraction). XIV 267–68 results from smoothing of unusual word-order and XV 156 seems the unconscious replacement of a less familiar term in this collocation. In XV 410 the form of Hm suggests that w could have read as WCr, while in the most indicative instance XIV 171, *hem greue* could have been intelligently or inadvertently omitted by Hm. Thus, although slight doubt remains, it seems likely that WCr, despite its size, is not a genetic group like WHm. In the case of M's agreements, however, a direct relation must be accepted at least for the half-dozen by visible correction, a conclusion congruent with M's other agreements with w (= γ) recorded in § 12 (see also § 35 on M). The general situation regarding w may be contrasted with that of the **A** manuscripts TCh discussed at *A Version* § 12, where (unlike Hm here) H[2], the dissident member of t's postulated genetic TH[2] sub-group, must have been corrected from a copy of another (sub)-family. In the present case, the corrected member of w seems to be Cr, not a partner in a genetic pair *WCr but a copy free of several presumed w errors retained in WHm, which are such a pair.[15]

§ 16. The group cannot be eliminated, however; for w or its component copies, severally or in pairs and sometimes with other-version support, attest solely some 10 readings that seem original and a further 17 (in square brackets here) where it is accompanied by one other manuscript or α.

Major w: [V 423 +GC]. X 57 +**AC**. XI 144 +**C**. WHm: XI 287 +**C**. XIX 321 +Cr³**C**. [XX 117 +**FC**]. W: XV 461; [III 283 +GC] (*both by felicitous conjecture*). I 54 +**ZAC**. Cr: I 152 (? *by correction from* C). [III 342 +GC]. Cr³: XII 270 (? *by conjecture; no // in* C). **Minor** w: II 90 +**C**. [VI 201 +GC]. [XIII 334 (+M *corr.*, FC)]. WHm: Pr 59 +**AC**. [XII 182 +FC]. [XVII 137 +α**C**]. [XIX 9 +L**C**]. WCr: [XIV 257 +Mα]. [XIX 437 (+FC)]. W: XV 552 +**C**. [V 638 +GAC. XVIII 234 +RC]. XIX 111 +**C**: *not adopted but possibly original*. Cr: [I 176 +GZAC. II 35 +YC. IV 94 +HC. XIII 223 +FM (*by erasure*) C].

All the agreed readings of w are recorded in the main Apparatus and those of WHm, WCr and W that are not included there are given in the Appendix in Vol. I.

Group **g**

§ 17. The second γ group, **g**, is a more complex unit having two lines of transmission from its postulated original. One is represented by **G**, its most important member, the other by a postulated source **y** from which the other seven manuscripts YOC²CBmBoCot exclusively descend, with further units formed within them. Neither g nor its sub-group y uniquely preserve an original reading by pure descent from the archetype or by other-version correction. Instead, they illustrate how rapidly the text was corrupted in the generation after the poem was composed.[16] In the discussion, greatest attention will be given to G, whose medieval ancestor adopted from an other-version source (**A**) some unique readings with a good claim to be original.

§ 18. The group **g** is established by some 230 agreements, about 100 of them major. Though strict reckoning yields around 210, this exceeds K–D's 'more than 190' (p. 52), even excluding readings where one member is absent through individual divergence or defect in the manuscript. In some 30 more instances, g's agreement with one other witness (of either family) seems coincidental, not genetic. In the list below, square brackets mark these, but not its 21 agreements with Cr²³. This is because Cr¹ was the source of Cr² (on which Cr³ is based), and the copy that Cr² was collated with was probably later than g itself. The group reads near-uniformly with w up to about V 234 (see § 13), a fact suggesting that γ itself or an accurate copy furnished the earlier part of w and g before two new sources were used that produced the distinctive text of each.

§ 19. The main characteristics of g are of a kind found in the sub-archetypes and the archetype as well as in its descendant y. These are, firstly, the omission of some 16 whole and four half-lines from γ and the insertion of four spurious lines. Next, g tends to simplify the style by omitting words, e.g. adjectives (XI 212, XVI 185, XVIII 36), adverbs (VIII 127, XII 143, XIII 131–32 [twice]), and especially 're-inforcing' pronouns (V 572, VI 50, 150, VIII 114 and XV 71). Signs of hasty copying are the repeated truncation of the stave-phrase, as at IX 75 and XVII 285, and the re-writing, virtually as prose, of IX 95–6. A tendency to modernise occasions substitution of *he* for *wye* at V 533, *barne* for *burn* at XI 361, XVI 180 and 263, *sweuene* for *metels* at XI 6 (with which compare the misunderstanding of this noun's number at XI 86), and *make* for β *macche* (itself an error for the rare and archaic *mette*). The g scribe often attempts to make the text more explicit, e.g. at X 159, 194, 467; XIV 2; XV 314; XX 163, 178 and 256) and sometimes changes the sense in seeking greater emphasis, e.g. at X 248; XI 49 and XIII 43, while not hesitating to remove characteristic rhetorical repetitions, as at X 287 and XVII 322. These features, taken together with g's omissions and spurious lines, indicate a group-original later than w, though not derived from it, since it contains, for instance, two lines w omits (XII 103 and XV 373) that were presumably in g. The manuscript is unlikely to have been much older than its earliest descendants, Bm and Bo, which date from *c*.1400.

§ 20. In the following list of line-references for all g variants,[17] a minus sign denotes agreement of a member with the other β copies wLM, a plus sign agreement of a non-member with g (these readings are in square brackets):

Major [V 255 +F], 433 -B. VI 23. IX 25, 41, 92*a*, 95–6, 97, [181 +Cr²³]. [X 23 +Cr²³], 47 -CB, 89, 194, 205 (Oure Lord) god), 219, 248, [251 (helþe) sake; +Cr²³)], 257, 287, 337¹·², *403, 438, 456¹·²·³, [466 +W], 467. XI 5, [6 +M], [47 +Cr²³], [49¹·² +Cr²³], [82 +Cr], 212, 291 -B, [339 +M], 358, [361 +Cr]. XII 16, 34, 50, [74 +Cr], 143, 154 (*spur. l. foll.*), 192. XIII 6, 15, 43, 52, 56, 132, 153 (*different. error* Y), 187 -Y, 279, 317, 343. XIV 2, 3, [70 +F], 111, [120 +Cr²³; *diff. error* CB], 277, [286 +Cr²³], [329 +F]. XV [23 +Hm], 66, [71 +Cr²³], 229 (*spur. l. foll.*), 253–4, 314, 316, [556 +Hm], 587 (knewe) knowe). XVI 30 -Y, 81 (CB *def.*), 126, 180, 182 (*om* OC²), 185, *210. XVII 123–4 (O *def.*), [285 +F], 322, 351. XVIII [9 +Cr²³], 11, 24, 221, 259 (*spur. l. foll.*), *279 (*spur. l. foll.*), 294 (*spur. l. foll.*). XIX *3–4, *5, 149 (hym) it), 167, *219b–27a *ll. om*, 228, [239 +Cr²³], *255, *287 (*def.* O), *340. XX [48 -C²+R], *95–6, 163, [182 +Cr²³], 191, 236 (-B; *diff. error*), 236 (siþen) seyen), 256, 346. **Minor** V [393 +Cr²³], [256 +F], 572. VI 50 -B, [51 +Cr²³], 81, 143, 150, [167 +Cr³], 183, 273. VII [152 +Hm]. VIII 50, 54, [97 þat) the +Cr²³], 114. IX 41 seide) seith, [91 +Cr²³], [154 +Cr²³], 204. X [18 +a], 25*a*, 34, 88*a*, 94 (Nouȝt) And n.), 97, 159, 188¹, 188² (neuere) no), 198, 206, 246, 309, 320 (wiþ) &), [327*a* +M], [355 +Cr], [376 +F]. XI 32, 46, 74, 87 (hem) *om*), 134, 146, [141 +F], 187, [199 +F], 209, 231, 252, 262, 321, 340, 378, 417. XII 49 (may) myght), 92, 102, 139, 159, 200, 226, [256 +F], 268, [273 +Cr²³]. XIII 34, 47, 79, 95, 120, [131 +M], [239 +R], 301, 308, [334 +L], 375. XIV 4, 14, 21, 46 (*diff. error* CB), 55, 86, [93 +Cr²³], 96, 111, 162, 191, 201, 244, 269, 293 (wiþ) *om*), 331. XV 50, 87, 118 -Y, 124, 130, 160, 195, 200, 252, 271, [327¹ +F], 327² (ise) þe), 370, 376¹·², 402, 509, 554, 581, 582, 604. XVI 69 (CB *def.*), 176, [181 +Cr²³], 186, 212, 248, 264. XVII 45, 46, 315. XVIII 35, 36, 83, [86 +Cr], 109, 145, [171 +Cr²³], 179, 2559, 364 (hast) *om*), 386. XIX 66, [121 +Cr²³], 135, 206, 318 (*def.* O), 320 (*def.*O), 364, [462 +Cr²³], [460 +Cr, *def.* B]. XX 18, 178 -O, 305.

§ 21. Group g cannot be eliminated; for though the whole unequivocally attests no unique right readings, such are preserved severally by individual members and sub-groups, whether directly or through correction from outside the **B** tradition (see §§ 22ff below). In the following list of eight where g is accompanied by one manuscript or α, a *plus* denotes support from outside g or from another version:

Major X 124 +MA. XI 130 +MR**C**. **Minor** V 533 +FZA**C**, 552 +αZA**C**. IX 11 -CB+F. XI 81*a* +Hm. XIX 15 +Hm**C**. XX 366 +CrF**C**.

Sub-group **y**

§ 22. The first large sub-division of g consists of YOC²CB(=BmBoCot). These seven manuscripts descend from **y**, an early copy of g postulated on the basis of 75 agreements in error not found in the remaining member G, which shares its 155 other distinctive variants. There are 28 major and 48 minor readings, tabulated here as for g above, and eight more (two of them major) where y is randomly accompanied by one or two other manuscripts.

Major V [111 -C+MCr²³], 166 (hele) holde), 254, [*268 (*spur. l. foll.*, +Cr²³], 283, 296¹·² [*spur. l. foll.*, +Ht], [331 (*spur. l. foll.* +Cr²³Ht], 397 (fourty) fifty), 416, 437, [540 +Cr²³], [557 +F], 560 (*spur. l. foll.*) VI 47*a* (*spur. l. foll.*), 66, 129¹·², 151, 216, 287, 288 (Lammesse) herueste), 294, 298, *307–8 (-CB, *ll. om*), *312. VII 30, 119¹·². XV 593. XVII 17, 179 (-C², O *def.*). **Minor** Pr 141 (-B, *def.*). II [92 +L-B *def.*]. III 209 (a²) the). V 131 (to²) *om*), 132 (þoruȝ) by), [142 +a], 156 (of) with). 176, 234, 256, 262, 290, 294, 335, [367 +Cr²³], 395, 481, [538 +Cr²³], 587, 593, 594, 629 (any) the). VI 45, [48 +Cr²³], 50, 55 (s. þe k.) *trs*), 57, 67, [147 +Cr³], 189, 200, 236, 257, 265, [306 +F-CB (*l. om*)], 309, [315 +FC], 317. VII 11, 44, [56 +Hm], 58, 69, 83, 123. VIII 81. X [85 -C+R], [205 +M], 439. XII 132, 176. XIII 77, 191. XV 7, 78. XVI [182 +Cr²³]. XVII 29, 200 (+C, *def.* O). XVIII 11. XIX 267.

It seems likely from the eight agreements of Cr^{23} with y, together with the 21 listed under g, that Cr^2 was collated at some stage with a manuscript of the y branch (see below). The sub-group y contains a unique minor right reading at VII 56 (-C+**C**) and two others (also minor) with F accompanying, at II 120 and VI 152. In addition, some members have right readings in two major instances, YOC^2Cr^{23} at IV 10 and GYC^2 at XVIII 160, both by presumed correction severally from **C**. Finally, there are about a dozen instances (noted below) where constituent members or pairs preserve an apparently superior reading. The sub-group therefore cannot be eliminated.

§ 23. A further division of y is into $<Y(OC^2)>$ and $<CB>$, each of which has an exclusive ancestor. K–D's judgement (p. 45) that YOC^2 probably form a genetic group is acceptable on balance; but it is noteworthy that amongst the 33 variants supporting it, only three appear significant. Of these, VI 307–08 may be reasonably inferred to represent y (CB missing the lines). In V 111 agreement of Y with OC^2 in *myn herte akeþ* could be a coincidental alteration to prose order of CB's ancestral reading **akeþ myn herte* (with which M coincides), while C substitutes a synonym *werkes* for the verb. Of Y's other agreements with OC^2 (listed in *K–D*, pp 44–5) the most impressive is XX 63 *siþ...was] than...to be* (so likewise Cr^{23}). Taken with the important corrected reading at IV 10 (also shared by Cr^{23}), this may indicate that the $<Y(OC^2)>$ ancestor was the very y-type manuscript consulted by Cr^2. But other OC^2Cr^{23} agreements, such as their omission of line XVI 202, suggest rather that this copy will have been the immediate ancestor only of the pair $<OC^2>$.[18] The individual manuscript **Y** cannot be eliminated, as it attests, possibly by contamination from **C**, one major right reading at Pr 171 and a minor one at VI 207 (confirmed by **ZAC**), a minor reading at II 35 shared by Cr, and a major one at XVIII 160 shared by GC^2.

§ 24. The two copies associated with Y form the most substantially attested pair after the α manuscripts R and F (§ 44 below), with some 330 agreements, 78 of them major. This is despite O's being seriously defective in XVII and XIX. **OC^2** seem to have had as their exclusive common ancestor an inaccurate transcript of the same manuscript from which Y was copied. Its main features are a spurious line instead of XV 122, two added Latin lines after Pr 39 and XI 277 (the latter = VII 87) and sixteen omitted lines: I 31, 135; II 66; V 174; *VII 174–81 (on the Papal power, possibly censored); VIII 7, 24; XI 264 and XVI 171. Major errors of OC^2 are found in Cr^{23} at XVI 202 (a line probably lost coincidentally through homœoteleuton) and in Cr^3 at VI 219 (*false men] fawti man*) and 226 (*god] go*). Since the OC^2 readings are of little interest, only a few are cited incidentally in the Apparatus as part of the complex variants of a lemma.

Pr 34, 67, 152. I 31, 37, 155, 206. II 80 +H. III 258, 284. V 181. VI 77, 198. VII 138, *174–81. X 50, 441. XI 49, 150, 284*a*, 402, 419. XII 17, 42, 60, 192. XIII 50, 135, 139, 223, 265. XIV 52, 171. XV 122, 126–7, 374, 528. XVI 110, 182*a*. C^2 *only*: II 3. IV 145, 193 (+M). V 179. VIII 101. X 153 (*a.h.*). XIV 101. XV 39. XVIII 12, 172. XIX 113–14. XX 256, 260, 261. *Individual* C^2 *readings cited at* X 139, 348 *show contamination from* **A**.

The sub-group OC^2 cannot be eliminated, however, as it or one member contains (mostly by benign contamination) seven unique right readings, four in which it is accompanied by one other g manuscript and eight supported by α:

Major IX 4 +**AC**. XI 398 +α. XIII [411 +**B**; *corrected from* **C**]. **Minor** Pr 159. VI 284 +**ZAC**. X 28 +**C**. [XV 577 +Cr]. *With* α: V 186 +**AC**. VI 80 +**C**. VII 93 +**ZAC**. XIII 50 +**C**, [255*a* +CotC]. XIV 41 +**C**, 131*a* +**C**. O *only*: **Major** XIX 181 +**C**. **Minor** [XV 317*a* +αC]. [XIX 46 +HmC]. C^2 *only*: **Major** I 200 +**ZAC**. [XVII 198*a* +CrC]. XVIII 160 +**C**.

Here there is a notable incidence of agreement with α and further agreement with it *in error* at XIII

97, 125, 135, 313 (+C), XIV 306 (+B), XV 319 (+G). OC^2's collation with a copy from the other family in the area of XIII–XIV, though antecedently not very likely, therefore cannot be ruled out.

§ 25. The other large sub-group in y is <**CB**>, made up of **C** and the three closely-related manuscripts BmBoCot, represented only in III–XX, which is given the group-sigil **B** by K–D. The genetic nature of <CB> is not seriously challenged by the existence of 87 agreements between B and a member of the α family, F. All but a half dozen of these K–D adequately account for as coincidental; but it is hard to agree with them that, had the errors of <CB> been significantly fewer in number, its genetic character might well have seemed less clear than that of BF, a group they (rightly) consider random. For they ignore the character of these errors which, even if reduced to the number of BF (i.e. by about two thirds), would still contain over thirty major examples, five times as many as those in BF. This example shows the importance of considering the quality and not just the quantity of readings when seeking to determine the genetic relationships of the manuscripts. For it is these agreements that will have been least credibly produced by 'convergent and specifically coincident variation' (*K–D*, p. 48). The group <CB> is established by some 263 agreements, of which about 100 are major. Its original would therefore appear to have been copied by a very careless scribe, who omitted 77 lines and 18 half-lines, his irresponsibility towards the exemplar being shown by the unusually large proportion of major errors. The readings of <CB> have even less intrinsic interest than OC^2's and are only occasionally cited as part of complex sets of variants.

III 154, 205. IV 33, 57, 67. V 422. VI 8, 280, 300, 303, 307. VII 27. IX 129, 130. X 124, 125, 353*a*. XI 370. XIII 415. XIV 101, 120, 141. XVI 30, 56–91. XVIII 161, 348, 389, 390. XIX 94.

But <CB>'s members severally contain seven unique right readings; and the group attests two supported by the other family and six more with support from one or two other manuscripts of both families:

Major [VIII 127 +α]. C *only*: XIX 391 +**C**. B *only*: [III 6 +α**ZAC**]. [X 172 +Hm?**GAC**]. XIII 2 (+**C**-Cot; *from* Bo, *over erasure* Bm), [411 +OC^2**C**]. XX 378 (+**C**-Bo; Bm *def.*). **Minor** [VI 128 +Cr**ZAC**; *def.* Cot]. [VIII 83 +α]. [XIV 198 +R]. B *only*) [III 3 +H**C**], [11 -BoCot+R**ZAC**], 12 +**ZAC**, [251 +HR], 322 -BoCot+**C**. VI 257 +**ZAC**, [277 +GF**ZAC**]. XIII 2 -Cot+**C**. C *only*: [II 113 +HmH**ZAC**].

It therefore cannot be eliminated.

§ 26. Among the two major components of this sub-group of y, the single manuscript C is cited only in the following instances as part of a complex set of variants:

Pr 29, 46. II 115, [130 +H]. III 150. IX 149, 169. XI 84, 125, 374. XII 228, 234. XV 69. XVI 252. XVII 214, 337*a*. XVIII 109.

§ 27. The other (composite) 'member' of this sub-group is **B**, of which the three constituent manuscripts (**Bm**, **Bo** and **Cot**) share over 800 agreements in error and may be safely taken to descend from a single exclusive ancestor. In the Apparatus 'B' is thus the sigil which follows readings where all three manuscripts agree, but it is preceded by a query sign when one or two diverge. Within the grouping, *BmBo* have 123 agreements, some 22 of them major, and *BoCot* 130, about 34 major, but *BmCot* only five, all minor. On grounds of date, Bm and Bo cannot derive from Cot; and while the former two are roughly coæval, there are codicological reasons for thinking Bo 'an incomplete copy of Bm'.[19] The latter appears to have been produced in a professional workshop from a specially prepared exemplar, using text from both **A** and **C** to meet the requirement presumably of a 'complete' *Piers Plowman*. For the three descendants of B are, like Bodley 851 (Z), the only 'conjoint texts' to have their two discrete versions linked by material from a *third*. Their **C** portion (which is given the **C** group-sigil b in this edition) runs from Pr 1 to II 128 and continues, after no visible break, with A II 86–198 (the end of A II). It now seems probable that the **B** Version proper begins around III 29, the first 28 lines of III being taken from an **A** copy of the same textual character as II 86–198.[20] The likelihood that this copy was descended from **A**-family **r** is shown by the variant *carien* at II 126; that it was of r^1-type, by *besette...sore* 105, *foolys* 144; and that its sub-group within r^1 was t, by the variants *trotten* 144 (Ch) and *quentely* 130 (H^2). Finally, that B's **A** source was H^2 or its exemplar seems suggested by the major agreement at II 190 *half...dayes*] *wit hem terme of here lyues* and the spurious line following (as noted in *K–D*, 1, n. 3).[21] There are also signs of contamination from **C** in B at XIII 2, XV 289, 549 (all by alteration in Bm); in Bm alone at III 322 (by alteration); and in Cot at XX 378 (where Bo preserves Bx, and Bm is defective). Correspondingly, contamination from the **B** Version appears in the **C** portion after Pr 133, where it adds B Pr 106; at Pr 231 *Reule*] *ryne*; at I 160 *comseth a myhte*] *a myȝte bygynneþ*; and at II 112 *and...manye*] *of Rutland sokene*. B's many variants are cited separately, or with one other manuscript, only a few times, as part of complex variants:

[V 494 +G]. VI 223, [318 +F]. VII 1. X 425, 429a, 461. XII 194 -Bm. XIV 52 -Bm, 73, [117 +G], 129 -Bm. XV [103 +α, 264 +α,] 280, [330 +F]. XVI 45 -Cot. [XVIII 2 +W, 431 +F]. XX 13 -Cot, 236 -Cot. Cot *only*: IV 86. XIII 119, 378. XVI 30. XX 236.

The right readings in B that prevent its elimination are given in the list at § 25 above.

Manuscript **G**

§ 28. A second line of transmission from the group-original is represented by **G**, a sixteenth-century copy whose medieval ancestor underwent extensive contamination from **A** (on which see further § 67). The independent descent of G's lost source from g is demonstrated by its freedom from the 75 group errors of y listed in § 22 above.[22] But the majority of its unique right readings are unlikely to preserve from γ readings corrupted severally by w, L, M and also α. In principle, these could be corrections from a **B** copy superior to Bx at certain points. But if so, that lost manuscript inexplicably failed to supply G's ancestor with the many other right readings solely preserved by α, which *ex hypothesi* it should have contained. For the one agreement with α, at XIII 195 (an unusually long Type IIa line inviting easy loss of the first stave), could be a rare case where G alone has accurately preserved γ. There is thus no logical necessity for positing such a lost source, as will become clear. Instead, G's corrections may be more economically attributed to 'benign contamination' from the other versions, particularly **A**. G cannot be eliminated, however, because it uniquely attests 15 right readings (12 of them with other-version support). It also has another 28 such where it is accompanied by one or two copies of both families, with other-version support in 24.

Major I 191 +**ZAC**. II 8 +**AC**. *With one other* MS: III 283 +WC. I 187, 206 +HZAC. *With two* MSS: X 172 +HmBAC. XIII 195 +a. XVIII 160 +YC^{2}C. **Minor** +**ZAC**: Pr 231. I 37, 125, 174. III 124. V 583; *with one* MS I 176 +Cr. I 191; III 160 +F. IV 99 +M, 105 +H; *with two* MSS I 199, II 75 +HF; VI 277 +BF. +**AC**: Pr 67. VII 109, 146; *with one* MS V 628 +F, 638 +W; VIII 38, X 70, 420 +F; *with two* MSS VII 194 +α; X 172 +HmB. +**C**: Pr 182; *with* R XIII 424; *with* α Pr 205; XI 129. +**Z,-A**: *with* LR V 382. *With no other-version support*: VI 161, XVII 86 (*both* +α).

Of these, only in Pr 182 is G supported solely by **C** (there being no **ZA** parallel) and here, given the line's 'T-type' metrical structure,[23] haplography could well account for coincidental loss of *þo* in w, y, L, M, H and α, thus obviating the need to presume *ad hoc* correction from a copy of **C**. For it is noteworthy that in the other listed cases[24] G's ancestor could in principle have derived all its correct readings from an **A** manuscript. This possibility is indirectly strengthened by half a dozen more where G has a reading that has been accepted in the edited text for **A** or **C** but is here rejected for **B**, or has an **A** reading judged erroneous for that version. In some 15 of the errors listed below, G is accompanied by one of the other manuscripts extensively contaminated from **A**:

Major Pr 62 +FA, 82 +A-MSS uHK. I 8 +HA, 41 +*A*-?duJ, 96 +Ax. IV 107 +*A*-U, 141 +A. VIII 81 +F (*so A*-MSS ChRUW: *visual error or induced by contextual suggestion*). **Minor** Pr 34 +HA. I 48 +HA, 109 +A. III 3 +F; (*so A*-ChVE). 46 +HA, 109 +HA, 115 +HA, 293 +A. IV 137 +A, 193 (*so A*-wE). V 481 +FC. 634 +FA. VI 56 +A, 204 +A-*r*ʲJLK. VII 56 +FC, 147 +FC, 180 +FA. X 180 +FA, 420 +A.

Of the remaining errors that G shares disjunctively with the two other manuscripts showing **A** contamination elsewhere (in all about 140 with F and 40 with H), the following few are recorded as part of a set of complex variants:

F: **Major** I 38 *L. om* (*probably homoarchy*). 136. **Minor** Pr 57. III 264. V 257, 628 (*cf.* **AC**). VI 94 (*cf.* **ZAC**). 196. VII 69, 177 (*cf.* **C**). VIII 93. H: **Major** I 186.

But despite their large numbers, G's agreements with both H and F are nearly all minor, and most are trivial.

§ 29. Finally, of G's numerous individual errors 76 are in the Apparatus amongst the complex variants of certain readings, major ones being asterisked:

Pr 42, 61, 76, 96, 212. I 139, 182, 196, 209. II 20, 166, 219. III 36, 118 +**ZAC**. IV 36, *155 , 190. V 84, 179, *283, 305, *469, 565, 609. VI 9, 124 +**ZAC**, *151, 180, 241, 318. VII 92, 152, 189. VIII 48. IX 149, 158. X 337, 342, 391, *459. XI 60, 79, 86, 138, 149, 178, *435. XII 138, 176, 202, 210, 212*a*, 288. XIII 3, 39, 96, 119, 300, 343, 394. XIV *89, 253, 267. XV 53, 78, *116, *443, 593. XVI 274. XVII 282, 295. XVIII 147, *423. XX 45.

Extensive contamination from **A** has given G not only several readings here rejected for **B** but also a number preferred as likely to correspond to an original corrupted in Bx. These suffice to make it the most significant γ witness (see further §§ 67–8 below).

(b) Three Individual Manuscripts

Manuscript **H**

§ 30. Outside the complex sub-family γ, manuscripts L, M and H each merit group status, since none descends from the others or from γ. **H** is a conjoint text made up of B Pr–V 125 followed by an A-text of the **m** family designated H[3] (*A Version* §§ 28–9 above). Notwithstanding K–D's hesitancy,[25] there is little doubt that H descends from β or that its right readings are indeed 'by correction'. As with G, on the most economical hypothesis these come not from a lost **B** source but from **A**. In its **B** portion H shares all the β family's major wrong readings except for those listed in § 31 below. Four individual errors are derivatives from β (I 70, III 32, IV 94 and V 15) and a fifth (V 76), while it could be a reflex of the reading preserved in α, is probably also a more explicit form of β. H cannot derive from L or M, as it lacks their distinctive errors; the only γ witness it accompanies is G, with which it has about 40 exclusive agreements in error; and its closest associate is F, with which it has some 90 agreements. Most striking of all, however, is the extensive contamination from **A** shown in H's individual errors and in those shared with F and G. This probably accounts also for its 26 right readings, some found in one α or β copy (§ 32, end), a marked feature explicitly noted below. H's postulated **A** source is shown by II 123 to have been of the r^l type; Pr 10 and possibly 213 agree with the r^l sub-group u; and V 15 with U, a member of this pair. Other agreements at Pr 7 and II 159 *segges*] *men* (with **A** manuscript V), and at Pr 225 and I 186 (with **A** manuscript M), seem to contradict H's r^l affinities. But on balance these contaminations, presumably present in its immediate source (*h*) and perhaps partly memorial in character, may be taken to come from an A-Text close to u (see further § 67 below). This conclusion is consistent with its date, a generation later than U.

§ 31. H shares some 90 errors with F, and in the following list of major agreements, ten omitted in the Apparatus have been added:

Major Pr 7 +Cr, AvW, 44 +**A**, 46 +AHW, 74 +ARUEH, 163, 213 +Au. I 1 merke] derke +**A**-duVK, 91, 123 garte] made, 162 +CF. II 159 segges] men +AV, 163. III 69–72 *ll. om*, 166 now] oure +AuChvM, 225 kynne] manere of +AH, CAG, 265. IV 16 to ryde] *om.* 189 Erles] Lordes. V 37 dide] seyde. 78 discryue] discry3e +AuChLJEAM, 114 dedly] euere.

Of the remaining 70, which are minor, 21 are listed in the Apparatus:

Minor Pr 23, 31, 42, 44 +**A**, 62, 73, 78 +*A*tuHE, 85, 107, 116, 124, 212 +*A*UK. I 183, 202, 209. II 29, 40, 149. III 94, 162, 265.

None of these, however, is of such a kind that it could not be coincidental. The most significant, omission of III 69–72, could have been mechanically caused by the repetition of 65 at 70 or be due to clerical censorship of an injunction to noblemen that was judged imprudent. No immediate reason appears for loss of I 91, unless this too was censorship provoked by taking the statement over-literally (the phrasing being uncomfortably close to that of C I 110). A genetic relationship between H and F would, then, seem unlikely.

§ 32. H also shares over 40 errors with G (*K–D*, p. 60), which are fewer and (more important) little more impressive in quality than those with F (cf. § 25 above). A dozen are given in the Apparatus, the parallel agreement of seven with **A** possibly explaining the link with G, which was similarly contaminated from **A** (§ 28 above):

Major Pr 34 +**A**. I 8 +**A**, 186^2 [*coinciding gloss of hard word*]. **Minor** Pr 111, 173. I 48 +**A**, 51 +**A**. II 5, 45. III 46 +**A**, 109 +**A**, 115 +**A**.

Finally, H has ten exclusive agreements with all or some **A** copies:

Major Pr 63. I 186 (= M). II 123 (= rE), 163, 197 *leeste*] *beste* (= **A**-TDuJWM). IV 160. V 15 (= U). **Minor** Pr 225 (= M). I 59. III 73.

H is the sole authority for no **B** readings without other-version support; but despite its brevity it remains a significant witness that cannot be eliminated, because it preserves, *with* other-version support, 26 readings that appear intrinsically superior to those of Bx. Of these it attests 15 alone and another 11 along with one or two copies of either family. Pr 99 may be a felicitous guess, a borrowing from α (R is defective here) or an echo of **C**; but the rest could all come from **A** (see § 67 below):

Major +**ZAC**: Pr 41, 59 (*here closest to* Ar), 76. I 11 (*so A*-uHE). 187 +G, 206 +G. IV 105 +G, 145 (*almost right; so* **Z**), 190. +**AC**: II 9 +F ?= α). III 41, 48. **Minor** +**ZAC**: II 75 +GF, 216 +αG. III 3 +B, 114 +G, 132 +G. IV 47, 90, 94 +Cr. +**AC**: III 226. +**A**: I 11 (*almost right; closest to A*uE), 186 (*almost right; so A*M). III 41 (*almost right*), 251 +R. +**C**: Pr 99 (α *absent*).

Of H's individual variants, all are recorded where a lemma is given for a line.

Manuscript **M**

§ 33. **M** is of less value than H, even though present for the whole text. Its affinities with L and H include probable loss of Pr 39b in its exemplar, for which it inserts a Latin half-line. But M cannot derive from either, being a generation earlier than H and lacking such major errors of L as the omission of I 37b–38a. This latter instance exemplifies M's extensive correction (at more than one stage) from γ sources; but it cannot derive directly from γ either, since it lacks the 40 γ errors (§ 12 above). M's immediate ancestor *m* is postulated in order to account for both its first-stage γ variants and for its handful of unique right readings. That *m* was a fairly accurate copy of β is suggested by four minor cases more probably due to accurate transmission of the family original than to collation with a manuscript of the α family: VII 20, XII 16, XV 121 and 196. Before M was copied, its source *m* received, at certain points, good corrections of two kinds. Perhaps the result of intelligent scribal conjecture are those at X 60, XI 41 and XII 245 (the right reading at VI 119, on the other hand, is visibly by addition in M itself). Others probably came from collation with a γ source, such as the three at I 31, XIV 106 and XVIII 31, one also found in g at X 124 (possibly coincidental) and two in w at Pr 2 and 31. Four further readings, agreeing with g and α at I 37 and X 124, with Crg and α at I 38, and with w and α at XX 306, may also be due to collation or, just as probably, transmit *m*'s correct β reading where L has corrupted it. By way of contrast, in VI 326 a later hand has restored a likely β (and Bx) reading earlier wrongly adapted to that of γ. At least seven other such alterations are to the right reading. Those at III 284, XIII 223 and XIX 117 erase, and those at VI 119, XII 161 and XIII 191 add to a probable Bx reading by looking to **A** or **C**. That at XVII 184–85 corrects (from the same source as Cr) the same mechanical error found in the reading of γ.

§ 34. M's transmission history was thus more complex than those of H or L. But unfortunately its borrowings from γ, whether made in *m* or after M was copied, mostly corrupted a manuscript that had begun as a reliable representative of β. The following 74 M variants (30 major) from the early stage of mistaken 'correction' are divided according to the γ branch sharing them and include in square brackets 18 where one other β copy or α accompanies. Readings omitted from the Apparatus are given in full:

Major γ: II 148. VI 326. XIII 283–4. XIV 1. XV 398, 506. XVI 50, 60. [XVII 339 +L]. XVIII 198, 390. g: V 166 -CB. XI 6.[26] [XIV 167 -Y+F]. w: X 61. [XI 398 -Cr+Bm]. XIII 411 (*a substitution for the senseless* Bx *reading properly corrected by* OC[2]B *from* **C**). XIV 179, [300 +L]. Cr: V 533 dwelleþ] wonyeth. XVII 304. XVIII 383. XIX 4 +F, [321 +L], 380, 399. XX 260. **Minor** g: V 210. [VIII 30 +F]. XIV 146. XV 36. XVI 27.[27] 221. XVII 11, 15, 104 -Cr, 166 -Hm. XVIII 354. g: VI 305. IX 130, 200. XI 233, 339, 372, 377, 416. XII [197 +Hm], 202, [211 +Cr, 289 +Cr]. XIII 131, [134 +Cr]. XIV [46 +F], 215. XV [22 +Hm], 353. [XVII 95 +Cr]. [XVIII 420 (+Hm)]. w: X 177. XIII 411. XV 455, 502. XVIII 84, 347. WCr: [XIII 203 (+G)]. [XV 207 +L]. XVIII 85. Cr: VI 213 (bi-] *om.*). VII 3 (hym] *om.*). XVI 110a. XIX 77.

The incongruence between M's agreement with both w or its components and with g requires explanation, since w and g are separate branches of γ (§ 11 above). Possibly *m* was collated early with exemplars of both w and g types, or all the agreements with either g (25) or w (26) at this phase may result from random variation. Given, however, that M has three times as many *major* agreements with w as with g and that the second phase of visible 'correction' is from a w source (§ 34), it seems likelier that the agreements with g are the random ones. The striking failure of M's source to agree with Cr at I 37 would then have to be ascribed to a particular form of homoteleuton in Cr (one shared by H) and not to the presence of the error in Cr's ancestor (the likeliest source for M's visible correction in I 38). The other three major cases could also be coincidental: the phrase-loss in V 166 due to the unusual line-length, the synonym in XI 6 to obvious substitution of a commoner term and the misunderstanding in XIV 167 to ambiguous spelling in the exemplar.

§ 35. At a second phase of correction, itself carried out in more than one stage, M was altered by erasures, insertions and over-writing in accordance with a copy of w-type. A notable case is XVII 184–85, where M has corrected its γ-type reading from an exemplar which was obviously not L. But since M's visibly altered readings also include at least six major errors shared with Cr and none with any other copy, it would be economic to identify that exemplar with Cr's manuscript original, in which the correction came from outside the γ tradition. No distinction is drawn between these stages of correction in the following list of 34 agreements (20 major), set out as in § 33 above. They include in square brackets six where M is accompanied by one or two other manuscripts:

Major γ: V 208. IX 98*a*. XII 245. XV 63. w: [Pr 149 +GH]. [VI 200 +?G]. XV 224. [XVI 125 +F]. XVIII 299. WCr: [V 492 +YOC²]. IX 118. XIV 317. XV 410. XIX 186. Cr: V 184, 185 me] hym (*both*). IX 101. 127. XVI 110*a*. XVII 160. XIX 76. **Minor** γ: V 441. XII 245. g: XIII 355. w: [III 267 +GHF. 351 +GH]. XV 200. WCr: V 248. 364. XIII 179. XIV 248, 288. Cr XI 288 (take] toke). XIII 413 (dedes *over erasure*). XIV 148 alle] yow a., yow +M).

§ 36. M also has some 35 agreements with F, all minor and most of them trivial. Its dozen agreements with L are rightly dismissed as very slight by K–D (p. 38) and the major instance they identify (*walweþ* VIII 41) is not accepted here as an error. More important is the presumed gap at Pr 39b in *m* which an enterprising later corrector has filled with a Latin version of the half-line, in a manner recalling another intelligent alteration at X 366. As this omission is shared with L and H, it may well be the reflex of a Ø-reading or of &c either in β or in a common source intermediate between <LMH> and β; for it is hard to see how each individual witness lost the English b-half independently. On the former supposition, γ can only have filled out the line here from **A**. Unfortunately, the exact α reading is unknowable, but if F's omission of the line is accurate, it may be that Bx was defective or contained only the first word and that the four branches of β each attempted to repair the gap independently. Of M's individual errors some 20 only are recorded, as part of a set of complex variants:

Pr 39. IV 20. V 410. 424. VI 9 +**ZA**. 204. IX 135. X 50. 366 (*over erasure*; *so* **A**-ms H³). 377. XIII 270. 284. XIV 316–17*a*. XV 92. XVI 90. XVII 1. 349. XIX 408. XX 271.

M's interest is less textual than bibliographical, in its pointing to activity at a possible single centre of copying responsible for w and its descendants, including perhaps also M. But it contains four unique right readings (III 284, VI 119, XI 41, XII 245), the first three implying knowledge of **A** or **C**, which show signs of an intelligent scribe at work. M therefore cannot be eliminated.

Manuscript **L**

§ 37. If the main interest of H is its felicitous contamination from **A** and that of M its infelicitous 'internal' contamination from γ, that of **L** is its preservation of a complete β text with neither kind of contamination. L has only a few major individual errors of omission, such as the second half of the Latin XVIII 410 and the English b-half of Pr 39 discussed at § 36 above (the first acceptably but the second mistakenly abbreviated to &c). Its only significant pairing is with R; there are no separative LF errors. The dozen agreements of L and α (congruent with those with R) might seem to point to an exclusive ancestor between < Lα > and Bx. But some of the minor ones are probably coincidental and the major examples more economically explained as preserving by pure descent readings where Bx itself was in error and γ corrected from another version (as suggested for Pr 39 at § 36).

Major *With* RF: V 261 (*possibly original and altered in* γ *on comparison with* **C**). XVIII 31 (*perhaps a coincidental misresolution of* *li3þ). *With* R: IV 28 (*need not* = Bx: *possibly coincidental through eyeskip from* fol- > for (*a) hadde). V 351 (?*smoothing of* Bx *trumbled). X 271 (*most probably visual confusion of* l *and* b). **Minor** *With* RF: [I 31 +G]. *With* R: X 425. XIII 338. XIV 106 (?Bx = Ø). XVII 296 (*eyeskip from* so*ry* > so). XVIII 39 (*possibly* Bx *over-explicitness, coincidentally levelled in* F).

§ 38. L's independent descent (< *l* < β < Bx) is, however, collaterally indicated by the more than 50 right readings it shares exclusively with α. In the following list of these, other-version agreement is noted as confirming their probable archetypal character. Agreements with one or two other β copies are in square brackets.

Major *With* RF: V 208 +**AC**, 209 +**A**, -**C**. XIII 158 (L *alt. to* g). XIII 283–84 +**C**. XIV 1, 239 +**C**. XV 398, 506 +**C**. XVI 50 +**C**. XVII 304 +**C**. XVIII 390 +**C**. *With* R: VI 200 +**ZAC**, 225. IX 98*a*. XII 245. XIII 270. XV 63, 494. XX 287. *With* F (R *def.*): XIX 190 +**C**, 217 +**C**. **Minor** *With* RF: II 148 +**ZAC**. VI 326. [XIV 85 +Cr]. XV 36 +**C**, 200. XVI 60, 221 +**C**. XVII 11 +**C**, 15 +**C**, [104 +Cr], 162. XVIII 349 +**C**, 354 +**C**. XX 6. *With* R: Pr 140, [143 +C]. V [383 +**BZAC**], [424 +Hm], 441 (= Bx; *a nearly right reading given parallel emendation in* **C**). VIII 30 +**AC**, 43 - γ**MA** *and* F**C**. IX 64. X 435 (F *def.*), [461 +Cr¹]. XII 196 +**C**. XIII 150, 300, 301, 355. XIV 258 +**C**. XV 187. XVII 81 -**C**. *With* F (R *def.*): XIX 47 +**C**, 94 +**C**, 309 +**C**. *Possible agreements where* L *has mechanical error*: VIII 127 (no] *om* L; +CB). XI 339 (*if* 3e *not an exclamation*). XIX 457 (*if* sowe *not p.t. of* sen).

Among these, one reading shared with RF (XIII 158) shows L visibly altering its exemplar to agree with γ, in a manner recalling M (§ 35 above) and is a case of coincidental error that tests the direct method to its limit. For if the reading *sen* is 'easier,' *deme* may equally be judged 'more explicit', so that, by two well-tried criteria for unoriginality, *either* could be of scribal origin and choice between them is evenly balanced. On the general assumption, however, that L in most cases = β, the complete Lα / ?α agreements specified here may be taken effectively as = Bx. They will therefore be included later among the archetypal readings given at § 57 below, without comment but with other-version support given where available.

§ 39. In conclusion, there are seven instances where L uniquely preserves what on intrinsic grounds has the best claim to be the original reading. In the major cases this may be that of β and thence of Bx; but contamination from **C** remains possible.

Major +**C**: XV 611; XVIII 198 (α *def.*); XIX 38. **Minor** XIV 181. 253 (α *def.*). +**C** XVI 27 (α *def.*); XX 6.

These alone would preclude L's elimination; but the examples in § 38 incidentally illustrate L's general reliability. Thus, though containing no unique material from β (as do both R and F from α), L is indeed what Skeat thought it, the best of the B-Text manuscripts. Its position somewhat resembles that of *r²* in the **A** tradition; but although L's agreements with α are only some two-fifths of those that *r²* has with **m**, this is enough to earn it the status of a group. With due allow-ance, then, for its necessary incompleteness, this edition accordingly treats L (like manuscript R in the **A** tradition) as the primary citation-source for the Bx lemma at all points where β is right but the copy-text W is in error (see IV § 56 below).

(c) *The β family: conclusions*

§ 40. The above survey of the structure of the β family has shown the groups and their constit-uent manuscripts severally to contain something like 116 variants (about 40 of them major) that, on intrinsic grounds and on comparison with the other versions, may be judged original. Some must preserve Bx by direct descent through β, but others appear to have come in by contamination from manuscripts of **A** or **C**. As none of the witnesses except Hm (which has no unique right readings but some interesting variants) can therefore be eliminated, all have been collated. The evidence for the postulated family manuscript β as the common source of γ, *h*, *m* and *l* is the body of 685 wrong readings, 248 of them major, shared by all four branches (three after H ceases). In about 515 of these, α with other-version support, and in another 110 α standing alone, has been preferred to the certain or likely β reading. The numbers of α variants adopted rise to 618 with other-version support and to 142 without it, if those also attested by some β witnesses are added (all are included in the list). But in about a dozen major examples of these, the text of β cannot be regarded as certain. It is interesting therefore that, in marked contrast, ten times as many of the *minor* α variants adopted into the text are readings shared by one or more other β manuscripts. In principle, therefore, perhaps only about three-quarters of the total minor category could be securely taken as representing the exclusive family reading of β.[28] Secondly, where consensus is lacking, direct analysis of the competing variants must be used to discriminate the probable family reading within the four branches, severally or in combination. Certainty as to what β reads here is thus effectively half of that which obtains for the α family, where only two representatives survive.

§ 41. That all the β variants in question are indeed agreements in error is clear when they are compared with α and the available **Z**, **A** and **C** parallels.[29] This situation closely resembles what we find in the **A** Version; so, allowing for occasional non-unanimous attestation, the secure evidence for β may be set out below in the form earlier used for the two families of **A** (see *A Version §§ 23, 47 above*). It thus divides both by major and minor instances and according to the other-version support for the readings adopted. The lemmata are from α unless noted otherwise, the variants from β. As with **A**, for reasons of space only major readings are given in full (the most important with *) and the minor ones by reference. A minus sign indicates agreement of R or F with the rejected β variant; a plus, agreement of another β witness with the lemma.

§ 42. **Readings with other-version support**

(i) Major

(a) *Both* **R** *and* **F** *present*

+**ZA**: I 70 +G bitrayed arn] bitrayeþ he (*cf.* C). 113 Til] But for. IV 194 he (þou F)] it. VI 103 -pote] -foot.

+**ZAC**: I 73 -R halsede] asked (haskede R). II 183 fobberes (fobbes **ZC**)] Freres. 210 -R feeris] felawes. III 6 +B world] moolde. 140 +H trewþe] þe trewe. IV 94 meken] ?mengen. V 15 pride] pure p. 469 +Cr knowe] owe. 521 Syse] Synay. 550 of hym] *om.* 557 peril (*om* F)] helþe. VI 30 bukkes (boores F)] brokkes.

+**A**: V 97 -F mayne] manye. 113 men (hem F)] *om.* VII 125 be fooles] by foweles. VIII 46 canon (þe comoun F)] Chanon. 50 -F self] soule. X 154 -F wel] it. 223 þe goode wif †F] Studie. 422 dide] *om.*

+**AC**: II 236 fere] drede. III 63 see] seye. V 84 wryngyede...fust †F] wryngynge he yede. 215 -F barly] b. malt. 326 Tho] Two. 588 -F þat] man. VI 76 -F aske] take. VIII 64 abide me made] brouʒte me aslepe. *X 291–302 *Ll. om.*

+**C**: II 200 Go] To. III 32 +Cr clerke] leode +A. 67 -F god] crist. 214 yerne] renne +A. V 76 shrewe (shryve F) shewe. 126 euere] *om* +A. 181 speche] riʒt. 238 a...Iewes †F] and I. a lesson. 370 and hise sydes] *om.* 495 it (*om* F)] was. VI 39 men] hem. VII 193 -F fyue] foure. X 78–9 *Ll. om.* 314 pure] *om.* *410–12 *Ll. om.* 429a +Cr[23] Sunt] Siue. XI 7 For] That. 8 -F and loue] allone. 41 graiþly] gretly. 59 -F dide] wrouʒte. *110 *L. om.* 121 saue] safly. 131b–32a *om.* 134 -F riʒt] *om.* 138 may al] al to. *159–69 *Ll. om.* 208 children] breþeren. 238 -F for sooþ] *om.* 265 segge] man. *382–91 *Ll. om.* 427b–29a *om.* 433 by my soule] *om.* XII *55–7a *om.* 104 lereþ] ledeþ. *116–25a *Ll. om.* 151–52 *Ll. om.* 218–21 *Ll. misord.* 229 kynde] *om.* 282 Ac] For. 287 trewe. (†F] *om.* XIII 35, 47 mette(s)] macche(s). 50 he; lif] I; as I lyue. 80 and] he. 103 best] wel. 104 drank after] took þe cuppe and d. *165–72a *Ll. om.* *293–99 *Ll. om.* 350 lef] wel. 394

(+BmBo) here (*om* F)] hire. *400–09 *Ll. om.* *437–54 *Ll. om.* XIV 204 þo ribaudes] þat ribaude. 217 Or; or] Arst; þan. *228–38 *Ll. om.* 273 neyȝ is pouerte] to hise seintes. 275 pacience (*om* F)] wiþ p. 292 poore riȝt] any p. 309 þat] and. 316 lered] lettred. XV 25 þouȝte (ofte F)] *om.*p 1116 wolueliche (foxly F)] vnloueliche. 188 .seche] speke.i *244–48 *Ll. om.* *303–04 *Ll. om.* *510–27 *Ll. om.* 528 And nauȝt to] That. 530 -F amonges romaynes] in Romayne; in greete roome F. *572b–75a *Ll. om.* XVI 121 iesus (crist F)] ich. 136 -F arne] was. 140 cene] maundee. 142 so(m)] oon. 199 alle] *om.* 220 pure †F] *om.* 250 buyrn] barn. 262 +HmGC wiþ] mid. wye] man. XVII brynge] bigynne. *69 *L. om.* 86 +G gome] groom. 103 outlawe is] Outlawes. 176 -F pulte] putte. *177b–79a *om.* 179 and] at. 196 he seyde] me þynkeþ. 207 warm] hoot. *218–44 *Ll. om.* 246 tache] tow. 290 semed] were. *309–10 *Ll. om.* 325 smerteþ] smyteþ in. 336 ouȝte] ofte. XVIII] 8 +HmB orgene] Organye. 14 -R on] or. 28 Feiþ…deye] he þe foule fend and fals doom to deeþ. 35 -F forbite] forbete. 87 Iesu (crist F)] hym. 101 deeþ…yvenquisshed] his d. worþ avenged. 129 kynde] kynnes. 156 vertue] venym. 193 -R of] *om.* 202 preie] preue. 269 Laȝar is] hym likeþ. 274 þis lord] hym. 283 I…iseised] siþen I seised. 295 he wente aboute] haþ he gon. 312b–13a *om.* 399 kyn] kynde. 410a (+g) *clarior…amor*] *om.* 411 sharpest] sharpe. XX *37 *L. om.* 38 Philosophres] Wise men. 39 wel elengely] in wildernesse. 55 made] *om.* 62 gladdere] leuere. 63 +HmCr[1]B leute] lente. 67 gile] any while. 102 lefte] leet. 117 -R+WHm brode] blody. 120 +Cr kirke] chirche. 126 -F suede] sente. 191 wange] *om.* 211 Weede; mete] *trs.* 249 lakke] faille. 253 telle] teche. 256 hem] *om.* 260 taken hem wages] hem paie. 263 parisshe] place. 291 shul] wol. 311 +Cr in þe sege] þe segg. 337 frere] segge. 351 here so] so it. 360 -F ben] biten.

(b) *With only* **R** *present*
(*Cf.* **C**): *XIII 170, 172 *Ll. om.*

(c) *With only* **F** *present*
+**ZA**: II 9 +H pureste on] fyneste vpon.

+**AC**: VIII 109b–10a *om.* +**C**: XVIII 426 carolden] dauncede. XIX 43 his] *om.* *56–9 *Ll. om.* 60 yeueþ] yaf. 68 wilnen] willen. 73 riȝt] *om.* 76 Ensense] *om.* 94 Erþeliche] Thre yliche. 117 +CrM oonly] holy. 118 fauntekyn] faunt fyn. 130 and…herde] to here & dombe speke he made. *152b *om.* 173 +CrCot *Dominus*] *Deus.* *237b–38a *om.* 250 +Hm pacience] penaunce. 269 yit…Piers] Grace gaf P. of his goodnesse. 275 aiþes] harewes. 276 Piers greynes] greynes þe. 285 meschief] muchel drynke. 286 out] ne scolde out. *337 *L. om.* 398 Or] That. 411 be…fode] þe comune fede. 457 sowne] seiȝe. 467 toke] seke. XX 7 lyue by] þi bilyue.

(ii) Minor

(a) *Both* **R** *and* **F** *present*
+**Z**: Pr 223. +**ZA**: II 122 +GYH, 171. III 12 +BGMH. IV 142 +HmCrH. V 545. VI 237, 285 +B. VII 62, 96. +**ZAC**: I 45[1], 80 +HmGM, 182, 199 +GH. II 131, 138 +GH, 216 +GH, 226. III 19[2] +CrB, 128, 130–1 +H, 162[1]. IV 103, 141. V 19[1,2], 35, 573 +G, 596. VI 42, 89, 120 +HmCr, 185 +G, 216, 218, 222 +B, 292. VII 57[1,2] +y, 68, 92[1,] 93 +OC[2], 100. +**A**: II 120 +y, 159 +G. V 111, 112. VII 106, 135. VIII 66 +B. IX 53 (*not* Cx), 188. X 20[2], 60, 128, 129, 133, 137 (*not* C), 147, 209, 221[2], 369. +**AC**: Pr 20, 37[2], 215, 216, 229. II 227 +Hm (*not* Z). III 39, 49, 214[1], 229. V 186 +OC[2], 194[1] +GCot,[2] 213, 305, 321[2] -F), 359, 575 +Cot. VI 67[1,2], 95 -RZ. VII 26 +GCB (*not* Z), 181, 186 +g, 194 +G. VIII 72, 89, 116. IX 176[1,2], 194 +B. X 223[1], 377[1,2]. +**C**: Pr 93[1], 109 +H, 205 +G. I 71 +Hm. II 91. III 8, 68, 122 +HmH (*not* ZA), 155 (*not* ZA), 214[2] (*not* A), 301, 327 +G. IV 62 +H-F. V 130, 148 +Hm, 151, 192, 195 -F, 274[2], 317 (*not* A), 321[1] (*not* A), 357, 369, 370[2], 386, 394, 398 +OCB, 403 +Hm, 407, 441a +BoCot, 442, 483, 494, 496, 502, 505 +GCot, 507 +CrG, 603a, 619 (*not* A), 620 (*not* A). VI 45 +Hm (*not* ZA), 52, 80 +OC[2],105, 161 +G. VII 8 +B, 199 (*not* A). VIII 43 -F (*not* A), 57, 59 +WHm. IX 20 (*not* A), 189. X 77, 87, 147 (*not* A), 384 +GM, 391[2], 399 +WCr, 458 (*not* A). XI 7, 20, 26, 37, 43, 58a, 84, 129[2] +G, [145; *cf.* C], 147[1], 200, 204, 238[1] +BM, 262, 288 +W, 348, 350, 367 +CrCot, 401, 415 -F. XII 138 +Cr, 203, 213[1,2], 244, 285[1,2.] XIII 4 +HmG, 56, 92, 93, 112, 330, 349, 364, 398, 410, 423 -F, 426. XIV [40; *cf.* C], 41 +OC[2], 51, 52[1], 66[1,2] -F, 67 +Cr, 72 -F, 205, 239, 257[1] +WCrM, 257[2] +CB-F, 265 -F, 289[2,] 292[2] -F, 295 -F, 301 -F, 307 -F, 310 -F, 313 -F. XV 5 +WCrBM, 18 -F, 20 +HmCrY, 55a, 73[1], 74 +G-F, 78, 88, 100, 115, 162a +M, 193, 256, 317a[1,2], 355, 359, 362, 494, 502, 529[1,;2] +W, 531[1,2], 575[1,2], 585, 587, 591. XVI 30, 76, 83 +Cr, 88 +Cr, 115, 123, 148, 176, 254[2], 275. XVII 1, 3, 10, 13, 14a, 15 +CrG, 23, 57, 65, 74, 85, 137 +WHm, 139, 141, 166, 176[2], 181, 202, 204[1,2], 264, 299[1,2], 302, 320, 329[1,2], 330 -F, 336[1], 339 +w, 348[1,2]. XVIII 12, 35a -F, 45, 51 -F, 85, 96 +HmCrOB, 147[1], 167, 170, 181, 192 +Cr[3]C[2]B, 241 +WCrO, 248, 261, 265, 271, 276 +Cr, 277 +wCB, 280, 319, 342, 360, 364, 376[1], 380, 384. XX 35 +CrG, 36, 38[2] +GC[2], 42, 60[1,2], 78, 87, 93, 97, 114, 119, 125 +g, 136 +Hm, 138, 139, 141, 142, 147 +Cr[23]g, 150 +W, 171 -F, 183, 194, 198[1,2], 207[1,2], 208, 210, 218, 221, 277, 283[1,2], 290 +Cr, 303 +WCr[1]B, 306 +w, 321 +G, 327, 343, 349, 357, 361 -F, 364 -F, 366 +Crg-R, 383.

(b) *Only* **F** *present*
+**ZA**: II 171. +**ZAC**: I 182, 199 +GH. +**A**: VIII 102[1]. +**AC**: Pr 20, 37[2]. +**C**: Pr 93[1,] 109 +H. I 141a. XVIII 429. XIX 24,

48, 64 +YBoCot, 77 +G, 91, 109, 120, 140^2, $145^{1,2}$, 149, 151, 151/2, 154, 158, 180 +GC^2, 209, 217, 224^1, 224^2 +Cr^{23}, 229, 279^1, 282^2, 314, 339, 384 +Y, 399 +g, 437 +WCr, $450^{1,2}$, 452, 461^2, 483a. XX 1, 3, 9, 11, 13^2, 26 +G.

§ 43. **Readings with no other-version parallel**

(i) Major

(a) *Both* **R** *and* **F** *present*

II 91 (cf. **C**) wenynges] wedes. 176 deuoutrye] Auoutrye. V 176 (cf. **C**) wel] wyn. 270 -F quod Repentaunce] om. 410 I late] l. I passe. 420 (it) clausemele] oon clause wel. VIII 127 no man (man *om* F)] womman (man L). IX 60 wiзt] man. 96^1 drad hym] om. X 47 worþ] зifte / value (cf. **A**). 239 -F propre] *om.* 284 manliche (soþly F)] saufly. 303 skile and scorn but if he] scorn but if a clerk wol. *368 *L. om.* 472 kunnyng] knowyng. XI 5 til I was †F] weex I. 179^2 -F oure lord] god. 184 -F iuele] heele. *196 *L. om.* 281 wise] parfite. 396 wrouзte] dide. [398 +OC^2 þolieþ] þolie. 419 þe to] to be. XIII 195 +G Marie] *om.* 267 bake] om. 272 grete] good. 290 bold] badde. 323 lakkynge] laughynge. 361 wittes wyes] which wey. 391 conscience] herte. XIV 28 which is] with his. 141 two heuenes for] heuene in. *183 *L. om.* 189 pouke] pope. 212^2 riche] Richesse. 274 þat...preise] ye preise faste. XV 89 muche (grete R)] long. 106 auзt †F] noзt. 337 ful] *om.* *395 *L. om.* 422 fyndynge] almesse. XVI 43 brewe] breke. 50 (cf. **C**) planke] plante. 119 þat] and. XVII *112a *L. om.* XVIII 76 þrowe] tyme. 109^2 lese] cesse. 356^2 þing] þo.

(b) *With only* **R** *present*

XI 339 зede] зe / þe. XV 460 keperes] cropers. *471–84, 489a *Ll. om.* XVII 190 ypersed] yperiss(h)ed.

(c) *With only* **F** *present*

Pr 122^2 lif] man. I 149 þat spice; vseþ] trs.

(ii) Minor

(a) *Both* **R** *and* **F** *present*

II 51, 229 +CrH. III 100 +H, 231, 235 +H. V 79 +BH, 219 +y, 274 -F, 279, 408, 491, 547. VI 48^1 +Hm, 132 +G, 157, 202. VII 14 +wB, 70. IX 35, 48 +W, 86^2, 119, 122 +Hm, 178, 190. X 114a, 218, 262a, 379, 473. XI 193^1 +g, 197, 214 +$WHmC^2$, 277 +$WHmCr^1$, 279 +CrM, 289 +WBM, 295 +B, 330. XII 16 +M, 30, 34, 49, 66, 73, 78. XIII 221, 229, 255a +OC^2Cot, 280, 376 +WCrM, 387 -F,424 +G, 455, 456. XIV 88 +HmCrB, 116 +Hmg, 119, 131a +OC^2, 135^1, 168, 182 -F, 186 +WCr, 198^2. XV 90 -F, 109, 121, 144, 196 +M, 147 +B, 207, 211 +W, 281, 282, 283, 323 +CrM, $342a^1$, 386^1. XVI 9 +Crg, 11 +Cr^{23}g, 45 +GCot, 77, 110a, 160, 184 +y-F. XVII 166, 171^2. XVIII 303, 313^2, 345, 356^1.

(b) *With only* **F** *present* I 153.

iv. *The* α *family of manuscripts*: R *and* F

§ 44. The second family has only two surviving copies, **R** and **F**, neither a complete representative of the α text. R is physically defective at three points and F's exemplar might have been so at one point. Of R's two extant portions Lansdowne 398, which formed the original first quire of Rawlinson Poetry 38, has lost folios 1, 2, 7 and 8 and thus lacks Pr 1–124 and I 141–II 40. The Rawlinson portion has lost all eight folios of quire 14, which contained XVIII 413–XX 26. Otherwise the surviving part of R is almost as complete as that of L, lacking only three and a half text-lines (VIII 101–2, 104 and 105a) and one citation-line (XVII 112a). Unluckily, however, the material in the lost leaves amounts to 764 text-lines and 14 citation-lines, a quantity comparable to that absent from the Digby 102 copy that is substantively the best of the **C** witnesses (see *C Version* § 19 below). These losses are partly made good by F in all R's defective sections, though F's own omissions include about 164 text-lines and four citation-lines. The largest of these, XV 428a–91, may have been due to loss of a leaf in its exemplar (here called *f*), and is fortunately present in R. Although their closeness in date does not totally preclude it, neither copy is likely to derive from the other. Sean Taylor[30] claims on palaeographical grounds that the scribe of Corpus 201 knew Rawlinson and judges the visible alterations in R to be in his hand. His further contention, that R may have served as F's exemplar, would be more plausible if it were the case that the F scribe had access to R in its undefective state. However, very few readings where F is superior to R and to β are such that they cannot be due to consultation of an **A** or **C** copy but must be ascribed to felicitous conjecture or to correction from a **B** exemplar independent of α or from outside the Bx tradition.[31] The omitted, the spurious and even the sophisticated lines are, to be sure, compatible with F's derivation from R. But it is hard to accept that its many contaminations from **A**, some of them necessary corrections of archetypal errors, were directly introduced by the Corpus scribe, for these have left no visible traces in F. The postulated exemplar *f* must therefore have existed, and this could have been based on R. But whether or not (as would seem likely) *f* also had such features, F as it now stands is a heavily sophisticated witness, with a text re-written wholesale in places, frequently 'improving' the alliteration and altering the style (see e.g. V 276*a*, 573). Where direct comparison is possible, F emerges as about ten times less accurate than R; so in most points of difference between them, R is the only reliable witness to the text of α. Nevertheless, F does sometimes preserve α where R is defective and sometimes even correctly against R. It is, further, the sole witness to five lines and five half-lines of the B-Text, mostly in Passus XIX, which are confirmed as authentic on comparison with the B[1] material preserved by **C**. Skeat was therefore mistaken to reject the manuscript outright, and K–D deserve full credit for making use of it. But to the present editor, they over-estimate F's value and sometimes misinterpret the nature of its distinctive readings.

§ 45. The intrinsic worth of manuscript **R** was, on the other hand, recognised by Skeat, who discovered it, and is much greater than that of F. For R is specifically the sole source of some eighteen lines of text and also a far more faithful general witness to α. Particularly important are XV 471–84, where F is defective, and without which the text of the **B** Version would be incomplete. R does not group significantly with any β manuscript except L, and these agreements, as already argued at §§ 37–8 above, seem due not to descent from an exclusive common ancestor but to each copy's independently preserving at these points its ancestral reading and thence that of Bx. Like L, R in the present editor's judgement preserves a pure B-Text uncontaminated from any other version (see § 39). Its many agreements with **C** against β may be interpreted as signifying that α often accurately transmitted Bx where β corrupted it. Finally, R contains no spurious material of its own, since the half-line after the corrupt form of XVII 8 and the three-line substitution for the presumably lost III 51–62 may both be inferred to have been present in α.

§ 46. By contrast **F**, as already noted, groups extensively with two β manuscripts, G and H, in about 140 and 90 readings respectively. However, where these agreements are not minor and probably coincidental, what they seem to indicate is common influence from **A** in all three copies (§§ 29–30 and 66–8). F is characterised first by contamination from **A**, benign at VIII 109*b*–10*a*, where the sense requires two half-lines presumed lost by Bx but possessing a slightly revised **C** parallel. In five instances elsewhere, the material does not belong in the B-Text: after Pr 94, F adds A Pr 95, and it inserts corrupt reflexes of parallel **A** lines in VIII after 49, 80, 101 and 102 (= A IX 45, 71, 93 and 95). The absence of these **A** lines from **C** (in contrast to VIII 109–10 cited above) indicates that they had been removed in the revision to **B**. It may be surmised that all of them, including the latter, were added in *f* before F was copied. The confused character of the presumptive α text round about 99–108, reflected in omission and misordering in both witnesses, might indeed have been what prompted *f*'s scribe to consult another copy of the poem. The line inserted after Pr 94 shows that he already knew the **A** Version, and it seems that he went on to adopt further readings from it at VIII 105b and 106b. For comparison of the latter with C X 104–05, a slightly revised form of the text in βR, reveals it to be not the original B-Text but that of A IX 98b and 99b. F also omits 164 text-lines and six citation-lines.

Pr 3, 33b–34a, 39, 41, 50–4, 98 (*spur. l. instead.*), 99. I 119, 157. II 11. III *69–72, 350. IV 52, 67, 193. V 275 (4 *spur. ll. inst.*), 296, 369, 471, 547, 583–84, 605. VI 161. VII 100, 176a. VIII 21, 99–100. IX 142, 221. X 21, 221, 279–80, 353a, 355, 397a, 435. XI 5 (6 *spur. ll. instead.*), 50, 247, *337–39, 414. XII 61, 167. XIII 170, 172, 301. XIV 22 (2 *spur. ll. instead.*), 41, 201, 212a, 215, 304. XV 218, 353, *428–91, 508. XVI 186, 248. XVII 186b–91a. XVIII 319a, 423. XIX 88b–89a, 161a–62, 205–07, 247, 439–40. XX 301.

Finally, F inserts some 50 spurious lines at 25 points (to the list in *K–D* 222–23 should be added its substitute for Pr 98). Like its contaminations and omissions, these evince less 'typical' scribal negligence than complete unconcern for fidelity to the original. Assuming the presence of these lines in *f,* it might thus seem more likely that this was produced by an amateur making over the text according to his own lights than by a professional scribe required to provide as accurate a copy as possible of his exemplar. A similar engagement with the poem's internal structure may underlie the manuscript's idiosyncratic passus-divisions.[32] Despite these deficiencies, however, F cannot be eliminated. Where R is absent, it attests against β some 90 right readings, 35 of them major, recorded in §§ 48 and 49 as potentially the readings of α. And where R is present but errs with β, F is right in at least the 21 instances listed, whether these are ascribed (as at V 23) to α or (as in VIII 109–10 and most cases) to contamination:

Major I 73. II 210. V 23. VII 174/5 (*l. div.*). VIII 109b–110a. XVIII 14, 193. **Minor** I 43, 45, [57 +Cr^{23}H]. II 51, [120 +y]. III 145. IV 15. V 32, 597. VI 95. VII 113. [VIII 83 +CB]. [XIII 223 +Cr]. XV 89.

§ 47. The special features of the α family are four. The first is the presence, among 625 exclusive right readings, of some 170 authentic lines and 15 half-lines not found in β. These have already appeared as lemmata at §§ 42–3, but for convenience they will be given together in a group at § 58 below. The second is the absence of some 203 lines and 18 half-lines found in the other family at 85 separate locations; these will be listed together at § 56. The third is some nine spurious lines occurring at three points where α lacks material present in β: III 51–62, IX 170–72 and XVI 270–73 (a tenth line after XVII 8 that K–D accept as authentic is also treated here as spurious; see the *Textual Notes ad loc*). The fourth feature is a body of some 411 other errors, about 255 of them major. In 245 of these (213 major) the α variant has been rejected for a β reading with other-version support, in the remaining 166 (41 of them major) for a β variant with no other-version support. Additionally, there is a body of readings where, as against the adopted β variant, α may possibly have been preserved in its one extant witness. In some 150 of these (85 major) there is other-version support for the β reading, but in 66 (about 20 major) none. Of the roughly 190 readings attested by F alone, it appears antecedently unlikely that more than about 10% preserve α, whereas of the 25 readings in R alone, most may be reliably held to do so. In this judgement, qualitative evaluation of specific readings is guided in part by the general character of F as a witness to α.

§ 48. **Readings with other-version support**

The evidence for α is set out in the same way as that for β at §§ 42–3 above. Unless specified otherwise, the lemmata represent β and the variants are from R as the presumed readings of α. A minus sign indicates agreement of R or F with the lemma, a plus sign that the β ms / other version denoted shares the rejected α reading, square brackets that R and F have divergent errors and so α cannot be reliably discerned:

(i) Major

(a) (*Both* **R** *and* **F** *present*)

+**Z**: VI 103² atwo] at / awey (*cf.* **A**).

+**ZA**: I 44 holdeþ] kepeth +**C**, *82 *L. om.* 134 siȝte of] *om.* II 108 which] þis +HC. 111 Rutland] rokeland. III 127 (*and cf.* **C**) false] faire. IV 118 an hyne] nauȝte / vanyte. VI 238 mnam] man +BoCot. VII 31 som] *om.* *41*a L. om.*

+**ZAC**: Pr 213 poundes] poudres / pownded. I 133 and troneþ] for to saue. 138 yet mote ye kenne me] I mote lerne. III 5 sooþ-] couth- / sotil-. *149b–50a *om* (*spur.* 149b F). 187 kyng] kniȝt. 205 blood] lond. IV 55 hewen] hennes. 65 my lord] *om* +CrH. 90 moore] be. V 41 preide] preued. 70 al] *om.* 73 þe Saterday] on þe day. 519 bolle] bulle. 552 hewe... euen] men þat þei ne haue it anone. 611 forþ] *om.* VI 86–8 *mis-div.* 88 defende it (*trs* b)] Ikepid it. for...bileue] *om.* *217 *L. om.* 245 wel] for. 301 wolde wastour] ne wolde no w. 307 noȝt] *om.* *309b–10a *om.* VII 37 marchauntȝ murie manye] manye marchauntz þat. 39–40 *mis-div. with padding*: mede] m. for þat craft is schrewed.

+**ZC**: I 41 seeþ] sueth.

+**A**: Pr 225 þe longe day] þe fayre d. F; here dayes here R (*cf.* **C**). III 219 biddynge] beggyng. VI 113 To] And ȝeed to. VII 133 þe Abbesse] *om.* 156 cleyme] reue. 182 renkes] thenke. VIII 51 sleuþe] soule +Hm. *103 *L. om.* IX 162 crist] Ihesus. X 14 on erþe] here. 72 tyme] *om* +**C**. 135 bolde] *om.* 167 speche] berynge. 185 sotile] sauȝtele. 189 Loke] loue. þee likeþ] þow thenke. 192 *simu-*] simi-(+Cr²³CotL). 217 founded] (by)fond. 376 witnesseþ] telleth.

+**AC**: III *51–62 *Three ll. like* A III 50–1. 63 of youre house] to ȝow alle. 277 ende] endede +Hm. V 316 dysshere] dissheres douȝter. 344 þat herde] *om.* VI 230 þee] god. 276 be þow] yow yow / þe. VII 125 he] or. 191 didest] dost. IX 2 kynnes] maner. 29 lisse] blisse +CrGBM. 135 ywasshen] Iwasted. 169 cheeste; choppes] iangelynge; gaying. *170–72 *Three spur. ll.* *200–03 *Ll. om.* X 1 hote] called. *424 *L. om.* +**C**: Pr 135 ius] vis. 171–72 *Ll. om.* I 119 *et...altissimo] &c.* II 85 cheste] gestes. III 91 loue] lord. 310 spille] lese. IV 26 Mede...erþe] on e. m. þe mayde maketh. 40 Reson] *om.* 104 (*cf.* **C**) crist] god (*cf.* **ZA**). 173 wiþ; loked] *om*; loke. V 261 heires] vssue +L. 406 feble] seke. 505 ruþe] mercy. VI 48 cherles] clerkes. IX *160–61 *Ll. om.* *166 *L. om.* *179–85 *Ll. om.* X 250 merite] mercy. XI 4 wo] sorwe. 6 mette me þanne] me tydde to dreme. *46 *L. om.* 58 *pecuniosus*] pecunious +B. 60 yarn] ran +Hm (ȝeede F). 108 if; it knewe] *om*; it knowe. 125 reneye] receyue. 129 rome] renne +Cr. 130 a reneyed] he renneth. 255 folwe] wolde / welde. 356 brouȝten] brynge (bredde R). 434 þyng] *om* (man F). 435 euery man shonyeth] no man loueth. XII 59 gras] grace. 99 eiȝen] siȝte. 107 witted] wedded. 131 (*cf.* **C**) marke] make (+Cr). 135 broȝt] bouȝte. *140–47a *Ll. om.* 159 what manere] whanere (ensample F). *169 *L. om.* 178 keuereth] kenneth. *185 *L. om.* 186 to book sette] sette to scole. 212a *Quia reddit*] And *reddite*. 215 assoille] telle. 233 iogele] iangele. 260 pureliche] priueliche. 266 logik] glosing. XIII *14–20 *Ll. om.* 45 and wepe] (with) many. 80 noȝt] *om* (yt F). 331a *Et alibi...acutus om.* 373b–74a *om.* XIV 52 gyues] feytoures. 59 bettre] leuere. *157–59 *Ll. om.* 212 heiȝe] riȝt +G. 213 preesseth] precheth. *252–3 *Ll. om.* 263 lond] lorde. 276a, 306 *sollici-*] soli- +OC²B. 288b *om.* 293 wiȝtes] wittes. XV 42 *-itanus*] -anus. *72 *L. om.* 107 vn-] *om* +WCrG. 111 dongehill] dongoun. 118 *-greditur*; *-tum*; *-docium*; *-andum*] -cedit; -ta; -dos; -atum. 156 saueour] god +Cr²³. 293 soden] eeten. 297 manye longe yeres] amonges wilde bestes. 317a *brutorum...sufficiat*] *om.* 503 and...bileueþ] to on persone to helpe. 528 mennes] *om* +Hm. *532–68 *Ll. om.* 584 men] it hem. XVI 27b–28a *om.* 198 children] barnes. 252 seiȝ] seyde. *264 *L. om.* 270–73 *Three spur. ll. inst.* XVII 7b *om.* 8 Luciferis lordshipe] sathanas power. *A spurious half-line after.* *37–47 *Ll. om.* 95 he] *om.* 107 seigh] seith (+GC²). 109 vnhardy þat] vn-. *113²24 *Ll. om.* 140 loued] leued. 148 at] and. 152 an hand] a fust. 160 -inne] *om.* *218–44 *Ll. om.* 254 *ingratus...kynde] ingrat...kynne. 296 now] nouȝt. 300 þoruȝ] to. 312 nounpower] nounper. *316 *L. om.* 340 cause] resoun. XVIII 31 lieþ] likth +L. 41 Iewes] *om.* 62 depe] here. 83 stode] stede. 86 vnspered] opned. 93 for] hem for. 109a *cessabit vnxio vestra] om.* 147 I] *om.* 157 fordo] do. *179 *L. om.* 182 my suster] *om.* *198 *L. om.* 216 ynoȝ] nouȝte. 218 murþe] ioye. 226 lisse] blisse +GY. 233 wise of] men in. 246 see] mone. 251 leue] ?leese (*om* R). *252–53 *Ll. om.* 276 he robbeþ] & robbe. 296 tyme] *om.* 363 widder] grettere. 383 iu-] *om* +YOCBL. XX 48 bide] bydde +g. 62 wel] *om* +G. 65 were] we. 91 Confort a] *om* (a komely F). 132 bright] rede. 151 kille] calle. 152 lepte aside] seith *occide*. 158 wo] *om.* 174 dyas] dayes. 202 me] my lif. 214 Conscience] *om.* 233 for] for no. *238–39 *Ll. om.* 256 newe and] *trs* 265 Hir ordre and] heraude. 269 out of] of / ouer on(y).

(b) *With only* **R** *present*

+**A**: X 221 wightly] miȝteliche. +**C**: VIII 21 sooþly] *om.* 100 oon] and. to...boþe] *om.* *No o-v.*: XV 218 The] To. 443 garte] and grete +B.

(c) *With only* **F** *present*

+**ZA**: Pr 27. I 145 be] is good. 146 after] soone. +**ZAC**: *Pr 3 *L. om.* 8 Vnder] Vpon. 9 watre*s*] wawys. 22 *L. mispl.* 42 Faiteden] & fele f. 43 to bedde] togydre. 46 pli3ten] pyght*yn* (+H). *53–4 *Ll. om.* 60 good] selue. I 175 ruþe] mercy. 184 no man] alle men. 186 feet] fewte. 196 no3t] *om.* 201 deele] d. with. II 5 lo] se. *11 *L. om.* 28 kam...bettre] am...b. roote. +**AC**: Pr 37 han] welden. 39 **L. om.* 62 Manye] Fele. freres] *om* +G. 71 -hede] oþis. auowes] fele a. 74 bonched] blessid +H. 75 rau3te] lawhte. 77 leneþ it] beleven on. 78 bisshop yblessed and] blessynge bisshop. 82 peple] men; poraille b. 83 parisshe preestes] vikerys. +**A**: Pr 33b–34a *om.* 205 also...heuene] it ys þe. gr. g. þat good into blisse. 208 þat...bettre] tak it if þou lyke. +**C** Pr 88 in tokene] to knowe. *94 *After this* A Pr 95. 96 sitten] þey Iuggyn. *98 *Spur. l. instead* *99 *L. om.* 103 alle vertues] hevene. 112 hym] he. I 155 þis fold] manhode. *157 *L. om.* 162 taxeþ] askeþ (+H). 202 þat(1)] date. II 12 þereon rede] set abowhte with. 22 bilowen h*ym*] she is lowly. 24 is a] bore. XVIII *423a *Iusticia... sunt] om.* XIX 3 holly] holyly. 4 yede] wente +CrM. 5 eftsoones; me mette] *om;* y drempte. 8 Iesu] hymselue. 15 called] named. *88b–89a *om.* 90 And...riche*s*] For it shal turne tresoun. 133 *Fili Dauid*; *Ihesus*] *trs* +g. 135 The burdes þo] þerfore men. 151 songen] konyngly s. 153 he yede] wente. *161a–62 *Ll. om.* *205–07 *Ll. om.* 239 thecche] þresche. 247 **L. om.* 282 That] For he. 306 þe...falle] þey men falle ageyn þe kyng. 318 kynde] *om.* 320 Grace] g. þat þy frut. 329 watlede...and(2)] he peyntede þe wallis with þe woundis of. 340 alle cristene] cristendom. 342 Surquidous his sergeaunt] surquidores were sergawntys. 343 spye; oon] *pl.;* &. 345 tyne þei sholde] þey wolde stroye. 357 on wikked kepynge] wikkednesse he meyntiþ. 377 as...of] I s. of toforehond. 381 wellede] walmede. 412 þei ben] þou art. 416 or an hennes] *om.* *439–40 *Ll. om.* 445 som] *om.* XX 23 fer to] fore.

(ii) Minor

(a) *Both* **R** *and* **F** *present*

+**Z**: V 74 +HmC²CAC. +**ZA**: II 161. III 23. IV 56. V 25. VI 234. VII 48, 92 +Cot. +**ZAC**: I 87, 88, 129. II 115, 143, 149, 155. III 19, 33, 36, 133. V 582. VI 130¹, 155, 168 +Hm, 171 +G, 203 +Y, 320. VII 19¹,²,³, 24. +**A**: I 78. II 237¹. III 80, 82. V 80 +H, 109, 118, 566, 627. VII 125, 136 +G, 138. VIII 35 +HmC², 36. IX 10 +CrC²C, [28 (*om* R)], 51, [175], 206. X 20, 66, 176 (*so* C). +**C**: Pr 153, 165, 175, 185. I 136 +G. II 68, 83. III 63 (*so* A), 328. IV [36], 161 +Hm. V 40, 154 †F, 250, 275 †F, 404 +w, 433, 540. VI 50, 193. VIII 92. IX [14], 110. X 75, 86, 88a +GC²M, 243 +L, 246, 246a, 248 +GOC², 391, 408. XI 21, 101, 124 +G, 147, [151], [153], 157, 210, 220¹,² +GCot, 245, 393, 402, 422². XII 137 +B, 138, 148, 153, 165 +HmCrGCotM, 176 +L, [181], 221, 227, 258, 265, 272, 284¹;² +CrL. XIII 41, 74¹ +G;² †F, 76, 84, 109, 116, 174, 257, [258], 427a. XIV 18 +?gL, 47, 47a, 48, 49 +HmCr, 60, 207, 216, 256 +B, 267, 289, 293, 299. XV 8, 14 +g, 53¹ +Cr;² 61 +Hm, 73, 81, 95, 103 +B, 121¹,², 154, 160, 162, 170 +Y, 172, 175, 181, 404, 603, 610. XVI 89, 103, [141], 152, 200 +Cr, 209, 252²,³, 254. XVII 9, 29 +GC², 50, 58, 96, 171, 245, 266 +Y, 290, 327. XVIII 22 +HmCrB, 30 +W, 50, [69], 73, 84 +Cr, 121, 189, 204, 213, 215 +HmGYOB, 220, 261a / 262, 269, 290, 298 +Cr, 302¹,², 320, 322, 323 +WHm, 348 +Cr, 350 +g, 354, 376²,³, 391 +G, 396, 403 +Cr²³GC². XX 45, 163 +BoCot, 166, 199, 212, 240¹,², 242, 249, 289, 379.

(b) *With only* **R** *present*

+**AC**: V 605 +wg**Z**. +**C**: V 275. IX 142. XI 247. XII 61. XVIII 319a / 320.

(c) *With only* **F** *present*

+**ZA**: Pr 14, 15, 23 +HC, 24, 60 +GC, 61 +GH, 73¹ +**C**. I 146, 152¹, 204, 209 +H. +**ZC**: Pr 44 +HA. +**ZAC**: Pr 4 +H, 5, 6, 31, 42, 48, 71, 72, 76. I 142, 166, 177, 180, 181, 183 +H, 186³ +G, 187, 190, 191, 192, 201, 203, 207. +**A**: Pr 15, 16, 66 +C, 69 +Z**C**. I 144. +**AC**: Pr 20 +GZ, 59 +GZ, 67, 77 (*cf.* Z), 78 +HZ, 82. I 175, 189. +**C**: Pr 73² +HZA, 102, 105 +WHm, 108¹, [108² +C)], 110 +WCr²³H, 117¹. I 152², 160¹;² +CrOC², 162, 202 +H. XVIII 422 +wg. XIX 9 +CrgM, 11, 30, 63, 64, 78, 108 / 09, 110 +?g, 113, 114 +WHm, 140¹,³, 146 (risen] vp r.), 152¹ +Cot, 153, 231¹,², 246 +Cr²³, 251, 279, 294, 321, 322 +Cot, 350 +W, 403, 404, 408, 414 +C²B, 419, 421, 454, 483 +CrO. XX 7, 8, 10 +CrYOC²M, 19.

§ 49. Readings with no other-version parallel

(i) Major

(a) *Both* **R** *and* **F** *present*

Pr *144 *L. om.* 208 Forþi] For. III 243 truþe] trewe. 352 mede] me. IV 181² wel] *om* (+CrGH). V 131 chaffare] ware. 139 abrood] *om.* 144 freres] *om.* 248 here] þere. 437 manye] myn (fele F). 639 knowe þere] welcome. VI 26 labours] laboreres (+Hm). VII 80 For] Forthi. VIII 100 oon] and (F *def.*). 101 That if] For if þat (R *def.*) *103 *L. om.* IX 74 of þat] *om.* 83 mebles] nobles (mone F) +Hm. 96 drede] loue. dooþ þerfore] to do. 101 siþþe] seche (all swiche F). *114b–17a *Ll. om.* 192 *propter fornicacionem] om.* X 69 kynnes] *om* +G. 204 suwen] scheweth +G. 219 to knowe what is] for to k.

255*a vel*] *aut.* 286 or to greue] *om.* 394 dide...oþere] and other dede. 395 holy writ seiþ] h. w. (s. þe book F). XI *47–9 *Ll. om.* 106 laude] lakke. 255 folwe] wolde / welde. 278 wille] wille With eny wel or wo (w. to suffre wo for welthe F). 279*a inpossibile*] *difficile.* 284 dide] *om.* 322 wondres] wordis (+B; worchynge F). 374 sewest] schewest (makst F). mysfeet] misfeith +BoCot; myschef F. 422 þi] in þi. to suwe] efte to sitte. XII 11 pestilences] penaunce(s). *13–13*a Ll. om.* L. om.* 48 baddenesse she] badd vse. *76 *L. om.* XIII 143 þow lere þe] to lere and. 214 confermen] confourmen +G. 268 wole] wel. 343 it] I (he F). XIV 14 word] thouȝt. 101 driȝte] lord (god F). 129 to lyue] to þe / of lif. 139 noȝt] *om* (ryght soo þe same F). 142 moore] huire. 143 hire] heuene. 152 rew-] riȝt. 144*a transire*] *ascendere.* 155–6 *Ll. om.* 174 lord] lore (lyȝn F). 190 He] Ho (We F). 198 But] And. 320 þe actif man þo] *om* (þanne F). 323 seweþ] scheweth. XV 254*a L. om.* 264 ne] þe (+B). 280 mylde] meke. 285 fond] fedde. 317 rule] ordre. 337 fressh] ful. 341 feeste] fede. 342*a Item*[2]*... rapis*] om. 386 suffiseþ] *sufficit.* 423 goode] lele. XVI 25 witen] kepen. 48 whan] what. 51 pureliche] priueliche. 189 The. light of al þat lif haþ] þat alle þe liȝt of þe lif. 192 knowe] *om* (owiþ F). XVII 163 is] *om* +HmGCB. 192 shullen] swolle +HmCr[23]M.

(b) *With only* **R** *present*
XV 218 The] To. 443 garte] and grete +B. here and] and to +g. 447 faste] *om.* 461 mynnen] take +C.

(c) *With only* **F** *present*
Pr *50–2 *Ll. om.* 62 Manye] Fele. freres] *om* (+GA; *cf.* **C**). 89 signe; sholden] charge; sh. at hom. 91 Liggen] & nowht l. 120 tilie; lif] swynke; skyl. I 204 selue] in heuene. II 14 enuenymes] enemyes. 22 bilowen hym] she is lowly. 32 loue] honowre. 36 How...kyng] See how dauid meneþ. 38 bereþ witnesse] ȝow techeþ. VIII 101 That if] For if þat. *102 A IX 95 *after it.* XX 387.

(ii) Minor

(a) *Both* **R** *and* **F** *present*
Pr 135[2], 143, 197 (*om* F), 210. II 98[1,2]. III 109, 236 +Cot, 324, 351 †F. IV 125, 156 +Cr[23], 181 +CrGH. V 142 +y, 254, 257, 272*a* +Cr, 277, 421, 426 +B. VI 196 (*om* F), 249. VII 74, 77[1,2]. IX 66, 76, 81, 86, 88, 107, 126, 149 +Hm, 158. X 26*a*, 94, 205 +Cr, 230, 254, 256, 263, 265, 274, 436, 468, 471. XI 81, 151, 179, 220[1,2], 245, 268, 397, 424. XII 21, 22, 23, 29, 29*a* +Cr[23], 38, 63, 69, 82 +HmB, 88, 192 (+M, *om* F), 273. XIII 123, 158[1,2], 187, 193, 203, 209, 210, 236, 239 +g, 240, 250, 279, 289 +Cr, 302, 312, 317 +GOC[2], 323, 344 +Hmg, 383. XIV 4 +Cr[23], 12, 14 +Cr[3]g, 19, 29, 47*a*, 97, 120 +HmY, 135, 139, 143[1], 144*a*, 187, 197. XV [85], 93, 121, [154], 162, 170 +Y, 263, 278, 284, 286, 294, 319 +GOC[2], 345, 417, 420, 421, 424 +HmCrCot, 426, 498, 501. XVI 4, 12, 17, 38, [59]. XVII 100, 104, 134, 307. XVIII [109], 109*a*, 255, [351].

(b) *With only* **R** *present*
XI 247. XII 61. XIV 76*a*. XV 430, 435, 454 +Hm, 461 +G, 467, 486, 491, 508.

(c) *With only* **F** *present*
Pr 36, 90[1,2], 106, 108, 111, 113[1,2], 115, 116[1];[2]+MH, 119[1] +HmGMH,[2], 121[1,2,3]+Cr, 123, 124[1,2]+H. I 150[1,2], 151, 153[2], 154, 158, 159, 160[1,3]. II 13[1,2,3], 16, 37. XX 13 +Cr.

v. *Comparison of the* α *and* β *families*

§ 50. It is now necessary to consider the relationship and comparative textual worth of the two separate lines of transmission of the B-Text that have been established. Skeat first recognised the α tradition as part of **B**; but as well as ignoring F he identified R as a 'transition stage' between **A** and **C**, 'the B-Text *with later improvements and after-thoughts*' (II, xii). Skeat based his view on R's additions and ascribed most of its omissions to carelessness. This last conclusion is acceptable, but not his judgement that R's 'mere *variations* are but few'. For there are at least 1725 cases where the Bx reading is in clear contestation between the α variant and that of β, the tradition from which all editors since Crowley have selected their copy-text. If the unique lines (individually or grouped) are counted as single readings, about 650 may be classed as major. In some 250 of these, together with about 370 of the minor ones, α alone appears to preserve Bx. Only about 38% of the readings adopted in this edition are therefore taken from α. But for a fairer estimate of the relative value of the two traditions it needs to be remembered that F, at points the only witness present, is significantly less reliable as an α source than is R (§ 44 above). Where both R and F are to hand, comparison will show the two families to attest a more closely similar number of right readings (675 for β and 625 for α). By contrast, over the roughly 780 lines with only F to represent α, the proportion of right readings is 155 to F's 37, over 4 to 1 in favour of β. Where β is absent, comparison of the two α sources over some 175 lines shows R (as already noted) to be about ten times more accurate than F. This proportion is borne out over the bulk of the poem, where both R and F can be systematically compared with β. In the light of these considerations, it is safe to suppose that if R had survived entire, the critical B-Text might have contained more nearly equal numbers of α and β readings and R even have proved suitable as the base-text, since its language is closer than W's to Langland's probable dialect.

§ 51. That R's omissions were due to scribal carelessness is the conclusion of K–D's account identifying various forms of 'eyeskip' as the main cause (pp. 67–9). But unlike Skeat, they consider the unique lines of R (and F) to be not additions to an earlier β form but part of the common source of both families that were omitted by β in the same largely unconscious ways as were the lines lost from α. This explanation has the advantage of simplicity, even if the operation of the suggested mechanisms is not always equally decisive or straightforward. Thus, it would seem unarguable that β left out XI 382–91 through homœoarchy: '*Holy writ...wye wisseþ* followed by Latin 38[2], *wise...witty...wroot bible* followed by Latin 39[2]' (*K–D* p. 66). By contrast, α's omission of XVII 113–24 through 'resumption at a wrong point' (ibid., p. 68) induced by a series of recurring key-words (*feiþ* four times, *felawe* three times, *folwen* twice) is more open to doubt. For despite the recurrence of such a situation at XVII 281–44, K–D's analysis will not satisfy a positivist editor as will one ascribable to mechanical causes. Questioning some of the mechanical explanations has led to a revival of Skeat's notion that R's text is an intermediate stage between β and C.[33] Ralph Hanna, for example, tries to accommodate K–D's ascription to β's scribe of its losses from the archetypal source with viewing some α passages, particularly in XI–XV, as revisions. He further urges the significance of thematic factors ignored by K–D, maintaining how XIII 400–09 and XIV 228–38 both deal with Gluttony and Sloth and appear to fill in 'gaps' in β's discussion of the deadly sins. K–D's ascription of the first of these losses to 'notional homœoteleuton (*grace...helpes* 39[9]; *mercy amenden* 40[9]' is indeed a little tenuous taken by itself. But it is much strengthened when *helpes* 399 is seen to be echoed by *helpe it* 408 (the penultimate line of the omitted passage), while the recall of *mynde...moore* 398 in *mercy amenden* 409 looks rather more like the 'verbal and notional homœoteleuton' of which K–D later speak (see § 52). Both the shape of the words and the likeness of the ideas might thus have contributed to the omission, and though this case is not classically simple, instances of eyeskip frequently fail to be. In the second instance, moreover, the first two lines omitted do not relate to the account of Gluttony and Sloth but to that of Wrath, of which they form the conclusion. So since these at least cannot have formed part of a postulated α addition, 'thematic' factors lose relevance. K–D propose 'resumption at a wrong point induced by homœoteleuton (*cheueþ* 227, *-chief* 238)', together with various 'internal correspondences' of recurring connective particles. Their explanation seems to the present editor to gain persuasiveness after observing that at the start of 239, where β resumes, α apparently read *And þouȝ*, i. e. lacked the repeated *if* which might have made a hasty scribe believe he had copied the intervening 230–38 and the two lines before them.

§ 52. There is of course no reason in principle to restrict the enquiry to unconscious scribal loss. For between 'copyist's inattention' and 'author's revision' lies a third possibility, that of' deliberate scribal intervention'. Thus, fourteen lines after this passage, α has an omission of two lines about brothels that K–D put down to homœoarchy (*A...stuwes* 252, *A...suwe* 254). But scribal censorship on prudential grounds could be the cause here, as in other passages dealing with similar topics. Examples of this are III 51–62, a loss K–D diagnose as due to 'verbal and notional homœo-teleuton', and IX 179–85, which they attribute to homœoarchy but which ends with a Latin allusion to brothels. (Comparable to this are α's omission of the phrase *propter fornicacionem* from the Pauline quotation at IX 192 and β's mention of prostitutes receiving mercy at XIV 183, which could however be mechanical). 'Notional correspondence amounting to homœoarchy' (*K–D*, p. 68) may account for loss of XII 185 from α; but so may scribal unease with Imaginatif's uncompromising attitude to the uneducated. Censorship, now for religious reasons rather than moral or 'political' correctness, may also be at work elsewhere. Examples are in α at XII 193 and XV 72 (if the latter is not mechanical), XVI 264 (possibly superstitious objection to an unlucky word) and XVII 316, and in β at XVII 309–10. The very first β loss, at X 78–9, is seen by K–D as due to homoarchy (*That* 77, 79); but it is interpreted by Taylor, a supporter of Skeat's view of R, as a topical addition in 1382 alluding to the plague of August 1381, which particularly affected children.[34] Here, however, it is not hard to suspect a scribal deletion of lines that might have seemed blasphemous to some readers. Indirectly favouring this view is the Bx scribe's censorship of a no less outspoken expression at line 53 of the same passus. Similar, if more remotely, is the poet's own removal of A XI 161, as perhaps open to various misinterpretations.[35]

§ 53. Proponents of the hypothesis of 'revision within the **B** tradition' also find in some passages an incoherence indicative of continuing authorial involvement at a post-archetypal stage of transmission. An example is XV 528, cited by Justice[36] as well as Taylor, who deems the later insertion of 510–27 in α responsible for syntactic nonsense at 528:

> He is a forbisene to alle bisshopes and a briȝt myrour,
> And souereynliche to swiche þat of Surrye bereþ þe name,
> *And nauȝt to* huppe aboute in Engelond to halwe mennes auteres...

For the italicised phrase β has *That*, which K–D understand as a scribal smoothing after omission of 510–27. But four successive relative clauses introduced by *that* (as in the β form of this passage)[37] are very uncharacteristic of Langland's syntax. Moreover, the supposed confusion in α's reading will disappear once the sentence's elliptical structure is grasped. For the sense here is: 'St Thomas sets a shining example [of faithful duty] to all bishops, [especially to those *in partibus infidelium*], and [he did] not [set an example] of gadding about the country where they have no business to be'. It is hard to credit that the poet, if he had caused a syntactical 'mess' or 'hash'[38] through hasty intervention, would not have put it right in the **C** revision, which generally aims at greater clarity and explicitness. And yet the line, except for a transposition of the verb and the adverbial phrase, remains unaltered at C XVII 279 (see p. 605 of Vol. I). As so often with Langland, the confusion lies not in what the poet wrote but in the minds of his readers. Taylor's objections to the Kane-Donaldson shift of XV 503–09, 528–31 and 532–68, which is accepted in the present edition, lose their force once the intelligibility of 528 has been demonstrated.

§ 54. Supporters of what may be called the 'revisionary' hypothesis further argue that more than one α passage could be removed without disrupting the sequence of thought as found in β.

An example is that on Saul and the Ark at XII 116–25*a*. Yet here Taylor's claim that the preceding line 115 'lead[s] quite logically' into 12[6][39] need not count against the contextual coherence of the α lines but in favour of that of the passage as a whole (114–30). For while Langland's reference to Saul undoubtedly amplifies his warning against interference with the priestly prerogative even by the highest in the land, mention of *his sones also* at 117 is making a pointed contrast with *preestes sone* at 115, the line before the α passage commences. Similarly, the allusion to priestly anointing of a knight at 126, the line *after* the passage ends, acquires sharper focus if seen as originally following *christos meos* 125*a*. This is because what the anointed clergy 'keep' is not only the sacraments but also 'sacramentals' such as the oils of anointing. Thus, if Taylor were right about XII 116–25*a*, its incorporation into the β text would actually exhibit a carefulness incompatible with its being an 'anomalous addition' made in response to events after the Rebellion of 1381.[40] It is a weakness of Taylor's analyses that they arise from a mistaken quest for topical allusion. But this is something Langland seems to have employed only if a more general moral significance could be drawn from a particular historical event. The classic case is the great wind of 1362, which is retained unaltered from **Z** through to **C**.[41]

§ 55. The 'revision hypothesis' also requires a complicated genetic scheme to account for the α passages apparently lacking from β without adequate mechanical explanation. Hanna's argument[42] is that from Langland's original (*O*) was made a copy (*O¹*), and from this another (*O²*), which omitted about 20 of the 37 unique α passages (and which corresponds to the source here called β). At a second stage, the <rf> passages were copied into O; from O thus augmented, into O¹; and from O¹ into both the copy used for revision to **C** (= 'B¹') and into O², from whence the RF source (= 'α') acquired them. Historically speaking, such a manuscript evolution is no more improbable than the simpler one preferred here; but it seems to the present editor analytically less persuasive. For since all the evidence lies within the text, the main issue would appear to be logical rather than historical: whether a two-stage authorial manuscript and one vertical axis of transmission or a one-stage original and two-branch vertical axis better explain the data. Hanna is no doubt right to hesitate over some of K–D's homœographic explanations (which may however be susceptible of further refinement) and also to maintain that, on distributional grounds, purely mechanical losses are unlikely to have occurred only from Passus X onwards. But this is not a decisive objection to the hypothesis of a 'unitary' **B** tradition,[43] given the demonstrable existence of such losses amongst β's omissions in XI–XX and α's in Pr–IX. For the first half of β could have been produced by a more careful scribe than the one who produced the second half (the converse situation to that hypothesised for the copying of the archetypal manuscript at § 5). What seems clear is that the idea that some α passages do not 'fit' holds up in none of the cases adduced.

§ 56. Even more unconvincing is Hanna's conception of Langland's attitude to his poem as that of someone who 'felt uncompelled to ensure the accuracy of his text' but 'placed his credence in a copyist, whose work he shows no sign of having supervised and corrected.'[44] The first assertion here conflicts with the poet's strictures in XI 305–06 upon the scribal *goky* who *parcelles ouerskippe[þ]*. The second is contradicted by the singular accuracy of the archetypal text in Passus XVI (see § 5 above), which can scarcely be explained except by authorial correction. But it is not hard to envisage circumstances that might have prevented Langland from exercising continuous supervision of the scribal efforts. Further, some **C** revisions could be, as K–D believe, direct responses to uncorrected B[1] errors. But if they are, these logically endorse rather than question the *a priori* likelihood of the poet's wanting a carefully copied text of his carefully written poem. Hanna's notion might once have seemed plausible, with only Skeat's text to rely on and before Langland's poetic technique had been explored. But it rests on the incoherent assumption that the author of so 'fine a literary document' had a 'general lack of interest in local textual detail' and a 'relative lack of interest in the text.'[45] Complementing Taylor's and Justice's notion of Langland's 'syntactical confusion', which has been shown to be mistaken, Hanna's comments reveal the imprudence of generalising on no firmer a basis than 800 lines from 'widely-scattered passages', which he confidently proceeds to 're-edit.'[46] For the many changes made throughout the **C** revision, especially in the b-verses, argue strongly against his view of Langland and show both the extent and the minuteness of the poet's concern with matters of 'local textual detail' affecting vocabulary, metre, style and expression. Without comparative scrutiny of the text in all versions, such sweeping statements about the poet's 'compulsions' are vain. For both editing the text and correctly interpreting its details demand a vigilant sense of the whole when dealing with any part.[47]

§ 57. It will have emerged from the above discussion that the notion of a *Piers Plowman* that never achieved or even aimed at a final form, but remained continuously subject to 'rolling revision', is unacceptable. It is a notion that confuses authorial composition with the quite distinct process of scribal transmission; and it arises out of a misunderstanding of the nature of Langland's poetic art and his entire undertaking seen in the context of the similar enterprises of his major contemporaries Chaucer, Gower and the *Gawain*-poet. To the present editor, the textual evidence affords no firmer grounds for belief in a two-phase B-Text represented by α and β than in a two-phase A-Text with earlier and later forms represented by **r** and **m** respectively. In each of the three universally accepted versions of the poem, three conclusions seem highly probable. First, the line of transmission has divided into two independent post-archetypal branches, between which there was no reciprocal interaction. Second, the subsequent variations attested, from individual minor readings to lines and passages, were not introduced into either sub-archetype by the author.[48] Third, none of the readings that appear original on intrinsic grounds have come in from a lost source superior to Bx. Since B[1] existed for Langland's use in revising to **C**, it could in principle have provided some of those superior readings for post-archetypal scribes who had access to it. But as has been argued above (§§ 25, 28, 32 and 46), all such preferred readings may be more economically ascribed to contamination from **A** or **C** (see also §§ 62 and 71 below). After analysis, the disjunctive readings listed in §§ 41–48, which massively differentiate two competing textual traditions, suggest only one cause: scribal intervention, conscious, partly conscious or unconscious, during the copying of a long and often provocative piece of 'making'. For in most major and in many minor instances of conflicting readings, clear grounds exist for judging that one variant is derived from a source represented by the other and consequently that in each case either α *or* β is likely to preserve the archetypal text. The **B** Version of *Piers Plowman* possessed a distinctive *telos* which its poet set out to realise as scrupulously as Chaucer did in his *Troilus*, however scurvily Langland's *scriueynes* fell short of being *trewe* (see *Intro.* V §§ 23–5 below). Before examining (in §§ 60–5) the damage they wrought, it will be convenient to complete this section by tabulating here the unique lines of α and β, which Skeat recognised as part of **B** and K–D first identified as partial witnesses to a single text.

§ 58. (*i*) The β family is the sole witness of six citation-lines and some 200 text-lines, consisting of 191 whole and 17 half-lines. (The presence or absence of other-version support for these is found in §§ 42–3 above).

Pr 3. 33b–34a. 50–4. 144. 171. I 82. 157. II 11. III 51–62 [3 *semi-spurious ll. in* a]. 149b–50a. IV *none*. V 474. VI 88b. 217. 309b–10a. VII 41a. VIII 14–17. 100b. 103. IX 114b–17a. 160–61. 166. 170–72 [3 *spur. ll.* a]. 179–85 [*citation ll. at* 183a]. 200–03. X 424. XI 46–9. XII 13–13a. XIII 14–20. 373b–74a. XIV 155–59. 252–53. 288b. 309a. XV 72. 254a. 402–03. 532–68. XVI 27b–28a. 264. 270–73 [3 *spur. ll.* a]. XVII 7b. 34–47. 113–24. 218–44. 316. XVIII 179. 198. 252–53. 423. XIX 88b–89a. 161a–162. 204–07. 211b–13. 247. 439–40. XX 238–39.

(*ii*) The α family is the sole witness of five citation-lines and some 187 text-lines, consisting of 167 whole and fifteen half-lines, nine spurious lines and three (enclosed in square brackets) here treated as a scribal confection from authentic **A** material.

(*a*) *In* RF: Pr–IX *none*. X 78–9. 291–302. 368. 380. 410–12. XI 110. 131b–32a. 159–69 (167 *om* F). 196. 382–91. 427b–29a. XII 55–7a. 116–25a. 151–52. XIII 165–72a (170, 172 *om* F). 293–99. 400–09. 437–54. XIV 183, 228–38. XV 244–48. 303–04. 395. 510–27. 572b–75a. XVI *none*. XVII [8]. 69. 112a. 177b–79a. 309–10. XVIII 312b–13a. XIX *none*. XX 37. [*Spurious: three ll. at* III 51 (*like* A III 50–1); *for* IX 170–72; *for* XVI 270–73].
(*b*) *In* R *only*: XI 167. XIII 170, 172. XV 471–84. 489a.
(*c*) *In* F *only*: VIII 109b–110a. XIX 56–9. 152b. 237b–38a. 337.

As stated at § 57, on the hypothesis that α and β are sub-archetypes of Bx, the readings that either attests in the other's absence are, when correct, presumed to be those of the archetype; when not, they are of necessity only possibly so.

vi. *The Archetypal Text of the* **B** *Version*

§ 59. In the two lists of family readings at §§ 42–3 and 48–9, the selected lemma has been tacitly understood to represent Bx, and the rejected variant a scribal corruption of the latter in one or other sub-archetype. The more important examples will be found discussed in detail in the *Textual Notes*. But the minor ones, too numerous for individual consideration, are mostly so similar that systematic notice here would add little to what is already familiar from the Athlone editions (some typical examples will be cited at the end of § 65 below). In the following list, lines are identified as certainly or probably archetypal where (*a*) α and β agree; (*b*) β agrees with R *or* F understood as preserving α; (*c*) of the constituent branches of β (§§ 9–10 above), one or more (usually L) agree with α, or with R / F understood as = α, a '?' indicating uncertainty due to absence of other-version support (these are already listed at § 38 above). Two unadopted Lα agreements which may be archetypal and are conceivably original appear marked '‡'. Otherwise the list includes all and only the archetypal lines judged correct, ignoring wrong line-division where no substantive error results. It excludes (*a*) readings attested by only one family even if, from intrinsic character and other-version support, they appear original and so presumptively archetypal; (*b*) readings judged correct but resulting from possible coincidence or other-version contamination. The latter category embraces most of the 116 right readings noted in the foregoing discussions of the β subgroups, which will be recorded in § 62 as equivalent to editorially emended readings, the 'editor' in such cases having been the scribe. Details of available other-version support are provided only for the readings in category (*c*). As those and most major archetypal errors corrected in the text are discussed in the *Textual Notes*, except where the rationale of emendation seems self-evident, only a few are singled out for mention in §§ 65–7 below. Because of the defectiveness of both α witnesses, it is clearly stated which manuscripts are present to attest this family at any point.

Square brackets denote readings where Bx has been editorially reconstituted from split variants. A plus indicates agreement with the adopted, a minus agreement with the rejected reading.

Pr (α = F): 1–2. 12–13. 18. 20. 23. 25–6. 30. 35–6. 44–5. 47. 49. 56. 63. 69–70. [77]. 79. 85–6. 92. 94–5. 100–01. 104–05. 123. (α = RF): 125–34. 136–9. ? 140. 141–42. 145–47. 149–58. 160–70. 173–78. 180–81. 183–4. 186–88. 193–96. 198–99. 201. 203–04. 207. 211–12. 214–15. 217–22. 224. 226. 230–31.

I 1–3. 5–10. 12–30. +**ZAC** 31. 32–6.36. 38–40. 48–53. 55–6. 58–9. 61–3. 65–9. 72. 74–6. 79–81. 83–6. 89–97. 100–03. 105–09. 111. 114–18. 120. 122. 124. 126. 128. 130–32. 135. 137. 139–40. (α = F): 143. 148. 156. 159. 161. 163–64. 167–73. 178–79. 183. 188. 195. ?199.

II 2–3. 6. 15. 17–18. 27. 33–4. 39. (α = RF): 42. 44–6. 48–50. 52–4. 56–67. 69–74. 76–82. 86–8. 90. 92–7. 99–100. 102–07. 109–10. 112. 114–19. 123–30. 132–37. 139–42. 144. [145]. 146–7. +**ZAC** 148. 149–53. 156–58. 160. 162–79. 182. 184–97. 199. 204–09. 211–21. 223–25. 228. 230–35.

III 1–2. 4. 7. 9–10. 13–14. 16–18. 20–31. 34–5. 37–8. 40. 42–7. 50. 64–6. 69–70. 72–4. 76–9. 81. 83–5. 88–90. 92–7. 99. 101–03. 105–08. 110–11. 115–16. 118–21. 123. 125–26. 129. 134–39. 142–44. 146. 148. 152–54. 156–59. 161. 163–74. 176–77. 179–81. [182]. 184–86. 188–204. 206–09. 211–13. 215–18. 220–21. 223. 225. 227–28. 230. 232–34. 237–42. 244–50. +**A** ?251. 252–54. 256–57. 259. 261–64. 266–76. 278–80. 282. 285–88. 290–91. 293–94. 296–97. 299–300. 302–09. 311–15. 317–18. 320–21. 323–26. 329–35. 337–41. 343. 347–50. 353.

IV 1–3. 5–6. 8–9. 11. 13–14. 16–25. 28–31. 33–5. 37. 39. 41–6. 48–54. 57–61. 63–4. 66–85. 87–9. 92–3. 95–8. 100–02. 107–08. 110–16. 119–35. 137–40. 142–44. 146–55. 157. 159–60. 162–72. 174–80. 182–83. 185–89. 191–93.

V 1–6. 9–14. 16. 18. 20–2. 24. 27–8. 30. ?31. 33. 36–9. 42–6. 49–69. 71–2. 74–5. 77–8. 81–3. 85–96. 98–108. 110. 114–17. 119–25. 127. 129. 132–38. 140–41. 143. 145–47. 149–50. 152–53. 155. 157–59. 161–64. 166–70. 173. 177–78. 180. 182–85. 187. 189–91. 196–207. +**AC** 208. +**A-C** 209. 210–11. 216–20. 224–37. 239–47. 249. 251–52. 255–56. 258. 260. +**C** ‡261. 262–64. 266–69. 271–73. 276. 278. 280–81. 283. 285–99. 301–03. 306–09. 311–12. 314–15. 319–20. 322. 324–25. 329. 331–37. 339–43. 345–50. ‡351. 352–56. 358. 360–63. 365–68. 371–74. 377. 379–82. +**ZAC** 383. 384–85. 387. 389–93. 395–99. 401–03. 411. 413–14. 416–19. 422. +**C** 424. 425. 427–32. 434–36. 438–39. 442–45. 447–50. 452–55. 457–62. 464–65. 467. 470. 472. 475–76. 478–82. 484–86. 488–90. 492–93. 498–501. 503–04. 506. 508–11. 513. 515–18. 520. 523–25. 527–31. 534–35. 537–39. 541–44. 546. 548–49. 551. 553–54. 556. 558–64. 568–72. 574. 577–80. 584–87. 589–90. 592–95. 598. 600–08. 612. 614–16. 618. 620–26. 629–31. 633–37. 640–42.

VI 1. 3–7. 9–25. 27–29. 31–2. 35–8. 40–1. 43–4. 46–7. 49. 51. 53–8. 62–4. 68–73. 75. 77–9. 81–2. 84. 90–1. 93. 96–7. 99–102. 104. 106–12. 114–18. 121–22. 124–27. 129. 131. 133–35. 137. 139–47. 149. 151. 153. 156. 158–60. 163–67. 169–70. 172–74. 176–78. 180–84. 186–92. 195. 197. 199. 204. 206. 208–09. 211. 213–14. 220. 224. ?225. 226–29. 231–33. 235–36. 239–41. 243–44. 246–48. 250–56. 258–70. 273–76. 279–80. 282–83. 286–89. 291. 293–300. 302–04. 306–08. 311. 313–19. 322–23. ?326. 327–28.

VII 2–6. 9–16. 18. 22–3. 27–30. 32. 35–6. 38. 40–4. 47. 50–5. 58. 60–1. 63–7. 69. 71–3. 75–6. 78–9. 81–7. 90–1. 97–9. 101–03. 105. 108. 110–19. 121–24. 126–32. 134–35. 137. 139–42. 144–45. 147–55. 157–67. 169–74. 176–80. 183–90. 192. 195–98. 200–01.

VIII 1–3. 5. 7–8. 10–11. 13. 18–20. 22–4. 26–7. 29. +**AC** 30. 32–4. 37. 39–40. 42. -**A** ?43. 45–7. 49. 52–6. 58. 60–2. 67–8. 71. 73. 75–6. 79–82. 84–8. 90–1. 94. 96. 98. 106. 111–15. 117–18. 120–24. 126. ?127. 128.

IX 1. 3. 5–6. 8–9. 12–13. 18–19. 21. 23. 25. ?26. 27. 30. 32. 34. 36–7. 40. 43–7. 49–50. 52. 54. 56–9. 61–3. ?64. 65. 67–73. 75. 77–80. 82. 84–5. 89–90. 92–5. 97–8. 100. 102–06. 108–09. 111–12. ?113. 120–25. 127–34. 136–40. 143–48. 150–53. 156–57. 164–65. 167. 173–74. 177. 186. 191. 195–97. 199. 205. 207.

X 2–13. 15–7. 19. 22–7. 29–35. 37–45. 48–9. 51–2. 56. 58–9. 61–5. 67. 73–4. 76. 80–5. 88–9. 91–3. 95–107. 109–23. 125–27. 130. 132. 134. 136. 138. 148–53. 155. 157–61. 164–66. 168–70. 174–75. 177–84. 187–88. 191–203. 206–08. 210–16. 220. 222. 224–29. 231–38. 240–41. 244–45. 247. 249. 252–53. 255. 257–64. 266–70. ?271. 272. 275–78. 280–83. 285. 287–90. 305–06. 308–13. 315–19. 321–22. 324–36. 338–41. 343–66. 370–75. 381–83. 386. 388–90. 392. 396–407. 414–20. 423. 425–33. ?435. 437–45. 447–48. 450–57. 459–60. +**A** 461. 462–65. 467. 469–70. 474–5.

XI 1–3. 9–20. 22–5. 27–36. 38–40. 42. 44–5. 50–7. 61–6. 68–80. 83. 85. 87–100. 102–05. 109. 111–20. 122–23. 126. 128. ?133. 135–37. 139–43. 146. 148–50. 152. 154–56. 158. 170–78. 180. 182–83. 185–92. 194–95. 198–99. 201. 203. 205–07. 209. 211–19. 221–37. 240–44. 246. 248–54. 256–61. 263–64. 266–67. 269–76. ?277. 279–80. 282–83. 285–87. 290–94. 296–300. 302–21. 323–24. 326–29. 331–38. ?339. 340–42. [343]. 344–47. 349. 351–54. 357–66. 368–69. 373. 375–81. 392. 394–95. 399–400. 403–14. 416–18. 421. 425–26. 431–32. 436–37.

XII 1–3. 5–10. 12. 14–5. 17–20. 26–8. 31–3. 35–7. 39–47. 50–4. 58. 62. 64–5. 67–8. 70–2. 74–5. 79–81. 83–7. 89–90. 92–4. 96–8. 100–03. 105–06. 108–10. 112–15. 128. 132–34. 139. 149–50. 154–58. 160–64. 166–68. 170–75. 177. 179–80. 182. 187–91. 194–95. +**C** 196. 197–201. [202]. 204–07. 209. 211–12. 216–20. 222–26. 228–39. 241–43. 245–57. 259–64. 267–69. 271. 274–81. 283. 286. 288. 291–94.

XIII 1. 3. 5–7. 9–10. 12–13. 12–13. 21–34. 36–40. 42–4. 46. 48–9. 51. 53. 54–5. 57–9. 61. 64–9. 71–3. 75. 77–9. 81. 83–4. 87–90. 94. 97–102. 105–11. 113–15. 117–19. [120]. 121–22. 124–34. 137–42. 144–49. 151–57. ?158. 159–64. 173. 176–86. 188–92. 194. 196–208. 211–13. 215–20. 222. 224–28. 230–32. 234–35. 237–38. 241–49. 251–54. 256. 259. 261–66. 269. ?270. 271. 273–75. 277–78. 281–82. +C 283–84. 285–88. 291–92. ?301. 303–11. 313–16. 318–22. 324–25. 327–29. 331–33. 335–40. 342. 345–48. 351–53. ?355. 356–60. 362–63. 365–66. 368–72. 375–82. 384–86. 388–90. 392–97. 413–22. 425. 427–36. 457–60.

XIV ?1. 2–3. 5–6. 10–11. 13. 15–17. 20. 22. 24–7. 30–5. 37–9. 42–6. 50. 53–5. 57–8. 62–5. 68–71. 73–84. ?85. 86–96. 98–9. 102–05. 107–15. 117–18. 121–22. 124–28. 130–31. 136–38. 140. 145–51. 160–73. 175–76. [177]. 178–80. 184–85. 188. 191–95. 199–203. 206. 208. 210–11. 214–15. 218–22. 224–27. +C 239. 240–51. 254–55. 258–59. 261–62. 264. 266. 268–72. 276. [277]. 278–83. 286–87. 294. 296–98. 302–03. 305. 308. 312. 314–15. 317–19. 321–22. 324–28. 330–32.

XV 1–4. 6–7. 9–11. 13. 15–17. 19–24. 26–35. +C 36. 37–41. 43–52. 54–6. 58–60. 62. ?63 (-C). 64–9. 71. 75–7. 79–80. 82–4. 86–7. 91–2. 94. 96–9. 101–02. 104–05. 108. 110. 112–14. 117. 119–20. 122. 124–25. 128–32. 134. 137. 139–43. 145–46. 148–53. 155. 157–59. 161. 163–69. 171. 173–74. 176–79. 182–86. ?187. 189–92. 194–95. 197–99. ?200. 201–05. 208–17. 219–23. 225–43. 249–54. 255. 257–62. 265–77. 279. 287–92. 295–96. 298–302. 305–11. 313. 315–16. 318. 323–36. 338. 340. 343–44. 346–51. 353–54. 356–58. 360–61. 363–69. 371–76. 378–85. 387–92. 396–7. ?+C 398. 399–401. 405–06. 408–16. 418–19. 425. 427–29. 431–34. 436–42. 445–46. 448–49. 451–53. 455–59. 462–66. 468–69. 487–89. 490. 492–93. ?+C 494. 495–97. 499–500. 505–05. +C 506. 509. 569–70. 576–78. 580–83. 586. 588–90. 592. 594–98. 600–02. 604–09.

XVI 1–3. 5–11. 13–16. 18–24. 26. 29. 31–37. 39–42. 44. 46–7. 49. +C 50. 52–8. ?+C 60. 61–75. 79–82. 84–8. 90–2. 94. 96–102. 104–10. 111–14. 116–18. 120. 122. 124–35. 137–39. 143–47. 149–51. 153–57. 159. 161–75. 177–88. 190–91. 194–97. 202–08. 210. 212–19. +C 221. 222–49. 251. 253. 255–61. 263. 265–69. 274.

XVII 2. 5–6. +C 11. 12. 14. +C 15. 16–22. 24–28. 30. 32–6. 48–9. 51–6. 59–64. 66–8. 70–3. 75–7. 79–80. -C ?81. [82]. 83–4. 87–9. 91. 93–4. 97–99. 101–02. ?104. 105–06. 108. 110–12. 125–33. 135–36. 142–47. 149–51. 153. 155–59. 161. ?162. 165. 167–70. 172–75. 180. 182–89. 191. 193–95. 197–98. 200–01. 203. 205–06. 208–13. 215–17. 247–53. 255–63. 265. 267–89. 291–93. 295. 297–98. 301. +C 304. 305–06. 308. 310–11. 313–14. 315. 317–19. 321–24. 328. 331–35. 337. 338. ?339. 341–43. 345–47. 349–52.

XVIII 1–7. 9–10. 13. 15–21. 23–7. 29. 32–4. 36–8. [39]. 42–4. 46–9. 52–3. 55–8. 60–1. 63–8. 70–2. 74–5. 77–81. 88–92. 94–5. 97–100. 102–08. 110–18. 120. 122–23. 125–28. 130–6. 148–50. 152–53. 155. 158. 162–64. 166. 168–69. 171–72. 176–78. 180. 183–88. 190–91. 194–97. 199–201. 203. 205–12. 214. 217. 219. 221–25. 227–32. 235–45. 247. 249–50. 254. 256–60. 262–64. 266–68. 270. 272–73. 275. 277–79. 284–89. 291–94. 297. 299–301. 304–05. 307–11. 314–15. 321. 324–41. 345–47. +C 349. 352–53. +C 354. 355. 357–59. 361–62. 365–75. 377–79. 381–82. 385–89. +C 390. 392. 393–95. 397–98. 400–01. 404–05. 407–10. 412. (**a** = F): 413–15. 418–21. 424. 427–28. 432–33.

XIX 2. 17. 33. 37. +C 47. 53–5. 61–2. 65–67. 69–70. 74. 84. 86. 95. 100. 104. 106. 107. 112. 115. 121–23. 129. 144. 147. 163. 166–67. 171. 178. +C 190. 193. 201. 208. 220–21. 226. 228. 235. 242–43. 257–58. 261. 266. 278. 291. 295–96. 300. 303. 305. +C 309. 331. 336. 338. 344. 358. 362–66. 368. 370–71. 383. 388. 393. 399. 410. 427. 438. 443. 447–49. +C ?457. 460. 462. 464. 475–76. 478–80.

XX +C 6. 12. 15–16. 18. 20. (α = RF): 28–33. 40–1. 43–4. 46–7. 49–53. 56–9. 61. 64. 66. 68–77. 79–86. 88–90. 92. 94. 96. 98–101. 103. 105. 107–13. 115–16. 118. 121–24. ?125. 128–31. 133–35. 137. 140. 143–49. 153–57. 159–62. 164–65. 167–70. 172–73. 175–82. 184–90. 192–93. 195–97. 200–01. 203–06. 209. 213. 215–17. 219–20. 222–32. 234–37. 241. 243–48. 250–52. 254–55. 257. 259. 262. 264. 266–68. 270–76. 278. 280–82. 285–88. 294–300. 302. ?303. 304–05. 307–08. 310. 313–20. 322–26. 328. 330–36. 338–42. 344–48. 350. 352–56. 358–59. 362–63. 365. 368–76. 381–82. 384–86.

vii. *Emendation of Errors in the Archetypal B-Text*

§ 60. The archetypal B-Text contains some 600 major and minor errors (six times as many as Cx and proportionally four times as many as Ax). To save space, they are referenced only by line-number, since all of the major ones will be found discussed in the *Textual Notes*. They are divided into whole-line and intralinear errors. About 55 major errors involve whole lines: two dozen misdivided, of which five are followed by scribal misexpansion or omission (denoted by *); a dozen misplaced; nine omitted; and fifteen spurious, in a dozen separate instances. Other-version evidence for emendation is indicated where available and emended readings are listed again below in the categories to which they belong. Half a dozen cases where absence of one family renders Bx undecidable are in square brackets.

(i) *Misdivided Lines*
III 223/24* (*em. from* **A**). V 149/50 *as* 3 *ll.* (*em. after* Cr^{23}; *cf.* **C**). 188* *as* 2 *ll.* (*em. from* **AC**). VII 69/70. ?174/75 (*correct* F; *so* **AC**). IX 41/2. X [297/8 *only in* α; *em. from* **AC**]. 446/47. XI 148/49. 204* *as* 2 *ll*; *em. from* **C**. 346/47 (*em. from* **C**). 371/72; *em. after* **C**). XII 129/30*; *rec. after* **C**. 183/4 (*em. after* **C**). 251/2. XIII 53a/4. 56/6a. 255* *as* 2 *ll*; *em. after* **C**. 330/31; *em. from* **C**. XIV 316–17a (*em. from* **C**). XVIII 32/3; *em. from* **C**. XIX 305–06 *as* 3 *ll*; *em. from* **C**. 317/18; *em. from* **C**. 345/46; *em. from* **C**. XX 33a/5 *as* 2 *ll*; *em. from* **C**. 62/3; *em. from* **C**.

(ii) *Misplaced Lines*
Pr 189–92 *after* 197. I 98–9, 100–03 *trs*; *em. after* **ZA**. II 203 *after* 205; *em. after* **ZAC**. VI 275, 276 *trs*; *em. after* **ZAC**. [IX 166 (*only in* β) *after* 168; *em. after* **AC**]. XIII 52, 53 *trs*. XIV 286, 286a *trs*. 304a, 306 *trs*. [XV 503–09, 528–31 *after* 532–68 b; *here in* α. 532–68 *after* 502a β; *om* α]*. XVIII 6–8 *after* 9.

(iii) *Omitted Lines*
I 112 (*supplied from* **Z**). [IV 10: *in* YOC^{2}Cr^{23}; ? *from* **A** *or* **C**]. V 328 (*from* **C**). 338 (*from* **A**). XI 371b. XII 129b. XVIII 161. XIX 441. XX 261 (*from* **C**).

(iv) *Spurious Lines*
After: IV 38. V 39a, 54, 193, 556. VI 17, 182. VII 59 (2 *ll*). X 266. XI 67. *In place of*: XVIII 82 (*suppl. from* **C**). XIX 373 (2 *ll*; *em. from* **C**).

§ 61. Some 550 instances (about 70% major) of wrong readings within lines involve individual words, phrases or half-lines; where more than one occurs in a line they are numbered by their position in the Apparatus. They are divided as corrected by restoration, reconstruction or conjecture (see *A Version* § 56 above). Superior non-archetypal readings that appear original and are also found in one or more **B** manuscripts are included with (i) if convincingly attributable to contamination, with (iii) if attributable to scribal guesswork. (These have already been listed above in the sections on each sub-family and its groups). Lines found defective on metrical grounds are marked ^. A plus sign denotes manuscripts containing the reading adopted in the text. Instances where through conflict between families or absence of one family the Bx reading is undecidable, and so cannot be judged certainly corrupt, are in square brackets.

§ 62. (i) *Restored readings*

Some 320 archetypal errors, of which nearly 155 are major, have been emended by restoration on the basis of secure readings in one or more of the other three versions. About 15% are made chiefly on metrical grounds; in the rest, for various reasons of sense, style or expression as well as metre. Around 119 corrections, 33 being major, are based on the agreed **ZAC** reading. The next highest number is 93 taken from **AC** (half of them major) and 90 from **C** (58 major and 32 minor). There are also some 24 cases where Bx seems undecidable, but some may be archetypal, including several in Passus XIX where F is the only α witness. Just over 20 are from **ZA, ZC, Z** and **A**. About 113 of the adopted readings are *also* attested in one or more extant **B** witnesses. Of these, some 83 are minor, and most could have arisen through felicitous coincidental variation. Among the 30 major ones, many are ascribable to contamination. Those in G, H, and F come from an **A** source (see §§ 28, 32, 46 above) and those in OC^2 from **C** (§ 24). But those from L or R are, on the general showing of these manuscripts, antecedently likely to represent β and α respectively, and thence by inference Bx (see §§ 36–7).

From **ZAC**: **Major** Pr 41^1;^{2}+H. 59^2(*cf.* H). [76^4 +H]. I ^165. 186 (*cf.* H). 187 +GH. 191^2 +G.^200. ^206 +GH. II 47. 180. 181. ^200. 210 +F. III 124. 132. IV 10 +YOC^{2}Cr^{23}. 109. V ^47. 468. [474]. 512. 514. ^557. 617. VI 179. 198. 200. 215. 221. 312. VII ^7. ^104. **Minor** Pr 29. 231 +G. I 4. 37 +G. 54 +W. 88. 104. 125 +G. 136. 142. 174 +G. 176 +CrG. 191^1

+GF. II ^28. 75 +GHF. 89. 113 +HmCH. 198. 201. 202. 222. III 3 +BH. 12 +B. 113. 114 +H; *added* G. 117. 124[1] +G;[2] +F. 132 +GH. 141. 160 +GF. IV 32. 47 +H. 94 +CrH. 105 +GH. 106. 117 +HmHF. 136. 184. 190 +H. V 17. 26. 35. 463. 473 +CrGF. 512. 533 +gF. 536 +y. 567. 575. 576. 583 +G. 588. 597. 609. 610. 613. VI 2. 8 +WHmYOC[2]. 34. 59–60–61. 65 +WCrC[2]CBoCot. 88. 92. 94. 119 +M *added*. 128 +BCr. 152 +yF. 205. 207[1],*cf.* YOC[2];[2] +Y. 210. 216 +M. 257 +B. 277 +GBF. 284 +OC[2]. 324. VII 33 +HmF. 48. 88–9. 93[1,2]. 94. 95.

From **ZA**: **Major** I 127 (*cf.* **C**). VI ^285. VII 49. **Minor** Pr 7. I 199. II 75 +GHF. III 15. IV 99 +GM.

From **ZC**: **Minor** I 64.

From **Z**: **Major** I 112. V 555.

From **AC**: **Major** Pr ^82. I 152 +Cr. II 8 +G. 9 +F=?a. III ^98. 151. 222. 281. IV 145 (*cf.* **HZ**). V 126. 188 *misexpanded* Bx. 193. 195. 214. 221. 223. 304[1] *misexp.* 310. 526 (*cf.* **Z**). VI +Z 271, 305. VII +Z 24. 109. 175. VIII 12. 25, 28 +F. ^31. ^93. 95. 107. 108. 119. IX 4 +OC[2]. 7. 17. 22. X 36. 53. 68. 171. ^173. 378. 385. 421. **Minor** Pr 59[1] +WHm. 67 +G. I 200[1] +C[2];[2]. II 229. III 41 (*cf.* **H**). 48 +H. 87. 147. 183. 210. *24. 226 +H. 265. 284 +M *corr.* 289. 295. V 34. 209. 304[2]. 318. 451. 466 +Hm. 471. 532. 628 (*cf.* GF). 638 +WG. VI 74. +Z 278, 321. VII 109 +G. 146 +G. 168. VIII 38 +G*F.* 70. 74. IX 169. 187. 193. X 21[1,2]. 54. 55. 57 +w. 70 +FG. 71. 156. 172 +HmB?G. *From* **A**: **Major** III ^71. 224. V 591. VI ^272. VIII 44. (100). X 124 +gM. **Minor** I 191[4]. II 120 +yF; *not* **Z**, *but cf.* **C**. III 251 +BHR =? α. VIII 78 +F. X 60 +M.

From **C**: **Major** [Pr 171 +Y]. I 11 (*cf.* **H**). II [22]. 84. 143. III 283 +WG. 292. 316. 322 +Bm. 342 +GCr. IV 90 +H. V 179. 330. 351. IX ^16. XI 110. 144 +w. ^287. [429]. XII ^129. XIII 2 +B. ^8. 96 +OC[2]Cot. ^175. 223 +CrF; *by erasure* M. ^341. 411 +OC[2]B. ^424. ^444. 454. XIV ^304. XV ^115. [^545. ^547. ^550. ^554]. 611 [+L = ?β]. XVI 27 +L. (136). XVII 234. ^316. ^326. XVIII 40. 54. 154. 160[1] +C[2];[2] +YGC[2]. 198 +L. ^402. ^406. XIX 38 [+L =?β]. [56]. [57]. 97. [^152]. [154]. [181 +O]. [183]. ^252. 304. ^317. 333. [337]. ^346. [367]. 433. [468]. [^483]. XX ^34. ^54. 67. 104. 106. 117 +WHmF. ^309. ^377. **Minor** Pr [99 +H]. 148. 182 +G. II 35 +YCr. 90 +w. III 226 +H. IV 90 +H. V 172. 176. 423 +wG. 441. 495. 497. 565. VI 201 +wG. VII 56 +y. X 297. XI ^127. ^287 +WHm. 325. XII 56*a*. [25]. XIII 45*a* +g. XIV 181 [+L = ?β]. 291*a* +Cot. XV 552 +W. XVI 27 [+L = ?β]. [142]. XVII 198*a* +CrC[2]. 199. 222 +CrGC. XVIII [151]. 231. ?234 +WR. XIX [9 +WHmL]. 46 +HmO. 83 +LCB. 181 +L. 297. 376. 391 +C. 432 +CB. 434. XX 6 +L = ?β. 8. 14. 19[1] +YC[2]M;[2]. 127 +CrM. 284.

§ 63. (ii) *Reconstructed readings*

Some 140 errors (all but about ten major) are identified from deficiencies of sense, metre and style. These, often on comparison with (near)-parallels in the other versions, may be securely reconstructed. As with restoration and reconstruction, the distinction between a 'reconstruction' and a 'conjecture' can be a fine one. Thus, in III 260 or V 171 a mechanical explanation of the metrical defect is at hand (here haplography). In IV 86, by contrast, the error is linguistic and stylistic (substitution of a commoner synonym causing damage to metre). The 'reconstruction' of the second of these seems hard to distinguish from the 'conjecture' at IV 91 (*wiþseide] seide*). But on closer inspection the latter will be seen to be more speculative than the former. For it competes with **C**, which arguably preserves (as K–D believe) a harder **B** reading supplanted by Bx; it assumes an unparalleled usage of the proposed word; and that word is presumed so unusual as to have prompted the same substitution from the **Z** as from the Ax and Bx scribes. Since editorial judgements inevitably differ about how to identify, categorise and rectify errors, archetypal readings judged corrupt will be examined in detail in the *Textual Notes*. Some fifteen reconstructions are not of a presumed original from the demonstrably faulty archetype but of the presumed archetype, where one sub-archetype is absent or both divergently defective, as in the 'split variation' at Pr 159 or V 456. These are placed in square brackets and not reckoned in the total of sure Bx errors. In others where a reconstructed Bx reading appears unoriginal, it can be emended only by conjecture; but all such instances (marked ‡) are nonetheless included here as reconstructions when based on direct manuscript evidence. Some 90 emendations (just over 60%) made wholly or partly on metrical grounds are preceded by ^. Of these, about 50 are further specified *trs* if corrected by intralinear transposition (in all but two cases in the b-half). About 60 are marked *v* (*f*) *s* / *a* / *o* where they involve verbal (formal) substitution / addition / omission, and four are by re-lineation (*rl*).

Major Pr ^117*vs* (*after* **C**). [^159]. I ^123*trs*. II ^43*vs*. III ^75*trs*. [^255*va* (*so for* // **A**)]. ^260*va*. ^344*trs*. ^345*trs*. IV 38*vs*. ^158*va*. V ^23*trs* (*after* F). ^149/50*rl* (*so* Cr²³). ^165*vs* (*after* Cr). 171*va*. 174*trs*. 194*va*. ^253*trs*. ^259*trs*. ^282*vs*. ^284*vs*. ^300*trs*. 364. 375. 405. ^412*vs*. ^415*vs*. ^441*trs;vs*. [456]. 487*vo*. VI ^123*vs*. ^242*vs*. VIII 44 (*after* A). ^69*trs*. ^99*trs*. IX ^33*va*. 38. ^39*vs*. 41/2. 42. ^55*vs*. ^87*trs*. ^91*trs*. 113*vs*. ^154*trs*. [155]. ^163 (*so* // **A**). ^188*vs*. X ^50*vs*. ^90*vs*. ^108¹ (*so* // **A**);² *vs*. ^131. 186*va*. ^204*trs*. ^274*vs*. [^301*vs* (*in* α *only*; *so* // **C**)]. 304*vs*. ^307*vs*. 320*vs,o*. ^323*trs*. ^337*vo*. ^367*vs*. ^411*vsf*. ^446*vs*. XI ^67*trs*. ^82*trs*. ^86*trs*. [^184]. [196; *in* α *only*]. ^239*trs*. 325. ^343‡*vs*. 385; 386; [388 (*in* α *only*)]. ^420*trs*. ^435. XII ^24*trs*. ^95*trs*. ^203*vs*. 210‡. ^251/52*rl*. 270 (*so* Cr³). 290*va*. XIII ^63*trs*. ^82*trs*. 96*vsf*. 407; [442 (*in* a *only*)]. XIV ^8*vs*. [36]. ^61*va*. [^123*trs* (*in* β*only*)]. [131*a*]. ^260*trs*. ^311*va*. XV ^111*trs*. [126–27]. ^314*trs*. ^320*va*. ^377*trs*. ^421*va*. [480 (R= α *only*)]. 504. ^551*trs*. XVI [142]. [158]. XVII ^78*trs*. [82]. ^164*trs*. ^294*trs*. XVIII ^281*va*. ^282*va*. 283‡. 306*trs*. ^343*trs*. XIX 90*vs,o*; 186; ^230*va*; 236*trs* (*so in* // **C**). 252*vs*. 317/18*rl*. ^348*trs*; ^446*trs*; XX 366*va*. 367*va*. **Minor** XI 148/49. [XIV 299]. [XV 520, 521 (*in* α *only*)]. XVIII [170].

After **K–D**: V 195. ^440*vs*. X 273*trs*. XI [^184]. 205/05*rl*. XII 183/84*rl*. XIII 299*vs*. ^326*trs*. XIV ^9*trs*. ^223*vs*. ^304*vs*. 316–17*rl*. XV ^138*trs*. ^352*vs*. ^394*trs*. [471*vs*. (R *only*)]. XVI ^192*trs* (*so in* // **C**). XVII ^116*trs*. XVIII ^32/3*rl*. ^165*vsf* (*so in* // **C**). 316–18*rl*. ^343*trs*. 423*vsf*. XX 301*vs* (*so in* // **C**). ^380*vs*. **Minor** V 420. VII 69/70. XI 202. [XIX 434].

§ 64. (*iii*) *Conjectural readings*

In nearly 90 instances where direct textual evidence is slight or completely lacking, intralinear errors have been emended by conjecture, 70 of them largely on metrical grounds. One follows Skeat and about fifteen K–D; the rest are new. The degree of confidence they command depends on six factors: the existence or otherwise of parallel usages in **B** or the other versions, the strength of lexical support within the poem and / or the period, the context of the emendation, its complexity, its implications for the neighbouring text, and the calibre of competing proposals. No attempt is made to sub-divide the emendations according to such features; but in the *Textual Notes* they receive detailed consideration, and in some important cases alternatives are examined. As all these readings are major and this section contains the most arguable textual decisions, the conjectured lemma and the rejected archetypal reading are given in full. In the list an * indicates a word not found elsewhere in Langland. As in (i) and (ii), square brackets indicate an uncertain Bx reading, and these entries, too, are not counted in the total.

^Pr 11 me] I. ^206 so] to. I ^121 for] *om*. ^160 inmiddes] bitwene (*so in* // **C**). III ^260 (*haplography*) fel fel] fel. ^298 lordeþ] ruleþ. ^319 moot] wole. ^346 tidy] good. IV ^86 suffre] lete. ^91 wiþseide] seide (*so in* // **ZA**). V 111 liþeþ] likeþ. ^171 (*haplography*) faste faste] faste. ^282 his] goddes. ^378 it] *om*. ^400 siþenes] yet. ^412 mengen I of] go to. VI ^138 *garisoun] amendement. ^148 receyue] haue. ^150 putte] make. ^223 norisse] help. ^281 ek] *om* (*so in* // **A**). ^325 merke] se. VII ^34 drede] fere yow. ^45 preue] leue. IX ^15 biddeþ] ruleþ. ^39 welde] hadde. X ^90 loke] rule. 190 kennyng] kynne. ^242 *animales] beestes. ^246 *Gospelleres] Euaungelistes. ^251 Siþþe] Thanne. ^301 *querele] chide. [320 biyeten] biten / beten hem]. ^393 men] þei. ^446 wiþ] and. XI 49 of þe leste] if þe leste. ^181 principally] souereynly. 301 at] and. ^430 noye] doute. ^438 *rauȝte] folwed. 439 craued] preyde. kenne] telle. XII ^60 gomes lowe] lowe. ^127 Com] Was. ^131 Olde lyueris] Lyueris. XIII ^85 preue] telle. ^136 by so] so. (245 alle is] alle; *so* M). ^300 go telle] telle. XIV 7 me was looþ] looþ . 23 *myte] myste. 196 wroȝten] writen. 284–85 and Ioye / Is to þe body] is to þe body / And ioye also to þe soule. [300 lowe] ?*lawde*]. ^311 so wel] wel. XV ^123 ech haþ] haþ. [126–27 his...haue²] seruice to saue / haue]. ^312 haþ ben] was. ^393 Lede] persone. ^421 Bernard boþe] Bernard. ^470 mowen] don. XVI ^201 leodes] persones. XVII ^38 *teeþ] gooþ . ^214 þat lowe] þat. ^392 clene wasshen] wasshen. XIX [12 hise] Piers / cristis; 90 *richels] riche gold. 186 To hym] Hym. 241 of noumbres] noumbres ^244 wel er] er. 255 þat...Grace] alle quod Grace þat grace. 306 any kynnes gilte] gilt or in trespas. ^372 right saue] saue. ^409 Saue] But. ^413 leode] man. XX ^292 pleyen] make. ^293 renkes] men. 367 and my] my. 377 come for] for (*so all in* // **C**).

After **K–D**: II ^36 caccheþ] takeþ. V ^128 *biggyng] dwellyng. ^165 purueiede] ordeyned. ^415 telle I vp gesse] vp g. shryue me. VII ^59 if I lye witeþ Mathew] holdeþ þis for truþe / That if þat I lye M. is to blame. IX ^99 Tynynge] Lesynge. X ^279 barnes] folk. XII ^4 mynne] þynke. ^193 graiþ is hem euere] and he is euer redy. 270 wisshen (*after* Cr³)] wissen vs. XIV 28 Haukyn wil] Haukyns wif. XV [^224 stille] tyl / so]. ^450 fourmed] seide. XVII 90 segge] man. XIX ^230 Somme wyes] Somme. XX ^378 adreynt and dremeþ] and d. (*both so em. in* // **C**).

After **Sk**: XIII ^86 preynte] wynked.

§ 65. As in the case of the **A** archetype (*A Version* § 57), these Bx readings include mechanical errors: simple visual slips at V 111 and XI 30, 49, followed by smoothing in XIV 28 and XIX 90 (the latter presumably reflecting B-Ø); haplography at III 260 and V 171; unconscious substitutions of easier, non-alliterating synonyms (V 400, XIV 196); and losses of a small stave-word (V 378, XIII 136, XV 123) or a prefix (IV 91). But the incidence of seemingly deliberate alterations of the exemplar reading is heavier in Bx than in Ax; and it indicates a scribe determined to clarify the sense of the text, where he found it difficult, with scant regard for the resulting damage to the metre. The second half-line, in particular the key-stave, was especially vulnerable, and some at least of **C**'s revisions seem motivated by recognition of corruptions here, as at X 90, XI 430 and XII 193. At times the Bx error diagnosed has required treatment by conjecturing a word not paralleled in the author but difficult enough to have occasioned the archetypal substitution: examples are at V 138, X 242 and XVII 38. Less drastic are cases where the proposed expression is a part of the poet's recognised vocabulary that has been supplanted more than once. Examples are the verb *rulen* for three harder conjectured synonyms (III 298, IX 15, X 90) and the noun *persone* for *leode* in reference to God at XV 393 and XVI 201. The claims of emendations like the second here are strengthened by evidence elsewhere of the Bx scribe's aversion to lexically-restricted alliterating synonyms for 'man', as at XVII 90 and XX 293. But the main justification for such editorial changes to the archetypal text lies in the 85% of securer restorations and reconstructions in §§ 59–60 above. Without that evidence, the 15% in § 64 would have been adopted more hesitantly, and in some cases not at all.

viii. *Readings of Indeterminable Origin*

§ 66. Like that of **A**, the **B** tradition also contains readings that are not evidently or inferentially archetypal or sub-archetypal but randomly distributed across both families. In these, often minor instances, the direction of variation must be ascertained mainly from their intrinsic character, something most reliably done with other-version evidence as a control. This is particularly necessary where R is defective; for the Bx reading can be certain only when R is present. A good example is I 127, in which the adopted harder variant *pult* LR (understood as = β and α respectively) is also attested by one member of the γ sub-family Cr and by **Z**. The reading of the remaining γ copies and F (*putte*) is, however, supported by Ax. For *pulte* to be original, therefore, an error in Ax must have been repeated coincidentally by g, by the immediate ancestor of <WHm> and by F, or (if Cr is understood as having been corrected), by γ and F together. The mistake could have arisen from misunderstanding the sense, which seems clear enough in **Z**, **C** (revised) and an **A** witness W that is contaminated from **C** (*A Version* § 18 above). The error's first stage was Bx's replacement of accusative *hym* with nominative *he* so as to generate *he pult*, a possible but contextually unusual reading. Its emendation has been classed as a 'restoration' at § 60 above, since *pokede* **C** appears the reviser's response to an exemplar with *pult* rather than *putte*. But it could arguably be considered a 'reconstruction', as the full adopted reading *hym pult* is not unequivocally instanced in either **Z** or **C**. At Pr 186 L, three y mss (YOC) and R have *cracchy*, which is both in **C** and is harder than the majority *cacchen*. Here F's participation in the error suggests that it was not γ but w and three g-group members that substituted the more obvious verb, under inducement from 189 and the general context. The agreement of the latter witnesses should therefore be seen not as genetic but as due to random convergence.

§ 67. Often, however, because so much new material is added in **B**, no parallel evidence from **A** or **C** is available, and the 'direct' method must operate virtually in a textual vacuum. An example is the fairly minor Pr 140, where L and R (again taken as = β and α respectively) read *answeres* against γF *answerede*. The direction of variation from present to past may be diagnosed as revealing a scribal attempt to balance *greued* in 139. But F and γ may have departed from their respective α and β exemplars because Bx's actual reading was not *answeres* but a tense-ambiguous **answeryt* (for *answeryth*) that has left divergent reflexes in both sub-archetypes (see Appendix One, § 2 (b)). Acceptance here of LR's resolution as accurate will therefore depend on judging the mixed-tense form of 139–40 at once harder than the unmixed and demonstrably characteristic of the poet's practice. Such examples are frequent, but limitations of space restrict consideration in the *Textual Notes* to only the more important ones

ix. *Possible* **A** *and* **C** *Contamination in the* **B** *Version*

§ 68. The manuscripts showing most contamination from the **A** Version are (as observed at §§ 28, 30–1 and 46 above) H, G and especially F. The close links of *H* with **A** may relate to its being (uniquely) a conjoint **BA** text. For it seems reasonable to assume that if the available **B** pas-sūs of H's postulated source *h* recommended themselves to its scribe as a 'fuller' form, he might then have been led to collate it with the corresponding **A** portion at points where the former's text seemed unsatisfactory. This would account for the presence of desirable corrections like *her wombys] hemselue* (Pr 59), *nayle] tree* (I 186), *erdyn* [for *erende*] (III 41). All of H's 'good' readings are in fact in **A** except for *hys] om* Pr 99, which is only in **C**. But this, the sole reading that might support for H a claim to descent distinct from β, could be a felicitous scribal guess prompted by the context. What confirms contamination as the source of these readings in H is the presence of sixteen major **A** tradition errors like *sweuenyd] sweyed* Pr 10 and *pountyd] poundes* Pr 213 (both close to group u at A Pr 10, 86). Of *G's* unique right readings, none are shared with **A** alone; but (like H) G has significant disjunctive agreements in error with **A**, and these two fac-tors together prove contamination. Major errors are those with Ax at I 96 (and at III 46, where H accompanies), while others are with particular **A** groupings, as at Pr 82 (with uHK) and I 41 (with r^{1}J). Minor ones occur at IV 193 (with wE) and at VI 204 (with r^{1}).

§ 69. Amongst these contaminations is an editorially challenging category in which, despite **A**'s soundness, the variant in question has been held to 'correct' mistakenly a Bx reading here judged a revision. Thus, H variants rejected include *mete* at Pr 63, a correct **A** reading but one understood as revised in **B** to *marchen*, which is retained in accordance with the canon of ratifi-cation (it is confirmed by **C**). Like some of H's minor errors, many of them shared with G and F, this one could have arisen (semi)-memorially. So might *wersse þan nouth* at Pr 186 which, while recalling the ending of a stock phrase, replaces the 'harder' stave-word *feblere* with a (non-scanning) synonym. In G a major example is III 46 *brocour] baud* and a minor one III 293 *ayein] to*, both of which K–D print.[49] Another major instance from G (where the reading is also that of **Z**) is IV 141 *helpe] saue*. This too is adopted by K–D but its metrical form suggests revision, since Bx here uses the rarer Type IIb (see *Intro.* IV, §§ 39–41). The general principle this case illustrates is that a reading (even when authorial in character) which is diagnosed as present by contamina-tion is *not* to be accepted unless that of Bx is demonstrably unsatisfactory. For while originality in the source-version is a necessary, it can never be a sufficient condition for preferring **A** to a Bx reading that is by 'intrinsic' standards relatively less good but satisfies the core-text criteria.

§ 70. The same proviso applies with particular stringency to F, the copy that draws on the earlier version most openly (and often to greatest advantage). The phenomenon has been discussed in detail at § 46 above, but its causes remain open to speculation. What seems clear is that it fits better with the principle of economy to judge F's specific superior readings not (as do K–D) corrections 'from a manuscript of the **B** Version' but contaminations 'severally from manuscripts of **A** and **C**.' For the Athlone editors' hypothesis of a lost **B** copy as the source of F's 'authoritative' readings becomes proportionally more tenuous as one questions the originality of many such instances 'where **B**'s text is unique' and others for which K–D claim the F reading's 'superiority to those of the archetypal **C** tradition' (*K–D* p. 172).[50] But there is nothing tenuous about the evidence of borrowing from **A** in F, and a phase of collation of its α exemplar with an **A** copy may be securely ascribed to its postulated source *f*. The latter explanation may be defended against the charge of multiplying entities needlessly, because Corpus 201 itself (unlike M and, less extensively, Bm or Cot) does not reveal visible correction by the main or other hands (see § 34 above). One striking example is the line A Pr 95 added after Pr 94, which doubtless left no residue in the **C** Version because it was in fact removed in the extensive **B** revision of **A**'s Prologue. The plain evidence of contamination here must raise a presumption that several of F's other (real or supposed) corrections to the readings of β and R have a similar origin. Some of this **A** contamination may be semi-conscious, but if a corrupt form of **A** appears, deliberate substitution may be involved. An example is at VIII 49, where the rhetorically more emphatic *fowle flesh3* replaces the theologically more exact *flesshis wil*. But for the one **A** contamination found in either sub-archetype, the three lines that in α replace β's twelve at III 51–62, a memorial explanation will suffice (*K–D* p. 67). This example, taken with the family's numerous other missing passages, offers solid evidence that α was directly based on Bx and lost these lines mechanically, as K–D suppose (see §§ 50–1). But it could equally be that censorship on grounds of propriety has operated here (as suggested at § 52 above) and that the α scribe inserted some imperfectly recollected **A** lines to fill a too-obvious gap.

§ 71. Likewise restricted to a few manuscripts are the contaminations from **C**, which occur mainly in two γ sub-groups (§§ 24, 27 above). Firstly <OC²> has six such readings (one major), and its constituent members O and C² each have three (respectively one and all major). The explanation of these lies less readily to hand than for those in the trio of conjoint **BC** copies that make up B. But in at least XIII 411 (shared with B), OC²'s source may have been trying to make sense of Bx's near-nonsensical *hys woman*] *is whan a man*, which γ, L and R seem to have despaired of. A similar enterprise is displayed by C² and O at XVIII 160 and XIX 181, in which *al* and *seest* are required respectively for the sense and for the metre; but neither presupposes direct scribal access to **C**. Such access was evidently absent at XX 261, where C²'s scribe has filled a perceived sense-gap either by half-recalling the lost **C** line or, more probably, by intelligently guessing its likely content. Felicitous conjecture may also explain C's right reading *Mighte* at XIX 391, and at XIII 100 F's *gan rodye* and Hm's *ruddud*. The latter, adopted by K–D (and *Sch¹*), is here rejected as a possible scribal recalling of **C**'s graphic revision of a syntactically difficult original. In the case of B, however, direct resort to a **C** copy seems a fair presumption; for this postulated group-original must have been a **B** Version with a defective beginning which was 'patched' from a copy of **C** (§ 27 above). The latter might well have been consulted additionally to make good a few readings that failed to give sense, such as XIII 2, even if more straightforward metrical corrections like III 6 need not presuppose this. But that the **C** Version was familiar to the scribes who copied B's extant descendants is indicated by such 'good' corrections in Cot as *adreynt* at XX 378 and such erroneous 'corrections' as *mercede* for *mercy* at XIX 76. K–D use the first in a reconstruction of the line followed here for both versions. They also (p. 160) accept the second as original, R–K duly following in their edition of **C**. This is rejected here; for while the word in question is undeniably what K–D call a 'Langlandian expression', very probably a coinage, its threefold occurrence is restricted to III 290–332, and it is not recorded anywhere else. The likelihood that Cot's scribe altered his exemplar to *mercede* after consulting a lost **B** copy superior to both Bx and B¹ (rather than through recalling its memorable introduction at C III 290) therefore seems remote. Correction from **A** or **C** is not restricted to OC²B, remaining at least possible in one other group-source, w, at X 57 *guttes fullen*] *gutte(s) been / is fulle*, and at XI 287 *lynnen ne wollen*] *trs*. Neither of these examples, however, seems beyond the capacity of the limited number of copyists of the extant **B** manuscripts. For these were predominantly London scribes who could have known the poem in one or more of its other versions, too.

x. Passūs XIX–XX *of* **B** *and* Passūs XXI–XXII *of* **C**

§ 72. It remains to consider Passūs XIX–XX of the **B** Version, with their unique body of supplementary attestation in the near-identical archetypal text of **C**. The following analysis fills out the brief account in §§ 2–4 above and will provide a transition to the next section dealing with the **C** Version. Firstly, in the poem's final two passūs it is clear that both Bx and B¹ (the basis of B² = Cx), descend from the same source, B-Ø. This is proved by fifteen shared errors, twelve of which are major. In the following list of these, the lemma is in all but four cases the editorially emended reading, and the variant the agreed reading of Bx and B². Where two variants appear, the first is Bx, the second Cx; and if the latter is uncertain, both contending sub-archetypal readings are given. In XIX, where R is absent, an F reading only doubtfully that of α is disregarded if Cx and β agree.

B XIX (**C** XXI) 12 hise] Piers β; cristis F(= ? α)Cx. 76 Encense F] *om* βCx (Rechels *C*-R). 90 richels] riche gold. 186 To hym] Hym (and ʒaf hym *C*-p). 236 buggynge and sellynge *C*-N²] *trs*. 241 of noumbres] noumbres. 305/06 *So div. C*-Y; *as* 3 *ll*. 348 caples tweyne] two caples. 372 right saue] saue. 409 Saue] But. 413 leode *C*-N²] man. 446 þe Pope; amende] *trs*. **B** XX (**C** XXII) 292 pleyen] maken. 293 renkes] men. 366 alle hem] al Bx; hem Cx. 367 and my Lady] my lady. 378 adreynt and dremeþ] and dremeþ Bx (adreynt Cot); adreint Cx.

Of the above, five require brief comment. In XIX, 12 could be another B¹ reading if F here = α and α = Bx. In 76 F's *Encense*, not supported by Cx, is taken to be (like the **C** witness R's *rechels*) a happy scribal guess and not the reading of α (< Bx). Both 236 and 413 are here judged similarly felicitous scribal improvements of B¹'s defective metre and not, as R–K believe, 'correction[s] from a pre-archetypal **C** copy.'[51] Finally, at XX 378 Cot's *adreynt* is interpreted as either a recollection of **C** or an attempt to correct a reading found faulty in sense by substituting that of the **C** manuscript posited as available for collation when Cot was produced (about a decade later than Bm).[52]

§ 73. As stated in § 3 above, it is clear that Bx does not derive from B¹, since it lacks nine certain or probable B¹ errors (six of them major) that are retained in B². There is no proof (as already noted) that these were not introduced by the scribe of Cx, who obviously cannot be held incapable of error. But since B^1 is in effect known only through B^2, an attempt to distinguish further between B^2 and Cx (assuming it feasible) would hardly affect the issue of Bx's independent descent from B-Ø. In the list of Cx errors below, the lemma is an emendation, unless specified as the reading of Bx.

B XIX (**C** XXI) 242 craftily Bx] *om.* 306 any kynnes gilte] gilt or in trespas Bx; Cx *uncertain*: þynge gulty *C*-**p**; agulte *C*-**x**. 342 Bx *uncertain*: Surquidous β] Surquidours Cx?α. 377 Bx; *line om* Cx. **B** XX (**C** XXII) 13 Bx *uncertain*: noon β] þat F; Cx *uncertain*: ?þat non. 120 kirke] α = Bx; churche Cxβ. 301 hij] he Bx; they Cx. 366 alle hem] al Bx; hem Cx. 378 adreynt and dremeþ] and dremeþ Bx; adreint Cx.

Of these, too, five require brief comment. XX 366 and 378 are listed again because these emended readings are based on what appear to be 'split' variants, each partially containing the reconstructed form presumed for B-Ø. XIX 342 may be a B^1 error for the reading which β has felicitously corrected (see *Textual Notes*). In XIX 377 and XX 120 alone can it be certain that Bx retains the exact form of the common original.

§ 74. The third point made at § 3 above was that B^2 is not derived from Bx, since it lacks the latter's 25 errors. These are now listed in full below:

B XIX (**C** XXI) 12 hise] Piers β*C*-N[2]; Cristes CxF. 56–8 Bx *uncertain*. 56 toek Lucifer þe loþly] Cx; þanne took he lotthly lucifer F; *l. om* β. 57 hym as he is bounde] Cx; his as his bondeman F; *l. om* β. 58 he (1)] he þat F. 59 lawe] Cx; lawes F. 97 comsede] Cx; gan to Bx. 154 Bx *uncertain*: and preide þo] and bisouȝte þe; al þo propre F. 181 seste] Cx*B*-0; doost Bx. 183 þouȝte] Cx; Bx *uncertain*: tauȝte β; took sone F. 230 wyes] *om* Bx; men Cx. 244 wel er] er Bx; ?*C revised*. 252 be] Cx; were Bx. 255 þat alle craftes quod Grace] alle quod Grace þat grace Bx; **C** *revised*. 297 plete] plede Cx; Bx *uncertain*: he pletede F; pleieþ β. 301 euene] Cx; euere Bx. 306 any kynnes gilte] Cx *uncertain*: any þynge gulty *C*-**p**; agulte *C*-**x**; gilt or in trespas Bx. 317/18 *So div.* Cx; Bx *uncertain*: *div. after* worþi β; *after* vertues F. 317 forþi] worþi ?Bx. 333 home Piers] Cx?Bx (hoom F = ?α; Piers = ?β). 337 lond; þe] Cx; Bx *uncertain*: loore; & þe F; *l. om* β. 346 Sire Piers sew] Cx; Bx *uncertain*: P. plowhman seew all F; P. þere hadde ysowen β. 367 in holynesse] Cx; Bx *uncertain*: in vnitee β; strong F. 373 a sisour and a somonour] Cx; And false men flatereris vsurers and þeuis / Lyeris and questemongeris Bx. 433 soudeþ] Cx; sendeþ Bx. 441 *So* Cx; *l. om* Bx. 468 wole he nel he] Cx; Bx *uncertain*: I wole β; to presoun F. 482 That þou haue þyn askyng] Cx; Bx *uncertain*: þat þou þyn lykyng have F; Take þow may in resoun β.

B XX (**C** XXII) 8 Was] Cx?Bx (& þat was F; As β. 14 cacche] Bx *uncertain*: cauȝte β; caste F. 19 deide for þurste] Cx; *trs* Bx. 34 God] Cx; and Bx. 54 it tid] Cx; it Bx. 62/3 *So div.* ?Cx; *after* lyue Bx. 67 hir] Cx; hem Bx. hir lemmans] Cx; lemmans of Bx. 126 suede] Cx?α; sente βF. 198 heo] Cx?α; she βF. 261 *In* Cx; *l. om* Bx. 309 pardon] Cx; *om* Bx. 366 alle hem] al Bx; hem Cx. 377 come] Cx; *om* Bx. 380 hij] þei Bx; ?**C** *revised*.

Despite the many uncertain readings here, especially in XIX, the proof afforded by XX 261 is (as at § 73 above) decisive. It is therefore inferentially probable that two copies of B-Ø were made, one (B-Øa) the immediate source of Bx, and the other (B^1) used in the revision to **C**. It remains possible in theory that some scribes had access to B-Øa down to the level of individual extant manuscripts such as O, C^2 and B, and found in that early copy (which would fill the rôle of K–D's 'lost superior **B** manuscript') the correct readings they now preserve where Bx is in error. But a more economical explanation, for which reasons have been given, is that all such readings have come in by contamination from copies of the **C** Version. After their generation, it seems to the present editor likely that the two traditions of Bx and B^1 never made any direct contact.

Conclusion

§ 75. From the above account it is clear that an edition of **B** must depend even more than one of **A** (and, as will emerge, of **C**) upon other-version evidence, here from both the prior and the subsequent texts. This assumption was implicit in the practice of Skeat (I, §§ 34, 37) but was fully developed only by Kane and Donaldson. The present edition takes the assumption to its logical conclusion, by attempting to establish the text of **B** in parallel with that of all the others, including **Z**. Consideration of the latter version will be kept until after discussion of **C**, to which the next section is devoted.

THE B VERSION: NOTES

1 Ll. 49–51, which are hesitantly retained, add little and are somewhat clumsily written (see *Textual Notes*).

2 See section on date at *Introduction*, V §§ 14–18 below. If the Ophni-Phineas passage in C Pr is in draft form, it may be a late addition, perhaps suggesting that Langland saw the Prologue as an appropriate location for material of topical interest.

3 This fact Langland would moreover have had to take into account in his final revision, which was presumably made available entire only after his death. See Schmidt, 'L's Visions and Revisions', esp. p. 7.

4 Other possible signs of this in **C** that K–D profess to identify (*B Version,* pp. 103ff) seem insufficiently demonstrable to figure in the present discussion.

5 An exception is the case of Passus XVI, on which see below at § 5.

6 The hypothetical projected figure represents a sixth of the total at the error-rate of the better Bx scribe.

7 The estimate here is less strict than in the Everyman *B-Text* p. lxi, since it includes marginal cases, lines attested by only one tradition, and citation lines.

8 *B Version*, pp. 62–9.

9 Recent revivals of Skeat's view that α represents a phase of the **B** tradition intermediate between β and **C** are examined and rejected at §§ 50–55 below.

10 See Blackman 'Some Notes', p. 517 and Adams 'Evidence for Stemma', p. 274. Though Blackman's ω corresponds to γ in the present diagram, she identifies β not as a sub-archetype but as what is here called Bx, and judges α a **B** tradition contaminated from **A** and **C**. Adams sees Cr^1 as descended from β^1, a derivate of β on the same level of transmission as LM, which was collated with M; WHm as descended from β^2, a derivate of β^1; B as descended from β^4, a derivate of β^3 (= γ); and C^2 as descended from O.

11 These readings are discussed under both w and M at §§ 13 and 34–6 below.

12 In most of these, w is accompanied by the rejected manuscript S, which derives from the same immediate ancestor as WHmCr and will be disregarded after the next note.

13 The number rises to 58 if four shared with S are added: X 155, XIX 286 (major); XIX 452, XX 234 (minor). K–D's figure of 43 (table, p. 21) is incorrect.

14 K–D's figure of 17 (p. 21) is thus seriously out.

15 Cr's one major right reading at I 152, unless it is an inspired scribal conjecture, is probably the result of collation with a **C** copy.

16 The complex changes of exemplar within y are discussed by K–D, pp. 44–8, 51–4.

17 Readings inadvertently omitted from the Apparatus will be given here in full.

18 Though ease of loss by homœoteleuton in this instance must be acknowledged.

19 Davis 'The Rationale for a Copy of a Text', p. 144.

20 Davis, 'Rationale', p. 149.

21 The *trotten* agreement with Ch at 144 would accordingly have to be dismissed as coincidental. It may be significant in this context that H^2 and its companions TCh are also conjoint manuscripts, although (unlike BmBoCot) their **A** and **C** portions have not been linked by material from the third version, here **B**.

22 Blackman, 'Some Notes', pp. 314–15, recognises both G's contamination and its independent value.

23 See *Intro*. IV *Editing the Text* § 40.

24 To these could arguably be added III 118 and VI 124, supported by **ZA(C)**, but not adopted for **B**, as Bx is not in these instances clearly inferior.

25 *B Version*, p. 61

26 In Apparatus for 'g' read 'gM'.

27 In Apparatus for 'G' read 'g'.

28 This is an indication that major agreements are much likelier than minor ones to be genetic in origin; for in most of the 120 cases of the latter, agreement of a β-ms with α appears coincidental.

29 See §§ 42–3 below for a list of β's errors.

30 In 'The F Scribe and the R MS of *PP*', pp. 530–48.

31 Examples are V 23, XII 49, XV 89 and XVIII 14.

32 See *Introduction* I, *The Manuscripts*, no. 23, for references.

33 Hanna, 'On the Versions of *PP*', in *Pursuing History,* pp. 221–22. The position is also argued by Warner in 'The *Ur*-B *PP*', pp. 20–21.

34 'The Lost Revision of *PP* B', p. 119.

35 See *Textual Notes ad loc.*

36 'Introduction' to *Written Work*, ed. Justice & Kerby-Fulton, pp. 5–8.

37 See *Sk* II, 283 n. Skeat's reconstructed sequence is probably that of Bx (see *TN* to C XVII 187–251); for the likely β form of 506–09, 528–29 see Justice, p. 6

38 The culinary figures are respectively from Justice, p. 6 and Taylor, p. 116. Warner aptly points out that the 'supposed hash' is also found in B I 100–1, XIV 138–9//.

39 'Lost Revision', p. 120.

40 Ibid., p. 119.

41 Z V 32–47; AB V 14–20; C V 116–22.

42 'Versions', pp. 223–29.

43 Cf. J. H. Newman: 'Now the test of an admissible hypothesis will be its incorporating without force the whole circle of statements of which it takes cognizance. Some of these may be *prima facie* adverse, and the difficulty may be reasonably solved; some may be at least accounted for, and their objective force suspended; others, it may be, cannot be explained, and must not be explained away' (*An Essay on the Development of Christian Doctrine* (1845) III, v, 5). The most radical account of the genesis of the **B** tradition, which speculatively reconstructs the transmission-history of α and β in the light of ms NLW 733, is Warner's, for which the author's term 'scenario' ('*Ur*-B' p. 23) might seem a better description than 'hypothesis'.

44 Hanna, 'Versions', pp. 219–21. Fletcher's objection ('Essential WL' pp. 62–3n4) that **L**, 'though taking trouble over his composition', might have tolerated scribal inaccuracy (over vernacular poetry as opposed to legal documents) 'within a certain latitude of reason' seems to the present writer not just 'paradoxical', as its author describes it, but self-contradictory.

45 Ibid., p. 226; an opinion succinctly described by Kane (in Alford, *Companion* p. 196) as 'pure nonsense'. Warner's similar notion of this poet's 'most distinctive trait' as a 'compulsion to tinker' ('*Ur*-B' 12) reveals basic misunderstanding of the nature of **L**'s art as a *makere* and of his activity as a scrupulous reviser. For demonstration of Langland's intense interest in the minute particulars of language and versification, see *The Clerkly Maker*, and the *Commentary* in this edition, both *passim*.

46 Ibid., p. 229.

47 'Re-editing' the **B** Version, as one who has done so might without impertinence suggest, resembles a medieval pilgrimage from Dover to Jerusalem more than one from Southwark to Canterbury.

48 An argument that accepts the integrity of the **B** Version but holds that **L** intervened in the tradition after the copying of the archetypal manuscript has been made by Adams in his important recent article 'The R/F MSS of *PP*'. For Adams, Bx was corrected, particularly in the second half of the poem, with loosely-inserted slips in the manner envisaged by R–K for the composition of **C** (see *Intro*. II §§ 107–9 above). Some of these additions were accordingly unavailable to α and others to β in what Adams discerns as a pattern of 'complementary' loss / inclusion. A unitary **B** Version is still proposed, though with Bx now seen not as a scribal fair-copy but as an authorially-altered manuscript evincing a kind of 'rolling revision' (though not the same kind as that proposed by disintegrationists like Taylor).

49 Reasons for retaining Bx in the former are given in the *Textual Notes ad loc.*

50 Among those discussed in the *Textual Notes*, see the note on B XIX / C XXI 76.

51 *C Version*, p. 102. R–K, it should be said, do not include these two particular N^2 readings in their list of such corrections.

52 K–D, *B Version*, p. 5; Davis, 'Rationale'. p. 143.

The C Version

i. *The Manuscript Tradition*

§ 1. It is unknown when and why Langland began his final re-writing of *Piers Plowman*.[1] This is unlikely to have been soon after the completion of **B**, as the notion of 'rolling revision' (rejected at *B Version* § 57 above) would allow. Time was required for the work to be read, 'received' and make the impact to which John Ball's famous allusion testifies.[2] The Peasants' Revolt of 1381 thus readily suggests a *terminus a quo*, an occasion and a motive. It cannot have been, as with **A**, the poem's imperfect state that prompted recomposition, since **B** is complete. Moreover, the low incidence of **C** contamination in the earliest **B** copies[3] argues against wide familiarity with **C** in the author's lifetime and accords with the general opinion that Langland did not finish it. The scale of **C** contamination in the **A** copies K and W, and the supplementation of **Z** and **A** by **C** rather than **B** in seven of the eleven 'conjoint' versions,[4] need not conflict with that supposition. For the relatively late date of the **A** manuscripts,[5] themselves witnesses to an unfinished version, is consistent with their having been produced to meet demand for a copy of the poem in any shape or form. This interest could have been aroused by the fame of **B**, possibly assisted by the posthumous release of **C**. The *terminus ad quem* of the final version is more unsure. Its unfinished condition, which was not remarked by Skeat, is commonly ascribed to the poet's death after completing the revision of B XVIII as C XX. But this event is dateable only from two literary sources outside the poem. One is the reference to it in the conclusion to A XII by John But, identified as the King's Messenger who died in 1386; the other, corroborating this, is the echoes of **C** in *The Testament of Love* by Thomas Usk, who was executed in March 1388.[6] More recently, a case for Langland's being still active in 1388 has been argued from supposed allusions to the Statute of Labourers of that year in the opening of Passus V, a passage thus judged to be the last-completed portion of the poem.[7] The case seems to the present editor unproven; but to accept those allusions, discount Usk's testimony or ascribe it to acquaintance with a work in progress, and attribute the A XII reference to another John But, would leave the year of the poet's death completely uncertain.[8] The only remaining downward constraint would be the date of the earliest **C** manuscripts, such as Trinity College, Dublin 212 (V), the copy containing the note about Langland's paternity. This is assigned to the end of the fourteenth century but stands textually at seven removes from the original,[9] a fact that implies strong interest in the work during the decade after the poet's death.

§ 2. As with **A** and **B**, internal evidence for dating is scanty and ambiguous. A new passage (III 200–09) criticising scandalous royal tolerance of wrongdoing suggests, as Skeat believed, Richard II's growing unpopularity in the 1390s; but it is not incompatible with earlier unease about the young king's behaviour in the mid-1380s. The lines need not be pressed too hard, as little of substance hangs on establishing the date of the author's death. For exactly how 'unfinished' the **C** Version is, and whether the last two passūs were deliberately left untouched, underwent minor revision, or were posthumously annexed as an ending because the author's working papers were too 'foul' to be copied, remain matters of literary judgement, about which major disagreement is possible. Positive knowledge of the manuscript tradition terminates in the archetypal source of the surviving witnesses. This was a copy either authorised by the poet or based on his papers as arranged by a 'literary executor' who was the work's first 'editor.' Russell and Kane's analysis of the archetype leads them to think of the poet's holograph not as a fair copy awaiting only a final touching-up in places but as made up of working drafts (*C Version*, p. 89). Consequently, for someone copying what they see as a heavily-altered B-Text interleaved with new material, there was far more chance of error than had been the case for the scribe of B-Ø, who presumably worked from the author's fair copy. Such an interpretation allows the Athlone editors an ample licence to intervene. But while it is naturally difficult to be uninfluenced in the process of editing by one's general sense of the probable process of revision, the richness of manuscript attestation in **C** and the relatively uncorrupt state of the archetype (compared with that of **B**) encourage editorial caution rather than boldness in its treatment.

§ 3. How and when the archetypal **C** manuscript (**Cx** hereafter) was generated remain uncertain. But in the case of two groups of the earlier manuscripts, linguistic evidence indicates copying in or near the poet's presumed place of origin, and within a period of at most fifty years. The first group belongs to one sub-archetypal family x^1, (from South-West Worcestershire). The second, p^2 (from adjacent South-East Herefordshire), includes all three witnesses of what may be the elder branch of **p**, a sub-division of the other family x^2.[10] Some members of p^1, the larger and probably younger branch of **p**, show linguistic features that relate them to other central south-midland counties, Gloucestershire and Oxfordshire.[11] In marked contrast with most manuscripts of **B**, those of **C** show no particular London connections. But whatever this might imply about Langland's place of residence when finishing **C**, the text itself reveals even more strongly than **B** what Pearsall calls a 'casual intimacy of London reference.'[12] Moreover, while **C** abounds in close observation of the life of the urban poor and refers in the Passus V 'Autobiographical Prelude' to the Dreamer's domicile in Cornhill and to 'lollers' dwelling in the capital, it shows no regional concerns, but retains its predecessor's national and universal outlook.

§ 4. To return to the manuscript tradition: by contrast with **B**, for Prologue to XX of **C** only one initial scribal copy of the authorial manuscript need be assumed as the source of all the thirty extant witnesses. For XXI–XXII the most economical supposition is that Cx was directly based on the last two passūs in the poet's revision copy, 'B^1' (*B Version* §§ 2–3, 71–3). The text of this could have been untouched, or lightly revised in places, the interpretation preferred here. In Pr–XX, Cx as now recoverable stands at two removes from the authorial revision-copy of **B**. But it has already been found valuably to supplement Bx in the the task of establishing **B**'s original form; and in XXI–XXII it is even illuminated by Bx where the latter lacks errors that Cx inherited from B^1. The final two passūs of **C** (where the substantive content of Cx is called 'B^2') accordingly attest some of the securest text in the whole poem. That they nonetheless contain proportionately twice as many errors as the earlier passūs may be due to their largely unrevised condition. This feature lends support to the opinion favoured here that the holograph of Pr–XX was nearer a fair copy than a working draft. But those passūs have to be edited mainly from **C** manuscript evidence alone, for all their differences from the earlier versions may be due to revision. The operation of the 'linear postulate' naturally remains subject at all times to the 'core-text' criteria relied on for assessing the authenticity of **A** and **B**. But much of **C**, particularly from the part corresponding to the middle of B XI onwards, has little or no close textual equivalent. Allowance has further to be made for lexical and rhetorical developments in Langland's style of a kind paralleled in the 'last periods' of his major contemporary Chaucer, later writers like Shakespeare and Milton, and 'revising' poets like Wordsworth, Yeats and Auden. These developments may be generally expected not to contradict the core-text criteria, themselves based in part upon the C-Text (in its *un*revised portions). But devices like *repetitio* are much commoner in new and revised **C** than in **B**, which in turn differs markedly from **A** in its more complex syntax and macaronic style. Such considerations have a part to play in the process of establishing the text of the final version.

ii. *The two families of* **C** *manuscripts*

§ 5. The archetypal readings of **C**'s 7354 text-lines are preserved uniformly or with fair certainty in only some 4350, about 60% of the whole.[13] In the remaining 3004, the Cx reading must be established firstly by comparing the testimony of traditions that originate from the two independent copies of Cx here called x^1 and x^2. In some 1180 of these readings, secondly, the text of each of these copies cannot be distinguished with complete security for such comparison, because of cross-family differences between their constituent witnesses. This problem arises largely with minor instances, in which the Cx reading must be sought amongst the competing alternatives by the direct method, with or without help from other versions. The archetypal text that emerges is still, to the present editor's judgement, much less faulty than it seems to Russell and Kane (R–K hereafter). For it has only 108 errors that demand emendation, about 1 in every 68 lines, or less than 1.5 %. This may be higher than the 1 in 58 (or 0.78) inferentially estimated for B-Ø, where this can be reconstructed in the last two passūs. But it is more than four times better than Bx's average error-rate of one in 16 (or over 8.5 %) of its firmly attested lines. These comparative figures give no reason to think that Cx was other than a direct copy of the holograph

§ 6. The distribution of Cx's errors, with the readily explained increase occurring in the little-revised XXI–XXII, points to the work of a single scribe, by contrast with the two scribes detectable in the archetypal phase of **B** (*B Version* §§ 4–5 above). Unlike Bx (but again expectedly, given the likeliest assumptions as to how it was produced), no individual passus or passage appears virtually error-free like B XVI, which seems to have been corrected by the poet (*B Version* § 5). Cx's typical errors (discussed at §§ 67–72 below) are mechanical or broadly unconscious. A few may reflect imperfectly-finished material, such as the half-dozen in Pr 108–23 and the single line XVII 73, unless this is spurious, as tentatively judged here (see the textual note). Emendation of **C**, however, is more speculative than in **B**, since only about 40 of the Cx errors diagnosed (fewer than half) occur where parallel material is at hand. Moreover, the **C** tradition reveals a surprisingly low proportion of assured archetypal lines, something that results from the tendency of the sub-archetypes attesting its readings to introduce variants on a wider scale than do α and β of **B**. The problem is exacerbated by the unavailability of a major x^2 group witness in Pr–XI, where **t**'s extant representatives TH²Ch preserve an A-Text. The archetypal character of agreed x^1t readings in the section from XII–XXII (usually also implying agreement of x^1 and x^2) is thus necessarily more secure than that of readings in Pr–XI supported only by x^1 or by **p**. Certainty about the character of x^2 in the earlier portion is therefore unattainable; but it seems likely that the ancestral manuscripts of x^1 and x^2, which have texts of comparable quality, were near-coæval products of copying in closely related centres. For their typical errors (and particularly x^1's) are 'negative', early-stage faults of omission due to carelessness and haste. By contrast, **p** not only has these (and shares them at times with t),[14] it also displays 'positive' scribal features like deliberate substitution, re-writing and padding-out that suggest prior acquaintance with the text.

§ 7. What seems fairly sure is that, as in the case of Bx, two early copies were made from Cx. The first, x^1, is clearly attested and has a simpler history, if one as complex as that of **r** in the **A** tradition. Its eleven extant representatives are the six single-version copies XYIP²UD, the four conjoint copies D²BOL and the fragment H. From the second family-original x^2, which has certain seemingly contradictory features, derive the remaining seventeen. These are the twelve single-version copies PEAVRMQFSGKN, the five conjoint copies TH²ChWZ, the fragment Ca and the **C** interpolations here designated K². The x^1 manuscripts fall into three groups, each with its own ancestor deriving independently from the family original. Thus XYIHP²D² descend exclusively from a single copy of x^1 (**y**) and BOL from one closely related to y (**b**). Both y and b may also possess an exclusive common ancestor (**i**) that would satisfactorily account for their shared errors; but the amount of text available for comparison is too small for this to be certain. UD descend from a third copy of x^1 (**u**), which is independent of y and b, and also of i. Three separate lines of transmission from x^1 are thus shown in the diagram at § 13 below. The unusual manuscript N² could derive from a fourth copy of x^1; but it is heavily contaminated from the **p** branch of x^2, and its anomalous position in the list of sigla is intended to indicate as much.[15]

§ 8. The line of descent from x^2 divides into two strongly contrasted branches with separate ancestors deriving independently from their common sub-archetypal source. The first, **t**, is preserved in the three conjoint manuscripts TH² and Ch, which descend from t via two intermediate sources.[16] The second branch **p** comprises the fourteen copies PEAVRMQWFSZGKN, but despite its large size and complex structure is to all appearances a sub-family like t. That is, **p** is less like β than like γ in the **B** tradition, since its ancestral manuscript seems not to have been immediately copied from Cx. It falls however into two further sub-divisions with major group-status, the exclusive originals of which derived immediately from **p**. These are p^2, represented by GKN, and p^1, consisting of PEAVRMQWFSZ. The eleven p^1 copies form two further distinct sub-groups: **m** containing three pairs PE, AV and RM, and **q** comprising Q, F and S, which are joined after Passus IX by Z (in its earlier portion the Z-Text) and after Passus XI by W (up to that point an A-Text). The readings of group p^2 are closer than p^1's to those of x^1 in Pr–XI and to those of x^1t in Passūs XII–XXII. This feature could result from inter-family contamination, but it is more economically ascribed to p^2's greater fidelity to **p**'s presumed original text. The appellation 'p^2' is thus not intended to signal the group's textually secondary character but only its numerically smaller attestation by three manuscripts (one seriously defective), in contrast to p^1's eleven. For if the numerical proportions had been reversed, GKN would stand in the line of sigla just after the x^1t copies that they are more closely related to. Both branches of **p** could have been coæval, though they were generated in different locations. But with the exception of one p^1 copy (A), neither is linguistically as near as family x^1 to the archetype's presumed place of origin. This, from the evidence of the more primitive x^1 copies, was SW Worcestershire around Malvern.

§ 9. Although the ancestor of the x^2 family was not descended from or influenced by x^1, one branch t, despite its limited attestation, reads so closely with x^1 that the Athlone editors treat both t and x^1 as belonging to a single family. Agreement of t with x^1 is admittedly about eight times more frequent than with **p**. But while 80 errors t shares with x^1 seem to imply an exclusive common ancestor, even the 25 of these that could be called major may be attributable to coincidence. The dependence of t on **p** is ruled out since it lacks **p**'s 400 errors (140 of them major) in this section. But by contrast with x^1, the sixteen major errors amongst the 55 that t shares with **p** do appear, after analysis, of such a kind as to suggest an exclusive common ancestor. This is most economically identified as the direct copy of Cx here designated x^2.

§ 10. In transmitting the ancestral text, t was nonetheless much the more accurate of the two postulated x^2 branches. This may be the reason why t's readings, even after allowing for its subfamily errors, are so much closer to x^1's than are those of **p**. It is therefore convenient to denote the x^1t readings in XII–XXII by the joint sigil **x** but to forgo 'x^2' in the apparatus for the agreed readings of **pt**. If t had been present as a C-Text in Pr–XI, it might have been preferable to use the sigils x^1 and x^2 throughout; but there is no way of knowing whether t shared more errors with **p** than with x^1 in those passūs where the t copies now preserve only the **A** portion of their conjoint text. This is purely a matter of procedure, therefore, which has as its corollary the use of '**x**' rather than 'x^1' for the readings of XYIP^{2}UD in Pr–XI. It implies neither doubt that x^2 existed nor belief that t would have agreed preponderantly with x^1 had it been present. Its practical purpose is that of highlighting the clearly observable contrast between **p** and **x** throughout the text, where both traditions may be compared on the basis of numerous complete witnesses. This contrast brings out the dual character of **p** as independent (in preserving through x^2 archetypal readings lost by x^1 and sometimes by t) but also as subordinate (in often corrupting x^2 at points after XII, where t's greater reliability can be confirmed by x^1). There is another reason for keeping the separate sigil **p** even when its agreements with t presumably attest their common x^2 source. This is that **p** is the only faithful witness to x^2 (and thence by inference to Cx) in nearly 300 instances (about 80 of them major) where it is x^1 that errs and another 80 (about 25 of them major) where t shares x^1's error. Thus in Pr–XI, where t is absent, **p** in effect earns the status of a manuscript 'family'. For where it is right against x^1, **p** must be judged to preserve the reading of x^2, the family original it is presumed to share with t. But **p**'s errors in this section may or may not have been present in x^2; for this can be known only from Passus XII on, when the degree of **p**'s accuracy can be gauged through comparison with t. The evidence from here on reveals **p** to be as proportionally corrupt as its showing against x^1 in Pr–XI would give reason to expect. Yet since **p** also preserves 300 right readings, it remains an indispensable authority for the text throughout. In contrast with the **B** family α's relation to β, then, **p** emerges as secondary in importance even in Pr–XI, where the competing variant is attested by x^1 alone; but its value is relatively higher than that of the **m** family of **A** in comparison with **r**.

§ 11. In conclusion, there are two direct lines of transmission from the archetype, x^1 and x^2. From x^1, y and b descend, perhaps through a shared intermediary source, i, and u immediately. Another three lines correspondingly derive from x^2, t perhaps immediately, p^1 and p^2 through their intermediate source **p**.[17] Although p^1 seldom and p^2 never uniquely preserves Cx, neither branch can be eliminated. For constituent pairs or individual members of each appear at times to be the sole faithful witness to their ancestral text **p**. The readings of **p** are accordingly registered in the Apparatus throughout. As with the sub-archetypes, however, the complex subsequent history of their further group-traditions, involving many intermittent losses, restricts the number of group-sigils it is convenient to cite. Thus 'm' and 'q', which appear in the diagram below, are not employed in the Apparatus. Conversely, among the p^1 groups, e, because persistently instanced by four witnesses, is the only one to be used or to have its variants frequently included. Of the x^1 branches, the briefly attested but closely knit three-member group b is recorded wherever **x** is seriously in doubt, since in its few hundred lines as a C-Text it is a co-witness to the hypothetical sub-family ancestor i that it may share with y. For if b had been present throughout, a sub-family i might have emerged that rivalled **p** in frequency of citation. Next t, because entitled to sub-family status like **p**'s, is cited wherever Cx is not virtually certain from the agreement of x^1 and **p**. But to save space, t's many (and often eccentric) individual variants are ignored where an Apparatus entry is not otherwise needed. Among the two-member groups, only u is cited to any extent, as it is an independent witness to the correct x^1 reading when y errs. By contrast r, though guaranteed independent by its unique preservation of one apparently authentic line,[18] is noticed only as part of a list of complex variants.

§ 12. As the parent-group of the chosen base-manuscript, y's readings are recorded where certainly or probably recoverable. Its most complete representative, *Hm 143* (X), has been favoured by all editors since its discovery in 1924 (II § 41). But while its one serious rival *BL Addl. 35157* (U) is of closely similar date and linguistic character, there is little reason to prefer it. The present edition thus takes X as the copy-text for a reconstruction of Cx on the basis of x^1 corrected from the x^2 tradition preserved initially in **p** and, from XII onwards, in **p** and t together. In something over 100 instances, corruptions traceable to Cx, the common source of both traditions, have been emended by restoration on the authority of individual witnesses or that of the parallel B-Text, especially in XXI–XXII, by reconstruction, or by conjecture where little or no direct evidence is available. The text is thus presented in the language of a manuscript dateable to within a decade of the archetype, with grammar and orthography fairly close to that reliably presumed for the original (see Appendix I §§ 1–2).

§ 13. On the basis of the foregoing account, the inferred relationships between the extant **C** copies and their hypothetical group- and family-ancestors may be diagrammatically expressed as follows:

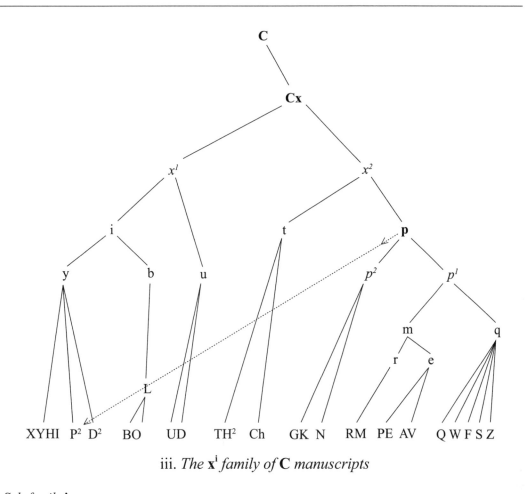

iii. *The* **x**ⁱ *family of* **C** *manuscripts*

Sub-family **i**

§ 14. The hypothetical sub-family **i** comprises **XYIP²D²BOL** and fragment *H* (which, from the scanty evidence available, belongs immediately after X).[19] It is described as a sub-family rather than a group because, like γ in the Bx tradition, it has two distinct branches containing several manuscripts. One, **b**, was the immediate source of BOL; but a combination of losses, re-arrangement and contamination make it uncertain whether further sub-divisions exist within the other, **y**, one possible arrangement being [{(XHYI)P²}D²]. The sub-family i is recognisable initially on the basis of six agreements in error between y and b. The exact relation of these groups is hard to specify with certainty because of b's brevity, the absence of YD² over the portion attested by b, I's partial absence in the Prologue and P²'s contamination from **p**, a feature indicated by broken lines. (N²'s position is too unclear to allow its inclusion in the diagram; see § 39 below). The character of the first three readings listed indicates, however, that the relation of y and b was close.

Major Pr 28, 183 +K². II 9 (*corr. a.h.* O). **Minor** I 152 (*so* I, *but* -P²), [174 +AVS]. II 66² (*add to App.*).

The postulate of a common source i presupposes that neither constituent group derives from the other. The <BOL> ancestor's *lack* of y's errors at Pr 107, I 102 and 192 need in itself imply only that b was at these points a more accurate copy of y than its other extant representatives, XIP^2. But more is indicated by b's unique right readings at Pr 224 and particularly at 216. Were *reik* at 216 only a brilliant scribal conjecture, b's descent from y would not be worth doubting; if original, however, it must be due either to correction from a superior pre-archetypal copy or to pure descent from Cx through x^1, the more economical explanation preferred here. For its part, y lacks b's major errors at Pr 133 and II 112, and this fact can be reconciled with the errors y shares with b only by positing an immediate common ancestor that contained both. These may seem slender grounds for positing i; but as b is present for less than 8% of **C**, they might in principle have been much strengthened had b preserved the whole text. The position of i in the diagram at § 13 above takes account of the clearly non-secondary character of y, both in Pr–II 128 and the rest of the poem (on the term 'secondary' cf. § 62). Whatever its defects, i must have been uncontaminated from **p** and other versions. For such is the case with its descendant y, though two y copies D^2 and P^2 exhibit this feature, the latter massively, and members of b are contaminated from **B** (see §§ 24–5, § 27).

a. *Group* y

§ 15. The first group includes the base-manuscript of this edition and so (as with groups w of **B** and t of **A**) receives extended treatment. Since i, the original of **y**, does not descend from b, and since X itself is earlier than L, the oldest of b's three members, y and b may be assumed to have been coæval. Apart from X the group includes three more single-version copies, one complete but damaged (P^2) and two with major losses (Y at the beginning, I in the beginning, middle and end); one conjoint copy of late date (D^2); and a fragment of 100 lines from between Passus I and III (H). The members of y cannot be ordered with precision because of substantial gaps in Y and I; but P^2 and to a less extent D^2 differ from XYIH in being contaminated from **p**. Nonetheless, after discounting D^2's absence from about half the poem, the five main witnesses can be reliably accepted as a genetic group on the basis of some 26 isolative errors, sixteen of them major. In 60 further readings, 30 major, one or two members lack the group error, or y is joined, seemingly at random, by one to three other copies. The group is imperfectly represented: (a) from II 157–XII 19 by XYIP^2 (joined by H for III 123–74); (b) from XII 20–XXI 79 by XYIP^{2}D^2; and (c) from XXI 80 to XXII by XYP^{2}D^2. Prior to II 157 there are four members XIP^{2}H, from I 199 to II 44. Before I 199 there are only three XIP^2, with I absent from the Prologue before 91 and after 157, a stretch in which no exclusive errors of those present are found. In the following list of y's agreements, a minus sign indicates that one member lacks the denoted error, a plus that a manuscript not a member of y shares it, the latter references being in square brackets.

Major (a) II 240. III 449, 451. IV 139, [158 +F], 178 -I. V 118^1, [118^2 -P^2+EA], [133 -I+G.] ?VII 300. VIII 20, 166, 315, 333. IX 38 [*def.* I, +AVG]. [265 +EK], 270. [XI 268 -Y+U].
(b) XII [35 +N^2], 140–41 -Y. XIII 112 -D^2, 123*a* -Y. XIV ?48 -Y, 125 -YP^2+N^2, 155 -Y. XV 1[44 +EQWN], 190 -Y (*in App. for* D^{2}D *read* P^{2}D^2), 2[42 -P^2+U,] 2[83 -Y+DQ]. XVI [128 -P^2+VR], 232^1 -Y, 315 -Y. XVII 210 -Y, 239 -Y. XVIII 33 -D^2, [60 -Y+U], 75 (*different error* Y), [139 *def.* I; -Y+D], 244 (*diff. error* D^2). XIX 174 -D^2; *om* X, 240, 245 (*diff. error* P^2), 2[97 +DM.] XX [75 +N^2], 307, [389 -P^2+F]. XXI 48, 58 -D^2, ?113 (*om* IP^{2}D^2), 317, 350/51 (*in App. read* ut *for* t *and* y *for* x^1).
(c) XXI [312 +N^{2}W,] [320 +N], *om* D^2, [347 +N^{2}N,] 3[49 +S,] XXII 13^3, 186 -D^2.
Minor (a) II 217^2, 238 -P^2. III 5, 205, 342 -P^2, 447. IV 4, [132 -P^2+U.] V 160 (*in App. for* P^2, **x** *read* P^{2}u, y). VI 376. VII 108, 239 -P^2, [281 +K]. VIII 87 (*om* I; *in App. del.* p^2 *and for* p^1 *read* **p**), 148 -P^2. IX 313 -P^2, *om* I. [XI 271/2 +N^2].
(b) [XV 37 +SWN, 167 -Y+U]. XVII 173 -Y, [263 -Y+F]. XVIII [97 -Y+Z], 207. XIX 8, 138 -P^2, 187 -P^2, [227 +N], 290 -D^2, *om* P^2. XX 270 †P^2; †D^2, [441 -I+PN], [457 +N (*see Textual Note*)]. XXI 57 [(*add to App.*) -P^2+DT], 82 [-P^2+?t], 86 -D^2, 225 [(*add to App.*) +D].

172

§ 16. In this list the copies outside the y group that share its variant (those in square brackets) lack persistence, so they do not disconfirm the evidence of the criterial readings. On the other hand, attention is due to three copies significantly free from the postulated group-error: Y, especially in the (b) section (in 17 cases, 13 major); P^2 (in 13, four major); and D^2 (in six, four major). P^2's right readings, which are here regarded as resulting from its collation with a **p** copy (§§ 24–5 below), are congruent with its also including several **p** errors. The D^2 evidence, which may be similarly explained, is too small for certainty, but the number of instances is proportionally high. The right readings of Y, though they could derive from a source such as u, may simply be more accurate reflexes of the group-original than those of the other members.[20] But major deficiencies in Y, I and D^2, and the indeterminate character of many variants, make it hard to be sure whether y's members should be ordered as given or as $[(XHIP^2D^2)Y]$. There is a case for treating b as part of y since their agreements in b's small attested portion, if sustained over the whole poem, might have outweighed the evidence of its unique right readings. But on the available data, these favour the arrangement $[(XYHIP^2D^2)BOL]$, denoting independent derivation of y and b from i, which was an immediate copy of x^1 (§§ 13–14). Such an explanation fits with b's origin as a defective **B** copy supplemented from a **C** copy that has left echoes in the manuscript's **B** portion (*B Version* § 27; and § 27 below).

§ 17. Despite its errors, y is the soundest identifiable Cx group. Its hypothesised parent manuscript i, presumably one of the earliest generated, thus warrants a place on the same level of transmission as the x^2 sub-families t and **p**. Group y cannot be eliminated, as it contains some 30 right readings that are unique, eight of them major, and eight more (given in square brackets) shared by one or two other manuscripts. In addition, some of its members uniquely possess right readings not derived from another version. These must therefore be present by pure descent, by intelligent scribal conjecture or by correction from outside the Cx tradition.[21] In the following list of y's correct readings, a minus sign before a sigil indicates a y copy's agreement in error with **p** or **p**u, a plus sign agreement with y of a **p** copy, U, or another version.[22]

Major -P^2 II 191. V 14 (*in App. for* **x** *read* y, *for* P^2 *read* P^2u), 35. VI 382, 410. XVI 183 (+ α of **B**). XXI -P^2D^2 449. -P^2 470.

Minor [Pr -P^2+b 13]. III 118, 316, [+FS 334]. V 90, -P^2 161, -P^2 190. VI 59^1, 82, 90, 381. VIII -YP^2 159^2, [-I+Q; *om* P^2 196,] 264^2, 282, 331. IX -IP^2 157, [+U 260]. X 189, -Y 229. XI 145. XVI 255, [-P^2+WN^2 347]. XVII -Y 67, -P^2D^2 77. XIX -P^2D^2 168, [+TW 233]. XX 328, [-P^2D^2+W 464]. XII +WN 25.

§ 18. The only complete member of y is **X**, chosen as the copy-text though substantively less good than Y, which is ruled out because it is defective before II 157. While X is comparatively somewhat less sound a descendant of its original than its counterpart W for the **B** Version, its x^1 text is intrinsically preferable for the half of the poem where x^2's only representative is **p**, and it shows no contamination from the other versions. The language of manuscript X is close to the poet's presumed SWM dialect. Its handwriting places it among the half-dozen oldest copies of **C**, and the many corrections by a second hand (except for one over erasure at III 176) do not seem to have involved collation with an exemplar from a different family, as was the case with P^2 (§§ 24–5 below). X is remarkable for its systematic erasures of the name *Peres*, which begin at VI 366 (fol. 28*v*), where the referent is not actually the eponymous ploughman. Their presence is unexplained, but is more likely to have had some precautionary political aim than to be a scribe's preparation for rubrication.[23] For reasons of space, they are not recorded in the Apparatus, and except where substantive issues arise over the exact reading, as at V 31, all small alterations by the corrector's hand are ignored (for these the Athlone apparatus should be consulted). The bulk of X's individual variants are removed to the Appendix in Vol I so as not to distract attention from the family and group readings that the main Apparatus seeks to record, though the facts of insertion or erasure are noted where relevant.[24] X suffers from the mislineation common in most copies of the longer versions, but its significant omissions are few and there are no losses of lines larger than of two at the most. It wants only Pr 232 and VII 304 in addition to the two lines and eight half-lines absent from its family ancestor x^1 and the one apparently missing from i at Pr 183. It contains one minor unique right reading at XI 295[25] and no distinctive spurious matter.

§ 19. Manuscript **Y** resembles R of the **B** Version in that it is potentially the best copy of **C** but for lacking, through loss of leaves, the first 600 lines (as R lacks 750). Carefully written in a clear script and set out as if prose, Y has no corrections or alterations by another hand and appears, from readings like XIX 59, a fairly sound descendant of the group-original. Thus it lacks the major errors found in the other y copies at XII 140–41, XVII 173, 239, and minor ones at XV 167, 283 and XVII 210a, 263. Collation of its immediate exemplar with an x^2 copy cannot be ruled out to explain this; but the four readings free from the x^1 error that suggest that possibility could be due to intelligent scribal conjecture (VI 51, XVI 76/7, 232 and XVII 78). This interpretation is confirmed by Y's careful spellings at III 492 (shared with P^2U) and VIII 184, which preserve exact sense, and its unique correct lineation at XXI 304/05.[26]

§ 20. By contrast with the neglected Y, manuscript **I** has had its fair share of attention. Skeat thought the I form of passages corresponding to IX 128–40 and 203–79 in some respects superior to the 'received text' as found in his base-manuscript P. Just as he had judged Rawlinson Poetry 38 a later stage of **B** than that in Laud 581, he saw Ilchester as an earlier draft of **C** with readings that sometimes '*point back* to the B-Text.' An example Skeat cites is XVII 94, where 'I alone keeps the right reading *Wederwise*, found also in the B-Text.'[27] But Skeat failed to notice that this is the reading of the whole family as attested by the four x^1 copies available to him, and the error *Wonderwyse* is a major piece of evidence for the postulated common origin of **p** and t.[28] Russell, too, formerly believed I's Pr 104–24 'a superior survival of an original...deformed in the version preserved by the other manuscripts' [i.e. the archetypal text].[29] This opinion, though abandoned, glimmers spectrally in R–K's speculation (p. 194) that the Prologue's weaving of discrete passages on hermits and bishops into 'an integral discourse on a distinct topic' suggests I's access to 'surviving loose revision material' (presumably Langland's drafts).

§ 21. It will be appropriate to consider I further here in its relationship to the conflated **ABC** copy **Ht**. For in Ht the interpolation of IX 66–279 and Pr 91–127 after B VI 158 has been seen by Wendy Scase as evidence for the existence of a 'second textual tradition' of **C** distinct from that of the archetype.[30] Observing the close similarity in the two copies' linking lines and pattern of omissions,[31] Scase takes their substantial agreements in error to indicate that manuscript I was an 'improvement' of 'something close to the Ht text,' noting that Ht and I lack the 'B-Text lines interlineated with this material in the C-Text' (pp. 458–9). These passages, she argues, were not excerpts from the received C-Text but were generated in the process of incorporating the new material into the poem. The lines on false hermits circulated in a form 'cued for insertion but not edited into the C-Text revision'; but it is less clear that the Ophni-Phineas passage did so, since in I it continues as a C-Text, whereas in Ht it ends with C Pr 125–7. The passages' imperfect alliteration, clichés, lack of amplification, and possible metrical experiment all point to an unfinished condition.[32] Finding support in the 'autobiographical passage' of C V (esp. 1–5) for 'early, separate circulation, and subsequent re-thinking and revision,'[33] she concludes that the IHt text should be taken into account in editing **C**.

§ 22. One unexpected editorial consequence of Scase's claim is that the received text's imperfectly alliterating Pr 105–24 would have to be seen as itself the product of a scribe's redaction 'from memory or from what [he] could decipher' (in Skeat's words) of an accidentally-defaced original copy.[34] This opinion is echoed in Brewer's statement that the 'chaotic state of the manuscripts' may reflect the process of the work's composition as much as that of its transmission.[35] But no such wide-ranging speculative inferences need be drawn from the evidence of the hermits / bishops passages in manuscript I. For the whole notion of I's text as an 'improvement' of a lost IHt original is over-elaborate and arbitrary and, as Pearsall has shown, both copies contain little that cannot be attributed to an enterprising scribe bent on 'alliterative embellishment.'[36] As now printed entire in the Athlone Appendix, the Ilchester Prologue reveals its true character as what R–K call a 'compilation' of 'passages from C IX...set within a conveniently simple frame of the **A** Prologue, with a little filling out from that of **C**.'[37] The I text itself shows typical scribal substitutions for words that lack alliteration in the Cx form, such as *peres* for *folk* at 116 and 118, with its unLanglandian contextual sense.[38] Such 'improvements,' like those in the **B** manuscript F, may in principle be distinguishable from a hypothetical earlier and other creation underlying them. But the prospects for its recovery are slight and its textual usefulness, as all editors except Skeat have eventually agreed, is minimal. There thus seems little reason to question Pearsall's conclusion that the I Prologue is in shape and substance a wholly scribal product. All that ms I yields of value here is one correct reading at 127 (shared with K^2's **C** interpolation), a felicitous conflation of seemingly 'split' **x** and **p** variants that may be what Cx actually read. And at VI 149, I uniquely attests one major variant judged original, so it cannot be eliminated. It is also the only x^1 copy with the correct reading at X 275.

§ 23. For the rest, ms I stands firmly in the y group, on the basis of all but four of the 26 agreements noted at § 15 above. More specifically, it has 22 disjunctive agreements with X (*R–K* p. 44) where Y is also present, of which three are major, VI 223[1] [in App. *read* 'XI' for 'X'], VII 148 and X 197. This grouping is not challenged by I's 17 such agreements with Y (*R–K*, p. 44), most of which are trivial spelling-variants. The one exception is *a pes*] *an ase* at VIII 166; but this is almost certainly a y-group reading, since *a mase* X is a derived individual variant and P^2 has altered *as* in another ink over erasure. The XI pairing is little more effectively challenged by the 38 agreements of XY (*R–K*, p. 44), since these are again largely of spellings. Perhaps no more than three where I is present are major (VII 8, XIX 91 and XXI 36), as are another three where it is absent (XVIII 147, XXI 135 and 249). So comparable a closeness between X and each of its partners permits, without imposing, the relation [(XY)I]; so R–K's explanation of 'sporadic consultation and "correction" in a single copying centre' (p. 44) seems very plausible. It is certainly consistent with both the orthographic and the textual evidence, e.g. the spelling *ou* for the diphthong |ɔɪ| in III 64 *cloustre* XY and XVII 224 *apousened* XI [in App. *read* 'XI' *for* 'X], which suggests a common exemplar, 'regularised' by I in the first case and by Y in the second.[39] These somewhat indeterminate data suggest that **XYI** (to which H should be added) are less like BOL (since no one member is based on either of the others) than like AMH[3] in the **A** family **m** (*A Ver-*

sion § 25). For within y these three copies effectively form a 'core-group' on the basis of some 18 agreements, half of them major. The reason for the great discrepancy between this figure and the 33 agreements estimated by R–K (p. 43) is that many of the variants they judge errors are not so regarded here. Moreover, half a dozen they include were shared by P^2 before its (visible) correction, so these are cited at § 15 above as evidence for y rather than for <XYI>. In other words, P^2's descent from y looks to be direct and not through any one of the three 'core' copies, their immediate exemplars, or their group original, if there was one. The same holds for D^2 which, as a conjoint text, necessarily shares many fewer readings with the core-group. In the list below, two XYI agreements inadvertently omitted are given in full [in the Apparatus to XII 237 and XX 197, 241 *for* 'XY' *read* 'XYI'; to V 160, 190 *read* y *for* **x**; and to VI 167 *read* 'XI' *for* 'X'].

Major IV 21^1 (*corr. a.h.* X). VI 167. IX 125 haue] *om*, + *a.h.* X. IX 331. XII 237. XIX 145 him] U&*r*; *om* XYI, 290 [*in App. for* y *read* ?y]. XX 197, 241. **Minor** II 238. III 447. IV 4, 21^2. V 160, 190. XVII 206 [*in App. for* **p** *read* **p**P^{2}u; *for* xG *read* XYI]; *possibly only a bad spelling if read as* religioues]. ?XX 239 [*in App. add* was þer I], 270 [*for* P^2 *read* P^{2}D^2].

These variants, few and unpersistent, are not incompatible with P^2's and D^2's membership of y (§ 15 above); for the ascription of their correct readings to exemplars collated with **p** copies is confirmed by their having several indicative **p** errors (§§ 24–6 below). The grouping XYI is questioned by some 20 agreements of XYU (*R–K* p. 45); but all of these save three are minor, and most are trivial, including the simple visual error at XX 240 (*h* for *b*). In the major crux at XI 124, the reading *mette* IP^{2}D is more probably a coincidental 'correction' of a phrase rendered difficult by prior corruption of the verb than a preservation (from y and u respectively) of the true x^1 form lost by XYU (see *Textual Notes*). The IP^{2}D variant cannot be archetypal, since *ouet* XYU is a mere spelling-variant of *out* **p**, which must therefore have been the reading of Cx. At Passus XI 218 the reading of XYU is once more that of x^1 concealed by further variation in P^{2}D; and in XXI 466 the same is true, except that D here corrects from its regular secondary **p** source. The challenge from XYU can thus be safely set aside.

§ 24. Among the members of y, **P^2** underwent most contamination from **p**, first in its immediate exemplar and then by visible insertion and alteration in the manuscript. The first phase reveals nearly 100 agreements in error, some 35 major. Most could be from either **p** branch, but whereas there are no exclusive agreements with p^2 some 19, of which four are major (II 126, III 54, X 275^2 and XIX 165), indicate collation with a p^1 copy. More specific pointers to P^2's conflation-source appear in minor readings and are correspondingly less reliable. XVII 228 suggests the p^1 group m and some 70 more (*R–K* p. 27) specifically manuscript M, a copy early enough to have been used by the scribe of P^2's exemplar. A dozen readings categorisable as major by the single criterion of affecting a line's scansion are of kinds sometimes caused by random convergence. These are the *kyrke*] *churche* substitutions at III 397, V 103, VIII 26, 53, IX 9, XI 246, 250, XV 11 and XVI 255; the inverse *ch-*] *c-* at II 89; and the apparently visual errors at XVI 266 and XVII 162. In the following list of P^2**p** agreements, those shared by up to three x^1 copies and, in one case, two aberrant members of t, are denoted by a *plus* sign. Illustrating the types of readings (including 14 major ones) where coincidental variation may have occurred, they are recorded here solely to furnish a yardstick of comparison with the exclusive agreements adduced as potentially genetic. Of P^2's many additions in a later hand, the few cited in the Apparatus are placed in square brackets here. While these prove collation with a manuscript of a different tradition, they say nothing about the character of P^2's main exemplar, so most are omitted.

Major Pr 230. II 89 +ID, 126. III 54, 223, 276, 357 +U, 415 +D. V 35^1 +u, [35^2], 66, 104, 105, 122. VI 55, 68, 149, 298^1

(*in App. for* **p** *read* **pP**^{2}), 436. VII 176, 247. VIII 26, 167, 220, 258, 322. IX 9, 202, 338^{1,2}. X 275^2 (=p^lK). XI 246 +D, 250, 270. XII 10 +D^{2}u. XIII 195. XIV 28 +t. XV 290. XVI 105 +DH^2, 183, 255 +D^{2}uCh, 266 +UG, 302 +Ch. XVII 136, 139, 162 +uCh. XIX 165 +D^{2}N^2. XX 34*a*, [140 (=p^l)], 203 +t. XX 471. XXI 453. XXII 323 +DTH^2.

Minor Pr 13 +u. [81]. I 99 (*in App.* read not P^{2}p^2 but p^lP^2), 177 (*in App.* read **x**p^2 for **x** and p^lU for **p**). II 27*a*^{2} +b, 73 (*in App. for* **p** *read* **pP**^{2}), 86, 136 p^l+U, 139 +D, 159^{1,3}. III 14 (*in App.* read **x**p^2M for **x** and p^l for ?**p**), 61, 109 +D, 191^2, 247, 305 +u, 324 (p^l). IV 37, 55 +D, 90^2, 105, 127. V 14 +u, 18, 51, [66], 78 +D, 192. VI 42^2 +I, 136, 235, 252, 269 +ID, 271 (*in App.* read p^lP^{2}D), 275 (p^lN), 278, 280^2 (*in App.* read **pP**^{2}), 317, 367, 394, 414. VII 22, 58, 61^1 (*in App. for* **p** *read* **pP**^{2}), 97, 115 +D, 144 +D, 147, 182, 223, 245^{1,2} (*in App. for* **p** *read* **pP**^{2}), 252, 255 +D, 257 +D, 286. VIII 30, 53 +u, 68 +D (*add in App.*). 91, 111 (p^l+N), 115 (p^l), 139, 148 +u, 159, 175 (=p^l) +D, 190, 227, 244, 301, 304^1 (p^l). IX 8 +u (*corr. App.* to read y *for* **x**, P^{2}u *for* P^2), 60, 105 +U, 153, 207, 230 (=p^lG), 247, 299, [345]. X 38 +D, 50 +X, 130 +ID, 175 (= p^lN) +D, 178, 268 +DN^2, 292. XI 171, 201 +DN^2, 210 (=p^l), 266, 316 +H^{2}Ch. XII 80 +D^{2}UN^2, 113 +N^2, 185 (=p^l)+Gu, 217 +T. XIII 89 +D^{2}ut, 107 (=p^l) +NN^2, 119, 136^2, 186 +D^{2}Dt, 236. XIV 39 +D^{2}t, 56 +u, 194 (=p^l; *add to App.*). XV 12 (=p^l) +D^2, 47 +Ch, 70 (=p^l *or* ?eRM), 151, 165, 214 +Ch, 243 +D, 250 +D, 257 +N^2. XVI 39 (?= e), 78 +Dt, 101 +N^2, 230 +D^{2}UTCh, 360 +tN^2. XVII 10 +D^{2}D, 28 +D^{2}DCh, 77 +D^{2}ut, 228 (= eRM). XVIII 271 +D^2. XIX 63, 65 (=p^l +U), 327. XX 8^2 +I, 82 +ChN^2, 106 +N^2, 112, 174, 229 +N^2, 231 +D^2, 320 +Ch, 354 +DChN^2, 395 +D^{2}Ch, 399 +U. XXI 11 +D^2, 13 +D^2, 42 +YD, 321 +Dt, 348 +D^{2}N^{2}t, 433 +Ch. XXII 95 +U, 245 +t, 266 +D^{2}Dt.

§ 25. From its **p**-type source, P^2 also took good readings such as the striking one at XXI 435, acquired at the visible second stage of correction (the same process appears in D^2 and D). But some 38 (six major), distributed fairly evenly through the text, must belong to the first stage and are therefore unlikely to preserve the reading of i. For the errors P^2 corrects are shared by the other y witnesses with u and so must have been in x^l, while attribution of its right readings to a **p** source correct at those points is congruent with the 100 errors P^2 shares with **p** (listed at § 24). In a further 35 cases, other x^l copies with the *right* reading have also been specified, not as evidence for **p** contamination in P^2 but to illustrate the frequency of random convergent variation. Where t concurs with them, the **p** reading in P^2 may be descended from x^2; but where D^2 and D concur, it is more probable that their exemplars were (like P^2's) collated with a **p** copy, as both (unlike t) also contain errors of this sub-family (see §§ 26 and 29).

Major Pr 20. VI 148, 359^2. IX 137. XI 266 +D. XIV 138. XVI 128 +uCh. XIX 301, 332 (*partial*). XX 389 +ut. XXI 247 +D^{2}t, [435] +D^{2}D, 480 +D^{2}t. XXII 51 +D^{2}Dt.

Minor Pr 33, 172, 208, 210. I 35, 46, 181, 182. II 60. III 262, 494. IV 15, 38, 56, 62. V 134, 151, 160. VI 6^2, 51^2 +Y, 59^3, 95, 104 +D, 312 +D, 320. VII 5 +D, 71 +D, 164 +D, 184 (*add in App.*), 240^2, 281 +Iu. VIII 42^2+D, 85, 303 +U, 314. IX [345^1]. X 45 +u, 136 +IDN^2. XI 55, 184^2 +N^2. XIII 173 +t. XIV 97 +Iut, 128 +Dt. XV 21 +t, 66 +D^{2}uN^{2}t, 261, 263*a* +D^{2}Ch, 296^1 +Ch. XVI 84, 330 +D^{2}t. XVII 117 +t, 261 +D^{2}DN^{2}t. XVIII 46 +IDt. XIX 187 +ut. XX 323^3 +D^{2}Dt, 373 +N^{2}t, 382 +Dt, 413 +U. XXI 82 +uN^2, 162 +D^{2}t, 246 +t, 287 +Dt, 381 +t. XXII 307 +D^{2}Dt.

These many correct(ed) readings give P^2 no special importance, but they illuminate the activity of scribes interested by the numerous differences between the two textual traditions. P^2 cannot be eliminated, since it has (probably by felicitous conjecture) the best verb-form at IX 311 and unique right readings at III 6 and XVII 147.

§ 26. The final member of y is the sixteenth-century conjoint text **D**^{2}. It is more loosely related to the 'core-group' than is P^2, which it resembles in that its lost exemplar also seems to have been collated with a copy of **p**. D^2's descent from y is indicated by 40 errors, some 30 major, shared with all or most of the group (see § 15). In seven cases (five major) where it lacks the y-group error, it is presumed corrected from an x^2 source. This conclusion is supported directly by its twelve x^l family errors (five disjunctive and seven more shared by other x^l copies in brackets): [XIII 186 +P^{2}D; XIV 39 +P^2]; XVII 84; XIX 41, [143 +u]; [XX 464 +P^{2}u; XXI 73 +P^{2}D, 185 +D]; and XXII 31 (to which should be added in the Apparatus [XII 88 +D], XVI 81^1, XIX 27), and collaterally by some 20 readings free from x^1 family errors (see § 33). That the former's source was t rather than **p** is indicated only by the wrong line-division at XXI 241/2 and by two other (non-exclusive) major errors, at XVII 125 (+I) and XXII 449 (+P^{2}u), one an obvious substitution of an easier synonym, the other an omission, but both perhaps coincidental. This interpretation is challenged by one major omission error (XIX 165) and two minor ones shared exclusively with **p** (XII 10, 176); but a link with t is collaterally indicated by the two major right readings at XXI 401 +N^2 and XXII 110. D^2 cannot be eliminated, as it has a unique right reading at XXI 410, possibly by happy scribal correction of an obvious gap in the sense.

b. *Group* **b**

§ 27. The major x^1 group **b** comprises the three conjoint manuscripts **BOL**, which share some 50 isolative agreements, about 20 of them major. So large a number of errors in only 560 lines (about 7.5 % of the poem) confirms R–K's view that b's **C** source was a poor manuscript.[40] It was also one contaminated from **B** at Pr 72, 133 (after which b has B Pr 106), 231 and I 5 (this last shared with I), while at 160 its error *a myȝte bygynneþ] comseth a myhte* is significantly that of Bx. This feature is unsurprising, given the circumstances of its origin (*B Version* § 27). Most of b's readings are not recorded except when part of a larger variant entry, as at Pr 183, II 84, 112 (major) and Pr 171, 192 (minor). But b cannot be eliminated, because of its unique major right reading at Pr 216.

c. *Group* **u**

§ 28. The third constituent group of x^1 is **u**, consisting of **U** and **D**. Arguably it should be treated as a sub-family on a line with i in direct descent from the family ancestor. But though perhaps as early as y, u is unlikely to precede i; for it shows signs of collation with an x^2 copy at Pr 181–83, where x^1 seems to have been defective, and possibly at XV 80–3, where only u and t have correct lineation. The group is established from 130 agreements in error, about a fifth of them major (listed in full *R–K*, pp 30–1). Only the following appear in Vol I, as part of a larger apparatus entry.

Major Pr 181, 183. II 9 (*for* U *read* u). III 479. **Minor** [I 133 +S]. IV 134. VI 376.

Group u's identity is collaterally confirmed by its unique attestation of eight right readings, which preclude its elimination. In three of these the group-reading is inferentially that of only one member, the other having erred with y. D's freedom from several x^1 errors, however, is better attributed to correction from an x^2 source, because it also shares some x^2 errors (see § 30 below).

Major VI 163. XI 208 (D), 269/70 (U), [306 +YN^2]. [VII 36 (D,+VQK)]. VIII 77–8a (*in App. for* 'so' *read* 'So u' *and for* 'All MSS' *read* 'X&r'). XIX 255/56.
Minor II [159 +QF], 217. VIII 135 (D; *in App. read* Ne haue] D), 247/48.

That u derives from x^1 is shown by its sharing 360 presumptive family errors with y (see §§ 33–4 on x^1 below). But it cannot descend from y, as it is free of the 86 certain or probable y-group errors listed at § 15, or from the postulated source of y and b, since it lacks the six i errors (§ 14). Of u's two constituents, **U** is a complete, early and uncontaminated x^1 witness and could if required have furnished the copy-text in the absence of X. U cannot be derived from D, which is both later and free from three of its errors where all other copies are also wrong. It does not group with any other copy than D, and when lacking the right readings preserved solely by D, it may be presumed to have erred from their exclusive common ancestor. U's one unique major right reading precludes its elimination, but as it otherwise requires no further notice except when supporting other witnesses as part of a longer apparatus entry, only a few of its individual variants are recorded, as at VII 276.

§ 29. Unlike U, **D** has substantial agreements with other copies: 45 with M (*R–K*, p.28), all minor and most trivial; 68 with P^2; and 60 with N, which R–K (p. 31) convincingly judge random. Of the last, one worth notice is X 275 *lely*] *trewly*, where D's exemplar probably replaced the contextually obscure x^1 reading *leix* with *lely* from a **p** source and D then substituted an obvious modernising synonym that happens to coincide with the p^2 copy N (as again at XX 307). The high number of D's readings cited is partly due to its frequent divergence from U when the latter appears as the citation-source for u:

Pr 216. II 217. IV 180. VIII 349. X 7. XI 218, 288, XII 98^2. XIII 125^1. XIV 150. XV 8 (cf. **p**), 89 (*after erasure*), 131 (*ins.*), 167. XVII 207–10. XVIII 75^2. XIX 290^2. XX 13, 107 +N^2, 114, 140, 177, 337, 413. XXII 215, 236, 282.

Like P^2 of y, D's immediate exemplar seems to have been collated with a copy of x^2, as shown by its sharing nine / ten x^2 errors:

Major XV 89 +D^2, *after erasure*; 106 +D^2. XXII 13. **Minor** XII 88 +D^2. XVI 328. XVII 82 +D^2. XXI 73 +P^{2}D^2, 185 +P^{2}D^2, 321. [XII 236].

This conclusion is supported collaterally by D's 17 agreements with x^2 in a right reading:

Major XI 44 (+ *a.h.*). XIII 39/40. XXI 365, 466. XXII 240 +D^2. **Minor** XII 37. XIV 47, 128 +P^2, 193. XVI 362. XVII 104 +D^2, 155^1. XVIII 46 +IP^2, 240 +IP^{2}D^2, 248 +IP^{2}D^2, 323^3 +P^{2}D^2, 382+P^2.

While in principle these may merely indicate accurate preservation of u where U erred, D's persistent co-occurrence with P^2D^2 strengthens the likelihood that its exemplar was similarly corrected from an x^2 source (see §§ 25–6 above). Two major instances, IV 180 and XV 89, prove a second stage of correction in D itself, like that in P^2 (§ 24 above), but also paralleled in D^2.[41]

§ 30. Of necessity, these errors are clearly attributable to x^2 only from Passus XII onwards, where t is also present; for any earlier agreements may go back only to x^2's descendant **p**. But the repeated specific agreement with either group p^1 or p^2 that would decisively confirm the latter interpretation is not found; so the exact origin of D's five agreements in error with **p** before Passus XII remains uncertain:

Major II 185 (= PMS +P^2). IV 180 (*over erasure*). **Minor** II 101, 174. VII 255 +P^2.

The same holds true in the dozen instances where D is free of the u-group and x^1 family error and where, for its right readings, an x^2 source must be presumed:

Major VI 125, 148 (*add* +P^2). VII 36 (= VQK), 164 +P^2, 177. XI 56. XIII 125^3. **Minor** II 187, 198 (= PEF, +P^2), VII 173, 201 +P^2, 213. VIII 42 +P^2.

Of these, at least XIII 125 confirms that D's x^2 source cannot have been t, which is here wrong; and that conclusion is to some extent supported by XX 321, where D's error is with **p** against x^1t. But this is minor and, like XXII 386, where conversely D's agreement in a right reading is with H^{2}Ch (=?t), could be coincidental. D is chiefly of interest as, like P^2, illustrating inter-family contact between an x^1 member and x^2 (probably in the form of a **p** copy). But it cannot be eliminated, as it has four unique right readings, Pr 138 and XI 56 (perhaps scribal conjectures), and two recorded at § 28 as representing u.

d. The x^1 family: conclusions

§ 31. The above survey of the structure of x^1 has shown its groups and individual members to contain nearly 50 variants (about 20 of them major) which appear original on intrinsic grounds and on comparison with the parallel text in one or more other versions. These readings, as in the case of the α and β families in **B**, include some that may preserve the archetype by direct descent through x^1 and others that may have come in from a source belonging to the family x^2. There are a few probable contaminations from **B** in individual x^1 copies; but none of these is drawn upon to emend the text. Since all the extant x^1 witnesses contain one or more unique right readings, none can be eliminated; so all have been collated, though to save space they are cited only selectively. But the readings of group y are recorded entire in the Apparatus and those of X either there or in the Appendix. The evidence for x^1, the exclusive common ancestor of y, b and u, is the body of 380 wrong readings, some 130 of them major, shared exclusively by all three branches. The variant preferred to x^1 in the list below is presumed to be the reading of x^2, as represented by **pt** in about 60 cases; by **p** alone in another 315; and by group t in some six where x^1 seems to have varied from Cx and **p** from the presumed reading of x^2. By contrast with what may be observed in the **B** tradition, which has no inter-familial contamination, in 180 instances of x^1 errors (about 30 of them major), the reading judged correct is shared by between one and four x^1 witnesses. The secure total of crite-rial x^1 readings is strictly therefore only 200, about half of them major. But it is quickly apparent that the copies containing most of the 180 right readings (P^2, D, D^2 and N^2) are all certain to have been corrected from an x^2 source (on N^2, see §§ 39–40 below). As few as about 20 such readings appear in manuscripts other than those four, and these may be explained as due to coincidental con-vergence. I's large number may perhaps result from memorial contamination; b's may either result from contamination or preserve an authentic x^1 reading lost by y and u (after b ceases at II 128, x^1 in effect denotes only yu). Except for a few cases, such as those where U and D are uniquely error-free (listed at § 28), right readings in individual members of y or u are therefore judged likely to have come in from an x^2 source. Discounting these, agreement of the uncontaminated copies XYI (the 'core-group' of y) and U (the older member of u) indicates the probable reading of x^1. Where this is lacking, direct analysis is needed to discriminate the family reading from amongst the three (after II 128, two) branches. But these cases are few and, as will appear later, uncertainty is much less than in **p**, which has twice as many fully attested groups as x^1.

§ 32. As with the α and β readings in **B**, judgement that all the rejected x^1 variants represent agreements in error has been made after comparison with not only the readings of the other family but also the available other-version parallels. Such comparison, however, is subject to one sig-nificant consideration that did not apply in the examination of **B**: that **C** may in principle embody a new authorial reading at any given point. On the postulate that revision was 'linear', **A** and **B** readings, and even agreements of **B** and its predecessor(s) against **C**, can therefore never do more than suggest possible correction of a 'suspect' reading. And it follows *a fortiori* by the canon of ratification (see *Intro.* IV § 22) that **B** readings retained in **C** are not to be emended (the Athlone edition suffers from frequently overriding both the postulate and the canon).[42] Otherwise, with allowance for non-unanimous or defective attestation (specified no further here), the secure evi-dence for x^1 may be set out in near-identical form as for **A** and **B** (see *A Version* § 23, *B Version* § 42). It is similarly divided by major and minor instances (the former given in full, the latter by reference only) and according to available other-version support for the readings adopted. Except in a few emended lines, the lemmata understood to represent the readings of x^2 are in Pr–XI taken from **p**, thereafter from **pt** or from **p** alone, a t agreement in error with x^1 being indicated by '-t'. The variants are the readings of x^1. A minus indicates agreement of an x^2 group-member (**p** or t) with the rejected x^1 variant; a plus, agreement of one or more x^1 witnesses with the lemma; 'so', agreement of another version with x^1.

§ 33. **Readings with other-version support**

(i) **Major**

(a) *With* y, b *and* u *present*

+**ZAB**: Pr 20 +P^2 ryche] pore. I 133 trone] tour. 179 wham...desireþ] when no man here couayteth.

+**ZB**: I 39 -Ax +?N.

+**AB**: Pr 184 lewed] l. thyng.

+**B**: Pr 61 marchen] maken. 141b–42a -AVS] *om.* 145 to þe puple] *om.* 182 *L. om.* 187 hym] vs. 191 +P^{2}B ybought] ybroughte. 192 +O non raton] *om* / (n)on. I 145 for] to abate. II 66 as] *om.*

(b) *With* y *and* u *present*

+**ZAB**: II 154 -RN soure] sore. 191^2 +P^{2}D of] and. IV 1 Cesseth] Sethe. 7 fecche] seche. 75 gat ich] was gyue me. 107 reson] Mede. 134 +?D it] (it) nat. 146 þat...confesours] *om.* VI 328 penaunce his] Repentaunce is. VII 177 +D the way] today. 180^1 ar] but. 224^3 nat] *om.* VIII 211 þow] hunger. 236 God] *om.*

+**AB**: II 158 -MSN go] to. III +D 280 go] *om.* 431 hated hym] *om.* VI 233 hath] hadde. 359 +P^2 dayes] d. y bouhte it. 401 wexed] wasche. 407 He] And. VII 164 +P^{2}D seten] sette. 170 sepulcre] s. of oure lord (*so* Z), 239 (*so* Z), +IP^{2}D 260 (*so* Z). VIII 18 wihtliche] wittiliche. 307 say] sayde. IX 24 techeþ] hem hoteth. 175 men] *om.* X 56 knowyng...Y] knowlechyng. 154 þat...hadde] bygynnynge h. he. XI 44 yn] *om.* 278 comended] comaunded.

+**B**: III 66 do] *om.* 70b–71 -EG *om.* 129 -MN Corteisliche] Fol c. 421/2 *misdiv.* 421 Mebles] That dwelleth in Amalek m. 456 Moises] The which M. 479 myddell] ? Ø (*see Textual Note*). 481 shullen] and. 482 For] *Quia.* V 163 +ID here] *om.* VI 125 +D-R spiritualte] spirituale. VII 35 ouht] hit. 133 -E fresshe] flesch. VIII 46 fro] or. IX 67 to gyuen] *om.* XI 164 me] *om.* 218 techen men] *trs.* XII 87 -t+D^{2}D masses] mo m. XIV 138 -t+P^2 so] *om.* XV 221 -t eir] *om.* XVI 260 -tN^2 men] *om.* XVII 254 -t turne] *om.* XVIII 169 -t+D^{2}D that ribaud; he] the ribaudes; they. XIX 291 -Gt Drede] Som d.; awey]. 301 +P^2-Wt on] *om.* 332 +D^{2}D-NTH^2 that his lyf] that is lyue and. XXI 161*a oportet*] *om.* 269 -Wt to harwen] to harwed. 344/45 -TH^2 *misdiv.* 365 +D and diche] a dich. -t+N^2 al] *om.*

+**A**: VII 170 sepulcre] s. of oure lord +Z?B.

+**Z**: VI 321 me] *om.*

(ii) **Minor**

(a) *With* y, b *and* u *present*

+**ZAB**: Pr 21, 33^{1,2}. I 24, 41, -N 62. II 6, 19, +P^{2}D-M 21, +b 111, 116. **+AB**: Pr -S 56 (*so* Z), 78, +b 82. I +u-N 49 (*corr. App.*), +P^2 181 (*so* Z). II -*p*^{2} 10 (*so* Z). **+B**: Pr +P^2 172, +P^2 191, -F 214. I +D-AVM 31, +P^{2}D 35 (*so* Z). II +P^{2}D 53, +I 59, -MF 60.

(b) *With* y *and* u *present*

+**ZAB**: II 163, -M 229, -GRM 231. III +P^{2}D 190, 191, 198^2, 262. IV 15, 56, +IP^2 62^2, 70^2, +D 128^1, -*p*^{2}+Y 128^2 (*corr. App.*), 129, 135. V -GM 116. VI +P^{2}D 312. VII 58, -RF+P^2 64, -K 166, 168, -G+D 173, +P^{2}D 201, 247. VIII -PAVQ+P^{2}D 42, 58, 97, 131, -*p*^{2} 153^2 (*in App. for* **p** *read* p^1, *for* **x** *read* xp^2), +IP^{2}U 180, +P^2 314, 323, 345.

+**AB**: II 145. III +P^2 173 (*so* Z), 178 (*so* Z). IV 126 (*so* Z). V -M 126 (*so* Z), -N 151. VI +I 93, +YI 219, 228 þe] Ac þe (*add to* App.), 319, +P^2 359, +IU 378, 383, -S 399, 417, 437^1 (*so* Z). VII 157, -K+IP^2 225, 260, +D 270, 285^2. VIII 83, 231 (*so* Z), 305, +ID 313^2. IX +D 62, 284, +P^{2}D 328. X 78, +D 81^2, -K 108^2, 108^3, 109, 111, 120, -Z+DN^2 146, +N^2 282, 284^1. XI -ZK 38, 51*a*, 53^1 (*in App. del.* G, *and for* KN *read* p^2), 106, +N^2 108, +N^2 119.

+**B**: III +P^2 59, +I 137, -M 474, 478, 483. IV +D 160, +ID 173. VI -AVRQG 36, +Y 59, +I-N 234, -R 248^1, -MSG 266, -AVM 344, 409, +U 416. VII +P^{2}D 5, 9, +P^{2}D 14, +I 70, 123, +P^2 184. VIII 208. IX +D-K 54. X +U-M 38^1 (*so* A), +DN^2-Q 234, +P^2 284. XI -F 159, +P^{2}N^2-K 184^2, +DN^2 280, 283, +N^2 296^3, +N^2 300. XII +N^2 83, +N^2 146^2. XV +D^2, -T 41^2, +D 165^2, 216, 226*a*. XVI -EQN 14, +P^{2}D^{2}D 46^2, 54*a*, 90, 102, +DN^2-TH^2 104, -R 115/15*a*, +N^2-tZWN 261, +Y-tVRZGN 271, +N^2-t 332, -t 334. XVII 20, 224, +D^2 278^1, 309. XVIII -G 131^1, +IN^2 258. XIX +P^2-N 112, +D^{2}D-TH^2 164^2, -t 189, +D-t 200, +D^{2}N^2 293^2. XX 12, -TH^2 13, +D-TH^2 69^1, -tAVWM 69^2, +N^2 85, 91, +YN^2-TH^2 158^1, +DN^2-?t

267, +P²U 413. XXI -W 91, +N² 159, +P²D²-N 162², -TH²F 162³, +D²N² 194, 212, +P²D 287, +D-TH² 378, +D²N²-tG 411. XXII -W 334 (*read* pt *for* p, *x¹ for* x).

§ 34. **Readings with no other-version parallel**

(i) Major

(a) *With* y, b *and* u *present*
I 88 thus] hit is thus (þys **p**). 148 hit²] hit first. II 90¹ he] and.

(b) *With* y *and* u *present*
III 95² sendeþ] sende. 316 +D ys] *om*. 319 -RMQSN douwe] do. 347 with] þat. 351 hol] holy. 366² sirename] name. 375³ fecche] seche. 387 relatifs] relac*o*ynes. 395 mene] nempne. 417 +D-QF bone] loue. 429¹ +D-EGN his] is. VI 51² +YP² y] a. 60¹, 148 +D-AVMGK wrathe] w*a*rthe. 173 +D loue] moder loue. 304¹ +D what] *om*. 307² by...made] *om*. 334 +D fonk] flonke. VII 145/46 *misdiv*. 172 and in Damaskle] y haue be in bothe. 207 as] *om*. 259 be] *om*. VIII 269 grone] greue. 283 ȝif power] ȝif thow pouer. IX 23 Treuthe nolde] no t. wolde. 71–9 *mislin*. 137 +P²-M lollares] lorelles. X 39¹ +DN² as] *om*. 202 hit] hym. XI 153¹ syre] fader. 155 ȝe...bokes] *om*. 160 Thus; leaute] Thus in; lel. 177 Clergies lore] clerkes techyng. 266² +P²D deuyned] deuyed. 273/74 *misdiv*. 287 -QFSZK wihtnesse] witnesse. XII 215 after] *om*; hertely t. XIII 231 For; and] *om*; or. XV 213 +Ch one] *om*. XVI 22 on...deydest] on vs alle; on þi renkis alle t. 273 Vnkynde] Vnkunnynge. XVII [116 *in* RM; *l. om*; *see Textual Note*]. 190–91 sethe...name; *Ite...mundum*] *trs*. XIX 147 Be he] Bote he be. XX 61 +DN²-H²M two] to. 293 mangonel] mangrel. 294 encloye] and cloye. XXII 240 +D²D felicite] felice.

(ii) Minor

(a) *With* y, b *and* u *present*
Pr -M 115. I 25. II 106.

(b) *With* y *and* u *present*
II +D 187. III +I 86, 87¹, 89¹, +D 91², 118¹, 375¹, +P²D 399, 496¹, +D 496². IV +P² 132¹, +P²D 132², 163. V +Y 96, +P² 97², 170. VI 15, +P² 95, +P²D 104², +U 137². VII 207, 231¹, 251¹. VIII 67, +P² 85, 166². IX 141², +I-*p²* 161², +D 197, -N 277, +P² 345. XI +P² 55, +I 77, +D 82, 200, 272¹. XV -t 154, +IP²D 242. XVI -tF 34. XVII +D²-TH² 145. XIX +D 19, -TH²+N² 134, 291, +D²-RW 332¹. XX -TH² 13, +N² 65, +N² 98, 105, +N² 112*a*, +D 176, -WG+N² 200², 203¹, +P²N² 373, +P²D 382. XXI +P²D²-N 162², +D²-PEAVZ 235, +P²-H² 246¹, +D²-*p²*QWFSZ 354, +D² 359, +D 365¹, +P² 381, +P²D²-*p²* 457. XXII 56 (*del*. D), +D² 91, -F 231, +D² 243, +P²D²D-EQ 307².

Among the minor variants in this list, among which some convergent agreement is to be expected, freedom from the family error is persistently attested only by P² (44 instances), D (46), and D² (18). For D², with allowance made for its absence in Pr–XI, the evidence of *x²* contamination is comparable to that for P² and D, but less than in N² (§§ 39–40 below), which has only some 23 minor right readings against *x¹* and has been provisionally placed with it.

iv. *The* x² *family of* C *manuscripts*

(a) *Sub-family* t

§ 35. The second sub-archetypal family is *x²*, the postulated ancestor of **p** and t. The sub-family t begins at XI 300*a*, where it takes up after A XI 313. As in their **A** portion, its members TH²Ch continue as an assured genetic group in XI 301–XXII on the basis of some 400 agreements in error (*R–K* pp. 38–9), about 175 of them major. The most important of these is the omission of 18 whole lines as well as three half-lines lost after misdivision (see below). Despite its status as a sub-family, t's individual variants, being notably aberrant, are not given entire in the Apparatus. The 80 recorded (usually as part of a longer list of variants) include the most striking instances. In the following list, 15 more are added in square brackets, where t is joined by one to three other copies. Though not criterial, these too are probably group errors, but of the type in which coincidental variation has also operated.

Major XII 4, 37, 41, 71^2, 74, 114^2, 176, 221, 226, 239–43 *Ll. om.* XIII 7, 10, 12, 124 *L. om.*, [125 +N^2], 203. XIV 23 *L. om*, 26, 29, 55, 62, 68, 108, 121/3, 122b *om*, 150, 158 *L. om*, [195 +K], 211. XV 6, 41, 58, 158. XVI 22, 92. XVII 21, 63–4 *Ll. om*, 74, 103, [108 +P^2], 126, [139 +WN^2], 157, 190, 251, 256, 259. XVIII [10 +N^2], 33 *L. om*, [50+Z], 52, 217^2. XIX 21b–23a *Ll. om*, 28, 59, [171 +QFN *L. om*], 237^2, 253. XX 55, 98, 122 *L. om*, + *a.h.* T, 263. XXI 178 *L. om*, 228, [+D^2 241, 242], 366, 389, 415, 429, 438–40 *Ll. om*, 482. XXII ?18, 174, 200, 231 *L. om*, [+XD^2W 270], 332, 360, 378, 380.
Minor XI 302. XII 18^2, 28. XIII 155, 179. XIV 99. 181^2. [XV 286 +N^2]. XVI [4 +N^2], 308. XVII [309 +WN^2]. XIX [15 +W], 104, 251. XX 106, 323, 460. XXI 31, [338 +W], [349 +WG], 410. XXII [12 +P^2].

It is unknown whether t's text of Pr–XI was lost and the present conjoint structure an attempt to make good its loss, or whether XII–XXII was 'cannibalised' from an x^2 copy to 'complete' A Pr–XI. If t had the earlier part of **C**, a proportionate number of exclusive errors might well have confirmed it as the most persistent of all the groups.

§ 36. Within t, the pairing TH^2 found in the **A** portion reappears in nearly 200 agreements, about 40 major. These are challenged by some 80 agreements of TCh, about 25 major, and some 40 of H^2Ch, perhaps six major (*R–K*, pp 28–9). The latter are too unpersistent (and minor) to be likely to be other than coincidental. Of the former, all save 25 occur where H^2 is defective, notably in XIV–XVI (as R–K note), and could otherwise have been further evidence for the <TH^2Ch> relation. Further, some TCh agreements where H^2 is present could easily be random, e.g (quasi)-orthographical variation, as at XII 134 *of riche*] *in liche* (*yliche* H^2), 198 *counteth*] *countede* (*counte* H^2), XVI 304, XX 68 *wyhte*] *wiʒ* XX 432 *ille*] *euele*; and non-significant registration of a quotation-form, e.g. *&c* mistakenly added after *carnis* at XI 312. In one seemingly major example at XVIII 289 *renne*] *þanne*, H^2 has altered what could have been *þan* to *cam*. In another, at XX 338, a different hand has inserted *men*, and at XXII 23 *is*, where the exemplar may well have read Ø with TCh. At XIX 226 *blowynge*] *bowynge* (*vowynge*) and at XXII 378 *adreint*] *& dryueliþ* (*& trayliþ*), the H^2 variant is identifiable as an individual departure from a shared t reading of obviously poor sense. Finally, in XX 86 *trinen*] *trien* the right reading (not so accepted in *R–K*) is retained by H^2 where TCh have a coincidental visual error. TH^2 may therefore be ascribed an exclusive common ancestor that was a moderately accurate copy of t. They remain necessary for the text as the joint witness to t in the unique right reading at XV 211. The more faulty third member Ch descends independently from t and lacks five further lines (XV 7, XVII 259, XX 122, XXI 82 and XXII 301). Its striking variant *mynne*] *make* at XXII 367 forms the basis of R–K's implausible conjecture *make...memoria*. But with the best lineation of a macaronic line and its supplement at XV 61–61*a*, as well as a unique right reading at XVI 123, Ch cannot be eliminated.

§ 37. The ancestral manuscript t seems to have been a very defective witness to its family original x^2, notably in its many line-losses. The cause of these is usually mechanical, as in the homoteleuton at XVII 62–4 (*charite*) and the homoarchy at XIV 23–4 (*Ac grace*); but censorship may have operated at XIII 124. A notable feature of t is its re-writing of whole phrases, e.g. *spouse to be byknowe*] *spousehod to beknowe* at XIII 11; *foleuiles*] *felouns* at XXI 247; *That*] *Trewþe wile þat* at XXI 482; and *dyas*] *dyetis* at XXII 174. Some of these could have appeared difficult, but others are not problematic, e.g. at XIV 15 (*man shulde* for *suche be*); at XIV 26, which alters the theology; or at XVII 21, with its humorously incongruous pragmatism. Elsewhere t will normalise alliteration, as at XIII 212, where *kyndely* inserted before *therwith* after misdivision turns a correct macaronic stave-phrase into an appended Latin quotation. Other examples are XV 41, where the line and its parallel are either two-stave or scan cognatively on *p* / *b*, and XIX 253, where *kid* is clearly scribal (Cx's possible corruption here is considered in the *Textual Notes ad loc*). Although this tendency can felicitously generate the reading that might have been conjectured (e.g. *lede*] *wyht* at XIII 59), t's independent value is small by comparison with **p**. But since **p**'s unique right readings occur mostly where t is defective, as presumptive x^2 readings they might well have supported it. Half a dozen that t uniquely preserves prevent its elimination:

Major XIII 59. XV 211. XVI 123 (Ch). XX 444. XXI 401^1, [401^2 +D^{2}N^2]. XXII 13^3 [*in App. read* 'noon] t']. **Minor** XII 5. [XXII 110 +D^2-Ch].

§ 38. The claim at §§ 6–7 above that t and **p** have an exclusive common ancestor x^2 is supported by 37 disjunctive agreements in error. Additionally listed here are another 40 (strictly non-criterial) readings in which **pt** are joined by one to three x^1 copies. That these are most often the usual suspects D^2 (20), P^2 (15) and D (10), confirms the earlier view of them as contaminated from **p**. As before, major readings are given in full, minor ones by reference. The lemma is the reading of x^1; a plus denotes agreement of an x^1 copy with x^2; a minus, agreement of an x^2 copy with x^1; round brackets, approximate agreement.

Major XII 88 +D^{2}D as] and, 213 +D^2-ChGS foel] foul. XIII 64 wyten] w. wel. XIV 28 +P^2 also] of (*om* VMQWSZK), 39 +P^{2}D^2-AVZ kyrke] churche, 209^2 +D^2 his] þe. XV 27 vp; and^2] *om*; for, 34 -RCh Ilyk] y. to, 51*a et orationes*] *om*, 89 +D^2 compacience] to pacience, 103 +D^2 (*om* Ch) a] þe, 106 -ECh+D(l *added* D^2) take] talke, 156 to] *om*, 308 -ECh er] here. XVI 81 +D^2 wel] *om*, (149 here] Ø **p** / he t), 183 +P^2 Mens] mannys, 219 -AVRMWZ wel] wol. XVII 82 +D^{2}D-N ȝe] þe, 84 +D^2 ȝe] þei, 94 Weder] Wonder, 136 +P^2 aloueth] loueþ, 268 +P^2 bissheinede] bisshopid. XVIII 38 werkes; wormes] *trs*. XIX 6 -EAVZG thy] þe, 100 o] *om*, 276 charite] leel c. XX 67 her] *om*, 96/8 -Ch *L. div.*, 272 +N^2 Principes] Princes. XXI 114 +UN^2 Bothe] *om*, 460 For] *om*. XXII 13^2 +D wyht] wot, 33 *a* /6 *L.d.*, 48 -AZ byde] bydde, (103 þat euere stured] sterede neuere (*trs* t)), 227 -RQWFSZ holynesse] holychurche, 236 cheytyftee] chaitife [*in App. for* **x** *read* x^1, *for* **p** *read* **p**t], 338 do bothe] done; bothe x^1.
Minor XII 6^2, -*p*^{2}+N^2 22, -QWFSZ 151, +N^2 192. XIII -M 41, +N^2 83, 98^2, +DN^2 171, +P^{2}D^{2}DN^2 186. XIV -AMSK 13, -K 213. XV -AVRM 83, 98, -W 101, +D^2 120^1, 146, 169. XVI +P^{2}D^{2}U 230, +N^2 318, -W 325, +D 328, 360 -G+P^2. XVII 35/6, 48, ?110, 179, 193. XVIII +P^{2}D 57. XIX +D^2 27, +D^2 36^2, -W+D^2 41, (+P^{2}D^2 241), (302), -RG+D^2 311, -F+D^2 331, 188, +UN^2 241, 396. XXI -RMFZ+P^{2}D^{2}D 73, -G 158, +D^{2}D 185, -MNZ+U 190, +P^{2}D 321^2, +P^{2}D^{2}N^2-*p*^{2} 348^2, 378, -ChSG+P^2 395, 476^2. XXII +D^2 31, 60, +U 77, +P^2 245, +D^2 290.

The readings cited as evidence for x^2 are collaterally supported by others where, on intrinsic grounds and in the light of other-version evidence, **pt** is judged to be right. In themselves these need imply no more than **pt**'s accurate preservation of Cx where x^1 erred but are congruent with the hypothesis of a single family ancestor containing both (see § 64 below).[43]

(b) *A transitional manuscript*: N^2

§ 39. Before proceeding to sub-family **p**, it is worth examining the unusual manuscript NLW 733B, **N**^{2}. Though closest to x^1 (as seen on comparing its readings with x^1's at §§ 33–4 above), N^2 has been conflated with **p**, contaminated from **B** and extensively sophisticated, so as to be almost unclassifiable. But it has a few superior readings that may be original. The only conjoint **AC** copy to become a C-Text at the end of the *Visio* not the *Vita de Dowel*, and with its Passus X's first 13 lines still of **A** type,[44] N^2 runs on to XXI 428 before becoming illegible. Several omissions between X and XIII of non-mechanical origin may be due to moral or theological censorship. N^2's substantial agreements with five witnesses include some 90 each with the **p** copies W and F, some 50 with P^2 (*R–K* pp. 32–3) and several with groups of both families.[45] Although the **A** portion of NLW 733B, N, forms a genetic pair with the **A** manuscript W, a qualitative scrutiny of the readings R–K list confirms their view that no such relation holds for the **C** portions of the two copies. The same is true of N^2's agreements with F, so both must presumably be due to convergent variation. As N^2 pairs indifferently in minor variants with copies of the other family, only major readings have been noted, of which some, but not all, are recorded in the Apparatus.

i With x^1: X 154. XI 44, 151^1, 273/4, 278. XII 5. XIII 39/40. XIV 46. XV 97. XVI 76/7. XIX 115. XX 34^1, 347/8. XXI 366.

ii With x^1+t: XV 221. ?XIX 147, 332^1. XXI 344/5.

iii With **p** only: X 39, 113. XI 164. XII 87. ?XIII 172. [XV 132 +Ch]. XVIII 169. XIX 301, ?332^2. XX 294, 470. ?XXI 161*a*, 269 (to) sholde), 365. With p^1: XIII 392. XIV 63. XIX 165. XX 114.

iv With **pt**: XVII 217, 262^2. XVIII 60. XIX 118, 261. XX 103^1, 260^2, 272, 293.

Amongst these 40 major agreements across half the poem, the proportions are very nearly balanced (x^1 14, **p** 16, x^1t 4, **pt** 9), so that it is hard to be sure whether N^2's exemplar was of x^1 or x^2 type or whether its scribe produced a conflated text by selecting readings now from one and now from the other. That N^2 does not derive from x^2 is indicated by its freedom from the major **pt** error at XV 89 (a crux where D, by contrast, shows visible collation with an x^2 copy). But that its exemplar was textually close to x^1 is indicated by its Ø-variant in the crux at XVIII 75, where the other four disjunctive errors strongly imply such a reading for the x^1 family original (though interestingly N^2 is accompanied here by the **p** copy W, its companion in the text's **A** portion). Against this, N^2 is both free of x^1's major omissions at XIX 261, 290^2 (the latter with D^2) and shares the important **p** error at XV 132. Its omission of XIV 63 may result from independent censorship; but its 14 agreements with p^1, four major (§ 42 below) and its many pairings with W and F, p^1 copies of a single genetic sub-group q (see §§ 51–3 below) need explanation. N^2 may therefore be most economically seen as deriving from an x^1 manuscript that was compared at the point of production with a p^1 copy (of q-type) and also, as argued below, a manuscript of **B**.

§ 40. With many lines omitted and others garbled, N^2 is a ready candidate for rejection; but it is retained for occasional collation on account of five major readings that answer to the conjectural form of the original:

XI 161 That doth] Doþ N^2; That maketh X&r. XX 94 haue ruthe] rewe N^2; haue mercy X&r. 400 gretter] N^2; wyddore X&r. XXI 236 buggynge; sullyng] N^2; *trs* X&r. 412 lede] N^2; man X&r.

These and some 40 more readings listed below convince R–K, who adopt all save XXI 236, that N^2's source was authoritatively corrected from a **C** copy superior to Cx. But in comparing this situation to that of the **B** manuscript F,[46] they presuppose a textual entity no more necessary here than the one they invoke to account for F's good readings. For like those, which evince contamination from **A**,[47] the 40 N^2 readings R–K list are better understood to be contaminations from **B**.[48] That the **B** manuscript consulted by N^2 was of the β family emerges from examination of ten examples in list (b), taken from those R–K find 'available as a control' where the Cx reading 'appears a scribal derivative of that of **B**.'[49] Most in list (a) are Bx readings R–K prefer to Cx readings that they judge unoriginal. But these, though acceptable, have no place in **C** and should be dismissed. In the list below, the variants are from N^2 and the line-number of parallel **B** is in brackets.

(a) X/IX [300 +M] goed^2] *om*; 308 Ac] *om* (202). XI/X 84 Wittes] his (141); 189 Elde] he (XI 28). XIII/XI 125 for] *om* (312); 199 amys standeth] mystandit (380). XIV/XII 96 to þe] to (152); 152 as] *om*; 198 as lewede men] lewde *only* B-Cr^{23}g (273). XVI/XIV 85 Pouerte] þe pore (245); 154 al] al goed (318); 168 heuene] þe (XV 19). XVII/XV 197 here] *om* (535), 199 pees; plente] *trs* (537); 219 dede and] *om* (537); 220 his] *om* (556); 225 myhte] may (561), 226 and] *om*. XVIII/XVI 289 And] I (272). XIX/XVII 90 þat] þe (98); 176 fyn] *om* (208); 188 eny] no (222); 232 and] *om* (265); 299 Ac] *om* (317). XX/XVIII 95 fouely] felly (92); 97 was a] *om* (94); 130 þerof] *om* (127); 138 ouer-] *om* (135); 229 ther-thorw] *om* (220); 256 Lo] *om* (247); 364 alle] *om* (322); 400 (363); 421 eny felones] a f. (380); 422 hy; tretours] he; a t.(381).

Additionally, R–K include as representing **B** ten β readings rejected in the present edition's B-Text in favour of α:

(b) XII/XI 74 þat heo ne may al] al to (138); 83 þe] *om* (147). XIII/XI 162 mony] how m. (350). XV/XIII 102 penantes] a p. (93); 121 ful] *om* (112); 255 And] *om* (XIV 52). XVI/XIV 4 deyeth] d. he (135); 127 his] *om* (292); 151 lered^2] letred (316). XVIII/XVI 129 and] *om* (95).

If all these agreements were decisively with the archetypal text of **B**, there might be at least *prima facie* grounds for thinking some of N^2's 'superior' readings to originate outside the archetypal tradition of **C**. But list (b) indicates that N^2 was contaminated specifically from a sub-archetypal B-Text of β type. For α's agreement with Cx against β in these ten examples tends to confirm the antecedent probability that the reading they share is original (the alternative possibility that α is contaminated from **C** has nothing to commend it). Further argument, if needed, would stress that, as there is no intrinsic objection to the adopted readings in list (a), the differences between Bx and Cx may be properly ascribed to revision, and R–K's claim for N^2's special authority rejected. N^2's few unique (nearly)-right readings are thus better seen, like those in certain other copies of both families, as products of happy scribal guesswork. For in each case, as shown in the relevant *Textual Notes*, the origin of the Cx error is readily explainable. Like P^2 earlier, N^2 indicates both strong interest in the text of the **C** Version and the relative ease of access in the early fifteenth century to x^1 and x^2 manuscripts at or around a single centre of copying. Whichever family it started from, N^2 is now to be reckoned a conflation of both, as well illustrated by XIII 39/40, where it has x^1's wrong line-division but in 39 p^1's omission of initial *Ther*.[50] For this reason, and because of its widespread corruption, N^2 is only selectively cited.

v. *The sub-family* **p**

§ 41. The 14 manuscripts **PEAVRMQWFSZGKN** derive from a single ancestor **p**, which is directly descended from x^2. It is characterised by some 1440 agreements in error, 275 major and 1165 minor. The manuscripts divide into two main groups, p^1 consisting of PEAVRMQWFSZ and p^2 of GKN. Neither derives from the other, so both must descend independently from **p**. They are differentiated by nearly 400 readings, about 75 of them major, which fall into two sets. In the first, either p^1 or p^2 is antecedently likely to represent **p** because it also agrees with x^1(t). In the second, either could preserve **p** but both differ from x^1(t) and both are wrong. When p^2 errs with p^1, it will reflect a **p** error here; when p^2 is right in its agreement with p^1, the **p** reading attested has presumably preserved Cx through x^2. In 220 instances, p^2 is right with **x** but almost never right against p^1 and **x** in combination. For this reason, **p**'s two distinct branches are treated first and the sub-family as a whole is discussed at the end of this section rather than at the beginning (as was done for γ in the **B** tradition). These **x**p^2 readings form the lemmata in the list of p^1 errors at § 42; p^2's half-dozen divergences from **x** are italicised and will be separately listed at § 61. The similarly few minor cases of **x** and p^2 agreeing in a *wrong* reading are considered at § 44.

a. *Branch* p[1]

§ 42. The branch *p¹* resembles the eight-member group g of the **B** sub-family γ (*B Version* §§ 17–21); but its structure is more complex and its distinctive variants much more abundant. It falls into two groups **m** and **q**, m dividing further into **e** and **r**, e into the two genetic pairs PE and AV, and r yielding one genetic pair RM, while no clear sub-division emerges within q. Seven members of *p¹* have major omissions: *AV* VII 236–83, XXII 88–end; *M* XVI 4–157, XVIII 244–XIX 32; *F* VII 264–IX 181, XIII 93–XV 179; *S* VIII 267–X 95, XV 82–157, XVI–XX, XXI 8–323; and *WZ* are conjoined with **A/Z** to XI/IX respectively. Thus, although no sub-division of *p¹* appears whole throughout, each is represented by at least one (near)-complete early manuscript, m by **P** (for e) and **M** (for r), q by **Q**. Between them these three copies, supplemented by R where M has gaps and by F where Q is damaged between V and VII, are indispensable. Given, therefore, that the *p¹* tradition is distinguished within **p** by its contrast with *p²*, and that the relative certainty of a *p²* reading depends on the degree of its three constituents' availability, the 224 readings below have been divided according to fullness of attestation in the latter. In the list, a minus sign before a sigil indicates a member's divergence from the presumed group reading; a plus, agreement of a *p²* or *x¹*(t) member with the rejected reading. Italicised numbers denote those readings where *p²* also differs from the lemma.

Major

(a) *Where GKN are present* (II 218–XIII 225; XIV 41–XV 66)[51]
III 54 -M+P^2. V 97^1. VI *40*, 338, 340, 388 and *390* +N (*over erasure*), 394^2. VII 232. VIII 98–9 *Ll. om*, *337*. IX 97 +D, 187 -Q *L. om*. X 274^2 -QZ, 275^1 +KP^2. XI 34, 96, 224. XIII (*ll. om* G: 39^2 +N^2, 40, 62, 63); 66 +D^{2}Ch. XIV 43, 62, 63 +N^2, 157^{1,2}.

(b) *Only GN are present* (Pr 154–II 217; XV 67–XXII 40)
Pr 195 -M, 226. I 40, 92, 165 -M. II 121^2 -M, 122 -M, 160 -M. XVI 75, 108, 266 +GP^{2}U [*L. om through homoteleuton*], 323^2 , 326^1 (*l. om* G), 371 +G. XVII 72, 151^1 -Z, 162 -QZ+uCh [*coincidental visual error*], 283. XVIII 244. XIX 10, 89, *94*, 165 +P^{2}D^{2}N^2. XX 73^1, 114 +ChN^2, 140 +P^{2}N (*alt.*), 200^1, 201, 390^2, 419, 430 -Z, 461 (*l. om*). XXI 110, 319^3, 340^2 (+P^2 *alt. a.h.*), 427, 447, 482 +GDt. XXII 6.

(c) *Only KN present* (XIII 226–XIV 40)
XIV 37 (*l. om* K).

Minor[52]

(a) *Where GKN are present* (II 218–XIII 225; XIV 41–XV 66)
III 14 +M, 360^1, 368. IV 10, 156, 190. V *152*, 168. VI 29 +N, 32 +G, 72, 99, 122 +G, *141*, 156, 177, 248^2, 251, 271 +P^{2}D (*l. om* G), 275 +P^{2}N, 382^2, VII 2^{1,2}, 18 +G, 20 +DG-MS, 48 +P^2-RM, ?95, 101 +N, 191, 196 -AV+N, 256, 291, 294. VIII 48^{1,2}, 73, 83 +N, 107^{1,2}, 112, 115 +P^2, 171, 175 +P^{2}D, 179, 192 -M, 216^1 -M, 246, 304^1 +P^2, 308, 313 +KN, 323^1 +N, 323^3, 324^1, 328, 332. IX 8^2+P^{2}u, 78 +K, 101^1 +U, 117 +N, 133 +N, 150, 153^2, 161^1, 162^2 -Q (=?q), 166, 167, 180, 188, 199, 200^2, 203, 218 +G, 246, 247^2, 254^{1,2}, 258 -M, 261 -Q+P^2, 262 -RQ+P^{2}D, 279, 297 -Q, 310. X 6 -Z, 68 -F+I, 99, 118, 133, 165 +N^2, 175 +NP^{2}D, 184 +GN^2, 264. XI 210^1, 210^2 +P^2, 269, 287^1, 304. XII 13 -F+N^2, 22 +N^2, 63^1, 64 -FW+t, 86 +N^2, 152 +YChN, 163, 164, 173, 204 +N^2, 212 +N^2. XIII 25, 103 +N, 107 +NP^{2}H^{2}N^2, 134, 136, 151, 177 +Ch, 185, 202 +D^2, 210, 223^1, 224. XIV 90^3, 91^2, 118 -S, 124, 150^2, 157^2 +H^2, 165, 194 +P^2, 198, 207, 212 (*l. om* G). XV 3 +D^{2}Ch, 12 +P^{2}D^2, 17 +N^2, 26, 33^2 +Ch, 46^1, 48, 58^1, 62.

(b) *Only GN are present* (Pr 154–II 217; XV 67–XXII 40)
Pr 212, 231 -M. I 66 -M, 76 -M, 98 -MF, 190 -M. II 12 -M, 38 -M, 40 -M, 55 -M, 70 -M, 79^1 -M, 136 +P^{2}U, 138 -M. XV 70^1 -MW, 70^2 -QSZ+P^{2}N^2, 76a, 92. XVI 57, 122, 182 -M+D^2, 281-QZ+TH^2, 316^2 +G, 341 -MW+YGN^2, 355 +ut. XVII 14^{1,2} +N, 61 +ND^2, 70 -WF, 82 +GD^{2}Dt [*coincidental visual error*], 171 -F, 184 -F+N, 193 -W+t, 251, 311 -W. XIX 37, 63^1, 65^1 +P^{2}U, 104 +G, 298 -WZ+D^{2}DCh, 311 +ND^{2}t, 334 +DChN^2. XX 4, 8^1, 20, 96^1 +N, 108, 112^1 +GP^2, 144 -M, 151, 198^2, 206, 208^2, 214^1 +D, 214^2 +N^2 (*a. h.* P^2), 287^1, 353 +DN, 365 +NCh, 390^1 -W+G, 457^1. XXI 186^2, 229 -F+P^2, 252, 289, 316, 319^1, 333 -F, 364 +N^2, 456^2 +X, 474 (*l. om* G). XXII 6.

(c) *Only KN present* (XIII 226–XIV 400). XIV 7^2.

(d) *Only N present* (Pr 1–154, XV 288–XVI 40, XXII 41–end) *None.*

§ 43. In this list p^1 is distinguished by some 200 exclusive readings, 40 of them major, supported by another 83, all but 12 of them minor, where it is joined by one p^2 and one to three **x** manuscripts. Most agreements with an **x** copy are likely to be random but the 21 with P^2 (six of them major) and 15 with N^2 (four major) may be ascribable to collation of these copies' x^1 exemplars with a manuscript of p^1 type (see §§ 24, 39–40 above). Conversely significant are 27 cases, six major, in which the p^1 copy M is free of the group error. Chiefly in Pr–II, these suggest close (if limited) consultation of an **x** or p^2 copy, similar to what occurs in P^2 in relation to **p** (§ 24 above and § 56 below). Also worth remarking are specific agreements with p^1 of individual p^2 copies: N (15, two major), G (10, two major) and K (one major). Most of these could be coincidental, but not N's two major instances at VI 390 and XX 140, which show visible alteration like that found at points in P^2, D^2 and D. What no p^1 copy reveals is any clear x^1 contamination in the form of definitely erroneous readings (see below).

§ 44. All in all, p^1 appears to have been a relatively poor copy of its original **p** and, as will emerge (§ 55 below), inferior to p^2. It lacked five lines: XX 461 for no evident reason, VIII 98–9 and XVI 266 through homoteleuton, IX 187 possibly through censorship. Otherwise, its only notable features are a tendency towards greater explicitness in expression and a preference for *noþer* over Cx's double negative *ne no* (e.g. XX 108, XXI 252, 289). But p^1 cannot be eliminated, since it contains a handful of unique apparently right readings, as well as those preserved in constituent members, some of which may go back to Cx through **p**.[53] The former, though minor and probably due to chance, require further attention because each contradicts **x** as well as p^2:

VII 253 in²] *om* **x**p^2EMFS. XI 53 hym] *om* **x**p^2. 115³ my] many **x**p2. XVI 362 þe] *om* x^1p^2. XXI 354 queyntise] pl. x^1p^2 +QFSZ [*correcting App.*].

The first example is a case of coincidental mechanical omission. In the second and fourth, the sense is arguably complete without the pronoun / article, which p^1 may have inserted for explicitness. In the third the rejected reading is acceptable and may even be original, echoing *many* in // B X 169. In the last the plural may have come in coincidentally under inducement from preceding *colours* (found also, after amendment of the Apparatus, in q). Together these instances, like the correction of the Latin at VIII 246*a*, XVI 54*a*, 115*a*, hardly raise serious doubt that when p^2 agrees with x^1t (or with x^1t before XII), the reading attested is probably that of Cx. There are two exceptions. One occurs at Pr 7, where the Cx reading is doubtful and must be reconstructed from the split variants preserved in p^1 and **x**, but where **x** is substantively, though not formally, supported by the sole p^2 witness N (see the *Textual Notes*). The more important case, in RM at XVII 116, will be discussed at § 49 below.

The p¹ *groups*

i Group **m**: *a. Sub-group* **e**

§ 45. The sub-division of p^1 called *group e* consists of **PEAV**, which with **RM** ('r'), make up a larger genetic group **m** characterised by some 75 agreements (see § 50 below). Before examining its structure, e's relationship to m may be illustrated by three examples. One occurs at VII 61 *no gult so greet*, where **p** transposed the first phrase to *gult non*, m next dropped *gult*, <AV> retained the noun-Ø nonsense-reading (< e < m), a later hand adding *gult* in V, and the others smoothed by inserting *synne*, <RM> after *non* and <PE> after *grete*. Secondly, at X 19, where

p had preserved Cx, e retained m's omission of *euere²*, while r smoothed by inserting *ȝet*. Here r may have substituted a synonym and only e omitted; but it is more economical to suppose that m read Ø, having shed the adverb through eyeskip (*eu*ere > *h*ere) or deliberately through stylistic objection. Finally at XX 287², though Cx was again correctly preserved in **p** (> *p²* and q),[54] m lost *oure* by near-haplography after *oute* and e faithfully followed its exemplar, but the more enterprising r plausibly substituted *thy*. To these three e readings may be added another 14, of which these six are major.

II 237 ones] one. III 45 man] frere. VII 180 *Extra Latin line.* XVIII 173 kissyng] cossyns, 176 wille] *om*, 219 And] As.

Of these, the Latin line *Hic primo comparet Petrus Plouhman* looks less like a textual than an *ordinatio* feature of its postulated group-exemplar. Together with the three instances examined, it questions R–K's judgement that these agreements are 'not strong support' [for a PEAV grouping]; for with no 'significant conflicting evidence' (*R–K*, p. 48) in the form of a group <PERM>, they are enough to endorse the sequence PEAVRM in preference to R–K's order PERMVA.

§ 46. The four copies deriving from e form two genetic pairs. The first <**PE**> has 270 agreements (listed in *R–K* pp. 24–5), 70 of them major. Among the most important are two additional lines of Latin, one completing the Scriptural quotation at IX 326*a*, the second (after VII 203) another *ordinatio*-like feature perhaps lost from its e-source by <AV>. Eleven lines are omitted: III 420, V 158, VI 204–5, VII 186 [?lost through eyeskip],[55] VIII 275, X 168, XII 138, 180 and XVII 135, 260. Most of these omissions are mechanical, though the first and last may be due to clerical censorship. The second group <AV> shows 'absolutely persistent agreement in 443 [*recte* 435] readings' (*R–K*, p. 22). About 100 of these are major, including the loss of the rest of Passus XXII after l. 87, where the common exemplar was defective, and of another 73 lines, 9 half-lines and 8 citation-lines.

Possibly through loss of leaf: VII 236–83; *homoteleuton*: Pr 188–89, III 391–92, IV 87–9, XIX 122–24, XX 5, 430–32, XXII 26, [*at mid-line*] VIII 130b–31a, XIII 108b–09a; *homoarchy*: VI 134 [?or censorship], XI 312b–15a; *eyeskip*: III 6b–7a (*man* > *men*), XXI 88b–90a (*Resones...Resoun*); ? XX 35b. *Citation-lines*: III 189*a*, XVI 54*a*, 357*a*, XVII 235*a*, 280*a*, XIX 319*a* XX 164*a*, 270*a*.

The source of neither <PE> nor <AV> appears to have derived from the other; but since V is one of the earliest extant copies (not later than *c.* 1400), the date of e might have been within a decade of the poem's composition. AV could be eliminated, as it contains no unique right readings, and e be represented by PE, which attest the best reading at II 190 (together with N, corrected over erasure).

Group m: *b. Sub-group* **r**

§ 47. As noted at § 45, e forms part of a six-member group m with **r**, the exclusive ancestor of <**RM**>. This pair's early member **M** lacks a further 235 lines through loss of leaves (XVI 4–157, XVIII 244–XIX 32). It also misplaces XVII 188–257 (the Mahomet passage) after 286, copying XVII 286 after 186 but following it with XVII 259–85*a*. Its order intriguingly recalls that adopted in the reconstructed text of **B** (see Vol I pp 602–3); but the notion that M might reflect knowledge of a pre-archetypal form of **B** begs too many questions to be useful. **R**'s immediate exemplar, to judge by the errors it shares with e, was a faithful copy of r, whereas M's underwent extensive lateral influence from *x¹* or *p²* (§ 43 above). That the pair have an exclusive ancestor is indicated by persistent agreement in some 275 readings (roughly the same number as <PE>'s), about 120 major. The most important are the omission of eight text-lines, two half-lines and two citation-lines, and the inclusion of two spurious lines:

Lost through homœoteleuton: III 239–41 (letten / leten), V 30 (hacches / churches), VI 60 (sounede / semede **p**). *Homoarchy*: VII 225. VIII 44a, XIX 134a [*both at end of* 44, 134 *in* e, ? *possibly in margin* r]. XVIII 162 [*eyeskip from* lewes 162 *beginning* > lewes 164 *end*]. XX 293b–4a [*eyeskip from* and > en-]. XVI 183 [*visual distraction*: mens ...mone...mem-]. *Two spurious ll. after* VII 217 (*R–K*, p. 185) [*the second a memorial reconstruction of omitted* VII 225].

Some 16 RM readings appear in the Apparatus as part of a larger entry:

Major VI 316, 384. VII 111, 152a. VIII 111. X 160. XVII 285 +Ch. XVIII 229. **Minor** VI 419. VII 138. X 197, 217. XII 164. XVII 107, 108. XIX 36.

§ 48. The genetic status of <RM> is not seriously challenged by the 70-odd errors M shares with F of p^1, N of p^2, and P^2 of the x^1 family. Among the few major ones with F *herte* for *thouhte* in VII 20 was probably induced coincidentally by *herte* at 17, while *god wot* for *tho gomus* at Pr 44 suggests parallel contamination from B Pr 43. Of the seemingly more impressive agreements with N, most major ones seem easy coincidences. Some are synonym-substitutions such as *Large* for *Grete* at Pr 53, *clepede* for *calde* at I 4, *thankede* for *merciede* at III 21, *dude* for *wrouhte* at VI 211 and *man* for *segg* at XII 163. Others are visual errors, like *gracioust* for *grathest* at I 199 (paralleled in the **A** tradition) and *cleymyng* for *cleuynge* at XVII 128. The striking *grace* for *Lukes* at VIII 109 may result from failure in both M and N to grasp the referent. The seven major errors shared with P^2 include synonyms like *legge* for *wedde* at IV 143, *liue* for *regne* at IV 171, *kuind* for *connynge* at XV 18 (induced by preceding *Kynd*) and *hurteþ* for *smyteth* at XX 385 (induced by 384). But as R–K note (p. 28), M's partner R does not pair significantly otherwise and only about 18 times with each of F, N and P^2. Conversely, while M joins the latter thrice more frequently than does R, it pairs with R in total four times more often than with any of them and in major agreements sixteen times more often than with all three together.

§ 49. The above brief account does not wholly exhaust the interest of r, which in some 25 variants agrees with **x**, in 20 exclusively, against a wrong reading not only of p^1 but of **p** (bracketed agreements are approximate):

Major Pr 49. IV 171. V 55. VII 34 +FN. VIII 257/8, 258^2. X $80.^{56}$ XV 284. XX 1 +WF. **Minor**: Pr 137. III 211 +F. VI 113, 129, 133^2, 181, 365. (VII 95). IX 52, (254), 281^3, (327). XIII 84 +G. XV 83 +AV. XVIII 70. XXI 11. XXII 331.

In the absence of agreements in error with **x** these, like M's at § 43 above, may simply be readings where r alone accurately preserved **p** ($< m < p^1$). But this cannot easily account for the presence of r's unique line XVII 116, which by every criterion, including comparison with the corresponding **B** lines, appears genuine in metre, style and sense (in contrast with, say, r's patently scribal pair after VII 217). It is also, unlike less obviously inauthentic lines such as M's after XII 249 and XX 98, the sole **C** line with no exact other-version parallel that is necessary for the sense. In principle, r's scribe could have confected 116a from the sense of 382b and 116b from that of 382a in parallel B XV. But this notion is harder to credit than that XVII 116 is authorial. Rejected by R–K alone among editors, the line is adopted here as the best solution to a major crux (see the *Textual Notes*). Either it stood in the group-ancestor m or was introduced into r from a source independent of Cx, an uneconomical hypothesis that generates more problems than it solves.

Group m: *c. agreed readings of* **e** *and* **r**

§ 50. It seems probable, therefore, that <RM> descend from a manuscript r more accurate at some points than any other in the x^2 tradition, and at one point than any in *either* tradition. That r nonetheless shares with e an exclusive common ancestor m is shown from the two groups' agreement in 45 errors, some 15 major. These are supplemented by 30, perhaps a third of them major, where M is free of the postulated group error (*R–K*, p. 47). In some, M's different error suggests merely random individual divergence, as at III 435, in which *oftest* echoes m's presumed superlative. But elsewhere intermittent recourse to or recollection of p^2 or of the other family occurs, as in M's word-order in the b-half of the same line. Because of these discrepancies, the Apparatus does not use the group-sigil r, but it records among larger variant-entries some 40 eRM readings, including (as indirectly confirmatory though not criterial) a dozen where one or two other manuscripts accompany m:

III 305,[57] 370, 484, 490. IV 124. V 88. VI 280, 297. VII 153, 284, 306. VIII 47 +D, 246 (= ?p^1), 337. IX 5, 24, 50, 162, 186 +N, 241, 299. XI 54 +Y [? *censorship*], 72, 183. XII 147. XIII 43, 187. XIV 84. XV 111, 176 +DW, 177, 303 +FN, 304. XVII 188, 228 +P². XVIII 2 +N², 14, 131. XIX 53 +F, 58, 65. XX 7 +W, (10), 50, 256 (+N *ins*.), 302 +N. XXI 20, 96, 286, 459, 468 +W. *Where* M *lacks the* m *error or has a different one*: III 435. IX 20 +N. XVI 31 (M *def.*), 140. XXI 152 +NT.

The group m cannot be eliminated because, apart from XVII 116 (in theory possibly of non-group origin), it has at IV 35 what seems the right word-order in the light of // **B**.

ii Group **q**

§ 51. The next group **q**, less solidly attested than m, is represented throughout by only one copy **Q** and contains two likely genetic pairs <**QF**> and <**WZ**>. As R–K note (pp. 49–50), **QWFSZ** are actually present together only in Passus XII–XXII; so where one or more members are defective, the 'group' reading is inferential, though there are good grounds for thinking the inference reliable. As with m, this restricted and intermittent attestation does not favour use of the sigil q in the Apparatus, which records its variants only occasionally in a larger entry, as at XIII 59 and XVI 31. Group q is defined by 56 major agreements, seven with all members present and unanimous; minor ones (*R–K*, 49–51) are disregarded because of the witnesses' extensive defectiveness. In the list, a minus = 'manuscript free of group error', '‡' = 'different error'.

(a) QWFSZ *present*: XII 93 louye...Lordes] for ȝoure lordus loue to. 96 [*L. om through eyeskip to* 98, *but without loss of* 97]. 193 mowe] dure m. 232 ariste] wexuþ.[58] XIII 28 ben] ben ful. 59 *As* 2 *ll*. 72 -W semeth] were. XXI 326 made] hadde. 385 ylette] bete. XXII 47 ful soure] some. XXII -WZ 228 or] for.

(b) W *absent*: X 114 -F vppon] for; 189 we] *om*; 241 synne] gult; 306b–307a -F and...lene *om*. XI 5 to Wyt] *om*. 160 -S Thus] Þis; 253 -F as] to make as; 286 ‡F many] my.

(c) F *absent*: XIII 201 -W so...profit] of felawe so fayre ne of profyt neuer þe mo. XIV 6 -Z defended] dystuted (-ted) -dyed S). 193 *Five spur. ll. added*.[59]

(d) S *absent*: XVI 31 ‡F. 144 -F treuth-] reson-. -F 247b–48a leues...nat] *om* [*homoteleuton at caesura*: bereth...bereth]. 362 -F commissarie] consayle & c. XVII 76 follynge] prente; 215 ȝow for] *om*. 258 -W in a fayth] mafay. 298 ȝut] *om*. 302 Tho] Lo. 312 oþer] and. XVIII 50 the pouke] *om* [?*censorship*]. 58 he sayde] quaþ he. 84 ‡W this] þi. 158, [159 +G], 161: *extra Lat. ll. after* (159 = B XVI 135a), 167 Fryday] f. nyȝt; 177 *Lat. l. added*. 246 age] gate. XIX

80 faste aftur] fast (*trs* W). XX 230 Adames] (a) man(nus). XXI 20 -F noen] *om.* 247 ‡F He]
Hit.

(e) WF *absent* XIII 163 egges] nestus & e.

(f) WZ *absent*: I 4 castel] clif. 95 lordene] inordine (disordeyned F). III 138 þis] þi. 276 therfore]
here. VI 46 fetures] feþerus. 364 Hewe] heruey. 428 nones] onus. VII 103 foul sage] falsage.

(g) WFZ *absent*: VIII 243–6*a om.*

§ 52. This list reveals a *p¹* 'core-group' <**QFS**> (somewhat like the *x¹* core-group XYI noted at
§ 23) which, allowing for significant absences, is attested throughout. Since all the major cases at
(f) and (g) occur before WZ appear, they could all in principle be group-readings of q; but within
the core-group a genetic pairing <**QF**> is strongly indicated by some 95 agreements, the 35 major
ones including the loss of XVII 151 and XXII 103 (*R–K*, p. 36). This is not contradicted by the
30 agreements of **QZ** in X–XXI (*R–K*, p. 37), which are all minor and could be coincidental.[60]
Rather more challenging to <**QF**> are the 65 agreements of **QS**; but of the twenty major ones ten,
including the important omission of VIII 243–6*a*, occur where F is absent and are thus potential
'core' readings. The remaining ten wither away on closer scrutiny. Four that may be mechani-
cally induced are II 64 *menye* for *eny* (by word-initial *me-* in *Mede, men, me*); X 245 *graye* for
grayth (haplography after *y / þ* confusion); XII 18 *hond* for *hed* (smoothing after *e / o* confusion or
deliberate correction);[61] and XXII 174 *drenges* for *drogges* (unconscious confusion with *drinkes*).
Among the six non-mechanical cases, in III 125 *brown* for unusual *blew* may be a coincidental
substitution like that of *blake* by both AV and GN (pairs belonging to separate divisions of **p**) as,
at VII 115, may *liken* for similarly uncommon *litheth*.[62] In VII 82, *falsages* for *foel-sages* is very
probably the q group-reading from which F's *fele fals folk* further varies by way of smoothing.
At VII 259, *lond* for *loue* may also be a smoothing after misreading of *loue* as *lone* (here inap-
propriate). In XI 212 *goed aftur*] *g. auntur aftur* the third word may have been mechanically lost
by F through haplography. The most striking example of all is the one most easily explained. At
VII 106 Cx *feste* is evidently wrong, q's *beste* an unsuccessful attempt to correct it and F's *geste*
a happy scribal guess prompted by recollection of *storye* at // B XIII 447. The preceding analysis
may be taken to confirm the grouping <(QF)>S. The 52 agreements of WZ in XII–XXII, over half
major, are 'relatively persistent' (*R–K* p. 37);[63] so if this pair is genetic, a better ordering of q's
components than the present edition's QWFSZ will be *R–K*'s QFSWZ. Group q is nowhere the
sole source of a *p¹* right reading against error in both **x** and *p²*; but it is a valuable supplementary *p¹*
witness both where **p** is uniquely right (§ 44 above) and where m has further diverged. Its member
F contains at VII 106 an indispensable major right reading.

§ 53. As with m (§ 42 above), some members of q appear to have been corrected from an **x** or
p² source. This is indicated by Q's possession of a line (IX 187) that *p¹* seems to have lacked. This
might have been coincidentally omitted in both m and F, by eyeskip or through censorship, but
Q's other right readings *serk*] *sherte* at I 99 and the Latin *sciunt*] *sapiunt* at XI 165 favour lateral
transmission to explain its presence in Q. The same explanation need not necessarily apply to W
in four instances, to F in six, and to Z in one (see § 51). For in each, if the correction came from
a copy of the other *p¹* group m, it might nonetheless have been Q alone that turned to *p²* or **x**. But
which of these alternatives is true cannot be established, since Q does not elsewhere agree in error
with the latter. Little can therefore be inferred from these features except that the source of Q, the
earliest member, like that of the slightly earlier m manuscript M, may have had access to copies

outside the p^1 tradition, and also that such access became progressively restricted. But certainly striking is the absence of solid evidence for resort to manuscripts of the other family. Thus, even if shared dialectal features suggest two early copying centres in Worcestershire (for x^1 and x^2), the origin of p^1 is likely to have been at a more central Midland location. This contrasts with the next major group, which was generated further to the west.[64]

b. *Branch* p^2

§ 54. The second branch of **p** consists of three descendants of an original produced in SE Herefordshire, just south of the poet's probable dialectal area. That p^2 was coæval with the other branch is suggested by the early date of its oldest member **G**, which is close to that of p^1's V and within perhaps a dozen years from Langland's presumed obit. G's value is, however, much reduced by its lacking over 600 lines through loss of leaves and another 100 through omissions, singly or in groups. The second early copy **K** is a mere torso, wanting the first 650 lines through loss of leaves and about the last 2900, perhaps because the exemplar was already imperfect. The only complete p^2 copy is thus **N**, the latest. The sequential representation of <GKN>, indicated analytically at § 42 above, is: Pr 1–153 N; Pr 154–II 216 GN; II 217–XIII 225 GKN; XIII 225*a*–XIV 40 KN; XIV 41–XV 66 GKN; XV 67–287 GN; XV 288–XVI 40 N; XVI 41–XXII 39 GN; XXII 40–387 N. Thus p^2 is fully instanced in about 25 agreements in error, nine major, across some 3730 lines or just over 50% of the poem.[65] A minus sign here indicates freedom from the group error.

Major V 125. VI 40. VII 1 -slob-] -slot-. 6 A...bolk] belkynge he b. 261 in thyn h.; sytteth] *trs*. VIII 50 with] *om*. 171. 337. XII 70 And...ere] And rewarde.
Minor IV 15 hym] *om*. 133 ens.] sg., 190. V 30 in] at, 44.[66] 66 and] *om*. 152. 159 places] *sg*. VI 438 in] on. VIII 14 the] *om*. 133 of] for. IX 308 And] *om*. 325 into] in. XIII 54 þat] þe. 119 is] is he. 190 day; nyhte] *trs*.

Secondly, in some 60 readings across nearly 3500 lines (just above 40% of the poem) where K is absent, **GN** could in principle represent p^2. The following ten are major:[67]

Pr 172 cloches] clawes. 189 roume] renne. II 13 rede] ryche. XV 188 Sobrete] Sobernesse. XVI 149 here] *om*.[68] XVII 118 nat(1)] *om*. XVIII 17 sethe] saide, 104 and] he. XXI 151 songen] swettely s. 246 vnrihtfulliche] wiþ wrong.

Finally, for 560 lines (some 7% of the poem), N alone may attest p^2, e.g. in Pr 110 and XXII 110, 198[2] and 212 (although each of these could be an individual error).

§ 55. Because of the defectiveness in the data establishing p^2, where one of the three copies is absent, collateral evidence may be looked for in the support of **x**. For when agreeing with **x** in a right reading, unless contamination is posited, p^2 inferentially preserves **p** and p^1 has erred. By extension, when the right reading appears in any one or two of its three members, unless this too is to be ascribed to contamination from **x**, it again may be judged to preserve p^2. The 270-odd instances listed at § 42 above where GKN join **x** to furnish the lemma imply that p^2 was a far more accurate copy of **p** than was p^1 (see § 44 above). If these may be interpreted as the presumed readings of their source-manuscript, it should be permissible to go on to identify the single or paired agreements of G, K and N with **x** in right readings as likewise representing the likely text of p^2. In the following list of some 40 a minus denotes a p^2 (and, where such occurs, an **x**) copy sharing the p^1 error; a plus, a p^1 copy with the right reading:

Major
(a) GKN *present*: VI 388 -N (*alt*.). 390 -N (*alt*.). VII 20 -G+M [*unconscious substitution of near-synonym*]. X 275[2] -KP[2].
(b) GN *present* XVI 266 -GP[2]U [*l. lost through homoteleuton*]. 371 -G [*visual error foll. by smoothing*]. XVII 14[1,2] -N,

82 -GD²Dt [ʒ / þ *confusion*]. XX 140 -N (*alt.*) +P². 256 -N (*ins.*). 353 -N [*eyeskip from* her > er̃the]. 365 -NCh. 418 -NDN². XXI 482 -G+Dt [*unconscious substitution of contextually commoner word*]. (c) *Only* N *present* XVI 31².

Minor

(a) GKN *present*: VI 29 -N, 32 -G, 122 -G, 71 -N. IX 218 -G, 230 -GP². X 117 -GY, 184 -GN². XI 109 ‡N. XII 185 -GP²u.
(b) GN *present* II 148 -N+R. XVI 259, 319 -GD², 341 -GY+MW. XVII 61 -N, 184 -N+F. XIX 234 -Gt+R. XX 96 -N, 112 -GP², 390 -G. XXI 190 -G+MZ, 390. XXII 25 -Gut+W. (c) *Only* N *present* Pr 10, 36, 58. XXII 63 +W.

Among the 43 instances listed here, G contains some twenty and N some dozen (eight major), which diverge from the presumed group-reading to share the p^1 error. If the minor cases are discounted as probably coincidental, G's remaining major ones all appear likely on analysis to have mechanical causes. K's single example at X 275 could be a coincidence prompted by *louye* in 274; for K, though defective, is generally very accurate. Only N seems to owe four major changes of its p^2 text to consultation of a p^1 copy. Four others may reflect earlier alteration in N's exemplar, but this looks likely only for XVII 14. The early G and K are thus pure examples of the p^2 tradition and only the late N seems aware of p^1. This need not imply that the relatively greater corruption of p^1 is due to its original's relative lateness, for an initial faultiness could have been compounded through successive copying by m, e and r, the group-ancestors of the extant copies. But the more 'primary' character of the p^2 witnesses may well be associated with the simplicity of their generation.

§ 56. None of the three copies derives directly from either of the others and only N need have had an immediate ancestor between it and p^2. As well as being much older than N, G possesses VIII 275b–76a (which K lacks); K, as early as G, has many lines G omits, e.g. V 21, XIII 39, 63, XIV 63, 212; but N cannot derive from K, as it too has VIII 275b–76, nor from G, since it has nearly all of G's missing lines. On the basis of some 100 agreements, about a dozen major, R–K find a genetic relation between G and N (p. 35). But while they acknowledge (n. 19) that 'an indeterminate number' *after* XV 66, where K breaks off, could also be evidence for the group KGN, they fail to note that K's absence *before* II 217 also entails ignoring in the number half a dozen GN agreements between Pr 154, where G begins, and II 216. As three of these are major (Pr 172 *cloches*] *clawes*, 189 *roume*] *renne*, II 13 *rede*] *ryche*), the total reduces to about 40, of which barely half a dozen can be called major. Further, perhaps 25 minor ones (e. g. II 15 *atyer*] *tyr*, IV 116 *reclused*] *reclosed*, VI 40 *enchesoun*] *chesoun*) are simply spelling-variants that should not count as substantive agreements. The genetic character of GN, in any case uncertain because of K's massive absences, is questioned firstly by 45 agreements of GK, some ten of them major (*R–K*, pp 40–1). But since K is present for comparison with G in less than half as many lines as N, a qualitative scrutiny of their shared variants is essential. What this reveals is that GK, as well as omitting III 172 and XIII 86, have at least one reading unattributable to chance, V 10 *inwitt*] *duite* (*vnite* p^1N ? = **p**). A second challenge to GN is the 19 agreements of KN, perhaps nine of them major. The most striking include the Latin form *rectis* for *rect* at III 333 and 35 (these, paralleled in M's *rectes*, may be evidence that M used a p^2 and not an **x** copy for its run of corrections in Pr–II, as suggested at § 43 above). Others include *kyssyng*] *cursyng* VI 187, *elde*] *colde* VI 200 and *hunte*] *oute* VIII 28. Given the logical difficulty of ascribing both GN and KN to convergent variation, simple acceptance of <GN> as genetic should perhaps yield to R–K's 'alternative explanation' of 'consultation in a single copying centre' (cf. § 23 above). In the case of N, this implicitly signifies not Harley 2376 itself, which is a generation later in date than G, but its postulated exemplar. All in all, there would thus seem little reason for preferring a genetic to a chronological arrangement of the sequence of sigils in p^2. The group cannot be eliminated since it has a unique right reading at XIII 120 (where the Apparatus should read 'GK' before '*trs*' and '*p¹*N' for '**p**') and a few superior single-member variants due perhaps to felicitous accident:

Major G: VII 131 sy3t] liht X&r (?Cx), 306 wel] ful (?Cx).
Minor G: VIII 148 what þat] what y; þat ?**pu**. IX 63 hi] he / they. N: I 187 +S hy] þei [*the metrically requisite pronoun-form*]; III 175 fle [*omitted from Apparatus*]; XXII 329 come [*the superior past subjunctive verb-form*].[69]

Finally, p^2 valuably represents **p** where p^1 is absent or in error (see § 42 above).

§ 57. This discussion has shown that the principal groups p^1 and p^2 and their constituent manuscripts between them preserve some thirteen readings, eight of them major, which appear original on intrinsic grounds and from comparison with the parallel text of the other version(s) where available. These are mostly to be judged happy scribal conjectures, except for the whole line XVII 116 (§ 49 and *Textual Notes*). There are no signs in **p** or its members (except M) of contamination from any earlier version, though occasional readings like G's at VII 131 or F's at VII 106 may reflect their scribes' knowledge of **B**. Several members of both branches could be eliminated as lacking unique right readings, e.g. E, A, V, Z and K, and **p** might be adequately represented by PRMQFGN. But since ten of its fourteen members (including four of the latter seven) are defective, collating all the witnesses increases the firmness with which sub-group, group and sub-family readings can be established. This is of consequence for the text of Pr–XII, where **p** is the sole representative of x^2, its readings often preserving the archetypal text and providing the lemma for x^1's defining variants at §§ 33–4 above. But since the certain evidence for **p** itself is the agreed readings of p^1 and p^2, a control must be sought where p^1 is *un*certain because its constituent groups conflict. This is found firstly in p^2, which can aid in discriminating the likely reading of p^1 as between groups m and q; secondly, in t and (before XII) in x^1.

§ 58. As with the earlier accounts (*A Version* § 45; *B Version* § 41), all the 1445 **p** variants listed below have of course been identified as agreements in error. Against the inescapable sub-jectivity of such a judgement the main defence lies in the comparative x^1 evidence, the available parallels in **Z**, **A** and, above all, **B**. But in cases of conflict between **C** families, especially in rela-tion to minor readings, the logic of the linear postulate is here regarded as overriding the joint witness of earlier versions. Thus, when **AZ**'s support for **p** is made to rank after **B**'s for **x**, a **Z** reading ratified by **A** is understood as a reading revised in **B**, not one retained in **C** from B¹ but corrupted in Bx. At other times, the presumption that **C** could be revised may endorse an intrinsi-cally harder (or simply acceptable) **x** reading even when **p** enjoys all the other-version support.[70] In the list below, the readings identified as shared errors of **p** and t are not given again, since these will be found at § 38 above, where they are cited as joint evidence for the readings of x^2. Unsup-ported **p** variants before XII, however, may be inferred to preserve x^2 only when they are judged authentic on their own merits, because any errors in this portion might be simply **p** divergences from the sub-archetypal source. Allowing, then, for occasional non-unanimous attestation, the full evidence for **p** is set out as earlier for x^1, divided according to major and minor readings and other-version support. There are 145 major and 634 minor instances where the adopted variant has such support, 130 major and 536 minor ones where it does not. The lemmata before Passus XII, unless indicated otherwise, are from x^1, denoted simply by **x** as in the Apparatus; but from XII to XXII the same sigil denotes *joint* readings of x^1 and t. As earlier, for reasons of space, minor readings are given by reference only, but the major ones in full. This is because **p**, as in principle representing x^2 in Pr–XII where t is absent, in effect acquires family status (unlike γ in **B**, which is never the *sole* witness to β). For the sake of completeness and convenience, **p**'s readings therefore continue to be recorded in full even after XII, when agreed x^lt is denoted by **x**. Round brackets signify a near but non-identical reading; square brackets one where, despite other-version support, **p** is still rejected. A minus sign before a sigil denotes agreement of an **x** witness / other version with the rejected **p** variant; a plus sign, agreement of a **p** member with the lemma; 'so', other-version agreement with **p**.

§ 59. Readings with other-version support

(i) Major

+ZAB: Pr 2 shroudes] shrobbis. shep] shepherde. I 33 yerne] wilne. 36 ȝut mote ȝe] ȝe mote. 197 carefole] cristine. II 72 standeth] stod. 73 vnfoldeth] vnfeeld; hath] hadde. III 6 were leuest haue] w. l. to h. P^2; is l. h. **p**; l. hadde **x**. 25 man] *om*. 165 and^2] alle. 181 +VM ones] one. 223 +F knowestou] knoweþ. IV 43 +M sulue] *om*. 61 +MF otes] oþer twelue. V 115 synne] s. to punyshe þe puple. 119 segges] to syggen ous. 137 forwanyen] forwene. VI 316 swythe] ful. VII 176 -P^2 calleth] clepeþ. 195 -AxP^2+P hewe] hyne. 204 way theder] (heye) w. þyderwarde wyteþ wel þe soþe. 229 se] *om*. 247 -P^2+G Biddeth] Rydeth to. VIII (25 tho thow louest] þe while þou lyuest). 93 this] *om*. 257/8 +RM *L. div*. 257 +RM shal] he shal. 258^1 -P^2+RM wel] *om*. 258^2 +RM bireue] b. for hus rechelesnesse. 322 -P^2 neyh] *om*. IX 41 many] somme.
+ZB: II 191 -Ax, u *fornicatores*] fornicators. III 17 [-Ax, *om*] +R wedde] wende. 29 þou myhte] we mowe.
+Z: III 225 weye] wyterly.
+AB: Pr 49 +RM wyse] vnwyse. 72 bounchede] blessed. 74 -P^2D gyue] ȝeueþ. 229 *til* hem] a tast for nouht. III 67 +MF se] (se and) seye. 70 An auntur] Leste. 73 +M lordes] l. loue. VI 197 Sire] *om*. 209 leef] lesyng. 382 -u Tho] Two. 393 louryng] lakeryng. 436 -P^2 lyf] lyuyng. IX 311 for defaute we shulle] we shulleþ for d. 338^1 dome] day of d. X 113 we] togederes we. 304 -U here] *om*. XI 21 gentele] g. and wys. 92 -XIP^{2}N^2 man] *om*. 107 wo] muche wo. 217 (ho tauhte men bettre] hij t. men boþe). 264 -N^2 Then] Also. 270 -P^2 to dethe] *om*.
+B: Pr 140 Myght] The muche m. III 269 ȝerne] renne. V 141 -ZA ȝe; ȝow] hij; hem. VI 55 -P^2 Y lye wenen] ȝe wene ich lye. 68 -P^2 chalengynge] *l*anglynge. 160 at euen] *om*. 163 cough] cowede. 228 -A ale] *om*. 248^3 his] *om*. 284 in a doute] *om*. 426 Godes; his] þy; þy. VII 41 So with] Þat with so. 43 his] *om*. 134 lup] lemed. 137 dame] moder. [138 so] *om*; *so* **B**]. VIII 197 proud] ful p. X 66 mouthes] murye m. 84 alle] herteliche a. 95 +K-u pulte] putte. XI 68 wynneth; hath] *trs*. 76 now] *om*. 148 Austin...bokes] Herof a. þe olde made bokes and b. 220 wisest] wise. 232 goed] worldliche g. XII 20^2 welde] wedde. 57 for...breste] of hus breste sauete for synne. 70 (And) for his (rechelesnes) rewarden hym þere] Rewardynge hym þer for hus r. XIII 161 made...moche] þerto m. a molde / With alle here wyse castes. XIV 66 -YDN^2 at] a. 103 yse] ich seye. 121/3 *mislin*. XV 106 +E-D^{2}DT take] talke. 249 oute of his poke; hente] *trs*. 258 +W etynge] ondyng. 282 -D rihtfullyche] do ryghtful. 284 +RM rychesse] riche. 299 somtyme sum] tyme of som. XVI 3 -D Hewen] Thei. 4 selde] shulle nat. 42 -F Cristene] cr. men. noon coueytous for] no couetise to. 58 haueth] shewith. 92 nat] nat ful longe. 114 Pacience] pacient. 120 by] quaþ. 246 in somur tyme; on trees] *trs*. 329 ȝerneth he into ȝouthe] he ȝ. into þouht. 356 recomendeth] comendeþ. XVII 220 +VZ-uH^{2}Ch kirke] churche. 254 ho so] þat. 305 studeden] fondeden. XVIII 209 alle] *om*. 286 Lollyng] Longynge. XIX 50 ȝeden] wente. 196 the...Trinite; 197 Melteth...mercy] *trs*. XX 34a -P^2 *morsus*] *om*. 96/8 *L. div*. 96 for euere] *om*. 105 lordeyns] lordynges. 255 soffre] s. deþ. 272^1 -tN^2 *Principes*] Princes. 272^2 place] palys. 276 Care] Colde c. 332 trolled] troiled and trauailed / In hus tyme. 393/4 *L. div*. 470 -N^2 caroled] daunsede. 471 -P^2 riht] *om*. XXI 28 knele; to hym] *trs*. 45 lyf] þe lykyng lyf. 60 ȝeueth] ȝaue. 127 folk] fele f. 181 me] *om*. 191 men] *om*. 401 while] t; *om x^l*; for. 444 þat^1] hem þat. 449 olde Lawe and þe newe Lawe] l. boþe old and newe. 459 -D alle] *om*. 463 of my reue; to take] *trs*. XXII 17 anoenriht nymeth hym vnder] nymeþ hym anon vnder his. 18 +F yf] ȝeueþ. 37 fele nedes] for neode. 70 hit baer] bar þat baner. 95 -P^2U he] *om*. 136 ȝede] hyede. 143 lowh] l. lowde. 156 his lemman; fortune] *trs*. 183 aftur] hastede a. 198^2 forbete] afeynted and f. 200 ney] and neihede. 208 othere] o. þynges. (293 remenaunt] r. of þe good). 297 Consience; assailede] *trs*. 323 -P^2DTH^2 sayde] quod.

(ii) Minor

+ZAB: Pr 4. -u 10. 28. 43. (50). 58. I -b 20. [-L 37 (*so* **ZAB**)]. 43. 79. +MF-U 84. [82 (*so* **ZAB**)]. 88. +F 101. [128 (*so* **ZAB**)]. 136. 160^1. 161. -D 167. 174^1. 182^{1,3}. 189. II +R 73^1. 73^2. 79^2. [93 (*so* Bx)]. -P^2 126. -P^2+E 159^1. +F 165^1. 165^2. -U 169. 179^1. 191^1. +M 192. +MF 202^{1,2}. 210. [+M 212 (*so* Bx)]. +M 216. (+F 220). 221. 223^1. 228. 229^2. 235. III (6). 7. -D 12. [16^1 (*so* **ZAB**); +AVM 16^2]. 27. 133. +P^2D 145. 152. +F 174. 179. 198^1. 199. 215. 227. 259. 260. [+F 262^3 (*so* **ZAB**)]. IV 21. 27. 46. +MF 62. 79. 82^1. +F 82. 84. 87. 90^1. -D 102. 103. 126. 177. V 130. VI 4. 438. VII 57. 58^1. -P^2 58^3. -D 60. -P^2 61^{1,2}. 64^1. 68. 164. 171. 180^2. -P^2 182. 192. 194. -D 205. (214). 217. -P^2 223. 228. 233. VIII 1. (25). 39. 41^1.

93. (+M; †Bx 101). 109^1. 112. 113. -D 143. (†Ax 149). 150. 156. 164. -D 172. -P^2+M 227. 257. +M 294. 312. -P^2 322. 325^{1,2}. 334. 346^1. -D 347.

+ZA: VIII 17. **-B**+S 18.

+ZB: II -DA+RSG 174. IV -A+MG 90. -UA+M 110. V -**A** 109. +FS; *l. om* 134. VII -IP^{2}A 245^1. VIII -**A** 219. -A+G 313.

+Z: Pr +N 36.

+AB: Pr -**Z** 25. 64. -OU 75 hit] hit to. 83. [84 *so* **AB**]. 161. 164. [221 *so* **AB**]. I 174^1 (*so* **Z**). -U 178 (*so* **Z**). 188 (*so* **Z**). II 252. III 21. [48 (*so* **AB**)]. 70. -U 448. IV -Z**P**^{2} 105. VI 215. 357. 358. 363. +RM 365. 380. 387. +M 391. +F 403. +Q-P^2 414. VII 155 (*so* **Z**). 269. 285^1. -P^2 286. VIII 16 (*so* **Z**). 27 (*so* **Z**). 50. 56. +S-P^2 68. 76^1. +MS 76^2. +G 83. 229^2. IX 177 (*so* **Z**). 281^1. [+AVF-**AB** 281^2]. +RM 281^3. -D 282. 290. 293. 297. -P^2 299. 302. 304. 305^1. 309. +D 313. 330. 331^1. 338^2. +M 343^2. X -ZN 11. 19. 29. 36. -P^{2}D 38^2. 38^3. 46. 64. 73. 77. 81^1. 108^{1,4}. +S-D 130.^{1}, +N-P^{2}D 130^2. -N^2 143. +G 230. 235. 277. 295. XI -U+R 3. 6. -N^2 15. -I 39. +S 87^1. (87^2). -Y 93. 115. -N^2 116, 119. 138^1, 222, 264. -P^2 266^1. 271^1. -N^2 293. +F 296^{1,4}.

+B: Pr 79. 89. 91. [+M-**B** 136]. +RM 137. 176-7. -b 190^2. I 78 And also kenne] Also to k. 139. 153. 159. [II -**B** 14]. 35. 52. 71^1. 86^2. +R-P^2 89. +M 94. 99. -P^{2}bD 108. -AD 141. III +F 31. 457. 477. IV -Z**A** 45. 111. -ZA 122. (127). -Z**A**U+MSN 159. V -P^{2}u 161. 165. 167^1. VI 41. 56. -D 57. 58^1. [-Bu 59; **p** *may be right here*]. +M 70. 72^1. -M 75. 77^1. -u 82. +F 88. -u 90. 94. +RM 129. +AF 133^1. 151. 156^2. 165. 178. 179. 201. 238. 245. -u 246^2. +PEM 249^1. 276. -P^2 278, 280. 282. 285. 327. 341. 347. 361, 379 (*so* **A**). +E 397. 427^{1,2}. VII 1. 4. 6. +M 7. 9^1. 16. 22. +S 26. +P^2 28. 29. 35^1. 38. 39. 40. 45. +I 47. 49. 72^2. 78. 80. 90. +F 92. +G 94. +MS-P^2 97. 111^2. 112. 124^1. +M 124^2. -AZ 235, 236^1, 245^2. +K-uA 271. VIII -Z**A** 3. 35. 37. 139. 154. -P^{2}Z**A** 301. IX -P^2 8^1. [-**B** 39]. -Y 42. -**A** 349. X 62^{1,2}. 66^2. +N-D**A** 105. XI 26. 28. 74. 157. 166. +N-D 167. 168. 169^1. -N^2 170. +S-P^2 171. 184. 186. 189. -N^2 190. +QM-N^2 192. -N^2 215. 236. 240. -N^2 244. 285^1. +F 285^2. 300^1. XII 23, 26. -N^2 33. 38. 69. 70. 71^1. 74^2. -P^{2}D^{2}UN^2 80. -N^2 111^2. -P^2 113^2. 121. -D 129. 130. 131. 142^1. -N^2 146^1. [-**B** 150]. XIII 110 -P^2 119^{1,2}. 121. 127. 158. 162. 176^1. 178. 212^2. -P^2 226. XIV 53. -P^{2}u 56. 66. 78. -N^2 87. 90. 108. 149. 151. 152. 156. +M-YU 209^1. XV +G 2. 11^1. 19^1. 69. +MWS 72^1. +G 84. 90. [-P^{2}D**B** 105]. -D^{2}Ch 135. -P^2 165. 166. 173^2. +MWS-Ch 209. 224. 228^{1,2}. 240. 252. -P^2 257^1. 257^2. +S 267^1. -Ch 269. 270. +SN-Yu 274. 292. +QSN-D 293. XVI 4^3. [+QF-**B** 38]. 39. +F 42. -D^{2}U 45. 48. +WF 49. 56. 73. +F 76. 79. +F 80. 85. 91. 93. 101. 102^1. 111. 128^1. 130. +G-Ch 144. 167. 186. 194. 205. +QWZ 207. +G 224. +M 234. +MF 264. 321^{1,2}. 328. [+EVRF-**B** 330^2]. +MWN-Y 341. 345^{1,2}. 356. XVII +W 112^1, 113. XVIII 35^{1,2}. [-**B** 45]. XIX +M 50. +MW-P^2 63. +FN 66. +FG 68. -P^2 69. +G 70. -D^{2}DH^{2}Ch 76. 84. [-**B** 148]. 153. 164. 171. 192. 204^2. 224. 252. 255. 285. 286. +G 310. 317. 319. +N-D^{2}Ch 325. -P^2 327. XX -Ch 52. 56. 71. 77. [-P^2**B**]. +G 96. 112^2. 125. +WN-I 126. -P^2 162. [-**B** 163]. 171. +EWF 208. 210. -Ch 215. 220. +F 227. -P^2 228, 229^2. -P^{2}D^2 231. 234. 254. 260. +W 270. [-**B** 273]. +MG 281. [-**B** 299]. 302^2. 321. 337. -ICh 362. 393. -P^{2}D^{2}Ch 395. +MQ-P^{2}U 399. 404. 413. 462. 474. XXI 3. +RM-P^2 11. -P^{2}D^2 13. 14. 21. +F 30^1. 30^2. 31. -ChN^2 44. 47. 63^1. [-**B** 63^2]. 76. 87. +F 114^2. 132. 137. 168. 188. 195. 208. 214. 220. 222. 224. 232. 233. 235^2. -D^2 259. 265. 278. 340^1. 342. 346. 348. 356. 380. 386. 389. +W 433. -P^2 437. 440. -D^2 471. 472. XXII 3. 7. 13. 15. 17. 35. 36. 42. 45. 46. 50. +W 55. +RW 60^1. 60^{2,3}. 65. 67. 71. 80. 95. -P^2 129. 136^1. 140. -ID^{2}DH^{2}Ch 151. 152. -D 172. 192. 196. +PE-Ch 212^1. 212^2. 215. 220. 222. 232. 235. -P^{2}D^{2}DCh 266. +F 290. +W 322. 327. +RM 331. -D^{2}Ch 337. +P 343. 346. 353. 364. 370^2. 374.

§ 60. Readings with no other-version parallel

(i) Major

Pr 46 also] synful. 50 aftir] *om.* I 67 and his lore] *om.* 99 fyghte and fende] feithfullich defende and fyȝte for. 110 That] He; þat was] god. II 68 hit were so] þer to. 78 Mede] And me. 83 þat hath a] hath with. 184 *rectores*] rectours. 191 -u *fornicatores*] fornicators. III 89 grayeth] grete. 153 Mede] maide. 255 *As two ll.* kyng] k. ycoroned by marye. 274 Bothe] *om.* 287 +AV sayth] sheweþ. 290 +F(M) and] a. 304 *As two ll.* dette] d. for þe doynge. 316 (+M) and to] *om.* 356 -P^{2}U kyrke] churche. 367 am] *om.* 369^2) alle] *om.* 376 to his lawe] þus to hym. 382 now] *om.* 385 Such...resoun] Al r. reproueþ such imparfit peple. 397^2) -P^2 kyrke] churche. 412 Ruth] reweþ. -P^{2}D derfly] delfulliche. 423/4 myhte / Spille hit] myhte spille. 427 and warnede hym by] by warning of. 499^2) recheth] recetteþ. IV 30 þe comune] þei couthen. 123 be] for. 125 ruyflares] robbers (*so* **B**). 140 *Nullum malum*; man] *trs.* V 14 -P^{2}u mywen] mowen. 21 They...fynden] Hem þat bedreden be bylyue to f. 44^{1,2}) so] *om*; opelond] on londone. 48 This Y segge] Thus y synge. 103 +AFN-P^2 louable] lowable. 104, 105 +VRF-P^2 kyrke] churche. 125 to heuene] ryght for (and hou) to lyuen. 167^2) +RM so] *om.* VI 29 +F clerk] lered. 39 -D couent] couetyse. 42 -IP^2 clerkysh] clerkes. 65 -P^2 corse-men] corsement. 67 -I pissede] passede. 147 heo^2)] ich. 258 weyhtes] wittes. VII 255 +M-P^{2}D payne] pyne. ?295 graytheliche] grettliche. VIII 53^2 -P^{2}u kyrke] churche. 74 lele] for l. 216 filial] ?fial. 349 schaef] shaft. viii] vm. IX 19 suche] sitthen. 71 Ac þat most neden] The most needy. 195 Noyther] *om.* 259 ar wroken] ben broke. X 37 so] *om.* 98 Sholde...to] That no bisshop sholde here byddinge. 100

demede] diuinide. 196[2)]] on rode] *om.* 217 *As two ll.* engendrede] e. and a gome vnryghtful. 249 makynge] of mankynde. 251 -N[2] seth[2)]] sitthen. XI 68 wynneth; hath] *trs.* 76 now] *om.* 78 þat loueth] lyuen. 178 manere] wyse. 203 sihte] sete. 208 -P[2]N[2] *prescite*] prechen. 246 -P[2]D kyrke] churche. 250 -P[2]N[2] kyrke] churche. 286 ʒe] ich. XII 93 oure] ʒoure. 106 hou beste to] how he may. 169 ʒut] Thus. 176 Ennedy] Ouidius. 186 grace] grete g. 217 lete] leue. XIII 9 *As two ll.* his hosewyf] hym ys h. and heeld here hymself. 42 fayre] *om.* 69 rychesse] grete r. 92 So þe pore] The porter. 148 ferddede] herdeyed. 200 soffre alle] *trs.* XIV 26 worcheth God sulue] g. hymself w. 45[2)] come] be. 179 pennes] feþeres. XV 8 -P[2] lotes] lockes. 72 eny] heuene. 80–3 *Mislin.* 82 mendynantz] m. and made eny sarmon. 126 +W techeth] telleþ. 132 -ChN[2] palmare ʒent] plouhman. 142–5 *Mislin.* 143 helpe] Hertely þou hym h. 232 Plente] Pure p. 238 helpe] heye h. 240 neuere was here] was þer neuere (*cf.* **B**). 248 quod Actyf; ay] *trs.* 290/1 *Misdiv.* 290 -P[2] puyre] *om.* XVI 31/2 *Misdiv.* 31 quyteth] soueraynliche q. 273 +QW curatours] creatures. 327 Worth; hit] Ys; wel. XVII 39 haue we] ʒe h. 124 letynge] lengthynge. 125 chere] *om.* 132 and gentel Sarresines] gentiles and s. 139 -P[2] lyue] louen. 241 mannes] *om.* 247 -H[2] hy] *om.* 247[2] -D[2] descendet] descendede. XVIII 80 *Actiua*...hit] lettred men in here langage *actiua* lif. 83 *Actiua*] That is a.; *Contemplatiua Vita*] *trs.* 98 hey heuene is priueoste] heuene buth most pryue. 155 *As two ll.* bere] Broke brede to b. 156 vnkunnynge] vnknowing. 200 leue] looke þow l. 247 when tyme cometh] what t. XIX 128 *As two ll.* And] Al. he] graythly he. hit] þat þat he gripeþ. 239 and a nythynge] *om.* 293 helpe thenne] hem h. XX 98 the dede] hym þat was d. 181 shal] shullen. 355 belyen] bygylie. 444 Þo ledis] t; Tho *x[1]*. Alle þo.

(ii) Minor

Pr -P[2]u 13. 67. 101[2]. 103. 108. 123. I 19. 23. 55. 64. 75. 103. 104. 110. 111. 113. 114. 121[1,2]. 122. 124. 125. 142. 149[1,2]. 175. II 7. 22. 28. -D 29. 33. +S 44. 57. 68. 78. +F 90. 107. 121. 123. +M 125. 129. 130. 135. -P[2]D 139. +MF 169. 172. 176. 179[2]. 198. 218. III 44. 61. 77. 91. 93. 96. +N 97. -P[2] 100. -I 108. -P[2]D 109. 128. 132. 134. +M 144. -P[2] 191. -D 200. 208. +F 209. 210. +RMF 211. 213. +MN 233. 240. +FS-P[2] 241. -I 244[1]. +F 246. -I 251. 252[1]. 254. +FS-u 334. 338. -IP[2] 346. 358. 366. 369[1]. +M 372. -IP[2]U 380[3]. 388. 392. 394[2]. 400. +R-D 409. 420. 444. 491. 494[1]. 499[1]. V 23. 37. 54. 55[1,2]. +FSG 66[1]. 66[2]. +M 68. 95[1,2]. 97[1]. 121. 157. 164. 166. +F-D 187. +M 188. V +A 1. 16. +M-P[2] 18[1]. 24. 35[2]. +F 40. -P[2] 51[1]. 51[2]. 54. +RM 55. 56. 60. 66. 67. 77. +AVR-P[2]D 78. +MFN 83. 88[2]. +S 90[3]. +EAM 95[1]. 95[2]. 105[2]. 114. -P[2] 122. 192. VI 1. 14. 18. 42[1]. 49[1]. 51[1]. 60[2]. +D 84. 107. -F 116. 126. -u 137[1]. -MFS 143[2]. 147[1]. -P[2] 149[1]. +RM 181. +M 186. 187. 188. 190. 192. 204. -P[2]D 252. +M 255. 256. 257. 290. 291. 292. 298[1,2]. 303. -P[2] 317. 332. 337. 381[1]. -u 381[2]. 409[2]. +M 421. 425. 427[2]. 429. 433. VII 23[1]. -P[2]u 23[2]. 74. 75[1]. 115. 118. -P[2]D 144. -P[2]u 147. 148. 153. +FS 202. -P[2] 252. -P[2]D 257. 271. +K-u 297. 302. VIII 49. 57. -P[2] 91. 160 -P[2] 167. 178. -P[2] 190. 197. 214. -P[2] 220. 237. -P[2] 244. 259. 264[1]. -u 264[2]. +M 271. 278. 282. 284. IX 16. 17. -P[2] 56, 60. 67[1]. 71. +G 74. 77. -IP[2]D 87, 90. 93[1,2,3]. -I 104. -P[2]U 105. 106. 109. 113. 120. 124. 130. -U 141. -P[2] 153. 159. -P[2] 162. 174. +MN 182. 193[1]. 195. 200. 201[2]. -P[2] 202. -P[2] 207. 208. 213. 214. 217. 221. -U 222. -P[2] 225. 236. +N 246[2]. -P[2] 247. +N 249. 260. 266. 268. 270[2]. 306. 307[1,2]. +G-P[2] 343[1]. +M-P[2] 345[2]. X 24. 25. -N[2] 37. 38[4]. -u 39[2]. 41. 42. -XP[2] 50. 51. +M 52. +F 54. 97. 110. 127. 161. 170. 171. +K-N[2] 171[2]. +FN-P[2]N[2] 178. -u 189[1]. 189[2]. 196[1]. 197. -N[2] 199. 206. 207. +S 208. 212. 213. 225. -u+N[2] 229. 242. 245. -N[2] 251, 262. 263[1]. 265[2]. -IU 267. 268[1]. -P[2]DN[2] 268[2]. 291. -P[2] 292. 296. +G 301. 311[1]. XI +M 12/13. 16. 27. 33. +SN 45. 50. -D 64. 80. -N[2] 95. 109[2]. -IP[2]N[2] 138[2]. 144. -u 145. 187. 154. +QMN-D 157. 163. +MS-N[2] 187. -P[2]N[2] 201. 238. 263. 271[2]. +MF-P[2] 272[2]. -u 272[3]. 274. 275 pyne **x**PN; payne **p**YU. 283[1]. XII 18. -WS 20[1]. +Y 28. 100. -N[2] 122. 127. 180. -N[2] 186. 191[1,2]. 195. 225. 227. 234. +M 236. -DCh 238. -N[2]D[2] 241. +MW 248. XIII 8. 12[2]. 14. 15. 19. 23. 24. +W-D[2] 37. +F 51, 58. -D[2] 60. 68[1]. 72. 74. 76. 77. +RMG 84. 96. 98[1]. -P[2] 98[3]. 99. -N[2] 105. 114[2]. 120. 122. 170. 172[1]. 175[1]. +M-D 175[2]. 190. 201. -Ch 209. +S-D[2] 217. XIV 7[1]. 8[1,2]. 10. 30. +AVS 34. 76. 134. 142. +M 160. 162. 182. XV +W-D 23. 28. -P[2]Ch 47. 52[1,2]. 68. 71. 81. +MW-P[2] 151. 157. 158. 167[1]. +MW 171. 186. 205. -P[2]Ch 214. 219. +WS 222. +SZ 225. +F 234. -P[2]D 243, 250. 295. +QZ-D 297. 308. XVI +F 36[1,2]. 63. 117. 141. 160. 164. 228[1,2]. 293. 304. 308. 311. 312. 313. 323. 329[1]. 363. 370. XVII +N 4[1]. 4[2]. +M 7. -P[2] 10. -P[2]D[2]DCh 28. 39[1]. +G 61. 74[1]. 75. +M 76. 81. +F 88[1,2]. 93. -ID[2]DCh 118. 140. 148. 153. -D 164. 168. 246. 254[2]. 260[2]. 292[1,2]. XVIII +MW 17. 18[1,2]. 21. 26. 47. 49. 50. 58. 63[1]. +RM 70. 73. 75[1,3]. 81. 84. 87. 94. 96. 106. 108[1,2]. 122[2]. 135[1,2]. 141. 142. +F 152. 163. 175. 181. 193. +PG-YD[2]Ch 197. 217. 222. -Ch 256. 269. XIX 18. 36. 64[1]. -P[2] 64[2]. 77. XX 63. 79. 93. 174. 229[1]. 272[3]. 336. +G-N 353. 358. 405. 420. XXI 175.

§ 61. A few features of these lists deserve brief comment. Among the contaminated *x[1]* copies, N[2], D[2] and D have 32, 20 and 41 agreements respectively with **p**. These are significant numbers when N[2]'s absence in Pr–X and XXII is noted, even if coincidence could explain many of the minor ones. Easily most striking is P[2] which, out of 207 **p** agreements attested by one or more *x[1]* copies (some 32 of them major), has 24 major and 96 minor, or 58%, and shares about 8% of the total 1445 for **p**. On the other side, no **p** copy lacks sub-family errors on this scale, though F is free of 50 minor and seven major errors, some 4% of the whole and M does even better, lacking 70 minor and twelve major errors, or 5.75%. Though these figures do not imply certain collation of F's and M's exemplars with an **x** or x^1-type source, they may point to the involvement of scribes who had already copied such manuscripts and sometimes preferred the verbal form or substance of remembered readings. Also worth remarking are the 20 rejected readings where **x** or x^1 stands alone but the **p** variants are shared by **B**. Any or all of these could (and for consistency arguably should) be preferred. But as noted at § 58 above, in this situation it is logically defensible to subordinate other-version support to the presumption of linearity, provided that the readings adopted meet the acceptability canon (see *Intro.* IV § 16 below). Since they do, and most of the instances are minor, any agreements of **p** with **B** (like those with **A** or **Z**, but where **B** confirms **x**) may be deemed coincidental. For without t to support their claim as potential readings of x^2, the case for thinking such **p** variants archetypal lacks weight.

vi. *Comparison of* **x** *and* **p** *and of* x^1 *and* **p**t.

§ 62. Straightforward comparison of the two sub-archetypal traditions is excluded because of the absence of full evidence for x^2 from the first half of the poem. What is possible throughout the text is to compare x^1 and **p**, with the constant recognition that in Pr–XI wrong **p** readings do not necessarily imply errors in its x^2 source, which might have agreed with x^1 had t been present. Analysis of the traditions thus requires three stages. First **p** is compared with x^1; then with x^1 and t agreeing; finally **p**t (taken as representing x^2) are compared with x^1. That x^1 and t are not a single family in simple contrast with another family **p** has already been argued (at § 38) on the basis that the errors shared by **p** and t indicate an exclusive common ancestor. But even with allowance made for the number of good **p**t readings in XII–XXII (not evidence for that ancestor), it seems unlikely that x^2 could have been superior overall to x^1. As matters stand, x^1 is easily preferable, though subject to frequent correction from x^2 as preserved in **p**t / **p**. The account of **p**t favoured here is regrettably less economical than one recognising only two sub-archetypal traditions for **C**, as for **A** and **B**. It depends, too, on the correctness of identifying the **p**t errors in XII–XXII as genetic. Their secondary character (first observed in relation to **p** by Carnegy 1934) shows through on a comparison of **p**t's divergences from Cx's presumed text with those of x^1, which appear more primitive and elementary. Thus both **p** and t are characterised by over-elaboration, sophistication, and occasional failure to understand the poet's vocabulary, thought and (particularly in the case of **p**) metre. These features are best explained if both **p** and t were copied not directly from the archetype but from an intermediate source, x^2 (which is what 'secondary' is intended to signify). The conclusion drawn is therefore that **p** and t arose independently from a sub-archetypal copy x^2, parallel in generation to x^1 (the common original of y, b and u) and in places free from its errors and omissions. This is as simple an interpretation of the text's early history as that of R–K, who accept only two families, **x** (= x^1t) and **p**. But it directly accounts for the observed nature of **p**t's joint errors and it indirectly explains why, taken severally, the latter also appear 'secondary' when compared with those of x^1 and even some of those preserved severally by its three descendants, y, b and u.

§ 63. Comparison first of x^1 with **p** in Pr–XI brings out their typical differences in respect of omitted or expanded material. Thus x^1 has mechanically lost Pr 141–42 (through eyeskip from *Kynde Wit > Kynde Wit*) and III 71b–72a (through eyeskip from *con- > cou-*).[71] Very similar factors explain omission of the relative clause in IV 146a (with consequential mislineation) and XI

155a, through eyeskip or phrasal haplography (*bokes...bokes*).[72] The reason for the loss of Pr 182 and probably also 183 (which u inaccurately supplies) is less clear; but there could have been visual distraction from *belle...beygh* in 180 or else some damage in the exemplar. For its part **p**, as in III 140–41, tends to expand two lines to three[73] or, more typically, a single line to two. Examples are III 304, VII 204 and X 217, and another five such occur later, after t appears, at XIII 161, XVI 92,[74] XVIII 155, XIX 128 and XX 332. These suggest that the inertness of the three earlier instances is not inherited from x^2 but specific to the scribe of **p**. The same cast of mind shows in several major and minor readings listed at §§ 59–60, ranging from the prosiness of Pr 2 *Y shop me into shrobbis as y a shepherde were* to the timidity at XX 270 of *daunsede* for *caroled*. Lesser idiosyncracies throughout **p** include omission of the line-initial connective *And*, substitution of a participle for a relative clause and alteration of *ne* to *nother*. Many of these features are neutral in themselves;[75] but the looseness and inaccuracy of **p** are borne out by the figures: in Pr–XI x^1 has 280 errors (104 major) to **p**'s nearly 900 (of which 196 are major). However, the most notable discrepancy is between the relative proportions of the different types of error. For whereas in the major instances **p** is less than twice as inaccurate as x^1, in the minor, at 700:176 **p** is four times more inaccurate than x^1. This fact is attributable to the practices noted above and is confirmed by the figures given in § 64. Nonetheless **p** attests, for most of x^1's 280 wrong readings, an x^2 text that seems to preserve the archetype.

§ 64. The 'secondary' quality of **p**'s errors, even more pronounced than that of **pt**, remains in evidence from XII onwards. The second stage of the comparison is that of **p**'s readings with x^1's (§ 38 above) where both x^1 and t are present. This reveals, however, only one distinctive feature **p** shares with t that could be a relict of x^2, the substitution of *ch-* for metrically necessary *k-* in *kyrke*. In this section, the error-ratio of **p** to x^1 is 80:26 for major, and 470:75 for minor readings. The figure for minor variants here is significantly higher, with about six times more **p** errors (as opposed to four in Pr–XI); but it is proportionately the same, relative to the major errors (three times as opposed to twice those of x^1 in Pr–XI). Neither the absolute increase nor the proportional consistency is likely to be connected with the presence here of t; for *ex hypothesi* t's agreement with x^1 merely implies faithful preservation of Cx by **pt**'s postulated source x^2. What the comparison brings out is, instead, that **p** was generally much more inaccurate than t in transmitting x^2. That this is a correct interpretation of the relationship between **p** and t is borne out by the third stage of the comparison, that between **pt** and x^1. Here, to begin with, there are ten major and 65 minor **pt** agreements that appear correct where x^1 has erred. It is, of course, not these but the agreements in error that provide evidence for their exclusive common ancestor; but they offer indirect support for **p**'s claim *before* XII to be in places an accurate witness to x^2 and, through it, to Cx. That claim itself is directly founded on the 335 instances, 120 of them major, where **p** alone possesses the right reading. These include *after* XII some 55, about 15 of them major, in which t's convergences in error with x^1 must therefore necessarily be judged coincidental (as argued above at § 38). As the unique witness to eight half-lines and two whole lines (one in RM only)[76] that are not found in x^1 or in t, **p**'s importance for the text of **C** is clearly beyond dispute. But among a total of some 1840 instances (affecting about 45% of the poem) where unambiguous family variants are in open contestation, **p** gives the right reading in only about 21%. It must follow then that even the best surviving representative of the **p** tradition, which is manuscript P, cannot serve as a copy-text for the final version of the poem. This analysis indicates that Skeat might have done better to adopt Y (supplemented where defective by D and I) in preference to the comely, complete but substantively defective P.

vii. *The agreed readings of* **x** *and* p^2.

§ 65. Because of the bi-partite structure of the **p** sub-family, the archetypal readings of **C** cannot be considered immediately, as was possible with the **B** Version. The situation instead resembles that of the r^2**m** agreements in **A** (*A Version* §§ 48–53). For there exists a body of 150 readings in which one branch of one family, here p^2 of **p**, agrees with **x** against the other branch in attesting what appear on intrinsic grounds the readings of the archetype. These already provide the lemmata in the list of p^1's distinctive readings at § 42 above. But it is convenient to document in this section (as earlier for **A**) the evidence that points to p^2 as the older and more faithful branch. Some half-dozen minor instances where **B** happens to support the rejected reading are here attributable to coincidence.

Readings with other-version support[77]

Major +ZAB: VIII 341. **+ZB**: -Ax I 92. **+B**: Pr 226 -**ZA**. XIV 63 -GN^2. 207. XVI 266 -GP^{2}U. XX 200. 201. 461. XXI 110. 427.
Minor +ZAB: VIII 175. 179. 192 +M. 308. 328. 332. **+AB**: X 115 -N. 117 -YG. 133. **+B**: IV 179. V 116. VI 251. 271. [392 -**B**]. VII 2. VIII 73. 141. 146. IX [310 -**B**]. X 68 -I. 274 +SZ. XI 210. 269. 315. XII 13 +F-N^2. 22 -N^2. [86 -N^2**B**]. XIII [103 -N**B**]. 107 -NP^{2}N^2. 177. XIV 124. 157. 165. 194. 212. XV 3 -D^{2}Ch. [12 -P^{2}D^2**B**]. 17 þat] *om.* 26. 48. 58. 100 +ZW. XVI 57. 75. 182 +M-D^2. 199. 354 +MQF. 355 -u. XVII 171 +F. 311 +W. XIX 89. [133 -**B**Ch]. 334 -DCh. XX 4. 108. 144 +M. 206. XXI 229 +F. 263. 275 +MW. 289. 316. 333 +F. 364 -N^2. 392. 447. 455 +M-ut. 474. XXII 6. 63 +W.

Readings with no other-version parallel

Major III 205. XIII 40. 62. XIV 43. XVI 108. 326. 371 -G. XVII 162 +QZ -P^{2}uCh. 283.
Minor I 40. 66, 76 +M. 98 +MF. II 12 +M. VII 232. VIII 48. 246. IX 78. 97. 117-N. 133 -N. 150. 155. 161^{78}. 166. 180. 188. 196. 199. 203. 218 -G. 246. 248. 254. 258 +M. 261 +Q. 262 +RQ. 279. X 6 +Z. 99. 160 -IU. 175 -NP^{2}D. 181. 184 -GN^2. 264. XI 96. 301. 304. XII 163. 173. 204 -N^2. 212. XIII 25. 66 -D^{2}Ch. 134. 185. XV 62. 70. 92. XVI 122. 281 +QZ. 360 -NP^2. XVII 70 +WF. 72. XVIII 144 +RM-G. XIX 10. 37. 65. 104 -G. 106 -t. XX 20. 73.

In these readings, of which some 20 (or about 2% of the text) are major, agreement of x^1 with p^2 (and t usually, p^2t here jointly representing x^2) is taken to indicate Cx. Lines attested on the basis of **p** and t are not similarly listed, since these have been identified not as separate families but as sub-divisions of the one family x^2.

viii. *The Archetypal Text of the* **C** *Version*

§ 66. After this consideration of the divergent post-archetypal lines of descent, the next section records some 4350 lines that reveal no certain divisions between families or sub-families. As with the **A** and **B** Versions, the selected lemma in the two main lists of family readings at §§ 33–4 and 59–60, unless otherwise stated, has been tacitly understood to preserve the archetype, and the rejected reading to be a corruption of it variously by x^1, **p** or **pt**. But in some 4320 of the poem's 7354 text-lines, just under 60%, Cx is certainly or probably attested, with little or no divergence from individual copies. In the 30 lines marked √, where the **x** and **p** readings remain unsure because of conflicts across family boundaries due to coincidence or contamination, Cx may be recoverable by immediate analysis of the direction of variation. All lines listed are accepted as original, except that incorrect line-division producing no major or minor substantive error has been ignored. The lines here included as archetypal are therefore those (*a*) where x^1 agrees with **p** / **pt** (= x^2); (*b*) where x^1 or an x^1 (sub)-group agrees with one or more branches of **p** identified as preserving the sub-family reading; (*c*) where up to three unrelated members of x^1 join a single two- or three-copy sub-group of **p** (with or without t) in an intrinsically harder reading from which the other variants appear to have been generated. Details of other-version support are not given here except for readings of category (*c*), where genetic character is hardest to determine; but most of these are discussed in the *Textual Notes*. Excluded from the list are (a) the 1825 readings in contestation between the two families, even where on intrinsic and other-version evidence x^I or **p** (whether or not supported by t) seem original (and so presumptively archetypal); and (*b*) particular right readings (noted in the accounts of the **x** and **p** sub-groups at §§ 31 and 57 above) which may have entered individual members of one family from another version, through felicitous conjecture or coincidence. The latter are noticed at §§ 73–4 and accorded the textual status of 'readings editorially emended by a scribe'. Archetypal text-lines judged to contain errors are examined in §§ 67–70 below.

Pr 1. 3. 5–6. 8–9. √10. 11–12. 14–19. 23–4. 29–32. 34–5. 38. 39–42. 44–5. 47–9. 51–5. 57. 59–60. 62–3. 65–7. 70. 73–7. 81. 85–8. 90. 92. 96–100. 102. 104–6. 109. 114. 116. 119. 121–2. 124–6. 128–35. 137–9. 147–60. 162–3. 165–8. 173–5. 178–80. 184–6. 188. 193–200. 203–7. 208–9. 211–13. 215. 217–20. 222–3. 225–8. 232.

I 1–2. √4. 6–7. √8. 10–18. 21–2. 25–30. 32. 34. 36. 38. 42. 44–7. 50–4. √56. 57–60. 61. 63. 65. 68–75. 77. 80–3. 85–6. 89–91. 93–7. 100. √102. 105–8. 115–20. 123. 126–7. 130–2. 134. 138. 140–1. 143–4. 146. 150. 152–4. 157–8. 163. 165–6. 168–9. 171. 173. 176. 180. 183. 185–6. 191–2. 194–5. 198–9.

II 1–4. 8. 13. 15–18. 20. 23–7. 30–2. 34–6. 38. 40–3. 46–51. 53. 58. 61–5. √67. 69–70. 74–5. 77. 80–2. 85. 87–8. 91. 96–8. 100. 102–5. 109–10. 112–15. 117–20. 122. 124. 127–8. 131–4. 136–8. 140. 142–4. 146–7. 149. 150–2. 155–7. 160–2. 164. 167–8. 170–1. 173. 175. 177. 178. 180–3. 188–9. 193–5. √196?. 197. 199–201. 203–9. 211. 213–15. 219. 222. 224–7. 230. 232–4. 236–9. 241–51.

III 1–4. 8–13. 15. 17–18. 20. 22–4. 26. 28. 30. 32–9. 41–3. 45–7. 49–58. 60. 62–5. 68. 74–76. 78–84. 88. 90. 92. 94. 97–9. 102–7. 110–17. 119–26. 130–1. 135–6. 138. 142–3. 146–51. 154–64. 166–7. 169–72. 177. 180. 182–89. 192–7. 201–2. √203. 206–7. 216–22. 224. 226. 228–32. √233. 234. 236–9. 243. 246. 248–50. 253. 256–8. 261. (262). 263–5. 267–8. 270. 273. 275. 277–8. 281–2. 284–6. 288–9. 291–303. 306–15. 317–18. 320. 322–7. 330–3. 336–7. 339–41. √342. 343–5. 348. 350. 352–5. 357. 359. √360. 361–3. 365. 368. 370–1. 373–4. 377–8. 383–4. 386. 389–91. 393. 396. 398. 401–2. √403. 404–6. 408. 410–11. 413–14. 416. 418–19. 425–6. 428. 430. 432–43. 445–6. 450. √451. 452–5. 458–60. 461–73. 475. 480. 484–9. ?492. 497–8.

IV 2–3. 6. 8–14. 17–20. 22. 24. 26. 28–9. 31–4. 40–2. 44. 47–51. 53. 57–60. 63–5. 67. 69. 71–2. 74. 77–8. 80–1. 83–6. 88–9. 91–4. 98–101. 104. 106. 108–9. 112–14. 116–9. 124. 130. 133. 136–9. 142–5. 148–9. 151–6. 161–2. 165. 168–70. 172. 176. 178. 181–5. 191–6.

V 2–9. 11. 13. 15. 17. 19–20. 22–3. 25–32. 33–4. 36–9. 41. 43. 45–7. 49–50. 52–3. 57–9. 61–5. 68. 70–6. 80–2. 84–7. 89. 92–4. 99. 100–2. 106. 108. 111–13. 117. 120–1. 123–4. 127–9. 131–2. 136. 139–40. 142–7. 149–50. 153. 155–60. 162. 164. 169. 171–4. 176. 178. 180–1. 183. 185–9. 191. 193–9.

VI 2–3. 5. 7–13. 16–17. 19–28. 30–5. 37–8. 43–8. 50. 52. 54. 61–4. 66. 69. 74. 76. 78. 81. 83. 85–7. 89. 91. √96. 97–8. 101–3. 105–6. 108–12. 114–15. 117–24. 127–8. 130–2. 138–9. 142. 145–6. 150. 152. 157–8. 161. 166–72. 174–7. 180. 182–5. 191. 193. 196. 198–200. 202–3. 206–8. 210–14. 217. 221. 225–6. 229–32. 236–7. 240–4. 247. 259–65. 267–8. 272. 277. 286–9. 293–6. 299–300. 302. 305–6. 308–10. 313–15. 318. 322–4. 326. 329–31. 333. 338–40. 343. 345–6. 348–56. 360. 362. 364. 366. 368. 371. 373–5. 377. 385–6. 389. 396. 398. 400. 402. 404–6. 411–12. 415. 419–20. 422–4. 428. 430–2. 434.

VII 10. 12–13. 15. 17–21. 24–5. 27. 30–3. 37. 42. 44. 46. 48. 50–3. 56. 59. 62–3. 65–7. 69. 73. 76–7. 79. 81–3. 84–9. 91. 93. 96. 98–105. 109–10. 113–14. 116–17. 119–21. 126–7. 129–30. 132. 135–6. 139. 141–3. 149–52. 154. 158–63. 165. 167. 169. 174–5. 179. 181. 183. 185–91. 193. 195–8. 200. 203. 206. 208–12. 215. 218–22. 226–7. 230. 234. 237–8. 241–4. 246. 248. 250. 254. 256. 258. 261–2. 264–8. 272. 273–80. 282–3. 287–9. 291–8. 301. 303–5.

VIII 2. 4–9. 11–14. 19. 21–4. 28–9. 31. 33–4. 36. 38. 40. 42–5. 47. 54–5. 59–63. 64 (+**B**). 65–6. 69–72. 75. 77. 79–82. 86. 88–9. 92. 94–6. 98. 100. 102–8. 110. 114. 116–17. 119–21. 123–30. 132–4. 136–8. 140. 142. 144–5. 147. 151–2. 155. 157–8. 161–3. 165. 168–71. 173–4. 176. 181–3. 185–9. 198–206. 209–10. 212–13. 215. 217–18. 222–6. 228. 230. 233–5. 238–43. 245. 247. 249–56. 260–3. 265–6. 268. 270. 272–4. 276–7. 279–81. 285–93. 295–8. 300. 304. 306. 309–11. 316–21. 338. 342. 348. 350–2.

IX 1–7. 10–15. 18. 20–2. 25. 26–7. 28–37. 43–51. 53. 55. 58–9. 61. 64–6. 68–9. 72–3. 75–6. 79–86. 88–9. 91–2. 94. 99–103. 107–8. 110–12. 114–16. 117. 118–19. 121–3. 125. 126–9. 131. 135–6. 138–40. 142–9. 151–2. 154. 155. 156. 158. 163–5. 168–9. 171–2. 176. 178–9. 181. 183–7. 189–92. 194. 198. 204–5. 206. 209–11. 215–16. 219–20. 223–4.

226–9. 231–5. 237–45. 250. 253. 255–6. 262. 263. 264. 267. 269. 271–6. 278. 280. 283. 286–9. 291–2. 294–6. 298. 300–01. 303. 308. 312. 314–15. 317–18. 320–6. 329. 332–7. 339–42. 344. 346–8. 350–1.

X 1–5. 8–10. 12–18. 20–1. 23. 26–8. 30–5. 40. 43–4. 47–9. 53. 55. 57–61. 63. 65. 72. 74–6. 79. 82–3. 85–6. 89. 91–3. 96. 101–3. 106–7. 112. 114. 116. 118. 119. 121. 123–6. 128–9. 131–2. 134–5. 137. 139–42. 144–5. 147–50. 152–3. 155–9. √163. 166. 168–9. 173–4. 176–7. 179–80. 182. 183. 186–8. 190–5. 198. 200–01. 204–5. 209–11. 214–16. 218–24. 226–8. 231–3. 236–40. 241. 243–4. 246–7. 248. 250. 252–4. 256. 259–61. 266. 269–73. 276. 278–81. 283. 285–7. 289–90. 293. 298–9. 302–3. 305. 308–10.

XI 1–2. 4–5. 7–10. 14. 18–20. 22–5. 29–32. 35–7. 41–3. 46–9. 52. 54. 57–60. 61. 62–3. 65–7. 69. 71. 73. 75. 79. 81. 83–6. 88–91. 94. 98–9. 101. 103–5. 110–14. 117–18. 120–5. 127–37. 139–42. 146. 149–52. 156. 158. 162. 172–6. 179–82. 185. 188. 191. 193–9. 204–7. 209. 211–14. 219. 221. 223. 225–30. 237. 239. 241–3. 245. 247–8. 252–62. 265. 267. 275–7. 279. 281–2. 284. 290. 294. 297–9. 302. 305. 307–11. 314.

XII 1. 3. 7–9. 11. 14–15. 19. 27. 31–2. 34. 36. 39–40. 42–5. 46. 48–56. 58–62. 65–8. 72–3. 75–9. 81–2. 84–5. 89–92. 94–6. 99–105. 107–10. 112. 115–17. 119. 123–6. 132–8. 140–1. 143–5. 147. 149. √151. 153–6. 158–62. 164. 165–7. √168. 170–2. 174–5. 177–9. 181–4. 187–9. 193–4. 196–203. 205. 207. 209–10. √211. 213. 216. 218–20. 222–4. 228–33. 237. 242–7.

XIII 1–4. 10–11. 16. 18. 21. 26–7. 29–36. 38. 43–50. 57–61. 65. 67. 70–1. 73. 75. 80–2. 85–8. 90–1. 93–5. 97. 100–02. 104. 106. 108–9. 111. 113. 115–18. 128–9. 131–2. 135. 137–40. 142–3. 145–6. 149–50. 152–7. 160. 165–9. 174. 184. 187–9. 193–6. 198–9. 202. 205. 207–8. 210–11. 213–16. 218–20. 222. 224–5. 227–9. 232–3. 235–7. 239–46. 248.

XIV 1. 3–6. 11–21. 25. 27. 29. 31. 32. 33. 35–6. 40–2. 44. 49–52. 54–5. 57–9. 61. 64–5. 67. 70. 72–5. 77. 79–81. 83. 85–6. 89. 92–3. ?94. 95–6. 98–102. 104–6. 109–13. 115–17. 119–20. 125–7. 129–33. 135. 137. 139–41. 143. 145–8. 150. 154. 155. 158–9. 161. 163–4. 166–7. 169–78. 180. 183. 187. 191. 192. 195–7. 200–06. 208. 210. ?211. 214–17.

XV 1. 4–6. 9–10. 13–16. 18. 20. 22. 24–5. 29–30. 32. 35–6. √38. 40–5. 49–51. 53–6. 59–60. 63–5. 73. 75. 77–9. 88. 93–6. 99. 102. 104. 108–10. 111. 112–14. 116–17. 119. 121–4. 128–30. 133–4. 136–42. 147–50. 152–3. 155. 159–64. 170. 172. 175. 177–85. 187–9. 190–204. 206–7. √208. 210. 217–18. 223. 227. 229–33. 235–7. 239. 241. 244–6. 247. 251. 253. 255–6. 260. 262–5. 268. 271–2. 275–81. 285. 287–9. 291. 293–4. 298. 301–2. 304–7. 309–11.

XVI 1–2. 5–13. 15–21. 23–30. 32–3. 35. 37–8. 39–41. 44. 47. 50–5. 59–62. 66–72. 77. 82–3. 86–9. 94–100. 103. 106–7. 109–10. 113. 115. 119. 124. 136–7. 129–33. 135–9. 143. 145–8. 150–3. 155–9. 161–3. 168–9. 171–2. 174–6. 179–81. 184–5. 187–93. 195–8. 200–04. 206–27. 229. 231. 233. 235. 237–45. 247–53. 256–8. 262–3. 265. 267–70. 272. 274–80. 282–92. 294–301. 303. 305. 310. 314. 317. 320. 322. 324. 331. 333. 335–44. 346. 348–53. 357–9. 361. 364–9.

XVII 1–3. 5–6. 8–9. 11. 13. 16–19. 21–3. 25–7. 29–38. 40–7. 49–52. 54–60. 62–6. 67. 68–9. 71. 79–80. 83. 85–6. 89–91. √95. 96–7. 100. 102. 105–6. 109. 111. 114 *?116. 119–23. 126–31. 133–5. 137–8. 141–4. 146. 149–50. 152. 154. 156–61. 163. 166–7. 169–70. 172. 174–5. 177–8. 180–1. 183. 185. 187–9. 192. 194–7. 199–202. 204–5. 208. 211–17. 221–3. 226–7. 229–38. 242–5. 248–50. 252–3. 257–8. 260. √267. 270. 273–5. 277. 279–82. 284. 286–91. 293–6. 298–304. 306–8. 312–14. 316–19.

XVIII 1. 3–9. 11–13. 15–16. 19–20. 22–3. 27–9. 31. 34. 36–7. 42. 44. 48. 51. 53. 54. 56. 59. 61–2. 64–9. 71–2. 74. 76–9. 82. 85–6. 88–93. 100–01. 103. 105. 107. 109–21. 124–5. 128. 132–3. 136–8. 140. 143. 145–51. 153–4. 157–62. 165–8. 170–4. 176–7. 179–80. 182–9. √190. 191–2. 194–6. 198–9. 203. 206. 208. 210–16. 218–21. 223–31. 232. 234–40. 242–3. 245–6. 248–55. 257. 259–68. √271. 272–3. 275–85. 287–8. 290–2.

XIX 1–9. 11–12. 14–15. 20–6. 29–31. 33. 38–40. 42–9. 51–8. 60–2. 67. 71–5. 78–83. 85–8. 90. 92–3. 95–9. 101–03. 107–11. 114. 116–7. 119–27. 129–32. 135–7. 139–42. 144–6. 149–52. 154–63. 166–7. 169–70. 172–3. 175–86. 187. √190. 191. 193–5. 198–9. 201–3. 215–19. 221–3. 225–6. 228–32. 235. 236. 237–8. 243–4. 247. 249–50. 253–4. 258. 259–60. 262–75. 277–84. 286. 288–9. 291. 292. 294–6. 298–300. 303–04. 306. 308–09. 312–16. 318. 320–4. 326. 328–30. 333.

XX 2–3. 5–7. 10–11. 14–19. 21–33. 35–6. √37. 38–49. 51. 53. √55. 57. √58. 59–60. √61. 62. 64. 66. 68. 70. 72. 74. 76. 78. 80–1. 83. 86–90. 92. 95. 99–102. 104. 107. 109–11. 113. 123–4. 127–31. 132. 133–7. 139. 141. 145–8. 150. 152–5. 157. 159–61. 164–7. 169–70. 172. 175. 177. 178–80. 183. 185–7. 189–99. 203. 207. 212–14. 216–17. 219. 221–5. 232–3. 235–40. 242–53. 256. 257. 258–9. 261–6. 268–9. 271. 274–5. 277–80. 282–3. 286–7. 289–92. 295–8. 300–01. 303–6. 308–10. 312–19. 322–5. 326. 327. 329–31. 333–5. 338–40. 342–6. 349–52. 356. 357. 360–1. 363–4. 366–8. 370–2. 374–8. 363–8. 392. 394. 396. 397–8. 401–03. 406–11. 414–17. 421. 423–43. 445–59. 463. 465. 467–9. 472–3. 475–8.

XXI 1. 4–10. 15–20. 22–7. 29. 32–8. 40–1. 43. 46. 49–57. 59. 61. 64–72. √73. 75. 77–81. 83–5. 88–9. 92–4. 96–109. 111–12. √113. 114–26. 128–31. 133–6. 138–57. 160–1. 163–7. 169–74. 176–80. 182–4. √185. 187. 189. √190. 192–3. 196–207. 209. 211. 213. 215–19. 221. 223. 225–8. 231. 234. 237–40. 243–5. 247–51. √252. 253–8. 260–2. 264. 266–8. 270–4. 276–86. 288. 290–5. 297–304. 306–7. 309–11. 313–15. 318. √319. 320–32. 334–9. 341. 343–5. 349. 350–3.

√354. 355. 357–8. 360–1. 363. √366. 367–70. 372–5. 377. 379. 382–5. 387–8. 391. 393. √395. 396–400. 402–06. 409. 413. 415–17. √418. 424–6. 430. 432. 434. 436. 438–9. 441–3. 446. 448. 452. 454. 458. 461–2. 464–5. 467–9. 473. 475. 477–9. 481. 483–4.

XXII 1–2. 4–5. 8–9. 11–12. 14. 16. 20–2. 24. 27. 29. 32–4. 38–40. 43–4. 49. 52–3. 57–9. 61. 64. 66. 68. 72–6. 78–9. 81–4. 86–90. 92–4. 96–102. 104–6. √107. 108–9. 111–19. 121–8. 130. 132–5. 137–9. 141–2. 144–50. 153–5. 157–61. 163. 165–9. √170. √171. 173. 176–82. 184–5. 188–91. 193–5. 197. 199. 202–7. 209–11. 213–14. 216–19. 221. 223–30. 233–4. 237–9. 241–2. 244. 246–62. 264–5. 267–75. 277–81. 283–9. 291. 294–6. 298–9. 302–21. 324–6. 328. 330–1. 333. 335–6. 339–42. 344–5. 347–52. 354–63. 365. 369. 372–3. 375–7. 379–85. 387.

ix. *Emendation of Errors in the Archetypal C-Text*

§ 67. There now follows a list of some 90 certain and 23 possible archetypal errors in the C-Text, amounting to between one in every 65 and one in every 80 lines. They are referenced by line-number only, set out in the same form as for **B** (*B Version* § 60 above) and divided into errors of whole lines and errors within lines. Amongst twelve instances of whole-line errors, seven are misdivided, of which three are followed by scribal misexpansion or omission (denoted by ‡); two and two halves are omitted; and one is judged spurious. Available other-version evidence used for emendation is indicated in brackets, and restored or reconstructed readings are listed again under those headings. Examples where the Cx reading is uncertain because both families are wrong or one is absent are given in square brackets and not counted amongst the total.

(i) *Misdivided Lines*
[I 97–100 *div. after* ordre, poynt, faste y; *as* 5 *ll. after* knyghtes, knyghthed, serk, treuthe **pu**]. V [114/15 (*em. after* **ZAB**)]. VI 223/4 (*em. after* **AB**). VIII ‡221/2 (*em. after* **ZAB**). [XI ‡312/13] (*em. after* **B**). [XIV 121–3] (*em. after* **B**). XX 54/5 (*em. after* **B**).
(ii) *Omitted Lines*
XI 312b, XIII 126b, XV 285, XXI 376 (*all added from* **B**).
(iii) *Spurious Line*
After XVII 73.

§ 68. (*i*) *Restored readings*

Some 30 certain and six possible intralinear archetypal errors, all but one major, have been identi-fied and emended by restoration[79] of a secure other-version reading accepted as the likely **C** origi-nal from which Cx has departed. Of these, 26 are made on the basis of **B** and ten of (**Z**)**AB**. Eight emended solely for metrical reasons are marked with the sign ^. Seven cases where Cx itself is undecidable from the split family variants are placed in square brackets. Six emended readings also appear in a single **C** witness, whether by felicitous accident or guess.

Major *From* **ZAB** VII 247. [IX 23]. *From* **AB** III 429. VI ^224. ^273. X [^7]. ^172. ^301. [XI 11]. *From* **B** I ^151. III 490. VII [111]. 131 G. VIII 77–8a. XI 56 D. 218. 312. XIII 126. XIV 121–3. XV ^273. 285. XVI 43. 199a. XVIII 94 *cf.* N². XIX 13. XX 400 N²· 412. 422 N. XXI 76. ^242 *cf.* F. 376. XXII [13]. 120. 329 N. [338]. **Minor** *From* **ZAB** [IX 23].

§ 69. (*ii*) *Reconstructed readings*

Some 30 certain and 16 possible errors, all but four major, are diagnosed in as many lines that appear defective in sense, style or metre. These are corrected through reconstruction of a hypo-thetical original reading on the basis of extant manuscript evidence and comparison with other-version parallels where available. Square brackets denote reconstructions not of the original from a corrupt archetype but of a presumed archetypal reading from the diversely defective sub-archetypes: an example is the 'split variation' in the very first emended reading at Pr 7. Such reconstructed Cx readings, when still judged inauthentic, are nonetheless included here if further proposed correction is founded on direct other-version evidence. Some 25 emendations on metrical grounds are marked ^. As with **B**, intralinear transpositions are marked '*trs*', relineations '*rl*', and verbal (formal) substitution / addition / omission by '*v (f) s / a / o*'.

Major [Pr 7 *after* **ZAB**]. ^108 *trs*. ^113 *trs*. ^116, ^118 *vs*. ^120 *trs*. 123 *vs*. ^138 D. I [88] *vo*. 97–100 *rl*. [113] *fs*. [122] *va*. III [6; *cf*. P²F]. ^139 *trs*. [321] *vs*. IV [175]. VI [205] *va*. [220] *vf*. VIII [90²] *fs*. 221/2 *va*; *after* **ZAB**. IX [316] *vs*. X ^22 *trs*. ^164 *trs*. ^267 *vs*. ^301 *vs*. XI ^143 *trs*. ^161 *vs*; *cf*. N². XII 206. XIII ^5,^6 *trs*. XIV ^23 *trs*. [68] *fs*. XV [120] *fs*. ^212 *fs*. XVI ^64 *fs* EWN. XVII [108] *fs*. [^190–1] *fs*. XIX ^91 *trs*. 94 N² *vs*.[80] 138. XXI ^347 *trs*, *fs*. ^445 *trs*. XXII ^301 *fs*. 378 *va*; *after* **B**. **Minor** Pr 127 VIII [90¹] *fs*. XX 91 fs. ^173 *fs*. [260] *va*.

§ 70. (*iii*) *Conjectural readings*

In 32 certain and one possible instance where there is little or no direct supporting evidence, intralinear errors have been conjecturally emended, 24 largely on metrical grounds (marked ^). The general factors governing the degree of confidence they can be expected to command have been already described above (*A Version* § 55). Since all of them are major, both the lemma and the rejected archetypal or presumed archetypal readings have been given in full. Square brackets indicate that Cx remains uncertain.

I ^109 luther] fals. ^112 lefte] north. ^155 inmiddes] bitwene (*so // **B**). III ^272 salarie] mede. ^329 cesar. V ^154 querele] chyde (*so // **B**). ^182 ryht] al. VI ^155 faste²] *om* (*so // **B**). ^336 myd] with. VII ^54 be] for. VIII 90 wordynge] worchynge (*so* Pe). XI ^17 leel] *om*. ^126 leide] caste. ^161 doth] maketh (*after* N²). XII 190 -sette] *om*. 208 Worthen] Then. XV [52 was as] as / Ø]. ^220 but] *om*. XVII 147 more] *om* (*so* P²). ^190–1 sethe...name; *Ite...mundum*] *trs*. XVIII ^202 his owne myhte to shewe] to se his o. m. XIX [^28 lich] body (lif t)]. XX [288 the carnel] the car / oure catel]. *So* // **B**): XXI 90 richeles] riche gold 230 wyes] men (*so* K–D). ^236 buggynge; sullyng] N²; *trs*. ^241 of] *om*. ^408 Saue] Bote. XXII ^292 pleyen] maken. ^293 renkes] men. ^301 hy] they. 366 alle hem] hem. 367 and] *om*.

§ 71. The archetypal errors and their emendations are fully discussed in the *Textual Notes*, so they require only brief general notice here. As in **A** and **B**, they will be found to illustrate both unconscious and deliberate scribal variation from the presumed original. Examples of smaller unconscious visual errors occur at III 90, VI 155, 224, VII 131 and VIII 90 (by anticipation). After XV 284 a whole line has been lost through confusion occasioned by word-initial similarities during the sequence *rede...rychesse...ende : renke...rychesse...rekene*. In the uncertain area between unconscious and deliberate errors belong the replacement of *k-* in *kirke* by *ch-* at Pr 138 (a frequent feature likewise of both **p** and t) and of *myd* by *with* in VI 336. So also do at least some examples of variation to prose order, as at III 139, X 22, XI 143, twice in close succession at XIII 5 and 6, at XVIII 202 (with further smoothing of the verb) and at XIX 91. Split variation of the kind also encountered in the sub-archetypes (e. g. at I 122) occurs in Cx at Pr 7 and IV 175. Very possibly deliberate scribal changes include substitutions of more familiar, non-alliterating synonyms as at Pr 116, I 108, III 272, V 154 and XIX 28. Attempts to identify a less than obvious referent or to puzzle out its sense appear at IX 23 and XI 11 respectively. Censorship was not a feature of the archetypal scribe, despite the forthright **C** Version attacks on royal and clerical abuses that might have provoked it. But a possible exception is XXI 376 (unless the poet himself struck this through as morally presumptuous). The archetype was also free of the spurious lines that afflicted Bx: even the one such example after XVII 73 could arguably be let stand after emendation (though its syntactical link with 73 is weak and it appears suggested by the last phrase of that line).

§ 72. As to the possible presence of material in draft condition, the only passage of any length that might seriously be thought to lack its final finish is Pr 95–124. Since the apparent failure in scribal accuracy here is ten times the average rate for the whole poem, and this could be more charitably attributed not to the scribe but to the rough character of his copy-text, the matter clearly deserves further comment. The errors diagnosed include three inversions to prose order at 108, 113 and 120; two substitutions of the same contextually more expected term at 116 and 118; and one failure to understand the referent at 123 (a line which is not certainly archetypal). All of these features, however, are fairly typical of the Cx scribe's performance in the rest of the work (§ 71 above). Generally speaking, therefore, while the presence of draft material here remains a possibility, the wider notion favoured by R–K of Cx's entire copy-text as an interleaved **B** manuscript with extensive insertions and deletions does not seem convincingly borne out by analysis of the evidence.[81] An essential factor for the Athlone editors, their judgement that the final passūs are a wholly unrevised B-Text, is also rejected here. Their opinion that Cx's source in XXI–XXII was the scribal **B** manuscript B^1 is, however, accepted, but with the modification that some small (possibly preliminary) changes had been inserted by the poet. This is consistent with seeing the source of Cx's Pr–XX not as a working draft but as an authorial fair copy that perhaps still required attention in a few places. As a consequence of this rather different understanding of the archetypal scribe's exemplar, nothing like R–K's practice of combining frequent transpositions and corrections of Cx with the retention of metrically imperfect lines has been permitted in the present edition. Nor have the numerous changes to Cx's minor details of wording and phrasing that R–K make on the basis of their (sometimes emended) texts of the **A** and / or **B** Versions. As already stated (§ 58 above), in the treatment of **C** the linear postulate must act with special force as a brake on editorial intervention. Alterations to the archetypal text have accordingly been restricted mainly to major instances, where the likelihood of corruption has seemed barely open to argument. **C** is thus treated, like **B**, as a work largely embodying its author's final intentions. Where readings only doubtfully archetypal are allowed to stand in the edited text, they are attributed not to presumed error in the archetype but to corruption in the course of sub-archetypal transmission. Only rarely do such readings receive emendation, as at XII 206–08, which is perhaps the most speculative example in this edition.[82]

x. *Readings of Indeterminable Origin*

§ 73. The **C** tradition has relatively few readings that look intrinsically authentic but are randomly distributed across both families and so are not evidently or inferentially archetypal. Much more common are cases where a single group or manuscript from either family contains a major right reading.[83] Thus in two cases of important group-variants, *reik* b at Pr 216 and *while Y can* t at XXI 401, the presumption of descent from Cx through i and x^2 respectively would seem to be tolerably secure. Many individual copies may be taken as uniquely preserving their group readings and thence those of their family and of the archetype, e.g. ms X at VI 382, Y at XXI 304/5 (< y) and D at XI 208 (< u). But in others, singular retention of a group-original is altogether harder to credit. Such readings can only arise (a) by contamination, (b) by felicitous accident, (c) by scribal conjecture or (d) by correction from a lost **C** manuscript superior to Cx. Among possible examples of (b) are *clawes* at VI 149, attested only by I; *more* at XVII 147 in P^2; *be thy comune fode* at XXI 410 in D^2; *craftily* at XXI 242 in F; and *siht* at VII 131 in G.[84] A second important F reading *geste* at VII 106 may belong to (a), (b), (c) or (d), and a third, *ne* at XX 462, could be simply a commonsense response, though again the scribe's awareness of **B** cannot be excluded. N^2 shares the latter correction;[85] but in the light of the evidence given in §§ 39–40 above, contamination probably accounts for this (and for other good N^2 variants like *grettore* at XX 400).

§ 74. Explanation (d), which R–K favour for the 45 N^2 readings they adopt into the text,[86] has been discussed and rejected at § 40. Instead, to account for N^2's four unique right readings with no other-version parallel, (c) is here preferred. The reading *ledis* in t at XX 444 is likewise not beyond an enterprising scribe, to judge by an identical N^2 instance at XXI 412 which, as parallel **B** makes clear, cannot have been the reading of B-Ø, the source of both traditions in these passūs.[87] The most noteworthy possible scribal conjecture occurs not in a single extant manuscript but in the genetic pair <RM> at XVII 116, which from the point of view of its origin is the most challenging crux in the whole text. If R–K's hypothesis of a 'lost pre-archetypal **C** manuscript' found support anywhere, it would be here. However, if the explanation of this line as present in Cx but mechanically lost is accepted,[88] grounds for belief in that source disappear. As with the **B** Version, it thus seems virtually certain that no copy underived from the archetype has left any trace in the manuscript tradition of **C**.

Conclusion

§ 75. Editing **C** has at many points required taking into account the evidence of the other versions. This is clear in particular from the lists at §§ 33 and 59 above, where discrimination of the Cx reading in contestation between the two families has been guided by the archetypal texts of **A** and / or **B**. But the use made of such evidence has been subject to an important constraint. Whereas **AC** unanimity creates a presumption that **B** was unaltered, the linear postulate keeps open the possibility at all points of revision in **C**. So any agreement not of Cx but of one or other sub-archetype with **A** and / or **B** as potentially confirmation of a reading's originality should be viewed very cautiously. For in this situation, every choice in effect requires use of the direct method; and while rigorous attention to the core-text criteria may mitigate, it cannot eliminate the *a priori* element in this procedure (see *Introduction* IV § 27). As a result, solving textual cruces in the final version is in some ways less straightforward than in **B**, especially when the material is entirely new. In compensation, the archetypal **C** tradition proves to be nearly six times less corrupt than that of **B**. And because minor readings are by nature hard to establish as certain errors, few such Cx readings ask to be emended simply because they seem intrinsically less good than those of parallel **B** and / or **A**. To that extent, the present edition of **C**, on comparison with the Athlone, will appear relatively more conservative than those of **A** and **B**. This is explained largely by its very different assessment of the quality of the available textual evidence, itself the product of differences sometimes in applying the same editorial principles, sometimes in the principles themselves. These differences, as will now appear, become acute in relation to the version to be considered next.

THE C VERSION: NOTES

1 For a fuller consideration of the question, see *Intro.* V below §§ 7–11.

2 See ibid. § 10.

3 Except for OC^2 and for B and its constituent members, on which see *B Version* § 71 above.

4 See above *A Version* §§ 17, 21 and *Intro.* I, *Manuscripts* 43–52. The **B** copies BmBoCot (nos. 43–5) are also completed by a **C** beginning before an **A** link.

5 Only one **A** manuscript, the Vernon copy (no. 4), is as early as 1400.

6 Donaldson, *C-Text*, pp. 18–19.

7 See Anne Middleton, 'Acts of Vagrancy...', p. 208.

8 J. Bowers's judgement ('*PP*'s William Langland') that these facts and the frequent surprising agreement of **AC** against **B** point to **C** as the form chronologically closer to **A** has nothing to recommend it. Whether the completion of **A** copies from **C** implies informed contemporary recognition of **C** as the final version or is purely opportunistic remains a matter of speculation. Bowers, in further taking John But to refer to Will's death while working on **A**, fails to see that the antecedent of *þis werk* A XII 103 can be read as inclusive of *þat here is writen and oþer werkes boþe* of 101. The undeveloped nature of A Pr–XI and the uncertain, sketch-like quality of A XII are incongruent with its being later than **B** or **C**.

9 I, *Manuscripts* no. 33; see Kane, *Authorship*, pp. 26–33, *Introduction* V, § 4, and the diagram at § 13.

10 I, *Manuscripts*, nos. 24–28 (x^l; cf. 32, 52); nos. 39–41 (p^2; cf. also 38).

11 *Ibid.*, nos. 30, 36 and nos. 31, 37 (p^l).

12 'Langland's London', in Justice and Kirby-Fulton, eds., *Written Work*, p. 191.

13 This compares with about 70% for **B** and 75% for **A**.

14 Unfortunately for the critical history of **C**, Skeat, like Whitaker, based his edition on a **p** manuscript, P (*Introduction* II, § 41). This was no doubt inevitable, since the two best complete x^l copies, X and U, had not come to light, and the substantively superior Y was less than ideal, because lacking the first 640 lines. But consultation of Digby 102 and Douce 104 (D), the companion of Additional 35157 (U), in addition to I, might at the least have improved Skeat's text and forestalled the misconception he made current of Langland's final phase as one of decline.

15 R–K by contrast place N^2 last in their list of the **p** family's witnesses. But its **p** readings could result from early comparison with a **p** copy in its immediate exemplar. They further propose (p. 102, n. 23) 'a pre-archetypal **C** copy' as the source of some of N^2's 'authoritative corrections'. But these, the only evidence for such a copy, can be explained as either contaminations from **B** or, in a half-dozen cases, enlightened scribal conjectures, as argued at § 40 below. The importance of N^2 is urged by Warner, '*Ur-B*'.

16 Were t extant for Pr–XII and ms T in contention to furnish the base-text, **C** might (like **A** and **B**) have been represented by a third Trinity, Cambridge manuscript in the same East Midland language as the other two. But better than such an appearance of Chaucer-like uniformity is the presentation of at least one of the longer versions in a dialectal form close to that inferred for the author.

17 The two families thus display a symmetrical relationship with each other at the upper level of their descent; see the diagram at § 13 below.

18 The line is XVII 116; see the *Textual Notes*.

19 H was examined and collated when Vol I was prepared; but permission to print its readings in the Apparatus was witheld by the then owner. Its substantive variants, consequently unrecorded in the Apparatus, are close to those of X (see *R–K* p. 46 n.).

20 This explanation does not contradict what is said of b at § 14 above, because Y's one unique right reading (XXI 304/05) is in fact a minor one.

21 E.g. Y at XXI 304/5, I at VI 149, P^2 at XVII 147, D^2 at XXI 410. The first explanation (direct descent) is preferred here as the more economical and probable.

22 For the following entries the Apparatus in Vol I should be corrected: read 'y' for 'x' and 'pu' for 'p' in III 118, 334; V 90; VI 59, 82, 90, 410; VIII 159, 264, 331^l; X 229; XVI 255; XIX 113; XXI 470; read 'y' for 'x^l' in XVII 67, 77 and XIX 168. In VIII 282 read In] **x**N; At **p**. ese in] **p**u; ese and in] y.

23 See Bowers, '*PP* and the Police', p. 26; idem, 'L's *PP* in Hm 143', pp. 160–66; Calabrese, 'Corrections...in Hm 143', pp. 195–99.

24 For a full list of 323 errors apparently introduced by the scribe of X see *R–K*, p. 176, n. 32.

25 In the Apparatus read 'X' for 'x'; for '?p...P^2' read 'Y&r (†G)'.

26 An interpretation strengthened by readings like XVII 78 and XIV 125 (so P^2).

27 *SkC*, p. xxxvii.

28 Skeat also adopted I's additional line after XI 79; his filled-out form of its extra half-line after XII 207 is accepted by Pearsall.

29 'Aspects of Revision', p. 29. For the passage see Appendix in Vol. I p. 743.

30 Wendy Scase, 'Two *PP* C-Text Interpolations'.

31 I. e. IX 85–95, 99, 113–14, 151–2, 161, 163–87, 211, 225, 275–6.

32 R–K, p. 194, agree that IHt have a common ancestor and that neither is a copy of the other.

33 Scase, p. 452. C V 5 in particular might well allude to a passage already known 'outside' the still-developing revision-text and obviously not present in **B**. But it scarcely strains belief that Langland should proleptically mention matter that appears only four passūs later (even if his earlier practice, as at B X 117, is stricter). The discrepancy may tacitly support Middleton's opinion that V 1–108 is the latest written portion of the text (see § 1 above); but that is not in itself proof of **C**'s unfinished state. For further comment on the HtI form, see Middleton ibid. 315n.

34 *SkC*, p. 450.

35 *Editing 'PP'*, p. 351; cf. p. 166. Compare the comment at *B Version* § 57 above.

36 'The "Ilchester" Manuscript of *PP*', p. 191; *R–K*, p. 194.

37 *R–K*, p. 192. The passages are C IX 75–254, A Pr 55–83, C IX 255–79, A Pr 84–95, C Pr 91–157 and A Pr 96–109.

38 Pearsall, '"Ilchester" MS', p. 191 and n. 50.

39 The first is retained as a possible true form influenced by Latin *claustrum*.

40 *C Version*, p. 40, where the agreements are listed.

41 Other examples are Pr 216 and IV 180. In D^2 at XV 106 an *l* has been inserted in *take,* the presumed exemplar-reading, evidently found difficult by the copyist.

42 This point is made again apropos of **p** at § 61 below. R–K, by contrast, emend extensively from **A**, **B** or **AB** in combination.

43 These agreements need not be listed here, since they have already appeared in the lemmata at the conclusion of iii above (§§ 33–4). See further §§ 62, 64.

44 The right reading *leode* at X 7 has accordingly not been included in list (a) below, as it occurs among lines not here regarded as a C-Text. The unique **ZC** copy Bodley 851 makes the juncture at the same point (see *Z Version* § 32 below).

45 For its agreements with p^1 against p^2 and **x**, see § 67. N^2 also groups with specific x^1 copies: XID^2 at XIV 125; UD at XVI 183; D at XX 107; XP^2+M at XI 169.

46 *R–K*, p. 102 n. 23.

47 See *B Version*, § 46 above.

48 See, for example, XI 287 and XIV 138 (with *om*).

49 *R–K*, p. 102 n. 23, end. The interpretation of N^2 given here is rejected by Warner, who views the manuscript as partly attesting 'the first edition of the C Version' ('*Ur-B PP*', pp.7, 11); but his argument mainly concerns the relation of N^2 to the sub-archetypal traditions of **B**, not those of **C**. Readers are invited to consider whether the account in paragraphs 39–41 of this section or the article expounding Warner's remarkable thesis better deserves the description 'tortuously complicated' (ibid. 10).

50 The sigil N^2 should be added in the Apparatus for both readings.

51 In G, lines are lacking at XIII 39, 40, 62, 63 and XIV 62, 63.

52 In the Apparatus to Pr 212 *add*: þat'] **x**p^2; *om* p^1; to I 99^1 *del*. 'P^2' and for '$p1$' read 'p^1P^2'; to II 40 for 'p^2' read 'p^2M'; to II 138 *del*. '?' and 'N'; to III 14 for 'M' read 'p^2M', for '?**p**' read 'p^1'; to VII 294 for '**p**' read 'p^1', for 'KN' read 'p^2'; to X 133 *del*. '?' and 'G'; to XI 34 for 'K' read '?p^2', for '**p**' read '?p^1 (lowed G)'; to XI 224 for '**x**' read '**x**p^2 (*alt. to* 3e G)'; to XII 173 for '**x**' read '**x**p^2', for '**p**' read 'p^1'; to XIII 224 *del*. 'G'; to XV 17 *add*: þat] **x**p^2 (y N); *om* p^1N^2; to XVI 355 for '**x**N' read '**y**$p2$', for 'G' read 'ut'; to XIX 63^1 for '**x**' read 'x^1', for 'U' read 'Ut', for 'G' read 'D^2'; to XIX 94 for 'N' read 'p^2', for **p** read 'p^1'; to XX 144 for 'N' read 'p^2M', *del*. 'G', 418 for '**x**' read 'yU', for 'H^2' read 'Yt', to 419 for 'Ch)' read 'Ch) p^2 (holy N)'; to XXI 252 for 'N' read 'p^2', *del*. 'G'; to 319 read 'p^2' for 'G' and 'p^1' for '**p**'; to 340 *del*. '?' and 'G'.

53 Examples are the dialectal stave-word *mid* at III 252 preserved by e, Q, K (but lost in **x** and the other **p** copies) and <RM>'s unique line at XVII 116.

54 In Apparatus, 'QW' should appear before 'FZ' not after 'e'.

55 In Apparatus, *del*. 'SK'. The error is shared by the C-Text interpolation in Digby 145 (K^2), which may derive from <PE>'s common source.

56 In Apparatus, for 'RM' *read* 'RM (of] halt)'.

57 In Apparatus to III 305 and XVII 188 *del.* 'Q', to VI 280, *del.* 'S', to XIII 43, XV 177 and XXI 20 *del.* 'QW', to XV 111 *del.* 'W', to IX 162, XIII 187, XIV 84, XVIII 32 *read* 'eRM' for '?p^{1}', to XVI 140 *read* 'eR; a lif F' for 'p^{1}', to XVII 269 read 'X&r' for '$\mathbf{x}p^{2}$MF' and 'eR' for 'p^{1}'.

58 Add to Apparatus: 'wexuþ QWFSZ'.

59 In Apparatus for 'S' *read* 'QWSZ'

60 Two that are potentially major require comment. First, in *is*] *is ful ofte* XVII 76 F could have eliminated *ofte* because it seemed metrically over-weighted (W lacks the error entirely). Second, at XVI 148 *swettore*] *sofly ys s.*, though more striking, could have been induced by *sothly* at 146 preceding.

61 This does not strictly belong in R–K's list as an exclusive QS agreement, since it is in substance shared by W (*hande*) and is therefore probably a q error independently corrected by F after recognition of its inferior contextual sense.

62 In Apparatus, for 'S' read 'QS'.

63 One of the most striking, the misplacing of XV 288 after 293, can hardly have occurred except in a common ancestor.

64 See I, *Manuscripts* 30–5, 36–8, 39–41.

65 See *R–K* p. 40, who reckon 32; but among variants they count are such as *leret* for *lereth* at III 212, which are better treated as non-substantive. Those omitted from the Apparatus are given here in full.

66 In Apparatus, for 'vpon G' read 'vpon p^{2}'.

67 They are absent from the Apparatus because they do not contribute to determining the reading of Cx; but they should have been included.

68 In Apparatus, for 'G' (*both*) read 'GN'.

69 The minor exceptions in N at III 175 (omitted from the Apparatus), XXII 329 and in G at VIII 148, IX 63 are probably felicitous scribal corrections *vp gesse*.

70 In these instances, mostly minor, logical consistency has yielded to the recognition of possible revision in **C** and **p**'s coincidental convergence with (an)other version(s). Thus, an **x** reading may be adopted if it appears the harder, as at I 128; but it remains possible that **p** here preserves Cx, as at I 37 and 82.

71 The purely mechanical nature of these errors is underlined by their recurrence respectively in the **p** copies <AV>S and the unrelated EG. This point is accurately noted by Carnegy 'C-Text of *PP*', p. 15.

72 R–K's emendation (eliminating *bokes / ȝe*), though elegant, is otiose.

73 Both versions of the line are rejected by R–K in a reconstruction that leaves an inauthentic masculine ending in 14[0] and alters the sense of 14[2].

74 This also undergoes major emendation by R–K, who reject both traditions for the reading of K–D's B-Text, a reconstruction based partially on evidence from **C**.

75 For an earlier comparison of **p** and **x** (requiring some modification in the light of the present examination), see Schmidt, 'C Version'.

76 It is understood here both that XVII 116 is authentic and that it was not inserted in the ancestor of <RM> from a source outside the archetypal tradition.

77 In Apparatus to VIII 161, 341; XII 173, XXI 392 for '**x**' read '$\mathbf{x}p^{2}$' and for '**p**' read 'p^{1}'; to XXI 455 for '**x**' read 'y' and for 'p^{1}' read '$p^{1}$$P^{2}$ut'.

78 In the text the sg. is preferable; correct App. to read 'beggare $\mathbf{x}p^{2}$'; pl. p^{1}'.

79 For details of the three main processes of emendation, see *A Version* § 56.

80 In Apparatus, insert 'N^{2}' after 'leue]'.

81 See *R–K*, p. 89. For further consideration of the status of the Ophni-Phineas passage see *Z Version* § 6 below.

82 See the *Textual Notes ad loc.*

83 Minor readings are ignored here since, as has been amply demonstrated in this *Introduction*, most of these could in principle be due to coincidence.

84 Examples where two or three unrelated copies agree in a right reading are *hy* SN at I 187, *cople* <PE> + N (by correction) at II 190 and *ben* EWN at XVI 64.

85 In Apparatus to XX 460, for 'F' read 'FN^{2}'.

86 *R–K*, p. 102, n. 23.

87 As this source, *B-Ø*, has already been analysed (at the end of *B Version* §§ 72–4 above), no further comparison of B XIX–XX and C XXI–XXII is necessary here.

88 See the *Textual Notes* for an account of the possible mechanism of loss.

The Z Version

i. *The* Z-Text *as a draft version or work in progress*

§ 1. An uncontroversial claim could be made for noticing the version of Pr–VIII in manuscript Bodley 851 (**Z**), which was dismissed by Skeat and ignored by Kane (*Introduction* II § 35). This is that **Z** is simply an **A** copy that lacks about 40% of the text but has some worthwhile variants suggesting possible descent from a non-archetypal **A** source. However, as stated above (*Intro.* II § 147), its peculiar qualities seem to the present editor to justify Rigg and Brewer's identification of **Z** as a separate version of the poem, earlier than **A**. A convincing demonstration of their claim that the text is not a finished work but a draft would create a presumption (though it could not prove) that it is also by Langland. An investigation might thus profitably begin with this question, because there are available for comparison with **Z** two other portions of text in what may be an unfinished state, C Pr 95–124 and A XII 1–98. It has already been argued (*C Version* § 72 above) that the Ophni-Phineas addition does not certainly reflect an unfinished original, because it displays typical characteristics of the archetypal scribe (even if concentrated to an unusual degree). So any examination of the issue should make explicit at the outset that inferior scribal work and authorial draft text are not always easy to tell apart. While application of the direct method has earlier favoured a 'scribal' interpretation of the state of this passage, the 'authorial draft' interpretation can be defended on the grounds that the level of transmission-error present is statistically improbable.[1] Given the uncertainty, therefore, comparison is also worth making with a second possible draft sequence, Passus XII of **A**, which is here accepted as authentic up to line 98 (*A Version* §§ 69–75). In relation to assessing the status of **Z**, this **A** continuation is arguably more relevant than C Pr 95–124; for it is some twenty years nearer in time to Bodley 851's hypothesised original and, like most of **Z**, attests material that the poet did not re-use (see § 6).

§ 2. The initial evidence that Rigg-Brewer ('R–B' hereafter) adduce for **Z**'s provisional character (pp. 13–14) is its internal inconsistencies. One such is its failure to mention at Pr 15 the dungeon that will be referred to 85 lines later. Here, though the text does not necessarily imply that the dreamer must have noticed the dungeon, the unprepared reference seems clumsy. It has perhaps only one major parallel ascribable to lack of final revision, the Dreamer's waking in **C** at XIX 334 without apparently having first fallen asleep at XVIII 180. The fact that no dungeon is referred to in **C** (*R–B* p. 13, n. 45) might even lead to suspicion of influence from the later version. However, comparison with C Pr 87–8 shows that **Z** differs completely from **C** in focussing not on the dale's diabolic inhabitants but on its weather. To turn from an 'inconsistency' to a redundancy: the phrase *as dym as a cloude* at Z 16b is reminiscent of A III 180 but also appears in **Z** at its proper place. Here it would seem less likely that this is an echo of **A** than that **A** eliminated an earlier use of the phrase in **Z** in order to avoid repetition, and inserted a dungeon reference to prepare for Holy Church's later mention. This example, though not proving the Bodley 851 text a draft, indicates its priority and possible originality. For since Z Pr 16b–17 do not derive from the **AB** or **C** forms of these lines, if they are scribal they must be what R–B call an 'unmotivated imitation' (p. 15).

§ 3. More cogent evidence of **Z**'s probable draft character is found in IV 122–30, lines that are absent from **A** at this point but recur as Z V 1–9 and correspond to A IV 140–49. R–B persuasively judge the first occurrence to be an earlier-written passage that was left uncancelled after the later one was composed, and for that reason was found in Bodley 851's immediate exemplar or in that exemplar's holograph source. Supplementary evidence for this conclusion is the three lines immediately before it (IV 119–21), which were presumably intended to be deleted as part of the larger transposition of this passage. These appear genuine in content and expression, for they make good sense, are in the poet's best manner and fit well with the preceding list of *impossibilia*. Moreover, the metrical form of 120 (Type IIa) and the cross-caesural wordplay on *manere* and *manes* in 121 are established Langlandian 'fingerprints' (see *Intro. IV Editing the Text* § 41 and Appendix I § 6. iii below). Also genuine in feel is line 124, and though part of its sense is found in A IV 143b, it can hardly derive from the latter. For A IV 143b looks like a reversion to **Z** IV 124 rather than to its re-written form at Z V 3, which compares the dumbstruck villains to a stone, not to a sluggish horse. The lines hypothetically deleted in **A** from the dialogue at Z IV 130–32 also exhibit authenticating features like the internally-rhymed b-verse of Type Ic at 131, which resembles such half-lines as B XIX 338 //. But one noteworthy sign of specifically draft character here is the grammatical ambiguity of 132. Another is the metrical awkwardness of 126, which must scan as *ab / ba* unless *seyden* is treated as an 'onset' or anacrusis and the stresses are placed on *Resoun* and *ryghtfullyche* to give a Type IIIa line. The passage as a whole would therefore seem to indicate re-working at two successive stages; and even on its second occurrence, at Z V 1–9, it has still not reached the form finally achieved in A IV 141–50. For **A**, as already noted, introduces new changes: at 143b, 149b–150a and, most importantly, 145a, where the needed stave-word finally replaces *seyde* at the metrically still defective // Z V 5. To assign these **Z** variants to a careless copyist of the **A** Version requires assuming that, though he had no problem at IV 124 with a rare dialectal word (*stuty*, recorded only here by MED), he twice substituted *seyde* for the familar *reherside*. For the latter is a lexically easy word used over a dozen times in like circumstances, as at Z Pr 113, V 76 and, in close association with *Resoun* and *seyde*, at B XI 413 //. It is much more credible, therefore, that the poet *first* wrote the obvious *seyde* but later replaced it with a suitable alliterating synonym (MED s.v. *rehersen* 4 (a)) in order to normalise the metre (even though finally he omitted the line in revising to **B**).[2]

§ 4. A similar situation suggestive of a still fluid text is found in the statement at III 1 that Lady Mede was alone, although at II 214 earlier it was said that Favel stayed with her. As R–B point out, the chance that this was scribally produced is slight, whereas a draft might well have contained such an 'uncancelled inconsistency.' The line-and-a-half here considered to have been revised in **A** are unlikely to be a scribal derivate from the **A** form, since the first has normative scansion and the second a 'small-word' stave (*to*) that is typical of Langland's practice from his earliest period (IV § 47 below). What the four **A** lines apparently do is to modify an original in which Favel was intended to be present throughout Mede's interview with the King. The exact point of Langland's changed conception can be located at the beginning of Z III. Here the first ten lines remain untouched in **A** except for line 10, the redundant b-half of which might have called for alteration. This line, of the rare variant-type IIa, has now been replaced by one of Type IIIa that again has a grammatical monosyllable (*be*) as its first stave.

§ 5. R–B's third separate example involves I 100–02, which they suspect may be a draft (note *ad loc*). But they are right also to obelise line 101, which appears a slip by the Bodley 815 scribe induced by taking *other alles* as conjunctive rather than adverbial and misconnecting it with the threat in 102. As relineated and emended here by insertion of *ye*, the line now corresponds exactly to its **A** equivalent. But **A**'s posited cancellation of the injunction to mildness in Z 100 removes a line of the Type IIa which, with its typically Langlandian structure, may be presumed authentic. The uncommon compound *loue-lawes* employed here is found in *Piers Plowman* only once again, in the singular, at C XVII 130. But the **Z** use is very unlikely to be a scribal recollection of that passage (on which see I § 133 above), as it differs completely from it in both context and referent (cf. § 2 above). The foregoing interpretation assumes *wo* 102, which gives poor sense in context, to be a visual error for *weye*. In the *Indexical Glossary* therefore the attested form has been conservatively glossed 'wretched', as in its other appearance at V 21 //; but it could be an aphetic spelling of the variant *wowon* recorded for the verb's past participle (MED s.v. *weien* v.), allowing a homophonic pun (as, perhaps, it also does at C IX 271, where the copy-text reads the standard *weye*). Alternatively, the lines in their manuscript shape could betoken a provisional phase at which the poet had not yet decided how to complete the b-verse of I 101. This explanation leaves them anacoluthic; but although this is an occasional Langlandian feature, scribal mislineation here could be just as likely. A final possible draft instance is VII 6, where the repetition of *heye weye* from 4 may have been eliminated in **A** as weak, though it looks like scribal dittography (*R–B*, note *ad loc*). These last two examples illustrate the point made at § 1 above about how hard it can be to tell faulty copying from authorial first thoughts. But the fact that in most of them unique **Z** lines that meet the core-text criteria appear *within* presumptive draft passages strengthens the likelihood that those lines are original.

§ 6. The total of **Z** material qualifying for direct comparison with **A** and **C** draft passages is nonetheless small. Apart from the lines showing inversions to prose order (II 141b and V 147b), the most impressive candidate for draft status is the complex at IV 122ff / V 1–10, and especially the repeated IV 126 / V 5, the particular metrical defectiveness of which does not look scribal. These lines somewhat resemble C Pr 116 and 118 where, if *men* in both b-verses had been expuncted in the exemplar and *folk* inserted marginally or supralinearly by the 'editor', the Cx scribe could have mistakenly copied the commoner word and thereby damaged the metre. Another suggestive similarity is the rhythmical parallelism between C Pr 124 *For ʒoure shréwed sóffraunce and ʒoure oune sínne* and Z VI 38 *That [yé] lóueyen hym léuere than yóure oune hértes*, which both also use contrapuntal alliteration in their a-verse (*abb / ax: abb / ab*). Somewhat more ambiguous are the inversions to prose order in Z II 141 and V 147, which recall those in C Pr 108, 113 and 120 but at the same time illustrate a more widely documented tendency of scribes when copying the b-verses (see *B Version* § 65 above). To turn now to a comparison with A XII, line 21 of the latter, unless read as a very rough Type IIIa, finds a parallel in Z V 152. For in both, a stave-word on *w* (*wikkednesse*) would normalise the metre (as effectively, in the latter case, as the more difficult original **wandedes* actually conjectured). But, as so often, it is hard to distinguish authorial from scribal 'meddling.' Much the same is true at 32, where the b-half again fails to alliterate. Lines 49–50 are passably lineated in manuscript J, and they have been so printed in the text. But if it is actually R not J that here preserves the <(RU)J> archetypal text, the original division might have come after the Latin, with the present 50b forming part of a new line that was never completed. Somewhat more compelling is line 62, which is at the limits of tolerable scansion and should perhaps be divided after *answered*, with insertion of *wye* after *welcome*. But here too the lineation could be either the result of scribal incompetence or the faithful reflex of a prose line waiting to be shaped into verse. All in all, a neutral verdict may have to be brought in; for A XII evinces few potential draft-lines as arresting as C Pr 108–15 though, like the **C** passage as a whole, it has many in acceptably finished form (*A Version* §§ 67–74).

§ 7. Some doubts, therefore, surround the question. But if the case for **Z**'s draft character could be sustained in relation to larger structural features (like those discussed in §§ 8 and 19 below), the local co-presence of unfinished with unimpugnable finished lines in **Z**'s unique passages would raise a strong presumption of its integral originality. For while even a proven draft text might be non-Langlandian, one with such lines could almost certainly not. However, acceptance of **Z** as a 'work in progress' need not rely exclusively on the evidence of instances like those examined. There are also the lines hypothetically removed in **A** that are not strictly identifiable as 'draft' work but resemble other (finished) lines rejected for assignable reasons during the process of re-composition. These have features that, without being conspicuously superfluous, may have made them seem otiose. One is II 40's reference to the notaries, along with Simony and Civil, which re-appears little altered at II 119 (retained in **A**), after a line on the latter as recipients of bribes (excised in **A**). A second possibly over-subtle example is Pr 53–6, which Langland might have feared would look odd in a passage satirising clerks if it failed to be read as ironic. Another is Pr 70–3 on justices, less liable to miss the mark but weak after the preceding shot at barristers. Thirdly, there are some lines evidently designed to effect a transition from one stage of the vision to the next. One is Pr 94, the point where **A**'s Passus I begins. Now in **ABC** the *mountain* ('hill' in **Z**) yields its symbolic significance to the *tower*; but **Z** mentions the 'hill' again at 99, the first of two lines removed and replaced in **A**. Together, these references may well seem to suggest the writer's initial uncertainty about the relative importance of the (high) hill: (deep) dale / tower: dungeon antinomies. This motivic issue is resolved only in **B**'s restoration of **Z**'s *castel,* but it reaches an intermediate stage with **A**'s *clyf* at I 4.

§ 8. Finally, three further passages suggest fluid first thoughts awaiting development or possible removal. One is II 1–3, which summarises what precedes and forecasts what is to follow. Another is II 163–70, noted *ad loc* by R–B, who find the uneven syntax an indication of the passage's draft character (as may be the mislineation of 165–66, if it is not scribal). A third is IV 157–59, some transitional lines connected with **Z**'s original passus-division after Reason's final speech. These become redundant with **A**'s new passus-division; but they in any case 'conflict with what follows', as R–B note *ad loc,* since the vision of Reason and the King in fact continues. Such larger passages of transition-marking material cannot easily be explained as scribal in origin. But they would fit well with a context where the poet was trying out his work-in-progress on an 'audience' unfamiliar with it, and so very different from that of his final version.[3]

§ 9. The lines discussed above sit at the boundaries of reasonably identifiable 'draft material.' Others might seem to tell against the draft-hypothesis, because they expand an idea in a way resembling known instances of enthusiastic scribal embellishment.[4] Their genuineness is, however, suggested by their both meeting the core-text criteria and containing in themselves sufficient reason for their later excision. Thus in Pr 57–8, after the passage discussed at § 7 above occurs an attack on religious provisors, coupled with a defence of poor unbeneficed clerks. The second line anticipates IV 118, which is paralleled in **ABC**. But the first line's lack of any echo in later versions may imply that Langland came to think the abuse not notorious enough to justify attacking (whereas the criticism of religious, absent from **A**, appears in a more moderate and traditional guise at B IV 120 // C 116). Another passage, II 163–70 (mentioned at § 8 above), strikes R–B as 'noticeably weak' and as a 'pastiche of earlier lines' (p. 15). But if the repetition of 164 at 168 suggests its 'half-written character,' the misdivision at 165/6 may be otherwise explained (see the *Textual Notes*). The revising poet could well have judged it 'not needed', as R–B say; but its original presence may have been due to his composing it for a primary audience of listeners, who would benefit from some reminder of what had happened. The passage is also defensible as building up to an effective rhetorical climax in the *t*-alliterating 169–70, with their characteristic polysemantic wordplay on two senses of *tene* (MED s.v. *tenen* v. 4 (a), 1). While these lines are thus not definitely proved a draft, they do have a provisional 'feel' which may be connected with their function in oral performance. This is something also suggested by I 86 // A 137, which was removed in **B**, a version apparently aimed at a reading audience.[5] The passage on words and wind at V 34–40 is also very good in itself[6] but could likewise have been excised as a narratorial digression that weakened the moral impact of Reason's sermon. Once again, anticipating an oral audience would account for **Z**'s tone of combined intimacy and urgency, a surmise supported by the use of the pronoun *vs* at line 43 (the line was presumably deleted in **A** as over-explicit and discrepant with *ye* at 41). Much the same seems true of II 1–3, whether this is taken as coming from the narrator or from Holy Church.

§ 10. The passage at VI 68–75 on Truth's elemental powers, by contrast, illustrates not *digressio* but *amplificatio*.[7] Its presumed rejection from **A** appears to initiate a larger process of *abbreviatio* continued in **B**, which names the intercessor-figures Grace and Amendment but not Truth, and even eliminates the residual mention of the tower at A VI 79. Coupled with this passage is the pair of lines on the Windsor masons at 77–8, which may have seemed too locally specific to suit the cosmic context of Truth's activities in 66–74. Here light is thrown on the **A** revision from the vantage point of **B**, which perceptibly heightens the tension by cancelling the 'lack-of-time' trope, a semi-oral feature still remaining vestigially in **A**.[8] But perhaps the chief reason for the passage's removal is its containing a quasi-contradiction that persists in **A** and is cleared up only in **B**. This is the notion of Truth as dwelling both in the heart and in heaven after death. The basic idea is already present in Z VI 92–3 as part of a passage left unaltered by **A**. But as the revision-sequence reveals a maturing conception of divine reality as apprehensible through spiritual conversion *in via,* this would render overt reference to the transcendent domain less appropriate here. Thus in successive stages the love and law of ZA VI 92–3/96–7 are superseded by the submissive charity of B V 607–08 and finally transfigured in the mystical ecclesiology of C VII 256–57. These signs of increasing theological refinement may not prove the originality of the more 'exterior' allegory in Z VI 68–73, but they highlight its 'primitive' character. Given, further, that these lines satisfy the editorial canon of intrinsic acceptability (IV, § 16 below), their independence of the version immediately following emerges clearly. This instance illustrates well how reading all four texts 'synoptically' can bring out a development of key ideas that is much less apparent when they are taken in separation.

§ 11. As noted above (II § 139), the three unique lines in Robert the Robber's speech at V 142–4 are hard to dismiss as scribal, so typical are they of the poet's characteristic modes of thought and expression.[9] Here, perhaps the most likely reason for **A**'s rejecting them might be the implausibility of so adroit a scriptural allusion in the speaker's mouth. For Robert the Robber is conceived both as a type of spiritual extremity and as a contemporary thief begging clemency from his saviour King 'mounted' on the 'palfrey' of the cross.[10] In A V 246, the **Z** lines may therefore have been replaced by one expressing a more generalised notion better fitted to the emblematic aspect of this character's compound identity. As macaronic verses with no later reflex, they invite particular comparison with A XII 50–7, which involve four occurrences of the same two Pauline phrases. The 'signpost allegory' in which those **A** lines occur was abandoned at that point in **B**; but they were recalled for other service in B III 339–44, a passage already in **A** at this point as part of what would be a postulated 80-line addition to the text of **Z**. However, the A XII line meriting closest comparison with Z V 142–4 is 28, which has no **B** parallel, and which cannot have been abandoned by **B** because its cited texts had been used in the Reason-Mede dispute.

§ 12. The longest of these apparent excisions in **A** is the satire on physicians at Z VII 260–78. Although this change is in itself not difficult to account for, the passage has one problematic feature that would seem to question **Z**'s authenticity at this point. This is that in the rhyming lines 258–59 just before it, 259b's last lift attests not the text of parallel **AC** but of a form of **B** here held to be suspect of archetypal corruption. However, if this is a rare exception to the operation of the linear postulate, it could possibly be **B** that restored a pre-**A** reading, and **C** that returned to **A**, not the **Z** scribe who substituted a (corrupt) Bx reading for one originally identical with **AC**. The textual consequence of that conclusion would of course be to support retention of the Bx form of the line as authentic. But as this example is one of several such cases, it will be more conveniently considered with the others at §§ 23–6 below. The main point here is that the passage as a whole seems to accord satisfactorily with the core-text criteria. There is, moreover, a resonance of Langlandian lexis at 276b in the phrase *medecynes shapeth*, which resembles *shop salue* at B XX 307, and a significant hint of the lines' provisional character in the repetition of 262a as 276a. One likely reason for the removal of 265–78 in **A** might be the later use of 271–72 at Z VIII 48, with reference now to lawyers, and preceded by the full psalm-verse earlier quoted in part as 270a (*R–B*, note *ad loc*). These lines, which are revised in **B** and are finally omitted in **C**, stand unchanged in parallel **A**; but it is very hard to imagine any 'scribal author' borrowing them from **A** for insertion at this earlier point. A second possible reason for the postulated cut is that **A**'s argument, which is made to concentrate on the benefits of moderate diet and the dangers of over-indulgence succeeded by ineffective physic, ignores the issue of payment for medical treatment so prominent in **Z**. The stress on doctors' mendacity in the subsequent versions is at odds with **Z**'s open-minded contrast between the *science trewe* and the *leches lyares*; but this need hardly presuppose more than a hardening of Langland's opinion on the topic. What seems beyond dispute is that 277–78 are both underived from any other extant lines of *Piers Plowman* and worthy of its poet. Their essence is kept in A VII 258, which remains unaltered through **B** and **C** despite successive changes to the a-half of the preceding line (Z 264/ A 257/ B 272/ C 296).[11]

ii. *The Content of* **Z** *compared with* **A**

§ 13. This analysis of the evidence for **Z**'s status as a work in process of composition pro-
duces on balance a positive result and opens the serious possibility that the text comes from Lang-
land's hand. It will now be helpful to set out its substantive content by way of a comparison with
A, the version of which **Z**, if it is not original, would have to be a deviant form. Since R–B (pp.
129–137) present these details in their running and tabular concordances, an analytical layout is
adopted here that will supplement rather than duplicate theirs. **Z** is some 40% shorter than **A**, con-
taining 1515 text-lines and three citation-lines to **A**'s 2545 text-lines and 50 citation-lines (count-
ing in Passus XII). The passus-divisions of **Z** and **A** correspond, except at three points: where Z
Pr 94–145 becomes A I 1–55; where V 1–18 becomes A IV 151–58 and V 19–154 is made A V
1–256; and where V 155–66 becomes A VI 1–12 and VI 1–102 becomes A VI 13–106. Otherwise
A Pr 1–109 = Z Pr 1–93; A II 1–198 = Z II 1–215; A III 1–276 = Z III 1–176; A IV 1–140 = Z IV
1–159; A VII 1–307 = Z VII 1–328 and A VIII 1–88 = Z VIII 1–92. Despite these differences,
the **Z** divisions do not betray the palpably scribal character of the passus-ordering in the **B** copy
Corpus 201 (*B Version* § 46 above); rather, they tend to confirm the impression of priority and
provisionality conveyed by the 'draft' passages examined in section i. The other main differences
between the texts, here taken as due to revision of **Z** by **A**, have been arranged under the headings
of omissions, alterations and additions. Major ones are asterisked and possible reasons for the
changes are suggested.

§ 14. (*i*) About 155 of **Z**'s unique lines are omitted by **A** without replacement, 122 in *groups*
of two or more:

Pr 35–6 replaced by one line 34; 53–8 (bishops and religious: see §§ 7–8 above, and with 54b cf. B VI 180b); 70–3
(justices: see § 7). II 1–3 (summarising 'oral' lines: see § 9); 40–2 (40 re-used later at 119 = **ABC**); 163–70 (summarising
lines). III 122–4 (the lady doth protest too much; 122b is almost repeated at IV 59 and with 124b cf. Z II 173 / A 156);
*147–76 (early conception of Conscience, superseded). IV 119–21 ('apodosis' of the 'impossible conditions': deleted as
over-explicit); [122–30] (?uncancelled first draft of V 1–9: see § 3 above); 157–9 (?uncancelled superfluous transitional
lines). V 34–40 (digression: with 39 cf. B XI 163, XVIII 322); 59–60;[12] 73–4 (needless elaboration of 72a; 74b used as
A IX 51b); 142–4 replaced by single new line. VI 68–72 and 74–5 (excision of cosmic details); 77–8 (topical details).
VII 107–8 (circumstantial details); 196–201 (unnecessary details; 197 repeats 175–6); 230–2 (digression: 230a repeats
V 48a; but 230 re-used entire as B IX 72); 260–2; 265–70; 274–8 (detailed attack on doctors: see § 12 above). VIII 75–6
(circumstantial details removed).

Some 34 more *individual lines* are omitted:

Z Pr 36, 64 replaced by a new line; 90 (?lost from **A** but restored in **B**; with 90a cf. VIII 64a //); 145. I 18 (tone perhaps
wrong); 23 (redundant); 39 (too general); 65 (inappropriate imagery); 100 (too indulgent: see § 5). II 10 (cf. 34); 45
(elimination of this characte's rôle); 47 (otiose detail); 100 (over-specific); 118 (redundant); 177 (potentially misleading,
mercy being the king's prerogative); 189 (too detailed here: but re-used at C III 78). III 96 (circumstantial detail). IV 50
(cf. II 45); 152 partly repeats III 92. V 43 (too explicit); 45, 70, 98, 101 (cf. B V 242), 130 (all too circumstantial). VII 31
(echoed in B VI 36); 49 repeats II 208, but changed attitude to minstrels also relevant; 59 (circumstantial detail); 64–8
replaced by 3 ll.; 170 (too circumstantial); 245 (as one l.); 263–4 taken up as A 257–8 (*abbreviatio*); 316 (over-emphatic
repetition; cf. 245 above). VIII 69 (qualified judgement dropped).

Lastly, there are also omitted 16 (half-)lines with identical or recognisable *parallels* in **B** / **C**:

II 16 almost = B 12 (but cf. C 13); 148 (148a = B 174a); 188 almost = B 207; Pr 5 (Pr 5a = C Pr 5a); 35; 189 almost =
C III 78 (discursive lines only part-restored in **B** but not here in **C**). III 18 = **BC** (see § 23 and note 30 below); 28b cf.
B 28 / C 29; 32a = C 33a, 33 = C 32 (details restored in revised form in **C**). IV 17–18 = **BC**. V 59–60; 75a = **BC**; 104a
= B 380a.

§ 15. (*ii*) Some 200 lines receive *revision* in **A**, for which possible reasons are again suggested. First, nearly 40 lines are variously *transposed* (line-references are to the corresponding line-position in **Z**).

Pr 47–8 → after 52, 49–52 → after 42; 59–60 → before 86; 61–3 → after 85; 74–81 → after Z 46 = A Pr 64 (after inserting 6 new ll.). I 116 → before 112. II 68–9 trs; 97 → after 99. III 71–2 trs.; 95 → after 99, 99 → before 95. IV 132–31 → V 1–9. V 139 → after 136. VI 47 → 53.

§ 16. Next, 70 lines and 37 half-lines undergo *total replacement* or *extensive re-writing*.

Pr 16b (repeated at III 131); 63b–64 (too circumstantial); 65 reduced to 2 lines; 89; 94 (see § 7); 98b; 99–100 as 3 lines (see § 7). I 21–3 as 2 ll. (with 23 cf. A III 108, C III 417, XVI 63); 104b; 121a (repeats ref. to Trinity of I 71). II 16; 56b; 60 as 2 ll.; 70–2 (70a and final lift, 71a retained in B 86); 80b (change of referent);[13] 85b (so **BC**: the b-verse of **A** is re-used at C II 156); 97; 99a (removes obscure word); 104 (repeats legal point about Meed's legitimacy already made at 90); 146 and 147b (improve metre); 148 (a-half = B 174a)*; 158b (replaces vacuous last lift); 160 (replaces lexically obscure line); 190a; 214–15 expanded as 4 ll. III 10 (redundant b-half); 28b (strengthens promise: cf **BC**); 39b (heightens dramatic irony). IV 20 (clarifies allegory); 24b (half-line repeated at 31); 62b–63a (the simple **Z** form unlikely to be derived from **A**, which is corrupt in Ax and may have read likewise: see *Textual Notes*); 78b (more exact); 85 (vocalic alliteration or else possibly a draft line with [*A*] *seyde* intended to stand after *me*); 100b (improves psychological allegory); 125; *130–2 (130 = V 9 = A IV 149; 131 = V 13 = A V 153, 132 = V 15 = A IV 117 / V 154): draft lines. V 3b (a version of Z IV 124 with added wordplay); 24b; 27; 54b (adds new idea); *91–103 replaced by 58–208, a major amplification adding 140 ll: with 96 cf. C XIX 276; 97a = A 107a; 99 = 100; 102–3 = A 142–5; 100 (more general); *124a (major crux: see *Textual Notes*); 129a (removes title to generalise sense); 136b; 140b rewritten; 142–4 replaced by 246. VI 16 (improves sense); 32 transposes line-halves and introduces reinforcing statement; 38 improves metre: for pattern cf. C Pr 124; 44 modifies Biblical sense; 62–3 makes allegory more theologicaly accurate; 65b replaced with richer content but re-used in new line at A 108; 101b (lechery rather than self-love; cf 88 above). VII 6b; 38b (more realistic promise); 48–9 (as 3 ll. strengthening criticism: with 49a cf. II 208); 52a; 54b–55 removes archaic word in 54b; 58 (dissatisfaction with this b-half shown in threefold revision); 61; 64–68 (as 3 ll.); 76–7 replaced by one line; 82b widens reference; 87b repeats 83; 88b changes metre; 91 (circumstantial detail: re-used at B XIX 315; and cf. A 103); 98b repeats 93b; 152b (cf. **B** which retains adv.); 163b avoids anticipation);[14] 165b; 166b; 193b; 234; 238 as A 236; 259b* (= Bx); 263–4 = A 257–8; 271–3 used as VIII 47–9; 286 removes wordplay; 287b; 302b; 310b* (= Bx); 311 (witty rephrasing); 325b (repetition: phrase re-used in B XIII 268a); as new line: 61, 76–7, 91 (b-verse used in A 103 revising Z 98b). VIII 32b (more exact balance); 61 removes obscure macaronic stave; 74 (criticism strengthened); 89b–90 (order changed).

§ 17. A further 107 are revised more selectively by expansion and / or substitution / deletion of a *single word / phrase*. (Non-lexical instances are ignored, and cross-references are given for lines not immediately parallel).

Pr 9a (less specific); 48b (less ambiguous); 50a (less explicit; normalises metre); 61b = A 90 (less mild); 80a = A 71 adds detail and normalises metre; 83b = A 74 (less obvious word); 96a, b (b less specific). I 7b (theologically more exact); 36b (less specific); 56a (more familiar form);[15] 69 gives needed contrast with *word* in 68; 91a and 92b give desired rhetorical repetition often preferred in **AB**; 127a and 128a (theologically more exact). II 7a (fuller phrase); 18b removes jingling rhyme; 49 (interesting re-phrasing with repetition of *myd*); 54b (different referent); 92a (more apt); 107b–8a (transposed for better distinction); 125; 130 (tautological); 132 (= **C**); 136a (not superfluous). b (2) = **B** (unspecific but apparently restored); 138 (liaisonal stave replaced by lexical verb); 143b and 183a (less limiting); 206b (less vague). III 13b moderates the criticism;[16] 34 improves metre; 36b (less broad);[17] 39b (less restricted); 48b (Ax perhaps in error); 54a (closer to wedding service); 76b removes inappropriate animal associations; 87a (less weak); 90b removes ambiguity;[18] 108b (neutral term contextually more apt); 115a = **C**;[19] 120a (sense more appropriate).[20] IV 4b (synonym provides rhetorical *repetitio* in **ABC**); 10 (perhaps not a revision if *wyl* is a spelling variant of *wel* as at IV 89); 51a alters chagrin to fear; 53a adds disambiguating word (later dropped in C); 71b (preposition typical of C); 76b (more exact: cf.135b; rhetorically repeated verb reduces over-strong possibility); 99 (explicit); 103 (strengthens condition); 141b (better balance of nouns); 143b (more precise); 144a normalises alliteration and gives paronomasia; 146a (less limited reference). V 5a improves metre; 7 (emphasis); 9b (stronger); 10a gives the repetition of verb; 14b (stronger synonym); 31a generalises the warning; 52a = B 25 (formal change); 58 (more explicit); 63b and 77a (lexically recessive synonyms,[21] the latter not favoured by L. elsewhere); 87a (type in place of personification: **C** reverts to **Z**); 104b (less general or spiritual); 109a (more logical); 111a (more economic); 113b replaces difficult archaic word; 118b (less general); 123b (more dramatic); 132a (better rhythm); 136b clarifies sense; 137a (restored in **C**); 149b (neutral, but avoids rhyme with *lay* 150);[22] 152b improves metre, but copy perhaps here corrupt: see *Textual Notes*); 154a (grammatically more explicit); 158b (general term more correct; but cf VI 11). VI 2b tightens metre and avoids obvious (cf. Bx); 3b improves metre; 41b (more specific); 46b strengthens warning; 50a (formal injunction for direct command); 53 (neutral synonym);[23] 56a (cf. 50a); 80b (more comprehensive physical and religious sense);[24] 85 reduces emphasis that **B** restores; 88b raises tone.[25] VII 3b removes unusual collocation;[26] 26a (the converse of the preceding); 45a (more concise); 46a (phrasing more polite); 53b (part of re-written 53–4); 70a distinguishes two acts; 75 alters viewpoint on judgement; 132b (more precise); 134b (synonym);[27] *139b = **C** (see *Textual Notes*); 166b (precise: removes redundant phrase); 176a and 179b (more exact); 182b drops idiolectal variant;[28] 202a (more emphatic); 208a improves metre; 212b strengthens oath; 219b (more exact); 240b (more intimate tone); 241a improves stress-pattern; 253a highlights different vice; 254b = **B** (perhaps revised for play on *longe* at A 247: see *Textual Notes*); 255b; 279b (sharper sense); 281b (cf. Z IV 135); 282a strengthens assertion; 283a (synonym); 298 adds idea; 308a; *310b = Bx (see *Textual Notes*); 313a (synonym replaced perhaps to avoid rhyme); 317 and 321 (same word replaced by stronger);[29] 323a; 326b replaces non-naturalised borrowing. VIII 22 (canonically more definite); *26a = Bx (see *Textual Notes*); 37b (changed metre strengthens rhetoric); 62b (more emphatic); 63a improves phrasing; 64–7 (original past tenses altered: uniformity restored in **B**); 70b (new idea); 91a (concrete for abstract).

Between them, these three categories cover the main cases where revision of **Z** by **A** may be postulated.[30]

§ 18. (*iii*) Some 343 lines of new material with no antecedent in **Z** are *added* in **A**.

Pr 35–9 *after* Z Pr 34 expand attack on false minstrels; 52–4 *after* Z 48 also expand attack on false minstrels; 59–64 *after* Z 46 and 77–9 *after* Z 85 expand criticism of friars and modify criticism of bishops; 96–7 *after* 85; 104–8 *after* 92 add London food-sellers. I 29 *after* Z Pr 119 explains 119; 40 *after* Z Pr 129 rounds off admonition; 162 *after* Z I 111 initiates rhetorical *repetitio*.[31] III 34–89 *after* Z III 36 introduce Meed's corrupt confession and the attack on simony; 196–276 *after* Z III 146 (*amplificatio* on benefits of meed and Conscience's *responsio*). IV 17 (practical wisdom as aid to reason). V 58–106 *after* Z V 91, 108–41 *after* Z 98 and 146–208 *after* Z 104 (amplification of Envy, Greed and Gluttony). VI 61 expands commandment from Bible; 107–126 *after* Z VI 102 (expansion on necessity of virtue as well as grace). VII 53 *after* Z VII 52, 62–9 *after* Z 61, 208–12a *after* Z 211 extend religious argument for charity. VIII 54a *after* Z VIII 55 (new Latin citation).

Finally **A**, although deleting four / five macaronic lines / staves at V 124, 142–3, VII 267 and VIII 69, introduces five new macaronic lines at III 54, 238, 258, V 191 and VII 67, as well as eight more citation-lines at VII 68a, VIII 54a and (amongst the new passages) at III 64a, 85, 221a, 228, 233a and VII 212a.[32]

§ 19. The way in which these hypothetical **A** revisions have been carried out seems to support the case for **Z**'s authenticity, because it is very like what occurs in the canonical revised versions. Although this assertion cannot be illustrated at length here, one example may be given of the 'direction of revision' revealed by the comparison.

> And broughtest me borwes my byddyng to *holde*,
> Wil thy lif lasted to loue me oure alle,
> And eke to be buxum my byddyng to *wyrche*.

A I 75–6 would seem to reduce Z I 21–3 to two lines by replacing *holde* with *wyrche* (so rendering the rest of line 23 redundant) and re-writing 22 with no change of sense. This closely resembles the **C** revision of B II 110–11:

> Bette þe Bedel of Bokynghamshire
> Reynald þe Reue of Rutland sokene

where the new material in C II 112b *and redyng-kynges manye* has been accommodated by transferring B 110b to C 111 and running together **B**'s two b-verses into a single new stave-phrase on *b, Bannebury sokene*. In the postulated revision of Z II 214–15 to A II 195–98 (a passage already touched on at § 4 above), it seems likelier that the earlier text should be the briefer one. For it is in **Z** that 'two' are said to be present and both to 'tremble' on arrest, whereas in the (identical) **ABC** parallel Mede is alone and the extra circumstantial detail (198a) is achieved only at the price of repeating *fere* (197b) and using a filler-phrase (197a). This example, however, recalls A II 51–2:

> And heo be *boun at his bode* his bidding to fulfille,
> *At bedde and at boord* buxum and hende

which a redactor could arguably have reduced to

> And to be boun at ys bede at bord ant at bedde

at Z II 60 by running together the two a-verses. It is thus conceivable that in Z II 214–15 such a redactor similarly condensed four **A** lines into two. What is hard to credit, though, is that he would have changed the plot so as to leave Mede with Favel as her companion and both in a state of frightened apprehension.[33] So if deliberate *abbreviatio* is in question at all, it is much more likely to have been authorial and the 'direction of revision' to run from **A → Z**. But this would reveal the poet not as uncertain what to write but as forgetting what he had written (cf. *Intro.* V § 17 below); for at the opening of the immediately following Passus III, Mede is found alone in **Z**, as in **A**. Thus, given the evidence of idiosyncratically Langlandian versification in Z II 215 (see § 4), the likeliest conclusion for an unprejudiced reader is that **Z** represents, as R–B argued, an authentic work in process of composition, with the dramatic situation of Passus II as yet undetermined in all its details.

iii. *Authenticating Features of Language, Metre and Style*

§ 20. After due allowance made for their occasional draft character, the **Z** lines that **A** omits or revises (with few exceptions) conform to the core-line criteria in language, style and metre. Bodley 851's linguistic coherence may not be in itself an argument for the authenticity of this (as it never can be for any Middle English) text. But its congruence with the poet's presumed original dialect, that of the South-West Midlands around Malvern, counts as a positive more than a neutral indicator.[34] Nor is the grammatical evidence contradicted by the nature of **Z**'s unique vocabulary. This, however, deserves analysis, as it contains (a) some 50 lexical words absent from **A, B** and **C**; (b) six words with senses not instanced elsewhere in *PP*; and (c) eight infrequent words found only once in the canonical versions:

(a) *annueles* Pr 63; *apropre* Pr 58; *asentaunt* III 152; *assch* [tree] V 45; **bewsoun* III 158; *bornet, blanket* III 159; *birch* Pr 9; *boten* v[1] III 158; *bourly* III 159; *caucyon* V 143; *cleken* III 36 (?= *clokken*); *clumse* VII 54 (cf. *claumsen* XV 254); *dekne* VII 231; *delys* III 161; *dollen* IV 124; **feym* VII 326; *fichen* II 160; *Flemmyng* VII 278; *helm* [tree] V 45; *lesewe* II 47; *lewdelyche* III 164; *logge* II 47; *lower* VII 270; *messe* V 37; *morgagen* III 96; *morthrare* VII 263; *nysot* II 99; *quellen* VII 263; *reyken* IV 158; *Schyr Thorsday* VIII 76; (*eny / som*) *skynes* II 180, VIII 34; *smethe* VI 80; *sowsen* II 100; *spanne* VI 78; *stat* Pr 55; *stemen* VI 75; *stowlyche* III 158; *stryuore* VII 196; **stuty* IV 124; *tetheren* III 76; *thondren* Pr 17; *tylen* VI 66; *to-bersten* V 39; *trental* Pr 65; *vnschryuen* VIII 76; *veile* VII 56; *ward* Pr 99; VIII 75; *worsted* V 100.
(b) *beten* VII 170; *foundur* III 176; *glorie* II 72; *multeplyen* III 120; *wellen* VII 286, *witen* VII 59.
(c) *apostata* I 65; *cammok* VII 91; *digneliche* Pr 54; *forsslewthen* VII 65; *pelour* I 65; *pyuysche* VII 139; *provendre* III 33; *staleword* VII 196.

Many of these terms are in keeping with the legal and ecclesiastical registers of Langland's lexis and the few archaic or regional ones are not at odds with it. Among a handful of the most uncommon, three instanced nowhere else[35] fit well enough with the generally recognised features of his usage. *Feym* is a borrowing from French; *bewsoun* is a mongrel form of the French *beau fitz* used at A VIII 146 //, resembling the anglicised (but rare) *beaupere* recorded only once before its appearances at B XVIII 230 and C IX 248;[36] and *stuty* is a restricted dialectal item. One other, *cammok*, occurs in *cammokes ant wedus*[37] at B XIX 315 which, despite a similar context, seems unlikely to have prompted a scribal substitution here, since the **Z** line is locally coherent and A's so far revised as to keep from its source only one stave-word, *colter*.

§ 21. The unique **Z** lines share four stylistic features with the core-text of the canonical versions. One is their juxtaposition of clerkly and colloquial motifs, often involving typically abrupt shifts of idea and image, as at V 34–40 and VI 65–80. Related to this is the use of macaronic lines that weld Latin and English elements into a semantic and syntactical unity, as at V 142–44 or VIII 61 (the former excised, the latter replaced by its native equivalent in **A**). Third, **Z** gives Piers's son at VII 64–8 an allegorical 'command-name' (a device apparently confined to Langland) at once too unlike parallel A VII 72–4 to derive from it and too well fitted to the constraints of the long line to come from an imitator's hand. Fourth, and even more striking, is a special type of homophonic wordplay on grammatical lexemes functioning as stave-words, e.g. *for* at VII 231 and *to* in Pr 64, which closely resembles B XVIII 148. It is hard to imagine these features (especially the last) appearing at all, let alone together, in the work of a scribal redactor.

§ 22. The metrical quality of **Z**'s unique lines is, finally, perhaps their most telling feature, because amongst editorial criteria it is metre that draws on the widest possible range of evidence.[38] These lines not only observe the verse-norms of the relevant core-text (the agreed readings of **ABC**),[39] they also illustrate eight specific features of verse-practice either restricted to or highly distinctive of Langland. These are 'microlexical' or 'small-word' staves; 'transitional', Type II and Type III lines; one- or two-word b-verses with clashed stresses; cognative staves; rhyme; and elastic line-length (on the presence of these in the core-text, see IV §37–9). The first is typically a monosyllabic modal verb, grammatical lexeme or bound morpheme forming a 'full' or, more commonly, 'mute' stave right after the caesura in a standard line. Examples are *be-* at IV 159, *by* at II 97, *for* at VII 231, 260 and *to* at Pr 145. The second exploits a mute key-stave to generate the unique 'transitional' or 'T-type' line scanning *aa[a] / bb*. Examples are II 118, VII 38, 245, 279 and possibly III 158.[40] The third and fourth illustrate unusual variant line-types: IIa (*aaa / xx*) at I 100, III 10, 165, IIb at VII 76 and possibly IV 120; Type III (*ax / ax*) at Pr 50, IV 144 and VIII 74 (all made standard in **A**), and also at IV 126 and V 96 (both possibly in draft form).[41] Fifth, there are examples of the 'monolexical half-line' (*Intro.* IV § 38), with a single word carrying the two final stresses, the first a full stave (as *déstréres* II 146), and of the 'duolexical half-line', with clashing stresses also in a trisyllabic final lift-pair (*tyl they bé thére* II 147).[42] Sixth, 'allophonic' staves appear (IV § 46), including *s / sh* at II 189, III 122, 152, IV 152 and *f / v* in V 142. Seventh, internal rhyme is used at IV 131, final at II 17/18, ?VI 80/1, VII 258/9, 262/3, 324/5, and identical at IV 49/50. Lastly, line-length varies in a manner typical of Langland, from the seventeen syllables of VIII 75 to the nine of VII 170 (the latter not necessarily, as R–B opine *ad loc*, 'an experiment, intended for expansion').[43]

iv. *Objections to the Authenticity of* Z

§ 23. The cumulative evidence of language, style and versification set out above creates a presumption that the text in Bodley 851 is a copy, perhaps at one remove, of a Langlandian text-in-progress (though not necessarily a *first* draft). Content, structure and thought are consonant with seeing in it a version more primitive than **A**, which has hitherto been thought the earliest. In its own terms, **Z** may even be 'complete', though obviously not 'finished'.[44] The text ends acceptably (if abruptly) with the sending of Truth's pardon, but before its dramatic tearing by Piers. In **A** this event both forms the climax of the *Visio* and initiates the *Vita*'s quest for Dowel (**Z** has no *Vita*). The one potentially serious objection to this view of **Z** is the presence in it of some readings that in principle could arise from other-version contamination and thus imply its secondary and inauthentic character. Given the weight attached to this process in such **C** manuscripts as N[2] (*C Version* § 40 above), the objection obviously needs to be addressed. Of the 45 possible examples, 18 are substantially attested in the **m** family of **A**, some 27 in **B** and / or **C**. All receive detailed treatment in the *Textual Notes*, but the major ones have been listed together here for convenience. The most important are three in which the Bodley 851 text agrees with archetypal B-Text readings that arguably show as unoriginal on comparison with the joint readings of **A** and **C** (*ii*, nos. 10–12 below).

(i) **Z** *readings found in the* **m** *family of* **A**[45]
(a) *Whole lines*: 1. Z V 59–60 // B V 32–3, C V 134–35. 2, 3. VI 76 (= A VI 82), 79–80 (= A VI 83–4) // B V 592–93, C VII 239–40.
(b) *Half-lines and phrases*: 1. Z I 54 (= A I 106) mene] *om.* 2. I 92 (= A I 143) tene] þyne **AB** (*so* **C**; *not adopted*).[46] 3. II 56 (= A II 47) sesed] feffid (*not adopted*).[47] 4. II 130 (= A II 120 // B) togeder] for euere (*not adopted*).[48] 5. II 155 (= A II 146 // BC) thys men] þis mene. 6. III 93 (= A III 146 // **BC**) hem the gate] ? hem / þe treuþe ofte. 7. IV 151 (= A IV 136 // **BC**) mekenesse] resoun. 8. VI 58 (= A VI 71 // **AB**) in no manere elles nat] loke þat þou leiȝe nouȝt (+ms A). 9. VII 60 leue] *om.* 10. VII 81 (= A VII 86 // **BC**) masse] mynde. 11. VII 165 (= A VII 168) Furst the fycycyan] *trs.* 12. VIII 84 leden] lyuen (*not adopted*).[49]

(ii) **Z** *readings found in* **B**
(a) *Whole lines*: 1. Pr 90 = B Pr 223 (*om* AC). 2. II 148 = B 174 (cf. A II 139). 3. II 188 = B 207 (om **A**).
(b) *Half-lines and phrases*: 1. II 16 = B II 12 // C II 13. 2. II 125 // A II 116 syre. 3. II 136 // A II 127 ynowe. 4. III 87 // A III 140 = B III 151 habbe. 5. V 10 // A IV 150 = B IV 187 ye bidde. 6. V 52 // A 25 = B 25 here wastyng. 7. V 104a // A 209a = B 380a Gloton. 8. VII 152 // A 155 = B VI 170 to mysdon hym eftsones. 9. VII 254 // A 251 = B VI 266 afyngred. 10. VII 259 // A 256, C VIII 294 = B VI 271 for lyflode ys swete. 11. VII 310 // A 290, C VIII 329 = B VI 305 in borw ys to. 12. VIII 26 // A 26, C IX 28 = B VII 24 that they scholde.

(iii) **Z** *readings found in* **C**
(a) *Whole lines*: 1. Pr 35 = C Pr 36. 2. II 189 = C III 78. 3. III 18 = C III 19 (B 18).
(b) *Half-lines and phrases*: 1. Pr 5a = C Pr 5a Ant sey many sellys. 2. I 92 = C 164 tene (see i (a) above). 3. V 124 Quod ye nan / yeuan = C VI 309.[50] 4. VII 139 = C VIII 151 pyuysche. 5. VII 202 = C VIII 223 herke. 6. VII 227 = C VIII 256 hym licuth] þere nede is / þere it nedeþ **AB**.

§ 24. In (i) above the situation is relatively straightforward. Agreements of **m** and **Z**, whether or not with other-version support, may be interpreted as archetypal **A** readings that underwent corruption in **r**. In the case of (b) *2, 3, 4* and *12*, reasons are given in the *Textual Notes* for their not being adopted in the text, and need not be repeated here. More extended comment is required for iii. Thus (a) *1* is judged on balance unlikely to be an echo, despite expressing the hostile attitude to minstrels of **C** (which excises **AB**'s distinction of 'true' minstrels from *iaperes*), because it is one of a syntactically-linked pair, of which the unique second is not clearly inauthentic. (For

2, see comment on ii (a) *3* below). Example 3 may be a case where Ax has lost the line through homoarchy. Under (b), *1* is a line which could have been excluded from **A** (followed in this by **B**) and later part-restored in **C**, where the b-half differs completely.[51] (On *2*, see i (a) above, and on the crux at *3*, note 50). Examples *4* and *5* could both be original first-thoughts revised (the former twice, differently) before final restoration in **C**.[52] Finally, in *6* the **C** reading has gone back from **AB**'s parsimonious to **Z**'s more generous treatment of industrious workmen, further heightening the contrast with that of the slothful by adding 252–53 and *ȝut* in 257. This particular reversion recalls the similarly comprehensive change of attitude noted in (a) *1* above.

§ 25. These examples may be accommodated without too much strain within a view of the revision-process as basically linear, but with occasional restorations of the text's earliest form. They are therefore not compelling evidence that **Z**, whether in its genesis or at its first or present copying, was contaminated from either the **A** Version or from **C**. Much the same appears to hold good for (ii), with only three exceptions which require special attention. One is the case of (a) *1*, where the line's absence from **C** signifies little since the preceding line in the source at B 222, which is in **A** and (in early form) in **Z**, has also been deleted in **C**'s revision. Possibly it was lost in Ax through attention-skip from *manye opere craftes* to *As dikeris* (see the *Textual Notes*). Next, in *2* the **Z** line could somewhat more plausibly be construed as a contamination from **B**; but this occurs as part of 144–47, which already reveal major reconstruction in **A**, with **Z**'s a-half being retrieved for use in B 174 and the replacement **A** line retained, after revision, as B 178. Lastly, in *3* the elements of 188 are (not dissimilarly) re-arranged to form B 207, and those of 189, at a later stage still, fused with B III 77b to produce C III 78. In (b) *1*, the second half-line is closer to **B**, of which 12b is revised in **C** to incorporate *ryche* from Z 16a. It could have been scribally intruded in place of one like A 12; but quite possibly the latter was meant to follow Z 16, which it may have lost mechanically, by eyeskip from *rede...glede* → *red...golde* (though the closeness of *derrest pris* to *pureste perreȝe* points to B 13–14 as here developing the thought of the clearly genuine A 12). In *2, syre* may be conjectured to have been originally present in **A** but haplographically omitted before *certis* and afterwards restored by **B** in later position. In *3* the Ax reading, with its 'strong' (trisyllabic) pre-final dip, could be a scribal substitution or a revision later retracted as over-emphatic (see *Textual Notes*). In *4*, revision of an original *habbe* to *holde* and then back to *haue* in **B** is credible; but this instance remains one where 'first draft' is not easily distinguishable from 'scribal substitution', and in the text the **AC** reading has been preferred for **B** as the stronger. In the case of *5*, the **A** line looks unchallengeable; but **B** could well be 'second thoughts' endorsing the 'first thoughts' in **Z** (cf. VII 254, VIII 26 below). In *6* the verb-phrase *þat he wastide* may be authorial revision or scribal substitution; but as it involves no difference of sense or style, it is retained. In *7* it would seem more probable that **B** is a fusion of **Z**'s a- and **A**'s b-half than that **Z** is an echo of **B**.[53] In *8* Ax is clearly corrupt and its unmetrical *next metten* needs emendation, perhaps even more radically to *mette eftsoone* as in **B**.[54] In *9* the **A** reading, though not easy, might (if scribal) be due to Ax's missing the irony in *afyngred* and replacing it with *alongid* as contextually more appropriate. Alternatively, if the latter was the poet's own 'second thoughts', **B** may here be a 'reversion to first thoughts', as at IV 187 and VII 24.

§ 26. In examples *10–12*, however, although **AC** has (as in (b) *4*) been preferred in the text as 'superior', the present editor, if allowed such second thoughts, might well acknowledge the existence of alternative readings between which the poet himself hesitated and, in all three cases, let Bx stand as what Langland had written in **B**. Thus in *10* the rhyming half-line *for lyflode ys swete* may be defended as having a genuinely Langlandian ring (cf. A Pr 83 //, not in **Z**); *11* on the grounds that its sense is not obviously scribal (though, as no reason for the substitution appears, it could be a coincidental visual error); and *12* as semantically and metrically neutral. These three examples illustrate that the direct method, even when aided by dual-version consensus and controlled by the core-text criteria, cannot distinguish with finality between the scribal and the authentic. Their actual treatment in the present text may nonetheless appear somewhat paradoxical in the light of these observations; but this is the inevitable result of acknowledging both the claims of the analytical criteria and the complexity of the possible historical situation (see further IV § 19). For (unattractively complex as this account appears) the actual copy of **Z** on which Bodley 851 is based, though substantially original, could have been contaminated from a post-archetypal **B** manuscript with readings different from those of agreed **AC**.

§ 27. The editorial uncertainty here acknowledged about those readings is at variance with the earlier largely positive assessment of **Z**. But on closer examination, it need not prove seriously damaging to the latter. For it will be realised that judgement of the authenticity of the text of Bx, although made in the light of the parallel **AC** readings, has had of necessity to be reached independently of a decision on the originality of **Z**. And this originality it is logically essential not to presuppose when attempting to resolve contradictions between the canonical versions that may question the postulate of linear revision (see IV, § 2). Now, since a decision as to the scribal character of Bx in these instances depends solely upon immediate analysis, it runs the risk (like all reconstructions) of being wrong, because the direct method is by nature hypothetico-deductive, rather than purely inductive. The possibility of a mistaken editorial decision therefore obviously cannot be excluded; for while a rigorously 'parallelist' procedure may yield relative certainty, it is not indefectible. All three Bx readings may therefore preserve revisions that the author later reversed, and should arguably not be altered to agree with **A** and **C**. But except where (as here) direct support comes from **Z**, their particular challenges to the general validity of the linear postulate do not seem decisive. For a weighty consideration to be borne in mind is the volume of Bx readings with no **Z** parallel to complicate matters that are convincingly identifiable as defective in sense, style or metre. And it is such general certitude about the scribal origin of their defectiveness that justifies general confidence in the linear postulate. Finally, the pervasive authenticating features analysed in §§ 1–12, 20–22 together point to a linear development in thought and expression from $\mathbf{Z} \rightarrow \mathbf{A} \rightarrow \mathbf{B} \rightarrow \mathbf{C}$,[55] if with occasional reversions (for reasons that may evade surmise) to an earlier condition of the text. On that deliberate but undogmatic note, it should now be permissible to close the enquiry into **Z**'s implications for the other versions, which has arisen in examining the issue of its own authenticity. The next issue to address is the question of presumed errors in **Z** and the best procedure for their editorial treatment.

v. *Emendation of Errors in the* Z-Text

§ 28. It has already been stated (II § 136) that the right way to present the text of **Z** is with minimal alteration to its language and substantive readings. For if Bodley 851 is a unique witness to a distinct version, it ought to be treated as would the archetypal **A**, **B** and **C** manuscripts, had these survived, since like them it is a copy of the original at no more than two removes. But **Z** requires even greater editorial caution because, unlike the canonical versions, it appears to be a draft of the poem in its first known form. Any differences between **Z** and **A** may thus be due to **A**'s revision of its (provisional) text rather than to scribal interference. That said, it will not be surprising, that in a manuscript based on a transcript of the holograph, scribal mistakes occur. But as already shown, these are not easy to distinguish from draft imperfections when only one exemplar survives. The present edition therefore aims to present not a 'reconstruction' of Scribe X's *source* but a readable form of the text in Bodley 851, conservatively corrected in the light of its immediate successor **A** and, where relevant, the later versions. How 'conservative' the treatment of **Z** is may be gauged from the fact that even agreements with Bx readings that are emended in the edited text of **B** are kept in **Z**, since they meet the core-text criteria and may in principle have been revised in **A** (see § 26).

§ 29. Amongst the mechanical slips in Bodley 851, those recognised by its first editors are corrected here, along with some 55 more. Other rejected readings of the copy-text occupy indeterminate ground between possible scribal errors and draft lines faithfully transcribed but unsatisfactory in sense or form or both. The general issue involved has been touched on at § 5; but these instances have been assembled in full at this point for convenience of comparison with similar examples in the three canonical versions (cf. *A Version* §§ 56–8 above). Finally, there are cases where a presumptively authorial text seems to have been altered, perhaps deliberately. Beyond this, only four major conjectures have been adopted, on the assumption that Scribe X or his exemplar substituted an easier reading for a plainly difficult original. Such changes to **Z**'s readings touch the limits of legitimate editorial intervention. But in order to present a text of **Z** that allows for the peculiar character of this version but also meets the 'core-text' criteria, these emendations have been regarded as defensible.[56]

§ 30. The readings given here, like those diagnosed in the archetypal A-text (*A Version* §§ 55–7), illustrate the commoner types of unconscious scribal error. The Z-Text nowhere omits or misplaces lines and so any such divergences from **A** are regarded as due to revision (see § 14). But it has half a dozen misdivided lines: at I 90/1, 95/6, with omission of the last lift at I 79/80 and with damage to metre also at I 101/2, II 165/6, III 133/4 and VI 87. Whether occasioned by ambiguity in the source-manuscript (see § 31) or of purely mechanical origin, this group perhaps overlaps with the final category, since division of long-lines may not have been marked with exactness in the manuscript at the composition stage. Amongst mistakes of visual origin is letter-confusion, as of *e / o* (common in Bodley 851): Pr 113; I 14 *woman*] *women* (?visual error for *womon*); IV 149 *renkes*] *ronkes*; VI 3 *-hem*]-*hom*, 81 *sothe*] *sethe*; of *l* and long *s* at VI 40 *wolt*] *wost*;[57] of *u / n* (common in all traditions) at II 199 *yhouted*] *yhonted*; and of ꝫ / þ at III 111 *ye*] *the* and VII 113 *be ye*] *bethe*. Non-specific visual errors occur at Pr 67 *nat*] *om* (confusion after *ant* I 13); I 13 *is*] *as* (?or relict of original *is as*), 29 *seynt*] *senne*.[58] Others perhaps due to simple misreading of the exemplar include at I 123 *For thise arn*] *Foryth* and the somewhat similar *troneth*] *tronen* (pl. for sg.) at I 71; *take hyt*] *taken* at I 131; *vp*] *vn* at II 50 (suggested by following -*(o) un*); *lost*] *?loft* at III 163; *me*] *one* at V 83 and *nas*] *was* at V 155. Dittography is fairly common, as at III 133 *pyte*] *thow pyte*; V 72 *filio*] *filij*; VII 148 *that y*] *thay y*. Haplography is even more frequent, involving omission of a single letter at Pr 112 *non*] *no*,[59] II 133 *bown*] *bow* and IV 141 *nullum*] *nllum*; of a word at Pr 129 *hit* (needed for sense), I 81 *thow*, 101 *ye* (cf. *ye* 100, 102), 114 *kyn*, 129 *Y*, II 192 *go*] (after *to*), III 109 *the*] (after -*eth*; cf. III 17), IV 117 *yt* (?or *yf yt*)] *yf* (cf. VII 12), V 18 *we* after *lib*be, VI 15 *kynde*, 35 *ant*; or of a whole phrase, as at IV 88 *man that*] *om.* and VII 312 *dyne a-*] *om* after *deyn-*. Several cases of eyeskip are illustrated, as at II 171 *the*] *om* → *tho* (or possibly haplography after preceding original **quath*); III 108 *the*] *om* (→ *thow*); IV 92 *mede*] *me* (→ *ma*de); VI 56 *no*] *om* (*Ploke* → *plonte*) and VII 35 *to my*] *om* → *co-*, *cro-*. Eyeskip sometimes also occurs through alliterative inducement and with omission of a whole phrase, as at II 117 *go gyue*] (after *gyle* → *gold* attraction). The two processes operate together at IV 32 *kyng thenne*, caused by *the* → *thenne* attraction or haplography after *the kynge* 31; at V 27 *thenne*, *y* (attraction to *then* and to *y* 28); at V 89 *that*] *om* after *wyth* and → to *a* and at VI 100 *thou*] *the* (attraction to following *efft*). A recurring omission with a visual and / or *auditory* origin is of the (pre)-final preterite morpheme *-ed-*, as at I 51 *knigted*] *knigten*, 97 *honged*] *hongen* (?for *hongeden*); III 144 *-edest*] *-est* and IV 34 *wordeden*] *worden*, 54 *pleyneden*] *pleynen*. Probably auditory are *bought vs*] *boughtes* at II 6, *ofsent hire*] *ofsentare* at III 38, *my by-*] *by my* at V 25 (unconscious consonantal transposition), *-ted*] *-ked* at VI 99, *he* after *yf* at VI 112, *wyght-*] *wyt-* at VII 22 and the substitution of *to* for *tho* at IV 149 and V 151.

§ 31. A smaller group of about a dozen errors could relate to the draft condition of **Z**'s exemplar. Pr 84 *blyssed*] *om* may arise from a gap in the copy (since eyeskip seems unlikely here) or be a sign of a work-in-progress, but is satisfactorily emendable from **A**. II 87 could be an expuncted authorial first thought (cf. **C**, which restores it with appropriate change in the last lift); 163 *to*] *to that* has anacoluthon; II 141b and V 147 have prose order, so are possibly scribal (cf. the Ophni-Phineas passage in C Pr 105–24 discussed at § 6 above). In VI 37 and 38 *ye* omitted without apparent mechanical reason, and in 77 *ne*] *om* after *-re*, are perhaps errors of haste, whether of a scribe or of the composing poet. In VII 6 *Ich wol*] *Ant schal* is possibly due to unconscious suggestion from *ant* 5, but the draft text may have wanted the pronoun and auxiliary. Other ambiguous cases are VII 50 *seide*] *quad*: ?unconscious substitution; 162 **boȝede*] *a yede*: perhaps not certainly an error (see note); VIII 33 *oure*] *om* (?or haplography after *for*); 44 *copiede*] *copede*: possibly auditory error; 68 *beggeres*] *beggaueres*: ?the false form a scribal or authorial slip; 71 *a*] *at*: caused by visual attraction to following *that* and 91 *For*] *Ful*: ?an auditory error induced by following *loue*. All these examples again illustrate the difficulty of telling authorial undecidedness from scribal inaccuracy. But in the light of the other versions, correction would seem to be relatively straightforward, except at VII 162, where the need for a parallel emendation in **A** doubles rather than halving the uncertainty.

§ 32. Finally, a handful of errors may be due in part to conscious scribal intervention. The simplest *þou*] *y* IV 132 perhaps arises from misconstruing the larger contextual sense, though conceivably from simple *ȝ* / *þ* confusion. Similarly *wil*] *wel* VI 61 may be motivated partly by a failure to grasp the allegory. Either deliberate or automatic is the substitution of the non-alliterating dialectal variant of a pronominal form at I 113, an error repeated in the archetypes of the other versions.[60] Perhaps the only controversial emendations are four where the sense is acceptable but the metre defective: Pr 12 *me*] *I* (*xa* / *ax*; so AxBx); IV 80 *withseyde*] *seyde* (*aa* / *bb*; so AxBx); V 152 *wandedes*] *mysdedes* (*aa* / *xx*); V 124 *Quodque mnam*] *Quod ye nan* / *yeuan* (possibly a mistranscription following a misunderstanding).[61] As the rationale of these conjectures is given in the *Textual Notes*, brief comment may suffice here. The first two exemplify 'simultaneous' emendation of metrically defective **AB** lines that the **C** parallel shows Langland to have eventually re-written as normative, but with use of the same stave-sounds. The third may well seem as 'adventurous' as the Athlone editors' reconstruction *purses and* at C XXII 219 // and the fourth as otiose as their Latin conjecture *in lateribus Aquilonis* at C I 112b, both rejected (the first in the *Textual Notes,* the second also at II § 111). Probably the best that can be said by way of defence (or apology) is that each of these conjectures aspires to what Russell and Kane call 'an absolute comparison between actual readings and abstractions' (II § 219 above). To follow where angels have not feared to tread is to act, like R–K, in the belief that it is better to have guessed and erred than never to have guessed at all.

vi. §§ 33–5 *Conclusion*

§ 33. Four authentic versions of the poem, only one of them likely to have been completely finished and 'published', have now been described and the sources of their texts analysed in such detail as the scope of this edition permits. To the **A**, **B** and **C** Versions accepted since Skeat has been added the work-in-progress that Langland put aside (but never wholly forgot) after embarking on **A**. Nothing is at present known as to how **Z** became accessible; but it is a fair presumption that interest in *Piers Plowman* was renewed by the release of a second long version soon after the poet's death. This could have stimulated the creation of the various conjoint **AC** manuscripts and thereby led to the discovery and copying of the present Z-Text's lost source. A contemporary reader encountering the latter might well have thought it (as do the Athlone editors) a truncated form of the shorter version **A**, which also now surfaced and circulated. This would explain why, as in the case of **A**, a text of the **C** *Vita* should have been annexed to **Z**; for it is revealing that at least one of the conjoint copies, NLW 733B, adds C X–XXII to its **A** portion at the same point (the end of the second Vision) as does Bodley 851.[62] But before doing so, the Q scribe of **Z** introduced the 100-line linking-passage (= A VIII 82–185) that R–B call 'Q¹'. This ends with a spurious couplet and a colophon that, spurious or not, is inaccurately positioned here.[63]

§ 34. R–B (pp. 28–30) favour seeing Q^1 as based on a second exemplar, distinct from **Z**'s source and textually affiliated with the **A** copies J and U, but not with the **m** family, the relation of which to **Z** is recorded at § 23 (*i*) above. This seems highly probable, and Q^1's addition may imply its scribe's awareness of the scene with which the Second Vision ended in the most familiar version **B** (as it does in **A**), the tearing of Truth's pardon, followed by a coda on the validity of dreams, pardons and dowel. R–B nonetheless find it 'arguable' that in lines 113–14 (= A VIII 111–12) '*Q* preserves Langland's original draft' because 'the hypermetrical 113 and the non-alliterating 114 would have been enough cause for scribes to rewrite the line' (p. 111, n.). But even if the Q^1 lines were the reflex of a draft, there would be no reason to suppose that they remained such in **A**; for except in Passus XII, **A** does not contain any draft lines. Moreover, as argued in the *Textual Notes* to A VIII 111–12, the **m** tradition has these lines correctly divided, and their substantive readings are supported by α of **B**. The aberrant Q form is thus recognisable as a variant of the corrupt **r** reading, not a reflection of an authorial draft.

§ 35. If this conclusion is correct, there is no obstacle to accepting R–B's wider judgement concerning the whole text, that 'the logic of the second vision is complete' (p. 29) and that **Z** finishes at VIII 91–2:

> [For] loue of here lownesse, Oure Lord hem hath graunted
> Here penaunce ant here purgatorye vpon thys puyr erthe.

What remains of the earliest version thus appears to end on a positive note. This, as subsequent developments prove, was not Langland's last word on the theme, and it may not have been his intended last word even at this early stage. But as it stands, **Z** could fittingly be followed by the colophon that Q¹ affixed to his continuation from **A**: *Explicit vita et visio Petri Plowman*. There, it is obviously wrong , but after VIII 92 would make very good sense.

THE Z VERSION: NOTES

1 See *C Version* § 72 above. In virtue of its possible draft character, the passage has a better claim to be a late addition than does the 'autobiographical' opening of C V, in which Middleton detects allusions to the 1388 Statute of Labourers ('C Version "Autobiography,"') but which shows no comparable stylistic or metrical deficiency.

2 Substitution of *seyde* for *reherside* is instanced in W and N (see *Ka* Apparatus to A IV 145); but the same phenomenon in **Z** requires another interpretation because of differences in the wider context and the double appearance at two locations. However, the case reveals how hard it is to tell scribal prosification from authorial first thoughts in (semi)-prose. (For a parallel, cf. the rhythmically smoother line produced by replacing *haued* at Z V 132 with the less easy *was*). The presence of *quad* in Z VII 50b is taken here as a scribal error, but it could be a first-thought revised to the less usual *seide* at A VII 50 (see § 30 below).

3 An audience that would include many familiar with the B-Text.

4 An example is the lines printed by Skeat from Harley 875 as A II 136–9, 141–3.

5 Despite occasional 'oral' features (e.g. *ye men þat ben murye* at B Pr 209). Other lines suggestive of such a situation include II 1–3 and 10.

6 Discussed in detail in Schmidt, 'Visions and Revisions', pp. 17–18.

7 Similar examples are III 122–24, V 142–44 and VII 196–201, 265–69. Amplification also occurs in shorter doses at I 18, 39, 64; II 10, 47; III 96; IV 50, 152; V 43, 45, 70, 73–4, 130; VII 59, 77, 107–08, 245, 316 and VIII 69, 75–6.

8 From these the moon, the wind and fire have already been omitted.

9 To these may be added *erit* at Z IV 141, which makes good macaronic syntax and is unlikely to be a scribal substitution for **A**'s *with*.

10 See the lyric in Gray, *Religious Lyrics* no. 28, ll. 13–14.

11 The Bx form must be conjectured from the split variants in α and β (*TN ad loc*).

12 These lines, found in **m**, could have been lost from **r**; but see *TN* to C V 134–5.

13 Similar thrice-repeated linear revision (mostly of the b-verses) is seen also at III 28, IV 100, V 9, VI 16, 65, 88, VII 38, 58, 287. Twofold revision is about twice as common: I 21, 69, 104, 127; II 92, 97, 146, 158; III 10; VI 41, 80; VII 3, 6, 25, 54, 87; in the cases of I 128 and VII 139, **C** harks back to **Z**.

14 The half-line better fits the effect of barley-bread and beans (see the *TN*).

15 See MED s.v. *bede* n. 1(c); cf. 2. 60 // A *bode*.

16 This is to take *somme* as 'some', not as a spelling variant of the adv. *same* 'together'; but the revision may imply both.

17 R–B (note *ad loc*) see it as a possible form of *clakken* 'chatter foolishly' (OED s.v. *Clack*); but more probably *e* is an error for *o*, as often in this manuscript.

18 I.e. *fallen* is presumably a West Midland spelling of *fellen* and *ryght* is a noun, not an adverb; the secondary sense works, but is distracting.

19 Possibly original in **A** and replaced by *Conscience* to avoid an internal rhyme here after Ax had corrupted *gabbe* to *leiʒe*.

20 The sense of the verb is presumably intended to be as in MED s.v. Ib (a) 'augment' (not 3, as at B VI 326), and of the noun as in MED s.v. *manhede* 2 (a) 'dignity' (not the scantly-attested 3 (f) 'manpower'). Meed would find little favour with the king if she were offering the proposed bridegroom a private army.

21 The former is not used by **L** elsewhere; *made* in **A** and **C** may be archetypal substitutions.

22 The phrase is found at Pr 118 // and III 87 //.

23 There is no semantic or metrical difference; the reading could also have been *hand* in the intermediate versions (cf. C III 75 //).

24 See MED s.v. *clene* adj. 2 (a), 4 (b).

25 The text is not unproblematic, since **A** might be expected to read *wyf*, as conjectured by Kane after **B** (pp. 445–46); but see *TN* to C VII 249.

26 Paul's association with Rome is correct but unexpected; the **A** revision is, like **BC**, more conventional.

27 The word itself is typical of **L**'s lexis; for the semantic overlap see MED s.v. *haunten* v. 4 (a), illustrated at C XV 198, which links them as synonyms. It seems inconceivable that a scribe would have substituted *haunten*.

28 For the verb's overlap in sense with *putte*, see MED s.v. *pilten* v. 2 (a).

29 Though *gruche* is eliminated from **A**, its return at B VI 314 and C 337 suggests the word's initial presence in the first version, since neither appearance in **Z** would seem to derive from these (wholly new) lines.

30 A handful of cases where **A** diverges from **Z** do not count as revisions but probably indicate an error in Ax, which is emended here from **Z**: A I 39, 94, 110*, 116, 183 (so **B**; perhaps emend **A**?); II 59, 142; III 18 (so **BC**; possibly lost in **A** through homoarchy and should perhaps be inserted in **A**), 101b (?possibly dittography), 116; IV 63; V 155 (so **BC**), 156 (so **C**); VI 30 (**Z** right; not clear whether Ax was corrupt, as it is unknowable), 66 (possibly revised out as obscure); VII 25b (Ax uncertain; cf. **BC**), 89, 90b (so **B**), ?139a, 160b (so **BC**), ?314 (so **BC**); VIII 13, 22. Others may be archetypal but are attested only in **m**, e.g. IV 17–18, which may belong in **A**, though on balance it is rejected here (see *TN*).

31 The line Z I 117, repeated in A 162 to introduce the 'avaricious parsons' sequence, is retained in **BC**, but **C** (like **Z**) uses it only once.

32 Most of the new citations are introduced in the three passūs of the **A** *Vita*.

33 Similarly, a scribe is unlikely to have turned A VI 75–6 into the theologically less exact Z VI 62–3: although baptism consoles, it is not consolation that saves.

34 The apparent counter-indication at I 113 is paralleled in the **AB** archetypes and is here understood in all cases as a scribal error. The form presumed original is attested in two **A** copies, J and N.

35 See MED s.v. *fame* n. (2), recorded *c.* 1425, *stuti* adj; *bewsoun* is not in MED.

36 Ibid. s.v. *beau* adj. 2 (d), (f).

37 Ibid. s.v *cammok* n.; MED's other citations are from encyclopaedias and herbals.

38 All lines have been classified and the results summarised in *Intro*. IV §§ 37–48 and Appendix I; see also Schmidt, *Clerkly Maker* ch. 2 and 'Z-Text: a Metrical Examination'.

39 See *Intro*. IV, 'Core-Text' § 11 (a). Obviously the primary core-text (= **ZABC**) cannot logically be invoked in this connection.

40 For discussion of these terms see *Intro*. IV §§ 37–49 and Schmidt, 'Metrical Examination' pp. 296–9.

41 It may be that **loue and* was originally present or intended to be present before *charite*; see *Textual Notes* for discussion.

42 With the first, cf. XIX / XXI 332(1) *déuisede*, 351/350 *Cóntricioun*; with the second, cf. *cán súlle* at BC XIX / XXI 402[1].

43 For short lines of similar sound, cf. A XI 83–4 / B X 127–28; several lines of seventeen syllables or more are found in the core-text (e.g. A I 98 // BC 100/97).

44 The Dreamer's awaking and some reflection on his dream (in the manner of A VIII 131ff) could have been envisaged; but without the dramatic quarrel between Piers and the Priest to wake him, something more perfunctory might have sufficed.

45 These are considered in detail by R–B, pp. 23–4. As the strength of attestation for **m** readings obviously fluctuates, only those supported by the 'core-group' AMH[3] are treated as securely preserving **m**, and variations in members present are noted. On this see *A Version* §§ 25, 29.

46 See *TN* on C I 164 for full discussion of this problem.

47 See *TN* on A 47.

48 See *TN* on C II 170.

49 See *TN* on C IX 173.

50 See discussion in *TN* to C VII 309–10.

51 Unlike **A** ms K, which inserts the **C** form of the whole line.

52 See *TN* on C VIII 151 and C VIII 223. L. uses *herke* only once.

53 R–B's remark on V 104 ('similar to B V 379; *om* **A**') is confusing. **Z**'s a-half = **B**'s a-half, but **B**'s b-half = **A**'s.

54 On the synonymity of the adverbs, see MED s.v. *eft-sone(s* adv. 2 (a).

55 For straightforward examples of linear three-stage revision see note 13 above. The postulated existence of Langland's 'repertorium' of half-lines (see Appendix III) may explain some of the exceptions to the general operation of the linear postulate.

56 The issues are fully discussed in the *TN ad loc*.

57 Unless *wost* is a possible abbreviation of *woldest*.

58 Or it could be a misreading as 'hold sin hard' (but the idiom is unattested).

59 Inadvertently omitted from the Apparatus.

60 JN of **A** alone preserve *hy*; but only in **Z** is it in fact metrically essential.

61 The emendation **boȝede*] *a yede* at VII 163 may also belong here; but possibly the text is not an error (see *TN*).

62 See *Intro*. I, *Manuscripts*, nos 46–51; NLW 733B is no. 51.

63 See *TN* to Z VIII 92 (under C IX 185).

IV. EDITING THE TEXT

i. *The Core-text of* Piers Plowman

(a) *Nature of the Core-text*

§ 1. The principles and procedures adopted in this edition have been frequently mentioned earlier in the *Introduction*; there now follows a direct examination of the theoretical and practical problems of editing the poem. Four independent versions have been accepted, and in the last section, in order to justify recognition of **Z** as a work by the author of **A**, **B** and **C**, the Bodley 851 text has been examined in the light of criteria derived from the poem's 'core-lines'. That these criteria are editorially relevant for much more than the authentication of **Z** (III, *Z Version* §§ 20–22) is clear from their use in relation to Passus XII of **A** (III, *A Version* §§ 69–71); but that they provide an empirical test of originality in all the versions makes them crucial to the idea of a parallel-text. Further, since each textual tradition shows corruption at every level of transmission, these criteria are almost as important for editing any one version on its own. The discussion therefore begins with the concept underlying the basis of the entire enterprise: that of the 'core' lines attested in common by two or more versions.

§ 2. If the 'originality' of a unique reading is certain only when it conforms with the core-text criteria, it would follow that *Piers Plowman* should ideally be edited 'in parallel'.[1] But since parallel-editing depends on the authoritativeness of these criteria, the lines that **Z** shares with the canonical versions can be considered to be part of the core-text only if **Z**'s authenticity is settled without reference to these lines. To escape circularity here, it would strictly be necessary to include in the core-text only those in **A**, **B** and **C**. However, there is at present no 'other' evidence that could prove **Z**'s authenticity; so if this is to be tested, it would seem reasonable to employ, provisionally, the portion of text in which **Z** attests lines shared with other versions, as part of a 'heuristic' procedure for discovering the status of its unique lines (for it is chiefly in lines unique to each version that authenticity becomes a major issue). The most important of these groups is **ZABC**; and from a purely logical standpoint, **Z**'s presence in this group may be discounted, the lines in question being regarded as part of a group[2] **ABC** that **Z** happens to join with. But from a procedural point of view, **Z**'s inclusion helps to distinguish, at the outset, lines attested by four independent sources from lines attested by three or two, without forgetting that the hypothesis does not presuppose **Z**'s authenticity. The **ZABC** lines have therefore been listed below at the beginning rather than the end of the core-text repertory. What they suggest is that the revision-process was 'linear' or uni-directional. That is to say, whether Langland added, omitted or altered, he rarely restored his poem to the form it had in the text prior to the one he was revising. For example, **C** very rarely 'revises back' to **A**, or **B** to **Z**.[3] This 'postulate of linearity', which acts as a control on emendation of the text by appeal to another version, is *a priori* in character to the extent that it relies on antecedent probability (see III, *Z Version* §§ 26–7 above); but like the postulate of the core-text, it can be empirically justified. Careful study of the versions as they evolve moves this probability close to virtual certainty.

§ 3. Now, if **Z** lines agreeing with either **A** or **B** or **C** are (provisionally) admitted into the corpus of core-text, those **Z** lines agreeing with all three, the largest possible number of versional witnesses (see § 5), will serve to constitute its 'primary' division. If after enquiry **Z** is not accepted as genuine, and its status in relation to disputed single-version readings becomes that of an unclassified **A** witness (important simply because not descended from Ax), the criterial value of the **ABC** common lines (§ 11 (a) below) will remain unaffected. In any case, the inclusion or exclusion of **Z** does not affect the ascription of special authority to unanimity between versions, since the text becomes increasingly securer where two or more agree. This assertion is not itself *a priori* as applied to any two versions that stand in immediate sequence; but it partly presumes their order determinable on grounds other than their sharing lines located in versions at different stages of development. However, the assumption that revision was linear is strengthened when unique lines are compared in the light of the common lines seen in their several contexts. What the core-text generates is the axiom that 'a line's textual authority is proportional to its versional attestation'. This is the 'principle of unanimity'; and from it arises a 'principle of acceptability' that certifies unique archetypal readings as authentic, without further argument, if they conform to the core-text criteria. These principles furnish the canons of guidance or 'methodological rules'[4] for editing that will be elaborated at §§ 16ff below. But first the rationale of the core-text needs to be explained and fully documented.

§ 4. To determine each version's archetypal text when the pairs of family witnesses disagree, to diagnose errors in that text and (where possible) to emend them, all demand an objective standard of reference as a counter-weight to inevitable editorial bias. But as is generally recognised, the high incidence of random variation at every stage in the traditions rules out systematic reliance on the most objective (because most impersonal) editorial technique, recension. 'Immediate' analysis accordingly proves indispensable in many cases as a means to ascertain the direction of scribal variation (see II §§ 66–7). But the 'direct method' is in essence a hypothetico-deductive procedure; and its key notion of the *lectio difficilior,* though rational in principle, is always partly intuitive in application. Moreover, this important traditional criterion (as those who have used it know) may fall short in practice even of the qualified degree of objectivity[5] to be expected when the text being analysed is a poem. And it is chiefly as a way of minimising the criterion's arbitrariness that the editor needs to look to the norms of language, style and versification that can be derived from the core-text. To qualify for the core-text, lines must ideally show no verbal or syntactic differences that affect sense or metre. But in this area it is possible for the textual critic to be rigorous without becoming rigid, e.g. in acknowledging a line's substantive identity across versions even when a near-synonymous lexical word may have been introduced in a metrical dip. And, after recognition that revision has occurred, common identity may be accorded to two parallel lines even when revision introduces a new stave-word (but without causing change of meaning) into the line's final lift, which is always metrically 'neutral'.[6]

§ 5. In the light of these observations and qualifications, a 'basic core-text' can be recognised in some 4140 lines preserved by two or more versions, of which 2680 (64·5% of this number) are wholly identical.[7] Its primary category **ZABC** is instanced in 530 lines (12·5%); a secondary category in the four three-version groupings **ABC**, **ZAB**, **ZAC** and **ZBC** (some 598 lines or 14·5 %); and a tertiary category in the six two-version groups **ZA**, **ZB**, **ZC**, **AB**, **AC** and **BC** (some 3020 lines or 73%). Of these, **BC** (even when Passūs XXI–XXII are omitted as possibly representing only one version) stands out, with some 41·5% of the common text and 24% of the fully identical lines. In the lists below these eleven groups have, however, been ordered according to the number not of lines but of versions that they represent. For this better indicates a group's relative weight as evidence for authenticity, given that the strength of textual testimony is proportional to its independence (see § 3). But since the manuscripts in each of the **ABC** traditions derive from a common archetype, each version constitutes only one independent witness to the 'common' inter-versional text. It follows that, if **Z** is shown to be authentic (III *Z Version* § 19), the lines of highest authority will be those in **ZABC**, which will have passed a threefold authorial scrutiny and attest an initial version retained to the end, while those in group **ABC** will rank next. On the supposition that **Z** is prior, the group **ZAB** will be of almost equal weight as manifesting a like unbroken linear continuity, again with one (here the final) revision to follow (**B** > **C**). The lines of group **BC**, where not newly added in either version, will witness to one re-working if **A** here retained **Z**, to two if **A** had already revised or added to **Z**. Those of **AB** will be lines revised either twice (**Z** > **A**; **B** > **C**) or, if not present initially in **Z** or finally in **C**, only once. The other large two-member group, also linear, is **ZA**.

§ 6. The remaining five groups ostensibly suggest an absence of linear continuity; but on analysis the discrepant member in each case will be found to disclose archetypal corruption, not to be a genuine revision later reversed.[8] The eight-line **ZBC** group, listed separately below for clarity, is actually part of **ZABC**, though this is concealed by archetypal corruptions in Ax. In the slightly larger **AC** (28 lines) and **ZAC** (20 lines), the fifty or so deviations of **B** may be similarly attributed to corruptions in Bx. In principle, **B** in all these instances could have revised, and **C** could then have reverted to the **A**(**Z**) reading. For even a high antecedent probability of linearity allows that the poet (who seems to have kept a topicalised 'repertory' of (half)-lines for use in different situations)[9] may have re-called or consulted earlier forms of his work. This is what happens at C X 60, which echoes A IX 52; at C X 184, which is nearer to A X 58 than to revised B IX 67; and at C XIX 134b, which corresponds to A X 28b. Of course, the conclusion that most **B** lines diverging from (**Z**)**AC** show not **B** revision but Bx corruption is bound to contain an element of 'subjectivity' arising from the method of direct analysis that diagnoses the corruption; but this can be reduced significantly under the guidance of the core-text norms.[10] Amongst the other two 'non-linear' groups, the **ZC** agreements (few of them perfect) could again be instances of **Z** readings abandoned in **A** and **B** but finally reinstated in **C**.[11] Similarly, **ZB** agreements could be readings removed from **A** and restored in **B**, only to be again rejected in **C**. But though the existence of both groups must qualify the absoluteness of the linear postulate, it does not undermine its general validity. Further, on the (admittedly more complicated) supposition advanced at III *Z Version* § 26, **ZC** and **ZB** breaches of linearity may even evince scribal contamination from **B** or **C** introduced by the copyist of **Z**'s exemplar. That explanation continues to remain possible since the **Z** manuscript Bodley 851 is not a holograph and could have been made by someone who read **C** while it was in progress or soon after its release; but it obviously does not impose itself.

The challenging readings of these small non-linear groups, which represent a mere 0·5% of the core-text, are therefore statistically of limited evidential value. This said, their problematic nature merits the detailed attention that they will receive in the *Textual Notes*.

§ 7. The numerically significant groups, by contrast, are the linear **ZABC**, **ABC**, **ZAB**, **ZA**, **AB** and **BC**. These add up to some 4074 lines that, with the non-linear groups' 66, give a basic core-text of 4140 lines, nearly twice the number of lines in **A** and some 22% of the four versions' total of 19,000. Two further classes of 'auxiliary' lines are also available to augment the core-text. The first is that in which one version diverges from its group in a single lift, most often the last, where a change has least metrical impact (cf. note 6 above) or, in a few cases, within a dip, where metre is again unaffected. A second class consists of half-lines that persist through two, three or four versions. These are illustrated only selectively at § 13, since the main corpus is large enough to satisfy its criterial function. The basic core-text is of fundamental importance for specifying the poet's linguistic and metrical practice in the way needed to provide a strong test of authenticity over the poem's stages of development. It is a convenient resource, in that it consists of whole lines accessible through the parallel-text format even where transposed (since all larger instances are printed twice). It is logically coherent, in recognising lines with multiple attestation as 'original' not *a priori* but on the basis of all and only those features exemplified in the corpus. And it is empirical, in that its analytic postulate of 'Langland' as 'the author of the lines recorded in the corpus' is validated by all and only those lines. The core-text norms, which are both permissive and stipulative, obviously cannot be applied mechanically. But they constitute the most reliable editorial guide for authenticating lines found in only one version, and for identifying those that are spurious or corrupt.

§ 8. The theoretical demands of 'parallel-editing' have now been indicated, and the aims and principles of this edition will be set out in detail in section ii below. But it may be helpful here to summarise them in relation to the core-text norms that provide their basis. The four editorial goals kept in mind have been: to determine and discriminate between competing family-variants in the received versions; to establish the archetypal texts; where essential, to emend them; and to test the **Z** text's claim to originality. For achieving these, appeal is made to criteria based on the 'Langlandian core-text'. The principle of *unanimity* derived from this corpus provides the necessary and sufficient basis for the two main tasks of the 'critical' editor. These are: to test the acceptability of the syntax, lexis, style and versification of unique lines in terms of their conformity with the core-text criteria; and to use these criteria in correcting the errors thus revealed in the archetypal texts of **A**, **B**, **C** and (allowing for the restraints imposed by its draft character) in **Z**. Such a method can never be sufficiently *a posteriori* to satisfy the positivist; for it presumes *a priori* that unanimous attestation is equivalent to unitary authorship of all four versions (or, if only the 'secondary' core-text is in question, the 'canonical' three). But though this presumption cannot be proved on internal evidence alone, it can be defended as a heuristic hypothesis with great potential for discovering whatever data are needed to confirm it. Moreover, conclusions reached by this method count as 'empirical', since they remain open to being falsified by possible future discovery of external evidence that **Z**, **A**, **B** or **C** is not from the hand of the author of the other two / three versions. The approach described, which may for convenience be described as 'critical empiricism', adopts a less simple notion of the substantive text than does the 'positivist' in any of its varieties. But its aim is to formulate criteria of comparable definiteness (see §§ 14–36) that retain the strengths of the recensional and the 'direct' methods, while remaining free of the main weaknesses of all three.

(b) *Repertory of the Basic Core-text*

§ 9. In the corpus of 4140 lines forming the eleven core-text groups, where one or two versions diverge, their sigil is recorded in brackets so as to acknowledge the possibility of revision. 'Ax', 'Bx' and 'Cx' (or '?**Z**') in brackets imply probable corruption in the respective archetype / exemplar, so such instances are not counted in the total. Lines marked + (or ++) are those where one or more versions display one / two variation(s) in (usually) minor lexical words that have little effect on sense or metre. Small differences in grammatical words or in word-order are not noted. Lines wholly unchanged are in italics and their numbers in brackets after each total; in categorising them, metrically neutral non-lexical variants (such as *a* for *on* or *he*) have been ignored. Line-references are keyed to the versions present in the order **CBAZ**.

§ 10. The *primary* core-text consists of some 530 (247) **ZABC** lines attested in Prologue–Passus IX (references to passus- and line-number are keyed to **C**). The list includes twenty given at § 11 (c), as cases where Bx was probably corrupt, and eight given at § 11 (d), where Ax was corrupt; but these are not counted in the total here.

Pr *1–3.* 6. *19.* 20. *21.* 22–5. 27. *30.* 31. *32.* 33. *34–5.* 41. 42 (Bx). 43. *47.* 49 (Bx). *51.* 66. 67. 68. *69.* 71. 73. 74 (Bx). *76.* 77. *162–63.* 232+ (**Z**). **I** *3. 10.* 12. *13. 20.* 30. 33–5. *36.* [39(1: Bx; 2:Ax)]. *41.* 45. 48–9. *50–1.* 52. *53.* 54. *57.* 58–9. *61–2.* 63. *68–9.* 70+. 71. *72.* 78. *79–83.* 85. 88. *89–93.* 98+. 101–02. *105.* 126. *127.* [*128–29* C *differs in lift* 2]. 134 (Bx). 136. *138.* 140 (?**Z**). 143. 161. 162. *165. 166–8. 169* +(Bx). *170. 171*+ (Bx). *172.* 174. *176.* 177. *178.* 179–80. 182+ (Bx). 188–89. ++190. 191. 194+ (1:Bx;**Z**; 2: Bx). *195.* 196+. 197. 200 (Bx). *201.* **II** 1 (?Bx). *2. 3. 5. 8.* 10. *19. 23. 30* (Bx). 47 (?Bx; *see* Textual Notes [*TN*]). *72. 79. 93.* 108–09. *113.* 114+ (Bx). 115 (?Ax). *116.* 118. 147. *151. 153.* 154. *155. 157.* 158 (**Z**). 159. *160. 162.* 168. *173.* 191 (Bx). *192–93.* 194. *195–96. 202–03.* 204. *208–10.* 211 (1:**ZA**; 2: Bx). 212 (Bx). *214–16. 220–30.* 231 (Bx). *232–33.* (234). 238 (?**Z**Bx). 240–41. **III** *1. 2. 3–5.* 8+. 9+. *12.* 13++. 14+. 15. *17.* 18 (**Z**). *20–22.* 23. *25. 27. 28. 34.* 36–7. *127.* 133. 137. 145–46. 147 (?Ax). 150. 151–52. 154. *155–56.* 157–58. 159 (Bx). *160.* 161. 163. *164–65.* 166. 167 (Bx). 170–71. 173. *174–84.* 185+. 187 (Bx). *188–90.* 191. *192–95. 197–99.* 214–17. *219–24.* 226–31. 258–61. **IV** *2–3. 5–9. 10* (Bx; *see* TN). *11.* ++12. 16. 20. +42 (**Z**). *57–8.* 59–61. *63–4.* 74. *75.* 78. *79–80.* 81. *88–91.* 94. *96.* 97. 100+. *101–03.* 105. 107. *108.* 109+ (**Z**). 110. 111–12. 124+. 133+. 135. *136–37. 144. 146.* 157. *158. 179.* **V** 115. *116–17.* 118. 119. 121–22. *123.* 128 (Bx). 130–33. 136. *137.* 141. *143–44.* 145 (Bx). 197. 199. **VI** 1+. 2+. *3.* 5–6. 7. *8* (**Z**). *310.* 311. *312.* 316+. *318–19.* 321 (Bx). *326.* 327 (1: Bx; 2: ?**Z**). 328–29. 438–39. 440+. **VII** 56–61. 62 ++. 64 (Bx). *65.* 66. *67. 154.* 155. 156 (1:**Z**; 2:Bx) 157. 158 (AxBx). 159. *161. 164–69.* 174–76. 178–82. 185–87. *188.* 192. *193.* 194. 201. 210. *213–14. 218–19.* 222–5. *226–7.* 228. *229.* 230+ (**C**). 231. 236. 239. *242–3.* 244. 245. 246+ (**C**). 251. *253* (?**Z**). *261–3.* 264. 265+ (**C**). 266. 268 (Bx). **VIII** *2. 3. 5. 6. 15.* 16. *18* (**Z**). *20.* 24. 26. 28–9. 32 (Bx; **Z**). *33.* 35. 36. 39. 40. 42. *62. 80.* 81. *92.* 94. *95.* 97. *100* (Ax). 101. 102. 103. 105. 106 (Ax). 107. *108. 113–14. 116* (Ax). *117. 119–20.* 121. 123. 125–27. 129++ (**C**). 133. 134. 141. *142. 149* (?Ax [*uncertain*]). 153. 154. 156. *161–2.* 164. *165.* 171. *172.* 173. *174.* 175 (Ax). 176 (Bx). *180–1. 183.* 188. 204 (Bx). 207 (Bx). 210 (Ax). 211. *212.* 217 (Bx). *218.* 223. *224.* 226 (Bx). 227. *228.* 231 (Bx). 238+ (**C**). 257+ (**C**). 258 (?**Z**). 273. 274. *276.* +277. 291 (Ax). *293.* [?294 (**Z**;Bx); *see* TN]. 301–02. 304. 312. *314–15.* 316. *317.* 318. 322. 326. 327++. *328.* 329 (**Z**Bx). 331 (**Z**). 333 (Ax). 334. 336+ (Bx). *343.* 346. 347. **IX** *1–3. 5.* 7 (Bx). *22.* 25. *27.* 28 (**Z**;Bx). 29. *36.* 37. 41. 46. 58. 61. 63. 167 (Bx). 170. *176.* 177. 185 (Bx).

§ 11. The *secondary* core-text of 588 lines consists of:

(a) Some 320 (272) **ABC** lines attested in Pr–XI; again keyed to **C**.

Pr 48. 53. *54.* 55+. *56.* 57 (Bx). *58. 62. 63.* 65. 78. 79. 80 (Bx). *82.* 84. 159. *160.* **I** *1.* 2. 7. **II** *145.* 215–16. 235. 249–51. 252+. **III** 31. *38.* 40++. *42.* 45. 47. 50. *51. 79.* 80. *82–4.* 85. *115–16. 127.* 249. 264+. 265 (Bx). *266. 267. 268.* 269 (Ax). *273. 279.* 280. *283. 312–13. 428.* 429 (Cx). *431–33. 436–39. 441. 443. 446–47. 452.* **IV** *1. 5. 92. 109. 140. 142. 145.* **V**

120. 140. 149. **VI** *63.* 94 (**A**). *196–97.* 198 (Bx). *199.* 203 (Bx). *205–06. 208–10.* 212. *213–17.* 219. *220. 223.* 224 (Bx; Cx). *227.* 229. 231 (Bx). *232.* 233 (Bx). *349–50. 354. 356–60.* 363 (Bx). *364–66. 371. 373–76. 378–79. 383. 387–93. 395–96. 398–400. 403–06.* 407 (AxBx). *414–15.* 417. *438–40.* **VII** 220. 267. *269–74. 278.* 280–87. 289–90. **VIII** *68–71. 75–9. 82–3.* 110. *232.* **IX** *62.* 166+ (Bx). *293. 295.* 296 (Bx). *297–99. 304* (Ax). *308–09. 311–14. 319–20. 324.* 325 (Bx). *327–39.* 342–44. *346. 348–50.* 352+. **X** *1–5.* 7 (Cx). 8–11. 12 (Bx). *19–20. 27–33.* 34 (Bx). *44–7. 57–8. 63* (Ax). *64. 68–70. 72–3. 77. 81.* 82++. *83.* 87++. *88–9. 103. 106–07. 113–21. 123–24. 128–40. 143–47.* 151. *155–56. 172.* 228. *230–31. 273.* 276 (Bx). *277–81. 295.* 298. **XI** *1. 3. 4. 7–9. 31.* 37 (Bx). 38–41. 47–8. 53–4. *85. 88. 90. 92. 102–03.* +116 (Bx). *117–24. 128–29. 210–11.* 222++. *255. 257. 259–60.* 264 (Bx) *278. 294.*

(b) Some 240 (120) **ZAB** lines attested in B Pr–VII = ZA Pr–VIII; keyed to **B**.

Pr *4.* 7. *12–14.* 24. *26.* 220. **I** 14. 16. *17–19. 23.* 24–6. *27–8.* 30. 34. *39.* 48+ (?Bx). *50.* 51. 59. *68. 73.* 76. 80. *82.* 103+. 104 (Bx). 105. 107–09. 110+. *111.* 112 om Bx]. 127 (Ax;Bx). *128–29. 132–33.* 134 (?Z). *135. 139. 143.* 144. *146.* 191+ (Bx;Z). 199+. 202+. 209+ (Ax). **II** 6. (9). 19. 45. 46. 54. 55. 74. *75.* 102. *105.* 110. 111. *118–19.* 120. 122–4. *125.* 126. *129. 131.* 133. 136 (A). 137. 139. *148. 150–51.* 152–54. 156. 158 (?Ax). 159. 161 (?Ax). 162. *164.* 165 (?Z). 167. 168 (**Z**). *171–72.* 180 (Bx). *187.* 189. 194. *195. 202. 227–28.* 233. **III** 6. 7. *15. 23. 25. 29.* 102++. 104. 105. 108. 165. 168. *187–91.* 192–93. +194. 195. *196–97.* 198–200. *201. 206–08.* **IV** 13. *14.* ++23. 27. *28–30.* 45. 46 (Z?Ax). 49. *51–2.* 59. *64.* +65. *66. 68–70.* +71. *72.* 73. *81. 87.* 91 (ZAxBx; *see* Textual Notes). 99 (Z). 118. 126. *128. 131. 142.* 191+. *192.* 193. 194. **V** *1.* 10+. *22.* 24. *57. 63.* 72. *73.* 224+. *226.* 227+. 381. 382. *460.* 528. 533 (Ax). *552–3.* 556. 560+. *561.* 565. *586.* 587+. **VI** *10. 15.* 44. 50+ (Z). 51. 55 (?Z). 56. *62. 66* (?A). 87. 108–9 (Ax). 124. 130. 153. *158. 160.* 166+ (**B**). 169+ (**B**). 183+ (**B**). *186.* 214. *220. 231–4.* 235++ (Z;B). 236 (**B**). 237. *239–40.* 246. 249. 252. +257. *258.* 269. 275. 285 (Bx). 293++ (**Z**). 299. 315++ (**B**). *318.* 322. **VII** *4. 9. 10.* 17. *19.* 26+ (**B**). 27. 29. 31+ (**B**). *47. 50.* 61–2+ (**Z**). 96–7+ (**Z**). 98.

(c) Some 20 (3) **ZAC** lines, keyed to **C**. This list includes lines also given at § 10 on the presumption that in original **B** these lines read as **ZAC** and that in all but II 146 Bx was certainly corrupt.

Pr 42. 49. 57. 74. **I** *50.* 84. **II** 146. 190. 191. **V** 145. **VI** 321. 327. **VII** 156. [158(Ax)]. **VIII** *176.* 204. 217. 226. 336. **IX** 7+. *185.*

(d) Some 8 (3) **ZBC** lines, keyed to **C**. These also appear under the 'primary' category on the assumption that Ax is here corrupt.

I *92.* **III** 19 (?Ax). 225 (?AxB). **V** *130* (Ax). **VII** 157 (Ax uncertain). **VIII** 175 (Ax). 210 (Ax). *291* (Ax).

§ 12. The *tertiary* core-text of 3023 lines consists of:

(a) 130 (60) **ZA** lines attested in Pr–VIII 80; these are keyed to **A**. In four cases Ax and in three cases ms Z are presumed corrupt.

Pr *45. 100.* **I** 101. 110 (Ax). 111. *119–20.* 136. 137+. 138. 169. **II** *22–3.* 24–6. *30–2.* 35. 36–8. *39.* 40+. *41–2.* 43–4. *46.* 48. 49. *50.* 53. *58.* 59 (Ax). *60.* 66. *70–1.* 80. 107. *130. 133.* 140. *186.* **IV** *28–30.* 53. 63 (Ax). *66.* 73. 89. 91. *107. 133. 136.* 137. 138. *140.* 147. *158* (Z). **V** 2. *11–12.* 53. 241. 242+. 254 (Z). **VI** *46.* 79 (Ax). 80. *81. 93.* 97. **VII** 10–12. 21. 26+. 30. 33. 43. 109. 115. 124. *125.* 127–28. 130. *131–4. 136.* 137+. 138. *141. 148. 176.* 223. 230. 232++. 227. **VIII** 11. 12. 14. *15.* 16. *17–18.* 28+. *29–30.* 33 (Z). 38+. *39–40.* 41. 43–6. *47–8.* 51. 55–9. 60. 61+. 62+. *74–5. 78.*

(b) 8/9 (1) **ZB** lines (keyed to **B**). In most of these cases the evidence that Ax may be corrupt is not decisive.

Pr 223 (? *l. om* Ax). **I** *36,* 79 (against **AC**; see *TN*). 127. **II** 136 (see *TN*), 163 (see *TN*). [207; *see* Textual Notes]. **III** 168. **V** 25.

(c) 3/4 **ZC** lines (keyed to **C**).

Pr 36 (*l. not in* **AB**). **II** 217 (*against* **AB**). **III** 32–3 (*ll. om* **AB**), 78. **IV** 69. *See* Textual Notes *on all.*

(d) Some 303 (156) **AB** lines; keyed to **B**.

Pr *16.* 35. 36+. 38+. *39. 66.* 222. **I** *30–1.* 64. 180. 198. 205. *208.* **II** *121.* (127). 128. *150–51. 157. 170.* 184. *188.* 190.

210. 234. **III** 10. *37.* 39+. *50. 63. 73.* 76–7. *80–1.* 82. *89–92. 94–5. 99.* 103. *216–21.* 222 (Bx). *223.* 224 (Bx). *227. 229–31.* +232. 233. *234.* 246. *247–49.* +250. *251–53.* 255 (?Ax; Bx). *256. 259.* 260 (AxBx). *262–63. 288.* 293. **IV** 111. 137. *146.* **V** *9.* 77.78–9. *80.* 83. *85. 93.* 94–6. 99–100. 103–05. 106–07. 108 (Ax). 109. 110. 111 (AxBx). 112. +113. *115.* 117. +118. *122. 124. 220.* 224. 225+. *226–27. 299. 302. 314–15. 325. 362.* 456 (?AxBx). +461. 468 (Bx). *562. 566.* 575 (Bx). *627.* **VI** 50. +58. 59–60 (Bx). *218.* 243. 272 (?Bx). 281 (AxBx). **VII** 80. *106. 114–18.* +119. *120.* +122. 123. +124. *125.* 127–8. ++129. *130–32.* 133. +134. +135. *137–9. 153.* +154. *156–57.* +159. 168. +172. 173. ++197. **VIII** *6.* +13. +32. 34–5. *36.* +37. +38. +45. *46.* ++47. *48.* 49–50. +57. *66. 73.* 81–2. 84. 89. 93 (Bx). +94. 95 (Bx). *98. 101. 102.* ++103. *104.* +109. 110. **IX** *28. 31.* 48–51. *52.* +54. 59. *119.* ++124. +129. *131. 136. 156.* 157–8+. 159+. *162.* 163 (AxBx). 164. *165. 167. 174–6. 186.* ++187 (Bx). *198.* +199. +204. *206.* **X** *5–7.* 8+. *12.* 14–16. *20.* ++21. 33–5. 36 (Bx). 46. +47. 48. *49.* 51–2. +59. *60.* +65. 66–7. *72.* +104. *107.* 108 (AxBx). +110. *115.* +116. *119–22.* +123. *124.* 126–29. *132–33. 135–6.* +140. *141. 143. 150.* +152. *154.* +162. *164–68.* 169. 170. 187. 197+. *198.* +200. 201. 209–10. 212. *215.* 217. *220–21.* 222. *223.* +224. 225. +227. +228. 229. 293. 295. 331. 332+. *333. 346.* +347 (?Bx). *348.* 349. 350 (?Ax). +362. +363. *368.* 369. 414. 424. 452–53. 462.

(e) 28 (13) **AC** lines; keyed to **C**. These are also listed in 11 (a) above and are there judged **B** lines that were corrupted in Bx.

Pr 80. **I** 76 (*see* Textual Notes). **III** 124 (*see TN*). 276. **IV** 142. **VI** 198. 203. 205. 224. *233. 357.* **VII** 170 (*see TN*). **VIII** *207.* 294 (*see TN*). *329* (*see TN*). **IX** 28 (*see TN*). *284.* 325. **X** *12. 34.* 106. *107. 134. 143.* **XI** 37. 116. *118. 211.*

(f) 2551 (1804) **BC** lines; keyed to **C**.

Pr *85–6. 89–92.* +94. +125. *126.* +127. *128–29.* +131. *132.* +134–35. 136. *139. 141.* +143 (Bx). *148.* +149. *150. 166.* 167. *168.* 169. *173. 180.* 182. 183. *184.* 185. *186–8. 190–93.* 194. *195–200.* 202. 203–5. *207–8.* 209–10. *213.* 217. **I** *31.* +139. *150.* 151–4. 155 (BxCx; *see TN*). *156–9.* **II** *24.* 49. 50. 51. *53.* 58. *59–62. 64.* +66. 67. 69. 71. *84–7.* 89. 92–4. 96. 97–9. +103. 211 (Bx). **III** *35.* +56. 57–9. *60.* 61–2. *63.* +64. +66. 69. *70–1.* 72. 422. 424. 425. 434. +435. *453.* 454. *459–60.* 461. 465. *467.* 468 (Bx). 469. 472. 474. 476. 477. *478–9.* 481–2. 486. 487–90. 492 (Bx). +494. *495.* **IV** *25. 86.* ++114. +119. *130.* ++148. +151. *160.* 169. *171–2.* 173–4. **V** 138. 152. *153.* 154 (BxCx). *160.* +161. *163–5.* 167. *169.* 170–1. *180. 191.* **VI** +36–7. 43. *55.* +56. *57–8. 69.* ++70–2. *73–4. 77–82. 85–8.* 90. 94. ++95. 97. 103. 125. *128–33.* 134 (Cx). *135.* 152. 153. *154.* 155 (BxCx). 156 (Bx). *157.* 160 (Bx). *161.* 163 (Bx). 164. *165–6.* 168. +178–180. *183.* +184–5. 200. 202. 228. *234–5.* 236. 239. *240–2.* 245. 248–9. *250.* 251. 254. +260–1. *262.* 264–6. 268. 269. *270–2.* 273 (Cx). +274. 275. 276. *277–9.* 280. *281.* 282. *283–4.* 288. *294. 296–7. 339. 341–3.* 343–5. 346–7. 408–9. *411–13.* 425. **VII** *1. 3–4.* 5. *6.* 8. *10.* 11–14. *16.* +17. *18–19.* 24. 26. 28. 30. 31. 32. 35. 36–8. *39–40.* +41. *42.* 43. *44–8.* 54 (Bx Cx). *55.* 69. 71–2. 72. *76–8. 80–2.* 83 (Bx). 84. *85.* 86–7. *88.* 90. *92–7.* +98. *99–103.* 104. *105.* +106. *107–14.* +115. *116.* 120–3. *124.* 125–6. *131–2.* 134. *137.* +138. 139. 141–2. 149. *151–2.* **VIII** *12.* 38. *72.* 73. *192.* +197. *270.* 351. *353.* **IX** *13.* 52. *53.* 54. 171. 310. **X** 14. *15–17.* 61. *62. 66. 74–5. 86.* 104–5. *122. 141.* 142 (Bx). 233. +234. *236.* 237. 257. +258. 286. ++287–8. 305. 308–9. **XI** *14–15.* 21. 51 (Bx). *164–5. 168–9.* +170. 171. *172.* +173. *174–5. 179–86.* 188. +189. *190–97. 205.* 210. +212. +214. ++218 (Cx). 223. 229–32. *239–40.* +245. 249. 252. 258. *281.* 284–5. 296. *308–09.* 312 (Cx). 313–15. **XII** *1.* +3. *7.* 9. *10–14.* 15. 19.*21.* 31. 33–5. *36.* 42–44. 45 (?Bx). *48–59.* 61–5 (63 (Bx)). *67–9. 73.*76. ++77. *82–3.* +86. 87. *91.* 110. *111–12.* 113. *114–16.* 119. 121. *124–5.* 128. +130. *136–9. 143.* +144. *145–9.* 150. *153.* 155–5a. **XIII** 100–05. *107–10.* 111–12. *116–21.* ++122. *124.* 125. 126 (Cx). *127.* 135–41. 142. 143–5. *147.* 149. +150. *156–8. 160.* +161. +162. +163. +166. *173–4. 177–9. 198.* +199. [204–5 French]. +209. 211. *212–13. 214–15.* +221. 222–6. +228. ++229. *235–7. 242–3.* +246. **XIV** *1.* 17. *18.* 44. *46–52.* 53–4. 56. *57–61.* +64. 65–7. +68. *77–86.* +87. 89. *92–6. 98–100.* +101. *103–4.* +105. 106–8. ++109. 110. *111–15.* 116. *117.* 118–19. *120–22.* ++125. *126–28.* 129. *130.* +131. 135–9. +140. 141–2. +144. *145–7.* 148. *149.* 150. *151.* 152. *153.* +154–5. *156.* ++158. *170–1.* +185. *187.* +190. 191. *192.* 194. +195. *196–7.* ++198. *199–200.* 202–7. +208. 209–10. +211. *212–13.* **XV** *1–3.* ++4. *5.* 9. + 10 (Bx). +12. *15–17. 31–2.* +39. *41.* +42. *43–5.* +47. *48–51.* +56. *57–8.* ++64–6. 67. 69. ++83. *84–5.* 88. 90. 93. *96–7.* 99–100. *101–2.* 104 (Bx). 105. *106.* +107. ++108. *110.* +111. *112.* 113. 121–2. +123. *124.* +129. 136. +144. *148–9. 159–60.* ++165–6. +172. *173.* 174. *176. 180–1. 187–90.* +191. *192–3. 203.* 204. *205.* ++206. *207–8.* +209. 210. *226–9.* +230. *231. 239.* +240. 241. *244–5.* +253. *254–5.* 256. *257–8.* ++259–61. *262.* 263. ++265. +266. *267–70.* 272. 273 (Cx). 274. ++282. *283–4. 289.* +290. *291–94.* 295. *298–9. 301.* 302. **XVI** *1–2.* +3. 4. +5. 7. 8. ?9 (*see TN*). 10. *11.* 13–14. 15. +38. *39–52.* 54–5. +56. *57–62.* 64 (Bx). *66–68.* +69. *71–5.* +76. *77.* 80–3. 84. +85. *86–7.* +88–9. ++90. 91. *93. 95–8.* 100–04. +107. +108. *110.* 115. *119. 122.* +123. *124–9. 131–32.* +134. *137–8. 142.* +143. *144–5.* +146. 147–8. *151.* ++154–5. 164. *165–7.* +168. 181. 182–3. +184. *185–90. 193–4. 196–213.* +214. 215–17. 220. +221. 222. +223. ++232. 233. +234. *236.* 237. +241. 244. *245–6.* +247. 250–2. +253. *254.* 257. 260. +261. *262.* 265. ++266. *267.* ++268. *274.*++275. 276. 277. 278. +279. +291. *292. 295. 297–8. 316.* 321–2. 329–30. 332. +334. 337. 341. *344–6. 348–53.* ++354. +355. *356.* +358. 359. *361.* 362.

++363. 370. **XVII** *13*. 14. *17*. +18. +19. *20*. 21. 28. ++55. *56*. ++77. +94. *96*. *100–01*. 102. 104. *105–7*. *109*. +111. *113*. *120–1*. 171. +182. 187. *188*. 189. *192*. *195–6*. 197. *198*. 199. 200. 201. *203–7*. 208 (Bx).+209. 210 (Bx). *211*. *213*. 214. ++215. *216*. 217. *218*. +219. *220–6*. 229. +232. 252. *253*. 254. *255*. +256. 257–9. +260. 262. *263–9*. 270. +271. ++276. *277–8*. 279. *280–2*. 297–9. +300. 302. 305–6. 310. *311*. 315–16. *318–19*. 320. **XVIII** *31*. 33. +34. 35. +36. *37*. 38. +40. *43–4*. *109*. 110. *112–17*. +120. *124–7*. 129. *131–4*. *137*. 155. 161. *164*. 167. 169. *177*. *182–3*. 185. *202* (BxCx; *see TN*). *203–06*. 207. *208–9*. 241. +243. *244*. +252. *253*. 254. 255. +257. +258. +259. *266*. +267. 270. +271. 272. 273. +274. 275. *276–79*. 280–1. *282–3*. +284. 285–6. *287–8*. 289–92. **XIX** *1–2*. 6. *11–16*. *19–22*. 25. +27–8. *29*. +30. *32*. 34. +36. *46*. 47. +49. *50–1*. 52. 56. *57–8*. 59–60. *61–2*. *66*. 67. 68–9. 73. *78*. ++83. 84. *85*. 90. 96. +97. *99*. *112*. +116. *117*. +118. *119*. *121*. *123–5*. *141–4*. +145. 148–9. +150. *153–7*. *162–4*. 165–6. *167*. 168. *169–70*. 171. *172–3*. +175–9. +180. 181–2. *183–6*. 187–9. *190*. *192*. 193. *194–6*. 197. *198–9*. 200. *201–5*. *207–220*. +221. *222–28*. *230*. 232. *233*. 249. 250. +251. *252*. +253. *254–62*. *264–7*. +268. *269–73*. *277–85*. +287. ++288. *291–2*. 293–4. *295–6*.+298. ++299–300. *301–4*. +305. *306*. *308* (Bx). *309–13*.314. *315–18*. *320–31*. 332. *333–4*. **XX** *1*. *3–4*. 5. *6–11*. 12. *13–19*. 21. 22. 23. *25–7*. 28–30. *31–4*. 34. *35–7*. 39 (Bx). *40–4*. 47. +49. 51. 52. 56. *57–60*. 64. *65–7*. 68. *69–70*. 72. 73. +75. 76. 77. *81–3*. +84. *87–9*. *91*. 92. 94 (Cx). *96*. 99. 101. *102*. *104–06*. 108. *113*. 115. *117*. 119. 120. 122 (Bx). *123–9*. 130. *131–3*. 135. *136*. 137. +138. 139. +140. *141–6*. 147. *148–9*. +150. *152–3*. 157 (Bx). *159*. 160. 163. *165–70*. *173*. ++175. *176*. 178. *179–80*. *182–4*. 185. *190–1*. 192. *193–4*. *199–201*. 203. ++204. *205–11*. 214. *219–23*. 225. 226. 227. 228. ++229. *230–4*. 236. *237–40*. 241. *242–7*. 248. *249*. *251–5*. 256. 257. *258–9*. 264. *265–6*. *268–70*. ++273. *274–80*. *295–8*. 299. *300–01*. 302. *313*. 321. *322*. 323. 325. *329*. *330–1*. *335*. 337. 341 (Bx). *342*. +344. *362–3*. 364. *365–6*. +367. 368. 372. *373–5*. *377–8*. 388. +389. +390. *391*. +393. 395–396. *397–8*. 399. 400 (Cx). *401–3*. *408*. 412 (Cx). 413. *414–15*. 417–18. *419*. 421–3. +424. *425*. 426. *427–8*. +429. 430–1. *438*. 439. 441. *443*. 444 (Bx). *445–6*. +447. 448 (Bx). 450. +451. *455–7*. 460–74. 476–8. **Passus XXI–XXII**: *these are assumed identical unless noted otherwise*. **XXI** 12 (BxCx). 21. 39. 43. 56–7 (Bx). 63. 76 (Cx). 90 (BxCx). 97 (Bx). 111. 134. 140. 164. 183 (?Bx). 186 (BxCx). 187. 206. 230 (BxCx). 236, 241 (BxCx). 242. [244b]. [252: *two changes*]. [254: *two changes*]. 256. 272. [281 *first lift*]. 286. 297 (?Bx). 303 (Bx). 305 [*both differently*]. 316 (Bx). 336 (?Bx). 345 (Bx). 347 (BxCx).360. 365. 366 (?Bx). 376 (Cx). 378–9. 384. 389. 402. 403. 408 (BxCx). 411. 413 (Bx). 429. 441 (Bx). 445 (BxCx). 467 (?Bx).482 (?Bx). **XXII** 8 (Bx). 13 (Cx). 14, 19, 34, 54 (Bx). 62. 97. 130. 167. 261 (Bx). 292–3 (BxCx).301 (Cx). 309 [*lift* 4]. 312.338 (Cx). 366 [*both*]. 367 (BxCx). 378 [*both*].

Auxiliary Core-text

§ 13. As noted at § 7, there is an auxiliary body of lines where two or more versions differ in only one lift-phrase, yet cannot be considered even substantively identical since the revision involves a major lexical change. For purely illustrative purposes, some 150 examples are given here from the portion of text (= C Pr–IX 186 //) where all four versions are present. Line-references are to the target version in the order **ZABC**.

(a) Differences occur most commonly in the *fourth lift* of a standard line:

From **Z** → **A**: I 4. 75. 120. 143. II 14 (*removing rhyme*). 121. 187. III 13. 27 (*with change from* Type Ia *to* T-type; *reversed in* **B**: cf. Z III 30). 160. IV 76.98. 120. 149. V 18. 223. 251. VI 53. 58. 82. VII 3. 135 (*changes* Ie *to* T-type). 169. 245. 252. 278. 296.
From **A** → **B**: Pr 37. I 103. III 39. 42. 102. IV 111. 186. V 10. 116. 197. 225. 229. 449. VI 24. VII 122, 124. 134 (Type I *to* T-type). VIII 33. 45. 111. IX 153. X 125. 130, 335 (*metrical change to* T-type). 138. 153. 197. 226. 294. 332. 343. 370. 459.
From **B** → **C**: Pr 130. 133. 165. 171. 174 (*internal rhyme*). 175 (Type Ia → Ib). 189. 218. I 145. 148. II 63. 65. 148. III 475. VII 70 (*by deletion of last lift in a* Type Ic, *giving 'clashed' b-verse*).

They occur much less commonly in the other stave-positions:

(b) in the first lift:

Z → **A**: III 172. VIII 72 (Type IIIa *to* Ia). **B** → **C** Pr 172.

(c) in the second:

Z → **A**: IV 131 (*changing* Ib *to* Id). VIII 62. **A** → **B**: III 41. IV 80. V 216. **B** → **C**: Pr 140. 178. 201. 216. III 76.

(d) in the third lift of an extended line:

A III 167 (← Z III 115) → B III 180.

(e) at the key-stave position in a standard line:

Z → **A**: Pr 51. II 8. 99. III 129. VI 92. VII 184. 259 (*changing* T-type *to* Ia). VIII 68. **A** → **B**: Pr 63. I 8. III 32.

The rare lexical changes in the dips usually occur in the a-verse:

Z → **A**: V 31a. 53a. VII 178a. 181b. 262a. 268a. **A** → **B**: III 299a. IV 71b. VI 169a. VII 167a. **B** → **C**: I 147a.

But identical half-lines are abundantly instanced, the changes being mostly in the b-verse. Significant metrical consequences are noticed:

Z → **A**: Pr 16. 82. II 51. II 137 (*clashing* b-verse *changed to* Type I *with removal of rhyme*). 149 (*changing keystave noun to verb*). III 92. 143. IV 23. V 6. 27. VI 78 (*re-written as* Type IIa). 105. VII 37. 55. 59. 82. 92. 93 (*changes* IIIb *to* IIIa). 103. 155. 166. 168. 194. 282. 304. VIII 22. 32. 86. **A** → **B**: III 36. 98 (Type Ia *to* IIb). 100 (Type I *to* Type IIa). IV 160. VI 28. **B** → **C**: Pr 137. 170. 179. 181. 214–15. I 149. II 88. 103a. IV 35–6.

ii. *Editorial Principles and Procedures*

(a) *The canons of unanimity and conformity*

§ 14. The above completes the corpus of evidence in support of the principle that agreed lines in two or more versions are to be understood as constituting 'what Langland wrote.'[12] The *unanimity principle*, as it has been called, makes only a 'minimal' assertion; for Langland as clearly, if not as surely, wrote in its surviving form much more of the material than just the core-text. But its positive substance (the core-lines are textual 'facts') and its analytic form (it covers all and only these facts) give the core-text the secure empirical character necessary for an edited text that seeks to win wide assent. Moreover, since the principle acknowledges the legitimate claims of the 'positivist' conception of the text, it is a fit starting-point for a work aimed at scholars with very different approaches to editing. Ascertainment of 'unanimity' cannot, of course, be absolute, since the poet did more in revising than simply add, subtract or transpose lines and passages. He altered the text in so massive and detailed a way as to make the successive versions appear (to some readers) more as stages in a process than as finished products. The appearance of 'process' is most striking in **Z** and (to a less extent) in A XII and C Pr 95–124. But while the parallel-text's juxtaposition of closely similar lines highlights *Piers Plowman*'s evolution as a 'life's work' with true spiritual unity, it should not be allowed to obscure how each text embodies a separate and distinct artistic intention. That this claim is not universally accepted of even the one completed version is shown by recent 'provisionalist' studies that question how finished and final the **B** Version is. But whereas these arguments have already, it is hoped, been adequately rebutted (III, *B Version* §§ 52–7), it is not being contended here that **C**, let alone **A** or **Z**, can be satisfactorily read in isolation. What is being urged is the recognition at succesive stages of an implied will to completion, notwithstanding that this 'will' was expressed through acts of (re)composition that produced **A**, **B** and **C**. As the enterprise lasted more than twenty-five years, it generated distinctive material at each stage. The effort to discover what Langland 'intended' at *any* stage therefore demands a firm empirical basis. This, it is argued, only the core-text can provide. For as all accept, the circumstances of copying prompted at *every* stage deliberate scribal intervention in response to the poem's content, form and language. So for nearly 40% of the **ABC** text, correcting transmission-errors involves direct analysis in order to find the archetypal reading that lies behind the extant variants.[13] By way of compensation, an editor can 'control' his analysis in the light of the scribal variation evidenced by reference to almost four times as many lines than the core-text itself contains. The core-text can, in turn, furnish an understanding of the poet's idiom reliable enough to justify emending the archetype when it too is suspected of error. But this 'rational' method of discerning the direction of scribal variation, though a vital editorial procedure, cannot be treated as a canon, even if its central *durior lectio* criterion may aspire to the rigour of a principle. For the irreducibly *a priori* element in this method is clear from the disagreements its particular applications can arouse. But if it is to remain the *primary* procedure, its criteria for judging a reading 'harder' must conform to the data of the core-text.

§ 15. Now 'difficulty', as stated at II § 74 above, can never suffice the editor as a means of discriminating the reading of the archetype among the conflicting sub-archetypal, group or individual variants. This reservation applies *a fortiori* when the archetype is suspected of having corrupted a 'harder' original, and a wholly conjectural emendation is proposed (cf. II § 77). For a criterion that is neither entirely logical nor entirely empirical can obviously never entail emendation. Accordingly, even an editor who relies on the core-text's authority cannot readily allow a procedure that is analytic ('rational') to risk becoming speculative ('radical'). Instead he should try where possible to preserve the reading of the archetype, on account of its 'logically positive' character. This is because 'editorial conservatism' is the only way to safeguard the reader's textual rights. And such conservatism should not be objected to as uncritical, let alone irrational, because the canon of economy that governs it is wholly rational (see § 19). In practice this means that if non-paralleled archetypal readings conform to the core-criteria, it is more logically economical to retain them, unless an overwhelming case for rejecting them can be made. When it is not necessary to emend, it is necessary not to emend;[14] an axiom that demands resistance to the lavish 'correction' of minor archetypal readings of rationalist editors like Kane-Donaldson and Russell-Kane. But conversely, conservatism of this kind does not imply concurrence with positivists of varying stripe like Skeat, Knott-Fowler and Pearsall, who restrict their interventions to choice of the 'best' readings but offer no arguments for believing that these are what the poet wrote. Excessive editorial confidence, whether in one's chosen base-manuscript, literary taste or sense of Langland's *usus scribendi*, tends to frustrate the reader's legitimate expectations from a critical edition. For while even a secure archetypal text is not beyond criticism, it should never be abandoned without misgiving.

§ 16. The second major editorial canon is the *principle of acceptability* of readings that meet the core-text norms. This is arrived at after analysing the unique as well as the common lines in the received versions and **Z**, and it admits few exceptions (see § 18). On its positive side, the canon presumes that unshared lines claiming authenticity will conform to the core-text criteria. Though this is not a logical stipulation, it is a presumption the strength of which will be clear from the extent of the tertiary core-group (f) of **BC** lines and the proportionally large size of both the secondary core-group (a) of **ABC** lines and the tertiary core-group (d) of **AB** lines (see §§ 11 and 12 above). For these groups show that the common lines' main features persisted unchanged from the poem's earliest accepted form, **A**, to its latest, **C**. And since this persistence increases if a primary core-group **ZABC** is provisionally recognised (and **Z** placed first in the group), the presumption of conformity is also favoured by the principle of economy (see § 19 below): i.e. the poet wrote the same types of line from beginning to end of his work on *Piers Plowman*. Now, not impossibly a Langlandian line could breach the core-criteria and still be authentic. As Shakespeare's late plays include lines with more than the ten syllables of his early ones, **C** might have introduced a new metrical type not found in **A** (none in fact appears). But this canon's permissive power is less restricted than its stipulative: for it allows as authentic all unique lines that conform to the core-criteria. If any of these lines were in fact proved inauthentic, it would follow that a scribe who wrote lines exactly like 'Langland' (the poem) would be, from an editorial standpoint, indistinguishable from 'Langland' (the poet). But the *principle of economy* raises the presumption that these lines (with few exceptions) are original, to near-certainty. On its negative side, failing the core-criteria will render such lines correspondingly likely to be corrupt. But as the canon of acceptabilty / conformity remains 'falsifiable' (by discovery of a holograph or externally authenticated text), it qualifies as 'critically empirical'.

§ 17. The acceptability canon is thus foundational for a parallel-text edition. Firstly, although not as analytic as the unanimity principle, it is derivable from the purely rational principle of economy (described below). For it must be more economical to hold that all 'acceptable' lines are likely to be authentic than that some are not. This is not to say that 'acceptable' lines defy scrutiny; but where they have no parallel, an editor should not be in haste to question them. Secondly, the criteria of acceptability envisaged here have been deduced not from an 'idea' of how the poet might have expressed himself (R–K's 'abstractions') but from a body of evidence even more 'logically positive' than that of a single versional archetype, namely the 'core-text'. This protects against the error of insisting that the poet conform at all points to his specific practice at *some* points; the present edition does not aim to be, in the Athlone editors' sense, an 'ideal' text (cf. *K–D* p.213). Further, since the acceptability canon formally authorises rejection of unparalleled lines that fail to observe the core-text norms, it is more fundamental for editing than the *durior lectio* criterion. For that criterion by definition operates rigorously only where there are two or more archetypal readings to compare; whereas a critical edition must both authenticate lines unique to each version and exclude spurious lines and corrupt readings.[15] This second canon, which is for the present editor what the concept of *usus scribendi* is for Kane and his collaborators, is thus stronger and more rigorous than the Athlonean standard. Its permissive power also exceeds that of the canon of unanimity; for it permits rejection even of lines *within* the core-text. At first glance this may appear a logical contradiction, since 'acceptable' lines are precisely those that meet the core-text norms. The paradox may be resolved as follows. Since some kinds of scribal error (especially mechanical ones) are liable to be made repeatedly at the sub-archetypal level, they might even occur in the core-text (as it is here maintained they do). But such cases of repeated archetypal error should be very few in number; and if each apparent exception can be adequately explained, the concept of 'core-text norms' will not be falsified but confirmed (see § 18). Nor is the anticipated objection that 'hard cases make bad law' apposite here, since the guilty party in these cases is not the poet but his scribes. As no lines that conflict with these norms in fact occur in the primary division of the core-text, it will be argued below that the few found in the other divisions do not undermine the theory's general soundness.[16]

§ 18. Now, of the thirteen examples of apparently corrupt core-text lines, the five that demand immediate attention occur in the secondary division.[17] In group **ZAB** are two, both revised in **C**, where a fairly complex process of successive archetypal corruptions must be posited. At Pr 11 // [*me*] *meten*] *I meten*, mechanical error in the form of haplography seems to have played an important contributory part. In the case of IV 91 // a thrice-repeated scribal substitution of *seide* for original *wiþseide has been supposed (though other 'harder' originals could explain the line's breach of the core-text metrical norms). At VI 407 *He thromblede at the thresfold and threw to þe erthe,* where **AB** appear corrupt on the showing of **C**, the Bx reading could have been *trembled*, a different error from the g-group's *stumbled*, or else both could be easier scribal reflexes of an archetypal (and original) *thrumbled*, which is here adopted on the showing of **C** (whence *A*-V has derived its correct reading). At III 225 *weye* **AB** (severally) and at VIII 329 *brewestares* **ZB** (jointly) conflict with **ZC** and **AC** respectively. But while both examples challenge the linear postulate, they do not undermine the validity of the core-text norms, because in all versions the acceptability criterion is satisfied. In III 225 no emendation is made, and there is almost as strong a case for so leaving VIII 329, which *is* tentatively emended, but not without some misgiving (see the *Textual Notes* and cf. § 15). The other eight cases appear in the tertiary division. Group **AB** has at III 260 an instance of presumed haplography (exactly paralleled at C VI 155) and two of specific visual error, at V 111 *liþeþ* (where there is ʒ / þ confusion) and at IX 163 *any* (which seems to show loss of -*y* through attraction to preceding *yong* or following *any*). At VI 281 *and* [*ek*] *an hauer cake*, the line's metrical defectiveness is ascribed to visually-induced loss of a grammatical word functioning as a mute liaisonal stave (K–D's restoration *a cake of otes* from parallel **C** ascribes the error to lexical substitution). At X 108 *bigiled*, a verb widely instanced in the text, is diagnosed as having ousted a less common variant-form *biwiled*. In group **BC** at I 155 the lexically easier *bitwene* is understood to have supplanted the rare preposition *inmiddes*. Finally, haplography is taken to account for the unanimity of the archetypes' faulty metre at VI 155 *faste* [*faste*] for *faste* and at VII 54 (*for* substituted for *be*).[18] The total of lines to be ascribed to convergent substitutions amounts to a mere 0·3% of the whole. So it does not seem excessive to claim that, since the validity of the core-criteria is unchallenged over 4140 lines, their general applicability for the remaining four-fifths is massively endorsed.

(b) *The principle of economy*

§ 19. The third editorial principle (mentioned at § 16 above), which is also foundational, is in theory conceptually prior; and it is not peculiar to works in several versions, but equally relevant for editing any text. The principle of *simplicity or economy* insists on employing the fewest assumptions that will adequately explain the available data. Obviously, the 'simplest' account of a textual tradition may not be the historically true one; for if some necessary evidence is unavailable, what is explained 'adequately' may be less significant than lost material that could be reasonably postulated.[19] Further, the possibility of a conflict between 'historical' and 'analytical' approaches may well prompt the wider question: whether to edit 'critically' means to deduce the original text from the evidence of the surviving witnesses or to reconstruct from bibliographical history the stages of its generation and corruption. These alternatives are somewhat artificial, however; for to avoid fancifulness, the analytical critic must know how medieval texts were written, reproduced and disseminated, and to escape triviality, the historical bibliographer needs to understand what a literary text is. The issue is too large to explore in detail here, but one negative proposition needs emphasis at this point. This is that the antecedent probability on which historical reasoning is based cannot achieve the certainty required by an editorial principle: it is thus unarguably more 'economical' to stick to the data and refrain wherever possible from speculation.[20] However, editing still remains at bottom a 'discipline' without self-evident first principles. For while it may aim to be empirical, to the extent that it is 'critical' it is also 'hypothetico-deductive'; so it cannot operate without some (indemonstrable) assumptions. And when account is taken of its lexical and contextual aspects, which are not successive steps in an experiment but interwoven threads in a fabric of interpretation, editing Langland properly cannot seek to be other than 'historically' informed throughout. The reader is invited to discover from the *Textual Notes* and *Commentary* how successfully this edition has balanced the historical and the analytical in establishing the text and interpreting its meaning.

§ 20. The key importance of the canon of economy emerges nowhere more vividly than in relation to one major textual issue that divides the Athlone editors from the present editor. Though it may seem phantasmal to the 'strict' positivist dealing non-critically with facts rather than explanations, it should engage the attention of rationalist and empiricist alike. The issue concerns the true authority of readings that appear, without other-version support, in individual copies or in the postulated source of an established genetic pair: readings found by 'direct' analysis superior to those of the archetype, but judged too good to be scribal conjectures. The most notable of these is C XVII 116, which is omitted from all copies except the RM group of family **p**:[21]

> Bote they fayle in philosophie - and philosoferes lyuede
> *And wolde wel examene hem - wonder me thynketh!*

The 'eclectic positivist' editors[22] of **C** happily include it; but Skeat, referring to parallel B XV 376 [382], observes only that his other collated copies 'leave the sentence incomplete' (*SkC*, note), while Pearsall asserts (incorrectly) that it is 'supplied from P'. If this line is considered non-archetypal yet essential, it could be explained as a correction from a 'superior lost **C** manuscript', though only at the cost of breaching the canon of economy. The present edition also admits XVII 116, on grounds of sense, but supports it only with a genealogical argument. This argument is not 'simple' in itself but is conceptually more economical than recourse to a second explanatory assumption; and by tacitly acknowledging a complex 'historical' situation behind the reading, it invites scrutiny of its 'analytic' claim in the light of the textual situation as a whole.[23]

§ 21. This particular case is one where the Athlone editors do not invoke a hypothetical lost source, because they omit the line without comment and leave the reader to conclude (as presumably they do) that the sentence at issue is not 'incomplete.' But they do hypothesise such sources for 'good corrections' in the **B** manuscript F[24] and the **C** manuscript N²[25]. And since in both sets of instances their interpretations have been rejected, the situation again raises the spectre of a conflict between 'historical' and 'analytical' understandings of the nature and origin of some important readings. Now the present editor has earlier countenanced what appears to be a hypothetical 'lost source' in the form of **C**'s revision copy (B¹), as well as a primary scribal **B** manuscript ('B-Ø') prior to both this and to Bx (III, *B Version*, § 2 above). But it needs to be stressed that 'B-Ø' has not been postulated as an antecedently probable cause of the agreements between Bx and B¹; it has been inferred as the logically necessary reason for those agreements. Thus, to affirm the existence of B-Ø as the source of Bx and B¹ while denying that it is the immediate or proximate correction-source of F is only to underline the axiom that simple deduction is always preferable to complex speculation. For while the cited analyses of certain superior F and N² readings suggest intelligent guesswork in the case of N²'s five instances, they demonstrate contamination in the case of F. Moreover, as both of these scribal phenomena are abundantly instanced in the **ABC** traditions, there is no call for a further editorial assumption (like the supplementary Ptolemaic epicycles) to explain the aberrant orbits of 'rogue' manuscripts. This may seem much ado, if not quite about nothing, then about textual trifles light as air; yet there is more at stake here than a theoretical point. For what the Athlone editors hypothesise is unnecessary entities to account for readings that they prefer on intrinsic grounds. But a more economic explanation is at hand; for analysis shows that F borrowed from an A-text and that N^2, besides making some felicitous conjectures, drew on a B-text, and one identifiably of β type. These instances undeniably confirm the value of the 'direct method' in discerning the superior originality of some of these readings; but the method falls short of explaining the origin of either set. It remains an indispensable 'critical' procedure; and its subjective element is virtually eliminated by 'historical' appeal to other-version contamination as explanation for the 'superior' readings in these two witnesses.

(c) *The linear postulate and the canon of ratification*

§ 22. As should now be clear, the economy principle underlies the canon of conformity / acceptability, making agreement with the norms generated by the unanimity principle the formally sufficient and virtually necessary criterion of authenticity. One special feature of its application that differentiates the present from the Athlone text is that the latter's editors often prefer the reading of an earlier versional archetype (**A** for **B**, or **B** for **C**) to a later one that they believe corrupt. They sometimes even adopt the minority reading in a later version if it agrees with the archetypal text of an earlier one that they consider superior. This edition agrees with theirs in sometimes choosing for **B** an **A** reading confirmed by **C** (assuming always that the core-text norms are satisfied). But such emendations are authorised primarily by the linear postulate and only secondarily by the *durior lectio* criterion. In this way the principles of economy and acceptability are both preserved; for though a lost **B** original *is* hypothesised to account for the readings preferred, only one reading is assumed for **A**, **B** and **C**. And since in these cases Bx is rejected only when it fails to conform to the core-text norms, neither the linear postulate as confirmed by the **AC** agreement nor the intrinsic 'hardness' of the adopted reading is being treated as sufficient justification for that decision. By the same token, no Bx reading that meets the core-criteria is set aside for an apparently superior **A** reading. This is because the same postulate that presumes **B** unrevised when **A** and **C** agree presumes it revised when **B** differs from **A** but **A** is not confirmed by **C**. And that conclusion obviously holds *a fortiori* when **B** is confirmed by **C**. For though the 'methodological rule' here called the 'linear postulate' cannot qualify (any more than the *durior lectio* criterion) as a 'principle', its congruence with the canon of economy allows the deduction of a third rule that does possess the stipulative and permissive force of a principle. This is the *canon of ratification*, which affirms that all readings retained by a subsequent version are implicitly ratified by it. Such readings may therefore be rejected as unoriginal only if they breach the core-text criteria. And this, analysis shows, is something that they never do.

iii. *Specification of the core-text criteria*

(a) *Linguistic and stylistic aspects*

§ 23. These criteria it is obviously desirable to specify as fully as possible, just as the Athlone editors describe their notion of Langland's *usus scribendi* on the basis of their total experience of editing the text. But how convincingly this can be done for a poem composed over at least as many years as Shakespeare's entire *oeuvre* is debatable. For there must exist an antecedent likelihood of some stylistic change between **A** and **C** (as is indeed borne out by examination of each version's distinctive material). It is therefore necessary to recall that 'core-text' norms derive by definition from the common features, those that remained constant. But the conformity canon does not so much stipulate all authentic features of each version as proclaim authentic only those features common to two or more versions. The details of how it does may be found by referring to the earlier discussions of such features in **Z** and in Passus XII of **A** (III, *Z Version* §§ 20–2; *A Version* §§ 69–71). In the present editor's judgement, the most secure aspect of any 'specification' is the versification. And the **ABC** core-text amply furnishes metrical criteria for assaying the originality of lines that lack other-version support, including those in **Z**. Lexical, syntactic and stylistic norms admit of less precision. And while appeal to the *durior lectio* helps to sharpen certainty, opinions can differ sharply as to what constitutes a 'harder reading'.[26] Consequently that criterion, even when guided by the core-text norms, cannot rule out the possibility that an 'easier' reading may come from the revising author and not a scribe. This caveat does not imply an automatic reluctance to accept non-archetypal harder readings. But regard for the economy principle as expressed in the acceptability canon dictates great caution when preferring them.

§ 24. It will be no surprise, therefore, that while the present edition sometimes emends, it remains in general much closer than the Athlone to the preserved or reconstructed archetypal forms of each version. This is because to establish the archetype from conflicting variants is not a purely analytical matter of applying the *durior lectio* criterion; for if the acceptability and economy principles are followed, it is to a significant extent an empirical matter. That is, it gives due weight to the genealogical implications even of non-straightforward variants. But to emend a preserved or reconstructed archetype, even by 'low-level' restoration of **B** from **AC**, must increase the subjective element, inasmuch as the linear postulate itself rests on an *a priori* assumption. For any rejection of an archetypal reading must occur along a continuum of relative *un*certainty. Every restoration, however well founded, qualifies the authority of the final text; every reconstruction, however prudent, lessens it; every conjecture, however brilliant, weakens it. This said, even an editor who prefers positive data to imaginative hypotheses, and demonstration to persuasion, will (if he also feels a dual obligation to his poet and readers alike) with difficulty avoid occasional resort to both. A 'definitive edition' of Langland, however desirable, therefore remains unattainable. And on that sober note, this account of editorial principles and procedure may conclude by summing up the main aim of the present work in a single word: economy. This amounts in practice to printing the recoverable archetypal texts of each version with the minimum of necessary emendation. And it has meant steering a course between the positivist rock and the rationalist gulf, keeping both ears open to the siren-song of the 'ideal text', but remaining bound by the core-lines' four-ply cable.

Minor readings

§ 25. The area of the text where for the most part the archetypal form has been retained without much difficulty, even where some divergent witnesses find support in one or more other versions, is that of minor readings. Here study of the entire tradition leads the present editor to reject the Athlone view of scribal and authorial characteristics as distinct enough to enable confident recognition of one minor reading as easier or harder than another. For as comparison with a text of comparable length such as Chaucer's *Troilus* readily brings out, the flexibility of word-order and word-choice allowed by the unrhymed alliterative long-line tempted scribes to far greater verbal liberties than when they copied rhyming stanzas made up of lines with fixed syllabic length. And that even apparently problematic cases can be dealt with satisfactorily if the canons of economy and acceptability are observed may be illustrated from an example of syntax relating to the juxta-position of clauses without any co-ordinating conjunction at C I 161–2 //:

> And þat falleth to þe fader þat formede vs alle,
> Lokede on vs with loue and let his sone deye.

Since all four versions here have no *And* before *Lokede*, the 'primary core-text' consensus points to this less common (and so 'harder') asyndetic usage as probably authorial. **Z**'s further omission of *and* before *let,* in therefore conforming with the strongest core-text criteria, will both count as acceptable and may even seem (relatively) 'harder' than the **ABC-p** reading *and let*. But it does not follow that the zero-form *let* in the **x** tradition of **C** must therefore be preferred to *and let* in **p**. For while it is undecidable which sub-archetypal variant preserves Cx, the **AB** support for **p**'s similarly acceptable if (relatively) 'easier' reading allows that **C** might here have been unrevised. This example is called minor because it does not affect sense, metre or style. But if, as is simplest to suppose, **p** preserves Cx and Cx the original, then **C**'s non-revision may be taken to ratify the archetypal reading *and let* in **A** and **B**. The linear postulate, because it deals in probability and not certainty, cannot by itself prove non-revision; but the economy principle it too embodies will in such instances favour it.

§ 26. At I 182, an example involving grammatical number, the Athlone editors prefer the singular *dede* as harder than the plural:

> And as ded as a dorenayl but yf þe dedes folowe:
> *Fides sine operibus mortua est.*

Here the textual evidence is divided across the traditions, with *dede* supported by *C*-**p**, *B*-G and *A*-**r**, *dedes* by *C*-**x**, Bx, *A*-**m** and **Z**. But while the plural may be preferred as closer to the Latin, the direction of variation cannot be convincingly demonstrated. The only basis for decision is therefore the weight of the genetic evidence: two archetypes and two sub-archetypes against two sub-archetypes and a contaminated individual copy, G. This clear situation contrasts with the less clear one of almost exact archetypal equipollence at II 223 *And byschytten hym in here* shoppes (Ax?Cx against **Z**?Bx), where there would arguably be a case for keeping the archetype in **ZAC** but adopting the base-manuscript's reading (supported by F) for **B** on the grounds that Bx is uncertain. However, in the comparable *weddyng(es)* at II 118 (Bx**Z** pl. against ?AxCx sg.), it would seem better to accept the lack of linear uniformity. For here the sub-archetypal readings of Ax are ambiguous, **m**'s substantive error perhaps concealing an Ax plural, whereas **C**, which revises the entire line, determines the number by using the indefinite article. On a surface exami-nation, this case seems to suggest a paradoxical conflict between two arguments both supported by the economy principle: one in favour of adopting *weddyng* in all four versions, the other of keeping the discernible archetypal form in each. But a deeper analysis reveals that in minor read-ings of this type it is not possible to distinguish decisively between the authorial and the scribal. The more economical course is therefore to prefer the archetype, because this makes it unneces-sary to emend **Z** and adopt a minority (GC^2) reading for **B**, while the difference of sense, though not trivial, is still minor. A parallel case where superficially it seems that the direct method *can* distinguish originality between competing minor readings is *Here myhtow se* ensaumples *in hym-*

self one at I 167, in which *C*-**x**?Bx**Z**A-**r** stand against *C*-**p**A-**m**. But on closer study this instance proves not to be a minor reading at all, as it involves a significant difference of meaning (see the *Textual Notes*). What the two previous sub-archetypal conflicts nevertheless indicate is that, since scribes apparently substituted a singular for no discernible reason, they might well have done the same in similar cases elsewhere. It is not being assumed, of course, that the major / minor distinction invoked here is always a hard and fast one, and there are borderline cases. Yet even where doubt exists, if the principle of economy is observed in relation to minor variants, it has been found to support the archetypal reading against that of a group or an individual copy.[27]

Major readings

§ 27. Matters are quite otherwise with respect to indisputably major readings, where the direct method plays a much more important part. At the lower end of significance, where only a metrical aspect is affected, is C VII 170: *'Fro Sinoye', he sayde, 'and fro þe* sepulcre' in which *of Oure Lord* is added at the line-end by **Z**, archetypal **B**, the **x** family of **C** and the **A** copies A, H[3] and K. Here the rejected variant is not in conflict with the core-text's metrical norms. But it is judged 'easier' because it is (and here very obviously) more 'explicit'; and the one judged harder has a b-verse with a double lift in a single word (*sepúlcre*) exemplifying a rare 'monolexical' stress-pattern confirmed as 'Langlandian' by the core-text.[28] What gives the *durior lectio* criterion its power here is that one of the two variants is so much more compressed, elliptical and metrically idiosyncratic that it can reasonably be claimed as the source of the other. In theory, *of oure lord* could have been removed in **A** and so, on grounds of intrinsic acceptability, should be kept for **Z** (as it is in the present text). But though the **C** traditions again divide, the **p** variant may here be defended as likelier to represent Cx, in part because the resultant agreement of **AC** will make it easier to interpret Bx and **x** as 'explicitation-glosses'.[29] In this instance the linear postulate is logically not strong enough to decide the outcome, since if AH[3]K preserved Ax, and **x** preserved Cx, then **AC** agreement would support the *rejected* reading. So here the *durior lectio* criterion acts valuably as a *schoriare to schuyuen hit vp*, and the decision is reached mainly by 'rational' analysis.

§ 28. In the case of major readings, most particular textual situations display special features; but leaving these out of account, it is possible to generalise the issue roughly as follows. In the contested variants of a major reading the (non-metrical) features that may be described as 'harder' or 'easier' include its style, lexis, meaning or syntax. Thus a word may be uncommon, or its local sense unusual, or the patterning of the entire phrase unexpected. These are not, of course, the sole areas in which scribal substitutions are found to occur, though they are the most typical; and more could be said about how the 'difficulty' of variants is to be assessed. But it must be recognised at the same time that, while major errors are antecedently unlikely to be unconscious, there may be factors to consider distinct from the lexico-syntactic character of the reading, for example censorship. What the example in § 27 does not imply is that a sub-archetypal *durior lectio* within one version should be always adopted when its rejected competitor forms the secure archetypal reading in another. For an archetypal reading is in effect the 'logical' *residue and remenaunt* of the 'positive' text. The same caution is therefore needed when it is rejected for a superior other-version reading as when no parallel exists and choice is between two sub-archetypal variants in a single version. For if, as seems likely, scribes who copied *Piers Plowman* could have half-consciously picked up features of Langland's idiom (something easily overlooked by a rationalist editor), discriminating originality becomes a delicate, even a hazardous business. So much seems evident from C Pr 216 *For hadde ȝe ratones ȝoure* reik *ȝe couthe nat reule ȝowseluen,* a classic case where a truly circumspect editor would probably not favour group b's minority variant *reik* against the majority (and potentially archetypal) reading *reed.* The main justification for preferring *reik* is that in this case **C**'s changing **B**'s source-line from the rarer Type IIIa to the normative Type Ia (as scribes like the *B-F* redactor frequently did) is identifiable not as a scribe's but as the author's choice of a second full stave, insasmuch as its sense closely answers to archetypal *wille* in **B**. On balance (and the *Textual Notes* spell out how fine the balance is), the lexically harder *reik* may be adopted for **C**. But while the semantic equivalence noted allows the possibility that **B** also read *reik*, this cannot justify emending Bx to accord with the critical reading of **C**. In doing so, therefore, K–D elevate the *durior lectio* criterion over the canons of economy and acceptability, which forbid unnecessary emendation. And that the emendation is unnecessary is shown by the fact that the core-text evidence authenticates the scansion pattern *ax / ax,* which the Athlone editors (mistakenly believing it scribal) use as metrical grounds for 'correcting' the archetypal text of **B**.

§ 29. The admonition against adopting *reik* for **B** may nonetheless appear at odds with the resolution of the crux at A I 110 as *And was þe louelokest of* [*l*]*iȝt aftir Oure Lord seluen,* where **Z** is used to emend Ax and the line in its **Z** form subsequently adopted into **B**, which omits it. The detailed rationale of this complex reconstruction is given in the *Textual Notes,* but it will be worthwhile here to draw out some of its wider implications. To the Athlone editors, who first adopted the [*l*]*iȝt* emendation (*Ka²,* p. 462; *K–D,* p. 205n), **Z**'s reading would have to be a happy scribal guess by an otherwise aberrant **A** witness, or else a correction from some 'lost **A** source superior to Ax'[30] (though, as already noted at I § 64, in overlooking **Z** they necessarily forgo both possibilities and emend by straight conjecture). The theoretical question is this: if retention of *siȝt* would yield a passable Type III line, how can the emendation *liȝt* be justified both in **A** and in the line as then restored in **B**? For the same principle of economy invoked against adopting *reik* for the text of B Pr 201 argues against emending Ax here. If Ax's form is acceptable, the unemended line should also (by the linear postulate) be preferred in the reconstructed **B**, on the supposition that it is likelier to have been retained in **B** than revised back to the form of **Z** ('When it is not necessary to emend, it is necessary not to emend'). In defence of the decision, *liȝt* has been judged 'superior' to *siȝt* in part as lexically harder but in part on 'positive' grounds; for the rejected Ax reading can be shown with near-certainty to be a visual error. But this makes its emendation from **Z** less a conjecture or a reconstruction than a 'restoration'. And this, being the class of correction that makes fewest assumptions about what cannot be proven, is least vulnerable to positivist objections. On a less superficial scrutiny, the 'rationalist' emendation can be claimed not to breach the 'positivist' principle of economy but to endorse it. For the emended line, now identical in all three versions, both explains the rejected form of Ax and fills the undoubted sense-gap in Bx. The example thus differs from that of C Pr 216 more than resembling it. For as the latter shows no mechanical reason why *reik* should have been supplanted, it must be less economical to read *reik* in **B**, when the rationale for rejection of Bx *wille* is largely (and mistakenly) metrical. But in **C**, as stated above, the main reason for preferring *reik* to *reed* is that its sense corresponds more closely to *wille.* Far from proving *wille* a non-alliterating scribal substitution for the same original, *reik* may simply illustrate **C**'s (well-documented) tendency to normalise the 'metrically harder' Type III lines of **B**.

§ 30. In the above cases it has been argued that the subjective element in the 'direct' approach to editing can be to a great extent controlled by appeal to self-consistent 'methodological rules'. But it must be conceded that an editorial 'reason' more closely approximates the soft-edged *ratio decidendi* of the law-court than the hard-edged conclusiveness of the laboratory. A case in point involves the word *hardere* itself, which has been preferred to archetypal *auarouser* in B I 191 *Are non* hardere *þan hij whan* [*hij*] *ben auaunced.* As the textual evidence here is both the agreed **ZA** reading and **C**'s revised *Aren none* hardore *ne hungriore then men of Holy Churche,* the grounds for decision will be partly antecedent (the linear postulate) and partly analytic (the canon of ratification). However, the rejected Bx reading *auarouser* cannot be deemed intrinsically unacceptable and, if annominative wordplay on *auaunced* is discerned, may even merit adoption. Likewise, its echo in C 187 Auerous *and euel-willed whan hy ben auansed,* which completes the line's re-writing, could imply not that *hardere* stood in original **B** but that the **C** Version is a new synthesis of **B** and **A** incorporating both words. As **C** would thus in part be confirming the reading while revising it, to reject *auarouser* as an over-explicit substitution by B-Ø's scribe would require a complicated explanation defying both the canon of ratification and the principle of economy. These 'positive' objections to the reconstruction adopted need answering, since any single abandonment of editorial principles requires defence, especially where the reading has a representative character (as this one has). What is relied on here to provide an answer is, it must be granted, not pure logic, but something analogous to the accumulated practical wisdom of the experienced judge: a broader (if less formulable) contextual understanding of Langland's probable train of thought that would justify challenging the credibility of the Bx witness. Thus in **ZAC** the speaker connects 'hardness' with the sin of *pride*, since it is clerks promoted to higher-paid posts who are being said to resist calls on their generosity. But this point is more telling if mention of *greed* (meaning both *coueitise* 'desire to get' and *auarice* 'desire to keep') is deferred until the metaphorical lines B I 196–7 //:

> Thei ben acombred wiþ coueitise, þei konne noȝt out crepe,
> So harde haþ auarice yhasped hem togideres.

If this argument from 'antecedent poetic probability' is reinforced by recalling the oral dimension postulated for the earliest text **Z** (*Z Version*, §§ 8–9 above), the more narrowly logical counter-case (which must be very carefully weighed) may be judged weaker than the one that is less formally rigorous. It should, however, be acknowledged that **C** abandons the 'deferral' noted and, like Bx, names the clerics' greed straight after declaring their want of charity. The matter, as said in the last paragraph, can be very uncertain; and so complete consistency, not to say 'definitiveness' (§ 24), is in such complex cases well nigh unattainable.

§ 31. In the last example, the archetypal reading at B I 191 was concluded to be scribal on the showing of agreed **ZA**, despite its echo in the two-line form of **C**. In another type of case, as at II 95 (= B II 91) *In* woldes *and in weschynges and with ydel thouhtes,* there is no **ZA** evidence to hand. Here the **C** reading is thus not a clear (if ambiguously interpretable) reflex of **B**. Instead, both archetypes must be determined on the basis of three substantive sub-archetypal variants, of which *wedes*] *woldes* appears in both traditions (in *B*-β and in *C*-**p**). On the one hand, the principle of economy as embodied in the canon of ratification would recommend *wedes*, which also satisfies the canon of conformity. But direct analysis identifies as harder *C*-**x** *woldes* which, though not identical with *B*-α *wenynges* (in K–D's attractive reconstruction, **wenes*), is close to it in sense. What the recurrence of *wedes* reveals is that scribes in both traditions sometimes responded to readings that they found difficult by means of convergent substitutions for what were discrete originals. As is brought out in the *Textual Notes*, the α reading of which revised **C** appears a reflex is (as in the similar case of *reik] wille* at § 28) lexically harder than that of the β family. So here, though the contention is less straightforward than if it were between two agreed sub-archetypal variants from each version, the plea of *durior lectio* will perforce carry great weight.

§ 32. Any notion, however, that a reading's 'hardness' can pass beyond the 'suasive' to the 'demonstrative' needs further elaboration. For it is not enough for a *lectio* that is *durior* in one of the ways described at § 28 to provide the best available reading in the context. It should also account for the other variants and, if possible, be supported by the linear postulate or the canon of ratification, or both. An example where a reading that may be lexically the hardest does *not* satisfy these other requirements is at A X 136 *Boþe maidenis and* martires*, monkis and ancris*. Here *r¹* reads *nonnes* for *martires* but the dissident t copy Ch has *mynchons*, which expresses *r¹*'s sense but produces a normatively alliterating line (and is, partly for that reason, adopted by Kane). However, to see *mynchons* as archetypal requires presuming, first, that *nonnes* was coincidentally substituted for it by the ancestors of TH², D and u, and a collocatively commoner stave-word *martires* substituted by both *r²* and **m**; second, that Langland used an *r²***m** revision-copy of **A** and allowed this corruption to stand in **B**. Now, the presence of *martires* in B¹ and perhaps also in B-Ø (like that of *auarouser* in Bx at B I 191) is suggested by its reflex in C X 206b *confessours and martres*; but by contrast with the B I 191 case (§ 30 above), there is here no semantic or other ground for objection to *martires*. By the canons of acceptability and ratification it should therefore be retained in both **A** and **B**. What this example indicates is that even so powerful a critical procedure as the *durior lectio* must be a less dependable resource than a basic principle. Serious methodological difficulties can thus arise from over-reliance on it. Firstly, Kane's complicated explanation of the textual evidence fails to satisfy the principle of economy. Secondly, Kane-Donaldson's retention of *martres* in **B** contradicts Kane's decision for **A**. Thirdly, there arises in consequence Kane's awkward notion that the poet's 'passing over' of scribal errors in his revision copy lends 'a kind of sanction' to **A** readings that he identifies as corrupt on intrinsic grounds (*Ka²*, p. 463). But if *martres* is read in both **A** and **B**, the canon of ratification can be followed and the principle of economy preserved.

§ 33. Kane's discussion of the other Ch readings he adopts (pp. 161–2) highlights what may be singled out as the central weakness of the 'Athlone' method. The reading *mynchons*, Kane holds, is harder than the alternatives, so can only be rejected outright if it is judged a 'brilliant scribal emendation'. And doing this 'seems to make nonsense of the basis of textual criticism by assuming a scribe capable of improving on the poet's work'. But Kane's assertion that the lexically harder reading is an improvement is open to question. For if, as he claims, *martires* could have been scribally substituted 'because of the suggestion of the common phrase of liturgy and ecclesiastical calendar', it could no less have been what the poet wrote, since it is contextually appropriate and conforms with the core-text criteria. Further, whereas martyrs *are* thematically important in Langland, nuns are not; *martires* offers a second distinct category, whereas *mynchons* comes close to repeating *maidenis*; and the unusual *mynchons* appears nowhere else in the corpus. Secondly, it is no less questionable that 'brilliant scribal emendations' are virtually impossible; for the Athlone editors themselves helpfully demonstrate that they occur. One such emendation that they adopt in place of the archetypal reading is *tripe* from manuscript F (CUL

Ff. 5. 35) at C IX 262 *The tarre is vntydy þat to þe* shep *bylongeth*. Here, though R–K (p. 164) recognise that Cx's key-stave could be *to*, they judge it unlikely that the relatively uncommon *tripe* 'small flock' would have been put in place of *shep*. The word is rare (see MED s.v. *trippe* n. 2), but this might not be sufficient reason why an enterprising scribe could not have substituted it. For that such things occurred is shown by the example of C VII 106 *And fithele the, withoute flaterynge, of God Friday þe geste*. Here Cx reads the inappropriate *feste* but F has *geste*; and if *geste* is not a 'brilliant scribal emendation' (prompted in part by recalling **B**'s contextually apt synonym *storye*), it can only be a 'correction from a superior lost MS', an explanation that (as always) violates the canon of economy. However, in VII 106, by contrast with *shep* at IX 262, the archetypal **C** reading fails of originality by the criterion of sense, and should be emended to the F scribe's reading on the grounds that the latter cannot be bettered by any editorial conjecture.[31] But if *geste* is not derived from a superior lost **C** copy and could be a 'brilliant scribal emendation', so might *tripe* (though the requirement of sense will not compel its adoption). Kane's third suspect claim is that the *durior lectio* criterion forms 'the basis of textual criticism' and that the notion of a scribal variant being other than 'easier' would make 'nonsense' of it. But the foregoing analysis has shown this conclusion to be mistaken. For the criterion of the harder reading is not a basic principle; however valuable, it is only a procedure (§ 21). And as examples like this must indicate to its most hardened advocates, it is a procedure that is by no means universally applicable.

§ 34. Kane is of course right to contend all the same that 'the editor must at the outset allow the possibility of originality to these readings' (p. 162). But it is one thing to take theoretical cognisance of possibly authoritative manuscript corrections 'at the outset', and quite another to reject archetypal readings that are confirmed by a later version. The Athlone editors regularly confuse the possible with the probable, because they do not appreciate the force of the canon of ratification (they appear wholly innocent of that concept as elaborated at § 22). Now *martires* is an example where both **B** and **C** confirm the majority and probably archetypal reading of **A**, whereas in the case of *shep* there is no comparative material because the line is unique to **C**. But there is massive evidence in the core-text to show that Langland used *to* and similar grammatical words as mute key-staves (see § 47 below), an idiosyncratic practice that might be overlooked by a scribe who formed his notion of 'correct' metre on more conventional alliterative writers. In the case of VII 106, by contrast, which has a parallel in **B**, F's *geste* is just what an editor might propose for **C** on the basis of the form of Cx *feste* and the sense of Bx *storye*. Further favouring such a 'conjectural restoration'[32] is the fact that *geste*, unlike *mynchons* or *tripe*, is a word instanced in the **BC** core-text (at XI 21 and XV 200) in the sense required of '(sacred) narrative'. The contextual suitability that licenses emendation of Cx *feste* is thus supported by antecedent lexical probability, since *geste* demonstrably figured in the poet's word-stock.

§ 35. Now in fairness to the Athlone editors whose methods and conclusions have been criticised, the present editor must confess to rejecting the very same small-word stave as R–K at C IX 262 in favour of a comparable 'conjectural restoration' at A VI 79. In *The tour þere Treupe is hymself* [*tyliþ*] *vp to þe sonne*, Ax reads *is vp to* for *tyliþ vp to* and, by core-text metrical criteria, scans 'acceptably' on *to*. The crux of the argument for nonetheless emending is that (in contrast with C IX 262) *to* is here unlikely to be the intended stave-word. For in its one other appearance elsewhere as a 'full' stave, it is in a context where the repetition of two discrete homophones has a clear rhetorical purpose, pointed up by the emphatic paronomasia. This is B XVI 148 *The whiche tokne* to *þis day* to *muche is yvsed*, where the first *to* is the preposition of A VI 79 and C IX 262 but the second is the comparative adverb, and the line's characteristic wordplay is enhanced by the homophone's prior occurrence as the first syllable of to*kne*. In A VI 79 there is no such contextual justification for particular stress on the particle, so a full-stave *to* in the b-half would be pointless as well as clumsy. The basis of the 'conjectural restoration' offered is the parallel Z VI 66, and it is here contended that A VI 79 read likewise and the Ax scribe (not the poet) substituted *is* for a verb that was lexically unfamiliar. This example well illustrates what may be called the 'normal' processes of corruption; and its emendation presumes *tyleth* antecedently unlikely to be a scribal substitution for *is* (though the striking examples discussed above have vividly shown that such a possibility existed). There is, therefore, justification for the apprehensions of Kane, or of any editor who resorts to the direct method. If a scribe could make such a 'brilliant emendation' as *tyleth*, the entire *durior lectio* criterion might be at risk of becoming as threadbare as Coveitise's cloak and leaving barely enough room for the louse-leap of a conjecture. But by way of answer: while *tyleth* superficially resembles *mynchons* and *tripe*, two important features distinguish **Z**'s reading here from those examples. First, like *geste* earlier, *tyleth* has a parallel, at C VI 220 // AB *Til ten ȝerde other twelue* tol[led] *out threttene*, where the *C*-**p** spelling *tilled* for *tolled* should be especially noted. Second, it yields a reading both semantically and metrically stronger than that of Ax. Either feature by itself might be inconclusive; but together they point to **Z**'s originality and furnish a defensible rationale for emendation of **A**. What should be remembered in these situations is that the linear postulate has both a retrospective and a prospective dimension. It presumes either that a revision will not reinstate the version before the one being revised, or that if a later reading judged inferior to its predecessor is not ratified by its successor, revision cannot be assumed to have occurred.

§ 36. A theoretical objection to this argument arises that must now be answered, and it is as follows. If the linear postulate measures not certainty but only probability, however high (§ 25), it must admit exceptions. Langland might therefore have been prepared, for the sake of intelligibility, to adopt the poetically lame *is vp to* in place of the lexically obscure *tyleth*. But this possibility clashes with the antecedent probability that the purpose of revision was to improve what he had written. Thus it has been the common critical view of the changes from **A** to **B** that, though Langland (for structural or thematic reasons) omitted some passages of high quality, his direct rewriting yielded poetry that is both more profound and more precise. Cases of (perhaps regrettable) omission might include A X 118–30 and Z V 35–40,[33] examples of successful revision, the development of *plante of pes* at A I 137a into B I 152–8. But *Piers Plowman* studies have laboured under the mistaken belief (induced by Skeat's edition though largely lifted by Salter's and Pearsall's pioneering work)[34] that **C** is often poetically inferior to **B**, because it privileges the religious message over the artistic medium. It is of course arguable that not all **C**'s detailed changes are improvements, as in the case of *yȝoten hitsilue* at C I 149 compared with (*y*)*eten his fille* at B I 154.[35] But the experience of parallel-editing has brought it forcibly home to the present editor how generally **C** improves on **B** in depth of thought, exactness of language and clarity of expression as much as **B** surpasses **A** in richness of imagery, complexity of style and variety of tone. There is little sign of poetic decline up to the very last point where major alterations are detectable (C Passus XX). Such a judgement will, it is hoped, become widely accepted in time as a result of reading this critical text of all four versions in parallel. It is stated here mainly to underline that an antecedent expectation of progressive improvement is borne out by the evidence, and assists the editor in discriminating original readings from archetypal corruptions at each stage of the linear sequence of versions. Whether that expectation ever justifies emending an acceptable archetypal reading is something better left to the judgement of the reader, who may object that the principle of economy should always override the claims of the *durior lectio* criterion. The same reader is asked to remember, however, that while to alter an archetype is to offend against economy, to emend by adopting the reading of an earlier version does not multiply entities but reduce them. The case of *tyliþ* discussed at § 35 thus illustrates *in nuce* the subtle and complex lexical challenges faced by anyone attempting to edit the poem in all its extant versions.

(b) *Metrical Aspects*

§ 37. In §§ 23–36 above, selected syntactic, lexical and stylistic examples have brought out how the core-criteria assist in the work of discrimination and emendation. The theoretical demands of parallel-editing have now been sufficiently explored to place the reader in full posses-sion of the textual principles relied upon in preparing this edition. The section will conclude with a formal account of the metre. This, though summary and illustrated mainly from the core-text, is based not on a representative sampling but on a complete analysis of the poem's 19,000 lines, one already cited selectively in an earlier study.[36] But as the confines of an edition do not allow for the listing of every line under its metrical type, the account below will mention only the lines of 'variant' type, the 87% not listed being of the *aa / ax* form rightly regarded as 'normative'. The aim of the following discussion is to 'fingerprint' the versification of all and only the lines of core-text, so as to provide a firm basis for recognising originality in singly-attested lines and a secure rationale for emending readings judged corrupt on metrical grounds.

Langland's Versification

§ 38. *Piers Plowman* is composed in accentual long-lines, which may be end-stopped or 'run-on' (enjambed),[37] and are divided into two halves ('a' and 'b') by a medial pause. The a-half may contain two or three stressed syllables (lifts) but the b-half must contain only two. Any lift may be followed, and the first lift in either half may be preceded, by a weak or a strong dip (of one or more than one unstressed syllables respectively). Rhyme and pararhyme of various kinds are used as ornamental or expressive devices, and their density exceeds that found in other allit-erative makers; but as they are not unique, they cannot qualify as textually criterial (in Appendix One, §§ 5–6, it will be proposed that *identical* rhyme and *full-word* cross-caesural pararhyme are potentially criterial). The metre's main formal principle is the use of structural alliteration to heighten or reinforce the stressed syllables and so give the line its characteristic metrical shape. But contrary to the claim of Hoyt Duggan's 'Metrical Rule II' (unfortunately ambiguous in its for-mulation) that 'Alliteration always falls on a stressed syllable',[38] Langland sometimes alliterates syllables without stress and stresses syllables without alliteration (see § 39 below). Langland's lines vary much more in length than those of such contemporaries as the authors of *Purity* or *Wynnere and Wastoure*, of whom the first seems to have read and the second to have been read by him. Thus they range from ten syllables (as at B X 127–8 // A, Z VII 170) to almost twenty (C XV 226 // B), the majority falling between these extremes, with an increase in length between **A** and **B** proportionally continued in **C**. Such elasticity could induce scribal mislineation at all levels of transmission;[39] but it is what allows the poet to adhere to the natural stress-patterns of ordinary speech or prose and so achieve both tense and relaxed utterance at will. This capacity for expansion or contraction, which makes possible the poem's fluid movement and flexible tone, depends on the number of slack syllables (varying from one to four) in the dips that separate the lifts in each half-line. 'Zero-dips' or clashing stresses can occur in the b-verse, either 'duolexically', in two words (*cán súlle* XXI 402 // B, *póynt ménes* Z VII 232) or 'monolexically', within a single word (*sepúlcre* VII 170 // A?B,[40] *bihéstes* XX 320, *déuisede* XXI 331 // B, *cóntricioun* XXI 350 //, *Iustície* XXI 400, 477 //; *vitáilles* B V 437, *decéites* B XII 130)[41]. Since the duolexical type is to be found elsewhere,[42] it is the monolexical variety of half-line that is criterial for authenticity. The lifts usually number four in the *standard line* of Types Ia and b, but augmentation of the a-verse by an extra lift gives the Type I variants Ic–e and Types IIa and b. The first lift always carries alliteration and is a 'full stave'. But in the commonest *extended* variant, Type Ie (as at IV 64 // ZAB),[43] the extra lift, whether analysed as occupying the second or third stave-position, may be 'blank' (unalliterated) or 'counterpointed' by a matching stave-sound in the second lift of the b-half (§ 39, end).

§ 39. The metrical term 'staves' has been customarily applied only to alliterating lifts; but Langland's practice over 19,000 lines requires formal recognition of three distinct types of stave. These are the traditional 'full' stave with stress and alliteration, the 'blank' stave with stress but no alliteration, and the 'mute' stave with alliteration but no stress. The blank stave appears not only in the extended Type Ie (scanning *aax / ax* or *axa / ax*) but in the 'reduced' Type IIIa (*ax / ax*), as at III 222 // ZAB.[44] In Types I and III, full staves stand in both halves of the line, but Type II is unusual in having them in the first half only, giving the 'clustered' scansion-pattern *aaa / xx*, as in II 227 //. All three Types may be alliteratively 'enriched' if a normally blank stave is made full. In Type I this decorative stave is the fourth, giving Type Ib (*aa / aa*), as at Pr 1 //; the third, giving Ic (*aaa / ax*), as at I 3 //; or the third and fifth together, giving Type Id (*aaa / aa*), as at III 174. In Type III the enriched lift may also be the fourth, giving Type IIIb (*ax / aa*), as at IV 12. But Types II and III yield two further enriched variants with a second repeated stave-sound. One of these is Type IIIc (*ab / ab*), as at VI 229 // where, despite the cross-caesural linkage, the alliteration is 'antiphonal', since the *a* and *b* staves have equal 'thematic' prominence and independence. This Type is very rare before the longer versions and is therefore not found in the primary core-text. The other enriched variant is the even rarer IIb (*aaa / bb*), as at IX 6 // B and B III 50 // A, in which the *a* and *b* groups also relate 'antiphonally' (not 'contrapuntally'), because the *lettres* or 'stave-sounds' are not *loken* or 'interwoven'. Type IIb, in which no mute staves feature, is the only one of the main line-types that is strictly criterial.

§ 40. The distribution of staves found in one enriched variant of Type Ie (*aab / ab*) produces a pattern of 'contrapuntal' staves that could be described as ornamental or decorative (as at X 150 //AB). But that found in Types IIb and IIIc establishes new structural types, because the primary and secondary staves (with their ratios 3:2 and 2:2 respectively) achieve (near)-equal prominence. Now in over 400 lines, both common or singly attested, the first lift of the b-verse, the 'key-stave', is unstressed ('mute'), as in *with* at Pr 24 //. But when by way of compensation the two lifts following this muted stave introduce a second stave-sound, a new pattern results, as at VI 322 //. This special type of *transitional* line ('T-type' for short), which shares features of the muted Type Ie and of Ib, is apparently unique to Langland and so strongly criterial. It is given a special notation *aa / [a]bb*, the brackets signifying that the key-stave is mute. Despite a superficial likeness to Type Ie, these *a-* and *b-* staves are not thematic and contrapuntal respectively (§ 39). But because the first of the b-staves carries part of the key-stave's function of stress (lost after muting), it is more than ornamental. Structurally, it may be thought of as forming with the second b-stave a sort of alliterative 'cauda', and this new pattern should be recognised as a separate category. Some thirty examples appear in the core-text, and the T-type is also abundantly illustrated in the non-paralleled lines of the poem's canonical versions. But since it is virtually confined to Langland, its occurrence in the unique Z III 158 and VII 38 serves to give the T-type line a significant part in the metrical case for **Z**'s authenticity.

Variant Line-Types

§ 41. As the patterns briefly analysed above provide firm guidelines for establishing the acceptability of lines attested severally in each version, their representation in the core-text is worth setting out here in full. Of lines that scan in one or other of the *ten anormative types* (non-*aa / ax*), the primary division of core-text yields some 60 or about 11.3% of its 530 lines; the secondary division of 598 lines, some 70 (= 11.7%); and the tertiary (totalling 2150 with the 870 of C XXI–XXII // excluded), some 286 (= 13.3%). Of the 3280 lines strictly qualifying (i.e. the total 4140 *minus* Passus XXI–XXII), some 416 or 12.6% are therefore 'variant'; so at some 87.4% of the core-text, the 'normative' lines can be seen fully to deserve their name. In illustrating the variant types, estimates have been conservative, no ambiguous examples or lines capable of normative scansion being admitted (a query recognises the possibility of alternative scansions). It will be observed that the degree of homogeneity displayed is very striking, **BC** indicating only a *marginal* increase in departures from the norm, while the small non-linear groups **ZB**, **ZC** and **AC** yield no variant lines. For ease of reference, the data have been set out by type, indicating the relative degree of representation in each core-text division. An '*' denotes counterpoint in extended lines, a '+' enrichment or supplementation in lines of Type II or III, 'm' = macaronic. Line-references observe the sequence **CBAZ**.

Type Ib *aa / aa* **ZABC**: Pr 1. I 61, 68, 190. II 220. III 166, 179, 194. IV 88–9. VII 59, 214, 225. VIII 2, 94, 153. IX 61. **ABC**: Pr 55, 84. III 50, 431. VI 196, 400, 414. VII 280, 289. VIII 78. X 19, 44, 77, 118, 134, 139. XI 4, 128. **ZAB**: Pr 12. I 17, 68, 209. II 123. III 108. IV 13, 118, 126. V 382. VI 165, 214, 246. VII 4. **ZA**: V 53. VII 12, 125. VIII 17. **ZB, ZC, AC**: 0. **AB**: III 217, 262. V 108. VIII 47, 101. IX 52. X 110, 119, 126, 167, 170, 333. **BC**: Pr 131, 217. II 84, 97. III 465. VI 58, 74, 260, 270. VII 18, 94. X 86, 309. X1 180, 181. XII 119. XIII 100, 173. XIV 8, 48, 51, 54, 60, 65, 77, 120, 138, 145, 185. XVI 4, 125, 148. XVII 105, 182, 216, 270, 281. XVIII 34, 183, 284. XIX 32, 57, 192, 230, 251, 261, 310, 330, 334. XX 145, 169, 180, 364, 375, 419, 447, 455, 473, 476. *Total*: 122 = 29.3%.

Type Ic *aaa / ax* **ZABC**: Pr 19. I 3. II 3, ?30, ?157, 202, 212. III 3, 23, 127, 176, 195. IV 16, 20, 91, 97. VI 8. VII 161, 268. VIII 123, 129, 164, 165, 224, 294, 318, 333. **ABC**: Pr 65. VI 63, 390, 417. VII 281. X 130, 155. XI 41, 47. **ZAB**: I 34, 105. II 129, 161. V 63. VII 62. **ZA**: II 22. IV 137. VII 128, 176. VIII 15. **AB**: Pr 16. VII 172. X 36, 295. **BC**: Pr 148, 183, 195. I 139. III 478. V 160. VI 56, 249, 277. VII 13, 48. 77, 80, *83, 98, 138. IX 54. X 15, 141. XI 190, 212, 314. XII 10, 15, 121. XIII 111, 137, 211. XIV 94, 97, 103, 171. XV 5, 260, 293. XVI 143, 144, 214, 257. XVIII 31, 292. XIX 193. XX 4, 36, 56, 59, 210, 225, 374, 431, 474. *Total*: 100 = 24.0%.

Type Id *aaa / aa* **ZABC**: III 174. VIII 207. **ABC, ZAB**: 0. **AB**: VII 156. **BC**: Pr 149. VI 262. *Total*: 5 = 1.2%.

Type Ie *aax / ax* etc. **ZABC**: I 82. III 18. IV 64, 74, 79 (*axa / ax*). *V 130 (*aba / ab*). VIII 317, 322, 347 (*aax / aa*). **ABC**: III 267. V 120. VI 395. VIII 76, 77. X 120, 135, *144. XI 38. **ZAB**: I 73. II *122, 202. V 227. VI *87. **ZA**: II 42. **AB**: V 83. VII 80. VIII *50. IX 54, 136, 204. X *66, 215. **BC**: Pr 90. II 49. III 422, 487. VI 69, 157, 236, 250, *275, 297. VII 19, 42, 71, 116. VIII *270. XI 165, 194, 196. 229, 239. XII 11, 49, 110, 111, 115, 136, 144. XIII 103, *104, 110, 119. XIV 18, *85, 104, 106, 121, 142, 194. XV 39, 43, 136 (m), 144, 203, 227, 231, 253, 263. XVI 3, 8, 66, 85, 90, *93, *96, 108, 110, 128, 130, 147, 168, 184, 194, 217, 348. XVII 13, 94, 100, 265, 316. XVIII 274. XIX 16, 46, *59, 83, 85, *142, 145, *223, 255, 267, 294, 298, 311, 312, 316, 332. XX 12, 42, 47, *49, 57, 94, 137, 143, 171, 176, *179, *185, 231, 245, 246, *254, 257, 268, 270, 342, 362, 388, 412, 425, 430, 472. *Total* 143 = 34.3%.

Type IIa *aaa* / *xx* **ZABC** II 227. IV 107. VII 97, 331. **ABC**: Pr 80. VIII 110. X 68. **ZAB**: V 72. **ZA**: VII 131. **AB**: †III 255. VIII 32, 36. X 47. **BC**: †VI 155. VII 47 (*enriched*), 151 (m). XII 114, 137. XIV 58, 213. XVII 120. [XVIII 124 (m)]. XIX 165, 279. 299. XX 68, 122, †157, 236, 398, 424, 466. *Total* 31 = 6.9%.

Type IIb *aaa* / *bb* **ZABC, ZAB**: 0. **ABC**: IV 145. X 72. **ZA**: VI 81n. VIII 78. **AB**: III 50. V †456. **BC**: XV 96. XVI 82, 182. XVII 203, 318. XX 229. *Total* 11 = 2.6%.

Type IIIa *ax* / *ax* **ZABC**: III 222. V 116. VI 319 (*axx* / *ax*). VII 178, 179. **ABC**: VI 199, 229, 376. VII 220. IX 289, 320, 335n. X 70. **ZAB**: II 105. IV 59. VI 248. **ZA**: VI 46. **AB**: II 127. III 10, 229. V 9 (*ext.*)n. X 162. **BC**: Pr 166. VI 345. [XII 12 (m)]. †XIII 126, 127, 198. XIV 99, 204. XV 41. XVI 210. [XVII 203, 318]. [XVIII 124.] XIX 34, 190, 299. *Total* 38 = 8.5%.

Type IIIb *ax* / *aa* **ZABC** IV 12. **ABC**: IX 309. **ZAB, ZA, AB**: 0. **BC**: XVI 223. *Total* 3 = 0.7%.

Type IIIc *ab* / *ab* **ZABC**: 0. **ABC**: VI 229. **ZAB**: 0. **ZA**: VIII 14. **AB**: V 627. X 201. **BC**: XI 46, 175. XII 3. XIX 190. *Total* 8 = 1.6%.

'T'-type *aa* / [*a*]*bb* **ZABC**: I 41. (V 135 ?†Ax). VI 322. IX 170. **ABC**: X 146. XI 124. **ZAB**: I 22. (?108). †IV 91. 194. **AB**: Pr 218 (cf. // **C**). **BC**: Pr 196. †I 155. VI 180. VII 36, 95. X 14, ?122. XII 34, 52, 70, 147. 192. XVI 51, 185. XVII 215. XVIII 287. XIX 15. XX 27, 132, 160, 408. *Total* 29 = 7%.

These lists show that (after the composite 'T-type') Types II and III, at about 10% each, are the rarest and Type Ie the most favoured variant, closely followed by Type Ib.

§ 42. The ten variant types are also exemplified in the unique lines of **B** and **C**, all but the very rare IIb in **A** and all but Id, IIb and IIIc in **Z**, which has, it should be noted, only about 200 non-paralleled lines (or 13% of its text). As supporting the common authorship of all four texts, this evidence is illustrated with one example per passus where possible. But because of its special importance for the authentication of A XII and **Z**, the data for these are given in full.

Type Ib C: Pr 175. I 27, 202–3. II 104. III 94. IV 65. V 7. VI 54. VII 148. VIII 178. IX 174. X 100. XI 74. XII 215. XIII 30. XIV 60. XV 98. XVI 23. XVII 127. XVIII 22. XIX 3. XX 196. **B**: Pr 50. II 18. III 306. IV 43. V 108. VI 46. VII 35. VIII 92. IX 44. X 24–5. XI 217. XII 41. XIII 6. XIV 11. XV 241. XVI 177. XVII 70. XVIII 252. **A**: II 137. III 31. IV 149. V 70, 97. VII 3. VIII 37. X 28. 45. 114. 137. 160. XI 81, 177, 183, 257, 272, 295. XII 23, 27, 34 (*s* / *sh*), 79, 80, 94. **Z**: Pr 57, 83, 100. II 60, 143. IV 146. V 3, 24, 39, 45, 140. VII 53, 58, 198.

Type Ic C: Pr 30, 37. II 41. III 351, 356. IV 195. VI 101, 118. 301. VII 13. VIII 89. IX 207, 273. X 79. XI 298. XII 88. XIII 29, 65, 187. XIV 21. 38. XV 122. XVI 17. XVII 67. XVIII 10. XIX 242. XX 317. **B**: Pr 45. II 107. IV 195. V 429. VII 36. IX 106, 178. X 329, 340. XI 63, 159, 172, 183, 227. XII 5, 20, 68. XIII 125, 224, 237. XIV 1, 18. XV 297, 348. XVI 20, 117. XVII 82. XVIII 95. **A**: X 75, 99, 152, 158, 159. XI 188, 222, 310. XII 20, 59, 61, 70. **Z**: Pr 94. I 116. II 167. III 150, 151. IV 1, 131. V VII 323. 74, 93. VI 74.

Type Id C: Pr 88. I 94. III 404 (m), 480 (m). X 77. XI 18. XII 119. XVII 126. XVIII 246. XX 112. **B**: III 72. X 95. XII 228. XV 433. XVII 139, 345. **A**: V 97. **Z**: O.

Type Ie C: Pr 96. I 103. II 18. III *96, 100. IV 170. V 68. VI 169. VII 204. VIII 41. IX 35. X 174. XI 67. XII *161. XIII 1. XIV 134. XV 119. XVI 8. XVII 32. XVIII 1. XIX 72. XX *98. **B**: Pr 129. I 115. II 36. III 245. V 131, 141, 242. VI 140. VII 53. IX 54, 67, 73. X 284. XI 26. XII 17. XIII 21. XIV 44. XV 66. XVI 6. XVII 37. XVIII 55. **A**: I 178. VI 27. IX 45. XI 252. **Z**: Pr *54, 99. I 113. II 91. III 54, 169. V 95. VI *70. VII 59, 286, 316.

Type IIa C: Pr 100, 117. I 113. III 122 (monolexical staves), 274. IV 62+. V 17. VI 96. VII 306. VIII 177. IX 130+. XII 233. XIII 230. XIV 31, 33. XVI 24, 160. XVII 40, 83. **B**: III 100, 265. IV 171. VIII 23. IX 70. X 302, 365. XI 153, 262. XII 51, 118. XIII 114. XIV 30. XV 3+. 250. XVI 73. XVII 43. XVIII 383 (*f* / *þ*). **A**: VII 235+. X 56+. **Z**: I 100. III 10, 165. IV 120. VI 3. VII 76. VIII 69.

Type IIb C: I 55. III 338. ?355 (m),494. VI 51. X 35, 215. XIII 192. XIV 161. XVIII 92, 219. **B**: Pr 95. V 370. 394 (*liaisonal*), 407. VII 30. X 274 (*em.*). XI 39. XII 227. XIII 32. XIV 48, 137. XV 71, 198. XVII 170. XVIII 46 (m). **A**: V 49. XI 213 (*mute 2nd st.*). **Z**: 0.

Type IIIa C: Pr 110. III 30, 342. V 53. VI *22. VIII *209. IX 261 (m). XI 109. XIII 63. XIV 4, 72. XV 158. XVI 191 (m). XVII 140. XVIII 119 (m). XIX 26. XX 20 (m). **B**: I 118. III *334, 341. IV 159. V 2, 38. VI 180. VII 73. IX 182, 200. X *98, 264. XI 50, 53. XII 30, 40. XIII 35. XIV 98. XV 117, 119. XVI 16 (m), 150. XVIII 71, 113. **A**: XI *163, 178, 254 (m). XII 28 (m), 49, 78, 83. **Z**: Pr 50. IV 144. V 96. VI 78. VIII 74.

Type IIIb C: III 335. VI 267. X 179. XI 33, 68. XV 215. XVI 270, 282. XVIII 7. XX *198. **B**: I 120. II 33. IV *36. IX 88 (or IIIa on *sh / j*). XI *7, 397. XII 146. XV 295, 444. XVII 101 (ext). **A, Z**: 0.
Type IIIc C: XIII 40. XVI 173. XVII 38. XVIII 61, 237. XIX 9. XX 216. **B**: V 101, 509. 275. VI 241. IX 71. X 438 (m). XI 52, 214, 397. XII 81. XV 69 (*Latin*). XVI 244, 257. XVIII 54, 308. **A**: IX 52. **Z**: 0.
'T'-type C: Pr 7. II 12, 27. III 296. IV 116. V 23, 111. VI 46, 180. VII 36. VIII 237. IX 180. X 56. XI 44. XII 5. XIII 245. XVI 219. XVII 291. XVIII 4, 24, 262. XIX 176, 206. XX 217. **B**: Pr 163. I 150. II 37. IV 157. V 421. VI 133, 240. IX 45, 55. X 118. XI 148. XII 16. XIII 346. XIV 274. XV 113, 484. XVI 49. XVII 107. XVIII 301. **A**: X 108, 126. **Z**: II 118. III 158. VII 38, 245, 279.

Of these ten variant-types, the eight found in other writers[45] obviously do not count as criterial. But the general showing from the four versions' typical patterns is congruent with their coming from the hand of the same poet, and the 'idiometric' (or metrically unique) Types IIb and 'T' indicate that this is likely to be the case.

§ 43. What is true of the 'straight' English line-types also holds for most of the Latin / French-English macaronic lines, as is shown by some 50 core-text examples from C Pr–XI, where **ABC** are all present:

ZABC: Pr 226 (*French*). I 48, 82, 92, 195. II 191. IV 140–1. VI 315, 320, 329. VII 56. VIII 95, 266 and 334 (*French*). IX 3, 23. **ABC**: Pr 40. III 311, 432. VI 398. VII 77. IX 311 and X 11 (*French*). X 134–5. XI 7, 51, 299. **ZAB**: II 123. V 475. VI 232. **BC**: III 463. V 171. VII 6, 116. (IX 69). X 20–1, 258. XI 165, 174, 178, 191, 249. **AB**: VII 127. IX 49. X 343, 346.

These are exactly paralleled by about 40 examples from C Pr–XI found in one version only:

C: II 185. III 299, 355–6, 405. IV 164, 188, 190. V 46, 86–8. VI 257. VII 291. IX 45, 186, 257–8, 261, 272. X 95, 175. **B**: III 350. IV 120. V 242, 276, 298, 419. VII 136, 151. X 44, 282, 320. **A**: VIII 135. X 50, 262. XI 254. XII 28, 56–7. **Z**: V 142–3. VIII 61.[46]

A mere handful of 'licensed' macaronic lines have only two full staves in the a-verse:

ZABC: V 199. **BC**: III 489, 493. VI 64, 153, 283. VII 152.

These too are paralleled in lines unique to a single version:

C VI 302. B XIII 196. A VIII 123. Z VII 267.[47]

The macaronics likewise support attribution of the canonical versions, A XII and the Z-text to one and the same hand.[48]

Stave-Types

§ 44. The variant types of line (especially IIb and 'T'), however useful for discrimination and emendation, are not the only available means to achieve a comprehensive metrical 'finger-printing' of the poet. The core-text also illustrates twelve distinct categories of *stave*. As well as the full, mute, blank, monolexical and contrapuntal, it offers examples of the supplemental, the internal, the liaisonal, the cognative, the dialectal, the macaronic and the microlexical (or 'small-word') types of stave. Consideration has already been given to the first three, the foundation of the variant line-types (§ 39 above); to the monolexical,[49] usually featuring one full and one blank stave in a single word (§ 38); and to the contrapuntal stave that functions both decoratively (§ 39)[50] and as a structural device for creating the T-type (§ 40). No less 'idiometric' than these is the interesting minor category of the 'supplemental' fourth stave. This is sometimes found when the line's *first lift* (invariably a full stave) is a word of low semantic rank such as a bound morpheme, grammatical lexeme, modal verb or the verb *to be*.[51] Occasionally it appears also when the *key-*

stave is such a word and is muted (C VII 197, X 172 //, XV 145; B XV 244), and sometimes to strengthen the stave-pattern in the b-half of a Type III line (*B IX 87).

Core-text: IX 283 // AB *by*-[1] → *bulle*, X 172 // B *y*- → -*ynne*, XIX 165 // B *For* → *fynger*, XXI 271 // B *Gregory* → *gode* and XXII 298 // B *In* → *heeld*.
Single-version: C V 198 *seynt* → *soules*, VII 197 *where* → *woneth*, X 41 -*ful* → *fallynge*, X 108 *so* → *spede*, XI 125 *con-* → *compas*, XV 145 *with* → *wynne*, XIX 135 *al* → *euere*, XX 71 *somme* → *assaie*, XXII 298 // *In* → *heeld*. **B** II 107 (in *a*-half) *wiþ*[1] ← *while*, IX 87 *Cristes* → *kynde*, XI 70 *Ac yet* → *konnyng*, XII 147 *But* → *beste*, XIII 321 *was* → *wille*, XV 247 (with *liaised* first stave) *Ac avarice* → *kynnesmen*. **A** VII 235 *He* → *hondis*.

Latin or French staves (§ 43 above) follow the same rules as native words. So does the rare 'dialectal' stave, a South-Western variant of the standard pronominal forms *they* and *she*, of which examples are *hij* at B Pr 66 // A and *heo* at B III 29 // ZA, B IX 55 (T-type).

§ 45. Also noteworthy are two 'licences' virtually unknown outside Langland that may be regarded as criterial. One is the internal stave, a sound that must be isolated from its consonant-group to furnish the structural alliteration of a formal line-type. An example is *l* [← *cl*] in III 35 // B, replacing an *l*-alliterating Type Ib line in A III 31 that itself revises a Type IIIb in Z III 34.[52] Others are:

V 153 // B [*k* ← *sk*]. VIII 67 [*g* ← *gl*]. X 105 // B [*r* ← *thr*], 269 [*k* ← *sk*]. XI 197 // B [*t* ← *st*] and the macaronic XXI 202 // B [*p* ← *sp*], XXI 152 // [*r* ← *Chr*], 202 // [*p* ←*sp*], 303 // [*p* ← *sp*]. B IV 23 [*w* ← *tw*]. B VII 39 [*l* ← *pl*]. B XVII 3 [*r* ← *wr*].

A second licensed variety is the liaisonal stave, a device through which a preceding word's final consonant provides the needed stave-sound by liaison with the next lift's initial sound (usually a vowel).[53] Examples are:

d at B V 394 (*quod he*). *f* at B II 194 // ZA, B V 627, IX 27, XV 289, XVI 231 (all three removed at // C X 153, XVII 15, XVIII 248) and A XI 46; *f* + consonant at B I 18 // ZA (*fw*, *fl*, *fl*). *k* at B XV 247. *n* at VII 217 and VIII 40 // ZAB, VI 128 // B. *s* at C III 104 (*this haue*), V 200, B XII 22, XIII 19 (*mac.*); *s* + consonant at B X 402 (*sw*, *s*, *s*). *t* + consonant at B V 287 *it were* (cf. XX 247). *þat* B X 233 *þe articles* (+ *f*), XVII 88.

Perhaps the most striking case occurs at XX 247 // B *Tho þat wéren in héuene token stélla comáta*, where the *t* of *þat* functions as the first stave, liaising with *weren*. With its mute key-stave in [*to*] *ken* and internal supplemental stave in *stella* [*t* ← *st*], this line demonstrates how a concentration of idiometric features helps to produce the peculiarly Langlandian tone of 'vernacular clerkliness'.

§ 46. Similar to the last two 'licensed' categories are the *cognative* staves, exploited by the poet to enlarge the range of his alliterative repertoire.[54] Occurring where voiced and unvoiced consonants (such as the stops *b, d, g: p, t, k*) are alliterated together, these may be thought of as 'metrical allophones'. Like them is *s / sh*, widely attested in all versions including **Z** (III 122); but this is not criterial, as it is found in other alliterative works.[55] Neither, strictly, are the labial spirants, since it seems likely that the poet's dialect levelled *f* and *v* as |v|, and possible that his idiolect did the same for the pairs |f| and |θ| (= *th*, *þ* in lexical words), |v| and |ð| (= non-lexical *th*, *þ*). But *f*, *v* and lexical *þ* alliterating together may be an instance of 'idiometric' allophony (see Appendix One, A.§2(a)). Examples from the core-text are:

Stops. **b / p**: V 165 // B. XVI 67 // B, 115 // B (m.). **k / g**: VIII 79 (*internal* 1st *stave*). XIX 279 // B. XXI 213, 323 // B. A IV 91 // Z. **t / d**: XX 182, 325.
Spirants. **f / v**: Pr 69 // AB. III 36 // ZAB. V 191 // ZAB (m.). XVI 221 // B (m.). XVII 109 // B. XIX 271 // B. XX 123, 154 // B. **f / v / th**: B I 23, V 382 // ZA. **s / sh**: Pr 221 // AB (*T-type*). II 24, 59 // B. III 429 // AB, 460 // B. VI 355 // AB.

III 460, VII 28, XIX 277 // B. **B** II 126; 159, 164, 168 // ZA [in these last three, the **C** revision alliterates only on |s|]. B V 73, VI 232 // ZA. B III 50 // A. **A** IV 28 // Z.

And examples found in the four versions severally include:

b / p in C XVI 263, 289; *d / t* in C XV 127 (cf. B XIII 117), B XVIII 379 (from liaison of *þat_is*); *f / v* at C XV 5, B Pr 190; *f / þ* at B V 410; *k / g* at C XIV 132, B V 136; *s / sh* at C Pr 13, Z III 122, 152, IV 152.

This evidence, which indicates that some kinds of metrical allophones formed a part of the poet's repertoire from the earliest stages, argues against any emendation of 'cognatively'-scanning lines on metrical grounds.

§ 47. Perhaps the most distinctive stave-type of all is the microlexical or 'small-word' stave, a grammatical morpheme that may appear in either half of the line as a full or a mute stave.[56] This type, which includes modal verbs as well as pronouns, prepositions and prefixes, was first recognised by Kane and Donaldson[57] and is best known for providing (very conspicuously) the key-stave at numerous points in the core-text and in each version severally. In itself, it is an indicative authenticating feature as well as being the structural basis of the strictly criterial T-type line (§ 40 above). Excluding such lines and equally all others with bound-morpheme prefixes like *con-, des-, en-, mys-, pro-* or *re-* occurring in Romance-derived words capable of variable stress, there are nearly two hundred mute key-staves to be found in the core-text. Where possible, one from each passus is given for illustration, reference being as usual to the 'senior' version in the grouping:

ZABC: Pr 24. I 54. II 209, 212. III 36. IV 57. V 119. VI 322. VII 56. VIII 105, 266 (*French*). IX 1, 61. **ABC**: II 252. III 283. VI 56. VIII 328. X 120. XI 1, 50, 90, 137. **BC**: Pr 85, 180. II 36, 66. III 51. VI 37. VII 4. **ZAB**: B I 23, 132. IV 28. V 25. **AB**: Pr 62. II 128. III 221, 227. X 107. **ZA**: I 120. II 30. VII 226.

Over 200 examples are also found in each version severally (for a full list of both classes see Appendix One):

C: Pr 85. I 18. II 12. III 65. IV 21. V 19. VI 16. IX 32. X 181. XI 1, 151. **B**: Pr 180. II 14. III 235. IV 34. V 86. VI 47. VII 55. IX 36. X 161. **A**: V 68. VII 236. VIII 33. X 57, 145, 206. XI 62, 64, 165, 224. XII 11, 19, 24, 567 (m). **Z**: Pr 145. II 148. IV 159. VII 59, 231, 261.

Mute staves in other than key-position include:

ZABC: I 43. III 190. IV 1.V 197. VII 187. VIII 54. **ABC**: Pr 48. VII 235. X 3, 144. **ZAB**: I 50. V 224, 200. VII 63. **BC**: VI 184. XIII 103. **AB**: V 110.

But even more striking than these mute staves are the much rarer microlexical full-staves, which contextually receive heavy stress. Like their mute counterparts, they are mainly grammatical lexemes and modals, and the same words tend to recur (*with, for*). But because their identification demands a higher interpretative element, only unambiguous examples are cited (some in non-key position are given):

ZABC: II 234 *with*. IV 50 *for*. 62 *bi*. VIII 110 *wol*. IX 167 *with*. **ABC**: Pr 78 *bi*. **BC**: X 237 *for*. XV 228 *but*. XVI 221 *emforth*. XVII 193 *so*. 268 *bi-*. XIX 164 *For*. 261 *to*. XX 70 *so*. 417 *my*. **C**: II 34, VI 26 *my*. IX 200 *by*. XI 75 *þe*. XIV 37 *with*. 91 *But*. **B**: III 353 *so*. XIII 321 *was*. XV 171 *kan*. 284 *by*. 324 *for*. 569 *by*. ?XVI 130 *so*. 148 *to* (1, 2). XVII 36 *so*. 154 *for*. 279 *to* (1). **A**: V 136 *be*.

§ 48. Close examination of this rough double-dozen of line- and stave-types suggests that, at the metrical level, the poem's textual transmission was much less unreliable than the Athlone editors suppose. The latter deserve full credit for their recognition of Langland's 'small-word' and monolexical staves and their illuminating metrical concept of 'modulation'.[58] But the unhappy textual consequences of shortcomings in their metrical theory appear in several groundless emendations of Type III lines and of cognatively, internally and liaisonally staved lines among those cited above.[59] Such mistakes can be avoided by heeding the authority of the core-text, which furnishes the editor with a broad range of metrical as well as syntactical or stylistic means for characteristing the poet's practice comprehensively and accurately.[60] But of these the *strictly* criterial features, as described and exemplified above, are five: among types of line, the IIb *aaa / bb* and 'T'-type *aa / [a]bb* pattern;[61] of half-line, the monolexical; of stave, the internal and liaisonal. To the 'intralinear' stave-types that feature at the line-level may now be added, at a level beyond that of the single line, the 'homolexical' translinear stave. This is the name for a stave formed by the same word appearing as the last lift of one line (usually blank) and the first of the next (always full). The thirty examples of this feature, which when read consecutively are so striking as to have a claim to being also criterial, are given separately here for convenience (they are included again in the complete list of translinear staves at Appendix I § 8 v).

Core-text ZABC III 2~3. 36~7. IX 62~3. **ZAB** IV [43~4]. 187. X 35~6. **BC** XI 284~5. XVI 47~8. XIX 254~5. XX 403~4. XXI 92~3. XXII 189~90.
Separate versions C VI 13~14. 62~3. 244~5. XIV 198~9. XVI 47~8. 243~4. XVII 173~4. XVIII 10~11. XIX 254~5. **B** IV 187~8. V 141~2. XII 165~6. 168~9. XIII 128~9. XIV 322~3. XVI 12~13. **A** X 52~3. **Z** IV 125~6.

One further feature unlisted above because not especially characteristic of Langland is the feminine ending required at the end of the line. The first 13 lines of the Prologue show this syllable to occur eleven times in inflexional *–e(s)*, once in *–ed* (7), and once in unstressed *hit* (11; cf. *sweuene* in // B 11). The practice is observed throughout the poem, and its editorial significance may be judged from the list of archetypal lines given in Vol. I pp 761–2 where a metrically needed final *-e* has been added to the last word in a line.[62] Although this feature is not criterial, its function as a constraint upon conjectural emendation is shown in its ruling out as acceptable any b-half emendation that does not end with a single unstressed syllable.

iv. *Presentation of the* Text *and* Editorial Matter

(a) *The Text*

§ 49. This explanation of the principles and methods used in preparing the parallel-text edition concludes with an account of the presentation of the **A**, **B**, **C** and **Z** *Texts* in Vol. I and its relation to the *Textual Notes* forming Part B of Vol. II. The treatment of the text has throughout aimed at ease of use by readers concerned with the structure and meaning of the poem. The main effort has therefore been to present for each version surviving in multiple copies the substantive readings of its reconstructed archetype, emended only where necessary, in the language of the chosen copy-text. But since each base-manuscript has been preferred less for its superior readings than for its completeness, early date and consistency of grammar and dialect, the linguistic forms have been carefully preserved and all emendations adapted to accord with them. In the case of **Z**, the object has not been to reconstruct the language of Bodley 851's exemplar, let alone of that exemplar's source, which analysis indicates was an authorial draft (III, Z Version § 28). For as there is only one witness for this version, except for correction of evident mechanical errors, its linguistic accidentals have been kept unaltered even where they may conceal substantive forms that were closer to the original.

§ 50. The copy-texts of the three main versions have been prepared after a full collation of each of the four manuscripts (*T, W, X* and *Z*). In preparing the selection of variants used in the Apparatus, it has fortunately been possible to consult the originals of nearly all the other manuscripts. But for a few, such as manuscript W of **C**, the former Duke of Westminster's copy, microfilms have been used. In the edited text, all manuscript contractions are silently expanded to accord with the prevailing forms of the copy in question. In Latin quotations & is printed as *et* and *&c* as '...'. One contraction of particular note that occurs in MS Huntington 143, the copy-text for **C**, is *ll* joined by a ligature. Though its significance is not certain, it has been interpreted as syllabic where a final -*e* is metrically required at the line-end (see § 48 above), but not in other positions. Elsewhere, when any of the copy-texts lacks such a final -*e*, it is supplied in italic (see Appendix Two in Vol. I). All exterior presentational features such as capitalisation, word-division, punctuation and paragraphing are editorial. No record is made of such features as they appear in the base-manuscripts, though they have occasionally offered interpretative guidance.[63] Skeat's Oxford Edition was inconsistent in its handling of Middle English letter-forms but preserved the manuscripts' paragraphing and medial pointing. The Athlone editions use modern punctuation but not capitals for proper names, and have no paragraphing. In contrast with both, this edition's treatment of presentational features, especially punctuation, is thoroughgoing and explicit; its basis is a conviction that the poet's meaning can be securely understood from the structure of his sentences, which shows the impress of training in Latin grammar. Although (as the present editor is aware) the author of *Piers Plowman* enjoyed wordplay, his ambiguities tend to be semantic or lexical rather than morphosyntactic. So it has seemed that this edition would best serve the reader's interests by using the resources of punctuation and paragraphing as Langland might have done had he been writing today. Those who believe that his metre and sense are better appreciated through attending to the layout of manuscripts prepared for readers close in time to the poet have the option of inspecting facsimiles of the copytexts, all of which except T have now been published.[64]

§ 51. The original spelling has, on the other hand, been kept, including the obsolete letters *ȝ* and *þ*.[65] Though no loss of sense would be sustained if these were replaced by their modern equivalents, as in standard editions of Chaucer (or the Everyman *B-Text*), an undesirable discrepancy would arise between the Text and the Apparatus and *Textual Notes* that could cause confusion.[66] Where particular spellings of the base-manuscripts are rejected because misleadingly ambiguous or unlikely to represent 'true' forms instanced in the period, they have been recorded in the Appendix (e.g. *selles* C Pr 5, *cussed* C Pr 95 or *bygge* C V 90). The same treatment has been given to Latin and French text, which is printed in italics even where the base-manuscript may have no rubrication, underlining or boxing. Critical readings taken from another manuscript of the version in question retain spellings where compatible with those of the copy-text or adapt them to the customary spelling of the latter (e.g. *kairen, cracchy* B Pr 29, 186). The same holds for all readings without manuscript support that are introduced as restorations, reconstructions or conjectures (e.g. *luther* C I 109 or *wiþseide* B IV 91 //). Readings 'restored' from another version have the form of the relevant version as printed in this edition, but adapted to the copy-text's spelling where appropriate (e.g. [*a*]*redy* A IV 155 or [*þr*]*umblide* A V 200). Square brackets in the text are used only around readings restored from another version (e.g. [*Til*] and [*were*] B Pr 41); reconstructed from extant evidence (e.g. *of-wa*[*ndr*]*ed* C Pr 7); or wholly conjectural (e.g. [*me*] B Pr 11 // ZA). Brackets are not placed around readings adopted from one or more extant witnesses to the version in question. When the emended reading's source is obvious from the parallel text(s), this fact is not repeated in the Apparatus, but its original proposer (where there is one) is acknowledged (e.g. 'K–D' at B Pr 76).

§ 52. The treatment of the copy-texts disregards most intralinear *ordinatio* features of the English text and larger interlinear ones like section-headings, as well as internal or marginal glosses and annotations by the main scribe, a corrector or a later hand. *Incipits* and *explicits*, however, as potentially informative, are recorded in the *Apparatus* under the manuscript form judged closest to that of the versional archetype. More often than not this is the inferential form of one or other sub-archetype. For example, in the rubric for Passus I of the **C** Version (p. 27), the wording of **x** as accurately preserved in the copy-text X is treated like a standard lemma and that of **p** as a normal variant. Significant positive variants usually appear in brackets, e.g. the divergent α rubrics at Passus III of **B** (p. 86), and major negative variants are also recorded, e.g. '*om* GC²' at the same point. Where the archetype apparently lacked a rubric but some copies supply one, these are noted, e.g. at the end of Passus VII of **B** (p. 354). There is probably no part of the rubrics that can be regarded with certainty as original (see the discussion in Appendix Two). But as the internal organisation of the text indicates that at least the numbered passus-headings are likely to derive from the author, these are given in an equivalent English form in the text.[67]

(b) *Apparatus*

§ 53. The main function of the *Textual Apparatus* (touched on briefly at *Intro.* II, § 6) is to record information relevant for the establishment of the archetypal text when the latter is not attested by the manuscripts with actual or virtual unanimity. When no entry appears, it is to be assumed that there are no variants or that the few which exist are so corrupt as to be useless for editing.[68] For each of the three main versions, when both family readings are certain and the text is based on one or the other, the Apparatus gives one as the lemma and the other as the variant. These families are **r** and **m** for **A**, α and β for **B**, **x** and **p** (or x^1 and **pt**) for **C**.[69] For **A**, the Apparatus also records the readings of the sub-families r^1 and r^2; for **C**, the major groups y, p^1 and p^2, with a query sign if there is uncertainty. For the **B** Version, where the main α witness R is defective at beginning and end, the numerous variants of the other witness F, which are often very corrupt or sophisticated, are not recorded entire but only when deemed likely to be a true reflex of α. These economies, the aim of which is to avoid cluttering the Apparatus with information of no value for establishing the text, involve a degree of editorial judgement. But the reasons for regarding F as of limited intrinsic value will be found set forth at length at III, *B Version* § 46 above.[70] By contrast, the variant readings of R, the only reliable α copy, are all given, either in the main Apparatus or, if F agrees with β in a reading judged original, in the Appendix. Among the other variants given, group-sigils are employed for all versions wherever they appear correctly to represent the shared readings of the manuscripts in question, divergent individual copies being noted within brackets. The rejected readings of each version's base-manuscript have been relegated to the Appendix if unique or supported by up to three unrelated witnesses. But those of the constant three-member variant groups are recorded in the main Apparatus (for the **A** Version TH²Ch, with the sigil t, and for the **B** Version, WHmCr, with the sigil w).

§ 54. The Apparatus uses the following conventions. *(i)* At the beginning of each passus the manuscripts collated are listed, then the opening rubrics (explicits are given at the end of each passus). *(ii)* The order of citation follows the initial list, whether manuscripts are cited individually or by their group sigils. Thus in A Pr 7, 'v' after 'TCh' indicates that 'VH' (and their inferred ancestral source) both support the reading *of-*. *(iii)* A group-sigil appearing immediately after the lemma indicates that the reading's specific manuscript-source is the first member of the group in its sigil-order as listed. Thus at C Pr 216, *reik* is cited from group b's first member, B. *(iv)* The *variants* are given in order of their degree of semantic distance from the lemma.

§ 55. *(v)* The lemma is ordinarily cited from the base-manuscript when this preserves the family reading, as at B Pr 6, where the family-sigil signifies that both lemmata are taken from β in its W form. *(vi)* When the family reading is not unanimous but is discerned in that of a group, the latter's sigil appears after the lemma, as at B Pr 2, where the group is w and the reading is being cited from W, its chief representative. *(vii)* When the adopted reading is supported by a minority of witnesses, these are listed as ordered in their respective genetic groups, with the base-manuscript first (unless it has an eccentric spelling, when another member of its group is cited). Thus in A Pr 7, the six copies supporting the prefix *of-* are cited after the lemma bracket, beginning with T. In this (fairly typical) case, 'R&r' after the rejected majority reading means that 'R and the rest of the manuscripts' read *for-*, and that this variant is cited from R. *(viii)* The abbreviation *&r* indicates that the reading of the cited source-manuscript is shared by all other copies save those for which other individual variants are specified. Thus in A Pr 2 'T&r' signifies that *a shroud* appears in all except the four copies with the adopted reading and the three with the two other discrete variants recorded.

§ 56. *(ix)* This procedure does not apply to the **Z** Version, which has no variants. For each of the other versions, a lemma or rejected family-variant not taken from the base-manuscript normally comes from a single 'citation-copy' chosen for its substantive superiority (and one otherwise qualified to serve as copy-text but for its defectiveness or inferiority in accidentals). The sigils of these manuscripts, which are R for **A**, L for **B** and Y for **C** (before C II 157, U), often precede '&r' signifying as described at § 55, e.g. at A Pr 8, B Pr 13 or C II 223[(2)]. *(x)* For **A**, ms R further functions as 'citation-copy' for the reading of its family **r** and also its sub-family r^1. But when the adopted or rejected reading is that of the other **r** sub-family r^2, the source cited is V and, after V ceases, J. When it is that of the other **A** family **m**, the citation-copy is **m**'s chief (and only complete) representative, M. *(xi)* When Ax is emended, the rejected form given after the lemma bracket is ordinarily that of the base-manuscript, T, e.g. for *I* at A Pr 11. If T diverges from Ax, R or the next manuscript in linear order is cited to represent the presumed archetypal reading. *(xii)* For **B**, ms L acts as citation-copy and provides the β lemma when W has an individual or group error. Thus at B Pr 231, a line that is missing from W and two other copies, the entry cites 'L&r', meaning that the text prints L (adapted to the spelling of W), *except* for the order of *I seiȝ*. This last follows ms G, which is cited in its exact form as the second entry, followed by 'K–D' to acknowledge the editors who first printed the adopted reading. The rejected variant is then cited in the form it has in L and the remaining copies other than G. The sequence in which the first entry records the three copies that lack line 231 follows the normal linear order of the individual sigils: after W comes Y from its sub-family γ and then F from family α.

§ 57. (*xiii*) In **C**, ms Y (and before it becomes available, U) functions like R and L earlier to represent the presumed **x** family reading when X errs or is absent. (*xiv*) For **C** the family **x** (= x^1 before Passus XII) and the group y are cited from the copy-text X, b from B, u from U and t from T. 'Family' **p**, sub-family p^1 and group e are all represented by P, and sub-family p^2 by G, K and N in that order. This may be observed at II 5, where the lemma is from **x**, and II 6, where it is from **p**. From Pr–XI the family-sigil **x** has the exclusive sense 'x^1'; for as the only 'x^1' witnesses present belong to **p**, it remains uncertain whether t would have agreed with **p** or with x^1. From Passus XII to XXII '**x**' is used inclusively for agreed readings of x^1 and t, e.g. at XII 2, where **p** cannot represent x^2. In this section, however, it becomes possible to use 'x^1', as at XII 5, where the correct reading is preserved by tp. But while such agreements of t and **p** in right readings might permit a sigil x^2 and such agreements in error as XVII 94 might stipulate it (see diagram in III, *C Version* § 13, and cf. III § 38), the sigil is avoided, for the reasons set out in III § 10. Instead, only '**pt**' is used for agreed readings, whether lemmas or variants, that stand in clear contrast to those of x^1, as at XVII 117 and 136 respectively. (*xv*) The order of citation of group-sigils is ordinarily that of the copies comprising the groups, as at II $9^{(1)}$, where 'yb' answers to the sequence XIP^{2}BOL. One special procedure to be noted is illustrated from the same entry. At II $9^{(1,2)}$ the sigil-order 'pu' is a deliberate acknowledgement that the readings (one a lemma, the other a variant) are supported first by a 'virtual' family,[71] then by a group of the other family. The aim of this procedure is to recognise the relative weight of attestation and to highlight the discrepant alignment between different branches of the Cx tradition.

§ 58. Three conventions of abbreviation in the *Apparatus* require comment: hyphens, italics, and query signs. A hyphen is used to indicate that in a compound word only the part immediately following the hyphen has variants among the collated copies. Thus in C Pr 7 '-wandred' indicates that the lemma's full form is as in the text and the variants' full forms are both preceded by *of*. But no hyphen appears before either variant because in the cited source both are separated from preceding *of*, the grammatical status of which is clearly different in the p^1 variant (gerund) and that of **x** (past participle). The italics in this case denote that the ending of the variant cited as 'walk*ed*' itself varies in some of the sources. If these variations are substantive, they will normally be specified after the lemma-bracket, as here in the internal entry after '**xMN**', where four copies attest a gerundial form. When no such further information is offered, it should be assumed that the other members of the family or group show a non-substantive, often merely orthographic difference from the form in the lemma or main variant, e.g. 'che*ff*ede' at Pr 33. A query sign has as its specific purpose to draw attention to evidence that may qualify the validity of the sigil immediately following the sign and to alert the reader to a problem in the text that may receive attention in the *Textual Notes*. A good example is Pr 49, an early instance raising the possibility that the RM ancestor may have been collated with an **x** copy or represent an independent line of transmission from **p** (cf. III, *C Version* § 48).

(c) *Format*

§ 59. In Vol. I (pp. xv, xiii), the basic features of the parallel-text format and the meaning of the sigla are described, and the latter more fully in the introductory sections of part III. Wherever possible, the texts have been arranged to make the parallel material start and end at points where the sense is substantially identical or closely similar. This applies also to transposed passages where the parallels are printed for a second time. Limitations of space have not always allowed such treatment for shorter passages or for the printing of both the **B** and **C** lines twice in their respective new positions. However, the location of this material has been signalled by page-references at the place where a form of it might appear. This happens particularly often with **Z**, which lacks several passages presumed added in **A** and may not resume for many pages after the point of expansion. There are similar problems, on a smaller scale, with **A**. Main entries in the *Textual Notes* therefore contain bracketed references to the related **B**, **A** and **Z** material, however close or loose the correspondence.

(d) *Textual Notes, Commentary and Indexical Glossary*

§ 60. The *Textual Notes*, like all the illustrative material in part IV, are keyed to the final version; but when lines or passages in **C**'s predecessors have been omitted in revision, reference is first to **B** and then to **A** for material confined to **A** and **Z**. Where the substance of the note has to do with **Z**, **A** or **B** but **C** possesses broadly corresponding material, the text-reference is again to the latter. The *Notes*, which have been designed to be consulted alongside the open parallel text, focus on issues concerning the establishment of the readings adopted in Vol. I. Where interpretative comments appear, these are sometimes on metrical or (mainly) lexical matters bearing on the text and involving cross-reference to the *Indexical Glossary* (e.g. XI 41). The *Commentary* and *Textual Notes* have not been combined, since (given the great length of both sections) it has seemed more convenient for the reader to keep them apart, as in the Everyman B-Text. All general interpretative information is therefore placed in the *Commentary* unless it directly relates to the resolution of textual problems (e.g. at X 294) or involves proper names (e.g. on A X 153). But by contrast with the procedure adopted in the Everyman B-Text (where textual and lexical notes formed one section), historical information on the sense and associations of glossed items, and also explanation of metrical points, is placed in the *Commentary*. The *Indexical Glossary* (the rationale of which is fully explained in its headnote) aims to be at once comprehensive and concise. It too is keyed to the **C** Version in the first instance but provides referenced glosses for all lexical items unique to each of the others. Unlike Skeat's *Glossary*, it contains only words occurring in the edited text; but variants found in the Apparatus that receive specific mention in the *Textual Notes* appear in a supplementary index of items. The *Bibliography* lists all works referred to (usually by short title) in Vol. II and a number consulted but not specifically cited in the *Introduction*, the *Commentary* and the *Textual Notes*.

IV. EDITING THE TEXT: NOTES

1 This is a matter of principle; whether the texts should also be printed in parallel is a pragmatic issue.

2 For greater clarity in examining metre, the two sets of readings are separately presented at §§ 10–11 below.

3 Although **C** does not revise a **B** line back to its **A** form, it sometimes uses **A** material omitted from **B**: e.g. A 2.166 at 2.248, A 10.125 at 13.23, A 11.306 at 3.395 and A 11.201 at 5.76. Likewise, **B** at Pr 223 may be restoring a **Z** line Pr 90 (unless this was omitted by Ax) and, at 2. 207 similarly, **Z** 2.188 (see further *Intro*. III, *Z*, § 23 (ii)).

4 In Karl Popper's phrase (*The Logic of Scientific Discovery* § 11) these 'are ...conventions...[that] might be described as the rules of the game' [*here*, of textual criticism].

5 'Objective' here answers to Popper's 'inter-subjectively testable' (op. cit. § 8).

6 It is 'neutral' even though a full stave in final position characterises the distinct metrical Types Ib and d, IIb, and IIIb and c; for these are all *variants* (of Types I, II and III respectively) and not base-forms defining the line-type in question. Examples would be *wente] ȝede* at C I 70 or *ouhte] sholde* at C VII 98.

7 Whole numbers and decimal fractions close to the decade by no more than two are rounded up or down to allow for ambiguous cases in the more numerous categories.

8 Each example is separately discussed in the *Textual Notes*.

9 For evidence of such a repertorium see *Intro.* V §§ 29–30 below and Appendix III ('Repertory').

10 The present edition therefore often follows the Athlone in correcting clear archetypal errors in **B**.

11 The most striking examples are Pr 35 and III 32–3, 78.

12 To adapt Popper (*op. cit.* § 21), the theory of the core-text is 'empirical' because it prohibits a class of 'potential falsifiers' [e.g. the metrical type *aa / xa*] and permits another class with which it is consistent [e.g. the type *ax / ax*]. This canon is obeyed in the present edition with only two exceptions where the common text of **ZAB** is conjecturally emended, B Pr 11 // and B IV 91 // (see § 18 below), both of which are discussed in full in the *Textual Notes*.

13 See *Introduction* II §§ 66f above.

14 Whether this is so in every such instance in the present edition may be open to debate; see for example § 29 below.

15 This is something that pre-Athlone editors rarely did, and Skeat included many such lines in his A-Text.

16 In the much-discussed *baches* at C VII 158 // (*Ka* p. 444, Adams '*Durior Lectio*', pp. 8–12), Bx is corrupt but Ax is *uncertain*, though it probably read as **ZC**; see *Textual Notes ad loc.*

17 All the examples cited are discussed in detail in the *Textual Notes*.

18 B V 456 cannot count here as a core-text anomaly, since both archetypes are uncertain and have to be reconstructed from sub-archetypal split variants, and Z appears corrupt.

19 This is a key difference between explanatory hypotheses in the humanities and in the natural sciences, since in principle lost documents may be unique and so permanently irrecoverable, whereas natural entities instantiate a class. Though Popper rejects the phrase 'principle of economy of thought,' his term 'simplicity' corresponds to what is meant here by economy: 'Simple statements, if knowledge is our object, are to be prized more highly than less simple ones *because they tell us more*; *because their empirical content is greater*; *and because they are better testable*' (op. cit. § 43).

20 Like that of Russell-Kane (*C Version* p. 89) and Hanna, 'Versions', pp. 236–8.

21 Discussed at *Introduction* III, *C Version* § 49 above.

22 See *Introduction* II, §§ 9, 18 above.

23 See *Textual Notes ad loc* below.

24 See *Introduction* II § 96 and III, *B Version* § 46.

25 See *C Version* § 40 above.

26 Adams, 'Editing and the Limitations of the *Durior Lectio*', p. 14 n. 3.

27 A similar position is taken by Adams, 'Editing *PP* B' pp. 40–4 and Brewer, 'Authorial vs. Scribal Writing' pp. 68–9, *Editing* 'PP', pp. 386–91.

28 Uninstanced elsewhere, this is as much of an authorial 'fingerprint' as the T-type line, and is found in the core-text as well as in each version severally (e.g. Z II 146 *déstréres*). Such a pattern is also found in the a-half, e.g. *pálmére* VII 179 // **ZAB**; see further §. 45 below.

29 For detailed discussion, see the *Textual Notes ad loc.*

30 This (theoretically possible) view of **Z** is to the present editor insufficient to explain the ensemble of **Z**'s textual features taken as a whole.

31 See the *Textual Notes ad loc.*

32 See III *A Version* § 56 above.

33 On the second of these see Schmidt 'Visions and Revisions', pp. 17–18.

34 See *Introduction* II § 18 above.

35 The Athlone editors would not agree, since they regard the Bx reading as a scribal corruption of an original identical with **C** and emend accordingly.

36 For a systematic account see *The Clerkly Maker*, ch. 2.

37 The scale of **L**'s use of enjambement can be judged from the following sample percentages from one passus in the two longer versions: C XVII 5.5%, B XV 3%.

38 See Duggan, 'Langland's Meter', p. 44. As Duggan would presumably exclude the fourth lift of a standard line of *aa / ax* type, which is by definition stressed but is also blank, his Metrical Rule II should have said 'Alliteration falls *only* on a stressed syllable'. Unfortunately, this would still not be true, as may be seen from *I myhte gete no grayn*

of Wittes grete wittes at C 11.84, where lift four (*wittes*) is 'notionally' blank but 'really' alliterates with unstressed *Wittes* before the key-stave. Duggan's earlier statement that 'Structural alliteration occurs only on stressed syllables' (1986:123n14) is unambiguous, but is also open to objection in not covering the very important category of mute staves, over 400 in total. For since these (nearly half of them in the core-text) have alliteration but not stress, they cannot be treated as 'non-structural' (see further Appendix One § 4 i). For further comment on defects in Duggan's metrical theory, in this case his 'Metrical Rule V', see at note 62 below.

39 Line XV 226 falls victim to mislineation in most **C** copies and in parallel Bx.

40 This is a line where emendation of **B** is justified on the basis of presumed linear agreement of **C** and **A** (*A*-family **m** being also 'filled out').

41 In VII 179a *pálmére* may not be a true zero-dip if the *l* is taken as syllabic.

42 See e.g. *warre sone* and *life dures* in *Wynnere and Wastoure* ll. 85, 108.

43 An extra lift occurs sometimes in an 'extended' Type IIIa, as at VI 319 //.

44 Unless specified otherwise, examples are from the primary core-text: the text-reference is to **C** and '//' = '// **ZAB**'.

45 E.g. Ib: *William of Palerne* 163, *Wynnere and Wastoure* 167, *Purity* 1; Ic: *WPal* 18, *WW* 386, *Pur*. 3; Id: *WPal* 386; Ie: *WPal* 14, *WW* 116, *Pur*. 23; IIa: *WPal* 62; IIIa: *WPal* 72, *WW* 429; IIIb: *WW* 103.

46 On the basis of this evidence Bx is conjecturally emended at VII 45.

47 In A XII 50 the first lift is blank, i.e. stressed but unalliterated.

48 Macaronic alliterative lines are found elsewhere only in poems heavily influenced by *PP*, such as *PPCr* 691, 713–14 and *MS*.

49 These are paralleled by, e.g., *couherde* and *stepchilderen* at *WPal* 4, 131, *onyȝed* 'one-eyed' at *Pur*. 102; but these are strictly compounds and so not truly monolexical like *deseites* at B XII 130 or *conqueste* at BC XXI 43. However, *manhede* at *WPal* 431 closely resembles *maleese* at B XVII 193.

50 These are rare but not unparalleled, e.g. *aab / ab* at *WPal* 429, *Pur*. 11.

51 An apparent parallel outside *PP* is in *WPal* 5536, where a grammatical morpheme stave formed by liaison with a preceding adverb is supplemented by a lexical fourth stave (*wil he* ← *lenges*): *ȝif þe lord god lif wil he in erthe lenges*.

52 An internal stave occurs in *WPal* 3150 (*p* ← *spayne*), and another possible case is 5533 (*n* ← *knowe*); but the line could scan as Type IIIa with a quadrisyllabic onset.

53 For a possible liaisonal line elsewhere see *WPal* 5531 *edwardes douȝter*. This core-text feature provides precedent for the conjectural emendations **any olde* at B IX 163 // A and **ek an* at B VI 281 (a line with a mute key-stave and a supplemental fourth stave).

54 The rationale for this type of stave is discussed in *Clerkly Maker*, pp. 40–1. The *f / v* staves, which are dialectally indicative, are listed in Appendix One, § 2 (a).

55 For *s / sh* cf. *WPal* 76; for *k / g* likewise *WPal* at 166, 2361.

56 Mute staves are not, of course, confined to such words and frequently consist of contextually de-stressed lexical words, some as important as *God* (as at I 46 // ABC, III 427 // BC, C Pr 117, 121). For a complete list see Appendix One, § 4. i.

57 *B Version*, p. 135; see also Kane, '"Music"', p. 53.

58 See K–D, *B Version*, pp. 135, n. 20 and 139, n. 43, Kane, '"Music"'.

59 Examples of Athlone emendations of Type IIIa lines appear at III 222, VII 178, B III 229; of lines having internal staves at X 105 //; liaisonal staves at B V 394, IX 27; and cognative staves at XIX 279 // XXI 213 // (with resultant confusion of the poet's theology of creation and grace).

60 See *The Clerkly Maker*, chs. 2 and 3.

61 This type is not found in other alliterative poems that have been studied from a metrical point of view.

62 On this feature see Cable, 'ME Meter', esp. pp. 53–4, 67–8 (it is recognised by Duggan in 'L.'s Dialect and final –*e*', p. 184n61); in other positions Duggan seems to be right that final –*e* may be properly treated as subject to elision and syncope. However, Duggan's Metrical Rule V (governing the shape of the b-verse) is only partly true of L's practice as instanced in the core-text and as confirmed throughout the poem's archetypal lines except for those listed in Vol. I, Appendix Two. For while L's 'line terminal dip' is indeed 'always weak', the core-text, massively supported by single-version evidence, shows that it is not 'optional' (Duggan, 'L.'s Meter', p. 45). The 'Rule' as Duggan here formulates it is actually self-contradictory in claiming that 'A strong b-verse dip is a string of one to four unstressed syllables. A weak dip has one syllable'; for if the second sentence is true, the first must be false (the latter needs to delete 'strong' or replace 'one' by 'two'). Duggan corrects this error in 'L's Dialect' (p.159, with no acknowledgment of the earlier

misformulation). However, his new statement mistakenly re-affirms the optionality of the line-terminal dip and fails to note explicitly the frequency of *zero*-dips before either lift in the b-verse (more commonly the first), as in the primary core-text line 1.167. This said, Duggan's 'Rule V' is broadly borne out by the core-text data, as is his case for sounding of final –*e* in such 'historically motivated' forms as plural adjectives like *hokede* (in the core-text line Pr 51), which must be trisyllabic to meet the requirement that 'One of the dips preceding either lift must be strong' (Duggan 1987:45).

63 For the **C** Version these may be found in the *Facsimile*, ed. Chambers; for **B** in Benson-Blanchfield and in the Electronic *PP* edition of Trinity, Cambridge B. 15. 17.

64 Unlike the *Confessio Amantis* and the *Canterbury Tales*, **L**'s originals have left no traces in the form of Latin *commentum* or *annotatio* that might conceivably derive from the author.

65 Except that in **B** the value |z| for *з* has been denoted by *z*, a vestigial inconsistency arising from a (misguided) wish to reduce the visible differences between the present and the Everyman text (*Intro.* I § 19), the second edition of which was being prepared for press simultaneously with Vol. I.

66 Retention of the obsolete letters carries no implication that **L** belonged to a 'provincial' school of alliterative writing (whatever that might mean); for if he was a 'maker', he was a maker of the capital.

67 For a detailed account of the poem's *Rubrics* see Appendix II.

68 The numerous such variants are given in full in the Athlone Apparatus.

69 The rationale for handling the last of these, which is somewhat complicated, is described in III, *C Version* §§ 10, 62–4 and § 57 below.

70 Many of F's variants have no more claim to special attention in relation to **B** than do those of N² in relation to **C**.

71 On the 'virtual' family status of **p** in at least Pr–XI cf. III *C Version* §10.

V. THE POEM IN TIME

i. *The Authorship of* Piers Plowman

§ 1. The quality of mystery that invests the titular hero of *Piers Plowman* extends to his creator, about whom little is known except what can be inferred from the text. This little is discounted by some scholars as either fictional or as too distorted by irony to serve in constructing the poet's biography. In Chaucer's dream-vision poems the protagonists are recognisably *personae* of the author, in the *Legend of Good Women* very clearly and closely so. But the Will of the **A** Version of *Piers* is perhaps to be better understood, like the Dreamer in *Pearl*, less as a self-portrait than as a representative figure, modelled upon the author, through whom the relation between human and divine love and between God's justice and mercy, compelling preoccupations of the age, may be dramatically articulated. Our ignorance of even the name of the Cotton Nero A. X. poet is understandable enough, because *Pearl* is extant in only one copy and cannot have been much read. But the mystery about the authorship of *Piers Plowman* is that it survives in as many manuscripts as *The Canterbury Tales* and the *Confessio Amantis*, it proved popular and controversial, and was even, arguably, the most extensively-circulated poem of its time. The paucity of our information about Langland[1] might be due to his prudent avoidance of publicity, since outspoken religious and political criticisms risked arousing conflict with both ecclesiastical and secular authorities.[2] But a more general reason could be that, whereas the English courtly poets (and before them Chrétien de Troyes, Dante, Wolfram and Machaut) named themselves as the authors of their works, the personal history of the writer of a non-courtly work, however wide its appeal, may have been regarded as of scant interest by medieval readers. Even in the case of Chaucer, though more is known of him as a poet from contemporaries, the details that make his 'literary biography' possible have been preserved largely thanks to his career as a public servant. This said, the 'Langland' *within* the poem still seems shadowy by comparison both with the 'Chaucer' who refers 'internally' to his various writings, and with the 'Gower' who declares himself as *auctor* in the Latin commentary-gloss surrounding his English text.[3] However, by way of compensation, Langland's 'self-revelation' in the Prelude to C V is more detailed than anything those writers give us. As such, it has come in for intense scrutiny, though scholars differ about how factually it is to be taken.[4]

§ 2. The Dreamer of *Piers Plowman* is named Will, a felicitous homonym of the common noun denoting in medieval psychology one of the three main *potentiae* of the soul. This is the power fundamental to the search (for Truth and Dowel) of a protagonist who is allowed to describe his experiences in the first person. The textual evidence is, even here, not free of uncertainty; for where the Dreamer is called 'Wil' by Thought at B VIII 126, that word may denote the faculty rather than a person (A IX 118); and *Wil* is changed to *oen* in C X 125, whether to conceal the author's identity or not to have it (mis)taken as a proper name. Conversely, at C I 5 'Wille' is substituted for 'Sone' of **ZAB**, though there too it is not contextually sure whether Holy Church means to name a person or a faculty, the revision allowing both.[5] On the other hand, three third-person references to the Dreamer-narrator as WILL occur in the 'core-lines', the most reliable part of the text. The one at C VI 2 // ZAB once again exploits the semantic-referential ambiguity of 'WILL'. That at B XI 45 alludes to the proverbial 'wit' / 'will' contrast and, in its revised form at C XII 2, generates a double pun on the senses of both the proper name ('William' / 'the will') and the common noun ('the faculty' / 'the object of desiring'). A third, found only at A VIII 43 // Z and perhaps meant to balance the first (at A V 44), effectually identifies author and protagonist. And this identification is sustained in the later versions' frequent mention of the poem's dreamer as the poem's writer (e.g. at C XXI 1 // B). Outside the core-text, references to WILL (apart from the unique one at C I 5) occur in portions of text that not all scholars accept as original. The two at A XII 51, within the part of that passus here judged authentic, seem to be no less equivocally 'personal' and 'faculty' denominatives than at any other point. The use of 'Wil' purely as a generic personal name is evident at VI 70–1 // B, where any ambiguity is between two referents rather than between a sense and a reference. A complementary univocal use of *Wil* for the faculty is at C VII 233 // ZAB, which provides the proverbial basis for equivoques like that at B VIII 126 // A.

§ 3. 'WILL' is, then, meant to be understood at once as the shortened form of 'William' and as a pregnant 'nature-name' proclaiming the Dreamer's embodiment of 'volition' and 'desire' (MED s.v. *wille* n. 1 (a), (a)). That this appellation is persistently punning is clear from its use at B XV 152 *'I haue lyued in londe,' quod I, 'my name is Longe Wille'* (removed in revision), where at one and the same time 'tallness' is ascribed to the 'WILL'-persona and 'patient perseverance' to the faculty he embodies.[6] The line was noted by a late C15th hand in the margin of *B*-ms Laud Misc 581 as giving 'the name of thauctour'; and this early reader's equation of Dreamer-persona with poet accords with both the reconstructed archetypal colophon of C IX and the established practice in the late work of Chaucer and Gower. That the author's name was WILL is also asserted in John But's conclusion to A XII, which claims knowledge both of his 'other works concerning Piers Plowman' (presumably the other versions) and of his death (A XII 101–5). Whatever the precise relationship between the poet's biography and its reflection in the poem, contemporaries are likely to have understood the Dreamer's Christian name 'WILL' to be the writer's. But the conclusion that B XV 152 also puns on the surname 'Langland' depends on information external to the text.

§ 4. Early traditions that attribute *Piers Plowman* to 'Robert Langland', as Skeat noted (*B-Text* xxviii), are likely to have originated in the corrupt reading of B VIII 1 *yrobed* as *y Robert* found in *B*-ms F (and also in *A*-ms M). An early 16th ascription on a pastedown in the *B*-ms Hm 128, like other ascriptions associated with the antiquary John Bale, expresses uncertainty as to whether 'Robert or william langland made pers plow[man]'.[7] But none attends the statement about the poet's paternity written in an early C15th hand on fol. 89v of the *C*-ms TCD 212 (reproduced as pl. 1 in Kane 1965):

> Memorandum quod Stacy de Rokayle pater willielmi de Langlond qui stacius fuit generosus & morabatur in Schiptoun vnder whicwode tenens domini le Spenser in comitatu Oxoniensi qui predictus willielmus fecit librum qui vocatur Perys ploughman.

> ['It is worthy of record that Stacy de Rokayle was the father of William de Langlond. This Stacy was of gentle birth and lived in Shipton-under-Wychwood, a tenant of the Lord Despenser in the county of Oxfordshire. The aforesaid William made the book that is called *Piers Plowman* '].

This note appears to be of independent authority, and its language and the type of interest it displays suggest a person involved in the legal profession.[8] It is unlikely to be an inference from B XV 152 (see § 3), since successful detection of an anagrammatised name would presuppose knowledge that the poet was called Langland. But as the correctness of the Dublin inscription is corroborated by B XV 152, acceptance of it reciprocally confirms the presence of an anagram in that line (and supports the case for finding the name also in A XI 118). A problem arises here as to whether the surname 'Langland' was the poet's; for if he was the son of Stacy de Rokayle, he ought by rights to have borne his father's surname (a matter, interestingly, accorded special importance by Conscience at C III 366). But the questions whether the poet did not call himself 'William Rokayle' because he may have been illegitimate or because (his work being too 'inflammatory' for him to risk using his family name) he adopted the *nom de plume* 'Langland', as maintained by John Bowers,[9] must remain unanswered in our present state of knowledge. A second, more circumstantial challenge comes from a rubric-reference (possibly archetypal) to 'Willelmi .W.' in the explicit to C IX (Vol I, p. 355). Kane (*Evidence for Authorship*, pp. 35–7) suggests that this '.W.' could be a scribal error occasioned by preoccupation with rubricating the letter or (more plausibly) may signify another surname beginning with *W* (e.g. 'Wychwood').[10] The use of an abbreviated form '.W.' would tend to suggest, however, that the author's actual name was common knowledge; yet none beginning with *W* has been found associated with *Piers Plowman*. Neither objection to the presumptive accuracy of the TCD ascription therefore holds much force; so, failing discovery of a 'William Rokayle' who could be shown to have written under an assumed name, it seems safest to accept 'William L.' (rather than 'Robert L.' or 'William W.') as the name of the author. How many versions the TCD ascription's 'liber' denotes remains disputed, as it was in the early twentieth century, when multiple authorship of those known (a theory going back to Hearne and Ritson in the eighteenth) was advocated by Manly and opposed by Jusserand, Chambers and others. But there now seems a consensus (arising perhaps more from indifference than conviction) that the **A**, **B** and **C** Versions, whatever their order or state of completeness, are the work of one poet, whom it is convenient to call William Langland.[11]

§ 5. In the absence of documentary evidence of Langland's relations with his family, all biographical inferences must depend on the text of the poem. But though as an allegorical dream-vision it is obviously a work of fiction, not everything in it need be 'fictitious'. In parts it more closely relates to the realities of the time than do comparable works such as *The Parliament of Fowls* or *Pearl*, which describe imagined worlds based on books and reflection.[12] For *Piers Plowman* mentions historically-recorded natural catastrophes like pestilences and storms, political and religious events like the French Wars and the Schism, and public figures like John Chichester, whose mayoral office helps to date the B-Text. Such factors predispose towards our taking WILL as an accurate depiction, if somewhat 'fictionalised' according to the dream-vision genre's conventions,[13] of the poet as an unbeneficed clerk in minor orders surviving precariously in the manner described in the Prelude to C V. Even more important than these outward details is what the poem conveys of its author's quality of mind and deepest concerns. His choice of an archaic (if 'reviving') metre need not in itself signify a deliberate effort of dissociation from the metropolitan cultural world. Alliterative verse, though provincial and regarded as alien to the South by Chaucer's Parson (*CT* X 42–3), was not restricted to one region, but was found in the South- and North-West Midlands, in Lincolnshire and in Yorkshire. It was used in heroic poems like the *Morte Arthure* and romances like *Sir Gawain and the Green Knight*, where the bedroom scene of

Fitt III is tonally much closer to the courtly sophistication of *Troilus* Book III than to the clerkly bluntness of *Piers* XXII 189–98. But whether Langland knew works belonging to this variegated tradition or only those with broadly 'moral' themes like *Winner and Waster*, he differs from his predecessors and followers in one striking respect. This is his fusion of immediate observation of contemporary social and economic life with an intensely individual re-imagining of 'holy writ' in his extended sense of Biblical, patristic and other religious and devotional writings (the figure of Piers most memorably exemplifies such a 'fusion'). It is at present unknown whether moral and religious poetry was all Langland wrote, or whether he commenced 'maker' in a more conventional way (as did Chaucer with the *Roman de la Rose*) by translating from a work in French. In this regard, David Lawton's speculation that Langland might have been the 'William' who translated *William of Palerne* (*WPal* 5521–6) deserves to be carefully examined, as the lexical and metrical evidence of affinity from all four versions is very suggestive.[14] In the case of *Piers Plowman* itself, however, even the rudimentary and tentative **Z** Version owes little to known vernacular or learned models. The poem's original language, as far as it can be ascertained, is consistent with its 'locating' the first vision on the Malvern Hills.[15] But in **B** and even more in **C**, the work comes across as decidedly not a 'regional' but a 'London' poem, from Haukyn's mention of the missing Stratford bread-carts at B XIII 266–7 to the Dreamer's at V 1–2 of his cottage in Cornhill, 'a narrow east-west street in the middle of a city of lanes'.[16]

§ 6. There is no evidence in *Piers Plowman* to indicate that its author ever belonged to a religious order, but some that he had studied Arts at a higher-level institution, and had attended lectures on the Bible, perhaps in preparation for the priesthood. Though wholly internal to the text, this evidence is more reliable than may at first be thought. In theory, the educational experiences that the Third Vision describes, leading through the trivium and quadrivium to the beginning of theology or canon law, need not have been the poet's own. But several passages show an understanding of syllogistic procedure (not paralleled in his poetic contemporaries) that can only have been acquired in a university or *studium generale*. Instances of this understanding, the most extended being WILL's disputation with the Minorites (C X 20ff //), support interpretation of the *laudes scolae* at B X 303–4 as recalling first-hand acquaintance. But the latter are linked with equally warm praise of the *cloistre*, and *Piers Plowman* shows more sympathy with what Morton Bloomfield called 'monastic philosophy'[17] than with formal scholastic theology, of which Langland seems suspicious. This circumstance may point to his association with a monastic house (possibly Little Malvern Priory) during his early years; and Bowers's suggestion that Langland had been a secular student at the Benedictine cathedral school at Worcester would be attractive did it not mistake the contextual sense of *scole* in C V 36 and fail to see the significance of the poet's familiarity with dialectic.[18] However, Langland's concern with the condition of 'English clerks' (B XV 414) is in no way confined to the religious orders but extends generally to the spiritual mission of the clergy, and specifically to the secular priesthood's pastoral rôle and its contemporary shortcomings. The whole text tacitly supports what the C V Prelude expressly states: that the creator of the Dreamer-persona was a 'clerk' who, whether owing to his marriage or some other reason, had a secure place in no canonical order within the Church. Langland himself may well have confronted at some point a crucial choice between the mendicant and the monastic ways of religious life, with their differing valuations of the place of thought, prayer and evangelisation. But while his poem might be defensibly read as the dramatised reflex of some such crisis, we can only speculate as to the extent of the spiritual autobiography it contains.

ii. *Audience, Date and Early Reception*

§ 7. If the poet cannot be disentangled from his poem, neither can the poem from its audience. This is because it is virtually certain that *Piers Plowman* was known to the leaders of the Peasants' Uprising and even seems to have been re-worked partly in response to its reception by them. In speaking of the poem's audience, a distinction needs to be made between the 'outer' audience of actual readers and the 'inner' audience implied by its content, language, form and occasional direct address, which Anne Middleton calls its 'public'.[19] By the time of **C**, Langland's final outer audience, some of whom had doubtless formed judgements about the author's intentions, might have had to be taken account of when constructing the new 'public' or 'internal' audience of the revision. About Langland's very first readers nothing is known;[20] but it seems a reasonable assumption that the audience of **A** and *a fortiori* of **Z** would have been his immediate acquaintances. *Piers Plowman* does not seem to have been commissioned but to have been a personal enterprise, perhaps stimulated by Langland's 'prophetic' response to growing social instability following the first Statute of Labourers (1351) and by such memorably 'apocalyptic' events of the 1360s as the plague, tempest and war described as early as **Z**. It has been maintained by Anne Hudson that **A** was the version known to the leaders of the 1381 Revolt.[21] If she is right, Langland could be imagined at an early stage of his career as writing for a 'primary audience' of reform-minded lower clergy. This would have included at its 'centre' men with views as relatively moderate as those of the later author of *Pierce the Ploughman's Crede*,[22] at its 'outer edges' as radical as those of John Ball (see §§ 9 and 10 below). But apart from the Vernon and Trinity copies dated *c.* 1400 there are no surviving **A** manuscripts from before the first quarter of the C15th; and given this version's unfinished state, it seems doubtful whether circulation of **A** could have been extensive enough for the allusions to the Plowman and the Triad in Ball's letter to the Essex insurgents to have been readily grasped (see *Intro*. III, *A*, § 1). Admittedly, interpretation of Piers as a 'peasant hero' challenging the authority of the Church (and perhaps by implication of the state) might be more easily encouraged by **A** than by **B**, with its simultaneously disconcerting and re-assuring transformation of Piers into a *figura* of Christ. But the completed and presumably 'published' **B** was a substantial work, of which the earliest extant copies were made in London, and this seems more likely to have been the version that achieved wide circulation. Its archetypal manuscript was presumably generated only a couple of years before the Rising, which some of its ideas and images may have unintentionally inspired (see *Intro*. III, *B*, §§ 1–3). It is of course quite possible that both versions were known to the rebel leaders, who took from **B** what they had already found in **A** and ignored the later, enigmatic evolution of the Plowman as 'something to their purpose nothing'. But there are no convincing reasons for thinking that they did not know **B** in summer 1381 because it was as yet unwritten.

§ 8. The 'implied' first audience of *Piers Plowman*, however, seems (on the same sort of internal grounds appealed to at § 6) to have been one of educated people like Langland. For from the earliest version to the last, this is indicated by its macaronic lines and quotations, many untranslated, which presuppose *litterati*, readers competent in Latin.[23] These need not have been clergy in the narrower sense, since there was a growing number of 'Latin-literate' laymen (Chaucer and Gower among them) who could have understood the poem without difficulty.[24] But what the texts suggest, progressively, is that wholly 'non-literate' readers were being 'headed off'. Thus, hazardous ignorance of the learned tongue is implicitly warned against in the *commune*'s capping of the Goliard's response to the Angel at B Pr 145, and more explicitly in the aside ('authorly' in its use of *write*) at B XIII 71–2:

> Holi Writ bit men be war - I wol noȝt write it here
> In Englissh, on auenture it sholde be reherced to ofte,
> And greue þerwiþ þat goode men ben - ac gramariens shul rede:
> *Vnusquisque a fratre se custodiat...*

The B-Text's projected 'public' is one of *gramariens* who know Latin and are intellectually mature enough to 'place' the work's strong criticisms of the clergy. The *lettred lordes* of III 124, by contrast, are doubtless so called ironically, since for them the Latin Biblical warning *is* translated. And at C III 340–42 the King himself amusingly voices to Conscience a need to have him explain his learned *mede / mercede* analogy that might have been shared by non-grammarians ('for En-glisch was it neuere'). It would have been only realistic for Langland to anticipate that a poem on the universal theme of salvation might reach a wider 'mixed' readership (including the *lewede* men addressed at XIII 25), and to allow for this at different points. Thus at B VII 59–9*a*, for example, the passage cited for the *legistres and lawieres* is left in the Latin, no doubt on the assumption that they can read it. From the **Z** Version to **C**, the poem may be said to assume a primary internal audience of the 'literate' in the accepted late-medieval sense.

§ 9. The internal audience is reflected in the 'external' one to the extent that recorded owners of *Piers Plowman* texts in the next half-century were in the first instance ordinary clerics, and secondly, educated laymen of modest background. This conclusion emerges from studies of wills bequeathing copies of the poem. The earliest wills include those of Walter de Brugge, Canon of York Minster, who died in Trim in 1396 and left his copy to John Wormyngton, an English priest in Ireland, and William Palmere, parish-priest of St Alphage, Cripplegate, who died in 1400 and left his to Agnes Eggesfield.[25] Moreover, the dominant classes in the 1381 Revolt, who were upper-rank agricultural workers and town-tradespeople (many of them literate in English) with lower clergy among their leadership, are thought by Anne Hudson to be recalled 'with fair congruity' by 'the kinds of men associated with copies of *PP*'.[26] Among identified contemporary non-clerical readers are writers like the A-Text epiloguist John But,[27] and Thomas Usk, who wrote *The Testament of Love*.[28] But the authors of the works that the poem most deeply affected, all of them written *c*.1395–1410, remain anonymous, and their status obscure. *Richard the Redeless*, *Mum and the Sothsegger* and *Pierce the Ploughman's Crede* are all composed in Langlandian metre and idiom and belong loosely to the tradition of social and political debate initiated by *Winner and Waster* nearly a half-century before.[29] Authorship of the *Crede* is claimed by the writer of *The Plowman's Tale*, a poem in rhymed stanzas assignable to the same twenty-year period:

> Of freres I have told before
> In a makyng of a 'Crede',
> And yet I coud tell worse and more,
> But men wold werien it to rede (1065–9).[30]

Yet of Langland's two imitators in the 1390s, the *Richard the Redeless*-poet inspired by his social / political concerns and the *Crede*-poet by his religious, only the former could be called close to Langland in spirit and outlook. Judging from these works by 'followers', and others such as *Patience*, *Purity* and *St Erkenwald* by contemporaries, Langland's influence was largely confined to the 'non-Chaucerian' writers (though if *The Plowman's Tale* is by the *Crede*-poet, it in a sense bridges the two traditions in its attempt to foist the poem off on Chaucer's pilgrim-Plowman).[31] In the manuscripts, however, *Piers* keeps company with a wide variety of prose and verse compositions, from *Mandeville's Travels* and *Troilus* (no. 53 in the list of *Manuscripts*) to the *Lay Folks' Mass Book* (no. 16) and Richard Rolle's *Form of Living* (no. 11). It is never found exclusively with alliterative pieces, and this may give some notion of the range of the poem's appeal.[32] It is, as it happens, mainly the later codices that include *Piers* with other works; and apart from the Vernon A-Text, the Trinity B-Text, the Digby 102 C-Text and the unique Bodley Z-Text (nos. 4, 11, 25 and 52), the important **ABC** manuscripts preserve the poem by itself.[33] These and other, later copies, with their annotations and signs of provenance and ownership, yield interesting information about what *Piers Plowman* continued to mean to its readers from within a decade of Langland's death to the period of Crowley's printed editions.[34] But since the audience they reveal is not the immediate one the poem may have been written for, what they illuminate is its transmission and reception, rather than its genesis.[35] Unfortunately, except for that of the Rebels, no closely contemporary reactions survive that might suggest motives, beyond the obvious one of improving the poem's quality, for Langland's continuing to work at it; so these motives can only be surmised from the nature of his revisions.[36] Since some of the poet's attitudes to the state of the Church resemble those of John Wycliffe, its most important fourteenth-century critic, it is not surprising that *Piers* should have interested and provoked imitation from Lollard writers.[37] But it is noteworthy that while those immediate responses that draw the poem into the fold of history are mainly responses to its perceived political attitudes, the author of the chief of these, John Ball, was (rightly or wrongly) also regarded as a disciple of Wycliffe by monastic writers like Walsingham and Knighton, who calls him Wycliffe's *premeditator* 'intellectual forerunner', and by the compilers of the *Fasciculi Zizaniorum*.[38]

§ 10. John Ball's letter to the commons of Essex in 1381 (given below from BL MS Royal 13 E.ix, f. 287) contains in the phrases italicised unmistakable allusions to names and ideas that appear in the poem:

> Iohon Schep, somtyme Seynte Marie prest of ȝork, and now of Colchestre, greteth wel Iohan Nameles, and Iohan þe Mullere, and Iohon Cartere, and biddeþ hem þat þei bee war of gyle in borugh, and stondeth togidre in Godes name, and biddeþ *Peres Plouȝman* go to his werk, and chastise wel *Hobbe þe Robbere*, and takeþ with ȝou Iohan Trewman, and alle hiis felawes, and no mo, and loke shappe ȝou to on heued, and no mo.
>
>> Iohan þe Mullere haþ ygrounde smal, smal, smal;
>> *þe kynges sone of heuene* schal paye for al.
>> Be ye war or þe [? *for* ye] be wo;
>> Knoweþ ȝour freend fro ȝour foo;
>> Haueth ynow and seith 'Hoo';
>> And *do wel and bettre* and fleth synne,
>> And sekeþ pees and hold ȝou þerinne;
>
> And so biddeþ Iohan Trewman and alle his felawes

So does a letter purporting to come from 'Jack Carter,' which is included in *Knighton's Chronicle* (from BL ms Cot. Tib. C.VII):

> Jakke Carter prayes ȝowe alle that *ȝe make a gode ende of that ȝe hane begunnen*, and *do wele and ay bettur and bettur*, for at the even men heryth the day. For if the ende be wele, than is alle wele. Lat *Peres the Plowman* my brother duelle at home and dyȝt us corne, and I will go with ȝowe that y may to dyȝte oure mete and oure drynke, *that ȝe none fayle*; lokke that *Hobbe Robbyoure* be wele chastysed for lesyng of ȝoure grace for ȝe have gret nede to take God with ȝowe in alle ȝoure dedes. For nowe is tyme to be war.[39]

These allusions are hard to explain except on the assumption that *Piers Plowman* was familiar to the leaders of the uprising. In both letters, the rhyming name 'Hobbe the Robber' recalls 'Robert the Robber' in B 5.462 //, Hobbe (MED s.v. *Hobbe* n.) being a familiar form of Robert. The context excludes any notion of an allusion to Sir Robert Hales, the unpopular treasurer killed by the rebels on 14 June 1381; and in the Carter letter, the phrase *for lesyng of youre grace* 'in order not to forfeit the divine favour [your cause deserves]' is evidently warning the peasants against indiscriminate looting. The 'do well and better' phrase echoes the first two stages of Langland's Triad (though in *Piers* the double-comparative form *better* occurs usually only in *non*-Triad references [cf. *IG* s.v. *bettere* av]). In the Ball letter, 'The king's son of heaven' is a characteristic group-genitive phrase little instanced outside the poem (B 18.321 //), and its conjunction here with the idea of 'paying for all' will recall the argument of B 18.341–2. In the Carter letter, the 'good end' phrase echoes B 18.160. A non-verbal 'echo' of a Langlandian thought is detectable in the 'even / end / well' collocation, which is reminiscent of B 14.134–9; the phrase 'ay bettur and bettur' recalls one of the sub-archetypal forms of B 18.363b; and 'heryn the day', which seems to mean 'hear what work was done that day and reckon the payment due for it' (MED s.v. *heren* v. 4d(b)) evokes B 5.421. Now, except for 'that ye none fayle' (echoing B 2.146 // ZAC), the absence of these phrases from **A** tells against Hudson's case (§ 7), pointing instead to **B** as the version the rebels knew. By making Piers Plowman his 'brother' (perhaps an allusion to B 6.207 // ZAC), 'Jack Carter' enlists in the rebels' cause a peasant hero who famously tore up an 'official' document *for pure tene* (B 7.115 // A), and thereby 'appropriates' the poem. Whether its author might have been more troubled than pleased by such 'appropriations', they obliquely illuminate changes in **C** that imply intense reconsideration of his poem in the light of the 1381 events and their aftermath.[40]

§ 11. Neither the TCD ascription nor the insurgents' allusions, however, give any firm indication of Langland's dates. His obit is indicated (somewhat uncertainly) by the third primary source, the reference in A XII 99–105, as not later than 1387, if what it says is correct and if its author was the John But noted as dead by April of that year.[41] This conclusion accords with at least one clear echo of **C** in Thomas Usk's *Testament of Love*, which was completed a year or two before his execution in March 1388. As this could in principle reflect Usk's knowledge of the final version while it was in progress (see *Commentary* on 6.21–6 and 18.60), it does not firmly establish Langland's own death-date as 1387 at the latest. The question has been thoroughly examined by John Bowers, who rightly objects that most of the Usk parallels with **C** observed by Skeat are also in **B** (though Usk could conceivably have known *both* versions). However, while Bowers places a genuine query over the indebtedness of *TL* III v 1–5 to *PP* 18.6, his dismissal of the echo of C 6.22–6 in *TL* I v 117–20 is not persuasive. For here 'wening his own wit more excellent than other' clearly recalls 'Wene Y were witty and wiser then another' (C VI 24). And a little less obviously, Usk's phrase 'scorning al maner devyse' looks to be derived from the poem's '*Scorner* and vnskilful to hem that *skil* shewede, / In *alle manere* maners my name to be yknowe', where in addition to the two verbal echoes, *skil*, though not the identical word, closely answers in sense to Usk's *devyse*.[42] Recent studies have argued, on the other hand, that Langland was alive in 1388, on the grounds that the C V Prelude reveals acquaintance with specific provisions of the Statute of Labourers enacted by the Cambridge Parliament in September of that year.[43] If this were correct, the statement in A XII 103–5 would be fictitious or, if factually true, have to come from another John But than the king's messenger. Its further consequence would be to leave the poet's date of death lying at some point between 1388 and the earliest assignable date of any extant manuscript. This could be as early as 1390 (see § 12 below) but not later than about 1409, the probable date of *MS*, which directly echoes the **C** Version (commonly assumed to have been left unfinished because Langland had died).[44] Accepting *c*.1388 as the earliest time for the cessation of work on **C** (to allow for copying of the text through its successive stages) might therefore favour 1389 as the 'notional' year of Langland's obit. And since that of Usk does not exclude this (if he read **C** in draft), Skeat's proposal of *c*.1393 for the C-Text cannot at present be ruled out. But the case for 1388 as an earliest limit is, though attractive, a matter of interpretation. By contrast, the A XII evidence offers a positive statement (with the same authentic ring as the TCD ascription) that cannot be lightly set aside, and the most plausible John But still seems to the present writer the one identified by Rickert. On balance, then, 1386/1387 is to be preferred as the likely date of Langland's death.

§ 12. For the poet's date of birth no external evidence has been found, and the best hope for it lies in the future discovery of certain documentary reference to a son of Stacy de Rokayle named William. Internal references to the Dreamer's age may, if we follow the accepted dream-vision convention of broad correspondence between author and first-person narrator, be cautiously drawn on to construct the 'biography' of the poet (that their oneness is intended is clear from XXI 1, with its distinction between *wrot* and *dremed*). Thus at B XI 47, Lust of the Eyes is said to follow WILL forty-five years; so, taking the date of **B** as 1378–9 (see § 16 below), on the straightforward — if somewhat disconcerting — supposition that the poet was afflicted by greed 'from the time of his birth' rather than (more charitably) 'from the time of puberty or adolescence', he would have been born *c*.1333. Langland would thus have been old enough to witness the social and moral effects of the Great Plague (1348–9), which he touches on at various points.[45] About his upbringing and education, the C V Prelude offers details in no way contradicted by the solid internal evidence of the work's thought and expression considered at § 6. Moreover, because of its gratuitousness, this passage is antecedently less likely to be pure invention than what Donaldson called in his pioneering study an *apologia* for the author's known (and troublingly ambiguous) manner of life. But the Prelude remains 'generic' in character, nonetheless. WILL informs his interlocutors in this waking episode that his father and family paid for his education up to what may be interpreted as the beginning of the theology course at a university or else at a cathedral or mendicant school in the capital (35–9) which 'provided training equivalent to that acquired at a university'.[46] But he does not say what sort of people they were, nor why, though he still wears clerical garb (41), he was not ordained. How closely this evocation of an amphibian persona moving between lay and clerical estates answers to historical 'reality' remains uncertain. The Langland whose 'represented life' has been recently re-told by Ralph Hanna may have deliberately chosen to depict himself *in persona alterius* (the greatest of portraitists, Rembrandt, sometimes painted himself *in many kynne gyse* — as St Paul, in oriental garb, and even as a friar). And even if this 'brilliant portrait of the personality of a man who knew himself well'[47] is no more 'truthful' than Rembrandt's self-depictions, then it has a great deal of value to tell us about the author. Unfortunately, as Langland (unlike Chaucer writing to Bukton and Scogan) nowhere addresses a named acquaintance through whom we might locate him in a specific social context, his immediate 'circle' remains a subject for conjecture. All, however, is not left in deepest shadow. For the poet's wider 'milieu' has recently been shown, through controlled 'historicising' speculation from the evidence of the text and manuscripts, to encompass a London readership with a taste for serious vernacular literature. This readership would have been made up of scribes and civil-servants, progressive clergy and religiously earnest members of the knightly class somewhat on the lines of the well-known 'Lollard knight' Sir John Clanvowe.[48] And it requires little effort to see the sort of audience who might have been attracted by Gower's 'In Praise of Peace' or Chaucer's Boethian Ballade 'Truth' being drawn to a longer work that makes God's first 'nature-name' *Treuthe* and concludes Christ's victory over Satan with a harmonious colloquy between God's Daughters 'Peace' and 'Truth'.

iii. *Sequence of the Versions*

§ 13. If the questions of authorship and audience cannot be wholly separated, neither can those of the date and sequence of the versions. It has been seen that 'The Book of Piers Plowman' has been traditionally ascribed only to an author called Langland. The notion, based upon supposedly major differences between the versions, that **A**, **B** and **C** are by more than one author, was much discussed in the last century; but it finds almost no support today. The **B** Version is ascribed to John Trevisa by David Fowler;[49] but Donaldson[50] tellingly cites C V 92–101 as evidence for single authorship of the three (or as the present editor contends, four) versions of the poem. And George Kane shows how the 'signature-line' B XV 152 is further evidence that one man wrote all the versions.[51] It has been maintained above (III, *Z Version*, §§ 20–2; IV §§ 1–8) that single authorship of the canonical versions **A**, **B** and **C** is indicated by the common linguistic, stylistic and metrical qualities that distinguish them from the work of the other alliterative makers, and that the presence of these qualities in the contested **Z** Version argues for its authenticity. The question of the sequence of **Z**, **A**, **B** and **C** ought ideally, of course, to be settled by appeal to external evidence for their date. But such evidence is not common in the period, and is hardly more forthcoming in the case of Chaucer, a public figure of some celebrity. At best, the four versions present a second kind of internal evidence, that of virtually certain allusions to dateable events; and these, when combined with the aforementioned features of language, form and expression, create a 'moral' certainty as to their order. That conclusion has been recently challenged, and the case for reconsidering the sequence must accordingly be examined. At this point, suffice it to say that if the received order for **ABC** is confirmed, and if **Z** is judged authentic on grounds of its intrinsic quality and assured 'core-text' characteristics, then its content and structure allow it only one possible place in the sequence. This is at the beginning, as the earliest (and in all probability draft) form of a more or less complete version of *Piers Plowman.* It will then follow that **A** revised and expanded **Z**; that it was abortively continued in Passus XII; and that it was then abandoned for the new start represented by **B**, which was completed and 'published.' This version, at least partly in response to its reception, was revised and reached its intended final shape **C**, in all but a few places, by the time of Langland's death.

§ 14. Before considering the objections to this account, it is necessary to look at the internal evidence for dating all four versions. As already noted, the date of each and the sequence of all cannot be separated; but they are in principle two distinct questions (see *Intro.* II, §§ 137–8). Failing other positive external evidence, the latest date of composition of a medieval text will be that of the earliest manuscript in which it survives, a matter that can now often be established with some precision. The period of 1390–1400 has been proposed for two copies of **C**, no. 33, TCD 212 (V), containing the Latin memorandum (in a much later hand) on the poet and his father, and no. 39, CUL Dd. 3.13 (G).[52] If *c.*1390 is correct, these copies come very close to the presumed obit of Langland, which is not later than 1387 (on the basis of John But's testimony) or earlier than 1388 (on that deduced from supposed echoes of the Cambridge Statute of Labourers in C V). Their very early date naturally argues a rapid process of generation (and degeneration) of the text of **C** (*Intro*. III, *C*, § 1). But if the date is tilted to the end of the decade, these manuscripts take their place as coævals with a dozen other important witnesses of approximately 1400: nos. 4 (V of **A**); nos. 11, 20, 22, 23 (W, L, R and F of **B**); nos. 24, 26, 28, 30, 31, 40 and fragment iii (X, I, U, P, E, K and H of **C**); no. 46 (the conjoint ms T of **AC**); and perhaps no. 52 (**Z**). With the addition of nos. 2 and 10 (R and M of **A**), these include most of the manuscripts essential for editing *Piers Plowman*. Considered together with the Langland-influenced poems *PPCr, RRe* and *MS*, which belong between the mid-1390s and 1410, this clustering indicates a marked interest in the poem during the last ten years of the fourteenth and the first ten of the fifteenth century. It is only a guess that the poet's death and the release of **C** provoked this interest; but the fact that copies of all versions were then produced, and the presence of at least one conjoint text, strongly suggest as much. The date of the earliest **C** manuscripts and the internal evidence that **C** was written after and partly in response to the Peasants' Revolt thus help to fix its composition within the decade 1381–1390.

§ 15. Desire to read the poem (in whatever form) at the turn of the century also best accounts for the production about then of the one early single-version copy of **A**.[53] But that **A** was early recognised as an 'incomplete' representation of *Piers Plowman* is implied by its having been supplemented from another version over the next two decades in at least six of the surviving copies (nos. 43–5, 47–8, 51). Now, if the A-Text was not circulated widely till after 1400, and if the version that Ball's letter alludes to is **B** (as seems likeliest from § 10 above), some time would have had to elapse between the 'publication' of the latter and its becoming well-known to the rebel leaders. This probable necessity accords well with the internal evidence. For though no early copy of **B** survives to provide a limiting latest date of composition, this is provided by the internal evidence of allusions in its final passūs to the Papal Wars. These are best understood as the campaigns of April 1379 that immediately followed the Great Schism (see *Commentary* on 21/19.430 ff and cf. C 22/20.127, which appears to be a revision). Kane's relation of these lines to *pre*-Schism papal conflicts in the 1360s and 1377 seems to the present writer implausible.[54] So too does the claim of Anne Hudson, who places **B** firmly after the Rising and judges that 'the simplest understanding' of these papal wars is as referring to the Despenser Crusade of 1383.[55] But her argument that, as the earlier territorial wars of the papacy did not involve England, they were unlikely to have struck Langland or his readers sufficiently to justify such an allusive reference (ibid. p.100n18) does not persuade; for the first hostilities between Urban and his opponents in April 1379 will have caused far the greater moral shock and are better reconcilable with the completion of **B** in that year, and well before the Revolt, of which this version has no convincing echoes (Hudson's comment on B 15.566=C 17.232 is answered in the *Commentary*). Finally, that B 15.525–7 refers 'almost certainly' to Archbishop Sudbury, who was murdered by the insurgents in June 1381, as maintained by Fowler (1962:174–5), has no evidence to support it. For the text shows the reference as plainly to Thomas Becket, to a generic category of bishops and to the sub-category of those *in partibus infidelium*.[56] (Sean Taylor's similar arguments for regarding **B** as post-1381[57] have been considered and rejected at *Intro*. III, §§ 52–4 above). On the other side, the extensive internal evidence for a *post*-1381 date for **C** indicates that **B** must have been completed well before that date.[58] The Rat Fable in B Pr 176–208 is commonly understood to refer allegorically to the Good Parliament of 1376, perhaps as seen from the standpoint of 1377 (when the boy Richard II became king) and B Pr 123–45 have been connected with the coronation celebrations in July of that year.[59] But since in principle both these sets of lines could have been inserted in the Prologue at any point before 1379 (the date of the Schism), only the *earliest* possible date for **B** can be securely established from a piece of solid internal evidence: the unusually exact reference at B 13.265–71 to the dearth of 1370 and John Chichester's mayoralty. That this 'long-to-be-thought-upon' event was 'not long passed' (268, 265) does not, unfortunately, help to establish when Langland began work on **B**. But this version's length and complexity suggest that it could have occupied him for much of the decade.

§ 16. The date of **A** has no such firm evidence as Chichester's mayoralty to fix on. Bennett argued on the basis of various allusions for *c.*1370, but some of these now seem insecure. One such is that in A III 185 to the death of Edward III's Queen Philippa in 1369; for the critical text (see *TN*) makes the 'mourning' here not the king's for his wife but that of the English army over their reverses (and the line is already in **Z**). That the phrase 'Rome-renneres' at A IV 111 would be an 'appropriate' use in the period 1367–70 (because the Pope was away from Avignon) is a more plausible point, but this detail is again in **Z**. The best evidence for 1370 is Lady Mede's description as an allusion to Alice Perrers, as proposed by Huppé, but this one is a matter of interpretation.[60] Certainly, **A** cannot come before 1362, because A V 14 mentions the great wind of Saturday 15 January of that year (see *Commentary* on C V 114–17); but since its latest possible date is only that of the oldest **A** copy (the Vernon MS of *c.*1400), there is no external proof that **A** is early. Internal evidence of a more subjective kind must therefore be cited in this version: its simplicity of outline and its stressing social and political rather than religious and spiritual issues more than does **B** (if less than **Z**), are features that have traditionally been taken to indicate its priority. For **B** reveals expansion of as well as addition to **A**, an increased complexity of thought on political and religious themes, and greater richness of style. All these indicate considerable development since the composition of **A** and a date for the latter in the early rather than mid-1370s.

§ 17. Recently **A**'s special features have been ascribed by Jill Mann to its being an abbreviated version, subsequent to **B** and **C**, prepared by Langland or someone else for a particular, less sophisticated audience of, perhaps, young people and women. The notion of **A** as an abridgement for a non-clerical audience, first proposed by Howard Meroney, seems counter-intuitive and unparalleled in the major writers of the period.[61] Thus, even without considering the positive internal evidence for lateness, the difference in depth and subtlety between the Short and Long versions of his younger contemporary Julian of Norwich's *Showings* (which *prima facie* resemble the case of Langland's A- and B-Texts) shows every sign of being due to revision over (or after) a long period rather than to the aim of addressing a different audience, which could be made to support a later date for the Short Version. Mann argues that the **A** Version lacks many of the Latin lines of **B** and **C**, but unfortunately for her case **A** also possesses Latin quotations and macaronic lines not found in the later versions; and while some of its unique quotations are translated (e.g. X 94*a*, at 93), others are not (e.g. VIII 123, X 41*a*, 90).[62] It is puzzling indeed to understand why in some copies **A** should have supplemented its text from **C**, 'the abridged text being preferred as far as it went' (p. 47). For this begs the question of whether **A** *was* an abridgement (incomplete, at that) and not simply the early version that was all the compilers could lay their hands on. It is *a fortiori* even harder to accept Mann's ascription of the **BC** echoes in **Z** to *its* being an abridgement made after both **B** and **C** had been written (p. 45), since **Z** like **A** contains unique Latin lines, translated or untranslated as may be (VII 271; V 142–3, VII 267). But more generally, it would be a strange 'abridgement' that not only restricted itself to the first two visions of **B** (where **A** had covered the first three) but revealed a fundamentally different conception of the second vision's action to that of **A**. For **Z** lacks the tearing of the pardon (so does **C**, but it retains Piers's *consequential* quarrel with the priest). Whatever the undertaking imagined by Mann might be, it could not credibly have had Langland's approval, implying as that would a poet with no idea of how he wanted to be understood, successively uttering contradictory deliverances in various states of development. Now, a negative judgement of **Z** as an enthusiastic but misguided scribe-author's memorial reconstruction of **A** (widely straying at some points, uncannily accurate at others) is less unintelligible than this argument, if no more persuasive. But it would envisage a very different entity from the authorial or, at best, authorised abridgement that Mann proposes the **A** Version to be. For **Z** (III, *Z Version*, §§ 1–12) reads not like the reduced form of a finished long poem but like the first draft of a new work with no antecedent, such as **C** has in **B**. Further, as well as lacking the clarity and assurance of **A** (which no one has ever claimed to be a draft), **Z** displays tentativeness, redundancy and repetition. It also contains unique material that it is scarcely possible to see being added in an 'abridgement'.[63] Mann's case for revising the order of the versions, which rests mainly on **A**'s supposed omission of Latin quotations, 'sexual' material, passages critical of the clergy and nobility, and metaphor, has been forcefully answered by Traugott Lawler and George Kane.[64] To the present writer, it defies credence that a version of *Piers Plowman* not merely shorter but concluded with challenging abruptness could ever have been produced for an audience deemed incapable of grappling with the demands of **B**.[65] For despite Mann's arguments to the contrary, there is very little sign of **A**'s having been purged of the characteristic difficulties of **B**. A vigorous and impressive poem as far as it goes, the **A** Version arguably offers in Passus XI a kind of 'ending', if not a true conclusion. But while it makes good sense as the first completed phase of Langland's life-work, it makes none as a simplification of that work after its completion.

§ 18. From the above it will have emerged, however, that even with the traditional sequence of the versions still in place, dating them with certainty is not possible at present. A set of 'ideal' dates would perhaps be 1365 for **Z**; 1370 for **A**; 1379 for **B**; and 1387 for **C**. But over-precision must yield to the obligation not to over-value the meagre external evidence or the inferences to be drawn from internal evidence. What can be asserted about the Ball, But and Usk testimonies, the order of the texts and the authenticity of **Z** has now been summarised. It hardly needs saying that varying weight will be attached to arguments for dating based on metre, language, style and structure, which are interpretative to a greater or less extent. It has been the purpose of this section, however, to refrain as far as possible from speculative reconstruction of the poet's life and milieu, which some scholars today would regard as a form of 'myth-making'.[66] This is not to deny that the poem's fictions mediate 'truths' about the poet. But there are self-validating truths and truths depending on antecedent readiness to believe; likewise, there are two kinds of inferences that may be drawn from them. That the poet (as in Donaldson's 'biography' and Hanna's 'represented life') was an educated psalter-clerk, or that his having a wife and daughter impeded his advance in the Church, is a possible truth of the second kind: a 'myth' that explains what it does not prove (as myths by their nature cannot). But that Langland's understanding of syllogism-structure implies that he had studied at university or equivalent level is a likelihood that it behoves the demythologiser to *dis*prove. However, in the present instance, while this probability does not strengthen, neither does it serve to challenge the larger 'myth', a consideration that will hearten those less eager to investigate Langland's way with words than his way of life.

iv. *Later Reception of the Poem*

§ 19. Langland's supposed relations with Wycliffe and his followers are a subject that currently attracts attention, if only because much more is known about those who might have read the poem than about the poet himself. And here lies scope for a further myth: that *Piers Plowman* was an inspiration to the Lollards *c*.1390 as it had been for the Rebels *c*.1380. If, however, the 'Lollard myth' is well-grounded, its origin (as in the case of the insurgents before them) is less likely to be what the poem says than the Wycliffites' antecedent readiness to believe that the poet was of their number, if not of their name. This would have found expression in those selective interpretations to which the poem's 'dialogic' procedure renders it vulnerable. Such Langlandian '(mis) reading-circles' might have elected to ignore, for example, the poet's uniformly attested vision of Christendom as a sacramental society where an authoritative priesthood is of the essence. More specifically, as has been observed, Lollard readers would have had to forget that Langland, though strongly criticising the fraternal orders, does not seek their abolition.[67] The influence of *Piers Plowman* on religious dissenting movements that persisted through the fifteenth century and resurfaced as Protestant reformation in the sixteenth has been amply surveyed by recent writers; so there is no need to recapitulate here what in fact belongs to the work's afterlife.[68] Langland's social as much as his religious ideas, in his own time and up to the Tudor age, were exploited for their own purposes by radical reformers from John Ball to Robert Crowley. And though his writing was misinterpreted, anyone who set out to compose an ambitious poem on the theme of religious salvation (as surely as one on the value of earthly love) was bound to run such a risk. The 'ideas' in question, moreover, were not being communicated as straightforward polemic, whether in verse or prose, like *The Simonie* or the 'Jack Upland' tracts.[69] Instead, they were embodied in a work of creative imagination as complex and original as the *Troilus* of Chaucer who, after being misunderstood by his (courtly) readers, supposedly recanted his supposed attack on love and women.

§ 20. It is not unreasonable, then, to envisage Langland's C-Text as a kind of 'response' to his readers. For it significantly modifies the B-Text's treatment of the relations between the individual and the religious authority that taught him to be a citizen of the heavenly kingdom, and those between the individual and the secular authority that told him how to behave as a subject of the king of England. It may well be that the Rising of 1381 and the condemnation of Wycliffe's teachings at the Blackfriars Council in 1382 gave Langland occasions to ponder his poem's potential for being misinterpreted. And it would not be difficult to agree with Anne Hudson that the 'actuality' and the 'aftermath' of the Revolt, together with its 'implication of his own poem in its course,' might have given him 'the spur to compose'. But on the other hand, it is not easy to agree either that the **B** Version expresses 'evidently very mixed feelings about the revolt' or that **C** constitutes 'a hasty, sometimes panicky, sometimes overingenious response to a text its author at times appears to disown'. The **C** Version indeed shows signs of urgent and deep reconsideration; one passage (C Pr 95–127) is unfinished (though that is not itself a sign of haste); and the *mede / mercede* distinction in III 332–406 is 'overingenious'. But how this connects with the poet's 'unease about his own responsibilities to the rebels'[70] is not clear, and the statement may suggest a misconception about what *Piers Plowman* is. To all who have edited it (and the present writer is no exception), *Piers Plowman* is above all a great literary work. Rather than speaking about Langland's responsibilities to the rebels (about which the poem says nothing), it might be better to speak of his responsibility for his poetry and to his poem (which he mentions first in B XII 20–22a and later, as the lines seem patient of interpretation, in C V 92–101).[71]

§ 21. For it could be argued without too much difficulty that Langland remained politically and theologically what Elizabeth Kirk calls a 'radical conservative'.[72] All the versions show, as Pamela Raabe recognises,[73] that what he 'evidently' desired was repentance for sin, the restoration of the divine image in man through sacramental grace and, to make these things possible, the renewal of social and (first and foremost) religious institutions by restoring them *ad pristinum statum*. Drawing his exemplars from *The Golden Legend* and Arthurian romance, Langland ends by evoking for his 'ideal bishop' the image of a martyr, and for his 'ideal king' (perhaps more surprisingly) that of a knightly hero. Proof of this appears in a passage added at XVII 283–92 that shows not 'panicky haste' but full-blooded re-commitment to his earliest principles:

> Euery bisshope bi þe lawe sholde buxumliche walke
> And pacientliche thorw his prouynce and to his peple hym shewe,
> Feden hem and follen hem and fere hem fro synne...
> And enchaunten hem to charite, on Holy Churche to bileue.
> For as þe kynde is of a knyhte or for a kynge to be take
> And amonges here enemyes in mortel batayles
> To be culd and ouercome the comune to defende,
> So is þe kynde of a curatour for Cristes loue to preche,
> And deye for his dere childrene to destruye dedly synne.

It was, however, precisely over how to define and attain this *status pristinus* that the similarities and differences between Langland and both rebels and Lollards would have required 'negotiation' when he was composing **C**. And while this negotiation ultimately led him to emphasise submission to authority so that 'the plant of peace' might flourish, his final revision neither renounced its critique of those entrusted with authority nor, to any degree, the 'option for the poor' that marked his outlook from **Z** onwards.[74]

§ 22. Inevitably, Langland would have had almost no control over the 'responses' of contemporary readers. The most significant of these readers were perhaps those who wrote poems modelled on his, like the author of the *Crede*, the centrepiece in what is known (not without irony) as 'the *Piers Plowman* tradition'. As an impassioned *dialogus* that articulates opposing 'positions' with equal vehemence, through visionary satire at once cerebral and demotic, sublime and coarse, *Piers Plowman* threw down a challenge to those 'strong' misreadings to which major poems seem susceptible.[75] The fate of Langland's work in his time (which is all that concerns the present discussion) suggests that the authorities regarded his 'vernacular theology' neither with hostility nor with favour, but with indifference. Archbishop Arundel's Oxford Council of 1408 did not condemn the poem along with works of heterodox theology (as the Bishop of Paris in 1277 had denounced the *Roman de la Rose* in company with the writings of the Latin Averroists); 'trial material', in Anne Hudson's words, 'produces no evidence of the confiscation of *Piers Plowman* copies from suspected heretics.'[76] But neither did they appreciate the fundamental orthodoxy of a work that some of the dissenting wing had made their own.[77] The defeat of Lollardy in 1415 and (perhaps even more important) the triumph of the 'Chaucerian' poetic line in the fifteenth century helped to push *Piers Plowman* to the margins of its culture. And for the next fifty years the centre ground was dominated by a supreme literary 'entrepreneur', the *un*radical conservative John Lydgate, who was in many ways Langland's antithesis in method and motivation and who shows no interest in Chaucer's great contemporary. Many of the paradoxes and contradictions that doubtless exercised readers of *Piers Plowman* in its time have continued to energise critical interest in ours, often at the expense of its literary qualities. The main danger for *our* time is not of *Piers* being 'misread' as of its not being, as a poem, read at all; and this may be the worst form of misreading. Elizabeth Salter's declaration that 'the most important reason for reading *Piers Plowman* is...that it contains a wider variety of fine poetry than any other work from the English Middle Ages' is, if true, one that deserves to be hung above every Langland scholar's desk, but with 'reading' emended to 'reading and writing about'.[78]

v. *The Composition and Revision of* Piers Plowman

§ 23. If the main postulates of this *Introduction*'s argument have proved acceptable, it should now be possible to give a concise account of Langland's methods of composition and revision and, for want of a better word, his 'sources'.[79] To the reader who doubts the authenticity of **Z**, the versions' traditional authorship and sequence, the poet's clarity of purpose, his seriousness about the details of his art and his concern with the accurate transmission of his text, what follows may draw only qualified assent. From the beginning of the present enterprise, however, all but the first of these assumptions have been embraced as the necessary basis for a parallel-text. And as it has been argued that editing in parallel validates these assumptions, including the first, the supporting evidence (set out in *Intro.* IV above) need not be recapitulated here. Volume I provides in a convenient form the primary materials for studying a work preserved in successive stages of completeness. But although contingently co-present as 'alternative' textual possibilities, the versions representing these stages (it may be assumed) were not intended by the author to exist essentially as such (in this they are unlike the 'states' of an etching, which the engraver, using a medium open to progressive — if irreversible — alteration, may approve as variant interpretations of his subject).[80] That this is true the conflicting scribal readings in the archetypal traditions amply bear out. These 'variants' were the price Langland had to pay if his poem was to be disseminated at all under the limitations of a manuscript culture, for 'l'écriture médiévale ne produit pas de variantes, elle est variance'.[81] But as contended earlier in this *Introduction*, it is the major 'variations' of *non*-scribal origin that distinguish one 'version' from another.

§ 24. This is not to deny that two versions of *Piers Plowman* might have been 'in competition' during the decade after **B** was put forth for copying, probably the last of the poet's life. For it would be unlikely that Langland lacked readers for **A** in the decade *before* he completed **B**. Possibly even, to hazard more (unavoidable) speculation, their mixed 'responses' to the circulated text 'spurred' his composition of **B**. As readers typically do, they may have admired and criticised, inquired of Langland if and how he intended to go on, and urged him to do so (with good effect, since *his* 'response' was an original masterpiece). But it is also hard to believe that Langland could have seen **A** as a viable alternative or have sanctioned its continued circulation after realising his project in the form of **B**: at which stage, comparison would show **A** as superseded by its expanded, extended and completed successor. For an important difference between **B**'s relation to **A** and **C**'s to **B** is that **B** was from the start a new venture. Carefully planned and executed, it is from Passus XI onwards not a revision at all, since there is no antecedent material in **A**. By contrast, **C** is a critical re-construction, comparable in length, of a completed poem that in places no longer said what Langland wanted to, or did so in a way he was no longer disposed to say it. **C**'s excisions and additions are made in reaction to a pre-existing text that is in a real sense its 'source', as **A** (after Passus XI) never was a source for **B**. That difference noted, the nature of the 'revision' nonetheless compels us to regard the C-Text as a poem in its own right. This poem Langland doubtless meant as the last word on his life-long theme of justice and salvation. But he could hardly have been unaware that it would be fated to 'compete' (in a way that **A** never could have) with the text that had made his reputation, if not his 'name'. For the situation in the later 1380s was significantly altered from the early 1370s, when Langland might have 'shown' **A** to an immediate 'circle'. The fact of **B**'s 'publication' with his approval (attested both by its complete-ness and his checking of the archetypal text)[82] would have imparted urgency to his rewriting: the 'responses' of some readers (after the 'reactions' of others) will have been sharper than in the case of **A**. So, even if 'fools' approval' did not sting Langland into re-writing so much as his own 'exasperated spirit', it cannot have been a negligible factor.

§ 25. It will be clear from what has been said so far that editorial experience, fortified by a modest measure of speculation, provides little ground for supporting any 'indeterminist' theories of composition. To the present writer the four texts of *Piers Plowman* do not declare themselves as 'photographs that caught a static image of a living organism at a given but not necessarily significant moment of time',[83] with the author impulsively altering the **r** form of **A** by adding or removing lines and phrases so as to create the **m** redaction for a particular group of readers; dangling before his interpellatory audience now the β and now the α text of **B**; and, during his massive re-construction of **B**, appeasing them with bleeding chunks of 'London' satire to make 'lollers' rage and cottars laugh through their tears.[84] On the other hand, it does not strain credulity that during his final labours Langland should have allowed (or even invited) certain *acutiores* to 'read' completed parts of his new version, if it was their criticisms that had 'spurred' him to attempt it (and these might have included Usk, Wells or But, though no evidence like Chaucer's 'Envoy to Bukton' lends substance to the speculation). For the Z, **A**, **B** and **C** Versions make much less sense as points of stasis in an 'endless' process of 'rolling revision' than as purposeful, if painful, steps (*passūs*) towards realising a grand and noble design. And that this was Langland's aim seems clear from his confident transformation of the **A** Prologue into that of **B**. Since the structural coherence of individual visions is now widely accepted (that of the Second Vision in **B** was demonstrated long ago, and an analysis of the Sixth Vision's intricate organisation will be found in the *Commentary*),[85] It would seem reasonable to assume that what Langland sought in the parts he aimed at in the whole. This was *unity* (neither the word nor the idea strikes as unLang-landian). But 'Langlandian unity' is not the same as the boldly foregrounded formal architecture seen in *The Parliament of Fowls* or *Sir Gawain*, works retaining a residue of 'Ricardian' ambigu-ity to 'saffron with' their tentatively affirmative endings. Had the **B** Version fallen silent after the Easter mass-bells, its likeness to the major Ricardian pieces would not have passed unremarked. Particularly noteworthy would have seemed its closeness to the most 'through-composed' of these poems, *Pearl*. For B XVIII 475–6 and *Pearl* 1208–10 both envisage the reception of Com-munion as the 'eschatological' symbolic act of *fratres habitantes in unum* (Ps 132:1 = B XVIII 425a), whereas now *Pearl* concludes virtually with an 'answer' to what is Langland's actual final passus. Indeed, that **B** may have ended at Passus XVIII, and that XIX and XX were *added* in the **C** revision, has been mooted by Warner as a 'startling possibility'.[86] Too startling, one may feel, to be really probable; for the building of Unity and the immediate attack on it would seem (to most readers) thematically indispensable if **B**'s conception of Grace's activity in time is to be completed and 'salvation history' shown as continuing into the present. Conversely, had Langland wished the poem to end at C XX, our sense of this version as a 'revision' would demand matchingly drastic revision. But those are possibilities to be pursued no further here; **C** offers the same disconcertingly dramatic end as **B**.

§ 26. In what is commonly acknowledged as the greatest religious allegory of the period, the *Divina Commedia,* Dante created a poem with its end potentially present in its beginning, and capable of accommodating a mass of historical material within its intricate *post-mortem* architectonic. By contrast, the recalcitrance of Langland's resolutely *in via* theme, and his lack of any guide or model, offered daunting challenges to the realisation of his enterprise. Most readers tend to agree that the sense of effort and striving conveyed by *Piers Plowman* is refracted rather than contained by the formal structures of its eight main visions. Langland has no envelope of eternity to restrict the energies of his poetry from flooding into the real world of late-medieval English society. His poem may well strike readers familiar with the *Commedia* as being carried forward through its revisions on an ever more rapidly-flowing stream of historical time, even as being 'about' the process of the Christian experience in time, or what is called 'the drama of salvation history'. However, the recent critical notion that will be rejected in the next two paragraphs is not that the poem's composition was other than a 'process' (and obviously, given the conditions, a protracted one) but that process could ever have been what Langland aimed at. 'Post-modern' interpreters, laudably eager to win friends for *Piers Plowman*, its time, and its culture, should be wary of projecting onto the life-work of a fourteenth-century *makere* the ambivalences of decentred pluralism.[87] Medieval religious allegories mirror the epoch's common understanding of history, personal and universal, as a linear movement with its *ende* (both 'purpose' and 'conclusion') in death and judgement. The 'death' is that of the author *whan þis werk was wrouȝt* (A XII 103), the 'judgement' not that of 'times to come' but of the Judge of all times. Thus C V 94–101 would make little psychological (not to say spiritual) sense unless Langland's 'end' was to get 'this work' finally 'wrought'.[88] Nor would John But have prayed for WILL's soul unless he believed the poet had reached his 'end', in death. Even Chaucer's *Canterbury Tales*, which seems to point down the road of indeterminacy with the author's invitation to 'turn over the leaf and chose another tale' (I 3177), finds itself sharply re-aligned with the age's central paradigm when the pilgrims arrive at their destination, the Parson reminds them that life is a journey to judgement, and the maker takes his leave of his book and of his readers. And to instance a piece of possibly unfinished work, the abrupt end of A XI should not be thought to imply that the author espoused a poetic of fragmentation, any more than does the more obviously 'broken-off' Book III of *The House of Fame* (Ricardian poets sometimes know they should leave off if they do not know how to go on). Though it may be granted that 'perfection of the work' was, for Langland, not disjoined from but co-extensive with 'perfection of the life', his poem attests what was a lifelong struggle for the humility to accept imperfection. But an aesthetic of 'accepted imperfection' is not the same as an aesthetic of indeterminacy. Despite its modern-seeming plasticity, *Piers Plowman* rests on the same late-Gothic structural principles as *Troilus, St Erkenwald, Pearl* and the *Confessio Amantis*. Nor does there seem much reason to believe that Langland's artistic principles were at odds with those of the Ricardian masters who wrote these poems.[89]

§ 27. The situation with regard to Langland's texts is nonetheless singular enough, and our knowledge of his compositional practices sufficiently meagre, to baulk further speculation (the present writer has exceeded his licence already). But by way of conclusion, it is perhaps worth saying that for even the one more recent work that is 'semblable somdeel to *Piers þe Plowman*', Wordsworth's *Prelude*, it was not a 'process' but a product that its author kept constantly in view. Langland's poem is admittedly in many ways less like that work than *The Recluse*, the unachieved larger work on 'nature, man, and society' to which Wordsworth's enquiry into the growth of the poet's mind was a 'prelude'. The versions of *Piers Plowman* that survive may be read today, according to taste, in some historically 'authentic' manuscript text, or in the form of 'critically' reconstructed archetypes. But the poem they transmit seems too publicly engaged, right from its opening scene in a 'field ful of folk', ever to have existed as the sequence of re-copied holographs that Wordsworth's (never-published) *Prelude* constitutes.[90] Langland may have praised, but there is little sign that he practised, the reclusive life; his represented isolation is an inward condition, not (like the later poet's) a deliberate rural seclusion. He left the Malvern Hills, instead of lingering there; *clerk þou3 he were*, he stands out in his time as the critical celebrant of *ertheliche honeste thynges*, 'active' to his inky fingertips. And in all this he is essentially *of* his time, which may have tolerated, even on occasion admired, but generally did not foster solitariness.

§ 28. Langland may therefore be envisaged as a thoroughly social, even a public writer,[91] showing or reading his work to friends from whom he received (and perhaps solicited) comments and suggestions. All poetry, insofar as it *is* poetry (and including even didactic religious writing), is meant to give people pleasure. And if the poet's own quarters proved too cramped for this purpose, he presumably knew people (they need not be called 'patrons') with space to offer, encouragement and refreshment.[92] His activity was also, from A VIII 89–XII 98, and from B XI until the crisis that provoked renewed work, one of composition rather than revision. Thus **Z** preserves a draft (not a first, it seems probable, but a second or later draft) of a work that was completed but not 'finished'; fit to be read out, but not to be read 'in'. This version Langland turned into **A** by adding the extraordinary Tearing of the Pardon after its closing 'beatitude' words on the poor. Our sole manuscript copy of **Z**, it may be surmised, is most probably the posthumous product of a time when interest in *any* form of *Piers Plowman* was strongest, and when Langland's literary remains were being preserved for and distributed to those who had supported him during life. These remains, it may be assumed, would not have included rough papers that showed his composing hand at work. For medieval aesthetics was not concerned with the preparatory stages of 'masterworks'; and the 'aesthetic of imperfection' mentioned above must be understood not in terms of the later idea of the inspired fragment, but of St Gregory's idea of 'perfection in imperfection'.[93] This notion betokens acceptance that no human work can be perfect (though man should nonetheless strive to make it so) and not the Romantics' acknowledgement (nourished by belief in the mysteriousness of poetic inspiration) of the *opus imperfectum* as a legitimate artistic category. Nor is the poet himself likely to have parted with the early draft texts, as opposed to finished portions, of any version. If **C** was known to Usk, this might simply imply that it *was* (like **Z**) virtually 'complete', though not 'finished'', when Langland died (see § 11 above).

§ 29. It seems a fair assumption therefore that Langland might have kept his draft materials with him, notwithstanding that he would have had to give up his final manuscript of **B** for copying and that the C-Text unquestionably reflects errors present in the text of **B** he worked from, which must therefore have been a scribal product. But there is no real evidence for thinking that he used a scribal manuscript in revising from **A** to **B**. And since **A** (by contrast with **B**) is likely to have undergone only limited scribal copying in the poet's lifetime, he could well have held on to his own fair copy or a pre-final draft. Quite possibly, if they contained anything of potential future value, he also kept working-papers of **A** (and later **B**) too extensively written-over to be of use as scribal copy-text. It is of course more than possible that, in the highly mnemonic culture of his time, Langland composed long passages of the poem in his head before writing them down (even in the age of print, Milton and Wordsworth did as much), and could subsequently recall the material he needed at will. But supposition aside, there is evidence recoverable through analysis of the text that he did indeed possess a 'repertorium' or 'poetic bank' of lines and half-lines, ready to be drawn upon in different situations.

§ 30. This document could have been alphabetically arranged for convenience like the Biblical and preaching concordances of the day, and it would not be hard to reconstruct it from the material given below in Appendix Three. From this it appears that some 65 lines and 250 half-lines (37% of the latter b-verses) are used more than once, whether in the same version or in a later one (not all are verbally identical, and where a small difference is found this has been duly noted). It is admittedly not usual to think of Langland as to any degree a 'formulaic' poet (although his use of rhetorical *repetitio* is well known).[94] But even according to the flexible rules of versification that he employed, he could hardly have composed nearly 19,000 lines without re-using units of verse-structure. What is surprising is not that Langland sometimes resorted to metrical set-phrases, but that he did so very rarely. With only the half-lines counted as properly formulaic (whole-lines belonging more to rhetorical *repetitio*), they amount to only 0.70% of the whole. The 65 full lines are, at 0.33%, an even smaller proportion, though their impact is necessarily greater. These figures explain why the style of *Piers Plowman* does not strike as 'formulaic', even though some half-lines are repeated as many as sixteen times.[95] For though Langland no more than Chaucer or Gower avoids common phrases and idioms in constructing half-lines, he relatively seldom repeats them, so that his style comes across as colloquial without being prosaic. By definition, most of these non-parallel *repeated* half-lines do not belong to the core-text, though a small number occur more than once in more than one version. But 'repeat-verses' distinguishable from parallel-lines are also to be found outside passages that (even after repositioning) appear parallel when compared with the relevant displaced material.

§ 31. Most studies of Langland's revisions have understandably focussed on the four larger procedures of omitting, adding, transposing and re-writing material from the immediately antecedent version. Useful analyses of **A**, **B** and **C** appear in the Athlone editions (Kane 19–24; Kane-Donaldson 72–8; Russell-Kane 63–4), and Malcolm Godden's pioneering study covers all four included in this edition.[96] A full examination of the revision-process would, however, require a separate volume, and none is attempted here, though the most important changes are discussed *ad loc* in Sections B and C of the present volume. But while it has been maintained that the poet's acts of revision were essentially 'linear' (IV § 22 above), analysis of repeated **C** half-lines shows that Langland felt free to restore what he had previously written if he so wished. For there is no reason to doubt that he had access to these earlier forms, and not only in the 'repertorium' form hypothesised. A representative example is the line 'And is to mene in oure mouth more ne mynne' (III 395), a somewhat 'formulaic' addition in a new passage of **C**. Here Langland was taking up A XI 306 'And is to mene in oure mouþ more ne *lesse*', the second and fourth lifts of which he had revised in parallel B X 456 to 'And is to mene *to Englissh men* more ne *lesse*'. But in **C** he both changed *lesse* to *mynne* in the b-half to make up a Type Ib line *and* he remembered to alter the b-half lift in parallel C XI 293 to read 'And is to mene no more to men *that beth lewed*', where only lift four contains a new idea. This is evidence that Langland re-composed with the texts of both **A** and **B** to hand (or, less credibly, in his head), since he was clearly taking into account the implications of re-using elements from a version anterior to the one directly under revision. Even more striking is a line from a part of the poem corresponding only to the B-Text, 'So is he fader and formeour, þe furste of alle thynges' (C XIX 134), which repeats A X 28 except for adding the onset-phrase. At B IX 27 he had revised the b-half of this line to *of al þat euere was maked*, presumably to avoid repeating the previous line's 'of alle kynnes *þynges*', and now he altered this b-half to 'of al þat *forth groweth*'. These lines suggest not recourse to a repertory-concordance but eye-access to the full A-Text. By contrast, C Pr 88b, which appears to repeat A II 45a, is more likely to be drawn from the repertory, as it is a formulaic half-line used a dozen times in **C** and three times in **B**, half of these falling in the b-verse.

§ 32. Another example that may point to similar access to **Z** when Langland was writing **B** and **C** is B IX 72 'Of þis matere I miȝte make a long tale', which is deleted in **C**, is absent from **A** but is first encountered in the earliest version as VII 230. To a sceptic of the authenticity of **Z**, this might seem evidence that the substantive text in Bodley 851 post-dates **B**. But the line's presence in **B** could also be explained by its having been in Langland's repertorium, not wanted in **A**, but re-activated later for use in **B**. For it is a transition-forming quasi-filler, repeated at B XV 89 except for substitution of *muche bible* for *long tale*. Again, in **C**, in a passage without parallel in **Z**, Langland picked up III 78 'Bothe schyreues and seriauntes *and suche as* kepeth *lawes*' from Z II 189 'As seriauntes and scheryues that schyres han to kepe', altering the last two lifts, the word-order and the sense. The strongest evidence that this might indeed be a 'repertory' line is that it does not appear in **A** or **B** and can scarcely have been inserted in **Z** by a compiler working with more than one text, because it is not present *at that point* in **C** (i.e. in the 'Drede' scene at C II 217–19). On a simpler explanation, Langland could have picked the line out directly from his copy of **Z**, which (as said at § 29 above) he is antecedently unlikely to have given away for keeping, let alone copying, to an acquaintance. But the 'repertorium' explanation here better accords with the other evidence produced so far. The widely disjunct appearance of **B** lines in **C** (i.e. in non-parallel positions both earlier and later than the **B** occurrences) also provides supporting evidence for the existence of the repertorium. Thus B 2.187 // ZC appears as late as C XVII 249, III 193a (modified) at C XIII 56, IV 32 at XV 37, XV 486 at C XVII 230; while X 121b appears in an *earlier* position at C X 104, XIV 182 at C XIII 57, and XV 120 at C III 228b. In all these cases, Langland is careful to make modifications to the corresponding passage in the later text, presumably so as to avoid unintended repetition. With these fitful but illuminating glimpses into the shadowy interior of Langland's 'cave of making', we may turn to the broader and vaguer question of the maker's 'sources.'

vi. *The Sources of* Piers Plowman

§ 33. To find a dream-poem framework as the setting for his vision in the Prologue, Langland need have looked no further than the opening of one of the few earlier alliterative works that he certainly knew, *Winner and Waster*. But apart from a delayed echo of that poem's symphony of birdsong in the transitional waking-sequence before the Third Vision (X 61–7 //), and the detail of running water in B Pr 8–10 // ZA (= *WW* 33, 44), the earliest version **Z** immediately strikes out independently to evoke a symbolic landscape that owes everything to the Bible and nothing to the *Winner*-poet (see *Commentary* on Pr 14–21). Langland's second major departure from his English predecessor's example was to construct two self-contained dream-visions, and make the first lead naturally on to the second. This was required so that he could answer WILL's great question to Holy Church, 'How can I save my soul?' The answer was, 'All who live a "true" life in their appointed state in our corrupt society will be certain to receive a pardon from TRUTH, and the patient poor of this world will receive the greatest pardon of all'. This 'answer' sums up the 'meaning' of the first version of *Piers Plowman*, and it takes two dreams to convey. Langland is thought to have got the structural device of multiple visions, as well as various aspects of his later treatment of the life of Christ, from a source not in English but in French, the 'vernacular of clerks'. This is the tripartite corpus of dream-visions by Guillaume de Deguileville, the *Pèlerinages de Vie Humaine*, *de l'Ame* and *de Jhesucrist* (*c*.1330–60), a work noticed by a number of earlier scholars and, most recently examined by John Burrow.[97] However, apart from these and Robert Grosseteste's *Chateau d'Amour*, which he seems to echo in IX 234ff, 269ff (see *Commentary*), Langland displays relatively little interest in the Continental dream-allegory tradition. He is indifferent to its *fons et origo* the *Roman de la Rose*, in strong contrast to Chaucer, who started his career by translating that work and found the *Roman* a life-long inspiration, or even the alliterative peer who adapted some lines of 'Clopyngnel' in so wittily 'Langlandian' a fashion in *Purity* 1057–64 (but see the *Commentary* on I 6). The language of 'French men and free men' (B XI 384) was apparently for him no more than an assumed accomplishment. Unlike Chaucer, Langland (who gives no sign of having travelled to France) shows little susceptibility to its siren-song, which he perhaps associated with the ostentatiousness of decadent knighthood and the luxury of papal Avignon. Langland obviously wanted this 'richest realm' left in peace and left to itself, and the throwaway insult of X 135 may obliquely hint at a reason why. His antagonism to France (if it is really that) seems to be based not on a sense of cultural inferiority but on suspicion of the exterior 'Gallic' polish that the spirit of *mondanité* could cunningly exploit in order to entrap a *cœur simple*. But if Langland's own poetry is not unsophisticated, it may be fairly described as *anti*-sophisticated. Thus even *courtoisie*, the emblem of French civilisation for his contemporaries, never simply 'means good' in *Piers Plowman*, which struggles to wrench this ambiguous token-term from the keeping of Lady Mede and enlist it in the lexicon of grace.[98] During Richard II's later years, Langland is no more likely to have approved *Troilus and Criseyde*'s painstaking endeavour to 'redeem' *fin' amour* than *Sir Gawain*'s painful transvaluations of 'chivalry' and 'courtesy'. For those central values of the time his defiant exemplar is a saviour 'without spurs or spear' in ploughman's garb.

§ 34. For all medieval poets 'social man' living in community formed the real, the principal artistic subject. So even when WILL has a vision of Nature from the mountain of Middle-Earth, he quickly turns his gaze from the blameless beasts to focus (with whatever chagrin) on the troubled world of fallen men and women. But typically, in an age without romanticism, Langland (unlike Wordsworth) shows no nostalgia for a lost childhood of visionary innocence. His quest is not for the rusty gate of Eden but the well-oiled drawbridge of the City of God. And this (following the dual model of 'Jerusalem' as bride and city in Apoc 21:2) is the 'spiritual organism' manifested to the Dreamer first as HOLY CHURCH and finally as UNITY. But the 'drawbridge' to be crossed is the 'material organisation' in which that organism had become historically compacted. For inescapably, the spiritual reality to which Christian learning and worship were held to grant access finds itself summoned into the poetry through the insistent citations from *holiwrit* that sound Langland's most distinctive note. These *tixtes* provide him a handhold on the attention of his more cultured and presumably influential readers; they are what might have impressed Wycliffe if that stern *doctour* ever read *Piers Plowman*. Together with the macaronic lines, which usually embed morsels of larger quotations, they stand in tension with the de-provincialised vernacular through which Langland probes a domain of discourse where it had no recognised rights, feeling with its fingers the fleshly heart of *clergye*. Highlighted in the manuscripts of the poem by underlining and rubrication, the Latin quotations conversely serve to 'prove' Langland's metropolitanised English. But to the reader today, as doubtless then, they resemble a door (whether locked or open) into the work's innermost recesses. For to Langland, 'þe Engelisch of oure eldres' is not in itself an alternative mode of access to religious truth; because salvation, to his thinking, lies in 'þe cofre of Cristes tresor,' to which 'clerkes kepe þe keyes' (B XII 108–9). So immediate, indeed, is Langland's sense of Christianity's 'Roman' lineage that he treats its arrival in England as a thing but of yesterday. He makes vivid to himself how the compassionate intercessor for the pagan Emperor Trajan was the same champion of the heathen English who with a legendary pun on his lips[99] resolved to send Augustine to Canterbury. He sees Christianity as a Latin 'thing', the *res Latina* as the *res Christiana*. Against this rooted conviction is set, to be sure, the other pole of the cultural dialectic, the simple faith of simple folk, 'pore peple as plouȝmen, and pastours of bestes'. Yet even this faith, we cannot fail to notice, must be formulated in the phrase *sola fides*; even these folk have no choice but to 'Percen *with a Paternoster* þe paleis of heuene' (A XI 310–12). For Langland never calls the Lord's Prayer the 'Our Father'; and he never recognises 'true' knowledge of religion without *clergye*.[100]

§ 35. 'Vernacular theology' may in some sense describe parts of *Piers Plowman*, even if to think of the poem as a 'theological' work risks the irrelevance that arises from generic misclassification.[101] But Langland seems to have employed 'þe Engelisch of oure eldres' because it was appropriate to *makyng*, not because he thought it able (as did Reginald Pecock a century later) to capture the Queen of the Sciences for the mother tongue. Thus, unlike the Lollards he does not even desiderate 'þe Bible in English' in order to 'expoune' Scripture, as one Wycliffite writer has it, 'myche openliere and shortliere...and myche sharpliere and groundliere' for the benefit of 'a symple man'. And this because for Langland, *clerkes kepe þe keyes*. Rather, his work resembles what David Lawton calls (in reference to Rolle) 'a limited form of functional bilingualism, enabling devotional and liturgical recognition of familiar text'.[102] *Piers Plowman* is not (as is *Patience*) a work of *translatio*, however 'free'; for somewhat like the anonymous author of *The Cloud of Unknowing* as Nicholas Watson describes him, Langland 'acts not simply as a clerical translator of learned material but as a fierce vernacular *critic* of the academic world from which his learning derives'.[103] These formulations may help to situate Langland in relation to certain aspects of his wider intellectual milieu. To the student of *Piers Plowman*, tension between the learned and the vernacular, foregrounded by a unique style forged in revising, is its fundamental dynamic and merits the close attention of all who approach it as a poem.[104]

§ 36. The Latin quotations mentioned above remind us that, whereas study of the medieval poet's method of composition tends to start with 'sources', Langland does not strictly seem to have any.[105] John Alford has argued, however, that he '*began* with the quotations, and from them, using the standard aids of a medieval preacher, derived the substance of the poem'. And his view finds support in Judson Allen's claim that 'the text of the poem obeys no logic of its own, but occurs as commentary on a development of an array of themes already defined elsewhere as an ordered set — usually by the Bible.'[106] But even allowing, as Allen does, that Langland might have come across major compilation-sources such as Hugh of St Cher's Psalter Commentary only *after* writing **Z** (which has barely more than a dozen quotations), both comments are surely much exaggerated. An unprejudiced reader of the poem in the sequence **ZABC** will not be quickly moved to abandon the traditional view of the Latin quotations as designed to reinforce and illustrate the sense of the English text, which is primary. They provide the germinal idea of particular thematic structures, suggest developments, create networks of allusion and broaden contextual meaning.[107] In this way, the quotations can resemble conventional 'sources', as when the Latin is translated or paraphrased before or after being given.[108] But textually speaking, they figure as the chief element of a cultural matrix furnished by the *Biblia glossata* and 'aids' to its study such as incipits, concordances and dictionaries. They provide a horizon of transcendental reference and ensure that the 'meaning' of the 'earthly honest things' of English 'experience' that form the poem's foreground is not lost.

§ 37. As a psalter-clerk, Langland will have been involved to some degree in the communal prayer by which monastic and other religious clergy 'sacralised' the hours of day and night. But even more important than the complete Divine Office for widening access to the words of Scripture beyond the circles of the *litterati* was the circumambient 'text' of *masse and houres* in which the people at large were able to participate and which (as Sr Mary Davlin puts it)

> exist[s] not to be read or heard passively, but to be participated in, played out, worked
> and played with over and over; their purpose...experience, both aesthetic and religious,
> [through which] they release an increasing fullness of connotative meaning.[109]

Langland evidently assumed, for example, that observance of the Sunday obligation implied attendance not only at Mass but also at the 'hours' of Matins and Evensong.[110] And while the exact meaning of the Missal or Breviary readings might have been lost on all but the few, in a broader sense the Church's daily worship formed a shared 'possession' of layman and clerk alike. The Latin of the liturgy was perceived less as a 'learned' than as a 'sacred' language, consecrated to a special purpose that elevated it above the mundane vernacular. In particular, the ceremonies of the Easter Triduum, a recurring communal 'immersion' in the most moving and dramatic texts of the New Testament, constituted a solemn rite of collective spiritual renewal. Preceded by Lenten sermons, and followed by the miracle plays of midsummer, the central days of the Church's year offered a religious experience of high intensity, at an emotional rather than an intellectual plane.[111] Langland could therefore expect the Passion narrative of B XVIII to be appreciated by an audience wider than the formally 'literate'; but understood, of course, at more than one level. It is not so much that (as the comments of Alford and Allen propose) the 'substance' of his greatest Passus is 'derived' from the fifty Latin quotations that vein its English text as that this substance, embodied in an 'earthly honest' fourteenth-century South-West Midland vernacular, is nourished by a flow of regionally and temporally unrestricted 'sacred' speech. This language is marked in the written text by rubrication, and invites (when read aloud) a change of pitch and tone. The pinnacle of Langland's 'clerkly making', Passus XVIII offers a model for comprehending the entire question of his 'sources', or what might better (if more loosely) be called his 'inspiration'. The resonant textuality that sustains this passus, together with the quieter reflectiveness of the one that follows it, furnish our widest perspective on his enterprise.[112] Langland, it clearly emerges, was inspired by the same sources as the community of believers whose corporate experience of sacred 'timelessness' he alone of his contemporaries managed to articulate 'in time'. English speech and Latin liturgy joined to give Langland an *os magna sonaturum,* a voice of great compass with unique expressive and communicative power.

§ 38. A distinction should perhaps be recognised, then, between the poet's sources in this broader sense and his reading as such. But Passus XVIII not only draws deeply on 'enacted scripture', the shared words of a rite of *anamnesis*; it also uses a text that the poet had presumably 'read', not 'heard sung or recited', the account of the Harrowing of Hell in the Apocryphal *Gospel of Nicodemus.* This Langland certainly knew in the Latin, probably also in the C13th English translation, and possibly through a dramatisation in the Corpus Christi plays that were taking shape in his early years (though Latin para-liturgical dramas had been composed since the thirteenth century and vernacular cycles were known by the last quarter of the fourteenth, the individual pageant-themes were probably in formation not earlier than *c.*1350).[113] Once again, to contrast Langland with his great contemporary, whereas Chaucer's personal discovery *Il Filostrato* was a narrative source that he could conceal from his audience under the fictitious name of 'Lollius', the *Harrowing* that Langland used was common cultural property. This story had no part in the formal Easter service, but popular tradition had made the *Descensus* narrative familiar enough to toll reminiscent bells through the measures of Langland's resonant verse, and invite attention to what was new and unexpected in its presentation. And unlike the more *recherché* Debate of the Four Daughters of God that precedes it, the *Harrowing* story worked with motifs that were widely known in the visual art of the time.[114] That Langland himself found this episode a continuing artistic challenge is clear from the significant changes he made to his treatment of it in Passus XX, the last fully revised part of **C**.

§ 39. Connected in principle (though not always in practice) with the liturgy and 'para-liturgy' (processions and devotions) was another public auditory experience, that of the preaching-sermon. A typical Sunday homily from the local *persone* might offer little to feed the poet's imagination; but London in his time had outstanding preachers, often mendicants, who could be heard in their own great churches or at St Paul's Cross (where the Gluttonous Doctor was heard to preach on fasting a few days before WILL met him in Conscience's house). The impress of sermon-like features is detectable throughout *Piers Plowman,* though modern readers may be less apt to see the poem (like G. R. Owst, the pioneer in this field) as 'the fine product of English medieval preaching'[115] or the sermon as the origin of its attitudes, images and ideas so much as something that encouraged the poet to express all these in particular well-known ways. Elizabeth Salter accordingly turned from Owst's concentration on thematic content to study the formal influence of the *ars predicandi* on Langland's poetic procedures. And A. C. Spearing followed her, arguing that the preacher's organisation by 'division' of the 'theme' provides the poem's main ordering principle, and offering an analysis of Reason's address to the Folk of the Field (V 125ff).[116] While this *sermo prelati ad status* is probably the only formal sermon in the poem, other longer discourses like those of Anima and Holy Church are similarly constructed. But as Siegfried Wenzel observes, though the structure of Holy Church's speech resembles that of a Middle English sermon he examines, 'its *mode of progression* and development' are uncharacteristic of fourteenth-century sermons and more reminiscent of devotional writings like the *Ancrene Wisse*.[117] This needs saying, since the influence on Langland of English and especially of Latin devotional prose, such as that of the Bernardine-Bonaventuran tradition, is easy to underestimate.

But sermons, it should also be noted, are not always accepted in *Piers Plowman* as authoritative instruction. Sometimes dubious characters are seen preaching, such as an unlicensed pardoner (Pr 66) and troublous mendicants (XI 54, 207). And even Mahomet is shown to exploit, as a means to deceive the gullible, the combination of oratory and personality that successful preachers depend on. Langland often voices suspicion of practised sermonists who 'prechen and preue hit nat' (XVI 262, XVII 383–4); and at B XV 448 he proclaims his preference for miracle-working over eloquence as a means of evangelisation. The cynical might not marvel if this should prove in shorter supply; but what Langland is really asking for is preaching valorised by holiness of life, as witness one of his best macaronic outbursts:

> '*Beatus*,' seiþ Seint Bernard, '*qui scripturas legit*
> *Et verba vertit in opera* fulliche to his power' (XV 60–1).

This exhortation is meant to apply to all who study the Bible, but *a fortiori* to those who make sermons on problematic texts, as do (ten lines later) the 'Freres and fele oþere maistres þat to þe lewed *prechen*' (B XV 70). As so often, the poet's key concern in highlighting the ambiguous relationship between Latin as the language of *holy loore* and English as that of *kynde understondyng* is the responsibility of the *lered* to the *lewed*.

§ 40. This said, Langland is by no means always the earnest moralist. Nearer to Dickens in some ways than to Milton, he can be humorously sceptical about the readiness of religious experts to leap up and preach, as witness Dame Scripture mounting her pulpit two steps at a time (XII 42). And the Z-Text Dreamer's wry response to Hunger's exposition of the 'theme' *servus nequam*, that 'hit fallet nat for me, for Y am no dekne / To preche the peple what that poynt menes' (Z VII 231–2) seems consciously ambiguous as to which response is invited: 'What a pity!' or 'And a good thing too!' None of this is meant to question that some of Langland's poetic figures of speech owe a genuine debt to the rich homiletic culture of the time, and Wenzel is probably right that investigation of unread Latin sermons may 'bear fruit for *Piers Plowman* scholarship'.[118] But while one may hope, one hesitates; for though Langland uses *sarmon* in the sense both of 'discourse' and 'preaching-sermon', it is the former that he seems most to have profited from. Indeed, his one favourable reference to the latter, in the line 'Patriarkes and prophetes, precheours of Goddes wordes' (VII 87), seems to envisage not churchmen but august scriptural personages like Jeremiah and John the Baptist. He had probably heard enough sermons to have reservations about them as a force for good, if what they taught was contradicted (as it doubtless often was) by the lives of those who preached them. And one suspects that though Langland scorned *idiotes preestes* who mangled the liturgy, his conviction that *sola fides sufficit* guaranteed a limit on the harm that *overskipperis* could do to the *lewed*. In regard to sermons, by contrast, for preachers to urge self-denial while living like epicures brought clerks, *clergye* and *the feith* into disrepute. On the whole, then, the tradition of interpretation stemming from Owst may have overstated the direct influence of the pulpit upon the poet's creative processes. For if participation in the Church's liturgy provided the *lewed* a comforting spiritual shawl, exposure to preaching could prove like standing in a cold east wind. The poet preferred the shawl to the wind.

§ 41. Sustaining what may be thought of as Langland's broadly communal 'inspiration' was, however, a select body of Latin writings that helped him to refine his understanding of the central Christian 'mysteries' as the medieval Church received them. These mysteries were the Incarnation, the Trinity, and the operation of Grace through time in the lives of the Saints whose memorial feasts formed a 'sanctoral' cycle intertwined with the 'temporal' cycle of the Church's Calendar. The terseness of the Gospel narratives, moreover, prompted in this period the writing of 'lives' of Christ that filled it out and 'pointed' it with colourful detail. Taking example from the impassioned eloquence of St Bernard, these attempts by (largely) Mendicant writers to arouse devotion among the laity readily found their way into the vernacular. The most influential was the *Vita Christi* of the fourteenth-century Carthusian Ludolf of Saxony, which is drawn upon in the **C** revision.[119] But one that might have had a special appeal to Langland was the *Philomena* of the thirteenth-century Yorkshireman John of Howden, a lyrical-epic Passion-meditation in rhyming quatrains of almost 'Metaphysical' pointedness and complexity that call Langland's methods to mind:

> *Scribe corde, quod lingua proferam:*
> *Scissae carnis loricam laceram,*
> *Seminatam in fronte literam,*
> *Quam cum lego, da corpus deseram* (*Philom.* XIX 61).

The 'unmeasurable' mystery of the Trinity, which some modern interpreters have seen as an organising structural principle of *Piers Plowman*, had received its fullest treatment in the 'books and books' of Augustine's *De Trinitate*.[120] But an unexplored further possible source is the *De Trinitate* of the twelfth-century mystic Richard of St Victor, whose strikingly original presentation of the divine nature as 'shared love harmoniously in community...fused into one affection by the flame of love' (III. xix)[121] furnishes an image that underlies passages such as XIX 169–71. For *seintes lyues redyng* Langland turned to the *Legenda Aurea* of the Dominican master James of Voragine, a favourite book that he mentions three times by name.[122] Such writings offered a key enabling him to 'decode' the text of salvation inscribed on the body of Christ in its 'mystical' extension through historical time, the Church. In a more general way, the entire range of man's moral life Langland found treated in another major authority that he refers to by name. This is the *Moralia in Job* written by the one of 'Peres foure stottes' he twice calls (among eight several mentions) 'Gregory the grete clerk', whose thought and theory pervade the entire poem. Such lofty doctrine, finally, he supplements with the *oother science* of Cato's thrifty couplets, a repository of everyday prudence.[123]

§ 42. The 'natures of things' also seem to have fascinated Langland, whether it was the way that birds and mammals copulate or the paradoxical means by which scorpion-bites are supposedly cured (XIII 143–66; XX 154–59). So did the natures of words, as revealed in his insistence on the etymologies of *loller* and *hethen* (IX 213–14, B XV 458–60.[124] But Langland is especially fascinated by the relationship between words and things, espousing not the 'conventionalist' theory standard among students of language in our day but (like the medieval *modistae*, who were 'Realists') a form of 'lexical Platonism', which posits substantive affinities between the referents of homophonous lexemes.[125] And in the same general tradition of metaphysical Realism, he embraces the 'sacramental' understanding of language and the world of the twelfth-century poet-theologian Alan of Lille, which goes back to the Augustine of *On Christian Doctrine*. More particularly, Langland's vision of creation as thrown into disorder by human sin owes much to Alan's *De Planctu Naturae* (a work Chaucer cites in *The Parliament of Fowls* 316), where the poet's encounter with Nature (not seen in a dream-vision but decidedly visionary) follows upon his anguished questionings in the opening elegiacs:

Heu! quo naturae secessit gratia? morum
Forma, pudicitiae norma, pudoris amor?...
Sed male naturae munus pro munere donat,
Cum sexum lucri vendit amore suum.

Other traces of Alan's ideas surface in the poem's sombre vision of how 'man and mankynde.../ Resoun reulede hem nat, noþer ryche ne pore' (XIII 181–2) but also, in a more hopeful vein, in its positive valuation of 'ertheliche honeste thynges' (XXI 94) as the *liber, pictura, speculum* and *fidele signaculum* of mankind's 'life, and death, and state and fate' (*Omnis mundi creatura*).[126]

§ 43. It has been shown by a number of scholars[127] that the 'monastic philosophy' of the twelfth and thirteenth centuries, especially the Bernardine tradition of interior self-understanding, becomes after the turning-point of the first inner dream the guide that directs the Dreamer's spiritual 'journey' through the *Vita*. This journey records his progress from preoccupation with intellectual knowledge (*scientia*) in the Third Vision to a fervent embrace of spiritual wisdom (*sapientia*) in the Fourth and Fifth. It may have been essentially a prolonged reflection on the 'nature' of his most original creation, Piers, that inspired the poet's transformation of Will from a fiercely contentious 'knight' of Pride to a silently attentive servant of Humility. Yet Langland's selective but impassioned reading may be allowed to have played a part in this. Whether or not a fresh discovery in the pseudo-Bernardine *Cogitationes piissimae* that *Multi multa sciunt et seipsos nesciunt* prompted his return to the 'affective' monastic tradition after a period under the spell of scholastic training, the Dreamer's attitude to the theology of the schools appears throughout the poem negative if not hostile, marked by the anguish of one who has 'ay loste and loste' (V 95). It is a matter of speculation whether this 'represented' disillusion is to be connected with a crisis in the author's life in which he turned from the disputes of the mendicant theologians *in scole* to seek relief in the wisdom of the *cloistre*, perhaps first encountered in youth on the Malvern Hills. Certainly, since Bloomfield, students of Langland's 'philosophy' (the present writer among them) have found the ascription of specific scholastic sources harder to establish than those from monastic tradition.[128] Langland criticises both mendicant and secular *maistres* for propounding 'materes vnmesurable to tellen of the Trinite' (B XV 71). But on this awesome subject the only authority he *quotes* is Augustine, 'highest of the four' (and fount of monastic sapience), recoiling from the schoolmen's obsession with 'insolibles and falaes' (XVI 229) and naming 'Coveytyse to conne and to knowe sciences' (XVI 222), the purpose for which in a sense the Schools existed, as the sin that drove man out of Eden.

§ 44. The strain of vehement anti-intellectualism voiced through Will need not, of course, convey Langland's own conviction. But it figures as the dialectical antithesis of a reverential awe before the majesty of Reason, God's Law at work in nature and in the structures of human society, including those of government and justice. Only a clerk, perhaps, could excoriate clerkish wrong-headedness, greed and mendacity with such force. But only a 'genuine poet' (see § 45 below) could adequately imagine the reckless viciousness and sordor of sublunary existence, see it, and 'in time' learn to suffer it. And it is not the least strength of *Piers Plowman* to escape at so many points (though not always) the 'immodest tone' of the indignant preacher. Partly he manages this through his other flexible and original creation Will, the wincing butt of those stern instructresses Holy Church, Study and Scripture, partly by articulating his punitive spleen through the voices of several variously authoritative protagonists, from Reason and Piers to Anima and Conscience.

But one particular clerkly poetic tradition it seems Langland also learned from is that of 'goliardic' Latin complaint, which lies behind some of his most memorable satire, as in the scenes of Glutton's Confession and the dinner at Conscience's house. In this same body of writing Langland could have satisfied his evident taste for puzzles, riddles, enigmas and pseudo-prophecies, none of which are prominent features of vernacular verse. The tradition of clever, coarse railing, not without a dash of *turpiloquium*, is loosely associated with the twelfth-century Archdeacon of Oxford, Walter Map. The latter's works appear in such manuscripts of monastic origin as Bodley 851 (bound up with the Z-Text), and have been aptly labelled 'interclerical', because they are 'written by clerics for clerics, targeting different clerical communities'.[129] Langland's 'translation' of this variety of learned vituperation involves a measure of softening to accommodate it to the ears of laypeople among his audience. But his lines on Glutton's excesses:

> A pissede a potel in a *Paternoster*-whyle
> And blew his rownd ruet at his rygebones ende,
> That alle þat herde þe horne helde here nose after
> And wesched hit hadde be wexed with a weps of breres (VI 398–401)

are perfectly in the spirit of goliardic writing. For the cream of the jest here is that the same image of the 'horn' recurs some 200 lines later, after Repentance's lofty prayer 'God þat of Thi goodnesse' at C VII 122ff:

> Thenne hente Hope an horn of *Deus, tu conuersus viuificabis nos*,
> And blewe hit with *Beati quorum remisse sunt iniquitates* (VII 151–2)

— lines that come from the Introit of the Mass. This contraposition of the sublime with what is customarily (if inaccurately) called the grotesque, the spotless eucharistic table and the tavern-floor slippery with urine and vomit, is characteristic and original. But it is still short of the perfect fusion of the *Philomena* and *Golias* modes that will form the true 'Langlandian grotesque' and that represents his supreme achievement as a clerkly maker. This unique kind of poetry is best illustrated (like much else that is best in the poem) in the great scene of the Harrowing of Hell. For here the chaotic quarrelling of the Devils (mirroring and magnifying that of the Daughters) is astonishingly transformed in the revised lines of C XX 275–94, where battle-poetry that would be at home in the *Morte Arthure* is embedded in a context that undermines even as it elevates:

> 'Ac arise vp, Ragamoffyn, and areche me alle þe barres,
> That Belial thy beelsyre beet with thy dame,
> And Y shal lette this loerd and his liht stoppe.
> Ar we thorw brihtnesse be blente, go barre we þe ʒates!' (XX 281–84).

§ 45. This last reference to another great alliterative poem of the period, of uncertain date but almost certainly later than Langland, brings us back full circle to the 'mystery' with which the discussion in this section began. Now, however, this is the mystery not of who Langland the Man was, but of where Langland the Maker 'came from'. What is known about this was first made explicit in a seminal study by Derek Pearsall: that the South-West Midlands were the original place where the alliterative tradition mysteriously *rekeuerede and lyuede*, yielding in time a rich harvest of longer poems, at least half a dozen of them masterpieces.[130] But a century of research has not dispersed the mist that hangs over the 'sources' and 'origins' of the Ricardian age's most controversial poet. How much is tradition and how much individual talent remains disputed, and there is still much to be done and discovered. Perhaps the most significant point is that Langland managed, apparently without help from any known predecessor, to produce what Wordsworth called in the penultimate sentence of his 'Preface' to the *Lyrical Ballads*

> a species of poetry...which is genuine poetry...in its nature well adapted to interest mankind permanently, and likewise important in the multiplicity and quality of its moral relations.[131]

There is evidence enough that *Piers Plowman* 'interested' readers in its time, for reasons about which it is difficult now to be completely clear. But if it continues 'to interest mankind permanently', it is perhaps most likely to be for the reason Wordsworth mentions: 'the multiplicity and quality of its moral relations'.

THE POEM IN TIME: NOTES

1 For a valuable overview of the documents, see Hanna, *William Langland* (*WL*), now updated in Hanna 'Emendations', whence they are cited.

2 As argued by Kerby-Fulton in Justice & Kerby-Fulton, *Written Work* pp. 69–70. Kane 'Labour and Authorship', p. 422, rightly maintains that the *PP* texts do not support her arguments.

3 See *The Legend of Good Women*, G Prol 255–661; *Confessio Amantis*, side-note to Bk I, l. 60.

4 The passage is examined by Middleton in a volume of essays that find in its 'apparent self-portraiture' what their editor calls 'an opening...into the character of vernacular authorship in Ricardian England' (*Written Work*, p. 2). The fullest account of the 'myth' of Langland is in Benson, *Public 'PP'*, pp. 3–41.

5 Scribal objection to a proper name is registered in the *C*-b variant *sone*, the product of contamination. For acute discussion of the referent of 'WILL' see Simpson 'Authorial Naming' in Hewett-Smith, *WL's 'PP,'* pp. 145–65.

6 MED s.v. *wille* 6 (a), citing the *MP Psalter* of 1350: 'Our Lord is...of *longe wille* and michel merciable'.

7 The Bale inscriptions are given in full in Hanna, *WL* pp. 158–9; on Bale (1495–1563) see Simpson, *Reform and Cultural Revolution*, pp. 17–31.

8 The note, with the annals it accompanies, has been placed by Lister Matheson and M. T. Tavormina, in Abergavenny *c.* 1415 (unpublished paper cited in Hanna, 'Emendations', p. 186). The Rokayle records collected in Moore 'Studies' (1914), pp. 44–5 are reprinted in Hanna, *WL*, p. 158, and the discovery of new information on Stacy's father Peter (**L**'s putative grandfather) and his associates is mentioned by Matheson in his review of this work (p. 194). That the author of *PP* was called William de la Rokele was first proposed by Cargill, 'Langland Myth' (1935). Hanna, 'Emendations', p. 186, notes Matheson's discovery (reported in an unpublished paper) of a William Rokayle ordained to the first tonsure [i.e. to a stage preparatory to the first canonical grade] by Bishop Wolstan de Bransford of Worcester, possibly at Bredon near Hanley Castle in 1339 (Wolstan's Calendar # 1021, 199b). Further documentary evidence that Stacy had a son William, and that he had received minor orders, would create a strong possibility that Matheson's Rokayle was the poet.

9 Bowers, 'Editing the Text, Writing the Author's Life', p. 80.

10 Kane, *Evidence for Authorship*, pp. 35–7.

11 See the useful bibliographical summary in Pearsall, *Annotated Bibliography,* pp. 45–64.

12 A specific social setting for *PF* has long been the subject of speculation, and Bowers ('Royal Setting') intriguingly locates *Pearl* in the context of Ricardian cultural-political conflicts of the mid-1390s. But the landscapes of both works are countries of the dreaming mind, Alanian or Johannine, and their air is that of neither the Malvern Hills nor Cornhill.

13 See Kane, *Autobiographical Fallacy*; Burrow, *Fictions*, pp. 83–9.

14 Lawton in Alford, *Companion* (AlfC), p. 245. See further in the *Commentary* the notes on C VI.46, X.289, XIII.148, XIV.295, XV.40, 205, XVI.174, XX.6, 395, 455, 463, 478, XXI.70, XXII.303; B X.268, 334, 360, XIX.82; A III.251, XII.73; Z III.158, 159, 160. For the most recent discussion see Warner, 'L. and the Problem of *WPal*'.

15 See Samuels in AlfC, p. 201, Samuels, 'L.'s Dialect', p. 234, and Appendix I on Language and Metre. That the Malvern Hills have symbolic rather than personal significance is plausibly maintained by Benson, *Public 'PP'*, pp. 203–6; but the choice of locale is unlikely to have been arbitrary.

16 Du Boulay, *England of PP*, p. 61; medieval Cornhill is vividly described in Benson, *Public 'PP'*, pp. 206–33. The poem has some thirty mentions of London and particular places within or near it; see further the *Commentary* on Pr

83, 89, 91; II.148, 169, 174; 5.1, 4, 44, VI.83, 96, 365, 367; XI.65; XV.71; XVI.286; B V.317; X.46; XIII.264; Z VII.274. On the 'London' aspect generally see Barron, 'London Poet', Simpson, '"After Craftes Counseil"', and Pearsall, 'L.'s London', and Hanna, *London Literature*..

17 The term used by Bloomfield (*Fourteenth Century Apocalypse,* pp. 68–97) for patristic and neo-patristic Biblically-based writings on moral and psychological topics, a field profitably harvested in Bourquin's pioneering *PP:Etudes*. The stress in this 'philosophy' (perhaps better called 'theology') on the importance of self-knowledge, and hence on 'moral psychology', is brought out in Wittig's important study of the 'Inward Journey' of the Dreamer. On the thought of the Cistercians and Victorines see Stiegman in Evans, ed. *Medieval Theologians*, pp. 129–55.

18 Bowers, *Crisis of WILL,* pp. 18–22; but against this cf. the *Commentary* note on V.37. See further the *Commentary* on X.21–9 and also on XIV.202–17, XV.263–5 and B X.343–6. For the C14th university arts course, see Courtenay, *Schools and Scholars*, pp. 30–6, and on the theology course ibid. pp. 41–3. A significant allusion to contemporary preoccupation with logic *in scole* (on which see ibid. pp. 221–40) occurs in the criticism of mendicants' applications of dialectic to theology; see *Commentary* on XVI.228–30.

19 For Middleton's distinction see her 'Audience and Public' in Lawton, ed. *Alliterative Poetry*; the present distinction between internal and external audience follows that of Dieter Mehl, 'Audience of Chaucer's *Troilus*'. For further consideration of the complexities involved, and the position of the author as reader of his own work, see Schmidt, 'Visions & Revisions', pp. 10–13.

20 By comparison with the specificity of a commissioned poem such as *William of Palerne*, 5521–40, the **A** Version's 'public' exists as a conventional construct at some remove from its real 'audience': cf. 'preche it in þin harpe / Þer þou art mery at mete, ȝif men bidde þe ȝedde' at A I. 137–8.

21 '*PP* and the Peasants' Revolt', pp. 87–8.

22 For a balanced estimate of this work as a deceptive link between **L** and the Wycliffites, from whom he stands distinct, cf. Von Nolcken, 'Wycliffites', esp. p. 85, and for a judicious and sensitive consideration of the whole question Pearsall, 'L. and Lollardy'. Cole argues that **L**. does not use *lollere* to mean 'Wycliffite' (with its necessary implication of doctrinal heresy) but to refer to 'a specifically lay oriented version of virtuous poverty and Christian discipleship' ('WL's Lollardy', p. 28).

23 See for instance Z V. 142–3; A X. 86*a*, 94*a*, XI. 154*a*.

24 See Parkes, 'The Literacy of the Laity' in Parkes, *Scribes*, pp. 275–97. On the poem's projected lay audience see Somerset, *Clerical Discourse and Lay Audience*, ch. 2.

25 For the wills see Burrow 1957, repr. 1984 with postscript. On Walter de Brugge, see Cargill, 'Langland Myth' pp. 36–9, Davies, 'Life and Travels', pp. 49–50, 56n20; for another clerical Yorkshire owner *c*.1410 J. Hughes, *Pastors and Visionaries*, p. 205; and on Palmere, see Wood, 'C14th Owner', pp. 85, 88n21. Their copies, like most of those mentioned in bequests, are not extant; but one ms Douce 104 (no. 29) is probably from Ireland (Pearsall, *Facsimile* pp. xii–xiii), where Brugge had worked.

26 Hudson, 'Revolt', p. 91.

27 The whole of the passus is ascribed to him by Middleton in her very full 1988 discussion, but he is taken by the present editor as author only of the A XII Appendix. Materials on the recorded John Buts are assembled in Hanna, *WL,* pp. 160–3, who favours ('Emendations', p. 187) another But than the traditional one on the strength of the arguments in Scase, 'John But's *PP* ', which seem to the present writer unconvincing. 'But' is argued to be a coterie code-name (like 'Longlond') by Kerby-Fulton and Justice (1997:73).

28 Usk, who was executed in March 1388, wrote the *Testament c*.1385–7.

29 The questioning of the traditional early dating of *WW* in the mid-1350s by Salter, 'Timeliness' and Trigg, ed. *WW,* does not seem persuasive to the present writer. The most recent editor of *RRe* and *MS* (following Kane, 'Some C14th "political" poems', p. 90) takes them as earlier and later compositions (*c*.1400 and 1409 respectively) by one author, and reaffirms the traditional date of *PPCr* in the late 1390s (Barr, *PP Tradition*, p.16; for the full supporting arguments see Barr, 'Relationship'). A pioneering study of the 'Piers Plowman' tradition is Lawton, 'Lollardy' (1981), which takes *MS* as the work of 'a Lollard sympathiser' (788); and a very detailed account of the poems mentioned and of a later alliterative piece *The Crowned King* (1415) is Barr, *Signes and Sothe*.

30 Ed. Skeat, *Chaucerian and Other Pieces*, no. II, who observes that against the *Tale*-author's claim 'there cannot be adduced any argument whatever' (ed. *Crede*, pp. xiv–xv). Barr's objection on the grounds that the *Tale* is in rhymed stanzas rather than alliterative long lines (*Tradition*, p.10) lacks cogency. The two Lollard poems have many phrases in common and 'alliteration is employed in the Tale very freely' (Skeat, *Chaucerian*, pp. xxxiii–iv); so the relationship of the two pieces is not unlike that of the long-line *Sir Gawain* and the stanzaic, rhymed and alliterative *Pearl*, poems accepted without difficulty today as by the same author.

31 This personage, together with the conception of the structural plan of the *General Prologue*, represent Chaucer's recognisable debt to Langland (*Sk* IV.ii p. 863; Cooper, 'L's & Chaucer's Prologues'). But it is also tempting to see in the dramatised encounter of the *Troilus*-poet with two questioners in *LGW Pr* (G 234–545) echoes of the *Piers Plowman*-poet's examination by Reason and Conscience in the 'Prelude' to C Passus V. Welsh writers of the 14th and 15th c. have been plausibly claimed to have read *PP* (Breeze 1990, 1993). Some influence on Hoccleve has been detected by Kerby-Fulton (in Wallace, ed., *Cambridge History of Medieval Literature* [*CHMEL*], p. 537), and later there are John Audelay in 'Solomon and Marcol' = Whiting no. 2 (*c.* 1426), discussed in Simpson, *Reform,* pp. 378–80, and Skelton, especially the figure of Drede in *The Bowge of Court* (*c.*1498). For the *Erkenwald*-poet's debt to Langland see Schmidt, 'Courtesy', pp. 153–6 (noticed by Morse, *St Erkenwald*, pp. 27–8) and for the *Purity*-poet's ibid. and Schmidt, '*Kynde Craft,*' p. 123n63. Hanna's conclusion from his belief that 'some passages unique to **Z** depend for their intelligibility on the reader's knowledge of other versions' seems to the present writer untrue. But given that he finds **Z** 'often logically disruptive to the sense of a passage', his judgement that the author of the Z-Text was 'an imitator, "editing" with a *Piers* reading circle in mind' (*CHMEL* p. 519) seems hard to credit.

32 Those it appears with include *Joseph of Arimathea* (see *Intro.* I, *The Manuscripts*, no. 4), *Susannah* (no. 6), *The Wars of Alexander* (no. 8), *The Siege of Jerusalem* (nos. 12, 31), *Richard the Redeless* (no. 18) and *Pierce the Ploughman's Crede* (no. 34). On the Vernon grouping see Lawton in *CHMEL* pp. 480–1. Langland is interestingly compared with Mandeville (and with Margery Kempe) in Benson, *Public 'PP'*, pp. 113–56

33 They are R, U and M of **A** (I, *Manuscripts*, nos. 2, 3, 10); L, R and F of **B** (nos. 20, 22, 23); and X, I, U and P of **C** (nos. 24, 26, 28 and 30).

34 See for the annotations on the mss of **B**, Benson & Blanchfield, *MSS of PP: B Version* and on **C**, Russell, 'Early Responses' and '"As They Read It"'. For what can be learned of **L**'s early readers see Middleton, 'Making a Good End', Scase, *New Anticlericalism*, Hanna, *WL*, Kerby-Fulton, 'Bibliographic Ego', Davies, 'Life, Travels and Library', and Kerby-Fulton and Justice, 'Langlandian Reading-Circles'.

35 Whereas, by comparison, *William of Palerne* is stated by its poet to have been written at the behest of Humphrey Earl of Hereford (*WPal* 164–8); cf. however Justice, 'Langlandian Reading Circles.'

36 See especially the *Commentary* on Pr 138, 140; I.75, 94–100; II.243–end; III.200–01; IV.174–5; V.181–3, 186–8, 195–6; XIII.25; XIV.35–7; XV.13–14; XVI. 22; XIX. 231–48*a*; XX.350–8; XXI.251–5.

37 See the *Commentary* on XVI.320, 338; and cf. Gradon, 'Ideology' and Hudson, 'Legacy' in Alf*C*, p. 261.

38 See Hudson in Alf*C*, pp. 66–8, Hanna *WL*, pp. 164–5. For Knighton's phrase, see his *Chronicle*, ed. Martin, p. 276.

39 The texts are given from Hanna, *WL,* pp. 165–6 (in the Carter text in the most recent edition by G. H. Martin, the phrase *for lesynge of* is mistranslated). Other accounts of the poem's real or supposed relations with the Rising are Bowers, '*PP* and the Police', Green, 'John Ball's Letters' (who compares them with *PPCr* and prints them in an appendix), and Rydzeski, *Radical Nostalgia*. The letters and other documents connecting *PP* with the 1381 Rising are carefully examined by Hudson, '*PP* and Peasants' Revolt', pp. 85–106; but her conclusions that **B** is a response to the Revolt and that **C** represents a hasty re-writing strike the present editor as implausible (see further n. 47).

40 For a judicious analysis of Ball's response to *PP* see Barr, *Signes and Sothe*, pp. 10–133, and for a detailed if at times tendentious account of the rebels' attitudes to the poem see Justice, *Writing and Rebellion*, pp. 102–39, 231–54.

41 See Rickert, 'John But'; among the materials concerning the known John Buts in Hanna, *WL* pp. 28–31 see esp. 5 (g). Hanna criticises Rickert's identification, though the evidence he cites for But's contact with the Despenser family (9. n. 18) tells for, not against it. He is right, however, that Rickert's interpretation of *duk* and *dedes* in A XII 87 as respectively 'king' and 'documents licensing an arrest' is unconvincing; but if Langland wrote XII 98 (as argued in *Intro.* III, *A Version*, §§ 68–70), it is also irrelevant. From within the poem itself, the circumstantial and favourable comparison of the *pore pacyent* to a messenger (C XIII 32–91) would have appealed to the John But of the traditional identification. Kerby-Fulton and Justice ('Langlandian Reading Circles', pp. 71–3) deduce from A XII that 'But' (the name being possibly assumed) was a member of a circle of scriveners and civil servants, probably with legal connections, who took an active interest in the poem. Bowers more specifically speculates ('Editing the Text', pp. 87–9) that But may be the man recorded as controller of customs at Bristol in 1399 (and a candidate for authorship of *RRe* and *MS*). But this presupposes acceptance of Jill Mann's re-ordering of the versions ('Power of the Alphabet') to make **A** the last, which is rejected below.

42 Bowers, 'Dating *PP*'. See also Lewis 1995, who presents non-Langlandian sources for Usk's tree-image.

43 Echoes are detected by Baldwin, *Theme of Government*, pp. 59, 101n9; Coleman, *PP and Moderni*, pp. 41, 66; Godden, *Making of PP*, pp. 171–2; and at adequate length by Middleton, 'Acts of Vagrancy'. Relevant extracts from the text of the Statute, with comment, are in Hanna, *WL*, pp. 163–5.

44 See the *Textual Notes* on 11.126 and *MS* 348; the echo is noted in Barr, *Signes*, p. 14n65. Coleman's view that C belongs to the 1390s (*Moderni,* pp. 41–20) has little to recommend it.

45 For **L**'s judgement of the Plague's effect on marriage, religious belief, sexual behaviour and the upbringing of children, see the *Commentary* on respectively X.273–5; XI.59–64, XV.219–25; XXII.98–120; B V.35–6.

46 Courtenay, *Schools,* p. 99. A comprehensive sketch of **L**'s likely course of education deduced from the text (and subject to the necessary reservations) is provided in Orme, 'L. and Education'.

47 See Donaldson, *C-Text and its Poet*, pp. 199–226.

48 Kerby-Fulton, 'Bibliographic Ego', pp. 116–7. Clanvowe's religious treatise *The Two Ways* is an isolated work; but readers might have found this knight's tone reminiscent of Langland's Knight Conscience in B XIII.180–211.

49 Fowler, *Literary Relations of the A and B Texts,* pp. 185–205.

50 Donaldson, *C-Text*, p. 226.

51 *Evidence for Authorship,* p. 70.

52 Doyle, 'Surviving MSS', pp. 42–3. A similarly early date has been proposed for no. 52 (the hand-X portion of **Z**), which Rigg-Brewer would place between 1376 and 1388, but Hanna (following Doyle) around 1400. See *Intro*. II § 137 and n. 242.

53 Cf. Adams, 'Editing *PP B*'; Hanna, 'Studies', pp. 19–20.

54 Kane, in AlfC, p. 185.

55 'Peasants' Revolt', p. 100.

56 Fowler, *Relations*, pp. 174–5.

57 Taylor, 'Lost Revision of *PP* B', p. 119.

58 See note 36 above.

59 See Huppé, 'Date of B-Text'; Bennett 'Date of B-Text', and the *Commentary* on Pr 152–7, B Pr 128.

60 See Bennett, 'Date of A-Text'; Huppé, 'A-Text and Norman Wars'.

61 See J. Mann, 'Alphabet'; Meroney, 'Life and Death of Longe Wille', pp. 22–3.

62 Cf. also A X.108, 111*a*, 120*a* (paraphrased); A X. 81*a*, translated at preceding 79–80, which is also in B IX. 94*a* but *not* translated there.

63 See Z III. 91–101 for 'draft' features; Z III. 147–76, Z V. 33–40 (the complicated but coherent argument of which is examined in Schmidt 'Visions', pp. 21–2).

64 Lawler, 'Reply', deals very fully with short passages, long passages, and 'characteristic **B** ideas'. Kane's 'Open Letter', which is decisive, adopts an uncharacteristically courteous tone towards Mann's (uncharacteristically implausible) piece that contrasts with that of his review of Rigg and Brewer's serious case for the authenticity of **Z**.

65 It is unknown which version William Palmere bequeathed to Agnes Eggesfield, as the copy in question is not identified among those extant.

66 *Public 'PP'*, pp. 3–107. Benson's notion of 'myth' does not tally with that of the present writer.

67 Hudson, *Premature Reformation*, p. 22; Barr, *Socio-literary Practice in the C14th* p. 151.

68 See Lawton 'Lollardy'; Jansen 'Politics, Protest'; Barr *PP Tradition*; and especially Hudson *Reformation*, pp. 398–408.

69 Salter, '*PP and The Simonie*'; *Jack Upland*, ed. Heyworth.

70 Hudson, 'Peasants' Revolt', p. 102. If one agrees with Hudson that the version the rebels knew was **A** (ibid. pp. 88, 90), it becomes slightly less easy to claim that they had misinterpreted Langland's Piers as challenging traditional notions of authority in society and the Church (Astell, *Political Allegory* ch. 2 claims that they had not misunderstood **L** at all). Hudson places **B** after the Revolt partly because she interprets B XIX.446–9 'as alluding to the 1383 Despenser crusade' (ibid. p. 100 and n. 17); but reasons have been given (see note § 15 above) for finding this unconvincing.

71 See Schmidt, *Clerkly Maker,* pp. 142–3, 'Visions and Revisions', pp. 22–6.

72 Kirk, *Dream Thought of Piers Plowman,* p. 9.

73 Raabe, *Imitating God: the Allegory of Faith in* PP.

74 Acceptance of spiritual authority for the sake of unity within the Church is stressed by Conscience in a notable new line at Pr 138; serious criticism of ecclesiastical abuses at Pr 95–127, and of misuse of civic and royal power at III.200–14; deep sympathy for the plight of honest poor people in IX.71–98. See the *Commentary* on all these passages.

75 The concept of a 'strong' or creative misreading was introduced by Harold Bloom in his seminal study *Poetry and Repression*; see further Schmidt 'Visions and Revisions', pp. 10–11.

76 'Legacy of *PP*', p. 255.

77 Lawton's pithy formulation 'The issue is really that Lollards had Langlandian sympathies' ('Lollardy', p. 793) has

been sharply challenged by Simpson, *Reform and Cultural Revolution,* pp. 371–2. A judicious summary of **L**'s relations with Wyclif and his followers is given in Hudson 'Legacy', pp. 398–408 and most recently 'L. and Lollardy?', pp. 93–105.

78 Salter, *PP: an Introduction,* p. 1. The pioneering appreciations of *PP* as poetry by Coghill, Lawlor and Salter (all published in 1962) and by Spearing (1963 and 1964) were followed after a decade by book-length critiques (Kirk 1972, Carruthers 1973, Aers 1975, Schmidt 1987, Davlin 1989, Godden 1990, Simpson 1990, and Burrow 1993). But over the 1990s the growing body of specialised studies has concentrated on the text, context, background, and theological and political ideas, rather than the poem's qualities as a great work of medieval literature, the assumption on which the Athlone and the present edition are predicated. Two encouraging recent exceptions have been Rogers, *Interpretation in PP* and (in the Salter tradition) Davlin, *The Place of God in PP.*

79 An account of the poem's structure, themes and literary art has not been attempted in this *Introduction*. What is possible within the limits of editions for the student and the general reader may be found in Schmidt, *Vision of PP*, pp. xxx–liv and *PP: a new translation,* pp. xi–xl.

80 The four versions of Rembrandt's masterpiece *The Three Crosses* (1653–1660) will aptly illustrate this point; see Boon, *Rembrandt: Complete Etchings* pls. 244–5.

81 Cerquiglini, *Eloge de la variante,* p. 111.

82 The basis of this inference is the virtual absence of scribal errors in Passus XVI; see *Intro. III, B,* § 5.

83 Donaldson, 'MSS R and F', p. 211.

84 Against Scase's claim that a passage of **C** circulated independently, see the arguments in the *Intro. III, C,* §§ 21–2, and notes 33, 35.

85 See Burrow 'Action of L.'s Second Vision' and the analytical headnote to the *Commentary* on C XX.

86 Warner, '*Ur*-B *PP*', p. 24.

87 One recent such critic is Rogers (*Interpretation in PP*), in many ways a judicious exponent of a lucid 'post-modern' hermeneutics (see the present writer's review in *RES* 55 [2004], pp. 446–7).

88 Cf. the discussion of these lines in Schmidt, 'Visions and Revisions', pp. 23–5.

89 A study conscious of **L**'s 'Ricardian' sense of human limitedness and 'Gregorian' awareness of imperfection in perfection is Nolan, *Visionary Perspective,* pp. 205–58. Another showing a firm conviction (not always well-articulated) of **L**'s artistic control and coherence of purpose is Raabe, *Imitating God.*

90 *The Prelude* achieved two-book form in 1799 as 'a limitedly private autobiography' (Stephen Gill, *Words-worth*, p. 231) and five-book form in 1804; was completed in thirteen books in 1805; revised in 1832; then brought to its fourteen-book form in 1839, the version printed after the poet's death in 1850 (see the Norton edition, ed. Wordsworth et al.). To Gill, 'Wordsworth's greatest poem encompasses and unifies many genres. Satire and narrative, description and meditation, the visionary and the deliberately banal — all are exploited in...the flexible blank verse he made his characteristic instrument...As an autobiography...it was written not only to present a self-image to posterity but to assist the writer to understand his own life so that the rest of it might be lived more purposefully and in accordance with truths perceived in the act of writing the poem' (ibid. 1–2). But Gill's claim that the poet could not bear the idea of finality is convincingly disputed by Leader, who maintains that Wordsworth 'held to the goal of mastery or perfection, or the attempt to come as close to it as possible' (*Revision*, p. 35). The analogy with Langland and his critics will not escape notice (for direct comparison of both poets as revisers, see Wordsworth, 'Revision as Making').

91 Following the pioneering work of Middleton, 'The Idea of Public Poetry', Benson has developed this notion as the central argument of *Public PP.*

92 The convention of soliciting a drink still mimicked in *WW* is avoided, as is the fiction of an audience 'present and *reacting*,' except at Pr 217 after **B**'s 'Rat Fable' addition, which might have provoked laughter.

93 'Quo se ipse imperfectum respicit, inde ad humilitatis culmen perfectior assurgat' (*Moralia* 5. 4.5). See the illuminating discussion in Straw, *Gregory the Great*, pp. 188–9.

94 For examples of *repetitio* see the *Commentary* on Pr 28; I.12, 20–1; II.11–12; III.94–100; VI.162–3; VII.111–15, 264–5; VIII.139; IX.44–5; X.18–20; XI.16–18, 235–8; XII.108; XIII.156–60; XIV.94; XV.18; XVI.120; XX.207; XXII.35–50. On B XI.218–26 see Schmidt, *Clerkly Maker,* pp. 55–7.

95 The phrase *al my (his / hir) lyf-tyme* (Appendix Three, C Pr 50b) is a stock expression not confined to literary use like *as the world askes*, which occurs only once but is also found in *SGGK* 530.

96 *The Making of 'Piers Plowman',* the first study to do so.

97 See Jusserand, *PP*, p. 173; Owen *PP: A Comparison*; Bourquin, *Etudes*, pp. 780–98 and Burrow, *L.'s Fictions,* pp. 113–18. For other French sources and analogues see Gaffney 'Allegory' (Nicole de Bozon), Cornelius '*Roman de Fauvel*' and Nolan, *Visionary Perspective* (Huon de Méri, Raoul de Houdenc and Rutebeuf).

98 See the very revealing French proverb quoted at XVII.163–4; and cf. *IG* s.v. *cortesye* for the 'redeemed' uses of the term beginning as early as I.20.

99 See B XV.442–3, C XII.82–9, and Schmidt, *Clerkly Maker*, p. 108 for discussion.

100 The limiting cases of Trajan and Dismas 'prove' this contention in the sense of showing it to be *generally* true, though admitting extraordinary exceptions under the principle *misericordia eius super omnia*; see the *Commentary* on XII 76.

101 The phrase, taken from Bernard McGinn, is explained and defended in Watson, 'Censorship and Cultural Change', p. 823n4. That **L**'s 'entire enterprise looks like' the 'vernacular theologizing' prosecuted by the ecclesiastical authorities is nonetheless urged by Middleton 1997:291; but if it does, the resemblance seems to have evaded record (see § 22 and note 77 above). On Langland's 'theology' see Hort, *Contemporary Religious Thought*, pp. 28–59; Coleman, *Moderni*; Harwood, *Problem of Belief*; and for a general survey Adams in AlfC, pp. 87–114 (with the caveats noted by Schmidt in *JEGP* 89 [1990] p. 214). It may nonetheless be better to speak of 'the use of theological ideas in *PP*' than of '**L**'s theology'.

102 Lawton, 'Englishing the Bible' in *CHMEL*, pp. 470–1 (the Wycliffite claim is cited by him from Hudson, *Selections* p. 69). Rolle's 'amphibian' negotiation of vernacular and Latin adumbrates Langland, who may have known some of his writings (see Schmidt, 'Treatment of the Passion', pp. 174–6).

103 'The Middle English Mystics', in *CHMEL*, p.553.

104 A contribution was made by the present writer in *The Clerkly Maker,* pp. 81–107. The fundamental work in this area was Sullivan, *Insertions*.

105 A good guide to **L**'s 'sources' is Pearsall, *Critical Bibliography*, pp. 74–110. The classic instance of the importance of source-study is Chaucer's *Troilus* as edited, with the Italian original *en face*, by Windeatt. *Patience* (based on Jonah) is another example, as is one of the earliest works of the Alliterative Revival, *William of Palerne*.

106 See Alford, 'Role of Quotations', p. 82l; Allen, *Ethical Poetic*, p. 275.

107 See the *Commentary* on Pr 40, 108; I.82110*a*, 121*a*, and *passim.*

108 See for example A X.80–81*a*; B IX.130–30*a*; C X.230–41.

109 Davlin, *Game of Heuene*, p.5. The specific contexts of **L**'s quotations in the *Breviary*, first noted by Skeat, emphasised by Hort (but see for criticisms Adams 'Liturgy Revisited') and highlighted in the notes to *Pe*, are amply documented in Alf*Q, passim*.

110 Although 'hearing matins and mass' is regarded by **L**'s Sloth as proper for monks (VII.65–60), but for him an act of special penance, the implication of other passages is that it should be normal practice for the laity (see C IX.227–9).

111 For an accessible account of the Holy Week ceremonies as performed in this period, see Duffy, *Stripping,* pp. 22–37; and on the contextual heightening imparted to the quotations in B XVIII see Barr, 'Use of Latin Quotations', pp. 440–8. The importance of the liturgy in shaping the structure of the last passūs is shown by Saint-Jacques, 'Conscience's Final Pilgrimage'; and for a persuasive argument that the Glutton scene is a satiric parody of the liturgy of the Easter Triduum see Wilcockson 1998.

112 This point is properly emphasised by Vaughan, 'Liturgical Perspectives', building on the germinal studies of St-Jacques (1967, 1969, 1970), and serves to counter the text-based approach to **L**'s Biblical sources in Robertson and Huppé's pioneering *PP and Scriptural Tradition*. The structural significance of 'enacted scripture', though not confined to B XVIII / C XX, especially centres on the services of *þe Saterday þat sette first þe kalender* (see for example the *Commentary* on VII.119–53a, which closely relates in 'pitch and tonality' to that passus). **L** seems fully aware that every Mass is interpretable as an epitome of the Easter Triduum.

113 See Kolve, *Play Called Corpus Christi*, ch. 10. **L**'s mediation between disparate sources and contemporary modes of interpreting this theme is examined by Taylor, 'Harrowing Hell's Half-acre'.

114 Because so much medieval art was destroyed by Reformers and Puritans, examples in England are few; but one from North Cove church, Suffolk is given as pl. 8B in Benson, *Public PP,* p. 180. For the relation of **L**'s poetry to late Gothic art, see Salter, '*PP* and the Visual Arts' in her *English and International,* pp. 56–66; Davlin, *Place of God in PP and Medieval Art.*

115 Owst, '"Angel" and "Goliardeys"', p. 271; the subject is treated in detail in Owst, *Literature and Pulpit*, pp. 548–75. A balanced and accurate formulation of the 'diffuse and widely dispersed influence' of sermons is furnished by Wenzel in 'Medieval Sermons and Study of Literature' and in his chapter on medieval sermons in AlfC.

116 See Salter, *Introduction*, pp. 24–30; Spearing, 'Verbal Repetition' and *Criticism* [rev. ed. 1972], pp. 107–34.

117 See Wenzel in AlfC, pp. 168–9, and the *Commentary* on XVI.264–5.

118 Wenzel, ibid. p. 161. See the *Commentary* on V.136–9, VI.337*a*, VIII.46, B Pr 145.

119 As noted by Pearsall (see *Commentary* on II.32); on Ludolf see Conway, '*Vita Christi*'.

120 Cf. the *Commentary* on XI.148. For the poem's structural embodiment of Trinitarian ideas, see especially Clopper 'L.'s Trinitarian Analogies' and 'Contemplative Matrix'; and for expansion of the 'trinity' idea more widely, Fletcher, 'Social Trinity' and Galloway, 'Intellectual Pregnancy'.

121 In *PL* 196:1–1378; tr. Zinn, *Richard of St Victor*, p. 292.

122 See 17.157, B 15.269, and *Commentary* on B 11.160.

123 On 'Cato', the name of an unknown C4th Latin writer who is quoted five times (cf. *Commentary* on 4.17), see Galloway, 'Two Notes on L.'s Cato'.

124 See the *Commentary* on these passages, in which the *kynde* meaning of words is emphasised.

125 See Schmidt, *Clerkly Maker,* p. 90, referring to Mann, 'Satiric Subject', who builds on Jolivet, 'Quelques cas de "platonisme grammatical"'. For a selection of examples see the *Commentary* on Pr 5; I.20–1, 35–6; II.235; III.403, 476, 495; V.134–5, 142; VI.87; VII.36–7; VIII.133–4; X.54; XI.128; XIII.67; XIV.136; XVII.10; XVIII.25; XX.266; XXI.86. This type of clerkly wordplay extends to proper names (X.251, XII.2) and across the Latin-English linguistic boundary (VIII.77, XV.50, 57; XVII.66–6a).

126 See *PL* 210:579.

127 Notably Bloomfield, *C14th Apocalypse*; Davlin '*Kynde Knowynge*'; Bourquin, *Etudes*; Wittig 'Inward Journey'; and Simpson, 'From Reason to Affective Knowledge'.

128 See Schmidt 'L. and Scholastic Philosophy'. L's general familiarity with scholastic ideas and arguments is nonetheless demonstrated in Coleman, *Moderni* and cogently argued in Harwood, *Problem of Belief.*

129 Kerby-Fulton in *CHMEL* p. 531. For the possible influence of Map, see the *Commentary* on 15.100.

130 See Pearsall, 'Origins' and Lawton, 'Diversity'. The argument is challenged by Hanna in *CHMEL* pp. 488–512.

131 Owen & Smyser, eds., *Prose Works of Wordsworth*, p. 159.

B. TEXTUAL NOTES

Reference is in the first place to the **C** Version; where **C** has no text, citation is from **B**. The other versions are denoted in brackets, ordinarily in the sequence **ZAB**. Lines with no corresponding material in **C** are discussed as near as possible to the point where they stand printed in parallel to the text of **C**. Notes on these, where they exceed a single entry, are indented for ease of reference. A few additions and corrections to the Text and Apparatus are included here if relevant to the discussion, but they are collected together for convenience at the end of this Volume. Abbreviations in the form '*A*-M', '*C*-**x**' etc signify a ms or family / group of the version specified in *italic*. Bold **L** = 'Langland'; &*r* 'and the rest'; Ø = zero-reading; ⊗ = 'contamination'; '⇒' = 'substitution'; ↔ = 'transposed'; < = 'deriving from'. For explanation of the ms and group sigla used see Vol. I, p. xiii, and *Introduction* II–III.

Title

The poem has no title *within* the text. All titles must therefore be presumed part of the extrinsic format (*forma tractatûs*) of any given ms. Although variously named *tractatus*, *dialogus* and *liber*, the work is most commonly called *visio*, as in *C*-ms P, a text with elaborate scribal layout. A title incorporating the Dreamer's / Author's name and the poem's chief subject must have been familiar in a form such as '*Visio Willelmi de Petro Plouhman*,' followed (as at **p** Passus XI = X in **x**) by '*Visio eiusdem Willelmi de Do-wel*,' at **p** XVIII [**x** XVII] by '*V. e. W. de Do-bet*,' and at **p** XXII [**x** XXI] by '*V. e. W. de Do-best*.' The rubrics in **B**, the only version certainly completed, are argued by Adams (1985) to be scribal rather than authorial, a view extended more tentatively to **C** in Adams 1995:51–84. They are nonetheless the most important element of the *forma tractatûs* and deserve to be recorded in an edition (as by *Sk* but not Athlone after A; see Appendix Two). Crowley entitled his first printing (1550) *The Vision of Piers Plowman*, and although both *Sk* and *K–D* have included 'Dowel, Dobet and Dobest' in their full titles, most explicits typically read '*Explicit (liber) de petro ploughman.*' Such a title, omitting reference to 'Do-wel', etc., accords with John But's reference to Will's 'werkes.../ Of Peres þe Plowman and mechel puple also' (A 12.102). Early wills of 1396 and 1400 speak of 'my / a book (called) Piers Plowman' (Davies 1999:49; Wood 1984). And while contemporary readers might have known the poem as 'The Book of Piers Plowman' (cf. Chaucer's 'Book of Troilus'), the only early reference outside a testamentary context (the inscription in TCD ms 212 of *c.* 1400) names it *Perys ploughman*. Outside the explicits and incipits, no other titles survive from between the presumed date of **L**'s death (*c.* 1387/8) and the earliest critical mention, by Puttenham (1589) following Crowley or Rogers (1561), who also calls the poem *Piers Plowman*.

Prologue

RUBRIC The heading *Prologue* appears only in *A*-ms R, in the form *Hic incipit liber qui uocatur pers plowman. Prologus*. This scribal contribution agrees with the (presumably authorial) numbering of passūs in **A**, **B** and **C**-family **x**, where *passus primus* prefaces the section immediately following the Prologue. Whereas the wording of the incipits and explicits varies somewhat, the number and order of passus-divisions in all versions seems secure, the most deviant copies being Corpus 201 (F of **B**), and to a less extent Bodley 851 (**Z**), on which see *Introduction* I, *Manuscripts*, nos. 23 and 52. In Pr the important mss of **A** are fully represented, but Y is defective for **C** and R for **B**.

2 (ZAB 2) *shroudes*: the corrupt variant *shrobbis*, in the **A** mss JK presumably by contamination ('⊗' hereafter) from a copy of the **C** family **p** (and also in *B*-Cr), will have resulted from mistaking *shope* 'dressed myself' (MED s.v. *shapen* v. 5) for 'betook myself' (ib. 6). *A*-Ch has an idiosyncratic near-synonym. The plural form seems assured from the **BC** readings, correct and corrupt; *C*-BOL *a shrowde* (so *R–K*) may be induced by the singular nouns with indefinite article in 2b and 3a. *B*-H (sg.) may show ⊗ from an *A*-source here, as so often later (e.g. at 42, 74). Possibly **A** read *shroude*, a form that might have invited addition of an art. or a pl. ending; *A*-W's *a shrowedes* can only be a slip; **Z**'s witness here favours the plural. *shep*: 'sheep' not 'shepherd', which finds no lexical support; **p**'s variant will be by ⊗, a scribal substitution ('⇒' hereafter) after failure to grasp the point of the comparison.

    Z 5 The a-half could be by ⊗ from **C** 5; but the b-half's characteristic semantic pun ('say' / 'see') does not look scribal, resembling but not imitating **C**'s *adnominatio* on *sel-* and *sel-*. The line would fit satisfactorily in both **A** and **B** at this point, but no reason for its loss appears, unless perhaps visual distraction due to homœoarchy / homœoteleuton (*many sellys...alle /...May...Hylles*).

6 (Z 6, AB 5) *But*: a revision of **Z** or an error in the **A** archetype (Ax), and in *B*-H by ⊗ from an **A** ms; emendation is unnecessary, since the sense is identical. **7 (Z 8, AB 7)** *of-wandred*: the **A** reading is confirmed by **Z**, several **A** mss showing a further smoothing to the form found in *B*-HF and Cr (? by ⊗ respectively from **A** and **C**). **B**'s *for-* may be a revision, since the *of-* form is very rare, although it could have been scribally altered as in *A*-R&r and later restored in **C**. The *-yng* variants in *C*-**p** show the same scribal smoothing as in *A*-DvWE, and the archaic construction with *of* + verbal noun in **x** may thus be identified as original. But the substantive reading is still likely to be **p**'s, since the moral implications of 'wandering' are lost in *walked* (cf. Bx *walke* for *wandre* **A**, a reading confirmed by **C**, at B 5.195 below). Against this, *walken* replaces *wandriþ* A 8.79 at B 7.95, C 9.172; but here the sense is neutral and **L** may have wished to *avoid* a moral implication.

   BA 10–12, Z 11–12 *sweyed* (MED s.v. *sweien* v. (1)) *or* its homonym *sweien* v. (2)) goes better with *murye*, and *sweyued* (MED s.v *sweiven* v.'whirl, sweep') could have been visually induced from *sweuene* 11, as presumably was *A*-RV *sweuenede*. *me (to) meten*: tentatively emending an unmetrical line in AxBxZ (*xa / ax*). The revised equivalent C 9 points to the solution, along with such instances of preference for the impersonal construction with *meten* (MED s.v. v. (3), sense 2) as C 10.67 (B 8.68, A 9.59); C 21.481 (B 19.485). A clue to the source of the ZAxBx error may be the reading of VJM *mette I me* for *mette me* (*mette I* A) at A IX 59. Whether or not preserving the Ax form split into those of A and of T&r, this later variant suggests how *gan I meten* could derive from an original **gan me meten* that had lost *me* through haplography before *meten* and with subsequent ⇒ in AxBx of a necessary pronoun (*I*). The likelihood of repeated error in the **Z** copy and successive archetypes is to be countenanced here, since *gan* with impersonal *meten* is not found elsewhere (Kane 1996:319) and could therefore have presented difficulty to scribes.

14 (Z 14, AB 13) In the light of **Z**'s Ø (so also *A*-HWM), *K–D*'s emendation *Ac* for **B** is rejected as unsure. *And B*-WCMH is a scribal intrusion; but *Ac* **A** may be a revision later dropped or else an Ax attempt to ease the transition. **Z 16b–17** are unique, 16b anticipating the *dymme cloude* of Z III 131 below. **20 (Z 19, AB 18)** *ryche*: although *pore* **x** makes sense if *mene* means 'of middle condition' (MED s.v. *mene* adj. (2)), it seems likelier that *alle* should imply reference to the whole range. Terms denoting the poles would be apter, *mene* thus signifying 'of poor or low status' (MED s.v. adj. (1), sense 2). The formula recurs at 219, clearly with the latter sense. **24 (Z 23, AB 22)** Support from **Z** points to *wonne þat* as the probable reading of Ax. *A*-M may here represent the common original of the family **m** or, like KUW, show correction of an **r**-type reading from a **B** or **C** source. Presumably **r**'s ambiguous **wonn* was mistaken for the

relative pronoun *w(h)om*, further smoothed or levelled in later descendants. *B*-F *þese* could here (in the absence of R) represent its family original α or else be derived from **A** or **C**. Its omission from **Z**, as from *B*-β, may be due to visual attraction from *wonnen* to *wastours*. **26 (Z 25, AB 24)** *of clothyng*: the expression caused little difficulty to the **AB** scribes and both **C** families support *of*. **Z**, which appears to distinguish face and dress, if not original, could show influence from a **C** source like PE. **27 (Z 26, AB 25)** *penaunces* **CZ** against *penaunce* **AB**: whether revision or scribal ⇒ is involved seems undecidable on intrinsic grounds. **28 (Z 27, AB 26)** *ful*: adopted as the **C** reading in the light of **ZAB** and the likelihood that the common original of *C*-yb (= **i**) substituted a synonym to avoid repeating *ful* in 22 and (with *harde* again) at 23 above. *harde*: repeating 23, though insufficient grounds appear for judging it scribal with *R–K* (29 is also revised). **31 (Z 30, AB 29)** Whether showing asyndeton after preceding *holde(th)*, or a suppressed relative pronoun, **ZAC** suggests that Bx *And* here is scribal. **33 (Z 32, AB 31)** A preterite for both verbs is preferable on stylistic grounds, conforming with the preceding past tenses and balancing the two present tenses in 34. The variation in the second verb here (as in other instances to be noted and discussed as they occur) could reflect an ambiguously-spelled original 3rd person sg. / pl. ending in *-yt*, a form capable of resolution as *-id* (*-ed*) or *-eth* (*-en*). **36 (Z 35, AB 34)** The **C** revision of **AB** could be a reversion to a first thought, or else **Z** here show ⊗ from **C**. But the following **Z** line 36 looks authentic (see *Commentary*). In **AB**, notwithstanding previous editorial consensus, *synnelees* is retained, giving a line of Type IIa, or of Type IIb in **B** (*B*-GH *trowe* for *leeue* shows possible ⊗ from **A**). Scribes variously aimed at conforming the alliterative pattern to Type Ic (*giltles*, *gyleles*); at doing this and also making a negative criticism (*gylefully* K, *gylously* W); or at the latter simply (*synfulliche* H²). But though not found elsewhere in *PP*, *giltles* was not uncommon (see MED s.v. 2 (b)) and would not readily have invited ⇒. **40 (AB 39)** *is...hyne*: absence of *B*-F here makes Bx indeterminable, the LMH readings suggesting the b-half's absence from β and its insertion from an **A** source in γ or severally in the ancestors of WHm, G, YOC² and B. Alternatively but less probably, γ here preserves β and LMH have a common ancestor that lacked the half-line. Its retention (revised) in **C** indicates its presence in **B**. **42 (Z 38, AB 41)** *bretful*: securely attested in **ZAC**, *breed ful* Bx being identifiable as smoothing of an ambiguous original *bred ful* (a spelling attested by H). The form of Bx's a-half is irrecoverable in the absence of α, but *Wiþ* (whether < Bx or not) is part of the smoothing process consequential upon misidentifying the sense of *bred*. The H reading, half-way between **ZAC** and ?Bx, could be the result of ⊗ from **A** in the b-half. *was* **ZC**: presumably original (with immediate antecedent thought of as subject); but *were* **A** may be kept and provide the standard form for **B**. **43 (Z 39, AB 42)** *Fayteden*: certain in **ZBC**, but in the A tradition conflict of variants for the first main verb cuts across both families (M against E). Despite *Ka* (p. 160), *K–F* are right here, since *faiten* was the rarer verb, little instanced outside *PP* (see MED s.vv.) and *flite* could have been a ⇒ to avoid repeating a word perhaps mistakenly understood as *fiȝten* (for the ambiguous variant spelling *feytyn* see MED s.v. *fighten* v. 1a (a)). On grounds of contextual sense, the beggars might have been less likely to *flite* after eating to repletion than to exercise deception as a general habit. **ZC** agreement in *and* may not be significant, as the conjunction could have been added independently in ms Z, as in *B*-HF, or be original and later omitted (cf. 67). *R–K*'s deletion of both is unwarranted. **45 (Z 41, AB 44)** *vp B*-HF: either coincidental or showing ⊗ from **A**. **46 (Z 42, AB 45)** *also* **x**: weak, as *synful* **p** is over-emphatic, though closer to **B**. *R–K* omit, but it is unlikely that **C** ever read as **AZ**. *suche*: M's *hem* perhaps echoes **B**. **49 (Z 51, A 48, B 49)** An intrusive pronoun in β may be recognised as scribal in the light of **ZAC**. The correct reading could have been in α, since F's *&* may be ⇒ for *∅* rather than *They*. The reading *on* **xZ** is rejected by *R–K* for *in* **p** agreeing with **AB**-β; at 15.186 **p** has *∅* (so *R–K*) while **x** divides between *in / on* (with the sense unaffected either way). **50b** reads in M as **ZAB** (so *R–K*), but this is likelier to be recollection of a familiar line than correction from a superior lost **C** copy (cf. 46).

B 50–2 are not in **AC** and were either omitted in revising **B** or are spurious (their metre correct if awkward, the clustering of Type Ib lines untypical). They begin five lines unattested by the sole α witness F and, while 53–4 are authenticated on **ZAC** evidence, 50–2 could potentially be a scribal interpolation in β. However, the metaphor appears at B 14.309 and the implied association of mendacious pilgrims with 'bad' minstrels through the image of 'tuning' sounds authorial. **55 (A 54, B 57)** Emendation of Ax *ermytes* by adding the (etymologically correct) central *-e* presumes scansion of *And...hem* as the three- or four-syllable prelude-dip of a Type IIIb line in **AB** rather than of *hem* by itself as the first stave-word. The smoother form of revised **C** allows *hemself* to be the first lift, easing the line's scansion to Type Ib. *R–K*'s emendation to **AB** *shopen hem* is groundless. **56–77, 81–4** Manuscript **I** is present here as a corrupt text made up of **A** lines interspersed with text from **C**; only the **C** lines 91–157 are fully collated. *R–K* (pp. 186–194) print the I *Prologue* in its entirety, with discussion. **57 (Z 44, A 56, B 59)** Agreement on **AC** as the probable original reading in all versions seems fairly secure. The participial form in WHm is by correction in their immediate ancestor and Bx will have read as L&r, having perhaps misconstrued a pr. pple

spelled *prechend* (a form attested in *A*-J) as the past pl. *precheden*. The source of the error could have been the unexpectedness of a participle in a sequence of preterites and the awkwardness of the transition. The easy reading *hemselue* in the b-half appears scribal in the light of **ZAC**; H's nearly correct variant may be derived from an **A** copy. **61 (A 60, B 63)** **A** and revised **BC** are very close in meaning: *meten* 'touch' (MED s.v., v. (4), 5(a)), *marchen* 'be in tandem'(MED s.v. v. (1), sense (c), with deliberate play on sense (a) 'adjoin'). Attempts to substitute a similar idea are *maken* 'mate' *C*-**x** (*macchen C*-O) *B*-Hm*A*-M. **B-H** shows ⊗ from an **A** source, *C*-M an attempt to replace one metaphor by another, although the homophony across the caesura already allows it.

Z 53–8 are unique and unexceptionable on grounds of metre, style and sense. 53–5 anticipate Z 8.13–15. The specific criticism of provisors in 57–8 is not repeated here in other versions, though it is made later in 4.125–30 //. 57b anticipates B Pr 146a, 2.62. **Z 63b–4** do not appear scribal so much as an early form of A 82–3; the *adnominatio* of *-to, to* in 64 is characteristic of **L** (cf. B 16.148). **63 (A 62, B 65)** The **A** line is virtually repeated at A 12.58. **64 (A 63, B 66)** *And* **CF** / *∅* **Aβ**: Bx is uncertain in the absence of R, but with little difference of sense involved. *hy*: the recessive Southern (S) pl. pronominal form (confirmed by **B**) and the Ax reading behind the **A** variants except for KW, which show influence from **C**, and *biginne* v, which perhaps misread *hi* as *bi* and smoothed by deletion of preceding *and*. **65 (A 64, B 67)** *vp*: in the light of **AC** the presumed **B** reading; but Bx is irrecoverable, and *vp* G is likelier to be due to ⊗ from **A** than to be a reflex of **g** (cf. also *falsnes* at 71, where β's *falshede* is acceptable). **67 (Z 75, A 66, B 69)** *And* **ZC** / *∅* **AB**: the conflict here that ostensibly argues against linear revision (or for **C** influence on **Z**) may be non-significant, as at 43 above, also involving *and* (cf. the reverse situation at 68 //, where **C** omits the conjunction, and see *Intro*. IV §25). **69** Here and in 72 the Apparatus records an I reading of interest as indicating its **A** character in the section 56–90. **70 (Z 78, A 69, B 72)** *wordes* **ZBC**: *A*-M's variant may be ⊗ from **B** or an accurate reflex of **m** (*A*-E here showing an **r** character); but no reason appears for seeing **A** as here having revised **Z**. **72 (Z 80, A 71, B 74)** The rare *bounchede*, not instanced in the C14th outside *PP* (MED s.v. *bonchen*), is presumed original as the harder and apter reading; *blessed* **p** was perhaps induced from 76 and occurs as a variant in all versions except **Z**. *B*-HF may show ⊗ from an **A** source of RUE-type (which have *blessed*) or a **C** source like **p**. The support of **Z**, in what seems an earlier form of the line, is conclusive for this reading. *bulles*: illustrating the *repetitio* common in **C**; so, despite the agreement of *C*-b and M, representing respectively **x** and **p** types, *breuet* (adopted *R–K*) should be rejected as ⊗ from **B**. **74 (Z 82, A 73, B 76)** *ȝe; ȝoure*:

discrimination of the 2nd person as the correct form in **A** is guided by **C** supported by **Z**, and *K–D*'s emendation of **B** is accepted on that basis. Bx might have read Ø for *ȝe* and *hire* for *ȝoure*, to judge by the variants. *geven A-E*: adopted as the **A** reading in the light of **ZBC-x** and the metrical requirement of a palatal stop (Ax presumably read *ȝeuen*). *helpe*: H's variant, whether derived from an independent **B** tradition or (as here judged) the result of ⊗ from **A**, appears right from **ZAC** agreement, *kepe* an arguably over-emphatic ⇒ by the Bx scribe. **76 (Z 84, A 75, B 78)** *yblessed*: supplied in **Z** for both sense and metre. **80 (A 79, B 82)** is clearly of the rare Type IIa in **AC**; *K–D*'s emendation may be safely accepted for **B**. Loss of one *p* stave, *peple* in Bx (so *A*-RH) and *poore* in *C*-X, was doubtless occasioned by eyeskip from *por-* to *par-*. The **B** variants *pouere*, *poraille*, *pore men* could all be reflexes of ?Bx **por :::le*. **84 (A 83, B 86)** *so / Ø*: revision here in **C** is uncertain, *swete* giving better rhythm (so *R–K*) but *so* being explicable as a consequence of revising *for* to *while*.

    A 84–102 In ms *A*-K (see *Ka* pp. 36–7) appears here an A-Text conflated with **C** readings, of **x** type in the sequence C 85–232 except at 164 (individual readings are recorded at 183, 216, 224). For notes on these lines see at 159 below (Vol. I, p. 19).

    B 94 The extra F line could have been in α (< Bx), but its absence from **C** points to ⊗ here from **A**, as is common in F (see on 8.49, 80, 101, 102, *Intro*. III *B* § 46).

91–157 appear on fols. 5r–6r of ms I immediately preceded by A 84–95 and followed by A 96–109 (end of A Pr; see *R–K* 186–92). The present editor agrees with *Pe* (1981) that it is a skilful scribe's work. The Cx text cannot be described as 'not in any recognisable alliterative form' (Donaldson 1949:246f) except at a few points, nor its sense as 'dubious' (Russell 1969:29, who in *R–K* 87 n.36 abandons his judgement of the I passage as much closer to the original). But since it recalls uneven work such as A XII and Z 4.129–59, 5.1–18, it could possibly derive from a late insertion that **L**'s death prevented from receiving its final form (see *Intro*. III *Z* § 6). Against this, some errors needing emendation for the metre are of a usual scribal type: variation to prose order at 108, 113, 120; ⇒ of similar but commoner idiom at 123; and of more familiar words at 114, 116–8. Only their relative density and the high number of Type III lines (some ten) suggest a provisional or draft character for Cx's source. *R–K* 87–8 see the passage as the content of a single-leaf draft misplaced by the 'editor' who prepared copy for Cx, leaving it unemended as 'the roughest of **L**'s drafts.' Why an 'editor' should have placed it here is unclear; but the *poet* may have done so because he wished to link the prelates attacked in 101ff with those of 85ff through the familiar Biblical association of greed with idolatry (e.g. Col 3: 5, Eph 5:5). The one-line addition at 138, support-

ing the authority of reforming cardinals and Pope so as to counterbalance the critique of avaricious prelates, favours the positioning of 95–124 as authorial. So does direct address adopted at 125 to make these lines fit in with the mode of 96ff. The I form of 105–24, the most textually distinctive portion, is given in Vol I, p. 743 (Appendix) but not drawn on in emending the text here. Scase (1987) holds that the Ophni-Phineas passage in I and the conflated ms Ht may have circulated in a form distinct from that in the Cx tradition, discerning in I and Ht a shared shape and content, with many substantive agreements in error. The argument, though of interest, is unpersuasive (see further Hanna 1989; *R–K* 193–4; *Intro*. III *C* §§ 21–2; Galloway 1999:72–80). **95** *cused*: the aphetic form, the likely Cx reading underlying both the **p** and the (contextually unacceptable) **x** variant. **107** *For Offinies synne*: the sense requiring *synne*, *sone* is explicable as a visual error for **sunne* (with *u* = |y|) in the immediate source (so b). The trisyllabic form of *Offinies* is preferred as providing the second (or first) stave in a line of Type Ia (or IIIa) and a characteristic chime with *Fines*, also to be scanned as trisyllabic *finees* as P suggests (cf. 123 below, where the stress is on *Óffni* and // B 10.281, where it is possibly though not certainly on *Offýn*). **108** scans as Type IIIa on *d* as emended or as Type I, reading *batáyle* with cognative second stave. The b-half in Cx shows presumed scribal inversion to prose order. *Dei p* is preferred after B 10.282 (so Vulgate). **111** scans as Type IIa on vowels (*as, it, hym*), with a vocalic 'supplemental' stave (*Intro*. IV § 44) on *Ísrael* (for consonantal Type IIa see 117). **112** scans like reconstructed 108. **113** The Cx line shows variation to prose order in the b-half. F's attempt to correct the metre is clearly scribal padding. **114** scans either on vowels, with rhetorical stresses on the pronominals, or on lexical keywords, with two liaisonal staves *his_chayere, his_nekke* (although *ch-* could have been sounded |ʃ| to alliterate as a metrical allophone of *s* (so *Sk* III, n.); for further *s / sh* alliteration cf. 119b (and on this type see *Intro*. IV § 46). F's ⇒ ignores **L**'s idiosyncratic consonantal approximations. **115** scans as extended Type IIIa on vowels with counterpoint (*abb / ax*) or (with muted key-stave *þat*) as Type Ia on |v| / |f|. **116; 118** lack in Cx a satisfactory key-stave. As here emended, they scan on |v|, |f| and have a closely parallel rhetorical structure (*for þei were prestis.../ Forthy Y sey, ȝe prestes*). Cx's replacement of *folk* by *men* may have been induced by the phrase's greater commonness (though **L**'s use of the conjectured expression at B 15.384 occasioned no difficulty for the scribe of Bx). 116 now scans as Ie, if both *for* and *þei* are full staves, as the sense seems to require, 118 as extended Type IIIa. Reading *segges* for 118 would yield a Type IIIa line with an arguably superior stress-pattern; but the collocation is unparalleled. A third possibility is to make *Hóly* the key-stave in both lines, with *hy* for *þei* in

116; but the stress-pattern produced is uncharacteristic. **119** scans on *s / sh,* the key-stave being *-schípe.* Wrenching of stress from root syllable to suffix is not elsewhere instanced in this word (unless perhaps at B 1.48), but parallels are *afterwárdes* B 10.224 and *welcómed* 15.31, 37, 16.170, 22.60. **120** could scan as Type IIIc on *here* and *hem,* but such unusual emphasis would seem forced here, and the emendation adopted presumes scribal inversion to prose order. **121; 122** scan as Type IIIa, the first on *sh / s,* the second on vowels (*hardere; on*), with rhetorical parallelism and cross-line variation of stress from *suche* to *on.* **123** scans after emendation as Type IIb on vowels and *f / v.* Both traditions show corruption, but the sense is largely preserved in **x**, while **p**'s *or on here* looks like a smoothing of the awkward *here,* a pl. possessive referring back to *both* men ('Ophni and Fineas their father' = 'O's and F's father'). *R–K*'s acceptance of **p** destroys the parallel between Christian bishop and Jewish High Priest emphasised by the rich rhyme through including the sons as objects of the punishment. However, the threat to the prelates is not defeat in battle but dislodgement from their 'chairs'. The error in **x** will have resulted from the awkward caesura, which separates Fineas from Ophni. **124** scans as a double-counterpointed line *abb / ab* on *ʒ, s / sh.* A more conventional structure might come from emending the b-half to *synne of ʒoure oune,* but this is much less effective rhetorically. **127 (B 99)** *his:* accepted on grounds of sense and supported by **C**, from which *B-H* does not elsewhere show ⊗; it could also have been the α reading, for which no witness remains. *Con(si)storie:* here used metaphorically (contrast *kyngdom* B 105, where there is no possessive in // C 133 but WHmF have incorrectly inserted one). In the b-half **x** has the right order but the wrong pronoun, **p** the wrong order and the right pronoun, with rhythm that appears suspect on comparison with **B**. I has both right, perhaps by lucky correction, as also has the **x**-type source of K^2, if that was not I. **133 (B 105)** *C*-b and also U here show ⊗ from **B**, as in the next line (cf. also *here* at 125 and *shonye* at 189). **135 (B 108)** *presumen:* if *B-F* preserves α, **B** could have been a present and β a mis-resolution of tense-ambiguous Bx **presumyt.* But since 134–37 are revised in detail, they may be here, and F be a coincidental agreement with **C**. **138** could be of Type IIa in ?Cx with *quod* as second stave; but more probably ⇒ for *Kirke* of the commoner *chirche,* which affects the metre of the b-half (as at 22.120, B 10.411), goes back to Cx. D's *kerk* (if < u) may preserve **x** or else be a felicitous scribal correction (cf. on 16.279). The form *kirke* is nearly always used as a stave-word (see *IG* s.v.), the exceptions being 17.276 and **B** 15.197, 545, 19.446 (*chirche* in // B 15.525, C 16.337, 17.202, 21.445 [no // for B 15.384]). **140** *men:* another hand in P^2 adds the controversial *mene* of I. **141–42** Loss of two half-lines in **x** (as also in **p**-AVS) will have been by eyeskip

from *wytt* 141 > *wit* 142. After 141 *R–K* unconvincingly insert B 115; but **C** must be understood as reducing Clergy's political rôle by replacing him with Kynde Wit in 142. **143 (B 117)** The Bx b-half is metrically defective, and reconstruction from // **C** presumes ⇒ occasioned by objection to the punning *repetitio* or else by desire to widen the scope of the *fyndyng.* **145 (B 119)** *to þe puple:* required on grounds of sense and confirmed by // **B**, though **x** will scan as Type IIIa; loss will have been by eyeskip from *-able* to *puple.* **B 122** *lif:* adopted as providing an adequate stave-word; but if F's reading was prompted by *lif* 120, α itself (< Bx) might have read *lede,* of which *man* β is an exact synonym (cf. N^2's happy conjecture *leode* for *man* Cx at 21.412).

> **B 125** *Hereafter the sigil* α *denotes the family reading understood as preserved in* **R**, *unless indication is given to the contrary.* **F**'s *numerous sophisticated variants, recorded only if judged possibly to represent* α, *will be found in full in the Apparatus to K–D.*

148 *Kynge:* an unceremonious address, modified in M (and in P^2 marginally *a.h.*) by prefixing *sire,* which *R–K* adopt. This is here judged an echo of **B**, not a correction from a superior **C** source. **149 (B 126)** *leue / lene:* the *B*-CrF readings are either ⊗ from **C** or visual errors for Bx *lene.* Arguably Cx *leue* is itself such an error (*R–K* interpret the mss as *lene*). On grounds of sense, Christ might be more plausibly asked to 'grant' than to 'permit'; but a cooler tone towards the 'King' would be in keeping with omission of *sire* in 148 (and see 156). **154 (B 134)** From this point until 2.216, when they are joined by K, *p^2* has *two* representatives, G and N. **156 (B 136)** Cx's omission of B 137 enables the sowing image to continue without interruption from images of stripping and measuring as in **B** and contains a warning to the King not present in the remaining lines (B 139–45, with their dialectical opposition of minatory and submissive political viewpoints, have been correspondingly dropped in the careful revision of this passage). *R–K*'s inclusion of it is accordingly unacceptable.

B 140 *answeres:* the present-tense form of L (? = β)R(? = α), perhaps a resolution of tense-ambiguous **answeryt* Bx, is here adopted as slightly harder in context; cf. on 135 and pr. t. *serueth* in C 160, which is p.t. in **ZAB** (*C*-P^2DG *serued* is adopted by *R–K*). **B 143** scans 'cognatively' on |g| and |k| (cf. B 18.48, *Intro.* IV § 46) and needs no emendation as in Sch (*can*) and *K–D* (*comsed*). **159–64** occur earlier at Z 65–9 / A 84–9 (Vol I, pp. 12–13) and later at B 211–16 (ibid., p. 24). The 'lawyers' passage' was evidently a highly mobile portion of the Pr. **159 (Z 65, A 84, B 211)** *selke:* final *-e* is added in both A and **B** to provide the necessary feminine ending; this type of formal emendation will not be noticed hereafter (all examples are listed in Vol I pp. 761–2). Z 65 forms the basis of **A**'s expanded 84–5. **161 (Z 66, A 86, B 213)** *poundes*: certain in **C** and perhaps the reading of all earlier versions, or else a revision of a difficult expression in **AB**. The form *poundes* could be noun or verb; if a verb, either *pounen 'expound' (not recorded) or *pounen* 'pulverise' (MED s.v. v. 1(a)), with a possible pun on both senses. If *pounen, it would be an unknown aphetic form of the verb *expoun(d)en* instanced at B 14.278 (the verb-form in MED s.v. *pounden* v. is cited from this passage in **A** only). Unless *poundes*, therefore, were an *ad hoc* Northern form, it could only be tentatively regarded as a present-tense verb; but though *poundyt A*-u*Ka*, B-F?H (*pountyd*), *K–DSch*[1], would fit well with the tense-sequence of all preceding verbs in **AB**, direct lexical evidence for *poun(d)en* 'expound' is lacking. Preferable would be either main sense of *pounen*, 'pulverise' or 'beat': the advocates 'mince' the law for their clients' money or 'belabour it' on their clients' behalf. Interpretation as the former is suggested by *B-R*'s corrupt *poudres*, either an attempt to make explicit the metaphorical idea of 'pounding' to dust or a pr. t. (Northern) form of *poudren* (MED s.v. 3c (fig.) 'season'), which would be not unapt in context. Much depends on whether *B-FH* transmit respectively the true α and β readings or show ⊗ from an **A**-type source. In the light of **C** and **Z** (the latest and the earliest reading), *poundes* in all its ambiguity is here accepted as punning on one or possibly two verbs and the noun. The main notion is that the greedy lawyers work only for money (164), whether the sums be small or large. Variants of the penny / pound collocation occur at 2.232 and 16.297; so, all in all, *R–K*'s emendation of **C** to *pounded* should be rejected. **162 (Z 67, A 87, B 214)** *nat*: Ø **Z**, perhaps expressing 'an incredulous aposiopesis' (*R–B*), to which 68 would be an answer; but more probably the negative particle has been inadvertently omitted through distraction from *Ant* preceding. *Vnlose*: adopted for **B** as the form favoured by **ZAC**, though *vnlese* L (< β)R(< α) may represent Bx; both forms are cited from this passage by MED s.v. *unloosen* v. 2(a), *unleesen* v. 2 (the earliest for the former). **164 (Z 69, A 89, B 216)** *er / til*: contextually intersubstitutable adverbial conjunctions evenly attested in the **ABC** traditions. But the sequence **ZB**-α**C**-**x** supports *er* as more probably primary in **L**'s dialect and as the original reading of **A** (cf. also 173). **166 (B 147)** scans either as Type IIIa or IIIc on *m* and *þ* (from liaison of *with hem*) or else as Ia with an internal *m* stave (*smale*). In either case, *myd* of *B-W* (so *K–D, R–K*) is as needless a scribal correction of the metre as *C-M*'s ⇒ of *among* for *with*. **167 (B 148)** *Comen*: *K–D*'s emendation of Bx's mistaken *And* is accepted in the light of **C**, since the number describes the whole gathering, not just one part of it, as *And* would require. **170 (B 151)** *somme*: more precise here, and a possible revision, *hem* (agreeing with **B**) being ⇒ of a more expected word.

B 152 *dredes*: 'something inspiring fear' (MED s.v. *drede* n. 5a; with special reference to the Rolle quotation). With no real tautology after *doute* 'fear', *K–D*'s preference for OC²'s feeble *dedes* is to be rejected.

171 (B 153) *sorre*: the hardest reading and the likeliest to have generated the competing variant, the comparative adverb meaning 'all the more grievously [*sc.* if they complain]'. Found in the early G and in M, it could easily have been adapted to the advancing comparative *sorrer* in most **p** copies or corrupted to the positive as in **x**.

B 159 *Sayde*: if with an absolute sense 'spoke' or 'narrated a story' (MED s.v. *seien* v. 6(a); 11 (a)), this needs a semi-colon after *alle;* if not, *quod he* 160 becomes pleonastic, though not perforce scribal. *hemseluen alle*: neither β nor α is metrical (*aa / xa; aa / bb*). The line here reconstructed as Type Ie with 'standard' counterpoint (*aab / ab*) presumes 'split variants', rendering superfluous such conjectural stave-words as *salue* (*K–D, Sch*) for *help*. **181 (B 166)** *here way roume*: *K–D*'s questioning of Bx *awey renne* does not seem justified, though *B*-β at 171 shows that confusion of *renn-* and *rom-* was easy enough (and lost α could in principle have read as **C**). Cx is hard to reconstruct securely in the absence of a clear **x** reading, but **p** is acceptable on grounds of sense and unlikely to derive from a **B** source, since 189 sounds like the deliberate *repetitio* typical of **C**. The group-original of b read *way briȝt siluer*, O having substituted *knowe* over an erasure after *way*. If b here preserves *x*[1] through i, the lacunae will have affected the last two words of 181, plus all 182, and 183 minus the last two words (K² in omitting all three lines clearly belongs with *x*[1]). The basis for thinking this right is the discreteness of the attempted corrections. Thus u and P² (which originally read as b) offer what seems the reading of B 174; but absence of 182 from u renders it unlikely that *way shonye* could represent what *x*[1] read, while 183 in u looks like an intelligent scribal attempt to fill out the imperfect *x*[1] source-line from the context. X first erased *way* and substituted *war,* then inserted *beyȝ* (a poorly spelled ?*be y-*), the sense intended being presumably '(hereby) be aware'. **185–87 (B 170–72)** The lines B 171–72 will have been lost by α through eyeskip from *mowen* 170 → *mowen* 172, and *pleye* 171 → *pleye likeþ* 173. G and sub-group w may have lost 170 through anticipation of 172. In B 171 Y's *rometh*, direct from g or by felicitous correction, is apter on grounds of sense and looks secure in the light of **C**. Confusion of *rem- / ren-* occurs at 20.103 in some **p** and **x** copies (and possibly at // Bx), as does *e / o* confusion, so an error-sequence *rom → rem → ren-* seems not improbable. But whether the error was in Bx remains unknown in the absence of α. **189 (B 174)** *ben*: an infinitive dependent on *mowe* understood (187), the **x** and **p** variants severally making explicit the sense OLU have corrected, perhaps by reference to a **B** source (in C-App. read 'be OLU' after 'ben]', and insert '?' before 'x'). *R–K*'s adoption of *shonye* b (like 133, another echo of **B**) has no warrant. **194** *R–K* add B 180 hereafter; but no reason for its loss appears, omission could have been intentional and there is no obvious gap in sense. **196 (B 182)** Whether or not the line is scanned as T-Type on |m| and |θ| / |δ|, *tho* improves the metre and could have been easily lost from Bx by haplography / homoarchy before the verb. *B–G* may have it from *C*, from a superior lost **B** copy (*K–D*) or by felicitous conjecture (*Intro.* II, *B Version* § 28). **202 (B 188)** *be we*: b and F are here taken to preserve the correct reading, by reference to **B** or by felicitous variation, as against the *x¹* error (shared by *B-H*). The pronoun will probably have been lost through *be* > < *ne-* attraction.

B 189–92 occur after 197 in Bx and presumably had that order in *B¹*, the poet's revision-copy of **B** (*Intro.* II, *B Version* § 2), since **C** 203 stands immediately *after* the equivalent **B** line (188), following these lines' removal in revision. *K–D* (p. 176) argue persuasively, on grounds of inconsequence in the argument, that they were misordered in Bx and (more speculatively) that their deletion in **C** was a sign of *L*'s dissatisfaction with the text he was revising. But if the lines' position in B¹ was as here reordered, and they were retained in **C**, it becomes at least possible that Cx lost them mechanically through homœoteleuton (*shewe...sh(e)rewe*).

211 (B 206) *so*: the key-stave in revised **C** is here conjectured as the **B** original for which the expected particle *to* is a Bx ⟹, producing a line of pattern *aa / xx*. *B-F*'s *slen* (adopted by *K–D*), a metrical 'improvement' characteristic of this ms, should be rejected as giving poor sense. For the mouse cannot be arguing that the cat be allowed to *kill* them at will (cf. 189 above), rather that if they do not vex the cat by some constraint, he might stick to *conynges* and not kill rats and mice. **216 (B 201)** *reik*: a conjecture of Onions in 1908 accepted by all subsequent editors, though its 'intrinsic merits' (Mitchell 1939) require support from the ms evidence and the reading of **B**. For b's *reik* 'way', D's meaningless *roife* over erasure may represent an exemplar spelled *roike*. X's *ryot* (*a.h.*) over erased *reed* is perhaps a reversed spelling for *royt*, a variant of *royke* recorded only in *Promptorium Parvulorum* (MED s.vv. *raike*; *roit*). Of this, U's *rued*, despite its 'unusual' spelling (Mitchell), can hardly be a reflex, MED giving it as a spelling-variant of *red* (though only of n. (3) 'reed' not of n. (1) 'counsel'). In the light of X's erased reading, P² and the **p**-family, it is thus possible that Cx read *reed*. On the other hand, *reik* b may be an **x** reading corrupted in D and perhaps contaminated from **p** in P². The appropriateness of its sense 'way, preferred option' is supported by that of Bx *wille* (also attested, perhaps as a synonym-substitute, by the **C** interpolation in K²). But *reed* 'way of proceeding, course of action' (MED s.v. n. (1), sense 3a) would be almost as suitable, especially if taken as

ironic. The mouse's notion is of the rats' wilful behaviour as a *reed* that is *reedles* (a 'plan' without 'counsel'), playing on closely-related co-polysemes in characteristic late-Langlandian manner. In **B**, the sense of *wille*, closer to *reik* than to *reed*, may indicate that Bx (and K²) substituted an easier near-synonym (so *K–DSch¹*); but since the Bx line scans as Type IIIa, and preference for Type Ia is a marked feature of the **C** revision, the case for emending Bx has little force (see *Intro.* IV § 28). **220 (Z 59, A 96, B 217)** Agreed **BC** *bondemen* may be seen as a revision, anticipated in some **A** mss, to a more readily intelligible word. The harder reading *bondage* of **A** is supported by **Z** and is unlikely to be scribal in either. **224** *of / þe*: split variants of the form attested in b.

B 223 (Z 90) is a line possibly lost from Ax, since it effects a better transition to A 102, *dikeris and delueris* being indeed *laborers*, not practitioners of *craftis*. **226 (Z 92, A 103, B 225)** No clear reason appears for the variants *longe* γA, *dere* B-L, *fayre* B-F, *here* B-R, Ø *B*-H (cf. *A*-M); but the closeness of *B*-R to **C** is evident despite the second (adverbial) *here*. If β had read Ø (as does H), *þe longe day* could have come into *B*-γM from an **A** source, in which case R could stand for α (< Bx), with L *dere* a visual error for this, and be preferred. The *B*-γ reading also appears in *C*-M, presumably by ⊗ from such a source. **232 (Z 93, A 109, B 231)** *Y say*: in the light of **ZAC** agreement, the order of *B*-G is to be preferred as original, whether by pure descent from g, ⊗ from **A**, or felicitous chance variation.

Passus I

RUBRICS In **B** the archetypal rubric's confirmation of this as Passus One may be regarded as also correct for the other versions, where one family omits (*A*-**m**) and one misnumbers through taking Pr as Passus One (*C*-**p**). The full form naming 'Piers Plowman' may go back to an authorial heading in **B** that was retained in **C**. **1 (AB 1, Z Pr 94)** *the / þis*: either **B** is a revision of **A** reversed in **C**, or a more explicit Bx ⟹, or else **A** read *þis* and **C** is a new revision. **3** *lere*: the variant *lore* appears a contextually prompted misresolution of a presumed original **leore*. **4 (Z Pr 96, AB 4)** *þe*: Bx's *a* appears a scribal ⟹ that misses the reference back to the *tour* of B Pr 14. *castel*: Ax evidently had *clyf* 'steep slope' (MED s.v. 1 (b)). **ZBC** agreement on *castel* suggests possible damage in Ax's exemplar after initial *c-*, and the variants indicate scribal dissatisfaction with the sense. The presence of *clif* in *C*-q may be due to memorial ⊗; it has no claim to represent Cx. **5 (Z Pr 97, AB 5)** *Wille*: a revision following the change of *faire* to *by name* in 4; *sone C*-Ib appears memorial ⊗ from **B** (as earlier in both at Pr 72).

Z Pr 98–100 The thought in 98b is echoed at Z 125 and perhaps for that reason removed in revision to **A**.

These unique **Z** lines seem authentic in both sense and metre: 99 is Type Ie with lift 2 blank, and 100 is Type Ib. **9 (AB 9)** *thei halde*: a word-order less usual in such a construction, so likelier to be original here, by revision. **11 (Z Pr 102, AB 11)** *may...mene*: ZAxBx have inauthentic *aa / xa*. If their exemplars had lacked *be* from a presumed original with the **C** form, the **Z**Ax scribes could have produced the attested wording with *is þis to* by ⇒ of *is*. *A*-RUHE and *B*-H, the latter perhaps by ⊗ from an **A** source (*Intro*. III *B* § 30), will then have corrected the metre by conjecturing *bemene* 'signify', a verb-form certainly used at Pr 217 // (line not in **ZA**) and 1.56. Bx either duplicates the **Z**Ax error or retains **B**, with the error overlooked by **L** in a presumed scribal copy of **A** used in revision. *B*-H may preserve **B** and γLMα all have varied from Bx; but this seems unlikely, and *is this to mene / may this bemene* are perhaps best seen as split variants of a common original later restored in **C**, the more explicit form of which seems to have been Bx's at 60 below. The **C** tradition, being free from uncertainty, is accordingly adopted for all versions. The unsupported reading *bemene* in *C*-D is more probably an echo of Pr 217 than a correction from a superior lost **C** source (as *R–K* judge in adopting it). **15** is either Type IIIa or Type I with two staves in *fáyfúl*. **21 (Z Pr 112, AB 21)** *thre*: omitted by *C*-MF, probably by haplography (*tho, thre*). The numeral gives the a-half a falling rhythm like that of 19a and the *repetitio* of 20 does not suggest unoriginality (as *R–K* hold), since it is common in **C** (e.g. *drynke* in 24, 25).

BA 24–5 (Z Pr 115–16) *And*: Ax *Þat oþer* may be scribal over-explicitness designed to avoid repeating *And*; but a revision later reversed in **B** cannot be excluded. *þow driest*: favouring the originality of *þe driȝeþ A*-t as a more archaic impersonal construction modernised in **B** (and anticipated in most **A** copies) is the support of **Z** (cf. also *the* for *þou* AB 26 in // Z). **25 (Z Pr 118, AB 27)** *Lo*: in the light of *For* **ZAB** to be judged the Cx reading lost in **x** by haplography before L*oot;* for the idiom, cf. 12.90, 221. The interjection forms a prelude-dip in a Type Ia or, if stressed, transforms the line to a Type Ic. **30a** *Genesis*: omitted by DS. **L** does not cite sources in the earlier texts, but comparison of 16.141a with // **B** leaves it uncertain whether both references or neither may be due to the scribe of Cx. **34 (Z Pr 124, A 34, B 36)** *Al is nat / Hit ys nat al*: in the conflict of **ZB** and **AC**, the latter have the slightly harder reading, and **Z** may show ⊗ from a post-Bx source or coincidental agreement with **B**. But as the sense is identical, emendation of so minor a variant is not justified (see *Intro*. IV §§ 25–6). **35–6 (Z Pr 125–26, A 35–6, B 37–8)** The **B** half-lines 37b, 38a have been lost severally in *B*-(WHm) CL, doubtless through eyeskip from *likame* to *liere*. Loss of 37 by *B*-CrH may result from haplography of the pre-caesural lift. **37 (Z Pr 127, A 37, B 39)** *Which*: the less

usual relative form, so likelier to be a revision than a scribal ⇒ (see *MES* 196). *wolde þe*: the Ø-relative **ZBC** form must underlie the reading of *A*-**m**, and attempted smoothing in **r** destroys the metre in the b-half. **39 (Z Pr 129, A 39, B 41)** **Z**'s verbal inflexion explains the origin of the ?Ax a-half *And þat shent þi soule*, where *s(h)ent* is a visual error for **seuth*, easily made if its immediate exemplar had *sh-* for *s-* (cf. *C*-X's *schenth* over erasure and *shende* in *C*-L's rewritten line *For thei wolde shende thi soule...*) and / or *-t* for *-eth* (*seut*). The probable *B*-β reading (in γM) elicited puzzled responses from L and Y, perhaps because spelled *seit* or *sees*; *B*-α shows the same orthographic or lexical error (*-ue* for *-eu*) found in **x** and one **p** witness N, while *C*-PG appear to reflect a hypothetical Cx form **seuth* (actually that of **Z**). *Sk* translates 'And that [i.e. *Mesure* 33] looks after the soul and speaks to you in your heart'. More naturally taken, *þat* is not the subject but the object of the verb: 'and the soul sees that [alliance of the devil, world and flesh against man] and speaks to you of it in your heart' (implying a distinction between rational and voluntary powers). In **Z** *hit* is presumed lost by haplography following *seyth*. In the b-half, only H²K of the **A** witnesses preserve what appears from **ZBC** the correct reading. If **m** is taken as a piece of scribal re-writing, the reading *set* looks like scribal smoothing after ⇒ of *shent* for *seeþ*, perhaps prompted by **r**'s having spelled it **seyt* (cf. *B*-C's ambiguous spelling *setth*). *B*-G's agreement here with *A*-**r** can now be explained (against *K–DSch¹*) as ⊗ from an **A** source, *B*-F seeming also to echo this tradition in its sophisticating b-half. The error *sleth B*-HmC-M can be seen (in Hm visibly) as convergent ⇒ for a difficult original, the posited Cx **seuth*, which has left a reflex in the back-spelled **sueþ-* forms (cf. *B*-α). Bx *This and* for *And* appears an attempt to find a pl. prn object for the verb (*B*-F taking the process a step further with *þese three*). Apart from this last error, Bx seems to have had the right reading as in **Z** and **C**. The latter adds in revision a line with *wysseth* (40) making clear that, as with both verbs in 39, there is only one subject. In the light of the preceding, *Sk*'s identification of this as *mesure* is unacceptable. For acute discussion of this crux in all versions see further Galloway 1999:79–82. **40 (A 40, B 42)** scans awkwardly in AxBx as Type IIIa on *þou, þe*, unless *war* belongs before *shuldist*. **42 (Z Pr 131, A 42, B 44)** *holdeth / kepeth*: a plausible genetic explanation is lacking for the clash *holdeth* ZAβ / *kepeth* αC; but no major issue of sense being involved, β is kept for **B**. Either α may represent a phase of the B-Text intermediary between β and **C** (an interpretation rejected in *Intro*. III *B* §§ 51–5), or it may show ⊗ from **C**, or be an easy coincidental ⇒ of a reading later adopted in revision (contrast 66 below). **43 (Z Pr 132, A 43, B 45)** *to wham*: Bx adds *madame*, which is rejected on the agreement of **ZAC** as scribal interpolation. F may show influence here from **A** or **C**, or have omitted independently, substituting a pronoun in the a-half (*ʒe*).

A 46 (Z Pr 135, B 48) The **m**-variant, with *Wheder* given here in the contracted form of **Z**, indicates for **A** likewise a Type IIa line scanning on *w* rather than a Ia line with wrenched stress on *-shipe* scanning cognatively on *sh / s* as at Pr 119 discussed above and as in *KaK–F* (Bx may, but need not, be scanned so as to give a 'T'-type line). The reading of GH is presumably from an **A** copy (see *Intro.* III *B* §§ 28–32 on ⊗ in these mss).

B 50 (Z Pr 137, A 48) Ax lacked the participial proclitic *i-*, which appears on the showing of **ZB** to form a mute stave two in a Type Ia line.

47 (Z Pr 138, A 49, B 51) *hym / Ø*: the rhythm of **ZA** in the b-half is smoother than that of ?Bx, but *hym* could be a revision to strengthen the sense and GH may have deleted by reference to a copy of **A**. **48 (Z Pr 139, A 50, B 52)** is revised from Type IIIa to Type Ia with muted second stave and from a double to a single macaronic (*R–K*'s *cesari* for *Cesar* is unwarranted). **50 (Z Pr 141, A 52, B 54)** *riʒtfulliche*: confirmed for **B** by **ZAC** and its correctness recognized by *B-W* in felicitously altering Bx. **55 (Z I 2, A 57, B 59)** *That* Bx: perhaps scribal over-emphasis induced by *That* 61, as suggested by *The* in Z**A**B-H (which shows the usual influence from **A**) and parallel (revised) **C**; but emendation is unnecessary. **56** The variants indicate difficulty sensed in the AxBx traditions over the form of *bymene*. The genetically-unconnected **A** copies R, HJK and M point to an Ax spelling *be mene*, and if Bx's exemplar had read the same this might have invited smoothing to *be to meene* (the reading accepted for **B** at 11 above on the showing of // **C**). *B-GFH* may all show influence from an **A** and C²Cr³ from a **C** source. But *bemeene* is here accepted for **B** on the evidence of **C** and probable Ax as well as the contextual appropriateness of the sense 'signify' (applied to the *dale*). **59** *þat... name*: 'whose name is Wrong'; on genitival *that* + possessive for 'whose' see MED s.v. *that* rel. pron. 1c. (b). *R–K*'s adoption of *is yhote* after MU, which show ⊗ from **B**, is unwarranted, as 58–60 are all revised. **60 (Z 7, A 62, B 64)** *fond*: agreement of **ZC** and the characteristic asyndeton suggest that Bx *and* is a scribal smoothing, whether of *a* (= he), as in **A**, or of a Ø-relative (HmF may show ⊗ from **A**). *hit*: perhaps lost in **Z** through attraction to *hymsylfe*. **63 (Z 10, A 65, B 67)** *byiapede*: agreement with **C** against *iapide* **AB** need not here indicate ⊗ in **Z**, since both forms were in free variation; *A*-M has the prefix and MED s.v. *japen, bijapen* records L's as the first use of both verbs. **66 (Z 13, A 68, B 70)** *he...sonest*: **C** is (? coincidentally) closer to β, while α, here joined by β-G (presumably by ⊗, but not from an α source), is identical with **A**'s revised form of **Z** (the reverse of the situation at 42). *B-H*'s unmetrical synonym reflects β. In **Z** *is* emends what is either a mechanical error or a partial reflex of **is*

as. **68 (Z 14, A 69, B 71)** *heo*: adopted for **A** on the showing of agreed **Z(B)C** as the AxBx form of which **m**α is a correct reflex and **r**β *it* a scribal corruption. **70 (Z 16, A 71, B 73)** *halsede*: judged the original **B** reading on the grounds of intrinsic superiority and **ZAC** agreement. F will presumably have here corrected its α (< Bx) source *f* by reference to a **C** or more probably **A** copy. For (*pace K–D* p. 168) *hasked* R is likelier to be a spelling variant of *asked* than a corruption of *halsede*, the heavy incidence of unetymological *h* in **Z** (as in *hasked* Pr 136) indicating a relict of a possibly idiolectal feature. *wente*: found as a ⇒ in *B-F* but in **C** probably revision of a lexically recessive form to give a verb alliterating translinearly with 71, so that *R–K*'s emendation to *ʒede* is unwarranted.

Z 18 appears original, with characteristic translinear alliteration from 17; but its omission in **A** (as superfluous, and to avoid anticipation of *fayth* at A 74) is no loss. **73 (Z 20, A 74, B 76)** The simple form *þi feiþ* is adopted for **A** on the showing of **Z** and **B**'s *þe*, which is less probably the pronoun than the article (in the latter sense the phrase makes up B 15.447b). The form of *A*-JM (*þe þi f.*) is also found in *B*-G (? by ⊗) and this or the vKW order may be original, though **C**'s revision of the b-half in the sense of *fre* found in B XIX 39 reduces certainty. **74 (Z 21, A 75, B 77)** *Thow / And*: **AC**'s pronoun gives the most satisfactory reading, *B*-GHF perhaps taking it from an **A**, *B*-Cr from an **A** or **C** source (cf. on 56 above). It is accordingly adopted for **B**; but a verb-form without pronoun (found e.g. at 20.379, also 2 p. pret.) may be the true **B**, as it is the **Z** reading (*B*-HmOC² more probably reflect smoothing of the latter than an original split into *And* and *thou*).

Z 21–3 show probable 'draft' redundancy after 21, the three lines being adequately contracted into two by **A**. **76 (Z 24, A 77, B 79)** *knelede / courbed*: agreement of **ZB** against **AC** may suggest scribal efforts to avoid the pleonasm of *knelide...knees*, *courbed* in itself being lexically harder (MED s.v. gives no other C14th use). If so, **Z** could be echoing **B**, the reading then belonging to the scribal layer of the **Z** manuscript's descent. However, in contrast Z 2.4 below is *with* **AC** against Bx, and the possibility of successive changes from **Z** to **A**, then back to **Z** in **B**, and finally back to **A** in **C**, though challenging the linear postulate, must argue for caution here in emending **B**. *B*-H shows ⊗ from **A**, its reversed word-order also appearing in *A*-vJ.

B 82 (Z 27, A 80) is omitted from *B*-α for no apparent reason, but from **C** presumably as a revision. *manne*: inflected dative for the required feminine ending. **79** In **C**-App. *add* no] p**O**+U *a.h.*; *om* x. **80 (Z 29, A 82, B 84)** *saynt art yholde*: a sense 'that hold sin firmly' is possible for **Z**'s *senne hard yholde*, but contextually not apt. More probably *senne* is a bad **Z** spelling for *seynt* (cf. *sent* 2.80, *seyn* 5.69) and *hard* for *art*, as *R–B* note.

HC is being referred to as she named herself at Z 19, and such specific reference to her power over sin (alluding to Mt 18:18) would be premature. **81 (Z 30, A 83, B 85)** *quod she*: possibly a Bx attempt to avoid running HC's answer into Will's question, or else an authorial explicitness deleted in **C**. **84 (Z 33, A 86, B 88)** *For*: required by the sense, and restored as the probable **B** reading on the showing of ZAC; no reason for mechanical loss in Bx appears. *who* CZ: possibly the original in **B** also if *B-R He* (smoothed further in F) is a visual error. **87 (Z 36, A 89, B 91)** *also*: a (characteristic) **C** synonym for *ek* (which is replaced by it at 2.252, 21.429 and dropped at 8.311, and which could have been lost by Bx through eyeskip to following *ylik*). **88 (Z 37, A 90, B 92)** *Pe*: possibly over-specific but clearly attested in Bx, less clearly in Ax, and perhaps deliberately dropped in revision to **C**. *B-H*'s reading may be by ⊗ from an **A** source like ChRVH(J). *thus / þys*: choice of reading is difficult since **x** seems to incorporate an element of ZA (*hit*) and an echo of **B** (*þis*), while **p** is identical with **B** (where *B-H* again follows **A**) yet too simple to have generated **x**. The reading adopted accounts for the form of **p** and instances a use of *thus* sufficiently uncommon to have prompted **x**'s expansion.

Z 39 Arguably lacking in appositeness here, the line seems to have been omitted as otiose in **A**. That *Treuthe* is valued by all has already been stated (38). **91 (Z 41, A 93, B 95)** Initial *And* is either the Ax reading or added in **r** (the **m** mss are here variously corrupt), and is omitted from the text in the light of ZBC. **92 (Z 42, A 94, B 96)** *transgressores*: the exemplars of Ax and *C-p¹* have replaced the Latin with an exact English equivalent (see *Commentary*), possibly as a marginal or intralinear gloss suggested by *trespas* 93. If **Z** is here not an echo of **B** or **C** it must be judged, as a harder reading not in the Ax tradition, a pointer to the original reading of **A**, and may be brought in as evidence for **Z**'s priority to **A**. *B-G*'s error shows ⊗ more probably from an **A** source than from **C**. The Anglicised form in P²b suggests the word's early currency, though MED has no prior record. **97–101** The first instance in **C** of long lines misdivided in the archetype of **x** and **p**. The division is correct in **p** for 97–8 but wrong for 99, where the b-half has been expanded. *R–K* adopt **p**'s lineation and adverb, reading *serk* (with the masculine line ending **L** avoided) and *thei* as first stave. But its inauthentic character appears on comparison with 15.226–27, where *pureliche* achieves the same padding-out as *feithfullich* here. In the Apparatus for **p** in place of *def.* read *defende and fyʒte for.* **98 (Z 50, A 102, B 104)** *passeth*: Bx's incorrect tense may result from a visual error in resolving its exemplar's **passyt*, a form actually instanced in *A*-ms J (cf. on Pr 33, B 140). *þe ordre* ZB: arguably also to be read in **A**, since Ax may have had Ø (so **m**) and **r** have supplied an appropriate modifier. **101–02 (Z 44–5, A 96–7, B 98–9)**. On grounds of incon-

sequence in the argument *K–D* (p. 104) convincingly give the lines the order they have in **ZA**. That **C** has them in Bx's order is due to a mechanical error going back to B-Ø, the source of Bx and **L**'s revision-ms B¹. **104 (Z 51, A 103, B 105)** *knigted* Z: the ms form *knigten* may be an incorrect reflex, induced by preceding *kynggen*, of an exemplar reading **kniʒteden. tene*: clearly disyllabic in ZAC, so **B** is given a final *-e* for the necessary feminine ending. **105 (Z 52, A 104, B 106)** The uniformity of this ZABC 'core' line argues against making *Cherubyn and* a prelude-dip and giving *Seraphyn* two lifts. Rather, a |ʃ| pronunciation may be presumed for *Ch-*, a 'metrical allophone' of |s|, giving a standard line.

B 108 (Z 54, A 106) *me(e)ne*: *A*-**m** contains the stave-word missing in **r**, which could easily have lost it through haplography if *mayne* had been spelled *mene*. *B-G*'s omission, if not coincidental, suggests collation with an **A** source of **r** type.

Z 58 (A 110, [B 112], C 106) The line, absent from Bx, is metrically faulty in *A*-**r**, which wants the key-stave and has a defective last lift. The lack of a second full stave was evidently seen as a deficiency, which group **t**'s reading seems an attempt to remedy (adopted by *Sch¹* in ignorance of **Z**). For *siʒt* can be understood as an Ax misreading of original *liʒt* caused by confusion of long *s* with *l* (the converse error occurs in *Pearl* 1050 [BL Cotton Nero A. x]; for a case of the same in *PP*, cf. App. at B 5.492). *Ka²* so concludes, following a conjecture of *K–D* for B 1.112, in unawareness that *lyght* is attested by **Z** at 1.58. But since *no* ms in the Ax tradition reads thus and the line was (inadvertently) omitted from Bx, **Z** must derive from an **A** or **B** source superior to Ax or Bx, or be a brilliant scribal guess, or be the original reading of a version prior to **A** (the interpretation favoured here as the likeliest). That **Z**'s *lord syluen* is shared by M does not argue against this conclusion, since M also reads *siʒt* with the other **A** copies and its *seluyn* may represent the family original without **m** having to be posited as the origin of **Z**. The loss of *seluen* in **r** will probably have been due to homoteleuton (the word occurring again at the end of 111) and that of the whole line in Bx to homœoteleuton (*heuene, sel*uen).

B 116 A Type III line like B Pr 147; *B-W* alone hypercorrects *wiþ* to *myd*. **109** lacks a key-stave with *l*. A possible original underlying unmetrical *fals* is *lyeres*, given the association of Lucifer's fall with lying in parallel B 1.118 and later in C XX 350ff. But *luther*, the conjecture preferred here, is another word favoured by **L**, though not otherwise common. It is applied to Lucifer at B 18.355 with special associations of deceitfulness and has the contextually synonymous sense 'false' at 19.246, while here it suggests treachery, as at 3.317 (see further *lu(y)ther* in *IG*). **111–13** are here taken as part of HC's speech,

314

R–K's ascription of it to Will being scarcely credible if their emendation of 112 is accepted (see below) and unnecessary in any case; HC is speculating rhetorically on the mysterious origin of evil. **112** The Cx line scans *aa / xx* and evidently lacks a key stave on *l.* The word conjectured here may have been supplanted by inducement from *northerne* 114 and (possibly) a marginal or interlinear gloss in the exemplar, although it could also have been visually mistaken as *lofte* and so replaced by an apt direction-word. It is the strangeness of the expression, given the aerial perspective of the description, that will presumably have prompted the hypothetical gloss. The reference to the quarter of sunrise in 113 anticipates HC's direction to look on the left (i.e. towards the north) at 2.5, where the speaker is standing in the east. *R–K*'s ingenious conjecture *in lateribus Aquilonis* for the whole of 112b (p. 169), diagnosing *north* as an intruded gloss upon a phrase drawn from Is 14:13, deserves respect; but such archetypal ⇒ for the Latin half of a macaronic has no parallel. **113** *Thenne to:* reconstructed as the original of the **x** and **p** split variants. **B 121** *for:* Bx scans *aa / xx* and *for* is conjectured as unconsciously omitted through preoccupation with the sense. *K–D*'s *ful* would seem to anticipate *togideres.* **B 123** Bx scans *xa / ax* and since simple ↔ of verb and object will give a Type IIIa line, *K–D*'s elaborate reconstruction is otiose.

122 *ne meuen:* reconstructed as giving both the verb needed for metre and sense and, as a consequence of the redundant negative particle, the form likeliest to have generated the *n*-variants, which were possibly written in Cx as ambiguous **nemeuen.* **126** *summe*[3]: adopted also for **B** on the strength of **ZAC** agreement. Bx presumably inserted *and,* whilst G omitted it after collation with an **A** source. **128 (Z 64, A 116, B 127)** The Ax reading *he put out* (from which only W varies) is supported for **B** by γMHF. But L's *pult,* taken as representing β (with the support of Cr derived from another source than w), and R's *pelt* (representing α) offer the harder reading. Bx may thus be reconstructed as *he pult out* 'he displayed' (a meaning illustrated only from this instance in MED s.v. *pilten* v. 3 (b)). The *B-*γ reading, to which HF have coincidentally varied (M perhaps by ⊗ from γ), will then seem an attempt to make sense of a probably unintelligible phrase (there is no real evidence for the sense 'display'). Much harder is the sense of **Z,** which cannot derive from an **A** or **B** source but which is very close to revised **C** (see MED s.v. *pilten* 1 (a) 'thrust' and *poken* 1 (b) 'push or thrust'). If its immediate exemplar read thus, Bx, having failed to grasp that 'pride' was the verb's subject, and influenced by the commoner phrase *he putte,* will have substituted *he* for *hym* and γMHF have then levelled to the more familiar expression. Finally **C** restored the original sense, but with a verb less liable to being mistaken. Thus, although the evidence from **Z** and **C** is more inferential

than direct, it seems fairly safe to conclude that the form of the phrase in both **A** and **B** was identical with that in **Z,** and to emend accordingly. At B 8.97 the verb *pulte* again caused difficulties, though there LR agreement (pointing to Bx) is supported by OC[2] and what appear attempted corrections in CrY of ?γ *putte.* In // **C** 10.95 **p** has *putte* against *pulte* **x,** as do *A*-DM for the difficult **A** original *pungen,* the only cited example of this sense in MED s.v. *pingen* v. **133 (Z 71, A 122, B 133)** That the key-stave of the b-half begins with *t-* (for which *c-* in the *croun-* variants would be an easy visual error) is evident from both **ZB** and revised **C.** The singular, making the Trinity the subject, gives a reading which may not be harder but is more apt. Construing the verb in **Z** and some **A** copies as plural may have been due to the influence of a series of pl. verbs after *þo* A 119 and to the ambiguous number of the *-iþ* ending. In **C** choice is evenly divided between *tour* (which recalls Pr 15 and collocates with *heuene* 132) and *trone,* echoing **ZAB** *troneþ* and relating more figuratively to *heuene.* Either could be a misreading for the other.

B 134 (Z 72, A 123) **Z**'s Type III line will pass but would make better sense if *Y seye as* were understood as a first lift lost through haplography as in Z 129.

134 (Z 74, A 125, B 136) *Lere:* a sg. imperative (as in ZC, more apt in context; but the addressee is implicitly pl. as much as sg., viz. the whole *lettred* audience of the poem. *pus:* emendation of Bx seems secure in the light of **ZBC.** **135** *That:* the objection of ungrammaticality (*R–K* p. 166) is irrelevant, since the whole clause is in effect elliptical: 'That "Truth" and "true love" — no treasure is better [than these]'. *That* clearly derives from **B** and editorial 'correction' to *than* is otiose. **136 (Z 76, A 127, B 138)** In the form of the a-half ZC stand against **AB,** in that of the b-half Bx seems fairly certain (supported by **Z** and *C-***x**), while in the Ax tradition one variant is that of *C-***p** (but *ʒe mote* **p** can hardly have generated *ʒut mot ʒe* as supposed by *R–K*). The version with double *ʒet* may seem the most attractive, with its discrimination of senses ('still'; 'even more'), but no emendation of **Z** or **C** is called for. **140 (Z 79, A 130, B 142)** The ms reading as it stands makes acceptable sense, and emendation of 79 could be avoided. Divided after *louy,* **Z** 80 will scan as a Type IIIa line on *þ* as the original draft reading. This would become a smoother Type Ia, reading [*Lord*] *God*; but the reconstruction of **Z** from **ABC** favoured here presumes that *in thyn herte* was accidentally omitted (perhaps through having been written in the exemplar's margin). **142 (Z 81, A 132, B 144)** The second *thow* will have been easily lost by haplography in copying **Z.** The prose order of **Z**'s a-half may reflect the draft stage of composition (for examples of prose order that could be either scribal in origin or due to the draft character of the text, see C Pr 108, 113). **145 (B 148)** The sub-archetypal readings *for* and *to abate* could be split variants of **for* to *abate* which, like **x**, would give a Type Ic line with an impossible b-half; but the form of // **B** reliably guides choice of **p** as representing Cx here. **147 (Z 86, A 137, B 152)** The reading *plente* stood in *A*-**m** and **Z**, probably in *B*-β (but H is absent) and possibly in *B*-α (but R is defective), *plante* in *A*-**r** and **C**. The latter is preferable on grounds of sense (see further Adams 1991:12–13) and its difficult referent may have prompted scribal ⇒ of a word often accompanying *pees* in common usage (see 17.93, 199 and cf. 13.170). More simply, *plente* could have resulted from *o / e* confusion (as in *C*-AR). But *plonte* was clearly the reading of **C** and quite probably of **A**, from one of which sources *B*-Cr will have derived its correction. *B*-Y's *planetes*, if not a simple misspelling, may have been induced by the association of one of them (e.g. Venus, Chaucer's 'wel-willy planete') with peace. **149 (B 154)** *eten* **B**: though α is uncertain without R, β seems to be *y-eten*, so that F's *h* may more plausibly be taken as an intruded aspirate (as in the **Z**-ms passim) not the indication of a spirant. Mechanically, however, *yeten* could be a reflex of *yʒeten*, a spelling variant of **C**'s substantive reading, with *his fille* to be seen as a Bx smoothing after misconstruction of the 'beget' verb as 'eat'. But *K–D*'s interpretation of Cr as a correction from a superior lost *B*-ms is an unnecessary hypothesis, since the reading is **C**'s, from which Cr shows occasional ⊗ (as at 147). The Bx form, though bold, is metaphorically coherent in itself and with later development of this image as the Tree of Charity (B 16.3ff), while avoiding anticipation of the incarnational statement in 155 and strengthening the pregnant figure of heavenly love drawing sustenance from human nature. **C**'s figure, more theologically explicit, is better seen as a new idea than as the **B** original underlying Bx. The pervasiveness of revision in this passage argues against *R–K*'s replacement of *As* 151, *Tho was hit* 152 by *And* and re-ordering of 150–51 to accord with the sequence in **B**. **151 (B 155)** *þis*: if a Type IIa structure with vocalic 'small-word' stave (theoretically possible) is excluded, the stave-word needed will have |v| or |f|, most probably *þis*, the metrical significance of which could have been missed by the Cx-scribe. The ease of *þe* ⇒ for *þis* appears from the identical error in *B*-OC² (and cf. Bx at 206, A 180). In Bx and Cx the 5-syllable prelude-dip is awkwardly long and both lines would be improved metrically by reading *tho* for *when*.

155 (B 160) If a vowel / *k* Type IIb structure is disallowed (cf. note on 151) and the lexical words are stressed as they seem to require, unoriginal *aa / bb* results. *K–D* emend by transposing the two b-half staves and finding the needed *m*-stave on *-múne*, but *R–K* adopt Cx. While variation to the commoner *order* of words in the phrase could well have occurred in both archetypes, the emendation proposed here presumes instead scribal ⇒ of a commoner word, viz. *bitwene* for original *inmiddes*. The latter had an

adverbial sense 'between' (see MED s.v. 2) but the sense here conjectured is rather 'in a mid-position (between)'. The resulting scansion, which manages to avoid *K–D*'s wrenching of stress, gives a 'T'-type line: *aa / [a]bb*.

160 (Z 88, A 139, B 165) *comseth a myhte*: Bx's b-half suggests scribal variation to prose-order and ⇒ of a commoner synonym for the verb. In principle, Bx would scan 'cognatively' with G's simple ↔ ; but in the light of **ZAC** agreement, it seems safe to emend. In **ZAB** (the normally monosyllabic) nominative is emended to a disyllabic form (by analogy with the inflected dative form, as in **C**) to provide the required feminine ending. **164 (Z 92, A 143, B 169)** *tene* **ZC** / *pyne* **AB**: perhaps due to Z's ⊗ from **C** or *A*-**m** during scribal copying of the draft, with *pyne* then being also the presumed original reading of **Z**, retained in **AB** and not revised until **C**. Alternatively, *tene* could be a **Z** original revised to *pyne* in **A** or (if ?**m** *tene* = **A**) in **B**, on the possible basis of a revision ms of **r** type, **C**'s being then a restored reading, not a revision of B[1]. On intrinsic grounds, *tene* may be judged both contextually harder (as ambiguous) and stylistically superior (as avoiding anticipation of *paynede* 166 //). There would thus be a case for adopting *tene* in both **A** and **B** and rejecting *pyne* as scribal in both *A*-**r** and Bx. Finally, though, despite lack of signs of major changes in 1.154–74, *tene* may indeed be a **C** revision back to an earlier form and *peyne* a reading **L** found acceptable for **B**, even if originating in a supposed scribal **A** copy. Retention of *pyne* for **AB** in the face of *A*-**m**'s witness is not very satisfactory; but emendation of the (unexceptional) *p(e)yne* hardly more so. Definitely unacceptable is to adopt *peyne* in **C** as do *R–K*, rejecting a Cx reading to which there is no intrinsic objection. **167 (Z 95, A 146, B 172)** *ensaumples*: the pl. to be preferred in all versions as harder and more exact, referring to the dual examples of power (shown in mercy) and humility specified in 168 //, and closely echoed in 171 //. **169 (Z 97, A 148, B 174)** *hengen...hye*: clearly preterite in tense, either strong or weak forms being suitable for emending **Z**'s (doubtless mechanical) error (for *e / o* confusion in **Z** see on 147 above). The adverb *hye* is clearly attested in the b-half, and *A*-**r**'s *by* a visual error for *hy*. Agreement of **ZAC** indicates that **B** is also likely to have read as in *B*-G, which presumably shows ⊗ from an **A** source such as v (itself more likely to have *heiʒe* by good correction from an **m**-type or **C** copy than to preserve **r** against all other members of the family). **170 (Z 98, A 149, B 175)** *ʒow*: the *A*-**r** error *þe* seems a misreading through *ʒ / þ* confusion of **ʒe*, which is found in two copies and may have been in Ax as it is in **Z**. But the *A*-**m** reading is clearer, is that of **BC**, and specifies *haue* as imperative pl. and not infinitive or subjunctive. **171 (Z 99, A 150, B 176)** *myhty*: apparently the original form of the adjective, Bx *myʒtful* probably anticipating B 173 (where it is securely attested in all versions). G presumably shows ⊗

from an **A**, Cr more probably from a **C** source. **172–73 (Z 101–02, A 151–52, B 177–78***)* R–B* suggest that Z 102 may follow directly from 100 (with 101 parenthetic) and offer a possible translation for the ms form: 'or else you will be sorry for it when you go hence'. But as it stands, 101 is unmetrical and the lines are better taken as meaning the same as **A** but as having suffered misdivision. The adverb *therewyth* must here have the sense 'as a consequence' (MED s.v. adv. 5(f)). The earliest thought, like the latest, is that of commensurability, for good as well as for evil; but though *wo* seems less fitting than what replaced it, the case for emending to *weiʒe* is not strong. *ʒe*: necessary for the sense and possibly lost in **Z** through distraction from *Ye...ye* in 102. **177 (Z 106, A 156, B 182)** *ʒow*: in the light of **ZBC** perhaps to be judged omitted from Ax's exemplar; but no emendation on grounds of sense and metre is needed. *goodliche*: with disyllabic suffix, since this is a core-text line, in contradiction to Duggan's claim (1990:179) that it is never so, since otherwise the b-verse will not fulfil the requirement of his Metrical Rule V that 'One of the dips preceding either lift must be strong' (Duggan 1987:45); cf. 18.58 and B 16.78 (neither a core-line) where *-liche* must also be disyllabic, for the same reason. **180 (Z 109, A 159, B 185)** *iugeth* **ZC**?*A-m*: perhaps present-tense in all versions since (while neither is clearly harder) both may be conflicting resolutions of a tense-ambiguous original ending in *-yt* (see note on 98). What does not seem in doubt is that the verb is 'judge'. *Ka*'s claims (p. 435) that *ioynide* 'is more pregnant, implying both judgement and injunction' lacks lexicographical support (see MED s.v. *joinen* v.(2)) and that '*iuggid* can scarcely have produced...its own unmetrical synonym *demys*' is incomprehensible. But the *A-t* reading may be only a scribal attempt to make sense of a word in which *u / n* confusion could have easily occurred. *R–K* sensibly abandon this notion, opting for *iuged* after MFN. **181 (Z 110, A 160, B 186)** *feet*: a word so spelled as to be interpretable as either 'deed' or 'feet', thereby allowing a pun on *folowe* in 182. *A-m*'s variant, which is also that of *B-F* (perhaps by ⊗ from **A**), is influenced by *feiþ* and is an attempt to make sense of a contextually difficult word. The article is here omitted on the basis of **ABC-p** against **ZC-x**, which is less vivid. *feblore*: in the b-half, Bx seems to have attempted to 'improve' the rationality of the original, and *B-H* is presumably based on a partially recalled **A** source; but emendation in the light of **ZAC** agreement seems secure. *nauʒt*: no final *-e* is added since the diphthong could have been realised disyllabically, as at 9.112. **182 (Z 111, A 161, B 187)** *dedes*: nearer the Latin, while *dede* corresponds more closely to the number and sense of *fait* and to the form of the adjective *ded* (see *Intro.* IV § 26); but revision of **Z** by **A** looks unlikely (*B-G* may show influence from an *A-r* source). **183 (A 162, B 188)** There seems little logical justification for Bx *Forþi* in a

strong sense and it could be caught up from the (justified) connective at 175. But if it has a weaker sense 'accordingly' (MED s.v. *for-thi* adv. & conj.), omission of it as scribal will be needless. **186 (Z 113, A 165, B 191)** *hardore*: judged the likeliest reading for **B** on the showing of **ZAC**, *Auarouser* looking like Bx over-explicitness, perhaps unconsciously motivated by the collocation of the positive forms of the two words at B197. G's *herder* is presumably by ⊗ from an **A** source. **187** *hy*: the older vocalic form of the pl. prn would seem metrically preferable for **ZB** in the light of **C**. Though revised, C 186 also alliterates on vowels, but 187b seems to have suffered from the same ⇒ in Cx, and *C-SN* to have corrected the metre independently (like *A-J*?*V*). The line will scan as Type IIa in all three archetypes (but not **Z**, which as here emended is a Type Ie). *R–K* retain Cx in 187, presumably finding the key-stave in *ávaunsed* (a credible Langlandian scansion); but reading *hy* here and emending to this form in **ZAB** enables the pronoun to function as a full stave, giving better balance with the a-half. For further discussion see *Intro.* IV § 30. **188 (Z 114, A 166, B 192)** *kyn*: the line may scan on |k|, with *Cristéne* containing two lifts or, more probably, on vowels, with the privative prefix and the strongly contrasted *here, alle* bearing full sentence-stress and alliteration. **Z**'s Ø-reading is just possible, but the nominal use of a pl. possessive is unidiomatic (contrast the sg. at 13.7) and loss through distraction from preceding *vnkynde* likely.

A 169 (Z 118, B 195) *For ʒe*: reconstructed in the light of **Z** taken as the original of which *ʒe* and *For* are split variants (A's an attempted smoothing of the postulated **m** reading). **190 (Z 119, A 170, B 196)** *out crepe*: perhaps the original word-order in **Z** as well, though emendation can be avoided by adding a final *-e* for the required feminine ending (see MED s.v. *out* (*e*) adv.). **194 (Z 123, A 174, B 200)** Agreement of **AC** in the a-half guides emendation of both Bx (where H has been influenced from an **A** source) and **Z**. For the latter *R–B*'s explanation of *Foryth* as *forgyt*, governed by *trecherye*, is possible but strained. More probably, it is a confused reflex of **For thy(se)*, with accidental omission of *arn*). In the b-half, agreement of **ZBC** furnishes an emendation of Bx's unmetrical synonym (for a case of a possible converse ⇒ cf. B 10.246). The line scans on |w|. **199** Here the **C** *fragment* **H** begins. In Passus I it attests 199–end and belongs with y (see *Intro.* III C §§ 15–17). **200 (Z 129, A 180, B 206)** *siht of*: seemingly part of the text in all versions, though a line without the phrase will scan as a vocalic Type IIa or a counterpointed Type Ie. Its omission in both Bx and *A-m* could suggest ⊗ of the latter from a **B** source or that the revision to **B** was made from a scribal **A** ms of **m** type. But no mechanical reason for the loss appears, other than distraction from preceding *seiʒe...seide*. B-GH have presumably corrected here from an **A** source of **r** type, as has *A*-E in its copying of this line for a second time (for full details see *Ka* Apparatus *ad loc*). The presence of the phrase in **Z** indicates the latter's textual independence here: it cannot be derived from a **B** source or from an **A** source of **m** type, while the preceding 127–28 show no other affinities with one of **r** type. *Y*: presumed lost in **Z** by haplography after *Forth*y.

Z 131–2 *take hyt*: MS *taken* is possible, but inferior in sense to the conjectured form of the original, one which could have been easily corrupted through unconscious ⇒ of *yn* for *hyt* under inducement from *in*, th*yn*. **Z 132 (A 182–3, B 208–9)** *the wyth* **Z**: perhaps a case of ⊗ from a **B** source, or else lost from Ax. The sense does not strictly require it, and in the absence of confirmatory evidence from **C** it is not adopted in the text of **A**. The final lift *Lord* may be realised as a disyllable without needing to sound the medial fricative historically found in *lauerd* (cf. on *nauht* at 181 above).

203 In the text *correct misprinted* that *to* the.

Passus II

Collation Fragment **H** continues to 44 and reads with **y** unless otherwise noted.

Z 1–3 are unique to **Z** save that 2b and 1b were retained at A 1.2, 182 respectively (**Z** has a different half-line for A 1.182 and omits A 1.2). **Z** 1a substantially repeats the first phrase of **Z** 1.131, the phrasing of 2b recurs at **Z** 5.145 // **A** and that of line 3 looks forward to C 8.229 //. Metrically correct, these lines exhibit the redundancy typical of a draft (as likewise at 10). They are probably to be assigned to the narrator-poet since HC has given a farewell blessing at 1.132, but they may have been intended for her if the original plan was that she should leave at a later stage. These are further symptoms of **Z**'s draft-character here.

1 (Z 4, AB 1) *courbed* **B** could be a Bx ⇒ for *knelide* or else a revision finally rejected in **C** for the earlier reading. **A** has dropped **Z**'s *For*, presumably after omitting the summarising transition **Z** 1–3. **3 (Z 6, AB 3)** *blissed / blisful*: the reading of Ax remains uncertain, neither variant being contextually the harder (*blisful* 2(b) = *blessed* 3(a); see *MED* s.vv). *B*-C² may show ⊗ from a **C** source here; unless **Z** has ⊗ from **B** at the scribal level, it serves to confirm *blisful* for **A**. The **C** revision is anticipated in seven **A** witnesses, while *blisful* is read by the five **C** mss ILDMN. *bought vs* **Z**: the obvious emendation for what here appears a possible aural error. **Z** 7 scans a little awkwardly as Type IIIc on *f* and *k*, unless there has been scribal ↔ of verb and object in the b-half. A 4 moves the stresses to lexical words and sharpens the sense of the a-half, both signs of a revising hand.

9 (Z 12, AB 8) *wonderly*: the majority **p** variant *wonder*-

lich riche is apparently an error for Cx *wonderliche*. The *B*-G reading adopted for **B** in the light of **AC** may be a ⊗ from an **A** source. However, Bx is uncertain since R is absent and F sophisticated. If it read as *B*-β and **Z**, the latter must be either an original form rejected in **A** and restored in **B** or else a **Z**-copy echo of a post-archetypal **B** source (as *A*-M may also be). The *worthely* variant could have arisen from *n / r* confusion induced by anticipation of B 19 (Z 19); the converse occurs at A 15, where uvN have *wonderly* for *worþily* (*Ka* App.) **10 (Z 13, AB 9)** *þe pureste*: preferred for **B** as metrically necessary, supported by **ZA** and confirmed by partially revised **C**. F's correct reading could represent α here or be (as H probably is) by ⊗ from an **A** source. That *pureste* was found hard is indicated by the three **A** variants, one of them (J) that of β. **13 (Z 16, AB 12)** The **Z** line could be echoing **B** in the b-half or else be a first form partially restored in revised **B** after being earlier replaced in **A** (perhaps to bring in a topical allusion to Alice Perrers). **20–1 (B 21–2)** *ylow*; *lakked*: transposed needlessly by *R*–K after **B**, though Cx's sense is acceptable and the new line at 22 indicates active revision at this point. *Leutee*; *hym*: masculine contextually even without reference to **C**. *B*-β's *hire* may stem from recalling the grammatical gender of this noun-type in French and Latin and suggestion from the local abundance of feminine pronouns (20, 23, 24). If F's Ø-reading = α and α = Bx, β's error becomes the easier to account for.

A 19 *she*: emended by *K*–FKa to *heo* to obtain a Type IIIa line scanning on vowels (a type now not recognised by *Ka*) or Type Ia with liaisonal third stave (*was hire*) scanning on *s / sh*. De-stressing of *Wrong* can be avoided if the line is scanned as Type IIa with 'supplemental' fourth stave (*aaa / xa*). B 24 revises to a smoother Type Ia, while retaining *s / sh* 'cognative' alliteration. **23, 30 (Z 22, 25; A 18, 21; B 23, 28)** In the case of **C** the base-ms representation of the feminine pronoun is corrected to the unambiguous standard SWM form. That of **Z** is left unemended in keeping with the treatment of its manuscript spelling throughout. In **B**, emendation is unnecessary in the first and, strictly, in the second instance; but a better stress-pattern results if 30 // is treated as an extended line of Type Ic with mute key-stave. Cases involving only spelling-emendation of the base-ms are not discussed henceforth unless they affect sense or metre. **27 (B 27)** **C** re-writes as T-type a Type Ib line with an awkward five-syllable onset and a (probably) mute key-stave (*as*). **B** would read more smoothly with ↔ of *after*, *hym* to give a liaisonal stave (*hym_after*) and a Type IIa line; but **C**'s retention of the word-order in its unrevised a-half cautions against emendation. **27a** *Talis...filia*: to be preferred as an authentic adaptation of the phrase influenced by the passage in Ezech 16:44 that is the probable source (see *Commentary*). **30 (Z 25, A 21,**

B 28) *a* **Z** may be an error for *of* (so *R–B*) or for *of a,* but the sense of the ms-reading will just pass.

Z 28 (A 24) *here*[2]: **Z** is revised in **A** to give sharper sense; in **Z** 'their' refers to both Fauel and Gyle.

B 33 scans awkwardly on vowels as *ax / aa* and would be smoother if pleonastic *He* were presumed lost before *shal* or *leef me* after *lord* (by eyeskip to *leef*).

34 *That what man*: '[with the consequence] that whatever man'; preferable to **p**'s abrupt form, which lacks any link with 33. **37 (B 35)** *lippe*: preferred for **B** as the harder reading to which YCr vary (perhaps by ⊗ from **C**) and for which Bx substituted a more familiar form, as did *C-p*.

B 36 *cacchep*: conjectured for the needed stave-word in the b-half as a less usual term for which Bx substituted a non-alliterating synonym. It is instanced at B 11.173 in a similar context, with which cf. also the metaphorical use at B 13.299.

44 (Z 29, A 25, B 43) The Bx line scans as Type Ie with counterpoint in the a-half but has an awkward stress on *is* in the b-half, the conjectured prn form *heo* furnishing a better stress-pattern. However, the stave-sound in **A** is |l| and it may be that Bx missed the irony in original *lady* (the key-stave in // **C**) and substituted *she* for it. *this*: Cx could have read as in P[2], with *that* and *this* as split variants in the two sub-archetypes. **ZAB** have the conjunction, but **L** commonly omits it (36 above). **47 (Z 33, A 29, B 47)** Emendation of Bx's b-half as evident scribal ⇒ seems justified in the light of // **ZA** and revised **C**. The error may be the result of conscious objection to repeated *alle* 45 and partially induced by the thought in B 48a below. **C**'s revision manages to eliminate the repetition in re-writing B 45b.

A 32 (Z 36) will scan cognatively on |k| and |g| as Type Ia or Ie.

53 *aslepe*: the **x** reading *as aslepe* could be original, suggesting a comparison in parallel with 54b. But while the vision may be 'as it were' in dream, the sleep is a fact and *as* probably a sub-archetypal dittography induced by *as it were*.

A 35 (Z 39) *ofsent*: preferred as giving better sense and corresponding to a line in parallel with *sompned* in Z 42 (deleted in revision); the verb recurs at B 3.102.

Z 39–50. 39–44 are reduced to A 35–7. **Z 40** recurs as Z 119 and is retained as A 110. **45** This anticipation of 159 is removed in **A** as otiose, with deletion of the following connective. **47** An authentic-sounding line dropped perhaps as superfluous amplification. **50** *vp*: mechanical error perhaps through eyeskip to *paneloun*.

A 42 (Z 51) *telid*: a rarer form of the same verb (*tylen*) instanced at Z 6.66 (see also *tollen* at 6.220) and more probably original, with sense 'spread out' as opposed to 'pitched' (*teldit*); see MED s.v. *tillen* v. (2) (c), *telden* v. (a). **A 47 (Z 56)** *feffid / sesed*: either is a possible visual error for the other. The former could have

been induced by co-occurrence of *feffe* with *mariage* at 37; but since the error (if any) would be mechanical, there is no strong reason to adopt **m** for **A**, despite the support of **Z**. The ⇒ of *feffyd* for *fastnid* by **m** at 48 may even be smoothing after recognition of the prior ⇒.

66 *R–K* unwarrantably omit *forth* and transpose 66b to accord with **B**; but the revision begun in 65 continues. **72 (Z 62, A 54, B 72)** *Thenne*: perhaps lost from **A** before *stondiþ* (its position in **Z**) or *Symonye* (**BC**) but not needed for sense or metre.

79 (Z 65, A 57, B 75) Either the jussive subjunctive or the imperative is apt; but the linear sequence **ZAB** with alteration in **C** seems the most likely, the subjunctive in most *A-r* copies being scribal anticipation of the revision in **C**. *erthe*: original in the light of **ZAC** agreement, with *þis* a Bx intrusion of the same kind as *C-p here*. GHF presumably reflect collation with an **A** source. **84 (Z 67, A 59, B 80)** *prynses* **ZBC** is conjectured as having been corrupted to *present* in Ax through visual error, giving weaker sense and losing the anticipation of 'the Prince of this World' at A 10.8. **88 (Z 69, A 60, B 84)** *Yre* could be a revision and Bx could scan (weakly) as standard with *and* as a mute key-stave. But emendation here is probably justified, as *wraþe* is quite likely to be a scribal ⇒ of the more familiar word for 'anger' used throughout Passus V. *Ire* does not otherwise occur in **B** but once in **Z** at 5.91 and twice elsewhere in **C**, at 20.435 and (problematically) at 11.110 (see note). **90 (Z 70, A 62, B 86)** appears in four distinct forms, **Z**'s b-half resembling **B**. The whole 'charter' section has undergone extensive re-revision. **91 (Z 71, A 63, B 87)** The form of the a-half is closely similar in **ZBC**, which lack **A**'s 'isle' metaphor; all four b-halves differ. In **A** *þe faste,* the hardest of the six variants, appears likeliest to have generated *laste* and *false*, which resemble it in shape. **L**'s characteristic view of this vice as 'gripping tightly' occurs at 1.191 //, with which compare 16.87//. A contextually apt sense 'hard-hearted, ?niggardly' (MED s.v. *fast* adj. 7(d)) appears to have been obsolete. **93 (Z 68, A 61, B 89)** *With*: in the light of **ZBC**, unconscious ⇒ of *And* in Bx is presumed, perhaps through eyeskip to 91.

Z 71–2 are lines apparently not derived from any of the other versions, 72 being unique, while 71a is closer to **BC**, 71b to **C**, than to **A**.

95 (B 91) *woldes*: the variant *wedes* C-p*B*-β is plausible enough in context and its (relative) unexpectedness, together with inducement from *wille wolde* 96 might have invited ⇒ in *B*-α and *C*-x of a word connected with thoughts and desires. But as *K–D* conjecture, the rare *wenes* 'hopes, expectations' (MED s.v. *wene* n. (b)), would explain the form of *wedes*, the form and sense of *wenynges* and the sense of *woldes*. The two attested variants are, however, not inferior in sense to *wenes*, though *woldes* is the less difficult, given the common collocation with *wisshes* (e.g. Gower, *CA* VI 923). The form of *B*-α could have been *wendynges, or else F, here accepted as having the right sense, may preserve α correctly (*wenynge* is securely attested at 22.33). That of H (*wendys*) might suggest likewise that β had a form *wendes (? an analogical verbal noun from a preterite, like *woldes*) which might have baffled scribes and invited the 'correction' *wedes*. Here it is assumed that C has revised B, though **p**'s ⇒ for *woldes* is harder to explain than if Cx read *wenynges*. *R–K*, notwithstanding *K–D*, read with **p**; while both **B** and **C** remain uncertain, emendation is necessary in neither. **101** *in...spene*: the second *speke* is here taken as a verb, though it could be a spelling variant of *speche* **p**u (to which IL*P²* should be added, emending the apparatus entry). Since OB share X's *speke*, and this is the harder reading, it is possible that two members of y (I and P²) and one of b (L) have severally varied from the group reading through interpreting *speke* as a noun (when the comma after *ydelnesse* would stand after *speke*). On the other hand, *speke²* as a repeated verb, closely coupled with another (*spene*) that requires a slightly different sense of *in vayne*, is a rhetorically effective *repetitio* with good claim to be original. **105** *R–K* remove the line to stand after 101, making *This lyf* the direct object of *spene*; but such re-writing cannot be justified. **106 (B 103)** *a dwelling*: the variants *a / þay* perhaps point to an ambiguously-spelled *a dwellyn Cx, in which *x¹* wrongly took *a* as the pronoun and *x²* (> **p**) rightly as the article, a reading supported by // B 103. **109 (Z 79, A 72, B 108)** *þis*: unusually for C giving a Type IIIc for a Type Ia line, unless *þis* is a Cx error for *which*, as *B*-α (here supported by H) could be for *which* ?Bx (> β, supported by **AZ**). In α's case, the ⇒ could have been induced by *þis* at 105 (a line deleted in C). **114–15 (Z 84–5, A 77–8, B 113–14)** If these lines are indirect speech, they would involve a (not unusual) tense-change from 109; if direct, would require that Simony or Civil or both be speaking in the third person about themselves. The present tense favours direct speech, most probably from the speaker of 74. Theology's rejoinder is to Civil (as last speaker) in **AB**, to Simony in C and (originally it appears) also in **Z**, though the latter alters to what is presumably intended to be Civil (*Cyuynye* ms). The form of the verb as third person passive is assured in **C** and **Z** and was probably that of Ax; but Bx seems to have had *I assele*, a reading arguably harder and, if original, a revision. The form of 85b in **Z** is identical with that of **BC**, from one of which it could derive; but if **Z** is original here, **B** will have reverted to a **Z** form later abandoned in **A** or retained in **A** and replaced by Ax with a (contextually-apt) reference to notaries. A's b-half here is used by C at 156 below, which may also preserve the **B** original. **118 (Z 88, A 81, B 117)** *weddyng(es)*: the sg. without article is arguably harder, but the pl. provides a contrast between the gen-

eral category and the particular example furnished by *þis weddyng* (118), so Bx may stand as one revision (reverting to **Z**), and **C** as another (reverting to **A** with addition of the article). **120 (Z 90, A 83, B 119)** *engendred* **B**: the *-th* spelling of *B*-YCLR perhaps pointing to that of Bx, paralleled in the *-t* endings of **ZA** (not in C), and indicating a past participle form (cf. B 120). **125 (Z 91, A 94, B 120)** *graunte*: the variation in tenses may derive from a tense-ambiguous *grauntyt* in the archetypes and the exemplar of **Z**, capable of resolution as present or preterite (cf. note on 1.180). In revised **C** the verb-form is again ambiguous, though a past tense is preferable following *plyhte*124: *graunte* C-**x** may be an assimilated present (<*graunteþ*) or preterite (<*grauntede*), with *were* meaning 'should be', or even a jussive subjunctive. The latter is possible, given the Ø-preterite variants in **A** (and see MED s.v.); but while the sense of B 120 is now contained in 124, 125 could refer to future events (*were* 128 balancing 125). The **x** form allows both.

B 123 (Z 94, A 87) In the absence of the *A*-ms A, the sole **m** witness is here taken as preserving the group-original (E here deriving from an **r**-type source), to be identified in the light of **ZB** as = Ax. Alternatively, **m** could here show ⊗ from a **B** source and **Z** derive from **m** or **B**. The line in **r** could scan on *is, his* as Type IIIb (a variation not acknowledged by *Ka*, who nonetheless accepts it with *K–F*; but the natural way of reading gives unmetrical *aa / bb*. It therefore looks like a scribal expansion-gloss and not, as *R–B* suggest, an **A** revision, while **Z**, **m** and Bx are highly unlikely to represent a contraction through omission of two half-lines. The witness of *B*-H at this point could in principle signify its distinct line of descent from **B**; but as this would have to be independent not only of β but of Bx, the reading is more economically interpreted as a case of H's ⊗ from an **A** ms of family **r**. **128** From here on, **b** (BOL) having *ceased* as a C-Text, the *x¹* group of C is represented only by XIP² and UD until 157, when ms Y begins. BOL here *continue* with a transitional passage of **A** material (2.186–98, not collated because of no textual interest) before taking up at the beginning of Passus III as a **B-Text** with the sigil B. **139 (Z 99, A 91, B 127)** Ax scans as an awkward Type IIIa line with two stresses on *nótóries*, unless it has transposed an original order as found in **B**. Revision in **A** could have been prompted by the rarity and potential difficulty of **Z**'s *nysotes*, of which MED s.v. has only one earlier example, from *WW* 410 (and no citation of Z 99).

B 135–6, Z 108–9, A 99–100 Agreement of **ZB** in *lawe* does not necessitate emendation of Ax. For the **A** reading (like **Z** having both *lawe* and *leaute* but in different order) looks a transitional stage between **Z** and **B**, which does not mention *leaute* here, doubtless because of the positively moral and non-neutral character of this term as used in the later versions.

143 (Z 102, A 94, B 130) *faythles / faytles*: the hardest variant on grounds of sense may well be *feyntles* 'untiring' (so *Ka*). However, *feytles* ?'without deeds' (a sense not recorded in MED s.v. but suggested by *R–B ad loc*, referring to Z I 110 //) could be the original, revised to *feiþles* **B**, which is retained in **C**. *Faytles* may, on the other hand, be only a spelling variant of the latter (*t* for the *th* ending). The **A** variants *feyth-* and *feynt-* would then be scribal attempts to resolve an orthographically unfamiliar form; those of V, R and E do not appear to be reflexes of any other. **150 (Z 109, A 101, B 137)** *iuggede* **Z**: past subjunctive, sitting awkwardly with the imperative that follows; while possible, it may be a mistaken reflex of the exemplar's **iugget = iuggyth* (see on 125). In **AB** and (revised) **C** the tense of the conditional clause is uniformly present. **154 (Z 113, A 105, B 141)** *soure*: the harder reading as well as fitting better with **L**'s thought elsewhere, as at 15.49 // and particularly B 10.359, though *sore* appears in one **A** family and in B-Crg (?by ⊗). **156 (Z 115, A 107, B 143)** In the **A** tradition, ms M is here identified, in the light of **Z**, as the reflex of **m** (< Ax) or else as a felicitous correction of an incomplete b-half like that of **r** (left unmetrical by *KaK–F*; the readings of E and particularly L may be by ⊗ from **C**). In Bx *seruice* clerical censorship may be operating, since the *seles* it substitutes for would presumably be a bishop's. In emending, the sg. is preferred as the line is reconstructed to accord integrally with **C**. Bx *also þe* is metrically possible, but its inconsequential character shows as scribal on comparison with **ZC**.

157 From here on, with the presence of Y, the readings of **C** group **y** are attested by XYIP²; XYIP²UD therefore now = *x¹* (representing **x**). When the readings of X are corrected from another **x** authority, this will be Y unless otherwise indicated.

158 (Z 117, A 109, B 145) *go*: the visual error *to* in C-**x** and in several **B** mss is one that recurs at B 2.200 in β (where **B** may be revising **A**). *Go* is preferably to be read as imperative not infinitive, if Fauel's speech is taken to run from 158–61 (and likewise in // **ZAB**). In **Z** omission of *gyue* through partial haplography after *gyle* would perhaps be more easily explained if *go* had not been present in the exemplar. But the phrase could have been lost by eyeskip from *Gyle* to *gold*, another contributory factor being misunderstanding of *bad* as meaning 'offered' not 'bade'.

Z 118 is a draft line (perhaps T-type), presumably omitted as otiose in **A**.

161 *with...speche*: a revision that *R–K* unwarrantably replace with B 148. It certainly anticipates 167 below, but such echoic *repetitio* is common in **C**. **165 (Z 125, A 116, B 152)** *syre* **ZB** has perhaps been lost from **A** by haplography (**sere* before **sertis*); but the line has satisfactory sense and metre. **166 (Z 126, A 117, B 153)** *wyt / wittes*

ZA / B: the sg. in B-GHF may reflect ⊗ from **A** more probably than a **B** tradition distinct from Bx. Since the pl. gives good sense, it is retained in the absence of counter-evidence from // **C**. **167 (Z 127, A 118, B 154)** *thorw*: preferred for **AB** in the light of **ZC**. Ax *wiþ* may have been visually induced from *wyt* 117, a mistake found in all members of B-β save H, which seems to descend separately from the family ancestor. *tonge*: C-M has *speche*, taken by *R–K* as a correction from a superior **C** source but here understood as probably ⊗ from **B**. **169 (Z 129, A 120, B 156)** *þat þe* **AB**: here judged the original form of which *þat* and *þe* are split variants (**C** is revised). **170 (Z 130, A 121, B 157)** *for euere* **AB**: perhaps a revision of **Z**'s *togydderes*; but the latter reading in **m** is hard to see as a coincidental ⇒ for the **r** variant supported by **B** (unless perhaps it was a modernised form of an Ax reading mistaken as **yfere*). **173 (Z 133, A 124, B 160)** *bowen*: final *-n* is added in **Z**, which has presumably lost it through haplography after *w* (or **u*). **174 (Z 134, A 125, B 161)** *hym*: the pl. *hem* occurs in at least one family in each of the later versions as well as in Ax; but in the light of **Z** and the b-half of **C** (*his*), sg. *hym* is preferable as the harder variant. Whichever is adopted, the expression in **C**'s b-half remains slightly awkward after the preceding pl. verbs *leten* and *bade*. M reads *þis* and F *þe* (so *R–K*); but both may be scribal responses to an awkwardness possibly of authorial origin. **175 (Z 135, A 126, B 162)** *cairen*: judged the original for **A** in the light of agreement between **Z** and B-αLM against AxB-γ. The easier *carien* has been induced by the form of preceding *caride* and contextual reference to carriage-horses. **C**'s revision (as at 4.24) reveals **L**'s awareness of the word's potential difficulty.

Z 136–8 136 (A 127, B 163) *ynowe* **Z** may show ⊗ from **B** or be an early reading restored in **B**, with *of þe beste* an Ax alteration of **A** after judging *ynowe* too close to following *al newe* or visually misconstruing it as identical with the latter. The **ZB** agreement challenges the linear postulate, but since the former phrase meets the criterion of acceptability, the case for emending it may be allowed to lapse. **138 (A 129, B 165)** scans as Type Ia with a liaisonal stave (*Fals_on*), perhaps revised in **A** (if *sat* has not been lost from ms **Z** through attraction to *that*.

A 130 (Z 139, B 166) *fetysliche*: the **A** groups VH (= **v**) and EM (= **m**) preserve the ostensibly harder *feyntliche* 'feignedly', which could have been the reading of Ax. H², however, may be seen as offering a synonym for *fetisliche* rather than as reflecting *feyntliche*, while Ch is an idiosyncratic ⇒ close in sense to *fetisliche*. The spelling of J and B-Cr (*fetelych*) suggests that the AxBx form was written with the *s* obscured or omitted. *Feyntliche* might seem to read better in context than the other variants, including ZBx; but the notion of 'fine words' (or of flattery) as akin to 'fair clothing' is characteristic of **L** (cf.

16.268) and intrinsically no less likely to be original. *B-G* may be a reflex, following loss of the nasal suspension, of a reading derived from an **r** source of v type or (less probably) one of **m** type, or simply a spelling-variant of *feetly*, a word closely related to the Bx form.

Z 141–8 141 (A 132, B 168) *on....goen*: in the light of **A**, the verb and adverbial phrase in **Z** appear to have been miscopied in prose order, whether at the scribal phase or in the original draft form (for parallel cases see C Pr 108, 113). The verb, here in fully expanded form, must be in final position to provide the required feminine ending. **146 (A 137)** *destreres*: not requiring to be scanned as tetrasyllabic, since the stress-pattern *déstréres* is authentic (cf. *sepúlcre* C 7.170 //), Z 147 repeating this rhythm and re-inforcing it with rhyme. A revises to Type Ib by adding *south dénis*. **148 (B 174)** **Z** here either shows memorial ⊗ from **B** or attests an early form of a line replaced in **A** by one about the Paulines, restored in **B**'s revision and omitted again from **C**. Scansion would be smoother with *hy* for *they*.

185 *vppon*: the expanded form as in 184 (conjectured or accidentally substituted by one ms, F), needed to furnish a first stave in the a-half (Cx evidently read *on*). **190 (Z 150, A 141, B 180)** *drawe*: in the light of **ZAC** agreement the probable original of **B**; Bx *lede* (perhaps anticipating 182) offers no difference of sense and will be an arbitrary or unconscious scribal ⇒. **191 (Z 151, A 142, B 181)** *oure* **ZAC**: the probable original, Bx's ⇒ attempting to avoid repetition of 180. *fornicatores* **ZBC**: while an English form (perhaps a coinage of **L**'s) could have been used in **A**, this is unlikely if **Z** was prior. A Latin term seems preferable in all versions, since the word reads as a quotation from a charge-sheet (cf. on *transgressores* at 1.92). If Ax's exemplar was unrubricated, the word could have been mistakenly understood as English (although it was not common and MED records no earlier example than this). The same error occurs in *C*-**p**, which makes a similar ⇒ for *rectores* at 184. **193 (Z 153, A 144, B 183)** *fobbes*: possibly the original form for **A** (so *Ka*), unless **Z** is a scribal echo of a **C** source. It is not clear from the **A** variants what Ax read, the *fo*- forms indicating either *fobbes* or *fobberes*, and the *-ers* forms favouring the latter, so *A*-K's reading (that of α < ?Bx) is adopted for **A**. No difference of sense is involved, and as both forms are cited by MED only from **L**, they may have alternated freely in the sequence **Z(AB)C**. The *B*-β*A*-Lw variant *freres* shows a scribal animus perhaps influenced by recollection of *Frere Faytour* of 8.73 and the collocation at 11.54 // **AB**. *rennen*: the Ax reading for the verb in the light of **ZBC**, with *iotten* (a presumed preterite of *gon*, idiosyncratically varied to *trotten* in Ch) a scribal ⇒ by group t. Despite *Ka*'s arguments (Notes *ad loc*), this seems a case where an ostensibly harder reading (if such it really is) shows from the other evidence as more probably scribal,

and *R–K* sensibly abandon it. *B-H yede* suggests ⊗ from a source of *A*-t type. Brewer's contention (1996:396) that *iotten* could be an original **A** reading rejected in favour of the 'clearer and more communicative' *rennen* is contradicted by the fact that **Z** already reads *rennes* (as noted ibid. p. 395n). It is more economical to presume scribal activity here. **195 (Z 155, A 146, B 185)** *this men*: preferred to *þis mené* 'this company' which, though *prima facie* the harder reading, is to be judged a misunderstanding of the sense through taking the presumed pl. demonstrative adjective form *þis* (clearly instanced in **ZC**) for a sg. and then smoothing with a sg. noun. *B-G* once again shows ⊗ from an **A** source of **r** type. *R–K*'s intrusion of *meyne* into **C** seems remarkable (cf. note on *rennen* at 193 above). **197** *sende*: read by *R–K* as *seude* (Ø-relative preterite), which is probably better.

Z 163–70 These lines of summary, to judge from the repetition of 164b at 168b, seem to be in draft form, and this would account for the anacoluthon in 163. But the misdivision of 165/6 may be due to the scribe of Bodley 851. The two lines will scan correctly as re-arranged here and *lach* is easily emended to the required disyllabic form by addition of final *-e* (for the phrase *lacchen mede* cf. C 3. 390 below).

200 The minority reading *wel* MF adopted by *R–K* is here taken as a reminiscence of **B**. The repetition (of *alle* in 201) is a characteristic feature of **C** (cf. on 161 above). **Z 171 (A 154, B 193, C 204)** *the*: omission in **Z** a scribal slip (perhaps wrongly emended as following *tho*) or reflection of the text's draft character (cf.3.17).

B 198–203 Bx makes several successive errors that may be emended in the light of **ZAC** and the context generally. In **198** *wol loke* illustrates scribal over-emphasis (here paralleled in *A*-H). In **200** *þyng* for *tresor* is a generalising idiomatic ⇒ for the agreed **ZAC** reading (in the a-half, despite the damaged state of R, the α reading can be divined in the light of **C** as that underlying F and so accepted as = Bx). In **201** the Bx inversion error, diagnosable on comparison with **ZAC-x**, is one also shared by *C*-**p**, the precipitating mechanism in both cases being attraction of the adverb to a position immediately after the verb. In **202** inserted *and* is a smoothing that reduces the immediacy of the command as recorded in **ZAC**. In **203**, misplacement of the line, which on the showing of **ZAC** belongs after 202, may have been prompted by a wish to dispatch the three named villains as a group before turning to the somewhat different treatment of Mede.

217 (Z 187, A 169, B 206) *dene / doom*: the **ZB** readings seem secure and Ax probably read *doom*, the variant *dune* VJL being explicable as memorial ⊗ from **C** (so *Ka*). Neither word is more obviously appropriate to the context: *din* was fairly rare, *doom* is perhaps contextually harder (*Ka*), if it possesses the sense 'command' cited by MED s.v. *dom* n. 3(a) (and see *R–K* 115), though the context might equally have suggested it to the Ax and Bx scribes. The *doom* reading in C-P[2] is visibly by addition, perhaps by ⊗ from a **B** source, while that in C-D (in App. *add* also N) could result from visual confusion of an exemplar read as *deme* and then smoothed; neither throws serious doubt on what Cx must have read. On balance, it seems best to accept that **A** and **B** could have had *doom* and **C** altered to *dene*, with subsequent revision of 218a. **Z** would then be either a first thought that was rejected in **A** or an echo of later **C** entering at the scribal stage of **Z**. The former, though challenging the linear postulate, would seem likelier if the sequence Z 188–90 is original, since this contains material used in the later versions but not in **A** (see next).

Z 188–90 are probably draft lines that anticipate rather than scribal lines that echo the later versions (188 = B 207, 189 = C 3.78). Although exhibiting the redundancy typical of scribal padding-out, they also display correct metre (with characteristic *s / sh* alliteration in 189) and syntax (with object / subject inversion in 188 as at 22.80 //). 188 could have been present in **A**, lost by Ax, and then restored in **B**. In the light of C 218a, which summarises the content of B 207–8 // Z, there is a case for inserting at least Z 188 after A 169; but since the Ax text makes adequate sense, it may be allowed to stand. **190** *fore*: probably 'beforehand' (MED s.v. *fore* adv. 1, citing *WPal* 4142), but possibly the preposition, if a following *fere* 'fear' has been haplographically lost (cf. 192).

219 (Z 190, A 171, B 210) *feres*: the assured reading in the b-half of **ZAC**, Bx's ⇒ (if βR *felawes* is so taken) perhaps arising from objection to the repetition necessitated by the wordplay at 211 (cf. on B 181 above; *for fere*[1] is removed in C 219). The F reading presumed correct, while it could represent α, is more probably due to ⊗ from C or A. **221 (Z 192, A 173, B 212)** *to* **Z**: an adverb of motion with an implied verb, a misreading of *go*, or the infinitive particle (with following *go* having been lost through visual assimilation), the possibility favoured here on comparison with **ABC** (cf. on Z 190 above). **223 (Z 194, A 175, B 214)** *shoppes / shoppe*: the collective sg. is more probably original, but nothing is to be gained by rejecting the advancing form here and elsewhere (cf. *churches* at 231). **225 (Z 196, A 177, B 216)** *thenne*: the potentially ambiguous original form ('from there') preserved in **ZC**, which would explain the mistaken reflex *þanne* β and is accordingly adopted for **A** and (from α) for **B** (*B*-GH show ⊗ from *A*-**r**). **227 (Z 198, A 179, B 218)** In all versions this is a Type IIa line with de-aspirated *wh* in the second lift, as clearly reflected in **Z**'s spelling *nawer* (cf. *wham* 17.89, scanning on |w| and the **Z** spelling *wam* at Pr 132). **228 (Z 199, A 180, B 219)** *yhoutid*: preferable to *yhonted* (so *R–K*) on grounds of sense as well as providing a characteristic chime with *yhote*; people who shoo Liar away are not likely to 'hunt' for him

only to tell their quarry to 'pack up and be off'. The error is a visual one, but the **m**-group variants point to the true reading preserved in RD of **A**. **Z**'s error must belong to the scribal stage of copying (or it may not be one, since the manuscript reading is not certain). **231 (Z 202, A 183, B 222)** *on...seeles*: the correct order, on comparison of **B** with agreed **ZAC**. Although unobjectionable in itself, Bx seems to have anticipated through visual attraction of s*enten* to s*eles*. *churches*: the pl. more probably original in all versions since the sg. formed part of a familiar set phrase. **233 (Z 204, A 185, B 224)** *thei*: for *thei* of // **BC**, Ax read either *hy* or *hy hym*, the form presumed to underlie **Z**, and the alternative preferred as likely to have generated the split variants *þey / hym*. A-TD show progressive corruption of *hym > he > be*, requiring the preterite to be read as the p.p. (though the grammar remains poor). **237 (Z 208, A 189, B 228)** *Ac* **ZBC** is conjectured for **A**, though (if Ax read Ø) the other mss could have variously substituted an appropriate connective. **238 (Z 209, A 190, B 229)** *withhelden / helden*: agreement of **ZBx** against **AC** is to be explained either as due to **Z**'s ⊗ from **B** or by positing the sequence: Ø-prefix **Z** (or omission in ms Z), *wiþ-* **A**, omission **B**, *wiþ-* **C**. Haplographic omission could have been induced by *with* in Z 208, 210 (B 228, 230). *half* **ZAC**: possibly also the original in **B**; but the α form is acceptable. **249–52 (Z 214–15, A 195–98, B 234–37)** The **A** revision of **Z** is retained unaltered and is an expansion comparable to that of Z 60 at A 51–2. In **C** it comes after six extra lines, incorporating A 166, a rare case (like 3.395) of an **A** line omitted in **B** being retained in **C** (though not after C 214, the parallel passage, which reads as **B**). Either **L** deliberately restored the line because of its intrinsic importance and new appositeness, or an earlier form of what became C 243–48 was drafted for **B** but then omitted by **L** or (whether accidentally or deliberately) by Bx.

Passus III

Collation *Fragment* H is present from 123 to 173 and reads with **x** unless noted.

2 (ZAB 2) *Thorw* X&r: a small example of preference for one preposition of agency over another. *R–K* mistakenly see as archetypal ⇒, but the usage is already found at A 1.107, 6.106, B 1.32 and in C's retention at C 2.248 of A 2.166, but with replacement of *for* by *thorw*. In C-MF *Wiþ*, correction from a superior *C*-ms seems remote and reminiscence of **B** likelier. *Kynge*: this word, particularly prone to loss of final *-e* (see 3.215 //), could have possessed the disyllabic bye-pronunciation that spellings like *kyingus* Z 2.161 suggest (cf. also *byhyend* Z 3.36 and contrast Z 3.126 // B 3.188). But the dative inflectional *-e* is overwhelmingly probable here to provide the feminine ending. **3 (ZAB 3)** *callede*: the present-tense forms in some

A mss may be wrong reflexes of an ambiguously spelled Ax *callit. (see 13, II 125 for parallels). *y can* **ZAC** is presumed original for **B** also, and Bx may have inverted through alliterative attraction to preceding *called, clerk*. **5 (ZAB 5)** *Y shal*: the **r**-variant *I wile* may represent *Ichul* (so V), a possible miscopying of Ax *Ischul (the substantive **m** form confirmed by **ZBC**) which was mis-resolved as *i(ch) wil(e)*. **6 (ZAB 6)** Either b-half **C** variant may represent Cx, but the form reconstructed here is proposed as the likeliest to have generated both. P²'s exemplar has corrected its **x**-type original from a **p**-type ms like F, a copy that here preserves *to* from its group-original but substitutes for *is* the subjunctive verb-form required for the key-stave on *w* (now mute not full as in **B**). U has for its group original *leuest hire were*, which is close to the **ZAB** reading.

8 (ZAB 8) The random **A** variants *þe / þis / my / here* may reflect a Ø-reading in Ax. For **B**, α's pl. noun is preferred in the light of **C**, *þis* being a spelling variant of the pl. demonstrative (common in **C**). *þe gilt B*-FB may reflect an **A** source. **9 (ZAB 9)** *thenne*: omission in **Z** may be due to the Z-scribe or a sign of draft character (cf. 20). **10 (ZAB 10)** The **B** line is revised in **C** as two, the first of which scans as Type Ia on *m* while the second perhaps echoes from **AB** the grammatical word *by*, used as key-stave in following 11b. The **Z** line, of the rare Type IIa almost exclusive to **L**, contains a redundant b-half suggesting its draft character. **A** revises to Type IIIa with a (semantically unjustified) main stress on *be*, which is retained in **B**, the vowel being presumably long (= *by*) in **A** also. *Ka²* judges *brouȝte* **AB** to be scribal and emends to the harder *mened* on the strength of *B*-F's variant *mente* (omitted from Apparatus), referring to MED s.v. *menen* v. (4), a use illustrated only from C15th. This presupposes that Ax substituted *brouȝte* (thus destroying the metre), that F corrected from outside the Bx tradition, and that B¹ was also in error (**C** retaining *brouhte*). This interpretation is rejected because of its incorrect understanding of **L**'s metre and uneconomical hypothesis of a superior **B** source for F, a copy here showing its habitual tendency to 'regularise' metre. But that **L** remained content to use *by* as a full stave is clear from 11b, and once the authenticity of the Type III structure is recognised the problem becomes non-existent and the solution gratuitous. **13 (ZAB 12)** *worschipede*: the second verb's present-tense forms in **A** and **B** mss may be mistaken resolutions of archetypal spellings with *-et* (the form actually attested in *A*-H²) for *-ed*. That each original had contrasted verb-tenses appears likely from the agreement of **Z** and **C**, the latter's *new* first verb (*wendeth*) still having a present tense. **15 (ZAB 14)** *dwelde*: final *-e* is added in **Z** for the required feminine ending (though the terminal *-l* may be syllabic here). Present-tense endings in the **AB** traditions may be aural reflexes of a p.t. ending with *-t*. **16 (ZAB**

15) *And*: a **C** revision or an *x¹* smoothing of an archetypal Ø-reading (so *R–K*) misconstrued in **p** as the participle. In **B** the pt. pl. form conjectured is that likeliest to have been corrupted to the ambiguous *conforten* through loss of the central preterite morpheme, before being smoothed to the unambiguous infinitive in Bx (cf. the inverse situation at **Z** 26 compared with // **ABC** below). *B*-HB's smoothings accord with the tense-sequence of their respective verbs in 14 to coincide with **C**. **18 (ZAB 17)** *the*: **Z**'s omission of the article may be a scribal slip or a sign of the text's draft status (cf. Z 2.171 above). **19 (ZB 18)** The identical form of this line in ZC allows that it may be in **Z** a scribal echo of **C**; but it is better judged an original line lost by Ax through homoarchy (*For* occurring at the beginning of the lost line in a different sense) and might well be restored in **A**. If the **Z** line preserves the original, it may be Bx that has varied in the first phrase and by addition of *and*. But since its form is otherwise unexceptional, and the sense of Ax acceptable as it stands, no emendation to either text is imperative. **20 (ZB 19, A 18)** *and*: the **A** variant *a* (also in *B*-BoCot) may be a mistaken reflex of ?Ax *or*, a substitution for *and* (the error is repeated in *B*-β). Agreement of **ZC** but chiefly superior sense ('ingenuity' and 'strength' being two separate resources) are here decisive in discriminating the **AB** variants. **23 (ZB 22, A 21)** *and* AB / Ø ZC: retention or omission of the conjunction is a matter of indifference, though the Ø-form attested by **Z** and most **C** mss of both families is arguably harder (cf. *Intro*. IV § 25 above), with *and* then to be presumed as archetypally intruded in (at least) Bx. *coppes* **ZBC**: *pecis A*-**r** could be original if it is scanned 'cognatively' as Type IIa (*k / g*) and if *A*-W is seen as showing ⊗ from **C** or **B** and **m** as a scribal attempt to avoid apparent duplication of sense. But **Z**, unless itself echoing **B** or **C**, supports *coppis* as the supplanted original, being not a 'repetition' (*Ka²*) but (with short vowel) specifying small drinking cups or bowls (< OE *cuppe*) as against large, chalice-like vessels (< OF *coupe*: see MED s.v. *cuppe* n). The annominative word-play is characteristic (see Schmidt 1987: 67–75). **24–5 (ZB 23–4, A 22–3)** have been lost by *A*-EM perhaps through eyeskip (*manye > man > mayne*); but on the evidence of A, they could have been in **m**. **29 (ZB 28, A 27); 31 (ZB 30, A 29)** The lines exhibit revision, **Z**'s reading *loke* 28 being replaced by one of uniform sense though variable wording. That **Z** *deureth* 30 is a scribal echo of *dure* at **C** 29b seems unlikely, since it could be an attempt to avoid repeating *lasteth* at 33b (// **C** 32). On the assumption that **B** is original, **C** here would apparently attest **L**'s readiness to re-use **Z** material rejected in **A** and **B**. **30 (ZB 29, A 28)** *heo þanne*: the word-order adopted here for **A**, only possibly that of **r**, is supported by // **ZB** and gives superior rhythm. The form *heo* is retained as the probable original, making the line of standard type. **C** revision to

Type IIIa is unusual; but for **C**'s replacement of a pronoun with a proper name cf. *Lyare* at 2.234. **31 (ZB 30, A 29)** *ȝow*: adopted in **AB** as the harder reading, **Z** confirming and *B*-L, R being taken to represent respectively β and α. The abrupt transition to direct speech, involving a mixed construction, would account both for the levelling to the indirect in *B*-γMF and A*x* (unless *A*-RU alone preserve A*x*) and for the deferral of direct address in **C** to the next line. The infinitive *make* without *to* (attested in WN) is adopted for **A** as the form likeliest to account for both the *ȝow* / *hem* variants in the other **A** mss and for the form with *to* in **B** retained in **C**. **Z** 30's b-half is identical with that of AB I 78/76, where the *equivalent* **Z** line 22 is of completely different shape, and appears to have been removed in revision. **32–3 (Z 32–3)** A form of these lines appears after A 33 in *A*-WN, a genetic pair with ⊗ from **C**. Though the **Z** lines could also derive from **C**, they are here judged draft material rejected in revising to **A**. Either **L** resorted to his text of **Z** or retained a 'repertory' of lines and passages which he drew on when revising to **C** (see *Intro.* V §§ 29–30 and Appendix Three). *pluralite*: a striking case of the unvoiced labial stop counting as a metrical allophone of |b|. *R–K* (p. 168) adopt F's unique *here bonchef* with the sense 'the prosperity that they [*sc.* the benefices] confer'. But, given **L**'s well-attested licence of 'cognative' alliteration (*Intro.* IV § 46, this must be mistaken 'scribal repair of alliteration'. **34 (ZB 31, A 30)** *atte*: adopted as the likely A*x*C*x* reading, of which *at*, *at þe* appear logical reflexes, and preferred for **C** in the light of **B**. *do*: the secure **ABC** reading (of which *A*-v**m** may be a phonic reflex) is rejected by *KaK–D* (p. 100) but on inadequate grounds, for it gives much superior sense: Meed is able to facilitate the canon lawyers' promotion, not cause it directly (cf. 66 // below). Possibly A*x* read *to don* (as in W) with *do* and *to* being split variants of *r²*, while *r¹* smoothed to Ø. **35 (Z 34, A 31, B 32)** *clerk*: in the light of **C**'s secure text preferred as the substantive B*x* reading, *B*-α plural being a scribal slip induced by 34. Loss of the line in *A*-A and agreement of *A*-E with **r** leave it uncertain whether *A*-M here preserves **m** (and thence possibly A*x*) or has ⊗ from a *B*-α source. If the former, *A*-**r** and *B*-β would appear scribal attempts to 'correct' *clerk* for one or other reason: failure to discern the internal |l| stave, censorship, objection to the repetition, or wrong perception of a contrast between *ledes* ('people' generally) favoured by Mede and the specific group of *clerkes* of 33 (34). But **Z**'s indefinite *hem*, perhaps echoed by *lede A*-**r**E, is another reason for accepting *lede* in **A**. In **Z** the caesura presumably comes after two-stressed *lówednésse* in a line of Type IIIb. **37 (Z 36, A 33, B 34)** The *absence* from **Z** after 36 of the 57 lines following in **A** (34–89), if due to loss of a leaf in the exemplar, would be evidence of **Z**'s status as a *scribal version* of **A**. That it does not have to result from deliberate omission seems

established from Knott's argument (1915: 393–94), cited *Ka* 56–7. However, **A**'s scene with the friar-confessor (34–52) and the didactic excursus it provokes (53–89) appear to form a self-contained piece of new material added to a source which, taken by itself, shows no obvious discontinuity. This tells not for but *against* mechanical omission of the lines and so against a scribal character for **Z**. **39 (A 35, B 36)** B*x* *melled þise wordes* is regarded by *K–D* (pp. 105–06) and *Sch*¹ as one of several ⇒ of a censoring kind in 36–46. But despite revised **C**'s closeness to **A** in phrasing and choice of adverb, the B*x* b-half is not obviously scribal, if less than strictly necessary before 37a. Likewise, **C**'s *myldeliche* could be seen as deliberate avoidance of a lexically restricted verb (see MED s.v. *melen* v.) dropped in the revision of B 3.105, a line (already present in **ZA**) that repeats B 36 entirely. B*x*'s supposed censorship could have been undone by restoring the verb as well as an adverbial synonym in **C**. But a more plausible motive for **B**'s revising out *loutide* could have been (as when replacing *baudekyn* at A 40) its exaggerated quality (one **C** ms, M, actually adopts *loutede* for *sayde*, doubtless in recollection of **A**). **40 (A 37, B 38)** *bothe*: the revision introduced in **B** disambiguates the scansion that in **A** requires elision: *léiȝe þe þ'ichóne*. It seems unlikely that either **A** variant *alle* or *boþe*, each apparently a dissatisfied response to the rhythmical pattern, is archetypal. **48 (A 45, B 46)** B*x* *brocour* is seen by *K–D* (p. 106) as scribal censorship of a reading preserved in G by correction from a source independent of B*x*. H's *on hand*, which makes poor sense, could be a visual error for **owen baud* (cf. *erdyn* at 41 above): following *after* indicates that the substantive reading was indeed that of G (and **A**). Both G and H may here, however, show ⊗ from an **A** source and *brocour* be a **B** revision making for greater obliquity of suggestion: cf. the ⇒ at B 41 of *bedeman* for *baudekyn*, a coined derivative of the word in question (see MED s.v. *baudekin* n. (2)). **48–9** transfer B 41–2 (already revised at 43–4), keeping B 42 unchanged. **48 (A 40, B 41); 51 (A 47, B 48)** *ernde*; *stande*: in the light of agreed **AC**, B*x* *message* and *sitten* look like scribal ⇒, and so emendation to *erende* and *stonden* is justified. Unless *B*-H derives from a **B** source distinct from B*x*, its right readings will be by ⊗ from an **A** copy (for a back-spelling similar to *erdyn*, cf. the variant *lenede* recorded in the App. at 13.172). **55–67 (A 50–2, B 51–63)** The **B** lines are found only in β, the three α lines corresponding to B 51–4 being unmetrical expansion of A 50–1. This is apparently the only case of either **B** family ancestor showing direct indebtedness to **A**. **66 (B 62)** *ho payede*: adopted by *Sch*¹ after *K–D* as the likely **B** original but now rejected, since B*x* *and paie* makes good sense and **C** may merely be continuing the detailed revision instanced in preceding 65. **67 (A 52, B 63)** *se:*

preferable on grounds of sense to *seye,* which is presumably a visual error for a similar form of the verb 'to see'. The appearance of *seye* both in sub-archetypes of Bx and Cx (coupled with *se* in C-*p¹*) and in the randomly grouped **A** mss VH, M, W indicates that it was an easy scribal ⇒, perhaps induced by preceding *segge* or the shape of *peynten, purtr*ayen in 66 (62). **70 (B 66)** *worlde:* final *-e* is added for the required feminine ending since, though *rl* could be syllabic, the oblique-case noun in line-final position is likely to have been inflected (cf. 10.48).

   B 69–72 No mechanical reason appears for the loss of these lines from FH, and all are present in **A**. A possible explanation is clerical circumspection: the admonition to *alle good folk* B 64 tolerable, but that to *lordes* too provocative.

73 (A 60, B 69) *writyng(es) / werkes: K–D* (p. 81) take **AC** agreement in *writynge(s)* as indicating that Bx *werkes* is a scribal ⇒ of a more general term, the motive being perhaps to avoid a jingle with *writen* in 70. However, since **C** both removes the jingle and restores the (now necessary) reference to *writynges,* furthering a process begun in **B**, objection to Bx as scribal cannot be sustained.

   B 71 (A 62) *gyue:* the Bx reading *dele* gives the inauthentic scansion *aa / bb* and suggests a scribal ⇒ of a familiar collocation, in part alliteratively induced. But that *A*-**m** also reads *dele* allows the possibility that this was the reading of Ax and that any archetypal corruption was rather the ⇒ of *men* for original *gomes* in the a-half of an extended line that would then have scanned as Type IIb. However, agreement of (the genetically unrelated) *A*-J with **m** points to the likelihood that *dele* is of scribal origin, and possibly influenced by awareness of the Bx tradition here. There may be a vestige of B¹ *dele* in revised C 76 *delest.*

75 (A 55, B 73) *hand:* certain for **C**, as is *half* for **B** (where H presumably again shows influence from an **A** source). The evidence for **A** is randomly divided, perhaps because scribes have variously identified the implied nominal referent of the Latin, which omits *manus.* The two terms are fully interchangeable, since *hand* is the subject (as in the Latin) of a verb of knowing (*be war, wite*) not of doing, and associated in **BC** with *syde,* which collocates equally well with either.

   B 75 The Bx line's defective *xa / ax* pattern and its omission from H may point to its spuriousness. But transposition of subject and verb gives an acceptable Type IIIa line, the sense of which recalls A 64 and is echoed in revised C 74–75b. Other possible emendations are *comaundeþ* for *bit* or *gomes* for *men* (cf. on B 71 above).

   A 65 (B 76) scans defectively in Ax (*aa / xa*), on the showing of **B**, through misdivision from 66. The emendation offered here (to the reading of **B**, but retaining Ax's original verb-complement order) is adopted by *Ka²* without notice.

77–83 (A 65–70, B 76–81) The **C** revision, which at 77 anticipates Mede's request of 115 (// B 87, A 76), recognises the anacoluthic character of the syntax in both earlier versions and normalises accordingly. A 69–75 / B 80–6 are effectively parenthetical, with a very idiomatic resumption of the main sentence at *mayr* A 76 (B 87) taking up *meiris* A 65 (B 76) [suggestion of J.A. Burrow to the editor]. C 78 apparently re-uses Z II 189 along with B 77b to form the new line. **95** *sendeth* **p**: ostensibly less strong than *sende* **x**, which if subjunctive and not indicative specifies the vengeance asked for; but a result-clause reads more smoothly, with *falleth* 97 in elaborative parallel, than a second purpose clause in parallel with *avenge* 93. However, *p¹* has weakened by losing the causal connection between the prayer and the divine use of punishment *on this erthe* (101) as an incentive to repent and so escape punishment *in helle.* **104** *Al this haue*: the first *s*-stave is generated by liaison of *this_háue.* **115 (A 76, B 87)** *a bisowte*: in the light of C*A*-**r** agreement, Bx*A*-**m** appears a plausible corruption which could have arisen through the scribes' taking the pronominal *a* as intended for *hath,* or perhaps through seeing the repeated subject as redundant and then smoothing to the form with auxiliary and past participle. The line's masculine ending betrays its scribal character and suggests the likelihood of **B** having read as **AC**.

118 (B 90) *And* **p** / Ø **x**: the **x**-reading either introduces asyndetically a purpose clause in indirect speech (like *Graunte* at 100 above) or forms the opening of the direct statement by Mede (so *R–K*), with 118a constituting a (dramatically) ironic self-undermining citation. But in // B 91 / A 80 her speech begins with the injunction to 'love' them, and this guides choice of the variant here.

   B 95 (A 84) *tolde*: the superficially harder *tok* of *A*-*r¹* may reflect stylistically-motivated scribal objection to *tolde...telle.*

123 From here to 175 *fragment* H of **C** is present. **124 (A 86, B 97)** *lordes*: secure in **C** and *leodes* unobjectionable in **B**. The variant *men* in four **A** sources may indicate that some scribes found *leodes* lexically difficult or objected to a source-reading *lordes* on grounds of sense (*leodes* Bx could be similarly explained). Presumably *lordes* is meant to cover people like mayors, who would be particularly vulnerable to bribery, and *office* in B 100 may argue for preferring it in **B** too. But while **C** reversion to an **A** reading is unusual, it undoubtedly occurs (cf. note on II 249–52). Retention of Bx challenges the linear postulate (*Intro.* IV § 22), but since Bx meets the acceptability canon, alteration of it to accord with **AC** is better avoided.

   A 89 (B 100) *or ȝerisȝiuys: Ka* shows the origin of the *r¹* variant *for here seruice* (retained by *K–F*) in visual confusion of *ȝ* and *s.* The other variants appear individual ⇒ of common synonyms for a harder reading.

125 (A 87, B 98) *forbrenne*: Bx has the inauthentic metrical pattern *aa / bb* and loss of the proclitic intensive, here stressed on the prefix as a stave-word in a Type IIb line, could have been through visual distraction from *fir-* to *for*. **129–30 (Z 40–1, A 93–4, B 104–05)** The tenses of one and perhaps both verbs in **AB** are in contestation. The present is here preferred as probably archetypal, though both past and present are possible resolutions of hypothetical forms spelled with final **-it* (for *comsit* Ch, *comensit* M, *mellyt* E in the **A** tradition, see *Ka* Apparatus). Evidence for this spelling as possibly original appears in relict forms such as *thechet* in Z 3.61; see on 2.120 above. However, the tenses of **Z** and (revised) **C** are clearly preterite and so retained. **133 (Z 42, A 95, B 106)** *woman*: accepted in **A** on the showing of agreed **ZBC**. *Ka*'s case (p. 164) for *wy* as the difficult original does not account for all the readings (as claimed). For the presence of a Ø-variant suggests that Ax was probably defective here and that NL (the latter transposing *woman* with *vnwittily*) have corrected independently, though perhaps by reference to a **B** source. **137 (Z 43, A 96, B 107)** The line would scan more smoothly in **B** and **C** if the key-stave were identified as |w| (so **Z** and possibly **A**); but in conjunctive use *þo* is more usual, *whan* being commoner as the interrogative adverb. Both **B** and **C** will scan on |v| (< *þ / f*) with four-syllable prelude-dip and possible wrenched stress on *neuére* as at 12.38 (expanding the enclitic pronoun-subject to *thow*). In **C** an alternative but less satisfactory scansion is as an extended Type IIIa, with *For* as stave one. Three **B** and two **C** mss (VN) have *whan*, by ⊗ from an **A** source or by independent correction (presumably on metrical grounds). **139** *a-take þe mowe*: an emendation to correct the metre in the b-half, which has been damaged through inversion to prose order. *R–K*, despite gratuitous and implausible reconstruction of 140–41, leave Cx unemended and 140 with a masculine ending. **140–41** The original is here seen as preserved in **x**, of which 141 is the rare but authentic Type IIa, with evident rhetorical emphasis, and **p**'s *marre þe with myschef* as characteristic scribal padding-out after misdivision of an unusually long line (cf. 15.226), rather than (as *R–K* hold) an authentic half-line omitted by *x¹* with subsequential smoothing (see further *Intro*. II § 130). *as an ancre*: unconvincingly rejected as a scribal gloss by Carnegy (1934:12–13) but defended by Mitchell (1939:486–8). It is necessary on grounds of metre (the line otherwise has a masculine ending) and of sense: without the mitigation of enclosure in an *anchorhold*, there could hardly *be* a 'wel wors woen' than (imprisonment in) Corf Castle. **146 (Z 47, A 100, B 111)** *to wyue*: R (? = α) preserves what is probably also the authentic Bx form, giving good balance with *haue*, and should be preferred in the text.
147–48 (Z 48–9, A 101–02, B 112–13) The **C** reading in 147 is certain and identical with that of **Z** and *B-R*

but conflicts with *B*-βF and Ax. Whether or not repeated *ellis* was a revision of **Z** in **A**, objection to it occurs in Bx which, however, seems secure in the light of C 148 (supported by **Z**). In 112 *B*-F may have coincidentally varied with β or show ⊗ from an **A** source, or else *B-R* may be itself an independent correction from **C**. There is no intrinsic objection to *ellis* in A 101, such cases of 'identical-rhyme' occurring elsewhere, e. g. at Z Pr 69 / 70, **B** Pr 127 / 8, 1.146 / 47, 7.36 / 7 and Appendix I, 5.ii.b). But Bx *soone* 113 is emended, despite support from one family in // A 102, since **m** (here accompanied by V) may in this case have ⊗ from a **B** source. In B 112, by contrast, it seems preferable on balance to see *B-R* as representing α and thence Bx, with β a (perhaps unconscious) variation to an associated parallel locution. **149 (Z 50, A 103, B 114)** *Thenne* **ZAC**: accepted as the probable reading for **B**, Bx having inserted *And* and GH having deleted it by reference to **A** (though G, unusually, re-inserts the connective). **152 (Z 53, A 106, B 117)** *What / To wite what*: the elliptical form of the question understood in *loutide*, here identified as original, is spelled out in **p**, Bx and variously in a few **A** mss. But the *C*-xAx reading, shared by **Z**, appears intrinsically harder. **153 (Z 54, A 107, B 118)** The **p** reading *maide* (so *R–K*) seems closer to **AB(Z)** *womman* (*lady*) but the tone of the unceremonious *Mede* **x** is more in keeping with the King's attitude as shown at 142–43 above. His plan is to make an honest woman of Mede by marrying her to Conscience, change of name (143) perhaps bringing change of nature. *quod þe Kyng* **B** (Ø **ZAC**): possibly a Bx intrusion, omitted in G (presumably following an **A** source); but it could have been added in **B** and deleted again in **C** as one of various (small) revisions in 153–54. **154 (Z 55, A 108, B 119)** *and*: omission in **AB** may be authorial or archetypally scribal; but **Z** need not here show ⊗ from **C**, since the intrusion could have been mechanically induced from **Z**'s *ant* (for *yf*) in 54 above. **158 (Z 59, A 112, B 123)** Of the **A** variants *She r / And* **m** either is acceptable and either may be an attempt to fill in a Ø-original. Alternatively, **m** may be a scribal reflex of Ax **a* or ⊗ from a **B** source. **159 (Z 60, A 113, B 124)** *In trist; (s)he* **CZA**: identified as the likely original readings for **B**, from which Bx will have omitted *In* with subsequent smoothing (omission of *she*). G's ancestor presumably inserted *In* after **A** but left the verb as in Bx, while F's *she* (in the b-half) is only coincidentally correct, being part of a wider re-writing of a type characteristic of this ms. *teneth* **CZA**: here judged the probable **B** original replaced in Bx by a more explicit verb through alliterative suggestion from preceding stave-words in *tr-* and the general context of allusion to betrayal (esp. of a king in 127), or by memorial ⊗ from B1.70. The scribal character of Bx is indicated by its abruptness in introducing a new grammatical subject for a verb that in **ZAC** parallels one preceding and two following with Mede as subject (*B-H* is presumably ⇒ of a near-synonym for Bx *treieþ*). **161 (Z 62, A 115, B 126)** *lereth*: confusion of tense in *r¹* resulting from mis-resolution of an **r** form spelled like M's *lernyt, louet* (cf. on 129–30 above). **163 (Z 64, A 117, B 128)** The verb-tenses are clear in **Z** (present) and **C** (past; present) but contested in **AB**. Confusion may have arisen because of the variation in tenses betweeen the two verbs, correctly preserved in **C**. The past (preterite in **A**, perfect in **BC**) is preferable for the first, the present for the second: Mede once poisoned popes but continues to harm the Church. This distinction, which appears a revision of **Z**'s draft original (unless *-th* in *Poyseneth* is there meant to represent a preterite *-t*), is lost in *A-r¹*, *B-βF* but correctly preserved in *B-R*, **C** and *A-r²***m**. **165 (Z 66, A 119, B 130)** *and²*: the several attempts of *B-FC*-**p** (*alle*), and of *B-β* plus a random group of **A** mss (*in*) to correct a supposed logical error miss the general sense of the half-line: 'anywhere, even if one were to look throughout the world'. Either *and* is a co-ordinating conjunction in an ellipsis for 'between heaven and hell and [between hell and] earth' or it is being used as a separable part of the conjunctive adverbial phrase *and thogh* 'even if / even though' (MED s.v. *and* conj. 5(b) gives examples which, though C15th, have just the sense required here). If *B-F*'s sophistication *þey men al erthe* is judged to show ⊗, it must have been from a **C** source of **p**-type. **167 (Z 68, A 121, B 132)** *þe*: preferred on the showing of **ZAC** as probably original against *a* Bx (GH presumably deriving from an **A** source). *knaues....alle* **ZAC**: the Bx b-half, acceptable enough in itself, seems scribal in the light of **ZAC** agreement, being over-specific in its mention of *walking* and missing the force of *alle*. **171 (Z 72, A 124, B 135)** *nere*: the contracted colloquial form giving better rhythm and likely to be original in all versions. **173 (Z 73, A 126, B 137)** *She*: presumed Ax *And* could have been a misreading of the exemplar's *A* 'She'; cf. on 181 below. *and*: presumed lost from *C*-x**Z** through alliterative attraction (cf. Z 79, 86, 105 below). **175 (Z 75, A 128, B 139)** *fle*: the Cx reading *and fle* appears also in some **A** mss and in *B-F* (possibly from an **A** or a **C** source). The prepositionless infinitive or (elliptical) 3rd person subjunctive is the hardest reading and seems the likeliest original, so Cx may be emended to read with **ZAB**. **176 (Z 76, A 129, B 140)** *And*: adopted for **A** in the light of **BC**, though both *And* **m** and *Sche* **r** may be scribal resolutions of Ax **A*, or smoothings of Ø (as in **Z**). *Treuthe*: the personified form is contextually more vivid, assigning to False's earthly opposite the same name as his heavenly one, as at 191 // below (and cf. also 14.209, 212, with similar sense). The variant *þe trewe* is perhaps induced by a wish to achieve parallelism with *þe fals* or to avoid confusion with *Treuthe* having the referent 'God'. *teieth*: the **m** variant *fetteres* gives a Type IIb line, but if **r** is not original this could be a scribal reflex of

Ax **tetbereth*, as in **Z**. In the **C** tradition the correct reading is that of **p** which, unusually, appears to have been adopted into ms X from a **p**-source over an erased reading **techeth hym f[a]l[s]te*. Clearly wrong on grounds of sense, this appears a visual error also underlying D's weak attempt at correction. **177 (Z 77, A 130, B 141)** *harmede*: in the light of **ZAC** agreement, Bx *harm dide* (so *A*-EH) may be diagnosed either as a scribal ⇒ to achieve greater emphasis, or as a visual reflex of the exemplar's **harmedede* (with erroneously duplicated preterite morpheme). **180 (Z 80, A 133, B 144)** The Ax reading is clearly *as,* but **ZC** agreement might indicate that **A** also read *thus* (so *A*-JN) and Bx made the same ⇒; or *as* could be a minor revision and right for **A** and **B** (so also *C*-P²M). **181 (Z 81, A 134, B 145)** *He(o)*: **ZAC** provide a firm basis for rejecting *And* (?Bx, unless F = α) as a scribal error for the form **A* presumed in the exemplar. *ones*: 'on a single occasion (in a month)' (cf. 21.391), more arresting and more probably original than *one* 'in a single month (as compared with four months)'. See MED s.v. *ones* adv. 1(a). **183 (Z 83, A 136, B 147)** *Heo CA* is likely to represent also the **B** original, with Bx having anticipated *For* in 148 (the same mechanism accounting for **Z**). It may be, however, that both the **Z** and Bx scribes were offering an *explanation*: Mede's privy access to the Pope gives her greater power than the King's privy seal. **184 (Z 84, A 137, B 148)** *For / Sire / For Sire:* all three are acceptable and **ZC** agreement here could be coincidental. The connective may however have been lost from Ax and it improves the sense by giving a reason for the provisors' knowledge. **185 (Z 85, A 138, B 149)** *thow*: the *A*-W spelling (*þif*), showing *þ* / *ȝ* confusion, helps to explain the error *ȝif* in several **A** mss. **186 (Z 86, A 139, B 150)** *prouendreth*: clearly attested in **ZC** and the extant **B** family, and also the probable reading of Ax. The verbal form *Prouendris* in *A*-H²RHE and *B*-C could well explain how **r**'s error arose: through mistaking a verbal sg. for a form of the nominal plural. **187 (Z 87, A 140, B 151)** Agreement of **AC** in the harder reading *holde* suggests that *haue* Bx is a scribal error, perhaps the result of misreading an exemplar form *halde* as *habbe* (the actual **Z** form, which could be scribal or original here), and of unconscious suggestion from the phrase *to have and to hold*. **188 (Z 88, A 141, B 152)** *bringeth*: **ZC** agreement points to the finite form of this verb (the fourth in a succession of such verbs) as original in all versions. Ax and Bx will have then varied towards the easier sense with an infinitive (or possibly an elliptical indicative pl. with understood subject 'they'). The latter would make the priests (or their concubines) and not Mede the implied subject of the verb. But while good literal sense, this is less striking than to make Mede, herself accused of bastardy at 2.24, the metaphorical parent of the clerical bastards (the Latin C 188*a* will allow either reading, the pl.

matres perhaps favouring the former). The minority of **A** and **B** mss with *bryngeth* are less likely to preserve Ax and Bx than to be independent recognitions of the correct sense. **191 (Z 90, A 143, B 154)** *falleth ryght ofte* **Z** makes good sense; if *ryght* is an adverb, then *falleth* = 'falls'; if a noun 'justice', *falleth* = 'fells' (see MED s.vv.). **192 (Z 92, A 145, B 155)** *þe* αC / *youre* **Z?A**B-β: possibly *A*-M preserves **m** (< Ax) and thence **A**, and Z*A*-r*B*-β have each substituted a more emphatic reading. **193 (Z 93, A 146, B 156)** *hym þe gate*: the only reading commanding assent on intrinsic grounds. The seven major **A** variants (including Ø) suggest a lacuna in **r** that the group-ancestors and individual mss variously tried to fill (t possibly, U clearly from 143b); Ax will then have been preserved only in **m**, as support from **Z** also indicates. But if **m** was also defective, its gap may have been filled from a **B** source, as occasionally elsewhere. **197 (Z 95, A 149, B 160)** *mote*: the absolute use of the verb appears original from secure **ZAC** agreement. GF have presumably corrected by reference to an **A** source, Bx to have missed the construction and H to have smoothed further.

Z 96 is a unique line, apparently authentic on grounds of metre and meaning, but omitted in **A** perhaps because of redundancy. Only the b-half adds anything (and that not quite apt to a *mene man* in **L**'s sense) while the main point is made again in 98. **198 (Z 97, A 150, B 161)** *ende*: the reading also for **Z**, where *hynde* with an intruded aspirate and raised *y* for *e* is unlikely to represent the adj. *hende*. The verb's *-n* ending (after eQK) is perhaps what helped to generate the **x** error. **199 (Z 98, A 151, B 162)** *he*: the sex of 'Lawe' may be masculine or feminine. Ax could well have been the latter, and *he* is also an ambiguous spelling in the **C** tradition (as at Z 99, 100). But given the habitual association of justices and barristers with the legal process, the masculine form is preferable (cf. 4.144 below). **200 (Z 91, A 144, B 163)** *in / to*: in **A** perhaps split variants of Ax *into* (so **Z**). **212** *lereth*: preferable to the more obvious *ledeth* in a context concerned with the corruption of the learned (*clerkes* 210, *witt* 211, and cf. *maister* 214). **213 (Z 103, A 155, B 168)** The first *hem* seems to have been lost from Ax, but the second *hem* may be an Ax error and *þei* a scribal ⇒ of the advancing form of the (nominative) pronoun (anticipating *þei* in **B**). **Z**'s *hey* is taken to reflect a presumed original *hy*, which is adopted here for **A**.

Z 108–11 *the*: accidentally lost, in 108 for no clear reason, in 109 through assimilation to preceding *-eth*. *schewen*: an acceptable contextual sense is 'proclaim' (MED s.v. *sheuen* v. 7 (c)), but this seems less appropriate than 'say' since Mede has not yet replied to Conscience. **111** *ȝe*: ms Z's reading presumably results from confusion of *þ* with *ȝ* in the exemplar and scribal inattention to the contextual sense.

222 (Z 112, A 164, B 177) is unmistakably of Type IIIa

in all four versions. *K–D* (p. 205n), rejecting this pattern as inauthentic, emend **B** to *most* on the basis of the **A** mss HL, which normalise to *aa / ax* (though *Ka²* inconsistently leaves **A** unemended, as do *R–K* C). The textual evidence the Athlone editors ignore serves to invalidate their theory of **L**'s metrical types, as their discrepant handling of **A** and **C** tacitly concedes. **225 (Z 115, A 167, B 180)** *weye*: unless **Z** here shows ⊗ from **C**, this will be a first form revised successively in **A** and **B**, to which **C** returned. Neither of the former is however suspect as scribal on the usual grounds. *gabbe*: not an especially difficult word (MED s.v. has many citations); but it may have been glossed in Ax's exemplar and the gloss copied in its place, or else *leiȝe* may be Ax ⇒ of a more explicit verb (*A*-H²'s late correction is presumably from a **B** or a **C** source). Although **Z** could be here echoing **C**, as with *weye*, there are no grounds for rejecting *gabbe* in **B** (as do *K–D*).

Z 122–24 These three unique lines appear authentic. The idiom of 122b recurs at Z 4.59 //,124b repeats Z 2.173b (and was perhaps removed in **A** for that reason).

B 190 (Z 128, A 177) *hym*: omission in **Z** gives the verb the sense 'were ashamed', lexically possible (see MED s.v. *shamen* v.1a (a)) and so accepted by *R–B*. But the key issue in all versions seems to be the effect of the two antagonists' actions upon the King, so *hym* is supplied here as needed for the sense.

A 185–8 (Z 136–38, B 198–200) Difficulty over sg. and pl. pronoun referents begins with the contested reading at A 185, where ?**m**, if it does not itself show ⊗ from **B**, may preserve (with inversion) the true reading corrupted in **r**. The source of the error would have been *þ / ȝ* (or *y*) confusion in *mery(ȝ)e*, read as *merþe* in **r**. Loss of *men* in **r** would have come through assimilation to following *mer-* and smoothing of the damaged reading to *hym* would have ensued. While A 186–87 is more easily read with a sg. or a pl. throughout, the whole referring to the king or to his men, the sudden change of referent at 186 (or 185), supported by **ZB** and here adopted, is more difficult and not untypical of **L**.

241 *þe Kyng*: possibly a Cx intrusion which produces an excessively heavy (five-syllable) pre-final dip; smoother would be an elliptical original without an object or reading simply *hym* or Ø for *þe...kyng*. In any case, it might be better to omit *to*. **244** *conquered*: the past participle in agreement with the pronoun subject as the hardest may be the likeliest original. The **p** reading makes explicit while **x**, correctly resolved by D, attempts to rationalise the sense but without taking in (from *Hit* 245) that the grammatical subject's referent is the territory and not the conqueror. **252** *thermyd*: the probable original, substituted by a few **p**-group copies for Cx *therwith*, illustrating loss of the lexically recessive stave-word to the advancing (but here unmetrical) form also found elsewhere in the text (see 5.135 and Apparatus). For other instances of *thermyd* in stave-position see 9.270, B 15.316, A 2.37 and 7.212. **261 (Z 143, A 192, B 205)** *Ye* Z: if this and not *3a* was the Ax form of the exclamation, **r** could have lost it through quasi-haplography induced by initial *þ / 3* confusion. Unless the same error occurred in Bx, **B**'s deletion was retained in **C**. The idiom is instanced at 11.155, 314; 16.137. **262 (Z 144, A 193, B 206)** *Vnconnyngliche*: the harder reading and probably that of Cx, since shared by the sub-group p^2 (G's *Vnwisly*, to which N's *Vnconnabelyche* should be added, is evidently a reflex of it). *conseyledest*: **Z**'s omission of the preterite tense-morpheme must be scribal, since the accusation refers to an act now completed; cf. Z 4.34 for a similar case. **265 (A 197, B 210)** *men mede* AC: adopted for **B** as a slightly harder reading that Bx (like *A*-VH) replaces with one bringing the relative pronoun into direct conjunction with its antecedent. **266 (A 198, B 211)** *and to*: reconstructed for Ax from what appear split variants in the light of Bx*C*-**x**, presuming *and* lost by attraction of *To > to alle*. **267 (A 199, B 212)** *be byloued*: giving an awkwardly long four-syllable dip in the a-half when compared with **B** (the line is Type Ie). Possibly *be* is Cx dittography following *be / by* in its exemplar (*R–K* omit, after P²uP (which lack *be*). **269 (A 201, B 214)** *3erne / renne*: there is no sense-difference contextually but *B*-α's rarer form seems likelier to represent Bx than does β, which scans *aa / bb* like Ax. The verb-form *3erne* also preserved in *C*-**x** is thus to be seen as the probable **A** original, too, and *A*-M's corrupt reading *Þei desiryt* interpreted as a scribal synonym for a word misread as its homonym *3erne* 'desire'. **272** The Cx line scans *aa / xx* yet appears to reflect an attempted revision of the vapid **AB** b-half (adopted by *R–K*), which scans as Type Ib. The last lift sounds authentic, though the construction *mede thei asken / And taken mede* may suggest that the problematic third stave in 272 is unlikely to have been also *mede*. To scan, this would require a preceding liaisonal stave on *seruantes_for*, theoretically giving Type IIa, but with an inferior stress-pattern and a weak anticipation of 273a. The conjectured stave-word *salarie* occurs, significantly collocated on both occasions with *seruauntes*, at 7.39 and B 14.142 (so also at *RRe* IV 46). It was unusual enough to have invited ⇒ under inducement from the form of 275b and the many local occurrences of *mede*, one of which might well have been inserted *parentrelinarie* as a gloss. (On the lexical distribution of *salarie* see MED s.v.; the main C14th appearances are in L). **276 (A 209, B 222)** *kenne clerkes* **B**: the form of the a-half in Bx appears corrupt in the light of agreed **AC**. The verb *kenne* was found difficult by the *C*-**p** scribe as by some **A** scribes and *A*-M's reading very probably shows direct ⊗ from a **B** source (though in the absence of A it is not certain if this represents **m**, E reading here with *r¹*). The form of the adverb in *C*-**p** could be tentatively

reconstructed from the variants as **herfore* 'for this', a form which might have been that of Cx (cf. *of hem* in // **AB**) or a ⇒ for the Cx form here accepted as preserved in **x**. **277–78 (A 210–11, B 223–24)** The form of Bx, with a Type IIa line in 223, is not obviously unoriginal (although the position of the caesura is untypical) and may seem to confirm the *A*-**m** form of 211 against *A*-**r** as the reading of Ax. However, **C** evidently agrees with **r** both in the form and in the sense of 278 (277b is revised from **B**) and this suggests that the Bx form is here scribal and that **m** may have ⊗ from a post-Bx source. The *A*-**r** form is therefore preferred here as likelier to have been also that of **B**. Having perhaps already undergone misdivision in Bx's immediate exemplar, it would have invited expansion of 224 by the Bx scribe. The new phrase *at...tymes* seems over-explicit and the rhythm of the b-half uncharacteristic. *A*-**r**'s *also* is accepted in the light of synonymous *bothe* **C** as a likely reading for the last lift in **B**. **279 (A 212, B 225)** *prentis*: the aphetic form adopted here on the evidence of both **p** and Ax, giving a single feminine ending as in the other versions. Grammatically it is either a plural with assimilated -*es* or a collective singular. **280 (A 213, B 226)** *Marchaundise* AC: the probable **B** reading for which Bx will have substituted the concrete pl. noun, perhaps through visual error induced by supposing parallelism with *preestes*, *men* (223, 225); H will have its reading from an **A** source. The line could be T-type, but is better stressed on *nede* to rhyme internally with *mede* and (in **C**) anticipate internally rhyming *lede*.

B 241 scans in Bx as Type IIIa with four-syllable prelude-dip, though the a-half may have inverted noun and verb to prose order under inducement from the b-half. **311 (A 233a, B 254a)** *recipiunt*: the present-tense form, evidently that of Cx, understood as a deliberate alteration of the familiar scriptural text, to which three sources (RM) (QFS) (P²) have severally 'corrected'.

A 234 (B 255) The variants divide between *lou3* and *lewed* in both traditions of each version, and *Ka²*'s diagnosis (p. 461) of split variation induced by virtual dittography of *low lewed* can be invoked twice just as appropriately as once. Alternatively, but less persuasively, one of the variants is right and the lost stave-word to be identified as a harder synonym of *folk* (*lede*, not instanced in any copy) or of *taken* (*lacchen*, actually substituted by the scribe of *A*-N).

319 *desauowe*: X's mistaken *desalowe* may be coincidental or result from comparison of its source with a **p**-type ms like QFS, and the same error may have been made in U before erasure and re-correction. A possible motive for X's alteration might have been scribal censorship of the notion that king, emperor or pope could break a 'vow'. **321** *hy...of*: the reflexes preserved in the readings of **p** and **x** are taken to be split variants of the Type Ic line here reconstructed as the probable reading of Cx (*hi* is the actual form of the pronoun in N). **328** *si ne*: the **p**-reading *synne*, which gives the implied sense 'without a qualifying clause "subject to not sinning"' would be acceptable, but looks like scribal smoothing of archetypal '*si* ne' (or '*sin* ne'), each a harder reading, with its elliptical use of Latin. The likeliest form of **x** is *sine* but the version in I (and probably Y and U), adopted by *Pe*, is the clearest and comes closest to the probable original, yielding the sense: '*if* you act justly [*ryhte* 324] you will enjoy divine favour'. The line scans as an extended Type IIIa with double counterpoint (*sgg* / *sg*) and *R–K*'s conjecture *grace* for *thing* is otiose. **329** *cesar*: the line reads unmetrically as *aa* / *xx* in all mss and is so left by *R–K*. But the variant *so may* YIU could preserve an archetypal form *rihte so sothly, so may*, in which each *so* had a distinct sense ('in this way' and 'also') and which would obviate the need for emendation. On the other hand, *so may* could be merely a scribal attempt to supply an extra stave-word in the a-half. The more drastic conjecture proposed here requires a form *cesar* elsewhere attested in stave-position (e.g. at B 1.51), gives superior rhythm and arguably collocates more aptly here with *pope* than does *kyng*. A reason for its loss would have been association of the *c*-form (instanced at B I 51) exclusively with the pagan ruler in the Gospels rather than the contemporary Holy Roman Emperor. The latter was usually *kayser*, as at 318, 322 above, and the form with |s| was used mainly as a titular name of the former (see MED s.v. *cesar* n). **335** *As:* seems more expected, introducing the comparison, and *ac* may have come in from a*cordaunce* 336. *Ac* is read by *R–K* as the ms and archetypal reading, giving a half-line identical with 393a, and is defended by Carlson 1991. It could arguably answer to the scholastic *Sed* '(But) now', introducing a middle premiss; but the syllogism would be left with no conclusion. So it might seem better to take **L** to have meant not the conjunction but the comparative adverb seen at 360b, since 360–1 echo, gloss and explain 335–6. **347** The undeniably awkward syntax of **x** may accurately reflect a Cx reading that was misunderstood by **p**; but a better parallel between the simile-example and the larger grammatical trope emerges if *beleueth* is read as 'remains' not as 'believes' (see MED s.v. *bileven* v. 3(b)). In 349 *To pay* is then to be read as an ellipsis, a verb '(and) expects (him)' being understood before it. **351** *hol*: the variant *holy* **x** looks like scribal over-emphasis consequent on failure to grasp that *hol herte = cor integrum*, the condition of *treuthe* in the righteous man. **364** *cause*: the context points to *cause* 'reasonable grounds' as the certain Cx reading. *Sk*'s and *R–K*'s preference for *case* is not supported by the summarising lines 370–71, which specify only two out of the three grammatical categories. **365** *and²*: evidently the reading of Cx, though possibly **C** read Ø, to which *Pe*'s emendation *to*] *and* would closely answer (cf. the simple infinitive *stande* at 245). **366** *sire²*:

presumed lost from **x** by haplography rather than added to **p** by dittography or deliberate correction. It derives from *sur* (< Lat *super*) where *syre* (n.) is from OF *seior* (< Lat *senior*). MED gives *sirename* as compound s.v. *sire* n. 3 but cites the present passage under *surname* n. (b), and the spellings here suggest that the two were probably not distinguished. **L** himself may have intended a pun while aware that *sire²* is but a spelling variant of *sur* (or *sor*) and not etymologically linked with *syre¹*. The context in any case clearly requires that it is not the father's personal or *kynde name* (10.69) but his family name that is in question. **368** *worliche*: evidently a pronunciation-spelling of a word that most copies give as *worldlich* 'human, of this world' (*Sk*) not of *worthli(ch)* 'excellent', as taken by *P²* and *Pe* (see OED s.v. *Worldly* a. (2), MED s.v. *worldli* a. 2(b), citing this passage). This sense is confirmed beyond doubt by 369, which refers to the bad as well as the good qualities of the speaker's natural offspring; cf. also *wordliche* 10.91, with loss of *l* but retention of the stop. **380–81** Both alternative pairs of readings make sense but *mere; lordes* seems contextually more apt than *myre; londes*. The word *mere* could mean either 'boundary' (MED s.v. 2a), such as a path or embankment, or 'lake, pool' (MED s.v. 2). Arguably an expanse of water between adjacent estates would have greater need of a single visible marker and fits better as a metaphorical image for the property to which two parties make claim. **387** *relatifs*: **x** here appears to have substituted *relacyounes* for the more apt *relatifs* under inducement from the contextually dominant set-phrase *relacyoun (indi) rect*. **394** scans very awkwardly with *in²* as key-stave, and *gendre* could be an intruded scribal gloss for *kynde*. In the text for *acordaunde* it would be preferable to read *acordaunce,* the better as it is the archetypal reading. (In C-App. for first entry *read instead*: acordaunce] Y&r (acorde E); acordaunde XP²). **396** The needed third stave on |m| is provided by wrenched stress on *wymmén*. **403** *is man*: I's variant *is he man*, adopted by *Pe*, is rejected in the light of the general sense of the passage, which refers to man, not Christ (see *Commentary* further).

A 239 (B 260) Both archetypes lack a stave-word on |v| in the b-half. *Ka²* following *K–D* p. 205n proposes *þat* as the first stave-word on the basis of *A*-vW, to produce a line scanning as Type IIa. But no plausible reason appears for the replacement of *þat* by *þe* in the other **A** mss, and it is more natural to suppose *þat* a reflex of the phrase *whi þat* 'why'. *Þat* would then arguably be metrically non-significant, and it could hardly be a demonstrative referring emphatically to a vengeance not yet specified (the expected *þe* is what both archetypes read). The more drastic emendation here proposed is the adjective *fel* in post-nominal position, presumed lost through haplography in Ax and Bx. The play on this homophone (here also a homograph) and the mechanism of loss are of the simplest (a similar case is conjectured for the CxBx readings at 6.155 // 5.171, *q.v.*; and for a parallel cf. the omission of *beste* by C-YA from the phrase *beste bestes* at 426 below). **412** *aftur Ruth* **x**: a hard and contextually apt reading, with **p**'s *rew(e)th* is a mere spelling-variant. *R–K*'s emendation *of þe reuthe* is doubly phantasmal in this regard. **415 (A 242, B 263)** *derfly*: lexically the harder, as *delfulliche* is stylistically the more emphatic reading. The base form of the latter is collocated with *deth* at B 15.521, which **p** may here be recalling, though the phrase is quasi-formulaic.

A 243 The omission from **BC** of this line (specifying the reason for the Amalekites' punishment) is not sufficient reason for suspecting it to be a piece of scribal elaboration of *eldren* 242. However, the cause of its absence from ?*r*[1] is not clear; presumably it will have been added to R from a ms of *r*[2] type, since d and U do not have an exclusive common ancestor allowing R alone to represent *r*[1] here. **417 (A 245, B 265)** *To*: adopted into **B** on the strength of **AC** agreement. Bx may have added *Thee* to its (Ø) source-reading and *B*-Hm(OC[2]) have independently substituted *to*. *bone* **p**: not strictly necessary on metrical grounds, since the line could scan as Type IIa like // **B**, but obviously preferable on grounds of sense to *loue*, which could be a visual error for *lore* or for *bone*.

B 267 (A 250) *Bernes*: in the light of **B** the minority **A** reading is adopted as the honorific word for 'men', which stands at the opposite end of the scale from *bestis*. It is unlikely that a synonym for *Children* 247 would be introduced again so soon. **421** *Mebles* **p**: *That dwelleth in Amalek* appears to be a gloss on the previous line mistakenly included in the text by the scribe of *x*[1]. **423 (B 269b, 271a)** The **C** line, which recomposes two **B** half-lines, here scans as an expanded Type IIIa with counterpoint (*abb / ab*). The somewhat awkward Bx 271, which seems to scan on grammatical words (*For*[1,2]; *þow*) may be corrupt. If the stave-sound in original B 271 was |m|, the key-stave could have been *man,* a word vulnerable to loss through assimilation to preceding *monee,* or else one such as *moste* for *loke*; but given the uncertainty, emendation is best avoided. In C 423–24 there may be split variation from Cx, **p** correctly retaining *spille* in 423b but omitting the first lift of 424, while **x** omitted the translineating *s*-stave but kept the (presumably repeated) *Spille* in 424. Each of the Cx sub-archetypes would thus exhibit translinear haplography, and Cx might be reconstructed to read *al that thow myhte spille / Spille hit*, giving two Type Ia lines. This possibility notwithstanding, the form of Bx 272, though itself open to doubt, points to **x**'s unusual (but authentic) metrical pattern as more probably retaining the form of the revised original. *R–K* insert *fynde* after *myhte*, but this reconstruction from **B** is unnecessary. **427** *and...by*: **x**, though syntactically somewhat elliptical, is acceptable if *warnede* is taken in close conjunction with *wolde* read as a full lexical verb. It probably

preserves Cx, the syntax of **p** showing signs of smoothing here. The sense is: 'in a manner other than God wished, and other than He had warned him [to do] through S.' **429 (A 255, B 277)** *seed*: the Cx line scans *aab / ba*, an extended and counterpointed variant of the *ab / ba* form avoided by **L** (or, with a liaisonal *s*-stave, *his_for*). But insertion of *seed* is warranted on the showing of **AB**. It is unlikely to be a revision distinguishing between Saul's family and his posterity (see 431) but could easily have been lost in Cx through distraction from *sayde* in 428a above. **430 (A 256, B 278)** *Saul* Bx, which seems unnecessary for the sense and weakens the force of the clashing stresses in cross-caesural pararhyme, could be a scribal insertion; but its presence in revised C 430 cautions against emendation here. **432 (A 258, B 280)** *culorum*: presumably pronounced *clôrum* to provide a first lift without wrenching of the stress. *cas*: the three substantive and the Ø variants in the **A** tradition may be due to **r**'s having had a lacuna; but *cas* could be a conjecture in ChN and in **m** preserve Ax or be a borrowing from **B**. **433 (A 259, B 281)** The line probably scans on *n* with first stave and key-stave liaisonal (*An auntur; noen ende*), though it could equally be vocalic, with the second stave muted. Bx *men* might easily have arisen through anticipating *noon* or from misapprehension of the sense; it is clear from 434–35 // that the speaker fears danger to himself, not displeasure to his audience. Emendation is on the joint witness of **AC**. **435 (B 283)** *sothest*: the Bx reading *sothes* is acceptable in itself but weaker than that of **C**, with its ironically balanced superlatives; loss of *-t* could have been induced by *-es* > < *is* attraction. *R–K*'s adoption of **B** destroys one of **L**'s local improvements. *B*-WG's appear to be individual corrections possibly made in knowledge of **C**. **436 (A 260, B 284)** *Wit me*: though the Ax reading could have been *wit it me* or *wit me it*, of which *wit me / it me* could be diagnosed as split variants, the joint witness of *A-r*[2] and **m** tells against this. A reading including both *wit* and *it* lies behind that of Bx; but agreement of **C** and (probably) **A** seems to justify omitting *it* also from **B**. **441 (A 265, B 289)** *vs*: the Bx reading *hem* is unacceptable on grounds of sense, unless it has the remote referent *reumes* 285, since the immediate one it repeats (288) denotes enemies. *A*-**m** could here show ⊗ from a **B** source, and agreement of *A*-**r** (? = Ax) and **C** indicates that *vs* was also in **B** and Bx a ⇒ of *hem* through inducement from preceding 288 and inattention to the sense. **444 (B 292)** *trewe men*: reconstruction of **B** in the light of **C** is needed to emend the unmetrical Bx line (*aa / xx*), into the b-half of which the familiar *trupe* has come through probable inducement from 293 (cf. C 456 below). **445 (B 293)** *treuthe*: should be capitalised as a personification (cf. 139). Its referent is implied by // **B** to be 'God', although in **C** it could be simply the quality. **446 (A 269, B 294)** *no lif*: though *A*-**m** and W could here show ⊗ from a **B** source, they may equally preserve Ax, **r** having misunderstood the line through unconscious association of *lif* with *lese* in contexts involving the administration of justice. This would have occurred more easily if Ax had read *no lif* for *and no lif*, a reading which would account for the variation *and / or* between the **A** mss. But the sense of A 270 makes clear that *lif* here = 'person' and is meant to stand in contrast with *Seriaunt*, so that there is no reason for doubting that **A** itself read the same as **BC**. **447 (A 270, B 295)** *þat:* the probable Bx reading *here* is not objectionable in itself but is rejected in the light of **A?C** *þat* as likely to be a more explicit scribal ⇒. The **C** variants may however suggest that the reading was Ø in both Bx and in B¹. **448 (B 296)** *paueloun / cloke:* against *K–DSch, cloke* is not here regarded as scribal, but *paueloun* **C** is taken as an alteration of **B** from a Type IIIa into a Type Ia line, a common feature of the revision (cf. B 3.10, 229, B 4.59). **449 (A 272, B 297)** *euel:* required by the sense in **C** if an uncharacteristically flat assertion is to be avoided; it will have been lost from y through partial haplography of *euel* after *Much*el, to the precise form of which the omission affords oblique testimony. **450 (A 273, B 298)** *lordeþ* **B**: the Bx line has the inauthentic pattern *aa / bb* and to emend it *K–D* (p. 195) propose *ledeþ* as the stave-word supplanted by *ruleþ* (so *Sch*). But *ledeþ* is not lexically difficult, as would be *lordeþ*, offered as an alternative conjecture here. This word is instanced transitively in Chaucer (*Complaint of Mars* 166) and is found in intransitive use at 11.69 //, the first recorded appearance (see MED s.v. *lorden* v.). Its rarity, together with presumed scribal objection to the adnominative repetition of *lorde(s)*, a characteristic feature, would account for the ⇒. *letteth:* a subject *a* 'she' is to be understood, with *Mede* not *euel* as the referent. **454 (B 302)** *wonder:* Bx gives the line a bumpy trisyllabic final dip, unless it is taken as the key-stave, providing wordplay with *wonder* 304a. Otherwise the word could be an intensifier induced by the latter and replacing original *wel* (= *so* in revised **C**). **456 (B 303)** *Moises:* despite an apparent parallel to **x** in 22.62a, *The which Moises* here appears to be a senseless scribal expansion of a seemingly short line when compared with **p** and // **B**, and resembles the one noted at 421 above. B 303 scans not as a T-type (*aa / [a]bb*) but as standard with a liaisonal key-stave on *m* (*come_into*). *K–D's* emendation *into [myddel] erþe* is quite unnecessary. **457** *briht:* a revision, of characteristically Langlandian type (cf. 20.100 for a similar phrase), which *R–K* incomprehensibly reject for *brode* **B**. **468 (B 316)** The line in Bx scans *xa / ax* unless, improbably, *commune* is two-stressed and preceded by a four-syllable anacrusis, giving an awkward and uncharacteristic Type IIIa line. Emendation from **C** seems justified here since *carke* was lexically difficult enough to be vulnerable to scribal ⇒. **471 (B 319)** *moot* **B**: Bx *wole*, giving an unmetrical

b-half, appears a scribal ⇒ for the needed stave-word in *m*. Of the two possible modal verbs, *moten* is here preferred to *mowen* as the stronger. But in the light of the **C** revision, Bx's ⇒ could perhaps have been of *truthe* for *trewe men*, as at 292, with subsequent smoothing. **476** *smethen:* an elliptical infinitive (with *shal* understood); but YIP²UR have the singular subjunctive *smythe*, which is closer to **B**, and Cx just as probably read the latter. **479 (B 327)** *myddel:* the first lift in **C**, to judge by // **B**; **p** presumably preserves Cx, P² having acquired the reading from a **p**-source. The omission in I and the insertions in X (*a.h.*) and P² suggest that **x** read Ø. The immediate sources of u and Y must have inserted their respective conjectures independently, since none of the substantive **x** variants alliterates or is derived from one of the others. **485–86 (B 334–35)** The **B** line scans as an extended Type III counterpointed in the a-half (*abb / ax*) with *þ / v* (perhaps pronounced |v|) as the 'thematic' stave sounds (see Schmidt 1987²:92). However, if the form of the pronoun in Bx was *hij* (as in YCLMR) the fricative stave-word would have to be *That* (1) or (2) in the a-half, producing an awkward stress-pattern. In the light of **C**, which is evidently a revision adding a third palatal lift, it might be conjectured that in **B** an archetypal *hij* was put for **ȝe* through failure to see an original *wynneþ* as 2nd pers. pl. (cf. the 3rd pers. pl. form *haueþ* adopted at 335 to account for the variants *haþ, haue, hadde*). But as so much uncertainty remains, **C** being 3rd pers. sg. (except *taketh*, which is parenthetical), this emendation is not adopted here. **489 (B 339)** *probate:* capable of being scanned with a cognative second stave in *próbáte* and a three or four-syllable metrical 'onset' (contrast 493//), unless the line is metrically anomalous because macaronic (see Schmidt 1987:101). **490 (B 340)** *lyne:* if Cx read *leef*, this could have represented a misapprehension of its exemplar's *lyue* (unconsciously induced by associations with *ende*), itself an easy visual error for original *lyne*. *Sk* (Apparatus) recognises the latter as the correct reading for **C** but prints *leef*, and the formal emendation is made by *Pe*. **491 (B 342)** The **B** line may scan vocalically with muted key-stave and contrapuntal *l*-staves or else (preferably) as Type IIIa on *l*, the theme-stave of revised **C**. **492 (B 342)** *felle:* for Bx *fele* 'many', which Cx might also have read, *felle* being a felicitous scribal correction in three **C** and two **B** mss. Since there is no // **A** here, *B-GCr*'s reading (if not a scribal guess) must be from either a thus-corrected **C** or (least probably) a lost **B** source. But since *felle* is the harder, more apt and so more probably original reading, YP²U could well represent **x** (< Cx). The precise sense here may be the relatively unusual 'subtle, wise' (MED s.v. *fel* adj. 2(a)) rather than 'fierce, harsh' (ibid., 3 and 5), the preferred (and commoner) sense at B 5.168. However, since 'more words' are indeed to follow and those quoted *are* shrewd ones, a homophonic pun may well be intended. **493 (B 343)** The a-half would seem to lack an alliterating first lift unless *Quod bonum est* forms a four-syllable onset before two-stressed *ténéte*, which is very awkward since the first vowel is short. More probably, the a-half is permitted to be anomalous because macaronic (see Schmidt 1987[2]:101). In both halves, though, a 'compensatory' extra stave appears (if the mid-line pause in **C** comes after *tixst*, a standard line results).

B 344–46 344 appears as the first of three corrupt lines and may point to scribal failure of attention on approaching the end of the passus (cf. *Notes* on B 2.198–203, towards the end of Passus II). The Bx form yields the scansion *ax / xa*, and *K–D* plausibly emend *ferde* to *mysferde* to provide a standard line (so *Sch*). Less drastically, inversion of verb and noun through promotion of the more important idea may be diagnosed in the a-half here and the line emended to scan as Type IIIa. **345** The Bx form could be Type IIIb with a four- or five-syllable onset and a two-stressed *Sápiénce*. But the normal pronunciation of the latter word, as is clear from 333 above, is *Sápiènce*, and the emendation here suggested presumes only Bx inversion to prose order in the a-half, producing a smoother line, still of Type IIIb. **346** is unmetrical as it stands in Bx (*aa / xx*). *K–D* propose *trewe*, but it is hard to see *good* as a ⇒ for this. The word here conjectured, *tidy* (OED s.v. 3(a) 'good, useful', and see MED s.v. 3b) occurs at 3.474 = B 3.322; 20.332, 21.442; B 9.105). In these cases *tidy* is used only with *man*, but this may tell for not against it here, since the novel usage might have been what prompted the Bx scribe to replace it. In the comparative form at 12.189, the context suggests the sense 'useful, profitable' that is exactly right at B 3.346. **494 (B 348)** C revises to the rare Type IIb what appears to be a Type IIIb line on |v| with liaisonal first stave *if ye* or a Type Ia line with a slightly awkward key-stave on a modal verb *shul* enclosed by asymmetrical contrapuntal staves (on such 'line-type ambiguity' see Schmidt 1987:37–8). **499** *recceth* **x**: in context the harder reading, avoiding a pointless repetition; for though *reccetep* **p** 'harbours' (MED s.v. *reccetten* v.) is apt enough, it could have been suggested by the noun in the b-half.

Z 147–76 The unique 30-line passage that concludes Passus III in **Z** shows no specific verbal ⊗ from **BC** and only 162b has left a trace in **A** (at A 3.236). But there are echoes of its thought in one or other later version. Thus 153a is like 8.185a; 166 recalls 21.456 and 151 is reminiscent of Conscience's actions in 22.228ff. A simple account of these **Z** 'echoes' as a *scribal* response to **C** (especially its final section) is challenged by the evident authenticity of the writing in **Z**. A second possibility, that the passage is post-**BC** but still *original*, leaves unexplained the no less evident primitiveness of its conception of Conscience and of Mede's relation to him. A third interpretation would see the passage as an early form of the ending of Passus III, cut from **A** because its lengthy attack on friars seemed irrelevant at this point, but later drawn on in the **B** conclusion when describing Conscience's fatal ambivalence towards the friars as confessors. The resonances of **B** and **C** would therefore be 'pre-echoes' or anticipations of material and ideas later to be worked up and pointing to the existence of a Langlandian *repertorium* of lines and phrases. **Z 163** *a lost*: *R–B* find the sense of ms *aloft* unclear and possibly concealing a corruption. But if *f* is a visual error for long *s*, the crux could be resolved as *a lost*, with wordplay on *lust* 'pleasure' and *lost* 'loss', the ME form of the latter paralleled at 5.97 below, and presumably an original spelling. **175–6** As punctuated, the sense is that 'without Conscience's knowledge, Meed does nothing of which he is not the prime originator'; but with a semi-colon after *sothe* it would be that 'she does nothing without his knowledge, but he is not the *prime* originator [of all human acts]'. Awkward as the shift is, it is possible to read 175 as spoken to the King (about Conscience) and 176 as directly addressed to Conscience (about himself). 175 would undoubtedly read more easily if *not* were a spelling of *noght*: 'Without his being privy to it, I perform no action of which Conscience is not the source'. For an acute discussion of the problem in these lines see Brewer 1984:216n7.

Passus IV

1 (ZAB 1) *Cesseth*: **Z** *seseth*[2] could be a scribal insertion, but is not paralleled in extant **ABC** mss and might be a first-version original. **C-x** *sethe*, perhaps a verb derived from the noun meaning 'satisfaction' or 'reparation', is not to be seen as a substantive revision of **B** but a visual error induced by following *sauhtene*. **4 (ZAB 4)** *rathir*: if **Z**'s *arre* shows ⊗ it may be from a **C** source of y-type. The adverbial *arre* is not elsewhere instanced but could be the form underlying *A-r erst*. If the **B** variant *for euere* were a reflex of **er* (for *arre*), then *are* might be preferable for **C**; but no difference in sense is involved and either could be original in **BC**. Substituted *are* presumably results from stylistic objection to repeated *rather* in two successive lines. **5 (ZAB 5)** *-tyl* **ZC**: a uniquely instanced non-substantive variant of *-to*, the advancing form used in every other occurrence (see *IG*). **6 (ZAB 6)** *pe* **AB**: omission of *pe* in **ZCx** (added in **C**-YP[2]D) is supported by six **A** mss randomly and one **B** ms (Y). Present in AxBx, it may be original in those (or all) versions. **10 (ZAB 10)** The line was probably in **B**, though no reason, mechanical or otherwise, for its loss from Bx appears. It was presumably restored in the ancestors of Y<OC[2]> from **A** or **C** and in Cr[23] from **C**. **15 (ZAB 15)** *hym; sayde*[2]: apparently absent from Bx and adopted on the joint showing of **ZAC** from F, which here may be corrected from a **C** source. Bx, which has a satisfactory Type IIIa line as it stands, presumably substituted *bad* through stylistic objection to repetition of the verb (cf. on *are* at 4). **16 (ZAB 16)** *the a:* adopted on the showing of *AB* as the probable Cx reading, preserved coincidentally in *C-F* (D actually reads *þere* not *þe*), of which **p** and **x** attest split variants. **17–9 (B 17–9, Z 17–8, A 17)** Ax could have contained *BC*18–19, from which *A*-**m**W might have preserved them, W by reference to a source of **m**-type. One possibility is that **m** could here show ⊗ from **B**, as could **Z**. Alternatively, the **Z** form could attest a first draft, from which Z 17–18 were then dropped in the revision to **A** (but with retention of *And cald*) to create the present 'Cato' line A 17, only to be subsequently restored after the latter in the revision to **B**. Given the uncertainty, 18–19 are omitted as not indispensable for the sense in **A**. **21–2 (Z 20–2, A 19–21, B 21–3)** Revision is apparent in each stage from **A** to **C**. *Wyl* **Z** may be original, a spelling variant of *wel* (as at Z 89 below) or a ⊗ from C 22, which introduces an allegorised 'will'. Burrow (1990:142) supports it as the original **AB** reading corrupted to *wel* in both archetypes, a possibility all the easier if *hym* had been present as a reinforcing appositional pronoun with original *wil*. But as the half-line is confirmed by **C**, the principle of ratification cautions strongly against emendation of **AB**. *Auyseth-þe-byfore:* continuous revision is again apparent. The Ax reading is uncertain and could have been *riȝt wytful,* of which *wytful* and *riȝtful* would then be 'split and fused' variants; but more probably the latter is a contextually induced aural error for the former. **23** *with peynted wittes:* found puzzling by Burrow (1990:141–2) but allowed as acceptable by *Pe* if *with* means 'against', *peynted* then being understood figuratively as 'specious' (like *coloured* at 21.349). But though ingenious, this seems unnecessary, as the notion is plainly one of 'will' being restrained by 'wit', here plural because a more specific sense like 'reason', 'judgement' (OED s.v. sb. 13, MED 6(a)) is intended. The allegorical detail is either secondary or else *peynted* here = 'florid [eloquent]', but in an innocent sense like that at 16.321 (MED s.v. *peinten* 5 (a) rather than 6 (a) 'specious'). *Pe*'s emendation of *wittes* to *withes* 'withies' is thus otiose.

  B 23 (Z 22, A 21) *he / we:* apparent revision in **B** makes it difficult to argue for the randomly-attested variant *he*] *we* as the original reading in **A**. The line scans more smoothly in both **A** and **B** with |w| as the sound of the key-stave (an internal stave in *twies* in **B**), though the sense is unaffected. The occurrence of the random variants *come* for *be* in *B*-CrGC²H) and *be* for *come* in *A*-N leave it uncertain if *be* **Z** is also original or a scribal variant, whether random or an echo of a **B** source. **25 (Z 24, A 23, B 25)** *ryt:* the majority form *ryȝt* could be that of Cx as the adverb used with an understood verb of motion. But more probably it is the contracted 3rd pers.

sg. (< *rydeth*) spelled with *ȝ* to indicate vowel length, but to be rejected on grounds of ambiguity (that the verb is intended seems confirmed from // **ZAB**). *swyþe* **A**: the six scribal variants reveal difficulty with the lexical use of the word ('quickly') though this was not uncommon (MED s.v. *swithe* adv. 3(a)). **28 (Z 26, A 25, B 28)** *for they* **ZAB**: no mechanical reason appears for loss in *B*-LR. If these two mss (as pure descendants of β and α respectively) preserve the defective reading of Bx, then γ (the source of *B*-wg) and F may merely be offering a commonsense emendation of a perceived gap in the sense, or correcting from an **A** ms (rather than another **B** copy of a tradition superior to Bx). **30** *þe comune* **x**: the **p** variant (conceivably a smoothed reflex of Cx **þe comen* misread as *þei connen*) is excluded on grounds of sense since, even if Conscience might complain to the king, there is no one for the king to complain to. **32 (Z 30, A 29, B 32)** *Ac:* on the showing of **ZAC** Bx *And* looks a scribal error for *Ac,* probably induced by initial *And* 33 (cf. C 41 below). *myle* **A**: preferable on grounds of rhythm and supported by **Z**. **35 (B 35)** The word-order of **p** is discriminated on comparison with **B** as that of Cx. **36 (B 36)** Bx scans as an extended Type IIIb with counterpoint (*abb // aa*). A better balance with 35 would arguably be obtained if, in the light of **C**, the line were taken as Type Ia with *l* as stave sound and a liaisonal key-stave provided by conjecturing *hij* for *þei* and inversion of verb and pronoun in the b-half (*wol_hij*). But the emendation is not strictly necessary and so is not adopted here. **38 (B 38)** Bx scans as Type IIIa and the unmetrical line following is rejected as scribal padding; but *K–D*'s extensive reconstruction is unnecessary. Though *chiknes* is not obviously unoriginal, the presence of *capones* in the spurious line suggests that its position in **B** was as in // **C**. **39 (B 39)** *his:* preferred as less probably scribal than the over-explicit *goddes* **x**. **41 (B 43)** *Ac:* the conjectured reading of Cx as indicated by the sense and form of the competing variants. **42 (Z 32, A 31, B 44)** *kyng thenne:* lost in **Z** through haplography (*R–B*) after 31b. *aȝen* **A**: adopted as the probable Ax reading preserved in **m** and **Z**, unless both (improbably) show ⊗ from **B**; *(in)to* **r** looks like a scribal attempt to remove a perceived ambiguity in the preposition that commonly signifies opposition (see 16.214, 20.262 and MED s.v. prep. 4(a)). **44 (Z 34, A 33, B 46)** In A, the word-order of **m** is adopted in the light of **ZB** but *wel* is retained as the adverb despite *ful* **Z**. Neither sense nor metre is affected and *wel / ful* seem to have been in free variation. *speke / wor4eden:* possibly present-tense in **Z**, but this seems unlikely given the sequence of preterites from 30 onwards and the ease of loss of the internal preterite morpheme *-ed* after *-d* and before *-en* (cf. Z 3.144, and note under 3.262). The error occurs also in *B*-C² and *A*-N (and cf. Z 54, where the syntax necessitates a preterite subjunctive). **46** *forleyen:* internal *-e* is

added to expand the participial morpheme as a full sylla-
ble (*ley-en*) for the needed feminine ending. **52** The prefix
a- is judged archetypal on the agreement of most **p** mss and
x, and *He* **p** is preferred to *And* **x** (contrast the **x**-reading at
56). It is possible that the original read *A wayteth (so
R–K; cf. 58 below). **56 (Z 41, A 40, B 53)** On the basis of
superior metre and **ZBC** agreement, **m**'s reading with
final *neuere* is discriminated as that of Ax. Although **A**
could have been unchanged from **Z**, Ax being preserved
in **r** with inversion of the adverbs to commoner prose
order, it is more economical to adopt an *A*-family reading
that needs no emendation on metrical grounds. **58 (Z 43,
A 42, B 55)** *hewen*: certain for **A** in the light of **ZBC**
agreement, *hynen* r^l and *hynes* *C*-DAVRMQFS probably
reflecting *n / u* confusion in copying a form spelled **hy(u)
en.* See also on A 94, 104 below. **61 (Z 46, A 45, B 58)**
otes: judged original on the showing of **ZAB**. Possibly **p**
misread the last word of the line as *other* and conjectur-
ally completed the sense while MF corrected from an **x**
copy or **B**. **62 (Z 47, A 46, B 59)** The **A** mss E and M have
corrupt attempts to fill a probable lacuna or make good a
damaged exemplar, and the **m**-group reading is likely to
have contained the contracted form *bat* (so **Z**, with
retracted vowel as in *rat* C 3.406), of which *bad* seems to
be a confused recollection. Of the two lines in *A*-E the
first may echo **C** (if *treth* = *threteth // manascheth* **C**), the
second (an alternative attempt to supply the line) either **B**
or another **A** source, while M corrupts further by adding
wyf. **64–6 (Z 50–2, A 48–9, B 61–3)** The unique line 50
in **Z** seems original, though of draft character (it could
have been dropped because judged redundant), as does Z
51a, forming part of a standard Type Ia line. The identical
rhyme with *tolde* 50 is exactly paralleled at A 5.9/10 and
recalled in the non-identical end-rhyme of C 65/6 // **B. 68
(Z 63, A 61, B 75)** is continuously revised, only **Z** and **C**
being metrically satisfactory as they stand. Both scan as
Type Ia on vowels and **Z** shows affinity in meaning but
no direct sign of ⊗ from **C** in its a-half. The **B** line gives
good sense, but the metre assumes somewhat awkward
scansion with lifts on *his*[1,2] against the natural expectation
of emphasis on the semantically salient nouns. *B*-F's nor-
malisation of the metre by inverting object and adverb to
prose order in the b-half is unlikely to represent α and
thence Bx, given the agreement of R with β**ZAC**. Most
probably the line's unusual pattern is due to its both echo-
ing and deliberately varying that of 64a. In the a-half
most **A** mss (the t-group excepted) attest *his / of his* with
no following verb, suggesting a lacuna here in Ax. The
conjectured verb *offride*, if miscopied from an exemplar
*offryt in the present-tense form *offres*, could have been
lost through occasioning eye-skip from *of his* to *handy*.
The source of t may have been recalling the b-half of B
64 in its attempt to repair the exemplar text; but it is
unlikely to preserve an Ax reading lost from **m** and from

most members of **r**. Although **Z** makes sense, it is argu-
able on comparison with the b-half in **ABC** that *payed*
should be seen in **Z** also not as a preterite but as a past
participle, Wrong specifying the conditions under which
he will pay, not those under which he is paying now; the
conjunction is accordingly treated as a probable scribal
intrusion. The identity of **Z**'s reading in preceding 62
with that of W at A 60 will be fortuitous rather than evi-
dence of some link between these mss, for the form of the
following line shows W's source attempting (like that of
the unrelated E) to produce sense from a presumably
damaged exemplar reading. W's adverb *fast* could thus
be explained as an attempt to complete a line which, hav-
ing lost *hym to helpe*, would have seemed defective in
both sense and metre. Not impossibly, however, *hym to
helpe* belongs in the a-half of A 61, the position occupied
by the closely parallel *And for to haue here helpe* **C. 70
(Z 54, A 52, B 66)** *pleyneden* **Z**: the preterite morpheme
added on the evidence of **ABC** and the tense-sequence of
53 (for similar omission cf. on Z 34 above). **73 (Z 65, A
63, B 77)** *nomen* **A**: the harder word adopted as the likely
A original on the showing of **Z**; *tok* will have come into
r^l and randomly into *A*-JWE as the more modern term
(and perhaps as that familiar from parallel **BC**). The Ax
form of this line also, however, shows a case of moderni-
sation: though scanning satisfactorily as Type IIIc (*ab /
ab*), it appears (like *B*-HmGC^{2}CB and*C*-xAS) to have
substituted *wiþ* for *myd*, which is accordingly adopted
though not strictly required for the metre. **80–1 (Z 73–4,
A 71–2, B 84–5)** The first line was lost in r^l, probably half
of the second in r^l and all of it in t, while both were added
to H^2 (or its immediate ancestor) from an **A** ms of r^2 type.
82 (Z 75, A 73, B 86) The Bx line will scan as Type IIIa
with an awkward five-syllable anacrusis, but *lete hym
no3t* looks doubtful in the light of **ZAC** *schal / sholde nat.*
Bx's possible reason for a paraphrastic ⇒ could have
been scribal unease at the sudden shift to direct speech.
Alternatively, **B** might have been a substantive revision
and Bx unconscious ⇒ of a (non-alliterating) synonym
for the lexical verb with *s* here conjectured. The **C** line
would then have to be seen as a wholesale revision, per-
haps prompted by defective metre in **L**'s ms (B^1), but in
any case reverting to a combination of modal verb with
Bx's and possibly **ZA**'s (?) indirect speech (the latter has
been treated as direct speech in the edited text but need
not be). **84 (Z 77, A 75, B 88)** *do*: here taken as a revision
of **B**, though not impossibly it has come in by eyeskip to
mysdo at 86 below. *R–K* adopt *make* after *C*-F alone,
though neither metre nor sense requires it and it is better
seen not as a correction from yet another superior **C**
source but as easily induced by the common collocation
maken amendes. **86 (Z 79, A 77, B 90)** The form of the
a-half in *A*-tL may preserve an archetypal and original
reading lost in the rest of the tradition and is unlikely to

have been a scribal alteration, as it is clearly the harder. An Ax spelling of the pronoun subject as in **Z** (*a*) could have been misread as a cardinal numeral, giving the sense 'that one wrongful action', and so omitted for reasons of censorship as seeming to encourage an attitude of laxity. That *mysdede* was a verb in **A** seems indicated by the form of both **Z** and of revised **BC**. *And* **B**: preferred to *And so* on the showing of **C** and presumably accidental in *B*-H, since it cannot be by ⊗ from **A** or **C**; *so* will then be a Bx scribal intrusion, perhaps visually suggested by *-sdo*. **87 (Z 80, A 78, B 91)** All versions before **C** have the inauthentic metrical pattern *aa / bb*, though there is no objection on grounds of sense. The proposal of *K–DKa²* that **C** *witnessede* was also the original of **AB** presumes a threefold occurrence of 'substitution of the common collocation by alliterative inducement' (*Ka²*, p. 461). This could also have occurred if the word for which *seide* was substituted was in fact an exact synonym *quod* (used only before or after direct speech, and not as main verb with noun-phrase object as here). The more drastic emendation here proposed traces the error to both a mechanical cause (loss of initial *wiþ* through haplography following eyeskip after final *-wiþ* in *þerewiþ*) and also to the hardness of the stave-word, which is instanced only once in any of the four versions (see A 4.142). If the original read *wiþseide þe same*, the sense would be 'made the same point in opposition' (i.e. to the king, while agreeing with Wisdom), with *þe same* as direct object, as at 3.30, or 'objected likewise', with *þe same* used adverbially, as at 3.27, which is perhaps the more likely with this verb. The reconstructed line has the 'T'-type structure abundantly instanced in all versions. The problem of thrice-repeated loss associated with *K–D*'s conjecture also remains here, but is offset by the greater difficulty of the supplanted word (for the converse case of a conjectured loss of the second element, the lexical morpheme, in a *wiþ-* compound, see on 12.190 below). **90 (Z 83, A 81, B 94)** *Thanne*: the probable reading for **B** on the showing of **ZAC**, *And* Bx appearing a scribal intrusion perhaps induced by *And* 95; *B*-Cr will have corrected from **C**, *B*-H from **A**. *she*: a word easily lost from Ax*C*-**p** if its form was *he* (as in *B*-R?C*x), through quasi-haplography before following *be-*. But as it is not necessary to the sense, it is not adopted in **A**. **91 (Z 84, A 82, B 95)** *puyre*: the (possible) *A*-**r** reading *purid* (so *C* -M) is acceptable in itself but on comparison with **ZBC** may look like scribal over-emphasis. **92 (Z 85, A 83, B 96)** The **Z** line scans either as Type IIIa on |ð| with stress on the possessive (paralleled in C 7.103), or vocalically as Type Ia with a mute stave in *amendy*. Loss of this stave-word in *A*-vJEM could have occurred more easily (through quasi-haplography) if Ax had read *of me man* as in *r¹* and the same omission could have affected **Z** in the copying of the ms. But in the light of the later revisions, the form with *man* in the a-half that

looks likeliest to be original in **A**, and the word-order of *A*-Aw is adopted as giving the smoother rhythm achieved in **BC**. **94 (Z 87, A 85, B 98)** The word-order of the a-halves in *A*-**r**, **m** records divergent reflexes of an **A** original presumed preserved in **ZBC**; either AxBx scribes added *to* or the ZCx scribes omitted it. **95 (Z 88, A 86, B 99)** *man that*: lost from **Z** through eyeskip (*that > that*) or haplography (*R–B*). *ofte*: Bx *so* is omitted (following *B*-GM) as perhaps visually induced by *so* in 97b. The metrical pattern of Bx, with a trisyllabic pre-final dip, is indeed that of the conjecturally restored A 5.130, but without the semantic justification of *so* in that instance. **97 (Z 92, A 90, B 103)** *Mede*: the Z-ms error is a mechanical slip induced by the proximity of *-de, my, me*. **99 (Z 93, A 91, B 104)** *God*: no emendation to *Crist* in **ZA** on grounds of metre is required, since the line scans 'cognatively' on |k| |k| |g|. The revision in **BC**, eliminating the 'cognative' stave, is extensive and progressive. **100 (Z 94, A 92, B 105)** *wendeþ*: the revision to *goth* in **C** alters the line-type from Id to Ia so as to throw the stress onto the adverb (see next note). If *goth* is a Cx error, no grounds for its occurrence appear, since *wendeþ* is hardly difficult. *ar* **ZAC**: on comparison Bx *erst wol I* suggests less an authorial revision finally rejected than a scribal heightening of dramatic tone or smoothing after miscopying conjunctive *er* as the adverbial *erst*. *B*-GH here are not witnessing to a better **B** tradition but ⊗ from an **A** source. **101 (Z 95, A 93, B 106)** *Lope*: preferred for **B** on the witness of **ZAC**, Bx *For* appearing a scribal attempt to ease a transition. *awey*: added in *C*-PEN (so *R–K*) as in *B*-F (presumably from **A**), but its omission in **BC** avoids ineffective repetition of *away* 100. **104 (Z 98, A 96, B 109)** *Y lyue* **CZA**: although *he lyueþ* Bx is not obviously wrong and revision in the line's b-half might sanction revision in the a-half as well, the phrase looks suspect in the light of agreed **ZAC**. The 3rd-person form may have come in through inducement from adjacent *hym, he, hym* (the same error appears in *A*-W, which has borrowed the whole line from a ms of the later version). **105 (Z 99, A 97, B 110)** *men*: either a scribal addition in *A*-*r¹*Bx*C*-**x** or else added in **A**, retained in **B** but lost in *A*-*r²***m**C-**p** through assimilation to the preceding plural morpheme *-(m)e* in *summe* (as judged here). **110 (Z 108, A 106, B 115)** In the absence of *A*-A, the Ax reading may be only probably and not certainly divined as that of **m**. But it is confirmed by **ZBC** and by *A*-W, though the latter may show ⊗ from **B** as at 96 (see on 104 above). The reading of **r**, requiring an awkward caesura and reducing two separate statements (generic + specific) to one, results from the recognised scribal tendency towards the simplest word-order and from anticipation of the post-nominal infinitive. The error might have occurred more easily if **A** had read as **Z**, omitting *al*. In **A** *it* (**ZBC**) is not added after *here* since not strictly needed for the sense. **113 (Z**

106, A 104, B 118) Though **C** completely revises the b-half, the **ZAB** readings are identical but for added *be* in **AB**. The figurative term for 'a thing of low value' is rendered as *hepyng* by *A*-Ch, a reading here judged a ⇒ for Ax *hyne* (cf. Ch's idiosyncratic *raike* at 153, *schregges* at Pr 2). *A*-M *heuene* is evidently an error for an exemplar-reading spelled conjecturally *hyuen (cf. 58n above), though in part perhaps unconsciously induced by preceding *holynesse*. **124 (Z 112, A 110, B 127)** *he*: lost from **Z** for no evident mechanical reason but needed for the sense; such omissions are characteristic of the manuscript, but may reflect the exemplar's draft-status. **125 (Z 113, A 111, B 128)** *ruyflares* **x**: not a sub-archetypal ⇒ for a Cx reading preserved in **p** (so **ZAB**) but a striking revision inserting a word found little elsewhere outside **L** (see 6.315, and for the verb 4.54, B 5.230, 234; MED s. vv. *riflen* v., *riflere* n., and Wilcockson 1983). **127 (Z 115, A 113, B 130)** For *croune* **A** *Ka* finds *r¹ coyn* 'stamp, impress' (MED s.v. *coin* n. 2a. (a)) 'harder and less obvious'; but agreement of *r²***m** and **Z** points to the former as the probable Ax reading. The likelihood that *koyne* at C 1.46 above bears the sense cited by *Ka* supports *coyn* here; but given the **BC** revision in the b-half, grounds for rejecting *croune* are not decisive. **129 (Z 117, A 115, B 132)** *it*: *yf* **Z** is corrected to *yf yt* as in **B** by *R–B* (diagnosing loss of *yt* by partial haplography) but here to the simpler *yt* as in **AC**.

Z 119–32 contain three groups of unique lines, all unexceptionable for sense and characteristic in metre. 120 is the very rare Type IIa; 121 may be either Type IIIa scanning translinearly from 120 on *m*, or Type Ia scanning on *n*.. Z 122–23 correspond to A 141–42, and 126–30 to A 145–49; they are re-written at the opening of Z V below, 126 here having the same defective metre (*ab / ba*) as its counterpart line at Z 5.5. This duplication strongly suggests the draft character of these lines, in which neither alliterative alternative to 'say', *rehersen* and *recorden* (A 145, B 172), was yet determined, although the former was soon to be used at Z 149 below (see Intro. III *Z* § 3). In 130 and 132, where the errors have mechanical causes, emendation is desirable since 'for grammatical reasons, either *y* or *schalt* (pres. 2 sg.) must be emended... Reason is saying that the king cannot rule justly while Meed is at court' (*R–B*, p. 75, n.).

133 (Z 134, A 119, B 136) *seyen* C: a revision, with unexceptionable sense, so *R–K*'s ⇒ of *shewen* has no basis. Alteration of *schewen* at Z 3.108 to *seiȝen* in A 3.160 indicates near-synonymy of the lexemes in some contexts. *othere*: correction of Bx *ouþerwhile* to *ouþer* on grounds of both sense and metre seems justified in the light of **ZAC** agreement. *B*-R may preserve the α (< Bx) reading with correct *ouþer* and scribally added *ouþerwhile*, which have been levelled convergently in β and F to a less awkward form. **139** *do*: elliptical, as part of

a revision, 'nor [shall I] grant mercy for payment'; but y's Ø-reading (retained by *R–K*) could be original and is closer to **B** (so I*Pe*). **140 (Z 141, A 126, B 143)** *þe*: **ZAB** is stylistically preferable, and perhaps lost mechanically from Cx by eye-skip from '*ma*lum' to '*ma*n'. In **Z**, loss of *u* (or *n*) in *nullum* will be by haplography. **142 (Z 143, A 128, B 145)** *in Englische*: in the light of agreed **AC**, loss of the preposition (*on / in*) from **Z** through quasi-haplography may be diagnosed (*on, En-*). B-H *englys* corrects, perhaps memorially from **A**, what appears an intelligent Bx attempt to restore from a badly-spelled *onglys what it took as an original insisting on the uncomfortable literal sense of a crucial Scriptural text. **152–53** It would be better to delete the stop after *thonkede* and place a semicolon after *speche* (*R–K*).

B 158–9 158 The Bx line scans either *aa / xa* or, if *And Wit* form the anacrusis, *ab / ab* (Type IIIc on |k|), an authentic pattern. If *Wit* forms the first lift, the simplest emendation would be transposition of *comendede* and *hise wordes* (considered and rejected by *K–D*). But their emendation *Kynde* for *And* is convincing in the light of revised **C**, for in this context the character Wit is indeed 'corrupt and venal' (*K–D*, p. 181) as at near-identical B 91, which might have unconsciously influenced the Bx scribe. **159** The Bx line scans as Type IIIa, and since there is no objection on grounds of sense and there may be a deliberate avoidance of repetition of 152, *K–D*'s emendation of *halle* to *moot-halle* is rejected.

155 (Z 151, A 136, B 160) *Mekenesse*: agreement of **ZBC** in the a-half supports *A*-**m** as representing the original and rejection of *A*-**r** as a scribal ⇒ giving inferior sense and metre. Repetition of *Resoun* is awkward, leading to the word's incorporation in a six-syllable onset and placing the caesura after *Mede*. What is at issue is whether repentance for wrongdoing or pecuniary means should procure the king's mercy: to obey *mekenes* is thus to follow Reason (cf. A 125 above). The agreement of E's reading suggests ⊗ from **r** (here preserving Ax) or ⊗ of **m** (represented by AM) from **B** (which seems improbable).

Z 152, 157–9, V 3 (A 143) 152 seems authentic but perhaps otiose. **157–9** look original but strongly suggest draft character; contradicting the opening of Passus V, they were presumably cancelled in **A**'s revision. **V 3** The b-half in **Z** has been revised in **A** to a form that echoes the comparison (to a dumb beast not a stone) at Z 4.124, which occurs in the earlier portion of **Z** corresponding to A 141–8

B 172 (Z V 5, A 145) The line scans as Type Ia in both **A** and **B** but lacks a first |r| stave in **Z** here and at 4.126, unmetrical *seyde* (a variant in *A*-w) being either scribal in both instances or a sign of **Z**'s draft character. **A**'s stave-word *reherside* has already appeared as part of the poet's repertoire at Z 4.149 above, but its use at A 145 could be a revision, so the case for emendation is not strong. **178 (Z V 7, A 147, B 184)** *And alle*: also the reading of Ax. Of the two words one is omitted in each of the phrase's appearances in **Z**, *alle* here (so also *A*-M), *And* at 4.128 (so also *A*-UVA, Bx). Emendation of Bx is on the basis of AC agreement. **184 (Z V 13, A 153, B 190)** *ryden*: clearly attested from **Z** to **C**. While unconscious replacement of *ryde* by a colourless non-alliterating synonym *wende* in *A*-d is by no means improbable, ⇒ of *raike* may be identified not (as by *Ka*) as the harder original behind d but rather as an idiosyncratic choice of the Ch-scribe (see on 113), notwithstanding that this word featured in the poet's lexicon (e.g. in the draft line Z 4.158, cancelled in **A**). *hennes* **ZAC**: to be preferred as the probable reading of **B**, *fro me* Bx illustrating scribal over-emphasis here. *B-H* presumably shows ⊗ from **A**. **187 (Z V 11, A 151, B 188)** The line scans as Type IIIa in Ax and **Z**. *Ka²*, rejecting this metrical pattern as inauthentic, emends *quaþ* to *seiþ*, the reading of *A*-N. But *seiþ* could be a **B** revision, re-inforcing the key-stave with a second mute *s*-stave. **L**'s Type IIIa lines avoid a mute key-stave, and it seems that names with 'Saint' could bear stress on the title (cf. 12.100, 14.136).

A 155 (B 192, Z V 15) *aredy*: reconstructed in the light of **ZB** as the probable Ax form of which *?als* **m**, Ø **r** are reflexes.

B 194 (Z V 17, A 157) The line scans 'cognatively' on *gkg* and *ff* as a T-type (*aa / [a]bb*). Emendation by *K–DKa²* of *graunte* to *graunte gladly* after *A*-V is agratuitous adoption of a plainly scribal attempt at metrical 'correction'.

Z V 18 (A 158, B 195) *libbe* **Z**: taken by *R–B* as an infinitive after *graunte*; but this seems somewhat strained and (without *to*) uncharacteristic both as an idiom and as an example of **L**'s practice. In the light of **AB**, *We* is accordingly conjectured as omitted through partial haplography after '*libbe*', such omission being typical of the Z-manuscript's scribe.

Passus V (ZAB V)

10 *inwitt* **x**: *vnite* **p** is an easy visual error for *inwitte(e)*, which is required on grounds of sense ('sound of body and mind'). The collocation of *inwit and his hele* at 10.182 confirms the reading here, though the sense 'mind' (see MED s.v. *inwit* n.) puzzled copyists in the **p** tradition (and that of P², who presumably found *inwit* and *vnite* in his **x**- and **p**-type exemplars respectively but rejected both). GK *duite* is striking evidence of an immediate common ancestor with readings distinct from those of N, the other representative of *p²*. *R–K* (p. 159) ingeniously suggest *unnit* 'vain idleness' (MED s.v. *unnit* n., not instanced after mid-13th century), for which the two main family variants would be scribal attempts at making sense of the word's minims. But their unawareness of 10.182 makes their conjecture, questionable on grounds of obsolescence,

superfluous. **19** scans with a mute key-stave *or*, though the line would be metrically stronger with *hogges* for *swyn* (M's *hogges* erroneously for *gees* seems unlikely to be a reflex of a Cx stave-word). The third *or* would also give better rhythm if expanded as *oþer*. **21** In this major crux the probable Cx reading is divined in the sub-archetypal variant judged harder and so less likely to be derived from the other. That *Hem þat bedreden be bylyue to fynde* looked simpler seems clear from its adoption by a later hand into P², which presumably had in its main exemplar a corrupted version of the form here proposed for **x**. In reconstructing, meaningless *the by* is here seen as an **x** error for Cx **therby*, with *r* damaged or omitted; **x** could have lost *be* through eyeskip from '*be*tered' to 'ther*by*' or (if the wording was *I be betered* as in ms I) through haplography (*be-, bet-*). I's reading is substantively nearest the conjectured Cx form but has varied to prose order, producing inferior rhythm. X's *marginal* correction (adopted by *Pe*) yields much the same sense as I: 'does the *comune* benefit from your way of life, since it provides you with the means of life?' But X's *inserted* correction, with an active construction = *they ybetered be*, is unlikely to be original, though witnessing to the perceived difficulty of **x**'s compressed syntax. The latter would have been clearer if preceded by *That*; but the sense can be ascertained without it: '(So that) those who provide you with your living have some advantage from what you do'. Alternatively, *to* is to be understood before *be*, giving a construction like those at 6.48 (*They to wene þat Y were*) and 21.233 (*They leely to lyue*). But **p**'s reading, adopted by *R–K* with insufficient discussion, could never have been found hard enough to give rise to that of **x**. **35** *ʒong²*: could have been dittographically added in y (or perhaps to normalise) or (like *syre* at 3.366 above) haplographically omitted in **pu**, with further smoothing in **p** to fill out the line. If instead u is taken as here preserving *x¹* and thence Cx (**p** having inserted *quath ich*), the line scans as a terse Type IIIa of a kind common in **A** and **B** (and still found, though less frequently, in **C**). On the other hand, *ʒong²* is more likely to have been (deliberately) omitted from P², the latter's main exemplar being a y-type ms. This may suggest that u (like **p**) omitted the word through missing its intensive force ('very young indeed'), a sense tacitly recognised by the surviving witnesses of y, none of which omits or deletes the second *ʒong*. *R–K*'s conjecture *ʒut ʒong* is in any case otiose, since either **x** or **p** will provide a metrically acceptable reading. **40** *y*: added in X in another hand but absent from YIU. **44** *opelond* **x** / *in londone* **p**: the **p** form of this line, long familiar from *Sk* (and adopted as *vp london* by *R–K*, p.154) offers attractive wordplay, and a punning allusion to the second half of the author's surname may be intended in the repetition of *lond* (cf. B 15.152 and the comparable allusion to the *first* half in 24a above). But the main point seems to be that he lives, in the manner described in 42–3, 'both in the capital and out in the country', a meaning supported by the internal 'facts' of the Dreamer's life and by the ease with which the corruption could have occurred if **p** had read *vpon londen* as in GKN (= p^2). **53** scans somewhat stiffly, as Type IIIa on *m*. R–K's *semeth* for *thynketh* will by their metrical criteria place the caesura before *syre*, giving a (very short) b-half with an unidiomatic stress pattern *Syŕe Résoun*. But the line thus emended would also scan satisfactorily as Type IIIa (*ax / ax*). **61** R–K re-order, placing hereafter 67–9, 62, 63–6, with full stop after the last. This gives acceptable, perhaps superior (certainly different) sense to that of Cx. But the repetition 'God' after 'Crist' (*R–K* 62) does not sound right, nor does recommending lords' *kin* (rather than lords) as the object of serfs' service. It seems safer to retain the text, taking *lordes kyn* in the wider sense of 'gentlemen's children' as at 73 below. **71** *barnes*: 'children', as in 70 (with which it balances), *bastardus* being postpositive, notwithstanding *R–K* p.154, who prefer *barones* YAP^2 (*o* + P^2). But the gradational move from 'lawful sons (of serfs)' → bishops, to 'the illegitimate children (of anyone)' → archdeacons reads better in the context of complaint about decline. **72** *sopares*: not a difficult, if a rarely instanced word. Both *soutares* X and *schipherdes* I are linked (though not disparagingly) at B 10.461 as *lewed iuttes*, and the XI scribes might have been independently distracted through recollection of this key passage. **78–9** *refused*; *taken*: better read (like preceding *han be, leyde, ryden*) as past participles dependent on the causal temporal clause that introduces this eleven-line sentence, and not as linked main verbs. The departure of sanctity (80) is seen as the consequence of a series of abuses, simony being the last of them. **88** *voluntas Dei*: likelier to represent Cx than the more familiar form of the *Paternoster*-phrase (as found at 15.252, with a b-half echoing this line). The <eRM> ancestor presumably 'corrected' to the usual wording. **91** *mynstre*: 'monastery', preferable, notwithstanding its ostensibly asymmetrical relation to *prior*, since metonymic for 'abbot (of a main monastery)'; *mynistre* (perhaps only a spelling variant here) gives inferior metre, though the sense 'superior of a religious order' is acceptable (MED s.v. *ministre* 2b, but cited only from here). The line scans either as Type IIa with *But* as first stave or as Type Ia with cognative staves |b| / |b| / |p|. **98** *wordes*: contextually the aptest reading, the 'words' being those of the Gospel quotation following. The variant *wyrdes* (adopted by *R–K*) may have been prompted visually by *wynnyng* and semantically by the cognate *warth* and preceding *happed* 95. **103** *louable*: either from (1) *louen*, with internal |v| (< OE *lofian*) or (2) (*al*)*lowen*, with internal |u| (< OF *alouer* < Lat *allaudare*), both meaning 'praise', 'commend', or (3) (*al*)*lowen* (< OF *allouer* < Lat *allocare*) 'assign (credit) to'. AlfG 4 notes that 'L's usage frequently suggests the blending of

award and praise', as here if (2) and (3) were in question. At 17.130 *allouable* appears, of which present *louable* may be an aphetic form (MED s.vv. *loven* v. (2), *louen* v. (4), *allouen* v. 1(a)). **104** *Y wente*: R–K's emendation to imperative *ywende* provides no reason for the second command, and the formula-like reprise at 105a may be original. **107** *Syȝing*: the form adopted has a modified spelling close to that of X. Possibly the (substantively erroneous) *Schryuing* I is attempting to make sense of a y reading with initial *sch-*, while Y's *smytynge* offers a more radical ⇒ for a word found unintelligible. Occasional initial |s| as *sch* in X may derive from a linguistic stratum close to the original (at 7.300, a range of variants have been generated from a conjectural form **s(c)hy(ȝ) en* in x) but this spelling is rejected here as potentially confusing.

AB 2 (Z 20) scans as Type Ia in **ZA**, as IIIa in **B**. *K–D* p. 88 adopt the **A** form, claiming that in Bx 'The piety of the occasion is increased [*sc.* by a scribe] by excluding a mundane detail' [viz. *þe mete*, the key-stave in **A**]. Even if this were true, the change may well be authorial, the tone of 'piety' being heightened not diminished in the **C** revision (105–08). *K–D* also find defective metre, rejecting the pattern *ax / ax* (well-instanced in the core-text) as unoriginal, while scanning it incorrectly as *xaay*. **BA 7, Z 25** *my bileue*: *R–B* consider that *by my leue* **Z** may be a scribal slip or an authorial joke. It is judged the former here and accordingly emended.

109 (Z 27, AB 9) The revised **C** line may scan as Type IIa or like **AB** as extended Type IIIa with counterpoint (|v|, |m|), the theme-staves being *þanne* and *byfore*. **Z** is either a (metrically imperfect) draft or has lost *thenne* through scribal eyeskip to following *then* (as here conjectured). **Z**'s *fore telle* may be a draft form further corrupted by visual mistaking of *o* for *e* and *d* for *l*, with omission of **Y** through haplography. Only the latter is here restored as necessary for the sense, and the awkward (but possible) reading 'than I tell above / before this' may stand (see MED s.v. *fore adv.* 1). *K–D* judge that the earlier versions read *mette me* with **C** and not *sauȝ I* (so *Ka^2*), but the sequence **Z** > **A** > **B** cautions against drastic emendation. **110 (Z 28, AB 10)** The self-rhymed *tolde* in **A** may reflect an earlier form corrupted in ms **Z** (but see note above and that on Z 4.50–2 under C 4.64–6) and it seems to be echoed by the *repetitio* of the verb (*mette*) in **C** 109–10. Bx *seide* could thus arguably register a scribal objection to the repetition. But as its sense and metre are unexceptionable, it is perhaps best taken as recording a stage in the process of revision (*tolde* in **B**-H would then be a characteristic ⊗ from **A**). For another case where revision, this time from **B** to **C**, eliminates identical end-rhyme, cf. B 7.36–7=C 9.40–1. **114–15 (Z 29–31, AB 11–13)** As divided in Cx, 114 has the unoriginal pattern *aa / xa* and could be simply emended by transposing the preposition and noun-phrase, to leave line 115 as Type Ic. But since the form of the **ZAB** lines points to *prechede* as probably the last word of revised C 114, re-lineation is justified. The cause of the misdivision will have been the unusual length, not of 114 as a whole, but of the immediate post-caesural dip (eight syllables). *C*-**p** presents a further stage of corruption, in effect the converse of that diagnosed in Cx: shortening of 115 and addition of a half-line to create a new line that looks a model instance of scribal 'over-explicitness'. **A**'s *pestilences* seems to revise **Z**'s singular while retaining the sg. verb-form (securely attested with pl. subject for **BC**), which was doubtless what led several A-Text scribes to smooth the noun's number.

Z 34–40, 43, 45 are unique lines of acceptable metre and sense. **Z** 37 *messe ant; the masse*: possibly dittography for the single phrase *the m(e)sse*; or an original form *the masse, the messe* (with reference to the Mass as both sacramental meal and liturgical sacrifice). For a similar doublet cf. *pays* and *pees* at 18.177.

118 (Z 44, AB 16) Either *poffed* or *possed* could, on grounds of sense, be original in one or all versions. If **Z** is authentic, so may be *possid* in *A*-EM (? = **m**, v *pass-ched* being a spelling variant) and *C*-yEA, *puffid* **B** being either a revision discarded in **C** or a Bx ⇒ coinciding with r^2, and *p*u*P^2*. Either variant could be a visual error for the other (*f* for long *s* or long *s* for *f*) and given the uncertainty, it seems best to retain **Z** and prefer *poffed* for **A** and **C** in the light of Bx. Against the originality of *poste* in **Z** may be adduced the greater appropriateness of 'puffed' in the context of preceding Z 40 on the 'wind' of God's powerful word that broke down the gates of hell (39; with which compare *breeþ* B 18.322). **119 (Z 41, AB 17)** *segges*: despite scant manuscript support, worth cautiously adopting for **A** on the strength of agreed **ZC** (**C** perhaps revising *ʒe segges* **B**). The latter reading, in an ambiguous form *ʒe segge*, probably underlies *A*-EA *I sey*; *A*-M *to men* (so coincidentally in v) will then be a smoothing that indicates the presence of *segge* in **m** and thus, inferentially, in Ax. The variants *seyþ* RUD and *sent* t reveal successive stages of smoothing after misreading *ʒ* (for g) as *y* / *þ* and point to the absence from r^1 of *ʒe* before the noun. The family-readings may therefore be reconstructed as *seʒʒe* **r**, *y seʒʒe* **m**, pointing to Ax *(ʒe) seʒʒe* (= *ye segges* **B**). In the **A** form here offered *ʒe* is omitted as more probably a **B** revision (if it is not a Bx ⇒). The *C*-**p** variant may be seen as a final stage in the corruption, the noun *segge* becoming *to segges* in x^2 (= 'to men') and then the verb-phrase *to segge* (*ous*) 'to say to us' in **p**. *that*: adopted for **B** on the strength of **Z?AC** agreement. **122 (Z 47, AB 20)** *hem* x: adopted for **C** in the light of **ZAB** agreement; for while *ous* **p** would seem the more logical choice after *we* 119, *hem* here resembles **ZAB** inasmuch as the latter have it (also asymmetrically) after *ye*. The shift in address from the outer to the

inner audience, superficially the result of inadvertence in revising, could be authorially intended, and the more 'correct' logic scribal. **125 (Z 50, AB 23)** On solely metrical grounds, the forms of **x** (Type Ia) and **p** (Ic) are both acceptable; but the major **p**-variant will have arisen from misreading *heuene* as *leuen* 'live', the divergent smoothings *ryght for* / *and hou* well illustrating the dual transmission of **p** through p^1 and p^2. The **B** line has clearly been revised from **A**; the reading of Bx was probably that of ?βR, which has the inauthentic scansion *aa / xa* (unless F here preserves α). But whether or not F's correct metrical form is original, the infinitive particle is to be included in the reconstructed archetypal text as having occasioned the variation to prose order in the b-half of β-R. **126 (Z 52, AB 25)** *þat he wastide* 25 may be an Ax corruption of an original identical with that of **ZB**, or **Z** may show ⊗ from or (as here presumed) anticipation of **B**. But **C** is too extensively revised to furnish evidence for emending Ax, which is acceptable. **128 (Z 53, AB 26)** *And* **ZAB** / *He* **C**: four **B** mss have anticipated **C** by substituting *He* for archetypal *And*, perhaps through misreading the ampersand as *A. leue*: Bx *lete* is metrically and lexically unexceptionable but seems pointless as a revision of **A** reversed in **C**, and so is rejected as a probable scribal ⇒. **130 (Z 55, AB 28)** *stowe*: the reading adapted for **A** from *A*-J, which was most probably derived from a **B** copy of BHF type, with *of* before *Stowe*. Ax's presumed loss of the surname, by eyeskip to *staues* at the line-end or through haplography induced by following *tauʒte*, would have been easy if the name had been spelt *staue*. **Z**, unless showing ⊗ from **B** or **C**, here points to the likely presence of a surname in **A**, since *Thomas* alone seems too formal to have been the authorial version. **133 (Z 58, AB 31)** *half*: the metre of Ax requires an awkward stress on a^1 and it may be that *half* has been omitted through auditory or visual error from an original **a half*. *A*-N's variant, here judged correct, is presumably by ⊗ from a **B** or **C** source. On the strength of **ZBC** agreement, *half* may be restored without the article.

A 31 Hereafter two lines resembling C 134–35 (B 32–3) appear in **mJ**. Their presence in Z 59–60 would argue for their having also been in **A**, a possible reason for their loss from **r** being eyeskip from *worþ^2* at 31 to *werche* at the end of the last phrase *wolde werche* (particularly easy if *a grote* had been written in the margin of the exemplar). Against this, J's agreement with **m** here points to its r^2-type exemplar having been collated with another source, less probably an **A** ms of **m**-type than one of the **B** Version (to judge from J's likely use of a **B** source at 28 above). Since, therefore, it is not impossible that **m** (and also **Z**) have added the lines, they are omitted from **A**. A major reason for caution here is that similar signs of 'farcing' in this passus appear in the **m** tradition after 42, 110 and 190, perhaps indicating desire to represent a popular scene in its fullest form from whatever source. The theoretical possibility that **m** descends not from the same archetype as **r** but from a different *redaction* of **A** is not strong. Firstly, **m** also *omits* lines found in **r** (viz. 74–5), something better explained if it is a sub-archetype of Ax, and most of its additional lines (which also appear in **B**) are shared by one or more **r** copies (e.g. K,W and U). Manuscripts such as these are more likely to have derived the lines from **B** than from **m**, with which they affiliate no further in the many readings where **r** and **m** vary disjunctively. The behaviour of these **r** witnesses itself strengthens the assumption (intrinsically more economical) that **m** likewise resorted to a **B** source in order to amplify the descriptions of the Sins. A second factor telling against **m**'s pure descent from Ax here is that the form of the present lines is not both authentic and distinct from that of **B**. But though this comment applies also to 87, 163 and 167, there are grounds for treating those lines differently. Thus at 87, mechanical explanations of the line's loss from **r** such as homoteleuton appear, while censorship might also have operated, suggesting that **m** *is* there derived from Ax rather than by ⊗ from **B**. **136 (Z 61, A 32, B 34)** *He*: in the light of (**Z**)AC agreement, *And panne* Bx may be omitted as a case of scribal over-explicitness. **138 (B 40)** *spryng*: expanded in the light of **B** from Cx *spryg,* which may show loss of the nasal suspension here in the x reading; a form *spryg* without *n* is attested in the same sense but MED s.v. *sprigge* n. (1) quotes only this example. (In *C*-App. *add*: hus] pU; here y; *pe* D). **139a (B 39a)** The line following in Bx scans *ax / ax* (Type IIIa) but seems otiose, 'prompted by [the] Latin line and...translat[ing] it' (*K–D* p. 193). **141–42 (Z 64–5, A 35–6, B 42–4)** The two later texts (**B** securely, **C** in x only) make the whole utterance direct speech, **Z** and *A*-**m** make it indirect, while *A*-**r** offers a transitional form (in *C*-**p**, coincidental agreement with **A** seems to have resulted from failure to see where the direct speech begins). This might be evidence for two lines of transmission in the **A** revision of **Z**, one leading to **m**, the other to **r**, from a ms of which the **B** revision was made. But the fact that *A*-H and (in part) W, both **r**-group witnesses, share the variant may indicate rather that **m**'s reading here is due to mistaking *ʒe* for *pei* (35) through *p / ʒ* confusion, with subsequential smoothing in the final pronoun and in 36. While the same explanation could be adduced for **Z**, the tense of *prechyd* in Z 64 suggests that the indirect speech-form may have been original in this version. In B 44 the spelling of the base-ms W (supported by C²CH and possibly M, which alters the *e* to *y*) has not been changed to that of L&r (? = Bx), since it better facilitates possible wordplay on *leue* in the b-half. **145 (Z 68, A 39, B 47)** *stewed*: adopted for **B** on the strength of **Z**AC agreement, *ruled* Bx appearing as a 'substitution of a more emphatic and easier reading, possibly with deliberate elimination

of the pun' (*K–D*, p. 82). The word is either the rare verb meaning 'restrain, check' (MED s.v. *steuen* v. (1)), with a homophonic pun on *steward*, or a spelling-variant, with semantic pun, of the more common *stowid* 'established (in order)' (see MED s.v. *stouen* v. 1 (c), 2 (b)). **146–79 (= A XI 204–13, B X 292–329)** For convenience, notes on the parallel **AB** passage in this first instance of *major transposition* in **C** are given here and not later. They are to be read with the Apparatus that appears in its normal place in the text of **AB** in Vol I (pp. 424–428). **149 (A XI 208, B X 296)** *lygge*: presumably also the Ax reading (< *r²***m**), for which *r¹* will have substituted the adverb *longe* after misreading *dreiʒe* as the verb. T will then have smoothed the reading of its group original t (*longe*) and DH² have corrected to *lyggyn*, whether independently or by reference to an *r²* source. **150 (A XI 209, B X 297)** The line that follows 297 in *B*-α (Vol I, p. 426, Apparatus, β omitting B 10.291–302) is rightly dismissed by *K–D* (p. 193) as a scribal intrusion. Though metrically acceptable, it is best diagnosed as a piece over-emphatic padding after 297 had been rendered too long by the addition of *quod Gregorie* and subsequent misdivision. *K–D* reconstruct B 297 to accord exactly with **A**; but in the light of **C**, it seems better to make *religion* rather than *it* the subject of the two verbs in **B**. The rare *roilep* of **A** is, however, to be preferred to *rollep* R (a probable visual error) and the imperfectly alliterating *trollyp* F, perhaps an anticipatory echo of B 18.298 (all three verbs have much the same sense). **153–54 (B X 300–01)** The retention of the **B** lines apparently unchanged in **C** indicates that **L** was willing to alliterate the |k| of *cloystre* in 153 (300) with the stop within the consonant-group *sk* in *scole, skilles* (cf. 8.67, 10.269 and see *Intro.* IV § 45). In 154 (301), however, no head-rhyme is possible between the a-half stops and the b-half affricate. A simple emendation would be cognatively-alliterating *gome* for *man*, giving a Type IIa line, but this has an unidiomatic feel here. It may therefore be presumed that a difficult original invited ⇒ of a commoner word in Bx and Cx successively. The intense revision, e.g. at 151, 155, argues against **L**'s inadvertent acceptance of *chide* from his scribal **B** ms (as evidently judged by *R–K*, who retain *chyde*). Their conjectural emendation *carpe* (MED s.v. *carpen* v. 3(c)) is described by *K–D* as 'lexically adventurous' (p. 207) and so, obviously, is the rarer word *querele* proposed here (see MED s.vv. n., v.). Repeated ⇒ in Bx and Cx could have occurred the more easily if *chide* had appeared as an intralinear gloss; but this does not strictly need to have been the case. **155 (B X 302–04)** corresponds to three **B** lines, the text of which is uncertain. The form of the sole **B** witness α at 302 scans (a little awkwardly) as Type IIa with the first lift on *But*, Bx possibly having read *bep* for *is* or had a second *but* before *to¹*. The resumption of β at 303 offers choice between its reading and that of R

(=α), F here being evidently corrupt on grounds of sense. β offers an acceptable metrical pattern like that in 300, but with the |k| stave in the b-half. However, R's variant is superior in stating both that reason prevails in a university (echoing but varying the sense of *skiles* 300), and that the clerk who refuses to learn deserves contempt. β could have missed the first point (which is not self-evident) and have supplied the needed third stave by substituting the obvious *clerk* for the indefinite *he*. In 304 the pointless Bx *loueþ* in the b-half, repeating *loue* in the a-half and plainly induced by it, appears scribal. The conjectural emendation here proposed on grounds of sense follows the rationale adduced above for preferring α at 303: that the activity of co-operative study is a *reason* why harmony and not discord should prevail amongst scholars. *K–D*'s suggestion *loweþ hym to* is prompted by the sense of **C**'s revision *louhnesse* and by its closeness in form to Bx's verb. But it seems likelier that *loueþ* came in through objection to repetition of the verb here conjectured (*lere*), after the earlier repetition (in identical rhyme) of its free variant *lerne*, as a result of failure to grasp the difference in sense (here *lere* = 'teach' not 'learn'). **158** *lawedays*: *R–K* read *louedaies* with P²DM, but these must show ⊗ from **A** or **B**. The Cx reading, in a line and passage revised in detail, is harder and insists more strongly on the monastic regulars' entanglement in secular affairs by dint of their position as major landowners. **159 (B X 307)** revises to a standard Type Ia a Bx line with the inauthentic scansion *aa / bb*. The conjecture *vpon* for *on* provides a second stave in the a-half, giving the line a Type IIb structure very close to that of A 11.213, with its second stave found (not very satisfactorily) in the unstressed second syllable of the verb *Póperiþ* (and the same emendation may be desirable). The ⇒ of *on* was presumably unconscious; see on 15.212 below and cf. on 2.185 above, where one **C** ms offers the required form. **165 (B X 313)** There are no metrical grounds for questioning the authenticity of the line (identical in **B** and **C**); *K–D*'s conjecture *þei purely* for *hemself* is thus otiose and *R–K* sensibly leave **C** unaltered. No difficulty appears once 'cognative' alliteration on *p / b* is discerned, with *be* as either preposition or subjunctive verb (more probably the latter, since it stands in contrastive apposition with indicative *ben*). The line scans as Type Ia with *ben* unstressed or as Type Ic with *ben* stressed. **166 (B X 314)** *chartre*: the occurrence of the variant *charite* in **p** readily suggests how it could also have been a Bx ⇒ for *chartre* **B**, the harder **x** reading here preferred for **C**: the sense of the half-line is 'though that is their very *raison d'être*'. *B-F charge* is closer in both form and sense to *chartre* than to *charite*, allowing the possibility that α read *chartre* and that R has varied coincidentally with β, which will then have gone on to corrupt further by omitting the stave-word *pure*. But revision in **C** is quite possible, the

blunt sarcasm of *pure charite* being replaced by a graver tone. **172 (B X 320)** The Bx line does not make sense, whether *biten hem* or *beten hem* is read. The present emendation *biyeten* replaces a more complex earlier one (*Sch¹* 1978), diagnosing the α and β readings as misunderstandings of a difficult phrase *biyeten hem* 'obtain for themselves', thus enabling 321 (in Bx a Type IIIa line) to remain unemended. The sense of *biyeten* is 'acquire possession of' (MED s.v. 1(a)), its direct object being *That* 321. The pronoun *hem* could be retained as dative reflexive 'for themselves' but on balance is better omitted as a scribal smoothing after ⇒ of a verb that required a direct object. In the context, it would seem likelier that the barons should reclaim the land on behalf of their *heirs* (the *barnes* of 321). **175 (B X 323–24)** The Bx line 323 scans anomalously as *aa / xa* and emendation is on the grounds of the unusual sequence, that of colloquial speech, being what have motivated the inversion that destroyed the metre. In 324, a Type IIa line, two staves are to be found in *Grégòries*. Since the second must be mute, this is to be regarded as a licensed exception, Type IIa normally requiring three full staves (cf. the closely similar *Poperiþ* at A 11.213, noted at 159 above). But it may render otiose a conjectural stave-word in the b-half ([*gan*] *yuele despende Sch,* [*vngodly*] *despended K–D*). **179** *kirke*: the Cx line scans as Type IIIa, but emendation of *churche* to *kirke*, proposed by *Sk* (and attested by D), while not strictly required, is adopted here as according with **C**'s tendency to normalise Type IIIa lines in revising. **182** *ryht so*: proposed to restore the metre and sharpen the sense of a line that scans imperfectly in Cx as *xa / aa* (and is so left by *R–K*). Nobles and commons should be at one with each other *just as* the king should be with his whole people.

[The parallel text returns to the main sequence here]

B V 54 The line that follows in Bx lacks alliteration and is rightly judged spurious, one of those prompted by, and introducing, a line of Latin (*K–D*, p. 193). **Z 70** is unique to this version and, while conceivably a piece of enthusiastic scribal elaboration, could well be an authentic line deleted as inappropriately expansive at this point. For three earlier such examples cf. Z 2.47, 189, 3.96. **199–200 (Z 72–5, A 42, B 58–9)** Z 75 is a line that appears to be a draft version of B 59 (itself later revised as C 200) and follows two lines of authentic appearance, the second of which introduces 75 in a manner without parallel in **B** or **C**. This suggests that the line was also originally in **A**, and a version of it in fact appears in KW and in EM, the latter pair perhaps representing **m** (A lacks the line). But this attestation by some **A** copies of two unrelated families may be due to ⊗ from a **B** or **C** source in each case. The line could have been omitted with Z 73–4 in the revision to **A** and have been later restored in **B**. But since the sense in the majority of **r** witnesses is satisfactory, its restoration here, though desirable, does not seem imperative. *Qui....Filio*: line 199 // has a blank first stave but a 'compensatory' fourth stave (like the 'supplemental' type described at *Intro.* IV § 44), a metrical licence that sometimes occurs in macaronic lines. *Filio* **Z**: correcting a simple mechanical slip. **200** *thus endede*: with key-stave formed liaisonally (*thus_endede*), one of the clearest examples of this stave-type to be found (*Intro.* IV § 45).

Passus VI (ZAB V)

2 (Z 77, A 44, B 61) *garte* **BZ**: perhaps replaced in Ax by the regionally less-restricted *made* which, as the probable original in **C**, will be a revision (the metrical usefulness of *gart* is clear from its appearance in stave-position at C 5.146). The variant in *A*-A may be due to ⊗ from a *B*-source, whereas *B*-HF may show ⊗ from **A** and Hm from **C**.

Z 83 *one*: apparently a visual error, perhaps induced by *o* in adjacent words.

16–17 The repetition in the a-halves, despite the varied word-order, will seem empty unless implying (a) 'to each parent in turn' and (b) 'over and over again'. A stronger if more obvious contrast would emerge if *vnbuxum* 17a were originally *nat buxum.* But reconstruction, by omitting *of mercy...ybe* and re-lineating, is to be resisted, as is *R–K*'s conjecture *bold* for *vnbuxum*[2]. **22** scans as an extended Type IIIa with counterpointed a-half if the stave-sound is *sk*, as unambiguously in 25, but if vocalic, as Type 1a with onset and 'echoic' counterpoint (Schmidt 1987:65). Either alternative obviates any need to posit a lost *s* stave-word such as *swiche* in position two.

30–62 The first of several passages of **C VI** and **VII** that revise material from **B XIII** as part of a more extended treatment of the SINS (though earlier 19a already echoes B 13.282). For notes on **B** see below *ad loc.* **32** *wilnynge*: the variant *wilned* here (as at 41) may be an erroneous reflex of a participial form **wilnende* in Cx. **37** In *C*-App. *add* my-] **p** (*def.* K)P[2]D; hym- ?**x**. Though the reading *hym*, which seems to be that of **x**, could be an oversight in revising from B XIII (*Pe, ad loc*), this would have the effect of making a scribal reading (that of **p**) 'correct' against an authorial one. More probably it is a family error, perhaps induced by unconscious recollection of **B** (as at 59–60). **39** The **p** variant appears a scribal slip perhaps prompted by an exemplar reading *couet* with nasal suspension. D's *couetes* may suggest an ambiguously-spelled exemplar: this ms has *couent* and *couetys(e)* elsewhere and the present instance may be intended as a plural of the former word. **40** Here *p*[2] seems nearer to the probable form of **p** and *p*[1] a secondary smoothing of an

exemplar presumably found meaningless. **46** has an onset translinearly alliterated with the blank fourth lift of 45 to form a T-type, though *for* could be stressed here to give a normative line. **51 (B XIII 305)** scans as Type IIb on |v| and |s| with a wrenched stress on *neuére* providing the second lift. **B** could be Type Ie, the most likely pattern, or Ib with a 'strong' (five-syllable) second dip. **56 (B XIII 309)** The word-order of **x** is preferred in the light of // **B**, but the pl. form of **p** is more probably original. The masculine sg. *he* of **x** is now not logical after revision of **B**'s second *hym* to *here* and is most probably an erroneous reflex of the original *hy* preserved from **p** in two members of *p*[2] (*R–K*'s unwarranted emendation of Cx *here* to *hym* should be rejected). Accepting the (gender-indeterminate) pl. pronoun *hy* gives a Type Ic line; but the line would also scan, as Type IIa, with *þei*. **59–60 (B XIII 312–13)** *Pe*, retaining **x**, takes these implicitly as authorial comment, as in the **B** lines under revision. But it seems preferable with *Sk* to follow **p** (to which Y has corrected) in seeing them as part of Pride's speech, the present tense of *seme* 60 in **x** going better thus, while treating the free-standing Latin of 60*a* as authorial commentary, as in **B**. The conflicting tenses of *sounen* in **p** and **x** may be the consequence of a tense-ambiguous Cx form *sounyt* (see at III 129–30). It is resolved as past here to accord more aptly with the a-half verbs, preterite indicative and subjunctive respectively after *tolde* 47, *swor* 51 (*take* 53, *sygge* 54 are infinitives, after *wolde* understood) and with the general sequence of past-tense verbs throughout the confession.

Z 89 *that*: necessary for the construction and securely attested in the other versions, but lost mechanically by eyeskip from the exemplar's *Wyth* to *a.* **Z 91–101** appear to form an early draft that was much expanded in A and progressively thereafter; to explain them as a garbled scribal summary of an A original is implausible. The collocation of Envy and Wrath in 91, though anticipating **C**'s hostile confrontation of these vices at 66, is independent, while evincing a like understanding of Envy's nature. Line 96 will scan as Type IIIa if the break is placed after *be*, though giving an uncharacteristic rhythm in the b-half, with its five-syllable final dip. Possibly a stave-word like *leel* (as conjectured at B 9.188) or the phrase *loue and* (as at 19. 276) has been omitted; but the awkwardness could be due to the draft character of the line.

64 (A 59, B 76) The direction of thought in the earlier versions is partly to be recovered from the final form of **C**. That Envy's cry is effectively a curse in **C** helps to discriminate *schrewe* as the bold **B** original, the β variant being a scribal relapse to the uncontentious **A** original and *B*-H a ⇒ nearer to the presumed form of Bx and the sense of α (F is here evidently a scribal reflex of α's verb). That *shrewe* was also the original **A** reading is undemonstrable, but not very likely if *cope* is the object. The chief problem in establishing **A** is the unusual noun that has generated the other four variants. This is distinguished by *Ka*, its hardness helping explain the revised **B** form, one more resistant to corruption by scribes. The emendation *comsiþ* in **A** is not vital on metrical grounds, as the line could scan cognatively, but seems safe enough (cf. B 1.165 // ZAC). **65** *corse-men*: **p**'s unique *corsement* is hard enough to be original and the form underlying D (='cursing'), and also, *pace Pe*, allegorically appropriate, because Langland's Sin is 'hostility, resentment, hatred' generally (*Invidia*), not just 'envy' in the narrower modern sense (the symbolic 'clothes' an ironically reversed counterpart of those in a passage such as Col 3:12–14). However *corse-men*, perhaps a transient personification, is even harder, and U's reflex, accepted (without conviction) by *Pe*, points to this as the probable *x¹* reading behind y. **66 (A 67, B 84)** The closeness in thought and form of **C** and **A** (anger; the strong verb *writhen*) may argue in favour of *K–D*'s emendation of **B** to read with **A**. But against this, the α form preserved in R gives the same sense as **AC**, only with a weak verb of OE Type 2 and omitting the pun on anger, while the line (notwithstanding *K–D*) scans as Type IIIc or counterpointed Ie. The β corruption of the presumed Bx reading may have arisen through mistaking the preterite morpheme for the verb *yede* and subsequently smoothing with a pronoun and a participial ending to the verb stem. (In *C*-App. *add* he] **p**; *om* **x** (+ *a.h.* X)). **67** *pissede* **x** / *passede* **p**: though either act might have provoked anger, it seems likelier that **p** is toning down the original than that **x** is strengthening it (cf. also the thought at 8.151). **69** It is possible that **A**'s 74–5 were originally here in **B**, since **C**'s 69 corresponds in position to A 74; however, **C** omits A 75 with no breach in sense, and its form is not that of A 74 but of B 13.325. **B 89** scans either as an extended Type III with rhetorical stress on *his* or, preferably, as Type IIIa.

A 74–82 74–5 appear original in sense and metre and will have been lost from **m** by homoteleuton (*ofte* 73, 75) and inserted in E's ancestor from an **r** source. *K–D* (p. 84) ascribe to the same mechanism loss of these lines from Bx after 93. But the omission seems deliberate, A 5.74a being used later as B 13.325, and no echo of the unused line-and-a-half appearing in **C**. **79 (B 97)** scans vocalically in **r** with mute key-stave or a full stave on *I*, and in **m** on *m*, the stave-sound of revised **B**. The latter gives superior sense, making Wrath the cause of dissension between his neighbour's retainers and other people. By contrast, **r** has the dissension between the neighbour and his own retainers, which while acceptable is further from **B** than is **m**. The Bx reading is to be discriminated as that preserved in R, while F is close to the *A*-**r** variant. **81–2 (B 99–100)** The verb-tenses are presumed in **A** to have been non-according with those in 83–4, their later accord in **B** being (variously) anticipated by H²JWN and by T&r. But a present tense for *hate* is to be favoured in the light of **B**.

B 102 (A 84) Bx scans not *aa* / *bb*, an inauthentic pattern, but *aa* / *ax*, with stress rhetorically thrown from *woot* to *my* in the b-half. The change, which makes the threat allusive rather than explicit, is in keeping with that in 101b from A 5.83b. **A 87–90 A 87 (B 105)** A mechanical reason for the loss from **r** might be the presence of *for* (...)*þe peple* in both 86a and 87b. But the presence of *aftir* at the beginning of 88 in **?r** would suggest that **r**'s exemplar had been damaged, leaving only the final word of 87, which was subsequently taken over to begin 88. The line's presence in **m** is thus less likely to be by ⊗ from **B** than by descent from Ax, since a clear vestige of it remains in **r**. But *A*-W may well be thus derived, since it has *Aftre* at the beginning of 88 as well as at the end of 87. **90 (B 108)** scans in **r**, leaving 91 as metrically possible but very abrupt. *Ka* convincingly explains Ax loss of initial *Awey* by attraction to preceding *awey* in 89a. *Also* **m** looks like a scribal provision of a first stave, but could be a reflex of a damaged Ax, and **B** a revision. Although **B** ⊗ in **m** has been recognised (5.133 //), recourse to **B** here seems to have been avoided.

B 109–11 B 109 (A 91) *Eleyne* Bx: if original, a revision for which no reason appears. A masculine name would fit more easily here, as the F variant evidently implies (though Wrath's dual sex is later instanced at B 5.155ff). In 111, 112 *his* must therefore have a generic force and cannot refer back to *Eleyne*. Possibly the feminine name, with the α spelling *heleyne*, arose as a visual error for Bx **he heyne*, with *he* either anticipatory dittography or a pleonastic pronoun of emphasis. **B 111 (A 93)** The reading *liketh*, probably that of Bx (and one among the five substantive **A** variants) seems scarcely hard enough to have generated the other four in **A** or the inferior **B** variant *aketh*. On grounds of sense, *lighteth* would be acceptable but seems insufficiently unusual to have invited ⇒. The proposed reading *liþeþ* is instanced at A 7.180 and C 19.71, though only in a literal sense, the first of these causing difficulty to some scribes; the sense here is 'alleviate, ease' (MED s.v. *lithen* v. (2)). If the original had been spelled *litheth*, the variant *lihteth* could have been generated by metathesis (as at C 19.71 in ms X); if *liþeþ*, then *liȝteþ* could equally well have arisen through þ / ȝ confusion. The hardness of the meaning and the mechanical ease of the ⇒ described combine to recommend choice of the conjecture over any of the attested variants.

A 95 (B 113) is reconstructed in the light of **B**, the required sense of **þere þat* (the presumed original of the split variants *þere*, *þat*) being equivalent to *þat* 'inasmuch as, because' in **B**. The pronoun form *hy* is likely to be the Ax reading underlying the **r** variants. The metre of **B** may be of T-type, *wel* having been added to produce *on do wel* (in **A** *on do bet*) a witty 'anti-pun' (on this see Schmidt 1987:111).

69–85 (B XIII 325–42) For the Apparatus to **B** see Vol I, p. 534.

70 (B XIII 326) The b-half in Bx has evidently undergone scribal inversion to prose order, and *K–D* 's reconstruction after revised **C** restores the metre. **72 (B XIII 328)** The stresses in **C**'s b-half are either *fíkel and fáls tónge*, or *fíkel and fáls tònge* with double feminine ending, or *fíkel and fáls tónge*, which makes a lexical word part of a 'strong' penultimate dip but is preferable. **74–5 (B XIII 330–31)** *K–D*'s re-division of **B** 330–31 in the light of **C** gives a more balanced pair of lines: though Bx 330 is not unmetrical, 331 has a clumsy a-half. However, their judgement (p. 90) that on comparison with **C** the Bx b-half shows 'miscomprehension induced by preceding context' is not compelling. For whilst the repetition is a little weak, it is not obviously unoriginal, and it seems to have invited the sort of changes typical in **C** (there is also revision in following 76). **76** is syntactically linked with 75 and introduces the Latin, which is better presented as authorial comment. *R–K* treat this line and 76*a* as the speaker's, but it seems incredible that the character Envy should quote these two psalm-passages and their homiletic introductory line. **77** The sense is unexceptionable and *R–K*'s emendation *with* for *such* gratuitous. **79** *an*: lost in **x** by haplography before *angre*. **84 (B XIII 341)** Bx scans as Type IIIa, but the lack of parallelism between 340 and 341 appears suspect: for in **C** 'God' corresponds to the Soutere, his 'word' and 'grace' to the latter's 'charm'. *K–D* reconstruct **B**'s a-half as *For goddes word ne grace*; the simpler solution here presumes *God* lost through visual attraction to following *Goddes*, with resultant smoothing of *ne* to *no*. **91 (B V 124, A V 103)** *the beste*: in **m** perhaps by ⊗ from **B**, *to goode* not being evidently scribal, and the **B** reading certainly more emphatic. But **r** equally may be attempting to tone down the optimism, which B 125 will stress more strongly than **A**. **93 (A 105, B 126)** *Enuye: þat segge* Bx looks suspicious on comparison with **AC**, which repeat the Sin's name, indicating vocalic scansion with counterpoint on *s*.

From this point the **m** *family of* **A** *is represented by a* fourth *ms,* **H**³ (Harley 3954), *hitherto a* **B** *copy* (**H**). *The* group-sigil **m** *henceforth (subject to the variations recorded in the Apparatus) denotes the agreed readings of* **EAMH**³ *and by inference those of their exclusive common ancestor.*

94 (A 106, B 127) *K–D* (p. 102) object to Bx *megre* (retained in **C**) as scribal, because Envy was earlier described as swollen. But his lean physique is compatible with his 'swelling' through emotional turmoil, and *bolniþ* AB 99/118 does not imply 'fatness'. **96 (B 128)** The Bx line has an inauthentic pattern *aa / xx*, revised in **C** with use of a different stave-sound. *K–D* p. 195 plausibly conjecture ⇒ *biggyng* 'residing' as unusual enough to have invited ⇒ of a commoner term (see MED s.v. *biggen* v.

1(a)). **99** The archetypal reading (< **x**p²) may be *þat,* or else *so* and *þat* could be split variants of the form reconstructed here, which yields a T-type line, as indeed does the p¹ reading (in *C*-App. for '**x**M' read 'XM'; for '**p**' read 'Y&r'). Arguably *and* should be omitted as a scribal insertion; Cx clearly lacked it. **105 (B 135)** The **B** line scans either vocalically as a variant of Type Ie with mute key-stave or as Type IIIa on *w*, the latter perhaps preferable in the light of **C**, which revises to Type Ia on *w* with mute key-stave.

B 136 scans as Type Ia on cognative staves (*k / g*); cf. B 18.48.

126–27 (B 149–50) Of Bx's three lines the first may be scanned as Type Ia (with liasonal *r*-stave) and the second as Type III on *l*, while the third is unmetrical. *K–D* securely adopt the corrected Cr² division, but its source is unknown. The simplest explanation is that it derives not from a **B** source superior to Bx but from collation with **C** which, though revised at this point, retains the presumed original structure of **B** clearly enough to have guided a corrector. Cr¹ could be an earlier attempt to correct from **C** and *K–D* (p. 91) may be right to omit *wikked* as overemphatic. **128 (B 151)** *abbesse*: containing both b-half lifts without intervening dip, originally perhaps uncontracted *abbodesse*. If so, this was presumably in **B**, where the β-tradition evinces dissatisfaction with the metre by supplying *boþe* as the final lift. **134 (B 157)** *ac*: sharpening the sense and here conjectured lost in Cx by haplography before '*a* cokewolde' (so also in *B*-HmCr²³G, where *B*-Cr¹y substitute *And*).

B 165 *purueiede*: providing for Bx's missing key-stave an 'alliterating synonym with a particular contextual meaning lexically well established but not actually instanced in the poem' (*K–D* p.197). This meaning (spelling out *forwit* 164) is either 'foresaw' (taking *for* as conjunction) or, more probably, 'provided' (the actual reading of Cr), with *for* as preposition, which would be merely an extension of the literal sense instanced at B 14.29. If *provided* Cr is from a lost **B** source superior to Bx, the word it is echoing would be *purveiede*, but it is probably an intelligent guess. Like the Bx and conjectural readings, Cr has a 'monolexical' stave-pattern paralleled by 128 (cf. also 4.172, 7.170 and see *Intro.* IV § 38). The Bx reading itself could be a marginal or supralinear gloss incorporated into the text, or ⇒ of a contextually more familiar word. **147** The general sense of the passage (taken along with Y, *bothe* 148) shows that **p**'s *ich* must be wrong (though understandably so, given the shifting viewpoint of the speaker from 145 to 148). But **p**'s *hue* furnishes the needed third stave and directs emendation of **x**'s first *and*, consequentially, second *she* to *heo*. This is a major instance of a recessive pronominal form having served as a useful metrical resource. *R–K* leave the line unmetrical by their criteria (not discerning a mute key-stave). **149** The **p**

reading makes as good sense as that adopted, though it is less vivid and fits less closely with 150. But the presence of *on* in the **x**-mss (altered in P²'s source and visibly in D) produces a nonsensical reading and suggests that Cx read *cloʒes*, the error having arisen through *ʒ* / *þ* confusion (cf. on B 111 and 163, 194). If *clopes* was archetypal, I's reading would be an intelligent response to the perceived lack of sense of *on with the clopes*. The form *cloʒes* is sparsely attested and its rarity may have contributed to the error (see MED s.v. *claue* n. (1)). *R–K* p. 161 argue for *clothes* (in the sense 'coverchiefs'), but *clawes* looks like a moderate reworking of **B**'s (perhaps exaggerated) *knyues*. **155 (B 171)** The form of the line in BxCx allows barely acceptable scansion on *don, -dayes* and *to* (cognative and mute). *K–D* conjecture omission of *perf* as the third stave-word before *bred*, thus restoring the stresses to their natural position. But no reason appears for its loss except inducement from the common collocation, and *R–K* abandon this conjecture, leaving the line unmetrical. The reading adopted here presumes mechanical loss of the following adverb through haplography; for similar examples cf. *ʒong ʒong* 5.35, *fel* B 3.260 (and for a parallel cf. 3.426 *beste bestes*, where YA have omitted *beste*). The adverb *faste*, identical in form with the verb, will here have the sense 'severely' or 'diligently' (MED s.v. *faste* adv. 4 (c), 6 (c)). **156 (B 172)** In the light of **C**, the **B** reading is reconstructed as that presumed for α, of which R and F preserve split variants. **158 (B 174)** The Bx line will scan as Type Ie on voiced fricatives (-*þi, haue_I, þo*) and so emendation is not strictly necessary. But a better correlation of staves and significant lexical words is achieved by identifying the stave-sound as *l*, as in revised **C**. The emendation, which presupposes Bx inversion to prose order, yields a Type IIIa line with *likyng* in the same first-stave position as its synonym *luste* in **C**. **160 (B 176)** *at euen* in **C** is judged original in the light of **B**; **p** may have omitted it through seeing the line as over-weighted (as is **x** at 173b). *and whan* **B**: reconstructed in the light of **C** from the split variants *and, whan. wel*: preferred to *wyn* on comparison with **C**'s revised adverb *late*. **162 (B 178)** is either Type Ie scanning on vocalic theme-staves or an extended Type IIIa with *w* as contrapuntal stave. **163 (B 179)** *couʒe*: suggested by the context as the substantive lexeme; a metaphor from the preceding image of overdrinking. The spelling of *C*-y is best construed as an idiosyncratic variant of that preserved in *C*-u rather than as a preterite of *couʒen* or an approximation of *coupe*. The latter is to be rejected on grounds of poor idiom and inappropriate tense, as is the former if *wiste* 162 is conditional (as *woet* implies) and not a simple past tense as **p** takes it. **C**'s revision increases the malice of Wrath's slanders by hinting that they are not surely based, whereas **B**'s two indicatives (*woot* 178...*woot* 179) imply that they are. **170–74** These lines left virtually unchanged through **ZAB** are

developed with material from B XIII into a much longer account of Lechery. **173 (B V 73)** *loue* **p**: the reading of **x**, semantically possible but metrically inferior, may have arisen through the scribe's unconsciously taking the petition as addressed to Christ; the more natural sense of *for thy moder loue* would be 'for the love of your mother' rather than 'because of your mother(ly) love'. **174 (B V 74, Z V 90, A V 57)** *myd* **BZ** and *with* **CA**: possibly in free variation in the author's dialect; so, since the word is not in stave-position, the form used in the base ms (for **A** and **C** also that of the archetype) is retained. **198 (A 109, B 188)** In the light of **C** the correct **A** form would appear to be that of *r²*. The line's unusual length appears to have led to expansion of the b-half in both *A*-**m** and in Bx; misdivision, sometimes with expansion, being common in all versions where exceptionally long lines appear, it seems right to emend Bx to accord with **C**. The phrase *as a blynd hagge* serves to create a Type IIIa line after a preceding Type Ia, and objection to it is not on metrical grounds but because the half-line adds nothing to the sense by comparing Greed to an old woman. Bx may have introduced the error, or the poet's *A*-ms could itself have been of **m** type; but more probably **m** here shows ⊗ from the Bx tradition, similar signs of desire to expand the Sins' descriptions appearing after A 110 (with which contrast A 87 above). **200 (B 190)** alliterates on *s*, treated as a metrical allophone of |ʃ| in **L**'s metrical practice (cf. *Intro.* IV § 46) and *ch*, the latter perhaps sounding close to |ʃ| in the liaising phrase *his_chyn*. A bye-pronunciation of *cheueled* with |ʃ| may also have existed, since it has left a reflex in *shiver* (see MED s.v. *chiveren* v. (c)). **202** *hat*: better than *lousy hat* B 192, which anticipates B 194. **203 (A 111, B 193)** The line following in Bx is rejected as spurious since it is over-emphatic, unmetrical and stylistically alien. But its *Al torn* seems to echo a presumed original epithet in 193a (preserved in identical **AC**), which is adopted in place of *tawny*, as the poet's concern seems to be the tattered state of Coueitise's coat, not its hue. **204 (A 112, B 194)** In **A**, the form of 112b is the unmetrical *aa / xa* in **r** (ms W of this family being perhaps a scribal 'improvement' influenced by an **m** source) and in all **m** witnesses except H³. The corruption may have arisen through the presence in the b-half of two verbs of supposition, *leue* and *trowe*, one of which the **r** scribe deemed superfluous. But the probable Cx form (*hit / hit as*) seems syntactically too simple in itself to have invited alteration; so it is inadvisable to emend both **A** and **B** to accord with **C** (as do *Ka²* p. 461, *K–D* p. 93). The readings here offered are somewhat tentative reconstructions. Evidence that Ax contained the phrase *I trowe* is its presence in some members of **r** as a variant of *leue*. In Bx a syntactically intervening stave-phrase is presumed lost through homoarchy from *lepe* immediately preceding at the mid-line; *þe bettre* is retained, but could have been a scribal ⇒ if *I trowe* was judged a repetition. The Bx form as emended now seems satisfactory in both sense and metre. In the light of the majority **x** witnesses, it would seem that *hit* was present in Cx, whether or not followed by *as* (so **p**). The XD reading then is lïkely to be an intelligent scribal guess, though arguably superior to the *hit / hit as* form deducible as that of Cx. **205 (A 113, B 195)** *He* in **C** may be masculine or an ambiguous Cx spelling of *Heo* (as may be the case in *B*-α). In **A**, however, the feminine forms are unlikely to have arisen from *He*, and Ax may be judged to have read *Heo*. A feminine form is securely attested in *B*-β and in *C*-P² (added *a.h.* in X). In **C**, however, the pronoun has been left in the gender-ambiguous form since the sex of the louse (doubtless here the flea) was perhaps of as little consequence to the poet as it is to the reader. In all probability y had no negative particle and u either retained *nat* from **x** or added it, perhaps by reference to **p**. The double negative *ne...not* is preserved in *B*-R (? = α). **216 (A 124, B 206)** The variants *lyser* and *list* are identical in sense (see MED s.vv. *liser* n. and *liste* n. (2)). In the Bx tradition the two copies supporting *list* are suspect of ⊗ from **A**, whilst in the Ax and Cx traditions the appearance of both words in mss of each family suggests that they were in free variation. *K–D* (pp. 153–54) suspect *lyser* as a scribal variant induced by attraction to following *lenger,* but against this, it seems to be the rarer word, and the distribution of manuscript support points to its having been archetypal in the later versions and probably also in the earliest. **218 (A 126, B 208)** All three traditions have manuscript support for a stave-word (*pak*) having *p* rather than *b*. It is attested by *B*-γ and also by *B*-M over an erasure of a word that may fairly be presumed *bat* as in α and L (and thus, quite probably, in β); the likelihood is therefore that Bx read *bat*. In **C** *pak* is attested by most **p** mss and by UD, suggesting that y (and possibly also *x¹*) read *bat*. In **A** the split is fairly clear, **r** reading *pakke* and *bat* being probably the reading of **m**. *K–D* (p. 205n) and *Ka²* identifying the key-stave as *p*, retain *pak* as the second stave-word and emend the first (*Brochide*) to *Prochide* on the strength of *A*-U. But *Ka²* is not convincing that U finds support in KW *Pryckede*, more probably a scribal gloss on a difficult original that could have been either (cf. *Prikede* M as substitute for the *second* stave-word *bat*, the probable reading of **m**). *K–D* rightly find *prochid* 'brought together' harder in sense than *broched* 'stitched loosely'; but it can also be construed as the *A*-U scribe's attempt to 'correct' the metre rather than as a survival of the original. But *bat-nedle,* which is also harder than *pakke-nedle,* cannot well be such an attempt, since the resulting line has a *p*-stave in the second half. The simplest solution is to see both **A** and **B** as intended to scan 'cognatively' with an unvoiced labial stop for key-stave and the voiced stop in the a-half (see *Intro.* IV § 46). **C**, if *bat* is here accepted as the sec-

ond stave-word, must then have been revised to scan on *b* only, exhibiting the tendency to a more uniform metrical practice common in the latest version. **219 (A 127, B 209)** *pressour(es)* **AC**; *presse* Bx: the lexeme is likely to have been *pressour,* whether pl. or sg. in **B**. *pynned*: in the light of **AB** best taken as past tense, *bande / playted* (218) and *potte* likewise not being infinitives like *brochen* but finite preterites. *C*-YI only possibly preserve the *x¹* reading here, the other members' present tense resulting from the tense-ambiguity of the first verb. The verbal lexeme's identity is clear in **C**, but whereas in the **AB** traditions *pyned* may be no more than a bad spelling for *pynned*, its metaphorical boldness supports it on intrinsic grounds as the probable archetypal and original reading in both. **C** would then be a revision in the direction of literalism (like *yʒoten hitsulue* for *yeten his fille* at 1.149 //). **220 (A 128, B 210)** The most precise and appropriate verb-form for **C** is that attested for **AB**, *tolled* 'extended, was drawn out to' (MED s.v. *tollen* v. (1)). The two **C** family readings are perhaps orthographic variants, or that of **x** may represent the preterite of *tellen* 'amount to, reach the number of' (MED s.v. *tellen* v. 17 (h)). The **p** spelling with *i / y* is arguably authentic, given a form such as *tyleth* at Z 6.66; but that with *o* is preferable, since the probable pun on *tellen* (preterite) would be best achieved by adopting the spelling of **AB** here. **221 (A 129, B 211)** *wynstere* **A**: the probable reading of **r**, providing a characteristic punning suggestion of profiteering (with play on 'win') along with the literal sense of 'one who winds threads (of silk or wool)' (MED s.v. *windestre* n., recorded only here; OED s.v. *Windster* has post-1700 examples). The fact that *webbester* was substituted for it in six **A** mss (three from group **m**) is inadequate reason for doubting, with *K–D*, the originality of Bx *webbe*. For **B**'s occasional replacement of a rare word with one more familiar anticipates **C**'s general tendency to seek immediate intelligibility. **222 (A 130, B 212)** The reading *oute* **BC** points to *out* **m** as derived from Ax, if it is not a ⊗ from **B**; but **r** *softe* 'loosely' (MED s.v. *softe* adv. 3(b)), unless original as *KaK–D* judge, cannot easily have been generated from *oute*. Some slight evidence survives in *so softe* R and *per owt* EH³ that Ax may have had *so* before *oute,* and this would better account for *softe* **r** by smoothing and *out* AM by elimination of *per*, EH³'s (if not **m**'s) ⇒ for postulated Ax *so*. The perceived metrical awkwardness of *so oute* could have prompted the revision attested in **B** and preserved in **C**, an improvement anticipated by AM. The contextual sense of *softe* 'loosely' is approximately that of *oute* here; the reference of *so* 'in this way' would imply that the thread was to be spun in a manner suitable for racking after the cloth had been woven (see *Commentary*). **223–24 (A 131–32, B 213–14)** In the light of agreed *A*-**r**Bx, it seems that *more* ended 223 rather than beginning 224. Misdivision will have occurred through ambiguous placement of the adverb in Cx's exemplar, as in that of *A*-**m**. This may have facilitated loss of the first stave-word in 224, but the main mechanism here will have been haplography before the first syllable of aun*cer*, as in all **A** mss save JEL (the JE spelling of 'own' is significantly *awne*). Though in error, *r¹* shows awareness that the line must scan vocalically. *payede*: a potentially ambiguous spelling like *A*-J's *payʒed*, cited as the lemma for *r²*, would account for the variant *peysede* (*ʒ* being read as *z*) and its unmetrical synonym *weid*. *whan I*: judged from **AC** agreement to be the **B** reading, altered in Bx to the more emphatic *whoso*. **227 (A 135, B 217)** The ⇒ of *hem*- for *hym*- occurs randomly in copies of all three versions through misconstruing demonstrative *þat* as a relative, with *laboreres* as antecedent; but *hym*, involving semi-personification of the ale, is the harder reading. **228 (A 136, B 218)** *ale* BxC-**x**: regarded by *K–D* (p. 86) on comparison with **A** as scribal explicitness; an addition easily explained as incorporating a marginal or interlinear gloss in the exemplar. However, since the a-half is revised in **B**, the explicitness may be authorial (compare the pronoun *he / a* in **BC** at 229, not present in A 137). **231; 233 (A 139, 141; B 221, 223)** On the strength of **AC** agreement *Whan* and *þis elleuene wynter* may be confidently restored as the original text of **B**. For since both Bx readings show on comparison as unambiguous instances of 'scribal over-emphasis', the linear postulate and the *durior lectio* criterion in combination may be allowed to outweigh the canon of acceptability.

A 142 (B 224, Z 99) An Ax reading with a form such as N's *so þike* would explain both the visual error *soþly* in **r** (< *soþlike) and the paraphrastic reflex in **m**. Restoration proceeds by resolving N's form into adverb + verb + pronoun on the model of *B*-β. The early **Z** reading (taken with B 235), confirms that a Norfolk dialectal oath is intended.

B 232 (C 238) The *B*-γ reading is the clearest, and the absence of *be* from LR and from M's exemplar could be due to Bx's having lost the verb through homoarchy (< following be*ttre*). F has independently corrected and is unlikely to represent α here; so unless Bx preserved an elliptical original, γ is to be preferred as a felicitous correction. The **C** revision incorporates *be* but the line now scans on vowels (unaspirated *h*), as Bx could have done (Type IIIa or Type Ia with mute key-stave).

242 The asymmetry in the archetype's verb-tenses has been adjusted in uRMF to the more logical sequence of **B**. But *lente* 243 shows **C** revising towards a consistent use of preterite finite forms, Greed describing what he did 'in his youth'. *R–K*'s alteration of both to infinitives is thus inadvisable. **245–46 (B 246–47)** Bx's verb-tenses are first present, then preterite, and Cx could have alternated likewise (mixture of tenses is not uncharacteristic: see on 3.13). However, the preterite attested at C 246 is

not certainly even sub-archetypal, and the revision may have deliberately held back a past-tense verb until 247 to contrast the occasional act of one of Greed's victims with his own habitual practice. Given the *repetitio* of forms of *lenen* (six times in seven lines), *R–K*'s alteration of *lene* 246 to *lede* is indefensible on grounds of sense or style.

B 253–61 B 253 The Bx line has the inauthentic metrical pattern *aa / xa*. As in C 3.139, simple transposition to prose order has occurred, with loss of the needed key-stave (here the voiced labial stop |b|). Both earlier emendations, *for pure nede* for *mote nedes* (*K–D*) and *purely mote* for *mote* (*Sch¹*), which it prompted, become otiose once 'cognative alliteration' is recognised as part of **L**'s practice. **261** *heyres*: γ+M, here accepted for **B**, although the agreement of L and (almost certainly) α suggests that Bx read *ysue*. Presumably all beneficiaries, whether bodily descendants or not, were intended, and γ's correction may have anticipated this by commonsense or in awareness of the **C** reading (cf. V 441); see MED s.v. *issue* n. 3 (a) and entries in *IG*.

258 *weyhtes*: the clearest spelling of what is, in context, almost certainly the precise sense of the original. The reversed spelling of XY (a reflex of their immediate ancestor's) and the more familiar uP² form indicate that *x¹* quite probably read *wyhtes*, an ambiguous spelling of the lexeme meaning 'weights'. The form of the **p** variants (with RFS here coinciding with uP²) would suggest that Cx likewise read thus. The contextually plausible majority **p** reading accepted by *R–K* could have been generated through the influence of a common collocation ('word and wit') and the proximity of *wit* (here 'intelligence applied to sharp practices'). But in context 'weights' is harder, more apt and avoids anticipating 261, 264, and so should be preferred. **267** scans as a Type IIIb on vowels, though it would read better with stresses on lexical words. Either the a-half could have verb and noun-phrase transposed in both archetypes or *on* could be emended to *vpon* (so *C-F*), with the break coming after *pynched*. **273–74 (B XIII 385–86)** The Cx line 273 scans *aa / xx* before and *xa / ax* after re-lineation. Both are inauthentic metrical patterns and on the showing of // **B** the parenthetical phrase *woot God* may be restored to provide the a-half's second stave, lost through eyeskip from *wi*lle to *wi*tterly, with resulting mislineation due to the wish for a line of adequate length. Following **B**, the word-order is **x**'s and the initial negative is omitted as in **p**. The line as emended forms one of 23 in succession only slightly altered from **B** (13.366–99*a*, with omissions). In B 385, unless coincidental, omission of *I* by L and R (possibly < β and α respectively) may indicate its absence from Bx; but the γF reading (that of **C**) is preferable. **280 (B XIII 394)** *with my*: possibly also the original reading in **B**, from which Bx could have lost *my* (like *C*-eRM). Alternatively, *with / my* β-R / F could be split variants of the same form in Bx, loss of *my* having been caused by semi-haplography before *moneie*. But the issue of sense is too slight to justify emendation.

B 266 (C 289) The form of Bx seems reasonably secure in the light of revised **C**. It contained the phrase *of þyne* before the mid-line break, so F's incoherent variant may be seen as attempting to provide a lexical *p* stave in the b-half, with consequential smoothing of the preceding phrase, which has partly determined its form. The wG reading is a (probably coincidental) levelling of the asseveration to a more familiar form. Once a mute 'cognative' stave on *bi* has been identified for the b-half as the Bx reading (< ?gLMR), conjectural emendations such as *For pyne of my soule* (*K–D*, p. 187) and *so God pyne my soule in helle* (*Sch¹*) become otiose.

290 (B 268) *Thow*: the **x**-reading with omission of the conjunctive particle seems more idiomatic and closer to the source-line. Pe's stop after *wiste* and retention of ms X's inserted *ȝif* gives a logical but (in context) inappropriate meaning. **297 (B 275)** *Ys haldyng / Beeþ holden*: not different in sense, but the more colloquial variant with a sg. verb after antecedent pl. *alle* at 296 // 273 and a form of the past participle resembling the present is likelier to be original. In **B**, the clear differentiation of γ from LM in relation to the verb is blurred over choice of the participial form, only R retaining the one identified as original. In **C**, support cuts across both families as to the form of both, implying substantive equivalence.

B 276a–82 276a Between the psalm-verse cited and 277 α has a line scanning *aa / xx* (cf. 282 below) that resists emendation and adds nothing, but disrupts the flow of sense from 276a to 277. It may be an intrusion by the α scribe prompted by memorial anticipation of Piers's rôle as 'servant of Truth' in 540–50 below. F corrupts further by omitting the crucial 276a *Ecce enim in veritatem* that elucidates 276b ('wher I mene truþe'). **277** is a satisfactory Type Ib with a full rhetorical stress on *wiþ*, a word often muted in key-stave position (e.g. at B Pr 22). **282** expresses an important motif which recurs, with the same quotation following and a line about mercy preceding, at B 11.139. In principle, the *aa / xx* scansion could indicate a typical scribal addition introducing a Latin quotation. But the defective metre is easily emended by conjecturing *His* (= *eius* in the Latin) as the original supplanted by an unmetrical and obviously more explicit term (for a parallel conjecture see C 6.307 and cf. 173 above). The line will now scan as an extended Type IIIa with counterpoint (*abb / ax*). Both are rejected as spurious by *K–D* (p. 193) on insufficient grounds.

306–08 *Pe* suggests that the original may have consisted of 306a and 307a, the first asseveration having come in from 296b and then been amplified in **p** by addition of a second in 307b. This would certainly give a more economical line. The twofold oath must therefore be

defended as expressing Repentance's indignation at Coveitise, as the tone of 294 sufficiently implies. Metrically, 307 is an acceptable Type IIIa line scanning on |k| in **p**. But there are reasons of sense and style for preferring vocalic alliteration in this line since *arste*, whether as here spelled or more suggestively as spelled in **p**, provides sardonic wordplay on both *ers* 305 and *errant* 306. The simple emendation *Hym* (with which may be compared the conjectured readings at B 282 and the parallel case at 21.12) presumes on grounds of sense that *Cryst* is scribal. For **L** normally keeps distinct the functions of the Persons of the Trinity and, though the Creator becomes creature in another context (B 16.215), does not speak of Christ the incarnate Second Person as 'Creator' (notwithstanding 16.165, where reference is to the theological notion of 'New Creation' through Baptism).

309–10 (Z 124–25, A 229–30, B 456–57) The lines on Evan the Welshman are a revised transposition of B 456–59, a passage of uncertain form that retains a text close to **A** and possibly **Z** (see Vol I, pp. 236–7), all three earlier versions appearing corrupt at the same point. On the face of it, the a-half of B 456 // A 229 (*And yet wole I yelde ayein*) preserved in the larger families *B-β*, *A-r* could be accepted as satisfactory in metre (Type IIa) and sense (as main clause taking a noun-clause object represented by B 457=A 230) and as identical with C 309–10 but for the latter's first two words *Hyhte ȝeuan*. The presumptive α reading *what I nam* R, of which F's variant is a modernising reflex, could thus be dismissed as an attempt to provide an object for *yelde* after failure to construe the grammar of the Bx reading preserved in β. What questions this account is the possible support of α by *A*-**m** and **Z**. The evidence for **m** is fragmentary: only H³ preserves the posited reading, but with *euer* inserted as an intensifier after *Qwat*; A lacks the line; E reads with **r**; and M rewrites the half-line under influence from following 232a (though *euerche man* could derive from **What euer ich nam*, the error being initiated by transposing the consonants in *nam*). Agreement of **m** and α could be due to ⊗ of **m** from a B-Text of α type; such ⊗, where identified in Passus V, is in principle as likely to have been from a source later than, as from one anterior to, the generation of the **B** sub-archetypes. Support for this diagnosis may be at hand in **Z**'s apparently senseless *Quod ye nan*, resoluble as a visual error for **Quad y nam*. Hanna (*YLS* 7:18n, following Kane 1985:919–20) reads *ye nan* in **Z** as *yeuan*, the line thus becoming a clear echo of C 6.309. On the other hand, *n / u* minim confusion is hard to settle definitively without recourse to the local context of meaning. Another objection to this interpretation is that the posited appearance of 'Evan the Welshman' in **Z** is neither prepared for as in **C** nor syntactically integrated with what precedes and follows in **Z**. Thus, if *yelde ayeyn* in **Z** is taken as part of the speaker's name as in **C**, there is no main verb; if not, it is an infinitive lacking an expected (but understood) verb of volition, such as **A** and **B** provide. If, then, the hypothetical reading underlying **Z**'s *Quod ye nan* is *Quad y nam*, and the speaker still Sloth (cf. Z 5.110), it may be explained either as an **m**-type **A** variant derived through ⊗ from an α-type **B** source, or as an authentic early reading forming, like those of **m** and α, *part* of the proposed reconstructed text of **AB** *And yet what I nam wole I yelde ayein*, with *And yet* and *what I nam* identified as split variants. The verb *yelde* will then have *two* noun-clause objects, one preceding and one following it, and the posited split will have been occasioned in both sub-archetypes by the line's length and the grammar's unexpected complexity. The **C** revision, which is textually unproblematic, now replaces the *whole* phrase *And yet what I nam* by *Hyhte ʒeuan* (naming a character new to the Sins-sequence who is introduced by the explanatory line 308), and not merely by *one or other* of the parts of the phrase preserved in **r**β and **m**α. There would thus be a good case for reconstructing **Z** to accord with the form now adopted for **A** and **B**. But an *alternative* interpretation is to see **Z**'s reading not as a corrupt reflex of this reconstructed form but as an early version having as the first two words of the a-half a difficult Latin phrase *Quodque mnam* (the noun perhaps ambiguously spelled *nam*). *R–B* (p. 83) offer this as their second explanation of the crux, detecting a reference to the text of Lk 19:11–27 cited at B 6.238ff. The form *Quodque* would result from mistaking feminine *m(i)na* as neuter. This difficult conjecture is tentatively preferred here as the form likeliest to have generated the surviving reading in ms Z, although corruption of a Latin stave-phrase is admittedly very rare in the *PP* tradition as a whole. The consequences for the textual history of the passage are accordingly as follows. **Z** is an early version, *semantically* difficult in character, which was revised to an **A** form exhibiting *metrical* and *syntactic* difficulty. Since the **Z** line is macaronic, its scansion could permit the licence often found in such lines, giving *xaa / bb* (*mnám, yélde, ayéyn; Ý, háue*). But a small emendation of *yf* to *yyf*, which is the **A** form (though not there strictly needed for the metre), makes the line one of Type Ia with muted key-stave and the Latin phrase now forming the anacrusis.

311 (Z 126, A 231, B 458) *my*: slightly less hard than *me* XY (supported by **Z**B-R). But whilst the reading with *my* could mean both (a) 'though I lack means to live' and (b) 'though my standard of living suffer', and that with *me* can mean only (a), both are compatible with the declaration in 313–14. **312 (Z 127, A 232, B 459)** *That*: in constructions like this often having a preclusive sense 'but that' (cf. 7.61, and K² in App; and see MED s.v. *that* conj.1 (d), with citation from Grimestone). Accordingly *shal* **p**, confirmed by **ZAB**, is to be preferred as correct. **316 (Z 132, A 236, B 463)** *And*: certain in **BC**

and presumably a revision to avoid weakening the adversative force of *Ac* in 317//. This 'improvement' is anticipated by **A** mss from both **r** groups and **m**, so need not be due to ⊗ from **B**, and *Ac* may be accepted as = Ax since it is supported by **Z**. -*wyth* **ZAC**: adopted as the **B** original, Bx being a pointless ⇒ of the contextually near-synonymous *of* (cf.the *contrast* between the two in 15.241). **317 (Z 133, A 237, B 464)** *Ac*: in A 237 assured on grounds of superior sense and support from **ZBC**; but here, by contrast, it is Ax that may have 'improved' and the VLN reflex could well show influence from **B**. **319 (Z 135, A 239, B 466)** reads identically in all three archetypes and also in **Z**, if *the* is there presumed lost by haplography. The only acceptable scansion is as extended Type IIIa (*axx / ax*) on |ð| (*Tho; the*). The *bismas* variants in *B*-R, *C*-UVK must be regarded as scribal attempts to make the line normative, not as reflexes of an original mistakenly 'corrected' by the other mss. The name of the 'Good Thief' is uniformly attested as Dismas (see *Commentary*). **321 (Z 137, A 243, B 468)** *me*: the certain reading only of **Z** but probable for **C** and possible for both **A** and for **B** (where F may have it from an **A** source, Hm more probably from **C**). **ZC** agreement need not in this instance be significant, since **p** could have supplied as a commonsense emendation a word that might have appeared omitted in Cx. *Robert*: firmly attested in **ZAC** and providing a better grammatical fit with the 1st person verb *haue* than does *Robbere* Bx, which may have been prompted through distraction from 462 above and the -*ere* ending of *Redd*ere. **322 (Z 138, A 244, B 469)** *with...knowe*: 'by means of any skill I have knowledge of', supported by **ZACB**-α, is preferable to 'that which I owe' (*sc.* the goods he has stolen). *A*-N may here show ⊗ from a **B** source of β-type. **323 (Z 141, A 245, B 470)** Ø **ZC** / *But* **AB**: presumably added in **A**, retained in **B** and then deleted again in **C** (cf. the omission of *Ac* Z 145 / A 247 at B 472 / C 326). **327 (Z 147, A 249, B 474)** *coupe*: harder than the competing variant *gilt*, which would give a cognatively-scanning line; firmly attested by **ZC**, it could well have been in *B*-α here (but the evidence is wanting). In the Ax tradition, *coupe* is likely to have been the reading of **m**, of which the genetically-related members <MH³> have varied to the **r** reading also attested by *B*-β (cf. 350, where *coupe* is secure in **BC** but subject to variation in **A**). *to...eftsones*: in **Z** the reading is as probably a scribal error as a metrically imperfect draft original; the metre of the b-half can be corrected by transposition to the **AB** order, which is confirmed for the final phrase by **C**. *R–K* adjust the direct and indirect objects in **C** to accord with **AB**, but revision may have occurred here (see next note). **328 (Z 148, A 250, B 475)** *penaunce* **p** (for *Penitencia* **ZAB**): only possibly archetypal, though preferable for sense to *Repentaunce* **x**, which was perhaps prompted by the appearance of this name at 330 below. In

315–29 the other four personifications have Latin names and, unless there is revision here, both **p** and **x** readings could be 'translation-splits' of a Cx reading identical with that of **ZAB** (so *R–K*), or perhaps one Englished from **C** as *penitence*, a word of quasi-technical register (see MED). *wolde* **ZC** / *sholde* **AB**: probably a non-significant clash, since **Z** here shows no ⊗ from **C**'s revised a-half. After 328 *R–K* insert B 476, presumed lost for no obvious reason, which completes but is not absolutely necessary to the sense. However, since the idea of 'walking in the right path' is taken up in *romest* 330, deliberate omission may be understood. **334 (B 284)** *fonk*: like *flonke* a rare word, each instanced only once outside **L** in the C14th, in Gower and the *Gawain*-poet (see MED s.vv. *fonk, flaunk*). D has doubtless drawn on a **p** source but P² has substituted an easier synonym. *inmiddes*: conjectured as the missing stave-word in Bx's unmetrical b-half on the showing of **C**'s *amydde* (with which cf. also *amed-des* 9.122). The word may have been lost because it is required to act as a full stave, whereas stressing *þe sée* in accord with sense and syntax will reduce it to a mute stave in a 7-syllable antepenultimate dip. **336–37** As divided in both **x** and **p**, 336 has the unmetrical form *aa / xx*, while 337 in **p** is Type Ie and in **x** Type IIIa. The basic **p** form of 336 is adopted since, after emendation of Cx *with* to *myd*, it provides a line with grammatically superior separation of the subject and anticipatory adverbial phrase from the three verbs that together convey a logically ordered moral sequence. (The recessive preposition *myd* as a stave is found at 4.73 and 16.180; here ⇒ of *with* in Cx may have been unconsciously induced by final *wille*.) **345** remains after revision of Type IIIc, despite replacement of *is* by *be*, the break being unlikely to fall after *beste*.

A V 148 (B 299) *Ac*: conjectured as the **m** reading underlying *Bot* EM. That of **r** was possibly Ø as in HN, the two variants in W and V appearing attempts to find an appropriate connective, whilst *And* T&r shows the obvious reading adopted by the majority under influence from preceding and following *And*.

353 (A 149, B 300) In both **C** and **A**, though occupying different halves of the line, 353a / 149b each have two full staves, **C** scanning as Type Ia, **A** as Type IIb. But to scan at all (on vowels), Bx requires that the adverb become a trisyllabic dip (as is possible but not necessary in **A**), giving an awkward rhythm and stress-pattern in the b-half. The reconstruction assumes transposition of the adverbial phrase and verb-phrase in Bx and gives a line scanning on |w| as Type IIIb, an extended variant with vocalic counterpoint in the a-half, if both verb and pronoun are stressed, as in **A**. **356 (A 152, B 303)** Although **C** deletes it in revising, *quaþ heo* is here judged to have been in **AB**, and omitted in **m** (though added in M) perhaps through eyeskip to 153 or 154. **357 (A 153, B 304)** *Hastow*: in **C** certain, in **A** almost so, on the strength of *r¹***m** agreement.

The shortness of the line may have prompted the needless scribal filler *ought* in several **A** mss; but the fuller and more explicit *ought in þi pors* seems due in vN to ⊗ from a **B** source, as elsewhere in Passus V (see below on 163). Bx itself appears more obviously scribal on comparison with **AC**, and is accordingly emended. **361 (A 158, B 308)** *Souhteres / sywestre*: either reading giving acceptable sense and metre, the former being perhaps the harder, since female shoemakers were presumably less common than seamstresses. *Sywestre* may thus be a scribal ⇒ of a more expected expression, and *B-B* (which has it) could have derived this reading from a **C**-source of **p** type, while *B-M*'s *sowsteresse* is an amalgam of both variants. If Ax read *sowsteresse*, it will have been revised in **B**, since Bx unmistakably has *souteresse*. **A-V**'s scribally explicit *souters wyf* is shared by **C**-P² and (with visible addition a.h.) **C**-D. **362 (A 159, B 309)** *warinar*: discriminated for **A** in the light of **BC** as the likely *r²* reading, itself possibly a correction (from a **B** source) of a damaged exemplar reading *we(r):::* or *wa(r):::*, variously supplemented or supplanted in *r¹* and **m**. **363 (A 160, B 310)** *Tymme*: a name of uncertain form in all versions, the extensive *Symme* variant in **A** and **B** mss probably pointing to the vowel as having been *y*, and the *Thomme* variant to the initial consonant as *t*. In either instance, a more familiar name has been intruded in place of one found nowhere else in the poem (*Tomme* appears at 5.130 //, *Symme* at 6.207 //). *knaues*: well-established in **AC** and so presumptively in **B**, *prentices* Bx being a seemingly pointless ⇒, though neither metrically nor stylistically objectionable. **364 (A 161, B 311)** The spelling-form adopted for *Hugh* in **A** is that of **B**, which is also instanced in *A*-E.

A 163, 167 (B 313, 317, C 366, 372) It is uncertain whether these (undoubtedly authentic) lines were in **A**. The main authority is **m**, from which in principle vN may have borrowed them. As they were not in **r**, both **m** and vN could have adopted them from a **B** source which, on the evidence of vN's reading at 153 and that of **m** at 109, was post-Bx. But against this explanation A 178, an authentic line (it is also in **C**) supported by both **m** and ?*r²*, is *absent* from Bx. If 163 was in Ax, its omission by **r** could be due to censorship; but no such reason appears for the omission of 167. This second case, and possibly also the first, may be instances of 'farcing' of Ax with lines from a section of **B** well known and popular (cf. the rejected lines in **m** and some other copies after 31, 42, 110 above and 190, 200 below). **366** *Peres*: this name is erased here in X, as very frequently in its later appearances, referring to Piers Plowman. The point is not noticed further and the reason for it (possibly precautionary) remains uncertain. **373 (A 168, B 318)** *of*: on the strength of **AC** agreement to be seen as lost from Bx (and from *A*-RUHJA) through failure to grasp the partitive genitive construction. *And* and *of* appear split variants of the Ax reading preserved in VH³. **382 (A 176, B 326)** *Tho*: erroneously supplanted by *Two* in one each of the **BC** sub-archetypes and four **A** copies. This is probably due to an ambiguous archetypal spelling *To* (attested e.g. in *C*-YI), the relative rareness of the pronoun (*tho* being commonest as temporal adverb / conjunction, as illustrated by the error in *B*-F), and (in the C-Text) by a contextual expectation of reference to the (two) *arbitreres* of the barter named at 381. **384 (A 178, B 328)** is securely preserved, in revised form, only in **C**. The **A** variants may point to a lacuna in Ax, **m** alone (with which H partially accords) giving a complete line. One sub-family (*r¹*) omits 178b and runs 178a into 179, while ?*r²* has an empty reading with *hoso* (W has its own equally vapid form). Finally, the line is lost from LK, perhaps through eyeskip from *togideris* 176, 179 (they have also lost 177). A mechanical explanation of Bx's almost certain loss of 328 would be haplography due to repetition of initial *And*; like 338, it was probably in **B**, since it is present in **C** (with revised b-half) as well as **A**; but its precise **B** form is undeterminable. Accordingly, since **m**'s reading may itself be a scribal conjecture (though a better one than *r²*'s), the **C** form is here adopted for **B** (contrast B 338 below). **385 (A 179, B 329)** The diverse a-half corruptions of the initial pronoun in the **A** mss may arise from Ax having read *Tho*. One variant *tweyne* suggests that **m** read *two*, an easy misconstruction of pronominal *Tho* spelled *To in its exemplar (cf. on A 5.176). Another, *þen* d, might reflect misreading of the same word as the adverb *tho* 'then' (cf. on *B*-F's variant at B 326), with subsequent insertion of a supposedly necessary pronoun *þey*. **386 (A 180, B 330)** *þei bysouȝte*: safely reconstructed for **B**'s b-half as a revision of **A** identical with **C**. The source of Bx's error will have been ȝ / þ confusion generating the contextually nonsensical *souþe*, perhaps preceded by *Hy* [for *þey*] *by*, giving the reading *by þe southe preserved in β. This was vulnerable to the further corruption witnessed in α following misconstruction of *souþe* as a noun, and β will then have smoothed the (now ungrammatical) infinitive to a preterite so as to produce a half-line with at least some surface sense. (For further examples of similar ambiguous spellings cf. 163 //). **390 (A 184, B 334)** Unless contaminated from a **B** source (on which see 394), **x** may be accepted as preserving the original a-half fragmentarily attested in GK (?< *p²*) and grammatically simplified in *p¹*, to which N has here varied (perhaps following comparison with a ms of *p¹* type). **391 (A 185, B 335)** *repentede*: clearly preterite in **BC**, the present-tense forms in **A** mss (and in *C*-MK, which *R–K* adopt) probably reflecting yet again a tense-ambiguous Ax reading *repentit or *repente* (as in **m**), each identifiable as a spelling variant of the normal past-tense form. **392 (A 186, B 336)** *of*: retained as acceptable, though *Ø* is probably original in **AB** and possibly also in **C** (to judge by the striking case at 335). **393 (A 187, B 337)** *louryng*:

the rejected *lakeryng* **p** is a uniquely instanced form, glossed by MED as 'noisy revelry', but suggested by *Sk* (*Gl.*, s.v.) as derived from *lakkeren, an (unrecorded) frequentative form of *lakken* 'reproach'. More probably it is *likeryng*, also a hapax, which MED implies may be a gradational variant of the latter. *Sk*'s guess 'frowning' (*Gl.*, s.v.) on the basis of Sc. *lucken* 'knit the brows' is, however, attractive, making it a contextually apt synonym for *louryng* which could easily have generated the other four **p** variants. But while as an obviously harder reading it could be judged a revision, *louryng* **x** is unlikely to be a ⊗ from **B** (for the opposition of 'laughing' and 'louring' cf. also A 8.107, which has no **BC** //). **394 (A 188, B 338)** No reason appears, except possibly anticipation of the verb in 339, for Bx's loss of this line, which may be confidently restored on the joint showing of **AC** (cf. B 5.328 above). The form adopted for the b-half here is **A**'s, though there is no serious question that Cx read *þo* (lost in **p** by partial haplography) and *awake*, a convincingly original revision, for which *p¹ aryse* could be a scribal ⇒ prompted by recalling the hypothesised **B** form (cf. on 390).

A 189 (B 339, C 95) *vmwhile*: easily borrowed by the **A** copies NJ from **B** or **C** to correct the Ax reading *sumwhile*. The latter, while not obviously wrong on grounds of sense or metre, is probably a scribal synonym for a regionally restricted term, and perhaps partly induced by the line's environment of heavy *s*-alliteration. **397 (B 341)** is present in *A*-**m** and could be argued to have been lost in **r** by eyeskip from *(v)mwhile* 189 to *Paternoster-while* 191 (though in that case 190 would presumably also have been lost). It is perhaps best regarded as another example of **m**'s 'farcing' the A-Text from a **B** source, as again after A 200. **399 (A 193, B 343)** *And* **p**: syntactically preferable here to *A* **x**, despite support for the pronoun against the conjunction from *A*-J?**m** and *B*-R. The latter all read *He*, a reflex of a presumed group-original *A*, which could have been smoothed to *And* in **r** and β**F** or else be a visual error for original *And*.

A 196 (B 347, C 403) The b-half could have been lost from **r** by *r¹* and the *r²* copies JK coincidentally, though no mechanical reason for the loss appears. Alternatively, vN may have corrected from **m** or, as elsewhere, from a **B** source, as has the *r¹* ms U, which shows definite signs of **B** ⊗ after 200. **A 198 (B 349, C 405)** *leiþ*: preferred for **A** in the light of **B** (confirmed by **C**), which is unlikely to be a revision. Ax could have read a tense-ambiguous form *leit (cf. on A 5.185 above) and vM have corrected from **B**. **407 (A 200, B 351)** *thromblede*: reliably established for Cx on the agreement of **x** and ?*p²*, N (randomly joined by <PE>, M and P²) having independently varied to the commonplace scribal conjecture *stumblede* also attested in *B*-γ and Ax. The form of the difficult word's first syllable is reliably suggested by the *C*-R<QFS> variant. Either *trom- or *trem- was the probable Bx reading (> Lα, *B*-M here having visibly altered from a γ source). The origin of *A*-V's right reading is unlikely to be a copy in the Ax or Bx traditions, so it must be either a felicitous guess or correction from a good **C** ms. The hardest reading in sense and form, it is on metrical grounds the only acceptable variant attested. It was possibly even an invention of **L** (MED s.v. *thrumblen* v. gives the only other example from Malory, in a different sense).

408–13 (B 352–57) The presence of these lines in *A*-m is most probably due to borrowing from a **B** source; despite corruptions, they transmit a text unmistakably that of **B**, not of **C** (see Vol. I, Appendix I). Their possible presence in Ax and subsequent loss by **r** are not explained by mechanical or other features. The lines are not in vN, which elsewhere in Passus V show signs of drawing on **B**; but their presence in U reveals at least one scribe of an **r**-type ms judging it worthwhile to incorporate a vivid and (after the success of **B**) doubtless popular passage in his text. In the light of the cases of probable 'farcing' in the Sins sequence noted above, it needs little prudence to reject them as not part of the original A-Text. **410 (B 354)** *greued*: here taken as a past participle (see MED s.v. *greven* v. 3a (a)), harder than the more obvious *gronyd*, a possible visual error. *R–K*'s ⇒ of the **B** reading *grym* has no warrant on grounds of sense or metre. **419 (A 206, B 363)** *spake* CA: forming either lift 2 of a Type IIIa line or, less probably, part of the dip in a Type Ia line, with *was* providing the second stave-word and a |w| pronunciation posited for *who*. Agreement of **AC** against Bx here might point to *warp* as a case of scribal over-emphasis perhaps prompted by finding *was* too weak as a second full stave. But the criterion of **AC** agreement cannot be applied mechanically; occasional 'non-linear' revision could have occurred. Whilst *warp* gives better rhythm, its very hardness might have prompted a **C** revision back to the form first used in *A* (the *B*-Hm ⇒ for Bx, if not ⊗ from **C**, might also be aiming at clarity); the criterion of *durior lectio* cannot be applied mechanically either (see *Intro.* IV § 28). *Warp* in this usage occurs earlier at B 5.86, of which 5.363 could be a scribal recollection. But since that line was not in *A* and is omitted from **C**, which thus contains *no* instances of *warp*, **L**'s early and later judgement of this verb as insufficiently plain does not preclude his use of it in revising A 5.206. The word also occurs in A 4.142 and 10.33, the former not in **BC** but supported by **Z**, the latter revised in **B** to *spak* (unless this is a Bx ⇒). **420 (A 207, B 364)** is textually certain in **C**, with its wordplay, and virtually so in *A*. That the metrically-required *wytyd* was the first stave seems sure from its being the probable **m** reading (> EA) reflected in H³ *wyssyd*, a weaker idea expressed in a word of similar form unconsciously influenced by the visual likeness of *witen* 'know'. M, the other member of **m**, in this case *joins*

r in ⇒ of the advancing synonym *blamide*. V's *warnede* corrects the metre while ignoring the available alliterating synonym for *blamide* **r**. The **m** reading strongly indicates its independent descent from Ax, since ⊗ from a post-Bx source, reliably inferrable elsewhere, is ruled out here. In the b-half, Ax corresponds partly to Bx and partly to **C**, but need not be judged to derive from the latter either. On the other hand, ⊗ from **C** or **A** could explain the reading *wif* in *B*-?w (from which M has here been visibly corrected), since Bx cannot have read other than *wit*. The latter, whilst a possible **B** alteration, later incorporated by **C**, that also echoed **A** (cf. note on 419 above), is likely to be *part* of a reading that included *wif* in the a-half, loss of *wit* being due to the length of the line, which was also revised in the b-half. As here reconstructed, **B** now contains a double subject for the reproach to Glutton, the line becoming Type Ic. **421 (A 208, B 367)** The a-half of the **C** line is so much closer to **A** (especially in its *r²*m form) than to **B** as to suggest 'non-linear' revision and direct reference back to the A-Text. However, the b-half clearly echoes the 'shriving' idea added in **B**, not that of **A**, and the **C** line now presents as a re-worked amalgam of the two earlier versions. Since no difference of sense arises, the word-order adopted is that of *r¹* supported by representatives of *r²* and **m**. **424** All copies save YIDQFS have *Y me* for *me*. The pronoun was probably in Cx, and while it could have been lost by haplography (as likewise in Bx) it is strictly redundant after earlier *Y*. **431 (B 374)** The reading of *C*-M might echo **B** or simply be offering a more familiar synonym for a harder word introduced in **C** apparently for the wordplay.

B 375–82 375 *feestyng*: the sin of *delicacye* envisaged here is contrasted with a different offence, against Church discipline, three lines later. Bx *fastyng* may be taken as a visual error for the conjectured word, partly induced by the presence of the more familiar phrase in 378. **377** scans cognatively with a mute key-stave on *to* as a T-type. No emendation is required on grounds of sense: Glutton eats in taverns for the sake of the drink (an idea echoed in // C 6.433b) as well as the scandalous gossip to be had there. **378** *it*: conjectured as the necessary stave-word (here mute) in a line with the pattern *aa / xx* in Bx. The idiom combines a generalising sg. subject (denoting a class of situations) with a pl. verb (following a noun-phrase complement in the plural). F's attempted 'correction' gives a line with an inauthentic pattern (*aa / bb*). **380 (Z 104, A 209)** has no // in **C** and is closer to **Z** than to **A** in the a-half, suggesting either reference back to **Z** in revising or an echo of **B** in **Z**, at the scribal stage of its production. The former alternative seems more probable in the light of the **C** echo of **A** at 421. But *sorwe* **Z** is not an echo of **B**, which retains *doel* from **A**. **382 (Z 106, A 211)** *faste* ZB; *to faste* **A**. The Ax reading eliminates the wordplay in **Z**?**B**, which would allow *faste* to be both adverb and infinitive (though *to* would be normal after *auouen*). Addition of *to* to *B*-M is presumably the result of comparison with a γ-source, the original M reading having been as L (= β) and R (= α). *for...furste*: the adopted form (**BC-p**) is in contention with *for eny hunger or furste* Z*C*-**x** as the reading for the b-half in all versions. Cross-family distribution of support amongst the **A** mss and the clear attestation of **B** may be allowed to decide. **436 (Z 105, A 210, B 381)** *lyf* **x**, which is confirmed by the witness of preceding **ZAB**, here has the sense 'living' (MED s.v. *lif* n.5(c)), which the **p** variant explicitly spells out, but at the expense of the polysemy.

Passus VII (ZA V, B V and XIII)

Collation For 176–269 the *C*-interpolations in Digby 145 (K[2]) are selectively collated after **p**. **7 (B V 392)** *romede* **x**: 'roared' as in **B** where *rored* could be a visual error or deliberate ⇒. MED s.v. *romien* v. (c) records the subsidiary sense 'arouse oneself', also appropriate in context, but not 'stretched' (*Pe* Glossary). The **p** variant *remed* 'yawned' or 'cried out' (MED s.v. *remen* v. (1), (4)) is also apt here and occurs in participial form at 20.103. But the rarer *romede* is the harder and so more probably original form (P[2]'s modernising ⇒ is a gloss on one of the sub-archetypal variants). **9 (B 394)** revises the b-half to give a Type Ia line in place of the Type IIb with a liaisonal stave on *quod_he* in **B**. There is no reason for suspecting the Bx b-half of being a ⇒ for an original identical with **C**, for Sloth here expresses *wanhope* rather than terror of death as in **C**.

B 400 (C 15) The Bx reading *yet* gives the inauthentic scansion *aa / xx*. But the point seems to be not that Sloth 'furthermore' or 'until this day' lacked sorrow for sins but that he felt no continuing sorrow for them *after* confession, as he should have (in order to be deterred from future sin). The ⇒ of *yet* for conjectured *sipenes* was evidently an easy one (cf. C 7.29, Apparatus, where it replaces *thenne*) and could have been induced by *foryete* at 398. If Bx's exemplar had *sennes* or *synnes* for both the adverb (as in Z 6.16, 7.266) and the noun, it could have been mistakenly deleted as dittography (as likewise in B[1]). This would have motivated both the Bx ⇒ and **C**'s revision of a now metrically imperfect line. **17** *ten*: officiously altered (after **B**) to *two* by *R–K*, who overlook the change of *two* B 415 to *ten* at C 29. **20 (B 405)** *puyre selde*: emending a Bx line with inauthentic scansion *aa / xx*, that has a ⇒ of the familiar (but here unmetrical) adverb *ful* for the rarer (and more characteristic) one of **C**. As with 15 (B 400), **C** correction of Bx's metrical defectiveness in the b-half seems to have prompted further revision of the last lift, here away from the T-Type of reconstructed **B** to a standard Type Ia, probably with muted key-stave. Cf. the revision of B 407 in C 22, which

follows **B**'s IIb structure but with a different stave-sound. **27 (B 412)** *mengen I of*: conjectured to emend a ?Bx line scanning imperfectly as *aax / xx*, and needing a stave-word on *m* in the b-half. F's variant (if not a reflex of α) offers a verb with implied sense of 'motion towards' which could have easily invited ⇒ of the obvious *go*, and is used by *K–D* for their emendation *moste to* (so *Sch*[1]). But the verb preferred here is one echoed in the revised **C** b-half, where the sense of the latter is less likely to be 'remember [to go to]' than 'be remembered at' (MED s.v. *memorie* n. 2(a), 4(b)). Sloth is here understood to *recall* that he can safely arrive late at the Friary Church without risk of the rebuke his parish-priest would give him. Bx, on this diagnosis, will have replaced a verb of intention with a more explicit verb of motion.

B 415–20 415 (C 29) *telle I vp gesse*: the Bx b-half is the fourth non-alliterating key-stave in fifteen lines. Bx seems to have substituted a more explicit and emphatic verb *shryue* (so as to augment the gravity of the offence) and then inverted adverb and verb as part of a process of smoothing. The conjecture of *K–D* (p. 181) adopted provides a necessary stave-word in *t* based on the revised b-half. The C Version, as in 15 and 20 above, has revision in the last lift. **420 (C 34)** *clausemele* **B**: the harder reading (the word is found only here), which β has smoothed after mistaking the adverb for a combination of the noun and a different adverb of similar visual shape (cf. *Parcelmele* B III 81). Revised **C**'s form and redundancy of sense indicate that *it* (omitted) may be an insertion in α. **34 (B 422)** *Catoun*: **x** supported by two **p**-sources is here judged likelier to be original than *canon* (e, q, GK), despite apparent support for the latter from **B**. The **C** line is revising two **B** lines, 420 and 422, increasing Sloth the Priest's ignorance to the point where he cannot read a Latin school text let alone the Psalter or a tome of Canon Law. It is unlikely that the <RM> ancestor here has ⊗ from an **x**-source or independent ⇒ of *Catoun* but quite possibly retains the reading of **p** (< Cx), from which e and q have each convergently varied. The likelihood of this is strengthened if N's reading (agreeing with RM) is that of *p*[2] and not an individual scribal correction, from whatever source. **35 (B 423)** *bygge*: 'buy', *ytayled* doubtless recording an act of borrowing connected with the purchase. Even if the original form of the verb was *begge* (so *C*-XUDG, *B*-Cr[1]GR), choice of the text-spelling is dictated by need to avoid ambiguity, the phrase 'beg or borrow' being irrelevant. **36 (B 424)** Choice is between (a) vocalic scansion of the line (reading *if*) as Type Ie or as an extended IIIb with counterpoint, and (b) scansion on |j| (reading *ʒyf*) as a Type Ia line with muted key-stave (in **B**) or as a T-Type line in **C**. The alternative (b) is preferable, since this allows a more natural emphasis, throwing the a-half stresses onto lexical words. The witness of LR suggests that Bx may indeed have read *ʒif*; but Cx seems to have read *yf*.

B 440 (53) *yarn*: conjectured as the necessary first stave-word in **B**, for which the advancing verb-form appears a Bx ⇒. This preterite is found in stave-position at B 11.60, and for a parallel case see *C*-**p**, *B*-β and Ax at 3.269 // (Apparatus). In revision, *yarn* is replaced with a near-synonym less vulnerable to corruption and the b-half of the line further revised (cf. note on 20 above). **54 (B 441)** *beggere...(y)be be*: both Bx and Cx have the defective scansion *aa / xx* as a result of the same presumed corruption either by haplography (*(y)be* < *be*) or by deliberate deletion of *be²* through failure to grasp its sense 'for, on account of' (MED s.v. *bi* prep. 7a), followed by ⇒ of the same non-alliterating synonym (for parallels see 5.35, 6.155). In reconstructing, the word-order of **C** (noun; past participle) is adopted, necessitating inversion (in emending **B**) of what appears the likely Bx order. The minimal form (without *haue I*) in LR is identified as archetypal, *haue I* having been added by γ (and visibly so added from a γ-source by M), whether by ⊗ from **C** or by independent anticipation of **C**'s expanded form. **58 (Z 113, A 218, B 445)** *fro*: the form preferred for **B** (against *Sch¹*) is that attested by *C*-**pu**, **Z** and probably Bx, but in contention in **A**. Discrimination of *fro* as a preposition requires *wolde* to be part of a relative clause with Ø-subject (*that* is actually inserted in *A*-**m** as in **C**) and not as introduced by the subordinating conjunction *for*. *wolde* **x**: preferred to *wol* for all versions on the clear showing of **B** + **Z**A-**m**. **61 (B 448)** *þat...is*: an apparently logically necessary *nys* could have been lost through assimilation to preceding *-nesse*, with *is* then an archetypal ⇒. But the conjunction of *-nesse / nys* is uneuphonious, and idiomatic use of *is* following *þat* with a preclusive sense 'but that' (so actually K²) is attested elsewhere (cf. 6.312 //). In **A**, by contrast, choice between the two forms is influenced by the reading of **Z**, though arguably here too the negative particle should be omitted. **64 (Z 119, A 224, B 451)** *make*: Bx *lette* appears in the light of **ZAC** a scribal ⇒ of a more emphatic and explicit verb.

Z 124, A 229, B 456; Z 135; B 468, 474 For extended discussion of these cruces see the notes on **C 6.309–10, 315–29** above.

70 (B XIII 411) On the evidence of GYC (? = g), L, and R (= α), the Bx reading was the nonsensical *hys woman*, a visual error based perhaps on aspirated spelling of the verb and misreading of **wan a man* as *woman* together with inaccurate recollection of Glutton's wife at B 5.358–64. The emendation by w has been borrowed by M but F's is probably independent. However the <OC²>B correction, though evidently derived from **C,** is likely to be what **B** read (cf. on B 14.28 below). **83 (B XIII 424)** *in hope*: supplied in **B** to provide a vocalic key stave-word presumed lost in Bx through semi-haplography (*liþen hem / in hope*). The line scans as an extended Type IIIa with double counterpoint (*abb / ab*). **101 (B XIII 442)**

If Bx also read *ryche*, the anacoluthic conjunction *þat* reconstructed as the form underlying the variants *at / men at* F may have been inserted by α (β is defective here); but it could be authorial. **103 (B XIII 444)** *thy*: evidently the second of two grammatical words (*for* 'in place of' being the first) that bear strong sentence-stress. The Bx reading cannot be known for certain in the absence of β, but α may have substituted *þe* through inattention to the unusual distribution of stresses. R's *þe hey3*, possibly an auditory error for *thye* (as *the hye*), is unacceptable on grounds of sense, since the rich man would presumably not breach decorum in this way (any more than does Conscience the knight with the poor hermit Patience and Will at 15.42). **106 (B XIII 447)** *geste*: a shrewd scribal conjecture in ms F rightly adopted on grounds of sense by *Sk*, followed by *Pe* (who misattributes it to **B**, of which it is not the reading) and by *R–K* (see further *Intro.* IV § 34 above). Cx *feste* is inappropriate as Good Friday is not strictly a feast and the precise point being made is that the 'story' of Christ's heroic suffering teaches a different message from that of the *foul sage*. An attempt to emend a damaged exemplar, inducement from the *f*-alliteration, confused anticipation of 115 or unease over the secular associations of *geste* may all have helped towards the corruption. There are no other signs of revision in C 7.96–116, so Bx *storye* could conceivably be a simplifying scribal 'gloss' for *geste*; but it is unobjectionable in itself. **111 (B XIII 452)** *liþed*: the likely reading of the sole **B** witness α, presumably that of Bx, is harder, gives good sense and should be original. In **C** the variant *leued* (or *lened*) **x** is unsuitable in context, since L's concern is not so much with 'believing in' or even 'giving to' minstrels as with 'listening to' them (cf. 115, 118) and has doubtless been suggested by immediately preceding *lyue*. *Sk*'s substantive suggestion is accepted but the tense judged preterite as in the b-half (and in the **B** source, now seen to be unrevised). This contrasts with the present in 109–10, isolating the moment of death, which provides the subject's envisaged viewpoint. **113 (B XIII 454)** *for...so*: not absolutely necessary for the metre in **B**, since the Bx line will scan as a clipped Type IIIa with two lifts in the first lexical word (*wélhópe*). But the sense is sharpened by its presence, which identifies heaven as *mede* for the right dispensing of *mede* on earth. B 450–57 are otherwise unrevised except for *loued* 456, unless that is a Bx error for *lythed* (cf.*C*-**p** at 111 above). **123 (B V 482)** *liche*: revising to a Type IIIa line what may be in **B** a Type I, if *man* falls before the caesura. This would be unusual, and more probably *man* **B** belongs in the b-half while **C**'s omission of *moost* makes the line smoother with little loss of meaning. Vocalic scansion with mute key-stave as Type I is possible but inferior. **128 (B 487)** *sone*: *and* after *sone* in Bx is to be rejected as a redundant scribal insertion resulting from misunderstanding of the sense. **129 (B 488)** *secte*: having the sense of *sute* 'guise, attire' at 16.98 (= B 14.259), so *sute* **B** is unlikely to be a scribal ⇒ for it here. *B-W*'s *secte* is presumably a coincidental agreement with the revised line. The two words have considerable semantic overlap; see MED s.vv. *secte* n. 1(c), *sute* n. 1(a), 2(a). **131 (B 492)** *siht*: providing the necessary key-stave with *s* (though a liaisonal scansion *lees_liht* is possible). Cx ⇒ of *l* is through visual confusion with long *s*, unconscious association of sun with light and inducement from *liht* 132 as in several **B** copies, visibly in M (for the converse error in Ax, see A 1.110 and note on Z 58 //). *C-G* is presumably a felicitous correction, perhaps made in knowledge of **B**. On this more pregnant (as it is unquestionably the harder) reading, see the *Commentary*. **134 (B 495)** *The / And þe*: In **C** the construction is clear, with *lihte* as subject re-inforced pronominally (*hit*); if identical in **B**, then presumably misread in the a-half by Bx, which inserts ungrammatical *þoruȝ*, *was* being a further smoothing introduced by β. The reading with *þoruȝ* and without *it* is quite possible (with 495b parenthetical); but grammatically this would require *blewest* in 496 and contextually *liȝt* needs to be the subject of this active verb (*blewe* B 496, *brouhte* C 135), which describes a first action completed by a second (both duly realised in 20.368–69 //). **136 (B 497)** The proclitic is not strictly necessary for the metre, though the b-half reads more smoothly if *ȝedest* bears the stress and *Thow* is muted. This does not occur in Type IIIa lines, but *þer-* may function as a 'supplementary' stave in the a-half. Its loss in Bx could have been occasioned by distraction from *þ-* in preceding *þridde* and following *þow*. **138 (B 499)** *so¹ / Ø pB*: here **x**, now scanning as Type Id, is seen as a **C** revision that stresses the privileged way in which divine consolation is vouchsafed to sinners. *C-p* has lost the significance of *so¹* 'in this way' (echoed by *so²* in the b-half), perhaps through reading *al* and *so* as *also* and eyeskip to the following *solace*, *soffredest*. **152a (B 508)** *C-IU* (for 'U' read 'IU' in Apparatus) probably preserve by chance rather than by reference to **B** the correct lineation of two macaronic lines with unusually long b-halves followed by a free-standing Latin line.

  Z 151–2 (A 253–4) 151 *tho*: the temporal adverb clearly attested in **ABC** and the probable reading of **Z**, which sometimes omits / adds *h* (see e.g. 4.149, 6.95), rather than the redundant adverb *to* in a compound verb meaning 'to throng together'. **152** The **Z** form of this line has the unoriginal metrical pattern *aa / xx*, though the 'monolexical' structure of *mýsdédes* (*Intro.* IV p. 38) is authentic. **A**'s *wykkide dedis* could be a revision of a line unmetrical in the draft **Z**, or the reading for which the **Z**-*mysdedes* is a non-alliterating scribal synonym (though arguably the harder reading). But another possibility is that the **Z** original was more not less difficult than *mys-*

dedes while both having its metrical structure and providing the needed stave-sound in key-position. The extreme rarity of the conjectured word *wandedes* would account both for the presumed ⇒ in ms **Z** and the revision in **A** (cf. **boȝede* A 7.165 //, *tyleth* Z 6.66 //; 22.308 and notes). Though OED has *wandeidy a.* cited under the prefix *wan-*, MED cites no example under the same; but it may be that the adj. *wan* is in question, used figuratively of deeds, as in *York Plays* 36/38 (cited in MED s.v. *wan* adj. 4). Another difficult synonym in *w*, with a metrical pattern like that of **A** but not of ms **Z**, is *weðer-dedes*, a compound found in Laȝamon's *Brut*, 10521, possibly here with sense 'evil' (MED s.v. *wither* adj. (b) but cited under (a) 'ferocious, hostile', which does seem the certain sense at *Brut* 8143). **156 (Z 154, A 256, B 512)** The **ZAC** reading, agreed but for **A**'s addition of *To haue* (revision of a terse original) allows secure reconstruction of **B**, of which Bx preserved most of the a-half (omitting *to* haplographically after *go*) but substituted for the lost b-half a filler-phrase of plausible sense but defective metre (scanning *xx*). **157 (Z 155, A VI 1)** *was*: erroneous in **Z** on grounds of sense, unless a following *noon* is to be inserted, on the showing of **ABC**. But a less radical emendation is to read *nas* and see *noon* as an **A** revision, perhaps of an exemplar with the grammatically faulty reading found in ms **Z**. *wye*: on the showing (here) of **ZBC** the first stave-word, revised in **B** to the near-synonymous (and evidently commoner) *wight* or replaced in Bx by this word. Ax, now irrecoverable from the divergent witness of **r** and **m**, was probably closer to *was nane* **m** than to **r**'s milder variant, with its look of a scribal filler, perhaps generated by misreading *weye non* as *we men*. **A-K** may have corrected from a **B** source or by intelligent guess, but its substantive reading is here modified to agree with **ZC** as giving the likeliest form of **A**. **158 (Z 156, A VI 2, B 514)** *baches*: firmly attested in **C**, from which *A-W* may have derived it, the hardest reading, with a good claim for all versions. The **A** variant *bankes* EA may show ⊗ from a post-Bx source; though the word's shape or the wish for an alliterating word could have suggested the ⇒, the sense could not have. By contrast both *dales* (perhaps representing **m**) and *valeis* **r** preserve the correct sense of the presumed original, but at the cost of the metre in the b-half. If **Z** is here original, and not showing ⊗ from **C**, it preserves an important reading that might have been lost to our **AB** texts in the absence of any stronger evidence than that of *A*-W. There is indirect support for *baches* in what seems an echo of this phrase at 10.232 // **B**, revising **A**, where *dales* points back to the presence of its rare synonym here in 7.158. The discussion in Adams 1991: 8–12 unfortunately ignores the witness of **Z** (see esp. p. 10).

  Z 160 (A VI 6, B 518, C 162) *wethewyse* 'withy-wise': possibly original, so loss of *-windes* **ABC** need not be presumed. *ywowden*: either an idiolectal spelling with assimilated medial consonant (cf. *Hensong* 5.123) or showing loss of *n* through haplography.

165 (Z 163, A 9, B 521) *Syse*: clearly attested in **CZ**, but causing difficulty in both the *A*-**r** and *B*-β traditions, where scribes puzzled by the aphetic form of Assisi (*asise* in *B*-R) have derived from A 14 (B 526) the name of a perhaps more famous pilgrimage destination. In the *A*-**m** tradition E and in the Cx tradition uF preserve a corrupt reflex of the correct reading, while H³ substitutes at random. **170** *þe sepulcre*: a 'monolexical' stave-word that furnishes both lifts in the b-half. Amongst the **A** mss, K may show ⊗ from a **C** copy of **x**-type, AH³ influence from the Bx tradition (which here however has an unmetrical form). If **Z** has ⊗, it is more probably from **C**. However, in each case where *of oure lord* has been inserted, the source may have been a marginal gloss in the immediate exemplar. The harder reading is undoubtedly *þe sepúlcre*, which is allusive and has a metrical pattern paralleled in 4.172, 7.70, 20.158, 21.331). while the expanded one gives a rhythm that is uncharacteristic. This reading is retained for **Z** alone as it may be original there; but where the sub-archetypal traditions offer a choice, it is omitted, and reconstruction of the clumsy b-half in **B** is directed by the choice made for **A** and **C**. **172 (Z VI 4, A 16, B 528)** *and in Damaskle* **p**: not an intrusive scribal ⇒ for the reading in **x**, which must be dittography of the entire 171b, but a revision that gives specificity to the vague half-line retained from **Z → B**. **174–75** make more logical sense in this order, and so *R–K*'s inversion of them to follow **AB** is completely unwarrranted. **176 (Z VI 8, A 20, B 532)** *quod they* AC/ Ø ZB: a speech-marker phrase possibly absent from **Z**, but on the showing of **AC** judged to have been probably lost in Bx on account of the line's unusual length. For the next 93 lines the *C-Text interpolation* in *A*-**K** is collated as another **p**-family witness, its exemplar having changed from the **x**-type ms used in Pr–VI and the opening of VII. **177** *wissen*: the probable original in **B**, which Bx has expanded (deliberately, given the identical error at 304), probably under partial inducement from *auȝt* at 532. *B*-gF have felicitously omitted, possibly but not necessarily after comparison with **A** or **C**. **178–79 (Z 10–11, A 22–23, B 534–35)** Apart from the single detail of **Z**'s present tense for preterite, *both* lines in all four versions are incontestable examples of Type IIIa (see *Intro.*, IV §§ 41–2). *K–D*'s emendation of *saw* to *ne saw* on the basis of *A*-V and *B*-B to make the line scan on *n* (p. 205n) seems little short of desperate (so *Ka²*). *R–K* retain this in 179 but abandon *K–D*'s adventurous emendation of B 534 (*me...helpe*] *God glade me*). This example shows the incoherence in the Athlone texts that arises from confusion about the nature of **L**'s metre, and its serious impact on the process of editing. In 179, *pálmére* may be interpreted as a 'monolexical' stave-word with two lifts in consequence if *l* is given

full syllabic value (cf. *folowáre* 188). **181 (Z 13, A 25, B 537)** The unapocopated **CZ** form *heued* (archetypally attested in **B** at 14.233) is adopted in **AB** to provide the required feminine ending. **183 (Z 15, A 27, B 539)** The **BC** readings and that of **A** are secure and satisfactory. **Z** scans awkwardly with two stresses in *Cónscyénce* as it stands, and *kynde* in post-nominal position is accordingly conjectured as having been omitted through haplography before *kened* (*kende being a likely spelling of the word in **Z**'s exemplar), a loss further induced by the presence of *kyndely* in 14 above. The sense is not strong, but that fact helps to explain why **A** substitutes another epithet (*clene*) in pre-nominal position and adds a second noetic figure as a guide. Persisting dissatisfaction with the half-line is attested by the further revision in **B**, retained in **C**. *A*-N is best seen as showing ⊗ from **B** or **C**, not isolated attestation of original **A**. **184 (Z 16, A 28, B 540)** The form of the a-half is secure in **C** and in **Z**, the earliest form, which cannot be derived from any of the later ones, having no factitive verb and the adverb as first lift. In **A**, the latter has been lost by *r¹* and (coincidentally) HE, presumably by eyeskip to *serue* (positing an exemplar form **sethe(n)*), but corrupted to *sothe* in M and further smoothed to *sothenesse* in H³. The form of **C** (*sykeren... sethen*) echoes both **A** and Bx, probably indicating that **B** had both the original adverb and a new one. The latter is here taken to have occasioned the loss of the former through homoarchy (*siþþen, sikerly*), but the length and sibilance of the resultant Type Ic line may have prompted the compact re-writing of **B**'s revised a-half. **188 (Z 18, A 30, B 542)** scans either vocalically as Type IIIa (or Ia with mute second stave) or on |f| / |v|, with *folowáre* as quadrisyllabic (and so to be expanded in **ZB**, where *l* may be interpreted as a syllabic grapheme).

A 32–9 (Z 20–7) 32 *eek*: presumably lost from **r** by haplography before its exemplar's postulated *yke*pide* and severally restored by UV; likewise individually lost by EA from **m** (here represented by MH³, their reading confirmed by **Z**). **35 (Z 23)** *his*: a revision, unless *þis* represents an original **A** reading. **39 (B 552, C 195)** *hewe*: to be judged the original form in **A** as in **ZBC**. J's unusual spelling suggests a possible Ax form *hyȝe to explain the majority *hyne*, a variant (perhaps induced by following *hyre*) also that of the *C*-**p** group (except P) and of P²D (over erasure).

197 (Z 29, A 41, B 554) *wy*: in the Ax tradition, the likely original of ?**m** *wiȝt*, though the form of Ax itself might have been a bad spelling such as *we*, that could have motivated the ⇒ *he* in the majority of **r** mss. In Bx the key-stave is now *where*, either full or mute, and *he* could be a revision in response to a sense of *wy*'s register as perhaps inappropriate to Truth (= God) as referent, not implying that **L**'s **A** copy was corrupt at this point. In **C**, the blank stave *Treuthe* carries the b-half stress and a mute stave *where* the alliteration, an added *w*-stave providing 'supplemental' alliteration' in the last lift (see *Intro*. IV § 44). **198 (Z 30, A 42, B 555)** *wel...place*: certain in ZC but uncertain in the Ax tradition and suspect in Bx. The **A** readings may be identified as split variants falling into three groups, the omitted word being *way* or *wel* or *riȝt*. Reconstruction proceeds under guidance from agreed **ZC**, the adverb *wel* being taken as modifying *ryht*. Bx *witterly,* though not unmetrical, seems empty and over-emphatic in the light of **ZC** (and reconstructed **A**) through losing the important idea of *directness* on the route to Truth. The revised **C** line, with alliterating *wol* for *shal*, retains the idea while omitting the word *wey* (presumably as understood).

B 556 The Bx line that follows should be rejected as scribal padding, despite its apparent 'pre-echo' of C 204. Although its metre could be corrected by reading *wonyng* for *dwellyng*, it adds nothing to the sense, does not fit syntactically and interrupts the movement from the pilgrims' ingenuous offer to Piers' angry response.

200 (Z 32, A 44, B 557) *þe...soule*: on the showing of **ACZ** the likely reading of **B**, which has been corrupted by Bx to give *ab / ba* instead of *ab / ab*. **201 (Z 33, A 45, B 558)** *nolde*: certain in **B** and probable in **C**; in **A** *nolde / wald noght* may be split variants of a doubly negative original that read as in **Z**. **203 (Z 34, A 46, B 559)** *lasse*: a **B** revision, retained in **C**, of *wers* **ZA**, which scan satisfactorily as Type IIIa. *A*-VLN have anticipated or show ⊗ from **B**. **204 (Z 35, A 47, B 560)** *Ac* ZBC: also likely to be the original form in **A**. *ant* **Z** 'if': conjectured as necessary for the sense and as the form likeliest to have been lost through visual error (assimilation to preceding A*c*). **206–07 (Z 37–8, A 49–50, B 562–63)** *ȝe*[1,2] **ABC**: omitted twice in **Z** for no visible reason, unless as a result of haste in copying. In Z 38 the scansion appears to be vocalic (Type III), with the rhetorical stress on *him* (Truth; Christ) and *loueyen* forming part of the prelude-dip, although a Type III scanning on *l* is possible with a final pattern *oúne hèrtus*. **A**'s revision (retained in **BC**) unambiguously promotes the lexical verb to chief position as first lift. **211 (Z 40, A 52, B 565)** *wolt* **Z**: an obvious emendation on grounds of sense for scribal misreading of *l* as (long) *s*, but *wost* could be an assimilated form of *woldest* and no emendation necessary. *hij / hy*: the antecedent being pl. in all versions, Bx *he* may be seen as a scribal misresolution of *a*, the number-indeterminate pronominal form found in **Z**, but not elsewhere instanced in the Bx tradition, so best rendered here in the plainest SWM pl. form. Ax *men* is acceptable, but in the light of **ZC** also likely to be a scribal ⇒ for a vocalic pl. pronoun. **212** R–K (incredibly) read with **B**; but the whole line is plainly revised. **213 (Z 42, A 54, B 567)** *Forto*: firmly attested in **ZA** and acceptably so in **C**, so likely to be the **B** reading for which Bx (like *C-p*[1]) has substituted the advancing conjunction,

perhaps in response to a transitional form *Fortil* (actually instanced in *C*-ms U) in its immediate exemplar. *ford*: the unusual spelling *forþe* in three distinct **A** sources, could perhaps reflect Ax, or have come in from *forþ* in 53, but is rejected as distracting and unlikely to be original. **214 (Z 43, A 55, B 568)** *at* ZC: either coincidental or showing **C** ⊗ in the copying stage of ms Z; but perhaps lost from AxBx by assimilation to following *þat*. **221–22 (Z 50–1, A 62–3, B 575–76)** *þou; thyn* CAZ: are likely to be also the correct original readings for **B**. β and Bx respectively will have substituted plurals under influence from the preceding forms in 554–69, failing to recall the abrupt change to the singular at 570 // and the subsequent unambiguous address to each individual pilgrim severally. Plurals resume in **B** and **Z** at 597 (83); but since the // lines in **AC** have the sg., it may be that no great significance attaches to the variation, all four becoming pl. again at 247 //. It seems on balance that the pronouns would have been sg. in **B**. **226 (Z 54, A 67, B 580)** *berw*: on the strength of agreed **ZBC**, discriminated from among the five variants as the original in **A**. Their number, range and grouping suggest that Ax had a badly-spelled form that was hard to interpret and that scribes variously conjectured an appropriate stave-word, some perhaps with recollection of **B**. **227 (Z 55, A 68, B 581)** *Is*: a subjectless verb, most probably original in all versions. In the Ax tradition, neither **m**'s relative / demonstrative nor **r**'s personal pronoun (like *B*-β) is evidently a reading for which the other must be a ⇒. Ax therefore is quite likely to have kept the original Ø-relative of **A** preserved in ZC and in *B*-α. **228 (Z 56, A 69, B 582)** *no* ABC: evidently better in **Z** also, despite the different construction there, since if what Piers meant was more a threat than an admonition, *vp* would be more natural than *for*. **229 (Z 59, A 70, B 583)** *þow*: adopted for **B** on the joint witness of ZAC; see note on 221–22 // above for discussion of the mistaken pl. number in Bx. *B*-G is quite probably the result of collation with **A** (see *Intro*. III, *B*, §§ 28–9). **230 (Z 58, A 71, B 584)** *In...nat*: on the showing of agreed **ZBC** to be discriminated as the probable reading of **A**. The **r** variant does not alliterate with the b-half and emendation of *manis* to *ledis*. So, either **m** has here preserved Ax and **r** substituted an unmetrical half-line prompted by the sense of the preceding line or Ax was here defective, **r** representing one scribal attempt to fill the gap and **m** another, drawn from a **B** source. **233 (Z 61, A 74, B 587)** *Wil*: on the evidence of **AB** and (revised) **C** likely to be the original **Z** reading, of which ms *wel* is an orthographic not a substantive variant, i.e. not the adverb, which is syntactically and idiomatically improbable. **234 (Z 62, A 75, B 588)** *The carneles ben of* ZAC: reconstructed as also the original in **B**, for which Bx has substituted a construction parallel to and perhaps induced by *Botrased* 589. **237–38 (Z 65, A 78, B 591)** The revision shows **A** rewriting the b-half of **Z** after adding a third full lift in the a-half to create a Type IIa line. This process continues, though in **B** only the third lift is revised. While Bx offers acceptable sense and metre, the line's expansion into two in **C**, the b-half of 238 identical with **A**'s, suggests that the latter's final lift was lost from Bx, perhaps through the need to write it in the margin. Decision here is thus more tentative than in straightforward cases of identical **AC** witness against a Bx reading defective in both metre and sense, and non-linear revision cannot be excluded; but on balance emendation seems justified.

Z 66–75 66 (A 79) *tyleth* **Z**: probably original as the key-stave in a Type Ie line. The widely attested verb (MED s.v. *tillen* (2) (b)) occurs at A 2.42 // Z 2.51 and, in its more commonly spelled form *tollide*, at A 5.128 //, with the identical form *tylyd* in *A*-E (see *Ka* Apparatus) and with *tilleth* as the **p**-family variant in // C 6.220. The Ax line could scan on |t| with a key-stave on *to* or else vocalically, both scansions scarcely improving on the form of **Z**. The problem for the Ax scribe lay perhaps less in the word itself, which caused no difficulty on earlier appearances in its directional meaning (as at A 2.42 //), than in its contextual application to stone rather than to a fabric, as in the other two instances. But it was uncommon enough for its ⇒ by the **Z** scribe for original *is* to be improbable. The present reading thus affords lexical evidence for **Z**'s authenticity, if not necessarily its priority; for even if **Z** represents a form of the **A**-Text, it must derive from a source distinct from Ax for which no manuscript evidence exists outside **Z** (see further *Intro.* IV § 3). **68–72** show no metrical or stylistic sign of being unoriginal (see also **77–8** below, and *Commentary*). They would seem to have been deleted in **A** as part of a progressive reduction of the **Z** account of Truth's tower till it is completely removed in **B**. **68** *A may se*: for the stress-pattern using this modal cf. 2.149, 3.252. **73 (A 81)** *þing*: adopted for **A** as giving a line of (the rare but authentic) Type IIb (|d| / |θ| |f|), though **m**'s Ø form with 'monolexical' *déféndiþ* is also characteristic of **L** (as in *désérued* 4.172, *sepúlcre* 7.170). **74–5** are unique lines, with integral metre and characteristic wordplay in 75.

A 82–4 82 (Z 76) is present in **m** only and could easily have been lost from **r** through homœoteleuton (*-endiþ* / *-ondiþ*). The distinctive form of its last lift tells against **Z**'s derivation of it from an of **m**-type **A** source or, conversely, of **m** from **Z**, Ax having *had* to read like **m** so as to occasion the postulated mechanical loss in **r**. The line, not being in **B** or **C** in either form, must be either original or a scribal addition in both cases. But the latter possibility would require a direct connection between **Z** and **m** for which there is little evidence elsewhere in the form of agreements in error. **84 (Z 80)** The b-half differs completely from the **BC** form, *clene* appearing on the face of it an **A** revision of **Z** *smethe* (for *smothe*).

Z 77–8 are unique lines that make good sense and have authentic metre (78 scanning as Type IIIa); perhaps omitted in **A** as too topical and circumstantial to be appropriate in a description of an allegorical building. **77** *ne*: inserted as necessary for the sense and presumed lost through virtual haplography after *-re* in *Wyndeles*ore. **239–40 (Z 79–80, A 83–4, B 592–93)** may be judged to have been lost from *A*-**r** for reasons perhaps connected with the prior, but more easily explained, loss of 82. They exhibit continuous revision from **Z** to **C**, *hatte* **C** being unusually a reversion to **A**, and the last lift in *A*-**m** a movement away from **Z**'s physical to **BC**'s completely spiritual image. Once again, the independence of **Z** and **m** from each other and from **BC** is manifest, both lines giving firm grounds for belief in **m**'s linear descent from Ax and, if **Z** 79–80 are taken with 77–8, the priority of **Z** to the latter. **239** *bydde* **BC**-**p** / *byde* **ZAC**-**x**: *byde* is presumably a bad spelling for *byd(de)*, the context favouring *bydden* in all versions; cf. the converse situation at 22.48 below. **242–44, 246 (Z 81–4, A 85–8, B 595–89)** *sothe* **Z** 81: a mechanical error, perhaps induced by *smethe* (a genuine spelling variant) at 80 above. *woot* **B** 597: the indicative (as shown by the context and the witness of **ZAC**) being the required mood for the verb, as *B-F*'s synonym ⇒ tacitly recognises (the subjunctive results from failure to grasp where the direct speech commences). **247 (Z 87, A 91, B 601)** The **Z** line is re-divided after *A*-**m**, **B** and revised **C** to provide the necessary feminine ending and, if *mayster* has its normal disyllabic pronunciation, a final lift (for an identical case of misdivision in **Z**, see 1.95/6, where *onus* is again at the line-end). *Grace* **C**: corresponding to *ones* in its correct position in **B**. *hym* **ZAB**: clearly demanded in **C** on grounds of sense. The error is unlikely to have been in **B**[1] and overlooked in revision; rather Cx, distracted by *ʒow* preceding, will have misconstrued the imperative as introducing another direct command. **249 (A 92, Z 88, B 602)** *wy* **A**: almost certainly the Ax source of the other substantive variants; for although on comparison with **ZB** this could seem a corruption of original **wy(ʒ)f*, that word was not difficult enough to prompt ⇒ or to need revision as was *wy*, with its more restricted and (contextually) indeterminate reference. The **C** revision ascribes the shutting of the gate to both Adam and Eve and the Ax reading here accepted may indicate **L**'s first wish to imply what is finally stated explicitly, after the more conventional assertion of **Z**. Conceivably **B**'s reading was influenced by the sense of 603*a* and (un)conscious anti-feminism. **253 (Z 91, A 95, B 605)** *in*[2]: lost through haplography in all traditions, but **Z** may be left since the need to emend on grounds of sense is not overwhelming. **260 (Z 94, A 98, B 609)** *Wrath-the (nat)*: the spellings with single or double fricative consonant alike are to be interpreted in this context not as the noun (as by *R–K*) but as the imperative + reflexive pronoun object. Omission of the latter by some **AB** witnesses (as by *C*-X) is due to the scribes of individual copies or lost group-ancestors; each of the archetypes and **Z** seem to have intended the verb. In **AC** it is not certain whether the imperative was negative; in **Z** it is negative, in Bx it was not, leaving original **B** uncertain. The **A** reading with *nou3t* conforms to the pattern of negative commandments at A 57, 60, 64, as *R–B* note *ad loc*, and taken closely with the prior imperative *be war*, the underlying meaning is 'beware not to get angry', even if the (seemingly illogical) surface sense 'beware of not-getting-angry' might have invited scribal deletion of the negative particle. The probabilities are hard to ascertain, but since no significant issue is at stake, the Z-ms form, Bx's and those likeliest to represent Ax and Cx are retained. **261 (Z 95, A 99, B 610)** *For*: on the joint witness of **ZAC** lost from Bx, for no clear cause; the conjunction sharpens the sense by citing Wrath's hostility to Charity as the reason for being on guard. **264 (Z 98, A 102, B 613)** *so* **ZAC**: unlikely to have been revised to *þanne* in **B** as this would pointlessly repeat the end of 612, whence it has doubtless come into Bx by unconscious repetition. **265** *close*: an instance of *repetitio* (after 264), an important feature of **L**'s style in **C** that *R–K*'s unwarranted emendation to **AB** *kepe* ignores. **266 (Z 100, A 104, B 615)** *thow*: *the* for *thou* in **Z** is paralleled at A 12.91. **268 (Z 102, A 106, B 617)** The **ZAC** agreement questions the authenticity of Bx. Although metrically emendable by transposition of object and verb in the b-half, it suspiciously repeats both adverbs and the main verb of 615. This may point to scribal censorship, perhaps prompted by unease at the laxism suggested by the condition set out in the a-half. *ac*: perhaps also the reading of **A**, and adopted in reconstructed **B** on the strength of **ZC** agreement; but Ax *and* being acceptable, no emendation is strictly required. **270 (A 108, B 619)** *ouer*: possibly the original preposition in Ax, although K is here judged to reveal ⊗ from **C**. The other three variants, of which *of* also shows as that of *B*-β, could be ⇒ for the reading with the fullest and most definite sense, one implying authority, not just duty. **271 (A 109, B 620)** *Vmbletee*: to be discerned in the light of **C** as the more probably original spelling, *B*-R here representing α (< Bx), with *B*-F having varied to the advancing β form also attested in Ax. **276** *places*: U *puttes* (so *Pe*) is a scribal ⇒ (possibly suggested by the allegory and recalling *prisones in puttes* 9.72) for a Cx reading with a contextually difficult sense 'field of battle' (see MED s.v. *place* 2(c)), and cf. *Commentary*). **278 (A 114, B 626)** has the somewhat unexpected structure of an extended Type IIIa line with a-half counterpoint scanning vocalically on *He* in **AB** and on *Is* in **C**. The remote possibility that a (mute) stave *wel* was lost before *faire* in all three archetypes cannot be ruled out, but no emendation is justified. **279 (B 627)** **C** re-writes as Type Ia a line

of apparent Type IIIa form scanning on |v| and |s| with a (liaisonal) first stave on *if_ye* and one on rhetorically-stressed *þise*. Scansion as Type I on *s* with the caesura after *some*, a five-syllable prelude, and two lifts in *séuéne* is barely possible; but the line would yield a satisfactory Type Ib structure if *but if* were diagnosed as a ⇒ error for *saue* in AxBx (cf. 21.408 //, where this emendation is proposed for a line that would otherwise not scan). **280 (A 116, B 628)** *eny of 3ow alle*: the elliptical form attested in AC is likely on 'linear' grounds to have been the reading of **B**, the Bx reading showing typical scribal explicitness (the omission of *quod Piers* from GF perhaps the result of comparison with **A**). **290 (A 126, B 638)** *so*: on the witness of **AC** the probable reading in **B**, with Bx *bi* apparently induced by following *bi-*. The reading of W judged correct is presumably coincidental, though G could, as at 280, derive from comparison with **A**. **297** The third stave is liaisonal (*þat_Y*) and *R–K*'s reconstruction *this to hym* as from split variants is (though plausible) otiose. **300** *sighen*: the reading of U (and D also, if *siggen* is only a spelling error for it), the least unsatisfactory of the five available variants, but going poorly with the mood and tone of 301. The y verb *chyden* fits better, but is evidently an anticipation of *chyde* in that line; the curious *shien[de]* of X (with the last two letters erased and written over) could be a back-spelling of a word intended for *chyden* but with the affricate represented, as often in X, by *s(c)h*). The **p** reading *synnen* (so *SkR–K*), presumably from an exemplar spelled *synegen* (whence the vapid PE variant), is to be rejected as incompatible with the sense of 301. The difficult original underlying y (and so perhaps **x**) could conceivably be **shien*, apparently unattested in ME, but found in OE. This is still extant as *shy* (OED s.v. *Shy* v.[1]) 'to take fright', and has a more appropriate sense in the context. The rarity of the word would have made for its loss as conjectured; but given the poor lexicographical evidence, it is safer not to emend. **306 (ZA VII 1, B VI 1)** In each of **ZAB** the line appears of Type IIa structure, with *(w)hoso* apparently scanning vocalically. But in Cx it seems to have the scansion *aa / xx*. A spelling such as *wo* in **Z** implies an alternative pronunciation with |w|, which would allow the Cx line to scan as Type Ia. But the presence of *wel* in **Z** may suggest that an adverb, absent from **AB**, was later added in **C** and that this was *wel*. Cx could then have substituted for this the increasingly common intensifier, perhaps under unconscious visual suggestion from *fol-* in 307 or objection to positively collocating *wel* with *wikked* when they are normally in contrastive relation (cf. *wel or wikke* at 16.175). The less obvious variant *so* eRM is unlikely to represent **p** and has probably been induced by following *hoso*. C-G thus provides here a felicitous scribal 'correction' in the interests of the metre which is adopted as giving a line of authentic character. **307 (ZA VII 2, B VI 2)** *myhte*: on the strength of **ZAC** agreement judged the probable reading of **B**, for which Bx will have substituted another, more emphatic modal verb.

Passus VIII (ZA VII, B VI)

3 (ZAB 5) *and...aftur*: lost for no apparent reason by *A*-**r**, the terse rhythm of which is found in (rare) later lines like A 11.83–4. While the filler in *A*-t is evidently scribal, **r** is not to be rejected out of hand as deficient, since the completed forms in **Z** and *A*-**m** could be derived from **B** or **C** (though no other line in *PP* has fewer than ten syllables). However, on grounds of sense it seems unlikely that **L** would have had Piers set off on pilgrimage without sowing the field he had ploughed. Most probably, therefore, **r** derives from a defective exemplar and **m** may be assumed to represent Ax here. **4 (ZAB 6)** *Y wolde*: correcting the Z-ms reading, which is anacoluthic after 5, the first-person pronoun being required. *Ant schal* could be an auditory error for an original *[I]ch wol* (with vowel missing), heard as *schal* and then smoothed by inserting the conjunction. **6 (ZAB 8)** *þe*: Bx probably read *þere* (> LMα) and γ will have felicitously varied or corrected to what is on the showing of **ZAC** the likeliest reading for **B**. **10 (B 11, ZA 19)** *on; sowen*: as taken here, *sowen* is a jussive subjunctive (with *That*) following the direct address of 9. Possibly **C** read not *on* but *an* (representing *han*) and *sowen*, which fits well with *to sowen* in Cx (so *PeR–K*, following the B-Text); but the reading adopted gives the same sense without need for emendation. In the Ax tradition, *þat* and *ʒe* show as split variants of the reading preserved in **ZBC** and reconstructed for **A**. The imperative mood of the verb in **r** is an evident scribal smoothing. *whan tyme is*: from the evidence of the ?**r** and ?**m** variants, Ax may have read *whanne it tyme is*, but v is preferred on the agreement of **ZBC**.

 ZA 12–15 12 *yt*: the Z-ms *yf* is intended for *yf yt* or for *yt*, as adopted for **A**. **15 (B 16)** *comaundiþ*: the *A*-**r** variant will yield a line scanning as Type IIa; but in the light of **B**, the MH³ reading may be discriminated as that of **m**, either by ⊗ from **B** or, on the witness of **ZB** agreement, from Ax. Like *wille* **r**, *biddes* EA may result from the scribe's objection to the corporal works of mercy being treated as 'commandments' rather than 'counsels' (see *Commentary* on 13).

 B 17 After this in Bx follows a metrically defective line that could be emended by transposition of *riche* and *poore* in the b-half to give a standard line scanning 'cognatively'. But in tone and content, it appears a scribal expansion, closely comparable to those that follow in Bx at 4.38, 5.93 and 6.182.

16 Cx perhaps read Ø and **p** made a plausible correction. The **AB** article is preferred, though **Z** agrees with *C*-**p**. **18 (ZA 22, B 20)** *hym*: on the strength of **ZBC** agree-

ment the minority variant is judged the likely original in **A**. Ax will have substituted a pl. prn through identifying *wynneþ* as pl. under influence from the two preceding pl. verbs. *to* **B**: possibly inserted by Bx and, though affecting neither sense nor metre, probably better omitted. *wihtliche*: judged original in the light of agreed **AB** and on grounds of sense. The Z-ms reading is clearly a mechanical error, but *C*-**x** has smoothed further, perhaps starting from a group-reading without the spirant (P²D corrupt to *witturly*).

 ZA 25 (B 23) The reading of the b-half in Ax is difficult to recover, given the number and range of variants, but perhaps the likeliest is *I wille conne erie* V. A spelling-variant of the verb *conne* (i.e. *gonne*) would explain the ?**mJ** variants *gynne / gon* and KN *comsen* (its form induced by *connen*, its sense by its synonym *gynnen*). The verb *leren* in **r** would then be an easy ⇒ of a commoner synonym for *conne,* while *eren* could have been introduced as a final lift under visual inducement from preceding *wille l*ere(n). However, this reconstruction is challenged by the agreement in the key-stave *be Cryst* of **ZBC**, each of which versions nonetheless has a distinctive *final* lift. This suggests that an oath was removed in Ax, through censorship or stylistic objection to repetition (23), leaving a lacuna that was variously filled (in L by a similar oath). **Z**'s verb looks the likely original that *assaye* **B** is replacing, while being the same as in **r**'s prefinal lift. The reconstruction furnishes a metrically and semantically satisfactory text for **A** identical with **Z**. **25 (ZA 28, B 26)** *labory*: the agreed reading for **ZAC** being the verb 'to labour', the phrase *labours do* could be a Bx ⇒ with subsequent smoothing by insertion of *opere*. But since sense and metre are satisfactory, and revision in both **B** and **C** possible, no emendation is proposed here.

 Z 31 is a unique line of acceptable sense and form, which **A** could have omitted either as not strictly necessary after 30 or because of the negative associations of the verb *meyntene* in such contexts. However, since B 36 has identical sense, the line has perhaps been inadvertently lost from Ax.

30 (Z 34, A 33, B 31) *wylde...culle*: an easy emendation of the Cx half-line, which scans *aa / xa*, on the basis of **ZAB**. Verb-noun ↔ to prose order may have been induced by attraction of *foules* to *diffoule* at the line-end in 31. **31 (Z 35, A 34, B 32)** *to my*: on the evidence of **ABC** and on grounds of sense presumably in **Z** and lost perhaps by attraction of *cometh > croft.* **32 (Z 36, A 35, B 33)** *þanne* **A**: restored on the showing of agreed **ZBC**; evidently lacking in Ax, though JE position their synonym correctly. *conseyued*: the hardest reading, clearly established only in *A*-**r**, for which the **m** and J variants appear evident scribal ⇒ in their failure to alliterate. The reading of Bx is *comsed,* as it is of three A mss and, in present-tense form, of a fourth and of ms **Z**. On intrinsic grounds, *con-*

seyuede is unlikely to be a scribal ⇒ for *comsed* which, while itself often replaced by a non-alliterating synonym (e.g. *C*-N *bygan*), was the more readily intelligible. But by that token, *comsed* could be a **B** revision, retained in **C**. The **Z** reading would then be explained as either a draft, replaced in **A** by *conseyuede*, or a mis-expansion of an exemplar reading thus, or a ⇒ by the scribe of ms Z under influence from a **B** or **C** source. Against the authenticity of *comsed* in **C** stand *C*–DM, which cannot derive from a post-Bx **B** source and are unlikely to show ⊗ from **A**. D could here represent u, as at 9.208, where its genetic partner U errs, and M likewise be the one accurate descendant of the p^1 source it shares (immediately) with R and (indirectly) with q, e. It is improbable that *conseyuede* is a scribal correction, whether by conjecture, by ⊗ from **A**, or by reference to a lost superior **C** source. D and M together are therefore reasonably likely to be witnesses (though isolated, mutually-supporting) to **x** and **p** respectively and so, by inference, to Cx. If *conseyuede* is judged authentic, **C** will here have retained or restored a **B** original lost in Bx. With no direct evidence, its adoption in **B** is perhaps nearer a conjecture than a reconstruction, supported by **C**'s probable and **A**'s virtually certain reading. The **A** variants *rehersede* and *answeryd* suggest that the relevant meaning here was taken as 'utter' (MED s.v. *conceiven* v. (8c)) not 'grasp, understand' (MED s.v. 6(a)), its evident sense at 10.56, where neither Ax nor Bx is in doubt because the word offers no contextual difficulty. This accepted, it seems reasonable further to reject Bx *quod he* 34, on the showing of agreed **AC**, as a scribal insertion. The case for also emending **Z** is as strong as (or no weaker than) that for emending Bx; but since **A** *could* be a revision of **Z**, it seems safer on balance for the 'acceptability' criterion to outweigh that of *durior lectio* and *comseth* to stand in **Z**. **35–53 (ZA 39(38)–49, B 37–54)** The alternation of sg. and pl. pronouns in **BC** may be non-significant, or intended to suggest the dual relationship of Piers to the knight, as servant and as authority. F's alteration of the Bx reading to a consistent singular may show ⊗ from **A**. **44 (B 47)** *sitte*: PEN's variant *(y)sette* is preferred on grounds of sense and in the light of // **B** by *R–K* (p. 167); but the past-participle of *setten* should be *(y)set*, and the disyllabic form attested indicates rather (with understood auxiliary *shal*) an infinitive form of a verb with the same sense as *sitten* (see MED s.v. *setten* v. 34 (d), *sitten* v.).

Z 48–9 (A 47, B 52) has a different form of the line that becomes A 47, though its idiosyncratically spelled *holde* may be the origin of the new verb in **A**. The extra line following is reminiscent of Z 2.208, but the b-half expresses a more cordial view of a group towards whom **L**'s attitude seems to have fluctuated considerably. **51** scans weakly in **ABC** with wrenched stress and an assimilated consonant group *ml* before the first lift. *R–K* (pp. 169–70) argue persuasively for *manliche (MED s.v.

mainli adv. 2(c) meaning 'especially', a word replaced by *nameliche* in the Trevisa instance cited, which has the spelling found in ms X at 9.335, and also in XUN at 2.162. This attractive conjectural reconstruction gives much better metre; but it has to contend with the securely established archetypal reading of all three versions in all three cases (a precedent would be *me meten in ZAB Pr 12). The possibility remains, however, that the *manliche* appearances in X could be scribal ⇒ for a stave-word found too licentious, though one **L** may have tolerated. See further 9.335n. **54 (ZA 50, B 55)** *sayde*: conjectured for **Z** in the light of **ABC** as the required key-stave, for which the familiar synonym will be an (? unconscious) scribal ⇒. **58–60 (Z 53–4, A 54–6, B 59–61)** In the light of agreed **AC(Z)** the Bx reading with the 1st person and present tense for 3rd person and preterite (*He; his; heng*) may be diagnosed as scribal ⇒ followed by smoothing. It was perhaps prompted by misreading *A 59 in the exemplar as *&*, as at 58 in *C*-**x**, though without the consequent errors and smoothing. **63 (B 64)** *pilgrimages*: an unexpected pl. (also found in *B*-CrMF, though not likely to represent Bx) perhaps induced by *palmeres*; but its sense being acceptable, it is retained here and again at 93 // below. **64 (Z 90, A 95, B 103)** *plouh-pote*: 'plough-pusher' (a forked stick), firmly attested in **ZA**, for which *B*-β and several **C** mss substitute *ploughfoot*, the 'foot' of the plough (*plough-bat = plough-staff* is a different instrument, a long-handled spade for cleaning the cutter). *pyk-staff*: the firmly established **ABC** reading, presumably a revision of **Z** *pik* (if this is original and *staf* has not been lost by eyeskip to following *pich*). The sense of *pik* is 'point', the abbreviation being synecdochic for the whole implement, the staff tipped with a metal point used by pilgrims (see 7.179 // **ZAB** for an earlier use of *pik* alone). But the form *pyk* t is unlikely to be original in **A**, while *potent* A could be an echo of B 8.97. *pyche a-to*: clearly established in **CZ**, but *a-to* is contested by *at B*-α and (possibly) Ax. The phrasal verb's somewhat unusual sense is 'thrust asunder', the action of the plough-pusher to facilitate the vertical cutting action of the plough. The variant *at* appears to be a reflex of *ato* suggested by the sense of *pote*, but overlooking the effect of the pointed instrument in thrusting both 'through' and 'at' the encumbering roots. This detail is spelled out in Z 91, a unique line that **A** revises to focus attention on the furrows being cleared (the b-half was preserved in L's 'repertory' and recurs in 21.314). The **A** variant *vp* expresses an understanding of *pyche* as equivalent to *pyke* 'dig up with a pointed instrument, hoe' as does, more remotely, *awey* (cf. C 118 // below). **65 (Z 91, A 96, B 104)** *clanse*: firmly established in **B** and in **C**, and possibly the reading of Ax, although each of the six **A** mss attesting it could perhaps show ⊗ from **B**. *Ka* argues persuasively for *close* on grounds of sense and *R–K* concur, following *C*-RM. But while *clense* 'clear' (MED s.v. *clensen* v. 1 (d)) gives a different contextual sense, it is equally apt; and if either alternative has been generated by visual error, *close* is the likelier, as it could result from failure to register a nasal suspension in the exemplar (the presumed explanation for <RM>). The possibility that **B** *clense* is a revision of an original **A** *close* cannot be ruled out. **66 (Z 58, A 59, B 65)** The b-half shows continuous linear revision in all four versions, with **ZBC** each specifying a single action among the necessary agricultural works Piers engages in (harrowing, sowing, weeding). Only for **A** is the witness divided, **r**'s *any þing swinke* appearing a scribal ⇒ for the reading preserved in **m** (here imperfectly attested), for one like that of **Z**, or for a lacuna in Ax. But the last of these explanations seems unlikely, since the **m** form is close to that of **Z** in its double vocalic alliteration, similar phrasing and rhythm, and also specifies a concrete action as do the other three versions.

Z 59 is a unique line, of Type Ie, with no echo in **ABC**; perhaps deleted as describing a work not so immediately appropriate to the season.

67 (ZA 60, B 66) *glene*: a revision of *lese* **B** replacing with a commoner synonym a word of more restricted circulation (*B*-Cr's variant may be ⊗ from **C**). The vocalically-scanning *A*-**r** reading appears a scribal smoothing after omission of the first stave word (*leue*). Perhaps realising that now the sense was weak (whether *here* was adverb or noun), the **r**-scribe further expanded *þermyd* 61 to provide, as an equivalent cause for the labourer's rejoicing (a product rather than an employment), giving metre as well as sense inferior on comparison with **ZBC**. The **m** variant by contrast appears to play convincingly on the noun ('leave') and the verb ('live' or 'remain'); but again the sense is poor, since *þermyd* 61 fits with neither. The emendation adopted here proceeds from diagnosing a visual error in **m** induced by preceding *leue*. The **C** reading, if it is not (as *R–K* assume) a C ⇒ for *lese*, requires in *glene* an internal *l* stave (a device paralleled at e.g. 5.153: see *Intro.* IV § 45). **68 (ZA 61, B 67)** *merye þermyde maugrey*: clearly attested in **BC** (the unique **Z** equivalent of this line having been completely replaced in **A**); the **m** variant selects itself on grounds of sense, metre and confirmation by **B**. The **r** ⇒ *wiþ þe corn* leaves the line as Type IIIa, a possibility considered by *Ka* but rejected by *Ka²* for the reading of **m**. In fact, **r** could be easily emended to Type IIa by adopting *myd* for *wiþ*; but **r**'s reading reveals itself on examination as a second stage of the smoothing begun in 60 with ⇒ of *haue...more* for *haue...leue to lesyn. bigruchen hit*: **BC** word-order and subjunctive mood, found together in the Ax tradition only in N (presumably by coincidence), with **m** having the right mood but no pronoun, **r** the wrong mood and order. It should be noted, however, that at 155 the same verb seems indicative, unless the *-eth* ending is a fusion of original *-e* and

hit, as possibly in D. In the present instance, *bigruchen* **x** can be interpreted as an elliptical infinitive after understood *may* or *sholde*; **pI** have *bygrucche*, which should probably be preferred. **74** is a 'Janus-faced' line in which the simple **x** reading *lele* without *for* (= 'as') allows a double sense. If the subject of *holdeth* is the *lollares and losels*, it means (a) 'Whom idlers and wastrels consider honest men', if *lele men* (b) 'whom honest men consider idlers and wasters'. The friars (the immediate antecedent of *That*) come off badly either way; but only sense (a) is permitted by **p**'s variant. **76 (A 66, B 74)** *forthere*: almost certain in **C** (only RM having *fourth*) and probable for Ax, providing the basis for emending Bx's ⇒ of a loosely similar word for one meaning 'more, to a greater extant'. *B*-B may have inserted *forþ* in awareness of **C** or **A**, but on metrical grounds (and despite possible syllabic *r*) the disyllabic adverb is preferable to the word familiar from the common phrase *telle forþ*. RM's variant may be a ⊗ or, more probably, a coincidence with the rejected reading of *A*-T&r. **77 (A 67, B 75)** scans as a macaronic Type Ie (with mute *de*) and the lineation here follows that in **u** (omitted from the Apparatus) and **AB**. Most mss treat the Latin a-half as 'appended' rather than 'enclosed' (see Schmidt 1987: 93–102). **79 (A 69, B 77)** The metrical pattern of the line is ambiguous, as it may scan vocalically with first stave on *áscaped* or on cognative palatal stops (|k| |g|), the second of these mute and the first 'internal' (*ascaped*). **82–3 (Z 64–8, A 72–4, B 80–2)** The name of Piers's son in **Z** is much longer than its equivalent in **A**, which has been completely revised, retaining only **Z** 66b. Given the difficulty of adapting composite allegorical nomenclature to fit alliterative metre, the **Z** lines constitute *prima facie* evidence of authenticity. They make good sense, are technically perfect and owe nothing to any of the accepted versions (even if the thought of 68a is like that of **B** 10.39b, 42a). **90** *And by*: reconstructed from the presumed split variants *And* (lost from **p**) and *by* (replaced in **x** by *aftur*, which has come in from 91). *wordynge*: *Pe*'s definitive emendation on grounds of sense. Cx *worchynge* is excluded by the meaning of 91 and may have been induced by the sense of synonymous *doynge* and the sense and form of immediately following *worche*. While the verbal noun itself is not instanced from before 1600, the verb was common (**C** 13.245, **B** 4.46, 10.427) and is found in participial form at **B** 17.48. **97 (Z 74, A 80, B 88)** *defenden...fende*: the agreed wording of **ZAC** (here in *prose* order) against which that of Bx, unobjectionable in itself, may be diagnosed as scribal (though the cause of the transposition is obscure). On the hypothesis of linear revision, Bx is accordingly emended, whereas in **C** 99 the same hypothesis supports *not* emending the order of the nouns in the a-half (against *R–K*, who make **C** accord with **AB**). *and* **C** / *for* **ZAB**: a **C** revision to Type IIa, unless *and* is taken as a Cx ⇒ for original *for*. **101 (Z 79,**

A 84, B 92) *my*[2]: on the showing of agreed **ZA** and prob-able **C**, omission of *my*[2] in Bx appears a scribal slip, per-haps induced by alliterative attraction (*corn > catel*). *my*[3] **ZC** / *þe* **AB**: though **C** could be restoring a more explicit reading, there is no real ground for thinking **Z** to show ⊗ from **C** or **AB** rather than being a first version restored after revision. **106 (Z 84, A 89, B 97)** *it*: in *B*-F inser-tion of a pronoun (*om* RM*R*–*K*) not strictly necessary for the sense, either coincidentally or by ⊗ from **C**. *douh-teres*: in itself Ax *frendis* is acceptable in metre and sense, offering a Type IIIa line and a contrast between 'friends' and 'children'. But in the light of **Z**, *douȝtres* challenges consideration not as a **B** revision but as the probable original reading of **A**, rejected by Ax for a supposedly more logical contrast. The **ZBC** reading may imply for *children* a specific sense it only acquires through coming after *douȝtres*; or else it implies no opposition, but merely appends the 'hypernym' (superordinate) to complete the sense specified by the preceding hyponym. **107 (Z 85, A 90, B 98)** *dette is*: the sg. appearing harder on grounds of sense (the 'debt' being what Piers owes to God), this is accordingly adopted for **BC**. But the Ax reading, though inferior, is acceptable, and emendation not imperative here. **114 (Z 94, A 99, B 107)** *digged*: in the Ax tradi-tion, whether the verb was *deluen* or (more probably) *dyggen*, the present tense was certain, misinterpreting an ambiguously-spelled preterite **dyggyt*. In the light of **ZBC**, the felicitous NA correction is accepted as likely to correspond to the original **A** reading. **115–16 (Z 95–6, A 100–01, B 108–09)** The b-half of 115 has been revised in **C**, but 116 confirms that the adverb *ȝerne* goes with *wrouhten* as in **ZB**, necessitating that *faste* qualified the verb of B 108 // (*preised*). This is preferable on grounds of sense to the reverse order attested in Ax, which pre-sumably results from visual error (ms W must here have corrected from a **B** source). **126 (Z 106, A 111, B 119)** *here*: although not strictly necessary, sharpening focus and appearing likely in the light of **ZAC** to have been in **B**. Bx could have lost it through alliterative attraction of *grayn* > *growith*, *B*-M have added from **A** or **C**. **130 (Z 112, A 115, B 123)** *pleynt*: the Bx line scanning *aab / bx* (an inauthentic pattern), *pleynt* is here conjectured on the showing of **ZA** as the **B** original and Bx *mone a* ⇒ under inducement from the common phrase *maken mone* and suggestion from preceding *made*. The revised **C** form indicates that this reading was in B[1], where it pro-vided the basis of a refashioned line scanning on *m*. **134 (Z 117, A 120, B 128)** *nother*: to be discerned from **ZAC** agreement as the **B** reading, with the simple negative a Bx ⇒ through failure to find terminal *-er* and confusion of *þ* with *ȝ*, followed by smoothing. The BCr correction will be from **C**. **135 (Z 113, A 116, B 124)** *Ne haue*: the presumed Cx reading (actually that of D), reconstructed from the surviving split variants as a revision of **B**; *We*

haue **p** is too easy to have invited ⇒ of *Ne* **x**. *ye* **Z**: the grammatically necessary plural securely restored in the light of **AB**, the Z-scribe doubtless having mistaken *ȝ* for *þ* in copying.

Z 120–5 (A 123–8, B 131–2) 120 *holde*: in **ZA** either a spelling variant of *olde* (with redundant pre-vocalic *h*) or a separate word (MED s.v. *hold* adj. 'loyal', 'trusty'), an interpretation indirectly supported by C 195 below. **B** takes it in the former sense and alters 'ought' to 'commanded' (which, though not an obvious improvement, need not be scribal). **121 (A 124, B 132)** *W(h)iche*: the harder read-ing on grounds of sense, following more naturally from *warne* A 123 // and likelier to be original in **A**. The erratic *A*-R spelling perhaps points to the underlying ?Ax reading from which the error *Suche* (= *Swiche*) derives. **125 (A 128)** *koes*: the hardest reading, from which *crowen* and *gees* probably come. In principle **Z** could originate from an **A** source of **m**-type, as does *A*-ms A, but since **Z** is known not to derive from Ax, its witness here independ-ently confirms the latter's probable reading.

B 138–50 138 (Z 129, A 132) *garisoun*: here pro-posed as furnishing a necessary key-stave word, Bx *amen-dement* being ⇒ of a non-alliterating synonym to give the unmetrical pattern *aa / xx*. The sense of the conjectured word is contextually appropriate to deliverance from both sickness and from imprisonment, the conditions specified in B 136 // above (see MED s.v. *garisoun* n. (b)), and it could have been suggested by the shape of the b-half in **A** (*gare hem to a*rise). **142** *afelde*: though *l* here could be syllabic, the inflected dative is more consonant with **L**'s practice, so final *e* is added for the necessary feminine ending. **148** *receyue*: providing the needed stave-word for which Bx seems to haue a (near-)synonym ⇒, producing a line with the inauthentic pattern *aa / xx* (the palpably scribal rewriting in F, as at 150, is characteristic of this ms). The present conjecture provides both better rhythm and a simpler explanation of the corruption than *riȝt noȝt* (*Sch*[1]), a phrase that occurs at 151 and is unlikely to have been repeated within three lines. **150** *putte*: conjectured as the required key stave-word, for which the Bx ⇒ is the common collocation *make at ese*. The F variant adopted by *K–D*, providing a metrical b-half that could scarcely have invited ⇒ by Bx's, cannot be other than flagrant sophistication.

148 (Z 131, A 134, B 146) The line as it stands in either ?**x** (reading *what*) or ?**p** (reading *þat*) tends to yield a Type IIIa pattern with vocalic stresses (*Y, hem*); for there to be sufficient notional substance and metrical weight in the a-half, the caesura must be located after *hem*[1] and the key-stave in *hem*[2]. But reconstruction here derives *what þat* from the split variants attested in **x** and **p** and scans the line on |w| as Type I with a mute second stave in *wolle*; a reading coinciding with that G preserves by felicitous scribal conjecture. **149 (Z 136, A 139, B 152)**

to wrath hym: from **ZBC** agreement, the probable reading of **A**. The **r** variant *arise*, which E derives from an **r**-source, yields a line of Type IIIa, while that of **m** suggests a lacuna in its exemplar, and thence perhaps in Ax. The **r** reading would be an attempt to fill it, while **m** achieves some easing of the rhythm by inserting the prefix *be-* before *gan*. **151 (Z 139, A 142, B 155)** *pyuische*: a rare word not found outside **L** in the C14th (MED s.v. *peivish* adj.), the presence of which in **Z** suggests possible ⊗ from **C** at the scribal phase, or else that this was a draft reading subsequently twice-revised. None of the four readings instanced is obviously scribal in character and accordingly no emendation is proposed. Since, however, *A*-**m** *pyned* could show ⊗ from **B**, while **r**'s *pilide* is arguably harder and cannot stem from it, the latter is retained for **A**. **153 (Z 140, A 143, B 156)** scans as Type IIIb except in *C*-**p**, which could be a scribal attempt to accord the line to Type I (here enriched with a fourth *w* stave as Ia) or a revision (as here judged), **x** having diverged to the more familiar version of the set phrase used in **ZAB**. **155 (Z 142, A 145, B 158)** *permyde*: the more archaic second element of this adverb, not strictly required on metrical grounds but appearing from **ZB** agreement to be the probable **m** form, is here taken to represent Ax, though preserved only in M.

B 162 (C 159) *while ilke*: adjective and noun (somewhat counter-idiomatically) ↔ to restore the metre damaged in Bx through inversion to prose order. In principle, the line could scan as an extended counterpointed Type III (*abb / ab*) but this goes against the natural tendency to stress the lexical words in both halves (for a similar error see B 13.82). F's correction shows cavalier disregard for sense.

A 151 (Z 148, B 166, C 163) *welde*: the harder **A** reading, supported by **Z**; *bere* in **B** is a revision, anticipated by *A*-t*r²*MH³. **166 (Z 152, A 155, B 170)** The b-half is revised from **Z** → **A** → **B**, and in **C** the whole rejected for a new half-line replacing B 169b. The **Z** form anticipates the adverb of **B**, which preserves **A**'s verb. The Ax order *next metten* gives an unmetrical structure *aa / xa*, unless (improbably) *hy* is read for *þei* and weak vocalic scansion on non-lexical words is posited. The conjectured emendation requires simple ↔ of verb and adverb, with addition of the required final *-e* found variably in the adverb. **170 (Z 155, A 158, B 173)** The metrical structure of the **C** line is problematic. Although scansion as a Type III on voiced fricatives is possible, the earlier versions point to lexical stave-words and thus scansion on |w|; but this gives a masculine ending, unless *nat* is expanded as a disyllabic form *na-uht, na-wiht*. (cf 9.112 and note below). However, a 'licensed' breach of the feminine-ending rule may be conceivable, given the special rhetorical emphasis suggested by the sense of the revised b-half, and two

juxtaposed monosyllables in 'clashing stress' are certainly very striking. **175 (Z 160, A 163, B 178)** *gottes*: on the showing of **ZBC** and as avoiding repetition, this is judged likely to be the original **A** reading, *mawis* having come in from 159. **176 (Z 161, A 164, B 179)** *hym byleue*: on the agreed witness of **ZAC** the last lift would appear to have been replaced in Bx by a phrase more emphatic and explicit, although in its α form metrically unexceptionable.

A 165–8 (Z 162–5) 165 On the evidence of *A*-*r²* ?**m** the reading of Ax was *he ȝede* or *heȝede,* and this would account for the form of **Z** *a yede*, in which *he-* has been taken as the pronoun subject. The line could scan as an extended Type III with counterpoint (*abb / ax*), the vowel staves being *a* and *hem*, an acceptable pattern, or as standard with two stresses in *bétwéne*, an 'idiometric' monolexical pattern (cf. *Intro.* IV § 38). The present emendation *boȝede* likewise provides full stresses on lexical words, the rationale of the conjectured corruption being the ease of *b* / *h* confusion and the relative rarity of the verb, which is found at B 5.566 // **ZA** (revised in **C**; see MED s.v. *bouen* v. (1), 6 (a)). **166 (Z 163)** *permyd*: preferred in the light of **Z** as the probable form in this (revised) line, giving in **A** a characteristic homophonic play with *amydde*. **168 (Z 165)** *defendite / yfet*: the *A*-W and K reading *fette* is presumably a chance variant coinciding with **Z**, since *defendite* appears a revision, doubtless due to realisation that water taken on top of beans would cause indigestion.

178 (B 182) After 182 Bx has an unmetrical line that could be emended by reading *mened* for *preied* but appears a piece of enthusiastic scribal expansion like those after B 4.38 and 5.193 (see *Intro.* III *B* § 60). The revised **C** line recurs in part at 192. **179 (Z 168, A 171, B 183)** In the light of **Z** and (revised) **C**, a temporal adverb is likely to have appeared in **A** having the form *þo*. In the Ax tradition, a reflex of *þo* appears in the demonstrative *þese / þo* of **m** but has evidently been lost from **r** and restored independently in V and, correctly positioned, in JN and H (as *þen*). The **B** reading *herof* could be a revision or a Bx ⇒ for the same word. **180 (Z 169, A 172, B 184)** *flailes*: the nonsense reading *fuales* in XY (< y) and D (< u), probably that of **x**, has been independently corrected in the other **x**-family mss, in P² probably from a **p**-source.

Z 170 is a correct unique line, presumed omitted in **A** as unnecessary elaboration.

182 (Z 172, A 174, B 186) *potte ful*: firmly attested in **ZBC** and more appropriate for a serving of *cooked* peas. No reason appears for its possible ⇒ for *potel*, a word which shows no variation to *potful* at 6.398 // **AB**. *ymakid* **A**: **ZB**'s expanded past participle form authorises emendation of **A**. **184** *Spitteden*: the past pl. of *spitten* 'to dig to a spade's depth' (see MED s.v. *spitten* v. 2). The tense-ambiguous **p** form, to which u varies, results from assimilative loss of the preterite morpheme. **188 (Z 175–76, A 177–78, B 191)** *blynde*: in **A** 178 supported by **Z**; the punctuation here aims to reduce what may be judged a weakness in the repetition. *Ka*'s conjecture *blereyed* on the basis of the RUE variant for *bedrede* at 177 is unjustified on grounds of sense or style. Concerning Bx, however, *K–D* may be right that some material is lost after 192, for the *brokelegged* idea of **ZA** 176/178 is retained at **C** 188, and that of *lame men* **ZA** 178/180 at **C** 189. However, after the change evident in **B** 192, reconstruction would be hazardous; so this must remain a possible case of 'non-linear' development, with **C** re-using **A** material omitted in initial revision to **B**.

ZA 177 (179) *ote*: preferrred here to *hote* on the strength of **Z** (and cf. *hauer* at **A** 266 below, and the w reading in its Apparatus). Either has acceptable sense and metre, and Ax was quite possibly spelled with unetymological *h* as at **Z** 120, 130.

196 *lone*: the harder reading (MED s.v. *lone* n. (1), 1(c) 'reward') and one that gives a characteristic internal rhyme in the b-half. It doubtless represents y and thence x^1, the **x**-witnesses I and u having varied to the **p** reading for the same presumed reason that **p** diverged from Cx, visual error partly induced by mistaking the sense as 'loaf' (*SkR–K*). But in its five other uses in the sg., four in **C** and one in **Z**, the 'loaf' word is spelled *loef* or *loof,* and the present instance must involve a lexeme of wider meaning (though no doubt the *lone* included a 'loaf'). The **p** ms Q has made the converse variation from its exemplar to the reading here judged correct on grounds of sense. **197, 203 (Z 182, A 184, B 197)** correspond to one line in each of the earlier versions. 197 is closer in the a-half to the word-order of **B**, 203 to that of **ZA**, possibly suggesting that the sequence subject / verb / adverb in original **B** might have been as in **ZA**; but since neither sense nor metre is affected, there is no case for emending Bx here (cf. **B** 198). The second line is rejected by *R–K* (p. 172) as a Cx error; but the repetition has a rhetorical purpose, need not have been supplied to provide a subject for *ʒaf* 204, and could thus be original (cf. the repetition at **A** 177–78 above). **204 (Z 183, A 185, B 198)** The Bx line has no obvious fault of sense or metre, and the acceptability canon ought perhaps to override the linear postulate here. But in the light of **ZAC**, scribal rewriting is strongly suggested by its caution about generosity to erstwhile feigned beggars, and the *K–D* restoration to accord with the other versions is consequently adopted. **207 (Z 185, A 187, B 200)** *erd*: certain in **Z**, the probable reading of *C*-**p** and, to judge by the **C** variants *erthe* and *ʒerd* **x** (replicated in the **A** and **B** traditions), also that of ?Bx (< L(M) = β, R = α). Of the **A** readings, four are easier reflexes and the fifth, *hurde* V, an orthographic variant of the same presumed form (the spelling is here adapted to that of ms T). *euere*: judged on

the strength of agreed **ZAC** as lost in Bx through partial haplography (*þere < euere*). **209 (Z 186, A 188, B 202)** **C** revises unusually to scan as a vocalic Type III or, if the caesura comes after *Hunger*, as Type Ie. **216** *filial*: recorded only here (see MED s.v. *filial* adj.), and so inevitably a cause of difficulty to the copyists. The **p**-scribe probably wrote *fial*, two of the reflexes (QS, M) suggesting that it was understood as connected with 'faith' and a third, *final*, being a desperate attempt at correction that produces virtual nonsense (D may have compared its **x** exemplar with a **p** ms here as often elsewhere). The required sense '[love] due from a child' would also have seemed odd, because the folk are not Piers's children but his brethren. But **L** may have meant '[love] due to me as a [fellow] child of Truth [i.e. as a sibling]', or, as MED s.v. glosses, 'expected of...a fellow Christian', an idea that fits well with *blody bretherne* in 217 (see further Hill 2002:67–72). The **p** reading *fial* 'trustworthy, genuine' (from OF *fiel*) defended by *R–K* (p. 151), though also a *hapax* in ME, is not quite as hard as *filial* contextually (and has left no trace in the language). **217 (Z 191, A 193, B 207)** *And*: on the showing of agreed **ZAC** restored to **B** as lost from Bx through visual assimilation to *And* 206, 209. If R here = α, this could be what Bx read, β and F having both levelled to the more commonly expected pronominal form, and Y(OC²) having introduced *& yet* as a further smoothing. *for* **ZAC**: the probable form of **B** (to which Y has felicitously varied), Bx having inserted an unnecessary attribution-phrase. **221–22 (Z 195, A 197, B 211)** In the light of agreed **ZAB** the Cx lines both appear scribal in form: they scan (221) as inauthentic *aa / bb* or, with some strain, as *aaa / bb* (Type IIb) on vowels, and (222) as Type Ia, but with the first lift requiring two full staves in *lyflode*. Reconstruction here presumes the **ZAB** phrase lost by eyeskip from *hem > hem*; correcting the damaged line, it improves the metrical structure of 222, which emerges as new and displaying translinear alliteration initiated by the (revised) last lift of 221. The sense is also superior to that of Cx, which has an unidiomatic phrase *amaystren to.*

Z 196–201 are unique and are presumed deleted in revision as yet another case of unnecessary elaboration (cf. **Z** 1.65, 2.47, 100, 189, 3.96, 122–24, 7.245). **223 (Z 202, A 198, B 212)** *herke(ne)* **ZC** / *here* **AB**: the small but real sense-difference suggesting a reversion to the first verb so as to heighten the urgency. The **Z** phrase, however, shares its word-order with **AB**, not **C**. **226 (Z 205, A 201, B 215)** *abaue*: in the light of **ZAC** identified as original **B**, a rare word inviting ⇒ of another with similar form (though different sense) that might have seemed contextually more expected (see MED s.v. *abaven* v. 4, but with no illustration of the required transitive use); in **ZAB** evidently seen as specifying the command *holde* 204 //. *Sk*'s reading of the word as *abanen* (MED s.v.

banen v., citing only this) gives an inappropriate sense ('injure'). The conjunction *And* in most **A** mss may be a mis-expansion of (perhaps detached) *A* in Ax, and in **C** a revision after alteration of the preceding line's b-half, and perhaps better omitted. **227 (Z 206, A 202, B 216)** *gromes* 'low fellows' (MED s.v. 3a), which is better in context; *R–K*'s change to *gomes* is groundless, though Bx read *gomes* and *B*-M's reading could come from either **A** or **C** (*A*-V, conversely, has *gomes*). **229 (Z 208, A 204, B 218)** *Fortune* **ZAB**-β / *Fals(hed)* / *fals men*) *?B*-α**C**: a conflict attributable not to α's ⊗ from **C** but to anticipation of *false* in 219, the substance of which becomes otiose if α is authentic. **C**'s condensation of two lines into one eliminates reference to Fortune.

B 219–27 219 Bx as it stands is a Type IIIa line with an awkward five-syllable onset; the expanded form of the conjunction *oþer* adopted here provides an internal voiced fricative stave eliding with *any* to form the first lift (a full stave). **221 (Z 211, A 207, C 231)** *kynde wolde*: discerned on the showing of **ZAC** as indicating the probable **B** original, for which *god techeþ* Bx appears a scribal ⇒ aiming to increase Hunger's authority. The injunction, coming from this speaker, would more properly express natural than divine positive law. **223 (A 209, C 233)** *norisse*: conjectured as the required stave-word in key-position to correct a Bx line scanning imperfectly as *aa / xx*. Its unusual extended sense here (see MED s.v. *norishen* v. 4(a) 'support, sustain') might have invited ⇒ of the alliterating near-synonym *help*; no wider reconstruction is required. **225 (A 212)** *þow*: necessary as the key-stave in a line of either Type IIIa or of Type Ia (with *Theiȝ* as first stave). L and R here appear to preserve β and α respectively, and thence Bx, M having varied with γ (though not in this instance by correction). **227** *bilowe*: here judged the likely Bx reading (< LM = β, + α) against *biloue* γ. The latter is admittedly closer to the Latin and to the translation of this in // **A**, but it may have been suggested by the former. On the other hand, the wordplay of LMα seems characteristic, and the rôle of humility in winning grace recalls the teaching at B 5.620. The form, a recognised variant of *bilouen*, is more probably a coinage based on the simplex *lowen*, found at 10.306 with reflexive prn (see MED s.v. *louen* v.1 4(b)). **236 (Z 212, A 213, B 228)** *good*: on the strength of **ZBC** agreement judged the probable reading of **A**, though perhaps not that of Ax (which may here have had an ambiguously-spelled **goud*). Five unrelated witnesses have corrected a reading obviously inferior in context. **241** *swoet and*: rejected as tautological by *R–K*, who for *swetynge* adopt *swetande* to account for Cx; but as the *annominatio* is typical, the reconstruction is unjustified. **242** *oure*: needlessly emended to *ȝoure* by *R–K*, who take the verbs as imperatives, whereas they are better read as infinitives dependent on *we sholde* understood. **242a**

The **p** order (preferred by *R–K*) is more logical, but not therefore necessarily original: **x** has the order found in the macaronic parallel **ZAB**, where *swynk* = Lat. *labor*, and this may have influenced **L** in revising. **244 (Z 219, A 220, B 235)** The **ZA** lines appear to be 'licensed' macaronics with a blank first stave, and the **B** line may be of the same type unless *frigoré* has two lifts and *Piger pro* forms a dip, giving a Type IIIa line. **L**'s 'conjugate' macaronics (Schmidt 1987:98) allow both lifts of a Latin half-line to fall in a single word only if this is a lexical compound, and do not base the second lift on an inflexional ending.

247/48 (Z 221/22, A 22/–23, B 237/38) The *?Cx* form of line 248 scans awkwardly with a five-syllable prelude-dip including an important noun (*suluer*). The original of 247 as here reconstructed makes the de-stressed lexical word the verb and reduces line 248 to one with a more normal shape in the a-half. The present re-division has been anticipated by u, which may represent **x** (as at 19.255 / 6), y having therefore presumably erred here with **p**, or be an independent correction. **248** *menyng*: treated as a verbal noun by *R–K*, who read *in*] *and* after P²RM, but easily interpretable as a participial adjective in an elliptical construction ('and [he did this] intending that...').

Z 230–32 seem authentic in both metre and phrasing, with typical wordplay on *for* as preposition and conjunction in 231. 230a had been previously used at Z 5.48 // and the whole line is re-used at B 9.72, which it seems hard to imagine a scribal redactor recalling at this point. The anecdotal character of the parenthesis may have led to removal of the lines in **A** as serving no useful purpose.

255 (Z 226, A 227, B 242) As it stands, Bx will scan as a Type IIIb line with *he* its first lift. But this gives the pronoun unnaturally heavy emphasis and may be diagnosed as the consequence of Bx's ⇒ of *wiþ* for the word here conjectured, in the light of **ZA** *senes / siþen* and **C** *thenne*, as the necessary vocalic first stave (*after*). **257–58 (Z 227–29, A 228–30, B 243–45)** The line-division of **C** may be securely accepted as that supported by **ZAB**. Since *p²* here agrees with e and q, and it is thus likely that *p¹* will represent **p**, <RM>'s source may have been collated with a corrected copy of **p** (see also on 17.116; *Intro.* III C § 49) or else compared with **x** (as suggested also by their substantive reading at 10.80).

A 235–36 (Z 238, B 250–51, C 260–61) 235 is of Type IIa on vowels with a 'supplemental' fifth vocalic stave, but it would scan more effectively on lexical words in the a-half if *get* were emended to *fet*, the contracted 3 sg. of *fetten* (MED s.v. 4(a)); **B**'s *fedeþ* may be a revision-echo of this (cf. note on *garisoun* B 6.138). **236** in principle scans vocalically with a mute stave in each half, but meaning and rhythm are greatly improved by conjecturing in position two the adverb *here* to balance *here* in 235. The sense is that the faithful worker with his hands is assured of reward from God in this world in the form of his sustenance. The first *here* will have gone by haplography before *here²*, a loss all the easier had Ax read as J, with *here²* immediately following *here¹*. In seeming awareness of the gap in sense, tR supply the postulated adverb *after* the object noun.

269 (Z 242, A 240, B 255) *groneth* **p**: arguably less likely to be original than *greueth*, which corresponds more closely to *akeþ* **ZAB**; but equally, it may have been moved back to take account of the revision of B 257 at 271. One or other variant is a visual error for Cx's reading (in *C-R* an original *grewith* is altered a.h. to *Gronythe*). **271 (Z 244, A 242, B 257)** *þat*: judged the probable **B** reading in the light of agreed **ZAC**, *and* Bx having been inserted to ease the transition, with *B-B* coinciding or else showing ⊗ from **C**.

Z 245 exhibits authentic metre and is less likely to be a scribal expansion of 244 than an original line omitted as over-specific in revision to **A**. Vestigial retention of *ofte* as the last word in A 242 is indirect evidence of the authenticity of Z 245.

274 (Z 250, A 247, B 262) *til* **BC** / *forto* **ZA**: certain in **C** as in **Z**; but the pair *for* and *to* in the AxBx traditions could be split variants of the form reconstructed for **A**. Since **B** nowhere instances the word, which is little found outside **L** (see MED s.v. *forto* prep. 1(a)), while **A** does (with minority support) at 7.2, the commoner form is preferred for **B**, the rarer for **A**.

A 250 (Z 253, B 265) *Leue*: in the light of **ZB** preferred for **A** as fitting better with the secondary sense of the final phrase ('persuasive to luxury'). *Loue* (though also apt here) is presumably the consequence of *e / o* confusion.

B 266, Z 254, A 251 The **A** reading *alongid* is harder than *afyngred* and more likely to be revision of the latter than a scribal ⇒ for it. Thus if **Z** does not here show ⊗ from **B**, it must preserve an original first revised in **A** and then restored in **B** (*B-F*, which is closer in sense to **A**, is here unlikely to represent α and thence Bx but may show partial ⊗ from an **A** source).

283 *be of* **p**: necessary for the sense, and producing a line with cognative staves (|b| |p| |p|); no reason immediately appears for loss of the phrase from **x**. *R–K* take the conjunction *ȝif* as the imperative of *ȝiuen* and read [*the pore be thy*] for *be of*, but no emendation is required for either sense or metre. **284** *in thy gate* **x**: rejected by *R–K* (p. 155) as having the contextually less apt sense 'way' (MED s.v. *gate* n. (2) 2(a)), while **p** is very close to 11.42 (*at þe ȝate*). But there is no reason why *gate* here should not mean 'gateway' (MED s.v. n. (1) 1 (a)), this use of *in* is harder than *at*, and the sense 'at the gate of your house' identical. **290 (Z 255, A 252, B 267)** *eres*: firmly established for **BC**, the minority **A** variant likely to be a

revision of **Z** *eyes*, for which *?Ax armes* may be a visual error (*eie* and *hede* seem random ⇒). **291 (Z 256, A 253, B 268)** *hodes*: in the light of agreed **ZBC** (only *C-DM* having *hode*) preferred as the probable original reading of **A**. The sg. may have been induced in Ax through the influence of *foode* in the b-half, parallelism with *cloke* 254, or judgement that a single garment was apt for a single actant (*A-L hodes* looks coincidental). **294 (Z 259, A 256, B 271)** *lest liflode him fayle* **AC**: tentatively adopted as the probable **B** reading, for which the Bx b-half seems a ⇒ conflating a word from the posited original (*liflode*) with a reminiscence of B Pr 86 (*for [...] is swete*). In principle, Bx could be revising the **A** form back to that of **Z**, and **C** revising **B** back to **A**. But as this would involve an unusual process of double restoration, it seems on balance preferable to see Bx as scribal, leaving the possibility that the Z ms reading here shows ⊗ from a post-Bx **B** source. Emendation of **Z** is however pointless, since the line gives acceptable sense and metre, and 'double restoration' cannot finally be ruled out.

Z 260–78 form a unique passage of nineteen lines, one of which (271) recurs at Z 8.47 // **AB** but is aptly deployed here between an English line introducing it and another translating it. 263–64 correspond to C 295–96 // **AB** (see esp. on **B 272**), but the rest of the digression on physicians has no parallel in the later texts. Stylistically, the lines cohere with **L**'s usual manner and the macaronic 267 seems of the 'intermediate' type (Schmidt:1987:100) found e.g. at 7.152, Z 7.219, scanning *aa / xx*. The passage's excessive length and over-particularity sufficiently explain its replacement by a pithy couplet in **AB**, only the first line of which is revised in **C**.

295 (Z 263–64, A 257, B 272) In the Bx tradition the line fails to scan both in β and in α (*aab / ba*) and to make sense in the a-half of α, unless R's *morareres* is a mere scribal slip for *morþareres*. In the light of Z 263, the substantive reading of β's a-half recommends itself as a basis for emendation; but **A**'s *mo* favours instead α's form and invites explanation of R's meaningless noun as misconstruing an α reading **mo:::eres*. (*B-F*'s *moraynerys* appears an individual attempt to make sense of a reading like R's). This is here reconstructed to accord with **A** *mo liȝeris*. **A** 257–58 may then be seen as rendering the two main ideas of Z 263–64 (that ignorant physicians are (a) murderers and (b) liars) in the reverse order, preserved in **BC**. The variant *murþereris*, β's attempt to make intelligible the problematic original attested in R (possibly a defective reading in Bx), will then be perhaps a coincidence with Z 263 (suggested by the sense of B 273) rather than a source of ⊗ in **Z** at its scribal phase. **297 (Z 279, A 259, B 274)** *Poul / Pernel*: secure readings in **Z**, **B** and **C**. The reading of **A** is likely to have been as in **Z**, since *Pernel* could hardly have been a ⇒ for *Poul*, and both **A** families attest it. The **A** variant *Poul* may reflect misreading of an abbreviated form of *Pernel* rather than showing ⊗ from a **B** source. **298–99 (Z 280–81, A 260–61, B 275–76)** In the light of agreed **ZAC**, the Bx order of these lines appears likely to be scribal, though no obvious reason for the error appears. **301 (Z 282, A 262, B 277)** *I¹:* necessary for the grammar of the sentence, and perhaps lost from Bx by distraction from *I* in 278 below. *B*-GBF may have added by collation with **A** or **C**, but the commonsense correction could have been independently made. *the* **ZC** / *God* **AB**: both acceptable, and the direction of revision uncertain. Most probably *God* is a revised form in **A**, *the* likewise in **C**, but either scribal intensification or censorship remains a possibility for *God* or *the* respectively. *ne wol* **x** / *nel* **p**: despite agreeing with **ZA**, **p** is less likely to be original, since the last two lifts are required to bear heavy emphasis so as to form the T-Type line in **B** that was retained in **C**: *ne wól I wénde*. For an exact parallel to this unique authentic metrical pattern (*Intro.* IV § 40) cf. *wél youre wórdes* Z 7.279. **302 (Z 283, A 263, B 278)** *Er* **AC** / *Til* **ZB**: the **Z** reading may show **B** influence, or **B** may have revised back to the first form, with **C** then restoring the reading adopted in **A**. But just as probably, since the two conjunctions were contextually in free variation, Bx *Til* may be unconscious scribal ⇒ of an advancing form. **305 (Z 286, A 266, B 281)** The **A** line is evidently a rewriting of **Z**, which seems original, but scans imperfectly in Ax, as in the light of revised **C** does Bx (*aa / xa*), though the last two lifts appear substantively authentic. In the emendation proposed here, the particle *ek* provides a mute key-stave in what now scans as a Type Ib line. The mechanism of loss could have been eyeskip from *an(d) > an* in both archetypes. *K–D*'s adoption of *cake of otes*] *haue cake* from // C VIII 305, attractive because a reconstruction rather than a conjecture, nonetheless presupposes ⇒ of a lexically easier expression (for the word's rarity see MED s.v. *haver* n. 2, where **L**'s is the only C14th citation other than proper names). **309 (Z 290, A 270, B 285)** The b-half reading in **Z** confirms that attested in *A*-family **m**, where *plante* is the past participle with the sense 'planted out' (see MED s.v. *plaunten* v. 1(a)). The **r** ↔ to an easier reading is repeated in *B*-β, which may but does not certainly here preserve Bx. The Z ms could have derived from *A*-**m** but more probably retains the original form of **Z**. The *B*-α variant appears to have been an unmetrical phrase involving *herbes*, F characteristically normalising the metre with an alliterating synonym for *queynte*; but the **C** revision's a-half indicates the likely presence of *plauntes* in **B**. **315 (Z 295, A 275, B 290)** *Thanne*: on the showing of agreed **ZAC** probably the original **B** reading, Bx having inserted *And* through inducement from *And* 289. *me*: the assured reading of **ZC** and superior on grounds of sense. *B*-F here shows either unconscious influence from preceding *þi*, as presumably does *A*-**r**, or ⊗ from an **A** source of **r**-type. **316 (Z 296, A**

276, B 291) *tho*: in the light of agreed **ZBC** likely to have been present in **A** and lost by Ax, perhaps through visual assimilation to following *pe-*. The *A*-R reading may be an attempted correction in awareness of *þo-*, but misunderstanding it as the demonstrative; w presumably corrected independently, perhaps by reference to a **C** source. **317 (Z 297, A 277, B 292)** *lappe*: in the light of agreed **ZC** the collective singular, the older and arguably harder form, is preferred as the probable original in **B** (> Bx > α > R) and in **A**, where Ax may have read *lappes*. **321 (Z 302, A 282, B 297)** *poysen* **AB**: here presumably replacing *peyse* **Z** as part of a complete revision of the b-half. **Z**'s reading is that conjectured by *Ka* (in ignorance of **Z**) as the original of **A**; but there is no serious reason for rejecting the boldly humorous metaphor of quelling Hunger with food. A motive for **A**'s revision could have been the poor logic of **Z**'s b-half; **C**'s exhibits characteristics greater directness. *opere erbes*: a b-half with awkward rhythm due to the heavy four-syllable dip before the pre-final lift. However, if this is *cresses*, **C** may have read simply *opere* or *erbes*, either word being a Cx insertion consequent on judging the sense incomplete. **322 (Z 303, A 283, B 298)** *and*: clearly the reading of **C** and adopted here for **B** as superior to the presumed Bx reading, possibly the asyndetic original. But on the showing of **Z**, where it is in a subordinate clause (co-ordinate in **C**), it is probably better in **A** to accept *þat* (functioning as a temporal conjunction), since the Ø-reading would make *cam* into the main verb. **323** *dentiesliche* XYD: here taken as a form of *deynteuosliche* (so *p¹*), but possibly an error for *deyntifliche* IUQK (preferred by *R–K*). Both adverbs are rare and their sense is the same (see MED s.v. *deintevousliche* and *deintifliche*). **325** *wandren*: the second of three infinitives in 325–26 dependent on *wolde*; the preterite in **p** is an easy error, attested also in several copies of **A** and **B**. **329 (Z 310, A 290, B 305)** *brewestares* **AC**: here tentatively judged the probable original for which *in burgh is to* will be a smoothing after a visual error. The sense and metre of Bx are unexceptionable, and it could be a reversion to the **Z** form of the b-half, like the case at C 294 //, challenging the uniform operation of linear revision. Alternatively, as tentatively concluded here, **Z** could show ⊗ at the scribal phase from a post-Bx **B** source (for discussion of the problem see *Intro.* III *Z* §§ 23–7). **330 (Z 311, A 291, B 306)** *to lyue on but* **C**: to be discriminated as the probable original in **B** and also in **A**. The variant *but lyue on / with* attested in some **AB** mss is a simplification (though acceptable) of the boldly figurative revision, returning to the form that might have been original in **Z** (unless the **Z**-ms here shows ⊗ from an **A** or **B** source). **331 (Z 312, A 292, B 307)** *Deynede...aday*: perhaps the identical reading in all four versions, and certainly giving the best sense; but as revision is possible, emendation of **Z** must be cautious. The verb will have been preterite in

ZBC, those **A** mss with the present probably reflecting a tense-ambiguous Ax form **deynet*. The negative particle was in **AC** and may be judged omitted from *B*-α through visual error (*-en to*) or through mistaking the verb 'to deign' for the one meaning 'to disdain' (see MED s.v. *deynen* v. (2); and cf. B 10.78). The latter could have been the intended verb in **Z**, but *not* could as well have been lost mechanically there, as it seems (on grounds of sense) that the phrase *to dyne a* was omitted through eyeskip from *Dey-* to *day*. In **AB** *dynen* is transitive 'eat' (MED s.v. *dinen* v. (2) 2 (a)), in **ZC** (with *of*) has the sense 'dine (upon)' (ib. (1)). **333 (Z 314, A 294, B 309)** *or ybake* **ZC**: supported by *B*-β and almost certain to have been the reading of **A**. Ax having read Ø / *bake*, *A*-**m** may have inserted / substituted *rostid* or have been contaminated from a **B** source (and then corrupted). The reason for the loss in *A*-**r** will have been the length of the line (Type Ic), causing misjudgement of the caesura as located after *flessh* and so of the line as of Type Ib. The sense requires *or ybake*, for the contrast is not between 'fresh meat' and 'fried fish' but between '(variously) cooked *fresh* meat or fish' (eaten hot) and 'smoked meat or fish' (eaten cold).

    Z 316 is a unique line of good sense and correct metre, presumably deleted in **A** as repeating too closely the sense of Z 310, 314 (for a similar case cf. Z VII 245). **336 (Z 318, A 297, B 312)** *waryen* **ZAC**: most probably also the original reading of **B**, for which Bx may be a censoring ⇒ of a milder, less hostile term in a politically sensitive context. **340 (Z 321, A 300, B 317)** *non* **ZC**: providing the most acceptable metrical form, though that proposed for **A** (on the basis of J's variant and that of R, which here reads *her non wolde*) gives the same sense and, with elision of *wolde* and *here*, smoother metre than Bx. The latter, in having both *þer* (?retained from Ax) and *of hem* (? = *here* **B**), requires muting of *wolde* and deferred stress on *noon* to avoid producing an uncharacteristically heavy four-syllable final dip. **341 (Z 322, A 301, B 318)** *his* xp^2 / *þe* p^1: the p^1 variant, supported by the majority of **A** and a couple of **B** witnesses, may be a pointed allusion to the demands of the Statute of Labourers that could have been censored in **x**, ?Bx and sundry **A** mss. But if **Z** is here original, the metaphorical sense of *statut* would appear to have been present from the outset, and it was failure to grasp this that prompted ⇒ of *þe*. The 'Statute' in question is that of Hunger, the labourers' 'master'. *so sturne* **C**: apparently an authorial transposition to prose-order so as to produce a Type Ib line with the rhythmic feel of a T-type. In the new b-half *lokede* does not now form a lift, but yields its stress to the alliterating non-lexical adverb *so*, and *R–K*'s alteration to the **AB** reading has no warrant whatever. **344 (Z 325, A 304, B 321)** *thorw* **CA**: judged likely to have been the reading of **B**. In principle, **B** could have restored the form first used in **Z**, or *wyth* could be a Z-ms ⊗ from a **B**

source, but more probably Bx is a scribal ⇒ of a synonym contextually in free variation with it. *wastours to chaste* **ABC**: **A**'s revised b-half following **Z** in its use of end-rhyme. That **Z**'s rhyme-word is different is diagnostic evidence of originality, this being a device no scribe could have imitated so closely. **346 (Z 328, A 307, B 324)** *sayth* **ZAC**: likely to have been original also in **B**, Bx's preterite being a ⇒ under influence from following *sente* and perhaps a tense-ambiguous exemplar form **seit*. The second verb *sente* is quite possibly a contracted present, rather than a preterite in a sentence referring to a current message but a past warning (since they are the same). **347 (Z 327, A 306, B 323)** *thorw²*: probably absent from both Ax and Bx, its presence in **Z** and in *C*-**x** (?< Cx) arguing for its inclusion in all versions, since it is more likely to have been scribally omitted as redundant than to have been added.

    B 325 The Bx line has the inauthentic pattern *aab / bx* and it seems likeliest that either the verb or the noun (rather than the adverb) has been supplanted by a non-alliterating word. Against an earlier conjecture *mone* (*K–D Sch¹*), the present suggestion posits scribal ⇒ of a commoner verb rather than the somewhat pointless replacement of one heavenly body by another, though C 350 could admittedly be interpreted as the reflex of such a reading. (The conjectured verb *merke* offers a possible emendation for *se* later at B 13.25, but the case there is less compelling). **349 (B 326)** *an viii* **x**: most probably the reading of Cx on grounds of sense (however elusive). The presumed **p** reading *an vm*, and MN *a vin*, both not just enigmatic but nonsensical, reveal progressive stages of misreading of the three minims after *v*. The line appears to scan as an enriched extended Type III with counterpoint on |θ| and |ʃ| (*abb / aa*), the second fricative stave being liaisonal (*with_an*) and muted, but with a 'supplemental' |f| stave in *fólwynge*. The substantive correctness of 'viii' is indirectly confirmed by the quoted form of this line in Crowley's preface, which gives 'eight' (see *Sk*, B, xxxiv), and more directly by *eighte* in B 326, the line under revision. *R–K*'s tentative conjecture *vii* for *viii* (p. 170) should therefore be rejected. *multiplied* **B**: elliptical for 'be multiplied', and most probably the reading of Bx (< Lα), M having here unusually *added* to a reading originally the same as that of γ (see *Intro.* III B § 34). But agreement of L and α will adequately guarantee Bx here, if *multiplie* is judged an easier reading induced by desire for parallelism with the preceding infinitive *haue*.

Passus IX (ZA VIII, B VII)

Collation In 75–281 a second text appears in I, selectively cited in the Apparatus with sigil *I*.

1 (ZA VIII 1, B VII 1) *sente* **ZAC**: discriminated as the probable **B** reading, Bx having inserted an unnecessary pronoun. **7 (ZAB 7)** *manere* ZAC: adopted in **B** as the necessary first stave-word, Bx *ooþer* being a ⇒ of the non-alliterating near-synonym common in the phrase 'or any *x*'. **10 (ZAB 10)** *reumes*: preferred also in **A** on the strength of agreed **ZBC** and greater contextual appropriateness of the plural. **13 (ZAB 13)** *yblessed that / yf*: **Z** is closer to **BC**, though the Ax reading is not easier or objectionable in metre or style. However, its sense is less appropriate in context, since it would seem more important that the bishops should be 'holy' than that they should bestow formal blessings. While **Z**'s a-half could show ⊗ from **B** or **C**, this seems unlikely since the b-half corresponds to that of the **A** tradition and not the revised **BC** form. Ax *þat* could originate from misreading *y* as *þ* and taking *blissen* as an original perhaps spelled **blissyt*, a form ambiguous between the past participle intended and the present indicative (*blissyþ*), with *and* a subsequent smoothing.

ZA 19 (B 17, C 21) *hey*: the right **A** reading on grounds of sense, doubtless adopted into *A*-HKM as individual corrections, perhaps in knowledge of **B**. Error could have arisen through inducement from the Ø-article form, by misidentification of the final consonant in *hiȝ* as *s* or *r*.

23 (ZA 21, B 19) *no a*: reconstructed in the light of **AB(Z)** as the probable **C** reading, of which *no* and *a* appear split variants. *C*-**x** *no pena* is identical with **Z**, a possible first draft, but *a* is unlikely to have been dropped in **C**, since it forms part of a formula. *nolde*: required in **C** as the key-stave in what is, after revision of the b-half, an extended Type IIIa line; either could be right in **ZAB**. **25 (ZA 23, B 21)** *and* **ABC**: adopted for **Z** on grounds of sense, as there are two oaths, not one, the Z-scribe mistaking *ant* for visually similar *ac*. **28 (ZA 26, B 24)** *And (That) bad / That they sholde*: either reading is acceptable on grounds of sense and metre, but the direct form attested in **A** and reflected in **C** indicates that Bx may here be a ⇒ of an indirect-clause construction suggested by the phrase *a lettre* in 23. If the Bx form is scribal, it is likely to be the reading present in **B**¹, the copy used in revision to **C**, since the latter's *That bad* appears to accommodate both **A** and Bx. The Z-ms reading could show influence from **B** here or be coincidental, although in principle this could be a case of non-linear revision: **Z(A)B(C)**. **29 (ZA 27, B 25)** *wynnynges* **CB**-α**Z** / *wynnyng* **B**-β**Ax**: either is acceptable, but one is likelier to be original in all versions, and Ax's singular is here judged an error caused perhaps through failure to register an abbreviated plural ending. **30 (ZA 28, B 26)** *men* **ZBC**: possibly lost from **A**, but as the sense of Ax is unexceptionable, no emendation need be made. **33 (ZA 30, B 28)** *Amende / bete(n) / do boote to*: progressively revised, but with unchanged sense ('repair'). The multiple variants in the Ax tradi-

tion suggest a difficult original, and while this could have been *bynde* d, the reading *bete* in *r*²?**m** (for which M *amendyn* is a synonymic ⇒) is closest to expanded **B** and revised **C**. But *aboute* could now mean 'in the region' as well as 'around their centres', as it probably does in *A*-d (see further *Intro.* II § 74). **35 (ZA 33, B 30)** again shows progressive revision (minor in **A**), with probably a 'non-linear' return in **C**'s a-half to the idea of God's love that is present in **ZA** but omitted in **B**. In **Z** *oure*, required for the sense and restored on the evidence of **A**, will have been lost by attraction of *for* > Lord*us*, as also in *A* -JWM.

B 33–4 (ZA 36–7, C 37–8) 33 *angel* **ZAC**: the probable original also in **B**, for which Bx (like *C*-I and *A*-M) will have substituted the more emphatic and metrically awkward *Archangel* (*B*-HmF's correction may show ⊗ from **C** or **A**). **34** Progressive revision (minor in **A**, from Type Ia to Ib) terminates in a **C** line of Type Ib that guides emendation of the unmetrical b-half of Bx (*aa / xa*). *drede*: the noun (close in sense to *despeyre* **C**), here conjectured as the necessary key-stave for which Bx *fere* is a non-alliterating synonymic ⇒, subsequently smoothed to a verb by addition of the pronoun *yow*. *deying*: judged also the reading of Cx on grounds of superior sense. **39 (ZA 38, B 36)** The *C*-**x** line is preferred as having the same metrical pattern as **B** (Type Ie); **p** will have lost se*the* through homoarchy before se*nde*. **41 (ZA 42, B 37)** *wopen / wepten*: either the strong or weak preterite is acceptable, the present-tense form in some **A** mss the result of *e / o* confusion with the former. **42 (ZA 44, B 38)** *preyde for* **C**: evidently a revision, and *R–K*'s ⇒ of *preiseden* **B** has no warrant. *copiede*: conjectured on grounds of sense as the correct reading in **A** and as necessary for the same reason in **Z**. A near-homophonic pun on *copede* 'provided with clothing' (i.e. metaphorical for 'glossed', 'laundered') may be intended in the light of preceding *clopis*, which could have induced the *copede* variant. *couth / couden*: 'made a return / recompense (of)'. *Ka*'s reading (p. 450) of the phrase as a 'somewhat unusual... assimilation of *connen þonk* to *don...mede*' is unconvincing; for while in ME one may 'feel thanks', and so 'offer it' (MED s.v. *connen* v. 6(g)), it is not possible to 'feel reward' and so, by extension, offer it (the construction *coude mede* is paralleled in *kydde reward* at *Purity* 208). The verb is therefore more convincingly identified as the pt. pl. of *kithen* (MED s.v. v. 4(a)), with loss of *th* through assimilation to following *d* and with *ou* the reflex of an original rounded central vowel |y| < OE *cyþen* (cf. the nominal form *couthe* at 17.196). The variant spellings *couþe* HN, *cowthin* J, *couth* **Z** may indicate assimilation of *d* to preceding *þ*. Either way, loss of one or other consonant from an original **coupden* has produced a form orthographically identical with the preterite of *connen*. **44 (ZA 45, B 39)** The identity of **C**'s a-half with **ZA** may suggest (on the 'linear' assumption) that **B** read the same;

but *pardon* in preceding C 43 indicates that the word was likely to have been present in B^1, so that this may be another case of 'non-linear' revision in **C**.

B 45 *preue*: Bx could have a 'licensed' macaronic structure (*aa / xx*), but is here judged a ⇒ of the more obvious 'believe' for a stave-word with the contextually-appropriate sense 'find [by experience]' (MED s.v. *preven* v. 4(a)).

47 (Z 51, A 50, B 41) *innócent(z)*: with wrenched stress to provide a required first stave, and bringing out the etymological sense, which each b-half further specifies; repeated in 19.270 //. The normal stress-pattern is exhibited earlier at 3.98 and B 3.242 (no //). **48 (Z 52, A 51, B 48)** *coueyteth nat here / hise*: the form of **ZAC** suggests that Bx, while unexceptionable in metre and sense, may have smoothed a defective b-half **coueiteth hise*; but emendation is very tentative, as non-linear revision in **C** cannot be ruled out (cf. 28, 35, 44). **49 (Z 53, A 52, B 49)** Since the a-half gives acceptable sense and metre, the whole **B** line could be rewritten and this be another case of 'non-linear' revision in **C**; but near-agreement of **ZAC**'s a-half favours emending the over-explicit reading of Bx. *lawe...declareth (shewiþ)*: the Bx line (Type IIa with an enriched fifth stave) looks like a scribal transposition of the main idea to the a-half, with subsequential smoothing.

A 54 (Z 55, B 51, C 50) *sykirly sauf* A: the order preferred on the evidence of **Z**, making the adverb a functional intensifier, not a mere asseveration. *þe...witnessiþ*: the **m**L order and wording, supported by **Z** and by (revised) **B**.

54 (Z 61, A 60, B 58) *mede* ABC: *mercedem* **Z** produces an authentic macaronic line; but while it seems to anticipate (or echo) the thought of C 3.290 ff, the Latin here bears the simple sense 'reward' of the Biblical text cited at C 3.311, and its use is neither inconsistent with nor necessarily derived from **C**'s elaborate distinction between *mede* and *mercede*. *here (his) / Ø*: possibly (in the light of **ZBC**) lost from Ax; but no emendation for metre or sense seems required. **57 (Z 58, A 57, B 53)** *nedede / nediþ*: both perhaps reflexes of a tense-ambiguous Cx form **nedyt*; the past subjunctive is preferred as slightly harder (cf. 87 and 19.34).

B 59 (Z 62, A 61) The b-half appears metrically corrupt in *A*-**r** and in Bx, where it is followed first by what seems a scribal expansion of the presumed original and a spurious line. Correction of *A*-**r** is by transposition of its prose order, and it seems probable in the light of *trowe* ?**m** that the verb, whichever it was, meant 'know' or 'believe' rather than 'blame'. The **m**-variant, though based only on the one witness present (M), is preferred as having the support of **Z** (its variant *now* for *ou3t* arguing against its deriving here from **m**). In Bx, *Mathew is to blame* indicates that the Bx scribe took the verb as the

imperative plural of the homograph meaning 'blame' (MED s.v. *witen* v. (3)). As here given, the **B** line is superficially closer to *A*-**r**; but since the reconstruction borders on conjecture (see *Intro*. III *B* § 61), it is best on balance to prefer for **A** the ?**mZ** form, satisfactory in itself and attested by two independent sources. **C**'s lack of any reflex of **B** may suggest that B^1 had a highly corrupt reading.

Z 69 is a unique parenthetic line of the rare Type IIb, perhaps dropped as too grudging in tone, given the strict conditions already laid down in Z 70ff.

63 (Z 71, A 69, B 66) *he*: on the showing of **ABC**, *at* **Z** is diagnosed as an error for *a* 'he' (induced by following *that*) rather than as the vocalic (mainly NE Midl.) form of the relative pronoun. *yf* **ZBC**: omitted from Ax but independently added by RJ, and likely to have been in **A** if it bears stress and *but* is mute. *hy*: adopted for **C** as the probable Cx reading, of which *he, they* are divergent reflexes (*hi* G being a happy coincidence or survival in this very early witness). The singular (randomly attested) will have resulted from objection to the mixed number of the verb-subjects in the line. **66–7 (B 69–70)** The **B** line is re-divided so as to avoid the awkward rhythm produced by the Bx lineation, which requires in 69 either a masculine ending (*3yue þát*), an untypical final half-stress (*3yue þàt*), or else emendation by transposition of the prose order to *þat 3yue*. The re-division here leaves 70 as a Type IIIa line, with a gradation established from 'the needy', to 'the more needy', to 'the neediest'. In *B*-M, the comparative morpheme may be a reflex of the β reading, eliminated by γ and (unusually) by L, and visibly erased by M too, though the double comparative seems the harder form. *to gyuen* **p**: preferred to Ø **x** as giving a characteristic T-type line; this is unlikely to be scribal in origin, whereas the last lift could have been lost in **x** by assimilation to *gyue* at 66 above.

71–161 The first *large-scale addition* of completely new **C** material to which there is no parallel in **B**; it ends with an echo of 63, 67 above. Parts of this are inserted into the *A*-type Prologue in ms I (75–162, 188–254 after Pr 54, and 255–81 after Pr 83) and lines 66–281, with some omissions, also appear in the conflated **BC** ms Ht after B 6.158. Scase (1987) argues that their versions of the **C** lines on hermits derive from a single source, distinct from the text in the Cx tradition, that circulated independently before being incorporated into the [received] C-Text, and should be taken into account in editing. But the imperfect alliteration, clichés, lack of amplification and possible metrical experiment, that Scase notes point rather to its unoriginal character as an extract transplanted by the scribes of Ht and I. The reason is adequately explained by Pearsall 1981:193 (with reference only to the scribe of I) as to promote 'matter that seemed to him of great importance to a more prominent position' (see further *Intro*. III *C* §§ 20–2). The text of the lines in Passus IX of I is collated here as I, and their repeated form in the Prologue as *I* (following *Sk*). In no cases do *I* variants provide distinctive readings justifying full citation in the Apparatus; they are given in full in Pearsall 1981:186–7, and *R–K* 186–94. **87** *hym*: more unexpected than *hem* since preceded and followed by a plural verb and possessive, but characteristic of **L** in focussing on both the individual and the group. ID are **x** mss that accord with **p** in making the 'fit' more logical. **101** *lorélles*: the variant *lollares*, which does not allow generation of the needed |r| stave, has come in apparently by anticipation from 103. **107** Here and at 213 the scribe of Y has written 'lollard' (Schaap 2001). **137** *lollares* **p**: preferred to *lorelles* here in part because the phrase deliberately repeats 107, and the point of altering the collocation would be obscure; ⇒ of *lorelles* was presumably to avoid repetition or the allowing of any creditable meaning to *lollare*, which could have acquired too specific associations of religious heterodoxy by *c.* 1395, when **x** was copied (see *Commentary*). **157** *han / an*: both variants representing either the contracted form of the verb or the indefinite article with intruded aspirate, the former being preferable. **161** *beggares*: better than the sg. with both *lollares* and *strikares* 59, *they* 161. **166 (Z 74, A 72, B 88)** *they* **ZAC**: preferable also in **B**, for which Bx gives (as in 89) the plural pronoun of direct address, a ⇒ either deliberate or due to ʒ / þ confusion, and followed by smoothing. *lyue*: a revision of **Z** *leuen* 'believe', unless that is a spelling variant of *lyuen*, and *in no loue* (which the sense would require) has been lost by visual assimilation to the preceding verb. *nouʒt in no* **A**: although *A*-VW agree with **BC**, a double negative seems likely in Ax, with VW, T&*r* having split variants of the reading preserved in MN. This might suggest that **Z** *nat* is a vestige of the same reading (see note above).

Z 75–6 These lines on the *lollares'* failure in their religious duties are an elaboration of *lawe* 74 and could have been dropped in **A** as inappropriately mild before the serious charges to follow in Z 77–85=A 73–81. They appear stylistically and metrically authentic (*ward* 75 if stressed has an understood final *-e* or a syllabic *r*) and the elliptical phrasing of 76a is similar to that of C 15.58. **167 (Z 77, A 73, B 89)** In the light of (substantially) agreed **ZAC**, the **B** line may be reconstructed, *Manye of yow* declaring itself a scribal interference with the categorical statement attested. The Cx reading could have been as in **x**p^2, rather than as reconstructed from the posited split variants *Thei* and *Ne*, and a like reading in **B** might more readily account for Bx intrusion of *Manye of yow*. On balance, however, it seems preferable to conform the phrasing of **BC** to that of **ZA**, which have the pronoun. **173 (Z 84, A 80, B 96)** *lyueth*: *leden* **Z** could be an original revised in **A**, and the **m** variant a scribal ⇒ for a near-synonym in a set phrase.

B 97 (Z 85, A 81) *he*; *was* **AB** / *war*; *they* **Z**: revised in **A**, the word-order *war they* pointing to an original form, to which the final version reverts (C 174 *Þai*). **177 (Z 88, A 84, B 100)** *in*: lost in *A-r***B**-β by haplography after *-brok*en. **183 (Z 89–90, A 85–6, B 101–02)** **Z**'s b-half in 89, which is syntactically and metrically coherent with following 90, shows as an original form revised in **A**. The b-half in Z 90 uses the idiom employed at Z 7.39 //, but with a different reference. This suggests its authenticity, while its implication that the humble afflicted may be *superior* to Piers could help account for its removal in the revision to **A**. In C, B 102 // has been revised to become the concluding line of the pardon's dispositions. **184 (Z 91, A 87, B 103)** *For*: on grounds of grammar and sense the agreed **ABC** reading is adopted for **Z**, whose scribe has anticipated the *l* of *loue*. **185 (Z 92, A 88, B 104)** *vppon this puyre*: adopted on the showing of **ZAC** as the probable reading of **B**. Amongst the sub-archetypal variants the form of ?α gives a line with a possible key-stave in *vpón* that could represent Bx; but omission of *pur* might have resulted from misunderstanding of its sense and consequent objection to its linking with *erthe*, a possibility the two substantive **A** variants confirm. Alternatively, the loss occurred through homoarchy (purg*atorie* > pur *erthe*), as in the Ø variant attested in some **A** mss. ?Bx's elimination of the characteristic homophonic wordplay is thus unlikely to represent a revision that was later restored to its **A** form in **C**.

After 92, the **Z** *Version ends*. ms Bodley 851 continues in a different hand (*Q*) as an *A-Text* to the end of Passus VIII (printed in full by *R–B*). This is collated here with the sigil 'Z' that is used later for this copy's **C** continuation. 'Z' has one unique reading *inproued* at 153 (for *inpugnid*); at 111 its variant *anoþir be foulys þat we ne sholde* conflates the readings of **m** and **r**; and in a few instances it groups with UJ. Otherwise Z displays no striking affiliations in major readings over the course of some hundred lines; after two unmetrical lines of scribal prayer for blessing, it ends on fol. 140v with the unique colophon *Explicit vita et visio Petri Plowman* (omitted in the Apparatus). Hand *Q* continues in the next leaf with a **p**-type text of the **C** Version.

186 (Z 90, A 86, B 102) *the* **x**β and *Peers* **e**RMN are unlikely, in the light of **AB** and the distribution of ms support, to be split variants of Cx *Peres the*. Rather the **e**RM group reading, to which N has varied, suggests an attempt to restrict the implications of what could be seen as an ambiguously generic term. **187** The presence of this line in Q suggests that it was also in q, unless added by reference to a p^2 source. Its omission from the common source of <**e**RM> could be due to a mechanical error caused by the presence of *ermytes* in 188 and 190; but possible scribal objection to the idea of 'holy hermits' as a category cannot be ruled out (*C-F* has presumably varied with <eRM> for one or other of these reasons). The line introduces *a second major new passage* of 92 lines that balances some 20 of material omitted from **B** 115–38*a* // **A**. **197** *here* p**D**: the logical number after *Summe* is plural (so twice in 198) but **x** could reflect **L**'s use of a distributive singular or Cx have had no possessive. **201** *they* **x**: with *holy ermytes* in apposition would appear the harder reading, and *þese* an attempt to smooth the expression to a more familiar phrase (plural *Alle* **p** must, however, be the correct form). **206** *Helden*: the contextually preferable resolution of a presumed Cx form **heolden*, of which *Holden* will be a tense-ambiguous reflex. **208** *That faytede*: a more characteristic expression, preferred here as at 71, where **p** again replaces a verb-phrase with a noun-phrase as subject. **212** *he lyueþ*: in the light of the Latin line that follows, with its general demand for observance of the law, the I-variant *of leuey*, less apt in context (*pace Pe*), shows as a scribal attempt to make intelligible an exemplar with a form such as **[Aȝen þe lawe] a liuie* (with *a* 'they' governing a plural verb). **214–18** Scase 1989:151 proposes elimination of the stop after *souneth* 216 and correlation of *As by* with *Rihte so,* a punctuation followed by *R–K* and argued for by Wittig 2001:176–7. But the translation proposed is forced, involving an unnatural comparison between a 'meaning' and a 'fact'. This does not fit well with the assigned referent of *hit* (the *word* 'lollen', not the *fact* of 'being crippled') or the meaning of Langland's habitual phrase *as by* 'according to' (see *IG* s.v. *as*). Wittig's understanding of the metaphorical sense of *lollen* 218 as 'lean idly upon [i.e. spuriously seek support in?] the belief and law of Holy Church' is accordingly unconvincing. **259** *wroken*: on the basis of two **x** variants *wriþen* P[2] and *wroþen* D (omitted from the Apparatus), *R–K* (p. 150) argue for the sense 'insinuate themselves' (OED s.v. *Writhe* v. 10 and 11 'move sinuously / with writhing motion'), which would be apt for a wolf slipping under a fence. They see *wroken* as 'probably not even a true form but a subconscious overlay of the family ancestor's *writhen* and *broken*'. But arguably the latter variant (**p**) points to *wroken* as the Cx form and *wriþen* / *wroþen* as intelligent scribal attempts to make sense of a very difficult original. OED records under *Wreak* v. the sense 'pass' (but used only of time) and the earliest sense (in OE only, and transitive) was 'drive, press' (1.a., c). Thus *writhen* must remain a possibility, and may be right. *Shep*: *R–K* argue for *tripe*, F's unique variant. With sense 'flock' (MED s.v. *trippe* n. 3a.) this, if ever, is a case where a particular scribe has failed to discern the mute stave on *to* and substituted a synonym in *t* to provide a full stave in key-position (see *Intro.* II § 131 for discussion). Another example of the F scribe's 'normalising' of an unusual alliterative pattern is *se* for *chayere* at Pr 114. **264** *shyt*: a contracted form of the verb, here

apparently having the sense (elsewhere unattested) of the compound (MED s.v. *bishiten* v.) and signifying that the wolf 'befouls' the sheep (see 266)) with his excrement (as a sign of how near them he is). The I-variant *bischit* may represent an attempt to disambiguate the verb, which normally means 'excrete', thereby illogically referring to the consequence of an act that has not yet occurred (see MED s.v. *shiten* v., which gives no example of the sense 'befoul' for the simplex). I's *Folde* carries this process a stage further, but *wolle* (repeated at 266 and translating *lanam* 264*a*) must be right. **264***a* The quotation, being proverbial (see *Commentary*), probably had an abbreviated form in Cx (like that at 20.453), but for convenience is given in full here. **284 (A 93, B 109)** *In*: adopted in the light of agreed **AC** as the probable reading of **B** (*B*-G may show its usual ⊗ from **A** here), *Al* appearing a piece of scribal over-emphasis in Bx. *lettre*: evidently preferable in context on grounds of sense, *leef* being a wrong expansion of contracted *lettre* or an unintelligent alteration for greater emphasis.

B 110a–b have been inconsistently numbered in the edited text of **B** as citation-lines, but should properly be treated as 'text-lines' in all three versions.

289 (A 98, B 112) The uniformly attested **ABC** line will scan as Type IIIa if *Bote Dowel* is made the anacrusis and *haue*[1] read as the first lift; but if stressed according to the natural sense, it yields two inauthentic patterns, *xa / ax* and *aa / bb* (on *w / s*). Possibly the form *wol* lies behind *shal* in each of the archetypes; but the absence of any attempt in the sub-archetypes so to emend, and the need to posit thrice-repeated loss would stretch probability. If this, the only apparently uncorrupt line not to scan, were deliberately unmetrical, some hidden symbolic purpose might be involved, connected with its sense and hinting at the virtual impossibility of obeying the pardon's condition (a parallel case might be the imperfect fifteenth stanza-group in *Pearl*, in which the extra stanza increases the poem's total to one more than the 'perfect' number 100). **291 (A 100, B 114)** *Bote* **C**: revising the 'preclusive' *Þat* of **AB** to give a more modern and unambiguous expression. *þe...soule* **AB**: either variant in the Ax tradition is acceptable on grounds of sense and metre, **r** scanning as an extended Type IIIa with counterpoint (*abb / ax*). The **m** reading could show ⊗ from **B**, but more probably **r** is a scribal attempt to avoid repetition of 98b (for a similar case later, in the Cx tradition, see 10.78, 80 and Apparatus *ad loc*).

A 101–12 101–02 (B 115–16) The Ax line-division is acceptable in itself but the ease with which the mis-division could have occurred and the superior rhythm attested (randomly) in HNH[3] support the form of **B**, which makes 116 (= A 102) a quasi-macaronic scanning as Type IIIa (*ámb-*, *vmb-*). Line 101, with *atweyne* preferred in the light of **B**, scans as counterpointed Type Ie (*ppt / pt*) with internal half-rhyme. **105 (B 119)** *belyue* ?**m**: preferred as a harder than *liflode* and in form closer to **B**'s revision *bely ioye* (if that is not a Bx visual error for *belyue*, as K–D judge). The **r**-variant will have come in from 107, 110. **109 (B 123)** *opere manye* ?**m**: here judged original in the light of **B**, *A*-**r** having inverted to prose order (as has the Bx sub-group y). **110 (B 124)** *ful mete* A: the four variants are of dubious value and may point to an obscure reading in Ax; but the one chosen, even if a scribal conjecture, may best approach the original, and points forward to the revised **B** form without being derived from it. The sense of *mete* is either 'pleasant' (MED s.v. *mete* adj 1b) or 'sufficient' (*s.v.* 3b), with a possible play on both and a further pun on the homophonic substantive meaning 'food' (with allusion to *panes* in the Latin quotation following). The variants *mochil, more* may point to an archetypal form **meche*, of which *mete* could also be a reflex (though here understood as the *correct* original that could have given rise to the postulated Ax form). **111–12 (B 125–26)** *be folis A*-**m** *B*-α: preferred as the harder and more pregnant reading, which looks forward to the idea of 'God's fools' developed at the end of the poem (22 / 20.61,74), but not without a play on *foweles* in alluding to birds' freedom from worldly cares (A 115–17, B 128–29). The difficult phrase seems to have been wrongly resolved in *B*-β while *A*-**r**, having likewise missed the correct referent, has smoothed to *anoper*. The surviving variants for A 112a may suggest that its form was not exactly as in AH³ but nearer to *Þat we be nou3t*; a conjectured archetypal form **Be nou3t* would more easily account for R's *are not* and the smoothed reflex of M. However, it seems safer to retain the AH³ reading, which is identical with **B** and lucid, than to attempt reconstruction. **296 (A 130, B 143)** *a myle* AC: restored as the original of **B**, for which Bx may have had an imperfect form as in R (?=α) which was later smoothed to make syntactical sense in β. **304 (A 136, B 152)** *book Bible* BC: reconstructed as the probable reading of **A**. As Ax stands, *bible* seems to have been misunderstood as a gloss and taken as the substantive reading with subsequent omission of *book* preceding. M has corrected the metre, perhaps in awareness of **B**; but only the **BC** appositive phrase-structure will have generated the Ax reading. The presence of *for* in the line makes the syntax of 305–10 // anacoluthic; lack of revision in **C** shows this was intentional.

B 156 (A 140) *cleyme*: clearly the correct reading on grounds of sense. A Bx spelling **cleme* could well have generated the ?β variant *cleue* (doubtless induced by *departed* 157). Thereafter **w** and three **g** mss will have corrected and α substituted a contextually appropriate term for one apparently meaningless. **311** *shulle*: adopted from P² as the plural form needed for the feminine ending. **316** *Israel*: convincingly proposed by *Pe* as the name given the patriarch in Gen 32:28

(presumably unfamiliar except as the name of the people) and as the likely Cx reading for which *Iacob* is a (substantively correct but unmetrical) ⇒, *Isaak* **x** a (mistaken) 'correction'. The line recalls A 3.243. **324–25 (A 158–59, B 174–75)** The line-division of AC is judged as that of original **B**, ?Bx having brought forward the object of the verb and F representing α or having corrected from **A** or **C**. **325** *ioye*: adopted on the showing of AC as the presumed **B** original for which Bx *heuene* appears a more explicit scribal ⇒, perhaps under influence from *celis* in 176a. That *ioye* is **L**'s short-hand for 'the happiness of heaven' is clear from an earlier passage such as B 7.36. **327 (A 161, B 177)** *Lord forbede* AC: Bx may be a smoothing after misreading the *e* of *forbede* as *o*; but the sense is identical. **335 (A 169, B 185)** *nam(e)líche*: with wrenched stress in all versions to provide an extraordinary first stave on |m| (the normal pronunciation, with stress on *ná*-, is instanced at 2.159 //). X has uniquely *manliche*, which may be right (see discussion of 8.51). **343 (A 177, B 193)** *fyue*: preferred to *foure* on the strength of **C** as the (harder) **B** revision, present in Bx, which F and β seem to have 'corrected' as a supposed error.

A 179 (B 195, C 345) *þe patent of þi pardoun*: here tentatively accepted as the Ax reading from which T&r have lost *of þi pardoun*, levelling *þe* to *þi* / *3oure* by homœoarchy (*pat*- / *par*). But the DRK(A) reading could be due to memorial ⊗ from **B**: the opening dip is long enough to suggest that *3iue* could be an Ax ⇒ for **paye* prompted by finding *paye* contextually inappropriate to the colloquial asseveration. The **B** term *patentes* is, perhaps significantly, absent from **C**. **351 (A 185, B 201)** *At* BCA-**m**: the inevitably correct reading in **A** since **r** gives no sense (*Þat* may have come in by visual attraction from 184). AM will here represent **m** (< Ax) and KZ have corrected independently on grounds of common sense.

Rubric The substance of the **C** *Explicit* is that the *vision* of 'Piers Plowman' has ended and that of 'Dowel' now begins. **A** concurs with the first part of **C** but declares that the *life* of 'Dowel, Dobet and Dobest' now begins. (On the unique form of the colophon in the **A** portion of ms Z, see the note at Z 92 above). The character of the **B** *Explicit* remains uncertain. It seems to have been lacking in γM, but the marginal note in L to the opening of Passus VIII suggests some indication in β that the 'vision' concluded with VII and a new section was now beginning (see note on **B** VIII Rubric; the term *inquisicio* used in M at VIII implies a common source with L, i.e. β). R's long title to VIII (see Apparatus *ad loc*) is very close in form to that of **A** and may well have stood as the general title in Bx, making clear that the new passus is the eighth of 'THE VISION OF PIERS PLOWMAN' and a beginning concerning 'Dowel, Dobet and Dobest', the content of the rest of the [same] work. It is unclear whether 'of

William' formed part of the postulated Bx rubric to VIII as it does in **AC**, but this must be at least probable. The letter 'W' after 'William' in one family of the **C** tradition finds no support in either **A** or **B**. It could preserve the form of the Cx reading which **p** went on to expand into 'William', as also did **x** (but without dropping the single letter, which stood for the same name, and became redundant after expansion). If it refers to a surname, no explanation has been forthcoming. (On the rubrics generally, see Appendix Two, and on **B**, Adams 1985, on **C** Adams 1994).

Passus X (A IX, B VIII)

RUBRICS On these see the terminal notes to C IX above. Selective collation of N^2 as a **C** ms begins at 14, as 1–13 are an A-Text (see 13 note). ms Z, after some transitional **A** readings, is now a C-Text, classed as a p^l member of the 'q' group.

6 *as I wente* **A?B** / *in þis worlde* **C**: Z here reads *as I wene* (the r^l variant in **A**) and N^2 *as I went*, the reading of A-r^2**m** and of **B**. N^2 here as at 13 is clearly an A-Text and so *R–K*'s rejection of *in this worlde* Cx is unwarranted. On the other hand, in the light of *B-F* support for β and **A**, R's variant may be seen not as representing α (and thence Bx) but as coincidental ⇒ of a semi-proverbial phrase (cf. 4.136, 15.167, 19.104, 20.242). For by contrast with *as I wen(t)e*, this expression is so common that no need arises to see R as in some way transitional between **B** and **C** (see *Intro.* III B §§ 52–5) or suspect of ⊗ from **C**. Nor need β as well as F show ⊗ from **A**, since there is no sign of this elsewhere in its tradition. **7** *leode*: restored on the strength of the **AB** witness and the contextual and metrical need (N^2, as an A-Text, reads thus here). It was probably lost by homœoarchy before l*onged*, and if Cx read as **x**, the **p** smoothing is easily explained. **9** *witte*: with doubled *t* and final *-e* added in **A** to provide the necessary feminine ending. **12** *aboute* **AC**: restored as the probable **B** reading supplanted in Bx by a more emphatic last lift, perhaps under suggestion from adjacent verbs of motion at 11, 14 and especially 6a above, which **L** is unlikely to have repeated here. **13** *dere...me*: C-N^2 here reads *doþ me to wisse*, the reading of **A**, which *R–K* (inconsistently with their practice at 6) do not adopt. Here, as in 6, **C** is revising and N^2 would appear to have made good a deficient opening to its exemplar's Passus X from an **A** ms, in a manner like *C*-I earlier (see on Pr 91–157). N^2 continues as a **C** witness of basically **x**-type showing strong ⊗ from a **p**-source. **14–17** Omission by α of these lines (which are not in **A**) need not indicate that α was an earlier and β a later form of the B-Text. The cause looks to have been eyeskip from *dwelleþ* 13a to *dwellynge* 18b occasioned by *dwelle* 17b. **18** (**A 14, B 18**) shows continuous revision from **A** → **C**, and the Bx form is unexceptionable on

grounds of sense and metre. *B-F* seems to have adapted the **A** reading, the first of some fourteen such instances in this passus, presumably by direct consultation of an **A** copy (see e.g. at 41, 48, B 49). The notion that these agreements of F with **A** against βR represent correction from a **B**-source of superior quality to Bx is rejected at *Intro.* III *B* § 46. A slight piece of evidence of possible scribal censorship in the source of BxB¹, recognised by **L** in revising, might be the mild asseveration *sothly* in the same position as **A**'s *Marie*. But against this, it is plain that **C** is aiming at its characteristic effects of rhetorical *repetitio* in prefacing Will's *Sothly* 21 with an earlier use of the word, which recurs 'traductively' at 22 (*sothe*). **22** Cx has varied to prose order, giving the inauthentic pattern *xa / ax*. The reconstructed line scans as Type IIIa, throwing heavy stresses on the alliteratively linked 'joy' and 'Jesus' (cf. C 21.25, B 11.184 where the conjunction of ideas recurs). *R–K* leave the line unmetrical, presumably judging it still in draft form, while Hanna (1998:184), ignoring the evidence of // **B**, drastically reconstructs by dividing 21/2 after *die* and omitting *falling* as scribal. **25** (**A 18, B 23**) The Cx line scans as Type Ia with a heavy stress on the negative particle to enable the feminine ending (*nát wèl*). The Bx line (scanning satisfactorily as Type IIa) preserves from **A** *as me þynkeþ*, but omits *sertis*. Restoration of the latter in **B** here is syntactically possible but not necessary on grounds of either sense or metre. The awkwardness of Ax is due to the absence of *dooþ yuele*, which is present in **B**, whether or not by addition, and is needed to give the syllogism its correct structure (see *Commentary*). The omission of the apodictic proposition in **A** could have been deliberate, so as implicitly to undermine Will's pretensions as a clerkly disputant. But the text remains doubtful here, and arguably *dooþ yuele* should be in **A** and *certes* in **B**, with the caesura coming (unusually) after the latter in both texts, which would then read as identical. Though this is supported by the appearance of *certes* as the (mute) keystave in revised **C**, on balance it is safer to leave **A** and **B** unemended. **29** (**A 21, B 26**) *other*- **x**: to be accepted on the showing of **AB** as the likeliest Cx reading, for which **p**'s synonymous *vm*- is a ⇒ later smoothed to unmetrical *sum*- in various copies. **31** (**A 23, B 28**) Bx scans satisfactorily as a Type IIa line, and could be a revision, but in the light of **AC**'s prose order is to be judged inauthentic. F may be an independent re-writing to produce a Type I line, but is more probably ⊗ from **A** or **C**, with *tyȝde* added by the F-scribe or his exemplar. **33** (**A 25, B 30**) *a* (3): one of the rare but significant instances where L (=β) and R (=α), supported by **AC**, agree in a minor reading against γ (here accompanied by F and M). See 43 below for another LR agreement, and cf. B 28 above (with M). **34** (**A 26, B 31**) *wagyng of the bote* **AC**: judged also the reading of **B**, which has become unmetrical in Bx (*aa / xa*) through promotion of the noun as main referent. **37** *so* **x**: needed on grounds of syntactical coherence and giving an expressive T-type line (in preference to scansion as Ia with four-syllable pre-final dip). N^2 omits with **p**. 38 scans either with a four-syllable final dip or, more satisfactorily, with *so* as a mute stave (to avoid repeating 37) and stress on *fareth* as in 41. **41 (A 33, B 38)** *hit fareth*: to be accepted on grounds of **AC** agreement as the probable reading for **B** also, *falleþ* having perhaps come into Bx through contextual suggestion (B 32–3); *B-GF* will here have ⊗ from an **A** copy. **46 (A 36, B 41)** *waleweth*: to be adopted on **AC** agreement as the probable original reading for **B** (see *MED* s.v. *walwen* v. 4 (a)). Presumably LM here = β but α has (untypically) varied with γ, owing either to the ease of *w / k* confusion (cf. C 10.160, App.) or the unusual nature of the verb, the *C-P²*RMN variant *walkeþ* (so *R–K*) being hard enough to be original (see *MED* s.v. *walken* v. (1).1). **48 (A 38, B 43)** *oure / þe / þi*: the **C** reading, which could be the source of *B-F* here, firmly established, like that of **A**. But *þi* is preferred for **B**, on the strength of L (=β) and R (=α), as a reading transitional between **A** and **C**, which has accommodated the modifier to preceding and following *þe* (M perhaps showing ⊗ from γ). *R–K*'s rejection of Cx *oure* and *þis* has no warrant. *þis* R: preferred for **B** as the reading confirmed by **C**, although βF *þe* (agreeing with **A**) could equally represent Bx here. *freel*: supported by **C** as the reading of **B**'s revision of **A** (from which F here shows ⊗). **49 (A 39, B 44)** is so revised as to offer no decisive confirmation for either **B** or **A**. But on metrical grounds **A**'s form is preferable as the likely original of **B**, although the superior rhythm of *a daye* suggests possible revision. The Bx line allows a Type Ib pattern with *a daye* as the b-half's first dip; but the uncharacteristic rhythm comes from the unidiomatic word-order caused by promoting the notion of 'every day' over that of 'seven times'.

B 49 The line that follows here in F appears a sophisticated version of A 45, added to or by its source with subsequent smoothing through insertion of *&* at the beginning of 50 as in **A**. Although it could in principle be derived from a **B** source independent of Bx (*K–D*), it finds no echo in **C**, is not necessary on grounds of sense and could as well have been deleted by **B** as omitted by Bx. **60 (A 52, B 61)** *with good ende to deye* **C**: closer to **A** than βR (? =Bx) *goode men to worþe*, and so perhaps supporting *B-F*'s *good ende to make* as derived from a **B** source superior to Bx. But despite its blunter tone, Bx is not necessarily scribal here but could represent revision, and F's reading a ⊗ from **C**. The **A** line scans as Type IIIc ('crossed' *ab / ab*) and while **B** clearly revises to Type I, emendation of Ax *ʒiue* to *giue* (*Ka*) is otiose. **62 (A 54, B 63)** *wilde*: the secure archetypal reading of both **C** and **B**, emended by *R–K* from D to *wyde*, which is likely to have come in from *wydewhare* in the previous line (if this seems implausible, their note at p. 165 on what **B** read is incomprehensible). **63 (A 55, B 64)** *abyde me made*

CB-α: an inevitable emendation (one of the few *Sk* makes to his base text) to provide a correctly scanning b-verse. **65 (A 57, B 66)** *lythen* **CB**: the reading that clearly underlies *lystyn A-***m**. While *lerne* would appear to give 'hard' sense, this does not justify its adoption here, let alone *K–D*'s emendation of Bx on its basis. It is hard is to know what 'learning' the birds' lays in this context might mean; but *lythen* is in any case the more uncommon word lexically. *þat þe*: preserved in *B-α* (< Bx) and here adopted as the Ax reading accidentally preserved in KA, of which *þat, þe* appear split variants.

A 60 (B 69) The **A** line, giving satisfactory sense and metre, is revised in **B** to scan on |w| and replace the obsolete *driʒt* and dubiously apt *doute*, a word difficult enough to generate four distinct variants. The *r¹* variants seem to be dissatisfied scribal responses to *in doute*, but *drouth* **m** is not one such and is hard to explain if Ax read *in doute*. Anne Middleton proposes in an unpublished paper on 'Langland's Language' that **L** wrote *in douth* 'in [a] company' (*MED* s.v. *douth* n.). This semi-formulaic expression, probably obsolescent by the time Ax was generated, would partly explain the form of **m** (though not its unapt sense), and its loose general sense 'anywhere' might account for the closely similar sense of **B**'s phrase *wiʒt in world* (an almost exact parallel is Laʒamon's *Brut* 9857, where ms Cotton Caligula A. ix reads *on dugeðe* and the more modernised Cotton Otho C. xiii has *on worle*). But βR (< Bx) has the inauthentic metrical pattern *xa / aa*, and the transposition here provides a correct if abrupt line of Type IIIb (*ax / aa*) which leaves the final lift in its **A** position. There is thus no need to emend the whole line on the basis of **A** (as *K–DSch*). F gives smoother metre, but its apposition of parenthetic and main verbs in the b-half is stylistically uncharacteristic.

69 (A 62, B 71) *kynde*: despite support for the majority **A** variant in *C-***p**, not only the harder but the only metrically correct reading (*C-I*'s *kynde righte* suggests that I has incorporated a gloss in its exemplar). The *A-***m** form could have been **kende*, thus easily generating the contextually inappropriate *kene* M. **70 (A 63, B 72)** The Ax line, scanning on |ð|, seems to have a mute key-stave, and if *quaþ_I* has a liaisonal second stave, the line will be securely of Type I, not Type III. The form *quod I* **BC** may conceal the same original with internal fricative, but both have in the pronoun *þow* a full stave in the b-half (*C-***p** has presumably lost this by haplography after *þow* in the a-half). *R–K* needlessly re-shape the line on the basis of *C-F* (which has *I þo*) to conform with *A-*tJ and *B-*βF. **71** The Cx reading *Wille* is here taken as a revision, from which six sources DEQZKN (four, if QZ = q and KN = *p²*) have varied, possibly through memorial ⊗ from **B**. The contextual appropriateness of the Dreamer's being named by his own Thought should not be doubted. **72 (A 65, B 74)** In **AC** the line scans by preference as the rare but authentic Type IIb on vowels and fricatives ($Y^{1,2}$, *art*; *Thouhte, thenne*). The speech-marker phrase *quod I* is thus restored in **B** as the second stave, having been lost through eyeskip (*I > I*). Bx *what þow art* appears a scribal ⇒ for the reading attested by **AC**, which in F is found presumably by ⊗ from **A** (or **C**). **78 (A 72, B 80)** After B 80, ms F has a line corresponding to A 71, its likely source (no trace of which remains in **C**). The sense of B 80a overlaps slightly with that of A 71a, a line anticipating the description of Dobet in A 77 (retained as B 85), considerations that may account for its deletion in **B**. **80 (A 74, B 82)** *and of his two handes*: a b-half perhaps suspicious since no clear reason for the repetition of 78b appears; as it could be a mechanical error in both **x** and <RM> (if e, q, p^2 here reflect **p**), the form of Cx remains undecided. The repeated half-line does not obviously improve on **AB** *takiþ but his owene* (to which *PeR–K* emend); but on the other hand, such rhetorical *repetitio* is found at 25/6 and 191/93 (cf. **B** 8.100, 105, 10.120, 127) and is a particular feature of **C** (e.g. at 262/65), while the half-lines each work to balance (with a requirement to act) two potentialities for 'truth'. Whatever the case, the **x** form of the b-verse is preferable to that of **p** which, despite a theoretically possible liaisonal stave in *halt_wel*, looks patently like a scribal attempt to *avoid* repetition. **81 (A 75, B 83)** *deynous C*-p**B**-α: preferred on the clear showing of **A** to the competing form *dedeynous*; no difference of sense is involved. **91 (A 84, B 93)** *ʒe (wordliche) wise* **CA**: Bx lacks a first stave and *Ye wise* is conjectured lost through distraction from *vnwise*, with *and* as subsequential smoothing. **93 (A 86, B 95)** *crose* **CA**: referring to the bishop's crook-shaped crosier and not his processional cross (as at B 5.12), and contextually preferable as also the original reading for **B**. Bx will have levelled to a more familiar word, perhaps as a consequence of a spelling like that attested in **C**. **94 (A 87, B 96)** In the light of the **C** line's b-half, which echoes that of **A**, original *to gode* in **B** could be judged to have been archetypally replaced by the more emphatic *fro helle*. But the Bx line scans correctly as Type Ib, the sense is satisfactory, and any emendation lacks certainty. *ille*: the harder reading. Coincidental cross-family agreement in error of X and M, if not a deliberate alteration of the restrictive sense of *ille*, could have been visually induced by the form of *halie*. *life* **A**: final -*e* is added to provide the necessary feminine ending, though the scansion *goód líf* is not ruled out. **95 (A 88, B 97)** *pulte*: a revision in **B** of *pungen* **A**, with much the same sense. The **ABC**-**pu** variant *putte* is either a visual error or a ⇒ of an easier, more familiar near-synonym. The sense here is 'thrust' (MED s.v. *pilten* v.1(a)); cf. also notes on B 1.127 and 19.143. **100 (A 90, B 99)** *demede* **x**: preferable here on grounds of sense, *diuinede* **p** being perhaps a visual error partly induced by eyeskip to 102b. *a* **x**: the harder and probably archetypal reading, the vari-

ants *and, as, at* all being attempts to clarify a difficult expression the form of which they cannot have generated. *ordeyned...amonges*: emending a Bx line with the metrical pattern *aa / xa* produced by inversion to prose order in the b-half. For a similar case likewise emended cf. *ayeines* at B 9.154 below.

B 100–10 The α family in this passage omits lines and half-lines, perhaps owing to material damage in the exemplar, which α seems to have tried to reconstruct from memory. The true state of α is presumably that reflected in R, since it contains three lines lost in F, which after 101, 102 shows recourse to another version [A], a feature instanced elsewhere in this ms. However, F's witness is valuable at 109–10 where it preserves, doubtless by reference to copies of **A** or **C**, the authentic half-lines 109b, 110a missing not only in α but also in β (and thus presumably in Bx).

101 (A 91, B 100) The **C** line scans on |k|, and β or Bx seems to have substituted *rulen*, as a more obvious and stronger way of specifying the king's function. This was perhaps by suggestion from following 106a, where *rule* follows a b-half (105) that repeats 100 with slight variation (a repetition added in **B** that C eliminates). **102 (A 92–3, B 101)** The revised **C** line may be merely amplifying the sense of B 101 (= A 92); but while the verbs of volition and admonition could reflect a **B** line lost in Bx that was close in sense to A 93 (*vnbuxum // wolde nat* **C**; *bidding // tauhte* **C**), they could equally be an echo of the latter. F inserts such a line, from either **A** or a lost **B** ms distinct from Bx. Given the corrupt state of the passage in α, as noted at B 100–10, the former explanation of F's line is favoured, since a lost 'superior' **B** source would *ex hypothesi* have been free of the omissions manifest in Bx as well as α in these lines.

B 102 (A 94–5) *sholde; prisoun*: preferred for **B** on the strength of α agreement with **A**, the superior coherence of the conditional with the tense-sequence of *dide* 101 and the more appropriate register of *prisoun* in the context. After the **A** line parallel to B 102 is one emphasising the severity of the king's justice, which is inserted here by *B*-F, presumably once again from an **A**-copy; it could have been eliminated in the revision to **B**. For while something of its harsh tone remains, C 101b is making a different point (about the king's rights rather than his attitude) and does not support the case for F's line as strictly necessary to the sequence of thought. Such instances of **B**'s *abbreviation* rather than expansion of material in **A** (as earlier by **A** of lines in **Z**) are not unprecedented (cf. B 7.30 // A 8.32–3, B 7.36 // A 8.38–9).

104 (A 98, B 105) *to kepen vs alle* **C**: corresponding, with slight revision, to the Bx b-half. F may be presumed to have adopted the **A** form as part of sustained ⊗ attested in 100–01 motivated by desire to correct a perceived damage to the exemplar in these lines. **105 (A 99, B 106)**

here thre wittes **C**: providing satisfactory scansion either as Type IIIa on vowels or as Type Ia (as it must in **B**), with *thre* treated as disyllabic with internal |r| stave (cf. B VII 39). Adoption of F, here showing ⊗ from **A**, or of the earlier conjecture *rede of hire wittes* (*Sch*[1]), cannot be justified. **106 (A 100, B 107)** *ne ellis nat* **AC**: to be adopted as the reading of **B**, from which Bx (scannable as Type IIIa) will have omitted as supposedly pleonastic. **107 (A 101, B 108)** *so* **AC**: preferred in **B** as the adverb for which Bx has substituted a synonym under unconscious influence from the preceding fricative monosyllables. F's sophisticated form conceals probable ⊗ from **A** or **C**. **108–09 (A 102–03, B 109–10)** On grounds of sense and metre the βR (=Bx) reading must be judged defective on the showing of **AC**. The error could have occurred through syntactic anticipation of 110. *B*-F will have inserted 109b and 110a by reference to an **A** rather than a **C** copy (*helpe, lerne* against *spede, here*); but the substance must of necessity have been present in original **B**. On comparison with *A* and Ø in C 109 / A 103, F's *For* might seem scribal; but since choice for **B** between **A** and **C** is undecidable, there is no need to emend. **111** A comma may be better after *dwelleth*, given the sense of *wole* 'is willing'. **112 (A 106, B 113)** The **C** line scans firmly on |k| and Bx is a Type IIIa with heavy stresses on *noon* and *now*. If Ax is also Type IIIa scanning on |n|, emendation of *wot* to *not* on the strength of V will seem gratuitous. But as double negation is common in **L** and there is a possible reflex of it here in the revised b-half of **C**, it could be that **A** had a standard line. The same may have been true of **B**, but the line is left unemended in the absence of ms support. **118 (A 112, B 119)** *a; speche* **AC**: adopted as the probable **B** reading for which Bx has substituted a noun suggested by the sense of the preceding half-line, with accidental omission of the article.

C X (continued); A X; B IX

RUBRICS The Ax tradition, following the colophon to VIII, seems to reflect an understanding of A IX as 'prologue' to the 'vita' of Dowel, &c., a recognition explicitly made by mss W and M. Passus X is accordingly treated in **A** as the *first* Dowel passus. But in **B**, where VIII is accounted *primus de dowel*, the present passus is made *nonus de visione* (so LMR). Attempts therefore to specify it as either about 'Dowel' (HmB) or about 'Dobet' (γ) cannot be reliably regarded as deriving from Bx. **130 (AB 3)** *is it* **BC**: preferred in this Type IIa line, since one or other word is probably a full stave and the inverted order, allowing full stress to the pronoun, gives a more speech-like stress-pattern. *A*-DKW diverge coincidentally from Ax under influence from the word-order normal in verb-phrases with preceding complement. **131 (AB 4)** *wittyly* **CA**: on grounds of sense the preferred

reading, for which Bx is ⇒ of a more emphatic term, possibly through misreading an exemplar form **witliche* as intending a contraction of *-er* after the *t*. The ancestor of <OC²> has presumably corrected from a **C** source. **134 (AB 7)** *to here hath enuye*: preferred to a Bx reading not obviously scribal on grounds of sense or metre, since **C** revision back to **A** seems improbable here. The unexpected word-order and delayed noun-phrase subject may have prompted the Bx scribe to make *enuye* a subject while *hateþ*, translating accurately the sense of *hath enuye*, could have been suggested by preceding *hatte*. The apparent paronomasia here seems pointless (cf. 15 below). **138 (AB 11)** *duk* **AC**: preferred also as the reading of **B**, with ?g and F having corrected a reading unobjectionable but unlikely to be a revision.

B 15 *biddeþ*: in the absence of **AC** evidence, rejection of Bx *ruleþ* as scribal is arguably unjustified, since the line scans vocalically as Type IIIb and gives a defensible pattern of stresses on rhetorically prominent *he* (1,2),*alle*. However, the context foregrounds the dual rôle of commanding and teaching (16), and a better stress-pattern emerges with lexical words on |b| as the staves. To this end *biddeþ* is conjectured in the absolute sense 'directs' to provide authentic-sounding polysemantic wordplay with *bit* 'commands' in the a-half (MED s.v. *bidden* v. 4(a), 4(b)).

141–42 (B 14–16, A 14–15) It is possible that two lines on Dobest are missing from Ax, since he is introduced at 14 along with Dowel and Dobet but without any prior account of his function. *A*-J adds here two lines: *dobest is in hir bowre & boldyth þat leuedy / and berith a batte on his honde lych a byschoppys mace*. These are not derived from either **B** or **C** though they are perhaps sufficiently Langland-like to be a reflex of a lost original, as noted in *Ka²* (p. 463). But not impossibly, line A 14 has a long pause at the caesura, introducing *Dobest* as a kind of afterthought not strictly governed by the logical force of the opening *Þus*. It would therefore be safer to treat the J lines as an accomplished scribal conjecture and not adopt them into the text. **142 (B 16)** The Bx line could scan *abb / ab* (stressed *hís léryng*); but on the showing of revised **C** it seems rather the result of inversion to prose order, and is therefore emended. **143 (A 16, B 17)** *hem alle* **AC**: judged also the **B** original replaced by a more emphatic idea, perhaps out of stylistic objection to repeated *alle* at 18a and at 22. A vestige of the presumed **B** reading seems to remain in Bx *al*. **148 (A 21, B 22)** *Goed-fayth*: a revision that *R–K* emend without warrant to **AB** *Godefray*. *alle* **AC**: preferred as the **B** reading for which Bx substitutes an empty intensifier from probable stylistic objection to repeated *alle* (see note above). **149 (A 22, B 23)** *fyue*: the secure reading of **C** and on the showing of βR evidently that of Bx, F having altered perhaps under influence from an **A** copy of r-type. In the Ax tradition one **m**-ms A has also varied to the **r**-reading, perhaps through inducement from the (secondary) alliteration on |s| in lexical words and the wish to count Inwit among the castle's outer defenders. Presumably Ax itself read **v*, which could have been easily misread by **r** as *vi*. In **A** the *sones* (= 'the sense-faculties with regard to their moral orientation') are posted to protect the *castel* (the body), while the rational / moral power Inwit guards *all* (soul, body and senses). This distinction having been eliminated in **B** (see 23), it might seem more logical to read *sixe*, though the textual evidence of Bx and **C** indicates that the senses' protecting rôle is still envisaged as separate from reason's supervisory one. However, the line scans on voiced and unvoiced fricatives and Bx either stresses *þis* or treats it as a muted key-stave. In the light of **AC**, which have *for* as key-stave, and of **C**'s *Anima*, Bx *lady* may be suspected as a scribal intrusion, with a preceding *for* (as in **AC**) omitted, and subsequential smoothing. But since the evidence is inconclusive and the line will pass muster, no emendation is offered.

A 23 The Ax line, removed in revision, has the pattern *xa / ax* and could be easily emended by diagnosing in the a-half inversion to prose order from an original *þis womman to kepe* (in a Type IIIa line). The J variant *kepe wel* appears a characteristic scribal 'correction' that does not recommend itself as the likely original (as it does to *Ka²*). The conjectural reading here proposed, however, is hard enough to have invited ⇒ of a commoner term, perhaps through desire to achieve parallelism with *kepe* in 24b. Moreover *wite* is well-established in **L**'s usage, as at A 67 (and at B 7.35, 16.25), and here enables homophonic wordplay on *wit* 'wisdom' suggested by *wise* in 23b and by the constable's own name.

150 (AB 24) *kepe*: in the light of agreed **AC**, the Bx reading *saue* may be diagnosed as a scribal ⇒ alliteratively induced by *sende, selue* and by the same tendency towards parallelism, here with *saue* 23, seen in Ax at 23. In the last lift *for euere* likewise appears as ⇒ of a more emphatic expression, perhaps under inducement from *euere* in 27b. F is here presumed to have derived both readings from an **A** copy. *and*: given the agreement of **AC**, perhaps preferable to Bx *to*, but no difference of meaning arises. **153 (A 28, B 27)** The shape of **C**'s revised b-half strongly supports the authenticity of Bx as preserving a **B** revision. The *B-F* reading could derive from **A**, but with characteristic sophistication based on the sense of Bx. The Bx line scans either with a mute stave on *þat* or more probably with a liaisonal stave on *of_al*, as Type I. While the b-half could raise doubts that *euere* has been suggested by following *neuere* and desire to intensify *al*, its rhythm (with a strong pre-final dip) is exactly matched at 40, which is not open to question, so it should be regarded as authentic. *þinges* **A**: the pl. preferred on metrical grounds as probably underlying revised B 26b.

A-RK will have severally corrected Ax's sg., which could have come in by visual anticipation of 31 and 34. **157 (A 32, B 31)** *shafte* **AB**: the preferred reading in **A**, where **r**'s *shap* seems to form part of a simplified understanding of the phrase as signifying 'feature and form' (as at B 11.395 and 13.297). But *shafte* is meant to imply both man's appearance and his (spiritual) nature as made in the divine image, a point explicit in the new **C** line 158 (see MED s.v. *shafte* n. (1) (d)). Despite an earlier view to the contrary (*Sch¹*: 277), *shafte* is better seen as the **B** original for which CrGC, independently or influenced by an **A** source of **r**-type, have an easier ⇒ of similar form.

B 32–9 32 (A 33) *warp / spak*: the former the harder reading and evidently that of Ax. H³W have either preserved the reading of **m** or filled a lacuna by reference to another **A** ms of **r**-type, the latter being likelier, given the randomly divergent AM variants. **B** must then have been revised, unusually to a Type IIIa line. The use of *warp* with *word* is, however, earlier instanced in **B**; at 5.86 **B** has no parallel, but in the parallels to B 5.363, *spak* is archetypally attested in **AC**. If the present instance is not a case of Bx ⇒ of *spak*, it may mirror **L**'s unease at using with reference to God a verb hitherto used only in connexion with the 'word' uttered by a Deadly Sin. But the **AC** parallels to B 5.363 tell against this, unless they too are scribal ⇒. Given the uncertainty, then, it seems prudent (against *K–DSch¹*) to let the archetypal reading stand in each case (as do *R–K* at C 6.419). After 32 there follow in *B-F* two spurious lines and another which appears an ungainly rewriting of A 34 unlikely to be (as *K–D* p. 171 hold) part of the original **B**. **33 (A 35)** *man*: likely to have been part of the Bx reading, on the showing of the **A** line under revision. *Adam* was probably a gloss in β, though omitted from γ, and possibly also present in α, though omitted from R and in F integrated into the text. If the gloss was in Bx, it was presumably inserted to provide an explicit parallel with *Eue* and an antecedent for *his* in 34. If Bx read like F, the line could scan (awkwardly) as a vocalic Type IIIb; but with the supralinear gloss here understood as scribal, it requires a third stave on |m|. This is found by diagnosing the simple superlative as a Bx ⇒ (perhaps deliberate, to avoid repetition of 31a) for the composite form, adoption of which provides a Type IIb line with vocalic b-half staves, alliterating translinearly with 34. **38** *ne*: conjectured as necessary for the elaborate simile to make sense and presumed lost from Bx through misunderstanding of *and* as 'if'. **L** is saying that, even if two conditions are fulfilled (parchment, ability to write), successful letter-writing requires a *third*, the instrument (*penne*). **39** *welde*: the Bx reading *hadde* yields an extended Type IIIa with two vocalic staves (*he, hadde*) and possible counterpoint on |w| in the a-half. But the line would read more strongly if the key-stave were also on |w| and both *write* and *wel* were thematic not contrapuntal staves in the a-half. The verb *welde* is therefore conjectured as providing an apt stave-word (attested in the sense 'possess' at 11.10, 72 //, 14.18 //, 22.12 //, B 10.29, 90). **160** *schalkes*: apparently the Cx reading and clearly right on grounds of sense; the comparision of sunshine to grace is a favourite one, as at 18.72–5, 19.194. The variant *shaftes* introduces a human referent to make sense of contextually inappropriate *schawes*, a mistake for *schalkes* by easy confusion of *w* with *lk* (cf. on 46). **162** *sheweth*: possibly a visual or aural error for *seweth* induced by *shewe* at 160 (an interpretation supported by 18.72 below). Alternatively, *seweth* is the ⇒ for *sheweth* of an easier phrase. The grammar, with *suche synfole men* as direct object, would require *sheweth* to mean 'look with favour upon', i.e. grant his grace (see MED s.v. *sheuen* v. (1)). But there may also be polysemantic play on the sense 'make revelation to' (MED s.v. 9(a)), establishing a closer parallel between 162 and 160. **163** *And*: the simpler reading and one expressing clearly enough the consequence of God's withdrawal of grace. However, it could be a ⇒ for an apter and more exact conjunction that is contextually harder, whether introducing a result, = 'so that' (MED s.v. *as* conj. 5) or a simple comparison with understood relative after *somme* = 'like some (who)' (s.v. 1(a)). Arguably therefore, *as* could be judged the more likely original and is so preferred by *R–K*. **164** *yworthe lat hem*: a reconstruction presupposing that the b-half in Cx has varied to prose order with loss of the key-stave in |w| (cf. 3.139 above). In principle Cx could scan as Type IIIc on vowel and approximant (*óf, wýte; hém, ywórthe*) or as Type Ia on vowels, as *R–K* presumably judge. But this would result in de-stressing the lexical verbs *wol* and *lat*, which seem crucial to the theological point of the argument concerning God's 'will' to 'know' [= acknowledge] man.

B 41–4 41 The Bx line could in principle scan vocalically on non-lexical words. But 42 would then count as a wholly non-alliterating macaronic, something **L** generally avoids. It is possible that *þere he seide* is a Bx scribal insertion, and that **B**'s Latin line was free-standing as in **A**. The alternative analysis proposed sees the mislineation as due to the postulated line 41's unusual length. The structure is then either Type II, with three vowel lifts as in Bx, *it, hym, as* (a structure closely similar to B 11.204) or that of a vocalic Type Ia with an unusually long five-syllable pre-final dip (*þe...he*). More speculatively, *Þe Bible* is a scribal ⇒ for *scripture* and the line scans on |s| as Type I (with omission of the final phrase). **42** *Faciamus*: the Bx reading *& facta sunt* is here diagnosed as a mistaken expansion of its exemplar's posited **&c*, since the scripture being cited (Ps 148:5) appears the wrong one, being concerned with the non-human creation. This may result from 'anticipatory recollection' of B 14.60*a*, where the psalm-verse is fittingly quoted after a line

describing the creation of the animals. The correct scripture in 41*a* (as *K–D* recognise) is Gen 1:26, the one cited in F, doubtless as a consequence of ⊗ from **A**. This appropriately concerns God's creation of *man* in his image and likeness, the pervading theme of this passage. **171 (B 48)** *þat* **x** / *and* **p**: possible reflexes of Cx Ø; but the pronoun is preferable in the light of **B**. *his* **B**: absent from β but preferable on grounds of sense and presumably added by W independently rather than by ⊗ from an α source. **172 (A 42, B 53)** *yclosed*: Cx, like *B*-β, apparently lacking the past-participle marker required to provide the line's key-stave, which is here mute (the fourth lift *-ynne* serves a 'supplemental' function).

B 55 (A 44) *heo*: conjectured as the metrically required form of the feminine pronoun, providing the key-stave in a T-type line. Bx *he* could well have been an incorrect reflex of a gender-indeterminate exemplar reading **a*.

176 (B 60) The **C** line revises by inverting the order of object and verb in the b-half and replacing the a-half noun-object with a pronoun *hym*. The latter is unlikely to have been the underlying Bx reading, since the line would not scan with it, whereas it will scan with either sub-archetypal variant, as Type IIa in α and Type I in β. The α reading is preferred as giving a rhetorically superior stress-pattern in both halves.

A 47–70 47 *help* Ax: somewhat weak, not in itself but in view of the repetition at 49b. On the basis of the t variant *Ka* conjectures *allie*, but *halle* is more probably a careless reflex of a group-original *halp* or possibly *hele*. With the sense '(spiritual) strength' *hele* (MED s.v. n.3(c)) would be appropriate as a difficult original for which *help* could be a scribal ⇒; but the case for emendation is not compelling (see further *Intro.* II § 71). **51** *reccheles*: little instanced as a noun (see MED s.v. 4(c)) but the hardest and most probably archetypal reading, the variants with *-nesse* being ⇒ of more familiar forms. **53** Unless there has been ↔ of subject and verb-phrase, the Ax line scans with two stresses in 'begýnnére', another example of a rare b-verse type earlier illustrated at A 6.14 // (and cf. 4.172, etc.). *going*: preferred on grounds of metre and harder sense as the probable **r** reading. The 'paternal' conception of Inwit established at A 17ff above is here developed, *good speche and going* corresponding to *Seywel* and *Go-wel* at A 19, 21. **68** scans *xa / ax* (thus in *Ka²*), with J's variant being a manifest attempt at scribal correction that does not account for the Ax reading *pore*. A simple emendation, giving a Type IIIa line, would be ↔ of *cateles* and *pore*, on the presumption that the more inclusive notion has been promoted by the Ax scribe with consequent damage to the metre. But *caitif* 'poor' (see MED s.v. adj. 2(b)) is conjectured as lexically difficult and providing a stave-word with the requisite sense. It occurs as a noun at 14.90 and semi-metaphorically at C

13.109 //, while the derived noun *cheitiftee* (with internal gloss *pouertee*) is instanced at 22.236 //.

186 The scansion of the line is uncertain. If *to* is adverbial = 'in addition' (MED s.v. *to* adv. 9(a)) it could be a scribal ⇒ for original *als*, making the line of Type IIa. As it stands, it scans as Type IIIa with presumed cognative alliteration of *ch* and *sh*: cf. the spelling *chingled* in ms X at 235 (Vol. I, Appendix One). But examination of 184–85 suggests that the **C** lines are drawing not only on B 67–8 but also on A 69–70: compare *helpe hem and saue / Fro folies* **A** with *and fram folye kepe / And...helpe to* **C**, where there is no close verbal parallel in **B**. Possibly therefore a verb *ouht,* corresponding to *awyng* in A 69, was lost by Cx before *to* in the a-half of 186, which would then be a Type IIa line. This is one of the more striking cases of (partially) non-linear revision. A final possibility is that *And* here means 'If', requiring a semi-colon after *kepe* but thereby promoting the first word to full-stave status, and again giving a Type IIa.

B 77–91 77 will scan either as an extended Type IIIb line with vocalic theme-stave and counterpoint on |p| or (preferably) as Type Ia with a cognative key-stave *but*, or, if this is muted, then as a T-type. A possible emendation of *haue* to *preue* here (*Sch*[1]) seems, by contrast with earlier B 7.45 (q.v.), insufficiently unwarranted. **87–9** The Bx form of 87 scans *aa / xa* unless *good* is taken as a cognative third stave in a Type IIb line, as it may be (leaving an uncharacteristically short b-half). The emendation here provides a Type IIIb line with *Cristes good* a unitary phrase given prominence as the key-stave (in either analysis there is a 'supplemental' fourth / third stave in *kynde*). The word-order here is such as to have easily invited inversion to the prose order evidenced in Bx. **88** scans most naturally as Type IIIa (possibly extended, if *ben* is a blank stave), with cognative alliteration between the key-stave *shame* and |tʃ| generated by liaison of *As* and *Iewes* in first position. **89** seems to scan vocalically on the morphemes *hir, vn-, I* the last mute), requiring a quadrisyllabic prelude-dip including the lexical word *commune*: the *vnkynde* Christians of 84 are being contrasted unfavourably with the *kynde* Jews of 86, whence the stress on the prefix. The alternative scansion as Type IIIa on *m* with wrenched stress in *commúne* and key-stave on *me* gives an inferior rhetorical pattern by comparison. An alternative to the above reconstructions would be to re-divide 87–8 after *Iewes* and read *aren* for *ben* in 88, scanning this line on vowels. **91** has the unmetrical pattern *xa / ax* in Bx and is here emended to a Type IIIa line by simple ↔ from prose order.

A 75–80 75 *wyt*: here taken as a spelling variant for *wyte*, which in context is more apt; *wyt* 'reason, understanding' may have been suggested by 71b (*wys vndirstanding*). Either way, chiming or annominative wordplay is to be discerned (see Schmidt 1987:113–16). **77** *miʒte*:

final *-e* added to provide the necessary feminine ending. **80** *douten* 'fear' (MED s.v.3) not 'doubt' (MED s.v. 1); evidently the harder reading for which **m**, here independently accompanied by V, seems to have substituted an unambiguous synonym. But 82, in which Ax is uniformly attested, implicitly bears out the exact equivalence of the verbs by equating the nouns (in **B** *dreden* alone appears between 93 and 96, very possibly in order to avoid the ambiguity).

B 98a–99 98a *verbo*: unlikely to be a scribal alteration of the well-known quotation from Js 2:10, the reading preserved in L (?=β) and R (?=α) probably representing Bx, which is here judged original. M has altered its β-type reading, perhaps following γ, and F has conflated the two readings. What is clearly in question is 'custody of the lips', and while *space* 98 allows that *any* misuse of time may constitute potentially grievous sin, *speche* 101 specifies the particular kind envisaged. **99** *Tynynge*: conjectured as the required first stave for which Bx has substituted a commoner non-alliterating synonym. The verb is well instanced in the relevant sense at 5.93 and at C 14.7–8, which recalls the present passage.

A 86–90 86 *þi seluen*: preferable on grounds of sense to the pointlessly repetitive *þe salme*, a visual error induced in part by preceding *Sauter*. **89** *wy*: the inevitable emendation of a word perhaps spelled **wheye* in Ax and so misresolved in *r*[1] and omitted as syntactically awkward in **m**, though necessary as the key-stave and squaring well with *hominem* in the Latin. *iudicat*: preferred on grounds of sense as the resolution of a visually ambiguous reading (for a parallel case cf. B 16.20 below); proposed by Alford (1988:74), who notes that the phrase is a legal maxim, 'the will or intention judges the man'. This gives stronger meaning than *indicat* 'reveals, manifests' and fits better with the sense of *acorde* 88, which has legal overtones (AlfG s.v. II), and the judgement motif of 94, which completes the argument on conscience.

197 *seth*: taken by SkPe (as by **p**) as the temporal conjunction, and providing an acceptable illustrative parallel with the envisaged loss of land and life in 194. But more probably the causal conjunction is intended, L's point being that Christ's preparedness to lose his life constitutes the *reason* for expecting martyrdom from the Church's leaders: their vocation to 'do best' involves facing death in order to spread the faith and obtain peace for the world (cf. the argument of 17.264–76). In mss XI (see Vol. I Appendix One) the reading *al* for *he lees* may be a truncated reflex of **a lees* 'he lost', *a* being a probable original form of the pronoun. **203** *defaute*: like *lacke* **p** a blank stave, but on balance more likely to be the original. It is well-instanced in identical context at 15.231, 273 and *lakke* in L has the sense '(moral) fault' (13.210, B 10.262).

A 91–130 The longest passage of **A** to have been omitted in **B** with almost no sign of its use elsewhere in revised form. Most of the material is unique, though two lines echo the end of the A *Visio*, 129 (= A 8.87a) and 130 (= A 8.183a). **A 94a** The second part of the quotation was probably omitted from Ax but is included for convenience as the sense is incomplete without it. **110** The variants *of*, *þat* and *how* all appear unlikely to be original, and Ax probably read Ø here. **119** *soueraynes*: here not the pl. of the concrete noun *souerayn* but a rare form of the abstract noun (MED s.v. *soverainnesse* n., which omits this earliest example). It stands in balance with preceding *suffraunce*, with which it 'chimes' annominatively (Schmidt 1987[2]:113–16).

204 (A 131, B 108) The Bx line, like C 205 which partly revises it, scans as Type IIIa and no emendation is needed, that of *Sch*[1] 95, 278 (after *K–D*) producing a line with unacceptable masculine ending. **206 (A 136, B 112)** *martres*: unquestionably the reading of **BC** and more unexpected in collocation with the three contemplative categories than *nonnes*, the non-alliterating *r*[1] reading. It is very improbable that *mynchons* underlies the latter (as *Ka* believes), since *martires* in the two unrelated families *r*[2] and **m** can hardly have been generated from it. Although lexically harder than *nonnes*, *mynchons* is not in context harder than *martires* and is best regarded as one of Ch's many idiosyncratic substitutions (here for the sake of the alliteration; see further *Intro*. IV §§ 32–3). **207 (A 137, B 111)** *cherles* B: possibly a scribal ⇒ suggested by the familiar 'oppositional' categorisations, the minority *clerkes* being more apt in a list of 'honourable' social orders; but BoCot and F may show influence from **A**, and *cherles* is otherwise acceptable.

B 113 *wye*: adopted as the clearest realisation of a word probably spelled in Bx as **wey(ʒ)e*, a form also attested in the Cx tradition (see *IG weye* n[2]). Deliberate ambiguity may here be intended, but on balance the unambiguous form seems preferable; cf. also C 18.229 below.

A 141 *heo*: convincingly conjectured as the Ax reading underlying *she* (a non-alliterating dialectal alternative) and *Eue* (a visual reflex that awkwardly repeats 140), a pair of variants randomly attested across the genetic groups.

B 121 (A 140) The Bx line scans as Type IIIc, on |k| and vowels, with a possible blank stave on *tyme* making this an extended variant of the type. *K–D*'s emendation *cursed* for *yuel* is gratuitous, since the metre and sense are acceptable. **B** appears to have replaced **A**'s *cursid* both here and at 123 (revising A 155), perhaps in order to avoid excessive use of *corsed* prior to its climactic appearances at 136 (A 170) and 138 (A 172). The restoration of *corsede* in C 215 (reinforced by the repetition at 220) represents a return to the **A**-Text, without calling in question the authenticity of **B**.

214 (A 150, B 122a) *in dolore*: clearly established in Cx, and perhaps running together Gen 3:16 with Ps 7:15

(*Pe*; see *Commentary*). The reading also appears as the β variant and could be archetypal and original in **B** too, but *dolorem* α is here preferred on the showing of **A**, as no major difference of meaning is involved. **216 (A 141, Ø B)** The **C** line corresponds to an **A** line either deliberately omitted in **B** or lost by Bx, presumably after 121. The former seems more likely since the **C** passage goes on to add a line (217) in the spirit of A 142, developing the account of Adam and Eve's intercourse after the Fall, of which no trace remains in **B**. *K–D*'s case for seeing A 141 as lost from Bx and requiring restoration is therefore not convincing.

B 124, 127 (A 153, 157, 159) The name *Seth* is clearly established in A 153 as *Seem* in B 124, and the same referent is intended, the son of Adam (Gen 4: 26) not the son of Noah (Gen 7: 13). In A 159 it seems likely that Ax read *Sem* and that Ch, M and the source of <RU> have corrected to *Seth*, presumably in the light of 153 (as also at 179 below). At A 157 it is also probable that Ax read *Sem* and *r*[1] has smoothed to *seye* perhaps on the basis of an immediate exemplar reading **seʒe* (with ʒ mistakenly for earlier þ). Since both *Seth* and *Sem* are instanced in the Ax tradition, it seems best to adopt *Seth* in all three cases so as to avoid contextual confusion with Noah's son. In the Bx tradition, however, only *Seem* is attested. At B 127 there is a possibility, realised by CrM, that *some* could be a corruption of *Sem*, and this certainly provides a closer parallel with the **A** line under revision (159). But *some* is acceptable as referring to the progeny of Seth (*þi* 126, *his* 128) and fits well with *hir* 129, so no emendation is required. The *authorial* confusion of names (if that is what it is) may be due in part to seeing the Flood as both the consequence of the sin of Seth's offspring and also as the occasion for the salvation of Noah's (of whom the most important was Sem). The error is decisively rectified in **C** at 251–55 where *Seth, Adames sone* is specified and the name twice repeated to obviate any risk of confusion. But since *Seem* in **B** could be an authorial rather than a scribal error, it is retained there.

A 154 The line could in principle scan on |k| as a Type IIIb but the resulting five- or six-syllable dip in the a-half would necessitate de-stressing the contextually prominent verb *mariede* at the expense of the meaning. The conjecture *manside* presumes ⇒ by Ax of a more familiar word under inducement immediately from *acursid* in 155b and more remotely from its earlier appearances in the vicinity (146, 148). The word occurs in an identical context in *Purity* 774 and though not instanced in **A** is found in **C**, in a non-restrictive sense, at 2.41 // and also in **B** at 4.160, 10.278, 12.84, 22.221. The edited line, scanning on |m| and |k|, is the rare Type IIb.

247a (B 152a) The grammar of the quotation in **C** is correct but that of Bx seems to have run together two constructions, one with a passive verb needing a nominative subject, and another with an accusative object which would require an active verb. Although **C** has this (as has *B-F* and, with different person, g), the passive form is adopted here for **B** as clearly archetypal and the noun is given in the correct nominative sg. form from w. **249 (A 180, B 154)** *makynge* x: apparently redundant before *made*, as is *of mankynde* p before *men*. Both could be reflexes of Cx **makynde*, a participial form erroneously substituted for a verbal noun, which was later restored in x. Cx itself could have been attempting to restore a damaged form (*ma...de*) of an original **mansede*, which would be without the redundancy of both sub-archetypes. *R–K* p. 160, objecting to the perceived tautology, propose *maugre kynde*; but the rhetorical *repetitio* is not ineffective, and no conjecture is warranted here. *Goddes wille ayeines* **B**: tentatively adopted for its more telling rhythmic pattern, though Bx could scan as an extended counterpointed Type IIIa, with wrenched stress giving the keystave *áyeìn* and a 'supplemental' |w| stave in position five. It presumes Bx inversion to prose order with loss of the important original key-stave (*wille*) and requires expanding the preposition to its trisyllabic form to provide the necessary feminine ending. **251** *seth²* x: a form presumed authentic as punning on the name *Seth*.

B 155–163 155 (A 181) The *B-β* variant gives satisfactory sense and metre, but in the light of the b-half of the **A** line under revision the sub-archetypes may be conjectured to preserve split variants of an original containing *men, now* (as in αA) and also *þat, so* (as in β). The length of the line as reconstructed would have been the main factor occasioning the split. **163 (A 187)** *any*: conjectured as providing the necessary key-stave (by liaison of *any_olde*), the AxBx lines scanning *aa / xx* as they stand. The conjecture *yolde* (*K–D, Sch¹*) for *olde* is attractive, the sense 'submissive' being attested in the period (MED s.v. *yelden* v.1a (c)), though the more appropriate '(sexually) exhausted' is only from a century later (OED s.v. *Yolden ppl.*, citing Dunbar; not recorded in MED). It is here presumed that *any* was twice replaced by the more expected *an*, the ⇒ being occasioned by the presence of *any* twice in 188 following (once in // **B**) and distraction from preceding |j| in *ȝiuen...ȝong*. Alternatively *olde* provides a key-stave if pronounced with a SW palatal glide (MED s.v. *old(e* adj.).

267 *ac*: conjectured as the liaisonal stave (*ac_late*), required in key position, for which Cx is presumed to have substituted the non-alliterating synonym *bute*. Emendation by inversion of *be knowe* (*R–K*) is excluded because it yields an unacceptable masculine ending. **269** Alliteration is on |k|, the first stave being internal to the consonant-group *sk* in *squier* (see *Intro.* IV §45). **273 (A 190, B 166)** On the joint showing of **AC**, where the line comes directly before 274 // (on the pestilence), it may be safely transposed to give in B 162–74 the identical sequence

preserved in A 186–98, without any revision. Omission of the line from α for no evident mechanical cause may suggest its absence from Bx also and restoration in β from memory (if so, more easily at the wrong point). **275** *lely* p: the reading that gives both satisfactory sense and metre and also accounts for the semi-nonsensical x variant *leix* (?= *leiȝes*). Presumably the x scribe perceived a clash of sense between *lyen* and *lely* through failing to grasp the adverb's asseverative-parenthetic function (cf. the oxymoronic effect of the similar combination of *lely* with *layne* in *SGGK* 1864). The idiosyncratic spelling is explained by *R–K*'s interpretation (p. 160) of *lyen* as 'lie (physically)', which allows the sense 'fallow' for *lei*, explaining *leix* as a homœograph; but on balance it seems better not to emend here. The **x**-mss I and D have both made individual commonsense corrections, the latter coinciding with **p**-N's 'normal' ⇒ of a less paradoxical synonym, while ms I was guided by the metre or referred to a **p** source to resolve the crux. **276 (A 192, B 168)** *many*: securely conjectured on the evidence of **AC** as having been present in **B** but lost in Bx through alliterative attraction of *forþ* > *foule*. **277 (A 193, B 169)** *choppes*: to be safely accepted on the showing of **AC** as the probable reading of **B**. The six diverse variants, which include a form *choppyng* close to the presumed original, suggest that both α and β (and hence Bx) may have read an unintelligible word (such as *cloppyng*) that prompted a range of scribal ⇒. **283 (A 199, B 175)** *togyderes*: discriminated as the presumed **A** original in the light of **BC**; the superficially harder synonym *ysamme* may have been induced by *same* 200. **286–90a (B 179–85)** A possible reason for loss of these lines in B-α could have been eyeskip from *man*er 179 to *man* and wom*man* at the end of 186, followed by resumption of copying at the next line; but censorship cannot be ruled out as another possible cause (see *Intro.* III B § 52). The omitted material, which is all new in **B**, is preserved entirely in **C**, where two Type IIIa lines (179 and 182) are revised to respectively a Type Ia and an extended Type IIIa with counterpoint, no question of emendation on metrical grounds arising in either case. **293 (A 203, B 187)** *bedbourde*: on the showing of agreed **AC** to be accepted as the likely **B** form for which Bx is a ⇒ of a more commonplace expression. **294 (A 204, B 188)** *Clene*: in the light of **AB** perhaps better placed at the end of 293, as no reason for changing the last lift appears. But since the **C** lines scan without difficulty and the enjambement is not uncharacteristic, no emendation is demanded. *leel* **B**: conjectured in the light of **C** (and secondarily **A**) as the necessary stave-word in |l| supplanted by the more obvious non-alliterating *parfit* (an epithet often collocated with this noun). **A**'s point is that the pair are legitimately married and love each other, **C**'s both this and also that they be faithful to each other. The phrase conjectured for **B** emphasises the Christian love of the spouses as based in marital fidelity, *leel* retaining, as usually, a residual semantic link with law (here divine positive law ordaining canonical wedlock). This is emphatic and explicit in **C**'s revision of the line and of B 190, which seems to revert in part to the argument of A 206–08. The possibility that *loue* was lost before *of soule* in Bx (since it appears in both **A** and **C**) is offset by the fact that *charite* has replaced *lawe* in the b-verse. **295 (A 205, B 189)** *dede derne*: a word-order assured in **C** and, as the harder, to be discriminated as the probable original in **A**, where the adjective has been lost from **m** and a majority of *r¹* and *r²* mss have normal prose order. However, as sense and metre remain unaffected, the Bx reading may be retained. **298 (A 209, B 193)** *That*: on the agreement of **AC** adopted also as the **B** reading, Bx seemingly having inserted *And þei* to smooth the transition. **300 (A 211, B 195)** *goed* (2) **p**: offering, of the two repeated words available to form the key-stave, both better sense (the repetition of *gete* being pointless) and characteristically contrastive wordplay on *goed* in the a-half; these 'gadlings' prosper neither materially nor spiritually. **301 (A 212, B 196)** *whiche*: providing the necessary key-stave in **C**'s b-half, the Cx line scanning *aa / xx*. In the light of **B**, however, *what* may be equally judged the *w*-word in **C** that was supplanted by *þat*, and the *what*-variants in the Ax tradition to support this inference. Though the conjecture *alle whiche* is proposed as likeliest to underlie the Cx form *alle þat*, the pronoun *al-what* (MED s.v. (c) 'whatever') may be preferable as involving only a 'reconstruction'. *R–K* leave the line unmetrical. **305–09 (B 200–03)** are not in **A** and could in principle have been added in β to a text already complete in the α form as it stands. But a mechanical explanation for the loss is at hand in the form of eyeskip from *Dowel* 200 to *Dowel* 204 (cf. on B179–85 above).

Passus XI (A XI, B X)

RUBRICS Like Ax, the Cx tradition ceases continuous passus-numbering with C IX, and seems (also like Ax) to regard Passus X as the prologue to Dowel (Dowel, Dobet and Dobest in **A**). None of the archetypes had a 'Prologus' rubric at the beginning of the poem, although a Prologue is implied through each one's managing to number correctly from Passus I onwards. Of the sub-archetypes only *C*-**p** errs by taking the untitled Prologue to be I and going on to number I as II. It may be safely inferred that this opening ∅-rubric form was authorial and it is quite likely, in the light of **AC** agreement around A X / C XI, that there was only intra-sectional numbering in the **B** original, if it was not introduced by the scribe of Bx. However, the practical convenience of continuous numbering in all versions is so great that it is adopted here and the manuscript rubrics are consigned to the Apparatus.

This is not to minimise their interest; but since only the passus-divisions as such are formally cognisable as units of the text, the remaining ms nomenclature, whatever its relation to the original, cannot be easily included in the text in modified form without distortion. **7 (AB 9)** *Nolite / Noli*: the pl. form, clearly established in **C** with appropriate change to a pl. addressee, is also that of the Biblical source-text. But (in the light of **B**) Ax is judged to have been made sg. to fit the local context. The pl. in *A*-**m** and the *r¹* sub-group d, may then be regarded as a scribal ⇒ of the form familiar from the Vulgate. **11 (AB 13)** *heo*: presumed the original reading from which the gender-ambiguous reflex **a* in Cx could have generated the variants *wit* **x** (misconstruing the referent) and *studie* **p** (construing it correctly). Neither is a likely ⇒ for the other. **12 (AB 14)** *a*: conjectured as the grammatically required pronoun lost in Cx perhaps through careless construing of the clause as one of relation not of result. **15–16 (AB 18–19)** The A-Text may here be securely accepted in the light of **BC** and on grounds of sense as that in **r**. From this passus on W derives from an **m** source but shows partial ⊗ from **r**, its source from Pr–IX. In 19 *can construe r¹* is to be preferred as the harder reading and the one partially confirmed by **BC** (*can*). The sense here is 'practise' (MED s.v. *construen* v. 5), and *Conterfeteþ ?r²* will be a scribal gloss of a difficult sense, while K's *contryven* could show ⊗ from **B** or **C**. **17 (AB 20)** *leel*: conjectured to emend the Cx line (which has the inauthentic metrical pattern *aa / xx*) on the presumption that the intensifying epithet was lost through homœoarchy (*let- >< lel-*) or through deliberate suppression of a qualifier supposed redundant. F's attempt to make the line scan correctly as *& lette trewþe with louedaies & begile þe leel trewe* is an intelligent scribal re-writing that may felicitously 'echo' the conjectured original. It might be simpler to take *treuthe* as an archetypal ⇒ for its synonym *lewte*; but the form of **AB** suggests that the collocation *lette treuthe* was retained in the revised **C** line. *R–K*'s conjecture [*lewed*] *treuthe* introduces a concept possibly though not necessarily implied by *peple* 19 but definitely not implied by *consayle* 18 and (even more strongly) *lordes* B 22. **18 (AB 21)** *That; are / ben*: in the light of **AC** agreement diagnosed as the original and Bx *is* a scribal alteration of the absolute relative pronoun to a more explicit form, with subsequential smoothing of the verb number. In the b-half, the word-order preferred for **A** is that supported by **B** and the *r¹* order may be seen as coincidental anticipation of the revised **C** form.

B 28 (C 27) As it stands, the (probable) reading of *B*-β in the b-half (<GYBL) is satisfactory in both sense and metre. But it does not account for the reading preserved in α which, on the showing of **C**'s revised b-half, would appear to have been present in **B**. The β and α readings may be diagnosed as split variants from an exceptionally

long line (though one not longer than B 13.255). In the form of Bx as reconstructed, *God* now appears twice as part of a dip (one and two), grammatically first as subject and then as object, having a parallel repetition of *good* as both key-stave and as stave one, with the verbs as staves two and three in the a-half (*Thilke þat God moost góod gyueþ, God moost gréueþ — leest góod þei déleþ*). **31 (A 24, B 32)** *Ac*: in the light of agreed **BC** reasonably supposed to have been present in **A** but lost in Ax, whence both the Ø-reading of **m** and **r**'s insertion, perhaps under inducement from *And* 25, of a connective judged necessary (V's felicitous variant is unlikely to represent Ax). **34 (A 29, B 36)** *or leet herfore (by)* **CA**: a phrase judged likely to have been lost from Bx and *C-***p** for similar causes, the length of the line being one. In Bx eyeskip from le*te* > le*sson* may have occasioned attraction of *loued* to (*þ*)*erfore*. Agreement of **AC** authorises restoring to **B**, here in its **A** form.

  B 37–50 37 (A 30) *daunted / dauncelid*: the **B** reading may be taken as a revision of **A**, the word in the sense 'made much of' (MED s.v. *daunten* v. 3(c)) being actually rarer. However, *dauncelen* appears the probable reading of Ax, and the **A** variant *dauntid* is presumed a tK ⇒ of a synonym later adopted in revision of the whole line. There is no need to postulate either that **L**'s *A*-ms was a scribal copy containing the variant *dauntid* or that tK here show ⊗ from **B**. **50 (A 37)** *game*: conjectured on the basis of // A 37b as the original for which Bx is a non-alliterating synonymic ⇒ under unconscious inducement from 48 and 52. *B-*M *glee* is an independent attempt to correct the metre and is unlikely to be the β and thence Bx reading.

37 (A 40, B 53) *how two slowe þe thridde*: to be safely adopted on the showing of **AC** as the **B** original for which Bx has a bland if metrically correct scribal ⇒ occasioned by objection to the blasphemous character of the image (not *authorial* censorship in response to readers' objections). **38 (A 41, B 54)** *take(n)* **AC**: preferred as the original also in **B**, apposition of main clauses without a conjunction being characteristic of **L**'s practice and *and* most probably a Bx addition to ease the syntax. **39 (A 42, B 55)** *presumpcioun*: on the showing of **AC** taken as the reading of **B**, the article being a Bx intrusion that eliminates the subtle play on the word's logical and moral senses (see MED s.v. n. (1) (a) and 2 (a), under the latter of which the present instance is cited). **41 (A 44, B 57)** *gnawen...gorge*: in both **B** and **C** plainly metaphorical, = 'defame God with their words' (*Sk*; see further Stanley 1976:445–6). This is probably also the sense of **A**, which has *in* for *with*. *K–D*'s argument (p. 103) that the sense 'bite God persistently in the throat' which they see as that of **A** 'was either missed or rejected as outrageous' and that the reading *gnawen wiþ þe gorge* 'is actually nonsense' is unconvincing, since the *with* form is retained

in **C** and presumably thereby given 'a kind of sanction' (*Ka²*, p. 463). But *K–D*'s claim (103n7) that the MED gloss (s.v. *gnauen* v. 3a) as 'disparage, carp at' is the result of being misled by the variant *in here* (tK) for *in þe* is mistaken. It makes no difference whether *here* or *þe* appears, *here* simply being more explicit and not generating another idiom. What the (indubitably irreverent) laymen do 'when their guts grow full' corresponds to what the gluttonous Doctor later does, in a less blatant manner, under similar circumstances, when challenged to speak 'of a trinite' (cf. 15.111). The word *gorge* here refers to the throat primarily as an organ of speech (as at B 66) and only secondarily (but with an apt quasi-pun), as an organ involved in eating. The possibility of a meaning such as that proposed by *K–D* for **A** is remote, though it may well have been in order to avoid the possibility of such unseemly literalism that **L** altered 'in' to 'with'. *gottes fullen*: almost certainly, on the showing of **AC** and as a harder reading, the original of **B** felicitously restored by w. Bx seems to have read *gutte is fulle* as a result of misconstruing the pl. subject as sg. noun + verb and pl. verb as sg. adjective.

43 (A 46, B 59) *afyngred*; *afurst*: the past-participial form attested in **BC** may also have been the **A** original and Ax could have substituted a noun in each case and then replaced the proclitic by a (more emphatic) preposition (*for*) under influence from *for* in the b-half. But as revision is possible here, emendation is rejected, DV *of*[1,2] being adopted as the closest in form to **L**'s later idiom. **44 (A 47, B 60)** The a-half of the revised **C** line, which condenses A 47–8, B 60–1 into a T-type, corresponds closely in sense to that of **A** (*haue hym in* // *nymen him in*), suggesting that Bx *neer* is a scribal error for **B** *in nor*, the felicitous conjecture of *B*-ms M. The meaning 'betake himself to, go (to)' for *nymen him* (MED s.v. *nimen* (v) 4a) is contextually possible but involves an awkward shift of referent between *hym* in the a-half and *his* in the b-half. More probably it is a Bx smoothing of *ne* or *nor* to *neer* after *in* had been lost through assimilation to the minims of preceding *hym*. The M-form *nor*, unusual in **L**'s language, is retained as obviating the need for emendation and as likelier to have prompted the postulated Bx ⇒. **50 (A 52, B 65)** The presence of *Mony* in revised **C** may be an echo of *Manye* in **A** which, as preserved in Ax, is an extended Type Ic line. *B-*F's variant *Manye mendynauntis* is either due to ⊗ from **A** or preserves *Manye* from α where *B*-R has joined β in omitting it by haplography before men*dinaunt*3. Because of the uncertainty, however, the Ax?Bx forms are each allowed to stand. **51 (A 55, B 68)** *in Memento* **AC**: here conjectured as the probable **B** reading for which *ofte* is Bx ⇒ of a vague general phrase, perhaps through failure to grasp the precise (but not obvious) reference to Psalm 131:6, quoted in 68a //. **51a** *i.e caritatem*: perhaps intruded in Cx (it is omitted by QFSZ = q) but possibly authorial and, as accurate and illuminating, worth preserving (see *Commentary*). **52 (A 56, B 69)** *knyhtes*: evidently a necessary coupling with *clerkes* in joint contrast with the *mene men* of 53. In **A** *kete men* seems the hardest reading and so likeliest to have generated the three substantive variants. Bx *opere kynnes men* thus becomes suspect as a vague phrase (of the type noted above at B 68) which does not provide any such effective contrast with *meene men* 70 and may well be a censoring scribal ⇒ for a **B** original identical with **A**. However, though capable of improvement, it is metrically acceptable and not impossibly (a weak) authorial change, so emendation is here avoided. **53 (A 57, B 70)** *hym*: preferable for the sense and in the light of **AB**, though possibly inserted by *p¹*. *here* **AC**: preferred to Bx as unlikely to have been revised in **B**, though there is no objection to *þe* (if it was lost in Bx's immediate exemplar, the definite article could have been supplied). *B*-FG either show ⊗ from an **A** source or independent ⇒ of (what is here) the more explicit word. **54 (A 58, B 71)** *vp* **AC**: judged to have been omitted by Bx as redundant; it is unlikely to have been removed by **L** and then restored in **C** since *fynden vp* is an integral phrase (see MED s.v. *finden* v. 21(b)). **55 (A 59, B 72)** *pestilences*: apparently a **C** revision taking account of more than one attack of the plague (cf. 60 // below). Two **C** mss U and M add *tyme* (pl. U); but while the sense does not require *tyme* in **B**, β is preferred on the showing of **A** and α judged to have omitted the noun, perhaps as metrically and semantically redundant. **56 (B 73)** presents problems of meaning in all **C** mss except D (and also F, which here reads *þei preche*). The **x** version gives poor sense, with both *prechyng* and *enuye* having to be objects of *haen founde* 54 as a consequence of reading *and* for the required *in*, as do also two **p**-mss K and Z. Omission of the line from the common ancestor of <eRM> and individually from Y may be due to censorship, whether from objection to the specific criticism of friars or from seeing the b-half as indiscriminately attributing *enuye* to clerks as a whole. The sense of the b-verse, however, appears to be 'because of sheer ill-will *towards* the clergy', with *clerkes* here implicitly having the restrictive sense 'the secular clergy' (MED s.v. *clerk* n. 1(b)), in contrast to the friars, who are regular clergy. Some evidence to substantiate this reading is the implied opposition between friars and 'clergy' in this sense at 22.376 (with which may be contrasted the contextually ambiguous use of the word at 22.228, where *friars* answer the summons addressed to Clergy). The form of the b-half phrase as preserved in q?*p²* (here supported by D) may well be that of **p** and thence of Cx, is the only acceptable one, and is confirmed by *for* in // **B**. In the a-half, while the Cx reading *prechyng* is grammatically possible after *haen founde*, it is inferior on grounds of sense to *prechen* **B**, for which it may be an uncon-

scious mechanical error. This has been corrected by D alone which, unless a felicitous conjecture, must derive from **B**.

A 67 See note below on B 108.

61–2 (B 78–9) The content of these lines suggests less that they are an addition to α than that their omission from *B*-β was due to censorship. In R the extended b-half, rendering the line of Type IIb, can be convincingly identified as scribal on comparison with **C**, and could result from misconstruction of an exemplar reading **hus here* as incomplete (F, unusually, may have retained the correct α reading). **79** *forgrynt*: a verb of extreme rarity, found only here and not in OED or MED. The **C** revision *togrynt* (also rare but not unique) is recorded in MED s.v. *togrinden* v. **74 (B 90)** The Bx line will scan awkwardly as an extended Type IIIb on vowels, with all the full staves falling in non-lexical words (cf. C 75); but a more satisfactory stress-pattern is provided if the important *litel* forms one of them. In the light of revised **C**, *loke* is therefore conjectured as the key-stave for which *rule* is a Bx ⇒ of a more or less apt non-alliterating synonym under unconscious suggestion from the sense of *weldeth*. The phrase *loke hym* here means 'behave, conduct himself' (see MED s.v. *loken* v. (2) 11(b)), whereas in **C** it has its commoner sense 'pay attention (to), find out (about)', as at B 15.185 (ibid. 8(b)). **76 (B 92)** *lettred*: almost certainly the reading underlying *p²* and the *p¹* mss F and Z (to which add Q, erroneously placed in the Apparatus with eRMS). The ⇒ *lewed* by the <eRM> ancestor and S suggests censorship aimed at protecting the clergy. But it is presumably of spiritual as well as secular lords, not only of upper and lower ranks of the laity, that greed is here predicated, and the collocation *lord and lewid* would be most unusual. **79** After this follows an extra line in I, adopted by *Sk* and *Pe*, which could have been dropped from Cx through scribal objection to its blunt criticism of *clergie* (cf. previous note). But it is not necessary to the sense and (by contrast with the case of RM at 17.11) its origin would remain difficult to account for textually. It is thus perhaps best taken as an indignant anti-intellectual outburst by the I-scribe that echoes A 11.19 (B 10.19). It is especially worth noting that *after* 81 ms I has, instead of a form of the Cx text, five lines corresponding to A 11.6, 9–12, B 10.6, 9–12. The **AB** line that I's extra line may recall occurs soon after this passage and could easily have suggested it.

B 108–39 (A 67–95) 108 (A 67) *biwilide*: a reconstruction (proposed by *Ka*, p. 156 and adopted by *K–D* but not by *Ka²*) to provide in both Ax and Bx the *w*-stave required in first position. The form posited is the rare verb of Norman-French derivation attested in *SGGK* 2425 (see MED s.v. *biwilen* v.) as that for which the commoner non-alliterating variant is an archetypal ⇒. *wye*: accepted on the showing of **A** as the original key-stave in **B** for which

Bx's non-alliterating synonym is a scribal ⇒, perhaps motivated by desire for a more emphatic contrast with *womman* (for a parallel, cf. 21.230 //). **119–20 (A 75–6)** In the light of substantially identical **B**, the true form of **A** may be established with reasonable certainty, though the VJ re-lineation probably comes from **B**. The mislineation in Ax will have been caused by the excessive length of 75, which resulted from inserting a prefatory phrase to introduce a line supposedly translating the quoted Latin 74 (the line expands and illustrates the sense of Rom 12:3 rather than translating it exactly). On the evidence of the majority of its members, **r**'s form of the first phrase was *That is to seyn*, and on that of AH³W, **m**'s was probably *That is*. The latter phrase, if included, would leave 75 scanning satisfactorily but is otiose and appears a scribal attempt to ease the juncture. **124 (A 80)** *whyes*: the ms evidence indicates *weyes* as the reading of Bx and probably that of Ax too. With sense 'ways' this would be an acceptable (if commonplace) echoing of, e.g., Is 55:8–9, and *whyys* A-K, B-gM could be seen as scribal 'improvement' suggested by the prominence of *why* at 66 (107), 75 (119) and 82 (126). However, since *weyes* is actually a common Cx spelling for *wyes,* and could be authorial (see *IG* s.v. *weye* n²), it may also have been used by **L** to represent the homophone *whyes*. The intrinsic hardness of the sense argues for preferring *whyes* and substantival use of *why* is little instanced outside **L**. The other main use is at C 14.156 //, where the **p** family and some **x** mss (I and the t-group) make the same mistake and where **x** is presumably an intelligent scribal re-formation of Cx *weyes*. (In the case of the sg. form at 18.147, the danger of ambiguity being much smaller, no problem appears in the ms tradition). **131** *ablende*: a verb securely attested at C 20.140 // and conjectured as providing the necessary (here muted) vocalic key-stave (initial *a-* could easily have been lost by aural or visual assimilation to preceding *to*). **135 (A 91)** *For*: the syntactically more complex reading preferred here as more appropriate on grounds of sense, treating the curse as conditional on the curious enquirer's doing well rather than as a blunt rejoinder to his enquiry. The Ø- reading may well have been prompted by the easier syntax and the lack of any original punctuation to make the syntactical structure explicit.

139 (A 95) *deep*; *arere*: both evidently revisions, *a dore nayl* and *on syȝde* having presumably come into F and C² by ⊗ from **A** (in C² by visible correction here, as again at 153 below).

92 (A 104, B 149) *man*: on the showing of Y and u possibly present in **x** or else lost from Cx and individually restored by scribes wishing to 'regularise' the metre. Its contextual appropriateness is obvious, representing Study's acceptance of Will's offer at 88 to be her 'man'.

B 153 (A 108) scans adequately on vowels in AxBx with *as* forming the first stave. But *Hij* for *Thei* would be better, placing emphasis on a word of higher semantic function vulnerable to replacement by the advancing pronominal form.

103 (A 111, B 156) *Gladdere*: on the showing of **AC** judged the original reading for **B**, *And* being presumed inserted by Bx under inducement from *And* 157, 158. **110** *ire*: rejected by *R–K* p. 167, who see it as an intruded marginal gloss for *enuy* (added by visible correction in V). But it is not clear why *wrothe* should have needed glossing by a *less* usual synonym (*wrathe* occurs nine times more often), and rhetorical doubling here is very possible.

A 124 (B 169) *þinges*: the majority and probably the Ax reading is confirmed by **B**. *Ka* prefers *wyttes* 'departments of knowledge' as harder in sense, but it is also the more explicit reading and could have been induced by preceding *wyt* 123.

115 *ouerseye*: ambiguously spelled *ouerse* in Cx, a form of preterite not elsewhere evidenced in the tradition. I's reading, though probably an intelligent scribal correction, furnishes both a better form and a characteristic play on preceding *sey* and should be preferred as the more likely original. *many*: agreement of **x** and p² here points to Cx as having read *many* (a possible reworking of B¹'s scribal reading at B 171), with p¹ having missed the contraction sign (in *C-App.* read many] xp² my p¹; his N²). **116 (A 126, B 171)** *a / the Bible* **CA**: in the light of virtual **CA** agreement, to be preferred as the probable **B** reading, for which Bx has substituted a vaguer phrase. The motive was possibly objection to the notion that the Bible could have had any other author than God; but *wrot* implies only agency, not authorship in the proper sense. *grette*: apparently archetypal in both later texts; while perhaps aurally suggested by following (and in **B** preceding) *sette*, it is the less expected and harder reading. **117 (A 127, B 172)** *yglosid* **AC**: to be preferred also for **B** on grounds of sense; it is the Psalms that Scripture studies with the aid of the gloss, not the glosses for their own sake. B and Hm could have corrected independently or have been collated here with **C**. G's uncertain reading *?glosse* falls ambiguously between **AC** and Bx, presumably through ⊗ from **A**. The error could have arisen from omission of the past-participle marker and / or the preterite morpheme.

118 (A 128, B 173) *al þe Lawe aftur* **AC**: to be preferred also as the probable **B** reading for which Bx has substituted a vague generalising phrase as at 171 above. **121** *opere*: *opere mo* FN², which *R–K* follow, is unnecessary for the sense and probably by memorial ⊗ from **B**. **124 (A 134, B 179)** *here / Ø*: if **r** and not **m** here represents Ax, **AC** agreement may suggest that the possessive could also have been lost in Bx through alliterative attraction (*-tr- > tooles*). But since no serious issue of meaning is involved, it is not adopted here. **126 (A 136, B 181)** As it stands the Cx line scans awkwardly on |b| as Type

IIIa, with both full staves in non-lexical words that lack normal sentence-stress (muting of *bothe* with consequent generation of a T-type line would be unlikely, since there is only one main stave in the a-half). A modest emendation making the line scan on |k| would be to read *ek* as the original for which the near-synonym *bothe* is a Cx ⇒. This would produce a liasional key-stave and thence an authentic T-type, the second |k| stave being located internally in *squire* (for an unambiguous parallel see 10.269). However, the present more radical emendation takes |l| as the stave-sound in the light of the **AB** form and proposes *leide* as having been replaced by one more familiar in connection with reckoning or construction (see MED s.v *casten* v. 20 (a), 25 (a)). This usage is paralleled in *ms* 348, which comes close to the form here proposed: *And laide leuel and lyne a-long by the squyre*. The line now scans as Type IIIb, with almost the same sound-pattern as the example of this type at 4.12. If *leide* is accepted as the original verb, it will form a phrasal construction with *ouet* 'out', which appears to be the Cx reading. IP²D *mette* (adopted by *PeR–K*) is then to be seen as an intelligent conjecture, 'cast measurements by means of the square, etc.,' prompted by dissatisfaction with the phrase *caste oute*. But whereas I and P² could derive from y, D's reading is more probably an independent emendation; for if it preserves u, then U will have varied coincidentally with y. The reading is, however, unlikely to be original since it gives the line the pattern *axx / bb* or *ax / (a)bb* (so left by *R–K*, presumably as a draft). In the upshot, there is little real difference of sense: 'laying out' [foundations and elevation of a building] with these *toles* is closely related to 'casting the measurements' [of a building] by means of the same.

B 186–88 186 (A 141) The Bx line scans as Type IIIa with internal rhyme, and the sense is adequate as it stands. Yet the context requires not simply the existence of love but the explicit presence of love 'within' Theology, as insisted upon in **A**; so it may be conjectured that *þerinne* has dropped out of the b-half. Arguably the adverb should be placed as the last word, this being the one most vulnerable to loss through homoteleuton, for the resulting identical *end*-rhyme would certainly be of a type well-instanced in **L**, e.g. B 1.146–47 // (and see Appendix I 5.ii). But against this, placing it pre-finally allows the main verb both the same relative position as in **A** and the Leonine internal rhyme favoured elsewhere by **L** (as at 21.325 // **B**). **188 (A 143)** *lakked*: the past tense in subjunctive function following an open-condition present, the harder reading in **A** and the one supported by both traditions of Bx. The scribal present-tense form, which aims at 'logical' uniformity, may have been suggested by a tense-ambiguous original spelled *lakkyt* (as actually in *A*-H³); but it follows **L**'s tendency elsewhere. Thus, the easy mixture of tenses in **A** is illustrated in the

four verbs of 138–39, with which contrast B 183–84, where the unified tenses seem to be the result of revision (so in // **C** 129–30).

134 (A 144, B 189) The Ax line (taking *vppon* as metrically preferable to *on*) scans as Type IIIa, without any need to conjecture a lost stave on |ð| in the a-half (as does *Ka²*, suggesting *þou*). Rhetorical stress here on *þérvppón* will appear justified because of its emphatic reference back to *loue* in 143 and the shift of full stress now to a word *(þere)* that did not carry stress in that line (contrast *þerwiþ* at A 162 // B 215 below). The **B** revision changes the action prescribed from 'believing' to 'loving'; but on stylistic grounds the plainer *Loke* β is perhaps preferable to the homonymically punning *loue* of α (though neither alternative is supported by the revised form of **C**'s a-half, which introduces a third verb *lerne*, echoing B 20.208). Both the β and α versions give acceptable scansions (Types Ic and IIa respectively) and in the b-half choice betweeen α agreeing with *þou þenke* **A** and β agreeing with *þe like* **C** is likewise evenly balanced (though *loke* at B 207 favours β here). Since no major question of meaning is at issue, β is accepted as closer to the final version.

B 190–204 190 (A 145, C 135) *kennyng*: an emendation not strictly necessary on grounds of sense or metre. But on comparison with **A** (*louis scole*) and **C** (*doctour*) the reading *kynne* seems contextually out of place, the word required being one that emphasises love's rôle as a teacher not as a relative, and this is just that of the Theology 'in which love is' (see note above and the verb *kenneþ* at 198 below). The noun *kennyng* here has the sense 'training, discipline': see MED s.v. *kenninge* ger. (b) and cf. 196 below, which contrasts Cato's *kennyng* with love's. The Bx form *kynne* could easily have been generated mechanically if the postulated reading in its exemplar had been cropped at the line-end (*kenn-*). **197** *yeme*: a revision, with Cr²³ a commoner synonymic ⇒ for the same reading in Cr¹'s lost ms source and F a ⊗ from **A**. **201 (A 153)** scans as Type IIIc, both scribal and editorial attempts to alter it to a standard (Type Ie) line being otiose. **201a–06a** revises **A** material occurring some eighty lines further on at 245a–255 (see Vol I, pp. 434–45). The whole passage on *ooþer science*, expanded in the first revision (B 191–219=A 146–65), is completely removed in the second. **201a** *habemus* β in the quotation (following the Vulgate) should arguably be *est* α, which is the reading at A 11.245a and fits better with the interpretation of the name of Piers's wife (*Dame Worch-when-tyme-is*) at 8.80 // (see *Commentary*). **204 (A 249)** *to swiche nameliche*: ↔ of indirect object and adverb to emend Bx's line scanning *xa / ax*. The adv. ('especially'), which is more restrained than **A**'s *souereynliche* 'supremely', is less likely to be an unmetrical scribal ⇒ than a revision. The stylistic motive could have been a wish to avoid undue repetition, since the adjective *souereyn* occurs in two different senses ('efficacious'; 'chief') at 208, 212, in lines newly added in **B**.

A 157–97 157 (B 211) *þre* **A** (*two* **B**): the 'unthrifty' *science* of **A** including astronomy, which **B** presumably excludes. While *two* could be an officious scribal correction, the awareness implied of a distinction between the practical science and judicial astrology could be authorial. **L** seems to have changed his mind about Albert in revising A 11.160 as B 214, so an altered attitude to astronomy may be plausibly maintained here. Study's less censorious tone about the natural sciences in **B** accompanies a more logical view of herself as their author, in keeping with the omission of **A**'s reference to conjuring the devil, which would seem to carry the joke too far. **159 (B 213)** *many / fele*: giving a liaisonal stave (*of_many*), unless *many* is an Ax ⇒ for the less common **B** form *fele*, which may otherwise be taken as a revision strengthening the alliteration at the key position. **161** As it stands, the Ax line has the inauthentic metrical pattern *xa / ax* (so left in *Ka²*), here emended to scan as Type IIIa. The two terms could have been transposed to give prominence to the seemingly more important word. **L**'s is the first recorded example of *pyromancy*, and the Ax scribe could have been ignorant of its exact sense 'divination by fire' and have thought it a high-sounding synonym for its more familiar partner. But it is the latter, understood pseudo-etymologically in its medieval spelling *nigromancie* as '*black* magic', that is primarily concerned with raising the *pouke*, and is therefore juxtaposed with the latter as here reconstructed. **163 (B 216)** The mislineations of *r¹* and **m** indicate scribal dissatisfaction with a line judged too short. But *r²* has preserved it in an acceptable if abrupt form, having the pattern *abb / ab* with vocalic theme staves and contrapuntal staves on |s|. *Sikir* could be a scribal filler after loss in Ax's exemplar of a b-half like that of B 216 or of a final lift **Studie* that Ax could have construed as a marginal gloss. But it resembles *soþly* at A 175 below, though 163 would scan without it, as a Type IIIa. **171 (B 224)** The form of the b-half in *B-F* is close to **A**, its inclusion of *hem* making it identical with *A*-U, and ⊗ from **A** is probable here. *boþe*: in **B** adjectival but in **A** adverbial in all mss except UVM (W has an adverbial synonym). Although *boþe* could be the adjective used pronominally if a full-stop is placed after *wyf* (as *Sk*'s medial point allows), mid-line sentence-separation is untypical of **L**. So it is better to regard **B** as a revision that by adding the co-ordinating conjunction establishes the construction anticipated by *A*-UVM. **177** *collide*: preferable contextually on grounds of sense, though the readings of H²Ch, of J and of V (presumably a synonym for *collide* in v) are most probably intelligent scribal corrections of an Ax reading *callide*. **178** scans as Type Ie with muted key-stave or as Type IIIa (on *w*). **180** scans 'cognatively' on |t| |d| |d|, the

first *t*-stave being either in *To*, stressing the purpose of his visit, or in the liaisonal *at_ʒów*, with stress on the instructors. As neither alternative is without awkwardness, Ax could have inverted to prose order a Type IIIa line reading in the a-half: *Dowel at ʒow to lerne*. **182** *she*: *he* mCh (omitted from Apparatus), very probably a correct reflex of an ambiguous Ax form misread as *heo* (so actually V). Since the equivalent of this speech is given to Clergy in **BC**, it would be more natural for him to reply to Will's words at 179–81, as is supposed by A 12.2; so on balance it would be preferable to read *he* here and take the speaker as Clergy (see Schmidt 2004). **191** *ben*: conjectured as the necessary second stave lost in Ax by distraction from preceding *Obed-*, bre-, and from beþ, bre- in 192. As it stands, the Ax line gives the scansion pattern *aa / xx* (so left in *Ka²*). A simpler solution of the metrical difficulty ('reconstruction' more than 'conjecture') would be to see *brethren* as having supplanted *sustren* in position two through unconscious inducement from the familiar phrasal order. **195** *ben in office* **m**: contextually superior on grounds of sense, the *office* being a bishop's and its discharge corresponding to the *facere* and *docere* in 196a that earn the term *magnus* (= Dobest). This reading and the correct lineation of 194–96 strikingly illustrate **m**'s independent textual value. **197** *beþ*: conjectured as the required first stave in a line with Ax ⇒ of a form normal for dialects other than Southern in the singular. As it stands, the Ax line gives the imperfect pattern *xa / ax* (so left in *Ka²*). But while the RUAW transposition will yield a Type IIIa line, this requires a syntactically unconvincing caesural pause after *is*, and so emendation here seems justifiable.

141–42 (B 232–33) The scansion of B 232 is here taken to be Type IIa, though it would read better if *Chirche* were *Kirke*. 233 may have vocalic staves, but since two Type IIa lines in succession would be uncharacteristic, it is better scanned on voiced fricatives, the first being generated from elision of *þe* and *articles* or liaison of *Wiþ* and *alle*. If both are treated as staves, the line becomes Type Ic. **143** *alyhte Goddes sone*: subject-verb ↔ providing the required key-stave in |l|. Cx has inverted to prose order (with damage to the metre) to promote the main idea to first position. *R–K*'s conjecture *loue* for *sone* may be 'elegant' (p.170), but it is also otiose.

B 242 *animáles*: conjectured as the original for which the common word *beestes* is here judged a Bx ⇒ giving the inauthentic pattern *aa / bb*. The rare synonym, with stress on the third syllable, provides the necessary key-stave in |m|. MED s.v. cites Trevisa's *Bartholomew* from *c.* 1398 as glossing *animal* 'a best'; but the Latin source-word should have been familiar enough for the term to be acceptable.

148 (B 243) *made*: despite αL agreement and the appearance of the pronoun in C's second version of the half-line at 154, *he* may be omitted from **B** on the showing of immediately // **C**, as sense and metre are unaffected.

B 246 *Gospellere*: conjectured as the necessary key-stave, here scanning cognatively with the |k| staves of the a-half, for which Bx is a ⇒ of the more familiar non-alliterating synonym. An earlier conjecture *same* explaining Bx *Euaungelistes* as a marginal gloss in its exemplar misread as a correction is now abandoned mainly because scansion on |s| necessitates reduction to a prelude-dip of two important lexical words in the a-half. The same objection holds against another conjecture *so þe*] *so* (presuming *so* (2) lost by haplography), which makes the line scan on |s|. Though not elsewhere instanced in **L**, the term *gospellere* is widely attested in the period (for the converse situation, with *gospel* as scribal ⇒ for *euaungelie* in Bx, see on B 1.200).

157 (B 248) *alle* **C** / *lewed* **B**: perhaps suspect for failing to make clear like **C** that belief is a universal requirement, and so as a scribal product induced by antithetical association with *clerkes* in 247. The g reading *men* could thus be viewed as a non-alliterating reflex of Bx *ledes*, closer in sense to *alle* but capable of suggesting or being mistaken for *lewed* in four lines of transmission (LMwα). On the other hand, g could be an attempt to counter misunderstanding, later carried through by **C**. So *lewed* may be allowed to stand in **B** as a loose first thought with the elliptical meaning 'ignorant (lay) people [and we are all, where understanding the Trinity is concerned, ignorant]'. **161** Two formally acceptable scansions of Cx are (i) as Type IIIb with two lifts in *Dówél* and a four-syllable prelude-dip or (ii) as Type Ib with a cognative first stave on *to* (cf. on A 180). However, reading with a more *natural* stress-pattern yields the inauthentic metrical schemes *aab / bb* (with |m| as theme-stave and |d| as counterpoint) or *xa / aa* (on |d|). The emendation here is anticipated by N² (one of the **C** mss that most often displays both **x** and **p** readings), but the relative pronoun is retained from Cx as probably original. The resulting play on two polysemes 'act', 'make' of the lexeme *don* (MED s.v. v. 1a (a), 4 (a)) seems characteristic but, if original, could nonetheless have provoked stylistic objection from the scribe of Cx.

B 251–90 form an unusual example of a long passage added in **B** and then deleted rather than revised in **C**. Ll. 279–82 provide the germ of C Pr 105–14, a newly-composed passage (see *ad loc* above), and the thought of 287–87*a* is echoed in C 9.260. **251** *Siþþe* 'next' (MED s.v. *sitthe* adv. (d)): conjectured here to provide a necessary first stave-word for a line scanning *xa / ax* or *xxa / ax* in Bx. *Dowel* has been described, without being named, starting with *It* at 232, and 251 now introduces the second of the three Do's in its proper order. **266** There follows in Bx a line of acceptable metre (Type IIIc) that nonetheless seems suspect from its lack of logical or syntactical connexion with 266 and over-emphatic listing of the ranks

of higher clergy. It exemplifies the same cast of mind found in such spurious Bx lines as those after 4.38, 6.17, 182 and 19.373. **271** *lost*: superior on grounds of sense to *boste* 'idle noise', the reading of R and originally of L (but altered to *lost*). Either both mss have coincidentally made the error through visual confusion of *l* with *b* or the RL agreement testifies to the reading of α and β respectively and thence of Bx (with γ and F having corrected independently); but M has not visibly altered an L-type reading to accord with γ, so the case for L as representing β is less compelling here and *lost* would appear anyway intrinsically preferable. **273** The Bx b-half has lost the key-stave by ⇒ of the order commoner in such phrases, and is easily reconstructed; see further B 8.99. **274** *no wi3t*: here reconstructed in the expanded phrasal form to provide the necessary third stave in this Type IIb line, for which Bx has a commoner non-alliterating ⇒. **B 279** *barnes*: conjectured as the necessary stave-word in *b* for which *folk* might have suggested itself as a more familiar synonym, giving a Bx line with the pattern *aa / xx*. Either *burnes* 'men' or *barnes* 'children' would suit, and scribal objection to the first will presumably have been on grounds of its restricted lexical distribution, to the second through failure to see its special Biblical sense. Both occur in **B** (at 3.267; 3.152); but reference to the **C** passage that develops these **B** lines provides convincing support for *barnes*: see C Pr 105, 111, where *children of Israel* occurs twice. **B 291–327*a* (A 202–18)** For notes, see above on C 5.146–79 *ad loc.*

XI 162–197 (B XI 1–36) For convenience, textual notes on parallel **B** are included at this point. **167 (B XI 5)** *warth*: in the light of **C** the inevitably required verb. Bx will have written *wraþe* by inducement from the noun in 4b above. **168 (B XI 7)** scans as an extended Type IIIa with standard counterpoint, the theme-stave being *f* and the contrapuntal stave *r*; or as Type IIa on *r* with liaisonal stave in *For Y*. **169 (B XI 8)** *and loue*: preferred on grounds of sense in both versions, where the same error has occurred, presumably for the same reason, i.e. mistaking the ampersand for the indefinite article and *u* for *n*, through the unfamiliarity of the notion of *þe lond of loue*. The mechanical ease of the error doubtless accounts for cross-family agreement in both traditions (*B*-F with β, *C*-M with XP²N²). It is just possible that the *C*-I reading may preserve that of group y, accounting for the levelled form of the other y mss but not for Y, which has corrected either independently or from a u-type source. Contextual and thematic arguments also support *and loue*, notably the balance between the false love of this first inner dream in **B** and the true love of the second (the *loue-dreem* in B 16.20), and the apparent echo of the phrase *longyng and loue* (C 169) at 180, *to lyue longe and ladyes to louye* (for discussion of B 16.20 see below). **177 (B XI 16)** *continence*: the Cx spelling of *contenaunce* **B** may involve a sardonic 'clerkly' pun on the homophone *continence*. M has *contynaunce* and R *countenance*, eliminating the pun. *clergies lore* **p**: preferred in the light of **B**'s *Clergie*; the T-type line generatied by reading *lore* 'compensates' for the excessively long prelude-dip. But *R–K*'s wholesale adoption of the **B** reading lacks justification. **193 (B XI 32)** scans awkwardly on fricatives with the first two staves *Couétyse of Yes*, (creating a long prelude-dip and stressing a semantically insignificant word), or on vowels, placing the caesura before *thow* and making *here* the key-stave (the latter preferable). **197 (B XI 36)** scans on *t*, the first stave being found internally in *stoupe*.

B X 337 *at nede*: *as nede techeþ* ?β / *at pure nede* α. Neither sub-archetypal reading appears to derive from the other, but both may be attempts to provide a last lift in consequence of mislocating the caesura after *nauȝt*. The reconstruction takes the line as Type IIb, with the midline pause coming after *it*, and *nauȝt but at nede* as an integral adverbial phrase forming the whole b-half. Thus *pure* α may be seen as an attempt to provide a fourth lift and *as...techeþ* β as a smoothing with the same aim. Both scribes evince unease with the Type IIb structure, authentic in **L** but rare elsewhere.

A 236–54 236 (B 347) The **A** line scans as standard, the **B** line either as extended Type IIIa with counterpoint on *s* or preferably, in the light of **A**, as Type I with *is_óure* as liaisonal key-stave. Though *þat* could be a Bx ⇒ for **A** *so*, with its characteristic wordplay ('of such a kind' / 'in such a way'), emendation is not required here. **237 (B 348)** *an*: the aptest reading in both versions on grounds of sense, one non-Christian being envisaged as at hand to baptise a dying pagan who requests it. Ax, to judge from **m** and u, could have read Ø, and ChK be a commonsense correction. But if *B-C²* gets its alteration from an **A** copy, it will be from one of d type. **239 (B 350)** *any man*: reconstructed on the basis of **B** as the true reading of **A**. Agreement with *r¹* of K, the only other remaining *r²* witness, may argue for the stronger theological statement as original; but generation of *an hy* from *any* is an easy visual (and even easier aural) error. J may therefore be judged to preserve one part of the Ax reading (*any*) and **m** another part (*man*), though M's *he* may suggest rather that *any* was the group reading. But the possibility of revision in **B** to tone down the original assertion cannot be securely ruled out. **240–41 (B 351–52)** scan either as Type IIIa or, preferably, as Type Ia with cognative staves |k| / |g|. *Ka²* inconsistently prefers J's *crist* to *god* in 240 on metrical grounds while accepting *degre* in 241 (on which see *IG* under *degree* n²). But J here is mistakenly attempting to correct the metre after failure to grasp the 'cognative' principle (as may KH³ with *decre* for *degre* in 241). **245** The line as reconstructed by *Ka* retains *suche* from **r** but omits *sone* from **m**, which is here kept as there is no reason other than euphony for rejecting

it. The characteristic wordplay on *shewiþ, sewiþ* (virtual homophones in **L**'s idiolect) suggests that it is not scribal padding designed to introduce the Latin of 245*a* (as evidently for *K–F*, who omit). So does the presence in **r** of *suche*, a hypermetric vestige of the line lost, as *Ka* notes, perhaps by inducement from *alle* in 244, 246. **245*a*–49** correspond to **B 201*a*–204** discussed earlier. **248 (B 203)** *giuen*: emending Ax *ȝiuen* as an unconscious ⇒ of the (here) unmetrical commoner form (though pointed scansion on vocalic grammatical words is possible). The line evidently proposes a characteristic polysemantic play on *good*, noun and adverb, like that at B 9.160. For confirmation of the emendation, see B 203, the revised form of A 248, which has *gyuen* as key-stave, though the pun on *good* has been removed. **254 (B 366)** *Non mecaberis*: 'thou shalt not commit adultery', evidently an authorial error in both versions for 'thou shalt not kill' (*non occides* in Lk 18:20, Ex 20:13, where it comes before *non moechaberis*). *Ka*'s complicated argument (retaining *Ne* from TH²) that this is a correlative use, with '*mecaberis*....not translated by *ne sle nouȝt* but parallel to it' (p. 456) is unconvincing. For *Non* is clearly the Ax reading and is repeated in B 366, where it cannot form any part of a supposed parallel construction. Further, the sole commandment in question in the context of A 252–55 / B 364–68 is the commandment not to kill. Neither A 254 nor B 366–67 can admit any interpretation but that *sle(e) no(u)ȝt* is being offered, albeit erroneously, as the translation of *non mecaberis*. Possibly **L** was confusing this uncommon verb with *necare* and misremembering the latter as deponent. Such appears the expedient (even more desperate than the Athlone editor's) of the *B*-mss Cr²³Y and GL, the latter pair going so far as to spell the root *necha-*, while Cr¹OC² opt for the correct future form of *necare* and M for the Vulgate verb, as does one *A*-ms, H³. But for the suggestion that **L** may have associated the fifth and sixth commandments in a particular way, see the *Commentary* on this passage.

B 367–70 367 *also*: conjectured to provide the required key-stave word from which Bx appears to have omitted the second element under inducement from the common expression *al for þe beste* (found earlier at B 5.484). **368** is presumably lost from β by homoarchy (*For* 368, 369). **370 (A 257)** The possible **m** readings *misdedes, lette* could be original in **A** or reveal ⊗ here from **B**; but no serious issue of meaning is involved.

208 *prescite* 'foreknown [*sc.* to be damned]': the reading preserved in D (< u); both right on grounds of sense and of a form such as to generate the attested variants. The nearest to it, *prescient* 'foreknowing', is not recorded in **L**'s day, though *prescience* is, from the 1370s (see MED s.v.), but U's error implies that it existed. Its sense is wrong here, but it may have been known as an English word, like the familiar noun, whereas *prescite* is still half-

Latin, as apparently indicated by the underlining in D. It is here treated as anglicised, however, so as to provide a better balance with the more fully English *predestinaet*, a word also (and wrongly) underlined in D. One of the earliest examples of *prescit* cited in MED s.v. (from Lydgate) collocates it with *predestinate*. But the absence of prior citations, other than one from an early C15th Wycliffite tract, suggests its C14th restriction to technical usage and L's use here could well have been the first in English. The spelling *precyet* in y may indicate descent from an **x** form spelled **precit*, and *prechen* **p** then be seen as smoothing a form misconstrued as *prechyt* under inducement from *prechen* 207. **211 (A 265, B 378)** *made*: preferred on the basis of **AC** agreement as the probable **B** reading for which Bx *tauȝte* is a deliberate ⇒ after taking *sapience* as the common noun 'wisdom' rather than as the title of a portion of the OT writings (see MED s.v. (a) and (f)). **215 (A 268, B 381)** *Dede* **A**: good sense in context, given that *in werk and in woord* 269 covers more actions than just Solomon's judgements (e.g., building the Temple, writing 'Sapience'). *Ka*'s emendation to *Demde* in the light of **BC** is therefore to be rejected as gratuitous. **B** is plainly a revision that saves Will's argument from appearing too obviously self-contradictory in stating both that Solomon did well and that he is damned (though what salvation requires is to *do* well). The revision of *wrouȝte* A 270 below (apropos of Aristotle) to *wissede* (B 382) supports this interpretation. For like *demed* at B 381 (retained in C just as *wissede* **B** is through its synonym *tauhte*), this verb points to the distinction between teaching 'dowel' (the fruit of knowledge) and living virtuously (the fruit of grace) that becomes crucial in B XIII. *techiþ* **A**: the **B** reading *telleþ*, which appears in MH³ as *tellit* (?< **m**) is either the original **A** reading or, as more likely here, ⊗ from **B** or coincidence with it. **218 (B 383)** *prechen*: in itself the **p** reading is unexceptionable; but the form of **x**, echoing **B** though wrong in repeating the verb from the a-half, prompts reconstruction of the line as (except for the order of object and adverbial phrase in the a-half) identical with **B**, which is needlessly adopted wholesale by *R–K*. The a-half form of *C-I* need not point to the presence of *prechen* in Cx but is either a guess or an echo of **B**. **221 (A 271, B 385)** *in helle*: agreement of AC suggests that Bx may be ⇒ of a milder phrase, perhaps through objection to the starkness of the original. **223 (A 277, B 387)** The A line makes sense as it stands, though the contrast between the sages' wisdom and their fate is not made as it is in **B** and **C** by the relative pronoun. Ax *And* may be ⇒ for original *That* under visual inducement from preceding *And* (twice); but the other signs of major revision in **B** here (see on 215 above) caution against emendation in this instance. In the b-half, *wonyn* H³ may show ⊗ from a **B** source; *wynne* **m** is likely to have come in by inducement from 276b. **224 (B 388)** *y* **x**p²: unlikely

to be ⇒ for *we* in p¹, contextually the more logical form after *we* 222; so if it is an unconscious relict of the B-Text under revision, perhaps original and to be retained. **233 (B 393)** *At*: following P², *R–K* read *Ac at*, which eases the transition (D has *Ac in* and RGK *Ac*); but there is no necessity for this and Cx may stand. *men* **B**: conjectured here as the required key-stave word for which Bx is ⇒ of a non-alliterating near-synonym. Possibly **B** read *hij* in an extended Type IIIa line scanning vocalically with standard counterpoint on *m* (*abb / ax*). But the stave-sound *m* in **C**'s revised b-half and the presence of two lexical words with *l* in Bx's b-half support the emendation. The line now scans as a normal T-type (*aa / [a]bb*). **251 (B 409)** *foles*: a possible spelling for *foules*, the word contextually most appropriate (cf. 242 above). But a play on the sense 'fools' is also apt, since the ark as type of the faithful remnant prefigures the *foles* of 22.61–2. The pun has been established as early as A 8.111 // B 7.125 (see the note *ad loc*). **252–54 (B 410–12)** The Bx lines have been lost from β very probably through homœoteleuton (-*ine* 409a, -*inne* 412). **253 (B 411)** *Kirke* **B**: conjectured as the necessary key-stave word, supplanted in α (and possibly Bx) by the commoner non-alliterating variant-form. In revised **C**, however, this is satisfactory, as the line scans on w. **262–63 (A 286, B 420)** **C**'s revision of **B** as two lines scans vocalically in 262 with strong rhetorical stresses on non-lexical words and has a secondary stave-pattern on *p*, the last lift alliterating translinearly with the first of 263. But if 262 was one of a pair scanning on *p*, Cx may have transposed the last two words to the present prose order. **264 (A 287, B 421)** *Then*: 'than' as in // **B**, but taken as 'then, next' and replaced in **p** by a synonym. *myhte do*: restored on the joint showing of **AC** as the likely **B** original for which Bx (scanning *aa / bb* or wrenching the stress in *wommán dide*) is presumed to have substituted *what womman*, perhaps under prompting from the (same mild) anti-feminism displayed towards the Magdalen by the narrator at 21.162 //. But **A** overtly and **B** tacitly establish an important contrast between possibility in 287 / 421 and actuality in 288 / 422 that depends in part on the syntactic contrast between 'mýȝte do' and 'díde' (abandoned in **C**'s revision of 422). **266** *deuyned* **p**: confirmed by the context and **B** *conspired*; **x**'s *deuyed* (? or *denyied*) being doubtless induced by *denyede* 265. **268** *lettere* **p**: apparently *leare* 'liar' in **x**; perhaps a scribal attempt to make sense of an exemplar misread to mean 'preventer' (as at 1.65), in consequence of missing the Biblical allusion and perhaps under unconscious influence from *gyle*. The YD corrections may as probably reflect independent recognitions of the allusion as recourse to a **p**-type source. **269–70 (A 289–90, B 423–4)** As it stands in **p**, the one-line version omitting *to dethe* is metrically unexceptionable. But the latter phrase, present in **AB**, weakens **x**'s b-half by de-stressing *peple* and benefits from the re-lineation actually offered by U. In **B**, 424 may have been dropped from α as a result of censorship (cf. the β omission of a comparably strong statement at B 78–9). In β, *Muche* seems inserted to fill out a line of untypical terseness (though in pattern paralleled at 127 // **A**) and may be safely omitted on the showing of **AC**. For **L**'s point is that 'even the (future) apostle was capable of *killing* Christians', not that 'he killed *many* rather than few'. **271 (A 291, B 425)** The Bx form of this revised line is metrically just satisfactory, being of Type IIIa with a five-syllable prelude-dip and two stresses in *sóueréyns*. A more regular shape closer to **A** could be obtained by diagnosing Bx loss of *so* by haplography before so*uerayns*, with subsequent smoothing to *as* (*so* seems to have been lost by the same mechanism in *A*-tH[3]). Alternatively, simple omission of Bx *as*, following **C**, would improve the rhythm, as would *swiche* for *þise*; but no emendation seems imperative. The **C** line, recast perhaps with direct recourse to the earliest version, reverts to the form of **A** in its b-half.

A 293 *am I forget*: RD, J, M (? representing respectively *r[1]*, *r[2]* and **m**); an idiom more unusual than the normal *haue I forget* preferred by *Ka* and thus unlikely to be derived from it. The meaningless TH[2] variant may well reflect t's visual error for *am I*, Ch the ⇒ of a familiar expression for that reading. K and H[3] have made the same ⇒ for the readings of their respective group-ancestors (*r[2]*, **m**), which was probably that of RDJM. If a preterite of *forgeten* formed with *ben* existed, its rarity would account for its replacement by the commoner construction with *hauen* and A's levelling to *I forgat*. B 441 is arguably abrupt, and the form of C 277 may suggest that Bx lost a line at this point. *K–D* accordingly insert A 293 before B 441 (so *Sch[1]*); but as evidence for reconstruction is uncertain, emendation is better avoided. The line's meaning being somewhat oblique, **L** may have preferred abruptness to obscurity in **B** but later have prepared more carefully in **C** for the introduction of the important idea in line 278.

274–75 could 'look like scribal padding-out into two lines of an original reading *Ho is worthy to [for] wele or to [for] wykkede pyne*' (Schmidt 1980:105; so *R–K*). But the punning *repetitio* characteristic of **C** seems detectable here. Thus *wele* 274 is to be read as a (deliberate) variant of the adverb *wel* (with long vowel) in an elliptical phrase 'well or wicked doing' (*Pe*), while in 275 *wele* is the noun 'happiness' (MED s.v. *wele* n.(1), 2 (a)) and *wikkede* means 'fierce, cruel' (MED s.v. *wikked* a. 2 (b)).

B 435 *wote*: the reading of L (?< β) and R (? < α), harder in conjoining present indicative with past subjunctive than the more logically concordant γ form, so likelier to be original. The form of g suggests w, its sense that of LR.

278 (A 294, B 441) *comended* **p**: on grounds of contex-

tual appropriateness and the support of **AB** to be preferred to *comaunded* **x**, which is not impossible but could here be no more than a bad spelling, one paralleled in *A*-KDMH[3] (*Ka* Apparatus). **283 (B 446)** The Bx division of 446 from 447 is acceptable in itself but syntactically the pronoun object falls better at the end of 446, rewritten **C** providing no firm guidance. Either way, 446 has a non-authentic pattern *aa / bb*, so *wiþ* is conjectured as the required key-stave for which Bx substituted the more obvious *and* (unless its reading was Ø as in R). The line now scans as a T-type. **287 (B 450)** *wihtnesse* **p**: the more unexpected and therefore harder variant, though possibly less appropriate here since it stands for physical strength which, like mental capacity, is declared unavailing without grace. The **x** reading, to which **p** group q has varied (*add* FS after Q), may have been suggested by the implied context of examination in a court (cf. *euidences* 286). But it presumably has a sense (MED s.v. *witnesse* n. 1) answering exactly to *wisdom* in **B** (so *C*-N[2]). **288 (B 451)** The reading of **x** is ungrammatical and that of **p** makes poor sense. For while *grace* and *fortune* evidently form the two lifts of the b-verse, the links between each, and between both and the a-verse, are obscure. The emendation here presumes loss of *is* in Cx through haplography before *his*; in **x** assimilation of the latter to *which*; and in **p** smoothing of *which* to *with* and of *to* to *and*. The sense of the reconstructed phrase *his grace of fortune* is something like 'God's grace granted for a specific occasion' (*sc.* the *meschief* of // **B**). The unconventional conjunction of two terms (*grace; fortune*) customarily contrasted with each other (as objected by *R–K* p. 155, who read *with*] *which / with his*) may well underlie the original corruption. **295 (A 308, B 458)** *kete* **A**: the Ax reading *grete* could alliterate 'cognatively' with |k| and *kete* 'distinguished' be no more than an attempt by KW to 'correct' the metre. But if a conjecture, it seems a good one, given the presence of *konnyng* in the **B** and **C** revisions and its earlier occurrence in a closely similar context A 11.56, where the same two mss, accompanied by V, preserve it (very possibly from Ax) and one of the erroneous variants is *grete* (see further *Intro.* II § 70). *in*: only in X ('x' is a misprint), preserving the intrinsically best reading; *and* Cx makes *konnyng* an adjective not a noun. **299** *paradys oper*: emended without warrant by *R–K* to read as **AB**, though there is no reason to doubt rewriting here. Thus B 463 is revised from A 313 and is in turn revised to C 300 so as to fuse B 463a and 464b into a single line (with minor alteration of the epithet), leaving *paradis* from B 464a to be re-used in C 299.

300a (A 313, B 465) At this point the majority of the **A-Text mss** break off, **RUJ** to be followed by Passus XII, **TH[2]Ch** and **K** by a C-Text of **x**-type (the Latin **300a** is in the former). **D[2]** joins y as a fifth member of this **C**

sub-group, its readings agreeing with y unless otherwise noted. TH²Ch now form a *C*-group **t**, readings of which are cited when agreeing with **p**, but only selectively when isolative. The four extant A-Text **rubrics** all appear to be scribal, the absence of an archetypal *explicit* indicating the unfinished state of this version. For convenience, notes on C 11.301–17 // B 10.469–75, 11.37–43 are given here, and notes on **A XII** after these.

306 (B 474) will scan as Type IIIa in the majority and perhaps archetypal reading. But the 'church' variant with *k* as in the **B** line under revision gives a firmer feel to it by linking the noun closely with the custodial verb *kepe* that for **L** defines the Church's providential function (cf. the shift at C 246 to *k* as key-stave sound from the vocalic stop of the **B** line it revises). **312** The **x** form of 312 will scan cognatively as Type Ib on |k| / |g| and, with two stresses on *bígýle*, 313 will scan as Type IIIa, while the **p** form has *aa / xx.* But in **x** the shortness of 313 and in **p** the uncharacteristic placing of the adverb clearly point to Cx's loss of a half-line after the macaronic a-verse of 312 and reflect sub-archetypal attempts to repair the omission by re-lineation. In the light of B 11.40, it therefore seems safe to restore *ne Coueytise of Yes* as the lost b-half and relineate accordingly. It is possible that *grettly* is a Cx error for an original *graythly*, as seems to be the case with *gretly* β in the Bx tradition. This is the reading of one *C*-ms, F, and is adopted by *R–K*; but as the Cx sense is acceptable and revision here is possible, no emendation need be made.

Passus A XII

On the authenticity of Passus XII see the *Introduction* III A §§ 67–74. It is here accepted as original up to l. 98; the last nineteen lines, headed *Appendix*, are to be ascribed to John But, and are given in italics. The rubric *Passus tercius de dowel* appears the product of the scribe of u and will not have been in the source of J or, presumably, in the common source of <uJ>. It could have been prompted by recognition that Clergy's opening words are a reply to Will's speech in XI 258–313. The metrical irregularities in the passus may be in part authorial if it derives from a draft (as occasionally with **Z**; see *Intro.* III Z § 6). But the text has been treated generally as if it were a finished fragment and emendations made on the assumption that some errors are likely to be scribal. The presence of two independent witnesses (R, J) for the first 88 lines makes comparative analysis of the readings possible, though there is no *parallel* material apart from some Latin quotations in any of the other versions. The copy-text is R, the only complete witness; for that reason, as in the case of **Z**, the ms spelling is retained. Only substantive variants are recorded in the Apparatus.

1–98 3 The <RU> line has the inauthentic pattern *xa / ax*, which could result from the u scribe's transposition to prose order of a phrase *betere don* in a Type IIIa line. J scans normatively, though with an unusually strong stress on *bene* after a six-syllable prelude-dip. This could be a scribal correction of the metre, but the fact that *don betere* would be the phrase expected supports its claim to be original. **4** *peryth* J: preferable to *put h(i)m* RU as the harder word, the verb being little instanced outside **L** (see MED s.v. *peren* v.(2)). As well as B 16.417, where it collocates with *apostles*, *peeris* (n) is linked with *aungeles* (the other category cited here) at B 16.71. **5** *seye*: presumably the preterite of *seyen* 'see' (= *seyʒ*; cf. C 11.115). The slackness of the b-half may be due to its draft character. **15** *fonte*: final *-e* is added to provide the necessary feminine ending. **17** scans as a familiar extended Type IIIa on vowels with standard counterpoint on *sk* (*abb / ax*). **21** scans very awkwardly as it stands as Type IIIa with the caesura after *ben.* But the tense-sequence of 20 suggests that the verb should be rather *were* 'should be', yielding a line of Type IIa. Alternatively, *synne* may have been substituted in the common source for *wikkednesse* under inducement from *synful* in 20a, 24b. Grounds for emendation are, however, not sufficient here. **32** scans *aa / xx* in the common source, but *lerne* may be diagnosed as a scribal ⇒ for a less expected word *cunne* 'know how to'. **34** *skele*: an inevitable emendation, R's variant perhaps an attempt to make sense of the reading attested by J rather than deliberately ⇒ for *sk(e)le*, a common word. **36** scans in J as Type IIa with the third stave *to* 'cognative' on *t*, the fourth lift *do* providing a 'supplemental' |d| stave and the b-half scanning *gó dó wèl* to give the necessary feminine ending. Less probably, *do* could form the key-stave with *wel* expanded to the disyllabic *wele*, which was mainly Northern in this period (see MED s.v. *well* adv.). **45** scans as either Type IIIa with caesura after *desyre* or as Type Ie with caesura after *him.* Both alternatives require a liaisonal stave *with_him* though in the second the key-stave becomes *for.* **48** The reconstructed form is proposed as generating the variants attested. J's inverted word-order is more probably original, though R's is exactly echoed at C 18.17; also preferable is the recessive lexeme *syþes* R, which is sometimes replaced by its advancing synonym (as in the subarchetypal **p** tradition at C 6.427). **49–50** As divided in J, the first is a Type IIIa with caesura after *me.* Final *-e* is supplied for the necessary feminine ending; but arguably *þan* should be placed before not after *a clerioun*, or *she* should read *Scripture.* Line 50 is to be read as an 'anomalous licensed' macaronic (Schmidt 1987:101) scanning either *xa / ax* cognatively or as Type I with two staves (one cognative) in *próbáte.* The apparent stress-pattern of this Latin phrase on its recurrence at 56 and its appearance in a macaronic at C III 489 // B argue for the former scansion of 50. **52** is either an anomalous macaronic scanning *xa / ax* on *b* or a licensed macaronic (Schmidt 1987:101) of Type IIIa with a mute key-stave on *Quod* (the latter in principle possibly a full stave). In the Apparatus read *Sk* for mistakenly printed J*Sk*; doubtless *Sk* is right, however, that J's spelling is an error for *borowhe*. **56** *And I*: conjectured as the original behind the split variants in J and R. **62** This sixteen-syllable line has five lifts and a caesura after *answered* and can only be scanned as a Type IIa with a 'strong' four-syllable dip before the final lift *be*. It looks to have been miscopied from two lines of Type Ib and Type Ia respectively divided after *answered*, with loss of a stave-word like*wye* after *welcome* (an error that could have arisen through scribal failure to see *I answered* as forming the whole b-verse of 62). **63** scans either as normative with a liaisonal key-stave *d* in *and_(H)unger* or like 17 as an extended Type IIIb with counterpoint on *d* (*abb / aa*). **67** *fentyse*: reconstructed from J's substantive form and R's spelling as the form of this word in 68, the one likely to underlie the two variants. The wish for internal rhyme in the b-half may have determined the precise form of the noun (cf. 74a below). **84** *house*: final *-e* is added for a feminine ending, but the stress pattern of 84b could have been *oúre hòus*, with strong internal rhyme. **85** is either Type IIIa or Ia with a liaisonal stave on *þat_oþer*. **88** is reconstructed from the split variants of R (*god wot*) and J (*quod he*), with *he* emended to *I* on grounds of contextual reference. The first three words form a prelude-dip before *Gód*, and the line scans cognatively as Type Ia (|g| |k| |g|). **90** The most natural scansion of this line is as a vocalic Type IIIa with the caesura after *lyf*; but it would doubtless read better if *l* were the stave-sound and *leue or *lede were inserted after *lyue*. **91** *Þou*: the nominative of the pronoun is obviously required by the grammar of *tomblest*. A similar slip occurs at Z 6.100. **92** *worþ*: a secure emendation, given the suitability of the sense 'will become' in connection with man's future happiness. **98** is here taken as the point where L's text breaks off, in a manner that recalls A XI 313 but is no more decisive as an ending (97–8 echo A 1.119–0).

99–117 Lines 99–105 are regarded by *Sk* as probably authentic; but **L** is unlikely to have ended the A-Text in this way with a reference (in 101–02) to what were presumably the later versions of *Piers Plowman*. John But's portion may thus be reasonably seen as beginning with the shift to the third person (though this is paralleled at A 5.44 // and A 8.43 where **L** is speaking of his dreamer-persona). On metrical and stylistic grounds 99–105 are in keeping with L's habitual manner, but if 104 is an echo of 22.100, 105 // (see *Intro*. III *A* § 68f and *Commentary*) this is evidence that But not **L** wrote it. **99** *þo wiste*: an obvious emendation on grounds of sense; the error could easily have arisen from an exemplar spelled *þoo wus*tt(*e*). **107** scans *aa / xx*; if *busyly* has been caught up from 106b above, the key-stave should perhaps be *sooþly* or *sik-*

erly. **113** will scan as standard on *r* if *Kyng* and *rewme* are transposed in the b-half; but it can also be read as extended Type IIIa with counterpoint (*abb / ab*) and *þis* as key-stave. **116–17** Two Type Ic lines in succession are unparalleled elsewhere in the poem, but would arguably be in place as a coda here. Although securely ascribable to But, they show him to have a very fair understanding of L's alliterative practice.

Passus XII (B XI)

Collation From here on, the sigil **x** is used to denote the agreed readings of the y-group (now comprising XYIP²D²), the u-group (UD) and the t-group (TH²Ch). A new sub-family sigil *x¹* is used for the exclusive agreed readings of y and u. Where t and **p** agree against *x¹*, they may be taken to represent the text of their postulated common ancestor *x²* (for discussion see *Intro*. III, *C Version* §§ 5–11, 31–2, 35–8). But a new sigil *x²* is not used in the Apparatus; instead, these readings are followed by the sigils **tp** (where the lemma or variant is cited from t) or **pt** (where it is cited from **p**).

Introductory Note

The content of **B XI** is revised and expanded in **C XII** and **XIII**, the material coming together in parallel again at **C XIV = B XII**. From approximately C XII 169 to 249 (the end of XII) and then from C XIII 1–99 appears a 180-line continuous sequence of unique C-Text even longer than the 'autobiographical' passage inserted at 5.1–108. As with the revision of B Passus V, Passus XI has been divided into two in **C** after expansion. These changes largely account for the final discrepancy in the passus-numbering of the two longer versions (20 in **B**, 22 in **C**). However, from C XIV (B XII) to XXII (B XX) the passus-content, despite extensive revision as far as C XX, runs almost in tandem, any gaps being of not more than thirty lines. There is one exception: from about **B XIII 264–460** there is no direct parallel-text in **C**, as most of the Haukyn material has been shifted to the revised Confession of the Sins. These roughly 180 **C** lines are reproduced on the right hand page of the text-volume (pp. 131–43). The Apparatus of the parallel **B** material appears below the main text of **B**; for discussion, see under the textual notes to C VI and C VII.

1–89 (B XI 44–152) 3 (B XI 46–9) The *B-β* lines are accepted as authentic, since 46 is retained as C 12.3, the substance of 48 in C 11.316 and part of the sense of 49b in C 11.317; they seem to have been lost from α by homœoarchy (*Couetise...con-* > *Coueitise...com-*). In 49, the probable β reading *if þe leste* gives a metrically acceptable line of Type IIa; while this could be archetypal, the sense is weak and the absence both of α and of parallel **C** leaves some uncertainty. The conjecture proposed here takes *þe leste* as a nominalised adjective ('the least') that was misconstrued by β (and perhaps Bx) as the impersonal verb *þe leste* ('you like'), either after misreading preceding *of* as *if* or through smoothing that word to *if* in order to make it fit the supposed syntactical form. As reconstructed, the phrase is to be taken as referring implicitly to the three Do's, though 48 names only two; the 'least' is presumably Dowel (for the thought cf. B 10.131–36). An alternative emendation would omit *of*, making *þe leste* refer not to Dowel but to ('the least bit of') knowledge about the three, as direct object of *knowe* (*ouȝt* being adverbial 'at all'). But the form adopted here, taking *knowen of* as a phrasal verb, better accounts for the presence of *if* in β. The g variant, which also takes *l(e)ste* as a noun (though a different one *lust* < *list* 'desire'), is clearly scribal in its redundancy, which further exceeds that of LMw. **4–6 (B 53–4)** Despite misdivision of 4 from 5 after *riche* to give an unmetrical line, t already shows its textual value both in retaining 5a (present in // **B**) and in the superiority of its text there to **p**, which also has the half-line, by descent from t**p**'s postulated common-source x^2. The misdivision, with consequent loss of 5a in x^1, appears caused by the succession of long lines, each of more than fifteen syllables. Line 5 scans as a T-type, *confésse* bearing its common accentuation (as in // **B** 54) and *good* being a cognative full stave (rather than forming part of the pre-caesural dip). In // B 53 the scansion is as Type IIIb with two lifts in *cónsciénce, goode* as cognative final stave, and a four-syllable prelude-dip. Though this is metrically acceptable, the line would read more smoothly as a Type Ib if *seide* were seen as a ⇒ for *quod*, which is not normally used introductively without a subject but could perhaps have originally been placed after *conscience* (cf. *IG* s.v. *quethen*, first entry). B 54 is Type IIb with the b-half scanning cognatively on |ʃ| / |s| and the a-half having *þee* as a cognative second stave or, possibly, is Ia, with *þi* as key-stave. **10 (B 58)** *pecuniosus* x**β**: linguistically the harder and rhythmically the superior reading. For another case of **p** anglicising a Latin stave-word, cf. *trespassours* p^1, *transgressours* p^2 for *transgressores* at 1.92 above. **12 (B 60)** *forȝat*: either 'forgot, lost recollection of' (MED s.v. *foryeten* v.1a) or 'lost, gave up' (MED s.v. 4(c), citing this passage). This second sense of the word (here given in the unambiguous form *forȝat*) is illustrated with relation to a *quality* (e.g. *myght, cruelnes*) only from early C15th examples; those from **L**'s contemporaries have only a *faculty* (mind, wit) as the object of loss in this sense of the verb. The later use could have been current earlier, but possibly **L** is here playing on two polysemes of the same lexeme, 'forgetting youth' having a special metonymic implication of 'forgetting the *sins* of youth (as one runs on into age)'. That is some-

thing Ymaginatif warns against at B 12.4–8, where Will's *fernyeres* are in effect the days of his youth, and this is the exact sense of the phrase in its second appearance at 22.155. *K–D* find no appropriate sense of *foryeten* here and emend to *foryede*, the preterite of *forgon* (MED s.v. v. 1b 'forsake, go from' or v. 2b 'lose, be deprived of'). Although contextually perhaps preferable, this reading is not clearly the harder, if wordplay on *forȝat* is accepted. The *C*-**x** reading *forȝet* need not (despite doubts in Sch^2) be seen as a reflex of a lost original **foryede*, since this is a well-attested spelling of the preterite of *forȝeten*. *K–D*'s emendation is thus hazardous in presuming 'corruption by visual error' (p. 111) in successive archetypes (it is rejected by *R–K*).

B 67–96 67 The Bx line scans as Type IIIa, with some awkwardness, reading two stresses in *crístnéd*. The inversion of p.p. and verb as emended here to give better rhythm presumes their ↔ to prose order in Bx (more speculatively, *man* could be seen as a Bx ⇒ for *gome* in an original Ia line, scanning cognatively). After 67 Bx has a spurious prose line transparently designed to underscore the axiom attributed to Conscience by extending it to cover a man's whole life or the part of it spent in the parish he may have moved to. **70** scans as Type IIa on |k| if a liaisonal first-stave is found on *Ac_yét*, with a 'supplemental' fourth stave on *konnyng*. *K–D*'s emendation on metrical grounds (p. 194) is otiose. **81** will scan stiffly as a Type IIIc line on |k| in *cóntrícion* and a 'strong' (three or four-syllable) pre-finale dip (*to...heiȝe*). But an alternative that seems preferable here takes |t| as stave-sound and *to* as a full key-stave, making the dip disyllabic or trisyllabic. A T-type line seems excluded since the a-half has only one full stave (cf. 82). Drastic emendation of *heiȝe* to *court / kingdom of* is to be avoided. **82** *be so*: the Bx line, reading *so be*, is metrically unobjectionable; but it seems clear that the chief idea in the b-half is expressed not by *be* but by *so* 'in this way' [*sc.* by contrition alone], which should thus carry the stress, giving a true T-type line (*aa / [a]bb*). It is probably desire to give *so* rhetorical stress that has caused the presumed Bx ↔, thereby changing the metrical pattern to the inauthentic *aa / bb*. **84** *louȝ*: preferred on the showing of C 23 as giving a better contrast with *loured*. Though not unacceptable in metre and sense, Bx *loke* may well have been induced visually from *loked* 85 or by a preterite of *louȝen* spelled with a stop *k* in the exemplar (cf. conversely the palatal variant *pouhe* for *poke* at 9.342 // B 7.192). **86** The Bx line scans with an excessively long prelude-dip of seven syllables (five in revised C 27) that may result from alliterative attraction of the phrase *amonges men* to *metels* in the b-half. The ↔ of adverbial and speech-marker phrase (the latter to its position in // C 27) reduces the initial dip to one of three syllables. **87** scans as standard on cognative staves |p| |p| / |b|. **89** scans, in the light of C 31 (which omits *quod I*), on vowels and cognative labial stops (|b|, |p|) as a free T-type line, the key-stave *and* being mute and *àllègge* accented on the first syllable. **93** The quotation appears convincingly in the light of // C 35 to be 'appended' or free-standing Latin (Schmidt1987:88–93) and so recognised by F (against Bx). Like the other two proof-texts in this sequence (93, 95 // 30, 35) but unlike 106*a* // 41*a* (a piece of Latin following the English which translates it), it deserves to be numbered as a 'text' not a 'citation-line'. **96** scans as Type IIIb on |s|, the first stave being either in *licítum* or by liaison of *is_licítum*; so there is no need to emend *segge* to *legge* (*K–D Sch*[1]).

38 (B 103) scans on voiced or voiced / unvoiced cognative staves, the first stave being in *neuéremore*, which is here taken to have 'wrenched stress' (cf. 3.320, 17.147, where it has normal alternative stress on first / third syllable). *C-*p and the two **B** copies HmF fail to grasp this and accordingly supply *þow* as a first stave, **p** losing *-more* in the process. **39 (B 104)** The revised **C** line has its caesura after *nat* and appears accordingly a T-type (scanning on *s* and *t*). **40 (B 105)** There is line-type ambiguity in revised **C**, which could be a Type IIIa like **B**, with cognative staves on unvoiced and voiced fricatives (*Thyng*; *thow*), or a Type Ia with cognative staves on labial stops |b| |p| / |p|. Given the rhetorical contrast between B 105 and 101, where *þyng* is respectively first lift and part of the dip, the former alternative may be preferred; but revision of *is* **B** to *wolde be* **C** supports the latter scansion. **41 (B 106)** *labbe it out* **C**: clearly a revision of **B**, which is closer to the Latin quotation. The reading of t, coinciding with the *B*-G variant, may express dissatisfaction with the failure of *labbe* to translate *lauda*, whereas G may be seen as ⇒ of a more familiar word for its β original (non-alliterating *B*-W *preise* is such another). The Gt reading offers characteristic paronomasia with *loue*, but the greater rarity of *lauden* is shown by MED, citing **L** here for its first appearance (*labbe* in // **C** is likewise so cited, s.v. *labben* v.). The *B*-α reading must remain uncertain, *lakke* R being nonsense as it stands but more probably therefore a faithful record of what prompted F to rewrite the whole a-half. Possibly α read like **C**, the R variant *lakke* being due to *k* / *b* confusion, and if so, *labbe* is in contention as the reading of Bx. But against this is the hardness of β *laude* and the ease with which α could have erred by inducement from *lakke* in the b-half as well as the presence in R of the negative particle, where *oute* would be expected after *labben* as in **C**. In sum, despite the distance in register between the two verbs, both illustrate **L**'s lexical adventurousness, and the originality of neither need be doubted. **45 (B 110)** *of Oure Lord*: restored (following *Sk* App.) as the likely **B** reading on the showing of **C**. Bx cannot be firmly established in the absence of the line from β (for which there is no obvious reason unless that the scribe misconstrued the syntax of 109 as

complete). But α very probably had the ungrammatical R reading, the result of anticipating *þat* in the b-half, which has prompted F's rewriting, in a manner similar to that at B 106. **57 (B 121)** *saue* xα: 'a decoction of herbs taken internally as a remedy' (MED s.v. *save* n. (1)); the harder and more appropriate reading in context (cf. *drynke* 58 //). Both *safly* β and *sauete* **p** result from failure to discern the noun in its spelling without *l* (that with *l* is found at B 17.76), which better enables paronomasia on the religious sense of *saue* (v) and *sauacioun*. *R–K*'s acceptance of *saue* here contradicts *K–D*'s preference (p. 152) of *sauete* in (needlessly) emending **B**. **63 (B 127)** *chatel*: required for the alliteration, the sense 'moveable goods' being that of the more familiar non-alliterating ⇒ *catel* in Bx and most **C** mss. **66** scans as Type IIIa, like the **B** line under revision, and *R–K*'s emendation to the reading of a single **B** source (w) is unwarranted. **74 (B 138)** *þat heo ne may al*: evidently a development, to a more explicit form, of the *B*-α reading with its characteristic Ø-relative (found at 76 // and B 152). The β variant appears a smoothing of the latter, which may be presumed the probable reading of Bx. It is adopted by *R–K* (p. 102) from N[2] as supposedly a correction from a superior lost **C** source, though much more likely to be by ⊗ from a **B** ms of β type (see further *Intro.* III *C* § 40). **75** The t-group and D[2] here read *beth...aboue* as in **B** for the apparent Cx reading *bothe...are aboue*. D has *beth* but includes *are*, as does P, which spells the former *beþe*. These latter mss suggest a variant spelling of *boþe* as the source of the D[2]t readings, though if t retains the reading of *x[2]*, this could in principle represent Cx. However, the revisions from 48 on are in matters of detail and the reading of **B**tD[2] is not obviously superior in sense to that adopted here. **77 (B 141)** *Hiȝte* **B**: making good sense (despite *K–D Sch*[1]), the somewhat abrupt mid-line shift to direct speech in 143, though unusual, being not unparalleled (cf. 10.13 // **AB**). *B*-Cr here strikingly shows ⊗ from **C**. **79 (B 143)** *Gregori*: the revised **C** key-stave replacing **B**'s |k| stave-pattern, in the interests of greater precision, with compound cognative staves |kr| |kr| / |gr| (contrast 80 //, where |kr| is used in all three lifts in **C** but **B**, treating |k| as the active stave-sound, has |kl| in first position against |kr|). *R–K*'s emendation to *clerkes* **B**, like their alterations of *helle* 78 and *thenne* 80 to read with **B** have no warrant on grounds of metre or sense. **84–5 (B 148–49)** 149 in Bx scans awkwardly with a seven-syllable prelude-dip that includes the important word *grace*. Re-division after *grace* restores this to prominence, making 148 a T-type. The revised **C** lines offer some support in their syntactic parallelism. **88 (B 151)** *as*: *x[1]*, preferable to *and x[2]* (< **p**t) if the phrase *my lawe rihtfol* means 'my own proper religion' (MED s.v. *laue* n. 4a (a); *rightful* adj. 4(b)), not 'my just administration'. **L**'s thought seems to be that 'love' was in effect (and so was effectually) Trajan's religion, even if he lacked *lele bileue* 'true Christian faith'; so *as* is less likely to be the ⇒ than is *and* (for the relevant sense of *as*, see MED s.v. *also* adv. 5d 'in the manner of' and cf. B 13.171). This interpretation is supported by **B**'s b-half; but an alternative, giving due weight to the explicitly legal *leele dome y-vsed* of 90, might associate *as* more closely with *lawe* than with *Loue* and understand the b-half 'in the form of / through the agency of my just administration (of the law)'. A play on both senses of *lawe* is not excluded here.

90ff (B 153ff) The ascription of the long speeches that follow (in **C** to 13.128, in **B** to 11.318) arouses editorial disagreement and raises larger questions of interpretation (for which see the *Commentary*). Despite difficulties about the appropriateness of some **B** lines to the Emperor Trajan, there is a strong textual signal at B 319 (*wiþ me gan* oon *dispute*) that the speech begun at 140 (*quod* oon *was broken out of helle*) is here concluded, though the only clear narratorial reference to a speaker is to Trajan at B 170. *Sk* ascribes B 170–72 to him as a quoted utterance within a long speech by Leute (153–318), making the *oon* of 319 more probably Leute (all line-numbers those of the present edition). But apart from the mention of *leautee* at 153 echoing Trajan's at 145, there is no justification for this ascription. For this is a reference not (like *quod Troianus*170) to a speaker but to a quality, one found in Trajan and as naturally to be predicated of himself in the exemplificatory third-person style as to be applied to him by Leute, who finishes speaking at 106*a* and is thus very unlikely to be the referent of *oon* in 319. *K–D* allow only 170 to Trajan, breaking the syntax to ascribe 171ff to the Dreamer, who is also given 153–169: consistent enough, apart from the abruptness of the syntactic interruption at 171, but inevitably limiting Trajan's direct part in the 'dispute' to lines 140–52 and line 170. This seems at variance with B 319, where the speaker says that the dispute was with *him*, whereas 140–52 are evidently aimed at Scripture (see 139 'oure bokes', 140 'baw for bokes') and 170 is *agreeing* with 153–69 (lines *K–D* ascribe to the Dreamer). The verb *disputen* could indeed signify 'engage in discussion, conversation, or reflection' (MED s.v. v. 2(a)), but in **L** is usually 'debate with...contradict' (ibid., 1(b) and see s.v. in *IG*), the sense indicated by Trajan's exclamation *baw* (140), an anti-clerkly equivalent of the *contra* introducing Will's earlier 'dispute' at B 8.20 //. But apparently favouring *K–D*'s interpretation is the fact that **C** ascribes its expansion of B 153–318 to *Rechelesnesse*. Earlier introduced at C 11.199 and, importantly, named at 276ff, he is specified at 13.129 as having *aresened* Clergy, and he is associated with Will by a verbal echo at 183 (*resonede*). On the other hand, it is Clergy, the object of Rechelesnesse's 'rage', who at 13.131–33 is *offered* Kynde's help (in **B** given to the Dreamer at //

B 320–25), and Will who *receives* it. A major revision has evidently transferred a speech largely by Trajan to a new speaker presumably meant to be a more suitable opponent of *clergie*. But the **C** transition from Trajan's speech to Rechelesnesse's, accepted here (with *SkPe*) as occurring at 12.90, is unfortunately little clearer, since no internal indication of the speaker is given and his naming as Rechelesnesse at 13.129 comes as a surprise (perhaps intentional). What is noteworthy is that **B**'s passage on Trajan's rescue from hell, culminating in the interjection at 170, is eliminated. (For further support of the interpretation here, see the *Commentary* on these omitted passages, B 159–69, 190–95, 211–29 and 268–72*a*.).

B 159–96 Loss of **159–69** by β may be explained as due to eyeskip from *Troianus*158a to *Troianus* 170a; but their omission from **C** is harder to account for. Possible reasons are that their suggestions of the Harrowing of Hell in 163–64 or of Trajan's having worshipped the true God (thereby seeming implicitly to identify the Natural with the Mosaic law at 167–69) were thought inapposite. The lines' authenticity is not in doubt, as 166–67 are echoed in C 98–9 and the thought of 168b in C 14.37. **167** One of three instances of individual lines (the others are 13.170, 172) where R is the sole **B** witness, F being deficient, and C having no parallel. **181 (C 101)** The presumed Bx line as attested in βR scans either *aa / bb* or, with *souereynly* as first lift, *xaa / bb*, neither being an authentic metrical pattern. The revised **C** *nameliche*, forming the prelude-dip in a Type Ia line, suggests that B[1] had its adverb in the same position, and the emendation proposes a word for which *souereynly* would be a non-alliterating ⇒ in Bx (and inferentially in B[1]). Both words are part of **L**'s standard lexicon, but *principalliche* is instanced in a closely similar context at B 14.195. The reconstructed B 181 now scans as Type IIb. The a-half ⇒ of F (adopted *K–D Sch*[1]), with acceptable metre and plausible sense, is here rejected as having been prompted by scribal unease at a double reference to the poor (181, 183) but no mention of one's neighbour in general. However, 182–83 merely elaborate 181 in reverse order, allotting a whole line to each half of it: **L** is here using the characteristic scriptural idea of a 'neighbour' as one's fellow-man in need (illustrated in Lk 10:30–7), which becomes for him specifically the poor (cf. esp. C 9.71). While BxB[1] were thus corrupt in at least the adverb, **C** keeps the remainder of 181 and uses B 183b to complete 101, excluding F's more commonplace notion. **184** *iuele*: understood as the harder reading for which the more obvious *heele* is a β ⇒. Cr modernises this as *helthe* and F coincides with β, doubtless after finding its α source *euel* contextually impossible, if construed as 'evil'. The βF line scans as Type IIIc, that of R as Type Ia. But the main argument for seeing R as a bad spelling for *iuel(e)* α (< Bx) is lexical, not metrical: for the sense 'a beloved person', well-illustrated from *Pearl*, see MED s.v. *jeuel* n. 2(c). **196** Loss of this line by β could have been due to eyeskip from *riche* at the caesura to *riche* at the same position in 197. With alteration of *hath* to *hadde*, the line would make grammatical sense in R; but the reconstruction interprets R's *Almiȝty* and F's *all* as split variants of an α reading with double wordplay on *Al-*, *alle* and *miȝty*, *myȝte*. The notion that God permitted inequality *for þe beste* and not through *nounpower* (B 17.312) seems characteristic of **L**.

112 (B 202) *gentel*: omission of *and* Bx, which makes the second half-line appositive rather than complementary, gives a better grammatical and semantic fit. **114 (B 204)** As divided in Bx, the two lines scan as Type Ia and Type IIIa, though the staccato structure of the second, with redundant *echone*, is untypical even of **L**'s shortest lines, such as B 10.127–28 // A 11.83–4, both of Type Ia. Parallel **C** suggests that Bx may have found the line excessively long and so divided it as two. The **C** form itself is not without metrical awkwardness, being a Type IIa with two of the three vowel-staves in non-lexical words (*ín; ás*) and the phrase *the...telleth* required to function as a five-syllable 'strong' dip. But a parallel instance is *þe Bible telleþ þere he* at B 9.41, where the rationale of reconstruction is similar to that invoked here, though there is no // **C** line. On the other hand, B 12.73 (no **C** //), which has the identical a-half, scans on *l*, and it is possible that the key-stave phrase should be **ledes sonnes*, an expresion unusual enough to have suffered ⇒ of *mennes sonnes* in both archetypes. **B 217** *alle synnes*: preferred as closer to Vulgate *peccata multa*, 'many' rendering a Hebraism for '(her) many sins', i.e. all her sins. **123 (B 231)** *lome* **C**: taken as a revision of *ofte*, **B** scanning vocalically with contrastive a-half stresses on *hir*, *oure* that remain as a secondary pattern in **C**. **131 (B 239)** The revised **C** line scans either as Type Ia with caesura after *louelich* and a trisyllabic pre-final dip, or as Type IIb (*aaa / bb*), which is preferable stylistically and metrically. The order of its a-half suggests that B¹ may have read as Bx, which gives an unmetrical line (*xa / ax*). The present reconstruction corrects a presumed ↔ of adjective and verb to prose order and gives a Type IIIa line. **140–41 (B 251)** All members of *C*-y except Y omit two half-lines apparently by eyeskip from *wille* 40 to *wille* 141, both occurring at the caesura (for a similar case see on B 196). The result, though unmetrical, gives plausible sense, but the retention in 140b of *hasteliche* from B 251a supports the originality of the two-line revision. Y either preserves y by direct descent or has collated with a **p**, t or u-type source. **150–51 (B 261–62)** Revised **C** renders *penaunce and pouerte* the double subject of *Maketh* and supports α's Ø-relative in 262 understood as subject of the verb (β being an evident smoothing). The order of nouns in **x** is a local revision, **p**'s reversion to **B**'s order promoting a more purely material understanding of the terms. **154**

by day: acceptable as a revision, and *R–K*'s rejection for *deth* **B** is unwarranted. **156** *churche*: *wrytte* in *C*-ms D, a reading preferred by *R–K* p. 162, who argue for the key-stave *hoso* as conventionally alliterating on |w|. This is implausible, since the D variant is explicable as an individual scribal response to the fact that 156–61 paraphrase Christ's words, which are directly quoted at 161a. **159** *logheth*: the variants in *g(h)*, *w* and *th* (X) indicate that Cx probably read ȝ, a form often represented as *gh* or misread as *þ*. **B 278** The β form of this line is accepted as giving good sense and fitting well syntactically with 279. The F reflex of α makes no sense and its b-half of 278 is patent scribal padding. The R reflex, however, might be made to yield sense if *For* 'despite' is read for *With*, and it could be that the missing b-half accurately records the condition of α, and α the reading of Bx. β will then have eliminated the a-half to produce the present (in itself satisfactory) reading. The a-half preserved in R could thus, in principle, be authentic and a conjectural reconstruction, taking into account both F and C 158, might read *[For] any wele or wo [in þis worlde to suffre]*. However, any completion of the line must be largely speculative in the absence of fuller evidence from **C**, so it is best avoided here and the half-line omitted.

168–249 are new in **C** and extend through **XIII 1–99**. Textual notes on **B** 11.285ff continue with the resumption of the parallel text at p. 480 of Vol I. **169** *ȝut* x: 'further, still more' (MED s.v. *yet* adv. 1 (a)); the difficult and contextually more suitable meaning, since self-denial is being affirmed as a 'counsel' to *all*, not just the *perfecti* of 164. *Thus* **p** may be a scribal ⇒ after misunderstanding the sense as 'nevertheless' (MED s.v. 2(a)). **176** *Ennedy* x: the **p** variant *ouidius* is doubtless the result of ⇒ of a familiar (if inappropriate) name after misreading Cx **enedie* (*e* as *o*, *n* as *u*). *Eneide* (the form in u) presumably represents *Ennedy* rather than Virgil's *Aeneid*. **190** *withsette* 'resist' (see MED s.v. *withsitten* v. 2(a)): conjectured as the needed key-stave, Cx having the inauthentic pattern *aa / xx*. The verbal part of the compound could have been lost by visual assimilation to following *forstes*, assisted by inducement from the common b-half rhythmic pattern /xxx/x, the occurrence of *with þe forst* in 194a, and the relative rarity of the word. The proposed verb's cognate *withsytte* is found at Pr 174, 8.202, 10.98 (preterite *withsaet* at 18.250), and that may have been the form of the word conjectured here too (the sense 'resist' is not recognised by MED before 1420, but see OED s.v. *Withsit* v.). The **p** repetition of *with* in following 191 is a further scribal corruption absent from **x**, which is thus fully compatible with the emendation in 190b, providing two further noun objects of the conjectured transitive verb. (For a parallel case of presumed corruption in a verbal compound involving *with*- cf. **wiþseide* at B 4.91 // **ZA**). A simpler emendation would be *shullen* for *mowen*, with the latter explained as having come in from 188 or 193. *R–K* p. 170 conjecture an omitted stave-phrase *in somer* after *þat* (ascribing its loss to inducement from the shape of 188) as one expressing the difference of farming procedure implicit in the context. But **L**'s point concerns not only *when* seeds are sown but what sort of 'seeds' they are: those able to endure 'winter' hardship (*soffry may penaunces*). **203–04** As here punctuated, 203 gives a multiple subject for the verb in 204; but no less acceptably, the three nouns could be objects of *soffren* as transitive verb (like its synonym in 206/7) and *Bito-keneth* have a Ø-relative subject; the sense is identical. **206–08** present a serious crux occasioned by corruption in 206 and, as here argued, in 208. The Cx reading in 206 is uncertain, though *so to* seems possible, given that a comparison of the suffering saints and the wheat-seed would be expected. This is taken as original by *R–K*, who adopt *Angeles* with **p** in 208, with the consequence that Christ's words in 209 are now spoken by unannounced celestial beings. But *Then* in **x** needs to be accounted for more fully. Manuscript I attempts to resolve the crux by inserting a half-line with the comparative adverb *more* to link it with *Then* (understood as 'than'). The missing b-half plausibly conjectured by *Sk* is adopted by *Pe* who also (unlike *Sk*) accepts I's variant *owen degre* (? < *aun gre*) for Cx *anger* and emends *to seyntes* 206 to *tho seyn-tes*. But though grammatically acceptable, this is not conceptually coherent; for the saints can hardly be *more* praiseworthy than angels 'at their own level of beatitude', which is logically not that of the angels. The confusion could be put right by reading *muche* for *more* in I's added a-half and *worthy* for *worthier* in *Sk*'s conjectured b-half, as well as emending *Then* to *As*. But the resulting reconstruction is not only fragile, it is otiose; for if I's half-line and 208 variant are both rejected as scribal, the archetypal text may yield adequate sense with a simpler emendation. That text is most probably represented by **x**, since omission of *þan* in **p** could easily have occurred by partial haplography before an*gels,* an*ger. Then* may consequently be analysed as the cropped remnant of the required verb *worthen*. This ought to be preterite subjunctive ('would become' after *saide* 206) but could equally be present indicative 'will become'. But either way, it requires *that* to be understood after *saide* and *so to / to / to his* to be seen as smoothings of absolute *so* '(that) thus / in that way' (referring back to the 'worthy' wheat-seed of 193). The phrase *Worthen angelis* may be taken as elliptical for 'would be(come) as (angels)', the thought being that saints would be, in their *anger* 'affliction' the equal of angels because they show perfect *obedience* to God's will, just as the holy virgins later are *euene with angelis, and angeles pere* (18.90) because they resemble them in *purity*. The ellipsis ought not, however, to obscure the boldness of the phrase's literal sense, since the notion

of man being transformed into something higher seems latent in that of sorrow (*tristicia*) being transformed into joy (*gaudium*) in 209, a thought to be echoed in 22.47 (cf. MED s.v. *worthen* v. 4(a)). Here the Latin points to the authenticity of *anger*, lexically characteristic of **L**, hard and apt, as against the easy and inappropriate *owen (de)gre*. *Worthen* thus becomes the first of three render-ings of *vertetur*, the second and third being *turne* (210) and *chaunge* (211). **213** *foel*: in the light of *stulte* 217a, obviously the right reading. **215** *hym after* **p**: on balance the best reading in context (see *Commentary*). The ?x^1 reading *hym* is metrically possible, but the enquiry seems directed to the audience *concerning* the fool in 215–16 (hence *he* 216), and only turns into direct address *to* the latter in 217. This parallels in reverse the shift from 2nd to 3rd person in Lk 12: 20 ff, **L**'s immediate source, which is quoted in a variant form at 217a, with conflation from Ps 38:7. The t reading (adopted by *Pe*) is a characteristic piece of scribal intensification comparable to that at 221. **217a** *egrediatur*: the subjunctive, though unexpected, is arresting enough to be original. **L** is here paraphrasing, and there is no need to emend the probable Cx reading in the interests of greater simplicity. **232** *ariste*: a contracted form not of the third person sg. but (analogically) of the third person pl., the spelling of which was identical in **L**'s dialect. **239–43** will have been lost from t by homo-teleuton (*þat hit kepeth* 238, 243). **248** *drede*: clearly occasioning difficulty to various scribes; but the sense is not 'strained' (*Pe*, preferring *grete*) so much as punningly ironic: the *drede* 'respect' that the rich get through money is not without *drede* 'fear' of losing that money to rob-bers. **249** The M line that follows (adopted by *Sk* in *PT*) is not totally unworthy of **L**; but unless it represents pure descent from **p** (< x^2 < Cx), it is likely to be a scribal attempt to round off the Passus more decisively.

Passus XIII (B XI)

5 scans imperfectly in Cx (*axx / xa*), probably through transposition of verb and complement to prose order in the b-half. As emended, the line is an extended Type IIIa with blank second and third staves. The **p** reading, for which the lemma is taken from M (*men rat*), is pre-ferred as giving a better placement of the a-half lift. **6** Cx has the incorrect scansion *xa / ax*, here as a result of promoting to first position the dominant idea of excess. The emendation adopted yields a normal Type IIIa line. More drastically, *mesure* could be conjectured as having been supplanted by *noumbre*. But this would be difficult to account for, as the phrase in question was a common idiom that posed no difficulty of sense: see MED s.v. *mesure* n. 8(a) and 9(b) for the phrase = 'immoderately, intemperately, excessively'. It is not found elsewhere in **L**, whereas the occurrence of *out of nombre* at 22.270 //

leaves no reason to doubt its authenticity here. *R–K* leave 6 and 7 unmetrical, presumably judging them not fully finished. **7** *his*: referring correctly and economically back to *mebles* in 6; *auʒte* t (so *PeR–K*) is a plausible filler, as is *al hus good* **p**, but both were doubtless prompted by the line's brevity (contrast 9, which is exceptionally long, and see on 14.211). **9** Although **p** offers in this instance two acceptable lines of standard type, it is much likelier that the Cx line's exceptional length (seventeen syllables) and the unexpected position of the caesura after *Abraham* led to misdivision followed by typical padding in **p**. **10** *spouse to be*: *spousehod to* t (so *Pe*), a smoothing, possibly after loss of *be* through haplography before *beknowe*. It gives acceptable sense and metre but looks scribal in the light of x^l**p** agreement. **12** *kynde kynge*: reconstructed as the probable Cx form of which *kynde* and *kynge* appear split variants. P^2 and N^2 and D may have consulted a **p** source, and the same could be true of YD^2, or they may have preserved y faithfully where <XI> have erred (and U by coincidence). Suspect as scribal, however, is the reading of t adopted by *Pe,* with its characteristic padding by the addition of *comely*. **20** *and*: *in here* **p** (stressing the internal virtue) may even imply that poverty in itself is bad, a reading with some support in 12.206–09 above. But the argument is that objective poverty *is* a good, as the condition if not the cause of the moral virtue of patience. **36** Even with final *-e* added to *messagere* to provide the necessary feminine ending, the line remains awkward to scan, perhaps the best of the alternatives being as a Type Ie; but it would read better if *nede* were omitted (as in 48a below). **40** shows as a clear instance of the rare Type IIIc (*ab / ab*) on vowels and *l.* **41** is an extended Type IIIa with counterpoint on *w* (*abb / ax*). **56** *mette*: likelier to be original despite the breach of tense-sequence, since such mixtures are characteristic of **L** and the 'logical' one more probably a scribal ⇒. **59** may scan with a liaisonal stave on *wole_hym* and *lede* be a felicitous conjecture by the t scribe. However, since *lede* occurs six times elsewhere in **C**, *wyht* could be a Cx ⇒ for this comparatively uncommon word meaning 'person' or 'man' (see MED s.v. *lede* n. (2) 1(a)) and the t reading may be cautiously accepted here. The QWFSZ variant here (which even in its corrupt two-line form implies *wiʒt* in **p** and thence in Cx) is the strongest individual piece of evidence for the existence of q, these five manuscripts' exclusive common ancestor. **63** *hostiele*: **p**t (=x^2), metrically preferable to x^l and, as elliptical, more likely to be original (contrast 64, where x^2 has the arguably redundant *wel*). **72** *treuthliche*: the spelling of X alone; *treuliche* in the remaining mss, which is presumably what Cx read, should preferably be adopted. **79** *ʒe*: preferred as the contextually harder reading, for which various witnesses across both families have substituted the more expected *þe* (in the text read *ʒe* for misprinted *þe*). *boþe two þe*: the presumed Cx form,

of which *boþe* and *boþe two* are imperfect reflexes. X will have read with ?y, lost *boþe* through visual distraction from following *þe*, then neglected to add it in the space provided. Y either preserves *two* direct from y or has corrected from a u (or **p**) source. *Pe's* conjecture *bowe to þe*, anticipated by N except for the article, could be justified by positing a Cx *boʒe miscopied as *boþe* through that commonest of single-letter errors, *ʒ / þ* confusion. But the context makes plain it is not submission to unspecified laws that is in question, but obligation (cf. *ybounde*) to the requirements of both charitable action and liturgical / penitential observance. **92** *So þe pore* **x**: *The porter [sc.* God] **p**, induced by unconscious suggestion from *gateward* 91 and difficulty over the sense. The question as to who 'performs the law' must relate to the poor (= the messenger), not to God.

100 *The parallel text of* B *resumes here* (XI 285)

102 (B 287) *lynnen ne wollene* C: the word-order presumed for **B** also, Bx having inverted to a more familiar one in which the chief fabric comes first, to give *aa / xa*. The immediate ancestor of WHm, or else each ms independently, has felicitously corrected. **104 (B 289)** *nyme*: adopted in **B** to provide the needed third stave in this Type IIa line, Bx's ⇒ of the familiar synonym being visually induced from *take* 290b.

B 299–300 are mistakenly judged by *K–D* (p. 114) to be 'untranslatable' and so in need of emendation. The text is not in doubt, and it may be that the idiosyncratic phrasing combined with the blunt explicitness of 301–02 seemed unsatisfactory to **L** and prompted omission of these lines in revision. The sense is: 'I think he has more faith in getting a benefice through [the mere fact of] his ordination than on account of his education or reputation for godly living'. **B 301** *at*: conjectured as necessary to give the phrase *wonder at* (found also at 346 // below), with *why* treated as a nominal direct object (for the appropriate sense see MED s.v. *at* prep. 7(a)). The Ø-reading of CrB makes sense but is more likely to be a correction of meaningless *and* than an accurate record of Bx, which presumably read *and*, a ⇒ for *at*, with *for* an intelligent guess at the intended meaning.

114 *shendeth*: clearly the hardest of the variants and a word strong enough to have invited scribal censorship on doctrinal grounds, whence the presumed Ø-reading of x^l required to explain those of ID^2(X) (all from y) and U (from u). The x^l mss Y and D have therefore presumably corrected here from an x^2 source, of **p** or t-type. If the sense here is 'ruin' or 'damage' (MED s.v. *shenden* v.1(b)), the implication that the Mass could become invalid on account of the priest's sins would be *prima facie* unorthodox and ill accord with the authorial-sounding words of Liberum Arbitrium at 17.117–21. But the latter envisages only *lewede vnderstondynge* rather than the fault of *luyther lyuynge* adjoined here, and **L** expresses elsewhere (through Haukyn) the view that intercessory prayer may be rendered powerless on account of the sin of the petitioner, including priests (*mannes masse* B 13.259, significantly revised however to *mannes prayere* in // C 15.230). It is remotely possible that the word replaced by Cx *shendeth* (not because doctrinally objectionable but because of its coarseness in context) could have been *shiteth*, with a sense ('befoul') attested only for the rare verb *beshiten,* but possibly so used by L, as arguably at 9.264, where two mss have an erroneous variant *schent* (perhaps induced by an exemplar form *shet) for *shyt*. However, there seems adequate reason for accepting *shendeth* here in a qualified sense of 'vitiate', 'spoil' or simply 'dishonour' rather than '(sacramentally) invalidate', a Wycliffite opinion even Rechelesnesse is unlikely to hold. **120 (B 307)** *is hit*: adopted on the strength of two *p*² mss (G and K) and **B** as the presumed Cx form (retaining **x**'s neuter subject and **p**'s word-order). **122** *For* **x**: needlessly emended to *To* by *R–K*; but the line is re-ordered and the sense is 'for the benefit of' (MED s.v. *for* prep. 3(a)). **125–26 (B 312–13)** In itself the **p** version of these lines could pass as acceptable in metre and sense, scanning as a cognative Type Ia followed by a Type IIIa line with two stresses in *sápiénter*. The **x** version can be re-divided after *nat*, as actually in D, with adoption of the spelling *nauht* to provide a disyllabic final lift (= *náwùht*). In discriminating between the two, therefore, **p** is to be rejected as showing in *clerkes as* a characteristic expansion of the **x** form that is supported by // **B**. But comparison with **B** also tends to suggest that the line's length led to misdivision and loss of 126b, though the precise mechanism of the loss is obscure; the b-half may thus be restored reasonably securely from **B**. The only attempt at a wholesale re-writing is by N², which reads for 125b–126: *þat can nouȝt wel her crede / þei sauoure nouȝt in sapienter to synge ne to rede.* **127 (B 314)** is a Type IIIa line with a six-syllable prelude-dip, scanning on *b*. It may be that *is* has replaced *beþ*, since sg. *beþ* 'is' occurs as a full stave at B 10.345, where the key-stave is *be* (cf. the emendation at A 11.97 above), and its adoption would give a smoother line here, of Type Ia. The rarity of the usage, *beth* being a plural form elsewhere in **L**, might account for ⇒ in both archetypes successively. Scansion as Type Ia on three non-lexical words in *n* is also possible (as presumably for *K–D, R–K*), but unlikely and unnecessary.

B 322 *wondres*: so clearly apt in context that the ?α reading may be no more than a visual error for it, perhaps unconsciously suggested by the nearer context of discourse (*dispute* 319, *ensaumples* 324 and *wit* 322). That α read as R is indirectly indicated by the shape and sense of *worchynge* F, a scribal response more probably

to *wordis* than to *wondris* (the source of ms B's reading remains uncertain since there is no // **C** and borrowing between the families is virtually uninstanced in the Bx tradition). In support of α as a harder and original reading is its possibly intended allusion to the 'book of creation', of which the 'words' would be the natural *ensamples* to be specified below (see *Commentary* further). It could then be *wondres* that was suggested by the dominance of this notion in the wider setting of the passage and the frequency of the word's appearance (at 328b, 346a and 349b) as an obvious ⇒ for the contextually obscurer *wordis* (for a parallel case, cf. at B 7.125 *foles* α, supported by *A-m*, against *foweles* β, again with no // **C**). **B 324** scans vocalically as an extended Type IIIa line, with counterpoint on |f| and *énsaùmples* stressed on the first syllable. *K–D* conjecture *forbisenes* as the key-stave for which Bx will have substituted *ensaumples*. In MED s.vv. sense 2 (b) of the former and 4 (a) of the latter overlap closely; but the required meaning of *forbisene* does not occur elsewhere in **L**, whereas that of *ensaumple* is instanced at 5.119 //. The emendation, which would yield a Type Ia line, should therefore be rejected.

133 (B 325) *creature*: *creature and* Bx; syntactically possible, making the two activities of 'knowing' through creation and loving God separate, the second perhaps consequential on the first. But this runs against the grain of the sense so clear from the **C** line, which is substantially identical: it is through discerning the wisdom and love manifested in the created world that man is brought to love the Creator. The error may result from the Bx scribe's taking the sense of *kynde* as '(type of) natural creation', in parallel with *creature*, not a Langlandian 'nature-name' for God, in apposition with *creatour*. **143 (B 334)** scans either as Type Ia with *sey* as first lift or as Type Ic, pronouncing *Resóun* as the first stave alliterating cognatively with unvoiced *s* following. **146 (B 337)** The **C** line alliterates as Type IIIa either on *they* or on *rótéyed* and *reste*, but awkwardly if the stem vowel is short. The former verb's rarity is clear from its being found only here, as likewise the noun *rotey* in // **B** (see MED s.v. *rutei* n., *ruteien* v.). **C** would scan more smoothly if auxiliary and participle were judged to have been inverted to prose order in Cx, and accordingly emended. Alternatively, *anon* may have lost preceding or terminal *riȝt* through distraction caused by its belonging syntactically to the b-half but metrically to the a-half as hypothetical stave two before the caesura. It is certainly very unusual for **C** to revise a **B** line from a Type I to a Type III; but *R–K*'s adoption of **B**'s reading here cannot be justified. **147–48 (B 338–39)** *a morwenynge(s)*: satisfactory in both sense and metre, Bx and Cx differing only in number. *K–D*'s imaginative conjecture *al mornynge* 'melancholy [*post coitum*]' (adopted *Sch*¹) appears to have the (ambiguous) support of *C*-ms D and possibly that of *B*-Hm (*all* *mornyng*). But the first could be a spelling variant and the second suggested by the sense of B 340ff. What is sure is that **C** makes no attempt to obviate recurrence of this supposed error but revises and tightens up B 339, characteristically shifting the position of subjects and verbs (as in the handling of B 325 at 133). The revision of 339 produces a closer parallel in both syntax and content, altering to Type Ia a line which is a vocalic Type IIa, or IIb (stressing *femélles*). This metrical change, *towards* the standard, is in the usual direction (cf. note on 146 above). *ȝede*: in **B** the presumed α reading, which was also the intended reading of L (the ms being marked for correction, as *Sk* notes). If L's source *l* was an accurate reflex of β, it is probable that γ misread *ȝe* as *þe* through *ȝ* / *þ* confusion. This verbless phrase was faithfully preserved in M and in g, while w smoothed by adding a verb (*ben*). The relative weakness of the Bx line, while helping to explain its revision, does not justify emending it. **150 (B 341)** is lost in some *C*-mss by homoteleuton (*þat...hadde* in 149, 151) and/or homoarchy (*Ther ne was*) and was presumably not in *p²* (it is also absent from G and inserted a.h. in K). **154–55 (B 343–44)** *token*: a form according with the preterite plural with short vowel (not present 'rýde') and wrongly emended by *PeR–K* after P²*Sk*. *drynkyng*: a participle, preferable to the gerund as modifying the circumstances of human sexual intercourse; t's intrusive *in* implies inebriation as a separate sin, not a specific, Lot-like occasion of *lost of flesch*, the only vice with which these lines are concerned (contrast 187–90 below). *mid* **B**: conjectured as the required key-stave, Bx *wiþ* being ⇒ of the advancing non-alliterating synonym, possibly under inducement from the a-half (for a parallel case later see B 12.203). F's b-half could be due to ⊗ from C 153a or suggestion from the identical half-line at 370 and is a typical attempt to regularise α, here preserved by R. **158–59 (B 346–47)** The re-lineation of Bx may be safely adopted on the showing of **C**, which is revised only in 159b. Although Bx 347 would scan adequately as Type IIIa, 346 might have been found too short because of the staccato character of the third and fourth lifts, both nonetheless disyllabic if *wher* is expanded as in **C**. (For a similar case of scribal difficulty with the disyllabic nature of *pye*, cf. the w-variant at B 12.252). **161 (B 349)** On comparison with **B**, the **x** form reveals **p** to have divided Cx on account of its length to produce a Type IIIb line and a characteristically padded-out Type Ia. **B 353** is an awkward Type IIa, which could easily be improved by reading *hij* for *þei*. **170** scans with a liaisonal stave on *toke_Y* or as an extended Type III with double counter-point (*abb / ab*). **172** *ledene* 'speech, song' (MED s.v. *leden* n. 2(b)) is obviously correct and *lenede* a back-spelling induced by *strenede* 171. U could have corrected by commonsense conjecture rather than from a **p** source, and P²'s variant is similarly explained. The reading of u

cannot be ascertained, because of D's illegibility (*R–K* claim to read *ledene*). **175** For *on*¹ it is arguably better to read *of* with DChRM (so *R–K*) as balancing *of* in the b-half. **180 (B 369)** C scans as Type IIIa on vowels or as Type Ia with stress on *Resóun*. **182–83 (B 371–72)** As they stand in Bx, the lines scan as respectively a Type IIIa with two lifts in *rébúkede* and as an inauthentic variant (*aa / bb*). The rewriting in F appears a scribal response, and an incompetent one, to a line of perceptible irregularity. Possibly 371a formed the b-half of 370; but in the light of C's revised lines, both of which alliterate on *r* as Type Ia, the phrase *neiþer riche ne pouere* may be fairly safely presumed to have been lost through eyeskip from *Reson*¹ to *Reson*². The lines as reconstructed scan as a Type Ia and as a T-type (here retaining *-seluen*, which *K–D* omit). **186 (B 374)** *sewest* **B**: in the light of revised **C** *reuledest* it is possible that *schewest* R (? = α) is the Bx and original **B** reading. The sense would be 'teach' (MED s.v. *scheuen* v. 8(a)), which is close to that at C 13.233. But since metrical allophony of *sh / s* appears a feature of **L**'s idiolect, the present case could be a simple spelling variant (by contrast with 10.162, where the same possible alternative is acknowledged but rejected). Here it is likely that *sewest* in Will's challenge balances *folwe* and repeats his earlier *folwede* 371, which is revised to *sewen* in // C 180 (cf. also the phrasing at B 422 and the revision at // C 233). **187** *sorfeten*: clearly archetypal and better in context than *forfeten*, the possible reading of IPEG, which *R–K* read for X and prefer, though their note (p. 148) is unpersuasive. **190–91** *oþer Bestes* **p** / *oþer bestes They* **x**: both variants possibly reflexes of Cx *oþer / Bestes þei*; but **p** is more satisfactory in its rhythm, which avoids too close a repetition of 186 and reserves the noun for contrast with *renkes* in the b-half. **192 (B 373)** As it stands in the two **x**-mss YU, this 19-syllable line is a Type IIb with an unusual strong dip after the third lift and another single-syllable dip after the caesura: *mérueileth me — for mán ıs móste_ylìche the // of wít*. The group original of t may be reconstructed as identical with that of <XIP²D²>, *the* having been lost through assimilation to preceding *–che* in TH² and padded out in Ch, which for *man...werkes* reads *man is most worthi / Boþe of wit and of werkes and most like to oure lorde*. Y and U may each have preserved by direct descent its respective group original (i.e. y and u), but it is just as probable that they (correctly) judged the line a single unit and copied accordingly. **193** *leueth* y: spelled *lyueþ* in **p**Yu. The words are identical (= 'live'), though the possible contextual ambiguity has been unequivocally resolved by M in the sense 'believe'. **197 (B 393)** *noli*: preferable on grounds of accord with preceding *te* and closeness to Vg. The form *noli te* is presumably a misunderstanding of the verb as reflexive: DtVRZKN have it as *nolite* (wrong here as a plural, and probably a mechanical error). **198 (B 379)** scans as Type Ia on cognative staves |g| |k| / |g| with a five-syllable prelude-dip and heavy rhetorical stress on *God*. For a parallel example of *soffrede* forming part of a strong (here four-syllable) prelude-dip cf. 3.327. **199** *amys standeth* **C**: here judged a revision, and N[2]'s reading *mystandit*, which R–K follow, ⊗ from **B**. **201–10 (B 382–91)** The **B** lines, partly retained and revised in **C**, are authentic and could have dropped from β by eyeskip from *wye wisseþ* 382 to *wise...witty* 392, where β resumes. The loss would have been facilitated by *Bible* 392 (= *Holy Writ* 382) inducing the β-scribe to believe he was resuming where he had stopped (after 381). **B 382** *wye*: preferred as the normal spelling in **B**, and to avoid the syntactical confusion that might arise from taking *weye* as 'way of living' (referring to God's *suffraunce* 378). **206 (B 385)** *þe quod* **B**: taken here as the presumptive α reading (< Bx) of which *þe* and *quod* are split variants. In **C** *þou* may be seen as part of a revision of the whole line. **207 (B 386)** *if þyn* **B**: reconstructed from *if þow* and *þyn* as giving the best sense in context after *my lif*. **209 (B 388)** *Crysten* **B**: reconstructed in the light of **C** as the likely original which Bx could have omitted, leaving a Ø-reading that merely repeated the sense of 387. This would have invited supplementation like that in R and F, which scan respectively as Type IIa and Type Ia, but each with suspicious phrasing, F anticipating 389a. The point having been made in 387 that man (like other creatures) cannot create himself, 388 now affirms, with use of deliberate wordplay on two senses of *make*, 'create' and 'render', that neither can he achieve salvation through his own powers. **B 397** scans as Type IIIb with two lifts in *creatúre*, but would undoubtedly be smoother if *bad* were seen as a Bx ⇒ for *comaunded*. **217 (B 406)** *chydde* **B**: possibly a Bx ⇒ for *sherewede*, as conjectured *Sch*[1] (cf. 6.75 // B 13.331). But if a pronunciation |ʃ| is assumed, a cognative stave for |s| may be found. At 423, 424 below the two phonemes |tʃ| and |ʃ| are kept distinct in successive lines; but **L** may have allowed them as 'metrical allophones' and so, by extension, |tʃ| as capable of alliterating with |s| (see C 7.300, Apparatus, though MED does not illustrate *chiden* spelled with *sh*). **B 420** The Bx line has anomalous scansion (*xa / ax*) or else a very awkward one with two lifts in 'likýng' and a four-syllable dip preceding. Emendation to *no likyng hadde he* presumes Bx inversion to prose order and gives a reconstructed line of Type IIIa. **230** *of* **p** / Ø **x**: either gives good sense, **x** requiring *preuete* to stand in apposition with *why* (so *R–K*). For *preuete* XIP[2]D[2] (?= y) read *preuede*; Y may here have corrected from a u- or t-type copy. **239 (B 429)** *To blame*: logically and syntactically required by the presence of *or* at the head of the α line, the phrase's restoration is inevitable, though no reason for its omission appears except eyeskip from *To bl*ame → *to bete*. **240 (B 430)** The Bx line could in principle scan vocalically on three non-lexical words; but the stress-pattern would run counter to

the flow of the sense and the evidence of **C**, the revised b-half of which suggests that |n| was the key-stave in the original B-Text (though perhaps also corrupted in B[1]). An earlier emendation *né stérue* (*Sch*[1]) posits loss of *ne* before following *he* and preserves the line's *n*-alliteration, though at the price of a clumsy (if not unprecedented) stress-pattern in the final two lifts. *K–D* conjecture *for nede*] *for doute*, making the adverbial phrase modify *sterue* rather than *nymeþ* and producing wordplay similar to that at 22.20 (though the repetition has less point here). The present conjecture gives a word with appropriate sense (MED s.v. *noi* n. (b) 'affliction' or (c) 'suffering'), which overlaps with sense 4 of *doute* 'danger, peril' (see MED s.v.). The latter might have been a Bx ⇒ made to give greater emphasis or because the grammatical construction and the sense 'lest he die on account of his suffering' were missed. **B 431** *Shame*: effectively a personification on a par with Nede (and fully such in 435), so probably also to be capitalised here. **244 (B 435)** is unmetrical in both sub-archetypes, and so the reading of Bx cannot readily be recovered from them without reference to **C**. The latter, however, strongly indicates that **B**'s b-half contained the verb *shonye* together with a noun meaning 'company'. The former survives in β, but in the wrong position, giving the inauthentic pattern *aa / xa*, while the latter is preserved in α as *felachipp*, resulting in the equally inauthentic *aa / xx*. β's *euery* has the sense of **C**, while α's *no* shows as a smoothing aimed at accommodating the substituted verb *loueth*. As reconstructed, there is still some awkwardness and Cr's *ech* would undoubtedly improve the rhythm. But this could have been a revision in **C**, and *euery* β is acceptable as the (likely) Bx form. **245 (B 436)** is in both **B** and **C** decisively T-type, with mute *was* as key-stave. **247–48 (B 438–39)** **C**'s revision of B 438b and of 439 (with a different stave-sound) may well be responding to corruption in B[1] perhaps as extensive as postulated for Bx. The latter is unlikely to have read *reuerenced hym after*, since *folwed* is presumably a ⇒ for a verb not of greeting but of motion, alliterating on *r*. The form here conjectured is the preterite of *rechen*, for which see MED s.v. v. 5(a), illustrating from B 8.35 (with *to*) and from *Purity* 619 (with *after*). Line 439 in Bx fails to alliterate (unless as vocalic Type III in *óf, hís*), so emendation here is wholly conjectural, **C** showing no trace of B[1]'s form except for *telle*, now as the blank fourth-lift. The verb proposed as the key-stave is suggested by the evidence of |k| alliteration in the surviving stave-word *curteisie* and is illustrated elsewhere in **L**'s usage (e.g. 7.91, B 15.161), as is *craued* (8.101, B 13.165). No clear reason for the presumed corruptions appears.

Passus XIV (B XII)

1 *Ymagenatyf*: to judge from the first appearance of this name at B 10.117 (in stave-position one) to be pronounced as five-syllables, with stress on the first; but the fourth syllable may also be stressed according to metrical requirement: *Ymagenátıf*. In none of its appearances (except possibly 15.21) is it stressed on *-má-*, an indication of the word's continuing link with its substantival root *ýmàge*, so pronounced in **L** at B 1.50 (cf. also on 15.21). By contrast the verb *ymáginen*, similarly derived, may be so accented in two of its three occurrences (21.278, B 13.289) though not in its third (B 13.358). **2** *sete*: 'should sit', the preterite subjunctive (if it is not a mere spelling variant of *sit(t)e*); preferred for **C** despite the alternative variant agreeing with **B** (adopted by *Sk*). The b-half has been revised and *sete*, the evident Cx reading, is unlikely to be a ⇒ for easier *sitte*. Here its tense is governed by the force of *was* 1, not *is* 2 (cf. a similar case at 6.99). **4** scans as Type IIIa, stressing *Dowél* as keystave, though a pun may have been lost through Cx ⇒ of *fol* for original *wel*, the ChR reading adopted by *R–K* (p. 163). The Bx line less doubtfully has the inauthentic pattern *aa / xx*, from ⇒ of a non-alliterating synonym for the less familiar word in key-stave position. The conjectured verb (MED s.v. *minnen* v.1 (a) 'remember or think about, call to mind, recall') also has a contextually more exact sense, since moral reflection based on recalling past actions is in question here (it is found at B 15.461 and at C 17.210 gives the emendation for // B 15.547). Derived from ON *minna*, it is etymologically distinct from *men(e) gen* (< OE *mynegian*) 'call to mind', 'remember' (MED s.v. *mingen* v. 3(a), (b)), which also occurs at 8.104 // and is conjectured at B 5.412. **12** The Cx reading is somewhat compressed and it may be either that *he* was lost through assimilation to following *be* or *and* inserted before simple *be*. The reading with *to be* in QSN² adopted by *R–K* is smoother but unlikely to be original.

B 13–48 Loss of **13–13a** from α may have been due to construing *strike* 14 as a translation of *castigo* 12a, but without noticing how *staf...yerde* translates *virga...baculus* 13a. **16** *makynge*: 'the composition of poetry', **L**'s use running together senses 5a(a) and 5b(a) (MED s.v. *making(e* ger.); to be preferred to the plural (= 'poems'). This is the form in John But's *medleþ of makyng* A 10.109, which probably echoes the present passage, and also of the word's other occurrence at A 11.32. **18** could scan cognatively on *t* and *d*, but is perhaps most satisfactorily read as having a five-syllable onset and the caesura after *Dobet*, with the stress shifted rhetorically in the final term of the triad (*Dobést bóþe*) to give a T-type. **22** scans as Type Ia with a liaisonal stave *as_I*; but conceivably *self* has been lost after *hym-* in what would then have been a Type IIa line. **24** could scan in principle as a Type IIa

with a 'cognative' third stave on |b| and a 'supplemental' |p| stave in position five. But *to ben* belongs closely with *parfiter*, having its normal unstressed structure as part of a strong dip after the second lift of a standard a-half. The b-half's adverbial phrase is thus presumed to have been transposed to prose order in Bx. **30** scans as Type IIIa, though this entails de-stressing of the first theological virtue and would be better as an extended Type III, with **þre* read after *alle*. **40** scans as Type IIIa with two lifts in *Lúcifér* that highlight the etymological sense of the name. **42** scans as Type IIa, since to take it as Type Ia with the caesura after *lew* would involve depriving the important adverb *deere* of stress and locating it as part of a strong pre-final dip (even if *he it* were omitted as a scribal intrusion). **48** *baddenesse* 'wickedness': first instanced here, α's more explicit ⇒ *badd vse* being possibly on account of the noun's rarity. A specifically sexual sense in this context is likely, given the associations of the adjective (MED s.v. *badde* adj. 1(b)).

17–18a (B 55–56a) The **B** lines may have been lost from β for reasons connected with repetition at 58 of *riche(sse) riзt so* from *riche...riзt so* 51a; but 'normal' eyeskip should also have produced loss of 52–4a. *Scientes...vapulabunt*: correcting the grammatically incorrect **C-x** form found also (in part) in α, the sole **B** witness. The source has a sg. reference, and to adopt *vapulabit* α and emend the participles to *sciens* and *faciens* would arguably give the most satisfactory reading (the immediate antecedent at 18 // 55 is sg. *hym*), but not perforce the original. The reading adopted in both versions is a compromise.

22 *Druyeth*: obviously superior on grounds of sense and contextual appropriateness (cf. *woky* 25), *Druyueth* being a mechanical slip producing the wrong meaning. **23 (B 60)** Both texts appear to have archetypal errors in the b-half that render the lines unmetrical. **C**'s inversion is *from* prose order (the converse of the error in **p** at 26b). In **B**, a stave-word seems to have been lost and the conjectured form, apt in sense and metre, is one easily prompting visual assimilation in Bx to preceding *amonges* if the latter were spelled aphetically in the exemplar with a nasal suspension, to yield in effect an anagrammatic form of **gomes*. **24 (B 60)** *gode-wil*: clearly indicated as the Cx reading (< *x¹* +**p**); perhaps censored on doctrinal grounds by those mss reading *god wole*. The thought parallels that of B 61–2; on the theological significance of the two readings, see the *Commentary*. **25 (B 61)** *woky*: 'moisten', a rare word (< OE *wacian* 'weaken') recorded in this sense only in **L** (MED s.v. *woken* v. 2(b)), and doubtless found difficult by scribes. The ⇒ *waky* is (loosely) apt to the context but destroys the metaphor of spiritual growth through the 'waters' of grace, which soften and break open the husk around the seed. **32** *wierdes*: 'destined (qualities)', = 'gifts of fortune' or *chaunce* (cf. 33), contrasted with God's gift of grace. The sense is not obvious and the majority variant *wordes* (that of **x** but unlikely to be archetypal, since it is inappropriate as well as easier) may be a visual error for Cx *werdes* (so Z). The N^2 synonym is presumably by ⊗ from its **p** source and not a ⇒ for an **x** form *wierdes*. (For elucidation of the wider sense and support for the reading adopted here, see *Commentary*). **37 (B 72)** *and Crist*: the elliptical harder reading, requiring an understood verb *wroet* not dependent on *witnesseth*. The key point is that two separate statements about 'writing' are being made, relating respectively to God and Christ. The p^1 source seems to have taken the b-half as necessarily governed by the main verb, its ⇒ an appropriate phrase qualifying *God wroet* and seeing 37–8 as concerned solely with the OT law written on the tablets of stone by the finger of God. As punctuated, the two statements of 37 are illustrated respectively by 38, the law of love here standing for justice (cf. B 1.151), and by 39, where the 'confirmed' law is that of grace. In the absence of GK, only one copy attests p^2; but N is unlikely here to show ⊗ from an **x** source. **42a** *Qui*: possibly *Quis* in Cx, but Vg has the (indefinite) relative *qui*, correctly rendered by *That* 41.

B 76 has presumably been lost from α by homœoteleuton, or by homoteleuton, if 75 had the form *dede* for the noun meaning 'death' (MED s.v. *ded* n.). **B 95** With normal stressing, Bx has the inauthentic pattern *xa / ax*, but with a four-syllable prelude-dip will yield a Type IIIa line. However, two lifts in *miroúrs* would be awkward (cf. *maister* at 101 below), and the conjecture offered presupposes Bx ↔ of verb and complement to prose order. The emended line scans as IIIa with stresses normally located. **46 (B 101)** The structure of the C line is certain on the showing of both **pt** (= x^2) and **B**; presumably x^1 lost 46a through eyeskip from *bokes* 45 to *God* after *bokes* 46. *mayster*: clearly attested in final position in both archetypes, yet problematic, since two lifts plus a final dip are needed and the word is normally disyllabic in **L** (and largely elsewhere). An *ad hoc* trisyllabic pronunciation is therefore presumed (as in the well-known case of *entrance* in *Macbeth* I v 39); but it is uncertain whether the extra syllable is to be found by smoothing the diphthong or by adding an unetymological final -e. The genetically separate *C*-mss V and GN (< p^1 and p^2 respectively) solve the difficulty by ⇒ of the Latin form, which will better tolerate a second stress on the central syllable (monolexical macaronic b-halves occur at 2.191, 12.10, 17.309 and B 13.198). In the revised C form, with *here* for *þe* B, an alternative scansion of the line is available as an extended Type IIIa with vocalic theme-staves and contrapuntal staves on |m|, and not impossibly the article is a Bx ⇒ for an original possessive as in **C**. *K–D*'s ↔ of subject and complement in the b-half, giving an unacceptable masculine ending, is abandoned by *R–K*. **48 (B 103)** *þe hye*

strete: firmly established on the basis of **p**, u (< x^1) and **B**. The y reading could have retained from x^1 the erroneous metathetic *sterre*, a vestige of which remains in Y's ↔ of adjective and article, and u have corrected its x^1 exemplar from an x^2 source. But more probably the error was confined to y, and x^1 read correctly here with x^2. The erased reading in X could have been *strete* and the alteration a scribal conjecture motivated by a wish to make sense of *hye þe strete*; but since the error also appears in P^2 and D^2, which do not derive from X, it was probably in y. **55 (B 110)** The metre of Cx's b-verse is awkward, whether *lewed* or *lered* is the key-stave. That *lered* is authentic seems confirmed by the naming of both categories in 71, so *R–K* are mistaken to omit it on the basis of N^2's *lewde men*] *lewed and lered*. But it is possible that *to helpe* is a scribal insertion, since without it the syntax connects as smoothly with that of 56 as in // **B 111**, *lewed and lered* forming the indirect objects of *3eue* (if this was missed, 55 might have appeared incomplete in sense).

B 116–25a could have been lost by β through eyeskip from *cheste* 114b to *cheste* 125a, though the scribe nevertheless managed both to copy 115 and to omit 125a.

58 (B 113) The line is either of Type IIa, with a second vocalic stave *in* (as in the closely similar 12.114) or standard Ia, with non-lexical *hit* promoted to key-stave for its contextual importance. **60 (B 115)** *prest*: preferable on grounds of sense and the support of // **B**; *prestis* may have been induced by the genitive second stave (the other following nouns are sg., as is *man* 59, which should appear in the text after *lewede*). **62 (B 117)** *hem bytydde* C: on the strength of x^1 and ?p^2 agreement the reading of Cx, which t, p^1, and N^2 independently reject, perhaps to avoid the near-exact repetition (but *sorwe* is muted). The easier readings of p^1 and N^2 are perceptibly derived from the one attested by x^1. That of t, *betau3te* 'allotted' (MED s.v. *bitechen* v. 4(b)) is hard enough to be original, though the only available subject is *Saul* (*R–K* p. 165 transcribe it as *becau3te*, p.t. of *bicacchen* 'trap; delude; get the better of'. But it is better judged an intelligent scribal variant in the light of x^1p^2 agreement and the appropriateness of such parallelism in a solemn admonition. The repetition, with the variation *hem* for *hym* and stressed pronoun, seems deliberate, and similar end-rhyme occurs at 17.39/40, 18.237/8, B 7.36/7. **B 119** scans awkwardly on grammatical vowel-staves in the b-half and would give a smoother Type IIIa line with ↔ of the two nouns. **67** *medle we* C: the B-α reading may be reconstructed from R and F in the light of C. **68** *chaufen* C: the hardest and on contextual grounds most suitable reading, a secure basis for emending B-α *chasen*, which presumably resulted from misreading *f* as long *s*. The infinitive form presupposes *we sholde* understood. *to wo*: of the **x** variants, *two* seems the likeliest original of x^1 since Ø without a sense-lacuna (as in **B**) would not have invited any ⇒, while in **C**'s b-half *and*, securely archetypal, shows revision of the syntax. The attested form *two* is here analysed as a running together of **to wo*, with *to* a spelling variant of resulting *two*, which has been subsequently misinterpreted as the infinitive marker in X, smoothed in P² and further expanded in I. The t variant will have preserved the postulated noun from x^2 but have replaced the preposition with *in*. Yu present no more than a correct spelling-variant of a word (the preposition) incorrectly taken as the numeral, but point to the reading of x^1. The **p** reading appears a scribal attempt to create acceptable syntax by replacing a functionless preposition with an adverb. On grounds of sense, the numeral is inappropriate here and the isolated preposition redundant, but the conjectured Cx form *to wo* provides both the apprehended outcome of an angry act and the textual explanation of the x^1 and x^2 forms reflected in the surviving variants *t(w)o* and *in wo*.

B 127–47a 127 Bx scans *xa / ax* and a Type IIa line could be produced by reading *Nas* for *Was* (cf. in the Apparatus the rejected variant at B 138 below). However, this would place the third stress on the negative particle rather than on the substantive *kny3t* that is alliteratively linked to the even more important key-stave *clergie* in the b-half. In the light of the parallelism in *cometh* 128, the line may be presumed to scan on |k| and *was* as the first stave to be an easy ⇒ for conjectured *Com*. **129–30** In the light of C 80 the form of Bx 129, run together with 130 to produce the inauthentic patterns *aa / xx* or *aa / bb(b)*, may be diagnosed as scribal. In principle, 129a could form the b-verse of 128 if this is scanned as Type IIb with two heavy a-half dips (*wit; si3tes*). But as reconstructed here in the light of **C**, 129 provides for the line a b-half from C 80b's important generalising statement on the sources of experiential knowledge. 130 scans cognatively as Type Ia with double lifts in *décéites* (on this 'idiometric' monolexical structure see *Intro*. IV § 38). **131** *Olde*: adopted as the required vocalic first stave in a line where the key-stave is *vseden* and Bx has the inauthentic metrical pattern *xa / ax* (the completely revised **C** provides no evidence on which to emend other than by conjecture). It is not clear why the word was lost, unless because deemed redundant in merely repeating *toforn vs*. In the line as now given, *Ólde lyueris* may be treated as a (single-lift) compound or as providing two of the three lifts in the a-verse of a Type Ie line. **140–47a** The β lines, which appear authentic on intrinsic grounds and on the showing of // C 84–91, could have been lost from α by eyeskip from *deum* to *diuersori*um, with an aural element contributing (*apud Deum / habet diuersorium*).
88 (B 144) *and of* **p**: possibly but not necessarily the Cx reading of which *and* t and *of* x^1 are split variants, since a comma in its place would give the same sense. The 'minimal' x^1 form could be that of **x**, *clennesse* appar-

ently repeating 86, where the referent is unambiguously the Virgin Mary. The **p** reading here adopted has the advantage of avoiding the ambiguity of x^1, which requires a particular punctuation. *hexte* **B**: on the showing of LM the probable β and possible Bx form, which gives better rhythm in this strong five-syllable dip than the one with long vowel commonest in this period. **95–6 (B 151–52)** The α lines appear authentic on grounds of their intrinsic character and presence in **C**; but no mechanical reason for their omission from β appears. **99 (B 155)** scans either cognatively as Type Ia on |ð| and |f| or as Type IIIa on |t|. **105 (B 161)** *B-γ sikerer* is grammatically correct and, with elision, rhythmically as acceptable as the probable Bx *siker*, which assimilates the comparative morpheme to preceding *-er*. **106 (B 162)** is identical in both archetypes, scanning vocalically as Type Ie with 'semi-counterpoint' on |k|. It is uncertain whether the first lift after muted *and* (1) comes in *swymmen* or the auxiliary *kan* treated as a lexical verb, the latter being semantically but not rhythmically superior. The unnecessary *K–D* emendation *kan* for *hap* is abandoned by *R–K* (inconsistently with their emendation of *han* 72 to *kan*). **109 (B 169)** Loss of the **B** line from α may have been induced visually by repetition of *swymme* 168 at the beginning of 169. **114 (B 174)** *a*: required as the subject for *knoweth* (Cx being ungrammatical) and here given the form likeliest to have generated the error under inducement from *And* 115. **121–23 (B 181–83)** The unusual length of these lines has led to misdivision in both sub-archetypes of **C**, **x**'s four lines being Type IIIa, Type IIIb, unmetrical, and Type Ia, and **p**'s three Type IIIa, Type IIIb (on vowels, after padding), and Type Ia. Reconstruction after **B** (which is identical but for the blank final lift of line 123 // 183) restores the presumed archetypal shape. The metrical structure of line 123, in its reconstructed **B** form, amongst the longest in the poem, is uncertain. But if *parauntur* is pronounced according to its spelling-form in **C**, it may be mute, or else *bothe* may be the key-stave and the a-half have the three full-staves that identify it as a Type IIa. Bx also appears wrongly divided, with the important *Vnkonnynge* placed as prelude-dip in 184; re-division accords with (revised and) reconstructed **C**. This case is a paradigm instance of the value of parallel-text editing of *PP*. **125 (B 185)** The **B** line, authenticated by its retention (revised) in **C**, will have been lost from α by homœoarchy (*wo / wel*). **128 (B 188)** is a macaronic line of Type Ie, stressing *Domínus*, and with the second stave blank (*herédıtàtıs*). **132 (B 192)** is shortened in revision, to scan cognatively on the consonant-groups |kr| |gr|, as *R–K* here tacitly (if inconsistently) recognise. **133 (B 193)** The Bx form of this line can only be conjectured, in the absence of α. Possibly it contained just the a-verse, which α omitted completely, while β filled out with the half-line attested in L&r. But the latter could reflect Bx's ⇒ of non-alliterating *redy* for harder *graiþ* and inversion to prose order with smoothing for a b-half having the form adopted here. The β form will scan vocalically as Type IIIa, but with poor syntactical connexion between the two clauses. The felicitous W emendation, understandably adopted by *Sk*, cannot be authentic, but W's pronoun *þat* (where Bx perhaps read Ø) is retained as necessary to make the construction clear. The key stave *graiþ* that *K–D* postulate is found earlier at B 1.205 //, AZ 8.41 and C 6.230 meaning 'direct' (MED s.v. *greith* adj. 2); and though the required sense 'ready' (MED s.v. 1(a)) is not instanced elsewhere in the poem, it was widely current (as at *SGGK* 448). As now given, the line scans on |g| like its revised **C** form, with stress on the conceptually significant word *grace*. **136 (B 196)** *as(s)erued*: the almost certain spelling of Cx and, on the showing of LR, the probable one of Bx. The aphetic form, although well-attested (MED s.v. *serven* v.(2) 2(b)), would be potentially ambiguous in this context. **142 (B 202)** *Seynte Iohn ne* **C**: adopted also for **B** as the reading of which β and α appear split variants (omitting respectively *ne* and *Seint*). **143 (B 203)** *mid* **B**: conjectured as the required key-stave (mute as at C 16.180), Bx scanning *aa / xx* and **C** revising the b-half to use the advancing form *with* and a new (lexical) word as key-stave. The form *mid* appears in probable stave-position at 4.73 // **ZAB** (where AxC-**x** both substitute *with*), at B 17.169 (where **C** revises to *with*) and at 16.180 (no //). The word also occurs at B 12.295, where only R (?< α < Bx) has it, βF read *with* and C 14.217 revises to *with*. **150 (B 210)** *leue* Y: established for **C** on intrinsic grounds and the support of **B**, the issue to the fore being the speaker's belief in graduated reward, not the nature of the thief's life in heaven. The t variant has presumably been influenced by the sense of preceding *telde* 149 and possibly also by *y / þ* confusion in its exemplar (*lyue y* read as *lyueþ*), as may have happened in <PE> N). *þat* **C**: simpler than the form reconstructed from the **B** variants, which yields good sense. The point in **B** is not *that* the speaker believes the Thief in heaven (as he could hardly not) but *what* he believes about the Thief's status. The exact reading of Bx is uncertain but is likely to have been that preserved in β, having changed *be* from a preposition to a verb by moving it from before *þe þef* to after it. If R is an accurate reflex of α (in which *þef* had been lost by haplography), F is an attempt to produce sense by substituting *it* for pointless *þe* (a **C**-variant identical to the one reconstructed here but for the reading *of*] *be*, which is that of *p¹*). However, an alternative and arguably superior possibility is that **B** lacked *by*, giving much the same form as **C**, which remains elliptical despite the addition of *þat*: '[as Trajan did not dwell in the depths of hell...], so I hold the Good Thief [does not occupy a high position] in heaven' The reconstructed form has however been preferred for **B** as that likeliest to have given rise to

the presumed reading of Bx, though there is no case for adopting it in **C** (as do *R–K*). **152 (B 212)** *los(e)li(che)* 'loosely, insecurely', not '*losel*-like'; though the thief *was* a 'rascal' in life (see MED s.v. *losel* n., with all C14 quotations from **L**) he is now one of the blessed in heaven. The t-variant *loueliche* 'gladly' or 'humbly' rationalises, perhaps because objecting to the notion that anyone could be in heaven 'conditionally'. But though theologically rather odd, this appears to be the sense here, as preceding 142–46a // make plain. The analogy would plainly work better if the thief stood for repentant sinners *in via*, not for the narrowly-saved blessed *in patria*. **153 (B 213)** displays 'line-type ambiguity' in that it may scan either as vocalic Type Ia (with *hym* as key-stave), as vocalic Type IIa (pronouncing *úppòn*), or as Type Ie on |k|, with *cryant* as key-stave, a liaisonal first-stave in *Ac_why* and a four-syllable dip before the third lift. None is fully satisfactory, but the last is to be preferred as allowing greatest metrical weight to the conceptually significant *cryant*. The primary sense is presumably 'vanquished', this being the aphetic form of *recreaunt* attested as the *x¹* variant at 20.103 // and as archetypal in **C** and probably **B** at 132//, which the present line echoes. MED s.v. *creaunt* adj. & n. acknowledges only this sense, but *Sk*'s gloss 'believer' points to a contextually appropriate secondary sense: it is the thief's faith that saves him, and 'entrusting his faith' to Christ precisely enacts the sense of the word's etymological root *recredere* (see OED s.v. *Recray*). Given the existence of a well-attested noun *creaunce* meaning 'belief', including religious faith (MED s.v. 1), it is possible that an adjective with the sense 'believing' was in use; but none of the MED examples cited under *creaunt* will bear this interpretation. **154 (B 214)** The **C** revision improves style at the expense of metre, leaving *þat* as mute second stave. That Cx has not lost *theef* appears likely from the similar revision in 155, which omits a lexical word *skile* present in **B** (perhaps as the first b-stave in a T-type line). *R–K* needlessly insert both words to make **C** accord with **B**. *woldest*: presumably monosyllabic [*wost*] rather than [*wold*], the subjunctive form in *B*-gL. **156 (B 216)** *whyes* **x**: preferred on grounds of sense and the support of **B** to *weyes*, a word semantically induced from *come to* 157, 158 and superficial conflict between 'why' and 'how' in 156b/157a. It is possible, though, that Bx had an ambiguous spelling, as suggested from B 10.124, where the preferred reading is not archetypal.

B 217–29 217 *a rebukynge*: either article + gerund (an absolute phrase appositively qualifying the verb) or preposition + gerund (taking final *-e* as inflexional and *a* as 'on'); if the second, *a-rebukynge* should be read. MED s.v. *rebuking(e* ger.), takes *aresounen a rebukynge* as a phrasal verb meaning 'to reproach', but cites this line only. The context (with *Reson* as object) implies the sense 'I engaged in argument with Reason, reproaching him', i.e. making two separate statements, the first of which appears rational (*skile* 215) until exposed as arising from passion (*willest* 218, *likyng* 219). **218–21** The α order of these lines gives a more logical progression to Ymaginatif's case, placing immediately after *aresonedest* the critically modifying *willest* (see on 217), then arranging 'birds and beasts', 'flowers', and 'stones and stars' (animal, vegetable, mineral) in a sequence that comes full circle with repeated 'beasts and birds'. **229 (C 162)** *Kynde* **B**: adapted to the spelling of W from α *kende*, which may be a pun and reflect the spelling of Bx (explaining loss of the noun in β by haplography). **164** scans as Type IIIa, cognatively on |g| / |k|. It is also possible that the stave-sound was |w|, if *goed* was a Cx ⇒ for *wele or if the a-half phrase shows ↔ from the less conventional order **of wykke and of goed* in Cx.

B 232–65 232 scans either as Type Ib with mute key-stave (*his*) and a strong trisyllabic pre-final dip, or Type Ie with enriched fifth lift. **B 240 (C 174–6)** Bx scans as Type IIIa on |m| with a five-syllable prelude-dip, but would read more smoothly with *he* for *þe pecok* (revised // **C** has a pronoun *þey*). **245** *taille* 'tally' (MED s.v. *taille* n. 3 (e)); the presumed Bx reading (< R = α, L = β) altered by M to that of γ, which F has independently varied. The homœograph *tail* and the influence of the dominant usage will have induced the variation; but it is better to keep the spelling distinct from the word for 'tail' (241, 248), while recognising that a punning figurative sense 'the end [of the rich]' is being evoked alongside the literal reference to their 'account' with God. The line scans as Type IIa or cognatively on |d| / |t| as Type Ic. **251–52** do not need re-division purely on grounds of metre, since 252 will scan as Type Ia (with caesura after *ere*). However, the final lift of 251 belongs syntactically with 252, *I leue* here being the main verb of the whole sentence, not parenthetic as at B 222 or semi-parenthetic as at C 166. In 251 *wille* thus requires the disyllabic oblique-case form attested in L, while in 252 the caesura may fall after *be*, giving a b-verse of near-minimal length (the w-intrusion *chiteryng* shows a scribe 'completing' a b-half judged too short) or after *ere* (resembling a 'longer' b-verse like 239). The rich man's *ledene* is being compared to the magpie's, which is *foul* like the peacock's (13.172). **255** is syntactically dependent on *leue* 254, *enuenymed* being the past participle with *shal be* understood. The γ reading, from which M shows ⊗, sits less well with 254, vouchsafing what the latter only supposes. It will have been induced through failure to grasp (as Cr does) the elliptical construction noted above, or else γ may be a wrong resolution of a β participle ending in -*yt*. **258** *witnesse(s)*: either reading could be original, that of βF being analysable as either sg. noun or present-tense verb. If the former, it recalls C 13.9; if the latter, Pr 120, with *and* in adversative sense (MED s.v. 4). **265** The Bx line scans with theme-stave

|t|, assuming pronunciation *Aristótle*, cognative semi-counterpoint in the a-half (on |g| |k|), and a 'supplemental' theme-stave in the b-half. In its other appearances, the Philosopher's name is stressed on the initial vowel (e.g. C 193 below); but a shifted stress here is plausible, since *Áristótle* is established as the standard pronunciation in Chaucerian verse (*CT* I 295). This makes the line formally an extended Type IIIb, and emendation (*K–D Sch*[1]) becomes unnecessary.

195 (B 270) *weyes*: either 'ways' or a spelling-variant of *wyes* 'men' (with a pun on the latter). The words were virtual homophones for **L** and wordplay is to be expected here (cf. note on 156 // above). *wenen*: presumably a revision of the conjectured **B** original, for which *wissen* (which gives no sense) appears a Bx ⇒ induced by its preceding occurrence, with *vs* as subsequential smoothing. Cr[3] must be a felicitous guess, not a ⊗ from **C**. The form *wisshen might have involved a play on *wissen* if *ss* had a sound like |ʃ| in **L**'s idiolect, as their frequent metrical allophony implies (see *Intro*. IV § 46). **198** *R–K* adopt t's reading (shared by GK), which is that of **B**; but while the majority variant may be anticipating 199a, *here bokes* is more likely to be by ⊗ from **B** and could well have been eliminated in **C** to avoid repeating 196b and to retain the rhetorical *repetitio* (*tho clerkes* 198 / *thise clerkes* 199) for its more pointed contrastive function in 198 / 99 (pagan: Christian). **200** *From* 201 **H**[2] is defective *until* 16.23 and t is represented only by TCh. **203 (B 278)** The **C** line scans as a 'licensed' anomalous macaronic *aax / bb*, unless the verb and adverb have been transposed in Cx from the order preserved in Bx, which is a correct macaronic Type IIb with a liaisonal stave on *vix_iustus*. **204** may scan vocalically as Type Ia with a mute key-stave *and* or as Type IIIa on *s*. **207 (B 282)** *Ac*: *For* β is preferred by Burrow 1993 on interpretative grounds; but the clear support of **C** for α makes this improbable as an original **B** reading. There is no contrast between *For* and *Ac* at B 284 (C 209), rather two senses of *Ac*, '(But) now' and 'However' (see *Commentary* further). **209 (B 284)** *trauersede*: identical in meaning with *transuersede*, a spelling variant; both first instanced here and possibly introduced by **L**. **211 (B 286)** *wolde*: the likely reading of Cx, implying the sense made explicit in **B**. The t insertion *leue*, accepted by *Pe*, is a characteristic attempt to fill out an elliptical phrase deemed incomplete (cf. on 13.7 above). *R–K* insert *amende* from **B**; but simple *wolde* fits in context with **L**'s stress on the paramount importance of the voluntary power, and is filled out by *wille* in the b-half. **213 (B 288)** The text is secure in both versions and its meaning, though not straightforward, is not in doubt: that if one's (moral) 'fidelity' (*treuthe*) produces a just way of life, it may be deemed in effect faith in the 'true' religion (*fides implicita*). Rejecting the possibility of sense in the archetypal lines, *K–D* emend to *And* *wheþer it worþ [of truþe] or noȝt, [þe] worþ [of] bileue is gret.* This is textually unnecessary, as there is no reason to believe **L** would have left unrevised a major reading that was scribally corrupted, and it is metrically unsound (in giving the line a masculine ending). The emendation is nonetheless sturdily and acutely argued for by Whatley (1984²); but its claim that 'the intrinsic value of faith is great, whether it actually comes to be faith in the true religion or not' would necessarily commit **L** to maintaining the value of *any* religious belief, provided it is sincerely held (and this can hardly have been his purpose in focussing on Trajan). The emendation is relinquished by *R–K* with a silence that is understandable.

B 290–5 The Bx order *eternam vitam* obscures the riddle concealed in the Latin name for God, DEVS: *d*ans *e*ternam *v*itam *s*uis 'giving eternal life to his own' (see *Commentary*). **B 295 (C 217)** *myd* **B**: not strictly necessary for the metre, since the line could be of Type IIa and is revised to scan on *w*; but as the new word *þerwith* in **C** bears stress on the prepositional suffix, *myd* in **B** is likely to have borne it as well.

Passus XV (B XIII)

Collation The **B** mss remain intact until XIX but both families of **C** mss have gaps. In particular, *x¹* has lost I of y, *x²* has lost H² of t, and **p** has lost K, which ends at 66, leaving *p²* represented only by GN (and for 15.288–16.40 by N alone).

2 *fay*: from the context probably the original in **B** too, ms B having doubtless corrected from **C** a reading found meaningless. If R's *fere* represents α it may be, like β *fre*, an attempt to make sense of a Bx form **fer*, a postulated miscopying of the exemplar's *fei*. The meaning here could be 'unfortunate, ill-fortuned' or even 'stricken' (MED s.v. *fei(e* adj. 3(a), (b)), given the immediate context (line 5). But the predominant sense is rather 'doomed to die' (MED s.v. 1(a)), since it is Will's thoughts of his coming end and subsequent fate that overshadow 11–15. In its only other appearance, at 16.195 (no //), the word has the related sense 1(b) 'dead' (so in comparing himself to a *mendenaunt* (3), Will appears as one destitute of earth's supports (5) and thus as incipiently dead to the world), or it may imply '(afflicted) with (a sense of) my life running out'. **6–8 (B 6)** The revised C 6 scans on |m|, unless auxiliary and infinitive in the b-half have undergone ↔ to prose order in Cx. The t variant yields a line that will scan as a T-type, but appears a re-writing after failure to grasp the parenthetical character of the conditional clause ('even if I should happen to live long') and the dependence of the elliptical *leue* 'that he would leave' upon *manaced*. The sense of *me byhynde* (7) is presumably itself elliptical, i.e. 'abandon, cast aside [my youthful state]' 'disregard me' (see MED s.v. *bihinde(n* adv. &

pred. adj., 3(h)). MED s.v. cites the present example as the first transitive use of 'vanish' (*vanishen* v. 4 (a) 'cause to disappear') but gives no other before the mid-C15th. This may be correct, or else a further ellipsis should be presumed for *vanschen* ('and [threatened me, that] all my virtues…would vanish'). *fayre lotes* 'attractive manners', as in *SGGK* 1116, cited in MED s.v. *lot(e* n. 1(a). The **p** variant *lockes* is a further corruption of the exemplar's presumed near-synonymous *lokes* (so instanced in D), the result of *t / c* confusion and possible memorial anticipation of a later passage involving Elde (22.183–84 //). **10 (B 8)** *peple*: the key-stave being clearly *pris*, the line requires a first stave on |p|. On the showing of **C**, *peple* may be securely adopted for **B** and Bx seen as ⇒ of a non-alliterating synonym through unconscious parallelism with 7b. **12 (B 10)** *byquath*: natural in this context of successive past-tense verbs, with *biqueþe* **B** presumably a spelling-variant of the preterite also attested in *p¹*. **17 (B 14)** scans either vocalically as a T-type with a mute key-stave (*in*) or (less probably) as a Type IIIb on cognative voiced and unvoiced dental stops, with the first found liaisonally (*þat_Ymaginatyf*).

B 14–20 These β lines show as authentic intrinsically and on comparison with **C**, with no mechanical reason for their loss from α unless eyskip from *Ymaginatyf* 14 → 19. **21** scans vocalically as Type Ia unless |m| is the key-stave in *Ymáginatif*, giving a Type IIIa line; the name is not stressed elsewhere on the second syllable (see *TN* on 14.1). **22–3** Both macaronic lines may be analysed as scanning normally, the second as Type IIIa, the first not as *aa / bb* but as Type Ia, with the stave-sound |dʒ| and a monolexical final lift (*iudicii*). They appear as a single line scanning *aaa / bb* in RMQS (so *R–K*), excessively unwieldly and unlikely to represent *p¹* (and thence **p**). **30 (B 25)** The revised **C** line scans as Type Ia on |m| and the **B** line could be a Type IIIa on either |m|, with two lifts in *máistèr* or on vowels, with *he* as key-stave and *I* as stave one (for a possible trisyllabic pronunciation of *maister* here cf. on 46 //). Another possibility is **merkede*] *seiȝ*, as conjectured at B 6.325. **31 (B 27)** On the showing of **B** and the repetition of virtually the whole line at 37, the *x²* reading may be judged secure, and *x¹* to have lost *wel and* by eyeskip from *wel → wel-* (as have QZGK). The line, scanned preferably as Type Ie to facilitate the play on *wel* (1, 2) shows the second verb to have had shifting stress. **34** *Ilyk x¹*: either the adjective meaning 'like, resembling' (MED s.v. *ilich* adj.1(a)), and thus the same in sense as **p**T *Ylike to* (cf. 1.87 //) or else the adverb 'likewise' (MED s.v. *iliche* adv. 1(c)), the sense illustrated at B 1.50 If the latter is accepted, and *ȝent* at 132 read as 'yond', Piers is to be understood as present and to be the referent of *him* 37 and the implied subject of the Ø-relative clause *Crauede and cryede* (Kane 1994:16). This reading failed to satisfy the scribe of x^2, who made the adjectival sense explicit by adding *to*; but it explains why Piers speaks at 139 without having been earlier introduced. The half-line *Conscience knewe him wel* (37) may then be seen as dramatising, in an act of recognition, Conscience's assertion at B 13.131b, which echoes *Piers*'s own earlier claim to acquaintance with the latter in B 7.134 and reliance on his 'counsel' in C 8.13. **40 (B 34)** The Bx line will scan as standard (like C 43b) with the caesura before *and*, Patience being the subject of the verb. But arguably *Pacience* has come in too soon by anticipation of line 35, which makes clear that he is not seated at the high table. **41 (B 35)** Agreement of Bx and x^1**p** is decisive. The adverb *prestly* (so *PeR–K*) has a kind of contextual appropriateness (Conscience *knowing* that Will needs Patience as a companion); but there is no reason for its loss and every reason for seeing it as a typical t intrusion to normalise the scansion. The line is either Type Ie with a cognative key-stave |b| or, preferably, Type IIIa, with caesura after *Y*. **51a (B 45a)** *effuderitis*: the grammatically incorrect (probable) Bx form altered in the γ sub-group g and then (visibly) in two unrelated copies Hm and M. **52** *was as*: reconstructed as the original from which the verb is postulated lost by haplography (assisted by the unexpectedness of the construction, which lacks a pronoun subject). The presumed **x** form is ungrammatical; I's *was* is grammatical but gives poor sense (who should advise Reason?) while **p** (which has the right sense) must be a scribal smoothing, as it is too simple to have given rise to the reading of **x**. **57 (B 49)** *Dia*: almost certainly the archetypal form in both versions, though *C*-**p**, some **x** mss and a group of **B** mss have officiously corrected to the form of the Latin adverb *Diu* what was doubtless a deliberate pun on the semi-naturalised English word for 'drug' found at 22.174 //. **L**'s image is that of perseverance as the 'medicinal potion' that sustains the constant exercise of a virtue. **61–1a (B 52–6a)** The C lines are shorter and simpler but still suffer from the difficulties scribes experienced in copying text with enclosed or appended Latin. Thus only one **C** ms (Ch) has a lineation that allows 61 to be scanned as a macaronic, while leaving the rest of the quotation free-standing, though D may also bear such an interpretation. Neither **B** family manages this, ?β dividing as in Cx and α rendering 56 unmetrical but treating the whole psalm-phrase as an appended quotation. Emendation here, as in **C**, is thus effectively conjectural. In B 52–4 re-ordering follows *K–D* in finding inconsequential the Bx order of the statements in 52 and 53 (*ooþer mete* presupposes that one course has already been served). The ↔ presumably occurred because both lines' first lift contained the verb-phrase *he brouȝte vs*. This is a reason for not dropping it from the text (as do *K–D*), since to have caused the mislineation diagnosed it must have been in Bx's exemplar (even if, arguably, not in the original).

The present 21-syllable macaronic line, with its seven-syllable prelude dip, is one of the the the longest in the poem, but is metrically a standard Type Ia. The following line, divided after *dissh*, is completely unmetrical in Bx, a macaronic with the English in the b-half (a feature that elsewhere occurs only in macaronic lines of correct metrical structure, as at B 139). As re-divided (again after *K–D*), 53a now forms with the second half of the Latin phrase quoted an 'appended' line closely similar to 56a (// C 61a). This enables 54 to scan as a perfect T-type macaronic, with the caesura after *Dixi* and the b-staves on *Confitébor* and *tíbi*. **63 (58a)** The macaronic **C** line scans cognatively on |t| / |d| as Type IIIa (*-trítum, Déus*), as could // **B**, which may nevertheless be treated as a normal citation-line of appended Latin. **68 (B 63)** The Bx line can theoretically be scanned, but in practice the dip before the key-stave (*with*) is excessively long, with two syllables before and another five after the caesura. Most probably Bx inverted participle and adverbial phrase to prose order; ↔ produces a b-half with a mute stave on the preposition and the two important lexical words as fully-stressed blank staves. **71–2** The past conditional *soffrede* 'would have to suffer' followed by the present *coueyte* is harder than the smoothed form of **p**. **72** *eny kyne* **x**: on the face of it illogical, **p**'s *heuene* presumably being an attempt to improve the logic, and *kyne* then requiring the further smoothing evinced in the unrelated <PE>, M and N. But for **L** *ioye* means '(one of) the joy(s) of heaven' (MED s.v. *joi(e* n. 2(a)) more often than 'a feeling of happiness or pleasure' (ibid., 1(a): the two senses are effectively contrasted in the identical-rhyming B 7.36–7). Here the phrase will thus signify 'any of the joys of / any kind of happiness in heaven'. **73** *how þat...what*: smoothed in *R–K* by omitting *what, he*; but the anacoluthic expression may be original. **80–3** The various mislineations here, with addition of a spurious half-line in **p**, will be due to erroneous division of 80/81 consequent upon mislocating the caesura. The only satisfactory division is in UD ($<x^1$) and t, presumably an accurate reflex of x^2; while **p** (also descended from x^2) goes astray only at 82, once again after mislocating the caesura in a line structurally similar to 80. **81** Cx seems to have read *diuerse*, a rare form recorded only here in C14 (see MED s.v. *diverse* adv.) and this is more likely than *diuersely* P^2D^2PQWS to be original. **88–9 (B 79–80)** present a major crux in both versions, requiring separate solutions that leave some difficulties unexplained. In C, choice between x^1 and x^2 (= **pt**) is unproblematic, since *compacience* is a reading so hard that it could hardly be scribal in origin. The metaphorical sense 'compassion, sympathy' is here first instanced, though not cited by MED s.v. *compacience* n. (quoting Trevisa from the C14th only for the literal sense of 'sympathy' between physical organs). The x^2 reading may thus be diagnosed as a scribal attempt to clarify an

expression found obscure, with subsequential smoothing of *and* in 89 to *he*. D, by erasing *com-* but without adding *to*, may have adopted it after comparison with a t or **p** source. Since the rejected x^2 reading is actually identical with that of Bx, it might seem better by the *durior lectio* criterion to diagnose the identical corruption in Bx and adopt the **C** reading for the presumed original of **B**, as do *K–D*. However, x^2 could here have coincided with Bx (or been influenced by it) but Bx itself attest a **B** reading (acceptable in itself) revised in **C** to the form attested by x^1 as probably original. The unusual contextual use as intransitive of the normally transitive verb is here presumably elliptical for *preueþ* [*pite* understood], the verb meaning 'demonstrate' (MED s.v. *preven* v. 9(a)), as in revised **C** (cf. the sense in the conjectural emendation at B 85 below). This Bx reading (as preserved in α), which now appears hard enough to be original and to have prompted revision to **C**'s syntactically more explicit (if lexically harder) form, may thus be accepted and the same punctuation adopted for **B** as for **C**.

B 82–6 82 (C 92) *þis ilke doctour bifore*: reconstructed as the original form of **B**, the Bx ↔ to prose order involving loss of the required key-stave (*dóctoúr* with two lifts is excluded as giving a masculine ending). **85 (C 94)** *preue*: conjectured as the required first stave in the a-half. In principle the Bx line could scan as Type IIIa with a four-syllable prelude-dip; but the verb *telle* seems weak in context, since what Will requires is for the Doctor to 'give a practical demonstration' that 'shows by example the truth' *of which he preched raþer*, not more *prechyng*. These are two senses of *preuen*, and a play on them here seems quite likely (see MED s.v. v. 9 (a) and (b), and for the association of *preue* and *preche*, 5.141 //, B 4.122). **86 (C 95)** *preynte*: the required key-stave, conjectured as having been in Bx but replaced in β by its non-alliterating synonym and in α by a word (*bad*) that alliterates cognatively but could not have generated *wynked*. The rare *prinken* is cited in MED from only two other C14th sources, recurring as a stave in a line with an identical final lift (122 // below), and in 20.19 //.

98 The construction is elliptical, *he shal* being understood (and accordingly inserted by N^2); *R–K*'s reconstruction after **B** is otiose. **104 (B 95)** *forel*: on the showing of **C** and the contextual reference to a book (*leef* 105 //) presumed the original in **B**, for which Bx substituted (or misread) perhaps under inducement from preceding references to food (a *fraiel* was a basket, especially for fruit; see MED s.v.). In its other appearance, *forellis* probably means 'boxes' (A 9.159 // B 10.213 *forceres* 'caskets'). But the sense here may be the 'bound volume' itself rather than its metonym 'a box for books', as in *ms* 1586, where the sense 'book' rather than 'book-cover' [Barr] is more appropriate. **105 (B 96)** *leef*: contextually the most appropriate word (cf. VI 209) which, especially in the variant-

spelling with voiced fricative *leue*, puns homophonically with *leue* in the b-half. *B*-g's ambiguous shape has been corrected in <OC^2>Cot either independently on grounds of commonsense or by reference to a C-Text. The readings of the other mss in this group suggest that g read *lyue* as does w, the other member of γ, and this could have been a visual error for Bx *lyne*, the reading preserved in LM (?< β) and α. That *lyue* was a variant of *leef* encountered in the *PP* tradition is suggested by the occurrence of the converse error at C 3.490, where Cx (doubtless under influence from *leues* at the *lyne ende*) apparently read *leef* for required *lyne* (see on // **B**). **106 (B 97)** *take*: 'take on, engage with', a metaphorical application of the sense classed under MED *taken* v. 5(a) 'make an attack'. The reading *talke* is weak here in conjunction with *appose* 'confront / dispute with' (MED s.v. *apposen* v. 1(a), (b)) and is unlikely to preserve x^2, despite its attestation in T, since Ch reads *take*, which is harder and therefore more likely to be the group reading of t (< x^2). The **p** ms E and the x^1 mss D and D^2 substitute independently the reading of the other family, presumably through contrasting judgements as to the appropriateness of the exemplar's reading. In the Bx tradition, α may have read as R, but F's re-writing, which substitutes the b-half's *aposen* and for the latter reads *pyttyn to* may reflect an α *take* for which *talke* could be a ⇒ in R (as in <OC^2>'s ancestor). The relatively unusual sense of *take* here involves wordplay with *take* at 103//. **107 (B 98)** *Dobest*: preferred for **C** on the showing of **B**; four individual mss and the source q correct independently, doubtless through identifying the Triad. **109 (B 100)** *rodded*: here taken as a revision of *rubbede* **B**, either a past participle (with redundant final *-e*) as in **C** or a preterite (necessitating insertion of a comma after *rose*). Though the revision is an improvement, this does not in itself call in question *rubbede* (as in $K–DSch^1$). *B*-Hm may thus be seen as prompted by antecedent *rody* in the a-half or as a ⊗ from a **C** copy, F as a further re-writing on the same basis. The passage running from 96–111 shows several signs of detailed revision (98b, 107b, 108a, 111b) and this may be an instance of a slightly larger one. It remains possible, however, that Bx under the influence of a sequence of preterites found the unusual *rodded* lexically difficult (see MED s.v. *ruden*, citing also *SGGK* 1695 for the p.p.) and replaced it with the simpler preterite *rubbede* (as did *C*-W). **114 (B 105)** scans on |n|, the first two staves in **B** being probably liaisonal (*noon_yuel*; *þyn_euen-*). **116–17 (B 106)** The Bx line scans as Type IIa with a liaisonal stave in *quod_I*, and there is no need to see *Dowel* as having undergone ↔ from key-stave position. Revised *saide Y* 116 and final *Dowel* 117 support both the stave-status of *quod_I* and the position of the object in the common source of BxB^1. *nouhte*: *nouthe* in three x^1 copies YIU and *now* in P^2N^2, which could be a reflex of *nouthe* y. This reading adopted by *R–K* requires *passen*117 to mean 'transgress' (MED s.v.10 (d)), whereas *nouhte* presupposes the sense 'surpass' (ib. 11a (a), as at A 12.4 or 'do' (13 (d)), the tone being sarcastic. In favour of 'not' is the presence of *noȝt* in B 106; *nouthe* may then be accounted for as a spelling error due to *ȝ / þ* confusion. **118** Y reads *louyeth* or *leuyeth* (so *R–K*) and arguably 'live' is better in context, since the Doctor's definition of Dowel at 114–15 has not mentioned 'love' as such; but positive charity seems to be implied by the quotation at 118*a*. **120 (B 110)** *But þat Dowel wol*: reconstructed as the presumed Cx reading from what appear to be the split variants *Bote dowel* in *x²* and *That dowel wol* in *x¹*. **123 (B 114)** C revises to Type Ie a line of Type IIa form, with normal stress shifted in the phrase *Sire doctour* in order not to mute the third stave (something **L** avoids in this position). *R–K*'s adoption of the **B** reading is thus ill-advised. **126–28 (B 116–18)** The scansion of the three **C** lines is as Type Ic (with cognative third stave on |t|), Ia (cognative key-stave on |d|), and either Ia (with cognative second stave on |t| and liaisonal third stave on *halde_hit*) or, alternatively, vocalic Type III with *halde* as key-stave and counterpoint on *d / t*. In 127 the preferred order is that of **p**, here probably representing *x²* (t having varied with *x¹* under inducement from the prose order in 128b); this provides a key-stave (*Dobet*) where *x¹*t have none (scansion of the line as Type II with *to* as second stave would seem unduly forced here). However, the indefinite article is retained from *x¹* as unlikely to be a scribal intrusion. Of the // **B** lines, 117 may be a Type Ia with a cognative first stave on |d|, although the caesura could come after *trauailleþ* and the line scan on |t| with a six-syllable prelude dip paralleling the five-syllable dip of following 118, which scans unambiguously on |s|. The latter two scansions produce lines that are not wholly satisfactory in their de-stressing of the second and third terms respectively of the triad. It may be therefore that in 118 *seiþ* is a Bx ⇒ for *techeth* intended to avoid repeating a verb that *actually* appeared in all three b-halves in succession, as in **C**. In that case 118 would also scan cognatively, with |t| in key-position. **129 (B 119)** *carpe* C: revising to an imperative what in **B** is an interrogative (with pronoun omitted), so emendation is unnecessary (as in *K–D Sch¹*). Cot could be an aural error or by ⊗ from **C**.

B 121 *hym*: preferred as giving better sense and as the probable reading of Bx, from α (> R) and β (> L, M). The γF variant *hem* reflects failure to grasp that the Seven Arts teach others (here Life, the referent of *hym*), not themselves.

132 (B 124) Despite its agreement with **B**, **p**'s reading *plouhman* (to which Ch and N² have varied, the latter probably by ⊗) is likely to be a scribal ⇒. The phrase *palmare ȝent* would have been found difficult because Piers has not been named as a palmer, and an epithet *ȝent*

(see MED s.v. *gent* adj. 1(a) 'noble') would have seemed unexpected in sense and spelling. Since the pronunciation (< Fr *gent*) must be with |dʒ|, *ȝent* would presumably then have been a Cx error for an original with *g*. However, Kane (1994:16) convincingly interprets it as a spelling variant of *yond* adv. 'over there' (P²'s re-spelling of the word). Thus *ȝet* YuT [correcting App. 'DTH²'] may be interpreted as a puzzled scribal response to an unusual spelling found, e.g., in the Harleian *King Horn* 68/1181 cited by MED s.v. *yond* adv. (d). The reading is to be taken with Kane's understanding of *Ilyk* at 34 as an adverb 'likewise' (OED s.v. *Ylike* adv., MED s.v. *iliche* adv.1 (c)), the required sense being found in B 1.50, where HmR omit final *-e*. This interpretation fits well with Piers' having been invited to join the company at dinner (37), so that his speech at 139–49 is now prepared for, and not wholly unexpected (see on 34).

B 128–39 128 scans unambiguously with a cognative key-stave on |t|. **136** *by*: conjectured to supply a cognative key-stave lost by *þo > < so* attraction. Bx would need to stress *displese hym* as third and fourth lifts, producing an unacceptable masculine ending. **139** scans as Type Ia with a cognative key-stave *tauȝte* (|d| |d| / |t|). **142–45 (B 137–46)** If the **p** form shows in 143 its characteristic padding after re-division and the other **x** mss' divergent mislineations variously result from judging 142 too short (XIP²D² divide 142–45 after *helpe, heued*, Dt treat 142–43 as a single line), Y's apparently correct lineation is likely to be by direct descent from *x¹* (< Cx). What seems secure is that Y's 142 corresponds closely with the form of B 137, now scanning as Type Ib but with *Deum* replacing *inimicos* (and the latter being translated in C 143a). **144** allows two alternative scansions, as Type Ie on |k| or as Type Ia on vowels, the first being preferable in treating *kynde* as (in context more appropriately) adjectival. **145 (B 146)** is Type IIa with a 'supplemental' *w* stave in both versions (cf. *Intro.* IV § 44); *with*, lost in eight **C** mss and replaced by a non-alliterating synonym in two, is metrically essential. **148 (B 147)** scans in the b-half with a normal feminine ending, as is clear if *lauhe on* is read with sounded final *-e* followed by an initial glottal stop. **154** *And*: possibly an intelligent **p** correction of an obvious error in *x²* (shared with *x¹* and thus presumably < Cx). **156** *to*: elliptical for 'to [that enterprise]', wrongly omitted by *x²* through being seen as redundant because connected with *wynnen*, a prolative infinitive dependent on *wolde*. **158** scans on *w* as a Type IIIa, t's *þe wy* for *he* (adopted by *R–K*) being a scribal attempt to adapt the less common pattern to the normative one. **162 (B 153)** The C revision confirms that Bx will have read *bere...aboute*, indicating that the **B** variants *abounte* and *a beaute* are mistaken scribal attempts to produce a grammatical object for the verb *bere*. That object is clearly *Dowel*; the referent of *þerinne* could be the pregnant Latin phrase

of 152b (on which see *Commentary*) but is more prob-
ably the *loue* of 147, 151. *K–D*'s bold conjecture *bouste*
'box', here specifically the pyx (MED s.v. *boist(e* n.1(a)),
accepted by *Sch*[1], is now rejected on grounds of contex-
tual meaning. Patience is not in holy orders, and only a
priest would be authorised to bear the Host. The revised
C 164 endorses this reading decisively, since it implies
that *anyone* is potentially able to carry *this abouten hym.*
Here the antecedent is explicitly *pacience* (161) and the
gloss *caritas* (166a), as in **B** (which deliberately leaves
the former obscure as part of the riddle).

   B 158 *se if*: reconstructed from L and α as the prob-
able reading of Bx, and one of two cases where L has been
visibly altered, perhaps by collation with a γ source such
as W (the other is 10.271, where the original L reading
is clearly an error). In the absence of // **C** it is uncertain
whether *deme* is to be interpreted as a more emphatic and
explicit ⇒ for *se*, or *se* as a ⇒ of the contextually more
obvious verb. The reconstruction presumes the former
but retains *if* against α *wher*, here virtually a synonym.

165 (B 162) *Ne nepere*: here judged the Cx source of
the split variants *Ne* **x** and *neiþer* **p**. The reading is actu-
ally attested by D, perhaps correcting by reference to a **p**
source, and is that of **B**. *Ne* will have been lost from **p** by
assimilation to following *neiþer* and *neuere* **x** induced by
aural confusion (possibly being an idiolectal homophone
of **neþer*) or visually from *neuere* 164a.

   B 165–72a may have been lost from β through eye-
skip from the Latin quotation 164a to that at 172a with-
out noticing that they were different. **167–68 (C168–69)**
Re-division of the (presumed) Bx lines after *þee* in the
light of **C** is preferable in order to prevent the object-
pronoun being isolated with its complement *Maister* in
168. The order of verb and pronoun in F is **C**'s, but gives
the b-half an awkward five-syllable pre-final dip. The
rhythm would be better with *ne* omitted, as was permissi-
ble after this 'preclusive' *þat*; but R needs no emendation.
170 The revised C 170 supports the authenticity of R's
line, which is required by the syntax and will have been
lost from F through misconstruing the sense of *and*169 as
'if' (MED s.v. 5 (a)), with subsequent smoothing in 171.
171 is a Type Ie line that scans on |ð| as theme-stave (*þee,
þei, þee*) with |j| as contrapuntal stave (*ȝyue, yemere*). **172**
is lost from F but original, leaving an echo in C 171b.
174 (B 175) *parfourme* **C**: judged also the probable **B**
reading for which non-alliterating Bx *conformen* (attested
in this sense at B 209) will be a ⇒ under aural induce-
ment from preceding *Kan* (see MED s.v. *conformen* v. 4
(b) and *performen* v. 4).

   B 196 scans as a 'quasi-macaronic' of irregular
structure (see Schmidt 1987:100). **B 203** The β reading
may be discriminated as *take conge to*, 'offer [his] fare-
well to', with *take* here meaning 'give' (MED s.v. *taken* v.
31a). The construction usually had *of* before the indirect

object and this is substituted by two members of w, one of
g, and M. The α reading is uncertain and was either *and*
R or Ø, the latter possibly the reading of Bx also, since it
is substantively equivalent to that of β.

191 (B 221) The b-half of **C** is revised to give a T-type
line and so does not direct choice for **B** as between α and
β. Bx may have read Ø for *and / þei*. **193 (B 223)** *hym*
(2): the Ø-reading of *B*-γ agrees with **C** which, however,
appears to have shortened the whole line by omission of
the adverb as well as of the pronoun (it seems that Bx
read *hem telle*, with the pl. pronoun obviously redundant
before *To Conscience* 224). The CrF removal of *hem*
could have been an independent commonsense alteration
(as with M, which erases); but F may well show ⊗ from
C, since it also omits *first*. **200** *and*: possibly Ø in y, to
judge by the four discrete variants. **208 (B 233)** *iogele*:
preferred on grounds of sense for both versions. The
word is first instanced here and is rare, whereas *iang(e)
le* (only randomly attested in the Cx tradition) was not
and will have come in by visual error aided by uncon-
scious suggestion from its common collocation with *iape*
(as at 2.99 //). **209 (B 234)** *sautrien* **C**: here taken as a
revision of **B** *saute*, a near-synonym of *saille* (lexically
as rare as *sautrien*). The latter has doubtless come into
B-C (and into F with alteration of word-order) by ⊗ from
C. **211 (B 236)** *furste to bryng*: to be judged the arche-
typal reading, preserved ($< x^2$) in the t form, of which x^1
and **p** present split variants. On the agreement of t and **p**,
bryng will have been in x^2 and, on the showing of **B**, in
Cx. **212** *vppon*: reconstructed in **C** as the form providing
the required key-stave (here mute). Its rarity in temporal
phrases would account for loss of the first syllable (but
cf. a similar emendation in a purely locative phrase at B
10.307, and on C 5.159). *parsche*: preferred in the light of
B 237–8 to *parscheprest* (which *R–K* read), *prest* having
come in from 214. **213** *one*: either added by **p** or (as here
judged) lost from T, to coincide with x^1 (it is in Ch). The
line scans as Type Ic; the rejected form is either Type Ib
(but with the caesura coming between the first and second
of the two main lexical verbs) or Type IIa. **220 (B 253)**
but: conjectured in **C** as the necessary first-stave lost in
Cx through syntactical inducement from the construc-
tion *founde Y þat* or through ⇒ of *þat*. In principle, the
line could scan vocalically on grammatical words, as B
253 probably does; but stress on these fulfils no useful
semantic function. The important words are *blessynge*
and *bulle*, which take up key elements from B 250, a line
also drawn upon here, and so it seems justified to regard
the **C** line as intended to scan on |b|. *R–K*'s major recon-
struction of the b-half after B 250 is without warrant.
221 (B 254) *luythere eir*: on grounds of sense the only
acceptable reading, as papal blessings and bulls could
not be expected to stop the activities of the wicked. The
word *eir* has been lost by haplography after *this luyth*ere,

which has been inattentively read in **x** as 'these evil men'. I spells this out but P²'s *morein* reflects its consultation of a **p**-copy. The // **B** line, which scans as Type IIIa on |l|, needs no emending, and the unidiomatic *K–D* conjecture *me thynkeþ* for *I bileue* is gratuitous. **226 (B 255)** is presumed a single line, the two-line forms being scribal products with characteristic padding in the b-verse (Bx, C-**p**). It seems likely on the showing of Y (< *x¹*) and t (< *x²*) that Cx preserved the line correctly and that I simply has a filled-out form of the misdivided y text (D² reveals consultation of a **p** copy). In Bx, the first of the two lines scans either *ax / ax* or *abb / aa*, the second *xa / ax*, the latter's b-half revealed as unoriginal on comparison with **C**. Bx *hymself* may be a scribal intrusion, as it is the only element differing from the smoother **C**, in which *Peter* is unmuted. F's omission may be due to ⊗ from **C** and is unlikely to preserve α. **231a–33** For a parallel, see B 14.75–6a.

   B 270–460 Substantive notes on these lines that involve *direct comparison* with **C** are given under C 6.30–7.118a. Lines *unique* to **B** and problems separable from the // **C**-Text are considered here, as are some already discussed in part under **C**. **270** *pritty*: the correct reading, preserved in L from β and in R from α. M seems to have corrected its error from knowledge of the true date, not by reference to an L-type source; but while metrically acceptable, its reading is unlikely to be that of Bx. **271** scans formally on |w| as Type Ia, but both staves two and three are mute, and the blank staves (*gésene; Chíchestre*) alliterate in cognative counterpoint (*a[a]b / [a]bx*). **276** scans either as Type Ia or as Type Id, placing the caesura after *plot* (2) and regarding *vnbúxom* and *spéche* as cognative and internal staves respectively (the latter scansion avoids an ungainly pre-final dip containing a major lexical word). **283** The loss of 283b–284a in wg and M is almost certainly a γ error that coincidentally occurred in M, as a consequence of eyeskip from *hymself* 283 to *hymself* 284. The retention of both half-lines in L points to their presence in β; α confirms their archetypal character and (slightly revised) // **C** their originality. **293–99** are attested in α alone and no mechanical reason for their loss from β appears. That they were present in B¹ is shown by their appearance in C VI; but α must have them from Bx and not by ⊗ from C 6.42–7, which extensively revise. **299** *loos*: required for the sense and given here in the spelling found at B 11.295 and 13.449 (in the phrase *good loos*), which indicates a long vowel (see MED s.v. *los* n. (2), here in sense 2 (b) 'praise'). The correct form is obscured by R's ambiguous spelling, one nonetheless attested for this word, that may indicate a variant pronunciation with short vowel (cf. conversely the spelling *loos* for 'loss' at C 6.275). F's sophisticated re-writing appears to reflect α *loos* in *loop*. **300** *go*: conjectured as the required key-stave, the lexical main words of the a-half scanning on |g|,

as does revised C 6.47. Loss of *go* will presumably have been by homoarchy after *gomes*. The line may be read as Type Ia or as a T-type with cognative b-staves (|t| |d|); scansion as Type Ie on vowels would place the stresses on *he* twice (or on *he, if*), whereas the sense requires that they fall on the verbs. **302** *on*: more probably lost through haplography (*ly* on) in α than added in β. **323** *lakkynge* α: in context more aptly specifying the cause of discord. **326 (C VI 70)** *to...it*: reconstructed after **C** to provide the key-stave omitted through Bx ↔ of verb and indirect object to prose order, with loss of the preposition. **330–31 (C VI 74–5)** On the showing of // **C**, the Bx lines may be securely re-divided so as to keep the adverb with its verb and prevent a metrically clumsy and semantically pointless prelude-dip in 331. The misdivision may have occurred under inducement from the apparent rhythmic parallelism between 330b and 329b preceding. **334 (C VI 77)** *swich*: adopted on the basis of unrevised C as the probable **B** original, *taken* here being the same verb appearing at 337 (MED s.v. *taken* v. 13 (a) 'be subjected to, suffer' rather than 14 (a) *taken with* 'submit to'). Possibly Bx read **wich*, with the *s* lost or obscured, and this was preserved in α and thence in R (corrected by F) and in β, whence it came to γ, L and M. The last altered correctly, as did w (or possibly only <WCr>, if Hm originally read *which*); but g and L seem to have taken **wich* as an error for *with* or else confused it visually with the latter. This case is unlikely to be one where w and M have referred to a **C** copy, since the passage occurs in a section of the **C** Version remote from its **B** counterpart. **341** *God ne*: see under C 6.84. **343–45 (C VI 175–78)** The α scribe wrongly rendered *it* 343 (with referent Haukyn's coat) as *I*; this was corrected by F; then α erred again in 344; finally in 345 R corrected the pronoun successfully, though F went astray this time. The initial mistake with *it* 343 could have occurred by a simple visual error (though one perhaps partly induced by the context and by confusion of *I* 342a with the *I* at 343a). **346–47 (C VI 179–80)** Both **B** lines may be T-type, though the first need not be, as is suggested by **C**'s omitting *tyme*. F's similar omission could be mechanical, the result of possible ⊗ from **C** or, less probably, an accurate reflex of α. **355–56** *of pointes his cote / Was colomy*: 'that his coat was grimy with spots of dirt' (MED s.v. *of* prep. 21 'with'). On the evidence of L, β read *his* and M has visibly added *of*, perhaps by reference to a γ-type ms. From R it appears that α also read *his* and F or its exemplar likewise inserted *of*, again through mistaking the construction as *parceyued of* and *Was* as a Ø-relative clause, whereas *parceyued* introduces a contact-clause with Ø-conjunction (*that* understood). The alteration of *his* to *þis* in w shows the latter diverging further from γ in this instance than has g. **358** scans vocalically as Type Ia or, if *ymágynede* is read here, as Type IIIc on |m| and vowels. **359** scans as an extended Type IIIa with semi-counterpoint on |m| in the a-half. Possibly Bx substituted *wiþ* for original *mid* as key-stave; but emendation is unnecessary and the counter-intuitive *K–D* conjecture *Thoruȝ* for *Wiþ* generates an a-half than cannot be scanned. **361 (C VI 258–59)** On the assumption that C 6.258–59 are a complete revision, *gyle* taking up *bigile* and *glosynge* echoing *wittes*, **B** may be established from the substantive reading underlying R. Thus F's *wit* correctly identifies the noun, R's *whitus* being a (perhaps idiolectal) variant with intrusive aspirate of the substantive *wittes*, the form given in the text. The alternative here rejected is that *whitus* is a back-spelling of *w(e)yhtes*, the substantive reading of revised C 258, for which *C*-ms X gives *whites* (*whit* in Y) and **p** sub-stitutes *wittes*. But in that **C** line *weyhtes* is contextu-ally the aptest and lexically the hardest reading (cf. also 16.128 //), whereas here it would be over-specific, and the more general *wittes* 'cunning devices' (MED s.v. *wit* n. 5, citing Br Pr 156) is also the more appropriate (cf. also *ymagynede* 358; *wit* 363, 366; and 21.453–58, especially the sense of *wit* 453, associated with *gyle* 458). The β reading appears a scribal smoothing after misreading as 'ways' of Bx *weys (a well-attested, possibly authorial spelling-variant of *wyes*). As it stands, the β line lacks an original stave-word (which may be conjectured to have been **w(e)yes*), presumed lost from the b-half through haplography, and yielding the sense 'ways to deceive'. But the evidence from α and **C** points rather to the form reconstructed here as the likeliest reading of **B** (see also 16.128 // B 14.293). **369** scans either as Type Ia on |b| or preferably as Type Ib on vowels with mute key-stave, in either event having both a-half staves on non-lexical monosyllables. **373–74 (C VI 269–70)** Loss of 373b and 374a, which appear authentic on intrinsic grounds and the support of unrevised **C**, will have presumably occurred in α through distraction from *rope(n)* at beginning and end of 374 and visual attraction from *neghebor(e)* to *or*. **376** scans vocalically as Type Ia with muted key-stave or, bet-ter, as Type IIIa on |b|. **391** *conscience* α: both (i) 'mind or heart as seat of thought, feeling and desire' (MED s.v. *conscience* n.1) and (ii) 'moral sense, conscience' (ibid. 2(a)), the latter being the dominant meaning in **L** (as at B 15.31–2 //). The β variant, taking up only (i) and scanning *aa / bb*, may result from objection to the use of *conscience* here in sense (ii). **400–09** appear authentic in themselves and on comparison with C 6.424–32, which retain ideas from only 402a (C 427) and 404 (C 428–29). The lines must have been in Bx, since they introduce the theme of Sloth developed in 410ff; their omission from β may have been occasioned by eyeskip from *helpes* 399 to *helpe it* 408, involving loss or subsequential deletion of 409. **407** *worþ*: the inevitable emendation of a meta-thetic α and possibly Bx error, exactly paralleled in Bx at 11.5; F's ⇒ was presumably suggested by *wende* in

the b-half. **437–54** are retained almost without revision (see on C 7.96–113) and could have been inserted in α at a second stage of **B**, or have been borrowed from **C**. But there is a clear gap in sense between 436 where β ends and 455 where it resumes that seems to rule out the possibility of β's constituting a distinct stage of the poem (see *Intro*. III *B* §§ 50–4). The passage may therefore be securely presumed lost by β, most probably through eyeskip from *wordes...amonges* (435–36) to *amonges... wordes* 454–55.

C XV cont'd; B XIV begins

B 14.1–28 are omitted in **C**; but for some material parallel to 16–22, see on C 16.25–31*a*. The ***main sequence of parallel text*** resumes at C 15.234.
1 *oon hater*: preferable on grounds of metre and sense, with *hool* best seen as a scribal intrusion. Though *hool* could have been lost from Lα by haplography, it over-weights the a-half and introduces the irrelevant notion (perhaps from recollecting 13.314) of Haukyn having other coats, whereas the allegory is concerned only with his one 'coat of Christendom' (13.274). M's exemplar will have derived its reading from a γ ms of w type. **5** allows two alternative scansions, on vowels or on *l*, both giving Type Ia. **7** The grammar of the b-half is defective in βR (= Bx) and F's variant is an attempt to make sense that has led on to complete re-writing of the following line. As reconstructed here, F's (presumably conjectural) *þat* and *me was* are retained to provide the result clause required by the sense, the ↔ providing smoother metre. The precise mechanism of loss of these phrases in Bx is obscure, but doubtless includes distraction from *þat* 6b, *losse* 7a. The line now scans as Type IIIc with cognative b-staves, the fourth translineating with *God* 8. **8** *gome*: conjectured as the required third stave in a Type IIa line, *man* being presumed a Bx ⇒ for the commoner non-alliterating synonym. The Bx line could scan vocalically as Type IIIa, but this would put the semantically most significant words into the metrically weakest positions. **9** Bx scans *ax / xa* and reconstruction here gives a Type IIIa line that restores the key-stave lost through ↔ to prose order. **21–2** As found in wLMR (= ?Bx), the line has an awkward six-syllable prelude-dip; F omits the Latin and expands *Dobest* into two lines which, though metrically correct, are unnecessary to the sense if not irrelevant (the first was adopted by *Sch¹* after *K–D* but both are now rejected as spurious). As in *Sk*, the final two words fol-lowing *after* are here detached to form a new quasi-macaronic line, though tentatively, since it is anomalous in lacking alliteration. Possibly *Dobest* belonged in 21 in place of *satisfaccion*; this would enable the Latin por-tion of the line to stand alone and in exact parallelism with the earlier 'parts of penance' at 17*a*, 18*a*. **23** *myte*:

conjectured as more appropriate to the sense than *myst*, which elsewhere in **L** signifies 'mist', is poorly attested as 'fume or cloud of smoke' and not at all, in this period, in the sense 'mildew' (see MED s.v. *mist* n.(1), 1b. (a) and (d) respectively). The *s* in Bx could be a mistaken reflex of *ȝ*; a spelling with medial spirant (signifying vowel-length) is recorded by MED s.v. *mite* n.(1) but not in the period. Association of mites with moths as damaging fabrics is found in Chaucer (*CT*, IV 560) and the stain the insect causes would be aptly denoted by the verb *bymolen*. **28** *Haukyn wil*: a reconstruction commending itself decisively on grounds of sense (as F has realised), since Haukyn is *Activa Vita* and comparing his *wife* with other minstrels would be bizarre. Bx is nonetheless defended by Alford 1977: 86n26 in the light of B 17.330–1, an explicit piece of allegorical interpretation of no relevance to the present passage, where the dichotomy is not between 'soul' and 'flesh' but between soul restored to a state of grace after confession and soul 'defiled' with sins committed since confession. It would be nonsense to say that 'no minstrel shall be more valued than Haukin's wife' [*sc.* 'flesh'] since the flesh may 'contrary' the soul (B 17. 331) but obviously cannot in itself be morally better or worse. Conscience in saying that no one will have a better 'garment' refers to Haukyn's improved spiritual condition if he assiduously uses all three parts of the sacrament of penance, as a result of which he will also be highly valued in his society (Benson's attempt [2004:54] to support Alford's criticism of the *K–D* emendation only makes confusion worse confounded). The present error could well be due to aural / visual suggestion from following *waf-*, reinforced by confused memory of the reference to his wife at 3 (and possibly of the exegetical trope found in 17.330–1). Smoothing to *Haukyns* will have followed, although if F's form *Haukyn* accurately preserves α, Bx may have had an uninflected genitive misconstrued as a nominative. For a closely similar mistake (nonsensical *hys woman* for *is whan a man* similarly induced in part by inaccurate association) see on B 13.411, under C 7.70. *which is* α: giving better sense even as the reflex of a Bx line with corrupt a-half reading, since *his* β is in any case grammatically incongruent with *wif*. Possibly *with his* originated as a visual error for a Bx form spelled *wich hys with an omitted and a wrongly added aspirate (cf. on B 13.334). **36** *yow eiþer*: reconstructed for α (< Bx) as semantically fuller than β, metrically superior to F and grammatically more correct than R.

240 (B 40) *here*: preserved only in XIP²D² (=?y) and accepted as a revision giving the semantically sharpest reading; but arguably it is the reading of the remaining mss ('t' in Apparatus should be 'Yut'), identical with the presumed reading of α (? < Bx), that is archetypal. **242 (B 42)** *þat*: adopted as giving the best grammar and sense, and as probably the reading of *x²*, to which three *x¹* mss have independently varied. The original *x¹ and* could perhaps be best explained as a reflex of a Ø-relative in Cx, *the worm wonte (unhistorical final -*e* in a contracted verb-form is common, e.g. in ms X at 21.435 *sente*). *woneth*: the reading of P² and the rest, XU having *wonte* and YID² *wond(e)*. The *wonte* / *wond(e)* readings have here been interpreted as spelling-variants of the assimilated 3rd pers. sg. of *wonen*. But *R–K* take them as the noun meaning 'mole', a rare word derived from OE *wand* (MED s.v. *wonte* n., citing only Trevisa in the period; OED s.v. *Want* sb.¹). This undoubtedly hard reading deserves serious consideration as possibly original. **249 (B 37)** The **C** line scans as Type IIIa with two lifts in *Pácién̄ce* and *R–K* needlessly insert *paciently* from B 14.37. **251 (B 48)** The **B** line scans as Type IIb with the third a-stave found in the suffix of *liflóde*, either with full stress, so that *it was* becomes the pre-caesural portion of the dip before *Pacience*, or else with half-stress (*liflòde ı̄t wàs*), the other half being found in the verb. This would be a special licence made acceptable because of the presence of the secondary |p| staves in the b-verse. **252 (B 49)** The **B** line is to be read either as a quasi-macaronic scanning *aa / xx* or, preferably, as a true macaronic of extended Type III with semi-counterpoint, the key-stave being the voiced fricative *voluntas* alliterating allophonically with *þanne* (*abb / ax*). **258 (B 55)** *etynge* **x**: preferable to *ondyng* **p** which, though harder lexically, is suspect as a scribal attempt to complete the listing of the senses (*heryng* MN² illustrates the same tendency). The less predictable *etynge* (unaltered from **B**) indicates an activity of the sense of *taste*, with its specific vice of 'over-delicacy' in the matter of food, and does not repeat *tonge* 257, which (as usually in **L**) refers to speech. **259 (B 56)** *Thar þe / Tharstow*: the form with *Th* is preferred in both versions as free from the semantic ambiguity of *Dar þe / Darstow*. The latter could be the reading of β and was almost certainly that of *x¹*, but the erroneous **p** *That* points to *Thar* as having been the form of Cx. The two verbs have separate origins but had become confused in usage (see MED s.vv. *durren* 2(a) and (b), *thurven* v. 2(b)). **L**'s original is indeterminable, since in this unique use the word occurs in non-stave position. **263a (B 60a)** *sunt*: adopted in **C** as the correct form of the verb; possibly Cx read Ø, **p** completing correctly, *x¹* and t incorrectly. **264 (B 61)** *boþe*: conjectured for **B** on the showing of revised **C** as a necessary second stave, the mechanism of loss being identified as *mowen > < men* attraction). Scansion of the Bx line as Type IIIc entails an awkward subordination of *men* to *bestes* that **C** avoids through having *bothe* as the (mute) key-stave (cf. also the metrical pattern of B 64b //). The emendation adopted counteracts this by making the nominalised numeral adjective precede the caesura, so as to anticipate the sense of *men* before the key-stave *beestes* that bears full stress. **270**

The **p** variant *telden* (*tolden* in MqN) may be a different lexeme *tellen of* 'discern, find' (MED s.v. *tellen* v.16(a), (b)). **273 (B 70)** *moore*: conjectured for **C** on the evidence of **B** as the required key-stave, presumably lost from Cx by quasi-haplography after *neuere*.

B 72–98 72 *Cristes*: possibly induced by 71b; but the more obvious *cristen* is the likelier scribal ⇒ (F coinciding with β), while parallel *Cristes* 72 underscores the contrast between ideal and actuality. **89** *ynliche*: lexically harder and theologically more precise, the variant *yliche* presumably resulting from scribal loss of the nasal suspension. **91** scans as a perfect macaronic, whether Type Ia on |p| with key-stave full or muted, or Type IIIa on |k|, stressing *peccáta* as in 93.
276 scans as an extended Type IIIa on vowels with a-verse counterpoint on |p|; *R–K*'s [*properly*] *parfit* is otiose. **281 (B 101)** *God almyhty*: a **C** revision of *Oure Driȝte*, which is presumed the reading of β and so of Bx. Both *lorde* R and *god more* F are to be taken as variant ⇒ for the same original, the latter perhaps showing ⊗ from **C**. Although apparently found difficult here, *Driȝte* in its other appearance with referent 'God' (B 13.269) caused no problem to the scribes. **285 (B 105)**: supplied from **B** as necessary to the sense, its absence leaving the sentence without a main verb. The line could have been lost from Cx through visual distraction (*rede...richesse* 284 / *renke...riche was... rekene*), and a copyist who paused at 284 and resumed at 286 could easily have lost the syntactical thread. The empatic connective *Then* (*Þat / And*) need not, however, be a scribal intrusion, since the rest of the line also displays revision. **286 (B 106)** *when he*: possibly revising an original that made the verb-subject the impersonal *it*; the latter, preserved in L (< β) and R (< α), will be the reading of Bx, γ a ⇒ of *he* as subject under inducement from *he*105b, 106b, and M an alteration from a γ-type ms. Alternatively, γ (preferred as supported by **C**) preserves a reading present in Bx (and in **L**'s revision ms B¹), and *it* is a coincidental ⇒ in LR. **299** *sende* pDX (t *alt. to* d): perhaps a form of the past subjunctive (*sente* would go better with *were* 300). **300 (B 119)** *elles were hit*: the order of **p** is preferred to that of **x** as preserving 'Platonic' wordplay on *ellis wher* and *elles were* (t agrees with *x¹* by varying coincidentally to prose order from the *x²* reading it would have shared with **p**). **B 123** *riche were*: the last two words requiring ↔ to provide the line's key-stave (Bx having unconsciously inverted to prose order in a manner akin to C 13.5). **310 (B 130)** Cx scans vocalically as Type IIIa on non-lexical words. It could easily be made a T-type like the **B** line under revision by insertion of *So* before *David* (corresponding to *as* in B 130); but grounds for emending are insufficient. **311 (B 131)** The Cx line introduced by *And sayth* presents as a metrically anomalous quasi-macaronic, whereas the **B** line under revision is a true macaronic verse of Type Ib. Possibly original **C**

had *And sayth Dormierunt* as the b-half, making 310 a (long but) regular Type Ia, and the supposed anomaly has arisen through misdivision (*R–K* follow W, which divides 311 from 310 after *inuenerunt*). In **B**, the last phrase of the quotation is reconstructed from the split variants of α to include the important words *eorum ymaginem*. The Bx form *sompnum* (accusative of 'sleep', where F following Vg reads *sompnium*) is retained as supported by Cx and so as possibly original. Doubtless it is intended metonymically to signify 'dream' (but for similar loss of a vowel, cf. the spelling *Eice* for *Eiice* at B 7.138*a* and 10.264*a*).

Passus XVI (B XIV–XV)

In the reconstruction of this section, B 14.319 corresponds to the point (16.155) where **C** makes a major break after omitting 14.320–32, the lines that end this passus in **B**. **3 (B 134)** *Hewen* **x**: retained from **B**, and not lexically difficult, so *Thei* **p** may reflect an exemplar spelled *Hyen* and mistaken for *Hy*, with D either having a coincidental error or showing ⊗ from a **p** source. **4 (B 135)** *to dyne* **C**: a construction, whether anacoluthic or elliptical, unlikely to be a scribal ⇒ for the easier *þat dyneþ* t**B**. Possibly it shows Cx smoothing by insertion of *to* in an exemplar reading with Ø-relative and number-indeterminate *a* for *he* (cf. the pl. pronoun *they* in **p**). However, the 'absolute' use of *to* + infinitive in an elliptical construction is instanced at 7 (*to fonge*, retained from **B**), so the originality of *to dyne* here need not be questioned and *R–K*'s adoption of t**B** should be rejected. **9 (B 141)** *here-beynge*: the firmly attested **BC** reading, and lexically just tolerable, though *and heuene herafter* B 141b which completes the thought, was perhaps omitted by Cx and should be restored. *R–K*'s retention of *K–D*'s emendation to *herberwynge* is baffling.

B 146–59 146 Choice between *alle*, the possible reading of Bx (> β > L, > α > R) and *hem alle* is not determinable on intrinsic grounds. But its broader scope (balanced by *alle*148), which is not restricted to the poor, suggests that *hem* γ is a scribal intrusion (M here presumably having ⊗ from a γ source [w]). **152** *rewfulliche* β: 'mercifully' (MED s.v. *reufulli* adv. (c)); preferable in context to the more obvious *riȝtfullich* α (though both *ruþe* and *leaute* are specified at 145, 146) and less likely to have been the ⇒, though this is exactly what occurred at A 8.10. The point is that acting *rewfulliche* is here something not confined to the rich, whereas acting righteously could never be so thought anyway. **155–59** were probably lost by α through eyeskip from *Ac* 155 to *Ac* 160.

22 (B 168) *þat on þe rode deydest* **p**: here taken as possibly preserved (through *x²*) from Cx. Presumably the mechanism of loss in *x¹* was eyeskip from the phrase *vs* *alle* 22a to its repetition at 23b and loss of 23a would have been expected; but since this half-line was noticed, the only consequence was mislineation (y divides after *mercy*, U after *mercy* and *meke*, D after *vs* and *meke*). If the lacuna was also in x^2 (and therefore in Cx), editorial choice between two completions of indeterminate authority must be made solely on intrinsic quality. The t variant *on þi renkis*] *on vs* (adopted by *PeR–K*), while metrically correct, is flat and has a filler-like redundancy; but **p** not only scans correctly, it is apt in context; while it echoes a line such as 6.318, it recalls the thought instead of merely the phrasing; and its linking of Christ's death on the cross with being *meke* 'humble' (23) is of a piece with 1.68 //. **25** scans as Type IIIa with two stresses in *cóntrición*, but it would give a smoother line (of Type IIIc) if noun and verb-phrase in the a-half were judged to have been inverted to prose order by Cx. *R–K*'s conjecture [*clereliche*] *to clanse* is wholly gratuitous. **30** scans as Type IIIa with two stresses in *cónféssio* (cf. on 25); *R–K*'s conjecture [*knowlechyng and*] *shrifte* is otiose. **31** *satisfaccio*: preferred as original since the three Latin penitential formulas appear to stand both in parallel together and in contrast with their English forms at 25–7. Underlining of *satisfaccion* in X and Y probably indicates recognition of its technical status; but this was obscured by omission of the *operis* part of the formula in Cx, for which no obvious reason appears (its intrusion in <PE> will have been encouraged by the presence of the complete formula at 31*a*). It seems likely that **p** read *satisfaccio* as in the text here and that the **x** mss correcting to this form did so independently or by collation with a **p** source. In the b-half, *soueraynliche* appears typical padding in **p** after erroneous division as two lines. **34** scans vocalically with mute key-stave and counterpoint on |b|. If *oþer* is mute and the stress on *bet*, the final lift in the b-half may be taken as compensating for the extra a-half muting (cf. *Intro.* IV § 44). **36** scans as Type IIa with *þat* as the third stave; if it is semi-muted (an irregularity), *defénde* may be meant as a 'supplemental' fricative stave.

B 174–96 174 *Lord*: in parallel with preceding *God* 170 and following *Crist* 179 as part of a prayer; *lore* 'lost' ?α is possible but inferior here. **177** *wynter tyme*: reconstructed in the light of // 178 as the underlying Bx form. **181** *his*: lost from γ and M but posited here for β on the strength of L, with indirect support from R *alle his*. The latter may preserve α's reading from which F has dropped the possessive, but *alle* is not necessary for the sense. For while the Ø-reading of γM is too indefinite, it is *Christ*'s 'nobility' or 'generosity' (MED s.v. *gentris(e* n. 2 (a)) that is the issue, so L's *his* may be safely accepted as preserving Bx. **190** *He*: the certain reading of β and probably also of α, *Ho* R being presumably a misspelling. F has doubtless altered to *We* to make the subject accord with the object of the devil's malice *vs* in 189; and the deed of

acquittal might well be carried by the recipient. But *this* document could be produced for the devil only at Judgement Day, where the appropriate person to bring it would be Christ the mediator, the understood referent of the pronoun here accepted. **196** *wroʒten*: conjectured as misread by Bx under unconscious inducement from *writeþ* 199 and references in the immediate context to written documents of various kinds. The error could have arisen if the exemplar read *wroten* (for *wrohten*), a current form of the preterite pl. of *werchen*. The reading *writen* is pointless here since what is in question is actions, especially devotional, on which money and effort are expended.

39 (B 198) *welle*: convincingly attested as archetypal in both versions and providing a homophonic pun on *wille* through using a dialectal variant of the latter (Kentish) presumably familiar in the contemporary language of London. **43 (B 202)** *þat þer ben*: to be accepted as original for **C** on the strength of support from **B**, *þat* (2) Cx being redundant, given that *For* is a conjunction, not a preposition. The collocation of *þat* with *ben* 'exist' here is slightly unexpected, and this will have led both to its omission in four **B** mss and to intrusion of *þat* (2) in the b-half there and in Cx. Possibly, however, the original (in **B** at least) had a Ø-relative clause in the b-half but a main clause in the a-half, and the a-half's relative pronoun was inserted in both Bx and B¹, whence it came to **C**. **46 (B 205)** *þere þat* **p**: to be discriminated on the showing of **B** as the form of Cx, attested *þere* and *þat* being split variants. **48 (B 207)** *And*: preferred also in **B** on the showing of **C**. The line expands but does not modify the argument of 46 (B 205), so *R–K*'s emendation to *Ac* is unnecessary. **50 (B 209)** The apocopated form *way* could also have been that of Bx (> ?α) but as no difference of sense is involved, β is retained. **53 (B 212)** *riche* α: the object of the verb, preferred in the light of the revision, which shows the *hey way* as a bumpy road to a man burdened with wealth; the alteration in **C** could have been prompted by the ambiguity of **B**. **64 (B 223)** *ben*: discriminated as the required verb-form for the key-stave, and so reconstructed in **B**, *arn* being an unconscious ⇒ in Bx and Cx perhaps under influence from the vowel beginning of *eueremore* and the vowel staves of 65 (B 224). The **C** mss reading *ben* are likely to show (like *B-F*) felicitous conjecture. **67 (B 226)** scans as Type Ia with a cognative first stave on |b| or as IIIa with two |b| staves. *R–K* sensibly refrain from *K–D*'s extravagant emendation of the b-half to *þe feblere is þe poore*.

B 228–38 look authentic on intrinsic grounds and from their appearance (lightly revised) in **C**. No mechanical reason appears for their loss from β, unless visual distraction induced by alliterative likeness in 229 / 238. **78 (B 237)** *more ful* **p***t*: the x^2 reading accepted as preserving Cx, x^1 having omitted both words through attraction of *neuere → mer(ye)*, with loss of the first stave on |m|.

For similar (conjectured) loss of *moore* in Cx, cf. 15.273 and on 17.147. **92 (B 252–53)** In the absence of these lines from α, no reason for which appears unless censorship, Bx must remain uncertain. It seems likely, however, that despite the two-line **p** form's likeness to **B** (and *pace* Schmidt 1980:105), it is **x** that represents Cx, with *ful longe* to be seen as a scribal filler. The **p** shape is metrically acceptable, but the second line also seems to pad out the material common to **x** 92b and to B 253a, while omitting the separate idea in B 253b. In **B**, the β form is here judged to have been preserved in the L variants, M having varied to the γ reading through influence from a w-type source. L could have substituted *were* so as to avoid repetition of *stoode*, but more probably *stoode* in 253 has come into γ from 252, the repetition being pointless here. The phrase *no þyng* seems to be an attempt to spell out the sense of the elliptical *noon* ('no custom[ers]'), which **C** will make explicit as *noen haunt*. *RK*'s reconstruction after **B** is without warrant, as the *C*-**x** line is satisfactory in both sense and metre (a Type IIa). **96 (B 257)** *is*: preferred as the harder reading in both versions, specifying the nature of Poverty's *rôle*, more than his *relationship* to God. Thus *is* and *his* are here unlikely to be split variants of **is his* (the actual reading of *C*-QZ); rather, *his* is to be judged a reflex of verbal **hys*, with intruded aspirate (of the type common in the Z-Text). **99 (B 260)** *asken and cleymen* **B**: ↔ of the order of the verbs in Bx to provide the key-stave (presumably Bx inverted the order so as to promote the concept (*cleymen*) regarded as more important). The line is now an extended Type IIIa scanning on vowels with semi-counterpoint on |p| (*abb / ax*) and the second b-half verb occupies the same position as in revised **C**, which makes |p| the theme-stave and has 'running' counterpoint on vowels (Schmidt 1987:63–4). An alternative scansion is as a vocalic Type Ia, with the second a-half lift in *is*. **105 (B 266)** *paramour*: preferred as avoiding the unintended number-ambiguity of the form with final *-s*, which is attested in the period for the sg. noun (see MED s.v. *paramour(e* n., where the sense 1(b) 'husband' corresponds to *make* in **B**). **106 (B 267)** Bx scans as an extended Type IIIa on vowels, and while *hym* could be a ⇒ for *man*, the latter, not being a difficult word, is more probably a **C** revision (to Type Ie) bringing the main stresses onto lexical words. **108** *persones*: one of several **C** revisions here. *R–K* adopt *parties* **B** without warrant, a word scarcely difficult enough to invite ⇒.

B 271–4 271 (C 110) scans as Type Ie, with the first stave in *So* (the comparative adverb carrying strong initial stress), the blank stave here in position 2 (*vch*) and a 'supplemental' |s| stave (*forsáketh*) in the fifth lift (see *Intro.* IV § 440). **273 (C 112)** *so neyȝ is pouerte* α: preferred as the more probable reading of Bx in the light of **C**'s *semblable bothe*. Perhaps β substituted the logically weak and contextually unapt *to his seintes* through

objecting to Bx's repetition; this is echoed in **C**'s revision which, however, varies *syb* instead of repeating *pouerte*. **274 (C 113)** The Bx b-half *þat here faste preise* is judged to survive in R, which mistakenly replaced the adverb *here* α with a verb *huyre*, but without a subject-pronoun. F substitutes one for *þat*, providing the basis for the *K–D* reconstruction *I here yow*. The phrase is here interpreted as an elliptical mode of address: an understood *ye* was supplied by β, which smoothed by dropping *here* (thereby damaging syntax and metre) to make the line scan *aa / bb*. **115 (B 276)** scans as a macaronic Type Ib line with two cognative Latin staves in the b-half (*odibíle bónum*). The list following is taken as prose and numbered as one citation line (115*a*) as in **p**. The **x** tradition erroneously appends the first item (*Remocio curarum*) to 115, thereby obscuring the character of the latter as a true verse. **115*a* (B 276*a*)** *solicitudine*: on grounds of sense and confirmation by the Latin source the preferred reading, *solitudine* being explicable as a visual error caused by assimilation of *-ci-* to following *-tu-*. However, if the presence of *semita* unconsciously suggested *solitudo*, the error may have been in Cx (and Bx) and corrected in *p¹* (and possibly β). But while it is repeated in α at 306, it seems to have been avoided in Cx at 141*a*. **116 (B 277)** scans like **B** as a counterpointed Type Ie, but with a mute key-stave on |k| (*aab / [a]bx*), while the **B** line has a full stave at key position (*kenne*) and treats *quod Haukyn* as extra-metrical. Despite the apparent resemblance to **C** of the R form of 277, this cannot be what **B** read, since the second line is prose and the first has an untypical full key-stave *quod*. **117–18 (B 278–79)** In the revised 117, *Pacience* is a full stave in position two. B 278 is a line of vocalic Type IIa with the semantically important *hard* as stave three and *quod Pacience* forming part of a strong dip before the second stave.

B 284–86*a* give inferior sense as preserved in Bx, and in 285 defective metre (*xa / ax* unless the caesura comes after *pure*, as it cannot). The reconstruction here follows *K–D* in making Bx 285a the b-half of 284 and in transposing 286 and 286*a*. This enables the first axiom cited from 276 to stand as a summarising conclusion of the preceding English, as occurs successively at 290*a*, 291*a*, 294*a* etc; in **C**, by contrast, at 121*a* and 126*b* the first two axioms *precede* their English, so *R–K*'s elaborate re-ordering after **B** has nothing to recommend it. In 285, the final phrase of Bx *And ioye*, replaced here at 284 by *is to þe body*, becomes the onset, the adverb *also* being inserted to provide a first stave. While loss of the latter through attraction to following *soule* is easy to conjecture, the mechanism of corruption remains obscure, and the rationale of the reconstruction is a general understanding of the total argument, the coherence of which should now be clear.

128 (B 293) *wightes*: 'weights', on grounds of sense and context the likeliest substantive reading; so *wittes B-R, C*-TH² may be interpreted as a reflex of the back-spelled *whittes* attested in y (< **x**), which was also the probable reading of *B*-α (*B*-F *wyʒles* is a near-synonymous ⇒ for α *whites* read as *wittes*). A parallel earlier occurs at C 6.258=B 13.361. **129 (B 294)** Since natural stressing might prefer the key-stave mute in what would otherwise be a Type IIIa line (such muting being avoided by **L**), it seems probable that *neyhebore* supplies a second stave by having stress wrenched onto its final syllable (a cognative 'compensating' final stave being provided by *paye*). However, if *but* is not here prepositional before demonstrative *þat* 'that which' but part of the conjunctive phrase *but þat* 'except, unless', it may carry both stress and alliteration. **130** *me*: the unstressed reduced indefinite pronoun (MED s.v. *me* pron. (1)), presenting no problem as the key-stave here, as it is mute. But in position 1 (always stressed) this form is not permissible. Undoubtedly the line would scan more effectively on |l| as a Type IIa, reading *ledes* for *men* (2), and the harder synonym could have been supplanted in Cx under inducement from preceding and following *men*. If so, the reduced form *me* (1), which would then fall into the onset, would be explained and acceptable. But on balance, major emendation here does not seem justified. **135 (B 299)** *is hit*: the verb-subject inversion here is probably due to omission of the numeral (*fifte*) and its replacement by an adverb. All the other 'points' from fourth to ninth follow the pattern *hit is a*, and **B** may be presumed to have done likewise, since it has the numeral (*fifte*) in conformity with all the others. Accordingly *it is* may be conjectured as the reading of Bx, to which α added the article and from which β omitted the pronoun (as in all the other cases from fourth to ninth). **136 (B 300)** *lowe*: conjectured as providing a reading in **B** that makes good sense and explains the form of the attested variants. Of these, *lawde* is nonsense, *lewde* over-specific and inappropriate (morality is in question, not learning), *land* vague and ill-fitted to the metaphor in *leche*, while *lawe* has no contextual relevance. The revised **C** form, making *foule eueles* the object of the *leche*'s ministrations, may point to a stave-word in **B** such as *luþere*, which could have lost its second syllable through assimilation to following *euere* in Bx. But a form *law(e) / *lewe* in B-Ø might equally have generated a postulated Bx *lawd* that would account for all four variants. The present emendation accordingly supposes the referent to have been 'the humble', since of two conjectured alternatives *luthere* and *lowe*, the second is more apt to the context: poverty promotes chastity in those whose position in society is a humble one. This affirmation may then be related to B 252–53, on the brothels, suggesting a correlation of this 'point' of poverty to the capital sin Lechery. **140 (B 304)** *liʒter*: conjectured on grounds of sense and the showing of revised **C** as the probable origi-

nal in **B** also. While *hardier* provides tolerable sense and metre, the Bx line being of Type Ib, repetition in *hardy man of herte* 305 is suspicious and suggests that *hardier* has come in by visual inducement from the following phrase. But *liʒter* goes better with the sense of *cantabit* in the parenthetical quotation. In **C** it is mute, so as to accommodate metrically the final adverb (though the text would be better without it). **141a (B 304a, 306)** The Bx lines provide an acceptable sequence as they stand; but if the emendation of *hardier* is accepted, the re-ordered sequence will appear preferable. Thus 304a now glosses the preceding and following English line (*liʒter // cantabit*; *þeues // latrone*) and 306 sums up the argument for the sixth 'point' by quoting (in full) the axiom given in part at 276a. Each of the nine citations listed occurs in this way at the *end* of its amplificatory English passage. **144 (B 309a)** The omission of the Latin line, the seventh of the 'points' of poverty, from both α and Cx may suggest its absence from both versions, since no mechanical reason for the loss appears. However, since *all* the other points are quoted in their proper places, it would seem best to follow β in including this one too in **B**. Among the **C** copies, F places it in the margin beside 143, R at the end of 145, PQWZ at the end of 144 (so *SkR–K*), and it should arguably be included in the text. **146 (B 311)** *so wel*: conjectured in the light of *sothly* **C** as the possible **B** reading from which Bx could have lost the required first-stave *so* by visual distraction from following *deserue*, so*mer*. Although the **C** lines are otherwise unrevised and *sothly* could be also what **B** read, a mechanical explanation is preferable in the absence of any adequate reason for Bx's change of that adverb. **150 (B 315)** The Bx line, just tolerable with two lifts in *sík(e)nésse*, would run better if the final phrase were transposed with *good leche*. **151 (B 316)** In the light of **C**, **B** may be re-lineated, improving the metre and removing the important name *Seint Austyn* from its (unstressed initial) position in the prelude dip of 317.

B XIV *ends here.*
C XVI *continues.* B XV *begins.*

Rubric in B The passus-heading in β is correct, R being out by one and F completely aberrant (F's rubrics are given in *Sk* II xxvii–xxx). B XV was perhaps intended to be the Prologue of *Dobet*, since the β rubrics at B XVI point to that passus (though with less than complete certainty) as being the first of *Dobet.* Similarly, the **C** rubric at XVII indicates that passus as the Prologue of *Dobet* (in **x**) but Passus I of *Dobet* in **p**, which has been one out in passus-numbering from the beginning of the poem. **165–66 (B XV 16–17)** 165b and 166b are transposed by *Pe*, following the arguments of *K–D* (pp 209–10) for such ↔ in **B** on grounds of 'contextually unsatisfactory sense'.

But even if 'physically simple' (*K–D*), altering a reading identical in both archetypes needs unusually strong justification. Here the presupposition of identical error in Cx strains credence and the arguments for emendation are tenuous (*R–K* abandon it). The sense of the text is that the souls of all were created by God; some are Christian; all are 'known' in heaven (in that Christ died for all); and some (the just) will enter there, including those who receive the faith or repent of sin at the end of life (*neuere so late*). For a relevant comparison, cf. the thought at 20.418–20. **172** scans as Type Ia on |f| with a liaisonal first stave (*Of_som*) or else as Type IIIa with *fihte* as first stave; *R–K*'s emendation *fele* for *som* is otiose. **173** Either order of the nouns in the b-half would give satisfactory metre, but **x** is preferred as varying the stress-pattern of *som tyme* from the preceding line. It is either Type IIIc or (if *to* is regarded as the mute second stave) Type Ia with counterpoint. **177** scans in Cx as *aa / xa* unless, improbably, the stave-sound is identified as |ð| and a cognative liaisonal-stave found in reconstructed **qua[th]_Y*, giving a Type IIa line. The felicitous variant of *C*-ms W, adopted here, enables the stresses to fall on three lexical words in |b|. Given that 177 is an unusually long line, the error could have come about if *quod he* had been found squeezed into the margin of the exemplar and then wrongly placed in copying by the scribe of Cx. **183 (B 25)** *Mens Thouhte*: reconstructed as the x^1 form (< Cx) on the evidence of XY's substantive reading and the u (and D^2) variant, as well as the form of *B-α*, accurately preserved in R and corruptly reflected in F. The x^2 reading involves smoothing after misinterpretation of *mens* as an English genitive plural. That of u has rightly recognised it as Latin, but like *B-β* has omitted the following gloss *thouhte* (presumably judging it marginal) to leave a line with a masculine ending (N^2, usually grouping with y, here reflects a **B** source of β-type). As here understood, the 'gloss' is internal and authorial, not scribal; for a parallel see on 22.236 // (*chey-tyftee pouertee*), where the gloss is not on a Latin but on a rare English word. **195** *body*: a blank stave in a Type Ic line scanning *aax / ax*. The revision of *flessh* **B**, to which FCh vary by alliterative inducement (mistakenly followed by *R–K*), is doubtless intentional, since **C** stresses death where **B** ambiguously suggests asceticism. **199a (B 39a)** *dum scit Mens est*: restored on the basis of **B** as omitted by the Cx scribe, perhaps after failing to recognise *Mens* in 183 as Latin (// Bx clearly had it). It seems unlikely that **L** dropped *Mens* from the Isidorean list simply because he had added *Liberum Arbitrium*, since the faculty Thought in any case appears in 183, whether that line originally contained *Mens* (as here in the edited text) or not. **215a (B 55a)** yields the pattern *aa / xx* with internal assonance 'compensating' for the omitted stave-sound |t| in the b-half. *opprimatur*: the Cx reading, supported by that of *B-R* (< α < ?Bx); perhaps an authorial alteration of the

source. *B-F* has changed to the future indicative form of Vg, while β has rationalised by substituting the present indicative (as has *C-N²*, presumably from a β source). But **L** could have intended to make the prophecy a malediction. **223 (B 63)** scans as Type IIIb on vowels with 'echoic' counterpoint (Schmidt 1987:65) on |p| in the a-half (*Pòtte / Páradys*). *Pulte* **B**: on the evidence of L (and original M) the reading of β, on R's that of α, and to be preferred on grounds of lexical hardness and contextually appropriate sense. The word has earlier caused scribal difficulties. At B 1.127 it is attested by LR (and Cr) against *putte* γMAx and supported by **Z** (**C** is here revised). At C 10.95, where y (< x^1) has *pulte* and **p**u *putte*, the variant *putte* in // **B** is only randomly attested, and *pulte* would seem secure as the original of w and g (< γ) as well as of L and α. In the present instance, the **B** variants leave it unclear whether γ or w and g severally altered to *putte* (visible alteration in M does not serve to establish whether γ or only w or g read *pulte*); for the <OC^2> ancestor has in *pullede* a reflex of postulated β *pulte*, though this could in principle be by correction from a ms of *l* or *m* type. Confirmation of *pult* as still part of L's active vocabulary in **C** is found at 11.208, a new line that refers to God's foreknowing, where no scribal difficulty has been experienced. It appears therefore that in the three uses of a word to denote acts of divine 'expulsion' (from heaven, from paradise and from the state of grace), L's characteristic choice is *pulten* (on which see MED s.v. *pilten* v. 1(a), (c)). Some grounds thus exist for seeing *potte* as a Cx ⇒ for original *pulte* and for emending accordingly; but as the sense-difference is small and revision possible, it may be let stand. **224 (B 64)** The **C** line is here accepted as a revised form that consists simply of **B**'s a-half, now scanning vocalically as Type Ia (the b-half could have been lost from Cx through inattention, as possibly at 16.9); but since the sense is complete and the following line largely revised, there is no real case for reconstruction. **227 (B 69) B** may be scanned as a Latin alliterative verse-line of Type IIIc (*ab / ab*) with an English prelude-dip *That is* (cf B 12.278 // earlier). Revised **C**, however, is a true macaronic of Type Ie in which three of the original four Latin words are again staves. Thus *sapere* (1) and (2) are full staves, *Non plus* the prelude-dip, *saide þe wyse* a phrase of the *quod he* type commonly treated as extra-metrical, *oportet* the second stave (blank), and *synne* the key-stave. An alternative scansion would make *saide þe wyse* intra-metrical and part of a strong second dip. Yet a third would have *pruyde* as key-stave, with the Latin a-half staves *plus* and *oportet* (words of high semantic prominence) and an eight-syllable dip. On balance, the first is to be preferred, since *synne of pruyde* appears an integral phrase with a full stave on the generic term, while both *oportet* and *sapere* can receive the major stress they require. The line's exceptional length, macaronic character and potentially ambiguous scansion not unexpectedly

provoked mislineation. But neither of its two-line forms provides acceptable metre for both lines, and the felicitous relineation of TN² imposes itself as correct. That of D may be interpreted as a single line and is so recorded in the Apparatus; but it is perhaps better seen as another case of division after *sapere* (2), since the scribe's usual medial colon does not appear after that word but after *wyse*. *Pe*'s division of the two lines after *wyse* leaves the first unmetrical, while *R–K*'s more drastic ↔ of the Latin and English phrases after *wyse* leaves *quam...sapere* as an isolated 'appended' line; both solutions are unsatisfactory in different ways. **228 (B 70)** *fele*: the revised **C** form suggesting that *fele* B-β derives from Bx and is not a ⇒ for a possible *manye*, and that the line is to be scanned on |f| / |v| with a cognative stave on |ð| (from *þat*, probably muted). **230 (B 72)** On the showing of revised **C**, this line was securely in Bx and may have been lost in α by eyeskip from *bileue* 72b to *bileuen* 73a. The wordplay on *bileue* noun and verb (abandoned in **C**) seems unmistakable. The *K–D* conjecture *lome* for *oftetymes* is rejected (despite its attractiveness) since based on an erroneous view of **L**'s metre as excluding Type III lines. While **C** 12.123 certainly has *lome* for Bx *ofte*, that line may be seen, like the present revised one, as a particular case of **C**'s generally increased preference for the Type I pattern. Where *lome* appeared in **B** (as comparative *lomere* at 20.238 //), it caused Bx no difficulty, though the scribe of ms **L** thought it worth a supralinear Latin gloss (*sepius*). **B 73 (C 231)** The Bx line is to be reconstructed from the evidence of both sub-archetypes as preserved in **L** (< β) and **R** (< α). The clue is the key-stave *by* 'as regards' (MED s.v. *bi* prep. 9a), which seems to have been lost by β through haplography after B*ettre*, b*ileuen*. The particle puns homophonically on the prefix *bi-*, which here carries sentence-stress, just as *bileuen* in turn puns semantically on preceding *bileue* (72). The sense of the line may be rendered: 'it would be better, in the case of several theologians, to give up that kind of teaching'. The line's metrical structure may be analysed as Type Ia, and it would be smoother if *by* were treated as a mute stave; but considerations of sense override those of rhythm here.
232–33 (B 76–7) *foliliche*: in the light of the **B** lines under revision, to be securely discriminated as the same adverb in both **C** lines, with neither instancing *folliche* 'entirely, utterly' (MED s.v. *fulli* adv. 1(b)). Both appearances of this variant are spelling errors for *foliliche*, caused by loss of *i* between syllabic-terminal and syllabic-initial *l*. The rhetorical figure used is *repetitio*, not *annominatio*. **234 (B 78)** *in to* **B**: here resolved as preposition + adverb in the light of *in* **C**, B-β offering the same reading as *into* B-α (presumably from Bx) but with an intruded conjunction. The *preposition* 'into' would be grammatically out of place after the verb *spenen* 77 and could not acceptably relate that verb to *shewynge*.

B 84–90 84 scans awkwardly either on |s| as Type IIa with a liaisonal stave on *as_ít*, or as Type IIIa on |f| with a wrenched stress on *fórsakeþ*. **89** *muche*: adopted as the probable Bx reading preserved (unusually) in **F**'s *mychil*, with ⇒ of one synonym (*grete*) in **R** and another (*long*) in β. Any of the three variants would give a Type Ia line, **F** one with a full stave, **R** and β probably one with a mute key-stave (*make*). The metrical argument is, however, weaker here than that from *durior lectio*, and the word *muche* can be cited as appearing at least once, at 21.368 //, in the relevant sense 'large' (MED s.v. *much(e* adj. 3(c)). **90 (C 240)** *ouer* ?α: preferred as the harder reading for which **F**, coinciding with β, has substituted *of* under visual or aural inducement from preceding *of* and *Of* 89. For a similar use see **B** 1.108 // **ZA** and for a case where β has *of* for α *ouer* (here confirmed by // **C**), see **B** 5.619.
248 revises to make explicit what is elliptically implied in *swiche* **B** 98 (cf. *wexe* 253 / Ø // **B**). This line could have been lost from Bx through visual distraction (*bowes...bereþ none / bowes þat bereþ nat*); but the semi-anacoluthic **C** line seems an afterthought, and the case for inclusion is not strong. **261 (B 109)** *þei* ?α: necessary for the correct sense and either lost coincidentally by **F** or re-introduced by **R**. The βF reading (Ø-relative standing for *þei þat*) is possible with a comma after *hem*, but is less close to the revised **C** form than is that of **R**. **263** scans as a Type IIa line with cognative alliteration (|p| / |b| |b|). **264 (B 111)** *in Latyn ypocrisie* **B**: the required ↔ restoring the first stave in what is now a Type IIIa line that scans on *l*, Bx presumably having inverted the order to give prominence to the dominant idea. In theory, Bx could scan vocalically with the initial stress on *ýpocrisie* and two mute staves (*in*, *is*) but in the light of **C**'s revision to a Type Ia scanning on *l*, the emendation seems justified (and cf. pronunciation of *Ypócrisye* in **C** 263). **266 (B 113)** Coincidental loss of the line in *p¹* and three mss from *p²*, **y** and **u** here provides a classic instance of homoteleuton. **267 (B 114)** *prélates*: pronounced with two full stresses. **268 (B 115)** *ben* **B**: emended on the evidence of (revised) **C** to provide the needed first stave in a Type Ia line. Bx might be scanned if both words of the French phrase ended the a-half (*paroles* then being a full cognative stave), but this would give a weak b-half with a full stress on *and*. **C** adds a second |b| stave to lengthen the b-half as if to ward off possible stave-loss through scribal ⇒ of *aren* in first position. **269 (B 116)** *wolueliche* α: on grounds of sense and metre and in the light of revised **C** the only possible reading, β being a visual error and **F** a capricious ⇒. **270 (B 117)** *Crísostómus*: two-stressed in both versions, **B** scanning as Type IIIa and **C** as Type IIIb. *R–K* add *and prestes*, creating a 'scribal' amalgam of **B** and **C**. **271 (B 118)** *corruptum*: the neuter form preferred on grounds of sense, since the presumed referent is

sacerdocium (the ordained clergy) not *tota ecclesia* (the Church as a whole). The error could have been induced from the following adjective ending in *-a* (*marcida*).

B 120–27 120 will scan as Type IIIa on |m| or, preferably, on |w| with *was* as stave one. The word *who* in **L** appears always to be vocalic, and the other two **B**-Text examples (10.436 and 11.346) cited by *K–D* (p. 13, n. 15) of its occasional pronunciation with initial |w| are Type IIIa lines that their metrical theory mistakenly rejects. (On a possible |w| pronunciation of *wham* see at C 17.89). **121, 122** may both scan cognatively on |p| and |b|, line 121 as Type Ib and 122 as Type Ie with vocalic counterpoint or as Type IIIc. **123** *ech*: conjectured as providing a key-stave *ech_hath* alliterating (cognatively) with |dʒ| in *Iohan* and *Geffrey*. The Bx line scans *aa / xx*, but a Type IIIa pattern remains remotely possible if *Iohan* is pronounced as a Latin name (with |j|) and *girdel* has the palatal sound reflected in (rare) contemporary spellings with *ʒ* (but MED s.v. illustrates *ʒirdel* no later than OE). Another emendation, involving heavy (perhaps appropriately sarcastic) stress on the titles, is the ↔ *of siluer a girdel* favoured by *K–D*. **126–27** The postulated Bx line, *Hadde he neuere seruice to *saue [haue R] siluer þerto, seiþ it with yuel wille*, scans as a Type Id (or Ie) but yields little sense. The thought is commonplace, the use of *þerto* unidiomatic, and the expression clumsy: the meaning would be that such a priest 'never saves money to buy himself a breviary', and only says his offices with grudging ill-will. The present reconstruction clarifies the syntax and explains how Bx could have been generated, identifying *his* as the key-stave in 126 and *haue* R as the verb, so as to relate the priest's activity to the 'tool' he performs it with. In 127 *saue he haue,* with *saue* as conjunction (MED s.v. *sauf* prep. 4(a) 'except, unless'), is offered as the origin of the β verb *saue* and in turn connected (but with greater appropriateness) to the priest's wish to receive payment for saying his offices (*þerto*). Loss of the postulated half-line will have been through assimilation of the second *haue* (127) to the first (126), and *haue* R (< α), *saue* (β) can now be distinguished as split variants of 127a. The reading is reconstructed only from material Bx is judged to have conflated from the proposed two-line original. Two copies respond to the perceived incoherence of Bx by adducing drink as a reason for the priest's dereliction of duty. F concocts *þat is betake to tauerne hows for ten schelyng plegge* after 125 to explain the priest's lack of a *porthors*, then re-writes 126 as *If he hadd no seruice ne siluer þerto with evil will he will synge,* which corresponds in substance to 127 as reconstructed here. But the <OC²> source's b-half variant *for spending at ale* cannot be what *seiþ it with yuel wille* was generated from or anything except explicit scribal invective against priests like Sir Piers of Pridie of B 5.313//. *K–D* adopt OC² into a two-line reconstruc-

tion, matching its inventiveness with *He syngeþ seruice bokelees,* their new a-half for 127. *yuel*: accepted on the evidence of α (recoverable from R and F) supported by L (< β), and on grounds of superior sense, as preferable to *ydel* γ, to which M (or its original *m*) has varied, no doubt by ⊗ from a w-type source.

273 *Vnkynde curatours*: the correct form of this phrase reconstructed from the split variants in **p** and **x**. Liberum Arbitrium's target here seems to be the clergy's pride and greed rather than their ignorance, and his phrase recalls Holy Church's words in I 186–88. The **x** variant could be due to recollection of the common term of criticism as used at, e.g. 15.16 //, that of **p** to mis-expansion of an abbreviated form, perhaps influenced by associations between *vnkynde* and *creature* like those at 6.294 //. **275** *ober wyse* C: treated as a pronoun followed by an adjective (here a full stave) agreeing with *God. R–K,* in treating *oþerwyse* as an adverb (with inferior stress-pattern), overlook the relevance of *witty God* **B**. **279 (B 136)** *Churche*: possibly revision to a Type IIIc line or else a Cx ⇒ for *kirke* as in *B*-β, to which *C*-YDChN² have independently altered. But the new pattern being acceptable, there is no need for emendation (for another case of *churche* C] *kirke* **B** see 337 //).

B 138 *entreþ þe bisshop*: ↔ provides the key-stave lost through presumed inversion to prose order in Bx (*aa / xx*). The line now scans as Type Ia. **B 140** Type Ia on |n| with a liaisonal first-stave *seyen_(h)e.*

282 (B 145) C revises a Ia line scanning on |g| to a vocalic IIIb, the type with a 'supplemental' stave in fourth position. Heavy rhetorical stress falls on *here* because it anticipates syntactically relative *That* in 283, which is wholly revised. **284 (B 149)** Both lines offer several possible scansions, depending on how the key-stave is identified and the sense of the whole line interpreted. **B** is either Type IIIa, scanning on |tʃ| like // C 296, Ia on vowels with a mute key-stave *A,* or vocalic Ie with counterpoint on |tʃ|. **C** offers no clearly superior option, and is either Type IIIa scanning on vowels, with *is* as key-stave; Ia on |ð| with *þat* as key-stave and a liaisonal stave derived by reading *quath _Y* for *quod Y*; or Ia on |t| |d| / |t| with *þat _is* as liaisonal key-stave, *quod_Y* as second stave (cognative and liaisonal) and *Charité* as first stave, with stress on the final syllable. The last alternative is probably to be preferred, as it avoids the de-stressing of the most important word consequent on locating it in the onset. (At B 156 the line's key-stave is not in doubt, but in revising it, C 288 restores the word's stressed position by establishing *Charite* as a full stave). **289 (B 157)** The revision, which detaches the Latin as a citation-line, scans either cognatively on |p| |p| / |b| or vocalically with *hym* as key-stave, the former being preferable as nearer to the pattern of normal speech stresses and to its source B 156, a Type Ic with a cognative third stave. B 157 may be scanned as a Type I Latin verse-line alliterating on |n|, with English *As* the initial dip. There is a case for including in the C-Text the third clause of the Biblical quotation, which is translated in the English of 291a; the truncated form in Cx could have omitted an *&c* present in the original (as in D²Q). **305** alliterates as an extended vocalic Type III with double counterpoint on |g|; so *R–K's* ↔ of *opere* and *ne greue* to give a Type I line is quite unnecessary. **330 (B 189)** *purtinaunces*: a revision to plural supported by the form of this expression at 2.108 //.

B 207–244 207 will scan on vowels but the stresses would fall more effectively if the stave-sound were |m| and *wiþ* a reflex of β *mid* (< Bx), the uncommon contextual sense of which might have invited ⇒ of *on* α, *yn* g (see MED s.v. *mid* prep. 6(a)). **213** Whereas easier scansion would be produced by reading *in lolleris nys he noʒt* in the a-half or *ne lyueþ* for *nys*, this will pass as Type Ie scanning on |n| with counterpoint on |l|, the (mute) key-stave being generated by elision of *ne + in*. F's *loveþ* is a characteristic scribal attempt to make the line normative. **224 (C 347)** *stille* **B**: conjectured by *K–D* as the required key-stave, *so* α being acceptable metrically but giving somewhat weak sense in context and failing to account for the form of the (equally unsatisfactory) β variant (see MED s.v. *stille* adv. 5 'continually'). It may be presumed that *tyl*, the *m*-reading altered to *for* in M by ⊗ from a w-source, was that of β, and *so* α could have resulted from mistaking the adverb for the adjective and judging the sense inappropriate here. Alternatively, *charite* had a by-pronunciation in |ʃ| furnishing a cognative stave for the |s| staves of the a-half. There is some spelling evidence of merging between *sh* and *ch* (see *TN* on 7.300), but the key-stave sound of the revised **C** line is clearly |tʃ|. On balance *stille* seems to offer the strongest sense, is seemingly echoed in *all here lyues* **C**, and could explain the form of β *tyl*. **234 (C 357)** Bx scans vocalically as a Type IIIa with strong sentence-stress on *hir* as key-stave and support in both half-lines from 'echoic' counterpoint on |w| and |l| (Schmidt 1987²:65–6); *pace K–D* and doubts in *Sch*¹, no emendation is needed. **244–48 (364–67)** The α lines seem genuine on intrinsic grounds and the showing of the (much-revised) **C** equivalent. No mechanical reason for their omission from β appears, but censorship may be suspected, since this is one of the most explicit criticisms of the hierarchy in the poem. **244** scans (after *Sk's* inevitable relineation) either vocalically with a mute key-stave (*and*) supported by 'supplemental' fourth stave (*Holy*), or else cognatively on |b| |b| / |p|, the latter alternative perhaps preferable in the light of (much-revised) **C**. **247** scans either as Type Ib on |k|, with the first stave found liaisonally in *Ac_áuarice*, or else as a vocalic T-type line with counterpoint on |k|, the latter perhaps more likely on the showing of C 365, which scans on vowels. **254a** β: lost from α perhaps through eyeskip from *moore* 254 to *mooste* 255.

[B XV *continues*]

Passus XVII (B XV *continued*)

RUBRIC See the note on the Rubric to XVI. It would appear that the **x** tradition regards XVII, the seventh of Dowel, as in effect a Prologue to *Dobet*, since XVIII is headed the *first* of *Dobet* (see Rubric to XVIII). But **p** sees Passus XVII as the *first* of *Dobet* and proceeds accordingly.

B 268 The F variant *verred* challenges consideration against *verray* as the possible α reading for which R may be a ⇒ of the same easier word as β (so *K–D Sch*¹). MED s.v. *averren* v. 1(b) 'cite' does not instance the unapocopated form before C15ⁱ or record *verren* separately, though OED s.v. *Aver* v. gives *ver* itself from *Destruction of Troy* (? early C15), and the word was lexically hard enough to have puzzled the βR scribes. On the other hand, the βR syntax is hard enough to be original and to have stimulated F's source to clarify (here felicitously). For *quod he* must refer both backwards to the quoted Latin phrase, as a parenthetic statement-index, and forwards to the English of the b-half, as a transitive verb taking a direct object. The point seems to be less that *many* examples are being cited than that they are *true*.

15 (B 289) *of_Austynes* **B**: providing the key-stave by liaison, so no emendation is required. The phrase *or ellis frerys lyen* in ms B seems to echo the revised b-half of C 16. **24 (B 295)** *souel* **p**: to be preferred as the etymologically more correct spelling (< OE *sufol*: see MED s.v. *souel* n.2.), avoiding confusion with *saule(e)* (< OF *saolee*: see MED s.v. *saule* n.), which occurs at B 16.11. Whichever spelling **L** used, the pronunciation is disyllabic, *souel* better facilitating the possible semi-pun on *soule* 'soul', 'life-principle' (see 22): the sustenance of heavenly grace for the contemplative takes the place of physical food.

B 303–07 303–4 (C 29–31) appear authentic on intrinsic grounds and on the showing of revised **C**, and may be presumed lost from β by eyeskip (*yfed þat folk* 302a → *foode by foweles* 305a, *beestes* 303a → *beestes* 305b). **307 (C 34)** Bx 307 scans *réligioús* and would give better rhythm with a final plural *-es* or an inserted *men / renkes* after *religious* (cf. *holy men* in // C 34).

37–8 Division after *saide* **p** is to be rejected as giving an anomalous Type IIa with third lift on (phrasally unstressed) *was* and the semantically important *blynde* then forming a dip (*To his Wýf whén hè wás blýnde*). As lineated in **x**, 38 scans as Type IIIc with crossed alliteration on vowels and |bl|.

B 312–14 312 *haþ ben*: conjectured to provide the needed key-stave for which *was* is a Bx ⇒ of a more obvious form. The theoretically possible vocalic scansion on monosyllabic grammatical words yields an unnatural stress pattern and verb-participle ↔ in the last lift (*K–D*) is ruled out as giving a masculine ending. **313** *foweles*: not to be taken as an error for *foles* (as by Cr), despite the apparently paradoxical notion of (metaphorical) 'birds' being fed by literal birds (though the *briddes* are also symbolic). A pun on *foles* is doubtless intended, as was the converse pun on *foweles* at B 7.125; but Anima's bird-imagery here is principally and directly related to that he uses at 471–79, and only secondarily and obliquely to that of 'God's fools' in B 20.61–2 //. As no case for emending appears, *K–D*'s conjecture [*by*] *goddes* [*behestes*] for *ben Goddes foweles* must provoke wonder (cf. *Intro.* II § 102). **314** *by lyue*: particle / infinitive ↔ necessary to restore the key-stave lost through Bx's presumed inversion to prose order (cf. closely parallel phrase *þat they with deleth* in C 9.167 //). **48** *grene-leued* **p**: perhaps preferable on grounds of contextual appropriateness, with further support to be found in its echo of 16.248, 253, referring to the tree of the Church. But though *grene loue* **x** could be an error caused by *e / o* confusion or partly induced by the sense of following *charite*, it is the harder reading, strongly and interestingly defended in Hill 2002:72ff by appeal to Gregory's exegesis of Job 44:24, and should be adopted. **50** *Holy Churche*: the evident reading of Cx, two mss altering to the normative scansion. While *kirke* could have been the original reading of **C**, the present Type IIIa structure promotes a functional stress on *Holy* that generates ironic tension between the sense of the epithet and that of the verb *amende*. **53 (B 317a)** The Latin text in **B** has the feel of a supporting citation and is printed as prose. That in **C**, being more the quoted utterance of a speaker first named in the English of 51, is set out as verse, following the layout in ms X. *Numquam*: either an authorial error for *numquid* (the reading of *B*-Cr²³F, *C*-DW) or to be taken as part of a statement, the question proper beginning only with *Aut*. In **C** either *eis* has been omitted after *cum* (preposition) or *cum* is here the conjunction ('whereas') with *eis* understood. **55 (B 320)** *moore* **B** 'further' (MED s.v. *mor(e* adv. 1 'to a greater extent'): conjectured in the light of revised **C** as the required first stave in a Type IIa line and presumed lost through partial haplography before *amortisede*. **C** has the word in stave-position two, creating a Type Ia line, and by forming a noun phrase with *eny* removes the last lift of **B**. But **C**'s retention of *chanouns* renders *K–D*'s conjecture *monyales* superfluous. **62** scans cognatively on |k| |k| / |g| as a Type Ia, so *R–K*'s emendation of *bigynneth* to *comseth* is not required.

    B 335–42a 335, 339 *robeþ*: in both cases the evidently right reading on grounds of contextual sense, Bx's error being presumably corrected by four mss severally (five in the case of 335, Y erring with the majority in 339). **342a** *Item* (2)...*rapis* β: lost from α by eyeskip from *Item* (1) → *Item* (2)...*Si autem*.

73 The archetypal line that follows scans cognatively *aa / xa* and could be emended without difficulty by ↔ to [*printe gode*] in the b-half. However, it looks suspiciously like a scribal expansion prompted by generalised ill-will against debased coinage and immediately by suggestion from the phrase *oþer worse* at the end of 73 and *printe(de)* at 75, 80). Thus the sense anticipates (and virtually repeats) that of 74–5 (*metal...nauhte = badde peny*; *printe puyr trewe = gode printe*). The thought flows better from 73–4 if the line is omitted, *Of...ygraue* elaborating the simile at 73b. Though identified as the sole spurious line in Cx, this one resembles the scribal line that follows B 5.193 (see Apparatus) and may be safely rejected from the text. **74** *moche moné*: the addition of the phrase *þat is mad* in t is a typical padding-out of a terse line doubtless felt to be too short. Instances such as this illustrate the untrustworthy character of the t-scribe's expansions (see Apparatus at 38 and 13.12). *nauhte*: 'worthless' (MED s.v. *nought* adj. (b)); the word is historically disyllabic and probably to be expanded as *ná-ùht* rather than having a diphthong + sounded final *-e* (cf. 1.181n and 9.112). **78 (B 352)** *of many of* **pt**: loss of the key-stave in x^1 will have been caused by eyeskip from *of* (1) → *of* (2), the scribe of Y making an attempt at correction that restores the metre but at the expense of the sense. *myd* **B**: conjectured as the required key-stave for which *with* is a Bx ⇒ of the (effectively standard) synonym. This emendation leaves following 353b saying the same as 352b, and a conjectured form such as [*myd*] *synne is foule*[*d*] would remove the redundancy and offer smoother metre; but on balance minimal interference seems advisable. **85 (B 355)** *vnresonable* **B**: 'against (the) reason(able order of things)', because a disordered macrocosmic reflection of human sinfulness, as in B 5.13–20 (MED s.v. adj. 3b). The mistaken citing of this example to illustrate (uniquely) the sense 'wild, inclement' (*ibid.* 4) is perhaps due to taking it as a supposed error for *unsesonable*). But the preferred sense is supported by the whole passage B 358–70 (on nature) and 371–83 (on man and society). Neither banal ⇒, *vnstable* F nor *vnseasonable* Cr²³ (adopted *K–D*) can be seriously considered a likely original. **87** *so* **pt** (= x^2): 'to such an extent' (MED s.v. *so* adv. 8(a)) establishes a more exact relation between the line's two clauses than does *and* x^1, even should this mean 'if' (MED s.v. *and* conj. (& adv.) 5(a)), as it probably does (the sense to be excluded is 'and'). For though this would neatly juxtapose 'unbelief' (lay) with 'wrong belief' (clerical) and challenge *so* as instancing scribal anti-clericalism, the thought recalls 16.272–73 and the preceding Latin, and is characteristic of **L**, with *erren* having a moral more than a purely intellectual sense (MED s.v. 2). **89** scans vocalically as an extended Type IIIa with a-half counterpoint on |w|, the key-stave being vocalically-pronounced *(wh) am*. It is possible that *wham* had a by-pronunciation in

|w|, but the relative pronoun is elsewhere sounded as an unaspirated vowel (see *TN* on B 15.120). **95 (B 357)** *lodesterres* 'guiding stars' (MED s.v. *lode-sterre* n. (b)). The sg. form appears a scribal attempt to specify a particular one, the Pole Star (ibid. s.v. (a)). **99 (B 361)** *while*: preferable on grounds of sense, since **L**'s theme is decline, the variant *wel* being a probable reflex of an ambiguous Cx spelling without *h*. **101 (B 364)** *sulle myhte* **x**: on the basis of the context and the identity with **B** to be preferred as the original in **C**, **p**'s variant being doubtless the result of misreading *sulle* as *sulde* and then smoothing *myhte* to the infinitive of an appropriate verb. **103 (B 366)** *follwares*: 'retainers, (farm) servants' (MED s.v. *folwer* n. 2(a)), i.e. the *tilyares* of 100 (the referent correctly identified by the scribe of P^2). The **p** variant *sowers*, which makes the line of Type IIb, may result from initial misreading of *f* as long *s*. But the (non-related) variants of P^2 and N^2 suggest that the word was found difficult in this sense. **106 (B 370)** *clymat*: '(region with respect to its) weather'; proposed for **B** on the assumption of a hypothetical Bx form **clemet* misexpanded as (meaningless) *clement* in α and then misread or rationalised to the plausible *element* in β (MED s.v. *element* n. 3 'atmospheric conditions; weather'). The latter is adopted by *K–D*, their line then scanning with two lifts in *cálcúled* but is securely to be identified as an error in the light of the lexical evidence and **C**. **108–09 (B 372–73)** Division of the lines according to **p** (as in **B**) leaves **x** lacking a second stave. This may be reconstructed from **p**'s *nouthe non* as *noon nouthe* which, in the form **non nou* in *x^1*, could easily have suffered haplographic loss of the adverb. The <RM> variant *no wye now* can be explained as a corruption of **p**'s reading, if a back-spelled form **nowhte now* is postulated (M's spelling *nowithg* may be a reflex of such a form). *Pe*, objecting to **p**'s 'padding', substitutes *of þise newe clerkes* from **B** to provide the omitted stave-phrase. But there is no justification for this, as the repetition of *nouthe* in 108a after 107b is characteristic of **L**'s late style. **110 (B 374)** *can*: necessary as the first stave in this Type IIa line and presumed lost by haplography before con*strue*. **112 (B 377)** *to fourmen hym vnder* **B**: reconstructed as an original phrasal form (partially) inverted to prose order in Bx, with consequent loss of the key-stave. F's attempt to remedy this loss results typically in altering the sense of the entire b-half. **115–16 (B 382–83)** In principle, line 115 as found in all mss except RM could make sense, if *bote* is taken not as a conjunction but as the noun meaning 'help', 'remedy' (MED s.v. *bote* n. (1)), with *and* having the sense 'and yet' (MED s.v. *and* conj. 4). But the presence in B 382b of the phrase *if swiche were apposed* and the greater completeness of the syntax with it argue for regarding line 116 as original. *Pe* follows *Sk* in printing the line but ascribes it to 'P', though it appears only in RM. It could in theory be a bril-

liant conjecture (partly inspired by **B**) on the part of the scribe of these copies' ancestral source r, since its absence from t and from the other **p** groups suggests that it was lacking in *x^2* as well as *x^1*. But if the line is genuine, its loss from *p^2*, e, q and t will be most simply explained as due to coincidental operation of the same mechanical factor as in *x^1*. This factor is the threefold occurrence of (near)-identical endings in the sequence of six lines of which it is the last: *maister*; *thynketh* (1); *maistres*; *-libet*; *lyuede*; *thynketh* (2). Such a lexical configuration is arguably singular enough to have occasioned an identical line-loss in five discrete sources. The metrical and semantic integrity of RM's line 116 argues against editorial scepticism based on unwillingness to accept so much convergent variation. Only one witness, F, recognises the lacuna in sense; but its distinctive b-half is probably a metrical filler borrowed from 112b rather than a partial reflex of the lost 116b, since the form incorporating the parenthesis *and...hem* gives superior sense. If it is authentic, the line's survival is most economically ascribable to independent descent of <RM> from *p^1* (< **p** < *x^2* < Cx). The alternative explanation, correction of r from a 'lost superior **C** ms', entails positing a textual entity for which there is no logical necessity. **118 (B 386)** *hastite* **x**: preferred as the harder reading for which **p** and some **x** mss substituted the easier near-synonym. MED s.v. *hastite* n. does not cite this occurrence, which is earlier than those recorded except for the one from *Cursor Mundi*.

124 *letynge* **x**: preferred as both theologically bolder and contextually apter than *lengthynge* **p**; but both words are lexically rare and first cited here, the former uniquely in this sense (MED s.vv. *leting(e* ger. (b) 'leaving or relinquishing', *lengthing(e* ger. (a) 'extension of life'). Salvation *in articulo mortis* by bare profession of faith might, however, seem more relevant to the situation of heathens than conversion towards the end of a long life, the presumed implication of **p**'s reading. (The inferior spelling *lettynge* is to be emended as inviting confusion with the gerund of *letten* 'hinder'). **125** *chere* **x**: to be accepted as the second stave in this Type Ia line and doubtless lost from **p** by visual assimilation to preceding ch(e)*r*che and following char*ite*. While not very uncommon (see MED s.v. *cher* adj. 2(a) 'dear'), the word has in three witnesses invited ⇒ of an existing synonym (*dere*). But in the rarer sense 'solicitous' (ibid. 2(b)) at 148, it seems to have caused no difficulty to the scribes. **131** *louye*: obviously the correct reading in the light of 136ff, and *R–K*'s emendation to *leue* (p. 174) mistakenly ignores the decisive sense of 130, 136–40. **L**'s subject is 'lawful love', love based upon *leaute* or righteousness. **132** *gentel Sarresines* **x**: 'pagans', i.e. non-Christians other than Jews. The **p** reading would distinguish pagans ('gentiles') from Moslems ('Saracens'), the former category presumably being thought of as covering such as the Prussians or Lithuanians. But **L**'s concern with contemporary 'heathens' is generally (and here quite specifically) with those of mono-theistic faith (see 134–35), viz. the Moslems. **136** *aloueth* x^1: 'commends' or 'sanctions' (MED s.v. *allouen* v.1(a); 3), preferred as being free from the ambiguity of *loueþ* x^2. If the latter is only an aphetic form of the former (MED s.v. *louen* v. (4)), then no pun on *louen* 'love' can be intended, other than perhaps a visual one. Given the concentration of references to law in the context (126, 130, 133, 136, 137, 139), the probable sense of the verb here is 'sanctions' (MED s.v. 3). That of the derived adjective at 130 will also be the legal one 'permissible' (MED s.v. *allouable* adj. (c)) rather than ibid. (a) 'praiseworthy, commendable', the sense under which this line is cited; but there is a recognised overlap of meaning. **139** *lyue* x^1: required on grounds of sense; only love that arises from a just *life* pleases God, and *louen* is interpretable as induced by preceding references to love, including the one at 136 in x^2. It might well have been the **p**-scribe's ⇒ for an original Ø-reading in x^2 (attested in t) misleadingly suggesting that the understood verb was *louyen* as at 137 and 138. The P^2 error both here and at 136 will be due to ⊗ from a **p**-type ms. **145** *the þy* pD^2Ch: preferred as maintaining **L**'s distinction between the willing self (*animus*) and the disembodied soul (*spiritus*) presupposed by the allegorical *interpretatio* in 143–44 of *amicum*140a. Failure to grasp this distinction (on which see 16.182//, 196//) has presumably led **x** to mistake the personal pronoun *þe* for the definite article and so to delete *þy* as redundant. The presence of the latter in Ch (but without *þe*) could indicate that it was in t but lost thence by the immediate ancestor of <TH²> and was accordingly also in x^2. **147** *more*: present in P^2 by felicitous variation and adopted as providing the key-stave in this Type Ia line; for while vocalic scansion is theoretically possible, it is rhythmically and semantically counter-intuitive. Presumably *more* was lost from Cx's exemplar through partial haplography after *neuere*, and *eft* is a ⇒ under influence from a parallel common locution. For a similar loss of *more* after *neuere* in x^1 (where x^2 retains it), see on 16.78, and cf. also 15.273, where Cx omits without ⇒. **155** *lente*; *sente*: either preterite or, in spite of final *-e*, contracted present-tense forms of both verbs, the latter preferable on contextual grounds since *lyf* and *lyflode* alike are continuing not momentary gifts of God. Metrically, it would be better to expand the second verb as *sendeþ*, since disyllabic *sente* pr. sg. is a 'false form'. *R–K*'s omission of *and* but retention of *sende* (now rendered subjunctive) confuses the issue: acknowledgment of God as provider, not supplication to God to provide.

   B 393–6 393 *Lede*: conjectured as the required key-stave for which Bx is judged a ⇒ of a non-alliterating synonym. The sense here (MED s.v. *led(e* n. (2) 1(a) 'person'), though also well-illustrated as applied to God

(ibid. 1(c)), could have troubled the scribe because of its accompanying epithet *almyȝty* (Cr's ⇒ of *god* suggests that even *persone* could seem to want dignity when thus collocated). That no difficulty was found in the same word at B 16.181, referring to the divine persons, may be due to its there denoting only a visual *representation* of the Trinity as human beings 'in one body'. The lost stave-word here cannot well have been *lord* (as *K–D* conclude), for this would neither have caused problems of sense or appropriateness nor have prompted *persone*, which is not a synonym of *lord* though it is of *lede*. **394** *bileueþ in oon God*: inversion of verb and noun-phrase, here unusually to prose order, is required to provide the lost key-stave. Bx's diagnosed ↔, perhaps from dissatisfaction with the metrical form of the presumed original, may have been induced in part by 395b. The line as emended does not have a masculine ending, since the last lift is the semantically important numeral of *ın oón Gòd* (by contrast, in the next line the stress-pattern is *oòn Gód*). **395** scans cognatively as a Type Ia line on |k| |k| / |g|; the vocalic scansion that *K–D*'s rejection of *k / g* stave-rime requires would both be intolerably awkward (through placing *Cristene* in the prelude-dip) and fail to achieve the b-half stress-variation from 394 (*oon* to *God*) that cognative scansion facilitates. Loss of the line from β will have been due to the simplest of mechanisms, eyeskip from Bx's identical 394 b-half to *mys*bileue in 396 (cf. 402–03). **396 (C 159)** The Bx line has two lifts in *myśbiléue,* a well-established 'monolexical' pattern (found in 273a) justified by the extra sentence-stress on this conceptually important key-word. Possibly, however, the original line-division came after *brouȝte*, as hinted by the verb's presence as final lift in 181 // 409.

165 (B 398) *Men* x^2: the stressed form of the indefinite pronoun needed for the first lift (cf. 3.477, 4.121, where *me* is not a stave, and 9.128, where it is mute). **174–75 (B 402–03)** The B lines, which seem authentic on intrinsic grounds and the support of **C**, will have been lost from α by eyeskip (*ere* 401 → *ere* 403). **182 (B 410)** *leuen*: preferred on grounds of sense, syntax (*on* **x** must require 'believe' not 'live') and the clear testimony of **B**. The *B*-M reading, which substitutes *lyued* not for *leeuen* but for the two adjectives, shows visibly as adopted from a w-source (unless Hm has been corrected).

   B 416–89a *have no parallel text in* **C.** **416–27a** have been suspected of not belonging in **B** but of being clumsily inserted by a scribe at the present point in Bx while actually forming 'a draft of matter perhaps originally intended for the opening of C XVII' (Warner 2004:122). This is unconvincing, since the lines show none of the characteristics of 'draft' material as it has been identified in the **Z**, **A** and **C** versions. Moreover, they form the opening of a much longer excised section (B 416–84), the rest of which Warner does not find suspect. 418 and

423 are indeed re-worked as C 17.35–6, 48, but the lines' interruption of 'a developing discourse about evangelism, not alms' (ib.120) should not be exaggerated. The comparison of the contemplatives to the *apostles* at 417 anticipates the lines on the (apostolic) evangelisers and their successors beginning at 437, and their life of intercessory prayer for peace (426–7) is clearly part of what **L** thinks of as effectual Christian 'mission'. **418** *þat*: providing the mute cognative key-stave in a standard line. **421** *boþe*: conjectured (following *K–D*) as the required third stave in what becomes a Type IIa line, and presumably lost in Bx by assimilation of *-þe* to following *þe* and *bo-* to preceding Be*rnard*. *K–D*'s positioning of *Boþe* as the first word of the line gives only half the explanation of the loss (attraction to following *Be-*). But attributing its omission to the difficulty of the word's probable sense here ('likewise') fits better with its position *after* the proper nouns, while a purely mechanical explanation would suffice (for a parallel quasi-adverbial use, cf. 7.51 // B 5.438). **422** *fyndynge* α: preferred as a more unusual (yet also characteristic) word found in a very similar context at C 6.293 and providing a pun on *fynde* 424a (see *Commentary* further). The contextually less exact *almesse* will have come into β from its appearance at the line-end in 419. **423** scans as Type Ic in β but as the rarer (and thus arguably more authentic) Type IIb in α. Choice is finely balanced, as *lele* could well have come in from 422b, and since no major issue of sense arises, *goode* may be readily adopted. **428a–91** Because of the gap in F here, presumably due to loss of a leaf in its exemplar *f*, α is represented solely by R, which at 471–84 provides the unique witness to fourteen **B** lines with no **C** parallel. **450** *fourmed*: conjectured as the required first stave-word in a standard line, Bx being ⇒ of a commoner word less apt in the context (see MED s.v. *formen* v. 5 'instruct'). However, as this sense has been instanced at B 15.377 without troubling the scribes, the emendation is less than wholly secure. Simpler solutions would be to read *fullynge* with two staves (an unattractive prospect), insert *was* before *and*, or conjecture mechanical loss of a stave word **fullyche* before *what* or after *fullynge*. **460** *keperes* α: preferable on grounds of sense and of coherence with the terms of the simile (= the Christian clergy: see the relevant use at C 16.273, and cf. 465). The (irrelevant) *croperes* may be a rationalisation of **creperes* β, a visual or aural error with reduplicated *r* for the reading identified as that of Bx. **461** *mynnen* W: on grounds of sense and metre a good candidate for originality, if in W probably a felicitous correction of *menen* w. Although *mynnen* could have been the reading of β and *nymmen* a metathetic error or the result of minim-confusion, it is just as possible that β read *nymmen* (as an accurate reflex of Bx), since α *take* (and so coincidentally C) can only be a synonym-substitute for the latter. A rare sense 'understand' for

nimen is, however, illustrated by MED s.v. 6b (a)) where the citation from *The Wars of Alexander* gives the Ashmole ms variant *mynned* for the correctly alliterating Dublin ms reading *nomyn* (the converse of the situation here). Theoretically the (presumed Bx) line could have the caesura after *man* or be of Type IIIa with a five-syllable dip; but *mynnen* is preferable as lexically more coherent with **L**'s usage (cf. C 17.210 where //*B*-β substitutes *Wite*, and 19.231 (no //). **470** *mowen*: conjectured to provide the required stave-word in position 1 where Bx ⇒ of the more obvious *don* is doubtless due to unconscious expectation of the verb that commonly follows the comparative adverb *so*. A more conservative emendation would diagnose simple ↔ of *men* and *rightfulle* to prose order in Bx. More radical is *K–D*'s *menen...after*, which finds its model in 404 and 474; but in those cases the idiom caused no difficulty to the archetypal (or to any other) **B** scribe, so their emendation corrects the error without explaining it. The present conjecture *mowen*, which gives the elliptical sense 'so may just men [be said to] desire mercy and truth', does so, since Bx *don* is no more than a simplification of that sense. **471–84** form the bulk of a coherent paragraph of text starting at 465 and constitute the first of two passages in B XV attested in only *one* sub-archetype (the other, 532–68, is in β only). There is no doubting its authenticity on grounds of thought or style, despite the lack of any **C** parallel, since it convincingly concludes a longer archetypally-attested passage (416–89a) with no reflex in **C**. As 471 begins with the first part of the fowls / calf simile and the lines in the second part are in β, the following fourteen, which elaborate the 'fowls' analogy, may be safely presumed to have been in Bx. The reason for their loss from β will most probably have been the scribe's resumption of copying at the wrong point in the text through inducement from four words or phrases at the beginning and end of the passage (*K–D* p. 67). **471** Since *understonde* is a past participle and *folk* a subject noun, the verb *is* would be expected. R's *his* is either one split variant from α **is his* (the possessive referring obliquely to God or Christ) or an idiolectal spelling of *is* with intruded *h*, as taken here. The line scans as standard with *fedde* as stave one or with a liaised cognative |ð| stave in *þe_honde*, or as vocalic Type IIIa with strong sentence-stress on *is*. **479** *wissynge*: 'instruction' or 'guidance', conjectured as providing superior sense contextually to *whistlynge,* which could be a visual error induced by homoteleuton (the identical rhyme in 478–79 does not itself indicate inauthenticity, being paralleled at, e.g., B 7.37, C 17.39–40). **480** *þe¹*: reconstructed to provide a subject for *bymeneþ*, which is transitive; *by* has either come in through anticipation of the verbal proclitic or else a pronoun *he* (with the Evangelist as referent understood) preceded the verb in α and was lost through visual assimilation to *by*. **489a** was omitted from β perhaps through a rubricator's oversight (*K–D*) or because the quotation at the end of 489, verse 1 of Ps 131, was thought sufficient indication of what follows (though 489*a* does not in fact appear till five verses later in the psalm). In context, the pronoun has as referent not the feminine nouns of preceding vss. 4 and 5 ('sleep', 'rest') but the *arca* of following verse 8. It is thus *eam* in Vg, as in its appearance at *C* 11.51*a* // AB, where it is glossed *'caritatem'*. The R or α scribe may have taken its referent as *locum* (vs 5) or even *David*.

C 187–251 (B 491–568) The re-ordering of **B 503–68** is based on arguments of *K–D* (pp. 176–79) for the lines' dislocation in the archetypal text. Their content and order in Bx is uncertain because of imperfect attestation and internal incoherence. Thus, each sub-archetype has lost *part* of this sequence for mechanical reasons. β has lost 510–27 by homoteleuton (*bere...names* 509, *bereþ þe name* 527) and α has lost 532–68 through mistaking in 'adjacent passages similar or related words or notions in approximately similar positions' (*K–D* 178n). The omitted passages appear securely authentic, both in themselves and as preserved (somewhat revised) in **C**, α at 17.262–78 and β at 194–251, though **C** inserts seventeen new lines between the main portion of the β passage and its last two lines (see Vol. I, pp. 608–9). Up to the gap at 532, α has the text in the order as here reconstructed and continues correct thereafter; but β, as well as losing 510–27, displaces the seven lines before it (503–09) and the four after it (528–31) to directly after 532–68. *Sk* inserts the α passage (510–27) between 509 and 528 as here given. The exact location in Bx (and in Bx's source) of the lines missing in α is likely, on the evidence of // **C**, to have been as in β. Consequently *Sk*'s order may be safely regarded as that of Bx and, as is clear in his parallel text, its closeness to **C** shows this order as likely to have been also that of the revision-manuscript B[1]. The displacement must therefore have occurred in B-Ø, the common source of <BxB[1]> postulated as the first scribal copy of the **B** Version (see *Intro.* III *B* §§ 2–6). It might thus appear unjustified to reject **C**'s confirmation of Bx in so large a matter, when it has been regularly accepted in smaller ones; but there is a difference of principle. For what is at issue here is not a textual reading, where **C**'s retention of Bx may be said to ratify it, but a textual *sequence*, where **C** could have accepted the scribal order while modifying the text in a way that takes cognizance of the incoherence produced by that sequence. That such was the case seems probable from *K–D*'s demonstration not only of the mechanism of dislocation but of the inconsequence in the argument of the passage, as well as from three revisions apparently designed to remedy it. The inconsequence lies in the separation of **L**'s criticism of the bishops for the failure of their mission to Moslems (and also Jews) from the reinforcing argument that such a mission *should* have a good chance

of success since both groups share part of the Christian faith (belief in one God). **L**'s first revision addresses this inconsequence in BxB[1] by placing B 500–02 as C 17.252–54 and following these lines with the 'reinforcing argument' referred to (C 255–82). A second revision, less compelling evidentially but worth noting, is the insertion at C 156–58 of lines on Mahomet as false mediator that anticipate B 505–06 (533–34 in *Sk* = Bx) // C 257–58. A third, more suggestive than demonstrative, is the addition of a new passage 233–49 just before the presumed point of dislocation 'as if to smooth an awkward transition' [i.e. to the lines now relocated as B 500–09, = *Sk* 492–94*a*, 532–38]. *K–D* recognise that the deficiencies diagnosed in the Bx sequence could be authorial in origin, but defensibly maintain that 'editorial decision must finally turn on assessment of relative likelihoods'. The Kane–Donaldson shift has been challenged on the grounds that α and β may preserve separate phases of the **B** Version (see *Intro.* III *B* § 53). But the gain in clarity and force would seem to justify their 'very simple rearrangement', which is accordingly adopted.

188–257 are transposed with 258–85*a* in *C*-ms M, a feature *Sk* rightly describes as 'not easy to follow or explain' (*C-Text*, xl) and *K–D* ascribe to either 'sophistication' or 'good correction' (p. 179n). Correction, if from **B**, would presuppose recourse to a lost **B** source independent of both Bx and of B[1] (which apparently had the same order as Bx) and thus of B-Ø (see above). But while the possibility of such a source may be accepted, its availability at the post-archetypal stage of copying is antecedently improbable. If from **C**, a source independent of Cx must be postulated, since M belongs to a distinct branch of the Cx tradition at five or more removes from the archetype (see diagram in *Intro.* III *C* § 13). But there are no grounds for hypothesising such a source, the case for N[2] having corrected therefrom being unsustainable (see ibid. §§ 39–40). The order in M must accordingly be put down to mechanical causes; the dislocation of both 286 and of 259–85b are noted in the manuscript. Though interesting, therefore, M's witness is unlikely to have any bearing on the arguments for re-ordering B 503–68. **190–91 (B 494–95)** The emendation is based on identifying the three major **C** variants as unoriginal on comparison with the Bx line under revision. In *x[1]*, which may fairly securely be taken to represent Cx, 190 has unmetrical *xa / ax*. Of t and **p**, either may represent *x[2]*, but more probably both are independent attempts to provide a missing stave, t more obviously by translating from the Latin sentence 191 (*mundum*). While the latter, uniformly attested as the reading of Cx, might be a 'mongrel' line not governed by the verse-rules of true-bred macaronics (Schmidt 1987:100), it could result from the Latin having been entered in the margin of the authorial exemplar and then misplaced by Cx in copying. Reconstruction starts from the fact that the b-half of the **B** line under revision (494) is a parenthesis placed between two parts of a single syntactic unit *wente...To be*. The English b-verse of Cx's 191 is made the b-verse of 190 and the Latin treated as a separate line amplifying the new 190b and syntactically dependent upon it, so that the whole phrase (190b–191) now forms the expanded parenthesis between 190a and 192 (the latter two syntactically identical with **B** 494a–495). The reconstruction, which eliminates the scribal phrases and restores the metre without altering the sense, is supported by the strikingly similar construction at 17.59–60, where a Latin imperative stands parenthetically between *bidden* and an infinitive.

B 500–31 *For notes see below on* **C** *252–82* in their *proper place.*

192 *prelates*: *R–K* alter to *pastors* after **B** to accord with *pastor* 193*a*; but given the revision in 190ff, there is no warrant to alter a reading satisfactory in metre and sense. **194–251 (B 532–68)** On the placing of these lines in **B**, see under **187–51**. **199** *pees and plente*: inverted by *R–K* to accord with **B** on the basis of N^2, though they do not follow N^2 in omitting *and* in 201. Both instances indicate ⊗ from **B**, not correction from a superior **C** source. **201 (B 539)** *and* **C**: a revision anticipated in WCrB; but asyndeton is a widely-attested feature of style in **B**. **206** The **x** variant *religiones* could be a visual error; although *religioun* in personal application is recorded (MED s.v. 1(a)), **L**'s usual form is that of **B**. **208 (B 545)** *clerkes* **B**: conjectured on the showing of unrevised **C** as the required key-stave for which β (or Bx) *men* is a (no doubt unconscious) ⇒ of a non-alliterating term very commonly collocated with *Holy Kirke / Churche,* as at 202b. **210 (547)** *Minne* **C**: conjectured on the showing of **C** as the first stave-word for **B** (cf. on **B** 461). Conceivably **C** revised to scan on |m| a **B** line with the stave-sound |w|, and the original key-stave was **wyes*. But on balance it seems likelier that β substituted *Wite* under inducement from following *wise*; and since, in the absence of α, the certain Bx reading remains unknowable, the emendation from **C** evidence (retaining *men*) is here to be preferred. **213 (B 549)** *dampnede* **C**: a revision strengthening the restrained **B** original, as at 215 below (**B** 551). **B**'s variant (with that of Bm visibly by correction) may be seen as a ⊗ from **C**, not a correction from a hypothetical superior lost **B** source. **214 (B 550)** *come auht* **C**: adopted also for **B** as the needed key-stave presumed lost in β, perhaps through failure to grasp the line's rhythmic structure (so that *Right* not *clerkes* was taken as first lift) together with unconscious influence from the common phrase *er longe*. **C** revises the syntax to give this and the following line a new subject (*coueitise*), a change better in keeping with the tone of *dampne* (**B**'s *þei* has as its referent 'Reason and rightful doom'). **215 (B 551)** *depose youre pride* **B**: verb-object ↔ (here to prose order, following **C**'s lightly

revised b-half phrase) provides the required key-stave. **218 (B 554)** *lese...euere* **B**: reconstructed on the basis of **C** to provide the required key-stave lost in β and possibly Bx through inversion of adverbial and verb-phrases. **228** *ȝe*: the reading of x^2, to which Y will have varied coincidentally, unless it alone preserves x^1. Either *ȝe* or *þe* could be a visual error for the other, but on grounds of sense *ȝe* is harder and so likelier to be original. The unexpected shift from one addressee (*lordes* 227) to another (*kynges* 228), though awkward, is not much more so than that from the same addressed subject to a new verb-subject making the *kings* potential beneficiaries of an action by the baronage. The sg. form *kynge* in ID, though pointed, cannot be original, as reference must be to kings generally (cf. *Alle londes* 237) or at the least to the English and French monarchs, not the King of England alone. **230** The added **C** line is of ambiguous metrical structure, either vocalic Type Ib with a mute key-stave *and* 'supplemented' by the fourth 'enriched' stave (*Intro.* IV § 44) or more naturally as Type IIIc with alternate staves on |ð| and vowels, the first generated by elision of *The* and *heuedes*. Standard scansion is excluded because *vnder hem* fails to provide a feminine ending (*ben* may be a Cx error for *aren*). To read *hem* for *tho* would make for smoother metre, but is stylistically clumsier. **231 (B 565)** *charite*: undoubtedly an improvement in style and metre; but the Bx reading with a four-syllable prelude dip is not necessarily scribal, since the rhythmic pattern, seen in 550 or 560 above, is a common one. **239** scans either as a vocalic Type Ie with mute key-stave and counterpoint or, preferably, on |m| with two lifts in *Mácométh*. **240** *quyete* x^2: preferred on grounds of sense, since acknowledging Mahomet's political astuteness (*gyle* 242), not ascribing Trajan-like qualities of justice to him. **247** *descendet* **x**: the present (possibly denoted by the *-et* ending) gives better sense, the reference being not to the single event of Pentecost but to the permanent offer of divine grace in response to devout prayer (specifically in the consecration at Mass). **252–82 (B 500–31)** See Vol I pp. 602–05 for the text and apparatus of the **B** passage and parallel text of the relevant **C** lines. **254 (B 502)** *turne* **p**: present in the **B** line under revision and essential for sense and metre, but lost from x^1 and t possibly through visual attraction of *sho*lde → *ho*so. **256 (B 504)** *grete holy God* **B**: reconstructed in the light of revised **C** as the probable form of **B**, that of Bx being not securely determinable. The α reading is metrically acceptable but would come very abruptly after 503, the sense of which it leaves incomplete (F's & is an obvious attempt to smooth the transition). On comparison with **C**, *On...greden* suggests the corruption of a hypothetical form **On a god þe grete* in α's immediate exemplar. In β *holy grete* may owe its metrical awkwardness to ↔ of the two epithets through alliterative attraction of *grete* to *god*; the same error occurs in C-N^2, which is probably by

⊗ from a *B-β* source (see *Intro.* III *C* § 40). In the Cx tradition, the underlying *x¹* reading may have been *grete god* as in YD²u (so *R–K*); but the form of X's *grethe* and t's added *of heuene* suggest a missing word between the first epithet and the noun, either *heuene* (in the possessive) or *hye*. The latter is preferred in the light of *B-β* and on the grounds of its contextual suitability (cf. *hy* 247, 262). **258 (B 506)** *lyueth* **C**: preferable also as the original for **B** (Bx < L = β, + α). The source γ (to which M varies, as frequently elsewhere) will have substituted *leue* through attempting to make explicit the elliptical construction whereby *leue* is 'understood' in the b-half as 'borrowed' from the actual verb of the a-half. The latter could have had the spelling-form *leue* (see MED s.v. *liven* v (1)); but annominative chime (Schmidt 1987:113–17) rather than exact homophony may have been intended. (One *C*-ms, Ch, has *leueþ,* adopted by *R–K* with the sense 'believe'). **264 (B 512)** *by sad resoen* **C**: adopted also for **B** as providing a stronger and more characteristic sense than the reading *þat by* for *by* α (which does not necessarily represent Bx here). The 'firm / serious ground *or* argument' in question is the literal *ensaumple* of Christ's acts of 'mercy and grace' [his healing miracles]. The *resoen* here is thus metaphorical (cf. MED s.v. *resoun* n. (2) 5(c)), whereas in α's reading it must signify 'reason' (ibid. s.v. 1a(a)). The relevance of this to the conversion of the Moslems could have prompted the variant; but 268 // and 270 // indicate that **L** has in mind 'suffering unto death' as the spiritual condition of both healing-miracles and the 'miracle' of conversion (on the linking of *ensaumple* with Christ's power, mercy and suffering see 1.167–69 //). **268 (B 516)** *bissh(e)inede x¹?α*: adopted as lexically harder, though its precise meaning in context is somewhat uncertain (*R–K* read *bisshemede* in XYI, but U has the unambiguous form *bishined* and D *bescyned*). MED has *bishinen* with only the strong preterite in all senses, of which the aptest is 2(b) 'enlighten' or 2(c) 'make illustrious' (with a metaphorical sense as of 'illuminating' a manuscript, or 'causing something to shine'); so **L** must here be using an otherwise uninstanced weak preterite. Alternatively, the word intended is **bisigned*, a (completely unrecorded) ?intensive form of *signen* 'to mark with a sign' (the actual ⇒ by F for the presumed α reading in R). Whatever the exact form of the lexeme, its extreme rarity caused difficulty. But *bisshopid x²* 'confirmed' has small claim to originality; for though also uncommon, it can hardly have generated *bissheinede* and is best judged a response to the implications of *metropolitanus* (267) as a title of Christ. The 'baptismal' significance of Christ's death on the cross was a familiar notion (see 21.325), whereas confirmation was associated with Pentecost (21.226–28 and see *Commentary*). **271 (B 519)** *enfourme*: clearly the right reading on grounds of sense (MED s.v. *enfourmen* v. 4 'teach or spread' [the Gospel]). The variant *enferme,* perhaps no

more than orthographic, might have been unconsciously induced by the contextual references to bishops (as, clearly, were *conferme* and D²B-F *ferme*). **275 (B 523)** The revised **C** line scans, like 276, on vowels, but as a Type IIIa. Four *C*-mss TVZN² severally read *kirke* for *churche*, which certainly provides effective contrast with the vocalic stress-pattern of 276. *R–K*'s adoption of this normalisation is at odds with their acceptance of Type III in 273, where the caesura is unlikely to come after *mony* and simple ↔ of the half-lines would yield a Type Ia line. **279 (B 528)** The variant *That* β for *And nat* **C**B-α is an attempt to achieve a juncture between 509 and 528 by borrowing the relative particle from the beginning of 509 and turning 528 into a second relative clause by reading *that* for the (now meaningless) *And nauȝt*. The sense of the **BC** line is elliptical: 'Thomas is an example to all bishops, and especially to titular bishops *in partibus,* [of martyrdom], not of wandering about England'. See further *Intro.* III *B* § 53 for fuller discussion. **B 572b–75a (285–86)** are attested by α and will have been lost from β by eyeskip (*goostly foode* (1) → (2)) but are clearly authentic on grounds of sense and metre (the 'patched' β line will scan but is defective in sense). **285 (B 572)** *follen*: 'baptise' (MED s.v. *fulwen* v.) rather than 'fill' (MED s.v. *fullen* v. (1)(b)), which is not appropriate here and will have been suggested by preceding *Feden.* The sense is not particularly apt, since baptism was specifically the parish priest's duty, and *fermen* 'confirm' might have been more exact. **286** On the order in M, see note on 186 above. **292** scans as Type Ia with a five-syllable prelude dip. **293 (B 578)** The **C** line, unless it has lost a |k| stave (whether an adverb **ek* or a first object before *haen* such as *clerkes* as in // B 580), must scan with a liaisonal stave on *Ac_we,* an unusual example of revision of a Type Ia to a Type IIa. *R–K*'s conjecture *crede* for *lawe* (p. 171) anticipates *bileue* 294, obscuring the specific meaning (*lawe = moral* teaching).

    B 583–611 583 is a 'licensed' macaronic with only one |p| stave in the a-half, the whole scanning *bba / ax,* unless it is a Type II with |dȝ| staves on *-gé* and on *Iéwen.* **584 (C 296)** is here taken to have *Messie* as key-stave (the revised line is a standard Type I). An alternative scansion on |t| would allow the α variant *it hem*; but in the light of **C** it seems better on balance to see |m| as the stave-sound. **604 (C 313)** *Grekes*: here taken as a reference to (some at least) of the pre-Christian Greeks, not to the Greek Orthodox, who were of course Christians as well as monotheists (MED s.v. *Grek* n. 1(a), not 1(c)). In spite of the revised **C** line's mentioning Jews and not Greeks, the WHm variant *Iewes* is likely not to be original but to have come in by visual error from 606, where *Sarȝens* also appears in the a-half as in 604. Possibly this happened coincidentally in WHm, and the w-group reading was correct as in Cr. **611 (C 320)** *rendren*: in the light of **C** the harder reading, preserved in **L** alone, and likelier to be original in **B**. Unusually α here reads with γM and, unless this is a reading of Bx which L has corrected by collation with **C**, is to be seen as a coincidental error. The mistake could have resulted from misconstruing the nasal suspension through failure to identify the correct lexeme. The precise sense is not certain here and the word's virtual restriction to **L** before 1400 suggests that it was found difficult. Thus, although the association with *recorden* 'remember' seems to favour the sense 'recite, repeat' (MED s.v. *rendren* (c)), there is room for doubt. To illustrate the only other sense of this verb acknowledged by MED 'translate' (s.v. (d)), the sole example cited is A 9.82 (= B 8.90, C 10.88), where the context suggests rather 'read aloud and expound' than 'translate'. Possibly, therefore, *rendren* here too means 'explain the meaning of', since what is in question is the progressive catechesis of adults with already-formed religious beliefs, not the instruction of infants learning by rote.

Passus XVIII (B XVI)

RUBRICS The Cx tradition (if accurately preserved in **x**) seems to make XVIII the *first* passus of *Dobet*, and XVII implicitly its Prologue. This fits with the *B-β* reading and points to the latter as representing Bx. Where *C-**p***'s numbering is one ahead, *B-**R**'s is one behind and *B-**F**'s completely anomalous.

25 (B 24) scans as a Type Ie line on |δ| and |θ| with mute key-stave *that* or as Type Ic with original **quath_he* for *quod he* to give a liaisonal stave on |θ|. This is not very satisfactory and it may be that Cx has substituted the commoner *bereth* for *shuyueth* to avoid too close repetition of 20.

B 20–8 20 *loue-dreem*: preferred on grounds of contextual meaning as well as metre, notwithstanding the argument for *lone* in *Sch*[1] and Schmidt 1986:29–30. The dream is produced by the *pure ioye* of hearing a beloved name, and the first-element stress of the compound phrase (*lóue-drèem*) would not be idiomatically possible with the reading *lone*. For a similar error see *allone* β for *and loue* αC at C 11.169 // B 11.8. **25** *witen* β: preferred as providing characteristic wordplay on *wite*. For although the α line could scan as Type IIa with *wiltow* as a full stave and *kepe* appears in revised C 28b, *kepen* is likely to be a ⇒ for this lexically less familiar verb, which is found also at B 7.35, A 10.67 (see OED s.v. *Wite* v. 2 'keep (safe)', MED s.v. *witien* v.(1) 'protect'). **27–8 (C 31–2)** *B*-α has lost two half-lines 27b, 28a through homoteleuton (*wynd...wynd*) at the line's mid-point. L's conditional is preferred in the light of **C** as likely to preserve β, M having varied to the γ reading.

37 (B 33) scans as Type Ia on |s| (|ʃ| and |s| in **C**) with a stress in *norisc(h)éth* seemingly wrenched from the root

syllable to the inflexional morpheme. The identical form of the line in both versions argues against *K–D*'s conjectural emendation of the key-stave *som* to *anoþer*. The metrical difficulty it posed is registered in the attempts to regularise by *C-G*'s and *B-F*'s adding *nyce* respectively before *wordes* and in place of *tyme*. **50 (B 50–1)** **C** unusually revises a Type Ia line to an extended Type IIIa scanning on |δ| / |θ|, possibly with counterpoint on |p|. *R–K* emend *palle* to *falle* (understood here as a scribal attempt to normalise the metre); but the likelihood of this verb's having been replaced in Cx (or in x^1, **p**) by the lexically harder *palle* (the assured reading of **B**) is remote. *thridde*: the right reading in both **B** and **C** (each shoring up the other), *B-M*'s source *m* evidently having erred by ⊗ from a γ ms. **55** *fayre* **x**: preferred to **p**, whose *wonder* may have been prompted by *ferly* 56. **60** *sonnere*: preferable on grounds of sense, with *somme* an easy visual error partly induced by its preceding occurrences in the a-half. The reading is clearly that of x^2 (> **pt**) and N^2 would seem to have been collated with a **p**-type source, as may D. It is not evident whether Y was too, or is a happy scribal correction, or an accurate independent reflex of y, as seems possible in the light of 75. The original of <XIP²D²> could have erred mechanically and U (< u) coincidentally. **63** *o*: 'one and the same [degree of]'; preferable on grounds of superior sense and presumably lost from several mss through haplography after *of*. **64** *sonnore*: though rejected as obscuring the wordplay on *sonne*, the *sannere* of XY is an authentic historical spelling-form derived from OE *sana* (see MED s.v. *sane* adv.), is instanced at Z 7.165, and could be original. **B 66** scans as Type IIIa on |s| and (*pace K–D Sch*[1]) no emendation is required. **70** *apples of o kynde*: 'fruit of one species'; the alternative without *o* preferred by *R–K* gives the sense 'natural fruit', which is acceptable, but does not repeat 62 so closely. **L**'s point is that whether the species is that of apples or of humankind, there is variation and difference, though one common species-nature. **75** *hete* x^2: judged original on grounds of sense and metre. Of the five x^1 variants, only the Ø-reading preserved in N^2 (and coincidentally in the **p** copy W) could have generated the others and thus be the group-original. The unrelated *þei* and *sonne* point to a Ø-form in u, as *thre* does to Ø in y, since it seems suggested by the threefold category specified in 74. Y's variant indicates independent descent from y, the group <XIP²D²> here sharing a disjunctive reading. It would appear likely, therefore, that x^1 read **These haen þe [ ] of þe holi goest* and that two mss of this family (Y and D) have omitted *þe* (1) in smoothing after insertion of their respective conjecture (U's *sonne*, being a noun, does not require such smoothing). The reading at 75 is one of the most decisive indicators of two major sub-divisions in the Cx tradition (x^1 and x^2), of a two-fold division in x^1 (y and u), and of a possible sub-division within y into < XIP²D² > and Y. **83** The ampersand here is expanded as *and* following DPAVMG in order to treat the line as a double macaronic (like 16.202) and better integrate it with the structure of the whole sentence. **94** For the preferred order in the b-half, cf. 123b. **B 71 (C 97)** The Bx line (*pace K–D Sch¹*) scans as a T-type with wrenched stress on -*hóde* giving the first vocalic a-stave, *and* as a mute key-stave, and the b-staves on *r*. **101** The a-half is treated by *R–K* as a parenthetical interjection; but this seems forced and is unparalleled in **L**'s usage, while the thought in 101b–03a is not such as to be unattributable to Will. **102** The epithet *faire* **p** is to be rejected as a scribal insertion for added emphasis (cf. *wonder* **p** at 55) which sits uneasily with *inparfit* 103. **B 78** Duggan (1990:180) argues for transposing verbal and adverbial phrases in the b-verse on metrical grounds; but though inversion to prose order is common enough in the Bx tradition, emendation is not strictly necessary, since the suffix -*liche* is disyllabic here (see note on 1.177 above). Nor does occurrence of monosyllabic terminal -*ly* at 9.329 // AB (a core-line) count decisively against this, since **L** could have used variant forms of the suffix at his convenience. **120–21 (B 87–8)** The C line as here punctuated requires *hit aftur* 'threw' (MED s.v. *hitten* v. 2(b), illustrated only from **L**) to have an understood object *it* (= *shoriare* 119). But possibly *fley* 121 is a Ø-relative clause and *Filius* the object of this verb, like *Filius* in // B 88. **126 (B 92)** *iustice(s)*: in each case what seems to be the archetypal form is given, since either may be intended; if *iustice* 'justice' (MED s.v. *justice* n. 1), then the pun is on 'judge' (ibid., 5(a)), if *iustices*, then it is on 'justice'. A second pun on *sone / sonne* also seems clearly intended (see *Commentary* further). **128** *That* 'at which time, when', corresponding to *And þanne* **B**. *R–K* place a full stop after *rype* and treat *That* as a demonstrative adjective, but the usage seems forced. **130 (B 96)** Understood in each case is an antecedent verb, hence 'to determine [who / which one]'; for a similar construction cf. 3.152 //. *fonge* **B** 'capture' (MED s.v. *fongen* v. 3): preferred on grounds of sense and closeness to revised **C**, though perhaps a felicitous correction. Either Bx read *fonde* 'try (for), attempt' (MED s.v. v. 8(a)) or else the reading of YCBLR is a ⇒ for Bx *fonge* 'undertake', 'endeavour' (MED s.v. 8), which overlaps semantically with *fonde*. The fittest meaning here however is 'get hold of' (= *fecche* C), since both Christ and Satan are to *try* for the fruit but only one will win it. **139 (B 103)** *hy*: the reading of x^2 and presumably also of x^1 (if Y = y and U = u). It is preferred on grounds of sense, 'the fullness of time' (MED s.v. *heigh* 6(b)) translating the Latin of the a-half (and cf. *plener* in // B 103). Therefore *by* is to be taken as a visual error, which D coincidentally shares with the exclusive ancestor of <XIP²D²> (though I's reading is unknown, owing to the loss of a leaf).

B 110–50 110 (C 143) In spite of earlier doubts (*K–D, Sch¹*), 110 can now be accepted as scanning cognatively, with the **C** line offering a complete revision of the b-half. There are no real grounds for questioning 108–09, which employ a type of repetition-with-variation (*sike and synfulle*) well instanced elsewhere in **L**. **110a (C 142a)** Choice between α *male habentibus* (Vg and *VL*) and β *infirmis* (*apud* Ambrose, *Apologia*) is evenly divided. But *sanis* (Vg *valentibus*) is common to *VL* and Ambrose (Alf*Q*). **115 (C 146)** *as*: revised to *ar* in the direction of greater fidelity to the Vg source Jn 11: 35 (though the phrasing is that of Mt 26: 37). Though possibly the result of miscopying *r* as *s* (*K–DSch¹*), Bx *as* could as easily have been an authorial misrecollection of the Biblical sequence, so emendation is not justified. The a-half shows further revision in *miracle*, and the preceding and following lines are both changed. **121 (C 152)** scans either as Type IIIa on *ch* or cognatively as Type Ia on the related unvoiced and voiced sounds |tʃ| and |dʒ|; emendation in either case is otiose. On grounds of sense *iesus* must be correct and β a misreading of the exemplar's Latin abbreviation *ihc* or *i ch* [= *iesus christus*]. **125 (C 154)** The numerically indefinite *fisshes* of **B** is revised to the literally inaccurate *fyue fisches and loues*. Amongst the **B** sources, w has unnecessarily altered *fisshes* to *two fisshes*, M following doubtless by collation with its w-type source and F independently changing α. But **L** may have recalled that the feedings of the Five and the Four Thousand gave different quantities for the fishes (two in Mt 14: 17 // Mk / Lk/ Jn, 'a few' in Mt 15: 34). **136** *arne*: to be securely adopted on the basis of sense and the showing of **C** as the strong preterite of the SWM form *ernen*, on all grounds likely to be **L**'s authentic usage. The R variant is an ambiguous syllabicised reflex that was probably the reading of Bx (as it is of *C*-YI) and generated the β preterite of a supposed verb *to be*, with F coincidentally following the same substitution-process. **140** scans on cognative staves (|θ| |f| / |ð|), the last of them mute. Either *cene* or *maundee* could be original, the latter giving a T-type line. But on balance it would seem preferable to judge *maundee* a scribal ⇒ aimed at avoiding repetition of *cene* in *soper* 141; for one co-polyseme of *maunde* (MED s.v. n. 2 (d)) is the washing of hands and feet (Christ's *mandatum* 'command' of love), and that may have been understood by the scribe. **142** *som* 'a certain one' (MED s.v. *som* pron. 1 sg. (a)), for which α has the spelling-form that normally represents the pl. and β ⇒ of a non-alliterating but unambiguous synonym. Given that the pl. sense is contextually excluded, *som* sg. is to be judged as the harder and therefore the likelier original reading. **150** scans as a Type IIIa line with the four-syllable prelude-dip by no means unusual in lines of all types (cf. e.g. B 79). Although original **B** could have read **Iudas þe Iew*, echoing B 10.128 still more closely than does Bx, no emendation is required, since the full staves are evidently the two proper names. *K–D*'s conjecture *pus*] *so* is otiose and weakens the line by locating all three staves in non-lexical at the expense of semantically more important words (for *pus* functioning with full semantic weight, cf. 160, where it is a full stave in key-position).

169 (B 151) *pat ribaud; he* ? **p**: to be preferred to the pl. on grounds of sense, since it is Judas who is in question, and the reference of the identical form in **B** is not in doubt. The mss suggest, however, that the correction may have been made in *p¹*, with D² agreeing coincidentally and D possibly by correction from a **p** source. In the absence of K it remains uncertain whether *p²* had the pl. noun, N's *pys* being potentially pl. though the noun is *rybaude* sg. The error could be due to retrospective smoothing of the sg. noun and demonstrative after earlier misconstruction of **a zede* as plural, while the noun in the exemplar could have had a number-ambiguous spelling **ribau(du)s*. But whether *p¹* here = **p** ($< x^2$) or shows intelligent correction, it is intrinsically preferable as representing the probable original of (here unrevised) C. **175** *vsen* 'practise': contextually more appropriate than *vysen* 'devise' (so X); either could be a visual error for the other, or the latter a spelling-variant of the former, with *y* a graphemic indicator of length. **176 (B 158)** *and at*: reconstructed for Bx after **C** from the split variants *and* α, *at* β, with a liaisonal stave (possibly mute) in *at_youre*.

B 161 *his name*: because he is known as 'Jesus' during the early stages of the Passion, becoming 'Christ' only at the crucifixion. Since the importance of the *name* of Jesus is later brought out in Will's remonstrance to Conscience at B XIX (esp. 15–25) // C, it is decidedly not a 'pointless homœograph [for **ynome*]' (*K–D* p. 185). F's variant seems an obvious ⇒ (unconsciously induced by preceding *taken*) for an exemplar misreading *y nome* of α **ys nome*, whereas βR (= Bx) make an important point about *Iesus*, who receives the further name *Crist* at 164. But if a past participle form *ynome* were read, the half-line *would* ('pointlessly') repeat 160b. The notion plainly underlying *K–D*'s reconstruction of F's exemplar reading, that it is taken from a postulated superior lost **B** ms, finds scant support from argument of this order.

177 (B 159) *pays; pees*: apparently no more than spelling variants (MED s.v. *pes* n.), as the ↔ by WCr etc suggests (the less common *pays* form is found elsewhere only at Z 4.52). Although the different graphs need not denote distinct senses of the same lexeme, such senses may well be intimated, e.g. 4 (a) 'freedom from molestation' and 5 (b) 'cessation of hostilities' ('alone'; 'in peace' [*Sk*]). After this q has a line: *Sinite eos abire etcetera* (= Jn 18:8). **181 (B 169)** *Estwárd*: requiring wrenched stress to provide the first stave; decisive support for its correctness appears in the key-stave of B 228 // below (*afterwárd*).

202 (B 192) Both archetypal lines have the same defective metrical pattern *aa / xa*. Emendation must therefore be tentative (*K–D* emend Bx, *R–K* leave Cx unmetrical), but scribal inversion to prose order may be discerned in each case. The sense of Cx *se* will correspond closely to *knowe* Bx if the latter is taken as 'know by experience' (MED s.v. *knouen* v. 4(a)), signifying that God (*potencia*) acquires *experiential* 'knowledge' of his power (as light / life) by exercising / manifesting it through an intermediary (*sapiencia*). This reading is theoretically possible but theologically tortuous. A more lucid interpretation of *knowe* in **B** would be as 'make known, reveal, show' (MED s.v. 7(a)), which is more appropriate to God's self-disclosure through Christ. In that case the **C** revision, which alters only the verb, might be expected to read not *se* but *shewe*, which is here conjectured as the original (perhaps ambiguously spelled **sewen*) for which Cx is presumed to have read **suen* (see for the spelling forms MED s.v. *sen* v. (1) and *sheuen* v. (1)). The source of error in Cx's exemplar could have been auditory as much as visual, since **L** may have sounded *s* as |ʃ| before front vowels (for an earlier example see on 1.39 // ZBC). But an equally important contributory factor might have been the semantic overlap between the two verbs (see MED s.v. *scheuen* 1(a) 'see'). The sense of *shewe* here will be 7(a) 'make known' or 9 (a) 'disclose, reveal', both close to the meaning of *knowe* preferred for **B**. **203 (B 193)** *soffreth hem bope*: the α reading confirmed by Cx as likely to be that of Bx, though the construction is idiosyncratic and the sense consequently difficult. Impersonal uses of *suffren* are not recorded in MED, which does not cite this example. Yet *hem bope* must be necessarily the subject of the verb, despite its object case, since *what* as subject yields no ascertainable meaning. Presumably, therefore, *hem* registers the continuing force of the verb *shewe* in 202 = B 192 *knowe* and is thus accusative, while logically it functions as a nominative. The sense of 202–03 (B 192–93) might be rendered tentatively: 'power, and a means / intermediary to manifest his own power and that of / proceeding from his agent, and what they both undergo / experience'. Although the unexpected grammatical form troubled neither archetypal scribe, *B*-β has regularised by making the verb-subject nominative, though with no substantive change in the meaning postulated here. **208–10 (B 198–201)** The punctuation adopted for these lines of somewhat strained analogical thinking assumes that **L** has in mind the notion of Christ as the Church's divine bridegroom, not her divine father. The *children of charite* of 207 (B 197) are 'fathered' upon the Church (their mother) by Christ. In B 199 a full stop after *Chirche* (*SkK–D*) would grammatically require *Crist, Cristendom and alle Cristene* to have the complement *Holy Chirche* or else, if *Holy Chirche* forms an integral phrase with *alle Cristene*, the (anticipatory) complement *children*; but neither reading gives satisfactory sense. In the light of // **C** 210, which replaces B 200 with B 210, the three subjects of B 199 (with *alle Cristene Holy Chirche* the third of them) are therefore better read with 200–01 and a verb *ben* understood before *In menynge þat*, the sense of which phrase then corresponds exactly to **C**'s *Bitokeneth*. The meaning is that the triad 'Christ', 'Christianity' and 'the [whole community of] Christians constituting the Church' signify [by their unity as Christ's mystical body] that man must believe in God as One who is also Three. If this reading is correct, *alle* C-**x**B-α is to be preferred against Ø in C-p**B**-β. The analogy, which is now theologically coherent, would gain in clarity if B 201 were a Ø-relative clause qualifying God (200): 'believe in one God who...revealed himself as a trinity', so initial *And* 201 may be a Bx error visually induced by *And* 202 or intruded in response to the compressed grammar of 201. This line is also not free of lexical difficulty, since the impersonal *louede* as a doublet of *lykede* is an idiosyncratic use (not illustrated in MED but recurring at B 17.140 below) with the second verb depending on the force of the familiar *hym lykede*. However, *K–D*'s desperate insertion of *he* before *louede*, making the line scan vocalically on three pronouns (or two and a preposition), is metrically and stylistically too much at odds with the sense to contend as a possible original. The conjectured stave-word **leodes*, used earlier at 181, has contextually just the required sense to have invited Bx ⇒ of a non-alliterating synonym in key-position (MED s.v. *led(e* n. (2) 'person'). However, even in the emended form of B 199–201 here given, the analogy suffers some loss of focus through being annexed to the earlier one in 198, where the Apostles are joined by two OT categories of 'children of charity' (patriarchs and prophets) who must be regarded as 'children of the *Church*' by retrospective adoption. This idea, theologically transparent in itself, was evidently judged important enough to be retained in C. The revision's clearer syntax, making the nouns of C 209 unambiguously the grammatical subject of *Bitokeneth* 210, was recognised by *Sk*, who nevertheless ignored its bearing on the punctuation of B 199 in his parallel-text. In consequence, where *K–D*'s line 201 scans poorly, *Sk*'s makes no sense. **215 (B 202)** The Bx line scans on |m| as an extended Type IIIa with counterpoint on |s| (*abb / ab*), so *K–D*'s emendation of the b-half is gratuitous. **B 213** *He*: the archetypal and probably original reading, wF severally correcting to a grammatically correct accusative after a transitive verb. But the phrase reads something like a free-standing title. **228–29** The sense is satisfactory, so that *R–K*'s re-division after *was* (following W) and emendation of *when* to *whom* seems unusually arbitrary. **229** *wye* ?*x²*: obviously right on grounds of sense, with *wey* a (possibly archetypal) spelling variant best avoided here since the potential

local ambiguity (with 'way') cannot be intended. For a closely similar case, cf. on B 9.113. **233–34** *Is and ay were*: the sg. *Is* relates solely to the Spirit in his procession from Father and Son (*of hem bothe is* translating B 223a); *were*, *worþ* (here pl.) refer elliptically to all three persons, with *þei* to be understood as subject. The t variant makes *was* and *worþ* appear to predicate eternity of the Spirit only. *and worþ withouten ende*: the final phrase echoing the doxology, and clearly necessary to provide the b-half of line 233, but apparently lost in *x¹* by assimilation of *worþ* to *were* in the a-half, and loss of *withouten ende* by homœoteleuton (*bote o mank*ynde). In theory, the *x¹* form of these lines would be metrically acceptable with division after *spirit*; but the notion of 'eternity' implied in *Is* and *were* feels incomplete without *worþ*. **236 (B 223)** The **C** line scans as Type Ia on |s|: *Só is Gòd Godes Sóne in thre persónes the Trinite.* The first word is the adverb (MED s.v. 1(a)), not the conjunction (ibid. 17), the subject of the verb being *Sone*, and the key-stave coming in the second syllable of *persónes,* which had shifting stress (cf. B 16.185n, Chaucer *CT* III 1161, Gower *CA* I 840, and contrast 234). *R–K*'s gratuitous emendation *God and godes sone is* yields strained sense, whereas Cx clearly gives two separate existential statements, one about the Son and the other about the Trinity. **242** scans cognatively as Type IIa (|g| |k| |g|) with a 'supplemental' |g| stave in position five (see *Intro.* IV § 44). *R–K*'s ↔ of *cam...thre* and *riȝt...gate* gives an unacceptable masculine ending or necessitates de-stressing the important word *thre.* **244 (B 228)** *her*: supported by **B** as also the probable original in **C**. The form *hes* (over an erasure in X, *he* in I) appears an attempt in y to harmonise the number of the possessive with sg. *hym* in 243, *he* in 245–46, whereas *they* 244b favours the pl. in this line at least, as in **B**, as referring to the 'angels' severally. **247 (B 230)** *when tyme cometh* **x**: preferred to **p**'s *what tyme,* since it alludes to an expected future meeting (to be achieved in the 'Harrowing' scene). It is not a mere memorial of the covenant as a past event, for Abraham is confident that he can point to his fidelity as grounds for his release from hell. The preterite verb-variant *mette* pu**H²** (adopted by *SkR–K*) clarifies the sense while compounding the error. **248 (B 231)** The **B** line scans as Type Ia with a liaisonal stave in *if_Í louede.* **249–50 (B 232–33)** The six-syllable prelude-dip in 249 is presumably justified because of the particular contrastive stress required on 'hým' (1) with referent 'Isaac', and 'hým' (2), with 'God'. It is possible that this pattern is being repeated in 250 (with a four-syllable prelude dip), although in that line *I* could equally well be the first lift.

B 246–73 246 *leneden*: on grounds of sense the best resolution of a word palaeographically and contextually ambiguous. 'Believed' goes well enough with Abraham the 'father of faith', but 'leaned' better suits the *foot of feiþ* metaphor of 245. **264 (C 281)** appears genuine on intrinsic grounds and the showing of near-identical **C**. Loss from α here will have been by the 'omission of [an] intervening syntactical unit through grammatical attraction between *may...no buyrn...brynge us* 262, 263 and *Til* 265' (*K–D* p. 68). **287–90 (B 270–73)** The spurious lines in α (printed on p. 751) bear little relation in sense to those of β, the authenticity of which is guaranteed by their intrinsic quality and their presence in (virtually unrevised) **C**. *Allas* and *longe* in α 270 indicate that its exemplar was damaged at this point and patched by the α scribe with doggerel prompted by the verbs of motion (*come, wolde*) in 274–75.

Passus XIX (B XVII)

RUBRIC Agreement of *B*-β with the rubric of *C*-**x** against *C*-**p** may point to the form of the heading in Bx. R is one behind in numbering the Passus and has no section-heading; F, having been previously three passūs out, here gives up the ghost.

8 *R–K* follow G to read *croes* in the a-half and adopt *crist* **B** for Cx *croes* in the b-half. But this looks like a case of revision, with *hym* rather than *seel* becoming the antecedent of the relative's complement. Thus *cristendom* and *croes* are now the joint subject of *hange*, which acquires a semi-figurative sense for the first of these subjects. **10 (B 8)** The extra line that follows in α, whether in its truncated R form or as expanded to a Type Ia line in F (and so adopted by *K–D*), is to be rejected on the evidence of **C**, which shows no trace of it, and on grounds of intrinsic want of content, as patently scribal patching after loss of 7b through eyeskip from *so* to *soþe*. **13** *on*: in the light of **B** the correct preposition (against *in* and redundant *and*). **15 (B 13)** *gome*: the ON-derived form with palatal stop (MED s.v. *gome* n. (4)) is preferred to that with the palatal spirant as providing the *cauda* of a T-type line. **22 (B 19)** Both lines could be of Type IIIa or, with wrenched stress on *wommén* to facilitate homophonic wordplay on *men...meny* (cf. *somme* at 33), of Type Ia. **24** *quod Fayth*: unnecessary, and perhaps come in by anticipation of 26 (GN[2] omit); but such repetition is found. **26 (B 23)** is revised, somewhat unusually, from a Type Ia to a Type IIIa. Possibly Cx *quod* is for *saide* or *mo* a ⇒ for *biside*; but emendation here cannot be justified. **27** *ȝow*: the clear reading of **B** and **C**, giving good sense; so *R–K*'s alteration to *hem* is indefensible. **28 (B 25)** *lich*: conjectured as the difficult original for which Cx's synonym is a non-alliterating ⇒ (see MED s.v. *lich* n.). Although t's *lif* is identical with **B** and could represent *x²*, it is not difficult enough to have invited ⇒ of *body*, though this is recorded as one of its meanings (MED s.v. *lif* n.7). **L** is therefore presumed to have recognised the semantic overlap between the dominant sense of *lif* 'animate existence; animating principle, soul' (MED s.v. *lif*. n.1a (a)

and (b)) and that of *soule* (= *anima*) and made explicit the benefits of faith that extend to man's corporeal as well as his spiritual nature. In **B** *lif* and *soule* are linked by *and* (as in t), allowing equivalence rather than difference, in *C*-*x¹***p** by *or*, which requires a contrast. In the light of these considerations *lich* is recommended as the substantive reading in the b-half which, like the a-half, appears revised in detail. **34 (B 31)** The identical **C** line confirms β as the form of Bx and this as original and of Type IIIa. *K–D*'s gratuitous emendation *now*] *þanne* is sensibly avoided by *R–K*. **35 (B 32)** The sound of the key-stave is |s| and while the **x** form can be scanned as Type IIa by reading *súfficéde*, *x²*'s *so* is preferable on grounds of sense (cf. B 36). But possibly Cx read *so to* (the actual reading of MW), of which *so* and *to* could be split variants, *so* then being mute. **36 (B 33)** The Cx line, of Type IIIa, scans awkwardly with a four-syllable prelude and an abrupt caesura after *hath*, and *speketh* has been lost by haplography after *Spes*, an omission all the easier if **C** had a Ø subject of the verb (thereby accounting for the variants *that* prn, *and* conj.). But the metrical weakness is not enough to warrant emendation.

B 37–47 These eleven β lines appear authentic on intrinsic grounds and the evidence of **C**'s (abbreviated) revision (cf. esp. C 43–7). Their omission from α is plausibly ascribed by *K–D* to resumption at the wrong point in the exemplar under inducement from repeated names and phrases in the sequence from 26–46 (*Abraham, thre... persones, lawe, Spes, beleeue and louye / louye and lene*), and eyeskip from *gome þat gooþ...heele* 37 to *Go...God helpe* 46 may have contributed. It is conceivable that the α version of **B** ran from 36 to 48 without break and that 37–47 are an addition in a second state of the text. But the transition would be very abrupt, and Will's objection to *Spes* in 31–6 insufficiently developed, as it lacks the two important points made in 40–1 and 43. **38** *teeþ*: tentatively conjectured as the lexically difficult stave-word for which the Bx ⇒ is a non-alliterating synonym caught up from 37. In principle, *Than he þat gooþ with* could form a dip before the heavily stressed *two*, but the Bx a-half is uncharacteristically flat in its repetition of 37a, and full stress on the grammatical word *to* in a Type III key-stave would be unparalleled. In the reading as emended, the key-stave *to* is now clearly mute, with *sighte* a blank stave carrying stress. If *sighte* were taken as key-stave, an alternative for the a-half might be *steppeþ*; but this would not seem difficult enough to invite ⇒, *gooþ* would not be an exact synonym, and the stress would be thrown off the semantically crucial *two*. On the conjectured verb, which is mainly SW, SWM or WM in distribution and well-illustrated from alliterative poetry, see MED s.v. *ten* v. (1), 1(a).

52 (B 52) *iaced* **C**: instanced only here (MED s.v. *jacen* v. 'hurry, rush') and of unknown etymology. If Skeat is right to link it with *jounce* 'bounce or jolt along', it may be a blend of the latter and the rare but attested *chacen* of **B**, 'a (partially) coined word, to make the alliteration more exact' (*Sk* IV:386). Given its presumed difficulty, *iaced* as the hypothetical **B** original could have invited ⇒ of the synonym *chaced* in Bx. But *iaced* did not cause wide difficulty to the C-Text scribes (U has *hased*, W *raked*), the line has detailed revision in both halves, *chacen* is apt in sense (see MED s.v. 5 (a) 'hurry') and cognative |tʃ| / |dʒ| alliteration in **B** may be safely accepted. *K–D*'s emendation of Bx to *iaced* is thus unwarranted (for similar revision of an originally cognative stave, cf. 20.48 B 18.48n). **54** *wilde wildernesse*: a collocation found earlier both at 10.62 (with // **B**) and at B 15.459. The Athlone editors gratuitously emend them all, reading *wide* here for *wilde*. **59 (B 58)** *of hym sihe*: the hardest variant, and clearly attested in the unrelated x^1 members YD^2 (< y) and D (< u). The sense is apparently 'perceived mentally' (MED s.v. *sen* v. 21 (a)), the implied notion being 'became aware of, grasped [the man's condition]'). It would presumably be a revision of **B**, a version of which is preserved with slight variations in t and (diversely) in **p**, both of which descend from x^2 (*R–K* read with **B**). The straightforward *hadde sihte of* attested at 63, 65 might in principle be divined as the reading of <XIP^2> and U, with loss of *hadde* (so Pe). More plausibly, *of hym siht* could be a back-spelled form of the contracted-present variant *of hym sith*. This would both explain the expanded x^2 form and be hard enough to have generated *of hym sihe*. But given that all eighteen verbs in the sequence 48–64 are in the past tense, this seems improbable, and *of hym siht* is perhaps best seen as no more than a perplexed response from the scribes of <XIP^2> and U to the rare construction preserved in YD^2 and D (< y + U, = ?x^1). The **p** variants except <RM> agree with t in *on* for *of*, so this is probably what x^2 read. But the adverb-verb order in x^2 is more likely to have been that of t than **p**. However, if *ferst had on him siʒt* represents x^2, it untypically has four syllables in the dip preceding the caesura and two following it. The adopted <YD^2>D form may therefore be read as a counterpointed Type Ie line (*aab / ab*) preserving y from x^1 (and < Cx). **63** *syke*: rejected for *segge* (with **B**) by *R–K* on the basis of D^2; but as this appears one of many revisions in the passage, there are no grounds for doubting Cx here. **70 (B 69)** The unquestionably authentic α line could have been lost from β by homoarchy (initial *And* the fourth successively in 66–9). **72 (B 71)** The **C** line's revised b-half shows the stave-sound to be |b| and provides some support for *K–D*'s conjecture *barm*] *lappe* in **B**. However, the Bx form will scan vocalically as a T-type with *Eńbawmed* as first stave, a blank second stave (*bond*) and the *cauda* in |l| after mute *his*. In its other two occurrences (13.106, 19.88) *enbaumed* bears stress on the root vowel; but with words of this type consisting of prefix and radical, the

stress was often shifting (contrast *ínparfitly* B 10.465, *inpárfit* B 15.95 //; *Éxperimentis* A 11.160 and its revised parallel *Expérimentʒ* B 10.214). **B 75–95 75** scans as a Type IIIa line with a three or four-syllable prelude dip containing a lexical verb, a pattern not uncommon in **L** (e.g. 33). In view of its appearance with stave-function in 76, *seide* here seems redundant, and without it the translineation from 74/5 would be smoother. But the repetition in 78 suggests a deliberate patterning and so the earlier conjecture *quod* for *seide* (*Sch^1*) is otiose. **78 (C 77)** will scan awkwardly if acceptably as Type IIIb on the vowels of non-lexical words; but if |s| is discerned as the stave-sound, an auxiliary **shal* may be conjectured as a mute key-stave lost before *make*, though there is no suggestion of this in **C**. Revision to consonantal scansion on lexical words is possible, but the simple reconstruction adopted merely presumes Bx verb-adverb ↔ to prose order. **81 (C 80)** *folweþ*: preferred on the showing of LR as the more likely Bx reading. Though this could be a mis-resolution of *folwet*, more probably γ and M have adapted the tense to fit the verb in the b-half. That tenses in co-ordinate clauses could be mixed is clear from *bystrideth* 78 (79) alongside *quod* preceding and *raped(e)* in following 80 (79). **C**, in eliminating one verb, keeps a simple preterite for the other. **82** *sprakliche*: adopted on the showing at 18.12 of α supported by **C** as the probable Bx form here of which *sparkliche* is a metathetised reflex. The sense could be 'quickly, at once' (MED s.v. *spakli* adv., quoting appositely *WPal* 3357 & *spakli gun ride*). But the identical form (s.v. *spakliche* adj.) appears as the β variant at 18.12 and *sprakliche* 'in a lively manner, quickly' (MED s.v. *sprakli* adv.) evidently existed, though cited only from here in the period. The more economic supposition is that **L** used one adverb with the form *spracliche* and the sense 'energetically, vigorously', which would fit equally well for Hope as later for the Samaritan. **86** *gome* α: to be identified (against *Sch^1*) as the Bx reading since it is contextually the harder, *groom* being a β ⇒ suggested in part aurally by the preceding and following stave-words in |gr|. There is overlap between a sub-sense of *grom* (MED s.v. 3(a) 'man of low station or birth' and (b) 'man') and the basic sense of *gome* (1(a) 'man'), and between a sub-sense of the latter (3(b) 'man servant') and sense 2(a) of the former 'male servant, retainer'. This may be illustrated from C 8.227 //, where Bx evidently read *gomes* for **ZAC** *grom(u)s* (with MED sense 3(a)) and only one **B** ms (M) has conjectured the correct word. **88** scans vocalically or, preferably, as a Type Ia line on |θ| |ð| / |θ| with *siþþe_Í* providing the key-stave by liaison. **90** scans *aax / xx* and lacks a key-stave. A possible conjecture would be *so* before *robbed*; but *segge* would seem safer, since the Bx tradition evidences ⇒ of *man* for *segge*, as at 11.265 in β. **92 (C 84)** *vnder molde*: confirmed for **B** by the secure reading of **C**, with the implied sense that no ordinary (herbal) remedy rooted in earth can save man, only *Loue...þe plonte of pees, most precious of vertues* (1.147). In the present figure, faith and hope are seen as 'earthly' virtues found in the old dispensation, whereas love belongs to the time of grace. *K–D*'s rejection of *molde* for *mone* (pp. 111–12) as 'contextually not meaningful' shows failure to understand the imagery and indifference to the textual evidence, and their claim that **C** 'here reproduces the corrupt reading of the **B** archetype' is self-refuting, since in 'reproducing' the reading **L** can hardly be inferred to have judged it 'corrupt'. *R–K* bow to fact and logic in abandoning the emendation. **95** *he*: syntactically necessary to provide articulation with the main clause in 97a and lost through visual assimilation to preceding *be* (cf. App. at C 91).

91 Cx scans in principle as a Type IIa line with cognative alliteration |b| |p| |p| and a 'compensatory' |p| stave in position five. However, this gives unnaturally heightened stress to *be* and it may therefore be safely supposed that verb-phrase and subject in the b-half have undergone ↔ to prose order. The order *priketh him* (adopted by *R–K*) is excluded as giving a masculine ending. **94** The phrase *And ʒut bote [he] leue* is to be construed as a second condition-setting clause dependent, if remotely, on *worth he neuere* 89. The first such clause (*And ʒut be plasterud* 91) requires *moot* to be understood, unless *be* is a p.p. = *ybe* (the former goes better with *leue* 94, the latter better with *haue eten* 90). But the syntax of 94 remains awkwardly elliptical, with an unexpressed apodosis ['he will never be saved] unless he believes faithfully...that the baby's body must be our ultimate remedy'. As here understood, *they* will be a mistaken Cx reflex of the exemplar's *a*, since a singular pronoun *he* fits better with the preceding *man* of 93 (the brackets are in fact otiose, since this is the reading of N²).

B 112a–116 112a Loss in β is ascribed by *K–D* (p. 67) to rubricator's oversight. **113–24** Despite the suggestive circumstance of **C**'s resumption just where α takes up (C 96=B 125), the twelve lines attested by β are not open to question as authentic. Nor is there real reason for thinking them part of a post-Bx stage of transmission unique to one tradition. Their mechanical loss from α is convincingly ascribed by *K–D* (p. 68) to resumption at a wrong point induced by a succession of recurring similar words and phrases before and within the omitted passage (*Feith; feloun; felawe; folwen*). **114** *out comune*: rejected as meaningless by *K–D* (p. 183), who argue for *outcom(m)en* Cr²³ (MED s.v. *outcomen* v. 2(a) p.pl. 'foreign, alien'). Though attractive, this interpretation is hazardous in the absence of α and any **C** parallel. Both Cr²³ and B which (on the imperfect showing of its members) may have read **vnkonnande*, could be attempted corrections consequent upon failing to see *kennen out* as a phrasal verb (= 'lead out') and *Which...Ierusalem* as a

noun-clause object of *knowen* 114 in apposition with its direct noun-object *contree*. As here understood, the point is the importance of a particular theological virtue to the ordinary *wye in þis world* who needs direction *þoruʒ þat wildernesse* (99): *Faith*'s guidance consists in teaching about salvation through the passion and death of Christ, allegorically represented as *þe wey þat I wente, and wher forþ to Ierusalem*. **116** The β line scans *aax / xa*, and presumed loss of the key-stave through inversion to prose order is remedied by ↔ of subject + verb-phrase with the adverbial phrase.

100 (B 130–31) *o God x¹*: preferred to *God x²* both on intrinsic grounds and on the evidence of the **B** lines under revision and 109 below (both apparently overlooked by *R–K*). B 130 has a 'double-stave' structure, being a vocalic Type Ib with rhetorical stresses on grammatical words and having a secondary sequence of |g| alliteration on lexical words; but only the vocalic pattern, in which the reduced numeral is important, is retained in **C**. (In *C*-H² *o* is added *a.h.*, possibly from an *x¹* source). **106** *venge*: an absolute use not illustrated in MED (s.v. *avengen* v.). Reflexive *me* could have been coincidentally lost in *x¹* and *p²* by assimilation to following *ve-*; but *x¹* and *p²* might preserve from Cx a harder reading with the generalised sense 'take revenge / act vengefully', changed in *p¹* and t to a commoner form.

B 140–64 140 *hym louede* β: presumed the reading of Bx, since R has a visual error and F nonsense. *K–D*, adopting *hym likede*, **C**'s revision to a more familiar phrase, compound their earlier mistake of re-constructing the same phrase at 16.201. But these widely separated appearances of so idiosyncratic a usage could hardly be scribal replacements of the commonplace *hym lykede*, so their emendation amounts to 'scribal rewriting' in its indifference to the evidence (*R–K* wisely desist from these excesses). **142 (C 118)** may be scanned as a T-type in both texts. *purely*: a highly characteristic term that recurs at 174 (identical in C). *K–D*'s adoption of **C**'s *the pethe of* in its place has no justification. *forþ*: in *x²* but lost from *x¹* by virtual haplography after *-fereth*. **151 (C 128)** *Al*: perhaps providing a basis for preferring *Al* **p** to *And* **x** in **C**. But the lines, with those preceding and following, have been extensively revised, a connective is in place here, and the rest of the p form of 128 shows extensive corruption. **153** *in oon shéwýnge*: a 'monolexical' stave-phrase, of the rare type (*Intro.* IV § 38) instanced at 7.170 // (*K–D*'s ↔ of *in oon* and *shewynge* is therefore unwarranted. The requirement of a feminine ending indicates that the word be not the participle but the verbal noun (MED s.v. *scheuing(e* ger.1(a) 'manifestation'). **154** scans on |f| with *for* as a rhetorically-stressed first lift ('because', 'for the reason that'). The ?α *paume²* (for which F substitutes *it*) will give a Type IIb line scanning *aaa / bb* on |p| and |f|; but it has an awkward caesura after *forþ* and an impossibly heavy final dip [*fúst*] *bòþě*. Though deserving consideration, R is therefore not to be preferred to β, which has the caesura after *fyngeres*. **164** The Bx line scans as Type IIIa with an awkward caesura after *in* (unless an even more awkward pattern with two lifts in *bilóngéþ* is accepted), and the semantically important *pre þynges* relegated to a prelude dip. The present emendation presumes subject and verb transposed to prose order, a very common occurrence in Bx. The line thus becomes an extended Type IIIa with semi-counterpoint (*abb / ax*), the important subject-phrase receives prominence as contrapuntal staves, and the caesura is located in its natural place before the preposition governing the indirect object.

133 (B 167) *As*: the probable reading of Cx, *And as* a p^l smoothing that happens to coincide with **B**. **134 (B 168)** *And* **x**: syntactically weak, and *So is* **p** (in the light of supporting **B**) likelier to represent x^2, with t having varied independently towards x^l. **136–38 (B 170–71)** The syntax of the **C** lines would flow more smoothly if *ne* were inserted before *worche*, since the two infinitives in 137 possess no subject or modal verb. As the text stands, they must therefore be read as indirectly dependent on *worche*, which is joined prolatively to *sholde*. Possibly a wider reconstruction is required for 138a: *Ne worche sholde no wriht*, which would make *wriht sholde* govern all three infinitives. However *no* u argues against *ne* y representing the reading of x^l (contrast 143) and reconstruction would accordingly be largely speculative. **138** *hy*: reconstructed as the probable Cx form underlying the variants *they* (plural) and *he* (vocalic). *awey*: pronounced either with stress wrenched to the first syllable *áwèy* (as at B 5.108) or preferably as trisyllablic *aweye* (as at 12.148 //), with inserted final *–e*. **143 (B 176)** *pulte* C-yB-α: 'extend' (MED s.v. *pilten* v. 3(a)); clearly the harder reading and thus an unlikely ⇒ for original *putte* in either version. Here y is presumed to have preserved the x^l reading, but since GN (= p^2) are also right, it seems less probable that x^2 had *putte* than that p^l, t and u severally varied to one more obvious. In the Bx tradition, only R retains the right reading (< α). Similar difficulties with *pulten* were experienced in earlier instances: in 10.95 **p** reads *putte*, but one p^l copy (K) has *pulte* with **x**; in // **B** *pulte* is almost certainly the reading of Bx; in B 1.127 *pulte* is preserved by L (= β), here accompanied by Cr, and by R (= α) against *putte* γM, while in the // passage Ax reads *putte* against **Z** *pulte* (see the notes on these lines, and esp. the discussion of 1.128 // B 1.127). **144–46 (B 177–79)** The lines B 177b–179a, attested only in α, unquestionably genuine on intrinsic grounds and the showing of (partly revised) **C**, will have been lost from β by homoteleuton at the caesura (*fust* 177, 179; cf. B 184–85 below). **147** *Be he* **p**: preferable on grounds of sense, the reading of **x** being awkward even with Ø-punctuation after *liketh*

and an understood object for *lat falle* supplied. Allowing this possibility, the noun-clause of 146 could be made the object of *liketh* 145 if **x**'s variant were seen as a visual error for *Bote be he*, yielding the same substantive meaning as **p** (so *R–K*, who put a stop after *toucheth*. But it seems safer to accept **p** as = Cx than to reconstruct.

B 184–85 (C 152–53) The two half-lines 184b, 185a have been lost from γ by the same mechanical error noted at B 177–79, homoteleuton at the caesura (*hand...hand*). M's error will probably have been coincidental, consisting in omission of 184b (followed by erasure and restoration) and complete loss of 185 (followed by restoration in the margin by the same corrector, whether by reference back to the exemplar or to an L-type source). Cr, as a γ-ms, can only have corrected from such a source or from a **C** copy. The error here identifies γ as a major genetic group, while the omission of 186 further distinguishes g from w as a sub-division within that group.

158 (B 190) *R–K* diagnose omission from Cx of original lines corresponding to B 190b–192 through homoteleuton very like that noted at 152–53 (here *hand...hand* again) and restore these lines to **C**. It is an attractive emendation, but since the sense of Cx is satisfactory this could be a case of *authorial* abbreviation, aiming to avoid the repetition of B 186 (= C 154) found in B 191. *ypersed* **B**: in context having the substantive sense 'pierce', so that the hypothetical β reading **yper(is)ched* may be seen as a spelling-variant either influenced by *perisshen*, a verb of distinct etymology, or reflecting a pronunciation intermediate between |s| and |ʃ|. (For spellings with *sh* see MED s.v. *percen* v. (derived from OF *perc(i)er, perchier*) and compare the spelling with *-iss-* under *perishen* v. (derived from the extended stem of OF *perir*).

163a, 164 (B 198a, 199) *Spiritum Sanctum* C-**p**: the accusative required on grounds of sense, Bx appearing to have erred in both instances, C-**x** in the first, perhaps by initially missing the nasal suspension in 'spirituı 'and then by smoothing 'sanctuı' to 'sancto'. The cause was presumably failure to grasp the sense of *in* 'against', though **L** so uses even English *in* (MED s.v. *in* prep. 20 (a)) at preceding 162 // 197 in free variation with *aʒeyn* 167 // (and see Apparatus to **B** for β's variant *in*). **171 (B 206)** *flaumynge fuyr* **x**: preferred on the showing of // **B** as the probable Cx form which **p** misread as a preterite, perhaps through missing a nasal suspension in an exemplar form spelled **flaumede* (that Bx had the *-ende* form of the present participle is indicated by the spelling *flaumende* in *B*-LR). Loss of 171 (and also 172) in t will have been caused by homoarchy and homoteleuton (*And...togyderes* 170, 172) and is paralleled in the **p**-group copies QF and N. **174** *se*: the probable Cx reading, for while *wirche* may point to **swynke* as the group-original of y, the Ø-reading of X suggests rather that the verb had been omitted and was independently supplied in YIP^2 (but in D^2 from another source of u, t or **p** type). The line, here taken to have been added in the revision to **C**, is held by *K–D* to have been lost by Bx 'through inducement to complete the correlative construction begun in 20[7]'. Though it was accepted for **B** in *Sch*[1], the reservation expressed there that the evidence is inconclusive is here held to tell against its inclusion (compare the cases of B 18.161, where revision still remains possible, and B 19.441, 20.261, where Cx preserves what appears a largely unrevised text of **B**[1]).

B 214–44 214 (C 180) Bx has the imperfect scansion *aa / xx* and *lowe* 'low' is conjectured as the required stave-word presumed lost through visual assimilation to *yb*lowe at 213a or to a preceding identical exemplar form of the word for 'fire' (MED s.v. *loue* n. 2(a)). This last is found as a t variant to *leye* in C 180, in ms C at // **B** and as the text form at 20.140 (in MED s.v. 3 '(flash of) light'; cf. *lei(e* n. (2) (a)). **218–44 (C 184–210)** The authenticity of these *B*-β lines is guaranteed by their presence (lightly revised) in **C**. This longest omission from α may have been occasioned by resumption at a wrong point induced by several words and phrases occurring in and just before the passage (*K–D* p. 69). But loss for purely mechanical reasons (215 and 249 being identical) would have been more certain had the omission run from 216 to 248, which is approximately the content of a single page (the average *PP* ms has about 38 lines to the page [Green 1987:307]). **224 (C 190)** The line scans as a vocalic extended Type IIIc with full counterpoint (*abb / ab*), or as a normal Type IIIc characteristically reversing the stress-pattern of the phrase *Holy Góest* in C 189 // **B** 223 and making the emphatic comparative adverb *as* the key-stave. *K–D*'s emendation *glede unglade* for *glede* takes W's *glade*] *glede* as descended from the postulated group original. But this conjecture illustrating their obliviousness (in seeking a metrically unnecessary stave-word) to the force of **BC** agreement, is unpersuasive, given its 'more than usually complex presumption of split variation' (p. 207), and the logic of their footnote 163 suggests its implausibility. For the W variant is explicable as an error for an exemplar form spelled *gl(e)ade* (one C15th example of *glad* is cited by MED s.v. *gled(e* n. (2)).

196–97 (B 230–31) The **p** form has defective metre in the first line (*aa / bb*) as a result of ↔ to prose order, perhaps arising from misreading *the grete myhte of þe Trinite*, the noun-phrase object of *melteth*, as appositional with *grace of þe Holi Gost* (on a possible fruitful ambiguity see *Commentary* further). The **p** form, however, gives the same sense as **x**, which is that of **B**. **200 (B 234)** *noȝt*: restored in **B** as necessary for the sense and presumed lost by Bx for a mechanical reason. This, if the form was *nat* as in **C**, could have been *þat* (1) > < *þat* (2) attraction. Alternatively, a negative particle *ne* could have been lost through visual confusion with either syllable of following *mowe*. The defect in sense went unnoticed not only by all

the scribes but also by *Sk*. **206 (B 240)** The **C** line retains **B**'s Type Ie or IIIc with counterpoint and mute key-stave (*aab / [a]b*) or (preferably) reads as a T-Type (*aa / [a]bb*). B-Y *faire* need not show ⊗ but accidental convergence with **C**'s revised epithet prompted by objection to the linking of *warm* with *flaumbe*. **212 (B 246)** *tasch* C**B**-α: a word instanced only here (MED s.v. *tach(e* n. (2) 'touch-wood') and too hard not to be the Bx reading, for which β *tow* is ⟹ of a more familiar term ('kindling made from hemp or flax'). **220 (B 254)** *ingratus*: preferred not because *ingrat* is the easier reading (it is instanced only here in MED s.v.) but because it is likelier that an abbreviation for *-us* in the α and **p** exemplars was overlooked in copying than that a naturalised word was made Latin by the scribes of *x*[1], t and β. The metre is unaffected either way, the line scanning with rhetorical stresses on both privative particles or as a macaronic T-type with its *cauda* alliterating cognatively on |g|, |k|. **231** has been added in revision, and there is no warrant for inserting it (as do *K–D*) after B 264. In **B** line 265 serves to direct the audience towards the example of Dives, which is not elaborated; in **C**, it introduces seventeen new lines and *Minne ȝe nat.../ That* is inserted to effect the transition and connect Dives with the rich men of 229. **232** *dampned*: evidently the reading of y and probably that of **p**, various **x** and **p** mss intruding the understood verb *was* (cf. 241, where **p** and t diversely fill out the terse syntax of Cx). The presumed Cx form here is close to that of B 265; but there is no need to omit *and*, which introduces a characteristic ellipsis. **237** *his lycame werie*: a second subordinate clause, having a new subject, dependent (like *lyue*) on the main verb *sotiled*, with *myhte* understood. The inserted *on* in Dt, paralleled in N (and adopted by *R–K* with omission of *on* in 236) smooths the abrupt but characteristic expression preserved in Cx. **240** *told*: preferred as harder and more precise in sense (MED s.v. *tellen* 18(b) 'consider'), *cald* y presumably resulting from *c / t* confusion. **242** *atymye*: a form of *atte(i)nen* in sense 1(a) 'attain' or (c) 'succeed in'. The spelling with *m* appears original, though it is unrecorded in MED, which does not cite the passage under *atteinen* v. Kane 2000:52–3 argues for derivation of the verb from OE *atemien* and the sense 'refrain from [fine living]'. But this is at variance with the entire context, since **L**'s point is that the rich should not be misers but should spend generously, so that others (including the poor) may benefit thereby. **251 (B 269)** *vnhynde*: 'ungenerous' (MED s.v. *hende* 2(c) + *vn-*), confused by several mss with its synonym (in this sense) under influence from the spelling-form and following *vnkyndenesse* 253. The word is probably, as **B** *vnkynde* must be, stressed on the privative prefix. **253 (B 271)** scans with two lifts in *vnkýndenésse* as Type IIIa, unusually revising a Type Ia, and possibly *þe contrarie* (as in **B**) has been lost through eyeskip from *kyn-* to *quen-* (so

PeR–K). The insertion by t of a stave-word *kid* (so *Sk*) is palpably scribal, since the 'making known' or 'recognition' of this vice has small bearing on the matter. The loss of **B**'s 'elemental' idea weakens the **C** line, but grounds for emendation are not strong. **255–56 (B 273–74)** The line-division in the majority of **C** mss is unsatisfactory in giving 255 a masculine ending, and re-lineation as in **B** is desirable. The correct u form could derive from x^1 (< Cx) but is more probably a happy scribal re-arrangement. Misdivision might have occurred through associating *this corsede theues* 255 too closely with its parallel subject *Vnkynde Cristene men* in 256. **268 (B 286)** The line could have been lost from γ by resumption at the wrong point following confusion of *mercy* 287 with *mercy...mercy* in 286. Cr^1 or its manuscript exemplar presumably restored by collation with a **C** copy or a **B** copy of *l* or *m* type. **270 (B 288)** *Innócence*: so stressed to provide the first stave in this Type Ie line. **275–76 (B 293–94) C** omits B 294 and revises as two lines a single **B** line of Type IIa structure with an extra *l* stave in position five. The sense and metre both being satisfactory, *K–D*'s reconstruction, a blend of **C** and **B**, amounts to the creation of a conflated text. **B 294** *þat he pleyneþ þere*: ↔ of the adverb and relative clause to prose order to restore the key-stave *pléynéþ* in final position, producing the unmetrical pattern *aa / xa* and giving in its two lifts an unacceptable masculine ending. The adverb *þere* has its normal disyllabic form with final *-e* to provide the required feminine ending (cf. **B** 4.23, 36). **277 (B 295)** *nouthe* **C**: quite possibly also the form in **B** (and Bx), thus accounting for ?γ **nouht*. The emphatic form conveys the sense 'at this very moment', also one sense of *nou* (MED s.v. adv. 1(a)), and may stand in contrast with the rhetorically emphatic *now* of 278 / 296 (MED s.v. *nou* 7(f)). *K–D*'s adoption of *nouthe* in **B** is thus defensible, but the metre does not require it here (contrast 244 or B 13.184 above) and since the sense difference is small, *now* may be allowed to stand. **278 (B 296)** The second *Y* of **C** is also preferable in **B** to the Ø-reading of LR, which could be coincidental or a reflex of Bx (this occurs also at B 13.385 and at B 18.202, where LR are joined by Y). Such omission of a subject pronoun could in principle be an original feature. However, in another (second-person) instance at B 5.494 (*Feddest*), **C** confirms the reading (C 8.133), while in *fettest* 20.379 **C** omits and **B** has the pronoun, but the verbs in the added **C** line 20.380 both *lack* it. The first *Y*, which is *not* necessary, has presumably been intruded in *B*-WHmM for the sake of emphasis; but in **C** it may be a revision. **279 (B 297)** scans cognatively as a Type Ic on |k| and |g|. *K–D*'s emendation *Crist* is metrically unnecessary and theologically inexact (cf. the 'economic' precision of *bouhte* at 267) and the note in *Sch^1* largely otiose. *R–K* sensibly retain **C**. **290 (B 308)** will scan satisfactorily as an extended Type IIIa on vowels with semi-counterpoint on

|l| or, preferably, as a T-type, with key-stave on |l| formed by liaison of *til_hem* (*aa / [a]bb*). *PeR–K*'s emendation to the form of **B**'s b-half *lif* is unnecessary and should be rejected: the D variant *lif,* coming before *hem*, clearly aims at 'regularising' the metre. The *sense* of Cx is virtually equivalent to that of **B**, while alluding to a familiar proverbial expression.

B 309–39 (C 291–321) 309–10 Loss of these (obviously authentic) lines from β is hard to account for on mechanical grounds. *K–D*'s explanation ('distraction by the corrupt copy preceding', p. 67) would be implausible even if 308b were corrupt as they judge. But deliberate censorship of the lines as too pessimistic cannot be entirely excluded and invites comparison with the converse situation at B 316 (where α omits). **316 (C 298)** The exact form of the b-half is unascertainable in the absence of α, but *K–D*'s conjecture *swich* may be safely adopted on the showing of (slightly revised) **C** as the necessary key-stave for which β (?or Bx) *hym* is a non-alliterating ⇒ suggested by preceding *His*. *K–D* (p. 69) attribute the loss in α to 'resumption at a wrong point induced by *restitucion* 31[5], *satisfaccion* 3[16]'. But a mechanical explanation is not less convincing here than deliberate censorship, α rejecting a theological position judged too lenient, as β at 309–10 may have rejected one thought too severe (either tradition displaying a consistent moral posture in the two cases). **326 (C 308)** The Bx line could in principle scan as Type IIIa, though stress on *be* would lack semantic or rhetorical justification. Neither of the sub-archetypal variants is likely to be the source of the other, though both could be reflexes of the relatively more difficult noun adopted by *K–D* from // **C**. MED s.v. *burre* n. (1) 2(b) 'hoarseness' cites only this one example of the word and OED has no further examples before *c.*1600. **336 (C 318)** *ouhte*: a stronger reading and the likelier to be original in both versions. **339 (C 321)** *ben* *B*-wαC: presumably lost from gLM by visual attraction of *ben* > < *in*. The error could have been in β (> γLM) and independently corrected in w, since convergence of g, L and M seems improbable. **332 (B 350)** *that his lyf amende*: tentatively discriminated as the Cx reading, *that* tightening **B**'s looser association of the will to charity with spiritual renewal. The larger divergence attested in **x** introduces a new notion, scribal in origin, of recovering from illness and then being converted, whereas the theme of 330–32 is patient endurance of illness as a spiritually meritorious act.

Passus XX (B XVIII)

RUBRICS *B*-β and *C*-**x** concur in regarding this passus, which is not through-numbered in **C**, as the third of *Dobet*, *C*-**p** as the fourth; *B*-α is out as before.

1 *Wollewaerd*: a rare word, only once instanced before **L**

(MED s.v. *wolward* a.). The probable Cx spelling (with -*ae*- for -*a*-), could account for **p**'s misunderstanding the sense of the second element as *weried* (as actually in QZ), with retrospective smoothing of the first element in some mss to an adverbial prefix (*wel, ful*); but the substantive reading is not in doubt. **2** revises to Type Ia a line of vocalic extended Type IIIc with counterpoint on |r| (*abb / ab*); for the pattern cf. B 19.452. Possibly Bx has inverted an original prose order (*récchep of nó wò*), which would give an acceptable b-half closer to **C** (so *K–DSch¹*); but since revision appears with the omission of B 6, it cannot be ruled out here. **6–7 (B 6–8)** Re-positioning of the **B** lines is required by the failure of sense in Bx (unnoticed by *Sk*), which has no verb governing the indirect object in 9a (Bx 6). **C** solves the problem by omitting 9 and drops 6 for good measure (as perhaps lowering the tone). **7** *by orgene*: preferred on the showing of **C** as the probable Bx reading, the β form *organye* being perhaps no more than a spelling variant. The special sense 'in *organum*' (vocal parts a fifth above or below the plainsong line, favoured by *Pe*), is instanced only from *c*.1400 (MED s.v. *organ(e* n.3); but the general sense in the period of *singen bi organe* is 'to sing to the accompaniment of instrumental music', whether the instruments are of strings or wind (MED s.v. ibid. 2., and see 1). Possibly, since the singers are processing, the instrument may be a portative organ (ibid. 2(a)). Trevisa's definition cited by MED s.v. *organum* shows the duality of contemporary reference ('general name of alle instrumentes of musik...specialliche...þe instrument...y-made of many pipes'), but omits the harmonic signification. **12 (B 14)** *and* **C**: a revision anticipated in *B*-g (and in Cr possibly by collation with a **C** source). The probable Bx reading *or* is unacceptable, since the shoes are not an *alternative* to the spurs, the significant item in the ceremony of knighting. F's *on,* an intelligent guess (unless it simply preserves α where R has erred visually with β), gives good enough sense to be adopted as the reading of **B**. **14 (B 16)** The superior spelling with final -*ous* is adopted to avoid possible confusion with the plural of the noun *auntur*. **24** *plates*: rejected for **B**'s *paltok* by *R–K*, who miss the pungent irony of one of **L**'s most forceful revisions. **30 (B 31)** The substantive sense is 'that he [Death] is lying', and αL *likth* may represent Bx in this sense (see MED s.v. *lien* v. (2), spelling-forms). The alternative sense 'what he [Life] pleases' is not so apt, and if β read thus, M could have altered from a γ-type source. But on the showing of *a lyeth* **C**, the αL reading is best interpreted as a spelling-variant, *likth* representing Bx **lyʒp* or **lyg(h)þ* with the same sense ('lies') as in γ. **34–34a (B 35–35a)** *forbite*: a harder reading lexically, the word being almost exclusive to **L** (MED s.v. *forbiten* v.), whereas *forbeten*, also in *PP* at 22.198 //, is commoner. The verb, describing Life's fatal 'bite' at Death, recalls its earlier use to describe the action of sin

upon charity at 18.39, where only X has the erroneous reading *forbet.* Its originality is confirmed by the Latin of 34a (*morsus*), with its mordant pun on *Mors*, on the strength of which the completion of the quotation may be accepted into **B** in a form reconstructed from F's evidence to accord with **C**. Therefore *forbite* may be safely identified as the Bx reading preserved in α, from which βF have varied convergently under inducement from following *adoun*. It remains uncertain whether *and* Bx has been misplaced, since its present position requires *bale-deeþ* to be a compound object of the phrasal verb *adoun brynge*. Placed after *adoun* in **C**, perhaps in revision, *deth* becomes the direct object of *brynge*, while *bale* 'death' (MED s.v. 2b) becomes its indirect object. This gives clearer sense and smoother style, but grounds for emending Bx are insufficently strong. More certain is it that *forbete* βF should be identified as a scribal ⇒ for the original **B** verb preserved in R. *R–K*'s adoption of *forbete* and re-ordering of the a-half to accord with **B** has nothing to recommend it. **36** *per x¹* (here **p**It): presumably an isolated spelling variant for the possessive, and not the adverb *þere*. It should be altered to *her* (*R–K*) as it is probably not archetypal. **37 (B 38)** *iustice*: pl. also in *B*-Cr²³YOCBF, but presumably an error in Cx, as the only judge is the Roman Pilate and the text cannot refer to the Jewish authorities Herod and the High Priest. **38 (B 39)** *þe court* **C**B-γMF: either LR *her*] *þe* is a convergent scribal error, heightening the hostility of the 'court', or it represents Bx (< β + α), where γ, M (< γ) and F (? < **C**) substitute the more neutral expression. But it is unlikely to be original. **39 (B 40)** *pelour*: lexically difficult and found first here, with a precise and apt legal sense (see MED s.v. *pelour* n.). The word's rarity doubtless provoked its replacement in Bx by one which, though contextually inappropriate, was loosely used as a term of abuse for 'ruffian', 'scoundrel' (MED s.v. *pilour* n. (1) (c)). The substituted word occurs in *PP* in its normal senses, (a) 'pillager' and (b) 'one who deprives others of money or goods by undue force' (ibid., senses (a) and (b)) at 22.263 // and 21.418 // respectively, in the latter with the well-attested variant spelling *pelours* in X. **46** revises to a Type Ia (or Ic) a Type IIb line with *quod* as stave two. *K–D*'s rejection of Bx's b-half for **C**'s because 'more emphatic' (p. 91) strains belief. **48 C** revises to a standard Type Ia a **B** line scanning cognatively with the same pattern (|g| |k| / |g|) but rhetorical *repetitio* of the epithet from 47. *K–D* 's diagnosis of *kene* as a scribal ⇒ induced by preceding copy (mistakenly accepted in *Sch¹*) fails to recognise **L**'s cognative staves. **49** *saide*: either in its normal sense (MED s.v *seien* 1(a)) with *quod* 50 pleonastic or, as preferable, absolute 'spoke' (ibid. 6(a)), as *K–D* take it (with a semi-colon better after *enuye*). **50** *þat ribaud* **C**B-β: *þe ribaudes* α, most simply accounted for as a mistaken pl. anticipating the implied pl. subject of *Nailed* 51

445

and the stated one of *þei putte* 52 (no pronoun in // **C**). In the light of **C** 50, however, it seems best to take the speaker of *Aue, raby* as the *other* of 47 who makes the crown of thorns. *vp*: reconstructed as the Cx form of the preposition in the relatively rare sense 'in physical opposition to' (MED s.v. *up* prep. 8 (b), 'in hostile encounter... attack on' (OED s.v. *Up* prep.[1] 3a). This was replaced in the **p** groups by *at* (as in // **B**) or *on*, while **x** treated *vp* as an adverb and added the preposition *to* (perhaps under suggestion from 52), thus overloading the dip. **51** *a*: one of two small revisions in this line; there is no reason to think Bx *þe* unoriginal (as *K–D* hold). **53** revises *deeþ-yuel...ydone* doubtless in consequence of a changed understanding of the purpose of the *poysen* (Mk 15: 36, Jn 19: 297; see *Commentary*). *K–D* (p. 91) again reject Bx for **C** because 'more emphatic'; but it could not fail to be (given what is being said), so as a reason for emending, this hardly signifies. **54 (B 54)** *saiden*: to be securely adopted in **B** on the showing of **C** as syntactically necessary after *And* before the quoted speech, and perhaps lost through distraction from preceding *beden* 53. **C** makes *saiden* a stave in revising to Type Ia a **B** line of Type IIIc that scanned on vowels and |s| (unless, as *K–D* judge, its b-half read *þiselue now þou helpe*, with the word-order of **C**). **55–6** In the light of near-identical **B**, Cx can be seen to have shortened two lines of unusual length. The product is three lines scanning *xa / ax*, as prose, *aa / ax*, only the last being of authentic form. Line 55 as now restored turns **B** *kynges sone* into a fully parenthetical phrase, sharpening up its theology to make Christ both Messiah and Divine Son. *R–K*'s replacement of *Crist, Godes sone* by *kynges sone* should be rejected; for being a king's son, as **L** seems to have realised, would not empower Jesus to come down from the cross, but being *God*'s son would. The wording of Mt 27:43 as well as 42 // is relevant. **61 C** revises a counterpointed Type Ie line, scanning *aab / ab* on |w| and |k|, to a form reconstructable from the evidence of the sub-archetypes. Thus *wal* moves from being stave one to being part of the prelude-dip, and the line's stave-sound is |t|, with staves three and five, *euene* and *peces*, blank not counterpointed as in **B**. It is presumed here on the evidence of y that x^1 contained a second adverb *al*, lost haplographically in x^2u before *a* 'in', the prepositional form still preserved in **p**. In P^2 both *al* and *a* were lost from y and *a* later added. The substantive key-stave, carrying full stress, is a numeral *two*, not the preposition; for *to* is the ambiguous orthographic variant (found also at 75) punning homophonically with *to* in the a-half, which bears rhetorical sentence-stress (contrast *to*- in 62). **63** *to-quasche*: the tense clearly past (*to-quaschete* in pUt) and the unique y spelling without preterite morpheme perhaps a 'false form', the verb being historically weak (it recurs at 257). **71 (B 69) C** revises **B**'s Type Ia to a Type IIIc scanning on vowels (*He*; *is*) and *s*. **73 (B 71)**

C revises to Type Ia a Type IIIc in **B**. *K–D* 's metrically unnecessary ↔ of *also* and *þat tyme* ignores **C**'s word-order, which confirms that of **B**. **75 (B 73)** In the light of **B**, the form of Cx may be discriminated as preserved in u ($< x^1$) and t ($< x^2$), **p** inverting the subject-verb order and padding out with an unnecessary adverb a line presumably judged too short. The intrusive phrase *of tho theues* (rejected as scribal after *Pe*) could have entered y from a marginal note in its exemplar designed to emphasize that only the thieves' legs, not Christ's, were broken (though its position misleadingly connects it with *cachepol*). This instance demonstrates N^2's primary descent from a y-type source. **78 (B 76)** *prowe B-α*: preferred for **B** as the harder reading, which **C** is judged to have revised to the more familiar *tyme*. *B-β* could have anticipated the change by ⇒ of a commoner synonym and need show no ⊗ from **C**. Conversely, α is unlikely to have substituted a lexically harder word for *tyme*; nor need Cx have replaced original *prowe*, as *R–K* judge, since the next line in **C** is also revised. **80 (B 78)** *blynde* **C**: an addition that anticipates 81b, for which reason *R–K* omit. However the threefold *repetitio* in 80, 84, 87 seems deliberate, and the word can be accepted as a blank stave in a Type Ie line. **84 (B 82)** *Iouste* x^1: more colloquial and arguably harder than x^2's form, though *To* could have been lost by haplography. The Bx line has a defective metrical pattern *xx / aa* and could be emended to give a Type IIIb by reading *jauelot* as a neologism for which the synonym *spere* was substituted. However MED s.v. has no evidence of this word before 1440 and this conjecture, though possibly less drastic than the one adopted, is lexically more hazardous. *K–D* (p. 94) may be right that the line was rewritten to exclude the notion of Longinus as a Jew, since he was honoured as a Christian saint (see *Commentary*); so the **C** reading is accepted, tentatively, for **B**. **86** is revised in both halves and *R–K*'s wholesale adoption of **B** has no justification. **91 (B 89)** *A*: the unstressed colloquial form posited as underlying *And* **x** and *He* **p**. **94 (B 91)** *ruthe* **C**: adopted on the showing of **B** as the likely original for which *mercy* is a non-alliterating ⇒ of a synonym commoner in this type of context. Although Cx, scanning as Type IIIa with a six-syllable prelude dip, could be a revision offering a more strictly rational antithesis to *riʒt* than the affective *ruthe* (see *Commentary*), the reconstruction seems safe, with a gain in metrical smoothness and little loss of meaning (for the standard mercy / right contrast cf. 439–40). N^2's variant, while not the basis of the emendation, indicates the intelligent scribal dissatisfaction with imperfect metre shown at 400; but that it was corrected from a 'pre-archetypal copy' (*R–K* p. 102) is a logically unnecessary supposition. **95** *fouely* **C**: a revision emphasising the force of the abuse rather than the ferocity of the motivation. N^2's *felly*, preferred by *R–K,* may be identified as derived from **B**. **96–8 (B 93–5)** The incorrect line-division in **p** and TH^2 (but in this instance not Ch) may directly reflect the reading of x^2, and was probably occasioned by eyeskip from *for* to *For þis*. The x^1 lineation, as well as giving more satisfactory metre, is supported by **B**. The form of the last phrase in 97 is reconstructed by *R–K* from **x** and **p** in the light of **B** as **to ʒow falle*, retaining the preposition of **B** and **p**, the verb of **p** and the imprecatory form of **x**. But this is unnecessary, since 97–8 show changes in detail, notably the removal of *alle*, so as implicitly to re-direct the ban towards the Jews present and their offspring rather than the whole nation or race. The reading *falle* in *B*-WHmGC^2 is, moreover, unlikely to be that of Bx and may show ⊗ from **C** (or merely influence from the common collocation *vengeaunce falle*), just as *to ʒow alle* Ch could be echoing **B**. Given the signs of revision, it is better to let the archetypal readings stand, without seeking a common underlying form for both. **98 (B 95)** *the dede x^1* (*hym þat was ded* **p**): 'the dead'. The singular t variant *þe dede þat ʒe dede* takes *dede* as 'deed' and *beten* as 'make amends for, atone for' (MED s.v. *beten* v. (2) 2(a)) or possibly *þat ʒe dede it* as an integral noun-phrase with *a boyes dede* as its complement (= 'that you did it was a rascally act'). M's flat extra line after 98 (adopted by *Sk*), while metrically and stylistically acceptable, is not necessitated by the syntax, and merely repeats 95, so is better interpreted as scribal over-insistence on the guilt of the Jews. **103** *ʒelde x^1*: a spelling variant of the contracted present found with its more usual unvoiced ending in x^2 and Bx. *recreaunt x^2* **B**: *creaunt x^1*, a well-attested variant that cannot be original here since a first stave in |r| is required. *remynge* **C**: of a visual form such that the erroneous **C** variants support *K–D*'s view of Bx as a visual mistake for the same reading. But since *rennyng* 'fleeing' (MED s.v. *rennen* v. (1) 4 (a)) is in keeping with the metaphorical figure and revision is continuing here, grounds for emendation are insecure. **106 (B 103)** *into x^1*: less smooth metrically than the monosyllabic *to* and *in*, the reading of **B**; but these could be split variants of x^1 *into* (< C*x*). **109 (B 106)** Both lines have 'dual' scansions, **C** as an extended Type IIIa on vowels with semi-counterpoint (*abb / ax*) or Type Ia with mute key-stave, and **B** as a Type IIb (with *But* as stave one) or as an extended Type IIIb on vowels with semi-counterpoint on |b|.

    B 109–19 109 Because of **C**'s revision in both half-lines, the Bx form cannot be decisively discriminated. The absence of the final word in L could indicate a Ø-reading in β, with γ having supplied an appropriate verb on the basis of the Latin *cessabit*. This will have come into *m* from γ, and from a w-type ms M will have added *of*, a word necessary for the line's grammatical coherence after adoption of *cesse*. The α reading *lese* is not self-evidently superior to *cesse*, though it fits more idiomatically with *crowne* than does *cesse*, and accords well

with B 7.159, where *The kyng lees his lordshipe* is close to the present *hir kyngdom þe crowne sholde lese*. (On the sense of *crowne* 'sovereignty', see MED s.v. *coroune* n. 5a, which exactly corresponds with that of *lordshipe* n., ibid., 3(d)). **113 (C 116)** is of Type IIIa and revised in **C** to a Type Ia by replacing *coste* with a filler-phrase providing a second stave. *K–D*'s insertion of *Where* before *Oute* to normalise the line is too arbitrary to deserve consideration. **119 (C 122)** While **C** scans as a Type IIa, Bx has the defective pattern *aa / xx*. The third stave *and a clene* is presumed lost by Bx on account of the line's length and the phrase's placing after a noun already provided with an epithet qualified by an adverb, the combined weight of which promoted expectation of a caesura following the noun. The line was lacking in t and T has supplied the gap not from another **C** ms but from a post-Bx copy of **B**, which lacked the adjectival phrase, adding *and* and substituting a synonymous expression for *she hihte*. **131 (C 134)** *K–D* (p. 90) diagnose homœoarchic loss of *wommane* (here understood as a **C** addition for explicitness); but this must remain speculative, as the sense does not require it and the line will scan as standard with shifted stress on *Wiþouten*.

140 (B 137) *lowe* **x**: preferred (as a revision in **C**), despite agreement with **B** of p^1, N and P^2 (the last doubtless collated with a **p** source). A sense '(flash) of light' is illustrated by two MED quotations s.v. *loue* n. (2); but in one it is that of a lightning flash and there seems no doubt that the sense here is the basic one, 'fire' or 'flame' (ibid. 1(a)), **C** stressing the light's fiery (sun-like) quality as much as its brightness. **141** After this *R–K* insert B 139 and read *And* before *That* in 142. But no mechanical or other reason appears for the omission, and since the sense runs on satisfactorily and the antecedent of *herof* can be the noun-clause of 136–7, the case for adding it is weak. **151 (B 149)** *parfit* **C**: revising **B** to emphasise Job's moral stature rather than his dual character as OT prophet and 'patriarch'. So despite the converse appearance of *prophete* as a variant in *C*-mss W and N, *K–D*'s ⇒ of **C** on the grounds that Bx misread a contracted form is to be rejected. **153 (B 151)** *heo* **C**: a stave-word here, so the ambiguously-spelled *he* of x^1α and the non-alliterating *she* of β are rejected for the W and S pronoun-form probably original in L's dialect. **157 (B 154)** Though Bx could scan (very awkwardly) on vowels as Type IIIa, this would be only if the important term *medicyne* is placed in the prelude-dip and the final lifts have the same structure as 155b. It seems safe therefore to suppose an original Type IIa structure as in **C** and Bx to be ⇒ of a non-alliterating semi-synonym. **158 (B 155)** Vocalic staves with semi-counterpoint seem intrinsically unlikely here, so the line may be scanned either cognatively on |t| |d| |d| as Type IIa (with a supplemental |t| stave in *destrúyeth*), or as Type Ia with 'monolexical' *déstrúyeth*, a pattern instanced at 320 (see *Intro*. IV § 38). *be*: omitted in ?**x** through *he* > < *de*d attraction but supplied (in different positions) by YCh and D²D. **162–64 (B 159–61)** The Bx form of these lines may be defended as not self-evidently defective in sense. But in the light of **C**, the contrast between the acts of guile and grace better prepares for the oxymoron of *good sleighte*; so a following line may be conjectured omitted by eyeskip from *good* 160 > *good* 161, with mechanical ⇒ of *sleighte* for *ende*. Its inclusion restores the lost antithesis between diabolic and divine *gile*, the stratagem (*sleighte*) being 'good' because its outcome (*ende*) proves so. In B 160 *al* is required for the syntax (since *bigan* is transitive) and for the sense (since the contrast with *ende* as restored otherwise fails). The **x** order is preferred for **C** as implicitly confirmed by 220 //; but because the position of *al* in **p** and B-C² (which may derive from a **p**-copy) would equally explain its mechanical loss from Bx (by attraction to preceding *þat*), it may also be accepted in **B**. The ⇒ of *ende* in 160 could be a happy guess in YG, since there is no definitive sign of ⊗ as already in C². The form of B 159 is metrically defective (*xa / xa*) and it appears thin in content, with no qualifying term to distinguish Satan's kind of *gile* from God's. *K–D*'s emendation replaces 159 with C 162, ignoring such signs of revision as the repetition of *formost* from 161 and vaguely ascribing the corruption to 'imperfect recollection' (p. 94). But reconstruction here, though guided by **C**, does not reproduce it, since the original passive construction in **B** could have been later made active in C 162. A passive construction in the b-half here accordingly subsumes the content of C 162b, while in the a-half a possessive *gilours* is posited as lost through haplography occasioned by *gile (bi)giled* following. **168, 173 (B 165, 170)** *heo*: adopted for **B** and **C** as the clearest form, for which both archetypes have the (possibly original) gender-ambiguous *he*, though the spelling conceals the rounded vowel (see MED s.v. *he* pron. (2)). **172 (B 169)** is revised to scan on |ll|, but Bx scans on |s| with a liasional key-stave *þis light* (the emendation [*Loue*] in *Sch²* has been erroneously retained from *Sch¹* and should read *he* as in *PT* Vol. I). **177 (B 174)** *And in*: the grammatically required form of the phrase (identical with **B**), of which *And* and *In* appear split variants; felicitously restored in D²Ch. **181–82 (B 178–79)** There is no good reason to question the authenticity of the archetypal b-halves *Mercy shal synge / haue* as do *K–D* (suggesting *merye shul synge* for **B**) and *Sch¹* (adopting *synge* for **B**); *Pe*'s note *ad loc* mistakenly suggests that *mery* is the reading of Bx, but it is that of only one ms, the **C** copy Ch. The phrase *I shal daunce þerto* in Bx presents no problem if the adverb means not 'also' but 'according with that [*sc.* the giving of Mercy]' (OED s.v. *Therto adv.* 2, MED s.v. 6c). *K–D*'s claim (p. 208) that *Mercy shal synge* makes 'poor sense because the speaker is replying to Righteousness, not Mercy' itself makes

poor sense, and *R–K*'s jocose restatement (p. 115) of their objection does not reassure. For that Peace should urge Righteousness to dance with her, declaring that (her close colleague) Mercy will provide the music of the *carole*, hardly baffles understanding. In the revision *þerto*, with *daunse* now immediately adjoined to *synge*, means 'to it [*sc.* Mercy's song]' or 'also, likewise' (OED s.v. 1 and 3, MED s.v. 11). The pl. *shullen* **p** may reflect misunderstanding of *Moises* as subject and *Mercy* as addressee. **B 179** has presumably been lost from α by homœoarchy (*daunce* 179, *dawe* 180). **195 (B 190)** In the light of **B**, the caesura in **C** could be located after *God*, or before it, with *God* forming the key-stave (mute or full) in a Type IIIa line. There is insufficient reason for omitting *of the world* as scribal with *R–K*. **198 (B 193)** could scan either as Type Ia on |ð| and |f| or as an extended Type IIIb on vowels with semi-counterpoint on |t|, *of* as key-stave and a supplemental vocalic fifth stave (a pattern also possible in **B**). Given the unusual importance of this tree, stressing *a* 'a single' or 'a certain' and *þat* 'that particular' (MED s.v. *on* num. 3(a), 9 (a); *that* def. art. & adj. 2b (a)), would be preferable (on *a*, cf. at 397–98 //). *K–D*'s acceptance (p. 161) of *the trees* Hm for *þe* as the **B** original finds no support in **C**, and *R–K* defy the testimony of Cx in adopting their emendation into **C**. However, F's *of þe*] *þe* βR may be safely taken in the light of **C** as preserving α (from which R will have varied to converge with β). **203 (B 198)** Reasons for the line's loss from α are obscure. *K–D* (p. 69) suggest connotational attraction (*fend* 197, *peyne...perpetuel* 199) or pseudo-grammatical attraction (*wille* 197 > *That* 199), the latter of these seeming the more probable. The presence of the necessary pronoun *I* in ms L, here presumably preserving by pure descent from β or making a commonsense correction of an erroneous β reading preserved in γM, may be contrasted with its absence at 202. In the Cx tradition **pt** (= *x²*) has made a similar error but smoothed by adding *and* to give a sense compatible with Righteousness's being the speaker. **207 (B 202)** *Y*: clearly necessary, since the speaker is now not Righteousness but Peace. The omission in L (? < β) and R (? < α) might not seem noteworthy, given that the γ ms Y joins them, save for the fact that these two copies have already made the identical error twice, at 13.385 and 17.296. Thus, though Y's convergence here may be accidental, it is quite possible that these errors were in Bx and that γF independently made a commonsense insertion (similar to that of L noted at 198), with M doing so by correction from its usual w-type γ source. But whereas in those earlier instances an idiosyncratic usage may be in question, comparable to the omission of the 2 pers. sg. pronoun at C 20.379–80, *I* would here appear to be indispensable. Its loss, which shows no mechanical cause, may therefore be due to misunderstanding *recorde* as imperative, after a prior failure to register Righteousness as the speaker. *preye* Cα: preferable on grounds of sense in both versions. The modal *moet* here and in 208 should be taken to mean not 'must' (MED s.v. *moten* v. (2) 2a) but 'may' (*ibid.* 1a), a sense which overlaps with *mouen* (v. (3) 3). There is thus no substantive revision in 207–08, **B**'s *moot / mowe* variation (which is not a contrast) being perhaps eliminated for that reason. A tone of humble entreaty seems more appropriate to Peace than one of demonstration. *B-β*'s misinterpretation of *moot* 202, together with the 'proof-like' appearance of the analogical argument in 204–16 and possible recollection of 152, may be what prompted ⇒ of *preue*. This is adopted by *K–D* and retained by *R–K* (partly on the witness of N^2's β–contaminated reading), but mistakenly. For whereas in 152 Mercy sets out to *preue by reson* a natural truth concerning poisons that involves *experience* (cf. *euydence* in // **C**), here the religious truth of man's coming salvation through Grace is a matter not of evidence but of faith and is therefore an object not of proof but of prayer. The suasive force of the analogies from experience in each case is a matter of their 'fitness' with God's nature as *Kynde*. **226 (B 217)** *gome*: the harder reading and necessary to provide the key-stave, assuming scansion on lexical words. The line as attested in x^1**p** could in principle scan on |f|, |v| with a liaisonal stave on *of_his*. *C*-t has either retained the correct reading from x^2 where **p** substituted the more familiar non-alliterating synonym convergently with x^1, or it has emended by felicitous conjecture. Influence from **B** here seems less likely, as it is not found elsewhere in t, whereas t's propensity for seeking metrical 'correctness' is widely evidenced. **231 (B 222)** scans on vowels, either as Type IIIa or, stressing *hath* and taking *soffred* as a blank third stave, as Type Ie (with *in* as muted key-stave). The line would undeniably read more smoothly with *see* for *wyte* (so *K–D*), and distraction from the preceding and following appearances of the latter verb in 229 (220) and 233 (224) might sufficiently explain its (unconscious) ⇒ here for a word not in itself difficult. But **C**'s ratification of Bx should quiet conjecture, especially given the pattern of rhetorical *repetitio* revealed in the mounting series [*To wite*] *what wele was...what he haþ suffred...what alle wo is*. To emend in such circumstances would be to interfere like a medieval scribe, as *R–K* seem to realise in not adopting *see*. **235** *loue*: a revision underlining the magnitude of concern shown in God's 'auntring' himself for man. *R–K*'s intrusion of **B**'s *langour* seems editorial *folye*, if not *synne*. **241 (B 232)** *Tho þat* **C**: apparently the only revision in a twelve-line sequence, unless Bx has inverted the words (as has *C-F*), seeing *þat* as a conjunction like the two following in 233–34; but no difference of sense arises. **242 (B 233)** *wyse* Cβ: contextually certain as the nominal adjective, not the noun *wyes* of which *B-α men* is a scribal reflex. **247 (B 238)** scans on |t| as a Type IIIa with a liaisonal first stave in *That_wéren* and a mute key-

stave in *token* 'compensated' by an internal full stave in *stella*, the word that contains the third lift, if the line is read with natural stressing. *K–D*'s conjecture *The oostes* for *Tho þat* is metrically unnecessary and textually unwarranted; the C-Text ratifies a reading in no way defective, as *R–K* apparently recognise by abandoning the emendation. **248 (B 239)** *tenden* **C**: preterite as in **B**, which has the uncontracted pl. form (MED s.v. *tenden* v. (3)). **250 (B 241)** *witnesseth*: preferred as giving a general statement about the elements' recognition of Christ's divinity (cf. 245 //). The preterite may be a misresolution of a tense-ambiguous BxCx form **witnesset*, induced by the tense of the preceding and following verbs. **252 (B 243)** After this C-F adds a line *Lord crist comaunde me to come to þe on watur* included by *Sk* which, though metrically acceptable, appears an evident translation of the following Latin with no claim to authenticity. **255 (B 246)** *heo*: the sun being feminine (*heresulue* 254) and as the clear vocalic form to be preferred here, though Cx probably read ambiguous *he*. *se* Cβ: preferred for **B** (although *mone* α gives a satisfactory T-type line) as both less obvious and more appropriate, the sun representing fire (along with the comet) as the third of the elements described in action so far. **260 (B 251)** *hit lihte*: conjectured as the Cx form of which *hit* x^2 and *lihte* x^1 are diagnosed as split variants. It may be presumed that D has retained the x^1 reading from u and U has converged with x^2, while N^2 has varied from its x^1 primary source to the reading of its secondary **p** source. As reconstructed **C**, which scans as a Type Ic, is to be regarded as a revision, since Bx appears satisfactory in sense and metre and need not be judged imperfect like identical x^2 on comparison with x^1. **261–62 (B 252–53)** Loss of these lines from α may have been occasioned by the successive occurrences of *And* in 250–51, 254, 256–59 (*K–D* p. 69). Alternatively, it could be due to wrong resumption at 254 through identifying *Iesus* as the key-word but omitting the two preceding lines that respectively begin and end in a similar or the same word (an error all the easier had **B** read *Iesus* for *Gigas*, as *K–D* suppose). However, **C** is completely revised, and nothing in **B** (with its characteristic macaronic stave and wordplay) suggests scribal corruption even if, in the absence of α, Bx's exact form is not recoverable. **263** The reading of tN^2 *of helle alle þo* (a. *þo*] *hem* N^2) for *alle of hem*, adopted by *PeR–K*, makes plausibly explicit the sense attested by x^1 and **p**; but it has no real claim to represent Cx. *K–D* (p. 90) hold that this line (in the t form) has been lost by Bx through homoarchy and homœoteleuton (*And...liketh, And...lyue*); if so, it would probably have been in B^1, not a revision as here assumed. But since the sense does not require it, the case for its inclusion in **B** remains speculative. **272 (B 263)** *Principes* x^1: preferred as the harder reading in a line seen as revised to macaronic form. The singular in IP^2U (and the English in **pt**) may result from the scribes' regarding Lucifer as the sole rather than the *immediate* addressee; but the Latin, being a direct quotation, should be given the pl. it has in the psalm-verse. *place* **x**: the likelier original, despite the possibility of irony in *palys* **p**, since **L** thinks of the devil not as ruler of a royal palace but as gaoler of a dungeon or overseer of a domain (it is *paradys* that properly bears the title of *palays* at 378). **288** *the carnel*: conjectured as the difficult but contextually appropriate original to which unsatisfactory *car(e)* '? chariot' (MED s.v. *carre n.* 3(a)) points as a reflex of a damaged or abbreviated original, while being itself the source of the smoothed and less apt variant *oure catel* of **p** (the word is found earlier in the description of Truth's court (7.234 //). The situation being one of war, it is the fortifications that they must first protect (*saue*), only thereafter the property within. Thus both *car* and *catel* should be rejected, while *Pe*'s conjecture *castel* seems too straightforward to have generated either. **293** *mangonel* **p**: the standard form of the word, perhaps spelled with omitted central vowel in x^2 (so tERQWF) and with *n* misread as *r* in x^1. **294** *And with*: the conjectured Cx form of which *And* and *With* appear split variants. Reconstructed thus, the syntax renders **x**'s third *and* redundant, but it may be a mistaken reflex of the proclitic *a-* **p**, here given in the fuller form (*en-*) attested in **M**. **299 (B 276)** *of his* **x**: preferred, despite **p**'s agreement with **B**, as offering characteristic wordplay on the grammatical particle (*of my, of his*). The motive for **p**'s ⇒ of the commoner *by* could have been to remove an apprehended ambiguity.

B 281–3 281 (C 304) *in deol*: conjectured on the showing of revised **C** as the required second stave in a Type IIa line, lost by *dwelle* > < *deueles* attraction in Bx, which scans *aa / xx*. **K–D**'s *driȝten* for *he*, providing the key-stave in a standard line, is unconvincing, since at 13.269, 14.101 (eliminated in **C**) the word has a tone of respectful loyalty inappropriate to the hostile speaker here. **282 (C 307)** *siþen*: conjectured not for the metre (since the line will scan as Type IIIa) but as giving the first of two reasons for Lucifer's confidence. It will have been lost by homœoarchy before *Soop-* or through anticipation of *siþen* (with different sense) in 283, and there may be an echo of it in C 308b, which revises the content of B 282. **283 (C 309)** *I sithen iseised*: the R form taken in the light of revised **C** as preserving that of α and thence Bx. F alters the subject + participle idiom to a full verb-phrase construction while β, omitting the first *I*, treats the second as a subject pronoun, not a participial proclitic, and makes the verb active. The two lines together give the sense 'And since he said...and I afterwards [was] given possession...' *seuenty hundred*: reconstructed in the light of revised **C** as closer to the traditional number (four or five thousand) and, being in the less usual form, easily liable to corruption. It is more likely that *seuene* was misread for *seuenty* than that *hundred* was substituted for

visually dissimilar *thousand*. (For a parallel formation cf. *ten hundred* at B 5.426//).

310 scans in Cx as Type IIIc on |n| or |w|. Possibly *þera-ȝeyne* has replaced *þerewiþ* in the same sense 'against it' (MED s.v. *therwith* adv. 1(a)) in a Type Ia line; but nothing is lost in the text accepted here. **R–K**'s emendation of *was* to *nas* is otiose. **320** scans with monolexical lifts in *bihéstes*, a pattern that is rare but authentic (cf. on 158 above) but reduces the effect of the lexical word *fals*. One possible emendation would diagnose b-half inversion to prose order and read *bihéstes fálse* with the prefix as a mute key-stave but with full stress on the root and the important adjective. Alternatively, *thorw* could be seen as a Cx ⇒ for synonymous *bi*, a word that would facilitate a characteristic wordplay on grammatical morphemes (cf. on 299). However, it seems that **C** favours the causal preposition *thorw* (as at 395, where it replaces *by* in B 350 twice), so it is best taken as authentic here. **322 (B 291)** should perhaps in the light of **C** be spoken by Gobelyn in **B** (as **K–D** judge). But revision here is possible and B 291 as naturally ends Satan's speech as it begins Gobelyn's (cf. 325, where the replacement of *Certes* **B** by *Forthy* is the basis for identifying the 'Deuel' with 'Gobelyne'). **323 (B 292)** *And*: a revision of **B**, with which t's *For* has coincided, perhaps under inducement from a wish to tighten the link between the two clauses. **325 (B 294)** scans cognatively on |d| |d / |t|, though *K–D* see Bx *wol* as an error occasioned by attraction to *God wol* 292. But their conjecture *do* is unconvincing in diagnosing the mechanism of error, inaccurate in judging the metre inauthentic, imprudent in ignoring the confirmatory force of **C** and implausible in reducing Christ's active rôle by supposing that he will 'have them fetched' (no one accompanies *Treuthe* to hell since no one can). On all counts, it is firmly to be rejected, and *R–K* are wise to refrain from emending. **332 (B 298)** **C** revises a Type IIIa to a Type Ia line by adding as second stave *like a tidy man*. **K–D** diagnose its omission from **B** on account of the length of the line; yet usually such length produces not loss of interior phrases but misdivision followed by padding (as here in C-**p**), and errors of this type are not easy to parallel in Bx. This **C** line, like the next, shows **L** actively revising **B**, and apart from their metrical objection, which is ill-founded, there are no grounds for the Athlone editors' emendation. **333 (B 299)** The b-half in **B** contains a 'hanging participle' that could have misled the scribe of w (through failure to grasp the reference) to judge the word an error for a visually similar verb of motion. M has probably altered from a w source. **336 (B 303)** could be a revision of a Type Ib to a Type IIIc scanning on |s| and |ʃ| or to a vocalic Type Ib with stresses on contextually important grammatical words. **341 (B 306)** *seillynge hiderward* **B**: Bx's Type IIIc line scanning on vowel / *s* is acceptable, but in the light of **C** suggests scribal ↔ to the order more familiar in b-verses, with the adverb before the participle. *seillynge*: with sense 'gliding' attested by MED s.v. *seilen* v. 4 (citing this passage), overlapping with one sense of *sylinge* in **C**. The latter more effectively plays on this verb's two senses of 'sink, drop' and 'proceed, go' (MED s.v. *silen* v.(3) (a), (b) respectively) and therefore fits well with the local perspective of the speaker, to whom Christ's approach would be from above. Occurrences of *silen* appear confined virtually to alliterative verse and it is lexically much harder than *seillynge*, which could be a Bx ⇒, if it is not simply a spelling variant (cf. *salid / syled* cited in MED s.v. ibid., from the two mss of *The Parliament of the Three Ages*, l. 657). On balance it seems better not to follow *K–D* in emending to **C**, since *seillynge* gives satisfactory sense and metre, and revision here cannot be ruled out. **343 (B 308)** *the fende* **C**: revising to Type Ia a **B** line of Type IIIc. *K–D* gratuitously judge *he* a Bx ⇒ under inducement from the rhyming monosyllables preceding. **344 (B 309)** *in his* **C**: a revision, taking the verb in the sense 'remain' (MED s.v. *abiden* v. 3(a)) rather than 'endure' or 'face' (ibid. 10(a), 12(a)). *B-F* could preserve Bx from α and R, like β, have lost *in* by haplography after preceding *abiden*; but the sense of βR is acceptable as it stands. **347–48 (B 312–13)** x^2B-α: on intrinsic grounds, the x^2 and α forms of these lines may be judged to represent respectively Cx and Bx, and x^1β to have lost the two half-lines as a result of homoarchy at the caesura (*lesynges* 347 [312], *lesing* 345 [313]). **349a (B 314a)** is possibly intended as a free-standing narratorial comment but is here taken as the clinching line of Satan's speech beginning at 341 and accordingly given in its expanded form as in the **C** copies RM and in **B**. **359–62 (B 315–20)** The revision is relatively free of uncertainty, the loss of 359b in x^1 being explained by eyeskip from *Lucifer* after the caesura to *Lucifer* 360 before the caesura; it drops the three pieces of appended Latin that seem to have occasioned the problems of order, lineation and metre in Bx and in both sub-archetypal traditions. The content is uniformly attested except for the omission of *soone* in R (corresponding to *aloude* in C 360) and sophistication by F of the phrase containing the adverb. *K–D* 's reconstruction yields a sequence logical in thought and correct in metre and is accordingly accepted as that of the probable original. Bx had defective metrical patterns in the lines here numbered 316–18, placing the first Latin phrase after present 317a and the second before 317b. The key to metrical correction is to recognise, in the light of // **C**, that none of the lines are macaronic but that the passage consists of English verse lines and Latin (prose) half-lines in alternation. Thus Lucifer's Latin question *Quis est iste* (316) answers Christ's command (315a), while Christ's Latin *Rex glorie* (318) answers Lucifer's English question (317a). Numbering these lines follows the practice

usual in this edition, only *Dominus virtutum* being treated as a 'citation-line' (319a), because it is syntactically free-standing. The sequence thus runs: 316 (*Quis*); 317 (*What lord*); 318 (*Rex*); 319 (*The lord*); 319a (*Dominus*). **365 (B 323)** *open*: either the adjective or the present-tense verb. Preterite *openede* is acceptable but easier and thus more likely to have been substituted under influence from the preterites *braek* 364 and *songen* 367. **372** *were*: a revision, referring to the original status of humanity. Posited Cx ⇒ for an original *be* (*R–K*) seems tenuous grounds for emendation. **379 (B 337)** *fettest*: containing no subject pronoun, the Ø-form of Cx presumably relying grammatically on the retained force of *thow* in 377. **381 (B 339)** While the revised line scans as Type Ia on |l|, **B** is a Type Ie with the key-stave generated by elision of *þ(e)_ólde*. **382 (B 340)** *be*: necessary for the sense and either by haplography in x^1 or through mistaking the verb as *giled*. **386** scans as Type Ic with the caesura after *lete* and with lyf^2 as key-stave. *anyentised*: spelled with -*issen* in Y, from the extended stem of OF *anientir* (MED s.v. *anientishen* v.); Cx may have read *aniente* as at 19.269 //. **B 343** The Bx line scans imperfectly *aa / xa* through fronting of the adverbial phrase, with consequent loss of the key-stave, and ↔ restores the metre. **393–94 (B 349–50)** The line-division in **C-p** gives an unmetrical 393 (*aa / xa*) with evident padding while that of **x**, though acceptable, awkwardly defers the adverb to the next line. In the light of B 349, which has an object pronoun after the verb, *here* is tentatively restored to the end of 393.

B 351–6 351 scans vocalically as Type IIIc on grammatical words (*in, álle*), the second bearing sentence-stress. The line would scan on |m| with *maugre* for *ayeins* (as in *K–D*) or *alle maner* for *alle*, the latter conjecture making the key-stave a lexical word. But given the lack of **C** support for either, Bx may stand. **356** *þyng* α: preferred as harder than *þo*, with the same terse stress-pattern as β (cf. B 10.127–28). But both may be split variants of Bx **þo þyng*.

397–98 (B 359–60) have *a* as a full stave, though 397 (359) is of Type Ia and 398 (360) of Type IIa (both vocalic). **400 (B 363)** *grettore* **C**-N^2**B**: required as the key-stave, Cx scanning *aa / bb*, and N^2's reading being a felicitous correction almost certainly from a **B** source. *wyddore* **C**β: preferable in **B** as providing a second dimension, *grettore* here (in the context of the metaphor of a growing plant or tree) denoting height. The α error exactly parallels that in Cx, ⇒ at the key-stave of a word familiar from a common repeating phrase, the consequence in both cases being to destroy the metre and conceal the locally discriminated sense of *grettore*. **405** *ne*: possibly unoriginal in its seeming to distinguish a metaphorical drink in the b-half from a literal one in the a-half, whereas the contrast intended is between *two* metaphorical 'drinks', one specific to the learned (*clergyse*), one shared by all (the *comune coppes* of 406). It could be that *ne* was shifted in Cx from a position before *wol* to one before *of*^{2}. **412** Y: required for the sense, as in **B**, and lost for no evident reason unless inducement from three preceding verbs in the 3rd person. **416 (B 375)** revises to Type Ia a **B** line of Type IIIa scanning on vowels (*át; -éuere*) or on |m| in the rhythmically parallel phrases 'mý bíddyng', 'mé líkeþ'. Conjecture of a Type Ia key-stave in |b| before *me* (*best K–D, be Sch*^{1}) is unnecessary. **419 (B 378)** *hole*: accepted on grounds of sense and the showing of **B** as referring to those who are 'entirely' Christ's brethren by sharing naturally in his humanity and sacramentally in his divinity. The ? t variant *holy* (shared by one **p**-ms, N) is a misreading of *hole* perhaps under influence from the sacramental aspect (baptism giving sanctifying grace); *halue* **p** a consequence of misunderstanding the sense (perhaps prompted by 436) or a smoothed reflex of a spelling variant *hale*; *owne* DF an attempt to simplify an idea found difficult. The line allows dual scansion as Type Ib on |b| or as a T-type on vowels and |b| (*aab / [a]bb*), varying 418 (which must scan on |b|), linking with it translinearly by making the latter's blank stave *alle* the first (full) stave of 419, and placing sentence-stress on *hole*. **420 (B 379)** revises to Type Ib a **B** line scanning either as Type Ia with a cognative liaisonal key-stave (|d| |d| / |t|) in *that_is* or, if the key-stave is also muted, as a T-type: *that_is withóuten énde* (*aa / [a]bb*), the latter preferable for its more natural stress-pattern. *K–D*'s *dureþ* for *is* presumes metrical defect where none exists. **422 (B 381)** *hy*: the presumed pl. prn in **C** (with scansion on vowels like **B**), the advancing non-alliterating form being a Cx ⇒ and N a felicitous correction for the sake of the metre. N^2 has *he were a treitour* following *a felown* in 421, readings accepted by *R–K* (p. 102) as corrections from a superior lost **C** source but here judged ⊗ from **B**. **424 (B 383)** **C** offers no obvious difficulty of interpretation, the contrast of *deth oþer iewyse* presumably being between the execution and the judge's passing of sentence, at either of which events the king could arrive by chance (both 'execution' and 'sentence' were primary senses of *juwis(e* (MED s.v. n. 1(a)). The probable Bx reading *deeþ or ooþer wise* appears unsatisfactory because there is obviously no punishment other than death for which *life* could be granted in remission. Thus it seems likely that **B** read *iuwise*, though WHmGC^2 will have corrected independently or by reference to **C**, *els* Cr preserving w's reflex of *oþer wise* and M deriving the same reading from its w-type secondary source. To adopt *iuwise* for **B** but retain *or* will make *ooþer* here an adjective, implying for *iuwise* a punishment other than 'execution' (its usual meaning), e.g. mutilation. But as this conflicts with the logical sense of 384, it may be that **L** deleted *or* in **C** to leave *ooþer* as the conjunction 'or' with the clearer meaning spelled out above. Alternatively, the **B** reading was identical with

C (as judged by *K–D*) and *or* was intruded by Bx or its exemplar through failure to register the sense of *iuwise* as 'sentence to punishment (usually by death)'. This, and not 'execution of punishment (usually by death)', its other sense, is the one supported by *doem* 427 // (which clearly envisages the act of final *judgement*). The smoothing *wise* would then have followed after rejection of *ooþer iuwise* 'other [death] sentence' as illogical. The confusion may have arisen in **B** if **L**'s first thought was indeed the act of execution itself as being interrupted by the king's arrival (421–22). It would thus be acceptable to find no revision in **C** 423–29b and to reject *or* from B 383 as a Bx error. **434 (B 392)** scans vocalically either with an abrupt caesura after *wol* that heightens the stress on the contextually significant stave-word *here* or (less expressively) with the caesura after *wykkede*. The Bx line has the imperfect pattern *aa / xx* and *clene* is here conjectured as the required stave-word lost haplographically after clen*sed*, cler*liche*. Although scansion of the emended line as Type IIa is possible, it reads better as Type Ia with muted key-stave and *clene* playing on its three main senses 'cleanly', 'properly' and 'completely' (MED s.v. *clene* adv. 1(a), 2(a), 3(a)). *K–D* justify their conjecture *keuered* as having been replaced by a 'more explicit' term (p. 198). But a mechanical explanation seems likelier, and the proposed phrase **clene wasshen* will recall an earlier reference to the purgation of sin by divine power at 10.228–29// (see *Commentary* further on the significance of this echo). **436** *halue-bretherne*: a reading adopted by K–D for **B** and defended by Donaldson (1982:72), though **B** contains implicitly what **C** will make explicit. **440 (B 398)** *and*: emended by *PeR–K* after **B**; but the latter is enforcing a deliberate contrast between *al helle* and *al mankynde*, both parts of which are eliminated in **C**. Accidental Cx ⇒ of *and* may be ruled out as improbable, so *and* may be taken as a revision of *al*, giving the non-trivial (and more certainly uncontroversial) meaning 'my mercy and my human nature [which I share with those I shall judge] will hold sway in heaven'. **444** *Tho ledis* t: possibly the x^2 reading from which *ledis* could have been lost by distraction from preceding *lede* (443) and following *leued* in both x^1 and **p**, then smoothed in **p** to *Alle*; or else a felicitous conjecture in the t scribe's manner designed to correct the metre (see 226). The x^1 reading scans as Type IIIa on *I* and in **p** (identical with *B-α*) as Type Ia with muted second and third staves; but both are unsatisfactory in throwing the stress off the important words that link Christ's *love* of the patriarchs with their *belief* in him. The *B-β* line (also Type IIIa) allows a more significant stress pattern (*me, my*), but likewise de-emphasises the verbs. On balance the t reading may therefore be tentatively adopted as the best on grounds of sense and as facilitating characteristic wordplay on *lede* 443 and *ledis*. It further guides conjectural reconstruction of

Bx, in which *ledes* must be presumed lost for the same mechanical reasons as in ?Cx. **448 (B 406)** *leste*: convincingly emended by *K–D* on the showing of **C** as the probable original in **B** for which *boldeste* is Bx's replacement of a non-alliterating term after failing (as did *Sch¹*) to appreciate that the 'fiendkins' (415) would have *less* to fear than the greater 'fiends'. Since **L**'s subtle logic here upsets the conventional expectation that 'daring' would be expected from the 'bold', this scribal (and editorial) error is unsurprising.

B 413 (C 457) For the next 532 lines the unique representative of *B-α* is F. But the readings of this wayward copy are cited in the Apparatus only where they appear intrinsically likely to represent α. Of the extensively sophisticated variants characteristic of F, a few are nonetheless considered when the text of **B** appears uncertain on the basis of sole β and // **C**.

460 (B 416) *That...ne*: adopted as the most unambiguous reading, though not impossibly *That* is elliptical for *But þat*, as seems to be the understanding of Hm, and this 'preclusive' use fits more naturally with the syntax of 461 (B 417). While the Bx reading cannot be finally established, it seems probable that Cx did not have *ne* (cf. on 6.312, 7.61 above). Like F, which may be an intelligent guess, N² also contains *ne* (probably from a *B-β* source). *louhynge*: read in XYI as *loulynge* by *R–K* and recorded as a substantive variant. But *louhynge* as an authentic (if little-instanced) spelling of the gerund seems quite possible as the underlying form of y, and may be accepted here. **464 (B 420)** The preterite *chydde* is unquestionably right on grounds of contextual sense; since Peace desires the sisters' smiles and embraces to cover all trace of their former discord, she cannot be intended to mean that they are still quarrelling. **466 (B 422)** must scan on |r| as a Type IIIa line with a five-syllable prelude, since scansion as Type IIa on |s| subordinates the speaker's name to the function-word *saide*, which will not naturally bear the stress required for position three in this type. **467 (B 423)** *here*: the spelling of the feminine sg. pronoun in Cx but modified in **B** to the normal spelling of the base ms (its potential ambiguity indicated by the substituted adverb in *B-G*). **470 (B 426)** *caroled C-xB-F*: discriminated as the harder and therefore more probably original reading in both **C** and in **B** (F < α = Bx), for which **p** and β *dauncede* is a neutral ⇒ unattended by ambiguous secular overtones (see MED s.v. *carolen* v., esp. the quotations from *Handlyng Synne* and *Cursor Mundi*). **473 (B 429)** *go*: accepted on the showing of **C** as the probable α reading (< Bx) lost in β by alliterative attraction of *Ariseþ* > reuerenceþ.

Passus XXI (B XIX)

In the last two passūs the texts represented, **Cx** (derived from *B²*, whether or not revised in details from *B¹*), and

Bx are here understood as independent witnesses to a single source from which both descend, *B-Ø*, the first scribal copy of the B-Text (see *Intro*. III B § 2). All the divergences between them are therefore noted, even if intrinsically unimportant, as each text contains potential evidence for the original reading of the other.

RUBRICS The Cx tradition is clear in regarding XXI–XXII as *Dobest* One and Two. *B-β* accords in part, implicitly treating XIX as the prologue of Dobest and denoting XX as Dobest One. But with no reliable evidence for α, the exact form of Bx remains uncertain.

12 *his(e)*: proposed in order to resolve the logical contradiction between the Cx reading *Cristes* (possibly *B-α*'s) and the adversative *ac* in 13b, which is supported by *B-β* (*om* F). *C-p* does this through ⇒ of the easier *and* (as have *B-CrC*, perhaps from a *C-p* copy). The *B-α* reading remains unknown, F having Ø in 13b; but there is no contradiction in β's *ac*, since the substantive β reading in 12 is *Piers*. It is uncertain, however, whether F *cristis* preserves α (and so represents Bx) or shows ⊗ from **C**. The reconstruction *his(e)* is difficult enough to have prompted two distinct and unrelated alternative readings. The 'logical' β variant depends on the figure's physical likeness to Piers and recalls Abraham's answers to Will's earlier question at 18.22–6. The 'theological' variant starts from the notion that Jesus after his 'conquest' on the cross bears the title 'Christ'. But since **L**'s understands his 'arms' (visible form) as belonging equally to the divine Son who assumed humanity and to the human nature he assumed, both of which are united in the person of 'Jesus Christ', the reading *Piers* would be satisfactory. Conversely, the contradiction in the *C-x* form would be avoided by reading with *C-p*, which could in theory preserve a revision in **C**. However, it seems improbable that **x** substituted *ac* for Cx *and* so as to render a lucid reading incoherent. On the assumption, therefore, that *ac* is the **BC** original, either *Piers* or the reconstructed form is likely to have been the common reading of B¹ and Bx. Although *Piers* would give good sense in **C** (and is so judged by *PeR–K*), *his(e)* better explains both *Piers* and *Cristes*, while allowing retention of the probable Cx reading *ac*. It is thus adopted as the postulated **BC** original for which Bx and B¹ substituted their respective resolutions. It should be noted that the **C** Apparatus entry omits to record that N² reads *Piers*. This N² reading, which *R–K* (p. 102) do not include with those they consider derived from a pre-Cx copy, is likely to be by ⊗ from a **B** source of β-type.

15 *callede* C: preferred on intrinsic grounds in **B** as almost certainly the reading of α, F's ⇒ being of a non-alliterating *preterite* synonym. *B-β calle(n)* may be a reflex of a tense-ambiguous form **callyt*, g an independent 'commonsense' correction. **18** The absence from **C** of the quotation later given as 80*a* indicates that its appearance here in F is more probably a scribal anticipation than a reflex of Bx. **21** *for to* **C** / *to* **B**: unlikely to be a revision; either could be the common original. **24** *more worthiore* **CF**: the harder reading, and if F = α here, likely to be that of Bx also (the *C*-mss ChQFG have *worþi*). **30** *Ac C-***x**?*B*-β: preferred to *And* **p**B-g on contextual grounds as contrasting the title of conqueror, which is 'special' because not received from another, with the previous two (cf. on *ac* at 13 above). **38** *Baptist* **C**B-L: self-evidently the right reading, with *B*-L's source *l* presumably deriving directly from β and M varying to γ under influence from its usual w-type secondary source. F has smoothed by deleting the article and could have varied through failure to grasp the allusion (see *Commentary*). Although L could be an independent commonsense correction of *baptisme*, or corrected from a **C** source, it probably preserves the reading of Bx; but the α form remains uncertain in the absence of R. **39** *and* **C**: possibly a revision in **C**, which commonly smooths such 'harder' asyndetic constructions. But if F preserves α, it may be that β has simply lost the conjunction by *fra-* > < *fre* attraction (*C*-N² also omits *and*, perhaps following *B*-β). **40** *Iesu*²: distinguished from *Iesus* (at 25), though it is unclear whether **x**'s repetition retains the reading of **B** (the same) or ?β preserves a varied form revised in **C**. (For similar variation between **C** and **B** see at 48, where F is taken to stand for α). **47** *was*: the less common form in pl. use and therefore more probably original, perhaps preferred because *fendes* is a collective pl., or under influence from the number of the following noun. *B*-L preserves from β, F from α, and M has varied with γ, while *C*-p substitutes the customary form, with inversion to prose order.

56–9 may have been lost from β by homoarchy of *And* 56, *And* 60 (*K–D*). In the absence of any control from β or from R, F's text as representing α is assessed in the light of its marked tendency to vary word-order and sophisticate phrasing and expression. **56** C's reading here does not appear a revision but the underlying form of **B**, which F may be judged to vary to prose order. **57** The **C** reading is more pregnant than that of F, even after correction of *his* (1) to *him*, the important idea being not that of Lucifer's *status* but of his actual *position*. F's reading may have been influenced by the preceding reference to *cherles* 55. **59** *lawe*: preferable since *lawe* here has the wider sense 'religion' (MED s.v. *laue* 4(a) or (b)) rather than the specific 'a (set of) rule(s) or ordinance(s)' (ibid. 1(a)).

60 scans as Type Ib with two staves in *lárgeliche*, or on vowels (*hé, álle*) as Type IIIc, so *R–K*'s object-adverb ↔ is unwarranted. *ʒeueth* **x**?α:preferred on grounds of sense to *ʒau(e)* **p**β as referring to Christ's continuing grant of heaven to the just. *Lege* **C**: the adjective as noun, marginally harder than the nominal form in **B**; either could be the common original or there may be a small revision here. **62** *be wel* **C** / *wel be* **B**: both acceptable, with no evidence of revision. **63** *his cros and his* **C** / *cros of his*

B-β: both acceptable, *þerwith* 64, 65 referring with equal propriety to the symbol alone or to the symbol and what it symbolises together (cf. B 14.190–91). If *his* (1) in F, which may reflect α, was also in Bx, it was presumably deleted in β to avoid the awkwardness of a reading **his cros of his passion*. The **C** reading could then be a revision to ease the latter (though **p** brings back some of the awkwardness by omitting *his* (1)). **74** *knelend*: preferable in **C** to the preterite, which may have come in by anticipation of 75 or failure to expand a nasal contraction in *kneléde*.

75–6 The context favours the presence of *(en)sense* in the common **BC** original, and its absence from Cx would indicate its omission from B¹. If F has here preserved it from α, the word will doubtless have been in Bx; but F could have provided at 76 a term judged necessary, as did *B*-Cot at the end of 75 (borrowing the β form at 86) and *C*-R at 76 (employing the native synonym conjectured at 90 below). The placing of the word in *K–DSch¹Pe* is at the end of 75. An explanation for its loss from that point might be failure to grasp the line's rare Type IIb structure; but an original positioning at the head of 76 as the prelude-dip in a long Type Ia line might more easily do so. (Lines with major lexical words in the initial dip are not uncommon, and one occurs below at 89). If L wrote the word in its apocopated form *sense*, it could have been lost in Bx / B¹ or their common ancestor B-Ø through being misconstrued as *sen(n)es* 'afterward' (MED s.v. *sitthenes* adv. (a), found at 78 below) and mistakenly deleted. The witness of B² here, as at 90, indicates that if L had indeed begun detailed revision of B¹, he did not make good all scribal omissions in his copy-text. **76** *withouten mercy askynge*: 'without asking for a "thank you" / 'any favour [in return]'. The text is entirely secure in both Bx and B² (< B¹) and the Cot reading *mercede* over an erasure may reflect both difficulty with this unusual use of *mercy* and acquaintance with an idiosyncratic term first introduced in C 3.290 and memorably elaborated there (*mede* registers similar awareness that the dominant senses of *mercy* would be inappropriate here). *K–D* (p. 160), however, support *mercede* on the grounds of likely direction of variation; they see it as capable of generating a gloss *mede* and a homœograph *mercy* and argue that lexical evidence for the sense 'thanks' is very poor and that the other uses in *PP* are non-analogous 'social gallicisms' (B 1.43 //; the other cases cited, at B 10.220 and 17.86, combine with 'graunt'). But analogous is exactly what this use is, as becomes clear if inverted commas are put around the word in the present instance. The Kings do not ask 'thanks' from their *conquerour noble* because they are subject rulers offering tribute to the *God þat al wrouhte* (20.246), who could say of their *ertheliche honeste þynges* what Christ says to Lucifer about the patriarchs: *Myne þei ben and of me — I may þe bet hem cleyme* (B

18.330). However, as well as 'thanks' (MED s.v. *merci* n. (1) 8(c)), there is present the sense 'favour' (ibid. *s.v.* 5(a)). The Kings seek *no* recognition from the *sovereyn /...of sand, sonne and see*, neither 'thanks' / 'favour' nor *eny kyne catel* (77) such as an earthly conqueror might be expected to offer tributaries in recognition of their homage. Thus while *mercede* could fit the context, there is insufficient reason to suppose it the original underlying *mercy*, and *K–D* 's emendation to **BC** should be rejected. **77** *knoweleched*: the preterite a better fit as the third main verb (coming as a climax after *knelede, offrede*) than as a second participle (after *askynge*). The correct form in F is presumably from α, that in G by felicitous conjecture. The β reading may result from misreading the pret. pl. termination *-eden* as *ende*, the older participial ending still attested in some copies as a relict form (e.g. at 3. 333 and at 74 above). **83** *Rihtfulness*: with the same primary sense 'justice' as *Rightwisnesse* (MED s.vv. 1(a)). Use of the latter (exactly synonymous, but more common) at 88 does not in itself argue against the former (uniquely instanced here in *PP*), as the virtues are assigned various synonyms between 83 and 93 (e.g. *Reuthe, Pite, Mercy* at 83, 92, 93). **84–7** are inserted in X in another hand; they may be presumed to have been lost by eyeskip from *offrede* 83 > *offrede* 87. **86** *sense*: the apocopated form preferred both as rhythmically smoother and as facilitating wordplay on the homophone *sense*, which overlaps semantically with *resoun* (MED s.v. *sense* n., *resoun* n. 10(a) 'meaning, signification'). **88–9** have an identical form in βC; F (? = α) will have lost 88b, 89a through eyeskip (from *gold* before the caesura in 88 to the relative *þat* at 89b after the caesura), partly induced by the presence of *Gold* as the initial word in 89. **90** *richeles*: conjectured as the harder native synonym for *(en)sense*, the word contextually required here (incense = 'reason', gold = 'justice'). The error was probably mechanical in origin, a superficially meaningless form **riche les* inviting ⇒ of a term (*gold*) often associated with the adjective *riche*. This confusion would have been facilitated by the further comparison of *Resoun* to *riht* and *treuthe, the* first of which forms the root of *Rihtwisnesse* ('Resones felawe'). *B-*F, after omitting 88b–89a, rewrites the a-half of 90 as *For it shal turne tresoun*. But the sequence of thought requires *it* to refer to *Rightwisnesse*, whereas the more natural referent would be *reed gold*, giving an unsuitable meaning here. *Resoun*, moreover, is left in F without any elaboration such as *Rightwisnesse* (B 88–9) and *Reuthe* (92–3) receive. *K–D* nonetheless argue for F's as the original reading supplanted through scribal censorship of a line 'mentioning treason in connection with kings'. Their objection to *riche gold* as unacceptable because at 86 incense signified 'reason' naturally holds; but the emendation offered above answers this, and is on all criteria one of the securest for any disputed reading

in the poem. By contrast, *K–D*'s adoption of F appears exceptionally weak, in itself and for the reasons adduced in support; *R–K*'s retention of it defies belief. **91** *cam þo* **C** (*trs* **B**): order of verb and adverb in the common original of Bx and B[1] could have been as here or transposed. *and kneled* **C**B-F: preferred as the Bx / B[1] reading, altered to a participle in β under inducement from *apperynge* 92, *knelynge* 95. **94** *Ertheliche* **C**B-F: preferred on grounds of sense as the common Bx / B[1] reading for which β will have substituted *Thre yliche* following mechanical ↔ of consonants in the first word (|r|, |θ|). **97** *comsed* **C**: possibly a revision of cognatively-alliterating *gan to*, but conjectured here as the original (cf. 106 below) replaced in Bx by a commoner synonym (Cx's ⇒ of *comsed* for *gan to* can be ruled out as improbable). **99** *For* / *Ø*: either could be original. **101** *durste*: presumably a revision of *hadde tyme to* Bx, which provides a cognative key-stave in a Type Ib line (with cognative b-staves). Conceivably Bx could be a ⇒ through objection to the tone of *durste*; but the motivation appears obscure. **108–9** *feste* / *Turned water into wyn* **C**: preferred as the probable reading of B-Ø and reconstructed as that of Bx. The latter appears with wrong line-division but correct word-order in ?α (though with insertion of *he* by F) and correct lineation but wrong word-order in β (here through inverting verb and noun to promote the idea judged most significant). *R–K*'s emendation of Cx to read with β (as presumably harder) surprisingly ignores the witness of F. **111** *lyfholinesse* **C**: rhythmically better and conceptually superior, but not impossibly a revision (*B-W*'s agreement with C is presumably coincidental). **113** *thus*: accepted here as a satisfactory original reading in both Bx and B[1], the variant *vs (B-g, C-y)* resulting from haplographic loss of initial *þ*. Conversely *B-*F's *þus vs* could preserve an original from which *vs* was lost by the same mechanism in B[1] and β; but the rhythm of the adopted form is clearly superior. **115** *þat* / *þe*: either could be original, *B-*WHm here converging coincidentally with C. **117** *only*: clearly right on grounds of sense. *B-*Cr's correction is possibly by collation with a C-Text, M's more probably independent. **134** *the* **C** / *Ø* β: either could be original, so F is not here adopted as representing α. C-WN[2] omit the article, the latter perhaps after comparison with a B-β copy. **135** is to be scanned as a 'licensed' macaronic with the anomalous pattern *aa / xx* found at 7.152 // above. The (possible) emendation of *et* to *sed et* would not be supported by the Biblical source in its well-established form. **140** *Herof* **C**: perhaps slightly preferable to *Wherof* β, but it is not a necessary stave-word and either could be original. *Ø* **C** / *of þe* **B**: either could be original, though the rhythm of the latter is smoother. **142** *on a* / *on*: either could be original or both reflexes of **a* 'on / one'. **148** *deuyned* **C**: 'foretold,' 'prophesied' (MED s.v. *divinen* v. 1(b)), found earlier in this sense at 17. 312 and B 15. 598; possibly a revision of *demede* **B** (MED s.v. *demen* v. 11b, c 'suppose, expect') with which senses 2(b), 3(b) of *divinen* partly overlap (*pace* the argument of *R–K*, p. 119). In both texts the referent of *men* is the *profetes* of 145, and *deuyned*, while an improvement in precision, is more in the nature of a repetition than *demede* (which could, however, be a visual error for the latter).

151–52 The *B*-β single-line form is plausible, but in the light of F unlikely to be that of Bx. F has, however, added an extra lift in the phrase *a mortuis* (independently accompanied here by the unrelated Cot) and substituted *he* in the b-half, perhaps through objection to applying a neuter *it* to Christ's risen body. Four unrelated **C** sources of the x^2 family insert *rex* in the a-half to make the line scan as a macaronic Type Ia, and this monosyllable could have been lost by haplography before *res-* (so *K–D*). But in the majority of **C** mss (= Cx) and in Bx the line will scan either as Type IIIa, with two lifts in *résúrgèns* or, preferably, as Type Ia with an internal |r| stave in *Chrístus*. The form of the Latin phrase, securely that of its Biblical source, is confirmed by its repetition at 160. **153** *Ø* CB-F /*he* β: either could be original (with F representing α), though more probably *he* was lost by *hem* > < *ʒede* attraction. **154** *preyede* (2) **C**: adopted for **B** as the likely original, with synonymous Bx *bisouʒte* (scanning in principle with a mute cognative stave *bi-*) a ⇒ following objection to the repeated verb (*K–D*, p. 95). The F line, except in preserving *þo*, appears not a reflexion of α but a scribal attempt to 'correct' the metre, *propre* having no ascertainable contextual appropriateness. There seems to be wordplay here on co-polysemes of *preien* (MED s.v.1a (a) and 1b (a)). But the repetition of a word with little real difference in sense has already been instanced at B 16.159 // (*pays; pees*), where F has characteristically sophisticated the b-half in a similar way. **159** *heo* p**B**: lost in **x**, perhaps through haplography if the exemplar form was *a.* **161a–62** C β: omitted by F for no immediate reason, unless eyeskip from *Christus* 160 to *Christum* 161 (though this does not explain loss of 162). **164** *Ø* / *for*: either could be original (cf. the converse situation at 21 above). **175** *Ø* / *Thow*: the 2nd pers. sg. preterite without pronoun, instanced earlier at 20.379–80 but not in // **B** and possibly a revision-feature in **C** or the reading of B-Ø, the <B¹Bx> source, smoothed to the more conventional form in Bx. **180** *be* CF: preferred to *alle be* β, here identifiable as a more emphatic scribal reading. **183** *thouhte*: to be preferred on grounds of sense as the original in **BC**, and not a **C** revision. Christ's intention is to perform an *act*, that of giving the sacramental power of forgiveness to the apostles; his *teaching* of them has been completed on Holy Thursday night. The Bx error could have been visual, though *t* for *th* is less frequent than *th* for *t* (cf. 239 below); the α reading is undiscernible through F's sophistication. **186** *To hym*: conjectured on the basis of

Hym B-βC-**x**, the presumed reading of both Bx and B¹, as the reading underlying both, from which B-Ø will have lost the preposition through homoarchy (*To* at 185). The key point is that 'forgiveness' (MED s.v. *pardoun* n. 1(a)) may be granted to all, but ability to 'release from temporal penalty' (ibid. 1(b)) to Piers alone, this being the sacramental *power* specified in 180. Since that is the inescapable sense of the lines, *K–D*'s more drastic transference of *Hym*186 to final position in 184 and transposition of 185 with 186 is quite unnecessary. Indeed, if absolute *Hym* were an acceptable prepositionless dative, no emendation would be required; but since the usage sounds unidiomatic and reads confusingly, it is not retained. **187** The present subjunctive in Bx is as acceptable as the preterite, though formally less correct than WHm strive to be (see Appendix). **C**'s preterite could be revision, or either might be original. **190** *to* / *Ø*: the probable archetypal readings are retained; again, either could be original. *elles*: preferred as both harder (MED s.v. *elles* adv. 5) and metrically smoother, β being presumably represented by L, α by F. For **L**'s use of this adverb in line-final position and in temporal sense, cf. Pr 89 //. The phrase *here or / ne elliswher*, found at 15.300 //, 19.163 // and *otherwhile elliswher*, found at 10.29 //, are placed only in the a-half. **194** *reddit*: the present tense, preferred to the future as the original since the second verb is also present, as is the English of 195 that translates it (*Payeth*). **197** scans as Type IIa, reading *dómesdáy*, with a supplementary stave in position five. **198** *Ø* / *þe*: the **C** reading arguably harder as implying the idea of *theosis*; but *þe* could have been lost through *gode* > < *God* attraction. **205–07** In Cβ; loss of these lines from F (though not necessarily from α) may have been by eyeskip from *Conscience* (205 end) to *Quod Conscience* (208 beginning). **206** *for* (1) **C**: with its characteristic wordplay arguably preferable for **B** as the harder reading (so *K–D*). In the absence of F, α is undeterminable, but *of* β makes good sense. The ?Bx line will scan satisfactorily as Type IIIc, as will Cx (which, however, has the alternative scansion *aab* / *ab* as Type Ie with counterpoint). **211–13** In Cβ, loss of the Latin in 211 after *wiþ* in F (perhaps through a rubricator's oversight), occasioned loss of 212–13, so that the scribe (whether of *f* or of α) picked up from *And thanne* 214 instead of *Thanne* 212. **212** *And...þo* C-**p** / *Thanne...song* B-β: the adverb seems confirmed as substantively archetypal on the showing of **p** and β; but *þo* could be an intruded **p** form (it substitutes at 214 for *And thenne* x**B**). Its position and the subject-verb order remain uncertain, though revision is unlikely here. *R–K* adopt the N² reading, that of B-β,(as again at 224 below). **213** scans as Type Ib on cognative staves (|k| |k| / |g| |g|). *K–D*'s emendation *Crist* for *God* is metrically superfluous and theologically imprecise, since it is the Holy Spirit who is being invoked in the Latin, not the Son, and *God of grace* appears an integral phrase.

214 *the*: a form that occurs in both versions at the end at 22.386 and is commoner than the Ø form. Cx gives, preferably, a Type IIb line and Bx can be scanned as Ia or T-type, so no alteration is warranted here. **217** *can* **C**B-LF: 'have mastery of' (MED s.v. *connen* v. 3(a)); required as the key-stave and self-evidently harder than *han*. F appears to attest α and L to preserve β, with M varying to the γ reading under presumed influence from its w-type source. *his(e)* **C**B-F: the harder reading, smoothed to the grammatically more logical pl. under the influence of *hir* 218 after *creatures*, which perhaps retains from the common source of <BxB[1]> a pluralised form of a collective sg. *al kyn creature. **224** *And...and* **C**B-F: agreement with **C** here supports F's reading as that of α. *B-β* may have lost the first two words through promotion of the dominant notion (*Pride*) and the conjunction through alliterative attraction (*Pope* > < *prynce*). *R–K* adopt the reading of N[2], which is, as usual, that of *B-β*. **228** The variant *gom* is metrically otiose but illustrates t's readiness to retain or substitute alliterating synonyms for 'man' (cf. on 20.226, 444). Group t also omits the article *a* and the phrase *to gye with*. **229** *hem* **C** / *hym* **B**: the sg. fitting better with *vch man*, but the pl. according correctly with *ʒow* 226. It could be a revision or either could attest the common original. **230** *wyes*: conjectured as the required first stave-word which Cx has replaced with the common non-alliterating synonym and Bx omitted; as they stand, both scan *xa / ax*. The Ø-reading of Bx could have been the result of distraction from *wit* at the end of the a-half and again at the beginning of 231 (if its source read *wyes*), or from preceding *som(me)* if it read *men*. That Cx had *men* seems virtually certain, despite the fact that three unrelated **C** copies and one group read Ø. Though in principle t could here preserve the reading of *x²*, while both *x¹* and *p* severally could have substituted *men* for Ø, it is more probable that tP²EW have all lost *men* for the same reason as has Bx. **231 C** could be revised, the sense being somewhat different. *K–D* reject Bx for **C**, but this is an unsafe emendation. For the former is not evidently scribal, and the small but significant change could easily have been made in **L**'s copy-text (B[1]) without causing disarrangement of the lines. **B** could be rendered more economical by deleting *hir liflode* and reading *þat* for *as* (the latter the reading of *C*-t). This would make the postulated **C** revision a mere matter of omitting initial *Wit* (as one *B*-ms Cot has done) and then inserting *treuthe*; but reconstruction of **B** on these lines remains too speculative. **236** Both Cx and Bx have an unmetrical line (*xa / ax*), which *K–D* emend by reading *By* (the preposition already instanced in 233 and 234) for *Wiþ*. But while this facilitates characteristic wordplay on the key-stave *bilyue*, which may have its prefix stressed, it unnaturally emphasises the particle in its proposed initial position (contrast the effect of stressed *by* at B Pr 80 // and B 3.10, the latter

revised in **C**). The reading adopted here, with ↔ of the *lexical* words in the a-half, yields a Type IIIa line while retaining a natural stress-pattern. The inversion, whether occurring independently in BxB[1] or present in B-Ø, could have resulted from promoting the idea thought most prominent in 'winning one's livelihood' by trade, i.e. *selling*. As in an earlier instance (20.400 above), a single *C*-copy N[2] anticipates the present emendation; but its citation in the Apparatus here does not imply that it is any more than a felicitous scribal correction. **237–38** are in **C** and *B*-F, and loss of 237b and 238a is attributed to Bx by Chambers and Grattan (1931:6). But the error pertains to β, which will have lost it through homoteleuton at the caesura (*laboure...labour*), aided perhaps by unconscious suggestion from the collocation of *lelly* to *lyue* with *by labour* at 233 above. The resulting line's acceptable sense and metre would have effectively concealed the error from detection, as it did from *Sk*. **239–40** Differences between Bx and Cx appear here which could be due to revision. 239 scans with a mute key-stave *to* or in **B** possibly with a cognative full stave *dyche*. C 240 rewrites a line which both repeats in its a-half the sense of B 231a (itself re-written in **C**) and supplies a correct if unforceful b-half. However, B 240 scans acceptably as Type I with two lifts in *liflóde* (as earlier at B 14.48) and both this pattern and the position of *wiþ* reveal variation here as well as repetition of 231a. In 239 *K–D*'s complex argument (pp 174–5) for *coke* in place of *dyche* relies on too many suppositions to justify emendation. In the Cx tradition, *theche* as the first verb is not seriously in doubt, with *teche* being, as *Sk* recognised (Apparatus), merely a spelling variant of a kind paralleled in Bx at 183 above. *R–K*'s re-arrangement of the verbs (p. 125) presupposes non-revision without arguing for it. In 240, their replacement of **C** by B 240 is radical interposition on the slenderest grounds. **241** has the inauthentic scansion *aa / xx* in both Bx and Cx. *K–D*'s emendation (p. 207; so *R–K*) provides in *figures* (MED s.v. *figure* n. 6(a) 'numerical symbol') an apt and rare lexeme for which *noumbres* could well be a scribal ⇒ (perhaps a B-Ø marginal gloss incorporated into the text in Bx and B[1]). An even apter and rarer term is *digit*, first instanced in Trevisa's *Bartholomew* (MED s.v.), which would give scansion on |d|. *Pe* omits *to kenne* after t, producing a line with cognative scansion (|t| |d| / |d|) but a stress-pattern with nothing to justify its deviance. The earlier emendation in *Sch*[1] with *diuerse* as a key-stave judged lost through a combination of homoarchy and the length of the line is here abandoned for a less drastic conjecture *of* 'concerning' (MED s.v. *of* prep. 23a). This provides a stave by liaison (*of_noumbres*) so inconspicuous as easily to have suffered loss in Bx and again in Cx (if not omitted in B[1]). **242** *some* **B**: easily omitted by homœoarchy before *com-*, its inclusion making the **C** line fit better with the pattern of the preceding categories introduced by *som(m)e*. But too little is lost by its absence for emendation of Cx here to be worthwhile. *craftily*: adopted from Bx as the second stave-word and judged lost through *com-* > < *col-* attraction in Cx (*C-F* has either conjectured independently or derived the adverb from comparison with a **B** source). The *first* stave *To keruen*, adopted by *PeR–K* (and by *K–D* for **B**), is attractive on grounds of sense and metre. But it appears more probably the t scribe's alteration of *to kenne*, which he omits from the end of 241, an easy mechanical error if his exemplar had the inconsequential reading **To kenne and to compace and coloures to make*. D²'s *keuer,* if intended for *keruen,* may be similarly accounted for, and H²'s *lernen* for *keruen* may point to *kenne* in t's source. It is possible that B¹ (and **B**) lacked an adverb, *cómpáce(n)* scanning with two lifts and *craftily* being a later Bx filler. But the insertion of adverbs is not a habitual feature of Bx, and as the sense of the whole phrase 'to practise architecture skilfully according to the rules of the profession' is convincingly non-trivial, it may be adopted as the intended reading in **C** (see MED s.vv. *compassen* v. 2(b) and *craftili* adv. (b)). **244** *wel* **B**: conjectured as the required key-stave presumed lost through *telle it* > < *it felle* attraction. The sense is either 'carefully' or 'successfully' (MED s.v. *wel* adv. 3a, 4a) or 'long' (ibid. 16). The b-half of **C** is adopted by *K–D* in place of Bx; but the former is scarcely hard enough to have invited 'substitution of a more explicit reading' (*K–D* p. 95). What this may be is a revision, perhaps to avoid the repetition in *er it fel* of *what sholde bifalle* 243, one that **L** could have easily made in his copy (B¹) by deletion of *telle...felle* and substitution of *and...bifore*. An alternative conjecture would be *wite*] *telle*, which is closer in sense to *be ywaer* **C** and could have been lost through partial haplography after *it* (and then smoothed). However, Bx's internal rhyme is demonstrably characteristic of **L**'s style (cf. B 1.33, 2.198 //, 3.265; C 10.303, 12.78) and the half-line may be judged substantively original, though having suffered mechanical loss of the adverb. **247** Either *men* **C** or *hem* **B**-β could be the common original, though *men* could have come in from 248 (*R–K* emend to *hem*). In the absence of F, lost doubtless through homoarchy (*And* 246, 248) assisted by the flow of thought from 246 (*recouere*) to 248 (*fecchen*), the α reading is irrecoverable, and it may be that Bx read as Cx. **252** shows what could well be revision, and despite Bx's imperfect metre, its substantive reading should not be rejected as 'more emphatic and explicit' (*K–D*, p. 95). The metrical defect in the b-half may be ascribed to Bx's ⇒ of the non-alliterating preterite under influence from the tense-sequence of the main verb (*forbad*). The construction may be understood as a mixture of indirect and semi-direct command, the present tense following without difficulty as in **C**, where it provides the key-stave conjectured here for **B**.

B 254–55 254 is followed by four lines of doggerel in F (printed *K–D*, p. 223) which the scribe has made no attempt to correct metrically and may represent an intrusion into its direct source *f,* or into α. But while in the absence of R their status remains undeterminable, they can be dismissed as of no textual interest. B 254 is judged spurious by *K–D* (p. 193) with no sufficient grounds and without discussion. But it scans satisfactorily as a Type IIIa with a six-syllable prelude dip, resembling in its rhythmic structure lines of unusual length like B 13.255 //. Moreover, its substantive content is not to be dismissed as due to 'scribal participation in the sense of a living text' (*K–D*); on the contrary, its quasi-egalitarian implications suffice to explain why, in a specific social context (see *Commentary*) **L** might have wished its removal. (It should emerge clearly from comparing B 254 with the pair after B 373, or with the other ten spurious lines in Bx [*Intro.* III B § 60 (iv)] why *K–D*'s judgement of it is rejected). C 254 now follows its omission of B 254 (as not 'scribal' but too radical) with a more conciliatory expression of the view that skill and knowledge are gifts of grace. **255** This line, to which C 254 actually corresponds, will scan acceptably on cognative staves (|g| |g| / |k|). But the a-half's sense is weak, *alle* referring unconvincingly to the addressees rather than to the *craft and connyng* that it qualifies in **C**. A simple reconstruction, bringing the line closer to the structure of **C** and incidentally generating characteristic homophonic wordplay, would be *þat al grace quod Grace* (the ease with which the Bx a-half could have been generated from such a reading is obvious). But the thought is banal and appears suspiciously like a dilution of the bolder idea that natural accomplishments and not just supernatural virtues are among the fruits of the Spirit's activity. The line as reconstructed is of Type Ia with a natural stress-pattern on cognative staves |k| |g| / |k|.

255 (B 256) Either *alle* Bx has come in from 255 or has been lost in Cx through visual assimilation to following *as* (especially if in the form *al*, the adverb). Revision seems unlikely here. **256 (B 257)** Either *he* **C** or *who* **B** could be original, although if both are reflexes of **ho*, it is **B** that will be substantively right (as judged by *R–K*). **268 (B 269)** *sethe* **C** / *yit* ?*B*-α: either could be original and revision is unlikely. Given the closeness of F and **C**, β's altered Ø-reading (which offers no help in discriminating) is unlikely to represent Bx, and *K–DR–K*'s endorsement of it is ill-founded. **269 (B 270)** The infinitive *to harwen* **C**-p**B** following an implied verb of command is preferable to the preterite *to harwed* **C**-**x**, since the action does not occur till 273 (on the construction cf. 233 above). Thus **x** will have mistaken *to* for the numeral and *harwen* for present indicative and smoothed the verb to accord with the tense of *gaef* 268 (P²uW omitting the 'numeral' presumably as contradicting *foure* 268). **271 (B 272)** scans cognatively (|g| |g| |k|) as Type IIa with a supplemental voiced stop in position five. Transposing *Ieroem* and *þe gode* (K–DR–KSch[1]) is accordingly superfluous. **272 (B 273)** Either *folewede* C or *folweþ* B could be a resolution of a tense-ambiguous original **folwyt*. The preterite goes better with 273, but mixing of tenses is frequent. **274 (B 275)** *aythes* C?α: preferred as the harder reading for which β will have substituted a commoner synonym that here alliterates acceptably. The word was very rare and is cited by MED s.v. *eithe* n. only from this line. F's spelling presumably reflects an α form **(h)ayptes*, with non-organic aspirate and subsequent *ȝ* / *þ* confusion. **276** *he*: lost in copies of B and C by haplography after preceding *set he*. **278 (B 279)** *þat* (2) xβ: preferred as the simpler reading, *frut* F being inappropriate in sense, *seed* p superfluous (though perhaps inserted to make the formula uniform with 283, 291, 300) but both scribal elaborations of a terse original. **281 (B 282)** *kele* C: a harder reading than *kepe* B, which could have been suggested by *saue* in the b-half. But the greater vividness may be due to revision, so rejection of Bx is unwarranted. The sense of B here is 'watch over, attend to' (MED s.v. *kepen* 14a). **285 (B 286)** scans cognatively on |ʃ| and |s| (found internally in the group |sk|), and failure to grasp this could have led β to insert an extra stave-word in |sk|. **286 (B 287)** *neuere* C / Ø B: added by Cx or lost from Bx by homoarchy (*ne*, **nere*). **296 (B 297)** The substantive reading is not in doubt, though evidence is evenly divided in C as between the infinitive and the preterite (*plede[d]*), the verb co-ordinating either with *soffre* 295 or with *keuered* 297. The former is favoured as more likely to underlie the present tense in β, which has the wrong verb (presumably a corruption of a form spelled ambiguously **pleit*), though F's tense has cross-family support in the Cx tradition. While the contending verb-forms are distinct (though etymologically cognate) words, their primary senses overlap exactly (MED s.v. *pleden* v. (a), *pleten* v.1(a)). The metaphorical reference here is to the man with fortitude who will 'go to law' only by enduring injustice patiently. The sense of β *pleieþ* 'deal with, handle' (MED s.v. *pleien* v. 1, 8(b), citing only this case), is undeniably hard, and in the form **pleit* could as easily have invited ⇒ of more obvious *ple(t)e*. But the legal metaphor, which is lost by *pleieþ*, seems decisively indicated by the quotation at 298, which both concludes Fortitude and effects a transition to the next virtue, Justice (now specifically concerned with procedure in court). N[2]'s *plaieþ* is presumably taken by R–K as correction from a lost superior C source (though not listed on p. 102) but is here judged yet another case of this copy's ⊗ from a B ms of β–type. **300–01 (B 301–02)** The resolution *euene* C is preferred to *euere* as more apt in context, its implications of balance, exactness and consistency (MED s.v. *even* adv. 3, 7, 15) marginally better fitting with justice (*trewe* / *With*

God) than that of constancy (*euere*) and echoed in the punning *eueneforth* at 310. Bx's error, doubtless visual, recurs in several C copies. **303 (B 304)** scans cognatively on |b| and the |p| staves internal to *aspyed* and *Spiritus*; emendation of *May* to *Shal* (K–DR–K) is therefore gratuitous. *thorw* C: preferred also in B as conveying precisely that justice is the agency through which good faith finds out guile. Although *for* overlaps with this sense (MED s.v. *for* prep. 4), the Bx reading is more probably an auditory error for *þoruȝ* than an original form revised in C, and if carrying a possible ambiguity (ibid. 1(a) 'on account of') that is better avoided. **304–05 (B 305–06)** Both Cx and Bx misdivide these two lines as three, presumably in consequence of their exceptional length, and only C-ms Y, probably by felicitous conjecture, gives the lineation adopted here. Of the Cx lines, the first scans as Type IIIb, the second is unmetrical and the third scans *aa / xa* (the final stave being cognative). In Bx the first and second lines are identical with Cx, the third (on the sole basis of β, since F is sophisticated) *ax / ax*, with cognative key-stave. Even after re-lineation, however, the b-verses of 305/306 remain discrepant, with a choice of C variants. The reconstruction here finds in the Bx and C-p expansions scribal reflexes of the postulated generalising expression *kynne(s)*, which now forms the key-stave. This involves taking *agulte* x, here uniquely (and doubtfully) attested as a noun (MED s.v. *agilt* n.), to be identical with *gilt* Bx (so C-DH[2]). The p variant *gulty* is then seen as a smoothing of this difficult word to the adjectival form, with *any þynge* p and *or in trespas* Bx being reflexes of the conjectured form *any [kynne]*. In the a-half, it may be that *kyng* (2) Cx was also in Bx; but this could have been a C revision of *he*, one easy to make by supralinear correction in B[1]. The construction with repeated subject has a close parallel in 20.55 //, where C repeats *Crist* in revising, and thus there is no sufficient reason to emend the a-half of B as do K–D (p. 95). The scansions of the two lines, with their (identically) reconstructed b-halves, are now *aax / aa* for B (Type Ie with cognative supplemental stave in fifth position), and *aaa / aa* for C (Type Id with cognative fifth stave). **308 (B 309)** *dede þe lawe*: 'carried out the law', rigorous adherence to the detailed requirements of the law being here stressed (cf. 310). L may be presumed in the light of Cx to preserve β, and F to preserve α, against the looser γ reading with which the two C copies DG converge. The wider sense 'administered justice' is expressed in 310. **310 (B 311)** The two words forming the last lifts overlap in their sense 'ability to do' (MED s.v. *knouing(e* ger. 5, citing this line, and *pouer(e* n. 1(a)). C could be a revision, either could be original and the other a scribal ⇒, or both could be synonym-reflexes of a common original *conninge* (MED s.v. ger. 1). Given the uncertainty, both should be allowed to stand, and K–D's judgement of Bx as 'more emphatic'

(p. 92) rejected. **316 (B 317)** *forthy* **C**: to be preferred on grounds of sense as the original for which Bx substituted a post-positional adjective, presumably through misinterpreting an exemplar form of the conjunction spelled *uorþi* (*u* representing the labial spirant with Southern voicing). The motivation for this could have been the apparently abrupt transition from exemplum to conclusion, an abruptness *C-p¹* eases by inserting *and*. The mislineation, giving an unmetrical line and an excessively long 318, will have resulted from mislocating the caesura after *vices*. **318 (B 319)** scans as Type Ia with a mute cognative key-stave in *cardinál(e)* rather than as Type IIa with wrenched stress on *aftúr*. *K–D*'s conjecture (p. 118) of *to* 'according to' (MED s.v. prep. 12a) for *after* (an easier reading) deserves consideration. **320 (B 321)** *Peres*: the obviously right reading on contextual grounds, *quod* in *B*-LMCr, *C*-y*B*-LM being a visual error induced by the immediate presence of *quod Peres* in the next line. *B*-WHmCr³ have corrected commonsensically, the last of these possibly by reference to a **C** source. **323 (B 324)** scans as Type Ic on cognative staves (|g| |g| |k| / |k|). *K–DR–K*'s conjectural emendation *garland*, having no metrical or other justification, is wholly gratuitous. **324 (B 325)** Despite the separate etymological origins of *peyned* **C** / *pyned* **B** 'suffered' (from OF and from OE respectively), one sense of *pyned* (MED s.v. *pinen* v. 3(b)) exactly coincides with that of *peinen* (s.v. 1(d)), and either could be original. *C*-D²ChG *pyned* endorse **B**'s (possibly intended) internal rhyme in the b-half (cf. 325b). **331 (B 332)** *déuýsed*: a rare but authentic 'monolexical' pattern found at 7.170, 20.158, 320 (and see *Intro*. IV § 38). **332 (B 333)** *hoem Peres* **C**: the securely conjectured original reading in **B** also, of which ?α *hoom* and *Piers* β appear as classic split variants. **334 (B 335)** scans on vowels with wrenched stress on *-hóed* and *hym-* as mute key-stave. **336 (B 337)** *londe* **C**: preferred as also the original reading for **B** on grounds of contextual appropriateness. Under inducement from preceding *trupe* and following *lawe*, F, perhaps not representing α here, appears to have substituted an abstract term through failure to grasp the metaphor of the 'land of faith' (on other allegorical 'lands' cf. 11.169, 15.190 and *Commentary*). The line may have been lost from β as 'a delaying syntactical unit through attraction between *Piers* 33[6] and *Piers* 33[8]' (*K–D*, p. 67). **337 (B 338)** Omission of *and* **B** (so *K–DSch¹*) gives a terser line; but the change to Ø **C** could have been made by deletion in B¹ and it is therefore retained. **341 (B 342)** The figure of Presumption as a single sergeant-of-arms accompanied by a single spy (*Surquidous; sergeaunt* β) would seem to make superior sense, the word being well-attested (MED s.v. *surquidous* adj. (a), though with no other certain examples of a personification), and C15th examples of the form *surquidour(s)* **C**?α are cited by MED s.v. *surquidrous*

adj. If the *s*-ending of the latter is, like that of *paramours* at 16.105, not intended as a sign of plurality, *seriauntes* pl. may be a Cx error based on wrongly inferring that it is. But if the pl. form attested in *B*-F's variant reflects α, the reading of Bx may well have been identical with that of Cx. As the texts stand here, *Thise two* 344 in **B** refers to the Sergeant and the Spy-with-Two-Names, in **C** more naturally to the spy and another companion or, if Spill-Love and Speak-Evil are one, less naturally to *one* of the 'sergeants' despatched by Pride. Probably the most satisfactory solution would be to see *Surquidours* as the (idiosyncratic) original form of the name (constructed on the analogy of a word such as *paramours*) with *sergeaunt* sg. qualifying it, and *Surquidous* as a β normalisation of an unfamiliar form. On the evidence of F, unless ⊗ from **C** is posited, revision is probably to be ruled out and Cx *seriauntes* could be fairly safely emended to the singular. **344–45 (B 345–46)** In the light of *C-p* the Bx*C*-**x** lines appear unoriginal in their misdivision, which leads to loss of the first stave-word. Bx has also lost the second stave-word, perhaps through *Sire > Piers* attraction, with subsequential smoothing of the a-half in β*F*, and reconstruction after *C-p* restores *sedes* to its proper position. The correct verb in **B** can be reliably discerned as preterite, but given the corrupt condition of β and the sophistication of α in F, the precise form of Bx is undeterminable except for the misdivision and loss of *Sire*. The reason for the latter was perhaps objection to applying the customary title of a knight or priest to a ploughman (as he was earlier), though it is poetically appropriate to Piers in his new capacity as a symbolic pope-figure. **347 (B 348)** *and* (1): probably the reading of Cx*B*-β and acceptable as extending the threat to include the addressee, but without prefacing his name with the personal pronoun *ȝe*. *K–DR–K*'s omission is arguably preferable on stylistic grounds. *caples tweyne*: ↔ (following *K–D*) restoring the key-stave doubtless lost in *B*-Ø (< Bx*B¹*) by inversion to prose order. The disyllabic form of the numeral, presumed altered in B-Ø to its usual pre-nominal form, is adopted to provide the necessary feminine ending. **348 (B 349)** The ↔ of the *partes penitentiae* in **p** to the more usual order is presumably a scribal 'correction'. But the Bx*C*-**x** order *Confessioun; Contricioun C*-**xB** has its own logical sequence: ritual act (personal and outward), spiritual disposition (personal and inward), religious condition (collective, outward and inward). **349 (B 350)** *oure*: clearly required by the sense; *ȝoure* may have come in mechanically by inducement from *ȝoure* in 347b, 348b. The Ø-readings may reflect deletions of *ȝoure* sensed (rightly) as inappropriate. **350–51 (B 351–52)** On the assumption that y has varied and that **p**ut preserve Cx (confirmed by Bx), the two identical lines appear to scan somewhat awkwardly (in the Apparatus 't' should be 'tu' and '*x¹*' should be 'y'). 350 is either a Type IIIb with the caesura after *nat* or (better) a Type Ia with 'monolexical' lifts in *Cóntricioun*, 351 a Type IIIc, with caesura after *ho* or *is,* or (better) a Type IIIa with caesura after *Cónfessioún*, (metrically balancing 350b). *K–D* (p. 119) object to the metrical inadequacy of the second line (but not of the first, which presents much the same difficulty) and to 'the bad sense of the two' if they 'understand the allegory correctly' (this they may not). Pride's emissaries are asserting that because their guile will throw a veil of deception and confusion over the practice and administration of Penance, Conscience will be unable to tell from men's outward behaviour or from (what they erroneously consider) their inner disposition whether they really are Christian or not. *K–D* judge that *be Contricioun / Ne be Confession* was a 'misguided gloss' intruded in the common ancestor [of BxB^1 = B-Ø] with 'consequent redivision' (and *Pe* favours this view, though without emending). By removing the 'gloss' they generate a single line of superior metre (and sense): *That Conscience shal nat knowe ho is Cristene or hethene*. But despite this improvement of the metre without significant loss of meaning, *K–D* have not explained why the 'gloss' was intruded in the first place. A possible mechanism accounting for this would be the presumption that B-Ø read *knowe þerby*, the referent being necessarily understood as the two elements of Penance, which the 'gloss' then specified. The latter could thus be held to have been 'intruded' without being 'misguided', since it would merely spell out what the adverb implied. But with so little to be gained, *K–D*'s invitation to improve the text is better declined. **358 (B 359)** The Bx reading *to*] *we* C (shared by *C*-MN^2) involves a change of construction in B 360, where *holde* becomes co-ordinate not subordinate, and the grammatically smoother form could be a revision. **360 (B 361)** *Ø* C / *And* B: the conjunction may have been added in Bx (as in *C*-t) to ease an abrupt transition. **365 (B 366)** Either *For* B or *Ø* C could be original, though *Ø* is usual in **L** after verbs of commanding, exhorting or entreating. *and diche*: harder than the nominal construction, induced by preceding *deluen*, which raises an expectation of an object. *al* C-**p**B-F / *Ø* C-x**β**: a small word that makes an important point about the protection (an encircling moat), and possibly lost by visual assimilation to ab*oute* following, under inducement from the phrasal rhythm of *deluen and dyche* and misassignation of the caesura. But the line is of the rare Type IIb with a strong pause after the adverb *depe*, which expresses KYNDE WIT's first order, and a heavy stress on the second adverb *al*, with its complementary and still more important order (see *Commentary* further). **366 (B 367)** *in holinesse* C: obviously apt on grounds of sense, as made explicit in 383. The Bx reading could have been either *Ø* (leading to variant ⇒ in β and α) or *Vnitee*, the product of stylistic dissatisfaction with the supposedly pointless repetition of *holinesse*, with F (or α) then replacing through objection

to the perceived wrong sense. *were a pile* C / *trs* B: either possibly original and both giving good metre, *pil(e)* having mono- and disyllabic base forms. The substantive reading is clearly *pile* (MED s.v. n. 4 sense 2(a) 'castle, tower, stronghold') not 1(a) 'pillar', as taken by t. The x^1 error *pole* will have resulted from mistaking the referent of *it*. **371 (B 372)** *riht* 'only' (MED s.v. *right(e* adv. Ib (d)): conjectured as the needed key-stave presumed lost in B-Ø by attraction of *synne* to *saue* one. *K–DR–K* make the line scan on *s* by conjecturing *forsoke* as first stave. But this emendation, which presumes deliberate ⇒ not a mechanical cause, is unconvincing as it both relegates the crucial word *Repenteden* to the prelude-dip and replaces *refusede* with a word which, being familiar in the phrase *forsaken synne*, is easier, and so unlikely to have been supplanted by one less common. **372 (B 373)** Bx here has two lines, the first scanning *aa / xa*, the second unmetrical. The former can in principle be corrected by ↔ of the b-half nouns; but while the second line retains the b-half of // C, it has clearly replaced the a-half's neutral nouns with a negatively-toned term (*questemongere*) and a term of general opprobrium (*Lyeris*). The four abusive categories thus suggest a scribe enthusiastically specifying types presumed capable of perjury. Since support for the authenticity of the first line and the a-half of the second is so weak, it seems safe to recognise C as retaining the text of B-Ø intact. **373 (B 374)** *thei* C / *Ø* B: not strictly required, but easily enough omitted from Bx (as by N^2), especially if the exemplar form was *hy*, before h*elden*. The two lines allow acceptable alternative stress-patterns, *with* being possibly a full stave in **B**, probably mute in C. **375 (B 376)** *ne was* C: the single negative arbitrating between the rival β and α variants, neither of which need represent Bx. **376 (B 377)** The Bx line does not appear scribal on grounds of sense or style and the meaning would be impoverished without it. Loss from Cx may be presumed for a syntactical and a mechanical reason, the parenthetical nature of the line breaking up the flow of thought from *Ther ne* 375 to *That he ne* (Cx 376) and eyeskip from *hadde* 375 to *halpe* 377. **378 (B 379)** *thorw* (1): preferred on x^1Bx agreement as the probable Cx form replaced in x^2 under inducement from following *be-, bi-,* and from *bi* in the b-half. *somme* (2): accepted on **p**Bx agreement as indicating the Cx form presumed lost in x^1 by bi*ddynge* > < *bi* attraction. *bi* C / *þoruз* B: natural stressing guides scansion of **C** as having cognative key-staves (|b| |b| / |p|), the last word being a two lift 'monolexical' (*pílgrimáges*). In principle 378 could also scan on |s| as an extended Type IIIa with cognative *b / p* counterpoint. Both alternatives are likewise available for **B**, and either preposition could be the common original; so *K–D*'s emendation of *þoruз* to *bi* becomes otiose. Either pl. *pilgimages* C or *sg.* **B**t could be original; but revision might have been made in order to produce a symmetrical balance with the two singular verbal nouns. **379 (B 380)** The corrupt state of F leaves it unclear whether *And B-β* = Bx or only β, but either this or *Or* **C** is acceptable. **384 (B 385)** *now* **C** / Ø **B**: perhaps lost from Bx by homœoarchy after *noȝt*; unlikely to have been added in revision or scribally for emphasis, like *now* in **p** at 386, but dropped by several C-mss, presumably because judged repetitious. **389 (B 390)** The title *the Plouhman* could have been added in revision or in Cx, or omitted in Bx as superfluous (so N²); but in either form the line scans as a T-type. **390 (B 391)** The bare noun *Myhte* in apposition with French-derived *power* (*C*-x*B*-?β) is more graphic and thus more likely to be original than the form with conjunction in **p**?α (the phrasing is reminiscent of 18.202). The pl. β is self-evidently inauthentic since only one power, that of consecration, is in question; *B*-C will have had the right reading by felicitous variation. *for to eten hit* **C** / *to ete it after* **B**: revision being unlikely here, choice between the variants is uncertain. Either *for* or *after* could have been added to a terse common original *to eten it* that exactly balanced *to maken it* in the a-half (Bx scans as a T-type). **394 (B 395)** scans either as a vocalic Type Ie with *vs* a rhetorically-stressed key-stave, or as a Type Ia on |k| with *quod* as first stave. The former alternative sits better with the tone of incredulity in 395[6], the latter makes a contrast with the vocalic alliteration of 395. **395 (B 396)** *or þat* **C**: perhaps a revision of *er* to achieve better balance as key-stave with *Ál þat* as first stave. **397 (B 398)** *Or CB*-F: 'beforehand, first' (MED s.v. *er* adv. 3), the first stage in a process of reconciliation with God, of which the next two are absolution and communion (398 [9]). The correct reading of Bx is retained by F from α, but β presumably mistook *or* for a conjunction implying (nonsensically) an *alternative* to the repayment of *debita* enjoined in B 396, and so rationalised the text by ⇒ of *That* to make the requirement of 398 parallel to that of 396, as it indeed is. *Or* is usually *er* in ms W, though at 10.417 it appears as *or*, perhaps punningly (see *Commentary*), and as *ar* in ms X; but both archetypes suggest that **L** spelled it *or* in stressed position. **400 (B 401)** The line scans as a standard macaronic of Type Ia with a characteristic 'monolexical' double lift in *Iústicie*, as at 477 (for this pattern see on 331 and *Intro.* IV § 38). The line repeats the (duolexical) structure of 399 (*bé (y)rúled*), though the usual stress-pattern in *Iustície* is that at 299, 303 and 408. *aftur* **C** / *wiþ* **B**: a small but significant change that could be a revision to produce symmetry with 401. N²'s *wiþ* (adopted R–K) will derive from a **B** copy. **401 (B 402)** *while Y can* t*B*-β: giving the best reading (so Pe), though t, joined by D² for *can*, may be an intelligent conjecture or (like N²) result from resort to a **B**-source to correct an exemplar reading found unsatisfactory. Agreement of **p** and x¹ in *couthe* suggests that the preterite was the reading of x² and so of Cx. The of x¹ reading Ø] *while* is more likely

to be archetypal than **p**'s *for*, which appears an attempt to link the clauses *Y wol nat* and *Y couthe*. In the Bx tradition, F has *but* for *while*, omitting *by Crist* and adding *wel* after *kan*. Here, if *but* could be filling out Ø in α, *wel* equally could be echoing *while*; but the sophistication in F precludes any certainty beyond the presence of *kan* in Bx. **402 (B 403)** Either *it* **B** was lost in Cx by assimilation to following *at* or inserted in β in anticipation of the direct object retained until 404. F's sophisticated reading *hole tappe* again conceals the form of α. The omission of *it* by O is presumably fortuitous. **403 (B 404)** The divergent conjunctions *and* **C** / *for* β arguably favour Ø F as attesting the common original. But F, which omits *ale* (2), could also have *lost* a conjunction (?*and*) by eyeskip from *þynne > þat*, so α must remain conjectural. N² again reads with β. **404 (B 405)** Either *to* **C** or Ø **B** is acceptable. **408 (B 409)** *Saue*: tentatively conjectured as the first stave in an extended Type IIIa line with semi-counterpoint (*abb / ax*). In principle, the line could be a 'licensed' macaronic (*aa / xx*), but in this passus it is noteworthy that **L** uniformly observes metrical norms where the names of the cardinal virtues appear. Alternatively, it could scan cognatively with a |p| stave found internally in *Spiritus* (|b| |b| / |p|), with which cf. 202 above. What seems virtually certain is that *Bote* was the reading of the common original B-Ø. However, this could have been caught up from *Bote* at 410 (411) or 407 (408), and the word conjectured here facilitates a characteristic pun on *ysaued* 409 (410). *Saue* as preposition occurs frequently (e.g. 371, 376); but it is not found as a conjunction in *PP*, though well instanced in the period (MED s.v. *sauf* prep., 4 [as conjunction] (a) 'except that, but; unless'). **410 (B 411)** *be thy comune fode*: reconstructed for **C** as the reading of **x** from the split variants *be* t (?=x²) and *thy* (x¹) and felicitously preserved in D², a member of C-y. The substantive reading adopted for **C** is also that to be discriminated as preserved by F from α, and in *B*-C² in a form identical with t's, perhaps following collation with a t-type **C** copy. The variant *þe comune fede* of *C*-p*B*-β gives the same essential sense and (in **p** at least) may be an attempt to rationalise an exemplar reading like t's after omitting *be*. **411 (B 412)** *wel*: lost in **x** and by coincidence in **p**-G by haplography before *we,* but to be accepted on grounds of style, idiom, and the support of **B**. *we* **C** / *þei* β / *þou* FC-D²: the referent of *þei* being somewhat obscure, this may account for F's (or α's) ⇒ of *þou*. Presumably in Bx Conscience must be thinking of the *comune* who speak at 395, not just the Brewer he directly addresses here. It is therefore unlikely that *þou* is original, since it is both easier than *þei* and cannot underlie both the latter and *we* (a better reading ȝe, is not attested). *C*-D² may here show ⊗ from a **B** copy like F; but N²'s reading is clearly that of *B*-β. **412 (B 413)** *many* **C** / *many a* ?**B**: the form without the article is attested in the Bx tradition by L (which may = β) but lacking support from R (here absent), is not adopted; the article also appears in *C*-mss ChRMFN (so *R–K*), but is clearly not archetypal. *lede*: conjectured as the original for which BxB¹ (= B-Ø) have the more familiar *man* under inducement from preceding *many*. As they stand, CxBx scan *aab / bx* and a key-stave in |l| is required. *K–D*'s conjecture *lif* 'with punning implications' (p. 118) [*sc.* on 412] is attractive; but *lif* caused no difficulty to the Bx scribe (as at 3.294, 10.262, 11.91, 213, 13.17, 282, 332, 15.6 and 20.92) or to the Cx scribe at 18.105 or 19.276, and the lexical evidence is overwhelming that in the sense 'living creature, man' (MED s.v. n. 6(a)) *lif* presented no problem; so it is an unlikely original for which *man* was a ⇒. But *lede* was both restricted and recessive, evidently so at 20.444 (where *C*-t may well not represent Cx) and // B 18. 402, where it is restored as the omitted first stave in the light of *C*-t (cf. also the conjectural readings at B 15.393, 16.201, where *lede* offers itself as the best emendation of a defective key-stave). On these grounds, the reading of *C*-ms N² may be confidently adopted as representing, by felicitous conjecture, the probable original in **B** and **C**. Here, the second case (cf. 21.236) where N² has a better reading than both archetypes and could in principle show correction from a 'superior lost **C** copy', *R–K* again choose *not* to adopt it. **413 (B 414)** *kirke*: not certainly the reading of either Cx or Bx and not strictly necessary on metrical grounds (its adoption making the line of Type Ia rather than IIIa), but preferred here, as the less common variant (and one widely instanced in stave-position). **414 (B 415)** The spelling *Cardinales* with final -*s* (modelled on French plural adjectives) is the form in both archetypes on its first occurrence at 275 //. But thereafter the -*s* is mostly dropped (318 //, 345 //, 396 //, 410 //), and as no special reason appears for its use here (or at 455), either could be right. **415 (B 416)** *or an hennes* Cβ: unlikely to be 'a more emphatic reading' (*K–D* p. 156, *Sch*¹) substituted independently in *x*¹**p** and in β. Rather, omission in the unrelated D, t and WF, as in *B*-F, will have been due to the length of the line and its apparent rhythmical termination at *fether*. Since the phrase was in Cx and is not a fixed expression inseparable from the preceding one, it can be taken as almost certainly the reading of Bx (and hence of B-Ø), so there are no grounds for deleting it from the text. **418 (B 419)** *pelours* C: here only a spelling-variant of *pilours* (the form at 22.263), not the separate lexeme instanced at 20.39, *pilour* in Bx (and see MED s.vv. *pilour* n. (1) 1(a), *pelour* n.). The form with *e* may have been deliberately employed here in B-Ø so as to allow a pun on *pelure,* but if so was regularised in Bx. **420 (B 421)** *þat / þer(e)*: possibly split variants of **þere þat*; but L's earlier use of *cometh ynne* has a simple relative pronoun (A 7.287 // Z). This reads more idiomatically here, and *þer* may have come in from 421, where it occurs twice. **424 (B 425)** *helden* ?**CB**: the best resolution

of a possible Cx form **heolden*, which must represent the preterite subjunctive. **425 (B 426)** scans awkwardly as a macaronic Type IIb with a wrenched stress in the third a-stave (*ámong*), and 425a might read better as the b-half of 424, with the Latin as a free-standing citation-line. **426 (B 427)** *wolde* C: more correct after the preterites *come, helden*; but since the obligation is perpetual, present *wole* **B** would be equally appropriate. **429 (B 430)** scans vocalically as a Type IIIb, the *B*-F reading (adopted by *K–DR–K*) being a characteristic attempt to 'correct' the alliteration. But the sense requires that the stressed words should be *newe* and *olde*, not *Peres* and *plouh*. This is only possible in a Type IIIb structure, which makes *newe* the second lift in the a-half (*his néwe ploùh*). *also* C / *ek with* **B**: either could be original, as revision is unlikely. **432 (B 433)** *soudeth* C: possibly a revision of **B** to increase force and precision. But the likelihood of visual error in Bx, partly induced by *sent* 436, is so great (it is also paralleled in three unrelated **C** sources) that the harder reading may be readily accepted as original in **B**. The implied point is not just that the Pope sends mercenaries against his opponents but that he misappropriates the *bona pauperum Christi* to pay them. **433 (B 434)** *Ac* C: reliably to be reconstructed for **B** on the evidence of F's sense and β's form (the latter doubtless induced visually by *And* 433). **434 (B 435)** A 'licensed' macaronic possibly scanning *xx / aa* (with *in-* stressed as key-stave) or, with five-syllable prelude-dip on *íus-, iniús-,* as Type IIIa. The fixed nature of the Biblical phrase will have rendered complete metrical adaptation difficult. **435 (B 436)** *sonne*: the obviously mistaken *soule*, a reading criterial for the group *x*¹ and visibly corrected in three of its members, probably induced unconsciously by associations of *God...sent...sonne* and *saue* with the Son's mission to save man's soul. **438–40 (B 439–41)** The same mechanical error (homoteleuton at 438, 441) has caused the loss of 439–40 in F (or α) as of 441 in Bx. The line is not absolutely necessary on grounds of sense, but there seems a parallelism intended between the activity of God (436), who is praised at 444, and that of his deputy Piers (438), who is 'blessed' at 441. **438** In the absence of α, *and wenches* β is not certainly the Bx reading, though *or for a wenche* C may revise to give a closer balance with the first phrase of the line. **443 (B 444)** scans as a Type IIIc line on |b| and |w|. Inversion of *gode, wicke* to a less expected order would yield a Type Ia line, but there is no necessity for this. *K–DR–K* (rightly) leave the line unemended, though inconsistently with their own metrical criteria. **444 (B 445)** *som x*¹**B**: omitted by *x*² presumably through *til* > < *tyme* attraction, reinforced perhaps by the sense of one syllable too many in the b-half, though the word is necessary to provide the (mute) key-stave in this Type Ia line. **445 (B 446)** *the Pope amende*: simple ↔ of a subject and verb inverted to prose order in BxB¹

(< B-Ø) creates from a line scanning *xa / ax* a satisfactory line of Type IIIa. *K–D*'s fertile speculations (p. 208) on possible forms of the a-half terminate in the conjecture *Piers* for *God*. Certainly, Conscience has been speaking of both (440, 443); but it is *He þat wrouhte all, boþe gode and wicke* who is also the one that *may al amende* (B 10.439). Indeed, most references in **L** to transitive amending (esp. morally) have God as their subject: see, e.g., 13.199, 18. 288, 19.295. The prayer *God amende* here is echoed below by *Crist...saue* at 452. But *Piers* at this juncture is distinct in identity-function from Christ, so *K–D*'s conjecture, far from having 'strong indications' in its favour, seems not only 'arbitrary' but wide of the mark. **449 (B 450)** In this line, the text of Bx helps effectively to discriminate the **C** variants. It clearly supports *lawe* (2), which is in only two members of y, against the rest as surely the reading of **x** and thence, against **p**'s sophisticated rewriting, of Cx. Conversely, in the b-half, **C** supports F (= α) as having here preserved the true reading of Bx. **451 (B 452)** scans as an extended Type IIIa on vowels with counterpoint on |r| (*abb / ab*), a pattern identical to that of B 18.2 or, if an oblique form with final -*e* is posited, as Type Ia, with two lifts in *rémenáunt(e)*. *He* ?**x**?α / *That he* **p**β: the form without *that* after *semeth*, being terser and more colloquial, is likelier to be original. Ø **C** / *ne* **B**: metre and sense are unaffected by presence or absence of the double negative. **453 (B 454)** *for þe* **C** / *of* β; *to* F: the rhythm of **C** preferable, though possibly a revision. On the other hand, *for þe* could have come in by suggestion from *For the* 454, β is satisfactory in itself and could represent Bx. **455 (B 456)** *Cardinale(s)*: see on 414 above. **456 (B 457)** *sowne* **C**B-F; the reading *sowe* of *B*-L is an ambiguous reflex of an exemplar spelling with suspension, not a form of the past subjunctive of *sen* (MED s.v. *sen* v (1) 8a(a), *sen to* 'look at'), to which *Sk* mistakenly alters. But γ appears to have misread under inducement from following *sighte* and M to have adopted accordingly from a w-source or by the same mechanism. *K–D* rightly take F as preserving from α the **B** original. **460 (B 461)** Either *For x¹*?α or Ø *x²*β is acceptable, and no reason appears for loss of the conjunction. But a connective eases the syntax, and the two Bx families offer split variants of the *C-x¹* form, with ⇒ by F of a synonym for *ech*. **466–67 (B 467–68)** The lines scan as follows: 466 as a T-type on |t| and |r| with wrenched stress on -*tus* (1) and -*tus* (2), giving *aa / [a]bb*; 467 as a Type IIIa with two lifts in *Fórtitúdinis* and a five-syllable prelude dip. *wolle he, null he*: conjectured also as the reading of **B**, with β appearing a smoothing after presumed loss of *he nel he* at the end of a long line. It is the lord's minions who will do the 'fetching' from his tenants. **471 (B 472)** Either *þat* or Ø: is acceptable, but **B** gives smoother rhythm (so P²H²ChR–*K*). **473 (B 474)** Either *And* **C** or *For* **B** could be right, **C**'s conjunction being repeated in the b-half, **B**'s repeating from 473b. **477**

(B 478) will scan as Type IIIa with two lifts in *Iústicie* as at 400. **481–82 (B 482–83)** The reading of Bx can be established in 481 on the agreement of βCx and scans acceptably as a normal Type Ia line, notwithstanding the objection of *K–D* (p. 175), mistakenly followed by *Sch¹*. For 483, *K–D* identify the Bx reading in that of β; but in the light of Cx *That thow haue al thyn askyng* it must be transparent that F's *þat þou þyn lykyng haue* is a reflex of α but with characteristic ⇒ of a synonym for the noun and a minor ↔ of the same verb-phrase. It is α, not β, that may best be judged to have preserved Bx, and it remains to show that the reading of the two archetypes, effectively identical, makes adequate sense. The difficulty in the lines is entirely grammatical. Normally, the conditional present subjunctive of the protasis *In condicioun...þat þou conne defende.../ And rewle* would be expected to be followed by an indicative, and this is what β has indeed substituted (*Take þow may*). But surprisingly it is here followed by another subjunctive, of the 'jussive' type (*That thow haue* CF), possibly as a way of expressing the appropriate combination of deference and firmness towards the royal addressee. It is therefore unnecessary to read 482a as a purpose clause and, in seeking a main clause for it to follow, to emend *riht wel and in* (an adverbial phrase further modifying *rewle*) to *riht wol and*. The only emendation required is the slight one of reconstructing from F the α form of B 483, which is identical with C 482 but for the omission of *al*. The case for and against this important little word is finely balanced. **L**'s habitual reserve towards absolute power would question it; but the *Omnia* of 482a, unless it has been anticipated by the Cx scribe, would support it. Otherwise it may be a late revision reflecting a significant change of attitude (see *Commentary*).

Passus XXII (B XX)

Collation In the final passūs, the main Cx traditions *x¹*, t and *p¹* continue to be well supported, but for *p²* only N remains. By way of compensation, Bx is reliably represented with the return of the one sound α witness R.
7 *to lyue by* **C**B-F: presumed original in **B** on the strength of CF (= α) agreement. *R–K*'s preference of the easier β reading is dubious, their ⇒ of it for Cx remarkable. **8** If *As* LMCr is the reading of β and **p** it requires *That* 7 to be a conjunction (following an understood verb of 'saying') and strongly favours *þat* F in 9 (omitted β) as also a conjunction. By contrast, the **x** reading *Was*, indirectly supported by *B*-α as reconstructed from F *& þat was* (and preferred as slightly the harder) presupposes *That* as a relative pronoun subject (= *That which*) and allows *þat* 9 to be either another such or, with change of construction, a conjunction. The line scans as a standard macaronic with the key-stave found either in *Spiritús* or, preferably, in *Témperáncie*. **11** The key-stave is apparently *for*, and

polysemous wordplay with initial *For* (see MED s.v. *for* prep. 5b(b), 1(a)) is facilitated if the latter bears full stress in a Type Ie line (*aax / ax*). Alternatively, *thre* may be the first lift and the wordplay less significant. **12** Either *for* **C** or *and* **B** could be original, or *for* a revision to sharpen the sense. **13** The b-half seems fairly secure for both texts on the agreement of ?Cx and ?α. In the a-half, the substantive reading of the first stave-word is *wight*, clearly established in Bx and discernible as that of C-*x¹*. The **p** reading (shared by D) would seem to be a smoothing of **wit(eth)*, a mistaken reflex of *with*, the common reversed-spelling of *wyht* actually instanced in U. The error may have been prompted in part by the unexpected change of subject between *weldeth* 12 and *wol be* 13. Once *wyht* is adopted, Cx *þat* can be omitted as redundant, the clause following being Ø-relative. The readings *noon* β / *þat* ?α may be split variants of Bx **noon þat*, but the relative pronoun is not strictly needed for the sense. As here understood, β's a-half is taken to preserve correctly both Bx and the presumed B¹ source of Cx. **14** *cacche*: reconstructed as also the correct form of Bx, which β has levelled to a preterite, perhaps through misconstruing the tense of *come*. But the latter, like *come* in 16, is present subjunctive, as is shown decisively by the present indicatives in the apodosis of 17 and the second verb in the protasis of 16 (contrast 21. 424). **19** *dysch*: preferred in **C** as the unambiguous form of the word, of which *dych* is a recognised spelling (see MED s.v. *dish* n.) evidently archetypal in **B**. The notion (unhappily implied by R–K's preference for *dych*) that the referent could be 'ditch' is obviously absurd. *deyde for furste* **C**: adopted also for **B** as the presumed common original, the alternative relying only on vocalic non-lexical stave-words *he, ech, er / he* (Bx has here, less usually, inverted an *original* prose order). The tense of the second verb is preferably past in **C** (as in **B**) after *wolde* 18, and in parallel with *dronke* in the a-half. **23** *be (v)er* C-**x**B-β: correct on grounds of sense, *for* being due to misreading *fer*. **25** Either *wel* ?**C** or *ful* **B** could be original, *wel* being perhaps even a y variant on *x¹ ful*; but no difference of sense or metre arises. **33a–36 (B 33a–35)** Both Cx and Bx evidently misdivided, although in neither case with the intrusion of spurious words or phrases as padding. The coincidence between *x²* and α may point to the respective forms of Cx and Bx; but the most satisfactory (and most probably correct) lineation is found by K–D, who treat 33a as a free-standing citation-line and not part of a macaronic. The first stave-word of 34 may be established for both versions as *God* on the showing of Cx, the Latin and the demands of sense and syntax (as antecedent of *hym* 35). It could have been lost from Bx by haplography before *gou-*, with subsequential smoothing. **35** Arguably *Ac* β yields a sharper contrast (when taken closely with *nexst*); but it may not stand for Bx here, given agreement of ?α and **C** in *And*. **37** In C*α*; omission of the line

from β will have been by homoarchy (*nedeþ* 36, *nedy* 38). **48** *byde* *x¹*β: with the sense 'wait patiently' (MED s.v. *biden* v. 5(a)), the harder variant and to be preferred to *bydde* *x²*?α*g*. Although late spellings with single *d* of the verb meaning 'to beg' are recorded (MED s.v. *bidden* v.), the word here appears to echo *abyde* 46 (so spelled D²U) and the erroneous variant may have come in by contextual suggestion from *abasched...to be nedy*. Need is urging Will to endure because Christ did, not to beg because he endured (which is illogical), and he has advocated taking, not begging, if dire necessity compels (20). The wider context of thought also supports *byde*, and any interpretation that depends on reading *bydde* is questionable (cf. further Nede's words against begging at 238–9). **54** *tyd* **C**: plausibly conjectured as having been lost by Bx through *it > < ti(t)* attraction. **62–3** Correct lineation and substantives are not found together in any (sub)archetype, but both can be satisfactorily reconstructed. (*The*) *whiche fooles* is confirmed by *x²*Bx, presence or absence of the article having no effect on metre or sense (*C*-W also lacks it). The initial phrase would seem to have been lost from *x¹* by haplography after *oneli*ch *foles* 61. The adverb *wel*, necessary as the key-stave, is confirmed by *x¹*β agreement; the mechanism of loss will have been repetition (after the caesura) of earlier *wel* (occurring *before* the caesura) in 61. The Cx misdivision may have been as in Bx; but *p¹*'s felicitous lineation must be correct, since it alone provides in *lyue* the needed first stave of 63, which scans *aa / xx* in BxC-**x**N. **67** *her(e)* **C**: adopted also for **B** as the common original for which Bx *hem* may be a simple visual error. Although in principle *gile* could be a verb, the phrase *hem gile* 'them to be practising guile' sounds unidiomatic, as the ⇒ in β attests. **70** scans cognatively on |p| |b| / |b| in B-βRC-**x** and the variants *bar yt bare* B-F and *bar þat baner* B-YC-**p** both appear attempts to lengthen the line and make it scan 'regularly' on |b| staves. K–D (p. 159) see the insertion of *baner* as an easier scribal reading (as indeed it appears), but judge the original to survive in F's *bare* with its 'superior meaning ..."uncased", "displayed as a sign of battle"' (MED s.v. *bar* adj. 13(a); accepted *Sch¹*). However, their observation that 'in the absence of R', F 'possibly represents its group (RF)', repeated on p. 165n86, is mistaken, since R (as K–D's apparatus correctly reports) is not defective but reads as β and, as presumably representing α, indicates the reading of Bx. Thus, while it remains remotely possible that *bare* was thrice lost by haplography in β, R and **x**, and twice smoothed to *baner* in **p** and (coincidentally) in B-Y, it is far more probable that BxCx read Ø and that F (or its exemplar) inserted *bare* to supply a supposed metrical gap. The principle of cognative alliteration proves the 'absent' stave-word to be an unnecessary entity here. **72** The ⇒ of *And* for *That* seems to have no motive other than stylistic aversion to repetition. Alternatively, the common original had a Ø-relative (as at 86) and this was supplied in Bx and in y, U, <TH²>, q and *p²*, while <eRM>, W and the two unrelated **x**-type mss D and Ch inserted *And* instead. **83** *scabbes* **C** / *scalles* **B**: effectively synonyms, *scalles* overlapping in sense with *scabbes* (MED s.v. *scale* n. (1), 2(a)), and neither more difficult, though **C** could be a revision. The reading *scabbes* in *B*-W is probably a visual error, since double *l* / *b* are easily confused and, as the same could have occurred either way in Bx and Cx, there is no case for reading *scalles* in **C** (with *R–K*). **87** Either *he* **C** or *hir* **B** is acceptable, and no reason for ⇒ of one for the other appears, though each could have been inserted to fill out a Ø-reading in the common original. **92** Hereafter *damaged readings of* ms **I** are not noted, and group **y** is represented by XYP²D². **97** *kyne* **C** / *kene* **B**: probably the same word (MED s.v. *kene* adj. 5(a) 'painful' and (d) 'noxious') with the *y* -spelling punningly alluding to Kynde, the author of the sores, and so possibly being the common original (on this grapheme of |e:| cf. *lyf* at 312 below). **103** The reading of the b-half in both versions is established on the agreement of Bx and *x¹*, with t representing the presumed text of *x²* (*neuere* for *euere*) and **p** a further stage of variation (↔ of verb and adverb). The substantive reading *euere* is not in doubt, the paronomasia on *euene* forming an essential element in the line's meaning. **104** *here lemmanes knyhtes* **C**: to be preferred on grounds of sense as the likely common original, the compound second subject of two apposed nouns ('lover-knights') being made to correspond with their ladies. In *B*-β, the b-half phrase effectively repeats that of the a-half and appears a mistaken alteration of the reading attested in R, that of α and probably preserving Bx. But Cx *hir*, giving sharper sense and smoother metre, does not look like revision and may be safely adopted for **B**. **106** *tho* **C**: yielding better sense, anticipating 109 and unlikely to be a revision, Bx *to* appearing a visual error for *tho* partly induced by *To* 107 (cf. *x¹* at 110). In other occurrences, the verb *bisechen* is always transitive (see 3.77, 115 and *IG* s.v.). **109** scans as a Type IIIa line, the *tho* of Kynde's response echoing that of Conscience's request (see note above). F's *sone* is a characteristic normalisation of the line to Type Ia unlikely to represent α: the sense 'immediately' (MED s.v. *sone* adv. 1a (a)) is inappropriate, 'shortly' (ibid. (b)) little less so; what matters is not the length of time but the fact that Kynde desisted *when* (or *after*) Conscience asked him and the people had begun to show signs of repenting. Adoption of *sone* by *R–K* (following *K–D*) is thus ill-advised, since both archetypes read *tho*. **110** *tho*: in the light of Bx, the Cx reading may be established as *to* (a poor spelling of *tho*), which *x¹* preserves correctly and P² etc. alter plausibly to the article (for the converse, *th* for *t*, cf. at 186). **113** *gaderet*: to be taken as a form of the preterite (= *gadered*); cf. 149. **117** *brode*: to be preferred as the

common original of both versions (cf. 226), *blody* being induced by the martial context. Presumably *B*-WhmF corrected independently upon registering the inappropriateness of their exemplar's reading. **120** *Kirke* **B**: securely to be accepted on the showing of α as the form of Bx (and inferentially of B¹), from which β and Cx have convergently varied to the commoner form, with loss of the keystave. Cr may well be an independent scribal correction. **126** *suede* **C**: to be accepted on grounds of sense as the **B** reading, perhaps found as *seude* in Bx, whence the form of R (< α). Thus spelled, it could have been misread as the preterite of *senden* (with voiced stop) and levelled to the commoner form *sente* found in βF. The context shows decisively that Symonye must be the one who 'preaches' and 'makes prelates', and who therefore first 'follows'. **127** On intrinsic grounds C's *presed on þe Pope* is a much stronger and bolder half-line than *prechede to þe peple* and may preserve the common original replaced in Bx by a more innocuous phrase. The scribe's motive could have been censorship: acceptance of Death as abstract universal leveller (101) was one thing, a direct charge of simony against the reigning pontiff another. Against this, it should be noted that the Bx scribe does *not* censor the even more forthright criticism of the (actual) Pope at 19.446; so since the metre shows no defect, there could well be revision here. Alternatively, misreading of *presed* as *preced* and insertion of *to þe peple* by way of smoothing is proposed by Barney 2006:214. But K–D's adoption of the **C** reading lacks conclusiveness and is not recommended (see also at 130). **128** Either a group sg. *temperaltee* or the pl. could be original. **130** The Bx reading *kneled to* is less vivid than *knokked* Cx, but cannot easily be a visual error for it, nor does any precise motive for ⇒ appear (K–D's explanation of 'misguided "improvement"' [p. 92] explains nothing). If 'submitted (hypocritically)' (*Sk*) is accepted as fitting well, there is no justification for rejecting *kneled to*, which may then be judged the second case within a few lines where a revising hand may be discerned (for another see on 380 below). **135** Either *vp* **B** or *on* **C** could be original, or both split variants of *vpon* (so P² with *on* added *a.h.*); but though *vp* is more typical of L's style, each may be allowed to stand. **140** The position of the adverb *tho* is less certain in Cx than in Bx, but affects neither sense nor metre. Agreed *C*-p*B*-F give a simpler form (so *K–DR–K*) that is unlikely to be the common original. **149** Either *priketh* **C** or *priked* **B** could be the common original, or both be reflexes of a tense-ambiguous form **prikyt*. *B*-W's present, coinciding with the majority of **C** copies, may have been induced by following *preiseþ*. **155** *ȝowthe* **C** / *sorwe* **B**: a change to normative metre, Bx scanning as Type IIIc, but also with change of sense. Reminiscence of C 12.12, 11.196f is evident; but this begins with 154, as *Pe* notes, and need not be 'scribal' (*K–D* p. 209). A metonymic sense 'the sins of youth' is entirely apt in context and would be natural enough as a revision of *sorwe* 'contrition'. The tR variant *þouȝt* may be interpreted as the result of *þ / ȝ* confusion. While the common original could have read Ø through eyeskip from *forȝete* to *forȝeue*, and both Cx and Bx have substituted independently a word judged appropriate, the change in thought and metre points rather to revision. *R–K*'s gratuitous rewriting of a Cx line sound in form and meaning as *And [s]o forȝete [sorwe] and [of synne ȝeue nouht]* invites comparison with the most intrusive scribal practice. **163** *sley* C / *war* B: an apparent revision of an extended Type IIIa line with semi-counterpoint on |w| to a Type Ie scanning on |s|. Both adjectives look authentic and there is no reason to see *war* as Bx ⇒ of a synonym by alliterative inducement (*K–D* p. 95), since *sley* is not a word of difficult meaning. However, *wex* g (so *K–D*) may indeed have been induced from *wax* 159 above and cannot be accepted as preserving β here against wLM. Its adoption by *R–K* (p. 127) for Cx is hazardous since, even if it is harder than *was*, a mechanical explanation of its appearance in g is at hand. **167** *shroef hym* C / *he shifte hym* B: here judged a revision in the direction of greater explicitness. The Bx verb (MED s.v. *shiften* v. 1(b), refl.) cannot well be a visual error for *shroef*, a verb of unmistakable sense that had no weak preterite *shrivede* at this period (see MED s.v. *shriven* v.). **171** The pl. *hertes* is judged the likely common original; for though less consistent than the sg., it conveys an intelligible distinction between the art of Physic personified and its practitioners severally, who become the subject of 172. **172** *gyuen*: to be accepted on the showing of Bx as also the probable form of B[1], the past tense having been induced from preceding *gaef* and a possible ambiguous Cx form (*g)euen*, as in T (cf. *wesched* 194 below). Mixture of present and preterite is characteristic of L and common in this section (e.g. 148–49). **183** As revision seems unlikely, the adverb *anoon* was either inserted in Bx or omitted by Cx. **198** *heo*: adopted on obvious grounds of sense as preferable to a possible B-Ø form *hee*. **202** Either Ø B could be original or *how* C a revision (in B-Text *delete misprinted* how). **212** Both *Y* C / *þere* B; Ø C / I ?**B**: are acceptable and neither more obviously original, though the **C** order is less usual. If the common source B-Ø read *þere I*; then *þere* Bx, *Y* Cx may be split variants, Bx having read Ø in the b-half (so α > R) and β having commonsensically inserted a pronoun subject. **215** *soethly*: not a strong reading but metrically adequate, and plainly that of B-Ø. *K–D* (p. 117) see it as a ⇒ for a near-synonymous *sikerly* (MED s.v. *sikerli* adv. 1 (a)), but here with the sense 'firmly' (ibid. s.v. 2(a)). However, as neither this nor *soorly* (*Sch*[1]), likelier as a visual error, imposes itself, Bx and Cx should be left to stand. **219** *pissares*: emended by *K–D* (p. 184) to *purses and* on the basis of the GC[2] variant *and gypsers*, and argued for again by *R–K* 135–36,

but founded on a nugatory objection to *Sk*'s explanation of the phrase as a cant term for armed retainers. The word, too vivid in itself to be scribal, could hardly have entered the common source B-Ø and persisted through both archetypal traditions if unintelligible to the copyists. Its allusion to such Biblical texts as III Kg 14:10, 16:11 or I Kg 25:22, 34 (where the Wycliffite Bible has *pissere* for Vg *mingentem*) displays **L**'s typical clerkly wit combined with the sort of humour shown in the established phrase *ballok knyf* at 15.124 (which compares a different part of the instrument and the male organ). Both examples re-prove the aggressive sexuality of the clerk who comports himself like 'a very good blade, a very tall man' (*Romeo and Juliet* II iv. 31). **225** *hym* C: perhaps present in B-Ø and lost mechanically from Bx by attraction of *aye*in to *wiþ*; but not strictly required for the sense, and possibly added in Cx (as in YOCB of *B*-g). **227** *holynesse*: preferred on the showing of Bx, the commonsensical *holy-churche* perhaps reflecting scribal unease with the idea of 'bringing down' a *moat* (cf. 21.383 above). **228** The rhythm of *or* C is better, but *ellis* could have been added in Bx or lost from Cx by *ell*is > < *falle* attraction. **236** *chey-tyftee pouertee*; on the showing of *C*-*x*[1] and *B*-WLα the probable reading of each archetype, *chaitife x*[2]*B*-?γ M attempting to turn the first noun into an adjective governing the *second* noun. *Sk* adapts **B** to the adjectival form of **p**, which gives acceptable sense and metre, while *Pe* follows *K–D* (p.117) in judging *pouertee* an early scribal gloss incorporated in the <BxB[1]> source (presupposing a phase before B-Ø). This gives a line with two lifts *chéytýftee*, an authentic 'monolexical' b-half pattern (see *Intro.* IV § 38). In its (older) variant AN-derived form *caytiftee* (9.255), the word caused no difficulty for the Cx scribe. Yet that fact argues not for but against viewing the present 'gloss' as scribal, since the spelling with central French *ch* is much the rarer (MED s.v. *caitiffe* n.). It is therefore accepted here as an (authorial) 'internal gloss' skilfully integrated into the metrical pattern of the line. **238–39** will have been lost from α either by eyeskip from *And siþen* B 236 > *And siþen* B 240 (though without the expected loss of 237) or perhaps by the 'notional correspondence' (*K–D* p. 69) in *liflode...begge / liflode...beg-geres* (238–39), *beggeres...foode* (241). **256** *newe* B: more probably omitted by **C** (or Cx) than added in Bx, though a mechanical loss would have been easier if *newe* came immediately before *nempned*, or else before *noum-brede* (as in α). However β is preferable to α, since it was the names not the numbering that would have been 'new'. The sense 'made or established for the first time, newly created' (MED s.v. *neue* adj.1 (a)) is appropriate, and Donaldson's objection to it as pointless (1949:242, followed by *K–D*) is misguided. **261** cannot be an addition, since it is needed to complete the sense of the sentence beginning in 260 (as recognised by the scribe of *B*-C[2]), and so must have been present in B^1. It could have been lost from Bx by distraction from similar corresponding ideas as at 238–39 (*nombre /...wages* 259–60, *nombre... ywaged* 261). The line scans vocalically as Type Ia on non-lexical words or as an extended Type IIIa with semi-counterpoint on |n|. **270** will have been lost from XD^2tW, as from *B*-Y, by homoteleuton (*nombre*). **271** Either Ø **C** or *þe* **B**: could be original, the noun in any case having shifting stress and the metre not being otherwise affected. **282** *They* C-t; Ø **B**: the correct reading is that of Bx, which requires *For* in 281 to be a conjunction, and that of t, which has presumably corrected by omitting *And*. The latter conjunction could have come into Cx as a consequence of reading *For* 281 as a preposition (MED s.v. *for* prep. 14 (a) 'as regards') or as a smoothing after addition of *þat* to a Ø-relative clause in the exemplar at 281b. **287** *leue* **C**: judged on the strength of L and α as the reading also of Bx, for which γ has ⇒ offers a more explicit expression. What the *folk* require is permission to postpone repayment of the loan, not a further loan (though the whole phrase will bear the equivalent sense 'extension of the period of re-payment of the loan'). The γ reading, which presumably arose as a visual error of a very common type (*lone* for *leue* by *e / o, n / u* confusion), and will have come into *B*-M from its usual w-type source, is shared by *C*-M (and adopted by *R–K*). **292–93** Both lines appear corrupt in the b-halves, having non-alliterating synonyms in place of the required key-staves on |p| and |r| respectively. The lineation is, however, correctly preserved in Bx and in $C-x^2$. *Pe* retains the x^1 reading but relineates after **p**, and *Sk* prints the **p** reading, emending P's *murþe* to *merye*. Both give lines scanning *aa / bb* and prose (unless *reménaunt* is pronounced with wrenched stress, making 293 a Type IIIa). *K–D* (p. 119) more drastically emend 292b to [*pleye*] *with þe remenaunt* and omit 293b. Hardly less drastic is [*purchace*] *hem mur*[*th*]*e* for 292 and *renkes* for *men* in 293, with omission from **B** of *þe residue and* in the light of // **C** (Sch^1). The present reconstruction of 292 accepts *K–D*'s original conjecture *pleyen* for the key-stave of 292 but retains *murye*, judging *maken* a B-Ø ⇒ under inducement from 289a as the expected word in this stock locution, where *murye* is an adjective not an adverb. Though there seems little likelihood of revision having occurred here, the a-halves of both archetypes are allowed to stand, since each gives a line acceptable in sense and metre. But there can be no certainty as to whether *þe residue and* was intruded in Bx or omitted in Cx. After adoption of the lexically restricted *renkes* as the key-stave in both lines (for which *men* is judged a B-Ø ⇒), the emended **B** line now scans as Type Ia and that of **C** as Type IIIc. **301** scans as Type IIIa in Cx, as Type Ia in Bx, but the sense requires a pl. pronoun subject. The vocalic form *hy* original in **L**'s dialect, which probably underlies the mistaken sg. in Bx, may be safely presumed to have been the reading of B^1, and its adoption for **C** makes the line identical in both versions. **306** Either *To* Cx or *Go* ?Bx could be the joint-original or both could be split variants of *To go*, the actual reading of *B*-W (cf. earlier 5.126//, and Apparatus for *to*] *go* ⇒); *R–K* read XYP^2D^2U as *Go*. **308** scans as a Type IIIa line on |v| (*For; þei*), though not very satisfactorily. *K–D* (p. 119) alter to a Type Ia by conjecturing *mysfetes* for *mysdedes*, citing B 11.37[4], where this word (MED s.v. *misfait* n.) uniquely occurs (though for all its rarity, *mysfeet* there caused the Bx scribe no difficulty). It is also possible that, if *wrouht* is the key-stave (as its significance merits), the first lift was a stave-word in *w*, the unrecorded **wandedes* conjectured at Z 5.152, a line unquestionably scanning on |w| (see note *ad loc*). A somewhat less speculative emendation would be a lexical word *wykkede* (so C-R) for the negative prefix *mys-*. More cautiously still, *hy* could be read for *þei*, giving a Type IIIb line with justifiable sentence-stress on *here*. This, however, involves accepting the vocalic allomorph of the subject-pronoun as the key-stave (but with full stress less clearly justified), so the line's scansion will still depend on non-lexical words. Given the want of a fully satisfactory emendation, the agreed reading (< B-Ø) should be retained. **309** *pardon* **C**: unlikely to have been added in revision of **B**, since it is contextually required for the sense, the line closely echoing B 19.393b–94, and for the metre, 309 being a true macaronic (of Type IIa) like B 19.394. Loss from Bx could have occurred by alliterative attraction (*Pi- > < pay-*). **312** *Lyf* CB-α: either a spelling variant of *leef* (so actually Z) or the substantive lexeme 'life', to be identified with the worldling Lyf of 143 ff, the name here meaning 'Life-to-be-lived-in-lechery', with a second (punning) sense 'Love-to-live-in-lechery'. If it is the former, as seems quite probable, the α reading should be preferred in the B-Text, β eliminating the pun and with it the link with the earlier character who had turned to earthly Physic for help against Age (169 ff). (On the spelling of the close |e:| sound, cf. the note on *kyne* at 37 above). **314** Either *the* Cx or *þis* Bx could be original, though Bx is the more explicit. **318** Ø **C** / *a* **B**: a sense-neutral variant of no metrical significance, the line being best taken to scan vocalically as an extended Type IIIa with semi-counterpoint on |m|. **326–27** scan as a Type Ia and Type IIIa respectively. *K–D*'s re-division after *haue* so as to standardise 327 and their omission of *a were* verge on editorial re-writing. **329** *coome* **B**: preferred also for **C**, where only N has (presumably by accident) the required form of the preterite subjunctive within an implied subordinate clause. The distinction between moods, generally preserved in Bx (*cam* 327, 330, 356, but *coom(e)* 329), is likely to have been original (but *coom* at 345 could be a non-significant local spelling variant). **338** *do boþe* **B**: accepted here as also the form of Cx (< B^1), *done* x^2 and *bothe x[1]* being diagnosable as split variants. **351** scans either as an extended Type IIIa on |s| with vocalic semi-counterpoint, or as a Type IIa on vowels. The former seems rhythmically preferable and its annominative chime between monosyllabic staves (*se, so*), is characteristic. **355** scans vocalically as Type IIIa, so *K–DR–K*'s noun-verb ↔ in the b-half to produce spiral alliteration is otiose. **356** Ø **C** / *in* **B**: either inserted in Bx or lost in Cx through minim confusion (ca*m* / *in*). **360** *ben* **CB**-R: preferred as giving superior metre, although *B*-βF could read acceptably as not Type Ia with quadrisyllabic prefinal dip but as Type Ic with cognative key-stave and the caesura after the second subject. However, it is likely that *biten* has come in from 362 (a similar desire to heighten the tone of the b-half is shown by the *C*-t variant *pynen*). It seems preferable that *byte* 362 should make specific, not merely repeat the verb of 360. **361** Either *chaungen* **C** / *change hem* **B** may be an auditory error for the other, but the absolute fully inflected infinitive seems preferable. **366** *alle hem*: reconstructed as the reading of B-Ø, of which Bx *al* and Cx *hem* appear split variants. The form adopted, as appropriate in this case, is the plural; word-play on *alle* / *al* is typical of **L** (cf. *alle* / *al* at 21. 394–95). **367** *and*: conjectured to provide a more natural-sounding pl. object for the pl. complement *freres* in 368 (*freres* is the BxCx reading (< B-Ø), obviously not impossible but nonetheless altered to the sg. by three **B** mss and one **C** ms). Presumably an ampersand could have been omitted by visual attraction of yo*w* > < *my*, or loss of *and* could have been by assimilation to preceding *And*. The referent of *Lady* should be the penitent's wife or mistress, Friar Flatterer here displaying his address as a 'lady's man' in what appears a conscious echo of 3. 38ff. *Pe*'s interpretation of *my lady* in the sense 'a particular object of my prayers' is very forced (and not at all supported by *Purity* 1084, where *my lady* refers, quite naturally in context, to the Blessed Virgin Mary). *K–DR–K*'s adoption for both versions of *B*-F's scribal re-writing of an ostensibly difficult line evades the issue. Their notion that *my lady* could be a misreading of contracted *memoria,* and subsequent emendation to the latter, is unpersuasive (though it has contributed a phantom Latin word which figures as a 'quotation' in Alf*Q*, p.117). As to *R–K*'s objections to *and my lady* (p. 136, n. 65), these are nugatory. The fact that Contrition is being addressed does not logically preclude a second addressee, the situation pointedly recalling that evoked by Peace at 346 above, while the construction *maken...as freres* reads contextually with naturalness and in no way violates Middle English idiom. The key to the crux is *As freres* in 368, here accepted on the strength of BxC-x[2] agreement as the probable reading of the common original. This necessitates that at least two persons are being promised tertiary membership of the order in return for their donation. While *al*[*le hem*] *that ye ben*

holden to are being promised the friars' prayers, they are not all being promised fraternity, a privilege reserved for Contrition and his Lady, and echoing 3.53–4, 67. **371** Neither *bifore* **C** nor *to doone* **B** is difficult nor does any evident motive for ⇒ or revision appear. It may be that Cx and Bx are split variants of B-Ø **wont* bifore to doone*, that Cx lost *doone* by visual anticipation of *For* 372, and Bx lost *bifore* by *wont* > < *doone* attraction. However, since both archetypes give acceptable sense and metre, with little to choose between them, they should be allowed to stand. **373** scans vocalically as an extended Type IIIa with *álle* as key-stave and double counterpoint on |s|. The superlative (*souerayneste* **B**) of an adjective already superlative in meaning (*souereyne* **C**) could be suspected as typical 'scribal over-emphasis'. But here the emphasis could equally be authorial (as at 1.146) and the *-st(e)* ending have been lost before following *s-* in Cx (TH[2] in fact have it). It is thus better to let each reading stand. The earlier emendation of *kynnes* to *skynnes* (*Sch[1]*) retains plausibility but lacks necessity, so is abandoned. *K–DR–K*'s more drastic *synnes of kynde* for *kynnes synnes*, with its wider unwarranted theological implications, amounts to editorial re-writing. **376–77** *Clergie...helpe* **C**: on balance marginally superior to *and bad Clergie...for to* **B**, the form of the request in C 376 more authentic than the explicit one in // Bx. The latter may have anticipated *bad* from 377 and then smoothed by substituting *also,* subsequently omitting *come*, perhaps to shorten the line. *K–D*'s reconstruction follows Cx in the a-half, omitting only *to*, but Bx in the b-half, omitting Cx *helpe* in B 377. The latter looks suspicious as pointless repetition of *help* 376 //. But given the uncertainty, it seems better to let both readings stand, except for the insertion in **B** of *come* as second stave (since, of the word's two appearances in Cx, this is the likelier to have been in the common original). The lines are not wholly satisfactory in either archetype; but both are open to fewer objections than a wider reconstruction, and the sense of both is clear. **378** *adreint and dremeþ*: reconstructed by *K–D* as the original form underlying what they identify as the split variants *dremeþ* Bx / *adreint* Cx. Possibly the latter was a revision of the Bx form (inferentially also that of B[1]) and both lines will scan acceptably as Type IIIa. But the sense of each seems defective and requires the other to complete the figure, 'drowned [in sleep] and dreaming'. If there has been revision, it was more probably to this reconstructed form, Cx (or B[1]) subsequently having lost the part (*and dremeþ*)) originally present in **B** and preserved in Bx. However, a mechanical explanation will best account for the readings: for if *and dremeþ* had been not conjunction + finite verb but a preposition + verbal noun (**adremeth* 'in a state of dreaming') the loss by each archetype of one word could have been the result of simple haplography through minim-confusion. **380** The difference in the a-halves *doth men drynke dwale þat men* **C** / *plastred hem so esily hij* **B** is so extreme that both may be original (**C** a revision), or one be a ⇒ for the other, or both a ⇒ for a lost form. The Cx version is striking enough to seem beyond suspicion; but that of Bx does not appear a variant of it, since its content is at once completely different and by no means patently scribal. The line's defective key-stave is easily remedied by adopting the vocalic allomorph of the plural pronoun and scanning the line on vowels (*hem, esily, hij*). *K–D*'s drastic adoption of **C**'s a-half is unacceptable, since the possibility of localised revision in **C** has never been stronger in these final passūs, and so the only proper course for the editor is to let each version speak for itself. **382** Either *wenden* **C** or *walken* **B** could be original, and revision seems improbable here: *wyde walken* appears as a set phrase at 7.175 //, 10.14 //, *wenden wide* at 10.200 and B Pr 4. *regneth* **C**: instanced only here in the sense 'extends' (MED s.v. *regnen* v. 4(f)), and so self-evidently difficult that there is no justification for *K–DR–K*'s emendation of it to *renneþ*. There is clearly some play on this sense, even if it is not uppermost, at 13.185 *as wyde as thow regneste*, which

alludes to the extent of Reason's immanence ('rule') in the natural world; so there would seem no grounds for questioning *regneth* here. But while *lasteþ* **B** could be an easier ⇒ for the latter, it could equally be the **B**[1] reading which **L** altered as a ?final act of revision. The sardonic pun on the prospects for Conscience in a situation where *þe world regneth* would strike experienced readers of *PP* as wholly characteristic. **386** The **B** form *þe Plowman* with the article, giving a T-type line, is preferred to Ø **C** as the sole one instanced in the last two passūs (21.6, 11, 188, 214, 259, 389, 433, 440, 22.77, 321). Its formal, quasi-titular quality is especially apt at this point.

Colophon The archetypal forms of the final colophon are not securely recoverable. It may have been in two parts, the first as in *B*-R (? = α)*C*-**p** ([*Explicit*] *passus secundus de dobest*), the second containing a form like *Explicit dialogus vocatus pers / liber de petri plowman*. The ?*C*-**x** form *liber vocatus pers ploghman* is fairly close to the ascription in the **C** copy V (Dublin 212) concerning the authorship of the poem, *librum qui vocatur Perys ploughman*.

C. COMMENTARY

The COMMENTARY is keyed to **C**; passus- and line-numbers for the other versions are given in brackets only when the relevant **Z/A/B** text is not immediately parallel. Comment on these versions is incorporated in the main sequence when no more than two short notes in succession appear. But when they are substantial and include separately-numbered notes *within* main entries, the initial note is indented. Works cited in abbreviated form are given their full references in the Bibliography. Biblical citations in Latin are from the *Biblia Vulgata,* ed. Colunga and Turrado; those in English are from the Douay-Rheims translation of the Vulgate. Citations from other Latin works are translated, but the original is given where the exact wording is important.

Prologue

The PROLOGUE consists in its original form of a waking 'prelude', 1–13, followed by a vision of human society placed in a mid-position between the spiritual poles of salvation and damnation: (i) [*a*] 14–164, (i) [*b*] 219–32. In the longer versions is added (ii) the exemplary *Fable of the Parliament of Rats and Mice* (B 146–210=C 165–218). Finally, Conscience's attack on idolatry is inserted at C 95–124 between the lines on clerics who take up secular work and those on the Pope and cardinals. Lines 1–13 form an outer 'frame' for the first two dreams (traditionally called the *Visio*). They are deliberately echoed in the opening of the third dream (10.2 // **AB**, but not in **Z**, which has concluded), the 'framing' effect being completed briefly in 9.293–6. The last 80 lines of Passus IX thus resemble a coda, and in all three versions could be read as the conclusion to an independent work. But as the mention of Dowel at 9.350 raises the prospect that this topic will be discussed in a third Vision, they effectively provide a preparation for / transition to it. The process of revision begins in 4 with *forth] wyde* suggesting a purposeful not an aimless journey and altering the line from a Type Ic to Type Ia. Though the May-morning opening goes back to the *Roman de la Rose*, **L** (unlike Chaucer and the *Purity*-poet) claims no direct knowledge of *RR*. And where Chaucer's dream-vision poems are verbally indebted to contemporary French masters, *PP* echoes earlier English alliterative pieces such as *The Simonie* (*c.* 1340), *Somer Sonday* (*SS, c.* 1327–50) and *Wynnere and Wastoure* (*WW, c.* 1352, though dated later by Salter 1978:30–65 [1988:180–198]). On the extent of **L**'s knowledge of earlier alliterative works see Hussey 1965 and Salter 1967.

1–13 PRELUDE to the First Vision. **1** A fusion of *SS* 1 'Opon a somer soneday se I þe sonne', which uses a Type Ib line (Robbins 1959:38), and *Parlement of the Thre Ages* [*PTA*] 2 'And the sesone of somere when softe bene the wedres' (which however is more likely to be echoing *PP*). *somer*: late spring or early summer, depending on whether *May* at 6 is 'May Day' or 'a day in May'. **L**'s 'summer' is usually 'the warm season' (see e.g. 15.295ff). **2** *shep*: 'sheep' (see the *Textual Notes* [*TN* hereafter])

because dressed in the coarse woollen garment characteristic of hermits (cf. *russet* 10.1 and *Wollewaerd* 20.1). On its possible Biblical resonance of 'exiled humanity as lost sheep' cf. Dyas 2001. **3** *vnholy of werkes*: hinting that the persona's 'countenaunce of clothing' is that of a 'wolf in sheep's clothing'; but this is ironic, because he is not *disgised* (B 24), though resembling many 'false hermits' (*gyrovagi*) who were. *Pe*'s rendering 'without holy works to his credit' and (after Mills 1969:186) 'but not, because of that, necessarily a man of sinful works', is lexically possible but unlikely. For the force of *un-* with evaluative epithets is negatively critical, not neutral (cf. *vnblessed, vnbuxum, vnrihtfole, vnsittynge, vntidy* in the *Indexical Glossary* [*IG* hereafter]), and Will is later seen as a (representative) sinner (6.2 and //). A diatribe against 'unholy hermits' is added in C 9.187–218. **4** The persona's journey superficially resembles a knight's on a quest 'wondyrs to seke', as in the *Alliterative Morte Arthure* [*AMA*] 2514, more than a lover's leisurely walk, as in *Romaunt of the Rose* [*Rom*]105. But he is more an observer, attempting to learn through listening, as is apt for one who will dispute like a clerk (10.20), so the 'mode' envisaged evokes a wandering scholar as well as a wandering hermit. The **ZAB** wording recalls *SS* 31: 'So wyde I walkede þat I wax wery of þe wey'. **5** Things marvellous and things rare or little known are linked in the mind through 'Platonic' wordplay, that which presupposes a real and necessary relationship between words (even when etymologically unconnected) and what they signify (see Jolivet 1962:93–9 and Schmidt 1987:90). **C** takes up much of the sense of **AB** 5–6 (*sellies = ferly, selkouthe // fairie*), but places the 'seeing' before the mention of the Malvern Hills, now become the site of Will's 'sleeping'. 5a appears in **Z** with a different b-half following: either a scribal echo of **C** introduced in the exemplar or, as here preferred, a draft form of a line that **AB** dropped but **C** recalled (and rewrote). **Z** also contains the *ferly* line (= **AB** 6), a redundancy such as might be expected in a draft (see *Intro.* III, *Z Version,* i; and cf. Z Pr 35, where **C** restores one line from a two-line draft on minstrels dropped in **AB**). **6** *Maluerne hulles*: a specificity rare in the dream-vision genre (cf. *The Crowned King* [in *PP Tradition,* ed. Barr] l. 20). The opening location of the *second* Vision (which in **C** now follows the new 'autobiographical prelude' to Passus V) will not seem necessarily at variance with 9.295 (which finds the dreamer on the hills again), if the 'cross' of 5.106 where he falls asleep is taken as located outside the building (Vision Seven in Passus XXI will occur *inside* a church). But since the Malvern Hills lack general symbolic significance, their mention may be just an 'authenticating' fictive detail, like Cornhill at 5.1, or included because corresponding to the writer's place of origin as known to his first audience. 'Malvern' may also be a 'cultural' flourish like the references to Western localities *WW* 8–9 and *Richard the Redeless* [*RRe*] 2. For as maintained by Kane 1965², the relationship between the author and the dream-vision persona involves a measure of historically accurate detail nonetheless meant to be ironically understood, the narrator being a poetic construct rather than an autobiographical self-portrait (Mills 1969; Burrow 1993, 6–27). Attempts have been made (e.g. by Bright 1928) to determine the actual site of the tower and field, and evidence for possible local connections is examined in Kaske 1968; but if **L** had wished this, he could have named the *kirke* at 5.105. **9** The Langlandian dream may be understood, in terms of the dominant medieval classification, as a *somnium*, open to both truth and falsehood and evoking a domain located between the mundane and the divine. See Kruger 1992, citing Macrobius: '[it] conceals with strange shape and veils with ambiguity the true meaning of the information being offered' (*Commentary on the Dream of Scipio*, I iii 10, tr. Stahl). On the number of the dreams in **A**, **B** and **C** see Frank 1951¹ and on their structural arrangement Weldon 1987¹. **13** *slepynge*: on the figurative significance of sleep see Johnson 1994.

(**i a**) **14–21** More important than geographical 'facts' are the symbolic orientations (on which see Davlin 1993); heaven as a tower and hell as a ditch are illustrated in Nolan 1977: fig. 22. Despite resemblances in the imagined scene and locale, the influence of the staging of morality plays like *The Castle of Perseverance* seems excluded by their later date (early C15th). **14** *Estward*: towards the sun, the earthly paradise and the holy city, all associated (Ps 26:1, Jn 23:5, Js 1:17) with God as the source of heavenly light (Ps 42:3 links light, truth and God's holy hill = *toft* in // **ZAB**; and see also Ps 15:1). When these locations re-appear in Passus XX, the east will again be the place of Truth. **15** *tour*: a traditional symbol of divine strength (Ps 60:4; Prov 18:10). *Treuthe*: the strength of truth being familiar from I Esd 4:41 and the previous verse in Esd. also speaking of the 'God of Truth'; cf. the phrase *turris alethiae* in the Archpoet's *Confessio*, which goes back to the *Ecloga Theoduli* (Raby 1965:226). While collocating the tower with truth, **C** asymmetrically opposes *tour* and *dale* where **AB** have *tour: dungeon; toft: dale*, retaining

obliquity in *Treuthe: Deth*. A reflex of **ZAB**'s mysterious description, *as Y trowed...as Y leue* 15–17 offset **C**'s new certainty in the assigning of names. Though *Treuthe* is at once proclaimed the tower's occupant (something postponed till the half-line B 1.12b // **ZA** that is 15b's source), this is still in part a 'nature-name' (the first in the poem), concealing as well as revealing, and designed to provoke thought. The word (on which see Davlin 1989: 29n8, 32n18; Green 1999:8–31) here signifies both *fidelitas* 'faithfulness', the nominal of the OT epithet for the Lord of the Covenant, *fortis et fidelis* (Deut 7:9; I Cor 1:9), and *veritas* 'truth(fulness)', the familiar NT term (Jn 1:14, 18:37, and esp. 14:6, quoted at 10.258 //, and 8:32, source of Chaucer's *Trouthe*). Though the Bible does not directly name God *Veritas* but *Deus veritatis* 'the God of truth' (Ps 30:67), Christ calls himself *via et veritas* in Jn 14:6 (quoted at 10.258 //), while Apoc 19:11 says of the one seated on the white horse [i.e. Christ] that he is *Fidelis, et Verax, et cum iustitia iudicat et pugnat*. The name here betokens God as object of both *ratio* 'the intellect' (i.e. of *belief* in / that) and of *voluntas* 'the rational will' (object of *faith* as trust, 'known' at a distance and only partially revealed). But the 'asymmetric' antithesis with Death (rather than Falsehood) implicitly associates Truth with Life, the **C** revision incorporating at an early stage the fruits of Life's 'case' against Death as a case for *treuthe* specifically as 'justice'. See esp. B 18.390=C 20.431 and 294=325, where the Devil calls Christ 'Truth' in recognising his divine strength, and C 14.212 //, which links God with *treuthe* as *fidelitas* at the end of the Trajan section. **AB 15** *dungeoun*: apt for a castle keep; the devil's prison is a 'pinfold' at B 5.624 (no //) and 16.264 // 18.281. **16** *Westward*: where the sun sets and earth becomes dark. **17** *dale*: aptly death's abode because now in night, but also recalling Ps 22:4, which is quoted at B 7.116 // **A** (though Vg has *medio* for *valle*) and Is 9:2 (with *regione* for *medio*). **18** *wones*: hell, to judge from its occupants. Though the vowel in *wo*- is sounded |ʊ| not |ɔ| its visual form 'Platonically' suggests the *wo* of this place (cf. 20.208, 209). **19** is of uncertain scansion: *fair* or *ful* or both carry stress, giving different (authentic) metrical patterns. **21b** A formula (cf. *Sir Gawain and the Green Knight* [*SGGK*] 530; *AMA* 2187), repeated at 21.23 but taken as raising the serious issue of *why* the world should 'require' men to wander by Dyas (2002), who shrewdly relates it to the traditional notion of man's 'exile' from his 'native land' following the Fall and sees Will as taught to re-interpret wandering in terms of 'life-pilgrimage' (on which see Dyas 2001).

Z 16b–17 seem original, and in 17b the caesura should probably come after *there*. They are replaced in **A** by the dungeon-image (mentioned at Z 100) but partly evoke its idea of darkness. **16** Anticipation of A 3.180 (// **ZB**) would explain the b-half's revision in **A**; but the hesitancy of *as me thou3te* has more the tone of **C** (11, 15, 17) and, if scribal, the lines could arguably be attempting to fill out an imperfectly written exemplar.

22–35 are virtually unrevised from **Z** to **C**. **26** *continance of clothyng*: the misleading appearance resulting from the garb adopted, whereas **Z** 25 seems to distinguish deceptive dress from deceptive looks and behaviour (MED s.v. *contenaunce* n., but sense 3a, not sense 3c). **C** makes the b-half refer to fashion rather than concealment. **28** *harde*: illustrating **C**'s propensity for rhetorical *repetitio* of key-ideas (cf. 23); the change blurs the suggestion in **ZAB** *streyte* of living by a rule. **29** *a good ende*: strengthening **ZAB**'s terse a-half with an idea that will become important in **C** (see 2.35, 3.339, 10.60), and is a pointer to its late date. **30** Anchorites lived enclosed in anchor-holds (Warren 1985), hermits more freely (Clay 1914; Darwin 1944), whether in solitary places, like those of the early Church (17.6ff), or as wanderers like the 'pilgrim-hermit' Patience (B 13.29–30). The Dreamer is first presented as resembling a suspicious example of the latter type; but it is the 'static' hermits living by roadsides who are actually criticised in 9.188ff. **33** *cheuede*: possibly punning on *cheuesaunce*, a dubious term associated with *chaffare, cheuen* at 6.252 (cf. B 5.245).

36–46 36–7 abolish any distinction between good and bad minstrels (on *japeres* see Schmidt 1987:5–11). The 'sinless' minstrels of **AB** 34 recall the *joculatores* in Thomas of Chobham's *Summa Confessorum* (ed. Broomfield 1968:291–2) 'who sing the deeds (*gesta*) of princes and the lives of saints, and make entertainments (*solatia*) for men in their sickness and trouble, and do not pour out scurrilous trash (*turpitudines*)': cf. 7.106 *geste*; B 7.85 *solas*; Pr 37 *foule fantasyes*. On 'good' minstrels, see further Du Boulay 1991:32–4 and Southworth 1989:57–100. While **Z** 35 could arguably be an echo of **C** incorporated by the first copyist of the **Z** draft, 36 seems authentic in its contrastive echo of 31b and its annominative cross-caesural pararhyme, resembling such lines as 13.92 (see Schmidt 1987:68–71). **C** may therefore be reverting here to an *original* comprehensive hostility to the minstrel-class and so have preserved one **Z** line while dropping the other (**Z** 36) in rewriting B 36ff. **AB** 35 *Iudas children*: a general term of obloquy (like *Caymes kynde* at B 9.128), not implying that the apostle was a minstrel, though (as the type of treachery through false words and 'fair countenance') aptly linked with minstrels who use disguise and tell lying tales (see B 16.149, 154–5). His name is collocated elsewhere with alliterating *Iew, Iesu, iape* and *iangle* as at 1.63, where he himself is the victim of the devil's *iape,* while B 9.91, which compares the minstrel's *patron* to Judas, reveals the thematic depth of the association. **39** The changes from *dar not* **A** through *wol nat* **B** to *myhte* **C** show **L**'s final moral posture as altogether more definite. **40** This first macaro-

nic line alludes to Eph 5:3–5; but *turpiloquium* is found in the Old Latin translation of the Bible, the *Vetus Latina* (*VL*), for the *turpem sermonem* of Col 3:8 in the Vulgate (Vg), a text closely related in thought and wording ('*turpi*tudo...stulti*loquium*...scurrilitas...non habet haereditatem in regno Christi et Dei'), and in patristic citations of that verse (Alf*Q* 33). Craun's discussion of the motif (1997:157–86), citing various manuals, argues that **L**'s use of the quotation 'invokes..both a Pauline verbal sin and a monitory pastoral discourse directed against it'. The phrase in 40b renders an idea from Hugh of St Cher's gloss on Jn 8:34 (*peccati* = *diaboli*: for the devil as personifying or embodying sin, cf. 20.388). If 39 alludes to I Thess 3:10 (*Sk*), the phrase *Qui....*would be admonishing *himself* not to speak obloquy; but the precise contextual sense of *turpiloquium* makes this unlikely. **Z 37** *as*: if 'in the manner of', then implying for *bidder* the sense 'one who prays' (MED *s.v.* n (b)); but since elsewhere that term is a synonym for 'one who begs alms', *as* is more simply 'like' (= 'and'). **45** *Robardus knaues*: a variant on *roberdesmen* found in statutes of Edward III and Richard II, and perhaps derived from the homophonic association of *robber* with the name Robert exploited later with Robert the robber at B 5.462 // (*knaues*, echoing 40, is another **C** *repetitio* like that at 28).

47–65 are little altered from **A** to **C** save for omission of B 50–2. But **A**'s revision of **Z** 43–52 inverts *friars-hermits-pilgrims* to *pilgrims-hermits-friars* and elaborates on the friars' special 'threat' to the church (anticipating the poem's climax in XXII/XX). Since the texts from **A** onwards emphasise less the friars' preaching than their activities as confessors, **Z**'s *lack* of this theme points to its priority. **47** *palmers*: strictly pilgrims to Jerusalem, who wore a palm-frond badge; here virtually = *pilgrimes* (on whom see Jusserand 1899:338–403, Sumption 1975, Finucane 1977, Adair 1978, Dyas 2001). The implication 'professional' pilgrims (*Bn*) is unsupported, for though the one such encountered 'in pilgrim's wise' (7.160) has never seen a 'palmer' seeking Truth (7.179), Piers on his last appearance is dressed like a 'palmer' (15.34), while Patience wears 'pilgrim's clothes' in // **B**. Holy Land sites, including Jerusalem, are mentioned directly only at 7.170–1 and Z 5.70 (omitted **ABC**); so perhaps *palmers* implied simply 'pilgrim-travellers abroad' (cf. Chaucer's *GP*13). **48** *seynt Iame*: the reputed burial-place of St James the Apostle at Compostela Cathedral in NW Spain (Galicia, specified in // **Z**, an anticipation of Z 5.163 removed in revision to **A**). It was the most popular foreign shrine for English pilgrims, who reached it by sea, enjoying special protection following the marriage of Edward I to Eleanor of Castile in 1254. *Rome*: site of the shrines of SS Peter and Paul and the many 'martired amonges Romaynes' (17.282). The Rome pilgrimage is mentioned again at 4.123, 7.166, 9.323, 16.38, 17.282. **B 50–2** seem otiose (see *TN*) and, though anticipating the 'professional' saint-seeker of B 5.530, they are cut with no loss. **51** *hokede staues*: as illustrated in Jusserand 1899:139. **52** *Walsyngham*: site of a shrine of the Virgin Mary in N Norfolk, popular since the C12th and second only to Canterbury as an English place of pilgrimage (Adair 1978:114–200). At Z 5.102 it is where Greed will go to do penance, and the reference to the latter's 'wife' there may have prompted **A**'s revision here to the more critical *wenches* (though presumably *wyues* Z 48, like *suster* at B 5.642, is heavily sarcastic). **54** *copes*: 'long clothes', unsuitable for manual work, such as the Dreamer wears at 5.41 (and cf. 8.185, 9.210). **55** *made*: removing the echo of Pr 2 in // **AB** *shopen*.

Z **53–8** describe bishops and religious in an ironic tone like that of the passage on the Pope's plenitude of power at 9.324–31 // (no **Z**); they are replaced in **A** by fuller criticism of friars. The lines intimate a gap between theory and common experience, though the scepticism implied in 56 is absent from later versions. The criticism of religious rectors at 57–8 is cut, though they are attacked for neglecting their churches (C 5.163–7). Here the charge is that the orders grow richer by drawing off the income while leaving the incumbent too little to live on, and so leading him to desert his pastoral duties (as described in 81–2 //). **Z**'s mild treatment of bishops is sharpened up in **A**, but the lines on religious are dropped. **53** *Bischopes blessed*: perhaps deleted here by **A** to avoid repetition at A 8.13. **58** *apropre*: the earliest use in this sense (MED s.v. *appropren* v 1(b)).

56–65 56 *freris*: the attack on their *confessional practices* (62–5) as the source of the Church's coming catastrophe, new in **A**, is unlikely to have been omitted by **Z** if that text were a scribal compilation. The friars' *preaching* is criticised for diluting the hard ethical (and especially penitential) demands of the bare Gospel text and authoritative commentaries on it (59b *doctours*). The repeated *shryuars* and the forceful language mark the change from hope of reform in **AB** to desire for some drastic action (more probably removal of their licences to hear confessions than their wholesale dissolution). *the foure ordres*: the Dominicans, Franciscans, Augustinians and Carmelites. The last, the White Friars, who were by no means a small order in C14th England (Lawrence 1994:92–8), get no further mention. The Dominicans (Order of Preachers or Black Friars) are alluded to at 22.252, and perhaps in the person of the Gluttonous Doctor, if he is modelled on Friar William Jordan (see at 15.30ff). The Austins (Augustinians) or friar-hermits appear at 17.15, a mildly satirical revision of non-satiric B 15.289. Though the mendicants are criticised collectively here and in 22, the Franciscans (Friars Minor or Grey Friars) are singled out (10.9ff //) for abandoning the ideal of poverty so warmly endorsed in XVI (see esp. 353–5, asserting that the charity

St Francis embodied is rare in his order now). The claim that **L** is writing from the position of reformers within the Franciscan order and even using a coded Franciscan discourse is overstated by Clopper 1997. **60** Mendicants in the universities had been a major force in the theological Faculties since the 13th c., and in the late 14th c. were conspicuous as defenders of orthodoxy against such radical seculars as Wyclif; most would have been trained at Oxford (Courtenay 1987:56–87). Franciscan 'masters' appear at 10.19 and a (possible) Dominican doctor at 15.30. **62** *charite*: metonymic for the friars ideally conceived (cf. 16.353–5), the sense of the line being 'since those whose special vocation was evangelical charity have become peddlers of cheap absolution'. **64** *choppe*: accrediting *charite* with a 'righteous violence' later found associated with *verray charite* in 19.273–4, lines that also link Holy Church and charity. **L**'s critique forms part of an English tradition of satirising the orders' mutual hostility that stretches from *WW* (156ff) to *Pierce the Ploughman Crede* [*PPCr*]. See Du Boulay 1991:80–6, 134–6; Szittya 1986:247–87. **65** *meschief*: related by Gwynn (1943) to the controversy (1356–60) between the friars and Abp. Fitzralph of Armagh. The new allusion in **A** may not be a direct reflex of this dispute, since **Z** notably lacks heavy anti-fraternal animus, though it must date from after 1362 (see on 5.116 below).

Z **59–85** contain the material afterwards expanded (with omission of 64, 70–3) in different order, the pardoner coming last (59–60 interrupt a passage on the clergy and are understandably moved in **A** to the end of the Pr). **A** 65–97 look like authorial tightening of a loosely-organised draft rather than **Z** being jumbled recollection by a scribe. The heavy irony of **Z** 70–3 is like that of 53–8 and seems unsophisticated when compared with the more pointed attack on judges and jurors at B 7.44–6. **63** *annueles...togyderus*: a two-year arrangement to say commemorative masses that would provide a handsome supplement (the generalised *symonye* at A 83 replaces two specific forms of it). *annueles* here predates the first-cited MED ref. in *PPCr* 414. **69/70** illustrate true 'rich' rhyme with polysemantic wordplay (cf. Pr 122/3, B 7.36/7).

66–80 The *pardoner* was empowered by the Pope to grant indulgences for the remission of temporal punishments due for sin (such as those of 69) after formal forgiveness of sins in confession, in return for payment towards the work of the Church; but he would need the diocesan's authorisation to preach in church for this purpose. Pardoners could not give absolution, since they were usually only in minor orders, nor were they licensed to give formal instruction 'like a priest'. Their sermons aimed to stimulate and intensify feelings that would arouse a desire to make confession and only after this make the penitents eligible to receive an indulgence. On pardoners see further 2.229–32, B 5.639–42; and on indulgences in this period, Swanson 1989:291–3, Lunt 1962: chs 9–12. **71** *kyssen*: as a sign of reverence towards the Pope understood as the successor of St Peter, from whom they have come (cf. the very different tone at 20.474). **72** *bounched...blered*: perhaps envisaging a sharp tap on the head that brings water to the eyes (*not* 'religious' tears, on which see 6.1–2). *bulles*: again illustrating **C**'s favoured *repetitio*. **Z 75** *bille*: a cognate derivate of *bulle* (MED s.v. *bille* n. 1(b)); *breuet* **AB**: differing in sense but with its referent either the same or else the bishop's (supposed) licence. *Bn* aptly notes how the *Visio*'s climax, a dispute over the validity of pardons, is here foreshadowed. Whether this pardoner's groundless pretension to absolve suggests that he is an unlicensed or even false pardoner with a forged bull (see Swanson 1989:248), the 'power' of his indulgence could hardly be less spiritual (cf. Haukin's sardonic complaint about *bulles* at B 13.244–55 below, slightly toned down in // C 15.218–26). **73** *rageman*: short for 'ragmanroll', a long parchment document with its ends cut into strips forming a tattered fringe, on which hung the leaden seals of the Pope and bishops authorising the pardoner (cf. B 13.247 and MED s.v. *rageman* n. 2(a)). Use of this word metonymically for the devil at 18.122 invests its appearance here with dubious overtones. *rynges and broches*: cf. Chaucer *CT* VI 908. **76** *yblessed...eres*: 'holy [as when he was blessed at his consecration] and worthy of his office / worthy to keep his ears [because he made good use of them]' (Johnston 1959). **78** *by*: 'in accordance with [*sc.* the intentions of]' (*Bn, Pe*; MED s.v. *bi* prep. 8b (a) 'with the permission of'; the sense 'against' [*Sk* IV i:13–14], is not illustrated in MED and seems out of place). The line need not be ironic, since the pardoner could have obtained the seal by bribing an official and be using it without the bishop's knowledge (see also Kellogg & Haselmayer 1951:267), a situation where the latter certainly needed to 'use his ears'. And such a situation is described in a Wycliffite text of the 1380s (Matthew 1880:154) cited by Fletcher 1990:136 as illustrating a simony-topos of the time. This pardoner evidently colludes with the parson (for a payment), and the poor are the dupes of both; but '*ignorancia non excusat episopos* nec ydiotes preestes' (B 11.315–6). **81–94 81–4** explain **A**'s added criticism of collusion. **Z 61–4**, on priests' attempts to augment their incomes, imply but do not state that they desert their parishes to hold chantry-posts. **Z 65** appears the basis of **A 84–5**, the wordplay on *houide / houuis* resembling that in **Z** 64, which is expanded into **A** 80–3, with omission of the *to / therto* pun. The relationship between **A** and **Z** here is hard to see except as that of one authorial version developing out of another. **81** *persones*: the rectors of parishes, who received the great tithe (on grain) and sometimes employed a vicar. The latter was allowed the lesser tithe (on hay, wool etc) and might in turn devolve his duties to

an unbeneficed clerk whom he paid a small salary (Swanson 1989:214–5); cf. also 13.100ff on the position of priests lacking sufficient financial support. 'Simony' here is the purchase or sale of a chantry-office (an abuse not explicitly mentioned in *PP* but known to have taken place) rather than its taking-on, as **Z** specifies with *annueles* and *trentales* (chantries were increasing at this time and were not confined to London). Will later may be envisaged (5.44ff) as doing part-time a job like that of a chantry-priest, who had not only to say his agreed mass(es) but 'to recite daily the office of the dead' (Cook 1947:14 and Kreider 1979), or of a clerk supported by a parish fraternity (Hill in Du Boulay & Barron 1971:242–55; Barron 1985:13–37). **82** *þe pestelence tyme*: the Great Plague in 1348–9, which killed a third of the population and perhaps half the clergy, leaving many parishes unable to support a priest from their drastically reduced tithes and leading to the admission of poorly qualified candidates to replace them. Three further attacks in 1361–2 (of fresh memory at the time of Z Pr 62), 1369 and 1375–6 (see 5.115, 11.60 and B 13.249 respectively) helped to keep the original allusion topical. (On the general character and impact of the plague, see Keen 1973:169–74; Ziegler 1971, Shrewsbury 1975, Bean in Williman 1982:23–39). **85–9** elaborate on criticism first made in **A**, introducing the theme (dominant in Vision Three) of the split between learning and holiness, and anticipating that of Vision Five, with its diatribe against worldly clergy as corrupting Christian society. **85** *Bisshopes*: the 'curial' bishops who were given their sees for serving the king, or whose secular duties kept them from their dioceses (Swanson 1989:80–1). The puns suspected by *Bn* on *cure* (with *curial*) and *crownynge* (their service to the crown supplanting the religious work their vocation calls for) are possible, but *curial* itself is uninstanced before the late 15th c. *Bachelers*: university graduates in theology (cf. // **A**) who had lectured on the Bible and Peter Lombard's *Sentences*. *maystres*; *doctours*: interchangeable terms for holders of the highest degree in theology or canon law. Working as civil servants or in the king's courts (A 95), they were rewarded with canonries, and some with bishoprics (hence the appropriateness of bishops at the head of the list). **BC** have shifted the emphasis from clerics already holding offices to those with 'heigh clergie' which they use to the neglect of their spiritual obligations. **A 92** *Archideknes*: the bishop's deputies who held courts in one of the divisions of the diocese; trained probably in canon law, they could end working in a royal law-court (see A 95). *denis*: here probably not the heads of cathedral chapters but rural deans responsible for a subdivision of the archdeaconry. **87** *with*: if taken with *Holy Chirche* making the latter an entity distinct from the clergy (and especially the hierarchy); but more naturally, forming a phrase *charged with* as at 22.237. The bishops and theologians are entrusted with the responsibility of governing and guiding the Church in order to 'cultivate' charity in the community (the figure echoes B 19.336–7). **89 BC** shift the stress from deserting the parish to neglecting the parishioners, who would especially need their confessors during the penitential season. **91** *Cheker*: the department of state that handled crown finances under the Treasurer, including both the treasury and the court of accounts; here specifically the Court of Exchequer dealing with revenue cases. *Chancerye*: the office of the Chancellor of England, keeper of the Great Seal, and effectively the King's first minister; here perhaps with special reference to the Court of Chancery, which issued writs for action at common law (Alford, *Glossary of Legal Diction* [Alf*G*]). *Bn* suspects an allusion to William of Wykeham, Bishop of Winchester, Chancellor from 1367–71; but both he and Bp. Brantingham the treasurer had been forced to resign in 1371 after the Commons demanded that churchmen be removed from government. The lines are not in **A**, so if **B** added them in allusion to Wykeham's prosecution in 1376, they will have lost their topicality by 1378–9. Although Simon of Sudbury, Abp. of Canterbury, became Chancellor in 1380 (which is conceivably not too late for a final version of **B** Pr), understanding **L**'s critiques of clerical abuses gains little from searching for particular targets. Both offices were largely staffed with clerics, who have the characteristic anonymity of civil servants (cf. Z 3.3, unchanged through **ABC**). **92** *wardus*: legal minors incapable of conducting their own affairs, here metonymically = 'guardianship-cases' (*Bn*); revenues from the estates of a deceased tenant-in-chief reverted to the crown during his heir's minority. *wardemotis*: meetings of citizens in city or borough wards, at which the Exchequer clerks claimed royal dues; the characteristic play on two senses of 'ward' is lost if *wardus* = 'city-wards' (*Sk*). *wayues*; *strayues*: lost property that reverted to the crown; though it included strayed animals, *strayues* may signify the property of 'aliens' (foreigners) dying without legitimate heirs (*Sk*; on these AF law terms see Alf*G*). **93–4** tighten up **B**'s somewhat repetitive lines, changing a rare Type IIb (95) to a Type Ia. **93** *seneschals*: the stewards of great lords (as opposed to the king), virtually their deputies in a manor's administrative and legal affairs (H. S. Bennett 1937:157–61). **94** *stewardus*: effectively synonymous with *seneschal* (Alf*G* s.vv.) **95–124 C** adds here (a) 95–106 (finished) and (b) 107–24, a re-writing of B 10.277–80 perhaps not in final form when copied into the archetype (see *TN*). The object of attack is not clerical venality in general but specifically prelates' encouragement of superstitious religiosity in order to raise money. It follows lines on the clergy's secular employment 'abruptly' (*Pe*) but not arbitrarily, the subject being their neglect of the laity's spiritual needs in encouraging thank-offerings for miracles supposedly

performed at shrines. The tone here is akin to that of near-contemporary Wycliffite criticism (Hudson, *Selections*1978:87); but the point is moral rather than doctrinal, attacking less image-veneration as such (cf. B 18.429=C 20.474–5, with a significant revision at 475a) than clerics' cynical exploitation of pious and gullible laypeople. In the analogy of the OT exemplum, Ely (Heli) = the prelates, his sons Ophni and Phinees = the priests, to whom the bishops are as 'fathers', the priests in turn being 'fathers' to the laity (120–22). The slight incoherence here, perhaps due to the text's unrevised state, may have partly prompted the scribes of mss I and F to substitute respectively *peres* 'lords' and *prelatus* for archetypal *men*. Defects of metre and thought might render the passage suspect as a scribal intrusion (see *TN* and *Intro.* III *Z Version* § 6); but the phrasing, if unpolished, is authentic, as in the play on *wrother* and *raper* in the Type II line 117 and the use of *soffraunce* in the counterpointed Type III line 124 in connexion with *coueitise*, which anticipates 3.206–07. **95** *Conscience*: appearing earlier than in **ZAB** and already having for **L**'s 'audience' (*Intro.* V § 7) the significance accorded him in B XX as a spiritual leader in the Church (his earlier 'social' identity as 'knight', retained in 3.145, is not made explicit at this juncture). Though he is identified by his name and action of 'accusing', whether Conscience is to be interpreted in precise scholastic terms has been much debated (by Hort 1938, Jenkins 1969, Carruthers 1973, Harwood 1992:91–138 and passim). **L**'s view seems closest to the Thomistic conception of conscience (Morgan 1987[1]) as the application of the rules of reason to a particular moral act, such as refusal to marry or to kiss Meed (and for Aquinas, conscience crucially *can* err in practical reasoning about an act, as will be seen in XXII when Conscience admits Friar Flatterer into Unity). What is here understood may perhaps be the disposition (*habitus*) responsible for this act, rather than the act itself, though in each of his three major appearances in **B** Conscience indeed carries out a definite and significant moral decision (cf. further 3.155–6, 20.242–5 //, B 13.180–83). However, **L** nowhere cites or alludes to any specific theoretical account of Conscience, a personification whose polysemous common name, long treated as equivalent to native *inwit* (MED s.vv. 2 (a) and 4, citing *Ancrene Wisse* [*AW*]), should be interpreted in the light of his own words. The equation of Latin *consciencia* with English 'Conscience' at 16.189–91, 199a is compatible with the Thomistic account, but coming from an older, less technical tradition should not be forced to yield a stricter sense than **L**'s definition requires. **97** *boxes*: for the offerings made at shrines. **98** *vntrewe*: i.e. 'false', by analogy with such 'sacrifices' in the OT, and unacceptable to God less because of the sin of the person offering (e.g. Cain) than because the 'miraculous' images are untrustworthy or 'lacking in (objective) validity'. **99** *wax*:

the votive-candles lit there (*Pe*) or, if *hangeth* is taken literally, waxen images of limbs for which a miraculous cure had been obtained or was being sought (Radford 1949:164–8, Finucane 1977:95–7, Swanson 1989:233–4). **103** *for...coueytise*: 'because of your love of greed / your covetous desire'. The thought 'al þe world be wors' (104) anticipates 'al euel spredeth' at 16.244, giving L's severest criticism of the clergy prominence by placing it near the poem's beginning. **104** *as Holy Writ telleth*: see I Kgs (= I Sam) 4:11, 18. The example of Eli's sons as representatives of priestly greed and incontinence is common in homiletic writing (Wenzel 1999:137–52). **107** *Fines his brother*: 'that of his brother Phinees'. **108** *Archa Dei losten*: the Ark of the Covenant, made of precious wood and plated with gold, and originally housing the stone Tablets of the Law. The most sacred emblem of the ancient Hebrew people and believed to represent the Divine Presence, it may here be taken as an allegorical figure of the Church, which risked the danger of being spiritually 'lost' through greed to the enemies of God as the Ark was to the Philistines. **109** *synne*: the covetous impiety of stealing from the sacrificial meats. **119** *maumettes*: such images as the Virgin and Child venerated at Walsingham (Adair 1978:119–20).

125–218 are substantially added in **B** and revised in **C**, only the short passage on lawyers having already appeared in A 84–9, which rewrote by expanding Z 65 into 84–5. **125–7** Coming now after the minatory Ophni-Phineas passage, this warning to priests adds their liturgical and devotional to their pastoral shortcomings and gains solemnity from the use of direct address (to fit in with 96ff), *constorie* and *acorse* taking on added irony from the allusion to Mt 25:31. *is... / Lest*: i.e. lest at the Last Day. *Con(si)story*: (a) the bishop's court for cases involving clergy (as at 3.34), presided over by the chancellor or the commissary (cf. 16.362 // below); (b) the Pope's solemn council of cardinals (alluded to at 134 below); but here (c) figurative for the *tribunal Christi* (II Cor 5:10) at Doomsday, with the Apostles as Christ's council of judges (Mt 19.28). It is a sign of the poem's structural cohesion that the eschatological note struck here will be echoed at the end with the appearance of Death and Antichrist. **128–38 128** *I parsceyued*: if given to Will as in **B** so as to fit with *fonde* 56 and *say* 231, this is free from the awkwardness found by *Pe*. But his (and *R–K*'s) ascription of 128–138 to Conscience is at variance with the context, and the abrupt change of speaker here posited at 138 may be explained by the need to avoid the ambivalent tone of B 111. The notion of the 'power of the keys' given to St Peter (and, in standard medieval acceptance, to his successors the popes) is based on Mt 16:19 (cited at 9.326*a* // and alluded to at 15.226 and 21.183–91). As *Bn* notes, the idea that Christians should see the 'cardinal virtues' (first so called by Ambrose) as forms of *love* goes back

to Augustine. Thus **L** can correctly affirm Christian rule as 'the exercise of power in a spirit of love'; otherwise, to make virtues of natural reason the 'hinges' of heaven's gates would be incongruous (the derivation of 'cardinal' from Lat *cardo* 'hinge' occurs in the Proem to the *Disticha Catonis* [*DC*], as noted by Baer 2001). The later allegory of Truth's 'court' makes the specifically Christian virtues of humility and love central (see esp. the manorgates 'hanging' on alms-deeds at 7.241). But here love appears a 'dimension' or a 'spirit' manifest in a proper exercise of the cardinal virtues, which are shown as capable of *im*proper exercise (in the spirit of covetousness) later at 21.458 ff. **130** Since Mt 16:19 does not explicitly describe Christ bequeathing the power of the keys 'with love', the true source may be Jn 13:13–16, with its lesson of Christian rule as a service of love. But the cardinal virtues may be emphasised because of the dominance of political and social concerns in this vision: they are *most vertuous* not, obviously, as higher than the theological virtues, but in their special function of fostering right order in secular governance. Their nature will be more fully explored in 21.275–320, where they are allegorically depicted as needing love to grow in their midst so as to protect them against vices (311–13). **132** *cardinales*: the *-s* pl. ending is imitated from French usage (cf. 7.82, B 11.316 and see Mustanoja, *Middle English Syntax* [*MES*] 277). **134–8** *Bn* sees in *court* 134 a specific allusion to the election of the anti-pope Clement VI in Sept 1378 by the French cardinals opposed to Urban VI (see also Bennett 1943:56). But this fits ill with the refusal at 136 to *impugne* 'find fault with', i.e. challenge the basis of their right [of election] (MED s.v. 2(b), with play on sense 2(a)); so the more probable referent is the general authority of the holiness and learning ideally to be found in a cardinal. **134** *caught han*: suggesting that actual cardinals do not deserve their name (as 'ideally' apprehended) because, while the Church as an organisation 'turns' on them as its structural hinges, their own lives do not 'turn' upon the spirit of the virtues (*Bn*). **135–6** The slight syntactical ambiguity (depending on whether or not the lines are run on) is well met by the rendering 'mak[e] a pope who will have the power that Peter had' (*Bn*). They have the right of election / the capacity (through it) to confer *plenitudo potestatis*. This 'power' of granting or withholding forgiveness of sins was held (on the basis of Jn 20:23) to be shared by the Apostles and their successors the bishops. But in 'high' papal theory it became associated with the Pope's prerogative of immediate jurisdiction in all parts of the Church and supreme spiritual authority over all, from peasant to Emperor. **138** The substituted line exhorts the post-1381 Dreamer (and the 'public' he represents) against disturbing the peace of the Christian community by disputation. *Contreplede*: a term perhaps introduced by **L** from Law French (Alf*G* s.v.). First used by Imaginatyf at B 12.98, it recurs in the new C 8.53 (echoing this line), where Piers defends the authority of Conscience 'counterpleaded' by the friars at B 20.385 (cf. also Piers's subtly-inflected advice to challenge *maystres and grete menne* at 8.87). This new view of Conscience's direct relationship with Will, further developed in 5.89ff, results from progressively absorbing the Dreamer's rôle as quester into Conscience's in the concluding passūs of **B**. The truth of 137 is *affirmed* by claiming that to *deny* it would cause harm. The addition may thus be (to modify *Bn*) a response to the papal wars of 1379 more than a pointed allusion to the Great Schism itself in Sept 1378 (at the time of the **C** revision, an event six or seven years past). But *Bn* is not wholly convincing in finding heavy reliance on the thought-sequence of II Pet 1:5–11; and any residual criticism of the cardinals in the Dreamer's words in **C** is counteracted by Conscience's interjection at 138 (while it is true that the referent of *hit* remains indeterminate). The provocative B 111 replaced implies both capacity and constraint, as do 217–8 below (see Simpson 1990:13–21).

139–64 139 *Knyghthede*: a distinct social order including the nobility and distinguished from the labouring, mercantile and clerical members of society by its responsibility for governing and protecting the realm; the earliest recorded use in this sense (see MED s.v. *knighthod* n. 2(c)). **L**'s main statements on the character and the duties of knights occur at 1.101–5, 8.23–53 and 17.287ff, which may be compared with the view of Gower in *CA* (on knighthood see Barber 1970, Bumke 1982; for the martial ideology of the medieval aristocracy, Keen 1984). **140** *tho men* (*Communes* **B**): the change of stress perhaps induced by awareness of the radical overtones of *communes* after 1381, when the peasant rebels sought an alliance between the king and what they called the 'true commons' against other lords secular and ecclesiastical. Or it may be no more than a recognition of the king's *de facto* dependence on the knightly estate for enforcing the authority he has directly from God. An extreme view that the C Pr revision presents 'the triumph of absolutism' is given by Baldwin 1981[1]:7–23. But the continuing (and increased) importance of Conscience (who is given the **B** Angel's lines at 151–7) demands a nuanced understanding of **L**'s robust stand for order (see further on B 145). **141–7** *Kynde Wit*: the 'natural reason' (Quirk 1953:182) that acquires knowledge through the data of experience; prior to formal reasoning, but also the *basis* of *clergie* 'understanding acquired through instruction' (see 14.34 and cf. A 12.41–6). This power seems more generally concerned with man's practical relations to the world than specifically with 'the moral aspect of human actions' (*Bn*), for the link with Conscience is not yet found in **B**. Kynde Wit has been more exactly correlated with the scholastic *vis cogitativa*, a power of the 'sensible soul'

that provides material for use by the 'rational soul' and is especially concerned to apprehend what is of benefit to man (Harwood 1976); but most commentators agree with *Bn*. Thus Baldwin too finds KW equivalent to *ratio naturalis* as described by Aquinas, 'which teaches [man] the Law' (1981[1]:22). Morgan (1987[1]) sees it as the natural understanding of the first principles of both the speculative and the practical intellect which serves as the *source* of the knowledge Conscience then applies to a particular act (Conscience acknowledges KW's 'teaching' at 3.436). And for White (1988:3–40) KW is both a (natural) faculty and the (natural) knowledge it has access to (especially regarding the pursuit of the good and doing well), though its meaning changes through the poem and between versions and is developed greatly in **B** and **C**. But like long-naturalised 'Conscience' (see 95 above), and unlike *Liberum Arbitrium* later, 'Kynde Wit' does not seem to be a technical term. Though found first in **L** (and elsewhere only in Trevisa), it comes from the common language and so is presumably meant to be intelligible from its first appearance at Z Pr 142 (MED s.v *kinde* adj. 1(e) cites Trevisa using the phrase to render Lat. *sensus*, and it correlates closely with this term at 16.187–8). The expression's meaning in different contexts should not be determined by a specific scholastic theory; but Morgan's study helpfully elucidates the relations between Kind Wit, Conscience and Reason. **143** *Comune*: 'the people, community' more than 'the Commons in parliament' [= burgesses and knights of the shire]. **B 120** *tilie*; *trauaille*: the first of many 'alliterating matched pairs', comparable to the 'copulative' alliterative phrases found in OE prose, which 'participate in a kind of mutual semantic assimilation' (Ryan 1969:267; these formula-like pairs are listed on pp. 272–3). **B 122** *knowe his owene*: 'recognise their true rights and duties' (*Bn*). **149** *Lewte*: the moral and spiritual dimension or pervading spirit of human law, which is meant to reflect divine justice (cf. B 11.153–55). The word is etymologically linked (< OF *lealte* < Lat. *legalitatem*) with ideas of the abstract essence of law; near-synonyms like 'fairness', 'equity', 'fidelity' and 'integrity' bring out various aspects of its meaning (see AlfG 84, 159); and a native equivalent is *treuthe* (cf. *SGGK* 2366). Lewte has been seen both generally as 'virtuousness of life', forming a 'triad' with *law* and *love* (Kean 1964, 1969), and even as corresponding specifically to the theological virtue Hope (Clutterbuck 1977). But perhaps the clearest gloss is **L**'s synonym *rihtfulnesse, rihtwisnesse* (21.83/89), emblematised by *gold* (which echoes the spiritual 'treasure' of *treuthe* praised at 1.81). This association, already present in its collocation with the king's *rightful ruylynge* at 150, supports Donaldson's gloss 'exact justice' (1949:66*n*). But its religious resonance aligns it with the *pietas* that clothes bare law (*nudum ius*) at 152ff below. Lewte is fleetingly again a personified character at 2.20 (as Holy Church's *lemman*), at 4.156 in close association with Love, and more extensively at 12.24–42, where his advice to Will is endorsed by Scripture. Here the term has been taken to imply 'the King's law-abiding subjects' by Kane (982:40), though perhaps this is only as part of its reference, not of its sense. **B 123–7** The *lunatik* could be an ironic persona of Will (cf. later his 'madness' at B 15.1–10). He could likewise stand for the 'unenlightened speaker' of what 'might have been spoken by a clerk' (*clergially*), addressing the King with the *thou* form of clerks 'careless of the pretensions of the world' (Burnley 1990:33, 36, 38), a touch echoed in **C**'s omission of *sire* 125. At 147 **C**'s replacement of the lean lunatic by KW makes for greater clarity.

151–7 151 *Conscience*: replacing, as befits the importance of his rôle in **C**, **B**'s lofty *angel* 131 (the low goliard who answers the latter being omitted). He is perhaps to be thought of here as a judge administering equity according to the dictates of 'conscience', in the light of later 4.186 (where it is however Reason who is envisaged as future 'Chancellor'). For increasingly the actual Chancellor's rôle in the Chancery Court was to correct law in individual cases where it was defective on account of its universality (J. H. Baker 1971:42; cf. also Baldwin 1981[1]:22–3). **B 128** *on hei3 an aungel*: perhaps recalling the one represented in a pageant at Cheap the day before Richard II's coronation on 16 July 1377 (Walsingham, *Historia Anglicana* 1, 331–2; Wickham 1980:54–5). But **B**'s collocation of angel and 'goliard' may have been suggested by the 'angels' who come to dissuade Golias from marriage in Walter Map's *Golias de conjuge non ducenda* (ed. Wright 1841:78), a work **L** seems to have known (see on 22.193–8 below). **152–7** The Latin Leonine hexameter and pentameter verses appear, added to the text of a 1315 sermon by Henry Harclay, Chancellor of Oxford, in Lambeth MS 61, f. 147v (*Bn*); whatever the source, the wordplay on *metere* 'measure / reap' will have appealed to **L**. Their use in an address to the king may allude to the sermon for the newly crowned Richard and for the peace of the realm preached by Thomas Brinton, Bishop of Rochester, on 17 July 1377 (ed. Devlin 1934: no.44; see also idem, xx, xxvii); but the sentiments have a general validity as well as a special aptness at the commencement of a reign. *Sum rex...metas*: '"I am King, I am Ruler;" one day you may be neither. You who control the lord Christ's lofty laws, The better to perform what you must do, Be pitiful as you are just; for naked law You must dispense in piety of heart. Sow such grain as you desire to reap. But strip law bare, the judgement you receive Will follow the naked letter of [God's] law. If you sow mercy, mercy you will harvest'. The verses oppose 'bare' justice to law administered with a sense of what is owed to God by his earthly deputy the king; 156 alludes to Mt 7:1–2, quoted at B 12.89*a*, and the thought echoes Js 2:13.

The sense of *pietas* here is close to that of ME *pite*, as in Gower's praise of Richard II for his 'justice medled with pite' in *CA* viii 2989–92 (*Bn*) and involves the religious awareness that should inform human law. Modern 'mercy', associated with but distinguished from 'pity' in Middle English, captures the sense, both terms being used interchangeably at 21.92–3 for one of the royal gifts the Three Kings bring Christ under the sign of myrrh. In Richard II's coronation oath was added (after the promise to maintain the laws) the phrase *iuste et racionabiliter* (McKisack 1959:399), the sense of the second adverb ('spiritually') coming close to *pietate* 155.

B 139–45 139 *gloton*: playing on the ultimate derivation of OF *goliardeis* from *gula* 'gluttony'. **141–2** 'As the name "king" is said to come from "rule", He who does not maintain the law with zeal Is but a king in name, and not in truth'. Though 'clothed' law is 'proper' law, the goliard's insistence complements rather than contradicts the angel's speech, highlighting the need to avoid arbitrary rule by linking the reality of kingly authority (*res*) with zealous maintenance of the nation's laws (*iura*). There is nothing Lollard-like about the sentiments (cf. *Bn*) and the ironic use of a speaker whose name is associated with gluttony is of a piece with the earlier recourse to a *lunatik* (this goliard is not especially loquacious). The Latin couplet has been related (*Sk, Bn*) to proverbial verses like those in Wright, ed. *Political Poems* (1859:278) stating that the king must rule himself rightly to be a true king, and to the fanciful derivation of *rex* from *recte agendo* (Alf*Q* 34). While this appears in a source **L** knew (Isidore's *Etymologies* 9.3), his own text speaks not of self-rule or right action but of kingship as nullified by neglect of law; so the lines in this form may be his own. **145** versifies the *Lex Regia*, the Roman law maxim *Quod principi placuit legis habet vigorem* (Justinian, *Institutes* 1.2.6; Alf*Q* 34) and appears in this form in Richard of Wetheringsette's C13th *Summa* as part of a 'vers of Latyn' (Wenzel, in Alford, *Companion to* PP [Alf*C*] 1988[2]:161). The commons' view of royal authority is extreme, and despite the invitation to interpret (*Bn* finding beneath the maxim a notion that power derives from the people), it seems that if *comune* here = the *lewed men* of 129, they do not know what they are saying. Fortescue, whose *De Laudibus Legum Angliae* IX *Bn* cites, *contrasts* the type of rule the maxim expresses ('regal') with that of the English monarchs ('political'), who cannot change the law without the people's consent (the type of rule both angel and goliard presuppose). The case for **L**'s shift from a 'political' to a 'regal' theory of government in revising to **C** is somewhat overstated by Baldwin 1981[1]:12–17.

158–64 correspond to **B 212–17**, giving the King a neat exit before the mice enter and illustrating **C**'s increased concern for smooth transitions. The 'court' is a court of

King's Bench for actions *coram rege* 'before the king' in criminal and other matters, where plaintiffs could bring a writ of *capias* against the accused (cf. 4.164, which cites the writ's opening words). **159** *houed...houes*: characteristic homophonic wordplay (cf. 61, 1.35–6). **160** *Seriantz...Barre*: senior barristers (*servientes ad legem*), who wore a coif of white silk covering the head and tied under the chin, and pleaded at a railed area in front of the judge's seat (cf. 3.447–48 and Alf*G* s.v. *sergeaunt* II, *barre*). **162** *for...Lord*: 'for pure charity's sake' (i.e. without payment). **164** *mum*: a non-committal sound through closed lips; the idea is personified in *Mum and the Sothsegger* [*MS*] 146 (*c.* 1410).

(ii) 165–218 The FABLE of the RATS, MICE and CAT, a traditional exemplum found in French and Latin, is used with a different purpose (urging action) by Brinton in a sermon (no. 69 in Devlin) before Congregation of 18 May 1376 (Owst 1925:270–9). It is depicted on a misericord in Great Malvern Priory Church (where the mice are hanging, not belling the cat). In the usual view, the fable's moral is the futility of attempting to curb royal power (Bennett 1943[2]), but any precise topical reference implied by 217–18 remains uncertain. If the *conseyl* of 167 alludes to the Good Parliament of 1376 (see Keen 1973: 261–64; Holmes 1975), the *cat* will be John of Gaunt, the most powerful man in England during Edward III's last years and Richard II's minority. The *rats* and *mice* then represent respectively the Lords and the Commons, the *rat of renown* 176 Sir Peter de la Mare, the Commons' speaker, and the *mouse* 196 a spokesman of the author's opinions. (By contrast, Orsten 1961 sees the mouse as a Gaunt-inspired 'mediator', whose argument for autocracy is *ironically* presented, and the events described as those of 1376 seen from the standpoint of 1377, when much of the Good Parliament's work had been undone). The *kitten* is usually identified as the young Richard, nine years old when his father the Black Prince died in 1376. Whichever interpretation is accepted here, there is no need for over-precision about the bell and the collar (180–4), presumably standing for constitutional restraints of some kind that might warn the commons of the King's threatening intentions. The popular animal fable, largely unaltered ten years after the event, is perhaps best regarded as a general allegory on the problems of balancing power within the body politic. **174** The small revision uses internal rhyme to enhance the near-formulaic antithesis of 'wit and will' found in an early alliterative piece of that name (and again collocated at 5.185, 6.167). **B 160** *Cite of Londoun*: stressing the independence of the capital, with its wealth, pride and political privileges. **C** generalises the location but, by specifying *segges* as knights rather than merchants and seeing them as a threat to the speaker, may evoke the liveried retainers of great lords such as John of Gaunt. **178** *Bn* notes the parallel with *Purity* 1638 (translating Dan 5:16); but the indebtedness, if any, is more probably to **L** (cf. Schmidt 1984:155–6). **184** *oure comune profyt*: a phrase with elevated moral and political overtones (cf. Chaucer's *Parlement of Foules* [*PF*] 47, 75, using it without *oure*, but here and at 201 denoting perhaps no more than the shared advantage of the rats and mice. **B 163–64** are omitted by **C** as perhaps allegorically over-literal (163) and because used later (164a) at B 8.26, which is retained in // **C** (cf. B 181 //, a line virtually repeated at B 17.247, which is also retained as // C 19.213). **B 189–92** The concreteness enlivens the allegory, but it is uncertain whether the rabbits and deer are great nobles or rich merchants. **190** *thise*: a sg. with intrusive -*e*; perhaps influenced by the pl. sense of *route*, though ms X conversely also uses *this* as a plural (see *IG* s.v., and on the pleonastic use of *this*, *MES* 138). **191–92** already hint that even a bad ruler is better than none. **204–05a** *kitoun*: implying that if the young Richard [only ten when he was crowned in July 1377] ruled in place of his uncle, life would be even worse. **205a** 'Woe to thee, O land, when thy king is a child' (Eccl 10:16), a text the chronicler Adam of Usk applied to Richard in 1382 when the king, though now married, was still under the guidance of a council. At the probable date of the **C** revision, little in the fable will have required changing. **217–18** imply a hidden (and dangerous meaning), and the drop in tone seems deliberate. *deuyne*: later used (9.305) of the prophet Daniel's interpretation of Nebuchadnezzar's dream (see Schmidt 2000:5–6).

(b) 219–32 219 The added line, with *ʒut* perhaps taken from B 211, illustrates **C**'s tightening of transitions (as in its deliberate echo of Pr 20). **220** *bondemen of thorpes*: perhaps serfs who had become free through spending a year and a day in a borough-town (see Du Boulay 1991:48). The phrase, revising unspecific **B**, takes up an expression used at A 2.45, from a passage omitted in **B**. **226** *Dew...Emme*: 'God save you, Lady Emma!' The song quoted may originally have been about Emma, Canute's queen, who survived trial by ordeal for a (false) charge of unchastity. But so edifying a tale fits ill with those who 'do their deeds ill', and this reference may be (by way of ironic application) to the 'wise woman' Dame Emma of Shoreditch (see on B 13.339). **230–31** *Oseye*: Alsace (Auxois). *Gascoyne*: ceded to England under the Treaty of Brétigny (see 3.241ff), and regained by France in 1372. *Reule*: La Reôle, a French wine-exporting town on the Garonne; *La Rochelle*: a fortified town on the Atlantic coast in Charente, and a major centre for the export of Bordeaux wines; cf. Chaucer, *Canterbury Tales* [*CT*] VI 571. **B 230** *Ryn*: the Rhineland, source of fine white wines ('Rhenish'), the change in **C** suggesting that they were scarce or little known.

Passus I (Z Pr 94–145, I)

Title. The term *passus* used as the heading for each of the poem's numbered divisions is a common Latin name for a section in a narrative or treatise (e.g. in a 1356 sermon of Richard Fitzralph noted by Dolan 1985:5–7), whence its use here (such poems as *The Wars of Alexander* may imitate the practice in *PP*). The familiar English form *pas* is found in *William of Palerne* [*WPal*] 61 and *The Destruction of Troy* 663 (see MED s.v. *pas* n.(1), (4b)). The **ABC** versions of PASSUS I, all of similar length, run closely parallel. It is occupied almost entirely by a single long speech of HOLY CHURCH, which may be divided into (i) 1–80 and (ii) 81–203, broken respectively by the Dreamer's questions at 11, 41–3, 55–6, 70–1, 79–80 and his *dotede* comment at 136–7. The main revision of **Z** in **A** is the more logical dividing of I from Pr after the vision of the Field of Folk. The sternly 'eschatological' tone of Z Pr 98–100 (its last line referring back to the dungeon of 16–17) is softened, the people now being described as in confusion (*þe mase*), as later they will *blostren* (7.158) like helpless beasts without guidance.

(i) 1–11 (Z Pr 94–100) 1 *montaigne*: God's 'holy mountain' in the OT is Mt Sion, becoming a symbol in the psalms (14:1) of heaven, and in prophetic writing (Is 2:2–3, 11:9) of the Messianic community of the last days, and thence inspiring the Gospel image of the Church as a city on a mountain (Mt 5:14). **3** *lady*: a personification of the Christian Church (see 72) as a woman, deriving from the image of the Lamb's Bride in Apoc 19:8, whose white linen robe is made of *iustificationes* 'saving acts' of the Saints (cf. also Apoc 7:13–14). As the 'Church Triumphant' she is conceptually distinct from the 'Church Militant' on earth (= 'Unity' in 21.330) and the 'Church Suffering' in Purgatory, though substantively one with it because the justified living and dead are united in 'mystic sweet communion with Jesus Christ their Lord'. This idea of spiritual continuity explains both **L**'s later seeing the *early* church as striving to separate itself from the World in the search for 'holiness' and also his having HOLY CHURCH (HC) speak of receiving Will in baptism (72 below). **L**'s personage may here owe something to such authoritative instructresses as Philosophy in Boethius's *Consolation of Philosophy*, 'descended from the sovereign seat' (Chaucer's *Boece* Pr 3, 9), Nature in Alan of Lille's *De Planctu Naturae* (*DPN*) coming from the *palatium* of the *impassibilis mundi* (*PL* 210:432), and Reason in the *Roman de la Rose* 'comen doun / Out of hir tour' (*Rom* 4615ff) and Deguileville's *Pèlerinage de Vie Humaine* (l. 1333. = *Pilgrimage* [Eng. trans.] ed. Henry 8/310). But the Bible, which offers the deepest dimension of the image, would by itself have sufficed as a model. Medieval iconography commonly contrasts the image of *Ecclesia*

with that of *Synagoga* or Judaism (a blindfolded woman); but at 2.9 below HC's opposite is to be her eschatological adversary *Babylon*, 'the mother of fornication' (Apoc 17:50), = unbelief or false belief (a richly-attired harlot). **5** *Wille / Sone*: the name not being indicated in **B** until 5.61 (confirmed at B 8.26 //), and **C** perhaps relying on readers' familiarity with **B** in exploiting its allegorical sense. He is by baptism a 'son' of Mother Church, a relationship reflected in her *thou* to Will and his *ye* to her. *slepestou*: that the 'sleep' implies 'spiritual torpor' (Robertson-Huppé [*R–H*] 37–8) is denied by *Bn*; but no other interlocutor sees Will as asleep *within* a dream, so a symbolic meaning would be apt here. **6** *mase*: either vain activity or a 'gret perplexite' like Amant's in *Rom* 4624, which anticipates Will's in Pr 8, worn out with wandering (see MED s.v. (b), (c)). While perhaps suggesting the labyrinth of existence, it is unlikely to allude to the mazes sometimes inscribed in cathedral floors as symbolic 'routes of pilgrimage' to the 'Jerusalem' placed at their centre (Santarcangeli 1974:215–20, 296–98, MED s.v. (d), with 'maze' here being the 'concrete' rather than the 'literal' [*Pe*] sense). **9** In its **A** form re-writes Z 99–100, keeping its vocalic alliteration and an echo of *dale* in its *tale. halde...tale*: 'make no account of' / ?'never talk about' (evoking the Pauline contrast of those whose 'conversation' is in heaven with those who 'mind earthly things' (Phil 3:20). Two distinct notions of 'heaven [here] on earth' will recur at B 10.299, 14.141=C 5.152, 16.9. **12–40 12b** redundantly repeats Pr 15, but in // **ZAB** is new information; a symptom of the didactic explicitness expressed in **C** through *repetitio*. **15** *fyue wittes*: the physical or outer senses, whose use should be moderate (cf. *sobre* 15.257 //); their 'right uses' will be personified as the 'sons' of Inwit at 10.145ff. **16** *worschipe...þerwith*: perhaps echoing Deut 6:5 (Mt 22:37). **17** *elementis*: presumably impying all four, earth, air, water and fire (see on 10.129–31, 20.245). **B 17** *erþe*: cf. Gen 1:29. **19** brings out as revised the concept of the *mean* as definitive of the virtues ('tempering' or giving proportion to each) by its use of the nominal form *mesure* (not introduced until 35 // in **B**) and stress on the need for it even in times of plenty (a theme introduced in **B** only at 6.257 //). **20–1** *comaunded*: the stress on the first syllable identical with *comune* hints at a 'Platonic' affinity between the divine will and the needs of human beings as a whole. *cortesye*: on this notion of God's kindness as a gratuitous gift, not a payment for desert, cf. at 14.215–16. *in comune*; *nidefol*: all men having a right to the necessary natural goods, which are provided by God's earth, not by human skill (contrast money at 42). In this idea ('rehearsed' by Need at 22.6–19) *Bn* discerns the medieval affirmation of *communis usus*, which is quite distinct from the denial of private ownership rejected at 22.277–80. To these three Ecclus 29:27 adds housing, which **L** does not see as absolutely necessary (wandering hermits do without it). **24** *tyme*: in place of **ZAB** *resoun*, by warning against lechery (cf. 10.291) rather than the danger to man's work (B 26 //, suggested by Ecclus 19:1), tightens the link to the Lot exemplum. **25–32** *Loot*: a familiar homiletic proof (cf. *CT* VI 485–7) that gluttony can lead to lechery and the further evil of wicked offspring, revealing **L**'s deep conviction (like the *Purity*-poet's) that sexual acts should only be performed in a way pleasing to God (cf. 10.215–304, especially 288–96). **25** *likerous drynke*: 'delicious drink that arouses desire'; translating Prov 20:1 ('Luxuriosa res vinum') and recurring at 10.178 in connexion with Herod and Lot, figures likewise linked at *CT* VI 485–91 by Chaucer (who uses the phrase ibid. 549). **30a** '[Come], let us make him drunk with wine, and let us lie with him, that we may preserve seed of our father' (Gen 19:32). The association of drink misused with wrongful sexual acts perhaps recalls Eph 5:18, since Lot's drunkenness potentially 'contains' *luxuria*. **C** blames *man* for his misuse of two *wyttes*, while **ZAB** sees it as a means whereby the devil corrupts man. **32b** removes a phrase (*do the bettre*) that will have acquired 'Langlandian' meanings by the time of the revision. **33** *Mesure is medecyne*: a paradox, since temperate use of natural goods will make physic unnecessary (19 has adumbrated the perils of *excess*: the medicines necessitated by *gluttony* are specified at Z 7.274–8; cf. 8.290–6). **L**'s *mesure* as a rational norm of moderate sufficiency, a 'law' governing even that need which 'has no law' (20.22–3), is close to Platonic *sophrosyne* 'temperance' (rendered *sobrietas* at I Tim 2:9). But it also recalls the Aristotelean conception of *all* virtue as a mean between extremes of excess and defect (*Nicomachean Ethics* II 6–9). This, though not directly in question, will emerge later in **L**'s presentation of the deadly sins and the virtue of poverty, where *sobrete* is described as *good leche in siknesse* (B 14.315). Finally, it shows influence from the Biblical teaching on God's creation of everything 'in measure [*mensura*], number and weight' (Wisd. 11:21). **35–6** The **C** form of the verb (*Leef*), which punningly brings out how men choose to believe what they like (*lef* 35), appears in **Z** too and may be the original in all versions. The homophones **L** 'Platonically' exploits ('whom we like we tend to trust') are, as often, etymologically unconnected. **37** *bigyle*: replacing **ZAB** *bytraye* and having the demonic overtones acquired in B 18.340–61. The devil, appearing to bring up the rear, in fact 'animates' the World instrumentally through the *mundi rectores* of Eph 6:12 (hence *wolde*). 'World' and 'flesh 'have the standard NT senses 'worldliness' and 'corrupt bodily desires' (as at B 16.48; 19.312, B 11.399). The evil triad re-appear as enemies of charity at 10.44 and 18.29ff. **39** **L**'s 'dualistic' anthropology, with its Platonic strain coming through Augustine and Gregory the Great (Straw 1988:107–27),

finds the spiritual soul threatened not only by outward foes (devil, world) but by the wayward body it must vigilantly govern. *seeth*: see *TN* on this crux. *herte*: the locus of the soul as life-principle (*anima*) under the rule of a rational moral sense (*inwit*); see 10.175 //. B 9.60–6 expand on the danger to *inwit* from drink.

41–53 41 is either a Type I line with muted key-stave and trisyllabic dip before the last lift or, preferably, a T-type line. **42** *moneye*: a man-made value, not one of the *bona naturae*, hence not self-evidently for 'common' use (cf. on 20–1). *Gospel*: Mt 22:16–21. **44–53 C** tightens the link between Will's question (perhaps originally prompted by doubts about royal taxation) and the scriptural answer, which in context concerns payment of tribute to Rome. **44** is either of Type Ia scanning on |g| with rhetorical stresses on *God* and *sayde* or Type IIb on |g| and |s| with 'cognative' third stave, but not an anomalous *aa / bb* type with its third lift on *se* (**ABC** may be T-Type). **46** *God*: startlingly underlining the authoritativeness of Christ's utterance on this important subject; paralleled at 3.74 and 12.140. **48a, 49a** 'Render [therefore to Caesar the things that are Caesar's]; and to God the things that are God's' (Mt 22:21). **C** turns from the image and inscription to the coin itself, arguing that the proper use of money, like other earthly transactions, falls to Reason and Kynde Wit, and should be determined by necessity and by thrift, the virtue of *mesure*.

Z Pr 145 A summarising conclusion echoing Z Pr 104, omitted in **A** after re-division of Pr / I at Z Pr 93=A Pr 109, and echoed at Z 1.121a, which A 1.172 revises. From here until VI, passus-divisions correspond in **ZA**; but Z II is preceded by similar summarising lines with a 'draft' feel (*Intro.* III, *Z*, i) and A VI opens with Z V 155–66.

54–67 55 Revision in **C** to the rare Type IIb omits the *dongeon*. **56** *bymene*: showing that Will grasped HC's explanation of the tower's symbolic meaning at 12. **59** *Wrong*: personifying all that is 'twisted aside' (*Wrynglawe* 4.32 reflects **L**'s awareness of the word's etymology). This second 'nature-name' obliquely denotes the Devil through his leading feature, comparably to the use of 'Truth' for God (for it is by his 'oppositeness' to truth that he is opposed to love at 65). *pat...his name*: on this use of 'that followed by a possessive' see *MES* 202–3. **60** *Fader of falshede*: the devil being from the beginning a murderer, a liar and the father of lies (Jn 8:44). **61–2** *Adam...Caym*: see Gen 3:1–7 (describing the serpent's temptation) and 4:1–17, where Satan is to be inferred as the source of Cain's anger from the enigmatic vs 7's crucial opposition between *agere bene...male* 'doing well and ill' and personification of sin. **62–3** *Caym; Iudas*: the first murderer and the archetypal traitor, exemplifying enmity to God (cf. 10.215–31 and 18.166ff, esp. 174–15). Like Cain, Judas is one 'by whom the scandal comes' (Mt

18:7): followers of Wrong will 'ban' the day as these did. **63** See Lk 22:3 and Jn 13:7 (on the Temptation), Mt 26:15 (on the silver). **64** *hellerne*: the tree on which Judas was traditionally supposed to have hanged himself, which has hollow branches. But the (possibly original) **ZC** spelling allows a grim 'Platonic' pun, making hell's lord responsible for suicide as well as treachery and murder. **C**'s addition of *hey* makes the event more clearly a counter-type to Christ's 'hanging' at 169. **66–7** give clearer sense than **ZAB**: inordinate desire for worldly wealth (*coveitise*) is the devil's instrument to undo mankind. The added 67 anticipates 190=B 196).

68–80 70 *hey name*: that of God, or of Christ (Phil 2:9). **72–5** will be recalled by Will as a comfort at 12.54–5 // when frightened by Scripture's 'Many are called, few are chosen'. This link is made possible because of her earlier rôle as authoritative interpreter of scripture ('this textes' 200), baptism entailing loyal commitment to Church and Bible alike. HC's rebuke for failure to recognise her recalls Nature's in *DPN* (*PL* 210:442). **73** *fre man*: drawing on the Biblical notion of Christ's 'saving death' as freeing man from sin through sacramental grace, which will be interpreted (metaphorically) at 21.39–40 in terms of a legal and social liberation. A more directly 'political' motive for the revision may be to affirm that the baptized need no other freedom and should not rebel against the authority of the Church they are pledged to obey (cf. on Pr 138). The line is probably not of T-type structure since *fré man* could be the quasi-compound (see MED s.v. *freman* n.). **74** *borewes*: the godparents, on whose duties see B 9.75–9. **75** *Leue*: the command to belief in the Church being perhaps a 'loyalist' response to the growth of the Wycliffite heresy (condemned at the Council of Blackfriars in 1382). The line is fuller now in content than // B 78. **77** retains the polysemous wordplay of **ZAB** and could be T-type in structure. **78** *kyndly*: perhaps qualifying both verbs, though more closely the post-caesural *bileue*. Believing 'properly, in the right way' is explored in Harwood 1992:11ff.

(ii) 81–203 The sermon-like character of HC's reply to Will is brought out by Wenzel (in Alf*C* 165–7), specifically with reference to // B 85–209. On the place of the speech in the structure of the poem as a whole see Kaske 1974, and for sensitive analysis of its linguistic texture Davlin 1989:25–46. For the influence of sermons on *PP* see Owst 1961:548–75, Spearing 1972:107–34, Wenzel in Alf*C* 155–172, Fletcher 2001:61–84.

81–124 81 *tresor(es)*: Will having denied interest at 79 in *tresor of erthe* (cf. 66), HC can affirm the worth of spiritual treasure. *tried*: 'assayed', like gold or silver. *treuthe*: divine wisdom as 'an infinite treasure to men' and 'more precious than any wealth' (Wisd 7:14; Prov 3:15). **82** *Deus caritas*: 'God is charity' (I Jn 4:8). Crucial

to **L**'s elaboration of the relationship between knowledge and love is the preceding clause in Jn 'He that loveth not knoweth not God'. HC links cognitive *veritas* with affective *caritas* through a value (*fidelitas, sapientia*) that offers a second Biblically authorised 'nature-name' for God. **83** *druerie*: playing on senses 3(a) and (b) 'love token'; 'treasure' (MED s.v.). *dere*: 'excellent / precious' and 'beloved' (MED s.v. adj. (1) 1–3, 4); cf. the collocation at 13.17. **84–5** perhaps derive from Cato's *Distichs* i. 3 (Galloway 1987:9–13). The revised 84b, echoing B 5.287, underlines the dual intellectual and moral senses of *trewe*, supports association of *treuthe* with *sapientia* and anticipates 10.78b (for the 'hand = action, tongue = speech' collocation, see also 6.109 and 19.257). **86** alludes to Jn 10:34, quoting Ps 81:6 ('I have said: you are gods'). The b-half improves on the **ZAB** filler-phrase, claiming the power of physical and spiritual healing as a mark of the perfected Christian. This recalls Ac 3:6, which contrasts 'healing' with 'silver and gold' (a passage recalled in 15.220–23a, quoting Mk 16:18). **87** The source is (loosely) Lk 6:40; despite possible allusions to mystical 'deification' (cf. Vasta 1965[2]) a doctrine with wider import for ordinary Christians seems intended here, to be graphically illustrated in the image of Piers at 21.8. **Z 39** is somewhat otiose, since it has just been stated that Truth is valued by all men. **92** *transgressores*: more probably 'wrongdoers', as in Js 2:8–9, than 'trespassers' in the narrower legal sense of those who commit breaches of the law short of felony, misprision or treason (see Alf*G* s.v.). **93** *Treuthe*: clearly now with the sense '[ideal earthly] justice' (rather than heavenly justice at doomsday); for the close scriptural connection of justice with wisdom, see Wisd 1:1, 5:6, 8:7. *termyned*; *trespas*: legal terms denoting the hearing to the end and the judging of a case in court (Alf*G*). **94–100** **C**'s focus on the duty of earthly justices to act without respect of persons (those who fail to are 'reproved by the law as transgressors' [Js 2:9]) may echo the breakdown of authority and morale among the seignorial class during the Peasants' Revolt, when they were paralysed into inaction (Harding, Tuck in Hilton & Aston 1984). The sixfold *repetitio* of *trewe* is notable. **95** *lordene loue*: on this form of the genitive pl. surviving from the weak OE ending *-ena* see *MES* 73. **97** *puyr ordre*: 'essential character' (but with *profession... appostata* perhaps playing on the religious sense), giving a second stave semantically richer than **AB**'s metrical filler (absent from **Z**, which is like *A-*m a Type III line); cf. on 86. **98** *poynt*: perhaps alluding to Js 2:10 'Whosoever shall keep the whole law, but offend in one *point* is become guilty of all' (*Pe*); but **L**'s stress is on truth as the *main* knightly quality (cf. *SGGK,* esp. 625–6). *appostata*: 'one who violates the code of an order (by quitting it without dispensation)' (MED s.v. 2), rather than 'violator of a code of ethics or morals' (MED s.v. 3, citing only this case from the 14th c.). **L** underscores less the 'religious character of the order of knighthood' (*Bn*) than the *parallel* between a religious vow and a knightly oath. **99** shows that **L** does not confuse knighthood with 'religion' but thinks of each 'order' as having a distinct sphere of action, though all must obey Truth in their different ways. *faste*: i.e. as a regular mortification, like monks. *forbere the serk*: and replace it with a penitential garment (see 6.6). **100** *leue*: the understood object in **C** being *treuthe*. **101–24 101** *Dauid*: a 'chivalricisation' of the warrior-king probably going back to I Par (= I Chr) 12:18 (*Bn*), where David creates thirty 'captains of the band'. To see him as having 'dubbed knights' flows naturally from the medieval conception of a king found in 21.29, 133–36, which affirms Christ's actions as *filius Dauid*, first knight, then king. But **L** cannot have been unaware of the romance tradition of tracing chivalry back to the Lord's warriors in the OT, such as those at 19.25 included amongst the 'Nine Worthies' of contemporary literature and iconography (e.g. *PTA* 451, *AMA* 3408–45; Keen 1984:265n64), and David himself, from whom the Grail knight Galahad was held to descend. See further Keen 1984:118–23 and (on the dubbing ceremony) 64–82. **102** *swere...swerd*: the chime of (etymologically unrelated) homophones hints at a 'Platonic' affinity between the associated virtues of fidelity and fortitude. **103** *God*: **C** is more straightforward theologically than **ZAB** *Christ* in not conflating the Son's post-Resurrection kingship (21.42) with his dominion as co-eternal Word before the creation of the angels. **104–5** *creatures*: (orders of) created being. *tene*: the 'number' of completed creation and that of the original orders of angels in apocryphal texts like II Enoch 29:3–4 (Russell 1984:94n). Lucifer may be envisaged here as head of a tenth order (?the highest), which fell with him, mankind's creation being meant to replace it and restore heaven's 'even number' (cf. 22.270). But Gregory the Great sees this order as a group drawn from the other nine, who fell with Lucifer (Hom. 34:6–11; cit. Russell 1984:94n, 237). The traditional *nine* orders as fixed by pseudo-Dionysius in the *Celestial Hierarchies*, proceeding downwards in choirs of three, were seraphim, cherubim and thrones; dominions, virtues and powers; principalities, archangels and angels. **L** names only the first two and last two and (as is clear from 107, B 108 // ZA) uses 'archangel' in a non-specific sense for all the higher orders above angels. His sequence need not imply the cherubim's priority in the hierarchy, since it echoes the standard phrase in the Preface to the Mass and the *Te Deum*. A depiction of seraphs leading the ranks of medieval society appears in the 'Orders of Angels' window in the church of All Saints, North St, York. *swiche...anoþer*: 'seven like them and one other'. **B 109** *by*: 'by means of' (= *thorw* ZA); knowledge and obedience (reason and will) are ordained together from the beginning. **B 110 (Z 56, A 108)** Cf. B

77: man's submission to the Church parallels the angels' to God; but the clergy's authority over the laity depends on their own obedience to God. **C**'s deletion of B 107–10 removes the echo, with some loss; but *appostata* 98 has already made the point.

A 110–11 (Z 58–9, B *112–13) *louelokest of lyght*: 'most radiantly beautiful' (*reliquis angelis eminentiorem*), as argued by Gregory the Great in *Moralia* 32:23. Light is a common Biblical symbol of divine glory (Ex 14:20, Ps 103:2; I Jn 1:5) and an apt image of truth (cf. Pss 35:10, 42:3; II Cor 4:6). Lucifer's name therefore signifies his original status as 'bearer' of the divine light / truth, losing which he falls into darkness / falsehood and *fendes liknesse*, though still able to transform himself deceitfully into an angel of light (II Cor 11:14).

107 *Goddes knyghtes*: cf. on 13.125 (applied to priests). **108–10** tighten the link between Lucifer's fall and his 'dubbing', to make his rebellion seem like that of a feudal knight against his liege lord. **109** *lothly*: chiming with *luther*, with outer form echoing inner will; the same term is used of Lucifer at 21.56. *luther wille*: 'treacherous intentions'; the conjectured sense is close to that in 3.317, used of royal feudatories. **B 114–18** The fiends are damned eternally, by contrast with man, and hell's occupants are unnumbered (cf. 20.374–5 //; 22.270 //). The whole passage shows influence from Is 14:4–15 as figuratively interpreted in patristic tradition (e.g. compare 114 with vv. 11, 15), **C**'s removal of these lines here silencing the echoes later in the B // to C 20.345, 22.270. *mo thousandes...forme*: as depicted by Bosch in the left panels of his Last Judgement triptych at the Akademie, Vienna and in the Haywain triptych at the Prado, Madrid; cf. also *Purity* 220–28. **110a** 'I shall set my foot in the north, and I shall be like the Most High', a *VL* abbreviation (Hill 2000:155) of Is 14:13–14, which has 'sedebo...in lateribus *aquilonis...similis ero Altissimo*'. **L**'s substitution of *pedem* for *sedem* echoes Isaiah's *solium*, and *sedebo* and may show the influence of Augustine's gloss on *pes superbiae* 'the foot of pride' (Ps 35:12; and cf. vs 13) as 'self-love' (A. L. Kellogg 1958:386). It is cited by Augustine in his comment on Pss 1:4, 47:2 (*Enarrationes in Psalmos*, *PL* 36:69, 534) and found also in Alan of Lille (*PL* 210:706), as noted by *R–H* 1951:44. **L** may have come on it there or through a commentary on Avianus's *Fables*, a work alluded to at B 12.256 (Risse 1966). **112** *lefte syde*: the north (see *TN*) if one is facing *the sonne syde* (113), the eastern direction which is that of heaven (132) and of Jerusalem, and to which churches were oriented. The 'left' was in popular tradition the weak or bad side (MED s.v. *lift* adj. 2; for *luft* as noun see B 4.62), where the 'goats' (= the unjust) will stand at the Last Judgement, to be sent thence to hell (Mt 25:41; see the Ravenna mosaic illustrated in Russell 1984:24). Lucifer is to be thought of as leaping towards God's throne from his station in the north

(112) and then falling out of heaven from there upon the northern part of the earth. The north is associated with hell in Job 26:6–7 and is the source of coming evils in Jer 1:14. The idea is related to the patristic notion of 'cold' as a symbol of malice, and hence of hell as a place of intense cold. **L**'s account may owe something to Gregory's *Moralia* 32:23 (see further Kellogg 1949:413–14 and Hill 1969), while Bonaventure's Commentary on Eccl 11:3 also places hell in the north. In 20.166–7, more benignly, it is the direction from which Righteousness, the eldest (but severest) Daughter of God, approaches. **113** *sonne syde...roweth*: theoretically the east, but in fact the south, to which the sun moves as it climbs (as at Pr 14, 9.294). **114–24 C** elaborates the directional symbolism, where **B** described the fall of the angels. HC's remark about northerners is superficially of a piece with the Norfolk references in Z 5.98, B 5.235 and familiar passages in Chaucer (*CT* X 42–3) and Trevisa (Sisam *C14 V&P*) illustrating conventional southern prejudice; but the provoking digression at 122–4 hardly improves on its source. **116** *þe sonne regneth*: doubtless with a pun intended, since this is where the Son of God (who is *sol iustitiae* 'sun of justice') sits in glory, waiting to do judgement. **118–19 A** parallel for this image is found by Hill (2000:156–7) in the C12th exegete Rupert of Deutz's *Commentaria* VIII:44 (*CCCM* 9:469). By a 'condign' punishment, Lucifer becomes king of the north (but not in heaven). **ZA 61/113** *hobeled*: an image possibly influenced by the folkloric notion that devils are lame and by patristic allegorisations of the 'feet of the soul' as 'love of God and neighbour', with 'lameness' being interpreted as 'sinfulness' (Hill 2000:158–60). **120** *helle...is*: cf. the parallel in Marlowe, *Dr Faustus* III 76 and Milton's *Paradise Lost* IV 75. *ybounde*: since the Harrowing of Hell; see 20.446, 21.57. **121a** 'The Lord said to my Lord: Sit thou at my right hand' (from the 'Messianic' Ps 109:1, alluded to at Heb 10:12–13). God speaks from a position in the west *facing* east, with the south on his right, where Christ (= *dominus meus*) sits as Lord (vs 3, 'from the womb before the day-star [*ante luciferum*] I begot thee,' has piquantly ironic aptness in this context). The south front as well as the west could sometimes be the location of cathedral tympana (as at Chartres) depicting Christ on doomsday. Once again, *dextris* has associations with the position of the just (see on 112), and with supreme authority conferred by God (Mk 14:62, Heb 1:3). **123–4** A piece of timeless popular lore used parabolically: suffering the 'cold' of earthly life will be worth it for the 'warmth' of heaven (cf. the use of similar imagery at 19.172–74).

    B 120–3 120 is to be read in the light of B 153a, which echoes it (*Bn*). **121** *but fellen*: an example of 'non-expression of the subject pronoun' of Type 1 (*MES* 140). *nyne dayes*: corresponding to the nine cosmic spheres and the nine orders of angels, from which he progressively

receded (Russell 1984:237n38). But the number of days could be distantly influenced by a tradition concerning the fall of the Titans found in Hesiod (*Sk*), which Milton may echo in *PL* VI 871, if he is not recalling **L** (see on C 120 above). **122–23** alliterate on *g* and *s*, the first a T-type, the second Type III with 'echoic' cognative counterpoint (see on *Intro* IV § 46 and Schmidt 1987:65).

125–35 125 *Holy Wryt*: 'early patristic tradition', rather than 'the Bible', a common sense of this phrase (MED s.v. *Holi Writ* n. (b)), as at 15.158, 19.288, A 10.94. The story of Lucifer's fall is based on Is 14:12 taken with Lk 10:18; but the scriptural origin of belief in demonic occupation of the elements is Eph 6:12 (other possible sources that develop the idea are Augustine, *Sunday Sermons* I 95 and Alan of Lille, *Anticlaudianus* IV 271ff [*Bn*]). These texts encouraged a view of natural disturbances as due to diabolic influence; but **L** commonly ascribes them to divine intervention for a moral purpose (e.g. 5.116–22), stressing the goodness of nature and its subjection to God (20.245–57). **Z 65** A line dropped in **A** and recalling Z 50, doubtless so as to underscore the parallel between fallen angels and false knights. *apostata*: taken up again in C 98, but in relation to knighthood (and so unlikely to be a scribal echo of **C**). *pelour*: either 'accuser' as at 20.39 or a spelling-variant for more common *pilour* 'robber', both apt names for the devil as enemy of mankind. **A 119** is substantially repeated at A 12.97 and **A 120b** echoed at A 12.98. **127** *Lucifer lowest*: since he fell from the 'highest' position (106), his sin being 'heaviest' and his condign punishment to end in the earth's centre: 'his fall was into a depth proportional to the height to which he aspired against his Maker' (Gregory, *Moralia* 34:21). **128** *ther*: the adv. partly filling in for the non-expressed subject relative *þat* **ZAB** (*MES* 205). **129–32** in effect translate the Latin of the Athanasian Creed quoted in Truth's pardon at 9.286–7 // (*Bn* aptly cites Jn 5:29 as the scriptural basis of this notion, as it is of the credal phrase). The references to the devil at B 7.114 // recall the present lines but are omitted in **C**. **131b** repeats 129b, showing **C** revising to a more explicitly formulaic mode. **132** re-stresses the directional symbolism of Pr 14, with assonantal wordplay on the eternity of heavenly bliss (*heuene; euere*). *Estward*: the direction from which just judgement arises (Is 41:2) and divine power is manifested (Apoc 7:2). **133** Whereas **ZAB** speak of God's 'enthronement' of the blessed, relying on Christ's promise at Apoc 3:21 (fulfilled at Apoc 20:4), **C**'s revision to make *truth* the throne of God anticipates the later view of the *heart* as the seat of Truth in Piers's allegory (7.254). The notion may be derived from texts about God judging with 'justice and truth' (Ps 95:13) and his throne as established on 'justice and judgement' (Ps 96:2), concepts close to **L**'s understanding of 'Truth' (cf. Ps 145:7 on how God 'keepeth truth for ever...executeth judgement for them that suffer wrong'). Both ideas come together suggestively in Is 16:5, on God as the merciful judge who 'shall sit upon [the throne] in truth...rendering that which is just'. **B 131** is a line already twice revised, but finally omitted in **C**. **135** The construction is elliptical: 'That there is no treasure better (than Truth).' **C** economically recalls *caritas* 82 and links *true* love with truth from the outset, obviating any possibility of misunderstanding *veritas* as sufficient. This replaces B 134–5 (Z 72–3, A 123–4), a summary recapitulating the opening of HC's homily on Truth (B 85 //).

136–44 form a transition from 'untruth' through 'truth and true love' to 'love' itself. **136** *kynde knowyng*: 'natural, instinctive knowledge or understanding.' It has been read as a vernacular equivalent to one or other scholastic or non-scholastic technical term: *synderesis* (Hort 1938:72–81), *ratio naturalis* (Erzgräber 1957:45), *sapientia* (Davlin 1981) and the *notitia intuitiva* of Ockham (Harwood 1992:9, who summarises its various non-technical senses; see id. 1983:246, and Strong 2003). But as with *kynde wit* (Pr 141–7 above) and *inwit* (6.420, 10.144 etc), a technical sense should not be insisted upon irrespective of context or even in any particular context. For the phrase does not translate any of the Latin names given to the soul or its acts at 16.199*a* (the power that 'knows' is *Mens* or 'Thouhte'). Nor is it personified as a character, and it may not have had the specificity of its congener Kynde Wit, the meaning being subtly inflected according to how, when and by whom it is used (see the helpful analysis in White 1988:41–59). Here Will disclaims direct knowledge of truth and asks to be instructed; at 7.182 Piers, having been 'instructed' by his whole way of life, will claim *kynde knowyng*. **137** The sense is: 'How truth grows up / originates, and whether it comes from / is beyond my capacities' (**C**); 'Through what power in a bodily organ it originates' (**ZAB**). The revision rules out regarding 'the faculty that knows Truth' as a corporeal power. **138–39*a*** HC seems to imply that if Will had bothered, he would have learned *how* Truth is known, by *ratio naturalis* or through the exercise of charity: '"kynde knowyng" pertains to love' (*R–H* 1951:46)). **139*a*** 'Alas, what a useless life I led in my youth'; a proverbial verse found in John Rylands Library Latin MS 394, which also contains part of the Latin at B 10.260*a* (Pantin 1930:81:114), and quoted again by Sloth at 7.54*a*. **140–2** make *kynde knowynge* a natural power (or *habitus* 'disposition' of a power) that teaches interiorly (the heart being the home of *Anima* at 10.175) what is part of divine positive law (Deut 6.5). It is here close to *synderesis*, the intuitive knowledge of the first principles of moral conduct to which the Commandments give formal expression. In action, this is *conscience*, as specified at 7.206–9, which repeat the two points made here: to love God above everything and to die rather than commit mortal sin. **142*a***

'Better it is to die than to live false' (cf. Usk, *TL* I vii. 61); new in **C** and repeated at 6.290*a*, 17.40*a*. This is not, *pace SkPe*, based on Tob 3:6 *Expedit enim mihi* mori *magis* quam vivere 'For it is better for me to die than to live' (which does not refer to sin), but on some proverbial utterance about death as preferable to an evil life, such as *Melius est mori quam vivere moleste* (Walther 38183, cited AlfQ 36), modified to yield an alliterating verse-line in Latin. Readiness to lose one's (earthly) life rather than commit a sin that 'kills' the soul ('the wages of sin is death' [Rom 6:23]) was standard doctrine, as in Piers's repetition of HC's teaching at VII 208–9. Here perfect obedience to the will of God, not formal profession of belief, is affirmed as the best evidence of 'treuth' (cf. Mt 7:21–4). **A 133–4** The tighter, more logical order indicates revision of Z 82–4. **B 147** is omitted in **C** with loss of an effective 'rich' rhyme. **A 137–8** The quasi-minstrel character of Will here is eliminated in the later versions' graduated critique of the minstrel class as a whole.

145–69 offer a direct treatment of love as exemplified in the life and death of Christ. Love of God having been described as 'truth' in living, Truth-as-God is now made to vouch for the healing efficacy of love.

145–53 145 *triacle*: a word derived from Lat *tyriaca* (< Gk *theriakon*) and denoting a supposed antidote to snake-bite made from the powdered body of a dead snake (a notion figuratively expounded at 20.153–59). The idea of a virtue as a *triacle* against sin is anticipated in *Ayenbite of Inwit* 144/28. **146** *souerayne salue*: foreshadowing 22.373, where the phrase refers to contrition (understood as sorrow for sin that arises from love of God). **147–53** The first instance of **L**'s *stylus altus*, introduced in the **B** revision and to be used later in describing the Passion (7.122ff, 20.8ff). **B 149** *seene*: leaving no visible trace of the wound of sin, an idea spelled out in B 14.95–6 on the effect of Satisfaction in Penance. *spice*: quite possibly 'species [of remedy]' (*Sk*) rather than 'spice' (see MED s.v. n (2)), since *triacle* was not made from plants (a confusion eliminated in **C**); but a possible link with the 'plant' image is noted by Pe. *R–H* 46 relate the *triacle* to the *unctio* of I Jn 2:27, which Bede (*PL* 93:96) glosses as *Dei charitas*, an interpretation supported by **C**'s substitution of *salue* for *spice*. But the lines may allude to patristic allegorisation of the brazen serpent the sight of which healed those bitten by snakes in the wilderness (Num 21:8–9) as Christ, who 'became a serpent to provide a *tyriaca* against the devil's poison' (Hugh of St Victor, cited by Smith 1966:21–34). **B 150–1** develop from A 136, the added Moses reference being subsequently omitted in **C**, perhaps to underscore the uniqueness of the NT revelation of divine love as *agape* (though *Bn,* citing Mk 12:29–31, brings out **L**'s sense of the continuity of Christian with Mosaic and pre-Mosaic teaching). **147** One of the poem's best-known lines, in this 'definitional' form giving due prominence to the idea even more strikingly than in **B** (the rich complex of imagery here is fully explored by Smith and by Kean 1965:349–63). Love is to be seen as both the chief theological virtue (I Cor 13:13) and the 'virtue' in the *plonte* (on the grounds for reading this in all versions, see *TN*). **148** Typical word-play (of the *lucus a non lucendo* type) on *heuene* and *heuy*, with // **B** ironically echoing B 120 (the 'gravity' of Lucifer's sin of *self*-love). Here the heavenly virtue paradoxically becomes 'light' only *after* taking on the weight that enables it to act in the material domain as Creator-become-Creature. **149** *yȝoten*: see MED s.v. *yeten* v. 3, 7b(b). The revision (see *TN* on the issues here) is from an image of *eating* to one of being *embodied*: earth = flesh, as in the allegory of 10.130; and cf. Gregory, *Sunday Sermons* 1.121 ('The King of heaven has taken into himself the flesh of our earth' [*Bn*]), both fitting the metaphor of love as a plant. The latter image is evidently to be associated with the great Messianic prophecy of Isaiah 53:2: 'he shall grow up as a tender plant, and as a root out of a thirsty ground', with perhaps an allusion to 'the leaves of the tree [of life]...for the healing of the nations' (Apoc 22:2). But Adams 1991:12–13 plausibly traces the phrase *plantam pacis* to the Septuagint reading of Ezech 34:29 as given in *VL* versions (where Vg has *germen nominatum* 'bud of renown'); this appears in, e.g., Augustine's Sermon 47 on Ezechiel in *Sermones de vetere testamento* (*CC* 41:601). Heffernan 1984 relates the imagery to two well-known Latin hymns *Rorate celi* and *Crux fidelis* associated respectively with Christmas and Passiontide. **152** The figure of the divine word as a piercing needle may derive ultimately from Heb 4:12 ('For the word of God is...more *piercing* than any two-edged sword...and is a discerner of the thoughts and intents of the heart'), with some echo of *wisdom* (equated in patristic thought with the Divine Word) as 'subtile...more active than all active things' (Wisd 7:22–4). The 'armour' and 'walls' symbolise the resistance of the human will armed with pride (a chivalric metaphor that will undergo characteristically paradoxical transformation in 20.21–4 and its climax 80–7). *Bn* finds an allusion to the Resurrection in B 158 (the 'armour' that of the soldiers outside Christ's 'high-walled' tomb) and to the Ascension in B 156. But the passage seems to be overwhelmingly about the Incarnation (*lyhter* in context = 'easier to handle' / 'more cheerful'), only prospectively concerned with the Passion (see above), and not at all with the events of Easter and after. When Christ breaks through Hell's gates he is seen by his adversaries not as healing Love but as conquering Truth (20.325, 362–65). **154–60** Another transitional passage between the lyrically heightened accounts of Christ's incarnation and the crucifixion. 'Love' is an intermediary between God and his people, as at 20.184, and is an oblique nature-name

for 'Jesus the mediator' of Heb 12:24 who is also 'God the judge of all' of vs. 23 (cf. further 18.202 on the Second Person of the Trinity as *mene*). But its reference is equivocal, since it also signifies the specific virtue to be found in man's heart. As *Bn* finely has it, 'Christ' who 'delivers judgement and assesses the fine...is the perfect king who clothes *nudum ius* with *pietas*'. **155** *mayre*: the choice of image perhaps reflecting the growing political influence of the Lord Mayor of London in the late 14th century. **157** *mercement*: a payment for pardon made to the king when a transgressor had been put 'in mercy' as a result of his offence (AlfG s.v.); the analogy is with the debt to God that man incurs through sin. The implicit play on 'mercy' and 'amercement' is later made explicit when Piers urges the knight to treat his tenants with mercy (8.37); Christ's justice is to be made the model for that of earthly lords. Mary (denoted by the nature-name Mercy at 7.287) herself becomes man's *mene* or mediatrix for grace at 9.347. **158–60** HC resumes the lesson begun at 140 and elaborates the oracular B 165 // into the triad of nature, heart and divine power (this last 'appropriated' to the First Person of the Trinity as at 18.34). The sense is roughly: God's power (*myhte* 158) operates in and through the heart, the seat of love, making it thus possible for man to 'know' God by virtue of the (created) nature he receives from (uncreated) Nature and the (recreated) nature he now sacramentally shares with God by adoption, following the Word's becoming incarnate. The syntactic balance of 161b and 163b reveals how God's creative and redemptive action are to be seen as continuous. On the relation of these lines to I Jn 4:7 see Davlin 1981:12. **159** *hed*; *heye welle*: 'chief source / origin', 'deep spring'; with perhaps some punning allusion to the contrast and complementarity of the intellectual and the affective. In order to 'know' God, man's 'heart' (in the Biblical sense of 'deepest spiritual self') must *be* his 'head'.

161–82a 162–63 echo I Jn 4:14, as *Bn* notes. **165–66** Two constructions are run together: Christ's beseeching God *for* mercy on those who crucify him, and *as* Mercy to have pity (cf. again the *pietas* of Pr 155 and comment on 154–57 above). This scene adumbrates the account at 20.89–94 of divine *pitee* shown in healing the blind Longinus without his asking: the allusion in pl. *hem* of 169b (Lk 23:34) is to all the executioners, but primarily to him. On the Passion theme in *PP*, see Bennett 1982:85–112 and Schmidt 1983[2]. **170–1** The injunction to the rich is to follow God's twofold 'examples' of power and mercy: their 'might' in the law courts is only a faint image of God's, so if *he* is humble, they should be all the more so. **171** *mote*: 'argue in court' (as at A 4.118), rather than 'cite, summon to court' (*Bn*), a sense not illustrated in MED s.v. **Z 100** 'Though you have charge of the laws, administer them [towards the poor] in a spirit of love'.

Despite being omitted in **A**, the line seems authentic in its use of the rare Type IIa and in its sense. Thus *loue-lawes*, a phrase used with a different sense at 17.130, here = *ius* + *pietas*, the key-ideas added in B Pr 135 and closely linked with the ultimate source of B Pr 137–38, which is that of Z 1.101//. **173a** 'For with the same measure that you shall mete withal, it shall be measured to you again' (Lk 6:38), repeated at 11.235a, B 11.226a (the first half of the vs is quoted at 195 // below). **174–8** HC sees simple obedience to the Commandments as insufficient for justification (*meryte* 178) without kindness arising from a love based on humility (cf. *meke* 171). **177** contains a favourite polysemantic pun (see Schmidt 1987:134–8): *good* (wealth) must be used *goodliche* (generously) in recognition of the 'metaphysical' affinity obtaining between the material and spiritual, which both derive from God. **179–82** Formal religion not finding expression in active charity counts as worth no more than a formal chastity untested by temptation. **179** *Malkyn*: diminutive of Mary or Matilda, the type-name of a homely lower-class girl (Cassidy 1948:52–3; Fletcher 1986:19–20). Chaucer's *Malkyns maydenhede* (*CT* II 30), perhaps ironically alluding to this line, implies a wanton rather than an ugly girl no one desires. *wham*: the sole instance in *PP* of the prepositionless oblique form of *who* (making the referent Malkyn), a small indication that **C** is later than **B**. **180** *gentele*: an alliteratively convenient epithet (as with Job at 11.21, 13.14; John at 21.266). **181** *feet*: both 'feet' and 'deed' (see *TN*). **182** *ded...nayl*: the earliest instance of this proverbial expression after *WPal* 628. *ded, dedes*: illustrating the contrastive *annominatio* seen at 148. **182a** '[For even as the body without the spirit is dead: so also] faith without works is dead' (Js 2:26, also 2:20); the basis for Dowel as good works that justify (all of Js 2:14–26 is relevant).

183–203 A revises **Z**'s order, **B** retains **A**, and **C** revises anew, removing the repeat of the 'motto' line B 188/194 to produce a tighter argument, generally echoing I Cor 13:1–3. **184** *laumpe*: an image derived from traditional commentaries on Mt 25:13. These include Chrysostom (Homily 78 on St Matthew), Augustine (Sermo 93:5) and the *Summa* of Frère Lorens, whose source might have been *Castitas sine charitate, lampas sine oleo* from St Bernard's Epistle 42 (*PL* 182:817), a text **L** probably knew (Schmidt 1983¹:108–10; see also *Fasciculus Morum* [*FM*] III.8, cit. Wenzel in AlfC 166n). **191** *yhapsed*: an image seemingly of the cleric being fastened by lock and chain to greed and shut up inside a treasure chest. **193** *luther ensaumple*: contrasted with Christ's *ensaumple* at 167; the first of many attacks on covetous clerics. **195** 'Give, and it shall be given to you' (Lk 6:38), in context preceding the second half of the verse quoted at 173a. 195b completes the Gospel injunction from Js 1:5 ('God who giveth to all men'), possibly suggested

by the verbal echo of Lk 6.38 in the last phrase of that verse (*et dabitur ei*). **196** *lok of loue...grace*: elliptical for 'love is the lock which (when opened by acts of charity) unlocks also God's grace (for the giver)'. The image is resumed at 7.250–52 // and seems indirectly indebted to Js 2:13, a passage directly recalled at 19.215–52 //. The possible sense 'river-barrier' for *lok* (Davlin 2001:76 citing MED s.v. n.(2), 2(a)), yields a different figure that compares interestingly with *Pearl* 607–8. **197** *acombred*: taking up the image of sin at 190, and ultimately derived from that of one's 'iniquities...as a heavy burden' (Ps 37:5). **198–9** are progressively revised, save that 199 remains unaltered in **AB**. **198** *leche of lyf*: looking back to the medicinal imagery of 145 but also, insofar as 'love' personified = Christ, forward to his rôle as healer of mankind at 19.95 (and cf. 20.403–4). **199** *graffe*: echoing the *plonte* of 147 and foreshadowing the tree of charity in 18.11–15. *way*: making plain the sense of *gate* in // **ZAB**, so as to suggest that the relevant source is not Mt 7:13–14 (*Pe*), which speaks of the *narrow* way, but OT texts about the *direct* way and *right* path of truth that is also the way of love (Pss 25:12, 26:11) and Christ's reference to himself as sole 'way' to God (Jn 14:6). **200** *this textes*: what she has been saying generally, or specifically the texts about *tresore* at 48–9, 82–3. **201** concludes the sermon whose theme was enunciated at 135, though the force of directly restating B 135 at B 207 is lessened in consequence of that line's revision in **C**. **202–03** *Loue hit*; *loue is*: making explicit what may be overlooked in **ZAB**, that as the inner meaning of truth, love should have (and be) the last word. The literal sense of HC's valediction is '*Love* Truth; I cannot remain to teach you what *love* is [because only experience can do that].' *Lette*: the word used in HC's second farewell in A 2.31 (*om* **BC**).

Passus II

PASSUS II divides into: (i) a tableau-like opening in which Will sees LADY MEDE and HOLY CHURCH explains who she is (1–52), followed by a dramatic sequence in five movements: (ii) the enfeoffment of Mede by SIMONY and CIVIL (53–115); (iii) THEOLOGY's demand for the King to decide if her marriage is lawful (116–154); (iv) the journey of the parties to London (155–99); (v) the KING's intervention (200–16); and (vi) the villains' desertion of Mede (217–52). This ends part one of Mede's 'Trial' (the second 'act' of Vision One), which the next passus completes.

(i) 1–7 form a *transition* between the discourse of HC and the 'Trial' of Mede. **2** *for...heuene*: 'for the love of Mary in heaven'; on this 'split group genitive', see *MES* 78–9; and on the uninflected form of *Marie* as showing the influence of Latin genitives, ibid. p. 72. **3** *barn*; *rode*:

the juxtaposition of 'crib and cross', Christ's Incarnation and Passion, anticipates the startling image of the bloody babe at 19.86–90 //, B 17.123 (no //). **4** *craft*: continuing the stress in B 1.139 // (revised **C**) on a power or capacity through which to know truth and (now) falsehood. The answer to Will's request is a 'vision', since he is instructed to look; and this enables 'falsehood,' an abstract idea, to become visible as a personification, *Fals*. **5** *left*: bodily goods are assigned to the left, spiritual to the right in St Bernard's exegesis of Ps 90:7 (Vasta 1965:77; and cf. Prov 3:16, though this refers to wisdom). The left is contextually the *north*, since Will is looking east (*Bn*); for the north as source of evil and destruction, cf. Jer 4:6, 6:1, Ezech 4:4 and see on 1.112 above). *he* (*a* **Z**): a pronoun pl. in **Z** (so *they* 10) but clearly sg. in **ABC**, causing surprise; but a plurality of 'false' persons appear because 'their name is legion'. **6** *Fauel*: an OF name (< Lat. *fabella*), here first used in English (see MED s.v.); perhaps derived from the *Roman de Fauvel* (see Yunck 1963:221–6). In **ZA** it is almost a synonym for False (though for *hise* the immediate antecedent may be meant) but the two are better seen as distinct, Favel being the 'enchanting' flatterer (see 43 below). *Lyare*: the antithesis of Sothnesse (24), but given a much more active rôle (see 225ff). **7** The repetition of the b-half at 19.22a describes the just. **Z** 10 is superfluous, even if 10a did not echo Z 2a (and recur at Z 6.29 //) or 10b repeat 8b; but the repetition at Z 31 may explain the deletions here from **A**.

8–18 The description of the 'woman' is continuously revised, **B** stressing the jewels (perhaps recalling Dame Richesse in *RR* 1053–1108 = *Rom* 1032–1128 [*Bn*]), **C** her wealth, with fivefold rhetorical *repetitio* of *riche*. **11a** A rhetorical device perhaps suggested by Apoc 17:4–5 (*inaurata auro*). **11b** hints at what **A** alone actually suggests (*perreiӡe* 12), an allusion to Alice Perrers, Edward III's mistress (see Huppé 1939:44–52, Bennett 1943[1] and for a recent interesting but tendentious account Trigg 1998:5–29); ZA 18/14 lends support. **15** In rejecting details of clothing, **C** loses the symbolism of scarlet, a colour suggesting the whore of Babylon in Apoc 17:4–5. The emphatic rhyme at 14/15 is a device anticipated in the assonance of A 6.81/2. **Z** 19 *worthely*: repeating Z 2.12, which is revised at A 2.8. **B** 13–16 *double manere*: the light (male) and dark (female) sapphires (Evans and Serjeantson 1933:101). *Orientals*: either the *margaritis* 'pearls' of Apoc 17:4 (cf. the adj. in Chaucer *LGW* Pr F 221) or sapphires (MED s.v.). *ewages...destroye*: referring to the supposed 'virtue' of the diamond, though here the gem intended is the beryl or the sea-coloured sapphire (see MED s.v., *AMA* 212–15 and *Rom* 1086–90 on gems that protect against 'venim'). *engreyned*: dyed fast in scarlet 'grain' (cochineal dye: cf. *coccino* in Apoc 17:4). **A** 14 *quen queyntere*: 'queen more elegantly dressed' / 'harlot more cunning' (see MED s.vv. *quene* n. (2), 1 (b),

queinte adj. 1(f), (c): a masterly line, but dropped perhaps because no longer topical. **B** 16 *reed gold*: the reddish tinge being imparted by copper used as a hardening alloy (cf. *Sir Orfeo*150). **16** revises **B** to stress the attractiveness of riches to Will. The woman indeed suggests cupidity (*Bn*; cf. 1.66 above), but the imagery more directly evokes the Pride of Life and by association Lust, as indicated by *raueschede*, a word with negative overtones used metaphorically in connexion with Fortune and excessive learning (11.168, 294) as well as literally of rape (4.47). **17** 'Whose wife she might be' (?*or* 'be about to become'). A woman's status depended on her husband's, hence the form of the enquiry. The revised line may still allude, if obliquely, to Alice Perrers, who in 1376 married William of Windsor, the king's deputy in Ireland.

19–52 *Holy Church's account of Mede* provides a moral frame within which to view the following action. **19** *Mede*: signifying both 'reward' in the neutral sense and 'dishonest reward' (e.g. payment for wrongdoing). *þe mayde*: MEDE (as plain 'reward') is technically a virgin and could remain chaste if she married Leute (see on Pr 149) but will become a harlot if she marries False, because her (married) name will then signify 'bribery'. HC implies that the neutral sense has been compromised in the real world and that Mede can now only be regarded as corrupt: she represents metonymically *tresor of erthe* contaminated by wrongful desire. Her clothing marks her as antithetical to the Bride of Christ and as HC's rival for man's loyalty. *Pe* points to the disintegrating effect of the new mercantile capitalist values upon traditional feudal society and the problems they raised for the older social morality, referring to Tawney 1926:14–55; but there is little direct treatment of economic issues as in *WW*. Discussions of Mede include Mitchell 1956:174–93; Yunck 1963; Benson 1980; Morgan 1987[1]; Simpson 1990:43–9; Eaton 1991; Carlson 1991; Burrow 1993[1]:34–50 and especially 2005:116, citing Noonan 1984:275 in support of his argument that Mede represents not *pecunia* 'money' (= coin) but *munera* 'bribery' (i.e. 'goods or money offered as improper inducements'). **21** *han to kepe*: taken unconvincingly in *MES* 531 in the sense 'be obliged to'; rather, the lords 'have the laws in their control', to watch over and admininster. **22** *kynges court*: the court of King's Bench, which heard cases concerning the Crown and trespasses against the King's peace. *comune court*: the court of Common Pleas, hearing most civil actions between subjects (see Alf*G* s.v. *court*, and Harding 1973). **23** *palays*: at Avignon, the seat of the papacy from 1309 until 1378, when Urban VI decided to remain in Rome; from June 1379 the seat of the anti-popes throughout the Great Schism. It was regularly attacked by satirists as a centre of luxurious living and clerical venality. **24** *Sothnesse*: the principle of truth(fulness) and esp. veridicity (so at 19.283); a 'nature-name' for God at B 18.282 and (in the form *Sothfastnesse*) for the Son at B 16.186. In the light of 31, the divine referent seems contextually more apt here than the transient personification of 2.200, A 4.138, Z 4.50 (see further on Z 45). *bastard*: illicitly begotten, *sc.* by the devil upon an unnamed mother (see AlfG 14 s.v. on the term's legal significance). *Bn* aptly notes antipathy to bastards voiced at 5.65, 71; 9.168 ff; but his doubts about Fals being Mede's father in **B** are unwarranted. However, since the Fals she is to marry is the devil's 'son', Wrong's 'incarnation' on earth (B 41) and hence her (half)-brother, the proposed union is incestuous, as *Bn* allows (see further Tavormina 1995:7n19). **C** clarifies the relation between Fauel and Fals, making the former Mede's father (25) and the one who persuades her to marry Fals (43). **A 20 / Z 24** *to wroꝑerhele manye*: 'to the harm / misfortune of many'. The first element of *wroꝑerhele* signifies 'anger' (hence = 'evil'), but **L** seems to have supposed an etymological link with *writhe* 'twist' (see 6.66 and cf. *croked* at 29 below). This archaic word (not found after 1400) returns once at 15.301 //. **26 C** revises to stress how the devil tells truth to pervert truth. **B**, as *Bn* notes, may allude to his lying temptation of Eve, a theme fully developed in 20.326, 376–81 //; but the direct reference is to Lucifer's fall to earth caused by his 'first' lie (B 1.118 and 18.310–12; B 26b is distantly recalled by the new lines on liars in C 20.350–58, esp. 353b). **27** *is manered*: 'takes her (moral) character' (for the phrase, cf. B 15.415). *of kynde*: 'about natural relationships' (in both human beings and plants); on *kynde* in *PP* see the wide-ranging discussion in White 1988 and Zeeman 2000. **27a** 'Like father, like daughter [son **B**]'. The **B** wording is identical with the opening phrase of the Athanasian Creed's 7th clause (AlfQ 36), giving an effect of mordant irony here; but **C** revises away from the credal to the proverbial form (Whiting F 80). The primary source, which *Pe* aptly cites, is Ezech 16:44 *sicut mater, ita et filia eius,* where unfaithful Jerusalem is denounced as *meretrix* (in **L** it is Mede's *father* who is evil). **28–9** 'virtually translate' Mt 7:16 (Tavormina 1995:11) except its first clause 'a fructibus eorum *cognoscetis eos*', where the 'fruits' are their works (the italicised words are apparently rendered at 47a). Also important is Mt 7:18: '*Non potest* arbor bona *malos fructus facere*,' where the good tree corresponds by implication to HC here. (The separateness of the purified apocalyptic Church personified in HC is later to be brought out in the application of this tree-image to the humanly flawed Church Militant, and specifically to its clergy, at 16.246–53). **29a** '[The] good tree brings forth good fruit' (Mt 7:17); the verse's wider context has relevance, notably the warning against false prophets in vs. 15, a notion linked with the 'falsehood' theme here. **30** *a bettere*: i.e. Christ, the 'father' of the Church which became the 'mother' of his 'children', all Christians (cf. 18.205–7). **31–3 (B 29–31)** This striking

figure provides the 'true' theological pattern of which the Mede-Fals relationship is an evil inversion. **B** less audaciously makes God the Father also the parent of HC, who is to marry Mercy (= the Spouse Christ). *BnSk* take 'mercy' B 31 as HC's dowry, while Tavormina 1995:12n26 understands *marie wiþ myselue* as 'with which to marry myself'. But the reading here preferred (which *Bn* notes) seems likelier on grounds of sense, and is supported by its other appearance at A 10.154, where the phrasal verb with reflexive means 'be married to' (MED s.v. *marien* v. 2 (c) cites both instances). **31** *Filius Dei*: 'the Son of God', a common NT phrase but perhaps with specific allusion to Mt 27:54 // Jn 19:34, where the moment of Christ's death is 'conterminous with the "birth" of HC' (AlfQ 36). **32** *neuere…lauhede*: a tradition recorded in the widely read *Vita Christi* (II xvii:45) of the C14th Carthusian Ludolf of Saxony (*Pe*); the ultimate Scriptural source may be the 'woe' addressed to the worldly prosperous who 'laugh' in Lk 6:25. The connection of lying with laughing may echo Gen 18:15, where Sarah denies that she laughed, a link that would have been closer still had **L**'s original verb-forms been *leiȝede…leyhede* (cf. the *liȝere / liȝen* pun in A 25). **33** *ducchesse*: i.e. 'sovereign duchess', a phrase avoiding possible confusion with the Marian title 'Queen of Heaven'. **33–5 C** distinguishes sharply between the heavenly and earthly church but stresses, in the first of many such passages of wordplay, that faithful believers will receive both earthly sufficiency and final grace. **B**'s radical contrast between the values of 'mercy' and 'meed' is formulaically reiterated at B 11.133=C 13.142. *good…good*: on this favourite wordplay of **L**'s see Schmidt 1987:34–8. **B 34** 'Whoever loves bribery / accepts Mede in marriage': allegorically, gives himself to her so that they become as one. **37** *here loue*: either a possessive genitive ('her love [of him]') or, more probably, an objective genitive 'his love of her'. *trewe charite / Caritatis*: **B**'s Latin is inflected (genitive), as elsewhere in macaronic staves (e.g. ablative after *with* at 7.116). That it denotes something more specific or technical than 'charity' (AlfQ 36–7) seems doubtful, as **C**'s translation with added adjective spells out its standard theological meaning. **38** *That…hevene*: in the context 'charity' (cf. I Cor 13:13, Col 3:14), though it is truth that Ps 14:2–3 commends in answer to the question in vs. 1. **39** *Dauyd*: King David (d. *c.* 970 BC), traditionally the author of the entire Book of Psalms (on the importance of the psalms in *PP* see Wurtele 2003, and on their general significance in the period Kuczynski 1995). *the doumbe*: an unparalleled usage; the Psalter, being a book, is without vocal speech and therefore *cannot* lie, though it is 'spiritually eloquent' (but at 20.240 the character Book ['the Bible'] is made to speak). **39a** 'Lord, who shall dwell in thy tabernacle? [...He that works justice...that speaks truth in his heart]' (Ps14:1). In the Latin of the answer *Qui...operatur iustitiam*; *Qui loquitur veritatem*, the two nouns correspond to the dual senses of ME *trewthe* (see on Pr 15). **B 37** A possible T-type line, closer to the Latin source (*Bn*). **40***a* 'He that hath not...taken bribes against the innocent' (Ps 14:5); indirectly indicating a negative action (refraining from bribes) where // B 37 (translating Ps 14:2–3) affirms a positive, if general one. **41–2** *Mede ymaried*: on the episode see esp. Tavormina 1995:1–47 and Fowler 2003, ch. 2. **B 40** *mansed sherewe*: applied to Mede at B 4.160, just as **C** makes its *Fikel-tonge* the attribute of another character, Fauel (25 above). *Bn* finds an allusion to Ps 5:11, quoted in Rom 3:13; the seminal Ps 14.3b is more likely (cf. C 26a, which inverts Ps 14:3a). **43** *Fauel*: Mede's father (25), who has planned her marriage to one with the attributes of the Antichrist (see on 21.220 below), being begotten of the devil as Christ is of God. The passage is recalled at the end of the poem, where Fauel's distinctive quality is embodied in a friar, B 42b being repeated at B 20.379, but the echo at C 22.379 is less direct because of the revision in 43b. **44** retains **B**'s revision, removing the pregnant pun on *Liʒeris* and *liʒen* that in **ZA** brought together verbal and sexual 'fickleness'. *this lady*: sarcastic politeness; the echo at 53 bringing out the 'bastard' character of Mede's position and claim (24 above). **45** (pre)-echoes B 11.410 / C 13.221. **46** *tomorwe*: a purely internal passage of time, events continuing without break at 54 // after HC's departure. The *division of this first dream*, introduced in **B**, serves to shift the viewpoint from the perspective of the Tower to that of the Field. **49–50** warn against premature, hence possibly ineffectual criticism. HC's reference to an ideal time when justice will prevail cautiously anticipates Leute's own sentiments at 12.39. **52** *consience*: 'conscience' in **C**, 'guilty conscience' (*Bn*) in **B**. The line, ending with the name the speech began with (which could be capitalised), conceivably warns against making gain out of criticising others' faults. **ZA 35a / 31a** HC's near-repetition of A 1.183 is cut in **B** doubtless as otiose.

(ii) 53–4 are transitional lines introducing a (strictly unnecessary) reference to Will's sleeping state that is perhaps the germ of the 'inner-dream' device developed first in B 11.5–6 (*aslepe...metels*). **53** *lyggynge aslepe*: this unusual reference to being asleep *within* the dream (absent from **ZA**) divides the vision of HC from that of MEDE and effects a shift from a world of supernal reality to one of sordid actuality.

55–66 56b–57 shift the focus of B 55 // from the parties to the parts of the country (north / south, east / west) or, possibly, of society (rich / poor), **C**'s change taking account of the B 56 repetition (added to **ZA** and not wholly apt here) of B Pr 18 (B 56b is re-used in a transitional line inserted as C Pr 219b). **A 38–9** are echoed in *Death and Liffe* 55–6: 'There was neither hill nor holte nor haunt there beside / But itt was plaunted fful of people, the plaine and the roughe'. **58** *knyghtes*: generally exempted from criticism by **L** and treated sympathetically when driven to pecuniary extremes (see 6.250). **A 43** *of cuntres*: suggesting perhaps local landowners not actually of knightly rank. **59** *sysores*: jurors of the assise, whose function at this time was more to give true testimony about the facts as known to them and the character of the accused than to evaluate the sworn evidence of witnesses (whence their susceptibility to financial pressure). *sompnores*: those who summoned defendants to trial in the church courts for offences against morality as well as marital, testamentary and personal property cases. They were notorious for taking bribes or exercising blackmail. *shyryues*: the king's chief administrative officers in the shires (see Baldwin 1981[1]:28–9). **60** *Bydels*; *bailifs*: manorial officials, the one summoning tenants to the manor court, the other representing the lord's interests there. *brokeres*: dealers in business or trade. **61** *Vorgoers*: purveyors who commandeered or bought up in advance goods, materials and labour for the king or, earlier, for a great lord, an activity forbidden in 1362 (Baldwin 1981[1]:43). *vitalers*: especially suspected at this period of dishonest practices in retailing (cf. 3.79–89). *voketes...Arches*: barristers practising in the Archbishop of Canterbury's provincial court at St Mary 'le Bow' (so called from the arches supporting the steeple; on the Court of Arches see Woodcock 1952:6–14). Like all lawyers, they were suspected of taking *munera super innocentem* (Ps 14:5). The passage will be echoed at 22.136–9. **62** recalls the rodent assembly at Pr 165. **63** *Simonye*: personifying the sin (named after Simon Magus in Ac 8:18–24) of buying and selling spiritual benefits (e.g. absolution), church offices, benefices or, in an extended sense, 'any divine gift intended for the common good (such as justice, knowledge, health)' (Alf*G* 145, citing 9.55). *BnPe*'s view of him as specifically a canon lawyer in collusion with his colleague (a civil lawyer) fits but does not impose itself, given the wide reference of the name. Salter 1967 [1988]:158–69 argues for **L**'s indebtedness to the early C14th poem *The Simonie*, preserved in the Auchinleck MS (ed. Embree & Urquhart, also Wright 1839, Robbins 1959). *Syuile*: Civil Law, the form of the *ius gentium* operative in England, mainly in the conciliar or prerogative courts, 'supplementary jurisdictions [of the crown] intended to provide remedies where the common law could not' (Baker 1971:50). Their law and procedure, deriving from Roman jurisprudence, resembled the Canon Law of the consistory (episcopal) courts and all subordinate tribunals of the universal papal jurisdiction, canon lawyers having first to undergo a training in civil law at the universities and civilians to be examined in canon law (Boyle 1964:136–8, 141–7). If *Simonye* here personifies '(corrupt) Canon law(yers)' it is because Mede's case involves marriage, a question for the church courts. Gilbert (1981:57) identifies *Syuile* as 'both canon and civil law' and finds a 'near identity of Civil and Simony' (see further Barratt 1982). Tavormina's interpretation of these two figures as 'metaphorical equivalents to the local priest' (1995:13n) presses the allegory too closely. *contrees*: juries drawn from the inhabitants of a judicial district (MED s.v. 6b). **66** *brokor*: Fauel arranges Mede's marriage; the arranged marriage is a practice in society that is criticised at 16.104–9 //, as *Bn* notes, because often done *for coueytise of catel* on the part of the bride's father (see Tavormina 1995:17–18). **B 66** *enjoyned*: 'joined in wedlock'; the earliest recorded use in this sense (cf. 2.150 below).

Z 40–57 / A 35–47 A omits Z 40–2 as partly redundant (Z 40 re-appears at 119). In Z 40–1 the comma after *fayle* could be omitted to make *sette* prolatively dependent on *fayle*. In Z 42 Civil's rôle is to *sese* 'take legal possession of' (MED s.v. *seisen* v. 1a) the lands that Fauel (her father) and Fals (her husband-to-be) are jointly to enfeoff her with (44), a jointure in lieu of a dowry. The **A** revision, dispensing with **Z**'s use of Civil, simplifies the procedure but with some loss of clarity, *chartres* 35 not *londus* becoming the antecedent of *halden* and the sense elliptical: 'charters [of entitlement to those lands that are to be granted].' **Z 45** disrupts the continuity and may have been cut so as to defer till A 150 (= Z 159) the introduction of a figure who remains a cipher (for the multiple referents of SOTHNESSE see on 24). This passage of rhetorical *amplificatio* that slows the action is reminiscent of *WW* 138–96; revised in **A** with omission of Z 47, it is omitted in **B**. **47** *lesewe*: see MED s.v. *leswe* n. (c). **56** (**A 47**) *meble*: the earliest uses cited in MED s.v. *moeble* n. are from **L**, but OED (s.v. *moble* a. and sb.) records several from the earlier C14th. **A 48 (Z 57)** *þe fyn is arered*: 'the fine is levied'. The *fyn* was a final agreement concerning property (rights) or the vesting of lands in a feoffee based on an agreed legal fiction of a supposed dispute between the parties requiring a material settlement (see AlfG 59 s.v. *fyn*).

67–108 69 *chartre*: a deed conveying landed property; in the allegory the 'territories' of the capital sins. Possible sources are pseudo-Grosseteste's poem on the marriage of the devil's daughters (Meyer 1900:54–72) and the early C14th *Roman de Fauvel* Bk II (Cornelius 1932). *Bn* considers **A**'s simple allegory slightly obscured in **BC**; however, the sins named in, e.g. 85–7, are not 'miscellaneous' but aptly specify 'locations' within particular symbolic regions such as the *chastel* of 89. The outline sketch of the Deadly Sins here will be elaborated dramatically in VI–VII and analytically in 16.43–96 (e.g. Gluttony at 97 is a summary foretaste of 6.349–432, 16.71–8). **70** *Gyle*: personifying a chief quality of the devil (see 20.377ff). **75–6** *vp lyking of*: 'at the will / pleasure of'. *Mede / mede*: the rich rhyme bringing out the relation between 'desire'

and 'bribery'; the explicit moral warning has dramatically ironic force coming from the vicious speaker (in **C** Simony). **76** *this*: i.e. the enactments of the charter (Tavormina 1995:24). *laste mede*: presumably alluding to the Last Judgement, though 79ff adhere to **B**'s pattern and do not recur to this theme. **78a** 'Let it be known to all present and to come', the standard opening of a charter of conveyance (AlfG 140). The device parodies the literary 'charter of Christ' of which Woolf (in Hussey 1969:57) cites a version from *c.* 1350 (and see further Spalding 1914:28–30, Keen 2002:27–49). **L** may also have had in mind the satirical form of the devil's *lettre* (83; cf. 107 below) such as the *Epistola Luciferi* of 1352 (Russell 1984:87–9), an ME version of which is discussed by Raymo in Pearsall and Waldron 1969:233–48. **80–1** Mede's allegorical marriage recalls the mercenary union criticised at 16.109; for the phrasing cf. 11.13, 18.13. **A 59 (Z 67)** *for...riche*: 'at all times, in all circumstances' (cf. B 102 // below); an ironic echo of the marriage service. Suggestions of the marriage ceremony (the reading of the *dotalium*) are found in this scene by Tavormina (1995:23). **84** *Pruyde...dispice*: the opposition between these two is developed at 16.57–9. **85; 87** For the phrasing cf. 16.361, 9.334. **88** *Enuye and Yre*: closely linked for **L**, the first having its broader sense of 'hostile ill-will' or *invidia* (MED s.v. 1(a)) as well as its narrower modern sense (ib. 3). The absence from **ZA** of a separate figure of Wrath after Envy in the Sins' confessions later may reflect an earlier view of 'Envy' as covering both sins, who appear effectively as a 'joint-sin' at Z 5.91 and the 'gloss' on this at 94. **90** *Coueytise*: generally 'greed', specifically 'desire for (obtaining) possessions' (cf. *auaryce* 91). *consenteth*: cited by MED as the only example of the sense '(agree to) concede something' (s.v. 2b(b)). **91** *vsurye*: lending money or goods at (exorbitant) interest (*usura*), which was not permitted to Christians, though loans (*mutua*) with agreed 'compensation' for any loss arising to the lender were (Gilchrist 1969:64–5, 68). See AlfG 162–3 s.v. for valuable refs. and for the distinction between bodily (or literal) and spiritual (or metaphorical) usury (on which cf. also on B 7.80–1a below). *auaryce*: though sometimes 'greed' generally, here specifically 'miserliness', greed *in* possession rather than *to* possess (= *coueytise*); see MED s.v. (a) and (b) and esp. *CT* X 744–5. **Z 71** *cheuysawnses*: 'trading in money or goods for profit, esp. by devious means, to circumvent the law (e.g. against usury)' (AlfG 27). In the context and in the light of 6.252 // B 5.245, illicit lending at interest would seem to be involved. **92** *bargaynes*: compacts or 'deals' setting out what each party is to give or take. *brocages*: business transactions, esp. by a third party (AlfG 13, 20), as in arranged marriages for profit (16.107–9); Fauel is a *brokor* 66. **93** *lordschip*: 'estate (belonging to a lord)', but with a hint that lechery is especially a vice of the higher classes (cf. 3.57, 22.90); see MED s.v. 4 (a) and cf. 5(c). **95** *woldes*: first recorded here and elsewhere only in Gower *CA* 6.924 (MED s.v. n. 2 misses this instance). **96** is recalled at 22.197; with the build-up to *wille* in a sequence of three lines alliterating on |w|, an ironic self-directed pun may be suspected. **97** resembles 6.360 below. *grete othes*: regularly thought of as a sin accompanying drunkenness (see on B 10.50); examples are at 22.226. **100** *before noone*: spelling out **B**'s *er ful tyme*; the fasting rule allowed only one meal, to be taken at midday, the normal time for the main meal being the evening (H. S. Bennett 1937:236). **A 65** is new, a Type 3 line scanning on *d* and reminiscent of Z III 163, but is replaced with expanded 89–92 in **B**. The linking of gluttony with lust in **A** recalls the Lot exemplum, as that with sloth anticipates B 14.76. **B 98** *breden*: either from *breden* 'live, dwell' (MED v. (3), 3(c), with apt quotation from *WPal* 1782) or from *breden* 'spread out, distend' (MED v. (2), 3) as maintained by Kane 2000:45, though the exact sense required 'grow stout [*sc.* from eating abundant town-refuse]' is not instanced). The sense 'breed' (s.v. v. (3) 3 (a)) does not impose itself, despite *bedden*, since the issue concerns gluttony as leading to sloth, not lechery; but polysemantic wordplay cannot be ruled out, even if a pun on two phonemically distinct verbs would be less effective. **103–04** *wanhope*: final impenitence, produced by 'despair of the mercy of God' (*CT* X 692) results from 'believing' in False and is the converse of belief in Truth, which will bring the grace of a good end (see on 35 above). The lines spell out that for persistent sinners the prospect of salvation through a long period in purgatory, though possible, is remote. **C** lessens the strict charter-like quality of B 102 //, with its legal phrases referring to permanent possession (*habendum et tenendum*) in fee-simple (Woolf 1969:57, AlfG 69–70) and also echoing the marriage service (Tavormina 1995:2). **104–05** Echoic end-chime replaces the full rhyme of **B 100–01** ending the list of sins. **105** *This lyf*: 'during this life'; like *fastyng dayes*100, an absolute time-phrase without preposition. **108** *appurtinaunces*: an accurate legal term for 'something annexed to another thing more worthy as principal, and which passes in possession with it, as a right of way or other easement' (AlfG 8). In context richly ironic, since those who go to hell will have no use for (purgatorial) 'easements' or rights of way (cf. Christ's hope-giving promise cited in Woolf 57). **B 105 (Z 76, A 69)** *one yeris ende*: 'the date fixed for the repayment of a loan [here = one's life] or the fulfilment of an obligation [= to serve God]' (AlfG 170 s.v. *yere*); cf. Piers's words to the knight at B 6.43–4. The sinner's soul is repaid to Satan rather than to God (contrast Piers's bequest at 8.96–7). **B 107** *wo*: removing the possible ambiguity of // **ZA** 78 (71), where 'Wrong' may have as referent both the Devil and his earthly surrogate, the human evil-doer who witnesses

the deed at 108 and will appear before the king at 4.46. **109–15 109** *Wrong*: see at 1.59. **110 (B 109)** *Peres*: a popular ME name (<AN), the commonest English form of 'Peter'; see also 6.366. *Paulines*: with B 178 below the only contemporary reference. Identification of these 'Paulines' with the Crutched Friars, one of the minor orders suppressed in 1370, whose house lay just within the City wall (Chettle 1949), is uncertain though possible, notwithstanding that pardoners were rarely friars (*Bn*). **C** *queste*: the jury of a church court (MED s.v. n.1); *Bn*'s suggestion 'a collection of alms or donations' is not illustrated in MED. **B** *doctrine*: i.e. metonymically their order, lit. 'the teachings of the [Order of Paulines]' (see MED s.v. *doctrine* n.2 (a)). AlfG 111–12 takes it as 'general instruction of knowledge in any field, including the law' and *Paulynes* as referring to suitors and witnesses in the consistory court, since the word's every occurrence [*sc.* in L] 'is in a legal context, pointing towards the ecclesiastical court of St Paul's'. B 178 (*Paulynes pryuees*) would support AlfG (see idem 111–12, 120–1), as would *queste* here. Du Boulay 1991:98–9 likewise takes *Paulynes* as 'the ecclesiastical lawyers who worked in St Paul's.' **A** *doctor*: i.e. learned member of the Paulines. *Bn*'s conjecture of an allusion to St Paul's and its neighbourhood is confirmed by **Z** *of Sent Poules chirche*, which fits with the present 'Piers' being a pardoner, yet not a friar (the revisions could allude ironically to a suppresssed order whose *former* members found employment on the margins of the Church in such rôles as the pardoner's). There is no lexical evidence for the term as referring to the cathedral or its court; OED cites 'Paulyns' for the crutched Friars from 1483 (s.v. *Pauline* a. and sb.) while Gregory's *Chronicle* (*c.* 1475) uses 'The ordyr of Powlys' (MED s.v. *Poule* n. 2(b)). **111** *Bette*: a man's name, recurring at B 5.32, with evident punning intent, here the assonance with *bedel* perhaps motivating the choice. Banbury in N Oxon. (Buckinghamshire in **ZAB**), like Rutland in B 111 (which kept its name 'Soke' until modern times), seems chosen for alliterative convenience, though gibes at particular regions occur (e.g. Norfolk at Z 5.98, B 5.235). **112** *Raynald*: 'Reginald'. *reue*: a manorial official elected by the peasants (Bennett 1937:166–78) and one who, besides being open to venality, would have a tendency to amass debts (11.301–2). *redyng-kynges*: here and at 6.371 found only in L; possibly a form of *rod-knight*, 'king' being a reversed-spelling variant of *knight* (MED s.v.). *Pe*'s suggestion that *redyng* may be from 'reeding', or 'redding' (i.e. dyeing red), or 'riding', the man being a master thatcher, a dyer or a lackey (with an ironic use of 'king') is little better supported. **113** *Munde*: a stock name for a miller (here a type of dishonesty), used again at B 10.44, where he seems a type of foolish ignorance. **114** *date...deuel*: a parody of the formula for dating a deed ('in the year of Our Lord', as at B 13.269), suggesting

Wrong's diabolic character, the document having been issued 'under the devil's aegis' (Tavormina 1995:22). A **78** *signes*: the marks appended to official documents by the public notaries, who dealt with ecclesiastical matters like papal provisions to, and exchanges of, benefices (whence the reference at C 185–6; see Gilbert 1981:58–9, Alf*G*). The phrase is re-used at C 156.

(iii) 116–54 116 *Teologie*: THEOLOGY, whom *Bn* rightly sees as taking over HC's rôle, is presumably here the Church's systematised (especially moral) teaching as applied in actual life, aimed at promoting the reign of truth and charity. Dame Study later contrasts this with the discipline's more problematic 'speculative' aspects in B 10.182–99. **117** *Symonye*: his replacement of Cyuyle **B** is logical, since arranging an illicit marriage could be regarded as coming under this sin (Alf*G* s.v.) and he has already taken the initiative at 74 above. **B 117** *wraþe wiþ*: 'with which to anger'. **120–26** Theology's view of Fikel-tonge (?Fauel) as Mede's grandfather (*belsyre*) and Fals as her father (so HC at B 25) contradicts HC in **C**, who makes Fauel Mede's father (25) and Fals her intended (42). The discrepancy between these two authorities could be intended to highlight Mede's ambiguous character; or *Fals* at 121 may be an authorial oversight for *Fauel.* The only way to avoid seeing the proposed union as one of father and daughter (though still incestuous) is to regard the suitor Fals as a distinct character, the (bastard) son and representative of the same evil principle as the father (2.42 // B 41). But in Theology's view, Mede is not a bastard (as HC accused her at 24) but legitimate offspring (on the word *moilere* see Bradley 1906–7:163–4; Alf*G* 102), because her *mother* was 'an honest woman deceived into making an alliance with Fals' (*Bn*), whence the daughter is canonically *mulierata* 'of legitimate birth'. Mede is thus given a dual ancestry, good and bad (*Amendes*, though possibly neutral in its sense 'compensation', is here viewed positively) and God is thought of as having pledged to reward Amends (= 'satisfaction for sin') by allying himself with her through marriage, so countering the influence of Fals. The interpretation of 124 depends on *treuthe* in its three other occurences with *plihten* (3.469, 8.33, 10.274) having the sense 'make a promise', so if thus taken here (as by *Pe*) *Treuthe* (1) will refer *non*-univocally to both God and his representatives (as Fals does both to the Devil and his). **C**'s explicitness, however, arguably blurs **ZAB**'s suggestion that Mede ought in an ideal world to be the daughter of Amends and therefore noble, while in the *actual* world (as what follows shows) she has a greater propensity for evil than for good (i.e. rewards tend to be given for the wrong reason or to the wrong people). Theology's equivocal perspective on Mede may be due to his being *in via*, in contrast to HC's eschatological standpoint (*in patria*); but seen in purely social terms, it helps account for Mede's plausible

posture before the King of an aristocratic lady worthy to be his 'kinswoman', like an heiress to one of the tenancies-in-chief (Baldwin 1981[1]:27, 33). In this passage the word-play on *treuthe* and *so* (124–25) amplifies that on *gyue* (126) in **ZAB** (see further Tavormina 1995:25–30, who finds in Theology's opposition to the marriage with Fals traces of objection on grounds of 'disparagement' and known enmity to Mede's lord). **127–8** The main attack is on Symonye himself, in **ZAB** on his crony Cyuyle, the corrupt ecclesiastical lawyer whose practices foster wrongful legal decisions that harm the Church. **129–30** *tixt*: in **C** not Scripture but the words of Lawrence the deacon (*Levita Laurentius* in the Magnificat antiphon at Vespers for his feast day, 10 August), who was believed to have been martyred by roasting on a gridiron at Rome in 258 for refusing to give up the riches of the Christian community and for referring to the poor as the 'treasure' of the Church (*Legenda Aurea* [*LA*] CXVII). Lawrence is cited again at 17.65–8, which echoes this passage in using *mede* in its 'true' sense of a just heavenly reward for a life of 'truth' on earth and *largenesse* in its honourable sense, by contrast with the suspect adverb at 138. *trewe doom*: the referent may be 'the reliable judgement' (of tradition) that what is described really happened thus. **132–3** His words echo the antiphon at Lauds (or *LA* 492): 'I thank you Lord that I have deserved to enter your gates' (on Lawrence and the liturgy see further Tavormina 1987). **B 123 (Z 94, A 87)** '[For] the labourer is worthy' (Lk 10:7, echoing Deut 24:14); the quoted words continue *mercede sua* 'his hire to have' (123b //). This 'text's' context concerns the right of apostolic preachers to food and shelter for preaching the gospel; but the wider reference here is to 'all who labour honestly with body or mind / do works of virtue' (anticipating the words of the pardon at 9.286). **Z 99** *nysotes*: a noun used as an adjective (*MES* 642–3), here in apposition with another preceding, with French pl. ending and even closer to French practice than B 11.316. **Z 100** *sowsest yow*: the lack of concord between sg. verb and pl. reflexive may be due to the attack being on Cyuyle both individually and in his complicity with Symonye and the notaries. *Seynte Marye rentus*: rents due for payment on Annunciation Day, 25 March ('Lady Day', the start of the New Year under the old scheme of reckoning the calendar); omitted as perhaps over-specific. **133–34** The rhyme-repetition of *diserue* 'earn by service' points up **L**'s singular quasi-Platonic notion of earthly institutions and practices as having their true ('authentic, original') archetype in heaven; cf. Schmidt 1987:117, and Simpson 1986[2] for a full discussion of this unnamed 'figure of thought' (which could perhaps be thought of as a form of 'transsumptio'). **136** *no man*: because those who live a life of 'truth' are one with 'Truth' and can be called by his name, just as followers of Christ are 'Christians'. Whether or not *treuthe* is capitalised here (balancing Fals 137), its (univocal) reference is to man, not to 'Truth (as God)'. **140** echoes 1.189, where destroyers of charity are also enemies of truth. **B 126 (Z 98, A 90)** *shenden*: licensed *s / sh* alliteration on 'metrical allophones' (*Intro.* IV § 46). **142** *Holy Writ*: presumably Jn 8:44, cited in note to 1.60 above. **144** *byʒete*: 'begotten', a puzzling expression if this is a simple adjective, since to have been born a bastard, Fals would have first to have been begotten. To make sense, *byʒete* must be given the meaning 'lawfully begotten' (so *Pe*), for which there is no lexical support, and treated as a nominal (as at B 41 above). The context implies that Fals = the Antichrist, the *false fende* who makes *fals sprynge* in 22.64, 55. **B 131 (Z 103, A 95)** *Belsabubbes*: the 'prince of the devils' in Mk 3:22–6; not mentioned by name later in the Harrowing of Hell sequence in Passus 20. **145** *moylore*: contradicting HC's assertion at 24 above that Mede is a bastard and so presumably a fit match for Fals. *a mayden of gode*: 'a lady richly left'; 'a girl of good family' (*Pe*). **ABC** suggest that 'maiden' merely = unmarried, as at 2.19 // (MED s.v. 1(a)), revising *Z*'s '(literally) a virgin' (ib. 2(a)). Theology's view in all versions does not square with Conscience's assertion of Mede's promiscuity at 3.164ff//, a discrepancy perhaps meant to signal the difference between theory and experience (cf. on 120–6). **148** *Londone*: implying, if literally meant, a hearing at the Arches in Cheapside (see on 61). They are intercepted by the king's officers (2.210, 3.1–2) and brought to the King's own prerogative court at Westminster (at this time a separate city); but at 174 Westminster is in any case their destination. This may be because Mede is envisaged as a royal ward, or the terms may be used without exactitude. The reference to journeying, however, is a reminder that the dream has occurred *opeland* (cf. 5.44 later) on the Malvern Hills, and the party are perhaps to be imagined as coming up to the capital from the west. **150** *iuroures othes*: testifying to their proclaimed character; see on 59 and cf. Z Pr 70. **151** *witty*: 'wise', a traditional attribute of God (cf. *witig god* in *Beowulf* 685). **152** *Conscience... consayl*: a member of 'Truth's privy council'; but the allegory does not insist on his function purely as the individual conscience, since he has already appeared both as spokesman of divine judgement (Pr 118–27) and (first in C) as a member of the king's Privy Council (Pr 158). **154** *soure*: a favourite transferred epithet describing the unpleasant consequences (= 'aftertaste') of a life of sin; cf. 15.49–51*a*, B 10.359 (see Schmidt 1987:91–2). **(iv) 155–74 155–6** The canon lawyer (Syuyle) is prepared to wait for his fee; the corrupt church official (Symonye) wants payment in advance for services to be rendered. The allegory allows that there may be a right use of the former, while the latter is always bad. **157** *floreynes*: gold coins imprinted with fleurs-de-lys on the obverse. The rare English florin, a gold piece with half and quarter, was

first issued by Edward III in 1344 with the value of 6s (see *Sk* IV 51, illustration in Poole I:292, pl. 34b–d). Italian florins (named from the city of Florence) were coined in 1282 and circulated widely, as were Flemish. Legal charges are high (*plus ça change...*), having to be paid in gold, not in silver shillings (see also 3.194, 7.227, where the cost of bribing false witnesses is again reckoned in florins). **161** *amaystrye*: presumably overcome her (real or feigned) scruples about marrying False by lying about his character. **B 148** *maken...wille*: a phrase with sexual overtones, as suggested by 22.197. **164** *comen*: with unexpressed subject (i.e. False-Witness, the notaries etc) understood (*MES* 142, 5c). **167** *mery tonge*: repeating with variation 161b, in C's characteristic way. Pleasant persuasiveness is needed to make Mede go happily (*with a goode wille*). **170** shows Mede subject to the desire which she tempts others with: greedy in herself and the cause of greed in others. **171–74** The party is swelled by supporters from the surrounding country drawn from classes especially prone to venality.

175–89 undergo continuous revision, not always in the direction of perfect clarity. **Z 143** *Symonye*: making a clear distinction between Symonye the master of summoners (who were church officials) and Cyuyle the (Canon) lawyer; **ABC** erase it. **Z 148** is either a scribal echo or an earlier form of a line dropped in **A** and revived for use as **B 174**. Though **C** omits these groups, it distinguishes between Mede's mount (a royal official) and the lawyers' (churchmen and church officials). The traditional 'riding' trope is found in Nicole Bozon's *Char d'Orguel* and in *The Simonie* 326, but derives ultimately from patristic commentary on Ex 15:1–4 and Cant 1:8 (Kellogg 1958). It recurs in 4.16–23 and, most strikingly, in 19.49ff (also B 17.108). **B 163** // *foles*: perhaps punning on 'fools', worldly wisemen who follow Wrong and are fools in God's eyes (contrast B 7.125, 22.61–2). **177** revises 'allophonic' *s / sh* alliteration to uniform *sh*. **178** *saunbure*: a word for a comfortable saddle or litter made of fine material, found only here (see MED s.v. *samburi* n., a blend of OF *sambüe* 'lady's saddle' and ML *saumarius* 'packhorse'). *syse to syse*: the twice-yearly progresses of the sheriff, when he could levy fines at the assize of bread and ale (*Bn*). **180** *righte faste by*: 'close on either side of'. **182** *prouisores*: those who held a 'provision' from the Pope to be appointed to a benefice when a vacancy occurred. Although strictly controlled by the Statute of Provisors of 1351 (confirmed and supplemented by *Praemunire* 1353), the system continued to function (McKisack 1959:272–85), even the stringent second Statute of 1390 remaining 'a dead letter' (idem, 282, and see further Pantin 1955:47–75, 82–9, Gee and Hardy 1921:112–25 for texts of the re-issued statutes, Swanson 1989:70–2 and refs. in AlfG 128). *serue*: i.e as mounts, but with a pun on 'serve as secretaries / assistants'. **184** *rectores*:

those who held as a benefice a church and the whole or best part of its endowment income (Alf*G* 128). The Latin form, as at 187, 191, characterises the learned speaker. *deuoutours*: an alteration from the usual form *auoutrie* (as at B 12.74), perhaps for metrical convenience, with a sardonic pun on *devout*. On the noun used as adj. see *MES* 642–3, and cf. on Z 148 below. **185** *permuten*: first found here and 'suggest[ing] a first-hand knowledge of the canonical pronouncements on the subject, e.g. Gregory IX, *Decret.* III 19' (Alf*G* 114). Exchanging benefices was considered simony if it involved a cash-adjustment (see on A 78). **186** *pore prouisores*: provisors *in forma paupe-rum*, who were granted precedence over other candidates for a benefice in the gift of a named *patron*, as opposed to those *in forma speciali*, who were granted a named *benefice* (Swanson 1989:70). *appeles*: metonymic for '[those who make] accusations alleging another's crime' or, more probably, 'supplications for mercy (Alf*G* 7) as at 244. The Court of Arches (see on 61) heard appeals from lower church courts of the province. **187** *Somnours*: apparitors, officers who summoned to a church court for offences against (mainly sexual) morality; see Woodcock 1952:45–9. *sodenes*: sub-deans (deputies of the dean), or rural deans acting locally for the bishop in testamentary, moral and other matters (*Bn*). The *south-* form (**AB**) shows *-th* standing for Norman French *-tz* (= *soutz* < Lat *subtus* 'under' [*Sk*]); see also 16.277. *supersedeas*: named from its first word, the Latin perhaps being used here as a false plural ('supersedeases'). The writ stayed or put an end to legal proceedings against persons accused of offences lying under its jurisdiction (here sexual misdemeanours). As it fell to the summoner to bring the accused to court, he might be dissuaded from doing so for a suitable payment (cf. *CT* I 653–7). The writ 'was meant to protect individual rights...but...was subject to abuses such as bribery' (Alf*G* 150; see also 4.190, 9.263). Mention of these writs, new in **C**, marks **L**'s increased awareness of and animosity towards abuses of the law. **188** *lyppeth... rydeth*: the satiric aptness of this image to the sin of *lech-erye* is obvious in the light of the 'mounting' imagery at B 7.90 and the use of *ryden* at 13.154, B 11.337 (MED s.v. *riden* v. 9 'copulate'). **189** The danger of 'false friends' to the testator's soul is stated at B 12.257. Why the *seca-tours* should be mounts for summoners is not clear, but the three groups are linked again at 16.277.

B 174–9 174 (Z 148) *Erchedeknes*: primarily eccle-siastical judges who went on parish visitations and im-posed fines for offences against sexual morality and church discipline (*Bn*). *officials*: officers presiding in a consistory court, e.g. as a bishop's chancellor; in **Z** per-haps in apposition with *Erchdekenus*, through being seen as a pl. adjectival form like *deuoutours* 184 (for an earlier reference see *The Simonie* 192). *registrers*: clerks of the church courts in charge of records, citations and receipts

(Alf*G* 129), who were always public notaries (Woodcock 1952:38). **175–77** The matters named fell to the arch-deacon and gave opportunity for bribery, e.g. to over-look charges of adultery. The practice of *derne usurie* or *occulta usura* was the lending of money (at exorbitant rates of interest) under colour of a trading transaction. An example would be the lender's purchase of goods from the borrower at an excessive price, the excess being a secret interest-bearing loan to the seller (on usury see Gil-christ 1969:108). **176** *diuorses*: not as today the dissolu-tion of a valid marriage but rather a canonical annulment or declaration that the marriage was invalid from the out-set (see Du Boulay 1991:97f). The modern sense existed (MED s.v *divorce* n. 1 (1402)) but is not, *pace* MED, that of either of **L**'s two uses (see also 22.139 and Alf*G* 48, *The Simonie* 199–203, Helmholz 1974:74 and Tavormina 1995:29n60). **177** The suggestion could be that profits from church fines helped defray the costs of bishops' visitations of their dioceses (there is an advance in preci-sion from **Z**→ **A**→ **B**, but **C** omits bishops, having men-tioned *prelates* at 182). **178 (A 139)** *Paulynes...consisto-rie*: taken as 'having to do with the consistory court of St Paul's Cathedral' by Alf*G* 120. However, while *Poules* as 'the ecclesiastical court of St Paul's' seems proven, no instance of *Paulines* itself supports this sense; so a reference to ex-members of the Pauline Friars remains a possibility (see on 110). *pryuees*: 'parties to suits in legal actions' (*Bn*); on the use of a French pl. ending with *s* in post-positional adjs. see *MES* 277, and cf. on 184. **190–99 190** *commissarie*: the bishop's adminstrative leg-ate exercising jurisdiction (particularly) in far-flung parts of his diocese. The supposition is that a living (*vitaliles*) is to be got from fining those summoned for sexual sins. This is the first clear case in **C** of alliteration on |f| and |v| with a Latin macaronic stave (cf. 61 above). *cart*: the motif of allegorical animals drawing carts is traditional, as *Bn* notes, citing Bozon's *Char d'Orguel* and a C12th illustration of Greed's chariot (Katzenellenbogen 1989, fig. 60); **L**'s is individual in making the 'beasts' not per-sonified vices but social types. **191** *fornicatores*: a techni-cal term covering both fornicators and adulterers (Alf*G* 62). Taking *mede* for overlooking such cases among the clergy is criticised in *The Simonie* 49–52. **192** *lang cart*: the four-wheeled *longa caretta* used for military and other transport. Allegorically, these deceiving characters are 'contained within' Liar, who appears as a separate type-figure at 225. **193** *fobbes / fobberes*: found only in **L** (see MED s.vv.), the back-formed verb surviving in the phrase 'fob off'. **196** *no...telle*: a variant on the allitera-tive formula (also found in *SGGK* 719 and in Z*A* 6.76/82, from where it has been deleted in // **B**, perhaps to avoid repetition). *tayl*: both 'number' and 'tail', stretching out behind them (cf. the pun at B 12.245). **197** revises and strengthens **ZAB**'s tag-like b-half. **198** *forgóere*: here, by contrast with 61 above, stressed on the second syllable. Gyle, the principle of diabolic deceitfulness (see on 70) becomes 'embodied' in one of the type-figures of Mede's *route* at 62. **199a** anticipates 7.177a, where the repentant folk of the field seek a guide to Truth.

(v) 200–16 200 *Sothnesse*: evidently the same quality named at 24, defined by 'clear-sightedness' (*Bn*), the ability to recognise Guile. His 'horse' vividly realises an abstract idea, a virtue especially appropriate to that *veritas* which 'prevails' in the long run (III Esd 4:41) and so requires patience. This substitution of a symbolic mount for **B**'s *palfrey* foreshadows an important development (later in **B**) of the major figure Patience, whose companion Conscience becomes (13.180–82). **Z 160** *fiched*: the earliest use in this (and perhaps any) sense, not cited in MED s.v. *fichen* v.(1). **202** *Conscience*: here 'perhaps conceived of as the chancellor, "the keeper of the king's conscience..."' (*Bn*). The rôle also fits well enough in the earlier versions, though in **C** he has already been introduced as the authoritative speaker of the words on the king's duties given to the angel in **B** (see on Pr 151–57).

Z 163–70 give an accurate (if redundant) summary of 'the action of Passus II up to this point' (*R–B*) that bears the marks of an authorial draft (see *TN*) rather than a scribal interpolation, the purpose of which would be inexplicable. **L** generally avoids passages of summary, an exception being 15.5–24 //, an occasion to recapitulate an important completed sequence and furnish a transition between dreams. **164, 168** *al togyderes*: 'the whole business'. **165/6** *lache / Mede*: the collocation occurs at C 3.390, though in sense 4 (a) of MED *lacchen* v. (1), which is distinct from the present one (id. 3 (a)). **166** *hym lette*: sense uncertain, but either 'and how he [Fauel / Falsenesse treated as one] conducted himself' (MED s.v. *leten* v. 17b) or, 'how to prevent him'; 'he was prevented' (*R–B*) does not seem a possible translation. **167** virtually repeats 117, **169a** repeats 86. **170** recalls Z 1.43; but the play on *tene* in 169 is characteristic of **L** (cf. 7.38, 8.36, 11.128).

207–16 207 *maynteyneth*: aids and abets them through money, protection or influence; alluding to the 'maintenance' of retainers by great lords (see AlfG 94–5). Baldwin 1981[1]:26–7 plausibly sees here the specific abuse of 'maintenance-at-law' (paying administrative officials fees and liveries for furthering the lord's interests) and in Mede herself 'a life-like example' of using bribes to sustain and increase her power. Z 177 supports this reading, which for **ABC** sits awkwardly with Mede's being the *object* of False's designs. But if at one level she signifies a 'corrupt great lady' (like Alice Perrers), such a reading seems right. The King's threat implies that maintenance is itself a crime potentially as grave as those of the actual criminal types 'maintained'. **208** *maynprise*: 'take in hand' literally, i.e. stand as personal surety or

maynpernour (= Lat. *manucaptor*) for a prisoner to be released on bail, who will be produced when required. See further 4.107, the figurative use at 18.281 and AlfG 93–4. **209b** This instance of internal rhyme has the effect of a performative utterance (here a 'doom') and marks a decisive moment. **Z 177** *For...Mede*: 'in spite of any request for clemency made by Mede [i.e. supported by the offer of money]'. **A**'s removal of this line (with its characteristic asseveration) makes sense, as the King has not yet met Mede, and the general point is made at Z 179. **210** *constable*: here 'an officer of the king's peace' (AlfG 35), a subordinate (*Bn*) of the Lord High Constable, who dealt with offences in or near the king's court. **211** *tyrauntes*: 'vicious rogues, villains' (again used at 22.60 of the 'fals fende Auntecrist'); it comes nearest to the Chaucerian political sense (*Legend of Good Women* F 374) at B 15.419. *tresor*: the first appearance since HC's last use of the word at 1.201 in answer to Will's question at 1.43, highlighting the fundamental antithesis between Truth and Falsehood in the widest sense being allegorically enacted. **216** *pylorye*: a device in which the offender stood with head secured; a standard punishment for breaching regulations of the purity and weight / quantity of bread and ale (see Benson 2004:228–36). Liar is here briefly associated with the peccant tradesmen to be mentioned at 3.80–3 for whom Mede will intercede with the mayor. **A 165–66 (Z 183–84)** A clear case of a revised **A** line omitted in **B** (perhaps as too mild after the preceding threats of death and imprisonment). The use of A 166 at C 248 is a unique instance of whole-line restoration, suggesting that **Z** lines might also have been re-used (see Z 189 // C 3.78).

(vi) 217–52 217 *Drede*: a fleeting personification of 'fear of earthly punishment', parallel to Wit's *drede of* [God's] *vengeaunce* at B 9.96. Dread is more positively viewed at A 10.80–4 as 'the beginning of goodness' (**L**'s figure, who appears briefly in *MS* 1262, may have suggested to Skelton the hapless hero of *The Bouge of Court*). *dene* (so **Z**; *doom* **AB**; see *TN*): a possible reference to the 'crying of names' of those summoned at the door of the royal council chamber (*Bn*, citing Baldwin 1913). **Z 188–9** (omitted in **A**), which anticipate B 207, lack **B**'s *And* 207, thus seeming to render the *dene* the King's angry series of commands. **C** makes 218a a parenthetical explanation of *dene* (otiose if **L** had retained *doom* in **C**). **219–20** *feres...fere...freres*: the wordplay hinting 'Platonically' at an affinity of the friars with False's cronies. *freres*: here first since Pr 58–65 singled out as exemplars of deceit, preparatory to their assuming that rôle in Vision Eight for sinners seeking 'easy penance' (22.285 will sharply recall 2.220). **222** *marchauntes*: found suspect later in Greed's confession and in the Pardon Scene, where they are guilty of swearing falsely to the quality of their wares (9.25–6) as Guile does here (with *shewen* 223 cf. *mostre* 6.260).

230 *cloutes*: less probably 'a child's small clothes' (*Bn*) than 'patched clothes' (MED s.v. 6 (a)), which Liar is put in to make him look like one of the common people (cf. Piers at B 6.59). **231** *senten hym*: i.e. as a pardoner, in appropriately humble attire (see on Pr 66ff). **232** *And*: elliptical for 'Where he / And there he' (see *MES* 142, 5(b)). **233–36** The *leches* and *spysours* (dealers in 'med'cinable gums') are naturally linked, as both seek Liar's services after noting his success as a fraudulent pardoner (the implications of *poundmele* 232). Physicians receive for their dishonest treatments brief criticisms at 8.290–6, digesting a longer attack in Z 7.255–78. **235** *aspye*: i.e. look carefully over (with the aim of carrying out some deception). The deliberate echo of *spysours* 'Platonically' intimates real affinities between the referents of homophonous lexemes. **237** *mynstrals*: this first reference since Pr 35–40 sitting better with the **C** and also **Z** forms of those lines than with the more positive **AB** view, which distinguishes these minstrels from 'japers' (see Schmidt 1987:5–11). *mesagers*: popularly associated with rumour and tell-tales (Chaucer's *Hous of Fame* [*HF*] 2128–129, and on the connection with 'meed', *PF* 228, cited *Bn*). But they are more favourably treated in **C**, which adds a long passage on them (13.32–91). **238** *half ȝere...dayes*: the exact length of Edward III's French campaign of 1359–60, from landing in France to signing the Treaty of Brétigny, 'a period when rumour was rampant' (*Bn*). **239** *freres*: the ones who ultimately succeed in getting Liar to join them, where his companion False already waits (220). **241** scans *abb / ab* as Type Ie on vowels with 'double counterpoint' on *l* (see Schmidt 1987:62-7). **242** ironically anticipates the Mendicants' claim about Dowel at 10.18–19. **243–48** break up the description of the rogues' dispersal, but enable Conscience to achieve the prominence he had by the end of **B**. Though clearly an addition in **C**, with Conscience's 'accusation' here echoing Pr 95 (also new), these lines conclude with one originally in **A** and before that in **Z** (see *TN* and on A 165–66 above). They represent Conscience's delayed response to Sothnesse's intelligence at 202 and explain why the canon lawyers are not frightened away with the rest of the villains but seek the intervention of the sovereign religious authority in the matter of Mede's marriage (against pending adverse judgement from the secular one). This evokes Conscience's warning against the danger that corrupt clerks pose to state and church, which reaches its climax in the solemn rhyme of 246–47 (cf. 75–6), followed by recovered A 166; and it may indirectly echo the hostility shown towards lawyers in the 1381 Rising. **Z 214b–15** The presence of Fauel before the council is incompatible with Z 3.1 and will accordingly have been removed in revision to **A** (*R–B*).

Passus III

PASSUS THREE is the thematic centre of gravity of the First Vision. Nearly twice its length in **A** and half as long again as in **B**, it is the longest passus in **C** (double those that precede and follow) and falls into three main parts. First a *prelude* (1–67) shows LADY MEDE at her work of corruption and making her insincere confession to a friar. There follow (i) an authorial digression on civic evils (68–126), and Mede's defiant offer to the mayor. The climax is her allegorical 'Trial' before the King (127–499), in five sections: (ii) a preliminary dialogue (129–54); three long speeches giving (iii) Conscience's 'case' for rejecting Mede as bride (155–214), (iv) her response (220–82) of similar length, and (v) Conscience's crushing dismissal of this (285–482), prompted by the King's finding in favour of Mede; as a conclusion (vi), her angry rejoinder and Conscience's sarcastic dismissal of her desperate appeal to scriptural authority (483–99). Despite the encounter's practical purpose (if Mede may not marry False, can she marry Conscience?) and its impassioned tone (reflecting the antipathy between the two principles of truth and falsehood the antagonists embody), the handling owes less to legal than to scholastic debate. This is evident in Conscience's recourse to a formal *distinctio* (285–406) between the concepts of *mede* and *mercede* (amusingly broken by the king's request for clarification at 340–2) and his confutation of Mede's 'text' by proving it incomplete and quoted out of context.

PRELUDE **1–37** describe the reception of Lady Mede alone at Westminster. Although she is arrested (2.252) and suspected of crimes (3.8), the respectfulness shown when she is brought for interview ironically underlines her power and influence. **2** *bedeles*: minor civic officials, often ceremonial. *baylifs*: lesser officers of justice under the sheriff. **3** *clerke*: perhaps the clerk of the King's Council, if the meeting is meant to resemble a blend of a law-court and that body (*Pe*). Kennedy (2003:178) sees the setting as one of a 'nascent Court of Chancery', but an over-precise interpretation of the allegory is probably misplaced. *name*: either official or personal (cf. *CT* I 284). **5–9** The King will 'assay' Mede as 'a ward in Chancery who has got into bad company' (*Bn*). The problem she anticipates is his refusal to let her 'wed at her will' (19) someone the King might disapprove of. **7** *wys men*: later identified as Reason and Conscience. **C**'s replacement of *my wit and my wil* suggests a more cautious assumption about the King's own understanding and inclination. **11** *boure* (*chambre* **AB**): an antechamber where Mede waits for audience. **13** *That*: on non-expression of the antecedent see *MES* 190. *wendeth to* (*wonyeþ at* **ZAB**) *Westmynstre*: the **C** revision, echoing 2.174, stresses the suitors' venality as much as that of the judges 'residing' and the lawyers practising there. 'Westminster', so called from its nearness to the Benedictine Abbey, is metonymic for the royal law-courts held in the great Norman Hall of the palace, which was extended by Richard II about ten years after the date of the C-Text (Baker 1971:29; Harvey 1944:59, with ills. and plan). The scene is directly recapitulated at 22.131–3, where Couetyse overcomes 'the wit and wisdom of Westminster Hall'. **14** *the iustices somme*: 'a number of the judges' (MED s.v. *som* adj. 2 (a); cf. *monye* **Z**). Judges are ill spoken-of throughout *PP* (2.150, 3.192, 22.134, B 7.44, Z Pr 70). **15** *Boskede*; *buyrde*: words from the standard alliterative lexicon (cf. *WPal* 1862–3) that **L** normally avoids, evoking ironically a courtly milieu appropriate for one like Mede. **16** *as they couthe*: 'as they well knew how to'. *clerkes*: if sg. and referring to the person at 3, this softens the insistence in **B** // that corrupt Law and Church go hand in hand. **21** *mercyede*: a very rare word perhaps punning on a sense 'bribe, reward'; MED s.v. *mercien* v. (1) aptly illustrates from Audelay (*Poems* 36/718: *Þay mercyn hem with mone and med preuely*), recalling this line. **22** *Of here*: 'for their'. **23** *Coupes*: alluding indirectly to the *poculum aureum* held by the Whore of Babylon in Apoc 17:4 (and see on 2.9–16). *clene*: 'pure', 'unalloyed' (cf. 4.91), but contextually ironic, since in Apoc 'full of uncleanness'. For this cup as a symbol of greed, cf. *De Mundi Cupiditate* 7–18 (Map, 167): 'Calix quem Babylon in manu bajulat est *avaritia* quae passim pullulat.' **24** *rubees*: the red, most precious 'oriental' variety that Mede herself wears at 2.13. *ȝeftes*: revision replacing the pararhyming wordplay on *manye* / *meynee* of **B** // with tartly euphemistic semantic punning (='bribes'; see *IG* for other examples). **25** *here mayne*: 'their retinue', but hers also, in the sense that Mede buys support by bribing servants and masters alike. *motoun of gold*: the *mouton d'or*, a gold coin stamped with the image of the Lamb of God, worth five silver shillings. **29b** A rare example of three-stage revision from **Z** → **C**. **32** *prouendres*: here the stipend of a canon-prebendary, but perhaps punning on the sense 'food for horses' (with a glance at the animal-allegory in 2.183ff). **33** *benefices*: 'bought' not directly but by such means as 'permutation' (see 2.185). *pluralite*: here with negative overtones (by contrast with its positive use at A 11.200). **34** *consistorie*: the court for hearing more serious and (for canon lawyers) lucrative cases, e.g. involving divorce or separation, usually before the bishop's legal officer (2.190–1; 16.362). Mede promises advancement to poorly qualified clerks if they can pay bribes for the privilege of being called to plead (cf. 'A satyre on the consistory courts' in Wright: 1839:155–9 and Alan of Lille: 'Modo non queritur quid sit in mentis armario, sed quid sit in aerario. Qui sunt qui assistunt palatiis regum? pecuniosi. Qui sunt qui excluduntur ab aula? litterati. Jam honoratur familia cresi, contemnitur familia

Christi' (*PL* 210:181); and see Swanson 1989:160–66; Wunderli 1981, Brundage 1987:409–10). **37** *clokke*: found only here. If the **Z** reading shows confusion of *e* for *o*, the word is the same and the sense 'limp, hobble'.

38–67 describe *Mede's confession.* **38** *confessour*: apart from the king's confessors (who were often themselves friars), the three who actually appear (cf. B 11.70, 22.372) are all friars, and all venal. Criticism of the corruption of mendicant confessors in the period is common, *CT* I 218–32, III 2089ff being only the best known examples. **43** *Consience*: an abstract idea, not inevitably to be regarded as personified at this point in **AB** but in **C** more convincingly so, since he has already appeared at Pr 95. **46** A possible T-type line, with the caudal *l* alliteration supplementing the allophonic alliteration on *sh / s* (cf. B Pr 34). **47** *noble*: an English coin (so named because made of gold), with half and quarter, introduced in 1344 and worth £1/3 (see Poole I:292–3, pl. 34 e–g). This most valuable single unit of specie is mentioned usually in contexts of illicit or morally dubious payment (see *IG*). **49** The re-use here of B 42 has the effect of repetition-with-variation, amplifying and focussing the thought; but removal of explicit *brocour / baud* (after running together B 41, 46) leaves ironic *bedman* to carry the full weight of the critique. **51** *ful heye*: with pun on the dimensions of the window and its cost. **52** *gable*: the triangular-topped end wall of the nave or of the aisle of the friary church. The Austin Friars' church in London had been rebuilt with large Curvilinear aisle-windows by Humfrey de Bohun in 1354, perhaps a decade before **A**; but this description may allude to the London Greyfriars church near Newgate, since the only religious order **L** ever names is the Franciscans (10.9). In the last quarter of the 14th c. a gable-window would be in the new Perpendicular style that extended the size and glass-area of the window-space. The passage seems echoed in *CT* III 2099–2106 and is imitated in *PPCr* 118–29, 162, 175–9. **53–4** promise daily commemoration of Mede's benefaction. *For Mede*: perhaps with a pun (*Pe*), obscured by modern capitalisation. *ordre*: a grander recognition than *house* **B**, because going beyond the confines of the building contributed to. Mede will be enrolled a member of his community by letters of fraternity entitling her to special privileges and benefits, and treated as an honorary nun, though the 'sin' she seeks 'release' from is lechery (cf. later 12.4–10 and 22.365–8). **57** *lordes...ladies*: that *luxuria* 'lust of the flesh' was a vice peculiarly incident to the higher classes is a point repeated at 16.90–3, 22.312. When the sin gets a more extended treatment in 6.170–95, the speaker is a lustful old man somewhat like Januarie in Chaucer's *Merchant's Tale*. **58** *this*: a common use of the demonstrative in 'generic', quasi-definite (or zero) function (*MES* 174). **59** *bokes*: a vague allusion suggesting some indistinct authority; but the notion that

Commentary

sexual sin was less serious because arising out of a natural impulse (i.e. to procreate) might be associated with such influential writings as Jean de Meun's continuation of the *RR*. **62** *seuene*: the seven deadly or mortal sins that destroy sanctifying grace in the soul. This was a common topic in prose and verse writings prompted by the Fourth Lateran Council's prescription (1215) of yearly confession, which made examination of conscience and understanding of the categories and sub-divisions of sin obligatory. Stemming from the early C13 penitential treatises of Raymund of Pennaforte and Peraldus, and the late C13th *Somme le Roy* of Frère Lorens, the main examples in English are the *Ayenbite of Inwit, Handlyng Synne, The Book of Vices and Virtues* and (from the late 1390s) Chaucer's *Parson's Tale*. This last, the best contemporary commentary on **L**'s treatment of the theme and extensively cited in Passūs V–VII below, defines 'the chief and spring of alle othere synnes' in Augustinian terms simply as 'whan man loveth any creature moore than...oure Creatour' (*CT* X 388, 357). *none sonner*: a construction that understands a relative of comparison ('than which... [is])'. Mede's view of lechery as mitigated by its 'naturalness' is rejected by the severer contemporary moralists: 'fornicacioun...is deedly synne and *agayns nature*' (*CT* X 864); '[that] lecherie is kyndeli...siche veyn wordis þat excusen synne done myche harme among men' (*Select English Works of Wyclif*, II:76). But it would be mistaken to suppose (as does White 1988:92) that the Samaritan in 19.314 supports Mede's position in 59, though assuredly citing what spokesmen of 'oure wikked flessh' maintain (the distinction is properly explained by Tavormina 1995:194). **66** *peynten and purtrayen*: have her picture as donor included in the window-glass. Examples from this period are the figures of a gentlewoman in the N nave window at Waterperry, Oxon, the knights of the Clare and Despenser families depicted at Tewkesbury Abbey, and Sir James Berners, from West Horseley, Surrey (Baker 1978: pls. 45; 27, 31; 40).

(i) 68–74a 68 *defendeth*: inferred from the text cited at 74a. **69** *writen...dedes*: not that such deeds are *described* in the glass, but as the making of the window is such a deed, the naming (and, even more, depiction) of the donor such a 'writing'. **72** *ho þe catel ouhte*: here *Pe*'s '"to whom the money that is spent properly belongs", viz. the poor' reads too much into the text's statement that God knows who paid for the window and how much it cost. Whereas **B**'s *þi* makes clear that God also perceives the donor's 'greed' [to be honoured as a pious benefactor], this is less clear in **C**, where the referent of *here* is the greedy friars. If **L** has no Lollard-like 'objection to beautifying churches' (*Pe*), he presumably had none to donors' giving for this purpose rather than 'giving to the poor and distributing alms', but only to their pride in wanting recognition. **74** *God*: **L**'s frequent way of refer-

ring to Christ as utterer of precepts with divine authority (cf. 1.46 above and contrast A 251 below). **74a** '[And when thou dost alms], let not thy left hand know what thy right hand doth' (Mt 6:3).

B 70–2 70 *wel-dedes*: i.e. in providing the windows. **71** *Goddes men*: here specifically the friars. **72** Echoing *mercedem suam* from Mt 6:5 (see 311 below).

77–114 The parenthetical / digressive **77–85 (89)**, 'never clearly related to the context in **AB**' (*Pe*), seem only loosely joined through linking of the *lordes* warned against *couetyse* at 72 with *suche as kepeth lawes* at 78, who are urged to punish commercial malpractices in the city arising from the same *couetyse*. The addition **90–114**, redolent of the 'London' character of many **C** additions (Pearsall 1997), has a free-standing quality and seems awkwardly inserted here (115–20 would fit more smoothly after 89).

77–89 77 *bysouhte*: taken as intransitive by *Pe*; but it has three direct objects in 78 and means 'entreated', though what Mede entreated them to *do* is deferred until the verb's repetition at 115, after the digression-parenthesis is completed. *mayr*: the senior civic official of a town, whose 'chief rôle was as a magistrate responsible for fair trade practices' (*Bn*; see Poole I 251–6 and fig. 56). **B 76** *maceres*: taken by *Bn* to denote merely attendants who preceded dignitaries, by Alf*G* in the light of **C** as 'sheriff, bailiff, or sergeant-at-mace' (see MED s.v. *sergeaunt* 2 (c)). But **L**'s usage is loose: only the mayors themselves could properly be 'intermediary' between the king and the civic community at large (as defined here and at 1.155 above). **78** re-works Z II 189, perhaps one of **L**'s 'repertory' lines (see Appendix III), not re-used in **A** or **B**. *seriauntes*: here the highly-paid and prestigious senior barristers (*servientes ad legem*) from whom the Common Law justices were selected (cf. Alf*G* s.v., *CT* I 309ff). **79** *To punischen*: a kind of 'predicative nominative' infinitive (*MES* 524–5) governing the three subjects in 78. *pilories*: see on 2.216. *pynyng-stoles*: likewise for punishment of breaches, esp. by women (see 5.131), of the assizes of bread and ale, by jeering, striking with rotten vegetables or ducking in the village pond. **82** *regraterye*: retail selling (esp. of victuals); legal but carefully regulated, and to be distinguished from the abuse of unlawful measure in 88–9. But **L** doubtless has in mind the practice of buying in rings from the wholesalers at depressed prices and re-selling dear at the expense of the poor purchaser, for which he has no good word (cf. 113). **85** *burgages*: tenements for rent, built in a 'row' (107) for several occupants (cf. the 'Rows' at Chester); then as now a major means of investing wealth from commercial profits. Their destruction by fire at 105 is seen as 'condign punishment'. **88** *þat...seled*: 'to the legal measure certified by the official seal' (see *Liber Albus* 233, 290; *English Gilds* 366–7; Lipson 1959:298–9).

90–114 This second major addition in **C**, 'on the suggestion of 121–6 [= B 93–6]' argues that the prayer of the poor may be answered by a vengeance of Biblical proportions that harms all alike, indicating 'the indivisibility of the community, in suffering as in true dealing' (*Pe*). The notion of indiscriminate divine *punishment* (paralleled in 11.62) may owe something to Lk 13:1–4; it finds its correlative in that of natural *benefits* extending to both just and unjust (21.435–6, commenting on Mt 5:45). **90–7** have been linked with John of Northampton's efforts in 1381–3 to reform the government of the City of London (Simpson 1993). **91** *thorw*[1–3]: the first and second denoting agency, the third, cause (as at 104). **93** *The whiche þat*: 'who'; a late, relatively rare construction (*MES* 199; also at 10.184). **95** *That*[1]: 'on those who'. *þat*: 'with the consequence that' (cf. *aftur* 103). **103** Cf. 11.62 below. **104** *breware*: see under gluttony at 6.225–33, where Coveitise's brewing wife Rose is a dishonest 'regrater' (cf. 82,113) and at 21.399ff. **105** *ybrent*: the construction fusing 'seen burgages burnt' and 'seen that...have been'. **106** *clemynge*: found only here in this sense (MED s.v. *clemen* v. 'stick'). **109** *for...siluer*: 'notwithstanding that money talks'; on the alliterative pattern cf. Pr 84. **111–14** *fre...freman...yfranchised*: all recorded here for the first time.

115–126 **118a** '[Take not away...my life with bloody men]: In whose hands are iniquities: their right hand is filled with gifts' (Ps 25:9–10), a text familiar from its use during the *Lavabo* prayer in the Introit of the Mass, contrasting 'innocence' (vs. 1; cf. 98) with 'vanity' (vs. 4); see further 287–9 below. **119** *for my loue*: 'for love of me', 'in order to have my favour'. **120** *aȝeyne þe lawe / reson*: effectively the same, the revision bringing out the semantic closeness of the two terms. That **L** sees 'reason' as the divine law within man and all human law as based upon reason is shown in Alf*G* s.v. *Resoun* and in Alford 1988[1]. **121** *Salamon þe sage*: Solomon, son of David, king of Israel from *c.* 970–930 BC. His reputation for the wise sayings that form the core of the Book of Proverbs led to his later being ascribed several of the other 'Wisdom' writings. **123a** '[For the congregation of the hypocrite is barren]: and fire shall devour their tabernacles, who love to take bribes'. The collocation of *munera* 'bribes' with *mede* 123 indirectly provides a Latin 'gloss' on the lady's name at 119 (cf. Schmidt 1987:91). Ascribing the Job quotation to the presumed author of all the sapiential writings was perhaps prompted by the similar sentiment in such texts as Prov 15:27 'Qui autem odit *munera* vivet'. **124** *lettred lordes*: presumably the rulers and judges of 122. **B 100** *yeresyeues*: gifts taken by a royal officer on entering office, and renewed on New Year's day, often as a cover for bribes to connive at the giver's malfeasance; here applied to civic and manorial officers.

127–499 The *'Trial' of Lady Mede*. **127–54** describe the King's *preliminary interview* with her, in which minatory finger-wagging at 139–44 does not wholly disguise his ambivalence (cf. *litel* 130). **128** *þat ladde here*: the official of 3 above, whom **L** was reluctant to name as the actual clerk to the king's council (*Pe*). The device may thus reveal more than it conceals, but like the Rat Fable has wider non-topical significance.

(ii) 129–54 **129–30** The criticism is sharp when read in the light of 207, where the indulgence of corruption must be impliedly in part the king's responsibility. **131–2** make clear the foreconceit of Mede as a royal 'ward' requiring the king's permission to 'wed'. Allegorically, this means that reward in the kingdom should be governed by the king's will operating under the rule of divine justice or *Treuthe*, whose ultimate referent here and at 139 will be 'God'. **140** *castel of Corf*: the dungeons at Corfe in SE Dorset, long of ill-repute (*Pe*, citing Pugh 1968:128); but 'forcible enclosure as an anchorite' somewhat lessens the seriousness of the king's threat. **144** *teche*: i.e. through the discipline of enclosure (dependent on *Y shal* 140; the king, not the women, will instruct Mede). **145** *Conscience*: his certain hostility to such a marriage has been foreshadowed in **C** by his attack on clerical avarice and deception advanced to Pr 95–127. Theology has already warned that Conscience is of Truth's council (2.152), while Conscience has informed the king of False's plan to marry Mede (2.202–3) and denounced corrupt clergy as a threat to order in the kingdom (2.245–8). The present plan for Mede's future, presumably discussed in the *conseyl* (127) at which Conscience was not present, presupposes (not wholly unreasonably) that the remedy for her wantonness lies in marrying her to an honest husband, allegorically that 'pecuniary reward is in effect neutral, becoming good if given to the virtuous.'

(iii) 155–219 Conscience's *diatribe against Mede*, most of it retained from **Z** through **B** but lengthened by a topical ten-line addition (203–12), contends in contrast that she is irreformable: allegorically, that 'all forms of "payment" other than strict retributive justice are tainted'. **151** *louted*: the words 'and asked' are implied in the action. **155b** echoes Mede's phrase at 147 with an ironic resonance of the *Kyrie* response. **159** echoes 1.66 to associate Conscience with HC's stance against Mede. *In...tresor*: qualifying *monye*. **162** *ȝoure fader*: at the time of **ZA**, when Edward III was reigning, this would have been understood as Edward II, and his gifts to favourites as a form of *mede*. By the time of **B**, the natural referent was the Black Prince, Richard II's father, and by **C** this would have seemed even more likely. In **B**, *false biheste* 127 might be meant to signify Edward II's wrongful promises (of advancement) to his favourites; those made to Edward's supplanters with the help of 'meed'; or (with a more contemporary resonance) the promise of Pedro of Castile to pay the Black Prince for helping him to recover his throne (see McKisack 1959:144), a reading perhaps supported by C 162b. But topically speaking, the line is a 'living fossil'; in Mede's reply at 220ff the only king envisaged is Edward III. **163** *apoisend popes*: on the historical level perhaps alluding to Benedict XI's alleged death by poison (1306); but figuratively, to Constantine's legendary 'Donation' endowing the Church with landed property (see on 17.220–4), an act held by many ecclesiastical moralists to have 'poisoned' its spiritual nature (*Sk*). **164–5** *baud...helle*: in the light of 166a perhaps 'harlot anywhere' (MED s.v. *baud* n. (b)); but some wordplay could be involved, since Mede is figuratively one who 'goes between' the Church and the devil ('heaven and hell'). **166** *tayl...talewys*: an annominative pun may be suspected, Mede's public words being as 'promiscuous' as her private parts. **167a** is proverbial, but with obvious play on 'common woman'. Though ostensibly 'lady' and 'maid' (capable of high and pure uses), Mede (as money) is really 'open' to all who want her. **168** *musels*: the implication being that Mede gives these diseases to others she lies with (leprosy in particular was believed to be venereally transmissible). **175–6** *Fals... Treuthe*: here not the Devil and God but 'collective personifications' of the unjust, like Mede's would-be groom, and the just, like Piers later, who at 7.199 is offered and refuses *mede*. **178–9** Users of *mede* care nothing about excommunication, because they can be sure either of bribing the responsible episcopal officials not to impose it or of getting absolution for the initial offence from a co-operative confessor. **181–2** A single operation by Mede will accomplish as much in a month as the king's most urgent commands in four months. **182–4** The king's personal seal went (for example) with a letter authorising a Chapter to proceed to an election, or a bishop to appoint to a royal benefice. It could be circumvented by a provisor who had established a prior claim through a papal licence obtained by payment (hence through 'Simony and herself'). Conscience is warning the king that his authority may be powerless against the influence of money. **188** *forbodene lawes*: an active use of the p.pl. explained as due to confusion with *forbode* n. (*MES* 571). **189a** 'They do not thrive, because their dams are drabs'; an added Leonine hexameter of unidentified origin. Although this refers to clerics' bastards, blaming only the women for the inherited bad qualities could be a reflex of **L**'s intermittent anti-feminism. **191** *the whiche*: a usage of native origin but influenced by OF *liquels* (*MES* 198–9); frequent in **C** and found earlier at B 10.475, etc (see *IG*) but absent from **ZA**. **193–4** The figure is of a straight path being blocked by heaps of coin. **193** *lyth*: 'lies (down)'; 'tells lies'. **194** *fayth*: here a collective personification of '(the cause of) honest people,' as with *treuthe* at 11.17, and perhaps to be capitalised like *Treuthe* at 176. *forth*:

'free course, way'; a substantival use probably introduced by **L**. It is overlooked by MED but recorded in OED (s.v. *forth* C. *sb.*), which cites only one later ME example (obviously recalling this one): 'These men of lawe...withdrawe them to...lette falshede haue his forth' (*Dives and Pauper* VIII.vii.320/1). **195** *leet*: contracted form (SW and S) of *ledeth*, but perhaps playing on the near-homophone *letteth* 'hinders' (cf. 193). **196** *loueday*: a day set aside by the manorial court for a meeting to settle a dispute amicably out of court; the meeting itself; or the reconciliation resulting from it (cf. 11.17 and see AlfG s.v.). Spargo 1940 holds that 'love' in the compound has the specialised legal sense 'licence or permission [of the court]', but J. W. Bennett 1958 sees the term as formed on the model of the older 'lawday' (used in revision of B 10.306 at 5.158). Surviving only as a proper name, it answers to Lat. *dies amoris* and AF *jour d'amour.* Lovedays often involved mediation by a priest, monk or friar (B 5.421, 10.306; *CT* I 258); but they had a bad reputation as occasions for bribery and intimidation (see the quotations from Wycliffite writings in MED s.v.), as the parallelism in 195 implies. *Leute*: see 2.20 and AlfG; here personifying 'the course of justice' and contrasted with *Lawe* 198 'the process of law'. **C** is conceptually more coherent than **B**, though syntactically less so, since the antecedent of *maʒe* is better if 'law' than if 'loveday'. **198** *lordlich*: 'haughty', with an ironical glance at lords' interference in the course of law. **200–14** add a dozen new lines with topical relevance. **200–01** *bonde*: a revision significantly eliminating the highest class and, with 201b reflecting a harsher view of the *comune* in the wake of the Peasants' Revolt, but also deploring the destructive effect of money-values on otherwise loyal (*trewe*) people. **202** A verb 'causes' is to be understood after *and.* **207** *Vnsittyng soffraunce*: unseemly tolerance, 'turning a blind eye' to wrong-doing, here personified as Mede's sister; repeated at 4.189, where it implies wrongful granting of privileges to individuals under the king's private seal. *SkP-T* xxxiv finds an allusion to Richard II's unpopularity in 1392 and cites his unsuccessful attempt to raise money from the London citizens; but the lines do not support so late a reference. **208** *Marye*: the king's plight being grave indeed to need so powerful an intercessor. **209** *no lond*: perhaps alluding to the fact that in 1385 Richard II was at war with Scotland, and in summer 1386 supported Gaunt's expedition to Spain and faced a great French host preparing at Sluys for what seemed imminent invasion. *thyn owene*: Parliament impeached Richard's Chancellor Michael de la Pole in autumn 1386 and established a continual council to govern for a year. *the; thyn*: the sg. for *Pe* showing 'familiar contempt'; but though a pl. to one person indicates polite respect (Mede's pl. to the king at 220), the sg. need not import the opposite (e.g. Kynde Wit's sg. at Pr 148–50, with which contrast Mede's sg. to

Conscience at 224). Conscience's tone here is of urgent, intimate admonition and entreaty. **210** *knet*: cf. B 15.242; revising *coupleþ* B 165, it implies the same 'wedding' metaphor. **211** echoes B 19.458–9. **214** *maister*: referring to Mede's sway over the rich, but with a pun on the sense 'teacher' (cf. *lereth* 212). Cf. the Vernon Lyric 'Mercy Passes All Things' in Brown 1957, no. 95, ll. 249–50: 'Who is a maister now but meede / And pruide þat wakned al vr wo'. **215–19** The 'head of law' must allow the accused to 'excuse', displaying here the impartiality of the king in *WW* 218–20.

(iv) 220–82 contain *Mede's response*, not only a self-defence but an attack on her accuser. **220–44 221** *in whom*: the dependent personal relative in place of impersonal *wher* forcing a direct choice between the two disputants. **223** Mede gives no specific reference, but presumably understands the monetary settlement accompanying the Treaty of Brétigny. **224** 'Nor to offer you personal insults in a posture of stiff intransigence'. Alf*G* finds legal resonances in *deprauen* (as in *famen* 231), and the presence of these allegorical characters to state their case has analogies with a court trial *coram rege*. But as personifying opposed principles, their closest predecessors are Winner and Waster. **229a** 'I [now] can, as I [then] could'. **232** *kulde...kyng*: presumably alluding to the murder of Edward II, an act 'counselled' by opponents Mede opportunistically identifies as Conscience's followers. **233–55 (B 186–200)** Mede's reply expands a more historically explicit **B** passage unchanged from **ZA**, but still argues that persistence would have won a victory against France, and great wealth. The anti-war policy she attributes to Conscience as 'cowardly' (B 206) is now 'unwise' (243, 262 indirectly answering the king's *vnwittiliche* at 133) and also 'unjust' (244–9), since the king's followers deserved a share in the spoils. Mede's notion of a conqueror will be ironically echoed by Conscience's in 21.30–3, only to be contradicted by its re-interpretation at 21.50–62 in application to Christ. **233** *sixty thousand*: an 'indefinite large number', as at B 17.23. If Mede means the lives of men rescued by 'bought truces and ransoms' (*Pe*), her argument is fallacious, since peace with France would have saved even more. **239–40** *fortune*; *wyrdus*: an adroit conjunction of two (often contrasted) notions, making it seem that in rejecting a chance-presented opportunity the king defied his God-given destiny. **242** *heritage*: the basis of the campaign being Edward's claim to the French throne through the female line in 1337 (although he had already paid homage to Philip of Valois in 1329). Since even those who favoured peace would have seemed disloyal to question the claim's validity, in his reply Conscience does not. **243** *sulle*: in the Treaty of Brétigny of 8 May 1360, whereby Edward abandoned his claim to France in return for the cession of Aquitaine, Calais and Guisnes, and agreed to send back the captured

French king John for a huge ransom (Keen 1973:139–42). **244** *ducherie*: a sovereign duchy. Throughout the war, the English refused to acknowledge French suzerainty over the duchy of Aquitaine.

B 189–200 (A 176–87, Z 127–38) 189 'In Normandy it was not on my account that he suffered trouble'; by alluding to the campaign of 1359–60 Mede blames the King's 'conscience' (moral scruple) for his decision to end the war. **191–3** *cold...cloude*: the hailstorm and cold of 'Black Monday' (14 Apr. 1360) that contributed to Edward's decision to quit France. **195–6** Mede's claim that the pillaging suffered by the French people (whose pots and pans the English soldiers carried off) was due to the abandonment of the campaign gets a new 'spin' in **C 239–40**, which turn a recognition that the campaign was faltering (**B**) into a bold assertion that it was succeeding. *Caleis*: the port of embarkation, held by the English, and doubtless full of dealers ready to buy the utensils cheaply (and sell them back to the French at a profit).

245–84 245–56 provide a stronger and more detailed argument for persisting with the war than do the preceding versions. Since Mede claims that those who fought for the king expected to share in the spoils of victory, she plainly sees the motive of a foreign war as gain (little has changed). Though referring to events of the 1360s, this passage written in the late 1380s may reflect disillusionment in England, after military defeats in Aquitaine during the previous decade, about the failure of the war to bring any long-term economic benefit or political security (see on 209). **247** *ladde*: even more extravagant than *brol* (retained from **B** at 261), where only the king's kin are envisaged. **249** *as a man*: 'as befits a man [of consequence]'; on this 'normative' use of *man* cf. 267 and *manhode* at 230. **251b–52** 'or else make [his men] grants of everything they can win, so that they might gain best advantage from it'. A conqueror should reward his followers himself, or leave them to acquire their own spoils from the conquered. **254** *coueiteth*: an audacious pun; cf. Conscience's 'benign' wordplay at B 164. **255–6** *constable*: in this context not 'chief officer of a ruler's household or court' (MED s.v. 2 (b), citing the line, and Alf*G* s.v.) but 'a high (or the chief) military officer of a ruler' (MED s.v. 4, with apt quotation from *The Siege of Jerusalem* 881–2: 'To þe kyng wer called *constables* þanne,/ *Marchals*...men þat he to tristiþ', and see *Sk*'s note *ad loc*, McKisack p. 265, Alf*G* s.v. *Marshal*). *marschal*: the king's commander-in-chief in the field, a term parallel in sense-development with *constable* (see OED svv.). Since Mede says that she would not entrust the (closely similar) duties of these officers to Conscience 'there [she] moste fyhte', a comma after *men* 256 would probably make this clearer. **262** *Vnconnynglich*: cf. 243; for 'cowardly' (B 206) see 241. **263** *a litel moné (siluer)*: actually three million crowns (in *gold*), never paid in full by the French.

A 196–276 form *this version's first major addition* and replace the vivid but conceptually somewhat uncertain 147–76 that conclude Passus III in **Z**. **266** *aliens*: in context perhaps referring to foreign mercenaries in the king's army. **269** *ȝerne...ryde*: i.e. on their service. **277** Internal rhyme here (and at 280–1 below) illustrates Mede's seductive rhetorical uses of *repetitio* (e.g. *mede* a dozen times; and compare also 275, 284 with B 220, 259). **279** *mede...prentis*: 'payment for training their apprentices' (on the sums paid, cf. Lipson 1959:414–16). The play of sound in *crafty...crauen, leueth...loueth* at 281 and the fourfold internal rhyme in 280–1 hint at a real ('Platonic') and not merely accidental affinity between the concepts of 'skill' and 'life' and that of 'meed'. **281–2** *mede...hire*: personified (cf. B 250) and better treated like B 227, where capitalisation formally recognises the word-play. **284** *me thynketh*: the repetition turning a Type III to a Type I line, while weakening (?intentionally) the King's assertion. *maistrye*: since she has won the debate, and deserves to rule.

(v) 285–482 *Conscience's rejoinder*, in **B** over twice and in **C** over three times as long as Mede's speech, decisively refutes her argument, supporting impassioned rhetoric with a quasi-scholastic structure.

B 230–58 separate two senses of the one word *mede* and propound a formal *distinctio* between 'reward' as God's proper recompense to those who 'work well' (= live a life of virtue) and the improper or 'unmeasured' reward the unjust give to wrong-doers, whom God will finally punish. This is supported by a bipartite scriptural *auctoritas* in the form of a question (234*a*) answered by another text (237*a*). Conscience does not rebut Mede's case point by point but answers 223–4 in 252–4*a*, 217–8 in 255–6 and 226 in 257–8 (on these lines see generally Alf*Q* p. 5, comparing the passage to B 7.40–51*a*). **234** *Prophete*: a Christian title for King David, the traditional author of the psalms (see Ac 2:25–35, esp. 30), based on his foretelling of the Messiah in Pss 15:8–11, 109:1, 131:11. **234*a*; 237*a*** 'Lord, who shall dwell in thy tabernacle? [Or who shall rest in thy holy hill?] He that walketh without blemish, and worketh justice' (Ps 14:1–2). **238** *of o colour...wille*: '[with his baptismal garment of innocence] spotlessly white [*sine macula* 'without blemish'], without hypocrisy or duplicity'. Alf*Q*, 6n highlights the phrase's legal connotations, citing the Latin vss in *CA* Pr ii: *Legibus vnicolor tunc temporis aura refulsit, / Iusticie plane tuncque fuere vie* ('Climate of law unclouded shone, / The paths of justice smoothly ran'); but it also has Biblical overtones (see Lev 19:19). **241** *enformeþ*: 'advises, gives [legal] counsel to' (Alf*Q* 7n10; MED s.v. 2). *truþe*: here and at 243 = 'justice' in a legal sense. **241*a*** 'He that hath not put out his money to usury, nor taken bribes against the innocent' (Ps 14:5, the *salmes ende*). The first two texts are translated after being quoted, the third before.

246–7 'A second meed, one without proper limits' (with *mesurelees* contrast *mesurable* 256). *desireþ...take*: the *maistres* craving and accepting such meed for wrongful 'maintenance'; but *take* may play on its antonym 'give' (the sense at C 3.350). **252** *plesynge*: 'a gift or offering (that will give them) pleasure', [rather than 'a sacrificial offering pleasing to God']; see MED s.v. (c), (a). **254** *hire...here*: the annominative wordplay underlining the semantic pun on *mede*: 'they get on earth the only enjoyable reward they will ever get'. **254*a*** 'Amen, [I say to you], they have received their reward' (Mt 6:5); Christ's condemnation of religious hypocrisy effectively applied to clerical greed.

285–313 285 *Nay...sothe*: translating a scholastic formula of denial (*nego*), adducing support from an authoritative Biblical text, and following it as in **B** with a *distinctio* introduced with *Ac* as an equivalent to the scholastic *sed contra* formula. **287–9** loosely paraphrase Ps 25:10 (B 249), quoted at 118*a* above and B 249 below. The 'large' or liberal-handed have 'gifts' in their right hands that they have won 'unlawfully' (= *iniquitatibus*) with their left. For a very full discussion of this passage see Adams 1988:217–32. **290–302** tactically define *mede* as 'payment in advance of work done', implying that such payment is neither wise nor just. **290** *mercede*: the King's objection at 342 that 'English was it never' holds for this word too, apparently coined by **L** from Latin *mercedem* and found only here, at 304, 332 and as a scribal variant in the **B** ms Cot at 20.76 (see *TN*). **293–5** The syntax is anacoluthic: 'It is neither reasonable nor just that (*That* 294)...nor that (*And for to* 295)...' **296–7** *Pe*'s explanation, that 'a man should be prepared to work even if he has no certainty that his employer will survive to pay him his proper reward' is mistaken: the referent of *he* 296 is the *he* of 294. What is 'against right and reason' (on the legal resonances of which, see Alf*G* s.v.) is for the workman to take or demand payment 'before the doing', when *he* may not survive to finish the job. **299** *pre manibus*: 'in advance' [= *avaunt la main*], a term 'often associated with usurious or unethical agreements' (Alf*G*); also at 9.45, and showing **C**'s heightened interest in legal practice. **300** *Harlotes*: the collocation with *hoores* may suggest one who either frequents or employs the latter, and a specific contextual sense 'bawds' or 'pimps'. **307*a*** 'The wages of him that hath been hired by thee shall not abide with thee until the morning' (Lev 19:13); 'a commonplace in canon law' (Alf*Q*, citing Brinton 2:364), alluded to by Piers at 7.195. **308** *reue*: the one who would pay the workmen their wages. **311** An unusual macaronic T-type line; see on B 254*a* above. **313** *permutacioun....peneworth*: presupposing not 'exactly equal exchange value' but a 'just price' for goods that takes proper account of the labour that went to producing them.

314–406 distinguish ingeniously (in some 90 added lines) between two *terms*, the familar *mede* and the newly-coined *mercede*. **C** grounds its distinction, more elaborate than **B**'s, in the nature of language, with grammar understood as an analogically ordered system reflecting the *ratio* or proportional relation between the human and the divine. But **C**'s conceptual procedure derives directly from **B**'s unmediated notion of a correct and incorrect *ratio* 'relacioun' between deed and desert. On the complexities and difficulties in this passage see Overstreet 1984.

314–31 321 *hardy to claymen*: elliptical for 'are to be so audacious as to claim'; cf. 13.9. **323** *Solomon*: although the prior warning was to the *lege* (316), this one seems addressed to the King (and indeed no heir of Richard was to be king of England). But perhaps **L** is alluding to Richard's youthful household counsellors (Keen 1973:276) and suggesting a parallel between the king and Solomon's son Roboam, who 'left the counsel of the old men...and consulted with the young men that had been brought up with him and stood before him' (III Kgs 12:8). *grace*: favour (as at 330) and not, despite the context, 'grace' in the theological sense. **326** *refte...mynde*: not strictly accurate, since Solomon's kingdom was lost only by his heirs. Nor does *ryhte mynde* here literally denote sanity (as claimed by MED s.v. *right* a. 6 (a), citing this line) so much as moral righteousness (cf. *ryhte* 324). However, when III Kgs 11:9 states that *aversa esset mens eius a Domino*, the 'turning away' is a religious one, and Solomon's rejection of moral wisdom may be meant to signify a metaphorical descent into unreason. **327** *mysbileue...leue*: the semantic pun pointedly implying that the speaker's belief *is* true. *helle*: because '[he] follow[ed] strange gods' (III Kgs 11:2); *Pe* notes contemporary 'uncertainty' about this because the idolatry has no mention in the parallel (later) account in II Para 9. But Will's words at 11.221 suggest no uncertainty, though Ymaginatif at 14.192 in urging prayer for Solomon's salvation will appeal to the absence of any *scripture* specifying his fate, and to the immensity of God's mercy. **328–9** *So... so*: both words carrying stress and playing on the senses 'therefore', 'in this way'. *si...glose*: 'without an implicit condition [that the recipient remain faithful to God]'. *Pe* aptly cites God's conditional offer of *grace* to Solomon: '*si* ambulaveris coram me...suscitabo thronum regni tui... *Si* autem aversi fueritis,...evellam vos de terra mea...' (II Para 7:17–19; cf. III Kgs 11:9 at 326). **332–406** propose an extended *distinctio* between *mede* and *mercede* by means of an analogy from grammatical relations, but initially define them simply as kinds of 'relation'. Of these *mercede* (the *second* 'relation' mentioned) denotes the direct or straight (*rect*) kind and *mede* the indirect. MED records *rect* as unique to **L** but illustrates only a grammatical sense that would necessitate translating *As* 335 (on which see *TN*) 'inasmuch as', thus deriving the moral 'ought' from the grammatical 'is' (value from fact). But the elaborateness of the analogy should not obscure the major ethical sense 'morally correct or upright' of *rect* at 366, which both OED and MED overlook and AlfG (despite recognising its cross-reference to *right*) leaves unsubstantiated. The basic *grammatical* sense of 'direct' applies to the nominative case, 'unbent' or uninflected, as opposed to the indirect or oblique cases, 'bent at an angle, inflected'. But while the argument illustrates an ethical *relacioun* that may be direct or indirect, this is conceptually prior to the analogy from grammar, in which the direct / indirect categories concern the relationships of nouns to their dependent adjectives. *Pe* explains that *mercede* (direct or proper reward) 'reflects the concord between God and man', whereas with *mede* 'the relationship is "indirect" and confused', though he concedes that since 'indirect relation' in grammar is not actually *incorrect*, 'some degree of propriety' is preserved for *mede*. But while the 'indirect relation' in grammar may not be confused, Conscience's analogy may (unintentionally) confuse, since in stipulating that a wage is *mercede* and payment for goods is 'exchange', he wants to exclude Mede from *any* rôle in human affairs. However, the coherence of the argument is ably defended with illuminating reference to the background of grammatical theory by Carlson 1991; and for a subtle analysis of the passage in terms of philosophical realism see Smith 1994.

333–42 333–4 The syntax is ambiguous, but *rect* must in this context apply to the nearer, *indirect* to the remoter antecedent. *reninde...hemsuluen*: rendered by *Sk* 'in a settled and secure (or regular) manner, agreeing with themselves (according to rule)', more closely by *Pe* as 'dependent on a firm and sure (concept of relation), in which both have a part' (the N form *reninde* is unusual in **L**). The metaphor of 'running on' suggests something like carriage-wheels over a road; but the notion of a 'basis' implied in *sikir* (cf. *fundement* 344) is not the relation itself (of *mede* and *mercede*) or its concept, but the condition that makes the relation possible and also 'resembles' it, in the way that adjective and noun achieve 'unity' and 'agreement' in the grammatical sphere. MED glosses *semblable* 3(c) as 'concordant', but with this example only, and presupposes a special 'grammatical' sense before the analogy from grammatical concord has been introduced. Under sense 2 'identical (in character) with', its illustrations cite the word with *wise*, *cas* and *manere*, but not with *relacion*. More naturally, it should therefore mean '(closely) similar to' (sense 1). Of the five other occurrences, the nearest to this (16.112), which states that poverty *is syb to Crist sulue and* semblable *bothe*, supports the latter reading. **337** *ayther...hem*: in grammar, the referents here are noun and adjective, which 'help' each other when they accord; but in the moral and religious sphere, they are the human will and the divine law which (when agreeing) generate the *retribucioun* 'reward' of final grace and heavenly happiness (cf. Carlson 1991). **339a** 'Be pleased, O Lord [for Thy name's sake] to grant eternal life to all of us who do good'; found in an early grace before meals (*Babees Book*, 382–5). The relevance of such a prayer here is to underline the 'habitual' character of Christian *lyuynge* (cf. 15.265). **340–2** Though the distinction between the two relations and the analogy that elucidates it is clear, the King not unreasonably wants this clerkly notion expounded in the vernacular (recalling Haukyn's request to Pacience at B 14.277).

343–61 343 *Relacioun*; *record*: the sense of 'a written account of legal proceedings kept as conclusive evidence' (MED s.v. *recorde* n. 5a) is worth noting as it reinforces the legal sense of *relacioun* 'the action of relating or narrating (an account....etc)' (AlfG 130) and 'reminds us of the historical basis of Christianity and the duty of the Christian to bear witness to it' (Martin in Vaughan 1993:173). **343a** 'Because it recalls a thing preceding it / its antecedent'. The formula explains the grammatical relation of a relative pronoun to its antecedent, as in Peter of Spain's 'Relativum *est ante latae rei recordativum*, quia...*relatio* est ante late rei recordatio' (Amassian and Sadowsky 1971:466). Such a fanciful etymology of *relatio* may have suggested use of grammatical analogy to explain a moral and spiritual *relacioun* (though Carlson 1991 throws light on the wider theological significance of Latin grammar in late medieval thought). A somewhat similar metaphor is found in a text by Henry de Harkeley in Lambeth Palace Library MS 61, ff. 143–147v (Kemp 1981:353–4). **344–5** 'Following (the course) and reaching down to the base of a stronghold, And (able) firmly (to) rise / ?project in order to strengthen the foundation (walls)'. The exact sense is uncertain, but 'direct relation' is envisaged as like foundation-course and buttresses that help support the walls (which themselves reach down to the base). Grammatical concord is imagined to 'strengthen' a linguistic, as a buttress strengthens a masonry structure. The rhetorical inversion of *fundement* and *strenghe* and the noun-verb conversion of the latter are noteworthy. **346** *In*: 'In respect of.' **347–50** *As...*: a second analogy to illustrate 'direct relation', which leads back ingeniously to the prior analogy from grammar. **347** *byleueth*: '(who) resides'. **348** *puyr treuthe*: 'absolute(ly) guaranteed) uprightness (in dealing with him)'. **349–50** describe the attributes of the perfect earthly master, which are modelled on those of the heavenly master. **351** *hol herte*: a sincere heart (*cor integrum*) with faith, from which arises the second theological virtue, hope (cf. its re-appearance at 7.257 as the place where charity will make its home). **351–3** *Pe*'s explanation can hardly be bettered: 'Man is here the adjective seeking direct relation, or concord, with the substantive [God], out of which

concord will come salvation...God is...antecedent, since all ...true concord depends upon him; yet...self-sufficient and...not conditioned by the relationship'. As *Pe* goes on to say, **L** refers indiscriminately to the noun / adj., antecedent / relative pronoun relation, two of the four types of grammatical relation (the others being subject / verb, partitive or superlative / genitive). *relacioun...sauacioun*: the rhyme (*concordantia sonuum*), which can hardly be accidental (see Appendix I § 5 ii), aurally echoes the grammatical agreement of adjective and noun. **352** *Seketh*: '(that) seeks'. *sustantif*: as here punctuated, a noun, the reading preferred because this is what 'God' must be in the metaphor as a whole. But there may be an elaborate clerkly pun, if it is also an adjective, as in MED s.v. *substantif* adj. (c), since God must also be man's 'substantive salvation'. **353** *ground of al*: the divine substance as the basis of reality, echoing Anima's exposition at B 15.371 of grammar as 'ground of all (learning)'. As *prima substantia*, God is metaphysically 'antecedent' to all created being, which may be said to relate to him 'adjectivally' (attributively). **354** *rihte*: playing on the two senses of *rect*, 'direct' and 'right(eous)'. **355–9** The influence of the *crede* (359) on the metaphor's development is stressed in *Pe*'s 'Grammatical agreement...correspond[s] to concord with Christ' through belief in the Creed's key articles, such as the Incarnation: *Verbum caro factum est* 'And the Word was made flesh' (Jn 1:14); the Church: *Credere in ecclesia* 356 (*Sarum Missal* 592); the forgiveness of sins: *remissioun to haue* = *remissionem peccatorum*, already quoted at B 15.611; and life eternal: *lyue...withouten ende* = *vitam eternam* (12th clause of the Apostles' Creed). But while *Pe* (with MED s.v. *kinde* n. 14b., uniquely citing this line from before C15) correctly glosses *kynde* in context as = *gendre* '(grammatical) gender' (394), he overlooks its root sense of 'nature', on which **L** plays (divine *nature* becomes human flesh, but the nouns *verbum* and *caro* do not have the same *gender*). Also overlooked is the wordplay on *case* 356, referring to 'situation' (MED s.v. *cas* n. 19a *as against* 10, the grammatical sense) of the *trewe* man as a member of the Church, and on *nombre* 357. The last is obscure unless *rotye and aryse* does not refer to a *post-mortem* corruption (MED s.v. *roten* v. 1a) and resurrection but to the manifold post-baptismal sinning and repentance (ib. s.v. 2 (a)) of even 'þe saddest man on erthe' (10.49). AlfQ rightly links 355b with the eighth article of the Nicene Creed (*Missal* 591) *Et homo factus est* 'And was made man'; but he overlooks the specific relevance of the Johannine sentence (not identical with the credal clause), in which *Verbum* punningly affirms the divine *Word* as the ontological and grammatical 'substantive' to which humankind must 'adjectivally' accord.

362–72 362 *Indirect*: a relation improper in grammar because the adjective is made to pair promiscuously with plural and singular nouns of all genders (e.g. 'hi pueri et puellae sunt Angli'). **362–3** The sense and tone alike recall B 15.48–9. **365** *gode and nat gode*: some of the concords will be fortuitously correct, as some forms of 'meed' may be genuinely deserved; but the analogy is again confusing (see above), since Conscience has sharply distinguished *mercede* from *mede*. Perhaps *in which...nat gode* should be in brackets and the antecedent of *which* understood as *nombres* (with no semi-colon after) rather than *cache to and come to. and...wille*: 'and (yet) give them what neither of them (actually) wants'; i.e. the attempt to have it both ways results in having it neither way. **366–9** The strictly logical force of these two analogies from family relationships is dubious. Thus it may well be 'unreasonable' to reject one's father's surname while insisting on one's rights as his son, or to take a wife but refuse to accept her bad qualities with her good. Yet accepting a 'plurality of obligations' would seem to sit better with *rect* than with *indirect* relation, even if it is plain how promiscuous 'agreements' might lead to the incurring of such obligations. *Pe*'s comment that 'social contracts, like grammatical relations, are binding in all their parts' since 'the parties to the contract cannot pick and choose which parts they are prepared to observe' expresses the gist of the argument perhaps more connectedly than the wording of the text itself allows. **370–2** *indirect*: here defined as desire for a plurality of benefits without acceptance of a plurality of obligations.

373–406 373–81 define a threefold reciprocal relation of king and community by *relacioun rect* corresponding to the triple categories of grammar. **375** abruptly shifts viewpoint in the b-half to accommodate the alliteration: but these are all things the king requires the *comune* to do for him. **377–8** The three terms cover the ruler's duty: to preserve customary law, adminster it with equity and keep the good of his people in mind. **378** *Lawe, loue and lewete*: 'agreement' of the *comune* with the king (adjectival 'concord' with the noun antecedent) is made conditional on his offering them these. While the phrase recalls both B Pr 122 and C Pr 149 (cf. 17.126–31), a theological resonance is perhaps suggested by the collocation of *lewete* with love (= charity) and law (= faith). *lord antecedent*: cf. 353. **379** *heued*: the parallel with Christ (as head of the Church) reinforces the equation of royal with divine in *antecedent*, so that Conscience here seems to endorse the quasi-absolutist claims of the King-figure at B 19.475 to be *aller heed* 'head of all' as well as *heed of lawe* 473). **380–1** Constancy as well as impartiality in the king mirrors his divine model. **382–92** The attack on personal self-interest involves a play on the senses of *cas*: the *puyr indirect* are 'defective in respect of (grammatical) case' (386) and so careless of 'the outcome of a case [law-suit]' (388), as long as they gain personally. **387** *relatifs indirect*: relative pronouns that do not agree cor-

rectly with their antecedents (e.g. *vir qui [for cui] librum dedi* 'The man *who* I gave the book to'). **389** *peccunie*: from Lat through OF; first used by L. **391–2** *noumbre*; *acorde*: both perhaps playing on grammatical senses. Conscience's ideal outcome in a legal case is 'unity', a reconciliation of the parties to the dispute on the basis of reciprocal concession, not the outright victory of one (usually the wealthier) through ability to pay a lawyer or bribe a judge. **394–9** The three categories are exemplified in reverse order: *alle maner* = number; *o kynde* [unity of faith] = gender, and *soffre penaunce* = case. **395** re-uses A 11.306 with change only of the last lift. **395–6** have running alliteration and a 'wrenched' stress on *wymmén*. **400** 'For love of that Lord who died for love of us'. **401** *kynde*: a polysemantic pun on 'nature' and 'gender'. **401a** echoes the Athanasian Creed's 'Ita *Deus* et *homo* unus est Christus' (*Sarum Breviary* 2:484); the bare juxtaposition (elliptical for 'God (became) man') is later literally rendered by the compound *God-Man* at 12.115. **402** *noumbre*: 'company' and '(grammatical category of) number'. **402a** '[God is charity: and] he that abideth in charity abideth in God, and God in him' (I Jn 4:16; so also at B 5.487a (2), B 9.64a). **403–5a** 'And so humanity is, as it were, a noun that requires an adjective with three real inflexional endings; [for] God [who is] one is a Trinity: namely, Father, Son and Holy Spirit'. The formula recalls B 10.239–40a. **403** *man...mankynde...maner*: the pun revealing L's 'Platonic' supposition of a 'real' relation between word and referent reflected in the felicitous homophonic overlaps between individual verbal items. **404** *hic et hec homo*: 'this human being (whether male or female)'; *homo* being a noun of common gender, the demonstrative can be both masculine and feminine. **405** *trewe*: because of God's nature as Truth (cf. *trewe Trinite* 11.151) but also 'genuine', 'authentic'. *termisones*: adapted from OF *terminaison* and found only here. It refers to the three distinct aspects or 'cases' (acc., gen., dat. / abl. of e.g. *verus* 'true') whereby the three persons of the Trinity may be thought to 'qualify' the *human* 'substantive' (through creation, incarnation and indwelling presence). **405a** *nominatiuo*: literally 'in the nominative'. *Pe* finds a pun on *in nomine*, 'in the name of [the Father, etc]', the opening words of the blessing when making the sign of the cross; but in context it is likelier to be on 'namely'. The nominative is the case of the *subiectum* 'the [verbal] subject' / '[divine] substance' which is 'one' but trinally 'inflected' by the three Persons. The final pun is of a piece with L's manner throughout this remarkable passage.

407–35 407–8 *Regum...Absoloun*: C takes up the revision of B with an added example from II Kgs [= II Sam] 14–18, describing the tragic ambition of David's son. Absalom was killed while caught in the branches of an oak (18:14–15); but L deliberately suggests an execution by hanging, the fate to which desire for *mede* has brought many (in 408 *heo* rather than / as well as *How* bears stress). **408** *sethe*: 'then, next', i.e. in order of the argument, not of the Bible, the story of Saul and the *kyng* (Agag, king of the Amalekites) being in I Kgs [= I Sam] 15, which follows immediately after the Book of Ruth. *for mede*: Saul's sin was to obey the voice of the people, not God (ibid. vs. 24); but Conscience, perhaps on the basis of 15:19, interprets his retention of the spoils as greed (425 below). **410–11** See 1 Kgs 31:2–4. *sone*: presumably Jonathan, though all three of Saul's sons died (see 429). *his knaue*: David (I Kgs 16:17–23). *lambren*: the commonest form, a 'double plural' (like *children*) with both the OE *-ru* ending and standard *-en* by analogy (Mossé § 59). **412** *Regum*: for *Liber Regum* 'the Book of Kings'. **415** *for dedes of here eldres*: their hostility to the Israelites in the wilderness, for which God promised to destroy them (Ex 17:8–16). A 245 closely recalls A 2.51, which may have been removed in **B** for that reason. **420** *woman*: in the contextually restricted contrastive sense of 'unmarried woman' (not recorded in MED). A 251 *Crist*: a loose synonym for *God* occasioned by alliterative necessity, as at A 10.151, 156 (cf. *WPal* 3148); **B** and **C** avoid such imprecision. **423** *mede of money*: 'payment in cash' (cf. A 249 'millions in cash'). **426** *beste*: **C** closely follows I Kgs 15:15 in making this detailed revision. **427** improves in substance and style on B 275. **429** *sayde... deye*: interpreting God's 'rejection' of Saul and his refusal to 'spare' at I Kgs 15:26, 29 as a threat of shameful death. **432** *culorum*: (pronounced *clórum*) 'conclusion', **L**'s 'clerkly' formation from [*per omnia saecula sae*]*culorum* 'for ever and ever', the ending of solemn prayers like the Offertory at Mass. Here it signifies 'full implications' (cf. Alf*Q ad loc*, referring to the echo in *RRe* 72: 'And constrewe ich clause with the *culorum*'). These implications remain obscure, but the examples of Absalom and Saul might seem in different ways applicable to King Richard, one suggesting his martial inferiority to his grandfather Edward III and father the Black Prince, the other warning that he might lose throne, life and line through succumbing to Mede (434–5 were however already in **B**). **433** Cf. Pr 217–18.

436–82 *Conscience's prophetic lines*, much extended in **B**, are little changed in **C** (on the 'prophetic' character of *PP* generally and **L**'s relation with the Biblical prophets, particularly Isaiah, see Steinberg 1991). The Samuel-Saul-David motif having been present from **A**, no more immediately contemporary references can be securely conjectured, except that the **B** source of 457–66 presumably warned against renewal of the war with France in the summer of 1377 just after Edward III's death, which brought many calamitous defeats and setbacks (Keen 1973:257). More positively, the **B** expansion may be connected with the jubilee proclaimed in the the 50th and last year of Edward III's reign (Feb. 1377) and the widespread

hope of peace and prosperity in that of his successor Richard, David being 'the type of the ideal king' (*Pe*). But the prophecy, like that at 5.168–79=B 10.316–29, remains indeterminate as to time and is generally influenced by the 'messianic' model in Is 2:2–4 (*Bn*), to which Baldwin (1981[1]:20, 95n37) adds Jer 30:8–10, Amos 9:11–15 and interpretations of them in the *Glossa Ordinaria* (*PL* 114:44, 580). **437** echoes Pr 150 in understanding reason as the basis of justice and so as fitted to rule and order the state (Alf*G* s.v. *Resoun*; Alford in Kennedy *et al.* 1988:199–215). **438** At the time of **A** this would have been seen to refer to Edward III and his son the Black Prince, then in his thirties (Richard was not born till 1367). **440** *alle oure enemyes*: the topical referent of this revised last lift (if one is sought) being perhaps Spain, France and Scotland, which were all at war with England in the mid-1380s. **441** *o Cristene kyng*: an 'apocalyptic' touch, since England already had 'one' king, and there was little prospect of a single monarch ruling all Christendom. **445** *taketh*: 'takes (or gives) money'. *treuthe*: probably best capitalised (with referent 'God as Justice'). *transuerseth*: a solemn word, first instanced here. **446** *Lewete*: 'Justice', clearly distinguishable from the process of law itself. **447** *for*: 'in order to do' / '(because of being richly paid) for doing'; in an ideal society no money would be made out of law as a profession. *werie*: the form of this weak verb (like *maky* 452) is characteristically SW (Mossé, *HME* 79). **450** *letteth*: the subject is either 'evil' or 'Mede'. **451–2** express sentiments to be re-iterated by Reason at 4.144–5 as a real possibility if the king himself espouses *treuthe*. **451** *kynde loue*: a phrase suggesting the basis of society in a common bond of mutual human concern. **452** *maky...laborer*: 'force lawyers to work with their hands for a living'. **454** *and...glade*: semi-parenthetical in both texts, though *so* makes it clearer ('and as a result become glad'). **456** *Moises*: the great Lawgiver, appropriately associated with the reign of perfect justice expected with the coming of the Messiah (cf. 17.295–7). That some Jewish sages expected his return is asserted at 17.312. *þat...trewe*: elliptical in **C** for 'on account of the fact that...' **459** *smythye*: with passive sense after factitive *don*. **460a** '[And he shall judge the Gentiles and rebuke many people]: and they shall turn their swords into ploughshares and their spears into sickles' (Is 2:4a); a key Messianic prophecy read in the Office of the first week in Advent. **462** *speke of God*: i.e. as a preacher (unless these words anticipate a person like Piers Plowman). *spille no tyme*: revision to a positive injunction of **B**'s threat of self-destruction against the slothful. The prevention of the sin of sloth is envisaged later by Reason (5.127) and Wit (10.187) as a practical matter, not a millennial ideal. **463** *Placebo*: 'I will please [the Lord in the land of the living]' (Ps 114:9). *Dirige*: 'Direct my way, Lord, in thy sight' ('Dirige Domine Deus meus in conspectu tuo viam meam' [*Breviary* 2:273], based on Ps 5:9b). These words that begin the antiphons of the Office of the Dead at vespers and matins respectively were contained in the prayer-book called the 'primer' and will be cited by the Dreamer as among the 'lomes' he 'labours with' in his self-defence against the charge of idleness before Reason and Conscience (45–6). Bp. Brinton's ironic contrast of *placebo* with *dirige* (1:204) cited in AlfQ does not seem relevant here, since Conscience names both psalms to exhort the clergy to pray to God 'at all times', i.e. for those in the land of the living and of the dead alike. **464** *seuene psalmes*: nos. 6, 31, 37, 50 (the 'Miserere'), 101, 129 ('De profundis') and 142, called 'penitential' because specially concerned with sin and repentance. They could be said as a private devotion or on behalf of others, as Will states at 5.47–8. **B 311–12** *hunte*: '"hunt" only in a way pleasing to God [with prayer]'. *dyngen*: '"strike blows" [cf. B VI 141 for literal sense] only by "hammering away" at saying the psalms'. The phrase occurs in two alliterative pieces, the mid-C14th 'Papelard Priest' (ed. Smith 1951:44, Revard 2001) and the late C14th 'Choristers' Lament' (ed. Utley 1946, Holsinger 1999, Appendix). **467–75** prophesy an ideal state of affairs in which 'He that speaketh truth in his heart: who hath not used deceit in his tongue' (Ps 14:3) will preside as sole judge in a single court, and, in a realm wholly at peace with itself and its neighbours, no corruption in the law will hinder the operation of justice. **470–1** *recorde...most trewe acorden*: unclear in reference, but Baldwin takes Conscience's rejection of corrupt jury assises to signify preference for 'the autocratic process of "judgement by record", and not the normal processes of Common Law' (1981[1]:20, 95n36, citing *Stat. Realm* 15 Richard II c.2). **472** *Kynges court*: the Court of King's Bench (originally sitting under the king), the chief forum for criminal actions and appeals from the Court of Common Pleas (which handled civil actions and appeals from local and manorial courts). *constorie*: see on 34 above. *chapitle*: the court of a cathedral, monastic or collegiate chapter, hearing disciplinary offences. **473** *a court*: echoing the Ciceronian idea of the unity and uniformity of all true law based upon right reason (Alford 1988[1]:203n21). **476** The wordplay again reflects 'lexical Platonism': a wrong kind of 'smiting' will lead to being 'smitten'. **476a** 'Nation shall not lift up sword against nation: neither shall they be exercised any more to war' (Is 2:4b); completing the quotation at 460a. **477–82** are unchanged from **B** and have no clearly ascertainable topical reference. Such riddling prophecies were common (e.g. 'John of Bridlington', in Wright, *Political Poems,* I) and an 'apocalyptic' sense, 'seriously meant' (*Pe*) but vague rather than exact, seems intended (see Thomas Wimbledon's 1388 Sermon at Paul's cross, 895–8, and Bloomfield 1961:211–12). **477** *worste*: indicating the calamities preceding the end of the

world. **478** *sonnes*: more probably an extraordinary portent than (metonymically) a time six years hence. *ship*: perhaps emblematising the Church (the *navis* or *arca Christi*). *half a shef*: i.e. twelve, since a full sheaf had 24 arrows (Bradley 1910). The figure may be meant to evoke the twelve apostles who will judge mankind with Christ on doomsday (Mt 19:28) and *half* the number of the 24 'ancients' in Apoc 11:16 (of whom the other twelve may be the Major Prophets). **479** *myddel of a mone*: most probably alluding to the Paschal Full Moon of Easter Week, a mysterious dramatic revelation of which will bring about the conversion of Jews and Moslems alike. The Jewish Passover celebrated on the 15th day of the first month (Lev 23:6) was reckoned by the Synoptic Gospels as the date of the Last Supper (in Jn 13:1 this is the *eve* of the pasch). The image metonymically evokes either 'the events of the crucifixion' (*Sk*) or, more probably, Christ's example of humble charity which, if followed by all Christians, should lead to the conversion of the Jews. Galloway (1995:87–9) interprets the line in the light of a well-known riddle contained in ms BL Harley 3362 as interpreted according to the methods of the *Secretum Philosophorum*, an early C14th English treatise on riddles. This *aenigma* is a Leonine couplet *Lune dimidium solis pariterque rotundum, / Et pars quarta rote: nil plus deus exigit a te* 'Half of a moon and equally the round of a sun, And the fourth part of a wheel: nothing more does God demand from you'. Here, the 'half of the moon' (according to its shape) will be the letter C, the 'round of the sun' O and the 'quarter of *rota*' the letter R, giving the Latin word COR 'heart' as the answer to the riddle. Ingenious and entirely in **L**'s spirit, its relevance to the riddle of Patience at 15.163 seems more than arguable. But the phrase *myddel of the mone* is unlikely to mean anything except 'half way point of the lunar cycle, full of the moon' (see MED s.v. *middel* n. 4), strongly suggesting the same sense at its later appearance in the **B** form of Patience's riddle (13.156). **480** *Saresines*: in the light of 481, this must mean the Moslems. *Credo..*: 'I believe in the Holy Spirit' (from the Apostles' Creed). **B 328** 'Glory to God in the highest: [and on earth peace to men of good will]' (Lk 2:14). The scriptural source of **B** evokes the birth of Christ as the peace-bringing event, **C**'s key article from the Apostles' Creed points to Pentecost; but since both texts occur in the Mass (the latter being the opening of the *Gloria*), the peace-bringing power of the Eucharist (cf. B 13.259) clearly underlies Conscience's entire plea for peace. The *syhte* that will cause the Moslems to sing their credal song is the full moon that will inaugurate the new order, or the conversion of the Jews (*Pe*). But since it is unclear why either event in itself would convince the Saracens, the 'sight' of 'Christians living virtuously in peace and charity' (*Bn*) is more probably intended (**L** associates both 'holy men' and 'helpe of the Holy Goste' (17.185) with the conversion of the Moslems). **481** *Machameth*: regarded here as an apostate Christian driven to found his own religion by a failed ambition to be pope (17.165–82), who will one day be punished in the demise of Islam; hence the association with Mede, with her promises to advance clerks (3.35–7). **482** 'A good name is better than great riches' (Prov 22:1); see on 486*a*. The point is that Mede, for all her wealth, has a bad name that she canot shake off.

(vi) 483–99 483 *As...wynd*: a stock comparison (*Patience* 411, stanzaic *Morte Arthur* 1144). **484** *Sapiense*: L's usual name for the *libri sapientiae* or 'Wisdom' books received by the medieval Church: Proverbs, Ecclesiastes, Wisdom and Ecclesiasticus, the first three regarded as the work of Solomon (see Davlin 1988:23–33). **486*a*** 'He that maketh presents shall purchase victory and honour' (Prov. 22:9). Mede both recognises the source of the Latin and adroitly answers Conscience's authority with a counter-citation from only a few verses later in the chapter; see 497 below. **487** Conscience courteously acknowledges Mede's cited authority before trenchantly denouncing her use of it as due to ignorance (a similar strategy of sarcasm is deployed in B 345, 347). **488** *lessoun*: suggesting (AlfQ) that the text is alluded to in its context as a *capitulum* at sext on Sunday (*Brev.* 2.64). **489; 493** *omnia...Quod...*: 'But prove ["put to the test"] all things: hold fast that which is good' (I Thess 5:21). The text provides 'sentence-names' in A 12.50–2 and is quoted by L's Christ at 20.233*a*. **490–1** The 'line' was at the foot of the recto and the rest of it was at the top of the leaf's verso (so strictly the action in 491b would precede that of 491a). **494** A line either of standard type with *s / sh* alliteration or, with *shal* de-stressed according to the sense-pattern, of the rare Type IIb. B 348 may be standard or (with liaisonal stave in *if ye*) of Type IIIb with a-half counterpoint on *s*. **495** *teneful*: more 'lexical Platonism', this time across languages; those who do *not* hold on (*tenere*) to what is good will find the scripture that enjoins this become a text that causes pain (*teneful*). **B 351** is either extended Type IIIa with counterpoint or standard with the third stave liaisonal *þat ye*. **497** scans like a standard English line and completes the verse quoted in part at 486*a*: 'but he carrieth away the souls of the receivers'. It both exemplifies the pre-scholastic method of arguing by setting one authority against another and satirises the attempt of hasty, poorly-informed or (as in Mede's case) ill-intentioned laypeople to justify their conduct on the authority of Scriptural quotations torn out of context. **499** makes clear that to 'receive' Mede is to receive 'Guile', the earthly representative of the devil (2.70, 17.111), under whose sway she stands (A 2.24).

Z 147–76 This 30-line passage that concludes III stands in place of 86 lines progressively extended from A → B → C and should arguably be printed immediately

after Z 146. Rounding off Meed's answer to Conscience with a sustained and at points puzzling attack on him, it lacks both the King's provisional decision for Mede (A 215–6) and Conscience's powerful reply (217–76). Though leaving no trace in A (except of 169 at A 213), it anticipates the longer versions in thought and verbal detail. **148** *Northfolk*: an emblem of close-fistedness, as is presumably Greed's 'Norfolk nose' later at Z 5.98. The remote East Anglian county's educational backwardness is implied in B 5.235, and a major satire on it is the Latin poem *Descriptio Northfolchie* (Wright 1838:93–106; see *R–B*, 17–18). *Normawndye*: alluding to her accusation at 144–6 of cowardly greed in abandoning the campaign for immediate monetary gains. *name was yfounde*: 'name / reputation [for prudential self-interest] was derived' (cf. *Foundour* at 176 below). **149** is taken by *R–B* as 'apparently a phrase for double-dealing', but just as probably it indicates his shrewdness about the value of his chattels. **150** The sense is 'Support now this person, now that, just as you please'. 150a resembles C 5.51. **151** *furst blamedest...shryue*: on this *R–B* observe that 'Conscience has not "blamed" the friars in this poem' but that having been 'rebuked by some authority, represented by Conscience' they 'have now been allowed to resume their old privileges, such as hearing confession'. 151–60, however, undeniably describe much of what happens in BC 20/22.230ff, where Conscience first 'forsakes' the friars (231), but later guarantees them their livelihood (249–50) provided they abandon speculative philosophy for practical charity, while 155 echoes Need's strictures at 20/22.231ff (for possible explanations of these '(pre-) echoes', see *TN*). **154** *couent couetyse*: the 'Platonic' wordplay is revealingly Langlandian. **156** *ant cumseth*: the subject *a* 'they' is understood. **158** A striking T-type line. *boted*: here some half-century before MED's earliest citation s.v. *boten* v. (2), with perhaps a homophonic pun on *boten* (1), 1(b) 'relieve'. *bewsoun*: analogous to *beau fitz*; a form of *bel sone*, with no pl. marker (see *MES* 57); a century earlier than the one citation in MED s.v. *bel* adj. (a). *bayard*: the familiar use of the name anticipating Z 4. 41 //. *stowlyche*: 'in fine style'; MED s.v. *stoutli* adv. 4, aptly citing parallel *WPal* 1950 *alle on stalworþ stedes stoutliche ihorsed*. **159** 'The thickest-woven brown [*burnet* < *brunet*] or white [undyed] woollen cloth for sale'. The *blanket* here is for wearing-apparel (cf. 9.254). **160** *bakken*: occurring elsewhere in this sense only at A 11.188; the noun *bak* (see *IG*) is rare outside L but found in *WPal* 2096. **161–2** The association of ideas is typical of L, as in the phrase *þe lecherie of clothyng* at 16.254 in a comparable attack on worldly and hypocritical clerks (with which cf. *in lykynge of lecherye...in wedes* at 6.176–7). *achoceth*: either *choken* with fused subject prn *a* or *achoken* with *a* omitted. **163–4** 'For lechery is sensual pleasure, and you also grossly inculcate [destructive] desire in clerk and layman alike'; for the possible pun on 'loss' and 'lust', see *TN*. **165–6** The thought is reminiscent of 21.454–6: 'The comune...counteth but litel...of conseyl... but if they sowne...to wynnynge.' **165** A line of Type IIIa or the rare Type IIa. **168** *at consayl*: 'in the Council' or 'in matters of an intimate and private nature'. *ful fewe*: cf. 3.199 //. **169** A counterpointed line of Type Ie (*aab / ab*). **170** The exact meaning is hard to determine, but clearly implied is the enrichment of friar-confessors by people suffering from a 'bad conscience'. Since Mede professes to see Conscience as the 'origin' of clerical greed in the sense of awakening scruples in rich sinners, the incoherence between this passage and her confession to a friar added at A 3.34ff would have required its removal. *robed*: with double reference; he has 'dressed' them in greed, and as a result of giving absolution for money they get the wherewithal to dress *themselves* in substantial clothes. **171** *soyleth*: the aphetic form of *assoylen* enabling a harsh homophonic pun on *soylen* 'soil, befoul'. *syluer... ouresylue*: the identical rhyme providing characteristic homophonic wordplay, with the sibilance of the Type Ib line aptly echoic. **172–3** argue that Conscience is the source of human action in the sense that he understands (*a wot hyt*) the nature of moral choices, whether good or bad, at their root. See the careful analysis of these lines in Brewer 1984:216n7. **174** *maistrye*: 'authority' (MED s.v. (c)) as well as 'power'; the idea survives at A 3.216 (not in **Z**). Mede with false modesty ascribes her duplicity to Conscience as her superior in human affairs. **175** 'God truly knows that without *his* knowing it, *I* can't accomplish anything of which *you* aren't the source and origin'. Mede's switch of addressee, from the king (apparently) at 167 to Conscience at 176, is paralleled, if less abruptly, at A 3.162 (*Nay, lord*) and 165 (*þou knowist*). **176** *foundour*: much earlier in this extended sense than the MED citations s.v. 4(b).

Passus IV (Z IV, V 1–18)

PASSUS FOUR is at 196 lines the shortest in **C**, following the longest, and describes the second half of Mede's 'Trial'. It presents allegorically the secular leadership's resort to the Church for wise counsel in the government of the realm: REASON will therefore emerge in V as personifying ecclesiastical authority in his *sermo ad status*. The Passus falls into: (i) the summoning of Reason (1–39); (ii) the Peace episode 40–107; (iii) Reason's admonition and prophecy (108–45); (iv) responses to it (146–65); (v) the king's rejection of Mede for Reason and Conscience as his councillors (166–96).

(i) 1–39 open with the King at Conscience's behest summoning Reason to advise him. **2** *sothe; bothe*: the internal rhyme suggesting the king's unrealistic and superficial

optimism: 'both' *cannot* serve him 'in truth'. **3** *Kusse here*: the kiss between former adversaries betokening reconciliation, something possible later between the Daughters of God (20. 463ff), because their 'conflict' is more apparent than real, but not here. The king naively desires the kiss of friendship to develop into that of love, the principles of conscientiousness and venality to 'marry' in his mind and domain. But Conscience as the practical application of *synderesis* (the knowledge of the first principles of moral action) should not be able to *sauhten* with the daughter of False. **4–5** *Nay*: the allegory enacts with precision **L**'s idea of Conscience as the soul's disposition to say yes or no to a particular line of action (*chepe or refuse* 16.189). *Pe* helpfully compares Alan of Lille's *Anticlaudianus* I viii–ix 'where Prudence defers likewise to the judgement of Reason'. *by Crist*: an oath here implying not irreverence (as with the brewer at 21.401) but serious purpose. The knightly speaker swears by his heavenly lord (cf. 8.19), whereas 'false' characters like Mede cannot invoke divine witness to their veracity. *But Reson...*: Conscience defers to Reason as the faculty of making general judgements in the light of the moral law (cf. 16.185). At the 'social' level of the allegory, **L**'s Conscience and Reason represent respectively the knightly and episcopal orders (this clarification coming only with **B**'s revision of A 5.11 where, as in **Z**, Conscience is confusingly a bishop). **7** *þat*: implying a verb of 'commanding' understood. **8** *consayle*: 'innermost thoughts', not 'advice'; Reason will advise *him*. **11** *acounte*: an apt term, since Conscience as God's *notarie* (16.190) will have to render a strict account to God on doomsday for the actions of the king and his subjects. **14** *Resoun*: personifying the intellectual principle that understands the *ratio* or divine order of the world; a norm in matters of moral praxis, both 'that which is apprehended and that which apprehends' (Alford 1988:204, an authoritative treatment of this complex idea). **17–23** The 'horse-riding' allegory is a counter-type to that of Mede's deceitful followers at 2.175–93. **17** *Catoun*: a symbol less of 'elementary learning' (*Bn*) than of 'everyday commonsense morality' or '(disillusioned) worldly prudence'. Aptly Reason's servant, he stands to him somewhat as Kynde Wit to Clergy, and is creditably associated with True-tongue. *Caton þe wyse* is approvingly quoted five times, only Study querying his *ooþer science* by comparison with Theology's more idealistic position at B 10.191–201 (deleted in **C**). 'Cato' denotes the *Disticha Catonis de Moribus ad Filium,* a C4th Latin collection in four books of two-line aphorisms in hexameters preceded by 56 prose phrases, attributed to 'Dionysius Cato' but of unknown authorship. With its edifying tone and simple Latin, it was useful as a basic school-text (cf. 7.34; see Galloway 1987, Baer 2001). **18** *Tomme Trewe-tonge*: the first personification with a self-characterising 'sentence-name'; already recommended as the ideal judge at 3.474. **20** *Soffre..*: his horse being the 'patient one waiting for evil to take its course', later named as Reason's special attribute and modelled on God's own *suffraunce* (13.194–200); an ideal 'suffrance' to be contrasted with the 'vnsittynge soffraunce' of 3.207. **21** *Auyseth..*: 'prudent foresight, to curb his will' (*Pe*); *providentia* is an aspect of prudence, and (Burrow 1990:141n9) taught by Reason's 'knaue' Cato in *DC* II.24: *Prospice qui veniant casus: hos esse ferendos; / nam levius laedit quidquid praevidimus ante.* The earlier forms *witty / wytful / witty-wordes*, surviving in *wittes* at C 23, place the same stress on the value of (listening to) words of wise counsel. **22** *wil...kyke*: ironically hinting at the Dreamer's refractory and argumentative character. **23** *wil*: the impulsive aspect of the soul requiring control by *suffraunce*; but the syntax (with *vpon* governing *Soffre...*) confusingly seems to identify the latter with the horse (will). This could be avoided by placing a comma after *vpon*, and reading *sette...vpon* as a phrasal verb with an implied object 'him' and *Soffre...* as the *complement* of 'saddle', as suggested by Burrow 1990:142 (see *TN* further). But the evolution of the earlier texts implies that the 'horse' *wil* is envisaged as being *transformed* into *Soffre...*(who is 'proleptically' so named) under the guidance of wise instruction; and this, despite awkward syntax, makes good theological sense. *peynted wittes*: suggesting that the horse's ornamental bridle signifies the persuasive eloquence sometimes needed to restrain 'wilfulness'; but unlike the example of *paynted wordes* at 22.115, the context here precludes an adverse sense. **27** The **C** alteration to *Waryn Wisman* qualifies the favourable overtones deriving from *Wisdom*'s association with Biblical *Sapience*. This character first appeared at B 4.154 and the contextual sense 'cunning and devious person' cited by *MED* s.v. *wise-man* (d) from *WBib* Job 5:14 (translating *sapientes* [Vg 5:13]) may be presumed here from Warren's association with *Wily-man*, who replaces **ZAB**'s more ambiguous Witty. **28–9** *Fayn...reed*: the lawyers turning to the authoritative spokesman of justice 'because they think that they have a special claim on Reason's help and advice' (*Pe*); but 29b shows why they will be disappointed. *that recorde sholde*: 'whose duty is to testify / declare (whether)'. **31** *Witty-man*: this **ZAB** figure's return in such company compromises his neutrality in **C**. *Wareyne Wryng-lawe*: a dishonest (?)barrister, perhaps identical with Wiseman, although in **B** the name Warren is given to Witty (67) as well as to Wisdom (154). A punning metonymic association of these characters' deviousness with the complexities of the burrows in a rabbit-warren cannot be ruled out, though 'Warren' was a common name and ME *wareine* (B Pr 163) denotes only the tract of bare land. **35–6** *wranglynge*: the symmetrical opposition with *leautee* (like *loue* with *wraþe*) suggesting 'engage in contentious law-suits'. **36a** 'Destruction and

unhappiness [are] in their ways: and the way of peace they have not known. There is no fear of God before their eyes' (Ps 13:3d); quoted in Rom 3:16–17 (*Pe*) during an argument on the inefficacy of the OT law to bring salvation.

B 29–41 // **ZA 29 29** *Cheker*: here the Exchequer of Pleas, a common-law court ancillary to the Exchequer and 'concerned with the enforcement of royal accounts and debts' (Baker 1971:35). *Chauncerye*: the Lord Chancellor's court of Chancery, now becoming 'a court of equity which served to correct the injustices of common law in individual cases' (Alf*G* s.v.) and dealt especially with grievances arising from other courts (McKisack 1959:199). Alf*G* doubts whether the *Pr* 91 ref. is to its equitable jurisdiction, and the most probable sense here is that Warren and Wily have financial liabilities to the Exchequer arising from a contract (*thyng*) and wish to be released from these by other means than payment in full, whether by appealing for special dispensation from the Chancellor's court, 'twisting' the legal process, or using bribes (B 31). See *MED* s.v. *thing* n. 11 (Alf*G* has no entry under *thing* but see s.v. *dischargen*); and see further Galloway 2001:122–5, Kennedy 2003:177. **32, 41** *knewe*; *knoweth*: Conscience 'recognises (the nature of)' but does not 'acknowledge (the worth of)'; a deliberate echo. The first use recalls B 2.47 and the second Christ's injunction in Mt 7:23 (*Bn*), with its resonance of Ps 13:4a.

(ii) 40–107 Mede's Trial modulates into a *Trial of Wrong*, who has injured PEACE and represents the same principle as her vanished would-be groom False; but Mede intervenes at 90. On the whole scene see Baldwin 1981:39–50, Simpson 1990:56–9 and Kennedy 2003:175–89, Giancarlo 2003;144–62. **40–63 41** *as...kennede*: despite conscience's being 'formed' upon the moral law of reason, specific decisions like 'recognising' *Wisman* may fittingly fall to the former; but over-strict interpretation of the psychological allegory should not be insisted upon. **42–3** The 'centrality' of Reason in royal governance (underlined by the identical rhyme) is more important than the topical referent of *sone* (at the time of **ZA** the Black Prince). In the illustrated MS Douce 104 f. 19 he is depicted here as a dignified seated figure, bearded and in riding-habit, with a hat, suggesting a judge (though 5.114 makes it clear he is a bishop). **45** *Pees*: personifying the spirit of amicable compromise that here may endanger the operation of legal justice (as later that of penitential justice at 22.335ff). He stands to Peace the Daughter of God (20.170) somewhat as the earthly institutional Church to the transcendent figure HC of Vision I (cf. on 17–23 above). *parlement*: not the Lords and / or Commons as a whole but rather (Baldwin 1981[1]:40–2) the Great Council of lords, a 'prerogative court' meeting under the king to hear complaints from private individuals, particularly against the administration of the law (*Pe*); see also 4.185.

This interpretation is challenged by Kennedy (2003:179–81), who argues for seeing Peace's action as exemplifying a 'common law' suit in Chancery. *bille*: a written petition (*libellus*) used to initiate a legal action, here one alleging 'assault on his person, property or land' by Wrong, which 'involved a criminal element' because 'the defendant was held to have committed a crime...against the King' (Stokes 1984:138–40). As allegedly perpetrated *vi et armis* and *contra pacem regis*, it would entitle Peace to seek a writ of *trespass* against Wrong (Alf*G* s.v., Baker 1971:82f). **46** *Wrong*: the earthly embodiment of the diabolic figure whom HC so named at 1.59; here perhaps referring more specifically to a class of civil and criminal *iniuriae* 'wrongs' against the king's peace (Alf*G* s.v.), those alleged including rape, theft, forcible entry and fraudulent sale. **46–8** tighten up **B** by making the three victims of rape represent the three female *status* of wife, widow and virgin in ascending order of moral gravity of the offence (see 18.56ff below). Both female type-names suggest purity and worth. **51–4** To Wrong's dishonesty and intimidation in **B** is added highway robbery, anticipating and replacing the description of Outlaw in B 17.99ff. **51** *Seynt Gyles doune*: the famous fair on St Giles's down near Winchester, mentioned at 6.211, 13.51. **57b** 'no matter what legal claim I made' (*Bn*). **58** *maynteneth*: supports with arms and payment; something made an offence by statute in 1377 (Kennedy 2003:182). **59** *forstalleth.*: he (forcibly) buys goods before they can come to the market-fairs, so as to re-sell for a profit at retail (see on 3.82) or avoid customs-dues (Alf*G* s.v.; Baker 1971:82f). Forestalling injured both wholesaler and purchaser, and the Edwardian statute against it was confirmed in 1378 (Kennedy 182n; see further Britnell 1987:89–102). *fyhteth...chepynges*: causing disturbances (to prevent the sale or bring the price down). **61** *tayle*: the tally-stick, an early form of duplicate invoice, marked with notches showing the amount due, and split so that both buyer and seller kept one half as a record of the transaction. Peace claims that Wrong never paid the money due. **64–107 65/6** The end-rhyme introduced in **B** replaces the identical rhyme in **Z** lost by revision in **A**. **67** makes clearer than **B** that Wisdom is a lawyer, whose services Wrong will pay handsomely for (with *largeliche* cf. 3.288–9). **68** *haue here helpe*: fitting better than *maken pees* **ZAB** (which sounds at odds with Wrong's subsequent defiance of Peace in 65–6) and making clear that he hopes to buy the court's mercy through the help of Mede. *handy-dandy*: a game in which one player shakes an object between his hands and then closes his fists, while the other must guess which hand it is in; so Wrong 'with closed hands' makes 'a privy payment' (cf. 22.265) to his lawyer to bribe the judges in his cause. **69** *the lord*: the king, as in **AB**. **72** The ambiguously semi-favourable presentation in B 69–73 // of the lawyers who

warn Wrong against the dangers of violent behaviour is removed in **C**. **73** *Mede*: money for bribery, personified as Lady Mede. **76** The tense-contrast between *knoweth* and *were* 77 leaves it uncertain whether this statement is from Peace or the narrator; but comparison with **ZA** favours the latter. **77** *Wyles*: replacing Wisdom is the cunning lawyer Wily-man of 31. **78** *ouercome*: to be recalled in Greed's attempt to overcome Conscience at 22.122 (*Bn*). **82** *seuene*: a favourite indefinite number symbolic of the completeness of the sentence (as seven days complete a week). **83** *a wys oen*: presumably Wisdom, the leader of the quartet. **84** *Maynprise*: personifying the principle or action of release of a prisoner to a *mainpernour* (107 below) on payment of a surety (see Keen 2002:92). **B 91** 'Wit put forward a counter-argument likewise'; see *TN*. **88–9** 'It is better that a payment of compensation should wipe out the wrong done than that the wrong(-doer) be punished and this remain the best compensation [the injured party gets]'. **96** *waged*: doubtfully glossed by MED (s.v. *wagen* v. 1(d)) '?indemnify, compensate for injuries', but taken by Baldwin in the double sense of receiving 'security [that Wrong "will do so no more"] / payment for agreeing to withdraw the case' (ibid. 1(a); 3 (a)), so that what is accepted is 'a bribe to Peace and the king to drop the case' (1981[1]:49). However, Peace is unlikely to be so open; he means rather 'guaranteed', and merely seeks the king's consent to his accepting the indemnity. **98** 'In this way, provided the King will agree, all my claims are satisfied'. But despite Peace's willingness to accept monetary 'amends', justice has for the king a wider scope than the settlement of personal grievances, since he is in part the party injured by Wrong's crimes (cf. *myn hewes* 102) and 'for the sake of (his own) Conscience' is obliged to enquire further. **C** agrees with **ZAB** in submitting to Reason (personifying the rule of right) the decision on whether to take 'pity' [i.e. allow the 'amends' Peace wants], but replaces the concession to a reformed attitude in Wrong with insistence on retribution for evil-doing. **103** *stokkes*: a wooden punishment-frame confining a seated prisoner's head and ankles (cf. *pylorye* 2.216). **105–6 C** revises the **ZAB** understanding of reason as 'informing' (the king's) conscience to one of conscience 'counselling' the king (in the practical decision of judging Wrong), implicitly in the light of (reason as) the principles of justice.

(iii) 108–45 *Reason's diatribe*, like Conscience's at 3.155–214, takes a severely 'normative' position, refusing 'pity' [in effect = compromise] unless and until a series of stringent conditions are fulfilled. **108–17** These *impossibilia*, implicitly a programme for reform at all levels of society, if idealistic, are not in themselves incapable of being implemented. **111** *Purnele*: short for Petronella, a female diminutive of Peter;

the name of a saint at A 7.259, though here and at 5.128, 6.3 a type-name for a proud rich woman, and elsewhere in *PP* usually unfavourable in implication (see *Proper-Name Index* [*PNI*]). **112** 'And the practice of indulging children [metonymic for 'the practitioners'] be itself sternly disciplined', i.e. the parents should be beaten for *not* beating their children; more simply (with *chasted* = *chastising*), the one activity should replace the other. **113** 'And the piety of (reformed) lechers be celebrated as a major festival'; *harlotes* in the light of *harlotrie* 110 is unlikely to mean 'scoundrels' (*Pe*). In **ZAB** the sense is 'be treated as no great matter', i.e. because it will be so common. The notion that the holiness could be the harlots' *present* 'superficial piety' (countenanced by *Pe* as a possible **AB** reading revised in **C**) depends on the misguided *KaK–D* emendation *hethyng* after *A*-ms Ch, which is a scribal error (see *TN*). **114** *clerkene*: an analogical extension of the old gen. pl. weak declension ending (*HME* 52, *MES* 73). **115a** echoes B 19.418a. **116** *outryderes*: first found here in an English text, and echoed in *CT* I 166. **117** *Benet*: St Benedict of Nursia (*c.* 480–*c.* 550), the founder of Western monasticism. The centre of the Benedictine way of life is the saying of the Divine Office; but while the Rule required a monk to remain attached to his monastery, it did not stipulate enclosure. *Dominik*: St Dominic (*c.* 1172–1221), founder of the Order of Preachers (1217), which followed the Rule of St Augustine. *Fraunceys*: St Francis of Assisi (*c.* 1181–1226), founder of the Order of Friars Minor (1209). Neither Dominicans nor Franciscans had to remain in their convents, so presumably Reason means 'live by the rule instituted by their founders'.

B 120–2 120 *Recordare*: elliptical for 'sing *Remember*, [*Lord*]' or, punningly, 'remember to sing *Remember*;' a common opening to Offertory antiphons in the Sarum Missal (*Bn*). **121** *Bernard*: St Bernard (1090–1153), Abbot of Clairvaux, the most celebrated Cistercian. The strict rule of his Order (founded 1098) was designed to foster enclosed contemplative life within monasteries built in remote situations. **122** *prechours*: not necessarily the Order of Preachers (*Bn*) but (as at 5.42) all whose office is to preach (**C** confirms this).

118–45 118 *lerede men*: probably the clergy, the reference being to their moral instruction to laypeople. **120–1** widens the scope from religious to all needy people and replaces the criticism of bishops' lordly ways with an injunction to practical charity. *ben*: 'be (replaced by)', 'become'. **122** *Seynt Iames*: the shrine of St James the Apostle at Compostela in Galicia (*Galys* 124), NW Spain, a favoured European destination of English pilgrims (cf. *CT* I 466). **122b** greatly sharpens the vaguer **B**. The *spirit* of St James is to be 'sought' by doing the *corporal* good works he commended, e.g. 'to visit the fatherless and widows' (Js 1:27), the image anticipating that of Piers's

symbolic 'pilgrimage' to St Truth. **123** seems to echo the developed 'pilgrimage' metaphor of B 6.102. *Rome*: with the tombs of St Peter and numerous martyrs, the chief pilgrimage-centre after the Holy Land. **C** somewhat uncomfortably interlaces figurative Rome with literal Compostela as a pilgrimage destination in recommending 'spiritual pilgrimages' in place of literal ones. The implication may be that money expended by pilgrims to *straunge strondes* could be more meritoriously used to relieve the needy at home. **124** *for euere*: suggesting one final pilgrimage at the end of life; but the logic is awkward and a metaphorical sense may be intended, 'go on a perpetual "pilgrimage" by means of a life of penance' ('inner pilgrimage' is discussed in Dyas ch. 9). **125** Here 'Rome' signifies the Papal Court, which was actually at Avignon in SE France at the time of **ZA** but had returned to Rome by the time of **B** (though the anti-pope Clement VII still resided there). The people vaguely denoted will be those seeking benefits from the Pope and willing to pay for them. *ruyflares*: officials at the Curia who took money for their services to papal petitioners. **127** *graue*: stamped coins. *vngraue*: blank coin or bullion. **128** *forfeture*: doubtless the objection voiced being to the impoverishment of the country's economy by the removal of money from circulation. *ouerward*: perhaps suggested by the sound of *Douere* **ZAB** and generalising its sense. At Dover, the chief port of embarkation for France, travellers could be examined to see if they were carrying gold or silver abroad, something forbidden by law (Statutes of 1381–2, ii 17–18; Lipson 1959:531–3) to all except the groups mentioned. **130** *prouisour*: a tolerance of provisors seemingly at odds with the view of them as simoniacs at 2.182 //, unless Reason means here those who 'go to receive benefices or offices already given' (*Bn*). Like the other classes mentioned whose journeying may be personally obligatory or beneficial to the realm, they would need cash for expenses. *penaunt*: revising **ZA** as apparently contradicting the tone of *Rome-rennares* 125; someone on whom pilgrimage had been imposed as a canonical penance for some grave sin. **Z 119–31** Partly cut and partly transposed in revision of a passage obviously in draft condition (*Intro.* III, *Z Version* §3). The lines allow the possibility of intervening for Wrong in the event of a general transformation of society; but **A**'s deletion recognises that Wrong can never be converted. **131** *by þe Rode*: an oath conveying solemn resolution, not irreverence; used only here (but cf. also 179) and perhaps especially fitting, since Reason later preaches with a cross (C 5.13, B 5.12). **132** *barre*: the railing before the judge's seat at which counsel stood to plead, hence metonymic for the profession of advocate ('barrister'). The revision hints at a special animus against the latter. **134–5** recall Mede's supposition at 3.257–8. **136** *Wrong*: standing for every type of wrongdoer. **138b** improves on **B** in precision and substance. **139** 'Nor [should I] grant him mercy in return for payment...'; on the revision's awkward syntax cf. *TN*. **139b** Though this oath is found elsewhere (see *PNI*), it is contextually ironic, since the Virgin Mary is usually identified as the merciful intercessor, as at 7.287–90. **140–1** *Nullum...irremuneratum*: from the definition of the just judge in the *De contemptu mundi*, iii 15 of Pope Innocent III (1160–1216): 'Ipse est iudex iustus...qui *nullum malum* praeterit *impunitum, nullum bonum irremuneratum*' (*Sk* IV 83); both parts will be quoted again as 20.433. Reason's stand for inflexible retributive justice recalls that of Conscience at 3.332–3, 350–1 and anticipates the wording of Truth's Pardon at 9.286–7. But the present use of negative personifications entails a witty transposition of the original predicates: 'The man *No-ill* encountered *unpunished* / And urged that *No-good* go *unrewarded*'. **142** *confessour*: perhaps implying that observance of the principle may require absolution for the king's past faults in this regard (variants of the phrases occur in penitential writings cited by Gray 1986:53–60). **144–5** If justice is followed, lawyers will have to turn peasant-farmers and the king will find himself loved, instead of disliked for his *vnsittynge suffraunce* of wrongdoing (3.207–9).

(iv) 146–65 147b *kyndeliche..*: the revision of B 150b and excision of (added) B 151 deleting a sharp criticism of the king's clerical advisers. **148–55 (B 150–56)** The change removes the Dreamer's guaranteeing presence (new in **B**) and tightens the contrast between law and justice with a mordant pun on *ryhte* 150 and *ryhtful* 151. In **B 154** Warren represents the misuse of legal expertise for profit (with 156a cf. B 3.157, B 5.580–1) and in **B 155–6** the lawyers' willingness to suppress facts they know might prejudice a client's case is the converse of their refusal (at B Pr 212–16) to speak a word without being paid for it. **151–3** All right-minded people acknowledge the truth of Reason's case, Conscience and Kynde Wit (companions at Pr 142) thank him for his virtuous sentence, and everyone hopes from his words that humble innocence rather than cynical wealth will prevail with the king. The interpretation here offered will require adoption at 152–3 of *R–K*'s punctuation, with no stop in 152 but a semi-colon after *speche* 153. **155** *Mekenesse...mayster*: allegorically signifying that only humble expression of sorrow for injury done, and not monetary compensation without remorse, will suffice as grounds for a truly '*sitting* suffrance'. **159b** Mutilation was an archaic penalty for certain offences (with the oath cf. 8.290, B 4.146). **161** A pungent polysemantic pun on two senses of *commune*, 'the community' and 'the commonly-used'. In 161b an arresting n. + adj. compound-epithet must be in question, since *queynte* as adj. could hardly be de-stressed, and the half-line cannot contain three lifts. There is surely however a homophonic pun on *queynte* adj. 'cunning' as in Chaucer *CT* I

3276/7. **164–5** *capias...custodias*: 'Take Mede and guard her securely' is 'the standard formula in writs of attachment,' addressed [by the king] to the sheriff and served by his clerk (AlfG), here relayed by the latter to the officers as Mede slips out. *set...carceratis*: 'but not with those in prison'. The ironically 'unsitting' substitution by **L** himself (*pace* AlfQ) for the usual *in prisona nostra* hints that the king's threats at 3.140–1 are unlikely to be fulfilled: house-arrest is the worst Mede has to fear.

(v) 166–96 166 *to consayl toek*: i.e. 'conferred privately with', but with the implication of making them (permanent) members of his Council. **169** *chetes*: the 'reversion of land or its appurtenances to the king...upon failure of heirs to a tenant in fee simple [i.e. one holding directly from the king as feudal lord]'; and also 'forfeiture of the lands and goods of a felon' (AlfG), this second situation being the one referred to at 10.242–4. The text implies that lawyers can be bribed to substitute 'false heirs', e.g. by providing bogus documentation of identity or legitimacy. **173** *ȝow*: strictly Wrong, who is in need of bail; but his counsel are being addressed on his behalf. **B 179** *þe Marie of heuene*: a rare use of the proper name in a phrase with the definite article (*MES* 239), outside 22.221 perhaps unique. **174–5** *leautee; lele*: the king requiring that the common law be equated with a strict regard for the principle of justice (*for* is even stronger than **B**'s *in* 'governed by'; cf. *euene* 178) and administered by faithful and virtuous men. The unfavourable contrast between (uncompromising) justice and (compromised) *lawe withouten leutee* recurs at 12.94ff, where the insistence on *loue* as well as *leute* echoes *lyf-holy* 4.175 (an expression that may imply involvement of churchmen in the administration of justice). The revision, doubtless reflecting circumstances after 1381, replaces confidence in the communal sagacity of *moost folk* with reliance on trustworthy judges hand-picked for their loyalty and probity. **180a** *alle reumes*: the purpose of *alle* perhaps being to extend the reference to just rule *over* Ireland and the remaining English possessions in France; but its repetition in 182 (echoed by the king in *al* 183) implies relations *between* countries. **180b** is an uncommon case of three-stage linear revision from **Z** → **C**. **185–6** The revision sharpens the looser sense of **ZAB**. *Chaunceller*: the use of *chief* indicating a parallel with the function of the Lord Chancellor of England, to whom the Chancellor of the Exchequer was a deputy. It seems to be implied at one level that the king of England is resolving to have a bishop as his chief minister of state (on a more abstract plane, Reason figures as 'chancellor' to the divine Wisdom in Nicholas Love's *Mirror*, p. 17 (AlfG s.v.)). *kynges justice*: Conscience will *judge* by the principles of equity in particular cases, just as Reason will *rule* by those of pure justice. **B 189** *Be... comen*: 'when my council has come.' **187a–90** Reason's reply is bracketed by the same phrase 'I assent', only with the qualifier 'but', a rhetorically tight utterance enclosing three strict injunctions that would seem to have had special relevance for Richard II. **187–8** *by so...partem*: 'on condition that you yourself *should hear the other side*'. The English conjunction is made to govern 188a and the subject *ʒowsulue* to fit with the Latin 2 pl. subj. in place of the usual imperative. **188** *Audiatis*: 'hear', in apposition with *yhere* 187 (hence the comma). This Roman law maxim was regarded 'as one of the self-evident propositions of natural law' (Alf*Q*). *aldremen and comeneres*: a set phrase specifically referring respectively to the chief officials of city wards, who were charged with holding the ward-mote (Pr 92), and the ordinary members elected to the common council of the city. **189** *priue lettres*: sent under the king's privy or personal signet or seal (in contrast to *letters patent* of public concern, sent under the Great Seal) and commonly granting a licence or favour. There may be an immediate allusion to a 1387 statute (11 Ric II c. 10, in confirmation of 2 Edw. III c. 8) that no such letters be sent in damage or prejudice of the realm, nor in disturbance of the law (Alf*G*); but the king had begun to use his personal seal as a warrant to the Chancery from 1383 onwards (Keen 1973:277). **190** *supersedeas*: 'you shall desist'; the opening word of a Chancery writ that stayed or stopped a proceeding in the common courts. While 'meant to protect individual rights...it was subject to abuses such as bribery, favouritism, etc.' (Alf*G*). **191** *loue...seluer*: i.e. 'if you rule justly, your subjects will be more willing to provide you financial subsidies.' **194** *Lumbardus of Lukes*: Lombards from Lucca (in N Italy), who after the expulsion of the Jews from England in 1290 became the chief bankers and moneylenders in the City of London and were especially useful to the king; Lombard St, just S of Cornhill, commemorates their residence there. For another criticism of Lombards, see Z 7.274. **196** *Resoun*: either the subject or the object of the verb; whichever way, only the just and upright are to be appointed to administer the realm. *Y wakede*: the second vision ends more logically with the dreamer waking, and so obviates the need for the poorly motivated waking at the opening of Passus V in **ZAB**.

Passus V

PASSUS FIVE, as concise as Four, has two balanced halves: (i) a *prelude* (1–108) introducing the Second Vision, and (ii) *Reason's Sermon* to the Folk (109–200), which precipitates the *Confessions* of the Deadly Sins in the next passus. The opening dialogue with two interlocutors foreshadows those described at 1 below and the one that initiates the Third Vision (10.1–60), 5.105–8 resembling the transition-passage at 10.61–7. **B** had added only about 20 lines to **A**, which remained the same length as the corresponding **Z** portion after halving Z 30–48 on the

great wind. **C**'s revisions have been necessitated by its expansion of **B**'s Sins-material from 400 to some 500 ll. and addition (from B XIII) of a 50-line passage on the origins of Sloth (7.69–118a). The *Confession Sequence* that fills **ZAB** V is now distributed in more manageable units over three shorter passūs (5–7) and embedded more firmly in the Dreamer's situation, turning the two waking episodes into a kind of didactic frame (on these changes see Russell 1982). The 'prelude' in certain respects replaces the exchange on *makyng* in B 12.10–28 but ranges more widely, and has attracted much attention as an ostensibly 'autobiographical' *apologia pro vita sua*. Middleton 1997 judges it **L**'s latest addition, reflecting provisions of the Statute of Labourers issued by the Cambridge Parliament of 1388. But little in Will's interrogation or replies could not have been written in 1382–7 (her main arguments are adequately answered in Wittig 2001:168–70). The 'historical' truth of **L**'s self-description is indeterminable, but the recognised convention of loosely modelling the narrator / dreamer-figure on the author (Kane, 1965[2]; Burrow 1993:82–108) certifies appearance and circumstances as likely to be authentic.

(i) 1–108 *The dialogue with Reason and Conscience.*
1–11 This waking encounter with personified abstractions resembles those with Hunger and Fever in A 12.59–98 and with Need in BC 20 / 22.1–50, containing rebuke and warning for the Dreamer and, through him, the audience. **1** *Cornehull*: a street in the City of London immediately S of the present Royal Exchange and Bank of England, and N of Lombard St (Du Boulay 1991: endpaper map). *Pe* notes the area's reputation as a resort for vagabonds, and cites the description in 'London Lickpenny' (Robbins 1959: no. 50, ll. 85–8). But as 'part of the city's commercial centre [it] always contained prosperous precincts' (Benson 2004:209, who has an illuminating account of medieval Cornhill [206–28]). **2** *Kytte*: a familiar diminutive of *Katherine*. If it has a meaning, it need not be as a type-name for 'a wife' (*Pe*, citing 7.303, and see *Vxorem duxi* following), but for a lascivious woman (MED s.v. *Kitte* n. 2(b), citing only *Beryn*). However, in 7.303 Actif may allude punningly to the name of his wife (and Will's own, B 18.428), who is *wantowen of maneres* 'undisciplined, wilful' (MED unconvincingly cites the latter under sense (d) 'lascivious'). *cote*: a dwelling of the poor (see *IG*). **3** *lollare*: a wasteful idler (MED s.v. *lollere* n.1), the earliest use of the noun in this sense being in B 15.213 (from *lollen* 'hang loosely', and confined to texts in the *PP* tradition). A possible pun on 'Lollard' (MED s.v. 2, a sense already in *CT* B 1173) cannot be ruled out; but this figurative use may be derived from a term for a hanging or trailing ship's rope (ibid. s.v. 3, c. 1356). **5** *made of*: commonly taken as 'composed verses about' (*Sk*, MED s.v. 5(b), *Pe*, Kane 1965[1]:64n1), in the light of which **C**

9.203–55 has been seen (by Scase 1987) as a specific piece of *makyng* about *lollares of Londone* that was separately circulated while **C** was being written (see *Intro*. III, *C*, §§ 21–2). But though there may be a secondary punning sense, in context *made of* (balancing *lytel ylet by* 3) more naturally means 'judge, regard' (Sisam 1962:233; MED s.v. *maken* 17 (a)). *Reason* is more likely to have 'taught' (5) the speaker to 'judge' than to 'compose poetry', and it is doubtful whether *lollers* who read clerkly satire would have given it a thought. This use underlies the phrase at 3.390 (and is how it was understood by the scribe of ms F, who substituted *rouȝte*). **6** *cam by*: 'acquired' (MED s.v. *comen* v. 4a. (e), a contextually apt sense proposed by Wittig 2001:270–1. But the association with *romynge* at 11 (rendered by Wittig 'moving in a desultory fashion') nonetheless implies a play on this phrasal use (earlier instanced at *WPal* 1688) and the literal sense 'pass by' found at 7.218, B 17.121. The idiom inevitably evokes an 'inward journey' like that described by Piers in 7.204ff, with its parallel expression *come into Consience* at 7.206 // **ZAB**. *Resoun*: in general terms 'the personification of the waking dreamer's own rational self-analysis...as well as the authoritative figure of Passus IV' (*Pe*); but the definitions at 16.186, 190 suggest here more specifically Will's examination of conscience in the light of moral law. Reflecting on his concrete moral decisions, he 'meets with' the principle of reason on which they are (or should be) predicated, which is *then* personified in the dream. **7–10** *hele...inwitt*: 'health of body and mind'; cf. 10. 182 and *TN*. **11** *Romynge*: a hanging participle (cf. B 18.299); it is Will who remembers. *aratede*: recalling the encounter with Reason in B 11.375.
12–34 12–19 specify three kinds of work: clerkly (12), 'crafty' (18a), and agricultural (13–19). **19** *Heggen*: either 'make / trim hedges' (*Sk, Pe*, MED) or the rare verb *eggen* 'harrow' (< OE *ecgan*; see OED s.v. *edge* v²) derived from *egþe* 'harrow' (= *aythe* 21.274), in which case it forms an alliterative doublet with *harwen*. The spelling *eggen* (in all **p** copies except MF) suggests that the *h* is inorganic, but is not decisive, though the verb's survival in rural usage favours the rarer lexeme. **21** '[So that] those who provide you a livelihood may be given some advantage [from doing so].' This construction with suspended subject pronoun, the infinitive as 'predicate nominative' (*MES* 524–5) is paralleled at 6.48, 21.233, 269; see *TN*. **24** *long*: 'tall'; alluding to the Persona's stature and punningly to one half of the author's surname, of which the second appears in 26a (he does *not* have 'lands'); for similar ironic self-references cf. B 15.152 and A 11.118 (*Pe* compares Hoccleve's *Regement of Princes* 981–7). **28** 'A compulsive spender or a time-waster' (*B&T-P*). **30** *Frydayes*: days of fasting, abstinence and alms-deeds, when the pious making their devotions would presumably be readier to give. *feste-dayes*: the many days of celebra-

tion, when the wealthier especially might be expected to feel generous. **31** *lollarne*: see on 4.114. **32a** '[God], Who will render to every man according to his works' (Rom 2:6; cf. Mt 16:27, Apoc 22:12). That the allusion is to Rom seems likely from the preceding verse's reference to 'the day of wrath...of the just judgement of God' (Rom 2:5). Alf*Q* traces the exact wording here to Hugh of St Cher's comment on Job 21:4. **34** *excused*: 'exempted (from working)'; the first use in this sense.
35–60a 35 *ȝong, ȝong*: 'very young indeed' (see *TN*). **36** *frendes*: 'family, relatives' (a ME set-phrase; see Olszewska 1973:205–7, who notes that in 12.157 the sense may be 'friends'). *scole*: 'university'. **37** *Holy Writ*: 'theology' (Bennett 1974:14). The context implies that Will had passed from the Arts into the Theology Faculty and was training for the secular priesthood (if he was a religious, he might have read Arts in the order's *studium* but would not have depended on his family for financial support). At Oxford, the Bible was studied during the first four years of the Theology course (Courtenay 1987:41–3). Bowers's preference for 'cathedral school' (1986:21–2) on the basis that the pl. form was used for the university in medieval times is mistaken; see MED s.v. *scole* n. (2), which shows the sg. as normal. **40** *foend...frendes*: echoes *frendes foende* 36 with polysemantic wordplay on *fynden*. The expense of the long university course required the support of a student's family or a patron (such as a bishop). **41** *longe clothes*: worn by clerks to distinguish them from laypeople; a wry hint at their aptness for one *long* (24) in stature as in name. **43a** 'In whatever vocation you have been called, [remain]'; loosely based on I Cor 7:20: 'Let every man abide in the same calling [i.e. type of work] in which he was called [*sc.* to be a Christian]' (cf. also vs. 24). **44** *London...opelond*: the present tense indicating alternating residence at the same period of time (on the reading see *TN*). Will receives hospitality (and possibly payment) in each household where he performs various clerical services (a line recalled at 16.286). **45–7** *lomes*: his 'tools of trade' are prayers of intercession. The 'Our Father', the psalms 'I will please the lord' (Ps 114:9) and 'Direct my way' (Ps 5:9), which are both parts of the Office of the Dead, and the seven penitential psalms (see on 3.463–4) all appear in the *prymer*, the standard book of devotion for laypeople (ed. Littlehales; see Duffy 1992:209–65). Will presumably said these prayers for (and perhaps with) his patrons. *Pater-noster*: on **L**'s understanding of this prayer see Gillespie 1991. **48** *here*: strictly redundant; for this duplicated possessive see *MES* 158 (and cf. 9.98). **50** *to be*: 'that I shall be / to make me' (on the infinitive as a predicate accusative see *MES* 527). **51** *on...begge*: i.e. he doesn't 'beg' at all [because he does a service for what he gets]. **52** *bagge or botel*: the visible attributes of the professional *loller*; free from them, Will associates himself rather with *Godes*

munstrals (see 9.136–40). **54** *constrayne*: anticipating the Latin maxim at 60*a* and answering Reason's implied 'constraint' upon Will at 13–21 to do (mainly) 'servile' labour. **55** *Levytycy*: 'of Leviticus', inflected in the genitive after *of*. The allusion is probably not to Lev 21 (*Pe*) but to such injunctions in Num 18:20–4 (*B&T-P*) as that the tribe of Levi should 'possess nothing in their land' but be content with 'an offering from the tithes'. The parallel here between the 'ministry' of clerks in minor orders and that of the OT Levites (cf. 60) sits loosely with Will, who could lawfully claim only voluntary 'offerings', not the 'tithes' reserved for beneficed priests. **56** *of kynde vnderstondynge*: 'as commonly understood', i.e it is self-evident, stands to reason. **57** *swerien...*: i.e. serve on juries; distrust of their probity recurs at 22.162. **58***a* 'Do not return evil for evil'. The nearest verbal source is the commentary on Lev 19:18 (the next vs of which is cited as 12.35), by Denis the Carthusian in *Op. Om.* 266 (AlfQ, who gives close parallels in I Thess 5:15, I Pet 3:9). **59** *hit ben*: on this 'formal' *hit* followed by a pl. vb (= 'they') cf. 8.217, 9.118 and see *MES* 132–3. **60***a* 'The Lord is the portion of my inheritance [and of my cup: it is thou that wilt restore my inheritance to me]' (Ps 15:5, quoting Num 18:20]; here cited in a less pragmatic context than at B 12.188. Though *hereditas* symbolises heaven, the verse's *b*-part may contain a hidden personal meaning for one who had renounced (or forfeited) an inheritance 'Crist for to serue'. *Clemencia....*: a maxim, possibly legal, of undiscovered origin. Despite a surface likeness to *Merchant of Venice* 4.1.179, it means not (*Pe*, AlfG) 'Mercy is not restricted' (which would require *constringitur*) but 'Mercy does not compel'. *B&T-P*'s 'it is perhaps intended to justify [clerics'] exemption from imposing legal or military sanctions on others' cannot be right, since clerics could only be required to 'impose' these if exercising *secular* office. The general reference is most probably to 'the privileges of tonsured clerks' (*Pe*); but a more specific contextual sense is: 'A generously lenient attitude (*clemencia*) [towards the obligation to earn one's livelihood] will not force [clerks to do such work as Reason described]'. The maxim authorises the sentiment in 54 and is illustrated by 61ff.

61–81 protest against the erosion of social distinctions (for **L**, guarantees of social order) following the Great Plague. The essential point is that if clerics (even unbeneficed ones) came only from the gentry, there could be no legal grounds for thinking that they should do servile work as when, right up to the highest levels in the church, they were being drawn from the estate of peasants (like Chaucer's Parson), and especially of serfs. **64** *frankeleynes*: free landowners below the knightly class; equated with 'ientel men' at 21.39. The one extant Langlandian life-record (*Intro.* V § 4) indicates that he came from this class, of which Chaucer's Franklin is the best-known lit-

erary example. **66***a* *Thyse bylongeth*: a very terse phrase, omitting both *it* before the impers. verb and *to* before the pronoun (on the synthetic pronoun-dative without preposition see *MES* 97). **66***b*–**67***a* 'and [it is the proper task of] noblemen's relations to serve God and the Christian community [as clergy], as befits their social position'; on the punctuation, cf. Sledd 1940:379–80. **68***b*–**9** envisage clerks who do not take holy orders performing 'clerical' and administrative duties for the nobility or the government. **70–81** *sythe*: governing all nine verbs before the main verb *hath be* in l. 80, *refused* etc being not linked main verbs but past participles dependent on the causal / temporal clause that introduces the sentence. In **73–4** *han be* is understood in 73a, *han* in 73b and 74b, where *ryden* is p.p. **71** Canon law prohibited the illegitimate from being consecrated bishop; but **L**'s objection extends to their appointment to the archidiaconate (often a stepping-stone to the episcopacy). *barnes bastardus*: 'bastard children', echoing 65a, with the second noun inflected adjectivally in the French manner (*MES* 277); against *R–K*'s preferred reading 'barons' bastards', see *TN*. **73–4** regard corruption of social harmony through the power of 'meed', and the departure of sanctity (80), as resulting from a series of abuses, simony being the last of them. **73** *lordes sones*: figuratively become the 'workmen' of newly rich merchant-traders by having to pledge their incomes to raise cash for the retinue and equipment needed for service with the king. This refers in part to events (**74–5**) affecting the previous generation; but there was war with France between 1369 and 1381, and against Scotland in 1385. Before the establishment of a national army in the 15th c., knights had to provide servants and equipment for war out of their own income; cf. the important new passage at 13.107–10 below. **76** expresses an opinion earlier voiced in A 11.201, a line not in **B**. **78–9** state that sons of the impoverished gentry have failed to win positions in the Church, which have gone to those using 'meed' to get them. **79** *Symondes sones*: those who sell and buy spiritual things; alluding to the sin of Simon Magus, who offered the Apostles money for spiritual power (Ac 8:18–24). In this period simony commonly denotes traffic in ecclesiastical preferment. **80** recalls Anima's assertion in B 15.92–102 that the return of virtue and charity requires reform of the clergy.

82–91 83 *consience*: the Dreamer's claim to know God's will for him echoing his statement in 6 above. **86–8** 'In truth man lives [*or*, man truly lives] not from the soil, or by bread, or food, as the "Our Father" testifies. It is *God's will be done* that provides us everything'. The source of the macaronic lines is the well-known 'Not in bread alone doth man live [*non in solo pane vivit homo*], but in every word that proceedeth from the mouth of God' (Mt 4:4, directly taken from Dt 8:3; quoted in full by Patience at 15.246*a*). Replacing the adj. *solus* by the ablative of the noun *solum* 'soil' furnishes a witty clerkly rejoinder to Reason's earlier implication that he should be doing manual (and especially agricultural) work. The '"word" from the mouth of God' that Will claims as sustenance enough for him is aptly one that he himself says for the providers of his *actual* food (46 above), but perhaps is here only synecdochic for prayer. The standard phrasing of the third petition occurs at 16.319, but the modified version here cited will recur at 15.252, where it receives a full 'commentary' in the form of an allegorical action (15.249–52) based on an original passage in // **B** to which the present addition is indebted. Another key scriptural text contrasting earthly with spiritual food that **L** may have associated with Mt 4:4 is Jn 4:34: 'Meus cibus est ut faciam *voluntatem* eius'. The present passage is a fore-taste of the 'transcendentalised' food-imagery that in **B** first appears only at 14.29, and in **A** not at all. **89** *lyeth*: taken by *PeB&T-P* as 'applies, is to the point' (MED s.v. *lien* v. (1), 11(b)). But the MED examples cited in support differ from this one in having an indirect object following; and *Ac* 90 would have to mean 'On the contrary, but rather' (MED s.v. *ac* conj. 2(a)). The context suggests more that Conscience concedes Will's assertion at 84–5 but interprets Will's action as 'begging' and then denies that this is *sad parfitnese*. Evoking the tone and manner of a scholastic disputation ('I agree; but I maintain'), Will's own concession at 92a balances Conscience's *Ac* at 90, while his qualifying response at 94 (where *Ac 3ut* can only mean 'But nonetheless') answers it. The general sense of 89–91 is thus: 'You say that Christ tells you in your conscience what work you should do; and by the same Christ, I can't deny that what you say is true. But it hardly counts as solid virtuousness of life to beg in cities.' The points of substance here, Will's appeal to his conscience as a guarantee of his integrity and his interlocutor's acknowledgement of this appeal, are lost if *lyeth* does not mean 'is (saying something) false'. It is thus possible to reject *Pe*'s rendering while agreeing with him that 'Conscience points out that **L**'s theory of the perfect life is not what he practises'. **91** *obediencer*: a monk in charge of one of the administrative offices, such as cellarer or sacristan (Lawrence 1993:121–4). Conscience's acceptance of monks' 'begging' as compatible with *parfitnesse*, and his tacit exclusion of friars', are striking.

92–101 The Biblically-inspired analogy could suggest the recklessness of the compulsive gambler as much as the calculated risk-taking of the merchant-venturer; but **L** may mean that to the prudential mind the two are hard to distinguish. **93** *ytynt tyme*: on this theme cf. B 9.99, borrowed for Ymaginatif's added warning in 14.5 on Will's special responsibility not to misuse speech or time (see the valuable discussion in Burrow 2003). **94** *I hope as he*: either anacoluthic, beginning a sentence not to be finished, or else *as he* = 'like a man who', initiating a comparison

not with *hope* but with *I*. As in 99 below, *hope* carries the senses '(go on) trust(ing)' and 'expect'. **95** *loste... laste*: the chime that links the ideas signified encouraging perseverance by suggesting that a temporary setback may be the parent of a final success. **96** *bargayne*: with literal referent of the metaphor indeterminable, but possibly 'the final version of the poem', as the artistic and moral vindication of **L**'s 'twenty years largely wasted' (cf. Schmidt 2000:23–6). **97** *leef*: a traditional emblem of worthlessness; perhaps also signifying the single leaf of paper 'lost' when the writing on it is deleted, a loss that will seem worthwhile when the work is completed. *laste ende*: 'end of the day' but also the 'final reckoning', when the lost time may be overlooked by the Judge if the final product was a decisive good. (The text quoted at 98a is preceded and followed [Mt 13:39–40, 49] by solemn references to the end of the world and the last judgement). **98** *wordes of grace*: the use of *wordes* as a spelling-variant of *wyrdes* (see *TN*), itself a derivation from *worthen*, might have appealed to **L** the etymologist. But while 'happy fortune' fits the lucky merchant of the analogy and its Gospel source, 'grace-bringing words' better suits the maker Will (the true subject of the analogy) and ties in more closely with the Latin following. It is the hopeful individuals of the parables cited who inspire him to persevere with his poetry and the way of life that sustains it, which both involve uttering 'grace-bringing words'. **98a** (i) 'The kingdom of heaven is like unto a treasure hidden in a field. [Which a man having found, hid it: and for joy thereof goeth and selleth all that he hath and buyeth that field]' (Mt 14:44). (ii) 'The woman who found the drachma'; alluding to Lk 15:8–9. These two 'parables of the kingdom' are complementary: (i) describes selling all you have to buy one supremely valuable thing, (ii) finding no joy in all you have until you recover the one thing you have lost, which thus acquires more value than the rest. An analogy with the persona as clerkly maker would not be far to find: he hazards everything to get one thing right (his poem), but then gets no profit from what he has achieved (the 'B Version') until every last bit of it is to his satisfaction (the ongoing 'C Version'). **99** *So*: less 'therefore' than 'in that way [i.e. like the merchant]'. **100–01** *gobet*: echoing the *micae* 'fragments' in the story of the Canaanite woman (Mt 15: 27). *tyme...tyme*: 'a period of time...every moment of my (life)time'.

100–08 100–04 *bigynne...continue*: if Reason's 'No more time-wasting' admonishes, Conscience's 'Persevere' encourages. **105–8** resume the parallel text with **ZAB V** but reduce the crudity of their transition by making the passage one that better motivates the second dream (through sorrow rather than regret) and prepares for its central theme (sin and repentance). The various pious actions, which recall Haukyn at the end of B XIII and imply no lack of sincerity, are typical of the more demonstrative kinds of medieval contrition (Vernet 1930:120–5). **105** reads, despite its deliberate repetition-with-variation (cf. *mette me / me mette* at 109–10), rather like a poetic 'catchword', and its removal would be a gain in economy. **107** *Pater-noster*: especially significant because of the medieval belief in the power of its seven petitions against each of the Deadly Sins and in its spiritual efficacy generally: 'This hooly orison amenuseth [lessens] eek venyal synne, and therfore it aperteneth specially to penitence...it avayleth eek agayn the vices of the soule' (*CT* X 1042; Gillespie 1994:107–11). **(ii) 109–200** *Reason's Sermon*. The structure of the vision in **B** as a fourfold action of sermon / confession / pilgrimage / pardon is illuminatingly analysed in Burrow 1984[1965]:79–101.

109–25 109–10 The opening of Vision Two amplifies through verbal repetition its echo of the opening of Vision One, a geographical supplementing of **ZAB**'s allegorical place-reference. *Maluerne Hulles*: recalling Pr 6 and in turn echoed at 9.295 by way of closure (though inconsistently, since the second dream occurs at or near Cornhill). Absence of further mention of the western locale suggests that the 'Visio' (= Pr–IX in its first form) envisaged an audience in the poet's home-region, but its **BC** continuations (with two dozen references to the capital and particular places in it) a London and national readership. **112–15** The **C** revision replaces the end-rhymes (different ones) of A 9/10, B11/12 with an assonantal echo of *prechede* 114 in *preuede* 115. But the substantive change is from Conscience as bishop in **ZA** (a function not coherent with his rôle as a knight able to marry Mede) to Reason as bishop in **B**, and then as supreme bishop in **C**, with Conscience intelligibly (if at the 'historical' level surprisingly) his cross-bearer. **112** *as a pope*: the conflict between this and his *addressing* the Pope at 191 below could be resolved by seeing him as 'a cardinal acting as papal legate' (*Pe*). But this is probably to be over-literal, since in the case of a personified abstraction 'rank' probably signifies allegorically 'importance'. Reason's higher position in **C** underlines his *universal* authority, the locale becoming both England (114) and the whole Christian world (111). **115** *preuede*: i.e. showed the truth of his claim by an appeal to a 'spiritual reading' of the 'book of Nature' akin to an exegete's of the book of Scripture (for a brilliant if overstated account of 'interpretation' as the poem's theme and method, see Rogers 2002). *this pestelences*: **C** preferring to describe attacks of the plague in the pl. (cf. 10.274, 11.60) and often with 'these', the force of which is both generic (plague is divine punishment for sin) and deictic (particular recent examples 'prove' this belief). After the Great Pestilence of 1348–9, three further attacks kept the subject topical (see on Pr 82); but by 1387 the 'proof by example' would be reminder more than demonstration. The unaltered re-

tention of this line from **Z** → **C** and the 'tempest' lines that follow imply as referent the outbreak of 1361–2. *was*: the subject being construed as a collective sg. (*MES* 62–3). **116** *south-weste wynde*: beginning on Sat. 15 Jan. 1362, lasting five days, and readily lending itself to the kind of moral *significacio* spoken of at B 15.482–3a. A figurative understanding of wind as an intelligible divine utterance is introduced as early as Z 34–6 after the line // to C 117, among seven lines deleted in **A** that provide the exemplum an apt commentary from *Holy Writ* [*that*] *wot muche bettre*. Storm symbolises God's anger against human pride in Is 28:1–3, 'Woe to...pride...the Lord is...as a *storm* of *hail*: a destroying *whirlwind*...'; Ezech 13:13, 'I will cause a *stormy wind*...in my indignation...and great *hailstones* in my wrath'; and Ps 148:8, '*hail*, snow, ice, *stormy winds*, which fulfil [the Lord's] word'. Along with the concurrent second plague and the hailstorm of 'Black Monday' (14 Apr. 1360), the great wind seems to have furnished motifs and perhaps even occasioned the composition of Vision Two in its **Z** form. **117** *for pride*: 'on account of / to check pride'. This 'general roote of...the sevene deedly synnes' (*CT* X 386ff) was seen as inviting direct divine retribution, as by John of Bridlington: 'propter luxuriam et *superbiam* fient istae duce destructionis et pestilentiae' (Wright, *PolP* I:82). *PP* regularly associates pestilence with pride (8.348, 11.58–60, B 10.72), and its indiscriminate effect on rich and poor alike needed no labouring. *poynt*: natural disorders having a moral 'reason' and (secondarily) 'purpose' (MED s.v. *pointe* n. (1), 6 (f) and (d)). **Z 34** Cf. *AW* 65/1: 'hwet is word but wind'. **118** *poffed*: hinting at what Z 40 makes explicit, that the *wynd of ys word* is the divine breath; as the MED exx. under *puffen* v. (a) show that the verb usually implies a human agent, a play on sense (b), found at 15.97, may be inferred. **119** *ensaunple*: for a later *ensanple...on trees* cf. 16.246, and for other 'natural' exempla B 7.128, 10.294, 11.324, 12.236, 15.472. These presuppose the 'sacramental' understanding of the world definitively expressed by Alan of Lille in 'Omnis mundi creatura' (*PL* 210:579; *OBMLV* no. 242). *do þe bettre*: the pregnant formula summing up the Vision's penitential intent, to effect attrition or repentance through fear of divine punishment (*drede...fordon*). This corresponds to simple conversion, not a higher stage in the life of virtue as will unfold in the *Vita* section later. **122** *hem alle*: despite **C**'s revision of **ZAB** *ye* to *we* 119, the pronoun's referent remains semantically disjunct, its immediate grammatical antecedent being the trees that emblematise diverse human types in the *felde of folk*, its more remote one his hearers. But *ous alle*, while more logical, might have seemed too sombre even for a penitential *sermo*. **125b** *to heuene*: 'to turn their minds to heavenly things'; likewise avoiding the repetition of B 11 in B 23 //. **126–45** now partly restate in a public sermon what Reason said to the King in his 'impossibilia' speech at 4.111ff. **126–7** recall Reason's stance towards the Dreamer at 26–8 above. *wastoures*: the pl. eliminating the first appearance of a personage who is to feature prominently at 8.149–78, but so as more exactly to echo the wording of Pr 24. In **ZAB** the sg. type-name signifies a caterpillar of the (rural) commonwealth, corresponding at a lower plane to the spendthrift of *WW*. **127** *tyme spille*: the eschatological character of 'honest work' is stressed in **C**, taking up the theme of 92–101. **128–33** describe three women who illustrate varieties of pride defined in penitential treatises. **128** *Purnele*: surnamed Proudheart at 6.3 (see on 4.111 above), with Wat's nameless wife embodying 'pompe and delit in temporal hyenesse and glori[ye] in this worldly estaat' (*CT* X 404), specifically as manifested in 'costlewe furrynge in hir gownes' (ibid. 417) and 'superfluitee...of clothynge' (431). **130** *Stoue*: a common name with no special meaning. **131** *Felyce*: the (?ironically) courtly name (cf. B 12.46) of a shrewish woman who exemplifies *inobedience, despit* or *janglynge* (*CT* X 395, 40). Timely discipline might save her from the punishment-stool reserved for scolds in the harsh world of village society (see on 3.79). **132** *Watte*: short for Walter; perhaps the same found with his wife in Betene's brew-house at 6.362. **133** *half marc*; *grote*: the value of a skilled workman's wage for a week (*Bn*); cf. the Wife of Bath in *CT* I 453–5. **134–5** The internal rhyme and assonance exemplify more 'lexical Platonism': the butcher is linked with his chopper and 'Betty' becomes her proper self when 'beaten'. *Butte* (or *Bette*): perhaps short for Bartholomew; a name given to a beadle and a butcher elsewhere. *Betene*: diminutive of Beatrice or Elizabeth; her sloth is 'ydelnesse...the yate of alle harmes' (*CT* X 713). *Sk* sees her as Butte's daughter, doubtless because children are mentioned in 136ff; but the only other Betene in *PP* is the *brewestere* of 6.352 who leads Glutton astray. **136–9** The **B** form (34–9) echoes a stanza preserved in *Fasciculus Morum* [*FM*], ed. Wenzel 1978:146, vs. 12. **137** *wynnynge*: well-to-do parents being commonly observed to indulge their offspring more. **C** omits the **B** line relating the collapse of discipline to parental indulgence of children who had survived the 1361–2 *mortalité des enfants* (so known because it especially affected children; see B 10.79 and McKisack 331). Also omitted is the common 'family' maxim (cf. Pr 203) having in the 'Proverbs of Hendyng' (Morris & Skeat 1873:36) the form *Luef child lore byhoueth* (and deriving from the b-half of the quoted Biblical verse). **139a** 'He that spareth the rod hateth his son: [but he that loveth him correcteth him betimes]'. The form of the Biblical a-verse's second part is closer to our 'spoil the child'. **142** *Lyue... leue*: 'Platonic' wordplay suggesting intrinsic relation between 'life' and 'belief'.

146–79 (B 10.292–329, A 11.204–13) move from briefly exhorting the secular clergy to warning the endowed religious at length in 35 lines expanded from B 10.292–308. Monastic foundations had been granted land and property by lay benefactors for the purposes of prayer and charity, and Reason's point here is that as the monks hold their lands from the crown, the king is entitled to take these over if they fail to observe their Rule. The lines were seen by some Reformation-period readers as a 'prophecy' of the Dissolution of the monasteries under Henry VIII (Crowley, *Address* in Sk *B-Text*, xxxiv; Jansen 1989); but they only advocate reform (Chaucer's more genial satire on the Monk in *CT* I 165–207 owes them several details). **C** here brings forward a passage from a longer critique of the clergy in B X to voice a positive ideal of enclosed religious life, with warm praise of monastic (and university) society, an attack on current failures in observance, and a warning of forcible change involving (without wholesale dispossession) a major redistribution of monks' wealth to the friars (173). **146** *Gregory*: Pope St Gregory the Great (*c*. 540–604), one of the four great Doctors of the Latin Church (21.317, B 9.73). Abbot at Rome in 585 and Pope in 590, he ardently promoted regular monasticism (then only a half-century old), exempting the orders from episcopal jurisdiction and making them directly responsible to the Pope (Lawrence 1989:19–22, 33). *grete clerk*: alluding to Gregory's learning, which had a pervasive influence on Western theological culture and spirituality (see Evans 1986; Straw 1988). *bokes (Morales B 293)*: the vaguer **C** is more accurate; Gregory's massive *Expositio in Librum Iob, sive Moralium Libri XXXV* (the *Moralia*) expounds *Job* in the literal, mystical and especially moral senses. The only patristic work **L** cites by name, it seems to have affected his thought more deeply than any book apart from the Bible. **147** *reule*: Gregory wrote no Rule as such, nor is the 'fish' simile in the *Moralia*; but the sentiment accords with his stress on 'stability of mind' (Straw 66–89). He is also an apt authority on the conduct of English monastic life, since his Prior Augustine, whom he sent to evangelise the English in 596, set up England's first 'Roman'-style monastery in Canterbury (see B 15.444). **148–51** The semi-proverbial 'As a fish without water lacks life, so does a monk without a monastery', attributed to Pope Eugenius by Gratian (*Sk*), occurs in the C4th *Life* of St Antony (reputedly the original founder of monachism) that was a source of *Legenda Aurea* [*LA*] 21.iv (see B 15.269ff // C 17.6ff) and is quoted in *CT* I.179–81. The proverb's warning against wandering or instability is here adapted to attack the worldliness arising from the monks' involvement in mundane business. **152–3** A sentiment found in Bp. Thomas Brinton, 'si sit vita angelica in terra, aut est in studio, vel in claustro' (Orsten 1970) and also in Petrus Ravennus, 'Si paradisus in hoc mundo est, in claustro vel in scholis' (Kaske

1957²:481–3), L's wording seeming to fuse the two. **153** *cloystre*: synecdoche for the religious house and thence metonymic for the enclosed contemplative way of life. *scole*: 'university' (Bennett 1974:14). The strong monastic influence on the layout of early collegiate buildings at both universities is evident in William of Wykeham's New College at Oxford (1379), with its original cloister still extant. **C** removes both the stress on learning given by the identical rhyme of B 302/3 (part of the 'praise' passage added in **B**) and the negative *scorn*, which sits ill with *ese*. **155** A full-stop is justifiable after *lerne //* as completing the double statement about cloister and school; but a semi-colon may be preferable if the primary contrast intended by *Ac* 156 is between the more rigorous academic and the lax monastic communities. Strikingly, no corresponding criticism of *scole-clerkes* follows that of the monks (on the relations between these cf. Lawrence 1989:141–6, and on the state of monasteries at this period McKisack 1959:305–9). **157** *ryde...aray*: doubtless with a pun on the literal meaning (that when monks hunt they do not wear their long habits). **158** *ledares..*: understand *ben* before. *lawedays*: days for holding a session of the manorial or sheriff's court, at which monks as major local landlords might be envisaged as involved (the revision recognises that monks, as opposed to parsons and friars, were not conspicuous in love-days). *ypurchaced*: buying more land out of their surplus revenues. **159–60** could refer to hunting when riding *out* to scattered estates (*Pe*), since some great abbots travelling on business even took hounds in their train (*Sk*), but more realistically perhaps to hunting when riding *over* adjacent fields of the same religious house, as the notion of leading a pack would imply (cf. *CT* I 90–2, 207). **A 11.213** *Poperiþ*: a word found only here and securely glossed from its variants (*pryken, ryden*). MED s.v. derives it from *poppen* v.1. 'strike' (as with spurs), itself instanced only a half-century later. **161–2** The lordly monk expects his serving-man to behave towards him as to a knight (cf. 21.28). The antonymic paronomasia on *lord(eyne)* anticipates that at 8.46 (*quene / queene*): the monk is not a real lord, so his servant has not failed in 'courtesy', as perhaps the real lords *have* (towards their children). **164** *ryne...auters*: a commonplace in Wycliffite criticisms of the regular clergy (Wyclif, *Select English Works*, 1.308–9, 313–15), as noted by *SkPe*. The altars being those of parish churches where the monastic corporation was the legal rector, to whom the greater (or agrarian) tithe was due, it is being alleged that absentee rectors neglect the state of the parish church's roof. **165–6** Resident regular canons (see on 170) look to their own comfort rather than the charitable work that is their calling. **168, 171** The metaphor is one of an authoritative priest-figure hearing the monks' confession of faults and imposing an appropriate collective 'penance'. But as Reason's 'prophecy'

is an indefinite, quasi-apocalyptic threat that the regulars' pride and negligence will one day be punished by a 'king' (who could be Christ), it need hardly imply a sacral rôle for a secular monarch. **169** *as...telleth*: a formulaic stave-phrase also at B 9.41 and varied at 3.426, 18.222, the reference being to the text about beating at 177a. **170** *chanons*: canons regular (as opposed to secular canons attached to cathedral or collegiate churches), who followed a semi-monastic mid-C11th rule drawn up from writings uncertainly attributed to St Augustine (whence 'Augustinian' Canons). Unlike monks, they could be parish priests, and were subject to the bishop's authority (see further Dickinson 1950, Lawrence 1989:163–9). Only the form from Central French *chanoine* occurs for the regulars, AN *canon* (B 10.46) referring to a secular canon. **171** *Ad pristinum...*: 'to return to the original state', first used by Isidore of Seville (*PL* 83:899–902) to refer to a penitent cleric's restoration to his rights. Alf*G* finds *status* to mean (a) 'grace, in which the penitent has to his credit as much merit as though he had never sinned', (b) '"good fame", with the restoration of all legal privileges'. But neither seems relevant here, since the phrase has a quite different application, declaring (within a metaphorical context) that the endowed regulars will be required *as a penance* to 'return to an original state' of material simplicity (*Pe,* Baldwin in Alf*C* 75) that will help them recover the spiritual purity of their founders (cf. Scase 1989:88–9, 202n14). Although used by Wyclif in 1378, the idea of disendowing the possessioners was not necessarily linked with heretical positions at this period (Gradon 1982:188–9). **172** *barnes*: the direct beneficiaries, if lands their ancestors gave the monks reverted to the original owners. **172a** 'Some trust in chariots, and some in horses: [but we will call upon the name of the Lord our God]. They are bound and have fallen; [but we are risen and are set upright]' (Ps 19:8–9). The psalm's omitted b-verses make clear the double analogy with the 'blameworthy' clergy ensnared by worldliness who are brought to a fall (the horses are especially apt after 157–60) and with those who trust only in God for their livelihood. **B 10.320** *Beatus vir*: 'Blessed is the man [who hath not walked in the counsel of the ungodly]' (Ps 1:1). The *techyng* of Ps 1 is that those who rely on God will prosper, while the wicked will perish, and it supplies 'prophetic' backing for the expected dispossession of the endowed regulars. This psalm-opening is cited again at B 5.418 and B 13. 52. **173–7 (B 10.322–6)** The general (and more optimistic) sense of **C** is that the monks' disendowment will release wealth for supporting the friars, whose valuable missionary rôle in society seems to be compromised by dependence on begging for a livelihood. **173** *fraytour*: the refectory where they ate; friaries were often laid out on the same plan as monasteries save for a cloister (Lawrence 1989:304). Although the word is etymologically unrelated, its derived form was near-identical with *frater* 'friar'. **175** *Constantyn*: a loose metonym for the future king who it is hoped will bring this about. Emperor *c.* 306–37 AD, he was the first ruler to provide land and property for the maintenance of the clergy, who had hitherto lived by their work and the gifts of the faithful (see also on 17.220ff). **176** *Abbot...*: a generalised figure of monastic rule; the Abbess may be his 'niece' (a vestige of *godchildren* **B**) because the female branches of religious orders generally followed the male as subsidiary foundations, but perhaps also because abbesses often came from noble and gentry families that had connections with the Church, through which they secured advancement (Lawrence 1989:216–17). **177** *knok...wounde*: surprisingly violent language if thought of as coming from Reason; but the suspicion that fierce tensions lurked beneath the convent's surface gentility emerges later under the sin of Wrath at 6.128–50. *crounes*: if 'shaven crowns', then 'a poor alteration' (*Sk*), being inapplicable to women. The sense should be 'top of the head' not 'tonsure' (MED s.v. *coroune* n. 10 (a), not 11); but with a probable pun on sense 1 'monarch's crown', the witty image of 'crounes' being struck by a 'king' is well purchased. **177a** (**B 327a**) 'How is the oppressor come to nothing, the tribute hath ceased? [**B**] / The Lord hath broken the staff of the wicked, the rod of the rulers, / [That struck the people in wrath] with an incurable wound' (Is 14: 4–6)'. Though *Pe* is right that 'altering of the syntax by omission' makes the 'rod' the object of the divine blow that causes an incurable injury, this does not necessarily render 'the relation of the second half of 177 to the idea of monastic reform' difficult. For in the analogy, the 'oppressor' ('the king of Babylon') is presumably 'the Abbot of England' (= monastic lordship) and his 'tribute' the income monks get on their property, while the 'rod' is a metonym for their economic and social power, which would indeed be incurably injured by reform as radical as that envisaged. **178** *as...tolde* (*Caym...awake* **B 328**): both versions have an 'eschatological' flavour, but **C** imagines a spiritual renewal of the Church prior to the advent of the 'king' (who seems increasingly like Christ), while **B** looks to the coming of Antichrist, figured as Cain. There is an obscure allusion to unspecified 'chronicles'; possibly pertinent here is the renewal of the Church's 'clothing' envisioned in Eph 5:26–7 (and cf. Apoc 7:14).

B 322–7 The ambiguity in the imagery of the source-lines could be what prompted the **C** revision; for since the 'coffers' of **323** stand for the royal treasury into which monastic revenues would first revert, the notion that friars will get the 'key' to this might be thought to contradict **L**'s point. **324** *godchildren*: 'spiritual children' (*Sk*); see on 147. **325** *Abyngdoun*: in Berks (now in Oxon), one of the oldest and richest abbeys, levelled at the Dissolution. As 'the house into which the monks...

were first introduced in England' it is 'representative of English monachism' (*Wr*). Galloway (2001[1]:22–4) proposes to find a specific allusion to the Abingdon townsmen's attempt to 'impeach' the Abbot before the king's council in 1368 for infringing on their ancient liberties, and takes the phrase 'knok of a kynge' as corresponding to the legal term *impetitus* 'impeachment'.

180–200 Returning to **B** V, the revision continues the text's expansion by deepening the theological content of Reason's teaching. **181** *tresor*: the disillusioned wordplay in **B** (*tresor / treson*) implying the people's possible unreliability is removed, perhaps because now realised in the 1381 uprising, which **L** may not have wanted thought of as a simple act of treasonable rebellion. *Conscience*: no exact allusion to specific words seems intended; but he had earlier urged the king against the pursuit of conventional *tresor* when arguing against Mede. **182–3** **C**'s counselling of accord between the different orders of society comes in the aftermath of the Peasants' Revolt and reflection on the reasons for it. *ryche*: presumably denoting secular and religious lords and the great merchants. *comuners*: craftsmen, tradespeople and peasants. **184–5** 'Let no machinations or greedy self-interest cause divisions between you and prevent the unanimity needed to discharge your responsibilities'. **184** *kyne counsayl*: 'kind of plan'; but as *kyne* is an archetypal spelling for *kene* 'sharp, harsh' (see 22.97), a semi-pun may be intended here, such counsel being likeliest to create dissension. **185** *That*: 'so that...not'; an idiosyncratic 'preclusive' use of *that* without *ne*. *ʒoure wardes kepe*: ambiguous in sense and reference, so as to allow some play on 'charges, responsibilities [i.e. to keep guard over]' (MED s.v. 2, citing this line) and 'city-wards [under your joint administrative care]' (ibid. 3 (b)). **186–8** The implied message is that everyone should keep his place, and that rebellion against the king's authority (not necessarily the same as the social status quo) is inspired by a devilish lie. *comune*: a more 'democratic' variant on the 'heavenly court' image at 1.104. **187** *Lucifer the lyare*: the stress on the Devil's lies, earlier introduced through his identification with Falsehood (1.60), is increased in **C**, as in the digression inserted at 20.350–8. It seems Reason finds diabolic influence at work in the 'lies' of those who provoked discord and rebellion against the king's authority, presumably the *wyse clerkes* (20.354) whose abstract arguments against private ownership (22.275–6) might have incited such as John Ball to teach the *lewed* disruptive doctrines of social equality. **189a** The repetition here of Conscience's injunction to the friars at B 20.246 may assume the audience's familiarity with UNITY as a 'nature-name' for the Church at the end of the B-Text. Although this sermon is addressed to all states and conditions of men, it may be implied that as the Church plays a special rôle in achieving social cohesion, its wealth is correspondingly a major source of divisiveness in the *comune*. **191–6 (B 52–5)** Reason's prayer to the Pope in **C** also has its admonition (B 51b) removed, no doubt in the same cause of fostering 'unity'. But it is unclear whether Wycliffite attacks on the highest ecclesiastical authority are being treated as analogous to (or even in part the source of) attacks on the authority of the state. **191** *haue pite*: hardly 'treat gently' (*Bn*), if the severe tone of B 19.432–3, 446–50*a* is borne in mind. The speaker in **B** is certainly here ascribing fault to the Pope, but the phrase fits less well in **C**, which shifts blame to secular rulers. **192–3** The injunction not to give pardons and indulgences to kings stipulates an end primarily to war between rulers (*alle...peple* being a single integral phrase), secondarily to antagonisms between rulers and their own people. **195b–6a** is not easy to interpret literally. Presumably not urging tolerance of evil-doing (cf. 4.94–104 above), it may be discreetly recommending pardon in perpetuity (i.e. no distraint upon their heirs) to those who took part in the Rebellion, and a more conciliatory approach than the harsh reprisals Richard's government took against the convicted rebels. But given that this is to be a 'penance', like that to be imposed on the monks (168–71 above), the king's own partial guilt seems inescapably implied. **B 52** *to kepe*: in your keeping (to administer), i.e. as rulers and judges (cf. B Pr 133). *Trupe*: Justice, as revealed by God. *youre coveitise*: '(the object of) your desire', with a punning implication as at B 3.164 (removed in revision) that, if they desire Truth, it will free them from that sin. **B 55** *Amen...*: 'Amen, I say to you, I know you not' (Mt 25:12); from the Parable of the Virgins, which appropriately teaches responsibility in one's office, with a possible reminiscence of Mt 7:23 'I never knew you', addressed to those 'that work iniquity'. **197** virtually repeats Pr 48. **198** *seynt*: both a title and an attribute 'holy' (as at 1.80, 11.204). The thought here is that the destination of a spiritual 'pilgrimage' should be God himself, here denoted by his primary 'nature-name' of Truth, like a saint the location of whose shrine may be known (as it is by Piers Plowman at 7.254). **199** *Qui...*: the formula-ending of many prayers and blessings, and appropriate here to Reason as a bishop concluding his sermon. If its well-known appearance in the Nicene Creed (*Brev.* 2:484) is being consciously echoed ('Et in Spiritum Sanctum...Qui cum Patre et Filio simul adoratur...'), then 'an identification of Truth with the Holy Spirit' (AlfQ) may indeed be intimated; but the poem's 'nature-name' for the Holy Ghost is *Grace*. Moreover, the early, fuller form of the line in Z 71–5, with its bracketing use of the 'Seek St Truth' phrase, clearly invokes the protection of Son and Spirit on those who seek (what can only be) the First Person, and this fits better with the pervasive use of 'Truth' to mean 'God (the Father)'. *pat...byfalle*: 'may good fortune come to those...' (a 'jussive' subjunctive).

Passus VI (ZAB V)

PASSUS SIX is the first of two in **C** dealing with the CONFESSIONS OF THE DEADLY SINS and the appearance of PIERS, which filled one passus in **B**. Though not dividing at the same point, it reverts to the more moderate size of **A**, breaking the massive B V into more digestible portions of about 450 (VI) and 300 lines (VII) each. It deals with Pride, Envy, Anger, Lust and Greed; but why Sloth begins VII instead of ending VI is not clear. **L** develops the Sins episode with over 100 lines of material from B XIII. He shortens Envy by 12 lines; leaves Gluttony and Sloth; but expands Pride by 50 lines, Lechery by 20, Wrath by 12 and Greed by 35. He thus obliterates the distinction in his earlier handling of the penitential theme between two separate phases of 'attrition' and 'contrition' (the Seven Deadly Sins; Haukyn's oblique 'confession'). But the loss in structural clarity is made up for by detailed improvements in expression. Haukyn's successor Actyf in C XV becomes a moderately virtuous character and, as a plausible contrast with the contemplative Patience, fitter to be the servant of Piers (who embodies both aspects). The passus falls into a brief prelude and six sections: (i) Pride 3–62; (ii) Envy 63–102; (iii) Wrath (103–69); (iv) Lechery (170–95); (v) Greed (196–307), followed by Evan the Welshman and Robert the Robber (308–14, 315–29), and Repentance's exhortation (330–48); (vi) Gluttony (349–440).

The moral scheme used derives from Gregory the Great's ordering, with the four 'spiritual' sins first and the three 'bodily' ones last: Pride, Anger, Envy, Avarice; Sloth, Gluttony, Lechery (Bloomfield 1952:105–21). It was familiar from vernacular works in the tradition stemming from the *Summa Vitiorum* of Peraldus (1236) and the AN *Somme le Roy* of Frère Lorens (1279). These included the early C14th English *Ayenbite of Inwyt* and *Handlyng Synne* and the later *Speculum Vitae* and *Book of Vices and Virtues* (see Pantin 1955 and Bloomfield generally). But easily the most accessible contemporary analogue is Chaucer's *Parson's Tale*, a schematic account of the 'parts' of Penitence and the capital sins in the sequence Pride, Envy, Anger, Sloth, Avarice, Gluttony, Lechery, a work that is close to *PP* in thought and phrasing and may reflect knowledge of it. **L** made some major changes in revising. **Z** treats Envy and Anger as a *joint* sin and **A** *omits* Anger. **B** *adds* Anger and ends with ROBERT THE ROBBER as a kind of 'summing-up' of all the sins before REPENTANCE returns to intercede for them all. **C** places Lechery after Anger, putting Robert (less subtly but logically enough) not at the end but after Avarice and a new character EVAN THE WELSHMAN. But no particular significance attaches to the final order where, after three of the five 'spiritual' sins (Pride, Envy and Anger), come a 'bodily' sin Lechery, the fourth spiritual sin Avarice, and the remaining bodily sins Gluttony and Sloth. The parallel version, where it differs, is discussed below *after* the initial commentary on the basic reference-text **C**.

1–2 PRELUDE: *Will's Repentance* **1** *Repentaunce*: envisaged here as an impulse of spirit ('ran') provoked by the sermon describing the effects of divine judgement, and personifying both remorse for sin and the recoil from sin that initates conversion of heart (on this very original creation, see Alford 1993). Despite the structural and conceptual change noted above, the **C** sinners are still moved to acknowledge and confess mainly out of a 'carnal' fear of punishment by an angry Lord rather than a 'spiritual' sorrow at offending a loving Father. **2** *Will*: the collective and individual *Animus* (16.182) that, *qua* guilty of all these vices, synecdochically 'represents' the folk of the field and is affected by the 'movement' of repentance. That the sinner-dreamer has the poet's presumed name is (even if fortuitously) an outstanding instance of the modesty-topos in medieval literature. But although reference to 'Will' in the third person here makes his symbolic rôle clear, the logically discordant (if dramatically striking) use of the first person at B 5.184–5 is abandoned, with a gain in clarity but some loss of tension (as often in the revision of **B** to **C**). *wepe*: recognised and encouraged in the period as an authentic outward expression of inward repentance (Vernet 1930:123–5), though its true meaning remains ambiguous for the beholder.

(i) 3–61 describe Pride, 'the beginning of all sin' (Ecclus 10:15); the only Sin allowed a proper name or presented as a woman (though both Envy and Anger include female examples). Gender is, however, indeterminate after the opening eight lines retained from **B**, and even these are not exclusive to a female speaker. All the capital vices had Latin names of feminine gender, but Superbia was the one most commonly presented as a woman (see *vanagloria* in Katzenellenbogen 1939: figs. 8a, 9, 15, 16, 66). Awareness of the categorisations in the penitential literature is obvious from the correspondence between **L**'s account of Pride and the sins Chaucer specifies under Superbia (*CT* X 390–405), e.g. *inobedience* 15–17a, 19, *swellynge of herte* 7b–18, *contumacie* 20–1, *despit* 22–3, *arrogance* and *pertinacie* 24–9, *veyneglorie* 30 (cf. esp. *CT* X 404), *ypocrisie* 31–3, *avauntynge* 34, *inpacience* 35, *elacioun* 36–7, *insolence* 38–41, 42–6, *presumpcioun* 50–60. The closeness in thought is seen at ll. 28–30 'wysor / To carpe...proud in port' compared with 'to regard of...his konnyng, and of his spekyng, and of his beryng' (*CT* X 399). **3** *Purnele Proud-herte*: very briefly treated in **ZAB** but most expanded in **C**, with 30 lines from B XIII and 18 new. *platte...erthe*: a symbolic self-abasement 'putting down' her high and mighty airs. **6** *hayre*: worn in place of a soft undergarment to discipline desire for bodily gratification. **7** *affayten*; *fers*: terms fig-

uring wilful self-love as a wild hawk that needs strict training to be tamed. (*ParsT* 479–80 offers not a physical 'remedy' against pride but 'suffering to be missaid' as the third form of 'humility of heart'). **8** *holde*: i.e. 'I shall hold.' **10–11** *of alle... hated*: either '*from* all whom I have despised' or '*on account of* all my contemptuous hostility against people'. The latter is likelier as the mercy is sought from God (cf. 16), and so *hem* for *that* in **Z** need not itself favour the former reading. For *hated* here denotes scorn or contempt (MED s.v. *haten* v. 1(c), not 1(b), under which this line is cited), forming *part* of the sense of 'envy' < L. *invidia*). This probably accounts for the word's original presence in **ZA**, the revision of which removes possible confusion with that later vice. **ZA 86/53** *þat*: 'to whom'; on this oblique use see *MES* 97. **12** *Resoun*: i.e. at 117 above. **13** *sharpeliche*: both 'in unsparing detail' and 'vigorously' (MED s.v. *sharpli* adv. 2 (a) and (b)); heartfelt confession of sin is to be as painful as its *scharp salue* (22.307), the *hayre* donned as penance. *shak of*: like the furred gown of 4.111. **14–29** These new lines progress from breaches of the 4th commandment ('Honour thy father and mother') to 'authorial' self-rebuke for satire on the clergy. That little of this relates to the *Vanitas*-figure of Purnele understandably prompts *Pe*'s question whether 'a separate personification of Pride begins to speak at l. 14'. Certainly, what he calls 'the eclectic nature of the text' accounts for the disjunction between 14–60 and 3–11; but such lack of 'fit' is already present in the shift from the masculine Will at 2 to the feminine Purnele at 3 (and cf. on Envy at B 109, revising A 91). Moreover, as some heterogeneity is to be expected in the drama of vices in action, Pride must be a composite figure with traits appropriate to different sexes and occupations, not a unique individual. The illustration of an extravagantly dressed young man in ms Douce 104 at f. 24r, although placed opposite the opening 'Purnele' lines, depicts the later, more obviously male figure suggested by ll. 30–5. **19–21** may be an oblique authorial self-accusation for Anima's criticisms at B 15.92–5 (though these are not in fact removed in **C**). **19** *Inobedient*: taking up B 13.282 and more accurately locating it in relation 'to his sovereyns and to his goostly fader' (*CT* X 393). **21–6** are clearly echoed by Usk, *TL* I. v. 117–19: '*wening his owne wit* more excellent than *other*; *scorning al maner devyse but his own* (see *Intro.* V § 11). **26** *in...maneres*: applying to the scorning or to the making known of his / her name. **30–61** take up the Haukyn section of B XIII, adding new lines at 38–40 and leaving only two unrevised; being based on the description of a man, they fit better if their speaker is male. **31** The false pretence to wealth or virtue is paralleled in *ParsT* 408–10 ('two maneres of Pride...withinne...and...withoute...that oon...signe of that oother'). **32** *Me* (*hym*) *wilnynge*: either an ethic dative 'desiring for myself' or a dative absolute phrase 'myself desiring', the participial adjective agreeing with the pronoun (*MES* 99–100, 115). The phrase is repeated as a nominative absolute at 41a without *me*. **36–41** describe *spiritual* pride taken 'in the goodes of grace...eek an outrageous folie' (*CT* X 470). **38** *secte*: probably in the light of *couent* 39 = 'religious order' (MED s. v. 2 (c)), the picture being of an itinerant whose lack of *stabilitas* would produce problems like those found under *Wrath* at 130, 162. **42** *And* (Or **B**): 'And / Or (that I was) the best...' **43** *strengest*: cf. 'pride...in his strengthe of body...is an heigh folye' (*CT* X 458). *styuest vnder gyrdel*: 'stoutest man alive' (*Pe*); but MED cites no other example of the phrase, and its positioning between 43a and 44 allows a *double entendre*, with *stif* here = 'potent' as well as 'valiant'. **45** 'And addicted to a way of living that no moral authority could commend.' **46** *fetures*: here clearly 'features' (MED s.v. *feture* n. (1) (b) or (c)), but in **B** either this or 'creatures' (ibid. 2 (b), as in its earliest use at *WPal* 2885–6: 'a mayde / *fairest of alle fetures* þat sche to-for hadde seie,' which is contextually ambiguous in the same way (contrast *WPal* 857 *so fair of alle fetures*). **47** *what*: i.e. charitable alms. **48** *They to wene*: 'so that they should suppose'; for the construction see on 5.21. **49–53** From boasting (as a branch of pride) comes exaggeration and thence outright lying. In 5.185–6 lying is connected with Lucifer's pride as the root of all sin, leading to his fall. **49–50** *And*: 'Even though (there was)...' *to telle*: dependent on *so bolde*. **52** *lyed on*: 'swore falsely by'. **59–60** 'I wanted people to know all that might occasion [particularly the] pride [I had] in getting people's praise' (**B**: 'that might please people and lead to his being praised'). Love of praise may come under *vauntynge* or *elacioun*; cf. 'desir to haue *commendacioun eek of the peple* hath caused deeth to many a busy man' (*CT* X 474). **60a** 'If I yet *pleased men*, I should not be the servant of Christ' (Gal 1:10); *and in another place*: 'No man can serve two masters' (Mt 6:24). A link between the two passages may be Mt 6:2: 'when thou dost an almsdeed [cf. 48–9 above], sound not a trumpet...as the hypocrites do...that they may be *honoured by men*'. **61** A variant of this semi-formulaic prayer for the sinner to be given the grace of repentance is repeated for Envy. While Repentance's responses illustrate the range of judgements open to confessors, from exhortation to refusal of absolution, these never fall to the indulgence shown by the friars who shrive Mede in IV and Lyf in XXII.

(ii) 63–102 The confession of ENVY replaces the 27-line **AB** passage with a revised form of B 13.325–42 that subordinates physical and social detail to the internal aspects of this 'spiritual' sin. **C** follows its source down to B 5.87 and then makes a deft textual suture with B 13.325 at 69. On the **ZAB** lines about Lechery at this point, see at 170. **62–8 63** *Enuye*: still with the wider etymological sense of its ultimate Latin source *invidia* 'evil / wicked will',

as at 87 // Z 94 (MED s.v. *envie* n. (1), = 'malice' in *ParsT*), to which the opposed virtue is *charite* Z 96, as well as the narrower moral theological sense of 'sorwe of oother mennes wele, and joye of othere mennes harm' that *ParsT* 483 derives from St Augustine (*Enarrationes in Psalmos* 104:17). *heuy herte*: reflecting the ambiguous 'sorrow' the envious feel, i.e. *dolor* not *contricio*, chagrin not remorse (*carefully* AB 59/76 shows how much it was the former). **64** *mea culpa*: through my fault; from the *Confiteor*, the priest's opening prayer in the penitential rite of the Mass. In **A** Envy simply declares his guilt, in **B** curses (?his sins) with the Latin formula (in the ablative), in **C** no less incongruously uses it to curse his enemies (a line indebted to the omitted B 106 //). **65** *clothes*: Envy's allegorical attire, itself a reified verb-phrase (infinitive or imperative), may owe something to the metaphor of Haukyn's sin-stained coat around which **B** developed this section, or be ironically inverting the Pauline garb of virtue and girdle of charity (Col 3:13–14). **66** *wroth*: a provocative action of twisting the raised and clenched fist around in the face of the other. *Wrath*: the only instance of one personified Sin interacting directly with another. The linking of envy with anger its companion sin, foreshadowed in the rudimentary sketch at Z 91–4, is confirmed at AB 66/83, 97/116, what joins them being 'hate' (cf. B 99, 114 below). **68** *Chidyng*: cf. the 'chidyng and wikkede wordes' noted in *ParsT* 525.

B 77–118 Lines 77–85 remain unchanged from **A**, 85–92 are new, and only 84a and 87 survive into **C**. **78** *kaury-maury*: a word of unknown origin found only in *PP*. **80** *foresleues*: cut from the long woollen outer garment of a friar; so he may be an ex-friar or, more straightforwardly, in another manifestation a friar in a *frokke*. The accusation of envy made against friars (that will later occur at B 20.273–6 despite the warning from Conscience at B 20.246) is cut from the **C** confession here as possibly a cheap gibe ill-suited to a portrait mainly of a layman (the half-line recurs in a complimentary context at B 15.230 //). **86** *neddres tonge*: a vestige of A 69; cf. 'the venym of Envye' in *ParsT* 530. **88** *bakbitynge*: a vice distinguished into five sub-species in *CT* X 493–5. *berynge... witnesse*: a phrase first instanced here and denoting not slander but perjury, a means of getting 'one's back' for which envy is a main motive. **89** *curteisie*: kindness and good-will being qualities against which calumny is a specific sin; but Envy remains capable of a 'false' courtesy at B 100 below. **91** *Gybbe*: familiar for Gilbert, here a type-name for any male neighbour. **91–2** Envy's 'joye of oother mannes harm' gives him more pleasure than his own prosperity, and is thus a 'synne ayayns kynde' (*CT* X491–2). *wey...chese*: the Essex wey of 3 cwt as opposed to the usual two-plus (*Sk*). The massive cheeses of ewes' milk (*Bn*), costing twopence in 1399 (see MED s.v. *wei* n (2), 1 (a), (a)), were brought to market in Cheapside through Aldgate and Bishopsgate (see Du Boulay, end-paper map). **A 69–72** These physiological details of sour and bitter secretions that cause flatulence and prevent Envy from eating may have been deleted as anticipating the imagery of A 99 (retained in **B**), 100–02 (also in **C**). *verious*: juice of unripe grapes or crab-apples, used in cookery and medicine. **93–118** have been excised in revision perhaps because material from them repeated in the Haukyn section is absorbed by **C** and some is not wholly suited to this sin (see on 108–10, 114, 118 below). Nevertheless, they illustrate standard aspects of envy paralleled in *ParsT*: thus with 93 cf. 'accusynge, whan man seketh occasion to *anoyen his neighebor*' (513); with 95, 97 'discord that vnbyndeth alle manere of *freendshipe*' (511); with 96 'Envye...is sory of alle the *bountees* of his neighebor' (489). **95** is virtually repeated at B 13.328, which is kept at C 72 below. **98** *speche*: removing the weak repetition of *tunge* in A 80. **101–2** On 'privy hate' or *malignitee* cf. *ParsT*: 'if he noght may, algate his *wikked wil* ne shal nat wante' (513). **106** *Crist...sorwe*: instead of prayer he 'curses men' (an idea retained in C 64–5). **107** *bolle...shete*: things of small worth; cf. 'grucchyng...agayns...los of catel' (*ParsT* 499–500). **108–10** seem more applicable to Greed than Envy (108 is very like Coveitise's admission at B 13.394–9 = C 6.281–5) and may have been dropped in part for that reason. **109** *Eleyne*: the switch to a feminine perspective is sudden, but unless this is a scribal error (see *TN*) the *his* of 111–12 will be a universal ungendered possessive. **110** *I wisshe*: a mark of covetousness rather than envy, which is strictly 'resentment at what another has' more than 'desire for it oneself' (see 116). **111–12** sum up the essence of this sin (see under C 63); with the laughter of *Schadenfreude* and the weeping of chagrin are contrasted the religious weeping noted at 2. **114** is substantially repeated at B 13.282, which fits in more aptly under Pride at C 6.35. **117** *loueles*: the mark of envy also at B 13.332. *dogge*: an image recurring at B 5.257. **118** *bolnep*: repeating 83. *for bitter*: on this use of the adj. as noun with *for* see *MES* 381.

69–102 The **C** revision seamlessly joins B 5.87 to B 13.325. **69** *blame*: 'to find fault with'; on the plain inf. as a predicate nominative see *MES* 526. **70–1** place malicious gossip under the sin of envy (as at B 13.333). *by*: 'about' not 'through'; *Watte* (Walter); *Wille*: stock type-names, **C**'s revision reducing the tongue-twisting quality of **B**. **73** *sleythes*: more appropriate than *strengthe* B 329, given that Envy is a coward. **74–5** describe a sin that destructively turns in upon itself when outward vengeance fails, the 'scissors' metaphor (suggested by the Latin *gladius acutus* of the second psalm-quotation) conveying the anguish of inward self-laceration. **75** *Lyke* (*As* **B**): 'As with'. *euen-cristene*: heightening the viciousness while avoiding the verbal repetition of 64–5 (*cursed hem* B 13.331b is pleonastic). **76** *Crist*: perhaps an inexact way

of referring to the Divine Teacher of the Prophet David more than a specific allusion to Christ's own prohibition of swearing (Mt 5:33–7). **76a** 'His mouth is full of *cursing*, and of *bitterness*, [and of deceit]: under his tongue are labour and *sorrow*' (Ps 9B (10):7). [And in another place]: 'The sons of men, whose teeth are weapons and arrows: and their *tongue* a *sharp* sword' (Ps 56:5). Both quotations aptly specify main features of envy. **77** *maystrie*: implying failure both to get one's way and to come out on top, hence frustrated expectation. *male(n)colie*: the sense shading from MED 3 (the emotional and spiritual sickness) to 4 (anger and gloomy anxiety), just as *angre* 79 implies both the inner state and the illness that attends it. The less common spelling without *n* shows the influence of mis-etymologising the prefix *male-* as 'evil, ill'. **78** *cardiacle*: for such palpitation caused by strong emotion cf. *CT* VI 313. **80** *twel-monthe*: perhaps alluding to the time since his last confession, this being obligatory once a year and usually made before the Easter Communion; cf. *ParsT* on the *rancour* that lasts 'from oon Estre day unto another' (551). **81** *Lechecraft...Lord*: spiritual healing through sacramental penance. On the pervasive image of grace as a holy medicine, cf. esp. the lines on Christ as *leche* at 18.138ff, 19.84ff, and for penance as medicine, B 17.96, 22.305ff. It is implied that Envy's physical symptoms will disappear if he receives medicine for the soul. *wycche*: here a maker of supposedly magical potions, rather than a sorcerer. **82–3** *ne can...To*: 'has no skill in comparison with...' **83** *Soutere of Southwerk*: an unknown but once no doubt familiar contemporary character. Southwark, just south of the Thames over London Bridge, was known for its brothels, breweries and alehouses (*CT* I 20), and lay beyond the reach of the strict City laws. *grace*: 'happy knack (of healing)', with ironic play on the theological sense (cf. 84). **B 13.340** *Shordych...Emme*: perhaps the person alluded to in Pr 226 which, present from **Z** through to **C**, may be the refrain of 'some low popular song' (*Sk*) that outlived its original subject (like the 'Mrs Porter' song in Eliot's *Waste Land*). The Lady Emma humorously named from Shoreditch, the area NE of Bishopsgate (Du Boulay, map), may have been one of those to whom Lechery resorted at times (189–91 below). **85** *chef hele*: echoing *cheef lyflode*, the revision at 68. The remedy Envy seeks for his sin is itself sinful, as consulting a 'witch' was strictly forbidden by the Church. **87** *euyl...euyl*: 'ill'; 'hard'; another piece of lexical Platonism, implying that just as the homonyms are semantically related, so are the conditions of soul and body. **88–90** The rhetorical question confounds physical and non-physical remedies, including the spiritually efficacious one of shrift's *scharp salue* (22.307). **88** *swellynge*: under Pride *ParsT* notes that 'Swellynge of herte is whan a man rejoyseth hym of harm that he hath doon' (398); but as this well describes Envy's attitude at

Commentary

B 111, his flatulent condition may be meant to signify the sin's 'condign' punishment. **89** *derworth drynke*: 'expensive cordial', perhaps including a tincture of gold (as in *CT* I 445), which was considered helpful 'agens cardeakle passioun' (Bartolomaeus Anglicus 16:4, tr. Trevisa 2:829). **C** avoids repeating the sense of *diapenidion* anticipated in B 121a. This rare word, which might have puzzled some readers, denotes a twisted thread of sugar used to relieve coughing. **91–2** The sense of 91 runs on to 92 and the revision improves precision and clarity, moving from the moderate hope of **A** through the incomplete and so potentially misleading **B** to the qualified two-stage penance in **C** (see 101–2). *ryht sory*: 'very / truly sorry', but also implying 'sorry in the right (properly religious) way' (MED s.v. *right* adv. 3(a), 9(a)). **93** *sory*: the first instance of a personified Sin 'carnally' misunderstanding a key theological idea (as Greed will 'restitution' at 237 //). **94** *megre*: revision of *mad* continuing the traditional motif of a vice given outward expression in its exemplar's physical appearance (cf. Pope's *Essay on Man* I. 217–8). Merchants are the only class for whom a specific form of sin is alleged to be not accidental but a trade. **95** is clearer, with the sinner as merchant acting as an agent for this sub-species of the vice, whereas in **B** it should properly be the Sin that designates a sub-species as its agent. **100** The internal rhyme neatly balances thought with action; (cf. 12.220, 18.292. 20.225, 258). **101–2** describe Envy's movement from remorse (*athynketh*) to seeking the grace of repentance as recommended at 91–2. *Lord...Lord*: simple affective *repetitio* with transposed lexical stress. **101b** *of thysulue*: not an objective genitive; hence, 'for the sake of that love which is yours by nature'.

(iii) 103–69 WRATH, defined in *ParsT* 535 as 'wikked wil to been avenged by word or by dede' (cf. 109b) and as arising out of envy (and also pride), seems to have been made a separate Sin in **B** so as to disengage the angry elements in *invidia* (see A 79, 97) from Envy's differentiating feature (see on 63 above). **104–17** are added, stressing the essence of Anger as the will to do bodily harm (see 109), whereas Envy's 'sword' is his tongue (cf. 77a above). In **C** a more general account of the fierce rebelliousness of this sin replaces **B**'s tendentious assault on the friars. **105** *wol*: on non-expression of the relative / personal pronoun see *MES* 204–5. **106** The same alliterative pattern recurs in 14.42 to express *invidia* as willed violence. **107** *to sle hym*: on the forms of manslaughter see *ParsT* 563–78. **110–13** *Inpacient...cause*: cf. *ParsT* on how the wrathful man 'blameth God of thyng of which he is hymself gilty' (580) and when 'amonested in his shrifte...wole he be angry' (584). **112** *somur...heruest*: if envy is incident to merchants, angry complaint could be specified as the husbandman's vice. **114–15; 117–18** The *repetitio* of 114a at 115a, shifting the stress from *alle* to *manere*, is typical of **C** (cf. on 101–02) as is the polyse-

mantic pun on by*fore / fore* (117b–118a). **116–17** 'Hearing harm' is not specified in *ParsT* but 'speaking harm' is, in the sin of 'double tonge, swiche as speken faire byforn folk and wikkedly bihynde' (644).

B 135–48 make the standard charge that friars' readiness to hear confessions encouraged by their successful sermons antagonises the parish clergy whose duty this is, and leads to that divisiveness within the Church adumbrated at Pr 64–5. The mendicants are regarded with some ambivalence; for despite **L**'s admiration for their founders' lofty ideals (see Clopper 1997), half a dozen major passages on them (2.220–42, 3.38–67, 10.1–60, 12.5–41a, 15.30–176, 22.230–384) offer almost nothing (if 5.173–5, 6.287–93 are excepted) favourable or friendly to the friars of his own day (Szittya, Du Boulay 1991:80–6, 134–6). But as **L** says little good about monks and parish clergy either, his emphasis on *Thyng þat al þe world woot* (12.36) may perhaps be best understood as part of the wider anti-clericalism of the period discussed by Scase 1989. **136** *gardyner*: of uncertain reference, possibly the master who instructed friars in preaching and hearing confessions. **137–8a** *lymytours*: a name applied later to the friar-confessor Sire *Penetrans-domos* at 22.347. The type is (for obvious reasons) the commonest butt of antifraternal satire, as in *CT* I 209, III 874. *lystres*: derived from OF *listre* 'reader' (< L. *lector*). Though *lector* usually signified a lecturer in theology (Lawrence 1994:128), *lystre* may denote contextually a friar who reads and preaches on a text, perhaps 'glosing' its hard moral demands 'to please lords' (as in B 20.355–72). *lesynges...lowe speche*: placed under *anger* in *ParsT*, these lies 'to the ese and profit of o man' (608) are presumably promises of 'esy penaunce' like those made to Mede in B 3.35–42. They produce an appearance of (false) humility, ironically anticipating B 16.6, where the leaves are *lele wordes*. The image suggests the potential for conflict in the Church arising from uncontrolled expansion of the mendicant religious foreshadowed in B Pr 66–7//. **140–1** *fruyt*: it is not obvious how friars' becoming confessors to *lordes* will make *folk* turn to them on such a scale as to antagonise the parish clergy. Perhaps the implication is that the nobility's favour encourages mendicants to preach critically about 'possessioners', so that ordinary people *in consequence* (hence 'fruit') prefer to confess to them, especially in Lent (and thereafter make their special Easter offering of alms to a friar rather than to the parson). Such sentiments as 'Thise curatz been ful necligent and slowe / To grope tendrely a conscience / In shrift' (aptly cited by *Sk* from *CT* III 1816–18) would understandably arouse the strife of which Wrath speaks. **147–8** *spiritualte*: their dispute about the value of parsons' earnings impoverishing both and forcing them to live on prayers and 'spiritual' things alone, or leaving one side with all the handsome donations from the faithful.

528

The text does not specify whether this refers to a present or future situation, or whether the friars want evangelical poverty for all or simply equal shares of the ecclesiastical cake (see on C 125–6 below). B 20.276ff suggest that **L** thought mendicants wanted the Church's wealth equally distributed amongst all the clergy. Compare *CT* III 1723, where the friar urges the people not to give alms to possessioners who have 'wele and habundaunce', i.e. the *spiritualte* or income from their benefice.

118–42 examine Wrath's life among the religious. **118 C** alters **B** to make the quarrel one between friars and bishops, who object to their hearing confessions without permission. The religious orders were under the direct authority of the Pope, but as the mendicants' work was in the dioceses, it could here be implied that if the ordinary refused his consent, they might persist without official approval and even criticise the bishop for lack of zeal. **123** *beggares and barones*: mendicant friars and the lordly prelates. **125–6** Wrath's assertion refers to an anticipated state of affairs, but arguably (notwithstanding the note on B 147–8 above) this is already the sense of **B** and could be expressed by placing a stop after *ooper* B 147 and a comma after *aboute* 149, the futurity being implicit in the present tense *reste*. An end to the strife Wrath foments between mendicants and 'possessioners' (including monks) will only come when one or other extreme solution is adopted. But at the end of the poem (22.384) Conscience proposes as a middle way the provision of adequate endowments to support the friars' ministry without any need for mendicancy. **127** *fortune*: glossing 'grace' in B 150 without repeating a phrase used at 83 by Envy. **130** *coek*: the 'convent-servant' figure effectively grows from *gardyner* B 136, but the latter has been removed in revision by **C**. **132** *pore ladies*: 'poor' because they vowed to own no personal property, 'ladies' because most nuns came from the upper ranks of society (Lawrence 1989:216–19) and had the same courtesy title *Dame* 'Madam' as their secular counterparts. Joan, Clarissa and Petronilla are all genteel-sounding names (though also borne by 'low' characters at 6.365, 366, 8.71 and possibly B 7.44). **133** *iangling*: spiteful gossip, one of the sins of the tongue (see *ParsT* 650) that lead to violence. These sexual insinuations refer to defects that would canonically debar a nun from becoming prioress. **136** *chapun-cote*: an undignified spot for the purpose, but perhaps hinting slyly at earlier dalliance with some *trede-fowel* in the same place. Purnele's situation would lead to her fitness for election being questioned at the convent's chapter-court. If the child's father were a priest, the case would come before the diocesan court and both might be declared *infamis* (see at B 166 below). **B 159** *chirie-tyme*: alluding to the licentious behaviour associated with the cherry-fairs held towards midsummer in the orchards. **137** The revision loses the *wordes / wortes* pun (Schmidt

1987:110) but avoids repetition of *ioutes* while creating the pungent irony of *sustres* and *lady* 138.

B 164–6 seem less Anger's sentiment than an authorial interjection 'voiced' through the immediate speaker, since it is echoed at B 19.162. **164** *Gregory*: here Gregory IX (Pope 1227–41), who forbade abbesses to hear nuns' confessions (cited *Bn* from *Decretals*, ed. Friedberg, ii. 887) because (the text implies) as mischievously gossipy women they could not keep them secret. **166** *infamis*: 'of ill repute', a term in canon law (AlfQ) for one formally pronounced guilty of *infamia* for serious irregularities (of which revealing the secrets of the confessional would be one), with resultant loss of the faculty to exercise holy orders.

143–63 By adding **143–50 C** replaces **B**'s clear 'religious' sequence of friars-nuns-monks with a 'three estates of womanhood' schema of (consecrated) virgins, wives and widows. No especially misogynistic animus need be suspected from this move to redress the sex-balance amongst the Sins. **144b–6** should perhaps be understood as in quotation marks; but the shift of Wrath from the standpoint of subject to that of observer is best sustained if the second pronoun at 147 is *she* not *Y*. **145** *Letyse-atte-Style*: a convenient type-name for (possibly) the wife of *Symme* at 207 below. **146** *haly-bred*: bread blessed and distributed after Mass to those who had not received Communion (i.e. most parishioners). One's position in the line to receive it, like the Wife of Bath's at the Offertory procession (*CT* I 449–52), could become a cause of dissension (cf. Duffy 1992:125–7). **147** *chydde*: under quarrelling *ParsT* 625, 630 cites such name-calling as 'thou harlot' and warns that a 'servant of God' should not wrangle (II Tim 2:24). **151–63** This favourable account may be meant to balance Reason's criticisms at 143–79 above by stressing that many monks pursue a life of tranquil order, disturbers of which are severely disciplined. **153** *Priour*: the head of a minor monastery (priory) or the deputy head of a major one (abbey). *Suppriour*: the Prior's deputy. *Pater Abbas*: the abbot (< Lat & Gk *abbas* < Aram. *abba* 'father'), having, as head of the monastic *familia*, the authority of a father over his spiritual 'children'. **154** *tales*: the penalty for malicious gossip being prison food and corporal punishment. *þe bare ers*: as illustrated in a representation of Patientia beating Ira at Southrop, Glos. (Kaske 1968: pl. 59c). **160** *otherwhile*: i.e. on special occasions such as feast days or founder's day, when he gets drunk and his pent-up anger pours out. **161–3** *flux...couʒe*: the slanderous utterances being like bouts of diarrhoea or vomiting that last for several days. **162–3** *couent*: the contrast between *eny* and *al* bringing out the nature of Wrath's injurious speech and justifying the *repetitio* so typical of **C**. **164–9 165** *Conseyl*: in *ParsT* 'biwreying of conseil, thurgh which a man is defamed' (645) appears among

Commentary

the 'synnes that comen of the tonge' (653). **166** *ouerdelicatly*: it not being obvious how concern with 'choice' drink promotes wrath, the idea may be rather of consuming *too much* from the range of drinks offered at a feast. *ParsT* includes under Gluttony 'whan a man get hym *to delicaat...drynke*' and also 'whan men taken to muche over mesure' (X 828–9). **167** *ne thy wit*: an improvement on **B**'s otiose second lift; as *ParsT* notes, 'dronkenesse bireveth hym the discrecioun of his wit' (825). **168** 'Be sober [and watch: because your adversary the devil, *as a roaring lion*, goeth about seeking whom he may devour' (I Pet 5:8). 'Soberness' here denotes seriousness of speech and behaviour as well as avoidance of drunkenness; but the connection between sins of the tongue's different powers (speech and taste) is made pointedly at B 10.165–8. The italicised phrase has special aptness to the sin of wrath. **169** *hym*; *his*: **B** *me*, *my*: misdiagnosed by *Bn* as scribal slips, but graphically reinforcing the persona's rôle as representative man at B 61, where use of the 3rd person brings out the dual sense of 'Will' as the name of both faculty and Dreamer.

(iv) 170–95 The brief confession of Lechery in **B** is expanded to 25 lines with ten from B XIII and ten new lines at beginning and end. *ParsT* places *Luxuria* as the last of the deadly sins, after *Gula*, its 'ny cosin' (836); but **L**'s Lechery needs neither food nor drink as stimulus, though appropriately vowing to fast as a penance. Positioned between anger and avarice, sins of the spirit, this sin of the flesh is the only vice pursued for pleasure rather than just as a (largely painful) compulsion, and is the one by which Will is led astray at 11.179–82. But Lechery alone expresses regret (*Alas*) and recognises that his *lycames gultes* originate in the *gost*, i.e. that the essence of lechery is a wilful assent to disordered desire (see 181). **170** *Oure Lady*: as the patron and exemplar of chastity, the best intermediary between himself and Christ (cf. 7.287). The sense of B 5.72, 'to bring about a state of mercy on God's part towards my soul', is much more clearly expressed in **C**. **171–2** The assonances in the b-lifts of both lines bring out the desperate urgency of his plea. **172** *putour* (< AF *putour*): one who makes a profession of his sin (cf. 186, 189–90), unlike Haukyn, a simple fornicator. Depiction of lechery in its most destructive form, making money by corrupting both women and the men who use them, is perhaps in answer to Lady Mede's argument that 'frelete of fleysche' is 'synne as of seuene noon sonner relesed' (3.59, 62). But Lechery is also a corrupter of virgins (178) and so 'cause of manye damages and vileynyes' (*ParsT* 870). **173** *Saturdayes*: days of special devotion to the Blessed Virgin. Water and a single meal will curb his propensities on the eve of the sabbath (cf. Wrath's Friday penance at 155 above); but in **C** the promised fast is to be perpetual. **176** 'The sins of my body in indulging in lechery'. **177–81** are closely parallelled in *ParsT* 851–62,

which describe in sequence the *fyve fingres* of lust: 'fool lookynge' (177), 'vileyns touchyng in wikkede manere' (179–80, 187), 'foule wordes' (186), 'kiss[ynge] in vileynye (187)' and 'the stynkynge dede of Leccherie' (181, 188). **177** *waitynge*: warned against in Mt 5:28. *wedes*: the link between provocative clothing and lust is made in *ParsT* under Pride rather than Lechery, which notes how 'scantnesse of clothyng...ne covere[th] nat the shameful membres of man, to wikked entente' (422) and women 'notifie in hir...atyr *likerousnesse* and pride' (430). **181** *wil*: the flesh's will or assent to 'lust in action'. *werk*: an early euphemism for the sexual act (like *dede*10. 295). **182** *fastyng dayes*: for laypeople the Wednesdays and Fridays in the Church's penitential seasons, especially Lent (cf. later under Sloth at 7.25–6). *Frydayes*: as well as the abstinence from meat prescribed throughout the year, other penances recommended in honour of the day of Christ's death included refraining from (lawful) sexual relations. **182** *heye-festes euenes*: the vigils of major feasts like Christmas and Easter, to be similarly marked; but the *forboden nyghtes* B 349 were sometimes taken to include periods of pregnancy and menstruation. Lechery was forbidden at all times, but the speaker's declared indifference to the religious seasons points up the lack of any restraint upon his indulgence. **183** scans most effectively on vocalic grammatical staves, with the *l*-words as an under-pattern. **193** *oold*: implying that he is looking back on a life of sin, and suggesting that in B 13.354 *hir* pertains to the lechers seen prospectively in their old age. *þat kynde*: proving that his lust was an act of will, not Mede's 'cours of kynde' (3.60). **194** 'I enjoyed listening to (people) talk about (their) debauchery'. **195** *lewete*: the appeal to God's perhaps alluding to Christ's forgiveness of the Woman taken in Adultery, a story elaborated at 14.41–2.

(v) 196–348 At 150 lines, the presentation of Greed is the longest, the confession of Heruy the miser being extended and supplemented by those of Euan The Welshman (308–14) and Robert The Robber (315–29), fraud and theft respectively (on the change in Robert's function see Introductory note, end), and concluded by an exhortation to Greed. Gluttony and Sloth following him bring comic relief after an episode which, despite humorous touches, depicts Greed (the sole Sin to have three representatives) as especially serious because it threatens the entire Christian community. Its gravity is emphasised in Ecclus 10:9 and 10 (the latter verse cited at B 10.336*a*) and *PP* presents it as the greatest vice of the time. **L** follows a model pattern prescribed in penitential handbooks (on their influence see Gray 1986[1]), with Repentance as confessor interrogating and rebuking Greed three times (six times in **B**) at 233–9, 248–57, 286–307 and finally *refusing* absolution until he has made restitution.

196–205 196 *Couetyse*: 'desire to have (wealth)', whether to get or to keep. *ParsT* more narrowly distinguishes *Coveitise* as 'to coveite swiche thynges as thou hast nat' from *Avarice* 'to withholde and kepe swiche thynges as thou hast, withoute rightful nede' (744). Though the special sense of *auarice* at 191 is apparently contrasted with *coueytise* in 190, both terms occur interchangeably, the latter three times more frequently. **197** *Sire Heruy*: this character (who seems to have suggested Heruy Hafter in Skelton's *Bouge of Court*) is neither knight nor priest, so no plain reason for his title appears. The grotesque image of the miser, the most fully visualised of the Sins, reflects the medieval belief that inner nature reveals itself in physiognomy, gesture and even dress. **198** *bitelbrowid*: the sense 'grim-browed, sullen' in MED s.v. would connect the first element with OE *bitol 'biting, sharp', which is phonologically possible but semantically unconvincing. More probably, Coveitise's shaggy overhanging eyebrows are being compared to the tufted protruding antennae of some insect (the common later understanding of the compound and the verb Shakespeare derived from it; see OED s.v. *beetle* a.). **199** *pors*: an emblem of Heruy's avaricious nature. **200** *ycheuelen*: a coinage or an idiolectal variant of *chiueren*, 'prob. a blend of *chillen* and *biueren*' (MED s.v.); a subject 'they' (= his cheeks) must be supplied as in **B**. **201** *yshaue*: cut so as to leave bristles sticking out as from bacon-rind after the meat has been removed; like the purse-cheek simile, an iconic emblem of miserliness that improves on **B**'s merely visual description. **202** *hat*: better than *lousy hat* B 192, which anticipates B 194. **203** *tore...twelue wynter*: the avaricious man's neglect of decent clothing is reiterated at 19.245–7, on the miserly rich. **204** *lous...lepe*: i.e there is so little material left that the louse would need to jump to get from one piece to the next; a variation on a semi-proverbial expression. **205** *He*: possibly a spelling-form for the feminine pronoun as in **AB**; but the louse's sex is not of pressing concern. *Walch*: metonymic for 'woollen flannel [made in Wales]', but doubtless reflecting a xenophobic English view of Welshmen as dishonest and mean instantiated by Evan at 308ff.

206–33 explore Greed's *commercial* frauds. **207** *Style*: cf. Lettyse at 145 above. **208b** affirms the apprentice's main obligation (repeated at 279). **209–10** *lerned...lessoun*: the sin being satirically envisaged not as an impulse or habit but as a skill, to be mastered in stages (cf. on 172). **209** *lye*: if with original vowel as in **A**, rhyming with *tweye* and with *waye* in the next line (and possibly with *Wy* in 211) to give an effect at once mnemonic and mimetic. *leef...tweye*: 'a page or two's worth [from the handbook of falsehoods]'. **210** *waye*: i.e. with fraudulent weights. **211** *Wy*: Weyhill near Andover, Hants, which had a week-long Michaelmas market for goods of every kind; Symme presumably dealt in foodstuffs. *Wynchestre*: where there

was also a great three-day autumn fair at St Giles's Down (4.51 above) under the patronage of the bishop. **212** *many manere marchandise*: cf. 'marchandise is in manye maneres....That...men haunten with fraude and...with lesynges...is cursed and dampnable' (*ParsT* 776, 779). **213** *grace of gile*: 'the devil's own luck', with some play on 'the grace of God', who is ironically invoked in 214b. **214** *this seuene ʒer*: perhaps signifying only an indefinitely long period of time (cf. 233 below, 10.73); but also the normal length of an apprenticeship, Greed implying that without the help of guile he might have failed to qualify as a master of his art. **215–16** *drow...drawe*: more 'Platonic' wordplay. *Donet*: 'the elements [of fraud]'; named after Aelius Donatus, the C4th Roman author of a basic Latin Grammar used in schools. Having learned to *read* (= 'lie') with a grocer, Greed studied *grammar* (= 'deception') with clothiers. **216–22** Avarice Draper's trick was apparently to stitch two widths of expensive striped cloth (*raye*) together loosely with a large stout needle, fasten the sewn piece in a wooden frame (*pressour*) and pull lengthwise on the selvage side (*lyser*) so as to stretch it, increasing the size of the piece but also weakening it. To make the operation easier, his wife Rose (see 232) caused her yarn to be spun loosely (*oute*), involving the spinners in the fraud. **218** *bat-nelde*: glossed in MED s.v. as 'bastingneedle'; but the variant *pak-nedle* in well over half the mss in all three traditions may suggest that the *bat-* element derives from OF *bast* 'pack-saddle' (the etymological root of *bastard*), as stated by OED s.v. **223–4** His wife's own deception of her gullible spinsters was to use a scale-balance 'pound' weight of 1¼ lbs; as they would have to put *more* wool in the pan to make it balance, she thereby paid for a quarter *less* than the weight of spun wool they brought her. Greed's own weighing-instrument was probably a 'steelyard', the bale being hung from the shorter arm of a lever and its weight determined by moving a counterpoise along a graduated scale inscribed on the longer arm, until balance was achieved. Although Greed's auncel measured accurately, it was ironically this device that was often banned by national and municipal regulations as open to fraudulent misuse (see C14th and C15th quots. in MED s.v. *auncel* n). So the text may hint at a more elaborate deception, whereby Greed used his *reliable* steelyard in order to 'con' his suppliers and purchasers into trusting that his wife's *false* scale-weights were also sound. **225–33** These brewery 'practices' follow a similar pattern of complex trickery. *Peny ale*: thin or small ale (cf. 21.403) sold at a penny a gallon. *poddyng ale*: thick ale sold at a groat or fourpence (the MED gloss 'cheap ale' s.v. *poding* n. (b) is misleading). The small ale stood in a separate barrel in the front shop, and customers who tried the best ale brought for tasting from the inner room paid the full price for this. But what Rose actually supplied was a mixture of the two, perhaps in 3:1 proportions (as with her weights), to evade detection. **229** *per-aftur*: both 'thereupon' (after sampling) and 'accordingly' (in the belief that they were getting what they had tasted). **230b–31a** The revision improves on **B** by adding a further deception (*ȝut*): when she filled her customers' cans by cupfuls, she gave them *less* as well as *worse*. Between them, husband and wife make accomplished use of the *false mesures and met* (B 13.359) condemned in Deut 25:13–15. **231b** *craft*: playing on MED senses 2(b) 'skill in deceiving' and 6(a) 'trade'. **232** '...was her actual name [*sc.* and rightly was she so named]'. **232–3** *regrater... hokkerye*: though the former could be neutral before the 15th c., the latter always had unfavourable overtones, reflecting people's distrust of those who bought necessities wholesale to sell at a profit. Rose uses the quality of her own ale to conceal her trickery (cf. the *false gyn* of Chaucer's Canon [*CT* VIII 1160ff], who uses real silver when pretending to transmute mercury). **233** *elleuene*: another (alliteratively convenient) indefinite period (cf. 203, 214); despite his gains, Avarice still wears his tattered twelve-year old jacket.

B 224–35 (A 142–5, Z 97–103) The **B** passage is cut in **C**, possibly because repetitive (225a repeats 200a) and over-specific (226–7). **224** *so thee Ik*: an asseveration in Norfolk dialect that may be the residue and remnant of *Northfolk nose* Z 98 (an obscure gibe seemingly not derived from it). Presumably the meanness or dishonesty of Norfolk people is implied (see on Z 3.148 above, Mann 1973:166 on Chaucer's Norfolk Reeve). **226** *Walsyngham*: see on Pr 52. **227** *Bromholm*: also in Norfolk, a day's journey from Walsingham, so Greed could visit both in one pilgrimage. The Cluniac Priory (close to Paston Hall) had a famous miracle-working relic of the true cross, brought from Constantinople in the early 13th c. and kept in a 'patriarchal' style processional cross, before which he will pray for release from his *debitum* of sin (MED s.v. *dette* n. 4(a)). On the cross (which disappeared in 1537) see Wormald *JWCI* 1937:31–45 (esp. pls. 6a–c, 7a–b; an ampulla depicting it is in Alexander & Binski 223, pl. 77); and cf. the contemporary mention in *CT* I 4286. **232** *haddest...hanged*: on this use of the infinitive after an adjective see *MES* 538. **235** *Northfolk*: meaning that Greed knew *no* French (*Bn*), because he lived so far from London and its environs that education would be supposed scarce there. Though the county capital Norwich was the third city of England, Walsingham stands at Norfolk's 'furthest end', so if Greed lived nearby, he would have been 25m from it.

234–44 concern Greed's *financial* deceptions. **237** *rufol restitucioun*: with Greed's failure to understand the word, cf. Envy and *sory* at 93; both examples figure spiritual obtuseness under verbal ignorance. The lines improve on B 232–3, which declare theft more serious than fraud, but lack the warning that failure to make restitution will

damn the sinner even if he is never found out. **239** *vsurye*: strictly, lending at (exorbitant) interest; more loosely, lending for profit (see on 2.91), which was regarded as a grave sin. But Greed uses it to describe banned commercial practices, from coin-clipping to credit-transfer. **241** *Lumbardus...Iewes*: see on 4.192. **242** Since any heap of current pennies showed small individual variations, after isolating the lightest and weighing the others against it, he would remove tiny quantities from the heaviest so as to bring them down to its weight, and on a large enough scale, there was profit in the silver thus collected. This practice may be the 'horrible crime' described in a Commons petition of 1376 (*Rotuli Parliamentorum* 2:332). **243 (B 240)** *loue of þe wed*: i.e. as opposed to charity towards the man. The loan is made in **B** from desire for the money to be got from selling the object pledged when it was forfeited, the *cros* being that inscribed on coins (Poole II, pls. 32, 34, and cf. 17.205). In **C**, it is for the pledge itself, which was more valuable than the loan or (the remaining wealth of) the man he made it to.

B 241–5 The sense of the elliptical B 240 is that Greed wanted the borrower to lose his security by failing to pay at the time agreed, and kept a written record in case this happened (241). The litotes of the macaronic 242 brings out his awareness of a charity he could have shown; but the irony works through *style indirect libre,* since knowledge of the psalm cannot be attributed to the *lewed* Greed as a 'character'. *Miseretur...*: '[Acceptable is the man that] sheweth mercy and lendeth' (Ps 111:5). Vs 9 shows that this psalm is concerned with charity to the poor, but **L** describes Greed's loan-making as directed towards the gentry in need of ready cash. **243** *chaffare*: either (a) he 'sells' (lends) goods (e.g. forfeited clothes or jewels from his pawn-store) and buys them back to furnish the cash they want) at less than their true value (*Bn*), so as to conceal what is really interest charged on a loan (this is the *derne usurie* of B 2.176); or (b) *chaffare* denotes a loan of cash to buy such goods elsewhere, which then formed the pledge he would later buy back at less than their value. Either way, Greed would make a good profit. **245** again concerns the financial side of his operations. *Sk*'s note that in an ordinance against usurers (38 Edw III) they are said to describe *occulta usura* as 'exhange or chevisance' suggests that the two terms are euphemistic synonyms for usury. Or Greed, like Chaucer's Merchant (*CT* I 278–82), may be making a profit on the currency-exchanges involved in his capital-transfer operations.

245–52 continue with Greed's crooked *financial* activities. **245** humorously extends his coin-clipping of silver to his lending, his interest being imagined as a piece clipped off each gold coin he advances; but *Sk*'s more literal view of Greed as lending his clients clipped coin is not excluded. **246** *Lumbardus lettres*: bills of exchange used by Lombard bankers in Rome to facilitate payments due to the papal exchequer (e.g. from English clerics on appointment to benefices or sees). The money would be handed to their agent in England [viz. Greed], who then provided a credit-note for the sum, which could be disbursed by their office in Rome. If conducted honestly, the only gain for him should have been a fee for service. **B 248** *took it by taille*: for the use here MED s.v. *taille* n. 3(d) has 'receive it on credit' (the only other example of the phrase, at *CT* I 570, meaning 'bought on credit'). Greed acted as factor and received the client's money (in exchange for credit abroad); but because he handled the credit-note, he could alter it to make it worth less there than made out at home. However, the new C 247 (which prudently replaces B 248's explanation of how this fraud was done) understands Greed to *lend* the client all or part of the sum; and if **B** also implied this, *took* will there mean 'gave' (MED s.v *taken* v. 31a). Greed will again have doctored the bill of credit so that less was handed over in Rome than he had advanced in England, but would make his profit only *after* his client paid him back (another variety of *usura occulta*). **248** *mayntenaunce*: 'support' (MED s.v. n.2(a)), something useful for a money-man in a society dominated by the land-owning classes, whose backing would be helpful in running the *manoirs* he got through defaults on loans. **250** He brought down his social superior's status to that of a trader in textiles by causing him to forfeit or sell back goods bought by 'feigned sale' (*Bn*). **251** *gloues*: a typical gift-offering by an apprentice joining a master to learn a craft. The cream of the jest is that Greed will have amassed them as forfeited pledges, while his clients 'learnt' nothing of his 'mystery'.

253–7a C removes the questioning about charity and hospitality in B 253–8 perhaps because implausible from a confessor who had heard so much of his penitent's attitude and acts (Greed treats people like cats and behaves like a dog, hates his neighbours and is hated by them). **C** warns that Greed's wealth lies under a curse: his executors will misspend it (cf. B 15.138–45, omitted in revision) and his heirs get no benefit. **B** is theologically sound enough, with Repentance *wishing* that Greed, unless sincerely contrite, should not receive the grace to make satisfaction with his ill-gotten goods (i.e. by acts of charity), but is more severe than **C**, where the confessor simply does not 'believe or expect' that Greed's sin will be forgiven without satisfaction. B 260–3 seem to echo *WW* 440–4. **256** Even the successor of St Peter, to whom Christ delegated all power to forgive (see on Pr 128–9), cannot remit sin unconditionally (cf. on 320 below). In terms of the *partes penitentiae* 'stages of sacramental penance', even after contrition and verbal confession, complete forgiveness and pardon for sin wait on the act of satisfaction (see at B 14.16ff). **257** *sine restitucione*: 'without restitution'. While on a naturalistic level the Latin should be even less

intelligible to Greed than the English at 234, **C** is stressing his moral not his educational *lewednesse*, and the Latin formulae are presumably directed to the audience. **257a** '[If the other man's property can be returned but is not, the penitence is not real but feigned; and even if there is true penitence], the sin is not forgiven until the stolen goods are returned' (Augustine, Epistle 153, sect. 20, in *Opera*, ed. Migne, ii.662). The given sentence (quoted in **B** at 272a) was a widely-cited maxim of canon law also found in sermons such as Brinton 1:27, *ME Sermons* 266 (see Alf*G*, Alford 1975:398, Gray 1986, Scase 1989:26). **258–85a** draw on B XIII, 258–61 dealing with Greed as *merchant*. **258–71 259** is echoed in 22.369 describing Friar Flatterer. **260–1** *Meddeled*: Greed's stratagems recalling on a larger scale his wife's petty deceptions (cf. the echo of 228 in 261a). *withynne*: (deep) inside the pile of goods (grain etc). **262–71** Greed's fraudulent activities as *farmer* grow directly into theft (265–6). **262** *hyne... beest*: alluding to the Tenth Commandment's prohibition against coveting one's neighbour's 'field, man-servant, ox, or ass,' (Deut 5:21, Ex 20:17). **267–71** *half-aker*: a normal small-holding of 16 furrows, a minimum capable of supporting a family. The fields lay in strips side by side divided by an unsown furrow, which offered Greed opportunities for adding covertly to his land. **268** *foet lond or a forw*: a foot's width was little in itself but (like the coin-shavings at 242 above) mounted up; since the field it ran alongside was a furlong (660 ft) in length, he could grab up some 3% of his neighbour's ground. **270** *over-reche*: cut his neighbour's corn on the other side of the furrow (something specifically forbidden in Deut 23:25).

272–85a return to Greed the *merchant's* constant concern with monetary rather than spiritual profit and loss. The whole passage, with its key-phrase at 279, implicitly comments on Mk 8:36: 'For what shall it profit a man, if he gain the whole world and suffer the loss of his soul?' **278** *Bruges*: at this time still a port, and a major centre of the Flemish cloth-trade, to which English wool would be sent. **279** *Prucelond*: Prussia, occupying most of present N Germany, 'the chief distributor of English cloth in Poland and West Russia' (McKisack 1959:359). **282b** The exact referent is unclear, perhaps 'anything in God's world that could delight the eye'. Greed cannot see properly because his eye is *nequam* 'evil', not *simplex* 'single' (cf. Mt 6:22–3). **283** *Paternoster*: the Christian's chief prayer, taught by Je sus in the part of the Sermon on the Mount preceding the *tesaurus* text. **285a** '[For] where thy treasure is, there is thy heart also' (Mt 6:21). The two verses before it, contrasting earthly and heavenly treasure, are directly relevant for understanding this passage. **286–307** Repentance's *refusal of absolution and his final warning* underline the seriousness of Greed's sin. **287** A possible T-type line revising one with cognative *þ / f* staves while turning the complimentary *good feiþ* into a mere asseveration. **C** disengages 'gold' from the powerful but not very lucid simile in **B** ('nor accept a penny from you as pocket-money, even if I were given a manuscript with leaves covered with a gold ground [*Bn*] for doing so'), which makes poor sense, since friars could not own such books as personal property. **290a** 'It is better to die than to live wickedly'; repeated at 17.40*a* (see on 1.142*a* and cf. 7.208–9). **293** *fyndynge*: friars are being obliquely admonished to follow Repentance and refuse absolution to 'false men' even if they offer handsome donations. **293a** 'Seek costly foods, another's slave you'll be; / Sup on your own plain bread, and you'll stay free' (source still unidentified). One friar who seeks such foods is the Doctor of Divinity of 15.66ff. **294** *vnkynde*: 'unnatural', because he preys on his own kind. **295** *by thy myhte*: 'as far as you are able'; if circumstances rule out exact restitution, he must make it up some other way, e.g. by charity. **296–300** The warning that those who knowingly accept money wrongfully obtained will 'share' in Greed's punishment as in his profits is directed in **C** not to a *werkman* (**B** 277) but to his parish priest (298, 304). It is assumed that the latter might have been persuaded by a rich tithe-offering to grant 'easy absolution' because, after the Plague, depopulation of parishes had reduced incumbents' income from that source. **298** On tithes, see at 8.101. **302** 'For behold, thou hast loved truth'; vs 8 of Ps 50, the fourth penitential psalm ('Miserere'), named at **B** 276: 'Have mercy on me, O God' (vs 3; and see **B** 13.53*a*). The *GO* interprets these verses as meaning that God will not compromise his truth (= 'justice') by leaving wrongdoers unpunished, but demands satisfaction from the sinner in the form of mercy shown to others. **B** 276 *I mene*: the exact referent of *I* should be God (addressed in vs. 8), on whose behalf Repentance speaks; but if it is the latter, then *mene* is to be understood as 'am referring to (a text that speaks of) truth'. **303** *vsure*: Ps 50 makes no direct reference to usury. **305/7** The sustained *annominatio* on ers-, err-, arste associates both groups (who are later linked at 16.259). *ers-wynnynge*: on current debate about whether earnings from prostitution could be tithed cf. Wycliffe (*EW*, p.433); 8.71 would imply that they should not. The less severe general view of the prospect for whores taken here may owe something to Mt 21:31 (which, however, contrasts them with Pharisees, not usurers).

B 278–82a 278 *Cum*...: 'With the holy thou wilt be holy;...[and with the perverse thou wilt be perverted]' (Ps 17:26–7). 'Construing' here involves more than translation: the text warns priests and religious against associating with the wicked for mercenary reasons if they would avoid their fate. **279** *wanhope*: Greed's reaction to Repentance's severity both echoes his threat at **B** 232 and prompts his injunction to pray for divine mercy, which

he declares illimitable. **282a** 'His tender mercies [*miserationes* Vg] are over [i.e. surpass] all his works' (Ps 144:9); repeated at **B** 11.139*a*=**C** 12.75*a* but removed here from its revised form (perhaps for that reason). **308–14** The introduction of EUAN THE WELSHMAN has no obvious explanation but is linked with the moving forward of the 'Robert' passage from after Sloth, the last Sin to confess in **B** (where, as *Pe* notes, it fits well as a warning against despair), to follow it immediately. Sloth's first two lines on repentance now form Evan's compound 'nature-name' (the first such in **C**) and the next two form the opening of his speech, which ends with his decision (alluding to the Mk 8:36 text cited under 272–85*a*) to renounce wealth for salvation. **308** *wonderly sory*: a sorrow, whether contrition (like Robert's at 316) or attrition aroused by Repentance's warning (which encouragingly replaces the *helle* threatened at 238 with *purgatorye* 299), accompanied by a resolve to make restitution at all costs. This suggests that Evan is a first manifestation of Greed, but now transformed by the incipient action of grace, while Robert in his new position is quite intelligibly the second. **309** *ȝeuan*: the form of the speaker's name perhaps punning on *ȝeuen* 'give'. On the textual problems of this passage see *TN*. It is here supposed that Evan's name is unlikely to have appeared in Z's first lift and so to be derived from **C**, since the speaker's resolution to amend is immediately followed not by **C** 313–14 but by the equivalent of **B** 461–2 // **A** 234–5, lines spoken by Sloth that the final version excises. **315–29** The passage on ROBERT undergoes continuous revision, **A** omitting three lines of **Z**, **B** two of **A**, and **C** one of **B**. Additionally, it alters the sinner's cognomen, which could (offensively) imply a 'Platonic' link of the common name *Robert* with robbery, and re-directs his prayer from himself to heaven. In **B** it forms a transition from confession to absolution. **315** *Robert*: not an 'eighth sin' or (recalling the *Roberdes knaues* of B Pr 44) 'a generic name for a slothful waster' (*Bn*) but typifying *all* sinners as spiritually 'in debt' to God and so 'at his mercy' like the first thief Lucifer of 477. *the ruyflare*: recalling *riflede* 236 and establishing this character unambiguously as an avatar of Greed. *Reddite*: 'give back', echoing *Reddite ergo omnibus debita* 'Render therefore to all men their dues' (Rom 13:7); quoted by Augustine in the discussion of restitution from which 257*a* is taken (*Pe*). The great importance of 'satisfaction' is later stressed by Conscience at 21.187–8. **316** *wherwith*: i.e. any good deeds to offset his sins; echoing 'And whereas they had not *wherewith* to pay...' (Lk 7:42). **318** *Caluarie*: the Roman name (Mk 15:22, Lk 23:33) for Golgotha ('place of a skull'), the hill of crucifixion outside Jerusalem. **319** scans weakly as an extended Type III on |ð| (*Tho*, *the*); but conceivably the anomalous *xa / ax* pattern produced by normal stressing on both a-half nouns may be meant (like stanza-group

XV in *Pearl*) to reflect symbolically its speaker's flawed spiritual state. Robert hopes that his prayer will likewise be received because he sincerely repents; but he lacks a good deed ('wherwith') comparable to his 'brother's' redeeming recognition that the robbers' punishment was just and that of Jesus unjust. In the two discussions at 11.255–63 and 14.131–55a, the Good Thief's salvation is ascribed in part to his acknowledgement of his guilt. In the earlier, Rechelesnesse (Will) adds that the thief *shrof hym* 'made his confession' to Christ (and thus received unconditional absolution, his mere acknowledgement constituting 'satisfaction'), while Ymaginatif affirms that those who implore God's grace will always receive it (14.131–2, and esp. // B 12.192). *Dysmas my brother*: the emblem of a last-minute penitence that won forgiveness and the promise of heaven from Christ himself. Only St Luke (23:39–43) distinguishes the characters of the two thieves. In ch. 10 of the apocryphal *Gospel of Nicodemus* (with which cf. also *LA* ch. 53, p.223) the one crucified on Christ's left hand is given the name Gestas and the one on his right the 'nature-name' Dismas (< Gk *dysmé* 'dying': cf. 'Longius' at 20.81); for the symbolism see on 2.5. **320** *mercy...man*: the **Z** form of this half-line is a 'repertory-phrase' used at 12.72 and elsewhere. *for* Memento *sake*: 'for (his words to you, "[Lord], remember [me when thou shalt come into thy kingdom]"' (Lk 23:42). **A 241–2 (Z 139–40)** The removal by **B** of these lines on hope, which interrupt the association between Dismas's case and Robert's, is a clear improvement. **321** *Reddere*: '[the where-withal] to pay back (the debt of sin)'. **322** *wynne*; *craft*: the spiritual 'skill' that will 'earn' (profit for his soul). **323** *mitigacioun*: a legal term, appropriate to the convicted robber appealing to his judge; first recorded here with this referent, but in the Wycliffite Bible (MED s.v.) translating Vg *propitiatio* ['forgiveness' Douai-Rheims] at Ecclus 17:28 (vss 20–8 of this ch. are relevant to the passage). The ground of Robert's plea in his defence (anticipating Christ's to Lucifer in 20.415–38) is not the circumstances of his own case but the precedent of Christ's treatment of Dismas. **325** *byfel...feloun*: a paronomastic phrase cautioning against complacency. Robert's eventual salvation would, however, seem to be implicit in the Lord's words at 20.426–7, and its basis is his being Christ's 'whole-brother' (20.419) through his 'baptism'. **326** *wepte faste*: signalising Robert's contrition (see on 6.2) and associating him with Will as a type of fallen humanity. As such he bears the 'debt' of sin and totally depends on divine mercy (320) and pity (321). The contrast of these correlative but distinguishable attributes (rational and affective) of the one Saviour God at B 478–80 is removed in revision. **328** *That*: i.e. 'saying that'. *penaunce*: less august than *Penitencia*, the concretisation of the sacramental 'support' of the wayfaring Christian that Robert has dulled with disuse. Omission of B 476 may be a simple economy,

but the staff-image tellingly anticipates a life of penitential 'pilgrimage' as proper satisfaction for a life of sin. **329** *Latro*: 'thief', synecdoche for *latrocinium* 'theft'; the puns on *lateo* 'lie hid' and *latus* 'side' supposed by AlfQ seem implausible. *aunte*: apart from making the relationship unpleasantly incestuous, no reason for his bad 'aunt' appears, though it balances with his good 'brother' at 319 (and foreshadows Glutton's worthy aunt Abstinence at 439). That **L**'s Lucifer is 'that first grand thief' is clear from B 16.40–5, 17.103–11, 18.351–4.

Z 142–44 wittily cite a parable about indebtedness that concludes (vs. 9) with an injunction to 'make friends of the mammon of iniquity' (i.e. use ill-gotten gains for charity, so as to gain the intercessory prayers of those helped). Robert's wish to identify with the unjust steward (*caucyon* echoing *cautionem* 'bill' in Lk 16:6) must fail, since he has spent the money. **A**'s removal of these lines sensibly recognises that they do not apply to Robert's situation and that 142b may tend to lighten the tone inappropriately. **142** 'To dig I am not able; [to beg I am ashamed]' (Lk 16:3); remotely recalled in C 5.23–4, 51. **143–4** 'If I knew how to, I would wish prudently to put a payment of security in place / So as not to have to beg, borrow or end my days in despair'.

330–48 330 *Rode*: an apt oath since Christ's saving death on the cross, the basis of all sinners' hope, is especially suited to one who identifies with the crucified robber. **334** *Temese*: a local image of hot embers tossed over the side of a ship into London's river by night, as vivid as that of boisterous swimmers at 14.104ff (another passage about escaping from despair through trust in sacramental penance). **335** *drop water*: a mere drop from the river of divine mercy having the power to extinguish the 'fire' of sin; on the appositive genitive, see *MES* 84. **337a** 'All wickedness, in comparison with God's mercy, is as it were a spark in the midst of the sea'; widely cited in penitential writings (Gray 1986:59), homiletic works like the *FM*, sermons by Holcot and John of Grimestone (Wenzel, in Alford 1988:156), and popular moral treatises like the *Speculum Christiani* 73, 115: 'sicut scintilla ignis in medio maris, sic omnis impietas uiri ad misericordiam dei' (AlfQ). It was generally attributed to St Augustine, ultimately deriving from *Enarrationes in Psalmos* on Ps 143:2: *Unda misericordiae peccati ignis exstinguitur* 'By mercy's flood sin's fire is put out' (*PL* 37:1861). **338–42** The wordplay in **C** allows a double reference to Greed's spiritual bankruptcy, as a result of which any use of his wrongly acquired 'goods' even to survive will only harm his soul further. The omitted B 287 spells out that he would have to beg or labour to feed himself. **338** *vsurer*: the central figure Greed, left alone after Evan and Robert leave. **339** *marchaundise*: something not evil in itself but become so in his hands. **343–8** The practical difficulty of making restitution with ill-gotten gains is overcome by leaving it to the bishop to dispose of them for charitable ends. Repentance almost envisages the latter as a religious stockbroker investing capital for a client; but at the same time he stresses that the bishop, as God's 'steward', is responsible for his people's spiritual welfare. The removal of **B**'s homophonic wordplay on *lente*, paronomasia on *lette* and contrast between wisdom (*Oure Lordes good*) and wealth (*þe good...geten...wiþ falshede*) increases the solemnity, but with some loss of colour. **348** *What*: the instruction that the priests under his authority were obliged to give their parishioners, notably when preparing for their annual confession before Easter.

(vi) 349–440 The (failed) confession of GLUTTON is expanded from **AB** with only some half-dozen new lines, four on drunken oaths from the Haukyn passage (C 6.424–7=B 13.400–03). Its humorous liveliness, which perhaps prompted some 'farcing' of the **m** branch of **A** with lines from **B** (see *TN* on A 163) suggests that its popularity may have preserved the passage from revision in **C**. Like all the sins save Pride and Greed, Gluttony receives only a type-name; but proper-naming his sixteen drinking-companions provides a dense social background for his decline and fall. The 'moral comedy' of this scene arises from Glutton's falling foul of his habitual vice even as he is on the way to confess it, and so receiving condign punishment for his behaviour. **349–74 351** *Friday*: a day on which some penance such as fasting until noon was recommended in Lent, when this scene may take place (recalling the day at 438 serves to enclose the scene as if in a frame). The relation of the Glutton scene to the Easter weekend by Wilcockson (1998) would make this 'Friday' that on which the events of 318–20 above took place. **352** *Betene...brewestere*: possibly the wife of Butte (5.134), who may be the butcher abetting Hick at the 'new fair' (but the name was common); on the split genitive see *MES* 78–9. **356** *good ale*: Glutton really being an illustration not of gormandising but of drunkenness, the gravity of which *ParsT* notes when calling *Gula* 'desordeynee coveitise to eten or to drinke' because 'whan a man is dronken, he hath lost his resoun; and this is dedly synne' (*CT* X 818, 823). **357–9** Fennel and peony seed could be chewed without breaking the fasting-rule but (ironically) would arouse thirst and were used to ease bladder-pains, a consequence of heavy drinking (cf. 398). **360** *grete othes*: notably blasphemous swearing by the parts of Christ's body, as acknowledged at 426 below and criticised by Chaucer's Parson and Pardoner (*CT* II 1171, VI 472–6); they are later coupled at B 10.50. **361–74** The two-dozen occupations found among Glutton's cronies give a cross-section of London low life, **C** 368–9 adding some criminal types. **362** *Watte*: cf. 5.132–3. **365** *Claryce*: on the name cf. at 134. *Cockeslane*: between Holborn and Smithfield, a haunt of prostitutes. *Clerc*: the parish clerk, possibly to 'Sire Piers' (that he *is* Piers [*Bn*] is syntacti-

cally possible but contextually implausible). Probably in minor orders and so charged with ceremonial duties like leading the responses, censing and receiving the offering, his companion is Claryce (cf. *CT* I 3312ff, esp. 3334–6 on Absolon's fondness for taverns and barmaids). **366** *Sire Peres of Prydie*: signifying 'a grossly incompetent priest'; one who when he reached the words *Qui pridie quam pateretur* 'Who, the day before he suffered, [took bread]...', a solemn moment in the consecration prayer during the Canon of the Mass, was obliged to start again if he had not properly prepared the bread and wine (John Mirk, *Instruction for Parish Priests* l.1902, noted by Oliphant 1960:167–8 in establishing the phrase's meaning). If Sir Piers's parish clerk was someone like the 'Clerc' of 365, the negligence might be partly explained; but doubtless his own head (aided by Betene's ale) was *toty of his swynk* with his concubine Pernele. *Flaundres*: many London prostitutes hailing from a region that Chaucer depicts as prone to riotous excess (*CT* VI 463ff). **367** *hayward*: about as popular in the period as game-keepers later. *heremyte*: like the 'unholy' one of Pr 3. *Tybourne*: the chief place of execution, where a permanent gallows stood at the junction of present-day Oxford St, Edgware Road and Bayswater Road (cf. B 12.189). **368** *Dawe*: a typical labourer with his hands; mentioned again at 8.352. **369** *Of*: 'consisting of' (MED s.v. *of* prep. 10(a)); on the partitive genitive see *MES* 79–80. **370** *rakeare*: in **B** from Cheapside, one of the 26 city wards, where vegetable and animal refuse from the market-stalls would have quickly filled his rubbish-cart. MED s.v. cites a 1384 Gild record naming a Richard Maillour of Cheap ward, so **C**'s revision could be removing an allusion that offended a particular raker. **372** *Garlek-monger*: Godfrey's place of work is similarly deleted; but the garlic he sells will have been brought up from France by ship to this landing-stage (*hithe*) on the upper Thames estuary. *Gryffyth*: a typical Welsh name. **373** *vphalderes*: based at Cornhill, where Will resided (cf. 12.220). *herly...*: the adverbial phrase referring to the whole group installed for a long day's drinking. **374** *Geuen*: a Ø-relative ('who gave'). *to hansull*: a free cup to get the drinking off to a good start. **375–440** The barter-session (375–92) seems harmless enough in itself, but inevitably leads to heavy drinking by the two participants (symbolised by the 'greeting' to Glutton at 392). **376** *newe fayre*: perhaps derived from a London fair thus named, of ill repute because barter gave scope for deception and / or squabbling if one party was drunk. The relative value of cloak and hood is assessed by some of the chapmen present (perhaps the experienced *upholderes*) and whoever gets the better deal is to make up the difference to the other (in money or ale); Hick has help from Bette, but Clement seems to need none. The swearing (384) is due to the assessors' being unable to agree the value; but the thing is settled amicably when

Robin is made umpire and decrees that, since he regards the hood as worth more, Clement should bridge the value-gap by buying a round for Hick (and presumably the other two). The penalty if either has second thoughts is to pay for a gallon of ale for 'Glutton' (this may signify 'a drink all round'). The explanation is not pellucid in **AB**, which state at 175/325 that 'the one who got the hood should be paid whatever more the cloak was worth', though this could not be known in advance but awaited independent valuation by the chapmen. **C** makes laboriously explicit (380–1) that whoever gets one won't get the other, but if one is judged to be worth more, its owner will pay the difference to the other party. Part of the satirical point is that the experts' judgement proves unacceptable, and a neutral non-expert arbitrarily decides the outcome: this is not proper trade (*permutacioun apertlich* 3.313) but just an excuse for drinking (394 couples them). **395** *euensong*: in monasteries the sixth canonical hour, vespers, commonly celebrated in parish churches only on Sundays. The time varied with the season, but the service was marked by the lighting of lamps and candles (hence its other name *lucernarium*) and the ringing of bells that would be heard (by the sober) anywhere. Here the phrase means in effect 'till sundown, all day'. **397** *two grydy sowes*: as illustrated in a carving on a choir-stall in Little Malvern priory Church (Kaske 1968: 59, pls. a–b). **398** *Paternoster-whyle*: the length would depend on how slowly and devoutly he said the prayer, which might have formed part of his penance. Like 'evensong', it illustrates how gluttons 'hire wombe is hire god' (*CT* X 820). **399–400** *ruet...horne*: a 'foul trump' that 'stank as the pit of hell' is described by Chaucer, *HF* 1654, perhaps recalling this scene; and cf. also *CT* VI 536. **401** *wexed*: MED s.v. *waxen* v. (2) (c), follows OED s.v. *Wax* v.², 2 in citing this (the only example), glossing it 'stop up [as with wax]'. But the line's ironic humour depends on the fact that the briars / furze would cause Glutton more pain if used to 'wax' his *ende* with the rubbing motion common to both polishing and the customary toilet-use. Hunters' horns were waxed to improve their tone, and the sense must be rather as in OED 1 '[polish with] wax', aptly citing *Master of Game* xxi (1400): 'A good hunters horne shuld be wele ywexede...after þat þe hunter þinketh þat it woll best sowne'. *weps*: straw or grass (not briars!) was commonly used for toilet purposes; see *ars-wispe* in MED s.v. *wispe* n. (c). **402a** Cf. the echo of this scene in 19.56 //, where being unable to *stepe ne stande* is (allegorically) the consequence of sin. **403–5** These comparisons with a performing dog and a trapper of birds (both highly trained) ironically highlight Glutton's drunken incapacity. **407** *thromblede*: first found here in **A**, and only here in this sense. **409–11** *knowes...lappe*: Clement gets him to his knees facing him and then Glutton vomits into his lap. **412** *Hertfordshyre*: unlike Norfolk, a county named

solely for alliterative convenience (cf. B 2.110). **416** The **B** revision reveals gluttony leading to the worst form of sloth, whereas **A** describes the fit of shakes following the drinking-bout. MED wrongly takes *exces*, a different lexeme answering to *surfet*, as a spelling-variant of *axesse* (a different word in **A**) and fails to record what is its earliest use s.v. 3. = 'intemperance'. *accidie*: glossed by MED as 'a spell of lethargy or apathy', citing only this example; but the pun on its main sense, 'the sin of sloth' is unmistakable, and the next Sin to follow (7.1) resembles his predecessor as the latter would look on awaking. **417** Glutton sleeps between Friday and Sunday evensong, a sign of his virtual transformation into Sloth. **420** *edwitede...synne*: **C**'s b-half showing reversion to the wording of **A**. *inwit*: the metrical stress on the second element highlighting this term's more general sense 'the rational power' (Quirk 1953); but since its moral colouring remains, it here virtually = 'conscience', which is what 'reproached' (*edwitede*) him. A 10.58–61 expresses **L**'s earlier view that drunkenness may quench awareness of right and wrong, but **C** shows Glutton moved by his own sense of shame (421 echoing A 208), rather than having first to be upbraided by his confessor. The reading of B 364 remains uncertain (see *TN*) and **C** may deliberately depict a sinner more susceptible to the 'ayenbite of inwit' than the total reprobate of **B**, whose conscience is almost extinct. **422–3** Glutton's prayer for pity replaces Repentance's admonition to purge his sins of speech and conduct by the 'verbal act' of confessing (B 366–7), for which he commends the penitent at B 379. In **C** the movement of repentance is thus spontaneous, rather than a response to priestly urging. **424–34** Glutton's inebriation leads to sins of inner and outer defilement by words and vomiting, and the comparison to a sick dog here is without the irony of 403–4. **C** omits the social harm caused by his waste of good food (B 374, with which cf. B 439). **426** In both **B** and **C** the first oath is blasphemous, the second a solemn one used improperly. **427** *falsly*: because too drunk to know what he was doing. Such defiance of the Second Commandment was seen as a direct offence against God. **428–33** Sins of eating before time, over-choicely or to excess are listed in *ParsT* 827–30 (and at 835 cf. 'to sitte longe at his mete'). The humorous but shrewd linking of gluttony with sloth in B 375–6 is replaced in **C** by typical *repetitio* of *foule* and the balance of excesses on feast and fast days dropped (neither a clear improvement). **428** *soper*: the evening-meal providing greater temptation to indulge, though excess at mid-day might be more serious, as it would prevent him from working (cf. Hunger's words at 8.274–5). **433** *bifore noen*: in effect eating the breakfast that the penitential regulations required him to forgo; but the sin is worse in **C** as it involves drink and bawdry. **B 379** *shewynge shrift*: 'making (your) confession'; a gerund governing a noun-object, as analysed in Tajima

537

2000:18–20. **437** *to verray God*: replacing the punning *faste* of B 382 ('to faste' / 'firmly'). His vow is presumably to keep from food before lunchtime on Friday, when abstinence from meat was always compulsory (hence *fysch*) but fasting so only in the penitential seasons. The penance that makes satisfaction for the sin is 'mesure..., that restreyneth by resoun the deslaue [uncontrolled] appetit of etynge' (*CT* X 835; cf. 1.32–5). **439** *Abstinence myn aunte*: for such 'relational' imagery cf. on 329. This authoritative figure is an abbess in B 7.133 and one of the seven sisters who serve Truth at 7.271. *ParsT* 832–3 notes that abstinence, the 'remedy' against gluttony, is spiritually efficacious only if accompanied by good will, patience and charity.

Passus VII (B V, ZA V–VI)

PASSUS SEVEN continues the Confessions of ZAB V and incorporates the rest of B V=ZA VI. It has six sections: (i) the Confession of SLOTH (1–68); (ii) a quasi-homiletic admonition to the rich (69–118*a*); (iii) Repentance's sublime prayer arousing hope among the sinners (119–153*a*); (iv) the penitents' setting out on 'pilgrimage' to St Truth and their encounter with the professional pilgrim (154–80); (v) the appearance of Piers Plowman to describe the way to *Treuthe* (181–281); (vi) the responses, mostly negative, to Piers (282–307). Adopted with little change from B 13.410–57, the 'admonition' (ii) considers SLOTH in relation to disreputable forms of entertainment that it contrasts with the figurative 'minstrelsy' of charitable acts. The effect is to make a vice that in its secular form corrupts society and government and in its spiritual form can induce resistance to conversion appear climactic or fundamental (see Wenzel 1960:135–47 and, arguing the centrality of *accidia* in **L**'s thought, Bowers 1986).

(i) 1–68 1 *Sleuthe*: here identified with *accidie* as the condition *consequent on* gluttonous excess of drink (**L**'s single use of that learned term at 6.416 lacks the full technical sense). This contrasts with Chaucer's use of 'sloth' not as the generic term but as a species of *Accidia* 'angwissh of troubled heart' (*CT* X 679) manifested in 'anoy of goodnesse' (*taedium boni*) or reluctance to do good. *ParsT* (like *PP*) understands the spiritual form of the sin as also physically enervating, for 'slothe maketh...feble and tendre' (689). **3** *stoel*: a faldstool or prie-dieu used for prolonged devotions. **4** *taylende*: metonymy for his need to evacuate; perhaps with an ironic pun on the homophone *taylende* (2) 'reckoning', alluding to his need for shrift. **5** *ryngyng*: i.e. of the church bells; confirming SLOTH's 'moral continuity' with Glutton, who was drunk asleep all Sunday till evensong (6.416–17). **6** *Benedicite*: 'Bless [me, Father, for I have sinned'; the formula for beginning confession. *bolk*: the belch (*eructatio*) produced by the build-up of wind after drinking, sardonically recalling the verse *Eructavit cor meum verbum bonum* (Ps 44:2). But Sloth's only 'good word' is *Benedicite*, a frequent exhortation in psalms (e.g. 102:21). *knokkede*: a standard penitential gesture; cf. 5.106, Z 5.97. **7** *romede*: 'uttered a noisy yawn' (see *TN*); but if it is MED *remen* v. 1(b) 'yawn', the whole phrase resembles *he gon ræmien and raxlede swiðe* in Laȝamon's *Brut* 12972. *rotte*: echoing Sloth's 'other half' Glutton's lapse into his sin on the point of confession at 6.355–60, as Repentance's rebuke does that at B 5.365. **9** *drede*: i.e. of unpreparedness for death; from Sloth 'comth *drede* to bigynne to werke anye goode werkes' (*ParsT* 690). **10** *Paternoster*: its recitation commonly forming part of penance; cf. 5.107 and *ParsT* 1043: 'This hooly orisoun amenuseth [*reduces*] eek venyal synne, and therfore it aperteneth specially to penitence' (see further Gillespie 1994). Sloth is here a layman but at 30 will assume the persona of a priest. *syngeth*: i.e. at Mass, between the Canon and the Communion. Because of the power ascribed to it as a 'sacramental' (a sacred act made efficacious through the Church's intercession), laypeople were encouraged to learn the Latin Paternoster from childhood so that they could join in with the priest when he said it at Mass (see B 13.237). **11** *can*: i.e. by heart, through having heard them so often; the line associates the speaker with the wealthy hearers of harlotry at 81ff. *rymes of Robyn Hode*: the first vernacular reference to the folk-hero (Gray 1984:3–4; for texts and discussion see Dobson & Taylor 1976, Knight 1994). *Randolf*: the Earl (1172–1232), another hero of popular ballads, whose story is told in the Percy Folio MS. He is usually identified with the third earl (Alexander 1982:152–7). **12** *maked*: devotional lyrics or such narrative poems as the *Stanzaic Life of Christ*, *South English Legendary* and *Miracles of the Virgin* in the Vernon and Auchinleck MSS. **13** *voues*: to break a vow or make one frivolously being considered a serious sin; cf. Eccl 5:3–4. **14–15** *penaunce...sory*: wilful refusal to perform canonical penance, the third *pars penitencie* (satisfaction). It was regarded as voiding absolution, though failure to feel true sorrow was not thought so grave as to invalidate confession. The correct attitude to the sacrament is described by Piers in words directly echoing these lines at 7.243–6. **16** *in wrathe*: his sole prayer being to ask God to curse somebody. **18–19** The irony of Sloth's nature is that he is 'busy' only about 'idleness', in church or tavern; this line reinforces his affinity with Glutton. **20** *payne...passioun*: subjects that might move to contrition, and often commended to penitents by confessors. **21** Sloth is now shown in its technical sense of failure to do good deeds recommended as penance: here the omission of two corporal works of mercy (cf. Mt 25:36), a motif illustrated in a window at All Saints, York (Swanson

1989:300). *prisone*: here with a wider sense than *putte*, in **B** the parish lock-up, often located underneath the church (as at Sleaford in Lincs). **22–3** *likene...vnlikyng*: typical 'late' semantic wordplay, echoing the attack on bawdy minstrels at B 10.42. **C** starkly opposes ribald tales and malicious mockery to the supreme fiction of Scripture, replacing the B 407 reference to the popular *ludi* of Midsummer Eve (June 23) condemned by churchmen for licentiousness and irreverence towards sacred personages (see MED's Mannyng, Rolle and Chaucer refs. s.v. *somer* n. (1), 3(c), and Wenzel 1989). **25** *Vigils*: times for fasting and watching in prayer, especially before major feasts. The other main *fasting-days* (involving abstinence from meat) were Fridays and Saturdays in Lent and the twelve Ember days marking the four seasons, i.e. the Wednesdays, Fridays and Saturdays after St Lucy (13 Dec.), Ash Wednesday, Whitsunday and the Exaltation of the Cross (14 Sept.). **26** *Lente*: Sloth's vice (compounded by lechery) is not intermitted even for the penitential season (cf. Pr 89). **27** Though failure to hear Sunday Mass was judged a grave sin, Sloth thinks his obligation discharged if the friars (at a church where perhaps he belongs to the fraternity) include his name in the community bidding-prayer (cf. Piers' expectation at 8.104 of such a mention from his parish priest for his lifelong payment of tithes). Friar Flatterer will later propose as much to Contricion, the type of those who 'wol nat suffre noon hardnesse ne penaunce'. *CT* X 679 and that passage favour this interpretation here. So does *MS* 630 'They haue a *memoire* of Mvm among alle other' (which MED s.v. *memorie* n. 2(c) misassigns in illustrating the phrase *haven memorie*). But as the **B** reading that **C** revises can only be conjecturally reconstructed, B 412 could mean 'recall [that there is a service at] the Friary church'. The point would then be that Sloth can arrive when the service is nearly over and still be held by his indulgent friar-confessor to have heard Mass. **B 413** 'Go, the service is finished', the priest's formula of dismissal of the people (from which 'mass' derives); 'sloth' is here negligent observance of the sabbath. **28** *seknesse*: with its concomitant fear of death; this illustrates the vice of tardiness, arising from 'a fals hope...that he shal lyve longe...that...faileth ful ofte' (*CT* X 719). **29** *ten 3er... haluendele*: stronger than **B**, which alludes exactly to the duty of annual confession imposed by the Fourth Lateran Council (1215) and to neglect of the requirement that 'shrift moste be purveyed bifore and avysed' (*CT* X 1000ff). **30–4** The abrupt alteration of Sloth's identity typifies the plasticity of **L**'s allegory (cf. Pride's changing sex at 6.14). A similar portrait is found in *The Papelard Priest*, an alliterative piece of *c.* 1350 (edited in Revard 2001, Appendix). **30** *prest and persoun*: 'ordained and beneficed'. **31** *solfe ne reden*: ignorant of Latin and unable to sing the notes of the scale, so unequipped to

perform his services properly or develop spiritually by reading the lives of the Saints. **32** A line perhaps echoed in *CT* I 191–2. **B 419–20** The comparison may have been omitted as too complicated for an audience including priests like those criticised under sloth, or simply as over-specific for the purpose, which is to assert that he is 'illiteratus'. *Beatus vir*: 'Blessed is the man ...'; opening both Ps 1 and 111, but here more probably alluding to the former, the second verse of which requires the just man to meditate 'on the law of the lord' (with which *Canoun* B 422 corresponds). *Beati omnes*: 'Blessed are all they [that fear the Lord: that walk in his ways]' (Ps 127:1). *Construe clausemele*: referring to evensong, when these psalms would have been sung or said, though even a zealous parson would rarely have preached then. **33** Presiding at the manor court, especially on settlement-days (B 421; see on 3.195–6); going through tenants' accounts with the reeve might both help his *parisshens* and provide profit on the side. **34** *Catoun*: further heightening of the slothful priest's incompetence; he is ignorant of elementary Latin grammar (see on 4.17) and cannot read with understanding. **B 422** *Canoun*: the *Corpus iuris canonici*, the body of ecclesiastical law. *Decretals*: either generic for a collection of papal decrees or specifically the *Decretum* of the great Bolognese jurist Gratian (d. *c.* 1160). Although two separate works seem envisaged, AlfG is not wholly persuasive that *Canoun* = specifically Gratian and *Decretals* = the *Corpus*. The latter denotes the C12th gathering of earlier conciliar canons and papal decrees together with the C13–14th papal decretals determining points of canon law: the *Decretals* of Gregory IX (1234), the *Novellae* of Innocent IV (*c.* 1254), the *Liber Sextus* of Boniface VIII (1298) and the *Constitutions of Clement V* promulgated by John XXII (1317). The *Decretum* or *Concordia discordantium canonum* (*c.* 1140) was an analytical compilation used as an authoritative reference work (and often thought of as part of the *Corpus*) but not adopted formally as the Church's official law (Brundage 1987:233). **L** does not quixotically expect a parson like the Doctor at 15.86, but *litteratus* enough to consult authorities when the need arose. **35–41** Sloth now metamorphoses into a dishonourable farmer who repudiates orally-agreed loans from trusting creditors but pays his own employees unwillingly and late (a sin against justice condemned in Lev 19:16, quoted at 3.307*a*). **35** *ytayled*: see on 4.61. **42–54** depict Sloth's decline into 'povertee and destruccioun...of...temporeel thynges' (*CT* X 721) through ingratitude and negligence. **42; 43; 45** *beenfeet; cortesie; loue*: forms of good that Sloth is as unapt to comprehend as to perform. The 'hawk' metaphor implies that he cynically appraises an act of disinterested goodwill to see what is in it for the giver (*he* always looks to his own advantage). **45** *luyred*: the lure was usually 'a bundle of leather and feathers resembling a bird' (MED s.v. *lure* n (1)), to which a piece of meat (= *ouht*) was sometimes attached. It was tied to a thong and swung round as part of training a hawk to return to the falconer. **47–8** *haue...speche*: i.e. both in forgetting to say 'thank you' and in not desisting from unkind remarks through remembrance of past kindnesses; sardonically punning on two senses of *sparen* 'refrain from' and 'save' (MED s.v. 2a, 5b). Burrow (2003:192–3), arguing with reference to B 435–9, would punctuate with a semi-colon after *sethe* 47 and *tyme* 48 so as to make *many a tyme* not an adverbial but a noun-phrase, yielding the sense: 'Have wasted many a moment of time in speaking or in failing to speak'. This misuse of time in relation to the gift of speech he persuasively shows to be specially apt to the sin of Sloth, illustrating from John de Burgo's manual for parish priests the *Pupilla Oculi* (cited from Wenzel 1960:197). **49–52** illustrate 'necligence, or reccheleesnesse, that rekketh of no thyng' (*CT* X 798), the serious consequence noted in 52b echoing 3.104–7 (which draws on first-hand observation). **53–4** Sloth's final transformation into a lazy vagabond who refuses to learn a trade and ends in beggary proves that if 'ignorance be mooder of alle harm...necligence is the norice' (*CT* X 710). **54a** The statement is quasi-authorial, not directly self-characterising as in its first appearance at 1.139a, the echo of which reminds that all the sins are implicitly those of 'Will' (6.2). **55** *swowened*: one harmful effect of sloth being 'sloggy slombrynge, which maketh a man be hevy and dul in body and in soule' (*CT* X 705). **56–68** formed the nucleus of the Sloth confession from **Z** onwards, and all survives save B 456–61 //, of which the first five lines are given to Evan, the last two omitted. **56** *Vigilate the veile*: 'Keep-Watch the Wakeful One'; a passing personification (unusually given words) of Sloth's near-extinct conscience, which produces tears sufficient to rouse him. The Latin name has resonances of texts on the need for alertness (lest death come suddenly), where sleep figures moral torpor, wakefulness spiritual awareness. These are Mk 13:33–7, 14:38 = Mt 26:41 (seeing sleep as vulnerability to temptation), I Cor 16:13, urging action, and I Pet 5:8, linking vigilance with sobriety (*sobrii estote, et vigilate*), a text preached to Glutton by Repentance at 6.168. Citing Wenzel 1967:102, Alf*Q* 13–14 notes that medieval commentators saw Mt 26:41 as warning specifically against *somnium accidiae*, the sleep of sloth. **58** *wanhope*: 'despair of the mercy of God, that comth...of to muche drede...that he hath doon so muche synne that it wol nat availlen hym, though he wolde repenten hym and forsake synne...' (*CT* X 692). As with Greed at B 5.279, this is Sloth's end-condition, identified at 80 as its extreme form. **63** *auowe*: undoing his neglected vows (13). *foule sleuthe*: formulaic *repetitio* of 54b. **64** *Sonday*: making 'condign' satisfaction for his breach of the Third Commandment (Ex 20:8) by observing all three services (mat-

ins, Mass, evensong) on the sabbath; cf. Lechery's special attention to Saturday and Gluttony's to Friday (6.173, 338). *seuene ʒere*: cf. B 5.73, removed in // C 6.173. *but... make*: 'unless sickness cause it to be otherwise'; ironically repeating 7.28 (fear has been transformed through attrition to a firm purpose of amendment). **66–8** *matynes*: said at dawn and followed by Mass and dinner at noon; he will not drink between midday and evensong at 3.0 p.m. *þe Rode*: the vow being made before the crucifix on the screen below the chancel arch.

B 5.456–61 (Z 5.124–30, A 5.229–34) will have come under Sloth originally because they deal with tardiness in restoring ill-gotten goods; but **C** improves in shifting them to the thievish Evan (see on 6.308–12). **B 460** *Rode of Chestre*: formerly on Rood Eye (Cross Island) in the River Dee at Chester; repeated by Piers at A 7.92, where // **BC** alter the oath. **461** Sloth's resolve is to use the money left after settling his debts to live virtuously rather than make satisfaction by a costly pilgrimage. These words adumbrate the major theme of 'true' pilgrimage as conversion of heart that will be developed in B VI = C VIII. **462–77 (Z 131–150, A 235–52)** See on **C 6.315–29**.

(ii) 69–118a consider the routes to sloth and specifically *wanhope*, regarded as the final stage of Accidia in *AI* (pp. 33–4), but digress into a diatribe against those who encourage idle entertainers, and an admonition to the rich to substitute the needy for such 'false' minstrels. In B XIII this ends the account of Haukyn's dire condition fittingly enough (he is a minstrel), but earns its place here as showing how works of charity can bring man to the opposite state of *welhope* (113) or confidence in final release from sin.

69–80 form a transitional passage of question followed by answer and prepare for the negative and positive exempla on false, true and figurative 'minstrelsy'. **69** *wheche been*: a shift to direct question recalling the didactic address of a *precheour of Goddes wordes* (87). But while the lines it introduces are perhaps 'not adapted to the dramatic situation' (*Pe*), they are hardly more abrupt than in their original location. *þe braunches*: the circumstances and acts that lead back / predispose towards the dark 'essence' of sloth, 'final impenitence', the unforgiveable 'sin against the Holy Ghost' (*CT* X 695). Sin was commonly symbolised as a tree with major branches and twigs (an image first found in *AI*, p. 17). Its conventional form occurs at B 15.74–5 (where the 'branches' grow *out of* the capital sins) and in *CT* X 388–9: 'everich of thise chief synnes hath his braunches and his twigges' (Katzenellenbogen 1989: ill. 66 depicts *Desperatio*, *Acedia* etc, the subdivisions of Sloth or *Tristicia*, as hanging fruits). **70** *Is*: elliptical for 'its origin is'; spiritual torpor leading to despair starts with lack of sorrow for sin, failure to do penance, and reluctance to hear or do good. **71** recalls

Sloth's admission at 14. **75** takes up B 13.350. *to* (1, 2); *of*: governed respectively by *likyng*, here 74. **77** *wordes of murthe*: 'amusing conversation', not bad in itself but implying lightness of mind when found with refusal to consider serious matters like one's mortality (cf. Eccl 7:5–7). **79** *carpeth*: replacing *telleþ* and echoing 76; an example of **C**'s typical *repetitio*.

81–118a 82 *foel-sages*: ideally 'sothseggers' (like King Lear's Fool) rather than *flateres and lyares*. But **L**'s animosity is explained by his wish to contrast *all* 'mysproud' jesters with skilled musicians (96) and religious preachers (87) and to recommend replacing them with another (metaphorical) type of 'minstrel', the poor (103). The passage is predicated on the higher classes' need to hear 'sad' words (grave truths from religious men) and see 'sad' sights (people in the poor estate that all must return to at the time of *deth-deynge*). **83a** '[Woe to you that are filled: for you shall hunger]. Woe to you that now laugh: [for you shall mourn and weep]' (Lk 6:25). The next verse is also relevant, intimating a parallel between these 'sage fools' and Luke's flattering 'false prophets', while the whole warning precedes injunctions to give generously to the needy. **85** echoes Sloth's words at 9 above. **86** *sorwe*: in hell. **86a** 'Those who consent [*sc.* to evil] and those who do [it] will be punished with the same penalty'; identified by Alford 1975 (following *Sk* and citing Lucas of Penna) as a canon-law maxim, also common in the 'penitential' tradition see (Alf*Q*): 'they that...*consenten* to the synne been parteners...of the dampnacioun of the synnere' (*CT* X 967). Presumably here the tellers of the bawdy *tales* (90) are the 'doers', their hearers the 'consenting partners'. **87** Despite the OT terms, the present tense shows that all three categories denote contemporary clergy. **89** *procuratours*: as later Piers is of the Holy Spirit (21.259; see Alf*G* s.v.). **92** *Dauid*: cited here as the model for 'God's minstrels' (David is discussed in Wurtele 2003). **92a** 'He that worketh *pride* shall not dwell in the midst of my house: he that speaketh unjust things [did not prosper before my eyes]' (Ps 100:7–8). **95** *mysproud man*: either the satirical *foel-sage* or another category of harmful companion (cf. the psalm quotation) like those at 11.38–41. **96** *kynges munstrals*: skilled professional musicians of the royal establishment, who were paid 20s. a year in Edward III's time (Southworth 1989:103). When coming to perform at the houses of bishops or the provincial nobility (Chambers 1903:i.53, ii.247), they would expect a warm reception for the respect due to their 'lord' (the king, but in the allegory God). **99** As the handicapped, sick and destitute are 'minstrels' sent by God, 'listening' to them (showing charity) will produce true *murthe* for the hearer (in heaven); cf. Mt 10:42 and 12.121–3. **100** *As*: 'for', 'inasmuch as' rather than 'just as', since Christ's words do not compare beggars to minstrels or refer to beggars at all, but to his disciples. A

later elaboration of the analogy at 9.128–38 calling God's minstrels his 'messengers' (9.136) refers to the infirm of mind who prompt charity, but affirms that they are *not* beggars. **100a** '[He that heareth you heareth me: and] he that despiseth you [despiseth me: and he that despiseth me despiseth him that sent me]' (Lk 10:16). The thought resembles Jn 5:23, 13.20 but **L** was more probably recalling Jn 12:48: '*Qui spernit* me et non accipit verba mea, habet qui iudicet eum*'. **102** *solace*: playing on the senses 'entertain' and 'comfort (spiritually)'; see MED s.v. *solasen* v. 1(a), 2(a). **103** *for*; *thy*: alliterating on metrical allophones, each word carries strong sentence stress: 'in place of / in the rôle of' (so, unstressed, at 107); 'your'. **104–5** As the enjambement bears out, the final infinitive *for to saue* depends syntactically and semantically on both *to lere* and *suffrede*: Christ's passion, and poetic accounts of it (in works like those mentioned under 12 above), will profit the soul of the prudent rich man. **106** *geste*: the MED exx. s.v. *geste* n.1 are exclusively secular in reference save for **L**, whose four uses all differ. But here the revision (see *TN*) emphasises that the Passion story is 'not less but more heroic' than the martial tales a knightly audience might favour. **107** *bordiour*: paradoxical, unless wholly figurative, since the blindness is not a subject for mirth (contrast the comic remarks of the natural fools at 9.136, who are 'mery bordiours'). **108** *crye...*: intercede with God for the rich man (now or at the Last Judgement) by citing his generosity. **110–11** *til...seyntes*: '...offer great comfort to him who during his life...' *here*: 'receive', 'welcome'. **112–13** 'settle into a state of confidence that he will join the saints in heaven because he did such deeds'. **L** is of his age in seeing a person's last hour as crucial, a time of despair or joyful hope of salvation, but realistic in judging that sloth (defined as reluctance to do good) severely lessens the chance of a person's 'death-bed conversion'. **115** The image is of a musician conducting a procession of merrymakers into a banquet. *lythed*: revision of **B** to achieve the *repetitio* of 111 again typical of **C**. **116** *turpiloquio*: inflected as ablative after *with*; the same word that in Pr 40 associates the low satirist with Lucifer, users of vile language being those who sing the devil's tune. *lay of sorwe*: ironically, composed of *wordes of murthe* (cf. 77); but its transcendental 'meaning' is misery, whereas (a favourite paradox of the poet) the literal 'lay of sorrow' about Christ's passion will lead to *murthe* (cf. 12.202–20). **117–18a** The conclusion added in **C**, which rounds off the argument with an admonitory patristic text on the danger of patronising immoral *japeres*, makes the inserted passage seem even more like a miniature sermon. **117** Hell's pain is 'unending' as well as 'ceaseless', purgatory's prescribed a limit; but though both are intense, neither is understood as unjust (for the same sense of *wikke* see 11.275). **118** *þat*: '[those] who(m)', a 'Janus-faced' relative, the nominative being principal. **118a** 'To give money to actors [is much the same as offering sacrifice to devils]', part of a statement attributed to St Jerome by Petrus Cantor, '*Paria sunt* histrionibus dare *et demonibus immolare*'(*PL* 205:155). This warning should be read beside the strong criticism at B 9.92a of bishops whose wrongful giving deprives Christ's poor of their due.

(iii) 119–53a have REPENTANCE as a priest interceding with God for the sins of the people. But in strict allegorical terms his action serves to demonstrate how spiritual change engenders humility and thence receptiveness to the grace of conversion (witnessed in amendment of life). The speech, with its liturgical resonances, closely relates in theme and tone to the Passion-Harrowing sequence in 20.57ff, which it anticipates, e.g. at 134 (Bennett 1982:85–112). It is as richly veined with scriptural quotations as Passus XX, and its echoes of the Holy Week services (*Bn*) help to locate the great repentance scene towards the end of the season favoured for compulsory annual confession and orientate it towards Easter, which completes the liturgical cycle of redemption begun at Christmas. The later passage that 'recapitulates' this scene is explicitly set towards the end of Lent (21.385). **119** The 'Platonic' play on 'readiness' and 'counsel' is typical of **C**. **123** See Gen 1:26. **124** *sykenesse*: i.e. in subjecting man to suffering and death. **125** *þe Book*: the Bible's account of death coming into the world through the sin of Adam (Gen 3:16–19, Rom 5:12), against which is set the hope of eternal life through Christ's death and resurrection. **125a** 'O happy fault, [which was blotted out by the death of Christ]! O [truly] necessary sin of Adam, [which earned so great a redeemer]'; from the canticle *Exultet* sung at the start of the Easter Vigil service on Holy Saturday: 'O certe *necessarium Adae peccatum*, [quod Christi morte deletum est!] O felix culpa, [quae talem ac tantum meruit habere Redemptorem]'. Strang 1963:208 suggests that **L**'s inversions derive from a lost lyrical form of this text; but it is typical of **L** that his quotations are free and fitted to their immediate context. The canticle's 'necessary' implies that the Fall, though caused by Satan's enmity, formed part of God's providential plan to bring forth a greater good. **126–8** The fault was 'happy' because it led to the Incarnation, a first 'new creation' that exalts man even more than did his original creation in God's image. This idea is fully developed by Peace the Daughter of God in 20.207–37. **128** *with*: here and at B 488 = 'through the agency / in the person of', not 'together with'. The prayer is addressed to God the Father, making clear that not He but the incarnate Second Person died on the cross (though *all* divine acts are to be thought of as done 'through the will of the Father' and 'by the working of the Holy Spirit'). **128a** '[Do you not believe that] I am in the Father and the Father in me?' (Jn 14:10); 'he that seeth me seeth the Father also' (Jn 14:9). The quotations

(of which the first is repeated at 11.155a during Clergy's speech on the Trinity) underline that Christ (though truly man) shares his divine nature with the Father, whom he manifests to the world in human guise (*sute / sekte*). **B 487a** 'Let us make man to our image and likeness' (Gen 1:26); 'And elsewhere, He that abideth in charity abideth in God, and God in him' (I Jn 4:16). The creation of Adam is associated with the *second* 'new creation' (see on 126–8), that of the Christian through baptismal grace, making possible the supernatural life of charity that incorporates redeemed mankind in the life of God, *quoniam Deus charitas est* (I Jn 4:8; cf.1.82). As *Bn* notes, the second quotation is the source of the hymn *Ubi caritas* 'Where charity and love are, there is God' sung as an antiphon on Maundy Thursday at the ceremony of the Washing of the Feet. **129** *secte*: 'fleshly form': a revision removing the polysemous wordplay on *sute* (B 488), which also signifies 'cause, action-at-law' (*Bn*) and 'pursuit'. The legal and chivalric senses apposite to Christ's encounter with Satan in the Crucifixion (20.393–5, 443, 408) are replaced by a simple emphasis on the truth of his incarnation. But neither *semed* nor *fourme* 130 implies the deceptive or illusory, rather the 'sensibly actual' appearance concealing the 'metaphysically real' truth (though the effect on the 'false' Satan is to deceive *him*). **B 489** *ful tyme*: 'noon', perhaps further suggesting Christ's death as the coming to fulfilment of his historical life at '*plenitudo temporis* tyme' (Gal 4:4: see 18.127); cf. C 2.100, which conversely substitutes *noone* for *ful tyme* B 96. The Synoptic Gospels' *nona hora* 'ninth hour' (Mt 27:46 //) was 3 p.m; but the canonical office of None originally fixed for that hour came to be said after the principal monastic Mass of *midday* (132 below), and this was the word's main sense by the 13th c. **130** Whereas **C** stresses the reality of Christ's suffering, B 490–1 affirm that the Godhead remained impassible while the human nature united with it in the person of Jesus endured the pain. **B 491** *it ladde*: the pronoun is double-referenced, since Christ led mankind to salvation, and humanity ('his capul that highte *Caro*' B 17.108) also 'led' or carried the divine nature. A sense 'endured' (MED s.v. *leden* 9(c)), with *sorwe* as object, is favoured in Mann's thoughtful discussion (1994[1]:44); but the *duxit* of 491a directs to the sense 'lead / carry (away captive)', with *secte* clearly the object. **130a** '[Ascending on high], he led captivity captive' (Eph 4:8, quoting Ps 67:19); sung as an antiphon verse on Ascension Day, and alluding to Christ's descent into *Limbo inferni* to release the souls of the just (a belief enshrined in clause 5 of the Apostles' Creed and based on I Pet 3:19 and Eph 4:9–10 9–10). The theme will be dramatically realised at 20.449. **131** refers to the 'darkening of the sun' between the sixth and ninth hour: *tenebrae factae sunt...Et obscuratus est sol* (Lk 23:44–5). *lees siht*: by *interpretatio*, 'became invisible' but literally 'became blind', since the sun is personified here, as later at 20.60. The phrasing echoes Rolle in his *Meditations on the Passion* (shorter version): *þe erþe þan trembled, þe sonne lost hys syȝt, þat al merk was þe weder, os it hadde ben nyȝt* (Ullmann 1884:462). *GO* states that 'the sun withdrew its beams either so as not to see the Lord hanging there or so that wicked blasphemers should not enjoy its light' (*PL* 114:348, following Bede on Mk in *PL* 92:290); and John of Hoveden writes that 'the sun refused to look upon / the suffering borne by the true sun' (original in *Poems*, ed. Raby, p. 188). On the rich Latin and vernacular poetic background to this motif, see Schmidt 1983²:185–8. **132** *mydday*: the normal time of dinner. The 'heavenly banquet' is here seen as celebrated at the time when on earth the Eucharistic *pignum* 'pledge' of that feast is re-enacted with the symbolic pouring out of the blood of Christ at the consecration of the wine. *Sk*'s doubt about making this connection, because Mass 'was more usually celebrated at an earlier hour,' is answered if what **L** had in mind is the major conventual Mass at noon (see on B 489). *most liht*: literally the sun's at full strength, but figuratively that of Christ the 'Sun of Righteousness' de-scending into the darkness of hell. *mel-tyme*: perhaps alluding to the legend in *St Patrick's Purgatory* (Day 1932:317–18, citing *SEL* pp. 216–17) that the blessed in the earthly paradise who have passed through purgatory are fed daily by a heavenly light. Wenzel (AlfC 164–5) notes a sermon passage used in *FM* that reads Christ's sacrificial death in the light of Cant 1:6 ('Indica mihi... ubi pascas, ubi cubes in meridie'). **133** Influence from the motif of the pelican sustaining its young with blood from its breast (*Pe*) conjoins with the well-known legend that the wood of the cross was made from the Tree of Life (Gen 2:30) and that its position on Calvary ('the place of the Skull') was directly above the grave of Adam, into whose mouth Christ's blood trickled. A C14th Italian crucifixion-fresco (Schiller 1972, II, pl. 504) comprehensively depicts the *arbor vitae*, the heavenly liturgy, the pelican (placed above the inscription) and the rock of calvary, while a C15th German Rood (ibid., pl. 489) also represents the tree of life. *tho*: the moment when Christ's blood was 'actually' shed, here envisaged as coinciding with that when it is made 'really' present at the priest's breaking of the Host. *forfadres*: all the patriarchs, beginning with Adam *oure aller fader* (B 16.205). Their participation in the feeding is graphically depicted in a wooden C13th German rood (Schiller 1972, II: pl. 479) where Adam holds a chalice to receive the blood. **133a** 'The people that walked in darkness have seen a great light: [to them that dwelt in the region of the shadow of death, light is risen]' (Is 9:2; qu. in Mt 4:16 with reference to the mission of Jesus). Read in the lesson for the Monday of the 4th week in Advent and the vespers of the Nativity, this text underlies the Introit of Christmas, associating

Christ's birth with his death as 'light-bringing' salvific events. Though not quoted in the Easter liturgy, it became the basis of patristic thought on Christ's liberation of the patriarchs from hell (*Bn* cites the *Sunday Sermons* of Pope St Leo, ii. 191), on which see *EN* 18:1. **134** *oute of The*: inspired by the Nicene Creed's description of the Son as 'Deum de Deo, *lumen de lumine*' (based on Jn 1:4–5, 9). *blente*: cf. 20.368. **B 496** *blewe*: the claim that 'strict syntax requires the action to be predicated of Lucifer' (*Bn*) is groundless, since *blewe* may be 2nd or 3rd pers. pret. (in the light of C 135 *brouhte* more probably the latter) and any difficulty must be semantic not syntactical. That the light, symbol of the divine power and presence, should 'blow' the souls out of hell is not much odder than that Christ's 'breath' should break hell's gates in 20.364 // (as *Bn* is aware), since this breath explains 'blew' (*Sk*). Fiery light and powerful wind together are traditional divine epiphanies from the OT to the Pentecost scene in Acts 2:2–3. For (uncompelling) speculation that the passage alludes to the theology of the generation of the Son by the Father and of insufflation by the Holy Spirit see Hill 1973:444–9. **136** *thridde day*: the morning of Easter Sunday being the third 'day' after the dawn of Good Friday, if this day is included. **137** *synful Marie*: Mary of Magdala, whose meeting with the risen Christ in the garden occupies half of Jn 20 (cf. 21.157–60). She was traditionally confused both with Mary of Bethany, sister of Martha and Lazarus (12.137), and with the un-named woman who anointed Jesus and had 'many sins forgiven her' (Lk 7:47). Since the 'seven devils' he had cast out of the Magdalen (Mk 16:9) were commonly allegorised as the deadly sins, she aptly emblematises the hope of forgiveness for the worst sinner (cf. 11.264–5). On the legend of Mary (*LA* xcvi) see Garth 1950 and Haskins 1993, and on the Magdalen hymns Szövérffy 1963. *Seynte Marye*: the usual ME style for the Blessed Virgin Mary (e.g. *CT* IV 2418), sometimes as part of *Oure Lady Seinte Marye* (*CT* VI 308). This appellation only became controversially contrasted with the title 'Our Lady' in Protestant usage at the Reformation. **138a** 'I came not to call the just, but sinners to penance' (Lk 5:32). Christ's appearance *first* to the Mary who typifies (converted) sinfulness rather than (unblemished) holiness is understood as offering special comfort to the truly penitent. **139–40** treat the evangelists as poets who composed the *geste* of Christ's heroic actions (see on 106, and cf. Lawton in Wallace1999: 478–9). *was don*: elliptical for '(related to what) was done' (*Bn*). *sekte*: with the same complex polysemy as at 129, 136. **B 501** *armes*: with both martial and heraldic senses (*Sk*), anticipating 20.21 where the referent is again 'humana natura'. **140a** '[And] the Word was made flesh, and dwelt among us' (Jn 1:14). **141** *by so muche*..: 'in virtue of the fact [that Christ now represents the human race he has become part of]'. **143** *fadur*: from 122 the prayer was to God the Father, from 129a to the incarnate Second Person, and now to the glorified Christ, in effect to God in his new relationship with mankind prophesied in the passage quoted at 147a. Formal Trinitarian exactitude is not to be looked for here, since for **L** it is the one God who makes and who becomes man (see 20.226, 230). **144–7a** affirm more clearly and explicitly than **B** that salvation is for those who are sincerely sorry for their sin. **147** *knowlechede*: understand 'our sins'. **147a** '[Whenever a sinner shall cry out], I will remember all [his] iniquities no more'; traced to pseudo-Ezekiel 33:12, by Marchand (1990), who notes that it was frequently cited in discussions on the necessity of confession and exhorting against the sin of despair. The possible source of this apocryphal OT passage is Jer 31:34b; certainly the whole of Jer 31:29–34 is relevant as a prophecy of the New Covenant established at the Incarnation. **148** *and... moder*: for the grammar see on 2.2. **151–6** This brief passage, dense with embedded and appended Latin, allegorises the awakening of the theological virtue of HOPE offered in baptism, lost by the *rybaudes* through persistence in sin, but now recovered through their formal repentance. A passing personification not to be simply identified with the *Spes* of XIX, Hope embodies positive trust in God that generates active will to do good. So as *welhope* (113), he signifies the metaphysical contrary to *wanhope*, the final stage of Sloth. **151** *horn*: understood by BnPe as suggesting the *tuba salutaris* 'trumpet of salvation' in the Easter *Exultet*'s opening sentence. But a verbally closer source is 'The Lord is...my protector and the *horn* of my salvation [*cornu salutis meae* = a powerful salvation for me],' from Ps 17:3, immediately after a reference to *hope* in God (*et sperabo in eum*), echoed by the canticle of Zacharias in Lk 1:69 (Alf*Q*). *Deus...*: 'Thou wilt turn, O God, and bring us to life: [and thy people shall rejoice in thee]' (Ps 85:7); the priest's prayer of general absolution (Burrow 1984 [1965]: 84) at the end of the public confession at Mass, after the *Confiteor* and the *Misereatur*. Though the context would suggest that Will and the repentant sinners have come to Mass and that **L** 'is here thinking of public liturgical, rather than private sacramental, penance' (Burrow), the two acts are complementary. Obligation to confess mortal sins personally to the priest remained, but those participating in the penitential rite of Mass could hope to be absolved from *venial* sins committed since receiving individual absolution at their last confession and receive help against falling into such sin (cf. *CT* X 385). **152–2a** 'Blessed are they whose iniquities are forgiven: and whose sins are covered' (Ps 31:1, the second penitential psalm). Assurance of sin forgiven is the 'breath' with which Hope fills his horn of God's life-giving presence in the Eucharist (a miniature scriptural allegory of the penitents' movement through Easter Confession to Communion that will be

dramatised in 21.367–93). The importance of this verse is shown by its return at 14.117a and B 13.52–53a, 14.93. **153** *alle Seyntes*: illustrating the dogma of 'the Communion of Saints', which precedes 'the Forgiveness of Sins' as the 9th clause of the Apostles' Creed; allusion is to Lk 15:7 on the joy in heaven over one repentant sinner. **153a** 'Men and beasts thou wilt preserve, O Lord: O how hast thou multiplied thy mercy, O God!' (Ps 35:7–80). **(iv) 154–80** describe the response of the Folk as emotional rather than rational, though **L** eliminates the more dramatic symptoms of this (AZ 254 /152) to stress their ignorance and bewilderment: now *thei wilneth bettre* but are still *aboute þe mase* (1.8, 6). **155** echoes HC's farewell at 2.51. **156** *to go to Treuthe*: remembering Reason's parting injunction at 5.198 that urged them to repent. **158** *blostrede; baches*: rare words, the former found first here in this sense and associated with the blind irrational movement of animals (as in *Pur* 886), the latter earlier only in Laʒamon (MED s.vv. *blusteren* v. and *bach* n.(1)). *bestes*: echoing *iumenta* 153a, but suggesting pity for 'distressed sheep without a shepherd' (cf. Mt 9:36, Ps 77:52–3). **159–60** give a merciless caricature of the professional religious tourist ostentatiously sporting souvenirs from the chief pilgrim-shrines in Europe and the Near East. **Z 158** *palmere*: originally a pilgrim entitled to wear on his hat palm-sprigs sewn crosswise, as a sign of having visited the Holy Places; by now denoting 'a pilgrim who had travelled overseas' (*CT* I 13). **160** *paynem*: because wearing the outlandish garb of *hethenesse*. **161** *bordoun*: a long staff carried by pilgrims travelling on foot. *liste*: perhaps for use as a bandage in case of accident (*Sk*). **164** *aunpolles*: lead or pewter flasks (*ampullae*) stamped with the saint's image (Alexander & Binski 1987:218–21, pls.43–53) and containing holy water from the shrine, in which the saint's relic had been dipped. **165** *Signes*: badges or insignia of having made a particular pilgrimage (Alexander & Binski pls. 54–67). *Syse*: Assisi, near Perugia, in Umbria, birth- and burial-place of St Francis. *shelles*: (Anderson 1971: pl. 60; Cutts 1925: pl. 163), commemorating a miracle of St James, through whose intercession a pagan knight saved from drowning in the sea emerged covered with scallop shells and was converted to the Christian faith (Cutts 169). *Galys*: see on Pr 48. **166–7** describe emblems of the pilgrimage to Rome (Sumption 1975:249–65). *crouch*: symbolising the martyrdom of St Peter. *kayes*: the crossed keys signifying Peter's spiritual authority (Mt 16:19). *vernicle*: a copy in cloth or metal of the napkin with which (according to her legend) St Veronica was believed to have wiped the face of Christ on the way to Calvary and on which his likeness was miraculously impressed; she was sometimes identified with the woman suffering from an issue of blood, whom Jesus cured (Mt 9:20–22). Gerald of Wales derived her name (probably a corruption of *Bernice* in Ac

25:13), from *vera icon* 'true image', the words inscribed under the Vernicle. The scene (Anderson 1971: pl. 38) became part of the Stations of the Cross performed in Rome (where the Vernicle was preserved in St Peter's) and is recorded in the *Legends of the Holy Rood* 170–1; but in the form **L** probably knew it (*LA* ch. 53), the incident occurs before the Passion (see further Lewis 1985). *bifore*: i.e. on his breast. **167–8** His 'carnal' attitude to pilgrimage is antithetical to Piers's spiritual understanding at 8.62–3. **170** *Sinoye*: Mt Sinai on the peninsula between Egypt and Palestine, where the great monastery claimed to preserve the body of St Catherine of Alexandria. *sepulcre*: Christ's tomb, the most sacred pilgrimage site, within the Church of the Holy Sepulchre in Jerusalem. **171** *Bedlem*: five miles S of Jerusalem, where the C4th Church of the Nativity stands over the traditional birthplace of Christ (Mt 2:1). All of these Holy Land sites were in the hands of the Turks, but intrepid pilgrims continued to visit them. *Babiloyne*: 'the Less' near Cairo (as distinguished from Babylon the Great in Mesopotamia), where 'a faire chirche of oure lady' (*Mandeville's Travels*, I 21) commemorated the time spent by Joseph and Mary in Egypt (Mt 2:14). **172** *Armonye*: where Noah's Ark had rested (Gen 8:30) on Mt Ararat (now in Turkey) and was still to be seen. *Alisaundre*: in Egypt, the main port of embarkation for pilgrims to the Holy Land and the place where St Mark and St Catherine had been martyred. *Damaskle*: capital of Syria, the legendary site where God created Adam before placing him in Eden (*Mandeville*, I..44; *CT* VII 2007; Comestor in *PL* 198:1053–1722). **176** *corseynt*: to the folk, 'saint' rather than 'saint's body [in a shrine]' (cf. Chaucer *HF* 117); but their very choice of term (MED s.v. *cor-seint* n.), implying a physical journey to a place like those the Pilgrim might have seen, shows them interpreting literal-mindedly Reason's injunction to seek 'St Truth' not 'St James or the saints of Rome' (metonyms for their shrines). Piers's response proves that he understands Reason correctly. **178–9** The pilgrim's ignorance of Truth's whereabouts echoes the charge against his ilk at Pr 47–50; but the harsh B Pr 50–2 having been cut, he is meant more probably as deceived than as deceiving. **179** *pyk*: like that in Cutts pl. 163, with the staff, hat and cloak part of the 'authentic' pilgrim's attire. **180** *ar now*: elliptical for 'before (you people) here just (have)'.

(v) 181–281 The sudden unprepared appearance of PIERS THE PLOUGHMAN opens the final section. His 100-line speech on the spiritual 'way' to Truth is only briefly interrupted twice by an entreaty at 199, but it provokes a set of cynical comments at 282–5. This is followed by two more substantial rejoinders, one negative and one positive, which round off the passus, initiate the second half of Vision Two and sharpen expectation of important events to follow.

181–98 181 *Peter*: a mild oath the thematic significance

of which will not be fully disclosed until 21.214, when Grace gives to Piers St Peter's NT rôle as guide and overseer of the Christian *comune*; but it is here appropriate as invoking the saint whose name he bears. *plouhman*: on the social status of the C14th ploughman, see Bennett 1937:183, Du Boulay 1991:44–51 and Dyer 1994. The best-known English literary type-portrait, in *GPCT*, is probably indebted to **L**, as is seen if B 545, 556–7 are compared with *CT* I 536, 538 and C 8.101–2 with *CT* 539–40. But Chaucer's giving his ploughman an idealised parson as brother eirenically counters the mutual antagonism dramatised in **L**'s Pardon Scene. Nothing in the text so far imports an allegorical reading, but a figurative relationship between ploughing and spiritual discernment was long established in commentary on the OT (e.g. Ecclus 6:18–20), and in the NT it symbolises religious commitment (Lk 9:62, I Cor 9:10, II Tim 2:6). *potte forth*: not necessarily implying pushing his head through a hedge on *over*hearing the question (*Bn*), but making better sense if Piers ('P.' hereafter) has heard the sermon along with the folk; for though P. never mentions REASON, 183 affirms his adherence to the principles formally expressed by the latter. **183** *Conscience*: first introduced in **C** as an unsparing opponent of 'carnal' religion, and properly acknowledged here as the source of P.'s moral and spiritual insight. But **C**, by removing the emphatic *re*-assertion of this point at B 7.134, offers no critique of clerical abuses beyond that of Conscience himself in Pr 95–124. *Kynde Wit*: see on Pr 141–7, which affirm both the priority of 'common understanding based on experience' to formal learning, and also its closeness to Conscience and Knighthood in providing for society's practical needs. **184, 189** *seruen; serued*: i.e. through his God-given calling as a ploughman (cf. *a potte me* 191; *hotep, deuyse* B 545, 547), which has a spiritual significance (cf. *withynne* 187) that the speaker holds certain. P.'s words affirm an unmediated acquaintance with Truth as a value through his faithful (*trewe*) practice of ordinary life in the world. **187** may scan with wrenched stress on *with-* or (more probably) on vowels, with natural word-stress and with sentence-stress on *his*; cf. the reversed form in 6.208, B 13.238. **188** *al...wynter*: 'many a long year' (*Bn*); despite 'olde and hoer' at 8.92, P. need only be in his fifties, and seems less decrepit than Will at 22.183ff. **189, 192** *to paye*: another example of **C** Version *repetitio*. **193–5** To speak of Truth as a just employer is situationally apt to P., who is rightly said to represent 'a peasant loyal to his manorial lord God in perpetuity' (Simpson 1987:99). At this point P.'s view of divine reward evokes Conscience's account of strictly just payment through 'wages' (*mercede* or *mesurable hire* 3.304=B 3.256) and corresponds to the theologians' *meritum de condigno* 'reward justly and absolutely merited' (Simpson, ibid. 93–60). But since P. claims to receive *hire* here and now

(193), he must believe not only that virtuous living is rewarded by God but that it brings its own recompense (a peaceful conscience), as well as assurance of divine favour (*paye*). **195** Cf. on 3.306–7; revision removes the (contextually inappropriate) allusion to the Vineyard Parable, where day's end symbolises death.

199–203 199 *mede*: a significant **C** substitution (reinforced at 202) of a dubious for a blameless term (*huyre* **ZAB**), in a field of discourse where even unintended ambiguity carries risks. **200** *bi...soule*: here, as at 4.137 and 8.102 (by contrast with B 6.117, 171), an oath that is thematically significant, not just expressive of anger. **201** *Seynt Thomas shryne*: at this time a veritable treasure-house because of pilgrims' grateful offerings. Abp. Thomas Becket (1120–70), who was murdered in his cathedral of Canterbury on Dec 29 1170, was canonised in Feb 1173, and his relics in the Trinity Chapel became the chief object of pilgrimage in England until the shrine's destruction by Henry VIII in 1538. The humour of P.'s paradoxical asseveration would not have been missed: as in *Pearl*, in the kingdom of *Treuthe*, a transvaluation of values must occur. The sin he here wishes to avoid would count as a form of simony.

204–81 P.'s elaborate 'signpost-allegory' of salvation (Frank 1953:237) conveys through its form a transcendental sense of 'the pilgrimage of human life', since as a 'figure of thought' *allegoria* bespeaks the spiritual dimension of historic existence and its record as narrative. It owes something to the French C13th poet Rutebeuf's *Voie de Paradis*, itself based on a work by Raoul de Houdenc (see Owen 1912, Nolan 1977:124). The somewhat mechanical *procédé* resembles the 'territorial' allegory in 2.88–96 (and similar homiletic expositions by the Minorite in 10.30–55, Conscience in B 14.15–28 and Anima in B 16.4–17); but the speech has didactic lucidity and is evidently grasped by its hearers. 205–30 describe how humility awakens consciousness of the divine imperatives (the Commandments); 231–59a how moral reformation in consequence of observing them lays the basis for a life of Christian devotion; 260–81 how, despite temptations to spiritual pride, the efficacious promptings of grace lead the pilgrim through ascetic discipline (the exercise of the virtues) to a state in this life that is a foretaste of beatitude in the life to come.

205–37 205 *Mekenesse*: specially connected with contrition, for which humility is a prerequisite (cf. B 4.142) and which alone earns not only royal 'grace' or favour (B 4.142) but also divine; cf. 'God resisteth the proud and giveth grace to the humble [*humilibus*]' (Js 4:6, I Pet 5:5, both quoting Prov 3:34, which has 'the meek' [*mansuetis*]). **206** *yknowe...sulue*: 'known by / recognised or acknowledged by' better brings out the presumed sense of the rather obscurely expressed B 562 'that Christ [who sees into your conscience] may know the truth

[about your spiritual state]' (for another rendering see Salter 1962:86n). Some allusion to the 'examination of conscience' preparatory to confession may be involved. **207–11** are based on Christ's summary of the two 'great commandments' of the Old Law in Lk 10:27, as given in Deut 6:5 and Lev 19:18 (cf. on 19.14a). **208–10** P.'s words paraphrase HC's injunction to Will at 1.140–4 (which she says derives from a *kynde knowyng* and constitutes truth), alluding to the text cited both there and at 6.290a. **209b** 'for fear [of some powerful man] or for entreaty'. **210–11a** *apayre* / *Otherwyse*: elliptical for 'harm / [nor treat] otherwise than'. **212** *brok*: the first watery barrier to be crossed, allegorically from the natural order into that of divine positive law. The b-half is not absolutely clear because elliptical, borrowing its verb from 213: 'until you find a kind of bridge across the brook.' *as it were*: because it is only a ford (a sense of *bridge* obsolete since OE). **ZAB** 'Be submissive (of speech)' may have been replaced because this is not one of the Ten Commandments, though it arises out of the virtue opposed to the root vice and is especially set against the 'inobedience' confessed to by Pride at 6.15–19. **213–15** Figurative 'immersion' in the habit of honouring one's parents is a 'baptism' in natural piety that prepares the individual for a successful and upright life. **L** stresses throughout the importance of early formation and the need for parental discipline, which produce strong limbs for running the race of virtuous living (the unquoted end of the 4th Commandment is relevant here), just as bad parenting does spiritual (and sometimes also bodily) injury to the children (cf. 5.138, 9.169). **215a** 'Honour thy father and thy mother, [that thou mayest be *long-lived* upon the land which the Lord thy God will give thee]' (Ex 20:12). **216–17** This expanded form of the 2nd Commandment (a marker or signpost?) may have suggested to **L** his idiosyncratic device of a *compound personal name* based on a *command-sentence*, such as those later at 8.80ff. The injunction counters a sin to which the drunken Glutton is especially prone (6.425–7), though it comes under anger in *CT* X 587–99). **218–28** The next four 'places' are for avoiding. **219–20** are the 9th and 10th Commandments, directed against Lechery (6.192) and Greed (6.262–4). **220** *pat...*: 'in such a way as to cause them any harm'. **221** *bere nat*: 'anything' understood. *but if...owene*: elliptical for 'nothing'. **223** The 7th and 5th Commandments, especially relevant to Anger (6.107) and Greed (6.265–71). **224** *luft hand*: where the evil-doers are positioned; another echo of HC's words (at 2.5). In Rutebeuf's *Voie* (150–1) the Dreamer is directed to keep the habitation of pride on his left as he proceeds to the House of Confession; and fragment G of the early C14th alliterative *Conflict of Wit and Will* contains the lines: 'þat bothe leute and loue louies with herte / And *leues on þat lefte hoende* alle lither redes' (ll. 5–6). **226–8** denote the 8th commandment, **229–30** perhaps also the 2nd. *ParsT* places all kinds of 'false swearing' under the sin of anger: 'Thou shalt swere sooth, for every lesynge is agayns Crist; for Crist is verray trouthe' (*CT* X 593). **231** *court...sonne*: envisaged as a fortified manor-house, the brightly shining court perhaps suggested by the Heavenly Jerusalem in Apoc 21:23 (cf. *Pearl* 1049–50). The image recalls the paradisal *tour* in the east of Pr 15 (see Davlin 2001:39–40 and ill. 2.7, from ms CUL Ee.iv.24, f. 35v). It may also owe something to Robert Grosseteste's allegorical poem *Château d'Amour* (Cornelius 1930:589; see *Sk* IV.i.150) and the tradition of interior dwellings represented by the C13th English *Sawles Warde* (on which see Mann 1994:200–03). This 'paradise within' is the state of sanctifying grace, that anticipates *in via* the heavenly condition of beatitude. **232** *mote*: a second watery barrier, suggesting baptism, through which man must pass from the OT domain of Law·to the promised land of Grace under the new covenant (of Mercy). **233** *Wyt*: natural reason, here not unaided but informed by the supernatural faith infused through baptism, which enables man to resist the siege of unruly desire (*Wil*). The traditional opposition between these two sides of the human soul appears in *The Conflict of Wit and Will*. **234** *carneles*: the embrasures between the merlions or uprights in a battlement, where the castle's defenders stood. *Cristendom*: baptism in the wider meaning of 'membership of the body of Christ'; not yet clear in the more diffuse **Z**, which may be paraphrased 'The crenellations offer a trustworthy assurance of salvation to the Christian' but somewhat confusingly makes baptism the buttress. *kynde*: '(spiritual) substance', i.e. the soul. **234–5** *saue / ysaued*: identical rhyme drawing out the martial metaphor's secondary spiritual meaning. **235** *Ybotresed*: qualifying *wallyng*, not its immediate antecedent *carneles*. The name of the buttress is the 'right belief' necessary to salvation; alluding to the final words of the Athanasian Creed recited at Prime on Sundays and some feast-days, 'This is the Catholic faith: unless a man *believes* it faithfully, he cannot be *saved*' (*Brev.* II 46–8). This Creed is quoted again in the crucial words of the Pardon at 9.288. **236** *houses*: the many mansions envisaged within this 'inner' replica of the Heavenly City. *yheled*: homophonically punning on *helen* 'heal, make whole', given that 'love *covers* a multitude of sins' (I Pet 4:8, and cf. Ps 31:1, Hope's text at 152*a*), an idea associated with healing of spiritual wounds through *satisfaccion* at B 14.96. **237** *lele*: significantly replacing *lowe* (**AB**) as a mark of the Christian community. Emphasis on trustworthy speech is part of **C**'s robust antipathy to lies and treachery.

Z 66–78 (A 79–82) The original description harked back to the *tour* of ZA Pr 14 /15 and contained interesting (but digressive) topical details. Reduced from 13 to 4 lines, the passage may have been finally deleted because

its stress on God's awesome power over the elements (perhaps suggested by Job 37:12) jarred with **L**'s desire to urge the accessibility of divine mercy. Reason's sermon having terrified the Folk into confessing their sins, P.'s task is to *encourage* their first steps towards a life of virtue aided by grace. **66 (79)** takes up Z Pr 103 / A I 12. **67 (80)** *day sterre*: echoing God's question in Job 38:32, with perhaps an allusion to his sovereignty over Lucifer whose name means 'day-star' (see Ps 109:3, Is 14:12 and cf. ZA 1.63/110). **68 L**'s notion of the moon as a mirror reflecting all mankind's thought seems to have no parallel. **69–70** With the linking of word and wind in this passage, cf. Z 5.34–40 above. **69** *word...wind*: a common Biblical image for God's sovereign power. **70** *blowe*: cf. Gen 8:1, Ex 14:21, 15:10. *be stille*: cf. Mk 4:39. *brethy softe*: cf. III Kgs 19:12. **71** *water...gloue*: perhaps echoing Is 40:12. **72** *fuyr...brenne*: the lightning, as in Ex 9:24, IV Kgs 1:10. **73 (A 81)** *Deth*: the opposition of Death to Life (= God) finds expression in the Crucifixion scene at 20.67, the subservience of Death to Kind (also = God) at 22.100ff. **74** *forst*: cf. Job 38:29. **75** *stere steren*: typical homophonic wordplay; *stere* may again, as in 67, allude to Lucifer. *steme*: cf. *CT* I 202. **77–8** *Wyndelesore*: alluding to Edward III's building works at Windsor from 1354 onwards (Walsingham, *Historia Anglicana* i. 288), which involved numerous workmen in 1365 (*R–B*, citing Salzman 1952:60). The master-masons were John Sponlee and (from 1360) William Wynford, pioneers of the Perpendicular style (Harvey 1984:280–1). **78** *spanne*: elliptical for 'a hand's-worth of work equal to it'; comparing earthly, external building with heavenly (and its homologue, interior) 'edification'.

238–59*a* 238 *barres*: either barriers without the gate or bolts to lock it (MED s.v. *barre* n. 1a, 4a); both should 'give way' easily in fraternal welcome. *bretherne of o wombe*: mutual consideration as typified by the (idealised) brotherly love of siblings, an OT norm of loyal affection, becoming in the NT a model of *charitas fraternitatis* (Rom 12:10) for those who through *cristendom* are *blody bretherne...of o body ywonne* (12.111). **239** *brygge*: the draw-bridge of earnest prayer. **240** *piler*: understood by *Bn* as one of the piers of the bridge across the moat (MED s.v. *piler* n. 1.j) or supporting a drawbridge; but the referent seems indeterminable. The later versions interpret the 'supports' of the spiritual life as penance and the intercessory power of the blessed united in purpose with the pilgrim or militant Church. This idea may derive from St Paul's description of 'the *house*...of the living God' as 'the *pillar* and ground of *the truth*' (I Tim 3:15). The earlier versions by contrast imagine the pillars (?supporting the gate-house) as like the Purbeck marble shafts common in early English C14th cathedrals (e.g. Wells or Lincoln), which took a polish. The image could have been dropped simply as repeating earlier

6.328 (= ZA 5.148/250). But although this is an effective symbol-allegory for the spiritual effect of penance on the soul, the reason for rejecting the architectural detail was perhaps its tacitly equating the ark of salvation with the Church as 'material organisation' rather than as 'spiritual organism'. **241** *hokes*: the fixed part of the door-hinge, let into the wall. **246** *parformed...*: reversing Sloth's sorry admission at 14. **247** *Amende-ȝow...Grace*: sanctifying *grace* being given to those who complete their confession by resolving to *amend* and by making due *satisfaction* through penance. P. urges the Folk to show that they have done this, are reconciled with the Church and now able to receive Holy Communion as a sign of it (the 'main' gate of heaven has as its additional immediate referent the door of the tabernacle where the Eucharist is reserved). The domestic *wiket* of the earlier versions, the everyday eating-imagery and the blaming of one or other partner finally disappear in the more solemn and abstract C 248–9. **B 603** *apples vnrosted*: because perfectly ripe, like all the fruit in paradise (labour, including cooking, being commonly seen as a consequence of the Fall). *eten here bane*: the death-bringing effect of the fruit (alluding to Gen 2:17) being reversed only when Christ (the 'Second Adam') comes to *drynken his deth-yuel* (B 18.53) on the cross, which was fabled to be fashioned from the wood of the Tree of Life. Paradise is here traditionally conceived as a walled garden with a wicket gate, a small gate in a larger one or a wall, like that in *CT* IV 2029–47 (see the 'Fall of Man' in the *Très Riches Heures du Duc de Berry* and Bosch's *Haywain* triptych). No *re*-admission is possible after the expulsion of Adam and Eve, who were condemned to die without hope; what the Redemption wins is the offer of entry into heaven. Mention of Eve (in the Latin) is thus due not to residual anti-feminism but to her theological significance as a type of Mary in the history of salvation. **249a** 'Through Eve [the gate of paradise] was closed to all, and through the Virgin Mary it was opened once again'; from the Antiphon of Our Lady sung at Lauds from the Monday within the Octave of Easter to the Vigil of the Ascension (*Bn*); see *Brev.* 1:dccclxx) As Eve's disobedience 'closed' heaven's gate to mankind, Mary's obedience to God's Word figuratively 'opens' it. But in patristic commentary on the sanctuary gate in Ezech 44:2 and the gate of justice in Ps 117:19 (*Pe*), the BVM was also herself figured as the *caeli porta* through which man might enter heaven and as the *regis alti ianua* 'gate of the high king' through which the Word entered the world (see the Candlemas and Assumption hymns 'Ave maris stella' and 'O gloriosa Domina' cited by *Sk*). **250–51** *leel lady*: the Virgin, 'who believed in the Lord' (responsory at Vespers of the Assumption). *vnlek...keye... clycat*: metonymic for the power to forgive sin, and usually associated with St Peter, but here emblematising the capacity to unlock the door of sanctification, and so effec-

tively making Mary co-redemptrix (cf. *vitam datam per virginem* in 'O gloriosa Domina'). *of grace*: 'by means of the grace [granted to her by God] / through her gracious kindness'; being herself 'full of grace' (Lk 1:28), she has been empowered to impart divine help and favour. **251** *keye*: found by *Bn* to recall David's in the Advent Vespers Antiphon for Dec. 20 'O clavis David' based on Is 22:22; here signifying Christ, whom the Virgin 'has' as her child. *thow...slepe*: the gloss 'i.e. in her womb' (*Pe*, following *Bn*'s 'felicitous reference to the immaculate conception') is not very apt, given the concessive *thow* 'even if'. The image suggests rather a noble chatelaine with full authority to admit or refuse entry to callers while her lord is resting. Technically speaking, Mary's intercessory (unlike her co-redemptive) power only becomes fully *active* after her assumption into glory. **254** The phrasing recalls St Augustine's 'in interiore animae habitat veritas' (cit. Spitzer, 1944:38), a figure echoed in *MS* 1225a 'in corde fidelis est habitacio veritatis', and there ascribed to *holy writte* (presumably in **L**'s sense of a patristic source). The basic theological idea is of the indwelling of the 'spirit of truth...[who] shall abide with you and shall be in you' (Jn 14:17) through *grace*, which **L** later employs as his 'nature-name' for the Third Person of the Trinity (21.214). *herte*: the centre of supernatural as of natural life because the seat of *Anima* 'soul' (cf. 10.175). **255–9a** 'Truth' is the subject of the three verbs in 255–6; and though 256 echoes B 607, 259 is closer in thought to A 97. All versions describe how Truth leads to Love, and knowledge of God's nature to ever more perfect performance of his will (growth in holiness). In **ZA** Truth teaches a law, in **B** unveils a vision, in **C** 'edifies' a habitation that becomes spiritually efficacious for others, a progression adumbrating the Dowel-Dobet-Dobest triad to come. **B 607–8** *cheyne of charite*: alluding to *charitatem...vinculum perfectionis* 'charity, the bond of perfection' (Col 3:14), an image that implies in context 'loving servitude' and 'love that binds [Christians together]' rather than a 'chain of office' (*Bn*). The actual phrase *vincula charitatis* occurs in the pseudo-Bernardine *Vitis Mystica* (*PL* 184:67), a work **L** seems to have known. *child*: an emblem of the simplicity and humility needed to enter the kingdom of heaven (Mt 18:3); cf. *Pearl* 721–2 and B 15.216 (*Bn*). 608 seems to *Bn* to 'make little sense in the context,' but the idea denoted is quite appropriately that of the complete obedience shown by Christ. *sires wille*: the Father's will, a main theme of St John's Gospel. **255** *payne*: not necessarily purgatory, since indwelling 'truth' helps the faithful believer to endure injustice and adversity here ('suffer' as God does). **256** *churche to make*: this virtue fashions an 'interior' equivalent of the visible Church whose exterior realisation in stone was itself commonly seen as an image of the Heavenly Jerusalem (Von Simson 1955:8–10); cf. I Cor 8:1: *charitas vero* *aedificat.* The symbolism, 'monastic' in flavour, reflects **L**'s sacramental view of a macrocosmic and microcosmic 'correspondence' between earthly and heavenly domains. **257–8** *hole*: playing on the senses 'healed', 'made whole' and 'sincere'; cf. *veritate et corde perfecto* 'truth and perfect heart' (Is 38:3). *herborwe*; *fynde*: perhaps denoting the contemplatives' intercessory prayer for the spiritual good of the faithful. **259** This triad seems an enigmatic periphrasis for the theological virtues in inverse order (charity, hope, faith). **259a** '(Whatever you ask in my name), (it shall be given to you)', a text conflating Jn 14:23 and Mt 7:7 (Alf*Q*). **260–8** warn against the spiritual pride (262) that menaces those whose advance in virtue makes them aware of others' relative sinfulness: a 'higher' (but deadlier) mutation of the vice described at 6.36–40. As these temptations incident to the spiritual life are treated not in penitential treatises but in ascetic writings such as *Ancrene Wisse*, P.'s awareness of them indicates the level of his religious maturity. **260** *Wrath-the*: 'Get(ting)-angry', i.e. 'pharisaic' resentment at one's neighbour's failings. In positive form, this command-name is syntactically clearer than the negative in **ZA**. **261a** anticipates the devil's siege of the soul at 10.134–5. **263** *boldnesse...beenfetes*: 'overconfidence in your own virtuous acts'. **264** *as dewe*: 'like dew in the sun', a typically vivid analogy (like the icicles at 19.194–5), but with a witty homophonic pun on 'as due'. **266** *hundret wynter*: 'a very long time (in purgatory)'; the heavy punishment for spiritual pride. **267** *to lete*: 'by thinking'; on this adverbial infinitive of cause see *MES* 536. **Z 101** may signify specifically the sin of Lust of the Eyes (one of Fortune's companions described in 11.175ff); or *wenche* may be used to draw an analogy with Eve (so called at Z 88) who tempted Adam *to lete wele by hymsulue*, whereby 'they lost [God's] love'. **268** *gifte*: some good deed(s) of the sinner, paradoxically imagined as like a 'bribe' to win God's favour (cf. 4.138). P. sees none such as possible and stresses the sovereign importance of grace at every stage of salvation, a teaching of St Augustine (as *Pe* notes) re-affirmed forcibly by Bradwardine against the so-called 'Pelagian' theologians in the 1340s. However, the assertion that after falling into grave sin one can regain God's favour only through a 'prevenient' grace that moves the will to repentance was not a distinctive tenet of Bradwardine's but the 'mainstream' teaching of Aquinas that became standard doctrine in the West. **269–81 269** *seuene susteres*: the seven Christian virtues developed in the soul through sacramental grace; customarily set as contraries to (and 'remedies' for) the seven capital sins. Distinct from the 'seven' composed of the four cardinal and three theological virtues, in this penitential context they are coherently opposed (as in *ParsT*) to the deadly sins treated in the Confessions: abstinence against gluttony; humility: pride; charity: envy; patience:

anger; chastity: lechery; generosity: greed (*CT* X 831, 475, 514, 658, 914, 810). The odd maiden out is Peace (*Pe*) unless, as the inner tranquillity that can counter sloth's 'angwissh of troubled herte' (*CT* X 676), she is to be equated with the 'seurtee or sikernesse...that...ne douteth no travaile...of the goode werkes that a man hath bigonne' (id. 734), i.e. the energetic diligence associated with sloth's usual remedy, fortitude. There is some overlap also with the twelve 'fruits of the [Holy] Spirit' (Gal 5:22–3), namely in the virtues of charity, peace, patience, kindness and chastity produced by the operation of sanctifying grace. The helpful maiden Peace returns as one of the 'Daughters of God' in 20.170ff, and an avatar of her companion Patience is the major (male) protagonist in Passus 15. (On possible influence from Grosseteste, see *Sk* IV i.152). **270** *porteres...*: for an illustration of these maidens defending a castle against the vices see Saxl 1942:104 (*Pe*). **274** *Largenesse*: specifically charitable giving, which was regarded as of great spiritual benefit. **275** The revision removes the (doubtless unintended) suggestion of possible release from hell, where *nulla est redempcio* (20.151a). **B 624** presumably refers to purgatory, or to the state of mortal sin, an interior constriction corresponding to the devil's 'pen'. **276** She ransoms and redeems souls suffering agony in purgatory, though the referent may properly include those wounded in the battle against sin while still *in via* who benefit from the intercessory prayer of the virtuous (cf. on 255–9). The line echoes in ironical answer Mede's dubious interventions at 3.173. **277** *sib*: a poetic figure of the individual's spiritual condition (like that of *aunte* at 6.329, 439); but at a deeper theological level, the 'relational' image intimates membership of the Communion of Saints, to which all in a state of grace are privileged to belong. **279 (B 627)** The revision eases the metre, perhaps to avoid ambiguously implying that possession of some virtue(s) cancels out one's remaining vice(s). For whereas 269–76 seem to envisage *each* virtue as able to secure a person's admission to heaven (e.g. 274), 279 requires 'relatedness' to them all, i.e. a completely sin-free state (cf. *eny gate* 281). The consistent position in *PP* is that any capital sin, if allowed to prevail, brings damnation (Js 2:10; see 13.121a). **280** P.'s asseveration recalls that of the King troubled by the difficulty of reforming society (4.177). *eny of ȝow*: '(for) any of you'; omission of 'inorganic' *for* (see *MES* 383–4) suggests that the phrase is being treated as a 'dative of person' (cf. *MES* 433–6).

(vi) 282–307 282–4 *cottepurs*; *hapeward*; *wafrestere*: professional thief and low entertainers. **284** *Wyte God*: 'May God know' = 'I'd have God know'. The female *wafrestere* (to judge by *CT* VI 479) may be assumed to sell not only cakes. **285** *frere prechynge*: an oblique tribute to the persuasive eloquence of the mendicants, renowned as outdoor preachers able to reach even those who never entered a church. **286** *3us*: 'On the contrary, you can!' **287** *Mercy*: a 'moat' at 232, but now personified and equated with Mary 'mother of mercy' (Office Hymn of the BVM). *myhte*: as chief intercessor before the throne of Christ at all times. **288** *syb...bothe*: through their identification (though sinless) with sinful humanity (cf. II Cor 5:21). **289b** 'Do not expect there is any other / it to be otherwise'. **290** *go bytyme*: i.e. not delay confession till the last moment, when the grace of repentance may not be offered. The Parable of the Supper warns against giving earthly concerns like possessions, work, or personal relationships priority over the demands of the Gospel. It replaces at a more plausibly 'average' level the (no doubt expected) refusals in B 639–42 of the Pardoner (afraid of having his credentials questioned) and the prostitute his companion. **B 640** *fecche my box*: presumably in order to get about his usual business, not use them as 'gifts' (cf. on 268 above) to bribe Truth's door-keepers. **291** scans on vowels or on *m* with liaised macaronic stave. *villam emi*: 'I have bought a farm [and I must needs go out and see it. I pray thee, hold me excused]' (Lk 14:18); rejecting P.'s invitation to a more active devotional life following the forgiveness of sins. **294** *falewe...*: cf. Lk 14:19. **298** *Actyf*: a personification of the practical life, destined to replace the B-Text's deplorable Haukyn in C XV, with most of his predecessor's viciousness having been peeled away in order to expand the portraits of the Deadly Sins depicted in C VI–VII. *hosbonde*: 'married man' (cf. the different sense at A 11.183, which this line recalls). Despite the appearance of 'Contemplation' at 304, 'Active' does not simply represent the 'active Christian life' of which Martha (Lk 10:41–2) was the traditional exemplar so much as 'the common body of sinning humanity' (*Pe*). **299** *wantowen*: glossed by MED s.v. *wantoun* a. as 'lascivious', doubtless in the light of the **p** variant *synnen*. But though possible here, the conjunction with *maneres* suggests that the sense 'self-willed', 'lacking self-discipline' is as apt (ibid. a, b), and the *maneres* pertain to her possessiveness. **303** *Kitte*: diminutive of Katherine, with contemporary overtones of lasciviousness (cf. Present-Day English 'moll'), as suggested by MED's quotation under *Kitte* n. (2) from *Beryn* 66: 'Goddis blessing have þow, Kitt! Now broke wel thy name!' **303a** '[And another said]: I have married a wife; and therefore I cannot come' (Lk 14:20). This text was often interpreted allegorically as signifying attachment to the pleasures of the flesh; but **L**'s rueful use of a name presumably to be recalled as that of Will's wife in B 20.193–8 implies rather that the married state must inevitably hinder single-minded cultivation of the spiritual life (cf. I Cor 7:27–34). **304** *Contemplacioun*: personifying in passing the same aspiration to ascetic devotion later found in PATIENCE, whose words at B 13.159ff are echoed in 304b–05a. The present juxtaposition with Actyf anticipates the encounter of those characters in 15.191ff.

550

Passus VIII (ZA VII, B VI)

PASSUS EIGHT, dealing with the ploughing of the 'Half-Acre', is a complete allegorical action, but minutely 'realistic' in its social detail. It shows the least alteration from **Z** to **C** of any passus, chiefly **A**'s omission of **Z**'s six elaborating lines 196–201 and 20-line attack on false *leches* and **C**'s extensions on beggars; major revision and expansion begin again only with C IX. One immediate change is the opening with Piers's reply to Contemplation's remark on the difficulty of reaching Truth without a guide, which in all but **C** begins the passus, in **ZAB** with no ascribed speaker. The **C** form better prepares to focus on the character and actions of PIERS, who dominates VIII, and this links it more closely with C VII. The initial change is matched by a cryptic addition at the end in both **B** and **C** illustrating the longer versions' increased complexity. The passus divides into three sections and an epilogue: (i) 1–111 on P.'s organisation of the ploughing; (ii) 112–66 on his difficulties with those who will not work; (iii) the Hunger episode (167–341) forming the core of the passus; and the short 'prophetic' conclusion 342–53.

(i) 1–111. 1–55 *Piers's dialogue with representatives of the gentry* enables him to act as spokesman for the duties of all members of society. **1** *Perkyn*: a diminutive of Piers (cf. *Watekyn* 6.70). *Petur*: P.'s asseveration recalling 7.181 points to the faithful and impulsive ploughman's relationship with his name-saint the chief apostle, whose rôle is to feed the sheep of Christ (Jn 21:15–17; see the illuminating discussion in Burrow 1993[1]:77–80, 119–22). **2** *half aker*: the average area (2420 sq. yds) of a strip in the open-field system of farming (*Pe*); the minimum needed to sustain one household. P.'s authoritative status makes it doubtful whether this signifies his entire holding, so the size may be symbolic, with the 'typical' half-acre field (commonly understood as 16 furrows each of a furlong-length) a microcosm of this world and P. standing for the ploughmen of Pr 22–4, 145 (*Bn*). The usual peasant-holding for someone like Piers would be about fifteen acres (Dyer 1994:161). *heye weye*: a position indicating P.'s closeness to the folk as they 'bluster' down the pilgrim-routes that ran alongside such fields. A real ploughman could have gone (like Chaucer's in the *GP*) to Canterbury or Walsingham after completing the annual sowing. But (as *Bn* notes) P. puts his vocation to provide food before his avocation to guide others, his own example of 'pilgrimage' being to remain in his calling and discharge it faithfully. **4** *way*: the spiritual 'way' to Truth that P. described in 7.205ff; a well-established scriptural figure of the Christian life, e.g. *viam Dei in veritate* (Mt 22:16) and *via veritatis / iustitiae* (II Pet 2:2, 21). **5** *lady*: perhaps the *wyf* (55) of the knight who speaks at 19. *sclayre*: a veil covering the head, lower cheeks and chin, worn by women of rank (Poole 1958: pl. 108, Baker 1978: pls. 38, 45). **7** *ladyes*: i.e. all the women present; slightly confusing in **C**, since the task in 8 was not for the *worthily wommen* (9), whose long fingers would work with finer stuffs, but for the ordinary *wyues and wyddewes* (12). As spinning was a task of women below the gentry class, the sack-sowing is presumably intended for them. **10** *on*: 'on a ground of' or 'with (thread)'. **11** *Chesibles*: ornamental embroidery for vestments that showed off the skill for which English needlework or *opus anglicanum* was renowned (see the 'orphrey' in Poole pl. 107a; Christie 1938). **12** *Wyues*: in parallel with *men* at 17. **13** *Consience conseyleth*: a change from divine command at B 16 (alluding to Mt 25:36) to interior counsel that is as noteworthy as the less utilitarian tone, P. becoming a means to persuade rather than admonish the knightly class. **15–16** P.'s promise to go on ploughing makes it unlikely that he should later intend wholly to 'give up' the active for a contemplative life at B 7.118–30 // (lines significantly cut in **C**); at this stage the work he stresses is mainly physical. *for...heuene*: the polysemy allowing both an asseveration and the reason for his labour; not only 'out of love for God' but 'in order to win God's love' (cf. A 3.223, which further signifies 'because of the love God has for them'). **17** *molde*: taking up *lond* 15; presumably all work other than husbandry is implied. **19** *knyhte*: the political rôle of knights having already been treated in Pr 139–43, this section explores their part in keeping order in rural society as local Justices of the Peace. **20** *teme*: a homophonic pun on *teme* MED n. 1 (f) 'team of draught animals' and n. 2 'theme' or 'topic' (of ploughing). **22** *for...were*: 'as a kind of relaxation, so to speak' (cf. B 12.22). **C** improves on its somewhat quixotic predecessors, the knight's light but friendly tone affirming solidarity rather than an unrealistic reversal of functional rôles. **23–4** firmly repudiate any notion (such as the 1381 rebels proclaimed) of replacing the traditional social orders with a single class of 'commons' under the king. **25** *tho thow louest*: P's warm support of the knight's position (going beyond a tenant farmer's obligation to his landlord) and his use of 'thou' here imply a relation of loyal trust rather than a claim to equality (P. shifts to the expected 'you' at 35ff). **26–31** P.'s 'condition' is that the knightly (first) estate should protect the clerical (second) and labouring (third) estate against those who prey parasitically on society and against the 'natural' threats to the food-supply all need. **27** echoes Pr 24, where the labourers' vulnerability is heightened by the lack of reference to the knightly class. *wastores*: with precise referent not clear, but including those who refuse to belong to any of the functional groups recognised since Anglo-Saxon times. **28** *hares*; *foxes*: beasts of the 'warren' (tracts of land set aside for small game), which only manorial lords could

hunt. **29** *bore*; *bokkes*: beasts of the forest, which peasants were nonetheless permitted to hunt over warren (Bennett 1937:64). *myn hegges*: dividing his strip from his neighbour's and from the road. That they are 'his' indicates his status as a self-sufficient peasant tenant (see Lister 1982; Dyer 1994). **31** *diffoule*: the revision introducing a wry pun on *foules* 30. **33** *treuthe*: a very solemn word from a knight, whose duty HC specifies as *to fyghte and fende treuthe* (1.99), and to be taken as binding (cf. *CT* V 1479). **34** This line's evolution is noteworthy, **C** retaining **B**'s b-half, **B** and **A** only the a-half of their immediate predecessor. **35–55** This striking account of ideal knightly conduct bespeaks special authority in P. as Truth's servant rather than merely as a 'representative' of the third estate. **36–7** *tene...mersyen*: homophonic and semantic wordplay (only the second pair are etymologically connected) indicating a lively awareness of the 'Platonic' power of verbal forms (Schmidt 1987:130–1). P. presumably does not mean that God *would* approve of causing deliberate distress to one's tenants. But as distress might indeed result from lawful impositions (*Bn*) like *tallage* (an arbitrary rate of rent), *heriot* (a customary claim on the best chattel of a deceased tenant) and *amerciaments* (discretionary fines), it is these that the knight is being urged to use with restraint. **39–40** P.'s advice accords with his own conduct at 7.200–3. **B 43** *one yeres ende*: taken by *Bn* as 'the end of one year or another, sooner or later'; but likening the privilege of rank during one's earthly life to a lease with a fixed date of *one* year is more telling. However, **C**'s motive for revision to a milder (and more intelligible) warning may have been not just the figure's lack of obviousness but the ambiguity of *perilous* B 44; for the **B** line confusingly echoes B 2.105, where the reference is to hell (and this too is deleted in **C**). **44a** 'Friend, go up higher' (Lk 14:10). The parable of the supper warns against all presumption, but here P. sees Christian humility as countering specifically pride that may arise from superior rank. The words are in Lk addressed to the humble man who has taken the lower place, and may elliptically be applied to the knight; but in the immediate context they appear to complete 44 and be addressed rather to the serf. This text's relevance to the feudal relation, though oblique, becomes more exact if read in the light of Js 2:6, which warns against oppressing the poor by force or law (see on 54), and more generally of Js 1:9–11. **45** *charnel*: the vault under the church for storing bones unearthed when the graveyard was dug over for new burials. Surviving charnel-houses are noted in Cook 1954:129–30. **46** *quene / queene*: a strong **B** addition further improved in **C** by arresting play on two words that differ in the sound-quality of the vowels but when written are as hard to tell apart in appearance as are royal bones from a commoner's (Schmidt 1987:113–4). The theme of Death the Leveller is a late-medieval literary commonplace, and this image, which goes back to St Ambrose, was widely used in preaching of the period (Fletcher 1993:350–4). **47** *corteys*: a significant addition (cf. 32) that softens the earlier text's austerity, suggesting fresh appreciation (in the wake of 1381) of how the common people were alienated by the nobility's purely authoritarian stance. A gentle and unassertive address was regarded by writers on chivalry as a feature of ideal knighthood (see *CT* I 46, 68–71 and Keen 1984:1–7). **48** *tales*: those recommended in **C** realistically including chivalric as well as didactic works. **51** On possible solutions to the line's metrical problem see *TN*. *suche men*: the 'japers' or 'false minstrels' attacked in Pr 35–40 (see Schmidt 1987:8–11); that P.'s opinion is the narrator's seems clear from comparison with 7.93–5, B 13.416–8. **Z 49** *messageres*: the contextual collocation implying the sense 'one who brings tidings in the form of an entertaining ballad' (MED s.v. *message* n. 1(a)). **53** This important addition, echoing the added Pr 138, may carry a generalised warning to members of the knightly class whose support for heterodox critics of the Church like Wyclif might have been read as weakening social and ecclesial order. **54** *Y assente*: representing the Knight's acceptance of P.'s 'prophetic' authority, in contrast with the disdainful attitude of the priest at B 7.131–2 (significantly deleted in **C**). *Gyle*: the C7th hermit-contemplative (*Egidie* 17.9), buried at St Gilles in S France; a popular saint in medieval England. His replacement of St James, the spokesman of '*doing well*' (cf. 1.180–2) who was appropriate to one thinking of pilgrimage (*Bn*), may intimate the knight's approval (like Conscience's for Patience at 15.184–5) of the ascetic simplicity that P. espouses. **55** *my wyf*: see on 5.

56–83 56b echoes 7.160 in its ostensive re-definition through a 'prophetic' donning of working-gear instead of the expected garb (scrip and staff) that symbolically enacts his rejection of conventional pilgrimage. On contemporary tensions between ideas of 'place pilgrimage' and 'life pilgrimage' see Dyas 2001:145–70. **58** *of*: 'pertaining to'. **59** *cokeres*: 'old stockings without feet, worn as gaiters' (*Sk*). *Kynde Wit*: echoing P.'s own claim at 7.183 that KW was his teacher. **Z 54** *clumse*: an adjective of probably Norse origin (OED s.v. *clumse* a.) related to the verb *clomsen*; the only known medieval instance, overlooked by MED. On this use of causal *for* with a semi-substantivised adj. see *MES* 381–2. **61** *buschel*: 8 gallons dry measure (enough to sow a half-acre), which could be carried in a wide shallow basket. *breed corn*: to be ground as bread-meal (for making 'whole-grain' loaves); here used as seed-corn. **62–3** *sethe...doen*: although in principle not necessarily meant ironically (i.e. 'if I do this, I *won't* then need to do *as palmeres doen*': see on 2), the new idea introduced in **B** that a life of *trewe* labour in the community suffices for salvation would preclude the need for literal pilgrimage. **64–5** are brought forward tell-

ingly from their position at B 103–4 // ZA (the end of P.'s speech) to complete the pilgrim-analogy. **64** *plouh-pote*: a stick with a pointed or forked end (Hassall 1954:fol. 6) used to clear the ground. Resembling the pilgrim's staff, it emblematises P.'s intent to 'guide' his fellow 'pilgrims' on the field by labouring in his calling. **65** *clanse*: clear of obstructions (see *TN*); the first recorded use with this referent. **66** *alle*: perhaps implying collective efforts on the common fields (Bennett 1937:44) or generally referring to those working the land. **67** *glene*: a revision eliminating the unintended ambiguity of *lesen* (MED s.v. 1, with which contrast senses 2 and 4). **68** *mery*: in the harvest feasting. **69** *crafty men*: the other main sector of the third estate (mainly in towns), skilled makers of specialised goods useful to all, for whom the special import of *treuthe* would be 'keeping to the standards laid down by the guilds'. **71–9** This added list of those excepted from sharing in the harvest seems meant to modify **Z**'s simple account of the well-integrated rural economy. The low characters enumerated ply their 'crafts of folly' (Owst 1961:371) typically in or around taverns like that described in 6.360ff or *CT* VI 465ff. **71** *iugelour*: 'Gesticulator...vbi harlott' (MED s.v. n. 1b, citing *Catholicon Anglicum* 68a). *Ionet...Stuyues*: possibly a stock name, since it recurs (once) in *Towneley Plays* 378/350; located in Southwark (home of 'Dame Emme'), outside the limits of the City's jurisdiction. The name is pronounced |sty:vəz| in **C** at least (MED s.v. *stive* n. 1) and refers to the small closets, heated by warm-air ducts, where the prostitutes met their clients. **73** P.'s hostility is ostensibly confined to *deceiving* friars, but the ambiguous breadth of *þat ordre* cannot be unintended, since no good is said of the mendicants anywhere in the poem. **74** The forceful added line illustrates polysemy without ambiguity in the normal sense. *lollares and loseles*: a coupling found in Clanvowe's *The Two Ways* (ed. Scattergood 1975:70). **75** *roust*: having a corrosive effect on the soul, 'rust' being a traditional homiletic image of sin (quots. in MED s.v. (d)). **76** *tolde me*: i.e. in the various scriptural texts echoed by this passage, which P. takes as a commission to 'prophetic' utterance. **77, 78a** 'Let them be blotted out of the book of the living: and with the just let them not be written' (Ps 68:29). The quoted text is correct in **A** but the **BC** modification integrating it more closely with 78 causes a lack of grammatical fit, as it needs an indicative mood for the verb after *Quia* (i.e. *scribuntur*) and is thus untranslatable. The psalm-text recalls Ex 32:32–3, and its eschatological overtones are clear from the use of the same image elsewhere, in Dan 7:10 and esp. Apoc 3:5 *non delebo nomen eius de libro vitae* (the 'book' holding the names of those who will be saved). P. seems to deny these characters the fruits of his labour because he finds their way of life incompatible with salvation. *dele*: the witty translinguistic pun generated from the Latin *del-*, *de l-* adding a 'Platonic' reason for avoiding the vicious to the Biblical authority of such texts as II Tim 2:15–17. **78** It was forbidden to accept tithe on immoral earnings (cf. 6.304–5). The 'just' to be rewarded at the Last Judgement are here associated with those who faithfully pay tithes (*Sk*; cf. 101). **79** *áscaped*: so stressed for the vocalic alliteration. *Bn* sees a reference back to the characters who disappeared from the scene at B 5.639–42; but *Sk*, following Whitaker, understands 'luckily escaped payment [*sc.* of tithes]', although 'it puts them in peril of their souls' (*Pe*). This is preferable, for the lines are dropped in **C** (which *cannot* therefore refer back to them) and P. does not name pardoners. The sense would appear to be: 'They (can count themselves lucky to) have got away with no heavier punishment (so far). May they find grace to repent (and live honestly, so as to be able to pay the tithes they owe and so be "written with the just")'. **80–3** P.'s family have allegorical nature-names rather than type-names like the bad characters just mentioned, the main change being his son's from **Z → A**. **80** *Worch...*: 'Act when the time is right to do so' and (alluding to Gal 6:10) 'Work while you have time to do so', both signifying 'Prudence'. **81** *Do...*: 'Disciplined obedience.' **82** *Suffre...*: 'Submission to authority'.

Z **64–8** This five-line injunction to industry and honesty has **L**'s stylistic 'fingerprint': no other poet produces alliterating 'name-lines' (though **C** improves by reducing the name to two lines). **Z 67** is recalled at 22.263, **68** at B 13.229a=C 15.204a. **68** *me*: either 'me' or 'people'.

84–91 incorporate at **86** the **AB** line 74 (82) omitted from the name, signifying 'Leave everything in God's hands as Scripture teaches'. Its new position slants P.'s admonition politically, perhaps associating his son with the younger generation of peasants who might have been among those most active in the uprising of 1381. The speech, which uses vocabulary close to Conscience's in Pr 95–127 and skilfully balances obedience to the king's authority with refusal to take the government and judiciary (who exercise it) at their own valuation, indicates P.'s moral standing, partly as for the poet's 'choric' mouthpiece. **86a; 90a** '[The scribes and the pharisees] have sitten on the chair of Moses. All things whatsoever they shall say to you, observe and do]: but according to their works do ye not. [For they say, and do not]' (Mt 23:2–3). This recurs in a similar context at 11.238a. **89** Strictly *hem* should be *hit* if *al* is sg., but if it = *alle* 'all things', then *hem* is acceptable. More probably, however, this is an elliptical construction: 'All they command you, allow them to (command you)'.

92–111 Despite the surface sense of **92–4**, reference to P.'s words at 64–5 suggests that he plans semi-retirement, not the complete 'rejection' of an active for a contemplative existence. **92** *myn owene*: enough saved through his lifetime's work to buy him food when he cannot grow his own. This indicates (contrary to what 303 would imply) that P. is not strictly a 'subsistence' farmer but has more than one strip to his holding. **94** *do wryte*: P.'s formal illiteracy requiring dictation of his will, in accord with his outward condition as an uneducated peasant. This fails to be at odds with his easy use of Latin scriptural quotations only because that is a purely symbolic device betokening *inward* closeness to the Gospel word. *biqueste*: on P.'s will see Perrow 1914:711–12, Bishop 1996:23–41. **95** 'In the name of God. Amen'; the standard formula for making a will. This was an act usual before setting out on pilgrimage, in case one never returned (*Bn*), but here signifies P.'s self-preparation for death. *I...mysulue*: declaring his will directly, not by proxy, and bequeathing (in order of importance) his soul, body and possessions. **96–9** reflect the common testamentary formula 'First, I bequeath my soul to God my creator' (*Bn*); but the language used is that of the feudal relation. P. returns what his 'lord' gave for the term of his life and trusts that at the individual judgement God will find his account in balance, his good deeds having discharged the penance due for his sins. **96** now scans better than **ZAB**, whether on vowels or on *sh / s*. **98** *crede*: neither the Nicene nor the Apostles' Creed, which do not refer to the individual judgement (at death). The allusion here may be to their mention of Christ as judge of living and dead on doomsday, and to the Paternoster's final petition. **99** *rental*: the record or register of rent due from tenant to landlord; here a figure for the creed, the last clause of which speaks of the eternal life promised to the just. Accompanying the stress on faith is P.'s trust that his good works will support his claim to salvation (cf. Js 2:22–6). Those in question here concern 'observance of the law', but 7.255–9a have shown the C-Text P.'s awareness of the greater demands of charity. **100** He will be buried in the churchyard and later his bones will be kept in the ossuary. *kyrke*: metonymic for the priest. **101** The greater or 'predial' tithe levied on the increase on grain-crops was given to the rector who, if not himself the incumbent, would give the latter a portion of it, or a stipend. The lesser tithe on the 'mixed' profits from livestock and on 'personal' profits from craft or trade went to the parish priest, even if only a vicar. The tithes on crops and animals were paid gross, those on craft and trade, net. *corn and catel*: probably referring to both tithes, *catel* here meaning '(income from) personal property or goods'. **102** *prestly*: like Truth (7.194), whose servant he is, and from whom he now expects final repayment. **103–4** *holdyng*: on this passive use of the present participle see *MES* 548. *masse...memorie*: the commemorative prayers (*Memento*) in the Canon of the Mass, perhaps those for the dead after the Consecration (*Bn*), and also those for the living before it, in which P. expects to be remembered by name. **105** *no more*: not implying that there *was* any more he had 'won' wrongfully. **106** *douhteres...childres*: on the authenticity of this unexpected collocation see *TN*. **107** *dette*: settlement of debts in making a will being imperative, failure to do so was regarded as a sin for which the debtor's soul would have to pay in purgatory. **108** *borwed...to bedde*: taken by *Bn* as alluding to Deut 20:10–13, though in fact that text enjoins a *lender* not to retain overnight a poor man's pledge (e.g. his cloak) against something he has borrowed and not yet repaid. The passage figuratively presents P. as free of all obligations and ready to leave this life with a clear conscience, his scrupulousness recalling his master Truth's at 7.195, and contrasting with the conduct of Wrong at 4.56. **109** uses a line that has already appeared at B 5.460, and is deleted in **C** at that point. *resudue... remenant*: the third portion of the net estate remaining after the widow had received one third and divided a second amongst the children. *Bn* sees this as 'equivalent' to 'the dead's part', which would cover overdue tithes and commemorative services or alms as specified by the testator. But P. must obviously be speaking metaphorically (cf. *pilgrym at þe plouh*); so *his* benefit from 'the dead's part' is to become 'dead to the world', by living more abstemiously and working for his neighbours. *Rode of Lukes*: a celebrated C8th wooden image of the crowned Christ on the cross in the cathedral at Lucca in N Italy; an unlikely object of pilgrimage for P. himself. **111** *pore and ryche*: the revision bringing out P.'s rôle of provider for all rather than 'champion of the poor' as in **B**, where 'the traditional bequest to the poor is transmuted into his labours for them' (*Bn*).

(ii) 112–66 offer a realistic description of contemporary agricultural practice. **112** *plouh*: literal, but also emblematic of *trewe* labours in the world (Lk 9:62). **114** *balkes*: the smaller ridges (produced by earth thrown up in ploughing, and now overgrown with weeds) rather than the wider unploughed strips dividing groups of furrows (see MED s.v. *balke* n. 2a and Poole 1958: I, fig. 2, pl. 1). **115** *apayed...payed*: typically 'Platonic' wordplay, 'satisfaction' and 'reward' being seen as reciprocal. **119** *hey prime*: the first break for refreshment, between dawn and noon. **120** P. stops either to supervise or to inspect their work, like a reeve (as he is later made in 21.259). **121** *huyred þeraftur*: 'paid accordingly'. **122** *ale*: usual at breakfast, often sweetened with honey. Ploughmen's food for the day was typically a loaf and a gallon of ale; but excess at mid-morning could make them like the gluttons at 6.395–6 (the ill-effects of over-drinking during the working-day have been warned against at B 1.25–6). **123** *trollilolly*: a refrain derived from *trollen* (MED s.v. v. 1 'rock', a word also first found in **L** with different sense at 20.332) and *lullai*; but it may be a meaningless cry of gaiety like modern echoic *tra la la*. The song recalls that of the bad workmen in Pr 225. **124** *in puyre tene*: an important revision in **B**, removing the unfortunate over-

tones of **ZA** *wrathe*. The phrase recurs at B 7.115, 16.86, with the effect of a *leitmotiv* in that version, and seems to denote the *ira per zelum* 'righteous anger' described in Gregory's *Moralia* (*PL* 75:726) and shown by Christ himself (*ST* II 2.158:2; III 15:9). But P.'s tendency to become quickly vexed (which associates him with Biblical personages like Moses and Peter) is almost eliminated in **C**. **127b** 'The devil take anyone who should care'; an execration paralleled in *PTA* 447. **129** *leiden...alery*: of uncertain origin, *alery* being possibly a cant word. The gloss 'acted as if paralysed' offered doubtfully in MED s.v. *aliri* cites the etymology proposed by Dobson 1947–8: 60 (OE *lima lyre* 'loss of [the use of] limbs'). But the explanation in Colledge 1957:111–13 convincingly shows (with the help of an illustration of a beggar from Bruegel's 'Fight between Carnival and Lent') that 'The object of the [*PP* beggars'] trick is to counterfeit a crippled or maimed appearance'. They do so not by sitting 'with the calf of one leg resting on the shin of the other' (*SkGl*) but by standing 'with the calf against the back of the thigh, so that it appears to be cut off' (*Bn*). This interpretation is supported by 135a and in turn supports *Sk*'s derivation of *alery* from OE *lira* 'fleshy part of the calf / thigh'. **135** *Lord...thonketh*: the humour of their hypocritical embrace of misfortune heightened by its deferral, the revised form suggesting that *lord...ye* in **ZAB** may have been intended as a parenthetical exclamation and not (*Bn*) as addressed to P. **136–40** vigorously re-write some rather slack **ZAB** lines and remove the echo in B 133 (itself a revision drawing on A 10.145 in the b-half) of the stock 'winner / waster' contrast, thus avoiding repetition of Pr 24. P. states firmly his belief that the prayers of the virtuous win practical blessings from God, already affirming the contemplative values later to be embodied in his *alter ego* Patience the Hermit. **B 131 //** *(h)olde hyne*: echoing Lk 12:42. **137–8** are perhaps an indirect allusion to Prov 20:4b, quoted entire at 246a; but no specific scriptural warning against false beggars seems intended. *a-beggeth*: from *on* + the old verbal noun *beggath*, a construction later replaced by the gerund (whence 'a-begging'); see *MES* 581–2. **139–40** This double *repetitio* is a form of paronomasia with subtle expansions of sense in the move from n. to v. and a. to av. *wastours*: an attack possibly prompted by social conditions after the Black Death, when a massive labour shortage led to large rises in workmen's wages that the government unsuccessfully struggled to control (McKisack 1959:331–42, Ziegler 1971, ch. 15). Despite crop failures and dearth between 1350–75 (Frank 1990), some preferred not to work at all. **141** *teme to dryue*: i.e. 'work the land'; the 'text of Truth' alluded to may be II Thess 3:10. **142–3** *barly...broke...bolted*: the minimum needed to survive. This was prison fare, to judge by *RR* 2757 (barley being valued mainly for malt to make ale, which they will *not* have); so here P. boldly promises better food to prisoners than to idle wastrels. **146–8** evolve continuously through the versions (see e.g. Z 132 → A 135 → B 146 → C 146), with wholesale abbreviation to avoid repetition (e.g. A 133 of A Pr 28 //). The revision includes sincere mendicants but excludes monks. **146** *nones*: the standard régime for a fast day, which (as *Bn* notes) they always observe. **B 147** *þat han* 'those who have'; **A 137** *þat* 'for him who'; on non-expression of the antecedent, see *MES* 190. **148** *What...what*: more exuberant paronomasia. *what þat*: on this combination see *MES* 195.

B 139–51 are developed from A 127–8 and describe the duties a serf had to perform for his lord (*Bn*). They may have been omitted after 1381 as potentially provocative, ll. 143–4 simply as over-emphatic (the sense of 139–40 is used to better effect in the ironic new context of C 5.13–19). **144** scans with cognative spirants (*þ / f / v*). On **L**'s notion of divine forbearance as 'vengeance', cf. Reason at B 11.378. **148** *Robert Renaboute*: perhaps a wandering hermit (*Bn*) and, since *Robert* seems always a 'bad' name in *PP*, a dishonest one (see B 187). **149** *postles*: mendicant friars, and perhaps also itinerant preachers maintained by bequests and licensed to preach within particular 'limits' in a diocese. **151** *vnresonable Religion*: a form of religious life lacking in rational proportion (Alford in Kennedy 1988:214). *Bn* finds an 'evident allusion' to the sending of the 72 disciples in Lk 10:7; but P. no less evidently declares 'unreasonable' a life dedicated to preaching the Gospel without some guarantee of sustenance from the laity, and Conscience makes a similar point at 20.264–7.

149–50 *Wastour*: a type-representative of all who batten unscrupulously on others' labours. The annominative *repetitio* in *yfouhte*, *fyhte* removes the impropriety of *gloue* coming from a peasant. **149** *gan...yfouhte*: on this use of the perfect infinitive 'to express a hypothetical action simultaneous with that of a non-auxiliary finite verb' see *MES* 517. **151** *pyuische*: after two changes the term of insult restored to its initial form in **Z**; a rare word of uncertain origin (perhaps < Lat *perversus*), first found here. **152** *Bretener*: a group reputed for boastfulness, as shown by *AMA* 1348. **155** The near-identity with 68 cannot be accidental, since the AB 145/158 b-half differs from AB 61/67b, the intention presumably being ironic. The earlier line was P.'s promise to those who *did* work; the present is Waster's insolent demand for the same reward *without* work. **157** *couenaunt*: an agreement that expresses (with feeling) a vision of ideal relations between labourer and landlord in feudal society; see on 26–34 above. **158** *dere*: the price of goods inevitably rising with scarcity. **159** The new line states how the failure of religious sanctions finally leaves no option but force. **163–6** The Knight's threat of resort to the shire court, though stronger in **C**, is no more effective: Waster will

not wait around to be tried. **166** *pes*: a stock expression of worthlessness, but piquantly apt in the light of 176, where P. judges Wastour 'worth' only a pease-loaf (which yet is better than nothing).

(iii) 167–353 The Hunger episode, a dramatised allegorical meditation on II Thess 3:10 (*si quis non vult operari, nec manducet*) presents a drastic solution to the problem of ensuring enough affordable food for all. This problem is seen as caused by the failure of many to work the land, with resulting dearth. The character Hunger may be derived from Faim in *RR* 10133ff (see Kaske 1988; and on the allegory, Hewett-Smith 1996). Piers's dialogue with him may be understood allegorically as part of an interior debate between his conflicting impulses to severity and permissiveness. **168** The shift from 'typical' narrative making complete sense at the literal level to personification-allegory continues the mode announced in the Confessions Scene, where type-figures interacted with the personified sins. The personification Hunger had re-appeared at A XII 63–76, and this repetition may have been among the reasons for abandoning the attempted continuation. **170** *Awreke me*: signifying that P.'s only means of controlling the wasters is to deny them any food at all. *wil nat*: a change indicating not that the wasters' behaviour is any less destructive but that the knightly class, their morale shaken after the Peasants' Rising, are now less willing (or able) to enforce the Statutes of Labourers. For if they try and compel the idle to work when they do not wish to, they might be refused their services at times like harvest. **175** *barste*: p. t. subjv. in revised **C**, but indic. in **ZAB**. **B 180** *doluen*: '(dead) and buried', omission of *ded* sharpening the sardonic contrast with *doluen* B 190: to dig for one's food is better than to dig one's grave.

A 165–70 (Z 162–7) The excision of this grotesquely vivid (if at points confusing) allegorical sequence is a loss, though undeniably speeding up the action. **165** *benene bat*: a long loaf of bean-flour, costing 1/3 the price of a wheat loaf (*Bn*, citing *English Gilds* 366). **168** Doctor Thirst paradoxically *forbids* them to drink (too much), whereas in **Z** he encourages it. This revision is doubtless due to realising that barley- and bean-bread rapidly swallowed down would swell if much water was drunk, causing acute indigestion. For a similar change (from **B** to **C**), cf. on 20.53.

178–222 178 is virtually repeated at 192, a possible oversight that might have been put right before 'publication' (cf. 197 at 203). **179** *faytours*: false beggars and hermits, distinct from the wasters (cf. 208, 210 below), who work for Piers *before* they feel the pangs of hunger. **182** *potage...wyf*: a more generous (and realistic) touch, perhaps implying that P. feeds them for their efforts with what he would willingly eat himself, thereby welcoming them back into the *comune*. **186–7** remove B 189b's repetition of 187b, *duntes* replacing *doluen* (see above at B 180) in a similar contrast with *flapton*. **188** *he*: of uncertain reference (presumably Piers); the allegorical inappropriateness of Hunger 'healing' (A 179) when he inflicts the *duntes* (C 187) may be the reason for the change (but cf. 225). **189** *longes*: perhaps synecdochic for the less tasty offal generally not eaten. **195** *holde hewe*: cf. ZAB 120. **198** *daubynge*: applying clay to wattle fencing or huts for sheltering livestock. **199** *pynnes*: used as nails, in wheel-axles ('linchpins'), and to fasten roof-tiles. **200** repeats 7.190, showing that to follow P. is to become Truth's servant like him (cf. 195). **202** The T-type line emphasises how animal necessity has taken on the coercive authority of the impotent knightly class, and with it the title (*Syre Hunger*). **204** P., like his master Truth, renders to each according to his works (Prov 24:12, Mt 16:27), 'justice' paying no more or less than what is due. **208** *awroke*: completing what he asked for at 170. **209** scans as an extended vocalic Type III with counterpoint (*abb / ax*). **214–16** P.'s words show the Half-Acre scene re-enacting the pattern of the Deadly Sins sequence on the social plane; though the 'wasters' are given up, the beggars, who seem redeemable, are not sorry for their conduct, only afraid of its consequences. P.'s hope, however, is for a society like a large family, founded through Christ's redeeming act and united by brotherly love, without which disintegration will occur. **216** *filial*: found nowhere else in ME and possibly introduced here. **217** *blody bretherne*: a paradoxical idea, false if taken literally but true in a spiritual sense, since their common baptism is a sharing in the sacrificial death of Christ. The sacramental mystery involved is elaborated at 12.111 with far-reaching social implications. **218** Perhaps the most important scriptural source is Mt 5:43–48, a text linking love of one's enemies with being children of the God who provides natural blessings for good and bad alike. But also pertinent is the text 'Every one shall...say to his brother: Be of good courage' (Is 41:6). **221** *amayster...louye*: the C revision moving the urgent debate about the 'means' to a productive and harmonious social order from plain obedience to 'filial' service, and from a 'Mosaic' to a 'Messianic' conception of human relations. **Z 196–201** are vigorous but repetitive elaboration (e.g. Z 175–6, 203) and understandably therefore dropped by **A**. **223–302** The discourse of Hunger, who is largely abetted by P. in his three interventions, deals with the problem of providing justly for those who cannot as well as those who will not work, and for distinguishing between them. **223–34 225** *houndes...breed*: of beans and bran; so unappetising that it should persuade able-bodied idlers to work for better. **226** *abaue*: 'confound' (OED s.v. *abave* v); MED does not record this sense or cite this instance. **229** *fals men*: replacing an awkward reference to Fortune that might have implied a criticism of Providence.

231 *lawe of kynde*: the natural law, but also punningly 'the divine law', *kynde* (as will be revealed at 10.52ff) being another nature-name for God, who has created all men. In **ZAB** the appeal is grounded on the brotherhood of Christians through baptism (cf. 217); here the 'law of Christ' is seen expressed in his epitome of Truth's Commandments (Mt 22:37–40) as the 'eternal law' in which 'natural law is contained' (Aquinas, *ST* I, 2, 71:6). **231a** 'Bear ye one another's burdens: and so you shall fulfil the law of Christ' (Gal 6:2). Hunger interprets Paul's text (on helping fellow Christians overcome the 'burden' of their faults by offering them mild instruction) as an injunction to share their want through 'filial' charity.

B 223–5a envisage (unlike C 232–4) misfortunes that men bring on themselves through their own actions as sins that God will punish. **223** *nouȝty*: judged 'ambiguous at this date' by MED (s.v. *noughti* adj. (a), citing *Pur.* 1359). But *Bn*'s apt citation of *SS* 115 'nedful and *nawthi*, naked and nawth' (not in MED s.v. (c)) confirms here the sense 'in want, needy' otherwise instanced only in the R variant at B 7.70. **224** *vengeaunce*: i.e. where any retribution is due. **225** 'Even if they *are* doing wrong, leave it to God to sort things out'. **225a** 'Revenge is mine and I will repay [them in due time]' (Deut 32:35, qu. Rom 12:19, Heb 10:30 which have *vindicta* for *ultio*). This is **L**'s most-often-cited Biblical text (B 10.206a, 368, C 17.235a, 21.449a), incorrect *vindictam* being a VL reading common in the period (AlfQ,Sk). Whereas **C** omits the important retribution-text, **B** probably implies awareness of Gal 6:5 ('For every man shall bear his *own* burden') as 'correlative' with Gal 6:1, which urges *not* condemning others' faults, through remembering one's own.

235–5a The sentiment preceding the quotation is altered in a more penitential sense, but with the same implication: charitable use of 'ill-gotten gains' will make satisfaction for sin and may gain the prayers of those helped. It is not suggested that P.'s gains are *untrewe* (cf. 105); but since all *tresor of erthe* is valueless when compared with *treuthe*, it should be used for others' good, the question of their 'deserts' being left to God. **235** *wiselich*: not just 'virtuously' but 'prudently' (cf. 223); Hunger does *not* advocate 'indiscriminate charity' (*Bn*, referring to Lk 6:27–38), nor can this be what P. has in mind at 236. **235a** 'Make unto you friends of the mammon of iniquity' (Lk 16:9).

236–315 *The dialogue between Hunger and Piers*. **237** *synneles*: i.e. give alms selectively (from even one's dubiously acquired riches); Hunger's appeal to three OT authorities and a rather OT-sounding Gospel parable shows that P. cannot think 'discriminate charity' might be sin. **240** *wyse men*: no immediate referent is apparent. The cognomen *geaunt* in **B** for *Genesis* refers to its being the longest book of the Bible (not counting Psalms) and the *engendrour* as it tells the origin of mankind (*Bn*). The clearer and more straightforward procedure in **C**, omitting the obscure *mnam* at B 238 // (but introducing two little-known *English* words at 242) and completing the quotations, suggests that readers might have found the macaronic syntax of B 232, 235 // difficult. **242** The first verb is unique, the second instanced in this sense only here; the construction requires understanding *we sholde*. **242a** 'In the sweat (and labour) of thy face shalt thou eat (thy) bread [till thou return to the earth, out of which thou wast taken]' (Gen 3:19). Inserted *labore* may have been prompted by Gen 3:17 *in laboribus comedes* (and cf. 261*a*). **243** *Salomon*: see on 3.121. **245** *sleuthe*: explicitly recognising idleness as one of the deadly sins (cf. 253, *CT* X 685). **246** *a-bribeth*; *a-beggeth*: see on 137–8; the identification of false beggars as failed labourers is confirmed by 9.203–10. **246a** 'Because of the cold, the sluggard would not plough: he shall beg therefore in the summer, and it shall not be given him' (Prov 20:4). To explain mistaken *yeme* 'winter' *Pe* suggests 'sympathetic association of winter and deprivation'; but 245 shows **L** aware that the text read *aestate* 'summer'. **247–58** The parable is told in Mt 25:14–30 and this reference may be recalling the specific mention of sloth in vs 26 *Serve male et piger* (*Bn*); but both the **ZAB** adj. *nequam* 'wicked' and the noun *mna* 'pound' come from Lk 19:12–27. **B 237** *mannes face*: alluding to the iconography derived from traditional exegesis of the 'four living creatures' in Apoc 4:7 (based on Ezech 1:10) as figures of the Four Evangelists (see on 21.263–7). Matthew was represented as a man because his Gospel begins with the human genealogy of Christ (see Schiller 1971:I, pl. 172). **249** *chele... hete*: signifying that the Christian should exercise his talents in all circumstances, including adversity. **Z 230–2** If this is a true autobiographical reference, it may reflect the fact that the author, though in minor orders, had not reached the rank of deacon, below which a clerk was not permitted to preach. See *Intro*, V § 4 and n. 8. **B 246–8** The rhyme-enclosed lines affirm almost catechetically that both nature and revelation require everyone to do some 'work', bodily or spiritual. *Bn* would have 'active and contemplative life' stand in parallel with husbandry and devotions, not as identical with them; though not exhaustive, these represent the two types of 'travail'. **259** *Sauter*: the psalm cited being concerned with the earthly blessings that will come to the just. **B 251a; 261a** *Beati... manducabis*: 'Blessed are all they [that fear the Lord: that walk in his ways]. For thou shalt eat the labours of thy hands: [blessed art thou, and it shall be well with thee]' (Ps 127:1–2). **Z** is here closest to the full original Latin, which 238 translates (a feature more in keeping with authorial draft than scribal adaptation). **A** is a paraphrase stating that work here gets a reward here. **B** and **C** variously add a moral and spiritual dimension to both work (*feiþful / lele* labour) and reward. While correcting **A**'s one-sidedness (the psalm promises prosperity for *righteousness*), both nonetheless foreground what the psalm only implies (*labour*). Hunger's argument is: 'man must work; those who do not are punished here and hereafter; those who do are rewarded likewise'. **C** ignores the positive aspect of the psalm-text to end on a note of sombre warning. **263** *be*: 'will be'. **264–5** resume the two problematic categories of *beggares* and *boys* that trouble Piers. **267** *fisyk*: a more dignified term than *lechecraft*, ironically implying that the 'learning' true medicine requires is spiritual rather than bodily. **270** *ʒow*: hardly 'P.s "servants" rather than P.' (*Bn*) since 268b candidly admits that he too can give in to the pleasures of harvest plenty. **B 253** *my deere*: 'good friend', the affectionate tone indicating P.'s sense of his interlocutor's moral value to him. **269** *Of...woke*: 'for a whole week'. **271** *manged ouer moche*: strongly recalling A 12.72–6, the only other recorded occurrence of *mangen*. The opposite pole of 'want' that disciplines sloth is here seen as 'over-plenty' leading to the related vice of gluttony (see on 7.1–68). This doctrine, of moderation not of deprivation, is that of HC in I 33 (*Mesure is medecyne*) and shows how consistent is the moral position developed through such authoritative figures as Hunger (the *in*consistency in his presentation at A 12.72–6 may be one reason for **L**'s abandoning that passus; see *Intro*. III, *A Version*, x). **276** *Sire Sorfeet*: another passing personification, specified in **B** as an epicure guilty of 'delicacy' and 'curiosity' (*CT* X 830). **277** Cf. Glutton at B 5.377. **278–89** The Biblical exemplum lends homiletic weight to Hunger's moral admonition and may be contrasted with the clever *forbisne* used by the Friars Minor at 10.33ff. **B 266** *many maner metes*: recalling Ecclus 32–3. **278** *Diues*: commonly treated as a proper name, from the parable in Lk 16:19–31 of the rich man (*dives*) and Lazarus the beggar covered with sores, whose proper name conversely gave rise to the generic *lazar* for 'leper'. (Dives is cited again at 15.303 and 19.232 as an exemplar of *unkyndenesse*). Hunger's advice does not presuppose that P. is 'rich' but urges all with more than they need to give to those in want, who are their true 'neighbours' (cf. 9.71ff). The counsel needs careful interpretation, since Hunger is telling P. to feed from his table all who like Lazarus (a beggar) are really needy, but to give only the leftover scraps to the suspect characters who call. **280** *culde hym*: the harsh tone recalling B 20.151; Hunger is part of the reality of Kynde as 'mortality', also manifested as age and disease. **282** *Abrahames lappe*: i.e. heaven; so at 18.272–3 (*sinus* in Lk 16:23 is usually rendered 'bosom'). **284** *grat*: the form with retracted vowel avoiding confusion with the contracted form of *greten*. **288** *bord*: a trestle-table, folded up after use and placed against the wall. **290** Hunger attributes most illnesses to excess, i.e. the deadly sin of Gluttony, through which 'the humours in [the] body been distempred' (*CT* X 825; cf.

also *CT* VII 2836–9, Ecclus 37:32–4). **291** *Fisyk*: a brief 'professional' type-personification like Cyuile at 2.63. **291–2** *hodes...cloke*: evidence of physicians' large fees, often paid in part with a gift of robes by their rich clients. Physic's fur cannot keep him warm against the attack of old age in 22.176–7. *of Callabre*: trimmed with fine grey squirrel fur from Calabria in S Italy. **292** *communes legge*: recalling Reason's words to Purnele at 5.128–9. The ironic *repetitio* of *legge* 290 is a device typically favoured in the revision to **C**. **A** 257–8 A two-line critique replaces **Z**'s impassioned 18-line diatribe against bad doctors, retaining only Z 263–4 (and later 271–3 at 8.46a–48). This revision is misunderstood by Kerby-Fulton (1999:519) as indicating difference of authorship. **296** *destyné*: not a power in its own right but what is foreseen for an individual as his allotted time on earth. The notion here is that temperate living is likely to ensure a longer life than medical treatment.

    Z 260–78 After Meed's attack on Conscience at 3.147–76, this is the longest passage of **Z** to be cut. Its complex and learned *distinctio* between true and false *leches* is also digressive and repetitive (271–3 recur as 8.47–9 apropos of lawyers), holding up the urgent dialogue between Hunger and Piers on the need for a morally balanced attitude towards the extremes of dearth and abundance to which the husbandman's way of life was subject. **260** *science...trewe*: cf. Gower on alchemy (*CA* IV 2598–9); Hunger's onslaught is upon ignorant practitioners, not on those who have properly qualified at the university, where a medical training took six years after completing the Arts course (Courtenay 1987:36–7). **261** accuses quacks of illiteracy (they cannot read even a manual of medicine). The tone of this line is very like that of B 15.375. **262–3** *hele / quelle*: for similar end-rhymes cf. Z 258/9 and C 8.343/4 (with identical rhythm), 9.92/3. **263** *maystres morthrares*: 'Masters of Murder' (cf. *doctour of deth* 20.402); for similar juxtaposed nouns cf. *maistres freres* at B Pr 62. **264** *lyares*: cf. Z 2.204–5, where Liar resides with the leeches. **265** *Ecclesiasticis*: ch. 38:1–9 deals with physicians and medicines as divinely ordained. The use of a single-word macaronic double-stave is characteristic. **267** 'Honour the physician for the need thou hast of him: [for the most High hath created him]' (Ecclus 38:1). The line scans as Type III on *n*. **268–70** are based on Ecclus 38:2, the phrasing resembling 14.85 (in a totally different context). **269** *ys*: perhaps better if 'thys', though the sense is acceptable. **271** 'Their reward shall be from kings and princes'; almost certainly from Hugh of St Cher's gloss 'id est, coram principibus et regibus' on Ecclus 38:3 (*R–B*; see further Alf*Q*). The notion that the cost of certain common necessities should be borne by king and lords is applied to lawyers' fees at B 7.42–3*a* (// in **Z** and **A**); but this earliest use in relation to doctors is closer to the source, as would be expected in a

first version. **274** *Lumbardes*: 'The Lombards notice that Londoners are gluttonous (and therefore prone to sickness) and see their opportunity to sell them medicines (which will turn out even more harmful)' (*R–B*, citing Thorndyke 1934:III, 526 on the Lombards' reputation for sorcery and poisoning). For London as a place of good eating see Pr 227–31. **276** *medecynes schapeth*: for similar phrasing cf. 'Shrift *schop* scharp salue' at 22.307. **277** *of the cardyacle*: 'by causing them heart-attacks [*sc.* through their toxic potions]'. **278** *Flemmynges*: residing in London, mainly in connection with the wool-trade. The line signifies 'people of all the different nations living there'.

297–341 The second half of this episode memorably evokes the cycle of the agricultural year, with its periods of want and plenty. 303–14 describe the 'hungry gap' before the next harvest (March to August), when the previous year's reserves were dwindling (Frank 1990:89–90) and the countryman's condition came near that of the urban poor all year round as described at 9.71–97. **297** *Poul*: a fitting name to invoke, since his teaching on work and feeding presides over the whole sequence (see on 141). *Pernel* **AZ**: St Petronella, the legendary daughter of St Peter (whence perhaps an apt saint for P. to swear by), who endured fever in order to grow in holiness, and fasted to death to avoid marrying a pagan lord (*LA* ch. 78). *poyntest...treuth*: part of the way to reality being through experience of *hoet hunger* (20.211). **299–300** The *repetitio* of *wel* in varying senses is typical of **C**. *awroke*: Hunger has done for P. what the knight (158) could not, and the past participle rounds off the sequence with an echo of the imperative at 170. **301** The only way to make Hunger (man's permanent companion) 'depart' is to feed him. **303–4** It is less likely that P. has only money enough to buy cheese, etc. (*Bn*), than that he has *no* money (to buy choice meats) but does have dairy produce, which he can provide himself (cf. *cow* 311), and oats for his cart-horse. **304** *grene*: unripe, because made (from the daily milk) for early eating. **306** *bred...peses*: the poor fare provided for beggars in 225 (the wheat having gone except for the seed-corn). **307** *ʒut*: he has not 'even' bacon and eggs, let alone fresh pork and poultry. **309–10** *parsilie*; *chiruulles*: cropped and eaten whole as salad-herbs (cf. *cresses* at 321 below). *sam-rede*: an improvement on *ripe chiries*, showing how hunger makes them eat the fruit (in early June) before it is fully ripe. **312** *drouthe*: of March (cf. *CT* I 2), the time for manuring the fields before the April rains (*Bn*). **313** *Lammasse*: < OE *hlaf-mæsse*; Aug. 1, the start of harvest-time, when a loaf made from the new wheat was offered at Mass. As this was also the feast of St Peter's Chains (see Ac 1:1–12), there is an apt parallel in the symbolism of P.'s release from 'imprisonment' by hunger. **317** *aples*: 'laid in hay or heather' (*CT* I 3262) to keep until the next September. **318** repeats 4.91 (ironically): this 'present' P. *will* accept or starve, since subsistence-farmers who depend on what they can put by have little money spare to buy food (but cf. on 92 above). **321** loses the witty 'poison'-image (on which see *TN*), doubtless to avoid the a-half's partially repeating 306b, 316. **322** *nyhed neyh*: either lito-tes ('by then harvest had come') or else this 'new' corn is the remains of last-year's, hoarded by merchants to sell dear and now released cheap to avoid a glut and provide space in barns (*Bn*). **324** *gode ale*: 'brewed from barley newly harvested' (*Bn*). **325–6** Another cycle of idleness begins with the arrival of plenty. *wandren*: dependent on *wolde*. **327** *clermatyn*: a choice bread of which nothing is known. *coket*: next in quality after *wastel* or cake bread (6.340), which came after *simenel*, the finest. **B 303** *ellis*: taken by *BnSch* as adj. = 'of other kinds' (MED s.v. *elles* adj. 1.b.) But the rhythm of the // lines and the unstress on the word suggest it is only an intensifier (ib. s.v. adv. 1a) used elliptically to mean that '(if not of the finest), their bread is (at the least) to be of wheat-flour alone.' **328** *halpenny ale*: 'feeble' ale like that drunk by the monks (6.159), costing half the standard brew (*peny ale* 332). **329** *brouneste*: thick, strong 'pudding ale', the darkest and dearest. **330** *Laborers*: taken by *Bn* to include crofters as well as unskilled town workmen of various kinds; cf. Gower, *Vox Clamantis* (in *Works* vol. iv) 5. 641. **331** *aday...wortes*: 'daily / the next day on yesterday's left-over greens'. **AB 292/307** *dyne*: here transitive (though **Z** has the same construction as **C**). **334** *chaut... pluchaut*: enticing cries from the cookshops (though not found earlier, the phrase sounds authentic), with perhaps some satire on the cooks' pretensions. **336** *ywrouhte*: making the discontented labourer's complaint about his wages one against his *destyné* (296) as ordained by God. **337** *Catones consayle*: see on 4.17. *gruche*: taking up a verb first used in **Z** (twice) but replaced in **AB** in both instances by *chide*. **337a** The second part of a Catonian couplet beginning *Infantem nudum cum te natura crearit*: '[Since Nature made you as a naked babe], Remember to bear the burden of poverty with patience' (*DC* I. 21). **338** *corseth*: not an outburst of bad temper but a rebellious challenge to authority. *iustices*: replacing *Counseil* so as to stress the royal judges' important rôle in punishing breaches of labour legislation during the unsettled period after 1381. **339** *lawes*: the Statutes of Labourers, beginning in 1349 and renewed again at about the time of **Z** in 1362, which required all workmen to take any employment available. Enforcement was at first successful, though the view voiced from **Z** onwards is that labourers' pay can be kept at a level in accord with the 'natural' (= divinely ordained) proportion between the value of goods and their price only through refusing excessive demands that subvert the providential social order. These laws designed 'to ensure a supply of cheap labour by pegging

wages [which nearly doubled between 1340–60] at pre-plague rates' (McKisack 1959:335) were much resented, and their restraint on peasants' economic aspirations contributed to the Rising of 1381. *lerne*: a revision with no change of sense; like *loke* here = 'prescribe'. **341** *statuyt*: a decree approved by parliament, addressed to all subjects and having the force of law, by contrast with an 'ordinance' passed by the king in council (Maitland 1974:186–8). The ironic figurative use implies a sanction more effective than those of the actual Statute.

342–53 This prophecy, spoken in 'authorial' voice but using a mode widely popular at the time and growing longer and darker in revision, seems intended (like much Biblical prophecy) as a moral warning rather than a prediction of disaster within a precise period of time. Thus 'before five years' would have indicated in **Z**, say, 1370, in **A** 1375 and in **B** 1383; but the alteration to 'few' in **C** safely covers the likelihood that some natural calamity would indeed befall. **343** *hiderwardes*: having temporarily quit the scene at harvest, but only to return in spring, in severer guise. **343/4** The rhyme's difference in **Z** is a strong indicator of its originality, the **A** revision both adding internal rhyme and eliminating the weak repetition of *werkmen*. **344** *water*: i.e. crop-destroying floods. **346** The grim message is to be inferred from the position of Saturn, the 'cold' planet farthest from Earth, which astrological lore associated with famine, flood and pestilence and (as in Chaucer) with social upheaval (*CT* I 2456, 2459, 2478). The *Prophecies* of 'John of Bridlington' (III c. 11, in Wright 1859:123–215) linked the pestilence of 1361–2 with 'the star most harmful to the earth and the bringer-in of plagues', while medieval astrologers believed that the Great Pestilence of 1349 had been 'brought about by an extraordinary conjunction of Saturn with the other planets, which happened scarcely once in a thousand years' (*Wr* p. xii). As *Bn* notes, the prophecy finds apocalyptic fulfilment at 22.80, where Kynde brings diseases 'oute of the planetes'. *sente*: 'sends [this message]'. **348–51** (**B 325–27**) The **Z** and **A** Versions end the passus here. The two riddling prophecies added in **B** and **C** could well be read as direct utterances of the personified planetary power. **348** The coupling of pride and plague directly recalls Reason's words in the sermon *ad status* that opened Vision Two, and the line anticipates 22.98 / echoes B 20.98: Pride arouses the anger of God, who punishes it with plagues. **349–50** 'are', as *Sk* observes encouragingly, 'of course, inexplicable', and as 'mysterious prophecies' they may well be incapable of sure exegesis. But in 350–1 it is hard not to see an allusion to the Four Horsemen of Apoc ch. 6, usually taken to symbolise destruction, war, plague and famine; and this (as with the earlier and very similar prophecy at 3.478–82) would favour a wider 'apocalyptic' context of interpretation. **349** *Pe*'s judgement that the line contains a cryptic date-reference is supported by 350a, all the more if the referent of 350b is not geographical 'in all parts of the world' (*Pe*) but temporal 'on both sides of the full of the moon' (i.e. throughout the month in question). If *schaef* (in the light of 3.478) is the true reading here, it would seem to refer to a sheaf of *arrows* (Bradley 1910:342; Bloomfield 1961:211–12), of which the usual number was 24. The line thus yields the *three* successive figures 3, 24 and 8, of which the first divides the second by the last and the last divides it by the first. This may darkly suggest the idea that 'The first shall be last and the last shall be first', echoing an eschatological saying of Christ (Mt 19:30) that is immediately preceded by a reference to the *twelve* apostles judging the *twelve* tribes of Israel (= 24; cf. on 3.478 above). If a specific time is being intimated, this would be the third *hour* of the 24th *day* of the eight month, August. And if Bradley is right that the word 'ship' is here meant to evoke the conventional medieval outline of a ship (x), *three* ships ('xxx') will yield the numerical value 30, and by adding 30+24+8 a *year* [13]62 is obtainable. This is a significant Langlandian date, but its precise relevance to a text written in the 1380s remains unclear. Bradley, however, observes that the **p** reading *shaft* offers another numerical rebus 'l' (= 50), and with *vm* as = *viii* we have 30+50+8, giving another date [13]88. The closeness of this to **C**'s probable date of composition (1385–7) would make the 'apocalyptic' events foretold (war, and famine in place of plague) not past but to come, and preventable only by an act of divine remission. However, while such interpretations are authorised by, e.g., the famous numerical cryptograph in Apoc 13:18, they may (have) seem(ed) to many readers a little forced.

B 325–6 are in some respects more obscure than **C** (which may be an effort to 'clarify' matters to some extent). **325** *þe sonne amys*: connected with an eclipse by *Bn*, who notes after Bradley that a total eclipse occurred in 1377. *two monkes heddes*: understood by *Bn* as 'curious shapes in the sky', such as the eclipse might well have suggested, with 'a covert allusion to certain religious — or to apparitions'. The image seems better to merit *Sk*'s resigned comment (cited above) than does **C**'s numerological riddle (which for *Bn* 'increases the obscurity'). **326** *a mayde*: possibly an allusion back to Mede the Maid; the half-line echoes B 3.169 and the prophecy recalls Conscience's concluding denunciation of Mede in B 3.325–30. *multiplied*: 'be' is to be understood, and the past participle may apply to all the preceding conditions of the prophecy or (as preferred here) only to the 'maid', whose 'multiplication' would presumably signify the begetting of offspring (the alchemical sense suspected by Bradley is hard to fit in). In **B** the numerological significance (if any) of the figures 2 and 8 is not easy to discern. **351–3 351** states that after a return of the plague, followed by war, famine will be inflicted as a divine punishment.

352 *Dawe þe Deluare*: a representative labourer 'with no land to live on but his hands', who would therefore be the first to feel the impact of famine. **353** *trewe*: 'respite'; a merciful cessation of God's punishments. The punning juxtaposition of this word with 'Truth' in its other appearance at 20.462 suggests a similar intention here, namely that moral reform such as the Confessions have depicted is needed, if divine punishment such as Reason described at the opening of this vision (5.114ff) is to be avoided.

Passus IX (B VII, ZA VIII)

PASSUS NINE, the 'Pardon Passus' is the second instance of major structural change in **C**. Here concern over the hostility towards the Church shown in the 1381 Rising may partly explain the removal of two passages implying a challenge to clerical authority. These are the Tearing of the Pardon and the quarrel between Piers and the Priest, an ambiguous and presumably controversial episode added in **A** as the climax of the passus (**Z** proper having *ended* before the Tearing). The present Passus divides into three: i. the main part on the receiving of the pardon by Piers and the account of its contents (1–279, with a major addition beginning at 187); ii. the response of the priest (280–91); and iii. the epilogue on dreams, pardons and the need to do well (297–351). In **ZA** the first section is unbroken, but **B** expands the lines on begging with a discussion of whether charity should be discriminating or not (74–84). **C** replaces this with a passage on the same theme some nine times longer, contrasting the worthy poor with deceitful beggars and *lolleres* (71–161). It also inserts a 90-line passage on true and false hermits (187–279), with the continuation or second half of the latter starting where **A**'s 'Tearing' began (see at 175). These additions, even after the removal of B 115–38a, make **C** some 40% longer than **B**; otherwise, the three sections remain about the same length, as do their proportions (4:1:2). The excision of the Tearing destroys the dramatic intensity of the **B** conclusion, while the additions unbalance the *Visio* in a way that the 'autobiographical prelude' arguably does not (see on C V above). Given the new material's thematic relevance and outstanding quality, this hardly amounts to a major failure of artistic judgement. But that the changes, both negative and positive, were motivated by some anticipation of the audience's likely response seems probable.

(i) 1–279 The Pardon. 1–8 In all versions the Pardon is sent by TRUTH, and in the later ones it is not to be confused with any earthly document. But the earlier leave it unclear whether those who earn Truth's pardon by the way they live have also a right to a formal plenary indulgence from the Pope without performing a specific penitential act like pilgrimage (the ambivalent excursus on papal pardons at A 158ff does little to dissipate this confusion). **1** *Treuthe*: the master Piers has served all his life, who hears about his work and promptly responds to it as P. had said he would (presumably by the gift of a good conscience giving assurance of salvation). *herof*: the work on the half-acre; *K–F*'s reference of the word to Saturn's warning of famine to come (in 8.346ff //) is unpersuasive, since the ploughing (as well as bearing its purely literal sense) emblematises the just life that earns pardon. **2–7** The message is implicitly that of St Paul cited at 5.43*a* (I Cor 7:20–23). **2** *taken his teme*: both 'take his plough-team' and 'understand his argument' (MED s.v. *taken* v. 22a 'understand'). **3** *a pena et a culpa*: 'from punishment and guilt'. In strict theory, personal guilt for sins was forgiven through sacramental confession, and what a pardon or indulgence remitted was the canonical punishment imposed for sin (e.g. a period of fasting). This remission was usually to be obtained through an act of satisfaction such as almsgiving. But the Latin phrase came to be understood loosely as signifying also guilt for forgotten (mainly venial), unconfessed or imperfectly confessed sins, and it was generally held that to receive a pardon efficaciously required prior absolution from all grave sins. Temporal penance not fully performed at a person's death would have to be made good in the next life; so the function of commemorative masses and other intercessory prayers for which the deceased left money was chiefly to shorten the time that the soul would spend in purgatory. The brief definition in Alf*G* is thus slightly misleading in conflating these two aspects, since **L**'s point is that a life of 'truth' will leave *no* punishment to be remitted (see further Dunning 1980 [1937]:109ff). In actuality, however, it was widely and mistakenly believed that a papal pardon in recognition of a major penitential act like a pilgrimage to Jerusalem or Rome not only remitted *all punishment* (thereby shortening time spent in purgatory) but absolved from *all guilt* without sacramental absolution (a misunderstanding that exposed the credulous to exploitation by such as Chaucer's Pardoner). But insistence on full confession (*pace* Hudson 1988[2]:405) is a major concern of the poet who, while understanding (and in principle accepting) the theory of pardon, is cool towards the practice. **L**'s development of a figurative *pardon* sent by Truth thus logically complements the figurative *pilgrimage* undertaken by Piers, his exclusive point in both cases being the spiritual reality (repentance and forgiveness) mediated through an external institution. **4** *For hym*: reversing expected social order in beginning with the husbandmen who provide food for all. *ayres*: not that salvation can be inherited, but that the promise, like the one to Abraham (18.256), holds for P.'s descendants if they serve Truth like him. The language is made to resemble that of a charter in order to bring out the pardon's (at least formal) likeness to conventional documents of the type (cf. also *seal* at 27). **8** *perpetuelly*: holding now and hereafter (cf. *for euere* 4) if, as is tacitly understood, the recipients live a life of *treuthe*. **9–12** *Kynges and knyhtes*: even upright nobles requiring time in purgatory, because their office unavoidably taints them with some failure in justice or humility. **13** *Bishopis yblessed*: in contrast, by the dignity of their divine office, granted immediate entry to heaven and a share as the apostles' successors in judging mankind at doomsday (Mt 19:28; with *deys* cf. Vg *sedes*). The phrase ironically recalls Pr 76, which criticises negligent prelates. **L**'s standard for episcopal excellence, however, being that of heroic martyrdom, his revision stresses the need not to fear the secular power of *lordes* (an ideal restated at 17.290–2). **14, 19** *fol of loue*; *lereth men*: corresponding roughly to **ZA** 14, denoting 'our duty towards God, and towards our neighbours' (*Sk*), and giving a fuller view than **B** of the episcopal 'mixed' life of contemplation and action (cf. B 6.248). The parallel **ZAB** lines allude to the two 'great commandments on which depend the law and the prophets' (Mt 22:36–40, and cf. 19.11–16*a*). The phrase *lereth men* is a rare direct echo of **A** in **C**. **20** *peres*: a proleptic pun seems possible in B 16 but less so here with *to* instead of *wiþ. alle...reule*: i.e. given rule in the next world by resisting the rulers of this one (cf. 10). **22–3** *Marchauntes...margine*: a more problematic category, because their motive is desire for profit (26); hence they are included as a concession, not by right. But though 'trade was dangerous for the soul' (*Bn*), what is here attacked is less the activity than the impiety and false swearing incident to it, and **L** may be assumed to have known the positive NT image of the merchant (Mt 13.450) as well as the hostile one (Apoc 18:11, 15). *many ȝeres...culpa*: i.e. off their time in purgatory, but not plenary remission, because the wholesale trader's way of life (as well as giving openings for serious crimes) was not self-evidently for the common good. **23** *Treuthe*: a revision removing the ambiguity that accompanies the irony of **ZAB**. *Pope*: perhaps implying that '[only] an ideal Pope would not, the actual Pope probably would'. **24** *haliday*: because selling on Sundays and feast days breaks the 3rd Commandment (Ex 20:8–11). **27** *secrete seal*: like the royal letters sealed with the privy seal, intended for their eyes only and not entitling them openly to defend their profiteering. **28–9** They are to turn their gains to benefits by works of general value to the community (maintaining hospitals, roads or bridges) and particular help to the neediest (the disabled, imprisoned, unmarried girls, orphan children, ?mendicant friars). On these works, many of which were provided for in bequests, see Thomson 1965 and Rosenthal 1972. **28** *boldly*: in the assurance that they can do some good even with the *mammona iniquitatis*. **37–40** These, the only words spoken directly by Truth, embody the Christian message of hope as *PP* understands it. **37** *Seynt Mihel*: often thought of as holding the balance that will 'weigh' souls at the time of judgement (cf. Jude vs. 9; and see Benson 2004:177–78). His protection was thus especially sought at the moment when the soul left the body and would be snatched at by the fiends, as described in *Prick of Conscience* 2216–373, 2902–19 (see Sheingorn 1995); the promise is an assurance that their prayer will be heard. **38** *despeyre*: effectively a gloss on **B**'s 'terminal fear' that undermines trust in divine mercy and engenders 'wanhope'. **ZA** 'whenever you die' acknowledges the possibility that sudden death (so common during the Plague) might prevent a final plea for grace. **39–40** The attitude to merchants has softened in **C** and the ban on 'professional' sins against *treuthe* is removed as perhaps out of keeping with the positive associations of a pardon. **40** The somewhat overweighted b-half removes the resonant identical rhyme of *ioye* in B 36/7. **42** *purchased*: through his confidential relationship with Truth.

    ZA 43–4 *Wille*: a breach of decorum, but less effective than at ZA 577/44 and with a touch of ironic lightness (cf. *mede*) out of keeping with the solemn tone of the scene. These lines imply that the poet-persona referred to in the 3rd person is a professional scribe who copies charters (as **L** himself might well have been, to judge by the insistence of 13.116–19). *here clause*: the part referring to them; as businessmen, they want a record of their quittance, for which they are prepared to pay handsomely.

43–57 The critique of lawyers, both shorter and less homiletically weighty than its immediate predecessor, replaces the modern-sounding proposal of 'legal aid' for those of low income with one of *pro bono* work by barristers. **44** *pat*: i.e. 'those among them who'. **44–5** *plede... pledynge*: the revision retaining the *repetitio* pattern of B 42. **45** *pre manibus*: 'beforehand', i.e. in advance of doing the work. Such payment, judged an usurious form of *mede*, had bad associations because sometimes done for immoral purposes (at 3.299 it is connected with prostitutes and quacks).

    B 39–51a 39 The key-stave is internal to the consonant group |pl|. **41** *innócentʒ*: stressed on the second syllable (as at 47), whereas the Latin stresses the third. *pat...*: 'who do not even know what evil is, [so do not suspect any].' **41a** Here as a commandment, 'thou shalt not take' but in Ps 14:5 (as quoted at 2.40a) a past-tense characterising statement '[he that hath not put out his money to usury], nor taken bribes against the innocent'. It is not clear from **B** alone whether reference is to lawyers taking inducements from people going to law against 'innocents' (e.g. in inheritance cases) or simply demanding pre-payment from their clients without consideration of the outcome. The second part of the quotation in **ZA**, from the gloss on Ecclus 38:2 noted under Z 7.271 above, affirms that lawyers should act for those who cannot afford fees and the State should pay them (*Bn* cites

ST II. 11.71), a sense to which *pre manibus* in **C** also points. **44–5** *Iohan*: 'a common fellow' (MED s.v. *Jon* (b)). Although it could also be 'Joan' (a type-name for a 'common woman'), prostitution was tried in the Church courts, not before a jury (whose members the lines presume open to corruption). **50–1** are removed in **C**, doubtless because repeating B 34–5. **51a** 'Lord, who shall dwell in thy tabernacle? Or who shall rest in thy holy hill?' (Ps 14:1); usually interpreted as referring to the temple of God in the heavenly Sion. *Bn* finds an allusion to Ps 14:5b (quoted in the **A** mss HW); but this merely sums up the five classes of righteous men specified in answer to the question asked at Ps 14:1.

51–69 52 *indulgences*: (intimations of) mercy from God, with perhaps an 'anti-pun' on the sense of 'formal papal pardon' (which would then be too late). **52–4** *ʒe...His... here*: a shift from direct address (echoing B 59) to impersonal generalisation that is more awkward than in **B**. *ful petyt*: only a slight remission of time in purgatory (cf. A 59). **56** *wit*: a surprising substitution for the expected *erthe*, ascribed 'to the frequent association of the five wits with the four elements' by *Bn* (with whom *Pe* agrees, suggesting *kynde witt* Pr 141 as the referent). But these 'wits' are the senses, not 'intellect(ual) knowledge', the argument here being rather that 'Human intelligence is a gift of God, like three at least of the four elements [*sc.* excluding *earth*, which was *not* owned in common], and is therefore free for all men to profit by. Just as we should afford the free use of [these] to all men, so should we give...advice and...counsel *even* to those who cannot afford...it' (*Sk*). This bold treatment of the faculty *wit* as an 'elemental' akin to a 'common' *tresor* enables a case by analogy for making its *fruits* ('knowledge') freely available to all. And if this notion of '*wit* got from others' (including an attorney's arguments in a law-court) as more than purely personal *catel* (cf. B 13.151) seems quixotic, the modern democratic institution of legal aid for the indigent shows it to have been prophetic. **B 53–4** *in commune*: recalling HC's teaching at 1.20. *Trupes tresores*: cf. C 10. 183. **A 57** *for prallis*: 'to be at our service'. **Z 67** *mercedem*: perhaps intended to recall *merces* at 47 (Alf*Q*). **Z**'s greater closeness to its source is a non-scribal feature supporting authenticity. **57** *alle...nedede*: cf. 1.21; 'necessary things' for 'common use' are (in modern terminology) a 'human right' (in **C** *alle* is more generous than **B**'s *trewe*). **B 59a** 'All things (therefore) whatsoever you would that men should do to you, do you also to them' (Mt 7:12). Christianity's 'Golden Rule' (cited again at 16.307) has special relevance for *legistris* because it was seen by canonists as the basis of natural law (Gratian *CIC* 1:1, cit. Alf*Q*). **55** *symonye*: since God's common gifts are akin to the religious goods ('of grace'). The revision removes the anacoluthon in B 53–6. **58–60** echo **8** in rounding off the list of those in the pardon and stressing again that honest labourers have nothing to fear and everything to hope for. **60** *Pardoun perpetuel*: cf. 8; the change from **ZAB** *absolucion* may be to exclude misunderstanding of a *pardon*, an 'indulgence' outside the strict bounds of the sacrament of penance, to which absolution pertained. **61–9** The passage on genuine and false beggars allows in a mixed class just this side of the 'wasters' (who are excluded). Their position is suggested by Z 69 ('Unless they are included on the reverse of the document, on the outside, separately)', the thought of which anticipates 14.144. **62** *sugestioun*: they are guilty of *suggestio falsi* (see AlfG). **63** *begeth or biddeth*: the distinction is not clear (*or* may = *vel* not *aut*). **B 67** *wiþ*: 'along with, like' (*MES* 419). **69** 'Take heed whom you give [alms] to' (*DC*, Pr., sent. 17). Baer (2001:131) cites from Hazelton 1956:10 a C13th commentary on *DC* that glosses these words 'et retribue affectionis illius dignis…quia…"qui *dat* mimis et *histrionibus* sacrificat demoniis"' (the text quoted in abbreviated form at 7.118*a*).

B 71–85 are omitted in **C**, signifying a hardening of attitude towards beggars; but the new passage on the deserving poor (70ff) is by way of compensation. **71** *Clerc of þe Stories*: Peter Comestor (d. 1179), whose *Historia Scholastica*, the major medieval authority on Biblical history, re-tells the sacred narratives with comments and patristic allegorical interpretations (on Peter see Daly 1957, Sherwood-Smith 2000). **73*a*** 'Let your alms remain in your hand until you have taken pains to find out whom you should give to'; not from Comestor but varying a proverb '*Desudet* eleemosyna in manu tua, donec invenias *iustum*, cui des' common in penitential texts (Gray 1986[1]:59). It is linked (Scase 1989:198n112) with the Cato quotation in Peter the Cantor's *Verbum Abbreviatum* (*PL* 205:150), perhaps misremembered here (AlfQ). This important passage, cut in **C** but for line 70, adduces in quasi-scholastic form (*Ac*) an opposing patristic authority, clarifies the issue by analysis ending in a scriptural quotation (76–81*a*) and draws a practical conclusion (*Forthi*) clinched by another patristic text. **74** *Gregory*: see on 5.146. **75*a*** 'Do not choose (for yourself) whom to take mercy upon, for it may be that you will pass over someone who deserves to receive (your alms); for it is not certain for which (act) you may please God more [*sc.* giving to the unworthy or the deserving].' This is not from Gregory as stated (*Sk*) but from Jerome's Commentary on Eccl. 11:6 (a text of which *Bn* notes the relevance to Piers in the present context): 'Ne eligas cui *bene facias*... Incertum est *enim quod opus* magis placeat Deo' (*PL* 23:1103). **78** *yarketh…reste*: 'prepares a place of rest for himself [*sc.* in heaven]'. **80** *beggeres borwen*…: cf. Ps 36:21, which contrasts the sinner who borrows with the merciful just man who gives. **81** *Bn* aptly cites Prov 19:17. **81*a*** 'And why then didst thou not give my money into the bank [*mensam*], that at my coming I might have

exacted it with usury [*sc.* interest]?' (Lk 19:23; cf. B 6.237–45). *Bn* finds that 'its application appears to rest on the interpretation of *mensa* as the table from which charity is dispensed, and is hardly congruous with that of 6.2[37]ff'. But **L**'s discretely idiosyncratic use of the parable suggests both that money is better given to beggars than to *nobody*, since it is thereby 'invested on behalf of God' who will repay with interest, and implies that the penalty for *not* doing so will be grave. **82** *Forthi* …: a conclusion not following logically from the injunction to the givers, but standing in parallel with it: all should give to all who ask; but not all *should* ask. *gret nede*: i.e. total destitution; a phrase taken up at C 67, 161 and illustrated at B 20.20=C 22.20. **83** *Book*: 'Bible' (though the source here is patristic), anticipating 86, where the quotation *is* scriptural; the revision eliminates this oversight. **84*a*** 'He is rich enough who does not lack bread'; from Jerome, Ep. 125 (*PL* 23:1085). A parallel possible source is I Tim 6:8 (*Bn*; also relevant are vss.18–190). **85** 'Let the practice of reading saints' lives be your source of comfort'. *LA* describes early desert hermits living *Withoute borwynge or beggynge bote of God one* (17.8; *Bn*); but omission of this idealistic exhortation reflects the increased realism in **C**.

70–161 There follows, introduced by a line retained from **B**, the first part of **C**'s longest insertion. Though retarding the episode's progress and (taken with the removal of the Tearing) lessening the drama still further, it is remarkable for 'unsentimental compassion and raw truth' (Pearsall 1988:180; see also Shepherd 1983:175). This passage on people who are truly destitute and those who feign to be, and then the second on 'lollares' and false hermits (187–279), are quasi-digressions. The short one they replace (B 74–86*a*, debating whether to give alms to all who ask) was added to the diatribe against false beggars in the summary of Truth's letter at ZA 44–5. Only the first is integrated into the Pardon narrative resumed at 166, and what mainly links them is the idea that something worthy in itself may be rendered suspect by a corrupt simulacrum. Thus, against both the genuinely needy who do their best to live honestly and the 'lunatic lollars' (neither of whom beg) are opposed the false beggars and hermits who are capable of work but ask alms deceitfully. **L**'s animus may suggest that his earlier attacks on the latter had struck home, perhaps even drawn a hostile personal reaction.

71–97 deal with households whose poverty arises from losing the bread-winner or having many mouths to feed. **71** 'But if we consider the matter carefully, it is the most needy who are our neighbours'; a conception drawn from Christ's parable of the Good Samaritan (Lk 10:30–6) answering the question 'Who is my neighbour?' and one destined to play a large part in the definition of charity at 19.48–79. **72** Cf. 4.123 on these places as objects of spiritual 'pilgrimage'. *puttes*: see on B 5.406. *pore*…

cotes: landless cottage-tenants and (to judge from 83) widows (*Pe*), whose earnings come only from whatever poorly-paid work they can do at home. **74** *hous-hyre*: rent due because they have no husbands who can work for the chief lord and so get a cottage to live in free. **75–6** *to...with*: 'for making porridge with which to satisfy'; the twofold use of phrasal *with* before the direct object of *maken* is noteworthy. **79** *reuel*: from OF *ruelle* 'lane', the narrow space for the cradle between bed and wall. **81** *rusches to pylie*: to make rush-lights from the pith by dipping it in tallow (the candles of the poor), for their own use and for sale. **82** *ryme*: either a reference (the only recorded one) to alliterative or 'head-rhymed' verse as *ryme* or, simply, 'verse as opposed to prose' (MED s.v. *rime* n. (c) and (b)). **84** *And...of*: 'And the woe of...'; a comma would be better after *cotes* 83. **87** *at* (1): 'from'. *hym*; *here*: typical alternation of sg. and pl. *noon*; *eue*: i.e. at both daily meals. **89** 'What other things are needed by the man [*hym* understood] who...' **91** *And...perto*: 'And many to reach for [what he earns]...' **92–3** *as for*; *as*: 'as if it were'. *ytake / bake*: end-rhyme lending a formula-like feel. **94** *ferthing-worth*: 'more than 12 quarts; a sufficient quantity' (*Sk*). **95** *were*: 'would be [if they could get it]'. **96** 'This would indeed be a worthwhile form of alms-giving'. **L**'s proposal for 'social benefits' places poor families and the disabled before the religious orders, the traditional recipients of alms.

98–104 form an introductory flourish on feigned beggars, to be developed in 139–58. *Ac beggares...they... he...suche*: 'But as for beggars...(except for those who are...), if one of them...even if that sort die of hunger'. The tortuous syntax leaves unclear whether those in 99 are among the pub-haunters. **98** *with bagges*: in which they hide away food beyond what they need to live (cf. 139). *þe whiche...churches*: 'whose churches are the taverns'; a grammatical construction that 'fuses' *þe whiche* '(for) who(m)' (functioning as an ethic dative) and *here* 'their'. Frequenting taverns is insistently linked with failure in religious duties (cf. Gluttton at 6.417 above). **101** *lorélles*: with wrenched stress providing the third *r* stave. **103** *lymes...*: as they denied at 8.135 above. *lollares lyf*: for detailed discussion of *lollare* see Scase 1989:149–60, Wittig 2001:175–80. **104** *Goddes lawe*: see Ex 20:9, and cf. Gen 3:17b. *lore*: cf. II Thess 3:10.

105–27a *opere beggares*: mentally disabled, and so not to blame for not working, *lollares* but not *lorelles*. **108** 'And become more or less deranged with the phases of the moon'. **109** recalls Patience's characterisation of Charity at B 13.161–2 and the Dreamer's at B 18.1–2. **110** *moneyles*: a word occurring only once again, at 295. **111** *will*: the pointed (pre)-echoes noted suggesting a pun on this word. *witteles*: cf. again 15.1. **112** *Peter*; *Poul*: referring to their missionary journeys. **115–17** argue (as about the rich at 16.19–21) that the all-powerful God's

allowing something suggests that he has a purpose for it. **118** *Hit aren*: see on 5.59. **119** *sent hem*: both verb and pronoun have duplex reference ('he sent [the apostles]'; 'he sends [these mad people]'). *seluerles*: cf. Lk 9:3. *somer garnement*: deduced from Christ's injunction not to take two coats (Lk 9:3). **120** *Withoute bagge*: cf. Lk 10:4a. **120a** 'When I sent you without bread or scrip'; running together Lk 22:35, *Quando misi vos sine sacculo, et pera* and Lk 9:3, *Nihil tuleritis...neque peram, neque panem, neque pecuniam* 'Take...neither scrip, nor bread, nor money'. **121** *Barfot*: cf. *watschoed* 20.1. **123a** '[And] salute no man by the way' (Lk 10:4b). **124** *Matheu*: possibly misrecalling Lk 10:5 'Into whatsoever house [*domum*] you enter' (Alf*Q*). **125a** '[Deal thy bread to the hungry and] bring the needy and the harbourless [*vagos* 'wanderers'] into thy house' (Is 58:7); the bracketed text is quoted at 11.67a. **127a** '[Let no man deceive himself]. If any man [among you] seem to be wise [in this world], let him become [*fiat* for *fiet*] a fool, that he may be wise' (I Cor 3:18).

128–38 describe the duty of the rich to welcome genuine minstrels, if only for the sake of their noble patrons (cf. 7.96ff above), and compare the 'lunatic lollars' to them (at 137 repeating 107 entire) and the minstrels' patron to God. **134** *ȝut rather*: 'all the more readily'. **138** If they have sinned, God knows the truth of the matter; it is not man's concern. This undisclosed divine awareness is metaphorically represented by a royal letter under the privy seal granting a privilege or exemption.

139–61 bitingly characterise the way of life of vagabonds who are commonly confused with the previous class by being called 'lollars', though neither sick nor feeble-minded but deliberately idle. **140** *lollarne...*: 'of lollars and (of) ignorant hermits, (who...)'; on the archaic gen. pl. see at 4.14. **149** *sode mete*: 'cooked food' or perhaps 'boiled meat' (MED s.v. n. 2d; cf. Z 7.316). **154** *a begyneld wyse*: 'in the manner of a beggar'; found only in **L**, though the *AW* (MED s.v.) has *beggild*. The original sense may have been 'beggarwoman' (from *beg-* + the female suffix *-ild*) but neither here nor at 10.266 does it have feminine reference. There is no evidence that the Netherlandish order of *Beguines* which OED s.v. connects the word with were familiar in England at this period. **155** 'And knows any trade, should he wish to put it to use'. **157** *han*: either the verb without following indefinite art., or the latter with intruded aspirate. **158** *Goddes lawe*: see on 104. **159–61** The 'conclusion' by Piers lends authority to the narratorial condemnation (lollars must reform, beggars be truly needy). **160a** recalls the opening of the 'Beggars sequence' at 61 and the lines provide a juncture with the 12-line section on their tricks and vices retained from **B**. *Sk* ascribes 162–279 to Piers, so that his diatribe against negligent clergy prompts the priest's intervention at 280. But although this passage seems like a digression, when punctuated as here the intervention seems appropriate by way of response to 159–61; and it is not easy to read 163–65 as coming from Piers. **160b** *til...amended*: bringing out the ploughman's moral authority in determining who should be 'in' the pardon.

162–74 An attack that ends with a new line 'deleting' false beggars from entitlement to pardon and benefit from the common prayer of the Church. **L** dislikes them for serving Truth's enemy False and harming the prospects of the virtuous poor who depend on *trewe* men's charity to live, whether widows or contemplatives (or marginal clerks like himself?) **162** *banneth*: presumably because begging implies a lack of faith in God's goodness. **162a** 'I have been young, and now am old: and [**B**] I have not seen the just forsaken, nor his seed seeking bread' (Ps 36:25). Donaldson 1982 speculates implausibly that *derelictum* can be read as the noun, making the line satiric ('I have never seen a just derelict…'). *And elsewhere*: 'My strength is weakened through poverty' (Ps 30:11b). Both psalms are impassioned expressions of trust in Providence under trial and adversity. **163–5** are somewhat digressive and repetitive. **163** *preche*: so as to 'gloss' the scriptural text, which does not explicitly 'ban' begging. **164** *this*: a generalising quasi-definite use of the demonstrative (*MES* 174), not a reference to the folk present. **168** *of kynde*: 'by nature'; beggar-children, begotten out of wedlock like animals, are here held to inherit a bent to idleness, which becomes habitual following the abuse they suffer from their parents. **B 90 (Z 78, A 74)** is excised as perhaps unsuitably low-comic in the context (*wehee* is used in *CT* I 4066 of a horse running after wild mares). **169** *of here children*: making explicit what is awkwardly expressed in **B**'s sudden shift from pl. to sg. **170** *faiten*: by pretending that their children were born disabled. **171** L's lack of sympathy for them arises from believing their disabilities to be self-caused (though this can hardly be true of the children). So austerely integralist a view of the family unit has an OT feel; but his divided attitude to the issue is suggested by Wit's argument at 10.236–47a.

175–86 This new form of the **ZAB** lines, expanded with a five-line parenthesis (178–82), ends with a macaronic containing the Latin that the Passus began with. But this *is* the end (however abrupt) of **Z**; and the Tearing scene added in **A** and retained in **B**, complicating the issue but rounded off with a musing epilogue on dreams and pardons, was plainly intended to give the *Visio* a conclusion at once more dramatic and more elegant. In **C** much more is to follow, beginning with lines on groups earlier omitted: the old; pregnant women whose inability to work makes the family poorer; those who have suffered misfortunes of natural or human origin. The passage makes its key idea a virtue that is to play a major rôle in the *Vita* because it earns divine mercy and complete pardon. *Patience*, especially as 'humble acceptance of suffering',

is seen as the product of true faith and therefore suffices (*sola fides sufficit*) to purge the soul of all remaining debt (cf. Pearsall 1988:181). Forming the passive counterpart to P.'s active work for his fellows in the Christian commonwealth, it is here found equally efficacious for salvation (in Z 90 even more so). A source for this notion that bodily distress meekly endured is spiritually purgative may be I Pet 4:1–2: 'for he that hath suffered in the flesh hath ceased from sins: That now he may live the rest of his time in the flesh, not after the desires of men but according to the will of God'.

187–279 The second major addition to Passus IX deals with 'false hermits', another category of *faitours* to be distinguished from a virtuous (at best, exemplary) group, the contemplative solitaries entirely devoted to *penaunce and pouerte* (B 15.270). The opening argument ('And alle holy eremytes...') follows the same procedure as at 128ff ('And alle manere munstrals...') and specifies this class of 'lollers' as *lewede ermytes* (192). **187** *holy eremites*: the successors of the *holy fadres* like Antony and Giles (B 15.272). **188–93** The sentence is not really incomplete (*Pe*), though the notion that 'they will not receive the pardon' is merely implied. For while it has two parallel subjects (*ermytes...thise lollares*), it is not anacoluthic. Punctuated (as is possible) with a comma after *Coueyten* 193, that verb may also be judged to have two parallel *objects* (*Al þat; þe contrarye*); but the latter is perhaps better explained 'as an adverbial phrase, with the force of "contrariwise"'(*Sk*). **188** *heye weye*: where the many who pass offer good prospects of alms; the model hermits by contrast *Woneden in wildernesse* (B 15.273), their solitude guaranteeing their sincerity. **193** *coterelles*: the *ouer-land strikares* who slink back to their *cotes* (151), misleadingly resembling the honest poor at 97. **196** *wonede whilom*: cf. 17.28. *lyons*: perhaps alluding to St Jerome, who is depicted in his cave with a tame lion at his feet; hermits with docile bears are not recorded. **197–202** stress the essence of the hermits' life as voluntary renunciation: they were not of low but high social class, *chose* poverty and either had income or worked to support themselves without imposing on others. **201** *were*: '(who) were' (Ø-relative). **203** *edifien*: glossed by MED s.v. 4(a) 'strengthen spiritually or morally', but this seems unlikely, since the point is that they *live* here (and construct their hermitages on the main road); so (as noted in Jones 1997:72n8) the sense will be 'build' (s.v. 1(a)), with an ironic 'anti-pun' on 'edify'. **205** *clerkes withouten grace*: perhaps like Will as he presents himself in Pr 3. **206** *Helden...hous*: for the phrase cf. B 15.142. **208** The sly implication is not that all friars are deceivers (cf. 8.73) but that, since those who deceive in friars' garb do well out of it, many *must* be. **210** *copes*: cf. Pr 54. **211** *oen of som ordre*: 'an individual belonging to some order or other'; read in the light of B 13.285, perhaps suggesting a (real or pretended) survivor of one of the obscurer orders suppressed in the C14th, though he is in fact its only 'member'. *profete*: 'used satirically' indeed (*Pe*), though a reference to Mt 7:15 seems out of place in this context. They are too *lewed* to set up as teachers, but not to ape the outward mannerisms of OT prophets (strange dress, behaviour and utterances) so as to impose on *lewed* hearers. **212** *þe lawe*: i.e. of the Church, though part of the meaning may be that feigned hermits in good health should do manual work as the Statute of Labourers required (cf. 245). *yf...trewe*: 'if (this) Latin (authority) is to be trusted'; a formulaic phrase (cf. 3.487). **212a** 'It is not permitted that we should make the law fit our wishes, but we should make our wishes fit the law'; untraced, but 'similar statements appear in Pseudo-Chrysostom's Commentary on Mt 23 and Innocent III's *De contemptu mundi* 2.4' (Alf*Q*), and the quotation is connected by Scase (214n59) with St Benedict's admonition against false hermits. **213–18** An ingenious deduction of the *lollares*' character from their name (or, proof of its aptness to their nature). **213** *Kyndeliche*: 'quite rightly', but also 'according to what they really are'. **214** *Engelysch...techynge*: implying that the verb, from which the noun indeed comes (MED s.v. *lollen* v.), was long familiar. But since **L** traces the sense 'loll about, move unnaturally' to the *fact* of lameness, *lollen* at **218** is not likely to allude punningly to Wycliffe's followers (as given by MED under 3 (b) 'to carry on as a Lollard' and as taken by *Pe* and also, with further speculations, by Kerby-Fulton 1999:523–4). The earliest use of *loller* with the referent 'Lollard' is *CT* II 1173, 1177, of the form *lollard* a 1395 close roll of Richard II (MED s.v. *Lollard* n. (a)). So despite suggestive contextual references to belief and law in 218, **L**'s insistence on the etymology (about which, in the light of his comment on *hethene* and *heeth* at B 15.458, he is unlikely to be wrong) and the strictness of the comparison (217a) indicate the correct meaning to be 'They lounge about idly in defiance of Christian doctrine and discipline' (cf. 104).

219–39 describe the civil and religious observance that the Church ordains for all members of society according to their estate. The best-known scriptural source for the doctrine of civil 'obedience' is Rom 13:1–6. **221** *religious*: perhaps not in its narrower sense but also including secular clergy who, being under formal obedience to their ordinary, have a 'rule' of life if not a Rule. **223–6** Cf. 5.65–6, 8.28–31. *fox...wolues*: their abundance in the woods and uplands making hunting a necessity and forming a main part of lords' perceived function in the rural economy. **227** *cese*: from both work and sport; it was obligatory to hear Mass on Sunday. **228** *mete*: the midday meal (dinner). **231** *haly...holly*: the emphatic chime stressing how Sundays and other feast-days were to be hallowed by attending all three services. **234** *Pouerte*:

allowing that the poor might find these observances difficult because of the pressure to work for basic needs. *trauayles*: those on necessary journeys might find themselves far from a church. **236–8** *this...dedly synne*: strictly only missing Mass on Sunday or a main feast-day; but regular non-attendance at the other Sunday services and breach of the fasting regulations ('this') were regarded as failure to fulfil the 3rd Commandment (Ex 20:8–11) and so potentially grave. **239** *acounted*: at the particular Judgement; cf. Pr 126–7.

240–54 This fine satire makes the serious point that such 'hermits' use their supposedly devotional manner of life as a cover for avoiding their basic religious duties. On hermits see Swanson 1989:271–3, Clay 1914: chs. 1–6 passim, Davis 1985. **240–1** *where*; *Yf*: 'whether'. *fer*: the assumption being that proper hermits would, if not ordained themselves, live in a community with a priest or near a church. **245** *þe lawe*: the Statute of Labourers. **246–7** *hem...he*: a switch from the collective to one typical individual. **246** *Y*: perhaps only representative, but the loss of normal narratorial distance heightens the sense of a digressive insertion. **247** *Come*: 'coming' (to dinner at some household); the form may be inf. or p.p. **248** 'He would have to be nothing less than an eminent divine or a venerable priest'. **249** *cloth*: russet; possibly his habit as a former friar. **250** *furste*: as an honoured guest like the *maister* of 15.39. **252** *syde...table*: cf. 14.139; this suggests that he may be an ex-friar, though never so distinguished as he now wishes to seem. **253** *wyn*: cf. 6.159–61 for the normal fare of professed religious and 15.66 for what they could get at a knight's table. **254** *blanked*: perhaps with the same sense as at Z 3.159, to fit with the white bread (both items implying 'the best quality'). **255–6** The accusation is like that of *vnsitting soffraunce* levelled at the king in 3.207. These *sottes* are not allowed to preach like the pardoner at Pr 78, but presumably stricter discipline is needed that would forbid them to go on wearing their habits. **257–8** *Simon...Vigilare*: 'It's as if the bishops were asleep; better wake up!' *Simon*: Simon Peter was regarded as the first bishop of Rome and (at least in high papal theory) his successors the popes as the immediate source of episcopal authority, which they delegated to the ordinary or territorial bishop. The quotation alludes to Christ's question in the Garden of Gethsemane: *Et ait Petro*: Simon, dormis? *non potuisti una hora vigilare?* 'And he saith to Peter: *Simon, sleepest thou? Couldst thou not watch one hour?*' (Mk 14:37). *charge*: a responsibility deriving from Christ's 'charge' or mandate (MED s.v. 7(a), first ex.) to Peter, 'Feed my sheep' (Jn 21:15–17), re-iterated in the Apostle's own injunction to priests to 'feed the flock of God' (I Pet 5:1–4) and 'watch' (*vigilate* 8). **259** *wakere*: ironically it is the wolves not the shepherds who 'keep watch'. *ben wroken*: 'have forced their way'; see *TN* on this apparently unique instance of the sense. **260** *berkeres*: allegorically, the parish clergy, who aid the bishops in their pastoral task. *as*: 'as if they were blind'. **261** '[I will strike the shepherd], and the sheep shall be dispersed' (Mk 14:27, quoting Zach 13:7). The NT reference is to the scattering of the disciples after Christ's death, the OT to the dispersion of the faithful remnant of Israel, a passage of Messianic intent. *þe dogge*: alluding to Is 56:10, quoted at B 10.287a. **262** *tarre*: mixed with lard for use against sheep-mange. The 'healing ointment' the people require for spiritual well-being is sound guidance in confession and good example from their pastors. **263** The best they can hope for however is that the archdeacon's summoner will, if bribed, stay proceedings against them over an offence (such as adultery) for which they have been summoned to the Church court; an invective against the desire for 'filthy lucre' (I Pet 5:2) corrupting the penitential system. *supersedeas*: see on 2.187. **264** *shabbede*: recalling A 8.17 (Kerby-Fulton 1999:524). *shyt wolle*: 'befouls the wool'; in the light of 266b the apparent contextual sense, although lexically the phrase ought to mean 'defecates (the) wool [of the sheep he has eaten]' (see *TN*). This 'has no literal sense' (*Pe*) unless the notion is that 'the proximity of evil clergy causes the laity to be spiritually defiled'. **264a** 'Under weak shepherds, the wolf befouls the wool, / The unprotected flock is torn by him'; *cacat* is glossed 'foedat' in Migne (= *fouleth* 266). The elegiac couplet is in Alan of Lille's *Liber Parabolarum* (*PL* 210:581), a work quoted at 20.452–3, and was a widely known proverbial saying (Whiting S241; Walther 30541; and cf. *CT* VI 101–2). **265** *herde*: i.e. the bishop. **266** *worye*: normally applied to the wolf; cf. 226. **268** *falsliche*: in a wrongful and deceptive manner (so the fleeces remain soiled). If *Pe* rightly interprets sheep-washing (on the basis of patristic commentary on Cant 4:2) as symbolising 'the purification of the soul of the faithful in the love of Christ', this protest will be against the compromising of sacramental penance by clergy whose bad confessional practice imperils the souls of the faithful. **269** *thy lord*: Christ, 'the prince of pastors', at the Last Judgement; the crucial source-text here is I Pet 5:2–4. **270** *moneye*: alluding to the large incomes of bishops, the purpose of which was in theory to further their pastoral work. **271** *weye*: implying that so many sheep will have perished that there will not be much wool. **272** 'Give an account of thy stewardship: [for now thou canst be steward no longer' (Lk 16:2); a text preached on by Thomas Wimbledon at Paul's Cross in 1388. Citing this parable is not just a warning but a threat: unworthy prelates will be punished in the next life, and may be dispossessed in this. **273–6** 'Your income, I believe, won't suffice to pay what you owe in that place where neither money nor mercy will avail you, but only "take this in return for the time *you* showed clemency for cash and broke my law"'. *lawe*: 'strict judgement by [the

divine] law'. **277** *lacchesse*: a variety of sloth manifested by those 'newe shepherdes that leten hir sheep wityngly go renne to the wolf that is in the breres' (*CT* X 720). **279** This tart warning reaches a dramatic end and skilfully returns to the *pardon*, which had slid into the background at 188. The digression has in principle been heard only by the outer, not the inner audience; but in provoking the priest's response, it in a manner accounts for (the otherwise unmotivated) *iangelede* at 292.

(ii) 280–91 *Piers's Quarrel with the Priest* The important **A** *continuation* (89–100) from where **Z** broke off is kept entire and little changed in **B**, but cut by about two thirds in **C**. **280** *a prest*: a type-figure, inevitably suggesting the local parish priest, who had official authority to examine and pronounce on a pardon received by one of his parishioners. **82** The contents have clearly been communicated to the folk (e.g. the merchants at 41, who are entered in the margin with 'many years' after them); but their details and the lawyers' were in the private letter, and the present document with its two-line text is the Pardon itself. **283** alliterates either as standard on *b* with stress shifted to the proclitic particles or (reading more naturally) as Type Ie with counterpoint (*aab / ab*). *Y*: a graphic reminder of the narrating persona as eye-witness of (but not, as in **A**, participant in) events at this crucial point. **284** This memorable line is quoted at *MS* 655 (changing *two* to *three*). **285** *in...Treuthe*: 'as Truth's own testimony'; therefore needing no further authorisation. **286–7** '[And] those who have done well shall go into eternal life; but those who (have done) evil (will go) into eternal fire'. Clause 40 of the Athanasian Creed ends a passage (vss. 31ff) on the Last Judgement that includes under 'doing well' the corporal works of mercy mentioned at 71–97 (see Mt 25:34–40). As a direct citation from a major Creed of the Church, the lines re-inforce HC's teaching at I 129–33, which is itself grounded on Scripture (cf. Mt 25:34, 41). The credal clause grafts a modified form of the phrases *supplicium aeternum* and *vitam aeternam* (Mt 25:46) onto a clause derived from Jn 5:29: '...procedent *qui bona fecerunt, in resurrectionem vitae; qui vero mala egerunt, in resurrecionem iudicii*'. **288** *Peter*: not an address to the ploughman (cf. *Peres* 280, *Perkyn* B 131) but the saint's name used in an asseveration (see on 7.181). *no pardoun*: in the document considered as a (formal) pardon or any (actual) 'pardon' in the wording of its text, which the priest now translates and expands. **289** The scansion of this (Type III) line is awkward in deferring the first lift until *haue*. The words echo exhortations to turn from evil and learn to do good in Ps 33:15 ('Diverte *a malo, et fac bonum*') and Is 1:16–17 ('Quiescete *agere perverse*, Discite *benefacere*'). Their eschatological resonance recalls II Cor 5:10 on how before the *tribunal Christi* 'the judgement seat of Christ' everyone will receive 'according as he has done, whether good or evil [*sive bonum, sive* *malum*]'. *haue thy soule*: cf. 'The Lord will redeem the souls of his servants' (Ps 33:23). **291** *euele shal ende*: an improvement on **B** in referring to both the wrong-doer's last moments and his final destiny; cf.'The death of the wicked is very evil' (Ps 33:22).

B 115–38a (A 101–25a) Apart from some small revisions (e.g. of the obscure verbs in A 107 and the provocative quotation in A 123), **A**'s mysterious and compelling continuation of the (presumably complete) **Z** Version is unchanged in **B** but excised in **C**, for reasons that must remain speculative. **115** *pure tene*: used again of P.'s other powerful and unexpected action at B 16.86 (removed in **C**). Earlier interpretations are surveyed by Frank 1957:28–9, who interprets P.'s tearing (1951:317–31) as symbolising acceptance of the content of Truth's conditional 'pardon' and rejection of the need for or value of formal paper pardons. P.'s action 'does not imply a rejection of the message from Truth' but shows that the pardon's efficacy 'is not dependent on...a piece of paper' but is conditional on the way one lives (*K–F*). The scene has generated diverse and conflicting views. Woolf 1969 sees the pardon as a quasi-legal document that only becomes a true pardon after P. has torn it. Schroeder 1970 ([=Carruthers 1973:70), like Frank and *K–F*, does not think P. rejects the pardon, and interestingly compares the tearing with Moses' angry breaking of the tablets of the Law: 'iratusque valde [= *in pure tene*]...tabulas...confregit' (Ex 32:19), an act seen in patristic exegesis as typologically signifying the change from the old law to the new (ibid. 71). Baker 1984[1] finds the pardon's emphasis on good works shown to be inadequate later in the poem by comparison with documents such as those of Patience, Peace and Christ. The theology is examined in subtle detail by Baker 1980, Adams 1983 and Simpson 1990:71–88; and for recent discussion see Lawler 2000. **116–17** '[For] though I should walk in the midst of the shadow of death, I will fear no evils: for thou art with me' (Ps 22:4). The Latin (part-quoted again at B 12.291 apropos Trajan and good works) will scan as two alliterative lines of Types III and I respectively. Vs 6 of this great psalm of comfort ('And thy *mercy* will follow me all the days of my life') is also closely relevant to P.'s situation. For while the psalm-text refers to 'mercies' shown in this life and not the next, *pardon perpetuel* (9.60) may signify a guarantee of unceasing grace to the faithful *in via* attempting to live in *treuthe*. **118** *cessen*: not permanently (cf. *so* 118, 119) but in order to leave more time for prayer and penance. Receiving Truth's message arouses urgent realisation that 'doing good / well' goes beyond fulfilling one's 'active' social duties (8.110–11); and awareness of the limitless demand of charity sharpens one's sense of the need for immediate attention to *preieres and penaunce*. These may be here equated with the Pardon's *bona opera* (*Bn*), though in this period prayer was normally contrasted

with 'acts' such as the corporal works of mercy described in the vss preceding Mt 25:46, on which the Pardon text is based. This injunction to active love of one's neighbour, which constitutes the *second* of the two 'great commandments', P. is fully aware of (8.218–19). But now he will give first place to the spiritual 'work' that providing for the community's (and his own) bodily needs has prevented him from doing, so as better to fulfil the *first* great commandment, to love God (cf. 124a below). **119** *bely ioye*: replacing *bélyue* and altered in turn in the revision of A 112 at B 126b. **120** *plouʒ*: like the pike-staff of penance at 6.328, an emblem of 'active effort' (in the ascetic life). **121** *wepen*: prayer in the penitential spirit of the dominant psalm-influenced tradition, which was authorised by Jesus' own practice (Heb 5:7) and, since the time of St Bernard, directed principally to meditation on the passion of Christ. There may be a clerkly 'visual' pun on the sense '(spiritual) weapon' against temptation (cf. 21.219). **122** *payn*: the chime on pen*aunce* inevitably suggesting a homophonic pun on the senses 'bread' and 'penitential suffering' (MED s.v. *peine* n. 2a; for similar wordplay, cf. B 14.314). The figurative sense of *eet* will then be 'fed inwardly upon, drew spiritual sustenance from' (MED s.v. *eten* v. 3b Fig. (a)). **124** *esy*: a revision that removes the polysemy of *mete* A which, while uncertain both textually and lexically (see *TN*), is perhaps too much after *payn* (though *mete* itself is re-used at B 129). **124a** 'My tears have been my bread day and night' (Ps 41:4). **125** *Luc lye*: the evangelist's veridicity is repeated at A 10.120, a line dropped in revision. *Be fooles*: i.e. to be 'fools for Christ's sake' (I Cor 4:10) but wise in the sight of God (I Cor 3:19), because free from desire for *worldes blisse*. Lk 10:21 echoes the Pauline contrast in setting the *parvuli* against the *sapientes* as receivers of the secrets of God's kingdom. The uneducated Piers numbers himself with the 'little ones' amongst those who receive the pardon. **127** 'Be not solicitous [for your life, what you shall eat...]' (Lk 12:22); on medieval discussions of the text see Frank 1957:31–33, Scase 1989:61–4. Alf*Q* relates P.'s decision to Phil 4:6 *Nihil sollicitiʒ sitis*, which advises reliance on prayer. The text's citation by Patience at B 14.34a directly recalls this scene. **129–30** are based on Lk 12:24. *foweles*: cf. as an emblem of *lowe libbyng men* the lark at B 12.264=C 14.187. **132** *lettred a litel*: reminiscent of the phrase *simpliciter litterati* applied by the Cistercian William of Rimington *c.* 1385 to those with a smattering of Latin whom the Lollards led astray (Aston in Hudson & Wilks 1987:311). The priest's gibe seems provoked by P.'s reliance on what he hears as a tag-phrase picked up from listening to such people. **133** P.'s answer uses homophonic word-play on *abbesse / a.b.c.* to suggest through phonetic identity a real ('Platonic') relation between the rudimentary education / Christian understanding of the *simplices* and the virtue of ascetic self-control (see further Simpson 1986³:51; Schmidt 1987:86–7; Tarvers 1988:137–41). **134** Conscience teaches, as it were, at the grammar-school of the soul. On conscience as a 'book', cf. the description of a Cistercian lay-brother, 'simplex et illiteratus', who had 'pro codice, conscientiam' and yet grew spiritually by reading 'in libro experientiae' (Kirk 1988:17). **136** *diuinour*: 'theologian' in all its four appearances; but perhaps here punning offensively on '(idle) soothsayer' (MED s.v. 1). *Dixit* …: 'The fool hath said [in his heart: There is no God]' (Ps 13:1). The Priest, as well as criticising what he takes to be the Ploughman's 'foolishness' in attempting to expound Scripture, alludes to Piers's injunction to *be* a 'fool', without grasping its spiritual sense. **A 123** 'Because I have not known learning, [I will enter into the powers of the Lord: O Lord, I will be mindful of thy justice alone]' (Ps 70:15–16). The Priest's use of this quotation, mockingly inverting the Psalmist's faith in divine support against his enemies, is replaced in **B** by an equally strong but less subtle insult. **137** *Lewed lorel*: showing that P. has understood the sarcasm and replies even more directly by calling his critic (in the vernacular) a spiritual ignoramus. *litel*: smartly taking up the priest's own word at 132. **138** *Salomons sawes*: the Book of Proverbs. **138a** 'Cast out the scoffers, lest with them quarrels abound' [Vg: 'and...quarrels and reproaches shall cease'] (Prov 22:10). The verse occurs immediately after the one quoted by P.'s teacher Conscience at B 3.335a = C 3.486a.

292–6 292 *iangelede*: now somewhat out of place without the quarrel as in **AB**. **293** *thorw here wordes*: the noisy exchange that wakes Will being part of the 'realism' of dream-vision poetry (cf. the clamorous birdsong in Chaucer's *Parlement of Foules* 693–4). **294** *southe*: a detail indicating the dream's length; 'it is almost noon' (*Bn*), six hours from the first dream's 'inner time' of dawn (Pr 14) to the present 'outer time' of waking. This, too, 'realistically' corresponds to the time it would take to read out the two visions' 3000+ lines. **295–6** *Meteles... meteles*: the near-homonymy yielding a wryly 'Platonic' suggestion that dreamers may go hungry, to be later realised at 22.3.

(iii) *Epilogue* **297–351 297–301** form a transition between the end of the vision and the semi-ironic coda on the validity of dreams (302–16) and indulgences (324–45). These two sections are linked by a 7-line passage (317–23), beginning with *meteles* and ending with *pardoun*, that bases its authority for preferring *dowel* to the latter upon the former. Its significance is underlined by *concatenatio* and its being linked to 296 by running alliteration and to 298 by translinear alliteration. The syntax is somewhat elusive, for while in 299 *fol pencyf* could be the second object of *maked* 297, the two noun clauses of 300–1 cannot be further such objects, and so must be read as dependent on *studie* 'reflect deeply about what /

how.' **298** *so be*: 'describe what is really the case' rather than 'turn out prophetic'. **299** *pencyf in herte*: although the gloss 'thoughtful' (MED s.v. *pensif* adj. (c) may be accepted here, the collocation with *herte* in quots. under (a) 'sorrowful' suggests an intended association with love-melancholy. This is confirmed by the tone of Will's later *love-dreem* after hearing Piers's name at B 16.18ff (a passage drastically revised in **C**, which replaces P. with *Liberum Arbitrium*). **301** *two propre wordes*: presumably *Dixit insipiens* B 136; ironically ambiguous, since these words 'pertain to himself' as well as being 'appropriate' and 'goodly' (MED s.v. *propre* adj. 1(a), 3(a), 4(a)). But in **C** the referent is not these but the two pieces of 'construing' at 289–90, *wordes* there meaning 'utterances' (MED s.v. *word* n. 2a (a)).

302–16 302, 304 *Ac*: the import of this *pro* / *contra* quasi-scholastic formulation being 'Now...but on the other hand'. **303** *Caton*: standing for 'common-sense worldly judgement'; see on 4.17. *canonistres*: perhaps adduced here as exemplifying a clarity and certainty of interpretation at variance with the vagueness and ambiguity of dreams (Macrobius I. iii. 10). **AB 135 /151** quote the passage: Somnia ne cures, [*nam mens humana quod optans / Dum vigilat sperat, per somnum cernit ad ipsum* 'Disregard dreams, because the human mind / Sees sleeping what awake it hopes to find' (*DC* II.31). **A 135** *by hemseluen*: '(that) in their judgement'. **304** *Ac...bereth*: the syntax is strictly anacoluthic (as also in **AB**); but if *for* is taken in the formulaic manner suggested at 302, the sentence can be read: 'but on the other hand, the Bible testifies...' **305** *Danyel...dremes*: cf. Dan chs. 2–4; for discussion see Schmidt 2000:5–8. **306** *Nabugodonasor*: King of Babylon (6th c. BC). **C** corrects **AB**'s misattribution of a prophecy (139ff/155ff) directed not to Nebuchadnezzar but to Belshazzar, his successor and reputed son (the sg. at 307 would be more correct). *Bn* wonders if the change may be due in part to the 'implications for Richard II that might have been read into it'; but in the mid-1380s the threat to the King was less from 'uncouth knights' than from his own 'lower lords'. **B 155** *þi dremels*: confusing Daniel's explanation of Nebuchadnezzar's dreams (Dan 2, 4) with his interpretation to Belshazzar of the writing on the wall (Dan 5:23–8). **B 156–7** *vnkouþe knyʒtes... lower*: the Medes under Darius, 'lower' because not of the royal house of Babylon. **308–16** are a loose re-telling of Gen 37:1–11. **308–9** *mone...sterres*: despite the def. art., denoting no particular stars (Gen 37:9), but symbolising Joseph's mother, father and eleven brothers (315–16). **310** *iuged*: an interpretation not in the Bible, though **L** may have thought that Gen 37:11 ('his father considered the thing [*sc.* dream] with himself') implied Jacob's belief in Joseph's dream as a true prophecy. **311–12** describe their coming to Egypt to look for corn during a famine (Gen 42–5); it is actually Joseph who foretells the famine (to

Pharaoh: Gen 41:15–37). **315–16** replace the repetition in **B** of 165a at 167a but neatly repeat 312b at 315b with changed word-order and tense. Otherwise the lines alliterate vocalically on non-lexical words in a clumsy way reminiscent of the possibly draft lines at Pr 112–13. **316** *Israel*: 'he strives with God', the name (see *TN*) that God gave Jacob after he wrestled with the angel.

317–45 again follow a 'semi-scholastic' procedure (see on 302), beginning at 324 with *3ut* '(Now it is) nonetheless (the case that...)', leading up to *Ac* 330 'However (on the other hand...)' and concluding with *Forthy* 332 'Therefore...' and *At* '(For) at' 338. This pattern is repeated in little within 321–3 ('*For...So..*'). **317** deliberately echoes 297 by way of summary. *Al this*: 'these Biblical examples and my own dreams.' **318** *And how*: governed by a verb implied in *studie*, 'And (reflect) on how the Priest asserted that "doing well" doesn't constitute a pardon'. The ironic sense 'that no pardon could be compared with "doing well"' is phantasmally evoked as a phrasal anti-pun (cf. the syntactical ambiguity of 319). *Dowel*: the first occurrence of a 'nominal verb-phrase' that is to provide a thematic structuring principle for the rest of the poem. **A 151–3** The leisurely 151–2 are dispensable; but 153 (with the cleric's *pure reson* counterweighing the Ploughman's *pure tene* at A 101) may have been removed as seeming to support the Priest, whereas **BC** *preuede* 'claimed [to find by experience of such things]' is fittingly ambivalent. **319** *demede*: with implied subject *I*; for though in principle in **AB** the Priest could be its subject and *indulgences* that of *passede* (an ambiguity allowed by the looseness of B 172), *For* C 321 removes any doubt that *Dowel* is the intended subject and governs all four objects. **320** *Bionales...*: legacies spent on such services that might have been better used (while the man was alive) in active 'doing well', thus obviating the need for them after his death (cf. 348–9 below). *lettres*: metonymic for the benefit to someone who supports the cause they promote (if the sense is as at B 5.640). **321** *dome*: again alluding to Mt 25:31–46 (see on 286–7). **323** *pardon and*: 'the pardon to be got from'. *Rome*: in // **B** 'the indulgence attached to visiting the basilica', i.e. *Seint Petres cherche* (*Bn*). **324** *hath þe Pope*: normal inversion after an adverb, not (as in *Ka*) a question. **325** *withouten penaunce*: if ironic, then hard to interpret precisely. There is no real contradiction between this and 328, as mistakenly judged in *Sch²*, which too closely associates 'pardon...with penance and prayer'. For the three categories are separate and distinct means of earning salvation (as might be brought out by punctuating with commas after each). 'L's view of indulgences' may then be read as 'orthodox enough' (*Bn*) if the sense of 324–5 is that 'a papal plenary indulgence [for some appropriate act of satisfaction] *is* able to save someone from purgatorial punishment [*penaunce*], if validly received [i.e. with

prior formal penance]'. Nonetheless, the mere survival from **A** to **C** of a phrase that risks misunderstanding and the exaggerated tone of 329 (which anticipates the friar at 10.31) may imply some reservations about the 'high' interpretation of the Pope's *plenitudo potestatis* derived from Christ's words to Peter quoted below. **326** *lettrede men...lawe*: theologians and canonists alike. **326a** '[And I will give to thee the keys of the kingdom of heaven. And] whatsoever thou shalt bind upon earth, it shall be bound also in heaven: [and whatsoever thou shalt loose upon earth it shall be loosed also in heaven' (Mt 16:19). The final bracketed part of this verse is the basis of the doctrine of canonical remission of punishment after death. **327** *so*: both 'therefore' and 'that is how'. **329** *Soules... dedly*: such a situation as when a dying sinner is absolved and through a major charitable benefaction receives a plenary indulgence for the temporal punishment he cannot now perform. **L** doubtless understands such apparent 'purchase' of pardon as an *in extremis* case (if by no means purely hypothetical) illustrating the 'mammon of iniquity' principle: that 'it is never too late to do well by yourself through doing well by others' (the point being to *do well*). **330–1** *to truste...so syker*: because active charity not only bespeaks an individual's humility, it benefits others, whereas this form of delegated piety does not. **333** *vp...tresor*: warning against the wrong inference that a virtuous use of money is a licence to sin in other ways. The word is resonant of its earlier charged occurrences, notably at 1.201–2. **335** Unless *nameliche* is a misreading for *manliche* (see *TN*) this line will require *maistres* to be trisyllabic and the pattern to be Type IIIa. **338, 341** *dede; dede*: the homophonic punning echo seeming to hint that what will matter to the dead at doomsday is what they did when alive (cf. *deth, dede* at 350–1 below). **338–9** *dome...acountes*: an image echoing that of Pr 126–7 and helping to draw together the *Visio*'s beginning and conclusion in a single eschatological perspective. **341** *day be day*: the judgement taking account not only of the end but of the course of each person's life, but concerning 'what' rather than 'how much' (342–3 scornfully dismiss the notion of quantity). **342** *provinciales lettres*: issued by the head of a religious order in a particular 'province' (e.g. England) and enabling lay people to participate in the spiritual benefits of its professed members, such as a mention in prayers for all members at Mass (cf. Wright *Pol. Songs* i. 256, ii. 21). The original idea behind religious confraternity was to share in the spiritual ideals of the order; but what **L** attacks here is a 'covetous' treating of salvation as a matter of *mede* rather than *treuthe* (as will become clear from Friar Flatterer's offer to Contrition at 22.366–7 below). **343** *fyue ordres*: the fifth order, first mentioned (*pace Sk*) in **B** not **C**, may be (as *Sk* thought) the Crutched Friars (*Fratres Cruciferi*, so named from the white cross emblazoned on their black habit), a non-mendicant order especially concerned with pilgrims and hospices. **342–5** The sentence is anacoluthic in all versions, but the sentiment is never in question: without good deeds, all the pardons in the world will prove worthless. This is not to condemn pardons as such, but a particular attitude of mind **L** seems to believe that they foster. **346–51** The convoluted concluding sentence encapsulates a prayer within an admonition and makes the object of the prayer the outcome of taking the counsel offered. **347–8** *And... That*: the verb *crye* is again to be understood after the first and before the second conjunction. **350–1** *deth...dede*: see on 338, 341. *reherce*: 'may be able to declare'.

Passus X (B VIII–IX, A IX–X)

PASSUS TEN initiates a Third Vision that in **C** fills the five passūs to XIV (XII in **B**, including an inner dream occupying most of XI) and at 1330 lines (1450 in **B**) forms the longest of the eight. Although the rubric ending IX is not securely authorial, the archetypal **C** *explicit* and **A** *incipit* both indicate a new start: this is the 'same' Dreamer's vision of the 'life' of doing well, better and best, beginning with the first of these. 'Life' here is at once 'life-story' (as of the saints in *LA*) and 'way or manner of life', both being explored through the Dreamer's search for a person 'Dowel' who lives it and is eventually to be identified as Piers / Christ. This is accomplished through the lively and often impassioned arguments of Will with type-figures and personified abstractions. The passus falls into three main parts. (i) a kind of 'prelude' to the dream describing an encounter with two Franciscan friars (1–60), is at 50 lines the longest waking-sequence after the 'autobiographical' episode (though unlike 5.1–108 it can be read as 'realistic' narrative). It is linked by a brief 'pastoral' reprise (61–7) of 1–5 to (ii), ll. 68–112, which consists of a calmer dialogue with THOUGHT. (iii) 128–311 is preceded by a short transition (113–27) where Thought introduces the Dreamer to WIT. The latter's discourse opens at a point corresponding to where A X / B IX began.

(i) 1–29 1–5 echo the Pr with references to clothing and summer (perhaps a symbol of Will's youth) during which his conviction (9.350–1) that Dowel is necessary for salvation drives his quest to 'give flesh' to this idea. **1** *russet*: the rough homespun worn by shepherds (the *shroudes* of Pr 2) and by the Minorites (called 'grey' friars after their garb of undyed wool), but also having associations with the Lollards (Hudson 1988:74–6,146–7). **3** *fraynede*: allegorically signifying his search for guidance; having seen Truth's pardon, he will try to find how to obey its injunction. **6–7** Will's rôle as 'representative man' is seen in the way his experience parallels that of the Folk in their quest

for St Truth at 7.157. *lasse ne more*: 'of whatever rank'; Will looks 'high and low' for Dowel. **8** *Friday*: a fasting-day (cf. 6.351), an apt time to meet mendicant religious vowed to ascetic self-denial. *two*: friars travelled in pairs (cf. B 12.19). **9** Franciscan theologians were amongst the greatest of the age, successive generations including Bonaventure (d. 1274), Duns Scotus (d.1308) and William of Ockham (d. 1347). On the Friars Minor in the 14th c. see Courtenay 1987:66–9, 185–90, 193–218. **11** *preyde hem*: echoing the request of the Folk to the Palmer at 7.169. **13** *frendes*: an initial attitude in keeping with his garb, which is like theirs; but Clopper 1997 overstates the case in thinking of the poet as a former Franciscan addressing a Minorite audience. **15** *courtes*: 'aristocratic households', like the one where Peace will say he met Friar Flatterer (22.345). **16** *cotes*: reflecting the Franciscans' mission to bring the Gospel to the urban poor. **17** *Do-euele*: a personified vernacular equivalent, never to recur, of the negative half of the Pardon formula *qui vero mala [egerunt]* (9.287). Will hopes they will be able to tell him what to avoid (as Piers told the Folk at 7.218–28). **18** *frere(s)*: the change from *Menours* works to widen the claim (which, while strong, need not be exclusive as Will takes it) to all friars instead of one order. **19** *hope*: the degree of unconscious arrogance in the claim depending on whether this ambiguous word is understood as 'believe' or 'hope'. **20** *Contra*: aggressive-sounding (at least in **C**, given the tone of 22b), but the normal abbreviated way ('contra dico') of stating the opposed position in a scholastic disputation (on the importance of this mode in **L** see Baker 1984). The procedure is preserved in *ST*'s standard formula *Sed contra* 'but on the other side of the question'. Like *ergo* at 28, this is its first appearance in a vernacular text, and it imparts a uniquely 'clerkish' tone to **L**'s writing. *despute*: 'argue the case', not implying quarrelsomeness; Will's interchange with the friars, his first real 'act' in the poem, differs from Piers's angry 'apposing' of the Priest after the latter had insultingly quoted a psalm-text at him (see B 7.136). His citation of authority follows the academic mode where controversial matters could be debated with calm courtesy, and it suggests that the *mony men* of 5 may be meant to include his teachers at the university or a religious *studium*. **21–9** Will's argument takes the form of a foreshortened syllogism: a major premiss of two propositions, the first assertoric (the scriptural dictum 21–4, treated as equivalent to a statement of fact) and the second (also bi-partite) apodictic (*whoso...euele*, necessarily true); a minor premiss (*Dowel...togederes*, again apodictic) linked by a copula; and a balancing two-part conclusion (*Ergo...freres* and its apodictic consequent *He...peple*). **21** *Sothly*: answering the friar at 18, with the force of 'It is a true proposition that....' *Septies...*: '[For] a just man shall fall seven times [and shall rise again: but the wicked shall fall down into evil]' (Prov 24:16). Will's opportunistic use of the first part of the verse is so like that for which Conscience rebukes Meed at 3.487 (after she has quoted from Prov 22:9b a commendation without the warning immediately following it) as to invite a cautious response to his challenge. The thought of the quoted verse is paralleled in Eccl 7:21, which omits mention of rising after sin, and 8:12, which warns against complacency, the greater pessimism of both passages according with the import of Will's truncated citation from Proverbs. **25–6** improve on the rhythm of **B** and the sense of **A**, deftly shifting the accent from the second to the first of the two words in the phrase. **25** The fourth lift is on *nat*. **26** spells out the meaning of 'not-well'. **27** Cf. 'But for to mowen don yvel ...ne mai nat ben referrid to good' (*Boece* IV. pr. ii. 247–9). **29** scans as Type I on *w* or as Type II on vowels.

30–60 'show', through an illustrative exemplum characteristic of the *ars praedicandi*, a more effective answer to Will than would be the purely analytical *distinctio* between senses of 'do well' and 'do evil' in a formal scholastic *responsum*. Clearly and memorably expounded so as to appeal to senses and emotions, the *forbisene* well illustrates the homiletic power of the mendicants. It is indebted to Augustine's Sermo 75, ch. iii (*PL* 5:247–9) on the account of Christ's stilling of the sea in Mt 14:24–33, which allegorises Peter's boat as the Church, the storm as temptation and the contrary wind as the devil who is trying to stop the disciples reaching the peace of heaven. *Pe* notes a Wycliffite sermon on Mt 24 (Arnold, iii. 375) attacking friars who apply the 'boat' image to themselves as the select vessel of salvation (cf. I Pet 3:20–1). **L**'s Minors refrain from doing so; but while not proving their contention that Dowel dwells with them, they demonstrate that occasional failures need not invalidate the claim they do make (18–19). *Pe* denounces their contention as 'a manifest falsehood'; but the friar's exposition takes full account of the text on which Will bases his argument, though quoting only the part that suits him. However, while he is neither presumptuous nor disingenuous (where Will is both), his subtle argument against *wanhope* fails adequately to recognise the need to avoid lesser offences and to see how the connectedness of venial to mortal can make of complacency the first step to presumption (these traits mark all the poem's friar-confessors at their worst). **33–5** *Lat bryng...*: a similitude that has something of the effect of a *distinctio* in that it accepts Will's major premiss (21–6), distinguishes between mortal sins and the venial sins of the just man so as to invalidate his minor premiss, and shows his conclusion not to follow. The result is to leave the friars' claim at 18–19 unrefuted (for an unusually positive reading of the friars see Strong 2003:255–75). *man...boet...water / water...bote...man*: the skilful inversion acting as a rhetorical substitute for the scholastic procedure of enumer-

ating and defining the key 'terms' of an argument. **36–43** correspond to **B** 45–50 // **A** 40–6 which, in describing the man's movements within the boat as necessary to prevent it capsizing (at 33–7 //), make sin appear inescapable, rather too promptly invoking a notion that Haukyn will find so 'hard' at B 14.322–3. **C** clarifies by assigning the boat a new meaning and arguing instead that to fall *within* the boat (= use the Church's sacrament of penance instead of despairing of God's mercy) preserves the just man. For his good works (*Dowel*) prevent him from falling *out* of the 'church' of charity that, as at 7.256–7, figures the state of grace (in // 35/30 the *stere*, like the pikestaff earlier, symbolises sacramental penance). The *rihtful mannes fallynge* (38, 41) is thereby distinguished from that of the *unrihtful* who forsakes the Church's ministry, and his good deeds (including his recourse to confession) are credited with power to protect him against mortal sin. Thus by the 'so' of *analogy* (38, 41), the friar arrives at the 'so' of *consequence* (43) and refutes Will's pessimistic contention that the just man 'falls out of joy' (52). **44–50** take up the earlier versions' understanding of 'the boat' as *oure body*, but now with the wider meaning of 'the conditions of our earthly existence'. They thus adapt **AB**'s conventional triad of man's three enemies, the world, the flesh and the devil, but blunt their sharp dichotomy between 'body' and 'soul' (or 'flesh'). **48–50** *That...lyf*: 'And so as a consequence, even the saint inevitably sins often during this life'. **B** 51 softens the bleak fatalism of **A** 47 with a phrase (*suffre...sleupe*) that indicates less 'laxism' (a mistaken emphasis of the Everyman *Commentary*'s note *ad loc*) than the notion of sin being (as in Julian of Norwich) *behovely* 'necessary / beneficial' (*Showings*, ch. 27) and divine sufferance as unfathomable. This idea is later developed in B 14.322–3 (lines removed in **C**) and is implicit in Ymaginatif's words at B 12.277–8=C 14.202–4, which need to be read alongside 21. **51–5** state that free will is given so that man can turn to sacramental penance during this life, where there is no evading sin. **C** is more optimistic than **B**, which in elaborating **A**'s brief reference to moral autonomy (*maistrie*) only increases the prospect of failure and the severity of punishment. **51** *foleweth*: cited as the only example of the sense 'urges' in MED s.v. *folwen* v. 5(e); but it could mean 'accompany' (ibid. 3(a)), with *To* 52 as elliptical for '(enabling him) to'. For while omitting **AB**'s negative view of freedom, **C** does not imply that freedom always and only prescribes *virtuous* action. *fre wit*: an obscure phrase possibly intended as a vernacular equivalent of *liberum arbitrium* 'rational free choice' (Schmidt 1968:168–9). The contrast between animals' unerring instinct as a kind of 'reason' to be contrasted with fallen man's frequently irrational behaviour is developed at B 11.34–49=C 13.143–6. **54** *rest...restitue*: 'Platonic' wordplay suggesting a connection between divine justice and peace of soul. **55** *lyf...lycames gultes*: not signifying 'sins of the flesh' as such; rather, that death is the price all men pay for the original sin of Adam *oure alle fader*. **56a–7b** are virually made up from 1.136. *kynde knowyng*: 'direct, immediate understanding'; though subtle, the argument has not been recondite, and the ambiguity of *bettere*, which is either adv. or adj. as noun, allows some value to the Minorite's demonstration that he *knows* where Dowel 'dwells'. **59–60** betray a vacillating attitude to the friars, *me* restoring the politeness of **A** (in one of a very small number of such reprises in **C**) lost with **B**'s mocking shift of the benison to Will. But the persisting ambiguity of *meschaunce* reveals Will as unsatisfied by the argument. **61–7** form a transition between the dispute outside the dream (20) and that within it (114), the added B 63 associating the conventional 'May' elements with the opening motif of *wildernesse* 'spiritual desolation' in B Pr 12 (omitted in **C**). The lines' musicality, ironically recalling the elaborate manner of *WW*, is enhanced by running alliteration (61–2, 65–6, 66–7), assonance (62–3), internal rhyme (63–4) and pararhyme (64–6). **61** directly recalls B Pr 4, more mutedly C Pr 4. **62** *wilde wildernesse*: deliberate derivational paranomasia, comparable to Dante's *selva selvaggia* in *Inf*. I.5 (Calí, 1971:35). Both the Athlone emendations are wide of the mark (see *TN*). **64** The triple chime in this line closely echoes *SS* 8–9: 'in launde vnder lynde me leste to lende / And lenede'. **66** recalls *SS* 15: 'ffor muche murþe of mouþ þe murie moeth made'. **67** brings the 'birds' sequence full circle with the echo-word *blisse*, finally fixing the **A** form still fluid in **B**. *merueilousliche.*: repeating Pr 7 to indicate how this new section is a continuation of the *Visio* (BA 68/59 similarly echo BA Pr 11, though less closely).

(ii) 68–75 68 The scansion requires *me* to be rhetorically stressed; if it is not, a 'compensatory' extra stave may be found in *mysulue*. *muche man*: a mirror image of the dream-narrator, to judge by his self-description at 5.24 and his nickname *Longe Wille* at B 15.152 (removed in **C**). Self-seeing or autoscopy when awake is a known pathological condition, but (rather more interestingly) encountering a personified aspect of oneself as a 'double' has been recognised as a feature of *dream*-experience (Freud 1954:505–6). Without literary parallel, this may be yet another piece of 'dream-vision realism' (Hieatt 1967). **69–70** *kynde...knowest*: the echo of 56a hinting that the encounter within the dream may help Will to *lerne bettere* through looking into his own soul rather than seeking Dowel in the world outside himself. On *kynde name* see the very full account in Middleton 1990. **70–5** The sequence of four questions follows an echoing rhetorical pattern suggesting an internal 'dialogue of one': *that...That*; *knowest...knowe*; *wost...woet*; *Thouhte... Thouht...***71** *Wille*: a revision (like that at 1.5) perhaps presupposing an audience now familiar with *PP*, for in

all three appearances of *Wille* in **B** a personification of the faculty rather than the dreamer's *kynde name* may be signified. However, A 12.89 indicates an earlier intention to name himself unequivocally in the course of the Third Vision. **72** *Thouhte*: the mind as knowing and reasoning power (MED s.v. *thought* n. 3(a)); the vernacular equivalent for *Mens* at 16.183, as it is Chaucer's for Dante's *mente* (*Inf*. II 7–90) in *HF* 2.523 (Schmidt 1969:151n99). **73** *seuen ʒer*: either a vague indefinite period or having reference to the time spent in grammar-school learning how to think (from age seven to fourteen, the normal age for beginning university studies). His challenge amounts to saying: 'You have finished your secondary education; have you not yet learned to reason to some purpose?' **76–106** represent through personification-allegory an internal debate on the nature of Dowel produced directly by Will's reflecting on the data of his experience. **76** Thought's answer, introducing the Dowel-Dobet-Dobest 'Triad' for the first time, concerns more than Will had asked about, as if it were impossible to state a positive value without also conceiving its comparative and superlative degrees. On this section see Kean in Hussey 1969:79–84. **77** *thre fayre vertues*: inescapably hinting at the three theological virtues of Faith, Hope and Charity, though their concrete social reference is uppermost here. **78–81** *Dowel*: described as a sober and upright Christian labourer. The omission of A 71 is an improvement, since his special quality is to be *trewe* 'honest, upright' rather than *mek* 'humble' (a quality usually associated in *PP* with religious). **78** repeats HC's words at 1.84 and again at 80, somewhat weakly varied without enough difference in the sense of the b-phrase. **79** The emphasis on charity clearly evokes the character of Piers (and seems echoed in *CT* I 531–7). **82–92** *Dobet*: signifying both the knightly and mercantile classes (82–7) and the clergy (88–90), though the use of a single pronoun *he* makes insufficiently clear whether the latter are first denoted from 88 or earlier. **84** *helpeth*: the charitable rôle of knights and monks alike. **85–7** may describe a knight's or merchant's use of his own wealth (perhaps dubiously acquired) for productive charitable ends. **86** *Erl Auerous*: cf. 2.90–1; representing the greed and ruthlessness of the aristocracy, which true noblemen are urged to renounce. **87** *Mammona*: possibly a type-name for the acquisitive merchant-class from whom charitable works such as those prescribed in Truth's letter would be appropriate (cf. 9.28–36). The allusion is to Lk 16:9, quoted at 8. 235*a* and 19.248*a*. **88** *religion*: 'the religious life' (MED s.v. n. 1(b), the sense also at 9.221, 22.264 (OED cites this passage under 1(a) 'religious order'). But as **L** is unlikely to be *excluding* the secular clergy, the word may cover all worthy clerks in holy orders (a sense securely attested, however, only in the phrase *man of religioun*, as in *CT* I 477). This would answer *Pe*'s difficulty as to whether being a religious is just one or the only form the life of Dobet can take. *Sk* favours this sense on the basis of Wycliffite attempts 'to extend the meaning...beyond its old narrow limits'. But his citation of *religious* 17.47 as = *men of holy Churche* 'clergy generally' at 17.41 is doubtful; for in the light of 17.35, the latter more probably bears the contextually specific sense 'friars and monks'. *rendred*: 'recited, repeated [the text of]' (MED s.v. *rendren* v. (c)); referring especially to monastic life, which focussed on singing psalms and hearing scriptural readings. But since MED s.v. (d), citing this line as sole evidence, wrongly glosses it 'translated' the possibility of contemporary misreadings cannot be completely ruled out (though OED s.v. *render* vb. 6 shows this sense not found before the 17th c.). **90** '[For] you gladly suffer the foolish; whereas yourselves are wise' (II Cor 11:19). The speaker mistranslates *suffertis* as *sufferte* 'allow', replacing Paul's irony with his own rather than indicating 'Thought's limitations' (*Pe*), though Thought's discourse is, of course, 'limited' in its scope. These *insipientes* correspond to the 'fools' of B 7.125 and of 22.61 who have (like Paul) given up the 'wisdom' of this world for the 'foolishness' of the Gospel, and whom the 'worldly wise' are being recommended to support with their charity. **93–99a** *Dobest*: embodying episcopal authority, with its special responsibility of standing up fearlessly against immoral and lawless nobles. The lines adapt **AB**'s attempt at relating the Triad to the political order, with the supreme secular authority (advised by the bishops) seen as exercising final control over the first and second estates. **C**'s change of their rôle from a political to a purely moral one may reflect an awareness that Archbishop Sudbury (murdered in the Peasants' uprising) had incurred popular enmity not as a churchman but as Richard II's Chancellor, and a judgement that a bishop's freedom to give moral leadership is hampered if he is in the service of the Crown. No immediate contemporary reference can, however, be identified. **93–4** *bere sholde*: the change from an indicative to a modal here and at 98–9 intimates uncertainty as to how likely this hope is to be fulfilled. *crose...halie*: crosier shaped like a shepherd's crook (cf. 9.255–79), symbol of the bishop's function as pastor of souls. **95** *preuaricatores legis*: those who evade the law, especially by means of wealth or position; a phrase common in glosses on Ps 118:119 'I have counted all the sinners of the earth prevaricators [*Praevaricantes*]' (AlfQ). **99** *as God hihte*: all the injunctions of inspired Scriptural writers being ascribed to God indifferently, whoever the immediate author (e.g. St Paul at B 8.94). **99a** 'And fear ye not them that kill the body and are not able to kill the soul' (Mt 10:28); from Christ's warning to his apostles (whose successors the bishops are) to expect persecution for preaching the Gospel. **100–02** are a significant addition stating that Dowel and Dobet (laity and clergy) have formally set up an episcopal order (Dobest)

to rule spiritually and a monarchy to guarantee that rule by force, while acting always in accord with all three orders' judgement and advice. On *demede* 'adjudged' or 'established' see MED s.v. *demen* v. 8(a). **101** *to kull... That...*: 'to put to death lawfully / Those who...'; a sombre stress on the duty of the highest civil authority to punish those who disobey the highest religious authority, perhaps prompted by the excommunications of Lollards in 1382. The death-penalty for heresy was not formally prescribed in England till 1401, but had been accepted in Europe from the end of the 13th c.

108–12 form a transitional passage like that at 56–60, in which Will again asks for a more direct intuitive knowledge of the nature of Dowel and the rest (in **AB**, specifically of how they *act*). But whereas the friars leave, Thought remains, as he is the necessary *mene* (120) in the strenuous mental activity leading to *wit* 'understanding through knowledge' (MED s.v. *wit* n. 2 (c) and 3(a)). **108** *sauereth*: whereas at 56 Will could not *conseyue* 'grasp' the friar's argument, here he 'has no taste for' Thought's. The response reveals a growing 'wilfulness' that builds towards the outburst at 13.179ff below, but for the present he is in control.

113–27 form a second transitional *passage* concluding what was in **AB** effectively a transitional *passus* preparing for a major new one; but in **C**, which tends to eschew disproportionate length or brevity, it introduces the last two-thirds of the same passus. **113** *thre dayes*: an indefinite period (like 'seven years' at 73) or with the Biblical sense of the 'third day' as decisive (cf. I Cor 15:4), so that meeting Wit becomes the climax of a crisis. **114** *Disputyng*: cf. on 20 above. **115** *Wit*: knowledge or understanding derived from reflection on what is experienced, primarily through the *wittes* 'senses', or learned from others in an informal way (the formal way being 'clergy'). A limit on the word's semantic range may be established from its use at 16.187–8 to render *sensus*, 'the understanding of what one is told and the source of every practical art and skill.' **116–18** Wit's appearance is that of a modestly dressed scholar, physically like the Dreamer (whose *wit* he of course is). **119** *iangle*: their *matere* (the nature of Dowel) not being one that will produce a quarrel like that between Piers and the Priest (over the nature of the Pardon) but will be an orderly exchange conducted through the 'medium' of Thought (who disappears as if absorbed into his successor Understanding). **121** The approach is still semi-scholastic (*purpos*; *preuen*), Will testing Wit's powers (in a line added in **B**) by requesting a formal *distinctio* between the three concepts. **122** *What*: 'As to what'. **125** *oen*: the revision removing (presumably) undesired echoes of the semi-proverbial antithesis between Will and Wit ('emotion and reason'; see on Pr 174).

C Passus X 128–311, A Passus X, B Passus IX

(iii) 128–311 Except for one question at 151, Wɪᴛ's 180-line speech is not interrupted by Will (who says nothing to deserve Study's rebuke at the opening of XI). It engages chiefly with the ordinary moral experience of lay-people in the family and society (see Tavormina 1995: 48–109 for a very full analysis of Wit's discourse).

128–58 Wit's starting point is man's situation as a material creature with a spiritual soul, and his traditional image of the Castle recalls the Friar's homiletic procedure in IX. While (as befits the speaker, a married layman) its flavour is secular rather than scriptural, its use in a spiritual allegory was long familiar from such works as *AW* (ed. Tolkien, 185/7). **128** *Sire*: a title relating this figure to Thought's earlier typology, with Dowel as the nobility, Dobest as the episcopate, and suggesting (somewhat awkwardly) that representatives of Dobet (the clergy?) should be descended from 'gentle blood' (a point earlier laboured at 5.63ff). The allegory signifies that Christians should receive elementary instruction in virtue from their natural parents, sacramental teaching from their priest, and wider authoritative guidance through life from their bishop. **129** *Kynde*: a new and arresting 'nature-name' for God the Father (cf. *Treuthe* earlier) in direct response to Will's demand for *a more kynde knowyng* at 109 (see 152–5). In technical language, Kynde represents *natura naturans* 'creating Nature' as contrasted with *natura naturata* 'created Nature' (on 'Kynde as God' see White 1988:60–88). **130** *ayer*: probably not 'air' (=*wynd* 131) but *aether*, the fiery 'upper air' above the earth, here treated as equivalent to the usual fourth element as the source of the body's heat. If the latter is the 'breath of life' of Gen 2:7 (Goodridge), called 'spirit' at 16.196 (cf. Wittig 1972:217n29), then this may be equated with the *aether*. **133** *lemman*: the image of God as a lover wooing the human soul, derived from patristic exegesis of the Song of Songs, was traditional in vernacular devotional writing. The classic chivalricised version in ME, with the soul as a 'lady' besieged by her foes 'inwith an earthen castle' is found in *AW* 198/18–20); see further Woolf 1962. *hymsulue*: because made in God's image and likeness (Gen 1:26, and cf. B 9.33, A 10.35). **134** *Anima*: the immortal Soul in its most comprehensive sense (16.199*a*), but with particular reference later (10.175) to its aspect as life-principle (16.181; see Schmidt 1968²). She is feminine as the 'object of desire' of both God and the Devil, not simply on account of the Latin noun's grammatical gender (for in B 15.23 Anima, the speaker who governs the whole passus, is male). *hath enuye*: not 'covets to possess' (*Pe*) but 'has malice [inspired by envy]', since she enjoys the love he has forfeited. **135** *Fraunce*: traditionally the national enemy; but the hostile

image does not bespeak Gallophobia, it simply evokes the stately pomp of French chivalry (see *Intro.* V § 33). *Princeps.*: 'the prince of this world', traditionally interpreted as signifying the devil (see A 10.62) and so used at 20.349*a*, quoting Jn 12:31 (see also Jn 14.30, 16:11). **136** *wyles*: especially the temptations of 'the world', i.e. *Pruyde of Parfyt Lyuynge* (11.176). **138** *marches*: perhaps specifically 'border territories' (MED s.v. *marche* n (2), 1(a)), a good place for a defensive castle against marauders (on **L**'s acquaintance with the Welsh Marches cf. Breeze 1993²). Man is being thought of as placed near the 'boundary' between two regions (of angel and animal). **140** *þat lady*: royal or at least a royal ward, having a duke's daughter as a handmaid and a bishop as tutor. **143** *constable*: as in the early C13th *Sawles Warde* where Wit, who as 'God's constable' (*SW* 43) corresponds to **L**'s Inwit, has the outer and inner senses ('wits') as his household servants (*SW* 15–23). **144** *Inwit*: a term varying in sense from the general 'mind' or 'the collection of inner faculties' (MED s.v. 1(a), 3(a)) to something identical with 'conscience'. Its neutral sense of 'the rational power generally' (Quirk), in opposition to *outwit* 'outer sense', allowed the possibility that *inwit* could be misused, as at B 13.289. But that meaning is here excluded; for Inwit is *wise* 144. Attempts restrictively to correlate so common a word as *inwit* with a technical term of philosophy such as *synderesis* (Harwood & Smith 1970) are less persuasive in relation to **AB** than to **C** (see on 177, and contrast the possible contextual relationship between the coined phrase *fre wit* and the technical *liberum arbitrium* conjectured at 51). But **L**'s *conscience* may have a more exact meaning, being chosen instead of 'Inwit' to translate *consciencia* at 16.199*a*. **L**'s 'Inwit' is thus perhaps best understood as a non-specific name for the rational power under its practical (moral) rather than theoretical (speculative) aspect, intended by God to guide man's use of his senses (as a father governs his sons). Murtaugh 1978:15 not implausibly detects in **L**'s conception some influence from the Augustinian-Bonaventuran notion of moral understanding as involving direct illumination by God. **145** *sones*: the bodily senses in respect of their 'right uses' (cf. A 10.52–3 below), or as Wittig puts it 'the sensual powers of man precisely as ordered to higher ends while justly supplying the needs of man' (1972:217). In *SW* 43–59 Wit's supports against the devil are not his own sons but four 'daughters of God', here the cardinal virtues. *furste wyue*: 'the flesh in its unfallen state, when the senses were uncorrupted' (*Pe*), 'the old law' (*R–H*; see also Wittig 1972:217–19); it would be vain to ask who the *second* wife was (in *SW* 10 Wit's 'wanton wife' is *Will*). More neutrally, the figure may signify *sensualite* 'the natural capacity for receiving physical sensation' (MED s.v. (a)), described in *The Cloud of Unknowing* as 'a miȝte of oure soule, rechyng & regnyng in þe bodely wittes, þorow þe whiche we haue bodely knowyng & felyng of alle bodely creatures' (118/7). **150** *come or sende*: at the moment of separation from the body, *þe deth of kynde* 20.219. **A 25** This question, omitted in **BC**, is answered at A 38–9=B 49–50 but dropped from **C**, perhaps because of doubt whether *Caro* should be equated with human nature in its entirety or only with the (animated) mortal part (see on B 49). **155** anticipates 20.59, which makes clear that the *payne* is not man's alone but has been shared by the Son of God in *membres and face*. **157–8** allude to the taking of human nature by the Son in Christ, through which man resembles God even more than do the angels. The resemblance was traditionally held to reside in the *gost* of the Man originally created for eternal happiness (A 36–7) and now in the re-born soul of each baptised person who does not forfeit sanctifying grace through mortal sin.

B 32–52 The threefold expansion of **A**'s straightforward account through an elaborate but rather awkward analogy is abandoned in **C** for one simpler and more intelligible. **32***a* '[For] he spoke, and they were made: [he commanded, and they were created]' (Ps 148:5). **A 34** The sense varies according as the stave-words are consonantal or vocalic: scansion on *w* makes the key-stave instrumental *wiþ*, on vowels the article *a* 'one single word' (i.e. *Fiat*). The latter seems preferable, but both are metrically clumsy and the line's omission is understandable since *al þing* repeats not only 31a but 28b. **34** *Eue... bon*: Gen 2:21–2. **35** *For*: an unexpected conjunction if the referent of *he* is God and the intended contrast one between God's 'singleness' and his use of a plural verb. But it is obviously in place if *he* refers to Adam (cf. Gen 2:18), for whom God made *Eue* 34 'because he was all alone by himself'. The same referent will also fit if *synguler* means 'unique [among creatures, through being made in the divine image]' (MED s.v. adj. 3(a), the sense at 6.36). The position of the mid-line pause tells against referring *hymself* to God, but the absence of a pronoun subject for *seide* argues for it: one of the awkwardnesses (another being the small-word staves of 36–7) that may have prompted removal of the whole passage. There is however an odd fitness in the ambiguity, which hints at the need for human plurality to mirror divine trinity. *Faciamus*: 'Let us make'; the opening of either Gen 1:26 'Let us make man to our image and likeness' (quoted in full at A 41*a* and earlier at B 5.487*a*) or of Gen 2:18 'And the Lord God said: It is not good for *man* to be *alone*: let us make him (*faciamus ei*) a help like unto himself', as seems more plausible in the light of 33–4. The *faciamus* phrase invited a 'Trinitarian' reading, as by Bede (*PL* 91:28–9): 'Faciamus, una ostenditur trium personarum operatio' (cf. also Raban Maur in *PL* 107:459), and some influence from the Victorine tradition has been suggested (Szittya 1986[2]). But in context it seems likely that the verb's pl. number (noted by *Sk*) is less important than its

sense, elaborated in 36–7, stressing not 'us' as opposed to 'me' but 'making' as opposed to 'saying' (the merely verbal act that sufficed to create the animals [32*a*]). **37** *wiþ*: here and at 42 meaning 'along with, as well as' not 'by means of' (cf. 51). **38–40** The tortuous analogy illustrates how as well as 'slime of the earth' (= *parchemyn*) from which he fashioned man's body, and his wisdom (*wit* 43), God needed to exert his *myȝt* to create man's immortal *goost*, something expressed 'instrumentally' by *penne* (see Schmidt 1980[3]; and for a different interpretation of the analogy, see Szittya 1986[2]). **41–2** *seide*: its sense repeated by, rather than translating *Dixit*; on the rationale of the reconstruction, which depends on the wider interpretation favoured, see *TN*. **43** 'He had to work actively as well as uttering his word, and thereby manifest his wisdom'. **46–7 (A 36)** *of þe (his) godhede*: 'by dint of his divine power'; *of* does not signify that man is a spark of the divine being but that his spiritual soul is akin to it because 'God is spirit' (Jn 4:24). **A 41***a* As under B 35. **49** *Caro*: 'human nature', 'the body animated by the life-principle', as at B 17.108 (the confusing dichotomy at A 50 is removed in **B**). **C**'s rejection of both lines suggests unease over a word elsewhere connected with disordered desire (11.174); but its neutral use, like that of English 'flesh' (MED s.v. 5a), has Scriptural warrant, as at Jn 1:14 where *caro* denotes the human nature, body and soul, taken by the Word. Hill 2001, citing Biblical, Patristic and medieval sources (and comparing the use at B 18.409), argues convincingly that *caro* is synecdochic for 'humanity'. **52** *myȝt...mageste*: 'his sovereign power'.

159–71 Retaining only B 48, the revision shifts attention from the creation of man in God's image to the marring of that image through sin. The tone is sombre, and in place of the exultant 148th psalm of B 32*a* comes Ps 80 which, though it begins in solemn rejoicing, modulates into solemn warning at vs 12. **162** *sheweth nat*: 'does not favour' / 'reveal (himself) to'; see *TN*. **166** '[So] I let them go according to the desires of their heart: [they shall walk in their own inventions]' (Ps 80:13); see B 66*a*. **168** *goed*: a sardonic pun (cf. 177; for **L**'s complex play on this word see Schmidt 1987:134–8). **170** echoes 152; the *luther* men are rejected for loving created wealth more than the creator. **171** *The which*: defining the creative God (*Kynde*) in Johannine terms as love and eternal life (cf. Jn 10:10, I Jn 4:8). For St John's influence on **L** see Davlin 1996.

172–86 revise and deepen the 'naturalistic' **AB** argument in a 'spiritual' direction, keeping the notion of mental and sensory powers as divine gifts to man (174) but adding the 'infused' virtues of love and trust in God (*leute* here may = faith-and-hope), which provide the supernatural life of the soul. **175** The main sources of **L**'s psychophysiology are the *De Anima* of Cassiodorus (*c.* 540) and the *De Spiritu et Anima* (C12th) of ?Alcher of Clairvaux

(Schmidt 1968²). In B 55–9 // A *Inwit* is 'the rational power' in its practical or moral aspect, the wording of B 59 suggesting however the inner law of 'conscience' in men, which is aided by but precedes the illumination brought by grace. His guidance of Anima can therefore be reconciled with his subordination to the religious authority Dobest (with *lat* B 58 cf. *is lad* B 16). However, the 'high' view of *inwit* in C 177 approaches the scholastic notion of *synderesis* (the soul's intuitive awareness of the first principles of moral action). So *grace* here perhaps signifies the 'actual' or 'prevenient' (as distinct from the sanctifying) grace given through the sacraments, which prompts good action and (it was thought) could exist in the unbaptised, as the Biblical examples show. **A 52–3** Cf. A 19–21. **177, 183** *tresour*: the term harking back to HC's teaching on Truth as the form of wealth that really matters (1.201). The underlying idea is that reason has an 'endowment' of moral intuition, which man can 'misspend' (176) through abuse of another divine gift, 'drink that does you good' (1.24). **178** *lykerous drynke*: repeating 1.25 and recalling HC's warnings at 1.25–40; association of these examples derives from Peter Comestor (Taitt 1976). **179** scans as a Type IIIb with a wrenched stress in the trisyllabic Latin form of the name *Herodés* providing the key-stave. The first stave *dede* alliterates translinearly with preceding *drynke*, the last stave of 178, as does the last stave *daffe* with the first of 180 (*douhter*). *Lote*: see on 1.25–31. *Noe*: on his drunkenness see Gen 9:20–7. *Herodes*: Herod Antipas, tetrarch of Galilee, who had protected the Baptist; inferred from the account of John's beheading in Mk 6:21–8 to have lost his *inwit* through over-drinking. **180–1** The dizzy syntax reflects the king's confused state: properly *bifore...gestes* modifies *daunsynge*, not *3af*. For the Gospel text makes clear that, while the king's rash promise was public (and therefore binding), the head was brought privately to Herodias his wife. *his douhter*: Salome, the daughter of Herod's wife by his brother Philip. **182** *hele*: good health and sound mind envisaged as all anyone could want; for the phrase cf. 5.10. **183** echoes the deleted B 7.54.

B 60–66a attack the morally corrosive effect of drink, repeating somewhat the argument of the Glutton sequence (B 5.366–7), which *glubberes* recalls. **61a** '[For many walk...whose end is destruction]: whose god is their belly; [and whose glory is in their shame...]' (Phil 3:[18]–19). **62** *hir soule*..: cf. B 7.113–4. **63** scans as Type I on *l* or as Type IIIa on *s* (cf. 71). **64a** '[God is charity: and] he that abideth in charity, abideth in God, [and God in him]' (I Jn 4:16). The unquoted end of the verse reminds how the abuse of Inwit can destroy the sanctifying grace that creates a 'church of charity' in the soul (cf. C 7.256–7). **65–6** *fordo...shoop*: because to quench reason in oneself is to unmake God's creation; anticipating the lines on murder at B 17.280–81 // (where Inwit

is again mentioned), as also that of God abandoning the morally abandoned at B 17.249–50a //, which likewise cites the *nescio vos*. **66** scans either vocalically on pronouns, with an exceptionally long prelude-dip of six syllables (including two lexical words) or, with greater ease, as Type IIIa on *s / sh* (cf. C 162). *liknesse*: found in reason, the power of moral judgement and self-control. **66a** 'Amen, I say to you, I know you not' (Mt 25:12). Verse 13 of Mt warns against the sudden arrival of death, which will find the drunkard unprepared for judgement.

184–6 C cuts **B**'s excursus on the decay of communal values and (unusually) looks behind **B** to **A**: 184 = A 58 and 185–6 rewrite A 69–70 rather than B 67–8.

A 58–75, B 67–71 The initial linking of the innocents with 'sots' and the ambiguity of *failiþ* (inwit is wanting in the one, extinguished in the other) make for confusion. But **A** goes on to distinguish quite clearly between the morally incompetent (58–65) and the morally adult (71–5) and between the drunk who fall under the devil's power and the innocents who do not sin even when they cause harm (*wykkide* 65). B 67–71 remove this unclarity but oddly lump together as incapable of rationally determining their lives the mentally defective with three groups of social poor (69 recalls A 8.32–3). Whether or not in response to readers' objections, C 185–6 wisely limit the point, while preserving in *folye* a polysemy free of real ambiguity. **A 66–70** strikingly stress parents' responsibility for their children's anti-social behaviour and the obligation of the community (here, of the Church as its organ) to protect the young from crime and ?sexual expoitation (*folies* A 70 = C 185). **A 75a** echoes the wording of Z Pr 71.

B 72–94a offer a negative exemplum (see 93–4) contrasting the failure in charity of the Christian community's 'spiritual fathers' with the mutual care shown by Jews. C's removal of this angry digression on a lordly and neglectful episcopate does not imply a more indulgent attitude toward the latter after 1381 (as the added C Pr 100–06 bear out), for the moral point is not weakened by concentrating on positive recommendations rather than hostile criticism. **72** re-uses Z 7.230. **73** *witnesses*: 'supporting texts'. *foure doctours*: the four great Western Doctors of the Church, Ambrose, Jerome, Augustine and Gregory. For their importance, see 21.268–74a. **74** *Luc*: Acts 6:1 refers to widows (Goodridge) but the true source (disallowed by alliterative necessity) is 'James the gentle' (1.180) whose injunction to help *faderlese children* and *widewes* (Js 1:27) draws on the precept of Deut 16:11–14 underlying the Jews' own *kyndenesse*. The rôle of *kyndenesse* in fostering unity within the Christian *commune* by economic means is explored in Galloway 1994. **77** An extended Type IIIb line with counterpoint (*abb / aa*) or a cognative Type Ia scanning on *pp / b*. **82–9 L**'s challenging praise of the Jews' solidarity and mutual concern is presumably inspired by reports (unless he had travelled in Europe), for they had been expelled from England in 1290. On **L**'s removal of these lines in **C**, see Narin Van Court, who argues that passages favourable to the Jews are 'revised, reduced, deleted or qualified in the last version' (1996:83). **85** *Iudas felawes*: that the Jewish nation was collectively guilty in perpetuity for the execution of Christ (and therefore condemned to the same fate as Judas) was an inference from Mt 27:25. This common belief, so alien to modern sentiment, accords with earlier OT ideas of racial guilt, the correlative of the Jews' belief in racial election; and the usual medieval understanding of this text seems endorsed by Faith's diatribe in 18.99–109a. **88** scans as Type IIIc (*ab / ab*) with cognative |dʒ| / |ʃ| alliteration. **91–2a** The notion of bishops who patronise low minstrels (rather than give charity to ragged beggars) as 'betrayers' of Christ is sharpened by awareness that Judas was the Apostles' purse-keeper (Jn 13:29), as bishops are keepers of the Christian community's possessions (for the collocation of Judas with 'japers' cf. B Pr 35). **92a** 'A traitor [worthy to be] set with Judas is the prelate who scants in distributing Christ's heritage'; *and in another place*, 'A ruinous giver is he who idly eats up what belongs to Christ's poor'. The Latin uses phrases from two passages traced by *Sk* to Peter the Cantor's *Verbum Abbreviatum*, ch. 47 (*PL* 205:135, 150); not quotations, and either drawn from another untraced source or recomposed (for the phrasing cf. B 15.244–6). **94a** 'The fear of the lord is the beginning of wisdom'; semi-proverbial (Ecclus 1:16, Ps 110:10, Prov 1:7, 9:10).

A **76–130** is (after Passus XII) the longest passage completely abandoned in revision to **B**, with only a little of the opening retained (79–81a) and many good lines never re-used, until **B** resumes with the discussion of marriage at 108ff. It defines the Triad as 'obedience (to the moral law),' 'sufferance', and 'humility', each closely linked with and following on from its predecessor. **76** *a duc*: referring back to A 11 (the image is dropped in the later versions). It actively destroys vice and enables virtue to begin and a parallel to the stages of penitence is unmistakable, with Dowel = confession and Dobet = satisfaction. *Dowel it makiþ*: though grammatically ambiguous, meaning 'fear of God generates (the will to) do-well', a sense in keeping with 80 and 118 as well as the general doctrine of Ecclus ch. 1 that underlies this passage. **78** *routen*: 'settle'; see MED s.v. v. (2) (c). **82** *For doute*: less 'out of fear' than 'as a consequence of fear': the doing-better (as 85 states) consists in awareness of possible (divine) punishment for sin as well as gratitude at having been justly punished for sin. *maister*: do-well being a discipline (Ecclus 1:34) that teaches virtue as well as avoidance of vice. **87** 'Thy rod and thy staff: they have comforted me' (Ps 22:4b); teaching the same lesson. **88–4a** The sense seems to be that if someone has

confessed his sins and is living by his (informed) conscience, he need seek nothing higher. **88** scans as Type IIa with a final cadence *-sélf dó wèl*. **90** 'The value of man's action is judged by his intention', a maxim of canon law cited in the *Summa Aurea* (1253) of the canonist Hostiensis: *Quicquid agant homines, intentio iudicat omnes* 'All men, whatever they may *do*, are judged by their intention' (AlfQ, proposing the reading; see *TN*). **91-4** form the poem's strongest assertion of the religious value of conscience enlightened by the Church's moral teaching. **L**'s omission of them could be linked with his later development of the idea of conscience's sense of right and wrong *possibly* conflicting with the words and judgements (at least of actual members) of the teaching Church, such as the Priest Piers quarrels with or the Doctor of Divinity in XV (B XIII) who angers Will. **94** *Goddis worde*: possibly Heb 10:26–7 (*Sk*); but the ultimate source is more probably St Paul's 'For all that is not of faith (*ex fide*) is sin' (Rom 14:23), where *fides* had long been understood as 'conscience'. *holiwrit*: the revered writings of the great Church Fathers, as distinct from the divinely inspired Biblical text (*Sk*; C 1.25 illustrates this use). **94a** 'The man who acts against (his) conscience is building (himself a house) in hell'; earliest attested in Gratian's *Decretum* (*CIC* 1:1088), and cited in Bromyard's *Summa Praedicantium* (1:130/1) s.v. *conscientia* as a gloss on the same text (AlfQ). Jean de la Rochelle (13th c.) uses this exact form in his *Summa de Vitiis* and Richard of St Victor, in his commentary on the *Song of Songs* (*PL* 196:481), a modified version of it in asserting that sins against conscience are mortal, citing Rom 14:23 (Schmidt 1967:366). The version in Alan of Lille's *Contra Haereticos* II xvi (*PL* 210:391) is not identical but could also be a source (Schmidt 1982:484). **95–102** The advice to *suffre and sit stille* defines Dobet as something to be received, not sought, and its warning against spiritual pride (101–2) echoes Piers's words at A 6.198–106. **98** 'As long as you live an upright life, care nothing for a villain's sneers / [What every fellow says is no concern of ours]' (*DC* III. 3). The line can be scanned as Type IIIa on *v*. **101** *herre*: 'something higher'. **102** *louʒnesse*: 'humility' (cf. 129), with a play on 'lowness' (inevitably 'lost' when one 'climbs'). **103–17** warn generally against restless instability, but in particular amongst those embarked on the religious life. **104** Whereas the common form of the proverb, 'a rolling stone gathers no moss', might argue against fixity in one's way of life, this witty variant argues *for* it in stating that a marble slab fixed in one place and trodden upon will keep its pristine condition. **105–6** Cf. A 11. 211, B 4.120. **107** *clergie*: a third authority added to the secular sages and folk wisdom. **108a** 'He who wanders from craft to craft / Belongs, be sure, to no craft'; learnedly varying the proverbial 'Jack of all trades and master of none'. A close analogue linking *genus* 'kind' with *ordo* 'religious order' is in Higden's *Polychronicon* I: 'Immo nonnulli *omne genus circumeuntes in nullo genere sunt, omnem ordinem attemptantes nullius ordinis sunt*'. Alf*Q* suggests a possible 'grammatical' context for the original (*genus* also = 'gender'); see Alford 1984. **111** *writen*: presumably as an edifying inscription in large letters on a wall. **112** 'Stay in whatever calling you were called to'; adapted from 'Unusquisque *in qua vocatione vocatus est, in ea permaneat*' (I Cor 7:20; see on C 5.43*a*). **115** *To... beryng*: 'so as to win heaven through the way you live [in that calling]'. **118** *to*: 'is to'. **119** *soueraynes*: '(true) elevation to a high rank (in heaven)'. This, the word's first occurrence, is overlooked by MED s.v. *soverainnesse* n. **120*a*** '[Because everyone that exalteth himself shall be humbled: and] he that humbleth himself shall be exalted' (Lk 14:11, 18:14). Wit's advice recalls that of Piers, who cites the preceding verse to the Knight at C 8.44*a*. **121** *his dede*: acts of humble submission to God. **123–8** The metaphor envisaging Dobest as the sweet-smelling flower with rough root and thorny stem, from which the attar of charity will be distilled, is probably indebted to the imagery of *Canticles* (cf. Cant. 4:16, 5:13). **125–6** are recalled at C 13:22–3, 12.179–87. The 'wheat' image is also Biblical in its overtones, evoking the abundant crop growing in the midst of surrounding adversity (Mt 13:24–30). The 'rough, ragged root' image anticipates the walnut figure of 12.146–52. **129–30** assert what is asked for at A 8.182–3a above: humility (*Dobet*) wins grace to perform works of charity (*Dobest*). Wit's doctrine here is identical with Anima's in B 15.168–9 and shows how Will's interlocutors function as partial revealers of a truth that the poet has already grasped as a whole, not one he is fragmentarily aware of and seeking to acquire.

187–203*a* The newly composed account of the Triad takes them as 'living a virtuous life according to moral reason,' 'loving one's enemies' (the distinctive ethical precept of Christianity), and 'making peace between all nations as a basis for spreading the Gospel universally'. **B** is closer to **A**, seeing Dowel as obedience to moral law from fear of God, obedience from love of God, and total contemplative self-dedication to God. **193** *Bishopes*: a new 'heroic' view of bishops as exemplary imitators of Christ the Lord rather than of secular lords. **194** *For to*: overtly (and perhaps with deliberate irony) an infinitive of purpose, 'in order to seek worldly loss and martyrdom by fearlessly preaching the gospel'; but the intended sense must be 'even at the cost of' (no parallel is cited in *MES*). **195** The Synoptics do not specify *thre clothes* (a number *Sk* regards as indefinite), whereas Jn 19:23 implies four garments (excluding the coat) divided between the four soldiers. This detail is indebted to Ludolf of Saxony's *Vita Christi* II.112 (ed. Boland et al., p. 639) and to a patristic tradition that Christ wore three garments before the crucifixion, of scarlet, purple and white (Hill 1978:200).

hit were: see on 5.59. **196** *ruyfled*: (< OF *rifler*), first recorded in **L** and possibly introduced by him (Wilcockson 1983). **197** *for*: 'in order that', but with a secondary sense 'because of' (explaining why Christ was put to death), with *sholde loue* meaning 'if love was to'. *wexe*: 'grow (up) into'; a distant echo of the lost 'rose' figure in **A**. **199** *dere зeres*: 'years of dearth'. Wit's point is that these 'princes' should visit the poorest parts of their dioceses so as to 'cultivate' men's souls, sow the grains of virtues like fortititude (cf. 21.275–6), and enable them to endure their material distress better (cf. the thought at 16.322–7). **200–01** echo B 20.382. *tulie*: cf. B 19.263; on this important trope see Barney 1973. **202** *loueth*; *leueth*: the 'Platonic' pararhyme emphasising the dependence of man's faith on the love God has shown man in Jesus who, though destitute on the cross, was raised to glory. *sterue... clothes*: not literally true, as Christ's death shows. But Wit's paradoxical claim (implicit in Ps 33) may be that 'starving' is the price of the heavenly banquet, or that clerical princes' deprivations must be measured against those of their *Lord Prince Iesu*. Certainly 198 implies that proper use of their wealth would soften the impact of *dere зeres* on the poor. **203*a*** '[The rich have wanted, and have suffered hunger: but] they that seek the Lord shall not be deprived of any good' (Ps 33:11); a warning to prelates (as to priests at B 11.280*a*).

B 95–107*a* The ascetic ideal of **B** is less specifically episcopal than in **C** and seems designed to cover ordinary laymen like Piers (cf. 105). It suggests the monastic régime that, in principle at least, sanctified each hour and left no room for *tynynge of tyme*. **97–8** *wiþdraweþ...To spille*: a use of the 'objective infinitive' in a sense ('from wasting') now expressed by the gerund. **98*a*** 'Who errs in one word is in all ways guilty'. The quotation, adapted *ad hoc* from Js 2:10 to give a Type IIIa line, is quoted again (correctly) at B 11.308*a*=C 13.121*a* (see *TN*). The wider allusion is to Christ's warning in Mt 12:36–7 of the punishment that awaits idle words. **100** With the awkward placing of the adverbial phrase cf. on 180. **101** *spire*: on this image see Shoaf 1987:128–33. **102–4** On the notion of God as the lord of the minstrel, cf. 9.126. Here he is thought of as having given all men speech in order to sing his praises. **102** *game of heuene*: because the blessed will sing praise to God for eternity, and because poetry is a divinely sanctioned form of serious play; see Davlin's illuminating study (1989:59–60, 111–22). **103** *feiþful...fiþele*: a likely 'Platonic' pun, a well-tuned fiddle making 'faithful' sounds, as a well-disciplined tongue speaks true words. B Pr 51–2 finds lying akin to discord in music. **104** *tauernes*: where speech is 'spilled' in oaths and bawdy songs. **105–7** *To...to hem*: pleonasm bordering on anacoluthon: 'God loves all upright men and gives them grace'. *loude ouþer stille*: 'at all times'; taking up the image of the instrument, playing or silent.

204–58 contrast at length *trewe* and *fals* people, Seth's progeny and Cain's, the exemplum of Noah's flood (222–58) incorporating a troubled meditation (236–47*a*) on the issue of whether moral guilt can be inherited. **204–5** cannot be a question as *Sk* takes it (with *so...As* proposing a comparison); *As* must here mean 'such as' (*Pe*). 204a is near to A 132a in wording but the last lift echoes B 108b, while 205 retains B 109b and re-writes B 108a, keeping the line's Type IIIa pattern. This definition of do-well as an outward 'state' (faithful marriage) introduces the topical theme of wrongful sexual relations to which Wit ascribes the disintegration of the social fabric. **206–7** concentrate on the contribution of laypeople in providing saints and clergy, omitting both earlier versions' nobles and churls and their 'naturalistic' OT view of the marriage 'goods' as *proles* and *adiutorium*, the peopling of the earth and the provision of marital support. C also cuts B's excursus on marriage, with its repetitions at 114a, 117a, and the 'paradisal' view of it at 118, the phrasing anticipating B 10.299 and the sentiment to be echoed in *Pur* 701–4 (Schmidt 1988:119–21). **B 117–18** *made...witnesse*: an allusion to Gen 2:18–24 as used at Mt 19:4–6. Since *witnesse* could imply 'present at' (*Sk*), the Marriage at Cana (Jn 2:2) may be intended to be recalled. **207** *maydenes*: i.e. virgin saints. The imagery of added 208–9 foreshadows the great figure of the tree of charity in 18.89–94, with virginity at the top. **208–9** are opportunistically adapted from Mt 7:18 (*Sk*) but vs 16 is also relevant, as that text's earlier and later citations at 2.28–9*a* and 10.247*a* indicate. **209** *sotil sciense*: because even the cleverest gardener cannot get sweet apples from a root-stock that naturally yields sour ones. Wit pessimistically implies that the best education cannot transform someone who is 'base' by heredity. **210** *no more to mene*: scarcely the contextual sense of the source-text's fruits ('deeds', not 'offspring'); but Wit's interpretation reflects one of the poet's strongest prepossessions. **211–12** That those born in wedlock have a 'lawful claim' to the grace by which men 'do well' sounds untypically unkind and also theologically unsound (the illegitimate, if baptized, being no more 'thralls' to sin than anyone else). But it might be charitably understood as presuming that 'unmarried parents are unlikely to baptise their children or teach them the faith' or, more speculatively, that 'the sanctifying grace imparted to Christian parents by the sacrament of marriage indirectly benefits their offspring'. **212** *lele legityme*: 'faithful lawfully-born people'. Wit at least acknowledges that if *all* the illegitimate can never do well, *some* of the legitimate may at times fail to do so. **214** '[Behold he (*sc.* the sinner) hath been in labour with injustice]; he hath conceived (in) sorrow, and brought forth iniquity' (Ps 7:15; Job 15:35, which adds 'and his womb prepareth deceits'; Is 59:4). *Pe* opines that *in dolore* is substituted for Vg *dolorem* (the form in the text

of // **AB**) under the influence of Gen 3:1 '*in sorrow* shalt thou bring forth children'. But the **C** reading is a known variant in both earlier traditions (see *TN*) and the change may be intended to stress the 'dolorous' issue of *careful concepcioun* more than the labour-pains that Gen imports (placing this quotation before the exemplum, however, frees the moral criticism from too close a dependence on the Biblical situation). The immediate context of the psalm-text (vss 14 and 16) could provide the basis for seeing 'lawless' sex as not only consequentially but intrinsically wrong: the 'arrows' of condign punishment for *ardentibus* 'them that burn [the lustful]' are suitably children who (like Cain) will carry on the cycle of wickedness. **215–21** allude to the tradition found in an OT Apocryphal text, the *Vita Adae et Evae* (ME trans. in Blake 1972:109–10), that Cain was conceived and born 'during the period of penitence and fasting to which our first parents were condemned for their breach of obedience' (*Wr*; see further Tavormina 1995: 84n59). Neither **A** nor **B** makes clear that this was why the 'time' was *yuel* or *cursid*. But **C**, though explicit, is not free of ambiguity, for 217a could mean 'without doing proper penance for their rash act [*sc.* of eating the fruit]' or 'without any regret for their rash act [of breaching the penance imposed for eating the fruit]'. What is clear is that the son's villainous character comes from the parents, their defiance of God's prohibition being like that of *sherewes* who couple outside marriage (for whom the *derne dede* is always *yuel*).

A 141–8, 151–6 are, despite a certain rhetorical vigour, rightly dropped in **B** as they are crude in feeling or expression (*wrecchide world*, *Crist / God*), slackly phrased (*se...likiþ* 149 after *whoso...knowen* 133) as well as repetitive and prolix (*Caym* six times, *cursid* four times, *Crist hatid*, *alle þat comen*, *Seþ and his sistir*, *couplide* twice, doublets in *wonen* and *libben*, *conseyuid* and *engendrit*). They are given final form at C 248–56 below; but from amongst the rejected lines 143a is reworked in another context at C 12.208 and 145b used twice at B 17.341//, B 19.218 //. **143** *aungel*: see Gen 3:23–4. **148** *Caym*: see Gen 4:1. **153** *Seth*: miswritten *Seem* at B 124. Adam's third son, born to take the place of 'Abel whom Cain slew' and father of Enos who 'began to call upon the name of the Lord' (Gen 4:25–6), is named in Lk 3:38 as the forefather of Joseph. **155** *alle þat comen*: Cain's descendants, who perished in the Flood (Gen 6–7); but symbolically 'Cain's kin' understood as the wilfully unrighteous in all generations (I Jn 3:12; Jude 11), who would be destroyed by God's anger (*Pe*). The verb here is preterite not present, but in // B 123 both verbs are tense-ambiguous. **157** *sente...aungel*: from Comestor's *HS*, Gen., ch. 31 as told in the C13th *Genesis and Exodus* poem based on it (ll. 517–54), an account going back to the lost Genesis commentary of the C3rd Greek Father Methodius of Olympus; see also Wilson, 1976:88–92.

Augustine in *The City of God* xv. 23 interpreted the sons of God and the daughters of men in Gen 6:2,4 as respectively the offspring of Seth and Cain. **161** *here werkis*: the coupling itself rather than the subsequent evil deeds of the offspring as cause of the divine anger.

219–21 This comparison from common life sees God as lord of the harvest: a feudal tenant (Adam) defiantly sows on a demesne fallow (Eve) and the crop (Cain) is cursed, because forbidden. The idea of the *hewe þat erieth nat* may be derived from Gen 4:12, where God tells Cain that any land *he* tills will be barren; the real-life referent would be a serf with no fields of his own who labours for wages. **220** *So...wreches*: because all illegitimate infants share Cain's curse and are marked out for destruction (Gen 4:11). This judgement, which affronts the modern notion of a child as a separate person with human rights, presumes instead the organic oneness of the family unit. It should be balanced by the assertion at B 78–9 of godparents' responsibility for the individual *litel barn er he þe lawe knowe*, which reflects the same medieval sense of 'collective identity' within the Christian *comune*. But the C doctrine (as at 246–7) is sterner than that of **AB**, which attack the coupling of the vicious and virtuous generations (the cause of the Flood), and make no overt link with the present-day situation.

222–35 describe the punishment of those who wilfully refuse to do well and the saving of an elect group to become the type and forerunner of the Christian Church. **224** '[I will destroy...from man even to beasts...: for] it repenteth me that I have made man [Vg *them*]' (Gen 6:7). The Bible text makes clear (as do 230–1) that the animals are cursed for the sin of man, under whose 'rule' they are (Gen 1:28): the 'subjects' share the lord's guilt as much as do his kin. The line is not translated here as in **AB** but at 255b–56a. **225** is repeated at 11.240, which relates the Ark to the Church and the Flood to the fiery deluge that will destroy the world (11.252). **228–9** *floed...bloed*: the trailed rhyme emphasising how the one is cause of the other, for the curse began when Cain made Abel's blood 'spring' and the pollution of the earth will end only with the 'washing clean' of his own 'blood'. **230** *Bestes...banne*: literally impossible, but symbolically including the humans (cf. the figurative use of *bestes* at 11.251). **235** *schingled ship*: with overlapping oak tiles; a common medieval English type. **236–47a** discuss in quasi-scholastic manner the problem of moral responsibility in the light of Biblical teaching and current legal practice. On the *pro* side is the OT supported by the law of England, on the *contra*, the NT; a *distinctio* resolves the clash of authorities by citing another NT text to elucidate or explain. **236, 238** *Here*; *hereageyn*: 'from this instance'; 'against (the maxim to be educed from) this instance'. **239** '[The soul that sinneth, the same shall die]: the son shall not bear the iniquity of the father, and

[B] the father shall not bear the iniquity of the son' (Ezech 18:20). *Pe* persuasively explains the 'mistake' (*Sk*) of Gospel (so at B 112*a*) by discerning 'a NT flavour' in the text and a prophetic foreshadowing of Christian moral standards in // Jer 31:29–30. Also relevant is Jn 9:1–3, where Christ implicitly endorses Ezechiel in denying that the blind man's physical ailment is due to his parents' sin, and Rom 2:6 which (quoting Prov 24:12b) states that everyone will be treated by God according to his own actions. No Biblical text is cited to support directly what the exemplum implied, but to Ex 20:5 (*Pe*), the rationale of which is explained at 220, may be added Pss 36:28b, 108:13–15, which see one's 'posterity' as one's 'property'. **242** *Westminstre lawe*: the common law administered by the royal courts. *worcheth....contrarye*: 'operates on the opposite principle'. **243–4** The heir to the property of an executed felon was deprived of the right of inheritance on the grounds of 'corruption of the blood', his chattels being escheated (forfeited) to the crown and his lands to his feudal lord. In theory 244 could mean 'It is for the King to decide what, if anything, the heir should be allowed to inherit'; but since felonies were 'unemendable' offences, they did not fall within the King's mercy (though this is how *Pe* takes *at þe Kynges wille*). **243** *thogh...and*: 'even if...if'. **245** *Ac*: 'But, against this' (= *Sed contra*). *glose*: taken (according to *Pe*) as 'a misleading gloss' by Wit, whose 'text-juggling...reveals the limitations of his understanding'. But this reading ignores the specific structure of Wit's argument. For the 'Gospel' authority referred to is not 239 but 247*a* (an actual 'Gospel' text), a *true* 'gloss' or clarification (functioning analogously to a *distinctio*) that enables Wit to explain how Scripture does not contradict itself. **245–7** may be paraphrased: 'The Gospel [which stated that sons should not suffer for their fathers' wrongdoing] provides its own commentary on that text (*ther*). And it veils what is the plain fact of the matter (*huydeth þe grayth treuthe*) under the fruit-tree figure that Christ used when speaking about offspring of this kind: namely that the offspring are always found to resemble the parents in natural disposition'. The unstated part of the argument would presumably run: 'If this text is true (and Scripture is always true if rightly interpreted), then it follows that the son would *not* really be paying for his father's sins but for those he would undoubtedly have gone on to commit himself (as Cain's descendants in the Bible exemplum did)'. **247***a* '[By their fruits you shall know them]. Do men [*Numquid* Vg; here lit. 'Never (do men)'] gather grapes of thorns, or [B] figs of thistles? *And elsewhere*: '[Even so every] good tree bringeth forth good fruit: and the evil tree bringeth forth evil fruit' (Mt 7:16–17). Christ's saying does not really teach hereditarian determinism, because it *infers* the nature of the tree from the fruits it bears (i.e. judges men good or bad by whether they do well or ill). But that is how Wit takes it, and there are no grounds for thinking that he is being criticised for doing so. For although **C**'s stance has hardened (*neuere* C 247 against *selde* B 152), the **B** evidence (*I fynde* 147, *sestow* 152) is that Wit is appealing to common experience.

B 143–52 are abandoned for the more powerful legal example, leaving a residue of their fruit-tree imagery at C 208–9. The lines verge on the bizarre, whether *appul* 149 denotes 'apple' (Tavormina 1995:91n77 remarking that apples were grafted on elders for the sake of colour) or generally 'fruit'. If the former, then marriages for greed are seen as *vnkynde* like those of the Sethites, who were morally a different *species* from the Cainites ('elders' in a 'Platonically' semi-punning sense, as Cain was the elder brother). If the latter, then grafting a superior elder-slip on an inferior stock could never make the tree's fruit sweet (since the elderberry is by nature sour). Either interpretation supports the conclusion that 'it would seem less of a marvel if an evil man produced a child who was not also bad'. The argument, new in **B**, is less nuanced than the issue demands and inferior to what replaces it in **C**. **145** *in o degree*: less likely to be 'in one respect' (Sch, *B-Text Translation*), since the cited scripture does not qualify but deny the traditional OT view, than 'in the same way, in the same degree' (MED s.v. *degre* n. 7(a), under the phrase *in o degre*), i.e. 'The Gospel for its part is correspondingly opposed to that view'. **149** *ellere*: see on I 64, where Judas is the 'cursed' NT antitype of the 'cursed' OT Cain, whose brother Abel was held to be a type of Christ.

A 178–9 have been removed in **B** perhaps as illogical in blaming Cain for the marriage between (as the text says) Seth's children and his sister's children 'against the law of our Lord [i.e. incestuously]'. The sense 'both married *others* [i.e. the Cainites]' rather than 'each other' would be unidiomatic for 179. **L**'s point has already been correctly made at A 151–4, which makes the crime the union of the children of *both* Seth and his sister with the descendants of Cain.

248–58 replace AB 178–85 / 153–9 to explain why the human race was destroyed, and not just Cain's descendants. It is because, when the Sethites intermarried with them, everyone (by a sort of moral Gresham's Law) became corrupted (the main rhetorical stress is on *world* not *why*). The passage therefore warns against 'mixed marriages' between the virtuous and the vicious and makes the object of God's regret his creation not only of man but of marriage (seen in A 134 as 'þe riccheste of reaumes, and þe rote of Dowel'). A and B both directly compare these OT 'adulterations' of good with bad to *vnkynde* contemporary marriages based on parental greed and ambition (153–59/178–85); these lead to the adulterous begetting of bastard children, so that the vicious cycle of social decay goes on and gets stronger (on the 'apoca-

lyptic' overtones of these comparisons cf. Tavormina 1995:90). C defers this application to the powerful new lines 259–72. **249–56** The outer and inner *m*-alliterating lines enclose five interlaced lines on *k, s, s, k, s* that metrically mirror the theme of intermarriage between the families and perhaps hint at the final triumph of the virtuous line (the *s / k* = virtue / vice dichotomy is adumbrated in **AB**). **251** *Seth*: see on A 153 above. *seth*: the 'Platonic' pun hinting that he is so called because conceived *after* Cain. **253** *catel...byheste*: phrases giving the exemplum its topical application, i.e. that neither actual wealth nor the prospect of it (or of the moral reform of the suspect partner) should tempt virtuous parents to give their sons or daughters to *sherewes*. **254** 'Let his offspring beget offspring on his brother Cain's offspring'. **255–6** may be echoed in *Pur* 285: *Me for þynkeȝ ful much þat euer I mon made*. **257** *goode* (2): i.e. any 'goods' except 'goodness'; on this strand of wordplay see Schmidt 1987:136–7. **258** *via..*: 'I am the way, and the truth, [and the life]' (Jn 14:6). *avauncen*: spiritually, in the first place, but implying that those who seek to 'wed' good, not meed, will wed Truth or Kind, to whom Anima belongs (cf. 133–4), and will not want for their worldly needs (see 202–3a, B 178 and cf. Mt 6:33). The term foreshadows the image of Christ as the 'conqueror' of sin who endowed his followers with true nobility (21.31ff).

259–80 energetically expand the diatribe against avaricious marriage-making but keep almost unaltered the memorable seven-line core AB 186–96 / 162–72. The attack, despite affinities with contemporary sermons, is individual in stressing how impecunious gentry degrade themselves by rejecting virtuous, well-bred (and attractive) girls without dowries for rich women of inferior origins. The passage complements the similar complaint on the rise of low-born clerks who bribe their way to the top (5.63–81 above). **259** *thei*: i.e. the majority, not the *fewe*. **260** *and connynge chapmen*: 'and because of the shrewd [arguments of] tradespeople'; *and* would read better if *as*. **262** *heo*: indef. for 'a girl'; its antecedent is not *kyn(rede)*. **263–4** *gode...goed*: see on 257 above. *haue*; *haue* 'possess' and 'take', because they seek 'the moneye of þis molde' (1.42) not 'the tresore of treuthe'(2.201); cf. the similar play on *bonde* and *hosebonde* in 270. **264** The landed nobility wish to augment their (diminishing) wealth even at the cost of debasing their lineage. **266** *bond...douhter*: 'A pack-saddle quean, a slave, a tinker's whelp'; indignant hyperbole for 'someone of servile origin'. **267** *Ac late*; **269** *squier*: examples respectively of liaisonal and internal staves. **270** The wordplay stands out in sharper relief if the line is scanned with *beden* muted and the final lifts on *-hére* and *-bónde*. **272** *wexe*: perhaps alluding to the practice of offering to the Church one's own weight in wax (*Sk*), often in the form of a 'man of wax' (*Pe*); see MED s.v. *wax* n.(1), 2b (b), citing C Pr

99 (though this probably refers to votive lights rather than a wax image). Whatever the exact sense, he would clearly exchange his wife for her weight in wax or a small sum of cash. *Pe* wonders whether *wexe* is the p.p. of *wexen* and *or* should be omitted. But perhaps it is the malleability of wax that is the issue: the *morwe* after their wedding-night, the deluded groom realises that his monied low-born wife *can of iangelynge* but not of *cortesye*. **274–5** The revised b-half and the added line stress the hollowness of a troth based on avarice. *lyen lely*: 'lie, truly', 'truly lie'; see *TN*. **274** *this pestelences*: the pl. taking into account the attacks of 1361 and later as well as 1348–9, after which there had been a brief rise in marriages and births followed by a resumption of the preceding decline in population (Postan 1972:43). Wit's judgement that the 'quality' of gentry marriages had deteriorated in the post-Plague years may be compared with Reason's on the spoiling of children at B 5.36. **275** No major lexical contrast of *lyketh* with *louye* 274 seems intended; the sense is 'neither of them affords any pleasure to the other'. **276–8** The implication is that their mutual revulsion rules out fulfilling the first purpose of marriage, offspring. **277** *Haen þei..*: possibly a question (rhetorical). **278** *Donemowe*: Little Dunmow in Essex, where a side of bacon was awarded to a couple wedded a year who could swear and prove they had never quarrelled or regretted marrying. The custom, dating back to the 13th c. and still kept up, is mentioned by the Wife of Bath, in an echo of these lines (*CT* III 217–18). *bote...helpe*: presumably to 'prove' by false testimony their entitlement to the flitch.

281–97 Wit's *conseyle* on marriage has three parts: a warning to all against marrying for the wrong reason, advice to the unwedded, and counsel to the wedded. **281–2** are half-composed of fixed phrases (281a = 9.346a, 282a = 260a) but re-invigorated by the lively wordplay on *coueytise* (Schmidt 1987:139). **282** *in...wyse*: not a strong half-line, but necessary for removing the contradiction between the **AB** b-verse and the approval of *kynrede* 'good blood' as a factor in choosing a wife at 261. **283–4** propose 'similarity of nature' as the criterion for good marriage: the one protects against aged lust (Chaucer's Januarie for May), the other against youthful greed (Jankyn for Alison of Bath). *maydones..*: virgins of either sex. **285** *more þe cause*: still idealistic, but less absolute than **B**. **286** *seculer*: 'lay' (MED s.v. *seculer* a. 1(d)), as opposed to clerical, not 'secular' as opposed to 'religious' (*Sk*). It is not being suggested that priests be permitted to marry. **287–8** *Wisely...lecherye*: echoing the Pauline text quoted below at 296a (and also vss 8–9), addressed to those *þat may nat contynue* ('sic *permaneant*, sicut et ego. Quod si non se *continent, nubant*'). **288** *lymʒerd*: a twig smeared with thick glue to trap birds, with an obvious polysemantic pun on 'penis' (MED s.v. *yerd* n. (2), 5(a)). The image is echoed in *PPCr* 564. **289** *wepene*:

the figurative use occurs only here, but cf. *ballok-knyf* B 15.124. *kene*: 'sharp, strong', as of a dagger (MED s.v. *kene* adj. 3(a), 6(a)), but also 'sexually ardent', as at B 13.348 (ib. 6(b), with apt citations from *WPal* 616 (*kene þouʒt*), 1011 (*kene kosses*). **290** *Awreke*: thereby turning the 'weapon' against the fiend. *Godes werk*: 'a divinely sanctioned act'; but with a pun on *werk* 'intercourse' (MED s.v. n.(1), as at 6.181 etc). The thought here may be echoed in *Pur* 697ff (Schmidt 1988:116–18). **290a** 'Thou lusty man, give not thy strength to whores: *The Gate of Death* is written on their doors'. **291** *out of tyme* (*in tyme* **B**): at the wrong / right time. **B 186** *vntyme*: e.g. those times named at B 13.349; see Brundage 1987:155–60. *bedbourd*: 'frolicking 'twixt the sheets'; a *hapax*, and a happy one in every sense. The conditions for lovemaking to be *Godes werk* are: to be free of mortal sin (esp. of a sexual kind), have real affection, and be properly married. The **B** reading is uncertain, but legitimacy in the act is stipulated. **295** *dede derne*: cf. *Pur* 697. The act is private between the spouses and their Maker who ordained it and works his purposes through it. **296** The revised form dissociates Paul's reluctant concession from the positive command alluded to by **B** (Gen 1:28, 2:24). **296a** 'It is good that for fear of fornication every man have his own wife' (I Cor 7:1–2). **299** *faytors*: the revision removing **A**'s concern over the inheritance of land and titles by people of ignoble character (possibly those begotten on serving-women and passed off as a barren wife's offspring, with consequent dilution of the gentry stock). Wit's is a 'pre-Chaucerian' belief that nobility of character is inherited. This view is soon to be significantly modified by Trajan's assertion (12.110–17) that grace won by Christ makes all faithful believers *gentil* in a deeper spiritual sense. But C 5.65–81 have shown the narrator convinced of the reality and necessity of social divisions based on inherited rank (and the qualities ideally supposed to go with it). **300** *Vngracious*: 'lacking the grace / luck'; the theological sense is secondary, since this is spelled out in 304: until God grants them the prevenient grace to repent, they will never be 'graced' with either the good deeds required for salvation or the goods needed for a decent life in the world. *goed*[1]: playing on the senses 'wealth' and 'virtue', neither of which they are 'favoured' to obtain. **301** *wasten*: the sexual licence of the parents being presciently seen to spawn an alienated and destructive 'underclass' destined for a bad end. **305–11** The final summary definition of the Triad, greatly expanded from **A**, sees *Dowel* as a life of obedience to the laws of Church and State, humility, innocence and benevolence (compatible with the Christian lay condition); *Dobet* as one of outgoing charitable action (that of the clergy); *Dobest* as one of abounding care for the whole *comune* (the true mark of the episcopal order). **310–11** make the important new point that the 'degree' of well-doing that people may achieve is in proportion to their (intrinsic) capacity: the more they are given, the more they are bound to give, and the better they become.

B 205–7 (A 217–8) *þe mody*: the 'proud prikere' of 135, the devil whose enmity to God is the chief threat to Anima. If the **AB** definitions imply an antithetical correlation of *drede* (faith) with 'the world' (= the sin of avarice) and *suffre* (hope) with 'the flesh' (= the sins of lust, gluttony, sloth), the undefined third (presumably the charity that grows from obedience and humility) stands against 'the devil' (= the sins of anger, envy and pride). **206** *wikked wille*: 'deliberate choice of evil', directly recalling the faculty in which well- and ill-doing alike are located (6.2). **207** In making explicit how the divine life in the soul is destroyed, the added line implies an equation of Dowel not only with virtue (the *habitus*) but also with the sanctifying grace (*gratia habitualis*) that creates it. *dryueþ away*: describing the failure of Duke Virtue's custodianship, a figure lost sight of in revision. It is through mortal sin that 'Mody' expels him from the Castle of Caro and wins possession of Lady Anima, a scenario to be enacted on a collective scale in the final passus of the poem.

Passus XI (B X, A XI)

PASSUS ELEVEN divides into: (i) DAME STUDY's diatribe (1–82), (ii) her dialogue with Will (83–105) and her reply (106–35), leading to his encounter with CLERGY and SCRIPTURE (136–61). This ends with a rebuke from Scripture (162–5) precipitating (iii) the fall into an inner dream and the vision of Middle Earth (166–94), followed by (iv) the vehement outpouring by RECHELESNESSE (195–317). Section (ii) cuts B 10.251–330, but the juncture of this shortened sequence with (iii), which takes over what in B XI is the first 'inner' dream (1–36), is unsatisfactory in leaving Scripture's hostility towards Will unmotivated. **B** has massively expanded **A**'s last completed passus by almost half, but **C** returns it to nearly the original length (about that of C X). The basic structure of (i) and (ii) as given in **A** is expanded in **B** largely with Clergy's long disquisition (B X 232–330). Of this, **C** omits the portion on Dobet and Dobest (251–90), including an attack on the clergy (although re-using some lines at C Pr 105–14), and shifts the criticism of the religious (B 10.291–327*a*) to C 5.146–179.

(i) 1–4 1 *wyf...Dame Studie*: personifying the disciplines preparatory to the study of philosophy and theology, i.e. at school, the study of grammar 'the ground of all' (17.107) and at university, of the seven Liberal Arts. But a deeper meaning is discerned by Harwood 1990 (who sees STUDY as both representing the teaching voice and as related to *lectio divina* in its spiritually formative function) and Zeeman 1999:193–5 (who also stresses how

'study' as *disciplina* in **L** signifies the intense effort, labour and difficulty of pursuing spiritual understanding). **2** *lene...lyf-holy*: the image, developing **A**'s b-half, suggesting a female religious instructing children in a priory school. Her allegorical 'marriage' to Wit plays on the senses of his name: as the 'knowledge' that the activity of study must unite itself to, and the 'faculty' (of understanding) that enables study to bear fruit. In her acerbic tone of a strict schoolmistress-figure is humorously contrasted with Wit's (still firm but) more relaxed 'voice of wise experience'. **4** *starynge*: 'glaring' (cf. *wroth* 3); but **C** improves by removing the over-stated AB 6/7 and changing 'man' to 'men' at 7.

5–27 6 The charge against the Dreamer seems unfair, since he is no more 'flatterer' than 'sot' (B 8), and it obviously has a broader target (cf. 11). However, Will does (if ironically) describe *himself* as a fool (B 15.3) or as so judged by others (B 11.68) and as 'nearly out of his mind' (15.1). **7** *Nolite...*: '[Give not that which is holy to dogs]. Neither cast ye [your pearls before swine; lest perhaps they trample them under their feet: and turning upon you, they tear you]' (Mt 7:6). Study envisages not so much violence against the teacher from brutish pupils as defilement of the proffered wisdom by those who cannot see what it is. **9** *dreuele*: metaphorical for 'defile by disrespectful treatment', a sense borne out by 11.40. **10** *preciouse...prince*: perhaps echoed in the first and last lines of *Pearl*. **AB 12** *paradis*: alluding to the belief (based on Gen 2:12 and richly elaborated in *Pearl* 73ff) that precious stones 'grew' in the Earthly Paradise. **12–13** The revision, in a tacit critique of *newe clerkes*, adds gluttony and lechery to avarice and pride as presumed motives for the pursuit of learning. *holynesse or hendenesse*: a coupling of religious and secular virtues as desired products of good education that recalls *SGGK* 653. **15** *cardet*: a metaphor from the combing-out of impurities in raw wool and the straightening of the fibres before spinning, by use of a metal tool furnished with teasel-hooks; it intimates that intellectual ability cannot now prosper unless 'dressed' with ambition and greed. **16, 18** The expansion of this troublesome line shows **C**'s liking for rhetorical *repetitio*, in contrast with the polysemantic punning on *serue* in A 22. **17** 'And put obstacles in the way of a just man's claim by settling the case out of court'. **18*a*** 'To those who know trifles and slanders, the law says "Enter"; those who know righteousness, it tells "Keep out".' This unidentified couplet highlights the corruption attacked in 4.148–50 / B 3.29–34, arguing that lawyers' careers depend on Lady Mede's favour. **19–20** describe how they win honour and wealth through manipulating the law or bribing juries. *yrobed...robbe*: more 'Platonic' wordplay; 'robed' specifically 'as a barrister' / 'judge'. **21** All three texts invoke the archetypical just man's moral authority, but (like the Psalter-citations following) they differ and are only partly from Job. **23** 'They spend their days in wealth. And in a moment [Vg *puncto* for *fine*] they go down to hell.' **B 25a** *Quare*...: 'Why then do the wicked live, [are they advanced, and strengthened with riches]?' (Job 21:7). *Bene*...: 'Why is it well with all them that transgress and do wickedly?' (Jer 12:1). **A 23a** 'Why doth the way of the wicked prosper?' (Jer 12:1, just before **B**'s *Bene*…, in **A** a variant of **B**'s Vg text). **A** is Jeremiah, **B** begins with Job and continues with Jeremiah, **C** is Job, possibly a deliberate correction. The source-chapters in both books ask whether the success of the wicked calls in question God's justice. **25** '[They] shall go into the generations of [their] fathers: and [they] shall never see light' (Ps 48:20). Vss 17–18 just before and the whole psalm are close to Job 21. *Et alibi*...: 'And in another place, "Behold these are sinners: [and yet abounding in the world they have obtained riches **B**]"' (Ps 72:12). **27a** 'For they have destroyed the things which thou hast made; [but what has the just man (done) **B**]?'

28–82 28 C does not specify *disours* or *iangleris* but shifts the critique from low minstrels to mocking clerks. **31** *he*: men like the author, who recounts *þe passioun of Crist* in XVIII–XX. **31** *ay...mouthe*: as does **L**, who cites it about once on every page. **32** *Treuthe*: a tacit allusion to the poet, who set out to tell of *treuthe and tricherye* (Pr 12). **B 33** *Tobye*: in a Vg book of *c.* 200 BC (Tobias = Tobit in AV Apocrypha). Its 'exemplary lives' of Tobias (cited at 11.70, 17.37) and his son provide models of household piety for 'lords at feasts' (34).

   B 38–50 (A 31–7) L's sharpest attack on the decline of minstrelsy (see Poole 1958:605–10; Southworth 1989:119ff; Schmidt 1987:5–11) into bawdy buffoonery. **44** *Munde þe Millere*: a type of the coarse, unspiritual man; cf. Chaucer's *janglere* who loved *harlotries* (*CT* I 560–1) and Mann 1973:160–1. *Multa* ...: 'God has done many [great things]'; loosely citing Ps 39:6. **46** *Seint Poules*: a canon there ranking among the wealthier clergy, with a large income from the benefices of which he might be rector. **49–50** Cf. the Vernon Lyric no. 95 (Brown 1957) ll. 133–4: 'Now harlotrye for murþe is holde, / And virtues tornen into vice'.

36–53 bitingly associate the higher classes' intellectual arrogance with lack of customary charity towards the needy. **36** *aȝen þe lered*: clergy perhaps present at table as at 15.39ff. **37** *Trinite*...: alluding to a story like Chaucer's Pardoner's Tale (*CT* VI), blasphemously applied to the Persons of the Blessed Trinity in speculations about the economy of salvation. *two*: the Father and Spirit. *thridde*: here the incarnate Son who is crucified. **38** *Bernard*: as almost a fifth 'Father' of the Church, a byword for theological orthodoxy, so that invoking his authority here is especially outrageous; see on B 4.121. **39** 'Reason presumptuously in probing the truths of religion / to prove the truth of their argument' (the latter alternative being

likelier in the light of 40b). **40** *dreule*: literally and figuratively, the 'pearls' here being the central dogmas of the faith; cf. 9. **42** *crye...ȝate*: avoiding **B**'s repetition of an earlier use at 9.80 (in a sequence omitted from **C**). **44** *go per God is*: euphemistic for 'drop dead;' but the added 45–6 turn the sarcasm against the speaker. **45** Either, 'in respect of those who utter such an order' or (from the suppliant's viewpoint), 'to those who ask alms in such dire need (it will be clear that...).' **47** *blisse*: ironic; the 'prosperity' is only temporal and will not become lasting if he uses it selfishly. **49** *riht*: 'very'; the insertion, making the line of T-type, evokes (by way of an 'anti-pun') only to exclude the notion that they are also 'righteous'. **B 66–7** are properly deleted as respectively repeating B 57=C 41 and anticipating B 70=C 53. **51** *Memento*: '[O Lord], remember [David: and all his meekness]' (Ps 131:1). **51a** 'Behold, we have heard of it [*that is,* charity] in Ephrata; we have found it in the fields of the wood' (Ps 131:6, with gloss). In the source the referent of *eam* is the Ark of the Covenant, which the Jews believed to house the divine presence and kept in a tabernacle-shrine before Solomon built the Temple; it here stands for holiness. *Ephrata*: otherwise Bethlehem, the city of David and the Messiah who it was expected would descend from him (see Mic 5:2); as the place of Christ's birth in a stable, an apt metonym for humility. The general point is that 'as the Ark was kept in the countryside, true Christian goodness will be found among simple people'. **52** *knyhtes*: a brave improvement on the weak **B** form.

54–69 54 *Freres and faytours*: guilt by alliterative association. Disturbing theological speculations characterised early C14th friar-theologians like Peter Aureole, a Franciscan, and Durandus of St-Pourçain, a Dominican (Leff 1958:272–9, Knowles1988:287–8). *questions*: 'theological conundrums'. *proude men*: possibly themselves. *pestelences*: perhaps (like 10.274 above) more recent (B 79) and prolonged attacks (60–1) provoking anguished uncertainty as to whether God wills or merely permits the innocent to suffer. **56** *Seynt Poules*: the great cross N of the E end of Old St Paul's, used for open-air preaching to large gatherings (cf. 15.70–1). *in...clerkes*: 'out of pure clerkly malice' (in allusion to bitter disputes between mendicant orders); or, as seems likelier, 'out of sheer hostility towards (the secular) clergy' (the friars themselves being 'religious' clerks; cf. 59, and *TN* further). The antagonism envisaged is between university theologians (more acute but no less arrogant than the lay would-be divines) and representatives of ecclesiastical authority like bishops and canons, whose acuity (like that of their modern successors) will have been dulled by routine administration. **57–8** *ne fre...ne sory*: implying that theological speculation undermines penance and charity, which for **L** go hand in hand. **60** *no power*: because the efficacy of prayer is related to the faith of the one who prays. **62** *gode men*:

more general than *girles* **B**, which directly evokes the *mortalité des enfants* of 1361–2, so called because specially fatal to children (McKisack 1959:131). Both idea and expression in **C** recall 3.103, the underlying notion being that since the *comune* is one, its innocent members suffer for the sins of the guilty ones. *togrynt*: a very rare word; the unique *forgrynt* that it replaces (unrecorded by OED or MED) may be a coinage. **63** *this...world*: 'these worldly wretches.' **64** *eny*: generalising the source of salutary fear beyond plague to death itself. **67a** 'Deal [thy bread **B**] to the hungry [and bring the needy...into thy house]' (Is 58:7). **68** scans as Type IIIb on *w* and vowels. **71a** 'If you have much [*copia* = *multum* Vg] give largely: if you have little, Take care even so to freely bestow a little' (Tob 4:9). **73–82** Six of these lines alliterate on *l* and two on *w*, the stave-sounds coming together in 82 to round off Study's speech, which concludes section (i) of the passus (80–1 echoing 7–10 at its opening). **76** *lettred man*: implying a well-to-do cleric, the phrase seemingly generated in revision of B 91. **79** recalls B 19.457.

B 92–136 combine spirited dialogue evoking contemporary debates on divine justice with details of manorial life (Colvin in Poole I:41–50; Girouard 1978:29–80, esp. 30; and see Tipping 1921: pls. 107, 206). The erosion of communal solidarity by the higher classes (through preferring domestic privacy) and of religious unity (in challenging the Church's teaching) are obliquely linked to suggest that ungenerousness and unbelief are 'reciprocal' vices. **C**'s excision of this major addition to **A** removes **B**'s telling association of theological presumption (fostered by friars' provocative sermons) with what the speaker views as lords' neglect of their social responsibilities. **94** *frere*: like Chaucer's in *CT* III 1709–60. **99** *for...sake*: an ironic homonymic pun, since they do it to shut out poor people in quest of scraps (42–5 above), not to help them. **102** *anoþer*: an heir (though it will finally make no difference whether miser or prodigal). **107** *worm*: see Gen 3:1–15. *in his blisse*: 'in his blessed state (which no imperfection could disturb)' or, 'in his happy place [Eden]'. **108–9** *biwiled; wiles*: dialectal variants (< AN) of *bigiled* and *giles*, words that will resonate in 20.322–7, 377–92a. **109–10** *helle...deep*: the sense is that 'Adam and Eve and their descendants after them were deprived of eternal life', not that 'all the just before Christ endure the torments of the greatest sinners'; so *helle* here = *limbo inferni*, the 'border land' of darkness adjoining Satan's domain (18.116–17). **112** *Of þat*: 'from / in relation to what'. **112a** See on 10.239. **114a** '[For] every one shall bear his own burden' (Gal 6:5). **115** *maistres*: ironic, their *glorie* 'vainglory'. **117** *Ymaginatif*: a unique preparatory reference to a character not introduced till the end of Passus XI, showing how each interlocutor serves a definite purpose in leading Will to understand 'Dowel'. But **C**'s deletion of this reference is small loss structur-

ally, since Ymaginatif will not actually explain why men must die (though he will defend the *clergye* attacked by the would-be *maistres*). **118** compresses two **A** lines into one, a feature marked in the revision of **B** to **C**. *Austyn*: see on 11.148. **118a** '[For I say...to all...], not to be more wise than it behoveth to be wise, [but to be wise unto sobriety and according as God has divided to every one the measure of faith]' (Rom 12:3); a critique of the demand for *kynde knowynge* by Will in 8.57–8, 110–11 //. As *Sk* notes, Augustine develops this 'theme' in *On Baptism* ii.5 (*PL* 43) when attacking the human temptation *aliquid sapere quam res se habet* 'to know a thing as in itself it is'. **119–20** recur (near)-entire at 126–7; the dense repetition-pattern (*wilneþ...wite* 124a, 126a, 133a; *wolde* 119, 125, 126, 129, 130) mimics a sustained catechesis. **121** Study firmly aligns herself with HC, whose tone and procedure at B 1.61–70 she recalls. **125** Study's anatomical curse vividly conveys her sense of how incongruous it is to probe the mysteries of Providence. **129–30** *as he wolde*: a stress on the supremacy of the divine will (honoured in the parenthesis), further implying the need to accept it through faith, not for the 'reasons' that 'arguers' seek and (as often as not) fail to find. Study may echo here Thomas Bradwardine's position in the 1340s against the followers of Ockham (Leff 1958:286–9). **131–2** *ablende...fro*: 'confuse men's minds as to the distinction between.' **134** *lyue*: the way to discover the meaning of the Triad being to *do* well, not try to define it.

(ii) 83–105 provide a transition between Study's attack on presumptuousness and statement of her own limitations and the need for Will (appropriately chastened) to progress to more advanced teachers. **83** *what ...menede*: signifying that if the will is to find *wit* 'understanding' (which as 'wedded to' can only be 'possessed by' *study*), it must submit to teaching, and not be headlong in its quest for answers. **84** *wittes*: 'wise judgements' (like those in Wit's allocution). **85, 87** *louted*: Wit's courteous bow teaches Will to show similar politeness to Study. **88** *ȝoure man*: Will's offer of allegiance reveals that he is ready for education, if it will bring real knowledge of the nature of Dowel (91). **92** *mekenesse*: the recognition of one's ignorance and the patient acceptance of instruction at the appropriate level. **93** *Clergie*: 'book-learning', with special reference to knowledge of the Bible. After a course of 'study' Will should be prepared to approach *clergie* (which is inseparable from God's written word, *scripture*). *cosyn*: here = 'brother-in-law', since he has married her sister (97). Wit, Study, Clergy and Scripture are all joined in a 'family-relationship' allegorically representing Will's progression through school to university. **94** *alle...of*: 'every theoretical and practical aspect of'. **96** *and ouer Skripture*: 'and (is placed in authority) over'; the 'authority' is that of the interpreting mind over the text, of *sententia* (theological interpretation) over *litera* (the grammatical relations of the words) and *sensus* (their immediate meaning); see generally Chamberlin 2000. 'Clergy' thus connotes 'formal religious doctrine' like that of a university textbook of theology such as Peter Lombard's *Sentences* (for a narrower interpretation see Harwood 1973[1]). *and ...trewe*: 'if the Bible texts copied by scribes could be relied on as accurate (for construing the *litera*)'. Study's concerns about inaccuracy are echoed by Rechelesnesse at 13.116–19. **97** *sib*: an aunt or older cousin. *þe seuene ars*: the Arts curriculum taken by all (except professed religious) before studying theology. Its classic form was the *trivium* 'threefold way', the mainly linguistic disciplines of grammar, rhetoric and dialectic or logic (which taught mastery in expression and reasoning); and the *quadrivium* 'fourfold way' of arithmetic, geometry, astronomy and music, mathematical subjects that taught the principles of scientific reasoning (on the Arts course see Piltz 1981:15–23). By the late 14th c. Arts graduates who were not seeking ordination, or those ordained but without a benefice (like Chaucer's Clerk) might go on to advanced work in philosophy based on Aristotle (*CT* I 294–5; Courtenay 1987:30–66). Holy Scripture or *sacra pagina* formed a main part of the higher ('post-graduate') course in divinity. **98** *wyf*: the Bible and the Fathers, the ideal 'marriage-partner', since the training in 'clergy' was for those seeking holy orders. *as hymsulue*: because Clergy's knowledge of doctrine and canon law derives from the Bible. **101** *kyndeliche*: meeting his condition at 91. Study's implication that there is no unmediated way to comprehend Dowel stresses the need for learning more than do parallel AB109 /154. But if she also tacitly challenges Piers's claim at 7.181–2 to direct knowledge of *Truth* (the presumed object of study), open conflict between her strengthened claim and the ploughman's bold defiance of the priest is avoided by C's excision of B 7.131–8a. **103** *gold*: Will's preference for wisdom over gold, echoing Prov 8:10, shows that he has heeded HC's exhortation at 1.81, 201. **105** *tyme is*: signifying that after a period of instruction, Will can move on to the next stage.

106–35 The second part of Study's speech gives practical guidance for Will's journey, but also defines the limitations of her competence, which does not stretch to matters within Clergy's province. **106** *hey wey*: the direct route to knowledge of divine things, through patient endurance of the vicissitudes inevitable in the scholar's vocation, which will become a major theme of Patience's teaching. It imports simplicity of life and avoidance of greed, gluttony, lust, anger and sloth. *Soffre..*: a 'signpost-allegory' recalling Piers's earlier to the pilgrims at 7.205ff, though the verbal parallel is closer in B 163–9 // A 118–24 (cf. also the 'domain'-allegory in 2.88ff). **109–10** warn against the remaining deadly sins (pride having been overcome at

92). But while *enuye* might be expected here (see *TN*), *ire* is probably a rhetorical repetition-with-variation of *wrothe* and the list not meant to be comprehensive (that **L** did not think clerks immune to envy is clear from his account of its driving the friars *to scole* at 22.273). **A 118** *longe launde*: possibly a sardonic pun on the poet's name, more obvious than the anagram at B 15.152 (and possibly too obvious to be in good taste).

B 164–8 164 *left half*: cf. B 5.578. *large myle*: cf. *WPal* 1732. **165** *court*: cf. B 585=C 7.231. **165–8** Truth, sobriety and modesty are the 'spiritual' *trivium* to understanding. On soberness as a fruit of poverty (a recommended state for clerks), cf. 16.150. **168** *That...*: 'in consequence of which everyone will be happy to impart his knowledge to you.'

110–11 *slewthe / treuthe*: the end-rhyme underscoring the formulaic character of Study's 'passport' conditions. **111** *hit*: with immediate antecedent 'sloth', though presumably all the named vices are intended. **115** The revision makes for better allegorical sense. Instead of merely claiming authority as Clergy's initial teacher, Study cites Will's 'qualifications': he has done the common foundation course (*my bokes*) and is now ready to go on. **116–17** Study takes credit for copying the scriptural texts (*wrot* 'wrote down') and perhaps even understanding their *litera* (cf. on 96), but not for interpretation and exegesis (*Bible...yglosed*). **118–19** Logic, like Music, formed part of Arts, whereas Law was a higher-degree course. Possibly Study *is* laying claim to civil law, which had to be studied before canon law (Courtenay 1987:40), while implicitly assigning the latter (with theology) to 'Clergy'. **118** *Logyk*: training in which was usually followed by courses in natural and moral sciences (Courtenay 1987:31–2). **119** *musons*: translating OF *moison* (< Lat. *mensionem* or *mensura*), defined as 'the measures or note forms in mensural polyphony' by Holsinger (1999:127), who quotes a definition of *mensura* as 'habitudo quantitiva longitudinem et brevitatem cuiuslibet cantus mensurabilis manifestans' from the English musical theorist Johannes Hanboys, *c.* 1375. The time and rhythm of 'mensurable' music was noted down by various signs, in contrast with 'immensurable' music (i.e. plainchant). University study of this 'art' was largely theoretical, and was based on Boethius's *Institutio musica*, which touched on practice only in Bk IV (Chadwick 1981:84–8). **120** *Plato* (427–347 BC): also called a 'poet' at 308 and 12.175, 14.189 (and indeed he wrote some fine epigrams). But since 22.275, tacitly alluding to *The Republic*, shows awareness that Plato was a philosopher, *poete* here may signify 'sage' as at 14.92, where the referent is the Magi (the sense 'any ancient writer' in MED s.v. *poete* n. is found only in **L**). **121** *Aristotel* (384–22 BC): whose writings on the rules of argumentative reasoning (the *Organon*) formed the basis of logic (as the Bible that of theology). **122** *Gramer*: the first stage of the university Arts course, though its rudiments were taught in the 'grammar school', attended by *gurles* '(male) children' from eight to fourteen (Orme 1973, 1982; Courtenay 1987:15–20). **24–7** *craftes*: here various skills connected with Architecture which, though not a 'liberal' art, required at its higher levels a knowledge of arithmetic and geometry. Murtaugh 1978:68 finds a precedent for this more extensive list of skills in Hugh of St Victor's *Didascalicon* 2:1, with its view of the entire system of study as designed to restore the divine image in man. **124–5** *contreuede*: not a strong instance of *repetitio*, but the accent-shift in the key-stave from -*treuede* in 124 (a T-type) to *con-* in 125 serves to vary the rhythm. **127** *loke demme*: from poring over the fine detail of these 'crafts'. **128–35** *Teologie*: a discipline pertaining to Clergy not to Study, who finds herself out of her depth. The reservations in all versions may reflect unease about the bold speculations on the soul, providence and free will of *moderni* like Holcot, Buckingham and Adam of Woodham (Leff 1958:291–3). But **C** at 131, rather than warning against these, asserts that theology is not a body of organised 'knowledge' but a matter of loyal 'faith', thereby removing the hostility in AB 141 (186). **128** *tened...ten*: the vexation seeming to be multiplied by the 'Platonic' chime, as it would not be if written 'two hundred.' **131–2** The *repetitio* of *soth-* and *bileue* (the latter with form-class variation recalling **AB**'s *loue*) is semantically stronger than that in 124–5 above. **132** loses the ironic **AB** pun on *best* and *bettere*, which half-retracts what it only half-concedes: that the 'Queen of the Sciences' sets most value on the crowning 'theological' virtue, charity. **133** *a lykyng thyng*: an ironic echo of 10.288. *loth...greue*: developing the thought of the deleted B 206a. **B 185** *to sotile in*: perhaps alluding to the fine-drawn distinctions associated with the school of Duns Scotus, the 'Doctor Subtilis' (d. 1308). **132–5 C**'s fourfold *repetitio* of *lou(i)e* (again with interwoven form-class variation) improves on its mantra-like sixfold **AB** source. **134a** anticipates 22.208a, 250b and echoes their source in **B**. **135** *doctour*: wittily paralleling the Triad-grades and the university hierarchy: above scholar, bachelor and master is a supreme teacher, at once 'precious' and 'beloved'.

B 191–219 (A 146–164) are excised in **C** as perhaps somewhat digressive and not wholly apt here. For Study both authoritatively supports Theology, which is not her proper province, and expresses (inappropriate) reservations about a respectable quadrivium subject, while taking ambiguous 'credit' for crafts dreamed up positively to mislead. **191** *ooper science*: here everyday moral wisdom, which lacks the special concern for others of the Charity taught by Theology. **192–3** 'He who in words would pretend, but in heart is no faithful friend - / Act like him, for your part: so art is beguiled by art' (*DC* I, 26). **194–6** paraphrase the Latin, strong proof (if any

were needed) that the **A** Version (which does not) cannot have been intended for an audience of *illiterati* (cf. *Intro.* V § 17). *gylours...bigile*: advice rejected here as the way to deal with one's fellow-men, but effectively invoked by Christ in the 'Harrowing' sequence (and incorporating at 20.392a a text close in sense to the Catonian couplet) as a way to deal with the devil. **197–8** *Ac...contrarie*: corresponding to the scholastic *Sed contra* (10.20), here setting a weightier (sacred) authority against a less weighty (secular) one. **199** *bidde...bidde*: replacing **A**'s plain statement with 'Platonic' wordplay hinting that 'command' and 'prayer' have the same (divine) origin. **199–201** *breperen*: cf. Mt 23:8, I Pet 3:8. *enemys...lene... good*: cf. 'But love ye your enemies: do good, and lend...' (Lk 6:35). **201** *do...yuel*: cf. Rom 12:21. *God hymself*: as inspirer of Apostolic teaching; less appropriate than in // **A**, where the words are Christ's own. **201a** '[And in *doing good*, let us not fail. For in due time we shall reap, not failing. Therefore], whilst we have time, let us *work good* to all men, but especially to those who are of the household of the faith' (Gal 6:9–10); cf. A 11.245a. This closely fits what follows, but as a text urging love of enemies and evildoers, less well than what it replaces. **A 154a** '[Woe to the world because of scandals. For] it must needs be that scandals come: [but nevertheless woe to that man by whom the scandal cometh]' (Mt 18:7); quoted in full at B 15.157a. **202–8** translate the Latin preceding (202–4) and following (205–6). **203–4** bring forward A 248–9 and are correspondingly deleted at that point. **206a** 'Revenge is mine, and I will repay [them in due time]' (Deut 32:35). The sense of only 206 is implied by the OT text, but since 205 is spelled out in Rom 12:19, which cites it and then the contextually apt Prov 25:21–2 (following it with the injunction translated at 201), that was probably the immediate source. **208** *science...soule*: a metaphor neatly bringing the argument back to the *artes*. **209–19** make some small but significant excisions from and improvements to **A**. **209** *Astronomye*: used indifferently in the period for the academic discipline of 'natural astronomy' and the pseudo-science of 'judicial astronomy' or forecasting from the heavenly bodies (='astrology'). The extensive overlap between the two is clear from 17.96–7, 21.245 (and well illustrated from Chaucer's Physician in *CT* I 414–18). *yuel*: possibly punning on the senses 'difficult' and 'bad', given the doubts at the mere mention of an 'art' that could lead easily to the more remunerative *astrologye*, as with Chaucer's Oxford clerk Nicholas (*CT* I 3191–97) or even to *magyk natureel*, as with his Clerk of Orléans (*CT* V 1273–96). 'Judicial' astronomy is also conjoined with the three mantic arts here named in Mandeville's description of the Great Khan's court (*Travels*, 154/2–3). **210** *Geometrie*: presumably not the respected second quadrival discipline (despite the reliance of magical conjuration on such complex geometrical figures as the pentangle) but *geomatria*, 'an occult art related to geo-mancy or a branch of geomancy' (MED s.v. *gemetrie* n. 2(b); see Herman 1991). *Geomesie*: 'divination by means of earth, dots and figures written in the ground' (MED s.v. *geomanci* n.); cf. *CT* I 2045n, Thorndyke II, 837–88. **211** *two*: the revision (perhaps responding to clerkly read-ers' protests) prudently safeguards astronomy from guilt by association. **212** *souereyn book*: the ultimate end of such studies, diabolic magic, subject-matter of the most advanced textbook in a notional academy of the occult. **213–14** refer to the deceits that attended the practice of alchemy (as revealed in Chaucer's *CT* VIII 1391–1425). **213** *fibicches*: a unique term possibly derived from *Pebi-chios*, an early alchemist and denoting '?some kind of alchemical manipulations or tricks' (MED s.v. *febic-ches*, citing R. Quirk). *in forceres*: i.e. secretly hidden away. *of...makynge*: fusing A 159b/160b, possibly as a concession to objections that Albert had been traduced here (see A 160–1 below). **215–19** Study rightly admits responsibility for *sciences* arising from *mis*direction of the 'virtue' she personifies, an activity that can never be a sufficient condition of true 'wisdom'; her duty is there-fore to warn against them as obstacles to *dowel*. **B** makes more robust Study's muted **A** farewell (A 165 recalling A 9.49b–50a). **217** *folk to deceyue*: an honest (if somewhat reprehensible) recognition that 'hydroptique immoderate desire for humane learning' [Donne] can lead astray. **218** *þise tokenes*: her recommendation of Will as now ready to begin Theology (allegorical shorthand for his having graduated in Arts). **219** *kyndely*: 'kindly, graciously'; al-though metrically in the a-half, crossing the caesura to form a phrase 'to know properly, in its true nature'. C 140 erases this dual meaning.

A 160–1 *Albertis makyng*: St Albertus Magnus, 'Doctor Universalis' (d. Cologne, 1280), the great Domin-ican theologian and philosopher, teacher of St Thomas Aquinas. He wrote widely on scientific topics, but was falsely ascribed various works on magic and alchemy. **161** *perimansie*: divination by looking at the flames of a fire. *nigromancie*: 'black' magic, the raising of demons and the spirits of the dead. This (usual) medieval spelling is by a false etymology, understanding *nigro-* as 'black' (it is a corruption of *necro-* 'dead'). *pouke*: an old unlucky name for the Devil (sanitised as Shakespeare's Puck); the line's removal seems an act of circumspection. **136–40** omit the point (A 176=B 229) that Will is hospi-tably received because he has native good sense and has done his educational groundwork. The drastic revision loses coherence by giving no reason why his hosts' good-will evaporates. **B 220–31** delete the redundant A 168 but remain leisurely (e.g. 222b repeats 221b, 224b is otiose). **140** reminds of the promise made at 101 in answer to Will's request at 91. **141–7** Clergy's response to Will's enquiry and what

follows are among **C**'s least satisfactory abbreviation-revisions. Scripture's animosity had made more sense in **B** in response to the Dreamer's harangue (greatly expand-ing **A**) which, despite some palpable hits, could fairly be judged bumptious. **141** *Clergie*: the official voice of the Church, proclaiming through its ordained ministers the Biblical teaching formally articulated by theologians (see Harwood 1973[1]). Clergy tells Will to follow the moral law of the OT and believe in the key Christian dogmas of the Incarnation and the Trinity, equating the Do's with the theological virtues of doctrinal belief, heartfelt trust, and selfless love of God and neighbour. The correspond-ing **B** passage (232–50) stresses the community aspect of Christian faith and lacks the final definition of the Triad, but goes on with a lively and digressive account (B 251–339) prompting the question from Will that motivates Scripture's rebuke. **141** *coueyte*: stressing intention and (at 147) action, rather than the intellectual understand-ing the Dreamer seeks. **142** *Kepe...kepe*: a 'Platonic' play on co-polysemes linking obedience to divine law with protection against evil. **144–5** The generation of Christ is virginal and, though accomplished on behalf of the human race, needs the agency of no male person. While the wordplay (*mankynde...mankynde*) is on co-polysemes of one lexeme, it also exploits complex phrasal antithesis (between *for* and *withoute*, *on þe* and *of þat*) to underline that 'a man' (Christ) is the sole true intermediary between man and God. **146–7** is close to the Doctor of Divini-ty's definition at 15.126=B 13.116. *al*: tersely replacing B 233–42, from which 234a, 240a survive as 147a and 154a.

B 232–42 begin with Dowel (*It*: **232**) defined as 'ecclesial faith', *bileue* in and through the Church. **235** *grete...neuere*: cf. B 2.30, 9.28, 16.194; **C** avoids these formulae. **237** *dedly deep*: the tautology hinting at per-manent 'spiritual' as against purely 'natural' mortality (*þe deep of kynde*). **238b** 'which is the spirit (proceed-ing) from them both'; the '*Filioque*' doctrine, first pro-posed by Augustine in *De Trinitate* (see on 148). **239–40** *Thre...al...oon...ech*: 'number stands appalled' as Clergy confronts Will with the cognitive impenetrability of the chief Christian dogma, that the Persons are distinct; not three Gods, yet wholly divine. **240a** *Deus...*: clause 15 of the Athanasian Creed, recited at Prime on Sundays; En-glished literally in 241, but also translatable 'The Father is God, the Son is God, the Holy Spirit is God' or 'God (is) Father, Son (and) Holy Spirit'. **242** Deferral of the title 'Maker' to the end links the Trinity active in history with the eternal Godhead of 235.

A 182–203 give a taut and vigorous account of the Triad, traces of which remain in **B** (186 underlies B Pr 120, 193 is behind B 15.169, 196a becomes B 13.118=C 15.128a). If the speaker at 182 is Scripture, her riposte at 225 will seem less of a sudden intervention, and in this version Clergy will then say nothing. But since he has the corresponding speech in **B**, *she* could be diagnosed as an **r**-tradition misreading as **heo* of *he*, the preferable reading of **m** (see *TN* and Schmidt 2004). **182–7** define *Dowel* as the honest, faithful way of life of uneducated working people. **188–94** define *Dobet* as a life of active charity, strongly suggestive of the pastoral ministry of the clergy, whether secular or (199–203) religious. **188** *to...bred*: 'to distribute bread to beggars' (cf. Is 58:7 qu. at 11.67–67*a* above). **190** *seken...seke*: characteristic 'Platonic' wordplay intimating that the sick are those whom we *should* seek out. **192** *þis*: either a pl. subject-form *þis* (common in **C** but not in **A**) or the complement of *þo* after pl. vb. *beþ* ('these are those who do better' / 'this is what those who do better are'). **192***a* 'Behold how good and how pleasant it is for brethren to dwell together in unity' (Ps 132:1); associated by Brinton [1:58, 114] with the unity of the Church (Alf*Q*). **193***a* 'Rejoice with them that rejoice: weep with them that weep' (Rom 12:12). **195–8** define *Dobest* as the life of the prelate, authorised to teach and govern clergy and laypeople alike. **196***a* '[But] he that shall do and teach, he shall be called great in the kingdom of heaven' (Mt 5:19). **199–203** return through the linking idea of 'endowment' to Dobet as the life of monastics, whose *stabilitas* is essential to the work of alms-giving for which they were endowed with wealth and rectorial incomes. The speaker strikingly emphasies community and charity rather than learning or contemplation as distinguishing their vocation. **201** is recalled at C 5.76. **203** both recalls Lady Mede's friar-confessor and anticipates Sir *Penetrans-domos* in B 20.341.

148–55*a* **148** *Austyn*: St Augustine of Hippo (354–430). *þe oelde*: 'venerable / early (Father of the Church)'. *bokes*: his 15-book treatise *De Trinitate*, completed *c.* 419 (see Clark in Stump & Kretzmann 2001:91–102); it influenced **L**'s treatment of the theme. **150** *Patriarkes...*: cf. *De Trin*. XII vii 12–viii 13; the texts will be Gen 18:1–2 (Trinity), Ps 109:1–3 and Jn 14:11–17 (Father and Son; cited below). **151–2** *apperede...seyh*: not the sense of 'Ecce *apparet mihi* in ænigmate *Trinitas, quod es Deus...*' (*Confessions* XIII 5); but that passage underlies the legend that a pious woman, while Augustine was saying mass, had a vision of him before the throne of God 'de trinitatis gloria...disputantem' (*LA* 124:564). It is a measure of Augustine's authority that Clergy turns to his mystical experience (as well as the Gospel) to support the Church's teaching on the Trinity. **155***a* 'I am in the Father and the Father in me'; *et qui...meum*: '[and] he that seeth me seeth the Father also' (Jn 14:10 / 11; 14:9).

B 244–9 B 244 This assertion of Augustine's purpose as being to confirm the faith of believers reflects his attack on the pride of intellectuals in mocking 'the mass of Christians who live by faith alone' (*De Trin*. IV xv 20). **B 246** *Crist...so*: either 'Christ declared himself to

be the authority [for this teaching]' or '...to be divine [as the Johannine text states]'. **B 249f** are echoed by a Lollard interpolator in *Jack Upland's Rejoinder* (Heyworth 1967:242–8).

156–61 156 is repeated entire at 14.155 below apropos of why some and not others are saved. **157** *alle*: spelling out what B 234 states but B 248 seemingly (and perhaps unintentionally) contradicts. **158** *fyn wit*: elliptical for 'intellectual subtlety *enough*'. **159** translates the following Latin, but the *repetitio* in *mouhte...mouhte* heightens the catechetical tone. **159***a* '[We must realise that divine action is not marvellous if it is understood by human reason; nor] is there any merit in believing only what can be tested by experience'. This much-quoted saying from Gregory the Great's *Homilies on the Gospels* II:26 (*PL* 76:1197) is found, e.g., in the first lesson of matins on the Sunday after Easter (*Pe*). **160** Elliptical for 'Thus faith [is the first virtue], trust [the second] and love the third.' *leute*: 'trust [in God]'; on this term's distinctive contextual referent 'hope' (especially in relation to the triad) cf. Clutterbuck 1977. **161** *That*: either assuming the qualifier 'respectively' (as seems likelier) or understanding the theological virtues (whose character as nominalised verbs is very evident here) as collectively empowering men to attain all three degrees of the Triad.

B 251–329 Of these eighty (at times somewhat loosely written) lines on DOBET and DOBEST, **C** omits the first forty, leaving only a few echoes elsewhere (e.g. 279–82, expanded at C Pr 105ff and 286–7*a* at 9.260–1), and transposes the rest to 5.146–79. It develops from a series of admonitory maxims for a general audience into a diatribe against unworthy clerics (266–90), then specifically monks (291–329). **252** *bit*: e.g. in such texts as Mt 5:9–12. **255***a* 'Seem what you are, or be what you seem' (Pseudo-Chrysostom, Homily 45 on Matthew [*PG* 56:885]); a frequently-cited adage (Alford 1975). The definition of Dobet as 'patient virtue' is close to that of Dobest by the Doctor of Divinity at B 13.118=C 15.128 (cf. on 146–7). **258** *Dobest*: exercise of rebuke (rightful only if one is righteous oneself) clearly fits with, though not strictly implying, formal authority in the Church. Clergy, like a preacher, translates or paraphrases the Latin before or after citing it. **260***a* 'If to blame others thou desire, / Beware lest thou blameworthy be; / Thy lore becomes befouled with mire / When thine own faults bite back at thee'. This anonymous Leonine hexameter circulated widely (sometimes either line separately) and first appears in the Rylands Lat. MS 394 that also contains B 1 141a [B 5.44a] //, a manuscript perhaps known to **L** (see Alf*Q* and Pantin 1930). **262***a* '[And] why seest thou [*vides* Vg] the mote that is in thy brother's eye; [and] seest not the beam that is in thy own eye?' (Mt 7:3). **264***a* '[Thou hypocrite], cast out first the beam out of thy own eye; [and then shalt thou see to cast out the mote out of thy brother's eye]' (Mt 7:5). Clergy 'grimly' warns priests guilty of gross sins not to rebuke laypeople for lesser ones; but while he holds that their *dogma* 'teaching' may be inefficacious, he avoids the Wycliffite opinion that priests in a state of mortal sin could not administer valid sacraments. **266** *blind bosard*: a proverbial phrase for 'a stupid, ignorant or worthless person' (OED s.v. *buzzard* sb.¹), of which this is the earliest cited example. The same word denotes 'buzzard', an inferior bird of the falcon family that cannot be trained for hawking, whence proverbially 'man [ne] may, for no dauntyng / Make a sperhauk of a bosard' (*RR* 4033, cit. MED s.v. *busard* n.). These 'blind buzzards' are like the 'dumb hounds' of 287 below. **268b** refers to both priests and parishioners; for the phrasing cf. *WPal* 2492 (*Many man by his miȝt*). **269** *This text*: the Latin of Mt 7:3–5. **270** *to..opere*: 'in order to bring salvation (effectively) to others.' **271–5** Clergy argues (somewhat tortuously) first (*For...yowselue*) that merely preaching the Gospel might have some value for the priest, even if it did no good to his hearers; next, that it now benefits no one (*Ac...Gospel*, the *lered* of 274 including the preacher) because he is *so* morally flawed he can't understand Scripture well enough even to preach on it. **275** *Marc*: not the only such misattribution; cf. B 6.237ff. **275a** '[They are blind and leaders of the blind. If the blind lead the blind, both fall into the pit' (Mt 15:14). Clergy's point is that the parishioners will be '(mis)led' by the priest's living (hence 'blind to moral truth') more than by his preaching. **277** *festu*: possibly introduced by **L** from OF (< Lat. *festucam* Mt 7:3); otherwise found only in Wycliffite writings (MED s.v.). **279–82** draw on I Kgs, chs. 2–4, esp 4:11–18. **281–2** Ophni and Phinees, sons of the priest Heli, were guilty of lechery (I Kgs 2:22) and greed that 'withdrew men from the sacrifice of the Lord' (2:17), so the parallel with contemporary 'bad priests' is not obscure. **282** *Archa Dei*: the Ark of the Covenant holding the Tables of the Law, which was in the care of the priests (see on C Pr 107 and on 51a). But there may also be a punning allusion to Noah's Ark, a traditional 'type' of the Christian Church, which was entrusted to the keeping of the clergy (cf. C 245–54). **285** '[These things hast thou done, and I was silent]. Thou thoughtest unjustly that I should be like to thee: but I will reprove thee, and set before thy face [= "lay the charge before you" RSV]' (Ps 49:21). The psalm ominously warns that God will withdraw his favour from the sacrificial priesthood (a type of the Christian clergy) and give it to 'his saints' (= right-living laypeople) 'who set his covenant before sacrifices' (vs 5). **286–7** *burel clerkes...carpen now*: these 'homespun scholars' may include mockers like the 'heiȝe men' of 103–5 above who 'carpen as þei clerkes were'. Clergy's impersonal 'voice' facilitates the utterance of radical sentiments without 'blame'. **287a** '[His watchmen are all blind. They are all ignorant]:

dumb dogs not able to bark' (Is 56:10). Isaiah's referent is Israel as a nation; but Richard Fitzralph in an Avignon sermon (Walsh 1981:216), had applied his image to the negligent members of the clerical estate (it is developed further at C 9.260–1). **289** *preiere*: 'mere asking,' but with a pun on the co-polyseme 'prayer', which is presumed to gain efficacy from the petitioner's virtuous living. **291** *pis rule*: i.e. of *holynesse*. **292–327a** See at C 5.146–177a. **162–4** On these transitional lines, see again after **B 370**. They link Clergy's address to Will with an inner dream of FORTUNE that in **B** occupies most of Passus XI.

B 330–70 The forty lines that at this point expand **A 11.219–57** are here annotated first. **330** *dominus*: '(being) a lord', i.e. 'lordship, high social rank.' This is the (*faux*)-*naïf* question, provoked by Clergy's apparent equation of Dowel with a future reforming king, that arouses Scripture's ire. But since its deletion in **C** leaves her 'scorn' unexplained, it may be that some new lines were planned to motivate the latter. **A 223** See on C 8.86a; the quotation recurs at 11.238a=B.10.397a. Will provokingly takes *principes* to mean secular lords, not prelates, the 'princes' of the Church. **331** SCRIPTURE represents the written word of the Bible, hence her appeal to the *scryueeynes* who copied the texts quoted at 336a, 337a. Her warnings against covetousness echo those of her sister Study at 161–2. **334** *reautee*: a word of which the only earlier occurrence is at *WPal* 5006. **335** *Poul*: the Pauline text in mind may be I Tim 6:6–10, 17–18, but *impossible* echoes rather Mt 19:24–6 (cited by Rechelesnesse at 11.203a). **336a** 'There is not a more wicked thing than to love money: [for such a one setteth even his own soul to sale]' (Ecclus 10:10). **337a** 'Money esteem, but not for its own sake' (*DC* IV.4a). The couplet continues *quam nemo sanctus nec honestus captat habere*, 'for virtuous men renounce the lust for wealth.' **338** *patriarkes and prophetes*: Job comes to mind, but also the Psalms, which praise 'God's poor' whose '*patience...shall not perish for ever*' (Ps 9:19). *poetes*: such as **L**'s anonymous contemporary who 'praises poverty with patience' at *Patience* 45. A 'spiritual' understanding of *pacience* is intimated by its collocation with *penaunce* in A 230. **340** *Apostles... witnesse*: a text especially apt being 'And we desire...that you become...followers of them who through faith and *patience* shall inherit the promises [*sc.* of eternal life]' (Heb 6: 11–12); cf. also Apoc 14:12. The blessedness of the poor is affirmed in the First Beatitude as given in Lk 6:20. **341–2** modify **A**'s overstated 'straw man' position by grounding the patient poor's right to heaven on a tacit understanding that (unlike the rich) they have had nothing here on earth; cf. 'Hath not God chosen the poor in this world, rich in faith and heirs of the kingdom...?' (Js 2:5). **342** is somewhat elliptical: 'whereas the rich cannot advance a claim [to salvation] as a right, but may only [appeal] to God to have pity and show grace'. The echo here of legal relations between subject and king, and the supra-legal character of divine compassion is unmistakable. **343** *Contra*: echoing 8 (10).20 and showing Will able to 'respond' scholastically to a theological assertion with a scriptural text that asserts the opposing view (and in a fairly radical form). *repreue*: 'refute' (answering *preueþ* 335); intellectually bolder than *wiþsigge* 'oppose.' **344** *Peter...Poul*: a deliberate riposte to Scripture's *Poul* 335. The authorities appealed to are not given here (though Scripture implicitly accepts their existence), and could be I Pet 3:21 ('baptism...now saveth you also...') and Gal 3:27–9 ('For as many of you as have been baptised in Christ...are...heirs according to the promise'). But while both texts may be taken to affirm the sufficiency (as well as necessity) of baptism for salvation, it was understood that the baptized must live out their Christian calling (by 'doing well'), and this opens a way for Scripture's reply. **345** *That is*: either, 'That is, (the) baptised are...' or, 'He who is baptised is...' **346** *That...extremis*: 'And *that* is (true, but) only in extreme cases...' Scripture too replies in scholastic mode, not directly denying Will's assertoric proposition (see on 10.29) but drawing a *distinctio* between (a) the narrow sense in which it *can* be absolutely true and (b) the wider sense in which it is not. Thus, when a Muslim or Jew at the point of death has no Christian at hand to perform the rite but receives baptism, he dies assured of salvation. *amonges*: 'in the case of...' or 'in the territories of'.

B 351–70 (A 240–57) 351 *Ac*: 'On the other hand, however...'; contrasting with (a), the wider case, (b), in which 345 is *not* true, i.e. for people born and brought up in a Christian society. **352–7** There is wordplay on both the senses of *confermed* 352 and the referents of *lawe*. In 352 the 'new law' of love is 'promoted' (MED s.v. *confermen* v. 7) and also 'ratified' (ibid. 1), in 354 it is at once the 'old law' that Christ fulfils and the new law that he establishes. Accordingly *That whoso* 353 can mean both 'Namely that / So that anyone who seeks eternal life...must [love]'. **353a** '[Therefore], if you be risen with Christ [*sc.* through baptism], [seek the things that are above]' (Col 3:1). **354** *and*: 'and in that way', as specified in **355–6** (which echo Mt 22:37–9, a passage quoted at A 11.242 and again at B 17.11–14 //). **A 242** '(Thou shalt) love [Vg *diliges*] the Lord thy God...[and] thy neighbour as thyself' (Mt 22:37, 39 run together). The first part is from Deut 6:5, the second a summary of the moral teaching of the 4th–10th Commandments. **357** *þat*: 'to those who believe (that they may) be saved', i.e. those who have faith must perform the works of faith. **A 243–4** *Godis word...enemys*: with reference to the distinctive Christian ethical precept 'Love your enemies' at Mt 5:43–4. **358–61** specify *Dowel* as almsgiving; but Scripture does not spell out the socially radical consequences of following Christ's precepts literally. **360** *bakkes*: rare outside *PP*

(though found in *WPal* 2096). **A 245a** See on B 10.201a. The sense of Gal 6:10 is paraphrased in A 246–50; but the eschatological vs 9 that precedes the Latin quoted is not developed till B 358–61. **362–3 B** alters **A** in specifying fellow-Christians and potential Christians; so Scripture, while affirming the Mosaic ban against killing one's fellow-men (on grounds of their 'likeness' to God), does not see the Gospel command of charity as answering to a 'human right' as now understood. Her priority is the moral renewal of Christian society and only then the conversion of pagans. **365** *þat ...liknesse*: 'that which is like my own likeness'; pleonastic for 'that which is made in my likeness' or (in the light of A 246b) 'that which is like (him who is) my likeness [i.e. the Son, who became a man].' **A 253** *ten hestis*: see Ex 20:1–17. **366** *tokene*: the chief such example in *PP* being God's command to Saul through Samuel to slay King Agag of Amalek (see A 3.238ff). *Non mecáberis*: i.e. for *Non moechaberis* 'thou shalt not commit adultery' (Ex 20:140); but since the speaker must intend 'thou shalt not kill', the error may be original (see *TN*). Donaldson, however, interestingly notes (1982:70) an echo of the collocation of adultery and killing in Js 2:11, following the important *offendit in uno* verse to be cited at B 11.308a (see also Goldsmith 1987:119–31); and AlfQ quotes from *FM* 681 an interesting comparison of adultery to manslaughter 'because husband and wife are one flesh'. **368** See C VIII under B 6.226. If this implies that capital punishment is forbidden to Christian authorities, **L** never states as much (cf. B 17.288–94=9.270–76, which envisage the severest divine punishment being for murder of the innocent). **369–70** do not translate any specific text but echo the familiar 'he shall render to a man according to his works' (Prov 24:12), especially as quoted in the eschatological contexts of Mt 16:27 and Rom 2:5–6.

11.162–13.215 The C revision distributes **B 10.371–475, 11.1–439** over two-and-a-half passus, reducing its dramatic intensity as well as its clarity and coherence in the interest of ascribing Will's angry speeches to Rechelesnesse, a personage whose substantial identity with the Dreamer becomes clear from 12.3–4. Lines 162–97 correspond to B 11.1–36, the opening of the first **B** passus that is entirely new (**A** having ended at 11.313). The revision here, which transposes as well as re-writes, involves loss of B 10.330–70=A 11.219–57 (discussed above).

162–5 162–4 now somewhat awkwardly link Clergy's address with Will's 'inner dream' of FORTUNE, which in **B** fills Passus XI. **162** recurs (with deliberate irony) at 13.130, where Scripture is the object, not the subject, of the same verb. **164** That this *Latyn* is meant to be (and is) understood by Will seems clear from his response at 166. **165** scans on *s* as a macaronic largely in Latin. 'Many know many things, yet know not themselves;' the opening of the *Cogitationes piissime de cognitione humanae* conditionis (*PL* 184:485), misattributed to St Bernard (see on B 4.121). This work belongs to a monastic tradition that saw 'self-understanding' as the knowledge of God's image in the soul, and the 'knowledge' of merely external things as vain (see Wittig 1972:212ff; Bennett 1982:145–6; Simpson 1986³:49–51).

166–317 The second half of the passus consists mainly of the vision of FORTUNE and her satellites, followed by the long speech of RECHELESNESSE (195–307) and the responses of Plato and Fauntelete (308–17).

(iii) 166–94 166 *for...wrathe of*: either 'because of the anger of her words' or 'from anger at her words,' the latter being more apt in **C**, which gives no reason for Scripture's 'scorn.' **167** *wynkynge*: initiating a remarkable dream-within-a-dream in which Will's *alter ego* Rechelesnesse appears to personify the extreme aspects of his 'lower' self responding to the experience of Fortune (rather as later in the second inner dream *Liberum Arbitrium* will function as wise spokesman of his 'higher' self). *wonder-liche*: removing B 11.6's echo of B Pr 11. **167–8** *mette / fette*: conspicuous end-rhyme marking Will's 'ravishment' from the outer-dream world of rational debate into an inner-dream world of emotional abandon. **168** *rauysched*: a word of ambiguous overtones (see MED s.v. *ravishen* v. 3) but always in *PP* with a negative sense (see IG). *Fortune*: the pagan goddess of worldly vicissitude, a 'merueylous monstre' who 'useth ful flaterynge famylarite with hem that sche enforceth to begyle, so longe, til that sche confounde with unsuffrable sorwe hem that sche hath left in despeer unpurueied' (Chaucer's *Boece* II, pr i, ll. 17–21); on *Fortuna* see Patch 1927 and Bartholomew 1966. Kaske 1968 draws attention to the iconography of Fortune's wheel at Kempley, Glos. and Leominster, and to an important depiction in the Arundel Psalter, which contains the inscription 'Vita decens seculi: speculo probatur' (165: pl. 60a). **169** *lond of longyng*: in part the allegorical terrain of worldly lusts (as the link with *loue* underlines), but less specific than *the launde...Lecherie* of B 10.163. For, as hinted by the phrase's sardonic inversion of the poet's *kynde name*, misdirected will 'ravishes' the soul into a *terra longinqua* 'distant land', where it becomes estranged from its defining object (God's image in the soul) and spiritually adrift in Augustine's *regio dissimilitudinis* 'land of unlikeness' (*Confessions*, vii, 10, 2; see Wittig 1972:232–4). **170** *myrrour...Myddelerd*: Fortune's mirror is the mutable world itself, particularly its transient pleasures (a like image occurs in Chaucer's Balade 'Fortune,' 10). But unlike the *speculum* of Nature in Alan of Lille's 'Omnis mundi creatura' (*PL* 210:579–80), as evoked by Kynde at 13.132, it 'reflects' only objects of selfish desire rather than acting as a *signaculum fidele nostrae sortis* 'a trustworthy token of our destiny' and a source of divinely guaranteed wisdom. Kaske 1969 traces **L**'s contrast of the two mirrors to that

between the deceptive mirror of Narcissus and the true mirror of Nature in *RR* 20416ff, 17468ff. He also draws attention (p. 164) to Honorius of Autun's 'imago mundi, eo quod dispositio *totius orbis* in eo, *quasi in speculo* conspiciatur' (*PL* 172; 119–20). *Myddelerd*: the world of man in medieval cosmology being thought of as placed in the middle of the universe, 'between' heaven above its height and hell at its centre (cf. 1.127). **171** *wondres*: cf. Will's 'unholy' quest in Pr 4 *wondres to here*. **172** *and... coueytest*: 'and recognise what (it is) you (really) desire.' **173** *fayre maydenes*: 'pretty girls', her handmaidens lust and greed; their implied virginity is no less ironic than their congener's (Mede the Maid). **174** *Concupiscencia Carnis...Pruyde*: avoidance of the English derivate for the Latin here directing attention towards its source I Jn 2:16, which condemns 'all that is in the world' [= Fortune's domain] as 'the concupiscence of the flesh and the concupiscence of the eyes and the pride of life,' because 'the world passeth away and the concupiscence thereof: but he that doth the will of God abideth for ever' (ib. vs 17). *ParsT* (*CT* X 335) relevantly warns how 'concupiscence...wrongfully disposed or ordeyned in man...maketh hym coveite, by coveitise of flessh, flesshly synne, by sighte of his eyen as to erthely thynges, and eek coveitise of hynesse by pride of herte'. On the background history of this unholy triad, see Howard 1966:43–53. **176** *Parfyt Lyuynge*: 'luxury,' as pursued by the dissolute Lyf in 22.143 and by the protagonist of the early morality play *The Pride of Life*; but here with a tart 'anti-pun' (Schmidt 1987:111n8) on the sense 'life of moral perfection' later instanced at B 15.417 (cf. 13.231). **177** The revision to a T-type structure groups the chimed staves in the a-half, the new pun sustaining the passage's sardonic tone: whatever rejecting Clergy's 'lore' does for Will's 'looks', it does *not* promote his 'continence.' **180–1** The cloying indulgence proffered is mimicked by the repeated Type Ib lines and the fricatives of 183, 185–6. **183–4** *wille / nelle*: perhaps originally a perfect rhyme; 'I won't give up keeping company with you'. **186** *frende*: the ability of Fortune to become one's 'foe' (12.13) or to 'fail' (15.5) was proverbial, as shown especially in her replacement of youth, wealth and rank by age, poverty and loss of position (prelude to VISION FOUR). **188** *Elde*: the 'olde elde' of B 12.8, a sombre figure who in *PTA* 290 warns Youth and Middle Eld, 'Make ȝour mirrours bi me.' He is here what the Dreamer becomes in 22.183, after age has taken its toll of the vital powers, and makes an intermediate appearance in the second inner dream at 18.106. On medieval notions of Old Age, see Burrow 1986:150–62, Dove 1986:26–42, 103–17. **190–1** *fayle*; *forsake*: see 15.5, 22.195–8. **193** scans on spirantal 'metrical allophones' (v, ð), with *of Yes* liaised.

(iv) 195–317 195 *Rechelesnesse*: 'heedless disregard of one's spiritual state.' Stepping forth as suddenly as Piers in 7.181, he is in **B** one of three (followed by Plato and Fauntelete) to adopt extreme positions expressive of the Dreamer's wilful *likyng* (B 1.45). In C 200–307 he is given Will's entire **B** reply to Scripture's long lesson and dark showing (B 372); but some extended prefatory lines make clear his character as a desperate extreme of folly (*wanhope* 198; *rybaude* 199). *ragged clothes*: indicating either the ravages of Fortune's enmity or scorn of outward show (as at 16.349 where they are, however, the garb of Charity). **197** scans with an internal *t*-stave in *stoupe* and chiastic assonance. **198** *Sir Wanhope*: 'despeir of the mercy of God' (*CT* X 692–5); at 22.160 not a knight but a prostitute. *sib*: seen in 7.58, 80 as the end-stage of sloth (cf. *CT* X 692); here defiant indifference to one's final destiny (200), a variety of spiritual sloth 'related' to this enemy of the soul. **200** has a vocalic structural pattern and echoic counterpoint on |g|. *myn one*: the majority choosing the former (cf. 1.7–9, 66–7). **201** *þat ʒe seyn*: a reference to Scripture's attack on *richesse* and *reautee* in B 332–42 which has, however, been deleted in C. Clergy himself does not attack wealth in either text (except implicitly, through criticising the worldliness of religious). So unless taken as an 'intertextual' allusion (to **B**), it is an oversight on the revising poet's part. **203a** '[Only] in this way is it possible for a rich man to enter [the kingdom of heaven] — as a camel [might pass through the eye of a needle]' (after Mt 19:23–4; Vg has *dives difficile intrabit* and *facilius est camelum....transire*).

204–24 return to the line of argument first proposed in **A** and maintained, with only a few careful changes, in **B**. **204–9a** evolve from a natural-sounding form, expressing the speaker's conviction in **A**, through an ascription of the predestination doctrine to Theology in **B**, then in **C** to the Gospel as cited by Clergy, i.e. from Will's conclusion out of Scripture, through the theologians', to the formal teaching authority of the Church. Of the three, **C** is the most aggressively technical; but though **A** seems the most coherent with what has gone before, its clarity is deceptive, since A 281 could imply that nothing men do throughout life affects their final standing in God's eyes. **204** sarcastically echoes the wording and sound of 203. *Clergie saith*: not directly referring to something Clergy said but generally to what Will understands the Church to maintain about the NT doctrine of grace. Similarly, *ye tellen* B 373 denotes the Biblical teaching as doctrinally formulated by her theologians, not any actual words of Dame Scripture. **205** *man ymaed was*: relating a man's lot to the moment of his creation, whereas **A** elliptically declares him 'marked out [to be saved or damned]', a destiny that removes the necessity for either dowel or grace. *legende of lyf*: the *liber vitae* of Apoc 20:12. **206–8** The speaker's sense that 'since God is all-knowing, he must foresee the evil each person may one day do' is undiminished by his awareness of a distinction between God's

'permissive' and 'constitutive' will, what he knows (and so must be understood to allow) and what he ordains (and so must intend). *predestinaet*: 'pre-elected to salvation,' a technical term from theology. It is contrasted with *prescite inparfit* 'foreknown to be one who would sin', a direct derivation from Lat. *praescitus* used of those 'þat are to be dampnid or are now dampnid [having died]' (MED s.v. *prescite* adj.). Both terms are first recorded here and perhaps introduced by **L**; see further Von Nolcken 1988:85. *pult...*: 'violently thrust out of God's favour and beyond the reach of his grace.' **209** *Vnwriten*: first instanced here and echoing *non...scriptus* in Apoc 20:15 (*Pe*). It evokes the NT notion (drawing on Dan 12:1) that only those *fore-ordained* to be saved are recorded, whereas Piers at 8.77 has employed the more archaic OT idea that God initially writes down in the 'book of life' all men's names but later blots out those of the wicked, retaining only those who will be saved because they *have* 'done well' (Ex 32:32, Ps 22:29 [quoted at 8.77], Ps 138:16). *for (som) wikked(nesse)*: elliptical for 'as going to be evil' / 'for doing evil [at some future time]'. **209a** '[And] no man hath ascended into heaven, but he that descended from heaven, [the Son of man who is in heaven]' (Jn 3:13). Since in context this refers to the divine Son's real pre-existence and not to the notional 'heavenly pre-existence' of the predestined, the speaker's arbitrary and extreme interpretation may be meant to be seen as deliberately provocative. **210–24** cite exemplary cases from sacred and secular history of the truth of 209a (the 'proof by illustration' favoured by the *ars praedicandi*). The argument runs: these men were great teachers of wisdom; yet the Church denies they are saved; therefore they were predestined to be damned, whatever they did (cf. *wrong oper ellis* A 260b). But the only valid conclusion from the first two premises is that wisdom is not sufficient for salvation (cf. 14.192–3). **210** *by Oure Lord*: both an asseveration and an appeal to his words just quoted. **211–16** restate Conscience's argument at 3.323–6, omitting his crucial point that God forsook Solomon not in spite of his wisdom but because of his disobedience. **211** *Salamon...Sapience*: see on 3.121, 484. **212** *gaf...goed*: 'favoured him with wisdom and wealth'; as at 3.323–4 *grace* does not have its precise theological sense. *aftur*: the gift of wealth being added to the wisdom he asked for (III Kgs 3:9–14). **215** *wymmen*: the two harlots on whom King Solomon passed his famous Judgement illustrating that 'the wisdom of God was in him' (III Kgs 3:28). **216** 'Let it be neither mine nor thine, but divide it' (III Kgs 3:26). The way in which Solomon's psychological insight was displayed resembles Christ's in the incident of the Woman taken in Adultery (Jn 8:3–11; see 14.40–2). **217** *Aristotel*: regarded as simply 'the Philosopher' by Aquinas and as 'the master of those who know' by Dante (*Inf.* IV 131). If Solomon stands for practical wisdom, Aristotle (the exemplar of 'wit' outside the revealed dispensation, whose works formed the basis of higher study in the Arts Faculty) emblematises theoretical knowledge (including natural philosophy). *tauhte*: avoiding like **B** the ambiguous and even contradictory *wrouȝte* of **A**. **218–21** argue, in the form of another imperfect syllogism, against the pursuit of *clergie*: 'Solomon and Aristotle were wise; both are damned; therefore wisdom leads to damnation'. Once again, the *valid* conclusion from the minor premiss would be that 'wisdom' as such does not suffice for salvation (without grace). **219** *wordes...werkes*: a return to the sense and wording of A 269, perhaps through dissatisfaction with the ambiguity of B 384 *Of hir wordes* 'as regards / on the basis of their words.' The *werkes* would presumably refer to such matters as Solomon's wise judgements and Aristotle's guidance of the young Alexander; the re-phrasing eliminates the unacceptable suggestion in A 270b that they lived lives of great sanctity. **221** *And*: i.e. 'And yet'; not intimating opposition between *maistres* and *Holi Churche*; rather that although the university theologians recognise both men's wisdom, they agree with the Church's standard view. *in helle*: neither sage being traditionally included among the pre-Christian just in the *Limbo Inferni* (8.116), the borderland province of Hell. Aristotle was not as a pagan automatically denied 'actual' or 'prevenient' grace to assist his natural *grace of wit*; but according to spurious medieval traditions, he had (like Solomon) fallen prey to lust (see the illustration from 1310–20 in Camille 1996:pl. 88 of him being 'ridden' by Phyllis) and had committed suicide (see on B 12.43 below). In III Kgs 11:1–11, Solomon's idolatry (following upon lust) in his later years provokes God to take away his kingdom from his descendants. **222–4** embroider the specious argument with rhetorical wordplay on *werkes*, *wys* and repetition of *w*, the speaker leaving it unclear which 'works' are to be imitated and which are cause of their being damned (as well as mixing up sg. and pl. persons). **223** *That*: improving on the looseness of *And* A 277. *for*: with polysemantic wordplay on the senses 'because of' and 'in spite of' (MED s.v. *for* prep. 1(a), 9(a): see *IG* for other examples), effective in leaving the opponent no means of answer.

225–54 225–8 enable a better transition to 229–32 (preserved from **B**) through use of *For* 231. But the scholastic concession ('I am not saying *contra* to your position: I allow that those who follow what the books teach "do well"') is at once retracted by an assertion of the extreme 'Augustinian' view that a morsel of grace ranks above the mass of traditional religious learning: *Ac* 225 = 'Now', *Ac* 227 = 'All the same'. **230** *vngracious*: a mordant pun intimating that because clever people may lack God's grace, they must lack the capacity to please him. **231** *mony*: i.e. many 'witty' men, the argument here being that since most clerks seek learning for profit, not for

love of God, they in effect represent that 'wisdom of the world' that is 'folly' in God's eyes. **232** *goed*: the anti-pun ('property not goodness') gains force from the adjacent 'chime' (*annominatio*) on *God* (Schmidt 1987:114; with 232 cf. 1.177, B 9.178, 13.357). **232–3** Although the present punctuation is defensible, the stop could be omitted (making the syntax as in **B**) and a colon be placed after *meschief*, giving the sense '(when) mercy would be the most valuable "good" — mercy, which is granted only to those who have given mercy'. The allusion is to Mt 5:7, but the contextual meaning of *mercy* is 'charitable generosity shown in selfless use of one's learning'. The removal of B 395 and revision of the ambiguously parenthetical 397a are improvements (the homophone *seyen* 237 is a different lexeme); for a chief strength of Rechelesnesse's argument in **C** is that much of it is indisputable. **235–238** More rhetorical *repetitio* that not only draws ammunition from Scripture's own *connyng* to make the case against 'learning without love' (*witnesseth*; *Goddes word*) but also allows sardonic anti-puns on the ethical sense of *wel*. **235a; 238a** *Eadem..*; *Super...*: see on 1.173a and 8.86a above. **239–44** again exemplify homily-like *repetitio*; for the rationale of this application of the ark-image to the clergy, see on 10.224–5. **243** scans on *s* with a liaisonal first stave *his wyf*. **245** *leue*: for this revision of *lene* **B** cf. Pr 149. **245** In **C** both *folk* and *faith* economically govern *Holy Kirke*, but whereas in **B** the Church is the subject of the verb, in **C** it is more explicitly the clergy. The *Churche* form of the noun-phrase, with stress on *Holy*, now appears in line 248. **247–8** *Archa Noe...Holy Churche*: a standard typological interpretation: 'Ecclesia dicitur *arca*, quia, sicut arca Noe eos qui in ea erant defendit a diluvio, ita *Ecclesia* suos a mortis aeternae periculo' (Alan of Lille in *PL* 210:707). It goes back to I Pet 3:20–1, a text of sacramental rather than apocalyptic emphasis that makes the equation obliquely in comparing the water of the Flood by which 'eight souls' were saved to 'baptism, being of the like form' that saves 'all Christian souls'. *herborw*: anticipating the image of 'the house Unity' in 21.330 (cf. *hous* B 405). **B 405** *and...saue*: elliptical for 'and have the reponsibility of protecting God's house(hold)'; **C** makes clear that 'Christian souls' are denoted. **250–1** *carpentares...bestes*: the 'proper' analogues being: churchmen ~ Noah's family, laity ~ the animals; but here the clergy are disturbingly equated with the Ark's builders, who were not saved. *vnder Crist*: the allusion to Our Lord's own 'craft' unsparingly highlights how, on account of their worldliness, clerks *fail* to 'build up' (edify) the Church. *Goddes foles*: both echoing the ironic sense 'fools to the world but wise before God' made explicit in 22.61 (but perhaps presumed as familiar from B 20) and playing annominatively on *foules* 'birds' (as at B 7.125–30). *fre bestes*: oxymoronic, since the 'lewed folk' are no more beasts, once liberated through baptism from the 'bondage' of sin. **251a** See on 7.153*a*; but whereas there the *bestes* are only implicitly equated with the Folk of the Field (cf. also 7.158), here the symbolic referent of *iumenta* is precise and the preceding words of the psalm-verse ('thy judgements are a great deep') clearly evoked by the eschatological context. Focus has now shifted from reform of the laity to reform of the clergy, and the poet's conviction 'that judgement should begin at the house of God' (I Pet 4:17) becomes relevant to the argument of this passage. **252** This notion derives from II Pet 3:5–12, which compares Noah's Flood with the 'fire against the day of judgement...of the ungodly'. *deth...ones*: either 'death and fire together' (with *deth* generic rather than specifically 'plague') or (more probably) 'deadly fire in one sudden instant'.

255–72 continue to argue from Biblical examples that mere faith can save not only without 'wisdom' but without 'do-well'. The probative instances mount from a common thief and a 'common woman', through a king driven by passion to kill a good man, to a (future) apostle who martyred Christians. But the proposition (suggestive of the 'Catholic' novels of Graham Greene) is again flawed: 'these "did worst" (not "best"), yet are saved; therefore to be saved one may (?must) live viciously, provided one has faith'. The argument ignores the crucial element of repentance, *followed by* good deeds: for even the Good Thief had a virtuous act (his rebuke of the Bad Thief's blasphemy [Lk 23:40–1]), and this was the fruit of (though uttered before profession of) his faith in Christ. The speaker here nonetheless has a point: that for all of them 'conversion' depended on the free proffer of divine grace, not on their own learning (or virtue). **255** *feloun*: see Lk 23:39–43 and on 6.319, and cf. 14.131–6. **256** *vnlawefulliche...lyued*: the 'positive' degree of 'do-ill', breaking the seventh commandment (the opposite of simple 'do-well' or keeping the law / comandments). **257** *shrof hym*: confession to and unconditional absolution and pardon from the 'great High Priest' himself (Heb 4:14), needing no penance in the form of (further) suffering or punishment (see on 262). **258** *sunnere ysaued*: on the strength of Christ's promise in Lk 23:43. In *GN* ch. 26 (ME version ed. Hulme 1573ff) the patriarchs liberated by Christ are surprised to meet the Good Thief in paradise. While his dramatic act of faith at the point of death would be properly interpreted as a limiting case, not a norm, Rechelesnesse as the spokesman of extremes is not disposed to take a balanced position. **258–60** Cf. 20.366–9. The choice of these figures is not arbitrary (they recur at 18.113–4): the first man, who is awakened from death by the blood of Christ (7.133), the great OT prophet of the Messiah (20.366), and the Messiah's forerunner. The text that probably underlies R.'s contrast of the Good Thief with the latter is Mt 11:11, 'he that is

the lesser [*v.l.* least] in the kingdom of heaven is greater than [John the Baptist]'. That Dismas *is* one of the 'least' will be maintained by Ymaginatif later at 14.131–48. **262** scans on vowels with an under-pattern of initial *p* sounds on the higher-ranking lexemes. *passioun*: the choice of this word suggesting that crucifixion with Christ (cf. Rom 6:6, Gal 2:19) constitutes a penance that needs no further *peyne*. **264** *Marie Maudelene*: traditionally identified with the 'woman...a sinner' who washes Christ's feet with her tears and is forgiven her sins (see on 7.137). Crucial to an understanding of R.'s argument is Christ's final words to the woman: 'Thy faith hath made thee safe' (Lk 7:37–50). **265** *denyede*: i.e. '(as she) said "no"' to'; C here (as with David) gives the sordid details **AB** only hint at. **266** Dauid's encompassing of Uriah the Hittite's death out of desire for his wife Bathsheba is told in II Kgs 11:14–17. Although losing **AB**'s fine gradational antithesis between *myȝte do* and *dede*, **C** provides one equally effective in its ironic *lelly...gyle / douhty...sleylokeste* paradox and its savage critique of ill-applied *connyng* by means of a graphetic 'Platonic' pun on *deuyned* (a visual transform of *denyede*). **269** *apostel*: not when he persecuted Christians; but the shocking juxtaposition of this title with *no pite* points up the impenetrable mysteriousness of divine election. R. here seems to echo disturbing contemporary speculations on such questions as 'Does God will only the good, or is a thing good only because God wills it?' **271** finally fixes this metrically troublesome line (which in **B** opens with a liaisonal stave on *þise ás*). Its great length (twice that of 269 or 270) formally mirrors Saul's abrupt but total spiritual transformation. **272** both obscures a truth (that grace abounded in these greatest of sinners) and suggests a falsehood (that they are saints because they did evil). **B 427–8** are rightly omitted in revision as repeating B 384–5. **273–5a** paraphrase the opening of the Latin quotation's omitted second part and offer a (not wholly satisfactory) revision of B 429–34, the form of which has been questioned (see *TN*). The **B** lines assert somewhat cryptically that two (seemingly unconnected) things are known to God alone: the fate of wise and virtuous men (or conceivably 'wise-and-virtuous men'); and whether people are to be judged on their good or on their evil acts and dispositions (the referent of *þere* 432 is 'God's hands', metonymic for his will). But the final conjunctive *for* does not readily follow; presumably the point of 434b is that 'the good *later* seen in Mary Magdalen, David and Paul shines all the brighter and better manifests the power of God's grace when contrasted with their former wickedness'. C 274–5 means 'Knows who deserves (what: whether bliss) for doing well or (pain) for doing evil'. Conceivably there is a pun on two senses of *for* 'because of'; 'in spite of' ('no one knows who is worthy [of heaven] — whether for his virtue or in spite of his sin'), as suggested by the following wordplay in 275 on *wele* '(heavenly) bliss' and *wykkede* (*pyne*) '(hellish) torment'. But the full scriptural text quoted does not support 'despite', stating rather that 'ill fortune and good befall all men alike in this life and so cannot be taken to signify divine (dis)favour'. **275** *he*: more probably reflexive than indefinite, since *no wyht woet wheþer he is* answers to Vg *nescit homo utrum... sit*. **275a** 'There are just men and wise men, and their works are in the hands of God: [and yet man knoweth not whether he be worthy of love, or hatred. But all things are kept uncertain for the time to come; because all things equally happen to the just and to the wicked, to the good and to the evil...]' (Eccl 9:1–2). **B 434** may be scanned as Type IIa to avoid an over-weighted b-verse.

    B 435–40 are cut in revision since they follow on directly from B 434 as part of an argument that **C** here omits. The colour-analogy is therefore not repeated at B 18.204–10, where Peace explains why suffering is necessary, but is used in variant form at parallel C 20.212–13. The argument moves from claiming that moral goodness could not be recognised without moral evil to contrast it with ('white cannot be perceived except in opposition to black') to asserting that we should tolerate evil men anyway, since even the virtuous are partly bad ('we are all neither white nor black but some shade of grey'). The ascription of 'complete white' to God alone implies that of 'complete black' to the Devil; and while this verges on dualism, the 'realistic' view of *man* it implies is scripturally based (440). **437** *goode*: see on 440 below. **438** 'When *must* steps onstage, there's nought but to *suffer* it'; a Latin-French macaronic scanning as a perfect Type IIIc line on vowels and *p*. This proverb, which is connected with the theme of judgement (AlfQ, s.v.), has the more usual form 'Quant *Oportet* vient en place, il convient que l'on le face', as in the *Roman des deduis* 3095–6 (cited Hassell 1982:183), and appears in an English poem on grammatical rules as 'And, when *oportet* cums in plas, / Thou knawys *miserere* has no gras' (Wright & Halliwell, ii.14, cited *Sk* II:163). **440** *Nemo bonus*: 'None is good [but God alone]' (Lk 18:19=Mk 10:18); Christ's reply to a rich man who addresses him as 'Good master', and whom he rebukes by asking 'Why dost thou call me good?' The implication in context is that only God may be called '(absolutely) good'. However, the use of *God* for Christ at 440 brings out that there *was* one man of whom 'bonus' could be strictly predicated, the divine Son (who is implied by the litotic *fewe* in 437). The text recurs at 15.137a.

276–307 276 firmly attributes the anti-clerical sentiment to R., who (ironically) bases his claim on his *reading*. The revision substitutes for the sharp contrast of *mouþ(es)* B 441, 445 the witty *clergie* of 283 to make the same point: that Christ replaced human learning by the superior wisdom of his Holy Spirit (A 301). The transition-

line A 293 ('And I cannot remember any more of what I learnt from my everyday practical experience') is well omitted in revision as both clumsy and inappropriate, since awareness that Christ did not commend learning is itself acquired from scripture (as C 276 acknowledges), not from *fyue wyttis techyng*. **280** 'When you shall stand before governors and kings [for my sake...be not thoughtful beforehand what you shall speak...For it is not you that speak, but the Holy Ghost' (Mk 13:9–11). **281** *clerkes* (*prestis*) *of þe lawe*: in context referring to the Jewish Scribes, though some readers of **C** might have thought of the ecclesiastical authorities, such as the Blackfriars' Council that condemned Wycliffe's doctrines in 1382. **283** *conclude*: like *disputen* B 447 a term showing how R. envisages his idealised *illiteratus* as able to engage the most accomplished scholastic theologian. It is not difficult to see why Lollard readers might have liked this. **284–5** allude to Ps 118:46, 'And I spoke of thy testimonies before kings: and I was not ashamed' (*Pe*). This text's keywords (*in testimoniis tuis in conspectu regum* echo those of 280 (*ante..reges...in testimonium*). **287** *wihtnesse*: an improvement on *wisedom*, affirming that theological victory is obtained neither by cleverness nor by compulsion. **288** *grace of fortune*: what is intended being apparently 'the divine gift of actual grace'; but the reading is unsure (see *TN* further). **290** *Austyn*: see at 148. *þat...wiste*: either parenthetical ('as far as anyone ever knew', he who said...was') or, as seems more idiomatic, completing the sense of *moste* ('for he who said the most that...knew...was...') (*Pe*). **B 453** *heiȝest....*: the chief of the Four Western Doctors of the Church, the *stottes* who harrow Piers's field in 21.268–74a. **291** *Saide*: '(Who) said.' *sarmon*: 'discourse', not 'sermon'. *for...clerkes*: an improvement in pointedness over **A**'s feeble and **B**'s flat b-half. **292** 'Behold, it is they, the uninstructed, who lay hold of heaven, while we the wise ones drown deep in hell'. This is loosely based on Augustine's *Confessions* VIII 8.1: 'Surgunt indocti, et *caelum rapiunt*, et *nos* cum doctrinis nostris sine corde *ecce ubi* volutamur in carne et sanguine.' Versions close to **L**'s circulated widely (AlfQ), so his omission of *sine corde* 'without heart' and substitution of 'hell' (= damnation) for 'flesh and blood' (= 'worldliness') may be of no particular significance; for **L**'s use of the quotation see further Benson 1976:51–4, Goldsmith 1987, and Lawton 1987;10n4 (citing the form in the Lollard *Lanterne of Liȝt* 5, which has *in infernum dimergimur*). *idiote*: 'ignorant simpletons', the sense of the English equivalent 'idiot' at B 16.170, as opposed to 'one (culpably) ignorant' (B 11.316). *rapiunt celum*: alluding to Mt 11:12, 'regnum *caelorum* vim patitur, et violenti *rapiunt* illud' ('the kingdom of heaven suffereth violence and the violent bear it away'), and tacitly equating impulsive *lewed* believers like Piers with the 'violent' of Christ's words. *sapientes*: an uneasy echo of 275a.

294–307 The formula-like contrast between simple and subtle is underscored by *repetitio* in end-position of *bileue* (294, 296, 300) and in first position of *selde falleth* (301a, 305a), enriched alliteration (295, 297, 300), frequency of the stave-sound *p* (cf. B 463–5) and identical rhyme at 297–8. **C** improves by prudently adding *lele* to the *pore* and *lewed* of **AB** (perhaps in consideration of post-1381 conditions), avoiding the awkwardness of vocalic grammatical staves in A 313 and B 465, and condensing B 463–4 into one firmly conclusive line. **300** *penaunceles*: 'without having to spend time suffering there'; expressing what may be only 'the views of Rechelesnesse' (*Pe*), but hardly much bolder than the Pardon it recalls, which equated humble acceptance of suffering with loyal service of Truth as '*purgatorie vppon this puyre erthe*' (9.185). The difference in sense between the three versions is less than maintained by Johnson 1991:86–7, especially if the **p** reading *passen* is adopted (although the sense in either case could be that the poor simply need a kind of 'passport-check' in the place of purgation but are, like their emblem the messenger at 13.89–91, admitted to heaven without 'toll'). *parfit bileue*: perfect (i.e. pure and total) faith taking the place of **B**'s 'imperfect knowledge' and (necessarily 'worldly') manner of living. **300a** 'A short prayer pierces heaven'; neatly balancing 292 in both wording and imagery (*penetrat celum ~ rapiunt celum*). This proverbial phrase is based on Ecclus 35:21: '*Oratio humiliantis se nubes penetrabit*' ('The prayer of him that humbleth himself shall pierce the clouds' (Alf*Q*)). But since the *Paternoster* is specified at 299 (and cf. B 468), allusion to Christ's teaching it to his disciples (Mt 6:7–13) and recommending short prayers is the likely source (*Orantes autem, nolite multum loqui* 'when you are praying, speak not much'). Also relevant is Mt 23:12–14 (noted by *Pe*), where Christ criticises the Pharisees because they do not humble themselves, but 'shut the kingdom of heaven against men' (by their hypocritical example) and fail in charity while 'praying long prayers (*orationes longas orantes*)'.

B 466–8 are probably well removed, as seeming (inadvertently) to imply preference for an ignorant clergy, whereas the target is the spiritual arrogance of the learned, not their learning. **467** *Credo..*: 'I believe in God the Father [Almighty]'; this, 'þe furste clause of oure bileue' [i.e. the Apostles' Creed] (17.316) is also cited by Liberum Arbitrium at 16.322 as *clergie* sufficient for his ideal figure of 'Charity'.

301–03 This image of the clerical office reflects current social practice in the manorial economy; but it also alludes to the steward (= 'reeve') representing the Christian minister in the eschatological parable at Lk 12:31–48, which concludes 'And unto whomsoever much is given, of him much shall be required'. **307** *lene hem*: significantly adding to the teaching of pure doctrine an obligation to dis-

pense literal 'tresor' (= practical charity) as an equal duty of the clergy.

B 475–75a *soule to saue*: 'soul that is to be saved'; on this passive future use of the infinitive see *MES* 525. **475a** 'Go you [also] into my vineyard [and I will give you what shall be just]' (Mt 20:4). As at B 15.499 the workmen in the Parable are understood to symbolise Christian preachers; but **C** omits this quotation at both points.

A 312–13 conclude the main text of the **A Version** and are obviously intended to echo the lines of the SECOND VISION (A 8.87–80) corresponding to the point at which the **Z Version** ended. They are extended at B 463–5, which are then further expanded to round off B X. In conjoint **AC**-mss like TH²Ch this forms the point of juncture between the **A** and **C** Versions (see *TN*).

*Passus B X ends here, but the **A Version** is continued in mss **RUJ** by **Passus XII**, which follows immediately here in the text. The last ten lines of **Passus C XI**, which are printed after **A XII** opposite their parallel **B XI 37–43** (Vol. I, pp. 452–3), are commented on here.*

308–17 (B 11.37–43) 308–9 *Homo...disponit*: 'Man proposes, God disposes', a common proverb (Whiting M162), which Hugh of St Cher cites in commenting on its Biblical source, Prov 16:9: '*Cor hominis disponit* viam suam, Sed *Domini* est dirigere gressus eius' ('The heart of man disposeth his way: but the Lord must direct his steps' (Alf*Q*)). *poete*: see on 11.120 (and cf. 12.175, 14.189). **310–13** 'All those whom Truth [= God] guarantees as virtuous do not, to my mind, act foolishly if they follow the will of Fortune. Neither lust nor avarice will afflict you or lead you astray, unless that is what you desire'. Something like the speaker's equation of 'principled indifference to circumstance' with 'resigned acceptance of Providence' (and concomitant protection from worldly vices) might well be deducible from the true Plato's account of *The Death of Socrates*. The tone, moreover, does not seem ironic, though Rechelesnesse has hardly taken it in the intended spirit when using (at 196a above) the same words as 'Plato' at 311, and immediately goes astray now, as might be expected. **314** *farewel, Fyppe*: 'bye, bye blackbird!' *Fyppe* is a name for a sparrow, imitative of its chirp (and later to be treated as the proper name 'Philip' by Skelton). *Faunteltee*: a personification of culpable naïveté, very different from the care-free Charity described at 16.296 as *a childische* [= childlike] *thing*. **316–17** *me thouhte*; *Y counted*: the tacit identification of Rechelesnesse with Will now becomes overt.

A Version: Passus XII

The first 98 lines of A XII are here understood as an attempt, later abandoned, to continue or, more probably, complete the text found in A Pr–XI; their authenticity is argued in III, *A Version* §§ 69–74. 99–117, printed in italics, are taken as John But's addition. The lines offer (1) a continuation of the interview with CLERGY and SCRIPTURE (1–54) and (2) a condensed account of Will's encounters with HUNGER and then FEVER, who urges him to do well for the remainder of his days in order to get to heaven. Line 97 repeats A 1.119 and the passus abruptly ends.

1–11 Clergy's reply does not take up Will's final point in A 11.309–13 that the simple faith of the uneducated is a surer way to salvation than much learning, but protests at his contentious questioning and doubts his integrity and diligence. **2** *do...deuer*: referring to 11.182–218 and thus evidence that those lines are better assigned not to Scripture but to Clergy (see *TN*). **3–4** are somewhat elliptical: 'one who desires a higher state than is taught by the Bible (desires something that) surpasses the apostolic life and equals the condition of angels'. **3** *bettere...tellep*: i.e. than may be learnt from studying scripture (something implicitly called in question at 11.308 as leading men into heresy). **5** *seye*: 'observed (before). **8** *apose*: like *asoylen* 11 a term from academic debate. *so manye*: i.e. problems. **9** *tene...Theologie*: cf. A 2.79 //. **10–11** 'If I knew for certain that you wished to act on what you learnt, it would be my wish to resolve your every question'.

12–33 13 Scripture calls on Clergy not to instruct Will further until he has been confessed and baptised, a measure of how dire she thinks his 'presumptuous' state to be. **15** *kynde cardinal Wit*: in the light of 41–3, this should be Kynde Wit, Scripture's cousin (43), who was earlier mentioned in A only once at 3.260 (this is the only favourable use of 'cardinal' in *PP*). Transposing *cardinal* and *kynde* would improve the rhythm but the present word-order need not be corrupt, since it may play on the senses 'natural' and 'gracious'. **16–17** Both *þat-* clauses depend on *seyde*, one as a result-clause, the other as a noun-clause object. 16 shows characteristic *s / sh* alliteration, 17 scans as an extended Type IIIb with counterpoint (*abb / aa*). **18** *tellen hit*: i.e. what do-well is. **19** *Godes derling*: traditional; cf. 'dauið, godes ahne deorling' (*AW* 14b). **19–33** Scripture supports her *skele* 'argument' that 'Theology forbids its doctrine to be imparted to slothful sinners' with three Biblical texts in rising order of authority (David, Paul, Christ) and emphasis (*also* 19, *often* 22, *neuere* 25). **19a** *Vidi...*: 'I beheld the transgressors, and I pined away; because they kept not thy word' (Ps 118:158). **20–1** Scripture applies the psalm-verse to the Dreamer with a tart pun on his name; Dowel cannot be taught to anyone who clings to his sinful ways. *I seyde*: elliptical for 'I said, (nor shall I say)...' **22** *often*: incorrect, since Pauline reference to such words (if 22a is the referent of *hit*) is rare. **22a** *Audiui...*: 'I [*he* Vg] heard secret words which it is not granted a man to utter' (II Cor 12:4); to be re-used in a much more powerful context

at 20.438a. **23–4** comment on rather than translating the Pauline verse, which speaks of a private revelation, not the public teaching of the Church. *þat....hit*: 'tell what I heard'; for the phrase cf. C 7.17. **25–6** The use of *God* for Christ (as at A 1.24–5) heightens the presumptuousness of Pilate's *aposing*, and relates it to Will's (8). **27** *an hundred*: assuming (wrongly) that the interview took place in public (see Jn 18:33). **28** *Quid..*: '[Pilate saith to him]: What is truth?' (Jn 18:38). *verilyche...vs*: an addition making the question more sarcastic than it is in context. An echo of this punning macaronic is heard in B 15.60–1 = C 16.220–1. **33** 'But when he talks to me, I am what he says I am — [a scold];' a dry intra-textual joke (he does so only in the next line).

34–54 34 *þis skele ysheued*: contextually 'brought forth this argument', but with a pun on the sense 'showed reasonableness' (cf. C 6.25), as a 'scold' does not. **35** Clergy's action echoes the behaviour of another berated husband, Wit, at A 11.94–5 and, more distantly and humorously, recalls A 3.178 (*Sk*). **38–9** The gesture expresses his offer of allegiance to Scripture, as earlier to Study at A 11.101–2. *For eueremore after*; a phrase found mainly in **L** (see MED s.v. *euermor* adv 4(a)) and perhaps a small indicator of authenticity. **41** *Kynde Wit þe confessour*: Will in fact meets quite another 'confessor', Fever, whose 'dwelling' is not with Life but with Death. It remains unclear why KW is given this sacramental rôle, unless because it is a matter of self-evident good sense to acknowledge one's faults before embarking on a life of virtue (in the later versions, he is *contrasted* with Clergy as a source of knowledge of the truth). **42** *low*: a friendly response to Will's new-found humility; confession is a *sine qua non* of beginning to do-well. **44** *Lyf*: the principle of life (cf. A 10.46), not yet a 'nature-name' for God, 'the lord of life' (20.59) who is its 'transcendental' referent. **49** *clerioun*: an emblem of the simplicity required for spiritual progress, denoting either a young clerk (Will must 'go back and 'start all over again') or a schoolboy (cf. Is 11:6 'a little child shall lead them', and Mk 10:15). **50–2** *Omnia-probate*; *Quod...*: '[But] prove all things: hold fast that which is good' (I Thess 5:21); quoted in a sense nearer to that at 20.233a and very different from that of Lady Meed at BC 3.339–43 / 489–93. **50** *Omnia..*: personifications named from hyphenated Latin scripture-texts are rare in *PP* (cf. the one-word cases *Vigilate* at 7.56, *Multi* 12.48, *Pauci* 12.50). There is one similar Latin place-name at 16.331, but those at 18.4, 19.73 are made-up noun-phrases, not Biblical quotations. *pore*: implying a submissiveness to whatever God sends, as at 15.33 (and cf. 58 below), but perhaps also smallness of stature MED s.v. *povre a.* 5(a)). **51–4** Scripture's advice signifies allegorically that Will must meekly accept his unavoidable peccability, confess his sins and seek to make satisfaction by acts of virtue. **52** *burgh*: a town next to a large manor-house (*court* 57).

The allegory here is not unlike that at A 6.67ff or 10.1–11: the place (= persistence in virtue) is one reached after experience of both good and ill, a notion associated with similar use of the Pauline text at 20.233–33a.

55–76 58 The close echo of A Pr 62 suggests that XII was an attempt to conclude rather than continue the poem. **59** *fyrste*: i.e. hunger; the second is fever. **60** 'As I was growing up, towards the start of day'. The reference may be to a particular experience of dearth in his younger days. **61** This heavily-stressed indication of dazed helplessness echoes A 4.143. **63–6** anticipate the onslaught of age and illness upon Life in B 20.169ff. **64** *weye*: 'manner of proceeding'; Hunger is one way in which Will has come near to death. **65** Cf. A 7.164–70. *helpe*: i.e. with spiritual remedies and counsel, which can aid Will to endure but not avoid death. **71** 'A beggar's bagful — I bought the whole lot at one go' (perhaps implying that this is the food of a beggar-man Hunger has killed). **72** scans on vowels, with the verb in the opening dip, as at 3. **73** 'Because of the meals I had missed / to avoid losing any food that was there, I could not restrain myself'. **74–6** recall the Hunger episode at A 7.239–52.

77–98 82 *Feuere..*: 'Quartan Fever', with bouts every fourth day. **84** *Cotidian*: quotidian fever, with daily attacks; the earliest use (missed by both OED and MED). **85** *Tercian*: tertian fever, recurring every third day (in modern reckoning 'quartan' is applied to fever recurring at 72-hour, tercian at 48-hour intervals). *trewe drinkeres*: because causing great thirst. **86** *letteres of Lyf*: 'letters concerning / addressed to Life, (saying that...)'; with perhaps a sinister pun on the sense 'injurer' (MED s.v. *lettere* n. (1)). **87** *dedis*: 'documents' (announcing his coming demise), with wordplay on the senses 'effects' and 'deaths'. **88** scans cognatively on *g / k*, the first three words forming a dip. **89–93** Fever tells Will that his hour has not yet come; he will be given more time to 'merit happiness (in heaven)' by doing well. This final phase of **A** will in effect be re-written as BC 20 / 22. 199–211, where he is eventually told the meaning of Dowel (*loue lelly*). **90** scans vocalically with secondary *l*-alliteration and the fourth lift on *fór*. **96a** The image and pararhyme anticipate B 18.327. **97** recalls A 1.119.

99–117 JOHN BUT's conclusion falls into a) the death of Will and wishes for his soul; b) the identification of the scribe; c) the formal farewell and loyal blessing on the King. **99–105** are unlikely to be by **L**, since they mention 'other works about Piers Plowman and numerous other characters'. Unless these are **Z** and some other (lost) version, they are most economically to be assumed the **B** and **C** Versions written after **A**. Warner 2005:13 plausibly argues for punctuating with a comma after *boþe* but is not convincing that the 'other works' mentioned must in consequence be taken to denote 'a category separate from *PP*' (17). At most, they *may* do so, for 102 could be

read quite naturally not as supplemental to but in parallel or apposition with 101, yielding the sense: 'Will composed what is written here and other works as well; [He composed works] about Piers Plowman and many [other] people too'. These 'many other people' need only be the numerous personages who appear in *PP*, not characters in some other Langlandian poem or poems supposedly being alluded to by But. **99** *Wille*: the author of the poem, whom the writer of these lines identifies with the protagonist of Passus XII and (presumably) of what precedes it. **103** *þis werk*: either just the text preceding *þat here is wryten* or including also the *oþer werkes* 101. **104** *Dep...dent*: seeming to echo *Depes dyntes* in BC 20 / 22.105, though the phrase was traditional (MED s.v. *dint* n. 1c (c)). This the writer may have inferred as answering Will's prayer to Kynde at 20. / 22.201–3; but since the text at that point does not report Will's death, only his reconciliation with the Church, John But may have had personal knowledge of the poet's death. **105** *closed vnder clom*: a unique phrase but paralleled by *closed under clay* (see MED s.v. *closen* v. 6a). *Crist...soule*: a standard prayer for the dead at or after burial; it is balanced by the prayers for the living at 115–7. **106** 'And that is how John But would often pray [for the author], when he read these writings of his.' His identification as the King's Messenger who died in 1387 (Rickert 1913–14:107) is supported by Middleton 1988:243–66 (whose attribution of the whole Passus to him is rejected here). Other John Buts in the period are listed by Hanna (1993:160–3), but none seems a better candidate than Rickert's, and his affirmation of loyalty to the King may be more than conventional. **108** *Iames... Iop*: suggesting acquaintance with **B** or **C**, since Jerome is not *alleged* in **A**. **107** *busyly*: presumably with a different sense here; but perhaps corrupt (see *TN*). **109** *for... makyng*: 'dabbles in versifying'; apparently an echo of B 12.16. **113** reads as *aa / xa*, but a copyist may have transposed the b-lifts to prose order. The line would give a time before Richard's deposition in 1399 as the *terminus post quem* for **L**'s obit. **114–15** should not be pressed too hard to yield a precise date when there were lords who might *not* love Richard *lely in herte* (such could be found from 1384 on). But's protestation of affection may, however, be contrasted with Conscience's exasperation with the King in C 3.207–14. **116–17** are two Type Ic lines that skilfully slow down the pace so as to 'make a good end'.

Passus XII (B XI 44–284)

PASSUS TWELVE consists of (i) a *prelude* describing Rechelesnesse / Will's moral collapse, his disappointment by the Friar and his exchange with LEAUTE and SCRIPTURE (1–75a); (ii) a 'bridge' passage (76–89) on the appearance of Trajan; and (iii) an extended tirade on divine mercy, the virtues of poverty and the dangers of wealth

(90–249), which from 170 onwards is entirely new. Continuing beyond the end of XII and up to 130 of XIII, this is one of the more awkward structural changes, devised seemingly to reduce the long and dense B X–XI to more manageable size. In **B** the material of (iii) is given to TRAJAN; but C 13.129 confirms that the whole 280-line speech has been transferred to RECHELESNESSE, who functions in part as the poet's quasi-dramatic mouthpiece, directly addressing an 'exterior' audience at 12.90, 221 (*lordes*), 13.25 (*lewede men*) and 13.64 (*wyse men*).

(i) 1–22 1 *Allas, eye*: 'Oh, the pity of it!' *Elde*: a reminder of a character who intervened from the wings at 11.188–94 but was silent during Rechelesnesse's long diatribe in 11.195–307 and the rejoinders of Will's bad counsellors. *Holynesse*: a conventionally appropriate companion to Elde (cf. 8.92–3) who has no further part to play. **2** On the traditional *wit / will* contrast, see at 7.243. Here the replacement of *likyng* **B** intimates 'Platonically' the relation between the dreamer's name and his chief propensity. **B 11.47** *fourty...more*: a basis, though somewhat slippery, for estimating Will's age (and by inference the poet's). If, contrary to modern notions, the dominance of LUST OF THE EYES is taken to begin from *birth* and the line is related to B 12.3, forty-five will be the Dreamer's total age (*Sk*); but the two references are not strictly parallel, since presumably we have imagination and memory from earliest childhood. More realistically in terms of the fiction, lechery's sway may be seen as extending from Will's abandonment of his studious search for Dowel, and 'forty-five' as loosely indicating the age *up to which* he languished under it. But the twofold mention may well be meant to hint at how old the author was at the time of the B-Text (see further Burrow 1993:92–3). **3** *me*: making clear that the Rechelesnesse in ragged clothes of 11.195 was but an oblique 'nature-name' for the narrator Will. **4/5** The rhyming revision (*were / frere*) refers to scruples as to how Will acquires wealth (the apparent sense of *good* 5, which is the referent of *hit* 6). But this is not necessarily the meaning in **B 50–1**, where the asymmetrical *mynde / dedes* contrast suggests rather that 'I continued to *think* about Dowel, although never acting it out'; and it is these scruples over how he may attain to virtue (53) that the wench assuages. **4** *reche / riche*: the sly pararhyme 'Platonically' hinting at the implied association of religious indifference with cupidity. **6** The new line, with its echoes of Lady Mede's 'easy' confessor at 3.42, 50, shows desire for money (shared by friars) as the clerk's main distraction from devoted study. **8** *fraternite... pardoun*: cf. 9.342–5, which couples these as equally useless on doomsday by comparison with Dowel. The words, recalling the friar-confessor's promise at 3.53–4, show Lust of the Eyes to be a true *damysele* (B 11.12) of Mede's patron FORTUNE. Her argument is that sin can be

pardoned without do-well and that *any* sin committed in acquiring money can be absolved by its judicious later use. **9** *Priour Prouincial*: the head of a mendicant order's whole 'province' (such as England). Having the status of a prelate, he might be prepared to grant pardons for a large enough donation. **10** *pol by pol*: 'each friar individually'. *pecuniosus*: for similar single Latin stave-words furnishing both lifts of a b-verse, cf. 2.191, 17.309, B 13.198. **10a** '[But] penance in the form of a payment of money does not suffice for spiritual faults'; a maxim of canon law, cited with slight variation in William Lyndwood's *Provinciale* of 1430 (AlfQ). Unattributable to the last speaker, it hangs suspended as if spoken 'aside' by Elde, the author, or the voice of conscience (cf. B 53), to which Will is not attending. **11–22** retain the core of **B** but remove the near-digression on burial and baptism (75–83). The passage takes Will in one line (12) from the condition of his summertime encounter with the mendicant masters in 10.9 to something like the decrepitude of 22.199–213. **12** *forʒat ʒouthe*: anticipating 22.155. *elde*: about 65 years, his notional age in the final passus. **15** is either an enriched Type IIa line (like B 63), with monolexical *cónféssede*, or a Ib, with the break after *Y*. *flittyng*: 'evasive', whereas in B 63–4 *flittynge...ayeins* chimes annominatively on the set phrase *fliten agaynes* 'oppose, contend against' (MED s.v. 2), suggesting that the friar tried to argue his way out of the original agreement (presumably, to give absolution on demand). **19–20** Cf. B 9.164. **20–22** The revision of B 74 *siluer* heightens the charge's formulaic quality, the repetition of *godes* forming a lexical triangle with the antithetical *rode* that friars should live by. **22** *Wher*: tartly punning on 'where' and 'whether', so as to accuse the friar not just of promise-breaking but of callous failure in his vocation, since burying the dead was the final 'corporal work of mercy' (added to the six in Mt 25:35–6).

B 75–83 76 *couent*: synecdoche for 'order' and more generally 'type of religious.' The 'Platonic' pun wrenches the verb from its neutral sense 'desire' (*IG* s.v. *coueiten*). *catecumelynges*: the idiosyncratic deformation of expected *catechumenes* (< Lat < Gk) 'a(ny) person newly receiving religious instruction,' with its diminutive suffix, links the term with children. Though *barnes* are not 'converts' in the usual sense, they must likewise (after baptism) be taught the elements of the faith (most actual baptizands would be infants). An instructional as well as a sacramental rôle may be envisaged for the friars; but the main point is that burial is a service that promises higher fees, gifts from the dead man's relations, and maybe legacies. Forfeiting the friar's readiness to absolve is the price Will pays for deciding to be buried not in the convent cemetery but in his parish church. The opinion his conscience prompts him to voice recalls Piers's words at B 6.91–5 (Conscience is the latter's instructor at B 7.134). **78** *Bapti3ynge*: as understood here to cover the subsequent instruction implied by *catecumelynges*, coming under the first two 'spiritual works of mercy' (converting and instructing). **80–3** claim that of the two sacraments, confession is the less valuable because, while there is no salvation without baptism, there can be without confession, if the baptised person is contrite. **81a** 'Contrition alone can blot out sin'; a common theological maxim cited in variant form by Brinton (1:81), who follows Aquinas (*ST* III Suppl. qu.5., art. 2) in illustrating it from the Good Thief (Alford in Vaughan 1993:21–2), and one featuring in controversies over the importance of oral confession (Alf*Q*; Gray 1986[1]). The opinion itself (complementing the maxim at B 11.59 above) does not *lye* against the Church's requirement of (annual) confession. Confession is urged at B 14.16–32=C 16.25–34 by Conscience, even if he equates contrition with Dowel; for though heartfelt sorrow rendered the mortal sin venial, the obligation to confess it remained (cf. 12.174ff). That such sorrow *suffices* for salvation (as affirmed by Repentance at B 5.125 and by the Samaritan at 19.298) and that baptism is *necessary* for salvation are notions that would have been unquestioned, though both prove not without difficulties. But less important than the doctrinal implications of what he says is Will's combative tone in objecting to pecuniary exploitation of the sacrament. **82** refers to a child who *dies* in a state of Original Sin and who, while obviously incapable of 'actual' sin, is likewise incapable of the contrition necessary to save the unbaptised. The wording closely echoes Scripture at B 10.347 but may be meant to verge recognisably on the *in extremis* position she distinguishes at B 10.346 (cf. also B 15.33=C 17.121). **82a** '[Jesus answered: Amen, amen, I say to thee], unless a man be born again [of water and the Holy Ghost, he cannot enter into the kingdom of God]' (Jn 3:5). **83** is addressed at once from Will to the friars and (through him) by the poet to the learned members of his audience (cf. C 17.210).

23–50 In this section **23–41a** show detailed revision of **B 84–106a** in the direction of greater explicitness, as at 25–6, finer discrimination (the *treuthe / trewe* quasi-rhyme at 27–8), and dramatic propriety, as in eliminating the reference to *metels* (unless **L** envisages a 'lucid dream' in which the dreamer knows he is dreaming); with B 86 contrast B Pr 209–10. B 94–100 are now transferred to Will and 96–100 shortened to C 28–9. **23** *Leaute*: personifying equitable fairness and disinterested good faith (MED s.v. (a); cf. on Pr 149, 2.20–1) rather than 'law-abiding people' (Kane 1982:40) or 'strict adherence to the letter of the law' (Donaldson 1949:66n). Though already mentioned at 3.446, 4.156 as a foe of untruth and Mede, he here seems as much an aspect of the Dreamer as the embodiment of his ideal audience that he is in **B** (Schmidt 1987[2]:12–13). **27–9** The answer to Will's wish would come better from

Leaute as in B 87; but the sequence of *s*-alliterating lines subtly distinguishes between truth as fact and truth as integrity: only an honest man may utter discreditable facts about dishonest men. **27** *were treuthe*: 'would be the truth (if I were to say it)'. **30** See on B 10.285. The context in Ps 49 is significant in making God threaten the man who 'declare[s] [his] justices' (16) even while 'speak[ing] against [his] brother' (20). **31** *also*: 'likewise', 'in their turn', i.e. in reply to the psalmist's accusation of hypocrisy they will cite an even more authoritative warning against hypocritical judgement. **32** 'Judge not (anyone), [that you may not be judged]' (Mt 7:1). **33** *And*: 'Yes, (but)'. **35** 'Thou shalt not hate thy brother (secretly) in thy heart: but reprove him openly, [lest you incur sin through him]' (Lev 19:17; cf. I Tim 5:20). The pl. *fratres* in B 88 is an adaptation to suit the 'implied referent' (Alf*Q* 19n33), the friars. **37** *retoryk*: 'poetry'; see Schmidt 1987[2]:108–41. **39** has the medial break after *nat*, whether *sum* is stressed or muted to give a T-type line. **41** *labbe..it out*: further from the Latin than **B** (but see *TN*). **41a** 'Praise moderately; blame more sparingly. [For too much praise deserves the same censure as too much blame]'; attributed to Seneca in Vincent of Beauvais, *Speculum Doctrinale* 5.69 and Alan of Lille, *Summa de Arte Praedicatoria* [*SAP*] 23 (*PL* 210:158). The Roman Stoic philosopher (*c*. 4 BC–65 AD) is quoted again at 16.141a.

B 96–100 are cut from **C** perhaps as irrelevant to an argument concerning public wrongs that affect the wider community. **97** *ech a lawe*: i.e. both civil and canon law permitting telling of the whole truth. **100** *synne*: presumably sins told under the seal of confession. Lewte is not authorising public exposure of individuals' faults; the text cited at 93=C 35 recommends not suppressing but taking up grievances face-to-face with one's fellow-Christians. **43** *matere*: the stern lesson that few will be saved. This would turn the many against religion if they heard it; but as the key-words remain in Latin, it can be grasped only by the few. **48, 50** *Multi*; *Pauci*: both words 'plucked' from the end of Scripture's preaching text (the parable of the marriage feast), 'For many [*multi*] are called but few [*pauci*] are chosen' (Mt 22:14). **50** *priueiliche*: not according to the Gospel; but perhaps meaning 'those chosen for salvation are known to God alone'.

51–75a The response of the clerk Will to this 'text' (51), as Kirk 1972:130 notes, both recalls (*tene*) and contrasts with (*tremblede*) the Plowman's to the 'text' of Truth's pardon (B 7.115), which led Piers not to *despute* but to *pulle it atweyne*. The debilitating effect of clerkly *wer* 'uncertainty' is ironically brought out by its 'Platonic' echo in *Where Y were*, the Latin *Utrum* 'whether' being a common opening to scholastic discussion of a *quaestio*. **53** *Holy Churche...fonte*: the most striking retrospective reference in the poem (to 1.72–3). Will understandably draws comfort from his associate membership of the

Communion of Saints, but remains doubtful about the sense of 'chosen': is it unconditional 'election' or only an offer of the means of salvation? (Cf. 60*a* and B 10.345 earlier). Scripture's *sompned* correlates with HC's *vnderfeng*, her *plihte* with *my biddyng to fulfille* (1.74). *R–H* 134–5 aptly note that in Augustine's interpretation of the parable, the marriage garment is not baptism but charity (to which baptismal grace opens the way). **56** *sismatikes*: anachronistic if taken literally; but Christ's 'call' is doubtless thought of as directly continued in historical time through the authoritative voice of his Church. **57–8** The powerful metaphor draws on the traditional image of Jesus as 'nursing mother' derived from texts like Is 49:15, 66:13 (Woolf 1968:189–90); for a possible source of the 'nurse' image Wenzel cites *FM* V, 7 (AlfC 162). The idea is vividly captured in the iconography of the 'Pelican in her Piety', which was fabled to feed its young with blood from its own breast; see Schiller II pls. 444, 451 (C13th), 504 (C14th). The present reference to Christ's blood as a healing remedy echoes 7.133 and seems directly derived from the penultimate stanza of the hymn *Adoro te devote* (traditionally ascribed to Aquinas): 'Pie pelicane, Iesu Domine, / Me immundum munda tuo sanguine, / Cuius una stilla salvum facere / Totum mundum posset omni scelere' ('O loving pelican, Lord Jesus, purify my impurity with your blood, one drop of which could save the whole world from all sin' (the original's *mundum / immundum* wordplay perhaps suggesting that on *saue* 57 'salve / safe(ly)'). But the context makes clear that the primary meaning is baptismal rather than eucharistic (cf. 60), and based on traditional interpretation of Jn 19:34 (see on 110–12 below). **58*a*** 'All you that thirst, come to the waters...' (Is 55:1). The text, used to open the Introit at Mass on the Saturday following mid-Lent Sunday, had special relevance to catechumens being instructed for baptism or penitents preparing for absolution at Easter. Wordplay on *sicientes* and *scientes* 'knowing,' a reading found in Bromyard 2:347–2 (AlfQ), is discerned by *R–H* 135, but not strongly supported by the quotation's form or context. **59** *perto*: with implied referent 'saving grace' (*bote*), whereas in B 123 *pere* refers to its source (*breste*) or, more widely, 'salvation'. **60** *bouhte...tauhte*: the annominative chime bringing out the need first for faith in Christ's saving death and then obedience to his command to receive baptism. **60*a*** 'He that believeth and is baptized shall be saved: [but he that believeth not shall be condemned]' (Mk 16:16). Read in the Gospel for Ascension Day, which ends the Easter season, the text concludes the sequence initiated by 58*a*. **62–6** The argument is that a Christian cannot *rihtfolliche* 'lawfully' renounce his religion, even if failing to practise it. For, after being freed through baptism from the devil's 'lordship', he is now a 'bondman' of Christ; and an attempt to escape from his new lord's service is like a serf's unauthorised flight from

the manor (the simile suggesting **L**'s endorsement of contemporary law and practice, which the 1381 insurgents were so strong against). **63–4** Villeins were not entitled to enter into legal agreements or to sell their moveable property without the lord's permission. The feudal analogy, with its tacit acceptance if not approval of servile status, would have won no friends among the rebels, who resented and wanted it abolished (see further on villeins, McKisack 1959:326–8, Keen 1973:189–98, Hilton 1969, and on the implications of this metaphor, Simpson 1990:122–4). **65** *rome fro home*: with this formulaic internal rhyme, cf. 60. **66** compares the apostate to a runaway serf who risks imprisonment if found. **67–8** *Reson*; *Conscience*: a coupling that recalls 5.11, where Will is *romynge in remembraunce* and, in answering Reason's 'rebuke', denies that he is a 'run-away' or 'caitiff' of any sort (5.82). Reason is envisaged as a 'moral reeve' who reckons up the dues of the lord's servants (cf. 3.308 and 13.34). **68** *acounte*: cf. 16.190. **69–70** He will pay for his lapsation by suffering purgatorial pains (believed to be akin to hell's in intensity though not duration) until the raising of the dead at the last day. **70** *rechelesnes*: this substitution for **B**'s third *arerages* is heavily ironic, coming from this speaker. *riht*: 'even until,' but punning on 'justly, lawfully'. **71** *and confessioun*: improving upon the inert *come and* of B 135 in fullness of sense and in sharpness, since *mouthe* must here suggest *oris confessio* more than just vocal prayer. The cautious orthodoxy contrasts with the boldness of B 11.81*a* (deleted in revision). **73–5*a*** The first revision (74*a*) makes for syntactic explicitness, *heo* anticipating the Daughter of God at 20.118–9 who personifies the 'feminine' side of the divine Judge. The second (on *bothe* see *TN*) recognises humility as in origin a divine quality, discernible in Christ's Incarnation and Passion and closely linked with *mercy*, as at 1.168, B 18.115. *mekenesse*: the penitent sinner's (cf. 7.247), which precedes the granting of God's mercy, though here imagined not temporally but as 'tending obediently upon' (and so assisting) it. **75** *bokes...werkes*: a perhaps intentional secondary contrast, since Trajan is about to show the superiority of 'well-doing' over 'wisdom' (cf. the tension in *soethnesse...werkes* at 83). Scripture's parting words fittingly cite the 'Books' whose study she personifies. **75*a*** 'His tender mercies [*miserationes* Vg] are over [surpass] all his works' (Ps 144:9); cited at B 5.282*a* but removed from its parallel in revision.

(ii) 76–89 are here treated as a 'bridge-passage' in **C**, spoken by Trajan, but in **B** as the opening of a long speech by him. On reasons for giving it to Trajan (who speaks of himself in the 3rd pers. from B 153–162) see *TN*; Rudd (1994:76, 179) notes the appropriateness of the examples used at B 189–95, 230–40, 248–56 to his character and status. **76** *bawe for bokes*: depending on the tone adopted, not necessarily implying rejection of scriptural authority

('Why refer to what "books" — even the Bible — say? I can vouch for this [God's mercy] from my own experience') so much as location of it in the *spirit* of Scripture, not its letter (cf. 98 below). *quod oen*: a memorable phrase clearly recalled in B at 319, which *closes* the speech and ratifies its ascription to the speaker of 76. *was...helle*: a sudden entry like Piers's at 5.537=C 7.181 (Rudd 1994:76); as Trajan is not *in* hell, the implied tense is pluperfect not preterite. The legend of his release from hell through St Gregory's intercession goes back to early lives of the latter, though the speaker himself refers us to L's presumed source, the *Legenda Aurea* (B 160 below; on the background see Wittig 1972:249–54 and Whatley 1984[1]:50–6). The story as used here has been found by Gradon 1983, Whatley 1984[2] and Burrow 1993:8–14 to express an unorthodox, 'Pelagian' view of Trajan as saved by good works alone. But Simpson 1990:125–8 persuasively sees it rather as 'semi-Pelagian', with Trajan's *leaute* and *trewthe* meriting salvation not *de condigno* 'condignly' (or 'absolutely') but *de congruo* 'congruently' (in the only manner appropriate to one in his situation), 'by doing what is in him' (a position developed and elaborated by Ymaginatyf at 14.205–17). Trajan offers a limiting case, not a norm, and the theological extremism of this example recalls that of the Good Thief at 11.255–263, a factor that may have prompted transference of the long 'disputation' based on it from the Emperor to Will-as-Rechelesnesse. **77** *Troian(e)s*: a well-recognised form of Trajan's name (Wenzel 1996:184). Emperor of Rome AD 98–117, he was known for his justice, integrity and concern for the common people. *trewe knyht*: for similar 'chivalricisation' cf. 1.101ff. **78** *dwellen in helle*: more *repetitio* underlined by internal rhyme in revision. **79** *Gregori*: the revision, requiring scansion on 'cognate' staves (*k / g*), and improving by referring directly to the agent not to the account of *clerkes* (which is incongruous coming from one who cries *bawe* to books). **80–1** The sense is obscure because elliptical in the revision of B 144. **B**'s 'all the erudite theological arguments under the sun couldn't find grounds for my salvation' contrasts learning unfavourably with do-well (as pardons had been in 9.317–45). But **C**'s sense ('it was not my being baptized that saved me — because I wasn't — it was only my righteous conduct') is more audacious theologically, going beyond the 'sufficiency-of-baptism' argument of 60*a* to a 'non-necessity-of-baptism' position even more *recheles* than that of Rechelesnesse. This *is* 'Pelagian', unless *myhte...onlyche* is only affirming Trajan's *treuthe* as a necessary, not a sufficient condition for his release. **82** *this*: 'this fact' or 'my righteousness', or perhaps both (cf. B 151). **83** *soethnesse...werkes*: affirming that though Trajan was ignorant of Christian *veritas*, his *fidelitas* was homologous to formal faith, and evidence that he would have believed, had he known what to believe.

84–5 *wilnede wepynge*: the intensity of the saint's prayer being signalled by his tears (cf. B 262–3) which, in alluding to Heb 5:7, equate the Pope's 'high-priesthood' with that of his exemplar, the Supreme High Priest Christ. *Y were saued*: avoiding B 148b's implication that prevenient grace might be available for one no longer *in via*. The distinction between that supposition and **C**'s *of his goodnesse* is a fine one, perhaps relying on contemporary notions of God's *potentia absoluta* as transcending the normal (*ordinata*) channels of grace, the Church's sacraments. **86–7** are doubtless not meant to question the efficacy of ritual intercession for the dead but to say that Masses (as part of the 'ordinate' dispensation) would have had no relevance for Trajan, since he was in hell, where *nulla est redempcio* (20.151*a*). **88** 'Love, in the absence of true faith (was what), as the "religion" proper to me / bringing me justification (*rihtfoel*), saved me'. In this reading, the 'love [*sc. of treuthe*]' is Trajan's, a man supposed to have served God like those in Mt 25:37–40, who are unconscious of having done so (cf. also Mt 7:21). But if the 'love' = the 'goodness' of 85, then the sense will be that 'God's own boundless charity, answering (indeed perhaps prompting) the intercessory prayer (of Gregory) saved me, though I lacked formal belief in the true religion to justify me'. The revision's removal of the potentially ambiguous *truþe* in B 151, 155 'as open to the possible misinterpretation that T's salvation was owing to his orthodox faith' is noted by Green 1999:23–4. **B 151** *by lernyng of*: either 'through finding out about' or 'by dint of the "learning" [= knowledge of Christian truth] tacitly implied in my just conduct'. The second rendering (complementary rather than alternative) is supported by *soethnesse* 83. For a similar interpretation see Doxsee 1988, who sees a 'desire' for baptism as implicit in Trajan's love of *trewthe*. **89** *Sarrasyn*: here = *paynym* B 162, with no implication that Trajan shared any part of Christian belief, e.g. in one God (cf. 17.315–6). Elsewhere its usual reference is to Moslem Arabs (e.g. at 3.480).

(iii) 90–249 This enormous speech, continuing for another 130 lines in the next passus (= B 11.153–318), is finally ascribed to Rechelesnesse at 13.129, and so may be taken to *begin* at 90 (where in **B** the speaker is likely to be Trajan; but in both versions much of it sounds quasi-choric in nature and tone. **90–3** retain B 153, 157–8 but drop 154 (redundant as repeating 143) and add one summarising line to replace B 159–69, which are slightly repetitive (161b = 151b, 164a = 156a), digressive (168–9) and anticipatory (168–9 // B 12.72–3=C 14.37–8). **93** *leute*: repeated four times up to 98 (as love is seven times in B 170–80).

B 153–69 are spoken by Trajan about himself in the 3rd person as an example, and at 170 he is not beginning to speak but resuming. **155** *pure truþe*: 'utter integrity'. **156** *witnesse*: an overstatement, as Gregory prayed in

hope, not certainty (**C** is less controversial). **159–69** are not without powerful moments, but omitting them makes for a tighter transition in **C**. **160** *legende sanctorum*: the macaronic title encompassing both its English name and the book's subject-matter. The *Legenda Aurea* 'Golden Legend' (*LA*) was completed *c.* 1265 by the Italian Dominican Jacobus de Voragine or Varazze (*c.* 1230–98; Abp. of Genoa in 1292). An immensely popular compilation of saints' lives and treatises on the Church festivals, much of it 'legendary' (see Reames 1985), *LA* is (with Gregory's *Moralia*) the only non-biblical book named by **L**, who relies on it in his accounts of various saints (as at 17.12, 21–4). **161** *leel loue*: contextually Trajan's, but also evoking God's reciprocal 'leaute'. **162** *peyne... paynym*: the 'Platonic' identical rhyme across the caesura pointing up his miraculous escape from the fate due to him as a pagan. **163** anticipates B 18.294, 322–3 and echoes Z 5.39. *truþe*: both Trajan's essential quality and the 'nature-name' for God / Christ cited at B 18.294; intimating that the virtue and the person are one. **165** *clergie*; *konnyng*: theology, which could not conceptually accommodate Gregory's *bone* with Trajan's unbaptized state. **166–7** *science...book*: in the ordinary sense neither, though the commandment of love *is* embodied in the written text of the Bible. **166** *Loue*: not strictly the 'theological virtue' of charity (the fruit of faith in God) but the Just Pagan's 'good-will towards men' that represents in terms of *de congruo* theology 'the best that is in him' (see on C 76). This is a notable advance from commendation of his perfect *justice*; but the association of truth and love has been foreshadowed by HC at B 1.148–51, here recalled. **168–9** *wrouȝte...wroot*: see Ex 32:15–16; cf. C 14.37–8.
94–109 94–100a move the stress in B 170–80 from love to *leautee*, from 'religion without love' to the more appropriate 'law without equity'. They tighten up the phrasing and eliminate otiose repetition (172a, 174a, 179b), but also lose the internal chimes of 176 and the effective rhetorical balancing of 176a / 179a. The eliminated **B** lines echo the sense of I Jn 3:17–18, 23. **100** *of his techyng*: referring to either the Apostle or the Lord. **100a** 'He that loveth not abideth in death' (I Jn 3:14). **101–2** shorten the somewhat wordy and repetitive B 181–8 (though losing the memorable 184–5, with their final assonance) and draw a double moral from the Gospel verses paraphrased in 103–9. These words echo HC's quotation from Js 2:26 at 1.186, and in giving them to Trajan, **L** may have recalled I Jn 3:10: 'Whosoever is not *just*, is not of God'. He proceeds here by a non-formal 'logic of negation': Trajan was not like Cain (who hated his brother); Abel was accepted by God; therefore Trajan, who did not hate his brothers, was accepted by God. Trajan can affirm that St John's *words* are *soþe* (B 175) because his own *werkes* are (B 147). **101** *pore peple*: that these 'represent'

Christ being implied in Mt 25:35. Trajan's 'love' for them is shown from his redress to a poor widow, which moved Gregory's compassion. But as he obviously had no love of his *enemies* during his life, he must be presumed to have learned this distinctive ethical precept of Christianity after his release from hell (cf. also I Pet on how 'the gospel [was] preached also to the dead'). **104** *knyhtes*: less close to the Biblical source-text, and losing the witty semantic wordplay on *kyn(nes)* at B 190. **104a** 'When thou makest a dinner...call not thy friends...[nor thy kinsmen nor thy neighbours who are rich: lest perhaps they also invite thee again, and a recompense be made to thee. But...call the poor, the lame and the blind. And thou shalt be blessed, because they have not wherewith to make thee recompense: for recompense shall be made thee at the resurrection of the just]' (Lk 14:12–14). **106–9** increase the *repetitio* (*paye* as well as *quite*) in place of the circumstantial detail of B 193a.
  B 196–9 may have been omitted as potentially provocative or liable to misinterpretation after 1381; but a similar comment, affirming God's wisdom in creating men different in fortune and talent, occurs at C 16.19–21=B 14.166–7. **198** *of...riche*: made rich from his treasure-chests (i.e. of grace); for the image cf. 1.194–7. **199** *breþeren...blood*: like brothers born of the same parents. All men are descended from Adam; but through sin, social divisions have arisen. Baptism in the name of the new Adam, Christ, restores this original equality.
110–20a Christianity was 'born' through the saving death of Christ, into which Christians are baptized (Rom 6:3–5). **110** The allusion is to the blood and water that flowed from the pierced side of Jesus (Jn 19:34), which in the light of I Jn 5:6 was understood in patristic exegesis as symbolising baptism and the eucharist. **111** *blody breth-erne*: 'brothers-by-blood' (*or* 'brothers through [Christ's] blood'), the Emperor's sentiment echoing the Plowman's (8.217–9) and anticipating Christ's at 20.418. **112** is a 'licensed' macaronic scanning *xa / ax* (Schmidt 1987:101–2). *As...vchone*: 'Each of us like noblemen, "like babes newborn"' (I Pet 2:2); spiritual re-birth through baptism frees men from the 'servile' status of sinners and makes them 'noble' (cf. on 62–6). The phrase occurs in the Introit for the Mass of Low Sunday (within the octave of Easter) and the Lesson of the day contains the passage from I Jn 5:6 cited above. **113** *but...make*: i.e. unless through sin we revert to the state of slaves. **113a** 'Whosoever committeth sin is the servant of sin' (Jn 8:34); cf. also vs 32. **114** *mennes sones*: a common OT phrase *filii hominum* found in e.g. Ps 4:3 (*Sk*), 'sons of Adam' only in Deut 32:8. The sense is 'human beings' but the implied contrast is with 'sons of God' (through baptism in Christ's name); cf. Gal 4:4–7. **115** *God-Man*: translating **L**'s own 'credal' phrase *Deus homo* at 3.401a. **116** *Redemptor*: here taken as Latin, though MED records

it as an English word 50 years later; 'redeemer' does not appear till the late 15th c. The Bible uses it of God (e.g. in Ps 19:14), but though ascribing 'redemption' to him (e.g. Mt 20:28, Rom 3:24, Eph 1:7), not Christ, whose Resurrection **L** sees as proof of his divinity, entitling him to this name. **118** substitutes for the gentle, tolerant phrasing of B 208b–09, with their repeated *man*, a harsher reminder of coming judgement. **120a** See on 9.286–7; the Creed recalls the sombre warning of Truth's Pardon on the necessity of 'do-well'.

B 210a–29a Most of this 20-line passage cut in **C** affirms the superiority of unlearned faith to logic and law (disciplines of the pre-Christian world that minister to the pride and avarice of modern clerks). But since the speaker's main theme is humility and the condition of poverty that favours it, these lines may be thought digressive. **210a** See at 8.231a. Gal 6:4, 9–10 certainly exhort to 'do-well', but 'in the spirit of 'meekness' (6:1), not with the monitory tone of C 120a (this text is cited at C 13.77a). **213** is cut here but re-phrased as C 15.80. **216–17** The reference is to Lk 7:37–50, where *mulier quae erat in civitate peccatrix* could be rendered 'a woman commonly known as a sinner'. The suggestion here is that since her sins were forgiven because of her faith (217) and not through baptism, *cristendom* 215 cannot be essential for salvation. But the parallel with Trajan is inexact, since the woman's faith is explicitly in Jesus, and the real likeness resides in her being forgiven 'because she hath *loved* much' (Lk 7:47), this love being understood as necessarily implying faith (in Christ), and Trajan's 'love [of *treuthe*]' conversely (if daringly) as implicit faith. **216** *commune*[1,2]: a dense pun on 'common / of the people' and 'in public'. **217** *Fides sua*: cf. '*Thy faith* hath made thee safe' (Lk 7:50); leaving this crucial text in Latin underlines its special relevance for clerks. *sauen; saluen*: another complex interchange of senses, salvation being a way of bringing 'health' to the soul (cf. 229b). **218** *logyk or lawe*: the implied referents being probably 'theological reasoning' (cf. *lesson* 221) and 'formal religious observance'; but the latter is quickly collapsed into its habitual sense, perhaps with a wry allusion to the lucrative practice of canon lawyers. **218–26** For an analysis of *repetitio* in these lines see Schmidt 1987:55–7. **223b** 'you who do not care for lies'. **225–6** *Feiþes techyng...That*: the implied referent of 'Faith' being the speaker of the quoted words, Christ, who is the antecedent likewise. **226–6a** *Johan*: actually Matthew (7:2) or Luke (6:38); see on 1.173a. **229** *Gregorie*: a text still untraced to Gregory (an especially apt authority for Trajan to quote), though the sentiment is his. **229a** 'It is better to examine our sins than the natures of things'. The exact source is untraced, but *R–H* 140n72 cite an analogue attributed to Augustine in Peter Lombard's *Collectanea* (PL 191:1601): '*For it is better to know our weakness than the natures of things. For wor-*

thier of praise is the soul that knows its own weakness than one that, heedless of this, examines (*scrutatur*) the courses of the stars, the foundations of the globe and the heights of the heavens'. They also note its closeness to the sense of the line cited at B 11.3=C 11.165. **121–249** This long discourse on the spiritual advantages of poverty and the dangers of wealth gains a different meaning through being transferred from Trajan to Rechelesnesse. **B** chiefly instructs the great to be humble (none was greater than the Emperor); **C** defends exterior poverty against the scorn of the rich (none was poorer than Christ). **124–9** This encounter on Easter day is narrated in Lk 24:13–35, which gives no reason for the two disciples' failure to recognise Jesus (his wearing mean clothing is **L**'s contribution). They know him at the breaking of the bread (vs 30), which for **L** signifies not only that Christ is to be 'recognised' as really present in the Eucharistic rite but that genuine faith is discerned through / expressed in charitable action, such as sharing food (*hem bitwene*). **126** *pilgrimes clothes*: the simple dress of such as Piers at 15.34, the true 'pilgrim for the love of God', not the distinctive garb of the 'professional' pilgrim at 7.160. **129b** lessens the 'works' / 'words' contrast of B 236–7, stressing the need not to judge by outward appearance. **130** *ensample*: hardly the obvious one; but the general lesson of humility and 'pacience' is certainly there, since Christ rebukes the two disciples who had thought him 'a prophet, mighty in work and word' (vs 19) for failing to grasp that the Messiah must suffer. **132** *pilgrimes...alle*: one of the key tropes of medieval religious thought (*peregrini et hospites / advenas*), deriving ultimately from such texts as Heb 11:13–16, I Pet 2:11; another famous literary instance is *CT* I 2847–8 (see Dyas 2001). **133** *pore likenesse*: 'the appearance of a poor man'. **134** The revision relies on the force of a specific *ensample* instead of the general statement of B 241–2, which may concede too much to poor appearance and contradict the godliness among the rich later acknowledged at 16.351–2. But its sentiment echoes St Benedict's admonition to receive 'the poor and pilgrims...for in them Christ is received the more' (*Rule*, ch. 53). **C** now says only that Christ was as one of the poor, but nothing about his being often encountered among them. *Holy seyntes*: the disciples who knew Jesus in the flesh. **B 244–5** are omitted in **C** doubtless as both partially inaccurate and as contradicted by Anima's rejection of begging at B 15.227. *Iohan*: presumably the Baptist (Mt 3:4) who, however, did *not* 'ask men for goods'. **135** *Matthew*: incorrect both here and at B 252, and in both cases probably induced by alliterative need rather than being ironically intended as the speaker's 'deliberate error'. **136** *pore...pore*: the literal poverty of Mary (if such is intended) may be an inference from Lk 1:48, where her 'humility' is primarily spiritual, that of Joseph from his failure to find room for them at the inn (Lk 2:7) 'because they were poor' (*LA* 41, the latter incident causing **L** some trouble at 14.90–1). **137** *Marie Maudelene*: identified with both Mary of Bethany and the unnamed woman who anoints Christ's feet at Bethany in the house of Simon the Leper (Mt 26:6) or of her sister and brother Martha and Lazarus (Jn 12:1–3); traditional since St Gregory the Great and re-stated in *LA* ch. 96, p. 408 (see on 7.137). **B 246** The revision removes not only a metrically awkward line with a strong dip in each half (the first containing the lexical word *aliȝte*), but also the variously problematic references to Jesus's mother (and therefore himself) as a 'Jew' (a term used elsewhere in *PP* to denote his opponents) and of 'pore gentel blood' (cf. 5.78). **139** 'Lord, hast thou no care that my sister hath left me alone to serve?' (Lk 10:40). **140** *God*: the full weight of divine authority being understood to inform Christ's answer (cf. 1.48). **142** *pouerte*: surprising if read literally (since the two women are sisters), but not if taken as 'poverty of spirit' (i.e. obedient humility), like that of the BVM. **140–2** *wel...betere*: the verbal echoing evokes the first two terms of the Triad (though the quoted Latin implies only a two-term opposition). **142a** '[But one thing is necessary]. Mary hath chosen the best part which shall not be taken away from her' (Lk 10:42). The 'best part' was traditionally interpreted as patient 'attending' on God, the contemplative as against the active life. **147b, 148a; 149a, 152a** The repeated formulaic phrasing recalls the manner of homiletic preaching (cf. 10.38a, 40a).

143–55a Poverty is further praised as providing freedom from care and the best conditions for penitential prayer and growth in holiness. The wholesale revision of B 11.269–84a (removing weakly repetitive lines like 270b, 272b, 280) adds 80 new lines on the superiority of poverty and the spiritual dangers of wealth, before resuming **B**'s critique of worldly priests. **144** *best* (*lif*): the exaltation of poverty by Rechelesnesse (Trajan) foreshadows Patience's praise of the state in XVI (B XIV). **149** *cornel of confort*: the loving mercy of God (152 below). The kernel (*nucleus*) is compared to Christ's divinity by Alan of Lille in his note on *nux* 'nut' (*PL* 120:871). **155a** 'Though poor, I play, but you, though rich, must brood' (Alexander of Ville-Dieu, *Doctrinale* 1091); cf. B 14.304a.

B 268–84a The argument here is that the OT doctrine of material sufficiency is spiritually inferior to the NT counsel of perfection through renouncing all possession. **269a** 'Give me neither beggary nor riches. [Give me only the necessaries of life]' (Prov 30:8). **L**'s variant wording (with *paupertates* for Vg *mendicitatem*) appears in *FM* 572. **270** *wiser...was*: cf. 'behold, a greater than Solomon here' (Lk 11:31). **272** *Luc*: a minor alliteratively-licensed inaccuracy (cf. B 252 above). **272a** 'If thou wilt be perfect, go sell [what thou hast and give to the poor]' (Mt 19:21); a text (minus the opening phrase) also found

at Lk 18:22. **278** *Dauid...Sauter*: alluding to Ps 36:25. **279a** 'Nothing is impossible to him who wills it'; a proverbial phrase (Walther 44445a1b) loosely derived from Mt 17:19 (which refers to faith, not will). **280** is repeated at 287 below. **280a** See at 10.203a. **284a** 'Judge me, O God, and distinguish my cause [from the nation that is not holy: deliver me from the unjust and deceitful man]' (Ps 42:1). Part of the Introit at Mass, the verse was especially associated with priests, a collection of treatises addressed to priests bearing this title (*Rolle*, ed. Allen (1927:93–113), cit.Alf*Q*). Deliverance from unworthy givers is sought in the *Lavabo* verses at the Offertory (Ps 25:10), taken from a psalm also opening with the words *Iudica me*.

156–78 156 *Holy Churche*: obviously not implying that this is the Church's teaching as opposed to Christ's (*efte* 162), since it merely amplifies the Gospel source of the following Latin. **161a** '[And] everyone that leaves [*reliquerit* 'hath left' Vg] [house or brethren or sisters or] father [or] mother [or wife or children or lands, for my name's sake, shall receive an hundredfold and shall possess life everlasting]' (Mt 19:29). **163** *segg...louede*: alluding to the account in Mk 10:21. **168a** See on B 272a above. **172a** 'So...every one...that doth not renounce all that he possesseth [cannot be my disciple]' (Lk 14:33, adapted). **173–8** constitute 'rhetorical amplification through random citation of learned "authorities"...probably little more than names to **L**' (*Pe*); echoing B 10.338–40, which is omitted at that point in **C**. **175** The line is repeated at 14.189. *Porfirie*: a voluminous Neo-Platonic writer (*c*. 232–*c*. 303) who espoused an ascetic contemplative life and, as the author of a treatise *Against the Christians*, may be here cited as an *argumentum a difficiliori*. *Plato*: see at 11.120. **176** *Aristotel*: see at 11.121. *Ennedy*: the Christian Latin writer Magnus Felix Ennodius (*c*. 473–521), Bp. of Pavia, author of hymns and epigrams. **177** *Tulius*: Marcus Tullius Cicero (106–46 BC); alluding perhaps to the austere Stoic philosophy expressed in his account of the 'Dream of Scipio', the last part of his *De republica* (cf. Chaucer *PF* 29–84). *Tolomeus*: Ptolemy, the Greek astronomer Claudius Ptolomeus (*c*. 100–179), whose *Almagest* in Latin translation had a preface with moral apophthegms by the Arab 'Albaguafe'. **178** *pacient pouerte*: both 'the patient endurance of poverty' and 'the state of poverty that exhibits endurance' (cf. B 14.101). These are linked in *Patience* 35–6.

179–211 argue that hardship fortifies and enables the Christian to produce more spiritual fruit, as hard winters encourage strong growth and abundant crops. The image of the farmer as a type of the faithful believer is in Js 5:7 (*Pe*), but the English distinction between winter and spring seeds is **L**'s. **180a** 'Unless the grain of wheat falling into the ground die, [Itself remaineth alone. But if it die, it bringeth forth much fruit]' (Jn 12:24–5); a text sung as an antiphon on the nativity of a martyr (AlfQ, citing *Brev.* 2:384) and seen by *Pe* as suggested to **L** by Lk 14:26. **187** *we lyuen alle*: the implication being that 'the blood of martyrs is the seed of the Church', and that all Christians benefit from the sacrificial lives of the saints. **199** *Fere*: probably 'danger' (MED s.v. *fer* n. (1).2; 'fire' would be possible (with raised SE vowel), though the word's usual (and presumably original) spelling in this text is SW *fuyr* (cf. 15. 166, and see Samuels 1985:241). **202–5** derive from Js 5:10–11 (*Pe*), which would perhaps support omission of the colon after *soffren* (see TN). **202** *this*: probably the pl. generic 'these', a common spelling in this text (*MES* 173) but possibly the sg. prn. 'this' as object. **208** *angelis...anger*: cf. A 10.143 with very different sense. **209** '[You shall be made sorrowful, but] your sorrow shall be turned into joy' (Jn 16:20). **212–49** use agricultural imagery to argue that material possessions ('sweet fruits') are really spiritual destitution and weaken men's ability to resist sin, while the 'easy' life of the rich ('fat land') predisposes them towards *alle vices*. **213** *Gospelle*: see at 217a. **215** The indirect form of the question in 215–6 would favour *after* here as a preposition 'concerning', though the source (Lk 12:20) shows the question to be direct, and the text here quickly moves into direct speech, concurrently evoking its adverbial sense. **217a** '[But God said to him]: Thou fool, this night shall thy soul depart [do they require thy soul of thee (Vg)]. [And whose shall those things be which thou hast provided? So is] he that layeth up treasure [for himself and is not rich towards God]' (Lk 12:20–21). *Tezaurisat...*: cf. also '[Surely man passeth as an image: yea and he is disquieted in vain]. He storeth up: and he knoweth not [for whom he shall gather these things]' (Ps 38:7). **219** *mothe*: cf. B 14.23. **220** *Hulle*: Cornhill, Will's place of residence (5.1), where second-hand clothes-dealers operated. The internal rhyme and final chime round off the mockery of the 'fool'. **227** *suche*: elliptical for 'is it with such'. **232** *ope*: '(heaped) on top of'. **234** *worth lygge*: 'will lie down (under its own weight)' (*Sk*). Taking *worth* as 'will be', *Pe* finds in *lygge* a form of an adj. unrecorded in MED but preserved in OED s.v. *ledger* adj. 5b, with a citation from Googe, not earlier than 1577 but very telling. **236** echoes B 14.73, which is removed in revision. **237** *how hit euere*: 'howsoever it'. **246–7** *hard...combraunce*: echoing the imagery and wording of 1.190–1. **248** *drede*: 'deference', with a tart pun on 'anxiety' (over losing it). **249** 'The wealth stored within them being the basic reason why there are robbers'.

Passus XIII (B XII)

PASSUS THIRTEEN (somewhat like books III and II of Chaucer's *Troilus*) is closely linked to XII, starting in the middle of a speech by Rechelesnesse (R.). XIII resembles XII in a certain symmetry, ending with the *start* of a speech by a new character that will continue through the *next* passus. Its emotional pattern is pyramidal, climaxing between 179–213 (where Will stands indignantly on a 'mountain'), then falling into a slough of embarrassed confusion (the 'ditch' of 235). In spite of its flowing dreamlike quality the three sections linked by transitional lines convey a sense of structural balance. (i) Ll. 1–97a continue RECHELESNESSE's diatribe against wealth and are new, the text parallel to Trajan's speech in **B** only resuming with the mention of unspiritual priests at 100 (for which a pair of link-lines 98–9 have been inserted) and going on for another 30 lines before the two parallel speeches end. The new material, now being designed not for the authoritative Trajan but for Will's 'doubled' persona R., mingles shrewd good sense with typical overstatements and mistakes of judgement (see on 11, 29, 77 and 114–15). (ii) consists of *a)* the vision of MIDDLEARTH (129–78), introduced by three connecting lines on KYNDE (131–3) and *b)* the dispute with REASON (179–213), also marked by such errors (e.g. at 191). (iii) Finally, there is the waking (214–18) out of the *inner dream* that began at 11.165, followed by the opening of a dialogue with a new interlocutor (YMAGYNATIF). The passus ends on a question from Will (219–48).

(i) 1–128 *Rechelesnesse on poverty and wealth* The rest of R.'s speech continues the praise of poverty (1–24), modulating into a comparison of it with wealth that modifies the original extremism through the extended exemplum / analogy of the Merchant and the Messenger (25–91). It concludes that poverty is spiritually superior (92–7a) and so preferable for priests, while importantly defining clerical 'poverty' as sufficiency, not destitution (98–128). **1–24** The two OT exempla cited argue better against wealth than for poverty, because in showing patiently-borne impoverishment rewarded by restoration of prosperity, they may prove too much, and cannot console those who were not rich in the first place. **1** *wel worth*: 'well may it be for'. *vnrobbed*: echoing *robbares* in 12.249. The thought here reflects that of the Latin line cited at B 14.304a and there removed in // **C**. **2b** repeats 12.144 but its logic is less than perfect, since presumably what saves the poor from being robbed is their lack of goods rather than their patience. However, **L** may simply see this virtue as what enables the condition of poverty to become a beatitude, not a curse. **4** Defying the OT (and modern) human expectation of getting richer over a lifetime's work, the saints grew progressively poorer through life, their ultimate exemplar being Christ himself (10.194–6). **4a** '[As sorrowful, yet always rejoicing: as needy, yet enriching many]: as having nothing and possessing all things' (II Cor 6:10). **5** *Abraham*: the story of how Sara was taken by the king of Gerara in the belief that she was Abraham's sister is told in Gen 20. **7** *for his*: 'because of his possessions.' **8** *pouerte*: in the sense of being deprived of his prize 'possession', his wife. *prince*: Abimelech; perhaps with an (unironical) echo of 3, for this 'prince' acts as an instrument of providence in teaching Abraham to trust God and not resort to deception. **11–12** *for he soffrede*; *criede hym mercy*: the speaker's (erroneous) interpretation of the scripture, where the 'kind king' in fact 'expostulates' with Abraham; but the happy outcome is indeed due to Abimelech's 'sincere heart' (Gen 20:6). **14** *gentele*: an epithet of alliterative convenience applied also to James and John (see *PNI*). **15** *the Book*: see Job ch. 1. **16–17** are composed from Job's reply to his wife: 'If we have received good things at [the hand of] God, [why should we not receive] evil [*mala* 'bad things']?' (Job 2:10). **18** Cf. 12.210 above *song*: L's way of assimilating Job's rebuking of his wife to the great psalm-verses of acceptance and hope (like Ps 112:5–8). **19** *newe*: both 'renewed' and 'new in nature', because now true 'spiritual joy' (cf. B 14.284–5). **20** *pacience*: Job is cited as the model of patience in Js 5:11, whereas Abraham in the NT is more commonly taken to exemplify faith. **22** *grayn*: the sense here, as at 12.186–7 above, is that humiliation (*greut*) can through the help of grace be the source of abundant virtue and even, if God so wills, be rewarded by further prosperity in this life. The underlying inspiration is again Jn 12:24–5. **23** *spredeth*: alluding to the abundant offspring of both (Gen 13:16, Job 42:16).

25–97a 25–31 are addressed to *lewede men* or *illiterati*, who risk drawing too extreme a conclusion about the dangers of wealth (perhaps L's response to post-1381 conditions). But they argue that even if Dowel is compatible with wealth, Do-*better* belongs to (the patient acceptance of) poverty, which acts as satisfaction for one's sins. The deeper meaning of the merchant-messenger *ensaumple* offered to prove this is, however, something for *wyse men* (64). **27** *fylosofres*: echoing B 20.38–9. **29** *lyues*: the comparison of wealth with poverty recalling that of active and contemplative 'lives' at 12.142–5. *large weyes*: showing that the speaker, in his eagerness to right the balance, has forgotten the warning of Mt 19:23–4. **30–1** Cf. 9.183–6, 11.300. **32** *merchant...mesager*: two categories of traveller liable to be stopped at toll-bridges and ports (cf. 4.129. **34** The literal referent of *Resoun* is obscure and is presumably some sort of official at a customs-post; but the anagogical sense of the allegory is made quite clear at 66 (on Reason as 'reckoner' cf. 3.308). **36** is a line of awkward scansion, having in the a-half the second stave mute, and blank staves in *nede* and *ylet*, and in the b-half a 'strong' dip before the 'monolexical' *méssagére* (see *Intro*. IV § 38). **37–8** *paper*: the merchant's documents emblematising the long list of sins to which the rich are thought prone during their lifetime. *dettes.../ lette*: a rhyme hinting 'Platonically' at the spiritual effect of sins as a hindrance to heaven. *pryué*: alluding to sharp

practices that weigh on his conscience. **38** 'Will cause him to be left, I warrant, a mile behind (the messenger).' **41–50** It was forbidden to cross a wheatfield, and the *haiward* (44) was the manorial official empowered to enforce this. Reason, judging it futile to take a pledge (of future payment of a fine for trespass) from a messenger who cannot pay, but reasonable to do so from a merchant (who can), notes that the common-law right is sometimes supported by local regulations for the payment of toll. **43a** 'Nede hath no lawe' (22.100), a maxim of natural law (*CIC* 1:374) that had become proverbial (see Alf*Q*). The precise interpretation of this first allegory at 64–91 tells against supposing that 'the messenger, because he has no money to pay the fine, commits no offence in breaking the law' (*Pe*). The point being made is that (though the messenger *has* broken the law) it is not *wys* 'sensible' (43) to fine him for a minor tort, while the toll stipulated by *lawe* (49) does not apply to him anyway, so he 'is let through at once' (40) without a pledge (cf. 22.13). There is thus little support for Harwood's opinion (1973:289) cited by *Pe* that R. seeks 'cheap grace' and settles for 'sinlessness for want of opportunity'; for it has been made clear that poverty patiently borne not only avoids 'occasions of sin' but disposes to humility. Since R. does not say that the poor are licensed to break the law, only excused from the legal obligations of the rich, it is not relevant that 'haywards could be extortioners, and were much hated' (*Pe*), this 'hayward' being the agent of 'þe Kyng of Heuene' (66). **47** *hatt...gloues*: items often taken as pledges. **49a** 'And on top of that, be held up'. **51** *o... to*: 'on the one road that leads to'. *Wynchestre fayre*: see on 6.211. **60** *moneye*: explained at 69ff. **63** *as safly*: '(he could travel) as safely'.

64–97a are ostensibly addressed to those who can interpret the allegory accurately, but also set out to explain it to those who cannot: the merchant = the rich, the 'way' = a righteous life, the 'toll' = charitable works. **65–77** recall the 'marginal' words of Truth's pardon on the obligations of merchants at 9.22–36. **66** *Aren*: '(who) are' (the construction being parallel to the later Ø-relative clause at 79). **67** *euene*: a 'Platonic' echo of *heuene* 66, indicating that steady, 'just' adherence to God's law will lead them to him. **77** *Crist hymsulf...*: the words are in fact St Paul's. **77a** See on 8.231a., where the maxim is cited as stating the *lawe of kynde*. **79** *Beth*: 'And who are'. *boþe...lawes*: earthly and divine. **84** *contumax*: '(held to be) in contempt of court', esp. for failure to answer a summons. The sense in question seems to be the legal one (Alf*G* s.v.) rather than that of someone 'thurgh his indignacioun...agayns euerich auctoritee or power of... his sovereyns' (*CT* X 401; cit. *Sk*). **86a** See on 12.60a; the understood completion of the quotation is 'will be saved'. **88** *seel*: the sender's imprint being allegorically 'the king of heaven's mark' (17.77), the spiritual 'character' received by the baptized (cf. II Tim 2:19). *lord*: i.e. Christ, who sends him to the Lord (87) 'God' with the *tale* that he is a true believer. **89–91** *byleue...leue*; *gate.. gateward*: the first pun is polysemic, the second homophonic (for the image cf. 7.242). **90** *lawe*: 'regulation', playing on the literal sense instanced at 49 and implying subordination of church discipline to the 'law' of faith (86). *lette...gate*: unlike earthly laws subject to bribery (3.193). **92–3** A poor man complies with the law of charity by feeling for others what he hopes they feel towards him, and not asking for himself more than he can give them. **92** *of*: 'through'. **93** *as*: 'as for'. **94–5** evoke scripture to claim that the beggar's will is in effect his 'all'. **97a** 'Amen, I say to you, this poor widow [hath cast in more than all they who have cast into the treasury...]' (Mk 12:43–4; cf. B 13.197–8).

98–9 are transitional lines that sum up R.'s new parable-argument and neatly link (*For* 100) with the discourse on priestly perfection that the revision broke into at B 11.280 (see on 12.16). **99** *pouerte*: a condition not of destitution, but like that of Chaucer's 'povre persoun' who 'koude in litel thyng have suffisaunce' (*CT* I 478, 490).

The parallel text resumes with
C XIII 100 = B XI 285

100–28 reproduce (with improvement at 114–15 of B 301–2 and no major alteration) Trajan's attack on unprovided and ill-qualified priests. But they make R. sound somewhat like a spokesman for Wycliffe's 'Poor Priests' (*Pe* compares 16.110 and cites Leff 1967:527–9). **100** *Spera*...: 'Hope in God, [for I will still give praise to him: the salvation of my countenance...]' (Ps 42:6–7); especially appropriate to priests (AlfQ) as forming part of the Introit Psalm *Iudica me* at Mass, the text cited at B 11.284a. Peter Lombard saw this verse as warning against *pressuras saeculi* 'worldly preoccupations' (*R–H* 143). However, it is not Ps 42 that makes the promises of 101–2 but Ps 36: '*Trust in the Lord*, and do good, and dwell in the land: and thou shalt be fed with its riches' (vs 3); cf. also Ps 36:16, 'Better is a little to the just than the great riches of the wicked'. **103–6** argue that a priest should have a guarantee of material support ('title') from a lay or clerical patron (*he* 105), or from his ordinary (106), that will enable him to concentrate on his spiritual responsibilities without needing to find money, e.g. through serving in a chantry (cf. Pr 81–4); see Swanson 1985, Revard 1987:116–27, Du Boulay 1991:24. **106** *blessed... enbaumed*: when ordaining him priest. **107–15** compare priestly ordination with the dubbing of a warrior-knight, who also needs to be properly qualified. **108** *or...strenthe*: either (a) 'or [if he did not], maintained him for his prowess in battle' (with *kyng* as understood subject), or (b) 'or provided [in some way] for his needs as a man-

at-arms' (with *knyht* as subject). The reference at 110b to a knight's reputation for valour shows that the parallel between bishop and king does not stipulate a knight's financial *independence* any more than a priest's (as made clear in parallel B 291b), provided each has support from the one who 'ordains' him. **112** *connynge ne kyn*: a complaint against ignorant clergy (of possibly unfree origin) reflecting conditions after the Great Pestilence, which reduced the number of priests by up to two-thirds in some dioceses. **112–13** Given the positive emphasis at 103, 106, *title* here more probably means '(mere) name of priest' or '(merely) verbal guarantee of support', i.e. something purely formal, like a tonsure (which in B 299–300 is contrasted with learning and virtue). **B 299–300** 'He has, I believe, more expectation of getting a benefice simply because he's been ordained than because of his learning or acknowledged piety'; omitted in **C** either as awkward or as partly repeating 297. **114–15** are much stronger than the vacuous B 301–2, and 'Wycliffite' in tone, while remaining formally orthodox. *shendeth*: 'does injury to', in a sense not far from 'dishonours' (MED s.v. *shenden* v. 3(b); see *TN*). R. seems to locate the *vitium* not in the rite performed but in the one who performs it, so that the charter-analogy (unaltered in **C**), where *formal* error invalidates, is logically inexact. **120** *goky*: 'a silly cuckoo (< *gok*)'; instanced only here and in works influenced by *PP*. **121a** '[And] whosoever [shall keep the whole law but] offend in one point, is become guilty of all' (Js 2:10). The Latin forms a perfect alliterative line scanning on vowels (the other such lines are 1.142a, 3.496a, 10.90, 15.142, 20.112a, 21.173, B 7.116–7, 10.438 [Lat./Fr. macaronic]). In context the reference is to an otherwise virtuous man's one (major) sin; but the application would be more apt if the text read *vno verbo* (see *TN* on the earlier appearance at B 9.98 with *verbo* for *vno*, a variant that looks original there). **122** *For*: 'For the benefit of'. **123** 'Sing praises to our God, sing ye;... for [the] God [of Israel] is the king of all the earth: sing ye wisely' (Ps 46:7–8). R. takes *sapienter* to refer to the way the priest performs the liturgy more than to his spiritual understanding of it. **128** 'Ignorance does not excuse [bishops] or unlearned priests'; in **B** denoting bishops' (culpable) unawareness of ordinands' deficiencies, in **C** the fact that lack of education does not excuse a priest for ill performance of the liturgy or the bishop for ordaining him. The phrase is a maxim of canon law echoed in Abp. Pecham's *Constitutions* (Lyndwood's *Provinciale* I) and quoted by Bromyard (1.35/4): 'Ignorance does not excuse a priest in those matters which pertain to his office' (AlfQ). **B 316** *ydiotes*: the adj. (< the loan-word *idiote* n.) given a pl. ending as if French (see *MES* 277).

(iia) 129–78 *The Vision of Middle-earth* **129–33** The lines' transitional intent is indicated by their mid-sentence introduction of an entirely new motif with a subordinating conjunction (compare *Til þat* 131 with *and siþen* B 320). Ascription of the speech is clearer than in B 317–19, with its sermon-like acknowledgement of *digressio* and indeterminate *oon*, which echoes and should refer to the *oon* of B 11.140. **129** *rage aresende*: ironic oxymoron 'placing' the preceding diatribe more critically than *dispute* in // B 319. **130** ironically recalls 11.162, which opened the rebuke precipitating the 'inner' dream. **131** *Kynde*: a benign character (see on 10.129) whose brief first appearance to help Clergy enlighten Will initiates the vision of MIDDLE EARTH. This focusses mainly on the non-human world and formally counterpoises that offered by Fortune at 11.170 (the echo of B 11.10 at B 11.322 is cut). **L**'s treatment of the 'plenitude of creation' theme is indebted to the C12th philosophical and poetic traditions associated respectively with the School of Chartres and Alan of Lille, and also to the Victorine contemplative writers (White 1986:241–8). The vision's specific aim is to show the sexual drive as an instrument of God's purpose and not an excuse for licentiousness. The account in **B 321–5** is more didactically explicit than C 132–3. It identifies KYNDE as the Creator (325, a repetition of B 9.26 avoided in **C**), recalls man's origin (Gen 3:9), declares that nature's 'wonders' provide parables for his instruction, and 'Platonically' chimes near-identical lexemes (325) in anticipation of B 16.215 (cf. also C 17.153, 18.94). **132** *myrour.*: see on 11.170. *hym*: identity with the Dreamer being implied by the shift to *Y* at 134 (in **B** the vision is shown to the latter) and confirmed by the 'reckless' tone of Will's remonstrance at 184ff, and by verbal echoes like *resonede* 183.

134–78 139–41 *bothe*: bringing out the 'mingled' nature of earthly existence. **143** *Resoun*: here representing the divine *ratio* embodied in the cosmic order, with some influence from the understanding in Roman jurisprudence of 'natural law' as 'that which nature teaches all things' (Alford 1988:211). **146** Despite the offered punctuation (presupposing two lifts in the verb), the caesura may come after *anon* and the line be of Type IIIc, or Type I on vowels. **148** *ferddede*: the only recorded intransitive use. **151b, 153a** illustrate **C**'s typical rhetorical *repetitio* (e.g. *nest* at 156, 159–60, the variations on *wonder* 137, 153, 158, 161). **152** *lykynge...flesch*: 'desire for sexual gratification'; cf. Z 3.163. **154** *out of resoun*: 'immoderately', because breaching the rational virtue of temperance. *rechelesliche*: ironically anticipating the motif of the Dreamer's discerning others' faults more readily than his own (B 386=C 207). **156/7** The rhyme heightens the formulaic character of the exempla. **165–6** Elaborate internal assonance / rhyme and fluid alliterative linking across the lines mirror the sense of order in nature seen in the earlier birds-passage at 10.63–7. **168** *Dompynges*: from *dompen* v. (MED s.v. (b)), possibly denoting the 'dive-dap' (moorhen or waterhen). **169** While the answer

is obviously 'from their Creator', its source is unlikely to be Job 39:13–17 (*Pe*), which remarks not on the birds' natural wisdom but on their *lack* of it; more relevant here is vs 4 of Ecclus 11, a ch. that influenced this passage. **170** *cauken*: from AF *cauquer* (< L. *calcare* 'trample'). **171–2** well illustrate 'Langlandian grotesque', the emblematic allusion to the rich, though muted, being elucidated at 14.178. Nature here functions as a 'faithful mirror of man's state', as in Alan of Lille's 'Omnis mundi creatura' (*PL* 210:579–80). **173–8** round off the vision of Middle Earth by recalling the opening (*see* 173=135; *colour* 178=138) and (more distantly) Pr 5 (*selcouthe*), with echoing phrases that again evoke the divine harmony through assonance and internal rhyme (174–7 on |oυ| and |ευ|). **175** *Ne...on*: 'Nor what (I saw by way) of'.

(iib) 179–213 record Will's challenge to Reason and Reason's authoritative answer, which induces a rush of shame that wakes him from his deep dream of God's paradisal world. **179–82** are no more than a response to what Will saw at 139–42; but his objection in **183–93** assumes that since Reason does *not* accompany man, the supposedly rational part of creation (cf. 192), he cannot after all be wise. On Will's confusion of two senses of *resoun* (191), 'natural instinct' and 'rationality' (involving freedom to choose), see Schmidt 1969:148, and on the theodicy underlying this scene, idem 1986:33–5. The contrast between fallen man's sexuality and the animals' is drawn by Alan of Lille's Nature in *DPN*: 'almost all things obey my rule, excluding man alone by an anomalous exception' (*PL* 210:448). **185** *Wherefore and why*: recalling B 11.301, words of Trajan omitted at that point in revision. **187–9** *sorfeten...wedes...wordes*: both warned against in Ecclus 11:4, 8. **191** *al*: both an adj. 'all' (contrasting with *fewe*) and an adv. 'entirely' (modifying *reule*). **193** *leueth*: possibly punning on 'believes' and 'lives'. **B 373** *witty*: applied to God as at B 15.130. REASON is another 'nature-name' for God and so replies with unique authority, while also being associated with the power in man's soul that made him the Creator's image and likeness. **194–213** retain the essence of **B**'s moral argument: that mankind's defective state need not import imperfection in God, and is his concern alone. **194** *Reche*: reinforcing this characteristic that makes *Will*'s 'nature-name' Rechelesnesse. **196** *Vch.*: signifying not 'everyone for himself' but 'mind your own affairs, not those of other people'; a position echoing B 10.263, where the *meuen mod* expression of 179 appears. **197** 'Strive not in a matter which doth not concern thee' (Ecclus 11:9). **B 378** superbly renders the French of B 384; but this oxymoronic line's omission in **C** seems due to a shift of emphasis towards *love* as what makes *soffraunce* (earlier criticised when *vnsittynge* at 3.207) a 'sovereign' virtue, supremely efficacious and 'sitting' for the king of kings. **198, 200** *soffreth*: 'puts up with' and 'suffers'; in both versions divine forbearance and suffering are to serve as models for man. **202** *soffrance*: the human virtue associated with God's mysterious tolerance of human sinfulness for his own hidden but ultimately 'reasonable' ends (cf. Ecclus 11:4, 14, 23). *for Godes loue*: distinguishing virtuous patience from craven acquiescence in wrongdoing. **B 382a** 'Be ye subject [therefore] to every [human] creature for God's sake...[for so is the will of God,...by *doing well*...as the servants of God... if, doing well *you suffer patiently*: this is thankworthy before God]' (I Pet 2:13–16, 20; cf. also Js 5:7–11). The omission before *creaturae of humanae* may, if intentional, signify that Will must learn to imitate the animals' *resoun* and so 'to tolerate the conditions of human necessity' (Kaulbach 1993:57). **203** *þe wyse*: i.e. 'Solomon', cited at 197. **204–5** 'Fine virtue is Patience, poor vengeance is Say-ill. Say-well and Suffer-well make a man speed well;' apparently proverbial (see Whiting S861), the thought being paralleled in *CT* V 773–80, which also translates the Cato tag quoted at 213 (*Pe*). **207** 'Before you blame anybody, consider whether there is anyone (including yourself) who deserves praise'. Reason's rejoinder echoes Leute's at 12.41*a*, which earned Scripture's approval, its 'Cato'-like prudence according with OT 'wisdom'. **B 386** *my lif*: 'the life of any man' as well as Reason's own observable 'behaviour' (for such double reference cf. on B 373 above). **208–9** argue that a man can no more create than he can christen himself: both require the action of another. **C** is milder in urging the Dreamer to reform his own life before others'. The revision replaces *lif* (at B 386, 389) with *repetitio* of *creature* at 208a, 209a and (with *variatio*) of verb-phrases at 208b, 209b. The omission of **B 394–9**, arguably digressive lines on bodily deformity as implying a criticism of divine perfection, improves the flow of Reason's argument that 'since *each* individual is imperfect, *none* should object that *all* are'. **B 396a** 'And God saw all the things that he had made, and they were very good' (Gen 1:31). **211** *matere*: presumably not implying that 'matter' *per se* is evil, but that man's 'fallenness' inevitably inclines him towards (especially sexual) sins he would be free from if he were pure spirit. **213** 'Cato agrees with me: "there's none from fault lives free"' (*DC* I. 5).

(iii) 214–48 open with the conclusion of the inner dream (Vision Three *b*) and return to the outer level of vision (Three *a*), which finishes at the end of C XIV=B XII. **214** *aschamed*: the violent access of feeling and surge of blood providing a psycho-physiological 'motivation' for the change of dream-state, which is not a true 'waking' but a receding from the stage at which greater things (*more* 216, 223) could have been dreamed. The phrasing recalls the moment when Will burst into tears and was plunged into the inner dream at 11.166 (on the association of states of emotional agitation with visionary experience, cf. *Pearl* 48–60, Carruthers 1998:170, 173). **217–218** The tone con-

trasts markedly with the confidence of **B**, the revision characteristically normalising the metrically licentious *s / ch* scansion of **B**. *grace*: here admitting of the theological sense, to hint that Will's access to deeper truth has been lost (like grace through sin) by his challenge to the divine wisdom personified in Reason. **219** *was...wyhte*: a phrase repeated from B 18.229 and replacing one at B 408 that echoed B 11.140, 319. **220** *What is Dowel*: the question to be repeated by Will at 15.112 but here addressed *to* him (and echoing his words at 218); his answer (the fruit of experience) is not rejected. The word is stressed *Dowél* as at 218, not *Dówel* as at 221. **221** *al*: a little word, but with a large change in sense. Will's repetition here shows that he accepts Reason's injunction to imitate God (200), whereas in **B** the repeated *moore* of 410 is meant to resonate with 405 and 412. *soffre*: in its double sense; see at 198. **223** *þat Clergie can*: intimating that the meaning of the Church's teaching would have been disclosed if the vision had been accepted without questioning. **223–5** *conseyued mor...forsake*: reminiscent of the *Pearl*-Dreamer's similar realisation (1189–94) after a similarly abrupt awakening. **225a** *Philosophus...*: 'You might have been a philosopher, had you held your peace'; adapted from Boethius, *De Cons. Phil.* II pr. 7, 74–6, and found in almost this form in Bromyard I 450:2. *Et alibi...*: 'And in another place: "it has sometimes embarrassed me that I spoke, never that I kept silent"'; adapted from *nam nulli tacuisse nocet, nocet esse locutum* 'for harm comes from speaking, never from having kept silence' (*DC*, I.12b). **226** *Adam*: a rather ill-suited exemplum, since Adam's sin was not to *speak* (about the fruit) but to *listen* to what Eve said (cf. Gen 3:6). The passage generally recalls the warning against imprudent and unconsidered utterance in Ecclus 11:7–9. **227–8** may echo *DC* I .3: *Virtutem primam esse puta compescere linguam; / proximus ille deo est, qui scit ratione tacere* (Baer 2001:139). **228** is of T-type, the b-staves being cognative on *p / b*. *wisdom... of God*: in forbidding Adam to eat a fruit that would bring him death (Gen 2:17). **230** *wyte why*: echoing B 10.124 (deleted in **C**), while // B 419 recalls Lewtee at B 11.105–6, and 419b Reason at B 376. **231** 'Because of the arrogant self-confidence that comes from your extravagant style of life'. *parfit lyuynge*: with sense as in the name of Fortune's damsel at 11.176, but with a sardonic 'anti-pun' on the contrary sense instanced at B 15.417. **232** *Reson*: a significant addition, this weighty figure's refusal inevitably entailing Clergy's also. **233** *connynge*: a revision avoiding repetition of the point at B 435. **234** *shame*: probably personified here (and at B 431), as later at 244. The quality denoted is fear of others' disapproval and implies the Dreamer's return to his condition at 6.2, illustrating the importance of the 'affective' element in disciplining the will when a purely 'cognitive' training has proved ineffective. Some influence from Richard of

St Victor's *Benjamin Minor* chs. xlv–xlviii (*PL* 196:51, ME tr. in Hodgson 1958:142–3) may be suspected here. *shrewe* (*man* B): the strongest reproach ever used towards the Dreamer by any of his interlocutors. **235–41** allegorise under the figure of drunkenness the rake's progress that the speaker finds illustrated in Will. **235** *daffe*: here as at 10.179 applied to a drunk displaying insolence and lack of reason (but earlier to Will by HC at 1.138). **237** *thenne*: when he has fallen from Fortune's favour but does not yet realise what has happened. *recheth*: linking Will's intoxication with worldly pleasure to his extreme attitude towards the wisdom of providence. While the phrase echoes 194, this is the wrong kind of 'failure to care'. **240** *Nede*: an important figure later in the waking prelude to Passus XXII, where his hostile tone recalls his rôle here as an extrinsic initiator of shame. **244** describes the reflex of shame seen in others' attitude, that which causes the 'smart'. **247** *aroes vp*: implying that Will has felt acute mortification, acknowledged his faultiness, and acquired a new readiness to be instructed.

Passus XIV (B XII)

This short but dense Passus consists almost entirely of a single speech by Ymagynatyf (Y. hereafter), who was introduced without being named at the end of PASSUS XIII when Will woke out of his inner dream. It pauses at 99–109, about mid-point, with a one-line question to Will (108), and is interrupted towards the close by a three-line objection from him (199–201) that Y. decisively answers, bringing the THIRD VISION to an end. C XIV is 80 lines shorter than B XII, with four main cuts at 16–54*a*, 81–96, 231–4 and 251–8. The chief of these is the first, Will's defence of his 'making' at B 20–8, which is compensated for by new matter on a similar theme earlier introduced at C V 92–104 (see Schmidt 1987:14–20, 142–3). Y.'s discourse defends *clergye* 'learning got from books' (specifically that concerning the way to salvation taught by the Scriptures) and 'the clergy' who have charge of it. He handles objections to the claim that knowledge of the Christian faith and acceptance of baptism are necessary for salvation, addressing the problem-cases of the Good Thief (131–48, 153–55*a*) and Trajan (149–50, 205–16), who were apparently saved without them. Ymagynatyf's argument employs vivid analogies based on experience that bear out his nature as the power of shaping mental images so as to draw spiritual understanding from them.

B 1–54*a* are considered first since they have been drastically revised and **C** is more conveniently commented on from where it takes up **B** to run continuously in parallel. Though in both versions Y. gives the Dreamer moral counsel, in **B** he does this much more explicitly through calling to Will's mind memories from the past,

thoughts of the present and imaginings of the future (e.g. of what it will be like to be old and unable to undertake penitential exercises for the sins of youth). **1** *Ymaginatyf*: a nominalised form of the adjective, signifying 'the ability to form images of things not experienced, e.g. of past or future events' (MED s.v. *imaginatif* adj. and n. 4 (c)). Corresponding to the *vis imaginativa* of late medieval epistemology, it encompasses acts now classed not under imagination but memory. In the tradition of 'monastic philosophy', however, *memoria* was considered not a passive but a 'shaping' and picturing power, especially in relation to the act of praying (cf. 16.184 and see Carruthers 1995). Literary personifications of imagination are rare, though one appears in the OF *Enseignement de la vraye noblesse* (cited in Keen 1984:152). **L**'s figure has been convincingly seen as the power of actively or vividly representing [images] to oneself (Wittig 1972:271); personifying the mind's capacity to make similitudes (Harwood 1975:249); providing images and examples as means to understand the truth (Minnis 1981); and functioning as the *sensus communis* to co-ordinate sense-experience under the direction of prudence and, eventually, grace (Gallacher 1991:49). At the opposite ends of usage, the devotional and the scholastic, are White's identification in Y. of 'imaginative contemplation' as understood in the Victorine tradition, leading to wonder and love of God (1986), and Kaulbach's (1993) of the human potentiality for thought (and especially prophecy) as understood in the 'Augustinised Avicennism' of the period. Undeniable resonances of each account indicating a synthetic conception drawn from many traditions argue against seeking too specific a source. Wherever **L** situated imagination among the mind's functions, he did not include it with Anima's names in B XV. So perhaps Y. represents less a spiritual faculty than (in the broadly 'Aristotelian' tradition) one mediating between the bodily senses and the rational soul in order to furnish images from which the intellect 'abstracts' general concepts with which to reason (cf. Gallacher 1991, 1992). That *Ymaginatif*, who in principle stands nearer to 'the knowledge derived from experience', should discourse on the value of *clergie* 'revealed knowledge' is ostensibly paradoxical. But the Dreamer having proved unable to learn *directly* from Reason (questioning his 'wisdom' on the basis of his own observations of animal behaviour), and having 'contraried Clergy' (see on 100 below), it seems ironically fitting to have him learn the 'limited value' of experiential knowledge from a faculty whose starting-point is likewise the data of the senses. **3** *fyue and fourty wynter*: if taken as covering Will's complete age at this point, denoting (as at B 11.47) the peak of 'middle life', which was seen as a time of critical decision for man's spiritual destiny (Burrow in Heyworth 1981:21–41). **5** *And how*: 'and (to reflect on) how...' **6** scans on |ð| and

Commentary

|w| as an extended Type IIIa with counterpoint (*abb / ab*). **9a** 'If not in the first watch nor in the second...'; after Lk 12:38: 'And if [the Lord] shall come in the second... or...the third watch and find them [watching], blessed are those servants.' As in Gregory's interpretation of this passage in his *XL Homiliarum in Evangelia*, Bk I, Hom. 13 (*PL* 76), three night-watches are here supposed. They correspond to youth, middle age and old age, when death and the individual judgement might come unexpectedly, and for which one must prepare (*R–H* 149 citing *GO* [*PL* 114:298]; see further Burrow 1986:69–70). **10–11** may have some personal significance known to the poet's earliest readers. The reference to the *pestilences* could betoken family losses; the *pouerte* agrees with the manner of life described in 16–17 and in C 5.1–4, 49–52; and A 12.81–7a record a (near-fatal) *angre*. **12** *baleyses*: natural affliction thought of as *virga Dei* 'the rod of God' (Job 21:9). **12a** 'Such as I love I [rebuke and] chastise' (Apoc 3:19, echoing Prov 3:12). In Lombard's *Commentary* (*PL* 191:243–4, cit. *R–H* 149n86) the 'rod' is interpreted as a light discipline, the staff as a stronger one (for older 'sons'). **13** *swiche...Iesus*: understood as prophetically applying to Christ's followers, who may expect persecution as a test of their faith. **13a** 'Thy rod and thy staff: they have comforted me' (Ps 22:4); a text encouraging the patient Christian to accept discipline as a sheep submits to the guiding blows of the shepherd: God's corrections become consolations (*Sk*). **16–17** *And;...and*: 'And yet'; 'when'. *medlest...makynge*: see Schmidt 1987:14–19. *seye...breed*: as a 'psalter-clerk', not qualified to celebrate Mass in a chantry (because not ordained priest), but authorised to recite the penitential psalms for the souls of the relatives of those who provide him sustenance. That this *may* reflect the poet's own circumstances is tacitly implied by his quoting from the psalms some 80 times severally. **17** *bokes ynowe*: semi-ironic, since books have clearly not given Will the *kynde knowynge* he has insisted on. **19** *peire freres*: alluding to the friars' custom of going about their mission in pairs, like those in 10.8 who answer Will's question about Dowel. **21–2** *pat... To*: running together two constructions to yield '(saying) that he should...' *solacen...make*: as Philosophy offers Boethius 'the sauasyoun of swetnesse rethorien' in *Boece* II pr. 141 (Rudd 1994:171). *sone*: alluding to the medieval view that the *Disticha de moribus ad Filium* (to give it its frequent title) was addressed by Cato to his son (Baer 2001:131) **22a** 'Give a place sometime to pleasure amid the pressure of cares / [That you might bear in spirit the burden of labour]' (*DC* III.6). **23–4** *holy men... Pleyden*: evoking the followers of St Francis, called *joculatores Domini* for their use of poems, tales and music in preaching the Gospel. **27** *wende...chirche*: i.e. adopt a contemplative life; the phrase 'foreshadows Will's arrival in Unity [at 22.212–13]' (White 1988:80). **27–8**

but; but: the semantic / metrical repetition-with-variation (mute and stressed co-ordinating / adverbial conjunction) is notable. **29a** '[And now there remain] faith, hope and charity, [these three]: and the greatest of these [is charity]' ((I Cor 13:13). **32** *lewte*: a quality, defining Dowel, that may here signify 'faith' in a wide sense of obedience to the commandments of God and the Church. Married man, monk and virgin all typify 'fidelity' to a chosen way of life that suffices for salvation, while the nine 'negative examples' following show what comes from varieties of infidelity. **35** *Ri3t so*: the first of three such arguments by analogical example (cf. 47, 51). **36** *Rome*: see on Pr 48. *Rochemador*: Rocamadour in Lot, S France, where the shrine of Our Lady was (and is) a favourite centre of pilgimage (illustrations in Jusserand 1899:338, 365). *but*: 'except' (i.e. not at all, since for a monk *stabilitas* is the 'main road'). **38** *continue*: used in this absolute sense of 'remain celibate' also at B 9.179=C 10.286 (MED s.v. *continuen* v. 6(b)). **39** *seint ferther*: the 'pilgrimage'-metaphor, with its wry pun on a non-existent 'St Further,' intimates that all the maiden needs for salvation is her virginity itself. **40** On the rhythm and alliteration in this line cf. B 2.33 above. *What made...lese*: answered in 45 (and repeated in 55), which also applies to the examples in 46–56a. *Lucifer*: see on 1.104ff. **41** *Salomon; Sampson*: whose loss of *sapience* 'knowledge of God' and *strengthe* '(divine) fortitude' was caused specifically by desire for foreign women rather than *catel* (III Kgs 11:1–10, Judges 16:4–21), though in 'Augustinian' terms, anything loved possessively may be so described. **42** *Iob*: whose loss of prosperity not being due to sin of any kind, *ioye* may signify the happiness ultimately restored to him (Job 42:12) more than the original wealth he 'paid a high price for.' **43–5** These four figures represent the summit of achievement in philosophy, science, literature and imperial conquest (*Wr*). **43** *Aristotle*: see on 11.121; held in popular legend to have fallen under the spell of a woman and said by Eumelus to have committed suicide (as did Socrates) by drinking hemlock (Chroust 1973, ch. 14). Like the next two, he presumably illustrates the moral weakness of natural intelligence (*kynde wit*) left to itself. *Ypocras*: the celebrated Greek physician Hippocrates (C5th BC), who was fabled to have died of dysentery sent as a divine punishment for murder (*The Seven Sages* 1040ff). *Virgile*: the great Roman poet (70–19 BC), bizarrely believed to have had himself cut to pieces in an attempt at magical self-rejuvenation, which failed (Comparetti 1966:367). **44** *Alisaundre*: Alexander the Great (356–23 BC), the archetype of earthly glory in medieval tradition and first among the 'Nine Worthies'; affirmed in his legendary history to have been poisoned (cf. *Kyng Alisaunder* 7850–93). The *combraunce* of *catel* is best represented by his case. *pat al wan*: with a possible grim secondary sense, punning on the homophonic noun-phrase ('that one who was utterly pale [after being poisoned]'). **46–8** These two instances prove the danger of over-valuing one's beauty as a 'possession' (*catel*). **46** *Felice*: heroine of the popular early C14th romance *Guy of Warwick,* who treated Guy with disdain when he wooed her and was left by him forty days after their marriage, the 'disgrace' presumably denoting what she felt as a result of this. **47–8** *Rosamounde*: 'fair Rosemund,' daughter of Walter, Lord Clifford, and mistress of King Henry II; allegedly poisoned by Henry's Queen Eleanor in 1177, she was buried at Godstow nunnery near Oxford. *bisette*: a reflexive *hir* is presumed by *Sk*, who makes 48a the inverted object; but an 'it' may be readily understood, though MED s.v. *dispenden* v. 1 (a) also cites (from Gower) an objectless use of this verb. **50** *wise wordes*: applying only to Solomon and Aristotle. **50a** 'Bad men there are, who about good speak well; [Reject the men, retain the truth they tell]'; from Epigram 169 by the C12th Anglo-Latin poet Godfrey of Winchester (Alf*Q*, citing Wright 1872:II 130). **53** *suffren*: 'indifferently accept the existence of' (with a polysemantic 'anti-pun' on 'suffer'); a similar point at B 15.138–45 is removed in revision. **54a** See on 1.195, where the reference is to specifically clerical avarice. Lk 6:38 ends with the warning at 1.173a, and the context implicitly evokes the verse after that quoted at 56a: '... unto whomsoever much is given [the rich, the fair or the wise]...much shall be required.'

(i) 1–109 move from a critique of the value of 'learning' and wealth to a defence of *clergie*, 1–16a forming Ymaginatyf's account of his own nature and of the Triad. **1–34 4** *Dowel*: Y. reminds Will of what he taught him before, his definitions of Dowel and Dobet coming not as answers to a particular question but as revived memories of what the Dreamer already knows (see on B 1 above). **7** *spille no speche*: recalling Wit's definition of Dowel at 10.187. **8–9** *tyne...tene*; *lowe...lawe*: hinting through the pararhymes that time wasted is opportunity lost for doing good, and that humility is the essence of obedience to the commandments. **13** defines love, morality and faith (the equivalents of the Triad elements) as 'facets' of a comprehensive whole, 'Charity', the modulated pararhymes (*louye, lyue, byleue*) 'Platonically' reflecting their referents' substantive relationship. **14** *Caritas*: 'Charity' (see on 2.37), appearing later as the fruit of the tree 'True Love' (of which *Kynde Loue* here is a synonym). The Latin term gains special resonance from such key Pauline texts as Col 3:14 (*Super omnia...charitatem habete*) and Rom 13:10 (on love [here actually *dilectio*] fulfilling the Law). **16a** 'It is a more blessed thing to give, rather than to ask [*accipere* Vg "receive"]' (Ac 20:35). **18** *weldeth*; *wel de*spene: more 'Platonic' wordplay, hinting at the 'ideal' relation posited between power and bounty. **18a** 'Those who know [God's will] and do not act [according to it] shall be beaten with many whips'; adapted from

Lk 12.47 ('servus qui...*non fecit* secundum voluntatem [domini sui] *vapulabit* multis'). **19–22** focus on disorder in Church and society and remove the potential ambiguity of B 57–8; for reference to the source (where Vg actually has *scientia*) does not favour giving *sapiencia* the meaning 'spiritual wisdom' as opposed to '(purely) intellectual or cognitive understanding' (*scientia*). **B 57a** '[...we know (*scimus*) that we all have knowledge (*scientia*)]. Knowledge puffeth up; [but charity edifieth]' (I Cor 8:1). The immediate Pauline context is important for correctly understanding **L**'s association of true wisdom with love: 'If any man think that he knoweth (*scire*) any thing, he hath not yet known (*cognovit*) as he ought to know (*scire*). But if any man love God (*diligere*), the same is known (*cognitus*) by him' (vss 2–3). The tacit logic of equivalence here is: if to love God is to be 'known' (acknowledged / understood) by him, then *e converso* to love ('acknowledge, obey') him is to 'know' (understand) him (a point reinforced at B 71b). **19–20** have a chiastic structure: *connynge → techares; rychesse → lordes. lewede men*: possibly alluding to the Lollard preachers, some of whom were laymen (though the term is sullied by association with *loreles*). **22** *Druyeth*: anticipating the figure of *graes* in 23–5; the abuses specified corrupt all, from peasants to prelates. **23–29** revise in the direction of greater metaphorical complexity and theological precision, tracing the operation of 'prevenient' grace, the arousal of the will to repent, and the 'softening' of the sinner's heart through the practice of virtues made possible by the gift of 'actual' grace. This excludes a full 'Pelagian' view that spiritually meritorious 'works' can proceed from human free-will without the action of grace, the imagery here more closely recalling B 1.152 and B 16.5–9. By contrast, B 59–61 locate the 'remedy' for pride of intellect and station in the 'patient poor' whose just living helps to heal the illnesses of society and the Church alike. **23** *grace...graes*: more 'Platonic' wordplay; nothing could be more natural than 'grass' (or less natural than 'grace'), yet the one answers homologically (as it does homophonically) to the other. **27a** 'The Spirit breatheth where he will [and thou hearest his voice...]' (Jn 3:8; see further at B 69a). The new rendering of *spiritus* as *Espirit* 27 highlights the Latin word's root sense of 'breath' and more readily enables the contrast of *spirat* with *inflat*, so that **C** keeps a residue of **B**'s conviction that the Holy Spirit especially favours the 'poor (in spirit)'. **28** *grace...grace...be*: i.e. 'the disposition to live virtuously cannot arise without (a specific intervention of) divine grace'. The meaning of *grace* (1) gains sharper outline in the light of the contrast at 33 below. **30–2** explain the origin of human learning in the senses, specifically sight, by which we read books (whence there need be no allusion to Jn 3:11 as found by *Pe*), and more generally experiential knowledge through 'natural intelligence'. The latter is properly a gift of nature, not of fortune (*Pe*), the gifts of fortune (= *wierdes*) being, e.g., position in society as determined by one's parentage. The notion that celestial influences shape character, one common in the period, was not held to necessitate strict determinism of the human will. **30** has contrapuntal staves in each half (*aab / ab*). **31** is a Type IIa with stress shifted to the prefix in *bygete*. **32a** 'What appears in this world is governed by what appears in the heavens'; a quotation (if such it is) of untraced origin. **33–4** fall short of perfect clarity, since *chaunce* may inadvertently suggest 'life-circumstances' (instead of 'what one has by nature'). **34** 'Clergy is knowledge acquired through natural processes of learning'.

B 64–9a 64 *siȝte and techyng*: in inverse order to their antecedents. **65a** '[Amen, amen, I say to you that] we speak what we know and we testify what we have seen' (Jn 3:11). In context, Christ appeals not to scripture but to 'direct' (= *kynde*) knowledge of God; but Y. exploits his text (which can only be understood through 'clergy') to support a contrast between 'learning from authority' and 'learning from experience'. **C**'s founding of *clergy* on sight provides a less subtle but more logical distinction (see on 30–2). **66** *of heuene*: because divinely revealed. **67** *of...peple*: 'through the observations [of natural things] made by a variety of human beings'. **68** *greet loue*: God's charity that makes him communicate knowledge of himself to his creature man (cf. Jn 3:16); but with a hint that human love, if strong enough (cf. Lk 7:47), can earn *grace*, 'God's favour', 'the supernatural means to live virtuously'. **69** *Knew neuere clerk*: grace as a supernatural gift being beyond the reach of learning and experience (85ff will nonetheless maintain the orthodox position that the clergy are divinely ordained as the ministers, though not as the source of grace). **69a** 'He knows not [thou knowest not *Vg*] whence he [the Holy Spirit] cometh and whither he goeth' (Jn 3:8); completing 63a.

35–71 are a defence of *clergie* or (the keepers of) sacred learning, as bringing salvation to sinners (35–42), instructing ignorant layfolk (43–57) and having charge of the religious cultus that sanctifies the people (58–71). **35–7** The revision is more awkward syntactically than B 70–1, since *clergie...for Cristes loue* must remain an integral phrase. But the important sense-change, perhaps reflecting revulsion from the 1381 rebels' attack on Church leaders, firmly installs (clerical) learning above the knowledge derived from experience. **35** *And ȝut*: 'Now, for all this'. **36** *clergi*: playing polysemically on MED senses 3(a) 'learning' (as at 35) and 1(a) 'the clergy'. **37–42a** remove the repetition of B 11.204a at B 73a and are more compressed, allusive and theologically dense, keeping the two scriptural exemplars but enforcing a more explicit understanding of Christ as the 'prophet' (Deut 18:15) who fulfils and ratifies the Mosaic

Law while seeming to challenge it. Yet at the same time it echoes the sound-pattern of the original in repeating **B**'s fourfold *Crist(es)* and relying on *k*-alliteration (though substituting an *s*-sequence for *w* at 40–2). **37** *Moyses witnesseth*: i.e. as the accepted human author of the Pentateuch. *God wroet*: alluding to the Commandments written in stone with 'the finger of God' (Ex 31:18). *and Crist... fynger*: not necessarily dependent on *witnesseth* so much as elliptical for 'and Christ *wrote*, using his finger' (after *Iesus...digito scribebat* in Jn 8:6). The syntactic parallel brings out not only how Christ is 'a law-giver like Moses' (*Pe*) but is like *God*, who gave Moses the Law in writing. **38** *Law of loue*: recalling HC's assertion in 1.45–53 that Truth gave this 'law' to Moses, a claim for the Mosaic law of *treuthe* 'justice' as being, when rightly interpreted, the same law taught by Christ. *Oure Lord*: the locution (evidently not used here from alliterative necessity) denotes Christ in its 20 other occurrences, save one at Z 6.46 (see *IG*). So its present reference to 'God' would seem meant to assert the ultimate oneness between the revelation of God as Truth in the OT and as Love in the NT (Christ will deliver 'tho that [he] louede' strictly 'by lawe' [20.369, 443]). *long...were*: in respect not of his eternal Sonship but of his temporal existence as Jesus of Nazareth. **39** *confermed*: i.e. the Commandments to love God and neighbour (Mt 22:37–40, cited at 19.11–20). *Holy Kirke made*: asserting the continuity of the Church of 'the new Israel' with the Assembly (Num 20:4, Deut 23:1) of the old Israel (Vg has *ecclesia* for both). **40** *in soend*: translating *in terra* (Jn 8:8). **42** adds the 'staff' and makes the Gospel's (married) woman a *strompet* (unless this is meant as sarcastically challenging her accusers, who are presumed able to recognise a prostitute). **42a** 'He that is without sin among you, [let him first cast a stone at her]' (Jn 8:7).

B 70–98 Although the retelling of the story of the Woman taken in Adultery (Jn 8:1–11) is prolix (cf. 75b, 76a, 80a, 81a), **70–81** are not without power in their insistent alliterating up to 83 chiefly on *k* (including its cognative *g* at 79) and *w*, to heighten the intensity of their six / fourfold repetition of *clergie*, *Crist(es)* and *womman*. **74–5** *auoutrye...deþe*: assuming (mistakenly) that the punishment for idolatry mentioned in Lev 20:2 was that enjoined for adultery (Lev 20:10), though Deut 22:23–4 specifies stoning for an espoused girl who is willingly unchaste. **77–80** *Ymaginatyf* (somewhat opportunistically) makes the 'learning' shown in the *caractes* the efficient cause of the act, though it is the mysterious but disconcerting *knowledge* revealed by Jesus through 'what he wrote' (not through 'the (f)act of (his) writing') that confounds the accusers. The interpretation of *Cristes writyng* as a list of the accusers' sins is found in Jerome's *Dialogue against the Pelagians* (PL 23:553). But *Sk* rightly traces this important parallel to Augustine's statement in Homily 33 on St John's Gospel, vii.6: 'Christ is the Lawgiver...What else does he signify when he writes on the ground? For the Law was written with the finger of God' (*PL* 35:1649). **81** *conforted*: a 'saving' (from physical and spiritual death) that prefigures the sacramental ministry of pardon. **84** *mansede...ende*: a warning to those excommunicated for some grave sin not to receive the last rites without confessing it; but obliquely aimed at the priest of immoral life who by celebrating Mass in a state of mortal sin 'eateth and drinketh judgement to himself' (I Cor 11:19). **85–9** propose that just as *clergie* (both 'sacred learning' and 'those ordained to apply it through their ministry') is a remedy 'comforting' the repentant, so its possession compounds the guilt of all who take their final communion unconfessed. **87** *yuele*: 'badly' (*av*) or 'in a state of sin' (*a*). **88–9** argue (in reverse order) that Christ's writing served both to prove the woman guilty of sin and to save her from it (as if aiming to ward off accusations of 'easy forgiveness'). The *expected* parallel would be between pardon for the woman and condemnation for her accusers, as in the retailing of the story at 78–9. **89a** 'Judge not, that you may not be judged' (Mt 7:1); an important injunction also cited in very different situations at 12.31*a*, 16.126*a*. **90–1** turn from the specific case of the viaticum to the general one of receiving the sacrament in a state of mortal sin. **90** *breþeren*: a momentary slip prompted by the original context (I Cor 11:33). **92–8** This loosely-focussed section will be reduced to one line (C 43) introducing the dominant metaphor of 'blindness'. But the connective *Forthy* is logically weightier at B 92, which gives a double reason for honouring clergy, its making possible (through the sacraments) both absolution and sanctification. Practical knowledge handed down traditionally and that which is revealed both deserve honour because they come from God. **95** The 'mirror' of Middle Earth (C 13.132) is that from which man, by 'kind wit', learns to love his creator KYNDE *in* the world; that of the soul is (in principle at least) unveiled by the clergy, who instruct 'kind-witted men' how to find CHRIST *through* the world (cf. B 15.162). There may be an echo here of Js 1:23–4; but these mirrors (of nature and scripture) are envisaged as reflecting divine truth itself, not just a man's outer self (see further Kruger 1991). **97** *logik; lawe*: dialectic as used to defend the faith / elucidate theology, and canon law, which both benefit *lewed men and lettred*. **98** *countreplede*: a legal term (Alf*G*) adapted from OF *contreplaitier* and, though suggested by *lawe* 97, used in a wider sense 'contradict'. **43–57** are carefully wrought of two negative similes introduced by *No more* and enfolding a positive (*riht as...riht so*), arguing that natural intelligence alone cannot lead men to Christianity and thus to the grace necessary for salvation. **45** A clerk who lacks books is aptly compared to a man without eyes, a trope more logically

anticipated at C 30 than at B 64. The connection of (scriptural) 'books' with 'eyes' will be later brought out in the 'broad-eyed' allegorical personification BOOK at 20.238–9. **46–7** refer clearly to the writers of Scripture and imply its literal inspiration. Men did the physical writing but received as it were a divinely-sent 'interior exemplar' to copy. **49** *lereth...to resoun*: 'instructs in wisdom' (the 'main road' to heaven). Y. here indicates why the *rude speche* (13.229) of Will's 'kind-witted' challenge to Reason (13.184–6) got such a dusty answer: intellectual presumption is the moral stumbling-block that the discipline of *lettrure* aims to remove. **50–1** read like an imaginary *reductio ad absurdum* of the effort to achieve salvation without *clergie*. But as *Sk* notes, they may allude topically to a real action of the blind King John of Bohemia who, though not wielding an axe in close combat, led his troops at the Battle of Crécy on 26 Aug 1346 and was promptly killed (Froissart's *Chronicles,* tr. Lord Berners, ch. 130). **54** *The whiche*: (membership of) the body of baptized Christians, the *arca* 'chest' / 'ark' that is the Church. *Cristis tresor*: sanctifying grace; the image earlier occurred at B 10.474, which was removed in revision at C 11.306. **55** *and lered*: removing any (doubtless unintended) suggestion that clerks may not themselves need grace and mercy (for confirmation of the thought cf. 71 below). The addition will not over-burden the b-half metrically if *the lewed and* forms the dip before *léred* (but see *TN* further).

58–71 offer a 'high' view of the sacredness of the priestly order. The *Saul* exemplum amounts to a rejection of the 'Wycliffite' view that the clergy could be deprived of their endowments for spiritual failings (64–6) and may even be implicitly warning the secular authorities against interfering with their prerogatives. **58** *Arca Dei*: 'the Ark of God' (see on Pr 108). The sudden shift in topic is not arbitrary, since the Ark of Israel was seen as a 'type' of the 'tabernacle' of Christ's human nature (Alan of Lille) and of the Eucharist (Bonaventure), of which the Christian priest was the custodian. *Leuytes*: ministers of the sanctuary in the early OT period chosen from the Tribe of Levi son of Jacob, who had special charge of the Ark of the Covenant (Num 1:50–1, 3:31, II Kg 15:24). Medieval Latin *Levita* was sometimes used by analogy for the Christian deacon (see MED s.v. *levite* n (b), and on 2.130); *L*'s exemplum speaks figuratively about ordained Christian ministers in general. **60** *Bote hit (he) were*: 'only someone who was'. **61–3** The patterned language, with subtly varied repeated b-halves and frequent pararhymes, produces a tone of ritual solemnity (see *TN*) lacking in the more circumstantial B 118–20, which alludes to Oza's sudden death after touching the Ark to steady it (II Kgs 6:6). **61** Even the anointed king of Israel was but a layman, and 'sacrifice' (the ritual hallowing of a victim offered to God, a type of the Christian Eucharist) belonged exclusively to priests;

see I Kg 13:9, in which the prophet Samuel rebukes Saul for his sacrilege and ascribes his coming fall to it. **64a** repeats 43a with small variation to complete the argument. **65–8** prepare Will for his encounter with the Doctor of Divinity in 15.39ff and recall the last (and only earlier) incident of such *cheste*, the 'words' between Piers and the Priest at 9.293. **69a** 'Touch ye not my anointed: [and do no evil to my prophets]' (Ps 104:15); often cited to support the notion of clerical privilege (AlfQ citing Hugh of St Cher). In context it refers to the 'holy people' of Israel, but is here applied to the Christian priesthood, whose rite of ordination included anointing (see 13.106). **70–1** replace the (not obviously relevant) mention of knightly 'ordination' with a wider, apter claim. *vycary*: stronger than *kepere*, and used most commonly of the pope (MED s.v. *vicare* n. overlooks this and other early uses).

72–83a describe broadly 'secular' knowledge of this world, acquired through the senses and associated with the pagans, who lacked a divine revelation. **72** *a clergie...*: 'a kind of "learning" of their own'. **B 129** repeats B 64 (also changed), **B 130** allows that experiential knowledge involves both truth and error. **76** *here sotiltees*: 'the intricacies / complexities of these things'; the revision implies a similar sense for *hir wittes* in B 133 (MED s.v. *wit* n. 6(d) 'meaning, significance'). **78** *bokes*: in which they recorded knowledge gained through the senses and reason. **79** *kynde knowyng*: the final occurrence of this expression. Y.'s point is that empirical 'science', being based on mere sense-data, cannot give the knowledge of God vital for salvation (whence Will's mistake in asking for it at 10.109). **81** *Patriarkes and prophetus*: an a-half set-phrase, referring here (the quotation is from St Paul) not to OT figures but to the Christian Fathers, who criticised pagan learning. **83** *clergie of Crist*: 'the learning taught by Christ', 'revealed truth'. **83a** '[If any man among you seem to be wise in this world, let him become a fool, that he may be wise]. For the wisdom of this world is foolishness with God' (I Cor 3:18–1). Here *sapiencia* signifies not just 'natural science' but 'earthly knowledge that measures the things of God by its standards'. Earlier I Cor 2:13–15 contrasts the intellectual arrogance of the 'sensual man' with the humble wisdom of the 'spiritual man'.

84–103 sets natural knowledge against the (revealed) knowledge of God that Y. regards as the essence of *clergie*. **84–5** show rich verbal patterning of internal rhyme (*heuene...cleue*), assonance (*cleue...lepe*) and chime (*cleue...loue*) that counter the agitated surface sense. The underlying image may be that of a fruit falling from the top of a tree and being caught by a child. **84** *Holi Gost*: alluding to the angel Gabriel's words at the Annunciation (Lk 1:35). **85** depicts not only a 'descent' but the act of Incarnation itself, directly echoing HC's speech on the 'plant of peace' at 1.148–9 and verbally 'pre-echoing'

Christ's *descensus ad inferos* (20.249), which completes the redemptive work this first descent began. On the basis of Cant 2:8, patristic exegesis had developed a notion of the 'leaps' of Christ recalled here (Smith 1966:30). **86** *clennesse*: at least in its primary reference a metonymic periphrasis for the Blessed Virgin (*R–H* 152), the type of this virtue (cf. *Purity* 1070–88); but it may at the same time denote 'the clean of heart' (= the shepherds) 'who shall *see* God' (Mt 5:8). *clerkes*: elucidated as the Wise Men by the quotation following 88, with 97 below; but 86a may conceal a translinguistic pun on the familiar figurative sense of *pastores* as 'the clergy' (cf. 16.203 and MED s.v. *pastour* n. 2(a)). Evidence for seeing the *pastours* 92 as symbolising those who seek Christ in the 'manger' of the sacred text is cited from the exegete Bruno Astensis by *R–H* 153 and decisive patristic evidence is given by Twomey 1991. Though 'shepherds' are only in Lk and 'Magi' only in Mt, both accounts are combined here to demonstrate how low and great alike qualify in different senses as *clerkes* if they humbly seek þe clergie of Crist. **86a** 'The shepherds said one to another: [Let us go over to Bethlehem and...see this word...which the Lord hath showed to us]' (Lk 2:15). **87–8** more exactly distinguish those who received God's favour (the Virgin, the Wise Men and the shepherds) from the rich and noble. Thus whereas B 144–5 rather illogically contrast the 'most learned' Magi (who were also rich) with both the rich *and* the very wise, C 87–8 contrast only purity and wisdom with wealth and rank. A small stylistic improvement in revision is to promote the *repetitio* from the adverb to the semantically more important adjective. **88a** '[When Jesus was born in Bethlehem...] there came wise men from the east [to Jerusalem]' (Mt 2:1). Believed to be 'three' because of the gifts mentioned at Mt 2:11, they were accorded the status of kings by the 3rd c. (cf. 21.75–95) and were venerated as saints, their supposed relics being royally enshrined at Cologne Cathedral. **89** This sarcastic side-swipe (which may be thought to mar the tone of Y.'s discourse) gets an ironic edge from its having been the Franciscans who promoted the cult of the Christ-child and the devotion of the Christmas Crib. The implication is presumably that the friars have now abandoned material and intellectual humility alike. **90–1** These superficially surprising lines must be meant to dissociate Christ not from the poor but from professional beggars, for whom *PP* has not a good word to say. Doubtless the **B** form is intended to support the attack on the mendicants, who believed their way of life based on the Saviour's, in asserting that Christ's family was respectable though *pore*, 'humble' not 'destitute' (cf. B 11.246–7). The softening of the hammer-like plosives in B 146–7 and their provocative quotation / comment are improvements. **B 147a** *Set...diuersorio*: '[And... she laid him in a manger]: because there was no room [for them] in the inn' (Lk 2:7). *et...diuersorium*: 'and a beggar does not have [any use for] an inn'; an untraced addition intimating that (since they were evidently *seeking* an inn) Joseph and Mary cannot have been 'beggars'. **148** *poetes*: a word perhaps determined by alliterative necessity; this earliest use bears none of the meanings given in MED s.v. and must in context denote 'sage'. *appered*: directly to the shepherds (Lk 2:9ff), but to the magi in a *dream* (Mt 2:12), whence possibly **L** the dream-vision poet got his hint for *poetes*. **94** *song a song*: rhetorical *conduplicatio*. *Gloria...*: 'Glory to God in the highest: [and on earth peace to men of good will]' (Lk 2:14). **95** *rotte...reste*: a non-literal sense perhaps being intended in the light of 15.305–9; since the Gospel is preached to the poor (Lk 7:22), the rich are likely to ignore it. **96** *sheware*: 'revealer' (MED s.v. *scheuere* n. (b), but with polysemantic wordplay on 'mirror', as suggested by the third *Aȝenbite* citation under sense (d): 'Ac þe filosofes yknewen god be writinge ase be ane *ssewere* huerinne hy lokeden'. **97** *comet...comen*: 'Platonic' wordplay, since the 'comet' was what made the magi 'come'. *comet*: 'a sterre wiþ a liȝt blasynge crest above' (Trevisa in MED s.v.); a common understanding of the *stella comata* [20.247] that appeared over Bethlehem, as in *LA* XIV:91.

99–103 are transitional lines linking the first part of Ymaginatyf's defence of *clergie* to the second, a *responsum* to the Dreamer's objection that learning hinders rather than helps salvation. **100** *contraridest*: 'said "contra as a clerk" to', 'put the case against' (specifically at 11.255ff, 278ff), in maintaining that the ignorant and wicked are saved more easily than the clever and wise. **101–2** are significantly revised, having added the *luyther* (the 'Good Thief' of 11.255) to the merely *lewede* (of 11.298–300); they clarify the somewhat confusing 158 (though attacking *kynde wyt* in passing at 11.228, Will has mainly targeted clerical learning). **102** 'Than clever scholars with minds capable of comprehending [theological truths]'. **103** In good scholastic fashion Y. concedes that Will is partly right (*soth of somme*), before arguing that he is mainly wrong. This 'partial truth' of the Dreamer's position will later be illustrated in Vision Four from the *Actyf* / Doctor of Divinity contrast, which is greatly reduced in the C Version. *in what manere*: an informal equivalent of the scholastic *distinctio*, 'What you say is partly the case, but only in a qualified way (*secundum quid*), as I shall make clear'.

104–08 tighten the argument by cutting the (strictly) otiose B 165–8. Y. continues in a manner recalling the Friar in 10.32ff, whose *forbisene* of the 'wagging boat' perplexed the Dreamer's *kynde knowyng*. He uses an *exemplum probativum per analogiam*, a particular example of a general truth, as the basis of a second, specific truth on another level (which Will now shows himself able to understand): 'Knowing how to swim saves a man from drowning;

therefore *kynde connyng* is of great *practical* value. By analogy (*Riht so* 110), knowing the theology of penitence saves the sinner from despairing. Therefore *clergie* is of great *spiritual* value.' *Sk* finds the swimmer-image possibly imitated from the Boethian comparison of a man who has feet and can walk with someone who lacks feet and must creep (*Boece* IV, pr ii, 105). But though this might have provided a hint, **L** speaks not of a natural *power* and its (unnatural) absence but of a *skill* that does not come by nature, and must be acquired. **105a** is repeated at 19.58 and used in *Siege of Jerusalem* at 365a. **110** *resoun hit sheweth*: 'it stands to reason', but alluding to the Resoun Will challenged at 13.183. **B 166–8** The image of despair as a 'river' that will yet not dismay the penitent man may have been suggested by Ps 31:6b, of which vs 1 is quoted at 177a. *dide*: an early example of emphatic pleonastic *do* in a metrically prominent position.

(ii) 110–217 110–29 111–15 again clearly echo 10.38–43: Y.'s example of the efficacy of sorrow for sin parallels the Franciscan Friar's of the distinction between mortal and venial sin. **114** *what is synne*: 'what acts are sins'; 'the (true) nature of (the state of) sin'. **115** *withoute*: 'even in the absence of'. The cause of 'comfort' is to know that contrition brings divine forgiveness, reducing a mortal to a venial sin without loss of sanctifying grace, though the obligation to confess it to a priest remains; see on B 11.81*a* and cf. the more qualified view of contrition at B 14.84–6, 92–3 (both deleted in revision). **116** *oen or tweyne*: Ps 6:7–9 and esp. Ps 50:19. **117** *contricioun... synne*: see Ps 31:3–5. **117a** 'Blessed are they whose iniquities are forgiven: and whose sins are covered.' This key text, first cited at 7.152, is specifically applied to 'contrition without confession' at B 14.92–3; but B 14.84–6 lay down the qualification that the penitent be too ill or weak to confess, and have lived as a faithful believer. **119** *floed*: see on B 166–8. **120** *Lente*: when confession before Easter communion was obligatory, and so some contrition prior to the act might be in place. **121** *hath no contricioun*: does not experience / express any sorrow until he gets to shrift (and can do as Repentance bids Sloth at 7.58–61). It is this that Y. doubts an uneducated *loresman* would be able to offer his *lewed* parishioners as a specific against 'wanhope'. **123–4** *parauntur...men*: reflecting **L**'s view of the low state of clerical education following the Great Plague. However explicit the Lateran norms on penitence, the seculars' theological backwardness left the field open for the expert ministrations of the friars. **124a** '[Let them alone: they are blind and leaders of the blind]. And if the blind lead the blind, [both fall into the pit]' (Mt 15:14; closely paralleled in Lk 6:39). The 'blind leaders' are ignorant clergy, the 'blind led' are ignorant laypeople, the 'pit' *þe put of helle* (B 10.369). **125–30** The defence of learning continues with a humorously 'minimalist' argument for education: that it can save not only a clerk's soul but his life in an emergency. **126–7** *þat*; *That*: 'the one who'; 'And the fact that'. **128** 'The Lord is the portion of my inheritance [and of my cup: it is thou that wilt restore my inheritance to me]' (Ps 15:5); a macaronic line that can be scanned as Type Ie (the famous Messianic psalm's opening '*Preserve* me, O Lord' is relevant in the context). An ability to read vs 5 of the psalm, 'quoted in the ceremony of tonsuring new clerics' (AlfQ), was a conventional test of literacy entitling a 'criminous clerk' to be tried in an ecclesiastical court (after conviction for felony by a secular court, but before sentence) and so escape hanging for such offences as theft. The 'neck-verse' was more usually Ps 50:1, but any psalm-verse could be prescribed. The basis of this privilege was the 1352 statute *Pro clero* which allowed a convicted clerk to be tried in the bishop's court by 'purgation', i.e. a supported oath of his innocence (see Swanson 1989:149–53). **129** *Tybourne*: in **B** the first recorded vernacular reference to Tyburn (see on 6.367 above); here metonymic for 'hanging'. **130** *lolled vp*: perhaps suggesting to some readers in the late 1380s a grim allusion to Lollardy (since heresy disbarred from 'benefit of clergy') but unlikely to do so in **B**, a decade earlier (see on 9.218). *saued*: the ironic exclamation leading naturally to the difficult case of Dismas, who did not save his life but his soul (though by faith, not 'learning').

130–55a deal with the problem posed by paradoxical instances of salvation *without* 'clergie'. **131–2** The syntax is either anacoluthic ('as for' to be supplied before 131 and 'that' before 132), or elliptical ('Was [*saved*]'). *toldest*: i.e. at 11.255–63. The argument Y. *answers* could be expressed as a syllogism: 'Dismas (= a criminal who could *not* claim benefit of clergy) was *lewed*; but he was saved; therefore *clergie* cannot be necessary for salvation'. Though logically correct, this is theologically misleading; for one (unique) example could hardly condone lifelong defiance of Christian moral teaching in expectation of the grace of final repentance. The argument Y. propounds is plainly not intended to disparage the Good Thief (the mystery of whose salvation is touched on at 153–5 below); but it counters Will's earlier extreme position, with its 'reckless' reliance on last-minute conversion and failure to see the need for constant striving after holiness. **134a** 'Is it my will that a sinner should die, saith the Lord God, and not that he should be converted from his ways and live?' The *VL* reading *peccatoris* [Vg *impii*] is more frequent (AlfQ), e.g. in the *N-Town* 'Death of Herod', l.1. **135–46a** recognise the perceived inequity of rewarding a felon equally with the greatest saint by positing a hierarchy of glory in heaven. Such a view at first glance contradicts that of the *Pearl*-poet (cf. Green 1999:371–2), whose baptized infant was raised to glory though she could neither sin nor do a virtuous act, whereas the Good Thief could respond to prevenient

grace in an act of faith, a kind of honorary 'baptism of blood' (see on 207–8 below), followed by confession and then 'communion' with Christ in paradise. Otherwise, though, their cases are symmetrical, both innocent child and repentant sinner dying soon / straight after their respective 'baptism'. **135** *noen hey blisse*: Y.'s acceptance (with modification) of Will's statement at 11.263 again exemplifies a quasi-scholastic *distinctio* procedure (cf. 103). **136** *aserued*: choice of this verb-form (see MED s.v.) enables a 'Platonic' polysemantic pun on senses 2 'deserve' and 1(c) 'minister to', the latter identical with the two verbs at 144, 147; equity requires equivalence of desert and service. **140** *beggare*: a slightly unhappy comparison in its (unintentional) suggestion that (in the *Pearl*-poet's phrases) the *gentyl cheuentayn* Christ is indeed a *chyche* or 'niggard' (and the ambiguity of 145 scarcely improves matters). The substantive point is that everyone in the hall, from beggar to chief guest, is fed on the same heavenly banquet. **142** *Iohn*: the Evangelist, widely seen as an exemplar of lofty contemplative spirituality *passynge alle opere* (21.267). *Simond*; *Iude*: the Apostles Simon the Cananean (Mt 10:4) or 'Zealot' (Lk 6:15) and Jude, brother of James (Lk 6:16), who share a feast day on Oct 28. **144** *soleyn*: wittily recognising the uniqueness of his case. **145–6** obviously can only apply to one *in via*, not to one *in patria*. Though *as þe lawe lyketh* does not mean that an ordinary thief lived under a suspended capital sentence, his prior conviction would raise a presumption of his guilt on any subsequent charge (a thief who escaped hanging might yet be branded with a 'T'). Here the analogy teaches the need to remember one's old offences in order to avoid complacency. **146a** 'Be not without fear about sin forgiven: [and add not sin upon sin]' (Ecclus 5:5); the following verses (6–9) warn against presumption, delay and the danger of sudden unexpected death. The inefficacy of sacramental absolution is not implied by this stress on the value of remembering sin for inducing humility and heightening moral sensitivity. **148** *resoun ne riht*: qualities essential to God as 'Truth,' which cannot be dispensed with in the next life. **149–52a** counter any notion that the Good Thief is in danger of ejection from heaven on a further offence (which would be impossible) by proposing a (somewhat whimsically) symmetrical relation between Will's two extreme examples of salvation without *clergie*: just as Trajan was 'only barely in hell', so Dismas is 'only barely in heaven' (but *vix iustus salvabitur* 203). **149** *nat depe*: because his only sin was ignorance of *revealed* truth. **151** *loweste*: the point made so vividly is moral rather than rigorously theological, with no suggestion that heaven has a 'limbo' corresponding to hell's and that the Good Thief is placed there. **152** *wel losliche he lolleth*: 'he dangles by a very loosely knotted rope'. The chosen verb is darkly ironic in its echo of 130, since the 'looseness' of the Thief's tie with heaven is the very reason why he is not choked to death ('damned'). The referent is contextually certain to be the Thief, not Trajan (as is claimed by Middleton 1997:316n85). *as by*: 'from the standpoint of'. **152a** 'For thou wilt render [*lit.* he renders] to every man according to his works' (Ps 61:13). This is an important and widely quoted text on the retributive character of divine justice (see Alf*Q*), earlier found glossing heaven as the place 'There *ryhtfulnese* rewardeth *ryht* as men deserveth' (5.32*a*). **153–5a** 'Why' grace was given to one thief rather than the other is not a *quaestio* capable of rational solution, the exemplum enabling Y. to return (from a matter bearing on the order of *grace*) to the issue that first provoked Will's challenge to Reason (why the order of *nature* is thus and not otherwise). **155a** 'Why seemed it well to him? Because he willed it'; loosely adapted from Pss 113B:3 and 134:6 ('Deus...omnia quaecumque *voluit* fecit'); and cf. Bonaventure: '*quia voluit, et rationem ipse novit*' (on *I Sent.* 44 1.1: *ad* 4). *Pe* aptly cites here Peter Comestor on speculating about why the Fall occurred: 'If it is asked why God allowed man to be tempted...we say..."because he willed it". But if it is asked *why he willed it*, it is pointless to inquire into the *cause* of the divine will, which is itself the supreme cause of every cause' (*PL* 198:1075). In **B** this passage has been alluded to by Study (at 10.126–7) just after her anticipatory reference to Ymaginatyf's forthcoming 'answer' to Will's *purpos* (both are removed in **C**).

156–67 considerably abbreviate (e.g. B 220–1 at 158) the vivid but somewhat circumstantial B 218–34, which illustrate how 'angels-on-a-pinpoint' speculations foster in laypeople the vice of idle *curiositas* (about which see Neuhauser 1988). Y. is less abrasive than Study at B 12.124, where *whyes* '(divine) causes or reasons' also appears; and rightly, since Will has only wondered at the intricacy of nature and loved the Creator for it. **156–7** *whyes...how*: though seeming to suggest hostility to scientific enquiry, indicating the sense 'the reasons why, the origins and final cause' (cf. B 224), so that what is really being opposed is indulgence in unfettered theological speculation. **161** replaces B 228, a line of Type Id, with one of Type IIa, the pattern of B 227. **162** *and* (2): i.e. 'as well as all the other animals'; no more implying that man is a beast than *creature* B 225 implies that *Kynde* is a created being. **163** *kynde...saue*: referring to the innate knowledge of sexual functioning needed for the species to survive. B 230 makes clothing oneself (usually associated with *culture*) an expression of human 'nature', although Genesis describes it as taught to man only after the Fall. **164** *goed...wikke*: recognition of God as the ultimate 'author' of evil requiring prudent distinction between what God has willed and what he has permitted for his own unfathomable purposes. But the sentiment, superficially at odds with 134*a*, is a Biblical commonplace: see

Job 2:10 (cited at 13.16–17) and Is 45:7. **165a** '[For] he spoke, and they were made: [he commanded, and they were created]' (Ps 148:5); repeated at 15.263*a*. **166** This statement implies that what seems *wykke* is part of the original creation, not simply a consequence of the Fall; and it widens the issue from 'why Man fell' to 'why there is evil in the world', the major problem of theodicy. **B 230** *hem*: either 'themselves' or 'them' (= their genitals). **168–84** shorten the richly detailed but repetitive beast-allegory of B 235–58, with some loss of colour but a gain in immediacy. The tempering of animosity against the rich is theologically securer and morally more benign. **168** *longe-lybbynge*: importing less the longevity of the ancients than their amassing wisdom over a long period of observation of animal behaviour (the 'examples' that underlie the fables of *poetes* B 236). **170** *foul foulest*: 'Platonic' wordplay humorously pointing up the grotesque contrast between different aspects of the birds in question (which may puzzle the 'curious' mind), to show that advantages of one kind are balanced by deficiencies of another. **172** *popeiay*: improving in sense on the plain not gaudy *pehen* B 239 (at 174 the hen is apt, since it *is* slow). **173** *Bytokenen*: 'stand for', echoing *Ensamples token* B 236; as *Pe* notes, Y. 'answers questionings of the order of nature with moralised lessons from "natural history"'. **176** *ful hey*: piquantly ironic, since the bird indeed symbolises the 'high' condition of those with wealth. **178** *ledene*: the peacock's unmusical cry being the price it pays for its glorious appearance. *careyne*: denoting at B 253 the bird's corpse as buried, but here more naturally the flesh as food (cf. B Pr 189). The taste for eating peacocks was on the wane, and their place at sumptuous banquets largely decorative. **182** *kyn*: the speaker's objection being to the respect paid to wealth, an accident of fortune (whereas birth and intelligence are natural gifts); the sentiment recalls that expressed at 10.261. **183–4** more concisely distinguish nobles (*rentes*) and bourgeois (*shoppe*). Thus: 'That is the way in which...' (ironic, because the poet's praise is ironic). *poete*: uncertain in sense because the reference is uncertain; but (in contrast with 92 above) the parallel of *poetes*189 with *grete clerk* B 265 may imply here a generic meaning 'authoritative ancient writer' rather than a title like 'the Philosopher' (for 'Aristotle').

B 244–60 vividly if somewhat laboriously elaborate the comparison between peacock and rich man, beginning and ending formally with *Right so* (244, 260). **245** *taille... sorwe*: the wretched end of a rich miser's life impeding his soul's ascent to heaven, as the peacock's long tail impedes its flight. **248** *tail...plukked*: i.e. after the 'bird' is dead. **249, 251** *þanne*: a warning against the perilousness of last-minute repentance induced by fear of hell, not love of God. **252** *pies*: rightly removed in revision; to introduce another bird of ugly cry is confusing, since the *peacock*'s has already been called 'unlovely' at 243. The comparison, however, also implies that the dying miser's desperate prayer will be (symbolically speaking) unintelligible gibberish (cf. the use of this image in the *York Crucifixion Play* 256). **253–5** The memory of the miser will stink like the peacock's decomposing body and infect all those who 'have contact with him', i.e. 'behave in like manner' (though this could possibly allude to some obscure popular superstition about not wishing to be buried next to a miser). **254** *flaumbe*: 'will smell'; *Sk*'s 'contaminate', which would anticipate 255, has no support, the only other MED example (s.v. *flaumen* v. 4) signifying 'smell'. **256** *po feet*: that the peacock has 'foulest feet and riueled' is ascribed to Aristotle by Bartholomaeus Anglicus (*Batman vpon Batholome* xii. 31, cit. *Sk*), but these details are not in Aristotle's comment on the peacock in *Historia Animalium* VI.9. Fletcher 1991 notes that the peacock's ugly feet were a homiletic commonplace, citing examples from *FM* 64 and a C14th Worcester sermon. The allegorisation of the feet as 'false friends' here (like that at 185 below) could be original. *Auynet*: a generic term for a collection of beast-fables (*Wr*); Avienus was a C4th Latin writer of fables (cf. *Donet* for 'grammar'). Fable 39 in Robert's *Fabliaux* (on the peacock who complained of his voice) contrasts the fate of the unjust rich (who will be 'poor' after death) and the just poor (who will enjoy the 'riches' of heaven). **257** *fulfille...wille*: for an inverted form of the same internal rhyme in the half-line cf. B 3.265. **258** *and...witnesse*: 'though they themselves were witnesses'.

185–98 185–90 somewhat implausibly attribute preference for the lark (= the humble poor) to various pagan authorities 'at random' (*Sk*), for alliterative convenience (with *poetes* 189 cf. *logik* 266). But the main point developed is that, although these were wise in their way, even 'great clerks', such wisdom based on 'kind wit' could not guarantee their salvation. **185** *larke*: much favoured as a dish (see *WW* 350). **187** *is resembled*: a comparison (again perhaps original) in keeping with the 'examples and terms' (236) L finds typical of pagan natural philosophy. **189** *Porfirie and Plato*: part of an evident 'repertory' line; see on 12.175. **190** *logik*: a loose alliteratively convenient term for 'philosophical writings'; neither this nor B 266 seems to refer to a specific work on dialectic, but *logik* is synecdochic for Aristotle's authoritative œuvre. **B 265** Aristotle observes (*Hist. Anim.* IX, 25) that the lark is edible, but does not draw this or any other moral *ensample*. **191** *clergie*: theological source, e.g. such as Gregory, whose successful intercession for the just but ignorant Trajan proves the emperor *saaf*. The remark seems designed to elicit Will's response at 199–201. **192** *Sortes*: a corrupt form of Socrates (*c*. 469–399 BC), Plato's 'mayster' who 'desserued vnrightful deth' (*Boece* 1.pr.3, 27). It is unclear whether he is mentioned for his wisdom or his justice, but the former seems likely. *scrip-*

ture: 'written [not specificially biblical] authority'. **194–8** The sense is: 'since the intellectual powers God gave these philosophers enabled them to write works of benefit to Christians, he must have intended their salvation, and so (it is fitting) that we should pray for it'. **194** *hope*: 'think' or 'believe' (governing *we ben yholde / That...*). **196** *And*: elliptical for 'And to be saved all the more effectively'. **198** *clerkes*: a revision that seems designed to provoke Will's denial.

199–201 This second speech of Will's is less compliant than his admission at 109 and presupposes an understood *Ac*: 'But *Christian* clerks assert in *their* books' (as opposed to *here bokes* 196). The strict requirement of baptism for salvation was not a theologians' opinion but the standard teaching of the Church (though special allowance was made for those before Christ who lived just lives); so exceptional rescues like Trajan's depending on recourse to God's *potentia absoluta* came close to threatening the necessity and sufficiency of the 'ordained' sacramental order.

202–17 The latent scholastic mode of Ymaginatyf's prior argumentation now becomes patent with his denial of Will's contention, supported by a Biblical *auctoritas* he will explicate as he attempts to integrate the case of Trajan (a just pagan who lived *after* Christ) into the existing paradigm of orthodoxy. **202** *Contra*: see on 10.20 where (as at B 10.343) the phrase is used by Will; here the Dreamer's own sympathetic imagination is being empowered to generate a 'solution' to the dilemma of how righteous non-Christians can be saved. **203** '[And if] the just man shall scarcely be saved, [where shall the ungodly and the sinner appear]?' (I Pet 4:18). *in die iudicii*: 'on the day of judgement'; L's addition. **204** *Ergo saluabitur*: 'Therefore (it follows that) he will be saved'. The salvation is not *entailed* by *vix* ('its difficulty') but would seem to be *implied* by it; and the assertion signifies broadly that 'while insisting that salvation is hard even for the just, scripture also guarantees it, whereas the prospect for the sinful must be a faint one'. The basis of Y.'s case for Trajan is that the Emperor does not really count as the *impius et peccator* of St Peter's question. But while *Sk* is right that L 'lays a stress upon *vix*', this applies only to the first part of the quotation; the consequent (his addition) stresses *saluabitur* and assumes an unstated middle proposition. This is clear if the statement is formulated syllogistically: 'The just man will be saved, if with difficulty. Trajan was just. Therefore Trajan will be saved (though with difficulty)'. Y. is thus intimating that if 'Aristotel þe wyse' (193) and other pagan sages are not found *un*just on judgement day, a matter that lies hidden with God ('Sunt iusti atque *sapientes...*' 11.275a), then they *will* (we may hope) be saved, however narrowly. *no more Latyn*: i.e. no further scriptural *auctoritates*. **205** *trewe knyhte*: an echo of 12.77 reminding the audience of the special appropriateness of 'true' conduct to the knightly order. Most pertinent to the Emperor's case is the judicial incorruptibility laid down in 1.94–5, which had made him an exemplar of *trewthe*. **206** *the boek*: the *LA* (see on 12.77 above). **207–8** distinguish three varieties of baptism recognised by the theologians (Dunning 1943:45–54): the ordinary kind *of fonte*; the 'baptism of blood' of a martyr who might not have received the sacrament but 'seals' his faith by dying as a witness to Christ; and the 'baptism of fire', a mysterious infusion of sanctifying grace direct into the soul of a *trewe* man that generates (if tacitly) the 'righteousness' (*trewthe*) needed for salvation. Obviously, one who received this last kind (which had no sacramental 'outward sign') lacked *clergie* in the sense of 'formal knowledge of revealed truth' (in Trajan, troublingly, this lack even prompted hostility to Christianity). But while ignorant of the theological virtues, the Emperor in some manner practised the first of them, so that 'justification' could be 'imputed' to him (as is argued by Whatley 1984²). **L**'s attempt to reconcile the supposed conflict between the positions of Paul and James (Rom 4:9; Js 2:20–6), depends on his seeing 'works of justice' like Trajan's as exemplifying (and therefore as constitutive of) *fides implicita*. For a similar account of Trajan's salvation as effected through an implicit baptism of desire distinct from the explicit desire for baptism described by St Thomas in *ST* III.68, 2 see Doxsee 1988. **207, 209** *Ac*: taken here as having the force of *Sed* '(but) now' in scholastic disputation, rather than of *Sed contra* 'but on the opposite side'. Following Whatley (1984²), Burrow (1993) understands the first *Ac* as introducing a way of salvation *distinct* from the three baptisms and (preferring at B 282=C 207 the β reading *For* to *Ac* αC) translates it 'but however that might be'. **208** *al*: either 'everything that has been said is a matter to be firmly believed' or 'each of these three modes of baptism constitutes real faith'. **B 283** *pat*: having as antecedent either baptism of fire ('and that is sure faith') or the whole statement from *Ac* to *fullyng* (3) 'and that is [a matter of] certain belief' (corresponding to the first alternative for C 208). **208a** 'There came a divine fire [at Pentecost, as told in Acts 2:3, but recalling also Mt 3:11], not burning but illuminating [and gave them the gifts of grace]'; from a Pentecost Antiphon in the *Sarum Breviary*, 1:mvi, mxvi (Hort 1938:167). **209–12** The anacoluthic construction well conveys the speaker's sense of urgency. Y. argues that Trajan's *treuthe* is a homologue to the third type of baptism, as it 'illuminated' his mind to do justice, and claims that the God who is Truth will therefore commend Trajan's *fidelitas* as equivalent to *fides* and as qualifying him to join the *fidelibus* of B 290. **209** *treuth*: a near-personification of 'a righteous man', like those at 2.136, 3.176, 191. *trespassed neuere*: remote as was the chance of such indefectibility in the absence of baptismal sanctification, **L** seems insist-

ent that it can be and has been found, his motive being perhaps to allay anxieties about divine justice arising from the fact that many, through no fault of their own, have never known or will know God's revelation in Christ. **210** *lawe*: 'religious principles,' but with some allusion to Trajan's exemplary administration of Roman justice. **211** *wolde*: i.e. 'would [choose it and] live according to it'; the inappropriateness of *amende* B 286 is plain enough. **212** *Ne wolde*: either preterite 'God never wished...' or, preferably, jussive subjunctive 'May God never wish...' (in which case Y.'s position need not appear 'heterodox' [Green 1999:369–70]). *trewe God...treuthe*: the close collocation reminding that Truth, the first 'nature-name' for God to appear (Pr 15), expresses the divine essence as knowable to man through the 'inner law' of conscience. **212** *alloued*: understood by Whatley (1984²) as 'given credit for' [i.e. the will or intention implied by *trewe lyuynge*], even as 'reckoned as efficacious for salvation'. This may be to overstate the matter, but there is little at stake in the difference between 'reward' and 'commend' since either way Trajan *has* been saved. **213** *wher...nat*: 'whether it will actually turn out so or not'. The final outcome remains *in manu Dei* (11.275*a*) because the working of God's free unfettered agency ('potentia absoluta') belongs to the innermost mystery of the divine will. *the bileue...treuthe*: '[it is nonetheless the case that] the faith found in a just man is great' (or, less probably, 'great trust can be placed in righteousness'). *bileue*: the first of the three theological virtues, here judged 'implicitly' present in one who *lives* justly without conscious awareness of revealed truth. **214** *hope*: the second theological virtue, here thought of as derived from and dependent upon the 'faith' implied in righteous living (though the Triad is not named here, it is tacitly evoked). **214a** '[Well done, good and *faithful* servant]: because thou hast been *faithful* over a few things, [I will place thee over many things. Enter thou into the joy of thy lord]' (Mt 25:23). A lucid scriptural passage replaces the enigmatic riddle-text of B 290, but still needs to be interpreted in order that its relevance to Trajan's situation may emerge. In the Parable of the Talents, the 'few things' may be understood as corresponding to the secular dominion entrusted to the Emperor, which he administered with a 'faithfulness' (integrity) justifying his Lord's trust in him (cf. Harwood 1973:288). Trajan's practical righteousness corresponds to Langlandian 'hope' (*leute*), which receives as its reward *multa* 'many things'. The latter are here construed in 'feudal' manner as a generous 'extra' exceeding what the 'faithful servant' expects, nothing less than the gift of *caritas*, the third theological virtue (215), which wins Trajan the *gaudium domini* in heaven. **215** *yf...trewe*: a phrase of set type (with parallels at 9.212, 14.151, 15.239, 274, 17.5) having the sense 'since it is indeed the case that' and implying that if a pagan lives justly *without* revelation, his reward should be all the more generous. **216** *cortesye...couenant...carpe*: i.e. the 'bonus' should exceed the 'agreed wage'; and though God's 'covenant' with righteous non-believers does not constrain him to grant them heaven, if this 'lord' *is* true to his nature, he will do so out of sheer kindness, whatever theologians might deduce from texts like Mk 16:16, cited at 13.86*a* above (see Schmidt 1984). **217** *al... wol*: a resigned acknowledgement of God's sovereignty, echoing (in a more hopeful tone) Study's words earlier at B 10.129–30.

B 290–5 291 'GOD is thus named as, so to say, "giving eternal life to his own", that is, to the faithful'. The key to the meaning of this quotation is an ingenious *interpretatio* of the Latin word DEVS as '*d*ans *v*itam *e*ternam *s*uis' found in a ms gloss in Evrard the German's treatise on rhetoric the *Laborintus*, ed. Faral 1924:65 (information from J.A. Burrow). The general sense may be paraphrased: 'God is wholly to be trusted, because the very letters of his NAME spell out his NATURE as the one who gives life to believers'. The exact source of this gladsome conceit is unknown, but the basic thought recalls Jn 17:2: 'ut omne, quod dedisti ei, *det* [Filius] *eis vitam aeternam*'. The promise of eternal life to the truly faithful forms a key part of the *dispensatio ordinata* mediated through Christ and the Church. **291** 'And in another place: "For though I should walk in the midst of the shadow of death, [I will fear no evils, for thou art with me]' (Ps 22:4). As this is the psalm of total trust in God quoted by Piers on tearing the Pardon at B 7.116–17, the effect here is to associate the *trewe* king / emperor with the *trewe* ploughman who will become in XIX–XX=XXI–XXII an emblem of the ideal Pope. This link is strengthened by the fact that the enigma-verse's phrase *vitam aeternam* echoes the first verse of Truth's pardon at B 7.110*a* (which promises the same reward to those who *bona egerunt*), thus in effect identifying Trajan as a 'pagan exemplar' of Dowel. The quoted psalm-verse needs to be read in the context of the preceding vs 3 ('He hath *led* me on the paths of *justice*') and the following vs 6 ('And thy *mercy* will *follow* me all the days of my life'). **292** 'The gloss on the basis of that verse concedes that a man of righteous life deserves a great reward'. The *GO* remarks on *mecum es* 'i.e. *in corde per fidem*, vt post umbram mortis ego tecum sim'; the source of this is Augustine's *Commentary* on the psalms (*PL* 36:182), noted by Davlin 1989:78. **293–5** Ymaginatyf's final commendation of 'wit and wisdom' comes somewhat unexpectedly after the praise of 'clergyless Dowel'. But its point would not be lost on a clerk, since it shows that *clergie* (informed by imagination as well as reason) has been required precisely in order to find a way to reconcile the salvation of righteous non-Christians with the Church's accepted teaching. **293** *wisdom....tresor*: specifically knowledge of *treuthe*, the tre-

sor praised by HC at B 1.208=C 201. **295a** closely recalls *so muche manhed & murþe* in *WPal* 97.

Passus XV
(B XIII, XIV 1–131*a*)

PASSUS FIFTEEN of **C** initiates VISION FOUR. In **B**, this vision *ends* decisively at 14.332 with Will awaking, and Vision Five begins with his falling asleep at 15.11 after a brief opening (15.1–10). The latter is neither a waking interlude nor a résumé of the preceding vision like the prelude to Vision Four, but a prologue summarising the Dreamer's life over a period of time between the episodes of Haukyn and Anima. An 'inner' dream (the second in the poem) is then made to form the deep heart's core of **B**'s Vision Five at 16.18–166; and from this Will wakes at B 16.167 into the containing 'outer' dream, which goes on to the end of B XVII. Though complex, the structure of **B**'s last five visions remains as coherent as that of the first three, thanks in part to the tight correspondence between vision- and passus-boundaries. Thus the Fourth occupies two passūs exactly (XIII–XIV), the Fifth three (XV–XVII) and the Sixth, Seventh and Eighth a single passus each (XVIII, XIX, XX). By contrast, **C** displays (at least superficially) a less clear organisation from XV to XIX, which may indicate a desire for a more dream-like fluidity of form (see on 28–9), or simply incomplete revision. Thus **C**'s Vision Four appears to run from 15.25 until 18.179, when the Dreamer awakes, though its action continues uninterrupted without his falling asleep again, and he wakes for a second time at the end of XIX. Close scrutiny of the revision suggests that **B**'s 'dream-within-a-dream' has been substantially retained. But as its opening is not formally indicated (it appears to be hidden away at about C 18.4–5), the fact that Will wakes at 18.179 is perplexing, though it corresponds to his 'waking' into the 'outer' dream at B 16.167. Nor is lucidity promoted by **C**'s abandonment of **B**'s tidy vision / passus correlation and (apparently arbitrary) decision to open XVI and XVII (at a point about halfway into the source of each, respectively B XIV and XV) with direct speech in reply to a speaker at the end of each preceding passus. The shortening of **B**'s XV recalls the splitting of B V into C V, VI and VII; but unsignalled transition to a deeper level of dream-experience risks creating confusion if, as is likely to happen, it passes unnoticed.

The first part of VISION FOUR opens with a prelude (1–24) and then divides into (i) the dinner at CONSCIENCE's house, from 25–185, linked by a five-line transitional passage (making clear Will's presence on the 'pilgrimage') and (ii) the opening dialogue between PATIENCE and ACTIVA VITA (HAUKYN of **B**), from 191–311. The two episodes narrated here focus on types of respectively *heigh clergye* (in the person of the Doctor of

Divinity) and *lewednesse* (in Actyf), between whom the Dreamer stands midway. The Vision begins as an attempt to reconcile Will with Clergy; but his bruising encounter with the learned friar confirms his rejection of the intellectual path to Dowel. He opts instead for an 'affective' approach to religious understanding ('seeing much and suffering more') in the company of his converse Patience, as a means to control the passions out of which most sins arise (on this see Simpson 1986[1]:14–19).

Prelude **1–24** are unusual in summarising the events of the preceding Vision (C XII–XIV, B XI–XII), from Fortune's entry in the first inner dream up to the disappearance of Ymaginatif. They retain B 1–10 intact but expand (and improve) most of 11–20. **1** *witteles*: a key word in the thematic development towards the *fooles* of XXI (see 18.179–80 //). Though Will is not about to go mad from the *wo and wrathe* that precipitated the inner dream (at 11.166), he has lost confidence in his reason after it has proved impotent before the mysteries of creation and the Creator. **2** *fay*: perhaps 'unfortunate, unlucky' or even 'stricken' (MED s.v. *feie* adj. 3(a), (b)), given Will's descent into near-destitution (5); but at 16.195 it means 'dying' or 'dead' (1a) and may imply here '(afflicted) with (a sense of) my life running out'. **3** *manere*: having a beggar's outward indifference to material welfare. **5–6** recall Elde's warning at 11.190 (now fulfilled) and spell out what is elliptically implied in B 6. *faylede*; *manaced*: seemingly parallel verbs and so, despite occurring in reflection on a dream that *foretold* this would happen, indicative (unlike subjunctive *lyuede* 7). **6–7** 'How Eld threatened me, saying that if I should happen to live to an old age, he would leave me in the lurch'. **10–18** use *repetitio* to link the key ideas of the summarising lines: *pore* (10, 11), *lewede, lord* (14, 15), *connynge* (18). **13–14** *al...boende*: 'all sections of society', generalising the sin of greed beyond the clergy, perhaps in the aftermath of 1381. **16** *curatours...incurable*: an angry pun 'Platonically' implying the dependence of the whole community's spiritual health on a virtuous clergy (a theme to be developed at 16.240ff). **18** *connynge*: a repetition (substituting for that of *bestes* in B 15–16) that shifts the sense from God's 'wisdom' to the 'instinctive knowledge' of animals by which they share in that wisdom, sardonically contrasted with *vnkunynge* 16. **B 15** *curteis*: see White 1986:244–6. **19** tones down the radicalism of B 17, which levels not only all men but all creatures. **20** removes the (unintended) restriction in B 16. **B 18** *creatures þat crepen*: cf. Ps 103–25, echoing Gen 1:25. **21–2** *iustus...vix*: 'That the just man before Jesus on Judgement Day / Shall not be saved, save by the skin of his teeth'. The lively new macaronics improve on the merely repeated B 19.
(i) *Conscience's dinner* **25–51a** The opening recalls that of the waking interlude prefacing Vision Two, which

occurred within a reverie of self-communing (5.9). For the indebtedness of this scene to traditional exegesis on Proverbs ch. 23, see Alford 1995, and to Mt 22, Lawler 1995; and cf. on 40 below. **26** *Clergie*: a figure not encountered since his single speech in Passus XI, to which Will had not been able to reply, though in B 10.330 his *faux-naïf* question (referred to by Ymaginatif at 14.100) was what provoked a tart rejoinder from Scripture. For discussion of the apparent incoherence at this point in the revision, see on C 11.162; B 24b shows Will, chastened by Ymaginatif's instruction, now ready to 'conceive more' (13.223) from Clergy and Scripture. **27–9** mimic the dream-like fluidity of the experience with its sustained verbal repetition (*rome...romede forth* twice, *Resoun* thrice). *Resoun*, the dinner-guest added in **C**, is especially relevant for the Dreamer's needs; for it is he, the companion of Conscience in Visions One and Two, whom Will finally *resonede* 'berated' at 13.183 after his *rage* against learning had remained unassuaged by Kynde's proffered evidence from experience (13.129–33). In **B** those present at Conscience's dinner are Clergy, his wife Scripture (who helps serve), the Doctor of Divinity, Will and the pilgrim Patience; in **C** are added Reason (as steward) and the pilgrim Piers. **27** *dyne*: an act symbolically marking Will's reconciliation with Clergy / Reason, whom he had offended by his *rude speche* 13.229. **30** *lyk*: ironically suggesting that he might *not* have been a friar (because he did not live up to the ideal), but of course *was*. **32** *woschen*: food being eaten with the fingers, the dust of the journey had to be removed. *dyner*: an afternoon meal, here at a knight's manor-house, with clerical guests at the high table and poor religious wayfarers receiving hospitality (rather than scraps) in the body of the hall (but not on the floor: cf. 42 below and 14.139–40 above). The arrangement is still clearly visible in the late-C14th halls of William of Wykeham's foundations at Winchester and Oxford. **33** *Pacience*: earlier the name of one of the seven sisters who watch over the postern-gates at Truth's castle. This important virtue, an active personification only in Vision Four, wears the garb of a 'pilgrim-hermit' and combines an 'inner journey' (Wittig 1972) of thought and prayer with an outward one of dependence on God and charity (Godden 1990; on the figure of Patience see further Baldwin 1990:80 and the learned and provocative but unconvincing account in Aers 2004: 122–33). His separateness from Piers in **C** (confirming and confirmed by the present understanding of *Ilyk* at 34) tells against seeing him in **B** as more than an analogue of the Ploughman. **34** Piers seems to be in Patience's company and to have literally become the poor pilgrim he had planned to be figuratively at 8.93. On the crux *Ilyk* 'likewise' and its implications for the meaning of the passage see *TN*. **35** *for...*: 'for the love of Christ in heaven'. **37–8** contain two important small variants in repeating 31–2, *him* (referring to Piers, someone 'known' to Conscience) and *alle* (a general welcome foreshadowing Conscience's hospitable posture in XXI). **37** *welcomede hem alle*: cf. 'When thou makest a dinner... call the poor' (Lk 14:12–13). **39** *maister*: a synonym for 'doctor' (66), the highest academic degree (here in Divinity, the senior faculty in the medieval university; cf. Pr 60, 10.90). The line may allude to Christ's warning to his disciples against losing spiritual humility by accepting honorific titles: 'Neither be ye called masters: for one is your master, Christ' (Mt 23:10); cf. *CT* III 2184–8. *furste*: like the Pharisees in Lk 14:7, who 'chose the first seats at the table' (the Doctor has the place of honour, on the host's right). B 34 rather confusingly implies an order of seating, but presumably Clergy sits on Conscience's left and Patience remains below with Will (see *TN* further). *worthy*: 'honourable'; with an ironic pun on the co-polyseme 'morally excellent'. **40** *styhlede...styward*: close in sense and wording to *WPal* 1199: *þat oþer was his stiward þat stiȝtled al his meyne* and id. 3841. The servitorial rôle of Reason (previously seen as a bishop at 5.112–13) graphically conveys how the apostolic calling is to service, not rule; see Jn 13:13–16, which is close to Lk 14:7–11, a passage that lies behind this whole scene. **41** *mettes*: suitably enough, since patience is what Will lacked in his *rage* against Clergy and Reason, and what will be tested as he listens to the Doctor speak. **42** *syde table*: a trestle table aligned with the length of the hall below the *deys* or platform for the high table (66). **43–5a** express allegorically how the priestly exponents of the Church's learning are ideally nourished on the Gospels and the writings of the Fathers (as more fully enacted later in the Ploughing allegory at 21.262–74). **45** *Austyn*: see on 11.148; allusion is to his commentaries on Scripture, such as the Tractates on the Gospels and Epistles of St John. *Ambrose* (339–97 AD): bishop of Milan, friend and mentor of Augustine; author of widely used hymns and important treatises on the sacraments and on ethics. As two of the Four Doctors of the Western Church (cf. 21.268ff), both are suitable 'meat' for this Doctor to 'chew on' (see Mann 1979:26–43). **45a** '[And in the same house, remain], eating and drinking such things as they have: [for the labourer is worthy of his hire...]' (Lk 10:7). Christ's instruction to his disciples to accept hospitality from a single household during their preaching mission was cited by friars as justifying this aspect of their manner of life. **46–51** improve on B's complicated contrast of one kind of literal food with another (luxurious with plain), instead clearly opposing 'this food' (spiritual sustenance such as Christ speaks of in Jn 4:34) to the literal 'food of more cost' preferred by the Doctor. The rapidly unfolding metaphor resembles that at 1.145ff in density and complexity, and the portentous moral is underlined by having the lines alliterate exclusively on *m* and *s*. **46**

myhte...chewe: 'didn't find to his taste'. **B 40** *man*: a junior friar accompanying the Doctor, as later at 22.341 (at 10.8–9 the pair are *both* 'masters'). *maner flessh*: 'plain, simply-prepared meat'. **47** *of more cost*: on the ironic suggestions, cf. *worthy* at 39. *potages*: something more elaborate than at 8.185, where it is ordinary labourers' food. **48** *þat...myswonne*: presumably not implying that his present host lives off ill-gotten gains but that the friar, like his predecessor at 3.38, customarily offers those who follow Mede 'easy absolution' in return for support of various kinds. **49–51** *sour...bittere...salte*: the final taste of their food proving unpleasant at the time of reckoning, unless they heal the offence with penitential intercession. *vnsauerly ygrounde*: i.e. if the spices have not been crushed finely enough to blend in the cooking. **50** *Post mortem*: 'after death'. Possibly 'the allegorical name of the mortar' is 'the whole expression from here to *teres*' (*Sk*); but the translinguistic echo of *mortem* in *morter* (and perhaps *mortrewes* 47) 'Platonically' implies a real link between wrongful enjoyment in this life and rightful retribution in the next. AlfQ interprets the phrase as 'in purgatory'; but purgatory is not mentioned, and if there is an allusion to 'sinful receipt and abuse of bequests ("*Post mortem*")' (Scase 1989:105), given the belief that heaviest punishment befell those with spiritual gifts they failed to use, the threat may be rather of damnation unless they pray for the souls of benefactors who *myswonne*. **51** *synge*: i.e. intercessory masses and penitential psalms. **51a** 'You who sup on men's sins — unless you pour forth tears and prayers on their behalf, what you devour with relish, you will retch up in pain'. The source is unknown, but the image and other details derive ultimately from Osee 4:8–11: 'They shall eat the sins of my people [*Peccata populi mei comedent*] and shall lift up their souls to their iniquity. And there shall be like people like priest... And they shall eat and shall not be filled...they have committed fornication...and wine and drunkenness take away the understanding'. Here the referent of *They* is probably *sacerdotes* 'the priests', as taken by Gratian (*CIC* 1:391, cit. AlfQ); but as used in the C13th anti-mendicant prophecy 'Insurgent gentes' (Kerby-Fulton 1990:156–7), the phrase is aimed at the friars. The image also appears in Huon de Méri's *Tournoiment de l'Antichrist* (*Sk* after Warton; see Owen 1912:104–7). Here the contextual allegorical sense of 'eat sins' will be 'profit from the vices of', i.e. by giving absolution in return for donations. **52–8 52** *as Resoun radde*: Reason is still counsellor to Conscience as at 4.5 above. **54** *breed*: a scriptural text, illustrating the doctrine of Deut 8:3 earlier appealed to by Will (see on 5.86–8). **56** *sour loef*: the sense here not unfavourable as at 49, since this leavened bread will be spiritually nourishing. *Agite penitenciam*...: 'Do penance: [for the kingdom of heaven is at hand]' (Mt 3:2); the message of John the Baptist, already found in the OT in Job

21:2 and Ezek 18:30, and repeated in the NT in Ac 2:38 and Apoc 2:5 (Alf*Q*). Conscience will prescribe penance again at 21.67, and its importance has been accepted by Will in the passage cited under 54 above. **57** *Dia perseuerans*: 'the potion of perseverance', playing 'Platonically' on the Gk *dia* 'medicinal drug' (used at 20.47) and Lat *diu* 'long', in allusion to Christ's assurance that 'he that shall *persevere unto the end*, he shall be saved' (Mt 10:22), and perhaps echoing his promise of the 'meat... which endureth (*permanet*) unto life everlasting' (Jn 6:27). See further Schmidt 1987:92, 1992:xli–ii, and *TN* for defence of the reading.

B 51–4 are removed in **C** as perhaps too metrically unwieldy and verbally complicated, with their array of quotations (mainly from Pss 31 and 50) laid out like items of food on a plate. As these and the other penitential psalms were specially prescribed for recitation during Lent (Alf*Q*), the scene may be meant to contrast the pilgrim-hermit's literal self-denial with the mendicant Doctor's facile verbal asceticism. **52** *he*: Conscience, in whom the act of penitential 'feasting' takes its origin. **52, 53a**[2] *Beati quorum*; *Et...peccata*: 'Blessed are they [whose iniquities are forgiven]: and whose sins are covered' (Ps 31:1). *Beatus vir*: 'Blessed is the man [to whom the Lord hath not imputed sin]' (Ps 31:2). *makyng*: the happy condition of being forgiven viewed (a trifle illogically) as the 'product' of *not* having sinned; but the absolved state in *PP* is, in line with orthodox teaching, thought of as restoring the condition of innocence (cf. B 14.96). 'Beatus vir' begins Ps 1, but as the second penitential psalm (already quoted), Ps 31 is the likely source here. **53a**[1] *Miserere...*: 'Have mercy on me, O God, [according to thy great mercy. And according to the multitude of thy tender mercies, blot out my iniquity]' (Ps 50:3); the central fourth penitential psalm. The prayer for forgiveness is served on the same platter as the offer of forgiveness, an assurance that sacramental penance is immediately efficacious. **54** *derne shrifte*: confession being an intimate transaction between the sinner and God; the dish is covered, so no one else can see what is in it. *Dixi...tibi*: 'I said: I will confess [against myself my injustice] to [the Lord. And thou hast forgiven the wickedness of my sin]' (Ps 31:5b). Annual confession was particularly encouraged before Easter. This scene shows Patience accepting the discipline that he will urge on Activa Vita in B 14.15–24 (a passage removed in revision to **C**).

59–77 60 Contrition is meant for all as the 'food' that sustains a sincere spiritual life. **61** *pytaunce*: a little portion (discreetly ordered by the host in **B** and provided by the 'cook' in **C**) appropriate to Patience, whose special vocation is to fasting and self-denial. **61b–61a** 'For this shall every one that is holy pray [to thee] in a seasonable time' (Ps 31:6). The contextual referent of *this* is 'forgiveness' or 'the grace of repentance' and that of *seasonable time*

'now, always' or more specifically 'the penitential season of Lent'. **62** *conforted*: 'cheered (with food, refreshment)'. *bothe*: 'as did'; the friendly service of this pair contrasts with their attitude earlier when Will impatiently disputed with them. **63** '[A sacrifice to God is an afflicted spirit]: a contrite and humbled heart, O God, thou wilt not despise' (Ps 50:19). **66a** '[Woe to you that are wise in your own eyes, and prudent in your own conceits]. Woe to you that are mighty to drink wine' (Is 5:22). The bracketed verse before the one quoted has special relevance to the Doctor's situation, as will appear. This Isaian 'woe' is linked with another familiar Pauline text against gluttony (Phil 3:18–19) in goliardic verses ascribed to Walter Map in his *De Avaritia et Luxuria Mundi* 89–90: 'Vae! vae vobis fortibus ad bibendum vina, / quorum deus venter est, hominis sentina' (Wright 1841:165). **71** *Poules*: the Doctor's sermon at St Paul's Cross outside the Cathedral (inside before the Dean, in **B**) having focussed on the Apostle's own sufferings, that in **C** more on the need for all Christians to suffer for love of God. **73** *how þat...what*: 'about Paul, and what suffering...' (anacoluthic). **74a** '[In labour and painfulness],....in hunger and thirst, [in fastings often...]' (II Cor 11:27). **B 67a** 'Thrice was I beaten [with rods]...' (II Cor 11:25)... '[And] of the Jews five times did I receive forty [stripes save one]' (II Cor 11:24). **77** 'There is danger in false brethren' (after II Cor 11:26).

78–85 are more obviously parenthetical in **B** (because of *write* B 71, with its breach of decorum) than in **C** where, with no intrusion of Will-the-author, the sentiments could arguably form part of Will-the-Dreamer's mutterings to his *mette* and continue without break at 86. **C** softens the tone, conceding that it could quote an elaboration on the Pauline text but will refrain so as not to upset brother-Christians, whereas **B** insists on giving the inflammatory text in Latin for the benefit of the *litterati*. **78–9** *Holy Writ...fals frere*: an opportunistic (and anachronistic) perversion of the Pauline *falsus frater* that uses St Francis' humble self-designation as 'brother' to attack the whole *secte* of mendicants. **80** The sentiment recalls that of Trajan at B 11.213, a line from a 20-line passage revised out at that point. **82** *fyue*: 'five (orders of)'. **83** *this*: the text quoted in **B** *with* introductory 'gloss'. **B 73a** 'Let everyone be on guard against a brother [= 'friar'], since, as they say, "there's danger in false brothers [friars]"'. No exact source is known, but similar utterances appear in anti-mendicant writings (Alf*Q*).

86–107 86–7 admiringly enunciate the friar's academic qualifications only to deflate them with a parenthetic gibe at his other less commendable kind of 'greatness'. **88** *vs pore*: echoing Trajan on the Christian gentry's duty of hospitality to the poor 'when [they] maken festes' (12.103). No direct judgement on the host can be intended, since he has invited a learned (and presumably devout) religious, and 'none kyne riche' (12.104). But since **L** later makes the hospitable Conscience evince blindness to the plausible 'falseness' of (at least some) mendicants at a crisis in the defence of Unity (22.242), he may have judged the knightly classes especially susceptible to the suave address of highly educated friars. **90** *wille*: the tart pun on his name bringing out the still unreformed character of the Dreamer, whose wish, even as toned-down in **C**, too readily recalls Envy's at B 5.102. **B 83** *Mahoun*: 'the Devil' (as at 20.293); the name of a pagan god (corrupted from *Mahomet*) popularly supposed to be worshipped by the Moslems. **93** *iurdan*: originally a vessel with bulb-shaped body and narrow neck widening at the top, used by physicians for urine specimens (whence applied to a chamber-pot). A coarse allusion to the Dominican William Jordan (Marcett 1938) may be allowed since it is Will who is speaking, though that would be hard to reconcile with Leaute's rules for moral satire in 12.33–41*a* (which are called forth in response to Will's anger against another friar). The contextual relevance of the dispute between Jordan and the anti-mendicant Durham monk Uhtred of Boldon is urged by Middleton 1987:31–2n. **94** *purgatorie on erthe*: penitential sufferings that will shorten a person's time in purgatory (cf. 9.185). **95–6** *Lat be...se*: advice to act on what Will asserted was Dowel: 'To se moche and soffre al' (13.221). **96** *may*: 'can (eat)'. **97** *penaunce*: Patience's humorous pun serving to counter, while sympathising with, his *mette*'s indignation. **98** *gothelen*: harshly recalling Glutton's porcine rumblings at 6.397. *gynnen*: '(he will) proceed to'. **100** *preuen hit*: implying that the Doctor has dialectical skill enough to argue a conclusion favourable to himself from the unlikeliest premisses. *Pocalips*: alluding to the goliardic *Apocalypse of Golias* attributed to Walter Map, which has a description of greedy abbots (Wright 1841:341–80). *Aueroy* (*Auereys* **B**): either Aurea, a Spanish solitary who drank only what she could distil from cinders, or Avoya, a saint fed with bread from heaven (*Sk*); or an imaginary saint (the **B** form echoing *Auarice*) suited to the Doctor, whose own 'passion' would presumably result from over-indulgence. Middleton (1987), favouring Marcett's proposed link with Friar Jordan, suggests that the name is a corruption of 'Averroes', the Spanish Moslem Aristotelian philosopher (*c.* 1126–98) whose preference for physical science over spiritual and moral had been supposedly espoused by the Dominicans, and that its use shows the Doctor to represent a purely carnal understanding of moral apologetics. But this does not fit well with 'Passion', and identification of the 'saint' remains uncertain. **103** *take...at*: in its earlier use at 12.77 clearly meaning 'appeal to' but here, in the light of B 94 *testifie of*, rather 'deliver testimony concerning'. *trinite*: taken as '*the* Trinity' by *Pe*; but *a* here (as at 111) indicates as referent rather the 'Dowel' Triad. **104** *of* (*after* **B**): 'concerning'; **C**'s removal of the punning *repetitio* on *after* is noteworthy.

108–38 110 *carpede*: presumably on 'the life of Dowel'. **111** *me* (*vs* **B**): a small revision showing Will's important rôle in this scene; Conscience's look down from the high table is an invitation to him to speak. **112** *Dowel... Dobest*: Will's question is the one Patience recommended at 107. **113** *dronke*: the deadly parenthesis demonstrating how much louder actions speak than words. The scene recalls Map's satiric parody of the sacred rites: 'Dum coenas celebrat abbas cum fratribus...vinumque geminis extollis manibus...calix inebrians in manu strenui' (*Golias* 361–7). **114–15** cover the prohibitive Commandments and express (in negative form) the same doctrine as Gal 5:14 (*Pe*), that 'all the law is fulfilled in one word: *Thou shalt love thy neighbour as thyself.*' This verse from Lev 19:18 occurs shortly after that quoted at 12.35 in the Leutee scene. **117a** echoes Study's words at 11.65 shortly after attacking friars who preach at St Paul's (11.54–69). *passeth*: either 'do, perform' or 'excel in, surpass' (MED s.v. *passen* v. 13 (d); 11a (a)). The sense 'transgress' (ib. 10a) would require *R–K*'s reading *nouthe* for *nouhte* in 116 (rejected in *TN*). **118a** '[Blessed be the Lord God of Israel]: because he hath visited and wrought the redemption [of his people]' (Lk 2:68); from the canticle of Zachary. Since the mission of all Christian preachers is 'To give knowledge of salvation to his people' (Lk 2:77), the sarcasm in this reference to the friar's visit (and 'redemption') is hard to miss. **119** *syke freres*: both these and the *yonge children* (?novices) of B 110 doubtless protesting if offered only 'penitents' food' while the doctor fed on *mortrews and poddynges*. **120** *in die iudicii...*: 'on judgement day', a standard Biblical phrase (e.g. Mt 12:36). The idea of 'Dowel' (Good Works) 'accusing' those who fail in the corporal works of mercy (of which the first was to feed the hungry) alludes to Mt 25:31–46 and echoes the earlier reference to Dowel as intercessor on Doomsday at 9.338–45. **B 111** *permute*: a witty choice of word, given its specialised canonical sense 'exchange of benefices between two clerics, one receiving compensation for the difference in value' (something regarded as simony; see Alf*G* s.v.). Will means that he stands to gain, at least in a material sense. **122/3** The full final rhyme (echoed by the identical rhyme at 126/7) restores a sense of 'courteous' calm to the dinner-table conversation by inviting repetition of the question, but without suggesting a provocative answer. **125** The answer, however, differs from his first casual reply and shows the Doctor rising to the challenge as he proposes 'obedience (in laypeople), instruction (by the clergy), and the union of obedience and instruction in a higher class of cleric'. **128a** '[But] he that shall do and teach, he shall be called great (in the kingdom of heaven **B**)' (Mt 5:19). The text was earlier cited by Scripture at A 11.196*a* in defining Dobest as 'a bishop's peer'; but the Doctor (ironically unapt an exemplar though he may be) more probably means learned mendicants like himself than the episcopal order as a whole. Alan of Lille's *Summa* evokes this text to warn: 'Qui enim docens non facit, Christo contradicit' (*PL* 210:184). **129** *þou*: the intimate pronoun used to Clergy (by contrast with the formal *ʒoure* to the Doctor at 123) suggesting familiarity such as that of a country knight with the parish priest of his church. **130–8** Clergy's reply, removing some of the obscurities of **B**, is adroitly adapted to prepare for the striking intervention of Piers. **130–1** 'As far as I am concerned, definition of Dowel is not a topic to be raised for discussion outside the theology faculties'. **B 120–1** The Seven Arts are at 11.97 Scripture's *sib*, a term not usually applied to one's children and (even if the constraints of metre are recognised) one inconsistent with their being *her* children (*Sk*). The inconsistency is certainly conceptual, as the Arts do not follow but precede Scripture in the order of studies. *castel...lif*: recalling Wit's allegory at 10.128ff where, under the authority of Dowel, Inwit and his *five* sons defend the *lady* Life. **132** Though it is not clear where Piers has been sitting, his presence at the end of the hall (*ʒent*) contrasts strongly with the B-Text's mere mention of him as *oon Piers*, 'a certain Piers' at 124; and Clergy's reluctance to analyse Dowel is now due to 'love' for Piers, not simply deference towards his objections. *inpugnede ones*: since **134** alludes broadly to such earlier passages as 7.196 (Truth as humble and faithful), 237 (love and *lele / lowe* speech), 8.43–4*a* (humility), 214–19 (love and fidelity), Clergy seems unlikely to intend one specific utterance of the Plowman (could such a passage be found). Perhaps he is meant to be recalling Piers' quarrel with the priest in B 7.130–38*a* (excised, however, in **C**) or the powerful case for love and against learning made by Trajan, Piers's surrogate. All three elements come together in the Emperor's speech (12.131, B 11.166) and *lowe herte* appears in the Pardon (9.184, B 7.62). **135, 137** *preue(th)*: Piers's position being based on authority rather than reason; but since Christ himself is cited, the 'text' is assumed without argument to be the essence of reason. **136** 'Thou shalt love [the Lord thy] God [with thy whole heart] and...thy neighbour [as thyself]' (Mt 22:37, 39); 'Lord, who shall dwell [in thy tabernacle?]' (Ps 14:1); see on 2.38–9*a*. As *Pe* notes, vv 3–4 of this psalm answer the question with a definition of Dowel in part identical with the Doctor's first at 114: 'He...that worketh justice...*nor hath done evil to his neighbour*'. **137a** '[And Jesus said to him: Why callest thou me good?] None is good [but one, that is God]'. **138** *lele...treuthe*: indirect reference to the 'double-natured' God whose sovereign transcendence Christ intimates by insisting that *he* should not be called 'good'.

B 122–30 122 Clergy finds difficulty in reconciling the idea of right action as understood by moral philosophy (based on Aristotle's *Ethics*, to which the Arts course immediately led) and religious morality as taught

by the Church. **124** Clergy's reticence in the face of Piers's objection seems to imply knowledge of Trajan's impassioned response to Scripture at 12.76ff (at which Clergy must be presumed present). *vs alle*: philosophers and theologians alike. **125** *saue loue one*: a sentiment like Trajan's at 12.94–6, even the wording echoing his 'ley þer a *bene* / Or *eny science* vnder sonne'. **128** *infinites*: 'limitless, boundless things' (Middleton 1972:169–78).

139–66a The two versions diverge considerably at this point and the revision, while equally dramatic, becomes even more obscure in its use of *aenigma*. **139–49** Piers's words are offered to 'prove' the assertions Clergy attributed to him and said he *could* prove; so in effect this passage of **C** not so much replaces as completes B 131–5*a*, where Conscience appeals to Patience's experience (of suffering) as a source of knowledge of Dowel. **139** *Pacientes vincunt*: 'the patient (or, 'those who suffer') conquer'; a phrase, quoted three times in each version, derived from the apocryphal *Testament of Job* 27:10 (Baldwin 1990:72). Paralleled in Chaucer (*CT* V 773–5: 'Pacience...venquysseth' and, recalling 13.198, *CT* X 658–60: 'Pacience...maketh a man lyk to God'), the thought is Stoic in origin and echoes the Dreamer's 'philosophical' definition of Dowel at 13.221. But it has a clearly religious resonance here, evoking NT texts that explicitly link this virtue with Christian Dowel: '[God] will render to every man...who, according to patience in good work (*patientiam boni operis*) seek[s]...eternal life' (Rom 2:6–7). Baer 2001 notes the similarity of thought to *DC* I.38: *Quem superare potes, interdum vince ferendo / maxima enim morum semper patientia virtus.* **140** *perpetuel pees*: synecdoche for *God*, which word glosses it in 141. Peace is a divine attribute in Ps 84:11, both 'peace of God' and 'God of peace' are common Pauline locutions (Phil 4:7, Rom 15:33), and it is conjoined with Patience at 7.273. *þat Y saide*: the maxim of 139, or what Clergy reported in 134ff. **142** 'Learn, teach, love God (your enemies **B**)'. As Alf*Q* notes, this has the character of a school maxim, to which **L** may have added 'enemies' from Mt 5:44 and 'God' from Mt 22:37. **B 140** *Loue*: a fleeting personification of Patience's beloved (and Peace's at B 18.181) that foreshadows the allegory of the Tree of Patience / Charity as Anima will describe it at 16.9–10. **143–4** *enemy...coles*: from Prov 25:21–2, quoted at Rom 12:20 by St Paul with the comment: 'Be not overcome by evil: but overcome evil by good'; the complementary command not to be unkind to one's fellow-Christian is taught by the Samaritan, a more fully 'emergent' version of Piers, at 19.217. Hot coals symbolise in context the 'mortification' of someone receiving only kindness in return for injury; but they were commonly interpreted as the heat of love that melts an enemy's hardness of heart (as in *AW* 206/10). **144–9** memorably convey the paradox of how human action is 'transformed' when its motive is charity (on the operation of this curious 'figure of thought', which might be called *transsumptio*, see Simpson 1986:161–83). **146** *eft and eft*: recalling Mt 18:20–1, 5.39, with the difference that in **L** the *suffering* of (literal or figurative) hostile blows undergoes 'transsumption' into the *giving* of (purely figurative) 'blows of charity'. **150–1** Piers's sudden departure distantly recalls that of Jesus at Emmaus (Lk 24:31) and is the first hint in **C** that he is a *figura* of Christ, a hint confirmed by the important final mention of him at 16.338 before his re-appearance at 20.8. But Piers here clearly possesses the same identity as in Vision Two and exists on the same allegorical plane with the Dreamer and the other personified figures, as Reason's ability to accompany him attests. **152** *ran after*: the immediate attraction of the personage who embodies Justice to the one who embodies Love anticipates a similar pursuit of the Samaritan by the Dreamer, Faith and *Spes* at 19.81. In the light of **B**'s ending, **C** might even hint at the need for the episcopate in a divided Christendom to 'follow' or 'look for' an *ideal* 'pope', if he can be found. Reason's disappearance from the poem leaves Conscience to work alone (Whitworth 1972) in the final two visions, which will concentrate on the spiritual integrity of the individual within the Church. *riht...yede*: 'went straight off with [Piers]'; the uncomfortable under-sense 'justice departed with [Reason]' cannot be decisively excluded. **153** *no mo*: the 'staff' having withdrawn, and of the guests, bishop and 'pope' departed, leaving only knight, priest, hermit, dreamer (and theologian) to continue the discussion. **154** *Pacience*: taking Piers's position (and his place), though not yet asked formally by Conscience to speak. **155** *litel thyng*: 'little'; '(something that is a) small thing'. *coueyteth*: simply 'desires', without the subtly punning *repetitio* of **B**. **156** *and...to*: 'if I really set my mind to it'. Patience's brag has nothing to do with 'diplomacy as opposed to war'; his way to 'win' France is to 'lose' the greedy desire to win it, the motto-phrase re-quoted at 158*a* proclaiming this paradoxical notion of 'conquest' to be that of Christ as later explained by Conscience at 21.50. **158** *a partye*: either (understanding *to* after *take*) 'a part (of authoritative tradition)' or (taking the phrase as *take...of*) 'partly, in part'. **160** *tonge*: metonymy for 'words of contumely', alluding to Mt 5:11. **161** *pacience*: here making explicit the referent of *it* B 164, as a 'little thing' (vouched for by the speaker who exemplifies the virtue) to be carried interiorly in all circumstances. Its closeness to heavenly charity is brought out by the gloss-citation 166*a*, which implies a view of the latter as essentially (not just accidentally) love that 'suffers all' (cf. I Cor 13:4, 7: 'Charitas *patiens* est,...omnia *suffert*,... omnia sustinet'). **163** *cart-whel*: an image alluding to the emblematic 'Wheel of the Virtues' familiar in the period as an allegorical diagram (Kaske 1963:55–7) in which Patientia is situated in the corner made by the spokes.

crow croune: possibly a crow's skull used as a charm, although the term 'head of the crow' is an alchemical term of art for the process of calcination (MED s.v. *hed* n. (1), 9(d)). Galloway 1995:94–6 ingeniously interprets the phrase in terms of the esoteric riddle-tradition of the early C14th English *Secretum philosophorum* to mean 'head [= *caput* or first syllable] of the Latin word for "crow" (*corvus*)', i.e. *cor* 'heart', and the '*cor*ner' of the cartwheel to signify a 'fourth part of the *rota* or wheel' i.e. the letter R which, when added to C and O, gives Cor. This explanation, which does not force the lexical sense overmuch, is rather more persuasive than his reading of 3.479 (see above and further on B 156 below), and accords well with the general meaning of the passage. 'Patience carried everywhere in the heart' is certainly what the speaker seems to have in mind. **166** *ne be*: elliptical for 'nor (will he) be'. **166*a*** '[Fear is not in charity: but perfect] charity casteth out fear, [because fear hath pain]...' (I Jn 4:18).

B 149–72*a* express the mystery of 'patient charity' in a riddle which, though entirely recast in **C**, remains enigmatic in the revision. **149** This perhaps self-evident assertion becomes in **C** a general statement of the contrast between true love and selfish desire. **150–1** *coueiteþ* (1, 2): the subject of a benign 'transsumption' of meaning like that noted under B 144–9. **151** *Kynde loue*: 'natural', 'true' and 'kind / gracious' are all meanings of the epithet in this phrase, which earlier occurred at 3.451; eight variants of the word *love* appear in 140–50. *speche*: a friend's precious conversation, the only 'possession' of his that true affection desires. **152–7** The basic image is that of a bundle tied with a strap on which is inscribed the tag of 152b. The riddle is correctly given by *Sk* 'the general solution...Charity, exercised with Patience' and the passage interpreted as 'a general reference to the great events of Christianity' (more particularly, the redemptive events of Passion Week that provide the ground-pattern of Vision Six). Detailed discussions by Smith 1961, Kaske 1963 (rev. 1969), Goodridge 1966:299–308 and Schweitzer 1974 provide more or less satisfactory attempts to 'undo it' in detail, and Baldwin 2001:102–4 attempts to relate the riddle to particular events in the peace-process between England and France in June 1377. **152** *half... lyne*: playing on both the grammatical and liturgical associations of the Latin b-half. One allusion is to the phrase *Tene hanc lampadem* 'hold this lamp' from Priscian's *Grammar* 'illustrating grammatical "rulership" by the *ex vi transitionis*' (Kaske 1963:240–1), the other to *half* of the priest's words to the baptizand during the solemn ceremony of the Easter Vigil, *Accipe lampadem ardentem [et irreprehensibilem: custodi baptismum tuum: serva mandata]* 'Hold the burning light that cannot be taken away; [keep your baptismal vows; observe the commandments]' (*Sarum Manual*, cited Schweitzer). The lit lamp is in the exegetical tradition a symbol of holy charity (see on 1.184). Galloway, however, sees the 'lamp' here not as an allusion to the grammatical expression but as a metaphoric substitution for 'moon' in the *Lune dimidium* phrase of the Harley 3362 riddle discussed under 3.479, and renders 152a as 'the "half-a-lamp" line in Latin' (1995:91). But this is unacceptable, for grammar, syntax and metre all show that **L**'s compound is not 'half a lamp' but 'half a lamp-line', and the indefinite *a* cannot be rendered 'the'. Another interpretation of *laumpe lyne* (Bradley 1910), as referring to the cord by which a lamp was suspended, conjectures a Latin word *cordella* as the key to the riddle, 'half' of this word being *corde* 'hert', an apt referent for *perinne* in 153 (and in harmony with Galloway's comment cited under 161 above). *Ex...*: '(drawn) from the (grammatical) power of transitivity', that 'by which [in Latin] a [transitive] verb "rules" [governs] its direct object in the accusative case' (Kaske 1963:236). The terminology for analysing syntax called *regimen* is discussed by Bland 1988, one given source (130–1) being Villedieu's *Doctrinale*, a work **L** cites at 11.267=C 12.155a. The exact interpretation of this compressed figure is hard to establish, but the general sense seems to be that 'the baptismal vows should "directly govern" Christians' actions and provide a secure "fastening" for the virtue (patience) that will sustain them through life'. The allegorisation of grammatical relations in B 13.151 anticipates that of the elaborate 'direct and indirect relation' in the *mede / mercede* figure of C 3.332–405a. Given the equal importance of the liturgical as of the grammatical context, *transicionis* may plausibly be taken as a punning allusion to *transitus* 'passage', i.e. the Hebrews' crossing of the Red Sea in Ex 12:11 (Schweitzer 315). This is the key event for the religion of the Jews, recalled in the Passover, and for Christians commemorated in the Holy Saturday liturgy as a 'type' of Christ's passion, death and resurrection. Galloway's interpretation of this phrase as 'the force of *transitio*' that 'may evoke the multiple procedures and "transitions" [of the riddle-tradition]' (1995:94) may register as over-ingenious. But Baldwin's rendering of the Latin phrase as 'from the passing over of power' and as perhaps referring 'to the transition of royal power (*vis*) from one reign [Edward III's] to the next [Richard II's]' must be impossible, since the phrase is *ex vi transitionis* not *ex transitione vis*. **153** *perinne*: here and at 158 having as referent *kynde loue* 151 (as *Sk* recognised), as does *herwith* 157. **154–5** 'As a symbol of [Holy] Saturday, which originally established the calendar [of the Christian year], together with all the significance of the [Mass of the] Wednesday of the following [Easter] week; the full of the moon providing the power of both [days]'. Baldwin's interpretation (2001:103–4) of Wednesday as 24 June 1377, the day on which the Treaty of Bruges (1375) expired and Saturday as 20 June 1377, 'the last complete day in the life of Edward III' carry lit-

tle conviction. But she is undeniably right that Patience's speech is urging on the government a 'patient foreign policy' in relation to France, which renewed hostilities in June 1377. **154** *signe*: perhaps with specific reference to the *sign* of Confirmation (Schweitzer), another sacrament customarily administered on the vigil of Easter (from the date of which the Church's moveable feasts were reckoned). **155** *wit*: 'meaning', i.e. the fulfilment of Christ's promises in the Second Coming and the Last Judgement, together with the necessity of Christ's suffering, as stated in Ac 3:18 (read in the Epistle of the day). **156** *myddel... moone*: the Paschal full moon, a metonym for the Christian Easter; the event from which stems the efficacy of baptism and confirmation, sacraments 'governed' directly by the *vis* 'power' of Christ's *transitus* 'passover' from death to life (Kaske 1969:245). *The myddel of the mone* must mean 'half-way point of the lunar cycle, full of the moon' (see MED s.v. *middel* n. 4); so Galloway's attempt (1995:87) to see it as equivalent to 'half of a moon' in the 'Oxford' riddle cited at 3.479, which has no lexical support, cannot be accepted. **157** *it*: i.e. *Charitas patiens* (I Cor 13:4), 'Charity, exercised with patience' (*Sk*). **158** *Vndo it*: 'Undo the bundle' / 'Resolve the riddle'. **164** *it*: as in 157. **164a** 'Charity fears nothing'; see on C 166a. **167–76** keep the essential sense of **B** 165–72, but remove some of the awkwardness of expression. The tone of the *impossibilia* recalls that of a text like Mt 21:21 (on faith) or I Cor 13:7 (on charity); in the end, patient charity is invincible and will reveal its power to those in power (for an interesting comparison of **L**'s posture with that of Wycliffite critics of Church involvement in war, see Somerset 2001). **B 168–9** *my3t...redels*: 'the power (that is the solution) of this riddle [i.e charity]'. The suggestion of E. Kirk (cited Somerset, 110n1) that it is the *Fiat voluntas tua* of B 14.49 is atttractive (if that comes somewhat late to be a gloss on a riddle 350 lines earlier); but 'obedience to the will of God as exemplified in the Passion' could well be regarded as the supreme act of *charitas patiens* shown by Christ towards mankind. *wicchecraft... wit*: because such influence, though commonly thought of as acquired through magic, is really a form of wisdom. **172** *dido*: found only here as a common noun; the name of the Queen of Carthage whose tragic story in Bk IV of Virgil's *Aeneid* moved Augustine to tears (*Conf.* I xiii 1). Its original use in **B** was perhaps suggested by Patience's *quene* at 170, and the Doctor's bright answer may imply, 'What you say has as little chance of happening as poor Dido had of getting Aeneas to stay with her when Jove was against it'. **173** *wit...worlde*: deliberately rejecting Patience's contention, but going further to deny that wisdom (even 'worldly') plays any part in the real world of passion-driven politics. **174** *Pope...enemyes*: an allusion to the Great Schism of September 1378, which was preceded by armed conflict at Rome between Pope

Urban VI and a mercenary army supporting the cardinals who sought to depose him. Freshly topical at the presumed time that **L** wrote **B** (1378–9), the Schism was to last another thirty years; and during the period of composition of **C** Urban led a major campaign against his former ally the King of Naples (1383–4). **B 176** *kynges*: Charles VI of France and Richard II of England. Political tension between the two countries during the Schism was heightened by English acknowledgement of Pope Urban and French support for the Avignonese anti-pope Clement VII, who was excommunicated by Urban VI in November 1378. The close entanglement of the two issues is seen in the last major C14th incident of the Hundred Years War, England's intervention in the Flemish revolt against French rule, culminating in the disastrous 'Crusade' of 1383 against the Clementists, led by Henry Despenser, Bishop of Norwich (McKisack 1959:145–7, 429–33; Houseley 1983). **C**'s excision of this line and revision of *peple* 77 to *parties* **C** 175 may reflect the truce with France of Jan. 1384, which lasted a year, and thus point to a date for the composition of this Passus round 1384–5 (when hostilities were renewed, they were largely confined to the struggle for supremacy in Spain). **175–6** *putte...conseyle*: a gesture of complacent superiority that will meet an unexpected check (albeit toned down in **C**).

B 179–99 179b expresses a commonly held view (see Pr 47–50), while failing to distinguish the speaker as an inner or spiritual 'pilgrim' (like Piers at B 7.120–1, who also chose penitential 'food') from such as the 'professional' pilgrim at B 5.515ff=C 7.159ff. *lye*: referring to his unrealistic claims for the power of patience at 166–78 (for assessments of these see Baldwin 2001 and Somerset's 'Response'). **180** *loude...curteisliche*: i.e. in rejecting the Friar's low-voiced (and discourteous) 'sidelining' of Patience. **182** *go*: in face of the Doctor's dismissal of the 'pilgrim', a surprising decision by the host to share Patience's journey (allegorically, adopt his manner of living). The omitted 17-line passage explicitly rejects 'learning' (keen intellect) for 'suffering' (good will) and heightens the emotional tone. The effect is to make Conscience seem reminiscent of such austere contemporary 'Lollard knights' as Sir John Clanvowe, author of *The Two Ways*. The tension in the interchange between knight and priest (Clergy), marked by the repetition of one speaker's phrases by the other (183a, 188a; 190, 202a), foreshadows a breach that lasts till the moment Conscience will call (in vain) for Clergy's help at 376, when it is too late. **184–8** Clergy's incredulous rejoinder shows him less worldly-wise than the Doctor, but still (despite his expressed respect for Piers 124–30) sceptical of Patience's seeming independence of institutional authority. **185** *yereȝeues*: implying that he will become a wandering minstrel (like Haukyn, whom they will soon meet). *rede...redels*: an etymological pun that stands out

if the line is read as T-type; clerkly interest in riddles as a part of rhetorical study is noted by Galloway 1995:93. **186** *bring yow*: an eirenic offer to meet the distinguished layman's desire for the pure milk of scripture to sustain his religious life. *book...lawe*: perhaps JOB, the 'last word' on the theme of 'patience'; an open but tactful hint that the knight (note the polite *ye* 184 as against Conscience's *þee* at 189) needs for this purpose nothing he could not learn from the Scriptures that are in Clergy's charge. But though Conscience seems driven by the same desire for *kynde knowyng* 'direct first-hand acquaintance' of Dowel as was Will, he seeks it not in books but in *preue*, i.e. in 'seeing much and suffering more' (B 11.421). **190** *proud*: Conscience 'speaks fair' to make clear he is not rejecting one 'sect' (friars) for just another (hermits), but responding as befits the spiritual 'timbre' he discerns in the two representatives of these ways of life. **191–2** *folk here*: the indefiniteness conveying a chilly politeness, since the *folk* can only be the Friar, just as *wight* 193 (echoing *wye* 191) can only be the Hermit. But the fourfold repetition of *wil* in 191–4, the half-rhyme on *fulle / wille* (countering Clergy's on *lawe / knowe* 186/7) and the emotive words *mood* and *moorne* leave no doubt that Conscience is firmly choosing the affective / volitional over the intellectual / cognitive as the best way to Dowel (on this key contrast see Simpson 1986:1–23). **193** *goode wil*: the importance of *bona voluntas* (Lk 2:14) to **L**'s thinking on the mystery of 'prevenient grace' (*gratia gratis data*) is preserved in C 14.24–5. Its synonymy with *trewe wille* here points up the crucial relevance of this concept to the situation of 'virtuous pagans', a point already made by Ymaginatyf at B 12.286–7=C 14.211–12 (with which cf. B 11.146–8=C 12.82–5). *was...fulle*: 'could never have an adequate price put on it'. **194** *tresor...wille*: the clear echo of Holy Church's words on *treuthe* (B 1.207) betokening less a shift in the poem's direction than a belated discovery through experience (*kynde knowyng* B 142–5) of their real meaning. **195** *Maudeleyne*: often identified with the 'woman...in the city, a sinner' of Lk 7:37–50 who anoints Christ with ointment and is forgiven 'many sins...because she hath loved much' (7:47); on 'Mary Magdalen' in *PP* see on 7.137. **196** *ȝacheus*: the rich tax-collector, 'a man that was a sinner' (Lk 19:7, paralleling Lk 7:37), whose dramatic disposal of his *tresour* is here judged less valuable spiritually than that of 'Maudeleyne' or the poor widow. *Dimidium...*: 'The half of my goods I give to the poor; [and if I have wronged any man of any thing, I restore him fourfold]' (Lk 19:8). **197–8** are omitted in revision here, having been used in the passage on poverty at C 13.96. **197** *poore widewe*: in Lk 21:1–4; like Mary Magdalen (as described later at 17.21–2), signifying passive acceptance of and total dependence on the divine will. **198** *gaȝophilacium*: 'the treasury' (Lk 21:1). **177–85** carefully revise **B 199–205**, adding fullness and weight to Conscience's speech, dropping the end-rhyme *frere / ere* and making small changes in tone, as with the harsh 'Platonic' self-rhyme Lett*rure* / lett*eth*. But since the words to Clergy are easily audible (not whispered as in **B**), they must (like *fol monye* 182) be meant as an oblique rebuke to the Doctor. The decorous **B** farewell (*curteisliche*; *first* 199) is replaced by the abrupt *sone*, a new asseveration-line added (179), and the good-humoured conclusion to the parting removed. **183** 'They can't recognise the nature of true patience (when they see it) / patience for the gracious thing it is'. **185** *to fynde*: 'discover the whereabouts of' and 'achieve (for myself)', but both implying that it cannot be found with the secular clergy or the religious orders.

B 203–15 203 *no congie*: because expecting to see him again betimes. Allegorically, this represents the priest's expectation that the lord of the manor will quickly tire of his pious whim and come back to his old friend and counsellor. 205b ominously anticipates Conscience's urgent cry at 20 (22).376, which will be followed by his second, desperate decision to 'become a pilgrim'. **205** *forwalked*: a rare word recorded only here and in *WPal* 2236 (also with *wery*). *wilne*: '(that you will) desire to have me advise you'. **206** *soop*: Conscience's acceptance here of his need for priestly support is completely dropped in **C**. **207** *oure partyng-felawe...bope*: a union of clergy and nobility (estates often at odds) in a spirit of loving charity could, he claims, achieve universal peace and 'conversion' of unbelievers. The possible pun on this phrase ('the fellow with whom we take our leave of each other') suggested in Simpson 1986³:64 is contextually improbable, since Conscience is about to *leave* Clergy and *accompany* Patience, and the condition proposed by *If* is an ideal one (hence the subjunctive). **212** The amicable repetition of Conscience's conciliatory phrase *That is soop* does not weaken Clergy's resolve to remain with his given duties in order to 'strengthen' the Christian community, simple and subtle alike ('sacramental confirmation', though reserved for the bishop [B 15.456], *may* also be implied under the *devoir* of the ordained clergy as a whole). But since he understands Conscience's intention (212), his tone in 215 must be taken as neutral, not sceptically ironic.

186–90 form a transitional passage between the two major episodes of Vision Four. **186a** The ironic echo of Pr 49 here and at 191 points the contrast between different kinds of 'pilgrim' and 'pilgrimage'. *grete wille*: 'intense commitment'; a phrase found otherwise only at 12.85, describing the fervour of Gregory's prayer for Trajan's salvation. That the Dreamer is inspired to identify his name with his action in a spontaneous response to the immediate situation need not imply the poet's unqualified endorsement of Conscience's action (here as later at the end of the poem) as normative. **187** *as...vitayles*: the com-

parison's ordinary meaning is 'transformed' (Simpson 1986²); for since Patience is not 'as' ordinary pilgrims, his food will not be 'as' theirs, but the sort he was content to be served at the dinner (cf. 57, 61 and 63 above). *hym and Consience*: patience and conscience are 'friends' in ch. v of Augustine's *De Patientia*: 'patientia amica est bonae conscientiae' (*PL* 40:611–27). **190** These vices are later coupled at 22.297, while the topographical allegory recalls that at 2.90.

(ii) 191–311 The *second episode* of Vision Four, that of ACTIVA VITA (Haukyn or *Actyf* in **B**), crosses the passus-boundaries to occupy half of C XVI (all of B XIV). Despite significantly altering **B**'s conception of Actyf (through transferring the descriptions of the sins on Haukyn's soiled coat to the Confession-sequence in Vision Two), **C** retains intact its threefold thematic purpose. This is, first, to contrast with the satirical portrait of a learned friar the more sympathetic (self-)portrait of a 'lewed' layman who, if also 'carnal' (though rather less in **C** than in **B**), is not closed to the call to penitence. Second, to offer Conscience a *preue* of how Patience, like his divine exemplar (13.198), 'suffers' sinners by encouraging rather than condemning their efforts to break free from the grip of vice. Third, more widely, to shift the focus of the poem's concern with salvation from the problem of learning that occupied Vision Three to the experience of *charitas patiens* incarnated in Christ, whose VITA will dominate the rest of the poem. The dialogue, opening with a question from Patience (197–8), is advanced by another three from Actyf (248, 276, 281–2) that break it into more manageable sections, is followed by Patience's massive homily on patient poverty, and ends with a final two questions expressing Actyf's (and in part the reader's) not unreasonable incomprehension (16.114,116). **194** *he²*: possibly referring to Patience; but if to Actyf, then the adverb marks how great the change in **L**'s conception of him is. **195** *Actiua Vita*: not 'the Active Life as opposed to the Contemplative Life' of contemporary religious discourse (cf. B 6.248) but 'a practical life based on and judged by purely temporal conceptions of goodness' (Maguire 1949 [1969]:195, 200). **196** *Peres prentys...*: the basis of this claim to a connection (allegorically, of the purveyors with the producers of food), one closer than in // B 238, being that Haukyn makes his bread from the corn Piers grows. It affirms the status of people like him as honest working members of the community. **197** *dere frende*: the warmth of Conscience's address here is to be contrasted with his sceptical coolness towards Will at 5.89–91.

200–33 200 *wafrer*: a maker and seller of ordinary *wafres*. In the immediate context, however, these appear to be the special wafers used for the Eucharistic host, and *godes gestes* are the communicants (*Pe*), an addition linking Actyf's rôle more directly with the Church's responsibility for 'feeding' souls. The Latin terms *wafferarius* and *menestrallus* were near-synonymous, since many wafer-sellers customarily provided entertainments (respectable or low) such as Haukyn says he *cannot* (see MED s.v. *minstrel* 2. 'servant, functionary', and cf. Southworth 1989:8–1). **201** *lauhe*: figuratively, since they take pleasure in his fare. **202** *payn*: the choice of the French form suggesting that these are fancy breads like those named at 8.327. **203** *robes*; *gounes*: gifts given only to the most distinguished of 'lords' minstrels', such as the King's (see Bullock-Davies 1978 and Southworth 1989, ch. 4). **204–9** Actyf unrealistically laments his lack of rich rewards for any of a jumble of crude and refined forms of amusement. **204** *lye*: make satirical gibes and innuendoes (about public figures), like the modern 'stand-up comic'. **207** *Farten*: the ability to do this at will was cultivated by low *japeres*, as shown in the marginal illustrations of certain medieval manuscripts. **210/11** The identical rhyme underlines his resentment at their refusal properly to recognise his services (such rhyme similarly heightens the catechetical flavour of the statement at 16. 265/6, 316/17, 17.39/40, 150/1). **214** Parallel **B 237** specifies the Paternoster (said at Mass before the distribution of Communion), a fitting prayer on behalf of the community's food-providers because its fourth petition is 'Give us this day our daily bread.' **216** The wider generality of **C** both removes **B**'s invidious collocation of tonsured clerics with false beggars and makes the important point that Actyf provides for all men, like his master Piers (8.24–5) and Piers's master Truth (21.433–6). **217** *Fro...Mihelmesse*: 'from one end of the year to the next'; the Feast of St Michael the Archangel (Sept. 29), a quarter-day, here also marks the end of one agricultural season and the start of another. *drynke*: a rhetorical exaggeration, obviously. **218** *þe Pope*: figuratively, in that Actyf and his kind provide for every level of society up to the highest, a fact that licenses him to complain about the 'practical' ineffectivenesss of the Church's ministrations. *Sk* takes this as an allusion to Peter's Pence, an ecclesiastical tax paid to the Pope by all; but the sum seems too small to support Haukyn's point. **B 244, 246** play on two senses of *provendre*, 'prebend' and 'provender' (for the Pope's mount, presumably better food than the bean-flour Hunger recommends for beggars at 8.225). But the jest is idle, for while Haukyn might (in hard times) realistically provide 'horse-bread' as a sideline, he could never be entitled to a clerical living. **220** *bulle*: the lead seal (*bulla*), stamped with the heads of SS Peter and Paul on one side and the reigning pontiff on the other, and attached to a papal pardon; 'solid' enough, but lacking any power to put an end to the plague. Actyf seems here to voice the disbelief engendered (as commonly happens) by natural disasters and scandals in the Church among laypeople who looked for material benefits from spir-

itual remedies received in a physical form. **221** *luythere eir*: expressing the belief that plague was caused by corruption of the atmosphere. **B 250** *bocches*: dark-coloured tumours ('buboes') in the groin or arm-pit; the commonest symptom of the bubonic plague, incurable and leading swiftly to death. **222** The wordplay on *bere* (like the *repetitio* on *myhte* in 220, 222) conveys the *lewed* Haukyn's disillusion, which parallels the *lered* Doctor's political cynicism at 173 above, though not excluding the possibility of self-criticism (227ff). **223a** '[And these signs shall follow them that believe]: In my name they shall cast out devils (**B**)...and they shall lay their hands upon the sick: and they shall recover' (Mk 16:17–18). **B 254** *as...sholde*: deliberately equivocal in tone, like the Dreamer-Narrator's remark at 9.327, poised between sullen doubt and a hunger for faith. **224** Actyf articulates an unwillingness to do anything for his fellow-Christians until the head of the Christian community does something for him. **226** *þe power*: 'the power of the keys' (see on Pr 136). *pot...salue*: an image of the healing power Christ gave to the Apostles. Actyf's initial point is that if Peter's successor, the Pope, possesses spiritual power (as Christians are expected to believe), then this should also enable him (as it apparently does not) to heal diseases, as did Peter. **226a** '[But Peter said]: "Silver and gold have I none, but what I have, I give thee. In the name of the Lord [Jesus...], arise and walk"' (Ac 3:6). No more than his master Piers's psalm-quotations at B 7.116–7 and 124a do these scriptural texts imply that Actyf is *litteratus* (16.116 makes it plain he is not). They function rather to convey symbolically his beliefs about Peter's power and the Sodomites' sinfulness: their content is Actyf's thought, their form directed to the capacities of the poem's 'literate' readers. **227–33** express an anti-mechanistic view of healing, one dependent on conversion of heart, that is hard not to see as authorial, just as the view of pride as punished by plague and dearth is of a piece with the stern prophecies of Reason and the narrator at 5.115–7 and 8.342–53. **231a–33** are adapted from B 14.75–7 and better integrated with the moral argument than **B 261–3**, which loosely connect the need to 'amend' with the need to work if one is to feed oneself. **231a** 'From too much bread and wine worst sins arise'; adapted from Peter Cantor's *Verbum Abbreviatum* CXXXV, 300: 'Et *abundantia panis* causa fuit *peccati Sodomorum*' (*PL* 205:331), and found in Brinton's Sermon 48 (p. 216); cf. also Comestor, *HS* (in *PL* 198:1099). It derives from Ezech 16:49, which significantly adds to excess of food both pride and sloth (*otium* 'rest' 233, = *ociositas* in B 14.76a) as causes of Sodom's sin (though lechery was more commonly linked with *gluttony*, as in *CT* X 839). A variant form of the quotation appears at B 14.76a.

B 261–460 Commentary *on the* transferred parts *of this* 200-*line passage omitted here will be found under* **C VI** *and* **VII**

B 261–460 261–71 Removal in **C** of these lines vividly localising HAUKYN in place and time (along with his personal name and vices) transforms the new character ACTYF from a fly-blown exemplar of quotidian viciousness into a blunt yet tolerably well-intentioned layman. But though avoiding some repetition and redundancy (e.g. 281 at 303, 295 at 297, 299b at 313b), the change entails loss of poetic richness and thematic subtlety. For Haukyn's capacity to achieve a measure of self-recognition serves dramatically in **B** to differentiate 'contrition' or repentance through sorrow (B 14.16–17*a*, 320–32) from the Deadly Sins' (often comically ignorant) 'attrition' or repentance from fear in B V. **262** *corn*: synecdoche for 'wafers'; referring to Haukyn's pre-dawn labours at the oven, not (by ellipsis) to Piers's work in the fields. **265** *no3t longe ypassed*: less than a decade, if the accepted dating of **B** (which the lines help to establish) is correct. **266** *Stratford*: Stratford-atte-Bowe in East London, residence not only of Chaucer's Prioress (*CT* A 125) but of many bakers supplying bread for the city. Places their carts stopped at included (according to Stow, p.159) Cheapside and Cornhill (*Wr*). **267–8** The beggars depend on *broke bred* (A 12.70–1), whereas the labourers can buy other food. **270** The year 1370 suffered a great dearth of corn partly because of lack of rain in the early growing season. **271** *Chichestre*: John de Chichester, a wealthy goldsmith, Mayor of London in 1369–70. **272/3** The terminal rhyme in effect marks off as a separate section of the passus a 'portrait' of Haukyn given variety by direct speech at 308–11, 329–42, 363–99 and 405–6; a question from Conscience at 314–15; shifts of narrative perspective to Will at 343 and Patience at 355; and a full-scale *digressio* (410–57) on the origins of sloth that quickly becomes an attack on the nobility's patronage of 'the fiend's disciples' and culpable neglect of 'God's minstrels'. In its first part, 275–313*a*, pride (including vanity and hypocrisy) is described as it appears on Haukyn's 'coat'; in the second, 314–409 deal with envy, lust, greed, gluttony and sloth; only anger is omitted, and therefore contributes no material to **C**'s revision of the Sins. **273** *Haukyn*: nowadays only a surname, but in origin a familiar form of Harvey or Henry (cf. *Watekyn* 6.70, *Perkyn* 8.1). Harley 1981:97–9 interestingly suggests that it may be a rhyming variant of 'Dawkin', a diminutive form of David, the archetypal repentant sinner, minstrel and exemplar of the active life. **274** *cote...bileueþ*: 'a tunic of orthodox Christian faith'; Haukyn's soul, allegorically figured as the white christening robe he was wrapped in at baptism (the scriptural background is discussed in Alford 1974:133–8). **275** *moled*: alluding to the 'spotted garment

[*tunicam maculatam*] which is carnal' of Jude 23 (Frank 1957:71n). **279** 'Pretending to inner or outer qualities that he did not possess'. **285–91** contain details that bring Haukyn's portrait disturbingly close to the Dreamer's own self-depiction (285a recalls B Pr 3, 287 applies to much of the poem's satirical writing, and 291 recalls B 11.414). The references to *wit* in 289 and 292–3 that strengthen this link are removed in revision, to leave Actyf a more *lewed* type of figure. **290** *as...name*: 'How best to get a reputation for sexual prowess'. **313** *and...hymselue*: 'and (serve as a means to win their) praise for himself'. **313***a* '[For do I now persuade men, or God? Or do I seek to please men?] If I [yet] pleased men, I should not be the *servant* of Christ' (Gal 1:10). 'And in another place: "No man can *serve* two masters... [You cannot *serve* God and mammon"]' (Mt 6:24). The texts are connected through this common theme: Haukyn's 'gospel' is *secundum hominem* 'according to man' (Gal 1:11) since, although he claims to serve Piers as his 'prentice', his behaviour reveals his true 'master' to be the spirit of this world. **323** *leue...chide*: '(and with) a tongue quick to quarrel'. **340** *of Shordych Dame Emme*: some notorious contemporary character, doubtless she of the workmen's song at Pr 226. Shoreditch lay just N of Bishopsgate outside the City wall. **357** *good...God*; **370** *gaderen...good*: on these significant chimes see Schmidt 1987²:135. **379** echoes B 1.192. **390–1** The sense of these difficult lines (cut in **C**) seems to be that 'even when performing a kind act, he clung inwardly to his grasping and loveless avarice.' As well as the contrast between the (reluctant) outward act and true inner attitude, the use of the polysemous *conscience* pointedly warns how the 'negative scruples' that the unconverted experience (about what they might lose through kindness) vitiate 'charitable' works and make them a further occasion for sin. It seems to be intimated here that only when restored to a state of grace can men produce acts which are truly virtuous, because arising from heartfelt love of God. **400** recalls B 5.307. **410–57** are transferred entire with small changes to C 7.69–118*a* (q.v.); they bring the argument round again through denunciation of the *mysproud man* (436) to the theme of the metaphorical 'minstrels' whose services comfort men at the hour of death. **458–60** return to where Haukyn was left at 409 as Conscience begins his characteristically 'courteous' enquiry into why Actyf has neglected to clean the stains of sin from his soul by making sacramental confession (see B 14.18). At one level, this encounter represents a way of broadening the knight Conscience's experience of the common man in preparation for his rôle as leader in Passūs XXI–XXII. The experience is made possible by the mediation of the hermit, the spiritual guide who moves between different levels of society.

B XIV *begins;* C XV *continues*

B 14.1–28 continue the dialogue of Conscience with Haukyn that will conclude at 320–32; both passages are deleted as part of **C**'s transformation of the latter from *l'homme moyen sensuel* to a morally more neutral type of the common man. Also much altered is Patience's almost lyrical assurance to Haukyn of spiritual sustenance, which ends by tellingly contrasting dearth, over-abundance and sufficiency (70–4). **2** *slepe þerinne*: suggesting spiritual slothfulness, of which unwillingness to change one's working clothes at night is an apt figure; allegorically, the robe of Christian living is to be worn at all times. **3a** 'I have married a wife; and therefore I cannot come' (Lk 14:20); the excuse of one of those invited in St Luke's Parable of the Supper, occurring shortly after the verses (12–14) quoted at 11.190*a*=C 12.104*a*, which lie behind 13.442–54=C 7.101–13. Alford (1974:133) interprets 'wife' allegorically as 'concupiscence'; but the collocation with servants and children suggests more widely 'preoccupation with the things of this world'. **5** *laued*: intermittent bouts of reform occasioned by illnesses and commercial setbacks, from which Haukyn always slips back into his old ways. **16–28** aim to show how Confession properly carried through will not only cleanse the 'garment' of the soul but enable a man to keep it 'clean' (in a state of grace). They draw on the standard penitential doctrine as found in the *SAP* of Alan of Lille, who states that *tria* 'three things' must be present for confession to be *vera* 'authentic': *cordis contricio, oris professio, operis satisfactio* (*PL* 210:173; see also AlfQ, and cf. *CT* X 106–9). Though these *tria* do not tally neatly with the Triad, contrition appears here as a (vital) preliminary *disposition*, loosening the impacted dirt from the coat (= the sloth that impedes initial recourse to the sacrament). Dowel is then the first properly good *action*, to confess (= washing the fabric clean). Dobet corresponds to a second action, the priest's giving of absolution (= restoring the original hue by steeping), which strengthens the penitent's will to virtue through the pouring-in of sanctifying grace. Finally Dobest (= the drying of the garment in readiness for wearing) signifies the expression of this renewed will in meritorious acts that discharge the debt of sin and protect the soul against defilements by the flesh, the world and the devil. This fluid but slightly confusing exposition is revised and clarified at C 16–31*a*, which exactly equates the graded Triad with the three parts of penitence (as described in *CT* X 106–9). **16–17** *of...make*: 'to construct something out of contrition'. **17a** 'Heartfelt sorrow (for having offended a loving God)'. **18a** 'Verbal confession (to a priest)'. **22** 'Making full satisfaction for the sin forgiven' (by prayer, almsgiving, devotions, pilgrimage). **23** *moþe*: from Mt 6:19–21, the last verse of which was quoted at B 13.399*a* above (Alford 1974). **28**

Activa Vita: a second occurrence of Haukyn's Latin cognomen (first used of himself at 13.225), but with deeper theological resonance, now more properly denoting a (normative) life of grace possible for laypeople who *be labour sholde lyuen and lyflode deseruen* (C 5.42; cf. B 6.248). This new reliance on *þe grace of God and hise grete helpes* (13.399) to 'walk worthy of the vocation in which [they have] been called' (Eph 4:1) is not to be seen as mechanical but as a real liberation from *vnkynde desiring* (356). **29–36** Coming after the account of sacramental confession, Patience's *paast...for þe soule* (29–30) may *suggest* the Eucharist; but what it *refers to* is God's word and patient acceptance of God's will (as confirmed by revised C 237–8). **34** and the following texts echo B 7.126–30, underscoring the close link between Patience and his avatar Piers, from whom the first two are virtually borrowed. **34a** '[Therefore]...be not solicitous [for your life, what you shall eat....Behold] the birds of the air, [for they neither sow, nor do they reap...and] your heavenly Father feedeth them' (Mt 6:25–6); immediately following the verse quoted at 313*a*. **L**'s *celi Deus* runs together *Pater...caelestis* (Mt) and *Deus* (in // Lk 12:24). *Pacientes*: see on C 15.139. **35–8** C's omission of this amusing interchange tends to flatten Actyf into something of a 'yes-man' and forfeit the telling connection between the *vitailles* Patience offers Haukyn and the penitential *mete* he himself ate in the first action of Vision Four. **37–8** *poke...vertues*: see 13.217–20.

C 234–52 Patience's reply to Actyf's last point at C 231 warns that since pride is so deeply rooted in human nature, it does not need wealth and plenty to nourish it, so dearth alone will not suffice to quell it. His own 'virtuous' remedy aims to heal rather than hurt, a measure of the difference between penitence based on fear and penitence based on 'verray sorwe' (see *CT* X 128–30). **238** *me hyder sente*: patience being the fourth of the twelve fruits of the Holy Spirit (Gal 5:22). **239** *yf...trewe*: both 'if what we believe is correct' (the usual sense, as at 14.151) and 'if our faith is genuine' (reminding that Christ's promises are not fulfilled automatically but in relation to the believer's disposition). In // B 39 the phrase is more tellingly a rejoinder to Haukyn's sceptical play on *leue* 36, which is echoed in *Leue...bileue* 246. **240** *here*: 'on this earth' rather than 'their'. **243** *cryket*: probably the salamander, fabled to live in fire (the Trevisa quot. in MED s.v. *criket* n. makes both points). *corleu*: the quail (*coturnix*), in exegetical tradition often a symbol of spiritual pilgrimage and the need to rely on faith in God (Spearman 1993:242–58); perhaps with some echo of the quails sent by God in Ex 16:13. **246a** 'Whatsoever you shall ask the Father in my name, it will be given to you' (adapted from Jn 14:13). 'And in another place: "Not in bread alone doth man live, but in every word that proceedeth from the mouth of God"' (Mt 4:4). The context of the first quotation is Christ's appeal to the Apostles at the Last Supper to believe in him, so that 'the works that I do, [they] also shall do' (vs 12). That of the second is Christ's rebuke to Satan during his fast of forty days, the scriptural model for the season of Lent; the citation of Deut 8:3 reminds the Israelites that during their forty years in the wilderness God fed them with manna and quails. Both the second text and the following *Paternoster* petition at 252 are used in the later-composed self-defence by the Dreamer at 5.82–8. **248** The rhythm of Actyf's mild enquiry ironically recalls that of Glutton at 6.357. **250** *pece*: continuing the metaphor of prayer as 'spiritual food' dramatised at 59–65. Patience's way of speaking has been anticipated by Piers at B 8.118–24*a*; but **C**'s removal of that passage weakens the link between these figures that is so strong in **B** (see on B 34) and was affirmed by **C**'s making Piers the first to utter Patience's motto-phrase (at 139 above). **252** *Fiat...*: 'Thy will be done', the third petition of the Lord's Prayer (Mt 6:10), quoted again by Liberum Arbitrium as a source of spiritual 'feeding' at 16.319, as is the fourth at 16.372*a* (see on B 168–9 above). A systematic association is made by Alan of Lille (*SAP* ch. xv) between seven types of patience, the seven petitions of the Paternoster and the Seven Beatitudes (*PL* 140–3). On the significance of the Paternoster in *PP*, see Gillespie in Minnis 1994:95–119.

253–75 form perhaps the frankest statement of the pilgrim hermit's philosophy of 'reckless' dependence on God alone for *lyflode*, and willing acceptance of deprivation. Taken as a whole, it may be understood less as rejecting earthly existence than as radically subordinating it to the spiritual life that lies beyond death. Moreover, the *social* radicalism of its conclusion shows that Patience is not denying the goodness of creation but asserting that man's sin is responsible for men's sufferings. **254** *claumsen*; *drouthe*: first recorded here in these senses. **256** *pacientes...*: see on 139 above. **262***a* 'One who cares for Christ will not covet this world'; the first part of a Leonine couplet that continues *sed quasi fetorem spernens illius amorem* 'but scorn the love of it like a sickening stench'. Taken from the *Cartula*, one of the grammatical texts making up the *Auctores Octo*, and also found as the *Carmen Paraeneticum* in *PL* 184:307 (Alf*Q* 88), it is based on I Jn 2:15, 'If any man love the world [*Si quis diligit mundum*], the charity of the Father is not in him', an important passage that underlies 11.162–97. **263–5***a* are couched as a quasi-syllogistic argument: 'God gave creatures life by his breath (= word) alone; therefore he must also keep them alive by his breath (word); if so, man too can be sustained by his word'. In strict logic the conclusion does not follow, since 'to be given life' is contained under 'to live' but not *e converso*. The argument's authority depends rather on the meaning of the scriptural texts adduced, which state that since God created all life by his word, he *must* have

both the power (and the will) to sustain it by his word. Patience takes literally the second part of the Matthean text quoted at 246*a* but ignores the first part, which tacitly modifies its extremism. **263***a* '[For he spoke] and they were made' (Ps 148:5). **265***a* 'Thou openest thy hand: and fillest with blessing every living creature' (Ps 144:16); part of a commonly used grace at meals (*Latin Graces* in *Babees Book,* ed. Furnivall 1868:382). **266** *founde*: three asymmetrically functioning examples from the OT and Christian legend; in the first and third, people favoured by God are fed by him; in the second, those who offend God are punished. *fourty wynter*: the period of the Israelites' 'journey in the wide wilderness' (Jos 5:6; cf. Ex 16:35). **267** *floed...dronke*: see Num 20:11, Ps 77:20 The rock struck by Moses is taken by St Paul (I Cor 10:4) as a 'figure' of Christ who is the sustenance of his people. **268** *Elies tyme*: see III Kgs 17:1ff. The prophet Elias (Elijah) 'closed heaven' by the command of God 'for three years and six months' (Js 5:17) to punish Achab king of Israel for idolatry. **270** *tylede*: on the basis of the *Sk* text *of no mete telden* explained by MED (s.v. *tellen* v. 1a (a)) as an ironic way of saying 'had nothing to eat'. But this gloss, like the **p** reading it is based on, is an error (see *TN*), since the verb (as is clear from B 67) is the same as at 266. **271** *Seuene slepen*: seven young men of Ephesus who were said to have remained asleep in a cave from the persecution of Christians under the Emperor Decius (*c.* 250) to the time of the Eastern Emperor Theodosius II (448); see *LA* ch. 101. They were cited first as proof of the resurrection of the dead, later as exemplifying God's miraculous preservation of his faithful. **273** *mesure*: the cardinal virtue of Temperance (to be described at 21.282–9). B 74 makes the witty point that 'moderation by its very nature can *never* be over-valued (become too costly), so that it cannot *ever* produce scarcity.' After extreme arguments for total dependence on God, Patience reverts to the moderate (and surprisingly modern) point of Holy Church at 1.33, that it is sins of excess like gluttony and greed on the part of the few (the rich) that produce scarcity for the many (the poor). **275** 'I will give to you according to your asking'; adapted from Ps 36:3–4: '[Trust in the Lord, and do good, and dwell in the land: and thou shalt be *fed* with its riches. Delight in the Lord]: and he will give thee the requests (*dabit tibi petitiones*) [of thy heart]'. The relevant NT parallel to this statement (which complements the 4th Paternoster petition) is less likely to be Mk 6:22 (*Pe*) than Jn 14:14. **B 72** *vnkyndenesse...makeþ*: 'a topos of medieval economic theory...Caristia* ['dearth'], which is not in Vg [Alf*Q*], occurs in writs and ordinances...directed against victuallers who in order to drive up prices created artificial scarcities' (Alf*G*).

B 75–96 are cut here and partly transferred, 75–80 to C 15.231–3 and 81–96 (in much modified form) to 16.25–35. **76***a Ociositas*: 'idleness', 'sloth'; see on C

15.231*a* above, which omits this. **77–80** are clearly if somewhat awkwardly expressed: 'Because (*For*)...(But) did...vengeance fell on them in such a way (*so*) that they sank...' **77** is a metrically clumsy line, understandably deleted. **78b** repeats B 1.28 (removed in **C**). **81–96** make (when read aright) a strong plea for recourse to sacramental confession, and 83 is only a little more explicit than standard penitential teaching on the power and worth of contrition-with-intent-to-confess (*CT* X 309 quotes the same Ps 31:5–6 cited at 93). Their deletion in **C** could be due to clerical readers' objection that emphasis on inward sorrow (though salutary) might inadvertently produce the opposite effect to that intended, but more probably to **L**'s awareness of the discrepancies between what they say and B 16–28. In Patience's three-stage move towards the act of confession (i.e. faith, contrition and conscience), the last presumably signifies the active awakening of the penitent's 'sad purpos to shryve him' (*CT* X 128). **81** *sheltrom*: 'protective battle-formation' (going back to the ancient English interlocking shield-wall); alluding to the *armatura Dei* of Eph 6:11–17. The figure is of a *collective* mode of defence, because the faith is not merely an individual's 'existential' commitment but that of the Church in which the baptized person shares (the moat of communal tears at 19.280–3 will carry a similar significance). **82** *conscience*: possibly alluding to Conscience's remarks at 16ff; but the collocation with faith and contrition at 87 argues against capitalisation here. **87** *Dowel*: at one with Conscience's analysis at 16.28; for since contrition arising from faithful assent to the Church's teaching and issuing in a resolve to confess is now equated with Dowel, so by implication Dobet becomes confession itself and Dobest satisfaction, as at C 16.25–35. **88** *surgiens*: a figure anticipating that in the dramatised allegory at 22.311ff. The three elements constitutive of Dowel can 'operate' on the sick soul, not just 'physic' it. But while weakening the illness, they do not destroy it, as maintained by Will at B 11.81*a* and by Ymaginatif at B 12.177 (89–91 however, which now ascribe destruction of sin to the act of confession, still insist on inward contrition *accompanying* it). **91** 'Through confession to a priest, sins are slain'; paralleled in Brinton 2:437, 'Peccata per confessionem delentur' (Alf*Q*). **92** *dryueþ it doun*: a figure from cutting off a weed above ground (cf. *roote* 94). **93** *et...*: see on B 12.177*a*. **96** *wounde*: returning to the 'surgeon' metaphor of 88.

276–82 276 The question, which assumes that patience' is what 'fed' the Israelites, Elias and the Sleepers, and serves to introduce the main theme of the next passus, is better integrated with the preceding discourse than Haukyn's about the whereabouts of *Charity*, a subject not hitherto mentioned. The latter echoes ironically the question of the Folk about the whereabouts of *Truth* at B 5.532–3 // (a point reinforced by *truþe* at B 99); but

Patience's answer recalls that of Piers rather than the Pilgrim. **277–8** The sense of this passage is that a will marked by a gentle spirit of reconciliation and harmony is conducted to heaven by Charity, here in effect identified with the patience that suffers every danger (I Cor 13:4,7). *wille*: the new explicit emphasis on the affective-volitional preparing the ground for the appearance of Liberum Arbitrium as Haukyn's *ledare* at 16.156. **279** *charite chaumpion*: taking up a memorable phrase at B 8.46, from an 8-line passage deleted by **C**. **280** *pore pacient*: 'poor person who has patience (enough)'; the first adjective is substantival, the second is the epithet. **282** 'Than spending one's wealth in a just and proper way'; what matters being not how wealth was obtained, but how it is spent. **283** 'Yes, but *is* there such a man? We'll praise *him* soon enough!' A split quotation from verses on the dangers of wealth and the rareness of virtuous rich men: '[Blessed is the rich man...that hath not put his trust in money nor in treasures]. Who is he, and we will praise him? [For he hath done wonderful things in his life]' (Ecclus 31:8–9). **284** *to...ende*: 'all over the globe' / 'till the crack of doom' (cf. 18.175). **B 107** *fel*: understand *ne fel* (*ne* borrowed from *ne dredde* 106) as in // **C**. **288** *of this ryche*: 'from among these rich people' rather than 'in this kingdom'. **289–90** *preue...haue*: 'prove that he should have'. *puyr resoun*: 'simple justice', the legal sense confirmed by *lawe* 290 and *iuge* 291. **291** *þat*: 'he who'. **292–6** Patience draws an analogy from observation of *kynde* 'the natural order' (B 119) that (like Ymaginatif's *ensample* of the peacock and the lark at 14.168–90) forms the basis of an ethical deduction. 'Even animals do not experience winter all year, so why should some men suffer the "winter" of hardship all their life? It therefore "stands to reason" (as well as being "a matter of strict legal right") that they should be granted *blisse*.' **300** In revising, **C** supplements **B**'s polysemantic verbal punning (on *som...som*) with homophonic phrasal wordplay (*elliswher...were*) so as to hint 'Platonically' that the very nature of things as ordained by God requires suffering in this life to be balanced equitably by joy in the next. **301** *þat*: '(for) who(m)'. **303–11** are more sombre and final in tone, and less sympathetic to the 'misfortune' of the wealthy (in having their 'payment' [heaven] in this life and losing it in the next), than are B 122–31*a*. For the latter's tacit implication that *if* all were equal in life, none need risk suffering 'beggary' after death, amounts to a questioning of Providence. **303** *Dyues*: 'Mr Rich'; see on 8.278. *douce vie*: the French phrase and the French derived *deyntees* (like the Latin name *Dives*) lexically mirroring the rich man's detachment from (and indifference to) the situation of his wretched opposite Lazarus. **304** *beggare*: because now destitute of all except suffering, a punishment ironically 'condign' (cf. also 309). **305** is like B 124 in alliterating on vowels; but though it likewise stresses the same homophone twice, **C** (perhaps in awareness of the vocally tricky *hir hire heer* of B 128) replaces the empty homonyms of B 124 with different lexemes menacingly coloured by the polysemantic pun (on 'here') in the second *here*. The suggestion is that even good deeds, if done in a state of sin, are spiritually fruitless for the rich: 'whan we doon deedly synne, it is for noght thanne to rehercen or drawen into memorie the goode werkes that we han wroght biforn' (*CT* X 237). **306** *ledes*: the ominous rhyme-echo of *dedes* 305 hinting at the transience of any treasure except *treuthe,* the Pardon having long ago pointed out that only those who '*do* well' will '*have* well' (9.289). **311** 'They have slept [their sleep: and all the men of riches] have found nothing in their hands' (Ps 75:6). 'And in another place, "As the dream of them that awake, [**B**] O Lord, *so* in thy city thou shalt bring their image to nothing"' (Ps 72:20). In the full form, the 'dream' denotes the rich men's life of *wele,* 'death' their awaking from it, the 'city' the place whence they will be judged to *purgatorie or helle* as the *puyre pore thynges* they are.

Passus XVI
(B XIV 132–XV 255)

PASSUS SIXTEEN continues to dissolve **B**'s bond between the structural units of passus and vision, carrying on directly with Patience's instruction to Actyf. It divides in half at about 156, with the appearance of *Liberum Arbitrium* (LA). But since this fails to coincide with a new vision as in **B**, the Fourth Vision in **C** goes on until 18.179, only implicitly indicating an inner dream at the point parallel to B 16.18–19, and with almost no revision between 37 and 155. From 210–83 LA delivers a diatribe against corruption in the Church, provoking Will's clerkly rejoinder on Charity's absence from the contemporary world, and from 284–372*a* a fervent homily on the nature of CHARITY that recalls and develops from Patience's disquisition on POVERTY in 43–155. This long instruction, lasting through 17.1–321, is punctuated by five (mainly) short questions and interjections from the Dreamer at 314–15, 334–7, 17.1–3, 125, 150. But most of XVII comprises a single speech like its source B XV where, after the Dreamer's 'charity' intervention at 148–62, ANIMA's vast discourse is broken by four similar instances of question / rejoinder / exclamation at 151–64, 175, 195, 197.

(i) 1–155 1–21 describe the spiritual danger of riches, omitting a passage (B 145–54) that tries to accommodate earthly wealth and heavenly reward with the justice of God, leaving the situation of the rich less hopeful in **C** (cf. also the omission of B 168–73). **4** *deyeth...to dyne*: 'does he die...who dines'. **9** is metrically acceptable as it

stands, but the incompleteness of the thought suggests a possible lacuna in Cx, which could be adequately filled by B 141b (see *TN*).

B 142–57 develop a semi-syllogistic argument by analogy from the world of experience in the half-acre and contemporary conditions of wages and desert. Rich men cannot justly get 'paid' twice, but if they use their wealth to help the poor, they get a second payment as a bounty (not a wage). However, since they rarely do that, wealth remains a serious danger; so *if* the rich receive heavenly reward, it is not as a 'just due' but only as a generous 'extra' for good service. **B** thus affirms the 'camel through the eye of a needle' view alluded to at B 212*a*, that their salvation (though not impossible) is very hard because of entanglement in worldly selfishness. **143** *at þe laste*: at death (as spelled out in the repetition at 147). **144** *Mathew*: alluding to Mt 19:23–4. **144*a*** 'From delights to delights is a difficult crossing'; based on St Jerome's *Epistola ad Julianum,* which has 'difficile, imo impossibile est...' (*PL* 22:965). **145** *rewarde*: playing polysemantically on the other main sense at 148, to hint at a 'Platonic' connection between human and divine munificence. **146** *lawe*: both secular and religious. **147** *curteisie*: an echo of B 12.177 resonant with theological significance, denoting the 'habitual grace' that protects the rich from the dangers of wealth, especially at death. **C** places this notion of 'courtesy more than covenant' (cf. 151) earlier, in Ymaginatif's account of how the just pagan is saved (see 14.215–6). **148** *double richesse*: 'a double helping of wealth'. **151** *cote*: a pointed choice of reward, since Haukyn complained at 13.228 of getting 'few robes' from earthly lords. It may be analogically implied that the sanctifying grace given through absolution, in returning him to the state of original righteousness conferred by baptism, is the 'courteous' gift of a second *cote of cristendom* (B 13.274). **153** *double hire*: ingeniously equating the lot of the rich with that of the rest, since all receive forgiveness and happiness. **154** *Here... hir*: for the stave-pattern cf. 124 and C 15.305. **155** *bokes*: whether the allusion is to *LA* or to ascetic writings, the scarcity of righteous rich men seems certain.

10–21 The seasonal analogy resumed from 15.292–301 is more rationally handled in **C** as the vehicle ('summer') is introduced *before* the tenor ('happiness'). **13** *myssomur*: around June 21, the summer solstice, and June 24, the Feast of St John. This marked the 'hungry gap' or period of scarcity between the last of the previous season's corn and that of the new harvest (Lammastide), when there would be little to spare for beggars (Frank 1990:89–90); cf. also B 178. The assimilated form (if original) may hint a sly pun on 'miss-summer'. **17** *somur somtyme*: the homophonically punning phrase from 15.299, here repeated in a prayer. **21** *for þe beste*: affirming that it is not from the 'nounpower' of God that wealth is unevenly spread, but for a providential reason (to give rich people opportunities for acts of charity).

22–36 22 *vs alle*: a striking revision; all need God's mercy and the virtue of humility, and **B**'s special concern for the souls of the rich may have appeared insensitive in the aftermath of 1381, when the authorities resorted to oppression but had no remedies to offer for social ills. *rode*: where the divine pity was supremely shown; recalling 1.164–6. **25–42** connect the wealth / poverty dyad with the confession triad through imagining sacramental penance as a kind of spiritual wealth that confers the power to endure literal poverty and, because equally accessible to all Christians, makes them in a sense all equal. **25–32** take up B 14.22, which was excised at that point in **C**. **25–6** *clanse...kulle*: cf. B 14.16–17, 91. **31a** 'Heartfelt contrition, oral confession, satisfaction through works'. **33–4** mimic echoically through internal rhymes the basic idea of 'sacramental wealth' through 'the abundant riches of [God's] grace' (cf. Eph 2:4–8) as a 'spiritual levelling' that makes all Christians potentially 'equals'. The Triad interpreted in terms of the grades of penitence creates a new spiritual hierarchy to supersede the 'carnal' one based on riches. **35** *charite*: perhaps personified, as a shared name for Christ and the Christian who is in a state of sanctifying grace. *chartre*: presumably of manumission from the 'serfdom' of sin (cf. on *acquitaunce* B 190 below). **36** *domesday*: recalling the intercessory rôle of Dowel described at 9.350–1.

B 168–95 Of these lines, **171–80a** are arguably dispensable because repetitive, 172 repeating 13.162 and 173 the sense of 171a, 179 that of 175; but omission of **174–80a**, with its skilful rhetorical patterning and delicate wordplay (*fulle...carefulle*, and *Conuertimini* 'Platonically' echoing *Conforte*), is a real poetic loss. **168** *rupe...men*: presumably through granting them grace to save themselves by acting *rewfulliche* towards the poor. *rewarde*: with perhaps a play on its other sense (cf. 145), since the rich have an opportunity to 'pay' the poor out of what God has given. *prisones*: visiting prisoners was recognised as a 'corporal work of mercy', but few could see the poor (see 174) as also figuratively 'imprisoned' by their want. **169** *ingrati*: 'ungrateful' in both legal and theological senses, 'refusing to reciprocate one's lord's kindness' (Alf*G* 73–4) and therefore (anticipating 170) 'ungracious', i.e. 'rejecting God's grace and so rejected by Him' (cf. B 17.254=19.220). Similar wordplay occurs in the *Floretus*, one of the *Auctores Octo* texts: *Non sis ingratus domino si vis fore gratus* 'Be not ungrateful to the Lord if you would be pleasing to him' (Alf*Q*). **179** *in þi riche*: a pun is possible here; for since both poor and rich may enter Christ's *kingdom*, he might be able to comfort the distressed 'in' or through the generosity of the *rich*, thereby comforting 'all'. **180a** 'Be converted to me, and you shall be saved' (Is 45:22). **181** *in...gen=*

tries: 'in virtue of his nobility of nature'; *in genere* 'in the kind or genus of'; a term in grammar and logic. **184** 'To receive baptism in the name of the Trinity'; cf. Mt 28:19. **185** *kynnes synnes*: the emphatic internal rhyme underlining the categorical assurance given by the sacrament. **186** *fille...folie...falle*: pararhyming *annominatio* hinting not that sin is trivial but that it is (in Julian of Norwich's term) *behovely* 'necessary' (*Showings*, ch. 27, p. 405) and so men should not be oppressed by a sense of hopelessness but always look to the mercy promised by God. **188** *as many siþes*: cf. Mt 18:22. **189** *pouke*: Walafrid Strabo in his *Expositio in Johannem* observes that 'homo percussus a *diabolo* qui credit *passionem Christi* liberabitur' (*PL* 114:906). *plede*: envisaging the Devil as counsel for the prosecution against man. *punysshe*: by making the sinner suffer from 'scrupulosity', the anxiety that he is not truly forgiven and reconciled to God. **190** *acquitaunce*: 'a document in evidence of a transaction...such as a release' (MED s.v.), here release from sin, obtained through baptism and penance. 'To be able to show a sealed release or acquittance was crucial; otherwise the law regarded a person to be still in debt' (Alf*G*). In the *Stanzaic Life of Christ* the Latin rubric after 6408 (on Christ's granting 'manumission' to mankind) defines *manumissio* as *litera acquietancie quando natiuus redimitur* 'a letter of acquittance when a serf buys his freedom' (ed. Foster, p. 215). **190a** *Pateat...*: 'Let it be manifest, etc.'; the first words of a deed, recalling a royal letter patent (192) declaring that the accused is released under surety (from Christ). *Per...*: 'Through the Passion of Our Lord [Jesus Christ]'; indicating the source of the reconciling sacraments' efficacy. This metaphor may derive from Col 2:14, which describes the forgiveness of sin through Christ's Passion in terms of the deletion of a document of accusation against the sinner. It is taken up again when the 'patent' becomes the tablet of the Old Law that awaits the 'seal' of *cros and Cristendom, and Crist þeron to honge* (B 17.10, 6). **191** *borwe*: mainprise, on which see Keen 2002:91–3 who, however, does not discuss this acquittance (cf. Steiner 2000:101–2). **192** *parchemyn*: the material of a letter patent from the king, figuring the disposition of humility needed for the saving power of Christ's Passion, accessible through the sacraments, to be 'written down' or made operative for man's soul. **194** *decourreþ*: from OF *decorir* 'to run or flow away from'; probably used by **L** to mean 'shun, avoid'. Kane 2000:50–1 takes the verb as derived from Lat. *decoriare* 'scrape clean from' (for which there is likewise no other ME instance); but though the sense would fit well with *principalliche...but*, the sudden shift to imperative pl. is unprepared for. The omission of the figure in **C** may register awareness that the line was obscure.

37–112 38 *preyeres*: a well-advised revision; since 'a piece of the Paternoster' was what Patience offered Haukyn at

49 (and cf. 372*a*), it would be unfitting to question its efficacy here. *Rome*: see on Pr 48, 4.123. **40–1** *writeth... freres*: i.e. the names of donors, as promised by the friar-confessor to Meed at 3.51–4. *fals*: if provided by absolved sinners who have no purpose to amend. **42** *in comune riche*: 'collectively wealthy' / '[live] in a society that is wealthy because each of its members desires the well-being of all'. This need not imply that all property must be owned in common, a theory of pagan origin attributed to the friars at 22.276 and repudiated at 277–9 as against God's law. It cannot be doubted that **L** knew the practice of the early Jerusalem community (Ac 2:44–5) was the basic model for religious orders and admired the spirit of mutual aid in *cloistre* and *scole*. But the b-verse stresses that Christians must *will* the common good above private or personal advantage, 'so distribution should undo excess' and 'all became poor' (Baldwin 2001:108), i.e. 'had enough'. Underpinning the social ideal advanced here is the same conception (see on 25–42) of the sacramental graces won by Christ as spiritual goods Christians share in, the 'common wealth' of the *holy comune in heuene* (5.86), on which the Church (Unity) is meant to be modelled. **43** *seuene synnes*: an account of the Deadly Sins attacking the individual soul that is transitional between the 'enacted' representation of them as types of 'Sinner' in Vision Two and as personified enemies in Vision Eight that *assailen* the Christian *comune* sheltering in Unity (21.337ff). The specific argument propounded here is that sin must be a greater threat to the rich than to the poor because vices are 'armed' by wealth, but 'disarmed' by patient poverty. In fact, although seven appear (in the order Pride, Anger, Gluttony, Covetousness, Avarice, Lechery and Sloth) the fourth and fifth are two aspects of Greed while Envy, a likelier vice of the have-nots than of the haves (except *in scole*) is prudently omitted as doubtless weakening the case. **44** *fend folleweth*: cf. 1.38. **47** *pore...ryche*: behind this realistic recognition that honour is valued by *all* human beings may lie the example of the technically 'poor' Doctor of Divinity (still present in Patience's and the audience's mind) who was 'maed sitte furste, as for the moste worthy' (15.39). **50–1** *fer...heuene*: Patience's placing of *wit*, a 'gift of nature', above wealth, a 'gift of fortune' (cf. *CT* X 452–43), may be thought to contradict Ymaginatif's linking of both as 'encumbrances' (14.17). But the collocation of wit with *wisdom* and of wisdom with *heauen* here suggests that the phrase denotes neither, but a 'gift of grace,' specifically the first of the Holy Ghost's seven gifts (Is 11:2); whence the indigent wise man's prayer is sooner heard than that of the wealthy fool. **53** The rich man's progress is slowed by changes in direction or gradient because of the weight of his goods ('worldly concerns impede spiritual growth'). **B 212***a* See on C 11.203. **54***a* 'For their works follow them' (Apoc 14:13); referring to the saints who

from their labours rest (vs 13). **55** *Batauntliche*: possibly coined by **L** from OF *batant*. **56** The joy is the reward not of the poverty itself but of the patience it is borne with. **B 215***a* 'Blessed are the poor [in spirit]; for theirs is the kingdom of heaven' (Mt 5:3). The wording may be influenced by Lk 6:20, which omits *spiritu*; but that is surely implied, since 215 and 220 make clear the necessity of the *patientia sanctorum* (Apoc 14:12) that brings heavenly 'rest' (cf. the identification of poverty and patience with respectively the first and last of the Beatitudes in *Patience* 34–45). **58** *mayster...man*: alluding to the arrogant behaviour of nobles' retainers. The phrasing recalls B 13.40, reminding that one can be proud of intellectual as well as material 'wealth', while conversely spiritual 'poverty' (humility) is possible, if difficult, for the literally rich. **60** *none*: because humility, the root of Christian virtue, is the specific against pride, the root of all sin (cf. *CT* X 475), and literal poverty disposes to meekness. **61** recalls *Rechelesnesse* at 13.2. **63** *breed...drynke*: avoiding the implication in *broke loues* 'scraps of bread' B 222 that beggary (cf. A 12.70) is being tacitly recommended. But since (against this) the change of *asken* B 229 to *begge* does suggest 'destitution' rather than 'basic sufficiency', it could be that poverty here is intended to signify only 'dependence on others for one's livelihood'. **64** *at werre*: the hostility between pride and humility (43), elaborated in traditional 'psychomachic' terms as a physical struggle between the deadly sins and (patient) poverty. **66** *wrastle*: an extended metaphor throughout which the vehicle is amusingly at odds with the tenor, since the poor man 'wins' the match by *not* wrestling (= 'getting angry'). *he*: i.e. Wrath. **68** *he*: i.e. again Wrath. **73** *glotonye*: i.e. even if he is able to indulge in drinking, he still has to 'pay' for it by sleeping on cold bed-straw. **76** *his...synne*: hendiadys for 'his great sin of gluttony'. **78 C** substitutes for **B**'s benign sympathy 'condign punishment': whether or not discomfort engenders contrition, it diminishes pleasure. **79–89** treat both aspects of Greed separately (see on 6.196), notionally making the total of sins up to seven, despite the omission of Envy. **84** *layk...neuere*: so the bout would be cancelled after the contenders had been measured. **88** *boest*: i.e. for the thief; but the poor man is better off because he has nothing to attract a burglar. **93** *serue nat*: fail in his religious observance. **95** *gretteste help*: cf. Haukyn's reliance on charms at 13.341–2. **96–7** Since the poor man always 'serves' another, he belongs to Christ's own liveried retinue, whether he is virtuous or not (cf. Js 2:1–6); and even where he *fails* to serve God (through sloth), his poverty means that he bears the Saviour's 'badge'. **99** *of puyr rihte*: 'as a matter of sheer justice' (cf. 15.290); categorical, where **B** is more tentative. **101** An unusual double-staved line with alternative scansion on *m* or vowels. **101–3** perhaps allude to the example *par excellence* of St Francis of Assisi, the son of a rich merchant, who renounced his wealth at the age of 24. **105** *paramour*: 'beloved'. The contrast in sense with 'husband' seen in Gower *CA* 4.1269 is negated here: as her *make* she feels for him *kynde loue of þe mariage* 'the affection natural and right towards a spouse', as noted by *Sk*, who finds an echo of Eph 5:31 (citing Gen 2:24). **110** *So hit fareth*: 'That is how it is', i.e. such a person greatly deserves love (from God). *persone*: possibly punning on 'person' and 'parish-priest' (cf. 13.99–102 above). **111** *weddeth*: as St Francis weds the Lady Poverty in the C13th Latin allegory the *Sacrum Commercium*. **112** *syb... semblable*: Christ's poverty as a model being stressed by mendicant rigorists.

113–55 113 *angryliche*: the only sign in **C** that Patience's unworldly idealism might set a nerve jangling in the representative of the common man. **114** *What is pouerte*: a translation of the question *Quid est Paupertas?* introducing the quoted Latin original that follows in answer. **B 274–5** 'For God's sake, Patience, you keep on singing the praises of poverty — but what exactly is it?' (For the contemporary social background to this discussion see Shepherd 1983, Aers 1983, Pearsall 1988, and the perceptive account of the oxymoronic character of the medieval concept of poverty in Scott 2001:141–53). **115–15a** 'Poverty is "a hateful good". It is the removal of cares; possession without calumny; a gift of God; the mother of health; a path free of worry; mistress of wisdom; business with no losses; [it is], amidst fortune's uncertainty, happiness without anxiety'; from the *Gnomae* of Secundus Philosophus, quoted by Vincent of Beauvais, *Speculum historiale* X, 71 and by others (AlfQ). Chaucer's paraphrase in *CT* III 1195–1200 may show the influence of **L** (e.g. the necessary association with patience at 1197–8) and the whole quotation appears as the Latin gloss to this passage in the Ellesmere MS. **115** scans as a macaronic Type Ib with cognative b-verse staves. *odibile bonum*: the oxymoron highlighting the contrast between poverty's superficial unattractiveness and its spiritual worth (see B 286a). Except for *donum Dei* (see on 134a), poverty's 'points' are of broadly non-Christian origin and not *prima facie* antithetically opposed to the seven sins severally but especially focused upon greed, envy, anger and gluttony. **116** *construe*: Actyf's perplexity amusingly recalling the King's at Conscience's learned 'grammatical' analogy of *mede* and *mercede* (3.340–2), and providing a motive for Patience to elaborate in ways that draw his exposition closer to the preceding one of the deadly sins, though they hardly qualify as a 'proper [strict] construing' of the Latin. **B 279** *by...vnderstonde*: 'so that you may understand'; see MED s.v. *bi* conj. 2b, citing only this example. **120** *goed*: rhetorical *repetitio* of co-polysemes, hinting 'Platonically' at the metaphysical oneness of ethical and logical categories. *greue a litel*: corresponding to **B**'s account of *odibile bonum*, which **C** does not cite directly

(in **B** the Latin 'points' come before, in **C** after their exposition in English). The subtle comparison of poverty with contrition in B 282–5 serves to link the Stoic ascetic values of the definition with the Christian penitential doctrine of B 14.81–96; but **C** is perhaps wise to confine the moral teaching wholly within the practical terms Actyf might readily understand. **B 286** *cura animarum*: 'the care of souls', i.e. a force that brings spiritual strength and encouragement. The canonical sense of 'the exercise of a clerical office...by a person legitimately appointed for the purpose' (AlfQ) seems to have no relevance in this context, but the expression's ambiguity may partly account for its deletion (on its relation to *remocio curarum* see Schmidt 1987:111). **122** *sothe to declare*: i.e. as a juror at the assise. **126a[1]** *Nolite...*: 'Judge not, that you may not be judged' (Mt 7:1); an opportunistic use of the 'commandment', which warns against individual 'judging' of one's neighbour's character, not against performing one's civic obligations. But a poet familiar with legal matters would be aware that medieval jurors often found on a defendant's (real or supposed) character rather than the facts of the case. **127** 'Poor people seldom become very well-off except through coming into a lawful inheritance'. The play on *rihte / rihtfole* recalls that on *wel* at B 278. **128** *wightes*: specified as a characteristic vice of the covetous at 6.258 and 19.246. *vnselede mesures*: like Haukyn at B 13.359; measures used by brewers and taverners had to to be sealed with the alderman's seal to attest their true capacity (*Sk*). The suggestion here seems to be that dealing honestly is likely to leave a man poor. **130** 'It's hard to raise a loan if people know you're badly off'; but in a society with inordinately high interest-charges, there were advantages in not falling into the 'credit-trap'. **133** *folies*: gluttony, lechery and sloth. **134** *collateral*: possibly alluding to the legal notion of 'collateral warranty' (AlfG); but a non-technical sense of the term (first used here) seems likeliest, these spiritual advantages being to the poor man unexpected gains or 'blessings in disguise'. **134a** *Donum Dei*: probably from the opening of St Augustine's *De Patientia* (PL 40:611), which states that 'Patience is so great *a gift of God* that it is even ascribed to Him who grants it to us' (Schmidt 1969:28, Orsten 1969, Baldwin 1990; and cf. 13.198–200). Augustine is explicitly acknowledged at 151. **136a** 'Mother of health' because poverty protects from excess, the cause of many illnesses (cf. 8.290–4); but since too *little* food would also undermine health, 'poverty' must denote 'sufficiency' rather than 'want'. B 299–300 make clear that the temptation is probably lechery (see *TN* on 136). **137** *pees*: because freeing from anxiety about violent assault ('wrath'). *pase of Aultoun*: a road or 'pass' on the Surrey-Hampshire border, at this time forested; a notorious haunt of outlaws (cf. B 17.103) who lay in wait for merchant-trains travelling to the fairs near Winchester (see 6.211,

13.51). **141** 'Given that he has no idea whom he might encounter by night'. **B 304***a* 'The povre man, whan he goth by the weye, Bifore the theves he may synge and pleye' (Juvenal, *Satires* X, 22 as translated by Chaucer in *CT* III 1193–4). The reading with *paupertas* for original *vacuus* is found in Bromyard, *SP* I:86/1 (Alf*Q*). **141***a Seneca...*: the Roman Stoic philosopher (*c.* 4 BC–65 AD), tutor of Nero. The exact source of this line (which will scan in both versions as a Type IIIb) is untraced; but the sentiment is in keeping with those in his Epistles 2 and 8 and with various remarks in the tract *De Paupertate* made up of quotations from Seneca's writings. **144** echoes B Pr 51, and the truth / treasure dichotomy is reminiscent of Holy Church's teaching in 1.81. Truth provides the poor man a perfect 'tuning-fork' for his speech in that, being free from cupidity, he is free to say what he really thinks. **147** *no loes*: 'not caring' about loss is a mark of the humility from which charity grows (cf. 288, where it is a mark of charity itself); seeking no material gain, he does not risk the *damnum* 'loss' of his own soul. *wynne*: either as the direct end of his *chaffare* or as a 'return' from others on his 'outlay' of unselfishness. **149** *here*: presumably the pronoun, with referent 'soul' (as is clear from // B 313 and would be clearer in **C** with *his* omitted). **151** *Austyn*: see on 134*a* above. **152** 'That true patient poverty meant humility in this life'; adding the more important positive part of Augustine's teaching, that the purpose of removing worldly anxieties is to free the soul to 'mind the things that are above, not the things that are upon the earth' (Col 3:2). **153** The added 152 removes an ambiguity in **B**, which might inadvertently imply lack of concern for *spiritual* 'business', the only proper *sollicitudo* (cf. also Rom 12:11). **153***a* The ninth point echoes and is the fruit of the first (121*a*): removing the wrong kind of *cura* brings the right kind of *felicitas*.

B 320–32 One of **C**'s chief structural omissions, in **B** ending the Fourth Vision with a dramatic emotional climax that plausibly motivates Will's awakening in the best tradition of medieval 'dream-vision realism' (see Hieatt 1967:89–97). **321** *for Dowelis sake*: 'because I could not do (anything for do-) well.' **323** *Synne...euere*: a sentiment echoed by Julian of Norwich (see on 186 above). *sory*: with polysemy perhaps intended, since Haukyn's melancholy is caused by thinking of 'the blight man was born for', though he also seems to repent with a new and comprehending contrition. **324** *wepte...eighen*: recalling earlier 'conversion' tears, those of Will (whose surrogate he in some manner is) at B 5.61, of Robert at B 5.463 and of Longeus at B 18.91. **326** *Swouned*: an extreme reaction reminiscent of such as Margery Kempe of Lynn (*Book*, p. 219). As with Will's faint at B 16.19, its removal may suggest doubts about emotional demonstrativeness as a true measure of spiritual sincerity. **327–8** Haukyn's judgement that possessions or superiority over others

minister to pride shows him as having fully accepted Patience's teaching at 59–61 above. *lordshipe*: here any kind of ownership of land. **330–1** *shame...couere*: his sinfulness being such that he should never be entitled to wear the clothes he coveted (at B 13.228–30), except for decency's sake. **331** *careyne*: the contemptuous term seeming apt because it is to *corpus mortis huius* 'the body of this death' (Rom 7:24) that Haukyn now realises he was enslaved. The whole of Romans ch. 7 (on man's 'carnal' incapacity to *perficere bonum* 'accomplish that which is good' has great relevance to this scene. **332** *wepte...awakede*: i.e. both at the noise within the dream (like that at 18.179 below) and at the intensity of the emotion, which Will shares empathetically with his surrogate Haukyn. The reverse-sequence (*falling* asleep through a strong access of his *own* feeling) has been illustrated at B 11.4–5 and will be again at C 5.108.

B XIV *ends here and* B XV *begins, running parallel with* C *to the end of* XVII

(ii) 156–372*a* contain the first part of an extended dialogue between Will and LIBERUM ARBITRIUM, who does most of the speaking. This large and significant revision divides B XV (which is only a little shorter than B V) towards mid-point, and redefines the relation between the Dreamer and his alter-ego Actyf, in whose 'free will' he now encounters an image of his own 'inner self'. The new structure is less monolithic but also less elegant than in **B**; for there Anima's passus-long monologue prepares for the Sixth Vision (an inner dream) to occupy (and lead to an awakening nearly coincident with the end of) Passus XVI, neatly balancing the opening's introductory material. **C**'s less tidy shape may be meant to reflect the fluidity of the dream state more accurately, but it makes for difficulty of comprehension and could be due to incomplete revision. The main structural boundary occurs clearly enough at the end of C 18.179; but another less explicit one seems intended at C 18.4, corresponding to the start of the inner dream in **B**. The re-naming of **B**'s ANIMA as Liberum Arbitrium may arise from an altered understanding of the traditional Isidorean powers of the soul (see Sanderlin 1941; Donaldson 1949:188–96; Schmidt 1969[2]; Harwood 1973[2]). But making him Actyf's 'leader' links this movement more closely to the encounter preceding it (Patience is presumed present throughout this dialogue, though never speaking again after 162). **156–71** The sudden transition lacks smoothness, as the new personage abruptly supplants Actyf (who never returns), and the 'interior' character of his interchange with Will is less obvious than in the dialogue with Anima in **B**. **156** *ledare*: a neutral term, but always positive in **L**, as is probably confirmed by the later Latin definition in 191–2. *Liberum Arbitrium*: 'Free Choice' more than simply 'Free Will', stressing the moral knowledge that gives rational decisions their 'freedom' rather than the 'existential' autonomy that *may* defy 'the dictates of that reason [or] recognition and observance of the will of God, [which] is for [man] true freedom' (*Pe*). The added definition at 199*a* (on which see Schmidt 1969²:134–43, Harwood 1973²:680–95), removes the ambiguity in the English at 191 and puts this beyond doubt. One motive for introducing a personification of the Soul's 'rationally determinative' power may be to counterbalance the affective/volitional thrust of the main arguments advanced in the Third Vision. **157** *Consience...Clergie*: because truly 'free' choice will be informed by both the innate moral sense and the teaching of the Church. **160** *Liberum Arbitrium* (LA) clearly supports Patience on the superiority of poverty, but his phrasing draws upon the omitted conclusion to B XIV. Thus the echo of B 14.327 in 158 is one of the poem's more striking 'intertextual' moments, almost as if Actyf's 'deep self' were speaking about his shallower ('Haukyn') self. **161** *preyde Pacience*: Will's new-found courtesy sits ill with the rebuke to him at 210 below (uncancelled from B 50). **162** The referent of *oper name* is obscure, since the Dreamer does not yet know any of his interlocutor's 'other names'; perhaps Patience means, 'Ask him by what other name he is known'. **164** *creature*: not by 'creation' (as all men are created by God) but by his 'new creation' through baptism. **166** *a party*: 'partly, in part', since not all who possess free choice are Christians. **167** *Peter the porter*: because traditionally thought of as gate-keeper of heaven, and represented in iconography as holding 'the keys of the kingdom' given him by Christ (Mt 16:19; cf. Pr 128–9). *fauchen*: his traditional iconographic emblem (see Baker 1978:pl.19), since as a Roman citizen St Paul was believed to have been executed by beheading with a sword

B 15.1–15 2 *Er*: implying that the knowledge eventually comes, when Will asks Kynde what *be best to lerne* (20/22.207) and receives the answer 'Love'. **3** *wit*: both 'knowledge' and 'understanding'. *fool*: contrasted with the dull 'daffe' of B 1.140 and looking forward to its ironic 'Pauline' use at the point where Will joins the 'fools' (the followers of Conscience) who seek refuge in Unity (22.61). At 10 Will's failure to show conventional 'respect of persons' leads perforce to his being held a worldly incompetent. **4** *lakkede my lif*: condign punishment for the behaviour Reason condemned at B 11.386; but the suffering it produces prepares him to receive further disclosures. **5–6** echo Js 2:1–3, an important vindicating authority for **L**'s entire enterprise. *and*: implying 'because'. **7** *persons*: like the *grete syres* of Pr 177. **10** *folk*: the *peple* on whom Holy Church comments at 1.5–9. *raued*: reflecting the judgement of 'the world' on those who give first place to 'the things that are above'. **11** *Reson*: the authoritative figure whose wisdom Will

'rebuked' at B 11.372; having 'suffred', he is ready to 'conceyue moore þoruȝ Reson' (B 11.411–12), who will now have 'ruþe' on him. *rokked*: implying that the Christian 'fool' is a kind of 'child'; as Will is to learn shortly, Charity is a 'childissh þyng' (B 15.149). **12** *sorcerie*: because raising bodiless spirits was the province of magicians; cf. *coniured* 14, where there may be humorous wordplay on MED sense 2(a). *wiþalle*: both 'to be sure', as at closely parallel B 18.115 (MED s.v. *with-al* adv. 1(c)), and 'altogether, completely' (1(a)). *sotil*: the soul (as noted by Simpson 1990:172n) being called 'subtilis et invisibilis' in the pseudo-Augustinian *De Spiritu et Anima* (*PL* 40:789). **13** *tolde*: an inward 'telling', since the soul has no bodily organs. **14–17** The insistent *k* alliteration underscores the catechetical character of this interchange.

171–80 are added to explain the new character's nature and function. **172–3** vary the phrase *somtyme* by shifting the stress from the first to the second element; 172 *may* be Type IIIa (see *TN*), 173 is probably IIIc. **174** *Layk*: i.e. '(consent to) engage in (some act)'; a submerged metaphor from 'play at a sport'. **175** *do wel or wykke*: making plain that both the virtue and its antithesis depend on the agent's free consent. *a wille with a resoun*: a loose but memorable rendering of the volitional and rational elements in *Liberum Arbitrium*; see further Harbert 1990. **178–9** 'It's like the way wood and fire support each other, and the same applies to [man's material nature and his] spiritual will'. LA will fit well enough in this figurative dichotomy if regarded as synecdochic for 'soul'. **180** presumably denotes the state of full possession of one's mental faculties.

181–99*a* provide a comprehensive analysis of the soul's multiple aspects by giving it ten (nine) different Latin names (see Schmidt 1969:151–2). Eight denote its vital, cognitive and affective powers, one a virtue of its volitional power (*love*), and one its condition in separation from the body (*spirit*). All are defined, but *Anima, Animus* and *Liberum Arbitrium* are given no vernacular equivalents, though presumably only the last lacked one (on the coined phrase *fre wit* as a possible such name see on 10.51 and Schmidt 1968¹:168–9). **181** *Anima*: the soul as life-principle, 'animans' (see earlier on 10.134 and Schmidt 1968²:363–4). **182** *Animus*: the appetitive and volitional capacity. **183** *Mens*: the mind in its active reasoning function, perhaps meant to recall the personification *Thouhte* at 10.72ff (*thought* is Chaucer's equivalent at *HF* 523 for his source Dante's *mente*). **184** *Memoria*: 'recollection,' in the sense of the spiritual function of 'calling to mind [God, one's past sins, one's benefactors etc]'. This is the only sense of English *memorie* in **L**, who more often uses *mynde* (MED s.v. n. (1), 2 and 3a) for 'memory' (see A 11.216 and cf. MED s.v. *memorie* n. 2(a), 4(b)). **186** *Racio*: a term with legal-moral resonances and a special association with justice fully explained in Alford 1988[1]. **187** *Sensus*: both 'sense-perception' (whence *welle* 'source') and 'understanding of the meaning of language' (whence *telleth*). The Latin term often answers to (*kynde*) *wit* in **L**'s customary usage (see on Pr 141–7 above). **189** *chalenge...chepe*: semi-figurative uses that signify acts of choosing to do or not do something. **190** *Concience*: see on Pr 95. *Goddes...notarie*: because divinely implanted in the soul, with the power and responsibility of 'reckoning' or evaluating all one's moral acts. **191** *gode...ille*: ostensibly expressing an 'Augustinian' understanding of free-will (see Schmidt 1969[2]:141). But if it is possible that *do* is meant to take *gode dedes* as its exclusive object and *do nat* only to govern *ille* (*dedes*), this syntactic ambiguity will find itself resolved in the purely positive conception of LA as given in the Latin definition at 199*a*. **193** *lelly*: in accordance with 'love' truly understood as charity. **196** *spirit*: the common formal term (= native *goest*) for the immaterial soul when separated from its body (as in Mt 27:50, Lk 24:39, I Pet 3:19). **197** *Austyn*: author of treatises on the soul; but the allusion here may be to the *De Spiritu et Anima* (see Schmidt 1969:143–4), which was ascribed to him in the period. *Ysodorus*: St Isidore (*c.* 560–636), Bp. of Seville, whose encyclopaedic *Etymologiae seu Origines* is **L**'s direct source for everything here except for **C**'s LA, which he may have added from Godfrey of Poitiers (Schmidt 1969[2]:142–3). **199***a* *Anima...Spiritus est*: 'The SOUL chooses for itself a variety of names according to its varying modes of operation. As giving life to the body, it is *Soul*; as willing, *Intention*; as knowing, *Mind*; as bringing to mind things past, *Memory*; as judging, *Reason*; as perceiving, *Sense*; as loving, *Love*; as turning from evil towards good, *Free Choice*; as breathing (the life-breath), *Spirit*' (Isidore, *Etymologies* XI.i.13). Like Patience's nine-fold definition of Poverty at 115–15*a*, this *divisio* (nine-part in **C** as well as **B** if *Mens* was accidentally omitted by **L**), is accompanied by an English paraphrase (181–96), here before not after the Latin. The influence of St Bernard's conception of free-will as reflecting the image of God in man is persuasively argued in Donaldson 1949:189ff. But the wording of the newly added clause on LA directly echoes Godfrey of Poitiers's '[liberi-arbitrii] est declinare a malo et eligere bonum', a formulation that itself conflates Ps 36:27 ('Declina a malo et fac bonum') and Is 7:15 ('reprobare malum, et eligere bonum'). For an analysis of this list see Schmidt 1969[2]:151–2.

200–39*a* **202** 'Prelate, Pontiff, Metropolitan [= primate of an ecclesiastical province], Bishop, Pastor'. **206** *and of myn*: a rebuke at odds with Will's having been *encouraged* by Patience to 'assay' LA's names (162), and perhaps reflecting imperfect revision at this point. **208–9** express a 'Faustian' craving for knowledge of everything, theoretical and practical (*sciences*; *craftes*). In exceed-

ing what is possible for a created being, it resembles Lucifer's *superbia* understood as desire for an omniscience leading to omnipotence. **211***a* See on 1.111*a*. **212** *a3eyns...resoun*: 'against every law of nature and of reason'. **213** *creature*: used not *proprie* of Christ but loosely as = 'being', or else with specific reference to his human nature (as divine, he would 'conne al'). **214** *Salamon*: see on 3.121. **215–215***a* 'Just as it is not good for a man to eat much honey, so he that is a searcher of majesty [*sc.* that of God] shall be overwhelmed by [his] glory' (Prov 25:27). On the reading *opprimatur* 'let him be overwhelmed', see *TN*. **216** The translation-response recalls Patience's words at 118 and reminds that the one whose 'leader' LA is remains the *lewed* Actyf. **218–19** do not improve on the compressed but pungent B 58–9, since the repeat of *worche* 218b, though skilfully stress-varied in the T-type 219 as *wél wórche*, is less telling than the sense-varied *do* of B 59 with medial pause before *double scape* (a notion correlating with that of 'double reward' at B 14.148). These lines do not cite but tacitly evoke Lk 12:47–8, which is quoted at B 12.56*a*=C 14.18*a*. **220–1** 'Blessed the man who does the Bible scan / And turns words into works as best he can'; from St Bernard's *Tractatus de Ordine Vitae* (*PL* 184:566), whose scriptural source is Mt 7:24: 'Omnis...qui audit *verba* mea haec et *facit* ea, assimilabitur viri sapienti...' (Alf*Q*). **223***a* 'Craving for knowledge deprived man of the glory of everlasting life'; from St Bernard's *Sermo IV in Ascensione Domini* (*PL* 183:311). The two quotations set against the Dreamer's (supposed) intellectual pride the spiritual humility, faith and love that St Bernard archetypally represents (Leff 1958:134–5; Stiegman in Evans 2001:129–39). LA's argument, somewhat ironically, echoes that of Will's *alter ego* Rechelesnesse at 11.276ff. **224–5** improve on B 64–5 (which repeat B 57) by correcting the awkwardly asymmetrical analogy between 'honey' and 'the reasoner' (instead of 'the knowledge derived from reason'). This revision replaces a warning against the worldly arrogance displayed in scholastic speculations on God's 'absolute' and 'ordained' power (*my3tes*) with one against plain intellectual disdain like the Priest's towards Piers at B 7.131–2. **226** *pat*: 'those who'. **B 67** *likynge*: 'desire [for such knowledge]', with a probable pun on 'licking' (i.e. of the *hony* that symbolises it) and a 'Platonic' linking of desire with the body (*licame*). *licames coueitise*: that *sapientia carnis* 'wisdom of the flesh' which is 'an enemy to God' (Rom 8:7). **227** '[For I say, by the grace that is given me],...not to be more wise than it behoveth to be wise, [but to be wise unto sobriety and according as God hath divided to every one the measure of faith]' (Rom 12:3). At 22 syllables, the longest line in the poem, scanning on *s* or *p* (see *TN*); // B 69 is a simple Type IIIc. **228** *Freres*: see on 11.54. *prechen*: an accusation not easy to substantiate from surviving examples of friars' sermons to lay people, and more guardedly expressed in **C**, which allows that points made in addresses to (say) a university audience might reach the non-*litterati* indirectly, as over the host's table in a lodging. **229** *insolibles and falaes*: taken by MED (following *Sk*'s preference) as adjectives qualifying *motyues*. But while such post-positioned French *s*-pl. endings amplify the same construction and may contribute towards an effective satirical point, it is more natural to take both as noun plurals (*Pe*), translating scholastic Latin *insolubilia* 'logical paradoxes' (on which see Spade 1975, 1982) and *fallaciae* 'logical fallacies'. The real cause of concern is the problems for believers produced when dialecticians speculate on dogmas of faith, in a form such as: 'God is all-good and so cannot do evil; but God is all-powerful and so can do anything; therefore God can and cannot do evil. *Quod est insolubile*'; or, 'Christ was God, so could not die; but Christ was man and so could die; therefore Christ could and could not die. *Quod est fallacia*'. **B 71** *vnmesurables*: perhaps suggested by *mensuram fidei* in Rom 12:3 (see at 227). These 'matters' moved for debate exceed the 'measure' appropriate for 'telling of the Trinity' (which is that of reverent faith). On the French adjectival form see *MES* 277. **231** substitutes simple rhetorical *repetitio* of *ten* for **B**'s 'Platonic' punning on *bileue...bileuen*, which subtly implies a link between faith and intellectual self-restraint. However, as well as being syntactically clearer than B 72–3, the adverbial phrase *ten sythe* (pointedly balanced against *fyue wittes*) economically modifies both *teche* and *were*, intimating that frequent *repetition* of basic truths is far more worthwhile than a quest for novelty. **B 74b–75** are well omitted; for though giving a neat descending pattern of 'ten, seven, (five)', they repeat B 14.219 and B 13.410=**C** 7.69. **234** *helynge*: perhaps 'clothing [themselves]' (MED s.v. ger. (2) 2(a)), as this corresponds to *haterynge* B 78; but the commoner sense 1 'roofing' would be as apt. **239a** 'Do not be respecters of persons'; a near-quotation from Js 2:1, which itself echoes Deut 1:17 ('nec accipietis cuiusquam personam') and Prov 24:23. While Ac 10:34 'Non est *personarum acceptor* Deus' may be verbally closest (*Pe*), it refers to God, not men. The 'judgement' context of the OT originals leads AlfQ to opine that **L**'s phrase was a legal maxim. But as the reference here is to friars' cultivation of the rich rather than the poor, a source that is conceptually closer if verbally remoter might be Lk 14:11–14, which 'records' what Christ said.

B 81a–85 81a 'Let them all be confounded that adore graven things' (Ps 96:7). 'And in another place: Why do you love vanity, and seek after lying?' (Ps 4:3). **82** *glose*: Cassiodorus on Ps 4:3 (*GO*), identifying 'graven things' with *lies* and false earthly goods that cannot fulfil what they promise (*PL* 113:849). The same authority's *Expositio in XX primos Psalmos* quotes without attribu-

tion the Augustinian comment on Ps 4 cited by *Sk* contrasting truth (which makes blessed) with *vanity* and *falsehood* (= love of worldly goods). **83** *If...wit*: 'If I'm grossly misrepresenting you because of my ignorant lack of understanding...' *brennyng*: a vivid asseveration like Book's later at B 18.254 (20.264). Heretics were already burnt at the stake in France, but in England not before the execution of the Lollard William Sawtrey a little before the statute *De Heretico Comburendo* of 1401, which confirmed a (long unused) canonical penalty.

240–83 severely attack the worldliness of contemporary priests and ascribe current moral decline to the laity's disillusionment with their hypocrisy. **240–53** paraphrase the Latin quoted at 271. **240** *holy writ*: not Scripture but authoritative traditional writings, as of the Church Fathers (cf. 1.125). **242** *enspireth*: 'fills with (religious) zeal'. **246** *ensample...trees*: cf. the earlier moral emblem of trees at 5.118–22; an inverted anticipation of the Tree of Charity at 18.9ff. **249** *stokkes*: an improvement in accuracy, since the root's disease will reach the branches from the trunk. **251** *to reule*: 'in which to govern'. **253–4** *leue... leue*: 'Platonic' *concatenatio* stating a condition for spiritual renewal in the Church. The image seems to echo St Bernard in *Sermones in Cantica Canticorum* 51.2: 'Itaque nec sine flore fructus, nec sine fide opus bonum' (cit. Stiegman in Evans 2001:149n58). **254** *lecherye of clothyng*: a metaphor pointing to the part played by fashionable dress in arousing admiration and desire; see 267–8 and B 15.123–4, and cf. *CT* I 156, 193–4, 262–3. **256** recalls 15.117; **257** echoes 10.78, 80; **259** adapts B 85. **260–2** The ellipsis here follows a complex construction (with incidental loss of tense-sequence in *amenden*): 'Laymen would be reluctant not to follow your teaching and renounce sin, more as a consequence of your example than (they would fail to do this) as a consequence of your not practising what you preach'. **263** scans cognatively on *p / b / p. braunche*: cf. *CT* X 393. **264–5** *in Latyn*: as in the C13th *Summa virtutum de remediis anime* where images of dunghill, wall and wolf-like behaviour all appear 'clustered in a passage on hypocrisy' (Wenzel 1984:94–6, and id. in Alford, ed. 1988:169). *dong-hep... snakes*: the nesting of snakes and worms in the warm interiors of dung-hills being a fact of natural history. This dunghill / snow image is found 'moralised' in *AI* 81: 'non uayr body ne is bote...ase a donghel besnewed'. But while the archetypal emblem of hypocritical deception is the 'subtle' serpent of Gen 3:1, the vice's best-known association with snakes is in John the Baptist's expression 'brood of vipers' addressed to the Pharisees and Sadducees (Mt 3:7), which seems to have been associated by **L** with Mt 23:27. **265/6** The identical end-rhyme reinforces the passage's homiletic-instructional tone. **266** *wal*: alluding to the 'whited sepulchres...full of...all filthiness' of Mt 23:27. **268** *enblaunched*: a loan-word found first here and only once later, and lexically at ease with the macaronic line's French stave-words. *bele paroles*: the fine words of their eloquent sermons which, like the whitewash on the surface of tombs, hides spiritual deadness within; to be contrasted with the *lele wordes* of B 16.6 (on these phrases see Schmidt 1983:139–41). *bele clothes*: in this context of 'hypocritical whitening', perhaps alluding ironically to the priest's alb (signifying 'integrity') and his *Asperges* prayer of purification before Mass ('lavabis me et super nivem dealbabor'), as much as to the inappropriate apparel implied by 254. The relevance of Js 2:2 (cited AlfQ) is not clear, since the rich man of that passage is neither hypocrite nor priest. **269** *lambes*: on vesting with the alb, the priest prays to be made white (*dealbatus*) with the blood of the Lamb, and there may be a learned anti-pun concealed here, since *dealbare* is Medieval Latin for 'whitewash' (see MED s.v. *whitlymen*). *wolues*: a Gospel image of 'false prophets' in sheep's clothing, the religious equivalent of the *wastours wolueskinnes* who destroy Piers's field in B 6.161. **270** *Iohannes Crisostomus*: St John Chrysostom (*c.* 347–407), Patriarch of Constantinople and Doctor of the Church; the widely-circulated homilies misascribed to him are classed as by 'Pseudo-Chrysostom'. **271** 'Just as all good comes out of the Temple, so does all evil. If the priesthood possesses integrity, the whole Church flourishes; but if it is corrupt, the faith of all withers up. If priests live in sin, the entire people turns to sin. Just as, when you see a tree pale and withered, you know it has something wrong with its root, so when you see a people undisciplined and irreligious, it is certain that their priests are diseased'. This passage from the Latin translation of pseudo-Chrysostom, Homily 38 on St Matthew (*PG* 56:839), is commenting on Mt 21, where the image of the barren fig-tree is at vs 19.

B 119–27 119 *lewed...Latyn*: this long and explicit warning to clerics, even fuller than that at B 13.71–3a, is veiled *only* by its being in Latin. **121–4** specify costly adornments judged unfitting for clerics to wear (cf. *CT* A 159–62, 195–7). **123** *Sire...Geffrey*: the common courtesy-title (= Lat. *Dominus*) for a priest (see also 6.366). **124** *ballok-knyf*: a fashionable ornamental dagger with a knobbed (testicle-shaped) haft (see Poole 1958:I, fig. 59c). **125** *porthors...plow*: recalling Piers's figurative use of 'plough' at B 7.120. *Placebo*: see on 3.463=B 3.311. **126–7** attack priests who insist on payment for their spiritual services. **272–83** affirm the 'poetic' justice or condign punishment whereby wealth that a man has unjustly obtained is spent unworthily after his death. This is a different attitude to the use of 'the mammon of iniquity' from that at 8.235–35a and 19.247–8a (each an injunction, not a description of the actual state of affairs). Laymen bequeath money to bad clerics, who leave it to people unwilling to use it to help the souls of the former. **272–3** Translinear 'trailing' rhyme

strengthens the protest and allows a mordant pun on 'provide' and '(later) discover to be' for *fynde*. **273** *Vnkynde curatours*: cf. 1.188–91. **275** 'God who is wise would never wish anything other than that...' **278** *pat*: 'that what'. **B 135** Bequests left to unworthy priests in the expectation of their prayers deprive the poor (*Goddes folk*) of a share in 'Christ's goods' (= wealth bequeathed to the Church). **280–1** *leue...Leueth...lyuen...loue*: the *concatenatio* transformed into *annominatio* as the staves move through the sequence of vowels; cf. 356. **B 147** *goode meteȝyueres*: the noun always accompanied by this adjective.

284–372a explain CHARITY through the actions of a personification of this virtue, **284–313** beginning with a sketch, on the basis of I Cor 13:4–7, of its passive or purely spiritual side. **284** The probing question about the nature of charity is triggered by a casual and 'unweighted' use of the word (like the riposte to a similar use of 'wille' at B 150). **286** echoes 5.44; **287** repeats 5.40 and 11.277. **B 152** stresses the length of the speaker's experience (*lyued* implies 'lived long'), C its social range (there seem to be echoes here of the 'autobiographical' passage). *Longe Wille*: 'Tall Will', 'Perseverance' (= *longanimitas*, the seventh fruit of the Holy Ghost); a memorable phrase intimating both his stature and his persistency. When forming an anagram with preceding *lond*, it also yields what has been taken as the poet's *kynde name*, in a manner reminiscent of the Preface to John of Bridlington's *Prophecies* (Wright, *Pol. Songs* 1859:127) explaining a verse '*Cantu* cantabit *ariae* plebs et jubilabit' ('The people of "Sing-an-air-ville" [Canterbury] / with the-singing-of-an-air will sing and rejoice'). **155** may just mean literally that 'they only give when certain of repayment (but otherwise never, however great the need)' or may relate more directly to expectations that their almsgiving will be re-paid by God in heaven. **289a** '[Charity...] is not puffed up, Is not ambitious, [seeketh not her own **B**]' (I Cor 13:4–5). **292** *nyme*: an infinitive dependent on an understood preceding *wolde*, omitted in revision. A similar auxiliary such as *wende* is needed before *fynde* and *thynketh* 294, which break the tense-sequence and ought to be preterite. **293** *sektes*: cf. 355; no Dominic, Francis or Clare is to be met with nowadays in the orders they founded. **294** *but figuratyfly*: i.e. *neuere sooþly* (B 162), only with the same relation to a body that a mirror-image has. **294a** 'We see here [*nunc* Vg] (through a glass) in a dark manner; but then face to face' (I Cor 13:12). The Pauline 'mirror' may signify the Creation or Scripture, both of which reflect, though dimly, the 'face' of God. **295** 'And I believe that is, as far as we can tell, how things really stand in relation to charity'. **296** *childische*: having the trusting innocence of 'newborn babes [who] desire the rational milk without guile' (I Pet 2:2); something very different from *fauntelte* (B 15.150). **296a (B 149a)** '[And Jesus calling unto him a little child,...said:...

Unless you [be converted and] become as little children, [you shall not enter into the kingdom of heaven **B**]' (Mt 18:2–3). That humility is the basis of charity echoes B 5.607, 11.208; saying so here serves dialectically to oppose spiritual 'childlikeness' to the childishness 'put away' by St Paul in I Cor 13:11 (the preceding verse). LA seems to urge mature Christians with a *fre liberal wille* ('open and generous, and so truly "free"') to be content to believe (in a childlike way) what they cannot see with their eyes and should not (in a childish way) ask to see. **B 164** 'In my opinion, Charity isn't something you get by force or by payment, as a prize or as a purchase'. **298** *russet*: as worn by friars and by the addressee (cf. on 10.1). **299** *cammaca*: a word from Arabic and ultimately of possible Chinese origin. **B 168** *Tarse*: Turkestan or Tartary (a region of Central Asia west of Chinese Sinkiang); first used here or at *SGGK* 571 (and cf. Mandeville's *Travels*, 24/17 linking 'cloth...of tartarie or of camaca'). **300–01** *glad...sory*: cf. Rom 12:15, quoted at A 11.193*a*, a line deleted there from **B** but retrieved for use here (B 169*b* also echoes Rom 12:14). **301–2** *childerne / Lawhe*: an image of approved (childlike) guilelessness. **304** 'It never occurs to him that anyone would lie on oath'. **306** *For... God*: 'such is his (own) reverent awe of God'. **306***a* See at B 7.59*a*, where C deletes. **308** *likene...scorne*: 'do imitations of people in order to mock them'. **309–11** recall Patience on *caritas* at 15.159–60. **312/13** *þat ilke / Þat*: 'the sort of person who'.

314–34*a* **314–15** The implication of Will's question, which verbally echoes Reason's to him at 5.26–7, is that to exercise practical charity presupposes economic independence. **316–34***a* LA's reply resumes Patience's teaching earlier on charity and on humility as the spiritual essence of 'poverty': as Charity's resources are spiritual, he can always draw on these even when he has no material means to succour those in need. **316/17** The identical rhyme added in revision underlines the quasi-catechetical character of LA's replies. **318–19** These two fleeting personifications of Charity's spiritual helpers affirm the oneness of OT and NT understandings of divine fidelity or *treuthe*. **318** *Aperis..*: 'Thou openest thy hand'; see on 15.265*a*, quoted before Patience illustrates from the case of the Seven Sleepers the efficacy of absolute dependence on God . **319** *Fiat...*: 'Thy will be done [on earth as it is in heaven]' (Mt 6:10); the third petition of the Lord's prayer and the same 'pece of þe *Paternoster* þat sholde fynde vs alle' offered by Patience to Actyf at 249–52. **320** *Credo...*: 'I believe in God the Father Almighty'. The revision here, perhaps in response to doctrinal turbulence in the 1380s, completes the list of the Church's four chief prayers that are the 'spiritual food' of Charity with the opening clause of the Apostles' Creed: sincere devotion must be complemented by right belief. **B 180** *Spera...*: 'Trust in the Lord, [and do good]' (Ps 36:3); a psalm of total trust in God,

on which see further at 13.100. **321** *purtraye...peynten*: a metaphorical evocation of the Rosary devotion; it envisages the Lord's Prayer as providing the 'outline' of faith in 'God the Father Almighty' that is 'coloured in' by the 'Hail Marys' focussed on the lives of Mary and Christ. The Rosary's three sets of five Mysteries for spiritual meditation (joyful, sorrowful and glorious), each contain ten 'Hail Marys' preceded by an 'Our Father' and followed by a 'Glory be'. *Auees*: from '*Ave* Maria, gratia plena', the opening of the prayer in Latin (Lk 1:26). **322** *pilgrimages*: symbolic ones like that of Piers 'atte plow for pouere mennes sake' (B 6.102); the wording echoes Reason's at 4.123 and Truth's at 9.34–5. **323–4** The provision of food and clothing were the first and fourth, visiting the imprisoned was the sixth of the 'corporal works of mercy' based on Mt 25:35–6. *pore men and prisones*: two separate categories, but regularly associated (and even identified) by **L** (see B 14.174). No nourishment was provided for prisoners save what was brought by *frendes* or by visitors as an act of charity. **B 183** is slightly obscure. If *hir* is a subjective genitive, the 'pardon' is something they give to their visitor, i.e. he obtains remission of *his* sins through the opportunity *they* provide. This meaning seems tonally at variance with the disinterestedness of Christian charity as defined at 157 above (*non querit que sua sunt*). However, if *pardoun* bears not its religious but its legal sense (MED s.v. 2 'release from penalty', not 1 'forgiveness of sins'), **L**'s point will be that those whom Charity visits find 'release' (relief) from the pain of their 'imprisonment' (literal or figurative) through the *bodily foode* or *goostly foode* that he brings. **324–7** Whereas **B 184–5** intimate that the mere fact of his visit and concern (*Thouʒ* 'even if') will have value, the revision (less subtly perhaps) stresses how Charity brings them, together with material help, the religious message that their condition provides an opportunity for the imitation of Christ. **329–34***a* After active good works, Charity turns to the contemplative side, weeping religious tears for the innocence lost in *ʒouthe* (metonymic for the sins of his own youth). An echo may be detected of the life of St Francis, a rich gallant before his conversion, who is named at 353–5 below. The 'washing' metaphor is that used by Conscience to Haukyn at B 14.16–28 (a passage excised in **C** perhaps to avoid confusion as well as repetition), and in the present allegory the soul is figured as a garment. The activity described here, however, is not sacramental confession but the *purgatio* that forms the first stage of the contemplative life; after sins have been forgiven, spiritual humility is to be renewed by regular acts of inner 'compunction'. **330** *hem*: the referent here (as at 331–2, B 192) being the 'accompanying attitudes' (vain self-regard, etc) of Pride (synecdochic for 'sin'), these strictly should be 'clawed' off (B 14.17) rather than 'laved'. But possibly **L** had in mind how spiritual writers like St Bernard believed that *amor carnalis* (= human love of Christ's humanity) could overcome the *vita carnalis* ('fleshly existence'), not destroying it but purifying and redirecting it towards *caritas* (*Sermons on Song of Songs* 20.9, cit. Stiegman in Evans 2001:148n26). **331** *Laboraui...*: 'I have laboured in my groanings, every night I will wash my bed: I will water my couch with my tears]' (Ps 6:7); from the first of the seven penitential psalms included in the Primer, the chief prayer-book used by lay people. This phrase provides the name of the spiritual 'laundry', anticipating the grange *Lavacrum-lex-Dei* at 19.73. **332** *breste*: the metaphorical source of his tears, and the referent of *hit* (revising *hem* B 190, which has the 'appurtenances' as referent). Striking the breast is the classic gesture of penitential sorrow (cf. 7.59–60, and Lk 18:13). **333** The stained breast is washed clean with tears; *hit* here too is altered from *hem* B 190 to make the 'washing' image fit better with the personal pronoun in the following Latin. **333a** 'Thou shalt wash me, and I shall be made whiter than snow' (Ps 50:9); familiar from the *Asperges* rite before Sunday Mass and conventionally associated with penitential tears, as by Brinton 1:84 (Alf*Q*); cf. on 268–9 above. **334a** is from the *Miserere*; see on 15.63.

336–38a 336 repeats 5.29, where Reason asks Will if this is indeed what he does. The sub-text may signify 'become a mendicant hermit (like Patience)'. **338** slightly moderates the negative tone of Anima's rejoinder at B 198, suggesting the same caution about criticising the official Church that is observable in the **C** line added earlier at Pr 138. The citation-gloss on 'Piers the Ploughman' is one of the most challenging moments in the poem; for discussion of the probable influence from Augustine's *De Trinitate* Bk XV, see Simpson 1986:9–13. **338a** 'And God saw their thoughts' (adapted from Lk 11:17 'Et ipse vidit cogitationes eorum' or the similar Mt 9:4). **L**'s arresting use of *Deus* for *ipse* makes explicit the divine nature of Jesus (to whom *Ipse* refers) and intimates that 'Piers' might be a 'guise' of Christ, just as the humanity of Jesus was of God (cf. Jn 14:9). The nuanced elaboration of this audacious idea at B 212 is omitted in **C**. **B 201–8** This attack on religious caterpillars may have been cut as both digressive and repetitive (204a=B 13.302a).

B 209–15 proclaim that Charity cannot be recognised by his outward appearance, learning (or lack of it), words or actions but only by his inner intent, something (*pat* 211) unknown to any human being except Piers, the Peter who 'is' Christ. **210** *wordes...wil*: a structurally important theme, on which see Burrow 1969:111–24 and the pertinent reference to Is 11:3 in Burrow 1993:120n4. Anima's loosely 'anti-intellectualist' position recalls Richard Rolle's in the Prologue to *Incendium Amoris*, p.147. **212** *Petrus...*: 'Peter, that is, Christ'; on this phrase see Huppé 1950:163–70, Davlin 1972:280–92 and for discussion of interpretations, Alford 1988[2]:55–6. Two

identifications are made here, of Piers with 'Petrus' and of 'Petrus' with Christ, the ambiguous term being the middle one, the Latin form of 'Piers' that inevitably suggests reference to the Apostle Peter. Separating the two names with *id est* invites a reading of the second as a gloss on the first, and hence their implicit identification at some level. The phrase itself has been thought to echo St Paul's allegorical interpretation of the rock (*petra*) from which Moses struck water in the wilderness: '*petra* autem erat *Christus*' (I Cor 10:4). This depends on accepting (Burrow 1993:121) that **L** deliberately substituted *petrus* for *petra* by way of allusion to Christ's punning promise to St Peter in Mt 16:18: 'tu es *Petrus*, et super hanc *petram* aedificabo ecclesiam meam', the scriptural basis of the Popes' claim to supreme jurisdiction in the Church (i.e. Christ the rock of salvation is present in Peter the rock of the Church). The particular divine power of seeing into men's hearts (Ps 7:10, I Par 28:9) is demonstrated in St Peter's detecting of Ananias's secret motivation (Ac 5:3–4), which Comestor (*PL* 198:1659) notes he did *praevidens in spiritu* 'through prophetic insight in the spirit' (Burrow 1993:121–2, acknowledging Goldsmith 1981:35–6). **215** *in ...*: 'on those who favour them'; a phrase with legal resonances (Gray 1986:60, Alf*G*). **216** *champion*: answering Will's denial at 164 above; Anima's use of the word involves a *transsumptio sensus* of the kind instanced at B 13.145 above.

339–72a 339–40 significantly alter B 210, rejecting appearance and words (but *not* actions) as reliable indicators of inner 'will' or intent. 339a repeats B 11.237 (on Christ at Emmaus). **340a** '[Though you will not believe me], believe the works' (Jn 10:38); Christ's works 'speak' for themselves and should suffice to create faith in those sceptical of 'mere' words. **342a** '[And when you fast], be not as the hypocrites, sad' (Mt 6:16). **344** *graye*: the colour of undyed wool, as worn by Franciscan friars. **345** *hit*: the implied referent is his clothing; but since one would scarcely give gilt armour to the needy, it may be indefinite ('he gave [alms]'). **346** *Edmond*: St Edmund the Martyr (*c.* 840–869), King of the East Angles, killed by invading Danes and interred at Bury St Edmund's. *Edward*: the Confessor (*c.* 1005–1066), the last Saxon king of England, who built and is buried at Westminster Abbey. Both were reputed to have lived a life of virginity. **347** *And...and*: 'And charity in an eminent degree was... and they were'. **348** *syngen and rede*: as a priest or deacon (cf. 5.68–9). **349** *clothes*: revising *wedes* here as at 12.126 (B 11.234). **351** *riche robes*: those of a prelate or great abbot. **352** *ycrymyled*: perhaps a form of *crimplen* 'curl, plait' as taken by *Sk* in IV I (p.348) and MED s.v. (a), which cites this as the earliest example (though all the others have medial *p*). Alternatively, it is a coinage from OF *cresmeler* 'anoint with holy oil' (*Sk* Gl s.v. and n. in IV II, p. 894) and alludes to *unge caput tuum* 'anoint thy head' (Mt 16:17, quoted at 342a above), to warn against judging outward austerity as a reliable sign of inner charity. **354** *Franceys tyme*: some 150 years earlier (see on 4.117). In the late 14th c. the Franciscan order was riven with dissension between the rigorist 'Observants' (1368, heirs of the earlier 'Spirituals' who had been condemned in the 1320s) and the 'Conventuals', who accepted the accumulation of property. **357a** 'Blessed is the rich man that is found without blemish' (Ecclus 31:8). The verse following this has already been quoted at 15.283. The present speaker's position may seem more optimistic about the rich than that of Patience the hermit, but in fact complements rather than rejects it, recalling B 14.145–54. **358–367** describe various public milieux in which charity is or is not to be encountered. **358; 360** *court*: the royal court; a law court. **361** virtually re-uses B 5.88 (on sins of envy), which is removed in C at that point. **362** *constorie...commissarie*: both criticised strongly at 3.34, 178–9. **363** *here lawe*: the complaint against the protracted nature of proceedings in the courts Christian echoes that against common-law courts in 3.198. **364–7** re-phrase in milder form the angry protest against ungenerous prelates in B 244–8. **366** *cardynals*: in L the objects of nothing but obloquy for their greed, notably at 21.225. **367** *coueytyse*: perhaps personified, like *auaris* at 365. The semi-formal repetition of the two terms may be meant to highlight their distinct special senses ('desire to keep'; 'desire to get'). **368** *coueyteth*: an ironic echo of 367, not unlike the wry humour of *eileþ* in B 251. **B 254a** 'In peace in the selfsame I will sleep [and I will rest]' (Ps 4:9); said regularly at compline and as an antiphon at matins on Holy Saturday (AlfQ). The exact referent of 'the selfsame' is not clear (it may be the 'light of God's countenance' mentioned at vs 7); but its connection with the resurrection of the just and with the peace and rest of heaven is made plain at B 18.186 below. **372a** 'Give us this day our daily bread' (Mt 6:11); another 'piece of the Paternoster', expressing Charity's dependence on 'God alone'. **B 255** recalls Z 1.127, a line perhaps stored up in a part of L's 'repertorium' (*Intro.* V §§ 29–30).

Passus XVII (B XV)

PASSUS XVII directly continues the dialogue with LIBERUM ARBITRIUM, making the division from XVI purely formal (even *borweth* 1 echoes *borwe* 16.372), and it does not end until 18.105. The Passus itself divides roughly into two halves, (i) 1–121 and (ii) 122–320. Its main theme is the essential reality of the Church as a 'spiritual organism' constituted by Charity, something shown supremely in its leaders' readiness to witness to Christ at the cost of their lives. This is contrasted with its actuality as a 'material organisation' subject to ambition and greed, which obstruct its mission of peace and salvation to the Christian and non-Christian world alike. LA's discourse is interrupted by Will's opening scepticism at 1–3 about whether charity exists, and his questions at 125 and 150, on the Church as charity and on whether pagans possess charity. The rest of B XV to which XVI corresponds is kept, except that 30 lines on the nature of the Church at 122–49 replace some 70 on the Church's mission (416–89a).

(i) 1–121 1–24 correspond to B 15.268–97, but only about seven lines remain unrevised. Answering Will's objection that this ideal is never found in experience, LA cites the Desert Fathers who, though hardly typifying normative spiritual life, serve as *exempla ab extremis* against the worldliness of contemporary churchmen. **1** *no such*: with no immediate referent in the passus, but denoting Charity as described in 16.288–72. **3** 'And, moreover, sometimes angry, without necessarily being to blame for that.' **5** 'He falls short of the highest level of charity'; on *cheef charite* cf. 16.347. **5a** '[Charity] beareth all things' (I Cor 13:7). **6** *Holy writ*: 'sacred tradition'; here specifically the *LA*. **8** links the argument with the end of the XVI (372).

B 258–71 begin with a deeply-felt defence of humble and peace-bringing charity that sees human suffering as providentially willed for a positive purpose, and go on to a detailed account of the hermit saints. They echo HC's eloquent praise of divine Love (1.160–9) and Reason's observation on how God 'suffers' (B 11.378–81), but alter the sense of that verb from 'tolerate' to 'endure'. A possible reason why C cut these lines is that 271b repeats 259a and has already been re-used at C 6.114. **267** See on 15.139. **268** *Verbi gratia*: 'By way of example'. *and*: 'and (cited)'. **269** See on B 11.160. The chapters of *LA* used are 15 (Paul the Hermit), 21 (Antony), 56 (Mary of Egypt), 96 (Mary Magdalen) and 130 (Giles). **277** *leons; leopardes*: emblems of the nobility, from whom Anima implies contemplatives should not seek support (this having caused the problem of the monks' possession of so much property). C's removal of the line suggests a softening of attitude towards this group after 1381, when they suffered the rebels' hostility. **282** *sondry tyme...book*: see *LA* p. 583.

9–36 9 *Egide...To his selle*: 'to Giles's cell' (anticipated indirect object). St Giles (d. ?700), a popular saint in medieval England, was said to have lived as a hermit and monk in Provence and to have been buried at present-day St Gilles, Rhône. According to St Jerome's *Vita Pauli*, Antony was his guest when a raven brought bread. *hynde*: the allegorical *significacio* of the 'mild beast' (B 280) is uncertain, either the monks (cf. B 468 below) or the Church generally, considered as custodian of 'Christ's goods'. **10** *selle selde*: 'Platonic' wordplay linking solitude with self-denial. *be*: '(itself) to be'. **12** *Antony*: St Antony of Egypt (?251–356), an early Desert hermit and the reputed founder of monasticism. *Arseny*: St Arsenius

(d. 449), a Roman nobleman, a follower of Antony. **B 283** *on a day*: 'once a day, daily'. **13** *Paul primus heremita*: 'Paul the first hermit', a phrase from the opening of his life in *LA* p.94. Most of what is known about St Paul of Thebes (†*c.* 340) is from Jerome's Life. **15–16** *frere Austynes...ordre*: the Augustinian Friars or 'Friars Hermits' (on the French adjectival *-s* ending see *MES* 276), who claimed Paul the Hermit as their founder. Several congregations following a common Rule said to be based on the precepts of St Augustine united to form the Order in 1256. Suspicion that this much-debated claim (Arbesmann 1943, Sanderlin 1943) might be untrue (*gabben*) seems excluded by *LA*'s reliance here on the friars' own tradition. **17** St Paul the Apostle's trade was tent-making (Ac 18:3); but like Chaucer (*CT* VI 445), **L** confuses him with the Hermit, who wove baskets (*PL* 23:28). **19** *Peter...Andrew*: see Mt 4:18. **21** St Mary Magdalene was believed to have come to Marseilles where, after converting the pagans, she lived 30 years in solitude on the 'heavenly banquet' of angels' song (*LA* 413), glossed here as 'contemplative love and faith'. *mores...dewes*: a tradition preserved in the early C14th Rawlinson lyric 'Maiden in the moor lay' (Sisam, p.167). **23** *Marie Egipciaca*: St Mary of Egypt, a C5th hermit (*LA* 247) who, like her namesake, having been a prostitute lived 47 years in penance and mortification. *thritty wynter* by confusion with the Magdalene. **24** *thre litle loves*: the *tres panes* she had brought with her (*LA* 248). **28** uses B 273, with annominative repetition as in 10.62. **30–1** Such events are common in the lives of the Desert Saints, e.g. the lion that 'mildly' (*mansuete*) helps Zosimas dig a grave for St Mary of Egypt (*LA* 249) and, most famously, St Jerome's amiable beast (*LA* 653–6). *foules*: betokening 'righteous' laymen whose duty it is to provide for contemplatives (in // B 306–7 the b-half noun-phrases are the verb subjects, *mylde* corresponding to *mansuetus*). From the fact that *LA*'s 'fierce beasts' (B 305), though 'courteous' to the saints, did not bring food, the speaker infers that they signify 'lords and ladies' (B 309) and such as merchants (cf. 46), who should not be relied on, as their wealth may be unjustly gained (C 36).

B 313–14 *foweles...briddes*: 'true' trusting believers are compared to birds, doubtless in allusion to Mt 6:26. But though this use of *foweles* allows a play on 'fools' (as with the converse pun in *Goddes foles* at 11.251), the whimsicality of the present lexical contrast with *briddes* may explain the lines' deletion.

37–64 37 *Holy Writ*: the book of Tobias, chs. 2–3. LA turns the story of Tobias's scrupulosity about the kid (here 'lamb') that his wife got for her weaving into a lesson to churchmen not to offer spiritual gifts (such as prayers of intercession) in return for material ones of dubious origin. His argument is that only an example like Tobias's *from* churchmen will succeed in altering the

behaviour of *rauenours*. **B 312** *yborwed*: a euphemism for 'extorted'. **39/40** The identical rhyme as usual heightens the exemplum's catechetical flavour. **40a** 'Take heed, lest perhaps it be stolen'; 'And elsewhere, "[O Lord, do with me according to thy will]...for it is better for me to die, than to live [badly]" (Tob 2:21; 3:60). The addition of *male* 'badly' in the second quotation is by contamination with a *worde* 'proverb' (Usk *TL* I VII 61) that **L** may have ascribed to Tob (see on 1.142a). **42** *riht...riht*: 'Platonic' wordplay underscoring the absolute character of *treuthe*. **48–9** The first metaphor for grace (*grene-leued*) echoes 16.248, and helps to determine the reading (but see *TN*); the second (*chield*), perhaps inspired by *refrigescet charitas multorum* in Mt 24:12, is related to images like that of grace as softening moisture at 14.23–5. On its eschatological overtones cf. Tavormina in Edwards 1994. **51** *parfite patriarke*: not technically one of the patriarchs of ancient Israel, but given an honorific title here (and at 20.151) for exemplary patience and humility. Authorship of the Biblical book was uncertain, and sometimes ascribed to Job himself. **52** *To make*: not directly; but the text can be so applied. *mesure*: the ascetic 'temperance' appropriate to professed religious. **53** *Nunquam...steterit*: 'Will the wild ass bray, *says Job*, when he hath grass? Or will the ox low when he standeth before a full manger?' (Job 6:5; *Numquam* 'never' is an error for the interrogative particle *Numquid*). *Brutorum...tua*: 'The very nature of brute beasts is a condemnation of you, since with them common [shared / ordinary] food suffices; your evil has originated from excess'. This second quotation probably comes from a commentary on Job such as the one *Sk* cites by Bruno Signiensis (*Expos. in Job* vi. 5, p. 329): 'Or else, let the very animals [*bruta animalia*] teach you, who don't go on bellowing or lowing when they have their fill of what they need'. The passage recalls 13.143ff, esp. 150. **54–8** form a significant outburst against pious laypeople who deprive their dependants in donating to religious orders. **59a** See on 7.215a. **62–4** replace the sarcastic attack on 'poore freres'. **62** alludes to the proverb 'Charity begins at home'. **64** *haste*: i.e. have means to do so.

B 326–45 undergo complete revision in **C**, criticism of contemporary religious yielding to praise for the early Church's bountiful clergy. **326** 'He hath distributed, he hath given to the poor' (Ps 111:9; quoted as part of St Paul's commendation of cheerful and generous giving in II Cor 9:9; for the second half of this psalm-verse see C 66a. **327** *it are*: see on 5.59. **328** *buyldynge*: of great 'preaching churches' like the London Blackfriars and Greyfriars (see on 3.52). **335, 339** Rhetorical *repetitio* underlines the speech's homiletic character. **338** recalls the Thames reference at B 12.160, and use of a similar analogy at C 6.334 may explain its removal here in **C**. **341–2** have characteristic repetition-with-variation (*riche ben, riche bén*). **342a** *Quia...*: 'For it is a sacrilege not to give to the poor what is theirs' (Peter the Cantor, *VA* ch. 47, in *PL* 205:147). *Item idem...*: 'The same [authority] also [says], "to give to sinners is to sacrifice to devils"' (ib. col. 149). *Item...*: '[He likewise says], "Monk, if you are in need and accept, you are giving rather than receiving; but if you are not in need and (yet) accept, you are stealing"' (ib. col. 152). *Porro...*: 'Further, a monk is not in need if he has what suffices for nature' (a reminiscence of I Tim 6:8); cf. C 7.118*a* and B 9.92*a*.

65–93 continue the critique of avarice with a pointed contrast between the model generosity of early clerics and the greed of contemporary 'false Christians' (not only but especially clerics). **65** *Laurence*: see at 2.129–30. **66–6a** *manhede...manet*: possibly an unusual 'Platonic' pun of a translinguistic kind. **66a** 'His justice remaineth for ever and ever' (Ps 111:9), the second part of the verse quoted as B 326, sung as a versicle on the feast of St Lawrence; for the biblical and liturgical context see Tavormina 1987:245–71. **67** *Goddes men*: here not 'the clergy' but the *pauperes Christi* (for the poor as God's special care see Ps 33:7–11). **70** *That*: 'Of which'. *here part*: sentiment and phrasing recalling 3.245; alms for the poor are a 'treasure' won by Christ's 'conquest' of men's hearts. **71** *of...lawe*: the duty of OT Jews to give tithes to the Levites (Num 18:26, Heb 7:5) being the scriptural basis of the Church's claim to the same. **72** *Purnele*: a type-name for a priest's concubine, as at 6.366. **73–84** The comparison of man's soul to a coin was traditional (Raw 1969:156–7). **73** *Loscheborw*: Luxembourg shillings and pence, light counterfeit coins the importation of which was forbidden as treason by Edward III in 1346 and later. **75** *þe printe*: the indelible 'character' held to be imparted to the priest's soul by his ordination. **77** *Kynges...Heuene*: on the group-genitive see *MES* 78–9. *marke*: here the sacramental 'character' conferred by baptism (*follynge*); but where the phrase occurs at // B 351 *crowne* (with its pun on 'tonsure' and the 'crown' symbol on coins) signifies Holy Orders. **85–6** stress the perceived inefficacy of churchmen's intercessory prayers for peace (86 recalls 15.230), **B 354** the collapse of fellowship in society. No topical allusion appears, but sin is more persuasively aligned with failures in the natural order via the declining competence of human agents.

94–121 95 *no byleue*: their lack of confidence in their technical skills inducing the same harmful anxiety as the doctrinal errors of theologians. **97** *byfore...aftur*: ascribing some measure of predictive capacity to judicial astronomy (see on B 10.209). **98–9** improve on B 360–2 in substance and precision. **98** *þe seuene sterres*: either the planets then known (*Pe*) or the Pleiades, in the constellation Taurus (a star-cluster when obscured would better indicate weather conditions than the widely scattered planets). **101** 'From the nature of the seed-corn the commercial value of the crop'. **102** *and*: i.e. 'and what'.

106 *clymat*: 'one of the regions of the earth dominated by certain zodiacal signs' (MED s.v. n. 1(b)); but the sense (c) 'often considered with respect to its weather' seems relevant, since weather-forecasting is in question. **107** *Gramer*: a discipline (see on 11.122) described by Isidore of Seville as the source and foundation ('origo et *fundamentum*') of the liberal arts (*Etym.* I.1.372). A complaint by Bp. Grandisson of Exeter in 1357 about the decline of grammar-teaching is cited by Moran (1985). **109** *versifye...endite*: on these two parts of *ars rhetorica* see Murphy 1974:135–93; Schmidt 1987²:21–7. **110** *construe*: the proper skill taught by *ars grammatica*. **B 375** *any langage*: i.e. French, the decline of which Trevisa observes in 1387 (Sisam 1962:149); on **L**'s knowledge of and use of French see Schmidt 1987²:102–7. **110–16** deplore the fall in educational standards from the most elementary level to the highest. **111–12** *Gyle...Flaterere*: an attack on the readiness of educators to debase standards (through venality, cowardice or stupidity) that has lost none of its timeliness. *þe seuene ars*: see on 11.97. **114** *quodlibet*: 'a question proposed for disputation on any academic topic' (MED s.v.). Presided over by a *maistre* in a higher faculty, these took place twice a year in Advent and Lent (AlfQ; see Piltz 1981:148–9 and Wippel 1982). **115–16** 'It would seem a miracle to me if they did not prove deficient in philosophy — assuming there were philosophers alive who were willing to give them a strict examination'. The tense-sequence is less clear than in B 382–3 (on **C**'s textual crux see *TN*). **117–21** assert that even if priests (culpably) mangle religious services, no blame falls on the laity attending who are (sincere) believers. **120** *Corpus Cristi feste*: the solemn commemoration, on the Thursday after Trinity Sunday, of the institution and gift of the Eucharist. Established *c.* 1263, it was celebrated by the 14th c. with processions and performances of religious plays. **121** *sola fides sufficit*: '[To strengthen the sincere heart], faith alone is enough', from vs. 4 of the hymn *Pange, lingua* (ascribed to St Thomas Aquinas) sung at Lauds on this day. **L** may derive *soethfaste byleue* 119 from *cor sincerum*; but Aquinas's point is that what *sheer faith* suffices for is 'accepting Christ's real presence in the sacrament (despite the defectiveness of the senses)', not 'salvation (despite the defectiveness of the priest)'.

(ii) 122–320a The important added lines **122–55** (half of them alliterating on *l* on account of the twelve-times recurring keyword 'love') attempt to explain how the theological virtue of CHARITY is substantially constitutive of the Christian Church as a 'spiritual organism' (cf. Tavormina 1994). **118** *hastite*: formed from *hasti a.* and first instanced here (earlier than the citations in MED). **122** *doen...wel...bettre*: almost accidentally alluding to the Triad, but more significantly echoing 92: '[if men did their duty as nature does, they would prosper materially]; if priests did their duty properly, laymen would thrive spiritually' (cf. 16.241–3). **123–4** The reference of *For...so* is to a *sola fides* posited as being given to an unbeliever on the point of death. Its linkage with **122** is oblique, however, since it cannot be that priests' good example might arouse faith in 'Saracens'; rather the elliptical meaning is 'For (given that even) pagans can be saved through a death-bed conversion, how much better would Christians' prospects be with a virtuous clergy to guide them!' **125–31** A crucial passage triggered by the question on the nature of Holy Church (one Will never addressed to HC herself). **126–9** A definition of HOLY CHURCH rather than strictly of Charity: 'Life, love and trust; one moral law based on a single religious faith; trust and true belief entwined together by love; Christians of every kind joined firmly together by a single purpose; [whether] giving, selling or lending — [doing] all without any falsehood or deceit'. The C-Text's emphasis on unity and orthodoxy appears to have been developed out of the idea of the Church as UNITY in B XX, perhaps as a response to the disunity produced by heresy and dissent in the 1380s. **130** *Loue-lawe withoute leutee*: 'a religion of love that is not founded on right morality.' **133** *here...diuerseth*: 'their religions differ (from ours / one another).' **134** scans either on |g| (as Type Ia or T-type) or on vowels as Type Ia; it echoes B 15.605, which is removed at that point. **136** *Ac*: perhaps 'It is, however, the case that' rather than 'but', since it is not being maintained that Jews and Saracens who worship 'with good heart' (*corde sincero*) love 'unlawfully', only that *here lawe diuerseth*. **137–40** bring out vividly the ambiguity of the supreme lexeme. 'Love' that is contrary to morality is condemned; only love based on obedience to God's will can issue as the charity that brings salvation (a tacit figuring of 'law' as the underground source of a spring, 'love'). **140a** 'Love God for his own sake, that is, for *truth*'s sake; / And your enemy for the sake of the commandment, that is, for the *law*'s sake; / And your friend for love's sake, that is, for the sake of *charity*'. The quotation (if such it is) remains unidentified; its substance, which is traditional, is paralleled elsewhere in the poem (AlfQ) and fully glossed by 141–3. But though truth, law and charity undeniably correspond to the theological virtues, they are here assigned their determining character in relation to their respective *objects* (God, enemy and fellow-Christian) and do not answer closely to the hierarchical Triad. The first line echoes A 11.242 and B 15.583 (*Dilige Deum et proximum*) but, perhaps prompted by Mt 5:43, LA distinguishes the expected *proximum* 'neighbour' as *inimicum* and *amicum*. The second recalls B 13.137, where Patience equates such love with Dobest. The third echoes B 13.149–51, on how *kynde loue* or *amor* can be transformed through grace into supernatural

caritas. **142** *entierely*: 'whole-heartedly', as in Patience's eloquent exhortation at B 13.143–8. *Goddes heste*: Christ's 'command' is the 'law' of the New Covenant (see Mt 5:44). **143** *thy fayre soule*: the soul as man's closest 'friend' recalls Patience quoting his *lemman* 'Love' at B 13.141–2. Much of LA's teaching re-works Patience's key deliverance on charity and (coming from him) must aim to reveal how deeply that teaching has entered Will's own *fayre soule*. **148** The stress on charity as involving true or proper *self*-love 'so...as to avoid sin and be kind to all' (*Sk*) is a measure of how far **C** (with its new material) has moved towards true interiority. *be cher ouer*: 'take loving care about', *cher* being evidently chosen not for the alliteration's sake but for its etymological tie with *charite*, than which nothing can be more 'dear.' Whether or not *Sk* is right that **L** mistakenly supposed native *chary* to derive from OF *cher*, a link with the *chierte* form of 'charity' seems plausible, and the present construction with *ouer* is cited by OED (s.v. *chere* a.) from the C15th *Dives et Pauper*. **149** LA's tone and phrasing recall Conscience's at Pr 138. **150/1** Identical rhyme heightens the catechetical character of the interchange. The question is crucial, as charity is a fruit of grace, which came only through faith in Christ and through the sacraments. Its answer concedes that Moslems *may* possess charity 'of a sort', a love of God based on the creature's natural veneration for the Creator. The revision (perhaps prompted by deeper reflection on the case of Trajan) alters Anima's judgement at B 389 that non-Christians may be saved through a sincere *faith* 'in some ways resembling ours' (392). **B 390–1** are deleted perhaps because repeating B 309, which // **C** retains. **153** The phrasing picks up on the lexical *annominatio* at B 16.215, which **C** deletes at that point. **B 392–3** are adapted from *LA*: 'But [Moslems] agree with Christians in believing in one sole all-powerful God who created everything' (p. 828; see also on B 605). **393** *For*: 'inasmuch as', i.e. *if* the clergy lived as they taught, they might win over those who share Christians' faith in one God; see Schmidt 1987[2]:73.

156–85 157 *Legende...*: referring to the account of Mahomet in the 'Life of Pope St Pelagius' forming ch. 181 of *LA* (pp. 827–31). The story is also told in the *Speculum Historiale* (*c.* 1260) of Vincent of Beauvais (IV.40), a Dominican contemporary of Jacobus de Voragine, whose expression 'chronica' (p. 827) may denote Vincent's work. **158** *a mene*: 'a (merely human) mediator' (*Sk*). **159** *Makemeth*: after 'Magumeth', the form of which may be influenced by the legendary tradition that he was 'pseudopropheta et etiam *magus*' (*LA* p. 827). *Messie*: as in *LA* pp. 828–9, which states that Mahomet declared *himself* to be the promised Messiah (not that *the Jews* so proclaimed him, as translated in Ryan & Ripperger 751). **160–4** argue that Moslems live by natural law and also by a positive law (the Prophet's teaching) that is for them what the

Commentary

Mosaic Law is for Jews. **161** *kynde...cours*: the echo of Lady Mede's *cours of kynde* (3.60) may be adventitious, for what is invoked to account for such Moslem practices as polygamy (*LA* p. 830) is the 'natural law' customs that Christian theologians held to have been superseded by the Law of Moses. **162** warns that where 'the *lawe* of kynde' is not restrained and over-ruled by a higher positive law, Mede's '*cours* of kynde' will prevail and moral order be unable to subsist. **163** *Beaute...*: 'Beauty without goodness', part of a well-known proverb (Whiting B 152); Fair Rosamund (B 12.47–8) would be a case in point. **164** *sanz cortesie*: 'without good breeding'; the unique choice of the courtly French language for these macaronics wittily reinforces the claim about the inadequacy of untutored nature. **165** *a man ycristened*: not stated as such in *LA,* which describes how a certain *gret clerk*, disappointed in his ecclesiastical ambitions, comes to Mahomet and shows him how to become a religious leader. **L** may have run together these two characters. **166** *cardinal of court*: 'in Romana curia' (ibid). *Pe* observes that **L** 'could have got all he needed from a popular handbook of exemplary stories like the *Alphabetum Narrationum*'; but the explicit reference and verbal details confirm *LA* as his chief source. **167** *pursuede*: translating *LA* 'cum...honorem...assequi non potuisset'; but *to haue be pope* may recall the description of a (Christian) magician greedily desiring to achieve high station and become pope ('exaltari magus hic et *pontificari* / Affectans auide') in another *Life of Mahomet*, by Hildebert of Lavardin. This C12th Latin poem cited by *Wr* may be the 'historia ipsius' referred to in *LA* (p. 827). **168** *Lossheborw*: 'impostor'; see at 73. **169** *souhte...Surie*: taken by *Sk* as alluding to the flight from Mecca to Medina in 622; but this is too specific, and **L** more probably refers to Mahomet's departure from Christian Palestine into pagan Arabia. **170–82** The version of the story as told in *Speculum Historiale* XXIII.40; in *LA* the trick with the dove is taught to Mahomet by the unnamed 'clericus quidam valde famosus'. **179** *God sulue...lyknesse*: a claim to divine authorisation modelled on the account in Mt 3:16 of how Jesus at his baptism received 'the Spirit of God descending as a dove' (it is invoked as the emblematic bringer of divine peace at 246–9). *coluere*: on the weak vocalic genitive sg. see *MES* 72. **183–6** argue by the logic of *e converso*: if a false preacher could successfully mislead, surely true ones could undo his work? **C** removes the symbolisation of greed as a dove in B 414 (problematic, given its association with guilelessness in Mt 10:16).

B 411–89a As part of the (conjectured) transposition of material in the revision of B XV (see *TN* on 187–251 and 188–257), this homiletic excursus rich in vivid parabolic detail has been excised, perhaps as digressive and repeating earlier material (see on 418, 423 and 431). However, 420b, 423a, 429 and 431 will be re-used at C 4.117,

17.48, 17.230 and 8.333. 416–50 deal with the contribution of personal holiness in the effort to establish peace in society and convert the heathen, 451–89 with ways of bringing faith and sustaining it. **411** *so*: 'to be thus'. **417** distantly recalls A 12.4. *parfit lyuynge*: i.e. their way of life which, if properly observed, equals the apostles'. **418** *ministres*: i.e. religious clergy (cf. *hem* 421); seculars would have 'title' to maintenance. **420–1** Antony represents the class of hermits (see on C 17.12); Dominic and Francis the order of mendicant preachers; Benedict and Bernard the monastic vocation (see on 4.117, B 4.121). **423** The metaphor of grace as growing among the humble echoes B 12.60–1, the phrase *be grene* B 102. **424** *fynde*: understand *hem* 'themselves'; the connection of the sense 'discover' to the verb's co-polyseme 'provide' at 422 hints 'Platonically' at a causal correlation between humility and healing. The key-stave is cognative *diuérse*. **425** *The bettre...*: as desired by Haukyn at B 13.248ff. **427** *Alle*: envisaging peace not only between nations but in society at large. *trewe*: specifically 'faithful to their vocation'. **427a** 'Ask and it shall be given you'; referring to prayer (cf. Jn 16:23, cited at C 7.259a). **428** The proverb is not recorded elsewhere. **428a, 430a** 'You are the salt of the earth. [But] if the salt lose its savour, wherewith shall it be salted?' (Mt 5:13). This scriptural insistence on the absolute need in the clergy for *holinesse and honeste* (= the power to 'save' souls) underlies Anima's categorical teaching at 92–5. **434** *heighe wey*: both 'direct route' and the *alta via* to heaven (*Boece* IV, m.7.70). **437–41** may echo Thomas Brinton's Sermon 91 (ed. Devlin 2, 413–14): 'Cogitent igitur...patres mei...*sal terrae*...quod si turba apostolica in omnem terram exiuit....*quanto magis* ipsi...laborarent vnanimiter...ut hostes nostri Iudei... transferentur in regnum filii Dei'(Warner 2003:128). **437** *Elleuene*: properly twelve (as *Sk* notes), counting Matthias, who was elected to replace Judas (Ac 1:25–6). **439** *Sholde*: i.e. be converted. *alle maner men*: implying people of different religions, just as 'all the world' signifies geographical terrains. **441** *saue*: with some play on the senses 'preserve (from corruption)', as at 428, and 'save (from sin)'. **443–44** *Gregory*; *Austyn*: see at C 5.146–7. St Augustine (d. 604/09) was the first archbishop of Canterbury. *þe kyng*: Ethelbert of Kent, converted to Christianity in 597. **445** *rede*: chiefly in Bede, *Historia Ecclesiastica* I. 23–2.3. **448** *Moore þoruȝ miracles*: the emphatic repetition here (echoing Haukyn at 13.256–7) points to the modern clergy's lack of the strong faith needed to work 'miracles' (of spiritual conversion: cf. Lk 17:6), however learned their sermons. **451–60** The comparison of a catechumen's baptism to the 'fulling' of cloth and domestication of wild animals seems inappropriate to the christening of an infant. But Anima correctly sees 'Christian initiation' as extending to confirmation, which took place when the child was older (though dependent on the availability of a bishop to administer the rite). **452–4** To prepare woven wool for tailoring involved raising the nap with teazles arranged on a frame, thickening the cloth by moistening and adding fuller's clay, then beating and pressing. **456–7** *and...hepene*: not strictly correct theologically, since a baptised infant who died was held to be in a state of grace *as to heueneward*. However, Anima may mean only that before confirmation (which ideally required prior instruction in Christian faith and morals), a child who had reached the age of reason remained in effect 'helpless' to perform the virtuous acts necessary for salvation. The passage may reflect the contemporary infrequency of confirmation; and while this was not confined to remote parishes after the Great Plague (see Swanson 1989:277–9), such considerations may have prompted the 'wilderness' analogy. **457** *hepene*; *heuene*: revealing 'Platonic' tension at the semantic level between these metrical homophones, with a hint at the need for transformation of one into the other through the 'fulling' process of Christian initiation. **458** *is to mene after*: i.e. is derived from (the etymology is correct); an allusion to the historical fact that outlying country districts were the last to be Christianised, as is registered in the parallel development of the Latin-derived synonym 'pagan' (< *paganus*, 'countryman'; see OED svv. *heathen, pagan*). **460** *vnresonable*: applying *analogice* not *proprie* to animals, which lack 'reason' in the usual sense. **461–84** form an elaborate beast-allegory only tenuously linked with the Parable of the Wedding Feast, but provide an opportunity to distinguish between the categories of instructed and upright laity, devout contemplatives and ordinary unlettered folk guided by the clergy's teaching and example. Though the analogy is characteristic, its quirkiness, whimsicality and lack of logical clarity could account for its removal. **461** *Mathew*: see Mt 22:1–14. *R–H* (p. 188n29) note that Bede interprets the *altilia* as the apostles; but in the present context the term seems rather to imply the Christian people at large, who are fed by the word and sacraments of Christ. **463** *foweles*: barnyard fowl, not mentioned in the parable. **463a** 'Behold, [I have prepared my dinner]; my [beeves and] fatlings are killed, and all things are ready' (Mt 22:40). **464** The calf is counted as one of the ritually pure animals at Lev 11:3, Deut 14:4 (*Sk*); and at B 16.229 Abraham will feed his angelic visitors with *calues flessh*. **465–9** are not easy to interpret as an analogical 'argument', but loosely, the calf signifies purity of life in the clergy, which nourishes the common people (*folk* 464, 471); they themselves are nourished by the milk of mercy and truth, as are the contemplatives (468), and upright laymen are sustained by love, justice, mercy and truth. **471–9** Ordinary uneducated people are compared to chickens and the clergy to their keeper, from whom they learn to live a life of Christian charity. **480–4** The giver of the feast stands for God. **481** *of*: '(who) of';

on the unexpressed subject-pronoun (Ø-relative) see *MES* 205. **482** *wederes*: cf. Reason's assertion at B 5.14–20. **485–8** *who...Thei wol*: 'those who...will'. **487** 'Without a tenth of the work honest men have to put in to get what they want'; the proportion ironically echoing the 'tithe' paid by laypeople to their priest. **488** *write*: the breach of decorum reminding the audience that Anima is a mouthpiece for the author's criticisms. **489–89a** *Mathew and Marc*: see 461 and 491. *Memento...Effrata*: see on 11.51. The psalm speaks of David's desire to care for the things of God above all else, and his trust in divine protection if he does so. Though the relevance of such zeal for 'English clerks' seems clear, the main point may be that to find *eam* (= 'charity' [11.51a], but more loosely 'receptivity to the Gospel') in heathen lands, would be an incentive for mission.

187–320a argue that 'apostolic' bishops of old lived ascetically and willingly gave their lives for the faith, and if their successors followed their example, they would convert the Moslems. But they have been corrupted by greed ever since Constantine endowed the Church, as appears from the case of the Templars (see on 209), whose fate is a warning to avaricious clerics. (On the transpositions of **B** material here, see *TN* to C 187–251; commentary on the parallel **B** lines will be found under **C**).

189–93 189 *Nasareth...*: representative names of titular sees *in partibus infidelium*, territories in Palestine and Syria under Moslem control. Bishops appointed to such sees, most of whom were friars (Warner 2003:112), rarely went near them, as the prospect of death was assured. **191** 'Go ye into the whole world and preach [the gospel to every creature]' (Mk 16:15); spoken just before the Ascension, after Christ rebukes the disciples for their lack of faith, and followed by his assurance that God will protect and empower them in their task of evangelising the world. **193a** 'The good shepherd giveth his life for his sheep...[But the hireling...leaveth the sheep and flieth...]' (Jn 10:11). These texts (the second repeated at 291a) show martyrdom as the price of properly discharging the apostolic office. **B 499a** 'Go you also into my vineyard [and I will give you what shall be just]' (Mt 20:4). This parable (here linked with such passages as Mt 9:37–8, Jn 4:35) is more often connected with proportionality of 'reward' and 'works' (as in *Pearl*) than with evangelisation of the world.

B 500–31 For commentary on these lines, see below on **C 17.252–82**.

194–232 194 *riht holy*: an improvement in precision in making the referent the hermits and missionary saints, not virtuous men generally. **197** *boek...consience*: 'nothing to read but their own innermost thoughts'. The trope of conscience as a written register of one's good and bad actions and thoughts to be publicly opened on the Day of Judgement may come from Alan of Lille's *SAP* (*PL*

210:118, 181), but it originates in Jerome's Commentary on Dan 7:10 (see Schmidt 1982:482–4, and Wilson 1983:387–9). **198a** 'But God forbid that I should glory, save in the cross of our Lord [Jesus Christ]' (Gal 6:14). **200–01** *rede...rede...rode*: self-rhyme linking adjectival with verbal *rede*, which itself repeats *rede* 194, but with a bitterly ironic sense-difference; heroic virtue is only 'read about' (in the past), whereas squalid venality is something to 'speak about' (in the present). The choice of 'red' for the coin (see on 3.47) starkly contrasts it with the blood-stained cross of Christ. **202** The added line condemns the use of money to 'buy' spiritual benefits in the contemporary church. **204–5** LA ascribes not only simony but war, and the distress that follows from it, to greed (a similar attitude to Chaucer's in 'The Former Age', ll. 60–3). **205** *couetyse...cros*: the noble bore a cross on the reverse. *corone*: i.e. the crown they seek being not the 'crown of justice' (II Tim 4:8), which may require martyrdom and is symbolised by the clerical *croune* 'tonsure', but the 'corruptible crown' (I Cor 9:25) of worldly success represented by the gold coin. The noble's obverse had a crowned king's head; but since the reverse's cross was also surrounded by crowns, **L**'s point may be that worldly churchmen choose the 'crown' but reject the 'cross' that goes with it (see Poole 1958:I, pl. 34e). **207** *grotes*: see idem, pl. 35a. **209** *Templers*: the great religious order of Knights Templar, given a rule in 1129 drawn up by St Bernard. The order was suppressed by Pope Clement V in 1312 under pressure from King Philip the Fair of France. **210–13** voice a widespread contemporary belief in the Templars' corruption, which they admitted under torture but which is now generally discredited. Ironically this attack on greed would have been better directed against the French king, who coveted their vast wealth in his domains. **211** *tresor...treuthe*: evoking a contrast first made in 1.135 by HC, who sees 'truth' as the distinctive ideal of knights (1.90–100). *dar nat*: perhaps alluding to the French charge against the Templars 'of cloaking under oaths of secrecy a system of organised vice and communal sacrilege' (Keen 1975:217). **215** *dampne dos ecclesie*: 'bring down condemnation upon the wealth the Church has accumulated through endowment'. The Latin phrase is either a quasi-personification or a metonym for 'those who hold the Church's temporal wealth', as at 223. **215a** 'He hath put down the mighty from their seat' (Lk 1:52). Spoken by the supreme exemplar of humility, the Virgin Mary, and familiar from its daily use at Vespers, this text underlines how greed is not being condemned as a separate sin but as a specific manifestation of the 'pride of life' held to afflict the clergy. **216–19a** seem to threaten that a faithful alliance between social groups who have overcome their own internal dissensions will strip the clergy of riches and force them to live simply on what the laity provide them. They overlook how the Church's wealth, which brought many positive benefits (e.g. educational), came from generous lay benefactors, and tend to confuse possession with greed. But the depth of LA's disillusionment with the institutional church is suggested by his ready assumption that the motives of those favouring disendowment would be disinterested. **219** *Leuitici*: the OT Levites here standing for the priesthood (see on 14.58). **219a** 'By first-fruits and tithes'; traced to Num 18 by Alf*Q*. **L** has run together Num 18:19 and 21, which prescribe respectively the first-fruits for priests and tithes for the Levites; but he uses 'Levite' figurally for the Christian clergy generally (as well as for 'deacons' specifically, as at 2.130). **220** *Constantyn*: see on 5.175. *dowede*: according to the fabricated C8th 'Donation of Constantine', whereby the Emperor granted Pope Sylvester I (314–35) perpetual primacy over the other churches of the empire and secular dominion over Rome and its Western provinces (see Southern 1970:91–3, and for contemporary citations, Smalley 1960:154–7). The story that an angelic voice was heard crying *Hodie venenum est effusum in ecclesiam Domini* 'Today poison is shed forth upon God's Church' goes back at least to the 13th c. It appears in *B*-mss OC² after 15.558, is cited in Higden's *Polychronicon* IV 26 and Gower *CA* Bk ii, and was favoured by Wycliffe (e.g. *Dialogue* IV, 18), who insisted on disendowing the Church as part of its reform. This inflammatory passage, which comes closer to Wycliffe's preaching in London in 1376 than any other in the poem, is associated with contemporary anti-possessioner polemic by Scase (1989:90). **222** *hye...crye*: the plangent internal rhyme heightening the speaker's anguish about an act from which he judges most of the Church's troubles to spring. **223** *Dos ecclesie*: i.e. 'the Church, by accepting endowments...'; see on 215. **225** *moste perto*: 'is needed for this'. *amende*: what worldly clerics have considered (202) the means to further the Church's position in society having become the problem for both the Church and society. **226** The thought, not fully expressed (but elucidated by the added lines 228, 233–8), seems to be that 'it is hard for prelates to pray sincerely / effectively for peace between those in conflict' either because of 'pre-occupation with looking after estates' or because 'as landlords, they may themselves be in civil or armed dispute about property'. **227** The exhortation here widens the call for dispossession beyond the religious orders (as in the 'prophecy' at 5.168–79) to the whole clergy. The underlying belief in material poverty as disposing towards 'spiritual poverty' or humility is paralleled in Wycliffe's tract on 'The Poverty of the Saviour' (*c.* 1378), but has a long and by no means 'heterodox' history (Gradon 1982). Hudson (1994:101) finds at B 15.563–6 a 'clear echo here of' the demands of Ball and Tyler during the Peasants' Revolt; but **L**'s 'echo' could be simply of a widely expressed opinion also voiced by Wyclif and the rebels (see *Intro.* V §§ 7–10 above). *dymes*: from OF *disme* < Lat *decima*); a policy advocated in Wycliffite writings (e.g. Arnold 1869:147, Matthew 1880:364–96). **233–49** develop an impassioned protest against war into a prayer for the true dove of heaven to bring about through sincerity what Mahomet with his false dove achieved through deceit. **233** *For...parfyte*: anacoluthic, since 236 reads *His* not *Hire*. *þe Pope formost*: perhaps alluding to Urban VI's wars against the anti-pope Clement VII in 1379, or against the King of Naples between 1383 and 1389, when Urban died, or (nearer home) the Despenser Crusade of April 1383 (see McKisack 1959:431–2; Houseley 1983). **234** *with moneye*: possession of wealth making war possible, just as desire for wealth causes it. **235–5a** *Luk*: an error; the OT text (Deut 32:35) is quoted in the NT at Rom 12:19, Heb 10:30; see on B 6.225a. **236** *with his pacience*: 'accompanied by patience [towards his enemies]'; echoing Patience at B 13.165–72a and Conscience at 13.207–11 (cf. Baldwin 2001:106–8). **238** *with alle prestes*: either 'along with the rest of the clergy' or 'with all those clerics who are at present his enemies [i.e. those who support the anti-pope].' *pax vobis*: 'peace be to you', Christ's first words to his Apostles at their last meeting (Lk 24:36, Jn 20:19), used by the priest in greeting the people after the 'Agnus Dei' at Mass. The allusion implies that the clergy have betrayed their Lord in not handing on his gift of peace to the world. **239–42** are not an accurate summary of how Islam spread among 'Sarrisines of Surie' (it was indeed *thorw mannes strenghe*) but reflect his source's claim that Mahomet won over through *sanctitatem simulatam* 'feigned holiness' those whom he could not overcome *per potentiam* 'by force' (*LA* 829). **242** *pacience*: coupling it with *gile* not to undermine the goodness of patience but to show how even the wicked can draw advantage from this most virtuous of virtues. **249** practically repeats B 2.187, which is accordingly revised at C 2.197. **250–320a** deal with the difficulty of converting non-Christians and the qualities needed for bishops in the apostolic work of building up the Christian *comune*. **250–61 250–1** Small revisions (*thus*; *now*) smooth the transition between the new material preceding and the section of // **B** with which **C** resumes (at Vol. I, p. 602; for comment on the major transposition of **B** material at 252–82, see *TN* on C 187–251). The syntactical ambiguity of *peple...That*, which could be a relative or a restrictive clause (leaving the intensity of the observation indeterminable), is perhaps best reflected with no punctuation after *amende*. The referent is probably 'the Christian people' (since **L** writes *amende* not *torne*) rather than non-believers collectively. **252** *scribz...Iewes*: presumably not meaning that the 'scribes' are *not* Jews; a carelessness (uncorrected in revision) perhaps resulting from alliterative necessity. **252** *lippe*: Islam being

seen (because monotheistic) as a partial, imperfect form of Christianity rather than as a religion in its own right regarded by its adherents as superseding Christianity. **B 502a** 'Seek and you shall find' (Mt 7:7), understanding in the original context 'an answer to your prayer'. Here the object could be 'that this is so' or, simply, 'the non-Christians, [whom you will find receptive to your efforts]'. **255** *alle paynymes*: here specifically 'all Moslems' (Bk IV of Alan of Lille's *Contra Haereticos* (*PL* 210:421) is directed 'contra paganos seu mahometanos'); but the ME term (< OF *paienisme*) normally implies 'non-Christian [other than Jew or Moslem]', as at B 11.162. **257** *shewe*: i.e. to God, in his rôle as mediator. **258** 'So those people live by one (and the same) faith (with us), but believe in a false mediator' (see *TN*). **259** *tho rihtfole men*: either specifically the Christians in Moslem lands, who have no clergy to minister to them, or generally all monotheists of good-will who have no one to preach the Gospel to them. **260–1** repeat with small variations 188–9 above. *perel*: i.e. to their souls, for not fulfilling their apostolic vocation. *Neptalym...*: names that are mere ciphers, as these places had no Christian missionary presence. **262–82** correspond to B 510–31 with a few small changes that remove repetition (e.g. B 521) or obscurity (B 524). **264–5** The ambiguity here entails no real contradiction: 'Christ performed miracles to show by a powerful "argument" that men are not saved through argument but through grace.' This assertion is of a piece with the poem's insistence that only the faithful witness of apostolic evangelisers (extending to 'miraculous' readiness for martyrdom) and not appeals to authority or subtle disputation could convince unbelievers of the truth of Christianity or lead lax believers to repent. **267** *metropolitanus*: '"chief bishop" of all the world; Jerusalem being the original Christian metropolis' (*Sk*). The unexpected application of this dignified ecclesiastical title to Christ (explained in the next line) brings out by implication the high demand made on prelates who *wilne þe name* (190). **268** *baptisede*: alluding to traditional interpretation of the water that came out of Christ's pierced side (Jn 19:34, I Jn 5:6) as a 'figure' of baptism, the sacrament of initiation into his death and resurrection (Rom 6:3–4; cf. Lk 12:50). See the *Homilies on St John's Gospel* of Augustine (1888:434) and Chrysostom (1889:319), cited in Weldon 1989:52–3. *bissheinede*: the 'illumination' is of the soul, both in the sense of 'enlightening' with divine wisdom and 'making bright or glorious' with divine grace. The blood is imagined as like the gold sometimes used to represent it in C14th works of art such as the Despenser retable in Norwich Cathedral or Duccio's *Maestà* (Davlin 2001:80n44; Alexander & Binski 1987:711). **272** illustrates the wide range of countries where missionaries in earlier times gave their lives for the faith. *Ynde*: held to have been evangelised by Thomas the Apostle, whose traditional place of martyrdom is near Madras ('Upper India' in *LA* 39). *Alisandre*: 'Blessed Alexandria, made bright with this triumphal blood' (*LA* 266), the place where St Mark perished in the Neronian persecution. *Armonye*: where St Bartholomew the Apostle was martyred at Albana (*LA* 546). *Spayne*: where those put to death *c.* 304 in the persecution under Diocletian included the protomartyr St Vincent of Saragossa (*LA* 117–20). **274–5** St Thomas Becket was murdered by knights of Henry II in his own cathedral church at Canterbury. **276** Cf. *The Simonie* 39 (Auchinleck text): '[Seint Thomas] was a piler ariht to holden vp holi churche' (cited by Warner 2003:122). **277–9** affirm that 'St Thomas is an example [of martyrdom] and *not* of wandering about the country and interfering in the affairs of local clergy' (see *TN*). **278** The 'pointed personal allusion' suspected by *Sk* is doubtful, pl. *suche* denoting the whole category of titular prelates. **280a** 'Put not your sickle into another man's corn'; a maxim in canon-law and penitential texts deriving from Deut 23:25 and used 'as the *auctoritas* prohibiting confessors from hearing the confessions of those...under another's jurisdiction' (Gray 1986[1]), and see Alf*Q*). The image of unconverted people as corn to be harvested is Biblical (cf. Mt 9:37–8, Jn 4:35); but there may be a sardonic allusion to the stealing of parsons' livelihood. **281** *amonges Romaynes*: including in the 1st century Peter and Paul (under Nero), in the 2nd Ignatius and Justin, in the 3rd 'Lawrence the Levite' (65 above). **282** *were*: the careful choice of the verb-mood contrasting a necessary condition with a fact (*was* 281).

283–92 rewrite B 569–77 to stress how the ideal Christ-like bishop is servant more than spiritual ruler. **284** *prouynce*: an exhortation implying poor pastoral care especially in the remoter parts of dioceses (cf. 292). **285** *Feden*: with 'spiritual sustenance' (B 572). **285a** 'By your staff's shape, let this be still your rule: / Drive, lead and goad your flock, heed law in full'. These Leonine verses (cited in Walther, *Initia* 8828), resembling those copied in BL MS Lansdowne 397, f. 9v (*Pe*), are anticipated at 10.93–5, which elaborate the symbolism of the bishop's crosier. **286** *enchaunten*: the only favourable use of this word, the crosier here being arrestingly imagined as a conjurer's rod. **287–92** draw an apparently original comparison between a priest / bishop and a knight / king as defenders of the whole community. **291a** See on 193a.

B 569–77 569 *cros*: the emblem here defining the bishop's responsibility, not that of authority (*crose* 10.93) but that of service, the cross worn on his breast or the processional one carried before him. **573** *Ysaie*: Isaiah, 'the Great Prophet' of the OT (8th c. BC). *of yow*: utterances of OT prophets applied 'in figure' to the Christian clergy, in a way illustrated earlier from the Psalms at 13.122–3a, 14.69–71. *Oʒias*: Osee [Hosea], a significant 'Minor Prophet' of the early 8th c. BC. The first passage has an unnamed man refusing to become king because he lacks

the wealth; the second, spoken by God, is here implicitly ascribed to the bishop. Hosea may have been confused with Malachy because their prophecies are similar, Hos 5:1 threatening priests in terms close to Mal 2 and 3 (in correcting **L**'s wrong ascription to Osee, *R–H* p. 189 misprint 'Mal' as 'Matt'). **575a** '[I am no healer and] in my house there is no bread nor clothing: make me not ruler of the people' (Is 3:7). **576** *for swiche*: 'in relation to / on behalf of'. What in context is a command from God to bring tithes to the temple is here made to relate to the use of the people's offerings to relieve *nedy folk*. **577** 'Bring all the tithes into the storehouse that there may be meat in my house' (Mal 3:10).

293–306 slightly shorten but greatly revise B 578–99, with loss of some powerful writing. **293** *of oure tonge*: i.e. bishops who preach in English and books written in English. **295** *Oure Lord*: 'God', not 'Christ'. **296** *maister...Messie*: i.e. the Mosaic Law is to hold good until the arrival of the divinely anointed deliverer foretold by Isaiah and Jeremiah (Is 9:6–7, 11:1–5; Jer 23:5–8, 33:14–26), whom Christians recognise in Jesus. **299–300** *saued*: the repetition bringing out how Our Lord's message of salvation from sin was underpinned by his acts of healing ('salvation' from disease). **301** *myracles...made*: as affirmed by Jesus himself a little before performing this one (Jn 10:37–8). **303** *Quadriduanus coeld*: 'dead for the space of four days' (Jn 11:39). **L**'s view of the crucial significance of this miracle for Christian faith is shown by the line's repetition in the second account of it at 18.145, where the last lift (the same as in B 16.114) takes up the second (*rome*) from B 594. **304** *soercerye*: an accusation made in Jn 7:20, 8:48, 10:20 *before* (not after) the raising of Lazarus (see 18.151a). **305** *studeden...struyden*: the self-destructive character of malice enacted 'Platonically' by the transformation of 'studeden' through 'struye' into 'struyden'. **306** *brouhte*: with *he* understood as in B 597; alluding to the destruction of Jerusalem in 70 AD, an event widely seen by medieval writers (e.g. in the alliterative *Siege of Jerusalem* 725–9) as divine retribution for the Crucifixion. **307** *ʒut*: both 'nevertheles' and 'even now.'

B 578–99 582 *stoon...stonde*: the rhyme-echo 'Platonically' enacting the commandments' permanence. **583** 'Love God and your neighbour', from '*Diliges* Dominum *Deum* tuum [ex toto corde tuo]...*et proximum* tuum [sicut teipsum]' (Lk 10:27), a text combining the *Iewen lawe* of Deut 6:5 and Lev 1:18 (where *amicum = proximum* in OT terms). **590–1** This miracle (Mt 14:15–21) was understood as fulfilling the Isaian prophecy of abundance in the Messianic age. **593–4** are replaced in **C** by two virtually identical with C 18.144–5, suggesting that the later lines awaited final attention, as this is the kind of exact repetition the revision tends to avoid. *stank*: a detail from Jn 11:39, removed as perhaps lowering the tone. **593a** '[He cried with a loud voice], "Lazarus, come forth".' **597a**

denotes in its final appearance 'suffering unto death', since Christ's *pacience* 'conquered' through his Passion. Anima's teaching re-inforces that of Conscience, Patience and Piers. **599** 'When the Holy One of Holy Ones shall come, your anointing shall come to an end'; a verse relating the end of the Jews' special relationship with God as his 'anointed people' to the death of Christ 'the Lord's Anointed' and the destruction of 'the city and the sanctuary', followed by 'the appointed desolation' (Dan 9:26). Derived from Dan 9:24, its wording (*Pe*) comes from the pseudo-Augustinian homily *Contra Judaeos* (*PL* 42:1124), which was read in a lesson for the 4th Sunday of advent (*Brev.* I.137). It is used in C at 20.112*a.* On the background see Cohen 1983.

307–20*a* continue on the rejection of Christ and on the prospects for preaching the faith to non-believers. **307** *Sarrasynes*: not strictly correct, since the Moslems saw Jesus as one of the great prophets, as **L** could have known from *LA* (p. 828). **309** *pseudo-propheta*: a phrase occurring during Christ's 'apocalyptic' prophecy of the destruction of the Temple (Mt 24:11, 24), which warns against deceivers and cites Daniel at vs 15; it was made familiar through its use in anti-mendicant writings (Szittya 1986:56). **312** The possibility that Moses would accompany (or actually be) the expected Messiah figured among Jewish expectations concerning this mysterious prophetic figure; but the notion has been projected onto the Moslems, who have no apocalyptic expectation of the return of Mahomet. **B 604** *Grekes*: not the Eastern Christians (MED s.v. *Grek* n.1(c), only from late 15th c.) but loosely used for 'non-Jewish non-Christians' (s.v. 1(b)), i.e. descendants of the pre-Christian 'Greeks' (Gentiles), who are distinguished from Moslems and Jews but supposed (like them) to be monotheists. **315–16** The thought here is close to that of Alan of Lille in *Contra haereticos* IV, 1: 'those called Saracens or pagans agree with Christians in affirming one God who created the universe, but with the Jews in denying that there is trinity in the divine unity' (*PL* 310:421). **316** 'I believe in God the Father Almighty' (first clause of the Apostles' Creed). **318** 'And in Jesus Christ [his only] Son, [Our Lord]' (2nd clause). **319** 'And [I believe] in the Holy Ghost' (7th clause). **320** 'the forgiveness of sins' (10th clause). **320*a*** 'The resurrection of the body and the life everlasting' (11th and 12th clauses).

Passus XVIII (B XVI)

PASSUS EIGHTEEN falls into (i) the TREE OF CHARITY episode (1–178), concluding with the formal end of VISION FOUR and (ii) the encounter with FAITH (179–292), which begins VISION FIVE and answers to the second part of the 'outer' dream (of Vision Five) in B 16.167–275. (i) is extensively altered, removing PIERS and adding a passage on contemplatives (60–80) in harmony with the revision's loftier and more spiritual tone. **C** abandons **B**'s bold but clear structure for a smoother if more elusive transition, so that any intended 'inner dream' in C XVIII that finished at 178=B 166 should have begun at 16 (a more likely point is 4, the entry into the secret place of the 'heart'). However, the dramatic break initiating the inner dream in **B** is neither needed nor possible; for whereas in **B** Anima is replaced by Piers, in **C** both figures coalesce into Liberum Arbitrium, who remains throughout with Will as custodian of the Tree. (ii) closely follows **B**, but with extensive re-writing.

(i) 1–178 The TREE OF CHARITY episode occurs in a 'quasi'-inner dream that ends with Will's being woken by the shouts at the arrest of Jesus in Gethsemane. **1–30** begin with an 'inward journey' (in Wittig's phrase) into 'the country of the heart' and have a more mysterious and suggestive quality than **B**'s 'prelude' (B 1–17). **1** *Leue...leue*: wordplay 'Platonically' linking Will's faith in the 'representative' power of his own Soul with LA's 'affection' for him (cf. 17.143). **2** *Charite*: last mentioned at 17.286, after forming the theme of the dialogue in 16.284–372. **4** *contre*: recalling the allegory at 15.190, but even more the heart as journey's end at 7.254–9*a*, where it was the seat of truth and the site of charity. *Cor-hominis*: 'the heart of man'; not a 'common phrase' in the Bible (Alf*Q*), though 'heart' by itself is, and denoting man's deepest centre of both understanding (I Kg 3:9) and will (Prov 6:18, Ps 44:21). The passage Alf*Q* cites as 'most pertinent to the context' (I Cor 2:9) speaks actually of what *cor hominis* has *not* conceived rather than of what is revealed to it. Perhaps more pertinent might be Prov 20:5, 'Counsel in the heart of a man (*cor viri*) is like deep water: but a wise man will draw it out' (as LA does from the well of Will's consciousness in this scene). **5** The image of the garden as a meeting-place with God derives ultimately from Gen 3:8ff, but as a place of *love*-encounter from Cant 4:12, 5:1. *pryuatees*: as the locus of man's secret thoughts (Ps 43:22). **6** *in þe myddes*: alluding to Gen 2:9, 3:3, where the Trees of Life and of Knowledge stand. *ympe*: recalling the tree whose 'ground' is 'free wil, ful in th[e] herte' in *TL* III vii 10, and suggesting that Usk may have read the C-Text while still in progress. On the tree-image see generally Smith 1966, and also A. J. Bowers 1975, Aers 1975:79–109, Salter 1988, Lewis 1995, Benson 1997:8, 2004:168–9. **7** scans as Type IIIb on |g| with final stress on *Ymagó* or, more naturally, as a licensed macaronic (*aa / bb*). *Ymago-Dei*: a title used of Christ in II Cor 4:4 (Alf*Q*); but the Genesis context evoked by *erber* would seem to allude to the account of man's creation 'in the image of God' (Gen 9:6). **9** *Trewe-loue*: an explicitness that seems designed to ward off ambiguity, the fruit's Latin name demanding a careful translation-gloss, and with *trewe* (like *kynde* at 14.14) here signifying 'real, essential'. (For the *English* term reciprocally defined 'aright' as charity, see MED s.v. *treu-love* n. 1(b)). *Trinite*: the tree's divine origin recalling the Incarnation passage in 1.147–53. But the point of naming the three-personed God is to match each enemy of Charity against a divine Person: the 'world' with the world's creator, the 'flesh' with God-made-flesh, the 'spirit of evil' with the Holy Spirit. **10** *louely lokynges*: the smiles of a mother to a child before it has speech, or of lovers before they have first spoken; for the phrase cf. *SS* 72. **12** scans cognatively on |k| |g| / |k|, with the lexical word *calleth* as key-stave. **14** *Caritas*: see at 14.14. *Cristes oune fode*: Christ's *cibus*, the will of God (Jn 4:34), and Christ as *cibus animae* (Jn 6:57). **15** *alle soules*: what solaces them being the *werkes* of 12, which the living may offer for their relief. **16** *siʒte*: a toned-down version of *swowned* B 19. **17** *Y...sithe*: using a phrase from A 12.48. **20** *schoriares*: a more exact term than *piles*; found only here and at *TL* II vii 87. **25–8** The exposition is more didactic than at B 24, where Will's question concerns the function, not the nature, of the supports. **25** *plonte*: recalling 1.147, where it emblematised Christ. **29** The Gregorian 'three winds' allegory of the soul's enemies in *Moralia* 13.25 (*PL* 75:980), noted in *R–H* 193 and Woolf 1968:408, is paralleled in Alan of Lille's 'four kinds of *pride*' that 'blow through the world like winds' (*PL* 120:133) and in Bonaventure's 'winds of pride and vainglory' that blow down the house of [man's good] intention (*PL* 184:665). On these winds' connection with worldliness see 31, and on their 'condign punishment' of the sin of Pride, cf. 5.116–7. The Three Temptations' re-appearance in this 'charity' inner-dream recalls their incursion in the 'concupiscence' inner-dream at 11.162–97, which was induced by *wrathe*, as this 'contemplative' dream is by *joye* (*R–H* 193). **30** *hit...myghte*: 'so that its strength should not fail'.

B XVI 1–25a The one-to-one symbolisation in Anima's speech is an 'allegory of equivalence' (Carruthers 1973:38) like that of Piers at 7.204ff. But Piers's own explanations of the Tree (a visible *shewynge* with a meaning) differ from his earlier 'signposting', which gave visual form to a purely inward 'journey'. **2** On the split or group genitive see *MES* 78–9. *Haukyns loue*: Will's 'What is charity?' at 15.149 having recalled Actyf's 'What is poverty?' at B 14.275, his taking-over of Haukyn's rôle is here underlined by his acceptance of Anima's teaching on behalf of all ordinary people. **4** *trie*: used of Truth and his tower at B 1.137, Pr 14, an epithet connecting the 'fruit' with the 'treasure', the divine as 'known' with the divine as 'loved'. **5** *Mercy*; *ruþe*: two distinct concepts, one rational, the other affective (Burnley 1979: Index s.vv. *mercy*, *pitee*). **6–7** The leaves-and-blossoms imagery here thematically inverts that of the false leaves and blossoms produced by Charity's antithesis Wrath at B 5.136–9 (a passage removed in

revision), as the *plonte* at C 25 reverses that at 7.228. The iconography of virtuous and vicious trees was traditional (see *R–H* 194, Salter 1988 [1971]:262–3, Katzenellenbogen 1989, Benson 1997:7–8). **6** *lele wordes*: those of the Church authorised by its Lord, as in 'The vine's leaves are the words of Jesus' from pseudo-Bernard's *Vitis mystica* (*PL* 184:651); on *lele wordes* see Schmidt 1983:139–41. **7** *buxom speche*: cf. 'A peaceable tongue is a tree of life' (Prov 15:4). **8** *Pacience...tree*: theologically coherent, since patience *is* the support on which the fruit grows. In *Vitis Mystica* humility [= **L**'s Patience] is called *radix crucis* (*PL* 184:733) and is so depicted in the tree of virtues in Katzenellenbogen 1989:fig. 67 (where the fruit is *Caritas*). But since the custom of language is to use the same name for the tree as for its fruit, the revision is clearer. **9** The probable source of the Tree of Charity image (Goldsmith 1981:59; Dronke 1981:214) is Augustine's *arbor caritatis* in his commentary on I Jn (*PL* 35:1993, 2020, 2033). **11** *saulee*: see *TN* on 17.24. **12–13** *groweþ...groweþ*: the *concatenatio* intensifying the catechetical tone; cf. the *complexio* of *groweþ* at 13a:15b and the purely dramatic *repetitio* of *Piers* at 17/18. **13–14** The allegory of the body as a garden may ultimately derive from Gen 2:9, where the Tree of Life corresponds in position to the heart; but the metaphor of the 'gardin in þe herte' is already found in *AI* 232/18. **16** *Liberum Arbitrium*: see on C 16.156. **17** *piken...weden*: apt images for LA's function of rejecting the bad as described at C 16.199a. **18** *Piers...joye*: marking the fulfilment of Will's desire to see Piers again that was implicit in *ful pencyf in herte* at B 7.146, a line it echoes. But the bold paralleling of his reaction to Piers's name with a devout contemplative's at that of Jesus might have provoked objections that prompted the revision. *pure*: 'sheer' and 'spiritually refined'. **20** *loue-dreem*: an exploitation of the love-vision convention reminiscent of *Pearl* 59–60, where the emotion precipitating the dream is grief. The compound phrase is unparalleled in the sense 'love-dream', the OED ex. under *love* sb. 15 from 'Swete Ihesu now' (*Minor Poems of Vernon MS*, p.449, l. 20) being a misclassification (now correctly glossed in MED as 'joy of love' s.v. *love* n.(1) 4b). The Vernon lyric's sense is accepted for the present phrase by Kane, who renders it 'ecstatic experience of the love of Christ' (1989:286n31). But given that what follows is the second 'inner dream', from which Will *wakes* at 167, the sense 'love-dream' must be primary, even allowing for a polysemantic pun (for rejection of the reading *lone dreem* see *TN*); cf. further Schmidt 2000:7–9. **24** Will's first words to Piers in the poem. **25** *wite...wite*: 'Platonic' *annominatio* strengthening the link between 'knowledge of God' and 'God's protection of man'. **25a** 'When *the just man* [VL, *he* Vg] shall fall he shall not be bruised, for the Lord putteth his hand under him' (Ps 36:24).

31–52 dramatise the deep enmity of 'the world' against charity, *concupiscentia mundi* against *voluntas Dei* in I Jn 2:15–17, and man's need for the support of the Trinity in his fight against evil (a foreshadowing of Pride's final siege of Unity). **31** *World*: corresponding loosely to *superbia vitae* 'the Pride of Life' at 11.176 (see on 29), whence arises Covetousness of the Eyes, the 'fair sights' that arouse desire for possession. **34** *Potencia Dei Patris*: 'the power of God the Father', the *propre myʒte* (see 54 below) of the First Person. Augustine refers in *De Trin.* Bk VI to I Cor 1:24 on 'Christ the power [*virtutem*] and wisdom of God' (AlfQ); yet as **L** does not seem to mean 'power shown in deeds' (*virtutem*) but 'power as capacity to create' (*potencia*), to make the latter's referent the *Second* Person would produce incoherence (cf. on 41 below). **35** *Flesch*: corresponding to *Concupiscencia Carnis* at 11.174. *flouryng tyme*: youth, when sexual desire is strongest. **37** *norischéth*: with wrenched stress on the third syllable (see *TN*). **39** The imagery suggests that when lust destroys charity, it leaves 'merely nominal adherence to the Church's teaching' (*bare stalke / leues*), rather than 'the bare text of God's scriptures' (as in Salter 1962:75, and cf. Aers 1975:91–2). **40** *Sapiencia...*: 'the wisdom of God the Father'. The Patristic association of the Verbum of St John's Prologue with the personified Sapientia of Proverbs 8:22–31 and Wisd 7:24–6 is most fully elaborated in the C15th *Macro* morality play of *Wisdom who is Christ*. **41** *The which*: drawing on the same Pauline text (I Cor 1:17–25) that finds God's unfathomable 'wisdom' exemplified supremely in the 'foolishness' of the Cross (a fit plank to 'ward' the tree of true-love). The deletion of B 38 dissociates the redemptive *power* (B 37 indeed echoing *virtutem* in I Cor 1:24) from man's actions and locates it entirely in the Son of God, whose 'penaunce' is not for any sin of his own. **44** *laddere*: the traditional 'ladder of vices' (Katzenellenbogen 1989:73n), inverting the *scala virtutum*. *ronges*: the 'steps' up towards strife being lies and falsehoods, as in the description of wrath's engendering at 6.138–42. **48** *this lordeynes*: with implied referent more probably as in // B 48 than in C 46. *lithereth þerto*: the revision introducing one of **L**'s happiest homophonic puns, 'to cast [lies, etc] at' (s.v. MED 1, < *lithere* n. (1) 'a sling'), 'to act wickedly' (s.v. 2, < *lithere* a. 'wicked'). **51** *Spiritus Sanctus*: 'the Holy Ghost', clarifying and (over)-simplifying B 46–52. In **C** the Third Person is denoted asymmetrically with the first two appellations, *Spiritus Sanctus* replacing **B**'s *Liberum Arbitrium*, which occurs where a Latin divine title would be expected (Murtaugh 1978:25) and more subtly distinguishes between the 'agent' free-will (the human faculty that responds to grace) and the 'instrument' grace (the bestowing of which is 'appropriated' to the Spirit, and equated with 'right belief'). The explanation could be perhaps that a Latin 'nature-name' such as *Gratia Dei Patris* might have

produced confusion through failing to affirm the crucial Western Trinitarian doctrine that the Spirit proceeds from the Father *and* the Son. **B**

B 47a–66 47a *Videatis..*: 'See [by this that] "He who sins against [*VL*; 'speaks against' Vg] the Holy Ghost, it shall not be forgiven him"' (Mt 12:32). *hoc...repugnat*: 'this is the same [as saying] that "one who sins through free will does not resist [sin as he should]"'. The unidentified maxim seems to take the 'sin against the Holy Ghost' as wilful refusal of the 'sufficient grace' given to resist the sins that destroy charity. **53–66** focus on the nature of the *postes*, whereas **C** re-directs interest from the three Divine Persons to the three 'degrees' into which humanity is disposed. **53** echoes Will's words to Anima at B 16.1; but as Will is to learn from Piers that the proper study of mankind is man, his theological curiosity is aroused only to be checked. **54** *propre myʒte*: the distinctive 'power-in-act' appropriated to each Person of the Trinity (respectively creation, redemption, sanctification). **56** *woxen...growed*: speculations about the generation of the Three Persons and the source of divine being; mysteries (as Piers will indicate) for devout meditation, not problems for intellectual probing. **60** 'That may indeed turn out to be the case'. By contrast with **C**, the three *piles* seem to 'grow' like trees, a feature *Pe* finds reminiscent of 'the three stems, also symbolic of the Trinity, which grew from the seeds planted by Seth, were found by Moses...and went to the making of the true Cross'. However, the relevance of this is unclear, since **L** presumably means that the one term *tree* may be predicated 'equivocally' of both God (goodness itself) and Man his image, who reproduces God's goodness in the *herber* of his heart. **61–3** may have been replaced because they lack perfect coherence. Piers describes the 'ground' the tree grows from, instead of saying what it is called, then claims he *has*; but Anima *named* it (as 'Patience') at 8, and the 'Trinity' that it *meneþ* 64 is not its 'name' or *significans* but its transcendental *significatum* 'referent' (the tree is in fact never named by Piers in **B**). The passage both dramatises man's intense desire to know about the being of God and affirms the need to rest content with analogical understanding: divine love is best 'known' through experiencing human charity, the image of God in man. **53–105** expand B 53–74 into a categorical exposition (not necessitated by the original account) of the three ways of life in which charity can reach different degrees of perfection. **53** re-uses B 22, deleted at that point. **56** *thre degrees*: a parallel with the Three Persons (*of o greetnesse* B 59 and *iliche grete* C 62); but not to be pressed. The tree of human life, with a man standing in it, is depicted in an early C15th spiritual encyclopaedia (Saxl 1942: pl. 22c). **59** may be scanned as Type IIa or as Ic with stresses on *is, al, o* and *Y*. **60** recalls 12.225, introducing a contradictory notion not resolved till 100 (*Pe*). On a natural level, sweet fruit is ripe fruit, therefore nearer

Commentary

to rotting than is unripe fruit (which is not sweet). But at a 'transcendental' level, virginity effects a transformation (a figure of thought described in Simpson 1986²) of the earthly state of affairs, managing to be sweet without becoming ripe, and never sour (because never unripe). **63** *suynge smale*: 'in regular gradation' (*Pe*); but the sense is rather of *successive sameness*, i.e. 'real apples are not all equally big, equally small or equally sweet'. **64–6** recall 1.116–17. *sonne...sonnore*: with a homophonous 'Platonic' pun ('copious grace brings quickly to perfection'). **67** *by oure kynde*: 'in relation to our (human) nature'. **68** *Adam...tre*: LA's tree is primarily metaphorical ('the tree of human nature'), but secondarily metonymic, for by tasting forbidden knowledge Adam left the guilt of his original sin to his 'fruit' or offspring. **69** *variable*: contrasted with the 'fast' or firm quality of truth, and so 'prone to falsity'. **71–80** form an addition that could doubtless have been more clearly expressed (for discussion see Tavormina 1995:118–40). They envisage one (normative) mode of active life, the married state and parenthood (78–80), but two of contemplative — continent widowhood (77) and consecrated virginity (73), arranged in ascending order of excellence. The 'grades of chastity' are specified in the pseudo-Bernardine *Vitis mystica* ch. 18 (*PL* 184:672); see also Bloomfield 1958:227–53. **72** *The whiche*: with antecedent *maydones*, glossed in 74 as both religious and other celibate clergy (not strictly 'contemplatives' alone); but if a colon replaced the stop after *sonne* 75, better to reflect the fluidity of ME syntax, then the widowed life could also be included (77). *seweth*: the Spirit, unlike the earthly sun, being able to move so as constantly to give these 'apples' warmth (grace) to 'ripen' or mature them spiritually. *sonne*: extending to the Holy Spirit the figure's commoner association with Christ as the Light that 'shineth in darkness' (Jn 1:5). The Spirit is 'sol' and 'radius' in a C13th *Veni Creator Spiritus* (Dreves-Blume 1909, *Jahrtausend* [*JLH*] II:169 = *Analecta Hymnica* [*AH*] XXI:52), 'lux beatissima' in the pentecostal sequence of 21.211, and 'ardens ignis' in another sequence (*JLH* II:64=*AH* X:34). **74** *men*: not in apposition, so understand '(and) men'. **77** *is lyf*: '(which) is a life'. **80** *That... hit*: 'which', with (redundant) supplementary object, a fusing of relative and co-ordinate constructions. **82** *as...techeth*: a polite quasi-scholastic appeal to learned authority in arguing *per contra*. **83** scans as a Type IIIa line on |t| (-*tiua*, -*témpla*-). 'Active Life and the Contemplative Life' puzzle the Dreamer, because LA has not invoked the familiar dichotomy of physical and spiritual *work* found at B 6.248 but three degrees in respect of the *exercise or restraint of* sexuality, a special kind of 'work' (see *IG* s.v.). **84** scans either as Type IIb on fricatives and |s| or as Type Ie on |g|. **86** *multiplieth*: see Gen 1:28 and Wit's praise of matrimony at 10.204–7. **87** *bettre...*

gode: an evocation of the Triad now in relation to the 'grades of chastity' paradigm. A similar analysis of 'the relative values of active and contemplative lives, with accompanying defence of the merits of the active life rightly lived' is noted in *Dives and Pauper* [*c*. 1410] 1/1, 65–9 by Tavormina 1995:139n50. **88/9** Identical phrasal rhyme underlines how the comparison requires the fruit to be seen *as in* 'from the perspective of' heaven (either *as* yields the same sense, which is not the simple comparative adverb understood by Tavormina 1995:139). **88** *Wydewhode*: regarded in the NT as favourable to prayer and closeness to God (e.g. Lk 2:36–7), its superiority to (second) marriage affirmed in I Cor 7:8–9. **L** mentions consecrated widowhood only once elsewhere (14.143), but urges charitable help for those who may wish to avoid re-marriage so as to achieve it (A 8.32). *more worthiore*: on multiple comparatives see *MES* 281. **B 69** *Continence*: a personified metonym for holy widowhood; its sense here is not, as wrongly glossed by MED s.v. 2(a), 'moderation in sexual intercourse (as between spouses),' but (b) 'abstinence from sexual intercourse' (as stated at C 77 and used at C 73). *kaylewey bastard*: possibly a grafted or cultivated dessert pear (*poire de caiollel*) from Cailloux in Burgundy; the comparison is obscure, beyond suggesting its excellence. **90** *euene with angelis*: a phrase 'Platonically' playing on its homophone *heuene* to intimate at once that virginity is 'for the angelic order the heavenly state' and 'the equal of the angelic condition' (a different co-polyseme of *euene* is later linked punningly with *heuene* at 22.270). *pere*: both 'equal' and (more mutedly than at B 71) 'pear'. **91–9** expand the praise of virginity. **91** *Hit*: i.e. Virginity (89); the tortuous attempt to make this refer to marriage in Tavormina 1995:126–39 is a misreading of the text. *furste fruyte*: in the religious sense 'first-fruit' (an earlier use than MED records s.v.), hence 'the choicest' (see 94). **93** 'Signifying that the Supreme Being aimed to honour the fairest being' (virginity being a necessary attribute of humankind in its original state). **94** *creature...creatour*: as at B 16.215 (revised out at that point), the *annominatio* hinting at the nearness of the one to the other. *furste*: with priority in rank, since they are equal to angels, and in time, since they are the first to see God. This latter 'eschatological' meaning of virginity reaches beyond the beatitude-promise (Mt 5:8) to the account of the 144,000 virgins in Rev 14:4 as 'the *first-fruits* to God and to the Lamb'. But there may also be an allusion to the supreme exemplar of virginity, whose Assumption into heaven is celebrated in 'Auguste in a hyʒ seysoun' (*Pearl* 39). **97/99** *on erthe / (as) of erthe*: paralleling the repeated *as in heuene* 88/9, though now the analogy implies that the way one lives in this life will be exactly reflected in the next. **97** *on erthe*: referring to *their* time on earth, since (except for Martha and Mary) neither category was prominent among Christ's followers during *his*. **98** *is*: the sg. with two pl. nouns, assuming them to be a collective or categorial subject and anticipating sg. *fruyte...hit* (99–100). **99** *as of erthe*: 'from the point of view of our life here' (cf. 88); the image is of choice fruit placed before a king. **B 70–1** *kynde*: in the light of C 99 'best, most excellent' (MED s.v. *kinde* adj. 5(c)), because 'truest [to its species]'. **71** *aungeles peeris*: 'the equals of angels / pears fit for angels [i.e. even choicer than the widow-*kayleweys*]' (see Biggs 1984:426–36 on the patristic sources of this image). **100** *swellynge*: from concupiscence or (its frequent consequence) pregnancy. The virginal state enjoys instead of 'the heat' of desire only the 'heat of the Holy Ghost', sanctifying grace. **101–5** allegorically express Will's desire for experiential knowledge of human existence in all its dimensions. They recall his words and LA's reply at 16.207–9, 212–13; but here within the 'quasi'-inner dream (an answer to his wish), he receives no rebuke. Owing to the replacement of Piers by LA and the transference of his actions to Elde, the passage holds less scope for drama, the echoic anger of the human Ploughman now being ascribed to his divine exemplar. But the Langlandian grotesque, a blend of humour and sublimity, remains.

106–17 enact the process of human development towards death (whence the aptness of Elde's 'shaking' the tree), though they run together the 'synchronic' falling (of the individual) with the 'diachronic' Fall (of just men from Adam to John). **107** *the rype*: '(so that) the ripe ones might fall.' **108** *Elde*: see on 11.188. *to...-ward*: on *to-ward* separated by its noun-object (*MES* 413) see at 16.144; the 'crop' is where virginity is placed. **108–10** The sounds uttered have a humorous fitness. *crye* 'cry out' (not 'weep'), because reluctant to be touched; *wepte*: as befits a widow; *foule noyse*: the unmusical clamour of a shrew (a touch of 'clerkly' anti-feminism heightening the strangeness of this passage). On the Bosch-like quality of **L**'s art see Salter 1988:263–6. **111** scans either as Type Ia on |d| (like B 79), with a six-syllable onset and a first stave by liaison of *hadde_eny*, or as Type IIa on vowels, the latter being perhaps preferable. **113–14** *Adam...Baptiste*: including patriarch, 'judge' and prophet, and extending from the first man, in the age of nature, to the last righteous man before 'the second Adam' Christ, in the time of grace. **116** *in ...Inferni*: 'in the borderlands of Hell', where the just remained until Christ led them out (20.364–9). Alf*Q* finds **L** here 'at variance with Church doctrine' (which was never very definite on this point). But as the 'Limbo Patrum' was often thought continuous with Hell (*ST* III, 52, Suppl. 69:4, 5), Satan may be understood to have a nominal (not a real) 'mastery' over the Patriarchs. Their 'darkness' is lack of the Divine Light that is soon to break in on them (cf. Adam's words in *LA* 54:243), and their 'dread' a continuing apprehension until they are liberated; but their *pleyinge* (273) clearly implies that they are not in torment.

118–37 118–23 signify that 'in the depths of the divine majesty' 118 (a stock phrase needing no source), 'anger' was provoked by the Devil's act, in consequence of which the Father as Power 'grasped' the Second Person to pursue and punish mankind's enemy. This sense for *lauhte* 119 is apt on the literal plane, but since the verb means 'assumed [human nature]' at 19.125, that would seem implied at the allegorical level. The difficulty of the phrase *Libera Voluntas Dei* (which corresponds to *Liberum Dei Arbitrium* at 20.20) is that it designates the *divine* will, Liberum Arbitrium the human power. What is clear nonetheless is that *þe Fadres wille* is expressed through the Second Person (*þe myddel shoriare* 119) who becomes man (*Filius* 'the Son' 121) by the 'grace and help' (B 51–2) of the Holy Spirit; in this way the Trinity works as one to redeem mankind through the Incarnation (see Hill 1975:531–2). **B 86–9** *for pure tene*: recalling the memorable use at B 7.115, a passage also removed in revision. Piers remains firmly human, while suggesting the potential in human nature to incarnate the eternal Word. The ambiguous syntax of 87–9 allows for *Filius* to be in apposition with 'Piers' or (more probably) with *pil* (as direct object of *hitte after*), a double sense barely possible in the revision at 120–22, which leaves a residue of syntactic-semantic difficulty (see *TN*). Hill (1975) detects an echo of the Communion prayer *Domine Jesu Christe* (in *Sarum Missal* 26–7), the phrase *by þe Faderes wille* echoing *ex voluntate Patris* and *frenesse of Spiritus Sancti* the words *co-operante spiritu sancto*. **122** The application of this earliest use of the word *ragman* (MED s.v. *raggeman* n. (b)) to Satan is **L**'s own (cf. 'Ragamoffyn' as a devil's name at 20.281). **123** *fals biheste and fruyt*: the promise to Adam and Eve of being as gods if they ate the forbidden fruit (Gen 3:1–6; cf. 20.320). The symbolism is deeply ironic, since Satan has both used fruit to deceive man and has won man's 'fruit' (offspring) as a prize. *furste*: beginning the period of his 'maistrie' over man. **124–5** See Lk 1:26–38; the Spirit speaks through the archangel when he proclaims his coming act (Lk 1:35). **126** *a iustices sone*: as Son of God, the Supreme Judge; there may be some play on *sonne*, since the title 'Sun of Justice' was applied to Christ as Messiah (Goldsmith 1981:6, 93n16). *iouken*: commonly used of birds (esp. hawks roosting) and alluding to the traditional image of Christ as a heavenly bird who descends to earth for a time (see Hill 1975:532). The association of the divine 'eagle' with the sun of justice is clear from the whole verse alluded to: 'Et orietur...Sol iustitiae, et sanitas in *pennis* suis' (Mal 4:2) and Alan of Lille's observation: 'Christ is called "eagle" because with irresistible penetration of mind he pierces the secrets of the *sun of justice*' (*PL* 210:706). *chaumbre*: cf. 'chambre of the Trinite' in William Herebert (Brown, *C14th Lyrics* 1957:32) and the Sequence on the nativity of the BVM, st.19 quoted by

Commentary

Alan of Lille in his *Distinctiones* (*PL* 210:980), that calls her 'totius trinitatis / nobile triclinium [couch]' (*AH* I.269). **127** *plenitudo temporis tyme*: '[But when the moment] of the fullness of time was come, [God sent his Son...]' (Gal 4:4–5). The 'moment' is that of Christ's death; but the pointed conjunction of this text with *Iesus...chaumbre* at 126 suggests the influence of Fortunatus's 'Pange lingua', which was sung on Good Friday at the Adoration of the Cross: 'And so when came the fullness / of the sacred time [*sacri plenitudo temporis*], / The Son who made the world was sent / down from his Father's clime / And went forth clothed in flesh assumed / within a virgin womb' (st. 4). **128–9** 'When Old Age should knock down the fruit, or when it should attain to ripeness, and Jesus have to joust for it, to settle by combat who was to get it'. **129** Since the sense of *j(o)uste* is figurative, a play on words (originating in the homophony of *justes* / *justice*) may be intimated ('(do) justly' / 'deal justice'). The decisive combat with Satan will be a 'judicial duel,' an action at once legal and chivalric. **131** could scan vocalically as Type Ie with a mute stave on (a)*doun*, but a preferable scansion is cognatively on |t| |t| / |d| with *adóun* as key-stave (for a similar pattern but with |t| as key-stave sound see 20.325 //). **133a** 'Behold the handmaid of the Lord: be it done to me [according to thy word]' (Lk 1:38). **134** *wenche*: a bold use of this slippery term (see *IG*), not elsewhere recorded in relation to the Mother of God, that proclaims her (outward) ordinariness (cf. 20.116). *fourty wokes*: the length of normal pregnancy, as in William of Shoreham's reference to 'Al hyre ioyen of *uorti woken*' (*Poems* 118/110). But as a number with significance in the Bible (the 'Wilderness years'; Jesus's desert fast) it suggests also a period of symbolic preparatory waiting for man's salvation preceding Christ's birth. **B 101–2** The (not quite decorous) implication that the Saviour displayed aggressive potential in the womb may account for the revision at C 135–6, which clearly refers to his youth. **136–7** *barnhoed...come*: alluding to the occasion when the twelve-year old Jesus disputed with the Doctors of the Law in the Temple (Lk 2:42–52) before his coming of age (which here figuratively = the dubbing of a knight). *bold... yfouhte*: 'bold enough to have fought'. In **B** the elliptical sense is 'knew enough about fighting to have fought'. **138–51a** describe Christ's miracles of healing, which evoke both faith and hostility. **138** *lechecraeft*: a metaphor for Jesus as a trainee physician, and not entirely lucid (whether with Piers Plowman or Liberum Arbitrium as his 'teacher'). It may have been prompted by Gal 4:1–7, which describe Christ as 'made under [i.e. subject to] the law' (vs 4), like one 'under tutors and governors until the time appointed by the father' (vs 2, referring to men generally but here applied to Christ). **B 104–5** The 'leechcraft' is initially that of learning how to dress battle-

injuries (a recognised knightly accomplishment, as in the *Histoire de Guillaume le Maréchal* ll. 1789–92), and the situation envisaged is that of an older knight acting as *mestre* to a younger (Burrow 1993:73–4). **139** The Latin phrase now signifies the climax (*hy tyme*) of Christ's life, his Passion, seen as initiated by his public ministry. **142a** '[The blind see], the lame walk, the lepers are cleansed...' (Mt 11: 5). **B 110a** 'They that are in health need not a physician, but they that are ill' (Mt 9:12); Christ's reply when the Pharisees ask why he consorts with *peccatores* 'synfulle' (whom he treats as spiritually 'sike'). The revision largely removes the metaphor in these lines (on which see Schmidt 1983:146–8), except for an echo in *clansed* 143, which answers to *mundantur* 142a. **B 111** *menyson blody*: alluding to the woman with an 'issue of blood' who was healed by Jesus after touching the hem of his garment (Mt 9:20); see also on 7.167. **144–5** See on 17.302–3, which these lines virtually repeat, the rhyme neatly contrasting the death natural to man with the supernatural life given by Christ. **146** *miracle*: not an improvement on *maistrie* B 115, which linked Jesus's miraculous act to the divine 'instruction' he received, the raising of Lazarus being his 'graduation-exercise' as a 'master' of the redemptive *ars*. The clear echo of these lines in B 18.276=C 20.299 is also foregone; but the replacement of *maistrie* by *miracle*, *selcouth* and *wonder* may be intended to avert an over-literal response to the metaphor. *mestus...*: 'Jesus became sad' (Mt 26:37); from the Garden of Gesthsemane narrative, replacing 'wept' (Jn 11:35) in that of the raising of Lazarus. At B 115 the chime-echo of *maistrie* in *mestus* 'Platonically' hints at the close union of divine power with human vulnerability in the person of the incarnate Son. **147** *yes...why*: the internal rhyme both echoing and differing from that of B 116, **C** intimating the deeper significance of this 'sign' and that Christ's sorrow is not just for the loss of a friend but for all men's subjection to death because of sin. **148–9** elaborate Jn 11:45 and 12.42 in the light of Jn 19:7. **147** The stock-phrase repeated here audaciously associates Christ with the three 'types of the common man' it is used of earlier, Will, Robert and Haukyn (6.2, 326, B 14.324). **148** *seyde þat tyme*: an inference from Jn 11:45, 12:11. **151** Despite this collocation, *Mahond* stands for 'Satan' (152) and not the founder of Islam (always 'Mahomet' in **L**). **151a** 'Thou hast a devil'; the exact form of Jn 7:20 and 8:48, in both of which Jesus is called mad (in the usual Biblical phrase meaning 'possessed'). But in only the third occurrence (*demonium habet*), just before the Raising of Lazarus (Jn 10:20), does the question arise of whether Jesus works wonders through the devil's agency. This accusation is provoked by his claim to have power over death (Jn 10:17–18), when speaking of his own resurrection, which the raising of Lazarus prefigures (Jn 11:23–6). **152–78** The halving of this 45-line stretch of **B** sacrifices vivid detail but keeps the substance intact, though with significant changes of emphasis. **152–3** condense four lines having repetition (B 124 of 109) and (in 121) prematurely voicing a theme that will be developed (in its proper place) at 18.104. **152** *saueour*: playing ironically on the sense of spiritual and physical salvation anticipated at B 109. **154** harks back to the form of B 15.590, a line omitted in revision at that point. **156** *Vnkynde*: because ungrateful for his various deeds of 'kindness'. *vnkunnynge*: in failing to recognise in these deeds the Messiah prophesied. **157** *ouerturned*: a small act but used (somewhat provocatively) at 163 as foreshadowing a much greater one, the meaning of which his listeners cannot grasp. **158** is a vocalic Type IIa having an unusual pattern of lifts, without intervening dips in the a-half: *hém oút álle* (cf. 22.307). **159** paraphrases the Latin at B 135*a*. **B 135*a*** 'My house shall be called the house of prayer; [but you have made it a den of thieves]' (Mt 21:13, quoting Is 56:7). In Mt this is said on Palm Sunday (and directly stirs up the Jewish rulers against Christ), in Jn during an earlier visit to Jerusalem at the beginning of his ministry. The two Gospel accounts may have been combined in order to connect this scene with the resurrection-motif pervading the story of Lazarus in Jn 11 (cf. on 146). **160–1** The ostensible referent of *hit* must be the *hous* so that, though Christ means the willing sacrifice of his life, his hearers' misunderstanding is hardly surprising (the source-account in Jn 2:13–22 is much clearer). **162** *iustice*: of uncertain reference, all the Evangelists making the official charge against Jesus before the Roman governor the political one of claiming to be King of the Jews. But since the accusation here is that before the Sanhedrin, the council of Jewish religious leaders (Mt 26:61), *iustice* (as at 178) may signify the High Priest and others authorised to judge in purely religious cases. **163** The a-verse cannot mean 'overturning [of the tables] *in* the Temple' but must refer to Christ's prophecy that he would re-build the 'temple' [of his body] if it were destroyed. *bitokened*: as noted in Jn 2:21; elliptical for 'the overturning symbolised his [crucifixion, the re-building his] resurrection', and what the overturning more widely 'betokens' is the end of the old dispensation. **164** *Enuye..*: repeating 6.87 and doubtless importing 'envy' as well as hatred. *Iewes*: with religious not racial reference; used by **L** (when re-telling NT material) in the regular Johannine sense of 'the religious leaders opposed to the mission of Jesus'. **165** *pans* (*siluer* B 143): see Mt 26:15. **165*a*** '[But they said: Not on the festival day], lest perchance there should be a tumult among the people' (Mt 26:5). **166** *Of*: 'from, through'. *Iudas þe Iew*: a regular collocation (see B 10.128, 15.264); more than an alliterative convenience, it aims to associate the disciple's treachery with that of the people he 'sells' Jesus to (cf. B 9.85), who are assumed to share his fate (see on 164). **167** *Pasche*: Passover, the

principal Jewish religious festival, commemorating the Exodus from Egypt, and celebrated on the night of the 14/15 in the month Nisan (here = the day after Good Friday). Although B 140 specifies *Þursday* as the day of the Last Supper, the Synoptic Gospels treat this meal as a Passover meal. **B 145** *Tu dicis*: 'Thou sayest it' (i.e. 'As you yourself say'), replacing Christ's reply *Tu dixisti* (Mt 26:25) to Judas's question 'Is it I?' with his words in answer to Pilate (Mk 15:2). **169** *Aue, raby*: 'Hail, rabbi. [And he kissed him]' (Mt 26:49). This is Judas's pre-arranged signal for the arrest of Jesus (Mk 14:44), as 170 explains. But the revision sacrifices the verbally complex digression on the insincere kiss at B 147–8, with its rich wordplay on three distinct homophonic lexemes (*to*), and its echoes tolling through 'tolde' and repeated 'tokne' (itself repeated in 'to kno*we*'). **170** *to be knowe*: 'in order that he [Jesus] might be recognised in that way', but with an ironic suggestion that the 'false kiss' will become a metonym for Judas's own treachery. **171** *sayde*: perhaps signifying 'spoke', since the Jews are not directly addressed till 176. **173** *kissyng*: the common salutation among friends in England at this time (cf. A 11.177). The revision is more appropriate, since Judas would not have been laughing. **B 155** *galle*: an ironic forewarning of the drink that will be offered Jesus on Calvary (Mt 27:34). **174** *myrrour*: a negative one, unlike St Thomas at 17.277. **175** The revision extends the condemnation from Judas to the whole class of friend-betrayers. **B 157** states that Judas shall be the worse for it (in becoming an example of how to destroy a friend through falsity). *worþe... þiselue*: the idea of evil 'recoiling' on itself, implicit in the Vulgate's verb-subject inversion of B 157*a* and the containment of *ve* in '*ve*nit'. **175*a*** '[Woe to the world because of scandals]. For it must needs be that scandals come; but nevertheless woe to that man by whom the scandal cometh' (Mt 18:7); in context not addressed to Judas, though the 'hanging' reference in Mt 18:6 may have suggested applying it to him. **177** See Jn 18:8.

B 160–66 This 'foreshadowing summary', with its ominous assonances, may have been cut because it reduces the tension of the coming drama through anticipating the chivalric account of the combat at B 18.28ff (itself an anticipation), 'giving away' its outcome (one not, of course, unknown to the audience) at B 18.35. **161, 163** The phrases composing 161b and 163b stand in apposition, person, act and name evoking joy for 'all', as Piers's did for one at 18. And the collocation of name and emotion, in echoing the latter, intimates how (despite the *difference* in name) person and mission are mysteriously one, as will be shown at B 18.25 (the importance of the name JESUS will be elaborated at B 19.18–22). **166** *Deide... day*: negative 'Platonic' *transsumptio* that in its creative wordplay discloses the creative power of the Word.

(ii) 179–292 The Encounter with FAITH takes place on a less profound level of dream-consciousness than the vision of the Tree of Charity. This is indicated by the retention of *wakede* from B 167 at 179, which argues for interpreting the preceding sequence as a deep (effectively 'inner') dream despite the lack of a 'swoon' at 4 like that at B 19. Unusually for **C**, Will's motivated awakening by *moche noyse* (see Schmidt 1986:25–6 and n9) is *more* dramatic than in **B**. The interchange following is an exposition through question-and-answer. The only 'vision' seen (Abraham's of the Trinity) will be an event *recalled* from the past, to be re-evaluated in the light of present understanding.

179–87 Vision 5*a* ends explicitly here in **B** at 167 and (virtually) in **C**. **180** The disappearance of *Liberum Arbitrium,* unlike that of his predecessor in **B**, is total, a clarification that foregoes the Piers-persona's rich capacity for progressive development. **B 170–1** *ydiot*: a word describing Will's sense of having lost rational self-control (cf. *frentyk* C 179) and affirming the continuity between the obsessions of his waking (B 15.10) and of his sleeping life. An 'idiot' is what the Dreamer seems to the world, even as he comes to understand spiritual truth (cf. I Cor 1:25, 3:19). The urgent pursuit for Piers (*souȝte*) actualises Will's desire at B 7.146 and will be recalled in Conscience's equally urgent quest at 20.386. **181** *waited*: contrasted with *souȝte* in B 171. Will cannot 'seek' his own faculty (because it has disappeared within his soul's *erber of pryuatees*) but must now turn for further enlightenment to the history of Christ's redemptive acts as unfolded, at the more 'communal' plane of the liturgically-oriented outer dream, in the scriptural readings of the Missal. **182** *mydde-Lentones Sonenday*: the fourth in Lent, called 'Laetare Sunday' after the Introit of the day, 'Rejoice, Jerusalem' (Ps 121:1). The time of ABRAHAM's appearance follows the liturgical sequence: he is the subject of the day's Epistle (Gal 4:22–31), which understands his two sons Ishmael and Isaac *per allegoriam* as signifying the Old Covenant and the New respectively. **B 175** is deleted as otiose, **174** as repeating B 5.525. **185** *with Fayth (of Abrahames hous* **B**): the inversion retaining ('with'; 'of') a separateness between the quality and the man, since the Biblical figure is a real person of 'exemplary' virtue, not the personification of an idea. **186** *heraud of armes*: one with the expertise to descry from a distance and accurately proclaim the blazons of those entering the tournament ground. **B 178–9** are properly removed because a 'quest' is more suitable to Will than to Faith, who as a 'herald' would wait for knights to arrive, not go out in search of them (but *seke* remains at 269, possibly with the sense 'ask about' (MED s.v. *sechen* v. 4(a)).
188–239 re-write **B**'s account of the Trinity with less assurance but perhaps more subtlety. As what follows

is continuously revised, it makes for clarity to break the commentary into smaller sections and deal *suyrelepes* with the two parallel texts.
188–96 188 revises B 181 in the words of B 17.27, at the cost of some repetition. *persones*: the choice of word implying the *interpretatio* of the emblem. *pensel*: 'a pennoncel or streamer identifying an individual knight' (MED s.v. *pencel* n. (1), (b)). The 'device' differs from that in B 181 in representing the persons as *departable*, signifying their unity not synecdochically by *lyp* but metonymically by *pensel*. **189** *speche*: i.e. the Word, the Second Person. *out of alle*: hinting at the generation of the Son, the double procession of the Spirit and the 'circumincession' or mutual interpenetration of the Persons (the *perichoresis* or 'dance' around the 'still point' described in T. S. Eliot's *Burnt Norton* II). **190** stresses total unanimity without conflict. **191** *se vpon*: 'consider theoretically'. *solus Deus*: '(one) only God'; despite the exact verbal parallels at Mk 2:7, Lk 5:21, 18.19 cited by Alf*Q*, the sense here is not 'God alone' but 'the sole God' as in the *Deus solus* of Ps 85:1 (*Pe*). **192** *suyrelepes... sondry names*: names *resulting* from the true distinction between Persons, not creating it; an indication of Will's metaphysically 'realist' view of religious truth. Though recalling his question on the soul's names at 16.201, this shows more tentativeness and respect. **195** The **C** line could be an extended Type Ia on |θ| with a mute stave on *þat* and vocalic semi-counterpoint (*hált ál*) or, in the light of the **B** line 188 under revision (which makes *a* the key-stave), a Type Ia (or Ic) line scanning on vowels. If the latter scansion is preferred for **C**, the word *a*, despite its semantic weight, must be treated as mute; but this is optional in **B**, which may be T-type (-*sóne*, -*sélue*). *halt al*: a rôle more commonly that of the Father, who 'contains' the whole Trinity. **196** *in alle*: conceiving the Spirit as divine immanence; *al* 'everything' and *alle* 'all (individual) beings' have 'the creation' as implied referent.
B 181–90 181 *noon...ooþer*: recalling B 57, as elements of the inner dream now 'surface' in the outer. **183** affirms both the unanimity of the persons and their self-sufficient divinity, a paradox hard to reconcile rationally with an 'appropriation' of functions that is not also a division of powers. **184** *makere*: 'Creator', the name of the Father as the generator who is not generated. **186–7** The special titles of the Son as knowable *veritas* (Jn 14:6) and guardian of rational beings derive from his nature as *Verbum* and *Sapientia* 'Word and Wisdom of the Father', revealer of God's hidden nature as Trinity. **189–90** *light*: source of understanding, as in *JLH* II:165, vs 2. *Confortour*: the *Consolator* sense of 'Paraclete' (Jn 14:16), which also means 'Advocate'; see the Pentecost hymns in *JLH* II 161, vs 2; 162, vs 1; 164, vs 8. *alle blisse*: the *beata gaudia* brought by *spiritus paraclitus* (*JLH* II:154).
197–239 form a (varyingly successful) attempt to throw

light on that *myrke thyng* the mystery of the Trinity (an object of trusting faith rather than *kynde knowynge*) by two analogies, of a lord and his servant, and of the human family of husband, wife and child.

200–14a compare the Trinity's act of self-disclosure to that of a lord who operates through an agent (for possible influence from Abelard here see Szittya 1986²). **202–3** 'Power, and a means to make known his own power, that of himself and that of his agent, and what both experience / undergo' (see *TN* further). **205** *seruaunt*: the term *servus Dei* 'servant of God', common in the OT for a prophet (I Par 6:49, Dan 6:20); but most relevant here is Phil 2:6–7, which state that Christ was 'in the form of God' but took on 'the form of a servant' for his redemptive work. **206–10** The relational image, which anticipates the second analogy in 215–39, is based on the theological emblem of the Church as the 'Bride' of Christ, whom he loves and who brings forth 'issue' (the saved). The immediate scriptural source is Apoc 21:2, 9, where the New Jerusalem (itself a 'type' of the Church as the City of God) is further figured as the Bride of the Lamb (Christ). **208** *Patriarches and prophetes*: OT 'servants of God' but placed with the apostles of the New Dispensation because the Church (like the Tree of Charity) has its roots in the past and extends to the end of time, so that the faith in God of the just before Christ (and the Messianic hope it engendered) are implicitly faith and hope in the Son who alone saves. **209–10** clarify B 199–200 by advancing B 210 to make more explicit how an 'incarnational trinity' (Christ the Head, the earthly society of the baptised co-terminous with the Christian world, and the Mystical Body that includes the blessed) may symbolise the Holy Trinity and the orthodox ('Trinitarian') faith. **211–14a** assert that the one Creator-God exists in Trinity (in 213 the a-half stresses fall best on *is*). That he made man in his likeness (212) inevitably raises an expectation (fulfilled in the next analogy) of a 'trinity' in mankind. **213–14** *bereth...werkes*: especially man himself, the Creator's chief 'work' (cf. the closely parallel Ps 8:6–7). While the world's proclamation of God's *triune* nature is not obvious, **L** may envisage it as divided into land, sea and sky, and 'created things' into lifeless, animate and spiritual, or 'animate creatures' into birds, beasts and fishes. **213** *A thre*: 'a trinity' or 'in trinity'. **214a** 'The heavens show forth the glory of God: and the firmament declareth the work of his hands' (Ps 18:2); a verse only loosely relevant to the argument about the created universe revealing the Trinity.

215–39 endeavour to show how humanity itself 'proves' (better, evidences) the divine triunity. For detailed discussion of this passage see Tavormina 1995:140–66.

215–26 215 *thre persones departable*: the three distinguishable divine Persons, seen as (necessarily) reflected in humankind, which is complete or perfect only when

male and female unite to engender offspring. *Y...by*: a claim less to demonstrate formally the truth of a proposition from data than to 'assay' the validity of a belief by submitting it to the test of experience (so as to acquire a *kynde knowynge*). **216** *o God*: the unity of the divine nature (shared by the three Persons) is shown *analogice* by the descent of human beings from Adam, so that they *aren bote oen in manhede* (220). **217** The phrasing is close to Bonaventure's 'Eva, quae fuit ab Adam sive de Adam deducta' in his Commentary on Bk I of Lombard's *Sentences*, 12.1.3, in *Op. Omn.* I:223 (Galloway 1998:130n16, citing Clopper 1997:119). **219** scans either as Type IIb on |ð| and |θ| and vowels, or as a vocalic Type Ib with a four-syllable onset. A vocalic scansion would seem preferable, since the first alternative would require a mute third stave in a Type II line, something **L** avoids. **221–6** The link between these lines and the foregoing is presumably the notion of unity as 'completeness'. A sterile union falls short of the norms of 'perfect' marriage, just as humanity would have been incomplete with only a male, or with a male and female but with no issue. **222** *Bible*: not a specific text; but the injunction at 223a accords with the 'Biblical' conception of an Israelite's duty to obey the divine command in Gen 1:28 (echoed as late as Lk 1:25). **223** *acorsede alle couples*: not, according to Tavormina (1989:155n81), a statement that individual childless couples are 'unblessed', since 'the command to multiply applies to the species as a whole'. But though this assertion need not be taken as universally intended, it remains dramatically apt in the mouth of Faith (Abraham), to whom God's *specific* 'promise' was of a child by his wife (Gen 15:2–6). **223a** 'Cursed is the man who has not left offspring in Israel'. The quotation appears in a lesson for St Anne's Day (*Hereford Breviary* II.266), addressed by the high priest to Joachim, father of the Virgin Mary, in the Temple (Tavormina 1989²:117–25).

B 201–19a offer a more complicated analogy, which though itself a little *myrke*, essentially takes the three *stat□s* seen (B 68–78) on the Tree that 'signifies' the Trinity (B 63) as constituting a 'collective human trinity' (203). This division derives from the familial 'trinity' of father, mother and child (205–6). But the ingenious (and somewhat tortuous) comparison of the *stat□s* to the *heavenly* Trinity fails to articulate the analogy of the third state, virginity, with the Spirit (which is not made explicit till C 18.74–5). **201** *in pre leodes*: an allusion to the three men who visited Abraham at Mamre (Gen 18:2; B 227) and were traditionally understood as an OT prefiguring of the Trinity revealed in the NT. **206** *of hem bope*: a happy 'betokening' by the 'human trinity' of the orthodox (Western) doctrine (*trewe bileue* 210) of the 'Double Procession' of the Spirit from Father and Son. **207** The mutual love of parents and child likewise figures that of the divine Persons. **208** *oon singuler name*: not the *same* name predicable univocally of God and Man, but one 'special' name predicable equivocally of *both* (i.e. *man-hede* 'humanity' of Man and *godhede* 'divinity' of God). But **L** may be punning on another sense of *singulere* 'unique' (MED s.v. 3(a)), if he also means to evoke the condition of the God-Man Christ who unites *heuene and here*. **211** *Might*: the generative power 'appropriated' to a father / the Father (see on 18.34=B 30). **212** Strictly, the subject of *bitokeneþ* is *might*, but obviously it is *marriage* that 'symbolises', power being predicated 'literally'. *trewely*: in part because the first human pair were given a 'marriage' blessing by God in the words 'Increase and multiply' (Gen 1:28). *dorste*: repeated at 214 and express-ing awareness of the audacity of the analogy. **213** *He*: an emphatic nominative instead of the expected accusative *Him* (see *TN*). **214** *widewe*: because separated by death (which occurs just after he utters the cry quoted) from his 'other half', the divine nature 'wedded' to his human nature. **214a** 'My God, my God, why hast thou forsaken me?' (Mt 27:46, quoting Ps 21:2). **215** *creatour weex creature*: the sense is that 'matrimony "becomes" widow-hood', power becoming powerlessness, through the death of the Creator'. The morphemic *annominatio* 'Platoni-cally' highlights **L**'s arresting ascription of Incarnation to God's analogical 'need' to experience the suffering and mortality that define creatureliness, so that his limitless perfection may be (paradoxically) 'completed' through limitation (cf. B 18.221–4). **L**'s wordplay recalls Walter of Châtillon's 'factor fit factura / et *creator creatura*' (ed. Strecker, no. 10, st. 3).

227–40 treble B 220–4 in the effort to elucidate the place of the Third Person, who had been left out of **B** (some-thing perhaps remarked on by an attentive early reader). They achieve this chiefly through omitting the awkward *statu̅s* analogy (though the elaborated 'marriage' model is not without difficulties) and insisting on an appeal to experience (240). **228** *in hymsulue*: in apposition with *in God Fader* 227. *simile*: the word, only half-naturalised, perhaps echoing Gen 2:18 ('faciamus ei adiutorium *sim-ile* sibi'), to suggest how Eve was both 'in' Adam and resembled him, and to compare her emergence from his side to the Son's leaving the 'bosom' of the Father' (Jn 1:18) at the Incarnation. **230–33** liken the 'springing' of the child from the first pair to the 'double procession' of the Spirit; but this *simile*'s weakness is that whereas they had further children, He is unique. **231** *spyer*: echoing the 'Eve-out-of-Adam' image to suggest consubstantial-ity more strongly than the slightly subordinationist 'Abel-out-of-Adam-and-Eve' image. **232** *of hem bothe*: perhaps better taken not as an adjectival possessive phrase but as an integral adverbial phrase qualifying *Is* 233 = 'proceeds / has his being from them both.' **233** involves a harsh shift from sg. subject (*Spirit*) to an implied pl. (*Thei*); for *were* could not be sg. (and so also subjunctive) if the 'double

procession' is eternal (*ay*) and necessary, not contingent and a 'consequence' of the Incarnation (see *TN*). **234–6** are somewhat elusive, but not unintelligible (see *TN* and at *Intro*. II § 133), though the comparison enforced by *as...So* is hardly exact, what is offered being a parallel under the guise of a likeness. But the thought becomes clearer if *mankynde* is seen as the 'human trinity' that is an analogue of the 'divine trinity' (see on B 201–19): 'Just as it is obvious that three persons — a man, his wife and their true offspring — are of absolutely one and the same human nature, so the Son of God is God, and the Trinity subsists in three persons'. **235** This insistence that the child be the 'legitimately begotten' offspring of mar-ried parents (an illegitimate child breaching both positive and natural law) is in place coming from the speaker; for Abraham sent away his servant's son Ishmael because only Isaac, as the child of promise, counted as his 'true' issue (Gen 21). But the sentiment is also of a piece with less specifically ascribable utterances, such as Wit's at 10.204–14. **237–8** The phrasal rhyme that seems to mimic the thematic content suggests a homology (cf. *encountre* 239) between divine and human trinities, as the verbal antithesis of *cam of* and *goth to* their complementarity. **237** scans as Type Ib on non-lexical words (*Ín, áren, ó, álle*) or, preferably, on |m| with two staves in *mátrimónie* and contrapuntal alliterating vowel staves (*áren, álle*). The line's breach of logic is only apparent, since the first man's name signifies equivocally both '(hu)man (nature)' and 'Adam' who, with Eve and Abel, 'came out of' it. **238** *alle thre*: the primary grammatical subject of *is* (like *Sone* in 236). **239** '"Three set against three" in the case of both the Godhead and humanity'. *Pe* notes that *treys* is an AN term for a throw of three in the dice-game of 'haz-ard' (MED s.v. *trei* n.(3)); but Tavormina (1982:162n) suspects a contracted form of *trey-as* 'three-ace', a two-dice throw of three and one. Though 'an excellent lin-guistic symbol of tri-unity', this requires greater metri-cal prominence for both *treys*, and scansion on *tt* / *d* as a macaronic Type IIa (with a cognative liaisonal stave in *quod̲ hé* or *Godhéde*). But with unwrenched stresses in the two opposed b-half terms (the key-notion being the mirror-symmetry of human and divine), preference would be for palatal-stopped Type IIe or IIIa (with cog-native main staves -*cóuntre*-, [*quód*], *Gód*). Perhaps noth-ing more precise is intended than a 'matched throw' that illustrates how an 'adventurous' Creator seeks 'equality' with his creature by becoming human so that man may become divine. **240** scans as Type III counterpointed and enriched (*abb* / *aa*).

B 220–4 222 *gendre of a generacion*: 'a species (springing) from a single act of generation'; somewhat loosely expressed, for though Adam's progeny 'proceed' from him, *he* was created, not generated. The phrase ap-plies better to the Trinity (see Tavormina 1989[1]). *bifore...*

heuene: an asseveration (cf. 1.140). **223** *So*: inaccurate, because the analogy ignores the usual theological opinion that essence and existence are identical in God, but distinct in creatures. The 'necessity' of a child's relation to its parent differs from that of the Second and Third Persons to the Father in being 'consequential', not 'ontological' (see on C 233). *Fre Wille*: adapting from Augustine (*De Trinitate* X, XII. 19, XV and XXI) the analogy between the Spirit and the human faculty that chooses and loves (cf. his *frenesse* at B 88 and association with *Liberum Arbitrium* at B 50–2). **223a** 'The Spirit proceeding from the Father and the Son'; the standard Western understanding of the dogma as expressed in the Athanasian Creed: 'Spiritus Sanctus a Patre et Filio...procedens' (Alf*Q*, p.105). **224** *alle* (1): loosely expressed, since *bothe* would be better.

241–69a bring the personification of Faith's 'historical' identity into focus as he retells the Biblical story of God's covenant with the Father of the Chosen People. The approach is doctrinal, with Abraham's experience seen as the first revelation of God's triune nature, but also typological and sacramental, his acts of circumcision and sacrifice being understood as figures of Baptism and the Eucharist. That Abraham's encounter is with one God 'gangynge a thre' is carefully sustained by the shifting number of the pronouns, e.g. *hym* 243, *they* 244 (Davlin 2001:93).

241–53 241 *somur...porche*: suggested by Gen 18:1; but the echo of Pr 1 and 10.2 hints at the general idea of 'new beginnings'. **242a** 'Three he saw and worshipped one'; from a Quinquagesima Antiphon (*Brev*.1:dxli) often cited in proofs of the doctrine of the Trinity (Ames 1970:56), and based on Gen 18:2 ('apparuerunt ei *tres* viri...quos cum *vidisset*...cucurrit...et *adoravit*'). Alan of Lille observes that 'in the three who appeared, [Abraham] understood trinity; and because *he adored one*, he understood a unity in the Trinity; and thus he is understood to have adored a God both three and one' (*PL* 210:404). In the 'liturgical' time-scheme that underlies Passūs XVIII–XXII and has reached the Fourth Sunday of Lent in 'dreamtime', this scene forms a 'prelude', since the fiftieth day before Easter is the Sunday before Ash Wednesday, when Lent begins. The OT readings of the whole week concern Abraham, those of the day itself dwelling on God's covenant with him that provides the substance of this section, and the day's hymn is one to the Trinity. **B 229** The details are from Gen 18:6–7. **247** *tokenes*: properly referring to circumcision, the *signum foederis* 'sign of the covenant'; but here related typologically to the patriarch's obedience in offering Isaac, and to God's providing the ram for sacrifice and swearing by himself to multiply Abraham's offspring for ever (Gen 22:13–18). The importance of Abraham extends beyond the OT rite of initiation to his figurative significance as 'father of faith' and his offering

as foreshadowing Christ's at the Last Supper and the Mass (see 264). *whan tyme cometh*: improving on the vagueness of B 230 and anticipating the encounter in Limbo (20.366). **249–50** both have unusually long 'preludal' dips and their first lift on the pronouns *hym* and *his* (with Isaac and God as referents). **251** *allowe*: alluding to St Paul's interpretation (Romans 4:3, citing Gen 15:6, 9) of Abraham's obedience as 'imputing' righteousness to him or 'justifying' him through his faith.

B 233–35 233 *bi hym*: with referent either God or Isaac; Abraham's 'will' as regards both is precisely the issue. *wol*: carefully balancing *wille* to bring out that God's attitude towards man depends in part on man's attitude to God. **235** The OT placing of the Covenant of Circumcision (Gen ch. 17) *before* the offering of Isaac is not incompatible with the Pauline view of this rite as a *signaculum iustitiae fidei* 'seal of the justice of the faith which [Abraham] had, being uncircumcised' (Rom 4:11). But **L**, taking the offering of Isaac as the *main* 'token' of that faith, places circumcision after it (*siþen*), signifying typologically that individual faith *precedes* baptism into the 'new Israel' of the Church. The *sone* of 252 could denote Ishmael (Gen 17:23–6), but *siþen* indicates the same *sone* as at C 248, Isaac (Gen 21:4), and B 234–5 put this beyond doubt. Presumably the point is that only Abraham's 'true' issue can be a fit type of Christ in the 'human trinity' model proposed as an analogy for the divine one.

254–69a 254 The bleeding at circumcision foreshadows that of Christ on the cross, which generated sacramental baptism (21.325 echoes the wording here). **255** *his bileue*: 'faith in him' (objective genitive). **257–9** *lyf...Mercy*: though neither promise is made to Abraham in Genesis, he here stands as a 'type' of the believer in the New Dispensation for whom these promises hold, subject to faith and repentance (the 'confessional' phrasing of 259–60 directly echoes 12.72). **B 242a** 'As you once promised to Abraham and to his seed'; a variant of the last verse of the *Magnificat*, based on Lk 1:46–55 and forming the regular first canticle at Vespers. **261–5a** As *Sk* notes, Abraham's sacrifice (Gen 15:9) has been confused with that of Melchisedech (Gen 14:18–19). But the 'confusion' may be intentional (*somewhat hit bitokneth* 264), since the 'altar' and 'worship of the Trinity' seem meant to prefigure the Mass where, during the Consecration prayer *Supra quae*, Melchisedech's sacrifice is mentioned (after Abraham's) as a type of Christ's. **261** *a sente me*: wihout authority in Genesis. **264** *so*: 'in this manner'; such stress on the elements that will be used in the Eucharist is part of the Church's seeing in 'the father of all them that believe' (Rom 4:11) a figure of Christ the perfect High Priest (as borne out by Abraham's 'prophetic' pre-consciousness that Christianity will extend God's revelation to all mankind). The entire presentation here is deeply influenced by the argument of Rom 4:16–25. **265a** '[And other sheep I have that are not of this fold: them also I must bring]... and there shall be one fold and one shepherd' (Jn 10:16); the main Gospel statement that Christ's mission is to unite the Gentiles and the Chosen Race as one people of God. **266–9a** condense B 249b–50a and omit 251 (a line repeated at B 18.324, but there retained by **C**). **266** Not only does Abraham's awareness of his rôle as a *figura* of the Christian believer pertain to his allegorical character as Faith, his words and actions are accommodated to the liturgical cycle's re-telling of salvation history, and find no parallel in the typologically-structured Miracle Plays. *here*: 'while alive on earth' (so at 269). *helle*: 'Limbo' (where he now dwells); for this sense of 'hell' see at 116. **269a** 'Behold the Lamb of God...[who taketh away the sin of the world]' (Jn 1:29). The Baptist's words convey his prophetic sense of the Messiah's redemptive mission as universal. But their image of 'Christ the Lamb of sacrifice' (correlative to Abraham's 'Christ the Shepherd') coheres with Faith's 'proleptic' allusion to the Mass, being the words the priest speaks as he holds up the Host before administering Communion.

270–92 enable Abraham to complete explaining his task as 'herald' of Christ's Incarnation and its purpose: to win back the 'fruit' that through the 'death of kind' caused by the Fall must fall into the Devil's hands (111–17). **270–3** are a fine specimen of 'grotesque sublime' in their allegorical 'realisation' of 'Abraham's bosom' (Lk 16:22), varying somewhat from the Biblical source's *chaos magnum* 'great gulf' between the place of the damned and the place 'afar off' where Abraham rests (Lk 16:26, 23). **271–2** *bosom*; *lappe*: synonyms translating Lat. *sinus*, which also meant a 'bay' or 'gulf' (resembling the open lap in shape). *blessede*: in his capacity as Father of those to be 'blessèd'. *lazar*: a word derived from the proper name of the beggar in the parable at Lk 16:19–31; denoting (MED s.v.) 'a poor person afflicted with a loathsome disease (often leprosy)'. Lazarus became the patron saint of lepers, and that **L** understood *lasar* as 'leper' is clear from 18.142, translating *leprosi* in Mt 11:5. **275** *I wolde ywyte*: renewing the inquisitiveness rebuked by Anima at 16.210, but receiving a more positive answer from Abraham. **278** *present*: the fruits of the tree (the just who have died before Christ), envisaged as a 'gift' intended for God but seized by the Devil without hope of redemption through ordinary means. The sense of their lying in the Devil's *daunger* (< L *dominationem* 'power') is in tension with their being at ease (*pleynge*), their situation seeming more like house-arrest than imprisonment. **279–86** The position envisaged is of remaining without freedom till the 'better pledge' (of Christ's life) has been paid, which exceeds any claim that even the just have upon God. A strict legal relation is judged to exist between God and the Devil and to govern their coming dispute for the posses-

sion of humanity; but Faith himself is (quite fittingly) unaware of the flaw in Satan's claim that Christ will expose in 20.370–92. For full discussion of this theme see Marx 1995. **281** *maynprise*: no simple payment of bail being able to effect their release. **282** *Crist...name*: in // B 265 a resonant re-working of B 161, a line omitted from **C** in revision. But the sense of 'Christ' as the right name for Jesus *after* he has conquered death is clear in context and will be made explicit at 21.62. **283** *þe deueles power*: in B 266 repeating B 10.237, also removed in **C**. **285** *or ligge*: 'or else we shall have to lie'; the *or...til* construction does not propose an alternative to deliverance by Christ, but repeats it. **286** *Lollyng*: a term more ambiguous in tone than *pleynge* 273, since their lot (if unrelieved) would resemble an eternal execution (cf. 14.130). *suche a lord*: not 'a lord such as' but 'that same lord' (MED s.v. *swich* adj. 1a (a)). **288** *myhte* (1, 2): the lexical-rhetorical noun → verb 'conversion' (polyptoton) underlies the Dreamer's sense of sharing Faith's frustration at mankind's plight in the grip of evil. But the **B** line's echo of B 420–5 (like Haukyn, Will weeps 'religious tears') is lost in **C**, since those lines have been removed in revision. **289** As at 13.219, a new character (*another*) who is to dominate the opening of the next passus is introduced at the end of this one. **290** The acceleration of the action is marked from this point and will continue at 19.50, 333–4. **291–2** *whennes...whoder*: increasingly urgent questioning that now concentrates on establishing the origin and purpose of all the speakers to be met. **292** *wolde...tolde*: internal rhyme producing through echo an effect of closure, and preparing for the passus to follow.

Passus XIX (B XVII)

PASSUS NINETEEN replaces vision with action and dialogue but is no less intellectually demanding than XVIII, with personification allegory supported from below by a typological one. It falls into (i) an encounter with *Spes*, who is figured by Moses (1–47), leading to an enactment of Christ's parable of the healing of the wounded man in Lk 10.29–37 (ll. 48–95). This is linked by the Dreamer's enquiry (96–107) to (ii) the Samaritan's discourse on God's *kynde* and the sin of *unkyndenesse* that blocks the operation of grace (108–334). It has expository and homiletic sections of roughly equal length: (a) an extended bi-partite *simile* (161) comparing the Trinity to a hand (113–167) and to a torch (169–225), then (b) a denunciation of *unkyndenesse* (226–334). The main change is to omit B 17.84–90 (perhaps as too complimentary to Will), 103–24 (a prophecy of 'Outlaw's' defeat not free of repetitions and redundancies), and 161–66 (some leisurely elaboration). B 17.180–352 remain (if with much local revision), but 234–48a add a condemnation of those who live luxuriously in indifference to the needy.

(i) 1–47 1 *Spes*: 'Hope'; the second virtue in St Paul's great 'list' at I Cor 13:13. *spie*: 'one who searches for someone / something' (MED s.v. 1(e)), with perhaps some allusion to Moses' spying of the promised land from afar off (Deut 34:1–5). *SPES* is not identified by name with the Hebrews' lawgiver as Faith is with their progenitor at 18.183. But though his figural relation to the 'theological' virtue of Hope, having no explicit NT basis, is necessarily more oblique than Abraham's to Faith, it is unmistakable (Lk 24:27 names him as the first to foretell Christ). *spere*: a probable translinguistic pun on F *espier* 'spy' (a word etymologically unconnected with the native verb *spere*) and *espeir* 'hope' (St Jacques 1977:483–5). There may also be a play on *spyer* 'sprout, scion' (18.231), hope being a virtue that 'grows out of' faith. *kny3te*: developing Faith's 'herald' image (18.186); *Spes* is envisaged as in pursuit of a 'knight errant' expected at the jousts but not yet arrived. **2** *maundement*: 'commandment', with a play on the sense 'writ' (MED s.v.1(b), 2(a); see Keen 2002:77). *Synay*: where the Ten Commandments were given (Ex 19:20; see on 7.170). **3** *alle reumes*: because the Commandments largely embody the precepts of the natural law (hence 'right and reason': cf. 21.481 and Alf*G*). **L** seems to think of even the non-Christian world as monotheist and to have no conception of a purely 'secular' society. **4** *lettre*: his *writ* (**B 3**), 'an administrative document used to order a particular action', here understood as involving 'a proclamation of law' (Keen 2002:77, 79). *Latyn... Ebrew*: the original Commandments being in Hebrew, but the reference to Latin signifying their translation for non-Jews into the official language of the Roman Empire, in which they are quoted at 22.279, B 10.366. The Bx line scans either as Type IIIc (on vowels and |w|) or as Type I on |r| with an internal stave in *writ* (see *Intro*. IV § 45); but the form of revised **C** as a Type Ib line and the fact that the *r*-staves would fall on lexical words recommends the latter. **5** *sey*: probably 'say' (cf. 23), but possibly with a play on 'saw' (cf. 29), alluding to Moses' vision of God on Sinai (Ex 19:20, 24:16). **6–7** The letters have not yet received their authentication, which is what 'nay' refers to; but as 'letters patent' (cf. 12), they are open to all, for the Commandments are not 'privy counsels' but universal laws (contrast Truth's 'secret seal' at 9.27). **6** *lettres*: plural because they are written on two tablets of stone, or because in both sacred languages. **7** *seel*: to validate the document; Christ's death will confirm God's promise of salvation to his people. **8** *croes*: often the form of a seal. *to hange*: after the Crucifixion, which will ratify man's hope of salvation by making available the sacraments of the Christian Faith. **9 (B 7)** Both lines have the same thematic and contrapuntal stave-sounds, but **C** scans as a Type Ie (*aab / ab*) and **B** as an extended Type IIIa (*abb / ab*). **10** *lowe...lygge*: the act of 'affixing the seal' (= the nailing of Jesus to the cross) will effect the

destruction of Satan's power, as will be seen in Passus XX. **11** *we...knowe*: 'so that we might know what the law says'. **12** *patente*: a newly promulgated royal edict addressed to the whole realm, which carried the Great Seal of England and was openly displayed for all to see. *roche*: alluding to the stone tablets on which the Law was written (Ex 24:12, 31:18). **13** *two wordes*: here 'a twofold command' (MED s.v. *word* n. 4 (a)). **14** 'Thou shalt love...God...and [love] thy neighbour [as thyself]' (Mt 22:37). The first part cites Deut 6:5, the central text of the Jewish religion, covering the content of the first two commandments. The second summarises the other eight, dealing with moral conduct, and recalls Lev 19:18 as quoted at Lk 10:27, which has *proximum* 'neighbour' for original *amicum* 'friend'. **15** *good gome*: reminiscent of 9.283–7, where Will reads the words of Truth's pardon, the first major 'divine document' in the poem. **16** *glose*: Christ's comment on the entire OT teaching. *gult penne*: metonymic for gold illumination, on the basis of the metaphor of the 'letter'. **16a** 'On these two [commandments] dependeth the whole law and the prophets' (Mt 22:40), i.e. they sum up the ethical teaching of the OT. **19–22** assert that the writ, though not *yet* sealed, is already effective, as if to say that those before Christ who 'loved God and their neighbour' *are* 'saved' (conditionally). Though in Limbo (cf. 24, 18.270–3), they will be released when his crucifixion 'seals' the document and makes it law. **20** recalls Truth's Pardon, esp. in its form at B 7.112–4. **21** *charme*: a metaphorical usage; but strict Jews wore the text on their heads (Deut 6:8), and medieval Christians often carried charms containing prayers (Duffy 1992:73), even if the practice was not approved (*CT* X 607). There is an ironic echo of the charm obtained from a 'wise woman' that Haukyn (13.341–2) relied on for *boote* instead of *Goddes word*. **23 (B 20)** The scansion of both lines may be vocalic, **C** an extended Type IIIa, **B** Type Ib; or each line may be read as a Type IIa on |s| with *saide* in **C** (or *þis_heraud* in **B**) as third stave. **25** These OT military champions extend from Mosaic times to the 2nd c. before Christ. *Iosue*: Joshua son of Nun, successor to Moses (Deut 34:9) as 'servant of the Lord' (Jos. 3:7, 24:29), whose devotion to the Commandments is shown when he renews and writes down the Mosaic covenant (Jos. 24:25–6). *Iudith*: the widow of Bethulia whose courageous beheading of the Assyrian general Holofernes is told in the apocryphal Book of Judith of the C4th–2nd BC. An exemplar of faith and piety (Jud 8:6–8, 16, 9:17), her song of thanksgiving formed the canticle at Lauds on Wednesdays. *Iudas Macabeus*: the pious hero (d. 161 BC) of I and II Maccabees. These last two books of the Latin OT were valued for affirming belief in resurrection and the efficacy of prayer for the dead (II Mac 7:9, 12:43–5, the latter said in the anniversary of the burial Mass) and their relevance in this context is clear from vs 45: 'they who had fallen asleep with godliness had great grace laid up for them'. **27** *Where...trewe*: 'Which if either of you can / Can either of you (be trustworthy)?' The question asks why, if *faith* in the Trinity together with repentance suffices for salvation, *love* of (one) God and one's neighbour is necessary? **30** virtually repeats 18.188, while its B 27 form is repeated exactly at C 98. **32** *sory*: '(were) sorry'. **33** *somme*; *somme*: the homophonic pun mockingly hinting at Will's incredulity. **35** now scans as revised on |s| not |v|. **36** *aspyed*: 'looked over / out'; the word plays on his rôle as *spie* (1). **38 (B 35)** may scan on |g| but furnishes a more effective set of contrasts on vowels, giving usually non-lexical *o* and *on* full semantic value (cf. *al(le)* in 39) and a first stave in *God-héde*. In **B**, *in* strictly belongs with *beleeue*, as *louye* takes a direct object. But Bx's order of the verbs can be justified, since 'belief' precedes 'love', and sound theology thus prevails over correct grammar. **C**, by contrast, with the line in its new position at 42, adopts the grammatically correct order, *belief* in (one) God having already been predicated at 38–9. **41** *as oureselue*: filling out the words omitted from the quotation at 14. **B 37–41** offer two examples from common experience to suggest that religion may just be too difficult for the ordinary man to understand, let alone to obey, so the 'simpler' it is, the 'easier' it will be to follow. **42** revises a syntactically awkward B 35 ('to believe in and to love'). The echo of 17.135 reminds that without its 'hard' doctrine of the Trinity (and its related doctrine of the Incarnation), Christianity comes much closer to Judaism and Islam. **43** *and for lered*: a change in the direction of intellectual humility recalls that at 14.55. **44–5** keep the objection ('to believe in the Trinity and love one's enemies...') but omit **B**'s observation that the second of these is *harder* than the first, and that Christianity's central ethical demand (Mt 5:44, explicitly extending Lev 19:18) is the chief obstacle to its acceptance. This, *pace Pe*, is surely in Will's mind; and Goodridge (p. 42) is mistaken that Will's problem is his inability to reconcile the doctrine that faith justifies with the command to good works and charity, a 'Pauline' dichotomy absent from the text. **46–7** Will's dismissive words to *Spes* (which in **C** also apply to Faith) clearly cue the arrival of one who will show that, however difficult, it *is* possible to *vse* 'practise' charity. What is not immediately clear is how this personage relates to the 'hard' teaching that forms half of his exposition; but he will emerge in Passus XX as the divine Son whose mission is to reveal the true nature of God to man, and the two crucial doctrines (Incarnation / Trinity; love of enemies) as inextricably connected.

48–82 The ultimate source of the SAMARITAN EPISODE is Lk 10:30–6, but it owes much to patristic exegesis as transmitted by medieval commentators on the liturgy of the 13th Sunday after the Octave of Pentecost (Saint-

Jacques 1969:217–30, Bennett 1981; Wailes 1987:210–12). The dramatised parable demonstrates concretely how efficacious religion must combine true belief and 'true' living, faith in the Trinity and service of one's neighbour, and how only through the Incarnation of one of the three 'lovely persons' can man receive the grace and example that equip him 'to love a shrew'. Though he has no abstract allegorical name, it is easy enough in the light of the preceding to divine the Samaritan's double function as a persona. 'Biblical', but not a 'straight' historical character like Abraham and Moses, this fictive type-figure serves as an oblique analogue *both* of Christ and of his faithful servant Piers (the 'transcendental' Plowman) in whom grace has actualised the divine 'image' (see Murtaugh 1978; Raw 1969). The Samaritan's supernatural Charity differentiates him from Faith and *Spes*, who are powerless to cure humanity incapacitated by sin. In the Gospel parable, the Priest and Levite reveal the limits of the OT religion. Bennett 1981 notes how allegorised representations of the Parable, in both literary and iconographic sources, were familiar in the period and show it to have been understood as a paradigm of the Fall and restoration of man. **L** has prepared for his specific identification of Priest and Levite with the Jews' progenitor and liberator respectively by his earlier stress on Abraham's sacrifice (a priestly function), and here by Moses's law-giving (historically the rôle of the Scribes rather than the Levites). A disturbing parallel may even be hinted at between Abraham / Moses and the contemporary Church establishment, with the 'outsider'-figure of the Samaritan possibly suggesting the devout layman of perfect integrity (Piers). This already complex pattern **L** further complicates by correlating the esteemed first two *Theological Virtues* with OT personages who can do nothing if they lack the third and highest Virtue, Charity. The normally expected relation between these virtues, all of them held to be infused by divine grace through baptism, was one of *interdependence*: being faith and hope *in Christ* (I Tim 1:1), they were the *fulfilment* of their OT types. But while ultimately reconcilable with the teaching of I Cor 13, **L**'s bold presentation arouses locally some intellectual and dramatic tension. **49** *Samaritaen*: a member of a race descended from the inhabitants of the ancient Kingdom of Israel whose 'impure' religion (mixed with some pagan practices) was regarded by Jews with hostile contempt. The Gospel parable shows those whose religion *is* ritually and doctrinally pure as nonetheless incapable of 'using' towards *their* 'neighbour' the 'law of love' taught to their leader Moses (cf. B 1.151). *muyle*: an apt rendering of Vg *iumentum*, since **L**'s re-telling blends the parable narrative with that of Jesus's entry into Jerusalem on an ass (Lk 19:35ff) to be recounted in 20.19. The unique 'Langlandian grotesque' will later be shown in making a humble beast of burden replace the powerful *destrier* ridden by this 'knight' (cf. 52), an instance of how 'earthly honest things' (in this case the supreme secular 'icon' of the age) must undergo a spiritual 'transformation of meaning'. **50** *rihte way*: judged by Bennett (1981:18) an echo of Christ's words 'Thou hast answered *right*' to the lawyer he addresses the parable to (Lk 10:28*b*). **51–2** The Lucan narrative makes clear that the traveller, the priest and the Levite (though not necessarily the Samaritan) were travelling *towards* Jericho. But **L** has them all going to Jerusalem (50), evoking the Gospel account of Christ's journey to his Passion (Jericho being named in Lk 19:1 as the town where Jesus stops on his way). **52** *ioust*: taking up a hint dropped as early as 1.152–3. Its prime religious source may be the Easter Sequence *Victimae paschali*, vs 3; but the image of Christ as a knight doing combat with Satan was established in medieval vernacular literature (see under 20.77). **53** *at ones*: more dramatic than in Lk 10:31–3, where the three pass the man successively at intervals. **54–5** improve the somewhat prosaic B 54 and their a-verses now echo 10.62a and 68a, evoking (as **B** does not) Will's state of moral perplexity at that earlier encounter. The traveller is understood in Hugh of St Victor's *Allegoriae in novum testamentum* (*PL* 175:814–5) as designating 'mankind gravely wounded by the evil of original sin' (*R–H*), the priest and levite as the 'fathers of old' who lived holy lives but were little able to heal the wounds of sin, and the Samaritan of course as Christ. In the C12th Lambeth homily *De natali Domini* cited by *Sk* (Morris, *OE Homilies* 1868:I, 78–85), the Levite is specifically Moses; and Bennett 1981 notes how St Bernard in his Sermon VII (*PL* 183:23) includes Abraham and Moses among several men who passed by the wounded traveller. **L**'s interpretation is redolent of the discourse of salvation theology (57a, 58b, 69b) and, as *Pe* notes (referring to discussions in Owst 1933:57–66, Coghill 1944:351–7, *R–H* 1951:2–3, 204–8, Salter 1967:5–7, Smith 1966:74–93), his handling of the parable can be usefully analysed in terms of the four levels of scriptural exegesis. **54** *theues hadde ybounde*: **L**'s addition, drawing on the common idea of persistent sin as incapacitating man from free action. The *latrones* (the devils or their instruments the deadly sins) are agents of 'that first grand thief' Satan. **55** *they*: '(whom) they'; on the Ø-relative see *MES* 205. **56a** recalls Glutton at 6.402. **57** *semiuief*: directly answering to *semivivo* in Lk 10:30; the word's one other appearance, in *Beryn* 2202 (*MED* s.v.), could be echoing this Langlandian coinage. **58** On the phrase see at 14.105. **60** 'And was unwilling to go anywhere near him' (the distance of 'nine plough-lands' is typical humorous exaggeration). The original significance of the 'passing by' in the parable is that the traveller might have been dead and, since touching a corpse incurred defilement, it shows both 'religious' men to place ritual purity above the law of

love (or *kynde*: see on B 72). By contrast, the 'impure' Samaritan does not recoil from handling and helping the desecrated image of the God both he and the Jews worship. **61–2** *ybosted...yholpe*: cf. 22, making clear that the 'carefole' man's 'care' is sin. **66** *lyard*: more grotesque humour, the mule becoming a grey horse as the 'joust' metaphor unfolds (by 72 its colour in **C** has changed to brown, returning to grey at 333). **68** *poues*: evidencing the physical contact the others avoided; this is the 'kynde knowynge' Will has been seeking, experiential knowledge of man's need by a *creatour* who becomes *creature*. **71–2** *wyn...oyle*: suggestive of the three healing sacraments (of baptism, absolution and unction). The wine is here used to cleanse wounds, not to drink; but *atamede* hints at its symbolic significance, and in the light of *embaumed* (88), the eucharist's healing as well as feeding power (*dronken*) is intimated. The Samaritan's act was often interpreted as prefiguring administration of the sacraments to someone whom simple faith and the observance of the moral law cannot help recover fully: restoration to God's favour comes only from the grace of Christ given through the 'mysteries' he instituted. **72** *on...sette*: an action seen by Bede to signify 'believing in Christ's incarnation, being initiated into his mysteries [sacraments], and at the same time being guarded against the onslaught of the Enemy' (*PL* 92:469–70). **73** *Lavacrum...*: 'the bath of the law of God', signifying the baptismal font (*Sk*); Alan of Lille in *SAP* XXX (*PL* 210:170) speaks of the *lavacrum baptismi,* doubtless echoing the *lavacrum regenerationis* of Titus 3:5, glossed 'Baptismum' by Hugh of St Cher (7:235b). The 'law of God' will cover the 'way of living' to which a Christian is committed by baptism, particularly the Mosaic Commandments as interpreted by Christ the new Moses in the Sermon on the Mount. *grange*: 'barn or outlying farmstead' (Vg *stabulum* 'stable', 'inn'); interpreted by Bede (*ibid.*) as the Christian religion found in the *Ecclesia praesens* where pilgrims on the way to their eternal *patria* are refreshed (cf. B 119). *Pe* (following Smith 1966:79) notes an anticipation of the barn of UNITY at 21.319. **B 72** *Lex Christi*: a phrase occurring in Gal 6:2: 'Bear ye one another's burdens and so you shall fulfil the law of Christ [*legem Christi*];' it is called the 'lawe of kynde' at 8.231*a* (cf. B 11.210*a*) and Christ is described as commanding it at 13.77. Alf*Q* observes that the Pauline verse was cited in glossing the Samaritan's action (e.g. by Hugh of St Cher 6:195) and was much discussed in the C14th (Coleman 1981:28). **74** The circumstantial details have no apparent allegorical significance, unless to imply the original separateness of the Christian community from the society in which it found itself. **75–7** indicate how the spiritual care of Christians falls to the ordained clergy until the Second Coming of Christ, who will reward his faithful ministers at the end of time (the vaguer *aʒeynward* is less confusing than **B**'s *come fro þe iustes*, which is bound to suggest the Resurrection). **75** *a-lechynge*: 'a-healing', < *on* + verbal noun. *to...myhte*: 'so that he should recover, if it was possible'. **76** *toek*: the construction takes a dative second object (cf. 2 above), but omission of usual *to* (stylistically one too many in this line) seems to follow the parallel construction with its commoner synonym *give*. The polysemantic *annominatio* on *toek...take* improves the somewhat vapid B 77b. **78** *lyard he bystrideth*: the phrase recalling Z 3.158. **79** The revision removes the split-preposition construction of B 80, with which cf. 16.144 above (*MES* 413).

   B 82–3 82 recalls *WPal* 5169 *hou þei* sped *hem to* spayne spacli *þerafter*; for the polysemantic *annominatio* in *spedde...spede* cf. on 76). **83** may be prompted by the account of Moses's talking to Christ on Mt Tabor (Mt 17:3) and Christ's speaking of himself ('beginning with Moses') on the way to Emmaus (Lk 24:27). **83–95** convey a sense of friendly intimacy unlike that between Will and any of his previous dozen interlocutors. The Samaritan's Piers-like courtesy (cf. 8.14–15 above), though less striking than in B 86–7, bespeaks his nature as the 'hidden' Christ. But as revelation is 'progressive', his Trinitarian teaching at 108–225 is presented as continuous with Abraham's at 18.199–239, though stressing not the metaphysics of triunity but the mystical bond between the virtue he embodies and the divine nature. Sins against charity strike at the centre of that nature and 'paralyse' the proffer of sanctifying grace, thereby leading to the specific 'sin against the Holy Ghost'. This is seen as extending from 'inhumane treatment of the needy' to 'wilful murder of the innocent', which destroys the grace of repentance whereby man has access to the divine life. At its deepest symbolic level, the Samaritan's discourse resumes the great penitential theme of the poem's earlier parts in sacramental terms, alluding to the phases of conversion and absolution that culminate in the Easter Communion, and implicitly equating the 'fruit charity' with Christ's presence in the Eucharist. **81** *sewede*: implying both Will's speed (explicit in B 84), which enables him to outstrip the two old men, and its cause, his direct response to St Paul's *Sectamini charitatem* 'Follow after charity' (I Cor 14:1). **B 87** echoes Will's poignant question at B 15.151; the answer is 'Here, in Christ'. Bennett (1981:23) convincingly finds an echo of Jn 15:15. **84** *medicyne*: on the image of Christ as physician and its structural significance in the poem see St-Jacques 1991. **85** *festred*: the earliest use, overlooked by MED. **86–8** scarcely improve on B 94–6, which memorably evoke demonic child-sacrifice, the better to force attention upon Christ's redemptive action as extending from his birth to death (cf. on 94). **86** *bloed...barn*: perhaps suggested by the thought that Jesus began his ministry to man when as an infant he bled the same blood he would shed on the cross: 'in his

circumcision...this pouring out of [Christ's blood] was the beginning of our redemption' (*LA* 82). **88–95** proceed in an order fitted to an ideal 'norm' for the time (chrisening in infancy and spiritual growth over a lifetime): 'Man cannot be saved without being baptised in Christ's name, believing firmly in Christ's saving Incarnation, resisting sin with the help of penance, and receiving the food of life in the Eucharist'. **88** *enbaumed*: as part of the rite of baptism (see on 72); yet **C** more comprehensively sees Christ's blood as not only cleansing (baptismal remission of 'original' sin) but as healing ('penitential' absolution from 'actual' sin). **B 95** Since the believer is baptized into the saving death of Christ (Rom 6:3–4), release from sin by Christ's blood is implicitly equated with this sacrament (I Jn 1:7; cf. also I Pet 1:2). But the most relevant scriptural context is provided by Jn 19:34 where, in the standard patristic understanding, the blood and water symbolically prefigure the first sacrament (see on 17.268). **90** The startling image of child-eating relates the greatest sacrament (the Eucharist) likewise to the infant Jesus by a sort of 'logic of backward inference'. This audacious way of speaking, where the unutterably sublime verges on the repellently grotesque, is modelled on Christ's own words in Jn 6:54–7, as noted by Bennett (1981), which alienate some of his disciples. But for **L** the high Eucharistic teaching of the 'pris' evangelist (21.267) is the spiritual centre of the Christian faith (see Schmidt 2006:306). **91** *plasterud*: taken up from B 96 to be applied not to Christ's suffering for sinners but to his followers' own resistance to sin through the power of grace (patience is the fourth 'fruit' of the Holy Spirit). **92** *this way*: the *semita vitae* or journey of life; the *wildernesse* of B 99 (eliminated from **C**) evokes more the perplexing 'region of unlikeness' of B Pr 12. **93 (B 101)** revises to Type Ia or Ic a **B** line of either extended Type IIIb with semi-counterpoint on |f| (scanning *abb / aa*) or (less probably) of Type Ia on *s* with a liaisonal stave *his felawe*. *such*: an improvement on *Feiþ...þiself* in B 101–2, which is theologically acceptable as indicating the necessity of Faith and Hope to protect against evil, but not in (apparently) affirming the adequacy of the Jewish religion. The conceptual discrepancy between these two dimensions of **L**'s double-named personification personages (Lawton's term 'actants' [1987:14–16] has a possible use here) may have been brought to his attention by critical readers, and is removed in revision. So is any hint of presumption in the somewhat Dantean 'thyself' and the (unintentionally) ambiguous reference in *oure werkes* at B 102, presumably denoting the acts of charity without which faith and trust do not suffice for salvation (I Cor 13). **94** *litel baby*: taking up B 96, but to be 'fed on' only 'in faith'. **94–5** *þat...That*: the double object of the verb, yielding the sense 'whose'. *lychame*: i.e. in the Eucharist, faith in Christ's Incarnation being a seamless whole from his birth to his death (cf. on 88), liturgically re-enacted from Christmas to Easter.

B 103–23 Excision of this realistic little allegory (foreshadowed at B 14.301–2) may have been prompted by its theological incoherences (see on C 93) and its anticipations of the next passus which, while arousing expectation, reduce tension. **103** *Outlawe*: an apt image for Satan, the rebel ejected from the 'holy comune' (5.186) of heaven, living outside God's order and preying on his people. **106** *hym...on horse*: contrasting the speaker with Faith and *Spes*; though a traveller on horseback might *escape* Outlaw Satan, a mounted 'knight' was a positive threat he would be wise to fear. **108** *Caro*: 'Flesh', last heard of as the 'castle' where Anima lived (B 9.49). The word evokes Jn 1:14 and probably has here the wider sense 'human nature' suggested by Hill 2001:216. The interpretation, familiar from liturgical commentaries (St-Jacques 1969), went back to Bede: '[The Samaritan's] beast is the flesh (*caro*), in which [Christ] saw fit to come to us' (ibid). **109** *in Inferno*: represented by the dark ditch into which the outlaw flees (cf. B Pr 15–19). **110** 'But within three days from now': in form a realistic 'chivalric' promise, but directly alluding to the time that Christ will lie in the grave (cf. B 18.42). **112** The words mean that for any who trust in Christ, the Devil's power is broken, not that the Devil will be powerless against any who sin wilfully. **112a** '[I will deliver them out of the hand of death. I will redeem them from death]. O death, I will be thy death; [O hell, I will be thy bite]' (Osee [Hosea] 13:14, and cf. I Cor 15:54–5, which alludes to it). The verse, which is repeated at B 18.35*a*=C 20.34*a*, implicitly understands Death and Hell as persons, and is liturgically associated with *Christ's* death, appearing as the first antiphon at Lauds on Holy Saturday. **113** *forster*: the rôle in which Faith after Christ's victory over death will direct men to the right path through the 'wilderness'. The idea here seems to be that Abraham's 'prospective' trust will reach fulfilment as the theological virtue Faith infused at baptism. Bennett (1981:25) notes the duty of a forester to keep the edges of the highway clear of trees and branches that might shelter brigands lying in wait. **114** *kennen out*: the prime task of Faith being guidance in what to believe about the things of God (*teche* 117). **116** *hostilers man*: an image from the parable being enacted, but needing to be read 'inversely' as personification- rather than symbol-allegory (Frank 1953), the virtue of hope bringing needed comfort to those for whom faith is not enough in the struggle against sin. **118** *lede*: the traditional rôle of Moses. *lettre*: the document of B 17.9 that contains the rule of life sufficient for salvation but has not yet been 'ratified'. **119** *bileue*: the *Lex Christi* of B 72. **120** *salue*: 'salvation', the goal of the Samaritan's journey to Jerusalem; the ointment is specified at 123, and the words indirectly reaffirm what the sacraments of healing intimated at B 70–1. **121** *come*

ayein: referring to Christ's post-resurrection appearance to the Apostles, when he gives them his spirit (Jn 20:22–3); but the 'salve' may be more narrowly understood as 'grace' (cf. 122), which will be released for *alle sike* on Pentecost Day (B 19.209 //). **96–107** rehearse the lesson Will has learnt from Faith and Hope. **98** virtually repeats 30, but in the form of B 27 (whereas B 127 *revises* the b-verse of 27), accentuating the effect of his speech as a 'lesson learnt'. **101** *for his loue*: 'for love of Him' (objective genitive). **103–7** express not a Mosaic but a Christian view of humility (influenced by Mt 7:3–4, Lk 18:13; Mt 5:11–12, 39.44) that reverses the self-conceit shown by Haukyn at B 13.287, 295–6. **105** *And*: 'And (to believe myself)'.

(ii)*a* 108–30 109 *as...o God*: 'according to *the way in which* A. taught you to believe in the One God [i.e. in God-as-Trinity]'. The Samaritan elides the teaching of Faith and Hope separately recounted by Will at 99–102: faith in divine (tri)unity and love of neighbour being inseparably bound together. **111** *Kynde Wit*: an unexpected reference to this elusive semi-personification of 'the knowledge derived from experience', evoking a mental world left far behind since the (quasi)-inner dream began at 18.4, but only to emphasise the distance between divine mysteries (Truth dwells in a high tower) and what commonsense expects or comprehends. The replacement of 'conscience' B 136 by 'eny kyne thouhtes' removes what could be a source of tension arising from **L**'s having used 'conscience' (which *should* always follow reason) to denote the conscientious scruples of someone unable to believe a doctrine that seemed against reason. The Samaritan's reply, like Ymaginatif's earlier, comes as two extended analogies of a hand (113–168) and a candle (169–77), the latter moving by an easy transition to describe the action of divine grace upon man. These rely on feeling and imagination rather than logic in attempting to answer such 'arguments' as that the dogma defies the principle of contradiction (cf. Alan of Lille in *PL* 210:401). **112** Anti-Trinitarian monotheism was not a current Christian heresy, so the Samaritan's real concern may be the objections of the Jews (whence his insistence that Abraham had knowledge of the Trinity). These Alan of Lille addresses in Bk. III of his treatise bearing the general title 'Against Heretics', first with scriptural and rational 'arguments' (*auctoritates et rationes*), then through analogies (*similitudines*), including one of a candle. *thien hoend*: see generally on this image Biggs 1991. **113** *bigynnynge*: connecting not God's own 'origin' but the Trinity's self-revelation with the 'origin' of the universe, prior to which (and during which) the 'fist' was ('and still is') folded or clenched. **114a** 'Folding the world fast in his fist', applied to the 'three-fold High deviser and designer' in the C6th Marian hymn 'Quem terra, pontus, aethera' sung at Matins in the Office of the BVM (*JLH* I:41, vs. 4). The Biblical sources of the image include Isaiah 40:12 (*Sk*) and Prov 30:4. **115** *fuste*: borrowed from *pugillo* in 114*a* but developed in typically idiosyncratic fashion. The clenched fist is an Augustinian 'natural sign' of *power* (the attribute appropriated to the Father at B 16.211–13); and in medieval art a hand with finger(s) outstretched often 'betokens' God's action: see Schiller I pl. 235, II pl. 531 (single hand with three spears), 527 (three hands). **116** *fynger*: as *Pe* notes (citing Bartholomaeus I. 21. 30), a traditional name of the Son; but see on 140*a*. **117** *as...paume*: 'as one does in the case of one's palm'. **118** *pethe*: in the light of // *purely* B 142 signifying more 'essence' than 'strength' (MED s.v. *pith* n. 2(a) not 3) and thus earlier than the recorded uses in this sense. Because the a-verse re-writes B 142a, C 141 avoids being repetition. **119** 'To perform whatever function the hand has strength and skill to accomplish'. **120** Parallel B 144 virtually repeats B 16.212, which **C** removes. **123** The basis of this apparently original thought may be that God 'touches' the world directly through the Word, by first creating and then by redeeming it (Jn 1:3, 10–11). **124** recalls *Cursor Mundi* 18940: 'Gaf to þaim þe haligast / Alkin wiit to *tuche and tast*'. *at techyng of*: the Divine Son being thought of as having undergone *kenosis* 'self-emptying' (Phil. 2:7) to become the obedient Jesus of history; an allusion to the power of the Holy Ghost overshadowing Mary (Lk 1:35). **B 149a** *Qui...*; **C 125a** *Natus...*: 'Who was conceived of the Holy Ghost, Born of the Virgin Mary'; the fourth and fifth clauses in the Apostles' Creed. The revision makes better sense, since the Son's birth, not his conception, is the main subject. **127** *huyde*: perhaps suggested by Is 40:12 ('Quis mensus est *pugillo* aquas...?'), which is strikingly linked with Dan 5:5 in a Trinity Sunday sermon by Jacobus a Voragine in Lambeth MS 43, col. 278 cited by Galloway (1998:138). The basic (and not quite satisfactory) assignation of fist, fingers and palm to the Persons severally may be original. **127a** 'For I, [if I be lifted up from the earth,] will draw all things to myself' (Jn 12:32). This is clearer in **B**, which can be made to refer back to the Son's action (the words being Christ's); but the 'drawing of all things' may signify God's resumption of Creation at the end of time. Better is the revision of B 154–6 which (though not at odds with physical fact) untheologically suggest that the 'palm' is the *source* of the Trinity, whereas the Spirit should proceed from Father and Son.

   B 160–3 160–1 echo 'aquas et caelos palmo ponderavit...molem terrae...' in Is 40:12 (Galloway 1998:138n28) and they may be recalled in *Patience* 206–8. **160** will scan either as Type Ia on |w| with a mute key-stave or as an extended Type IIIb on vowels with semi-counterpoint on |w| and first stave on either *halt* or a rhetorically-stressed *al* (abb / aa). Whichever pattern is recognised, the metrical structure of the b-half is identical: *wiþinne hém þrè*. **163** scans as Type IIIa on |t| with a liaisonal first stave (*it_is*) or, preferably, as Type Ia on |n| with a trisyllabic prelude dip. **131–52** affirm how all Three Persons possess 'full' godhead ('þe same myhte' 149) equally (131, 136, 141), **153–68** how God's grace is incapacitated by man's deliberate sin against his nature as Love. **132** *furste*: prior not in order of dignity but conceptually, and in order of time only insofar as God was initially known to *man* as 'Creator' and as 'One' before his final self-revelation as Three Persons, which had to await Christ's appearance in time (hence *ar* 133). **134** retrieves the form of A 10.28 (from the description of Kynde) to emphasise again that God is the originary source (as *fader*) of uncreated and (as *formeour*) of created being. **134a** 'Thou art Creator of all things', from the Compline hymn 'Jesu salvator saeculi', st. 2 (*Brev.* 2.234). **135 (B 169)** scans either as Type Ia on |w| with a four-syllable prelude dip and with the caesura before *and* or, preferably, on vowels as Type IIa with a 'supplemental' stave in position five. The **B** line may be either a vocalic Type Ic with mute key-stave or else a standard Type Ia on |m|. The latter is preferable since potency (*myʒt*) is associated closely with creative action (*makynge*) in the b-half, whereas **C** stresses the sempiternity of the Father's power. **136–40a** lack some clarity since they compare the Son with the thumb, implying an unintended analogy of the fingers with the Father (who is figured by the entire hand in an inclusive sense). **139** *be ne myhte*: a paradox (that the Father *depends* on the Son) resolved at 140, which states that the Father could not operate (*holde*; *hente*) without the *agency* of the Son, through whom he made the world. **B** expresses the same thought in calling the Son the *science* 'Wisdom' of the Father (cf. Wisd. 7:24–7). Though appearing to contradict the 'fullness' of power affirmed of each person (149), the explanation is that *failed þe Sone* presumes what is not even an 'ideal' but an *impossible* condition. **140a** 'Finger of God's right hand', from st. 3 of 'Veni creator spiritus' (*JLH* I:80), the hymn sung at 21.211–12. There, however, its referent is the Holy Ghost, whom the Pentecost Hymn quite logically calls the 'finger', thereby understanding the Son as the 'right hand' and 'God' as the Father 'containing' the Trinity as a whole. The motif is clearly illustrated in Schiller I: pls. 356–7, where the Spirit descends on Christ as a dove directly below the outstretched index finger of a right hand. **L**'s idiosyncratic departure from the customary use of the 'hand' image could have been prompted by the famous 'proof-text' *Sede a dextris meis* (Ps 109:1), which Alan of Lille in *CH* says 'pertinet *ad Filium*, qui existens Deus, sedet *a dextris* Domini, id est aequalis Patri' (*PL* 210:404). **142** The 'natural' function of the clenched fist is to strike, of the fingers to handle. **147** *greued...grype*: 'pained with what they grasp'; the Spirit is imagined as the Trinity's 'feeling' aspect, the *amor medius* 'Love between Father and Son' (*JLH* II:191, vs.5) that suffers from the sinner a direct *injuria* (like that to a King when a criminal breaks his peace). **149–50** *of...o God*: cf. 'Unum esse deitatis / Et *eiusdem potestatis*' (*JLH* II:191, vs. 2). **158** An economical fusion of B 190a and 193b allowing omission of 192 (as over-particular) and 191 (as repeating 186). **B 192** *toshullen*: taken as the p.p. of a verb the simplex of which is glossed 'break' by MED, rejecting the *Sk*, OED derivation from OE **scelan* (p.p. **scolen*) 'peel'. But *kynde wit* may well wonder whether someone with four fingers and thumb broken *could* 'help himself in many kinds of ways'. **161** 'On the basis of this analogy I find grounds for believing...' *simile*: a term from rhetoric here used to mean 'an analogy for use in an argument'; recalling Alan's *CH*: 'by a likeness (*similitudine*) the same [the doctrine of the Trinity] is proved' (in *PL* 210:406). **162** *in*: 'against' (167), a usage conditional upon the Latin quotation's *in* (cf. 'sinnyng in the Hooly Goost' at *CT* X 694). **163** *elleswhere*: i.e. in purgatory. **163a** See on B 16.47a; repeating Piers's teaching in a **B** passage removed from **C** at that point. A deliberate, free act of evil involves rejection of grace and contempt for the divine goodness, attitudes which, persisted in to the end, send the sinner straight to hell. *R–H* 208 understand the 'irremissible' sin as denial of faith and loss of hope leading to despair; but B 215–17=C 181–3 present it as wilful sin against charity. **165 (B 200)** scans either vocalically as Type Ia on *is* (1, 2) and *as* or, preferably, on |f| as Type IIa, with *For* as stave one and a supplemental |f| stave in position five. **168** *quenche*: 'extinguish', providing a transition to the image of the *torch* (cf. *R–H* 209).

169–225 use an *argument* and a dominant *image* that are ascribed to Augustine by Jacobus a Voragine, though deriving partly from Tertullian (Galloway 1998:139). The patristic comparisons familiar from medieval hymns (e.g. *aenigma radius* in *JLH* II:191, vs. 5), are all with the *sun*, its ray and its heat, not a candle and its wax and flame, to which there are closer analogues in Bartholomaeus XIX, 63:10 (*Sk*) and *LA* 164–5 (*Pe*). Images of candle *and* sun are, however, juxtaposed by Alan of Lille specifically as *similitudines* that 'prove' the doctrine of the Trinity: 'The Father is called spiritually...light, because he shines from himself...and because from him shines the light that illuminates, the Son, and the light that enkindles, the Holy Spirit' (*PL* 210 406–7). But it is **L** not Alan who envisions the 'sin against the Spirit' as a 'quenching' of the *lux inflammans* and who brings together 'divine light' and its 'extinction' by wilful sin. It may be assumed therefore that while the double *similitudo* is 'deeply rooted in clerical materials' (Galloway 1998:138), it is the poet's own imaginative synthesis of reading and experience, *kynde wit* and *clergye*. **169** *torche*: a large candle of twisted hemp soaked in wax. *taper*: wax candle. **174** *this*: a collo-quial use of the demonstrative for the definite article; see *MES* 174. **176** revises to a T-type a **B** line of the rare line-type IIb. *fyn loue and bileue*: infused by grace in baptism and penance, the sacraments that 'cleanse from sin'. With *fyn loue* compare *fyn hope* at 85: 'excellent, pure, refined, noble', this is God's unmerited love that alone can heal fallen man. **178 (B 212)** scans as Type Ia (*sómt□me*) or as Type IIIc (*sôm týme*). **180–1** mean that the divine life which can never be entirely quenched is blocked when opposed by man (cf. Jn 1:5, 11). The 'fire' in the wick that continues to smoulder is the obverse of the 'spark' of a repentant person's sin that can *not* remain alight in the river of unlimited divine forgiveness at 6.333–7a. **181** *grace withouten mercy*: a paradoxical phrase, since one sense of *grace* was 'mercy' (see *IG*); God's *kynde* cannot change, but its help to *unkynde* man can be blocked by deliberate resistance. **183** *lycame and*: a revision making clear that murder is envisaged (265–7); the univocal application of *leel* to 'body' and 'life' is noteworthy. **187** *togyderes*: the whole Trinity being the source of grace (divine life), the Spirit its form and agent. **191** *blowe*: the first of three witty inversions, here of the usual image of the Holy Ghost himself as *spiramen* 'breath' (*JLH* II:191, vs 3); for now the 'breath' is man's free assent (i.e. the will to 'love and believe' that makes for repentance) in the work of redemption. **192** *flaumeth he*: a second inversion, making the Spirit's fire 'melt' the 'solid' power of the Father and Son, and proving **L**'s 'grotesque sublime' sturdily underpinned by *kynde wit*. For since ice is water in another state, God's 'true' nature as merciful love rather than severe justice may be communicated through this image without offence to sense and reason. *Sk* aptly cites from Morris, *OE Homilies* (1868) ii.150: 'The tear of compassion is warm like the water of snow that trickles down in the sun's heat' (original in Latin). **194** *hete.. sonne*: the same Alanian metaphor for the Spirit (*solis... calor* in *PL* 210:407A) as at 18.75, there denoting 'sanctifying', but here 'habitual' grace. **196** *the...Trinite*: clearly the object of *melteth* 197, and thus denoting 'Potencia-Dei-Patris', with *al* being adverbial. But the syntax allows this phrase to be read also in apposition with the subject (*al* now becoming pronominal, and having reference to the Three Persons); for Love is, in the last resort, the 'sublime power' of God. **198** *wex*: a third unexpected inversion; with the human will now required to immolate itself like a candle-end flung on a sinking fire. **200** *derkenesse*: symbolically signifying 'sin', both echoing the canticle of Zachary said at Lauds (Lk 1:79) and foreshadowing 20.365. **204** *þat...deyeth*: recalling Trajan at 14.211, a passage where the Spirit's power as illuminating grace is invoked. *þat*: 'for someone who'. **206** An unusual T-type with the caudal b-staves anticipated in the a-verse after a muted a-stave in position 2. **208** *cortesye*: 'gracious generosity [beyond one's desert]'; also echoing the end of the Trajan passage (14.216). **209–10** The speaker's authority for this claim is 1.164–9, where Christ forgives even those who do *not* ask him pardon. **211** *fuyr at a flynt*: a cry for mercy from one who refused to show any. **212** *tasch*: i.e. 'willingness to repent'. **213** recalls Pr 195 and is echoed in *CT* VIII 781. **214** *flaume make*: i.e. 'bring mercy and grace'. *faile...kynde*: 'if what its very nature requires is absent' (fire needs something to burn); an example that shows common experience to argue against the possibility of forgiveness for the unforgiving. **215–225** warn against trusting in external 'religious' acts while remaining at heart *vnkynde* 'uncharitable' to one's fellow Christians. **215–16a** repeats 181–2a, a measure of the importance attached to the idea expressed here. **216a** 'Amen, I say to you, I know you not' (Mt 25:12); addressed by the Bridegroom (a parabolic *figura* of Christ) to the wise and foolish Virgins whose 'oil' represents deeds of active charity that prepare them for the arrival of their lord (cf. on I 183–4). **217** scans either on lexical words in |k| or, preferably, on vowels with *al* as key-stave, the important prefixes *vn-* and *em-* (*euene-*) bearing sentence-stress, and a secondary alliterative pattern on |k| (for other 'dual-scansion' lines cf. 19.3, 23, 38, 280 and B 17.3). **218** *Dele*: an echo of I Cor 13:3. The spiritual attitude envisaged is little more strained than that of its (deliberately) hyperbolic Pauline source, since those presumably intended are rich people who can 'buy' pardons while remaining unkind to their kind. **219** *Pampilon*: referring to indulgences for remission of sin granted by the Bishop of Pamplona in Navarre for issue by the Abbot of St Mary's Rounceval at Charing Cross (the house of Chaucer's Pardoner in *CT* I 670), a dependency of the Augustinian hospital of Our Lady of Roncesvalles on the pilgrim route to Compostella. These would be granted for actually 'seeking St James' or for a monetary composition for the same. The house had a bad reputation for pardon-mongering (Bloomfield 1956). **220** *ingratus*: '(personally) unkind, cruel', though the use of the Latin word was perhaps suggested by St Paul's description in II Tim 3:2ff of the *ingrati* who 'resist truth' (cf. 230a, from Christ's warning against those without true inward religion). The presence of *dele* at 218 precludes the sense 'ungrateful, mean' of *ingrati* at B 14.169, used of the rich who refuse alms to 'men þat it nedede'. **223** *blowynge of vnkyndenesse*: recalling the imagery of 'wicked winds' in 18.29ff and inverting the wind of love spoken of at 191. The very strong word *vnkyndenesse* (White 1988:95–110) here denotes the spiritual 'wind' of hell that blows fiercely against the clear flame of divine love. **224** *where*: 'whether (or not)'. **225** 'If I speak with the tongues of men, [and of angels, and have not charity, I am...nothing]' (I Cor 13:1–2). The famous Pauline passage is less an attack on uncharitableness than a declaration that salvation is impossible without charity; so a more relevant

(tacit) authority for seeing *vnkyndenesse* as a destructive force that quenches the divine light may be I Jn 2:9–11.
(b) 226–76 form a diatribe against 'unkindness' directed especially towards the wealthy (see on 218). **228** scans either on |k|, with two stresses in *cristéne* or on vowels, with *Y* as second stave (mute) and two stresses in *é(m) cristène* (cf. 217). **230a** 'Not every one that saith [to me], Lord, Lord shall enter into the kingdom of heaven: [but he that doth the will of my Father...]' (Mt 7:21); a warning against formal religion without 'do-well'. **231–48a** This elaboration of **B**'s perfunctory warning to complacent rich men may result from seeing the events of 1381 as a summons to social reform rather than the occasion for repressive reaction that it became. **232** *Diues*: sometimes taken as a proper name for the selfish 'Rich Man' (*Dives*) of Lk 16:19–31 already alluded to at 18.272. This second Lucan parable is cited to show not that Dives's wealth was ill-gotten but that he used it selfishly; and reference to the original makes clear that he is not condemned by 'a newe lawe' (19.34) but by that of Moses (Lk 16:31), who taught the love of neighbour the Samaritan Parable was told to illustrate (see on 49). **235** *as men rat*: an assertion with no explicit scriptural basis, but an important part of **L**'s warning that since lawful possession of wealth does not justify ignoring the higher law of divine justice, the lot of those who win *un*lawfully then fail to spend 'well' is desperate indeed. **238a** 'He feasted sumptuously and was clothed in linen'; adapted from Lk 16:19. **240** *Godes*: an objective genitive, here = 'to, against'. **241** With this minatory internal assonance and rhyme compare 265; Dives is not in limbo. **242** scans either as Type Ia with six-syllable prelude or as Ic with stave one found (unusually) in *with*. **242–3** *atymye..lyue*: 'might properly enough go about living like a lord'. **245–6** *ʒut...ʒut*: 'moreover... still further'. **247** *sitte*: i.e. at table; the implication being that if they ate as befits their wealth, there would be some left over for the needy, whereas their miserliness mars all. **248** echoes 16.274, where the thought concerns not *good* use of ill-won wealth but its inevitable *mis*use by the vicious. *frendis*: i.e. in heaven, who will intercede for him after death. **248a** See on 8.235a. **250** The sense is less that money should be given to the Church than to the 'needful poor', who are in a special sense *hise* 'God's' (cf. 12.133–4). **251–63** are effectively a commentary on I Tim 6:9–10 and equate *vnhyndenesse* with *vnkyndenesse*, the sin against God's own nature as life-giving love, both as literal murder and as the 'killing' of a man's reputation by slander so as to obtain his wealth. It is this that forges a link with the foregoing address to the rich: the 'thieves' are not all outlaws, nor the 'banks' they lurk under only of earth. **256** *Vnkynde Cristene men*: an arresting oxymoron highlighting the special unnaturalness of such a sin amongst believers; cf. *sed vos fraudatis...fratribus* (I Cor 6:8). **257** *for his mebles*: making clear that the meta-

phorical 'slaying' is not 'murder of the soul through evil example' (*R–H* 210) but slander, which ruins a man's livelihood through destroying his reputation. **258** *hath to kepe*: a clear allusion to 'your members are the temple of the Holy Ghost, who is in you, whom you have from God' (I Cor 6:19). **259** *loue*: the divine life of sanctifying grace identified with the Holy Spirit. The argument refers at once to the physical 'life' of the good man and the virtues ('fruits of the Spirit') that make him good. **260–1** neatly develop from 169: as the true 'mirror-image' of the Trinity, a virtuous man can be fitly compared to the same light-giving candle; cf. 'Sic luceat *lux* vestra...ut videant *opera* vestra *bona*...' (Mt 5:14–16). **261** scans as Type IIIc on |r| and |t| (*ab / ab*) with the first stave by liaison in *Or_élles* or on |t| as Type Ib with first and third stave (mute) in *to* and a 'compensating' fourth stave to supplement the latter. *to...Trinite*: 'such as are lit in honour of / as an image that duly honours the Trinity'. **262** *morthereth...man*: an act especially heinous because it destroys the physical 'temple' that houses the super-natural life of the Spirit. **267** *þat Crist dere bouhte*: 'that which Christ bought at so dear a cost'. The argument now defines the supreme sin as 'destroying the life of one redeemed by Christ', not only the 'good' but any (or per-haps any baptized) person. **268**; **269** *mercy* (2); *mercy*: the divine 'mercy' as personified in Christ and (mirror-wise) in the redeemed person; a striking analogy to the notion of the Spirit's 'love' as personified in the 'good' man (259). **269** *anyente*: possibly introduced by **L** from Fr. *anienter*. **270** Though technically not one of the moral virtues, Innocence here signifies something more posi-tive than 'freedom from guilt', and in its allusion to Abel implies the moral purity associated not only with infants but with those specially 'near' to God, like the virgins (cf. *priueoste* at 18.98). **271** *hit*: the understood referent being 'the act', but metonymically the agent. **272** *forschupte*: 'deformed, mutilated' (MED s.v. *forshapen* v.) according to well-supported glosses; but 'unmade' (*Sk*) better hits off the contextual sense of 'negating' the Creator's work. **272a** 'Avenge the blood of the just!' Alluding to Apoc 6:10, the phrase runs together the texts cited in AlfQ from the versicle for Holy Innocents' Day 'Vindica sanguinem nostrum' (*Brev.* 1.306) and the antiphon 'Vindica...san-guinem sanctorum tuorum' followed by the versicle 'Jus-torum animae' (*Brev.* 1.239). That there is an allusion to the blood of 'Abel the just' (Mt 23:35, Heb 11:4; cf. Gen 4:10), the first man to be murdered and a familiar type of Christ (Heb 12:24), seems certain. But the liturgical echo is equally clear, with no formal distinction made between the guiltlessness of murdered children and that of the 'good man' (the feast of the Innocents follows two days after that of Stephen the first martyr). **273** The exact referent of *verray charite* would seem not to be the virtue *per se,* since its supreme exemplar Christ asked

forgiveness not vengeance for his murderers. Rather, the virtuous and the innocent who are murdered could be envisaged as 'embodying' or 'personifying' the divine love (cf. on 268–9), and destruction of this love demands retribution as part of justice. The text invoked may be Rom 12:19 (citing Deut 32:35), which at once urges forgiveness for wrongdoing and promises that God will punish it. **274** *Charite...is*: recognising in 'Charity' the Church's inner essence as a 'spiritual organism', and so identifying the sin against the Spirit as also a direct attack on Christ. For the doctrine in this line, which improves on B 292 in depth and precision, cf. Piers's words at 7.256 expressing the poem's basic conception of the 'mystical body of Christ' as realised within individual believers in a state of grace. The verbal echo of Piers's *charge* in *chargeth* strengthens the conceptual link between these two passages. **275** *laste ende*: 'the (individual's) moment of death' (as implied by Will's *nouthe* at 277–80), or 'the Last Judgement'; still ambiguous, but clearer than B 294 *þere*. **276** *lyf*: a careful synonym for 'person' that ironi-cally highlights the evil of extinguishing 'life and love' (259) and warns against the consequence.

277–98 277 *pose*: the question broaching less Will's own immediate concern than the issue of the moral value of 'death-bed repentances', as a counter-case to the *Pearl*-Dreamer's view of the supposedly 'easy' salvation of those dying in infancy. The 'optimistic' view is reflected in *CT* X 94. **282** *repentaunce*: the sinner's conversion, which 'converts' divine justice to pity, as described at 193. **283** *selde yseyn*: not that God *cannot* offer the grace of final repentance (294), but that a hardened sinner is unlikely to change enough to be able to alter the course of justice. With its appeal to experience (cf. 20.153), this passage between 282–8a contains a dozen terms from the language of the law courts. *sothnesse...witnesse*: both 'to tell the truth' and 'where witnesses tell the truth (and judges aren't bribed)'. **284–5** *be; Be*: 'be found'; '(And) be'. **286** *þat partye*: i.e. the 'dead' man (hence the dif-ficulty of any 'accord'); but if the 'murder' was of a man's reputation, then forgiveness and compensation are theoretically possible. **288** *That...equitee*: 'So that each party may get what is his just due'. The king's mercy (remission of the lawful punishment) cannot properly be given without the agreement of the injured party, who is envisaged at 271ff as demanding retribution. The sever-ity of the Samaritan's argument here will be echoed by that of Truth and Righteousness at 20.145–51a, 195–206; but 297–8 obscurely adumbrate the miraculous 'letters' sent by Love to Mercy and Peace at 20.184–91. *holy writ*: 'sacred tradition'. **288a** See on 6.257a; St Augus-tine's maxim contains a dire warning that explains why to 'murder a good man' is such a heinous act. **290** *til... synne*: i.e. at death, when they have no more power to do wrong (cf. *CT* VI 286, which quotes this familiar saying, and *CT* X 92). **292** *mercy...mynde*: a harsher view of the prospects for repentance than that at 6.339, but some measure of how much graver the sin against the Holy Ghost is than greed (or any other). **293** *hope*: 'expectation', which can be qualified by 'good' or 'ill'. The sight of the evils he has done blocks out the thought of God as anything but the sternest judge (a state of mind later dramatised by Marlowe in Dr Faustus's last soliloquy). **294–8** re-state Scripture's words at 12.73–5a and recall Repentance's to Greed at B 5.281–2a. **294** *And...myhte*: 'and not because God isn't fully able...' **296a** See on B 5.282a. **297–8** '...it is restitution that will make this happen, in the form of heartfelt *sorrow*, which serves as *satisfaction* for those who are not in a position to pay what is due to justice'. This remarkable elision of the first and third *partes penitentiae* proves both the authority and the *kyndenesse* of the speaker. It tempers the warning to those who *euele lyuen and leten nat* with an echo of the promise to the truly repentant at 201–10, and it provides a crumb of comfort even for the desperate sinner, if not an actual guarantee of 'prevenient' grace.

299–334 The final part of the Samaritan's homily reduces the intensity that has reached its peak at 298 by using homely proverbial images of the 'picturing-model' type (Aers 1975:13–14) that serve to distinguish clearly between different spiritual conditions and to warn against falling into the one that leads to despair. **299** *thre thynges*: recalling the didactic method of HC expounding another 'three things' in B I 20ff. The best-known version of the exemplum, as *Sk* noted, is in a widely-cited passage from Pope Innocent III's *De Contemptu mundi* I, 18: 'There are three things that drive a man from his home: smoke, dripping water, and a wicked wife'. This is based on Prov 19:13, 27:15 (which *compare* the wrangling wife to the dripping roof), 10:27, which uses the smoke image, and 21:19, which declares the wilderness preferable to a quarrelsome woman. But two other likely sources are Map's *De Uxore non Ducenda* (ed. Wright 83) and another late C12th text, Peter Cantor's *Verbum Abbreviatum* (in *PL* 205:331), which offers similar (not the same [*Sk*]) interpretations of the 'three things' as his: *carnis tentatio* for the wife, *peccatum ignorantiae* for the smoke and *suggestio extrinseca* for the dripping water. **L** changes the order and significance of the second and third of the 'three things'. **300** *oune house*: 'domo propria' (Map). *Holy Writ*: with dual reference to the medieval authorities and to their Biblical source. **301** *wikkede wyf*: 'mala uxor' (Innocent). **306** 'It mars his sleep even worse than his wife or the wet' (a sardonic comparison of the 'wicked' wife's insistence to the drip of rainwater). **310** Elliptical for 'who should bring (and did not)', i.e 'for not bringing'. **311–16** cover all sins of the flesh resulting from the propensity of fallen human nature to give in. Awareness of the difference between weakness and

wickedness is evident from the careful use of *kynde* in 313, 322 to show how sins arising from these two sources are forgiveable, while those due to *vnkyndenesse* are not, as wet wood, though kindled, *cannot* 'foster' a flame but suffocates it. However, the phrasing (*cleueth on hym*) also recalls 7.303 and implies a sexually demanding as well as a nagging wife, while 314 with its echo of Mede's words at 3.59–60 also suggests specifically sexual sins. The passage expresses the imagined speaker's own laxism (cf. the Samaritan's use of *lihtliche* at 323), but its echo in 315–16 of 208–10 is nonetheless encouraging. **318** *seeknesses...sorwes*: recalling Ymaginatif's words on the power of *angres* to punish for sin and arouse conversion, but less warning against the loss of faith shown by Envy at 6.77–85 than encouraging the sufferer not to be too hard on himself. **319a** '"[My grace is sufficient for thee]: for power is made perfect in infirmity"' (II Cor 12:9); referring to the power of divine grace to enable men to make their weakness an occasion for developing the needed virtues (here, patience). **324** *euele may suffre*: recalling B 12.8, which is removed in **C**. **326** *coueytise and vnkyndenesse*: a significant coupling, seeing in unbridled greed the sin furthest from the boundless generosity of God. **327** *contrarie*: a different kind of 'oppositeness' from that of the afflicted who *contrarien* (322). **328–32** seem to argue that whereas the 'vnkynde' *reject* love, the afflicted and the fallen remain capable of inner or verbal generosity of some kind, which initiates their recovery. **331** anticipates 21.185 in its entirety. **332** *that...amende*: 'so that his own life may thereby improve'. **333–4** *prikede / awakede*: half-rhyme sealing the end of the passus (cf. the similar use of internal rhyme to end at 18.292 above). *awakede*: in B 352 ending the *outer* part of Vision Five (which began at B 15.11). But since there is no new dream at the corresponding point in C 16.156, the one that Will woke out of at 18.179 may be the presumed / implied 'inner' dream beginning at 18.4 (see *ad loc* on this problem). The 'outer' dream (if such it is) that he wakes from at 19.334 must therefore be the one that began at 15.25.

Passus XX (B XVIII)

PASSUS TWENTY (Vision Six) is the last fully revised portion of **C**; but it adds only some 45 lines, mainly on the devils' attempted resistance to Christ (281–94, 308–11), and omits B 255, 351–2, 355–7. The *additions* include 45, 212–13, 216–17, 314, 338–40, 346 and a not entirely happy semi-digression on lying, the sin of which Satan is seen as arch-exemplar (350–8). The many *verbal changes*, though minor, are mostly improvements and show no hesitancy, e.g. at 2, 34, 46, 48, 50, 53, 55, 61–2, 75–9, 86, 90, 93, 95–8, 100, 154–6, 186–9, 250, 303–7, 336, 345, 347, 360–1, 369, 379–85, 434–6, 458–9. The Passus contains echoes of a number of texts which are noted in detail to bring out the wide-ranging nature of **L**'s treatment of this sequence. The origins of its narrative material are mainly Latin: the canonical scriptures; the Easter liturgy (St-Jacques 1967); ch. 54 of *LA* (*Sk*), which **L** certainly used; and the latter's direct source the 'Gospel of Nicodemus' (*Evangelium Nicodemi*, hereafter *EN*). This last is the name given from the 13th c. to the Latin version of an apocryphal Greek Gospel of about the 5th century. It is made up of two works by separate authors, the *Gesta Pilati* 'The Acts of Pilate' and the *Descensus ad inferos* 'Descent into Hell' (which survives in two Latin versions, A and B). The first of these texts is an elaborated synthesis of the canonical Gospels, the second an imaginative work purporting to be the testimony of the sons of Simeon (Lk 2:25–35), who were released from hell when Christ rose from the dead and who witnessed the liberation of the patriarchs. **L** also shows awareness of the late C13th English verse-adaptations of *EN*, the *Harrowing of Hell* (*HH*) and *Gospel of Nicodemus* (*GN*), on the background of which see Izydorczyk (1997), as well as AN poems by Nicholas Bozon (*Vn rei estei jadis ke aueit vne amy*) and Robert Grosseteste (*Le Chasteau d'Amour*). The Debate of the Four Daughters of God that **L** inserted into his account is not part of the 'Harrowing' story but derives from a homiletic tradition widely popular in C12th France. First found in a sermon by St Bernard of *c.* 1140 (*PL* 183:383–90), it goes back to a lost Latin translation of the *Bereshith Rabbah*, a Hebrew *midrash* (commentary) on Genesis (Tveitane 1980).

As well as uniquely combining elements of the sublime and the earthy, Passus XX (as first noticed in Waldron 1986:75–6, discussing the B-Text) reveals a complex patterning and carefully balanced argument. Its *two linked main sequences* have a 'triptych'-like structure, each flanking an episode that forms its thematic and dramatic centre: (i) CHRIST'S CRUCIFIXION (his seeming defeat by Death) and (ii) the HARROWING OF HELL (Christ's real victory over Death). This novel design enhances the poetic spaciousness and theological perspective in what becomes, following successive reductions and sub-divisions of earlier passūs in **B**, the longest passus in **C**. The central portion of (i) occupies ll. 35–94 (b); it is 'framed' by (a) a tense interchange between Will and Faith (8–34*a*) prompted by the Samaritan's arrival in Jerusalem (which links Vision Six with Vision Five), and by (c) Faith's stinging rebuke to the Jews his descendants for rejecting Christ (95–112*a*). Before (a) comes a brief *prologue* (1–7) on Will's increasing alienation from worldly affairs as his thoughts focus on the liturgical mystery that reaches its doctrinal and emotional peak in Passion week. **L**'s final treatment of the Crucifixion in ll. 35–94 (Bennett 1982:85–112) combines its scriptural and literary sources with striking originality (Marx

1995:100–13). Sequence (ii) occupies ll. 113–478 and its 'central episode' (b) the HARROWING OF HELL (271–451), is framed by (a) the 'debate' of the FOUR DAUGHTERS OF GOD at ll. 116–270*a* (with its brief lead-in lines on the Dreamer's quasi-Dantean 'descent' into Limbo) and (c) their reconciliation (452–70). Further enclosed in (a) at 238–68 is a *sub-episode* (a¹), the intervention of BOOK to attest Jesus as Messiah, ending in a nuanced transition from what the Daughters *hear* to an event the audience *witness* with them (269–70*a*). The splendid central scene (271–451) divides into 1) the Devils' panic-stricken reaction to Christ's summons to open hell (274–94); 2) their 'frantic colloquy' (295–349*a*), a parodistic mirror-inversion of the 'Daughters' dispute' (Russell 1984:239); and 3) Christ's great speech (370–446*a*) justifying God's action as one not of force but law. This last is linked to the 'Devils' debate' by the 'Liar-digression' (350–8), is prefaced by Christ's liberation of the souls of the just (359–69), and closed with an elegant two-line transition to the sequence's outer frame (c), the *reconciliation* of the Daughters in a cosmic round-dance that echoes the divine harmony (452–71). The entire passus ends with an *epilogue* (471–8) in which joyful bells, heralded by dream-music balancing the pre-dream *prologue*'s organ and choir, wake the Dreamer for the first matins and mass of Easter Morning. In complexity of organisation, sustained dramatic irony, clarity of exposition and variety of style, Passus XX represents the summit of **L**'s art, and it could have served as not only the climax but as the conclusion of the whole work.

PROLOGUE 1–7 1 *Wollewaerd and watschoed*: Will's shirtlessness indicating his poverty (MED s.v. *wolle-ward*). But as the phrases coupled commonly describe penitents' garb (cf. *Prick of Conscience* 3512: 'And fast and ga *wolwarde*, and wake' [*Sk*]), 'wetshod' may indeed signify 'barefoot', the manner of the original Franciscans. *R–H* 212 note the contrast with his unholy hermit's apparel in Pr 2–3. *wente...aftur*: echoing *wente aweye* 19.334 and hinting a sense of Will's journey as one he does not expect to return from. **2** *recheles*: recalling the spokesman of total dependence on God last named at 13.129 and his sentiments at 13.94–5, 98, 101–2. **4** *wilnede*: his desire being for vision rather than instruction, spiritual wisdom more than theological learning. *eefte*: the adv. going with both verbs. **5** *lened me to*: echoing the beginning of Will's dream-visions at Pr 8b; but since 'Lent' is nearly over, perhaps also importing 'relied upon', i.e. 'lived in a penitential manner [befitting my advancing age]' ('lent myself to' [*R–H* 212] is unidiomatic). **B 6** is omitted perhaps because its tone conflicts with that of *gretly* following; earlier *rotte* at 14.95 had indicated not openness to, but ignorance of heavenly revelation (the angels' song), and at 7.7 was comically unedifying. *Ramis palmarum*: 'with palm-branches', short for *Dominica in r. p.* 'Palm Sunday' (so named after the responsory phrase 'Cum *ramis palmarum*: Hosanna, clamabant in excelsis'). Holy Week, the sixth and last of Lent, began with clergy and people processing round the church carrying blessed palm-branches and singing the hymn *Gloria, laus* on re-entering. **6** 'Glory, praise [and honour to thee, Christ, Redeemer King, / To whom their noble cry *Hosanna* Israel's children sing]'; the opening verse and antiphonal response of the hymn. *greetliche*: its use with *dremede* unparalleled and the exact sense uncertain, but perhaps (as in *WPal* 1248) 'with deep and powerful feeling' (MED s.v. *gretli* adv.), or else referring to the lofty content of this passus (contrast its one other occurrence at 11.313). But *long tyme* (5) and *faste* (B 6) also imply the length of time spent in single-minded pursuit of the vision's profound meaning. **7** *Osanna*: 'Save, we beseech Thee'. This Hebrew word, found only in the accounts of Christ's entry into Jerusalem (Mt 21:9 //) read in the first Palm Sunday Antiphon, underlies the *salvum me fac* of Ps 117:25–6, from which the Gospel acclamations quote; repeated in the Palm Sunday liturgy, it concludes the *Sanctus* at every Mass. *by orgene*: possibly a portative instrument accompanying the procession rather than the main one played in the church. But an organ seems intended, since the liturgical chant recalls the familiar ending of the last psalm, sung at Lauds on Saturdays: 'Laudate eum...*choro*...et *organo*' (150:4); see *TN* further. *oelde*: 'adult' rather than 'aged', contrasted with the *gurles* of 6 (perhaps singing antiphonally in a choir). B 9 *ofrauȝte*: 'obtained possession of', i.e. 'redeemed' (though most recorded instances mean 'reached to'). But whether the antecedent of *þat* is 'Christ' or 'his passion', the meaning is much the same, and the b-half's echo of B 7.147 faintly audible. The somewhat strained sense may account for the line's deletion. **(i) 8–112a** THE CRUCIFIXION SEQUENCE **(a) 8–34a** *Will and Faith* **8** The loss of partial resemblance to the actually encountered Samaritan is made up for by the partial recognition of Piers. Both effects are attributable to the interval between the Fifth and Sixth Visions, which has given the Dreamer time 'to studie / Of that [he] seyh slepynge' (9.297–8). **9–12** are deliberately paradoxical, the figure being both like and unlike knight, Samaritan and ploughman, yet by a conceptual *transsumptio* the true 'heavenly' norm of chivalric *kynde* (on 'earthly things which signify the supernatural' and the positive reflections in 'earthly concepts' of 'their eternal counterparts' cf. the valuable discussion in Waldron 1986:72). Weldon 1987[2]:119 interestingly compares the unrecognised Jesus to the 'fair unknown' of chivalric romance. **9** *asse bak*; *cam prikye*: an endingless 'positional genitive' and infinitive of manner after *comen*; see *MES* 73, 536–7. *boetles*: 'without boots' but not 'without remedy' (*boet*)

for man's sin, which depends not on 'piercing with' but on 'being pierced by' a spear; an echo of 1.152–3 and a foreshadowing of 20.80–8. **10** Cf. 'Withouten stedes and hors of prys / He haþ ouercome his enemys' (from the C14th *Meditations on the Life and Passion of Christ*, 1605–6, based on the C13th Latin *Philomena* of John of Hoveden, XIX 52). **12** *galoches*: possibly an alliterative synonym for 'shoes' (of the kind that could be pattern-cut) rather than signifying the specific type with wooden soles and leather fastening thongs. A knight armed for battle would have steel 'sabatouns' (*SGGK* 574; Cutts 1925:350, pl. from BL MS Royal 2. B vii); so this is peaceful footwear (like that worn by the figure being dubbed at court in Keen 1984:pl. 14). **13** 'O, Son of David!' Faith here momentarily speaks for those of his descendants who recognise in Jesus the promised 'Rex justus salvator' riding on an ass (Zach 9:9, quoted at Mt 21:5) and accordingly utters his 'herald's' cry to alert the spectators. Though immediately prompted by the context of Mt 21:9 //, the words are addressed to Jesus (*Fili* being vocative as in the Palm Sunday Antiphon); but since they are also those spoken by the blind men Christ heals *secundum fidem* at Mt 9:27–9 (AlfQ), they may be meant to evoke that stark image of 'blind' faith. **14** *heraud of armes*: see Keen 1984:136–7 on their duties. *auntrous*: the adj. used nominally (here pl.), paralleled only in *Ywain and Gawain* 3399. *ioustes*: single combats between mounted knights, often for a prize (here mankind). **15** *Olde*: referring not to their personal 'age' but to the ancient times they lived in, and contrasting the Jews who welcomed Jesus as the Saviour with those of the present time who still look for another (17.295–7). **15a** 'Blessed is he that cometh in the name of the Lord' (Mt 21:9, 23:39); ending the Antiphon *Pueri Hebraeorum* sung during the distribution of palms before the procession, and forming the second part of the *Sanctus* at Mass. Christ's own 'Messianic' sentence (Mt 23:39) is a direct allusion to his Second Coming. **17** *sholde iouste*: 'was going to joust'. For the full working-out of this metaphor see Waldron 1986:66–74, who shows *L*'s indebtedness to two allegorical crucifixion poems in AN by the C14th Franciscan poet Nicole Bozon, and Warner 1996:129–43 on the contribution of the tradition of 'Round Table' sermons. Even more important is the devotional tradition represented in the *Meditations* and the *Philomena*. **18** *þat...claymeth*: as prophesied at 18.129–30. *Pers...Plouhman*: on the split genitive see at 2.2. **19** *preynte*: a wordless sign recalling Piers's look that silences Will's questioning in B 16.64–5 (removed in C); on such signs see Burrow 2000. **20** *Liberum-Dei-Arbitrium*: a composite 'nature-name' suggesting both the figure who showed Will the Tree of Charity and the *Libera Voluntas Dei* of 18.129, there the equivalent of Piers in // B 16.86 and here corresponding to 'Jesus' at B 18.22. The referent is the divine Word who unites with human nature in the person of Christ (for whom 'Piers'/ 'Jesus' is an outer vesture) to make possible the one-to-one combat with Satan. *vndertake*: alluding to the Prophets' promise of a Saviour to Israel (e.g. Isaiah, chs 40–1). **21** *of his gentrice*: 'out of the nobility that is his by descent' (cf. B 14.181 and the quotation from Oliver de la Marche in Keen 1984:150). *Pers armes*: his human body, not the *conysaunce* described by Faith at 18.188, which might give his identity away and frighten his adversary off. Outlaw Death must be 'beguiled' into thinking he is fighting an adversary he can defeat. **22** *haberion...natura*: cf. 'þis *haberion* is þy body fre' (*Meditations* 1603, = *loricam carnis* in Hoveden XIX 61). **23** The motif of the disguised Christ as a chivalric figure appears in the AN poems attributed to Bozon, *Vn re esteit iadis ke avait vne amye* and *Coment le fiz deu fu armé en la croyz*, both found in the commonplace book of his fellow-mendicant William Herebert, ms BL Addl. 46919 (the former printed by Wright from BL Cotton Julius A V in Langtoft, ii 426–37, ll. 17–24; also in Jubinal II, 309). The first has been proposed as a specific source by Gaffney 1931, the second by Bourquin 1978:702–7; see further the discussion in Waldron 1986. *consummatus Deus*: 'supreme God' (*Pe*) but, though recalling the insistence on the Son's full divinity at B 17.172–3, also ironically anticipating the 'supreme' or consummating moment of his *human* existence at 57 below. **24** *plates*: on plate-armour, a late C14th development, see Poole 1958:I, 324–5 and pl. 53b, Keen 1984:221. The metaphoric *transsumptio*, based on the radical claim that Christ's 'kingdom' is not of this world (Jn 18:36), widens the gap between tenor and vehicle, since a ploughman would wear a simple woollen jacket (as in **B**), not armour. **B 25** *paltok*: cf. Walter of Châtillon, I.7: 'Dei prudentia.../ cum in substantia cerni non potuit, / nostre *camisia* se carnis induit' ('God's wisdom, that in substance went unknown, / A shirt of flesh put on, and that our own)'; and see also Wheatley 1993:135–42. *prikiare*: ironically contrasting this rider's humility with the pride of the two others this word is used of (10.135, B 10.307). **25** *in..*: 'in the divine nature he has from the Father'; a stock expression for which no source need be sought. **26** *or*: not implying 'logical' alternatives, but rather a set phrase as at B 15.389, hence, 'the Jews generally or the scribes of the Jews in particular'. 17.252 nonetheless seems to imply that **L** sees them as a separate (racial or religious) group among Christ's opponents. **28** *Deth*: a 'nature-name' for the embodiment of evil, first mentioned in C Pr 17 as the ruler of hell (*dux mortis* in *EN* 423, *LA* 243). He is the 'last enemy' of I Cor 15:26 (and see on 34*a*). The opposition here between a personified Death and Life (which inspired the later ME poem of that name) is indebted to vs 3 of the Sequence *Victimae paschali laudes* by Wipo of Swabia (11th c.) sung before

the Gospel on Easter Sunday: '*Mors et vita* duello / Conflixere mirando: / *Dux vitae* mortuus regnat vivus' ('Death and Life in wondrous duel strive: / The Lord of Life has died, yet reigns alive'). **27** *fals doem*: referring primarily to the unjust sentence of death passed upon Jesus the second Adam, secondarily to the curse of death laid on man (through the Tempter's 'falsity') for the first Adam's sin. **29** contains 15.19b and an a-half earlier used at B 14.32 but excised at that point in // **C**. **30** *Lyf*: a personification drawn from the Easter Sequence, and hence a contrastive nature-name of the quality characterising the WORD in Jn 1:4 (the allusion is to Christ's prophecy in Mk 8:31). *lyeth*: Death's claim being ultimately a 'fals doem', which Truth will controvert decisively. *to wedde*: as a gage thrown down in fulfilment of the 'undertaking' at 20 (cf. Mede's use of the phrase at 3.258). **31** *That...to*: 'that he will walk' (anacoluthic). **32** is either IIb or, like 18 more certainly, Type Ia. **34** largely retains **B**'s sense in the b-half: 'and bring eternal death to death' (also possible for B 35; see *TN*). **34a** '[I will deliver them out of the hand of death]. O death, I will be thy death: [O hell], I will be thy bite' (Osee 13:14). Already part-quoted at B 17.110*a* (removed in revision), it is here imagined as spoken by God, but with contextual relevance for Life's chivalric 'vaunt' to his enemy. Christ the Lion of Judah (Rev 5:5) will 'bite down' the fatal Tree of Good and Evil (20.206) that brought 'bale' into the world and from which the Doctor of Death harvests his poisonous wine, in return for Man's fatal 'bite' from its fruit. The 'death / bite' pun is possible only in Latin, so the whole quotation is needed: 'swallowing down death [*deglutiens mortem*] that [men] might be made heirs of life everlasting' (I Pet 3:22). The text is used in Alan of Lille's discussion in *CH* of Death's loss of 'jurisdiction' over man, cited at 36 below. It is illustrated along with its companion text from I Cor 15:54–5 in Schiller II pl. 531, and even more strikingly in pl. 385, which shows a lion-headed shoot from the cross 'biting down' Death.

(b) 35–94 describe CHRIST'S CRUCIFIXION in a free-flowing and richly macaronic style that keeps to the fore the words and imagery of the Holy Week readings. **35** '[Pilate], sitting in the place of judgement'; based on *sedente illo pro tribunali* (Mt 27:19). **36** *demen...rihte*: 'pass judgement on the claims of the two'; perhaps suggested by Alan of Lille's 'Because the presumption was unjust, when Death assaulted one over whom he had absolutely no legal claim, he rightly lost the jurisdiction he had obtained over man' (*PL* 210:419). **37** *iustice aȝeyns Iesus*: an ironic echo of *Iesus a iustices sone* at 18.126 that points up the difference between earthly and heavenly notions of right. **38** *court*: used loosely for those present before the *tribunale* (Mt 27:17–22). *Crucifige*: 'Crucify (him)' (Lk 23:21, Jn 19:6), read on Wednesday and Friday of Holy Week. **39** *pelour*: one who makes an *appeel* 'charge or accusation before a judge' (Alf*G* s.v. *appel*); corresponding to the two 'false witnesses' (Mt 26:60–1) who make the deposition of 40–5 before the Sanhedrin. As the Trial before Pilate had no 'accuser' figure, **L**'s version (which does not exonerate the governor) makes the event more like an anarchic English lynching than a Roman judicial process. **40** *despised*: i.e. 'it', the verb being transitive and not constructed with *of*. **41–5** are based on Mk 14:58 (and cf. Jn 2:19–21). **46** *Crucifige*: not given to any individual in the Gospels. *wycchecrafte*: a detail from *EN* II. para. 1 (*magus*), 4 (*maleficus*); cf. English verse *GN* (MS Addl. 32578, ed. Hulme) ll. 215–16 (*bywichid*). **47** *Tolle..*: 'Away with him: Away with him: [Crucify him]' (Jn 19:15). **47–8** are based on Mt 27:29 / Mk 15:17; the paradoxical 'garland' image appears in the early C14th *Northern Passion* 1110: 'Yiet a nomen *þornes kene* / And made him a *gerlond*' and the 'coronam de spinis' is represented as a victory-garlond in the early iconography of the *crux invicta* (Schiller II pls. 1, 9). **49** *enuye*: 'sheer malice', perhaps echoing the chief priests' *invidiam* suspected by Pilate at Mk 15:10 (a text read on Tuesday of Holy Week). **50** 'Hail, Rabbi [Master]' (Mt 26:49), the words of Judas to Christ in Gethsemane, which strikingly replace the 'Ave rex Iudaeorum' of Mt 27:29, making those who insult Jesus his own people, not the Roman soldiers. *redes*: with which the soldiers beat his head after placing one such in his right hand in mockery of a sceptre (Mt 27:30). *shot vp* (*þrew* **B**): the precise action envisaged is not clear in either version. **51** *thre nayles*: the manner of representing Christ's crucifixion standard in Western iconography after about 1250 (Schiller II pls. 480–532); cf. *AW* 129/2–3; Furnivall, ed. *Pol. Poems* 111; *Joseph of Arimathie* 262. The number may be symbolic in an indeterminate way, like the *thre clothes* at 10.195–6. *naked*: the (historically correct) early tradition (Schiller II 91) found in Berchorius, *Op. Omn.* (Cologne 1731:340) and mostly avoided in later depictions (see Schiller II pl. 310). **52–3** *pole*: a reed in Mt 27:48, Mk 15:36, a hyssop stick in Jn 19:29. *poysen*: the drink offered to Christ on the cross (a different mistake in each version); see Hoveden's 'the venomous people offer him a drink' (*Cythara*, st 33, ed. Raby) and 'for wine poison (*pro vino virus*) you would offer him' (*Canticum Amoris*, xxix 195). In **B** the drink is meant to hasten Christ's death, in **C** cruelly to prolong it. The first interpretation is found in devotional writings such as the Latin prose *Meditaciones* (ed. Stallings 1965:115), the English verse *Meditations*, and Hoveden's *Philomena* sts 194–5 (see Schmidt 1983²:176–85; Ruffing 1991); the second appears in *LA*. One expresses the wish of Satan, the other that of Hell (cf. Goblin's words at 335). **54–5** *hymsulue...rode*: based on Lk 23:35; the vocative form of B 54 is closer to Mt 27:40. **55** *Yf...sone*: a fusion of Lk 23:35 ('si hic est *Christus*') and Mt 27:40 ('si *Filius Dei*

es, descende de cruce'). **B 55** *kynges sone*: suggested by Mt 27:42 ('si *rex Israel* est, descendat nunc de cruce') and perhaps by *Meditations* 1868: 'Whi sleþ venym þe kynges sone?' **56** *thenne...leue*: conflating Mt 27:42 ('descendat...et credimus ei') and Mk 15:32 ('descendat... ut videamus, et credamus'). *Lyf*: a 'nature-name' for God, the 'lord of life' (59), whom they cannot recognise in the dying figure of Jesus (see on 30 above). **57** '[Jesus...said]: It is consummated. [And bowing his head, he gave up the ghost]' (Jn 19:30). The words refer both immediately to the end of Christ's ordeal and beyond that to his completion of the eternal plan of *consummatus Deus* (23): 'opus consummavi quod dedisti mihi' (Jn 17:4). In the liturgy of Good Friday this text, marking the most solemn moment, is followed by silence. **59** may be exceptionally a line with three lifts in the b-verse, symbolically representing a unique closure, or normative with *leyde* muted or with *his eyes* as part of a 'strong' pre-final dip. *lord...liht*: a title running together two divine 'nature-names' given at 20.306, 403 (cf. *Philomena*, sts 64–5) and supremely ironic in its echo of 10.155 as the title of 'God grettest'. Especially relevant among the images of Christ as Light in St John's Gospel are Jn 12:35–6 (alluding to his coming death) and 46. *leyde...togideres*: a phrase unparalleled as a way of saying 'lowered his eyelids / closed his eyes'. Kaske 1968 refers to depictions of Christ's half-closed or closing eyes in C14th windows at Preston, Glos. and Mamble, Worcs. **60** and **62b** re-enact the earlier crucifixion account (at 7.131) based on Lk 23:44–5, which was read at Mass on the Wednesday of Holy Week: 'tenebrae factae sunt....Et obscuratus est sol'. **61–5** are based on Mt 51–2, but **L** seems to have creatively (mis)read *velum templi* 'the veil of the Temple' as *vallum templi* 'rampart, wall' in the light of Mt 27:51–2 (and cf. *GN* ll. 691, 705–6). **61b–2a** *euene...to-roef*: 'in duas partes.... et petrae scissae sunt' (Mt 27:51). *hard roch*: echoing 19.12; the tearing of the Temple curtain was understood by the Fathers as symbolising the end of God's Covenant with the Jews, who had rejected his Son. The splitting of the Temple *wall* (fulfilling Christ's words at 18.160 and verbally recalled by the revision *to-cleue* at 112) is here perhaps meant to be associated with Moses' breaking of the Tablets of the Law in anger against the Hebrews for rejecting God (Ex 32:19). **63** adds an element of paradox in contrasting the 'quik' earth with the 'dede' men; the Gospel source is Mt 27:51–3. **64** Cf. *GN* l. 709. **65** *tempest*: a familiar Biblical symbol of God's anger (see on 5.121–2); here virtually a mythicised struggle between divinity and chaos symbolised by upheaval of all the elements, with one nameless 'dead body' being made a substitute for the herald Faith, who cannot see what is happening. **66** *bataille*: specifically interpreted as a 'civil duel of law' by Baldwin 1981²:66–72 (cf. the interesting comparison with the judicial duel in *Ywain and Gawain* in Clifton 1993:126–8). But the basic image of a conflict between death and life comes from vs 2 of the Easter Sequence (see at 28); the outcome is left uncertain to create tension for the events that follow Christ's death. On the iconography of *Mors* and *Vita* see Schiller II 114–15 and the important pl. 385. **69–70** The sound-repetitions in '*Sone*day', and '*Godes sone*' hint at further 'theopoetic' wordplay in '*sonne*-rysynge': the *sol iustitiae* and the *iustices sone* are one. Dawn is the time of the resurrection given in Mt 28:1–2, Mk 16:2. **70** *Somme*: based on the statement in Mt 27:54 of the centurion 'and the[m] that were with him', and interpretable as expressing awe at the earthquake rather than faith in Christ as in // Lk. *so fayre*: suggested by the quieter statement that 'the centurion...seeing that crying out *in this manner* he had given up the ghost...' (Mk 15:39). **70a** 'Indeed this was the son of God' (Mt 27:54). **71–2** An invented linking of the concern of Christ's enemies to ensure his death (Jn 19:31) with their reported charge (Jn 7:20) that he cast out devils by Satan's power (see on 18.150–51*a*). *soercerie*: cf. 17.304, stating that the Jews suspect Jesus of raising Lazarus by magic (whence their worry here). The term is not sharply distinguished from *wicchecraft* (used interchangeably at 46), but more strongly associated with raising the dead. **73–9** re-work the Gospel source, here mainly Jn 19:31–5, so as to give the 'gentries' of Jesus as the reason why he receives a spear-thrust from a knight and not the same insulting treatment as the thieves from a *cachepol*. **74** *so...lawe*: meaning little more than 'as the common [Roman] practice was, [to crucify several malefactors together]'. **75** *craked...legges*: so as to hasten their death (*armes aftur* is an addition). **77–9** The descent from *Godes body* to *knyht* somehow produces not bathos but ennoblement: as a man, the champion who has fought by the laws of chivalry deserves honourable treatment from his enemies (the present statement that he was a knight will form the basis of Conscience's words at 21.28). **78** *Kynde*: with primary reference to God, but with a secondary sense of 'the nature of things, what was fitting for someone who had *the kynde of a knyhte*' (11). **80–94** The story of the *blynde knyhte* (following *GN* 626) who reluctantly pierces Christ's side undergirds the thematic stress on *gentries*, the 'nobility' granted the Chosen People but which (as both 'redeeming grace' and 'social rights') the Jews have lost through 'ignoble' treatment of their rightful king by descent from David. **81** *Longius*: 'Longinus miles' (*EN* XVI 4), a name derived from Gk λονγχη 'spear(man)' (= Lat *lancea*) in Jn 19:34, and given him in *GN* ll. 625–30. In *LA* 202–3, St Longinus is the Roman centurion of Lk 23:47 (*videns signa quae fiebant...credidit* echoing *videns quod factum fuerat*); see also Comestor, *HS* (in *PL* 198:1633–4) and for the background, Peebles 1911, Kolve 1966:218–21, and Burdach 1974. **82** *place*: suggesting a jousting arena with the

ruler watching; but as Pilate was not present at the Crucifixion, reference here may be to prior events before the judgement-seat (Jn 19:13). **83** *mony teth*: a peculiar nonce-variant on the idiom *maugre his chekes*, perhaps darkly alluding to the *LA* statement that 'his teeth were torn out' for refusing to worship idols after his conversion. *was made*: by the Jews in *GN* 625, at Pilate's order in *LA*. **84** *Iouste*: the *bataille* being over, it is a dishonourable act to inflict wounds on a dead knight's body. *blynde Iewe*: L's alteration (he is a Roman centurion in *LA*) serving to illustrate this people's spiritual blindness, which he figures specifically as a lack of *gentries* (Clifton 1993:125 aptly notes how his literal blindness symbolically corresponds 'to the blindness of those who executed Jesus, not knowing what they did' [Lk 23:34]) and rightly stresses that in the *bataille* he 'cannot represent Satan...only the influence of Satan on the souls of men'). Longeus's essential *gentries*, revealed once he realises what he has done, proves that L does not regard the Jewish lack of faith in Christ as insuperable (see further on 88). **85–7** *alle they...Bote*: Longeus alone knowing neither that Jesus is dead nor that he is a 'knight' of royal descent. **87** *herte*: as in the earliest representation (*c.* 430), where Longinus thrusts his lance into Christ's heart (Schiller II pl. 323); C14th iconography shows a spear-wound in the right side (Schiller II pls 509, 518). The sacramental significance of the Saviour's *herte-blood* (cf. 21.58 below) as miraculously healing seems plain. **88** *vnspered*: a sovereign instance of L's serious wordplay, metaphorical and symbolic at once; the wounded hero's blood seeking not vengeance but virtue, and its effect being both to heal the body and inspire faith (see further Clifton 1993:126–7). But while the immediate written source *LA* describes how Longinus by chance touched his eyes *de sanguine Christi per lanceam decurrente* (see Schiller II pl. 525), agency is here ascribed to Christ's blood, as at 7.133. The scene may be viewed as exemplifying the Samaritan's words at 19.86–8, for in offering his knightly submission Longeus implicitly seeks to be *ybaptised*. L's making him a Jewish 'knight' may be influenced by the iconographic motif of the blindfolded 'Synagogue' with a pennoned lance that breaks when Christ dies, as in Schiller II pl. 529 (Synagoga is usually female, as in Mâle 189, Schiller II pl. 450, but male in Schiller II pl. 528). At a more literal level, it may be a (somewhat bizarrely) ironic inversion of the Jewish leaders' cry 'His blood be upon us and on our children' at Mt 27:25. **89** *fil...knees*: for an interesting connection of this action with response motifs of 'kneeling and naming' in relation to the metaphor of Christ as knight, see Weldon 1987[2]:119, and for illuminating association of Longinus's kneeling with the service of Good Friday, Weldon 1989:60–65. **91** *forthenketh*: as in the C13th OF *Passion,* source of the early C14th English *Northern Passion* (II.61), a text often accompanied in manuscripts by the *Harrowing*. **92–4** erupt in a spate of serious puns characteristic of the later versions (*do; licame / likynge; rihtful / riht*). **92** The cry for mercy is also a tacit prayer for the sacramental grace that will confirm his faith (this whole speech may be compared with Robert the Robber's at 6.323–4). The poem is silent about how Longinus's conversion bore fruit in missionary work and a martyr's death in Caesarea of Cappadocia *c.* 58 AD (*LA*). **93** offers not feudal service but surrender of all he owns as a forfeit for his crime. **94** *riht with þat*: 'immediately' and 'rightly thereupon'; the weeping is an appeal from Christ's *riʒt* 'justice' to his *ruthe* 'pity'. **(c) 95–112a** *Faith's denunciation of the Jews* for rejecting his and their saviour stresses that their action was as ignoble as it was wrong-headed (the small revisions at 95, 97 underscore the crime against Christ's *gentries*). The severe tone of Abraham Father of the Jews is clearly related to their *lack of faith,* not their race (as is confirmed by the preceding instance of the mercy shown to the Jew Longeus, who believes). **98** *dede...dede*: the *annominatio* exposing this deed stands as an extreme form of the *failure* of Priest and Levite to act towards another stripped and wounded man (in the parable of the Samaritan). **101** *gre*: the paradox of Christ's victory effectively 'chivalricised' in Longeus's submission. **102–3** *chaumpioun... recreaunt*: an action customarily taken as signifying cowardice, to judge by the tone of *CT* X 697, which describes the despairing man as 'lyk the coward champioun [not *victor* but *combatant*] recreant, that seith "creant" withoute nede'. There may be an etymological pun on *recreant* 'giving up one's religion', since the Jew Longeus in acknowledging his 'defeat' by divine Love *acquires* faith in his conqueror. **104** *derkenesse ydo*: i.e. by the Light's descent into Hell (to defeat Death) and his subsequent resurrection (to show how Life has *þe maistrie*). This association of Death with the darkness of hell is anticipated by the early revision at Pr 1–8. *Deth...yvenkused*: vividly illustrated in Schiller II pl. 531, where a 'Trinitarian' hand thrusts three spears into Death, Satan and Hell. **105** *lordeyns*: an 'anti-pun' on etymologically unrelated 'lord' (it is < OF *lordin*) may be suspected, since what their 'vileyns' behaviour has cost them is 'lordship' (spiritual election by God *and* the right to own land). **106–10** The Jews had been expelled from England in 1290 and, being without civil rights in most European states where they could reside, they had to live by money-lending, which the Lateran Council of 1215 had allowed them. But since the Jewish law forbade 'usury' (see on 110), contemporaries often saw their disabilities as condign punishment brought on the whole race (no more a nation after AD 70) by their own wish after Pilate's refusal to condemn Jesus (Mt 27:24–5), rather than as a (remediable) human injustice. (On the conditions of European Jews in the period see Cohn 1972:76–81, Cohen 1983,

Stow 1992). The central irony of the passage is that the Jews' progenitor Abraham was himself allowed to live in Canaan, and their law-giver Moses to authorise re-settlement of this 'promised' land, by conquest; so 'a father's curse' in effect reverses 'God's blessing' to him and his descendants at 18.255–7. **109** *as bareyne*: 'as if totally unproductive' (OED s.v. *barren* 4), i.e. unable to raise crops, rear livestock or engage in trade (the instance is misassigned by MED s.v. *barain* adj. 5 'destitute'). The word's use here may assume the Scholastic conception of money as 'barren' in nature, i.e. not a form of true property but only a medium of exchange, use of which was held to be adequately repaid by return of the original sum to the lender. Further reason for resentment against Jews was inevitable when, through taking interest, they made 'breed of barren metal' (*Merchant of Venice* I iii 132). *vsure*: see on 2.91; their 'ability' to practise this fitted in with Christians' need for money that other Christians were forbidden to lend them (the hypocrisy this gave rise to was to be excoriated by Marlowe in *The Jew of Malta*). Medieval writers say no good about a people they regarded not simply as 'unbelievers' but (95, 113) as *false*; and that the whole race had deceitfully *betrayed* Christ is implied in the Good Friday Collect asking God to deliver them not only from spiritual *obcaecatio* 'blindness' but from *perfidiam* 'treachery'. **110** Lending at interest was formally proscribed at the Second Council of Lyons (1274); but *alle lawes* may allude to Ex 22:25, Deut 23:19–20, which only forbids such lending to other (poor) Jews. **111** *Daniel*: an OT book especially important in Christian disputes with the Jews about the Messiah because Jesus's adoption of its term 'Son of Man' (7:13–14) in the Synoptic Gospels was understood as an oblique self-designation as the Messiah (see Schiller I 19, pl. 33). **112a** See on B 15.598a, an earlier use to describe the 'undoing' of Jewish hopes of a kingdom, removed at that point in revision. The Daniel passage (9:24) stating how '[vision and prophecy may be fulfilled and] the Saint of Saints may be anointed (*ungatur Sanctus sanctorum*)' was a key anti-Judaic text, discussed by Alan of Lille in *CH* in his proof that Christ was the expected Messiah (*PL* 210:411–12).

(ii) 113–478 THE HARROWING OF HELL SEQUENCE is preceded by a brief *transition* into what resembles another 'inner dream' (113–15), concluded (471–8) by Will's literal and spiritual awakening, and framed within the debate of THE FOUR DAUGHTERS OF GOD (116–270; 452–69). The scriptural source of this last motif is Ps 84:11, which is finally quoted at 467a, and among writers who use it, only **L** positions the argument at this point in salvation history (Traver 1907:147; discussions of its development are Traver 1929, Mäder 1971 and Tveitane 1980). Each of the Daughters has a leading trait: Truth's courage, Righteousness's firmness,

Mercy's gentleness and Peace's patience paralleling the complementarity of the four Cardinal Virtues, Fortitude, *Justice*, Temperance and Prudence. Their debate's two halves (between Mercy and Truth at 113–73, Justice and Peace at 174–237) are abruptly followed by BOOK's intervention, dissolving into 'vision' at the Latin command spoken by Christ's voice (269–70*a*). It is not resumed but it is resolved (at 462) with another Latin cry, that of angels affirming Christ's triumph. **L** does not so much dramatise a debate in the 'heart' of God, as understood by the C12th Julian of Vézelay (Tveitane 1980), as articulate the contradictions attending human attempts to understand the divine purpose. Popular in later drama (*The Castle of Perseverance* 95–111; the *N-Town Play* I 111–23), the motif is not found in the liturgy itself like that of the 'duel' of Life and Death (though the image of 'darkness' provides a linking element). The chief Latin source, St Bernard's Sermon I on the Annunciation (*PL* 183:383), which is much later than that of the Devils' debate (already in *EN* XVIII–XX), is a fruit of the special emphasis on Christ's humanity that marked the 'new devotion' of the early Gothic period. This is drawn upon for illustrations in a mid-C12th English Bible (Schiller I pl. 35), and the four figures are later depicted as part of the paradoxical image of 'Christ crucified by the Virtues' (Schiller II pls. 453, pairing Justice / Peace and Mercy / Truth above and below the cross; Saxl 1942:pl. 25b). The motif's first appearance in a vernacular text is in the AN *Château d'Amour* of Robert Grosseteste (ed. Murray; ME translations ed. Sajavaara). **L** may also have known an early C14th English variant, the Parable of the King and his Four Daughters in *Cursor Mundi* 9517–9752.

113–15 *A Transition* **113** *ferly*: the marvellous events culminating in the darkness at Christ's death. *false Iewes*: a measure of Will's self-identification with Christ (against whom the *vyl vilanye* has been perpetrated), but echoing a wider contemporary anxiety that Jews might actually repeat their first 'wounding' of Christ by desecrating his sacramental body in the Host, as in the mid-C15th 'Croxton Play of the Sacrament' (in *Non-cycle Plays*). **114** (*with*)*drow* (*me*): an action both literal and potentially symbolic, this deeply spiritual vision lacking only a formal indication that it is an 'inner dream'. *derkenesse*: evoking also the liturgical stress on mourning in the Office of Tenebrae said in the darkened church on Wednesday, Thursday and Friday of Holy Week. *descendit*...: 'He descended into Hell' (article 8 of the Apostles' Creed); an allusive periphrasis for 'the depths of hell'. The outward disappearance of the sun's light at Christ's death provides an awe-inspiring entry into the infernal domain where there is 'darkness and dread and the devil master' (18.117). **115** *seyh sothly*: the adverb affirming the truth less of the narrator's personal witness (cf. 116, 120) than of the dream's content, which rests on author-

ity. *secundum scripturas*: 'according to the sacred writings'; a phrase from the Nicene Creed said at Sunday Mass, but evoking its original source I Cor 15:4, which affirms that the key events of Christian faith fulfil OT prophecy. Insertion here of the *descendit*-phrase from the other familiar creed (it is absent from the Nicene) aligns the elaborated narrative of the apocryphal *EN* with that of the canonical scriptures, which contain the seeds of the story in I Pet 3:18–20.

(a) **116–270*a*** *The Debate of the Daughters of God* **116** *west*: the direction of sunset and of death (Russell 1984:139). In cathedrals the Last Judgement portal stood on the west or main front (e.g. Chartres in Schiller I pl. 62), and in parish churches the Doom was depicted in the west window, as at Fairford (Baker pl. 17) or on the chancel arch facing west (Benson 1998:18–20). Mercy's symbolic association with the Last Things portends what is hoped will be the final attitude of the Creator to his creatures. *wenche*: possibly neutral, but usually implying low social status. Its ironic conjunction at 119 with *buyrde*, a term from alliterative high style used of Lady Mede at 3.15, is a striking example of **L**'s 'grotesque sublime', superbly explored in Coghill 1988 [1962]). **117** *to helleward*: i.e. 'downward' (MED s.v. *helle* n. 1 (g)), the metrically required stress on the suffix favouring a polysemantic pun on *ward* 'stronghold' (MED s.v. n. 3(a)). Though in Pr 16–18 hell lies westward, and in 1.111–13 northward, the sisters seem to approach from all 'the round earth's imagin'd corners' towards a *centre* beneath which Hell lies. But *Sk*'s sense of the scene's resemblance to a stage-play where actors come from the four quarters and meet in the middle of an open space, though justifiable, lends no support to his inference that *helleward* means 'eastward'. For this 'stage' is no wooden platform but a theatre of the mind, and the directions' symbolic meanings are therefore crucial. **118** *Mercy*: a personification of the *misericordia* that is 'aboue Godes werkes' (Ps 114:9, qu. at 12.75*a*, 19.296*a* and cf. 6.337*a*). *mylde*: the revision modifying the complete verbal repetition at B 115b of B 16.91b without concealing the allusion to the Blessed Virgin Mary, the 'mater misericordiae' who at 7.285 is signified by Mercy the 'mayden, hath myhte ouer hem alle'. **119** *benyngne...speche*: retaining the verbal echo of B 16.7 in B 18.116. **121** *eest*: the most important symbolic 'direction', as the location of Truth's tower (see on Pr 14–15), and thus the only proper place for her to come from. **122** *Treuthe*: the *veritas* of Ps 84:11, God's self-revelation, under the limitations of time, history and language, as the object of human understanding. This, the first 'nature-name' the poet assigned to God, has special authority, even if the 'whole' truth of the divine nature is not known to the speaker and can only be grasped as a harmony eventually realised by the reconciliation of all four sisters. **123** *vertue*: a hint at the cardinal virtue *forti-*

tudo, the *myht* especially associated with God the Father. A parallel between the daughters and the cardinal virtues is suggested by their depiction in a mid-C12th crucifxion enamel (Schiller II pl. 446).

124–73 *Mercy and Treuthe* are regularly coupled in the Psalms, e.g. at 24:10, 88:14. **125** scans either as Type IIa with *of* mute or, perhaps preferably, as Ia or Ic with *of*, here meaning 'about', as a full-stave, thus facilitating repetition with variation in following 126 (123), where *Of* is unstressed. *this grete wonder*: the darkness above and the light below. The subject of the Harrowing is taken from Part II of the *EN*, ll. 1160–1536 in the ME translation. The version in *LA* 242–5, observing that the canonical Gospels say nothing about what Christ did in Limbo, refers to *EN* as authority for the story, along with an unspecified sermon of 'Augustine' (not used by **L**) that it retails at length (identified by Marx 1997:218 as pseudo-Augustine, Sermo 160 *De Pascha*). **126** *þe day roued*: 'day was breaking'; not the outer natural dawn of Easter morning (still to come) but the supernatural light before hell, which seems associated with the 'day' that 'withdrew' at 60. **127** *lihte*; *leem*: the doublet echoing *lux... luminis sempterni* (*LA* 243) or *illuxit...lux magna* (*EN Descensus* [Latin B] , XVIII.1). The light shining in darkness that cannot overcome it inevitably evokes the Biblical image of the Son's divine radiance (Jn 1:5). **130–1** A 'Platonic' association of the stave-syllables seems intended, given the earlier use of 'mercy' as a nature-name for the Virgin (see on 118). **132** *speche*: Gabriel's 'thou shalt conceive...Because no word [*verbum*] shall be impossible with God' and Mary's answering 'be it done to me according to thy word' (Lk 1:31, 37; 38). In iconography the virginal conception is often represented as taking place through the ear (Schiller I pls. 108, 111). **133** *grace...Gost*: cf. Lk 1:28–30, 35. **134** *wommane wem*: the loss of virginity (with Mary as referent); but **L** may more widely understand the stain of original sin contracted by all at conception (Ps 50:7, a verse following that quoted at 420*a*), but from which Mary was held to be free. On the weak subjective genitive in *wommane* see *MES* 73. **135** *witnesse*: referring to the prophecies (141) that this would happen, above all Is 9:2, quoted at 7.133*a*, foretelling this very event (7.134–5), and again here at 366. **136** *thritty*: the 'ideal' age (perfect manhood) traditionally said to have been Christ's at his death; it is more precisely specified (perhaps not accidentally) at line 3*32* below. **137** *Deyede*: a Ø-relative with *Who* understood. The homophonic play on *dey* and *day* echoes that at B 16.166 and recalls the *lyf* / *liht* collocation at 59. *mydday*: the ninth hour (*nona hora*), commonly reckoned today as 3 p.m., but understood as noon (see on 7.132) by **L**, who connects the earthly sun's disappearance with the heavenly Son's *aureus solis color* (*EN* XVIII.1, *LA* 243) before the gates of hell. **138** *clips*: no simple covering-over

with clouds but a unique planetary occurrence. Earlier crucifixion iconography often depicts the lesser and the greater light in the corners (Schiller II pl. 435 shows sun and moon weeping). **139** *In menynge*: the natural event having symbolic significance, as at 15.245, 5.121–2 above, because the 'book of nature' (see Alan of Lille in *PL* 210:579, Raby *OBMLV* 242) is the first part of God's ordained revelation to man. *merkenesse*: firstly that of the patriarchs in Limbo, but more widely of all humanity; Christ's resurrection brings a 'light' to the Gentiles and Jews as in the prophecy (Lk 2:32) that Simeon recalls at *EN* XVIII.2, *LA* 243. **140** re-presents as coming what was recalled in Repentance's great prayer at 7.134, reminding how liturgical ritual combines diachronic and synchronic axes, narrating salvation history and enacting an 'existential' drama. **141** The most specific prophecy concerning the second tree is Is 11:10, 'In that day, the root of Jesse... the Gentiles shall beseech: and his sepulchre shall be glorious' (qu. Rom 15:12). Although the symbolic image of the 'Jesse Tree' was commonly connected with the Incarnation, it is found 'combined with the tree-Cross as the *arbor vitae*' in the remarkable 'Jesse Cross' illustration in a mid-C14th *Speculum humanae salvationis* (Schiller II 135, pl. 442). **142–3** The notion of the 'tree of Christ's cross' (Ac 5:30, 10.39; I Pet 2:24) as the means to 'lift up' Man subjected to death through eating the fruit of the 'tree of good and evil' derives from the *Pange lingua*, sung during the ceremony of the Adoration of the Cross (and directly quoted at 164*a*). The tree's becoming the subject of the victory shows influence from the Good Friday liturgy's metonymic treatment of the 'crux fidelis', the alternating response to the verses. But the figurative theology of Venantius Fortunatus's great hymn is enriched from the medieval legend telling how the wood of the Cross grew from the seeds of the first *tre* in Gen 2:17 (see *Legends...*1871, *Legend...*1894). On the *arbor vitae* / *arbor crucis* iconography, see Schiller II 132–6, pls. 431 (C11th) and 443 (C14th), both including Adam and Eve; Saxl 1942:pl. 27b. **142** *tynt...wynne*: cf. 'To undo the loss inflicted by that wood' (*Pange lingua*, st. 2). **143** *deth*: the expected antithesis would be *lyf*, but the essence of the Christian paradox lies in this ultimate *transsumptio*, wherein the referent becomes the 'obedient' (and thence 'redemptive') death of Christ. **144** *walterot*: a humorously 'Platonic' nonce-creation from the elements of *troteuale* (a word of unknown etymology that MED cites four times from Mannyng's *Handlyng Synne*), rendering the 'nonsense' Truth accuses Mercy of even *more* nonsensical. The insulting tone, which makes the argument parody the calm politeness of scholastic disputation, is not without a touch of 'clerkly' anti-feminism. **146–7** The syntax is ambiguous, allowing *leue* to be indic. pl. governed by the noun-phrase subject in 145–6 or, as more likely, imper. sg. addressed to Mercy, with the noun-phrase as anticipated object in apposition with *hem* 147. **147** *brynge*: 'could bring'; a 'subjunctive of unreality' (*MES* 455). **149** *truyfle*: perhaps meant to recall *troteuale* (though not derived from it). *Treuthe...sothe*: a (deliberately) banal b-half with an ironic echo of Piers's words at 7.244; Truth's 'pre-Easter' *tokene* is the solemn OT certainty of 151*a*. **150** corresponds closely to its source *Sic qui descenderit ad inferos, non ascendet* 'so he that shall go down to hell shall not come up' (Job 7:9) and implies that Job, as one of the suffering patriarchs, can speak from experience. But the speaker is unaware of the words' ironic deeper sense: for *Christ's* 'descensus ad inferos' is that of one who has already 'descended' (to earth from heaven) and therefore will 'ascend' (from hell to earth); see on 11.209*a*. The same sentiment is ascribed to Solomon in the Towneley 'Harrowing' play (XXV/295–7). **151** *Iob*: strictly neither a patriarch nor a prophet, so not a 'perfect' example with which to rebut Mercy's claim to authority at 141. **151***a* 'For in hell there is no salvation; [have mercy on me, O God, and save me'; from the Office of the Dead, Nocturn 3, response 7 (*Brev.* 2:278). This paraphrase from Job 7:9 was widely cited in vernacular literature (e.g. *Prick* 7248) and in the penitential tradition (Alf*Q*). **152–64***a Mercy's reply* is (in good sermon fashion) an *argumentum per analogiam* ('For...and so...and as...so...'), its thrice-repeated instrumental preposition *thorw* (153, 159, 162) answering Truth's repeated 'never' (147, 150). **153** *experiense*: an earlier use than any recorded in MED, appealing to what Will has constantly sought as *kynde knowyng*. **154** The folk-belief in the contrary action of similars (on which see Bartolomaeus Anglicus 1249–50) had an 'experiential' basis, the lethal / recuperative action of herbal drugs (e.g. those derived from belladonna and digitalis) depending on the dosage and manner of administration. Mercy's implication that there are two kinds of death, corporeal and spiritual (one temporary, the other not necessarily eternal), will be taken up by Christ at 373–5. On the important link of this idea with Holy Church's *tryacle* figure at 1.145 see St-Jacques 1991:114–15. **155** *bote*: a 'remedy' for death won through death (itself the punishment for sin, not a means to *further* punishment), by God's sharing man's mortality through the Incarnation. **156** *scorpioun*: an apt choice for the analogy, as its barely visible bite made it an emblem of deadly treachery, and therefore of the Devil. **157–9** A common belief, found in Lanfranc's *Chirurgie* 344/11: 'scorpiouns...ben brent þat we mowe vse hem in *medicyns*'. **158** 'Until, dead, he is placed against the injured spot'. The *vertu* of Christ's death has already been learnt 'thorw experiense' in the healing of Longeus' blindness (symbolically, the consequence of sin) when he pierced Christ's already dead body (cf. 98). The image of Christ himself as the 'healing medicine' echoes the Johannine understanding of his Cross as the 'antitype' of

the brazen serpent set up by Moses in the desert, which cured from serpent-bite all who looked on it (Num 21:8–9); cf. Alan of Lille's *Distinctiones* citing Jn 3:14–15: 'Serpens...dicitur Christus' (*PL* 210:942) and Fortunatus in the stanza quoted at 164*a*: *Et medelam ferret inde, Hostis unde laeserat* 'Fetching healing from the place Where hostile malice left its trace'. **159** *vertu*: a deliberate 'anti-pun' as well as a play on co-polysemes; the hidden 'virtue' or strength that God as *parfit practisour* will draw from Satan's *dede* is unknown to the devil and obviously not due to *his* exercise of 'virtue'. **160** *this deth*: Christ's. But as ironic ambiguity is of great significance in this context of divine disguising and table-turning, the noun-phrase may also be resolved grammatically as '*this* shall destroy death', the antecedent of 'this' being the scorpion Christ (see on 158), and the whole of 161 then standing in apposition to *deth* 160. **161** suggests almost as strongly as B 158 Death's separate, near-dualistic existence alongside Satan over against God / Life, a way of thinking evidenced in the later iconography (Schiller II pls. 531, 532, 536). **163** *goed ende*: balancing the implied good beginning, the Creation (cf. Gen 1:31). The Apocalypse (21:1) strongly emphasises the creation of 'a new heaven and earth'. **164** *goed sleythe*: the wordplay operating as at 159, with oxymoron a pointer to God's final transformation of diabolic evil (which lacks substantial reality) into divine good. **164***a* '[That God by stratagem should foil / The shape-shifting Destroyer's guile'; from *Pange lingua*, st. 3. The *ars* is the Son's assuming human form, as Satan did a serpent's, with the difference that Incarnation is no disguise but a mysterious reality (including acceptance of death), a 'sleight,' yet not 'guile'.

165–173 *Righteousness and Peace* **166** *nype...north*: the region of 'biting cold', darkness and wintry night, here freed of the specifically diabolic associations of 1.110ff but in the OT often where 'evil and destruction' will come from (Jer 1:14, 4:6, 6:1). As in the OE *Wanderer*, cold is a 'natural' symbol of the end of time, pointing to the Judgement in which *justice* will reign. *nype*: possibly a back-formation (earlier than that of 1551 in OED s.v. *nip* sb. 1) from the verb *nyppen* at 6.104 (also first instanced in **L**) derived from OE *genip* 'darkness' or (*Sk*, MED s.v.) **hnipa* 'crag, peak' (peace and justice are both associated with mountains and hills in Ps 71:3, and in 84:12 'iustitia de caelo prospexit'). **167** *Rightwisenesse*: Justice, one of the Cardinal Virtues (21.219); a prime attribute of God in both OT and NT (Dan 9:7, Job 36:3; Rom 3:21). **168** Righteousness's seniority to Mercy in age and wisdom is obvious enough, her seniority to Truth less clear. That the eldest sister somehow reflects God's unrevealed essence and Truth his self-revelation in time seems out of keeping with her palpably limited knowledge at 192ff below. **169** is the only other Type Ib line alliterating on *s*, recalling Pr 1. The pararhyme with *soth* and half-rhymes with *bothe*, *yclothed, opere* create an effect of calm and reassurance. *southe*: the 'sikerore' region, according to HC (1.116). **170** *pacience*: 'an heigh vertu certeyn' (*CT* V 773) that promotes peace between human beings. It has a theological character in relation to the God who 'soffres' and as the fourth of the Twelve Fruits of the Spirit (Jn 14:27; Gal 5:22). But a further association of Peace's special 'clothing' or 'outward sign' *patience* with the Cardinal Virtue of prudence is suggested by Prov 14:29, a text cited by Chaucer's Dame Prudence (*CT* VII 1510). **171** *Loue*: an oblique 'nature-name' that is now empowered to take the place of 'Truth' in consequence of the full and final revelation in Christ that 'God is Love' (see on 1.82 above). In contemporary iconography it is represented metonymically by the singular motif of 'Caritas [*or* Ecclesia] embracing / piercing Christ on the Cross', as illustrated in Schiller II pl. 447 and most strikingly (because she embraces Christ *in the midst of* the Four Daughters) in the C14th stained-glass image in Schiller II pl. 453. Relevant to Love's 'mediatory' relation with the Daughters (through his 'love-correspondence' with Peace) is Alan of Lille's comment (*In cant. cantic.*) on the text *media charitate constravit propter filias Jerusalem* (Cant 3:10): 'Charity is, so to speak, the other virtues' mediatrix and form,...illuminates and informs the rest, and relates equally to them all' (*PL* 210:76). So too is his interpretation of 'Jerusalem' as 'the mind of Christ in which is the vision of "the peace which surpasseth all understanding" [Phil 4: 7]'. Love's 'desire for Peace' aptly figures God's wish to reconcile the world to himself through Christ (II Cor 5:18–19).

174–237 174 *When...oþer*: elliptical for 'when Peace [and Justice] approached each other'; the B 171 form has Peace being intercepted by Justice as she approaches the *other* two sisters. **175** *in*: the small revision of *for* removing **B**'s unjustified anticipation of an understanding that Righteousness does not yet possess, and making her bow an act of ordinary courtesy (see further on 466). **177** *garnementes*: such as a lover or bride wears; echoing Ps 44:9–12 and Is 52:7. **179** *merkenesse*: the dark enveloping them in Limbo, now pierced by the light of Love. **181** In the revision, the song of Mercy (see *TN*) provides the music for Peace to dance to; in B 178 the verb *haue* is two-way-facing, the subject being either *Adam...Moses* or *Mercy* (with sense either 'obtain' or 'take'). *Moises*: making clear that *Spes* was always to be understood as a *figura* of the hope of salvation from sin offered by the Commandments, rather than the 'historic' Moses who saw the vision of the 'promised land' [of heaven] but never entered it (he is still in Limbo). **183a** '[For wrath is in his indignation; and life in his good will]. In the evening weeping shall have place: and in the morning gladness' (Ps 29:6)'; to be read in the context of vs 4, where the psalmist's praise of God for 'saving his soul

from hell' makes the psalm especially apt for the vigil of Easter, the time of the action to be narrated. **187** As the office of condemning man was granted to the two elder sisters Justice and Truth, so that of 'saving' him is to the two younger. The rôle of Mercy and Peace as speakers for the defence is very explicit in the revised form of 186–7. *maynprisen*: see on 2.208, and the valuable discussion in Keen 2002:91–4. **190** *patente*: the New Covenant 'sealed' in Christ's blood and sent to Peace as an open letter to all mankind; fulfilling (as well as ratifying) that of *Spes* at 19.12, it is the same *acquitaunce* relied on by Patience at B 14.190a (not in // **C**). In keeping with the episode's pervasive 'legal' character, the patent combines the language of a charter of enfeoffment (offering entry to heaven) with the action of a writ of mainprise (offering the prerequisite release from hell), the first clause (190b) making the grant, the second (191b) the warranty (Keen 2002:91); see further Steiner 2000:106–7. **191** *In... requiescam*: 'In peace in the selfsame I will sleep and I will rest' (Ps 4:9); the understood referent of 'selfsame' is presumably 'the presence of God', and Love's letter is properly addressed to *Peace* because Love itself is what HC called the 'plant of peace, most precious of virtues' (1.147). Sung at Compline in Lent and (divided as versicle and response) at Matins on Holy Saturday (*Pe*), the verse denotes in its liturgical context Christ's own 'rest' in the tomb before his resurrection, and thus stands as an analogue to the imperfect *requies* of the just in Limbo, which is soon to become *pax* (the vision of God in heaven). **191** *And...duyre*: 'And to guarantee the lasting validity of this document'. There may be a pun on two polysemes of *dede*, since an 'action' (Christ's crucifixion) is what has permanently validated the 'document', and his sacrificial death needs no repeating (I Pet 3:18). **192–3** The tone of pitying incredulity, together with her condescending use of 'low' terms (*rauen, dronke, chewe*) suggests an elder sister convinced of her superior rationality and (taking into account Mercy's appeal to 'experience' at 153), the sheer weight of cause-and-effect ('if...then'). At 193 she repeats as a question what Truth stated at 147. **195** *bigynnynge...world*: a superficially puzzling phrase that echoes 19.113 and contains an implication unknown to the speaker. *doem*: the valid (but incomplete) OT view (Gen 2:17) of the divine plan for man. **197** *downriht*: the adverb here perhaps answering to Vg's emphatic *morte morieris* 'die the death'. Though there is only one *deth of kynde* (natural death), the speaker may imply *peyne perpetuel* (spiritual death) as well: the forfeiture not just of immortality (as in *Purity* 245–6) but of *any* hope of reconciliation with God after the loss. *euere*: a revision of **B**'s more accurate (and moderate) *after* 'as a result' that highlights Righteousness's imperfect understanding of even the Old Law, making her anticipate verbally Lucifer at 303–4 and, more generally, the *Spiritus Iusticie* of 21.299–310 (which while acting *euene trewe* acts only *eueneforth his knowyng*). **199–200** The internal rhyme in the b-verse and the emphatic pararhyme in the next a-verse underline the catechetical tone (Peace responds in kind at 225). **201** *loue*: a concession to Mercy's claim that Love is the power behind *зone lihte*, but also an assertion that the Fall was a wilful abandonment of that Love for a different teaching and love. **203–6** have strong associations with the language of the courts, and figure the two elder sisters as judges sitting on the bench to proclaim the law of heaven's King in all its rigour (*resoun, recorde, preyer, boteles bale*). **204** *is*: better than *be*, since they are not passing the sentence but recalling it.

207–37 *Peace's plea* **207** *preye*: 'petition'; its substance is the necessity, for both man (214) and (somewhat surprisingly) for God (216), of first-hand knowledge of suffering and death, and the verb *witen* is repeated ten times in Peace's speech. The same ground appealed to by Mercy at 153 is now supported and ratified by God's own wish to know *kyndeliche* 'through experience' (i.e. in his Son the man Jesus). The claim that such 'knowledge by contraries' (happiness, repletion, colour, light, wealth) is part of the divine plan is now extended *analogice* in the manner of the preacher, more than *logice* in that of the clerk, from the sensory domain (where the analogy is persuasive) to the moral (where it is doubtful). For Peace's argument risks blurring the distinction between God's choosing to experience what he is free to and man's choosing to know what he was forbidden to. **210** *woet*: 'really understands'. **212–13** take up (in inverted order) B 10.435, which is omitted at that point in revision. **213** scans either as Type Ia on |w|, with mute key-stave, or as an extended Type III on vowels with counterpoint on |w| and main stresses on *álle* in both halves. **216** is best scanned as a Type IIIc on vowels and |s| or as a Type Ie with blank second stave (*God*) and mute third stave. *ysoffred of*: 'undergone experience of'; contrasted with 'consented' in 222, 228, but both occurrences intimating 'suffered' (231, though even here not explicitly). **217** *wist*: the 'limitation' on God's capacity arising from his unlimitedness (i.e. it is impossible to God *as* God); but that this is not absolute is shown by the fact (and arguably necessity) of the Incarnation. *sour...*: an apt metaphor, since death came in from tasting fruit. **222** *sorwe of deynge*: thereby identifying entirely with Adam's race, since to be human is to have to die. The scriptural basis for the doctrine of Christ's *kenosis* 'self-emptying' to take the form of one 'enslaved' to death is Phil 2:6–11. **224** is unusual in replacing a macaronic line (if with one of somewhat weightier import). *moreyne*: the plague-image well suggesting the suddenness of the encounter with Death, and recalling so early a passage as A 12.81ff. The knowledge that we must die may teach us to live with restraint even more effectively than will want (*modicum*). **224** *mete with*: 'encounter', as at 18.182, but

in B 215 possibly with some play on the sense 'equate' (MED s.v. *meten* v. (1)), as at B 4.143. Peace offers a negative version of HC's 'measure is medicine': learning the evil of *too much* ('sin') through experience of *too little* ('suffering'). **225** has internal rhyme modelled on the Latin 'Leonine' line as at Pr 152–7. **227** *hym*: an emphatic 'popular' pleonastic use; see *MES* 137–8. *furste*: an important addition indicating that the Fall was part of God's providential plan. **229** *ther-thorw*: i.e. by 'felyng', as God, who knows only *wele*, will come to know *wo*. The final answer to the Dreamer's quest for direct knowledge of God is found in this assurance of God's direct knowledge of Man: *wyte* becomes *kyndeliche to knowe* 'to know by experience / as in itself it really is' through the intermediary of *fele*. **230** *auntred*: a resumption of the chivalric metaphor introduced at 14. The Son's becoming Man involves a transformation of all the categories, since this is an 'auntur' that cannot be lost, and can be 'won' only by losing. (On **L**'s use of the chivalric metaphor see Gaffney 1931, Waldron 1986 and Warner 1996). *Adames kynde*: more specific than *mankynde* in stating that Christ is the 'second Adam'. **231** God's 'knowledge' in heaven of man's suffering on earth is not yet a *kynde knowynge*, but it is what makes him desire such *knowynge*. However, the Incarnation seems hardly conceivable without 'precompassion' on the part of the Son, in whose image man was made (cf. the tone of 372). *in...places*: the adverbial phrase qualifying 'God's knowing', not 'Adam's suffering.' **233** *þat*: with antecedent *he* 232. **233a** See at 3.489. The application of this injunction to Christ is audacious but encouraging, since he can actually fulfil it. **234–7** are richly paradoxical: folly 'teaches', Peace proclaims the necessity of war, and men must lack prosperity to understand it. The 'Platonic' pun in 237 builds on the popular etymology that understood the exclamation *wei-la-wei* as meaning 'weal away'.

a¹ **238–68** The *Book episode* continues the fusion of comic and sublime, 'personifying' not an idea but an object (it has an article at 245), as in the prosopopœia of the OE Riddles and *The Dream of the Rood*. Yet this 'book' is the loftiest of all, God's own word, here *holiwrit* in its wider sense of both Scripture and patristic tradition (MED s.v. (a) and (b)), the latter especially as preserved in the service-books of the Church. **238** *two brode yes*: symbolising the Old and New Testaments, the literal and spiritual levels of interpretation (Kaske 1959:127), or (recalling Alan of Lille *In Cant. Cantic.* on the two eyes of the BVM) the active and the contemplative lives (*PL* 210:81). See also White 1995. **239** *bolde*: 'audacious' and 'forthright', as his oath and first words prove. **240** *Goddes body*: a common 'great oath', often with eucharistic reference (MED s.v. *bodi* n. 5), and not a little incongruous in a *beaupere*'s mouth. *bere witnesse*: an assertion that gains authority from the custom of swearing oaths on the Bible in court. **241** *blased a sterre*: see Mt 2:1–10. The verb has hitherto been used only in the torch-simile in 19.189, which re-surfaces in the echo of 19.260–1 at 248. **242** *That*: 'of such a kind that'. **243** *Bethleem þe citee*: (Lk 2:4); a word-order common in ME with ancient cities (*CT* I 939, VII 2147). **244** *saue*: as told to the shepherds in Lk 2:11 (the prophecy made to the 'wise' in Mt 2:2 was of a king). But the earlier Christmas narrative at 14.84–98 (verbally recalled at 249b) likewise unites as a single manifestation of *claritas Dei* 'God's radiance' (Lk 2:9) the appearances of the star to the Magi and of the angels to the shepherds, which are found severally in Mt and Lk. **245** The elements' witness to the Saviour's birth goes back to St Gregory the Great's C6th commentary on Mt 2:1–2 (Kaske 1959:119); their witness at Christ's death is found in Pope St Leo's Sermon 8 on the Passion, read as the ninth lesson in the third nocturn of Matins on Good Friday: *unam protulerunt omnia elementa sententiam* 'all the elements gave unanimous judgement'. In recalling HC's reference to the elements at 1.17, the line effectively links the divine work of creation (246) with that of redemption (244), revealing how the events that attest Christ's godhead extended from his birth through his ministry to his passion and death. *hereof*: effectively, 'to his divinity.' **246** *God...wrouhte*: acknowledging the Jesus who was to be put to death as being the divine VERBUM through whom 'omnia...facta sunt' (Jn 1:3). *welkene*: the 'upper air' or aether of the region above the moon; sometimes used for the element of 'pure fire', as in the listing of all four at B 17.161 (MED s.v. *ether* n.) but not here, where it denotes 'air'. **247** *Tho...*: the angels, whose association with the star relates to **L**'s running-together of the complementary Lucan and Matthean accounts of Christmas and Epiphany. *stella comata*: the specially-created 'long-haired star' (*stellam eius* 'comet' 14.97), understood in medieval interpretation as what the Magi saw (*ME Sermons* 227, cit. Alf*Q* 111; clearly thus depicted by Giotto *c.* 1305 in Schiller I pl.288). **248** See 19.261, which uses the same mute stave *to*. **249** The divine 'torch' inevitably suggests the 'High Holy Ghost' (14.84–5) who splits heaven so that Love can leap out 'into this low earth' (see the dove-nativities in Schiller I 183, 198 of mid-14th and early 15th c.). **250** *druye*: a small addition serving to link the Redeemer's subjection of the water under his feet with the Creator's mastering of the waters in Gen 1:9, Ex 14:29, 15:8. **253** 'Lord, [if it be thou], bid me come to thee upon the waters' (Mt 14:28). St Peter's words ironically contrast him with Christ, since he *fails* to walk on the water. **254–5** The sun's refusal to look on her creator's suffering is a major motif in Latin and vernacular devotional writing (Schmidt 1983²:185–88). In medieval iconography the sun is more usually depicted as a man and the moon as a woman (e.g. Schiller II pls. 381, 385); that *sonne* is feminine here (*heresulue*)

and elsewhere in later ME (Schmidt ibid. p. 187) may be a survival from OE literary tradition (*MES* 46n1). **256** *heuynesse*: the earth's, though the syntax allows it to be Christ's, and *soffre* to be both transitive and intransitive. The choice of word mutedly echoes (by way of an 'anti-pun') the 'love-heaviness' of I 148–9. **257** recalls 63 above. *quyk*: an eschatological, not animistic suggestion, evoking the Pauline idea of the whole creation 'groaning' in anticipation of the final consummation of things (Rom 8:93). But it seems appropriate enough that a 'wide world' held in the hand of the Trinity (B 17.159–62) should 'quake' when that hand is 'herte...in the myddes' (19.153). **258** *helle*: not mentioned in Mt 27:51; but the conjunction with *roches* 257 may be a recollection of the 'rock' and 'gates of hell' in Mt 16:18, the death of Christ being the birth of the Church that will continue his work of subduing Satan's kingdom. *holde~tholede*: the sonorous internal rhyme bringing out the profound theological antithesis between Christ's power and his suffering. **259** *Symondes sones*: named in *GN* as Carinus and Leucius (Lentinus) and identified as the sons of Simeon, the 'just and devout' old man who utters the *Nunc dimittis* in Lk 2:29–32. Raised at Christ's descent into Hell (which immediately follows the moment of his death and therefore implies they were among the *dede men* of 64 above), it is their written account of the events that is claimed as the source of the *GN*. **259a** '[And he had received an answer from the Holy Ghost], that he (*sc.* Simeon) should not see death [before he had seen the Christ of the Lord]' (Lk 2:26). Simeon's privilege is mirrored in that of his sons, who are released *from* Death at the moment of Christ's death. For the positioning of this verse here cf. *EN* (Latin A) XVIII:2. **260** *hit*: that the elements' witness proves Jesus 'Christ, and Christ God's son' (55). **261** *Iesus (Gigas)...geaunt*: a description that presents Christ's breaking down of Hell-gates as a typological fulfilment of Samson's carrying-away the Gates of Gaza (Jg 16:3; see Anderson fig. 11, Schiller II pls. 428, 488 from *c.* 1370, Kaske 1968:168). Kaske 1957 finds a reference to the common interpretation of Ps 18:6–7 ('Exsultavit ut gigas ad currendam viam; a summo caelo egressio eius') as referring to Christ's indomitability and more-than-human origin and nature. *gyn*: glossed for **B** 'siege-engine (figurative)' in MED s.v. *ginne* n. 4(a); but unless the allusion is to his cross, there is probably a polysemantic pun on sense 2 (a) 'trick, ruse'. For Christ's victory is not, like Samson's, a feat of physical strength but (in apparent weakness) one of superior wisdom, and his *gyn* (< L. *ingenium* 'intellect') is 'his double nature, true God and true man...whence he is called a *Giant*' (Hugh of St Cher, 6.138v, cit. Alf*Q* 111). **264** *brente*: alluding perhaps to heretics' punishment for teaching false doctrine (cf. Anima at B 15.83), and assuredly 'condign' for any *book* found to tell lies (cf. *CT* III 790–1). *bote*:

'unless' (Donaldson 1966:265–6) as against 'but' (Kaske 1959:136). *to lyue*: 'to life' (Kaske ib. 134–5; considered by Wittig 1986 an infinitive, but this is the same construction as at 398). Donaldson takes the verbs in B 255–6 as 'subjunctives, becoming infinitives [at 257]' (ib. 269); but both verbs in B 257=C 266 may be intransitive, with 'will' understood and their respective senses 'become dislocated' and 'split apart' (svv. 1b(a); 3(a)). **B 255** No reason appears for this line's excision, unless that the risen Christ possessed *more* than 'man's' powers, and a special reference to his mother seemed otiose (the Gospels do not mention an appearance to her). **266** *ioye vnioynen*: a 'Platonic' play on near-homophones, suggesting that since true joy 'gynneth dawe' from faith in Christ's divine power, the false 'joy' of his adversaries will come apart like a badly made piece of furniture (the MED gloss 'destroy' s.v. is too imprecise, given the conjunction with *vnlouken*). **267** *And bot*: still dependent on the main verb in 264a; Book is solemnly foretelling their destruction and damnation unless they believe. *newe lawe*: not itself a Biblical phrase but corresponding to *testamentum novum,* the 'new covenant' that supersedes the old (Heb 8:8 [citing Jer 31:31], 22).

269–70a provide a second skilful *transition* (cf. 113–15), this time from the debate outside to the debate inside hell. Somewhat confusingly, from the standpoint of infernal geography the *Limbo Patrum* where the just are held is now envisaged as enclosed by the Devil's walls, as if in an outer courtyard, whereas earlier it had seemed a territory adjacent to (but under the sway of) hell. **270a** 'Lift up your gates, O ye princes', [and be ye lifted up, O eternal gates]' (Ps 23:7). In the dialogue between Christ and Satan at B 315–19a (a major casualty in the revision to **C**) the remaining verses of this royal processional psalm are drawn upon, vividly evoking the liturgy of Holy Saturday, when Ps 23 was sung in the second nocturn at Matins. The psalm's 'palace gates' are conflated with the *portae inferi* of Mt 16:18 (so *EN* A. XXI:1) and the 'brazen gates' of *EN* A 21.2 (*LA* 244).

(b) 271–94 describe in ironically physical terms the *Defence of Hell.* **271** The theme of 'the Light of Christ' (*Lumen Christi*) is dominant in the vigil service of Easter (especially the canticle *Exultet*), which is insistently echoed: 'This night, of which it is written [cf. Ps 138:13]: And the night shall be lit up like the day [*nox...illuminabitur*]'. The phrase's more distant allusion is to the lightning and thunder (the most familiar combination of 'voice' and 'light') in Ex 19:16, which herald a theophany. More immediately, it recalls the *vocem virtutis* of Ps 67:34, the voice of God resounding in Job 37:2–4, and shaking the doors in Is 6:3–4, and the *vocem magnam* proclaiming the Devil's defeat and Christ's triumph in Apoc 12:10. The *liht / Lucifer* opposition (as at 359) seems deliberate, if B 1.112 // is recalled (cf. the *York* 'Fall of the Angels'

49–50). **272** *Principes*: the Latin investing Christ's command with a liturgical solemnity that heightens its irony; hereafter, the true *Princeps* 'speaks no more Latin'. **273b** translates the Latin quoted at B 318 and omitted in // **C.** **274** *Satoun*: a character elsewhere in *PP* presumed identical with the chief of the rebel angels (and cf. *N-Town* Passion I, 1–3), but here *distinguished* from 'Lucifer' as one of three (or possibly four) major fiends who may be meant to 'correspond' to the Daughters of God. In *EN* A. XX.3 (and *LA* p. 243, which is based on it) Satan is *princeps et dux mortis* and doubtless identical with Lucifer (Marx 1997:244–5). *Helle*: answering to *Inferus*, a personification of the place as in *EN* (deriving from Apoc 20:13–14); but here seemingly a metonymic title for a major devil, possibly Lucifer, who replies at 295 (on the devil's names see further Russell 1984:247–9). **275** Satan presumably means not that Christ's glorified soul entered hell in the days of his flesh but that he recognises coming from this 'lyht' the same 'stif vois' (B 15.593) he once heard summon Lazarus. (On the relation of the latter's raising from 'the pains of hell' [*Towneley* XXXI 204] with the Harrowing of Hell, see Pilkinton 1975:51–3). **277** Christ's assault is seen as like that of a medieval king besieging the gates of a fortified city, and the martial imagery of the added passage 281–94 (recalled in *Paradise Lost* VI 570ff) heightens the ironic incongruity of the devils' material defence against so irresistible a force as light and the purely spiritual 'lord' it manifests. Satan's military tactic is to provide inner protection for the chief devils, and to station lesser fiends on the battlements to do the fighting. **278** *per...is*: presumably heaven (which is what Christ intends), though Satan seems unaware that Lazarus is in the world of the living. *lihtliche*: 'easily', but with an unintentionally humorous homophonic pun on the effortless ease with which the heavenly *liht* performs its office. **279** *parled*: a word possibly introduced by **L** from OF. **280** The main allusion is to Isaiah's great prophecy, quoted in part at 20.366 (see at 7.133a). **281–4** introduce a note of grotesque comedy suggesting affinities with (and possibly influence from) the way in which this episode was treated in the earliest Miracle Plays (these are not extant, but cf. the early C15th *York* XXXVII = *Towneley* XXV). **281** *Ragamoffyn*: found only here as a contemptuous name for a lesser demon, with the etymological sense 'ragged lout', and once earlier as a surname (MED s.v.). *barres*: the *vectes ferreos* of *EN* [A] XXI.1. **282** *Belial*: from the Hebrew for 'wickedness' or 'destruction'; an ancient name for a false god, but used of the Devil in this addition's probable source II Cor 6:14–15: 'Or what fellowship hath *light* with darkness? And what concord hath Christ with *Belial*?' He appears in the Miracle Plays (e.g. *N-Town* 23/5), and this insertion may be a response to contemporary readers' 'Who he?' on first encountering B 322. *beelsyre; dame*:

the notion of 'families' among demons further heightening the parodic inversion of the Daughters; perhaps suggested by *filii Belial* at Deut 13:13 where, however, the referent is human (cf. *kyn* at 288). **284** *blente*: see Mercy's words at 140; the devils who dwell in 'darkness and dread' fear as a destructive weapon the light that mankind will welcome (cf. the ironic echo of *blente* 284 in *blende* 292). **285** perhaps refers to movable wooden louver-slats worked from below with a chain. **286** evokes a castle in the latest style: hell's dungeon is an inverted version of the Tower of Truth. *louer*: (< Fr *l'ouvert*), 'a lantern-like structure placed on the roof over the central hearth, with side openings for the escape of smoke' (Wood 1965:277; and see Salzman 1966:219–22). An early C15th louver survives at Lincoln College, Oxford (*RCHM Oxford* pl. 121). *loupe*: cited in MED s.v. n. (2) (a) as 'loophole...for the protection of archers, gunners. etc' (as at *SGGK* 792). But the word's conjunction here with *louer* (MED s.v. *lovere* n. (1)) suggests that this (earliest) example should instead come under (b) 'an opening for ventilation, a louver' (effectively a synonym); for if the devils are to hide *inside* in darkness, it is light coming from above (not through battlement-loopholes) that they would fear. **287–8** The internal and end-rhymes underline the sense of ritualised panic. **287** *Astarot*: originally 'the (moon)-goddess of the Sidonians' (III Kgs 11:33), usually coupled with Baal among the 'strange gods', as in Jg 2:13; a devil-name found in the Miracle Plays (*Towneley* XXV 107). **288** *Coltyng*: an unparalleled devil-name, probably invented as a patronymic (< *colt* + *-yng*) for this expendable 'fiendling'. *kyn*: 'tribe', extending the relational metaphor of 282. **289–94** describe forms of artillery, old and new, deployed against a supposed force of besiegers (Poole I pl. 12b). **289** *Brumstoen*: sometimes used in repelling sieges (*Siege of Jerusalem* 675), and abundant in hell's 'stagno ardenti igne et sulphure' (Apoc 21:8) to provide explosive materials for the cannon (the resemblance of which to hell-mouth needed no spelling out). *boylaunt brennyng*: two juxtaposed participles, the first with the rarer French ending, mimicking the speaker's desperation. **290** An ironic recall of the bold *transsumptio* at 15.143–4. **291** *bowes of brake*: 'cross-bows of the largest size and strongest tension' (*Sk*), worked by a crank or lever (*brake*); see Poole I fig. 41. *brasene gonnes*: an up-to-date touch, perhaps influenced by knowledge of the King's authorising large supplies of ordnance and ammunition for the Tower in 1382–7 (Poole I 161–2, fig. 48). **292** *sheltrom*: the infantry formation, originally with over-lapping shields and often a wooden platform-cover, which Satan (with comic literalism) expects to be used in the assault. His aim is presumably to smash this, fire the fragments and pick off the attackers as they run out and stumble on the iron obstacles. **293** *Mahond*: popularly thought to be a pagan deity (*Towneley* IX 9, 122), but for

L another devil-name (MED s.v. 1 (d)), at 18.151 translating Vg *demonium*. *mangonel*: heavy artillery piece like the *trébuchet* (Poole I fig. 42).

295–349a Since it is no use physically resisting Christ, Lucifer's ultimate 'line of defence' is *legal*: his 'rights' over a mankind justly condemned for sin and sentenced to die and go to hell for ever. According to the main Patristic 'devil's rights' theory of atonement, the Devil had been granted (B 283) possession of mankind after Adam's sin. This could be lawfully removed only if he tried to seize a sinless soul (the 'abuse of power' theory as formulated in Augustine *De Trin*. XIII [*PL* 42:1025–31]) *or* if such a soul were offered in place of the souls of men (the 'ransom' theory). Marx (1995) holds that this theory was modified rather than repudiated in the new 'atonement' theory of Anselm (*Cur Deus Homo*), who argued that since the Devil had deceived man, he had no right of possession over man, only (as argued by Simpson 1990:213), the power of a gaoler allowed him by God in respect of man's enthralment to sin. The aim of the Incarnation was that Christ should win back ('redeem') mankind from the Devil and effect a reconciliation ('atonement') between God and man. The 'compensation' (*amendes* B 18.343) he offers is not to the Devil (who has no true right to it) but to God (the 'satisfaction' theory). Marx 100–13 shows that while L is familiar with the older theory (as found in *EN*), he is basically in accord with the Anselmian understanding. This view has been vigorously disputed by Green (1999:362), who considers the notion of Lucifer's 'title' to mankind as unfounded not a rejection of but 'a weak form' of the pre-Anselmian soteriology. However, as Simpson convincingly maintains (1990:215), Langland does not promote but 'does, nevertheless, shape his narrative around [the 'Devil's rights'] theory, precisely as a way of refuting it, and...insisting on the legal aspect of the Atonement'. **297** echoes (with rich dramatic irony) 19.20, where *Spes* proclaimed how obeying God's law is the perfect protection against death. **298** *perelles*: i.e. the moral trap of being called a tyrant (in over-ruling his own law). **299** *robbeth*: ironically exposing his lack of self-understanding. *maistrie*: i.e. force, like the king's use of 'prerogative' to overrule the ordinary courts' judgement (rather than to supplement the insufficiency of existing precedent for the just settlement of a particular claim). But unbeknown to him, the word accurately predicts Christ's 'mastery' of the very legal argument Lucifer relies on. **300** *riht... resoun*: 'a well grounded right in law'. Lucifer's appeal is to the common-law principle of unevadable precedent (endorsed by Truth and Righteousness), implicitly as against those of equity (in its embryonic beginnings in the court of Chancery), which invoked a wider concept of fairness in judgement (Birnes 1975; Kennedy 2003). **301** A claim contested by Christ at 372 below. *bothe...ille*:

the devil's own excessive claim already (unintentionally) creating space for an 'equitable remedy'. **303–5** repeat Righteousness's words at 196–8; so Lucifer's claim might seem strong (see Simpson 1990:214–16). **304** *here dwelle euere*: Lucifer's 'unwrast' interpretation of the *þretynge* in Gen 2:17, the correct one being God's in 3:19 (which pronounces death, not eternal punishment). **309** *sesed*: a legal term; on the devil's 'seisin', see Alford 1977:944–5. *seuene thousand*: a figure perhaps metrically determined; usually (in relation to the supposed date of the Fall) 4000 (see Gray, *Selection*, no.2) or 4,600 (*York* 'Harrowing' 39–40, *Towneley* XXV 27–8)). **310** *neuere...now*: a misunderstanding of the law (as Christ makes clear at 375), which gives Lucifer no such 'right'. Consequently, the precedent he appeals to (the essence of customary law) and its length (something of weight in medieval courts) are irrelevant (see further Alford 1977²). **B 282** *Soothnesse*: see on 2.200; perhaps not formally a personification so much as a definition. **311** echoes Book's words at 240; despite the irony of the Father of Lies relying on God's veracity, the absolute truth of Scripture was common ground between all medieval disputants.

312–49a Save 312–13, 329–31, 335–7 these lines (divided between Satan, Gobelyn and a 'Devil' who may be Lucifer) are extensively revised in both substance and expression. **312** *That*: the precise antecedent being perhaps their long possession, which is certainly a fact. *doute*: a small revision allowing the fruitful double sense that the reason for Satan's 'fear' is the 'dubiety' of the devils' case. **314** *on his londe*: Lucifer has committed trespass as well as fraud. **316** is more elegantly expressed than B 288, which misleadingly suggests (*hem*) and then denies (*hirselue*) that Satan tempted Adam. **316a** 'Woe to him that is alone: [for, when he falleth, he hath none to lift him up]' (Eccl 4:10); referred to Eve's supposed wilfulness in going off by herself, so that she was alone when the Devil tempted her (cf. Milton, *PL* IX 380ff). **317** *aftur to knowe*: 'that after [eating the fruit] they would know'. **318** paraphrases Gen 3:5, 318b ironically repeating 301b, which states the consequences of their 'knowledge'. **319** *treson and tricherie*: 'falsity and deceit' (as in *SGGK* 4–5), given the known intention of the tempter here (and at 323). But part of his 'promise' was undeniably fulfilled, in that their eyes were opened, though they also died the death (Gen 3:4–7). *troyledest*: a rare verb (< OF *troiller*), elsewhere only in the *Trental of St Gregory* (*c.* 1350) 1, 11: '[Þe fend] *truyled* hire wiþ his tricherye'. **320** *bihéstes*: a very striking 'monolexical' b-half (see *Intro.* IV § 38). **322** Arguably this line should be given to the same speaker in **B**. *gyle*: a word that with its derivatives echoes insistently round the walls of hell through the rest of the passus. **323** *Gobelyn*: already a proper name *c.* 1325 ('Of Rybauds', in Wright, *Political Songs* 1839:238), but adapted from a word of unknown etymology meaning a demon or incu-

bus. Wenzel (in Alford 1988:163) relates him to 'a demon popularly called *goblin*' in *FM* VII.16 who specialised in leading travellers astray; but his rôle here seems too important for 'a puckish sprite'. In B 294 'the Devil' could have been meant to be distinct from Gobelyn, and the change of *Certes* to *Forthy* at C 325 provides the latter a more heroic function as executive officer in the field, while Lucifer (who originally tempted Eve) now lurks in headquarters planning a counter-attack. **324** *trewe title*: valid legal claim, *titulus iuris* (Alf*G*). Alford (1977²:945) notes that Gobelyn's point is that of a canonist, recognising that the devils do not possess man 'in good faith' but through fraud. *maketh*: 'invalidates it'. **325** *Treuthe*: God's first nature-name (see at Pr 15), now derived to the Son *e deitate Patris*. **326** The exquisite irony in God's 'deception' of Lucifer arises from his assuming the likeness of his own likeness (cf. Gen 1:27), whereas Lucifer's was performed under the disguise of another species. Where God's 'sleight' honours man, Lucifer's debases the serpent. **327** *in...weye*: 'in the form of a man' / 'in carrying out his plan of action' (cf. *way* at 298). **328** *gome*: on the *s*-less positional genitive see *MES* 72–3. **329** *thritty*: cf. *HH* 74–5 and see on 136. **331** *askede... answere*: during the Temptations in the desert (Mt 4:3– 10). Gobelyn alludes to the recognition of Christ's divine origin by 'unclean spirits' (Mk 3:11–12) whom he commanded 'not to make him known'. The text suggests that for **L**, God's 'deception' is to make the fiends see Jesus simply as a holy man whose good work must be frustrated (though in **C**, Gobelyn's suspicions (333) make him more active in seeking to prevent Christ's death). **B 299–300** *slepynge*: a notable early 'hanging participle'; the speaker of course went to Pilate's wife ('Claudia Procula') in *her* slumber, not his (**L** perhaps remembering Gobelyn's original nature as an incubus who pressed down upon his sleeping victim). The story, an elaboration of Mt 27:19 that ironically ascribes the Roman governor's and his wife's scruples to (unsuccessful) diabolic intervention, earns a play to itself in the York Miracle cycle (XXX, ll.158–76; see Kolve 1966:228–30). *done*: 'make of' (= kind of), here with uninfl. gen. (*MES* 86). **333b** repeats 19.236b.

341–49a are spoken by Satan (cf. 350), who is distinct from Gobelyn and Lucifer, and improve in clarity on B 306–14. **342** *grete lihte*: the *lucem magnam* of Is 9:2 (qu. Mt 4:16). The association of Christ's soul with the divine *Shekinah* or 'glory' evokes such texts as Ezech 43:2 and esp. Heb 1:3, which describes him as 'splendor gloriae et figura substantiae [Dei]'. **344** *abyde...sihte*: cf. Ps 5:6. **345–7** See on B 1.111–19; the **C** revision at that point omits the 'lies' motif for a digression on 'northern men'. **349a** 'Now shall the prince of this world be cast out' (Jn 12:31); spoken by Christ here in *EN*, and cited in a sermon of Pope Leo read in Lesson 8 at Matins on Good Friday. This may be a free-standing 'speakerless' quotation like 438a below; but it is ironically piquant to have Satan cite an (as yet unwritten) scripture against Lucifer (*princeps huius mundi* is used of the Devil at 10.135 and in a separate unparalleled text at A 10.62). The devils are not to be cast out of hell or even banned from the terrestrial region, but to lose their uncontested dominion over it.

350–69 350–8 The lively digression on liars may have been prompted by reflecting on 'dishonest' utterances of clergy and lawyers that were thought to have encouraged the commons' violent action against royal and ecclesiastical authority in the Rising of 1381. But it reduces the intensity of the scene and loses some splendid alternating Latin / English lines that make **B** read almost like a liturgical drama. **352** *at þe laste*: on Judgement Day. *lyares here*: 'people who tell pernicious falsehoods in this life'. **354** virtually repeats 9.51, again in a context of final judgement. **356a** 'Thou hatest all the workers of iniquity: thou wilt destroy all that speak a lie' (Ps 5:7). **357–8** This disarming interjection lowers the tone by comparison with **B**, but is perhaps aesthetically defensible as a *reculer pour mieux sauter* before the sublime scene to follow. **B 316–19a** *Quis...virtutum*: 'Who is this [King of Glory? The Lord of hosts, he is] the King of Glory' (Ps 23:10); quoted in *EN* 21:3, *LA* 244 where David (its supposed author) answers Hell's question. The great royal processional psalm, usual at Prime on Mondays, was sung at Matins on Holy Saturday (see vss 7–10 entire). **360** *lord*: Lucifer's use of the title (repeated three times before 371) tacitly recognises his coming defeat. **361** translates *virtutum* concisely but omits **B**'s wordplay for the dismaying affirmation anticipated at 342. **362** *Dukes... place*: an ironic courtesy from 'the King's Son'; cf. Alan of Lille's 'O vos *principes tenebrarum*, attollite portas...' (*PL* 210:907), 'duke of dethe' (*GN* 1453). *anoen*: more urgent than *prest* at 272 above. *ʒates*: Alan (ibid.) interprets *portas* as 'potestas diaboli qua detinebat captivos in inferno'. **363** *Kynges...Heuene*: see on 2.2. **364** *breth*: a metonym for 'spoken word' (as at 15.263) but directly implying that Christ blew the gates in; see B 5.495–6 and Z 5.39, which **L** seems to draw out of his 'repertory'. **366** *populus...*: see on 7.133a. **367** *Ecce...*: the Baptist's prophecy at 18.269a now fulfilled. **368** *Lucifer...ablende*: echoing 7.134 so as to bring out the circling recurrence of the liturgical cycle based on the solar year.

370–446 *Christ's vindication of the Redemption* A direct speech of Christ to the Devil is not found in *EN* or *GN* but in the ME *Harrowing*, which is virtually a drama. The indebtedness of **L**'s feudal language to Grosseteste's treatment is emphasised by Waldron (1986:79–80). **370–1** *soule(s)* and *bothe*: to be read with stresses in each line. The repetition is ripe with irony: for it is Christ's possession of a human body and soul through his Incarnation that will enable him to dispossess Satan of his

supposed 'right' over man. *to saue*: the change in sense from B 329 defers the outcome till the end of Christ's speech. **372** *þe bet*: '(the) better for that / than you.' **373** *resoun...mysulue*: 'simple justice and my own edict'. **374** The verbal repetition of B 280 in B 332 is here avoided by rewriting of the latter as C 305. **375** forms the crux of the legal issue: Lucifer (like Daughter Truth at 145–51a) has misconstrued a 'point of law', the nature of the punishment inflicted by God on man. The correct interpretation awaits the perfectly just judge who is also perfectly equitable through 'wyt[yng] what al wo is' because he 'woet of alle ioye' (233). **376** *dedly synne*: as when 'man turneth his herte fro God...that may nat chaunge... to thyng that may chaunge and flitte' (*CT* X 266, after Augustine *De libero arbitrio* 1.16). This is the sin that brought man death; but the familiar theological term is at once questioned by the speaker's claiming that Adam's sin was not self-suggested, a change that adds precision and removes **B**'s near-repetition of 18.90. **378** *my palays Paradys*: as depicted in the C13th *Mappa Mundi* at Hereford Cathedral (Kaske 1968). **B 338** *lusard*: the shape of the serpent in some iconographic depictions, e.g. the Rheims Cathedral Eve (ill. in Russell 1984:258); **L** may envisage a serpent (378) with hands (cf. Prov 30:28 on the lizard). *a lady visage*: an idea popularised by Peter Comestor (*HS*, Genesis 21): '[the devil] chose some sort of serpent having the face of a girl' (see further Bonnell 1917). In the 'Fall of Man' from the *Très Riches Heures du Duc de Berry* (c. 1420) at Chantilly and in the left panel of Bosch's *Haywain* triptych at Madrid (c. 1500) the 'visage' resembles Eve's own, and in both the whole upper body is human (and female). **381–2** *Aʒeyne...leue*: 'in defiance of my love [for them] and without my permission to do so.' *Olde...falle*: cf. Prov 28:18, Ps 9:16. *be*: 'should be', as an inference ('based on a sound principle' B 340) from 385a. *gylours...gyle*: on the 'folk-lore' aspect of Christ's trickery of Satan the trickster see Ashley 1982:133–4. **383–5** derive from Ex 21:26–7. **385a** 'Eye for eye, tooth for tooth' (Ex 21:24, inverting the Vg order); the legal principle of retribution (*lex talionis*). **386–7** 'Thus a living man must lose his life when he has destroyed a life, so that one life shall pay for another': see Ex 21:12. In citing this authority, Christ appeals to the law against the prosecutor; on his rôle more of an 'advocate' than judge, see Birnes 1975 and Baldwin 1981[2]. **B 344–5** make explicit that mankind is *owed* to God by Satan (because he was slain by 'Death'), and they come near to stating that Satan 'caused' Man's Fall, rather than merely making it possible by deceiving him into disobeying God. This doctrinally delicate point is abandoned in revision for the simpler and clearer assertion that Christ's life, which was not forfeit for sin, now 'quits' or makes recompense for Satan's (qualified) 'right' to the *justi* in limbo. **388** *Ergo*: a sign that the speaker must defeat the

Devil in argument, to show (for an alert and serious readership) that divine authority resides not in sheer power but in true justice ('right and reason' 395). The passage may therefore be understood as robustly affirming God's *potentia ordinata* in the face of contemporary questioning: 'Therefore my soul shall pay for man's, and only (that which is) sin will henceforth go to (the abode of) sin'. This utterance leaves open, as Julian of Norwich would later, whether Hell will *finally* possess any occupants other than the devils for whom it was created, or who created it (see further Watson 1997[2]). **389–90** *mysdede...fordede*: presumably a deliberate echo; Christ will make 'amends' for Adam's disobedience, which empowered Death to destroy (in him and his race) the original entitlement to eternal life that the death of Jesus will now restore. *mysdede*: the preterite is more circumspect than the perfect of B 342, which could suggest that Christ will pay for 'every (person's every) sinful act' (rather than 'the entire consequence of one sinful act') and thus undermine the Samaritan's firm teaching in 19.270–6 by implying that wilful sin without repentance could be overlooked. *to amenden*: a 'predicative infinitive expressive of futurity' (*MES* 525), here replacing a finite future (or perhaps volitional) in B 342 (cf. 2.84, 98ff). **391** *quykie and quyte*: 'give life to and make recompense for'; the satisfaction of the claim of divine justice will be accompanied by the gift of heaven. *queynte*: echoing the 'torch' image in 19.168ff; it is assumed that the just from Adam to the Baptist have sought God's mercy, not rejected it 'wickedly and wilfully' (19.269). **392** spells out, in close correspondence to the following Latin, that God's 'guile' (*grace*), is a deception without deceit. **392a** confirms Mercy's citation of the text at 164a; the immediate context of Fortunatus's hymn is relevant to Christ's present claim that his action is just because 'the true order of things demanded that in the work of man's salvation craft should undo the craft exercised by the betrayer in his many shapes.' **393** *aзeyne þe lawe*: Christ's case being (obliquely) addressed as much to Righteousness (representing a possible theological position: see 195–204) as to Lucifer, both of whom took their stand on strict law. **L**'s closeness to Grosseteste (*Château*, 1068–71) is noted by Waldron 1986:70n8. **394** states that Christ has come only for the just (the 'lege' who lived 'subject to his laws', i.e. obeyed his commandments) and is not acting by *force majeure*. A pun on *souereynliche by maistrie* is nonetheless inescapable: Christ *has* exercised 'supreme mastery' in correctly interpreting the divine decree that both he and Lucifer are bound by. **395** *raunsome*: with the root sense of 'release (a prisoner) by payment' here to the fore, since part of Christ's 'gracious guile' is to make the 'payment' of his soul one that Lucifer must accept but cannot keep (for closely similar wit in relation to a ransom, cf. *WPal* 1248–51: 'But gretly y þonk god þat

gart me achape, / & dede þe wante þi wille for þou wrong outest. / but, sire, in þe same seute sett artow nouз, / & I am prest as þi prisoun to paye þe my ransum'). *my lege*: 'my lawful subjects, [not yours]'; the act observes the laws of chivalry, it is not spoliation following conquest. **395a** 'I am not come to destroy the law but to fulfil' (Mt 5:17); from a passage emphasising observance of the law in its entirety. **396** *grace*: Christ's act being in essence not a deception at all; for since Lucifer's claim to absolute lordship of man (= his eternal *damnation*) is ill-founded, God no more needs to trick him out of it by superior guile than to force him out of it by superior power, but offers man eternal life through pure generosity. **B 351–2, 356** are omitted perhaps because repeating B 337; but the balanced irony of 355, 357 is thereby lost. **397, 398** *and alle*: reminding of the 'apples' on the Tree of Charity at 18.112. *a tre*: see on 142–3; the senses of *a* are at once 'a single' and 'one and the same'. **B 361a** '[He hath opened a pit and dug it]: and he is fallen into the hole he made' (Ps 7:16). The reference has an ironic appropriateness, since the 'pit' (= prison) of hell is presented as a literal not a figurative place. **399–400** The implied figure is of the sea or a tidal river; though dropping the text quotation, C 399 here draws on vs 17 of the same psalm: '*Convertetur* dolor eius in caput eius'. **401–2** The 'bitterness' is the cup of death 'brewed' for the second Adam by the Devil, which Lucifer will now have to drink forever. Cf. the 'cup of death' imagery of the English C14th *Meditations*: 'Of deþes cuppe he [Christ] dronk a drauзt / þorw which he haþ oure lyf ylauзt' (881–2) and see the discussion in Ruffing 1991:105–8. **403** *lyf; loue*: not an accidental collocation, since Christ gives those who love him a life that overcomes death (cf. 59), and continues to live in and through those who believe in him. For the equation of love with the essence of the Church as spiritual organism, see on 7.256–7, and on the Latin and vernacular sources and background of the imagery, see Schmidt 1983[2]:181–4. *loue...drynke*: the present image being of (man's) love as something Christ desires (the only drink that will satisfy his divine thirst), but as also implying a reciprocal offer of his love as the *vinum spirituale* 'the hot wine of sweet love' (Rolle, *Incendium* 279; *Mending* 129) that will sustain man's life on earth. **404** *as it semede*: a statement hardly intended to be gnostic but meaning that Christ's death was not the final defeat it appeared to be to his enemies. **405–7** A remarkable addition affirming that Christ died not for the powerful and educated few but for the powerless and ignorant many, identifying himself with the 'pore symple of herte' spoken of by Anima (B 16.8). The a-verse will be echoed by Need at 22.19. **406** *comune coppes...soules*: the image of the *poculum mortis* here undergoing a complete 'sacramental' *transsumptio*, as well illustrated by representations of Ecclesia holding a cup beneath the wound in Christ's side to collect his

Commentary

blood, such as the mid-C14th 'Jesse Cross' in Schiller II pl. 442. *depe helle*: an ironic reminder to Lucifer that his 'deep clergyse' has been defeated by the 'foolishness' of the cross. **408** *for...sake*: the adverbial phrase going with both preceding verbs, as cause and object respectively. **408a** 'I thirst' (Jn 19:28). The context makes clear that Christ's word on the cross is in fulfilment of the scripture of Ps 68:22; but it is also linked with his words to Peter in Gethsemane (Jn 18:11). The common OT symbol of *thirst* as 'desire for God' seen in Ps 41:3 (which Alan interprets as 'desiderium' in *PL* 210:947) is here transposed to Christ in a striking example of *communicatio idiomatum*. The allegorical interpretation of *sitis* as a 'love-thirst' for the souls of men was developed in devotional and mystical works of the 12–13th c., e.g. in the *Vitis Mystica* of Pseudo-Bernard: 'we believe that his thirst was a most burning desire for our salvation' (*PL* 184:662). The thought is itself genuinely Bernardine, as in the *Meditation on the Lord's Passion and Resurrection*: 'Sitio, I thirst. For what? For your faith, your salvation, your joy' (*PL* 184:744). **409–10** The added line contrasts worldly values (as emblematised in luxurious beverages) with celestial, providing a prolonged pararhyming chime through *fulle*, *valle* and *vale* that connects Christ's desire for souls with the decisive outcome of his effort at the end of time. **411** *ventage... Iosophat*: 'Yahweh has judged', the name of the valley near Jerusalem where it was believed that the Last Judgement would take place. The prophet's grapes of wrath in the source-text (Joel 3:12ff; cf. Apoc 16:19) on the coming destruction of the wicked are transformed by Christ into a metaphor for God's merciful love towards mankind (see further Lunz 1972). **412** *riht...resurrecio mortuorum*: 'wine newly pressed [from grapes] fully ripened, the resurrection of the dead'; on the English phrase see Wirtjes 1987. *must*: cf. *Vitis Mystica*: 'Musto quippe illo nobilissimo charitatis Dei' (*PL* 184:738). The chief reference is to the figurative 'wine-harvest' at the end of time, when God's plan will reach fulfilment with the rising of the dead for judgement (a scene vividly depicted in an Apocalypse scene from Bodl. MS Auct. D. 4. 17, f. 13r reproduced in Saxl 1942:pl. 32). On this motif the best comment comes at the end of the same work (ch. 46): 'The Spouse drinks his own *wine* from the vine in his vineyard, the Church;...drinks the *blood of the ripest grapes, the souls of his saints*, pressed and separated from the lees in the wine-press of the cross, in labour and thirst, cold and nakedness, vigils and other spiritual exercises.' The Latin phrase summing up the foundation of Christian belief comes from I Cor 15:12–13 and provides the 11th clause of the Nicene Creed. **413** *kynge...angeles*: alluding to the 'apocalyptic' conception of Christ's Second Coming in glory as an everlasting king (Dan 7:13) and judge (Mk 14:62), with a crown (Apoc 14:14) and with angels (Mk 8:38). **414**

out...soules: i.e. 'the souls of all men who are there'; it is not implied that all men are in hell (some would be in purgatory), but that the fate of many coming to judgement remains to be decided. **415** *fendekyns*: a coinage; not perhaps quite an affectionate diminutive, but perhaps a pitying recognition that even minor demons like Ragamuffin from dysfunctional diabolic families (281–2) might have a remote chance of getting out of the pit. **416** The revision of this half-line (like that in 429) does not automatically imply the doctrine of *apocatastasis* or universal salvation, which had been condemned at the Second Council of Constantinople in AD 543; but equally it does not rule out a final offer of grace to the fallen angels as impossible for an all-powerful God. For without trivialising evil or cheapening the cost of redemption, **L** has re-imagined the redemption in terms of the older 'glory-centred' theology of *Christus victor*. The result is a Lord of Life with 'auntrous' and royal qualities that outweigh the period's dominant late-medieval 'passion-centred' theology of *Christus patiens*, which will re-surface dramatically in the final passus. **417** *kynde*: 'very nature', soon glossed 'nature as man'. **418–20** affirm that Christ *may* pardon all men and *will* pardon all baptised Christians. The basis of this (not self-evidently 'orthodox') statement is the intense conviction pervading *PP* that God, as man's 'father and brother' (7.143), cannot be less loving than a human parent or sibling, any more than he can be less just than a human king. Waldron (1986:73) aptly notes the 'reciprocity' between Christ's words here and those of Piers at 8.217–18. **419** *hole brethren*: 'entire brethren', through divine adoption in baptism, as opposed to 'half-brethren' through their shared human nature (see 436 below): humanity makes men brothers of Christ as man; baptism, brothers of Christ as God. For if only the baptized are strictly God's adopted 'children' by grace (Gal 4:5), the Incarnation has established grounds for considering all Adam's offspring Christ's 'brethren' by *nature* (cf. I Cor 15:21–2). **420a** 'To thee only have I sinned' (Ps 50:6). The 'legal' force of this maxim resides in the very nature of sin as an offence against God, which he may remit if he so wishes (and that he does is implied by *Nolo mortem peccatoris* at 14.134a). **421–5** describe a startling appeal to the 'experience' argument invoked by Mercy at 153. **422** *Ofter than ones*: inasmuch as mankind has already suffered one 'hanging' (*death*), and so should not be punished with a second (*damnation*). Now as then it is a principle of the common-law tradition that a person cannot be punished twice for the same offence. **424** *thief*: a change perhaps meant to recall Robert the Robber (6.315–24) and his 'brother' the Good Thief crucified with Christ, the King who indeed gave him (eternal) life when he 'looked on him' (Lk 23:43). *deth oper iewyse*: 'execution or condemnation to be executed' / 'death or some other punishment' **B** (see *TN* further on the problems of this reading).

425 *Lawe*: here the ancient custom of pardoning a criminal who had survived hanging and had the good luck to have the king pass by; possibly alluding to the pardoning by Edward III of Walter Wynkeburn at Leicester in 1363 (*Sk*). *he...hym*: the respective referents being determinable from 428, though the contextual ambiguity is suggestive. **428** Christ's acceptance of the constraint of human custom (*lawe*) is a measure of how closely the Incarnation identifies him with man. **429** *dede...ille*: an alteration (which can hardly have seemed uncontroversial) appealing less to the notion of God's unlimited power than to the necessary limitedness of all human judgement in ignorance of the sinner's interior state, which is accessible only to God (the best gloss on this is the next two lines). **430–1** recognise that an earthly court cannot pass a perfectly just condemnation, since only an all-knowing judge can consider every mitigating circumstance relevant to equitable judgement of an individual. **430** *Be... abouhte*: 'if it be at all adequately paid for [i.e. by Christ's sacrifice]' (*Pe*) cannot be right, since *enythyng* would be inapplicable to that 'full and perfect sacrifice'. **L** must therefore refer to such people's virtuous acts, which are known to God alone: against the *boldenesse* of their *synne* must be set that of any *beenfetes* (7.263) to their credit. **431** *of*: altering a somewhat opaque original 'through' into 'from out of, on the basis of', which also allows the daring alternative sense 'I have the power to turn my justice into mercy [not arbitrarily, but on taking everything into account]' (cf. 19.196–7 above). *and...trewe*: 'while at the same time preserving the veracity of everything I have said in the Scriptures'. **432** recalls the words of the Pardon (9.286–7). *Holy Writ*: not scripture in the quotation itself, but doubtless evoking texts such as Mt 16:27 or Rom 2:6. *wol*: not implying constraint upon Christ but presuming that his *wordes* and *workes* will accord. *wreke...ille*: cf. 19.270–6. **433** See at 4.140. **434–5** 'And so [though] I wish to take vengeance on wrong-doers, for all my sharp anger [as God], my nature [as man] will exert restraining pressure on my will'. Christ's point is that though man's offence against an infinite God is in a sense 'infinite', he himself as a finite man can only feel a finite anger (*ire* answering to *ira* in the unquoted second part of the text following). *here*: at the place of judgement. **435a** 'O Lord, rebuke me not in thy indignation, [nor chastise me in thy wrath]' (Ps 6:2 and 37:2); another 'speakerless' quotation (the sentiment cannot be Christ's), like the resounding one to follow at 438a. **B 392–3** express a ground of traditional hope (the purgatorial 'work' of suffering that will satisfy justice), replaced in **C** by total reliance on grace. *til...hote*: 'until a command *Spare them* bid it be otherwise'; adapted from the first lesson of the Office for the Dead (Matins, first nocturn), taken from Job 7:16: '*Spare* me, Lord, for my days are nothing' (see Alford 1972). **436** *halue-bretherne*: much more precise than **B**,

and with reference presumably to non-Christians, *monye* delimiting those who (like Trajan) lived just lives according to their conscience (cf. Rom 2:14–16). **437–8** 'For while you might see your kinsman go cold and thirsty, you could not behold him bleed without feeling pity' (see on 418–20 above). The passage plays on the 'unspoken' sense of *blood*: Christ, having bled for mankind, can feel compassion for its suffering (cf. *Pearl* 1135–44). **438a** 'I heard secret words which it is not granted to man to utter' (II Cor 12:4). This enigmatic 'speakerless' quotation (on which see Donaldson 1982) is associated in St Gregory's *Moralia* (*PL* 76:630), commenting on Job 39:29, with I Cor 13:12 (Goldsmith 1981:97). If the voice is meant to be the poet-visionary's, the verb's first-person subject identifying him with St Paul would seem to involve allusion to the apostle's privileged 'visions and revelations of the Lord' (II Cor 12:1). The words' content remains mysterious (so they are called 'secret'); but the context implies that they concern the boundlessness of divine mercy, a persistent theme of the poem (19.294–8 anticipate this passage). For a very acute discussion of theological problems arising out of this text see White 1995. **439–40** *in*; *and*: small but crucial revisions linking God's absolute justice with his judgement upon hell (the angels who fell were tempted by one of their own) and his mercy with his incarnation (man fell tempted by a superior spiritual being). **B 398–400** *al mankynde*: not necessarily implying that all men *will* be saved but (if the contrast of *mankynde* and *vnkynde* is related to B 389–90) then certainly 'a hope hanging therein' that they *may* be. **442a** 'Enter not into judgement with thy servant: [for in thy sight no man living shall be justified]' (Ps 142:2); vs 3 following could be spoken by one in hell. **443–5** The intricate verbal patterning (*lawe...low*; *lede... ledis*; *louye(ede)...leued*, with the threefold *l*-alliteration followed by a sudden plosive outburst on *b*) endows with ritual finality Christ's final words to his adversary. **446** *bonde...chaynes*: an action based on Jude 6 which, with II Pet 2:4 (its source), is one of the few NT references to the fate of the rebel angels; cf. the elaboration in *EN* B. 24.4. **447–51** effect a third *transition*, this time from 'deep derk helle' (B 1.115) to the upper region where 'most shene is þe sonne' (455). This is the proper abode of the Four Daughters of God, who are now fully enlightened as to 'what this wonder means' (129) and inspired to share in the heavenly concert. **447** *Astarot*: chief of the 'fiendkins' (see on 287), whose panic recalls the *smale muys* of Pr 166 and Mede's terrified followers at 2.249. **448–9** echo Col 2:15: 'et expolians principatus, et potestates traduxit confidenter, palam triumphans illos in semetipso'. **450** The angels' song that announced the start of Christ's redemptive work (Lk 2:13–14) now marks its completion. **451** '[The angels quake to see / Man from death's doom made free]: Flesh sins, flesh frees from sin; / God reigns,

God's flesh within'; from vs 4 of 'Aeterne rex altissime' (for a translation insisting on *dei caro* as 'the humanity, body and soul, of God' cf. Hill 2001:217). Though sung on the vigil of the Ascension, forty days later, it fits well in a scene initiating the *triumphus gratiae* (vs 1) that the feast celebrates.

(c) **452–70** resume the *Debate of the Daughters of God* suspended at 270. Only three speak, but Mercy can afford to remain silent after the eloquence of her spokesman Christ. **452** *of ...note*: 'a song in Latin'. *poetes* (*poesie*): applied by **L** (the first writer to use either) solely to learned Latin poetry, in this case verses by Alan of Lille (see Schmidt 1987²:145). **453** *Clarior...amor*: 'Sun after storms often we brighter see, / Love also brighter after enmity'; from Alan's *Liber Parabolorum* (*PL* 210:581–2) and found in this exact form (with *nebula* for correct *nubila*) in the collection *Auctores Octo* (Alf*Q*). The quotation echoes a Biblical verse of some relevance in this context: 'For thou art not delighted in our being lost; because *after a storm* thou makest a calm, and after tears and weeping, thou pourest in joyfulness' (Tob 3:22). **455** *shoures*: with some play on the sense '(storm of) blows, battle' (MED s.v. 5), as in *WPal* 4514: '& many a *scharp schour* for þi sake þoled'. **458** Her appeal is naturally enough to the one who sent her the 'letters' that would explain 'what this marvel signifies'. Love's irresistible power and Peace's unbreakable patience are to be the *maistres* ('teachers' as well as 'governors') of man's life on earth. **462** *Trewes*: the light-hearted pun showing this sombre sister who called Mercy's 'trewe tale' (135) a 'truyfle' (149) joining the revelry and conceding, in another piece of sacred wordplay, that 'soeth by Iesus' (as Righteousness also grants at 466) goes deeper into the mystery of God's *kynde* than rigid adherence to 'truth'. **463** *Cluppe...kusse*: the kiss of peace being the symbol of reconciliation for Christians, exchanged at every Mass. The origins of the 'reverence' the Daughters now show each other is the Cross that Will urges his family to reverence with a kiss at 473–4 (for the phrasing, cf. the reconciliation of William and Alphons in *WPal* 4526). *in couenaunt*: 'as a sign of our agreement'; but with more than a little resonance of the 'new covenant' of which 'Jesus [is] the mediator' (Heb 12:24). **465** recalls Gabriel's words to Mary at Lk 1:37; the Incarnation has 'made possible' man's release from hell. **466** *reuerentlich*: cf. her greeting to Peace at 175; she now understands the meaning of her younger sister's 'rich clothing' of divine patience. **467** *per secula..*: 'for ever and ever', 'world without end', the standard concluding formula of longer prayers in the Mass, but with an echo of Heb 13:20–21. **467a** 'Mercy and truth have met each other: justice and peace have kissed' (Ps 84:11). The deferral until now of this crucial verse, from which the whole allegory of the Daughters arises (Traver 1925:44–92; Owst 1961:90–2), imparts a clinching authority to the argument. **468** On **L**'s presentation of the Easter triumph see Vaughan 1980:87–153 and Harbert in Phillips 1990:57–70. *Te Deum laudamus*: 'We praise you, God'; the great hymn of rejoicing, in rhythmic prose, sung at the end of Matins on Easter Sunday morning and on greater festivals. **469** *Loue*: the mysterious and much-anticipated figure whose brief entrance provides music that tunes the dancing and harmonises the four aspects of the divine Providence; the earthly presence of the risen Lord who has now returned to heaven. The image recalls depictions of angels singing and playing musical instruments, as in the *Très Riches Heures* (Schiller I pl. 292). **469a** 'Behold how good and pleasant it is [for brethren to dwell together in unity]' (Ps 132:1). The statement foreshadows **L**'s presentation of the community of believers under the 'nature-name' of UNITY in Passus XXI; cf. the discussion of this text in Brinton's *Sermons* 2:58, 114 (Alf*Q*). **470** *caroled*: 'danced in a ring'. The secular dance aptly (if boldly, given its associations) expresses the communal joy at Easter, while symbolising in its circular shape the cosmic harmony of 'sacred mirth' at the fulfilment of the divine plan for humanity.

EPILOGUE **471–8** The exultant coda of Passus XX is linked to the dream by the sounds of music, which express how 'terrenis coelestia, humanis divina junguntur' (*Exultet* canticle of Easter Saturday), passing from the heavenly 'symphony' of the Daughters into the familiar earthly summons to awake and worship. **471** *rang*: the bells rung on Easter morning in the parish churches of London linking the music that accompanies the mystic circle of the vision (a figure of eternity) with the linear human life that continues from year to year and will terminate in individual death and the final end of historical time. (On the Easter bells, the first to be rung since the start of Lent, see St- Jacques 1977¹). Being woken by a sound within the dream is a feature found earlier at 18.179, but a sound from the waking world outside is paralleled in Chaucer's *Parliament of Fowls* 695. **472** *Kitte*; *Calote*: as much (and perhaps as little) fictions as Will himself, though some wryly humorous lines are devoted to the former at 22.193–8 that might have carried a special resonance for the original audience. The possible pejorative associations of these two names are explored in Mustanoja 1970:51–76. **473; 476** *Godes resureccioun / blessed body*: the unusual phrases robustly conveying **L**'s understanding of the 'theology of glory', the act on which Christian faith is based having for him only one author (cf. Rom 4:24, 6:4, Col 2:12 I Thess 1:10, I Pet 1:21). **474** *crepe...*: the penitential ceremony of 'creeping to the cross' (Duffy 1992:29), that took place on Good Friday (and survives as the rite of the Veneration of the Cross); also sometimes performed on Easter Sunday (Harbert 1990:68). Will's summons to this devotional act aptly expresses how the continuance of Christ's victory over death requires his followers to share in the suffering that made it possible. *iewel*: because a symbol of Christ himself, 'our joy and jewel' (B 11.184). Harbert's insistence that 'it is a cross that he goes to kiss, not a crucifix' (ibid.) separates the suffering from the glory, something which for **L** can only occur at the end of time (cf. the imagery of *Pange Lingua* vs. 1: *gloriosi / Lauream certaminis* 'the laurel wreath of a glorious strife' and the theology of Gal 6:14). **475** This added line stresses the unique value, among all the relics revered by Christians, of the True Cross that had been stained with the blood of the incarnate God. Most churches possessed a supposed fragment of it, to be venerated annually at Eastertide and at the feast of the Invention of the Cross (May 3). **477** The significance of the Cross as the potent symbol of Christ's conquest of evil had been a familiar part of Christian tradition since the Dream of Constantine, in which he was said to have seen a great cross in the sky with the words *in hoc signo vinces* 'you will conquer by this emblem'. **478** *grisly goest*: a phrase also found in a somewhat less solemn context in *WPal* 1730. After celebrating the victory of Christ as 'Lord of Light', this magnificent passus ends with a climactic paradox: if the shadow of Christ's cross frightens the fearsome occupants of 'deep dark hell', its substance must be of incomparable power indeed.

Passus XXI (B XIX)

XXI and XXII contain only light revision and either awaited further changes or were regarded as finished. Though the contrast with the energy of revision in XX suggests a sudden cutting short, little here would seem to need alteration, and these passūs bring the **C** Version, like its predecessor, to a satisfactory (if troubled) close. XXI is structurally less complex and emotionally less elevated than XX, more didactic and expository (the calm before the storm), but lucidly planned and executed. It falls into three main sections, the echo of the first line by the last bringing the passus full circle. (i) 1–199 form the encounter with Conscience (a key figure in the last two passūs), introduced and ended by a repeated formulaic half-line at 12a (the entry of Jesus) and 208a (the coming of Grace). Its Prelude is a four-line waking scene of Will's visit to Church on Easter morning (as anticipated from the end of XX) and the singular yet strangely familiar vision of Piers-Christ (5–8). The vision opens (9–25) as a *dialogus* in the poem's customary mode that quickly becomes an authoritative discourse by Conscience like those of Anima and Will's other interlocutors, most recently the Samaritan in XIX. Conscience offers an 'inner narrative' that substantially re-tells the life of Christ, dealing from lines 149–99 with the events after his Crucifixion, leading to his Ascension, the last

event narrated in any gospel (Mk 16, Lk 24), its distinctive standpoint being an understanding of Christ as successively knight, king and conqueror or emperor. This section parallels the liturgical sequence from Christmas to Easter, the Age of the Son. (ii) 200–336 continue the outer narrative with the descent of the Holy Ghost, propelling a recapitulation of the Gospel account onwards to events told in the Book of Acts. Conscience introduces the Third Person of the Trinity (the Paraclete) under the poem's final divine 'nature-name' of Grace and invites the Dreamer to kneel and be caught up in the scriptural-devotional action, thus blurring the border between 'inner' and 'outer' narratives. This Pentecost sequence is the Age of the Spirit active in Christian history, which points forward eschatologically to the end of history. Section ii's account of the founding of the Church emphasises Grace's granting of two gifts: to Piers (a figure now strongly suggestive of the Apostle Peter and his successors) the power of pardon (i.e. spiritual dominion), and to the rest of society the earthly and spiritual gifts needed to do well. The allegory of the spiritual 'sowing' and the building of the Barn of Unity represents the Church's outward expansion through time, sustained by Scripture (the Four Gospels) and Sacred Tradition (the Four Doctors), authorities **L** has coupled throughout as *holiwrit*, and both incorporated in the annual cycle of readings used in liturgical worship. (iii) 337–484 describe the preparation of Unity under Conscience's leadership to withstand the siege of Pride (337–93), with the resistances and challenges to ideal Christian oneness of heart offered by different orders of society, from Commons to King (394–484). This section, which brings events firmly into the authorial present, answers to the liturgical time after Pentecost (from Trinity Sunday to Advent) and then the season of Lent once again. It also recapitulates in reverse the action of Vision 1 and (to some extent) of Vision 2, in particular Passūs VI–VIII and III–IV.

(i) 1–199. PRELUDE **1–8 1** *Thus Y wakede*: an opening that recalls the major section-division at 10.1 (Vision 3) and, like that of XXII, hints that the work's main argument is drawing to a conclusion. *wrot*: a verb the repetition of which at the end of the passus will indicate the character of the whole experience as something recorded for posterity and now being completed. **2** *derely*: in honour of the chief feast of the Church's year, so perhaps 'in my best clothes'. **3** *holly*: as urged at 9.231. *hoseled*: reception of the sacrament at Easter was compulsory for all. If it may be assumed that Will has made his confession, it is not necessarily implied that he misses communion by falling asleep, as contended by Weldon: 'Non-participation in the Eucharist symbolises the dreamer's spiritual deficiencies, which are compensated for and mitigated by the dream which follows...the body of Christ-Piers, the "host' he had evaded by falling asleep during the mass' (1987:275). For a dream need occupy little real time, and there is no sign in the text (nor is it plausible) that Will seeks to 'evade' communion, any more than that he immediately seizes up his writing-materials on waking (484). The dream is rather a profoundly 'eucharistic' vision, entirely appropriate at a point before the formal reception of communion. **4** *in myddes of*: 'at the mid-point of', when the assistants brought the bread and wine up to the priest for the Offertory. A point between the reading of the Word and the Canon is thematically fitting for a vision of Christ, though in pictorial tradition this more usually occurs during the Consecration when, according to the legend of the 'Mass of St Gregory', Christ as Man of Sorrows was seen poised above the Pope (Schiller II pls. 805–7). **L**'s version recalls the less familiar image of Gregory kneeling before the Man of Sorrows, which in a striking Swiss wall-painting of *c.* 1400 follows an unambiguous image of Christ as Artisan (Schiller II 226 and pl. 691). Most relevant here, given the liturgical setting, is the variant called the 'Eucharistic Man of Sorrows' (Schiller II pl. 760). **6** *Peres*: the sudden presentation of the Plowman with the marks of the passion and exactly resembling ('riht lik') Jesus resumes and makes explicit the earlier partial resemblance ('semblable somdeel') at 20.8, despite Will's uncertainty at 10–11. *peynted*: suggesting the devotional sculptures of the time painted in bright colours. **7** *cam...cros*: recalling B 5.12, where Reason preaches divine wrath and the need for repentance; but what is seen proclaims the triumph of mercy witnessed in XX. The best-known examples of Christ carrying his cross *after* the Passion, like Bellini's and Giovanni di Paolo's (Schiller II pls. 710, 713), are C15th; but the image probably existed earlier (ibid. 688).

9–14 9 *Conscience to kenne me*: the traditional function of this power, as **B**'s echo of line 7.134 (removed in // **C**) suggests. The discreet visual allusion to the iconographic motif of *Christus in torculari* [*crucis*] 'Christ in the Winepress [of the Cross]' derives from patristic commentary on Is 63:1–6, a key text that opens with the same question *Quis est iste* asked by Lucifer at B 18.316. Elaborated in works of passion-mysticism like *Vitis Mystica* (*PL* 184:739: see on 20.412 above and cf. Schmidt 1983²:181–2), it metamorphosed from an emblem of divine vengeance into one of divine mercy, the blood now being that of Christ and not of his enemies. Doctrinally this image (like that of the bleeding Lamb in *Pearl* 1135–40) serves to intimate his *compassio* or co-suffering with the members of the Mystical Body of which he is the head. Superimposing the 'chivalric' element drawn from another devotional tradition therefore restores some of the martial quality of Isaiah's *propugnator*, with an effect of startling paradox. The 'winepress'

image became a popular motif in art (Schiller II 228–9, pls. 808, 810–12); but the knight / ploughman aspects seem to be of **L**'s creating. **10ff** Will's questions to Conscience recall the interchange with Faith at 20.17–34. **11** *paynted*: the repetition from 6 pointing up the fictive character of this vision, which evokes images like those in wall-paintings of the time (on the significance of these for **L** see Benson 2004:157–201). **12** *armes*: echoing 20.21. The 'Arma Christi' (instruments of the Passion) formed a familiar iconographic motif (Schiller II pls. 654–7); but *armes* here metaphorically denotes the 'insignia' that enable Christ to be recognised by a 'herald' with the eyes of Faith. **13** *colours*: Christ's 'armorial' *gules on argent* may allude obliquely to the crusader knight's red cross on white (and cf. the short lyric in Gray 1975, no. 20). *cote armure*: recalling Will's question at 18.187. **14b** proclaims Christ both his people's champion and the benign 'conqueror' of their hearts, like the kingly wooer in *Ancrene Wisse*. 'Conquest' forms part of the theological theme of 'Christus triumphans', in which the Cross symbolises his victory over sin and death.

15–68 15 *Crist*: the Gk for Hebrew *Messiah* 'the Anointed One', by which title the Son's rôle in salvation history is specified as 'both the divinity that anoints and the humanity that is anointed' (*ST* III 16.5). Denied to Jesus by the Jews who rejected him, and by their descendants (cf. 17.307–14, 20.55), it is the *nomen credentium* insistently used by St Paul, though (with a few exceptions such as Mt 1:16, Jn 1:17) not by the Evangelists, who speak only of 'Jesus'. On these two names see Bernard's *Sermo I in vig. nat. Dom.* (*PL* 183:88). **16–18** allude to Phil 2:10 quoted at 80*a* below. On the significant 'pattern of kneeling' in this passus see Weldon 1989. *prophecied*: referring to the expectation in the Psalms and Isaiah (46:24) of God's salvation through a Messiah; no actual OT prophecy concerns the personal name *Jesus* ('Yahweh saves'). **18** *þe...Iesu*: 'the divine name, Jesus' (which replaces God's OT name Yahweh), 'the name of Jesus, God'. **19** *Ergo*: because the man who bore it has now been revealed as divine. **21** *deueles*: alluding to its use by the disciples in driving out evil spirits (Mk 9:37–8) and in the Church's rite of exorcism. *hit*: the name Jesus (not the title Christ), the object of a devotion popularised by Richard Rolle in his *Emendatio Vitae* (see Schmidt 1986:31–2). The feast in honour of the Holy Name (Aug. 7) began to be celebrated by the mid-14th c. and a special Mass was in existence by the 1380s (Pfaff 1970:66). **22** *saued*: see I Cor 6:11. **23** Will's insistence recalls his attitude to Liberum Arbitrium / Anima's many names; but here his curiosity receives no rebuke as at 16.205. **25** *Iesu*: the vocative case; used as a simple alternative form of the name at 44. *ioye*: brought simply by uttering the name, according to Rolle in his *Form of Living* (ed. Ogilvie-Thomson 18/610–20). **26–30** all scan on *k*, underscoring the 'catechetical' tone of the lines. **26** *kunne resoun*: an allusion back to Will's encounter with Conscience and Reason in 5.1–104. **27–30** The three grades inevitably suggest the Triad, here to be understood perhaps in relation to Christ's ministry, passion, and resurrection / ascension to glory. **32** *lordes of laddes*: the uniqueness of the conqueror (as evinced in the history of England) being the power to transform the social order by dint of his total control. The notion of divine grace 'freeing and ennobling' the slaves of sin has Scriptural origins (Rom 8:21, I Pet 2:9) and is echoed in the doctrine of 'theological nobility' [that of God's elect] taught by the C14th legist Bartolus of Sassoferrato (Keen 1984:149). **34–41** elaborate in more measured terms the denunciation of the Jews by Faith at 20.95–112*a*. They express the common medieval view that Christian baptism confers both spiritual and legal 'freedom' and that the Jews' legal and social disabilities (Cohn 1972:79–80; Gilchrist 1969:111) were the result of rejecting Jesus as the Messiah (as they were certainly the usual consequence of the Jews' unwillingness to give up their religion). **36–7** *worlde*: the referent being essentially 'Europe' or Christendom, since the Jews were spared these disabilities in Muslim lands. **38** *þe Baptist*: see Lk 7:29–30; implying that since many Jews followed John, who acknowledged Jesus as Messiah (Jn 1:26–37), it did not contravene their Jewish faith to do likewise. **39–40** could mean simply that Jews who received baptism in Christ's name were freed from sin; but the mention of Christ's being baptised (by John) seems pointless unless the referent of *follyng* 39 is the baptism performed by John. This would imply **L**'s awareness that John's disciples who became followers of Jesus were not baptised (a second time) in his name. *frankeleynes*: a term answering to *generosus* in the TCD ms 212 note on Stacy de Rokayle (see *Intro.* V §4). **41** *ycrouned...Iewes*: alluding to the crown of thorns and Pilate's mocking inscription above the cross, which were transformed into symbols of lordship after the resurrection (in the NT the divine title 'king [of kings]' is applied to Jesus only in Apoc 17:14). **42–3** 'It is fitting for...a conqueror to maintain [and protect] his bounty and his dominion with the revenues from his act of conquest / conquered territory' (MED s.v. *conqueste* n. 1(a), 2); the conqueror's chief duties are largesse and protection. Of the two verbs in 42b, *kepe* strictly governs the first and *defende* the second noun in 43 (a line that scans as a Type IIb with a monolexical stave-word *cónquéste* in position 2 and 3). **44–5** 'He brought them the means of justification by teaching them the law of eternal life [faith in himself as redeemer]' (cf. Jn 17:3); this is Christ's 'large'. **46–7** *fended hem*: Christ's protection against his people's foes, seen as deliverance from disease, sin and error (see Jn 4:52, Mt 9:20–2, Mk 5:1–14, 10:1–12). **48** *gentel prophete*: cf. 'propheta magnus' (Lk 7:16). **50** *con-*

querede he on cros: a general theological formulation, but also evoking the emblematic 'knightly' submission of the representative 'believing Jew' Longeus at 20.93 above. **51** echoes 20.28. **52** *regnede*: Christ's sovereignty being exemplified, even before the Ascension, in his conquest of hell. **53** *quyke...dede*: echoing the 6th clause of the Apostles' Creed. **55** *cherles*: a 'social' term substituted for the usual 'prisoners' in keeping with the metaphor of sin as slavery and liberation as ennoblement. **57** *bonde him*: an idea deriving from Apoc 20:1–3 (and cf. *EN* B 24). **58** *herte blood*: recalling 20.87–8; the blood from Christ's heart ('side' Jn 19:34) was traditionally interpreted as symbolising the sacrament of baptism by which 'all folk are made free' (cf. 12.110–11). **62** *Crist to mene*: not necessarily implying belief that the name signifies 'conqueror' (*Sk*) so much as the 'superlative degree' of the 'knight, king, conqueror' triad and is hence uniquely fitted to the 'Lord's Anointed' who was son of God as well as of David (Ac 2:36, I Cor 1:24). **63–8** recapitulate the teaching of Rechelesnesse at 12.205–11, of his *partyng-felawe* Patience on *Passio Domini* at B 14.189–93, and of Anima at B 15.270–1.

69–95 69 *cam...name*: for this type of internal rhyme within the b-half cf. 19.265. **70** *Faythly*: found in this sense (MED s.v. *feithli* adv. (c)) only here and at *WPal* 209 (*f. for to telle*). **71–95** re-tell the Infancy story to prove that Jesus was 'knight and king's son', stressing the recognition of his noble origin by the traditional representatives of the Gentile world. **72** The Magi ('Kings') in C14th nativity paintings are sometimes shown led by an angel, as by Giovanni Pisano (Schiller I, pl. 287), while in Giotto's 'Adoration' (ibid. pl. 288) an angel holds the gold vessel and the first king kneels. **74** An elaboration of the Lucan account common in late medieval pictorial representations (e.g. Schiller I, pls. 202, 206). **74*a*** 'Glory to God in the highest' (Lk 2:14); the text that opens the *Gloria* at Mass. **75–9** are based on Mt 2:11–12. **75** *Kynges*: after *LA* 89, which assigns the *sapientes et reges* their traditional names of Caspar, Balthasar and Melchior. The royal status of those who bring Christ gifts for which they ask neither thanks nor return (thus in effect 'tribute') adumbrates his appointed rôle as 'conqueror'. **79** *kyngene*: on the subjective genitive from the OE weak ending see *MES* 73. *by... angelis*: an inference from Mt 2:12 in the light of verse 13. **80** *word...speke*: at 16–20 above. **80*a*** '[God hath given him a name...above all names: That] in the name of JESUS every [knee] should bow, of those that are in heaven, on earth, [and under the earth]' (Phil 2:9–10). The 'earthly knees' here include those of the kings of the earth. **81** See at 74 above. The 'heavenly ones' recognise Christ's divinity at his birth, the 'infernal ones' do not, their submission coming only after his entry into hell (20.449–50). **82** *wit... world*: not *sapiencia mundi* but 'every kind of knowledge under the sun'. **83** The Magi are imagined almost in folk-tale terms as fairy godfathers bringing the royal child 'gifts of character' that he will need to fulfil his calling. These symbolised qualities recall the Four Daughters and anticipate the seed-symbolism of the cardinal virtues, e.g. 'Reason' suggests both Truth (cf. 90) and Prudence; but they are especially appropriate to a king-conqueror (cf. Pr 153–7). L's allegorisation alters the Biblical order of the gifts and differs from that of *LA* 93, which not unexpectedly sees *gold* as a 'tributum' of love to Christ's 'regia potestas', *incense* as a 'sacrificium' of worship to his 'divina majestas' and *myrrh* as a burial-offering 'ad sepultura mortuorum' acknowledging his 'humana mortalitas'. **85** *Magi*: pleasingly if incorrectly etymologised as 'quasi in sapientia magni' in *LA* 88, which also recognises its parallel senses of 'magician' and 'sorcerer'. The common view was that the Magi were Mesopotamian or Persian *secretorum inspectores* 'students of the occult' or astrologers (*LA* 89). Their esoteric learning enabled them to understand the significance of 'his star in the east' as the *signum* (cf. Gen 1:14) of a divine king's birth, and thence to offer him precious gifts of mystic signification. **86** *Resoun*: not *intellectus humanus* but *divina ratio* (the quality personified in the authoritative figure of 13.194ff), in apt recognition of Jesus as the *Logos* incarnate of Jn 1:14. *sense*: a 'Platonic' pun may be hinted by the aphetic form, since what a 'sensory' mode conceals (the mystical meaning of the gift) is revealed to the light of spiritual understanding. **88** Medieval jurisprudence stressed the close bond between equity and justice, reflecting 'the basic premise of natural law theory — that the rules governing human conduct should be in conformity with the natural order. Reason is the name given both to that order and to the faculty that apprehends it' (AlfG 134). *reed gold*: see on B 2.16. **89** 'It is to gold that justice is compared, because both are imperishable'. Gold was regarded as the perfect metal and a fit emblem of immortality because (unlike iron or copper, say) its appearance and chemical properties survive contact with the four elements. *Lewetee*: 'Justice'; see AlfG s.v. II and on Pr 149. **90** *richeles*: the emendation (see *TN*) removing the apparent 'contradiction' (*Sk*) in 90. *to...treuthe*: the more natural reading is to take both terms as synonyms for Reason; but Lewetee and Resoun are probably parallel subjects, *riht* glossing the first, *treuthe* the second. **92** *Pyte*: a word having the range of *pietas* (see on Pr 157); a near-synonym of *reuthe* 83 and *mercy* 93, which are mutually distinguishable as respectively affective and rational in the period (Burnley 1979, Index s.vv.). **93** *mirre is mercy*: a 'Platonic' pun, the connection being the use of myrrh to anoint the dead, an act of compassionate piety (cf. Jn 19:39). *mylde speche*: especially in passing judgement; the opposite of harshness or severity. **94** *Ertheliche honeste thynges*: 'natural objects of honourable use'; the key-phrase encapsulating L's 'sacramental' vision of the world. *was*: sg. because

the gifts are one gift offered 'at ones'. **95** *thre kyne*: i.e. from three different countries.

96–107 summarise the ministry of Jesus, which is then expounded in terms of the Triad as acts of power (108–23), compassion (124–82a) and pardon (183–199). **96** *for all*: i.e. because, though they were gifts for a king, Jesus had yet to earn that title by his own acts. The lesson is that though Baptism makes all Christians members of a 'royal priesthood', they cannot enter into their inheritance without actively 'doing well', as their Lord had to. **97** *comsed...man*: the implied reference being to his qualifying as a skilful knight, a stage towards winning his kingly title. **100** *wyles and wit*: alluding to Christ's mastery in argument (see e.g. Mt 22:35–46). **101** *whoso... hit*: 'if one might make bold to say'; a filler-phrase (cf. 3.235). **102** *soffrede*: in the desert (Mt 4:2). *hudde hym*: see Jn 8:59. **103** *fauht*: perhaps alluding to his driving the money-changers from the Temple with a whip. *fley*: to escape from his enemies (Jn 10:39). **104** *gaf goed*: perhaps referring (as Christ did not give alms) to the 'good wine' of the Wedding at Cana (Jn 2:1–10); see 108. *hele*: on Christ's miracles of healing cf. 18.140–45. **105** *Lyf and lyme*: see Mk 5:22ff; Mt 12:10–13. *as...wrouhte*: cf. 20.449. **107** *alle hem*: alluding to the Harrowing of Hell but echoing the eschatological 20.414.

108–23 describe and in the expository manner of catechesis (cf. 116 repeating 110) symbolically interpret Christ's turning of water into wine. **108** *iuuentee*: a fancy of L's in keeping with his 'Christus victor' triad (27–30). The scriptural source describes Jesus with disciples and implies his full maturity (Jn 2:2); but L makes Cana a 'wonder' of the Lord's *enfances*, performed 'before' (and impliedly 'for') his Mother. Unless meaning simply 'a Jewish celebration' (cf. 115), the phrase *Iewene feste* would seem to make 'this beginning of miracles' (Jn 2:11) a *public* 'sign' at the start of Jesus's mission, asserting his claim to be the Messiah (the Gospel account makes clear that it was quite the opposite). **110** *of his grace*: 'out of gracious kindness'; for Jesus's apparent reluctance, cf. Jn 2:4. **111–14** The general sense of the allegorisation (perhaps of L's devising) is clear, but the expression *wyn is likned...a* little awkward, since properly water should correspond to 'lawe' and wine to 'lyf-holinesse' (of which the sublime test is love of one's enemies). **112** The Old Law forbade wrong against all and allowed (though without encouraging) retribution against enemies, but it did not urge *love* for them. This, the distinctive ethical teaching of the New Law, was defined by Wit as 'do-better' at 10.189–90, but tacitly correlated with 'do-best' by Piers at 15.144. Christ's comment at Mt 5:43 assumes a common contemporary understanding of Lev 19:18 which that text need not itself assume. **113** *consayleth*; *commaundeth*: normally contrasted as precepts for the *perfecti* and the *incipientes* respectively;

but Christ's injunction at Mt 5:44 is a universal command like those that preceded it. **117** aims (rather inelegantly) to state that he was called not only Jesus but 'Christ', i.e. in recognition of his Messiahship revealed in the miracle. **118** *fauntekyn*: inappropriate, given Christ's actual age, unless the term is to be taken as referring to his lack of public position and his still being known (Mk 6:3) as *filius Marie* 'Mary's son' (it is she who asks him to perform the act). **120** *bileue*: not questioning that she did (Jn 2:5 presumes Mary's complete faith in Jesus), but openly confirming what she believed in her heart. **121** *Grace*: the first use of this new 'nature-name' for the 'high Holy Ghost' (14.84) working in and through Jesus. *of no gome*: 'not by any man'. **122** *no wyt*: not from the learning Jesus had to acquire in a normal way (such as knowledge of Scripture), but from his nature hidden 'in deitate Patris'. *thorw word one*: recalling the Creator's *dixit* (15.263a), so as to indicate Christ's divinity. **123** *Dowel*: treated as a noun here ('embarked upon [the knightly life of] Dowel'). **124–82a** Christ's ministry, Passion and resurrection are all treated under Dobet (kingship), accommodated with the new parallel triad enunciated at 27. This makes good sense, since the sending of the Holy Ghost obviously = the Conqueror's distribution of his 'large'. But it remains an imperfect correspondence, given that the *act of conquest* (the defeat of Satan's kingdom) takes place *before* the resurrection / ascension. So it is best to see the stages as continuous, rather than disjunct. **124–62 124** scans either as Type IIa on |w| or as Type IIIb on vowels. *wexen...absence*: figuratively speaking (see on 118), referring to his departure from Nazareth. The account is re-shaped to accord with L's imagining of Jesus as a Percival-like figure leaving his mother's household to perform the acts of war against Satan's dominion on earth that will win the kingdom rightfully his as the son of God. **125** *lame ...blynde*: see Mt 11:5. *liht*: not a mere alliterative necessity, but stressing how those miraculously healed could now fully 'see' who Jesus was. **126–7** Cf. B 15.590, and see Mt 14:17–20=Mk 6:38–44, Lk 9:13–17. **129** scans either as Type IIIb (with natural stress-pattern) or (stressing *was*) as Type Ie with an enriched final lift. *Dobet...wente*: suggested by *Bene omnia fecit* 'He hath done all things well' (Mk 7:37). **130** See Mk 7:32–5. *doynges*: deliberately stressing Christ's *acts* of kingly 'maistrie' (cf. *word one* at 122). The NT sees illnesses as signs of Satan's sway over man, and to overcome them as requiring *greater* power than that exercised over the non-human world in the wine-miracle. **132–3** See Mk 9:26–31; the people recognise in Jesus the promised Messianic king by observing his actions. **133** *Fili...*: 'Have mercy on us, O [Jesus] Son of David' (Mt 9:27, 15:22; cf. 21:9). This cry of the blind men / the Canaanite woman is associated here with the acclamation of the crowds at Christ's entry into Jerusalem on

Palm Sunday, and both of them with that of the women after David's defeat of Goliath a thousand years before Christ (see next). Jesus is called 'son of David' as a title of honour (because he is the Messiah) and also because his legal father Joseph was of the house and lineage of David (Mt 1:6, 16). **135** *Saul...*: '[And the women sung as they played. And they said]: Saul slew his thousands, and David his ten thousands' (I Kgs 18:7). **136** The people's recognition of Jesus parallels that of the women who acknowledged his 'ancestor' David. **137** *nempned... Nazareth*: 'called him [Jesus of] Nazareth, King of the Jews' (see Mt 21:9–11=Lk 19:38, Jn 12:13); the *titulus* placed above the cross in Jn 19:19 (the Synoptics omit the name). **137–9** *no man...Iesus*: after the Feeding of the Five Thousand (Jn 6:15). **138** *cayser*: here in part for alliterative convenience, but doubtless appropriate as anticipating Christ's universal spiritual *imperium*. **138** *Iuda*: the ancient kingdom of David, in Roman times part of the province of Judea, with an imperial governor but no native king. **139** *iustice*: an office occupied in reality by the Roman governor (cf. 20.37). **140** *Cayphas*: the Jewish high priest, chief mover in the plot to put Jesus to death (Mt 26:3–4). *enuye*: implied as a motive for their hostility in Jn 11:47–50. **142–3** The crucifixion (Pilate's act) is here ascribed to the moral agency of Christ's enemies among the Jews, as is his burial (which in Jn 19:38–42 is ascribed to the Council-members Joseph of Arimathea and Nicodemus, who were secretly his disciples). **144** *knyhtes*: the guard placed at Christ's tomb by the Jewish religious leaders (Mt 28:62–6). **145** *profetes*: alluding to Ps 15.10, understood at Ac 2:27 and 13.35–7 as applying to Christ. **147–8** *goen...deuyned*: not part of the psalm-prophecy but spoken by Christ at Mt 26:32. **148** *Marie*: a separate appearance of Jesus to his mother not being recorded in the Gospels, this addition is presumably on the basis of *LA* 241–2, which affirms the 'common belief' and cites St Ambrose in support. **149–56** are based on Mt 28:11–15. **150–1** The phrasing (confirmed by the end-rhyme) clearly recalls the account of the nativity scene at 74. *day spronge*: an echo of Christ's incarnation-title of 'dayspring' that hints at his resurrection as a birth to a new life (see Mt 28:1). **152** 'Christ, rising again [from the dead, dieth now no more. Death shall no more have dominion over him]' (Rom 6:9); sung as a Vespers antiphon during Eastertide. **154** *preyed...pees*: 'begged them to keep silent'. **155–161** The fourfold repetition of *cam* and the annominative com*pany* seems deliberate. **156** *bywiched*: recalling the accusation at 20.71–2 as colour for the fabrication put abroad. **157** *Marie Maudeleyne*: the first to see Jesus after his resurrection (Mk 16:9, Jn 20:14). **158** *Galilee*: see Mt 28:10; the account also contains echoes of the Easter Sequence ('Sepulcrum Christi viventis...Scimus Christum surrexisse'). *in...manhede*: complementing *Verray man* at 153; the risen Jesus is now manifestly the divine Son. **159** *lyues and lokynge*: 'alive and in full possession of his faculties'. *aloude cride*: see Jn 20:18. **160** 'Christ has risen', the Easter Sunday greeting. **161a** 'Thus it behove[s] Christ to suffer and [so] to enter [into his glory]'; a conflation of 'Nonne *oportuit haec pati Christum, et ita intrare* in gloriam suam' (Lk 24:26) with '*sic oportebat Christum pati* et resurgere a mortuis' (Lk 24:46), the latter verbally concording with *resurgens* 160 (AlfQ after *Pe*). **162** ironically inserts 'clerkly' anti-feminism (cf. B 5.166) in a solemn context, while echoing the Jewish reluctance to credit women's testimony in Mk 16:11 and Lk 24:11. The line is seen by Richardson 2000:180 (citing [p. 164] 'cum mos sit mulierum / Cuncta revelare' from the C12th Latin *Lamentations of Matheolus*1596–7) as 'a mocking application of proverbial misogyny'.

163–99 163–82a are based on the account in Jn 20:19–29. **163–5** The Gospels record only Peter (Lk 24:12) or Peter and John (Jn 20:2–10), not all the Twelve, going to the tomb to investigate. **165** *Taddee*: the apostle (Mt 10:3, Mk 3:18) commonly identified with the author of the Epistle of Jude and the brother of James 'the Less'. According to the 'Passion of SS Simon and Jude', he was martyred in Persia with his companion Simon 'the Zealot' (*LA* 710). *Thomas of Ynde*: said in early tradition going back to the C3rd 'Acts of Thomas' to be the evangeliser of India, who was martyred there (*LA* 39). **166** *wyse weyes*: referring to their prudent self-concealment 'for fear of the Jews' (Jn 20:19). **167–8** Christ's entry into the locked dwelling is a peaceable version of the breaking through hell's gates at 20.364–5, the repeated *al* bringing out his effortless power. **169** *Pax vobis*: 'Peace be to you' (Jn 20:19); read as the 'Alleluia' verse at Mass on the Sunday after Easter, and providing the greeting of the celebrant to servers and people before every Communion. **170–1** are resonant with spiritual meaning; Christ is 'teaching' Thomas to *believe* by entering deeply into the 'heart' or innermost purpose of his coming in the flesh (for the symbolic positioning of the spear-wound, see on 20.87 above). The scene is superbly illustrated on the Syon Cope of *c.* 1300, a masterpiece of *opus anglicanum* now in the Victoria & Albert Museum, London (Camille 1996: pl. 77). **172a** 'My Lord and my God'; the only explicit acknowledgement in the Gospels of Christ as God, rounding off and experientially 'proving' the opening affirmation at Jn 1:1. **174** *Y bileue*: an inference from Christ's words to Thomas at Jn 20:29. **176** *lyuynge...lokynge*: cf. on 159. **179** *Yblessed...euere*: an addition bringing out Christ's gratuitous kindness or 'courtesy' in giving Thomas more than he deserves (the source contains no such blessing). **182** *Y...hem*: a special assurance to the Dreamer (cf. B 15.162) and to the audience of the value God attaches to belief founded on trust rather than physical evidence. **182a** 'Blessed are they that have not seen and have believed' (Jn 20:29).

183–99 are based on Lk ch. 24 and Ac ch. 1, but differ from the scriptural accounts in stressing the forgiveness of 'actual' sin through sacramental penance rather than of original sin through baptism. They compress the events described in the liturgical lectionary from Easter to Ascension Thursday forty days later, which follows Ac 1:3, in the light of the account in Lk 24:50–1, which places the Ascension on the evening of Easter Day (see 192–3 below). **183** *Dobest*: specifically the commissioning of the Apostles, as the first step in the founding of the Church, the act of dobest itself. **184** *Peres*: here as at 202 below unequivocally identified with the Apostle Peter (Burrow 1993[1]:119–22), the spiritual 'ploughman' of all lands awaiting salvation (on the evangelical 'ploughing' motif the fundamental study is Barney 1973). **185–8** The power to *forgive* sin is granted solely to the bishops and the clergy under their authority, who receive it by a line of ordination reaching back to the Apostles. But the capacity to *be forgiven* is offered to all who are willing to confess their sins and 'satisfactorily meet the terms of Piers's pardon'. The sense of *knowleched to paye* as 'agreed to pay' is convincingly supported in MED s.v. *knoulechen* v. 7(g) by a 1343 ref. combining the two words, a legal usage not noted in AlfG. **188** *Redde quod debes*: 'Pay what you owe' (Mt 18:28); not without ironic humour, the words of the Unjust Servant in the parable here being turned against him. **189–90** are based on Christ's words to St Peter at Caesarea (Mt 16:19); see on Pr 129–30. **189** *his...payed*: 'the terms of his pardon met'. **190** *elles*: i.e. in heaven; Peter's acts of granting or witholding absolution will be ratified by God. **191** *dette*: not 'the sin of debt' but 'the binding obligation to make satisfaction for sin'; Peter and his successors cannot grant pardon for nothing. **192–9** echo the end of the second clause of the Apostles' Creed; on 192–3 cf. Lk 24:50, Ac 1:9. **194–5** *reddit...*: 'pays what he owes'. Line 196, glossing this, stresses that satisfaction must accord with strict equity. **197** expands 9.21 in lines that echo the wording of B 7.112–14. **199** may be scanned as Type Ia with caesura after *wonye*, as a T-type, or best as Type IIb dividing after *wo* and providing the most solemn conclusion to Conscience's *carpyng*.

(ii) 200–335 The *Grace Sequence* deals with the Founding of the Church and carries the liturgical time swiftly forward to Whitsun's celebration of the Descent of the Holy Ghost 'in spirit and power' on the 120 disciples (Ac 1:15). The final scene with Conscience describes this event, which fell on the fiftieth day after Passover. It is also an allegory of the (inward) experience of devout Christians communally re-enacting that of the disciples (preface to Mass of Pentecost), and the poetry draws deeply on the language and imagery of the seasonal readings. **200–13 201** *perto*: continuing the worship of Christ's cross begun at 20.475–6. Still at 325 below the cross remains the 'structural form' of the Church as the Mystical Body of Christ. **202** is a Type IIIa with two lifts in *Paraclitus* or, preferably, a Type Ia variant with mute second stave and internal first stave in *Spiritus*. That serviceable Latin lexeme scans with |sp| at 304, with |s| at 277, with |p| at 458 and on its final syllable with |t| at 466. *Paraclitus*: 'the Comforter'; based on the Johannine conception of the Holy Ghost as 'advocate' and 'strengthener' of believers (Jn 14:26, 15:26, 16:7). The phrase occurs in the Pentecost Vespers hymn 'Beata nobis gaudia' (st. 1) and 202–5 are influenced by the wording of st. 2; but the Spirit's action as Comforter is most fully elaborated in the Whitsun Sequence 'Veni, sancte spiritus'. *Peres...felawes*: this second appearance again contextually implying St Peter and his fellow apostles (cf. Burrow 1993:77–80). **203** *lihtnynge*: an imaginative variant (lightning is also forked) on the *dispertitae linguae tanquam ignis* 'parted tongues, as it were of fire' of Ac 2:3 (cf. 206), with some recollection of *ignis vibrante lumine* from the 'Beata' hymn, st. 2 (*JLH* 154). *lihte*: 'Platonic' wordplay relating the fire from the skies to the heaven-sent Spirit; but **L** stresses its illuminating as well as enkindling force (as in the Pentecost Sequence). **204** See Ac 2:4–11; the ironic echo of 16.208–9 reminds that God is the source of all *sciences and sotil craftes*, which must be learnt in humility and faith. **205** *wondred*: Will shares the 'amazement and wonder' (Ac 2:7, 12) of the Jews who hear the apostles preach after receiving the Spirit. **206** *lihte*: figuring the divine (as at 20.127) by an overwhelming radiance that arouses awe in those who behold it. **208** The a-half repeats 21.12 above (see introductory note), symmetrically 'signing off' the Dreamer's instruction by Conscience. *messager*: because sent by Christ to bring the Apostles knowledge and understanding of all they have to preach (Jn 13–15); cf. Mahomet's claim at 17.177–80. **209** scans either as Type Ia on |g| with a four-syllable prelude-dip or as Type Ic on cognative *k / g*, the first stave being |k| in *cometh. fro...God*: cf. Jn 15:26, the basis of the Western doctrine of the Double Procession, but a text interpreted by Eastern theologians as supporting their objection to the *Filioque* clause. Following Truth and Kind for the Father and Christ for the Son, the final divine 'nature-name' Grace (for the Holy Ghost) comes as no surprise, his rôle as bringer of all grace having been explained by the Samaritan at 19.181–217; see sts 1 and 7 of the hymn quoted at 211. **211** *Veni...*: the C9th Vespers Pentecost Hymn, ascribed to Raban Maur, which inspires much of the action and imagery in section iii of XXI (see *JLH* I, 80). **212** *many hundret*: evoking the interior of a great church such as St Paul's.

214–62 214 Grace's accompanying of Piers accords well with the latter's intimate knowledge of him displayed at 7.242ff, when he was seen more in terms of his action in prompting men to penitence and the pursuit of *treuthe*

or righteous living. *Peres the Plouhman*: the third appearance of the name now explicitly equating not Christ (as *Sk* holds) but Christ's apostolic vicar with his own successors in historical time, the popes and bishops (of whom the poem's eponymous hero is the type) and *pari passu* the first Christian community with the worshippers assembled to celebrate the feast. **215** *Conscience*'s allegorical rôle in this summoning of the *ecclesia* is not precisely determinable; but in the light of his first and persistent signification, he is likely to suggest the secular authority in its capacity of 'joint' religious leader with the clergy. **216** *today*: the liturgy associating each day of Pentecost week with one of the Seven Gifts of the Holy Ghost enumerated in Is 11:2, beginning with Wisdom on the Sunday itself. **L**'s elaboration at 230–62 departs from this list in both sequence and content, extending the Spirit's bounty to the whole range of necessary human activities ('tresor to lyue by' 218; 'alle craft and connying' 254), and blurs the distinction between religious and secular. For the argument that **L** envisages his ideal community as modelled on the parish fraternities of various occupational membership, see Simpson 1993. *grace*: not in the strict theological sense of the 'supernatural' gift (distinguished as 'prevenient', 'actual' and 'habitual') but as something nearer to 'talents or endowments' (254 below). **217** *his*: understanding 'to every individual of every kind'. **218** is a Type Ia sub-variant with *to* mute in both the second stave, as the unemphatic infinitive particle, and in the key-stave, where as the preposition 'until' it puns polysemantically. If both are mute, two of the four stresses fall on annominating lexical words, providing a contrapuntal pattern on *l*; but possibly *to* (2) is meant to be a full stave. The line recapitulates rather than merely repeats Wit's declaration at 10.182–3: *tresor* (repeated in a semi-catechetical manner at 226) exists in the new dispensation on a more exalted level. **219** scans as either a Type Ia on |w| or, as preferably here, with natural stress on lexical words, as Type IIIc on |w| and |f| (cf. 227 below, where *with* is best stressed in this Type Ia line with its necessarily muted key-stave *when*). **220** *Auntecrist*: a Johannine expression used for those who deny Christ's incarnation, Messiahship and divinity (I Jn 2:18–22, II Jn 7–11 cf. 4:3). It covers both Jews and Christian heretics already actively at work (II Jn 4:3), whose presence has an eschatological significance ('it is the last hour', I Jn 2:18). St Paul in II Thess 2:3–9 (without using the name) speaks in similar terms of 'the man of sin, the son of perdition' who seduces into error, envisaging him as a diabolic wonder-worker whose appearance will precede the Second Coming of Christ. On medieval developments of this figure see Cohn 1972:33–6 and Emmerson 1982. **222** *false profetes*: foretold by Christ himself (Mt 24:24), the same phrase denoting heretics and schismatics in II Pet 2:1 and I Jn 4:1. **224–5** *Pryde*:

the chief sin, thought of as assisted by Greed (a single vice, often second in the list of the Deadly Sins), denoted comprehensively by both the 'cardinals' who advise him (cf. 19.326). *Vnkyndenesse* here = *avaritia* or miserliness. **227** *wepne*: on the weapons of spiritual warfare see I Cor 10:4. **228–9** The elucidation given in 230ff indicates that these graces are the talents that make possible the skills of practical life. Worthwhile and useful activity is certainly thought of as a remedy against sin; but on a wider scale the line attests **L**'s vision of 'Unity' as a social ideal encompassing both secular and religious values. **229** *Ydelnesse*: indolence predisposing to amorous indulgence; he is porter of the garden gate in *RR* 1273ff / *CT* I 1940. **229a** '[Now] there are diversities of graces, [but the same Spirit...of ministries, but the same Lord...of operations, but the same God]' (I Cor 12:4). The spiritual charisms Paul refers to are 'transsumptively' interpreted by **L** as 'earthly honest things' (234). **230–4** describe the work of those who use speech to explain, argue and instruct, all tasks that meet real needs. **231** An echo of the opening (Pr 21), modified to emphasise the importance of justice in the pursuit of one's living. **233** *They... lyue*: on this 'predicate nominative' use of the infinitive see *MES* 524–5. **235** *syhte*: as used in activities like the scribe's or the architect's. **236** Perhaps the craftsman's skill in making and the merchant's in assessing the quality of goods are meant. **237–8** refer to farming and fishing; cf. 17.20. **239–40** are among the few fully revised lines in the passus. **241** *deuyne*: 'find out about, investigate (mathematical) matters'. **245** *astronomye*: see on B 10.209 and MED s.v. n (1). **246–8** Knights are envisaged as enforcers of justice in society who should use 'forcible means' to recover goods stolen by force; the example of the Knight's failed courtesy at B 6.164–8 proves this the only 'law' that law-breakers will heed. **248** *with*: 'by means of'; the sense 'against' given by MED (s.v. *with* prep. 1b.(a)) would deprive the line of its sardonic bite. The 'grace' in question here corresponds to the recognition at 1.91–100 of an obligation to compel rather than persuade when circumstances demand it. *Foleuiles lawes*: 'rough justice', a phrase found only here. Despite a possible pun on 'Foolville' ('Fool Town'), *Sk*'s preferred conjecture of a proper name 'Folville' is well supported by Stones (1957) and Bowers (1961). The allusion is to the practices of the Folville clan, a notorious criminal gang active in Leicestershire in the 1330s. See further Green 1999:165–205. **249** *longyng...Cristene*: monastic and solitary contemplatives (cf.16.110–12), not 'the poor' (Hewett-Smith 2001:240). **251–5** may allude to the conflict and rivalry amongst the contemporary London gilds (see Simpson 1993). The sentiment recalls Trajan at B 11.213–14. **256** *myldest of berynge*: cf. Mk 9:33–4, Jn 13:13–16. **257** *crowneth...kyng*: the quality that is to prevail in the governance of the Christian community and be

assisted by practical wisdom ('craft' virtually = *prudentia*). **259–62** recall and recapitulate Passūs VII–VIII. But Piers's 'ploughing' is now wholly spiritual, since he will administer Grace's moral economy and 'cultivate' justice in the Christian *comune*, his rôle emblematising those of the pope and bishops as successors of the Apostles. **260** refers to the bishop's duty as *prowour* or 'overseer' (the literal sense of *episcopus*) of the system of penance, from confession to pardon. *registrer*: literally the clerk of an ecclesiastical court (AlfG). He receives an 'account' of what those 'on earth' have done to make adequate satisfaction for their sins (for the Latin phrase see at 188). **261** *prowour*: a variant of *purveiour* (MED s.v. n 1(b)). **262** *to tulye treuthe*: for the scriptural origin of the metaphor cf. I Cor 9:10–11, which envisages the preaching of the Gospels in term of ploughing, sowing and harvesting. **263–74a** On the image of *spiritual ploughing* see *R–H* 17–19 and Barney 1973. The figure recapitulates 'mystically' the original sequence of literal ploughing in Passus VIII, where Piers attempted to create an orderly and productive régime to meet the community's need for food. **263** *foure grete oxen*: as seen on f. 170r of the Luttrell Psalter, reproduced in *R–H* title-page and Blanch 1969:21, and discussed in Camille 1987; also (with two beasts) f. iiib in Cambridge, Trinity R. 3.14 (frontispiece to Vol. I). A full team usually had eight, but the number here is evidently symbolic. The image of the four Gospel writers as oxen pulling the plough of evangelization appears (*R–H* 18) in a commentary on Lk 9:62 attributed to St Jerome: 'quatuor boves, id est, quatuor evangelistae' (*PL* 30:591). The traditional symbolisation, also going back to the 5th c., derives from the 'four living creatures' round the throne of God in Apoc 4:6–10 and was familiar in iconography of all types (Mâle 1961:35–7; Katzenellenbogen 1939: fig. 69; Schiller II 108–9, pl. 442 [*c*. 1350]). **264** *large... lou-chered*: perhaps alluding to the meek appearance in depictions of the bull that is St Luke's emblem (as in the very early image in Schiller I pl. 425) or, more obliquely, to his Gospel's special emphasis on the Virgin Mary's humility (Lk 1:48–52). **265** *Marc*: emblematised by a lion. *Mathewe*: his emblem a man (see on B 6.237). **266–7** *Iohan*: specially honoured for the theological depth of his Gospel (for his influence on *PP* see Davlin 1996). John's emblem is an eagle (often fashioned into the lectern supporting the Gospel book), because of the loftiness of the bird's flight and its fabled ability to look directly at the sun (an allusion to the description of the Word as the Light in Jn 1:4–9). **268** *stottes*: heavy work-horses often used for harrowing; an apt metonym for the arduous interpretative labours of the Four Great Doctors. **269** *erede*: ploughing understood allegorically by Raban Maur (*PL* 111:610–1) as the preaching of the Gospel through which the 'earth' of human hearts is prepared to receive the 'seeds' of the virtues. *they to harwen*: 'it would be their task to harrow' (for the construction see on 233). The action of reducing the tilth to a finer and smoother condition before sowing is a fit emblem of the Fathers' exegetical work on the Bible. **270–1** The four named had a special authority in the Western Church, were revered in the monastic as well as the scholastic traditions of Biblical study, and had a general and in some instances strongly specific influence on **L**'s understanding of doctrine, moral teaching and spirituality. **270** *Austyn*: see on 11.148. *Ambrosie*: see on 15.45. **271** *Gregory*: see on 5.146. *Ieroem*: St Jerome (*c*. 345–420), translator of the Hebrew and Greek scriptures into what became the standard Latin text (the Vulgate), and erudite commentator on a large part of the Bible. *þe gode*: alluding to his ascetic life as a hermit-monk at Bethlehem. **272–4a** Their Commentaries used Scripture to interpret itself, a comparative method with its roots in the practice of St Paul (e.g. in Gal 4:22–31). Jerome adopted the literal, Augustine and Gregory the allegorical approach. **273** *handwhile*: scant exaggeration, since the three great contemporaries commented on most of the Scriptural texts, while Gregory later synthesised, developed and transmitted their achievement to the medieval Church. **274** *aythes*: a word of extreme rarity (< OE *egþe* 'harrow'), as is its cognate verb *heggen* (see on 5.19). *oelde...newe*: perhaps an allusion to Mt 13:52; the 'thesaurus' of the OT (like that of the pre-Christian Cardinal Virtues) retains its moral and spiritual value even under the time of Grace. **274a** 'That is, the Old Testament and the New'; Alf*Q* (comparing B 15.212) finds that this 'suggests the language of a biblical commentary'. Scripture itself will help exegetes penetrate and smooth over the sometimes rough and difficult sense of particular Biblical texts and passages.

275–310 describe the sowing of the *Cardinal Virtues*. **275** *graynes*: since the virtues are the 'food' of the soul. The image has been traced to Homily I.3 on Ezechiel (*PL* 76:807–9) by one of the *foure stottes*, St Gregory, which with Jerome's Commentary forms the gloss in *GO* (Kaulbach 1993:136n119), and to Gregory's *Moralia in Job* II.49, ll.37–9, which describes the Spirit as forming the four cardinal virtues in the mind; see also Hugh of St Victor, *Summa Sententiarum* III xvii (*PL* 176:114), cited by Burrow 1993[1]:69. *cardinales vertues*: treated as if French, with the adjective having a plural inflection (see on Pr 132), but as a normal English phrase at 339. The notion of the four chief virtues of practical reason on which the other virtues 'turn' (*cardo* = 'hinge') was taken from Plato and Aristotle into the mainstream medieval view of divine revelation as building on the ground of human nature created in the image of God (*ST* I–II qu. 61). The traditional order moves from wise foresight, through the moderate way of life it makes possible, to the capacity to endure hardship, and finally to the ability to judge without fear or favour. The virtuous circle thus

turns from one cognitive through two affective virtues to a second cognitive virtue now informed with the knowledge derived from experience (*kynde knowynge*). Christian understanding of the cardinal virtues (something particularly important for those entrusted with secular or religious governance) was influenced by the list of the Spirit's seven gifts to the Messiah in Is 11:2–3, the wording of which is echoed in the names 'spiritus intellectus...spiritus fortitudinis' (see Burrow 1993[1]:69). Of these seven, 'consilium', 'fortitudo' and 'pietas' are seen by Aquinas as 'corresponding' respectively to prudence, fortitude and justice. **276** *sewe...soule*: not a new image in *PP*, but recalling 14.23–7a. As *Creator Spiritus* (211 above), the Third Person is fittingly made the author of the natural (cardinal) as well as the supernatural (theological) virtues. The sowing is performed by Grace as an example for his 'prowour' to imitate, clearly indicating that the Church's mission is not simply individual and other-worldly but aims to transform society as a whole. **277** 'The Spirit of Prudence': the virtue of planning and foresight (< *providentia*). Though called *spiritus intellectus* at 466, it signifies not 'speculative understanding' but sagacity or 'practical moral insight', with which it was often linked (Eph 1:8; cf. Prov 8:12, 14:8ff). Personified as 'Dame Prudence' in Chaucer's *Melibee*, it is never a purely 'secular' virtue, and is commended in Christ's exhortation to measure the 'cost' of discipleship (Lk 14:28–32). **278** The 'seeds' are imagined as growing in the soul and bearing fruit in wise foresight. **280–1** illustrate prudence from everyday experience, pointing up the virtues' affinity with *kynde wit*. **282** 'The Spirit of Temperance': more than mere moderation, this is restraint and self-control, much valued by the ancient Stoics but also seen as the basis of Christian asceticism and as a remedy for anger, greed and pride. Among the virtues, it is close to both the 'abstinentia' and 'patientia' urged in II Pet 1:6 and the 'modestia' and 'continentia' that are among the Spirit's 'fruits' in Gal 6:23, and its special importance will emerge later in the speech of NEED at 22.6ff. **284** *swelle*: with either repletion or rage; the possessor of this virtue will be able to handle *utraque fortuna* 'good hap or ill'. **288** *curious cloth*: attacked as a sign of extravagant pride in *CT* X 416–20. **289** *Maister Iohan*: an ironic 'learned' title for a skilled 'master chef'. **290** 'The Spirit of Fortitude': not the *wihtnesse of handes* of 247 but the courage to endure pain and distress without yielding. **296** *plede...pacience*: 'go to law only by patient acceptance'; *al* is either nominal or adverbial. *Parce...*: '[I have done with hope. I shall now live no longer]. Spare me, [Lord]' (Job 7:16); the text part-quoted by Christ at B 18.393, and in the Commentary on Cato's distich 'Parce laudato' (Alf*Q*). Job is the prime OT exemplar of patient fortitude, but the quotation comes from a passage that can hardly be called 'murye'. **297** *Caton*: see on 4.17. **298** 'Be [glad and] of stout heart when you are unjustly condemned' (*DC* II, 14). The text has *libens* before *cum* and the couplet concludes *nemo diu gaudet qui iudice vincit iniquo* 'None rejoice long who through a false judge win'. **299** 'The Spirit of Justice': the capacity to judge oneself and others with fairness, a virtue especially suited to those in public office. Described by Conscience as the 'chief seed' at 409, in a sense it incorporates the discernment of prudence, the fearlessness of fortitude and (as 'equity') the moderation of temperance, providing (as *treuthe* or *rihtwisnesse*) an organising concept of the poem (Stokes 1984:1–31; AlfG 76–7). **302** *gyle...priueyly*: as at 2.70ff. **303** *thorw*: 'by [those sitting in judgement]'. **304–9** lay down the need for adherence to the law and judicial impartiality in adminstering it, even if the wrong is done by the highest in the land. L's apprehensions about the likeliest source of interference seems prescient. **308** *dede*: a grim 'Platonic' pun, hinting that death might be the price of such scrupulous justice under a tyrant. **310** *eueneforth his knowyng*: 'to the best of his ability'; because the judge's knowledge of the truth should be his sole guide in making a just judgement.

311–36 describe through the figure of 'harrowing' the development of Christian theology. **311** Harrowing prepared the soil by removing troublesome weeds and covered the sown seeds to protect them against birds. **312–13** Though the 'natural' virtues of reason need the help of Scripture (interpreted by the Fathers) to grow, the task of destroying evil in the world falls to *Love*, the 'plant of peace' (1.147) that has now been 'sown' on earth through the Incarnation of Christ described in 69ff. **314** *cammokes*: the tough-rooted weed *Ononis spinosa* or *resta bovis* 'rest-harrow', which 'arrests' or obstructs the harrow's movement. *wedes*: '(other) weeds'. **317** *alle þat conneth*: 'all you who possess practical understanding'. Those addressed are not the clergy specifically but the Christian people at large, whose practice of the virtues should be directed by the Church's teachings. **320** *hous*: an image for the Church perhaps suggested by the capacious medieval tithe-barn (like the one still extant at Great Coxwell in Oxfordshire), which resembled in shape the mendicant 'preaching-church'. A patristic source for the idea appears to be Augustine's *Sermo* 73 (*PL* 38:471). *herborwe in*: an inf. verb-phrase allowing the object to stand at the line-end. **323–30** allegorically present the Church not as a material organisation but as a spiritual organism, the 'Mystical Body of Christ'. In accordance with traditional thought, the Cross (metonymic for the Passion) is made its central foundation (an idea that found its physical counterpart in the cruciform ground-plan of larger Christian edifices). **323** *cros*; *croune*: 'tokens' of the Passion signifying how the Christian community must suffer like its Lord in order to win the 'crown of glory' that the personified female figure of Ecclesia often wears

in depictions of the Crucifixion (Schiller II pls 446, 450). **325** *bapteme and bloed*: hendiadys for 'baptismal blood'; alluding to patristic understanding of the blood and water from Christ's side as emblems of the sacraments, especially baptism (see on 12.110–11, 21.58). *bloed...rode*: for the Leonine internal rhyme across the caesura, cf. Appendix One § 5.ii.(c). **326** *morter*: the bond holding together the members with their Head, the divine mercy shown in Christ's dying for mankind and the Church's sharing in his redemptive suffering. **328** *wateled and walled*: 'made a wall of wattle-and-daub' (a rural building-method using woven branches and lime-mortar). **329** *alle Holy Writ*: perhaps here signifying the authoritative patristic tradition. *roof*: Scripture 'covering' the harvested virtues against the elements and so protecting the Church against false belief, but not forming its foundation, which is Christ himself (Eph 2:20). **330** *Vnite*: a synecdochic 'nature-name' (itself *an Englisch*), unity being one of the 'marks' of Christ's mystical body as described in Eph 4:1–16. As an oblique designation of the Church for whose unity its Founder prayed (Jn 17:11), the name would have had special poignancy in 1378, when Christendom was divided by the Great Schism (see *Intro*. V § 15). The idea of 'unity' as a protection against the deadly sins, and much of the local imagery and verbal detail, are convincingly traced by Wilkes (1965) to *Ancrene Wisse* (ed. Day, 109–10). **331** *And...doen*: see 183 and cf. 279. **332** *cart*: for an earlier allegorical cart (of vices) see 2.190. *Cristendoem*: both 'baptism', which cleanses from original (as confession from actual) sin, and 'the Community of Christians' into which the baptized are initiated. *sheues*: human souls as a spiritual 'harvest' to be reaped by preaching the Gospel; cf. Mt 9:37–8, Jn 4:35. **334** *hayward*: the person assigned to watch and protect the crops against 'pickers and thieves' (cf. 5.16, 13.44). The ordinary clergy are envisaged as having a stable ministry to the local community (the parish), the prelates as having a wider call to evangelize. L does not see the latter's rôle strictly as missionary, except for bishops *in partibus*, but stresses the need for diocesan visitations in order to 'feed' the people with 'ghostly food' (see 17.277–92, B 15.572, and cf. I Pet 5:2–3). **335** See on 19.36 above. **336** covers both faith and morals, doctrine and edification, 'truth' and 'love' (cf. B 1.76, 16.6). *londe of bileue*: for another such allegorical terrain, cf. 11.169.

(iii) 337–484 deal with the *preparation for the Siege of Antichrist* that occupies the final Passus. It resembles that for the Harrowing of Hell in XX, and the tone of lines like 340 suggests a darkly ironic inversion of Christ's effortless triumph (20.364) over those who resisted him. The Deadly Sins first encountered in distorted human guise in Vision 2 now return in nakedly diabolic form to assail the barn of Grace, their eventual triumph reversing the fragile success of the original Piers in Passūs VII–IX.

337–93 describe the building of *the spiritual defence-works*. **337** *Now...plouh*: this 'spiritual ploughing' recalling the 'literal ploughing with a spiritual significance' at 8.110–12. *Peres*: signifying at the existential plane Christ's 'faithful pastors and teachers' (*Sk*), but at the historical, 'all who resist the enemies of Christianity'. These range from the first to be identified as Antichrist, the Roman Emperor Nero (when the Piers-figure correlates closely with St Peter), to all bringers of heresy, schism and worldliness into the Christian *comune*. *Pryde*: the root of the Deadly Sins and their determined leader. While assuredly an emblem of the contemporary clergy's material-mindedness, he perhaps typifies historically less the persecutions of the pagan Emperors (which hurt Christians but failed to corrupt the spiritual *ecclesia*) than the Church's more perilous temporal success under Constantine, after these persecutions had ceased. **340** The virtues are understood as a crop still growing in *þe londe of bileue*. **341–2** The simplest and most satisfactory solution to the problem of the number of villains present would probably be to see only two, Pride's sergeant-at-arms (sg.) and his spy (see *TN*). **341** *Surquidou(r)s*: an embodiment of arrogance or presumption, 'whan a man undertaketh an emprise that hym oghte nat do, or elles that he may nat do; and this is called *surquidrie*' (*CT* X 403). *seriaunt(es) of armes*: officers (usually armed) attending on the king; a class at this time in ill-repute for extortions and oppressions (Alf*G*). **342** *Spille-Loue*; *Speke-euele-bihynde*: 'command-names' like Amend-you, Dowel (or Modern English 'spoilsport' and 'killjoy'). The second, a gloss on the first explaining how back-biting and slander destroy charity, recalls Wrath at 6.115–17. **345** *Sire*: the title (contemptuously) acknowledging his 'priestly' status. **346** *broke*: as a result of the dissension to be caused by arrogance and slander in the Church; words well fitting both the heresies and schisms spoken of in the Epistles (e.g. I Cor 1:10–11, 14:33) and contemporary animosities between the supporters of Pope and antipope. **347** *come out*: a sign of defeat and surrender. *caples tweyne*: for another allegorical horse cf. B 17.108. That these particular *caples* are made to draw the cart of Belief serves to underline the crucial link between righteousness and orthodoxy. For **L** corrupt conduct and false belief (vice and heresy) both flourish when the sacrament of penance is abused. **350–1** The individual's conscience will become morally confused by mistaken guidance from his confessor, and in consequence the body of Christian believers will progressively go astray. The referent of *Conscience* may ironically include the conscientious priest confessing a penitent previously misled by one less scrupulous. **351** *Cristene or hethene*: a grim warning that the conduct and faith of Christians will have so decayed that the distinction becomes blurred. **352–3** *marchaunt*: a single example illustrating how and where

moral uncertainty can generate serious consequences for society as a whole. **354–7** The allegory enacts the nobility's special temptation of luxurious self-indulgence, the 'lord' being a type-figure later named at 22.312 as the recipient of a Friar's emollient ministrations. **358–62** Conscience's advice is that strength lies in unity and that dissension among Christians will help only the enemies of the Church. The contemporary resonance of the lines will have lessened only slightly a decade after the B-Text, since the Schism was still unresolved and the Lollards (who opposed obligatory confession) were gaining adherents (cf. Pearsall 2003:19). His stress on the need for Grace in order to oppose sin implies in this context the necessity of the sacraments (the usual channels of grace), something also challenged by Wycliffite teachers. **360** *pees*: recalling St Paul's reference to '*unity* of the spirit in the bond of *peace*' (Eph 4:3); a quality vital for the survival of the Church. **L**'s 'prophetic' awareness reflects the deepening impact of the Schism as well as echoing scriptural warnings against divisions (cf. I Jn 2:19). **362** *goen agayn*: i.e. set out from Unity to *attack*; they must therefore go on the defensive. **363–6** A close association with Conscience has been evident from as early as Pr 141–6. Since *kynde wit* 'intuitive good sense' is conceptually 'prior' to the moral reasoning that issues in a concrete judgement of *conscience*, his 'teaching' (cf. 3.436) may be understood to 'inform' the constable of the situation (MED s.v. *techen* v. 2(b)) and of the urgent need for an 'outer' spiritual defence (made up of pious works). **364** *comaundede*: the actual command coming from the 'officer' Conscience (367), with Kynde Wit as a sort of NCO conveying what needs to be done. **365** *diche depe*: recalling the abode of Wrong in B Pr 15–16; the onslaught of infernal powers on earth demands a matching resistance. **366** *Holi Churche*: the Church Militant, the whole body of Christian believers. *holinesse*: not impossibly with a 'Platonic' pun. The 'hole' is hollowed out for a spiritual stronghold that is an earthly simulacrum of Truth's tower, vividly expressive of the common medieval understanding of a cathedral church as an earthly 'replica' of the heavenly Jerusalem (cf. Von Simson 1956:8–11). *pile*: an image traced by Wilkes (1965:334–6) to *AW* (see at 380 below). **368** The Church's outer structure as a sacred society must imitate its inner nature as a spiritual edifice; hence the *moche moet* will correspond to that described at 7.232, the outward tears that fill it paralleling the repentance experienced inwardly. The passage recapitulates 10.128–36, where Anima within the Castle of *Caro* was represented as besieged by the Prince of this World. **369** *hem*: its 'ordained' defenders. **370–5** recapitulate various moments in Visions 1 and 2 (e.g. 2.59, B 5.641), as the world depicted reaches forward to the actual present and increasingly comes to resemble the *Visio*'s Field of Folk. **370** *comune wommen*:

because 'professional' sinners; Conscience does not contradict the teaching of Mt 21:31–2 and the recognitions at 18.143, B 11.216 of harlots who *will* 'repent and refuse sin'. **372** *sisour; sompnour*: a pair associated with the archetypal 'common woman' at 4.161–2 and condemned throughout *PP* (see 2.59, 3.170). **373–4** bring out how 'their sin's not accidental but a trade' (false testimony that a guilty person was innocent); heavily-stressed *sothly* highlights sarcastically their true awareness of their sin against truth. *with...helden*: recalling 2.179–80. **377** *wexe*: implying a change of metaphor (to that of a growing plant); but the notion of sanctity as the 'water' of spiritual life, outwardly manifested as 'religious tears', is soon resumed. **378–9** Prayer, pilgrimage and alms-giving are the traditional works of 'satisfaction'; the personal penances will include fasting and other forms of self-denial of a less visible kind. **380** recalls the action of Repentance in Passus VI, beginning with Will's weeping. *walled water*: the magnified image recalling such Biblical parallels as 'Let tears run down like a torrent day and night' (Lam 2:18). Wilkes aptly cites *AW* (ed. Day, pp. 109–10): 'ase ofte as þe ueond asaileð ouwer castel & te soule buruh, mid inwarde bonen worpe ut uppon him schaldende *teares*…þu hauest forschalded þe drake heaued mid *wallinde watere*…kastel þæt haueþ deope dich a buten & water be iðe dich þe kastel is wel kareleas aʒen his unwines…ah habbe ʒe depe dich of deope edwurdinesse & wete teres þerto' (Wilkes 1965). Although *wallinde* here must mean 'boiling' rather than 'springing', the verbal and contextual affinities are arresting. **382–3** The purgation effected during the penitential cycle aims to restore the Church each Lent to its pristine condition at its founding. For the idea of holiness as especially associated with chastity, cf. 18.95–6 above, *Purity* 7–16 and Alan of Lille's praise in *AP* of the blessing of a pure conscience 'that purges the mind of uncleanness' and is 'the image of eternal life' (*PL* 210:139). **385** *lord of lust*: the principle of sensual pleasure as something governing men's lives, the *exercitus carnis* 'army of the flesh' seen by Alan of Lille as fighting against the soul (*PL* 210:141, quoting Gal 5:17). *Lente:* The poem's 'liturgical time' has now shifted back (or forward) to the Lenten season with which the redemptive sequence began at 19.1. It commences and climaxes in the space of 386–7, as the Christian community perform an *anamnesis* or 'calling to mind' of Christ's redemptive death and resurrection. **386** *dyneth*: a figure evoking Biblical images of the Messianic banquet; the food is to be not, as at Conscience's / Reason's dinner (B XIII / C XV), the *words* of scripture but the consecrated 'bread of heaven'. **387** *labored...Lenten*: the discipline of self-denial recapitulating at a higher plane the bodily labours commended in Hunger's sermon to Piers (8.250–63). **388** *bred yblessed*: the Easter Eucharist, which was seen in a special way as the reward of

Lenten abstinence (cf. I Cor 5:7–8, the Communion verse for Easter Sunday). *Godes body*: the normal phrase for the sacred elements (cf. B 12.85), asserting their identity with the crucified Christ (cf. 20.77, 476, which the phrase echoes); a stronger sign of **L**'s rejection of Lollard beliefs than recognised by Pearsall 2003:13. *þervnder*: cf. *sub panis specie / Velaris divinitus* from the Corpus Christi sequence hymn 'O panis dulcissime' (*JLH* II, 210). **389** *Godes word*: the words of consecration instituted by Christ at the Last Supper (Mt 26:26–8). **390** states elliptically that Grace gave the ordained priesthood the *power* to consecrate the Eucharist and all Christians the *capacity* to receive it (cf. on 185–8). **391–3** propose a frequency of communion (perhaps also tacitly assuming confession before it) more like the clergy's than the once-yearly reception usual for laypeople (Duffy 1992:93–4). **393** *Redde...*: see on 188.

394–461 report the opposition Conscience meets with as a series of tense exchanges, first with the *comune*, next with a fractious brewer and an uneducated (but very vocal) vicar, and then (462–84) at the opposite end of the social scale, a nobleman and a king. **394–5** echo Christ's words at Mt 5:23–4 (together with I Cor 11:27–9 the scriptural basis for requiring confession before *housel*). The sacrament of 'communion' between Christ and the believer requires accord between the latter and all other Christians, an aspect of the rite especially stressed in the period, with its close-knit pattern of social organisation (Duffy 1992:127). **397a** 'And forgive us our trespasses'; the fifth petition of the Paternoster. **398** *assoiled*: obligatory confession before Easter Communion offering an opportunity to settle grievances between neighbours or more widely in the *comune*. **399** *Bawe*: ironically recalling Trajan's interjection at 12.76. *breware*: connected by profession with both the provision of drink and the deceits and abuses that went with it, as described in 6.225–31 above. **399–400** *be...Iesu*: the ironic syntactical ambiguity underlining the speaker's wrong disposition. **400** The 'justice' involved here is the sale of goods at a price reflecting their true value. **402** *at on hole*: i.e. pretend that both qualities are drawn from the same barrel of (superior) ale; a trick like that of Greed's wife Rose the Regrater at 6.225–33. **403** *Thikke...ale*: see on 6.226. **404** *hacky aftur*: found only here; it is possibly a phrasal verb, or else *aftur* may mean 'in accordance with'. **408–9** *Saue...ysaued*: with 'Platonic' wordplay depending on the emendation (on which see *TN*). **409** Though justice is here declared the 'chief' of the four cardinal virtues, a subtle claim for Temperance will be put by Need at 22.23ff. **411** *we*: a small revision bringing out the interdependence of everyone in Unity, and how the failings of one affect all. **412** *lewed vicory*: a shrewd observer like the prudent mouse of Pr 196ff. The acerbic commentary of this second 'lower-class' figure (whom Conscience significantly does not rebuke) articulates the *comune*'s grievances, his criticisms of the shortcomings of the highest orders in the Church recalling the narrator's at Pr 134–7. The ill-educated vicar's real-life counterparts would have been the priests rapidly ordained without proper training to make good the massive loss of parish clergy after the Black Death (see on Pr 82). Gasse 1996 relates the vicar to the earlier priest at 9.280=B 7.105 and sees him too as an object of satiric scorn. **414** The speaker's ignorance of what the Cardinal Virtues are intimates economically both his lack of learning and the absence of these qualities from the society of the time. *Cardinales Vertues*: the French form allowing a tart pun on 'virtuous cardinals'. **415** *a...hennes*: one of many such phrases ('bean' 12.94, 'pie-crust' 9.345) denoting a thing of little value; semi-proverbial in ring but not parallelled. **416–26** The attack on cardinals expresses resentment at their grand manner and cost to the ordinary diocesan clergy who had to contribute to their maintenance. Cardinal legates in England exercised 'extensive authority...with their own miniature curia, including a penitentiary' (Swanson 1989:150) and contemporary criticism of their luxurious living rivals that of the Avignon Papacy itself (Ullmann 1948:7n). There may be a specific allusion here to Cardinal Simon Langham (d. 1376), who was papal nuncius to England in 1371–2 and 1373 (Barney 2006). **418** *pelure...pelours*: a 'Platonic' pun relating luxury to legitimised extortion; the half-line recalls 4.115. **419** is the poem's only macaronic Type IIb line. *clamat cotidie*: 'cries out daily'; this is 'a formula used to initiate proceedings against a public enemy' (Alf*Q*, Alf*G*). **424–5** mordantly express ironic praise, suggesting that they both 'will and will not' be corrupted by the company of the Jews. **425** *Auenoun*: the papal residence until 1377, when Gregory XI removed the curia to Rome (though still intending to return there, when he died in April 1378). As the centre of papal taxation and litigation it required the ministrations of several curial cardinals, who raised the loans they needed from moneylenders, possibly including Jews (Gilchrist 1969 s.v. 'Avignon'). In 1379 a Jew transported to Avignon (which belonged to the papacy) the cardinals who supported the anti-pope Clement VII (Bennett 1943²:63); but the text need not be specifying these, as opposed to Pope Urban's supporters. *Cum sancto...*: see at B 5.278. **426** *Rome*: where the cardinals had their titular churches, the important relics of which were in their keeping. *as here reule wolde*: the 'rule' being their general responsibility as the Pope's immediate helpers in administering the universal Church. The speaker's objection is to the presence of cardinals as papal legates and nuncios (fiscal officers collecting papal taxes) in other countries, including England. *relikes*: sarcastically intimating that some of the holiness of these important relics of Roman martyrs and

saints might rub off on them. **427** *in*: '(should remain) in'; as desired by the King at 4.186. **428** *gredest so of*: cf. at 362, 389ff. **429** *newe plouh ...olde:* 'the ploughs of B VI and XIX respectively: the old plough for the growing of wheat on the half-acre and the new one for the cultivation of the virtues on the manor of Grace' (Burrow 2007:124). **430** *Emperour*: presumably not in a juridical but in a religious sense of 'supreme spiritual ruler'. The vicar, for whom the Pope's dominion stretches over the souls of all believers, is clearly no follower of Wycliffe, who had himself, however, written to Pope Urban VI a more or less conciliatory letter in 1378 (*Fasciculi* 341–2; Workman ii.315 for date). But his criticisms echo Wycliffe's in their negative contrast of papal conduct with Scriptural standards and in their admonitory repetition of 'Christian' (446–8). *alle...Cristene*: implying that such a Pope could work for the conversion of the Moslems, Jews and heathens with hope of success.

431–51 turn from cardinals to contrast the ferocity of the actual pope with the forebearance of a true *servus servorum* worthy of the name of Peter / Piers. **431–2** probably allude to Urban's use of mercenary soldiers against Clement VII in April 1379 (Bennett 1943:63; cf. *Intro*. V § 20). **432** *suche*: his Christian subjects who support the antipope. **433** *pat...doynge*: 'who follows the example of God in the way he conducts himself'. The vicar imagines an 'ideal pope' as guided by Reason's teaching at 13.194–200 and clearly implies that the reigning Pontiff would give far more effective spiritual leadership if he exercised *spiritus fortitudinis* through patiently enduring his enemies' opposition instead of asserting his rights by seeking to crush them through force (see on 467). **434** '[Love your enemies: do good to them that hate you... That you may be the children of your Father who is in heaven], who [maketh his sun to rise upon the good and bad and] raineth upon the just and the unjust' (Mt 5:44–5). **437–9** conflate the present allegorical sense of Piers's ploughing with the literal sense as enacted in Vision 2. The Pope, clergy and faithful laypeople must work for the good of all, including the worst, while keeping a proper distinction of dignity in the sacramental community between themselves and the wasters and prostitutes (who are not, however, excluded from Unity). **443–4** echo the words of Study at B 10.129–30. **444** *soffreth*: cf. 13.200, which gives another reason for putting up with evils. *til som tyme*: not implying that all *will* repent, only that they may (and at times and in ways known to God alone); a more benign interpretation of God's 'syttynge' sufferance than that in the parable of the cockle and wheat to which allusion is perhaps made (Mt 13:24–43). **445** *the Pope*: the obvious referent being Urban VI, whom England acknowledged. **446** *And*: 'Even though'. *pe Kynge*: with no specific reference being necessarily intended, only the Pope's standing claim to immediate universal spiritual jurisdiction unlimited by the temporal authority. **449a** 'Thou shalt not kill' (Ex 20:13), quoted at Lk 18:20; 'Revenge is mine' (Deut 32:35). In **B** there is a summary echo of B 10.366–8 (a passage **C** omits), which juxtaposes the quotations. Both Testaments concur in reserving to God the right to punish by force; but while **L** clearly has the clergy in mind, he does not necessarily deny its use to the civil power (cf. on 248). **452–61** insist that cardinals' ingenuity in acquiring *wele* has led all to care only for getting rich, by whatever means. **460** The climax of the complaint is that in the hypocritical moral ethos engendered by the clergy's example, virtues are manipulated as disguises for the concealment of vices.

462–84 *The response of nobility and king.* **462** *lord*: a type-figure, one with or cousin to the pleasure-loving noble later to be met with at 22.90–2. **463** *of my reue*: and thence from his tenants, from whom the reeve collected manorial dues. The lord presumably means that under the guise of prudent management he extracts the last ounce from his feudal dependents (whatever their conditions of life at any given time), an attitude Piers warned against at 8.36ff. **466** *Spiritus Intellectus*: 'the Spirit of Understanding', an ironic synonym for Prudence (see on 275), as the lord obviously 'understands' what is to his advantage. It is taken as a synecdoche by AlfQ, who cites from *FM* 589 'understanding of present things' as one of the three elements of prudence, and the discussion of the cardinal virtues in the Proem to Cato's *Distichs*. **467** The 'spirit of fortitude' here is nearer to 'aggression' than to the 'endurance' specified at 292–6. *fecche hit*: cf. 242. *he*: the person from whom the reeve reckoned the payment due. **468** *bi his corone*: by his authority as king; that the phrase is an oath and does not mean 'with reference to his crown' (*Sk*) seems supported by parallel 462. The king's speech concludes, from the proposition that he is head of law, that all he does is lawful (cf. the cry of the Commons at B Pr 145). **469–70** echo the words of the coronation oath of medieval English kings, but significantly omit all reference to ruling *justly*. **471** *to lyue by*: on this phrasal infinitive used as noun-subject (with 'the means' understood) see *MES* 523. **472** *heed*: either 'source' or 'controller' or both; in either case, the claim is to absolute authority. **476** *ʒow two*: addressed to the clergy and the people; the king is lawfully entitled to tax both. **476–7** Though nothing on these lines is said at 304–10, the king evidently considers himself (as supreme judge) to be above the judgement of all others and hence *potentially* above the law. For he fails to mention his duty of observing the ancient laws and customs of the realm as stated in Edward II's coronation oath, to which Conscience alludes at 480–1 below (see Maitland 1908:100–01 for further clarification of the issue, and Baldwin 1981, Firth Green 1995:232–7). **478** *borwe neuere*: and therefore need not 'pay what he owes' (since he owes nothing).

hoseled: cf. 394–8. **480–1** *defende...rewme...treuthe*: Conscience's 'condition' echoes the coronation promises of King Richard's great-grandfather Edward II to confirm the ancient customs and laws of England, to defend 'the laws and righteous customs which the community of the realm shall have chosen' and to do 'equal and right justice and discretion in mercy and truth' (on the oath see Richardson 1949 and 1960). The 'condition' is meant to exclude any conflation of public authority with personal power, the crucial issue in the later years of Richard II. **482** *thy lawe*: the constitutional precedent he cites in support of his claim. **482a** 'What's yours is yours to keep and defend, and not to seize for your own end'. An analogue is found in the *Summa de Vitiis* of Peraldus cited by Wenzel 1974:367: 'Likewise, if slaves' possessions are said to belong to their lords, this is in the sense only that they are to be defended by him, not plundered [*ad defendendum et non ad depredandum*]'. **483** *fer hoem*: 'a long journey home'; the suggestion is of a return from the cathedral to his village-parish. **484** brings the vision full circle by closely echoing line 1 of the Passus.

Passus XXII (B XX)

PASSUS XXII opens with an important waking Prelude (1–50). The remainder is given over to *Antichrist's Siege of Unity*: (i) the preparations (51–73); (ii) the siege itself, with counterattacks (74–142); (iii) the Lyf-Elde episode with the Dreamer (143–211); (iv) the Confession crisis, followed by the entry of Friar Flatterer (212–386); and (v) a Finale, the departure of Conscience, with which the poem abruptly ends (381–7). Will's falling asleep after a rebuke, and the beginning of Vision Eight, recall the opening of **C**'s Vision Two after its allegorised predream encounter with two somewhat aggressive personified figures at 5.1–108. The Need Episode (1–50) can now be seen to echo that revised opening, which was perhaps designedly added in the light of what had already been done in B XX. Both instances are interior dialogues of the waking self, the earlier one complacent in plenty (5.6–9), in the later wretched with want. NEED, personifying the 'necessitous deprivation' (Burrow 1993:95–100) mentioned by Piers at 9.62–3=B 7.66, is vocal in asserting the common right of all to share in the earth's produce that (as noted in Simpson 1990:233) was recognised by HC in I 17–19. His argument is regarded with suspicion by Adams (1978:273–301), who connects Need with the Antichrist of the following dream and with the *egestas* of Job 41:13 as understood in Gregory's commentary, and sees him as voicing the questionable views on poverty and mendicancy associated with friars. Simpson (1990:232–4) also sees Need as encouraging 'the poor, and Will in particular…to manipulate temperance', a view shared by Godden (1990:162–4). Yet this is surely not what he is doing by urging temperance even in a situation of 'necessitous deprivation'; and when Need appears within the dream at 232, he insists on the friars' adherence to the poverty they profess. This however has led Frank (1957:113–14) to interpret Need's speech as an ironically intended warning against the theory of poverty espoused by the friars. Here Frank is partly misled by reading *bydde* for *byde* at 48, and Simpson (239–40) makes the same mistake, as does Barney (2006:195, 204), who is misled by failure to recognise the irony in *begge* at V 51 (but see *TN*). In fact Need does not support begging and does oppose (what he regards as) the friars' covetousness, much as Conscience (233, 246) opposes their envy. For earlier and later discussions of this controversial figure and the themes articulated by the episode see Carruthers 1973:160–66, Hewett-Smith, 2001:33–53, the studies cited in Kim 2002:160n and most fully and insistently Barney 2006:186–96. A more positive interpretation of Need in the light of traditional treatments of the 'paupertas crucis' motif will be found in Schmidt 1983²:188–92, and of medieval natural law doctrine on the common ownership of earthly goods in Mann 2004:3–29.

Prelude **1–50** Need's rebuke articulates the Dreamer's own misgivings about the way of life described at 5.42–52, in which material necessity (in age) results from failure to do paid (physical) work. But his earlier robust reply to Reason at 5.82–8 is replaced by an oblique (and quietly subversive) defence of his position as conforming with Temperance. Need first claims (6–22) that 'winning' (obtaining) the bare necessities, even by dubious means (*sleithe*), is acceptable if it is the only way to survive and if it respects the cardinal virtue which, as it controls and moderates the others, *cannot* be 'manipulated'. Though Simpson is right to stress the importance of law for **L**, in a situation of extreme need natural law takes precedence over positive law, because no man-made decrees can be just that deprive man of the prospect of life, a gift of God. The 'law of kind' (the urge to preserve one's life) thus becomes indistinguishable from the 'law of reason' (the requirement to respect others' property), *insofar as it observes* Temperance. **4** *noen*: dinner-time; see on 2.100. *Nede*: personifying a condition always for **L** associated with feelings of shame, whether the want is self-caused, as at 13.240, or results from adverse fortune, as at 9.84–7, where the noon meal is again mentioned. **7** *to lyue by*: i.e. the minimum necessary for survival. **8** *techyng... tellyng*: not that Temperance *enjoins* 'taking', but will justify it if this virtue's precepts are followed. *Spiritus Temperancie*: see on 21.282–9; commended as protecting against the colourable excesses to which prudence, fortitude and justice were shown as exposed at 21.455–79. **10** *nede*: either grammatically identical with *nede* at 9

or the nominal adjective *nedé* meaning 'needy (person[s])'. *ne...lawe*: 'is not subject to the constraints of (positive) law'. It translates the Natural Law maxim *Necessitas non habet legem* earlier quoted at 13.43a in an addition insisting that a messenger who passes through a cornfield (and perhaps picks ears of corn) is not obliged to give a pledge to the hayward. Alf*G* 103 aptly cites *Dives et Pauper* 2:141, with its allusion to Mt 12:1–8, and Szittya 1986:270, 277 notes the phrase's special association with friars (for a standard discussion of the idea, see *ST* IIa–IIae, lxvi, a. 7, also a. 8 and q. lxxvii–viii). The implication of the parallel is that the Dreamer's harmless (if materially unproductive) mode of existence is like the errand-bearer's, in that he 'carries' the 'message of eternal life' to society by constantly writing about it. Thus he tacitly defends his poetic 'work' as partaking in Piers's cultivation of the field of Truth with the 'ploughshare of the tongue' (Barney 1973). The 'sleight' by which he 'comes to cloth' and 'drinks at a dish' is his *makynge*, the life of non-manual work that he defends in the Prelude to V. *dette*: i.e the 'debt' of sin. One in extremity who contravenes (positive) law to save his life does not sin if he takes only what he needs: so he does not 'owe' anyone anything. **11** *thre thynges*: these (food, drink, clothing) recall 1.20–4, where HC (like Need here) enjoins moderation in using gifts ordained by God *of his cortesye* 'bountifully' for the benefit of all (*in comune*). The burden of this timeless moral message concerning what are now called 'human rights' is that those who deny their fellow human beings these basic needs (whether through force, economic control, or law) are the ones who offend divine justice. **15** *synegeth*; *wynneth*: a 'Platonic' anti-pun signalled by the internal rhyme; for this kind of 'winning' is not a form of 'sinning'. **17** The personification generates a potent and paradoxical figure: a man reduced to dire need *has* no 'surety' in the usual sense. **18** *lawe of kynde*: perhaps with a dual reference, depending on whether the implied human subject of *wolde* is the needy man or other people. For it signifies both the natural instinct of self-preservation found in all creatures and the *lex naturalis*, the principles of moral reason forming part of man's nature as the image of God. **21** *Cardinale Vertues*: see on 21.275ff above. Need's claim is that temperance (unlike the other three virtues) intrinsically cannot be perverted, because one cannot by definition be too temperate. It is tacitly endorsed by the pragmatic Vicar in his not including temperance among the 'fayre vertues' that can be made to seem 'vises' (21.459); but it also recalls the idealists HC on *mesure* at 1.34–5 and Patience at B 14.74; and it is close to the teaching of Alan of Lille in *AP*: 'O what a glorious virtue is *temperance*, which makes virtue hold *the middle*, lest it should fall into *diminution* or develop into *excess*' (*PL* 210:162); cf. 27. Since Need's claim could arguably be extended to 'ideal' (as *rode*: not scripturally correct, the words being spoken to a scribe who asked to be Christ's disciple (Mt 8:20=Lk 9:58). But their appropriateness to Christ's ultimate 'poverty' on the cross may have licensed the misattribution, already found in the first version of Rolle's *Meditations on the Passion* (Horstman I, 1895:88), a work in the main 'affective' tradition. Also plainly recalled here is Mt 16:24, on 'bearing one's cross daily', and in a broader sense the Christian ascetic aspiration to 'crucify' every desire for worldly 'wele'. Need's speech draws not only on learned Bernardine-Franciscan devotional writing but on the vernacular tradition represented by Rolle, the C13th *Southern Passion* (1605ff) and the Harley 4196 text of the C14th *Northern Passion* (804ff); see Schmidt 1983²:174–96. **47** Thought and wording recall the paraphrase of Jn 16:20 at 12.211–12 but are also close to the 'Meditation A' (*De Passione secundum Ricardum*) ascribed to Rolle: 'it falleth to him that is grete to *suffre gret thinges* but soone thilke gret peynes shal be gone and after *shal ioye comme* withowten ende' (ed. Ogilvie-Thomson 65). **48** *abasched*: claiming on Christ's authority that the indigent should not feel shame or even embarrassment at their plight (as do the decent upright poor of 9.86–7). **48/9** The climactic identical rhyme imparts catechetical finality to Need's injunction. **49–50** The unparalleled extremity of divine love teaches all to endure their (comparatively) lesser privations, the crucified Saviour (1.167–9) being their 'example'. The thought here is close to that of a Latin passage ascribed to Augustine in the margin of Hoccleve's *Regement of Princes* 1079–85: 'Consider the Saviour's life from the time of his birth to his death on the cross, and you will find in it nothing save the marks of poverty'.

(i) 51–73 The *Eighth Vision* begins with Antichrist's siege of Unity. **53** *A(u)ntecrist*: see on 21.220. L here develops Mt 13:24–30, 39, with some influence from the early C13th French allegorical poem *Le Tournoiement d'Antéchrist* (Owen 1912:145–7; Jung 1971:268–89). His use of this figure lends a broadly 'apocalyptic' character to the attack on Unity, since Antichrist was thought of as a harbinger of the Second Coming of Christ; but no 'prophecy' of specific events need be intended. (On the 'apocalyptic' dimensions of the poem and their implications for its form see Bloomfield 1961). L's outlook seems closer to the 'reformist apocalypticism' described by Kerby-Fulton 1990 (recalling the reading of Frank 1968) than to the chiliastic 'end-time' apocalypticism of Emmerson (1981:193–203), which sees Antichrist's coming as ushering in the Last Judgement. **52** *mette ful merueylousely*: the introductory phrase to the final dream mirroring that of the first (Pr 9). **53–4** recall the eschatological imagery of Reason's speech at 5.120–2. *crop of treuthe*: as sown by Piers at 21.311; cf. 21.262. **55** *fals*: recalling (like *gyle* in 57) Meed's wooer in 2.42,

opposed to 'actual') justice, fortitude and prudence considered as each a 'mean' between extremes, and so as each a form of *mesure* (with all virtue being 'temperate' in its essence), his argument does not perforce entail 'depreciation of the other virtues' (*Pe*). **23–32** criticise the cardinal virtues other than temperance, here tacitly equated with Need and elevated in status as conducing to humility, which God himself displayed in the Incarnation. **23** *bi ver to*: 'by a long way comparable to'; cf. Conscience's comment on the primacy of Justice at 21.409. **25/6** The identical end-rhyme underlines the catechetical quality of the exposition. **29** scans as a macaronic Type IIIa with two lifts in *Iústicie* (cf. 21.477). *shal*: 'is constrained to'. **33** distinguishes between *insight* into the nature of things (true wisdom, a gift of the Spirit) and *foresight* about likely future outcomes (prudence), which can always prove mistaken. *ymaginacioun*: cf. 21.278–9. **33a** See on 11.308–9. **35–50** are marked by emphatic *traductio* of *need* and its derivatives over a dozen times. **35–7** The argument here echoes Patience's about the value of Poverty at 16.69–70. **35** *nexst hym*: cf. 18.98; because need removes any material obstacle between the soul and God. **36** *as*: '(is) as'. *louh...*: a comparison used in describing Dobet at 10.83. *pat*: '(of) that (which)'. **37** 'For of necessity Need makes the needy feel humble of heart'. **38** *Philosopheres*: such as Diogenes the Cynic (4th c. B.C.), cited as an authority on poverty in Chaucer's 'Former Age' 35, the 'wise men' who praise poverty at 12.143–5 and those mentioned at 12.175–8. Asceticism as the means to wisdom was central to such Christian 'ways' of holy living as the eremitic, the monastic and later the mendicant (cf. B 15.416–22). **40** *goestliche*: its position after the mid-line break favouring the sense 'really' (MED s.v. *gostli* adv 3(b)) rather than 'as a spirit' (ibid. 1 (c), citing this example); the stress is unequivocally on the physical truth of the Incarnation. **41** *nedy*: through abandoning his boundless 'wealth' as God for the limited condition of human existence. But on Christ's birth into a poor family, see 12.135–6, and on his praise of poverty 12.156–72; and for key scriptural texts on the special blessedness of 'the needy and the poor' cf. Pss 39:18, 40:2 and 68:30. **42** *the Boek...places*: the Gospels make little of Christ's personal poverty, but record his judgement of wealth as an obstacle to holiness in Mk 10:17–31. The desert of the Temptation is among those 'many different places' (taking the phrase as modifying *was* not *saith*) where his 'wilful' privation reached an extreme (Mt 4:1ff). **41–3** The inspiration for relating the idea of *paupertas Christi* to the cited Gospel text may be the pseudo-Bernardine *Vitis Mystica*: 'The king of kings... who alone lacked nothing...became so poor that, as he himself bears witness, he was found to be poorer than *the foxes...and the birds*...Poor in his birth, poorer in his life, poorest of all *upon the cross*' (PL 184:638–9). **43** *on...*

who was also 'a devil's offspring'. *sprynge and sprede*: echoing 13.23 and 16.242 on the growth and extension of goodness and holiness. *nedes*: not now the bare necessities Need spoke of but the unruly desires from which greed, envy and the other capital vices arise. **57** *growe*: the metaphor inverting positive earlier images of love and grace as plants (1.147, 13.22–3, 14.23ff, 17.47); after uprooting the virtues, Antichrist sows his own seeds of evil. *a god*: Antichrist's status as a false god depending on people's mistaking him for the representative of the true God. While no direct identification with a leader of the Church (such as the Anti-pope) is made, his strongest support is shockingly asserted to lie amongst clerics. Antichrist, Pride and *Lyf* (the diabolic, the worldly and the carnal) stand as an unholy trio set against Grace, Piers and Conscience, who signify heavenly, ecclesiastical and secular right order. **58** *Freres*: the most explicit condemnation of the 'corrupted' mendicants since the warning at Pr 56–65, which may now be seen as being fulfilled. *copes*: echoing the charge made as early as Pr 59 (and already in **Z**) of a kind of vain covetousnesss among them. **59** *religious*: used habitually by **L** for monks *as against* friars (see *IG* s.v.). **60** scans as a standard Type Ia line, reading *welcóme*. In this word, metrically necessary wrenching of stress occurs in five instances, normal accentuation on the first element in three (see *IG*). *tyraunt*: a word used earlier of False and his accomplices at 2.211 (another example of how the final vision 'recapitulates' the first). But the presentation here suggests the head of an invading army going about the country to raise support (69ff). **61** *foles*: the spiritually wise who are unwise in the sight of the world for not wishing to 'spede' through 'gyle'; see on B 7.125. **62–3** They find 'the shorter life the better' (15.262), while waiting for the promised end 'in longing to be hence' (21.249). The élite remnant of ascetic 'pilgrim-hermits' like those of Pr 25–30 may be envisaged. **63** *Leautee*: collectively standing for all (perhaps especially lay) people who live in accordance with *treuthe*; see on Pr 149. Friend of Holy Church, enemy of Mede, critic of the friars, Leautee vigorously affirms the right and duty to expose 'falsenesse and faytrye' (12.34) among clerics. **65** *þat* (1): an indefinite sg. for pl. 'those' understood. *mylde...holy*: without the sharp contrast between layman and religious contemplative intended at B 15.306–7 (revised in // **C**). **67** *hem*; *here*: i.e. 'false folk'. **68** *here*: i.e. 'these kings'. **69** *at*: 'serving under'. **70** The chief Deadly Sin holds 'pride of place' as his leader Antichrist's standard-bearer in the attack. **71** *a lord*: one like those favoured by Mede at 3.57 and perhaps to be identified with the 'lord of lust' of 21.385 and with *Lyf* at 143. **72–3** *kepar...gyour*: his rôle here seeming closer to a bishop's than a secular lord's, though his name permits equivocal reference with univocal sense.

(ii) 74–164 The *Defence of Unity* begins with Conscience

appealing to *Kynde* to help the Church (understood as co-extensive with all sincere believers) against what is now conceived more as a concerted onslaught by the forces of evil than as the individual's habitual yielding to weakness as in the Sins-sequence in Vision 2. **74** *foles*: Pauline irony, the worldly-unwise gladly adopting their enemies' mocking appellation. **75** repeats the invitation addressed to 'all Christians' at 21.359. The failure of *al þe comune* to answer the call to Unity may signify allegorically the ongoing dissension occasioned by the Schism, which in dividing the Church strengthens its enemies. **76** *crye... Kynde*: recalling the threat from *Princeps huius mundi* to the individual soul enclosed in the Castle of Caro at 10.134–6, though the Barn of Grace here is a purely spiritual organism and the threat to it collective. Conscience's 'cry' to Kynde (76) is less a direct request for punitive calamities than a forceful attempt (78), as in Reason's sermon at 5.114–22, to arouse men's instinctive dread of age, illness and 'the death of kind' (20.219) as a means of bringing them to repent of their sins. **77** The contemporary ordeal of the Church existentially recapitulates that of the early Christian community in the time of St Peter, its 'eschatological' dimension being something realised in everyday experience throughout every age. *Foles*: 'Fools that we are'. **79** *Beliales childrene*: human beings who have rejected God and embraced sin; see on 20.282. **80–7** distantly remember the approach of Death in the abandoned ending of **A** (A 12.62ff). This sequence also 'recapitulates' Piers's summoning of Hunger in 8.167–70, though here the instrument of chastisement is not famine but disease. **80** *Kynde Conscience*: juxtaposition of grammatical subject and object to bring out their closeness and suggest how men's moral sense is sharpened by taking proper account of mortality. KYNDE is the poem's 'nature-name' for God, author of endings as well as beginnings. *planetes*: an allusion to the notion of illnesses being influenced by planetary 'aspects' at birth, but also to that of a major malign conjunction as the origin of macrocosmic catastrophes (see on Saturn at 8.346). **81** *forreours*: because making preliminary inroads on the body in preparation for its demise; with this list of ailments cf. at 6.78–9. *feueres and fluxes*: suggesting a gastro-enteritic infection. **83** *radegoundes*: a disease (*gutta rosacea*) marked by inflammation and swellings (MED s.v. *red-gound* n). **L**'s spelling may suggest he thought that cure of the disease was sought through the particular intercession of St Radegund, the ascetic C6th abbess of Poitiers (*Sk*) who ministered to 'women covered with various kinds of leprous spots' (*LA* 953); but there is no direct evidence for this association. **84** *bocches*: implying in the light of B 13.250 plague-boils (*bubones*); the citation of this instance as figurative in MED s.v. *bocche* n. is wrong. **85** *Freneseyes*: attacks of delirium thought to be caused by an imbalance of the humours. *foule eueles*:

a recurrent set phrase (3.96, 16.136 and 21.46) possibly indicating a specific ailment, though there is no positive evidence for the 'epilepsy' suggested by MED s.v. *ivel* n. 5(b). **86** *Hadde*: '(Which) had'. **87** *a legioun*: the large figure for deaths evoking the aftermath of epidemic plague, when even survivors' resistance to lesser ailments was weakened by secondary infections. **89** *Deth*: see on A 12.63. L's DEATH says nothing but wreaks havoc on the population. The *Mors* who in Apoc 6:8 rides a pale horse was commonly interpreted as 'Plague', and in this quasi-apocalyptic context Death is perhaps meant as a version of the adversary *Mors* mastered by LIFE (Christ) in 20.67–9 (though the *Lyf* of 143 is very obviously to be distinguished from the latter). Iconographic representations of the Triumph of Death, a motif particularly popular in the early 15th c., are discussed in Tristram 1976:158–83. **91** *Conforte*: Lust's first line of defence against the approach of Death, who finds in his opposite number Old Age a foe with the power to lessen the efficacy (and attractiveness) of physical pleasure. **92** *alarme*: a military call to arms (< It *all'arme*); Kynde leads a counter-attack for Conscience against the forces of Antichrist, his officers being Elde and Death, his fighting-men the bodily ailments. *vch lyf*: 'everybody'. **93** *munstrals*: as if at a free tournament over open ground, a scene ironically illustrating how the Death who seemed to defeat Christ in a joust now sides with his Church against the sensual and proud. **95** *Elde*: the sombre figure first met at 11.190–4 (and perhaps recalled in Chaucer's Old Man of *CT* X. 713ff), whose warning to Will in the dream of Fortune is now realised; see also at 18.106ff. **96** *baner*: cf. 70, 91; if worldliness is essentially embodied in the 'lord' (= the Pride of Life), his adversary is Death, and the standard-bearers of the two hosts are respectively Comfort and Age. *bi riht*: as 'nearest' to Death; the task was an honourable one. **97** The violent ferocity of this scene, which draws on the imagery of the Book of the Apocalypse, recalls OT passages like that paraphrased at 3.416–24. *kyne*: the spelling, if original, supports annominative play on *kynne* 'kinds'. **98** *pokkes*: pustules of smallpox; distinguished from the large *bocche* of the pestilence. **99** *corupcions*: infectious diseases whose grim symptoms are a sign to the living to do penance in time. **100** Death is imagined as a mounted warrior whose single blow immediately strikes the enemy into the dust / into dust. The pregnant phrasing hints at the fulfilment of the warning in Gen 3:19 (*in pulverem reverteris*), which is used on Ash Wednesday in the rite of imposition of ashes. On the motif of the Triumph of Death in Europe in the half-century after the Black Death see the illustration of the fresco by Traini in the Camposanto at Pisa of *c.* 1350 (Meiss 1951: pl. 85). **101** echoes the imagery of the Dance of Death known to have been depicted in the Pardon Cloister at Old St Paul's. **103** *euene...euere*: 'Platonic' wordplay equating Death's blow with perma-

nent loss of control and movement. **104–5** *lady...duntes*: on this motif cf. such ME lyrics on the *Ubi sunt* theme as 'Where beth they...' (Brown *C XIII Lyrics*, no. 48). **106–9** intimate that the prayers of conscientious believers obtained an intermission of the diseases, enabling those whose sin had occasioned them (5.115–17) to repent. **106** *his*: with referent Kynde. **108** *priueyliche*: in the confessional; no humiliating public avowal is demanded. **109** *to se*: an infinitive either of purpose, 'to see (if) the people (would) amend' (cf. 107), or of cause, 'at seeing' (*MES* 536, citing B 2.117); but if the latter, not necessarily 'ironical' (*Sk*), since the 'few' might (initially) have repented.

110–64 *The Rallying of the Vices.* **110–13** The siege resumes with the reviving complacency (expressed in renewed dissipation) of those who have survived the disasters. The assault of these confident DEADLY SINS recapitulates in reverse their earlier avatars' repentance in Vision 2. **110** *Fortune*: here apparently a male character (unless *he* 111 is a B-Ø error for *heo*), whereas earlier Fortune was female, as commonly in medieval literature (see at 11.168ff, and Patch 1927). **111** *Lecherye*: also male, in contrast to Fortune's companion *Concupiscencia Carnis* at 11.179ff. **113** *greet oest*: that lechery is the commonest 'sin as of seven' was cheerily maintained by Mede at 3.58–60. **115** *priue*: ironically contrasting with 108. **116** *ydelnesse*: see on 21.229. **117** *bowe...arwes*: the traditional attributes of Cupid, classical god of desire (as in Chaucer *PF* 211–17, *RR* 923ff); but their presence in a military allegory is especially apt. **118** *fayre biheste*: recalling the arrow 'Faire-Semblaunt' carried by Cupid's squire in *RR* 963. *fals treuthe*: though the sense of *treuth* here is 'troth' or 'love-promise', the blunt oxymoron strikes home. **119** *vntidy tales*: 'louche gossip', the enemy less of ascetic holiness than of ordinary decency.

121–42 The lines on GREED recapitulate the extended account in Vision 2 (6.196–307), but with clear echoes of the Mede episode in Vision 1, esp. 3.77–127, and a heightened sense of this endemic vice's strength and persistence. **121–3** *Couetyse...Auarice*: for the distinction in sense, see at 6.196. **123** *hungriliche*: revealing how this special foe of Temperance is an inordinate desire that fails to satisfy; the poem's misers hoard without enjoying. **126** *Symonye*: see at 2.63. **127** A precise referent for this revision cannot be ascertained, but if Pope Urban VI (himself a reformer of prelatical excesses) is meant and if Antichrist *is* equated with the Antipope, then **L** may have in view attempts to bribe his opponents (for or against him). But at a more general level, the criticism seems directed against higher clerics who side with the *princeps huius mundi* in order to hang on to their wealth and status. **128** *temperaltee*: see on *spiritualte* at B 5.147. **129** *Kynges consail*: sometimes functioning as a final equitable court of appeal (see Kennedy 2003:179ff). **130**

knokked: a more explicit statement of what *kneled* **B** ironically implies (bespeaking corruption through the 'force' of bribery) and better in keeping tonally with *kene* 129, *baldeliche* 132 and the 'jousting' metaphor of 132–5. *Court*: the law courts, where conscientious testimony is vital for justice to flourish. **131** *Goed Faith*: at 10.148 one of the sons of Inwit (an avatar of Conscience) appointed to guard the soul 'till Kind come or send'. *Fals*: given the surname 'Faithless' at 2.42. *to abyde*: reversing his ignominious flight through 'dread' of strict justice at 2.220. The picture now is of a darkening world very different from the ideal society hoped for at the end of Vision 1. **132** *noble*: replacing the expected word *spere*; but the metaphor of money as a weapon against 'faith' or honesty here recalls 3.194. A sardonic pun here on the senses 'enlightened' for *brihte* and 'noble(man)' for *noble* (MED s.vv. a. 5(b)), n. (1) (a)) cannot be excluded. **133** *wit... Westminstre Halle*: metonymic for the senior justices of the King's Court, who sat there (see on 3.13). It is not implied that the money has been licitly spent on fees for the most learned counsel. **134** *iustice...iustede*: a trenchant 'Platonic' pun that hints at the ease with which judges can be 'borne down' by a heavy bribe. **135** *ouertulde*: a word appropriate to the allegorical context of jousting ('tilting'). *on amendement*: i.e. 'in payment for amending your judgement in my favour'. **136–7** recall 2.61–2. **136** *Arches*: metonymic for the appeal court of the Canterbury province held at St Mary le Bow Church in Cheapside (see on 2.61). **137** *Syuyle*; *Symonye*: see on 2.63. *Official*: see on B 2.174. **139** *Departen...come*: alluding to the marriage vows pledging 'good faith' for life: 'to have and to hold from this day forward...till death do us part'. *deuors*: the assumption being that the Official will falsify the grounds (e.g. consanguinity) of the annulment (see on B 2.176). **141** *were Cristene*: so that his power could be turned to good use instead of bad.

(iii) 143–82; 183–211 The LIFE episode, seamlessly joined with that of the Dreamer's encounter with ELDE (183–211), brings out Will's inescapable Haukyn-like involvement in the Sins until the point where he renounces them for the narrow way into Unity. **143** *dagge*: a sign of worldly vanity to contemporary moralists, who criticised 'the cost of...the degise endentynge...and...*daggynge* of sheres' because 'the moore that clooth is wasted, the moore moot it coste to the peple for the scarsnesse' (*CT* X 416–18). **145** *wastour*: 'idle good-for-nothing'. **146** *Lyare*: earlier encountered at 2.9 as a companion of False. The contrast may be simply between 'bond' and 'free', but as with all the terms used by Lyf, their values are reversed morally, a licence to sin being called 'freedom' and a willing acceptance of the moral law 'bondage'. **147** *folye*: a term willingly accepted by Conscience and his followers at 61 that sums up how spiritual values appear to the worldly wise. **150b** recalls 21.193, with its

reference to the *Parousia*, the Second Coming of Christ. It is not necessarily implied that the end-time has come, but rather that when it does, it will be like this, so that Kynde's action in the Plague is to be interpreted prophetically as an apocalyptic sign of the Last Days. **151** *saue... one*: not of course an explicit affirmation that all conscientious Christians will escape death, but its eschatological character confirmed by its echoing a statement in I Thess 4:16 that at the Parousia the just will be taken alive into heaven. The moral point is uppermost: that since the hour of Christ's Second Coming is unknown, believers must stand prepared at all hours. **152** describes Lyf's act as resembling that of a military leader halting in his advance to pick up a prostitute. **153** *Hele*: good health and the sense of well-being that comes with it (cf. the Dreamer at 5.7, 10). *heynesse of herte*: the vice rejected by Purnel Proudheart at 6.8. The present protagonists deliberately reverse the repentance of the Deadly Sins in Vision 2. **155** *forȝete ȝowthe*: either 'forget that you are no longer young' or 'forget the sins of your youth' (which should be repented in age before the onset of death); see *TN* further. **156** *Fortune*: here female again (cf. 110 above). The emblem of both sensuality (11.168) and of transience (15.5), Fortune's treacherousness is shown in her using Lyf's short respite from death to distract him from repentance. **157–8** allegorise the genesis of a particular deadly sin from the union of natural vitality and thoughtless surrender to sensuality. **159** could scan on *w* but (given the metrical stress on *was* in 158) is probably to be read as an extended Type III line with counterpoint (*abb / ax*). The repetition of this pattern at B 163 may have prompted revision in C. **160** *Wanhope*: somewhat surprisingly a woman here (having been male at 11.198); but 'marrying a punk' seems appropriate enough as an act of desperation or sheer sloth. **160b** The echo of 21.438b is ironic, given the name of this 'wench'. **162** *Tomme Twotonge*: the antithesis of Tomme *Trewe*-tonge (Reason's servant at 4.18), and standing for a class found hopelessly corrupt at every appearance. For the origin of the name, cf. the statement in Ecclus 5:11 that 'omnis peccator probatur in *duplici lingua*'. *ateynt*: possibly 'convicted...for perjury or...false verdict' (AlfG); but as such conviction would have put an abrupt stop to Tom's career, 'corrupt, perjurious [but *not* found out]' (MED s.v. *atteynen* v. 3 (b)) seems likelier. **163–4** Though the siege-engine is large, the distance it could hurl projectiles is somewhat exaggerated. **167** *good hope*: like the *wel hope* of 7.113, based on good deeds done in life and the positive expectation of forgiveness arising from these. The situation of Lyf here is that described by the Samaritan at 19.291–3. *hym*: with double referent, 'eld' being the state in which both 'hopes', one prompting to, the other away from confession, conflict. The allegory depicts the subject rejecting the temptations (especially sexual) that distract the old, despite illness and impotence, from preparing well for their coming death. **169** *Fisyk*: on this avaricious and cynical figure see at 8.291. **172** *glasene houe*: a proverbial phrase (Whiting H624); cf. MED s.v. *houue* n. (c) citing from *c.* 1300 'Þ[ou] madest me an houue of glas', and *TC* 5.469. The physicians' nostrums do not protect against danger, but may even increase it. **173** *lechecraft*: an untrustworthy physic, to be contrasted with the sober way of life recommended by Hunger at 8.270ff and the true (spiritual) healing offered by Christ at 18.138–45. **174** *dyaes*: from Gk διά 'through, made of', and standing for 'a drug made of (some specified ingredient' (cf. *diapenidion* at B 5.122); the first recorded use of the prefix as an independent noun. Lyf's material weapon ('drugs') is used against Elde's spiritual weapon ('good hope'). **175** has a complex metrical pattern *aab* / [a]*ba*, settting Elde's vocalic sounds against the liquids associated with Lyf. **176–7** *fisician...aftur*: poetic justice in the light of 8.291–6 (this physician cannot heal himself), and ironically echoing 18.161. **180** *in...hente*: 'expecting better fortune on the basis of his [present] good health, he plucked up courage'.

183–211 *Will's Encounter with Elde.* **183** *myn heued*: the Dreamer-Persona's startling reference to his own body bringing him into the forefront of the narrative. On *Elde* as a figure who urges repentance and warns of approaching death, see Burrow 1981. *ʒede*: the result of Elde's riding over the supine Dreamer being to leave him bald. **186** *vnhende ...the*: 'may discourtesy go / may [it] go discourteously with you'; *vnhende* is either an (unparalleled) nominal form of the adj (*Sk*) or the adv (MED s.v.). **189** *leue*: the repetition from 188 putting it beyond doubt that this is the same word, and not *leef* 'dear' (*Sk*). **190** Use of Leonine rhyme here anticipates the 'Goliardic' flavour of the following passage on Will's impotence. **191** *boffeded...wangteeth*: recalling Hunger's treatment of Waster and the Breton at 8.173–5. **193–8** A possible source of this ruefully mock-ironic passage is Walter Map's *Golias de conjuge non ducenda* 149–56: 'Omnem suscipiet virago masculum / omnemque subdita vincit testiculum. / Quis potest conjugis implere vasculum? / nam una mulier fatigat populum. / Insatiabilis vulva non deficit, / nec unam feminam vir unus reficit; / iccirco mulier se multis subjicit, / et adhuc sitiens non dicit *sufficit*' (Wright 1841:83). **193** *reuthe*: the tone of the next line showing the 'sorrow' to be chiefly on her own account. **194** *in heuene*: so that she could marry someone younger and more virile. **195** *fele*: on its sexual sense cf. 20.131. **196** *a nyhtes...naked*: the usual custom being to sleep wearing no night-clothes. **197** *maken...wille*: cf. B 2.148 above. **198** *Elde and heo*: more clerkly anti-feminism, implying that she is partly responsible for his condition. **199–203** are reminiscent of *CT* VI 720–38; 'the death of kind' would be a welcome relief from the 'care' of decrepit age.

201–11 The *Dreamer's dialogue with Kynde* concludes his encounters with figures of divine authority (Holy Church, Reason and Piers / Liberum Arbitrium in Visions 1, 3 and 5). His interlocutor's message is (unsurprisingly) to take refuge within the Church, the *schola amoris*, as the best place in which to 'learn to love'. **203–4** *Awreke*: 'heavenly vengeance' upon the body's enemy, age, properly taking the form of spiritual preparation for death. The Dreamer has learnt from 'worldly' experience what the ascetics of 21.249 made their deliberate choice in life. **205** *sende for the*: echoing 10.150; the messenger that Kynde will send is Death, now conceived more positively than as first at A 12.81–7. **206** *ar...thennes*: before the time of death. **207–9** This crucial interchange, which contains the germ of such later allegorical dramas as *Everyman*, serves to set in perpective the temporal skills and qualifications that will not help man 'in his most need'. The 'best craft' here is not distinct from the one commended by Christ to Mary 'Magdalen' at 12.142*a* above, since spiritual poverty or disengagement from worldly concerns is the ideal condition for learning the craft of love. **207–8** *beste...alle othere*: recalling Patience's '*Dilige*, and Dobest' at B 13.139. **210–11** echo Patience's promise at 15.159–66 that perfected love of God and neighbour (the craft of charity 'mastered') overcomes such fears as those about bodily necessities.

(iv) 212–27 *The Resumption of the Siege.* **212** *conseil of Kynde*: the divine voice communicating to the soul through the medium of ordinary human experience, which awakens the conscience to a sense of the need for repentance. **213** *Vnite*: here a 'nature-name' for the 'church of charity' in the heart, the state of spiritual union with God through confession followed by holy communion and the entry on a renewed life of active virtue. **214** *constable*: the same office in the Church community as INWIT performs in the soul of the individual Christian at 10.143ff. **215** *geauntes*: the Seven Deadly Sins. Though the term was used of Christ in his assault on Hell, the proverbial reputation of 'giants' was for wickedness. Alan of Lille's *Distinctiones* (*PL* 210:803) relates them to the *obstinati*, citing Job 26:5 'Gigantes gemunt sub aquis'; and the Wycliffite Bible gloss on Prov 21:16 understands *gigantum* as 'of men yuele rulid, ether of fendis' (MED s.v. *geaunt* n. & adj. 1(b)). The image may distantly echo the siege of Thebes by seven giants or that of heaven by the giants in *Boece* III Pr 12:144. **216** *helden aʒeyn*: 'stood in support (of A.) against'. **218** *prestes*: corrupt clerics, first seculars then religious, exemplars of both sloth and greed. **219** recalls the description of a worldly priest at B 15.121–7 (a passage removed at that point in revision), such attire emblematising lust and vanity. *paltokes*: unsuitable dress for one who should wear the clerk's 'long clothes' (5.41). These short jackets of fine cloth such as satin, usually worn with hose, are like the *hayneselyns*

attacked by Chaucer's Parson 'that thurgh hire shortnesse
ne covere nat the shameful membres of man, to wikkede
entente' (*CT* X 421). *pissares*: 'cocky swaggerers', their
knives probably of the type mentioned at B 15.124 (see
TN for defence of this reading and fuller explanation of
the phrase). **221** Swearing by Mary is common in *PP*,
but the oath with the definite article is paralleled only in
the phrase 'by þe Marie of heuene' at B 4.179. *march of
Ireland*: presumably a byword for bibulous uncouthness.
Satiric comment on Irish priests is found as early as *The
Owl and the Nightingale* 322 from the late 12th century.
222 *cache suluer*: i.e. for saying religious services (cf.
B 15.126–7). **223** *Then...ale*: 'at no more than the price
of a drink'. **225–6** The image of 'great oaths' like those
here and in the text cited by *Sk* (*WSEW* 3: 332) as sharp
weapons tearing the body of Christ was a homiletic com-
monplace, as in *CT* VI 472–5. **226** *nayles*: those used to
crucify Jesus. **227** *holynesse*: at 21.383 the water in the
moat, but here loosely understood as part of the barn's
outer defence-works.

228–41 *Conscience's summons of help: Nede.* **228** The
summons to *Clergie*, personification of the sacred learn-
ing that enables secular clerics to discharge their duties
properly, is answered (in their absence) by the chief
contemporary exponents of such learning, the friars,
who were not slow to 'preuen inparfit prelates of Holy
Churche' (6.119). The passage seems to imply that the
educational shortcomings of 'ydiotes preestes' (B 11.316)
after the Plague (see at Pr 82) contributed to the success
of the (highly educated) mendicants. **231** *crafte*: the one
referred to at 207 and at 250–2 (cf. B 15.422–2, a pas-
sage removed in revision). **232** *Nede*: a figure ironically
well-fitted to voice the discrepancy between the friars'
profession and their practice (see the headnote; for the
phrasing, see at 4). **233** *cure of soules*: presumably not
full responsibility for parishes; but their superior preach-
ing often prompted their hearers to make their confes-
sions to the friars, with the consequences foreseen at
56–65 (for an earlier account of the antagonism between
parochial clergy and mendicants removed in revision cf.
B 5.137–50). Need's remarks have been found to echo
not only the anti-mendicant criticisms of such as Fitz-
ralph, but also points made within the internal Fran-
ciscan reformist tradition (Clopper 1990). **235** *to fare
wel*: because they are as worldly as other clerics, but
desire the reputation for holiness that goes with a habit
of ascetic poverty. *folk...riche*: cf. B 5.137–9. **237** The
a-half's assertion that friars should eat their chosen 'food'
of poverty ominously echoes Righteousness's words at
20.205. **239–41** reject the argument that 'since friars flat-
ter because of their poverty, they would not flatter if they
were not poor', maintaining instead (on the basis of their
having freely chosen poverty) that 'since those who must
beg from poverty lie the more readily to avoid its dis-

comforts, let them live like beggars or, having renounced
material happiness, like the angels'. While initially he
turns down the friars' help (231), this proves unacceptable
to the magnanimous knight Conscience; but events prove
his trust misplaced. **239** *he þat laboreth*: the seculars, the
monks or laypeople; but reference to the latter seems con-
textually inappropriate. **240** *forsoke*: according to the rule
of Francis and Dominic, who followed the example of
the 'holy hermits' (9.201–2). **241** *angeles fode*: a phrase
used of the Eucharist (*panis angelicus*), or as a proleptic
metonym for Christ, as in the 'panem angelorum qui de
coelo descendit' of the *Vitis Mystica* (*PL* 184:646). But
its likeliest referent here should be 'loue and lele byleue'
(17.21–2), eked out (as by Mary Magdalen) with roots
and water. Need's assumption is that if the friars trusted
in God alone, he would not leave them without food (cf.
the 'authorial' attack on *beggarie* at 9.162–5, citing Pss
36:25 and 30:11b).

243–72 *Conscience's admission of the Friars into Unity*,
though guarded by qualifications that go some way to
meet Need's misgivings, is shown to be an error. This is
some measure of the poet's disillusionment with their
pretensions to evangelical charity and zeal. **243** *cortey-
sliche*: recalling the Knight at 8.161 rather than Con-
science's own earlier, less tolerant self in the First Vision
(3.155). *calde...freres*: allegorically representing the his-
torical welcome given the mendicants by popes, kings
and nobility into the formal structure of the Church, espe-
cially after 1256, when the dispute about the friars' posi-
tion was settled in their favour by Alexander IV. **246** *in
vnite*: a polysemous phrase meaning 'in a state of [spirit-
ual] unity with the whole Church, between your order and
other orders, and within your own order'. The admoni-
tion alludes to rivalries between seculars and mendicants;
between Franciscan and Dominican styles of theology
and mission; and within the Franciscan order itself *c.*
1370, when the Observants insisted on poverty and the
Conventuals accepted property and papal privileges. Con-
science's sympathies lie with the former, to judge by his
exhortation, but this seems contradicted by 384 below.
249 The third of these *necessaries*, possessing a place to
live (something implied by HC's *vesture* at 1.24), was
what most troubled rigorous interpreters of evangelical
poverty (cf. B 15.325–30). **250** repeats Kynde's advice
to Will at 208 and so would appear to be authoritative.
The command (*lerneth*) is not part of the condition (*leue*)
but follows it separately. *logic*: perhaps with the wider
sense 'philosophy' (as at 14.190). But Conscience's re-
quirement that they give up this discipline may allude to
the fact that its greatest C14th masters were indeed fri-
ars, like the Franciscan William of Ockham (who how-
ever supported the rigorists against Pope John XXII on
the question of poverty). The contextual implication is
that such study is at odds with the practice of charity,

though the overt criticism of logic by Trajan at B 11.218–29 (which the B-Text here would be echoing) has been removed in revision. **251–2** Francis of Assisi renounced his family wealth, but not study, as he was never himself a student; and while the young Dominic sold his books to help the poor during a famine, he also authorised the founding of a *schola* for his friars attached to the University of Paris in 1217, one that proved of major importance to the development of theology. Conscience's stance (which resembles St Bernard's towards Abelard in the 12th c.) is one of opposition to the university mendicants' deep involvement in theological debates, which Anima / Liberum Arbitrium denounces as undermining the faith (B 15 70–2=C 16.228–30). **253** *coueiteth cure*: a piece of ironic wordplay, Conscience at once warning the friars against desiring pastoral responsibility and recommending restraint as the 'cure' for the over-recruitment consequent upon their success as preachers. **254** *mesure*: understood as 'a rule of reason that limits', in accord with a correct judgement of the 'proper' number of any class of entitites, natural or human. **255** *hit*: the implied referent being 'all created things'. *serteyne...syker*: the notion that the number of every class of being should be fixed and determinate stemming from a view of the creator as a 'cosmic architect' who allows no arbitrary alteration or excess. **256a** '[Praise ye the Lord...] who telleth the number of the stars: [and calleth them all by their names]' (Ps 146:4). **262** scans as IIIc or as Ie with cross-caesural counterpoint on *b*. **266** refers back to the two categories mentioned, soldiers and monastics. *lawe*: the relation of numerical limit with equity is discussed by John of Salisbury, *Metalogicon* 2:20. **267** *A...certeyne*: 'A definite number for a definite purpose'. **268** *kynde wit*: 'simple common sense'. **269/70** Identical end-rhyme imparts a catechetical tone to the speech, which concludes with the eighth repetition of the keyword 'number' in ll. 253–72. **269** *wage*: plainly figurative, since friars were no more paid wages than were monks. *wexeth*: a reflex of their growing numbers. Although the mendicants in England formed, at some 2000, perhaps only a third of the regular clergy (Swanson 1989:83), their presence in towns would have made them much more 'visible' than the monks, who remained in their monasteries. **270** *euene*: apparently the earliest instance of this sense, but not cited in MED s.v. *even* adj. 5. The allusion is doubtless to the notion in Apoc 7:4 that there is a fixed (and 'even') number of the blessed, the homophony with *heuen* providing some noteworthy 'Platonic' wordplay. *withoute nombre*: not specifically mentioned in Scripture, but expected far to exceed that of the elect. In the 'darkness and dread' of hell, where there was *nullus ordo* (Job 10:22), the number of the damned would be impossible to count. **271–2** The source of Conscience's worry is that (unlike the monks') the mendicants' total number, being hard to discover, has

'no order'. The nature of the friars' mission meant that at any given time not all members of a convent would be resident, so no 'natural' limit was imposed on them by the number of religious houses available. According to the Biblical and neo-Platonic notions of *nombres proporcionables* (Wisd 11:21, *Boece* III m. 9, 18–19; Chadwick 1981:75, 234), 'limitlessness' would be interpreted as a sign of chaos and evil.

273–6 *Enuye*: not yet encountered among Antichrist's host at 215ff, but the 'giant' identified by Conscience (246) as the mendicants' special vice and the root both of their desire for influence and their resentment of the possessioners' advantages. *scole*: the friars' quest for pre-eminence in the university (cf. 250) here being traced to the vice ('enmity' or 'hatred' as well as 'envy') most directly opposed to love. **274** *lawe*: Canon Law, which with logic was unfavourably contrasted by Trajan with the 'law of love' at B 11.227. *contemplacioun*: 'consideracioun or speculacioun in þe resoun' (MED s.v. 2(a), citing Pecock), the present use ironically conjuring up by way of a polysemantic 'anti-pun' the commoner sense 'meditation on things divine' specified as the goal of 'monks and monyals' at 18.74. **275** *of*; *by*: 'out of / about'; 'by reference to'. Neither philosopher (see on 11.120 and 16.141a) taught pure communism, though Plato (*Republic* III 416e) restricted his Guardians' property to the 'necessaries', while Seneca (Ep. IX 3) held that greed had destroyed the Golden Age, when possession was believed to have been shared (cf. Chaucer, *Former Age* 5–15). The doctrine of primeval common ownership was attributed by Froissart to John Ball, a leader of the Peasants' Revolt (*Chronicles*, tr. Berners 1913:251), who was not unsympathetic to the mendicants (McKisack 1959:421); but such ideas have not been found in their extant sermons (Owst 1961:288).

277–94 form a narratorial interjection reminiscent of Will's outburst at 15.105, though less clearly distinguishable from the 'authorial' voice. **277** *lewed*: the friars' popularity with 'lewed peple' (B 15.70–2) making their excursions into novel social doctrine (like John Ball's) seem to the authorities a threat to the existing order. **278** *Moyses hit tauhte*: 'taught it to Moses / Moses taught it'. **278a** 'Thou shalt not covet thy neighbour's goods' (Ex 20:17); cited as a maxim of canon law (Alf*Q*) in Richard Fitzralph's polemic against the friars' claims to jurisdiction (Scase 1989:24–31). **280** *euele...yholde*: inasmuch as the people themselves enable the friar-confessors to 'covet' (successfully) the parson's 'goods' (his parishioners). **281–7** The syntax is somewhat loose but the sense is clear enough: shame (as commonly at this time) is seen as an integral part of the penitential process, and flight from it to the anonymity of a friar-confessor as undermining the moral influence of the sacrament. **282** *curatours*: whose task is to 'take care of' souls (by 'knowing' their condition) and to 'heal' them by absolution; see 14.70, 326–7 below, and cf. MED s.v. *curen* v. 2, 3(a). **283** scans cognatively as a standard Ia line on |b| |p| / |p|. **285** *Westmynstre*: metonymic for the royal courts of justice, where the suitors pretend to take the money under colour of pursuing a legal claim, only to squander it while asking for repayment to be waived or postponed. But an insincere confession to the friars, it is intimated, will no more remit sin than a misspent loan will settle an outstanding suit at law. There may be an allusion here to the abuse of the Westminster Sanctuary by debtors fleeing their creditors, with an echo of the 1378 statute governing its use (Baldwin 1982:106–8). **288** *be bifore*: 'be quick to make the most of it'. **290–4** claim that jurymen and executors purchase absolution and intercessory prayers from their friar-confessors with some of the misappropriated money, while they spend the rest on themselves. **294** *soffren...dette*: i.e. by not disbursing what the deceased bequeathed for charitable purposes in order to make satisfaction for their sins and shorten their time in purgatory.

295–324 *The Crisis of Contrition.* **296** *to...scole*: 'made provision for friars to study philosophy at the university'. Some of these contemporary friar-philosophers are discussed in Leff 1958:279–94 and Coleman 1981:151–8. **298** scans vocalically as a Type IIa line with a 'supplemental' stave in position five (see *Intro.* IV § 45), *In* 'within', 'inside', having full sentence-stress. **299** *Pees*: an appropriate gate-keeper, able to neutralise the harm of scandal-mongers and malicious gossips; but one whose eirenic posture proves vulnerable to a flatterer's subtle address. **302** *at þe ȝate*: the significance of Hypocrisy's closeness to the entrance of the Church being that he wounds those whose task is to form the conscience of the Christians within (cf.16.263–9). **303** For the phrasing cf. *WPal* 1218. **305–24** The Confession Crisis occurs when the sinners, represented by Lechery, recoil from the severe formal penance (figured as a biting treatment applied by a doctor) that their confessors enjoin. **305** *leche*: the old native word (repeated by Conscience at 319), carrying overtones of the necessarily painful nature of sincere shrift, but also echoing the metaphor as used of Christ in 18.138ff (see St-Jacques 1991). **307** contains a strikingly mimetic a-half with clashing stresses and falling rhythm in the third lift: ′′′ ˋ. **308** On the scansion see *TN*. **309** *redde...*: see on 21.188. **311** *Yf*: 'to find if'. *in the sege*: 'present at the siege' (so at 314), i.e. outside the barn, since 'Lyf' is within it. Paradoxical as it might seem (at the literal level) to seek medical help from amongst those *outside* Unity, at the allegorical a distinction is being drawn between the occupants of the Barn ('fools' vowed to holiness, including virtuous examples of the parish clergy) and those outside (who should be opposed to the besiegers but are soon discovered to be of their part). Lyf belongs with the former only inasmuch as

during Lent his thoughts turn customarily to changing his ways (he becomes a 'seasonal fool'). But like Lady Mede (who got 'easy penance' from a friar), he is a pliable character, always looking for a painless remedy. *softur*: on the adverbial use of the adj. here and at 315 see *MES* 315–16. **313** *fastyng...Fryday*: a usual, fairly mild penance for sins of the flesh, given to Gluttony at 6.351 and to Lechery at 6.174. Because of the link commonly perceived between 'thise two synnes...so ny cosyns' (*CT* X 836), fasting was deemed a fitting discipline for the irregular motions of the flesh, especially during Lent. *deye*: cf. 6.129 on the difficulty some felt in doing bodily penance. **314** *can*: 'knows how to'; the verb also (as 'know') directly governs *fysyk*. **315** *more*: 'knows more'. *fayror*: i.e. than Shrift. The allusion is to the confessional expertise of the friars, whose preaching had much increased use of this unpopular sacrament; cf. Bonaventure's 'Quare fratres minores praedicent et confessiones audiant' (*Op. om.* 8:375–83). **316** That 'Lyf / Lechery' should be unaware of (or indifferent to) the true nature of someone named *Flatrere* makes good allegorical sense; but the similar ignorance of Contrition and his 'cousin' Conscience (358) may hint that a 'blind-spot' of the pious gentry was susceptibility to the winning address of highly-educated mendicants. *is*: '(who) is (both)'; on 'non-expression of the subject pronoun' (Ø-relative clauses), see *MES* 204–5, which notes it as especially common in poetry. *fiscicien and surgien*: able to treat both diseases and wounds, and thus supposedly a complete master of the healing art (penitential theology and its practical application). The deeply ironic echo of 18.140–1 seems unmistakable. **317** *Contricion*: here personifying the important prior stage of penance; but his unawareness that a flatterer is hardly the right person to cure hypocrisy is disturbing. **319–21** The vehemently stressed negatives underline that the existing penitential system provides adequately for the confession and release of even the gravest sins (like incest, sacrilege and murder); friars, it is implied, can offer nothing further. **321** *Piers...alle*: the Pope as the ultimate recourse of the excommunicate, able to override any lower authority's decision to withhold absolution. **322** 'And may grant full remission, unless prevented by a refusal to make due satisfaction'. *dette*: see on 21.191; the internal rhyme emphasises how the only true obstacle to forgiveness lies in the will of the sinner. **323–4** The tone of these lines is as unclear as Conscience's apparent *volte-face*, some word like 'however' needing to be understood, along with his supposition that *any* kind of confession might be better than complete avoidance of sacramental penance. *soffre*: a word ambiguously echoing both the divine tolerance of 13.198–200 and the *vnsittynge suffraunce* of 3.207. Just as Conscience's earlier stiff opposition to Mede at 3.155–6 was modified by a concession at 4.4–5, so here his declaration of principle is undermined by the *hendenesse* that is always willing to find good even in one suspected of being untrustworthy. At the plane of personal allegory, it seems suggested, an individual's moral faculty can make wrong concrete judgements if the 'rede' of right Reason is weakened. The passage is obscure, but the reader may be intended to recall Christ's mysterious 'suffrance' of Judas's treachery as recounted in Jn 13:27. For a general discussion of Conscience see Jenkins 1969:124–42, and on the problem of his admission of Friar Flatterer, Simpson 1990:241–2 and Harwood 1992:136.

325–54 *The arrival of Friar Flatterer.* **325–30** describe how the Friar obtains, from a local magnate who knows him, a letter of recommendation to the ordinary for the right to hear confessions within his diocese (the latter's consent may obliquely imply some obligation to the lord for his own position). For an analysis of the following scene see Schmidt 1983:161–83. **326–7** *curen...curatour*: 'to heal like / exercise the powers of'. The polysemantic wordplay brings out L's sense of a theological as well as lexical link between the priest's ministry of spiritual healing and possession of the temporal rights that go with his office. **331** This rôle of Peace is foreshadowed in Eph 4:3, where Paul exhorts 'to keep the *unity* of the Spirit in the bond of *peace*'. **333** *profyt*: a term (distantly echoing Pr 57) the ambiguity of which is disguised by its association here with the positive idea of health. **336** *yf thei*: either 'for them to' (*hard* = 'difficult') or 'if they are to' (*hard* = 'painful'). **338** On a general plane, the claim to acquaintance with Conscience acknowledges the fact that scrupulous penitents *were* attracted to mendicant confessors and found them (at some point) helpful. On the more direct level of the poem's 'action', it finds support from 15.31, possible evidence that this 'knight' is one who regularly 'welcomes' friars at his table. Friar Flatterer may even be meant to be associated with the Doctor of Divinity's silent 'man' (he too has a *felawe*). *and...bothe*: possibly implying that as a knight who may have inflicted injuries in war, Conscience has himself benefited from this or some other friar's 'salves' in confession. **341** *felawe*: see on 10.8, 12.19. *Penetrans-domos*: 'Piercer-of-homes', alluding to the text 'in novissimis diebus...erunt homines...habentes speciem quidem pietatis...ex his enim sunt qui *penetrant domos*, et captivas ducunt mulierculas oneratas peccatis, quae ducuntur variis desideriis...' (II Tim 3:1–6). The Pauline text was commonly invoked in writings against the friars (Scase 1989:32–9), and in 1255 the secular master William of St-Amour's polemical tract on 'The Perils of the Last Days' accused them of breaking into the *domus conscientiae* 'the dwelling of conscience' (Szittya 1986:305). But the context, the evocation of 'foolish women' (like Lady Mede) and the metonymic symbolism of *oute* at 347 below make it hard to doubt the presence of 'clerkly' sexual innuendo in the phrase. **342–3** *fisyk*; *craft*: contrasting 'theoretical knowledge of penitential

theology' like that of the Franciscan friar at 10.30ff and 'effective practical skill in dealing with penitents' like that of Chaucer's Parson (*CT* I 515–23). **345** *thus ycoped*: i.e. under a similar guise as a confessor (and cf. Pr 61 for an instance of a literal reference). **346** *leche*: '(spiritual) physician'; but in context the *annominatio* with *lechour* seems unavoidable (see Schmidt 1983:143–4). *oute*: 'not at home', thus leaving 'my lady' and 'our women' exposed to the fraternal attentions of Flatterer Prickhouse. **348** *salued*: presumably the verb *salven* 'treat with medicaments' (as at 306), though if it were *salúen* 'greet' (not found elsewhere in *PP*) the satire would be no less pungent (ibid.141–3). *so*: 'in such a way', 'to such a degree' (MED s.v. 1a (a), 8 (a)). **349** *Hende-Speche*: another attribute of the graciously-disposed knight Conscience, personifying the courtesy obligatory for Christians (16.242–3). Unhappily, it admits the persuasive friar possessed of the same quality (*thorw* 355) when the suspicious roughness of Peace might have been preferable. **350** *make...chiere*: 'greet them with a smile'. **351** *here here*: i.e. in confession; understand 'such things as may, perchance, bring it about that...' **352–3** *Couetyse...Pruyde*: two of the other sins (along with Lechery and Sloth at 156–66) most incident to him. The speaker's hope is that the friar's example of voluntary poverty will inspire Lyf to renounce luxurious indulgence. **353** *be adrad of Deth*: like the Dreamer at 200 and in contrast to Fortune, who makes Lyf's survival of the Plague grounds for thinking he might 'drive away Death' (174), like 'this wreches of this world' of 11.63–4 (lines anticipating the present scene). **354** *acorde...oper*: echoing the King's attempt at 4.2–3 to reconcile Conscience with Mede.

355–73 355 *thorw*: 'by means of'; with its dual referent ambiguously suggesting that the 'entry' is effected through the mutual courtesy of the friar and the knight, who forgets his experience of mendicants at the dinner in Passus XV (the important lines B 13.191–2 having however been removed in revision, the link becomes 'intertextual' rather than 'intratextual'). A parallel to the friar's admission has been found in Prudentius's *Psychomachia* 667ff (Barney 1979:82–104). **357** *welcóme*: stressed as in 15.31. **358** *cosyn*: an allegorical relationship, recalling that of Study and Clergy, which might be expected to be less indirect, with conscience as the *parent* of contrition. **359** *Conforte*: though innocently intended, replete with unconsciously ironic resonances of Lyf's house of revelry at 182, as is confirmed by its appearance at 372. **359/60** The 'rich' rhyme here would seem to hint at desperation more than determination. **360** *plastres*: the penances, some perhaps literally physical (like fasting, or the hairshirt of Purnel at 6.6–7). **361** *lat*: '(he) lets'; on 'non-expression of the 3rd person subject pronoun' see *MES* 138–42. **362** *Lente to Lente*: the severity of the penances being evident from their allowing no respite even for the festive seasons. **363**

ouerlonge: the Friar's echo of Conscience's own criticism hinting at a tacit complicity in the relaxation of austerity that the latter favours. *amenden*: another 'innocent' word with unfortunate overtones of venality (cf. 135). **364** *gropeþ*: a word equivocally referring to the surgeon's and the confessor's intimate examination. **365–8** The Friar's promise to Contrition recalls that of Lady Mede's confessor at 3.38–44. 'Payment' purchasing the intercessory prayers of his convent will take the place of the arduous penances imposed by the parish priest and, it is implied, permit Contrition to share in the complacent delusions of Lyf (whose spiritual self he signifies). *payement...preye*: the internal rhyme associating material and spiritual realms in an audibly *vnsyttinge* manner. **366** *holde to*: 'obliged to (pray for)'; an 'offer that cannot be refused'. **367–8** Friar Flatterer undertakes to include Contrition and his lady in the prayers offered by the whole convent for those who have membership in it. *fraternite*: see on 3.54. **368** *a litel suluer*: how little is not clear, but it seems that this friar is not asking (like his predecessor and avatar in Vision 1), a major benefaction for a 'perpetual licence' to go on sinning, so much as a 'sweetener' for his good offices in formally mitigating the penitent's obligations. Unlike Mede's substantial gift recorded in window-glass, this 'payment' will be a secret between Contrition and Sir *Penetrans*. **369** *gedereth*: suggesting a large-scale operation that takes the friars right through society, commuting strict canonical penances in return for payment. *gloseth*: cleverly interpreting Contrition's sins (along the lines that Mede suggested finds support in 'books' at 3.59) as less grave than they were judged by his customary 'penitencer' (22.320). **370–1** *crye...wake*: austerities like those espoused by Piers at B 7.120–24*a*, endorsed by his 'prentys' Haukyn at B 14.324–32 (both passages removed in revision), and seen as practised by the ideal figure of Charity in B 15.186–93*a*=C 16.328–34*a*. But it is clearly not to be assumed that Conscience, whose request for 'comfort' at 359 seems to imply a *tempering* of penitential severity, would approve the 'clean forgetting' of contrition (370) offered by the Friar as 'comfort' at 372. **370** *forȝete*: 'forgotten (how) to'; implying not only that a specific obligation is neglected but that a virtuous habit is undermined (*woned* 370). **371** *wake*: a standard penance being to keep vigil in prayer (cf. the personage *Vigilate* at 7.56 who urges Sloth to active 'breast-beating'). **372** *confort*: here signifying 'relief from the rigours of mortification' rather than 'spiritual consolation arising from a good conscience'. *contricioun*: specifically the continuing sense of a *spiritus contribulatus* and *cor contritum* (Ps 50:19) that was thought to constitute the essence of penitence, is expressed in acts like those at 21.380–1, and alone justifies his name; he is now no longer 'himself'. **373** *kyne synnes*: for the tone of this concluding internal rhyme cf. on 322, 324 above.

374–80 374 *Sleuth*; *Pruyde*: waiting in the wings (see 149ff) and now renewing the assault, with an access of new strength from Contrition's descent into spiritual torpor. **376** *efte*: see at 328–9. He earlier received no help from the regular clergy (whose inadequacy had prompted his recourse to the friars) and their silence now testifies to the dire condition of the institutional Church. **377** The guardian of the entrance (*ȝate*) is the sacrament of penance; if this is rendered inefficacious, Christians are unable to receive the Eucharist, the sacrament that establishes Unity Holy Church as a 'spiritual organism'. **378–80** On the possibility of revision here see *TN*. The C form is both stronger in itself and better in keeping with the idea that Friar Flatterer has administered a 'benign' sleeping potion to neutralise the salutary fear of sin that the entire poem insists is indispensable to repentance. The essence of the friar's 'flattery' is to convince the sinner that he is not such a bad fellow after all. In this way the 'inevitabilist' and 'mediocritarian' stance of the Friars Minor found so unsatisfactory by the Dreamer at 10.49–50 is shown decaying into a moral insensibility that threatens to fulfil the prophecy of B Pr 66 (the ferocious C revision of which is now explained). **379** *enchaunted*: the unfavourable earlier uses of this word at 2.43 and at 17.176 (in connection with flattery and heresy respectively) indicating a sombre view of the friars as potential agents of the Antichrist, 'corrupted in mind, reprobate concerning the faith' (II Tim 3:8). **380** *dwale*: a bitter narcotic made from gall dissolved in wine with such (potentially poisonous) herbal ingredients as hemlock, henbane or deadly nightshade (see MED s.v. 4 (a)). Its function as a pain-killer makes it ironically appropriate here; but as the 'sleep' induced is a symbol of spiritual ignorance, a grim pun on the sense 'deception', 'error' (ibid. s.v. 1 (a)) seems likely in the context.

(v) 381–7 *Finale*. **381** *pilgrime*: an echo of Conscience's earlier resolve at B 13.182, a passage removed in revision to C (and more distantly of Piers's resolve at B 7.120). A second disillusionment with the prospect for spiritual renewal offered by the mendicant orders leads the figure of the conscientious knightly layman to recommence his urgent personal search for Piers, the sole 'kynde' exemplar of truth and charity in the world. **384** *þat freres hadde*: if this is dependent on *seke* 383, understand 'and [to look for some way in which] friars might be endowed [for their mission]'. The responsible spokesman of Christian laypeople now sees it as a prime problem of the Church that 'need' (in the sense of lack of assured income) is what induces the friars to lower the spiritual threshold and encourage people in general and the gentry in particular to evade the stricter demands of their faith as traditionally understood. But that Conscience rejected the unrealistic solution proposed by Need at 236–41 and sought some relaxation of traditional penitential rigour (359–62) has shown that he still valued the work a reformed mendicant movement might accomplish in the world. *fyndynge*: argued by Dolan 1988:37 to refer specifically to the Franciscans. The term, as Frank argues (1957:117), attests L's wish for 'some kind of reform...of the friars' and 'establishes a certain limit for interpretation of the more obscure elements in the conclusion'. **385** *countrepledeth*: a term importantly associated with Conscience in two lines added in revision (Pr 138 and 8.53). Without necessarily carrying the 'legal' force discerned by Simpson (1990:243), it reveals the speaker's sense of the dangerous power of mendicant learning and eloquence when used to advance a bad cause. **385–7** The conclusion of the poem has proved controversial: see Frank 1950 and the representative discussions in Harwood, Simpson and Godden, who all find it 'dark and despairing' (Godden 1990:164). The end is perhaps intended to be a deliberate challenge to interpretation, but it would seem mistaken to think of L's Conscience at the end of the existing form of **C** as personifying the intention of the conscientious layman literally to 'leave' the Church, let alone set up 'an ordre by hymselue' (B 13.285). This would be out

of keeping with his upright and loyal nature, especially as brought out by the added **C** lines insisting on 'Holy Church's rights' at Pr 138 and 8.53, which are obviously subsequent to the completion of B XX. The possibility therefore cannot be excluded that the ending was to receive further revision, perhaps on the scale of the text up to Passus XX. However, the circumstance of Conscience's apparent deception by the friars, on the other hand, remains a disturbing acknowledgement that human limitedness can only cry out for divine grace, and go on hoping for less flawed human vessels through which that grace may be mediated. The final collocation of KYNDE, PIERS and GRACE ('nature-names' for the Father, Son and Spirit) brings the work to its close with an impassioned plea to God for success in finding a true leader for the Church, an 'angelic' pope who might bring about the reform of the material organisation needed to save the spiritual organism. **385** *me avenge*: the sense is more 'do justice for me', 'vindicate me' than 'take vengeance [on my enemies]'. **386** *Piers þe Plouhman*: the articulation of the name functioning as a valedictory 'title' for the poem at its end.

D. BIBLIOGRAPHY OF WORKS CITED

The Bibliography includes all books and articles that are referred to by short title or author / date in sections A–C and a selection of the other main works consulted but not specifically mentioned (where revised and reprinted, they are cited in their latest published form except where otherwise stated). It is arranged under two main headings, **Primary** and **Secondary Sources**, the latter sub-divided into Reference Works; Textual, Linguistic and Metrical Studies; Critical and Interpretative Studies; Historical and Background Studies. The place of publication is London, unless otherwise specified.

I. PRIMARY SOURCES

A. Manuscripts

For a descriptive list of the *Piers Plowman* manuscripts see section A, *Introduction*, I, *The Manuscripts*. Studies of the manuscripts cited there by short title are given under II. B below.

B. Printed Primary Sources

1 Printed Facsimiles

Bennett, J. A. W., ed. *The vision of Pierce Plowman, now fyrste imprynted.* 1505 [1550].
Benson, C. D. & Blanchfield, L. S. *The Manuscripts of PP: the B Version.* Cambridge, 1997.
Brewer, C. & Rigg, A. G., eds. *PP: A Facsimile of the Z-Text in Bodleian Library, Oxford, MS Bodley 851.* Cambridge, 1994.
Chambers, R. W. *et al. PP: The Huntington Library Manuscript (HM 143) reproduced in Photostat.* San Marino, 1936.
Doyle, A. I., ed. *The Vernon Manuscript: A Facsimile of Bodleian Library, Oxford, MS. Eng. poet. a.1.* Cambridge, 1987.
Matsushita, T. *PP: the A-Text. A Facsimile of the Society of Antiquaries of London MS 687.* Tokyo, 2007.
——*PP: The Z Version. A Facsimile of Bodleian Library, Oxford MS Bodley 851.* Tokyo, 2008.
Pearsall, D. (with Scott, K.), eds. *PP: a Facsimile of Bodleian Library, Oxford, MS Douce 104.* Cambridge, 1992.

2 Electronic Sources

Adams, R., Duggan, H., Eliason, E., Hanna, R., Price-Wilkin, J. & Turville-Petre, T. *The PP Electronic Archive, Vol. I: Corpus Christi College, Oxford MS. 201 (F).* CD-ROM. Ann Arbor: University of Michigan Press, 1999.
Turville-Petre, T. & Duggan, H. *The PP Electronic Archive, Vol 2: Cambridge, Trinity College, MS B. 15. 17 (W).* CD-ROM. Ann Arbor, Michigan. 2001.
Heinrichs, K. *The PP Electronic Archive, Vol 3: Oxford, Oriel College, MS 79 (O).* CD-ROM. Boydell & Brewer for the Medieval Academy of America and SEENET. 2005.
Duggan, H. & Hanna, R. *The PP Electronic Archive, Vol 4: Oxford, Bodleian Library, MS Laud Misc. 581 (L).* CD-ROM. Boydell & Brewer for the Medieval Academy of America and SEENET. 2005.
Eliason, E., Turville-Petre, T. Duggan, H. *The PP Electronic Archive, Vol 5: London, British Library, MS Additional 35287 (M).* CD-ROM. Boydell & Brewer for the Medieval Academy of America and SEENET. 2005.

3 Editions of *Piers Plowman*

Bennett, J. A. W., ed. *PP: The Prologue and Passus I–VII of the B-Text.* Oxford, 1972.
Kane, G., ed. *PP: The A Version. Will's Visions of Piers Plowman and Do-Well.* 1960. 2nd edn. 1988.
——& Donaldson, E. T., eds. *Piers Plowman: the B Version. Will's Visions of PP, Do-Well, Do-Better and Do-Best.* 1975. 2nd edn., 1988.

Knott, T. A. & Fowler, D., eds. *PP. A Critical Edition of the A Version*. Baltimore, 1952; repr. 1964.

Pearsall, D. *PP by William Langland. An Edition of the C-Text*. 1978; repr. with corrections, Exeter 1994.

Rigg, A. G. & Brewer, C., eds. *PP: The Z Version*. Toronto, 1983.

Robertson, E. & Shepherd, S. eds. *William Langland. Piers Plowman*. Norton Critical Edition. New York & London, 2006.

Russell, G. & Kane, G., eds. *PP: The C Version*. 1997.

Salter, E. & Pearsall, D., eds. *PP: Selections from the C-Text*. 1967.

Schmidt, A. V. C., ed. *William Langland. The Vision of PP: A Critical Edition of the B-Text*. 1978; repr. 1987 with added Glossary. 2nd (revised) edn. 1995.

Skeat, W. W., ed. *The Vision of William concerning Piers Plowman, together with Vita de Dowel, Dobet, et Dobest, Secundum Wit et Resoun*, by William Langland. 5 vols. I: Text A, EETS o.s. 28 (1867); II: Text B, EETS o.s. 38 (1869); III: Text C, EETS o.s. 54 (1873); IV, i: Notes, EETS o.s. 67 (1877); IV, ii: General Preface, Notes and Indexes, EETS o.s. 81 (1885).

The Vision of William Concerning Piers the Plowman by William Langley (or Langland). 1869. 2nd edn rev. 1874.

The Vision of William Concerning PP in Three Parallel Texts. 2 vols. Oxford, 1886; repr. 1954.

Whitaker, T. D., ed. *Visio Willí de Petro Plouhman Item Visiones ejusdem de Dowel, Dobet, et Dobest*. 1813.

Wright, T., ed. *The Vision and the Creed of Piers Plowman*. 2 vols. 1842; rev. edn. 1856.

4 Translations of *Piers Plowman*

Covella, F. D. *The A-Text. An Alliterative Verse Translation*, intro. D. C. Fowler. Binghamton, NY. 1992.

Donaldson, E. T. *PP: An Alliterative Verse Translation*, ed. E. Kirk & J. Anderson. 1990; repr. ed. E. Robertson & S. Shepherd. New York, 2005.

Economou, G. *William Langland's PP: The C Version: A Verse Translation*. Philadelphia, 1996.

Goodridge, J. F. *Piers the Ploughman*. Harmondsworth, 1959; 2nd edn. 1966.

Schmidt, A. V. C. *PP: A New Translation of the B-Text*. Oxford, 1992.

5 Editions of other Texts

i ENGLISH WORKS

Ancrene Wisse. The English Text of the 'Ancrene Riwle': 'Ancrene Wisse', ed. J. R. R. Tolkien. EETS o.s. 249 (1962).

The English Text of the 'Ancrene Riwle': Cotton Nero A. xiv., ed. M. Day. EETS o.s. 225 (1952).

Ancrene Wisse: Parts Six and Seven, ed. G. Shepherd. Rev. edn. Exeter, 1985.

Audelay, John. *Poems*, ed. E. K. Whiting. EETS o.s. 184 (1931).

The Babees Book; see F. J. Furnivall, *Early English Meals and Manners*.

Barr, H. ed. *The Piers Plowman Tradition*. 1993.

Bartholomaeus Anglicus. *On the Properties of Things*. John Trevisa's translation of *Bartholomaeus Anglicus De Proprietatibus Rerum*, ed. M. C. Seymour. 2 vols. Oxford, 1975.

Batman vppon Bartholome. 1582.

Bennett, J. A. W. & Smithers, G. V., eds. *Early Middle English Verse and Prose*. Oxford, 1966.

Blake, N., ed. *Middle English Religious Prose*. 1972.

Brown, C., ed. *English Lyrics of the XIIIth Century*. Oxford, 1932.

Religious Lyrics of the XIVth Century. 2nd edn. Oxford, 1957.

Burrow, J. A. & Turville-Petre, T., eds. *A Book of Middle English*. 2nd edn. Oxford, 1996.

Geoffrey Chaucer, *Troilus and Criseyde*, ed. B. A. Windeatt. 1984.

——*Works. The Riverside Chaucer*, ed. L. D. Benson. Oxford, 1988.

Clanvowe. *The Works of Sir John Clanvowe*, ed. V. J. Scattergood. Cambridge, 1975.

The Cloud of Unknowing and the Book of Privy Counsel, ed. P. Hodgson. EETS o.s. 218 (1944).

The Conflict of Wit and Will, ed. B. Dickins. Kendal, 1937.

Cursor Mundi, ed. R. Morris. 7 vols. EETS o.s. 57, 59, 62, 66, 68, 99, 101 (1847–93).

Death and Liffe, ed. J. M. P. Donatelli. Cambridge, MA. 1989.

'Deonise Hid Divinite' and Other Treatises on Contemplative Prayer related to 'The Cloud of Unknowing,' ed. P. Hodgson. EETS o.s. 231 (1958).

Dives and Pauper, ed. P. Barnum. 2 vols., EETS o.s. 275, 280 (1976, 1980).

Dobson, R. B. & Taylor, J., eds. *Rymes of Robin Hood*. 1976.

Early English Meals and Manners, ed. F. J. Furnivall. EETS o.s. 32. 1868.

English Gilds, ed. Toulmin Smith & L. Toulmin Smith. EETS o.s. 40 (1870).

English Medieval Lapidaries, ed. J. Evans & M. Serjeantson. EETS o.s. 190 (1933).

Genesis and Exodus, ed. R. Morris. EETS o.s. 7 (1865).

Gower, John. *The Complete Works of John Gower*, ed. G. C. Macaulay. 4 vols. Oxford, 1899–1902.

Gray, D., ed. *A Selection of Religious Lyrics*. Oxford, 1975.

Greene, R., ed. *A Selection of English Carols*. Oxford, 1962.

The Romance of Guy of Warwick, ed. J. Zupitza. EETS e.s. 42 (1889).

Herebert, William. *The Works of William Herebert, OFM*, ed. S. R. Reimer. Toronto, 1987.

Hoccleve, Thomas. *Regement of Princes*, ed. F. J. Furnivall. EETS e.s. 72 (1897).

Hudson, A., ed. *Selections from English Wycliffite Writings*. Cambridge, 1978.

Jack Upland, Friar Daw's Reply, and Upland's Rejoinder ed. P. L. Heyworth. 1968.

Joseph of Arimathea, ed. D. Lawton. New York, 1982.

Julian of Norwich. *A Book of Showings to the Anchoress Julian of Norwich*, ed. E. Colledge & J. Walsh. Toronto, 1978.

Kempe, Margery. *The Book of Margery Kempe*, ed. S. B. Meech & H. E. Allen. EETS o.s. 212 (1940).

Kyng Alisaunder, ed. G. V. Smithers. 2 vols. EETS o.s. 227, 237 (1952, 1957).

Laʒamon. *'Brut'*, ed. G. L Brook & R. R. Leslie. 2 vols. EETS o.s. 250, 277 (1963, 1978).

Lanfranc. *Lanfrank's Science of Cirurgie*, Part I, ed. R. Fleischhacker. EETS. o.s. 102 (1894).

The Lanterne of Liʒt, ed. L. M. Swinburn. EETS o.s. 151 (1917).

The Legend of the Cross, ed. A. S. Napier. EETS o.s. 103 (1894).

Legends of the Holy Rood, ed. R. Morris. EETS o.s. 46 (1871).

Love, Nicholas. *A Mirror of the Blessed Life of Our Lord Jesus Christ*, ed. L. F. Powell. 1908.

The Macro Plays, ed. M. Eccles. EETS o.s. 262 (1969).

Mandeville, Sir John. *Mandeville's Travels*, ed. P. Hamelius. 2 vols. EETS o.s. 153, 154 (1919–23).

Mannyng, Robert. *Robert of Brunne's 'Handlyng Synne' and its French Original*, ed. F. J. Furnivall. EETS o.s. 119, 123 (1901–03).

Meditations on the Life and Passion of Christ, ed. C. D'Evelyn. EETS o.s. 158 (1921).

Michael, Dan of Northgate. *Dan Michel's 'Ayenbite of Inwyt'*, ed. R. Morris. EETS o.s 23 (1866). Vol. ii, Introduction & Notes by P. Gradon. EETS o.s. 278 (1979).

The Middle English Harrowing of Hell and Gospel of Nicodemus, ed. W. H. Hulme. EETS e.s. 100 (1907).

Middle English Sermons, ed. W. O. Ross. EETS o.s. 209 (1940).

Minor Poems of the Vernon Manuscript, ed. C. Horstmann & F. J. Furnivall. 2 vols. EETS o.s 98, 117 (1892, 1901).

Morris, R. & Skeat, W., eds. *Specimens of Early English*. Oxford, 1873.

Morte Arthure: A Critical Edition, ed. V. Krishna. New York, 1976.

Le Morte Arthur, ed. J. D. Bruce. EETS e.s. 88 (1903, repr. 1959).

Mum and the Sothsegger, ed. M. Day and R. Steele. EETS o.s. 199 (1936).

Non-cycle Plays and Fragments, ed. N. Davis. EETS e.s. 1 (1970).

The Northern Passion, ed. F. Foster. 2 vols. EETS o.s. 145, 147 (1913–16).

The N-Town Play, ed. S. Spector. 2 vols. EETS s.s. 11,12 (1991).

Old English Homilies and Homiletic Treatises, 1st series, ed. R. Morris. 2 vols. EETS o.s. 29, 34 (1868).

The Parlement of the Thre Ages, ed. M. Y. Offord. EETS o.s. 246 (1959).

Pearl-poet. *The Poems of the Pearl Manuscript,* ed. M. Andrew & R. Waldron. 1978; rev. edn. Exeter, 1987.

Pierce the Ploughmans Crede, ed. W. W. Skeat. EETS o.s. 30. (1867).

The Plowman's Tale, in W. W. Skeat, ed. *Chaucerian and Other Pieces* (Oxford, 1897) 147–90.

The Plowman's Tale: the c. 1532 and 1606 Editions of a Spurious Canterbury Tale, ed. M. Mc. Rhinelander. New York, 1997.

The Pricke of Conscience, ed. R. Morris. Philological Society, 1863.

The Promptorium Parvulorum: the First English-Latin Dictionary, ed. A. L. Mayhew. EETS e.s. 102 (1908).

The Prymer or Lay Folks' Prayer Book, ed. H. Littlehales. 2 vols. EETS o.s. 105, 109 (1895–7).

R. H. Robbins, ed. *Historical Poems of the XIVth and XVth Centuries*. New York, 1959.

Rolle, R. *English Prose Treatises of Richard Rolle of Hampole*, ed. G. G. Perry. EETS o.s. 20 (1866).

Yorkshire Writers: Richard Rolle of Hampole and his Followers, ed. C. Horstman. 2 vols. 1895–6.

Bibliography

The Fire of Love and the Mending of Life (tr. by Richard Misyn, 1434–5), ed. R. Harvey. EETS o.s. 106 (1896).

[Rolle] *Meditationes de Passione Domini*, ed. H. Lindkvist. Uppsala, 1917.

Writings Ascribed to Richard Rolle, ed. H. E. Allen. New York, 1927.

English Writings of Richard Rolle, ed. H. E. Allen. Oxford, 1931.

Richard Rolle: Prose and Verse, ed. S. J. Ogilvie-Thomson. EETS 293 (1988).

St Erkenwald, ed. R. Morse. Cambridge, 1975.

St Erkenwald, ed. C. Peterson. Philadelphia, 1977.

Sarjent, H. J. & Kittredge, G. L., eds. *English and Scottish Popular Ballads*. Boston, 1932.

Sawles Warde, in Bennett & Smithers (1966) 246–61.

The Seven Sages, ed. K. Brunner. EETS o.s. 191 (1932).

The Siege of Jerusalem, ed. R. Hanna & D. Lawton. EETS o.s. 320. Oxford, 2003.

The Simonie, ed. D. Embree & E. Urquhart. Heidelberg, 1991.

Sisam, K., ed. *Fourteenth Century Verse and Prose*. Oxford, repr. 1962.

The South English Legendary, ed. C. D'Evelyn & A. J. Mill. 3 vols. EETS o.s. 235, 236, 244 (1956–9).

The Southern Passion, ed. B. D. Brown. EETS o.s. 169 (1927).

Speculum Christiani, ed. G. Holmstedt. EETS o.s. 182 (1933).

A Stanzaic Life of Christ, ed. F. A. Foster. EETS o.s. 166 (1926).

The Towneley Plays, ed. A. C. Cawley & M. Stevens. 2 vols. EETS s.s. 13,14. Oxford, 1994.

Usk, Thomas. *The Testament of Love*, in W. W. Skeat, ed. *Chaucerian and Other Pieces* (Oxford, 1897) 1–145.

William of Palerne, ed. W. W. Skeat. EETS e.s. 1 (1867).

William of Palerne: An Alliterative Romance, ed. G. H. V. Bunt. Groningen, 1985.

William of Shoreham. *William of Shoreham's Poems*, ed. M. Konrath. EETS e.s. 86 (1900).

Wimbledon, Thomas. *Wimbledon's Sermon: Redde Rationem Villicationis Tue: a ME Sermon of the 14th Century*, ed. I. K. Knight. Pittsburgh, 1967.

Wordsworth, W. *Prose Works*, ed. W. J. B. Owen & J. W. Smyser. Oxford, 1974.

——*The Prelude: 1799, 1805, 1850*, eds. J. Wordsworth, M. H. Abrams and S. Gill. New York, 1979.

Wright, T., ed. *The Political Songs of England, From the Reign of John to that of Edward II*. Camden Society 6, 1839.

——*Political Poems and Songs Relating to English History*. Rolls Series. 2 vols. 1859–1861.

John Wycliffe. *Select English Works of Wyclif*, ed. T. Arnold. 3 vols. Oxford, 1869–71.

The English Works of Wyclif hitherto unprinted, ed. F. D. Matthew, EETS o.s. 74 (1880).

Wynnere and Wastoure, ed. S. Trigg. EETS o.s. 297 (1999).

The York Plays, ed. R. Beadle. 1982.

ii LATIN WORKS

Alan of Lille. *Alani de Insulis Opera Omnia*, ed. J-P. Migne. *PL* 210. Paris, 1855.

Alexander of Ville-Dieu. *Das* Doctrinale *des Alexander de Villa-Dei*, ed. D. Reichling. Berlin, 1893.

Aquinas, St Thomas. *Summa Theologica*. 6 vols. Madrid, 1961.

Auctores Octo cum Commento. Jacobus Myt, 1514.

Augustine, St. *Augustini Opera Omnia*, ed. J-P. Migne *PL* 32–47. Paris, 1861–65.

Homilies on the Gospel of John, ed. P. Schaff. 1888.

Bede. *Venerabilis Baedae Opera Omnia*, ed. J-P. Migne *PL* 90–5. Paris, 1862.

Historia Ecclesiastica, ed. B. Colgrave & R. A. B. Mynors. Oxford, 1969.

St Bernard. *Sancti Bernardi Opera Omnia*, ed. J. Mabillon. *PL* 182–5. Paris, 1859–60.

Opera, ed. J. Leclercq, C. H. Talbot & H. M. Rochais. 8 vols. Rome, 1957–77.

Bible, Vulgate. *Biblia Sacra iuxta Vulgatam Clementinam*, ed. by A. Colunga & L. Turrado. 4th edn. Madrid, 1965.

Glossed Bible Facsimile. *Biblia Latina cum Glossa Ordinaria*, 1480/1. Intro. K. Froelich & M. T. Gibson. 4 vols. Brepols-Turnhout, 1992.

Bible, English. *The Holy Bible: Douay-Rheims Version*. New York, 1941.

Bible, Old Latin (*Vetus Latina*). *Bibliorum Sacrorum Latinae Versiones Antiquae, seu Vetus Italica*, ed. P. Sabatier. 3 vols. Rheims-Paris, 1743–51.

Boethius. *Tractates & Consolation of Philosophy*, ed. H. F. Stewart & E. K. Rand. Cambridge, Mass., 1918, rev. edn. 1968.

Bonaventure, St. *Opera Omnia*. 10 vols. Quaracchi, 1882–1902.

Brinton, Thomas. *The Sermons of Thomas Brinton*. 2 vols, ed. M. A. Devlin. 1954.

730

Bromyard, John. *Summa Praedicantium*. 2 vols. Venice, 1586.

Bruno Signiensis, *Expositio in Librum Job*. Venice, 1651.

Cato, Dionysius. *Disticha Catonis*, ed. M. Boas & H. J. Botschuyer. Amsterdam, 1952.

Chobham, Thomas of. *Thome de Chobham Summa Confessorum*, ed. F. Broomfield. Namur, 1968.

Chrysostom, St John. *Homilies on the Gospel of St John and the Epistle to the Hebrews*, ed. P. Schaff. 1889.

Corpus Iuris Canonici, ed. A. Friedberg. 2 vols. Graz, 1955.

Corpus Scriptorum Ecclesiasticorum Latinorum. Vienna, 1866-.

Denis the Carthusian. *Dionysii Cartusiani Opera Omnia*. Montreuil and Tournai, 1896–1912.

Dreves, G. (rev. Blume, C.), eds. *Ein Jahrtausend Lateinischer Hymnendichtung: Eine Blütenlese aus den Analecta Hymnica*. Leipzig, 1909.

Faral, E. *Les Arts Poétiques du XIIe et XIIIe Siècle.* Paris, 1924.

Fasciculus Morum: A Fourteenth-Century Preacher's Handbook, ed. S. Wenzel. Pennsylvania, 1989.

Fasciculi Zizaniorum Magistri Johannis Wyclif cum Tritico, ed. W. W. Shirley. Rolls Series, V. 1858.

Glossa Ordinaria, ed. J-P. Migne. 2 vols. *PL* 113–14. Paris, 1852.

The Gospel of Nicodemus, ed. H. C. Kim. Toronto, 1973.

Gower, John. *Vox Clamantis*. See Gower under I above.

Gregory the Great. *Sancti Gregorii Opera Omnia*, ed. J-P. Migne. 4 vols. *PL* 75–9. Paris, 1849.

    Moralia in Job, ed. M. Adriaen. CCSL 143. Turnhout, 1979.

Hervieux, L. *Les Fabulistes Latins, III: Avianus*. Paris, 1894.

Higden, Ralph. *Polychronicon*, ed. C. Babington & J. R. Lumby. 9 vols. 1865–86.

Hildebert of Lavardin. *Hildeberti...Opera Omnia*, ed. J-P. Migne. *PL* 171. Paris, 1893.

Hugh of St Cher, *Postillae in Universa Biblia*. 7 vols. Lyons, 1667.

Hugh of St Victor. *Hugonis de Sancto Victore Opera Omnia*, ed. J-P. Migne. 3 vols. *PL* 175–7.

Innocent III, Pope. *De Contemptu Mundi*. See Lotario dei Segni.

Isidore of Seville. *Etymologiarum sive originum libri XX*, ed. W. M. Lindsay. 2 vols. Oxford, 1911.

Jacobus a Voragine. *Legenda Aurea*, ed. T. Graesse. 3rd. edn. Leipzig, 1890.

The Golden Legend tr. by G. Ryan & H. Ripperger, 1941, repr. New Hampshire, 1991.

John of Hoveden. *Nachtigallenlied* [*Philomena*], ed. C. Blume. Leipzig, 1930.

The Poems of John of Hoveden, ed. F. J. E. Raby. 1939.

John of Salisbury. *Metalogicon*, ed. C. C. J. Webb. Oxford, 1929.

Knighton, Henry. *Knighton's Chronicle, 1337–1396*. ed. G. H. Martin. Oxford, 1995.

Liber Albus. The White Book of the City of London, ed. H. T. Riley. 1861.

Peter Lombard. *Petri Lombardi Opera Omnia*, ed. J-P. Migne. 2 vols. *PL* 191–2. Paris, 1854.

Lotario dei Segni. *De miseria condicionis humane*, ed. and tr. R. E. Lewis. Chaucer Library, 1978.

Ludolph of Saxony. *Vita Jesu Christi*, ed. A. C. Boland, L. M. Regallot & J. Carnandet. Paris and Rome, 1865.

Lyndwood, William. *Provinciale*. Oxford, 1679.

Macrobius. *Commentary on the Dream of Scipio*, tr. W. H. Stahl. New York, 1952.

Map, Walter. *The Latin Poems commonly attributed to Walter Mapes*, ed. T. Wright. Camden Society, 1841.

Meditaciones de Passione Christi Olim Sancto Bonaventurae Attributae, ed. M. J. Stallings. Washington, D.C. 1965.

Migne, J-P., ed. *Patrologiae Cursus Completus. Series Latina*. 221 vols. Paris, 1844–64.

Petrus Cantor. *Opera Omnia*, ed. G. Galpin. *PL* 205. Paris, 1855.

Petrus Comestor. *Opera Omnia,* ed. J-P. Migne. *PL* 198. Paris, 1855.

Prudentius, Aurelius. *Works*, ed. H. J. Thomson. 2 vols. Cambridge, Mass., 1949–53.

Rabanus Maurus. *B. Rabani Mauri Opera Omnia*, ed. J-P. Migne. 6 vols. *PL* 107–12. Paris 1864.

Raby, F. J. E., ed. *The Oxford Book of Medieval Latin Verse*. Oxford, 1974.

Rolle, Richard. *Incendium Amoris*, ed. M. Deanesly. Manchester, 1915.

    Emendatio Vitae: Orationes ad Honorem Nominis Ihesu, ed. N. Watson. Toronto, 1995.

Rotuli Parliamentorum Anglie, 6 vols. n.d.

Sacrum Commercium, ed. S. Brufani. Medioevo Francescano, Testi, I. Assisi, 1990.

Sarum Breviary. Proctor, F. and Wordsworth, C., eds. *Breviarium ad Usum Insignis Ecclesiae Sarum.* 3 vols. Cambridge, 1857–86.

Sarum Manual. J. Collins, ed. *Manuale ad usum percelebris ecclesie Sarisburiensis*. 1960.

Sarum Missal. F. H. Dickinson, ed. *Missale ad usum Sarum*. Oxford, 1861–83.

Schneemelcher, W. *New Testament Apocrypha*. 5th edn. 1987.

Thurot, C. *Notices et Extraits de divers manuscrits latins, pour servir à l'histoire des doctrines grammaticales au Moyen Age.* Paris, 1869, repr. Frankfurt, 1964.

Tischendorf, C., ed. *Evangelia Apocrypha.* 2nd ed. Leipzig, 1876; repr. Hildesheim, 1966.

Walsingham, Thomas. *Historia Anglicana*, ed. H. T. Riley. Rolls Series, 2 vols. 1864.

Walter of Châtillon, *Die Gedichte Walters von Châtillon*, Vol. I, ed. K. Strecker. Berlin, 1925.

Walther, H., ed. *Proverbia Sententiaeque Latinitatis Medii Ævi.* 6 vols. Göttingen, 1963–9.

Wright, T. ed. *Early Mysteries and other Latin Poems.* 1838.

    The Anglo-Latin Satirical Poets and Epigrammatists of the 12th. Century. 2 vols. 1872.

——& Halliwell, J. *Reliquiae Antiquae.* 2 vols. 1841–3.

Wycliffe, John. *Dialogus sive Speculum Ecclesie Militantis*, ed. A.W. Pollard. Wyclif Society, 1886.

iii FRENCH WORKS

Bozon, Nicolas. *Deux poèmes de Nicholas Bozon*, ed. J. Vising. Gothenburg, 1919.

Deguileville, Guillaume de. *Le Pélerinage de Vie Humaine*, ed. J. J. Stürzinger (1893)

    Le Pélerinage de L'Ame, ed. idem (1895).

    Le Pélerinage Jesucrist, ed. idem (1897).

    The Pilgrimage of the Lyfe of the Manhode, ed. A. Henry 2 vols. EETS o.s. 288, 292 (1985, 1988).

Froissart, Jean. Tr. Lord Berners. *The Chronicles of Froissart*, ed. G. C. Macaulay. 1913.

Gervais du Bus. *Le Roman de Fauvel*, ed. A. Langfors. Société des Anciens Textes Français 31. Paris, 1914–21.

Grosseteste, Robert. *Le Château d'Amour de Robert Grosseteste*, ed. J. Murray. Paris, 1918.

    Le Mariage des neuf filles du diable, ed. P. Meyer, in *Romania* 29 (1900) 54–72.

    The ME Translations of Robert Grosseteste's 'Château d'Amour', ed. K. Sajavaara. Helsinki, 1967.

L'Histoire de Guillaume le Maréchal, ed. P. Meyer. Paris, 1891–1901.

Huon de Méri, *Li Tornoiemenz Antecrit*, ed. G. Wimmer. Marburg, 1888.

Jubinal, M., ed. *Nouveau Recueil.* 2 vols. Paris, 1839–42.

Langtoft, Peter. *The Chronicle of Pierre de Langtoft*, ed. T. Wright. 2 vols. 1866–68.

Lorris, Guillaume de & Jean de Meun. *Le Roman de la Rose*, ed. F. Lecoy. Paris, 1965–70.

Robert, A., ed. *Fabliaux inédits.* Paris, 1834.

Rutebeuf, *La Voie de Paradis*, ed. E. Faral & J. Bastin. Paris, 1959.

    Œuvres complètes de Rutebeuf, ed. A. Jubinal. Paris, repr. 1974.

II. SECONDARY SOURCES

A. Reference Works

a. Bibliographies

Colaianne, A. J. *PP: An Annotated Bibliography of Editions and Criticism 1550–1977.* New York/London, 1978.

Middleton, A. 'XVIII. *PP*,' in Hartung, A. E., ed. *A Manual of the Writings in Middle English* 1050–1500, vol 7. New Haven, Conn. (1986) 2211–34, 2417–43.

Pearsall, D. *An Annotated Critical Bibliography of Langland.* New York and London, 1990.

Proppe, K. '*PP*. An Annotated Bibliography for 1900–1968', *Comitatus* 3 (Los Angeles, 1972) 33–90.

The Yearbook of Langland Studies (Michigan, 1987–): 'Annual Bibliography'.

b. Dictionaries, Concordances, Glossaries and Grammars

Alford, J. *PP: A Glossary of Legal Diction.* Cambridge, 1988.

    PP: A Guide to the Quotations. New York, 1992.

Hassell, J. W. Jr. *Middle French Proverbs, Sentences and Proverbial Phrases.* Toronto, 1982.

Kane, G. *Piers Plowman: Glossary.* 2005.

Kurath, H., Kuhn, S. M, Reidy, J., & Lewis, R., eds. *Middle English Dictionary.* Ann Arbor, Michigan, 1964–2001.

Matsushita, T. *A Glossarial Concordance to William Langland's The Vision of PP: The B-Text.* 3 vols. Tokyo, 1998–2000.

Mossé, F. (tr. J. Walker). *A Handbook of Middle English.* Baltimore, 1952.

Mustanoja, T. *A Middle English Syntax. Part I: Parts of Speech.* Helsinki, 1960.

Oxford English Dictionary. Oxford, 1971.

Whiting, B. J., ed. *Proverbs, Sentences and Proverbial Phrases from English Writings Mainly before 1500.* Cambridge, Mass., 1968.

Wittig, J. S., ed. *A Concordance to the Athlone Edition of 'PP'.* 2001.

B. Textual, Linguistic and Metrical Studies

Adams, R. 'The Reliability of the Rubrics in the B-Text of *PP*,' *MÆ* 54 (1985) 20–31.

'Editing and the Limitations of the *Durior Lectio*,' *YLS* 5 (1991) 7–15.

'Editing *PP* B: the Imperative of an Intermittently Critical Edition', *SB* 45 (1992) 31–68.

'L's *Ordinatio*: The *Visio* and the *Vita* Once More', *YLS* 8 (1994) 51–84.

'Evidence for the Stemma of the *PP* B Manuscripts', *SB* 53 (2001) 173–94.

'The R/F MSS of *PP* and the Pattern of Alpha / Beta Complementary Omissions: Implications for Critical Editing', *TEXT* 12 (2002) 109–37.

Barney, P. 'Line-Number Index to the Athlone Edition of *PP*', *YLS* 7 (1993) 97–114.

'Line-Number Index to the Athlone Edition of *PP*: the C Version', *YLS* 12 (1998) 159–73.

Barney, S. 'L.'s Prosody: the State of the Study', in Tavormina and Yeager (1995) 65–85.

Benson, C. D. & Blanchfield, L. S. *The MSS of PP: the B Version.* Cambridge, 1997.

Black, M. 'A Scribal Translation of *PP*', *MÆ* 67 (1998) 257–90.

Blackman, E. 'Notes on the B-Text of *PP*,' *JEGP* 17 (1918) 489–545.

Blair, C. 'The Word "Baselard"', *Journal of the Arms & Armour Society* 11 (1984) 193–206.

Bowers, J. M. '*PP*'s William Langland: Editing the Text, Writing the Author's Life', *YLS* 9 (1995[1]) 65–102.

'L.'s *PP* in Hm 143: Copy, Commentary, Censorship', *YLS* 19 (2005) 137–68.

Bradley, H. 'The Word "Moillere" in *P the P,*' *MLR* 2 (1906–7) 163–4.

'Some Cruces in *PP*', *MLR* 5 (1910) 340–2.

Breeze, A. '"Tikes" at *PP* B. XIX. 37: Welsh *Taeog* "Serf, Bondman"', *NQ* 238 (1993[2]) 442–45.

Brewer, C. 'Z and the A-, B- and C-Texts of *PP*', *MÆ* 53 (1984) 194–219.

'Some Implications of the Z-Text for the Textual Tradition of *PP*.' Unpublished D.Phil. thesis. Oxford University, 1986.

'The Textual Principles of Kane's A-Text', *YLS* 3 (1989) 67–90.

'Authorial vs. Scribal Re-Writing in *PP*,' in Machan (1991) 59–89.

'George Kane's Processes of Revision', in Minnis & Brewer (1992) 71–92.

Editing 'PP': The evolution of the text. Cambridge, 1996.

Britnell, R. H. '*Forstall*, Forestalling and the Statute of Forestallers', *EHR* 102 (1987) 89–102.

Brooks, E. St J. 'The *PP* MSS in Trinity College, Dublin', *The Library*, 5th ser., 6 (1951) 5–22.

Cable, T. 'Middle English Meter and its Theoretical Implications', *YLS* 2 (1988) 47–69.

'Standards from the Past: The Conservative Syllable Structure of the Alliterative Revival', in J. B. Trahern, ed. *Standardizing English: Essays in the History of Language Change in Honor of J. H. Fisher.* Tennessee Studies in Literature 31 (1989) 42–56.

The English Alliterative Tradition. Philadelphia, 1991.

Calabrese, M. '[P] *the* [P.]; the Corrections, Interventions, and Erasures in Huntington MS Hm 143 (X)', *YLS* 19 (2005) 169–99.

Carnegy, F. A. R. *An Attempt to Approach the C-Text of PP.* 1934.

Cerquiglini, B. *Eloge de la variante: Histoire critique de la philologie.* Paris, 1989.

Chambers, R. W. and Grattan, J. G. 'The Text of *PP*: Critical Methods', *MLR* 11 (1916) 257–75.

'The Text of *PP*,' *MLR* 26 (1931) 1–51.

Clopper, L. 'L.'s Markings for the Structure of *PP*,' *MP* 85 (1988) 245–55.

'A Response to Robert Adams', *YLS* 9 (1995) 141–6.

Colledge, E. 'Aliri', *MÆ* 27 (1958) 111–13.

Crawford, W. R. 'Robert Crowley's Editions of *PP*: A Bibliographical and Textual Study'. Unpub. Diss. Yale University, 1957.

Bibliography

Dahl, E. 'Diverse Copies Have it Diversly: An Unorthodox Survey of *PP* Textual Scholarship from Crowley to Skeat', in Vaughan (1993) 53–80.

Davis, B. P. 'The Rationale for a Copy of a Text: Constructing the Exemplar for BL Add. MS 10574', *YLS* 11 (1997) 141–55.

Dobson, E. J. 'Some Notes on ME Texts', *English & Germanic Studies* I (1947–8) 56–62.

Dolan, T. P. '*Passus* in FitzRalph and L.', *ELN* 23 (1985) 5–7.

Donaldson, E. T. 'MSS R & F in the B-Tradition of *PP*,' *Transactions of the Connecticut Academy of Arts & Sciences* 39 (1955) 177–212.

'The Grammar of Book's Speech in *PP*' [1966], repr. Blanch (1969) 264–70.

Doyle, A. I. 'Remarks on Surviving MSS of *PP*', in Kratzmann and Simpson (1986) 35–48.

——& Parkes, M. B. 'The production of Copies of the *Canterbury Tales* and the *Confessio Amantis* in the Early 15th Century', in M. B. Parkes and A. G. Watson, eds., *Medieval Scribes, Manuscripts and Libraries. Studies Presented to N. R. Ker* (1978) 163–210.

Duggan, H. 'Final –e and the Rhythmic Structure of the B-Verse in ME Alliterative Poetry', *MP* 88 (1986[1]) 119–45.

'Alliterative Patterning as a Basis for Emendation in ME Alliterative Poetry', *SAC* 8 (1986[2]) 73–105.

'The Authenticity of the Z-Text of *PP*. Further Notes on Metrical Evidence', *MÆ* (1987[1]) 25–45.

'Notes towards a Theory of L.'s Meter', *YLS* 1 (1987[2]) 41–70.

'L.'s Dialect and Final -*e*', *SAC* 12 (1990[1]) 157–91.

'Stress Assignment in ME Alliterative Poetry', *JEGP* 89 (1990[2]) 309–29.

Edwards, A. S. G. 'The Early Reception of Chaucer and L.', *Florilegium* 15 (1998) 1–22.

'Two *PP* MSS from Helmingham Hall', *Transactions of the Cambridge Bibliographical Society* 11 (1999) 421–6.

Fisher, J. '*PP* and the Chancery Tradition' in Kennedy & al. (1988) 267–78.

Fletcher, A. J. 'The Essential (Ephemeral) WL: Textual Revision as Ethical Process in *PP*', *YLS* 15 (2001) 61–84.

Flom, G. T. 'A Note on *PP*,' *MLN* 23 (1908) 156–7.

Fowler, D. C. 'A New Edition of the B-Text of *PP*,' *YES* 7 (1977) 23–42.

'Editorial "Jamming": Two New Editions of *PP*', *Review* (Blacksburg, Va.) 2 (1980) 211–69.

Galloway. A. 'Uncharacterizable Entities: the Poetics of ME Scribal Culture and the Definitive *PP*,' *SB* 52 (1999) 59–84.

Green, R. F. 'The Lost Exemplar of the Z-Text of *PP* and its 20-line Pages', *MÆ* 56 (1987) 307–10.

Greetham, D. C. 'Reading in and around *PP*,' in P. Cohen, ed. *Texts and Textuality* (NY, 1997) 25–57.

Greg, W. W. *The Calculus of Variants*. Oxford, 1927.

'The Rationale of Copy-Text', *SB* 3 (1950) 19–36.

Griffiths, J. and Pearsall, D. eds. *Book Production and Publishing in Britain*, 1375–1475. Cambridge, 1989.

Grindley, C. 'The Life of a Book: BL MS Add. 35157 in an Historical Context', Glasgow PhD. Diss. 1996.

'Reading *PP* C-Text Annotations: Notes towards the Classification of Printed and Written Marginalia in Texts from the British Isles 1300–1641', in K. Kerby-Fulton & M. Hilmo, eds. *The Medieval Professional Reader at Work*. 2001.

Hailey, R. C. '"Geuyng light to the Reader": Robert Crowley's Editions of *PP* (1550)', *PBSA* 95 (2001) 483–502.

'Robert Crowley and the Editing of *PP* (1550)', *YLS* 21 (2007) 143–70.

Halamari, H. & Adams, R. 'On the Grammar and Rhetoric of Language Mixing in *PP*,' *NM* 103 (2002) 33–50.

Hanna, R. 'The Scribe of Huntington Hm 114', *SB* 42 (1989) 120–133.

'Studies in the MSS of *PP*,' *YLS* 7 (1993) 1–25.

'MS Bodley 851 and the Dissemination of *PP*,' in *Pursuing History* 195–202.

'On the Versions of *PP*,' in *Pursuing History* 203–43.

Pursuing History: ME Manuscripts and their Texts. Stanford, 1996.

Harley, M. P. 'The Derivation of *Hawkin* and its Application in *PP*,' *Names* 29 (1981) 97–99.

Hill, T. D. 'Green and Filial Love: Two Notes on the Russell-Kane C-Text: C 8.215 and C 17.48', *YLS* 16 (2002) 67–83.

Horobin, S. "In London and Opelond": The Dialect and Circulation of the C Version of *PP*', *MÆ* 74 (2005) 248–69.

'The Scribe of Rawlinson Poetry 137 and the Copying and Circulation of *PP*', *YLS* 19 (2005) 3–26.

——& Mooney, L. 'A *PP* Manuscript by the Hengwrt / Ellesmere Scribe and its Implications for London Standard English', *SAC* 26 (2004) 65–112.

——& Mosser, D. W. 'Scribe D's SW Midlands Roots: A Reconsideration', *NM* 106 (2006) 32–47.

Jansen, S. L. 'Politics, Protest, and a New *PP* Fragment: the Voice of the Past in Tudor England', *RES* 40 (1989) 93–9.

Johnston, G. K. W. '*PP*, B-Text, Pr 78–9', *NQ* 204 (1959) 243–4.

Kane, G. 'Poetry and Lexicography in the Translation of *PP*,' *Medieval and Renaissance Studies* 9 (1982) 33–54.

'The "Z Version" of *PP*,' *Speculum* 60 (1985) 910–30.

'The Text', in Alford, ed., *Companion* (1988) 175–200.

734

Review of Schmidt, *PP: A Parallel-Text Edition*, in *NQ* 43 (1996) 315–21.

'An Open Letter to Jill Mann about the Sequence of the Versions of *PP*,' *YLS* 14 (1999) 7–33.

'Word-Games: Glossing *PP*,' in S. Powell & J. J. Smith, eds., *New Perspectives in Middle English Texts: A Festschrift for R. A. Waldron* (Cambridge, 2000) 43–53.

Kennedy, E. J., Waldron, R. & Wittig, J., eds. *Medieval English Studies Presented to George Kane*. Woodbridge, 1988.

Kerby-Fulton, K. 'Langlandian Reading Circles and the Civil Service in London and Dublin, 1380–1427', *New Medieval Literatures* 1 (1998) 59–83.

'Professional Readers of L. at Home and Abroad: New Directions in the Political and Bureaucratic Codicology of *PP*,' in D. Pearsall, ed. *New Directions in Later Medieval Manuscript Studies* (Woodbridge, 2000) 103–29.

'"L. in his Working Clothes?" Scribe D, Loose Revision Material and the Nature of Scribal Intervention', in A. J. Minnis, ed. *ME Poetry: Texts and Traditions. Essays in Honour of D. Pearsall* (Woodbridge, 2001) 371–92.

'The Women Readers in L.'s Earliest Audience: some Codicological Evidence', in S. R. Jones, ed. *Learning and Literacy in Medieval England and Abroad* (Turnhout, 2003) 121–34.

——& D. Depres, *Iconography and the Professional Reader: The Politics of Book Production and the Douce 'PP'*. Minneapolis, 1999.

Kiernan, K. *'Beowulf' and the Beowulf Manuscript*. Ann Arbor, Michigan, 1996.

King, J. N. 'Robert Crowley's Editions of *PP*,' *MP* 73 (1976) 342–52.

Knott, T. A. 'An Essay toward the Critical Text of the A Version of *PP*', *MP* 12 (1915) 129–61.

Lawler, T. 'A Reply to Jill Mann, Reaffirming the Traditional Relation between the A and B Versions of *PP*,' *YLS* 10 (1996) 145–80.

Maas, P. *Textual Criticism*. Oxford, 1956.

Machan, T. 'Late ME Texts and the Higher and Lower Criticisms', in Machan, ed. *Medieval Literature: Texts and Interpretation* (Binghamton, N.Y. 1991) 3–16.

Mann. J. 'The Power of the Alphabet: A Reassessment of the Relation between the A and the B Versions of *PP*,' *YLS* 8 (1994¹) 21–50.

Minnis, A. J. & Brewer, C., eds. *Crux and Controversy in Middle English Textual Criticism*. Cambridge, 1992.

Mitchell, A. G. 'The Text of *PP* C. Prologue l. 125', *MÆ* 8 (1939) 118–20.

'Notes on the C-Text of *PP*,' *London Medieval Studies* 1 (1948 for 1939) 483–92.

Moore, S. 'Studies in *P the P*,' *MP* 11 (1913) 177–93; 12 (1914) 19–50.

Mustanoja, T. F. 'The Suggestive Use of Christian Names in M.E. Poetry', in J. Mandel and B. A. Rosenberg, eds. *Medieval Literature and Folklore Studies: Essays in Honor of F. L. Utley*. New Brunswick, N.J. (1970) 51–76.

Oliphant, R. 'L.'s "Sire Piers of Pridie"', *NQ* 205 (1960) 167–8.

Olszewska, E. S. 'ME "Fader and Frendes"', *NQ* 218 (1973) 205–7.

Onions, C. T. 'An Unrecorded Reading in "PP"', *MLR* 3 (1907–8) 170–1.

Parkes, M. B. 'The Influence of the Concepts of *Ordinatio* and *Compilatio* on the Development of the Book', in J. J. G. Alexander & M. T. Gibson, eds., *Medieval Learning and Literature: Essays Presented to R. W. Hunt* (Oxford, 1976) 115–41.

Patterson, L. 'The Logic of Textual Criticism and the Way of Genius: The Kane-Donaldson *PP* in Historical Perspective', in Patterson, *Negotiating the Past: The Historical Understanding of Medieval Literature* (Madison, Wis., 1987) 77–113.

Pearcy, R. J. 'Langland's *Fair Feld*,' *YLS* 11 (1997) 39–48.

Pearsall, D. 'The Ilchester Manuscript of *PP*,' *NM* 82 (1981) 181–93.

'Editing Medieval Texts: Some Developments and some Problems', in J. McGann, ed., *Textual Criticism and Literary Interpretation* (Chicago, 1985) 92–106.

Revard, C. '*Title* and *Auaunced* in *PP* B. 11. 290', *YLS* 1 (1987) 116–21.

Rouse, M. & R. H. '*Ordinatio* and *Compilatio* revisited' in M. J. Jordan & K. Emery, eds. *Ad litteram: Authoritative Texts and their Medieval Readers*. 1992.

Ruggiers, P., ed. *Editing Chaucer: The Great Tradition*. Norman, Oklahoma, 1984.

Russell, G. H. 'Some Aspects of the Process of Revision in *PP*,' in Hussey (1969) 27–49.

'Some Early Responses to the C Version of *PP*,' *Viator* 15 (1984) 275–303.

'"As They Read It": Some Notes on Early Responses to the C Version of *PP*,' *LSE* n.s. 20 (1989) 173–89.

——& Nathan, V. 'A *PP* MS in the Huntington Library', *HLQ* 26 (1963) 119–30.

Samuels, M. L. 'L.'s Dialect', *MÆ* 54 (1985) 232–47; with corrections in *MÆ* 55 (1986) 40.

'Dialect and Grammar', in Alford, ed. *Companion*, 201–21.

Bibliography

Scase, W. 'Two *PP* C-Text Interpolations: Evidence for a Second Textual Tradition', *NQ* 232 (1987) 456–63.

Schaap, T. 'From Professional to Private Readership: a Discussion and Transcription of C15th and C16th Marginalia in *PP* C-Text Oxford, Bodleian Library MS Digby 102', *Studies in Medieval and Renaissance History* 16 (2001) 81–116.

Schmidt, A. V. C. 'The C Version of *PP*: A New Edition', *NQ* 225 (1980) 102–110.

'The Authenticity of the Z-Text of *PP*: A Metrical Examination', *MÆ* 53 (1984) 295–300.

'A Misattributed Speech in *PP*, A XI 182–218', *NQ* 249 (2004) 238–40.

'*Ars or Scientia?* Reflections on Editing *PP*,' *YLS* 18 (2004) 31–54.

Sebastian, J. Review of Turville-Petre & Duggan, *PP Electronic Archive Vol. 2, YLS* 15 (2001) 219–27.

Shepherd, S. Review of Duggan et al., *PP Electronic Archive Vol. 1, YLS* 14 (2000) 199–207.

Skeat, W. W. *Parallel Extracts from Twenty-nine Manuscripts of PP.* EETS 17 (1866); reprinted in revised form as Index VII in EETS edn. of *PP*, IV ii 831–62.

Sledd, J. 'Three Textual Notes on C14th Poetry', *MLN* 55 (1940) 379–82.

Spargo, J. W. 'Chaucer's Love-Days', *Speculum* 15 (1940) 36–56.

Spearman, A. 'L.'s "Corlew": Another Look at *PP* B XIV 43', *MÆ* 62 (1993) 242–58.

Stanley, E. G. 'The B Version of *PP*: a New Edition', *NQ* 221 (1976) 435–7.

Tajima, M. '*PP* B. V. 379: A Syntactic Note', *NQ* 245 (2000) 18–20.

Taylor, S. 'The F Scribe and the R MS of *PP B*,' *ESt.* 77 (1996) 530–48.

'The R MS of *PP B*: A Critical Facsimile'. Unpub. Ph.D. diss. Univ. of Washington, 1995.

'The Lost Revision of *PP B*', *YLS* 11 (1997).

Thorne, J. R. & Uhart, M. C. 'Robert Crowley's *PP*,' *MÆ* 55 (1986) 248–54.

Turville-Petre, T. 'Sir Adrian Fortescue and his Copy of *PP*,' *YLS* 14 (2000) 29–48.

'Putting it Right: The Corrections of HL ms HM 128 and BL Additional ms 35287', *YLS* 16 (2002) 41–65.

Uhart, M. C. 'The Early Reception of *PP*.' Unpub. Ph.D. diss. University of Leicester, 1986.

Vaughan, M. F. 'The Ending(s) of *PP* A' in Vaughan (1993) 211–41.

Warner, L. 'The *Ur-B PP* and the Earliest Production of C and B', *YLS* 16 (2002) 3–39.

'*PP* B XV 417–28a: an Intrusion from L.'s C-Papers?', *NQ* 249 (2004) 119–22.

'John But and the Other Works that Will Wrought (*Piers Plowman* A XII 101–2)', *NQ* 250 (2005) 13–18.

'The Ending, and End, of *PP* B: the C Version Origins of the Final Two Passus', *MÆ* 76 (2007) 225–50.

Weldon, J. F. G. '*Ordinatio* and Genre in MS CCC 201: A Medieval Reading of the B-Text of *PP*,' *Florilegium* 12 (1993) 159–75.

Westcott, B. F. & Hort, F. J., eds. *The New Testament*. 2 vols. Cambridge and London, 1881–82.

Wilcockson, C. 'A Note on "Rifling" in *PP* B. V. 234', *MÆ* 52 (1983) 302–5.

Windeatt, B. A. 'The Scribes as Chaucer's Early Critics', *SAC* I (1979) 23–35.

Wittig, J. S. 'The ME "Absolute Infinitive" and the Speech of Book', in Groos et al. (1986) 217–40.

C. Critical and Interpretative Studies of *PP* and related works

Adams, J. F. '*PP* and the Three Ages of Man', *JEGP* 61 (1962) 23–41.

Adams, R. 'L. and the Liturgy Revisited', *SP* 73 (1976) 266–84.

'The Nature of Need in *PP*,' *Traditio* 34 (1978) 273–301.

'Piers's Pardon and Langland's Semi-Pelagianism', *Traditio* 39 (1983) 367–418.

'Some Versions of Apocalypse: Learned & Popular Eschatology in *PP*,' in Heffernan (1985) 194–236.

'*Mede* and *Mercede*: The Evolution of the Economics of Grace in the *PP* B and C Versions' in Kennedy & al. (1988) 217–32.

Aers, D. *PP and Christian Allegory*. 1975.

Chaucer, Langland and the Creative Imagination. 1980.

'*PP* and Problems in the Perception of Poverty: a Culture in Transition', *LSE* 14 (1983) 5–25.

Sanctifying Signs: Making Christian Tradition in Late Medieval England. Notre Dame, Indiana, 2004.

Alexander, J. W. 'Ranulph of Chester: An Outlaw of Legend?' *NM* 83 (1982) 152–7.

Alford, J. '*PP* B XVIII 390: "Til Parce It Hote"', *MP* 69 (1972) 323–5.

'Haukyn's Coat: Some Observations on *PP* B XIV 22–27', *MÆ* 43 (1974) 133–8.

'Some Unidentified Quotations in *PP*,' *MP* 72 (1975) 390–99.

'The Role of the Quotations in *PP*,' *Speculum* 52 (1977[1]) 80–99.

'Literature and Law in Medieval England', *PMLA* 92 (1977[2]) 941–51.

'The Grammatical Metaphor: A Survey of its Use in the Middle Ages', *Speculum* 57 (1982) 728–60.

'More Unidentified Quotations in *PP*,' *MP* 81 (1984) 146–49.

'The Idea of Reason in *PP*', in Kennedy et al. (1988[1]) 199–215.

Ed. *A Companion to 'PP'*. Berkeley, Los Angeles, London, 1988[2].

'The Figure of Repentance in *PP*', in Vaughan (1993) 3–28.

'L's Exegetical Drama: the sources of the Banquet Scene in *PP*', in R. G. Newhauser & J. A. Alford, eds., *Literature and Religion in the Later Middle Ages: Philological Studies in Honor of Siegfried Wenzel* (Binghamton, NY, 1995) 97–117.

Allen, J. B. *The Ethical Poetic of the Later Middle Ages*. Toronto, 1982.

'L.'s Writing and Reading: *Detractor* and the Pardon Passus', *Speculum* 59 (1984) 342–62.

Amassian, M. and Sadowsky, J. 'Mede and Mercede: a Study of the Grammatical Metaphor in "PP" C IV 335–409', *NM* 72 (1971) 457–6.

Ames, R. M. *The Fulfilment of the Scriptures: Abraham, Moses and Piers*. Evanston, Illinois, 1970.

Arn, M-J. 'L.'s Triumph of Grace in Dobest', *ESt.* 63 (1982) 506–16.

Ashley, K. M. 'The Guiler Beguiled: Christ and Satan as Theological Tricksters in Medieval Religious Literature', *Criticism* 24 (1982) 126–37.

Astell, A. W. *Political Allegory in Late Medieval England*. Ithaca, NY. 1999.

Baer, P. 'Cato's "Trace": Literacy, Readership, and the Process of Revision in *PP*,' *Studies in Medieval and Renaissance History* 16 (2001) 123–47.

Baker, D. N. 'From Plowing to Penitence: *PP* and C14th Theology', *Speculum* 55 (1980) 715–25.

'The Pardons of *PP*,' *NM* 85 (1984[1]) 462–72.

'Dialectic Form in *Pearl* and *PP*,' *Viator* 15 (1984[2]) 263–73.

'Meed and the Economics of Chivalry in *PP*,' in D. N. Baker, ed. *The Hundred Years' War: French and English Cultural Studies*. Albany, NY 2000.

Baldwin, A. *The Theme of Government in Piers Plowman*. Cambridge, 1981[1].

'The Double Duel in *PP* B XVIII and C XXI', *MÆ* 50 (1981[2]) 64–78.

'A Reference in *PP* to the Westminster Sanctuary', *NQ* 29 (1982) 106–8.

'The Triumph of Patience in Julian of Norwich and L.', in Phillips (1990) 71–83.

'Patient Politics in *PP*,' *YLS* 15 (2001) 99–108.

Barney, S. 'The Ploughshare of the Tongue: the Progress of a Symbol from the Bible to *PP*,' *MS* 35 (1973) 261–93.

Allegories of History, Allegories of Love. Hamden, Conn. 1979.

The Penn Commentary on 'Piers Plowman', Vol. 5: C Passus 20–22; B Passus 18–20. Pennsylvania, 2006.

Barr, H. 'The Use of Latin Quotations in *PP* with Special Reference to Passus XVIII of the B-Text', *NQ* 33 (1986) 440–8.

'The Relationship of *RRe* and *MS*: Some New Evidence', *YLS* 4 (1990) 105–33.

Signes and Sothe: Language in the PP Tradition. Cambridge, 1994.

Socio-literary Practice in the Fourteenth Century. Oxford, 2003.

Barratt, A. 'Civil and Theology in *PP*,' *Traditio* 28 (1982).

Barron, C. 'WL: A London Poet', in Hanawalt, ed. *Chaucer's England: Literature in Historical Context* (Minneapolis, 1992) 91–109.

Bennett, J. A. W. 'The Date of the A-Text of *PP*,' *PMLA* 58 (1943[1]) 566–72.

'The Date of the B-Text of *PP*,' *MÆ* 12 (1943[2]) 55–64.

Chaucer at Oxford and at Cambridge. Oxford, 1974.

'L.'s Samaritan', *Poetica* 12 (1981) 10–27.

'*Nosce te ipsum*: some Medieval and Modern Interpretations', in Bennett, *The Humane Medievalist*, ed. P. Boitani (Rome, 1982) 135–72.

Poetry of the Passion. Oxford, 1982.

Middle English Literature, ed. D. Gray. Oxford, 1986.

Benson, C. D. 'An Augustinian Irony in *PP*', *NQ* 23 (1976) 51–4.

'The Function of Lady Meed in *PP*,' *ES* 61 (1980) 193–205.

'*PP* and Parish Wall Paintings', *YLS* 11 (1998) 1–38.

Public PP: Modern Scholarship and Late Medieval English Culture. Pennsylvania, 2004.

Benson, L. & Wenzel, S., eds. *The Wisdom of Poetry: Essays in Early English Literature in honor of M. W. Bloomfield*. Kalamazoo, Mich., 1982.

Bibliography

Bertz, D. 'Prophecy and Apocalypse in L.'s *PP*, B. XVI–XIX', *JEGP* 84 (1985) 313–28.

Biggs, F. M. '"Aungeles Peeris": *PP* B 16.67–72 and C 18.85–100', *Anglia* 102 (1984) 426–36.

    '"For God is after an Hand': *PP* B 17. 138–205', *YLS* 5 (1991) 17–30.

Birnes, W. J. 'Christ as Advocate: the Legal Metaphor of *PP*', *AM* 16 (1975) 71–93.

Bishop, L. 'Will and the Law of Property', *YLS* 10 (1996) 23–41.

Blanch, R. J., ed. *Style and Symbolism in* PP: *a Modern Critical Anthology*. Knoxville, Tennessee, 1969.

Bloom, H. *Poetry and Repression: Revisionism from Blake to Stevens*. 1976.

Bloomfield, M. W. *The Seven Deadly Sins*. Michigan, 1952.

    'The Pardons of Pamplona and the Pardoner of Rounceval: *PP* B XVII 252', *PQ* 35 (1956) 60–8.

    '*PP* and the Three Grades of Chastity', *Anglia* 76 (1958) 227–53.

    PP as a Fourteenth Century Apocalypse. New Brunswick, 1961.

Bourquin, G. *PP: Etudes sur la Genèse littéraire des Trois Versions*. Lille and Paris, 1978.

Bowers, A. J. 'The Tree of Charity in *PP*: Its Allegorical and Structural Significance', in E. Rothstein & J. Wittreich, eds. *Literary Monographs*, vol. 6: *Medieval and Renaissance Literature* (Madison, Wisc., 1975) 1–34.

Bowers, J. M. *The Crisis of Will in* 'PP'. Washington, D.C. 1986.

    '*PP* and the Police: Notes toward a history of the Wycliffite Langland', *YLS* 6 (1992) 1–50.

    '*Pearl* in its Royal Setting', *SAC* 17 (1995²) 111–55.

    'Dating *PP*: Testing the Testimony of Usk's *Testament*,' *YLS* 13 (1999) 65–100.

    Chaucer and Langland: The Antagonistic Tradition. Notre Dame, Indiana, 2007.

Bowers, R. H. '"Foleuyles Lawes" (*PP* C 22.247)', *NQ* 206 (1961) 327–8.

Braswell, M. F. *The Medieval Sinner: Characterisation and Confession in the Literature of the English Middle Ages*. Rutherford, N.J., 1983.

Breeze, A. 'The Trinity as a Taper: a Welsh Allusion to L.', *NQ* 235 (1990) 5–6.

    'A Welsh Addition to the *PP* Group', *NQ* 238 (1993¹) 142–51.

Bright, A. H. *New Light on 'PP'*. 1928.

Burdach, K. *Der Gral: Forschungen über seinen Ursprung und seinen Zusammenhang mit der Longinuslegende*. 2nd edn. Darmstadt, 1974.

Burnley, J. D. *Chaucer's Language and the Philosophers' Tradition*. Cambridge, 1979.

    'Langland's Clergial Lunatic' in Phillips (1990) 31–8.

Burrow, J. A. 'The Audience of *PP*', *Anglia* 75 (1957), repr. in id. *Essays* (1984) 102–16.

    'The Action of L.'s Second Vision', *EC* 15 (1965) 247–68, repr. in *Essays* 79–101.

    'Words, Works and Will: Theme and Structure in *PP*', in Hussey (1969) 111–24.

    Ricardian Poetry. 1971.

    'L. *Nel Mezzo del Cammin*', in Heyworth (1981) 21–41.

    'Autobiographical Poetry in the Middle Ages', *PBA* 68 (1982) 389–412.

    Essays in Medieval Literature. Oxford, 1984.

    The Ages of Man. Oxford, 1986.

    'Reason's Horse', *YLS* 4 (1990) 139–44.

    Langland's Fictions. Oxford, 1993¹.

    Thinking in Poetry: Three Medieval Examples. 1993².

    'Gestures and Looks in *PP*,' *YLS* 14 (2000) 75–83.

    'Wasting Time, Wasting Words in *PP* B and C', *YLS* 17 (2003) 191–202.

    'Lady Meed and the Power of Money', *MÆ* 74 (2005) 113–18.

    'The Two Ploughs of Piers Plowman (B XIX 430)', *NQ* 252 (2007) 123–24.

Calí, P. *Allegory and Vision in Dante and Langland*. Cork, 1971.

Cargill, O. 'The Langland Myth', *PMLA* 50 (1935) 36–56.

Carlson, P. 'Lady Meed and God's Meed: The Grammar of *PP* B 3 and C 4', *Traditio* 46 (1991) 291–311.

Carruthers, M. *The Search for St. Truth*. Evanston, Illinois, 1973.

——& Kirk, E., eds. *Acts of Interpretation: the text and its contexts 700–1600. Essays on medieval and renaissance lierature in honour of E. T. Donaldson*. Norman, Oklahoma. 1982.

    'Imaginatif, Memoria and "The Need for Critical Theory" in *PP* Studies', *YLS* 9 (1995) 103–14. *See* Schroeder, M.

Cassidy, F. G. 'The Merit of Malkyn', *MLN* (1948) 52–3.

Chamberlin, J. *Medieval Arts Doctrines on Ambiguity and their Place in Langland's Poetics*. Montreal and Kingston, 2000.

Clifton, N. 'The Romance Convention of the Disguised Duel and the Climax of *PP*', *YLS* 7 (1993) 123–8.

Clopper, L. M. 'L.'s Trinitarian Analogies as Key to Meaning and Structure', *Medievalia et Humanistica* n.s. 9 (1979) 87–110.

'The Contemplative Matrix of *PP* B' *MLQ* 46 (1985) 3–28.

'L.'s Franciscanism', *ChR* 25 (1990) 54–75.

'Songes of Rechelesnesse': L. and the Franciscans. Michigan, 1997.

Clutterbuck, C. 'Hope and Good Works: *Leaute* in the C-Text of *PP*', *RES* 28 (1977) 129–40.

Coghill, N. 'God's Wenches and the Light that Spoke: some notes on Langland's kind of poetry,' [1962], repr. in D. Gray, ed. *The Collected Papers of Nevill Coghill, Shakespearean and Medievalist* (Sussex, 1988) 199–217.

Cole, A. 'WL's Lollardy', *YLS* 17 (2003) 25–54.

Coleman, J. *PP and the Moderni*. Rome, 1981.

Cooper, H. 'L.'s and Chaucer's Prologues', *YLS* 1 (1987) 71–81.

Cornelius, R. D. *The Figurative Castle*. Bryn Mawr, Pa. 1930.

'*PP* and the *Roman de Fauvel*', *PMLA* 47 (1932) 363–7.

Craun, E. D. *Lies, Slander and Obscenity in Medieval English Literature*. Cambridge, 1997.

Davies, R. 'The Life, Travels and Library of an Early Reader of *PP*', *YLS* 12 (1999) 49–64.

Davlin, Sr. M. C. '*Kynde Knowynge* as a Major Theme in *PP* B', *RES* n.s. 22 (1971) 1–19.

'"*Petrus, id est, Christus*": P. the P. as "The Whole Christ"', *ChR* 6 (1972) 280–92.

'A Genius-Kynde Illustration in Codex Vat. Pal. Lat. 629', *Manuscripta* 23 (1979) 149–58.

'Kynde Knowynge as a ME Equivalent for "Wisdom" in *PP* B', *MÆ* 50 (1981) 5–17.

'*PP* and the Books of Wisdom', *YLS* 2 (1988) 23–33.

A Game of Heuene: Word Play and the Meaning of 'PP' B. Cambridge, 1989.

'*PP* and the Gospel and First Epistle of John', *YLS* 10 (1996) 89–127.

The Place of God in PP *and Medieval Art*. Aldershot, Hants. 2001.

Day, M.'"Mele Tyme of Seintes": *PP* B, V, 500', *MLR* 227 (1932) 317–18.

Dolan, T. P. 'L. and FitzRalph: Two Solutions to the Mendicant Problem', *YLS* 2 (1988) 35–45.

Donaldson, E. T. *PP: The C-Text and its Poet*. New Haven and London, 1949.

'L. and some Scriptural Quotations', in Benson & Wenzel (1982) 67–72.

Donna, R. B. *Despair and hope: A Study in Langland and Augustine*. Washington, D.C., 1948.

Doob, P. R. *The Idea of the Labyrinth from Classical Antiquity through the Middle Ages*. Ithaca & London, 1990.

Dove, M. *The Perfect Age of Man's Life*. Cambridge, 1986.

Doxsee, E. '"Trew Treuthe" and Canon Law: the Orthodoxy of Trajan's Salvation in *PP* C-Text', *NM* 89 (1988) 295–311.

Dronke, P. 'Arbor Caritatis', in Heyworth (1981) 207–43.

Du Boulay, F. R. H. *The England of 'PP'*. Cambridge, 1991.

Dunning, T.P. 'L. and the Salvation of the Heathen', *MÆ* 12 (1943) 45–54.

'The Structure of the B-Text of *PP*', *RES* n.s. 7 (1956) 225–37; repr. in Blanch (1969) 87–100.

Piers Plowman: An Interpretation of the A-Text, 2nd edn. rev. and ed. by T. Dolan. Oxford, 1980.

Dyas, D. *Pilgrimage in Medieval English Literature, 700–1500*. Cambridge, 2001.

'A pilgrim in sheep's clothing? The nature of wandering in *PP*,' *ELN* 39 (2002) 1–12.

Dyer, C. '*PP* and Plowmen: A Historical Perspective', *YLS* 155–76.

Eaton, R. 'L.'s Malleable Lady Meed', *Costerus* 80 (Amsterdam & Atlanta, Ga., 1991) 119–41.

Emmerson, R. K. *Antichrist in the Middle Ages*. Seattle, 1981.

Erzgräber, W. *William Langlands 'PP'. Eine Interpretation des C-Textes*. Heidelberg, 1957.

Fletcher, A. J. 'Line 30 of the Man of Law's Tale and the Medieval Malkyn', *ELN* 24 (1986) 15–20.

'A Simoniacal Moment in *PP*,' *YLS* 4 (1990) 135–8.

'The Hideous Feet of L.'s Peacock', *NQ* 236 (1991) 18–20.

'The Social Trinity of *PP*,' *RES* 44 (1993) 343–61.

Preaching, Politics and Poetry in Late-Medieval England. Dublin, 1998.

Fowler, D. C. *P the P: Literary Relations of the A and B Texts*. Seattle, 1961.

'A Pointed Personal Allusion in *P the P*,' *MP* 77 (1979) 158–59.

'Star-Gazing: *PP* and the Peasants' Revolt', *Review* 18 (1996) 1–30.

'Annotating *PP*: The Athlone Project', *TEXT* 10 (1997) 151–60.

Fowler, E., *Literary Character: The Human Figure in Early English Writing* Ithaca, NY, 2003.

Frank, R. W. 'The Conclusion of *PP*,' *JEGP* 49 (1950) 309–16.

'The Pardon Scene in *PP*', *Speculum* 26 (1951[1]) 317–31.

'The Number of Dreams in *PP*,' *MLN* 66 (1951[2]) 309–12.

'The Art of Reading Medieval Personification-Allegory', *ELH* 20 (1953) 237–50.

Piers Plowman and the Scheme of Salvation. New Haven, 1957.

'The "Hungry Gap", Crop Failure, and Famine: the C14th Agricultural Crisis and *PP*,' *YLS* 4 (1990) 87–104.

Gaffney, W. 'The Allegory of the Christ-Knight in *PP*,' *PMLA* 46 (1931) 155–68.

Gallacher, P. J. 'Imagination, Prudence, and the *Sensus Communis*', *YLS* 5 (1991) 49–64.

'Imaginatif and the *Sensus Communis*,' *YLS* 6 (1992) 51–61.

Galloway, A. 'Two Notes on L.'s Cato: *PP* B. I. 88–91; IV 20–23,' *ELN* 25 (1987) 9–13.

'The Rhetoric of Riddling in Late-Medieval England: The "Oxford" Riddles, the *Secretum philosophorum* and the Riddles in *PP*,' *Speculum* 70 (1995) 68–105.

'Intellectual Pregnancy, Metaphysical Femininity, and the Social Doctrine of the Trinity in *PP*,' *YLS* 12 (1998) 117–52.

'Making History Legal: *PP* and the Rebels of C14th England', in Hewett-Smith (2001[1]) 7–39.

'*PP* and the Subject of the Law', *YLS* 15 (2001[2]) 117–28.

The Penn Commentary on 'Piers Plowman', Vol. I: C Prologue–Passus 4; B Prologue–Passus 4; A Prologue–Passus 4. Pennsylvania, 2006.

Gasse, R. 'L.'s "Lewd Vicory" Reconsidered', *JEGP* 95 (1996) 322–35.

Giancarlo, M. '*PP*, Parliament and the Public Voice', *YLS* 17 (2003) 135–74.

Gilbert, B. B. '"Civil" and the Notaries in *PP*,' *MÆ* 50 (1981) 49–63.

Gill, S. *Wordsworth: A Life*. Oxford, 1989.

Gillespie, V. 'Thy Will Be Done: *PP* and the *Paternoster*', in A. J. Minnis, ed., *Late-Medieval Religious Texts and their Transmission: Essays in Honour of A. I. Doyle* (Cambridge, 1994) 95–119.

Godden, M. *The Making of Piers Plowman*. 1990.

Goldsmith, M. E. *The Figure of Piers Plowman*. Cambridge, 1981.

'Piers' Apples: Some Bernardine Echoes in *PP*,' *LSE* n.s. 16 (1985) 309–25.

'Will's Pilgrimage in *PP* B', in M. Stokes & T. L. Burton, eds., *Medieval Literature and Antiquities: Studies in Honour of Basil Cottle* (Cambridge, 1987) 119–31.

Gradon, P. 'L. and the Ideology of Dissent', *PBA* 66 (1982 for 1980).

'*Trajanus Redivivus*: Another Look at Trajan in *PP*,' in D. Gray and E. G. Stanley, eds. *ME Studies Presented to Norman Davis* (Oxford, 1983) 71–103.

Grady, F. '*PP*, *St Erkenwald*, and the Rule of Exceptional Salvations', *YLS* 6 (1992) 63–8.

Gray, D. 'The Robin Hood Poems', *Poetica* 18 (1984) 1–39.

Gray, N. 'L.'s Quotations from the Penitential Tradition', *MP* 84 (1986[1]) 53–60.

'The Clemency of Cobbleres: A reading of "Glutton's Confession" in *PP*,' *Studies in English* n.s. 17 (1986[2]) 61–75.

Green, R. F. 'John Ball's Letters: Literary History and Historical Literature', in Hanawalt (1992) 176–200.

'Friar William Appleton and the Date of L.'s B-Text', *YLS* 11 (1997) 87–96.

A Crisis of Truth: Literature and Law in Ricardian England. Philadelphia, 1999.

Groos, A. et al., eds. *Magister Regis: Studies in Honor of R. E. Kaske*. New York, 1986.

Gwynn, A. 'The Date of the B-Text of *PP*,' *RES* 19 (1943) 1–24.

Hanna, R. *William Langland*. Aldershot, 1993.

'Annotating *PP*,' *TEXT* 10 (1994) 153–63.

'Emendations to a 1993 "Vita de Ne'erdowel"', *YLS* 14 (2000) 185–198.

London Literature, 1300–1380. Cambridge, 2005.

Hanawalt, B. 'Ballads and Bandits: C14th Outlaws and the Robin Hood Poems', in idem (1992) 154–75.

ed. *Chaucer's England: Literature in Historical Context*. Minneapolis, 1992.

Harbert, B. 'Langland's Easter', in Phillips (1980) 57–70.

'A Will with a Reason: Theological Developments in the C-Revision of *PP*,' in P. Boitani & A. Torti, eds., *Religion in the Poetry and Drama of the Late Middle Ages in England*. Cambridge, 1990.

Harwood, B. J. 'Clergye and the Action of the Third Vision in *PP*,' *MP* 70 (1973[1]) 279–90.

'*Liberum-Arbitrium* in the C-Text of *PP*,' *PQ* 52 (1973[2]) 680–95.

'Imaginative in *PP*,' *MÆ* 44 (1975) 249–63.

'Langland's *Kynde Wit*,' *JEGP* 75 (1976) 330–6.

'Langland's *Kynde Knowyng* and the Quest for Christ', *MP* 80 (1983) 242–55.

'Dame Study and the Place of Orality in *PP*,' *ELH* 57 (1990) 1–17.

'*PP*' and the Problem of Belief. Toronto, 1992.

——& Smith, R. F. 'Inwit and the Castle of *Caro* in *PP*,' *NM* 71 (1970) 48–54.

Hazelton, R. 'Two Texts of the *Disticha Catonis* and its Commentary, with special reference to Chaucer, Langland and Gower'. PhD. Diss. Rutgers University, 1956.

Heffernan, C. '*PP* B I 153–8', *ELN* 22 (1984) 1–5.

Heffernan, T. J., ed. *The Popular Literature of Medieval England*. Knoxville, Tennessee, 1985.

Hench, A. L. *The Allegorical Motif of Conscience and Reason, Counsellors* University of Virginia Studies 4, 1951.

Henry, A. 'Some Aspects of Biblical Imagery in *PP*,' in Phillips (1990) 39–55.

Herman, J. P. 'Gematria in *PP*,' *Connotations* I (1991) 168–72.

Hewett-Smith, K. M. 'Allegory of the Half-Acre: the Demands of History', *YLS* 10 (1996) 1–22.

 '"Nede ne hath no lawe": Poverty and the De-stabilisation of Allegory in the Final Visions of *PP*,' in Idem (2001) 233–53.

——ed. *William Langland's PP: A Book of Essays*. 2001.

Heyworth, P. L. '*Jack Upland's Rejoinder*, a Lollard Interpolator and *PP* B. X. 249f', *MÆ* 36 (1967) 242–8.

——ed. *Medieval Studies for J. A.W. Bennett Aetatis Suae LXX*. Oxford, 1981.

Hieatt, C. *The Realism of Dream-Visions*. The Hague, 1967.

Hill, T. D. 'The Tropological Context of Heat and Cold Imagery in Anglo–Saxon Poetry', *NM* 69 (1968) 522–32.

 'Some Remarks on the site of Lucifer's Throne', *Anglia* 87 (1969) 303–11.

 'The Light that Blew the Saints to Heaven: *PP* B V 495–503', *RES* ns. 24 (1973) 444–9.

 'A Liturgical Allusion in *PP* B XVI 88', *NQ* 220 (1975) 531–2.

 'Christ's "Thre Clothes": *PP* C.XI. 193', *NQ* 223 (1978) 200–3.

 '"Satan's Pratfall and the Foot of Love: some Pedal Images in *PP* A, B and C', *YLS* 14 (2000) 153–161.

 'The Problem of Synecdochic Flesh: *PP* B.9.49–50', *YLS* 15 (2001) 213–18.

Holsinger, B. W. 'L.'s Musical Reader: Liturgy, Law and the Constraints of Performance', *SAC* 21 (1999) 99–141.

Hort, G. *PP and Contemporary Religious Thought*. 1938.

Howard, D. R. *The Three Temptations*. Princeton, N.J., 1966.

Hudson, A. 'The Legacy of *PP*,' in Alford, *Companion* (1988[1]) 251–66.

 The Premature Reformation: Wycliffite Texts and Lollard History. Oxford, 1988[2].

 '*PP* and the Peasants' Revolt: A Problem Revisited', *YLS* 8 (1994) 85–106.

 'L. and Lollardy?', *YLS* 17 (2003) 93–105.

Hughes, J. *Pastors and Visionaries: Religion and Secular Life in Late Medieval Yorkshire*. Woodbridge, 1988.

Huppé, B. F. 'The A-Text of *PP* and the Norman Wars', *PMLA* 54 (1939) 37–64.

 'The Date of the B-Text of *PP*,' *SP* 38 (1941) 36–44.

 '*Petrus, id est, Christus*: Word Play in *PP*,' *ELH* 17 (1950) 163–70.

Hussey, S. S. 'L., Hilton and the Three Lives', *RES* n.s. 7 (1956) 132–59.

 'L.'s Reading of Alliterative Poetry', *MLR* 60 (1965) 163–70.

——(ed.): *PP: Critical Approaches* (1969).

Izydorczyk, Z., ed. *The Medieval Gospel of Nicodemus: Texts, Intertexts and Contexts in Western Europe*. Tempe, Arizona, 1997.

Jenkins, P. 'Conscience: The Frustration of Allegory', in Hussey (1969) 124–42. *See* Martin, P.

Johnson, D. F. '"Persen with a Pater-Noster Paradis oþer Hevene": *PP* C 11.296–98a', *YLS* 5 (1991) 77–89.

Jones, E. 'Langland and Hermits', *YLS* 11 (1997) 67–86.

Jones, H. S. V. 'Imaginatif in *PP*,' *JEGP* 13 (1914).

 '*In somnium, in visionem*: the Figurative Significance of Sleep in *PP*,' in L. Houwen and A. Macdonald, eds. *Loyal Letters: Studies in Medieval Alliterative Poetry and Prose* (Groningen, 1994) 239–300.

Jung, M-R. *Etudes sur le poème allégorique en France au Moyen Age*. Berne, 1971.

Jusserand, J. J. *PP: A Contribution to the History of English Mysticism*. 1894; repr. New York, 1965.

Justice, S. 'The Genres of *PP*,' *Viator* 19 (1988) 281–306.

 Writing and Rebellion: England in 1381. Berkeley & Los Angeles, 1994.

——& K. Kerby-Fulton, eds. *Written Work: Langland, Labor, and Authorship*. Philadelphia, 1997. *And see* Kerby-Fulton.

Kane, G. *PP: The Evidence for Authorship*. 1965[1].

 The Autobiographical Fallacy in Chaucer and Langland Studies. 1965[2].

 'Music "Neither Unpleasant nor Monotonous"', in Heyworth (1981) 43–63.

 'The Perplexities of WL', in Benson & Wenzel (1982) 73–89.

Bibliography

'Some C14th "political" Poems', in Kratzmann & Simpson (1986) 82–91.

Chaucer and Langland: Historical and Textual Approaches. Berkeley & Los Angeles, 1989.

'Reading *PP*,' *YLS* 8 (1994) 1–20.

'L., Labour and Authorship' (review article), *NQ* 243 (1998) 420–5.

Kaske, R.E. '*Gigas* the Giant in *PP*,' *JEGP* 56 (1957[1]) 177–85.

'L. and the *Paradisus Claustralis*,' *MLN* 72 (1957[2]) 481–3.

'The Speech of "Book" in *PP*,' *Anglia* 77 (1959[1]) 117–44.

'L.'s Walnut Simile', *JEGP* 58 (1959[2]) 650–4.

'"*Ex vi transicionis*" and Its Passage in *PP*,' *JEGP* 62 (1963) 32–60, repr. in Blanch 228–63.

'*PP* and Local Iconography', *JWCI* 31 (1968) 159–69.

'Holy Church's Speech and the Structure of *PP*,' in B. Rowland, ed. *Chaucer and ME: Studies in honour of R .H. Robbins.* 1974.

'The Character Hunger in *PP*,' in Kennedy & al (1988) 187–97.

Kaulbach, E. *Imaginative Prophecy in the B-Text of 'PP'.* Cambridge, 1993.

Kean, P. M. 'Love, Law and *Lewte* in *PP*,' *RES* n.s. 15 (1964) 241–61, repr. Blanch (1969) 132–55.

'L. on the Incarnation', *RES* n.s. 16 (1965) 349–63.

'Justice, Kingship and the Good Life in the Second Part of *PP*,' in Hussey (1969) 76–100.

Keen, J. A. *The Charters of Christ and 'PP': Documenting Salvation.* New York, 2002.

Kellogg, A. L. 'Satan, Langland and the North', *Speculum* 24 (1949) 413–14.

'Langland and Two Scriptural Texts', *Traditio* 14 (1958) 385–98.

——& Haselmayer, L. A. 'Chaucer's Satire of the Pardoner', *PMLA* 66 (1951) 251–77.

Kellogg, E. H. 'Bishop Brunton and the Fable of the Rats', *PMLA* 50 (1935) 385–98.

Kennedy, E. D., Waldron, R. & Wittig J. S., eds. *Medieval English Studies Presented to George Kane.* Woodbridge, 1988.

Kennedy, K. E. 'Retaining a Court of Chancery in *PP*,' *YLS* 17 (2003) 175–89.

Kerby-Fulton, K. *Reformist Apocalypticism and 'PP'.* Cambridge, 1990.

'"Who Has Written this Book?" Visionary Autobiography in L.'s C-Text', in M. Glasscoe, ed. *The Medieval Mystical Tradition in England* V (Cambridge, 1992) 101–16.

'L.'s Reading: some Evidence from MSS containing Religious Prophecy', in C. Morse, P. Doob & M. Woods, eds., *The Uses of MSS: Essays in memory of J. B. Allen* (Kalamazoo, 1992) 237–61.

'L. and the Bibliographic Ego', in Justice & Kerby-Fulton (1997) 67–143.

Piers Plowman, in Wallace, ed. *CHMEL* (1999) 513–38.

——& S. Justice, 'Langlandian Reading Circles and the Civil Service in London and Dublin, 1380–1427', *New Medieval Literatures* 1 (1997) 59–83.

Kim, M. 'Hunger, Need and the Politics of Poverty in *PP*,' *YLS* 16 (2002) 131–68.

King, J. N. *English Reformation Literature.* Princeton, 1982.

Kirk, E. D. *The Dream Thought of* PP. New Haven & London, 1972.

'"Who Suffreth More than God": Narrative Re-definition of Patience in *Patience* and *PP*,' in G. Schifforst, ed. *The Triumph of Patience* (Orlando, Fla., 1978) 88–104.

'L.'s Plowman and the Recreation of C14th Religious Metaphor', *YLS* 2 (1988) 1–23.

Kirk, R. 'References to the Law in *PP*,' *PMLA* 48 (1933) 322–8.

Knight, S. *Robin Hood: A Mythic Biography* (Ithaca, NY, 2003)

[Mentions L and Folvilles]

Kolve, V. A. *The Play Called Corpus Christi.* Stanford, 1966.

Kratzmann, G. & Simpson, J., eds. *Medieval English Religious and Ethical Literature: Essays in Honour of G. H. Russell.* Cambridge, 1986.

Kruger, S. F. 'Mirrors and the Trajectory of Vision in *PP*,' *Speculum* 66 (1991) 74–95.

Dreaming in the Middle Ages. Cambridge, 1992.

Kuczynski, M. *Prophetic Song: the Psalms as Moral Discourse in Late Medieval England.* Philadelphia, 1995.

Lawler, T. 'Conscience's Dinner', in Tavormina and Yeager (1995) 87–103.

'The Pardon Formula in *PP*: Its Ubiquity, its Binary Shape, its Silent Middle Term', *YLS* 14 (2000) 117–52.

Lawlor, J. 'The Imaginative Unity of *PP*,' *RES* n.s. 8 (1957) 113–26, repr. Blanch, 101–16.

PP: An Essay in Criticism. 1962.

Lawton, D. 'Lollardy and the *PP* Tradition', *MLR* 76 (1981) 780–93.

——ed. *Middle English Alliterative Poetry and its Literary Background.* Cambridge, 1982.

742

'The Subject of *PP*,' *YLS* 1 (1987) 1–30.

'Alliterative Style' (1988) in Alford, *Companion* 223–49.

'The Diversity of ME Alliterative Poetry', *LSE* n.s. 20 (1989) 143–72.

'Englishing the Bible, 1066–1549', in Wallace, ed. *CHMEL* 454–82.

Leader, Z. *Revision and Romantic Authorship*. Oxford, 1996.

Levy, B. S. and Szarmach, P. E., eds. *The Alliterative Tradition in the C14th.* Kent, Ohio, 1981.

Lewis, L. 'L.'s Tree of charity and Usk's "Wexing Tree"', *NQ* 240 (1995) 429–33.

Lindemann, E. 'Analogues for Latin Quotations in L.'s *PP*,' *NM* 78 (1977) 359–61.

Lister, R. 'The Peasants of *PP* and its Audience', in K. Parkinson & M. Priestman, *Peasants and Countrymen in Literature* (1982) 71–90.

Lunz, E. 'The Valley of Jehoshaphat in *PP*,' *Tulane Studies in English* 20 (1972) 1–10.

Mäder, E. J. *Der Streit der 'TöchterGottes': Zur Geschichte eines allegorischen Motivs.* Bern, 1971.

Maguire, S. 'The Significance of Haukyn, *Activa Vita*, in *PP*,' *RES* 25 (1949) 97–109; repr. Blanch, 194–208.

Mann, J. *Chaucer and Medieval Estates Satire.* Cambridge, 1973.

'Eating and Drinking in *PP*,' *E&S* 32 (1979) 26–43.

'Satiric Subject and Satiric Object in Goliardic Literature', *Mittellateinsches Jahrbuch* 15 (1980) 63–86.

'Allegorical Buildings in Medieval Literature', *MÆ* 63 (1994[2]) 191–210.

Marcett, M. E. *Uthred de Boldon, Friar William Jordan and PP.* New York, 1938.

Marchand, J. W. 'An Unidentified Latin Quote in *PP*,' *MP* 88 (1990–1) 398–400.

Martin, P. *'PP': the Field and the Tower.* 1979.

'*PP*: Indirect Relations and the Record of Truth', in Vaughan (1993) 169–90. *And see* Jenkins, P.

Marx, C. W. *The Devil's Rights and the Redemption in the Literature of Medieval England.* Cambridge, 1995.

Matheson, L. Review of *William Langland* by R. Hanna, *YLS* 8 (1994) 192–4.

Mehl, D. 'The Audience of Chaucer's *TC*', in S. Barney, ed., *Chaucer's Troilus: Essays in Criticism* (1980) 211–29. *Geoffrey Chaucer.* Cambridge, 1986.

Meroney, H. 'The Life and Death of Longe Wille', *ELH* 17 (1950) 1–35.

Middleton, A. 'The Idea of Public Poetry in the Reign of Richard II', *Speculum* 53 (1978) 99–114.

'Two Infinites: Grammatical Metaphor in *PP*,' *ELH* 39 (1972) 169–88.

'The Audience and Public of *PP*,' in Lawton, ed. *ME Alliterative Poetry* (1982) 101–23.

'The Passion of Seint Averoys [B.13.91]: "Deuynyng" and Divinity in the Banquet Scene', *YLS* 1 (1987) 31–40.

'Making a Good End: John But as a Reader of *PP*,' in Kennedy et al. (1988) 243–66.

'William Langland's "Kynde Name": Authorial Signature and Social Identity in Late–Fourteenth Century England', in L. Patterson, ed. *Literary Practice and Social Change in Britain, 1380–1530* (Berkeley, Los Angeles and London, 1990) 15–82.

'Acts of Vagrancy: The C Version "Autobiography" and the Statute of 1388', in Justice & Kerby-Fulton (1997) 208–317.

Mills, D. 'The Rôle of the Dreamer in *PP*', in Hussey (1969) 180–212.

Minnis, A. J. 'L.'s Ymaginatif and late-medieval theories of imagination', *Comparative Criticism: A Year Book* 3 (Cambridge, 1981) 71–103.

——ed. *Late-Medieval Religious Texts and their Transmission: Essays in Honour of A. I. Doyle.* Cambridge, 1994.

Mitchell, A. G. 'Lady Meed and the Art of *PP*,' (1956), repr. in Blanch (1969) 174–93.

Morgan, G. 'The Meaning of Kind Wit, Conscience and Reason in the First Vision of *PP*,' *MP* 84 (1987[1]) 351–8.

'L.'s Conception of Favel, Guile, Liar and False in the First Vision of *PP*,' *Neophilologus* 71 (1987[2]) 626–33.

'The Status and Meaning of Meed in the First Vision of *PP*,' *Neophilologus* 72 (1988) 449–63.

Murtaugh, D. M. *'PP' and the Image of God.* Gainesville, Fla. 1978.

Narin van Court, E. 'The Hermeneutics of Supersession: the Revision of the Jews from the B to the C-Text of *PP*,' *YLS* 10 (1996) 43–87.

Nolan, B. *The Gothic Visionary Perspective.* Princeton, 1977.

Orme, N. 'Langland and Education', *History of Education* 11 (1982) 251–66.

Orsten, E. M. 'The Ambiguities in L.'s Rat Parliament', *MS* (1961) 216–39.

'*Patientia* in the B-Text of *PP*,' *MS* 31 (1969) 317–33.

'"Heaven on Earth"—L.'s Vision of Life Within the Cloister', *American Benedictine Review* (1970) 526–34.

Overstreet, S. A. '"Grammaticus Ludens": Theological Aspects of L.'s Grammmatical Allegory', *Traditio* 40 (1984) 251–96.

Bibliography

Owen, D. L. *PP: A Comparison with some earlier and contemporary French Allegories.* 1912.

Owst, G. R. 'The "Angel" and the "Goliardeys" of L.'s Prologue', *MLR* 20 (1925) 270–9.
    Literature and Pulpit in Medieval England. 2nd edn. Oxford, 1961.

Pantin, W. A. 'A Medieval Collection of Latin and English Proverbs and Riddles, from the Rylands Latin MS 394', *BJRL* 14 (1930) 81–114.

Papka, C. R. 'The Limits of Apocalypse: Eschatology, Epistemology and Textuality in the *Commedia and PP*,' in Bynum, C. W. & Freedman, P., eds. *Last Things: Death and the Apocalypse in the Middle Ages* (Philadelphia, 2000) 233–56.

Pearsall, D. 'The Origins of the Alliterative Revival', in Levy and Szarmach (1981) 1–24.
    'The Alliterative Revival: Origins and Social Backgrounds', in Lawton (1982) 34–53.
    'Poverty and Poor People in *PP*,' in Kennedy et al. (1988) 167–85.
    '"Lunatyk Lollares" in *PP*,' in P. Boitani & A. Torti, eds. *Religion in the Poetry and Drama of the Late Middle Ages in England* (Cambridge, 1990) 163–78.
    'L.'s London' in Justice and Kerby-Fulton (1997) 185–207.
    'L. and Lollardy: from B to C', *YLS* 17 (2003) 7–23.
——ed. *New Directions in Later Medieval Manuscript Studies.* York and Woodbridge, 2000.
——& R.A. Waldron, eds. *Medieval Literature and Civilisation: Studies in Memory of G. N. Garmonsway.* 1969.

Peebles, R. J. *The Legend of Longinus in ecclesiastical art and in English Literature.* Bryn Mawr, 1911.

Perrow, E. C. *The Last Will and Testament as a Form of Literature.* Transactions of the Wisconsin Academy of Sciences, Arts & Letters 17 (1914) 682–753.

Phillips, H., ed. *Langland, the Mystics and the Medieval English Religious Tradition: Essays in Honour of S. S. Hussey.* Cambridge, 1990.

Pilkinton, M. C. 'The Raising of Lazarus: a Prefiguring Agent to the Harrowing of Hell', *MÆ* 44 (1975) 51–3.

Quirk, R. 'L.'s Use of *Kind Wit* and *Inwit*,' *JEGP* 52 (1953) 182–9.
    '"*Vis Imaginativa* "', *JEGP* 53 (1954) 81–3.

Raabe, P. *Imitating God: The Allegory of Faith in PP-B.* 1990.

Raby, F. J. E. '*Turris Alethie* and the *Ecloga Theoduli*', *MÆ* 34 (1965) 226–9.

Raw, B. 'Piers and the Image of God in Man', in Hussey (1969) 143–79.

Raymo, R. 'A ME Version of the *Epistola Luciferi ad Cleros*', in Pearsall & Waldron (1969) 233–48.

Revard, C. 'The Papelard Priest and the Black Prince', *SAC* 23 (2001) 359–406.

Richardson, G. 'L.'s Mary Magdalene: Proverbial Misogyny and the Problem of Authority', *YLS* 14 (2000) 163–184.

Rickert, E. 'John But, Messenger and Maker', *MP* 11 (1913–14) 107–116.

Risse, R. G. 'The Augustinian Paraphrase of Isaiah 14:13–14 in *PP* and the Commentary on the *Fables* of Avianus', *PQ* 45 (1966) 712–17.

Robertson, D. W. & Huppé, B. F. *PP and Scriptural Tradition.* Princeton, N.J., 1951.

Rogers, W. E. 'Knighthood as Trope: Holy Church's Interpretation of Knighthood in *PP* B.I', *Sewanee Medieval Studies* 9 (1999) 205–18.
    Interpretation in 'PP'. Washington, D.C., 2002.

Rudd, G. 'The State of the Ark: a Metaphor in Bromyard and *PP*,' *NQ* 235 (1990) 6–10.
    Managing Language in PP. Cambridge, 1994.

Ruffing, J. 'The Crucifixion Drink in *PP* B.18 and C.20', *YLS* 5 (1991) 99–109.

Russell, G. H. 'The Poet as Reviser: The Metamorphosis of the Confession of the Seven Deadly Sins in *PP*,' in Carruthers & Kirk (1982) 53–65.

Ryan, W. 'Word Play in Some OE Homilies and a Late ME Poem', in E. Atwood & A. Hill, eds. *Studies in Language, Literature and Culture of the Middle Ages and Later.* Austin, Texas, 1969.

Rydzeski, J. *Radical Nostalgia in the Age of PP: Economics, Apocalypticism, and Discontent.* New York, 1999.

St-Jacques, R. 'L.'s Christ-Knight and the Liturgy', *Revue de l'Université d'Ottawa* 37 (1967) 146–58.
    'The Liturgical Associations of L.'s Samaritan', *Traditio* 25 (1969) 217–30.
    'Conscience's Final Pilgrimage in *PP* and the Cyclical Structure of the Liturgy', *Revue de l'Université d'Ottawa* 40 (1970) 210–23.
    'L.'s Bells of the Resurrection and the Easter Liturgy', *English Studies in Canada* 3 (1977[1]) 129–35.
    'L.'s "Spes" the Spy and the Book of Numbers', *NQ* 222 (1977[2]) 483–5.
    'L.'s *Christus Medicus* Image and the Structure of *PP*,' *YLS* 5 (1991) 111–127.

Salter, E. *Piers Plowman: an Introduction.* Oxford, 1962.
    '*PP* and "The Simonie"', *Archiv* 203 (1967) 241–54, repr. in Salter, *English and International*, 158–69.

'*PP* and the Visual Arts' (1971), repr. in *English and International*, 256–66.

'The Timeliness of *Wynnere and Wastoure*', *MÆ* 47 (1978) 30–65, repr. in *English and International*, 180–98.

'L. and the Contexts of "PP"', *E&S* 32 (1979) 19–25.

English and International: Studies in the Literature, Art and Patronage of Medieval England, ed. D. Pearsall and N. Zeeman. Cambridge, 1988.

Sanderlin, G. 'The Character "Liberum Arbitrium"', *MLN* 56 (1941) 449–53.

'John Capgrave Speaks up for the Hermits', *Speculum* 18 (1943) 358–62.

Sargent, H. J. and Kittredge, G. L., eds. *English and Scottish Popular Ballads*. Boston, 1932.

Scase, W. *PP and the New Anticlericalism*. Cambridge, 1989.

'"First to reckon Richard": John But's *PP*,' *YLS* 11 (1997) 49–66.

Schmidt, A. V. C. 'A Note on the A-Text of *PP*, X.91–4', *NQ* 212 (1967) 355–6.

'A Note on the Phrase "Free Wit" in the C-Text of *PP*, XI 51', *NQ*. 213 (1968[1]) 168–9.

'A Note on L.'s Conception of "Anima" and "Inwit"', *NQ* 213 (1968[2]) 363–4.

'Two Notes on *PP*,' *NQ* 214 (1969[1]) 168–9.

'L. and Scholastic Philosophy', *MÆ* 38 (1969[2]) 134–56.

'L. and the Mystical Tradition', in M. Glasscoe, ed. *The Medieval Mystical Tradition in England* I (Exeter, 1980[1]) 17–38.

'L.'s Structural Imagery', *EC* 30 (1980[2]) 311–25.

'L.'s Pen / Parchment Analogy in *PP* B 1X 38–40', *NQ* 225 (1980[3]) 538–9.

'L.'s "Book of Conscience" and Alanus de Insulis,' *NQ* 227 (1982) 482–4.

'L., Chrysostom and Bernard: A Complex Echo', *NQ* 228 (1983[1]) 108–10.

'The Treatment of the Crucifixion in *PP* and in Rolle's *Meditations on the Passion*', *Analecta Cartusiana* 35 (1983[2]) 174–96.

'*Lele Wordes* and *Bele Paroles*: Some Aspects of L.'s Word-Play', *RES* n.s. 34 (1983[3]) 161–83.

'A Covenant more than Courtesy' [*recte* 'A Courtesy more than Covenant']: a Langlandian Phrase in its Context', *NQ* 229 (1984[2]) 153–6.

'The Inner Dreams in *PP*,' *MÆ* 55 (1986) 24–40.

'"Latent Content" and "The Testimony in the Text": Symbolic Meaning in *Sir Gawain and the Green Knight*', *RES* n.s. 38 (1987[1]) 145–68.

The Clerkly Maker: Langland's Poetic Art. Cambridge, 1987[2].

'*Kynde Craft* and the *Play of Paramorez*: Natural and Unnatural Love in *Purity*', in P. Boitani and A. Torti, eds. *Genres, Themes, and Images in English Literature*. Tübingen, 1988.

'L.'s Visions and Revisions', *YLS* 14 (2000) 5–27.

'"Elementary" Images in the Samaritan Episode of *PP*', *EC* 56 (2006) 303–23.

——& Jacobs, N., eds. *Medieval English Romances*. 2 vols, 1980.

Schroeder, M. C. '*PP*: The Tearing of the Pardon', *PQ* 49 (1970) 8–18. *And see* Carruthers.

Schweitzer, E. C. 'Half a Laumpe Lyne in Latyne" and Patience's Riddle in *PP*,' *JEGP* 73 (1974) 313–27.

Scott, A. 'Never noon so nedy ne poverer deide: *PP* and the Value of Poverty', *YLS* 15 (2001) 141–53.

'*PP*' *and the Poor*. Dublin, 2004.

Shepherd, G. T. 'Poverty in *PP*', in T. H. Aston et al., eds. *Social Relations and Ideas: essays in honour of R. H. Hilton* (Cambridge, 1983) 169–89.

Shoaf, R. A. '"Speche that spire is of grace": a Note on *PP* B.9.104', *YLS* 1 (1987) 128–33.

Simpson, J. 'From Reason to Affective Knowledge: Modes of Thought and Poetic Form in *PP*,' *MÆ* 55 (1986[1]) 1–23.

'The Transformation of Meaning: a Figure of Thought in *PP*,' *RES* 37 (1986[2]) 161–83.

'The Role of *Scientia* in *PP*,' in Kratzmann & Simpson (1986[3]) 49–65.

'"*Et vidit deus cogitaciones eorum*": A Parallel Instance and Possible Source for L.'s Use of a Biblical Formula at *PP* B XV 200*a*', *NQ* 231 (1986[4]) 9–13.

Piers Plowman: an Introduction to the B-Text. 1990. Rev. repr. Exeter, 2008.

'The Power of Impropriety: Authorial Naming in *PP*,' in Hewett-Smith (1991) 145–65.

'"After Craftes Conseil Clotheth Yow and Fede": L. and London City Politics', in N. Rogers, ed. *England in the C14th: Proceedings of the 1991 Harlaxton Symposium* (Stamford, 1993) 109–27.

'Grace Abounding: Evangelical Centralization and the End of *PP*,' *YLS* 14 (2000) 49–74.

Reform and Cultural Revolution: The Oxford English Literary History 2, 1350–1547. Oxford, 2002.

Smith, A. H. 'The ME Lyrics in Additional MS 45896', *London Mediaeval Studies* 2 (1951) 33–49.

Smith, B. H. 'Patience's Riddle: *PP* B XIII', *MLN* 76 (1961) 675–82.

Traditional Imagery of Charity in PP. The Hague, 1966.

Bibliography

Smith, D. V. 'The Labors of Reward: Meed, Mercede and the Beginning of Salvation', *YLS* 8 (1994) 127–54.

Smith, G., ed. *Elizabethan Critical Essays*. 2 vols. Oxford, 1904.

Somerset, F. 'Response' to Baldwin, 'Patient Politics in *PP*,' *YLS* 15 (2001) 109–115.

Spalding, M. C. *The Middle English Charters of Christ*. Bryn Mawr, 1914.

Spearing, A. C. 'Verbal Repetition in *PP* B and C', *JEGP* 62 (1963) 722–37.

   Criticism and Medieval Poetry. 2nd edn. 1972.

   Medieval Dream-Poetry. Cambridge, 1976.

Spitzer, L. *L'Amour Lointain*. Chapel Hill, 1944.

Steiner, E. 'L.'s Documents', *YLS* 15 (2000) 95–115.

Steinberg, T. L. '*PP* and Prophecy: an approach to the C-Text*. New York, 1991.

Stock, L. K. 'Will, Actyf, *pacience* and *Liberum Arbitrium*: Two Recurring Quotations in L.'s Revision of *PP* C-Text, Passus V, XV, XVI'. *Texas Studies in Literature and Language* 30 (1985) 461–77.

Stokes, M. *Justice and Mercy in PP: A Reading of the B-Text Visio.* 1984.

Strang, B. '*PP*, B-Text, Passus V, 491–2', *NQ* 208 (1963) 286.

Strong, D. 'The Questions Asked, the Answers Given: L., Scotus and Ockham', *ChR* 38 (2003) 255–75.

Sullivan, Sr C. *The Latin Insertions and the Macaronic Verse in '*PP*'*. Washington, 1932.

Swanson, R. N. 'L. and the Priest's Title', *NQ* 231 (1986) 438–40.

Szittya, P. R. *The Antifraternal Tradition in Medieval Literature*. Princeton, N.J., 1986[1].

   'The Trinity in L. and Abelard', in Groos, A. et al (1986[2]) 207–16.

Szövérffy, J. '"Peccatrix Quondam Femina": A Survey of the Mary Magdalen Hymns', *Traditio* 19 (1963) 79–146.

Taitt, P. 'In Defence of Lot', *NQ* 216 (1971) 284–5.

Tarvers, J. K. 'The Abbess's *ABC*', *YLS* 2 (1988) 137–41.

Tavormina, M. T. 'Kindly Similitude: Langland's Matrimonial Trinity', *MP* 80 (1982) 117–28.

   '*PP* and the Liturgy of St Lawrence', *SP* 84 (1987) 245–71.

   '"Gendre of a Generacion": *PP* B. 16.222', *ELN* 27 (1989[1]) 1–9.

   '"Maledictus qui non reliquit semen": The Curse on Infertility in *PP* B XVI and C XVIII', *MÆ* 58 (1989[2]) 117–25.

   Kindly Similitude: Marriage and Family in PP. Cambridge, 1995.

——& R. F. Yeager, eds. *The Endless Knot: Essays in Honour of Marie Borroff*. Cambridge, 1995.

   'The Chilling of Charity: Eschatological Allusions and Revisions in *PP* C 16–17', in R. Edwards, ed. *Art and Context in Late Medieval English Narrative: Essays in Honour of R. W. Frank, Jr.* Cambridge, 1994.

Taylor, S. 'Harrowing Hell's Halfacre: Langland's Mediation of the "Descensus" from the *Gospel of Nicodemus*' in Frantzen, A. J., ed. *Four Last Things: Death, Judgment, Heaven and Hell in the Middle Ages. Essays in Medieval Studies* Vol. 10 (Chicago, 1994) 145–58.

Thorne, J. B. 'Piers or Will: Confusion of Identity in the Early Reception of *PP*,' *MÆ* 60 (1991) 273–84.

Traver, H. *The Four Daughters of God*. Bryn Mawr, 1907.

   'The Four Daughters of God: A Mirror of Changing Doctrine', *PMLA* 40 (1925) 44–92.

Trigg, S. 'The Traffic in Medieval Women: Alice Perrers, Feminist Criticism and *PP*,' *YLS* 12 (1998) 5–29.

Tristram, P. *Figures of Life and Death in Medieval English Literature*. 1976.

Turville-Petre, T. *The Alliterative Revival*. Cambridge, 1977.

Tveitane, M. 'The Four Daughters of God: A Supplement', *NM* 81 (1980) 409–15.

Twomey, M. W. 'Christ's Leap and Mary's Clean Catch in *PP* B. 12.136–44a and C. 14.81–88a', *YLS* 5 (1991) 165–74.

Ullmann, J. 'Studien zu Richard Rolle de Hampole', *Englische Studien* 7 (1884) 415–72.

Utley, F. L. 'The Chorister's Lament', *Speculum* 21 (1946) 194–202.

Vasta, E. *The Spiritual Basis of 'PP'*. The Hague, 1965[1].

   'Truth, the Best Treasure, in *PP*,' *PQ* 44 (1965[2]) 17–29.

Vaughan, M. F. 'The Liturgical Perspectives of *PP* B XVI–XIX', *Studies in Medieval and Renaissance History* 3 (1980) 87–155.

   ed. *Suche Werkis to Werche: Essays on 'PP' in Honour of David C. Fowler*. East Lansing, Michigan, 1993.

   'The Ending(s) of *PP* A', in Vaughan (1993) 211–41.

Vershuis, A. '*PP*, Numerical Composition and the Prophecies', *Connotations* 1 (1991) 103–39.

Von Nolcken, C. '*PP*, the Wycliffites and *P. the P.'s Crede*', *YLS* 2 (1988) 71–102.

Waldron, R. A. 'Langland's Originality: The Christ-Knight and the Harrowing of Hell', in Kratzmann and Simpson (1986) 66–81.

Wallace, D., ed. *The Cambridge History of Medieval English Literature*. Cambridge, 1999.

746

Warner, L. 'Jesus the Jouster: the Christ-Knight and Medieval Theories of Atonement in *PP* and the "Round Table" Sermons', *YLS* 10 (1996) 130–43.

'Becket and the Hopping Bishops', *YLS* 17 (2003) 107–34.

'L and the Problem of *William of Palerne*'. *Viator* 37 (2006) 397–415.

Watson, N. 'Censorship and Cultural Change in Late-Medieval England: Vernacular Theology, the Oxford Translation Debate, and Arundel's Constitutions of 1409', *Speculum* 70 (1995) 822–64.

'Conceptions of the Word: the Mother Tongue and the Incarnation of God', *NML* 1 (1997)[1] 88–124.

'Visions of Inclusion: Universal Salvation and Vernacular Theology in Pre-Reformation England', *Journal of Medieval and Early Modern Studies* 27 (1997)[2] 145–87.

'The Middle English Mystics' in Wallace (1999) 539–65.

Weldon, J. F. G. 'The Structure of Dream Visions in *PP*,' *MS* 49 (1987[1]) 254–81.

'Sabotaged Text or Textual Ploy? The Christ-Knight Metaphor in *PP*,' *Florilegium* 9 (1987[2]) 113–23,

'Gesture of Perception: the Pattern of Kneeling in *PP*,' *YLS* 3 (1989) 49–66.

Wenzel, S. *The Sin of Sloth*: Acedia *in Medieval Thought and Literature*. Chapel Hill, N. Carolina, 1967.

'The Source of Chaucer's Seven Deadly Sins', *Traditio* 30 (1974) 351–78.

Verses in Sermons. Fasciculus Morum *and its Middle English Poems*. Cambridge, Mass., 1978.

'Medieval Sermons and the Study of Literature', in P. Boitani and A. Torti, eds., *Medieval and Pseudo-Medieval Literature*. Cambridge, 1984.

'Medieval Sermons', in Alford, *Companion* (1988) 155–72.

'*Somer Game* and Sermon References to a Corpus Christi Play', *MP* 86 (1989) 274–81.

'L's *Troianus*', *YLS* 10 (1996) 181–5.

'Eli and his Sons', *YLS* 13 (1999) 137–52.

Whatley, G. 'The Uses of Hagiography: the Legend of Pope Gregory and the Emperor Trajan in the Middle Ages', *Viator* 15 (1984[1]) 25–63.

'*PP* B.12. 277–94: Notes on Language, Text, and Theology', *MP* 82 (1984[2]) 1–12.

Wheatley, E. 'A Selfless Ploughman and the Christ/Piers Conjunction in *PP*,' *NQ* 238 (1993) 135–42.

White, H. 'L.'s Ymaginatif, Kynde and the Benjamin Major', *MÆ* 55 (1986) 241–8.

Nature and Salvation in PP. Cambridge, 1988.

'Book's Bold Speech and the *Archana Verba* of *PP* Passus B XVIII', *BJRL* 77 (1995) 31–46.

Whitworth, C. W. Jr. 'Changes in the Roles of Reason and Conscience in the Revisions of *PP*,' *NQ* 217 (1972) 4–7.

Wickham, G. Early *English Stages:1300–1600*. 2 vols. 2nd edn. New York, 1980.

Wilcockson, C. 'Glutton's Black Mass: *PP* B-Text Passus V 297–385', *NQ* 243 (1998) 173–6.

Wilkes, G. L. 'The Castle of Unite in *PP*,' *MS* 27 (1965) 334–6.

Wilson, E. *The Gawain-Poet*. Leiden, 1976.

'The "Gostly Drem" in *Pearl*', *NM* 69 (1968) 90–101.

'L.'s "Book of Conscience": Two ME Analogies and another possible Latin Source', *NQ* 228 (1983) 387–9.

Wirtjes, H. '*PP* B XVIII.371: "Right Ripe Must"', in M. Stokes and T. L. Burton, *Medieval Studies and Antiquities*: *Studies in Honour of Basil Cottle*. Woodbridge (1987) 133–43.

'*PP* B XVIII 364–73: the Cups that cheer but not Inebriate', in D. M. Reeks, ed. *Sentences: Essays presented to Alan Ward*. Southampton, 1988.

Wittig, J.S. '*PP* B Passus IX–XII: Elements in the Design of the Inward Journey', *Traditio* 28 (1972) 211–80.

'"Culture Wars" and the Persona in *PP*,' *YLS* 15 (2001) 167–201.

Woolf, R. 'The Theme of Christ the Lover-Knight in medieval English Literature', *RES* n.s. 13 (1962) 1–16.

The English Religious Lyric in the Middle Ages. Oxford, 1968.

'The Tearing of the Pardon', in Hussey (1969), 50–75.

Art and Doctrine: Essays on Medieval Literature, ed. H. O'Donoghue. 1986.

Wordsworth, J. 'Revision as Making: *The Prelude* and Its Peers', in R. Brinkley & K. Hanley, eds., *Romantic Revisions* (Cambridge, 1992) 18–42.

Wurtele, D. 'The Importance of the Psalms of David in WL's *The Vision of PP*', *Cithara* 43:1 (2003) 15–24.

Young, K. *The Drama of the Medieval Church*. Oxford, 1933.

Yunck, J. A. *The Lineage of Lady Meed: the Development of Medieval Venality Satire*. Notre Dame, Indiana, 1963.

Zeeman, N. 'Studying in the Middle Ages — and in *PP*,' *New Medieval Literatures* 3, ed. D. Lawton, W. Scase & R. Copeland. Oxford (1999) 199–222.

'The Condition of *Kynde*,' in D. Aers, ed. *Medieval literature & Historical Enquiry: Essays in Honour of Derek*

Pearsall. Cambridge (2000) 1–30.
'PP' and the Medieval Discourse of Desire. Cambridge, 2006.

D. Historical and Background Studies and Works of Reference

Adair, J. *The Pilgrim's Way.* 1978.

Adler, M. *The Jews of Medieval England.* 1939.

Alexander, J. & Binski, P. *Age of Chivalry: Art in Plantagenet England 1200–1400.* 1987.

Anderson, M. D. *History and Imagery in British Churches.* 1971.

Arbesmann, R. 'Jordanus of Saxony's *Vita Sancti Augustini,* the Source for John Capgrave's *Life of St Augustine',* Traditio 1 (1943) 341–53.

Ashworth, E. J. *The Tradition of Medieval Logic and Speculative Grammar.* Toronto, 1978.

Aston, M. 'Wyclif and the Vernacular' in A. Hudson & M. Wilks, eds. *From Ockham to Wyclif* (Oxford, 1987) 281–330.

Baker, J. *English Stained Glass of the Medieval Period.* 1978.

Baker, J. H. *An Introduction to English Legal History.* 1971.

Baker, T. *Medieval London.* 1970.

Baldwin, J. F. *The King's Council in England during the Middle Ages.* 1913.

Barber, R. *The Knight and Chivalry.* 1970.

Barron, C. M. 'The Parish Fraternities of Medieval London', in C. M. Barron & C. Harper Bill, eds., *The Church in pre-Reformation Society* (1985) 13–37.

Bartholomew, B. *Fortuna and Natura.* 1966.

Baum, P. F. 'The Medieval Legend of Judas Iscariot', *PMLA* 24 (1916) 481–632.

Bean, J. M. W. 'The Black Death: the Crisis and its Social and Economic Consequences', in Williman (1982) 23–39.

Bennett, H. S. *Life on the English Manor.* Cambridge, 1937.

Bennett, J. W. 'The Medieval Loveday', *Speculum* 33 (1958) 351–70.

Bolton, J. T. *The Medieval English Economy,* 1150–1500. 1980.

Bonnell, J. K. 'The Serpent with a Human Head in Art and in Mystery Play', *American Journal of Archeology* 21 (1917) 255–91.

Boon, K. G. *Rembrandt: The Complete Etchings.* 1977.

Boyle, L. *Pastoral Care, Clerical Education and Canon Law, 1200–1400.* 1981.
'The Curriculum of the Faculty of Canon Law at Oxford in the First Half of the C14th', in *Oxford Studies presented to Daniel Callus.* Oxford, 1964.

Brundage, J. A. *Law, Sex and Christian Society in Medieval Europe.* Chicago & London, 1987.

Bull, M. *The Miracles of Our Lady of Rocamadour.* 1999.

Bullock-Davies, C. *Menestrellorum multitudo*: Minstrels at a Royal Feast. Cardiff, 1978.

Bumke, J., tr. W. T. H. & E. Jackson. *The Concept of Knighthood in the Middle Ages.* New York, 1982.

Bursill-Hall, B. L. *Speculative Grammar of the Middle Ages.* The Hague, 1971.

Camille, M. 'Labouring for the Lord: the Ploughman and the Social Order in the Luttrell Psalter', *Art History* 10 (1987) 423–54.
Gothic Art. 1996.

Carruthers, M. *The Book of Memory: a Study of Memory in Medieval Culture.* Cambridge, 1990.
The Craft of Thought. Cambridge, 1998.

Catto, J., 'Wyclif and Wycliffism at Oxford 1356–1430', in Catto & Evans, eds., *Late Medieval Oxford,* 175–262.
——ed. *The Early Oxford Schools: The History of the University of Oxford,* gen. ed. T. H. Aston, vol. 1. Oxford, 1984.
& R. Evans, eds., *Late Medieval Oxford*: The History of the University of Oxford, gen. ed. T.H. Aston, vol. 2. Oxford, 1992.

Chadwick, H. *Boethius.* Oxford, 1981.

Chambers, E. K. *The Mediaeval Stage.* 2 vols. Oxford, 1903.

Cheney, C. R. *Notaries Public in England in the Thirteenth and Fourteenth Centuries.* Oxford, 1972.

Chettle, H. F. 'The Friars of the Holy Cross', *History* 34 (1949) 204–20.

Christie, A. G. I. *English Medieval Embroidery.* Oxford, 1938.

Chroust, A-H. *Aristotle.* 2 vols., 1973.

Clark, M. T. *'De Trinitate',* in Stump & Kretzmann, 91–102.

Clay, R. M. *The Medieval Hospitals of England.* 1909.

    The Hermits and Anchorites of England. 1914, repr. Detroit 1968.

Cohen, J. *The Friars and the Jews: the Evolution of Medieval Anti-Semitism.* 1982.

    'The Jews as Killers of Christ in the Latin Tradition, from Augustine to the Friars', *Traditio* 39 (1983) 1–27.

Cohn, N. *The Pursuit of the Millennium.* 1972.

Comparetti, D., tr. E. F. M. Beneche. *Vergil in the Middle Ages.* 1872; Eng. tr. repr. 1966.

Conway, C. A. 'The *Vita Christi* of Ludolf of Saxony and Late Medieval Devotion', *AC* 34 (1976).

Cook, G. H. *Medieval Chantries and Chantry Chapels.* 1947.

    The English Parish Church. 1954.

Courtenay, W. J. 'The Effect of the Black Death on English Higher Education', *Speculum* 55 (1980) 696–714.

    Schools and Scholars in 14th century England. Princeton, N.J. 1987.

Cross, F. E. & Livingstone, E. A., eds. *The Oxford Dictionary of the Christian Church.* Oxford, 1997.

Cutts, E. L. *Scenes and Characters of the Middle Ages.* 1925.

Daly, S. R. 'Peter Comestor: Master of Histories', *Speculum* 32 (1957) 62–73.

Darwin, F. D. S. *The English Medieval Recluse.* 1944.

Davis, V. 'The Rule of St Paul, the first hermit, in late medieval England', *Studies in Church History* 22 (1985) 203–14.

Dickinson, J. C. *The Origin of the Austin Canons.* 1950.

Du Boulay, F. R. H. & Barron, C., eds. *The Reign of Richard II: Essays in honour of May McKisack.* 1971.

Duffy, Eamon. *The Stripping of the Altars: Traditional Religion in England 1400–1580.* New Haven and London, 1992.

Dyer, C. *Standards of Living in the later Middle Ages.* Cambridge, 1989.

Emmerson, R. K. *Antichrist in the Middle Ages.* Seattle, 1981.

Evans, G. *The Thought of Gregory the Great.* Cambridge, 1986.

    ——ed. *The Medieval Theologians.* Oxford, 2001.

Finucane, R. C. *Miracles and Pilgrims: Popular Beliefs in Medieval England.* Totowa, N. J., 1977.

Freud, S. (tr. Strachey). *The Interpretation of Dreams.* 1954.

Friedberg, E., ed. *Corpus Iuris Canonici.* 2 vols. Leipzig, 1879–81; repr. Graz, 1959.

Gallais, P. & Riou, Y.-J., eds. *Mélanges offerts à René Crozet.* 2 vols. Poitiers, 1962.

Garth, H. M. *St Mary Magdalen in Medieval literature.* Johns Hopkins, 1950.

Gee, H. & Hardy, W. J., eds. *Documents Illustrative of English Church History.* 1921.

Gilchrist, J. *The Church and Economic Activity in the Middle Ages.* 1969.

Girouard, M. *Life in the English Country House.* New Haven, 1978.

Glorieux, P. *La Littérature quodlibétique.* 2 vols. Paris, 1925–35.

Glunz, H. *History of the Vulgate in England.* Cambridge, 1933.

Hamilton Thompson, A. *The Historical Growth of the English Parish Church.* Cambridge, 1913.

Harding, A. *The Law Courts of Medieval England.* 1973.

Haren, M. *Medieval Thought: the Western Intellectual Tradition from Antiquity to the Thirteenth Century.* 1985.

Harvey, J. *Henry Yevele: The Life of an English Architect.* 1944.

    English Mediaeval Architects: a Biographical Dictionary down to 1550. Gloucester, rev. 1984.

Haskins, S. *Mary Magdalene: Myth and Metaphor.* 1993.

Hassall, W. O. *The Holkham Bible Picture Book.* 1954.

Hatcher, J. *Plague, Population and the English Economy 1348–1530.* 1977.

Helmholz, R.H. *Marriage Litigation in Medieval England.* 1974.

Henisch, B. A. *Feast and Fast.* Pennsylvania, 1976.

Hill, R. M .T. '"A chauncerie for soules": London chantries in the reign of Richard II', in Du Boulay & Barron (1971) 242–55.

Hilton, R. H. & Aston, T. H., eds. *The English Rising of 1381.* Cambridge, 1984.

Holmes, G. *The Good Parliament.* 1975.

Houseley, N. 'The Bishop of Norwich's Crusade, 1383', *History Today* 33 (1983) 16–20.

An Inventory of the Historical Monuments in the City of Oxford. Royal Commission on Historical Monuments, England. 1939.

Jolivet, J. 'Quelques cas de "platonisme grammatical" du VIIe au XIIe siècle', in Gallais & Riou, eds. II 93–9.

Jusserand, J. J. *English Wayfaring Life in the Middle Ages.* 1899.

Kaske, R. E., with Groos, A. & Twomey, M. *Medieval Christian Literary Imagery: A Guide to Interpretation.* Toronto, 1988.

Katzenellenbogen, A. *Allegories of the Virtues and Vices in Medieval Art.* 1939; repr. Toronto, 1989.

Bibliography

Keen, M. *England in the Later Middle Ages*. 1973.
    Pelican History of Medieval Europe. Harmondsworth, repr. 1975.
    Chivalry. New Haven and London, 1984.
Kemp, E. W. 'History and action in the sermons of a medieval archbishop' in R. H. C. Davis & J. M. Wallace-Hadrill, eds., *The Writing of History in the Middle Ages: Essays presented to R.W. Southern* (Oxford, 1981) 353–4.
Kirschbaum, E. & al., eds. *Lexicon der christlichen Ikonographie*. 8 vols. Rome, 1968–76.
Knight, S. T. *Robin Hood: a Complete Study of the English Outlaw*. Oxford, 1994.
Knowles, M. D. *The Evolution of Medieval Thought*. 2nd edn. Ed. D. E. Luscombe & C. N. L. Brooke 1988.
——& Hadcock, R. H. *Medieval Religious Houses: England and Wales*. 2nd edn, 1971.
Kreider, A. *English Chantries: the road to dissolution*. Cambridge, Mass & London, 1979.
Kretzmann N., Kenny, A. J. P. & Pinborg, J., eds. *The Cambridge History of Later Medieval Philosophy*. Cambridge, 1982.
Lawrence, C. H. ed., *The English Church and the Papacy in the Middle Ages*. 1965.
    Medieval Monasticism. 2nd edn, 1989.
    The Friars. 1994.
Leff, G. *Medieval Thought: St Augustine to Ockham*. Harmondsworth, 1958.
    Heresy in the Middle Ages: The Relation of Heterodoxy to Dissent, c.1250–c.1450. 2 vols. Manchester & N.Y., 1967.
Lewis, F. 'The Veronica: Image, Legend and Viewer', in Ormrod (1986) 100–119.
Lewis, C. S. *The Discarded Image*. Cambridge, 1964.
Lipson, E. *The Economic History of England, Vol. I: The Middle Ages*. 1915 (12th edn. 1959).
Loewe, R. 'The Medieval History of the Latin Vulgate', in G. W. H. Lampe, ed., *The Cambridge History of the Bible*, II (Cambridge, 1969) 102–54.
Lunt, W. E. *Financial Relations of the Papacy with England, 1327–1534*. Cambridge, Mass., 1961.
Macy, G. *Theologies of the Eucharist in the Early Scholastic Period*. Oxford, 1984.
Maitland, F. W., ed. H. A. L. Fisher. *The Constitutional History of England*. Cambridge, 1908 (repr. 1974).
Mayr-Harting, H. & Moore, R. I., eds. *Studies in medieval history presented to R. H. C. Davis*. 1985.
McKisack, M. *The Fourteenth Century, 1307–1399*. Oxford, 1959.
Mâle, E., tr. D. Nussey. *The Gothic Image*. 1961.
Meiss, M. *Painting in Florence and Siena after the Black Death*. Princeton, 1951.
Moran, J. A. H. *The Growth of English Schooling 1340–1548*. Princeton, N.J. 1985.
Murphy, J. J. *Rhetoric in the Middle Ages*. Berkeley, 1974.
Myers, A. R., ed. *English Historical Documents, 1327–1485*. 1969.
Neuhauser, R. 'Augustinian *Vitium Curiositatis* and its Reception' in B. B. King & J. T. Schaefer, eds., *St Augustine and his Influence in the Middle Ages* (Sewanee, 1988) 99–124.
Noonan, J. T., Jr. *Bribes,* New York, 1984. pp 275–9.
Orme, N. *English Schools in the Middle Ages*. 1973.
Ormrod, W. M. ed. *England in the 13th Century.* Woodbridge, 1986.
Pantin, W. A. *The English Church in the Fourteenth Century*. Cambridge, 1955.
Partner, P. *The Murdered Magicians: the Templars and their Myth*. Oxford, 1982.
Patch, H. R. *The Goddess Fortuna in Medieval Literature*. 1927.
Pfaff, R. *New Liturgical Feasts in Medieval England*. Oxford, 1970.
Piltz, A., tr. D. Jones. *The World of Medieval Learning*. Oxford, 1981.
Poole, A. L., ed. *Medieval England*. 2 vols. Oxford, 1958.
Popper, K. R. *The Logic of Scientific Discovery*. Rev. edn. 1980.
Postan, M. M. *The Medieval Economy and Society*. Harmondsworth, 1972.
Pugh, R. B. *Imprisonment in Medieval England*. Cambridge, 1968.
Putnam, B. H. *The Enforcement of the Statute of Labourers*. New York, 1908.
Radford, U. M. 'The Wax Images found in Exeter Cathedral', *Antiquaries Journal* 29 (1949) 164–8.
Reames, S. L. *The Legenda Aurea*. Madison, Wisconsin, 1985.
Reuter, T., ed. *The Medieval Nobility*. Oxford, 1978.
Richardson, H. G. 'The English Coronation Oath', *Speculum* 24 (1949) 44–75.
    'The Coronation in Medieval England: the Evolution of the Office and the Oath'. *Traditio* 16 (1960) 111–202.
Rickert, M. *Painting in Britain: the Middle Ages*. 1954.
Rosenthal, J. T. *The Purchase of Paradise: Gift-Giving and the Aristocracy, 1307–1485*. 1972.
Roth, C. *A History of the Jews in England*. 3rd edn. Oxford, 1964.

Roth, F. *The English Austin Friars, 1249–1538*. New York, 1966.

Rotuli Parliamentorum. 6 vols, 1767–83.

Russell, J. B. *Lucifer: the Devil in the Middle Ages*. 1984.

Salzman, L. F. *Building in England down to 1450*. Oxford, 1952; revd. repr. 1966.

Santarcangeli, P. *Le Livre des Labyrinthes*. Paris, 1974.

Saxl, F. 'A Spiritual Encyclopaedia of the later Middle Ages', *JWCI* 5 (1942) 82–142.

Schiller, G. *Iconography of Christian Art*. 2 vols. 1971–2.

Sheehan, M. M. *The Will in Medieval England*. Toronto, 1963.

Sheingorn, P. '"And Flights of Angels Sing Thee to Thy Rest": The Soul's Conveyance to the Afterlife in the Middle Ages', in K. L. Scott & C. G Fisher, eds. *Art into Life*. East Lansing, Mich. (1995) 155–82.

Sherwood-Smith, M. C. *Studies in the Reception of the 'Historia Scholastica' of Peter Comestor*. Oxford, 2000.

Shinners, J. & Dohar, W. J., eds. *Pastors and the Care of Souls in Medieval England*. Notre Dame, Indiana, 1998.

Shrewsbury, J. F. *A History of Bubonic Plague in Medieval England*. Oxford, 1975.

Smalley, B. *English Friars and Antiquity in the Early 14th Century*. Oxford, 1960.

    The Study of the Bible in the Middle Ages. 3rd edn. Oxford, 1983.

Southern, R. W. *Western Society and the Church in the Middle Ages*. Harmondsworth, 1970.

Southworth, J. *The Medieval Minstrel*. Woodbridge, 1989.

Spade, P. V. *The Medieval Liar: a Catalogue of the Insolubilia Literature*. Toronto, 1975.

    'Insolubilia', in Kretzmann et. al., 245–53.

Spargo, J. W. 'Chaucer's Love-Days', *Speculum* 15 (1940) 35–56.

Statutes of the Realm. 11 vols. 1810–28 (repr. 1963).

Stiegman, E. 'Bernard of Clairvaux, William of St. Thierry, the Victorines', in Evans (2001) 129–55.

Stones, E. L. G. 'The Folvilles of Ashby Folville, Leicestershire, and their Associates in Crime 1326–41', *Transactions of the Royal Historical Society* 7 (1957) 117–36.

Stow, J. (ed. C .L. Kingsford). *A Survey of London*. 2 vols. Oxford, 1908.

Stow, K. *Alienated Minority: The Jews of Medieval Latin Europe*. Cambridge, Mass., 1992.

Straw, C. *Gregory the Great: Perfection in Imperfection*. Berkeley, Los Angeles & London, 1988.

Strutt, J., ed. Cox, J. *The Sports and Pastimes of the People of England*. 1903 edn., repr. 1969.

Stump, E. & Kretzmann, N., eds. *The Cambridge Companion to Augustine*. Cambridge, 2001.

Sumption, J. *Pilgrimage: An Image of Medieval Religion*. 1975.

Swanson, J. 'The *Glossa Ordinaria*', in Evans (2001) 156–67.

Swanson, R. N. *Universities, Academics, and the Great Schism*. Cambridge, 1979.

    'Titles to orders in medieval English episcopal registers', in Mayr-Harting & Moore (1985) 233–45.

    Church and Society in Late Medieval England. Oxford, 1989.

Talbot, C. H. *Medicine in Medieval England*. 1967.

Tawney, R. H. *Religion and the Rise of Capitalism*. 1926.

Thompson, A. H. *The English Clergy and their Organisation in the Later Middle Ages*. 1947.

Thompson, D. *A Descriptive Catalogue of Middle English Grammatical Texts*. New York, 1979.

Thomson, J. A. F. 'Piety and Charity in late medieval London', *Journal of Ecclesiastical History* 16 (1965) 178–95.

Thorndyke, L. *A History of Magic and Experimental Science*. 6 vols. New York, 1923–64.

Tipping, H. A. *English Homes, Vol. I*. 1921.

Toulmin, S. & Goodfield, J. *The Fabric of the Heavens*. Cambridge, Mass., 1963.

Tristram, E. W. *English Medieval Wall Painting: the C13th*. 2 vols. Oxford, 1950.

Tuck, J. A. 'Nobles, Commons and the Great Revolt of 1381', in Hilton & Aston (1984) 194–212.

Ullmann, W. *The Origins of the Great Schism*. 1948.

    Law and Politics in the Middle Ages. Ithaca, N.Y., 1975.

Vale, M. *Piety, Charity and Literacy among the Yorkshire Gentry 1370–1480*. York, 1976.

Vernet, F. *Medieval Spirituality*. 1930.

Von Simson, O. *The Gothic Cathedral*. 1956.

Wailes, S. L. *Medieval Allegories of Jesus' Parables*. Berkeley, 1987.

Walker, D. M., ed. *The Oxford Companion to Law*. Oxford, 1980.

Walsh, K. *A C14th Scholar and Primate: Richard FitzRalph in Oxford, Avignon and Armagh*. Oxford, 1981.

——& Wood, D., eds. *The Bible in the Medieval World*. Oxford, 1985.

Warren, A. K. *Anchorites and their patrons in medieval England*. Berkeley, Los Angeles & London, 1985.

Webb, J., ed. *A Roll of the Household Expenses of Richard de Swinfield, Bishop of Hereford* [*during*] *1298–90*. Camden Society, 1854.

Williams, A. 'Relations between the mendicant friars and the secular church in England in the later 14th century,' *Annuale Medievale* 1 (1960) 22–95.

Williman, D., ed. *The Black Death: the Impact of the Fourteenth Century Plague*. Binghampton, N.Y., 1982.

Wippel, J. F. 'The Quodlibetal Question as a Distinctive Literary Genre' in *Les genres littéraires dans les sources théologiques et philosophiques médiévales*, Publications de l'Institut d'études médiévales, 2nd ser. vol. 5 (Louvain, 1982) 7–84.

Wood, M. *The English Mediaeval House*. 1965.

Woodcock, B. L. *Medieval Ecclesiastical Courts in the Diocese of Canterbury*. 1952.

Wood-Legh, K. *Church Life in England under Edward III*. Cambridge, 1934.

    Perpetual Chantries in Britain. Cambridge, 1965.

Workman, H. B. *John Wyclif: a Study of the English Medieval Church*. 2 vols. Oxford, 1926.

Wormald, F. 'The Rood of Bromholm', *JWCI* 1 (1937) 37–45; repr. in J. Alexander, T. Brown & J. Gibbs (eds), *Francis Wormald: Collected Writings* (2 vols., 1988) 123–38.

Wunderli, R.M. *London Church Courts and Society on the eve of the Reformation*. Cambridge, Mass., 1981.

Ziegler, P. *The Black Death*. Harmondsworth, repr. 1971.

E. INDEXICAL GLOSSARY

The **Indexical Glossary** includes all separate words appearing in the texts in Vol. I; rejected variants recorded in the Apparatus or discussed in the *Textual Notes* are listed in a Supplementary Index. Grammatical words are illustrated extensively so as to bring out their full range of senses; but coverage of these, as of the commoner lexical words (*be, have, come* etc) is necessarily selective. Other lexical words are cited in all their independent appearances. Reference in the first place is to the **C** Version; where a word is not found in **C**, it is cited from **B**, and where not in **B**, then from **A**. All the unique words of **Z** are likewise listed, but the more wayward spelling variants of items otherwise found in **A**, **B** or **C** only where they may present particular difficulty. Instances of words in lines exactly or closely parallel to **C** are not recorded unless the line in question occurs at some distance from the **C** (or occasionally **B**, or **A**) original that is the point of reference. In the sequence of numbered references it is always stated whether a text other than **C** is in question; if two or more such follow in succession, the version is specified in bold type (**B, A, Z**) for the sake of clarity.

The order followed in each entry is as follows: the lemma in **bold** type, with spelling variants, if any; the word's grammatical class in *italics*; its forms, where any are given, in brackets; the gloss; the line-reference. Concise grammatical explanation as required is given in italics within round brackets, and further explanatory comment, where appropriate, is placed in square brackets. For convenience, entries will often include extensive examples of set or characteristic phrases in which the given lexeme appears, particularly where it is one with numerous indexed references. Additional information, e.g. specifying the referent, is also sometimes supplied, but no attempt is made to expand the glosses into full dictionary entries, and lexicographical detail must be sought elsewhere (the more difficult cases are discussed in the notes). The order of senses follows that used in the MED, with figurative meanings being given within each sequence of referenced literal senses on first occurrence. Where particular words are discussed from a textual or interpretative point of view in the *Textual Notes* the letter 'n' is appended to the cited line-number, where in the *Commentary*, 'c' is similarly appended.

The order of words is strictly alphabetical, except that in a few instances a derivative is moved up a position or two so as to follow immediately upon its radical and thereby enable the lexeme's semantic range to be more conveniently grasped. Each head-word is given in the spelling that occurs most commonly, but where the latter does not coincide with the first referenced gloss, the variant form is noted by being bracketed after the main form (e.g **althow** 2.121 bracketed after **althouh**). Words are listed in their standard lexicographical citation-form, whether or not this is instanced in the text, e.g. infinitives for verbs, such as *thuruen* (although only *thar* appears) and nominative sg. for nouns.

For the sake of simplicity, the following graphemes are treated as identical. Yogh (ȝ) as velar spirant |ɣ| is treated as equal to *gh* in medial and terminal position; in initial position as the palatal glide |j| it is treated as equivalent to consonantal *y*, with which it appears in the latter's normal alphabetical position; as |z| it is placed with *s*. Vocalic *i* / *y* are treated as one letter, but words beginning with consonantal *i* representing initial |dʒ| are grouped together at the end of the sequence. Where two common spellings exist in the texts, e.g. in words beginning with both *k* and *c* (such as *connen* / *konnen*), preference is given to the forms dominant in the C-Text. Cross-reference is made for the form not adopted for the head-word so that occurrences can be readily traced. Thorn (þ) and *th* are treated as one letter. The consonantal and vocalic values of *v* are distinguished in the same way as those of *i* described above: thus words with initial |v| occur in a group together at the end of the entry. This letter has the peculiar added feature of using non-initial *u* for |v|, e.g. *vuel* 6.20. Where *u* has this value, its order is always that of *v* in the modern alphabet, wherever it occurs; thus, e.g. *hauen* appears after < *hauk* → *hauthorn* > but before *hawe*.

Latin and French words are grouped in a separate list, but a few words of indeterminate status appear in the main Glossary, even if this means that they appear twice (e.g. *simile, q.v.*)

753

The following ABBREVIATIONS are used:

a	adjective		*masc.*	masculine
acc.	accusative		*meton.*	metonymic (sense)
app.	apposition			
art.	article		*n.*	noun
assev.	asseveration		*num.*	numeral
assim.	assimilated			
attrib.	attributive		*ord.*	ordinal
auxil.	auxiliary			
av; avl	adverb; adverbial		*parenth.*	parenthetic
			p.; p.p.	participle; past participle
card.	cardinal		*part.*	particle
coll.	collective		*p.t.*	past tense
comb.	combination		*pers.*	person(al)
comp.	comparative		*person.*	personified
cpd.	compound		*phr.*	phrase
conj.; conjv.	conjunction; conjunctive		*pl.*	plural
constr.	construction		*poss.*	possessive
contr.	contracted		*pr.*	present
correl.	correlative		*prec.*	preceding
			pred.	predicative
dat.	dative (case)		*pref.*	prefix
def.	definite		*prep.*	preposition(al)
dem.	demonstrative		*prn*	pronoun
dir.	direct		*prnl.*	pronominal
ellip.	elliptical		*ref.*	reference
emph.	emphatic		*refl.*	reflexive
et p.	*et passim*		*rel.*	relative
ex.	example			
excl.	exclamation		*sel.*	selected
			sg.	singular
fem.	feminine		*spec.*	specific(ally)
fig.	figurative (sense)		*subj.*	subject
foll.	following (followed)		*subjv.*	subjunctive
Fr	French		*suff.*	suffix
fut.	future		*sup.*	superlative
gen.	genitive		*tr.*	transitive
ger.	gerund		*trs.*	transposed
imp.	imperative		*uncontr.*	uncontracted
impers.	impersonal		*uninfl.*	uninflected
indef.	indefinite			
indic.	indicative		*v*	verb
inf.	infinitive			
infl.	inflected		Ø	zero reading
interj.	interjection		†	conjectural reading
interrog.	interrogative		*	word recorded only in *PP*
iron.	ironic (sense)		#	word first recorded in *PP*
It	Italian			

a¹ *a* (*as def. num.*) one 1.27, 3.473, B 3.258; *a* (*as indef. art.*) a Pr 1 *et p*; = a certain 12.77, 15.103, 17.158, 205, 258, 20.305, **B** 12.76, 18.193; (*before proper name*) 7.137, 303, (*foll.*) **al** ~ a whole 6.80, 8.269, 10.2; **vch** ~ every 6.245, 7.307, 12.106, B 13.68, **which** ~ what 9.300, 19.231, 20.127, which A 11.68 (*sup.*) ~ 20.475, (*av.*) ~ 22.87; *with n. of multitude / quantity / kind, foll. by* Ø *of*: ~ **doseyne** 4.38, ~ **drop** 6.335, ~ **galoun** B 5.336, ~ **payre** 6.251, B 12.19; ~ **seem** 3.42

a² *pers. prn* (*unstressed*) he Pr 72 *et p.*, Z Pr 121; she 2.17 *et p.*, Z 1.17; they 3.89, Z 5.154

a³ *prep.* on 2.56, 3.51, 259, 11.255, 14.131, 141, 15.19, 18.182, 20.44, 349, 21.237, B 16.189, 17.106, 18.314, A 4.32; in 3.51, 259, 9.154, 11.164, 13.147, 18.213, 242, 19.151, 193, A 5.215, 8.115; to A 9.58

a-⁴ *pref.* (*forming av*) = on 7.13, 52, 8.138, 197, at 6.236; ~ **daye** a day, daily B 8.44; = in 6.44, 7.26, 19.75, 22.196; at, by 19.174

a⁵ *excl.* ah, oh! 1.41, 20.13, Z 5.140

abaschen *v* be upset, lose one's composure [through shame *etc*], *p.p.* ~**ed, -et** ashamed 6.17, 9.86, 22.48, B 10.286; at a loss 15.164, B 10.445

abaten *v* lessen (difficulty of digesting) A 7.169; alleviate B 12.59

abauen *v* confound 8.226

a.b.c. *n* alphabet, a.b.c. B 7.133

abbesse *n* abbess [superior of convent of nuns] 5.176

abbot *n* abbot [superior of monastic abbey] 5.176, B 10.325

abedde *av* in bed 6.44, 7.26, 10.262, 265, 273, B 5.389

abeggen Z 7.66 *see* **abuggen** *v*

(a)-beggeth *av* (a-) begging 8.138, 246, Z 7.220

abyden *v* remain 1.132, 2.199, 250, 4.35, 9.40, 10.227, 22.79, 131, A 9.96; wait 8.288, **B** 11.377, 15.313; linger 10.63; continue A 7.138; endure 20.344, 22.46; *pr. p. a* ***abydyng(e)** steadfast 18.136, 21.295, 22.142

aby(y)en 20.446, B 3.251, **abyggen** 2.141 = **abuggen** *v*

abite *n* dress, habit Pr 3

abiten *v* bite / nip off 18.32

ablenden (*p.t.* **ablende**) blind 20.140, 368, † B 10. 31.

***abosten** *v* arrogantly defy 8.152

abouhte *p.t.* 10.262 *etc; see* **abuggen** *v*

aboute(n)¹ *av* around, about 7.162, B 11.17, A 6.73; in all directions 9.107, A 2.39; from all quarters 2.172; from place to place Pr 31, 5.29, B 2.177, A 10.105; here and there B 15.328; everywhere 4.183; this way and that 10.46, B Pr 151, *in phrr.* **al** ~ to everyone 2.158, 232; **comen** ~ come into existence A 10.217; *av as a* surrounding, neighbouring 10.12, 20.337, B 2.86; round about B 5.145; *in phrr.* **ben** ~ be diligent / active 4.77, 10.191, B 13.369; **comere** ~ visitor A 2.43; **rennere** ~ vagabond A 11.202

abouten² *prep.* enclosing B 5.586; (clasped) around Pr 178; in attendance on 2.62; near 19.58; about, upon

6.180, 8.173, 15.164, 22.191; throughout, all over 1.91, B 12.254; at approximately (the time of) 7.132, 9.246, 16.13, 20.69, 137, B 15.283; involved with 1.6, B 7.119; concerning 13.227, B 13.252, ? 1.88*n*

abouen¹ *av* at a higher level 18.87, *in phr.* **bringen** ~ bring to prosperity 13.21; *av as a* on top 21.281, B 5.192

abouen² *prep.* superior (in authority / rank) to 10.141, 21.473, B 8.95, Z 3.174; beyond, surpassing 12.75, 16.34, 19.102; over and above B 14.151

a-bribeth *av* a-scrounging 8.246

abroed *av* forth widely 15.263; out wide 9.143; (forth) away from home **B** 2.177, 5.139

absence *n* absence 21.124

absolucioun *n* remission B 7.63

abstinence *n* self-denial, *esp.* fasting, (*person.*) 6.439, 7.271

abuggen (*p.t.* **abouhte** 10.236, *p.p.* 20.430) pay for [at the cost of labour / suffering] 2.141, 8.41, 83, 16.219, 20.446, **B** 3.251, 12.42; pay the penalty 10.236, 13.15, 20.430; pay interest on B 13.376

ac *conj.* but Pr 78 *et p.*; nevertheless 10.51; but on the contrary/ rather 3.233, B 10.121; except / but (that) B 8.55; however Pr 62, A 5.247

acale *p.p. a* afflicted with cold 20.437

accidie *n* (the) sin of / bout of sloth 6.416

accion *n* right to go to law, grounds for a suit 1.94; act(ion) 5.196

accordyng *pr.p.* A 10.91 *see* **acorden** *v*

ac(c)usen *v* charge, indict 2.245, 3.219; *and see* **cusen** *v*

achocen *v* choke Z 3.161*n*

acombren *v* encumber, burden 2.52, Z 7.91; oppress 21.221; weigh down 1.31, 190, 197; *see* **(en)combren** *vv*

acordaunce *n* (grammatical) agreement 3.336, [394*n*]

acordaunde *pr.p.* 3.394 *see* **acorden** *v*

acorden *v* come to agreement 3.392, 6.385, 11.315, 13.213, 19.287, 22.304, B 13.122; be reconciled 5.183, 22.354; agree 3.273, 471, (grammatically) 355, 361, 371, *pr. p.* in (grammatical) agreement (with) 3.394*n*; concur [in judgement] (with) 4.87, 8.243, 9.69, 12.162, 20.242, **B** 3.319, 4.158, A 4.144, 10.88, Z 4.125; conform (with) *pr. p.* A 10.91

acorsen *v* excommunicate 22.263; interdict 20.96; declare anathema 18.223; damn Pr 127; condemn B 18.107; *p.p. a* wicked, execrable B 15.412. A 10.155

acountable *a* responsible 13.66

acounte *n* account, reckoning 7.40, 13.34, 21.465, A Pr 91; (*fig.*) final reckoning acquitaunce B 14.190. settle accounts 4.11, 7.33, 11.302, 13.34, (*fig.*) 12.68, Z 7.75; take account of, esteem 3.392, 8.159, 10.96; regard 9.239; value (at) 21.415

acoupen *v* accuse (of sin) B 13.459

\#**acquitaunce** *n* document of acquittal B 14.190

actif *a* active [= practising the life of activity in the world] **B** 6.248, 13.226, A 11.183, (*person.*) 7.298, 15.215 *et p.*, **B** 13.239, 273, 458, 14.26, 320, 16.2

acumbren *v* Z 7.91 = **acombren** *v*

acuth *pr. sg.* Z 7.242 *see* **aken** *v*

aday *av* on the next day, ? daily 8.331

adaunten *v* put down 3.440

ad(d)ere *n* serpent 20.315, 326, 378

#**adiectif** *n* adjective 3.335, 342, 360, 393, 404

a-do *n* business 5.163

adoun(e) *av* down Pr 64, *esp. in phrasal vv.* 1.91, 3.43, 4.88, 8.29, 10.95, 18.50, 20.28, 22.132, **B** 5.7, 9.205, 10.329, 16.73, 17.65 *etc*

adreden *v* (*p.p.* **adrad**) frighten 21.307, 22.353

adrenchen *v* (*p.t.* **adreynten**, *p.p.* **adreynt**) drown 10.163, B 10.407; inundate 10.248; befuddle 22.378

af(f)ayten *v* train 8.30; discipline 6.7, B 11.384

afe(e)ren *v* frighten, make afraid 1.10, 4.66, 8.128, 179, 11.282, 15.166, 19.82, 20.123, 477, 21.206, 22.166, **B** 11.63, 15.384

afeld(e) *av* (in)to the fields 4.144, 8.198, 312, B 6.142

afellen *v* (*p.t.* **afelde**) bring down, destroy 3.162

aferes *n. pl.* affairs, doings 6.152

affiaunce *n* trust 18.255

af(f)raynen *v* ask B 16.274, ~ **at** enquire (of) 20.16; *see* **fraynen** *v*

afyngred *p.p.* (< *of-hungred*) very hungry 9.85, 11.43, 50, 16.15, 17.68, B 6.266, A 12.59

afore *av* in advance B 14.134; earlier Z 5.28; *prep.* in front of B 5.12, 23, **as** ~ in the sight of B 12.79; ahead of Z 2.160

afrounten *v* insult 22.5

after[1] *av* after A 12.39; following Pr 52; in succession B 2.102; after that 12. 215, 14.85, 20.41, B Pr 140; in consequence 3.103, B 3.314; afterwards Pr 50, 9.181, 12.204, 215, 20.230, 22.103 *etc*, B 1.68, A 12.35; later B Pr 218; hereafter, to come Pr 207; accordingly 12.150, A 12.7; as well 11.118, 13.13, 15.26, 169, B 3.262, 5.110;

after[2] *prep.* after 2.106, 10.303, 12.200 *etc*; following B 5.261; towards Pr 14; for 1.123, 189, 8.279, 13.73, 14.120, 16.276, 18.180, 22.387, B 3.71; next to A 1.110; about B 13.95, A 12.79; in keeping with 2.27; according to 3.470, 9.110, 14.123, 127, 17.160, 19.19, 21.123, 22.247, A 12.94; in the likeness of B 17.138;

after[3] (*conj.*) ~ **(that)** according as 22.30, A 7.195

afterward(es) *av* next, after that B 10.224, A 11.181

afuyre *av* on fire 16.178

afurst(e) *p.p.a* (< *of-þyrst*) afflicted with thirst 9.85, 11.43, 16.15, 20.437, A 12.82

agayne (**aȝe(y)n(e)(s)**)[1] *av* back (again) 3.331, 6.309, 7.268, 20.399, 21.247, **B** 6.43, 17.121; again 9.29; in return 22.172, B 10.201;

agayne (**aȝe(y)n(e)(s)**)[2] *prep.* in front of 3.193; towards

B 4.44; contrary to 17.280, 20.377, A 10.160; against (= in opposition to, in defiance of) 3.188, 409, 445, 7.73, 8.341, 9.26, 65, 16.214, 238, 19.266, 20.262, 393, 21.362, 22.72, 113, 154 *etc*., **B** 5.608, 6.314, 8.46, 9.127, 10.39, 13.132, 15.68 *etc*, Z 6.75.

agasten *v* (*p.p.* **agast(e)**) frighten 2.221, 21.301, B 13.268; frighten off B 14.281

age *n* age 18.246; old age 22.189; *in phrr.* **myddel** ~ B 12.7; **of** ~ old enough 10.252, 22.159, **of twelue wynter** ~ twelve years old 6.203

ageyn(e)(s) B 6.314, A 10.160 *etc*; *see* **agayne** *av*

aglotyen *v* satisfy (with food) 9.76

ago *p.p., in av phr.* B 15.231 *see* **ygon** *v*

agrounde *av* on the earth B 1.90; *and see* **ground** *n*

agu(w)e *n* acute fever 6.79, 22.84

agulte *n* guilt, fault 21.305

agulten *v* sin 17.44; offend 6.17, 19.278, **B** 14.7, 15.391

aye Z 4.32, **aȝe(y)n(e)(s)** 7.73, 8.341, **B** 4.44, 10.201 *etc*; *see* **agayne** *av, etc*

aȝeynes *conj.* as soon as 21.319

aȝeynward *av* again, once more 19.77

ay *av* always 12.102, 115, 13.58, 14.133, 214, 16.62, 17.146; all the time B 8.49; eternally 18.233; for ever B 9.48; constantly 11.31, 15.247, 16.94, 20.400; every time 5.95, 10.40; in each case 8.219, Z 3.150, ~ **the lengere** in each case, the longer 13.4, the more often 3.136

#**aiel** *n* forefather, ancestor B 15.322

ay(e)r (eir) *n* air 1.126, 10.130, 15.221, B Pr 128, 14.44

aylen (eilen) *v* ail, afflict 8.134, 270, B 15.251

ayr (ey(e)r, heyr) *n* heir 3.321, 431, 5.59, 163, 6.255, 9.4, 10.86, 18.246, **B** 2. 102, 15. 322, A 10.210

aysches (askes) *n.pl.* ashes 3.125

*****aythe** *n* harrow 21.274

ayther (either) *prn* each of two B 13.348, 16.207; both 16.346, Z 5.91; each B 18.74; of each one 12.140, B 13.348; *as a* each, both 19.288, B 13.177; *in phrr.* ~ **of hem bothe** each of the two 16.197; ~ **oþer** each other 6.188, B 7.139, A 10.179; ~ **... oþer** each one... the other 6.149, 16.65, **B** 5.147, 9.86; **here; oure; yow** ~ **oþer** each of (the two of) them 22.354, us 6.188, you †B 14.36; *conj.* either (**or...eyþer** either ... or B 17.136)

aken *v* (*p.t. subjv.* **oke**) ache B 6.255, should ache **oke** 19.160

aker *n* arable field [of acre size], *in phr.* **half** ~ 6.267, 8.2, 3, 113, 123

aknowen *v* acknowledge, *p.p.* **aknowe**, *in phr.* **ben** ~ acknowledge, admit 9.86

al(l) (*pl.* **alle** Pr 56, B Pr 103, A 2.137) *a* all Pr 10, 3.473 *et p.*, *with prns* = them all, all of (them *etc*) *a* **hem** ~ Pr 68, **vs** ~ 7.124, **they** ~ 20.85, **we** ~ 12.132, **yow** ~ B 1.14; ~ **þat** 19.244, B 5.233, ~ **þise** B 9.71; (*placed after n / prn*): 2.219, 9.309, B 3.12, *before n* B 11.198;

whole, ~ **a** a whole 8.269, the whole of Pr 50, the entire Pr 192, A 7.134; *in n. phrr.* ~ **nacion** every nation 18. 102; ~ **þe reame** Pr 192, 5.114, 125, 11.59, B 15.524; ~ **þe world** the whole world 21.430, 22.49, B 15.437, Z 5.40; everyone Pr 100, 104, 12.36, 21.220; ~ **(thy etc) lyf-tyme** the whole of (your) life (long) 1.75, 2.32, 6.239, 436, 440, 7.215, 8.25, 10.169, 11.256, 15.198, 18.200, 20.3, 22.366, **B** 5.476, 13.142

al(l)(e) *n (gen. pl.* **al(l)er(e)** 21.474, B 16.205) everything Pr 13 *et p.*, B 3.269, Z 2.164; all things B 10.355, Z 5.36; all creatures 15.296; all people, everyone 2.249, 16.19, B 3.242; *in prnl and avl phrr.* **oure aller** of all of us B 16.205; **ouer** ~ everywhere B 9.55; **youre alere** of all of you 21.474; **wiþ** ~ moreover B 15.288

al *av* all, entirely Pr 28, B 2.125, A 7.183, Z Pr 28; purely, simply 7.139, 10.237, 12.51, B 4.150, A 10.179, Z 5.43; quite, absolutely B 2.164, A 7.170, Z 5.105; *(as emph. part.)* 8.124, 11.4, 13.166, 20.290, B 16.18; *in phr.* ~ **aboute** right round Pr 178, 7.162, 21.365; everywhere 4.183, in all directions 13.134; to everyone 2.158; ~ **aloude** out loud 6.23

alay *n* alloy of base metal B 15.348

alayen *v* alloy *(fig.)*, debase 17.79, B 15.352, 353

#alarme *interj.* to arms! 22.92

alday *avl phr.* time and again 17.96

aldreman *n* alderman [member of govering body of city] 4.188

ale *n* ale [beer brewed without hops] 6.159, 228, 392, 433, 7.51, 67, 8.122, 328, A 10.60; **bred and** ~ 7.51, 9.156, **feble** ~ 6.159, **good** ~ 6.356, 374, 8.324, 16.73, 22.223, **halpenny** ~ 8.328, **peny** ~ 6.226, 8.332, 9.92, **poddyng** ~ 6.226; **thikke...~ thynne** 21.403; ale-house / - drinking Pr 43, 7.19, 9.194

a-lechyng *ger. av* 19.75 *see* **lechen** *v*

aleggen *v* B 11.89, A 12.107 *see* **allegen** *v*

alere *n. gen. pl. see* **al(l)(e)** *n*

alery *av* twisted across, ? bent backwards 8.129*n*

aliche B 16.57 = **yliche** *av*

alien *n* foreign resident 3.266

alyday Z 6.47 = **holyday** *n*

alyhten (aliȝten) *v* alight, come down (upon) 11.143, B 11.246

alyue *a* alive 22.110, B 8.113; **o lyue** A 2.14 *see* **lyf** *n*

alkenamye *n* alchemy B 10.214

allas *interj.* alas! 12.1, 17.56, ~ **þat** 16.1

alle *a, n. pl.* Pr 20 *etc; see* **al(l)(e)** *a, n*

al(l)eggen *v* adduce [text] as proof 12.31, A 12.107

aller *n. gen. pl.* B 16.205 = **alere**; *see* **al(l)(e)** *n*

alles Z 1.101 = **elles** *av*

alleskynnes *gen. phr.* of every kind Z 3.172

allouable *a* permissible 17.130

allouaunce *n* allocation of funds [for expenses], repayment 9.269; acknowledgement, approbation 15.290, B 11.220

al(l)ouen *v* commend 12.141, 16.143, B 15.4; esteem 16.143, B 10.432, 434; recognise as valid 17.136, 18.82, 14.212*n*; permit 3.74; tolerate 3.204, 7.95; reward 8.250, 12.196; hold to (someone's) credit 18.251

almarie *n* cabinet 16.87

almesdede *n* charitable work, *esp.* almsgiving 7.72, 241

almesfull *a* generous in almsgiving 6.48

almesse (almusse) *n* alms 8.133, 9.141, 191, 13.78, 17.47 *(pl.)*, **B** 3.75, 7.73, 15.84, 311, 419, *(spec.)* food from table for distribution to poor B 6.146; act of charity 9.96

almest (almo(o)st) *av* almost 3.208, 22.227, B 4.174

almy(g)hty (almyhten Pr 218) almighty, omnipotent 1.110, 5.99, 14.98, 17.135, 20.465, B 15.393; *in phr.* ~ **God** B 10.431, **God** ~ Pr 218, 1.26, 6.426, 7.217, 13.101, 15.281, 17.152, 18.96, 211, 216, 19.38, B 5.132, 7.80, 9.64, 93, 190, 10.124, 15.295, **A** 10.132, 12.26; **Lord** ~ 17.135, 19.42

almusse *n* 9.96 = **almesse** *n*

alofte (olofte) *av* (up) on high 1.112, 6.423, 20.44, 147, B 1.90, (up) above **B** 12.219, *(fig.)* Pr 157; up(right) 6.409

alogh B 12.233 = **alouȝ** *av*

along *av* out, lengthwise 6.216

alongid *p.p.a* desirous, eager A 7.251

alosen *v* praise 19.103

aloud(e), alowed *av* out loud 6.23, 20.360; with a loud voice 2.131, 21.159

alowed *p.p.* 3.204 *see* **al(l)ouen** *v*

als *av* as 16.350, **B** 4.195, 6.36, A 2.122

alse *av* 17.92, B Pr 217, 3.46, 72, 5.226, 7.233, **A** 3.211, Z Pr 59 = **also** *av*

also *av* too, also, likewise Pr 46 *et p.*; (just) as 16.345, 21.441, B 3.331, A 11.95; so, in such a way †B 10.367

althouh (althow, alþeiȝ) *conj.* although 2.121, 12.146, 14.46, 20.373

alway, alwey *av* always, at all times 10.28, 16.96, B 15.313

am *1 sg. pr.* 1.72 *et p.*, *(without prn subj.)* 19.278, 20.129, B 5.599 *see* **ben** *v*

amayst(e)r(y)en *v* master, get control of 2.161, 167, 8.221

ameddes 9.122 = **amydde(s)** *prep.*

amendement *n* correction, ? improvement 3.122; **on / vp** ~ by way of compensation, [for taking trouble] 22.135; repentance 6.102; conversion B 10.363

amenden *v* put right 4.86, 12.74, 13.199, 17.202, 19.295, **B** 3.57, 94, 6.272, 10.60, 439, 11.104, 377, 12.95, 13.208; repair 3.65, 9.30, 31, 33, 19.160, 20.389, 22.363; improve B 12.286; heal 20.157; make amends for 4.92, 19.203; relieve **B** 9.83, 10.60, 11.209, 14.188; restore (peace in) 4.182; reform [morally] 1.77, 2.103, 141, 246, 3.100, 135, 6.61, 169, 7.121, 8.79, 9.16, 160, 237, 10.304, 15.229, 16.261, 17.50, 225, 250, 19.316,

332, 21.445, 22.109, **B** 5.132, 7.15, 10.123, 268, 11.424, 12.7, 15, 194, 14.20, (*person.*) 'Be converted' 7.243, 247; save, redeem 1.163, 7.127, 16.23, 18.288, **B** 13.409, 15.249; discipline Pr 212, 5.170, B 3.94

amendes *n* reparation, amends 4.84; (*person.*) 2.120 *et p.*; compensation 4.97, **B** 5.325, 18.343; **to ~ in** satisfaction B 18.328

amercyen *v* (impose a) fine (on) B 6.39; *see also* **mersyen** *v*

amydde(s) *av* in the middle [of it] B 13.83, 247; *prep.* in the middle of 6.334, 9.122, 10.33, 14.137, B 16.14; amidst 10.67, B 10.407; through the midst of 13.42; straight in the A 7.166

amys *a* wrong, amiss 19.295; in a disordered state B 6.325; *av* wrongly 1.172; amiss 13.199, Z 7.45

amonge *av* along with [it] B 14.238

among(es) *prep.* among 3.49 *et p.*, Z 7.287; in among 22.112; in the company of 6.241, 434, 9.189, 10.28, 11.34, 17.28; between 21.252; amidst 17.288, B 11.365; with Pr 131, B 10.48

amorteysen *v* alienate in mortmain 17.55

amorwe *av* (on) the next morning 3.307

amorwenynges *av* in the mornings B 11.338 (**amorwenynge** 13.147)

amounten *v* add up [to saying] A 3.86

ampulle *n* B 5.520 = **aunpolle** *n*

an[1] *indef. art.* (*before vowel and silent* h) Pr 3 *et p.*

an[2] *prep.* in 3.70, 7.217, 9.281, 14.7, 14, 16.186, 19.4, **B** 13.402, 17.116; on 2.134, 5.186, 6.124, 12.42, 17.222, 18.106, 21.192, **B** Pr 13, 11.107

an[3] *v* = **han** ~ Z Pr 99, *conj.* = **and** Z Pr 91 *etc*

ancre (**anker**) *n* anchorite / anchoress Pr 30, 3.140, 8.146, B 15.214, A 10.136

and (**ant** Z Pr 5 *et p.*, **an** Z 1.41) *conj.* and Pr 5 *et p.*; and yet Pr 162, 16.103, B 14.12; but Pr 195; if 2.204, 3.44, 4.34, 6.289, 8.160, 9.71, 238, 11.96, 12.194, 13.56, 15.156, 19.208, 22.14 (1), 210, **B** 2.193, 4.88, 5.90, 9.81, 10.360, 11.100, 12.240, 13.110, 15.427, 16.73, A 11.218; even though Pr 120, 3.114, 6. 49, 21. 446, B 10.407

angel *n* angel 9.37, 10.156, 11.150, 12.208, 14.92, 15.302, 17.222, 18.90, 20.413, 450, 21.72, 74, 79, 81, 150, 22.241, **B** Pr 128, 131, 9.124, 16.71, **A** 10.143, 157, 12.4, 95

anger, angre *n* anguish, affliction 6.79, 114, 12.208, 16.150, 19.320, 21.292, **B** 12.11, 15.259, 271; wrath A 10.143

angr(y)en *v* afflict, trouble 16.85, B 5.116

#**angrylyche** *av* petulantly 16.113

anhengen *v* hang 1.64

anhouren Z 6.42 = **honouren** *v*

any *a, n* 17.282, 21.305, B Pr 156 *et p.*, A 2.32 *et p.* = **eny** *a, n*

#**anyent(is)en** *v* utterly destroy 19.269, 20.386

†**animal** *n* animal B 10.242

anker 8.146 = **ancre** *n*

#**annuel** *n* payment for annual commemorative-service Z Pr 63

ano(e)n, ano(o)n(e) *av* at once Pr 113, 1.114, 6.338, 9.163, 13.40, 214, 217, 240, 18.106, 19.66, 20.362, 22.35, 136, B 16.19, A 12.35; presently 3.320, B 9.131; soon B 11.46; *conj.* ~ **as** as soon as Pr 111, 21.18; ~ **riht** *av* right away 4.150, 7.293, 15.52, 22.17; immediately B 11.337

anoyen *v* offend, irritate B 2.167; harass A 3.176; trouble B 5.93

another *prn* a second (person) 13.35, 18.289, 21.270, A 12.35; another Pr 199, 6.38, 17.104, B 9.84; another person, someone else 3.319, 7.293, 301, 18.197, 20.47, B 10.102; anyone else 6.24, 9.123; someone 3.295; one more 1.105; *a* a second B 3.246; another B 14.131

answere *n* answer, reply 20.331

answeren *v* answer, reply B Pr 140, 11.251, 18.315, A 12.62; give an answer [in explanation] B 10.117, [to interrogation] **A** 11.299, 301, 12.29, [in dispute] B 15.381; be accountable B 5.293

#**antecedent** *n* (grammatical) antecedent (*fig.*) 3.353, 361, *a* 3.378

apayen *v* please, satisfy 2.45, 8.115, 9.178, 15.64, B 6.195; *see* **payen** *v*

apayren (**ap(p)eyren**) *v* (do) harm (to) 3.163, 7.210, 8.229, Z 2.3; damage [by reducing] 5.144

(a)p(p)aray(l)le (**parail**) *n* dress, wearing-apparel 6.30 (B 13.278), 10.117, 12.126, 133, 17.72

(ap)parailen *v* clothe, attire Pr 25, 2.224, 7.160, 8.56, **B** Pr 23, 2.171, 215, 5.516, 6.57, 11.240

a-parceles *n. phr.* as (distinct) parts 19.98

apart *av* privately 6.383; ~**ye** separately 15.54

ap(p)e(e)l *n* formal charge 19.286; appeal [to a higher court] 2.186, [for protection] 2.244

apeyren Z 2.3 = **apayren** *v*

apenden *v* belong 1.97, B 1.45, Z Pr 55

ap(p)eren *v* appear 11.151, 14.92; show, reach 16.83; present oneself Pr 188, 3.149; be symbolised (by) 21.92

(a)pertly(che) *av* plainly, manifestly 3.313, 5.117, B 1.100; openly, in public B 5.23

apeward *n* ape-keeper [juggler with trained monkey] B 5.631

(a)poisenen *v* (kill by) poison 3.163; corrupt fatally 17.224; grievously harm B 3.82

ap(p)osen *v* confront with question 3.5, 5.10, 14.154, 15.94; (put a) question (to) 1.45, 15.193, 16.161, **A** 11.298, 12.26; dispute (with) B 7.139; ask question(s) A 12.8

ap(p)ostata *n* apostate, violator of the code of one's order 1.98, Z 1.65

(a)postel *n* apostle 9.20, 11.32, 150, 12.34, 13.3, 18.177,

208, 21.147, 155, 169, **B** 10.340, 15.417, A 12.4; **(Peter þe)** ~ 20.251, **(Poul þe)** ~ 11.269 *etc*; *(fig.)* 9.118; (itinerant) preacher B 6.149

appel (appul) *n* fruit 10.208, 20.305, 374, **B** 12.232, 16.73, A 10.141; apple 8.317, 18.62, **B** 5.603, 9.149, *(fig.)* 18.68, 70, 18.122, ~ **tree** 18.61, B 18.287

appelen *v* accuse (formally) B 11.421

appetit *n* appetite (for food) B 6.263

(ap)purtinaunce *n* subsidiary right / privilege *(iron.)* 2.108; appendage, accessory 16.330

Aprill *n* (the month of) April B 13.269

aprochen *v* approach 18.139, 20.174

apropren *v* acquire right to endowment and income (of) Z Pr 58

ar¹ *av, comp.* **arre** Z 4.4 the sooner, *(sup.)* **arst(e)** first (of all) 6.307, A 4.29; *and see* **or**¹ *av*

ar² *prep.* before 5.122, 17.61, *etc*; *and see* **or**² *prep.*, **er**²*prep.*

ar³ *conj.* before Pr 164 *et p.*; *and see* **or**⁴ *conj.*, **er**³ *conj.*

ar(e)n *pr. pl of* **ben** *v* Pr 93, 126, 11.237, **B** 3.80, 17.165, *etc.*; *with* **hit** *and pl. subj. following* there are 8.217, 15.288, A 7.49, Z 7.263; they are 9.118, 126; *(trs)* ~ **hit** are they 15.309

aray *n* order, *in phr.* **riden out of** ~ *(fig.)* behave in disorderly manner 5.157; clothing 2.16

arayen *v (refl.)* get ready 4.16; robe B 5.11

araten *v* reprove, berate 5.11, 12.37, B 11.375; scold B 14.163

#arbitrere *n* arbitrator, **be ~s** through the mediation of a third party 6.381

arc(h)a(u)ngel *n* archangel 1.107, 21.150, B 1.108

archidekne *n* A Pr 92 = **erchedekn** *n*

arch *n* arch, *in* **þe Arches** [*meton.* for the ecclesiastical court of appeal for Canterbury held at St Mary of the Arches (le Bow)] 2.61, 186, 22.136

are *pr. pl.* 8.217 *et pl.*; *see* **ar(e)(n)**, *pr. pl.*

arechen *v* get hold of, hand 20.281

aredy *a* prepared 6.97, 7.119, Z 6.69

aren *pr. pl.* Pr 93 *et p.*; *see* **ar(e)(n)**

arerage *n* B 10.470 = **arrerage** *n*

arere *av* back (wards) 6.404, B 10.139

areren *v* make, set forth A 2.48

(a)reso(u)nen *v* rebuke, berate 13.129, 183, 194, 245, B 12.217

arguen *v* dispute 16.113; expound an argument 11.121

arguere *n* disputant, critic B 10.118

argument *n* (formal) argument [in a disputation] 19.112, B 15.381

aryht *av* in the right way 17.157

arysen *v (contr. pr.* **ariste** 12.232, *p.t.* **aroos** 6.62 *etc)* get up 5.15, 6.62, 386, 391, 8.125, 13.247, 15.28, 20.281, **B** 6.263, 8.35, Z 4.158; rise [from the dead] 20.264, 21.52, 152, B 10.353, A 8.172, [from sick-bed] A 7.132, [from sin] 3.357, 10.52, 14.111; grow up 3.452;

originate (from) 11.234, 12.232, 17.139, 19.250, A 10.119, 121; be obtained A 8.47; occur 8.345; take place A 5.188

arm¹ *n* arm 16.82, 20.76, **B** 9.165, 15.122, *pl.* = embrace 7.26, A 12.42

arm² *n (in* **armes** *pl. only)* armour B 5.501; battle, *in phrr.* **iugement of** ~ trial by combat *(fig.)* 18.129, **seriaunt of** ~ (royal) officer commanding an armed force *(fig.)* 21.341; armorial bearings, coat of arms *(fig.)* 21.12, *(also)* B 5.501; *in phr.* **heraud of** ~ herald [at tournament] 20.14, *(fig.)* 18.186, 22.94

armen *v (p.p.* **y-armed**) arm, equip with weapons 21.144, *(fig.)* 21.354, 22.116

armure *n* armour *(fig.)* 1.153, *in phr.* **cote** ~ coat of arms *(fig.)* 21.13

arn *pr.pl.* 9.137, 10.298, B Pr 98 *etc*; *see* **ar(e)(n)** *pr.pl.*

arnde *n* A 3.40; *see* **er(e)nde** *n*

†arne *p.t.* B 16.136 = **ern** *p.t.*; *see* **rennen** *v*

arre *av comp.* the sooner Z 4.4

aro(e)s, aroos *p.t. see* **arysen** *v*

(a)r(r)erage *n* debt, arrears, *in phrr.* **casten in** ~ find (sb.) short in his accounts 12.68, **fallen / rennen in** ~ fall behind with payments / run into debt 9.272, 11.301, 12.65, 15.288, B 5.242

ars *n. pl.* 11.97 *see* **art** *n*

arst(e) *av* first, soonest 6.307, A 4.29

art *n (pl.* **ars, artȝ**) art, discipline, *in phr.* **the seuene** ~ the seven branches of higher study (at university) 11.97, 12.95, 17.114

art *2 sg.pr.* art, are 1.80 *et p.*

article *n* article [of Creed] B 10.233

artow *assim.* *2 sg. pr.* (= **art thow**) 13.225, 16.210, 18.184, 20.360, B 19.408

arwe *n* arrow 3.478, 22.117, 226

arwen *v* daunt, make fearful 3.236

as *conj.* as Pr 8 *et p.*; such as Pr 30, 220 *etc*, B 3.89, A 8.169; as for example 3.374, 6.276, 8.261, 13.51, 155, B 13.402, Z 7.91; = as if Pr 2, 66, 3.54 *etc*, B 5.100; = though 13.184; *av* = like Pr 3, 2.28, 3.387, 4.194 *etc*, B 10.350, A 10.212, Z Pr 37 inasmuch as 7.100; *in phrr.* ~ **by** to judge by, according to 3.306, 9.214, 11.268, 13.27, 97, 14.152, 201, 17.157, 21.456, B 14.155; as if from 8.88, 17.152, as if through 16.108; ~ **for** as if as 2.146, 9.92, 12.197, 15.39, 171, 18.205, 22.20, with regard to 7.191, B 15.457; ~ **in** in respect of 6.32; ~ **þee** as if to treat you B 13.171; ~ **to** in regard to 6.36, in comparison with 14.83; ~ **who seiþ** as if to say B 9.36; ~ **whoso** like someone who B 15.337; *(pleonastic for emph.)* 3.62, 6.32, 36, 11.265, 285, 12.81, 191, 17.149, 202, 18.88, 99, B 2.58, A 10.206, Z 2.131; *(as intensifier with av)* ~ **ȝerne** right away 7.36 (~ **quyk** B 14.190, **swiþe** ~ B 3.102, ~ **tyd** B 13.319, 16.61) *(in comb.)* **theder** ~ where...to 1.118; **ther** ~ where B 2.92

asayen 3.5= **assayen** *v*

ascapen 8.79 = **askapen** *v*

ascuth *3 pr. sg.* Pr 21, 1.34, *imp. pl* 6.56 = **asketh** *see* **asken** *v*

as(s)elen *v* seal [with official mark to authenticate] 2.114, 19.6, 9, Z 3.84

asentaunt *a.* willing Z 3.152; *and see* **assenten** *v*

aseruen *v* deserve, merit 14.136

aseth (**assetȝ**) *n* adequate satisfaction 19.204

as(c)hamed *p.p.a* filled with shame 6.421, 13.240, 22.284; mortified 13.214

asyde *av* sideways 6.404; out of the way, apart 19.59, 63, 22.152; off to one side A 11.95

askapen *v* escape 2.215, 3.61, 8.79; avoid B 3.57

asken *v* ask (question) (of) 6.353, 17.204, 18.78, 20.330, 22.332, **B** 3.236, 10.310, 11.408, 12.233, **A** 11.178, 12.27; (~ of) enquire (of sb.) (about sth.) 1.46, 10.5, 11.104, 18.24, 20.125, **B** 13.309, 16.65, A 12.11, ~ **after** enquire concerning 7.180, 12.215, A 12.79, ~ **at** 6.56; (make) request (for) 22.188, **B** 7.75, 10.203; ~ (**of**) beg, pray for [grace, mercy *etc*] (from) 6.14, 8.319, 9.237, 14.56, 132, 17.256, 18.260, 19.280, 19.268, 21.131, B 14.229, 17.334; demand 3.272, 275, 299, 301, 4.97, 7.36, 8.78, 15.291, 16.291, B 14.260, A 1.178; call for 1.34; claim 3.245, 13.49, 16.101, 17.70, 20.387, 21.482, 22.266, *ger.* request, claim 21.482; seek A 1.100; require Pr 21, 3.335, 404, 5.67, 18.78, 19.273, 20.417, 442, 21.231, 479, **B** Pr 120, 2.27, 18.348

askes *n.pl.* B 3.98 = **asyshes** *n*

aslepe *av* asleep 2.53, 5.108, 21.5, 22.51, **B** 11.5, 15.11

asoilen *v* 12.6, A 12.11 = **assoylen** *v*

asondry *a* separate B 17.165

asparen *v* spare B 15.140; *and see* **sparen** *v*

(a)spelen *v* save 6.431, 13.76

aspyen *v* (*p.t.* **aspy(e)de** 9.207, 21.337) observe (secretly) 4.53, 6.152; examine 2.235, 19.36; find out 2.46, 3.109, 12.143, 14.167, B 6.129, A 11.226; seek B 16.170; discover 8.232, 9.207, 21.303, B 8.127, Z 7.274; descry, catch sight of 15.153, 21.337, A 12.103

assay *n* trial, testing B 10.255

as(s)ayen *v* try 6.356; try out B 16.106; examine 3.5; find out 16.162, 20.71, B 16.74; have a go 8.22

assail(l)en *v* attack, besiege 13.62, 21.227, 22.126, 297, 375; afflict 2.297; tempt 20.330

assche *n* ash-tree Z 5.45

asse *n* ass ~ **bak** back of an ass 20.9

asselen *v* 19.6 *see* **as(s)elen** *v*

assemblee *n* gathering B Pr 218

assemblen *v* come together B 2.57

assent(e) *n* mutual agreement 16.108, B 9.116; sentiment, opinion B 4.187

assenten *v* assent, agree Pr 190, 2.68, 155, 170, 3.153, 4.98, 187, 190, 8.54, 10.106, B 4.182, 188, A 4.89; consent 19.266; approve 8.36

assignen *v* indicate, specify B 4.126

as(s)oylen *v* absolve [sacramentally] Pr 68, 3.42, 50, 180, 358, 6.168, 257, 294, 9.4, 12.16, 19.162, 21.186, 191, 398, B 5.272, Z 3.171; solve, explain 11.156, 14.155, B 11.221; answer, resolve 12.140, 17.114, B 3.237, A 12.11

ast *2 sg. pr.* Z 3.156 = **hast**; *see* **hauen** *v*

asterten *v* avoid 13. 211

astronom(i)en *n* astronomer 17.96, 21.245

astronomye *n* (the art of) astronomy 21.245, B 10.209

aswagen *v* lessen, relieve 6.88

at *prep.* at 2.68, 3.490, 5.29 *etc*, B 4.131; at the value of 5.97, 8.166; behind 22.69; from Pr 205, 2.176, 3.254, 375, 7.56, 292, 12.57, 13.158, 15.103, 19.211, 21.402, 22.19; in 20.416, B Pr 85; in time of 5.129, 10.190, 11.233, 15.5, 22.20; of 1.203, 3.26, 6.56; on 6.324, 9.21, 154, 321, 351, 11.252, 12.110, 16.54, 21.197, B 7.17, A 2.40; to 3.417, 7.214, 9.87, 16.63 *in phrr.* ~ **þe ale** Pr 43, **þe barre** 3.448, ~ **bedde** A 2.52, ~ **ese** 3.44, **þe freres** 7.27, **þe furste** 2.210, ~ **herte** 9.183, ~ **heste** 3.148, ~ **ynne** 10.4, ~ **large** 22.192, ~ **lykyng** 15.168, ~ **þe newe feire** A 5.171, ~ ... **nombre** 22.255, ~ **ones** 11.252, 13.31, ~ **þe stuyues** 13.74, ~ **wille** Pr 38, ~ **worthe** 14.66; *in names* = living at / by ~ **þe-Noke** A 5.115, ~ **þe-Style** 6.207

at(t)achen *v* arrest 2.211, 252; sequestrate 18.278; vouch for 11.310

a-taken *v* catch in the act, *p.p.* 3.139

atamen *v* broach 19.70

ateynen *v* find false or corrupt 22.162

athynken *v* (*impers.*) cause remorse, grieve 6.100, B 18.89

aþrest *a* afflicted with thirst A 12.82

atyer *n* fine apparel 2.15

atymyen *v* attain, manage 19.242, 246*n*

atiren *v* dress up, attire B 2.19, 166

a-to *av* in two 8.64, 20.75, 21.340

atones *avl phr.* B 17.53; *see* **ones** *av*

atte *prep. phr.* (= **at the**) 3.34, 4.132, **B** 5.197, 6.102, 115, 10.52, 11.118, **A** 7.48

attese *prep. phr.* 1.19 = **at ese**

attyf Z 7.235 = **actif** *a*

attre *n* poisonous, rotten matter B 12.255

atw(e)(y)n(n)e *av* in two Pr 114, B 7.115; apart 18.190

auctour *n* B 10.245, 15.120, 374 = **autor** *n*

audiense *n* a hearing 7.93

auditour *n* auditor, accountant 21.464

auȝte *p.t.* A 2.21, 5.71, 7.123, **aughtest** *2 sg.* A 1.73 = **ouhte(st)**; *see* **owen** *v*

auht (**ouȝt, ouht**) *prn* anything 6.111, 7.35, 8.235, **B** 11.49, 13.300, 416; something 7.45, 15.12, = everything 7.123; *in phrr.* **ar come ~ longe** before very long 17.214, **by ~ (þat)** as far as 7.283, 12.143; *av* at all 7.176, A 8.61

auncel (**auncer**) *n* weighing-balance 6.224

aungel A 10.143 *etc*, B Pr 128 *etc* = **angel** *n*

aunpolle *n* flask, ampulla 7.164

aunte *n* aunt 6.128, (*Abstinence*) 6.439, (*Latro*) 6.329

au(e)ntur(e) *n* chance, luck, *in phrr.* **an** ~ in case, lest perchance 3.70, 433, 8.40, **B** 3.72, 13.72, **good** ~ by good luck 8.79

aunt(e)ren *v* (*refl.*) venture, dare 10.218, 20.230, 22.175

auntrous *a as n* adventurous (knights) 20.14

auter *n* altar [of church] 5.164, 17.279, **B** 5.108, **A** 3.50, [of sacrifice] 18.263

autor (aucto(u)r) *n* authority 11.149, **B** 10.245; (Latin) writer **B** 15.374

auaylen (availlen) *v* help, be of use to 9.7, 274, 19.83, 22.179, **B** 10.272

auaryce (auaris) *n* avarice, (the sin of) greed 1.191, 2.91, 16.365, **B** 15.247, **A** 8.40, (*person.*) 16.85, 22.123

auarous(e) **B** 15.85 *see* **auerous** *a*

avauncen (avaunsen) *v* benefit, cause to prosper 10.258; promote 1.187, 3.36, ? 13.103 (*or* appoint), **A** 4.116

avengen *v* avenge 22.385n; (*refl.*) avenge oneself 6.74 (**B** 13.330); take vengeance upon 3.93

auenture *n* **B** 3.72, 13.72 *see* **au(e)ntur(e)** *n*

auer *n* wealth, property 6.32

auerous *a* avaricious, greedy 1.187, 16.279, **B** 15.85, *a as n* 14.21

auysen *v* (*refl.*) reflect, consider 17.54, (*person.*) 4.21

auoutrye *n* (the act of) adultery **B** 12.74

auowe *n* solemn vow 7.63, **B** Pr 71, 5.398; *and see* **vowe** *n*

avowen *v*[1] affirm 3.312, 15.115, 20.224, **Z** 3.162

auowen *v*[2] vow **B** 5.382

away (awey) *av* away 4.100, 10.229, 14.117, 17.144, 19.334, 22.56, 174, **B** Pr 166, **A** 4.93, 7.183; off, away 3.422, 4.60, 7.221, 8.118, 10.136, 12.240, 18.49, 155, 19.291, 21.156, **B** 5.107, 14.83, **Z** 7.59; aside 22.168, **B** 17.89; to the side **B** 5.108; along 19.52; *in phrr.* **fer** ~, **wel** ~ far and away, very much **B** 12.262, 14.209, 17.43; (*as predicate*) removed 12.148; absent, missing 19.138, **B** 1.190

awayten *v* waylay 10.301; watch stealthily 4.52, **B** 13.361; attend to 6.279; find out 17.63, **B** 10.332; look for **B** 16.257; wait / watch for **B** 16.138

awaken *v* (*p.t.* **awaked(e)** 5.1 *etc*, **B** 16.167, **awoke** 9.293, *p.p.* **awaked** 22.1) awake 2.103, 5.1, 9.293, 13.215, 15.1, 272, 16.77, 19.334, 22.387; wake up 7.8; wake, rouse Pr 214, (*fig.*) 15.308; arise 6.103, 139, 394; spring up 8.344

awey 2.225 *etc* = **away** *av*

a-werke *av* to work 8.197

awreken *v* (*p.p.* **awreke** 2.206, 17.4, **awroke** 8.208 *etc*) avenge 2.206, 8.158, 170, 208, 300, 17.4, 22.203, (*refl.*) vent (oneself) 10.290

ax *n* axe 3.458; battle-axe 14.51

axen *v* 7.180, **A** 11.178 = **asken** *v*

#**axesse** *n* attack of fever **A** 5.203

bab(e)len *v* mumble, mutter **AB** 5.8

baby *n* baby 19.94, **B** 17.96

#**baburlippid** *a.* with thick protruding lips 6.198c.

bacbiten *v see* **bakbiten** *v*

bache *n* valley 7.158

bacheler *n* (bachelor) knight 20.87, **B** 16.179; bachelor (of divinity) Pr 85, 9.248, **A** Pr 90

baco(u)n *n* bacon 6.201, 8.332, 9.148, 10.280, 15.68, 101

bad(e) *p.t.* 2.158, 219 *et p.*, **A** 12.106, **baed** 22.377; *see* **bidden** *v*

badde *a* wicked, vicious 9.16, **B** 10.280; ~**lyche** *av* poorly 4.55, 17.197; #~**nesse** *n* wickedness **B** 12.48

baed *p.t.* 22.377 = **bad(e)** *p.t.*

baer *p.t.* 18.115 *et p.*; *see* **beren** *v*[1]

ba(e)r *a* 22.184 *see* **bar**

bagge *n* bag, sack Pr 42, 5.52, 7.163, 9.98, 120, 139, 154; wallet 10.85; money-bag (*meton.*, = money) 22.142

bayard *n* (bay) horse [*as name*] 4.56, 8.178, 192, 19.72, **B** 4.124, **Z** 3.158

bail(l)if (bayl(i)e) *n* bailiff [sherrif's under-officer] 2.60, 3.2

bak(k)(e) *n* back 6.69, 9.154, 169, 20.9, **B** 2.172, 3.196, 199, 13.317, **A** 8.15, 12.70; cloak, outer garment [to cover back] 13.71, **B** 10.360

bakbiten *v* slander, detract [from someone's good name behind his back] 2.85, ger. 6.95, 16.361, **B** 5.88; **bakbitare** *n* detractor 18.46 (**B** 16.43)

baken *v* (*p.p.* **(y)bake(n)**) 8.178, **B** 6.292) bake 8.178, 192, 317, 333, **B** 6.182, 282, 15.432, ? roast 9.93n, **B** 15.462n

bakere *n* baker Pr 222, 3.80, 4.120

bakken *v* clothe **A** 11.188, clothe oneself **Z** 3.160

bakstere (baxter) *n* baker **B** Pr 219, 3.79

balayshen *v* beat with rod 6.157

bald(e)li(che) 16.55, 18.115, 22.70, 132, 328, **Z** 7.61 = **boldely** *av*

baldore, ~ere *comp.* 4.102, 9.334 *see* **bold** *a*

bale *n* wrong, misdeed 4.85, 88, 89, 20.206; evil **A** 10.147; sin 12.58; death, the life-destroyer (*semi-person.*) 20.34; misery 13.21, 141; ~ **deeþ** (*semi-person.*) baleful death **B** 18.35

baleyse *n* rod [for flogging] 11.123, (*fig.*) scourge, tribulation **B** 12.12

baly **Z** Pr 38 = **bely** *n*

balk(e) *n* ridge of unploughed land 8.114n

balled *a* bald 22.184, (*fig.*) crafty, glib 11.38

*#**ballok-knyf** *n* knob-hafted knife **B** 15.124n

bande *p.t.* 6.218; *see* **bynden** *v*

bane *n* destruction (of life) 8.350, **A** 6.93

baner *n* banner, military standard 22.69, 96; (bishop's) banner [*sc.* the Cross] **A** 8.15

banyer *n* standard-bearer **B** 15.435

banisshen *v* drive away **A** 3.274

bank *n* bank, slope B Pr 8; embankment B 17.103

bannen *v* curse 1.58, 10.230, 11.192; condemn 3.143, B 15.252; reproach B 10.7; strongly forbid 9.162

bapte(w)me (baptisme) *n* (the sacrament of) baptism 12.60, 14.201, 20.418, 419, **B** 11.82, 14.184, Z 6.63; = the water from Christ's side [symbolizing baptism; *see* Jn 19.34] 21.325

baptisen (baptiʒen) baptise B 16.250, = (administer Christian baptism to) **B** 10.345, 11.77, 79, 80, (*fig.*) 17.268, 19.88, *ger.* **baptiʒynge** administering baptism B 11.78

baptist *n* baptist 10.181, 21.38, *etc. see* **Iohan, St** (the Baptist)

bar *p.t.* 2.3 *et p.*, **baren** *pl.* 6.415, B 5.107 *see* **beren** *v¹*

bar(e) *a* bare 6.150; naked 6.157; devoid of hair 22.184; (*as intensive*) the very 18.39; **~fot** *a* barefoot 9.121, 20.9

bareyne *a* barren, unproductive 20.109

bargayn *n* business transaction 2.92, Z 2.97; purchase, bargain 5.96; agreement (to barter / sell) 6.394

barke *n* shell, husk 12.147, 148

barly *n* barley-meal 6.225, ~ **breed** 8.142, A 7.169; barley-sheaves Z 7.170

barn(e) (bern) *n* offspring, descendant 3.188, 5.70, 172 (B 10.321), 17.58, *in phr.* **~es bastardes** bastard offspring 5.71; (young) child 8.306, **B** 9.78, 165, 15.455, A 10.147, *spec.* = the infant Christ 2.3, 19.86, 90, 20.136, 241, 243, B 12.146, A 12.117; young person B 11.77; person 14.126, B 11.82, A 12.117; *pl.* people, *in phr.* **†barnes of Israel** children of Israel B 10.279

barnhoed *n* childhood, ? warriorship (*fig.*) 18.136

baro(u)n *n* lord, nobleman Pr 220, 5.172, 6.123; peer, great baron 22.129; baron [noble ranking between knight and earl] 3.261, **B** 10.320, 13.166; judge B 3.321

barre *n* barrier [outside gate] (*fig.*) 7.238; the Bar [rail before judge's seat in law court] 3.448, 4.132, 169, 9.45, **B** Pr 212, 4.169; bar [for bolting door] 20.281, 364

barren *v* (*p.p.* **ybarred**) bar 20.284, 21.167

barste *p.t.* 8.175; *see* **bresten** *v*

#bas(e)lard *n* (fashionable) dagger [worn at the girdle] 3.457, B 15.121, 124, A 11.214

basket *n* basket 18.155

bastard *n* bastard 2.24 (Mede), 2.144 (Fals), 6.133 (Ione), 5.65, 9.168; *a* illegitimate 5.71*n*; ? grafted, ? cultivated B 16.69

bat *n* clod, lump 18.92; loaf A 7.165

bat *contr. pr.* Z 4.47 = **bet(eth)**; *see* **beten** *v*

batayle *n* Pr 108, 112, 8.49, 14.50, 17.288, 22.262; warfare 3.475, 8.350; (single) combat 20.66, B 16.164

*batauntliche *av* with noisy eagerness 16.55

baþen *v* bathe B 17.95

*bat-nelde *n* pack-needle 6.218*c*

batren *v* thump, slap B 3.199

#baud(e) *n* procurer 8.72; procuress 6.189; go-between A 3.45; ?harlot 3.164

*baudekyn *n* little go-between A 3.40

baw(e) *interj.* (*expressing scorn*) bah! 12.76, 21.399

baxtere A Pr 98 = **bakstere** *n*

be *inf.* Pr 54, *p.p.* Pr 62, 3.259 *etc*, *subjv.* Pr 104, 150, *etc*; *see* **ben** *v*

be (by) *prep.* 12.145, B 3.15, Z 8.69; close to 7.218, 8.2, A 5.136; of 10.241, 14.72, 18.195; on 10.232, 20.316, B 18.45; to 1.116, 20.7, 169; in 9.214, 243, 11.74, 12.37; along 22.188, 22.1, B 10.305, Z 1.109; past 5.6, 11.108; alongside 2.180; with 3.40, 4.62, 7.30, 11.126; in relation to 13.229, 14.141, 16.110, **B** 1.28, 4.71, 10.187, 12.210; with reference to A 12.108; in regard to 6.36, 7.267, B 11.153, 418, A 11.209; in the case of B 15.73; through 1.158, 3.413, 7.54, B 1.139, A 10.157; for 6.40, 16.120; by means of 2.4, 6.381, 10.105 *etc*, B 7.128, A 7.21; on the basis of 2.122, B 10.332, 344, A 8.153, 11.196; according to 1.86, B 6.251, A 8.135; in accordance with Pr 78, 1.90, 2.147, **B** 3.7, 10.386, A 10.91, 11.276; concerning 3.287, 6.70, 162, 10.165, 11.11, 13.111; from the example of 3.142, A 11.275; from 4.154, 17.104, 22.275; = to the extent of 7.141, 19.60, A 4.29; in, on 6.373; during 7.64*n*, 111, B 6.101; *for phrasal vv.* **setten** ~ *etc, see main entries; in phrr.* ~ **dayes...** continually 9.222; **day** ~ **day** 9.341; ~ **fer** 22.315; ~**... myhte / power** according to one's power 6.295, 9.17, B 10.268, A 5.75; ~ **siht of** by the witness of 1.200, 2.115; ~ **that** from what 16.295, by that time 8.314, 322*n*; ~ **þis day** today 7.9, 8.302, (?*oath*) 4.172; *in oaths:* 3.141, 8.234, A 2.92, Z 4.152; *conj. in conjv. phr.* ~ **so** provided that 4.98, 5.39, 6.331, 12.4, 15.256, 21.450, 22.222, B 12.166; ?**so that** 14.279*n*

beaupere *n* elder, reverend father 20.239; venerable priest 9.248

beaute *n* beauty 13.10, B 12.48

beche *n* beech-tree 5.120

become *p.t.* A Pr 91, 7.181 *see* **bycomen** *v*

bed *imp. sg.* Z 7.45; *see* **beden** *v*

bed *n* (*dat.* **bedde**) bed Pr 44, 6.415, 7.4, 8.108, 9.145, 254, 19.303, B 10.65; *in phrr.* **a- (on)** ~ in bed 10.273; **at** ~ **and at boord** = in all conjugal duties and relations A 2.52; *in cpds.* # ~ **bourde** *n* bed-play, sexual relations 10.293; ~ **chaunbre** *n* bed room 6.228; ~ **rede(ne)** *a* bed-ridden 7.107, 9.34, A 7.130, Z 7.197*a* as *n* 9.177, B 6.191

bedden *v* provide with a bed, *p.p.* 17.197; (*refl.*) go to bed B 2.98

beddyng *ger.* bedding, somewhere to sleep Z 7.199; bed 16.73

bede *n* prayer 7.16, **B** 5.8, 12.28, ~**(s) biddyng** saying of prayers 12.86, 21.378, *in phr.* **peire** ~ set of rosary-beads B 15.122; command Z 1.56, 2.60

bedel 2.111, 3.2 = **bydel** *n*

bed(e)man *n* messenger, spokesman 3.43, 48; bedesman [one who prays for another, *esp.* religious] 3.274, B 15.205, 427

bedredene *a* 7.107 *etc*; *see* **bed** *n*

beden *p.t. pl.* 3.28, 15.27, 20.53, 21.143, *p.p.* 2.56; *see* **bidden** *v*

beden *v* (*p.p.* **bede(n), boden**) offer 10.270; invite 2.56

beel-syre 20.282 = **belsyre** *n*

beem *n* beam, plank B 10.264, 276

been *inf.* 5.15, *pr. pl.* 7.69; *see* **ben** *v*

beenfeet *n* good deed 7.42, 263

beer *inf.* 22.91; **beere** *p.t.* B 5.138, *subjv.* B 15.121; *see* **beren** *v*

beest B 3.267 *etc* = **best** *n*

beet *p.t.* 8.175, 20.282, 22.191 *see* **beten** *v*

*****befloberen** *v* muddy, soil B 13.401; *see* **flobren** *v*

before *av* 21.115, A 7.226; *prep.* 2.100, 13.124, 15.211, A 8.39; *see* **byfore** *av, prep.*

begeneld 10.266 = **begyneld** *n*

begen *v* 9.63 = **beggen** *v*

begere 3.274 = **beggare** *n*

beggare *n* beggar 2.173, 3.274, 5.65, 6.49, 7.54, 99, 8.193, 201, 210, 224, 279, 326, 9.61, 98, 161, 171, 12.117, 13.71, 94, 14.140, 15.297, 16.13, 55, 89, 350, 22.239, 241, B 3.219, 6.194, 7.80, 82, 10.360, 11.276, 13.267, 15.341, A 12.71, *in phrr.* ~**s and biddares** Pr 41 (*trs*), 8.210, 9.61, B 15.205, ~ **of kynde** natural beggars 9.168*n*; destitute person, pauper 6.123, 125, 16.103, 364, B 4.124, 9.90, 10.84, 11.197, 199, 13.303, A 10.115, 11.188; rascal, knave 8.265, 12.113, 15.304 (*with prn*)

#**beggarie** *n* (the practice of) begging 9.162, 165

begged Z 7.220 = **(a)-beggeth** *av*

beggen *v*[1] *v* beg (for) 5.29, 51, 90, 174, 6.313, 9.62, 121, 161, 189, Z 3.160; ask for alms (for) 9.86, 10.186, 16.70, 336, 22.238, B 6.192, 15.328 *in phrr.* ~ **(and)** / **or bidden** 9.63, B 6.236, 11.276, 15.256, 16.370, **borwen** 16.372, Z 5.144, *ger.* 17.8, 27

beggen *v*[2] Z 4.78 = **byggen** *v*

*****begyneld** *n* beggar 9.154*c*, 10.266

#**begynnere** *n* originator A 10.53

begynnyng *ger.* first stage A 10.80

begon *v* beset, overcome, *p.p.* A 2.24

begruchen 8.155 = **bigruchen** *v*

beʒonde (biyonde) *av* beyond, *in phrr.* **fro** ~ from abroad 3.145, **of** ~ abroad, in foreign lands B 4.128

byhyhte *p.t.* 3.30 *see* **bihoten** *v*

beheld *p.t.* Pr 14, 13.156, Z 4.159 *see* **byholden** *v*

behynde 16.49, A 5.74 *see* **byhynde** *av, prep.*

behoten 8.301 = **byhoten** *v*

behouen A 8.116, 10.74 = **bihouen** *v*

beygh (*pl.* **beyus**) *n* necklace, collar Pr 178, 180, 191

beyre *prn* (*gen. pl. of* **bo**), *in phr.* **þer beyre** of both of them 20.36

bek(e)ne *n* beacon, signal fire 19.230

bekennen A 11.165 = **bykennen** *v*

beknowen 5.92 = **byknowen** *v*

belauʒen *v* laugh / rejoice about, *p.t.* A 8.107

beleue 8.97, 15.239, 16.230, **beleuen** 7.125, 11.132 = **byleue(n)** *n, v*

bely *n* stomach Pr 42, A 12.70, 74, *in phr.* ~ **ioye** pleasure in eating B 7.119, A 8.112

belyen *v* (*p.p.* **bylowe(n)** 9.181 *etc*) tell lies against, accuse falsely 9.181, 20.355, B 2.22, 5.408, 10.22, A 5.76

belle *n* (church) bell 22.59; (ornamental) bell Pr 180 *et p.*

belouʒ *p.t.* A 8.107 *see* **belauʒen** *v*

*****belouren** *v* scowl / frown at A 8.107

belowen *p.p.* A 5.76 *see* **belyen** *v*

belsyre *n* grandfather 2.121, 20.282; forefather 10.236

belwen *v* bellow B 11.341

be(n) *v* (*pr. sg.* **am** 1.72, **art** 1.80, **best** (*with fut. sense*) 7.235, Z 7.238, **beth** B 10.345, †A 11.197, **is** Pr 40, *pl.* **ar(e)(n)** Pr 93, 126, (*after sg. subj.* 5.59, B 9.121, **ben** A 10.210), **ben** Pr 87, **beth** 3.28, A 6.110, **buth** 9.160, *imper. pl.* **beth** 1.171, (*with prn.*) be 3.85, *subjv.* Pr 104, *pl.* Pr 202, *p.t.* **was** Pr 15, *pl.* **were(n)** Pr 53, *subjv.* Pr 2, *p.p.* **(y)be(n)** Pr 62, B 11.242, A 11.195) be Pr 1 *et p.*; (*subjv.*) may be Pr 150, is 1.124; let it be 3.422; if... / are 5.165; let us be Pr 202; *in constrr.* *without* **to** = to be 3.28, = (he *etc*) will be 2.104, + *p.p.* = once (sth.) is done 3.247, 389, 8.211, 20.104, 21.189; *with p.t. of* **hauen** = would have been 6.214 *etc*; (have) exist(ence) 18.217; become, be made 5.71

bench *n* bench [at table] Pr 200, 6.361, **syde** ~ bench at side table 9.252; *in phr.* **Kynges** ~ court of ~ [= highest law court] A Pr 95

benden *v* bend, stoop 10.37

bene *n* (*gen. pl.* **ben(e)en(e)** A 7.165 / Z 7.162) bean 8.177, 226, 306, 317, 326, B 6.182, 194, A 7.169, made of beans A 7.165; (*fig.*) = thing of little value 12.94

benefice *n* ecclesiastical living 3.33, B 3.314, Z 3.32

beneth 18.85 = **bynethe** *av*

benigne *a* gentle, kind 18.11, 20.119, B 16.7; *av* ~ **lyche** with good will 14.57

benyson *n* (priest's) blessing B 13.236

berd *n* beard 6.201

bere *n* bear 9.196, B 15.299

beren *v*[1] (*p.t. 2 sg.* **bere** B 3.196, **bar** A 3.183), *3 sg.* **ba(e)r** 7.161, 18.115, *pl.* **baren** 6.415, **beren** Z Pr 53, *p.p.* **(y)bor(e)(n)** 1.58, 2.144, 14.31) carry 2.177, 3.422, 4.60, 126, 6.344, 415, 7.161, 163, 221, 8.108, 288, 9.139, 10.93, 13.54, 15.162, 222. 16.176, 18.115, 155, 271, 20.476, 21.49, 22.70, 96, 117, 286, *ger.* 8.198, **B** 3.41, 5.107, 6.142, 14.304, 15.97, **Z** Pr 53, 7.61, (*fig.*) A 8.15; support 2.3, 20.476; wear Pr 178, 16.97, 21.71, B 15.569; bear (weapon) 3.457, 475, 14.50; hold B 6.166; maintain, bear B 15.171, ~ **witnesse** 2.85, B

7.51 *etc*, *ger.* 16.361, B 5.88; thrust (through) 20.87, (down) 22.132; have [name] 3.143, 16.201, 17.261; give birth to B 9.165, *p.p.* **(y)bore(n)** 1.58, 2.144, 14.31, 90, 20.136, 241, 21.71, **B** 15.455, 17.123; bear [leaves, fruit] 2.28, 16.247, B 16.70; **beryng(e)** *ger.* behaviour, conduct 21.256, 22.116, **B** 10.256, 11.300, 13.277, A 10.115; demeanour B 15.202

beren *v*² bellow 13.150

berye *n* grape 2.28

berken *v* bark 9.261

berkere *n* barking dog 9.260

bern¹ 18.280, A 3.250 = **bu(y)rn(e)** *n*

bern² 17.58 = **barn(e)** *n*

bern(e)³ *n* barn 4.60, 8.179, 12.216, 21.346, 360, Z 7.61

berne 3.237, 422 = **brennen** *v*

berthe (burthe) *n* birth 14.93, 20.248, 21.81

berw *n* hill 7.226

beseken A 11.99, *ger.* A 11.108 = **bisechen** *v*

beside *av* nearby A 2.42

best *2 sg. pr.* 7.235, Z 7.238 *see* **ben** *v*

best(e) *a. sup.* best 6.41, 345, 10.191, B 13.314; finest 3.426, 6.228, 8.329, B 5.267; most excellent 21.436, B 13.171; most advantageous 3.383, 5.38, 11.233, 22.207, **B** 13.290, 14.30; *a as n* B 6.299, A 5.136, (= the best thing) 1.201, 4.9, 83, 8.19, 220, 12.144, 14.91, B 1.42, 4.30; one's best 3.252; *in phrr.* **for the** ~ as the best (thing) 12.144, 15.128, 17.297, A 11.154, in the best interests of (someone / everyone) 7.125, 12.168, 16.21, B 10.367, 11.197; **of þe** ~ of the best quality A 2.127, **to þe** ~ (in the) best (way) / to the best end B 5.124, A 8.62

best(e) *av* best 8.120, 9.248, 12.106, B 5.24; most B 6.87, A 11.195; most thoroughly 5.43; most highly 8.250(2), B 15.156; *in phr.* **don** ~ 10.110, 16.34, B 9.97, **þe** ~ in the most advantageous way A 10.95; ~ **liken** be most pleasing 9.28

beste *n* living creature [*incl.* man] 10.230, 14.162, 15.264, **B** 9.32, 13.15, A 10.27; animal 7.158, 10.233, 11.242, 13.143, 180, 186, 191, 14.80, 169, 15.18, 244 *et p.*, B 10.32, A 10.175; (*spec.*) = (wild) animal 9.224, 13.136, 16.10, 17.28 *et p.*, **B** 6.140, 7.90, A 10.67; = (farm) animal (*pl.* cattle, livestock) 3.420, 426, 7.186, 8.189, 9.269, 11.251, 14.88, 21.264, B 3.267, **A** 3.252, 4.153, 7.181, 11.310

bestryden Z 3.158 = **bystriden** *v*

bet(te) *av* better A Pr 63; *in phrr.* **don** ~ 14.10, 16.34; **þe** ~ the more satisfactorily B 11.174, A 10.82, the more successfully 7.239, 8.42, the more properly 20.372; **ben þe** ~ be better off 5.96

bet *p.t.* Pr 115, *p.p.* A 4.80 *see* **beten** *v*

beten *v*¹ (*contr. pr.* **bat** Z 4.47, *p.t.* **be(e)t(te)** Pr 115, 8.175, *p.p.* **(y)bet(e)(n)** 4.89) beat, flog 5.135, 7.60, 8.81, 11.123, (*fig.*) B 12.12; punish Pr 115, 4.89, 5.169, 8.163, 22.27; chastise 13.239; strike 20.98, B 16.127;

belabour (with blows) 4.102, 6.141, B 4.59, *ger.* (*fig.*) 15.149; flail, thresh Z 7.170; lay low 3.237; overcome 20.262; beat [cloth in cleaning] B 14.19, (*fig.*) 16.332

beten *v*² repair A 8.30; relieve 8.246

bet(t)(e)re *a* better (than), superior (to) 1.135, 2.11, 6.243, 381, 12.145, 16.50, 177, 231, 18.87, 19.310, 20.344, 22.16, 319, **B** Pr 191, 1.208 15.73, A 12.3, Z 7.55; greater 3.164; easier 16.88; more valuable 18.284, B 12.294; more powerful B 17.173; *a as n* the superior 12.142; superior 2.30, B 11.381, *in phrr.* **no** ~ nothing better 1.8, 14.210, 15.125, B 4.193, **þe** ~ the better 15.262, better off 4.86, B 15.425, A 7.210, **neuer þe** ~ no better off 4.89

bet(t)(e)r(e) *av* better 1.143, 7.275, 10.57, 71, 11.217, Z 5.35, (*ellip.*) (to do) better 8.162; more satisfactorily 5.145, 9.36, B Pr 66, A 11.165, 206; more successfully 14.196, A 11.31; more fittingly Pr 120, B 13.51; more thoroughly 1.136, 5.142, 10.57, B 11.385, A 8.121, Z 3.169; more easily Pr 163, B 5.419; **þe** ~ the better 10.137, the more successfully Pr 33, 3.424, **wel þe** ~ much / all the better A 7.138, *in phr.* **do (þe)** ~ 5.119, 14.11, 17.122, **B** 1.34, 9.96, A 10.89; more 11.132, 210, 14.136, **B** 5.232, 11.253, 16.231, A 6.35, 12.31, **þe** ~ the more B 10.187

beteren *v* give advantage / benefit (to) *p.p.* 5.21

beth *imp. pl.* 1.171 *et p.*, *3 pl. pr.* 3.28, 16.200 *et p.*, Z 3.158, *3 sg.* (*with fut. sense*) 19.86

betrauaillen 15.211 = **bytrauaillen** *v*

bette¹ 8.42 = **bet** *av*; **bette**² *p.t.* B 6.178 *etc*; *see* **beten** *v*¹

betwene *av* 10.120, *prep.* A 7.165, **betwyn** A 5.55, 10.206 = **bytwene** *av, prep.*

beuerege *n* drink (to seal bargain) 6.394

bew-pere 9.248 = **beau pere** *n*

#bewsoun *n.pl.* fine fellows Z 3.158n

by¹ Pr 78 *et p. see* **be** *prep.*

by² Z 2.57 = **be(n)** *v*

bible *n* book B 15.89; **þe** ~ the Bible 3.426, 484, 5.169, 8.238, 10.88, 11.116, 18.222, **B** 6.234, 7.137, 9.41, 10.279, 327, 11.269, 392, Z 7.269; copy of the Bible B 13.186; *in phr.* **þe boek** ~ the Book of Scripture 9.304, B 10.88

bicam *p.t.* 7.127 *et p.*; *see* **bycomen** *v*

bycause (of) *avl phr.* by reason of B 3.100

byc(c)he *n* bitch 6.403

bycomen *v* (*p.t.* **bycam** 7.127 *et p.*, **bicom** B 10.138, *pl.* **bycome** 12.111, A 1.112 *etc*) go to 15.151, B 5.642; become 7.127, 11.145, 12.111, 13.19, 17.267, 18.135, 20.60, 221, 21.38, 22.41, **A** Pr 91, 1.112, 2.32, 7.181; ~ (**to**) be fitting / suitable for 3.264, 5.61, 21.42

bid *contr. pr.* 17.62 *see* **bidden** *v*

biddare 8.210, 9.61, Z Pr 37 = **bidder(e)** *n*

bidden *v* (*contr. pr.* **bid** 17.62, **byt, bit** 3.306, 20.270 *etc*, *p.t.* **bad(e)** 2.158, 219, *pl.* **beden** 3.28, *p.p.* **beden (boden** B) 2.56) ask 6.344, 14.29, 22.286, B 3.219;

make a plea for B 8.103; pray 7.16, 142, 239, 14.57, 196, 19.217, **B** 5.227, 10.199 (2), 11.263, 12.9, 17, 28, 13.237, 15.323, A 12.106, Z 7.240; ~ **of** pray for 7.60; supplicate 19.209; ask for alms, (go) beg(ging) (for) 9.63, 16.350, 370, 17.2, **B** 6.236, 7.79, 82, 11.276, 15.256; command, direct 3.306, 8.227, 11.45, 15.78, 17.190, 20.270, **B** 4.187, 9.15, 92, 10.199 (1), 252, 12.54, 15.185, 219, Z 7.269; advise Z 2.41; urge 7.247, 8.227, B 15.312, Z 7.248; invite 2.56, A 1.138; wish 6.69; **biddyng** *ger.* praying, prayer 12.86, 16.350, **B** 11.152, 15.425; entreaty B 5.584; command, bidding 1.74, 3.417, 10.98, 16.63, 20.416, B 1.110, A 9.93, Z 1.23

bidder(e) (biddare) *n* one who asks for alms, beggar Pr 41, 8.210, 9.61, B 13.242, 15.205

bydel *n* beadle, under-bailiff 2.60, 111, 3.2

byden *v* (*contr. pr.* **byt** Z 7.135) remain B 9.134; remain in, endure B 18.309*n*; continue (working) Z 7.135; wait patiently 22.48, *pr. p. a* **bydynge** = steadfast B 20.142

bidowe *n* short curved sword or long broad knife A 11.214

bidrauelen *v* cover with spittle, *p.p.* B 5.191 (*and see* **dreuelen** *v*)

#**bidroppen** *v* besprinkle B 13.321

byfallen *v* (*p.t.* **byfel** 6.325, **byful** Pr 7, *subjv.* **byfulle** 6.27) happen 9.313, 10.8, 17.97, 18.167, 21.243, 22.351, B 7.167; befall, happen (to) B Pr 6, ~ **of** 6.325, B 9.159; (*subjv.*) may befall 5.199, 20.97, might / should befall 6.27, Z 4.135; belong / pertain to 1.48, 20.379; befit 13.108, **B** 11.293, 15.104, 16.60; be the duty of 9.129

byfore¹ *av* in front 7.167, 20.127, 22.184, **B** 13.316, 17.105; ahead 16.54, B 15.435; = openly 6.117*n*; in a superior position 12.142, **ben** ~ be forward, take advantage 22.288*n*; earlier 5.109, 21.115, A 7.226; previously 22.371, B 16.140; in advance 3.302, 4.21, 16.3, 7, 17.97, 21.16, 55, 148, 244, B 14.142; *in phr.* ~ **and / ne bihynde** anywhere B 15.153, (*trs*) ? 6.117*n*

byfor(e)² *prep.* in front of 5.106, 9.254, 22.96, B 13.82; before 15.211, B 13.74; in(to) the presence of Pr 197 *et p.*, 13.124, A 8.39; in preference to 17.60, 201; before (= prior to) 2.100, 6.433, 18.167

byg(ge) *a* sturdy 8.224, 18.136

bigan *p.t.* 1.103 *et p.*; *see* **bygynnen** *v*

bygare Z 2.53 = **buggere** *n*

bygat *p.t.* 1.29 *see* **bygeten** *v*

bigerdel *n* purse 10.85

bygeten *v* (*p.t.* **bygat**) beget 1.29; conceive, *p.p.* 10.210, 14.31 (*and see* **byȝete** *n*)

†**biggen** *v* dwell, *pr.p.* **biggyng** B 5.128

byggen (bu(y)ggen) *v* (*p.t.* **bouhte** 2.3, *p.p.* **ybought** Pr 191) buy Pr 183, 6.225, 8.303, 9.28, 16.72, 18.158, B 5.244, 7.52, A 12.71, Z 3.160, *ger.* 21.236; make

purchases 3.86, 7.35; acquire, obtain 3.33, 82, 85, 4.85, 5.96; pay for 6.229, B 13.193; pay (penalty for) 15.304, ~ **the tyme** (interest on loan) 6.247; get hold of 18.165; redeem 2.3, 8.217, 12.60, 19.267, **B** 9.65, 11.207, Z 5.93

byggere A 2.44, 11.212 = **buggere** *n*

bigilen *v* deceive, delude 20.164, 323, 326, 327, 380, 382, 392, B 10.195; defraud 3.92, 95, 11.17, 14.5, B 13.361; perplex 17.107; lead astray (into sin) 1.37, 11.313, 15.79, 16.45, 20.162, B 10.120, 127

bigynnen *v* (*p.t.* **bigan** 1.103, *pl.* **bigonne** B 5.338, *subjv.* B 14.149) originate (with) 6.341; bring into existence 1.103, 17.134, 19.113, 20.163; begin, start 5.100, 102, 6.180, 349, 394, 7.6, 8.164, 9.243, 17.62, 20.183, 310, 399, 21.110, 116, **B** 2.74, 13.347, 14.149; set about 7.122, 20.48, 21.214, 327

bigynnyng *ger.* beginning (of existence) 18.204, (of the world) 19.113, 20.195, (of man) 8.239; origin 14.159, 19.113, 20.195

*****byglosen** *v* persuade with specious arguments 20.380

bygon Z 2.28 = **begon** *v*

bygonne *p.t.* **B** 5.338, 14.149 *see* **bygynnen** *v*

bigruchen *v* complain (at) 8.68, 155

byhe(e)ld *p.t.* 9.283, 13.156, 16.350, B Pr 13, **bihelte** 13.134 *see* **biholden** *v*

byheste *n* promise 10.253, **fayre** ~ fine promise 12.13, 22.118, **fals** ~ deceiving promise 18.123, 20.320, B 3.127

bihyhte *p.t.* 6.5 *etc*; *see* **bihoten** *v*

byhynde *av* behind 15.7, 21.342, *in phrr.* ~ **or bifore** secretly or openly, anywhere 6.117, (*trs*) B 15.153, **leuen** ~ abandon 15.7 **putten** ~ push aside B 14.208, *as pred. a* in the rear **B** 15.436, 17.105; overdue 7.39; *prep.* behind 6.69, 9.283, 16.49

byhofte *n* benefit, use 12.189

biholden *v* (*p.t.* **byhe(e)ld** 9.283, **bihelte** 13.134) look Pr 14, 13.134, **B** 7.138, 11.9; catch sight of 9.283; see 13.156, 16.350, B 5.109, Z 4.159; look to 19.67

bihoten *v* (*p.t.* **bihyhte** 6.5 *etc*) promise 3.30, 6.5, 7.68, 8.301, 18.246, 258, 20.317, 375, 22.111

bihouen *v* (*impers.*) be necessary 7.294, **B** 17.315, 18.400, A 8.116; be compelled to B 8.34; (*pers.*) need 9.89, **B** 5.38, 9.71

byiapen *v* deceive 1.63

bykam *p.t.* 13.19 *see* **bycomen** *v*

bykennen *v* commend (to) 2.51, 10.58, A 2.31

bikeren *v* contend, fight 22.79

byknowen *v* (*p.t.* **byknewe(n)** 11.257, 21.149, *p.p.* **byknowe** 3.36) know 3.36; make known Pr 210; recognise B 18.24; admit 21.149; acknowledge 5.92, 13.10; confess 6.206, 11.257

bile *n* bill B 11.357

byleue¹ *n* (religious) faith 11.296, 14.213, 16.230, 17.87, 126, **B** 11.218, 220, 13.211, 15.347, 392, *in phrr.* **false**

~ 21.47, **ferme** ~ 14.208, B 17.133; **good** ~ 11.307, **lele** ~ 12.88, 15.246, 17.22, 127, 158, B 15.438; **parfit** ~ 11.300, 17.266, B 14.193, **rihte** ~ 11.294, **sothfaste** ~ 11.131, 15.188, 17.119, 18.51, **trewe** ~ 18.210; (*spec.*) (the virtue of) faith 11.160, 19.176, 191; faith (in God) 18.255; = the Christian religion (þe ~, **oure** ~) 7.73, 9.218, 12.45, 17.294, 316, 18.255, B 10.204, **Holy Kirke** ~ 13.89, B 17.119, **londe of** ~ 21.336; creed 21.348, B 5.7; trust, confidence 17.95; belief B 11.299; = what I / we believe 8.97, 14.151, 15.239, B 7.176

byleue² 5.21, 21.236 = **bilyue** *n*

byleuen *v*¹ (*imp.* **byleef** 11.143) (~ **in, on**) believe (in) 1.78, 2.75, 3.356, 7.235, 10.192, 11.132, 17.135, 187, 255, 269, 286, 19.28, 42, 44, 96, 20.268, 21.182, **B** 10.121, 232, 234, 14.86, 15.393, 394, 395, 15.571, 578, 17.35, 42; believe, have faith 13.86, 14.13, 16.357, 17.123, 133, 18.250, 19.32, 35, 110, 21.174; accept as true 11.152, 157, 21.178, 182, **B** 13.274, 15.476; place one's trust in 10.169; hold as certain, think 7.125, 14.122, **B** 6.88, 13.254

byleuen *v*² dwell 3.347; remain (? leave) behind 12.214; leave off 8.176

bilyen B 5.408, 10.22 *see* **belyen** *v*

bilyue *n* livelihood 1.18, 5.21, 8.260, 16.336, 21.236

bylyuen 10.169 = **byleuen** *v*¹

bille *n* (written) petition / complaint 4.45, B 13.248

bille Z Pr 75 = **bulle** *n*

bylongen *v* belong 1.43; [as right] B Pr 110; be incumbent on / the duty (of) 5.66, 9.230, 11.157, B 10.357; be due (to) 9.262, B 9.78; be proper for 18.201; be an attribute of B 17.164; pertain to 19.144

bylouen *v* love, admire, *p.p.* 3.267, Z 5.96

bylowe(n) *p.p.* 9.181; B 2.22 *see* **belyen** *v*

†**bilowen** *v* (*refl.*) humble (oneself) B 6.227

bymenen *v*¹ mourn B 15.147

bymenen *v*² (*p.t.* **bymente** 20.16) mean, signify Pr 217, 1.1, 56, 20.16, 172; symbolise B 15.480

*****bymolen** *v* stain, spot B 14.4, 22

bynam *p.t.* B 6.240 = **bynom**

bynden *v* (*p.t.* **bo(e)nd(e)** 19.72, 20.446, *p.p.* **(y) bounde(n)** Pr 193, 21.57) tie up 19.54, 20.100; wrap 7.161; bandage 19.72; bind (with fetters) 20.33, 446, B 2.208, (*fig.*) A 10.56; trim [chest] with bands Pr 97; make subject (to law) B 3.353; impose penance Pr 129, 21.190

byneth(e) *av* lower down 6.180 (B 13.347), 18.85; underneath B Pr 15

bynymen *v* (*p.t.* **byno(e)m** 8.254, *p.p.* **bynomen** B 3.314) take away (from) 3.320, 8.254, B 3.314

bionales *n. pl.* masses said over a two-year period 9.320*n*

byno(e)m *p.t.* 8.254, 13.9 *see* **bynymen** *v*

biquasshen *v* (*p.t.* **biquasshe**) shatter B 18.248

biqueste *n* will, testament 8.94

biquethen *v* (*p.t.* **byquath / byqueþe**) bequeath 15.12

birch *n* birch-tree Z Pr 9

bireuen *v* take away (from) 8.258

birewen *v* repent, regret B 12.249

byschytten *v* shut up, (*p.t.*) 2.223, (*p.p.*) 21.167

bis(c)hop *n* bishop Pr 76, 78, 81, 85, 3.185, 4.120, 193, 5.70, 6.344, 9.255, 10.98, 141, 193, 12.227, 13.106, 124, 127, 16.200, 201, 364, 17.217, 277, 283, 294, 22.320, 328, **B** 2.177, 6.149, 11.301, 15.138, 456, 574, A Pr 90, 94, Z Pr 53, *in phrr.* ~**es bayardes** B 4.124, ~ **crose** 10.93, ~ **lettres** 9.320, B 5.640, ~ **names** B 15.509, ~ **pere** 10.141, ~ **selys** Pr 67

bysechen, biseken *v* (*p.t.* **bysou(g)hte** 1.165 *etc*) entreat, beg 1.56, 3.77, 115, 4.107, 6.16, 92, 319, 386, 7.120, 142, 11.86, 18.141, 22.106, 170, A 12.11, *ger.* entreaty A 11.108, Z 4.121; pray for 1.165, 4.90, 6.10, 273, 323, 12.8, B 5.281, A 12.116; pray (to) 17.154, 244

bisegen *v* besiege 22.215

byseye *p.p.* 22.202 *see* **bysen** *v*

biseken 6.92, 7.120, A 12.116 = **bysechen** *v*

bysemen *v* befit 9.248

bysen *v* deal wih, treat 22.202

bysetten *v* bestow, invest 6.254, 345, B 5.260; employ B 12.47

bisherewen *v* scold, curse B 4.168

bishut *p.p.* 21.167 *see* **byschytten** *v*

bisy (**besy, busy**) *a* (pre)occupied 1.6; industrious 15.224; concerned **B** 7.119, 126, 14.34; ~**liche** *av* diligently 11.155; earnestly A 12.106; ? carefully, scrupulously A 12.107; ~**nesse** *n* anxiety 16.153

byside(s) *prep.* next to 6.54, 20.74; from 19.74

biside *av, in phr.* ~ **forth** in addition B 17.73

bisitten *v* afflict B 2.141, 10.359

#**bysloberen** *v* soil (with saliva) 7.1

bismere B 5.88, 19.296 = **busmare** *n*

bysnewed *p.p.* snowed-over 16.265

bisperen *v* lock up (in chest) B 15.143

bysou(g)hte, bisowte *p.t.* 1.165, 3.115 *etc*; *see* **bysechen** *v*

bis(s)h(e)inen *v* illuminate 17.268

bistowen *v* bestow, give B 7.73

bystriden *v* mount 19.78, Z 3.158

bisweten *v* (*p.t.* **biswatte**) cover with saliva (*lit.* sweat) B 13.403

byswynken *v* (*p.t.* **biswonke**) work for, obtain by toil 8.224, 260, 22.293, B 15.487

byt *contr. pr.* 3.306 *etc*, B 3.75, A 11.151, Z 7.269 *see* **bidden** *v*

bite *n* mouthful 20.206

bytechen *v* command (to) 15.184

byten *v* (*p.t.* **bo(o)t** B 5.83) cut 21.340; bite 6.141, B 5.83; smart 22.362; eat 15.54; *pr.p.a* (*fig.*) **bitynge in** severely critical of 9.16

#**bitelbrowed** *a* with beetling (prominent) brows 6.198*c*

bitere 22.27 = **bittere** *av*

bythenken *v* think up 6.107

bytyden *v* (*contr. pr.* **bitit**, *p.t.* **bytydde**) happen to, befall 3.156, 13.212, 14.61, 62, **B** 2.118, 3.167, Z 7.281

bytyme *av* in good time 7.290

bytok(e)nen *v* represent symbolically 14.173, 18.26, 210, 264, 19.120, 123, **B** 15.465, 16.212; presage, be a sign of 12.204, 18.163, 20.130, B 7.155; *and see* **tokenen** *v*

bytrayen *v* betray **B** 10.128, 16.150; deceive, lead astray 1.66, 7.58, **B** 1.39, 11.302

#**bytrauaylen** *v* get by labour 8.242, 15.211

bitt(e)r(e) *a* bitter(-tasting) 12.147, 148, *a as n* (= bitterness) B 5.118; harsh B 12.12; grievous 4.181; severe 15.50, B 11.152; fierce 20.66; *av* dearly 13.15, 15.304, 20.446, **B** 3.251, 10.280, (*comp.*) **bittorere** 16.219; severely 22.27; ~**liche** bitterly, harshly 3.143, 11.192; ~**nesse** *n* bitterness (*fig.*), = wickedness 20.401

bytulyen *v* gain by tilling 8.242

bytwene *av* in between Pr 19, 6.157; (*prep.*) between 3.165, 381, 4.43, 8.157, 10.277, 16.84, 17.248, **B** 5.72, 97, 9.186, 13.175, 176, A 7.165, *in phr.* **mene** ~ 10.120, **B** 3.76, 7.197; amongst 12.127

bywichen *v* cast a spell upon 21.156

†**biwilen** *v* deceive by cunning B 10.108

byȝete *n* (truly) begotten / legitimate progeny 2.144n; offspring B 2.41

†**biyeten** *v* take possession of B 10.320

biyonde B 3.110, 4.128 *see* **beȝonde** *av*

blak *a* B 10.435; murky 16.266

blame *n*, **to** ~ at fault 3.305, 5.132, B 8.55; to be censured 13.241, B 14.1; ~**les** *a* free from reproach 13.127, ~ **worþy** guilty, blameworthy B 10.260

blamen *v* rebuke, scold 3.435, 5.172, 13.239, **B** 10.7, 15.252; find fault with 6.69, 95, A 5.74; censure 9.162, 165, 12.38, B 10.258, 260, 286, Z 3.151; hold to blame 3.439, 13.124

blanket (blanked) *n* (white or undyed) woollen cloth Z 3.159; blanket 9.254

blase *n* flame 19.179

blasen *v* burn vigorously 19.186, 199, (*fig.*) 189, 223, 230; shine brightly 20.241

blasen *n* coat of arms B 16.179

blaunmanger *n* creamed stew 15.101

bleden *v* (*p.t.* **bledde(n)**) 18.254, 20.438, 21.107, 325, A 12.117; cause to bleed A 7.167

blenchen *v* turn aside 7.226

blenden *v* (*p.t.*, *p.p.* **blente**) blind 7.134, 20.284, 292

#**bler-eyede** *a* with watering eyes 19.308

bleren *v* cause to water, *p.p.a* watery 6.198, ~ **yes** cause eyes to water, (*fig.*) = hoodwink Pr 72

blessed *p.p.a* blessed (by God), holy, pious Pr 76, 7.135, 9.13, 10.181, 11.242, 14.15, 16.201, B 11.167, Z Pr 53; sacred 20.476, 21.146; pleasing to God 17.163,

Z 7.238; (chosen to eternal) blessed(ness) 11.248, A 10.115, *a as n* 7.135, 17.59; consecrated 21.388; happy, fortunate 16.153, B 14.36, (*comp.*) 12.145

blessen *v* bless, bestow (God's) favour on 18.91, B 19.182, (*invoc.*) 8.260, 21.179, 180, 440; make sign of 12.127, 18.271; ask God's blessing (on) A 11.151; consecrate 3.185, 13.106, 12.127; say thanks for 14.126, 18.254, (*invoc.*) 8.260, 21.179, 180, 440, B 11.163

blessyng(e) *n* divine favour A 7.236; (formal papal) blessing 15.220, 229, B 13.250

bleten *v* bleat 17.38

blew (bloo) *a* pale, blue-grey 3.125

blew(e) *p.t.* 6.399, 7.152, B 5.496 *see* **blowen** *v*

blynd(e) *a* blind 7.107, 8. 128, 143, 201, 9.97, 99, 177, 260, 14.50, 15.149, 17.38, 20.80, 84, 87, B 16.124, A 7.178, Z 7.197, *a as n* the blind 8.188, 18.142, 20.98, 21.125; unable to see 19.308; spiritually blind 7.263; giving out no light 19.229

blis(se) *n* (state of) happiness / well-being / good fortune 11.47, 13.141, 228, 14.80, 15.292, 296, 297, 20.347, 416, B 10.107n, 11.26, 16.190, **worldes** ~ B 7.126; the blessedness of heaven, beatitude Pr 29, 7.135, 9.40, 11.263, 12.160, 14.78, 16.100, 20.347, 21.54, **B** Pr 106, 1.113, 9.47, 10.464, 11.167, 14.85, 154, 215, 15.175, 481, 16.180, 17.32, **A** 2.30, 4.91, 11.313, Z 7.76; *in phrr.* **hey** ~, **more** ~ a high(er) degree of beatitude 14.135, B 6.47, **Lord of** ~ blessed Lord B 11.188; (God's) glory 1.103, 11.203, 14.96, B 3.232; ceremony B 3.103; rejoicing 3.11; joyful singing 10.63, 67

blisful *a* blessed B 2.3

blissed(e) B 11.167, A 10.115, **blissen** 18.254, A 11.151 *see* **blessed** *p.p.a*, **blessen** *v*

blythe *a* joyful, glad 2.171, 3.28, Z 3.39

blo(e)d (blood) *n* blood 18.254, 19.272, 448, ~ **of gees** 15.68, [= the blood of Christ] 7.133, 12.60, 110, 17.268, 19.86, 88, 20.88, 21.58, 325, [in Eucharist] 19.90; *in phrr.* **flesch and** ~ human form 1.151, ~**(s) (c)hedyng** bloodshed 15.157; shedding one's blood [= martyrdom] 14.207; (*spec.*) the 'humour' blood A 10.55, 56, 61; (blood) kin, family 3.261, 20.418, 419, 437, 438, B 11.199; lineage, race 10.229, **gentil** ~ people of gentle birth 5.78

blody *a* bloody, **menyson** ~ B 16.111; covered with blood 4.74, 6.150, 21.6, 13; (related) by blood 8.217, 12.111, 117

bloo *a* pale, bluish-grey B 3.98

blosme *n* blossom (*fig.*) 18.10, 11, B 16.7, 35; ~**n** *v* (*fig.*) flourish B 5.139

blostren *v* wander aimlessly 7.158

blowen *v*[1] (*p.t.* **blew(e)** 6.399, *p.p.* **(y)blowe(n)** 5.120) blow 5.120, 19.179, 310, 21.340, B 5.496, Z 6.70, (*fig.*) 18.36; ~ **to** blow upon (*fig.*) 19.191; *ger.* (*fig.*) 19.223; play [horn] (*fig.*) 6.399, 7.152

blowen *v*[2] blossom (*fig.*) 18.101, *ger.* B 16.26

#**bo(c)he** *n* plague-sore 22.84, B 13.250

bocher(e) *n* butcher Pr 222, 3.80, 6.378

bode *n* command A 2.51; message A 3.251

boden *p.p.* B 2.55 *see* **bidden** *v*

body(e) *n* body 5.33, 38, 12.22, 111, 13.134, 16.176, 177, 195, 17.146, 20.100, 337, 21.143, 146, **B** 5.83, 118, 12.48, (**dede**) ~ 3.105, 20.66, B 18.97, *in phrr.* ~ **half** front half B 13.317; **Godes** ~ 20.77, 476, [= Eucharist] 21.388, B 12.85, 86, 90, (*in oath*) 20.240; [*as opp. to* soul, = the 'flesh') 10.37, 47, 12.207, **B** 8.48, 14.284, 317, 15.425, *in phrr.* **labour of** ~ B 14.129, **lykynge of** ~ fleshly pleasure 9.202, 11.12, 16.102, **lust of** ~ 21.355, ~ **and soule** 1.58, 9.40, 20.301, 21.180, B 6.251, (*trs*) 1.146, 7.128, 12.89; person, self **B** 13.290, 16.124, anyone B 10.260, **no** ~ B 10.256, 16.83, **som** ~ one person 22.27

bodily *a* for the body B 15.575

bodyward, into þe *avl phr.* into the stomach A 7.167

bo(e)k(e) *n* book 17.197, **B** 5.267, 10.302, *in phr.* **to** ~ to studying 14.126, 157; (authoritative) writings, written authority 3.59, 5.146, 7.182, 11.115, 148, 154, 155, 228, 276, 12.75, 76, 13.128, 14.45, 46, 78, 169, 196, 201, 15.181, 17.294, **B** 10.427, 458, 12.17, 273, 14.155, 15.278; **the** ~ the written authority B 15.342, = the Bible Pr 129, 3.306, 5.38, 6.76, 7.125, 9.120, 127, 162, 10.23, 11.67, 13.15, 15.222, 17.59, 19.236, 21.71, 22.42, **B** 3.251, 6.251, 7.83, 10.252, 11.275, 12.65, (*person.*) 20.240 *et p.*; *in phr.* **the** ~ **Bible** the book of Scripture 9.304, = book (of the Bible) 1.180, 18.222, B 13.186; **Sapience** ~**s** the Book of Wisdom B 3.333; [= (*spec.*) the *Golden Legend*] 14.206, 15.269, 271, 17.27, B 15.282; = the books of law A 2.80; = service-book, psalter B 15.122; (*fig.*) = source of knowledge 12.98, **B** 5.146, 10.212, 11.167

boend *p.t.* 19.72 *see* **bynden** *v*

boende 15.14 = **bond(e)** *a*

boer 13.150 = **bor(e)** *n*

boerd 15.175 = **bord** *n*

boest 16.88, 21.252 = **boost** *n*

boet *n* boat 10.33, 39, 47, 227, B 8.36

boetles *a* without boots 20.9

boffaten (boffeden) *v* buffet, strike (with hand) 8.173, 22.191

†**boȝen** A 7.165 = **bowen** *v*

boy(e) *n* fellow (*contempt.*) Pr 78, A 11.61; churl, 12.113; low / common fellow 20.77, 79, 98; rascal 8.265, 9.194; jester 9.127

boylen *v* boil *pr. p.* **boylaunt** 20.289

boyste *n* box A 12.69

boke Pr 129 *et p.* = **bo(e)k(e)** *n*

bokke *n* buck [male fallow deer] 8.29

bold *a* daring, courageous 18.136, 21.295, B 16.179, *a as n* Z 4.142; confident 20.239, B 10.135, 258; presumptuous, forward Pr 202, 4.55, 8.201, 224, 18.46,

20.77, A 9.93, (*comp.* 4.102, 9.334); rash 6.34; impudent 2.87, 6.49, B 13.303, A 11.61; powerful 22.142, A Pr 90; mighty B 13.290

bold(e)ly *av* confidently 9.28, 16.55, 21.478; freely 18.115, Z 7.61; insolently 22.70; vigorously 22.132; promptly 22.328

bolden *v* embolden, cheer B 3.199

bold(e)nesse *n* gravity 20.430; assurance 7.263

bole *n* bull 13.150

bolk *n* belch 7.6

#**bollare** *n* tippler 9.194

bolle *n* drinking-bowl / cup 6.419, 20.407; bowl 7.163, B 5.107, A 7.167

bollyng (bollnyng) *n* swelling 8.226

bolnen *v* swell B 5.118

bolten *v* fetter 8.143

#**bommen** *v* guzzle 6.229, A 7.138

bon *n* bone 9.169, *pl.* limbs Z 5.142, body 8.100, 9.157, *in phr.* **gon on** ~ **es** walk about (alive) 20.337

bond *n* fastening (of straw) 5.14; fetter 21.57

bond(e) *a* of servile status 10.266, *a as n* 3.200, 10.270, 15.14

bonde *p.t.* 20.446, 21.57 *see* **bynden** *v*

bondage *n* (*coll.*) bondmen A Pr 96

bondeman *n* bondman, villein [customary tenant] 5.65, 70 (*gen. pl.*), 6.201, 8.42; ~ **of thorpes** Pr 220, ~ **of tounes** A 10.138

bone *n* prayer 12.86; command 3.417

boord *n* A 2.52 = **bord** *n*

boost *n* arrogance 16.64, A 1.111, ~ **of** pride in B 3.314; noise (= cause for boasting) 16.88; noisy argument 21.252

boot[1] B 8.36 = **boet** *n*; **boote**[2] B 7.28 = **bote** *n*

boot *p.t.* B 5.83 *see* **byten** *v*

bord *n* plank 10.225; side of boat 10.40; dining-table 8.276, 288, 15.175, B 13.36, *in phr.* **at bedde and at** ~ = at all times A 2.52*n*; ~**les** *a* without a table 14.140

bordiour *n* jester 7.107, 9.127, 136

bordoun *n* (pilgrim's) staff 7.161

bore *n* boar 8.29, 13.150

bore *p.p.* 14.31, 21.71 *see* **beren** *v*[1]

borewe 1.74 = **borw** *n*[1]

borewen 6.247, 16.129 = **borwen** *v*

borgeys Z Pr 59 = **burgeys** *n*

borgh *n* B 7.80, 10.135 = **borw(h)** *n*[2]

born *p.p.* 1.58, B 12.146 *etc*; *see* **beren** *v*[1]

bornet *n* fine brown woollen cloth Z 3.159

borre *n* bur, (*fig.*) hoareseness 19.308

borw[1] borough 2.92; town 9.189, B 2.98, A 12.52, Z 7.130; ~ **town** *n* town incorporated by royal charter 3.112

bor(e)w(h)(e) *n*[2] surety, guarantor 4.85, 18.280, 22.13, 248, **B** 7.80, 10.135; sponsor 1.74; **vnder** ~ under the protection of a surety B 14.191

borwen *v* borrow 2.176, 4.55, 56, 6.247, 342, 7.35, 8.108, 16.129, 313, 370, 372, 17.1, 21.478, 22.286, *ger.* 17.8, 27, **B** 5.253, 7.79, 13.376, 15.256, 312, (*fig.*) 6.342, B 5.289; stand surety for B 4.109

bosard *n* buzzard, (*fig.*) **blynd** ~ stupid oaf B 10.266c

bosch *n* bush 13.156

bosken *v* (*refl.*) hasten 3.15, 10.227

bosom *n* lap 18.271; bosom [front inside part of robe] 15.162

bost A 1.111 = **boest** *n*

bosten *v* brag, speak arrogantly 2.85, 6.34, **B** 13.281, 306, 15.252; (claim) boast(fully) 19.61

bostere *n* braggart B 13.303

bot(e) *conj.* Pr 36, 2.136 *etc, as prep.* 2.175, *av* 6.93 *etc; see* **but** *conj., prep. and av*

bote *n* good, advantage 15.229; remedy 4.85, 88, 89, 12.58; relief B 13.341, 14.116; cure 8.178, 192; salvation 20.476, B 12.86; repair B 7.28; *in phr.* **to** ~ in addition 16.108, B 14.238; *a* ~ **les** irremediable 20.206

botel *n* (leather) bottle / flask 5.52, 9.139, 19.70

#boten *v*[1] provide with boots Z 3.158

boten *v*[2] be added to [so as to equalise value] 6.381

botenen *v* cure 8.188

bothe *num., n* both 1.28 *et p.*, B 2.68, *in app. with prn.* **hem** ~, **they** ~, **vs** ~, **we** ~ both of them / us 2.90, 6.125, 8.24, 20.168, B 13.207; *after infl. prn.* **here** ~(**er**) 2.67 (B 2.68), **oure** ~, ~ **oure** 20.371, 6.181 of both of them / us; *a* both Pr 76 *et p.*; (*in deferred position*) 3.40, B 5.375, Z 6.3; (*emph.*) ~ **two** the two of them 13.28, B 2.55, Z 2.215; *as av* too, as well Pr 10. *et p.*, B Pr 116, A Pr 100, Z 3.163; *as correl. conj.* ~...**and** 2.252 *et p.*, B Pr 163, Z 1.18, (*with more than two subjs.*) = not only...but also **B** 15.489, 17.161

boton *n* stud B 15.124

botresen *v* buttress, support 7.235

botte Z 7.162 = **bat** *n*

bouken *v* cleanse with lye 16.332, B 14.19

boun A 2.51, 124, 3.245 = **bow(e)n** *a*

bounchen *v* strike (*fig.*) Pr 72

bounde(n) *p.p.* 21.57, A 10.56 *see* **bynden** *v*

bounte(e) *n* virtue 17.163; (chivalric) valour 8.49; reward B 14.150

bour *n* private room 3.11, 15, 6.228, **B** 2.65, 3.103, 139, Z 4.159; dwelling-place A 10.55

bourden *v* jest 16.200

bourdeour B 13.448; **bourdyor** *n* 9.127 = **bordiour** *n*

bourly *a* stout, excellent, *sup.* ~**okest** Z 3.159

bourne *n* stream B Pr 8

bowe[1] *n* bow 20.291, 22.117

bowe[2] 16.247 = **bow(h)(e)** *n*

bow(e)n *a* ready 2.173; willing **A** 2.51, 3.245

bowen *v* bow 21.17; submit 4.181, 10.270, 15.149; drop down 10.37, B 8.48; bend (down) 13.134; go B 5.566, †A7.165

bow(h)(e) *n* bough, branch 5.134, 16.247, 248, **B** 5.575, 15.98

box *n* jar B 13.195; case 9.263 [*with play on* jar], 13.54, B 5.640; collecting-box Pr 97, B 15.214

braek *p.t.* 20.364 = **brake**

#braggen *v* brag, boast noisily 6.34, 8.152, B 13.281

#braggere *n* braggart B 6.154

brayn *n* brain [as seat of mind] A 10.54, 56

braynwood *a* mad, crazed A 10.61

brak(e) *p.t.* Pr 114, 12.127, **B** 1.113, 10.282, 11.163; *see* **breken** *v*

brake *n* winch [of crossbow] 20.291

braken *v* vomit 6.430

bran (bren) *n* bran B 6.182, 282

bras *n* bronze Pr 183; (utensils of) brass / bronze 20.291

brasene *a* made of bronze 20.291

brast *p.t.* B 6.178 = **barste**

#braulen *v* wrangle, *ger.* 16.361

#braulere *n* quarrelsome person 18.46

braunche *n* branch, (*fig.*) = (sub)-species (of sin) 7.69, 80 (B 13.410, 421), 16.263, B 15.75

braw(e)n *n* meat 15.68, 101; boar's flesh B 13.63

brech *n* drawers 6.157

bre(e)d *n* bread 5.174, 8.306, 326, 9.120, 200, 11.67, 12.127, 15.54, 211, 18.262, **B** 12.85, 13.236, 242, 261, A 11.188, Z 7.199, *in combs.* ~ **corn** grain for making bread 8.61; ~ **yblessed** (= Eucharist) 21.388; **bake** ~ B 13.267, **barly** ~ 8.142, A 7.169, **broke** ~ A 12.70, **haly** ~ 6.146, Z 8.75, **hors** ~, **houndes** ~ 8.225, **whete** ~ B 6.137, 7.121, **whyte** ~ 9.254; ~ **and ale** 7.51, 9.156, ~ **and clothes** 22.248, ~ **and drynke** 16.63, B 13.252, ~ **and water** 6.155; food 5.174, 8.224, 16.63, 22.248, **B** 7.83, 84, 12.17, 85, *a* #**bredles** without food 9.121, 16.13

brede *n*[1] breadth 2.93, 3.259

brede *n*[2] roast meat Z 7.199

breden *v*[1] (*p.t.* **bredde(n)** 13.165) breed 13.165, B 11.358, *ger.* (manner of) breeding B 12.218; rear young **B** 11.347, 12.227; live ? B 2.98c

breden *v*[2] grow stout ? B 2.98c

breef *n* letter of authorisation 22.328

bre(e)re *n* briar 2.28; branch covered with prickles 6.401; dog-rose stem A 10.124

breiden *v* hasten B 17.69

breken *v* (*imp.* **brek** Z 6.50, *p.t.* **br(a)(e)k(e)** Pr 114, 20.313, 364, *p.p.* **(y)broke(n)e** Pr 69) break Pr 114, 2.87, 9.276, 334, **B** 5.575, 10.282, (into fragments) 18.155, B 14.222; tear **B** 5.107, 9.92; distribute (bread) 11.67, 12.127, A 11.188, Z 7.287; break into 16.88, 20.313, 21.346, A 9.79; be broken into / break open 16.88, 20.364; cripple 5.33, 9.169, 177; break down, destroy 8.29, 20.262, 21.340, B 11.163, ~ **vp** 4.60; ~ **out** escape from 12.76; fail to keep Pr 69, 9.236, 241, 20.320, **B** 1.113, 5.241, *ger.* 5.169

breme *a* vigorous, powerful B 12.223, *sup. comp.* A 10.55, 56

bren B 6.182 = **bran** *n*

brennen *v* (*imp.* **bern** 3.422, **bren** B 3.267, *p.t.* **brente** 19.310, **brende** B 17.328, *p.p.* **(y)brent** 3.105, B 5.267) burn (*tr.*) 3.105, 422, 20.264, B 3.267, Z 6.72, *ger.* B 15.83; (*intr.*) 12.69, 19.179, 199, 223, 230, 310, 20.289, ~**ynge aguwe** acute fever 22.84; make pure by fire, refine B 5.267

brest(e) *n* breast 5.106, 7.6, 60, 12.57, 16.332, Z 5.97; heart A 5.99

bresten *v* (*p.t.* **barste**) crush 8.175

Bretener *n* Breton 8.152*n*, 173

bretful *a* brimful Pr 42

breth *n* breath(ed) utterance 15.263, 264, 20.364

brether(e)n(e) *n.pl.* brothers [by blood-relationship] 7.238, 9.315, 21.255, B 10.199, 11.199, A 11.191, (*fig.*) B 11.207, 18.394; **blody** ~ (*fig.*) 8.217, 12.111, 117, 20.418, **halue** ~ 20.436, fellow human-beings / Christians 15.81, B 12.90; fellow religious 16.293, B 5.178

brethyen *v* Z 6.70, *ger.* (exchange of) breath B 11.357

bretil *a* fragile, brittle 10.47

breuh-wif *n* female brewer 6.353

breuet *n* letter 13.54; letter of authorisation B Pr 74, 5.640

brewen *v* (*p.t.* **brew**, *p.p.* **browe**) brew 6.225, 20.401

***brewecheste** *a* trouble-brewing B 16.43

brewere *n* brewer Pr 222, 3.80, 104, 4.120, 21.399, 407

brewestare *n* brewer 8.329, 9.189, B Pr 219; female brewer, alewife 6.352

brewhous *n* brewery-tavern 9.98

brybour *n* thievish impostor 22.262; *and see* **a-bribeth** *av*

brid *n* bird 9.200, 10.63, 13.156, 162, 15.292, **B** 11.357, 12.223, 14.44, 15.284, 314, *in phr.* ~**es and bestes** 11.242, 13.136, 14.80, 169, 15.292, B 12.218

bridale *n* wedding celebration 2.56, B 2.44

brydel *n* bridle B 4.22

brygge 7.239 = **brugge** *n*

bry(g)ht(e) *a* bright, shining Pr 178, 183, 3.457, 17.277, 20.100, 22.132; vivid, brilliant **B** 12.221, 14.19; *av* brightly 21.436; ~**nesse** *n* radiance 13.10, 20.284

bryngen *v* (*p.t.* **brouhte** 3.10, *p.p.* **(y)brouh(t)e** 3.2, 8.61, 15.11) bring 1.74, 2.214, 3.10, 4.56, 7.86, 7.135, 8.61, 317, 350, 9.200, 15.54, 211, 17.32, 19.84, 310, 20.34, **B** 10.309, 12.89, 13.52, 186, 15.308, A 12.87; introduce 11.169, 19.34; convey B 14.85, **A** 2.138, 10.147, Z 6.63; *in phrasal vv.* ~ **above** make prosperous 13.21; lead 3.408, 7.80, 11.194, 14.78, 17.236, 20.147, B 15.75, 426; lead out 9.260, B 11.152; ~ **(a)doun** overcome 3.43, 4.88, 20.28, 143, 340, 20.28, 21.51, B 9.205; ~ **a slepe** put to sleep A 9.58, ~ **forth** produce Pr 67, 1.18, 2.66, 3.188, 9.168, 10.276, 11.36, 15.61,

18.79, **B** 9.151, 13.236; give birth to 13.166, 18.223, A 10.147, (*fig.*) 2.31; display 6.141; ~ **(hit) to hepe**, ~ **herto** bring it about, succeed in (doing) 10.191, 193, 4.177; ~**in** bring into 6.415, 7.4, 8.163, 10.33, 17.181, A 3.144, 5.74; ~ **into world** give birth to 20.134; ~ **out of** release from 18.280, 20.265, 22.201, B 5.227; make (sb.) lose 21.285; ~ **to care** cause harm to 19.55; ~ **to louhynge** turn to laughter 20.460; ~ **to nauhte** destroy 2.139, 3.200, 17.306, B 14.95

#**brocage** *n* arrangement through an intermediary 16.107; business deal 2.92

broche *n* splint 19.212; brooch Pr 73, B 15.121

brochen *v* stitch loosely 6.218

brocour *n* **B** 3.46, 5.244 = **brokere** *n*

bro(o)d(e) *a* wide 7.161, 10.33, 20.238, B Pr 8, Z 2.47; extensive B 13.243; stout (? wide-spreading) 5.120, Z Pr 9; broad-headed 22.117, ~ **hokede** wide-barbed 22.226; broad-bladed B 3.305

brode *av* extensively 5.167

brok *n* brook, stream 7.212, (= water) 8.142

broke(n) *p.p.* 9.177, 18.155, 21.346, **A** 9.79, 12.70 *see* **breken** *v*

brokelegged *a* lamed in the leg 8.143, 188, 12.76, Z 7.197 (~ **sshankid** A 7.130)

brokere, broko(u)r *n* agent 2.60, B 5.244; purveyor 6.95; go-between 2.66, B 3.46

brol(le) *n* brat 3.261

brood 7.161 *etc*; *see* **bro(o)d(e)** *a*

brother *n* brother Pr 107, 1.62, 12.171, A 3.243, **Caymes seed his** ~ Cain his brother's offspring 10.254, (*fig.*) 7.143, **B** 5.466, (= fellow Christian) 10.263; *and see* **brether(e)n(e)** *n pl.*

brouken *v* drink 12.58, 20.401

broun *a* dark (= strong) 8.329

browe *n* eyebrow A 12.12

browe *p.p.* 20.401 *see* **brewen** *v*

brugge *n* bridge 7.212, 239 (drawbridge), 9.32

brumstoen *n* sulphur 20.289

brusshe *n* brush B 13.460

bruttenen *v* destroy 3.237, *ger.* destruction 15.157

buggen 4.85, 9.28, 16.72, 21.280 *etc*; = **byggen** *v*

buggere *n* purchaser B 10.306

buggynge *ger. see* **byggen** *v*

buyen 15.304 *see* **byggen** *v*

buylden *v* build B 12.227, *ger.* B 15.328

buyrde *n* lady 3.15, 20.119; damsel 21.135

bu(y)r(e)n(e) *n* man 6.247, 18.280, **B** 3.267, 11.361, 12.65; *pl.* people 18.11, Z 5.38; soldier 15.157; lord, baron 3.473

buyrielles *n sg* the grave 21.146

bulle *n* papal bull [edict of pardon] 3.184, 9.337, 15.220; (document of) pardon 9.42, 61, 160, 283; episcopal edict Pr 67, B 5.640

bummen A 7.138 = **bommen** *v*

bungen Z Pr 80 = **bounchen** *v*

burel *n* coarse woollen cloth (*fig.*, *attrib.*) = half-educated, ? lay B 10.286*n*

burgage *n* house in town [held by burgage tenure, directly from king or lord without feudal obligation] 3.85, 105

burgeys *n* (*sg. & pl.*) burgess (freeman / citizen of town) Pr 220, 3.200, 14.91 (*gen.*) **B** 5.128, 15.202, 342, **A** 3.144, 10.138

burg(h) B 2.98, A 12.52 = **borw** *n*

burien *v* bury 12.22, 21.143, **B** 11.65, 67, 74, 12.253, 13.9; bury the dead B 11.76, *ger.* B 11.78

burionen *v* sprout, burgeon B 15.75

burn B 3.267, 11.361, 12.65 = **bu(y)r(e)n(e)** *n*

burthe *n* birth 20.248, 21.81

buschel *n* bushel [= 8 gals.] 8.61

busy B 13.252, **busiliche** 11.155, A 12.106 *see* **bisy ~ a, av**

busken Z 4.159 = **bosken** *v*

busmare *n* calumny 21.295, B 5.88

but(e) *conj.* (*with subjv. clause*) unless Pr 64 *et p.*, B 4.142, A 4.96, except 10.120; (*with* **that** *and conditional cl.*) except that 3.396, unless †15.120; only that †15.220; (*with inf.*) except 5.9; (*with av.*) except 16.294; than (that) 10.210, 16.275, (*in constr. with* **yf**) unless 1.176 *et p.*, B 2.129, A 9.96, ~ (...) **hoso** unless one 7.306, 10.39; but (rather) (*with cl.*) 1.79, B 6.311, A 3.253, (*with inf.*) 8.335, B Pr 206; (*with n. phr.*) 1.99, 3.304, 17.265*n*; *in correl. conj.* but also 21.117; however 6.10, B 3.180, A 12.5; and, furthermore 12.200, B 5.470, A Pr 5; (*as av.*) only Pr 204 *etc*; nothing but 11.9, 13.239, B 11.429, Z 5.34; *as prep. with n.* except 1.21, 13.65*etc*, 9.289*n*, B 5.235; anything except 7.77; *as quasi-a.* only 2.200, 4.61, B 8.82

buth *3 pr.pl* 9.160; *see* **ben** *v*

buttre *n* butter B 5.438

buxum *a* obedient 3.417, 9.220, 16.63, B 1.110, **Z** 1.23, 6.41; submissive B 15.202, A 2.52; willing 15.224, B 6.194; modest, mild 20.119, **B** 5.566, 16.7; ~ **liche** *av* humbly 14.57, B 12.194; graciously 17.283; ~ **nesse** *n* humility 16.64; kindness 7.238, B 10.302; obedience 20.320, **B** 1.113, 4.187

caas B 10.348 = **ca(e)s** *n*

cabane(e) *n* tent B 3.191; cell A 12.35

cac(c)hen *v* (*p.t.* **cauhte** 13.214, *p.p.* **cauht** Pr134) get hold of 10.301, B Pr 207, 14.239; pick up, ? filch 22.14; capture 2.204; catch 14.174, 18.170, B Pr 189; snatch (at), pursue 3.364; take 6.408, †B 2.36; obtain **B** 11.173, 13.299; get 3.388, 6.78, B 12.221; ~ **of** get (sth.) from A11.87; receive Pr 134, 14.86, 21.128, ~ **colour** blush 13.214; drive, chase 14.117, A 7.128, 183

cachepol *n* catch-poll [minor law officer] 20.46, 75

ca(e)s *n* state of affairs 9.48 (?*or spec.* suit, law-case), 22.14, B 10.348; event 3.432, **in** ~ in the event that 9.155; (grammatical) case 3.336, 346, 356, 386, 388*c*, 394, 398*c* (*with pun on* condition)

cayren *v* wander Pr 31; proceed B 4.24; (*refl.*) betake oneself 6.350; convey B 2.162

cayser *n* emperor 3.314, 318, 22.101, B 9.111, A 11.219; lord 21.138; *and see* †**cesar** *n*

caytif (kaytif) *n* wretch 6.206, 8.244, 12.66; poor man 14.90; scoundrel 10.222, 20.96, 99, 21.406, Z 7.261; *a* worthless 13.109; poor †A 10.68; ~**liche** *av* wretchedly 3.241; meanly (clad) 12.129; ~**tee** *n* vileness 9.255; *and see* **cheytyftee**

cake *n* flat cake, loaf 8.305, Z 7.107; ~ **breed** *n* ? griddlecake B 16.229

cald(e) *p.t.* 1.4, *p.p.* Pr 132 *etc*; *see* **callen** *v*

calf *n* calf 8.311, B 15.465, 466, **y** ~ with calf Z 3.149, **calues flessh** veal **B** 15.464, 16.229

callen *v* (*p.t., p.p.* **cal(l)(e)d(e)**) call out B 17.74; call on 21.9; summon 3.3, 127, 149, 4.17, 20.472, 22.305, **B** 4.171, 15.593, A 12.49; invite 12.105, 22.243, B 13.31; (call by) name Pr 132, 1.4, 4.161, 5.162, 7.176, 9.213, 249, 10.69, 11.174, 175, 12.114, 14.14, 16.181, 199, 18.11, 12, 14, 19.51, 20.96, 21.15, 23, 85, 117, 136, 330, 22.5, **B** 7.91, 10.287, 11.173, 15.430, 16.135, 245, **A** 4.140, 10.25, 148, 12.84, **Z** 2.169, 6.41; greet B 1.4; **do** ~ have announced 3.34

cam *p.t.* Pr 95; *see* **comen** *v*

cammaca *n* fine (? silken) fabric 16.299

cammok *n* rest-harrow 21.314, Z 7.91

can[1] *pr. sg.* 2.236 *et p.*, *pl.* 1.190, 8.267, 11.18, 228, 14.11, 15.174 *see* **connen** *v*

can[2] *p.t.* (*modal v.*) did, proceeded to 15.191, 19.71

candle *n* candle 3.106; taper 19.186

cano(e)n (canoun)[1] *n* canon law 15.86, B 5.422; #**canonistre** *n* expert in canon law 9.303

cano(u)n[2] *n* cathedral canon B 10.46, A 11.33; *and see* **chano(u)n** *n*

canst *2 sg. pr. see* **connen** *v*

cantel *n* portion 14.163

capel (capul) *n* riding horse 4.24, **B** 2.162, 17.108; cart horse 21.333, 347

capon *n* capon 4.38, B 15.473

cappe *n* hat 7.173

caract *n* written character B 12.78, 88, 91

carden *v* comb [wool for spinning] 9.80, (*fig.*) spruce up 11.15

cardiacle *n* heart-disease 22.82, Z 7.277; heart-pains / palpitations 6.78

cardinal *n* cardinal Pr 134, 16.366, 17.166, 21.225, 416, 420, 423, 452, ~ **wit** A 12.15

cardinal(e) *a* (*pl. form* **-es**) cardinal, chief [of the virtues] Pr 132, 21.275, 318, 339, 396, 410, 414, 423, 455, 22.21, 73, 122, 304

care *n* sorrow, misery 1.57, 20.265; vexation 22.165;

distress, hardship 3.201, 372, 19.55, 20.276, 22.201, **B** 13.161, 14.175; harm 18.173; misfortune B 9.153; anxiety 20.223, B 2.151

car(e)fol(e) *a* sorrowful B 13.266; wretched, miserable B 9.158, 11.294; *a as n* wretched 11.42, 18.267; distressed 1.197, 12.105, 19.65, 21.128, B 14.179

carefully *av* wretchedly B 5.76

careyne 14.178, B 14.331 = **caroyne** *n*

caren *v* care 1.124, 9.109, 21.384; worry 22.150; be solicitous 15.259, B 2.162

caryen *v* carry 9.151, 21.332, A 6.32, Z 6.20

carnel *n* crenel, embrasure 7.234, †20.288

caroyne *n* corpse 8.100, 16.195; carcass B 12.253; (wretched) body B 14.331; flesh B Pr 189, 14.178n

carolen *v* dance and sing a *carole* [round dance] 20.470

carpen *v* speak, discourse Pr 209, 2.27, 4.32, 6.29, 7.76, 79, 11.52, 13.178, 15.110, 191, 16.270, 17.69, 18.219, 282, 21.69, 177, 200, 22.334, **B** 10.51, 104, 13.58, 180, 15.301, A 12.33, *ger.* B 10.140, manner of speaking 16.339; say 14.216, B 11.215; tell 2.203; object 19.111, B 10.106; find fault B 10.287, *ger.* carping talk B Pr 204, cry out B 10.58

carpentare *n* carpenter A 11.135, (*fig.*) 11.250

carpentrie *n* the craft of carpentry 11.125

carse *n* cress, (*fig.*) = jot, anything 11.14

cart *n* cart, wagon B 13.266, (= hay-wain) 5.13, (*fig.*) 2.190, 192, 21.332, 333, 348; *in cpds.* ~ **mare** 8.311, ~ **way** 3.167, ~**whel** cart-wheel 15.163

carten *v* work as a carter 5.62

cartere *n* cart-driver 9.205

cartsadlen *v* place cart-saddle [small saddle for cart-horse] upon B 2.180

cas 3.336 *et p.* = **ca(e)s** *n*

cast *n* skill 3.20

castel *n* castle, fortified tower 1.4, 3.140, (*fig.*) 10.129, 143, **B** 9.49, 13.120, A 10.22, 25; dungeon-stronghold 1.57, A 11.189

casten *v* (*contr. pr.* **cast** 9.151, *p.t.* **caste** Pr 143) throw 6.375, 14.104, B 16.128, Z 7.277; hurl 15.144, 20.289, B 16.42, 75; put 8.58; place B 15.401; place forcibly 4.81, B 8.102; ~ **vp** lift B 11.408; devote, apply 6.264, B 13.357, (*refl.*) apply oneself 9.151; provide B 6.16; think about 22.121; intend, plan 21.281, B 15.333; plot 11.16, 18, 21.141, B 16.137; ordain Pr 143; reckon (to be) 12.68; write, draw up B 13.248; *ger. phr.* **castynge of ei3en** looks, glance B 11.187

cat *n* cat Pr 168, 185 *et p.*, B 5.254

#catecumelyng *n* catechumen B 11.77n

catel *n* property 3.322, 425, 7.219, 8.157, 9.181, 10.195, 253, *in phr.* **coueytise of** ~ 10.260, 282, 12.243, 247, 16.109, B 9.157; goods B 7.22; money Pr 210, 3.72, 4.78, 5.129, 6.288, 8.230, 9.90, 13.107, 17.212, 22.209; income (from property) 8.101; treasure B 10.323; wealth 10.170, 12.216, 19.245, **B** 10.29, 11.211; *in*

phrr. ~ **and kynde wit** wealth and native ability 14.17, **lordes** ~ B 10.471, **losse of** ~ B 14.7, **trewe** ~ honestly earned wealth 19.240, **worldly** ~ material wealth 21.293, = reward 21.77; cattle, livestock B 3.273; possession **B** 12.294, 13.151; provisions [*sc.* food] B 15.428

*****cateles** *a* without property / money A 10.68

caucyon *n* surety-payment Z 5.143

caudel *n* hot drink, (*here* = mess) 6.411

cau(g)ht *p.p.* Pr 134, 18.170, 19.186, ~**e** *p.t.* 6.408, 13.214, 21.128 *see* **cac(c)hen** *v*

*****cauken** *v* tread the female, mate 13.170, 14.161, B 12.228

*****caurymaury** *n* rough cloth A 5.61, (B 5.78)

cause *n* cause 5.190, 9.255, B 12.224, 225; reason [for sth.] 3.316, 9.255, 16.205, 20.138; reason [for action], motive 10.285, 21.23, 63, B 11.173; justification 3.364, 17.131, 136, 19.322; side, case [in argument] B 13.126; responsibility 6.113; *in phrr.* **by** ~ **of** as a result of B 5.183, **by** ~ **to** in order to B 11.173, A 12.32

caue *n* pit B 12.253

cene *n* supper B 16.140

certeyn(e) *a* fixed, definite 19.33, 22.255, 265, *in phr.* **som(me)** ~ prescribed sum 19.33, B 13.377; indubitable B 10.429; sure 3.85, 9.165, 19.221

certeyne (*a as*) *n* fixed number 22.258, 267 (1); definite amount B 13.377; particular (order) 22.267 (2); **of** ~ as a secure sustenance B 6.151

certes *av* certainly, truly 9.331, B 2.152, A 9.18; surely, to be sure 5.22, 13.221; of course 13.246; indeed 9.257, 18.58

cesar (= **kayser**) *n* emperor 3.329n.

ces(s)en (sesen) *v* desist from, leave off 9.227, 14.41, 22.107, 109, B 7.118; stop 2.165, 4.1

chacen *v* rush, hasten B 17.52

†**chafen** B 12.125 = **chaufen** *v*

chaffare *n* trade, business Pr 33, **B** 5.225, 15.164; transaction involving exchange 6.379, B 5.245; merchandise, goods in trade 2.60, **B** 5.131, 243, 13.380

chaffaren *v* (engage in business or) trade for profit 5.94, 6.252, 8.249, 12.229, 16.147, **B** 6.238, 15.165, 16.129; gain through trade B 15.107

chayere *n* raised seat [of office] Pr 114

chayne *n* chain, fetter 20.446, B 17.111; ornamental chain (*fig.*), = 'bond' B 5.607

chalengen *v* rebuke 6.156; object to 6.136, *in phr.* **wiþouten chalangynge** without question B 15.344; (lay) claim (to) Pr 91; (make) claim / demand 16.189, B 15.165; scold, *ger.* **chalengynge** 6.68, B 11.423

chaleniable *a* open to objection 13.116

cha(u)mbre *n* private room 2.65, 7.93 (B 13.434), 236, **B** 3.10, 4.124, 10.100, Z 4.158; bedroom B 4.124; (*fig.*) womb 18.126

champion B 8.46, 15.216 = **cha(u)mpio(u)n** *n*

Chancerye *n* Chancery [office of Lord Chancellor of England] Pr 91, B 4.29

changen 6.146 = **chaungen** *v*

chano(u)n *n* canon [cleric living under canonical rule] 5.156, 170 (B 10.318), 17.55, A 10.113

chapeleyn *n* priest (officiating in a chapel) 1.185, 8.11; bishop's assistant priest 13.127

chapitre (chapitle) *n* (body of members of a) convent-chapter 3.472, B 5.159 ~ **hous** chapter-house 6.156

chapman *n* merchant, trader Pr 62, 5.136, 6.235, 379, 10.260, 12.229, B 15.85

chapun-cote *n* capon-shed 6.136

charge *n* (burden of) responsibility 9.96, 258; blame A 10.73

chargen *v* burden 9.73, ? 22.237; enjoin 5.136, 7.256; insist on, treat as important 19.274; care (about) 16.147, 288; appoint A 10.23; entrust (with) Pr 87, ? 22.237 (*or* burden)

charite *n* (the theological virtue of) charity Pr 87, 1.183, 185, 15.279, 16.284, 347, 17.49, 62, 64, 140, 148, 150, 151, 286, 19.276, **B** 1.194, 5.264, 12.30, 31, 15.156, 250, 343, 344, 16.3, 17.293, A 1.164, Z 5.96, (*person.*) 7.256, 272, 16.288, 295, 348, 18.2, B 14.97, 100; *in phrr.* **cheef** ~ 16.347, 17.5, **cheyne of** ~ B 5.607, **children of** ~ 18.207, **þe fruyt** ~ B 16.9, **ful** ~ B 15.153, **Holi Chirche and** ~ Pr 64, 2.140, 16.35, 19.274, †**leel** ~ B 9.188, **loue of** ~ 16.283, **parfit** ~ B 15.148, **puyr** ~ 11.65, **B** 10.314, 15.79, *pur* ~ for charity's sake 8.169 *et p.*, **trewe** ~ 2.37, **verray** ~ 19.273; ~ (þe) cha(u)mpion 15.279, B 8.46; (people's) love / affection 16.147, B 13.110; charitable act 17.231; (what is given out of) charity 1.189, 2.140

charme *n* magic spell (for healing) 6.85, (*fig.*) 19.21, B 17.21

charnel *n* charnel-house 8.45

chartre *n* deed granting rights 2.69, A 2.35; legal document 13.116, 119; legal contract 12.63, (*fig.*) agreement 16.35; charter of foundation 5.166

chast(e) *a* virgin(ally pure) 1.175, 185, 16.347, (?*av*) 18.77

chastite *n* chastity, sexual purity (*person.*) 7.272; sexual abstinence 1.183

chastel *n* castle 2.89

chastilet *n* little castle B 2.85

chasten *v* discipline Pr 212, 13.234, 19.301, 312, B 6.51; reprimand A 11.198; chastise, punish 4.112, 5.136, 8.344

chastisen *v* punish Pr 110, B 4.117

chatel *n* personal property, chattels 12.63

chat(t)eren *v* rant 2.89, 16.68

chaufen *v* grow warm 17.49; inflame (*fig.*) 14.68

chaumbre 7.93, 236, 18.126 = **cha(u)mbre** *n*

chaumbrere *n* confidant B 14.100

cha(u)mpio(u)n *n* chosen warrior 20.102, B 15.164;
(supreme) champion, protector knight 15.279, **B** 8.46, 15.216

chaunce *n* good luck 6.85 (B 13.342); (a matter of) one's luck / fate 14.33

Chaunceller *n* chancellor [king's chief executive and administrative officer] 4. 185

Chauncerye B 4.29 = **Chancerye** *n*

cha(u)ngen *v* change, alter (*tr.*) 5.81, 13.179, 22.361, B 16.129; (*intr.*) (for the worse) 6.146, (for better) 12.211

chedyng *ger.* shedding, *in phr.* **bloed** ~ [*sc.* as a martyr] 14.207

cheef *a* highest, supreme 4.185, A 10.72; foremost Pr 62; principal 6.68, 85, 7.272, 21.475, B 10.100; pre-eminent, most important 15.279, 20.102, 21.409, ~ **charite** 16.347 charity in the highest degree, ~ **iustice** judge of the supreme court 13.116, ~ **lord** immediate (feudal) lord 9.73; *a as n* leader B 14.100

chees *p.t.* 13.3 *see* **chesen** *v*

cheeste B 13.110 = **cheste** *n*[1]

cheyne B 5.607, 17.111 = **chayne** *n*

cheynen *v* fetter 1.183; *pr. subjv.* chain up [entrance] 20.285

cheytyftee *n* destitution 22.236; *and see* **caytiftee** *n*

cheke *n* jaw B 5.162; cheek 6.150, 199, 8.173, 9.208, 15.87, 109, B 5.82; *in phr.* **maugre(e)...chekes** despite all (sb.) can do 8.38, **B** 4.50, 6.158, 14.4

#**cheken** *v* (*pr. subjv.*) barricade 20.285

Cheker *n* Exchequer [royal court of accounts] Pr 91, 4.185, B 4.29

chele *n* cold 22.236, B 1.23, 10.59, *in phr.* **in** ~ **and in hete** at all times 8.249

chepen *v* bid to buy B 13.380; (*fig.*) = choose 16.189; *ger.* ~**yng** market 4.59, 8.322

cherche B 7.173, 10.252 (*uninfl. gen.*), A 12.17 *see* **churche** *n*

chere *n* mien, countenance, expression 11.188, 22.114, B 11.186, A 11.2, Z 3.39, **glad** ~ friendliness 6.374, B 16.155; *in phr.* **maken...** ~ show (...) expression 4.160, 17.30, 22.350; **chered** *a* with a (...) expression 21.264, 22.2

cher(e) *a* dear 17.125, *in phr.* ~ **ouer** deeply concerned about 17.148

cherie *n* cherry 8.310, 12.223, ~ **tyme** time of cherry harvest B 5.159

cherl *n* bondman 8.45, 12.63, 20.107, 21.35, 37, 22.146, B 9.111, A 3.247; slave 21.55; boor 1.29; villain B 16.121 (*with play on* bondman); fellow 6.410

cher(is)sen *v* indulge, *ger.* 4.112

cherubyn *n* cherubim 1.105*n*

chese *n* cheese 7.51, 9.150, **Essex** ~ B 5.92, **grene** ~**s** 8.304

chesen *v* (*p.t.* **chees** 13.3, *pl.* **chosen** Pr 33, 22.236, *p.p.* **(y)chose(n)** 6.379, 12.53) choose 6.379, 16.198, (as) a

way of life Pr 33, 20.205, 22.236; decide 16.174; elect
to eternal life 12.53; *p.p. as n* 12.54

chesible *n* chasuble 8.11

cheste *n*¹ strife, contention Pr 105, 2.89; quarreling
10.277, 14.68, B 13.110

cheste *n*² chest, ark 14.68

chete *n* escheat [reversion of estate to lord] 4.169

cheuen *v* fare Pr 33, (*impers.*) 16.68; succeed 6.252;
thrive 8.248, 20.107

cheuentayn *n* head, lord 21.475

cheuesaunce *n* way of acquiring (sth.) 22.16; agreement
to lend money with (concealed) payment of interest
6.252, B 5.245, Z 2.71

#cheuisshen *v* guard against A 10.73

chewen *v* eat 8.286, 15.46; consume 1.189, 2.140; subsist
20.205, 22.237

chibol *n* spring onion 8.310

chidare *n* troublemaker 18.46

chyden *v* (*contr. pr.* **chy(h)t** 1.175, 16.288, *p.t.* **chydde**
6.147) rail 3.223, rail against B 11.406; nag 7.301;
dispute 3.389; quarrel 1.175, 6.147, 20.205, 464, B
13.323; complain 8.335, 340, 12.229, 16.68, **B** 4.52,
13.380; *ger.* fault-finding 6.68, B 11.423

chief Pr 62, 7.272, 9.73, 13.116, 20.102, B 5.87, A 10.72;
B 14.100 *see* **cheef** *a; n*

chieftayn B 19.476 = **cheuentayn** *n*

chield 17.148 = **child** *n*

chield *p.p.* 17.49; *see* **chillen** *v*

chiere 22.350 = **chere** *n*

chyht *contr. pr.* 1.175 *see* **chyden** *v*

child(e) *n* (*pl.* ~**erne** 10.277, ~**ren(e)** Pr 105, 3.396 (*gen.
pl.* 4.112) ~**res** 8.106) child 1.175, 3.420, 6.156, B 5.38;
baby 6.136, **with** ~ pregnant 9.176, 20.133, 22.348; *pl.*
children Pr 115, 4.112, 5.136, 138, 8.106, 9.73, 89,
169, 10.259, 12.118, 158, 16.301, **B** 3.268, 9.68, 155,
11.384, 14.3, 15.248, **A** 3.247, 7.267, 10.103, 179,
Z 7.201; schoolboys 17.107; descendants 20.107, **B**
3.260, 16.121; offspring 5.65, 10.277, B 16.221, (*fig.*)
18.207, 208; = people Pr 105, 111; (adopted) children
of God 17.291, B 12.12; (spiritual) children 17.291;
followers 22.79, B Pr 35; *in phr.* **wymmen and** ~
3.396, 9.226

childhod *n* childhood A 10.73

childisch(e) *a* childlike 16.296, B 15.149

chillen *v* grow cold, *p.p.* **chield** grown cold 17.49; *ger.*,
for ~ to prevent...from growing cold 8.334

chymenee *n* fireplace B 10.100

chyn *n* chin 6.200

#chine *n* chink, crack 20.285

chirch(e) Pr 64 *et p.* = **churche** *n*

chirie-tyme *n* B 5.159 *see* **cherie** *a*

chiruul *n* chervil 8.310

chyt *contr. pr.* 16.288 *see* **chyden** *v*

chivaler *n* man-at-arms, knight 20.102

*chyuelen B 5.190 = **ycheuelen** *v*

chop *n* blow 10.277

choppen *v* strike Pr 64, 14.68, A 3.247

chose(n) *p.t. pl.* Pr 33, 20.205, 22.236, 237, *p.p.* 12.53; ~**e**
p.p. as n 12.54 *see* **chesen** *v*

churche (**cherche, chirche, kirk**) *n* church (= local
church-building) 2.231, 3.64, 5.12, 30, 60, 104, 6.272,
288, 354, 365, 7.65, 8.11, 45, 100, 9.189, 228, 241,
21.2, **B** 1.180, 5.1, 103, 11.65, 12.27, 13.9, 16.129,
Seint Petres ~ B 7.173, **Sent Poules** ~ Z 2.80, (*fig.*)
= spiritual temple 7.256; = the (Christian) Church [as
teaching, governing and sacramental body], **Holy** ~ Pr
64 *et p.* (*see* **Holy Churche** *for full refs.*), *person.* 1.72;
= the Christian clergy, *in phrr.* **curatours of** ~ 16.279,
folk of ~ Pr 118, **lawe of** ~ 9.218, 326, 14.152, **legates
of** ~ 7.81, **love of** ~ 9.104, **men of**~ 17.41, **prechours
of** ~ 16.250, **prelates of** ~ 6.119, 16.243, 22.229,
princes of ~ 10.198, = the community of Christian
believers (**Unite Holy** ~) 21.366, 22.75, 245

circumcisen *v* circumcise 18.252

cyte(e) *n* city Pr 177, 3.90, 112, 203, 5.90, 20.243, B
14.80, ~ **of Londoun** B Pr 160

Cyuyl(l)e *n* Civil (Roman) law, (*person.*) B 2.116 *et p.*;
and see **Syuyle**

clayme *n* demand 4.98

claymen *v* demand 3.377, 17.71, B 14.142; (lay) claim
(to, by right or title) 3.321, 374, 10.212, 12.59, 15.290,
16.99, 17.58, 71, 18.201, 20.18, 372, 21.446, 22.96, **B**
7.156, 10.321, 342, 18.344; declare (oneself) 21.446; ?
claim to possess 1.89

clannesse *n* (moral) purity, integrity 7.76 (B 13.417),
21.382, **B** 14.11, 15.465; virginity 14.86, 88, B 14.300

clansen *v* clear 8.65; purify 16.25, B 18.392; purge, ab-
solve 3.358, 18.143, 19.177

claumsen (**clomsen**) *v* become numb 15.254; *and see*
clumse *a as n* Z 7.54

clause *n* clause 17.316, B 7.106; sentence 4.147; (short)
text 11.249; letter (? *or* clause) A 8.44

*clausemele *av* clause by clause B 5.420

clawe *n* claw (= nail) 6.149, Pr 172 (**clee**)

clawen *v* claw, lacerate B Pr 154; scrape B 14.17; clutch
Pr 172; grasp 19.157, (*fig.*) B 10.283

clee Pr 172 = **clawe** *n*

cleef *p.t.* B 18.61 *see* **cleuen** *v*²

cleer *a* bright 7.231; pure B 12.221

cleymen B 7.156, 10.342 = **claymen** *v*

cleken *v* Z 3.36 cluck (*or* = **clokken**)

†clemat B 15.370 = **clymat** *n*

clemen *v* gutter 3.106

clemp *p.t.* 18.108 *see* **clymben** *v*

clene *a* (*comp.* **clenner,** *sup.* **clennest**) unmixed 8.327;
pure 3.23, 10.294, (*sup.*) 18.94, ~ **lyuyng** 21.382, 461;
clean **B** 14.2, 12, 15.190, (*fig.*) **B** 14.185, †18.392;
chaste B 1.195; ~ **moder** virgin mother 2.51, 7.155; ~

consience good, right conscience 9.26, **A** 6.27, 10.88; upright 21.382, 461, **B** 10.259, 11.300, (*comp.*) 13.296; ?elegant 20.122n; refined (*sup.*) 18.95, (*comp.*) 21.253; wholesome (*sup.*) **B** 14.44, 16.70; ~**nesse** *n* **B** 14.11, 300, 15.465 = **clannesse** *n*

clep(i)en *v* speak **B** 10.246; call (by name) 6.149, 21.117, 22.182; summon 11.18; invite 12.55, 104

clerc 5.54, 6.365, **B** 7.71, 13.248, **Z** 7.265, (~**us** *pl.*) **Z** 3.170 = **clerk** *n*

clere *av* brightly 19.223

clerg(i)(e) *n* the clergy 15.170, 21.470, **B** 3.165, **A** 11.65, (*person.*) **B** Pr 116, 3.15; learning 11.278, 283, 12.99, 14.30, 34, 35, 43, 70, 71, 72, 83, 191, 16.234, **B** 11.144, 165, 12.66, 71, 77, 81, 83, 85, 92, 15.209, 380, (*person.*) Pr 151, 11.93 *et p.*, 13.129 *et p.*, 14.100, 15.26 *et p.*, 22.228, **A** 12.1, 13, 35; doctrine 16.320, **B** 12.171; wisdom **A** 10.107

#**clergialiche** *av* in a scholarly way 8.34

clergyse *n* learning 20.405; the clergy **Z** 3.100

clerioun *n* young cleric **A** 12.49

clerk *n* cleric, member of the clergy 1.88, 121, 2.58, 246, 3.44, 49, 4.114 (*gen. pl.*), 146, 5.54, 56, 61, 63, 179, 7.91, 9.205, 210, 247, 11.306, 12.228, 14.54, 86, 199, 216, 16.263, 270, 279, 337, 17.69, 120, 175, 208, 214, 19.238, 20.354, 21.382, 417, 428, **B** 10.106, 112, 396, 411, 12.98, 233, 13.116, 14.180, 15.68, 104, 198, 331, 412, 443, 580, **A** 4.105, 10.137; = (higher) ecclesiastic 3.150, 12.228, 22.68, **B** 4.189; secular cleric 11.56; cleric (in orders below priest) **B** 13.11, 15.117; lawyer, ~ **of the lawe** learned lawyer 11.281, ~ **of þe Kinges bench** royal justice **A** Pr 95; parish clerk 6.365; educated person 11.236, 14.114, 118, *in phr.* ~ **and / or lewed** 'clerk or layman', educated or uneducated 6.29, 16.290, 22.68, **B** 10.51; learned man, scholar Pr 141, 3.27, 35, 210, 5.146, 6.76, 82, 7.182, 11.137, 156, 236, 291, 295, 12.162, 14.11, 45, 52, 64, 88, 97, 100, 114, 155, 198, 17.166, 21.271, **B** 3.347, 7.154, 10.104, 286, 466, 12.265, 15.82. 90, 211, 356, 372, 414; university student 10.20; student 3.276, **B** 10.196, 12.21; secretary (of records / accounts) 2.59, 3.179, 4.164, 21.465, **B** 10.471, **A** Pr 91; (*fig.*) 16.190; (royal) official 3.3, 16, **A** Pr 95; *in phrr.* **connynge** ~**es** 3.37, 14.102, **B** 10.458, **A** 11.273, **knyhtes and** ~**es** 3.44, 49, (*trs*) 7.96, 11.52, **A** 4.105

****clerkysh** *a* clerkly, apt for a scholar 6.42

clerliche *av* completely **B** 18.392

#**clermatyn** *n* a fine white bread 8.327

cleuen *v*[1] (**on**) cling to 7.303; hold together in 17.128; inhere in 19.313; devote (oneself) to **B** 11.224

cleuen *v*[2] (*p.t.* **cleef**) split **B** 18.61

cliaunt *n* (lawyer's) client 3.392

clycat *n* locking latch 7.251

clyf *n* hill **A** 1.4

****clyketen** *v* (shut locking) latch 7.265

clymat *n* region of the earth [considered with respect to its weather] 17.106

clymben *v* (*p.t.* **clemp**) climb 18.106, 108; aspire **A** 10.101

clingen *v* shrivel up 15.254

clippen *v* grasp 19.157; (*pr. subjv.*) embrace 20.463

clips *n* eclipse 20.138

clyuen **B** 11.224 = **cleuen** *v*[1]

cloches *n. pl.* clutches Pr 172; *and see* **cluchen** *v*

cloystre *n* monastery 4.116, 5.151, 153, 154; monastic building, cloister 3.64, 6.163, **B** 6.147

cloke *n* cloak 6.375, 380, 388, 7.166, 8.292, 9.139, **B** 3.296

****clokken** *v* limp 3.37

clom *n* clay **A** 12.105

clomsen **B** 14.51 = **claumsen** *v*

closen *v* close, shut (up) Pr 132, 7.264, 265, 15.268, 21.168, ~ **with** close...with Pr 133; **do** ~ have confined 3.140; enclose 10.132, 172; cover over **B** 18.135; = bury **A** 12.105

cloth *n* cloth 5.18, 8.13, **B** 6.14, **lynnen** ~ **B** 14.56, **wollone** ~ 6.221; clothing 4.114, *in phr.* **corn and** ~ / **breed and** ~**es** food and clothing 8.145, 15.259, 22.248; cloth garment 10.195, 22.16; garb 9.249, 21.288, *pl.* clothes 5.41, 8.58, 263, 10.203, 12.126, 16.268, 349, 19.238, 22.7, 143, **B** Pr 199, 6.16, 11.431, **A** 8.43, **Z** 7.48, 199, (*fig.*) 6.65, **B** 14.177, 329, *in pl. phrr.* **bele** ~**es** 16.268, **broke** ~ **B** 9.92, **holde** ~ **Z** 7.48, **longe** ~ 5.41, **pilgrymes** ~ 12.126, **B** 13.29, **raggede** ~ 11.195, **wyde** ~ 18.270

clothen *v* dress Pr 54, 1.3, 2.9, 5.2, 9.210, 15.81, 19.243, 21.258, **B** Pr 62, 5.78, 13.273, (*fig.*) 5.179, 20.170, 174; provide clothes for 9.90, 13.83, 16.324, 17.196, 22.209, **B** 4.119 *ger.* **clothyng** garb, clothing 9.208, 12.129, 16.339, 20.175, **B** 14.157 *in phrr.* **continance of** ~ Pr 26, **lecherye of** ~ 16.254, **rich** ~ 20.175

clothere *n* cloth-maker 11.15

clotus **Z** 7.199 *see* **cloth** *n*

cloude *n* cloud 10.159, 14.73, 20.456, **B** 3.193, **Z** Pr 16

cloustre 3.64 = **cloystre** *n*

clout *n* rag 2.230; lining **B** 13.63

clouten *v* patch 9.80, **B** 6.59

cluchen *v* close (fingers) into a fist 19.122; clutch 19.157; *see* **cloches** *n*

#**clumse** *a* (*as n*) numb(ness) **Z** 7.54n; *and see* **claumsen** *v*

cluppen 20.463 = **clippen** *v*

coblere *n* cobbler, shoe-repairer 6.375

cock *n* cockle 9.95

coek 6.130 = **coke** *n*

coeld 17.303, 18.145 = **cold** *a*

coest 3.372, 384 = **cost** *n*[2]

coffe *n* mitten 8.59

cof(fe)re *n* chest (for valuables) 5.129, 12.216, 16.87, 89, **B** 13.301, (*fig.*) 14.54, **B** 10.323, 11.198

coghen **B** 17.327 = **cou(ȝ)en** *v*

coyne (koyne) *n* image (on coin) 1.46, (*fig.*) 17.80, 81

cok *n* cock, ~ **es fether** = thing of no worth 21.415; (pea) cock 13.171

coke *n* cook Pr 227, 3.80, (*fig.*) 5.175, 6.130

#coken *v*¹ cook (*fig.*) 15.60

coken (koken) *v*² make haycocks 5.13, 21.239

cokeney *n* (?small) hen's egg 8.308*n*

coker *n* legging 8.59

cokere *n* haycock-maker, harvestman 5.13

#coket *n* bread of fine flour 8.327

cokewold(e) *n* cuckold 4.59, 6.134

col *n* cabbage B 6.285

cold(e) *n* cold 9.109, Z 7.200; **for** ~ because of the cold 8.244, 15.254, 16.77, B 13.161; to keep off the cold (from) 13.71, **B** 3.191, 6.60, against the cold Z 7.53; *a* 1.124, 9.93, 16.73, B 13.262, Z 3.157

cold *a* cold 1.124, *quadriduanus* ~ four days dead 17.303, 18.145

cole *n* coal 9.142, (*fig.*) 15.144

coler *n* (ornamental) neck-chain Pr 179, 209, B Pr 204

#collateral *a* concomitant 16.134

collen *v* embrace B 11.17, A 11.177

colloppes (colhoppes) *n. pl.*bacon and eggs 8.308, 15.68

colomy *a* grimy B 13.356

colour *n* colour 13.138, 175, 18.21, 20.212, B 12.221; specious argument / appearance B 15.209; coloured dye / pigment 21.242; armorial bearings 21.13, (*with play on* 'specious appearance') 21.354; (*fig.*) manner, guise B 3.238

colouren *v* colour, speciously present 21.349; make (sth.) appear 21.461

coltur *n* coulter [vertical-cutting plough-blade] 3.460, 8.65 (B 6.104)

coluer(e) *n* dove 17.173, 175, (*gen.*) 179, 246, B 15.406, (*fig.*) 414

com *imp.* 7.218, *p.t.* 2.30 *et p.*; *see* **comen** *v*

coma(u)ndement *n* command 3.409; precept 16.126; commandment 11.142, 16.231

com(m)aunden *v* command 13.77, 21.113, **B** 6.16, 11.180; order 2.210, 4.6, 8, 81, 195, 8.88, 15.53, 21.364, 367, *p.t. 2 sg.* Z 3.154; ordain 1.20

comaundour *n* master A 3.274

combraunce *n* trouble 5.190; misfortune 12.247, 18.173, B 12.45; distress 20.276

combren *v* overcome 1.67; **burden** A 10.93; *and see* **acombren** *v*

comely *a* beautiful 20.122; fit(ting) B 15.451

comen *v* (*imp.* **com** 7.218, *pl.* **cometh** 21.386, *p.t. sg.* **cam** Pr 95, **com(e)** 2.30, *pl.* **cam** 18.4, **come(n)** Pr 71, 10.206, *pr. subjv.* **come** 4.8, *p.t. subjv.* 7.169, 22.329, *p.p.* **(y)come(n)** 3.455, 5.63, B 4.189) come Pr 71 *et p.*; should come 17.296, 21.423, 22.329, B 17.83; get to arrive 12.49, 18.127, 137, A 4.21; arise 13.234; call 5.50, 9.125; be created B 12.127; *in phr. vv.* **~aȝen**

attack 22.72, 220, approach B 4.44; **ar ~ auht longe** before very long 17.214; **~by** pass 7.218 (1), (through) B 17.121, ?acquire 5.6n; **~ in** arrive (at) 6.231, 15.189, 17.173; enter 6.337, 7.218 (2), 9.253, B 11.50, take part in 13.84, 16.359; be (put) in A 7.287, **~ into** arrive in 7.206, 18.4, B 3.303; **~ of** be descended (from) 2.30, 3.60, 6.58, 10.206, 222, 14.182, 21.123, B 9.123; originate (from) 14.45, 79, 18.237, 21.25, 254; **~ til** attend 8.98; **~ to** arrive on B 2.26; reach 3.364; get to 6.307, 7.231, B 5.413; obtain 9.156, 21.69, 22.14, 16, 209, B 10.351; attain to 14.53, 157, 15.72; **~ togyderes** match (in contest) 16.79;

comen 18.143 = **comune** *a*

co(m)menden *v* praise 11.278, 14.117, 16.285; approve B 4.158; **to ~** to be commended 14.35

comenere *n* burgess, citizen [*spec.* member of town council] 4.188, B 15.331; one of the common people 5.183

comere *n* caller 2.240, **~ aboute** visitor A 2.43; *and see* **nyhte-comare** *n* 21.144

com(e)sen *v* originate 1.158, 160, *ger.* origin Z 3.172; begin 21.97, 106, 123, Z 3.156, *ger.* beginning 20.223, origin Z 3.172; proceed to 4.24, 8.337, 10.20, 14.202, 21.97, 22.212, B 3.104; undertake, *ger.* 11.94; utter Z 7.36

comet *n* comet 14.97

comfort 22.182; **comforten** 6.281, 20.265, 21.128 *see* **confort(en)** *n, v*

comyn 3.167 = **comune** *a*

comyng(e) *ger.* (Christ's`) coming (into the world) 18.267, 20.444

commen 12.169 = **comune** *a*

comissarie *n* bishop's legate 2.190, 3.179, 16.362

commune 21.370, B 5.641; B Pr 113 *et p.*; *see* **comune** *n, a*

compacen *v* design 21.242; establish B 10.180

#compacience *n* compassion 15.89

compaignie B 5.641, 11.422, 13.161 = **companie** *n*

companie *n* band 21.155, B 13.161, Z 2.163; body of followers 22.120; (social) gathering 16.342, 21.160; fellowship 22.182; company 13.244, **folwen ~, suen ~** keep company (with) B 5.641, 11.422; **compenable** *a* companionable 16.342

compas *n* compass (for measuring) 11.125

compasen B 10.180 = **compacen** *v*

compeny 22.182 = **companie** *n*

comsyng *ger.* see **com(e)sen** *v*

comune *n* people, community, nation Pr 95, 143, 144, 147, 1.155, 3.206, 374, 377, 384, 4.176, 5.20, 75, 180, 186, 17.289, 21.215, 394, 419, 469, 475, 479, 22.78, **B** Pr 115, 9.89, 10.29, 272, 12.294, 13.262; common people, populace 3.201, 468, 4.30, 76, 161, 8.84, 9.10, 15.170, 17.216, 308, 21.155, 382, 454, 22.30; free citizens [meeting as court] 16.360; fellowship 5.186; *pl.*

comunes the common people B Pr 114, A 3.66; sustenance Pr 143, 5.144, 8.292, 21.417

comune *a* common, *in phr.* ~ **profit** common good Pr 167, 184, 201, 4.119; of the whole community *in phr.* ~ **helpe** 3.244, 4.176*n*; open to all 3.167; *in phrr.* ~ **court** Court of Common Pleas, ? county court 2.22, 3.472; ~ **fode** food shared by all, ? ordinary, normal 21.410*n*; ~ **lawe** law of the land 20.74; ~ **peple** common people 2.58, 11.297, 21.7, 132, 423; þe ~ **speche** the familiar / well-known expression A 11.241; ~ **woman** prostitute 18.143, 21.370, B 11.216; *a as n, in phr.* **in** ~ (shared) in common 1.20, 16.42, 22.276; universally B 10.356; in public B 11.216

comunely(che) *av* usually 16.139; frequently, commonly 14.19, 21.314; in general 11.295

conceyuen (conseyuen) *v* conceive 10.215, 220, 13.149, 151, 20.132, **B** 9.121, 11.357; comprehend 10.56, 13.223; utter 8.32

concepcion *n* procreation, mating 13.145; offspring B 9.158

concience 3.254, (*person.*) 15.26 *et p.*, 16.190, 21.26, 22.106 = **consience** *n*

concluden *v* confute 11.283

condicion *n*, **in** ~ on condition 21.480

confermen *v* ratify 14.39, B 10.352; (administer sacrament of) confirm(ation to) B 13.214, 15.456

confessen *v* (*refl.*) (make one's) confess(ion of sins) 6.337, 12.5, 19.279; hear confession (of) 5.168, 12.15, 17.280, (*fig.*) B 10.316

confessio(u)n *n* (formal) confession of sins (to a priest) 10.53, 12.71, 14.115, 16.26, 21.333, 348, 351, 22.213, 329, B 14.187

confessour *n* confessor [= one who affirms Christian faith under persecution] 10.206, 12.198, B 12.203; [= priest who hears confessions] 3.38, 4.142, 146, 5.194, 22.372, **B** 11.70, 14.18, A 12.41, 77

conformen B 11.180, 13.209, 15.343 = **confo(u)rmen** *v*

confort *n* consolation 7.110, 16.134, Z 6.62 (? *or* trust); relief 22.372; pleasure (*person.*) 22.91, 182; benefit 5.75, B 4.151; strengthening 12.149, 152

confortable *a* consoling B 14.282

confortatif *a* cheerful B 15.219

conforten *v* inspire with spiritual strength 17.50, 18.73, B 11.264; reassure B 12.175; encourage 14.118, B 12.21; abet 22.67; refresh 15.189, 196, B 14.147, 179, 180; cheer (up) 2.164, 3.16, 27, 18.267, 20.265, 22.243, B 13.22; relieve 14.115; console 1.197, 6.281, 14.70; minister to 9.48, 15.196, 16.324, 22.359; succour 8.230, 9.97, 15.147, 21.128, B 12.81, 14.175; entertain 15.62, B 13.58

confortour *n* bringer of strength / refreshment B 16.190

confounden *v* cause harm to 5.190

confo(u)rmen *v* (*refl.*) consent, agree 3.397; submit to B 15.343; dispose **B** 11.180, 13.209

confus *p.p.a* discountenanced B 10.138

congie *n* leave, farewell B 13.203

conieyen (congeyen) *v* take leave of 15.177; order to leave, dismiss 3.219, 4.195, 11.163, 16.367

conyng *n* rabbit B Pr 189

conyon *n* fool, oaf A 11.87

conysaunce *n* heraldic device 18.187

coniuren *v* solemnly charge B 15.14

connen (konnen) *v* (*pr. sg.* **can** 2.236 *et p.*, *pl.* **can** 1.190, 3.496, 8.267, 11.18, 228, 14.11, 15.191, **conne(n)** 8.69, 13.125, 14.11, 17.316, **conneth** Pr 35, (*subjv.*) **conne** 14.111, 21.480); *p.t.* **couthe** Pr 196, **coude A** 2.188, 8.44, 12.73, *assim. 2. p. sg. p.t.* †**coudestow A** 6.21; *ger.* **connyng** 11.283, *pr. p.* 10.260) be able 3.218 *et p.*, A 11.185; have ability 6.82, 8.69; be capable of 6.58; know how to Pr 35, 3.496, 8.129, 14.111, 21.401; have mastery of 2.236, 16.209, 17.114, 22.231, Z 7.49; have knowledge of 7.157, 8.267, 16.213, B 2.227; know 3.3, 16.205; recognise, come to know 11.101, †A 12.32; grant A 8.44

connyng *ger.* skill 11.285, 14.106, 15.133, 21.235, 254, B 13.293; knowledge, understanding 11.295, 14.34, 36, 15.18 (2), **B** 10.472, 11.165, 211, 12.66; learning 11.228, 13.112, 233, 14.19; science, (branch of) knowledge 11.94, 15.133; wisdom 11.283, 15.18 (1), 21.461, B 11.300; prudence 21. 235, A 10.50

connyng(e) *a* skilful 6.42; clever, shrewd 10.260, B 11.70; learned 3.37, 14.102, 114, B 10.458, A 11.273

conqueren *v* acquire by force of arms 3.244 (*p.p.*), 254; ~ **on** win victory (over) 3.250; (*fig.*) be victorious 21.50

conquerour *n* conqueror [= one who subjugates a people] 21.27, 30, 43, 99, 106, (*fig.*) 21.50, 53, 62, 97; victorious leader 21.14

conqueste *n* conquered territory 21.43

conseyl, consayl *n* assembly Pr 167; council 11.18; (meeting of) (royal) council (of advisers) 3.127, 156, 4.119, 5.144, 16.358, 22.30, 68, 129, B 4.189; adviser, counsellor, **be of** ~ be counsellor to 16.359, B 4.193; be in the confidence of 2.152, **taken to** ~ take into one's confidence 4.166, 15.176, B 13.178; counsel, advice Pr 208, 3.7, 253, 375, 6.76, 8.337, 11.100, 317, 16.238, 367, 17.56, 21.38, 79, 258, 297, 317, 358, 396, 455, 22.21, 212, 242, B 9.115; plan, scheme 2.119, 5.184; secret / private matter(s) / concern(s) 4.8, 6.165, 21.162, B 5.166, Z 3.168*n*; wise judgement 22.147

conseilen *v* counsel, advise Pr 201, 3.232, 241, 253, 262, 4.106, 5.180, 6.29, 8.13, 9.346, 10.281, 14.5, 43, 64, 19.228, 21.201, 215, 394, 465, 22.74, **B** 11.224, 15.343; give (divine) counsel 12.169, 21.113, 394, persuade, prevail upon 1.62

conseyuen 10.56, B 9.121, *etc* = **conceyuen** *v*

consenten *v* agree to give 2.90

cons(c)ience *n* (inner) attitude of mind / feelings 3.71, B 13.391*n*; ? conscientiousness B 14.87; conscience

2.52, 5.83, 9.26, 17.197, 216, **B** 14.82, 189, 17.136, **A** 10.88, 91, 93, 11.309, (*person.*) Pr 138 *et p.*, **B** 7.134, Z 3.147; scruples 12.5; *in phrr.* **as in** ~ truly 17.149, **bi here** ~ in fairness, 'in all conscience' 6.385

conspiren *v* plot secretly B 10.19, 422

constable *n* constable, king's high or chief military officer (*fig.*) 3.255n; = warden of royal castle (*fig.*) 10.143, 22.214; = officer of the king's peace 2.210, 4.81, B 2.207, Z 2.188; justice of the peace 3.467

constillacioun *n* planetary / lunar position (in relation to the ascendant zodiacal sign) 14.31, A 10.146

cons(is)torie *n* consistory [bishop's] court 3.34, 178, 472, 16.362, (*fig.*) the court of God [judging mankind at the last day] Pr 127

constraynen *v* compel 5.54; restrain 20.435

constru(w)en *v* translate 4.142, 9.281, 16.116, **B** Pr 144, 5.278; explain 4.147, 7.34, B 5.420; interpret 17.110, B Pr 61; (pass) judge(ment on) B 2.36, A 8.134; practise A 11.19n

contemplacio(u)n *n* contemplation (of divine things) 18.73, 77, (*person.*) 7.304; rational speculation 22.274

contemplatif *a* contemplative (= devoted to contemplation of God) B 6.248

contenuen 5.39 = **contynuen** *v*

continaunce (continence) *n* outward show Pr 26; looks 11.177, Z Pr 25; meaningful look 6.165, 11.163, 15.121

continence *n* sexual abstinence 18.73; (state of) sexual abstinence (within widowhood or marriage) B 16.69

contynuen *v* persevere 5.104, 10.286, B 12.38

contraye 8.206, 21.314 = **contre(ye)** *n*

contrarie *n* opposite 1.121, 9.193, **B** 10.198, 395, 12.50; reverse 10.242, 17.106; contrary [element] 19.327, B 17.271; opposition 17.161

contrarien *v* oppose, act against 17.149, 19.313, B 5.54; violate 17.251; feel resentment 19.322, contradict Pr 59, 2.22, 14.100

contre(y)(e) *n* region, place 8.206, 9.111, 10.12, 269, 17.164, 21.136, 22.56, **B** 13.224, 16.170, 17.114, 121, (*fig.*) 15.190, 18.4; area of jurisdiction [ecclesiastical] 22.329; country, realm 2.56, 3.238, 17.164, 21.420, 22.224, B 15.519, A Pr 95; shire A 2.43; town 19.51; country district Pr 31, 10.15, **sysores of c** ~ **s** district jurors 2.63; the countryside 21.314

#contrepleden Pr 138 = **countrepleden** *v*

#contrerollor *n* keeper of the counter-roll (= accountant) 11.302

contreuen *v* plan, devise 14.160; establish Pr 144; fashion 11.124, 125; discover 14.73; scheme 6.39, 11.16, B 16.137

contricio(u)n *n* contrition [religious sorrow for sin] 10.53, 12.71, 14.115, 117, 121, 16.25, 21.348, 350, 22.213, **B** 11.81, 14.16, 82, 84, 87, 92, 282, (*person.*) 15.60, 21.333, 22.317 *et p.*

contrit *a* contrite, filled with sorrow for sin B 14.84

conuthe *pr. pl.* Z 8.13 = **conneth**; *see* **connen** *v*

conuerten *v* reform 18.143; convert 17.186; transform 20.188

cook 5.175 = **coke** *n*

co(o)me *p.t. subjv.* 17.296, 21.423, 22.329, B 17.83

cope A 5.59 = **coupe** *n²*

cope *n* cope [sleeveless clerical cloak] Pr 54, 59, 8.185, 9.210, 247, 22.58, Z 3.153

#copen *v* provide / dress with (in) a cope 2.240, 3.38, 179, 6.288, 22.345, (*fig.*) Z 3.156

copien *v* copy A 8.44

coplen 2.190 = **couplen** *v*

coppe *n* drinking-cup 3.23, 5.161, 6.389, 20.406; *av* ~ **mele** a cup(ful) at a time 6.231

corecten 21.305 = **cor(r)ecten** *v*

corleu *n* ?quail 15.243n

corn *n* (crop of cereal) grain 5.17, 8.31, 101, 244, 322, 17.173, 21.320, **B** 6.140, 15.401, **A** 6.32, 7.128, Z 7.65, 108; corn-fields 13.45; (as food) bread 15.259, B 13.262, A 7.183; **breed** ~ wheat-grain 8.61

cornel *n* kernel 12.149, 152

corner *n* angle (formed by spokes) 15.163

coro(u)ne 17.205, 21.468, B 2.10 *see* **croune** *n*

corps B 13.9, 19.151 = **cors** *n¹*

Corpus Cristi (feste) *n* the feast of Corpus Christi 17.120

cor(r)ecten *v* set right by rebuke 21.305; punish B 10.283

correctour *n* one who rebukes / punishes (for misconduct) B 10.283

cors *n* body [dead] 15.11, 21.151, [living] 16.181, B 1.139

cors 13.145 = **cours** *n*

corseynt *n* saint [*lit.* 'holy body'] 7.176

*****corse-men** *n. phr* 'curse-men' 6.65n

corsen *v* curse, invoke evil upon 6.64, 8.338, 22.68, **B** 10.466, 13.331, 15.171; utter an imprecation 19.309; excommunicate 3.178, *ger.* 8.159; *p.p.a* **corsed(e)** damned, accursed 10.220, 229, 231, 250, A 10.140, 146, 148; wicked 17.212, 19.255, 21.406, 435, 470, B 6.160, Z 2.163; ill-fortuned, wretched 3.106, (*comp.*) 21.420

corteys *a* well-bred, polite 4.17, 8.47, B 13.459, A 4.105; gracious, generous 14.160, 16.255, B 13.15, A 3.59; **~liche** *av* politely 8.161, 15.121, 194, B 13.31, 46, 180, 199; graciously 3.9, 129, 4.42, 152, 8.32, 161, 21.177, 22.243, 356, A 11.177; respectfully 2.164

cortesye *n* (refined / good manners 10.267, 17.164, B 10.310; courteous behaviour B 5.89; generosity, kindness 3.314, 7.43, 17.220, B 11.439, Z 2.7; loving-kindness, merciful graciousness [of God] 1.20, 19.208, 21.452, 22.106, B 12.77, 14.147; gracious gift 14.216; respect B 15.303

corupcion *n* disease 22.99

corue *p.t.* (*2 sg*) Z 3.153, **~n** *3 pl.* 8.185 *see* **keruen** *v*

cosyn *n* kinsman 11.93, 22.358, **B** 2.133, 12.93, A 12.41, 43, 53

cost *n*¹ disposition (? *or* expense) 3.72*n*

cost *n*² expense ? 3.72, 372, 384, 15.47, 19.238

costen *v* (*p.t.* ~ed(e), -e) cost Pr 209, 210, B 13.383

coste *n* region 10.12, B 2.86; quarter (of the heavens) B 18.113

costnen B Pr 205 = **costen** *v*

costume 14.73 = **custume** *n*

cote *n*¹ small cottage 4.123, 5.2, 9.72, 83, 151, 10.16, 14.90

cote *n*² tunic 16.299, **B** 5.109, 11.283, 14.151, (*fig.*)**B** 13.274, 314, 355, 403, 458, 14.17, ~ **armure** tunic with heraldic devices (*fig.*) 18.187, 21.13

*****coten** *v* provide with tunic 3.179

#**coterel** *n* (lesser) cotter, subtenant 9.97, 193

#**cotidian** *a* daily-recurring A 12.84

cottepors *n* cut-purse, thief 7.282

coude *p.t.* A 2.188, 12.72 = **couthe**, *2 sg.* †**coudestou**, **coudest thow**; *see* **connen** *v*

couden (**couth** Z) *p.t. pl.*; *see* **kithen** *v*

couen 19.309 = **couȝen** *v*

couert 1.104 = **court** *n*

cough (**cowh**) cough B 20.82 (22.82)

couȝen *v* cough 19.309; clear throat 15.110; vomit 6.163, 411

counforten A 11.189 = **conforten** *v*

counsayl 5. 184, **counseil** B Pr 144 etc = **conseyl** *n*; **counsei(ll)en** B Pr 115 etc, **A** 10.97, 11.222 = **conseilen** *v*

counte(e) *n* county, earldom 2.90

counten *v* number, reckon Z 3.168; regard, esteem 3.178, 9.303, 10.261, 11.177, 317, 12.198, 13.238, 14.83, 22.147, 222, A 7.154; take account (of), care (for / that) 9.109, 21.306, 447; make reckoning A 4.11; *and see* **acounten** *v*

#**co(u)ntrepleden** *v* plead in opposition to (a demand) 8.53, 88; argue against Pr 138, 22.385, B 12.98

countreseggen *v* contradict 11.225

coupable *a* (found) guilty 19.284; guilty (of sin) B 12.88

coupe *n*¹ guilt (for sin) 6.327, 350, A 5.59

coupe *n*² drinking bowl 3.23

coupen *v* slash (for decoration) 20.12

couple *n* married pair 18.223, B 9.162; pair (of male and female animals) B 9.141

couplen *v* unite in marriage B 9.126, 128, A 10.156, (*subjv.*) 158; join in league 4.146, **B** 3.165, 10.162; put on a leash B Pr 207; (be) hitch(ed) [to a vehicle] 2.190

courben *v* bend, kneel B 1.79, 2.1, Z 1.24

#**courrour** *n* courier, messenger A 12.84

cours *n* movement (of planets) 17.104; sequence 3.346; (proper) conduct, ? progress 3.388; process 3.60, 13.145; way 17.161

court *n* enclosed yard B 15.473; manor-house 10.15, 22.345, **B** 8.15, 13.23, (*fig.*) 7.231, B 10.165, A 12.57; royal residence Pr 168, 16.358, 18.95, A 4.29, Z 2.163; royal household Pr 204, 215; heavenly court of God 3.455, B 15.21, 22; (of judgement) 16.166; royal council 21.427, 22.130; papal court, curia Pr 134, 17.166, B Pr 111; law court, (royal) court of justice Pr 158, 2.22, 202, 3.34, 468, 472, 473, 20.38, 21.306, **B** 2.63, 4.166; manorial court 7.33; ? county court 16.360; church tribunal 3.34

courteysly(che) 2.164, 8.32, 161, = **corteysliche** *av*

courtepy *n* short jacket 8.185, B 5.79

couthe 17.196 = **kuth** *n*

couth(e) *p.t.* Pr 196 *et p.* (*2 sg.* **couthest** 10.74, 18.2) B 1.116, A 4.142, Z 5.143 *see* **connen** *v*

couth *p.t.* Z 8.44 *see* **kithen** *v*

coueiten *v* covet [*esp.* goods], desire unrightfully Pr 31, 3.425, 362, 5.151, 7.219, 9.48, 193, 10.281, 11.109, 16.144, 291, 15.155, 19.182, **B** 29, 11.76, 13.150, 14.309, 15.159, A 3.248; desire strongly, long (for) 3.254, 398, 401, 10.109, 11.18, 141, 12.61, 170, 15.72, 16.199, 368, 17.80, 228, 19.182, **B** Pr 189, 3.164, 10.337, 11.125, 13.151, 15.175, 254, 17.216, 22.253, **A** 10.101, 12.3; desire sexually (*fig.*) 20.171; yearn for 11.172, B 15.469, 17.122

coue(y)tise *n* covetousness, greed (y desire for wealth) Pr 59, 103, 1.67, 190, 2.52, 247, 3.72, 201, 210, 430, 5.184, 10.260, 282, 12.243, 247, 16.109, 17.205, 208, B 9.157 *in phr.* **counte** of ~ 2.90, **custumes** of ~ 3.206, **licames** ~ B 15.67; (*spec.*) the deadly sin of Greed 2.90, 4.33, 11.15, 15.13, 190, 17.214, 18.32, 19.256, 326, **B** 10.281, 13.356, 391, A 2.32, Z 3.154, 156, 170; (*person.*) 6.196, 16.79, 81, 367, 21.225, 22.141, 220, 297, 352, B 15.414, Z 5.97; ~ **of Yes** 11.175, 312; (strong) desire (*with pun on* 'greed') 4.114, 16.222, **B** 5.255, 14.11, A 7.183

coue(i)tous *a* covetous, greedy for wealth 6.206, 16.42, A 3.59, *as n* 14.21; eager for B 13.184

couena(u)nt *n* binding agreement 8.157, (*fig.*) = divine pledge 14.216; pact (of peace) 20.463; agreed payment B 14.151; condition, *in phr.* **in** ~ **þat** on condition that 6.389, 8.26, 21.187

couent *n* religious community (living under a rule) 6.39, 130, 162, 22.60, **B** 5.136, 11.76, Z 3.154; (the) convent(ual buildings) 5.151

coueren B 14.331 *see* **keueren** *v*

couerour *n* repairer / provider of roof 5.175

couetyse 3.72 *et p.*, **couetous** 6.206 *see* **coue(y)tise** *n*, **coue(i)tous** *a*

cow *n*¹ (*pl.* **kyen** B 6.140) cow 8.311, 13.149, **B** 6.140, 15.466, Z 3.149; *in cpds.* ~ **calf** female calf B 15.469, ~ **kynde** female of (any) cattle 13.149

cow (**ko**) *n*² chough A 7.128 (Z 7.125)

cowardly *av* in a cowardly manner B 3.206

cowh 22.82 = **cough** *n*

cow(h)en *v* 6.411, 15.110 = **couȝen** *v*

crabbed *a* ill-tempered 14.100, B 10.106

crachen *v* scratch [with claws] Pr 200, B Pr 154, [with fingernails] 6.140; comb [cloth to raise a nap] B 15.453; snatch, tear away 12.80

cradel *n* cradle 9.79

craft *n* power B 1.139; skill 6.322, 7.190, 9.90, 155, 16.188, 21.254, 22.206, 207, 343, B 5.25, (*person.*) 21.257, 258; ingenuity 3.20; (business) acumen 21.235; trade, craft Pr 144, 2.236, 5.20, 6.322, 7.190, 11.124, 8.200, 9.90, 155, 15.194, B Pr 222, 5.547, 7.31, 19.254; profession 4.170, 22.231; branch of learning 15.133; art, (applied) science 16.208; ? craft guild 21.251*n*; way, means 2.4; trick 6.231, B 10.21; activity 8.58, B 17.171

crafty *a* skilled in / master of a craft, ~ **men** 3.279, 8.69, A 11.185, ~ **connynge** skill in a craft B 13.293; skilfully wrought Pr 179

craftily *av* ingeniously 10.132; skilfully B 19.242

#**craym** *n* cream 8.305, 321

craken *v* break 20.75

crammen *v* cram, stuff full Pr 42

crampe 22.82, B 13.335 = **crompe** *n*

crauen *v* ask 16.55, †B 11.439, 13.165; ask (to have) 3.274, 276, 279, B 13.242, 15.254, 17.122; implore 12.151, B 14.187; beg 6.49, 15.35; demand (as one's due) 8.101, 21.479, B 15.165

creatour *n* (the) Creator [God] 10.152, 17.153, 18.94, B 11.325, 16.215

creature *n* created thing 17.153, B 16.215; creation 16.164, 165; living creature 13.133, 18.94, 21.17, 22.151, B 11.397, 13.18, 16.190, A 11.246; (order of) living creature 1.104; person, 'body' 6.294, 10.215, 13.209, 14.5, 43, 157, 15.225, 16.170, 213, 19.284, 20.122, 132, 21.217, 375, B 11.180, 12.83, 225, 276, 14.175, 180, 15.171, 195, 211, A 12.110; *in phrr.* ~ **vnder Crist** anyone anywhere 13.208, 14.159, **Cristene** ~ Christian person 15.274, 21.375, B 9.80, 84, 10.356, 362, 15.578, **Cristes** ~ 16.164, 165, B 11.198, **vncristene** ~ non-Christian 12.79, B 11.154; **vnkynde** ~ in-human person 19.182, 216, B 5.269

creaunt *a* (confessed as) vanquished, i.e. submitting [to Christ] in faith 14.132, 153; *and see* **recreaunt** *a*

crede *n* Creed, *spec.* the Apostles Creed 3.359, 8.98

crepen *v* (*p.t.* **crepte** A 12.35, **crope** (*pl.*) B 3.191) crawl 15.20, B 13.18, (*fig.*) B 16.28; creep Pr 200, 1.190, 22.44, [on knees as devotional act] 20.474; withdraw cautiously B 3.191, A 12.35, insinuate (oneself) 17.280

cresse (carse, kerse) *n* 8.321, **welle** ~ water cress 6.292; (*fig.*) thing of no value (? *with pun on* 'curse') 11.14

cryant 14.153 = **creaunt** *a*

crien *v* (*p.t.* **cri(e)d(e)** 1.76, *pl.* **criden** 21.213) shout out Pr 227, 17.222, 19.270, 20.13; ~ **on** shout at 7.57, B 11.70, 18.39, A 12.13; scream 6.140; cry out 4.157, 6.4, 64, 17.222, 21.213, 22.140, B 18.262; ~ **after** summon 22.90, B 15.279; demand B 15.254; call (upon) 22.78, 165, 376; wail 11.42, 18.108, B 9.80; lament tearfully 22.370; beg (for) 6.337, 7.155, 9.346, 13.12, 15.35, 17.246, 19.208, 279, 20.89, B 14.331; ~ **(to)** supplicate (in prayer) 2.1, 3.93, 6.170, 7.147, 155, 19.270, 22.201, B 5.106, 17.222, *pr.p.* Z 5.153; proclaim 7.108, 21.159, 364, B Pr 143; command publicly 4.164

cryket *n* house-cricket, ? salamander 15.243

crimylen *v* ? curl / plait, ? anoint (with oil) *p.p.* 16.352*n*

Crist *n* Christ, *in oaths:* **by** ~ 2.204, 246, 3.283, 4.4, 79, 99, 5.89, 7.282, 304, 8.19, 21, 167, 264, 308, 9.213, 11.141, 15.130, 179, 16.290, 21.401, 22.268, 381, B 5.163, 9.162, 10.343, 13.189, 272, 314, 14.12, 15.301, A 4.144, Z 7.108; *in imprecations:* **ȝeue hem sorwe** 19.309, B 5.106, **so me** ~ **helpe / spede** 4.11, 10.108, B 4.104, Z 7.200; *in assevs:* ~ **haue his soule** A 12.105, **for ~es loue** 15.35, 16.164, B 15.523, **for** ~ **sake** 14.5, B 12.92, **vnder** ~ anywhere (alive / in the world) 11.156, 12.80, 13.208, 14.155, 159; *in phrr.* **Cristes owene beestes** (= the Christian people) B 10.409; ~ **clergie** (= spiritual wisdom) 12.99; ~ **court** 16.166; ~ **creature(s)** 16.164, B 11.198; ~ **cros** 17.203; ~ **fode** 18.14; ~ **good(es)** (= the Church's wealth) B 9.87, 15.104; **~lawes** 17.251; ~ **loue** 17.281; ~ **messager** 21.208; **mynistres** 5.60; ~ **mouth** 11.278; ~ **name** B 15.456, A 12.13; ~ **passion** B 18.9; ~ **patrimonye** (= the Church's wealth) B 15.246; ~ **pees** 17.228; ~ **peple** B 14.72, 15.22; ~ **sonde** 16.134; ~ **tresor** (= the Church's doctrine and sacraments) 14.54, B 10.474; ~ **vycary** 14.70; ~ **wordes** 15.274; ~ **writyng** B 12.82

Cristen(e) *a* Christian 13.89, 16.165, 21.351; *in phrr.* ~ **bloed** 21.448; ~ **clerk** B 15.412; ~ **creature(s)** 15.274, 21.375, B 9.80, A 12.110; ~ **kynde** (= Christian people) B 10.424; ~ **kyng(es)** 3.441, B 13.176; ~ **man** 12.61, B 15.398; ~ **men** 19.256, B 10.351, Z 6.62; ~ **peple** 5.193, 11.270, 13.77, 15.230, 21.343, 364, B 12.158, 15.90; **~prouinces** B 15.608, ~ **reumes** B 15.524; ~ **soules** 11.246, 12.152, 20.406, B 15.430

Cristendo(e)m *n* Christianity, the Christian religion 12.80, 110, 14.53, 17.186, 282, 298, 18.209, 19.8, B 15.446, *in phr.* **cart** ~ 21.332; (the) Christian doctrine B 10.447, faith B 14.11, way of life 12.61, 17.251, baptism 7.234, 12.61, 14.205, 17.77, **B** ?11.215*n*, 12.276, 14.320, 15.351, *in phr.* **cote of** ~ (= baptismal regeneration) B 13.274

Cristene *a as n* Christian 17.183, *pl.* 1.89 *et p.*; *in phrr.* **alle** ~ 1.188; **alle kyne** ~ 17.128; **corsede** ~ 17.212; **euen** ~ 6.75; **false** ~ 17.76; **kynde** ~ 22.73; **parfyt** ~ 22.108; **vnkynde** ~ 17.275, 19.256; **we** ~ 17.293; **ȝe** ~ 21.386

crist(e)nen *v* baptize (into the Christian faith) 17.165, **B** 10.348, 11.67, 15.444, 456, A 12.15, *ger.* (the act of) christening B 14.185

croce A 9.86, †B 8.95 = **crose** *n*

crocer *n* cross-bearer 5.113

#crod *n* curd 8.305, 321, Z 7.286

cro(e)s(s) *n* cross [of crucifixion] 11.257, 14.153, *spec.* the cross of Christ 6.318, 10.58, 20.74, 21.14, 41, 50, 63, 200, 323, B 16.164, A 11.28, (*meton.*) Christ's death on the cross 17.203, 20.112; **on ~ wyse** stretched out on a cross, by crucifying 21.142; ornamental cross / crucifix 5.106, 20.474; (bishop's) cross (of office) **B** 5.12, 15.569, A 5.23; (*meton.*) the Christian faith 17.282, B 15.446, 578; (cross stamped on) coin 17.205, 208, B 5.240; cross-shaped seal 19.8, B 17.6

croft *n* (small enclosed) field [for cultivation] 5.17, 8.31, 314, Z 7.108, (*fig.*) 7.218, 219

crois A 11.28 = **cro(e)s** *n*

crok *n*¹ grappling-iron 20.294

crok *n*² (earthen) cooking-pot 21.281

croked(e) *p.p.a* crooked 2.29; crippled, deformed 9.97, *a as n* 12.105, B 16.109

crompe *n* cramp [disease with painful spasms] 6.78 (B 13.335), 22.82,

cronicle *n* chronicle, history 5.178

croos 17.282, 20.112 = **cro(e)s** *n*

crop *n* top 18.75, **B** 16.42, 69, 70, 75, **to þe ~ ward** towards the top 18.108; crop 22.53

crope(n) *p.t.* Pr 200, B Pr 186, 191 *see* **crepen** *v*

croppen *v* eat up **B** 6.32, 15.401

cros 14.153 *etc.*, = **cro(e)s(s)** *n*

crose *n* crosier 10.93

crouch *n* cross-emblem 7.166

croume *n* scrap (of bread) 8.279, 288

croune *n* (royal) crown 4.79, 135, 20.273, 413, 21.468, 469; crown-image (on coin) 17.205 (*with pun on* heavenly crown of glory), A 4.113; **~ of thornes** 21.49, 323; (crown-like) tiara 2.11, 15.163; (*meton.*) messianic sovereignty B 18.109; clerical tonsure 13.112, **B** 13.243, 15.351, (*meton.*) = priestly ordination B 11.299; hair on the top of the head 11.197, 16.352; top of the head 5.177, 22.184

crounen *v* crown (as king) 10.101, 104, 21.41, (as heavenly king) B 18.372, (*fig.*) 21.257, (as pope) 3.318; bedeck with diadem 2.11; tonsure (cleric) 5.56, 59, 63, 13.125, *ger.* Pr 86

crow *n* (*uninfl. gen.*) crow's 15.163

cruwel *a* pitiless B 13.391

cullen (killen, kullen) *v* (*p.t.* **culd(e)** 8.280, **kild(e)** B 5.163, A 3.251, *p.p.* **culd(e)** 17.289, 21.447, **ykuld** Pr 199, **kulled** B 16.152) strike, **~ to dethe** strike mortally 11.270; kill Pr 199, 1.62, 3.232, 8.30, 280, 10.250, 12.243, 21.447, 22.99, 151, B 5.163; slay

10.101, 17.289; put to death 21.142, B 16.137, 152; destroy 16.26

cultour B 6.104 = **kultour** *n*

cumsen Z 3.156, **cumsyng** *ger.* Z 3.172 *see* **com(e)sen** *v*

cunnen A 11.185, †12.32, Z 7.49 = **connen** *v*

cuntre A Pr 95, 2.43 = **contre(y)(e)** *n*

#curato(u)r *n* churchman with 'cure of souls' 17.290, 22.327, B 15.90; priest with spiritual charge of a parish 11.249, 15.16, 16.273, 279, 17.280, 21.413, 454, 22.282, B 1.195; spiritual authority 21.223,

cure *n* spiritual responsibility Pr 86; **~ (of soules)** pastoral responsibility (in a parish) 22.233, 237, 253; benefice B 11.300

curen *v* exercise pastoral responsibility 22.326 (*with pun on* heal); heal (? *with pun on latter*) 14.70

curious *a* artfully cut 21.288

cursen *p.p.* 3.106, 178, B 13.331, A 10.140, 148 *see* **corsen** *v*

curteis(e) *a* B 13.15, 459, **A** 3.59, 4.105; **curteisie** *n* B 5.89, 10.310, 11.439, 12.77, 14.147, 15.303; **curteisli(che)** *av* B 13.31, 46, 180, 199, A 11.177; *see* **corteys** *a*, **cortesye** *n*, **corteysliche** *av*

†cusen *v* charge with an offence Pr 95

custe *p.p.* 20.466; *see* **kissen** *v*

custume *n* usage, law 3.373; practice, behaviour 3.206, 9.18; traditional practice 14.73, B 12.97

cuueren 3.64 = **keueren** *v*¹

daffe *n* fool, idiot 1.138, 10.179, 13.235

daggen *v* ornament by cutting at the edges 22.143

day(e) *n* day Pr 226, 2.98, 238, 3.182, 303, 6.161, 7.18, 8.277, 10.228, 16.319, 18.283, **B** 1.121, 3.312, 5.489, 10.96, 13.415, **A** 7.135, 12.66; **thre ~es** 10.113, 15.70, 18.161, 20.31, **in / ar thre ~es aftur** within the space of three days 18.161, 20.41, 22.177; daytime 1.32, B 16.166; daylight 12.154, 20.215, 470, 21.150, (*person.*) 20.60; dawn, daybreak 1.113, 7.65, 20.126; day of the ecclesiastical year **B** 5.2, 11.313; day appointed / agreed upon B 5.241; *in pl.* **daies** = time 1.101, 20.111, 21.101; life 20.53, B 18.53, A 12.94, Z 5.73; *in phrr.* **~ after other** day after day 10.114, B 16.138, A 11.92; **~ bi ~** every day B 15.281; **~ and / ne / or nyghte(s)** at all times 1.32, 9.222, 11.192, 13.190, 17.29, 92, 171, 245, 19.218, (*trs*) 19.270, 21.20, 141, **B** 9.97, 13.369, 18.97; **~ of dome** Judgement Day 9.321, 351, 12.70, 22.294, **B** 7.17, 172, 10.358, 12.91, (*and see* **domes ~**) **~ withouten ende** for ever 2.106, 19.252; **~es doen** days ago 15.70; **~ es iourne** day's stint of work 16.5; **~ sterre** morning star A 6.80; *in time phrr:* **many ~** many a day, often A 5.71; for a long time (now) 5.156, 20.179; **this ~** today 17.223, 20.137, the present time B 16.148, **~ þre ~es** three days from today B 17.110; **a ~ hennes** a day's walk from here 10.128; **prime ~es** prime of the day (= 6–9 A.M) A 12.60; **firste ~** B 5.166; **thridde ~** 7.136,

ferþe ~ A 12.82; *in n. phrr.* **deth** ~ day of one's death 1.130, 9.350, 10.303, **B** 7.114, 12.245, 14.106; **domes** ~ Judgement Day 5.122 *et p.*; **fastyng** ~ day (appointed by Church) for obligatory fasting 2.100, 6.182, 433; **feste** ~ religious feast day 5.30; **haue gode** ~ farewell A 12.75; **haly (holy)** ~ feast-day of (obligatory) religious observance 6.272, 359, 7.25, 9.231, 13.85, A 7.12; **lyf** ~ day of one's life 3.187, B 1. 27; **loue** ~ settlement-day 11.17; *in prep. phrr.* **a** ~ one / a certain day 1.27, daily / ? on the next day 8.331; **be þis** ~ today 7.9, 8.302, 17.223, (*as assev.*) = 'I swear' 4.172, **B** 13.106, 17.63, A 7.170; **a** ~ one / ? in (the course of) one day 20.41, daily B 15.283; **on þe** ~ daily / ? during one day 10.31

dale *n* hollow Pr 17, 1.1, 55; valley, *in phr.* **bi ~s and hulles** = everywhere 10.232

dame *n* mother 2.120, 7.137, 8.81, 9.316, 20, 282, B 5.37; (*as title*) Lady, Madame 6.133, 11.1, B 10.229, Mistress Pr 226, 8.80

dam(o)ysele *n* noble maiden 20.470; young woman B 11.12; handmaiden 10.139

dampnacion *n* damnation B 12.87

dampnen *v* condemn 9.158, 17.213, 215, 19.285; condemn to hell, damn 6.324, 7.146, 12.78, 245, 17.137, 215, 20.308, 427, **B** 2.103, 12.91, 18.293, 379; *p.p.a* damned 19.232, 241, B 10.428

dar *pr. sg.* Pr 218, B 5.101, A Pr 38, Z 6.75, *pr.pl.* B Pr 152 *see* **durren** *v*

date *n* date [of execution of a document], ? name 2.114; year, time B 13.269

dauben *v* daub (with clay), *ger.* 8.198

dauncelen *v* make much of A 11.30

daunger *n* power [of the devil] 18.280; danger / risk (of death) 14.145

daunsen *v* dance 20.182, *ger.* dance 10.180

daunten B 3.288 = **adaunten**, B 15.400 = **endaunten**; cherish B 10.37

dawen *v* dawn 20.470, (*fig.*) arise 20.183

deba(e)t(e) *n* dispute 6.387, **at** ~ in dispute 6.123, B 15.427; strife 21.252, B 5.97

deceite (deseyte) *n* deception 20.376, B 10.19; **in** ~ **of** to deceive Pr 77; trickery 2.128; false appearance B 12.130

deceyuen *v* play tricks on B 10.214, 217; cheat, defraud 11.16, B Pr 79; lead astray 1.40, 17.184, 18.123, 174

declaren *v* determine [matter of law] 2.148, [verdict] 16.122; plead [legal case] 9.49

declynen *v* decline grammatically A 4.133

***decourren (of)** *v* depart from B 14.194c

decre(e) (degre) *n* law, edict A 11.241; canon law 17.113

decretal *n* papal decree, *pl.* (collection of) decretals B 5.422

#decretistre (of canoen) *n* expert in canon law 15.86

ded 1.182 *etc* = **de(e)d(e)** *a*

ded(e) *p.t.* Pr 123, 12.56 *etc*; *pl.* 12.245, 14.98, Z Pr 54; *see* **don** *v*

dede *n* act(ion), deed 1.30, 3.470, 6.333, 7.3, 146, 150, 10.240, 12.245, 16.191, 20.92, 98, 21.183, **B** 4.68, 5.506, 11.51, A 5.254, 10.121; transaction B 5.241; heroic deed 7.140, 21.133, 134; (sexual) act 10.295, 13.155; (virtuous) act(ion) 1.182, B 11.51; sin(ful act) 3.415, 10.232, **B** 12.76, 14.325, 18.334; work, task Pr 225, 3.303, 5.9, 21.279, 331; fact, reality B 13.133, *in phr.* **don in** ~ really do (sth) **B** 5.43, 10.358, A 4.108, Z 4.144; written document (*with pun on* 'effect') A 12.87; charter, legal deed 2.114, 20.191, **B** 2.161, 5.241; *in phrr.* †**wan** ~ evil action Z 5.152; **wel** ~ virtuous action 3.69, 15.305, B 3.70

de(e)d(e) *a* dead 1.182, 12.78, 186, 13.56, 20.64, 66, 72, 158, **B** 3.193, 14.321, 15.593, 18.97; *a as n (sg.)* 20.98, 22.294, (*pl.*) 9.21, 338, 21.53, 197

de(e)dly(ch) *a* destructive B 10.237; mortal (to the soul) 1.142, 5.122, 6.276 (B 13.388), 7.209, 9.238, 10.43, 12.37, 17.203, 291, 20.376, **B** 8.50, 9.207, 13.406, 14.78, 83, 88, 90, 95; *av* grievously, mortally B 5.114, A 10.156, (*of sin*) 9.329

deef *a* (*pl.* **deue**) deaf 11.61, B 10.132, *a as n* the deaf 21.130

deel *n* part B 15.487

deelen B 1.199, 10.215 = **delen** *v*

deen *n* dean [= head of cathedral chapter] B 13.65, [= official in charge of deanery, sub-division of arch-deaconry] B 2.173, A Pr 92, Z 2.146

de(e)p(e) *a* deep Pr 17, 1.55, 126, 20.64, 407, B 1.115, Z Pr 100; profound 20.405; *av* deep(ly) 6.166, 9.145, 11.301, 305, 14.149, 15.99, 21.365, Z 7.245, (*comp.*) **deppore** 11.130, B 15.199

deere *a*¹ B Pr 210 *et p.* = **dere** *a*¹

deere² *a* severe B 14.171 (*or* = *a*¹)

deere B 9.65, 12.42 = **dere** *av*

dees-playere *n* dice-player 8.72

dee† B 3.109 *et p.*, = **de(e)th(e)** *n*

defamen *v* dishonour A 11.64, Z 7.260; speak against B Pr 190, Z 3.121; *and see* **famen** *v*

defaute *n* want [of clothes, food *etc*] 7.305, 8.145, 213, 245, 352, 9.100, 206, 311, 10.203, 11.43, 14.16, 15.273, 294, 298, 17.68, 20.211, **B** 5.7, 9.82, 10.361, 14.165, 15.135; **payn** ~ lack of bread 15.231; defect B 11.214, 391, 12.95, 15.346; mistake 13.121; sin 12.38, B 10.277, **in** ~ guilty (of crime / sin) 2.153; (morally) to blame B 5.144; fault, responsibility 17.89

defenden *v* defend, protect 8.34, 97, 9.9, 16.133, 17.289, 19.268, 21.42, 470, 480, 22.76, 257, B 16.246; speak in defence of 16.36; forbid 3.68, 14.6, 16.168, 20.110, A 6.81, 7.168, 8.40, 12.18, 19

defense *n* prohibition 20.199, Z 6.75

#defyen *v*¹ reject (contemptuously) 22.66

def(f)yen *v*² digest 6.429, 16.224, (*fig.*) 6.87; be digested 6.438; help to be digested Pr 231

def(f)oulen *v* trample on 3.191; treat shamefully A 11.60; mortify 17.195; damage 8.31; sully B 14.24

defrauden *v* defraud 9.64

degre(e)[1] *n* level 18.56, 84; stage A 11.90; rank (in society) 5.67, 17.111; respect B 9.145

degre[2] A 11.241 = **decre** *n*

d(e)yen (d(e)iȝen) *v* die Pr 102, 1.142, 162, 2.221, 3.400, 5.40, 149, 6.318, 7.9, 129, 8.107, 127, 296, 352, 9.238, 10.58, 60, 196, 12.115, 14.211, 15.260, 16.4, 22, 17.192, 19.68, 204, 232, 277, 20.56, 58, 70, 137, 197, 304, 335, 404, 21.175, 22.19, 50, 177, 313, **B** 10.352, 11.283, 12.87, 13.406, 409, 15.138, 16.166, **A** 8.37, 9.47, 10.177, **Z** 3.131, 5.144, (*fig.*) 12.183, 20.429; = become subject to death 20.374, 397; be put to death 3.410, 415, 428, 4.5, 7.208, 10.232, 14.146, 17.271, 20.27, 22.62, B 15.518, 521; = give one's life 17.291; be extinguished 6.335

dey(i)ng(e) *ger.* dying, (time of) 9.38, 20.79, (moment of) 17.144; (experience of) 20.222, *in phr.* **deth** ~ hour of death 7.85, 110, state of spiritual death B 11.176; death 17.276 (B 15.525)

dey(e)s *n* dais, raised seat (of judgement) B 7.17; high table 11.40, 15.66

deilen A 11.162 = **delen** *v*

deynen *v*[1] deign 8.331, 11.61

deynen *v*[2] ?disdain Z 7.312n

deynous *a* disdainful, arrogant 10.81, 16.226

deynte(e) *n* delight 11.316; luxury 15.303; delicacy 15.92

deitee *n* divine nature B 10.56

dekne *n* deacon Z 7.231

delen *v* (*p.t.* **delt** A 12.104) give 1.195; give (as) alms 3.76, 11.69, 71, 13.95, 19.218, 21.379, **B** 10.28, 11.275, 12.245, 13.300, A 11.243; apportion 21.216; share out 8.106, B 15.246; deliver (blow) A 12.104; (have) deal(ings) (with) 8.77, 19.226, 21.352, B 5.245; have sexual intercourse 9.167

delicat *a* luxurious, ~**ly(che)** *av* choicely, fastidiously 6.166, 16.91, B 5.375

delys *n* sensual pleasure Z 3.161

delit *n* pleasure B 10.361; sensual delight A 2.65, Z 3.163

delitable *a* pleasurable 1.32

deliten *v* (*refl.*) take pleasure in B 1.29

delyueren *v* free 18.283, B 15.345; discharge 13.40; hand back to 13.13

delt *p.t.* A 12.104 *see* **delen** *v*

deluen *v* (*p.t. pl.* **doluen** B 6.190, *p.p.* **(i)doluen** B 6.180 / A 6.33) dig 21.365, 367, **B** 5.545, 6.141, 247, A 11.187; bury B 6.180, A 7.170

deluer (deluare) *n* digger Pr 225, 8.114, 198, 352

deluuye *n* deluge 11.252

demen *v* (pass) judge(ment on) Pr 94, 4.172, 11.215, 16.185, 21.307, **B** 4.181, 15.551; pronounce (judgement) B 13.306; censure, criticize 6.20, 8.83, 16.226,

B 5.113; adjudicate between 20.36; condemn 3.459, B 15.549; administer 4.175, *ger.* 12.81; judge (at Last Day) 9.21, 21.175, 197; direct B 13.172, Z 5.73; ordain 10.100; think, hold 3.290, 9.319, **B** 3.188, 6.180, Z Pr 54; believe B 19.148; tell 1.82, B 13.306

demme *a* dark 20.362, B 3.193, Z Pr 16; *av*, **loke** ~ have poor eyesight 11.127

dene[1] *n* din, clamour 2.217, 20.64, 126

dene[2] = **deen** *n*

denyen *v* refuse 11.265

dent A 12.104 = **dount** *n*

#**dentiesliche** *av* with choice food 8.323

†**deol** B 18.281 = **doel** *n*

dep 1.55 = **de(e)p(e)** *a*

departable *a* distinguishable 18.215, 19.30, 98

departen *v* part company 17.147; divide B 7.157; dissolve 22.139

depe Pr 17, 1.126 *etc*, Z 7.245 = **de(e)p(e)** *a, av*

deposen *v* remove from office 17.215; put down B 15.551

deppore (deppere) *comp.* 11.130, B 15.199 *see* **de(e)p(e)** *av*

deprauen *v* vilify 3.224, B 5.143

dere *a* excellent, (most) honoured, [of God] Pr 218, 1.83, 13.17, 168, **B** 11.407, 14.325, [of the Church] 7.65, [of a person] 10.127, (*a as n*) B 6.253, [of love] 11.135; (*sup.*) precious B 2.13; expensive B 14.74, [through scarcity] 8.158, 10.199, B 14.171n; dear, beloved 2.33, 8.91, 106, 15.197, 17.291, B 12.12

dere *av* dearly, at a high price 19.267, ~ **abyggen** pay a severe penalty for 8.83, ~ **liken** be well pleasing 8.315, A 6.80

derely *av* in the best manner 21.2

derfly *av* violently 3.415

der(i)en *v* harm 9.38, 19.20, 20.25, 297

derke *n* darkness 12.154, 13.56

derk(e) *a* (*comp.* **derkore**) dark 1.55, 20.62, **B** Pr 16, 1.115; darkened 20.60; black, ? wicked 21.21; hard to understand 11.130; ~**nesse** *n* darkness 18.117, 19.200, 20.67, 104, 114, 126, **B** 5.494, 16.251; ~ **liche** *av* obscurely B 10.372

derling *n* dear one, beloved A 12.19

derne *a* secret 3.291; hidden B 2.176; private B 13.54; intimate 10.295, 13.155; *av* ~**(ly)** inconspicuously 13.163

derrest *sup.* B 2.13 *see* **dere** *a*

derste *p.t.* Pr 193 *see* **durren** *v*

derthe *n* (period of) scarcity / high price (of food) 8.351, 16.311, B 14.171, 176

derworth(e) *a* (most) excellent 13.17; precious 1.83, 6.89

#**desauowen** *v* disclaim 3.319

descenden *v* (*p.t.* ~**et**) come down 17.247

deschargen *v* relieve 17.231, ~ **of** relieve (of liability for) B 4.29

descreuen (descryuen) *v* describe 6.196, 20.212, B 5.78; say the names of 22.94; explain B 16.53, 66, Z 3.147

deseyte Pr 77, 2.128, 20.376 = **deceite** *n*

desert *n* reward earned 3.291

deseruen *v* deserve, merit 2.133, 134, 3.294, 4.172, 5.32, 8.40, 204, 14.214, 16.4, 6, 146, **B** 6.87, 14.138, **A** 5.241, 12.92; earn 3.297, 301, 5.42, 45, 8.228, 13.85, B 14.126

desiren *v* wish 22.323, B 9.105, A 12.45; wish (to have) **B** 3.246, 252, 14.188, A 10.125; long for **B** 3.99, 15.468, A 10.47, Z 3.167, (*ger.*) craving B 13.356; desire (sexually) 1.179

#despeyr(e) *n* despair (of salvation) 9.38, 22.164, Z 5.144

despen(d)en *v* spend 8.235, 12.237, **B** 5.263, 10.324; employ 14.18, B 12.48; *and see* **spen(d)en** *v*

despicen, despisen 14.64, 6.80 *etc, see* **dispisen** *v*

desplesen *v* cause offence to 8.84, B 14.325, (*refl.*) take offence B 13.136

despoilen *v* rob 13.57

desputen 10.20, 12.52 = **disputen** *v*

dessallouwynge *n* refusal of credit 16.7

desseyuen *v* 1.40 = **deceyuen** *v*

destyne *n* destiny, providence 8.296

destrere *n* riding-horse (of noble breed) A 2.137

destruyen (destroyen) *v* destroy B 3.271; wipe out 9.17, 12.236, 16.172, 17.291, 22.383; kill 14.22, 19.182, 258, 266, 276, A 11.288; ruin welfare (of) 3.206, A 7.30, 124; take away 18.43; damage Pr 213; overcome 20.244, **B** 10.329, 16.165, 18.348, A 10.76; neutralise 20.158 B 2.14; drive out 21.313, B 13.250; squander Pr 24

de(e)th(e) *n* death 2.106, 8.187, 9.17, 52, 15.260, 286, 308, 17.203, 19.20, 20.34, 53, 137, 143, 160, 217, 297, 390 (2), 407, 21.51, 175, 308, 22.139, (*person.*) Pr 17, 20.28 *et p.*, 22.89 *et p.*, A 12.63 *et p.*, (death by) execution 3.459, 17.270, 20.424, 427; death-dealing calamity 11.64, 252; (= the plague) 8.351, ? 10.199, 16.311; spiritual death, perdition B 12.87; *in phrr.* ~ **day** day / time of (one's) death 1.130, 9.350, 10.303, **B** 3.109, 7.50, 12.245, 14.106, ~ **deynge** time of dying 7.85, 110, = condition of (spiritual) death B 11.176; ~ **yuel** fatal potion (*fig.*) B 18.53; ~ **of kynde** death (in the course) of nature 20.219; **bale** ~ baleful death B 18.35*n*, **doctour of** ~ death-dealing physician (*fig.*) 20.402; **to** ~ **e** 1.166, 3.476, 11.270, 14.42, 21.10, 141

dette *n* debt, what is owed (by / to sb.) Pr 91, 3.304, 8.107, 13.37, 75, 15.12; obligation (to God / one's fellow man) 9.273, 13.37; debt (to God) incurred through sin 6.299, 22.10, B 5.227; obligation to make satisfaction for sin 21.191, 22.322, *in phrr.* **in** ~ in debt 22.294; into debt B 7.79; **out(e) of** ~ free of debt / obligation 16.4, B 14.107

deuk 21.308 = **duk** *n*

deul[1] 8.127, 19.320 = **doel** *n*

deul[2] Z 2.84, 8.54 = **deuel** *n*

deuren Z 2.72, 3.30 = **du(y)ren** *v*

deue 21.130 *see* **deef** *a*

deuel *n* the Devil [Satan] 8.127, 278, 10.278, 302, 15.260, 18.111, 117, 19.241, 20.161, 297, 325, **B** 1.28, 29, 2.103, 7.114, 9.63, 14.78, 16.165, **A** 2.65, 11.22; (one of the) devil(s) 9.38, 19.20, 20.340, 21.21, **B** 7.50, 16.120, 18.158, 281; *in phrr.* ~**es dysors** 8.52, ~ **power** 18.283, B 10.237, ~ **punfolde** B 5.624; **date of þe** ~ 2.114

deuer (deuoir) *n* duty 17.122, **B** 11.284, 13.213; appointed task 16.5, 17.92, B 14.150, 153; best A 12.2

deuyden *v* divide arithmetically 21.241; distribute 21.216

deuyn *n* divinity, theology A Pr 90

deuinen *v* prophesy 17.312, 21.148, **B** 7.158, 15.598, 603; interpret Pr 218, 9.305; ponder 11.130; find out (about) 21.241; contrive 11.266; expound 15.99; determine 10.102

deuynour (dyuynour) *n* theologian 15.86, 124, **B** 7.136, 10.452

deuisen *v* consider 21.279; plan, specify 7.190, 8.200; fashion 21.331

deuocion *n* devout adoration B 15.295

deuoir B 11.284, 13.213, 14.150, 153 = **deuer** *n*

deuors *n* annulment 22.139, B 2.176

deuouren *v* devour (*fig.*) 2.140; consume 8.139; squander 16.280

deuouteliche *av* fervently 17.245

deuoutours *a pl.* (*or a as n*) adulterous / adulterers 2.184

deuoutrye *n* adultery B 2.176

dewe[1] *n* dew 7.264, 17.21*n*

dewe[2] *a* owed, owing 3.304

dewen A 11.199, 201 = **dowen** *v*

#dya *n* pharmaceutical preparation 22.174

*diapen(i)dion *n* sweet cough-medicine B 5.122

*dyademen *v* crown, *p.p.* 3.440

diamaund *n* diamond B 2.13

diche (dykke) *n* ditch [defensive] B Pr 16, [drainage] 13.235

dych B 20.19 = **dysch** *n*

dichen (dyken) *v* dig a ditch [defensive] 21.365, [boundary / enclosure / drainage] **B** 5.545, 6.141, 190, 19.239, **A** 6.33, 11.187

dyde *p.t.* 6.9, **dide(n)** B 1.28, 5.540 *et p.*; *see* **do(o)n** *v*

*dido *n* old wives' tale 15.172*n*

dyen Pr 102, 5.149 = **d(e)yen** *v*

dyeten *v* (*refl.*) regulate diet 8.290

diffoulen 8.31 = **defoulen** *v*

diggen (*p.t.* ~**ed**) dig 8.114

digneliche *av* honourably B 7.172; worthily Z Pr 54

dignite *n* position of authority A Pr 92

dyhten *v* (*p.t.* **dihte**, *p.p.* **di3t(e)**) prepare 8.315; get ready 21.2, A 2.137; have sexual intercourse with 1.27

dyk(ke) 13.235, A Pr 16 = **diche** *n*

dyken B 5.545, 6.141, 190, A 11.188 = **dichen** *v*

dyker(e) (dikare) *n* ditcher Pr 225, 6.368, 8.114

dym B 3.193, Z Pr 16 = **demme** *a*

#**dyme** *n* tithe 17.227

dymmen *v* grow dim 6.406

dynen *v* dine, have dinner Pr 228, 7.5, 8.331, 15.27, 16.4, 91, 21.386, B 5.377; eat 6.174, 8.277, 302, A 5.72

dyner *n* dinner 4.38, 8.315, 15.32

dyngen *v* knock (at door) 16.168; ~ **adoun** knock down B 10.329; ~ **vpon (Dauid)** pound away at (reciting) the Psalms B 3.312, (**sheues**) thresh grain B 6.141

dynt B 18.26, 20.105 = **dount** *n*

disalowen *v* refuse credit (*fig.*) B 14.130; *and see* **dessallouwynge** *n*

disceruen 13.85 = **deseruen** *v*

disceuen 17.184 = **deceyuen** *v*

disch(e), dysch *n* bowl [for drink] 20.405, 22.19; dish [for food] 15.92, B 13.54; platter 10.180

disciple *n* disciple 9.118, 18.166, **B** 13.430, 15.88, A 11.295

discomfiten *v* (*p.p.* **disconfit**) defeat Pr 108, 112

discrete *a* discerning, prudent 5.84

discryuen B 5.78, 16.53, 66 = **descreuen** *v*

diseruen 2.133, 134 = **deseruen** *v*

disgisen *v* deck out B Pr 24

dyso(u)r *n* minstrel 8.52, 15.172, A 11.30

dispayr 22.164 = **despeyr(e)** *n*

dispenden 12.237 = **despen(d)en** *v*

#**disperacion** *n* despair (of salvation) 19.291

dispisen (dispicen) *v* look down on 2.84, 21.34; despise 9.190; treat with contempt 6.80, 14.64; regard as worthless 7.118; disregard 17.251; revile 6.122, 20.40, 95; disparage 16.214

dispit *n* spite 8.184

displesen B 13.136, 14.325 = **desplesen** *v*

disputen *v* engage in (formal) debate / controversy 6.122, 10.20, 114, 12.52, **B** 10.447, 11.319; reason about 11.36; argue 6.137, B 10.111, 130; maintain / defend by argument 11.158

disseyuen 11.16 = **deceyuen** *v*

dissh B 13.54 = **disch(e)** *n*

disshere *n* dish-seller 6.371

distru(y)en Pr 213, 9.17, 12.236, 14.22, 19.258, 20.244, 21.313 = **distroyen** *v*

ditten (dutten Z) *v* shut A 7.176

dyuen *v* plunge, dive 13.168, 14.106, B 12.165

dyuer 16.5 = **deuer** *n*

diuerse *a* various, different 2.98, 14.79, **B** Pr 152, 12.67; various kinds of B 15.424; ~**ly** *av* variously, differently 15.81

diuersen *v* differ 17.133

diuinen B 7.158 = **deuynen** *v*

diuinite *n* theology 17.113, B 7.136

dyuynour 15.86 *etc* = **deuynour** *n*

diuors B 2.176 = **deuors** *n*

don Pr 109 *et p.*; *see* **do(o)n** *v*

dobben *v* dub, create (sb.) knight 1.101, (*p.p.*) 20.11

dobelar *n* plate, platter 15.92

Dobest *n* Do-best 10.76 *et p.*

Dobet *n* Do-better 10.76 *et p.*

docto(u)r *n* Doctor of the Church [one of the four great Latin Fathers] 21.317, B 9.73; theological authority Pr 59, B 10.452; learned theologian Pr 85, B 15.73; doctor (of divinity) 15.66 *et p.*; authoritative teacher 11.95, 135, 15.126; doctor (of medicine) 22.177; *in phrr.* ~ **of decre** 17.113, ~ **of lawe** B 15.243 (= doctor of Canon Law); ~ **of deth** (*fig.*) teacher of death 20.402; **Poulynes** ~ expert theologian / canon lawyer of the Pauline order A 2.73*n*

doctrine *n* teaching 11.226; profession, order B 2.109

doel (deol, deul) *n* suffering 8.127, 20.304, †B 18.281; lamentation 19.320, **B** 5.380, 15.146; ~ **ful** *a* miserable, painful B 15.521

do(e)m *n* judgement 2.129, 17.213; judgement at law, (judicial) sentence 3.470, 9.341, 20.27, 195, 427, 12.90, B 2.206, 11.145; (moral) judgement / decision 16.185; = the (Last) Judgement 6.297, 346, 9.321, 338, 351, 12.70, 20.427, 22.294, **B** 7.17, 10.358, 12.91; **domesday** *n* Judgement Day 5.122, 6.324, 9.21, 11.252, 16.36, 21.197; **domesman** *n* judge 21.307

doen 15.229, *pr. pl.* 6.155 etc, *p.p.* 15.70 etc, **doest** *2 pr.sg.* 8.83 *see* **do(o)n** *v*

dogge *n* dog 9.261, B 5.117

do3ter B 11.246 = **douhter** *n*

doynge *ger.* (performance of an) act 3.291, 292; action 8.91, 21.130, 433, B 15.476

doysayne (do3eyne) 22.164 = **doseyne** *num.*

doke *n* duck 6.174, B 17.63

dol *n* alms B 3.71

dollen *v* become dazed / stupid Z 4.124

doluen *p.t. pl.* B 6.190, *p.p.* B 6.180, 14.321

dombe 21.130 = **do(u)mbe** *a*

dome *n* 6.297 etc = **do(e)m** *n*

domen *v* Z 1.31, 5.73 = **demen** *v*

*****dompyng** *n* dabchick, moorhen 13.168

do(o)n *v* (*infl. inf.* ~**e** 3.232, 7.229, 8.117, 210, B 4.28, 6.203, 11.376, 419, 13.291, 20.371; *p.p.* (**y)do(e)n(e)** Pr 126, 2.128, 7.140, 20.111, **B** 3.263, 18.53, A 6.33; *a as n* (*infl. gen.*) **done** B 18.300; *3 pl pr.* **doon** B Pr 224; *3 sg. and pl. pr.* **do(o)th** 1.24, 6.335, *imp. pl.* **dooþ** B 5.43; *p.t.* **dede(n)** Pr 123 *et p.*, 14.98, Z Pr 54, *p.t. subjv.* 10.189, 17.92, 20.429, **dyde** 6.9, **dide(n)** B 1.28 *et p.*, 5.540 *etc*) do (sth.), perform an act(ion) Pr 126, 3.81, 319, 4.41, 6.53, 276, 7.140, 146, 10.43, 295, 12.90, 245, 15.229, 17.92, 122, 20.161, 376, 21.279, B 1.28, A 4.108; complete [task] 16.5, 21.183, 331; make 19.255; cause (to / to happen) 1.102, 2.221, 3.172, 6.155, 8.296, †11.161, 14.23, 16.91, 226, 17.303,

18.145, 19.299, 20.320, 21.311, 22.380, **B** 3.200, 5.94, 241, 540, 14.83, 15.405, **A** 5.77, 9.90; cause (not to) / prevent (from) 19.306; place 10.138; provide 7.110; (*refl.*) betake oneself 2.221, 10.278, 21.2; put 21.10; give 9.132, **B** 6.54; act, behave 3.331, 6.324, 9.321, 341, 351, 10.110, 11.226 (1), 12.11, **B** 8.101, 10.422, 12.234, 15.420; fare **B** 1.34; (*as emph. auxil.*) do 9.328, 19.175, Z 7.268, did **B** 12.168; (*as subst. for specific v.*) Pr 123, 9.112, 10.179, 16.55, 17.209, 219, 307, 21.44, 101, 212, 22.6, 374, **B** 5.37, 7.123, 10.406, **A** 4.53, 5.132; *in phrr.* ~ **equite** dispense justice 21.310, ~ **hit vpon** appeal to 2.39, ~ **lawe** enforce the law 3.446, 21.308; **what done** what kind of **B** 18.300

donet *n* elementary grammar (*fig.*) 6.215*n*

dong(e) *n* dung, manure 4.144, 8.184, 198, 312, 12.226, 231, 233, **B** 3.310, A 7.176, ~ **hep** *n* dung-heap 16.264, ~ **hill B** 15.111

donge(o)n *n* fortress **B** Pr 15, 1.59, Z Pr 100

doom B 2.206 = **do(e)m** *n*

doon B Pr 206 *et p.*, **doone B** 4.28 = **do(o)n** *v*

dore *n* doorway 6.406; door 67, A 11.95, 12.36; ~ **nayl** *n* door-stud 1.182

dorste *p.t.* 20.448, **B** 5.90, 11.86, 16.212, 214 *see* **durren** *v*

doseyne (dosoyne) *num.* dozen 4.38, 6.368, 22.164

doten *v* behave foolishly, *p.p.* foolish 1.138

doth 3 *pr. sg., pl.* Pr 225, 1.24 *etc*; *see* **do(o)n** *v*

double *a* twofold [= of amount] **B** 14.148, 153, 156, 15.59, [= of kind] **B** 2.13; ~ **fold** *a* / *av* double / twice over 9.344

doubler *n* platter **B** 13.82

do(ug)hter *n* 1.27 [Lot's], 2.33 [Truth's], 2.124, 3.368, 6.134, 8.81 [Piers'], 106, 10.139 [Dowel's], 10.180 [Herod's], 266, 20.472 [Will's], **B** 6.14, 11.246

douhty *a* valiant 11.266, (*comp.*) **B** 5.101, *sup.* ~ **(ok)est** 7.140, 21.134, = most formidable **B** 10.452; ~ **lyche** *av* valiantly 20.36

do(u)mb(e) *a* dumb, *as n (pl.)* the dumb 21.130; speechless **B** 10.139; failing to bark **B** 10.287; *as n (sg.)* the mute one [*sc.* the Psalter] 2.39, 40

doun *n* hill 4.51; upland A 10.173

doun (down) *av* down 1.4, 18.34, 111, 20.72, 86, 143, 340, 21.340, **B** 1.95, 6.30, 13.21, 14.92, **A** 5.215, 10.217; downward 20.88, ~ **riht** *av* utterly, ? certainly 20.197c

d(o)unt (dynt, dent) *n* blow, stroke 8.187, 20.25, 22.105, A 12.104

doute *n* (state) of uncertainty 6.284,(**B** 13.398), A 9.60*n*; doubt 16.32, **B** 12.32; fear 14.69, **B** Pr 152, **A** 10.82, 11.299

[**douth**, ~ **in douth** in the world, anywhere ? A 9.60*n*]

douten *v* doubt 16.230; fear 10.127, 199, 20.312, A 10.80

douue (dowue) *n* dove 17.171, 239, **B** 15.408

do wel *v. phr. as quasi-n.* 9.289, 21.116, **B** 13.111; (*person.*) Do-well 9.318 *et p.*

#**dowen** *v* endow 3.319, 17.220, A 11.199, 201

down 18.34, 111 *etc* = **doun** *av*

drad *contr. pr.* **B** 9.96, *p.p.* 21.21,~**de(n)** *p.t.* 6.276, 15.286, 16.311, 22.65, **B** 13.406, ~ **dyst** *p.t.* 2 *sg.* Z 3.131 *see* **dreden** *v*

draf *n* pig-swill 11.9; lees of ale 21.402

dranke *p.t.* 15.66 *see* **drinken** *v*

drap(i)er *n* clothier 6.215, 250

drat *contr. pr.* 7.72, 12.154, 22.380, **B** 9.93 *see* **dreden** *v*

drauht *n* draught, measure 22.223

drawen *v* (*p.t.* **drow(e)** 6.215 *etc*, *p.p.* **(y)drawe** 8.288, 20.139, **B** 10.37, A 11.145) pull 2.190; draw 15.57, 21.402; stretch 6.216; bring 11.314, A 11.145, ~ **forþ** advance **B** 10.37; lead **B** 5.43; attract 8.52, A 4.108; carry 8.312; remove 8.288, 20.139; ~ **(to)** approach 6.406, 8.190, 9.52, 13.99, 148, 15.286, 22.200; turn 19.63; (*refl.*) betake (oneself) 6.215, 9.145, 13.147, **B** 18.111

drawere *n* 6.369, 8.287 *see* **lach** ~, **toth** ~

dred(e) *n* fear 7.209, 8.187, 11.64, **B** 15.413, A 10.82, (*person.*) 2.217, **B** 2.209; anxiety 12.239, **B** Pr 152; terror 18.117, 20.60, 22.200, Z Pr 100, †**B** 7.34; ~ **of dispayr**, ~ **of disperacion** terror arising from (spiritual) despair 22.164, 19.291; awe (of God) 16.306, A 10.79, 118, 122; respect 12.248; = doubt 14.10; = danger, risk Pr 126, 5.121, 7.307, 14.108, 16.7, **B** 12.168

dreden *v* (*contr. pr.* (= **dredeth**), *sg.* **drad B** 9.96, **dred B** 13.413, **drat** 7.72 *etc*, *pl.* 22.380, *p.t.* **dradde(n)** 6.276 *etc*, 2 *sg.* **dreddest** 3.193, *p.p.* **drad** 21.21) (*refl.*) be afraid 7.9, 72, 85 (**B** 13.426), 9.238, 12.239, 20.325, **B** 9.89, 18.285, Z 3.131; fear, be afraid (of) 6.276, 9.17, 10.99, 12.154, 13.56, 15.260, 16.311, 22.154, **B** 3.193, 9.96, 10.288, 13.406; stand in awe (of) 9.14, **B** 9.93, 95, 204, A 10.216; (regard with) respect 8.159, 10.127; shun 1.32, 22.380

dredful *a* dread, terrible 9.338, 22.89, **B** Pr 16, 1.59; ~**ly** *av* fearfully 19.64; **dredles** *av* without doubt A 11.194

#**dregges** *n. pl.* dregs, lees 8.193, 21.402

drem *n* dream 9.305; **loue** ~ **B** 16.20*n*

*dremel(e)s** *n* dream 15.17, **B** 7.155, 13.14

dremen *v* dream †22.378, **B** 8.69, 20.378; (*impers.*) 20.6

drenchen *v* drown **B** 8.50, A 10.60, (be) drown(ed) **B** 12.168

dreuelen *v* slobber 11.9, **B** 10.41, (*fig.*) prate wildly 11.40; *and see* **bidrauelen** *v*

drye (druye) *n* dry weather Z 7.292, **in wete and in** ~ in all weathers 7.175

drye (druie) *a* rainless **B** 13.269; high and ~ 5.149; *in phr.* **drynken** ~ drain (the pot) dry 9.145; without getting wet 19.304, 20.250

drien *v* feel thirsty **B** 1.25, (*impers.*) A 1.25

driȝt *n* man, anyone A 9.60*n*

driȝte *n* lord (*sc.* God) B 13.269, 14.101

drink(e) *n* drink, beverage 8.193, 15.57, 20.403, 404, 407; [= alcoholic] drink 1.24, 10.178, 188, 15.217, 259, 16.63, **B** 1.29, 9.65, Z 7.316; potion 8.296; *in phrr.* delitable ~ 1.32, derworth ~ 6.89, likerous ~ 1.25, 10.178, B 10.166, swete ~ 16.150; breed and ~ 16.63, B 13.252; cloth ne ~ 15.259, mete (and) ~ 10.188, 15.217, **B** 5.256, 6.19

drynken *v* (*p.t.* **drank(e)** 15.66, **dronk(e)(n)** 15.113, 267, B 13.404, *p.t. subjv.* 22.19, *p.p.* **dronke(n)** 15.99) drink [water] 6.174, 8.142, 15.267, 22.19, [wine / ale] 1.24, 2.98, 5.9, 6.159, 166, 362, 8.277, 9.145, 13.144 (*ger.*), 155 (*pr. p.*), 15.99, 113, 16.91, 20.409, 22.223, **B** 5.375, 13.404, 14.77, [potion] 20.53, 402, 22.380, (*fig.*) 12.58, 20.405, 412, 22.380

drinkere *n* drinker A 12.85

drynkyng *ger.* drinking [of strong drink] 13.144, 155

drit *n* manure, ? mud A 7.176

driuen *v* (*p.t.* **drof** 18.158, A 12.104, *p.p.* **dryuen** 7.264) drive, chase 6.89, 7.264, 18.158, 19.291, 22.174, **B** 6.190, 14.83; thrust B 14.92; drive [team] 7.295, 8.141, B 9.207; herd 5.19; ~ **forth** pass Pr 226; charge 22.100; strike A 12.104

drof *p.p.* 18.158, A 12.104 *see* **driuen** *v*

#drogge *n* drug, medicament 22.174

droghte B 14.171, 176 = **drouthe** *n*

dronke *p.p.a* drunk 20.192, **~ne** drunken 13.235, ~ **lewe** *a* given to drink 10.81; **~nesse** *n* drunken state 1.27

drop *n* drop (of) 6.335

droppen *v* drop B 16.79

*****drosenes** *n. pl.* lees 8.193

drouthe *n* dry weather 8.312; lack of water 15.254, B 14.171, 176

druerie *n* treasure, ? love-token 1.83

druie *a* 9.145, 19.304, 20.250; *n* Z 7.292 = **drye** *a, n*

druyen *v* dry 14.22; become dry Z Pr 116

duc A 10.76 = **duk** *n*

ducchesse *n* sovereign duchess 2.33

ducherie *n* sovereign duchy 3.244

duellen A 12.81 = **dwellen** *v*

du(y)ren *v* last 1.106, 5.25 12.224, 20.65, **B** 10.91, A 12.94; *in phr.* **as longe as (my) lyf (may) duyre(th)** 11.90, 15.58, **B** 1.78, 6.56, 10.147; continue 16.11; go on B 15.240; live 3.29, B 10.207; remain (in force) 20.191

duk *n* lord, ruler 10.138, 20.362, **A** 10.76, 12.87; great lord 21.308

dung A 7.176 = **dong** *n*

dunt 8.187, 22.105 = **d(o)unt** *n*

duren 3.29, 20.65, **B** 1.78, 6.56, 10.91, 13.50, 15.240, A 12.94 = **du(y)ren** *v*

durren *v* (*pr. sg.* **dar** Pr 218, *pl.* 3.213, *p.t.* **dorste** 20.448, **durste** 2.250, *subjv.* **derste** Pr 193, **durste** 3.235) dare Pr 218, 2.250, 3.213, 9.261, 10.119, 17.29, 69, 19.64, 211, B 15.382, A 6.81, Z 6.75, *p.t.*

subjv. would have dared Pr 193, 3.258, 6.413, 8.202, (*with pr. sense*) should dare 3.235, 9.257, 21.101; (*as assev.*) venture to 2.36, 4.191, 8.290, 15.115, 289, 20.160, B 10.135

durste *p.t.* 2.250, 3.235 *etc*; *see* **durren** *v*

dust *n* dust, ? small pieces 22.100

dust *p.t. 2 sg.* 20.320 (=**dudest**) *see* **do(o)n** *v*

dutten Z 7.174 = **ditten** *v*

dwale *n* a sleeping draught 22.380

dwellen *v* (*p.t.* **dwelte** 3.15, **dwellede** B 3.14) reside, live Pr 83, 1.130, 5.151, 9.39, 10.13, 17, 27, 75, 111, 128, 303, 11.104, 12.78, 13.88, 19.241, 252, 20.197, **B** 4.34, 5.533, 554, 8.18, **A** 7.182, 12.46, 63, 81; remain 20.304, **B** 1.115, 13.213, 18.192; stay 3.15, 22.345

dwellyng *n* habitation 2.106, 6.115

Ebrew *n* (the) Hebrew (language) 19.4

ech(e) 5.196, B Pr 122, ~ **a** B Pr 51, ~ **one** 1.89 *see* **vch, vch a, vchone** *prn, a, n*

edifien *v* build [*sc.* hermitages] 9.203, [temple] 18.161, 20.42

edwiten *v* reproach 6.420, B 5.364

eefte 20.4 = **eft** *av*

eek A 6.32 = **ek(e)** *av*

eer 1.200 = **er** *av*

eest *n* east 20.121, B Pr 13

eet *contr. pr.* 16.217, *imp.* 15.253, *p.t.* 6.430, 8.319, 15.47, 17.23, 173, B 7.122, 12.232, 13.404 *see* **eten** *v*

eft(e) *av* again, once more 3.475, 7.266, 14.23, 15.146, 17.146, 20.4, 42, 420, **B** 3.348, 14.96, 15.603, 17.112, A 11.82; back (again) 3.331; then, thereupon 4.102, 13.132, 18.24, 128, 20.359, 22.376; likewise, moreover 12.162

eft(e)sone(s) *av* a second time, again 21.5, B 6.170; **ȝut ~** over and over again 6.327; next time Z 7.152

eg *n* egg [hen's] B 13.63, [wild bird's] 13.163

egge Z 7.33 = **hegge** *n*

eg-toel *n* sharp-edged weapon 3.475

eggen *v*[1] urge A 10.52; incite 1.61, B 18.288

eggen *v*[2] cover over, harrow Z 7.58; *and see* **heggen** *v*

egre *a* fierce, bitter 15.90, **~lich(e)** *av* bitterly 21.381; sharply B 16.64

eye (**eiȝe**) (*excl.*) oh! 12.1

eye (**eiȝe, eighe**) *n* 6.2, 20.383, B 10.125, 263, (*pl.* **~n** B Pr 74 *etc*) 13.344, **A** 10.52, 12.96 *see* **ye** *n*

ey(e)r 3.431, 5.59, 10.244, A 10.210 *see* **ayr** *n*

eyhte (**eighte**) *card. num.* eight 8.349 [*in form* **viii**], 22.344, B 6.326, A 10.175; *ord. num.* eighth 16.145 (= **eighteþe** B 14.310)

eylen B 6.128, 256, 15.251 = **aylen** *v*

eir 15.221, **B** Pr 128, 14.4 = **ay(e)r** *n*

eyþer 19.288, B 5.147 *etc*, A 10.179 = **ayther** *prn*

ek(e) *av* likewise 22.274, **B** 2.237, 10.465, 13.165, 15.324, 19.430, **A** 1.2, 166, 3.40, 169, 7.28, 8.71, Z

3.163, 7.245, 8.76; *also* B 6.†281, 286, **A** 1.79 *etc*, 6.32, †7.266, **Z** 1.7, 23, 7.201

elde *n* (old) age 6.200, 10.268, 12.12, **B** 11.60, 13.354, **old** ~ B 12.8, A 3.89, (*person.*) 11.188, 196, 22.95

eldre[1] *n* ancestor 3.415, 9.214 (*pl.* ~n) A 3.242

eldre[2] *a* elder 11.174

eldir A 1.66 *see* **(h)eller(ne)** *n*

eleccio(u)n *n* election by voting [of pope] Pr 137, [of prioress] 6.136

element *n* element [one of the four simple substances earth, air, water, fire] 1.17, 20.245

elynge *a* miserable Pr 204, 22.2; desolate B 10.96; **~ly(che)** *av* in lonely poverty 22.39; wretchedly B 12.44

el(l)eue(ne) *card. num.* eleven 2.238, 3.226, 6.233, 9.309, 315, 12.176, B 15.437

elle Z 1.121, 2.75 = **helle** *n*

eller B 1.68, 9.149 = **(h)eller(n)e** *n*

elles[1] **(ellis)** *a* besides 6.262, **B** 7.84, 10.400, 12.225, 234, 13.364, 15.6, 18.353, A 10.177, 208; other 3.446, 5.117, 7.230, 268, 9.197, 16.95, 17.61, 21.121, **B** 1.110, 3.306, A 10.211; *a as n* anything else **B** 11.215, 16.143; otherwise, of some other kind 3.291, A 3.59

elles[2] **(ellis)** *av* else 1.49, 3.94, 251, 298, 7.2, 75, 8.238, 9.99, 211, 13.47, 17.16, 19.261, 20.383, 21.464, **B** 5.149, 287, 387, 6.182, 303, 10.376, 433, 20.228, **Z** Pr 17; otherwise 1.172, 8.335, 10.106, 112, 16.37, 40, 19.151, A 11.260; (*ellip.*, = but that it should be so) 3.148, 9.327, 15.300, B 15.579, A 3.101; elsewhere 21.190; at other times Pr 89; under other circumstances 13.155

elles (ellis) wher(e) *av* elsewhere, in other places 3.234, 10.29; in another place 15.300, 19.163

emcristen(e) 2.99, 7.46, 10.79, 19.217, 228 = **euencristen** *n*

emforth 15.143, 16.221 = **euenforth** *prep.*

emperesse *n* empress B 13.166

emperour *n* emperor 3.268, 21.430, **B** 11.153, 13.166

#enbaumen *v* apply (sacramental) oil (to) 13.106, (*fig.*) 19.88; treat with oil 19.72

#enblaunchen *v* make white (*fig.*) 16.268

enchaunten *v* place a spell upon, bewitch (*fig.*) 2.43, 17.176, 286, 22.379

enchesoun *n* cause, reason 6.40

#encloyen *v* cripple (by snaring feet) 20.294

enclosen A 10.42 = **closen** *v*

encombren *v* overcome 21.229; *and see* **(a)combren** *v*

encreessen *v* multiply B 11.397

endaunten *v* tame 17.171

ende *n* end 1.93, 128, 3.198, 302, 13.24, 15.284, 18.175, 19.323, 20.207, 21.218, B 2.105; (moment) of death, dying 10.53, B 12.4, 84; conclusion 3.433, 5.97, (of book) A 12.109; last part B 3.248; purpose 21.279; extremity 6.3cf.10.333; edge 3.490, B 5.235; limit

17.105; *in phrr.* ~ **til oþer** 5.111; **good** ~ virtuous death [in state of grace] Pr 29, 2.35, 3.339, 10.60; happy outcome 20.163; **laste** ~ end of (one's) life 12.196, 16.2, 158, 282, ? 19.275n, ? final state B 2.101; **maken** ~ conclude (legal) action 3.198; **worse** ~ worst of it 16.66; **(day) withouten** ~ for ever 2.106, 3.359, 10.171, 18.233, 257, 19.252, 20.235, 21.199, B 18.379

enden *v* (come to an) end 3.303; finish 5.200; die 3.429, 9.291, **B** 1.131, 12.44, A 9.52; *ger.* **endynge** death 16.100

enditen *v* compose poem / letter 17.109; accuse formally 15.120, B 11.315

enemy(e) *n* enemy [one who hates sb.] 6.64, 106, 10.190, 15.143, 166, 17.142, 21.112, 114, **B** 10.199, 11.177, 181, A 11.244; foe in battle 3.242, 250, 440, 5.74, 14.51, 15.174, 17.288; foe (of mankind, = the Devil) 7.105, B 16.105

enfo(u)rmen *v* counsel B 3.241; teach 17.271, 19.97, B 15.519

Eng(e)lisch(e) *n* (the) English (language) 3.342, 4.142, 9.214, 281, 16.118, 186, 21.330, B 5.278, 13.72, 74, 14.277, 278, 15.375, A 11.254; *a* English 16.216, **B** 10.456, 15.414

engendren *v* beget 10.217, 251, **B** 2.119, 9.185, A 10.148; procreate 14.170, *ger.* procreation 13.144

engendrour *n* (pro)creator, beginner (*fig.*) B 6.231

engynen *v* contrive B 18.252

engleymen *v* cloy, constipate 16.217, B 15.64

engreynen *v* dye fast B 2.15, (*fig.*) B 14.20

enhancen *v* increase, advance 11.58

eny (any) *a* any Pr 174 *et p.*; any at all 9.48, 12.122, B 2.136, Z 5.106; any kind of 11.64, 14.182, 15.112, 21.294, A 2.32, *infl. n. phr.* **enys-kynnes** of any kind 2.212, 3.113; *as n* any(one) 6.162, 7.280, 18.111, 20.385; either 19.27; ~ **thyng** *n phr. as av* in any way, at all 20.430

enioynen *v* appoint 16.123; prescribe (for), impose on (sb.) 5.195, 7.71, 22.283, B 5.598; join together [things] 10.131, [persons in marriage] 2.150, B 2.66; *see also* **ioynen** *v*

enleuene 3.226, 12.176 = **el(l)eue(ne)** *card. num.*

enpugnen (inpugnen) *v* call in question validity [of a document] 13.117; find fault with 15.132

enqueste *n* trial by jury 5.57, 13.84; *and see* **queste** *n*

ensa(u)mple (ensaunple) *n* typical instance 4.133, B 10.469; sign, symbolic lesson 5.119, 12.130, 17.264; parabolic comparison / exemplary image 10.246, 11.291, 16.246, **B** 7.128, 10.294, 469, 11.324, 12.236, 15.472, A 10.110; model instance 1.167, 193, 13.26, 200, 16.261, B 15.261, 266, 433, A 11.274

ensense *n* incense 21.†76, 86, B 19.76

#enspiren *v* inspire (with zeal) 16.242

entente *n* aim, desire B 8.128

#ent(i)erely *av* whole-heartedly 10.190, 17.142

entermetynge *ger.* 13.225 *see* **entremet(t)en** *v*

#**entisen** *v* incite, tempt 7.90 (B 13.431), 20.316; *ger.* provoking B 13.322, tempting B 18.158

entre(e) *n* entry 12.59

entremet(t)en *v* interfere B 13.291; presume B 11.416; *ger.* intervention 13.225

entren *v* come in, enter 7.266, 20.290, 22.355, B 3.238; take possession [of estate, by entering it] B 15.138; enter, record 11.205

*****enuenyme** *n* poison B 2.14

enuenymen *v* infect, poison 12.255

enuye *n* enmity, hostility 6.87, 7.261, 10.134, 11.56, 18.164, 20.459, B 10.433, A 5.53; malice, spite 12.41, 20.49, B 13.322; envy 19.256, 21.140, 22.246, (*person.*) 2.88, 6.62, 63, 93, 21.229, 22.273, 295, Z 5.91

epistel 19.319 *see* **pistul** *n*

equite(e) *n* impartial justice, just / fair judgement 19.288, 21.310

er[1] *av* formerly 15.308; previously 1.200, 3.393, B 1.131, 134, *in phr.* **whil** ~ some time ago 10.292

er[2] *prep.* (= **ar, or**) before **B** 5.536, 6.146, 15.539, 17.110

er(e)[3] *conj.* before **B** Pr 155, 5.5, 51, 346, 373, 390, 461, 6.65, 11.221, 13.261, 15.2, 17.83, A 12.57, 103

erbe *n* plant 8.321

erber *n* (pleasure)-garden, arbour 18.5, B 16.15

erchebisshop *n* archbishop B 15.244

erchedeken *n* archdeacon [bishop's chief administrator] 5.71, 12.228, B 2.174

erd *n* dwelling-place 8.207

ere[1] *n* ear Pr 76, 4.14, 8.290, 16.143, 17.172, 175, 22.134, 190, **B** 4.146, 12.226, 252, 13.200, 15.401, A 12.23

ere[2] A 12.57, 103 = **er**[3] *conj.*

erede *p.t.* 21.269 *see* **er(y)en** *v*

er(e)mite Pr 30 *etc*; *see* **(h)eremite** *n*

eremore Z 8.4 = **eueremo(o)re** *av*

eren A 7.125 = **eryen** *v*

eretike *n* heretic 19.112

eryen *v* (*p.t.* **er(i)ede**) plough, till 8.2, 66, 113, 123, 9.5, 6, 10.218, 15.236, 21.269, A 7.125

eritage 10.244, 16.127, B 10.341 = **heritage** *n*

erl *n* earl 3.268, 7.11, 10.86, 12.228, **B** 10.320, 13.166; great noble 21.223, **B** 4.189, 11.199, A 11.219

erldom *n* estate(s) of an earl (*fig.*) 2.88

er(e)nde *n* message 3.48, 13.40, A 3.40, †B 3.41

erly *av* early 5.15, 6.373

ermyte 5.4, 9.188 *et p.* = **heremite** *n*

ern *p.t.* 18.164, **ernynge** *pr.p.* 21.381 *see* **rennen** *v*

erraunt *a* arrant, downright 6.306

erren *v* go wrong, err 17.87

ers *n* rear 5.160; buttocks 6.157; anus B 10.125; ~ **wyn- nynge** *n* gains from prostitution 6.305

erst *av sup.* first B 5.461; *and see* **arst(e)** *av*

erthe *n* the (physical) earth [contrasted with heaven and hell] 1.7, 126, 3.165, 14.85, 17.262, 18.99, 19.123, 20.232, 249, 256, **B** 1.17, 18.367, A 11.273; this world [as dwelling of man and other creatures] 1.66, 2.79, 135, 6.287, 7.126, 8.236, 10.160, 231, 11.202, 20.353, 421, 21.73, 261, 22.240, **B** 2.26, 3.303, 4.26, 9.100, 118, 153, A 11.273, 12.44; *in phrr.* **as of** ~ (considered) as (an) earth(ly) creature) 18.99; **in / on** ~ anywhere 2.10, 20.475, **B** 1.137, 15.211, Z 2.104, (alive) anywhere 10.24, 49; **(vpp)on (this)** ~ in this life 3.94, 100, 101, 323, 5.152, 9.185, 332, 13.14, 14.173, 15.94, 16.152, 18.97, **B** 4.26, 8.38, 10.14, A 9.52; the people of this earth / world B 16.211; ground 5.118, 6.3, 407, 15.242, 20.63, 69, **B** 3.230, 12.204, 13.240, [as burial place] A 12.104; (cultivable) land Pr 224, 6.269, 9.2, 12.185, 186, 17.100, B 15.458, A 10.126, A 11.184; = flesh [earth as man's material substance] 1.149, 18.92; the primary 'element' earth 10.130, 15.242, 18.92, 20.256, B 17.161

erthely(che) *a* belonging to (this) earth(ly) existence 21.94, 22.151, B 15.175

#**eschaunge** *n* exchange / conversion of money / or commodities [for profit] 6.280 (B 13.394), B 5.245

eschewen *v* avoid, shun 8.51

ese *n* comfort Pr 55; spiritual comfort / peace 5.152; *in phrr.* **at / in** ~ in comfort 5.165, 8.282, 9.143, 152, **B** Pr 157, 10.227, 18.209, **maken / putten at** ~ make comfortable 1.19, 3.4, 15.48, **B** 6.150, 13.42; treat hospitably **B** 15.340, 16.227, A 11.174; **with** ~ easily 13.53

esy *a* pleasant B 7.124; effortless B 15.207

esily *av* in comfort B 2.98; gently B 20.380

espien B 19.304 = **aspyen** *v*

estward *av* towards the east Pr 14, 1.132, B 16.169

eten *v* (*contr. pr.* **eet** 16.217, *p.t.* **eet** 6.430, **ete(n)** 15.67, 18.244, B 14.77, A 12.74, Z 7.166, *p.p.* **eten** 19.90, B 1.154, *ger.* 13.144, 15.258) eat 6.86, 159, 8.142, 146, 272, 326, 12.40, 41, 15.67, 18.244, 19.90, 20.198, 206, 316, 374, 21.278, 283, 291, 300, 390, 22.3, **B** 5.375, 376, 603, 6.263, 10.98, 101, 11.235, 13.107, **A** 6.93, 7.125, 10.141

#**eua(u)ngelie (ewangelie)** *n* the Christian Gospel 1.194; the Gospel record 11.204, 12.103, B 11.189; (one of the) Gospel(s) 15.45

euaungelist *n* evangelist B 13.39

eue 3.307, 9.87, B 3.312, Z 6.47, 8.76 = **euen** *n*

euel *n* evil B 10.201; wickedness 16.244; harm 3.449, 19.107; disease 3.96, 16.136, 21.46, 22.85

euel (yuel, vuel) *a* wicked, sinful 6.20, 21, ~ **wil** *n phr.* illwill 6.87, 18.164, B 10.433; wrongful 16.259; accursed B 9.121; difficult 6.87 (2), 8.45, 16.224, B 10.209

euel-willed *a phr.* full of ill-will 1.187

euele *av* wickedly 9.290, 291, 10.26, 302, 15.88, 19.290, 21.342; with evil consequences 13.114; badly 5.157, 7.71, 17.196, 22.186, 280, B 5.166; with difficulty 19.324, B 12.8

eue(n) *n* evening 7.225, 8.180, **B** 3.312, Z 6.47; *in phrr.* **at ~** in the evening 5.116, 6.160, 9.87, 142, **B** 5.552, 14.15, Z 8.76, **ouer ~** overnight 3.307, 7.195; eve of a feast-day 6.182, **A** 7.12; **~ynge** *n* evening **B** 11.339; **~song** *n* evensong, vespers 6.395, 7.68, 9.229, 244

euene Z 5.130 = **heuene** *n*

euene *a* equal 18.90; even, definite 22.270; **~ cristene (emcristene)** *n* fellow-Christian 2.99, 6.75, 7.46, 10.79, 19.217, 228, **B** 2.95, 5.434, 13.105, 390, 17.135, 262

euene *av* directly 20.121, A 8.128; squarely 22.103; right, exactly 1.121, 18.6, 19.153, 20.61, 121; evenly (*fig.*), = justly 4.178; steadily 13.67, 16.53; consistently 21.300

eueneforþ *av* equally **B** 13.144, 17.135; **~ (emforth)** *prep.* to the extent of 15.143, 16.221, 21.310

euer(e) *av* (*selected refs.*) always, at all times Pr 46, 1.102, 3.431, 6.93, 7.245, 8.299, 10.19, 51, 13.206, 15.146, 16.43, 19.218, 20.337, 21.291, 22.205, **B** 1.99, A 4.67; perpetually 1.132, 7.269, A 11.286; permanently 3.219, 5.96, 6.93, 7.184, 8.207, 9.4, 22.185, **B** 4.192, A 2.166; continuously 15.65; progressively 16.140, 18.111; ever, at any time Pr 123, 6.100, 7.12, 9.4, 11.193, 12.143, 20.45, 22.103, **B** 7.97, 8.69, 10.440, 14.304, **A** 2.12, 12.110; for ever 3.197, 4.70, 14.29, 17.93, 18.27, 19.135, 20.197, 21.45; *in phrr.* **for ~** 2.248, 3.219, 4.124, 7.184 *etc*, **B** 1.115 *etc*, = in perpetuity **B** 2.157, A 2.50, = permanently 4.124, Z 7.302; **how (so / ...) ~** in whatever way 12.6, 237; **what ~** 7.125; **where ~ B** 5.89; **~ after** 5.174

euermo B 7.80 = **eueremo(o)re** *av*

euereche *prn* both 20.76

euer(e)mo(o)re *av* always 3.286, 12.93, 16.3, 64, **B** 17.135; at all times 14.145, **B** 15.179, Z 7.38; for good 4.86, **B** 6.239, A 12.39; for ever 3.402, 17.66, **B** 15.484; **~ after** continually, permanently 3.249, 9.170, **B** 7.80, A 12.39; in perpetuity **B** 7.4, 18.184

euery *a* every 17.283, **B** 5.246; **~ creature B** 11.397, **Cristene cr. B** 10.362; **~ man** 9.229, 10.182, 12.119, **B** 11.435, 15.263, **~ manere...** 10.286, 19.260; **~ seg(ge)** 3.67; **~ wiȝt B** 8.53, Z 1.39

euesynges *n. pl.* eaves 19.194

#euidence *n* (piece of) evidence 19.161; authority for belief [from experience] 20.154, [from Scripture] 8.262; example [furnishing proof] 11.286, [of conduct] **B** 15.436

euyl 6.87, A 11.155 = **euel** *a*

#ewage *n* sea-coloured sapphire **B** 2.14

ewangelie 1.194 = **eua(u)ngelie** *n*

examenen *v* test for knowledge 17.116

excepte *prep.* except (for) 10.234, 16.213, **B** 11.98; *conj.* except 17.9

#exces(se) *n* surfeit, intemperance 6.416

exciten B 11.189 = **exiten** *v*

excusen (excucen) *v* exonerate 3.218, 9.239; defend, justify 22.6, **B** 12.20, 15.485; pardon **B** 9.183, *in phr.* **haue me / hem excused** forgive me / them 15.130, 19.83; let off, exempt 5.34, 7.297, 13.82

executour B 5.262, 12.257, 20.291 *see* **secatour** *n*

#exiten *v* stir up 6.20, 188; urge **B** 11.189

#experiense *n* (appeal to) practical observation / experience 20.153

experiment *n* feat **B** 10.214

expounen *v* explain the sense **B** 14.278

face *n* face 7.57, 8.241, **B** 1.15; facial appearance 1.10, 10.157, **B** 6.237, A 12.77; presence A 8.39

fader, fadur *n* (*gen.* **fad(e)res** 18.121, *uninfl. gen.* **fader** 16.27, Z 2.97) father Pr 123, 3.162, 5.36, 6.15, 7.213, 9.311, 313, 316, 10.243, 12.157, 16.105, 17.60, **B** 9.115, 147, A 10.66, Z 2.97, (*fig.*) 2.25, 121; ancestor **B** 16.205; patriarch 13.23; originator 1.14, 60, 10.153, 19.134, **B** 10.105; early Christian Father **B** 15.272; spiritual father, priest Pr 120, 122; (of God) the Father (of Jesus) 18.121, 227, 19.126, 132, 165, 192, 201, **B** 10.241, 16.223, 17.139, 150, 159, 168, 172, 173, A 8.39, (*fig.*) Father of Holy Church 2.31, **B** 2.29; (of God as) heavenly Father (of man / all creation) 1.161, 7.143, 10.153, 18.91, 19.210, **B** 7.53, 9.103, 10.105, 15.262, 418, 605, 16.213, A 11.64, *in phr.* **þe ~ wille of heuene** the will of the heavenly Father 16.27

faderlese *a* fatherless, orphaned **B** 9.68

fay *a* doomed to die 15.2, 16.195

fayere 22.350 = **fair** *a*

fayful 1.15; **fayfulleche** 8.70; *see* **faythful** *a*; **feiþfulliche** *av*

fail(l)en, fayl(l)en *v* forsake, fail, let down (sb.) 3.56, 11.190, 15.5, 16.317; neglect 12.122; be, prove wanting 2.96, 3.349, 17.144, 18.30, 21.219, **B** 14.88; fail (to do sth.) **B** 4.194; go wrong, err 9.302, 17.96, 103, 22.31; fail to produce (crops) 8.15; fail to grow 8.347; miss one's footing 1.119; leave out (words) 13.120; lack 2.159, 19.136, **B** 9.81, 11.26, 14.33, 15.431; be lacking (to / from) 1.185, 5.148, 6.256, 8.294, 10.168, 11.232, 15.227, 19.156, 214, 22.234, **B** 2.129, 146, 3.347, 7.121, 11.277, 12.7, 14.33, A 10.58; be absent, missing 19.139; run out of **B** 4.156, 10.295

fayn *a* happy, delighted 2.171, 8.323, 11.102; willing **B** 11.390; content 8.293, Z 6.74; desirous (of) 2.82, 3.154; eager for / to 4.13, 28

fayn *av* gladly, willingly 18.103, **B** 8.127, A 12.67

faynen (feynen) *v* fashion **B** Pr 36, (*refl.*) **B** 10.38; (*refl.*) pretend (to be) 8.128

fayre[1] *n* fair 6.211, 13.51; opportunity to sell 4.59; **newe ~** London fair [of low repute], (*fig. use for*) game of barter 6.376n

fayr(e)[2] *a* beautiful Pr 19n, 1.10, 11.173, 13.42, 175, 14.158, 177, 16.253, 18.29, **B** 15.333, (*comp.*) 18.55, (*sup.*) 14.170, 18.99; handsome 6.46, B 11.394; attractive 15.8, 18.33, 54, 55, *a as n* = fair side 9.85; pleasant 21.28, 22.350; bright 11.102, 19.173, 206; (deceptively) agreeable [of speech] 2.239, 8.216, 12.13, 18.172, 22.118, **B** 2.42, 15.350, A 2.130, [of expression] B 16.149; dear 17.143, 18.248; good 3.369; excellent 10.77, 13.201, 14.180, 21.459, B 11.193, (*sup.*) 18.89; splendid 2.163, 12.248, B 16.1 (2); fine 9.268, 10.145, 15.206, (*sup.*) 18.93; seemly (*comp.*) 9. (physically cleanest) B 19.254; ~**nesse** *n* beauty 13.172, **B** 2.77, 12.46

fayre³ *av* beautifully B 16.66; courteously 1.54, 7.278, 9.129, 322, 13.247, 15.31, 16.170, 17.31, 18.243, 21.73, 483, **B** 1.4, 6.24, 13.181, 15.9, 16.65, (*comp.*) B 10.227; properly 17.109; nobly 20.70; eloquently 17.83, **B** 1.74, 16.53 (2); favourably, *in phr.* ~ **hem / yow** (be)**falle** good luck to them / you 5.199, B 16.1, 53 (1); aptly 10.32; exactly 6.325; well 17.109; moderately (*comp.*) 22.315; clearly 1.2, 10.32

fairye *n* (the land of) supernatural beings B Pr 6

fayten *v* beg under false pretences Pr 43, 5.30, 9.170, 208, B 15.214; *ger.* **faityng** B 10.38

fayth (**feiþ**) *n* religion 16.251, 17.258; religious faith, belief (in God) 1.14, 17.258, **B** 15.605, 16.245, 17.133; the Christian faith 1.181, 11.57, 17.271, **B** 1.76, 13.211, 15.346, 447, 521, 522, 579, A 11.60, 63; Christian doctrine 11.158, 245, 21.272, B 10.233; (*spec.*) (the theological virtue of) Faith **B** 12.30, 13.129, 14.81, 82, 85, 87, 15.450, (*person.*) B 11.225 (= God), 18.185 *et p.*, 19.23 *et p.*, 20.13 *et p.*, B 17.81 *et p.* (= Abraham); trust 18.255; loyalty, constancy 3.157; honesty, truthfulness 3.194, Z 1.18; *in phr.*: **be my** ~ truly, assuredly 8.293, 12.19; **in** ~ truly 4.13, 50, 5.40, 8.34, 215, 11.229, 277, 14.3, 16.287, 20.128, 22.333, B 5.235; **good** ~ sincerity 4.37, 21.302, 22.28, B 5.264, Z 3.176 (*person.*) 10.148, 22.131; true justice 22.28, B 18.348, 352; (*as assev.*) **in, by good** ~ in all sincerity, 6.287, 340

faythful *a* sincerely religious 6.291; honest B 6.250; trustworthy 17.35, 18.141; loyal 1.15; just, true B 9.103

faythles *a* perfidious 2.143, **B** 9.119, 10.195, (*person.*) **Fals** ~ 2.42

faythly *av* truly 21.70

faytles Z 2.102 = **feytles** *a*

#**fayto(u)r** *n* deceiver, cheat 2.193, 8.73, 179, 10.299, 11.54, 22.5, B 15.215, A 2.94; false beggar, [esp. one feigning injury or illness] 8.128, 9.64, B 13.243

#**faytrye** *n* deception, imposture 8.138, 12.34

#**fal(l)a(e)s** *n* (*sg. or pl.*) deceptive legal stratagem 11.20, (*pl.*) sophistical argument 16.229

falewen *v* plough 7.294

fallen *v*¹ (*pr. subjv.* **falle** B 16.1; *p.t.* **ful** Pr 106, **fel** B 1.114, A 10.185; **fil** B 14.79, A 1.112, *pl.* **fullen** 1.125, **fellen** B 1.121; *p.t. subjv.* **fulle** 18.128, **felle** B 16.94,

fille B 14.186; *p.p.* (**y**)**falle** 2.102, 7.112, **fallen** B Pr 65; *pr.p.* **fallynge** 10.22, *ger.* 10.41) fall Pr 106, 113, 1.119, 3.102, 107, 6.334, 10.39(2), 13.235, 16.211, 18.48, 107, 19.147, 20.89, 346, 21.5, 22.51, 176, **B** 1.121, 8.32, 14.79, 15.300, A 5.215; *ger.* 18.30, B 16.25; fall (morally / spiritually) 2.102, 10.22, 39(1), 42, 11.305, 15.288, 19.314, *ger.* 10.41, 21.65; *in phrr.*: ~ **for** be proper for B 11.99, 394, Z 7.231; ~ **in** fall into 7.112, 9.272, 11.301, 15.288, 21.305, 22.10, 176, B 18.103; come into 19.292; come into contact with B 4.156; ~ **of** become of 6.325; afflict A 10.185; ~ **to** pertain to 1.161; be necessary (to) B 10.233; ~ **to be** become 18.128; be suitable / fitting (for) 18.185, ~ **for** B 11.99, 394, Z 7.231; fall down B 15.405; collapse 9.100; be brought low 20.106, 382, 22.228; issue as a consequence B 5.140; descend 3.125, B 10.277; alight upon 2.209; happen Pr 63, 3.90, 477, 17.232, 20.411, 22.32, B 7.158; befall B 16.1; turn out 3.97; turn (out) to (be) B 12.46

fallen² Z 3.90 = **fellen** *v*

fals *n* deceit 22.55; (*person.*) 2.6 etc

fals *a* deceitful, treacherous 2.91, 3.91, 114, 300, 9.64, 10.299, 16.274, 17.183, 20.320, 22.64, 285, B 10.195; *a as n* the deceitful 2.4, (*person.*) 3.175; untrustworthy 16.41, 22.285, B 12.257, A 10.210 (2); deceptive A 9.38; dishonest, corrupt 2.55, 6.293, 11.20, 20.27; wicked Pr 106, 3.102, 8.229, 12.199, 240, 21.248, **B** 9.147, 14.24; mendacious 2.83, 85, 6.72, 258, 7.226, 15.79, 18.123, 21.222, 373, 22.118, **B** 3.127, 9.119, 13.401; counterfeit (*fig.*) 17.76; misbelieving 17.258, 20.95, 113; erroneous 21.47; inaccurate 6.258, 13.117, 16.128, B 13.359; *in phrr.*: ~ **doem** 20.27; ~ **mesure** B 13.359; ~ **w(e)yhte** 6.258, 16.128; ~ **witnesse** 2.85, 7.226, 16.361, B 5.88, 13.359, (*person.*) 2.160

fals(h)ede *n* deceitfulness 1.60, 6.341, B Pr 71, (*person.*) 2.149, 3.41, A 2.50, Z 2.3

falsli(che) *av* treacherously, deceitfully 20.379, B 18.352; wickedly B 17.307; mendaciously 6.427; fraudulently 9.268*n*

falsnesse *n* deceitfulness 12.34, 22.66, Z 1.18, (*person.*) 2.70, 171, 212, Z 2.165; wrong B 15.262; mendacity Pr 69

fame *n* ill-repute A 5.74

famen *v* slander 3.231

famy(e)n(e) *n* famine, dearth of food 7.305, 8.215, 345, Z 7.326; extreme hunger 12.199

fand *p.t.* A Pr 17 = **fond**; see **fynden** *v*

fangen B 5.558; *see* **fongen** *v*

fantasie *n* fantastic notion A 11.63; extravagant amusement B Pr 36

fare *n* commotion 20.16, 128

faren *v* (*p.t.* **ferde(n)** 10.237, 13.229; *p.p.* **faren** 8.112) go on one's way **B** 2.184, 5.5; betake oneself 8.112; depart, **hennes** ~ depart this life **B** 7.97, 15.145; go by B 12.5; behave, act 12.19, 18.96, 19.114, 22.313, **B** 3.344, 10.94, 15.332; ~ **by** / **with** behave towards 13.229, 15.119, 22.313, B 13.149; fare, live 5.8, 6.334, 10.237, 11.75, 22.235, **B** 13.51, 15.185, A 11.178; go, happen, turn out 10.41, 11.245, 14.141, 16.110, 20.234; *in phrr.*: **it fareth bi / with** it goes with 10.38, 41, 16.110, 17.76, 18.67, 19.289, 22.290, **B** 12.201, 14.271, 15.350, 455; **fare(th) wel** farewell, goodbye 11.314, B 13.181

fast(e)[1] *a* tight-(fisted) A 2.63.

faste[2] *av* firmly 1.42, 3.176, **B** 13.153, 15.242, 17.133, 157, Z 2.160; securely 1.92, 2.212, B 17.111; soundly B 18.6; stoutly 21.103; closely 2.180; earnestly 7.57, **B** ? 5.382, 14.274; diligently B 15.447, **A** 7.10, 13; heartily B 6.108; faithfully †6.155(2); eagerly Pr 41, 4.77, 8.214, 11.176, **B** 4.167, 14.331, 16.169, A 4.133, 7.192; many times B 10.69, A 5.222; steadily 6.326, 15.66, **Z** 4.62, 5.91; speedily Pr 65, 4.28, 8.343, 17.209, 19.52, 80, 22.325; quickly B 4.30, 33, 42; instantly B 4.24, A 1.113

faste Z 2.95 = **fest** *p.p.*

fasten *v* fast [abstain from food and drink as a religious discipline] 1.99, 6.155, 351, 13.80, ? B 5.382*n*, A 5.211, ? Z 5.106; *ger.* **fastyng** Pr 69, 9.233, 20.313, ~ **day** 2.100, 6.182, 359, 433, 7.25, 9.94

fastened *p.p.* Z 2.57, **fastnid** A 2.48, 88 = **festned**; *see* **festenen** *v*

fatte *n* fat, grease 21.281

fat(te) *a* plump 9.208, (*comp.*) B 12.263; fertile 12.226

fauchen *n* falchion [broad sword with curved blade] 16.167

faucon *n* falcon 8.30, B 17.63

fauht *p.t.* 3.246, 20.408, 21.103; *see* **fy(g)hten** *v*

faumewarde (vawwarde) *n* vanguard, forefront 5.58, 22.95

faunen *v* fawn, ~ **with þe tayle** show fondness (by wagging the tail) 17.31

faunt *n* child 9.170, **B** 6.282, 16.101, A 10.58, 64, 66

#**faunt(o)kyn** *n* little child 9.35, 10.184, 21.118, B 13.214

***fauntelte(e)** *n* childishness, puerility B 15.150; (*person.*) 11.314

faut *n* reproach (for wrong) B 10.105

fauten *v* be lacking B 9.68; lack 10.184

fauel *n* flattery (*person.*) 2.25 *etc*

#**fauerable** *a* showing favour 3.191

feble *a* (physically) weak Z 5.142; weak (in contest) 16.67; infirm 7.21, B 15.576, (*fig.*) B 17.117; lacking in power B 17.173; impotent (*a as n*) B 9.163; ineffective B Pr 180; thin 6.159; debased B 15.349; (*comp.*) weaker (in faith) B 15.347, worse 1.181; (*sup.*) least powerful 14.171

fec(c)hen *v* (*p.t.* **fet(ten)**) 2.65, 239, A 5.216; *p.p.* **fet** 22.324) fetch 4.7, 8.316, 22.324, B 5.29, 640, A 7.281; bring B 11.56, A 7.33; come for 11.168, A 3.91; carry

away 2.239, 18.286, 20.275, 277, 325, 393, 21.467; carry off 8.154, 21.145, **B** 4.51, 16.49; steal 6.268 (B 13.372), 20.379, B 18.351; carry off to death 8.348; obtain, win 10.279, 18.130, 20.18, 32; draw 7.56; take away B 11.56; collect 20.154; *in phrr.*: ~ **at** seek (from) 3.375; ~ **away** carry off 12.240, 18.49; ~ **forth** bring forward, produce 2.157, 179, **B** 2.163, 11.324, Z 2.58, 136; ~ **fro, out of** rescue from 18.281, 286; recover 21.248; ~ **of** obtain from 2.191; *see also* **fetten** *v*

feden (*p.t.* **fedde** 6.433, *p.p.* **fed(d)e**) **B** 15.471, 16.125, Z 7.316) feed 6.433, 7.133, 17.171, 18.153, 21.126, **B** Pr 190, 15.462, 464, (*fig.*) 7.133, B 15.414; keep supplied with food 8.320, 323, 9.90, 17.11, 15, 57, 68, 21.258, 22.209, **B** 4.119, 14.10, 15.306, 339, A Pr 93; provide with meals 12.106, B 11.192, (*fig.*) B 15.484; sustain, support 7.82, B 6.250; nourish spiritually 17.285, B 14.30

fe(e) *n* estate, **knyhtes** ~ 5.77; money 4.128, (*pl.*) 7.227

feeld B Pr 17, 6.235 = **feld** *n*

feele B 17.151 = **felen** *v*

feend B 7.67, Z 7.133 = **fend** *n*

feerde *p.t.* 22.313; *see* **faren** *v*

feere B 2.194, 13.163, *see* **fe(e)re** *n*[1,2]; *pl.* B 5.168 = **aferes** *n*

feeste B 15.341; **feestyng** *ger.* †B 5.375 *see* **festen** *v*[1]

feet[1] *n* deed, act (*?with pun on* feet) 1.181

feet[2] 2.193 *etc*; *see* **foet** *n*

feffament *n* document of enfeoffment [investment with an estate] 2.73

feffen *v* enfeoff [put in legal possession of estate] 17.57; endow by way of gift, (*fig.*) 3.369, A 2.37; present with a gift 2.160; affiance, join sb. to another in a marriage contract 2.137, A 2.37, 47, 58

fey(e) 16.195, B 13.2 = **fay** *a*

***feym** Z 7.326 *see* **famy(e)n(e)** *n*

feynen B Pr 36, 10.38 = **faynen** *v*

feynte *a* faint, exhausted B 17.117

fe(y)ntise *n* exhaustion B 5.5, A 12.67, 68

feyr 19.173 = **fayr(e)** *a*

feytles *a* ?perfidious (= **faythles**, ? *with pun on* 'without deeds') A 2.94, Z 2.102

feiture *n* feature, ?creature B 13. 297c; *and see* **feture** *n*

feiþ B 1.76, 10.233, 13.211, 15.450, A 11.60, 63; ~ **ful B** 6.250, 9.103, 15.418; ~ **lees B** 9.119, 10.195; *see* **fayth** *n*, ~ **ful** *a*, ~ **les** *a*

feiþfulliche *av* honestly B 6.69 (= **fayfulleche** 8.70)

fel[1] *n* skin B 1.15

fel[2] *a* treacherous (?destructive) 18.35; terrible †B 3.260 (1); **felle** (*pl.*) severe (? *or* shrewd) 3.492, 6.152; ~**ly** *av* fiercely B 18.92

fel[3] *p.t.* B 3.260 (2), B 7.158 *etc*; *see* **fallen** *v*

felawe *n* companion 15.103, 21.202, 22.341, 350; associate 1.119, 2.183, B 7.12; intimate companion 19.80, 97, 21.88, **B** 17.87, 89 *et p.*, 18.197; fellow-servant 8.254; ~ swimmer B 12.167; ~ fisherman B 15.292; ~ freeman

3.111; accomplice 2.205, 4.27, **B** 9.85, 15.377; *in phr.*
partyng ~ partner B 13.207

felaws(c)hip(e) *n* company 11.185, B 11.435; partnership
(as spouse) 3.154; revelling 2.102; armed crew 4.50;
band of associates B 2.208, A 1.112; (heavenly) com-
munity B 1.114

feld *n* plain Pr 19, 1.2, 5.111; (arable) field 7.32, 12.194,
21.315, B 6.140, 235; open country 13.175, B 7.129;
surrounding country district A 2.39; *in phr.* **a~** to the
field 8.312

felde *p.t.* 3.239, 18.128; *see* **fellen** *v*

fele (vele 6.74) *indef. num. a* many 6.118, 9.95, 11.229,
13.138, 21.222, **B** 9.73, 10.213, 12.5, 15.70, 288; *in
phrr.*: **bi ~ fold** *av phr.* many times over **B** 12.263,
13.320; **~ tyme(s)** 6.74, 118, 16.228; **~ ꝫer** 16.354; *as
n* many 9.91, B 15.332, 519, Z 7.278

felen *v* (*p.t* **felede** 6.114, *ger.* **(v)elynge** 20.131) feel (by
touching) 19.146, 21.171, 22.195, *ger.* touch, con-
tact 20.131; feel, experience (emotion) 6.114, 7.130,
20.228, 22.37; perceive 16.187, B 17.179

felicite *n* well-being 22.240

felle *a. pl.* 3.492, 6.152 *see* **fel** *a*

felle *p.t. subjv.* **B** 16.94, 19.244; *see* **fallen** *v*

fellen *p.t. pl* **B** 1.121, 18.311; *see* **fallen** *v*

fellen *v* (*p.t.* **felde** 18.128, **felled** B 3.127) make sth.
fall 18.128; bring down B 3.127, A 3.41, Z 3.90; slay
3.239, A 12.66

felly *av* B 18.92 *see* **fel**², *av*

felo(u)n *n* criminal [*esp.* perpetrator of a felony, *e.g.*
treason, theft, murder] 6.325, 10.243, 11.255, 14.141,
20.421, **B** 17.111, 18.383

felonliche *av* feloniously 12.240, B 18.352

felowe 15.103, **~schipe** 11.185; *see* **felawe** *n*, **~s(c)hip(e)** *n*

femel(l)e *n* female 13.148, B 11.339

fend(e) *n* (the) Devil 1.38, 118, 2.42, 143, 8.97, 10.48,
14.119, 16.44, 18.43, 120, 130, 137, 20.18, 27, 32,
202, 477, 22.58, **B** 7.67, 11.399, 15.141, 16.48, **A**
7.136, 10.64; fiend, demon 20.315, 343, 21.47, 22.58,
64, B 14.24, A 1.112; *in phrr.*: **~es biyete** B 2.41; **~
disciples** B 13.430; **~ kynne** 2.42; **~ liknesse** B 1.114;
~ lymes 22.77, **~ procuratours** 7.89

***fendekyn** *n* small/lesser devil 20.415

fenden *v* defend, protect 1.99, 21.46, ?prevent 21.65

fenestre *n* window 20.13; glazed window 16.41

fen(k)elsede *n* fennel-seed 6.359

fentyse A 12.67, 68 = **feyntise** *n*

fer *a* far 9.241, 10.77, 12.239, B 10.473; long ago 16.354;
in phrr.: **~ (a)way** far and away 16.50; **~ and fele ꝫer**
many long years ago 16.354; **be ~** by a long way 22.23,
315; **(ful) ~** a long way 11.196, 20.166, 21.483

fer *av* far 14.176, 177, 17.196, B 10.473

ferde(n) *p.t.* 10.237, 13.229 *etc*; *see* **faren** *v*

ferden *v* assemble together 13.148

fe(e)re *n*¹ partner 17.19; comrade (in crime) 2.219, **B**

2.6, 194, 4.27, A 4.141; husband 19.302 (1); mate
13.164

fere *n*² fear 2.220, 249, 251, 8.191, 202, 215, 320, 12.199,
19.302 (2), 20.113, 22.169, **B** 2.210, 4.52, 6.183,
11.354, Z 6.74; danger 12.199, B 2.210

feren *v* frighten away 17.285

ferie *n* week day, **heye ~** holy day [church festival] fall-
ing on weekday 4.113, B 13.415

ferly *n* wonder(ful occurrence) Pr 63, 11.229, 18.56,
20.113, B Pr 6, A 12.58, 59; *in phrr.*: **(a) ~ me thyn-
keth** I should be astonished 15.119, 16.294, 17.112;
hauen ~ (of) be astonished at 11.229, 20.128

ferme¹ *n* use, **hauen lond to ~** have use of land (for fixed
payment) B 16.16

ferme² *a* steadfast 11.57, B 15.347; firm, steady 14.208,
18.255, **B** 15.579, 17.133; *av* firmly 21.120

fermen *v* strengthen B 10.74

fermerye *n* infirmary B 13.109

fern *av* formerly, **~ ago** long ago B 15.231

fernyere *n* past year B 12.5; *as av* in past years 7.46

fers (fiers(e)) *a* bold, fierce 6.7; savage B 15.305

ferst A 7.168 = **furst** *n*

ferste A 10.28 = **furst(e)** *a*

ferst(e) A 10.131, 11.135 = **furst(e)** *av*

ferþe (furthe) *ord. num. a.* fourth 21.299, A 12.82; *as n.*
9.56, 16.131

ferþer(e) B 2.202 *etc*, A 7.188 *etc*; *see* **forthere** *av*

ferþest *sup. a.* farthest, most distant B 5.235

ferthyng(e) *n* farthing 4.57, 7.201; **~ worth** farthing's
worth 6.359, 9.94

fesaunt *n* pheasant B 15.462

fest *p.p.* B 2.124 *see* **festen** *v*²

feste *n* religious feast [commemorative church celebra-
tion] 17.120 (**heye-festes** 6.182; **~ day** 5.30); feast, ban-
quet 6.291, 7.97, 115 (*fig.*), 9.95, 11.34, 12.103, 15.207,
21.108, 115, **B** 10.94, 11.216, 15.461, 480, A 11.60

festen *v*¹ entertain at a feast B 15.341, (*fig.*) 16.319, B
15.484; *ger.* feasting B †5.375, 11.193; feed abun-
dantly B 15.589

festen *v*² join (in marriage) B 2.124

festenen *v* attach (to), establish (in) 12.8; join (in mar-
riage), *p.p.* A 2.48, 88

#festren *v* fester 19.85

#festu *n* mote B 10.277c

fet *p.p.* 22.324, B 11.324; **feteth** *imp.* Z 7.34; *see* **fec(c)-
hen** *v*

fet(e) *n pl.* A 11.215, 12.47 *see* **foet** *n*

fet(t)eren *v* fetter, shackle 2.212, 7.21, 16.328, **B** 2.208,
17.111

fether *n* feather 13.138, 14.172, 177, 183, 21.415

fetisli(che) *av* elegantly B 2.11, 166

fette(n) *p.t.* 2.65 *etc*; *see* **fecchen** *v*

fetten *v* (*p.t.* **fette**) fetch 5.131; **~ forþ** bring forward A
2.49; **~ of** obtain from A 2.142; *and see* **fecchen** *v*

feture *n* feature 6.46c

feuer(e) *n* fever 3.96, 6.79, 21.46, 22.81, (*person.*) A 12.82

fewe *a* few Pr 63, 8.295, 305, 9.91, 10.259, 13.191, 15.203, 288, 16.130, 142, A 12.58, 66; *as n* 9.244, 18.147, 22.110, **B** 10.437, 11.390, 12.5, 15.4

fy (*excl.*) fie! 2.137, B 15.215

*fibicches (febicchis) *n. pl.?* alchemical tricks B 10.213c, A 11.159

fichen *v. refl.* brace (oneself in the saddle) Z 2.160

fierse B 15.305 = **fers** *a*

fifte *ord. num. a.* fifth B 11.47

fiftene *card. num.* fifteen A 3.38

fifty *card. num.* fifty B 3.39

fyge *n* fig 2.29

fight *n* combat B 15.164

fy(g)hten *v* (*p.t.* **fauht** 3.246, *pl.* **foughten** Pr 43, *p.p.* **yfouhte** 8.149) fight 1.96, 99, 3.236, 256, 5.58, 8.34, 150, 14.50, 21.219, 227, 448, 22.141, 166, 168, 302, (*fig.*) 18.137, (*ger.*) B 16.101: quarrel, brawl Pr 43, 1.175, 4.59, 5.154, **B** 4.52, 13.322; struggle spiritually 16.172, 21.65

#figuratyfly *av* in a figurative manner, ? as a hazy or indistinct image 16.294

fykel *a* deceitful 2.25, 3.157, 6.72, 11.20, **B** 2.79, 130; ~ **tonge** treacherous-tongue 2.6, (*person.*) 2.121, B 2.41

fil (= **ful**) *p.t.* **B** 14.79, 15.300 **A** 1.112, 5.215; **fille** *p.t. subjv.* **B** 14.186, 16.107 *see* **fallen** *v*

fyle *n* concubine 6.135

*filial *a* filial, as from child to parent 8.216

fille (fulle) *n* fill **B** 1.154, 6.263, 16.11

fillen (fullen) *v* fill 3.88, 6.389, B 15.337

filosophye 22.296 = **philosophie**

fylosofre 13.27 = **philosophere** *n*

filþe *n* dirt B 14.17

fyn *n*[1] fin 22.45

fyn *n*[2] fine [final agreement relating to alienation of property (rights)] A 2.36, 48

fyn[3] *a* excellent, perfect 19.85, 176; *sup.* Z 7.316; subtle 11.158

fynden *v* (*contr. pr. 2 sg.* **fynst** B 3.266, *3 sg.* **fynd(e)** 5.27, 16.317, **fynt(e)** 4.121, 5.88, 19.314, B 4.131; *p.t.* **fo(e)nd(e)** Pr 19, 1.60, **foond** B 11.293, **fonden** A Pr 36; *p.t. subjv.* **founde** 6.22, 15.220, B 15.311; *p.p.* **(y) founde(n)** 8.138, B 10.255) find Pr 19, 56, 3.492, 4.121, 128, 5.173, 6.76, 7.213, 8.229, 10.77, 13.164, 14.89, 15.104, 16.293; come upon 14.86, 17.161, **B** 3.266, 15.478, **ben founden** be met with 9.343, B 15.230; come across in books, read about 3.59, 494, 11.255, 277, 15.266, 17.84, 165, **B** 3.344, 9.67, 145, 11.154, 225, 277, 12.76, 15.278; discover [by enquiry] 6.22, 7.32, 8.138, 9.288, 12.212, **B** 3.269, 13.318; find out [by experience] 3.477, 11.186, 190, 12.15, 25, 15.185, 220, 16.353, 17.106, 18.172, 19.23, **B** 4.71, 6.58,

9.147, 11.390, 15.153, 230, 311, 424, 17.87, **A** 11.168, 12.59, Z 3.151; discover [by thinking] 1.60, 5.153, 15.138, 19.314; provide, supply Pr 143, 5.21, 27, 49, 88, 7.258, 8.70, 148, 13.71, 15.202, 217, 16.149, 314, 317, 318, **B** 7.30, 129, 130, 9.68, 73, 14.32; devise (for) A Pr 36; provide for, maintain 3.41, 375, 5.76, 9.30, 35, 10.183, 185, 13.108, 15.237, 252, 16.272, 317, 17.34, 21.448, 22.296, **B** 10.93, 15.285, 307, 572; determine and declare [as guilty] 2.153, B 5.144; originate 1.60; ~ **out** think up Pr 37; *pr.p.* explore 3.344; attain to B 13.129; ~ **vp** introduce, formulate 11.54

fyndyng(e) *ger.* (source of) maintenance 6.293, 22.384, B 15.422

fynger *n* finger 2.12, 8.9, 13.106, 14.37, 19.115 *et p.*, 21.171, **B** 10.125, 17.142 *et p.*, Z 7.54

fynt *contr. pr. 3 sg. see* **fynden** *v*

Fyppe *diminutive of* Philip [*name for* sparrow], *in excl.* **farewel** ~ come on, let's be off! 11.314

fir B 7.52 = **fuyr** *n*

firmament *n* air A 8.115

firs *n* (*pl.* ~**es**, ~**en**) furze B 5.345, A 5.194

first 1.23, B 3.244, A 12.59, *av* 1.60, B 1.76; *see* **furst(e)** *a, av*

firsen *n pl.* A 5.194 *see* **firs** *n*

fys(c)h *n* fish 5.148, 15.242, 264, 22.45, B 8.54, A 10.174; [*as food*] 6.159, 438, 7.49, 8.333, 9.93, 15.102, 18. 154, 21.126, **B** 15.431, 590

fischen *v* (catch) fish 17.19

fiscuth *3 sg.* 9.153 *see* **fisken** *v*

fis(c)i(s)cian *n* doctor of medicine 22.176; physician 18.141, 22.316, A 7.168

fysyk(e) *n* medical science 22.178, 342, **B** 15.383, Z 7.260; medical practice 8.267, 293, 22.315, 379; the medical profession (*person.*) 8.291, 22.169

fisyken *v* treat medically 22.324

#fisken *v* wander idly 9.153

fythele *n* fiddle, viol (*fig.*) 7.116, B 9.103

fythelen *v* (play the) fiddle 15.207; recite (to music) 7.106 (B 13.447)

fiþelere *n* fiddle-player B 10.94

fytheren *v* fit with tail-wing (of feathers) 22.118

fyue *card. num. a* five 1.15, 2.12, 10.145, 14.89, 15.82, 18.154, 21.126, B 12.3; *as n* 10.149; ~ **score** B 1.101; ~ **thousend** 18.154, 21.127, B 15.590; ~ **daies** 6.161, B 15.319; ~ **loues** 21.126, B 15.590; ~ **ordres** 8.191, 9.343; ~ **wittes** 1.15, 15.258, 16.232, 21.217, A 11.293; ~ **woundes** A 11.215; ~ **yer** B 6.322; ~ **ȝokes** 7.294

flail *n* flail [for threshing grain] 8.180

flappe *n* stroke B 13.67

flappen (on) *v* beat, thresh 8.180

flatere *n* flatterer 7.82, 89, 21.222, B 13.455

flateren *v* flatter, beguile with pleasing words 8.147, 12.25, 22.110, 235, 384; *pr.p.* 2.43; *ger.* flattering 7.106, 15.79

flaterer(e) flatterer 7.114, 11.6, B 2.166; (*person.*) 17.112, 22.316, 324

flatten *v* (*p.t.* **flatte(d)**) splash 7.57

flaum(b)e *n* flame 19.173, 206, 214

flaumen *v* blaze 19.171, 192; smell B 12.254

fle(e)n *v* (*p.t.* **fley(h)** 2.220, 21.103, **fleiȝ** B 17.89, **fledde** 2.249) flee, run away (from) 2.219, 220, 249, 17.144, 19.302, 22.44, 169, 285, B 17.318; escape 3.175, 21.103; depart 16.195, 20.343, 22.131; *and see* **flyen** *v*

flees *n* fleece 9.268

fley(h)[1] *p.t.* 2.220, 21.103 *see* **fle(e)n** *v*

fley(h)[2] *p.t.* 18.121, 19.59 *see* **flyen** *v*

fleysche 3.59 = **fles(c)h(e)** *n*

#flekede *p.pl.* spotted 13.138

Flemmyng *n* Fleming [person of Flemish birth / ancestry] Z 7.278

fles(c)h(e) *n* (human or animal) flesh B 12.242 (1), Z Pr 106; (flesh) meat 6.159, 7.49, 8.154, 333, 9.93, 14.180, 15.102, **B** 12.242 (2), 263, 13.40, 14.44, 15.431, 464, 16.229; (the human) body 17.195, B 16.101, A 11.215; bodily nature 7.143; man's sensual nature 3.59, 6.7, 16.133, [esp. as enemy of the soul] 1.38, 10.48, 19.312, 20.202, B 11.399, **A** 7.136, 9.45, (*person.*) 18.35; man's sexual nature 13.152, 18.79; *in phrr.*: ~ **and blode** human nature 1.151; **lost of** ~ lust of the flesh 13.152

flescheliche *a* of flesh 21.171

fleten *v* (*contr. pr.* **flet**) drift B 12.167; swim 22.45

flex *n* flax 8.12

fly *p.t.* 1.118 *see* **flyen** *v*

flicche *n* flitch, side (of bacon) 10.279

flyen (*pr. pl.* **fleeth** 10.233, *p.t. sg.* **fl(e)y(h)** 1.118, 18.121, 19.59, *pl.* **flowe(n)** 2.249, 19.82, *pr.p.* **fleynge** B 8.54) fly 1.118, 10.233, 14.171, 176, B 8.54; hasten 2.249, 8.179, 18.121, 19.59, 82, 20.369, 22.285

flyht *n* power of flight 14.171

flynt *n* hard rock 15.267; flint [for striking fire] 19.211, Z 6.72

flitten *v* change, *pr. p.* **flittyng** changeable, shifty 12.15

***flobren** *v* dirty B 14.15 *and see* **befloberen** *v*

flo(e)d, flood *n* river 5.148, B 14.43; river-current B 12.167, (*fig.*) 14.119; sea B 15.366; flood 3.91, 8.347, 9.182, 10.228, 15.166, B 10.407; stream (of water) 15.267

flore *n* floor 14.137

flor(e)yn(e) *n* florin 2.157, 160, 3.194, 7.227, B 4.156

florischen *v* adorn, ? cause to prosper 16.131

flour *n*[1] flower 13.175, 14.158, 16.253, B 16.26, 45, (*fig.*) A 10.122

flour *n*[2] flour 8.154, B 14.30

flouren *v* flower 18.35, B 16.94

flowe(n) *p.t. pl.* 2.249, 8.179, 19.82, 20.369 *see* **flyen** *v*

#flux *n* morbid discharge (*?fig.*) 6.161*c*; ?dysentery 21.46, 22.81

fobbe *n* cheat 2.193

fobbere *n* cheat, impostor B 2.183

fo(o)d(e) *n* food, sustenance Pr 43, 1.23, 5.27, 49, 6.293, 8.18, 70, 284, 291, 9.76, 15.102, 16.314, 323, 17.19, 22.15, **B** 7.30, 15.305, 478, 575, **A** 8.33, 116, 11.185, 186, (*fig.*) 7.258, 18.14 (?*with pun on* offspring) 21.410; *in phrr.*: **angeles** ~ ?= contemplation, ?manna 22.15; **goostly** ~ B 15.572, 575(2)

foe *n* (*pl.* **foes** 3.239, **fo(o)n** B 5.95) enemy 5.58, 6.72, 12.13, **B** 9.201, 15.262, Z 6.72

fo(e)l, fool *n* fool, stupid person 22.61, 62, 74, 77, B 7.125 (?*with pun on* **foules**), B 11.68; (natural) fool, half-wit 10.184, **B** 10.6, 15.3, 10, A 10.64; morally / spiritually obtuse person 12.213; (professional) buffoon / jester ? Pr 37, 7.89, 114, ? 11.6; ~ **sage** wise fool 7.82, 103

foend(e) *p.t.* 5.36, 40, 22.296, **foond** B 11.293, **fonden** A Pr 36 *see* **fynden** *v*

foet, fo(o)t(e) *n* (*pl.* **fe(e)t(e)**) foot 1.118, 19.56, B 15.452; **a foote** on foot *n* B 17.106; feet 2.193, 4.82, 18.244, **B** 12.242, 256, 15.300, **A** 11.215, 12.47; foot's distance 7.285, 307, **B** 5.6, 6.2; ~ **lond** foot-wide strip of land 6.268; foundation (*fig.*) B 16.245

fol 9.14 *etc*, 3.159 *etc* = **ful** *a, av*

fold *n* sheepfold (*fig.*) 9.259

fold(e) *n* earth 1.151; world 9.153, B 7.53; ground B 12.254

-fold *suff.* fold, times 12.160, B 11.256, B 13.320

folden *v* close, clench 19.115, 122, 131, 151, 155

fole *n* foal (? *with pun on* fool) 11.251, **B** 2.163, 11.343

foles 10.184, 22.61, 62, 74, 77 *see* **fo(e)l** *n*

fol(e)wen *v* follow 1.38, 2.196, 3.492, 494, 4.28, 8.349, 15.186, **B** 3.342, 15.463, 474, 16.162; advance along 6.118, A 12.91; accompany 6.127, 7.307, 10.51*c*, 81, 11.173, 12.74, 144, 13.62, 14.3, 15.307, 16.44, 46, 61, 139, 20.123, 21.272, 418, **B** 6.2, 11.47, 371, 14.266, 15.224, A 12.67; share, keep 11.185, B 5.641; obey 2.34, 77, 105, 3.246, 375, 7.305, 8.213, 11.311, 12.172, 13.2, 212, 15.9, 16.260, 17.143, 18.79, 19.289, 20.202, 21.33, 59, 22.58, **B** 3.7, 11.26, 39, 17.124, A 9.45, Z 6.74; observe 10.259; take after 10.247; approve B 11.251; ~ **for,** ~ **after** pursue 19.80; aim for 10.279; search for 3.344, B 15.250; afflict 16.78, B 11.374, A 12.68; consort with 3.363, B 3.39; result 1.182

fol(o)ware *n* 7.188; (farm) servant 17.103

folfillen 16.27 = **fulfillen** *v*

folye *n* (act of criminal) foolishness 10.185, A 10. 70, B 13.149; nonsense 14.82, 22.147; sinfulness, wrongdoing 11.311, 20.234, **B** 14.186, 15.76, 150; lechery 16.133; madness B 15.10

foliliche *av* sinfully 16.232, 233

folk(e) *n* people Pr 19, 1.2, 5.111, 6.245, 7.258, 8.323, 9.57, 10.3, 259, 11.57, 15.237, 16.187, 232, 17.83, 18.102, 19.176, 201, 22.64, **B** 5.144, 8.38, 10.217, 11.268, 15.10, 347, 447, 16.245; human beings 15.267; people (of a region), nation 17.258; [*of a group of*] people 7.169, 8.73, 138, 213, 216, 229, 9.95, 11.245, 282, 15.9, 266, 288, 16.328 (1), 17.103, 19.201, 289, 20.234, 21.59, **B** 4.181, 5.140, 150, 406, 6.2, 9.159, 11.99, 13.191, 214, 243, 15.302, 346, 350, 405, 424, 464, 471, 605, 16.246; *in phrr.*: ~ **ywedded** 5.64; **Lordes ~ of heuene** (= the blessed) 1.154; ~ **of Holy Chirche** (= the clergy) Pr †116, †118, B 15.384; **fals** ~ 10.299, 12.240, 22.285, **B** 9.119, 10.195; **felde of ~** Pr 19, 5.111; **Goddes ~** B 15.135; **good ~** 3.68; **lewed** ~ 11.251; **lou(h) ~** 6.227, 13.82, B 3.255; **myseise ~** B 7.26; **nedy ~ B** 12.53, 15.572; **oelde ~** 20.7; **pore ~** 8.147, 320, 9.72, 16.328 (2); **trewe ~ B** 7.54, B 9.108; (members of) army 3.246, 21.448

follen *v* baptize 17.285, 21.40, **B** 15.447, 450; *ger.* **follyng** baptism 14.207, 208, 17.76, 21.39

follware 17.103 = **fol(o)ware** *n*

folowen 2.105 *etc* = **folewen** *v*

fond(e) *p.t.* Pr 19 *etc*, B 15.285, **A** 11.168, 12.59 *see* **fynden** *v*

fondement 16.41 = **foundement** *n*

fonden *v* test 18.248; put to trial (by tempting to sin) 14.119, *ger.* **fondyng** temptation 10.42, 16.136, 19.91, B 11.399; try to find 12.106, B 15.333; try (to) 15.145, 16.44, 18.43, 22.166, **B** 6.219, 17.81, Z 2.165

fondlyng *n* bastard, little rogue 10.299

fongen *v* get hold of B 16.96; receive 15.203, 16.7; accept 7.201; partake (of) 9.91

fonk *n* spark 6.334

font(e) *n* baptismal font 12.54, 14.207, A 12.15

foo 12.13, B 9.201 = **foe** *n*

foold B 7.53 = **folde** *n*

for[1] *prep.* because of, on account of Pr 7(2), 28, 1.128, 2.227, 3.447, 4.50, [63], 5.115, 7.303, 8.127, [182, 213, 244, 251,] 9.68, 10.149, 12.34, 13.7, [225,] 14.196, 15.149, 16.261, 17.14, 19.223, 20.64 [, 123, 179, 348,] 21.107, 206, 22.11, [105, 148, 165, 195,] 313, (*with* **to** + *inf.*) 16.262, **B** 1.27, 3.193, [200,] 5.36, [112, 233,] 9.89, [155,] 10.263, [290,] 11.225, 13.333, [405,] 14.177, 15.178, [208, 425,] 18.172, A 2.166, A 10.66; *in phrr.*: **what ~...and** both because of .... and 20.113; (*with a*) ~ **bitter** B 5.118, ~ **cold** B 3.191, ~ **wykkid** A 11.263 because of bitterness / coldness / wickedness; by reason of 6.200, 9.249, [312,] 10.268, 11.209, 12.126, 13.10, 15.254, 17.65, 18.289, 22.36, B 5.83, [10.73,] **A** 4.143, 12.73, [76,] Z 2.170; [7.267;] by dint of B 10.140; for the sake of Pr 43, 1.54, 6.173, 8.7, 10.237, 11.177, B 15.146; out of Pr 59, 3.177, 6.47, 8.132, 14.197, 22.251, B 7.115, [16.86,] A 12.111, Z 2.7; [Z 6.74;] *in assevs.*: 1.54, 2.2 [4.137, 7.201]; on behalf of, for the good of 3.53, [99,] 4.93, 8.46, 11.122, 13.122; for use as / on 5.129, 6.359; as, in the capacity of Pr 145, 3.114, [267, 381,] 4.159, [174,] 5.195, 6.40, [387,] 7.103, [107,] 8.223, 9.238, 10.243, [298,] 11.291, [310,]

12.54, [142, 144, 174,] 13.119, [125,] 14.76, 15.126, 16.303, [309,] [371,] 17.159, [201, 297,] 18.99, 19.240 (1), 20.23, [474,] 21.461, **B** Pr 159, 1.151, 2.133, 4.118, 6.195, 11.300, 13.305, 15.5, 16.112, **A** 8.57, 10.81, 111, 11.304; *in phrr.* **as ~** 2.146, 9.92, 12.197, 15.39, 171, 18.205, 22.20; concerning, with regard to B 11.230, 430, 13.290, **A** 10.65, 11.72; **as** ~ 7.191; ~ **me, mysulf** as far as I am concerned Pr 207, 4.134, B 12.15; (*in excl.*) 12.76, 16.92; for the space of 7.131, †B 1.121; for the purpose of 5.129, B 2.178; (*pleonastically before* **to** + *inf.* Pr 187 [2.221, 6.345] *et p.*, B 11.45; *with* **as** 14.7; in order to get 3.367, 16.63, [17.19, 20.404, 22.239, 326,] B 5.267, A 2.126; in exchange / return for 2.232, 3.42, 5.72, 8.196, 9.276, 12.205, 18.285, 19.205, 22.138, [267,] B 18.343; in payment for 12.17, B 2.105, A 8.43; in reward for 10.180; in punishment for 14.79[, 16.76]; as a remedy for 12.57, Z 5.93; to prevent 2.240, 8.8, 226, 334, B 1.24, A 10.85; to protect against 13.71, B 6.60, Z 7.53; against A 10.73; in spite of 2.211, 216, 3.20, 109, 113, 4.23, 6.35, 437, 7.209, 8.216, 12.13, 14.53, 15.305, 19.240, 244, 20.31, 101, 365, 21.96, 294, 309 (1, 2), 400, 22.342, **B** 5.90, 9.40, ? 10.433n, 17.294, **A** 2.32, 3.249, Z 2.177; in place of 7.103; *with* **to** + *inf.* at the cost of 10.194; ~ **no** in spite of any 7.230, 285, 9.17, 10.253, Z 4.121; ~ **nouhte** in spite of anything 4.57, A 11.258; ~ **hought** Z 4.42; instead of ?7.103, 107, B 15.121; (appropriate) to, (fitting) for 3.264, 5.61 (1), 9.129 [230, 13.108, 17.287, ? 19.144, 21.42, 99] **B** 3.346, [11.99, 15.104], Z 7.231; *in set phrr.*: ~ **pouere or ~ riche** A 2.59 (*marriage vows*); ~ **(the) beste** 7.125, 16.21, **B** 10.368, 11.197, A 11.154; ~ **þe nones** for the occasion (*or as tag*) A 2.41; ~ **sothe** truly 3.112 *et p.*; ~ **treuthe** in truth 6.386

for[2] *conj.* for (the reason that) Pr 101, 109, 137, 168, 1.36 *et p.*, B 2.25, 123, **A** 2.138, 11.273, 12.109; (+ **that**) since **B** 4.68, 10.352, Z 5.150, Z 7.77; (*introductory*) because 20.78, 183, 347, **B** 5.101, 9.35, 62, 14.77; (*amplifying*) inasmuch as, seeing that Pr 79, 203, 216, 1.14, 2.104 *et p.*, **B** Pr 193, 1.27, 98, A 11.138, Z 5.34, (*pleonastic*) Z 2.4; (*indicating aim*) so that 7.167, 13.164, 21.145

*****forager** *n* (*fig.*) harbinger, forager 22.85, 81 (**forreour**)

forbad *p.t.* **B** 10.206, 19.252 *see* **forbeden** *v*

forbar *p.t.* 3.426 *see* **forberen** *v*

forbeden *v* (*pr. subjv.* **forbede** 3.147, *p.t.* **forbad** B 10.206, *p.p.* **forboden** 3.188) forbid 3.147, 155, 9.327, B 10.206, B 19.252; *p.p.* prohibited B 13.349, *in phr.* **forbodene lawes** laws that forbid (sth.) 3.188; *and see* **forbode** *n*

forberen *v* (*p.t.* **forbar** 3.426) refrain (from killing) 3.426; give up 1.99; do without, spare B 11.209, Z 3.169

forbeten *v* wear out, *p.p.* 22.198

forbis(e)ne *n* model, example 17.277; allegorical parable 10.32

forbiten *v* (*contr. pr.* **forbit**) bite 20.34; eat away 18.39

forbode *n* prohibition, *in phr.* **Goddes (Lordes)** ~ God forbid (that) 3.138, **B** 4.194, 7.177, 15.579

forbrennen *v* (*p.p.* **forbrent**) burn up 3.107, 125

force *n* importance, *in phr.* #**no** ~ it does not matter 14.10

forcer *n* chest, coffer **B** 10.213

ford *n* crossing-place (in stream) 7.213; (*fig.*) way through (**forth**) 3.194

fordede *p.t.* 20.390, **fordide B** 16.166; *see* **fordo(e)n** *v*

fordo(e)n *v* (*p.t.* **ford(e)de** 20.390, *p.p.* **fordo** 15.231) destroy 5.122, 15.231, 20.28, 41, 154 ('neutralise'), 390; kill 20.67; ruin **B** 9.65; undo 19.255; defeat, overcome 20.160, 21.51; extinguish 19.263

fore[1] *n* track, footsteps 6.118

fore[2] (*stressed form of* **for** *prep.*) on account of 9.68, 21.107, 22.195

fore[3] *av* in advance Z 2.190; forth Z 5.27*n*

foreyn *n* stranger 9.199

forfader *n* forefather 7.133, 10.237

#**forel** *n* case, box [esp. for books] 15.104, A 11.159

*****foresleue** *n* fore-part of sleeve **B** 5.80

forest *n* forest 9.224; ?(enclosed) wood **B** 15.332

foretellen *v* mention beforehand A 11.168

fore-teth *n pl.* front teeth 20.383

foreward A 2.50 = **for(o)ward** *n*

forfader *n* forefather 7.133, 10.237

forfaren *v* perish 8.234, **B** 15.135

forfeten *v* go wrong, transgress 22.25

forfeture *n* loss of property, *in phr.* **vp**~ on pain of losing 4.128

forfreten *v* (*contr. pr.* **forfret**) eat up 18.33

forgen *v* join firmly A 2.23

forget *p.p.* A 11.293 *see* **for3eten** *v*

forgeuenesse 19.188 = **for3euenesse** *n*

forgyuen 3.8, 138, **B** 4.101, *p.p.* 3.134, 20.186 *see* **for-3euen** *v*

*****forglotten** *v* greedily consume 11.66

forgon *v* forfeit 13.48

forgoere *n* leader, guide 2.198; harbinger 2.61 (**vorgoer**)

*****forgrynden** *v* (*contr. pr.* **forgrynt**) utterly destroy **B** 10.79

forlyen *v* (*p.p.* **forleyen**) rape 4.46

forlong *n* square furlong of land 7.32; furlong's walk (1/8 mile, = small distance) **B** 5.5

formallych *av* correctly 17.109

forme *n* figure **B** 13.297; body 7.130; likeness 1.109, 20.315, 22.52

formen *v* create 1.161, **B** 1.14, 10.105, 11.387, 16.213, Z 1.7; prepare, appoint A 8.39; give instruction **B** 15.377; teach † **B** 15.450; make up, form **B** 17.170

form(e)our *n* creator 10.153, 19.134

formest(e), formost(e) *av* first 1.73; originally 20.161, 162, **B** 10.217; first of all 17.60; to begin with 17.233; ~ **and furste** first and foremost 6.15, 21.120 (*trs*), A 10.131 (*trs*)

for(o)ward *n* pledge 4.13; agreement **B** 6.35, 11.64; **in** ~ on the understanding A 2.50

forpynen *v* torture, *p.p.* = wretched **B** 6.155

forren *v* trim with fur, *p.p.* 8.291, 15.203, 22.176

forreour 22.81 *see* **forager** *n*

forsa(e)ken *v* (*p.t.* **forso(e)k(e)**, *p.p.* **forsake**) disown 17.81; reject 20.200; abandon 13.225, **B** 9.66, 15.35; renounce 9.202, 12.156, 168, 16.110, 22.38, 240, **B** 11.274, 16.11; give up 17.195, 18.76; deny (oneself) 12.171; shun 22.231; refuse **B** 15.84, 311; deny 15.141; repudiate (debt) 7.37, depart from 16.110, 19.290; leave behind 16.104

forschuppen *v* (**forshapen B**) unmake, disfigure (the work of creation) 19.272

forsleuthen *v* spoil through lack of use 7.52; delay Z 7.64

forsothe *av* truly 4.2, 16.284, **B** 10.185, A 11.291

forst *n* frost 12.190, 194, A 8.116, Z 6.74

forstallen *v* 'forestall' [intercept or buy up goods in advance, to re-sell at profit]

forster *n* forester, officer in charge of a forest (*fig.*) **B** 17.113

forsweren *v* (*p.p.* **forswore(n)**) swear a falsehood, *p.p.* guilty of breaking an oath 10.280; perjured (in court) 21.372, 374

forth *av* forth Pr 49 *et p.*; forward 11.195; away 12.167; out Pr 4, 67; out of 19.171; after 2.102; ahead 4.34; along 3.107; on, further Pr 226, **B** 10.437; (in succession) thereafter **B** 13.210; ~ **with** along with 10.233. **wher** ~ in what direction 16.340; *in phrasal verbs* (*see s.vv*): **beren** ~ 18.115; **blostren** ~ 7.158; **bowen** ~ **B** 5.566; **bryngen** ~ 1.18, *et p.*; **cairen** ~ **B** 4.24; **comen** ~ 20.80; **drawen** ~ 11.314; **dryuen** ~ Pr 226; **faren** ~ **B** 2.184; **fecchen** ~ 2.157; **fynden** ~ A 11.63; **flaumen** ~ **B** 17.206; **flyen** ~ 10.233; **folowen** ~ 11.196; **fostren** ~ 19.173; **gon** ~ 4.162; **growen** ~ 10.153; **lepen** ~ **B** Pr 223; **lyuen** ~ **B** 10.437; **loken** ~ A 7.13; **luppen** ~ 2.69; **passen** ~ 11.263; **plukken** ~ 19.12; **poken** ~ 7.262; **potten** ~ 2.50; **pryken** ~ 2.201; **proferen** ~ 19.117; **rennen** ~ 18.290; **ryden** ~ 2.194; **romben** ~ A 4.30; **springen** ~ 18.231; **standen** ~ 2.72; **strenen** 13.171; **stryken** ~ 7.223; **suen** 2.102; **trollen** 20.332; **walken** ~ 15.2; **wenden** ~ 6.351; **wexen** ~ **B** 9.32; **yeuen** ~ 12.167

forthenken 20.91 = **forthynken** *v*

forthere *av* further 7.285, 10.11, **B** 2.202, 5.6, 12.35, 39, **A** 10.99, 11.293, 12.30, 68, 76, 89; onwards A 7.188; afterwards, ?more widely 8.76

forthermore *av* in addition 9.232

forthy *conj.* therefore, for that reason Pr 118, 201, 11.232 *et p.*; because **B** 10.396; ?accordingly **B** 1.188*n*

forthynken *v* (*impers.*) repent, **hit me ~eth** 10.255, 20.91

forto[1] *part. (with inf.)* = to B 14.7

forto[2] *prep.* till Z 7.250, ? A 7.247

forto[3] *conj.* until 7.213, A 6.54

fortune *n* fortune, *in phr.* **grace of ~** prosperity due to chance 11.288; (*semi-person.*) 3.239; (*person.*) 11.168, 173, 185, 186, 190, 196, 311, 12.7, 13, 15.5, 22.110, 156, B 6.218; good luck 22.148; state (brought about by chance) 3.477, 16.131; lot 6.127

forwalked *p.p.a* exhausted with walking B 13.205

***forwanyen** *v* weaken morally 5.137

forw(e) *n* furrow 8.65 (B 6.104, A 7.96), furrow's width (of land) 6.268 (B 13.372)

forwhy *conj.* for which reason B 13.281

forwit *n* foresight B 5.164

forȝaf *p.t.* 20.78 *see* **forȝeuen** *v*

forȝat *p.t.* 12.12 *see* **forȝeten** *v*

forȝelden *v* reward, repay; Lord / God **(it) þee forȝelde** may God reward you (for it) 8.298, B 13.189

forȝeten, forȝyten *v* (*p.t.* **forȝat**, *p.p.* **forȝete(n)**) forget 7.13, 36, 47, 12.12, 19.209, 315, 22.155, 370; A 11.293

forȝeuen *v* (*p.t.* **forȝaf**, *p.p.* **forȝeue, forgyue(n)**) forgive 19.201, 209, 271, 315, 21.397; pardon 3.8, 134, 138, B 4.101; grant, vouchsafe 20.78, 186

forȝeuenesse *n* forgiveness 6.435, 19.188, 210, 331, 21.185; pardon 5.195; excuse from payment 22.287

fostren *v* produce A 10.122; **~ forth** generate 19.173, 176

fote 1.118 *etc*; *see* **foet** *n*

fouchensa(e)f *v* undertake 5.49; grant graciously 18.18

fouely 20.95 *see* **foule** *av*

foughten *p.t. pl.* Pr 43 *see* **fy(g)hten** *v*

foul sage 7.103 *see* **foel** *n*

foul, fow(e)l *n* (wild) bird 6.405, 8.30, 10.233, 11.102, 13.137, 164, 14.170, 171, 185, 190, 17.11, 15, 32, 22.44, **B** 7.129, 8.54, 66, 9.140, 15.302, 313, Z 7.59; (domestic) fowl B 15.463, 471, 478

foul *a* dirty B 13.318, B 15.113, (*comp.*) dirtier B 13.320, (*sup.*) dirtiest, ? most menial B 19.254; unpleasant (-tasting) B 12.242; filthy, horrible 6.161, 432, 16.136, 21.46, 22.85, (*comp.*) 3.96; repulsive 18.54; ugly B 11.394; hideous 13.174, 18.110, B 16.77; rough, stormy 8.347; vile, indecent 7.114, 10.276, B 10.40; sinful, wicked Pr 37, 7.54, 63, 114; disgraceful 16.371; low, wretched 21.33; vile, base B 18.94; bad 3.369, (*sup.*) worst, most noxious 12.226, B 18.153; shameful B 11.391

foule *av* filthily **B** 13.401, 14.15; foul 13.243, B 12.254; harshly 20.95, 350, **B** 10.321, 11.214; (*sup.*) in the most repulsive way 14.170; hideously B 5.82; wickedly 2.43; disgracefully 3.231; shamefully 16.15; rudely 22.5; grievously 11.305; basely B 15.352

foulen *v* dirty, soil 9.266; defile (with sin) A 7.136; injure B 3.154; choke 22.315

founde *p.t. subjv.* 6.22, 15.220, B 15.311; **founde(n)** *p.p.* 8.138 *etc*; *see* **fynden** *v*

fo(u)ndement *n* foundation 21.327, (*fig.*) 3.344, 345; basis, motive (for action) 16.41

founden *v* build B 1.64; found B 15.289; provide for, endow 17.57, B 15.324; devise B 10.217

foundo(u)r *n* patron, benefactor A 11.216; originator Z 3.176

foure *num. a* Pr 56 *etc*; **~ dayes** B 13.65; **~ doctours** B 9.73; **~ Euaungelies** 15.45; **~ fyngres** B 17.158; **~ ordres** Pr 56, A 8.177; **~ oxen** 21.263; **~ sedes** 21.311; **~ stottes** 21.268; **~ thynges** 10.129; **~ vertues** Pr 131, 21.313; **~ hundred wynter** 19.211; *as n* 9.57, 21.272, B 7.53

fourme 7. 130, 20.315, 22.52 = **forme** *n*; **fourmen** B 15.377, †450, A 8.39 = **formen** *v*

fourty *num. a* forty 3.41 *etc*; **~ daies** 10.228; **~ voues** 7.13; **~ wynter** 3.41 (*perh. as indef. number*), 7.188, 14.3 (**fyue and ~** B 12.3), 15.266; **~ wokes** 18.134

fox *n* fox 8.28, 9.224, 22.44

fraynen *v* ask, inquire of 1.54, 7.169, 10.3, 18.291, B 18.18

fraytour *n* refectory 5.173

fram *prep.* from Pr 54, 2.178, 3.127, 132, 5.111, 131, 159, 6.348, 7.88, 255, 8.46, 145, 9.241, 10.185, 15.237, 16.133, 211, 18.188, 19.51, 82, 98, B 15.345; away from B 15.463; out of B 11.417, 16.263

franchise *n* condition of freedom 20.106

#franchisen *v* make (sb.) a freeman, *p.p.* 3.114

frankeleyn *n* franklin [landowner ranking below nobility] 5.64, 10.243; gentleman 21.39

fraternite(e) *n* religious brotherhood, order (of friars) 9.343, 12.8, 22.368

fre(e) *a* free [of rank / condition, not slave / serf] Pr 106, 5.64, 21.33, (*fig.*) 21.39; free of the bondage of sin 1.73, 11.251, 21.59; free, unrestricted in action 19.122 (**~ wil** 10.51, B 16.223, **~ wit** 10.51); noble 20.106, 22.146; of the gentry / nobility **B** 2.77, 11.383; generous 11.57, B 15.150, 151; freely available 9.57; = as a freeman of a corporation #3.111

freek 15.82 = **freke** *n*

freel 10.48 = **frel(e)** *a*; **freeletee** 19.314 = **frelete** *n*

freet *p.t.* 20.200 *see* **freten** *v*[1]

frek(e) *n* man, person 6.152, 9.153, 11.158, 15.2, 82, 18.185, **B** 4.13, 156, 6.218, 250, 11.26, 13.65, A 12.66

frel(e) *a* weak 3.157; changeable 10.48

frelete *n* frailty, weakness 3.59, 19.314

#freman *n* freeman [member of a town corporation] 3.108, 114

frem(me)de *a as n* stranger 12.157, B 15.141

Frenche *a* French B 11.384, Z 7.278, *as n* 13.203

frend(e) *n* friend 6.72, 10.13, 305, 12.106, 15.197,

17.125, 144, 20.457, **B** 5.100, 9.201, 11.177, 193, 12.257, 15.151, 17.87; intimate 17.143; benefactor 3.56, 9.199, 16.314, 317, 22.286; supporter 16.136, 21.145, Z 3.151; ally 10.87, 11.186, 12.7; relative 5.36, 40, 10.185, 12.157, 16.105, **B** 7.167, 9.115

frendli *av* amicably, *comp.* **frendloker** B 10.227 (**frend-liere** A 11.174)

#freneseye *n* (bout of) frenzy, delirium 22.85

frenesse *n* gracious generosity B 16.88

Frenssh *n* French (language) B 5.235

#frentik(e) *a* crazed, deranged 11.6, 18.179

frere *n* (*uninfl. gen.* frere 7.285, 9.208, 15.104, 16.353) friar 2.220, 240, 3.38, 56, 5.173, 6.287, 147, 191, 9.249, 10.8 *et p.*, 11.54, 12.5 *et p.*, 14.89, 15.30, 79, 16.228, 233, 287, 17.35, 52, 60, 22.58, 230, 240, 267, 273, 290, 296, 368, 384, **B** 5.80, (Envye), 135 (Wrathe), 144, 10.94, 11.68, 12.19, 13.199, Z 3.151; **the Freres** the Friars' church 7.27, 16.41; the Friars' convent 2.220, 22.285; ~ **Austynes** the Augustinian Friars 17.15; ~ **Faytour** Friar Deceiver 8.73; ~ **Fla-trere** Friar Flatterer 22.316 *et p.*; **faythful** ~ 6.291; **fals** ~ 15.79; **maistres** ~s B Pr 62; **mendenaunt** ~s Pr 60; **poore** ~s B 15.311; **syke** ~s 15.119

fresen *v* freeze 12.194, A 8.116

fres(s)h(e) *a* fresh 8.333, B 15.431, Z 7.316; freshly shed 7.133; fresh-flowing **B** 10.295, 15.337

freten *v*¹ (*p.t.* **freet, frete**) eat 2.100, 20.200; chafe 6.74 (**vrete**); *pr.p.* destructive 20.156

freten *v*² (*p.p.* **fretted**) adorn B 2.11

Friday *n* Friday 6.351, 438, 7.130, 10.8, 18.167, 21.142, 22.313, *pl.* 5.30, 6.155, 182, 9.94, **B** 13.349, 16.162; **God(e)** ~ Good Friday 7.106, 11.255, 14.131, 141, B 5.489

frien *v* fry, *p.p.* **yfried** 8.333, B 13.63

frith *n* wood(land) 9.224, 14.158, 17.11, **B** 11.364, 17.113

frithen (in) *v* hedge in, enclose 7.227

fro *prep.* from Pr 114, 1.4, 2.47 *et p.*; out of 7.300; against 10.287, 16.132; in distinction from 10.122; away from 7.17, 15.175, 16.335

frokke *n* long gown 16.353, B 5.80

from *prep.* from 7.105, 19.30, B 1.4 *etc*, A 7.128, Z 7.268

#frounce *n* wrinkle, crease B 13.318

fruyt *n* produce of crops 8.347, 16.253, 21.315; fruit (of Charity) 18.12 *et p.* (B 16.9 *et p.*) 20.18, (of Eden) 18.123, 20.198, 200, (of Piers) 20.18, 32, B 16.94, (*fig.*) B 5.140, A 10.122; offspring 10.276, 18.79

#fruyten *v* (*p.p.* **yfruyted**) come to fruit B 16.39

fuyr(e) *n* fire 6.334, 19.171 *et p.* Z 6.72; destructive fire, conflagration 3.103, 9.182, 11.252, 15.166; flame 21.206; (=) lightning 3.91, 96, 102, 125; the element fire 9.56, 15.243; mystical fire (of the Holy Spirit) 14.208; *in phr.*: **a-fuyre** on fire 7.52

ful¹ *a* full Pr 19, 1.2, 8.182, 10.272; full to capacity 3.88, 18.155, B 15.337, **A** 7.167, 12.71; well-supplied 12.226, 13.58, 19.294, 21.118, B 15.333; complete 19.131, **B** 15.153, 17.167, 168, 170, 173; ~ **tyme** fully time B 2.96; ? the moment of completion, noon B 5.489; the (appointed) time of fulfilment 18.137; *as n. in phr.* **to þe fulle** completely, in full measure 17.57; fully 20.410; in full B 13.193; one's fill B 14.178, A 12.72

ful² *av* fully, entirely 16.78; most 20.119; very (*with a and av*) Pr 23, 28, 204, 2.12, 19, 154, 164, 3.51, 85, 199, 495, 4.52, 5.123, 7.175, 250, 274, 9.11, 53, 141, 206, 11.2, 196, 317, 14.99, 15.90, 19.50, 52, 22.52, **B** Pr 26, 161, 3.251, 4.74, 6.44, 204, 7.124, 146, 10.186, 211, 11.78, 351, 12.254, 13.204, 15.116, 201, 16.179, 230, 234, 18.119, **A** 6.84, 8.110, 12.78, **Z** 3.157, 168, 5.45, 6.80, 7.298

ful³ *p.t.* Pr 106, 113, 1.119, 3.107, 6.334, 10.39, 16.211, 20.89, 21.5, 22.51, 176, Z 5.110; **fulle** *p.t. subjv.* 18.128, *p.t.* Z 1.60; **fullen** *p.t. pl.* 1.125; *see* **fallen** *v*

fulfillen (fulfellen, fulfullen) *v* carry out 1.74, 2.127, 3.417, 9.233, 16.27, 17.142; fulfil (prophecy) 21.80; elapse 8.345, 10.228

fullen *see* **ful** *p.t.*

fullen¹ 6.389 = **fillen** *v*

#fullen² *v* grow full 11.41

#fullen³ *v* full (woollen cloth), *ger.* **#fullyng (stokkes)** B 15.452

fullyche *av* fully, *in phr.* ~ **to his power** to the limits of his capacity B 15.61

fullyng *ger.* 14.208, B 15.450; *see* **follen** *v*

fundement 3.344, 345 *see* **foundement** *v*

furst(e) *ord. num. a* (**first** B 1.76 *et p.*, **ferst** A 1.74, 10.132) first 6.210, 419, 10.145, 15.105, 16.119, 187, 17.316, 18.34, 20.226, 21.70, 277, **B** 3.244, 5.166; original 20.159, B 11.64; primary, ultimate 18.93; *as n* **the** ~ 1.23, 2.65, 109, 12.38, 19.35, 132, 134, B 16.184; the originator 14.164, A 10.28; the chief person(s) 9.250; **at þe** ~ straight away 2.210, 8.168

furst(e) *av* first 3.36, 5.110, 6.210, 7.169, 11.120, 122, 15.5, 39, 18.94, 248, 291, 21.439, **B** 1.76, 5.51, 9.115; beforehand 12.183, 15.211, B 10.283; origi-nally 11.120, 14.160, 19.114, 20.227, 345, B 9.191, A 11.135; in the first place 7.143, 169, 9.221, 20.246, A 12.113; in the beginning 18.123, B 18.158; *in phr.* **formost and** ~ above all, first and foremost 6.15, A 10.131

furst *n* thirst 6.437, 20.410, 22.19, A11.46 (**þrest**), (*per-son.*) A 7.168 (**Ferst**)

fursten *v* (*impers.*) be thirsty 20.408

furthe 16.131 *see* **ferthe** *ord. num. a*

furwe B 6.104 = **forw** *n*

fust(e) *n* fist 6.66, 19.114, 126 *et p.*, B 17.139 *et p*; **a** ~**wyse** in the manner of a fist 19.151

ga *subjv.* Pr 228 *see* **gon** *v*

gabben *v* lie 3.225, 17.16; *ger.* **gabbyng** lying, deceit 17.129, 21.457, deception 22.125

gable *n* gable (-window) 3.52

gad(e)lyng *n* scoundrel B 4.51; rascal B 9.104; bastard, base fellow 10.298, 22.157

gaderen *v* muster 21.338, 22.113; seek, amass (wealth) 6.259, **B** 12.51, 250, 13.370; gather 18.112; collect (money *etc*) 16.71, 22.369

ga(e)f *p.t.* 21.268, 22.171, **gaf** 2.232 = ȝ**af** (**yaf**); *see* ȝ**euen** (**yeuen**) *v*

gay *a* fine 20.177

gayler *n* gaoler 3.174

gaynesse *n* luxury 11.66

galle *n* bile, ? rancour B 5.118; (*fig.*) malice B 16.155

galoche *n* shoe 20.12n

galon *n* gallon 6.230, 392, 396

galpen *v* open (one's) mouth wide 15.98

game *n* delight, ? pastime B 9.102; pastime A 11.37, †B 10.50; play B 5.407; sport Pr 171

gan *p.t.* 1.168 *etc*; *see* **gynnen** *v*

gangen *v* go 16.14, 18.177, B 2.168; *pr. p.* walking 18.242

gapen *v* stare open-mouthed B 10.41

gardyn *n* garden 20.313, 380, (*fig.*) B 16.13; ~**er** *n* gardener B 5.136

garen *v* (*p.t.* **gart(e)**, **gerte**) cause, make 5.146, 8.324, 11.122, 22.57, 131, **B** 1.123, 5.61, 129, 15.443, A 7.132 (**gere** Z 7.129)

†**garisoun** *n* deliverance B 6.138

garleek *n* garlic 6.358; ~ **monger** *n* garlic-seller 6.372

garlond *n* wreath, crown 20.48

garnement *n* garment, attire 9.119, 20.177, **B** 13.400, 14.25

gasten *v* frighten Z 7.325; *and see* **agasten** *v*

gat *p.t.* 4.75, B 1.33 *etc*; *see* **geten** *v*

gate *n*[1] gate 2.132, 7.241, 248, 281, 11.42, 12.49, 16.365, 18.242, 20.272; gateway 8.284; *see also* ȝ**ate, yate** *n*

gate *n*[2] way 19.46, 22.342, **B** 1.205, 17.112, A 12.88, **heiȝe** ~ main road B 4.42; path A 12.88; *in phr.* **letten hym þe** ~ obstruct his progress 3.193, 13.91; going 20.251

gateward *n* gatekeeper 7.242, 13.91

geaunt *n* giant 20.261, 22.215, (*fig.*) B 6.231

gedelyng B 9.104 = **gad(e)lyng** *n*

gederen 22.369 *see* **gaderen** *v*

gees Pr 228, 4.49, 5.19, 15.68, B 6.280 *see* **goos** *n*

gef Z 3.117 *p.t., ?or* = **gyue** *p.p.*; *see* ȝ**euen** *v*

#**gendre** *n* kind, species B 16.222; (grammatical) gender 3.394

generacion *n* (act of) generation B 16.222

gentel, gentil *a* belonging to the nobility or gentry 5.78, (*fig.*) 12.112, 21.34, 40; noble, gracious 1.180, 11.21, 13.14, 24, 21.48, 266, **B** 10.35, 11.246; gentile, pagan 17.132

genteliche *av* courteously 3.14; pleasantly 15.208

gentrice (gentries) *n* nobility, gracious generosity 20.21, B 14.181

geomesie *n* geomancy [divination from dots and figures on the earth] B 10.210

geometrie *n* geometry (= *geomatria*) B 10.210n

gerl B 1.33 = **gurl** *n*

gerner *n* granary, grain-store B 7.130

gerte Z 5.77 = **garte**

gerþ *n* saddle-girth (*fig.*) B 4.21

gesene *a* scarce B 13.271

gesse *n* consideration, **vp** ~ without thinking B 5.415

gest *n* guest, visitor 10.181, B 15.285; **Goddes** ~ stranger 15.200

geste *n* chivalric tale 15.206; heroic story 7.106; tale B 10.31; writings 11.21

geten *v* (*p.t.* **gat** 4.75, **gete(n)** 20.313, 22.157, B 18.354, *p.p.* **(y)gete(n)** 6.341, 20.101, 322) get, obtain Pr 164, 4.138, 6.340, 7.268, 281, 290, 11.84, 16.278, 18.52, 20.313, 322, 377, B 18.356; win, earn 20.12, 101; beget 10.298, 21.121, 22.157, A 10.160

geterne *n* gittern 15.209

geuen *pr. or p.t. pl.* 6.374; *see* ȝ**euen** *v*

gyde *n* guide 7.306, Z 2.158; leader B 15.435

gyen *v* guide, lead 2.198; (*refl.*) conduct (oneself) 21.228

gif *pr. subjv.* A 12.111 *see* ȝ**euen** *v*

gyft 3.338, 4.138, 7.268, 9.133, 11.288, 14.33, 15.210, **B** 5.53, 12.63, A 3.229 *etc* = ȝ**efte** *n*

gyle *n* guile, deceitful behaviour 6.190, 213, 259, 11.268, 16.278, 17.242, 20.162, 313, 377, 382, 396, 399, 21.457, 22.67, B 13.370, 18.361; deceitfulness, treachery Pr 12, 2.26, 125, 3.130, 211, 286, 12.242, 17.129, 20.322, 392, 21.301, 302, 458, 22.57, B 16.155, A 8.41; (*person.*) 2.70 *et p.*, 3.499, 17.111, A 2.24

gylen *v* deceive 9.65, 16.305, 22.125

gylle *n* gill (= 1/4 pint) 6.396

gylour *n* deceiver 20.162, 164, 382, B 10.194; defrauder 3.100, B 2.121

gilt[1] B 3.108 *etc*, A 3.8 *etc*; = **gult** *n*

gilt[2] **B** 15.221, 17.14, 18.14 = **gult** *a*

gilty *a* B 5.368, 10.258, 12.76, 192, **giltier** *a* (*comp.*) B 5.368, 12.79 *see* **gulty** *a*

gyn *n* device, engine (of war) 20.261

gynful *a* crafty, treacherous B 10.210

gynnen *v* (*p.t. sg..* **gan** 1.168 *etc*, *pl.* **gonne** Pr 145) begin 6.397, 15.98, 19.189, A 10.127; proceed (to) 2.176, 4.90, 5.105, 6.403, 22.110, B 10.111 *etc*; (*as weak auxil. + inf. = simple p.t.*) did / does 1.168, 2.139, 3.11, 4.148, 6.146, 179, 351, 430, 7.200, 8.149, 10.115, 11.87, 314, 12.52, 110, 18.8, 36, 19.63, 20.95, 254, 22.200, 302, 387, A 12.29, (**gonne(n)** Pr 145, **B** 8.116, 13.267, (*2nd pers.*) 7.122); *ger.* **gynnyng(e)** *n* beginning (in time) 10.154, **B** 2.30, 16.187, 194; *and see* **bigynnynge** *n*

gyour *n* (spiritual) guide 21.428, 22.72

gyrdel *n* girdle, belt B 15.123; *in phr.* **styuest vnder ~** most valiant 6.43

girl B 10.79, 177, **A** 10.160 = **gurl** *n*

girte *p.t.* B 5.373; *see* **gurden** *v*

gyse *n* dress, fashion Pr 26

gyuen[1] Pr 74 *et p.*; **gyuere** B 7.68; *see* **ȝeuen** *v*, **ȝeuere** *n*

gyuen[2] *v* shackle (*fig.*) 22.192

gyues *n.pl.* shackles 15.255

glad *a* glad, joyful, merry 3.282, 454, 16.300, *a as n* A 11.193; happy, pleased 16.298, A 10.100, *comp.* **glad(d)er(e)** 11.103, 22.62, B 5.91; cheerful 6.374, B 8.94; pleasant B 16.155

glad(i)en *v* gladden, make joyful 9.300, B 18.255; cheer 19.184, 22.171; comfort 8.126, 21.147; entertain 20.177, B 10.43; please A 10.201

gladliche *av* gladly, willingly 6.105, 16.345

glasen *v* glaze, fit (window) with glass 3.52, 65

glasene *a* (made of) glass, **gyue a ~ howue** delude with an imaginary protection 22.172

glede *n* live coal 19.184, 190, 198, B 2.12; fiery spark B 5.284

glee *n* music(al entertainment) B Pr 34

gleman *n* minstrel 6.403, 11.103, (*fig.*) B 9.102, 104

glenen *v* glean [gather corn left by reapers] 8.67

glyden *v* glide, pass through 20.478

globben *v* gulp, *p.p.* **yglobbed (yglupid** A) 6.396

glorie *n* glory 20.273; splendour 20.342; pride (in worldly renown) B 10.115, Z 2.72; vainglory 22.157

gloriously *av* splendidly 19.16

#**glosar** *n* sycophant 21.222

glose *n* gloss, explanatory comment (on text) 10.245, 15.83, 19.16, **B** 5.275, 12.291, 15.82, (*fig.*) 3.328

glosen *v* gloss, write explanatory comment on (text) 6.301, 11.117, 13.119, 19.13; interpret speciously Pr 58, *ger.* B 13.75; speak deceitfully 22.369, B 10.194, *prp.* *a* flattering 4.138; *ger.* smooth talking 6.259, cajoling words 22.125

gloto(u)n *n* glutton Pr 74, 15.87, **B** 9.61, 13.400, Z 2.92, (*fig.*) intemperate talker B Pr 139; **Goddes ~** 'godly glutton' B 13.78, 400; (*person.*) 6.349 *et p.*, 8.324, **Z** 5.104, 7.275

glotony(e) *n* gluttony [intemperate desire for / indulgence in food and / or drink] Pr 24, 44, 1.29, 2.97, 11.66, 16.73, 76, **B** 1.33, 10.50, Z Pr 82, (*person.*) 16.71, B 14.235, A 7.285, Z 2.72

gloue *n* glove 6.251, 13.47, B 6.153, Z 6.71

glowen *v* glow 19.189, 190, *prp.* 19.184; **~ on fuyr** catch fire 3.102

glubbere *n* gulper, **glotons glubberes** gulping gluttons B 9.61; *and see* **globben** *v*

gnawen *v* gnaw, (*fig.*) talk irreverently about 11.41

#**gnedy** *a* stingy 15.87

gobet *n* morsel, small portion 5.100

god *n* deity, divine being 1.86, 20.318, 22.57, B 9.61, Z 7.275

God (*main refs. only*) God Pr 117, 121, 1.26, 103, 177, 2.128, 132, 3.95, 323, 338, 353, 409, 413 *et p.*, 462, 5.67, 105, 6.16, 84, 111, 169, 424, 7.150, 206, 8.217, 236, 9.115, 289, 322, 346, 10.99, 158, 162, 202, 223, 252, 304, 11.27, 41, 46, 52, 61, 149, 212, 230, 309, 12.85, 151, 13.91, 124, 198, 14.37, 133, 194, 217, 15.141, 260, 299, 16.93, 95, 184, 306, 17.59, 80, 90, 131, 141, 152, 18.204, 211, 227, 236, 242, 19.31, 99, 148 *et p.*, 250, 270, 279, 20.186, 195, 216, 220, 226, 230, 246, 250, 258, 318, 323 *et p.*, 21.292, 433, 445, 22.34, 40, 254, 278, **B** 1.122, 2.120, 3.232, 5.53, 72, 6.138, 224, 228, 314, 7.76, 124, 130, 8.51, 9.46, 64, 65, 66, 95, 129, 204, 10.28, 66, 119, 364, 11.242, 272, 279, 395, 12.12, 14.100, 125, 15.66, 260, 263, 285, 16.9; (*with* Christ *as referent*) 1.46, 3.68, 10.208, 246, 12.102, 140, 163, 179, 213, 18.149, 20.446, 21.18, 110, 116, 174, B 10.261, A 12.29; *with standard epithets*: ~ **almyhty** 7.217, 15. 281, 18.96, 19.38, **B** 7.80, 9.93, 190, 11.196, 15.295, A 11.32; **dere ~** 1.83, **fayth-full** 17.35; **fol** 19.132; **gode ~** 6.435, B 15.250; **grete** 21.209, B 2.29; **grete hye** 17. 256; **grettest** 10.154; **myȝtful** B 11.277; **verray** 6.437; ~ **of grace** 21.213; *****God-man** God-made-man B 11.205; ~ **sulue** 14.26, 17.179, **hymselue** B 7.55, 9.117, 10.37, 201, 240, 16.13; ~ **Fader, Sone, Holy Goost** B 10.241; **Lord ~** 8.135, B 5.563; **o, oon ~** 11.154, 17.134, 18.211, 238, 19.31 *et p.*, **B** 2.30, 15.395; *in phrr.* ~ **and good(e) men** 5.67, 6.18; **gifte of ~** 11.288, 14.33; **grace of ~** 6.285, 14.28, 131, 15.228, B 9.59, 178, A 11.300; **wisdom and wit of ~** 13.228; *in assevs:* so me ~ helpe, *etc.* 2.126, 5.22, 6.296, 7.284, 20.240; *in poss. phrr:* **Goddes berthe** 14.93; **body** 20.77, 476, (*sacramental*) 20.240, 21.388, B 12.85; **boys** 9.127; **champion** B 15.216; **chosene** B 11.118; **clerk** 16.190; **derling** A 12.19; **foles** 11.251; **folk** B 15.135; **foweles** B 15.313; **gestes** 15.200; **gloton** B 13.78; **goed(es)** 10.177, 17.67; **grace** 10.168, B 14.20; **herte** 22.226; **heste** 17.142; **hous** B 10.405; **ymages** 20.326; **kynde** 19.254; **knyghtes** 1.107, 13.125; **lawe** 7.118, 9.104, 158, B 15.93; **loue** 6.47, 8.284, 9.66, 10.203, 16.103, B 11.276; **mede** A 3.223; **men** 17.67, B 3.71; **mercy** 11.218, 18.288; **munstrals** 7.99, 9.136; **name** B 13.402; **payne** 7.20; **passion B** 15.255, 16.38; **peple** A 11.198; **resureccioun** 20.473; **salt** B 15.441; **secret seal** 9.138; **seruice** 9.227; **sihte** 11.203; **sone** 18.149, 236, 20 55, 70, 331; **tretor** 19.240; **veniance** 14.69; **werk(es)** 10.290, 12.75; **wille** B 9.154; **word(es)** 6.84, 7.87, 94, 11.235, 21.389,

godchild *n* godchild, *pl.* B 9.75; (*fig.*) B 10.324

godfader *n* godfather B 9.75

godhede *n* the divine nature 18.227, 238, 239, 19.38, 21.158, 198, B 9.46, A 10.36

godmoder *n* godmother B 9.75

go(e)d, good *n* good (*as opp. to* evil) 14.164, 20.318; strength, power B 17.130; good deed(s), right conduct 7.286, 10.94, 16.110, **B** 10.203, **A** 4.108, 10.52; (þe) ~ good / virtuous people 9.15, 10.311, 11.310, 15.216, 20.301, 21.198, 443; benefit 1.24, 34, **B** 8.94, 11.381; good thing 3.365; blessing ?21.104, B 14.318; goods, possessions, property 1.177, 2.35, 145, 3.95, 214, 4.158, 6.258, 275, 284, 296, 8.144, 236, 251, 10.45, 168, 177, 257, 264, 300, 11. 57, 66, 12.20, 22, 240, 244, 13.72, 16.86, 282, **B** 9.164, 14.169, 270, A 3.248; wealth, money 6.340, 9.31, 135, 10.257(3), 11.27, 69, 72, 77, 212, 232, 12.5, 13.4, 16.255, 19.250, 21.104, 22.289, **B** 5.260, 11.276, 13.357, 370, 15.140, 175, A 11.248; (*fig.*) **B** 5.296, 9.87; useful knowledge Pr 196

go(e)d, go(o)d(e) *a* good 6.102, 435, 17.90; worthy 5.67, 7.108, 242, 21.271, **B** 2.30, 10.223; fine, ?strong 6.356, 374, 8.324, 16.73, 22.223, B 6.300; excellent Pr 228, 13.28, 16.120(1), 18.12, 87, 22.34, **B** 10.292, 12.30, Z 7.49; careful 9.71, 12.46, 14.99, 19.15, **B** 11.111, 17.104; right 11.307, 18.204; sound 16.120(2), 17.58, 18.84, 20.164, **B** 5.164, 14.315; valid B 15.349; solid B 5.286; effective B 15.435; honourable 3.302, 13.110, B 15.436; well-bred B 15.216; virtuous Pr 29, 2.35, 3.68, 92, 103, 339, 5.192, 9.50, 10.60, 257 (1,2), 263, 11.62, 14.25, 16.191, 19.260, **B** 8.61, 9.64, 10.436, 437, 13.73, 15.146, 423, 433, 16.9, **A** 9.52, 87, 10.53, Z 7.82; pious 17.134; holy 7.174, **B** 7.74, 10.202; kind 14.194, 19.330(2), 20.220, B 15.147, 169, 250; prosperous 22.111; fortunate 20.163, B 5.96; favourable 6.260; *in phrr*: ~ **auntur** by good luck 8.79; ~ **day** farewell A 12.75; ~ **fayth** trustworthiness, integrity 4.37, 21.302, 22.28, (*person.*) 131; **by** ~ **fayth** truly 6.340; ~ **Friday** 7.106, 11.255, 14.131, B 12.201; ~ **herte** courage 22.180; ~ **hope** (the virtue of) hope 19.293, 22.167; ~ **is, were** it would be well 20.71, B 15.565; ~ **wille** sincere intention; **with** ~ **wille** willingly 2.168, 7.295, sincerely 6.336, with benign intent 9.111; ~ **woen** in abundance 22.171; **maken** ~ repay 19.77, 205, B 5.272

good *av* well Pr 58, A 7. 131, 11.248 (2)

go(e)dnesse, goodnesse *n* goodness B 16.62; virtue, piety A 10.80; generosity 3.22; merciful kindness 6.61, 7.61, 122, 8.353, 12.85, 20.226, 21.116, **B** 1.122, 14.170, A 12.111

goodly(che) *av* graciously 11.138; gladly 1.177, B 11.279

goelde 22.171 = **gold** *n*

go(e)n *v* (*imp. pl.* **goth** 7.212, *p.p.* **go** 6.213, *p.t.* (1) **ȝede, yede** Pr 41 *etc*, (2) **wente** (*for refs. see under* **wenden**) walk 22.192, *p.t.* **ȝede** 9.296, 20.3, 22.2, 183, 185, 192, B 17.100; go Pr 44, 2.158, 168, 5.105, 6.213, 349, 7.156, 253, 290, 11.200, 16.73, 19.46, 64, 20.337, 21.147, 395, 22.273, 342, B 7.130, 9.107, *p.t.*

ȝede 6.417, 7.53, 136 (**ȝedest**), 8.108, 13.136, 15.152, 263, 18.169, 19.50, 20.314, 21.4, 153, 22.136,B 1.73; travel 4.124, 7.205, 11.200, 13.52, 14.93, 21.158, **B** 13.182, †300, 15.435, 443, *p.t.* **ȝede** Pr 41, 6.417, 7.53, 12.124, B 16.170; travel along 10.113, 17.111; go away, depart 2.213, 221, 7.295, **B** 9.92, 10.61, *p.t.* **ȝede** 4.162, 10.113, **B** 1.73, 11.339; lead **B** 1.205; spread 3.194; pass, *p.t.* **ȝede** B 15.304, A 12.60; *in phr.* **Lat** ~ **the coppe** let the cup pass along; move 6.403; engage in (sth.) 8.138, 246, 9.170, *p.t.* **ȝede** 6.267; live 9.117, 10.148, 17.196, *ger.* (way of) living 10.304, B 9.82, A 10.53, *p.t.* B 13.74, A 11.273; live 17.196; dwell 21.214, A 11.273; (*inchoative or semi-expletive*) proceed to, set about (sth.) Pr 228, 5.126, 6.181, 8.28, 67, 151, 227, 9.170, 266, 10.57, 225, 287, 12.50, 165, 18.122, 20.284, 473, 22.369; **B** 5.640, 6.31, 300, 11.54, 12.16, 13.32, A 12.36; turn to, refer to 1.44, 8.239, (*subjv.*) 18.227, ?B 10.194 (*see note*); be 6.213, 20.328, 22.186, *p.t.* **ȝede** 20.337, = go 11.50, B 10.360; remain free 3.136; (go) dress(ed) 19.247, *p.t.* **ȝede** 12.129, 17.196; be in form of 20.326 (*ger.*), 327; *in phrr*: ~ **agayn** rush to attack 21.362; ~ **gile ayein gile** let guile oppose guile B 18.358; ~ **hennes** die 9.348, **B** 3.245, (*ger.*) 14.165; ~ **ther God is** = to the next life; ~ **(to)gederes** belong to(gether) 18.238, 3.280

goere (to) *n* frequenter (of) B 9.104

goest 18.75 *etc*; **goestliche** 22.40 *see* **go(e)st-(liche)** *n, av*

goyng(e) *ger.* departure B 14.165; (outward) appearance 20.326, 327; conduct 10.304, A 10.53

#goky *n* fool 13.119, 120

gold *n* gold Pr 178, 4.127, 6.287, 10.168, 21.76, 88, 89, A 2.13; *in phrr*. **brent** ~ B 5.267; **clene** ~ 3.23; **puyre** ~ 4.91; **reed** ~ 21.88, B 2.16; **knappes of** ~ B 6.269; **motoun of** ~ 3.25; **pounde of** ~ 16.297; **rybanes of** ~ Z 2.17; gold money Pr 74, 2.158, 162, 3.174, 227, 9.133, 11.103, 17.205, 22.171, **B** Pr 34, 5.53, Z 2.167

gold *a* (made of) gold 17.207; ~ **wyr** B 2.11

goliardeis *n* buffoon B Pr 139

gom(e) *n*[1] (*uninfl. gen.* 20.328, *pl.* **gomus** Pr 44) man 7.178, 13.119, 198, 20.226, 328, 21.121, **B** 2.74, 5.368, 13.182, 357, 15.285, 17.37; man-servant B 17.86; person 13.91, 16.95, 305, **B** 10.226, †12.60, †14.8, 17.112; *pl.* people Pr 44, 10.238, 16.345, **B** 13.300, 17.130

gome *n*[2] heed 19.15; *and see* **ȝeme (yeme)** *n*

gomme *n* aromatic gum 2.236

gongen = **gangen** *v*

gonne *n* cannon 20.291

gonne(n) *p.t. pl.* Pr 145, *sg.* 7.122; *see* **gynnen** *v*

good 1.24, Pr 29, *see* **go(ed)** *n, a*

goos (*pl.* **gees**) goose 8.304; **goose wynge** goose's wing, = thing of small value B 4.37; *pl.* geese Pr 228, 5.19, 15.68, B 6.280

gorge *n* throat 11.41, B 10.66

gospel *n* the (teaching of the) Christian Gospel Pr 58,

1.86, 12.102; = (the text of one of) the Gospel(s) 1.44, 3.74, 10.238, 245, 11.235, 12.31, 213, 13.97, **B** 3.75, 5.54, 6.226, 7.127, 10.112, 261, 275, 475, 12.63, A 12.25; the Gospel (passage) read at Mass 13.120

†**gospellere** *n* evangelist B 10.246

gossip *n* friend 6.47, 356, A 5.154

go(e)st, **goost** *n* devil, demon 20.478; (divine) Spirit B 10.238; spirit (ghost) 12.214, B 15.145; soul (of man) 1.34, 6.175, 11.230, B 9.46; (=thought) 7.150; **Holy ~** the Holy Spirit of God 14.84, 18.52, 75, 196, 19.121, 147, 148, 166, 181, 189, 190, 196, 215, 221, 254, 258, 264, 20.133, **B** 10.238, 241, 12.63, 16.224, 17.156; *see also* (**Seint**) (**E)spirit**; **~ly** *a* spiritual B 15.572, 575; **~liche** *av* ?truthfully, really, (*or a*) ?spiritual 22.40*n*

goth(e)l(y)en *n* rumble 6.397, 15.98

gott(e) *n* gut, stomach; *pl.* 6.397, 8.175, 11.41, 15.98, A 12.76, Z 7.163; *sg.* stomach as seat of gluttony 1.34

goudnesse A 12.111 = **go(e)dnesse** *n*

goune *v* gown, robe 15.203, 16.298

gouernen *v* hold sway (over) 3.437; control, have mastery of 22.34; discipline, restrain B 5.51

gowte *n* gout, swelling at joint 22.192

grace *n* God's grace / favour 1.196, 199, 3.339, 5.98, 100, 6.285, 7.156, 268, 281, 290, 9.348, 10.168, 11.227, 14.33, 17.256, 265, 19.250, 20.428, **B** 9.101, 12.68; (*spec.*) grace as divine gift 10.177, 11.212, 15.228; as grace of repentance 3.100, 6.61, 7.120, 10.304, 11.232, 14.23, 28 (2)*n*, 131, 19.279, 291, B 14.20, 170, Z 5.95; as grace of a virtuous life **B** 5.260, 6.227, 8.61, 9.178, 10.188, (*pl.*) **B** 2.29, 15.66, A 10.129, Z 1.128; the state of grace 11.208; (quality of) virtue 14.28(1)*n*, 17.48, 21.321, B 15.423; ~ as special attribute of the Holy Spirit 19.168, 181, 188, 215, 279; ~ as divine power 18.52, 20.163, 392, 396, B 16.51, A 11.300, (*person.*) 7.247, 253, (= the Holy Spirit) 21.121, 209 *et p.*, 389, 428, 22.387; ~ as divine help in secular affairs 2.35, 3.323, 6.84, 8.132, 9.55, 10.211, 11.288, 12.186, 13.22, 17.256, 21.131, B 9.107; God's goodness, *esp.* mercy 1.76, 2.1, 132, 244, 6.319, 7.60, 250, 14.28(2), 57, 132, 197, 20.92, 189, 21.110, 116, 213, 22.140, **B** 10.342, 11.148, Z 5.93; ~ as natural gift 21.216, 228, 234; fortune, luck 6.83, 213, 13.217, 14.2, **B** 5.96, 150, A 10.100; good will / favour 3.330, 6.344, 11.86, 20.428, B 4.73, A 9.95; forgiveness 3.134, 4.138; pardon 5.192; permission 3.217; grace before meals 15.265; *in phrr*: **~ of amendement** 6.102; **~ of a good ende** 3.339, 9.50, 10.60; **~ of þe Holy Gost** 18.52, 19.196, 254, 20.133; **withouten ~** out of favour (with the Church) 9.205; **wordes of ~** gracious, blessed words 5.98

gracen *v* thank, *p.p.* B 6.124

gracious(e) *a* merciful 3.353, 14.133; pleasing B 6.226; **~ liche** *av* by means of grace / beautifully 18.7; by means of grace / mercifully B 18.358

gradde *p.t.* 22.387, B 16.78 *see* **greden** *v*

graes 14.23 = **gras** *n*

graffe *n* graft (*fig.*) 1.199

graffen *v* graft B 5.136

gray *a* drab, unbleached 16.298; *as n* 16.344

grayeth 3.89 = **graiþ** *a*

grayn *n* crop (*esp. of* wheat) 8.126, 132, 12.179, 186, 13.22, B 14.31, (*fig.*) 21.275, 319, seed, (*fig.*) particle, jot 11.84

graiþ *a* ready †B 12.193; direct B 1.205, (*sup.*) 1.199; plain 10.245, Z 8.41; exact, true 3.89, 6.230; **~(e) li(che)** *av* straightway 7.295, 11.138; quickly B 11.41; properly 22.322

gramarien *n* one who can read Latin B 13.73

gramer *n* Latin (grammar) 11.122, 17.107

grange *n* farm-house 19.73

grape *n* grape B 14.31

gras *n* grass 6.430, 13.176, 15.244, B 11.365; (as cattle-feed) 4.49, Z 7.66; healing herb 14.23

gras 6.84 = **grace** *n*

grat *contr. pr. pl.* 8.284 *see* **greden** *v*

graþest *sup.* 1.199 *see* **graiþ** *a*

graunt mercy *excl.* many thanks! B 10.220, 17.86

graunten *v* grant, give 1.168, 3.100, 134, 330, 6.102, 435, 8.353, 9.184, 19.188, 287, 20.186, 21.104, **B** 3.232, 9.47, 11.148; concede B 12.292; permit, allow 7.253, 12.64, B 11.97, A 12.25; consent, assent (to) 2.168, 18.131, B 4.194, A 2.24; yield (to) 3.365; allot A 8.87; decree **B** 2.120, 18.339, A 10.206; ordain A 11.196; grant (land, privilege, pardon) 2.70, 2.88, 3.251, 5.192, 9.8, 19, 23, 324, 21.184, B 16.241; promise A 3.233; undertake, offer B 17.86; *in phr.* **God ~** may God grant 2.125, 16.154, B 14.318

graue *n* grave 17.302, 20.64, B 16.113

grauen *v* bury 20.86, Z 2.72; engrave 3.52, *ger.* engraving 3.68, 74; stamp 4.127, 17.75, 207 (B 15.544)

gre(e) *n* prize (for victory) 20.101

grece *n* fat B 13.63

greden *v* (*contr. pr. 3 pl.* **grat** 8.284, *p.t.* **gradde** 22.387) shriek B 16.78; **~ after, to** pray fervently for 8.284, 14.133, 22.387, cry for 9.76, call for B 3.71; cry a proclamation B 2.74; go on (noisily) about 21.428

gredyre *n* gridiron 2.130

greet 3.222 *etc*; **greetliche** 20.6; **greetnesse** B 16.59; *see* **gret(e)-** *a, etc*

gre(e)ut *n* earth, ground 13.22, 176

greyn[1] B 14.31 = **grayn** *n*

greyn[2] *n* colour B 16.59; *and see* **engreynen** *v*

Grek *n* gentile, pagan B 15.604

grene *a* green 15.244, **B** 6.297, 11.365, 16.59; vigorous 16.253, B 15.423, **~ leued** 17.48; freshly cut 20.48; fresh(ly made) 8.304

gret(e) *a* (*comp.* **gretter(e)**, **grettore**, *sup.* **grettest(e)**) large, big Pr 53, 6.410, 10.45, 18.62, 112, 20.400, **A** 8.44, 12.69; long B 4.46; fat 15.87; pregnant 20.133;

powerful 21.263, 22.215, **B** 13.399, 14.38; abundant 2.162, 19.295, **B** 9.47, 17.313; numerous 21.338; great 3.22, 339, 7.110, 9.50, 10.9, 16.19, 95, 18.56, 19.148, **B** 5.380, 10.304, 12.292, 14.129; of high rank / authority Pr 177, 2.176, 3.282, 8.87, 9.133, 10.148, 15.210, *a as n* B 4.159; good, excellent 6.261, B 17.37; important B 9.59; mighty 6.285, 17.256, 18.149, B 15.66; solemn Pr 137; eminent 5.146, 17.166, 21.128, B 10.66; sublime 1.103, 10.154, 20.125, 21.198, 22.40, B 12.68; holy 21.209, **B** 2.29, 9.28; serious 7.61, 9.258; grievous 3.222, 20.101, (*as comp. av*) 22.28; angry 6.18; vile, wicked Pr 36, 16.76, B 12.79; strong 12.85, 15.186, B 11.262; deep 14.213, B 15.146; bright 20.342; pressing, extreme 9.67, 13.8, 22.20, B 7.82; *as n* much 3.89, B 12.250; *in recurring phrr.* ~ **clerk** 5.146, 11.291, 15.82, 21.271; ~ **lordes** 9.133, 10.148, 15.210, 255; ~ **myhte** 6.285, 19.196; ~ **othes** Pr 36, 2.97, 6.360, **B** 10.50, 13.400; ~ **witte(s)** 10.9, 11.84; ~ **wonder** 18.149, 20.125; ~**ly(che)** *av* seriously 11.313; at length / ? deeply 20.6; ~**nesse** *n* width B 16.59

greten *v*¹ (*p.t.* **grette** 11.116) greet 4.42, 11.116, 138, 18.184, 22.356; pay one's respects to 18.243, B 18.174; bid farewell (to) B 10.220; address 12.208; reward 6.392

greten *v*² weep B 5.380

grette *p.t.* 4.42, *etc*; *see* **greten** *v*¹

greut 13.22 = **gre(e)ut** *n*

greuaunce *n* affliction, disease B 12.59

greuen *v* hurt, injure Pr 171, 3.92, 5.58, 10.306, 11.27, 16.120, 288, 305, 19.147, 167, B 15.257; cause injury 11.133; offend 8.236, 16.207, B 10.28; oppress, harass 4.95, 8.339, 13.59, 15.165, 255, 16.71, 21.220, 22.28, **B** 10.206, 17.112; afflict 15.293; cause discomfort (to) 6.410; anger B 13.73, (*refl.*) get angry **B** Pr 139, 6.314; trouble 6.111, 11.313, 19.20, **B** 10.286, 11.279, Z 7.275; disturb Pr 208; agitate B 5.96

greuous *a* bitter 16.76

grewe *p.t.* 13.176, 18.56 *see* **growen** *v*

grydy *a* ravening 6.397

gri(e)s 8.304 = **grys** *n*¹

grym *a* terrible, monstrous(ly heavy) B 5.354; ~**ly** *av* sternly B 10.261; pitiably A 5.209

grype *n* grasp 19.147

gripen *v* (*p.p.* **grepe, grypen, griped**) grasp 19.128, 168; take 3.89, 227, B 3.250; receive 3.282

grys *n*¹ young pig 4.49; pork of young pig Pr 228, 8.304

grys *n*² grey (squirrel) fur 16.344

grynden *v* grind, *p.p.* **ygrounde** A 7.169; mix by grinding 15.49; sharpen 20.80; *and see* **for-, to-grynden** *vv*

grisly *a* fearsome 20.478

grochen *v* (**ageyn, of, on**) complain, grumble (at) Pr 171, 6.111, 8.227, 337, B 6.314, A 10.116, Z 7.317, 321

grom *n* (low) fellow 8.227

gronen *v* groan (with sickness), ? feel ill 8.269, 22.312, *ger.* A 12.76

gropen *v* feel, touch 19.128, 21.170; play with (sexually) 6.180; examine medically (*fig.*) 22.364

grote *n* groat, silver coin [worth fourpence] 3.174, 5.133, 6.230, 17.207, B 10.47

ground *n* fundamental principle 3.353; source 17.90, 141, B 2.29; basis 17.107, [of a claim] B 5.286; (surface of the) ground 5.120, 13.166, 14.140, 144, 20.44, B 10.140; earth, world 10.45, 60, **B** 5.260, 6.228, 10.226, **A** 1.88, 11.173; soil (*fig.*) B 16.62

grounde *p.p.* B 13.43 *see* **grynden** *v*

grou(e)n Z 7.59, 106, 108 *see* **growen** *v*

growen *v* (*p.t.* **grewe** 13.176, **growede** 18.7) grow, spring up 8.126, 10.153, 12.179, 13.176, (*fig.*) 14.23, 24, 18.7, 23, 56, 22.57, **B** 14.31, 15.423, 16.9, 12, 13, 56, 58, 62, Z 7.59, 108; thrive 10.209, (*fig.*) 17.48; increase 20.400; grow, be found 12.226, 21.315, (*fig.*) 18.56, 84, B 12.60

growel *n* gruel [soup containing meal] A 7.167

gruc(c)hen 8.227 *etc*; = **grochen** *v*

gult *a* gilded 16.344, 20.12; **with a ~ penne** with a golden pen (= in letters of gold) 19.16

gult *n* sin, transgression 3.8, 103, 134, 138, 6.176, 275, 7.61, 10.55, 236, 11.62, **B** 4.101, 10.280, Z 5.93; fault 15.228, B 19.306; **withouten** ~ undeservedly 4.75

gulty *a* guilty, blameworthy [for sin or crime] 6.175, 424, 21.304, **B** 10.258, 12.76, 192, (*comp.*) 99

gulten *v* offend 7.150

gurden *v* (*imp.* **gurdeth**, *p.t.* **girte**) cut 2.213; vomit B 5.373

gurl *n* child 1.29, 9.76, 11.122, 16.300, 20.6, B 10.79, A 10.160

gut B 1.36 *etc*; *see* **gott(e)** *n*

habben B 14.148, *etc* Z 1.107; *see* **hauen** *v*

haberion *n* coat of mail 20.22

habite B Pr 3 = **abite** *n*

habiten *v* dress, *p.p.* **yhabited** B 13.285

hacche *n* hatch [lower part of divided door] 5.29, 16.336

hachet *n* small battle-axe 3.458; hatchet A 7.59

hackenayman 6.364, 377 *see* **hakeney** ~ *n*

hackyen, hakken (after) *v* keep toiling away (at) 21.404

had *p.t.* 6.146 *etc*; **hadde** Pr 50 *et p.*; **hadden** 10.216 *et p.*; **haddest** 6.320 *et p.*; **haddestow** (= **haddest thow**) B 20.188; **haen** *pr.* 3.269 *et p.*; **haeth** 19.324 *etc*; *see* **hauen** *v*

hayl(l) *n* hail 15.165, B 14.172

hayl *interj.*; **al** ~ your health! hello! A 12.62

haylsen *v* greet (respectfully), salute 9.309, 10.10, B 5.100, A 12.79

hayre *n* (penitential garment of) haircloth, hairshirt 6.6

hayward *n* hayward [manorial field-keeper] 5.16, 6.367, 13.44, 46, (*fig.*) 21.334

hakeney *n* hackney-horse [small saddle-horse] 2.175; ~ **man** *n* keeper of hackneys for hire 6.364, 377

halden (holden) *v* (*contr. pr* **halt** 3.386, B 17.106, *p.t.* **he(e)ld(e)** 10.86, 22.145, 298, *pl.* **helden** 9.206, *pr.p.* **haldyng** 3.379, **holdyng** 8.103, *p.p.* **halden** 13.119, **(y)holde(n)** 1.80, 3.267, 6.40) grasp Pr 172, 19.127, 140, 157; hold 5.161, 6.400, 419, **B** 1.44, 17.157, 160, Z 7.58*n*; sustain 18.195; retain possession (of) 10.86, B 12.248, (*ger.* **holdyng**) 12.246; ~ **togederes** stick together 1.53, keep together 17.22; hold in (legal) possession A 2.36, 67; keep in 1.148, B 1.120; keep out 16.365, B 5.587; detain, keep back 7.67; restrain, hold 6.8, 20.148, 21.404, (*subjv.*) 424, A 12.29, **B** 4.22, 12.37, 15.265, A 12.75; oblige 6.297 (**haldyng** = **holden**), 8.103, 14.196, 19.39, 22.366, B 15.569, A 11.247; preside over 7.33, B 5.421; maintain, keep 3.187, 9.206, B 15.142, A 9.87, Z 2.209; defend 21.359, 22.75, 205, 298; ~ **vp** raise A 12.38; preserve B 6.214; ~ **with** support 1.94, 108, 2.153, 3.379, 8.50, 22.128, 216, 220, B 3.242; observe, keep 5.143, 157, 7.225, 9.24, 166, 221, 22.280, **B** 5.579, 10.291, 13.414; obey 9.166, A 6.97; practise 6.233; follow, keep to 13.67, 16.53, A 12.88; (*refl.*) remain Pr 30, 5.189, 8.207, 9.5, A 7.133, 10.114; hold firm, stand 20.258; ~ **(for)** regard (as), consider 1.80, 3.87, 267, 386, 6.40, 390, 8.74, 223, 9.336, 10.298, 11.311, 13.119, 184, 239, 14.76, 15.126, 127, 128, 16.371, 17.64, 111, 159, 21.373, 463, 22.145, 262, **B** 4.118, 5.257, 413, 11.68, 12.294, 15.10, 16.112, 17.106, **A** 4.136, 8.75, 11.62, Z 7.196; judge, believe 10.290, 11.221; ~ **no tale** have no regard for 1.9

hale Z 2.46 = **halle** *n*

hales 8.60 = **hals** *n*

hal(e)wen *v* consecrate 17.279

half *n* (*pl.* **half** 2.56; *and see* **halue(n)**) half 5.133, 15.181; side (of page = verso) 3.491, **body** ~ front side B 13.317, (*fig.*) 3.226; hand [direction] 2.5, 8; quarter [direction] 18.66; *in phrr.* **bothe** ~ **þe contre** both parts / sides of the country 2.56, **bothe** ~ **the mone** both parts of the lunar cycle 8.350

half *a* half (a / an), ~ **aker** 6.267, 8.2, 3, 113, 123; ~ **a laumpe lyne** B 13.152; ~ **loef** 9.150; ~ **marc** 5.133; ~...**pak of bokes** B 13.202; ~ **peny** 8.328; ~ **a shef of arwes** 3.478; ~ **ȝere** 2.238; *and see* **halue-**

haly, haly- 6.146, 272 see **holy(-)** *a*

halidome *n* (the) sacred relics (*in oath*) B 5.370

halien *v* draw, pull 10.94

halle *n* hall [large (royal or manorial) residence] A 2.38; = large communal room for meals 7.93, 236, 14.139, 15.40, B 10.96, 100; law-court B 4.159, A 4.118, **West-ministre** ~ 22.133; the company (assembled) in the hall B 4.162; *and see* **moet** ~

halpe *p.t.* 21.131, 377, A 11.31 see **helpen** *v*

hals *n* neck Pr 185, 194, 8.60

halsen *v*¹ embrace, *ger.* 6.187

halsen *v*² (**halsenen** Z) adjure 1.70; salute A 12.79 (= **haylsen**)

halt *contr. pr.* 3.386 *et p.*; *see* **halden** *v*

halue-bretherne *n* half-brethren (*fig.*) 20.436

haluendele *n* half-portion, half of it 7.29

hammard Z 3.132 = **homward** *av*

han *pr.pl.*, *3* Pr 63 *et p.*, *1* 3.51 *et p.*, *2* 8.271 *et p.*; *inf.* 9.157, B 20.265, A 3.189 *see* **hauen** *v*

hand (ho(e)nd) *n* 1.84, 3.75, 4.82, 143, 6.109, 8.261, 10.147, 14.59, 63, 16.82, 19.56, 66, 112, 118 *et p.*, 21.170, 22.117, **B** 15.122, 454, 17.138 *et p.*, **A** 7.235, 12.38, Z 7.67; power 3.242; keeping B 10.431; manual work Pr 223, 8.259, 330, 9.58, 198, A 7.232; manual skill B 13.298; action, conduct 6.109, 10.78, 13.110, 19.257, 21.247; *in phrr.* ~ **fedde** fed by hand B 15.471; ~ **mayden** maid-servant 18.132; ~**while** short space of time 21.273; **luft** ~ 7.224, **riȝt** ~ A 3.56; **large handes** liberal hands (for bribery) 3.288; **riche** ~ ? great wealth, ? money-making abilities 3.118; **two** ~ 1.84, 10.78

*****handy-dandy** *n as av* secret bribery 4.68*n*

hand(e)len *v* treat wounds 22.314; deal with, dispense, *p.p.* **yhandlit** A 2.99; *ger.* **handlynge** touching 15.258; caressing 6.187

hangen, hongen *v* (*p.t.* **heng** 8.60, *pl.* 1.169, **hongide** A 1.148, *p.p.* **hanged** Pr 194, **hongen** Pr 185) hang Pr 185, 191, 7.241, 8.60, **B** 15.214, 16.66; fasten B 4.22; be suspended Pr 99, 20.259, *pr.p.* sagging B 5.134; (put to death by) hang(ing) 2.207, 3.177, 6.238, 10.163, 243, 17.138, 20.421, **B** 1.68, 5.232, 279, (*in assev.*) 3.148, *ger.* 3.407; hold to (sb.) 3.226; cling, hold fast (to) B 13.391; depend on 14.214, *pr.p.* B 12.289

#**hangeman** *n* hangman 6.367

hankres Z Pr 29 = **ankeres** *n*

hansull *n* earnest of good fellowship, **to** ~ as a treat 6.374

hap *n* (one's) luck, fortune 3.297; (stroke of) luck 14.51, B 5.96; good fortune 22.386, A 12.111

hapeward 7.283 = **apeward** *n*

hap(pi)liche *av* perhaps, maybe 7.266

happen *v* happen, have the chance to 11.113, 13.46; (*impers. without* it) befall 3.438, 5.95, 9.113, B 6.46; turn out 15.6, 18.120

hapsen *v* fasten; *p.p.* **yhapsed** 1.191

hard *2 sg. pr.* Z 1.29 = **art**; *see* **be(n)** *v*

hard *a* hard 19.12; miserly 12.246, (*comp.*) 1.186; painful, rigorous B 14.322; severe 3.399, 12.200; fierce 22.217, 301; difficult 4.177, 7.280, 16.118, 22.336, **B** 10.209, 17.41, 42

harde *av* tightly 1.191, B 17.157; austerely Pr 28; sternly B 11.85; (*comp.*) more severely Pr 122; (*sup.*) most grievously 14.119; violently 22.185; fiercely 22.216, 302; hard, strenuously Pr 23, B 7.118

hardeliche *av* boldly, strenuously 8.28; (*comp.*) **hardiloker** more boldly 6.305

hardy *a* stouthearted, fearless 3.236, 9.265, 13.61, 21.291, B 14.305, (*comp.*) 21.58; bold (*comp.*) B 17.106; ~ **(to)** so bold as to 3.321, 4.63, 8.181, 13.9, A 12.23; **ouer ~** rash 3.298; firm 3.351; ~ **nesse** *n* stoutness, courage 21.31; audacity 20.79

hardy *av*, (*comp.*) **hardyore** more boldly 16.101

hardien *v* embolden B 15.436

hare *n* hare 7.32, 8.28

harewen 21.311 = **harwen** *v*

harlote *n* villain, knave 19.258, B 17.109; base fellow B 18.77; low jester 7.93, 8.50, 11.28, B 13.416, Z 7.48; lecher 3.300, 4.113, 22.144, **B** 14.183, 15.134

harlotrie *n* ribald jesting 4.110, 11.28, B 10.45, A 11.31; obscenity 16.258; obscene tale 7.22; lechery 7.75, 7.90, B 13.354

harm *n* harm 3.81, 6.109, 9.47, 15.114, Z 7.245; injury A 5.83; damage(s) B 4.31; calumny 6.117; suffering Z 7.201

harmen *v* injure A 11.252; (do) damage (to) 2.248, B 13.107, A 2.166; do wrong 3.177

harneys *n* armour 16.344; **pyken ~** plunder (dead men's) armour Z 7.67; **pyke ~** *n* plunderer of armour 22.263

harow! *excl* a distressed cry for succour 22.88

harpe *n* harp; **in þin ~** to the (accompaniment of the) harp A 1.137

harpen *v* play the harp 15.207, 20.450

harpour *n* harp-player B 14.25

harwe *n* harrow Z 7.58

harwen *v* (cultivate with a) harrow 5.19, (*fig.*) 21.269, 273, 311

hasche(h)t Z 1.48, 3.155, **hascuht** Z Pr 124 = **asketh**; *see* **asken** *v*

haspen, *p.p.* B 1.197 *see* **hapsen** *v*

hast(e) *2 sg. pr.* 2.137, 3.418 *et p.*; *see* **hauen** *v*

haste *n* haste, **in ~** in a hurry 8.319; quickly, speedily 8.171, 206, 14.175, 22.136, 144, 332

hast(e)li(che) *av* quickly 12.140, 165, 21.359, 22.167, *sup.* **hastilokest** most promptly 21.472

hasten *v* (*refl.*) go speedily 3.418, A 3.181; come quickly, soon 8.343

#hastite *n* haste, **for ~** through hurrying 17.118

hastow 3.133, 5.26 = **hast thow**; *see* **hauen** *v*

hat *3 pr. sg.* Z 4.133 = **hath**

hat *n* hat 6.202, 7.164, 13.47, B 5.529

hatchet A 7.59 = **hachet** *n*

hater *n* garment 9.157; cloak B 14.1

hateren *v* clothe, *ger.* **haterynge** clothing B 15.78

hath *3 sg. pr.* Pr 62 *et p.*, *pl.* Pr 38 *et p.*; *see* **hauen** *v*

hat(i)en *v* hate 15.215, 16.65, 119, 22.295, **B** 5.99, 114, 13.420; loathe 6.440, B 12.52; despise, scorn 4.110, 6.11*c*, 7.79, 9.190, 16.258, 17.138, **B** 6.50, 13.226, 239; show enmity towards 3.431, B 11.182

hatrede *n* hatred 3.177

hatte *3 sg. pr.* 3.496 *et p.*, *pl* 7.223 *et p.*; **hatted** Z 6.82,

hatteþ A 6.60 *etc* (= **hatte**); **hattest** *2 sg.pr.* 22.340; *see* **hoten** *v*

haubergeon B 18.23 = **haberion** *n*

hauȝt Z 6.8 = **auht** *av*

hauk *n* hawk 7.44, B 4.125

hauken *v* hunt with a hawk, *ger.* 3.465

haumpelles Z 5.162 *see* **aunpolle** *n*

haunt *n* resort, frequentation 16.92

haunten *v* practise, engage in 15.198, Z 7.134; indulge in Pr 75, 3.57, 63, 11.111

hauthorn 18.183 *see* **hawe-** *n*

hauen *v* (*1 pr.sg.* **habbe** Z 5.137, **haue** Pr 177 *et p.*; *2* **hast** 2.137 *et p.*, *3* **haeth** 19.324 *etc*, **hath** Pr 62 *et p.*, *pl 1, 2, 3* **haen** 3.269, **han** 3.51, 8.271, Pr 63, **an** Z Pr 91, **haue(n)** 2.167, 6.296, 9.174, *2 and 3* **haueth** 1.178, 5.166, **habbeth** Z 1.107; *pr. subjv.* **haue** *sg.* 2.50, 6.295, *pl.* 1.8, B 6.11; *imper. sg.* **haue** *pl.* **haue** A 1.149, **haueth** 1.170 *et p.*, **habbeth** Z 1.98; *p.t. 1,3 sg., 1 and 3 pl.* **had(d)e** Pr 50, 128, 6.146, **haued(e)** 3.40, 8.3, 14.150, Z 1.14, *2 sg.* **haddest** 6.320 *et p.*, **hauedest** Z 5.136, *p.t. as conditional* B 5.232; *1 and 3 pl.* **hadden** 10.216 *et p.*, **haueden** Z Pr 52, *p.p.* **(y)had** 7.44, 11.303 *et p*) have, possess Pr 136, 6.259 *et p.*; have (sb.) under one 15.306; have charge of 4.84; enjoy 3.194, 8.314; use, perform B 15.126; hold, keep 5.16, 6.339 *et p.*; remember 8.103; get, obtain Pr 83, 2.35, 3.101, 9.289, 22.328 *et p.*; accept 3.146; receive 6.293, 9.70, 13.169; take (back) 3.331; win 6.77, 17.240, 21.107; experience 6.416, 20.211; bear 6.136; take (pity) 3.86 *et p.*; feel (hate) 7.261, 18.270; have (sth.) to look after Pr 128, 3.51, 8.2; *as auxil., finite with p.p.* Pr 177 *et p.*; *infin. + p.p., with zero meaning*: **to ~ be** to be 17.167; **to ~ yfouhte** to fight 18.137; *after modal verbs*: **connen** B 15.301, 19.254; **mowen** 16.19, B 11.196; **shullen** 3.259; **willen** 6.418; *after* **durren** Pr 193, 3.258; *as infin. compl.* 3.6, (*with* **to**) 14.214; *as subst. for another (understood) v.* 10.19; *in phrr*: ~ **a-do, to doone** have business (to do) 5.163, dealings with B 4.28; ~ **(a)down** bring down 18.111, 22.227; ~ **excused** forgive (sb.) 15.130; **to ~ and to holde** possess and hold (of sb.) B 2.102; ~ **þe maistry** get the upper hand 20.68; ~ **out** carry away 20.321 (capture), 20.148 (release); bring out 20.287; ~ **at wille** have at one's disposal 13.226; *in assevs.,* **God ~ þe, devel ~** may God / the devil take 6.296, 8.127

hauylon *n* trick(y argument) B 10.131

hawe *n* haw(thorn berry) 11.8, 81; **~thorn** *n* hawthorn(-blossom) 18.183

he[1] *pers. prn.* (*acc.* **him** 4.64 *et p.*; *gen.* **his(e)** Pr 70 *et p.*, B 7.167 *et p.*, *dat.* **him** 4.64, **hym** Pr 111 *et p.*; *pl.* **he** Z 7.14, **hy** 1.187 *et p.*, A Pr 63 *et p.*, **hij** †B 1.191, *acc.* **hem** Pr 68 *et p.*, *gen.* **here** Pr 30 *et p.*, **hir** B 1.99 *et p.*, *dat.* **hem** Pr 54 *et p.* (*qqv*)) he, (him; his; (to) him; they; their; (to) them); *with indef. ref.* a man, (some) one 5.91, 8.143

he² Z Pr 101, 1.14, 16, 2.20 *et p.*, 3.29, 55 *et p.*; *see* **heo** *pers. prn.*

he³ Z 7.14 = **hy** *pers. prn.*

he(e)d (heued) *n* head 2.213, 6.150, 202, 10.175, 180, 12.18, 16.74, 19.72, 20.49, 290, 22.183, 185, 187, **B** 4.22, 6.325, (*fig.*) 13.145, A 10.60, Z Pr 80; (*meton.*) head-gear 5.133; **putten forth** ~ show oneself 4.74, 7.181; ruler, controller 3.379, 17.230, 21.?472, 474, **B** 15.429, 486; origin, source 1.159, 17.140, ?21.472; = life B 2.34; *in assevs:* **by myn** ~ by my life 4.177, 7.280; **hefdes** persons 17.85

heddere 22.334 = **hyddere** *av*

hede *n* heed, note; **nymen / taken** ~ take note (of), observe 9.71, 11.70, 247, 12.46, 221, 14.99, 17.108, 239, 18.19, **B** 6.15, 11.321, 13.316, 319, 15.91, **A** 8.78, 11.149, Z 5.98

heeld *p.t.* 22.298, B 11.70 *see* **halden** *v*

heele B 14.172, 17.37 = **hele** *n*

heelen B 6.192, 16.112, 17.119 = **helen** *v*¹

he(e)p *n* company 6.235; crowd Pr 51, 6.373, 8.183, B 14.305; great pack 5.160; spate 6.384; long list 16.203; *in phr.* **bringen to hepe** bring about 10.191, 193

heer¹ B 14.128 = **her** *av*

heer² *n* hair; **oone heeris ende** = the least little bit B 10.333; *pl.* **heres** hair Z 5.9

heet(e) *p.t.* 18.249, 22.273, 349; *see* **hoten** *v*

heeþ *n* heath, wasteland B 15.458

hef Z 4.96 = **efte** *av*

hefdes *pl.* 17.85 *see* **he(e)d** *n*

hegge *n* hedge 3.168, 8.29

heggen *v* ?harrow, make / cut hedges 5.19

hey! *interj.* used in burden of song 8.123

heigh- B 12.37, **heiȝ-** B Pr 13 *et p.*; *see* **hey(h)(e)** *a*

hey(h)(e), hy(e) *a* (*comp.* **herre** A 10.101, **herrore** 2.30, **hyere** B 2.28, *sup.* **heiȝest** B 10.453, A 10.45) high 1.64, 153, 14.176, 15.66, 18.98, **B** Pr 13, 7.17, 18.311, **Z** Pr 99, 2.49, 5.45; divine 1.70, 8.137, 14.84, 17.247, 262, **B** 2.33, 11.81, 12.40, 16.118; heavenly 17.256, A 11.313; exalted 14.135, (*comp.*) A 10.101; great, ~ **dome** Last Judgement 6.297, 346; chief, principal 1.159, ~ **gate** supernal gate 7.248; high road B 4.42, ~ **strete** main road 14.48, ~ **wey** 8.2, 9.32, 188, 203, 11.106, A 7.178, Z 7.6, (*fig.*) 13.67, 16.53, **B** 12.37, 15.434; (of) noble (rank) 2.81, 9.201, 16.33, *comp.* 2.30, B 10.103, 364; solemn 4.113, ~ **festes** solemn (religious) festivals 6.182; deep, lofty 16.234, *sup.* B 10.453; important 14.76; arrogant, haughty 6.8, 22.116; full, ~ **prime** = 9 a.m. 8.119, ~ **tyme** the appointed / fullness of time 18.139; *in phr:* **an** ~ on high, up above 5.186, 17.222, 18.106, 21.192, B Pr 128, 140; to a high position 12.42; aloud A 12.27

heye *av* high 1.169, 6.238, 14.176, B 11.360; to a great height 3.84; at high cost 3.51; loudly B 2.74; (*sup.*) most highly B 12.144, most intensely A 10.45; *in phr.* ~ **til** right up to 7.225

heyli(che) *av* munificently 3.251; at a high wage 8.335; greatly B 15.525; completely 8.89; strictly A 11.247

heihte 18.4 = **hihte** *pr.*, *see* **hoten** *v*

heynesse (of herte) *n* presumption 22.153

heyr 5.163, 6.255, **B** 2.102, 16.232 *see* **ayr** *n*

held(e)n *p.t.* 1.108, 6.400, 10.86, 17.22, A 4.136 *etc*; *see* **halden** *v*

hele *n*¹ (good) health 5.7, 10, 9.102, 105, 10.182, 16.12, 20.218, 22.153 (*person.*), 180, 386, (*fig.*) 19.84, **B** 6.258, 14.172, 17.37; healing 21.104; spiritual health 1.86, 19.84, 21.391, A 6.19; comfort 6.85; prosperity, good fortune 9.116; protection 21.474; salvation 17.140, B 5.266

hele *n*² heel A 11.81; crust, **pye** ~ (= thing of little value) 9.345

helen *v*¹ heal [physically] 8.225, 10.309, 21.131, **B** 6.192, 16.112, Z 7.262, (*fig.*) A 7.179; recover (*ger.*) B 17.116; heal [spiritually], free from sin 22.282, 357, B 17.119

hel(i)en (hilen) *v*² cover 7.236, 9.157, 13.163, *ger.* roofing, ?clothing 16.23(1), **B** 5.590, 11.351, 12.230, 232; conceal 22.340; keep secret B 5.166

helle *n* hell 1.120, 126, 183, 3.327, 6.238, 337, 7.88, 133, 9.278, 10.288, 303, 11.200, 221, 12.76, 78, 246, 14.149, 193, 15.302, 304, 309, 18.266, 19.241, 244, 20.127, 148, 150, 173, 180, 193, 232, 258, 270, 349, 364, 375, 407, 414, 420, 439, 21.52, 56, 22.270, (*person.*) 20.274, **B** 1.115, 198, 8.96, 10.109, 369, 11.144, 14.80, 15.75, 16.247, **A** 1.113, 5.242, 10.177, 11.68, Z 1.65; *in phrr:* ~ **pouke** 15.165; ~ **yates** B 11.163, Z 5.39; **heuene and** ~ 3.165, B 17.162; **peyne(s) of** ~ 2.108, 3.101; **to** ~**ward** towards hell 20.117

(h)eller(ne) *n* elder-tree 1.64, B 9.149

helm *n*¹ helmet 20.22

helm *n*² elm-tree Z 5.45

help *n* help, assistance 6.169, 7.289, 19.58, 83, 20.442, **B** 10.238, 15.196, 16.52; relief 22.169, B Pr 159; favour, good will 11.46; support 3.337, 4.68, 176, 8.256, 15.238, 16.95, 17.185; sustenance B 4.125; source of strength 21.391, B 13.399; supporter 16.95, 21.475, **B** 8.46, 11.218, A 10.47, 49

helples(e) *a* infirm 9.175; useless, lacking (in) B 7.98; unable to act for themselves B 9.70; abandoned, hopeless B 15.457

helpen *v* (*p.t.* **halp** 21.131, *p.t. subjv.* **halpe** 21.377, **holpe** 20.441, A 11.31, *pl.* **holpe** 8.123, 9.6, *p.p.* **(y)holpe** 11.28, B 5.624) help, assist 3.208, 4.192, 6.297, 299, 7.275, 8.18, 65, 66, 113, 123, 257, 9.6, 344, 10.278, 14.55, 15.12, 23, 19.62, 221, 21.377, 407, 22.228, 230, **B** 9.37, 10.333, A 11.31; assist (in fight) A 12.65; succour 15.143, 18.13, 21.131, **B** 5.430, 6.20, 142, 7.42, 9.77, 113, 16.124, A 4.60; save, preserve 7.273, 10.43, 14.55, 15.15, 19.57, 20.54, 204, 21.369, 431, B 17.286; rescue B 5.624; relieve 6.84, 8.233, 10.190, 11.30, B

7.70; avail, be of use / benefit (to) 1.17, 3.222, 8.137, 12.101, 19.159, 293, **B** 7.54, 13.390, 408, A 8.7; support Pr 74, 3.444, 9.33, 11.187, 12.119, 13.131, 16.44, 19.140, 22.376, **B** 3.242, 243, 15.336 (2), 16.26; provide for 3.251, 260, 8.219, 9.96, 125, 10.84, 186, 14.21, 15.224, 17.60, 62, **B** 7.26, 9.86, 15.336 (1), A 10.69; *in assevs.*: **so ~ me God / Crist ~** so help (preserve) me God / Christ 3.8, 4.11 *et p.*

helthe *n* (bodily) health 16.135, 22.333, Z 7.268; (spiritual) health, salvation 17.174, **B** 10.251, 11.229, 12.39

hem *pers. prn. 3 pl.* them Pr 39, 68 *et p.*; (*refl.*) themselves Pr 22 *et p.*; (*after impers. v. 3 pl. acc., dat.*) to themselves Pr 58; **~ þat** those who Pr 106, 1.169 *etc.*

hemself *emphatic pers. prn.* (**~selue(n)** B 10.83, A 4.107, **B** 3.216, **~ sylf(e)** Z 1.59, 5.64, **~sylue** Z 5.30, **~ sulue(n)** 9.77, 21.149) themselves Pr 55, B 10.397; (*as refl. obj. of v.*) 10.163 *et p.*, B 4.40, A 5.35; (*without parallel subj.*) (they) themselves **B** 10.313, 18.305

hen *n* hen; **hennes** hen's 21.415, *pl.* Z 7.287

hende *a* well-bred 8.47, 22. 188; courtly 10.146; polite 22.349, 355; well-behaved B 15.216; courteous A 2.52; generous 11.44, B 5.257; **~li(che)** *av* courteously 3.30, 18.184; politely 10.10, B 5.100; meekly 18.132; **~ nesse** *n* nobility 21.31; virtue 2.81, 11.13, 18.13, (*person.*) 22.145

hendret Z 5.162 = **hundred** *num.*

heng(en) *p.t.* 1.169, 8.60; *see* **hangen** *v*

henne(s) *av* from here 4.184, 5.80, 8.301, 10.128, 20.166, 280, 343, 21.322; (away) from this world / life 1.173, 6.312, 9.53, 348, 21.61, 249, 22.203, **B** 3.245, 7.97, A 8.18; from this time B 3.109; ago 5.35; **~ goyng, ~ partyng** *n. phr.* departure from this life **B** 14.165, 10.463

hensong Z 5.123 = **euensong** *n*

henten *v* (*p.t.* **hente(n)** 8.171, 183) take hold of 8.171; grasp 16.80, 19.140, 22.167; take 7.151, 15.249, 22.180; entrap 6.8; get hold of 8.183; overcome B 5.5, A 12.67

heo *pers. prn. 3 sg. fem.* (*acc.* **her** 1.54, **hire** B 1.58, *gen.* **her(e)** 1.10, 2.25, **hire** B 1.10) she 1.68 *et p.*, B 3.29 *etc*, A 1.10 *et p.*

hep Pr 51, **hepe** 10.191; *see* **he(e)p** *n*

her(e)[1] *pers. prn 3 sg. fem. obj.* her 1.54 *et p.*; for her 6.225; **for ~ loue** for love of her 2.37; (*refl.*) herself 4.90, 6.3; for herself 16.149; **by ~ one** alone by herself 20.316; *dat. after impers. v.* **~ were leuer** she would prefer 6.129, **~ were leuest** she would best like 3.6; **~ lef lyketh** it pleases her 7.252; **~ luste** she pleases 3.195

her(e)[2] (**hire** B 2.25 *et p.*) *poss. prn. fem. sg.* her 1.10, 2.25 *et p.*

her(e)[3] (**hire** B 2.150 *et p.*) *poss. prn. pl.* their Pr 30, 2.163 *et p.*, Z Pr 36 *et p.*; *in partitive constrns* of them: **~ either** each of them B 5.163; **~ aytheres / bothe / noyþer wille** the desire of each / both / neither of

them 12.140, 2.67; **~ ayther oþer** each other 22.354; **~ neyther** neither of them 10.275, B 4.33; **~ no(e)n** neither of them 14.105, 16.80, none of them A 7.300; **~ oen** each of them 20.67

her(e)[4] *av* here, in this place 2.69, 3.94, 231, 6.206, 8.126, 133, 15.116, 239, 18.97, 19.4, 18, 24, 92, 20.42, 169, 190, 273, 300, 304, 370, 375, 395, 434, 21.388, 22.88, 318, 351 (2), 358, **B** 5.248, 448, 6.65, 66, 13.191, 276, 14.274, 15.443, 16.24, 17.3, 23, 76, 113; at this point (in book) **B** Pr 38, 13.71, A 12.101; in this fact 1.167; in this matter B 10.111; in this world 1.9, 16, 6.238, 8.43, 9.321, 340, 348, 349, 10.304, 11.202, 272, 12.130, 165, 14.173, 15.300, 305, 16.100, 101, 18.206, 266, 269, 19.163, 20.352, 21.190, **B** 3.72, 233, 254, 8.38, 9.63, 10.123, 465, 11.188, 14.154, 165, 173, 176, 15.106, 486, 16.208, 18.24, **A** 3.63, 7.211, 235, †236 (1), 11.79, 12.92; now, at this time 13.225, B 5.233; *in cpd. avv.* **~ aboute** about this; **ben ~** be active about this 10.193; *and see* **ben aboute** 10.191; **~ aftur** in future 10.19; in the next life B 14.141; later on Pr 221, B 17.78; from now on **B** 7.120, 18.345, Z 7.38; **~ afterward** later on B 10.117; **~ agayn, ~ aȝen** against / opposed to this 10.238, 19.111, B 14.189; **~ beynge** *n. phr.* life in this world 16.9; **~ by** by this means 6.121; **~ fore** on this account 11.34, 22.295; **~ ynne** in here 17.39, 40, 22.343; **~ of** about / concerning this 9.1, 11.146, 148, 154, 16.35, 18.213, 19.249, 20.141, 279, 22.325, B 5.114, 6.183; **~ on** about this matter B 13.131; on this matter 12.97, B 10.283; **~ to** to this 2.15, to this point 4.177; for this B 9.36; **~ with** with this 12.162, B 13.157, by means of this 18.28

herayein B 14.189 = **heragayn** *av*; *see* **her(e)**[4]

heraud (of armes) *n* herald [at tournament, announcing knights] 18.186, 266, 20.14, 22.94, **B** 14.25, 16.177, 17.20, 53, 132

herber B 16.15 = **erber** *n*

herberwen 6.235 = **herborw(en)** *v*

herborw *n* place of refuge 11.248

herborwen *v* lodge 6.235, B 17.74, A 2.38, (*fig.*) 7.257; store 21.320

herd *p.p.* 13.128; **herde** *p.t.* Pr 95 *et p.*; *see* **heren** *v*

here A 6.37 = **huyre** *n*; Z 4.14 = **ere** *n*

hereaboute; hereaftur; hereagayn; hereayein; herby; her(e)ynne; herfore; her(e)of; heron; herto; *see* **her(e)**[4] *av*

hered *p.p.* Z 7.5 = **(y)ered**; *see* **eren** *v*

(h)er(e)mite *n* hermit [religious solitary] Pr 3, 30, 51, 55, 5.4, 6.367, 8.146, 183, 9.140, 187, 188, 190, 192, 195, 203, 217. 240, 17.6, **B** 13.30, 285, 15.213, 276, 416

heren *v* (*imper.* **yheer** B 17.138, *p.t.* **herde(n)** Pr 95, B 15.558, A 12.27, *p.p.* **(y)herd** 7.68) hear 4.157, 20.269, 21.21, 22.190, *ger.* (the act of) hearing A 10.52; understand 10.146, 11.221, 16.216, Z Pr 94; listen (to) 4.8, 110, 6.116, 434, 7.22, 77, 111, 8.48, 50, 16.16, B 12.243;

hear, attend 6.354, 7.66, 9.227, 229, 231, 242, 21.3, B 5.2; answer (prayer) 11.61, 19.221; hear (accounts read) 7.40; hear about (sth.) 7.74, 79, 10.109, 11.76, **B** Pr 164, 11.390, 15.58

her(e)of 9.1, 18.213 *etc*; *see* **her(e)**[4]

heres Z 5.9 *see* **heer**[2] *n*

herien *v* honour A 11.247

heryen Z 7.93, 8.5 = **eryen** *v*

herynne 17.39, 40, 22.343 *see* **her(e)**[4]

heritage *n* (sovereign) inheritance 3.242; (legal) inheritance 16.127, (*fig.*) spiritual inheritance (= place in heaven) B 10.341, 350

heresulue (~ **self** A, ~ **selue** B, ~ **silf** Z) *emphatic prn. fem. sg.* herself 20.254; she herself 3.180, 207; **by** ~ all by herself, all alone B 18.288

herken(en) *v* listen carefully 8.223, Z 7.20

herne *n* corner, secret hiding place 2.249 20.447

heron B 13.131 *see* **her(e)**[4]

heroudes 22.94 *see* **heraud** *n*

herre A 10.101, **herrore** 2.30 *comp.*; *see* **hey(h)(e)** *a*

herrys Z 2.74, *see* **ayr** *n*

herte *n* [physical] heart 1.169, 10.175, 12.51, 17.268, 20.87, 21.58, 171, 22.226, **B** 9.57, 16.15, **A** 6.50, 12.48; = stomach 6.214; (true, inner) self, soul 1.39, 6.331, 7.17, 254, 9.183, 11.53, B 10.433, A 10.78; heart [feeling(s)] 2.16, 3.489, 4.36, 6.11, 63, 89, 146, 7.261, 16.140, 19.329, 22.2, B 15.218, A 12.114; mood, spirits 22.171, B 5.111, A 5.97; mind, understanding 1.140, 159, 160, 6.289, 16.209, **B** 3.304, 6.49, A 11.259, Z 1.131; courage B 3.199; character, disposition 3.224, 351; desire 11.231; *in phrr.* **at, in** ~ to heart, seriously **B** 10.290, 15.259; **fre** ~ generosity B 15.151; **gode** ~ sincerity 17.134; courage 22.180; **hardy** ~, **hardinesse of** ~ valour 9.265, 21.31; **heyh** ~ 6.8, **heynesse of** ~ arrogance 22.153; **(with) heuy** ~ grudgingly 6.63;**hol(e)** ~ true, upright heart / dispostion 3.351, 7.257; **louh-herted** humble 22.37; **lowe** ~, **lowenesse of** ~ humility 9.184, B 7.62; **milde** ~**s** kind, gracious hearts 19.201; **poore (of)** ~ humble **B** 14.195, 16.8, humility B 14.99; **rewful** ~**s** merciful hearts B 14.148; **sorowe of** ~ heartfelt sorrow (for sin) 16.29, 18.260; **wil of** ~ heartfelt intention **B** 13.141, 14.14; **wikkede** ~**s** evil hearts 14.25; **with** ~ inwardly, in truth B 13.279; **with mouthe and** ~ in words and sincere intention 12.72, 18.260

herten *v* hurt, injure (*p.p.* **hert(e)**) 19.153, 20.384, 22.318, 336

herthe Z 1.62 = **erthe** *n*

herto 2.155, 4.177, B 9.36 *see* **her(e)**[4]

heruest *n* harvest-time [early autumn, ?August] 5.7, 6.112, 8.121, 322, B 6.66; = the ripened crops 8.314, 12.201

herwith 12.162, 18.28, B 13.157 *see* **her(e)**[4]

hest(e) *n* command, bidding 3.148, 17.142, 18.250, A

10.142, 160; instruction 8.213; Commandment 2.87, 9.334, 13.67, A 11.253

hete *n* heat 9.109, 16.179; warmth 18.75, 19.194; drought 15.165, 261, **B** 14.172, 15.271; hot weather 1.123; *in phr.* **in chele and in** ~ = in all circumstances 8.249

hete *p.t.* A 12.74; *see* **hoten** *v*

heten *p.t.* Z 6.89, 7.307 = **eten** *v*

hethen(e) (heþen(e)) *a* heathen, pagan 21.351, B 15.457, 458; *as n* a pagan B 10.348, (*collective*) heathens A 11.251, B 10.363; ~**esse** *n* a pagan country B 15.442

†**hetyn** *v*[3] Z 4.108 = **hat(i)en** *v*

hette *p.t.* 1.17, *pr.* Z 7.44 *see* **hoten** *v*

heued 3.379 *et p.*, B 14.233, **A** 4.64, 6.25, 10.49, Z 2.181 *et p.*; *see* **he(e)d** *n*

heuen(e) *n* heaven Pr 133, 150, 1.103, 132, 148, 2.38, 132, 3.98, 5.186, 6.307, 330, 8.43, 11.200, 222, 12.99, 14.84, 135, 206, 16.51, 211, 17.149, 247, 20.247, 346, 440, 21.74, 81, 192, 22.270, **B** Pr 128, 1.111, 120, 123, 151, 3.50, 9.100, 10.335, 351, 14.141 (2), 165, 15.479, 16.208; **A** 1.113, 8.38, 10.46, 11.173, Z 5.130, 6.63; (*fig.*) = (place of) supreme happiness 1.9, 5.152, **B** 3.72, 9.118, 14.128, 141 (1); (*euphem.*) **in** ~ dead 22.194; the (natural) heaven, sky 15.268, 22.276; *in phrr.* ~ **blisse B** Pr 106, 14.154; ~ **dore** 16.168; ~ **gate(s)** 2.132, 7.248; **hey** ~ 18.98, **B** 2.33, 12.40, 16.118; **as in** ~ from the stand-point of ~ 18.88, 89; **while God is in** ~ for ever B 2.107; **to** ~**ward** toward heaven 16.53, B 10.333; **as to** ~ **ward** in respect of heaven B 15.457; ~ **and erthe** 20.232; ~ **and helle** 3.165, B 17.162; **helle or** ~ 14.193; **archangel of** ~ 1.107; **blisse of** ~ 7.135; **court of** ~ 3.455; **ducchesse of** ~ 2.33; **eyres of** ~ 5.59; **eritage in** ~ B 10.341, 350; **fader of** ~ 18.91, 227, 19.210, **B** 7.53, 16.213; **game of** ~ B 9.102; **God of** ~ 15.406; ~ **godhede of** ~ B 9.46; **Holy Goest of** ~ 19.121, 166; **(Iesu) Crist in / of** ~ B 11.184, 12.126, 16.222; **Kyng of** ~ 13.66, 17.262; **konnynge of** ~ B 12.66; **Oure Lord in / of** 12.161, B 17.164, 18.357; **loweste of** ~ 14.151; **messager of** ~ 17.178; **munstrals of** ~, **munstracie of** ~ 9.126, 16.310; **paleys of** ~ B 10.462; **paradys oþer** ~ 11.299; **prince of** ~ 17.248; **reume of** ~ 5.125; **Registre of** ~ B 5.271; **Oure Saueour of** ~ B 9.127; **Seintes in** ~ B 5.509, 10.425, **A** 3.223, 8.33; **sire of** ~ 20.302; **sonne of** ~ 18.72; **souereynes in** ~ 11.271; **thef in** ~ 14.150; **triacle of** ~ 1.148; **Trinite of** ~ 18.26; **way(es) to** ~ 1.199, 13.29, B 12.37; *in genitival phrr.* **þe Fader wille of** ~ the will of the heavenly Father 16.27; ~ **riche blisse** the blessedness of the kingdom of heaven Pr 29, 16.100, B 15.175; **the Kynges marke / sone of** ~ mark / son of the King of Heaven 17.77, 20.363; ~ **the Lordes / Cristes loue of** ~ the love of the Lord / Christ in heaven 8.16, 15.35, **B** 6.220, 13.143; **Mary loue of heuene** the love of Mary in heaven 2.2; *in other assevs.* **by deere God in** ~ B Pr 210; **by Marie of** ~ 4.139, 173, 11.189, B 3.201

heuegore (*comp.*)14.105; **heuegeste** (*sup.*) 6.242 *see* **heuy** *a*

heuy *a* heavy 1.148, B 4.22; *comp.* **heuegore** heavier 14.105; **heuegeste** heaviest 6.242; sorrowful, dejected 6.63, 11.188; ~ **chere** mournful face 4.160; ~ **chered** with a gloomy expression 22.2; ~ **nesse** *n* grief 20.256

hew *n* colour 13.176, 14.158

hewe *n* (*pl.* **hewes** 1.123, **hewen** 16.3, B 14.3) servant 3.307, 4.58, 102, 7.195, 8.195, 10.218

hewen *v* chop (wood) A 7.59; strike 19.211

hexte *sup.* B 12.144 *see* **hey(e)** *av*

hy[1] *pers. prn. 3 pl.* they 1.187, †3.321, 6.56, 9.63, 14.191, †19.138, 20.422, 22.261, †301, A 1.165, 2.25, 126, †185, 3.24, 74, †155, 4.25, 5.†95, 256, †6.52, 7.125, 131, 190, 192, 277, 8.73, 10.16, 213

hy[2] 17.247, 18.106, 139 = **hey(h)(e)** *a*

hidde(n) *p.t.* 20.447, B 11.351, 17.109 *see* **h(u)yden** *v*

hyd(d)er(e) *av* hither, to this place 15.238, 18.17, 20.321, 336, 346, 22.334 ~**ward(es)** in this direction 8.343, 20.341

hyden 22.124 = **h(u)yden** *v*

hye 1.169, 17.222, B 3.48 = **heye** *av*; 7.248, 14.48, 17.256, 262 = **hey(h)(e)** *a*

hyen *v* hurry 22.325, B 3.194, 5.378, (*refl.*) 8.206

hyere B 2.28 = **herrore** *comp.*; *see* **hey(h)e** *a*

hif Z 6.91 = (ȝ)**yf** *conj.*

highte *3 pr. sg.* B 16.15, 61, 188, 17.108, Z 6.21 = **hatte**; *p.t.* B 17.134 *etc*, **hiȝte** B Pr 102 *et p.*, A 1.17 *et p.*, **hyȝt(h)e** A 12.49, 53; *p.p.* B 18.79; **hihte** *p.t.* 3.9 *et p.*, *p.p.* 6.309, 7.298, 20.81, 21.332 *see* **hoten** *v*

hij B Pr 66, 1.191, 5.565, †20.261, †301, †380 = **hy** *pers. prn.*

hilen B 12.232 *see* **helen** *v*[2]

hil(le) B Pr 5 *etc*, Z Pr 99 = **hul(le)** *n*

hym, him *pers. prn. 3 sg. masc. as dir. obj.*: him Pr 70 *et p.*; *as ind. obj*: to him 3.193, 4.15, 11.115, 13.90, 14.18, 125, 18.97; for him 9.3, 16.314, 318, B 13.248; from him 8.254, 258, 19.208; *after impers. vv.* Pr 187, 189, 2.241, 5.95, 9.87, 10.176, 16.68, 18.204, 19.144, 20.438 *etc*, B 8.34, 9.38, 16.201, 17.140; (*refl.*) himself 2.221, 6.390, 421, 7.62, †247, 8.194, 207, 9.5 (2), 90, 144, 237, 10.87, 11.257, 12.159, 13.89, 244, 246, 14.132, 153, 16.75, 111, 17.154, 284, 18.206, 20.39, 103, 21.102, 297, 440, 22.116, 123, 144, 22.167, B Pr 190, 1.29, 5.11, 89, 7.78, 9.97, 12.192, 13.291, 16.201, 17.82, 109; for himself 10.87, 21.338, 22.152, B 13.60, 18.14; to himself B 1.30; *semi-refl., dat. of interest, usu. not translated*: 2.116, 6.197, 7.72, 8.68, 149, 156, 166, 9.151, 10.218, 15.286, 19.79, 20.298, 22.289, B Pr 139, 10.90, 13.136; (*with v. of motion*) 6.350, 8.206, 343, 9.145, 11.64, 15.286, 18.118, 19.63, 22.175, 353; *in absolute constr.* ~ **wilnyng** while he desires B 13.280

hymsulue(n) (**himself** A 6.96, **himselue(n)** A 10.35, 1.44, **hymsylf** Z Pr 76, **hymsulf** 7.100, 13.77, 91, 15.236) *emph. pers. prn.*: himself, *appositive* 3.416 *et*

p., Z 1.7; (*refl.*) 8.117, 10.183, 13.208, B 3.310; *with prep.* 3.132, 4.43 *etc*; **by** ~ by itself, separately 6.227; on his own 10.241, 14.144; on its own, in itself 19.141; in himself B 13.283; **of** ~ of its own accord 17.49; (of) its own 20.159; in itself B 14.283; **with** ~ himself with 21.228; *as subj.* he himself Pr 68, 5.187, 7.112, 17.193, 240, 18.256, 20.302, 21.334, 450, B Pr 206, 9.118, 16.145, A 10.167; *as obj.* 10.133, 18.203

hynde Z 3.97 = **ende** *n*

hynde *n* hind, female deer 17.9

hyne *n* servant 6.262, B 6.131, 14.149, A Pr 39; (*fig.*) thing of little worth B 4.118

hippynge B 17.60 *see* **huppen** *v*

hire B 2.123, 3.72, 256, 6.139, 195, 14.128, 143, 149 = **huyre** *n*

hir(e)[1] *pers. prn. fem. obj.* B 1.58 *et p.*, A 2.24 *etc*; *see* **her(e)**[1]

hir(e)[2] *poss. prn. fem.* B 4.50, 9.56, 10.152, 12.46, 226, 14.266, 16.101, 17.320 (1,3), **hire** A 1.10 *et p.*; *see* **her(e)**[2]

hir(e)[3] *poss. prn. pl.* B Pr 28, 1.99 *et p.*, **hire** A 3.137, 252 *et p*; *see* **here**[3]

hireself A 3.133, **hirselue** B 3.148 *see* **heresulue** *emph. prn.*

his *poss. prn. masc. sg.* his Pr 70 *et p.*, (*with pl. n, infl. as a*) **hise** B 7.168 *et p.*; *as n* his people / dependants 19.251; his followers 21.220, 22.61; his possessions / wealth A 4.61

hit (**it**) *prn. neut. sg.* it Pr 11, 39, Z 1.79 *et p.*; *as subj. with pl. antecedent* 16.92, A 7.46, *as obj.* 9.57, 16.309, 18.11; *as subj. of pl. v with following pl. n.*, = there 15.288, = they 5.59, 8.52, 217, 9.118, 126, 194, 12.98, 15.309, Z 7.49, 263; = he 13.120, 19.271; *as anticipatory compl.* 15.237; *in ref. to understood subj.* 14.87, 165, *or obj.* 22.363, Z 7.58; *as grammatical obj. emphasising real obj.* [things] 4.177, [the consequences] 6.276; *or a foll. clause*: 3.147, 6.289, 7.4, 144, 8.212, 10.191, 12.100, 20.302, *or prec. clause*: 9.331, 13.239, 15.126, 16.280; *as subj. of imper. v.* 6.100, 7.50, 9.163, 19.34; *in pleonastic uses*: 14.58, 16.53, 131, 17.130, 18.80, 215, 20.147, 150, 337 (2), 21.476, 22.28, 54, 147, 275, B 10.441; *in phr.* **don** ~ **vppon** appeal to 1.82, 2.39

hitsilue *emph. refl. prn.* itself 1.149

hitten *v* (*contr. pr.* **hit** 20.383, *p.t.* **hit(te)** 6.377, 22.103) hit, strike 14.51, 22.103, 175, 190, B 5.162, A 7.166; knock 20.383; ~ **aftur** strike at 18.120, throw 6.377, ? B 16.87n; ~ **on** encounter 11.113

†thywe A 6.39 = **hewe** *n*

ho *prn* (*see also* **hoso, wham, who(m), whos**): *interrog. prn* who 3.66, 72, 6.419, 9.70, 10.72, 110, 11.149, 155, 217, 264, 274, 12.215, 13.198, 16.34, 314, 17.63, 18.130, 20.17, 26, 68, 212, 21.11, 58, 351, B 3.235, 7.129, 132, 10.245, 310, 422, 436, 11.360, 15.120, 325, 17.105; *rel. indef. prn* whoever, any(one) who 1.84

(who), 3.61, 7.277, 279, 11.16, 17.4, 19.153, 20.383, 21.58; *with understood conditional conj.* (if) 3.235, 14.10, 17.108, 254, 19.120, B 1.145, ~ þat B 19.257; those who B 15.485; *in phrr.* **as** ~ as if one B 9.36; as if to B 15.307; **maugre(y)** ~ in spite of any who, whoever may 8.68, 155; **~es** whose, of whom 1.46

hobelen *v* hobble, limp A 1.113

ho(e)d *n* hood 5.133, 6.202, 377, 380, 390, 13.47, Z 7.48; [distinctive] academic hood [of physicians] 8.291, 22.176 (*and see* **houe** *n*)

hoem 5.131 *etc* = **hom** *n*

hoen (on) *v* shout at B 10.61

hoend 19.112 *etc* = **hand** *n*

hoer 8.92, 18.183 = **hoor** *a*

hoerd *n* hoard, collection 18.116

hoes 1 46 *see* **ho** *prn*

hoet 20.211, 290 = **hot(e)** *a*

hoet *imper.* 20.287 *see* **houten** *v*

hogge *n* pig 11.8, B 6.181

hoke *n* crook (fixed part of hinge on which gate hangs) 7.241

hoken *v* bend like hook, *p.p.* hooked Pr 51, 10.94, Z 7.67; barbed 22.226

#hokkerye *n* retail trade 6.233

hold(e)[1] Z 7.48, 69, 8.86; = **old(e)** *a*

holde[2] *a* loyal 8.195, A 7.123

holden *v* 1.148 *etc*, A 10.114 = **halden** *v*

holdyng[1] *pr. p.* 8.103 *see* **halden** *v*

holdyng[2] *ger* grasping 12.246

hole *n* hole (in cask) 21.402; lair, den 22.44

hol(e) *a* entire, untorn B 6.59; whole, sincere 3.351, 7.257; full 20.419; **~ly** *av* together 19.29; completely 3.148, 9.231, 21.3

holy (haly) *a* (*of God*) holy 14.84, B 15.504; consecrated, hallowed (*of festivals, etc*) 1.123; (*of saints*) blessed 12.134, 173, B 3.235; pious, devout 6.40, 48, 9.187, 190, 201, 17.34, 185, 194, 18.116, 22.65, 252, B 12.23, 13.296, 15.429, 437; *in phrr:* ~ **bred** blessed bread 6.146, Z 8.75; ~ **chirche** the / a church 6.272, 354, 17.275, B 12.27; ~ **Chirche, Kirke** (*see below*); ~ **clergie** sacred learning, = scripture 16.238; ~ **comune** sacred community, society 5.186; ~ **day** holy day [church festival incl. Sundays] 1.123, 6.272, 7.18, 225, 9.24, 231, 13.85, B 13.415, A 7.12; ~ **eremytes** devout hermits 9.187; ~ **euene** eve of a holy day 13.85, A 7.12; ~ **fadres** (Desert) Fathers B 15.272; ~ **God** B 15.504; ~ **Go(o)st** the Holy Spirit 14.84 *et p.* (*see* **go(e)st**); ~ **hilles** (*fig.*) = heaven B 3.236; ~ **let(t)rure** holy scripture 11.26, 15.74; ~ **lore** (the) religious teaching (of the Church) 11.36; ~ **men** men of virtuous and pious life 17.34 *etc*; ~ **name** sacred name A 12.13; ~ **Scripture** 21.273; ~ **seintes** B 14.155, 15.269; ~ **water** blessed water (in church) Z 8.75; ~ **wordes** divine teaching B 15.449; ~ **writ** (*a*) sacred scripture, the Holy Bible Pr

104, 205, 1.69, 2.142, 3.486, 5.37, 8.86, 10.240, 248, 296, 11.31, 80, 209, 235, 253, 13.27, 15.78, 265, 17.4, 37, 190, 19.127, 247, 296, 300, 21.109, 329, **B** 1.130, 10.381, 395, 11.396, 13.132, 432, **A** 8.56, 12.97, **Z** 5.35; (*b*) authoritative (patristic) writings, Church tradition 1.125, 15.158, 16.240, 17.6, 19.288, 20.432, A 10.94; **lyf** ~ 9.195 *see* **lyf** *n*; **pop** ~ pope-holy, affectedly pious 6.37

Holy Chirche *n* the (institutional) Christian Church Pr 64, 87, 116, 118, 1.186, 2.140, 248, 3.163, 397, 5.191, 6.19, 119, 7.81, 8.78, 9.24, 104, 218, 219, 10.186, 198, 11.146, 221, 248, 253, 12.120, 156, 14.9, 21, 152, 16.35, 241, 243, 244, 250, 279, 296, 337, 17.5, 41, 50, 71, 124, 125, 167, 202, 230, 286, 18.74, 207, 209, 19.274, 21.224, 330, 336, 369, 383, 445, 22.75, 229, 245, 298, (*uninfl. gen.* Holy Church's 17.231, 21.475, **B** 10.252, 17.119) A 2.166, 12.17; (*person.*) 1.72, 12.53; **B** 6.242, 10.121, 232, 11.98, 159, 14.86, 15.244, 429, 486, 16.6; ~ **Kirke** Pr 138, 3.356, 5.179, 8.26, 53, 159, 9.9, 11.246, 250, 306, 13.89, 14.39, 17.77, 220, 276, 21.413, 470, †22.120 (Holy Church's 8.53, 13.89, 16.255), **B** 10.411, 12.82, 13.274, 15.136, 384, 545, Z 8.9

holynesse *n* (Christian) holiness (of life) 16.241, 18.5, 21.366, 377, 383, 404, 424, 22.145, 227, B 19.111; devotion, piety 4.113, 11.13, 18.159; virtue 2.81, 18.13, B 10.290; (*person.*) 12.1, 22.145; **lyf** ~ 5.80, 21.111 *see* **lyf** *n*

holiwrit A 10.94 *see* **holy** ~ *a*

holpe *p.t. subjv.* 20.441; **~(n)** *p.t. pl.* 8.113, 123, 9.6; *p.p.* 11.28, **B** 5.624, 7.70, 15.134, 16.124 *see* **helpen** *v*

holwe *a or av* hollow(ly) B 5.187

hom *n* dwelling 3.126, (*fig.*) B 9.56; *in phrr:* **at** ~ in (his) dwelling-place 9.5; present 10.28; **fro** ~ away from home 12.65; **~liche** *a* (making oneself) at home; **~ward** *av* homewards B 3.194

hom *av* (back) home 4.56, 5.131, 8.108, 207, 9.151, 21.332, A 7.33; *in phr:* **fer** ~ a long way to go home 21.483

homage *n* homage, **don** ~ acknowledge allegiance 14.98

hond 16.82, B 5.287, *etc*, A 3.55 *etc*; ~ **mayden** 18.132 *see* **hand** *n*

hondred 22.69 *see* **hundred** *num.*

honerably *av* reverently 14.98

honeste *a* virtuous 17.34; worthy, honourable 21.94

honeste(e) *n* virtue 16.241

hony *n* honey 16.217, 224

honouren *v* honour, show respect to 6.40, 7.213; respect 14.43, A 11.247; worship 5.105, 17.134, 153, 18.93, 19.39, B 15.605; show reverence for 17.206, 210, 282, 18.249, 20.267, B 15.446; venerate 14.93; celebrate 2.174; enrich 3.266, admire 14.179; bless 17.276; adorn 8.11

honten 9.223 = **hunten** *v*

hood 6.202 *etc* = **ho(ed)** *n*

hoolden 8.50, B 6.214 *see* **halden** *v*

hoom B 9.56 = **hom** *n*

hoor *a* hoary-headed, grey 6.193, 8.92; white (-haired) 9.175, 18.183, *a as n* 22.95, 202

ho(o)re *n* (*pl.* **hores** 16.259, **horen** 14.21) prostitute 3.300, 6.305, 14.21, 16.259, B 14.183, 15.85, 134; whore 4.161, 6.149; ~ **dom** *n* lechery 7.75, B 13.354

hoost B 20.113 = **oest** *n*

hoot B 18.206 = **hot(e)** *a*

hope *n* hope 3.135, 7.289, 9.142; expectation 1.100, 7.83, 22.180, B 3.200, 10.363; trust Pr 29; (the theological virtue of) hope in God 3.351, 14.214, B 12.30, A 5.242, (*person.*) (*a*) 7.151 (*b*) 19.61, 85, 100, B 17.53, 116, 118, 134; *in phr.* **gode** ~, **wel** ~ positive (attitude of) hope (in God) 7.113, 19.293, 22.167

hopen *v* hope 5.94, 14.194, 17.118, 146; trust 5.99, 12.200, B 15.479; think, believe 20.153, 21.385, *in phr.* **as I** ~ I believe 6.255, 8.103, 137, 9.273, 10.19, 16.21, 17.185, 18.1, B 10.153, Z 7.268; expect 8.314, 9.290, 14.11, 18.250, 254, 19.251

hoppen *v* leap, dance B 3.200

hopur *n* seed basket 8.60

hor Z 1.16 = **or**² *prep.*

hore 4.161 = **ho(o)re** *n*

hore 9.175, 22.95 = **hoor** *a*

horen *pl* 14.21 *see* **ho(o)re** *n*

horn *n* horn 5.16, (*fig.*) 7.151; horn-blast (*fig.*) 6.400

hors *n* (*pl.* **hors**) Z 4.124, *pl.* 2.176, 13.61, B 11.342; horses' 8.225; **on ~e** on horseback B 17.105, 18.83

hos(e)bande *n* husbandman, farmer 7.298 (*with pun*), 12.200, A 11.183; husband 10.270

hosbondrye *n* thrift 1.53

hosel *n* Holy Communion; ~ **en** *v* give Communion, **ben hoseled** receive Communion 21.3, 398, 478

hosewyf *n* wife 13.9, B 14.3

hoso (whoso) *indef. prn.* whoever, anyone who 1.57, 98, 3.406, 445, 494, 5.138, 6.380, 391, 8.120, 9.236, 321, 10.25, 78, 11.72, 226, 12.58, 156, 170, 212, 18.155, 19.5, 19, 120, 162, 167, 262, 20.383, 21.66, 278, 291, B Pr 144, 1.88, 3.283, 4.70, 5.54, 6.65, 67, 7.83, 10.211, 353, 13.376, 15.91, A 12.3; anyone (*with implied conditional conj.* if) Pr 205, 1.143, 4.128, 7.197, 204, 10.202, 16.368, 17.204, 254, 18.155, B 5.116, 275, A 5.97, 10.133; one B 6.1, 10.197, A 8.78; (some) one 3.362, 6.90, 405, 7.306, **as** ~ as if someone B 15.337; someone who 10.39

hostelen *v* provide lodging for (*fig.*) B 17.119

hostiele *n* lodging-house 13.63

hostiler *n* innkeeper 19.76, B 17.116; ostler, stableman 6.388, 390

hostrie *n* inn B 17.74

hot(e) *a* hot Pr 227, 5.7, 9.142, 15.144; peppery-hot 6.357, A 5.154; biting, burning 20.211

hoten *v* (*1 pr sg.* **hote**, 2.211, *p.t.* **hi(g)hte** 7.14, B 17.134, *p.p.* **yhote(n)** 8.78, 2.20, B 1.63, *passive pr. 1 sg.* **hatte** 3.496, **hote** 16.196, *2 sg.* **hattest** 22.340, *3 sg.* **hatte** 7.219, **hette** Z 7.44, **hoteth** 2.31, **hattiþ** A 6.60, **highte** B 16.15, **hyȝthe** A 12.53, *3 pl.* **hatte** 7.223, *p.t.* **he(e)t(e)** 18.249, 22.273, 349, **hi(g)hte** 7.14, **hyȝte** A 12.49, *p.p.* **hi(g)hte** 7.298, B 19.333) name, call 2.20, 7.298, 11.1, B 1.63, 10.150, Z 3.10, 174; be named, called 3.496, 7.219 *et p.*, 8.80, 10.134, 144, 11.170, 188, 308, 16.156, 196, 182, 184, 17.159, 18.9, 18, 183, 292, 20.81, 118, 122, 131, 239, 21.270, 277, 282, 326, 332, 22.340, B 6.44, 9.49, 10.163, 16.8, 61, 62, 188, 17.108, A 11.183; command, order 1.17, 2.211, 3.416, 4.3, 7.14, 246, 8.78, 89 (1), 9.219, 10.99, 13.44, 14.41, 18.249, 22.273, 349, B 5.545, 6.258, 8.94, 10.201, 364, A 12.74; bid 8.85, 89 (2), 272, 11.44, 67, 18.106, B 16.134, 17.134

hou Pr 130, 1.6, 12.106 *see* **how**¹,²

hound *n* dog 6.412, 430, 8.225, B 5.257, 10.61, 11.342; (hunting) hound 5.160, B 4.125, 10.308; herdsman's (watch)dog 9.265, B 10.287

#houpen *v* shout out 8.168

houre *n* hour B 14.12; *pl.* (Divine Office for) the canonical hours B Pr 97, 1.183, 15.385

hous *n* (*pl.* **houses** 3.96 *et p.*, **hous** Z 6.64) house 3.96, 102, 126, 6.352, 7.52, 19.303, 21.167, B 10.95, A 12.53, (*fig.*) 7.236; shelter, lodging A 2.38; shed (for corn) A 6.32, (*fig.*) 21.320, 330; building B 14.253; (consecrated) place 18.159; religious community B 3.63, 5.264, 267; buildings (of a religious house) B 11.65, 15.422; family B 16.177; household (*fig.*) B 10.229, A 12.84; establishment 9.206, B 15.142; ~ **hyre** rent for housing 9.74; *in phrr:* **burgeis** ~ 14.91; **caytyfs** ~ 14.90; **Goddes** ~ the Church B 10.405; **hungry** ~ = establishment with little to eat 9.206, (**in)to** ~ indoors 2.229, 9.125

housen *v* house, *ger.* **housynge** building (houses) 16.234

houswif B 14.3 = **hosewyf** *n*

houten *v* shout at; ~ **out** shout out 20.287; *p.p.* **yhouted** 2.228; ~ **out** shout out 20.287

houe *n* lawyer's coif Pr 159 (B Pr 211, A Pr 84), 3.447; **glasene** ~ glass hood (= a delusive protection) 22.172

houen *v* hang suspended Z 3.146n; wait about in readiness Pr 159, 20.82

how¹ *interrog. av* how 1.80 *et p.*

how² *conjv. av* how 1.6, 125 *et p.*; the manner in which Pr 130, 11.71, B 10.137, A 6.82; that B 5.109; (as to) how 6.264, 19.236, 20.333, B 16.147; (saying) how / that 8.130, B 5.364; (to hear) how 11.77; ~ **euere** all the ways in which B 12.223; ~ **so, so euere,** ~ **... euere** in whatever way 12.6, 237, 18.120, 19.152, A 11.260; ~ **þat** how 11.139, 13.142, 15.9, 73, 16.232, 18.162, B 13.353, A 8.17; **Lo / loke** ~ see the way in which 12.248, 13.20, 14.130, 22.202

how³ B 6.116 *see* **hey** *interj.*

hucche B 4.116 = **whicche** *n*

hudde(n) *p.t.* 13.163, 21.102 *see* **h(u)yden** *v*

huge *a* severe, grave 19.286; vehement 12.137

h(u)yden *v* (*p.t.* **hudde** 21.102, **hidde** B 17.109, *p.p.* **yhudde** B 10.430) hide 13.163, 21.460, **B** 10.430, 11.353; (*refl.*) 21.102, B 17.109; keep secretly 22.124; wrap round 19.127; state in a cryptic manner 10.245

h(u)yre *n* payment for service 3.301, 14.215, B 3.72; wages 3.307, 7.193, 195, 8.115, 9.273, 16.3, **B** 2.123, 3.256; rent 9.74; hire, **to** ~ for hire 2.175

h(u)yren *v* pay, *p.p.* 8.121, 335

hul(le), (hille) *n* hill 7.158, 10.232, Z Pr 94, 99; þe ~ Cornhill 12.220; **Maluerne Hulles** Pr 6, 163, 5.110, 9.295

Humylite A 6.109 = **Vmbletee** *n*

hundred *card. num.* hundred B 13.270; †**seuenty** ~ B 18.283; (*as indef. large number*) 7.164, 266, 12.176, 21.212, 22.218, **B** 15.374, 18.408, A 12.27, *pl.* 22.69; **enleuene** ~ 12.176, **foure** ~ 19.211, **seuene** ~ B 14.68, **ten** ~ 7.38, **þre** ~ B 13.270, **twenty** ~ B 16.10, ~ **fold** *a* hundred times over 12.160

hunger *n* (feelings of) hunger 6.437, 8.246, 272, 20.211, **B** 3.194, 15.281, A 11.46; lack of food 9.77, **B** 6.328, 15.271, Z 7.201; starvation 15.237, 261, (*person.*) 8.168 *et p.*, A 12.63, 74

***hungirly** *a* hungry-looking A 5.108*n* (*or* = **hungrily-(che)** *av*)

hungren *v* be hungry 8.225, (*impers.*) 15.253

hungry *a* hungry 6.412, B 18.395; (*as n*) hungry person(s) 8.192, B 5.374; meanly provided with food 9.206; greedy, avaricious 15.190, (*comp.*) **hungriore** 1.186; ~ **li(che)** *av* (*or a*) greedily 22.123, ?hungry-looking, emaciated(ly) 6.197

hunsen *v* abuse, insult A 11.48

hunten *v* hunt, ~ **to** hunt after 8.28, *ger.* hunting 3.465, (*fig.*) B 3.311

huppen *v* leap, gad (about) 17.279; *pr.p.* dashing, hurrying 19.61

hure A 12.41 = **her(e)**²; A 12.48 = **her(e)**¹

hurten *v* injure B 10.364

husbond A 11.183 = **hos(e)bande** *n*

huserye Z 8.40 = **vsurye** *n*

hutten 14.51 = **hitten** *v*

huxterie A 5.141 = **hokkerye** *n*

Y, I (**Ich** *before vowels, emph.* A 9.65, Z 8.62, *dial.* **Ik** B 5.224n, **Yc** Z 3.35) 2.216, 8.2, 3, 11.311, 13.128, 14.138, 15.89, 218, 16.286, 343, 348, 20.330, 342, 22.190, **B** 5.258, 7.143, 11.75, 12.28, 13.226, 248, 369, 370, 379, 384, 15.24, 36, *pers. pr. 1 sg.* I Pr 2, 56 *et p.*

y Z 3.149, 5.110 = **yn** *prep.*

i-, y- *prefix marking p.p.* Pr 42, A 2.9 *et p.*, *inf.*, 1.71, 4.187, 6.200, B 17.138, *av* 6.183, 10.116, 14.148, 21.442; *see under root-form entries*

y-armed *p.p.* 21.144 *see* **armen** *v*

ybake *p.p.* 8.333, **B** 6.182, 282, 15.432, 462 *see* **baken** *v*

ybaptised *p.p.* 19.88 *see* **baptisen** *v*

ybarred *p.p.* 21.167 *see* **barren** *v*

ybe *p.p.* 6.17, 7.54, 188, B 14.95 *see* **ben** *v*

ybedded *p.p.* 17.197 *see* **bedden** *v*

yberied *p.p.* 12.22 *see* **burien** *v*

ybete *p.p.* 4.89 *see* **beten** *v*¹

ybetered *p.p.* 5.21 *see* **beteren** *v*

yblamed *p.p.* 3.435, 439 *see* **blamen** *v*

yblessed (yblissed) *p.p.* Pr 76, 7.135, 8.260, 9.13, 11.248, 16.201, 21.179, 180, 388, 440, B 11.163, Z 7.238 *see* **blessed** *p.p.a and* **blessen** *v*

yblowen *p.p.* 19.179 *see* **blowen** *v*

ybore *p.p.* 2.144, 14.90, 20.136, 241, 243 *see* **beren** *v*

yborwed *p.p.* B 15.312 *see* **borwen** *v*

ybosted *p.p.* 19.61 *see* **bosten** *v*

ybotresed *p.p.* 7.235 *see* **botresen** *v*

ybought *p.p.* Pr 191, B 11.207 *see* **byggen** *v*

ybounde *p.p.* Pr 97, 193, 1.120, 7.161, 13.79, 19.54, 20.100, **B** 13.153, 18.95 *see* **bynden** *v*

ybrent *p.p.* 3.105 *see* **brennen** *v*

ybroke(n)(e) *p.p.* Pr 69, B 19.347 *see* **breken** *v*

ybrouhte *p.p.* 3.2 *see* **bryngen** *v*

ycald *p.p.* 9.213, 11.175, 14.14, 15.82, 16.181, 183, 190, A 4.140 *see* **callen** *v*

ycalled *a* wearing a cap 16.352

ycaryed *p.p.* Z 6.20 *see* **caryen** *v*

ycarped *p.p.* B 15.301 *see* **carpen** *v*

ychaffared *p.p.* 5.94 *see* **chaffaren** *v*

ychaunged *p.p.* 5.81 *see* **cha(u)ngen** *v*

***ycheuelen** *v* tremble 6.200; = **chyuelen** B 5.190

iche A 2.39, 7.135, 10.71, 207, 11.61, 250, **ichone** A 3.37, 249 *see* **vch** *a*, **vchon(e)** *prn*

ychose *p.p.* 6.379 *see* **chesen** *v*

yclansed *p.p.* 3.358 *see* **clansen** *v*

yclyketed *p.p.* 7.265 *see* **clyketen** *v*

yclosed *p.p.* 7.264, †10.172, 15.268 *see* **closen** *v*

yclothed *p.p.* 1.3, 2.9, 5.2, 17.196, 20.170, 174, B 13.273 *see* **clothen** *v*

yclouted *p.p.* B 6.59 *see* **clouten** *v*

ycome *p.p.* 3.455, 12.49, 18.127 *see* **comen** *v*

ycongeyed *p.p.* 16.367 *see* **conieyen** *v*

ycoped *p.p.* 3.38, 22.345 *see* **copen** *v*

ycouped *p.p.* 20.12 *see* **coupen** *v*

ycoupled *p.p.* B 9.126 *see* **couplen** *v*

ycrammed *p.p.* Pr 42 *see* **crammen** *v*

ycrimyled *p.p.* 16.352 *see* **crimylen** *v*

ycrouned *p.p.* 5.56, 59, 21.41 *see* **crounen** *v*

ycursed *p.p.* B 20.263 *see* **(a)corsen** *v*

ydampned *p.p.* 12.245 *see* **dampnen** *v*

ydel *n* vanity, **an** ~ in vain 7.217, B 13.402; to no purpose 14.7, 16.37, 21.405, 22.300

ydel(e) *a* worthless 7.19; sinful 2.95, B 14.13; idle, without work 5.27; *a as n* idle people B 13.226 (*? or n* **ydel**); ~ **nesse** *n* vanity 21.287; idle / worthless words 2.101; idleness, indolence 9.152, 15.215, 22.116, (*person.*) 21.229

ydyademed *p.p.* 3.440 *see* **dyademen** *v*

idyked *p.p.* A 6.33 *see* **dichen** *v*

ydyned *p.p.* 8.302 *see* **dynen** *v*

ydiot *n* ignoramus, simpleton B 16.170; #~**es** *pl. a* unlearned B 11.316

ydo(e)(ne) *p.p.* 2.128 *et p.*, 20.111, B 18.53, A 6.33; *see* **do(o)n** *v*

idoluen *p.p.* A 6.33 *see* **deluen** *v*

ydrawe *p.p.* 18.217, 229, 20.139 *see* **drawen** *v*

ydremed *p.p.* 21.1 *see* **dremen** *v*

ydronke *p.p.* 6.418, 8.302, 17.223, Z 7.245 *see* **drynken** *v*

ye (**eye** 6.2, **eiʒe** B 10.125) *n* eye 6.2, 236, 406, 7.1, 8.172, 16.333, 18.49, 147, 19.305, 325, 20.50, 88, 238, 21.381, B 10.125; sight Pr 72, 14.44; ~ **syhte** eye-sight, (good) vision 9.102; *in phrr.* **blered here ~s** hoodwinked them Pr 72; **Coueytise of ~s** Lust of the Eyes 11.175, 193, 312, 12.3; **lokyng of an ~** instant, twinkling of an eye A 12.96; **waitynges of ~s** watchings-out, observations 2.94

yentred *p.p.* 11.205 *see* **entren** *v*

yf, if[1] (**ʒif** 6.343 *et p.*, A Pr 37 *et p.*, B 9.77, **ʒef** 7.259; **yif** B 5.424, †**yyf** Z 5.124) *conj.* if Pr 171 *et p.*; provided that 4.171, 7.147, 9.13; assuming that 2.129, 9.212; if only, supposing that Pr 38, 80, 12.55, 18.216; that 22.336; whether 2.169, 9.298, 10.4, 15.107, 16.164; (to learn) whether 22.311, B 2.136; *in phrr.* ~ **þat** whether B 2.156; **but if** unless 1.176, 3.459, 5.161 *etc*, Z 4.130; **parauntur ~** if perchance 7.296

yf[2] *3 pr. subjv.* Z 3.101, *imper.* Z 7.48, *p.p.* Z 5.108 *see* **ʒeuen** *v*

yfalle(n) *p.p.* 7.112, 9.179, 182, 13.70, 20.106 *see* **fallen** *v*

yfed *p.p.* B 15.302 *see* **feden** *v*

yfere *av* together Z 5.63

yfet *p.p.* Z 7.165 *see* **fecchen** *v*

yfolde *p.p.* 19.115, 131 *see* **folden** *v*

yfolled *p.p.* 21.40 *see* **follen** *v*

yfolwed *p.p.* B 3.39 *see* **fol(e)wen** *v*

yfouhte *p.p.* 8.149, 18.137 *see* **fy(g)hten** *v*

yfo(u)nde(n) *p.p.* 3.41, 492, 16.285, 19.23, B 10.255, 15.230, Z 3.148 *see* **fynden** *v*

yfranchised *p.p.* 3.114 *see* **franchisen** *v*

yfried *p.p.* 8.333, B 13.63 *see* **frien** *v*

yfruyted *p.p.* B 16.39 *see* **fruyten** *v*

yftus Z 1.49 *etc*; *see* **ʒift** *n*

ygadered *p.p. see* **gaderen** *v*

ygete *p.p.* 20.322 *see* **geten** *v*

ygyue *p.p.* 2.162 *see* **ʒeuen** *v*

yglobbed *p.p.* 6.396 *see* **globben** *v*

yglosed *p.p.* 11.117, 19.13 *see* **glosen** *v*

ygon *v* pass, **longe ygo** a long time ago 20.296; **fern ago** in the distant past B 15.231

ygraced *p.p.* B 6.124 *see* **gracen** *v*

ygraunted *p.p.* 9.184, B 7.8, A 10.206 *see* **graunten** *v*

ygraue *p.p.* 4.127, 17.75, B 15.544, Z 2.72 *see* **grauen** *v*

ygreued *p.p.* 16.207 *see* **greuen** *v*

ygrounde *p.p.*, 15.49, 20.80, A 7.169 *see* **grynden** *v*

yhabited *p.p.* B 13.285 *see* **habiten** *v*

yhad *p.p.* 7.44 *see* **hauen** *v*

yhandlit *p.p.* A 2.99 *see* **hand(e)len** *v*

yhapsed (**yhasped** B 1.197) *p.p.* 1.191 *see* **hapsen** *v*

yhated *p.p.* B 9.100 *see* **hat(i)en** *v*

yheeled *p.p.* B 14.96 *see* **helen** *v*[1]

yheer *imper.* B 17.138 *see* **heren** *v*

yheled *p.p.* 7.236 *see* **hel(i)en** *v*[2]

yherd(e) *p.p.* 7.68, 16.51, B 10.103 *see* **heren** *v*

yheren *v* hear Z 2.86; hear (legal argument) 4.187

yhoked *p.p.* Z 7.67 *see* **hoken** *v*

yholde *p.p.* 1.80, 3.267, 5.157, 14.196, *see* **halden** *v*

yholpe *p.p.* 19.62 *see* **helpen** *v*

yhote *p.p.* 2.228, B 1.63, Z 3.10, 174 *see* **hoten** *v*

yhouted *p.p.* 2.228 *see* **houten** *v*

yhudde *p.p.* B 10.430 *see* **h(u)yden** *v*

yhuyred *p.p.* 8.335 *see* **h(u)yren** *v*

Ik (**Yk** Z) B 5.224 = **Ych** *pers. prn.*

ykald *p.p.* 9.249, 18.14 *see* **callen** *v*

ykeyed *p.p.* 7.265 *see* **keyen** *v*

ykept *p.p.* Z 6.20 *see* **kepen** *v*

ykyuered *p.p.* 21.86 *see* **keueren** *v*[1]

yknyt *p.p.* B 15.242 *see* **knytten** *v*

yknowen *v* recognise 4.71, 7.206, 12.123, 16.166, 20.23; admit Z 3.35; find out 13.223, B 11.405; *p.p. a* familiar 16.169, Z 2.70

ykud *p.p.* 12.198 *see* **kithen** *v*

ykuld *p.p.* Pr 199, 10.250

ylabored *p.p.* 8.255 *see* **labouren** *v*

ylasted *p.p.* B 3.192 *see* **lasten** *v*

ile *n* island, domain A 2.63

ylefte *p.p.* 17.162 *see* **leuen** *v*

yley(e) *p.p.* 11.260, B 5.81, 16.113 *see* **li(gg)en** *v*

yleyd *p.p.* 3.258 *see* **leggen** *v*

yleke Z 1.36 = **lyk** *av*

ylered *p.p.* 10.10, 11.127, *as a* B 13.214 *see* **leren** *v*

ylet[1] *p.p.* 3.204, 5.3 *see* **leten** *v*

ylet(te)[2] *p.p.* 13.36, 49, 21.385 *see* **letten** *v*

ylettred *a* educated 11.236

yleued *p.p.*[1] 16.248 *see* **leuen** *v*[3]

yleued *p.p.*[2] 16.286 (= **ylyued**) *see* **lyuen** *v*

ilych(e), ylyk(e) (to) *a* like, resembling 7.128, 10.68, 116, 13.192, 18.70, 20.3, B 1.91, 18.338

iliche, ylik(e) *av* likewise 15.34, B 1.50; alike, equally 14.148, 16.20, 18.22, 62, 21.442, B 13.350; as, equally with 10.133, 19.332

ylikned *p.p.* 16.264, 17.82 *see* **liknen** *v*

ylyued *p.p.* 11.256 *see* **lyuen** *v*

ilke *a* very, same 7.244, 10.142, 18.265, **B** 6.162,

9.189, 17.112; *prn* same (thing) 1.79; very person 16.312

ille *n* evil 20.318; wrong Pr 109, 1.49, 20.432, **B** 5.113, 10.26, A 9.93; sin 1.61; harm 1.85, A 10.68

ille *a* wicked 10.94, 16.191, 20.301

ille *av* wickedly 6.324, 20.429, B 2.195; badly Pr 225, 8.211

ylore *p.p.* 6.193, 12.185, **ylorn** B 18.313 *see* **lesen** *v*

ylost *p.p.* Pr 195, 12.96, 20.268, 349, 21.412 *see* **losen** *v²*

ylow *p.p.* 2.20 *see* **lyen** *v*

ima(e)d(e) *p.p.* 5.77, 6.250, 295, 7.139, 11.205, 16.19, A 2.26, **ymaked** 2.73, 8.289, 10.87, B Pr 14 *etc*; *see* **maken** *v*

ymage *n* image, representation B 1.50; likeness 20.326, A 10.35

Ymagenatyf *n* the imaginative faculty of the mind, *person.* 14.1, 202, 15.17

ymagenyen *v* think ahead 21.278; brood over B 13.289; form a plan B 13.358

ymaginacioun *n* forethought 22.33

ymaymed *p.p.* 5.34, 9.216, B 17.190 *see* **maymen** *v*

ymaked 2.73 *etc*; *see* **ima(e)d(e)** *p.p.*

ymanered *p.p. as a* 10.263 *see* **maneren** *v*

ymaried *p.p.* 2.41, 46 *see* **marien** *v*

ymartired *p.p.* B 15.522 *see* **martiren** *v*

ymedled *p.p.* 10.130 *see* **medlen** *v*

ymorthred *p.p.* 12.244 *see* **mortheren** *v*

impe, ympe *n* scion, graft B 5.136; sapling 18.6; **~n** *v* graft B 9.149, (*fig.*) B 5.137

impugnen *v* call in (question the validity of sth.) 9.301, 15.132, **B** 11.304, 13.124; find fault (with) Pr 136

yn *n* dwelling, **at ynne** at home, living 10.4

in (**yn** 5.44, 11.44, 13.70, **ynne** 1.133 *etc*) *prep.* in Pr 3, 1.133 *et p.*; inside 1.184, 12.219, 21.346; within 18.164, 20.254, 271, 21.82; on 1.112, 123, 2.172, 3.491, 6.284, 285, 9.75, 10.24, 11.202, 231, 12.151, 15.186, 16.234, 322, 17.207, 18.64, 19.48, 194, 21.356, **B** 12.48, 15.76, 328, 16.160; at 2.153, 8.284, 10.123, 11.71, 232, 17.120, **B** 6.66, 9.121, A 10.202; at the time (of) 7.85, 110, 9.38, 14.58, 17.124, 144, 20.79; to Pr 27, 8.198, 13.8, 84, 15.189, 16.360, 17.173, B 10.255 (1); toward Z Pr 14; in a state of 21.249; amongst 11.59, 16.47; into 2.102, 3.201, 6.337, 7.4, 113, 8.163, 9.253, 10.33, 11.167, 12.52, 65, 13.70, 14.104, 17.181, 19.292, 20.420, 21.289, 305, 420, 22.10, 176, **B** 5.279, 7.79, 10.278, 15.396, 18.103, **A** 3.144, 5.74, Z 4.35; within (the course of) Pr 63, 5.50, 6.398, 7.29, 12.219, 17.23, 36, 237, 20.41, 21.273, 357, 22.284, B 1.101, **A** 12.58, 66; during 1.25, 101, 6.183, 19.185, **B** 10.122, 14.24; under, subject to 14.9, 31, 17.295, B 7.62 (2), A 10.51, 146, Z 7.77; in (with) respect of / to 6.30, 13.144, 188, 16.102, 21.8, **B** 7.149, 15.497; according to B 11.397; of 20.108, B 17.181, A 2.66; against 9.16, 19.162; by 22.254, **B** 10.288, 15.304; by means of, through 3.159,

6.177, 7.190, 14.207, 20.110, 326, 382, 418, 21.433, A 9.28, Z 6.101; with 1.58, 14.211, 19.66, 204, 20.469, 21.181, 22.116, 144, **B** 9.125, 13.21, 15.174, 521, Z 2.14; as (a / an) Pr 86, 2.109, 4.149, 5.119, 13.200, 16.325, 17.264, B 10.294; *in phrr.* ~ **amendement / confort / deseyte / helpe / sauacioun of** to amend / support / deceive / give strength for / save Pr 3, 3.122, 5.75, 21.391, 5.198, 17.274; ~ **his bileue** in belief in him 18.255; ~ **couenant (foreward)** on condition 6.389, 8.26, 21.187, A 2.50; ~ **hope to** in the hope of (getting) Pr 29, B 10.363; ~ **lenghe and ~ brede** in every direction 2.93; ~ **menynge (signe, tokenynge) of / þat** as a sign / signifying that Pr 99, 5.121, 15.245, 17.33, 18.93, 20.139, B 10.143; ~ **point** ready B 13.111; ~ **my power** as far as I'm able 4.137; ~ **werke (dede)** actually 4.143, B 7.158, A 4.108; ~ **wete and in drye (chele and in hete, somur or ~ wynter)** at all times 7.175, 8.249, 16.146; ~ **wille** willing, desirous **B** 10. 168, 11. 278, 12.194, A 12.21; ~ **witnesse of** as a witness to 2.109, 9.285; ~ **þat** in as much as 13.93, 15.117; ~ **as moche as** as far as 19.203, B 7.15; **as ~** with regard to, in the case / matter of 2.94, 6.176, 11.265, 12.81, 13.155, 17.149, **B** 10.259, 13.278, 14.157, from the standpoint of 18.88, 89, 20.25, (as it were) in 19.164

in (**yn(ne)**) *av* (*with phrasal vv.*) within, inside 6.231, 360, 7.252, 11.44, 12.50, 20.286, 21.320, 22.345

incurable *a* beyond cure 5.177; irrevocable 15.16

#indepartable *a* indivisible 18.27

indirect *a* not direct (*grammar*); **relacioun =** ~ syntactic relationship between words not indicated by inflexional agreement 3.333, 341, (*fig.*) 3.362, 370, 382; **relatif ~** relative (pronoun *etc*) not agreeing with its antecedent 3.387

#indulgence *n* divine mercy / forgiveness for sin granted to the penitent 9.52; formal remission of punishment for sin [obtained by penitential act] 9.319, 344, 19.220, 22.322

ynempned *p.p.* B 9.54, 16.203, A 10.43 *see* **nem(p)nen** *v*

infinite *n* (*? or a as n*) unlimited (thing) B 13.128, 129

ingang (ingong B) *n* entry 7.281

inhabiten *v* dwell 9.188

inliche *av* deeply, earnestly 3.370; inwardly B 14.89

†inmiddes *prep.* in the middle of B 5.284; in between 1.155 (B 1.160)n; *and see* **amydde(s)** *prep.*

ynne 1.133, 184, 12.219, 17.198, 21.420, 22.193 = **in** *prep.*, 22.345 = **in** *av*

ynne *n* 10.4 *see* **yn** *n*

innocence *n* innocence, = (people of) guileless simplicity 3.98, 19.270

innocent *a* unoffending, guiltless 9.47, *a as n* **B** 3.242, 7.41

inobedient *a* disobedient 6.19; ~ **to ben** resentful at being B 13.282

yno3 B 14.33, 15.315, 317 = **ynow** *n*

ynome *p.p.* 22.46, B 11.212 *see* **nymen** *v*

ynow (yno(u)ʒ B) *n* enough 20.225, **B** 7.84 (1), 15.317; ~(e) *a* plenty of 2.157, 160, 11.179, 19.220, 20.292, **B** 2.163, 12.17; enough 2.35, 9.43, 10.183, 14.138, 15.239, 18.257, 22.249, **B** 7.84 (2), 9.178, 13.262, 15.315; *in phrr.* **moore þan** ~ B 12.198; **tyme** ~ soon enough B 11.36; ~ **þat** enough for one who A 7.137; **þat** ~ that in abundance / sufficiency B 14.33

inpacient *a* incapable of bearing suffering 6.110, 19.321

inparfit *a* morally faulty, sinful 3.385, 6.119, 11.208, 16.210, 245, 276, 17.229, 19.105, 21.431, 22.229; imperfectly formed (*fig.*) 18.103; defective, wanting in virtue 15.137

inparfitly *av* imperfectly B 10.465

inposible *a* impossible 20.465, B 10.335

inpugnen *see* **impugnen** *v*

#insolible *n* insoluble (logical) problem, logical paradox 16.229

intestate *a* without making a will B 15.138

intil *prep.* into B 13.211

into *prep.* into Pr 2 *et p.*; onto 14.85, B 3.303; (down) onto 20.249; to 7.206, 8.207, 11.18, 21.79, 147, B 1.205; toward B Pr 13; *in phrr:* ~ **þe bodyward** into the body A 7.167; ~ **pursward** for the making of money Pr 101

inwit *n* mind, understanding [esp. the moral reason] 6.420, (*person.*) 10.144, 174 *et p.*, 184, B 9.59, 60, 71, A 10.47, 56, 60; *in phrr:* **to / bi myn** ~ to my mind 9.117, 19.262, **þurgh** ~ through reflection A 12.99; **in** ~ in sound mind 5.10; will, soul 17.269; the inner faculties 18.180, B 13.289

ypay(e)d *p.p.* 3.305, 389, 22.309 B 19.393 *see* **paien** *v*

yparayled *p.p.* 7.160 *see* **(ap)paraillen** *v*

yparroked(e) *p.p.* 6.144, 17.13 *see* **parroken** *v*

ypassed *p.p.* Pr 203, 15.154, 16.369, 20.136, B 13.265 *see* **passen** *v*

ypersed *p.p.* B 17.190 *see* **persen** *v*

yplyht *p.p.* 6.208 *see* **pli(g)hten** *v*

ypocrisye *n* religious hypocrisy [pretence of virtue] 16.262, 263, (*person.*) 22.301 *et p.*

ypolsched B 15.111, Z 6.80 = **polishid** *p.p.*; *see* **poleschen** *v*

ypot *p.p.* 16.125 *see* **potten** *v*

ypresed *p.p.* 10.311, 12.197 *see* **pre(i)sen** *v*

ypreued *p.p.* 11.159 *see* **preuen** *v*

ypriked *p.p.* 22.86 *see* **priken** *v*

ypurchased *p.p.* 5.77, 158 *see* **purchacen** *v*

yquited *p.p.* 8.107 *see* **quyten** *v*

yrad *p.p.* 11.276 *see* **reden** *v*

yraueschid *p.p.* 11.294 *see* **raueschen** *v*

yraunsomed *p.p.* 11.261, 19.285 *see* **raunsomen** *v*

ire *n* anger 2.88, 11.110, 20.435, (*person.*) Z 5.91

yre(n) *n* iron 21.57; iron bands Pr 97, 16.87; ~s shackle(s), iron chain(s) 4.81, 8.143

yrented *p.p.* 10.268 *see* **renten** *v*

yreuestede *p.p. see* **reuesten** *v*

yrynged *p.p.* 2.12 *see* **ringen** *v*

yrobbed *p.p.* 9.180, 12.154, 21.447 *see* **robben** *v*

yrobed *p.p.* 10.1, 11.19, Z 2.17 *see* **roben** *v*

yron 4.81 = **yre(n)** *n*

yr(u)yfled *p.p.* 19.92 *see* **ruyflen** *v*

yruled *p.p.* 21.399 *see* **reulen** *v*

is, ys *3 sg. pr.* Pr 40 *et p.*, 1.145 *et p.*; *see* **be(n)** *v*

ys Z Pr 78 *etc* = **his** *poss. prn.*

ysaide *p.p.* 15.24 *see* **seyen** *v*

ysaye 18.140 = **ysey(e)n** *p.p.*

ysaued *p.p.* 7.235, 10.235, 11.241, 244, 255, 258, 296, 12.84, 14.77, 101, 201, 18.152, 19.32, 86, 21.409 *see* **sauen** *v*

yschape *p.p.* 15.301 *see* **shapen** *v*

ysey *p.t.* 12.85 *see* **ysen** *v*

yseide *p.p.* 15.125 *see* **seyen** *v*

ysey(e)(n) *p.p.* 16.343, 348, 18.240, 19.283, B 5.4 *see* **ysen** *v*

iseised *p.p.* B 18.283 *see* **sesen** v^2

isekel *n* icicle 19.194

ysen *v* (*p.t.* **ysey** 2.67, 12.85, *p.p.* **ysey(ʒ)e(n)** 16.348 *etc*) see 18.240, B 5.4, Z 4.75, 6.92; observe 14.103, 16.343, 348, 19.283; discover 2.67; witness B 16.216; look at 19.6; find (in books) B 14.155; take cognisance of 12.85; see to it Z 7.198; *and see* **sen** *v*

ysent(e) *p.p.* Pr 77, 7.126, 20.172, A 10.100 *see* **senden** *v*

yserued *p.p.* 3.309, 6.390, 7.189, 14.144, 21.439, B 5.413 *see* **seruen** *v*

yset *p.p.* Pr 97, 7.52, B 15.224, A 10.22 *see* **setten** *v*

yshaue *p.p.* 6.201, 16.352 *see* **shauen** *v*

ysherewen B 13.331 = **shrewen** *v*

ysheued, yshewed *p.p.* A 12.34, B 2.135 *see* **shewen** *v*

yshryue *p.p.* B 5.90 *see* **shryuen** *v*

ysyne(g)ed *p.p.* 10.216, A 8.163 *see* **synegen** *v*

yslepe *p.p.* A 5.4 *see* **slepen** *v*

ysoden *p.p.* B 15.432 *see* **sethen** *v*

ysoffred *p.p.* 3.449, 13.114, 20.216 *see* **soffren** *v*

ysoiled *p.p.* B 13.458 *see* **soilen** *v*

ysouʒt, ysougwth *p.p.* B Pr 50, Z 6.3 *see* **sechen** *v*

ysowed, ysowen *p.p.* 8.3, B 5.543 *see* **sowen** *v*

yspended, yspened *p.p.* B 14.102, 16.278 *see* **spenen** *v*

yspilde, yspilt *p.p.* 7.48, **B** 5.374, 436 *see* **spillen** *v*

yspoused *p.p.* B 9.126 *see* **spousen** *v*

yspronge *p.p.* 10.263, B 16.209 *see* **spryngen** *v*

issue *n* progeny, offspring 10.246, 12.115, 18.206 (*fig.*), 220, 235, 246, 256, 258, 20.196, 303, **B** 9.125, 16.206, 18.345; (*fig.*) = successors in office B 10.325

it Pr 34 *et p.*, **yt** Z 2.162 *et p.*, B Pr 10 *et p.*, A Pr 10 *et p.*, Z 3.176, 6.57 = **hit** *prn*

ytayled *p.p.* 7.35 *see* **taylen** *v*

ytake *p.p.* 9.92, 12.150, 16.326 *see* **taken** *v*

ytauhte, ytauʒt *p.p.* 8.20, 300, 22.186, A 11.172 *see* **techen** *v* yteynted *p.p.* B 15.454 *see* teynten *v*

ytempted *p.p.* 21.64 *see* tempten *v*

ythryuen *v* prosper Pr 34; *and see* þryuen *v*

ytilied *p.p.* B 15.107 *see* tylien *v*

ytynt *p.p.* 5.93 *see* tynen *v*

ytolde *p.p.* 3.132, 7.202 *see* tellen *v*

ytouked *p.p.* B 15.454 *see* touken *v*

yuel(e) 9.290, 10.302, B 7.41 *et p.*; *see* euel(e) *n, a*

yvsed *p.p.* B 16.148 *see* vsen *v*

yvenkused 20.104 *p.p. see* venkusen *v*

ywa(e)r *a* aware 10.115, 11.83; careful 1.40, 2.151, 9.51, 19.226, 20.354; warned 7.80, 11.63; on guard (against) A 10.85, Z 6.94

ywaged *p.p.* 22.261 *see* wagen *v*

ywalked *p.p.* 7.175 *see* walken *v*

ywasche *p.p.* 9.268, 10.228, B 13.315 *see* waschen *v*

ywedded *p.p.* 2.44, 5.64, 12.136 *see* wedden *v*

yweten (ywiten) *v* know Pr 181, 3.76, 18.275, 20.215, 219; learn 10.125; *and see* witen *v*[1]

ywhitlymed *p.p.a* lime-washed 16.266

ywis *av* certainly 13.220

ywitted *a*, wel ~ provided with good sense 11.236

ywoned *p.p.* 17.89 *see* won(y)en *v*

ywonne *p.p.* 3.247, 6.258, 12.111, 237, 19.245, 20.396, B 5.92 *see* wynnen *v*

yworded *p.p.* 15.150 *see* worden *v*

yworthen *v* be (left alone) Pr 201, 8.86, 10.164, B 6.225

ywounded *p.p.* 19.82, 22.306, 358 *see* wounden *v*

ywounden *p.p.* B 5.518 *see* wynden *v*

ywrye *p.p.* 16.74 *see* wryen *v*

ywrite(n) *p.p.* 1.194, 9.285, 17.84, B 10.412 *see* writen *v*

ywrithe *p.p.* 7.162 *see* writhen *v*

ywrouht(e), ywroȝt *p.p.* 1.131, 8.336, B 3.239, 4.68, 9.114, 117 *see* worchen *v*

yȝoten *p.p.* 1.149 *see* ȝeten *v*

*iacen *v* hurry 19.52

iang(e)len *v* chatter idly 2.99, *ger.* spiteful gossip 6.133; grumble B 6.313; dispute, argue 9.292, 10.119, (~ to) ~ with 15.93, B Pr 130, 4.155, *ger.* 180; *ger.* 10.273, 21.400; object B 16.119; protest B 16.144; cry out *pr.p.* B 9.82

iangelere *n* teller of (ribald) tales B Pr 35, 10.31

iangle *n* disputing 4.174

iape *n* trifle 22.145

iapen *v* deceive B 1.67; ~ mock (at) 20.40; tell jokes 2.99, 15.208, B 13.353

iapare, iaper *n* trickster 17.308; scoffer B 15.237; professional jester B Pr 35, 9.91, 10.31

ielosye *n* jealousy 10.273

ientel 21.40, A 1.159 = gentel *a*

ieroures Z Pr 70 *see* iurour *n*

Iesu(s) Jesus, *in oaths* by ~ Pr 180, 3.192, 20.462, 21.400, Z 5.130

Iew *n* (*gen. pl.* Iewen(e)) Jew [person of Jewish race / religion] 3.454, 479, 4.194, 6.241, 12.56, 14.200, 17.156, 252, 295, 315, 21.425, B 9.82, 85, 10.346, 13.210, 15.583; (Palestinian) Jew(s) [of the Old or New Testament, esp. their leaders] 1.63, 14.40, 17.304, 18.150 *et p.*, 20.15, 37, 40, 95, 113, 266, 21.10 *et p.*, 108, 139 *et p.*, B 10.35, 11.246, 12.42, 73, 78, 91, 15.264, 594, 16.127, 18.301; Iewene of the Jews 1.63, 20.266, (*as a*) Jewish 20.40, 21.108, B 15.583, 18.41)

iewel *n* jewel, treasure 3.192, 20.474, (*fig.*) †B 11.184

i(e)wyse *n* judicial sentence, (death) penalty 20.424n

#iogelen *v* entertain [with jesting, conjuring *etc*] 15.208

iogelour *n* jester, clown 8.71, B 10.31; illusionist 17.308

ioggen (iuggen B) *v* hurry, dash off 22.134

ioy(e) *n* happiness 13.14, 19, 15.299, 301, B 2.157, 12.42; pleasure 6.255, 15.295; satisfaction 20.266; joy 9.41, 18.16, 20.15; (spiritual) joy / happiness (*esp.* of heaven) 3.339, 9.50, 325, 10.22, 13.24, 14.78, 15.72, 291, 16.17, 56, 17.145, 20.183, 233, 345, 21.25, 66, 198, 22.40, 47, B 7.36, 11.167, 184, 14.285, 16.207; rejoicing 3.14, B 3.103, (cause of) rejoicing B 16.163; *in phr:* bely ~ pleasure(s) of eating B 7.119; ~les *a* joyless, unhappy 10.273

ioynen *v* hitch (*fig.*) 21.266; join (in marriage) 2.66

ioynte *n* joint (of leg), out of ~ dislocated 9.215; finger 19.143

ioyntly *av* together (in marriage) B 2.157

iolyf *a* joyful, happy 13.19

ionette *n* early ripening tree 12.223; *see* pere ~

*iot A 11.311 = iut(te) *n*

iouken *v* rest 18.126

iourne *n* (day's) stint of work 16.5

ioustare *n* jouster 21.10

iousten *v* joust (*fig.*) 18.129, 19.52, 20.17, 21, 26, 84, 183, 22.134, B 16.163;

ioustes *n pl.* jousting [single combats of mounted knights] (*fig.*) 20.14, B 17.52, 75

ioute *n* broth (*fig.*) 6.133

†iuele *n* B 11.184 = iewel *n*

iuge *n* judge 9.335, [of Christ] 15.291

iugement *n* judgement, of ~ armes trial by combat 18.129

iug(g)en *v* try in a court of law 16.123, Z Pr 70; pass (moral) judgement on 2.99; decide (concerning sth.) 2.169, 22.29, B 16.119; adjudge, assign B 2.137, 157; deem B 9.85; form the opinion, judge (that) 1.180, 17.132; express the opinion (that) B Pr 130; interpret 9.310; rule, act a final judge (over) 21.477

iu(y)ste *n* vessel with long neck and large bottom, *in phr.* ~ womb bottle-belly 15.93

#iurdan *n* chamber pot (*with pun on name* Jordan) 15.93n

iurour *n* juror [sworn witness in court of law] 2.150, B 7.44, Z Pr 70

iusten B 16.163; **iustes** B 17.52, 75 *see* **iousten** *v*, **ioustes** *n pl.*

iustice *n* judge, justice 2.49, (= Chief Justice) 150, 3.14, 192, 473, 16.123, 22.134, B 7.44, Z Pr 70, (*fig.*) 8.351; (= God) 18.126, (= the Roman procurator), 162, 178, 20.37; *in phrr*: **chef ~** presiding judge (at Courts of Common Pleas or King's Bench) 13.116; **kynges ~** presiding itinerant judge 4.186, 8.338, 19.284; ruler 9.314

iustifien *v* judge matters (for sb.) 21.44; ?govern, ?vindicate B Pr 130*n*

***iut(te)** *n* person of little consequence, nobody B 10.461

#iuventee *n* (time of) youth 21.108

kaes 3.432 = **caes** *n*
kaye 7.166 = **keye** *n*
#kaylewey *n* dessert pear B 16.69*n*
kayren 6.350 = **cayren** *v*
kayser 3.322, B 9.111 = **cayser** *n*
kaytif 6.206, *pl.* **kaytyues** Z 7.261 *see* **caytif** *n*
kalculen *v* learn by calculations 17.106
kald *p.p.* 3.401; **kalde** *p.t.* 4.17; *see* **callen** *v*
kalender *n* the ecclesiastical year B 13.154
kalketrappe *n* caltrop [spiked iron ball placed on ground to impede enemy] 20.294
kam *p.t.* 2.202, 22.327 = **cam**; *see* **comen** *v*
kan Pr 205, B Pr 111 *et p.* = **can**; **kannen** Z 7.261 = **konnen**; **kanst** 2.47 = **canst**; *see* **connen** *v*
kattes Pr 193 *see* **cat** *n*
kau3te *p.t.* B 13.405 = **cauhte**; *see* **cacchen** *v*
***kaurymaury** *n* rough cloth B 5.78
keye (kaye) *n* key 7.166, 251, 14.54, B 10.322, 15.247
keyen *v* lock with a key, *p.p.* **ykeyed** 7.265
#kelen *v* keel [cool liquid by stirring and skimming to prevent boiling] 21.281
kemben *v* comb [disentangle threads from] 9.80, 11.15
ken *imper.* A 12.53; **kende** *p.t.* 18.17, 21.235, A 11.135; **kenet** *3 pr. sg.* 1.140; *see* **kennen** *v*
kene *a* bold 22.129, 141; fierce 16.81, 22.375, B 18.415; sharp 2.29, 6.140, 20.47, 80, B 9.182, (*fig.*) 10.289; bitter, acrimonious 6.65; painful 18.173, 22.97; strong 20.435, B 13.348; earnest B 12.251
kenis A 10.2, 26, 27, **kenne** A 12.110, = **ky(n)ne(s)**; *see* **kyn** *n*
kennen *v* make known 1.88, †B 11.439; teach, instruct 1.136, 140, 2.4, 3.276, 4.41, 7.91, 11.91, 21.9, B 6.14, 23, 7.71, 10.112, 198, 337, 14.16, A 11.135, 222, *ger.* teaching B 10.†190, 196; explain 9.281, B 5.420, 14.277; direct 7.183, 11.93; guide B 17.114; come to know, learn 11.140, 21.241
kepar(e) *n* guardian 16.273; protector 21.446, 22.72; governor B 12.126; (**~ of bestes**) herdsman 14.88, B 15.460
kepe *n* heed, attention, notice 13.145, 165, 170, 15.177, B 13.272, A 10.97; care, concern 19.76, 22.359

kep(i)en *v* (*p.t.* **kept(e)** 3.411; *p.p.* **(y)kept** Z 6.20, A 10.50, **kepide** A 6.32; *ger.* **kepynge** 21.356) want B 4.193, A 1.8; wish, care (to) 3.432, 13.233; hold Pr 128, 1.42, 12.216, 14.54; **~ wiþouten** prevent from entering B 5.614; restrain B 10.165; possess 12.238, 243, B 10.359; keep 8.274, **B** 1.195, 15.247; preserve 5.129, 8.100, 145, 11.306, 19.258, **B** 14.11, 15.580, A 10.158; guard 10.137, 143, 21.144, 149, 22.257; defend 22.377, B 7.9; protect Pr 148, 2.47, 8.26, 157, 18.28, 21.144, †B 8.100, Z 7.65, 200; take care of, look after 1.51, 3.264, 411, 4.135, 5.17, 10.150, 19.7, 21.426, 22.92, **B** 15.346, 17.75, **A** 6.32, 7.181, Z 2.189; (keep) watch over **B** 10.471, 474, 19.282; administer 2.21, 3.78, 12.91, 16.337, **B** 5.52, 15.465; govern 3.441, A 8.149; obey, observe 11.142(1); abide by 1.90, 7.73, 9.340, Z 8.74; *ger.* behaviour 21.356
kerke 8.26 = **kirke** *n*
kernel[1] †B 5.588, **kirnel** A 6.75 = **carnel** *n*
kernel[2] B 11.260, 264 = **cornel** *n*
kernen *v* form grains 12.182
kerse B 10.17 = **carse** *n*
keruen *v* (*p.t. pl.* **coruen** 8.185) cut 8.185, Z 3.153; cut (furrows in) soil 8.65; *ger.* **keruynge** carving B 17.171
keruer *n* carver, sculptor 11.125
kete *a* distinguished A 11.56, 308
keueren *v*[1] cover 9.249, B 14.331; build / repair roof 3.64; protect 21.297; hide 9.138; conceal by disguise 21.349; mystically represent 21.86
keueren *v*[2] recover 22.336; deliver 14.118
kychene *n* kitchen 6.130, B 5.257
kidde *p.t.* B 5.434 *see* **kithen** *v*
kyen *n. pl.* cows ('kine') B 6.140 *and see* **cow** *n*[1]
#kyken *v* kick 4.22
killen (*p.t.* **killed** B 3.187, **kilde** B 20.99, A 3.251; *pl.* **killeden** B 19.142; *p.p.* **kild** B 5.163) = **cullen** *v*
kyn *n* kindred, family 1.188, 2.42, 57, 3.260, 5.66, 77, 6.58, 10.261, 13.112, 14.182, 16.166, 17.62, 196, 20.265, 441, **B** 12.93, 13.379; race A 10.156; kinsman, relative 7.282, B 11.190; parentage, stock 9.201, 10.261, B 2.131; kind, sort 3.279, 363, 5.183, 20.288; **kyn(n)e** kind(s) of 3.458, 8.69, 10.15, 11.124 *et p.*, **B** 2.201, 8.15 *et p.*, **(s)kenne(s), skynes** A 2.162, 8.34, 10.2, 26, 27, 84, 12.110
kynde *n* (essential) nature 3.401, 18.57, 19.254, 20.188, 230, 417, 435, B 15.14; natural disposition Pr 147, 9.168, 13.212, 19.313; character 21.403; physical nature 6.429, 10.47, 12.149, 20.219, B 15.14; natural power / force 15.243, 19.214, B 14.44; natural form 13.178, 18.21; way, manner 20.11, B 12.228; natural instinct(s) 6.193, 17.161, 18.78; instinctive behaviour 17.164; the innate moral sense 8.231; habitual / proper / customary action / occupation 3.250, 16.368, 17.287, 21.106; the natural / proper order (of things) 2.247,

3.397, B 11.67; the nature of things 16.212, B 14.119; nature [as source of created things] 3.60, 19.255; (*person.*) God as ~ 10.129 *et p.*, 13.131, 14.160, 15.18, ? 19.255, 20.78, 22.76 *et p.*; kind / class (of thing) 7.234, B 15.316; species 10.234, 13.151, 14.163, 18.62, B 11.397; race Pr 200, 18.67; people B 10.424; one's fellow man 19.220; stock 2.27, 81, 10.206, 21.123, B 9.128; parentage 10.247 (2); station / rank (by birth) 3.129, 21.479; progeny 10.247 (1), 13.151, 171, 18.223; gender 3.336, 371; grammatical aspect 3.361; *in phrr*: **aȝeyns** ~ 16.212; **by** ~ **of** owing to the nature of 19.322; **cours of** ~ 3.60; **deth of** ~ 20.219; **lawe of** ~ 8.231, 17.152, 160, 22.18

kynde *a* natural 20.132; innate, instinctive 3.71; proper, suitable by nature 2.29; correct, own 10.69; right A 11.254; (its) own B 15.466; genuine, real 15.183, 16.109, 22.73; kind, loving 15.144, B 11.187, A 11.250; generous 16.255; gracious, noble 13.12, A 12.15; ?excellent B 16.70n; *in phrr*: ~ **knowynge** natural knowledge [instinctive not learned] 1.136, 140, 160, 10.56, 109, 14.79, *pl.* B 12.136; ~ **loue** 3.451, 16.109, B 13.151; ~ **vnderstondynge** intuitive grasp 5.56, 14.102; ~ **wille** inward intent 3.71; ~ **wit** natural reason [practical understanding based on experience not education] 11.228, 14.17 *et p.*, 163, 17.216, 21.317, B 12.45, 14.125, (*person.*) Pr 141 *et p* 1.51, 3.436, 4.152, 7.183, 8.59, 13.238, 19.111, A 12. 41, 53; ~ **witted** endowed with ~ **wit** 14.52

kyndeli(che) *av* correctly 4.147, 17.110; properly 9.213; truly 20.212, 229, B 14.87, 15.2; rightly 1.78, 11.91, 101; thoroughly, completely 16.209; ?familiarly 7.182n; kindly, pleasantly B 3.15

kyndenesse *n* (acts of) kindness 7.46, B 13.390; kind feeling, benevolence A 3.274

kyndly *a* in accordance with (the law of) man's nature 17.153

kyne 22.97 = **kene** *a*

kyn(e)dom, kyngdoem *n* kingdom 2.247, 3.243, 411, 20.112, 423, 21.49, 138, B 7.156, (of heaven) Pr 133, **(of Coueitise)** A 2.62

kyneriche *n* kingdom Pr 148, 10.112, B 7.156, (of heaven) 12.170

king *n* (*gen. pl.* **kyngene** of (the) kings 21.79, B 1.105) king Pr 90, 1.155, 3.246, 250, 255, 260, 264, 314, 318, 322, 374, 377, 379, 412, 441, 467, 4.126, 135, 5.193, 194, 9.9, 305, 10.101, 11.281, 13.107, 109, 15.170, 16.124, 17.287, 19.287, 20.423, 441, 21.27, 29, 42, 97, 223, 257, 305, 306, 468, 22.67, 101, **B** 4.150, 151, 10.46, 13.166, 170, [= the Messianic king] 3.441, 5.168, 178, B 10.326, [= the Jewish Messiah] 3.455, [= Christ] 20.273, 277, 413, 426, B 1.105, ~ **of Iewes / Iuda** 21.41, 49, 138, **(of Heuene)** [= God] 7.251, 13.66, 17.262, 20.78, 363; *particular kings*: [Abimelech] 13.12, [Agag] 3.408, [Caesar] B 1.48, [David] B 2.36, [Magi] 21.72 *et*

p., [Nebuchadnezzar] B 7.154, [Saul] 3.430, = the King of England Pr 90, 139 *et p.*, 2.11, 146 *et p.*, 3.3 *et p.*, 4.3 *et p.*, 5.113 *et p.,* 8.338, 21.446, 468 *et p.*, B 15.444, Z 4.125, A Pr 91, [Richard] A 12.113; *in phrr*: ~**es bench** A Pr 95, ~**es consayl** 4.119, 22.30, 129, B Pr 144; ~ **court** 2.202, 3.472, 16.358, 18.95, 21.427; ~ **iustice** 4.186, 8.338, 19.284; ~ **munstral** 7.96, ~ **sone** 20.78, ~ **tresor** 5.181, ~**es wille** 2.218, 3.246, 10.244; ~**es and knyhtes** 1.90, 3.44, 9.9, 22.101, 257, **B** 7.9, 9.111, A 10.137

kinghed *n* kingship A 11.219, (**kynghod**) B 10.332

kyngryche B Pr 125 = **kyneriche** *n*

kynnesman *n* kinsman, relative B 15.247

kynneswomman *n* kinswoman 2.146

kynrede *n* family, kindred 10.261, B 9.174; progeny A 10.158

kirk(e), kyrk(e) *n* church Pr 138, 3.64, 5.60, 104, 179, 6.288, 8.26, 100, 11.246, 250, 306, 13.89, 14.39, 17.220, 276, 21.413, 470, †22.120, **B** 5.1, 103, 10.409, 411, 12.82, 13.9, 274, 15.136, 197, 384, 545, 19.446; **Holy** ~ 3.356, 397, 5.179, 8.26, 53, 159, 9.9, 11.246, 250, 306, 13.89, 14.39, 16.255, 17.77, 220, 276, 21.413, 470, 22.120, **B** 12.82, 13.274, 15.384

kyrkeward, to, *n. phr.* towards church 6.350

kyrkeȝerde *n* churchyard 15.11

kirtel *n* (man's) outer garment, tunic B 5.79, 11.283

kissen (cussen, kussen) *v* (*p.t.* **kiste, kuste (custe))** kiss 2.146, 4.3, 18.170, 20.463, 474, 22.354, **B** 16.152, 18.430, **A** 11.177, 12.47, *ger.* kissing 6.187, 18.173, B 16.149

kithen *v* (*p.t.* **kud, kidde** *p.p.* **ykud**) show (towards) 7.46, B 13.390, B 15.303; *p.p.* illustrious 12.198

kyto(u)n *n* kitten Pr 204, 208, 215

kitten (*p.t.* **kitten** B 6.188; *imp.* **kitte** A 4.140) = **kutten** *v*

kix *n* hollow stem [of hemlock *etc,* used for lighting] 19.186

knappe *n* button B 6.269

knaue *n* fellow A 12.77; servant, serving-man Pr 40, 227, 3.411, 4.17, 5.161, 6.363, 370, 9.205, 20.287, B 5.115; common labourer 1.124, 5.54, 62, 8.46, 9.209, A 7.181; wastrel, rogue Pr 45, 3.167

kne(e) *n* knee 1.76, 2.1, 3.93, 5.106, 6.409, 20.89, 474, A 12.47

knelen *v* (*p.t.* **kneled** 2.1, *pl.* **knelede** Pr 71; *pr.p.* **knelend** 21.74, **knelyng** 3.151) kneel 1.76, 3.45, 5.161, 7.3, 119, 17.177, 21.12, 17, 28, 81, 91, 95, 201, 208, 210, B 5.103, A 12.47

knet *p.p.* 3.210 *see* **knytten** *v*

kneuȝ *p.t.* A 2.188, 4.48, 66 = **knew**

knew(e) *p.t.* 4.64 *et p.*; *see* **knowen** *v*

knew(e)lichen B 12.192, 19.187, = **kno(we)lechen** *v*

knyf *n* (*pl.* **knyues**) knife 20.219, B 5.79, 163

kny(g)ht(e) (kniȝt) *n* knight Pr 179, 190, 1.90, 97, 101, 2.58, 467, 3.44, 49, 5.72, 77, 6.250, 8.21 *et p.*, 46, 9.9,

11.52, 12.104, 13.107, 16.210, 17.287, 20.11, 21.27 *et
p.*, 149, 22.101, 104, **B** 7.156, 10.146, 12.107, 15.331,
A 4.105; *with spec. ref.* (= Conscience) 3.145, (= Inwit)
10.144, (= Trajan) 14.149, 205, (= Longeus) 20.80 *et
p.*, (= Confort) 22.91, *(fig.)* (= angels) 1.104, 107, (=
clergy) 13.125 (= Christ) 20.78; *in phrr.* ~**es court**
7.33, ~**es douhter** 6.124, ~**es fees** 5.77, ~**es of cuntres**
knights of the shire A 2.43

kny3ten *v* to make (sb.) a knight B 1.105

knyghthed(e), knyhtho(e)d(e) *n* the knightly class Pr
139, 142, 17.216, B 10.330, 332, A 11.219; the order of
knighthood 1.98; (ideal) knightly conduct 20.99

knytten *v (p.p.* **knet)** fasten Pr 184, 3.210; bind, unite,
p.p. B 15.242

knok *n* blow *(fig.)* 5.177 (B 10.326)

knokken *v* knock (at gate) 8.287, 22.330; beat (breast)
5.106, 7.6, Z 5.97; strike a blow (against) B 16.128,
(fig.) 22.130

knoppe A 7.254 = **knappe** *n*

knotte 17.127 *see* **loue** ~ *n*

kno(we)lechen *v* acknowledge 21.77; confess 6.327,
7.147, 13.89, B 12.192; agree 21.187n; *ger.* B 14.187

knowen *v (contr. pr. 2 sg.* **knowestou** 3.223, *p.t.* **knew(e)**
4.64, *pl.* **knewe(n)** 16.366, *p.p.* **(y)knowe** Pr 54,
20.209) know (as true) 3.436, 5.83; perceive [with
senses] 14.97, [with mind] B 16.229; grasp, under-
stand 1.158, 7.167, 11.40, 14.74, 76, 16.183, 17.54, **B**
10.209, 12.133, *p.p.* 13.223, 20.209; get to know, find
out 10.75, 13.133; be skilled in 6.322, 19.119, *pr.p.*
11.295; be familiar / acquainted with 2.129, 7.182,
15.31, 16.166, 17.292, 298; know about B 10.466, *pr.p.*
22.67; (know by) experience 15.292, B 16.215, Z 2.70;
encounter 12.123; recognise 1.72, 2.4, 4.32, 71, 8.45,
12.125, 20.23, 21.350, *p.p.* Pr 54, 4.159; make (sth.)
known B 16.192; acknowledge 7.206, 11.95, B 4.41;
acknowledge (with honour), observe 9.232; have con-
sideration for 22.282, B 6.219; have sexual intercourse
with A 10.146

knowyng(e) *ger.* knowledge, acquaintance, **kynde** ~ direct
natural knowledge, intuitive understanding 1.136,
140, 160, 10.56, 109, 14.79; recognition, **for** ~ to pre-
vent recognition 2.240; ability 21.310

koes Z 7.125 *see* **cow** *n²*

koyne 1.46 = **coyne** *n*

koke 5.13 = **coken** *v²*

konne 21.204, B 6.149 *et p.*, A 12.7, Z 1.119 *see* **con-
nen** *v*

konnyng 11.295, 21.235, **B** 11.165, 211, 300, 12.66,
13.293 = **connyng** *n*

konnynge B 10.458, 11.70 = **connynge** *a*

konstable Z 2.188 = **constable** *n*

koude B Pr 129 *et p.* = **coude; koudest** B 8.76, **koudestow**
B 5.533 = **coudest(ow);** *see* **connen** *v*

kounten Z 4.11 *see* **acounten** *v*

kouþe B 1.116 *et p.* = **couthe; kouthest** 7.177 = **couthest**
(thow); *see* **connen** *v*

kud *p.t.* 7.46 *see* **kithen** *v*

kullen *(p.t.* **kulde** 3.232, 22.99, *p.p.* **kulled** 10.101,
16.26, B 16.152, 232 = **cullen**

kultour *n* coulter **B** 3.308, 6.104

kunne 11.101, 21.26, A 8.13 *see* **connen** *v*

kunnyng 11.228, B 10.472, *(pl.)* 11.94 = **connyng** *ger.*

kussen *(p.t.* **kuste** 18.170) 2.146 etc = **kissen** *v*

kuth (kiþ, couthe) *n* people 3.260, **here kingene** ~ the
land over which they ruled 21.79; *in phr.* ~ **and kin**
country and kinsfolk 17.196, B 13.379

kutten *v (imper.* **kut** 4.159) cut 5.134, 22.56

labben *v* blurt 12.41

laberen 11.254 = **labour(i)en** *v*

labo(u)r *n* (hard) work 5.42, 85, 16.145, 21.233; (physi-
cal) work 8.196, 9.207, 21.238, B 8.81; (piece of) work,
task B 6.26; activity 14.107; type of work 5.43; effort
Pr 195, 15.201, 16.40, 19.213; *in phrr.* ~ **of body** B
14.129; ~ **of handes** 9.198; ~ **of tonge** 21.233; **feiþful**
~ B 6.250; **lel(e)** ~ honest work Pr 146, 8.261, 10.79,
16.145

labo(u)r(i)en *v* (do) work 5.8, 45, 66, 8.25, 135, 214,
222, 250, 294, 9.103, 223, 245, 11.254, 21.237, A 7.13,
Z 7.77, *(fig.)* 21.387, 22.239, B 15.187 *ger.* **laboryng**
(hard) work (done) 8.251

labo(u)rer *n* manual worker, (esp. agricultural) labourer
[of lowest social class] 3.309, 347, 452, 4.144, 6.227,
8.330, 339, 9.58, 11.254, **B** 3.255, 10.460, **A** 2.45, 6.35;
servant 5.73, B 15.329; *in phrr.* **leel** ~ 3.347; **lewede** ~**s**
11.298, 304; **libbynge** ~**s** 9.58, B Pr 223

lac(c)hen *v (p.t.* **lauhte, laghte)** ensnare Pr 169, 6.405;
catch 2.215; seize 18.119, B 16.50; take 22.152, B 1.30,
Z 2.165; assume 19.125; get, obtain 1.100, 2.138, 3.390,
9.141, 15.204, 16.363, **B** 6.227, 11.222, 299, Z Pr 63;
catch up, remove B 18.327, A 12.96; take (leave) 1.203,
3.26, A 12.55; *ger.* **lacchynge** receiving B 1.103

lach(e)-drawer *n* beggar from door to door 8.287, 9.192

lac(c)hesse *n* laziness, remissness 8.253, 9.267, 277, B
8.37

la(c)k(i)en *v* lack B 9.71, 13.265, 17.293; be lacking /
wanting 6.311, 21.112, 22.249, B 10.188; *(impers.)*
lack 3.386, 13.102, 21.471, 22.210, 249, **B** 9.38, 10.188,
ger. lack, want 22.36; disparage 2.21, 13.25, 15.80,
B 10.205; find fault (with) 6.98, 7.23, 13.207, 14.6,
17.310, 19.103, 21.255, **B** 10.262, 11.394, 13.323
(ger.), 15.249, 253; criticise 1.115, 2.49, 3.58, 11.164,
12.41, **B** 6.224, 11.2, 213, 419, 12.97, 13.287, 15.4,
204, Z Pr 72

lacles *a* without fault 13.210

lad *p.p.* 10.142, 15.15; **ladde** *p.t.* Pr 139, 3.128, 9.340,
18.3, 178, 19.66, 73, B 5.247, 491, Z 3.10, *2 sg.* **lad-
dest** B 7.190 *see* **leden** *v*

ladde *n* male servant, attendant 3.247; low fellow, churl 8.194, 21.32

laddere *n* ladder 18.44

ladel *n* ladle 21.280

lady *n* mistress of household B 10.97; (*in ref. to*) nun 6.132, 142; woman of high birth or rank 3.488, 8.5, 7, B 6.10, A 11.203; (knight's) lady-love 22.104; nobleman's wife B 10.97, (*in title*) **my ~** 22.346, 367; (*of allegorical figures*) (Holy Church) 1.3, 115 *et p.*, 2.53, (Mede) 2.44, 3.26 *et p.*, (Largenesse) 7.274, (*Anima*) 10.140, (Scripture) A 12.42; (*as title of Virgin Mary*) **Oure ~** 3.99, 141, 4.39, 6.170, 7.12, 250, (*in assev.*) B 4.188; *in phr.* **lord(es) and / or lady(es)** 4.109, 6.249, 9.130, 11.202, 15.306, 17.44, 56, **B** Pr 95, 15.6, 309; woman 11.180, (*uninfl. gen.*) woman's B 18.338

lafte *p.t.* **B** 3.197, 20.251, 372 *see* **leuen** *v*¹

laghynge *pr.p.* 3.55 *see* **lauhen** *v*

laghte *p.t.* Pr 169 *see* **lacchen** *v*

lay *n*¹ song 10.65, (*fig.*) 7.116

lay *n*² law 21.43

lay *p.t.* Pr 8, 1.28, 2.130, 6.192, 227, 228, 261, 9.284, 18.144, 20.127, 22.312, B Pr 9 *et p.*; *see* **liggen** *v*

layd(e) *p.p.* 12.185, 17.302; **layth** *pr. sg.* 6.405 *see* **leggen** *v*

layȝe *p.p.* 6.329 (= **layn**) *see* **liggen** *v*

laiȝes *pl.* A 8.5 *see* **leye** *n*²

layk *n* sport 16.84; **~ en** *v* play, sport Pr 187, 16.174

layn *p.p.* 3.40 *see* **liggen** *v*

laynen *v* conceal 2.18

layth *3 sg.* 6.405 *see* **leggen** *v*

lak *n* fault, failing B 10.262; *and see* **lacles** *a*

lakken *v* 6.98 *etc*; *see* **la(c)k(i)en** *v*

Lammasse tyme *n. phr.* the time around Aug. 1, the feast of St Peter ad Vincula [harvest time] 8.313

lamb(e), lomb *n* (*pl.* **~es** 16.269, **~ren** 3.411, 9.260, B 15.206) lamb 17.38; *in phr*: **as louh as a ~** as meek / humble as a lamb 7.196, 10.83, 22.36

lame *a* lame, crippled in the feet 8.189, 9.215, *a as n* lame people 21.125

land (lond) *n* land, country, kingdom Pr 149, 3.209, 212, 234, 247, 259, 376, 419, 4.145, 10.192, 16.163, 17.237, 20.108, **B** 3.221, 7.157, 10.25, 13.209, A 11.203, Z 6.78; territory 3.419, 20.314, 21.32; land(ed property) 3.172, 315, 5.26, 158, 163, 167, 9.202, 10.194, 285, 11.184, 13.110, 15.168, 17.218, 221, 227, 20.93, 22.251, **B** 4.73, 10.86, 306, **Z** 2.42, 3.96; (farming) land 8.15, 294, 330, 12.226, 233, 20.108, **B** 6.271, 8.81, (*fig.*) 16.16; field 6.67; strip of ploughland 6.268, 19.60; the earth 17.102, 20.349, (*fig.*) = life B 5.476; the world, **in / on ~** in this world Pr 146, 10.124, B 15.152; land [in contrast with water] 15.19 *etc*; *in cpds*, **~ lepere** *n* as a vagabond B 15.213; ***~ tilynge** *a* engaged in husbandry 8.140, 11.298; **foet ~** 6.268, **leye ~** 10.219, **ouer ~**

9.159; *in phrr.* **~ of bileue** the kingdom of faith 21.336; **~ of longyng** domain of desire 11.169; **a ~ and a watre** on land and sea, everywhere 15.19, 20.29, 21.237, **B** 16.189, 18.314; **~ and / or lordschipe** estates and rank 3.315, 9.202, 11.12, 16.102, 158, 18.257, B 14.327

lane *n* lane, alley 2.226

lang 2.192 = **long** *a*

langage *n* language 18.80, 21.204, B 15.375

langour *n* sickness 18.142; suffering 15.298, B 18.226

lankart Z 2.152 = **lang cart** *n*

lanterne *n* lantern B 6.177

lapen *v* lap (up) 6.413; take a drink 22.18

lappe *n* lap 6.411; folded skirt / loose sleeve 8.317; bosom B 17.71, (*fig.*), (**Abrahames**) **~** 'Abraham's bosom', = the Limbo of the Fathers 8.282, 18.272, 275, 19.24, 33

large *n* munificence 21.43; freedom, **at ~** freely 22.192

large *a* munificent 11.73; generous 3.248, 14.215, B 13.299; prodigal 3.288; lavish 3.315, 450; large, big 18.70, 21.264; wide, broad 18.22, 20.44, (*fig.*) 13.29; **~ myle** a full / good mile B 10.164; *av* fully, *comp.* **(more) largere** (more) fully B 11.160; **~ liche** *av* munificently 12.109, 21.60; copiously 2.138, 4.67; fully 22.87; **~ nesse** *n* munificence 17.65, generosity (*person.*) 7.274

largesse *n* generous gift, **crien a ~** call out thanks (*sc.* for a generous gift) 7.108

larke *n* lark 14.185, 187

lasar, lazar *n* leper 18.142, 272

lasse *n* a smaller amount 8.286, 16.71, 140, B 5.248; **at ~** at even less 9.303; **no ~** (at) no lesser price B 5.220; *a* smaller 14.185, 16.88, B 16.57; less 3.136, 289, 11.69, 13.4; less (in importance) 2.48, 3.258, 19.148 (**lassore**); *av* less 4.156, 7.203, 8.165, 12.44, 154, B 11.69; **þe ~** the less 7.204, B 11.69, 14.1; *in phrr.* **more oþer ~** more or less (in quantity) 3.289; to a greater or less extent 9.108; of whatever rank / status 10.7, A 4.135; all of them 15.201; more or less (in number) 22.272; of whatever kind B 14.327; **~ other / ne more** the greater or the less(er) 2.48; the smaller or the bigger B 10.265; less or more B 13.17

lassore 19.148 = **lasse** *a*

last(e) *conj.* lest 5.144, 7.86, 11.254, 14.68, 20.325, 334, Z 7.133

last *a* latest B 18.313; final 2.76, B 2.101; *in phrr.* **at þe laste** finally, in the end 4.155, 7.7, 22.157, **B** 12.26, 52, 14.143, 15.14, 16.20, A 3.87; eventually 5.95, 9.207, 12.187, 13.22, 15.272, 17.138, 20.208, 321, 22.175, 347, B 13.21; as a last resort 6.265; at the last day Pr 126, 2.154, 12.67, 17.137, 146, 20.352, 355, 21.193, B 14.147; at the end of time 20.392, 22.150; at death 20.321; **at þe ~ ende** at the end of the day 5.97; at the time of death 12.196, 210, 16.2, 158, 282, 19.95; at the last judgement 19.275

lasten *v* (*contr. pr.* **last(e)** 10.171, 16.11, Z 3.124, *p.p.*

ylastede B 3.192, **last** A 3.179) last Pr 146, 10.171, 21.45, 22.211, **B** 4.195, 13.332, **A** 3.27, 10.37, **Z** 1.22, 5.73; continue 8.312, 16.11, A 12.93; endure 3.204, 12.161, 17.66, 21.89, B 9.45, A 2.60; keep 12.222; live 21.176, B 3.28; hold out 3.32, 11.73, 22.142, Z 3.33; persist **B** 15.258, 17.8; extend B 20.382

lat(e)¹ *contr. pr.* 3.173, 19.147, 22.361, 362, A 11.142; *p.t. sg.* 6.261; *imper. sg.* Pr 201, 2.49, 3.75, 4.21, 5.137, 6.393, 7.274, 8.37, 10.33, 11.309, 13.235, 15.95, 17.227, 18.105, 20.464, 22.241, **Z** 7.67 *etc*; *imper. pl.* **late** 4.174, 5.137, B 2.171 *etc*; *inf.* **lat(e)** Pr 201, 20.56; *pr. indic.* 3.136, B 5.410, *pr. subj.* B Pr 155 *see* **leten** *v*

lat(te)² *contr. pr.* 13.55, 15.278, B 9.58, A 11.142, Z 3.99 *see* **leden** *v*

late *a* tedious, protracted 7.159; *comp.* **lattere** subsequent 20.348

late *av* (at a) late (hour) 4.48, 10.140, 16.168; late in the day, only slowly B 10.211; recently 3.145, B 16.249; ~ (...) **longe** a long time later 6.160; ~ **and rathe** late and early (= at any time) 10.140, 11.89, B 3.73 *comp.* **latter** less readily, more tardily B 1.199

Latyn *n* (the) Latin (language) 1.139, 14.204, 15.80, 16.194, **B** Pr 129, 143, 3.332, 11.213, 13.152, 15.375; **a** ~ in Latin 11.164, 19.4; **fals** ~ incorrect Latin 13.117; piece of (writing in) Latin 3.124, 487, 9.164, 212, 10.92, 16.194, 17.54

laton (= **laten**) 10.202 *see* **leten** *v*

lauchen Z Pr 63 = **lacchen** *v*

lauden *v* praise, commend B 11.106

lauȝen, laughen B 5.111, 11.208, 13.353, 14.35, 15.172, **laughyng** B 16.155, 18.416 *see* **lauhen** *v*

lauȝte, laughte, lauȝþe *p.t.* **B** 1.30, 18.327, A 12.42, 55 = **lauhte**; **lauȝth** *p.p.* A 12.96 *see* **lacchen** *v*

lauhen, lawhen *v* (*p.t.* **lauhede** 2.32, **louh(e)** 12.23, 18.3, **lowh** 21.462, 22.143, **louȝ** A 4.137, **low** A 12.42) laugh 2.32, 4.101, 7.83, 15.204, 18.3, 21.462, B 13.353, A 4.137, Z 7.68, ~ **of** laugh at 4.19, 7.22, B 5.111, ~ **on** / **vp** rejoice with 15.148, B 11.208, smile at 12.23, A 12.42; *pr.p.* laughing 6.23; merry 22.114; smile 22.242; be happy 7.109; express pleasure (at) 15.201; *ger.* (**leyhing**) laughing 6.393; cheerful manner B 16.155; (**louhynge**) amity 20.460

lauhfollyche *a, av see* **laweful** ~ 9.59

laumpe *n* lamp 1.184; ~ **lyne** inscription on a lamp B 13.152

launce *n* lance 3.457

launcen, launsen (**vp**) *v* spring up 12.187, 224; bring forth 18.10

launde *n* glade, clearing Pr 8, 10.64, B 15.298, 304; (tract of) ground Z 2.47; plain (*fig.*) B 10.163

lauen *v* wash (*fig.*) 16.331, B 14.5

#**lauendrie** *n* laundry 16.331

lawe *n* the law [*generally* = (the body of) rule(s) governing human conduct] **B** Pr 122, 12.97, 18.284; specific law(s), statute(s) 21.33, **B** 5.52, 15.465, 16.119, Z Pr 72; [*with ref. to* the Mosaic law] divine (positive) law 10.197, 221, 17.295, 297, 18.186, 19.11, 36, 47, 21.112, **B** 15.583, 585; the (Christian) law (esp. the moral law taught by the Church) 6.45, 7.73, 259, 9.276, 277, 10.305, 11.99, 12.33, 13.86, 90, 92, 17.126, 136, 137, 139, 162, 292, 293, 20.110, 393, 22.266, **B** 10.352, 354, 12.34, 14.146; (divine) command(ment) or prohibition 20.306, 22.278, B 17.15; moral law (of reason) 12.88, 14.209, 210, B 9.78; the law (of the land) 3.293, 376, 378, 4.174, 175, 8.85, 165, 9.425, 12.64, 91, 94, 13.49, 117, 14.146, 20.425, 428, 443, 21.472; = prerogative, right 3.271, 21.471, 482; the (system / process of civil) law (as administered / executed) Pr 161, 2.21, 137, 148, 169, 209, 3.78, 195, 4.169, 12.81, (*person.*) 3.198, B 4.174; *in phrr.* **declaren** ~ practise the law 9.49; **don** (**þe**) ~ administer / execute legal justice 3.446, 21.308; (the process of ecclesiastical) law 16.363; law [as body of knowledge] 11.118, 22.274, B 11.218 *et p.*; the law [as a profession] 3.452, B 11.222, (*person.*) 4.144, B 4.174; **Wryng-lawe** the abuse of legal process (*person.*) 4.31; faith, religion 10.192, 17.133, = (Mahomet's) doctrine B 15.410; way of life / behaviour 10.126; *in phrr.* **aȝeyne þe** ~ in breach of the law (of land / Church) 3.120, 193, 9.212, 17.280, 20.393; **by goed** ~ with justice / with a sound legal claim 17.58; **by puyre** ~ by sheer right 15.290; **by þe** ~ in accordance with the law 8.165, 10.212, 17.283, B 14.109; **for** ~ as legally required 3.88; **bothe** ~**s** canon and civil law 13.79, B 7.14, A 8.13; **konnyng of** ~ expertise in law B 11.165; **men of** ~ lawyers (barristers and judges) 4.67, 148, 168, 9.44, 51, 17.46, 20.354; **clerkes of þe** ~ those learned in the law 11.281; **doctours of** ~ experts in canon law B 15.243; **þe comune** ~ the custom of the state 20.74; **Cristes** ~ the law / commandments of Christ, Christian moral teaching 9.340, 17.251; **Goddes** ~ the law of God 7.118, 9.104, 158, 166, B 15.93; **Newe** ~ the doctrine / moral law of the New Testament 18.265, 19.34, 20.268, 339, 21.35, 59, 111, 312, 449; **þe olde** ~ the (Mosaic moral) law of the Old Testament 12.114, 14.58, 17.71, 18.222, 20.381, 387, 21.312, 449; **Treuþe** ~**s** the laws of divine Justice A 6.97; **Westminstre** ~ the (common) law (of England administered in the king's courts) at Westminster 10.242; **wickede** ~**s** unjust ordinances 3.205; ~ **of Holy Churche** the moral teaching and / or discipline of the Church 9.218, 220, 326, 10.96, 13.82, 86, 14.9, 152, 21.336, B 16.6; ~ **of kynde** natural law (of reason) 8.231, 17.152, 160, 22.18, B 9.78; ~ **of Levyticy** Mosaic law in Leviticus 5.55; ~ **of lyf** teaching leading to (eternal) life 21.45; (**the**) ~ **of loue** the divine doctrine of love 12.121, 14.38

laweday *n* day for meeting of law-court 5.158

laweful *a* just B 11.145; upright B 15.308; ~**lyche** *av* in accordance with law 9.59

lawiere *n* lawyer B 7.59

lawnde Z 2.47 = **launde** *n*

lazar, laȝar 18.272 (B 16.255) = **lasar** *n*

le(a)ute(e) (lew(e)te(e)) *n* uprightness, honesty 17.127, 162, B 15.467; faithfulness, honour 6.195; (*person.*) Loyal Faithfulness Pr 149, 2.20, 4.156, 12.23 *et p.*, 22.63, 146; lawfulness, respect for law 17.130, 138; legal justice B Pr 122, (*person.*) A 2.100; right, justice 3.378, 4.174, 12.90, 94, 21.89, B 14.146, (*person.*) 2.20, 49, 3.196, 446; trust 11.160n. *in phr.* **loue and ~** love and uprightness / integrity 3.443, 4.36, 7.259, 12.81, 96, 98, 15.134, 17.126, **B** 11.166, 15.467

lecche 1.198 = **leche** *n*

lec(c)herye *n* lechery, lust(fulness) Pr 75, 2.188, 3.161, 6.194, 9.18, 10.161, 288, 17.79, 18.36, 21.421, 22.312, **B** 1.30, 6.143, 10.49, **Z** 3.161, 163; (*as allegorical domain*) 2.93, B 10.163; (*person.*) 6.170, 16.90, 22.111, 114; *in phr.* **likyng of ~** lustful pleasure(s) 6.176, 11.265, B 13.344; extravagance 16.254;

lec(c)herous *a* lustful **B** 2.125, 6.265

lec(c)hour *n* lecher, lustful person 6.195, 17.137, B 13.353, A 7.250, (*person.*) = Lust B 5.71

leche *n* physician 2.233, 3.300, 8.295, (*fig.*) 16.136, 22.305, 310, 319, 346, **~ of lyf** 1.198, B 16.118; medicine B 14.315

lechecra(e)ft *n* medical art 18.138, 22.173, B 6.253, (*fig.*) 6.81

lechen *v* cure 15.221, 18.142, **B** 13.254, 16.113, (*fig.*) 8.189, 19.95; *ger. phr.* **a-lechynge** to be cured 19.75

lecuth Z Pr 130 = **lyketh** *see* **lyken** *v*

ledare *n* ruler 21.100; principal, chief 1.154, 156, 15.171, B 10.188; person in charge 8.251; guide 16.156, B 12.96; *in phr.* **~ of lawedays / louedaies** one who presides at court sessions / settlement days 5.158 (B 10.306)

ledden *p.t. subjv.* B 9.190 *see* **leden** *v*

lede *n* man 3.281, 6.301, 7.159, 10.178, 13.59, 17.40, 19.78, **B** 1.141, 3.97, 5.174, 8.7, 17.64, 18.357, A 3.31; person 11.73, 13.210, 20.444, 21.412, **B** †15.393, 16.181, 201; retainer 17.221; subject 4.178; (*pl.*) = landed property 11.69, 17.221

leden *v* (*contr. pr.* **lat** 7.274, 15.278, **latte** 13.55, **leet** 3.195, *p.t.* **ladde** Pr 139 *et p.*, 2 *p.* **laddest** B 7.190, 3 *p. pl. subjv.* **ledden** B 9.190) conduct Pr 139, 2.148, 3.128, 7.274, 11.182, 15.278, 21.225, Z 3.10; guide **B** 10.22, 17.118; bring 7.115, 252, 15.15, 18.3, 178, 19.73; direct 4.12, 12.96; lead 19.66; rule, govern Pr 149, 4.145; manage 3.195, *ger.* **ledynge** management, plan 2.44; **~ forþ** preside over B 10.20; bear, carry 2.192, 4.144, 13.55, 16.140, 20.278, 280, 443, 449, **B** 5.247, 15.83; carry away (captive) B 5.491; **~ lyf** pass / live one's life 9.340, 16.18, 18.77, Z 8.84

ledene *n* cry (of a bird) 13.172, 14.178, 185, B 12.252

leed *n* lead [for seal] B 13.83, [for roofing] 7.237, B 13.247

le(e)f (leue) *n*[1] (**leues** *gen. sg.* 3.490, *pl.* 16.247, 18.48, B 5.267 *etc*) leaf 1.150, 16.247, 253, 17.14, B 12.230, (*fig.*) **B** 5.138, 16.6, 28, 35; page 3.491, 15.105, B 5.267; (*fig.*)= a small amount 6.209, B 6.253, A 8.160, *in phr.* **setten at a ~** regard as worthless 5.97; *and see* **leuen** *v*[3]

leef (leue) *n*[2] beloved B 2.33; pleasure (**leue**) 9.146

le(e)f[3] *imper. sg.* 1.36, 193, 5.24, 6.158, 275, 10.307, 13.210, 19.18, 22.208, Z 7.253 *see* **leuen** *v*[2]; Z 6.53 = **leuen** *v*[1]

le(e)f (leue)[4] *a* (*comp.* **leuer** 6.129 *etc, sup.* **leuest(e)** B 1.151 *etc*) dear 2.18, 17.148, 20.57 (2); beloved 6.171, 11.74, B 5.38; good 3.73, 7.199, 12.24, 18.1, 105; pleasing 1.35, B 9.58; precious, valued 20.457 (1), **B** 1.151, 17.281, A 1.136; agreeable, acceptable 3.6, 5.85, B 10.14; willing, eager, glad 6.116, 22.195, 312 (**Lyf**), B 13.323n; affectionate 12.118; *in impers. constr.* **me / þe / h(e)m is / were leuere / leuest** I / you / (t)he(y) (would) rather (most) prefer 6.129, 292, 313, 11.9, 227, 15.180, B 10.14, Z 3.123; *in pers. constr.* (*with* **hauen**) would prefer 7.22, B 5.140

le(e)f[5] *av* willingly 6.183; *in impers. constr.* **the / here leef li(c)keth** it well pleases you / her 3.19, 4.145, 7.252, *comp.* **leuere** more dearly B 1.143, A 6.50; more willingly **B** 15.195; *sup.* most dearly 1.141, **B** 5.563, 10.355

le(e)ge *a* (true) subject [of a sovereign] 3.414; **~ ledes** loyal subjects 4.178; *as n pl.* 3.316, 317, 20.395

le(e)k *n* leek B 5.81; **~ sed** leek seed 12.192

le(e)l(e) *a* loyal, faithful 12.131, 16.24, 21.60, †B 9.188, (*a as n*) 3.316, 317; true 7.196, 8.140, 10.212, 12.90, **B** 15.581, 16.6; honest 8.74, 295, †11.17, 21.238; just 17.131, 20.307, (*a as n*) 13.68, 19.45; virtuous, upright 9.14, 14.188, 17.139, 20.338, 21.251, **B** 10.432, 15.422, 467; trustworthy 19.28, **B** 11.166, 218; lawful 10.294, 22.138; worthy 7.250; sound, good 5.103, 19.183; excellent B 13.295; *in phrr.* **~ bileue** true faith 12.88, 15.246, 17.22, 127, 158, **B** 10.349, 15.438; **~ labour** honest toil Pr 146, 8.261, 10.79, 16.145; **~ laborer(es)** honest workm(a)n 3.347, 11.298; **~ lif** virtuous life 21.238, B 13.288, A 11.182; **~ lyuynge (men)** men of virtuous life 3.338, **B** 12.62, 15.93; **~ loue** true / faithful love Pr 88, 15.138, 16.194, **B** 11.161, 17.217; **~ speche** truthful speech 7.237, B 11.69

le(e)l(l)y(che) *av* wholeheartedly 7.207, 11.143, 147, 15.155, 17.217, 18.200, 19.94, 21.182, 22.210, **B** 7.124, 10.121, 13.142, A 11.144; sincerely 9.327, 11.268, 19.191, B 13.150, A 12.114; faithfully 3.31, 8.255, 10.140, 21.387, **B** 1.78, 2.32, 15.155; honourably 3.309, 8.140, 9.59, 21.233; virtuously 16.357; assuredly 2.76, B 12.173; in fact 10.275; rightly 16.193, 17.133; accurately 8.298, 17.117

le(e)me *n* radiance 20.127, B 18.137

leene B Pr 123 = **lene** *a*

leep *p.t.* B 2.69, 216 *see* **lepen** *v*

lees *p.t.* 7.131, 10.197, 13.152, 22.87, B 7.159 *see* **lesen** *v*¹

leest(e) *sup.* 3.209 *etc*, B 13.187 *see* **leste** *a*

leet¹ *p.t.* 3.195 *etc*, B 1.167 *etc*, **leete** *inf.* 8.293 *see* **leten** *v*

leet² *contr. pr.* 3.195 *see* **leden** *v*

leeue *v* B Pr 34 *etc*, *a* B 4.39 *see* **leuen** *v*², **le(e)f**⁴ *a*

lef *imper. sg.* 5.24, 6.158 *see* **leuen** *v*²

left(e)¹ *a* †1.112, 2.5, B 2.7 *etc* = **luft** *a*

lefte² *p.t.* Pr 130 *etc*, B 4.153 *etc*, A 3.184; *see* **leuen** *v*¹

leg *n* leg 8.129, 9.143, 215, 20.75, A 12.78

legate *n* (papal) legate 7.81

lege 20.395 = **le(e)ge** *a*

legende *n* written account (of lives), ~ **of lyf** the list of those predestined to eternal life 11.206; ~ *Sanctorum* the *Lives of the Saints* 17.157, B 11.160

leggen, leyen *v* (*3 sg. pr.* **layth** 6.405, *p.t.* **leyde** 5.73, *p.p.* **layd** 12.185, **yleyd** 3.258) lay, set 6.405, 409, 8.129, 14.59, 63, 17.302, 20.33, B 17.71, 18.77; lay (eggs) B 11.347; *in phrr.* ~ **eyes togederes** close eyes 20.59, ~ **ere to** listen to 16.143; place (in position) 6.405, 13.159, B 16.44; ~ **on** beat upon (*fig.*) 15.148, 22.114, 189, B 15.191; give as security, ~ **(to) wed(de)** 5.73, 20.30, 22.13, B 5.240, 16.267; pawn 8.292; wager 8.290, 12.94; ~ **lyf** stake one's life 3.258, 4.191, 20.160, ~ **heed** B 2.34; ~ **fautes on** ascribe blame to B 10.105

legion *n* legion, great company B 1.111; myriad, throng 22.87

legistre *n* expert in law B 7.14, 59

legityme *a as n* legitimate (people) 10.212

ley¹ *imper.* 12.94; **leid(e)** *p.p.* 20.30, B 15.592, *p.t.* 14.63 *etc*; *see* **leggen** *v*

ley² *p.t.* 13.159 *see* **liggen** *v*

l(e)ye *n*¹ flame 19.173, 180, (*fig.*) 259

leye *n*² field 9.5; ~ **land** fallow ground 10.219

leye(n) *p.p.* 21.55, B 3.38, *pr. pl.* Pr 89, **leyʒe(n)** *p.t. pl.* A 7.178, 10.180 *see* **liggen** *v*

leighe *p.t.* B 18.403 (= **low**); *see* **lyen** *v*

leyhing *ger.* 6.393 *see* **lauhen** *v*

leiþ A 3.146 (= **lyth**); *see* **lyen**; **leyth** 18.44, B 16.44 *see* **leggen** *v*

lek-sed 12.192 *see* **le(e)k** *n*

lel 16.145, **lele** Pr 88 *etc*, **lelest** B 13.295; **le(le)lyche** 16.357, 17.217, 19.191, **lely** 9.327 *etc*, **lelly** 2.76 *etc*; *see* **le(e)l(e)** *a*, **le(e)l(l)y(che)** *av*

leme B 18.137 = **le(e)m(e)** *v*

lemman *n* lover, ~**es knyhtes** lover-knights 22.104; mistress, paramour 7.26, 16.277, 22.152, 156; concubine 3.187; (spiritual) beloved 2.20 (*Leaute*), 10.133, A 10.46 (*Anima*), 20.184, B 13.140 (*Loue*), B 14.300 (*Poverte*)

lene *a* lean 10.116, B Pr 123; spare 11.2; emaciated 8.279; lank B 5.82; skinny A 12.78; scanty 8.263

lenedestow *p.t. 2 sg.* 6.248 (= **lenedest þow**) *see* **lenen** *v*²

lenen *v*¹ support oneself B 16.246; recline Pr 8, 10.64, (*refl.*) lie down (to rest) 20.5

lenen *v*² (*contr. pr.* **lent(e)** 11.47, B 9.106, *p.t.* **lened(e)** 6.244, 16.312, **lente** 6.243, *p.p.* **lent(e)** 6.249, 15.240) give Pr 75, 8.286, 10.92, 11.47, 15.240, 17.129, 155, 19.329, B 5.296, 7.75, 9.106, 10.42, 11.179, 13.17, 299, 15.86, 155; grant B Pr 126, 5.259, 10.404; give (as alms) 11.307, 12.118, 13.80, 22.239; afford 8.15, Z 7.107; lend (to) 4.191, 6.243 *et p.*, 277, 8.247, 16.130, 312, B 13.360; *in phr.* **lou(y)en...and** ~ 1.176, 8.231, 10.307, 12.109, 13.68, 14.13, 19.40, B 10.200, 354, 11.178, 15.170, 17.45, A 3.223

lengen *v* reside, dwell 6.158, 21.421, B 8.7; remain B 1.209

lenger, lengur *comp.a* longer 3.490, 6.216, 22.287; taller B 16.181

lenger(e), lengore, lengur *comp. av* (for a) longer (time) 1.202, 3.136, 4.1, 13.4, 36, 19.333, 22.63, B 17.8

lenghe (lengþe) *n* length 2.93, 3.259, 16.82 (**lenthe**), 18.20, 19.60, B 16.182; (time taken to walk) the distance (of) 13.38, B 15.187

lenghen *v* prolong 20.53, 335

lent(e) *contr. pr.* B 9.106, *p.p.* 6.249, 15.240, *p.t.* 6.243 *etc*; *see* **lenen** *v*²

lente(n) (lenton) *n* spring; ~ **sedes** seeds sown in springtime 12.192; (the liturgical season of) Lent Pr 89, 6.183, 7.26, 13.80, 14.120, 20.5, 21.385, 387, 22.362, *pl.*13.80 *in phr.* **mydde-Lentones Sonenday** mid-Lent Sunday 18.182

lenterne *n* lantern 8.174

lenthe 16.82 *see* **lenghe** *n*

leode †10.7, B 1.141 *etc*; *see* **lede** *n*

leon B 15.277 *see* **lyoun** *n*

leopard *n* leopard B 15.277, 298

lep *p.t.* 2.225, *inf.* 2.241 *see* **lepen** *v*

lepare, lepere *n* hopper; ~ **aboute** vagabond 9.107, 137; ~ **ouer lond** wandering (mendicant-) confessor A 11.203

lepen (lyppen, luppen) *v* (*p.t.* **lep** 2.225, *pl.* **lepen** 1.109, **lope** B 4.153, *pl.*, **lopen** B 1.117, *pl.*; **lup** 2.69, 7.134, **lepte** 22.152) hop 6.204; rush forward 2.69, B Pr 223, 4.153; travel B 5.476; run 7.215, 21.125; *in phrr.* ~ **alofte** leap on high (= aspire upwards) 1.112; ~ **asyde** dart away 22.152; ~ **from** digress from B 11.317; ~ **in** shine in, penetrate 20.286; ~ **out** leap out 1.109, 14.85, B 5.161, 18.312, radiate 7.134, roam abroad 2.241; ~ **vp** mount 2.186

lere *n* face 1.3, B 10.2

leren *v* teach 1.203, 3.212, 5.142, 6.348, 9.164, 11.146, 237, 15.95, 118, 16.33, 151, 19.101, 20.235, 338, 21.237, 249, 251, 280, B 7.125, 10.196, †304, 13.187, 15.390, 16.104; teach (to) 1.134, B 6.253, A 8.14; instruct 4.118 (2), 9.19, 11.127, 14.122, 124, 17.318, B 5.44, 11.169; *ger.* **leryng** instruction 10.142, 174,

17.160; [by example] A 1.173; *p.p. as a* **lered** learned, educated 16.226, instructed B 13.214; ~ **man** cleric 7.104, wise man 16.151; ~ **men** the clergy, clerics 3.40, 4.118, scholars 16.192, 18.82; bid 11.132, 17.131, 19.45; advise B 3.69; relate 7.104; inform 9.326, B 11.160; tell 8.222, 14.6, **B** 9.74, 11.420; learn 6.215, 10.10, 22.207, B 1.146, A 1.109, 9.103, 11.278, Z 7.25, *refl.* ~ **hym**, þe learn B 13.121, 143; *in phrr.* **lered (and) lewed** educated and uneducated (= all men) Pr 88, 3.169, 4.12, 9.230, 14.55, 15.14, 17.182, 21.114, 22.102, 247, **B** 10.234, 274, 15.394, A 2.45; **lewed... (and)** ~ 6.116, 11.36, 14.71, 16.33, 230, 281, 19.43, 22.266

lernen *v* learn, receive instruction 11.123, 13.80, B 10.303, A 10.84, 12.6; acquire knowledge of 1.139, 144, 6.241, 11.107, 12.121, 19.47, **B** 1.111, 5.205, 17.41; learn (how to do sth.) 5.43, 6.209, 7.191, 8.294, 11.134, 13.159, 14.107, 22.208, 250; study 22.274, **B** 5.234, 440, 10.302, 11.172; find out 10.57, 11.77, **B** 8.110, 10.231, 12.256, *ger.* **lernyng** B 11.151; teach 11.118, **B** 4.12, 5.295, 7.132, 10.181, 373, *ger.* example **B** 1.199, instruction, guidance B 15.472; prescribe 8.339; *in phr.* **lykyng to** ~ pleasure in receiving instruction 5.155, 7.74

lesen *v*¹ (*p.t.* **le(e)s** 7.131, *pl.* **loren** 14.63, *p.t. subjv.* **lore** 16.312, *p.p.* **(y)lore** 6.193, 20.81 **(y)lorn** Pr 112, B 18.313) lose Pr 112, 10.197, 14.63, 22.87, B 12.40; be dispossessed of 17.218, **B** 7.159, 18.109; forfeit 2.37, 3.466, 7.267, B 5.240; suffer the loss of 3.172, 4.169, 6.245, 314, 9.267, 10.194, 16.312, 20.81, **B** 3.159, 5.94, 12.54, A 10.102, *ger.* **lesynge** loss(es) B 5.111; give up 13.152; waste 16.272; destroy 10.178; *and see* **losen** *v*²

lesen *v*² glean B 6.66

lesewe *n* grassy place Z 2.47

lesynge *ger.*¹; *see* **lesen** *v*¹

lesyng *ger.*² lie B 10.414; falsehood 2.138, 17.310, 18.44, 20.345 *et p.*, 21.293, **B** 5.137, 10.22; fiction 15.105; idle tale 4.19, 7.22, B 10.166

lesse *a, a as n* B 5.220, 10.456, A 4.135, 8.143 *see* **lasse** *a, n*

lesso(u)n *n* scriptural text 3.488, B 11.221, Z 1.36; sermon **B** 10.36, 371; lesson [to be learned] B 17.40, (*fig.*) 6.217; lesson [for guidance in action] 12.91, **B** 6.275, 10.92; piece of instruction 6.210, 241

lest *conj.* lest, so that (not), for fear that Pr 127, 8.294, **B** 11.430, 12.7, 13.427, 15.385, A 7.136; *and see* **last(e)** *conj.*

lest *contr. pr.* B 11.97, 12.173 (= **lust**) *see* **lusten** *v*

lest(e) *sup. a* smallest 14.190; (very) least, slightest B 13.187, Z 6.49; lowest A 11.90; lowest (in rank), least important 3.25, 247, 261; *a as n* least (= smallest amount); smallest (one) 13.157; briefest poem 7.12; least important (one) 2.208, 20.448, B 11.49

leste *av* least 3.209; the least bit (of all) B 17.41, 18.284, Z 7.64

lesten A 12.93 = **lasten** *v*

let *contr. pr.* 10.161; *see* **letten** *v*

leten *v* (*contr. pr.* **lat** 3.173, A 11.142 *etc; imper. sg.* 3.75 *et p.*, *pl.* **late** 4.174, *p.t.* **lat** 6.261, **le(e)t** 1.162, 8.119 *etc*, **lette** 4.156 *etc*, *pl.* **leten** 2.172) give up 2.104, 3.263, 6.101, 8.293, 11.22, 12.217, 19.290, 20.386, **B** 5.224, 10.393, A 12.21, Z 3.154, 5.95, *ger.* **letynge (of lyf)** moment of death 17.124; leave 3.241; leave behind B 18.407; forsake, desert 11.184, B 4.191; cause (sb. to do sth.) 2.172, 209, 213, 215, 4.84, 142, 17.227; cause (sth. to be done) 2.172, 190, 22.143, **B** 2.171, 4.21, A 7.210; allow Pr 173, 1.162, 3.75, 173, 5.137, 6.393, 8.119, ?276, 12.50, 18.276; consider Pr 195, 4.156, 17.297, (*refl.*) conduct oneself, behave ? Z 2.160*n*; *in phr.* ~ **bi** esteem 3.204, 5.3, 7.267, B 10.187; let, may 20.205, 464; (*in supposition*) let (us suppose that), ~ **bryng a man** suppose a man were to be brought 10.33; cease, ~...**that** (not) cease until 6.311

letherne *a* of leather 6.199

leþi *a* empty, vain B 10.186

#**letynge** *ger.* 17.124 *see* **leten** *v*

letten *v* (*p.t.* **lette** 3.238, *p.p.* **(y)lette(d)** 21.385 (B 19.386)) hinder **B** 15.562, 16.46; prevent 17.168, 18.115, B 10.370, ~ **that** prevent (from) 3.35, 238, 10.161, 12.73, ~ **to** 14.177, 15.167, B 10.265; impede 4.170; obstruct 2.38, 3.450, 11.17, 13.90, 18.287, 20.283, 21.385, **B** 10.288, 14.212, 15.66; put a stop to B 3.198; stop 11.60, 13.9, 49, 15.221, 20.334, 22.173, 322, ?Z 2.166*n*, (from piercing) 1.153; delay 1.202, 13.36, 38, 19.78, 333, 20.53, B 9.131, *ger.* **lettyng** delay 8.5, 11.136

lettere *n*¹ obstructor 1.65

lettere *n*², 22.310, A 12.86, Z 7.261 *see* **lettre** *n*

let(te)red(e) 14.198, 16.254, Z 3.164, A 8.45 *see* **lettred** *a*

lettre *n* character (of the alphabet), letter 9.284, Z 7.261; letter (private) 2.233, 4.129, 13.59, 22.310, **B** 9.38, 40, 15.375; official document [recording agreement, granting rights or privileges] 2.83, 107; = charter 13.117; = licence 22.326, 327; = privy letter 9.27, 20.172, 184; letter patent 19.4 *et p.*, **B** 17.34, 118; written orders 11.268; authorisation, credentials 13.40, 88; (written) authority 20.81; scriptural text 12.114; inscription B 1.49; *in phrr.* **bisshopes** ~**s** licences for preaching of indulgences 9.320, B 5.640; **Lumbardus** ~**s** bills of exchange 6.246; **prinses** ~**s** letters of intercession or pardon 21.309; **priue** ~**s** letters sent under king's privy seal 4.189; **prouinciales** ~**s** letters of fraternity 9.342; ~**(s) of (oure) lif** written assurance of (length of) life B 10.91; communication concerning Life A 12.86*n*

lettred *a* educated (*esp.* in Latin) **B** 7.132, 12.96, 144, A 8.45, *a as n* 1.134; *in phrr:* ~ **leodes** learned men B 3.97; ~ **lordes** educated noblemen 3.124; ~ **men**

learned men, the clergy 9.326, 11.76, 12.45, 17.73, 87, 210, 18.80, 21.85, **B** 11.83, 12.157, 15.476; ~ **(men) (and) lewed (men)** 14.198, **B** 13.287, 15.353

lettrure *n* learning Pr 137, 9.195, 198, 11.99, 14.49, 127, 15.182; authority 11.210; **holy** ~ Holy Writ 11.26, 15.74

leute(e) 4.36, 7.259 *etc.*, *(person.)* 2.20 *see* **le(a)ute(e)** *n*

leue[1]*n* leave, permission 2.241, 3.16, 131, 6.439, 12.64, 13.82, 22.188, 189, B 3.231, A Pr 94; right Pr 50, 8.67, 9.146, 14.59; authorisation 2.115, 22.326, B 16.47; *in phrr*: **aʒenes** ~ in defiance of authority 20.275, 314, 381; **lengore ʒeres** ~ longer period of grace 22.287; **licence and** ~ formal permission Pr 83, 6.121, Z Pr 63; leave (to go), farewell 3.46, 4.15, 7.292, 21.483, A 12.55

leue[2] 2.18, 3.73, *etc*; *see* **le(e)f (leue)**[3] *a*

leuele (lyuel A) *n* mason's level [T-square and plumb line] 11.126

leuen *v*[1] (*p.t.* **lefte** 2.53 (**lafte** B 3.197), *p.p.* **ylefte** 17.162) cease (from) 9.209, 22.372, ~ **to** desist from B 7.150; leave off 16.174, A 3.185; abandon 15.7, 16.195, 17.162, 22.40, B 4.153; renounce 3.73, 5.128, 16.103, B 14.264; give up 6.339, 12.217, 16.254, 256, 22.108, 250, 251, 352, B 3.207; leave behind 18.155, 19.75, 20.449; *ger.* **lyuynge** vomit 6.413; allow 22.102, grant, **God / Lord / Crist** ~ may God / the Lord / Christ grant 7.156, 11.245, 17.40, 117, Pr 149; leave 2.53; pass by 7.224; put by 17.102; bequeath Pr 130, 6.254, 16.280, B 15.322; remain B 3.197

leuen *v*[2] (*imp. sg.* **leef** 1.36 *etc*) believe, have faith 14.199, 15.225, 17.124, 158, 182, 297, 19.94, 20.444, B 17.25, A 11.144; believe (sb. or sth.) 2.76, 3.220, 487, 5.3, 6.55, 275, 9.173, 267, 11.210, 13.193*n*, 210, 15.105, 17.217, 18.58, 198, 200, 19.18, 20.260, **B** 9.201, 11.49, 176, 12.94, 14.36 (1), Z 8.74; believe (that) 9.327, 11.202, 226, 14.150, 18.265, 19.103, 275, 20.56, 214, Z Pr 56; ~ **be** that he / there / it is 2.104, 14.210, B 5.275; trust (in) Pr 70, 1.36, 75, 2.105, 5.142, 6.81, 8.99, 19.24, 20.347, **B** 1.118, 6.265; think that, be sure Pr 103, 3.46, 4.169, 6.82, 253, 8.214, 298, 10.202, 16.281, 18.1, 19.137, 20.351, 21.411, 22.363, **B** 3.337, 9.40, 10.437, 12.252, 254, 13.264, 14.36 (2), 15.155, 18.314; suppose, think 1.139, 3.327, 5.187, 6.204, 301, 9.173, 12.44, 13.25, 38, 14.166, 17.168, 20.147, 171, 193, 307, 335, 393, 22.173, B 5.295; *(subjv.)* **no man** ~ let no one suppose 1.117; *in phr*: **as Y leue** in my opinion, as I think Pr 17 *et p.*

leuen *v*[3] (come into) leaf, *p.p.* **leued** in leaf, leafy B 15.97; **grene yleued** covered with green leaves 16.248

leuen *v*[4] 3.281, 419, 4.194, 5.44, 8.16, 12.230, ? 13.193*n*, 14.9, 15.180, 246, 17.182, Z Pr 36, 7.88 *see* **lyuen** *v*

leuer *comp.* 6.129 *etc*; **leuere** *comp.* B 1.143; *see* **le(e)f**[4] *a*; **leef**[5] *av*

leues *gen. sg.* 3.490; *pl.* 16.247, B 5.138 *etc*; *see* **le(e)f** *n*[1]

leuest(e) *sup.* 5.85, B 1.151, A 1.178; **leuest** *sup.* **B** 5.563, 10.355; *see* **leef**[4] *a*, **leef**[5] *av*

leuestow B 18.188 = **leuest thow**; *see* **leuen** *v*[2]

lewdeliche Z 3.164 *see* **lewed** ~ *av*

lewed *a* uneducated, ignorant Pr 70, 102, 1.134, 3.185, 6.23, 9.164, 14.20, 49, 101, 113, 120, 124, 125, 130, 198, 16.260, 272, 17.87, 21.412, **B** Pr 129, 7.137, 10.472, 12.96, 144; *a as n* uneducated / ignorant person 15.14, 17.182, *pl* 17.292, B 3.255; untrained 14.123, Z 7.274; ~ **of** ignorant of 14.107; unable to read Latin 11.293; lay (= non-clerical) 1.193, 11.307, 12.43, 13.25, 15.15, 17.54, 19.43, 20.355, **B** 12.231, 15.70, 119; *a as n* layman 14.59, 63, 113, 16.290, **B** 10.276, 11.96, 108, 302, 15.144, 391; laymen **B** 12.233, 15.353; lay people B 10.248; ordinary, common 9.223, 11.251, 298, A 10.103; useless, idle 1.184, A 11.141; *in phrr*. ~ **counsayle** worthless advice 17.56; ~ **ermytes** idle hermits 5.4, 9.140, 240; ~ **iuttes** uncouth nobodies B 10.461; ~ **knaues**, ~ **laboreres** ignorant workmen 9.209, 11.304; ~ **(men) and lered (men)** educated and uneducated / people of all kinds 3.40, 6.116 *etc*, **B** 3.38, 12.96 *etc* (*see also under* **lered**); ~ **peple** ordinary lay people 1.193, 17.121; ~ **preestes** ignorant / incompetent priests B 11.317; ~ **vnderstondynge** poor understanding 13.115; ~ **wit** untrained mind B 15.83; **clerk and / n(oþer)** ~ cleric and / (n)or layman 16.290, 22.68, B 10.51, A 11.38; ~**liche** *av* ignorantly, foolishly Z 3.164; ~**nesse** *n* lack of learning 3.35

lew(e)te(e) Pr 149, 3.378, 443, 446, 6.195, 21.89, B 12.32, Z 2.107 = **le(a)ute(e)** *n*

lyard *n* [name for] horse (spotted with grey) 19.66, 78, 333, B 17.72

lyare *n* liar, deceiver 1.36, 5.187, 7.82, 10.299, 21.293, **B** 9.119, 13.288, Z 7.253, *(person.)* 2.6, 69, 77, 192, 205, 215, 225, 234, 237, 22.146; charlatan A 7.257

libben 6.125, 8.70, 9.193, 17.249, 20.109, B 2.187, **A** 4.158, 10.144, *pr. p.* **libbyng(e)** 9.58, **B** Pr 223, 9.108, 10.430, 15.93 = **lyuen** *v*

liberal *a* magnanimous, bountiful B 15.150

lycame *n* body 6.52, 10.221, 19.95, 237, 20.93, B 12.233; flesh [as seat of sinful passions] Pr 32, 1.35, 36, B 15.67, Z Pr 36, 3.161; *in phrr*: ~**es gultes** sins of the flesh 6.176, 275; sins of (one's) life 10.55; ~ **and lyf** body and life 6.52, 15.58, 19.183, A 12.93; *see also* **lich**

licence *n* authorisation, *in phr*: ~ **and leue** formal permission Pr 83, 6.121

lich *n* body B 10.2, †19.28

liche 7.123, B 9.63, A 11.246 = **lyk(e)** *a*

licketh 3.19 = **lyketh**; *see* **lyken** *v*

lycour *n* juice 12.222

licud Z 8.26 = **likede**; **licuth** Z 3.150 *etc* = **lyketh**; *see* **lyken** *v*

lye 19.173 = **l(e)ye** *n*[1]

lief 17.126 = **lyf** *n*

lyen (liȝen) *v* (*p.t. 2 sg.* **low(e)** 20.348, 445 (**leighe** B 18.403), *p.p.* **(y)low(en)** 2.20, B 5.94) (tell a) lie 2.32, ? 3.193*n*, 6.55, 98, 138, 20.348, 445, 22.238; speak falsely Pr 50, 1.65, 6.52, 14.6, 16.304, 18.185, 22.277, 20.30, B 13.179, *ger.* B 13.323; make a false claim 10.275, 16.236, 19.224, 227, B 1.118, A 8.61; ~ **on** slander 2.20, **B** 5.94, 10.42, 200; tell lies about **B** 10.39, 205, 15.172; misinform, mislead 8.238, 17.27, **B** 3.251, 7.125, 9.74, 10.331, 11.83, ~ **on** B 15.83; be false to, deceive **B** 1.69, 14.144; speak untruthfully 2.39, ? 5.89*n*, 6.301, 15.179, B 11.223; tell tall stories 15.204, Z 7.68; be mistaken B 10.111

lieutenaunt *n* deputy B 16.47

lyf *n* (*gen. sg.* **lyues** 19.323, 21.218, *dat.* **lyue** 1.25) life, animate existence Pr 146, 173, 2.104, 3.172, 466, 6.101, 10.55, 174, 194, 197, 11.22, 90, 14.63, 15.58, 240, 17.124, 155, 18.285, 19.183, 259, 20.387, 425, 21.105, 22.11, 87, **B** 1.78 3.197, 4.73, 195, 5.98, 6.56, 8.37, 9.45, 54, 10.349, 393, 16.189, 17.308, 18.344, **A** 2.14, 10.46, 12.86, 93, 112; vital spirit A 6.50; *in phr.* ~ **and (of / for) soule** 6.314, 14.127, 17.22, 20.268, 370, 21.411, **B** 9.188, 17.25; (*person.*) = (principle of) earthly life **A** 12.44, 64, 86; = Pride of Life 20.30, 22.143 *et p.*, 312, 352; = (principle of) divine life, God 20.56, 67, 105; (span of) life 1.25, 9.340, 12.201, 15.262, 298, 16.18, 18.77 (1), 19.323, 21.218, 22.111, **B** Pr 49, 1.27, 5.366, 10.414, 14.24, 97, 124, 15.234, 17.307, A 10.145 *in phrr.* **o lyue** alive A 2.14; duration of (one's) life 7.111, 8.110, 174, 9.173, 12.92, 20.335, B 10.91; (the present) life 2.105, 6.313, 12.71, B 10.122; (the future) life (in heaven) 12.161, 18.257, *in phr.* **lawe of** ~ 21.45; divine life 10.171, B 9.48; state / way of life Pr 88, 5.31, 9.103, 140, 12.164, 13.98, 16.153, 18.77 (2) 20.110, 339, 21.238, **B** Pr 120, 10.134, 232, 11.255, 272, 13.288, A 11.182, 12.4, 90; (moral) conduct of life 6.45, 436, 10.294, 19.332, **B** 9.63, 64, 13.296, **A** 9.87, 11.217; manner / way of life 5.103, 8.278, 10.50, 126, 13.29, 18.81, **B** 3.166, 9.190, 11.386, 15.4, A 9.52, *in phr.* ~ **of usurie** B 3.240; living creature 15.19, B 13.17; human being, one 3.233, 446, 6.67, 423, 7.50, 9.197, 11.265, 12.33, 13.73, 207, 17.131, 18.105, 19.276, 20.386, 22.92, **B** 10.262, 11.213, 389, 13.282, 332, 15.6, 249, 354; (written) life (= biography) 7.31, B 7.85, 15.269; *in assevs.* ~ ...(**to**) **wedde** 2.36, 3.258, 20.30, **legge** ~ 4.191, 20.160, **by thy lyue** on your life! 8.234, 11.74; *in phrr:* **Actiua** ~ 18.80; **Contemplatif** ~ B 6.248, ~ **of contemplacioun** 18.77; **lec(c)he of** ~ 1.198, B 16.118; **legende of** ~ 11.206; **lord of** ~ 10.155, 20.59, 403, B 13.121; *in cpds.* ~ **dayes** (days of one's) life 3.187, B 1.27; ~ **holy** of holy life 4.175, 9.195, 11.2, 14.188, **B** 12.62, 15.206, 308, ~ **holiest** 10.50, ~ **holynesse** holiness of life 5.80, 21.111; ~ **tyme** lifetime, course / duration of (one's) life Pr 50, 1.75, 2.32,

6.239, 436, 440, 7.215, 8.25, 10.169, 11.182, 256, 15.198, 17.36, 18.200, 19.110, 20.3, 22.366, **B** 5.236, 476, 13.142, 15.142

liflode *n* sustenance, living 1.35, 3.466, 4.115, 5.42, 45, 6.311, 8.15, 222, 242, 9.245, 17.36, 22.239, **B** 8.81, 9.107, 14.34, 15.255, 19.231, 240, **A** 7.236, 8.110; food 8.15, 196, 263, 313, 9.100, 197, 13.102, 15.239, 272, 22.238, **B** 1.18, 11.280, 14.32, 15.184, 277, 308, 17.77, Z 7.107; the necessities of life 8.294, 17.155; means of living / to a livelihood 6.68, 13.113, 15.240, B 7.124; way of life Z 1.127

lyft[1] *n* sky, **byleue to þe** ~ trust in weather-lore 17.95

lyft[2] 3.75, B 5.578 = **luft** *a*

lyften *v* (*p.t.* **luft** 17.302 (**lifte** B 15.592), *ger.* **luftynge** 6.410) lift 6.409, 410, B 12.120; raise (from the dead) 17.302, 18.144

liges B 18.350 *see* **le(e)ge** *a*

ligge ? *a* flattened 12.234*n*; *see next*

li(gg)en *v* (*contr. pr.* **lith, lyth** 1.127, 4.62, *p.t.* **lay** Pr 8 *et p.*, **ley(ȝe)** 13.159, A 7.178, *p.p.* **layȝe** 6.329, **layn** 3.40, **(y)ley(e)** 11.260, 21.55, **B** 5.81, **(y)ley(e)n** B 16.113, A 11.284) lie (down) 5.149, 7.26, 22.378, **B** 13.21, 16.20, *pr.p.* **lyggynge** 2.53; recline, lie at ease 9.143; lie (fallen) 12.234*n*, 13.236, (sick) 22.312, A 7.130, 178, (buried) 13.22, 15.11, 18.144, B 12.255, (prostrate) B 5.63, (in torment) 1.127, 2.130, 20.146, Z 3.123; stay 14.120, 18.285; remain 19.180; remain in place 22.361; rest idle 8.160; be found 3.221, 6.227, 261; reside, lodge Pr 89, 4.122, 21.421, **B** 6.15, 17.116; spend (night) 5.16; lie hidden 7.45; *in phrr:* ~ **aȝeyn** ? obstruct 3.193*n*; ~ **by, togideres** sleep with, have sexual intercourse with 1.28, 3.40, 169, 4.62, 6.192, 329, B 2.136, A 2.25 (*subjv.*); ~ **in** depend on Pr 137, 20.428, B 4.73; ~ **on** bend forward above B 17.225; exist A 11.141; be 18.272; stand 20.127; consist 9.284, A 10.188; ? be relevant 5.89*n*

liȝt, light B 1.189 *et p.*; *see* **lyht(e)** *n*

lyht(e) *n* light 7.132, 134, 10.155, 20.59, 127, 140, 147, 172, 193, 271, 275, 280, 283, 286, 296, 306, 342, 359, 368, 369; radiance [of comet] 20.249, [of sun] 20.254, [of spiritual substance] Z 1.58, [of Paraclete] 21.206; flame [of lamp / torch] 1.184, 19.180; (the realm of) light (= heaven) A 12.96; sight 21.125, *in oath* **bi this** ~ 21.462; (*fig.*) = human life 19.263; (divine) source of life

lyht *a* light (in weight), *comp.* **~ere** 1.150; easy 19.43, *comp.* **~er** B 17.40, 44; cheerful, *comp.* **~ere** 16.140

lyhte *av* lightly, *in phrr.* **acounten** ~, B 11.16, **leten** ~ **of** 8.165, **setten** ~ **by** 11.164 set small store by, hold in low regard; easily, quickly 20.260

lyhtli(che) *av* (*comp.* **lyhtloker** 7.215, B 15.438 etc) mildly B 14.35; easily Pr 169, 4.101, 14.101, 17.253, 19.315, 323, 20.278, B 15.438, 501; nimbly 7.215; quickly 9.11, 12.224, 16.280; smartly 2.225; readily

16.130; promptly 4.168; immediately B 15.137; without good reason 7.301

lihtnynge *n* flash of flame 21.203

lyk(e) (**liche** 7.123, B 9.63) *a* like, similar (to) 1.87, 110, 2.224, 3.488, 6.75, 7.123, 10.45, 157, 21.8, B 5.117, 8.117, 9.63, 12.252; *and see* **ilych(e), ylyk(e)** *a*

lyke(y)liche 19.332, **ylike** 20.3) *av* like, in the same way (as) 2.224, 6.75, 403, 8.174, 9.158, 12.19, 19.332, 20.3, 332, B 15.348, 17.131

lyken *v* please 1.41, 22.156, B 1.28, 14.78; (*as impers. constr. with subj.*) 4.36, 22.156, B 11.24, (*without subj.*) Pr 168, 170, 188, 1.41, 2.241, 3.19, 175, 180, 227, 5.41, 8.154, 9.28, 20.33, 449, B 8.51, 11.97, 14.167, 16.230, 18.375, A 10.149, 12.37, 51, Z 3.150; (*subjv.*) 3.44, 11.134, 185, 19.329, B 9.190, 13.187, A 8.122, 12.1; like Pr 70, 3.330, 10.275, 22.30, 310, B 10.97, 13.264; (be) please(d) 14.146, 15.260, 19.120, B 12.166, 167, 15.91, A 8.58, 12.112; wish, desire 6.45, 12.164; *in phrr:* **lyketh and luste** pleases and wishes 9.146, 19.116, B 11.97, 12.173; **dere lyketh** best pleases 8.315, **lef lyketh** pleases well 4.145, 7.252, B Pr 163, 206; **good / best lykede** pleased well / best Pr 58, 9.28

lykene 16.308 *etc*; *see* **ly(e)knen** *v*

likerous(e) *a* lascivous B 10.163; luxurious(ly self-indulgent) Pr 32, B 6.265; delicious 1.25, 10.178, B 10.166

lykhame A 12.93 = **lycame** *n*

lykynde *pr.p.a* 18.78 = **lykyng** *a*

lykyng(e) *ger.* pleasure (in), enjoyment (of) 2.75, 11.12, 16.102, B 1.27, 14.129; sensual pleasure 11.182, B 9.181, 16.32; wish, desire 5.155, 6.194, 7.74, 83, 13.152, 16.308, B 5.174, 11.45, 49, 420, 12.219, 15.67, **in ~ of** affecting a desire for B 13.288; affection B 10.304; *in phrr:* **at...~** as one likes 14.55, 15.168, 16.174, 20.93, B Pr 62; **lust and ~** 16.211; **~ and lust** 11.82; **~(s) of body** 9.202, 11.12, 16.102, 22.71; **~ of lecherye** lustful pleasures 6.176, 11.265, B 13.344

lykyng *a* pleasing 11.133, 18.78, B 11.272; sexually stimulating 10.288, *sup.* 6.44

#**lykyngliche** *av* attractively 19.243

likken *v* lick, *ger.* licking B 15.304

lyk(e)nen *v* liken, compare 14.168, 190, 16.264, 17.73, *p.p.* **likned** analogous to 10.44, 47, 19.169, 260, 21.89, 111, Z 1.116; make derogatory comparisons (of) B 10.276; mimic (satirically) 7.23, 16.308, B 10.42

lik(e)nesse *n* guise, shape 12.123, 133, 17.179, 20.328, 21.203, 206, B 1.114, 121, 11.186, 231, 241, 18.355, 357; likeness, image B 9.66, 10.365

lyme *n* limb 8.261, A 7.180; member 22.195; *in phrr:* **in alle ~es** in every part 21.8; **fendes ~es** instruments of the devil 22.77; **lif and ~** 21.105, B 5.98; **~es to labory with** 5.8, 8.135, 9.103

lymytour *n* licensed mendicant friar 22.347, 363, B 5.137

lymȝerd *n* stick smeared with birdlime (*fig.*) 10.288

lyn *n* flax, **~sed** seed of flax, linseed 12.192

lynage *n* good birth 9.195; descendants B 9.48; family 9.197; **~ riche** well-to-do relatives 5.26, 13.110

lynde *n* linden (lime) tree 1.150, 10.64

lyne *n* cord (set as snare for birds) 6.405; (mason's) line 11.126, B 10.181; line (of writing) 9.284, B 3.340, 5.422; *in phr.* **laumpe ~** inscription on lamp B 13.152

lyn(n)en *n* linen cloth 1.3, 18, 13.102, B Pr 220, 11.280, 14.56; linen yarn A 7.13

lyo(u)n *n* lion 9.196, B 13.302, 15.204, 277

lippe *n*[1] lip, *pl.* Pr 162, 6.104, 245, 8.273, 11.227, 17.253, 20.52, B Pr 214, 5.83, A 7.166

lippe *n*[2] little bit (*lit.* mouthful) 2.37, 17.251

lyser *n* selvage 6.216

lysse *n* comfort 6.314; joy 10.155, 20.235; relief 1.198

list *n* strip of cloth 7.161

listen (*cont. pr.* **list** B 3.158, *subjv.* A Pr 37, *p.t.* **liste** B 1.150) = **lusten** *v*

lyst(e)nen *v* listen 15.251, 20.295, B 14.308

listre *n* lector, ? preaching friar B 5.137c

lite *n* little B 13.150, Z 2.159

lyte (**litte**) *a* little 1.139, 8.263, 9.207

lytel *n* little 2.200, 5.163, 11.74, 14.121, B 10.90, 12.250, A 10.116; (*as semi-av*) **a ~** a little, somewhat 16.120, 17.54, 20.357, B 13.268, 14.35, 15.422, a short time 18.167

litel *a* little 3.130, 263, 390, 11.229, 304, 12.26, 15.10, 155, 16.85, 90, 17.237, 19.94, 22.148, 368, B 10.472, 11.220, 15.475; small 17.24, 18.70, B Pr 191, 9.78; short 1.106, 12.224, 16.369, 17.237, 19.47

litel *av* 4.69, 5.31, 6.145, 11.34, 47, 16.143, 22.27, B 7.137, 10.371, 441, 17.91; *in phr.* **(a)counten ~** make small account (of), care little (for) 3.392, 10.261, 11.317, 21.454; **leten ~ by** have small respect for 5.3; **~ um** a little at a time 17.318

lyþ *n* body (*lit.* limb) B 16.181

lith *contr. pr.* Pr 137 *et p.*; *see* **liggen** *v*

lithen *v*[1] ease (pain of) 19.71, A 7.180

lythen *v*[2] listen to 6.194, 7.83, 97, 115, 10.65, 11.77

liþer B 10.166, 437, **lyther** 10.167 *see* **lu(y)ther** *a, av*

litheren (to) *v* attack (with sling) 18.48c

litte 9.207 *see* **lyte** *a*

lyue (*dat*) 1.25, 6.313, B 5.366, A 2.14 *see* **lyf** *n*

lyuen (**leuen** 3.281 *etc*, **lybben** 3.202 *etc*) *v* live, be alive Pr 102, 1.16, 3.281, 8.194, 15.171, 17.115, 248, 18.198, 20.29, B 2.187, 14.32, A 12.112; (continue to) live 3.296, 6.67, 10.50, 57, 11.180, 202, 13.4, 14.146, 15.180, 264, 266, 270, 272, 19.44, 75, 20.30, 264, 21.161, 22.63, B 6.181, 14.322, Z 5.123, 6.44; live eternally 3.359, 20.398; dwell 5.44, 16.286, 17.7, 292, 20.29, B 4.195, 8.93, 10.298, 14.43, A 10.144; live (in some state / condition) 6.314, 9.158, 159, 166, 173, 212, 15.298, 16.103, B 10.437, 11.176; live (in some manner) Pr

28, 175, 3.249, 288, 324, 4.118, 5.142, 7.73, 8.57, 70, 9.43, 159, 173, 193, 10.96, 126, 11.237, 256, 12.230, 14.9, 210, 15.273, 298, 303, 16.20, 269, 357, 17.158, 182, 19.237, 243, 290, 20.218, 21.355, 22.71, 90, 123, 312, **B** 3.227, 5.117, 10.134, 434, 14.152, Z Pr 36, 83; conduct oneself [according to / against a law / religion / rule] 3.202, 7.73, 8.69, 9.104, 291, 10.204, 15.95, 246, 262, 16.103, 17.139, 160, 258, 295, 18.73, 78, 21.249, 408, 22.247, **B** 3.164, 5.381, 10.25, 38, 12.34, 15.390, Z Pr 56; live (by feeding on) 5.174, 6.121, 292, 8.313, 9.200, 10.79, 173, 174, 12.187, 13.78, 15.241, 246, 17.21, 102, 18.10, 22.7, **B** 6.19, 15.255, 314, 422, (*fig.*) 15.246, 22.241; get a living [from benefice, interest *etc*] 4.194, 5.26, 6.125, 342, 17.219, 227, 20.109, 21.218, B 2.125; earn living [from work] Pr 146, 8.330, 9.58, 198, 17.20, 21.233, 238; *in assev.* **as longe as I ~** 4.104, 8.16, 11.89, B 4.191, 6.36, Z 7.88

lyuere *n* living person, †**olde ~ is** people who lived in the past B 12.131

lyues *a* alive 21.159

lyuyng *n* living, life 14.127, B 11.151, 161; way of life, conduct 2.55, 6.33, 286, 12.97, 115, 231, 461, 14.168, 15.104, 16.37, 21.382, 461, B 13.95, 15.391, 417, 423; (*person.*) **Pruyde of Parfit ~** the Pride of Life 11.176, 194

lyuynge (libbyng) *a* living, alive 9.58, 21.176, **B** 9.108, 13.282; *in phrr*: **lele ~** righteously living **B** 12.62, 15.93, *as n* 3.338; **lyther ~** evil-living 10.167; **lowe ~** humbly living B 12.264, 14.187, *as n* 16.152; *as n* **wel ~ B** 10.430

lixt 2 *pr. sg.* (= **liest**) *see* **lyen** *v*

lo *interj.* behold, look 2.5, 69, 6.55, 8.259, 11.26, 12.90, 221, 248, 13.20, 15.239, 292, 16.40, 236, 240, 17.65, 18.132, 239, 276, 19.4, 24, 20.254, 370, 22.202; see how 1.25, 5.186, 20.256, 258; *in phrr*: **~ here** look, here is 20.190, **B** 17.76, 18.328; **~ me here** here I am 20.370

lobi *n* lubber, lazy lout Pr 53

locud *p.t.* (= **lokede**), **locun** *pr.* (= **loken**) *see* **loken** *v*

lode-sterre *n* guiding-star 17.95

loef, loof *n* (*pl.* **loues**) loaf of bread 8.286, 9.150, 15.56, 17.24, 18.154, 21.126, **B** 14.222, 15.590, Z 7.107; **~ of benes** loaf of bean-flour B 6.282; **pese ~** loaf of pea-flour 8.176

loerd 20.283 = **lord** *n*

lo(e)s(se), loos *n* loss 6.275, 16.147, 21.293, **B** Pr 191, 13.387, 14.7

loest *p.p.* 16.40 (= **lost**) *see* **lesen** *v*

lo(e)th *a* hateful, unpleasant 15.80, 20.260, B 9.58, 12.243; spiteful 15.80; unwilling, reluctant Pr 53, 3.198, 8.48, 265, 9.44, 11.133, 12.217, 16.145, 260, 17.44, 22.361, **B** 11.222, 13.260, 15.5, 144, 309, A 12.6; *comp.* B 15.391; **me was ~** I was unwilling **B** 14.7; difficult 15.138

lo(e)thli(che) *a* fearsome 1.109, 21.56; disgusting 14.178, 16.264

l(o)oft *n* upper chamber Z 3.10; *in phrr*: **a ~e** on high Pr 175; **a ~ and o grounde** high and low, in every direction 20.44; **agrounde and o ~** on earth and in heaven B 1.90; *and see* **alofte** *av*

logge *n* encampment, shelter Z 2.47

loggyng *n* lodging A 12.44

logh 10.83 = **lowe** *a*

loghen 12.159 = **lowen** *v*

logyk *n* logic [the liberal art of reasoning] 11.118, 22.250, 274, **B** 11.218 *et p.*, 12.97; treatise on logic 14.190

lok *n*[1] lock [on chest or door] 6.266, *fig.* (*or* river-barrier) 1.196c; *and see* **louken** *v*

lok *n*[2] expression (of face) 11.268

loken *v* look Pr 187, 2.5, 8, 131, 6.4, 44, 7.50, 8.181, 11.170, 13.132, 15.251, 18.54, 272, 20.117, 368, **B** Pr 123, 18.118; gaze 13.173; glance 15.111; peer 11.127; stare 8.341, B 11.85; glare B 15.204; look about 4.63, B Pr 152; look up **B** 5.63, 10.138; *in phrr*: **~ on** look at 1.162, 4.67, 106, 167, 6.44, 315, 10.262, 11.85, 18.54, 20.425, 428, 448, **B** Pr 9, 4.173, 11.408, 186, 13.302, 16.64; **~ þerafter** look towards (it) 7.224; **~ vp** stare B 15.253; (be able to) see B 10.265, Z 3.28, *in idiom* **lyuen and ~** live and have the use of one's faculties 10.57, 20.29, 21.159, 176, B 14.32; appear, look 5.162, 8.174, 9.141, 11.2, 16.69, 269, 20.10, **B** 5.82, 15.206, 348, (*with ethic dat.*) 6.197; see, find out 2.169, 7.292, 15.251; look at, read 6.301, **B** 3.345, 7.137, consult A 8.14; examine 2.234; **~ forþ** search out A 7.13; see, consider 9.240, 277, 13.207, 14.130, B 11.83; be concerned (about), take heed (of) 8.234, 11.74, ?**B** 5.394, 15.185, 318; pay attention to 13.236, B 9.57; watch over 8.85, **B** 1.209, 7.166, 15.9, 16.47, Z 1.100; protect 20.379; see to it / take care (that) 1.144, 7.221, 228, 8.36, 277, 10.285, 11.147, 19.110, 21.255, 22.206, **B** 3.271, 5.575, 10.189, 207, 254, A 3.248, 10.92, 116; (*refl.*) conduct oneself †B 10.90; decree, decide 2.209, B 6.316; **~ after** wait for 14.120, 18.267; expect 3.248, 9.269, 13.73, 19.263

lokynge *a* fully conscious 21.159 (*and see* **loken** *v*)

lokyng(e) *ger.* looking, gazing (at) B 13.344, Z 6.101, *in phr.* **~ of an eye** twinkling of an eye A 12.96; expression 18.10, B 16.7; judgement 2.122; glancing at, referring to B 11.317

#lollare *n* idle vagabond 5.2, 4, 8.74, 287, 9.103, 107, 137, 158, 159, 192, 240, B 15.213, *gen. pl.* (*or a*) **lollarne** of a loller (idler) 5.31, 9.140

lollen *v* hang loosely 6.199; dangle (sb. from noose) 14.130; rest 14.152, 18.286; limp / ? act as a Lollard 9.215, 218*n*

lolly B 6.116 *see* **trollilolly** *excl.*

lomb(e) 7.196, 10.83, *pl.* **lombren** 9.260 *see* **lamb(e)** *n*

lome[1] *n* tool 5.45

lome² *av* frequently 10.167, 12.123, *comp.* 22.238

lompe *n* lump, piece 9.150

lond 3.172 *etc*, B 4.73; #**londleperis** B 15.213 *see* **land** ~ *n*

lone *n* (money-)lending 4.194; gift (of food from employer) 8.196

long *a* long (*spatially*) 20.44, 21.280, B 16.57; extensive A 11.118; *in phrr.* ~ **clothes** (= cleric's garb) 5.41; ~ **day** the whole / livelong day B Pr 225; ~ **lenthe** extensive reach 16.82; tall Pr 53, 5.24, 10.116, (*in name*) 15.152, (*a as n*) 16.84; long (*temporally*) long-lasting 7.203, 8.5; *in phrr.* ~ **labour** 9.207, ~ **lesson** B 10.371, ~ **lyf** 22.111, ~ **sorwe** B Pr 191, ~ **study** Pr 195, ~ **tale** B 9.72, ~ **tyme** 7.203, 20.5, 65, Z 6.44; ~ **trauayle** 19.213, ~ **while** 4.44, ~ **ȝeres** 11.260, 16.286, 17.26, **ouer** ~ of excessive duration 16.363, 22.363; **woke** ~ all week long 9.253; late, delayed 6.277, 7.159

long(e) *av* long, (for) a long time 3.296, 5.80, 123, 8.274, 11.180, 206, 12.194, 222, 13.178, 14.38, 15.7, 58, 16.60, 17.187, 18.287, 20.81, 171, 20.279, 339, 21.55, **B** 4.191, 195, 5.63, 81, 376, 6.36, 10.207, 13.21, 265, 268, 15.1, 191, 16.20; *in phrr.* ~ **ygo** a long time ago 20.296; ~ **lybbynge** long-lived 14.168; **as** ~ **as** as long as 4.104, 6.342, 8.16, 11.89, 15.58; **or** ~ **or** for a long time before 6.277; **ar come auht** ~ before long 17.214; **late and** ~ a long time later 7.159; **ouer** ~ for too long 22.361

longe *n* lung 8.189

longen *v*¹ be fitting (?*or* obligatory) B 11.419; appertain B 10.134; be characteristic (of) B 10.212; be appropriate (to) Z 6.65; belong (to) 7.270, B 2.46, A 12.64; live, dwell 10.7, (as part of retinue) 3.247, 9.130

longen *v*² (**after**) long (for) 8.279

longynge *ger.* yearning, desire 11.169, 21.249

loo 2.5 *etc* = **lo** *interj.*

loof 8.176 = **loef** *n*

loofte *n* height; *in phr.* **on** ~ 20.44 = **alofte** *av*

loore B 5.38, 9.71, 10.121, 14.86, 15.357, 19.240, ~**sman** B 15.390 *see* **lore(sman)** *n*

lo(o)s *n*¹ reputation 7.108, 13.110, B 13.299

loos *n*² 6.275 *see* **lo(e)s(se)** *n*

looþ B 9.58, 11.222, 13.360, 14.7, 15.5, 144, 309, 472 *see* **lo(e)th** *a*

lope *p. t. subjv.* 4.101, **lope(n)** *pt. pl.* **B** Pr 223, 1.117, 4.153, 5.161, 18.312 *see* **lepen** *v*

lord *n* (*infl. gen. pl.* **lordene** 1.95) head of household, lord of manor B 10.97; (*as title*) **my** ~ 22.346, 347; master Pr 175, 19.18; employer 7.97, 8.251 *et p.*, 9.269, 13.88, (*fig.*) 14.215; owner of property 13.87, 14.20, B 3.297; rich man 3.31, 11.26, A 3.273; ruler 3.259, 378, 4.69, 18.201, 21.56, **B** 10.25, 334, A 12.44, Z 7.270; governor 16.281; lord justice 2.21, **B** 3.25, 5.94; sovereign 7.207, 15.168, 171, 290, 21.174 (1), B 3.298; (*fig.*) ~ **of lyf** B 13.121, (*as title of king*) 3.147, 220, 4.69,

B 3.197, 231, 244, A 3.222; feudal lord 1.95, 3.309, 5.167, 9.73, 10.219, 11.184, 12.64, 15.14, B 10.92, 470; (ecclesiastical) authority, bishop 22.326, **lettred** ~ (senior) churchman 3.124; priest A 11.217; nobleman, man of rank Pr 62, 93, 3.57, 73, 268, 282, 381, 5.160, 163, 7.91, 95, 9.14, 18, 223, 230, 10.96, 148, 11.34, 76, 78, 202, 12.90, 117, 14.87, 15.210, 211, 16.143, 236, 17.227, 21.32, 355, **B** 3.346, 5.138, 7.157, 9.38, 10.22, 111, 11.188 (1), 12.144, 13.227, 15.86, 202, A 12.114; leader A 11.143; *in phrr.* ~**es kyn** 5.66; ~**es munstrals** 15.205; ~**es sones** 5.73; ~ **of lust** 21.385; **grete** ~**es** 9.133, 10.148, 15.255, 17.67; **ryche** ~**es** 14.87; ~ **and ladies** 4.109, 6.249, 7.81, 12.221, 15.306, 17.44, 56, **B** Pr 95, 5.243, 15.6, 309; ~**es and lorelles** high and low 15.216; noble warrior 18.286, 22.94; (*as general honorific title*) 20.280, 295, 297, 307, 360, 21.462, 22.71, 90, 92, B 18.88; (*as polite term of address*) B 6.124, 15.9; (*as title for God*) 1.110, 141, 11.47, 17.155, 157, 18.265, 19.44, 20.249, A 2.31, 12.112; **oure** ~ Pr 28, 130, 162, 1.87, 154, 2.131, 3.240, 419, 5.55, 85, 7.108, 9.49, 184, 10.221, 12.93, 98, 196, 13.11, 29, 73, 14.38, 150, 15.15, 74, 118, 278, 16.2, 151, 193, 17.26, 136, 168, 219, 235, 295, 18.78, 82, 198, 19.183, 263, 275, 323, 20.110, 201, 352, **B** Pr 214, 1.204, 209, 6.233, 9.106, 10.39, 205, 11.174, 188 (2) 15.170, 185, 354, 17.131, A 1.110, 10.129, 180; (*address to God*) 6.101, 195, 423, 16.17, **B** 3.235, 10.129, 14.174; *in phrr.* ~**es ere** B 12.252, ~**es good** (= grace) B 5.296; ~**es loue** love of our Lord (God) 3.400, 4.39, 12.93, 15.74, 16.151, 17.26, 18.254, B 11.172; (**the**) ~**es loue of heuene** the love of Heaven's Lord 8.16, B 13.143, A 3.223, 8.33; ~ (....) **almyhty** 17.135, 152, 19.42; ~ **God** 8.135, 10.55, **B** 5.563, 10.355; ~ **Treuthe** 9.19, 59; ~ (...) **of heuene** **B** 16.118, 17.164, 18.357; ~ **of lyf** 10.155, 20.59, 403; ~ **of liht** 20.306; ~ **of myhte** 20.361; *in oaths:* **by oure** ~ Pr 103, 6.292, 8.67, 11.210, 227, 15.180, B 6.66, 14.36, Z 3.123; *in excls:* 1.111, 6.4, 18.276, B 15.249, 16.12; *in prayers and wishes:* B 1.209, 10.129; *in assevs:* 3.147, 8.298, 9.327, 17.40, 117, **B** 6.272, 11.179; *in execrations:* 3.212, B 3.166; Christ 3.400, **oure** ~ 3.75, 99, 4.39, 6.81, 7.12, 74, 104, 12.45, 121, 123, 159, 161, 15.246, 20.369, 370, 443, 448, B 12.54, 94, Z 6.2, 46; ~ **Iesu** 21.8, 96, 174 (2)

lordeyne *n* evil-doer 18.48; rascal 5.162, 22.189; villain 20.105

lorden *v* govern †B 3.298; ~ **in** act as lord in / be owner of 11.69

lordene *gen. pl.* 1.95 *see* **lord** *n*

lordliche *a* haughty 3.198, B 13.302; *av* luxuriously 19.237, 243

lords(c)hip(e) *n* retinue B 2.46, A 6.35; ownership 17.218, 20.108; kingdom 3.263, (*fig.*) A 12.64; sovereignty B 7.159; dominion 2.107, 19.10, 22.251; *in phr.* **lond (and)** ~ territory and dominion 3.315, 9.202, 11.12,

16.102, 158, 18.257, B 14.327; authority B 16.191; (feudal) estate 3.248, 17.221, (*fig.*) 2.93; favour 2.48; power 20.349, B 9.40

lore *n* instruction 11.127, 15.262, 22.352, **B** 5.38, 9.71; teaching(s) 1.67, 9.104, 11.36, 177, 13.193, 16.260, 283, 17.235, 310, 20.201, 21.35, 408, **B** 10.111, 121, 14.86, A 2.17; learning, knowledge 11.99, 14.198, B 15.357; wisdom 11.76; guidance B 19.240; religion 17.182; narrative 17.65

lore *p.t. subjv.* 16.312, *p.p.* 20.81; **loren** *p.t. pl.* 14.63; **lorn** *p.p.* Pr 112 *see* **lesen** *v*

lorel *n* scoundrel Pr 75, 8.129, 9.101, 14.20, B 17.45; wastrel B 15.5; beggar 6.313, 15.216; fool 20.3

loresman *n* instructor 14.122, **B** 9.88, 15.390

lorken *v* lurk, creep stealthily, *pr.p.* 2.226

los 13.110 = **lo(o)s** *n* B Pr 191; = **lo(e)s(s)e** *n*

Loscheborw *n* (counterfeit) light coin from Luxemburg 17.73, 168, B 15.348; *as a* ~**es sterlynges** (counterfeit) silver pennies from Luxemburg 17.82

losel *n* scoundrel 8.74, **B** Pr 77, 6.122, 10.49; wastrel 16.280

losen *v*[1] praise **B** 11.419, 15.253

losen *v*[2] (*p.t. pl.* **losten** Pr 108, 20.345, *p.p.* **(y)lost** Pr 195, 2.104 *etc*) lose (possession of) Pr 108, 195, 3.196, 5.95, 6.277, 9.181, 20.345, 347, **B** 5.98, 8.37, 13.389; let slip B 18.310; forfeit 3.196, 20.349; waste Pr 195, 12.96, 16.40, 19.213, B 10.271; destroy 11.254; damn [of soul] 2.104, 14.71, 134, 20.268, 21.411, 412; fail to gain 5.95; lose (fight) 20.105; *and see* **lesen** *v*

losengerie *n* deceitful flattery, ? idleness **B** 6.143, 10.49

losliche *av* at ease (*lit.* loosely) 14.152

losse 21.293, **B** 13.387, 14.7 = **lo(e)s(s)e** *n*

Lossheborw 17.82, 168 = **Loscheborw** *n*

lossum *a* delightful (= 'lovesome') 10.262

lost[1] *n* loss 5.97

lost[2] *n* 13.152, ? Z 3.163n,c *see* **lust** *n*

lost *p.t.* 9.181, *p.p.* 2.104 *etc.*, *see* **losen** *v*

lote *n*, (*pl* ~**s**) manners, bearing 15.8

loteby *n* concubine 3.187

loth, loþ Pr 53 *etc*, A 12.6, *comp.* ~**er** B 15.391; *see* **lo(e)th** *a*

lothen *v* (*impers.*) be hateful to, **vs lotheth** we hate Pr 173, **eche lyf hit lothed** everyone felt disgust 7.50; hate 6.142, B 7.96

lotien *v* lurk B 17.103

louable *a* praiseworthy 5.103

loud(e) *a* loud 20.469; *av* loudly 18.36, 20.271, A 4.138, 12.16; with a loud noise 20.38; aloud B 13.180; *in phr*: ~ **ouþer stille** at all times B 9.106

loueliche 16.69 *see* **lou(h)liche** *av*

louȝ *p.t.* A 4.137, †B 11.84, **louh(e)** 12.23, 18.3 *see* **lauhen** *v*

louȝ A 11.2, **louh(e)** 6.227, 7.196, 12.185, 16.152, 22.36 *see* **lowe** *a*

lou(h) 21.264, 22.37 = **lowe** *av*

lou(h)liche *av* humbly 9.141, 16.69

louhynge *ger.* 20.460 *see* **lauhen** *v*

louhnesse 5.155, **louȝnesse** A 6.78, 10.102, 129 *etc*, *see* **low(e)nesse** *n*

louken *v* lock up, hide 20.254

lound Z 6.78 = **land** *n*

#**loupe** *n* loophole, ?louver 20.286c

louren *v* scowl 2.233, 6.98, *pr.p.* **lourynge** 5.162, B 5.82 (**lourande** A), *ger.* 6.393; frown 14.202; ~ **on** scowl, lower at 12.23, 24, B 10.310; look angrily 4.168, 7.301, B 13.265; look sad 16.302

lous *n* (head-)louse 6.204

#**lousy** *a* lice-infested B 5.192

louten *v* bow 11.85, 87, **B** 13.26, 15.9, *pr.p.* A 12.55; make obeisance 3.151, 5.171, B 15.86, A 3.35; intercede 3.99, 6.171

loue *n* love Pr 130, 3.316, 376, 378, 443, 4.191, 11.75, 12.88, 14.215, 17.136, B 13.357, A 4.96; friendship 4.69, 7.267, 11.75, 15.145, 20.201, 457; amity, concord 3.452, 8.214, 17.237, (*person.*) 4.145, 156; the (Christian) virtue (of) love, charity Pr 137, 1.65, 145, 162, 198, 203, 5.80, 7.45, 237, 9.14, 166, 10.197, 204, 11.133, 14.27, 85, 15.148, 278, 17.22, 24, 139, 19.191, 276, 20.20, 235, 403, 458, **B** 1.150, 9.95, 10.186, 187, 188, 190, 432, 11.170, 12.68. 13.125, 14.47, 15.218, 255, 17.118, A 1.136, 178, Z 1.116, (*person.*) 1.154, 156, 20.171, 172, 184, 460, 469, B 13.140; love [between the sexes] 10.285, 11.169, 16.104, A 10.204; a loved one B 4.49; partiality 1.100, 12.41; sake (*in* **for** + *gen. or of* -*phrases*), = for the sake of / on account of Pr 28, 103, 162, 3.400, 6.101, 173, 243, 248, 7.97, 9.49, 184, 12.159, 167, **B** 3.159, 5.240, 377, 6.26, 7.75, 9.54, A 10.129, **no lordene** ~ no lords' sake 1.95; **for a mannes** ~ 16.104; **for Haukyns** ~ for the sake of Haukyn; **for Piers** ~ **þe palmare / plouhman** for P. the p.'s sake 15.132, 22.77, A 8.132; *in set phrr.* **for Cristes** ~ **(in heuene)** for the sake of Christ (in heaven) 14.35, 15.35, 16.164, 17.281, 290, **B** 6.220, 15.15, 523; **for Goddes** ~ for the sake / love of God 6.47, 8.284, 9.35, 66, 13.202, 16.103, **B** 10.203, 11.276; **for (oure / the) Lordes** ~ **(of heuene)** for the sake / love of our / the Lord (in heaven) 3.400, 4.39, 8.16, 9.130, 12.93, 15.74, 16.151, 17.26, 18.254; B 13.143, A 3.223, 8.33; **for Marie** ~ **Thi Moder / ~ of heuene** for the sake of your mother Mary 7.148 / Mary in heaven 2.2, 8.16; *in cpds*: ~ **drem** love-dream B 16.20; ~ **knotte** love-knot 17.127; ~ **lawe** law of love 17.130, Z 1.100; *in phrr*: **dere** ~ 11.135; **filial** ~ 8.216; **fyn** ~ 19.176; **good** ~ pure, virtuous love 5.192, 10.300; **kynde** ~ true love 3.451, 14.14, 16.109; **lele** ~ faithful love Pr 88, 15.138, 16.194, **B** 11.161, 17.217, 225; **parfyt** ~ 15.219; **trewe** ~ 1.135, 18.9; ~ **and leue** permission and leave 20.314, 381; ~ **and lewetee** love and faithfulness / loyalty

3.378, 443, 4.36, 7.259, 10.173, 11.160, 12.81, 96, 98, 15.134, 17.126, **B** 11.166, 15.467; ~ ~ **and lyf** 10.171, 19.259; ~ **and lownesse** 3.443, 5.155; ~ **of charite** 16.283; ~ **of soule** spiritual love 10.294; ~ **of þe worlde** love of worldly things 11.82; **lawe of** ~ 12.121, 14.38; **lok of** ~ 1.196

loueday *n* (meeting on) day for settlement of dispute out of court 3.195, 196, 11.17, **B** 5.421, 10.306

louelees *a* without love, unloved **B** 5.117

loueli(che) *a* friendly, kind 12.131, 18.10, **B** 11.186; agreeable 10.83, **B** 5.553, 11.239; lovely, beautiful 1.3, 10.65, 262, 22.104, **B** 6.10, 8.66, 12.261, *comp.* **louelokere** pleasanter 14.185, *sup.* **louelokest** most beautiful 1.106, 6.44, 192, **B** 1.112; excellent 16.84, **B** 6.275, 17.44, *av* kindly 16.69*n*; graciously 3.55, **B** 13.26

lou(y)en *v* love [feel affection / friendship / warm esteem (for)] 3.35, 209, 4.153, 196, 6.145, 249, 7.203, 252, 8.25, 10.133, 11.279, 12.163, 16.106, 17.131, 19.93, 276, 329, 332, 20.56, 334, 338, 369, 444, **B** 9.106, 11.88, 13.140, 15.464, 16.2, 231, 17.281, 18.337, 356, **A** 3.199, 6.23, 12.114; show love (friendship, kindness) to 2.75, 3.57, 119, 5.180, 196, 8.218, 221, 231, 10.79, 92, 189, 192, 201, 202, 306, 307, 11.34, 132, 134, 12.7, 93, 109, 118, 13.68, 86, 14.13, 15.118, 16.90, 357, 17.138, 142, 143, 19.40, 45, 101, 21.112, 114, 251, 255, 22.208, 210, 250, **B** 9.201, 10.200, 205, 207, 357, 11.176, 178, 180, 182, 195, 222, 12.54, 13.143, 15.170, 185, 354, 472, 476, **Z** 5.96; *pr.p.* kind, generous 15.19, 16.24; love [God / Christ] (= worship, obey) 1.141, 11.47, 13.133, 16.170, 17.135, 141, 152, 157, 19.42, **B** 7.124, 10.355, 12.13, 15.393, 17.129; serve loyally [Church, king] Pr 149, 1.75, 2.34, **B** 9.94; love (sth.) 3.161, 7.118, 11.12, 13.29, 21.66, **B** 10.50, 336; desire 19.140, **Z** Pr 36; love, esteem, care for [quality] 1.202, 2.36, 48, 188, 3.58, 130, 144, 281, 4.19, 109, 6.142, 12.44, 13.193, 14.188, 17.52, 21.66, **B** 4.32, 10.187, 202, 12.92, 94; love / enjoy doing (sth.) 5.8, 7.111, 11.78, **B** 10.92, 11.223; love [person of opposite sex] 6.192, 7.301, 10.274, 11.180, 16.106, 22.195, **B** 12.33; make love 17.137, 18.225, **B** 13.353; *impers. use:* **hym louede** it pleased him **B** 16.201, 17.140; *in phrr:* ~ **and byleuen** 10.169, 19.42, 110, **B** 15.476, 17.35; ~ **lelly** 1.176, 3.31, 7.207, 15.155, 16.193, 17.217, **B** 1.78, 7.124, 10.189, 13.142, **togideres** ~ **lelly** love each other mutually **B** 15.553

#louer *n* louver [smoke-turret] 20.286c

loues *pl.* 17.24 *etc, see* **loef** *n*

low *p.t.* A12.42 *see* **lauhen** *v*

low(e) *p.t. 2. sg.* 20.348, 445, **lowen** *p.p.* **B** 5.94 *see* **lyen** *v*

lowe[1] *n* flame 20.140

lowe[2] *a* low, *sup.* (*a as n*) lowest part 14.151; (*as av*) (down) below 14.85, 20.249; (of), low (social rank) 21.35, (*comp.*) **B** 7.157, 159; *a as n* 16.33, **B** 6.227, 10.364; ~ **folk** simple common people 13.82, **B** 3.255,

6.227; humble, meek 7.196, 9.184, 10.83, 12.131, 16.69, 17.30, **B** 5.138, 591, 7.62, 11.239, 12.60; **lowliche** *av* humbly **B** 14.228

lowe[3] *av* low 5.24, **B** 13.26, *sup.* 1.127; down **B** 4.22; *in phrr:* ~ **chered** of humble countenance 21.264; ~ **herted** humble-hearted 22.37; ~ **lyuynge** of humble life 14.187; **lyggen** ~ lie in ruins 19.10; **potten...lowe** humble, bring down low 12.14; humbly 6.8, **A** 7.26

lowen *v* descend **B** Pr 129; humble 10.306, 12.159; make obedient to 8.194, *ger.* submitting (oneself) **B** 15.304

low(e)nesse *n* humility, meekness 3.443, 15.134, **B** 4.109, **Z** 8.91; lowly state 16.18

lower *n* recompense **Z** 7.270

low(h) *p.t.* 21.462, 22.143, **A** 12.42 *see* **lauhen** *v*

lowten A 12.55 = **louten** *v*

luft[1] (**left, lyft**) *a* left †1.112, 3.75; ~ **half** / **hand** left-hand side 2.5, 8, 7.224, **B** 10.164, verso side (of page) 3.491; *as n* villain **B** 4.62

luft[2] *p.t.* 17.302, 18.144, **luftynge** *ger.* 6.410 *see* **lyften** *v*

lu(y)ren *v* lure (*fig.*) 7.45

lu(y)ther *a* wicked, evil †1.109, 193, 4.104, 10.161, 14.101, **B** 10.437; sinful 6.436, 8.253, 9.18, 13.115, *a as n* wicked men 15.216, 17.82, the bad **B** 10.434; wrongful 17.36; deceitful 8.295, 9.181, **B** 10.166, 18.355; treacherous 3.317; false 19.246; foul, ~ **eir** = pestilential air 15.221; vicious **B** 5.117; *av* wickedly, ~ **lyuyng** evil-living 10.167

lunatik *n* madman **B** Pr 123; *a* suffering from recurrent madness [believed due to varying lunar phases] 9.107, 137

lup(pen) *p.t. pl., sg.* 1.112, 2.69, 7.134 *see* **lepen** *v*

lusard *n* serpent **B** 18.338

lust(e), (lost) *n* desire 1.110, 6.158, 11.82, 16.211; bodily appetite 21.355, 385, 22.90; ~**es of synne** sinful sexual desires 17.79; sexual pleasure 13.152, **Z** 3.163; sexual gratification 18.36, **A** 2.65

lusten (lesten, listen) *v* (*contr. pr. i(ndic. and subjv.)*) **lust(e)** Pr 175, 187, 3.169, 9.146, *p.t.* 15.25, 19.116, **B** Pr 130) *impers. without subj.* **me** / **us** / **hym** / **hem** / **here luste** it please(s) me *etc*, I *etc.* wish(ed) Pr 175, 187, 3.169, 195, 10.96, 13.236, 15.25, 20.449, 460, 22.18, **B** 1.150, **A** Pr 37, *in phr.* **liketh and** ~ please(s) and wish(es) 9.146, 14.113, 19.116, **B** 11.97; (*pers.*) wish, like 11.76

lustnen 20.295 = **lystenen** *v*

#luten *v* sing to the lute 20.469

luther 1.193 *etc* = **lu(y)ther** *a*

ma 2.250 = **mo** *n*

maad **B** 5.95, 398, 8.89, 9.44, 113, 10.101, 11.196, 220 = **(y)ma(e)d(e)** *p.p.*; *see* **maken** *v*

macchen (togideres) *v* marry (each other) **B** 9.175

macere *n* mace-bearer, ? sheriff **B** 3.76

#mache *n* wick 19.180

macuht Z 7.276, **macuth** Z 7.262 = **maketh** *see* **maken** *v*

mad[1] *p.p.* 3.208, A 2.22, 11.174 *see* **maken** *v*

mad[2] *a* (*pl.* **madde**) mad, insane B 9.70; furious A 5.106

madame *n. phr.* my lady (*polite term of address*) 1.11, 41, 56, 2.2 (*Holy Church*), 11.88, B 10.220 (*Studie*), B 3.344 (*Mede*)

madden *v* suffer fits of madness 9.108

made *p.t.* Pr 55 *etc*, *pl.* **maden** 7.184, *2 sg.* **madest** 6.234 *etc*, *p.p.* 4.97, 5.70; **maed** *p.p.* 10.130, 15.39 = **made**; *see* **maken** *v*

mageste B 9.52, 15.480 = **maiestee** *n*

may *n*[1] maiden, virgin A 12.116

May *n*[2] (the month of) May Pr 6, 16.10

may *pr. sg* Pr 9 *et p. see* **mowen** *v*

mayde(n) *n* maiden [(young) unmarried woman] 2.19, 145, 250, 3.1, 4, 39, 115, 4.163, 9.33, 12.136, 16.104, 106, 107, 18.92, 20.118, 124, B 2.44, 57, 3.105, 6.326, 9.70, 14.268, A 2.196, 3.35, 10.15, Z 2.104; unmarried person [of either sex] 10.283; girl 6.178, 11.174; virgin 7.127, 10.263, 11.144, 145, 17.267, 18.125, 131, 135, 19.87, 125, 20.131, B 12.38, 18.128, 139; consecrated virgin 10.207, 14.143, 18.71, 97, B 9.112, 15.468; lady-in-waiting 7.287; waiting-woman 11.173; maidservant 4.62, 7.272, A 4.46

maydenhe(e)d, ~hod(e) *n* virginity 1.179, 4.48; (consecrated) virginity B 16.71

maymen *v* maim, injure 5.34, 9.216, 20.384, B 17.190

mayne *n*[1] power 20.361

mayné *n*[2] household 18.253, B 10.93; retinue 3.25, B 5.97; company, troop B 1.108

maynpernour *n* (one standing) surety [for sb. to appear in court] 4.107, (*fig.*) B 18.184

maynprise *n* (*lit.*) release of a prisoner to a maynpernour, *here* = bail (*fig.*) 18.281, (*person.*) 4.84; *in phr.* **nymen vnder ~** act as surety for 22.17

maynprisen *v* arrange release (of prisoner), stand surety for 2.208, 4.173, (*fig.*) 20.187

mayntenaunce *n* support, backing [*esp.* at law] 6.248

maynte(y)nen *v* uphold 3.230, 271, B 2.37; support B 3.90; help 3.186; aid and abet 2.207, 4.58, B 3.167, 247; pay for 17.234; defend B 6.36, 13.126, Z 7.31

mayntenour *n* aider and abettor 3.286

mayr(e) *n* mayor (of a town) 1.155, 3.77, 108, 115, 122, 467, 8.87, 9.122, 335

maister *n* governor, ruler 3.442, 444, 8.340, 12.219, 15.169, 17.100, 170, 296, 18.117, 20.458; leading civic official 2.176, 8.87; magistrate 9.335, B 3.246; important person 3.214, 4.26, B 10.115; master (= superior) 4.155, 5.188, 7.247, 8.38, (= employer) 3.273, 6.212, 11.303, 16.58, B 3.255, 6.239; teacher, instructor 3.276, 14.46, 17.111, B 11.359, 14.255, 15.439, A 10.82; learned man, theologian Pr 60, 10.9, 11.218, 15.30, 39, 46, 91, 16.285, 17.312, 21.85, B 10.66, 11.80, 12.231, 15.70; master of arts / divinity Pr 85,

17.113, B 11.173; (*as title of master craftsman*) 21.289; expert (practitioner) Z 7.262, 263, 276

maistrie *n* control 4.132, B 6.326, 14.328; victory 3.284, 11.287, 18.52, 20.105; upper hand 6.77, 20.68; force 20.299, 394; remarkable feat B 4.26, 16.112; miracle B 16.115; skill 21.256; cunning 6.191; power, ability B 5.102, A 9.47, Z 3. 174

maiestee *n* sovereign majesty, sovereignty B 1.107, 16.184; þe ~ the divine majesty (*as title of God*) B 9.52, 15.480

make *n* spouse, wife 3.154, B 12.33, 14.124, 266; mate 13.139, 153, 18.224, 225, 235, B 11.343, 355, 374

mak(y)en *v* (*p.t.* **made** Pr 55 *et p.*, *pl.* **maden** 8.130, 17.30, B 10.407, A 9.57, *2 p. sg.* **madest** 6.234, 7.123, 128, 20.402, (*uncontr.*) **makede** B 9.130, *p.p.* **maad** B 4.103 *etc*, **mad** 3.208, A 2.22, 11.174, **ymad** 6.295, **maed** 10.130, 15.39, (*uncontr.*) **(y)maked** 7.12, 9.297, 10.87, B 6.186, 13.215) create 3.164, 6.5, 7.122, 123, 8.96, 239, 10.256, 13.208, 211, 17.314, 18.211, 19.279, 20.255, 361, 22.254, B 9.27, 33, 130, 10.226, 12.22, 15.170, 16.13, A 10.35, 142, 11.64, Z 5.37, 40; *in assevs*: **by / for Hym / God þat me / her made** 1.54, 3.164, 6.307, 15.159, B 2.128; establish 14.39, 18.265, 22.278, 367, B 7.53, 9.117, 191, A 8.28; construct, produce Pr 145, 3.64, 452, 7.256, 8.185, 10.129, 11.250, 13.156, 161, 17.17, 18.116, 19.206, 21.326, 329, 22.163, B 3.297, 9.72, 14.72, 73, A 10.79; make 2.192, 3.452, 5.14, 6.221, 263, 8.13, 13.121, 18.116, 20.48, 21.32, 242, 390, 22.337, B 6.142, 9.122, 13.251 14.16, 16.166, Z 7.262; cook 6.133, 182, 8.308, 9.75, B 6.186; draw up 8.95, 12.63, 16.35; write 7.12, 24, 11.148, 154, 14.46, 17.110, B 3.343, 9.38, 10.284, 15.89, A 11.274, 12.109; compose (poetry) B 12.22, ?5.5c; produce (sound) 18.110, B 4.23; make (look, gesture) 6.178, 11.163, 15.121; bring about 13.75, 15.230, 17.86, 202, 238, 248, 20.163, B 3.221, 4.64; arrange 10.249, B 15.241; hold 3.195, 7.101; obtain B 5.72; give 12.103, B 15.461, 480, 16.140; make (vow) 7.63, B 5.398; utter (threat) B 18.281; decree (law) 20.306; provide 16.88; cause 2.86, 7.4, 28, 64, 109, 9.317, 10.119, 19.297, 20.324, 21.284, B 4.70, 142, 5.97; inflict (wound) upon 20.90; cause (to be) 1.19, 3.4, 31, 267, 6.94, 7.128, 263, 8.158, 212, 271, 9.317, 11.214, 12.113, 241, 13.209, 15.294, 16.23, 17.229, 21.59, 294, 22.184, 197, B 2.148, 3.198, 5.95, 7.29, 10.116, 12.127, 13.215, 15.218, 16.133, A 10.83, 12.59; cause to be otherwise 9.233, 10.158, 20.324, B 4.72; turn (into) Pr 37, 1.73, 6.72, 15.233, B 14.81; cause to do 3.158, 479, 6.2, 7.109, 8.117, 221, 271, 9.297, 317, 10.35, 63, 66, 11.119, 170, 12.151, 16.94, 20.83, 346, 376, 21.125, 204, 383, 22.37, 127, 138, 307, B 3.278, 12.40; ~ **of** regard 5.5n, **~lytel tale of** have little regard (for sth.) 3.390; form 19.155; compose 10.130; win 10.87; *in phrr*: ~ **amendes** make reparation 4.97;

~ **at ese** entertain 3.4, 15.48, **B** 15.340, 16.227; ~ **deul** lament 19.320; ~ **ende** conclude 3.198, 433; ~ **fayere chiere** give pleasant reception (to) 22.350; ~ **good** pay, compensate 19.77, 206, B 5.272; ~ **heuy chere** lament 4.160; ~ **mencioun** mention, speak of 8.247, 11.284; ~ **merye, murþe** enjoy (oneself), have a good time 8.68, 22.289, B 15.139; entertain 15.199; ~ **mynde** mention 15.310, B 9.122; ~ **mone** complain 8.130; pray 16.184, 17.257; ~ **pleinte** make (a) complaint; ~ **restitucion** make restitution 6.295, 19.202, B 5.270; ~ **sacrefice** offer sacrifice 18.249; ~ **sawt** make an assault 22.217; ~ **sorwe** lament 3.17, B 13.411

maker(e) *n* creator **B** 10.242, 16.184

makyng(e) *ger.* creating B 17.169; making, construction 3.66; devising B 10.213, A 11.160; contracting 10.249; preparing B 13.52; writing, composing 3.493; (writing of) poetry B 12.16, **A** 11.32, 12.109; dubbing 13.109

male *n¹* male (animal) 13.147, B 11.339

male *a* male 18.253

male *n²* bag 6.236, 13.55

male(n)colie *n* melancholic rage 6.77 (B 13.334)

mal(e)ese *n* hardship 8.233; suffering 15.85; pain 19.158

malt *n* malt(ed barley) Pr 213

mamelen *v* babble 5.123, 13.227

man *n* (*gen. sg.* **mannes** 6.73, 7.88 *etc*, *gen. pl.* **men(ne)** 3.7, 102, 5.29, 13.45, 14.168, 15.277, **mennes** 3.103, 9.214, 12.114, 199, 20.414, *dat. sg.* **manne** †B 1.82) (human) person Pr 212, 3.197, 294, 6.86, 7.70, 80, 95, 109, 243, 10.33, 310, 11.187, 13.19, 14.15, 44, 52, 15.305, 16.217, 327, 17.154, 165, 281, 19.316, **B** 8.18, 127 (1, 2), 10.350, 351, 432, 11.67, 80, 277, 423, 12.99, 13.409, 14.84, 89, 15.58, 158, (*collective*) 3.421; *in phrr.* **eny** ~ anybody 6.117, 7.36, 42, 8.37, 21.18, **B** 14.328, 17.42; **euery** ~ everybody 9.229, 10.182, 12.119, B 15.263; **Y** ~ I, this person 2.133, I man 20.389; **many** ~ many people / a person 10.5 (B 8.5); **many oþere** ~ many another group of people 9.172; **no** ~ nobody 1.85, 117, 2.136, 4.40, 5.154, 8.246, 257, 9.47, 70, 121, 10.186, 295, 15.150, 16.207, 17.14, 20.214, 21.137, 22.102, **B** 4.127, 5.439, 10.364, 11.212, 13.136, 333, 15.257, 17.163; **sum** ~ somebody 14.137; **vche (eche)** ~ everybody 3.461, 5.196, 6.312, 8.117, 12.131, 13.244, 14.68, 20.338, 21.228, 397, 419, 460, **B** 5.272, 10.356, 370, 11.208, 209, 17.104; **what** ~ whoever 2.34, 36, 4.10; who B 13.25; what kind of person 4.10, 10.5; *pl.* **men** people Pr 34, 119, 214, 217, 1.42, 67, 2.64, 78, 189, 195, 3.63, 81, 158, 168, 170, 172, 265, 266, 289, 435, 456, 4.105, 170, 181, 5.5, 29, 6.69, 244, 295, 7.23, 69, 90, 92, 154, 167, 8.52, 296, 9.19, 30, 68, 84, 97, 126, 179, 180, 10.5, 84, 94, 97, 201, 249, 261, 11.127, 132, 161, 198, 217, 218, 236, 293, 12.28, 241, 13.65, 142, 14.46, 47, 56, 181, 15.48, 78, 199, 204, 227, 245, 270, 273, 277, 16.19, 40, 45, 70, 91, 123, 124, 130 (2), 155, 301, 302, 308, 17.97, 170, 178, 187, 222, 265, 273,

300, 18.95, 174, 19.62, 207, 208, 232, 264, 320, 324, 20.338, 21.4, 28, 112, 186, 191, 247, 280, 390, 430, 22.12, 27, 28, 264, 275, 278, 307, 380, **B** 2.36, 3.159, 219, 5.113; human being 7.127, 130, 11.145, 205, 15.264, 17.267, 18.135, 216, 19.39, 20.221, 21.153, **B** 8.127 (1, 2), 16.217; **to** ~ as a human being B 1.82; anyone 8.200, 11.213, 290, 15.160, 19.92, **B** 1.116, 5.283, 10.451, 14.98, 188; man(kind) 1.157, 2.38, 134, 3.354, 7.123, 10.51, 157, 256, 11.159, 12.151, 13.181, 192, 211, 14.119, 15.85, 17.263, 18.123, 211, 20.139, 162, 389, 417, **B** 8.47, 55, 9.33, 44, 52, 130, 11.398, 16.200, A 12.116; man (= adult male) 1.179, 3.45, 271, 420, 469, 475, 4.95, 140, 6.320, 347, 7.21, 95, 8.51, 69, 247, 9.132, 10.35, 68, 147, 11.197, 13.6, 15.30, 195, 16.106, 17.31, 159, 210, 18.92, 182, 237, 19.55, 82, 84, 287, 299, 20.239, 21.98, 22.93, **B** 3.24, 94, 8.127 (3), 9.21, 112, 12.33, 15.280, 415, 480, 574, 16.204, 17.75, 116; (*collective sense*) 13.139, 153, 18.224, 235, B 11.370, 374; *in phr.* **m(e)n and wom(e)n** 2.7, 7.205, 9.106, 17.181, 19.22, B 9.186; soldier 3.236, 252, 256, 257, 475, 17.234, 22.259, **B** 3.198, 221; man of rank / means 3.249, 267; vassal 11.88; retainer 4.58, B 3.167; (man-)servant 3.25, 4.129, 7.243, 15.215, 16.58, **B** 4.155, 13.40, 17.116; *in phrr:* **actif** ~ B 13.273, 458, 14.26, 320, 16.2; **badde** ~ 9.16; **beste** 21.436; **blynd(e)** ~ 7.107, 14.50; **crafty** ~ 3.279, 8.69; **Cristene** ~ 12.61, B 15.398, **cursed** ~ 21.470; **dede** ~ 20.64; **Englische** ~ 16.216; **fals** ~ 3.102, 8.229, 21.248, B 14.24; **fre** ~ 1.73, 5.64, 21.33, 39, 40; **Frenche** ~ B 11.384, Z 7.278; **gentel** ~ 12.112, 21.34; **God-Man** 12.115; **good(e)** ~ 3.92, 302, 5.67, 7.242, 10.263, 11.62, 19.260, 262, **B** 3.75, 7.74, 10.223, 436; **hardy** ~ 13.61, B 14.305; **holy** ~ 17.34, 185, 194, 18.116; **honest** ~ 17.34; **ydel** ~ 5.27; **ille** ~ 10.94; **kynde-wittede** ~ 14.52, 72; **lame** ~ 8.189; **lele** ~ 8.74, 140, 17.139; **lered** ~ 3.40, 4.118, 7.104, 16.151, 192, 18.82; **lettred** ~ 9.326, 11.76, 12.45, 14.198, 17.73, 87, 210, 18.80, 21.85; **lewede** ~ Pr 70, 102, 1.134, 3.40, 6.23, 9.164, 223, 11.307, 12.43, 13.25, 14.20, 49, 101, 124, 198, 15.15, 16.260, 272, 17.54, 87, 20.355, B Pr 129, 1.199; **longe-lybbynge** ~ 14.168; **lowe-lyuynge** ~ 14.187; **luyther** ~ 3.317, 9.181; ~ **lyuyng** ~ 10.167; **mene** ~ 9.54, 11.49, 53; **mylde** ~ 22.65; **myseyse** ~ 9.30; **northerne** ~ 1.114; **olde** ~ 9.175; **parfit** ~ 5.84; **pore** ~ 3.213, 7.78, 84, 194, 8.39, 12.136, 15.36, 16.126, 323, **B** 3.195, 241, 5.253, 254, 6.195, 11.241; **riche** ~ 2.184, 7.98, 12.107, 13.57, 97, 14.87, 95, 173, 184, 16.12, 356, 19.227, 229, 20.218; **rihtfole** ~ 17.259; **sad** ~ 10.31, 49; **seculer** ~ 10.286; **synnefol** ~ 7.145, 10.162; **tidy** ~ 3.474, 20.332, 21.442; **trewe** ~ 3.444, 7.38, 17.33; **wedded** ~ 10.205, 296, 18.71; **wiȝt** ~ B 9.21; **wykked** ~ 4.65, 8.27, 14.134, 16.275, B 16.146; **wys** ~ 3.7, 7.94, 8.240, 9.51, 336, 13.64, 19.226, 21.84; **world-riche** ~ 16.216; ~ **of gode** men of wealth 3.214; ~ **of lawe** lawyer 4.67,

148, 168, 9.44, 17.46, 20.354; ~ **on (þis) molde / of (this) worlde** (any) living person 2.208, 3.6, 10.14, 11.231, **B** 2.37, 3.80; *in vocative uses*: 4.92, 11.7, 92, 189, B 10.253

mana(s)c(h)en *v* threaten (sb.) 4.62, 15.6, B 6.170; threaten (to) B 16.49, 127

maner(e) *n*[1] manorial estate 5.159, B 5.242, Z 5.101; manor-house 7.232, (*fig.*) A 10.15

maner(e) *n*[2] kind / sort (of) 3.110, 332, 304, 6.282, 8.282, 9.7, 33, 10.286, 17.151, 19.260, 20.384, 21.326, **B** 2.13, 3.256, 5.25, 6.219, 266, 7.95, 13.40, 14.164; **al(le)** ~ every kind of 20.43, 22.254, **B** 14.224, 18.319, Z 7.31, **al(le)** ~ **men** Pr 20, 3.396, 4.121, 5.196, 8.17, 232, 9.219, 13.70, 17.249, 19. 41, 331, 21.185, 22.112, **B** 10.268, 278, 11.177, 15.439, Z 3.167; type 8.248; kinds / sorts (of) 3.268, 21.186, **many** ~ **men** 2.57, 197, 6.26 (1), 212, 7.86, 109; 9. 128, 17. 156, **suche** ~ 9.124, 10.246, 16.249; 16. 310, 106, B 3.244, A 10.63; **B** 3.231, 256, 6.266, 14.38, 183, 15.259, manner 3.403; form 21.98; nature, habit 7.44; character 2.7; fashion 15.3, B 13.459; way, manner (of doing sth.) 6.26 (2), 7.23, 230, 8.117, 9.162, 11.178, 14.74, 103, 17.170, 22.197, **B** 1.118, 5.280, 9.44, 10.275, 15.207, 397, A 2.47, Z 2.166; measure, degree B 1.19

maneren *v* have certain manners, *p.p. in phrr.* **is manered after** takes after 2.27, B 15.415; **wel ymanered** with good breeding 10.263

*****mangen** *v* eat 8.271, A 12.72

mangerye *n* feast 12.48; meal B 15.591

mangonel *n* siege-catapult 20.293

manhede, manhode *n* human nature 18.220, 239, 21.158; humanity, the human race B 16.202, 209, 220; human value / excellence B 12.295; dignity, honour 3.230, 17.66

many(e) (mon(e)y(e)) *a and n* many Pr 5, 60 *et p.*; (*with uninfl. pl. n. foll.*) 6.151, 9.297, 15.3; (*following n.*) Pr 96, 2.112, 7.227, 11.181, 14.189, 15.44, 16.133, 17.12, **B** Pr 219, 2.6, 3.23, 102, 6.293, 7.123, †13.44, 15.268; *in phrr.:* ~ **kyne** many kinds of Pr 26, 10.15, 13.55, 19.159, 22.97; ~ **manere** many kinds of 2.57, 197, 6.212, 17.156; many a Pr 212, 3.236, 310, 5.156, 7.243, 12.219, 244, 13.50, 15.305, 17.270, 281, 18.61, 20.179, 21.412, 22.318, **B** 2.57, 6.266, 8.5, 9.206, 13.134, 15.121, 200, A 4.21; (= many, *with ref. to antecedent or understood n.*) 9.41, 11.239, B 4.64, A 12.8; *as n* (= many people) Pr 27, 127, 2.226, 3.13, 159, 7.274, 8.113, 14.17, 15.182, 18.174, **B** 14.169, 16.116, A 5.104; ~ **of** many of 13.162, 19.229, 20.436

manyfold *n* abundance, **by** ~ by much, many times over 12.145

mankynde *n* (*uninfl. gen.* 11.144, B 16.162) mankind, the human race 3.403, 7.127, 13.181, 187, 16.98, 18.135, 215, 19.101, 20.185, 186, 221, 277, 21.324, **B** 10.236, 242, 16.209, 17.108, 18.398; human nature 18.234, 19.125, 20.440, 21.72, 22.41; the male sex 11.145

manlich *a* generous B 5.256

manliche *av* boldly B 10.284, 16.127; generously B 10.89, 93

manoir B 5.242, 586 = **manere** *n*[1]

manschipe *n* act of courtesy 12.107

mansen *v* curse, *p.p. a* **mansed(e)** accursed, damned 2.41, B 4.160; ? excommunicated, ?vicious 22.221, **B** 10.278, 12.84, †A 10.154

mansion *n* abode 16.58

manslauht *n* killing of men in battle 4.182, 17.241

mantel *n* mantle [sleeveless outer robe], cloak 15.205, 22.138

marbil *n* marble A 10.104

marc[1] mark [money of account worth 13s 4d], **half** ~ 5.133

marc[2] B 9.31 *see* **mark(e)** *n*

marcat (market) *n* market 19.74, B Pr 221; market-place B 5.99

march *n* province 22.221; territory, region 10.138, B 15.445

marchal B 3.201 = **marschal** *n*

marchaunden *v* trade, do business 6.280 (B 13.394)

marcha(u)n(t)dise *n* trading, commerce, buying and selling 3.110, 280, 312, 6.339; merchandise, wares Pr 61, 6.212, 260, 13.50, 52

marcha(u)nt *n* merchant, wholesale trader 2.222, 4.129, 193, 6.96, 9.22, 41, 13.32 *et p.*, 17.46, 21.352, Z 3.169

marchel 3.257 *see* **marschal** *n*

marchen (togyderes) *v* go reciprocally Pr 61

mare[1] *n* mare, **cart** ~ mare for drawing a cart 8.311

mare[2] 4.93 = **more** *comp. av.*

mareys *n. pl.* marsh(es) 13.167

margerie perle *n* pearl 11.7

margine *n* margin 9.22

mariage *n* marriage 10.249, B 9.155, 158; ~ **of wedlake** bond of matrimony A 10.207; marriage ceremony, wedding A 2.22, 26; woman's dowry, **feffen in** ~ endow with marriage portion A 2.37, 47; **lachen to** ~ take in marriage Z 2.165; **loue of þe** ~ marital affection, ? desire to marry 16.109

marien *v* give in marriage 16.107, B 9.155, A 10.181, 183; marry 2.54, 80, 170, **to** ~ able to marry; *p.p.* **maried** B 12.33, A 10.113; ~ **togyderes** marry each other 10.283; ~ **wiþ** get married to B 2.31, A 10.154; witness / attend wedding (of) B 2.57; provide for marriage (of) B 7.29

mark(e) *n* boundary-post 3.381; stamp (on coin) B 15.349; sign, **the kynges** ~ **of heuene** the token of heaven's king 17.77 (B 15.351); feature B 9.31; note B 17.104

marken *v* note, observe 14.74 (B 12.131), †B 6.325; note down (= predestine) A 11.261; allot, ordain 14.125

market B Pr 221, 5.99 = **marcat** *n*

marl *n* marl [clay mixed with calcium carbonate] 12.233

marschal *n* commander-in-chief 3.256, 257

martir *n* martyr [witness by death for the Christian faith] 10.206, 12.197, 14.143, 18.97

mart(i)ren *n* (put to death as a) martyr 17.281, 20.334, **B** 15.265

mas-pens 3.278 *see* **masse** *n*

masager A 12.83 = **messager** *n*

maȝe B Pr 192 = **mase** *n*

mase (maȝe) *n* confusion 3.197, B Pr 192; vain activity 1.6

maso(u)n *n* mason [builder / worker in stone] 13.161, **B** Pr 222, 10.180, **Z** Pr 89, 6.78

masse *n* Mass, the Eucharist(ic celebration) Pr 125, 1.178, 3.310, 5.68, 6.272, 354, 8.103, 9.243, 12.87, 13.104, 114, 17.117, 21.3, 4, **Z** 5.37; *in phrr*: ~ **and / or matynes** mass and / or morning service Pr 125, 3.53, 6.282, 7.27, 66, 9.228, 13.121, 22.367, **B** 5.2, 11.282; ~ **of þe day** mass of (a specific) day (in the church calendar) 13.126; ~ **pens** pence offered by the faithful at mass 3.278; **mannes** ~ mass said by a man **B** 13.259

mataynes 3.53, 7.66 = **matynes** *n*

matere *n* physical substance 13.211; business, event(s) 5.110, 15.25; subject 5.123, 19.48, **B** 9.72, 11.159, 15.89, **Z** 7.230; subject-matter, **good** ~ edifying matter **B** 15.58; *in phr*: **meuen** ~ discuss subject / question 1.122, 10.119, 12.43; broach topic **B** 11.230, 15.71

matynes *n* matins, morning service [before mass of the day] Pr 125, 3.53, 6.282, 7.27, 66, 9.228, 13.121, 22.367, **B** 5.2, 11.282

matrimonye *n* (the state of) marriage 10.211, 18.86, 110, 221, 237, 22.138, B 16.209, 211; (a) marriage, matrimonial union 2.149, 10.256, B 15.241

maugre(e) *n* blame, reproach **B** 6.239, 9.155

maugre(y) *prep.* in spite of 2.214; ~ **my / his / hire chekes / teth** in spite of all I / he / she could do 8.38, 20.83, **B** 4.50, 14.4 ~ **ho** no matter who 8.68, 155

maumet *n* idol Pr 119

maundement *n* writ, law (= the Commandments) 19.2, 62

maungen A 12.72 = **mangen** *v*

mawe *n* stomach 6.90, 432, 8.334, 15.91, 16.217, **B** 6.266, 15.64; belly 8.171

me¹ *impers. prn (reduced form of* **men** *prn)* one, people 3.406, 412, 477, 4.121, 5.54, 7.76, 9.128, 132, 133, 302, 11.29, 12.114, 13.5, 16.123, 130, 288, 293, 295, 17.73, 18.61

me² *1 p. prn (as dir. obj.)* me 1.4, 71 *et p.*; *(as indir. obj.)* to me Pr 182, 207, 1.43, 74, 3.147, 156, 4.61, 5.36, 49, 6.292, 313, 7.42, 11.137, 227, 16.168, 18.251, 258, 261, 19.2, 107, 20.281, 379, 408, 21.471, **B** 6.253, 7.121, 10.225, 11.148, 13.85, 190; for me B 5.278; from me 4.180; on me B 5.598; *(as refl.)* myself Pr 2, 4.16, 6.8, 10, 28, 74, 94, 175, 215, 288, 424, 433, 7.53, 65, 8.56, 19.279, 20.5, 92, 21.2, **B** Pr 7, 12.20, 17.84, A 12.75; *(as dat. of interest)* for me / myself, on my behalf 6.32,

7.9, 46, 85, 9.238, 20.312, B 10.386; *(in impers. constr. after impers. v* Pr 7, 9, 180, 196, 5.41, 6.27, 7.292, 294, 11.187, 13.153, 162, 15.25, 18.185, 20.6, B 16.230, A 12.37, Z 3.123; *after* **ben** 13.215, B 14.7; *(with prep.)* Pr 207, 1.75, 203, 2.214, 4.56, 11.164, 15.131, 22.200, 372, B 13.333, A 5.241, Z 7.231; **as for** ~ as far as I am concerned B 12.15

meble *n* (movable) wealth (*pl.* personal possessions or property) 9.270, 10.97, 13.6, 14.181, 15.169, 16.12, 19.257, B 9.83; *in phr*: ~ **and / ne vnmeble(s)** movable and immovable wealth / possessions 3.421, 10.188

mechel 6.332, A 12.102 = **muche(l)** *a*

meddeled *p.p.* 6.260 *see* **medlen** *v*

mede *n* reward, payment B 3.331; material reward / payment [in money or kind, for services] 2.52, 3.248, 265, 281, 294, 297, 310, 423, 7.84, 199, 202, 9.54, 274, 276, Z 3.96; fee, ? bribe 2.138, 3.123, 287, 289, 290, 292, 304, 312, 332, 390, 495, 498, **B** 3.245, 247, 352, 7.58; *(person.)* 2.19 *et p.*, 3.1 *et p.*; material wealth 3.408, 430; (final) spiritual reward [for life of vice or virtue] 2.76, 133, 134, 13.96, 17.66, B 12.289, 292; retribution 20.356

meden *v* reward B 3.216

medicyne *n* healing substance 19.84; medicine, medicament 20.157, Z 7.276, *(fig.)* remedy 1.33, 17.225; healing, treatment 19.77

medlen *v* mix, commingle 10.130; blend together (illicitly) 6.260; have to do 14.67; engage in A 12.109, *(refl.)* involve (oneself) B 12.16; fight 22.179; couple (sexually) with B 11.343

meekliche 3.265 = **mekeliche** *av*

meel B 1.24 = **mel(e)** *n*¹

meene B 1.108, 10.67 = **mene** *a*¹

mees *n*¹ *(pl.)* B Pr 147, 198 (= **muys**) *see* **mous** *n*

mees *n*² course, dish (of food) **B** 13.53, 15.316; (**messe**) ?meal, ? Host Z 5.37n

meeten B Pr 215 = **meten** *v*¹; B 15.251 *see* **meten** *v*³

#**megre** *a* emaciated 6.94

meynee B 1.108, 10.93 = **mayné** *n*²

meynpernour B 18.184 = **maynpernour** *n*

meynte(y)nen 3.271, 4.58, Z 7.31 = **maynte(y)nen** *v*

meke *a* kind 1.171; gentle B 18.115, **A** 9.71, 10.83, 128; merciful 1.168; humble, meek 16.23, 18.125, B 15.306; *a as n* the humble 9.15; submissive 8.212; tame 15.294

mekeliche *av* humbly 1.163, 237; obediently 3.265; uncomplainingly 9.183, 12.180; courteously A 3.35; mercifully 1.165

meken *v* humble 6.10, 17.154; become humble 22.35; submit, incline 4.90, 7.247

mekenesse *n* humility, meekness 7.205, *(person.)* 4.155, B 4.160; contrition 12.74, 19.205, B 4.142; kindness, generosity 8.38; courtesy 11.92

mekil A 6.111 = **muche(l)** *a*

mel(e) (meel) *n*¹ meal 12.107, **B** 1.24, 10.101; *in phrr*: **a**

~s **mete** food at a meal 6.289, 15.36; ~ **tyme** meal-time 7.132, 9.246

mele n^2 ground wheat, meal 9.75, B 13.261

mel(l)en *v* speak B 3.36, A 11.94

melten *v* (*p.p.* **molten** B 13.83) *intr.* melt 19.195, *tr.* (*fig.*) melt, soften 19.193, 197, *p.p.* molten B 13.83

membre *n* limb 5.33, 9.177, 216, 10.157; part (of the body) 20.384, B 12.229; (subsidiary) part 21.473; *in phr.*: ~ **for** ~ 'an eye for an eye', limb for limb B 18.343

memorie *n* memory, recollection (*esp.* in prayers) A 11.216; commemorative mention (in bidding prayers at mass) 7.27, 8.104

memprysen Z 2.175 = **maynprisen** *v*

men *impers. prn* one, people Pr 181, 214, 2.27, 3.165, 7.167, 176, 9.302, 11.174, 15.269, 284, 16.6, 81, 130, 17.222, 18.12, 19.6, 51, 20.471, 21.18, 28, **B** 3.325, 5.424, 12.75, 13.318, 14.150, 278, 445, 17.227, 263, **A** 1.138, 10.96; *and see* **me** *impers. prn*

men *pl.* Pr 20 *et p.*; *see* **man** *n*

mencioun *n* account, **maken** ~ give an account, tell 8.247, 11.284

mende (*pl.* **mendis**) *n* reparation, amends A 4.90, (*person.*) satisfaction A 2.83

menden *v* put right 3.61; cure, redeem Z 1.91; repair 6.288, A 3.51

mendena(u)nt *n* (*pl.*) orders of mendicant friars 13.78, 15.82; beggar 5.76, 9.179, 11.50, 15.3, **B** 10.65, 15.154, A 11.201; *n as a* mendicant Pr 60

mene *n* means 18.202, state (causing sth.) 16.94; intermediary 1.155, 9.347, 10.120, B 3.76; intermediary means B 9.34; mediator 17.158, 258

mene a^1 poor, of low rank Pr 20, 219, 3.81, 197, 9.54, 11.49, 53, B 10.67; (*comp.*) poorer B 14.166; lesser B 1.108

mene a^2 intervening, mean 6.281; intermediary B 9.114

men(e)gen *v* commemorate 8.104; ~ **of** remember †B 5.412

menen v^1 mean, signify 4.147, 5.37, 9.164, 11.83, **B** 10.89, 275, 13.212, 15.119, **Z** Pr 94, 1.3, 5.43, 7.232, *in phr.* **be to** ~ mean, signify 1.11, 3.124, 395, 6.303, 10.92, 210, 11.72, 247, 249, 293, 13.64, 65, 14.4, 16.155, 216, 17.41, 20.129, 215, 225, 21.62, 93, **B** 9.50, 11.273, 14.275, 319, 15.450, 458, **A** 8.139, 11.297; symbolise B 16.63; intend 11.114, *pr. p.* 8.248; aim for, seek, *pr.p.* 17.176; assert B 5.276; be caused by 20.129; *ger.* **menynge** understanding (*pl.*) 1.137; *in phrr*: **(in)** ~ **(as) after** in desire / search for 17.176, B 15.474; **in** ~ **of** in commemoration of Pr 99; **in** ~ **þat** in token that 15.245, 18.93, 20.139, **B** 15.306, 16.200

menen v^2 (*refl.*) complain 3.215, B 6.2

meneuer *n* fur (of grey squirrel) 22.138

mengen v^1 **B** †5.412, 6.95 = **men(e)gen** *v*

mengen v^2 mix (= adulterate) B 13.362

meny 19.22 = **many(e)** *a*

menyng *pr.p.* 8.248 *etc*, *ger.* Pr 99 *etc*; *see* **menen** v^1

menyson (blody) *n* ? dysentery, ? morbid menstrual flow B 16.111c

menne (*uninfl. gen. pl.*) men's 2.122, 4.115, 6.95, 293, 7.219, 9.191, 10.16, 13.45, 75, 78, 14.168, 15.173, 16.336, 21.381, 22.55, 187, 289, Z 7.179

mennes (*infl. gen. pl.*) men's 3.103, 9.214, 12.114, 199, 20.414, **B** Pr 198, 6.102, 10.95, 131, 213, 11.245, 15.422, 473, 476

Meno(u)r *n* Minorite, Franciscan friar 10.9, B 8.18

mensioun 11.284 = **mencioun** *n*

menthynen Z 2.174 = **maynte(y)nen** *v*

*****mercede** *n* wages [(due) payment for work] 3.290, 304, 332

mercement *n* fine, penalty 1.157, 4.182

mercer *n* mercer, dealer in textiles 6.250

mercy *n* forgiveness 1.165, 168, 6.16, 92, 274, 337, 7.147, 232, 9.237, 346, 12.72, 13.12, 14.56, 19.208, 268n, 292, 316, B 11.263, 14.187, 331, 16.5; *in phr.* ~ **for mysdedes** forgiveness for wrongdoing 6.274, 7.232, 12.72, 14.56, 18.259, B 5.72; pardon 19.287, 20.89, 21.185, Z 4.78; mercy 6.339, 17.265, 19.181 *et p.*, 324, 331, 20.431, 440, 21.93, 185, 326; (*person.*) 7.287, 12.74, 20.118, 124 *et p.*, B 2.31; clemency 3.471, 4.73, 90, 95, 139, 6.323, 332, 8.37, 9.274, 276, B 10.370; favour 2.133, 6.323, 21.76; charity, kindness 11.49, 13.142, 16.23, **B** 10.67, 15.468, 439; grace B 10.123, 13.409, A 11.261; *as excl.* pardon! 1.11, 2.2; have mercy! 6.4; *of thanks* 1.41; *of surprise* 18.276; *in phrr*: **do** ~ grant forgiveness 7.121; exercise clemency 4.139, 20.431, 440, **Goddis** ~ 11.218, 18.288, 19.326, ~ **of God** B 5.284; *excl.* **for ~s sake** to gain (oneself) mercy, at all costs B 10.253; graunt ~ many thanks **B** 10.220, 17.86

merciable *a* merciful, forgiving 9.15, 20.417, 436, *a as n* the merciful 19.197; compassionate B 5.504; generous, charitable 17.46, B 15.154

#**mercyen** *v* thank 3.21

merciful *a* forgiving, compassionate B 2.32

mercymonye *n* reward B 14.126

mere *n* ? lake, ? boundary 3.380n

mery(e) 2.167 *etc*; *see* **mury(e), (mery(e))** *a*

meryte *n* merit, spiritual credit 1.178, 11.159; (cause of) spiritual reward 16.327, **B** 5.379, 11.182

meritorie *a* suitable [in terms of desert] 9.68; spiritually profitable B 11.79

merk *n* stamp, imprint B 15.349

merke[1] *n* darkness 19.207

merke (myrke)[2] *a* dark 1.1; obscure, mysterious 18.197, B 11.159; *n* ~**nesse** *n* darkness (of hell) 20.139; (*fig.*) darkness of sin 20.179

†**merken** B 6.325 = **marken** *v*

mersyen *v* levy fine (on) 8.37; *and see* **amercyen** *v*

merthe 20.227, A 12.92 = **murthe** *n*

merueil *a*, (*sup.*) **merueilleste** A 9.59 = **merueillouseste**; *see* **merueillous** *a*

merueyl(l)e *n* wonderful work B 15.589; wonderment, astonishment, **hauen** ~ be astonished 20.130, B 11.75; cause of astonishment, ~ **me þynkeþ** I find it astonishing B 9.150

merueyl(l)en *v* (feel) wonder 15.21; (*impers.*) **me ~ed** I marvelled 13.162, 18.23, I wondered B 11.359, **me ~eth** I am astonished 13.192

merueillous *a* wonderful, astonishing **B** Pr 11, 11.6, (*sup.*) B 8.68

merueylousli(che) *av* wonderfully, **mette** ~ had an astonishing dream Pr 9, 9.308, 10.67, 22.52

mesager 2.237, 9.136, 13.32 *see* **mes(s)ager(e)** *n*

meschaunce *n* calamity 6.69; evil fate 19.231; adversity, misfortune Pr 105, 3.97; ill-luck **B** 3.167, 5.91; wrong-doing, sin 10.59, B 14.75, Z 5.74

mesch(i)ef *n* misfortune, calamity Pr 65, B 12.84; trouble 3.222, B 4.72n; affliction Pr 212, 9.183, 12.180, 203, 16.310; misery 15.160, 16.78, B 14.238; harm 22.65, *in phr.* ~ **and / or male(e)se** misery and suffering 8.233, 15.85; penury, distress 9.179, 10.203, 13.70, 16.94, B 14.174; want (of food) 8.212, 21.284; (spiritual) need 11.233, *in phr.* **at** ~ in need **B** 9.76, 10.451, 11.298, A 11.201; wickedness, sin ? **B** 3.278, 14.75, *in phr.* **at** ~ wrongfully A 10.181; infirmity 9.216; disease 16.249

mese(y)se *n* suffering, illness 15.160, B 9.76; starvation B 1.24; ~ *and see* **myseise** *a*

mesel (musel) *n* leper 3.168, 9.179, **B** 7.101, 16.111

meson-dew *n* hospital (for the poor) 9.30

mesour A 12.73 = **mesure** *n*

message *n* communication (*sc.* to God), prayer 17.257

mes(s)ager(e) *n* messenger, courier 2.237, 4.129, 13.32, 36, 39, 42, 53, 58, 63, 78, 87, *in phr.* **mynstrals and ~s** 2.237, 9.136, Z 7.49; (divine) envoy 9.136, 17.178, 18.131, 21.208, B 15.407

messe¹ B Pr 97, A 3.211 = **masse** *n*

messe² Z 5.37 *see* **mees** *n*²

Messie *n* Messiah 3.456, 17.159, 296, 301, B 15.603

mester 9.7 = **muster** *n*

mesurable *a* moderate B 1.19; appropriate B 3.256

mesure *n* measure [instrument / vessel for measuring quantity] 6.230, 16.128, B 13.359, (*fig.*) = amount 1.172; size B 16.182; proper quantity 22.254; what is appropriate / in proportion 22.26; moderation, temperance 1.19, 33, 15.273, 17.52, B 14.74, A 12.73; *in phr.* **out of** ~ immoderately 13.188

mesurelees *a* immoderate, without (proper) limit B 3.246

mesuren *v* (*refl.*) moderate, control (oneself) B 14.77, 81

met *n* (instrument / vessel for) measurement B 13.359

met *p.p.* 13.216 *see* **meten** *v*², B 11.242 *see* **meten** *v*³

metal *n* metal (of coin) 17.74, (*fig.*) 17.78 (B 15.349, 352)

mete *a* ? pleasant, ? sufficient A 8.110n

mete *n* food 3.278, 6.289, 7.84, 9.251, 10.188, 203, 13.85, 188, 227, 14.137, 15.33 *et p.*, 217, 233, 247, 16.72, 17.32, 176, 18.155, 21.284, 289, **B** 1.24, 5.256, 6.19, 266, 7.129, 11.277, 282, 13.53, 404, 14.157, 15.207, 474; *in phrr.* ~ **tilien** get one's food (by tilling) 15.270, B 6.232; ~ **and / or moneye** 8.204, 16.70, 19.232, B 11.195, A 7.210; sustenance 22.211; dish 15.44, 67, 91, B 13.108; meat ? 9.149, Z 7.316; meal, *in phr.* **at (þe)** ~ at table 8.51, 11.35, 16.341; dinner 6.147, 7.67, 9.228; banquet 21.418

#**meteȝyuere** *n* provider of hospitality B 15.147

metele(e)s *a* without food 9.295, B 10.65

metel(e)s *n* dream Pr 217, 9.296, 297, (*pl.*) 317, 15.4, **B** 2.53, 8.68, 11.6, 86, 405

meten *v*¹ measure Pr 163 (B Pr 215); measure out 1.172

meten *v*² (*p.t.* **mette** Pr 9 *etc*) dream 9.308, 22.52; (*impers.*) dream Pr 9, 219, 5.109, 110, 10.67, 11.167, 21.5, 484, B 11.6, †B Pr 11 (A Pr 11, Z Pr 12); **metyng(e)** *pr.p.* dreaming 2.54, *ger.* dream **B** 11.319, 13.4, A 9.59

meten *v*³ (*p.t.* **mette** 2.237 *etc*) come across 4.48, 6.178, 7.159, 296, 10.3, 8; meet, encounter 15.30, 17.30, 18.247, 19.53, 20.124, 21.157, **B** 5.99, 13.6; come upon 18.168; come together 20.124; meet (in battle) 22.93; enter the presence of 4.41; keep a rendezvous with B 16.146; catch up with B 17.81; ~ **togidere** meet one another 13.32, join, run (together) A Pr 60; ~ **with** meet, encounter 2.237, 4.140, 5.6, 9.122, 10.115, 11.189, 13.56, 61, 15.30, 192, 16.141, 18.182, 20.224, 22.4, B 15.251

methet Z 1.101 *see* **meten** *v*¹

mette *n* table-companion 15.41, 55

meuen *v* (*tr.*) move 19.160, shake 18.110; (*intr.*) move **B** 8.33, 17.166, *pr.p. a* **meuynge** shifting, changeable 9.110; arouse, stir up 13.179, 14.67, 21.287, **B** 10.263, 13.192, (*refl.*) 18.118; raise, *in phrr.* ~ **matere** raise topic, question 1.122, 10.119, 12.43, **B** 11.230, 15.271, ~ **motif** advance a proposition 15.131, 16.229, B 10.115; urge B 12.4

myche **Z** 2.3, 8.89 = **muche** *a*

my(n)(e) *poss. prn* (**mi** A 12.82, **myen** 18.255, **myn** 20.431, A 3.51, 11.261, *and before vowels and mute* **h** 4.58, 6.75 *et p., pl.* **myne** 4.97, 6.152) my Pr 203, B Pr 203, A 1.69, Z Pr 93, *et p.*; mine *sg.* 6.263, *pl.* (**myn**) 8.148, 16.206, B 5.110, (**myne**) 20.301, 372, B 6.148, 18.351

myd (myt) *prep.* with 4.73, †6.336, **B** 5.74, †12.203, †15.352, Z 5.90, 6.11, 7.58, 139, 177, 304, 8.18; at the same time as, **riȝt** ~ **þat** at that very moment B 12.295; accompanied by 16.180; in (the keeping of) B 17.169; ~ **fole** in foal †B 11.343

myd *av* by means of it Z 7.299

mydday *n* mid-day, noon 16.169; *in phr.* **aboute** ~ round about noon 7.132, 9.246, 20.137

mydde-Lentones (Sonenday) Mid-Lent Sunday *n. phr.* [4th Sunday of Lent] 18.182

myddel(l) *n* middle 19.158; waist 3.10, 6.408; full (of moon) 3.479

myddel *a* middle 18.119, B 12.7, 16.5

myd(d)elerd (~erthe) *n* the earth 11.170, 13.132

myddes *n* middle 2.195, 7.232, 21.4, A 2.40, *in phr.* euene in þe ~ right in the middle 18.6, 19.153

mydmorewe *n* mid-morning A 2.40

mydnyht *n* midnight 16.169, A 8.151

myen 18.255; *see* my(n)(e) *poss. prn*

myght Pr 140, 18.30, B 9.52, 16.182, miȝte 18.202, A 10.63, 64, 77, = myht *n*

myghte *p.t.* Pr 100, (*2 sg.* myghtest Pr 163), 174, 181, 1.148, B 1.82, 17.191, A 3.224, 8.123, 10.59, 86, 119, Z 3.169 = myhte; *see* mowen *v*

myghtful B 11.277, 17.312 = myhtfull *a*

miȝtiest *sup.* A 10.54 *see* myhty *a*

Mihelmasse *n* Michaelmas day [Sept 29] 15.217

myht(e) *n* (supernatural) power [of God] 1.158, 6.285, 9.115, 17.314, 18.288, 19.135, 149, 193, 196, 294, 20.477, 21.24, 186, 390, B 1.107, 5.132, 9.37, 44, 52, 10.104, 16.54, 184, 18.255; *in phrr.*: ~ **and mayne** power and might 20.361; ~ **of miracle** power to perform miracles 15.227; power [of devil] 18.151, B 10.329, 16.120, 165; potency B 13.156, 168; dominion 16.59; control 7.287; authority, warrant Pr 140; force 6.73, 8.208; firm severity B 4.173; capacity 16.85, 19.119, B 5.102, 12.7, 18.255; ability 18.202, *in phrr.* **by ~...**, **emforth ~...** according to (one's) capacity 6.295, 15.143, B 10.253; faculty 1.160; vigour 16.135; (physical) strength 18.30, B 16.182

myht(e) *2 sg. pr.* 1.144, 3.29, 423 *etc* (myhtow = myht þow 1.167); *1 and 3 sg. p.t.* Pr 68, 3.128, 229 *et p.*, *pl.* Pr 175, 4.78 *etc*, *2 p.* myhtest 16.19; *as cond.* Pr 39, 2.118, 146, 3.294; *2 p.* myhtest(e) 16.206, 19.281 *see* mowen *v*

myhtfull *a* possessed of (supernatural) power 1.168, B 17.312; mighty B 11.277

myhty *a* powerful 21.265, (*sup.*) A 10.54; capable of possessing power (to) 1.171

mylde *a* kind, gracious 9.15, 19.201, B 15.306; humble 14.143, 20.118, 22.65, (*sup.*) 21.256, B 15.468; ~ speche humble / diffident language / address 11.92, 15.277, 21.93, A 9.71, 10.83; gentle 17.239, B 15.280; tame 15.294; ~liche *av* kindly 3.10, 39; graciously 3.21, 77, 20.152; humbly 18.131, 19.280, Z 1.91; obediently 9.183; gently 17.30; ~nesse *n* humility B 15.174, 258

myle *n* (*pl.* myle) mile 7.17, 19.74, 22.164, B 5.373, 402, 16.10; *in phrr.* ~ way distance of a mile 9.296; large ~ full mile B 10.164; lenghe of a ~ time taken to walk a mile 13.38, B 15.187; arst...be a ~ a mile ahead A 4.29

myleliche Z 1.91 = myldeliche *av*

mylion *n* million A 3.249, 10.152

mylk *n* milk 7.51, 9.75, B 15.280, 466, 469; ~en *v* milk 17.10

myllares Z Pr 89; millere B 2.112 = mullere *n*

myn(e) 4.28, 62 *et p.*; *see* my(n)(e) *poss. prn*

mynde *n* mind 6.339, 12.91, 16.180; thought(s) 6.284, 19.292, B 11.50, A 11.216; memory, remembrance, hauen ~ in remember, think about 12.151, B 15.147; meditation B 15.295, 16.38; mention 15.310, B 9.122; reason 17.154; understanding B 16.58, ryhte ~ sound judgement 3.326

mynistre *n* minister B 15.418; (Cristes) ~ priest 5.60, B 15.418; official 16.124

ministren *v* render service / minister (to) 18.97; serve 19.119; administer (estate) B 12.52

mynne *a as n* less, *in phr.* more ne ~ no more or less, nothing else 3.395

minnen *v* (re)call to mind 17.210, B 15.461, †15.547; reflect †B 12.4

mynour *n* miner B Pr 222

mynstra(l)cie *n* music(al entertainment), minstrelsy [the minstrel's art] 3.12, 275, 15.197, 199, (*fig.*) 16.310, B 10.48; ? singing, ? story-telling B 10.43

mynstre *n* monastery 5.91

mynstrel (munstral) *n* minstrel (instrumental / vocal) musician, musical entertainer Pr 35, 2.237, 3.275, 9.128, 11.35, 15.195, B 3.133, 14.27, Z Pr 89, 7.49; kynges ~ 7.96, lordes ~ 15.205 minstrel retained by a king / lord; trumpeter 22.93; (*fig.*) Goddes ~ = the poor 7.99, 102, 109; the half-witted 9.136; ~s of heuene 9.126

myn(u)t(e)-while *n* space of a minute (= a very short time) 12.219, 13.199, 19.195

myracle *n* miracle Pr 99, 9.113, 15.227, 17.263, 301, 18.146, B 15.445, 448, 589

myre *n* bog, swamp 13.167

myrke 18.197 = merke *a*

mirre *n* (ointment of) myrrh 21.76, 92, 93

myr(r)our *n* mirror B 15.162, (*fig.*) 11.181, B 12.95, ~ of Myddelerd mirror of the world 11.170, 13.132; = example 17.277, 18.174

myrthe 3.12, B 3.220 = murthe *v*

misbeden *v* insult, maltreat 8.42

mysbileue *n* false (religious) belief 3.327, 17.273, 18.151; superstition Pr 102; *in phr.* bryngen / maken in ~ lead into false belief / heresy 17.181, B 10.116, 15.396

myschaunce 19.231 = meschaunce *n*

myschief B 9.76 = mesch(i)ef *n*

mischeuen *v* come to grief B 12.117

mysdede[1] *n* misdeed, transgression 1.157, 163, 3.45, 6.274, 7.70, 121, 12.72, 14.56, 16.261, 18.259, 22.308, B 5.72, 10.370, Z 5.136

mysdede[2] *p.t. see* mysdon *v*

mysdoer(e) *n* wrongdoer B 3.247, 297

mysdon *v* (*p.t.* mysdede 20.389, B 4.99, A 4.77, *p.p.*

mysdo 4.86) do wrong, transgress 3.158; do (sth.) wrongfully 4.86, 20.389, **B** 15.109, 18.342, A 4.77; wrong, injure **B** 4.99, 15.257, 18.97; beat up Z 7.152

myseise *a* infirm 9.30, *a as n* A 8.28; *see* **mese(y)se** *n*

myself 6.74 *etc*, **myselue** 3.233 *etc*; *see* **mysulue** *prn*

mysfaren *v* come to grief 10.162

***mysfeet** *n* misdeed B 11.374

myshap(pe) *n* accident 5.34, 12.203

myshappen *v* meet with bad luck, come to grief 3.481, 11.187, B 10.282

mysylfe Z 7.61, 198 *see* **mysulue** *prn*

mysliken *v* be displeased 16.312

myspenden *v* waste 10.187; misuse B 15.76

myspenen *v* misuse 5.93, 10.176, 16.232

mysproud *a* arrogant 7.95 (B 13.436)

mysrulen *v* misuse, abuse B 9.60

misseyen *v* insult, disparage 6.9; revile, rebuke 20.350, B 16.127

missen *v* be deprived of 14.44; be free of B Pr 192; *ger.* lack 10.203, A 12.73

mysshape(n) *p.p.a* deformed 9.171

myssomur *n* midsummer 16.13

***mysstanden** *v* be amiss B 11.380

myst *n* mist Pr 163; vapour 19.195

myst(y)(li) *a* obscure, hard to grasp, *comp.* **mysti(lok)er** 11.129

mysulue (**mysulf** 4.134 *etc*, **myself** 6.74 *etc*, **myselue(n)** 3.233 *etc*, A 11.163, **mysilfe** Z 7.61, 198) *emphatic prn* (*as appositive to subj.*) myself 2.183, 3.5 *etc*; (*as refl. obj.*) 6.74, 8.26, 19.159; (*as obj. of prep.*) 10.68, 12.52, 13.217, 14.140, 15.213, 19.93; (*indep., as subj.*) I myself 8.268, 18.253, B 10.228, (*as v. obj.*) (me) myself **B** 2.179, 13.122, 15.162, (*as obj. of prep.*) 20.373, **B** 6.137, 16.47; *in phr.* **for** ~ for my part 4.134

mysturnynge *ger.* going astray 7.307

***myswynnen** *v* (*p.t. pl.* **myswonne**) gain wrongfully 15.48

myt Z 5.50, 90 *etc* = **myd** *prep.*

myte *n*[1] mite [insect] †B 14.23

myte *n*[2] mite [coin] = (1/2 farthing) 13.96; (*fig.*) jot, whit 9.274, 22.179, **B** 7.50, 13.197

#mitigacioun *n* mitigation, lessening of punishment [i.e. for sin after death] 6.323

mytren *v* (invest with) mitre, *p.p.a* **mytrede** 4.193

mywen *v* stack (hay, grain) 5.14

***mnam** *n* mina [Greek coin = 100 drachmas] B 6.238, 240, 241, †Z 5.124

mo *n* other(s) 2.250, 3.1, 6.347, 15.153, 19.26, 22.272, B 15.334

mo *a* more (in number) Pr 166, 9.171, 14.3, 21.127, **B** 1.116, 5.242, A 7.257; additional, further 19.37, 264; *in phrr.* ~ **othere** others besides 4.10, B 12.118, **other** ~ 20.180, 21.54, B 10.176; **withouten** ~ without further 12.86

mo *av* to a greater degree B 14.328; besides, in addition 2.7, 113, 20.181, 21.165, B 17.282, A 10.152

moche 6.309 *etc*, Pr 196 *etc*; *see* **much(e)(l)** *n, a*

mochel 6.323 = **muche(l)** *a*

moder *n* (*uninfl. gen.* 21.124) mother 6.15, 16.104, 20.131, B 16.217, (*Amendes, mother of Mede*) 2.122, 123, (*Mary, mother of Christ*) 2.51, 4.39, 7.148, 155, 8.21, 9.347, 12.135, 21.119, 21.124, 148, B 18.255, A 12.116, (*fig.*) 16.135, (*the Church*) 18.207

mody *a* proud, *as n* (**þe**) ~ the proud one [= the Devil] B 9.205 (A 10.217)

modiliche *av* angrily 4.167

moebles B 3.269, 17.275 = **meble** *n*

moed (**mood**) *n* spirits, attitude 13.179; heart, feelings, **meuen** ~ stir up (one's) feelings , prompt (one's) heart B 13.192; anger, **meuede hym** ~ wrath (be)stirred (itself) 18.118, **meuen** ~ get angry B 10.263

moes *n* moss 17.14

moest (*sup.*) *a* 17.63, 19.237, 21.256, 421, *av* 16.119, 19.105 = **most(e)** *a, av*

moet 21.368 = **mote** *n*[2]

moet-halle 4.163 = **mot-halle** *n*

moet *pr. sg., pl.* 11.234, 302, 12.171, 16.70, 20.207, 208, 21.321, 368, 22.46, 238 *see* **moten** *v*

moeuen B 15.71, 19.288 = **meuen** *v*

#moilere (**moylo(u)re**) *a* born in wedlock 2.120, 145, 10.211; *as n* (legitimate) offspring 18.221, 235

moist *a* juicy 18.86

moisten *v* refresh 20.410

mok (**muk**) *n* dung B 6.142; (*fig.*) (landed) property 10.97

mold(e) *n*[1] earth 8.17, 19.84; world Pr 65, 1.42, 3.444, 12.180, 19.84, **B** 9.83, 11.273, A 3.233, Z 2.18, *in phr.* **man (...) (vp)on** ~ (mortal) human being 2.208, 9.172, 10.14, 11.231, 14.167, 17.249, **B** 2.187, 3.80, A 10.128

molde *n*[2] pattern, model 13.161

#mol *n* stain, mark B 13.315; *a* ***moled** spotted B 13.275

molten *p.p.* B 13.83 *see* **melten** *v*

mom B Pr 216 (A Pr 89, Z Pr 69) = **mum** *n*

mone *n*[1] complaint 8.130; prayer 16.184, 17.257

mone *n*[2] moon 9.108, 110, 308, 17.91, Z 6.68; *in phrr.* **on bothe half þe** ~ ? both before and after the full moon 8.350n; **myddel of a** ~ full (of a) moon 3.479, B 13.156

mone (**moneye**) *n*[3] money Pr 61, 164, 2.170, 3.263, 423, 6.244, 280, 9.270, 12.244, 13.48, 60, 97, 15.36, 169, 205, 17.234, 19.233, 21.352, 22.12, B 16.129, A 3.249, Z 3.95, 5.101; coinage 17.74, B 15.349; wealth 1.42, **Mammonaes** ~ ill-gotten gains 10.87; payment, ? bribe B 15.241, *in phrr.* **mede and / ne** ~ reward and / nor payment B 3.253, 271, **mete and / or** ~ food and / or money 8.204, 15.36, 16.70, B 11.195

moneye *pl.* 2.226 = **many(e)** *a, as n*

#moneyeles *a* moneyless 9.110, 295

monek 3.168, Z 3.69 = **monk** *n*

monewen A 7.87 = **men(e)gen** *v*

mony(e) Pr 27, 60, 2.113 *etc*; *see* **many(e)** *n and a*

moniale *n* nun 5.76, 170, 18.74, 22.264

monk *n* monk 3.168, 6.131, 151, 158, 7.66, 17.35, 52, 60, 18.74, **B** 6.325 (~es heddes), 15.274, A 10.113, 136; *in phrr.* ~es and / or chano(u)ns 5.156, 170, (B 10.318), 17.55, **and freres** 17.52, B 15.416, **and moniales** 5.76 *etc*

mont (mount) *n* mount(ain) 19.2, B 11.169

montai(g)ne *n* mountain 1.1, B 11.323, A 2.40

month *n* month 3.181, 5.50, 6.131, 21.391, B 10.151 *and see* **twel~**

mood B 10.263, 13.192 = **moed** *n*

moolde B 2.37, 9.83, 11.273 = **molde** *n*[1]

moone B 13.156 = **mone** *n*[2]

moore B Pr 52, 111, 2.76 *et p.*; moost B 1.151, 3.80 *etc*; *see* **more, most(e)** *n, a, av*

moornen B 13.192, 386, 411 = **mournen** *v*

moot *sg. pr.* B †3.319, 9.15 *etc*; *see* **moten** *v*[1]

moot-halle B 4.135, 152 = **mot-halle** *n*

mor *n*[1] marshland 13.167

mor *n*[2] 13.223, A 12.92 = **more** *n*[2]

more *n*[1] root 16.249, 17.21, 21.340, B 16.5, 14, 58

more *n*[2] (*comp. of* **muchel** *n*) more (= greater amount) Pr 219, 232, 1.122, 4.97, 100, 7.193, *in phr.* lasse ne ~ less or more B 13.17, the smaller or larger B 10.265; (= an additional amount) 1.189, 3.218, 5.109; something further B 9.36; þat ~ what further amount 19.77 (what...moore B 17.78); [*ref. to social rank*] *in phrr*: lasse other / ne ~lower or higher / greater 2.48, 10.7, 15.201; [*ref. to quantity*] ~ or lesse greater or smaller amount; a poynt of ~ one thing further 8.35; no ~ nothing else 13.39; ~ ne lesse nothing else but B 10.456; is no ~ to mene signifies nothing else 10.210, 11.72, 247, 293, 13.65, 17.41; withouten ~ forthwith 19.198; without any further action B 10.351

more *comp. a* bigger 21.124; more (in quantity) 1.178 *et p.*; greater 7.61, 281, 13.97, 14.216, 15.47, 17.232, 21.24, **B** 5.282, 284, 6.47, 7.81, 9.150, 16.133; longer 11.136

more *comp. av* more (= to a greater extent / degree) 2.80, 3.230, 7.98, 9.108, 11.49, 17.211; further 13.162, 21.69, **B** Pr 111, 11.47; eny ~ any further 3.138, ʒut ~ still further 12.241, 13.75, 16.132; no ~ not again Z 8.32; rather 16.261, B 15.448; longer B 3.290; (*comp. degree, with positive a*) 10.109, **B** 12.261, 14.27, 89, 101, (*as intensifier with comp. a.*) 18.65, 88, 21.24, B 7.70, (*with comp. av*) B 11.160, 15.199

moreouer *av* besides, in addition 5.53, 18.225

moreyne *n* death, mortality 20.224; plague 3.97

#morgagen *v* mortgage Z 3.96 [= pledge in return for loan], 5.101 [= accept as pledge in return for loan]

mornen 4.160 = **mournen** *v*

mornyng[1] Pr 6 = **morwenyng** *n*

mornyng(e)[2] 12.205, 21.294 = **mournynge** *ger.*; *see* **mournen** *v*

morreyne 3.97 = **moreyne** *n*

morsel *n* mouthful B 13.108

mortel *a* deadly 17.288

morter *n*[1] mortar [grinding / mixing bowl]

morter *n*[2] mortar, cement B 6.142, (*fig.*) 21.326

mortheren *v* murder 4.58, 19.262, A 5.84; slaughter A 3.249

morthrar *n* murderer Z 7.263

mortrew(e)s *n* stew(s) of pounded meat 15.47, 67, 101, B 13.108

morwe(n) *n* morning 6.352, 373, 8.180, 9.243, 11.102, B 14.15, Z Pr 6, 2.49; the next day 10.271, B 6.146; a-~ on the next day 7.13

mor(we)nyng *n* Pr 6, B 13.262; a-~ in the morning(s) 13.147

moskele *n* mussel 9.94

mosse *n* moss B 15.287

mossen *v* become mossy A 10.104

most(e) (moest 16.119 *etc*, moost B 3.80 *et p.*) *sup. a* most (= greatest, largest in size) 1.7, 3.382, B 10.93, (= largest in number) B 4.159, 181, (= largest in quantity) 7.132, 11.27 (1), 21.421, B 10.29 (2); *a as n* 11.289, B 8.55 (1); greatest Pr 65, 3.81, 11.190, 233, 14.108, 15.5, 17.63, 19.238, B 11.398, A 10.54; chief **B** 9.56, 15.255

most(e) (moest 16.119, 19.105, moost B Pr 158 *et p.*) *sup. av* most (= to the greatest degree) 2.38, 9.71, 11.27, 13.179, 16.119, **B** 5.99, 8.55 (2), 9.100, 10.28 (2), 12.52; (*with a*) Pr 131, 145, 176, 2.64, 3.471, 9.68, 10.157, 11.295, 13.192, 15.39, 21.266, **B** 4.166, †9.33, 10.29 (1), 11.272, 13.298, 15.156; (*intensifying sup. a*) 12.225, B 14.44; (*with av*) 10.14, 16.338, 19.237, (*with sup. av* 12.225); principally 13.179, **B** 11.230, 15.295

moste *p.t.* 3.256, 15.11, 16.161, 18.126, B 4.112, A 12.39, Z Pr 71, (*with pr. sense*) 7.2, 291, 9.280, 17.225, 243, **B** 5.150, 7.21, 13.315, 14.192, 277, 16.200, 19.67 *see* **moten** *v*[1]

#mo(u)stre *n* show, display 6.260 (B 13.362)

mote *n*[1] mote, speck B 10.263

mote *n*[2] moat 7.232, 21.368

mote *n*[3] assembly Z 4.150

moten *v*[1] (*pr.* mot(e) 1.136 *etc*, *pl.* mot(e)(n) 3.86, 7.205, *p.t.* moste 3.256, B 4.112 *etc*, (*with pr. sense*) 7.2, **B** 5.150, 7.21) be allowed, may 7.156, 20.207, 208, (*p.t.*) might 13.33, 16.161, **B** 4.112, 15.398, A 12.39; must 1.136, 7.2, 205, 291, 8.313, 9.280, 12.171, 13.48, 67, 21.67, 321, **B** 9.15, 37, 43, 109, 12.185, 14.192, 16.200; be compelled to †B 3.319; have to 6.127, 11.302, 16.70, B 13.261, will have to B 14.277, 21.321, would have to 18.126, B 13.179, should have to 3.256; (*absolute*) is necessary 17.225, B 9.36; ought 17.243,

B 13.315; *in phr.* ~ **nede(s)** must needs / of necessity 3.280, 11.234, 13.36, 19.87, 22.46, B 5.253; insist on 5.28; (*in asseverations, blessings, curses*): may 2.117, 7.156, 9.25, 15.149, 21.179, 180, B 10.132

moten *v*² go to law, plead a case 1.171, 3.197, A 4.118; *ger.* **motyng(e)** legal pleading, advocacy 4.132, 9.54

mo(o)t-halle *n* court-room, court of law 4.148, 163, B 4.135

mothe *n* (clothes)-moth 12.219, B 14.23, ~ **eten** motheaten B 10.360

#**moty(e)f** (*pl.* **motyues**) *n* proposition, argument, **meuen** ~ formally propose an argument for discussion 15.131, 16.229, B 10.115,

motyng(e) 4.132, 9.54 *see* **moten** *v*²

motoun *n* gold coin [stamped with image of Lamb of God] 3.25

mouhte *p.t.* 11.159, 267 = **myhte**; *see* **mowen** *v*²

mount B 11.169 = **mont** *n*

mountai(g)ne B 11.323, A 2.40 = **montai(g)ne** *n*

mounten (*vp*) *v* increase, ? spring up Pr 65

mo(u)rnen *v* grieve 6.274; sorrow 7.70; be troubled, anxious 3.17, 215; lament, complain 4.160, 15.65; *ger.* **mournynge** sorrow, grief 12.205, 17.147, 21.294, B 14.238

mous *n* (*pl.* **muys** Pr 166 (**mees** B)) mouse Pr 196, 207, 213

mouth *n* 6.180, 22.191, [*as organ of eating*] 6.432, 21.289, B 12.232 [*as organ of speech*] Pr 164, 1.165, 3.395, ? 6.161, 10.66, 11.31, 53, 278, 13.39, 58, 15.223, 16.30, 18.124, B 4.155, 5.281, 367, 10.445, 14.88, 90, A 3.240, 4.105, 11.306; speech, words 6.73, 16.341, B 15.257, A 9.71, *in phrr.* **with ~e and herte** with word and will 12.72, 18.260, **with ~e or with handes** by speech or action 19.257

mouthed *a* mouthed, **merye** ~ 9.126 *see* **mery(e)** *a*

mouthen *v* utter, speak 4.110, 20.152, B 6.237

moued *p.t.* 18.118 *see* **meuen** *v*

mowen *v*¹ mow 5.14, *ger.* 8.186

mowen *v*² (1, 3 *sg. pr.* **may** Pr 9, 1.11 *et p.*, 2 **miht** 1.144 *etc*, *subjv.* **mowe** 8.233, *pl.* **mowe(n)** Pr 185, 10.211 *et p., **may** 7.173, 8.130, 134 *etc*; *p.t.* 1, 3 **myhte**, (*with pr. sense*) **mouhte** 11.159, 267, 2 **my(g)htest** Pr 163, 16.19, 206, 19.281, *pl.* **my(g)hte** Pr 174, 4.78 *etc*): **may, myhte(e)** have power (to) Pr 68, 1.80, 148, 3.222, 229 (1, 2), 7.252, 10.258, 12.16, 74, 101, 15.229, 16.60, 19.83, 287, 20.157, 297, 431, 478, 21.29, 51, 22.179, 197, 322, B 5.57, 10.439, 17.166, A 6.80; can, be able (to) 1.80, 153, 167, 2.161, 3.61, 181, 194, 252, 319, 329, 390, 406, 4.84, 97, 133, 5.34, 6.77, 88, 94, 305, 7.3, 173, 267, 275, 303, 8.130, 134, 232, 332, 9.74, 148, 10.27, 57, 84, 160, 212, 238, 286, 310, 12.65, 87, 108, 195, 13.1, 52, 53, 92, 95, 14.44, 126, 176, 15.58, 16.65, 79, 80, 99, 101, 121, 147, 285, 327, 17.73, 86, 123, 18.61, 85, 19.78, 154, 193, 214, 260, 292, 298,

324, 329, 333, 20.204, 224, 372, 437, 438, 21.27, 303, 472, 478, 22.44, 190, 192, **B** Pr 196, 1.149, 3.227, 269, 5.132, 272, 10.276, 11.80, 82, 209, 361, 377, 12.49, 240, 13.171, 408, 14.74, 171, 15.389, 16.218, 17.92, 104, 117, 255, **A** 5.112, 7.37, 12.68, **Z** 6.68, 7.266; may be able (to) 6.332, 7.290, 11.171, 181; will be able 1.144, 3.249, 7.290, 8.178, 315, 9.274, 11.197, 15.159, 16.6, 340, 20.409, **B** 2.45, 15.561; (*sg. sbj.*) **mowe** (should) be able 3.139, 8.40, 233, **B** 14.312, 18.203, (*pl. sbj.*) 7.141, **B** 4.88 **mowe(n)** (*pl.*) can, be able 3.273, 8.342, 9.176, 10.211, 301, 12.188, 190, 16.216, 19.200, **B** 1.132, 6.39, 7.15, 10.347, 14.61, 15.86, will be able B 10.284; (*p.t. with pr. or fut. sense*) **myht(e)** could, might / should (be able to) Pr 39, 174, 181, 2.204, 3.61, 4.136, 5.123, 6.151, 7.220, 307, 8.137, 221, 11.77, 159, 12.73, 13.199, 15.159, 220, 245, 16.101, 138, 206, 17.225, 18.198, 224, 288, 19.11, 159, 265, 268, 280, 281, 282, 22.383, **B** 1.82, 6.139, 7.135, 9.72, 10.93, 272, 11.388, 12.16, 14.84, 15.89; (*p.t.*) could, was / might (be) able (to) 3.128, 196, 216, 4.150, 6.39, 86, 264, 281, 402, 429, 431, 7.185, 9.7, 11.84, 159, 285, 12.16, 80, 13.60, 14.167, 15.46, 16.19, 17.14, 169, 265, 18.55, 198, 224, 288, 19.56, 106, 236, 242, 20.179, 258, 333, 368, 21.293, 312, 22.93, 121, 197, **B** 1.120, 5.6, 255, 283, 439, 9.83, 116, 10.141, 11.196, 405, 13.313, 15.140, 334, 591, 16.137, 217, A 12.103; could have B 5.374; may, be allowed to 1.202, 2.123, 134, 136, 149, 3.245, 12.63, 15.297, 16.198, 18.281, 20.363, 22.20, B 10.30; may possibly 22.351; *p.t. with pr. sense* **myht(e)** might (be allowed) to 2.146, 3.61, 8.237, 16.206; be entitled 12.59, 16.99, 17.58, 70, B 10.342; must []; shall, will Pr 9, 1.58, 2.148, 3.29, 4.133, 8.42, 11.187, 12.212, B 7.96; (*p.t. with pr. sense*) **myhte** should Pr 175, 2.118, 6.167, B 15.251; *p.t.* should 3.294, 4.107, 8.204, 11.267, 18.120, 21.368, B 13.6; would 11.50, 12.58, **B** 1.120 (1), 15.140; ?ought 17.101; (*neutral use* = do) 4.157, 8.204, 13.139, 16.146, 22.93; (*with implied inf.*) 3.423, 4.78, 10.136, 16.292, 17.317, 19.75, B 11.152, 16.137, 17.82, A 10.212; (*absolute uses*, = be capable of) 6.185, 15.96; *in phrr.* **may ...be (to)** can possibly 1.11; ~ **be so, so ~ be** possibly 5.34, 8.41, 17.151, B 16.202; ~...**wel** can easily / readily 3.312, 13.211, 14.126, 16.129, 20.224, 21.62, 162, 22.323, **B** 6.46, 12.38, 14.311, 15.263, 591, ~ **þe bet** might more easily Pr 163, 20.372; ~ **nat be** is impossible 14.29, **be ne** ~ could not exist 19.139, B 12.85, **if hit ben** ~ if it were possible 9.298

much(e)(l) *n* much, a great deal Pr 207, 1.19, 33, 3.181, 6.309, 11.213, 13.94, 15.199, 16.52, 272, 21.405, 22.133, **B** 5.456, 10.89, 14.74; size B 16.182; *in phrr.* **as ~ to mene** = signifying B 9.50, A 10.39, 11.296; **by so ~ to** that extent 7.141, B 3.353; **in as ~ as** to the extent that 19.203, B 7.15; **ouer** ~ too much 8.271

muche(l) *a* much, a great deal (of sth.) Pr 99, 3.486, 4.65, 170, 5.109, 7.86, 9.77, 206, 13.53, 96, 14.138,

15.4, 16.217, 17.74, 19.320, 21.68, 76, 22.158, **B** 5.254, 7.134, 8.84, 14.74, 15.448, **Z** 2.3, 8.89; many, ~ **peple (folk)** 7.273, 8.348, 17.299, 20.35, 22.98, 290, A 12.102, *a as n* = so many things B Pr 202; tall 10.68; large 21.368, B 15.89; great 6.323, 7.148, 9.84, 10.176, 11.72, 194, 12.205, 13.7, 161, 14.125, 16.10, 12, 327, 18.179, 277, 19.55, 20.43, 21.98, **B** 9.150, 10.123, 11.75, 12.295, 13.263, 14.157, 175, 15.120, 378, A 10.147; utter A 4.136

muche *av* much, greatly 14.67, 15.199, 16.106, 285, 18.23, 199, 19.41; (*with comp. a*) 16.101, (*with comp. av*) 7.98, **B** 11.79, 11.319, 13.383, Z 5.35; (*with inf.*) 18.221; utterly 19.328; frequently 11.53, B 10.66; *in phrr.* **as ~ worthe** worth as much 13.94; **to ~** B 16.148

mu(y)le *n* mule 19.49

muynde 6.284 = **mynde** *n*

muys *pl.* Pr 166, 213 *see* **mous** *n*

muk B 6.142 = **mok** *n*

mulere A 2.96, **mul(l)iere** B 2.119, 132, 16.219, 221 = **moilere** *a, n*

mullere *n* miller 2.113

mulleston *n* mill-stone 20.293

multiplien *v* multiply, *p.p.* B 6.326; cause to prosper / augment Z 3.120n; increase 8.132, 18.86; produce (off-spring) 18.225; populate B 16.211

#**mum** *n* 'mmm' [murmured or mumbled sound] Pr 164

munstracye 15.197, 16.310, **munstral** 3.275 *etc*; *see* **mynstra(l)cie** *n*, **mynstrel** *n*

muracle 9.113 *see* **myracle** *n*

murgust *sup.* Z 2.104; **mury(e)** 8.155, 9.41 *etc*, 13.216, **murie** B 2.154 *etc*, **murier** B 1.107, **murieste** 16.341 *see* **mury(e)**

mury(e), (mery(e)) *a* cheerful, in good spirits 2.167, 13.58, A 1.138, (*sup.*) 16.341; mirthful 9.136; glad, happy 9.41, 16.78, 21.294; festive 22.181; pleasant, agreeable 2.161, 167, 14.180, (*comp.*) B 1.107, (*sup.*) Z 2.104; cheering 14.128, B 13.58; bawdy 6.185 (B 13.352); ? lively, ? keen Pr 217; **maken ~** cheer up (sb.) 15.199, B 3.198, (*refl.*) enjoy (oneself) 8.68, 155, 15.65, 22.289; **~ mouthed** of cheerful speech 9.126; (*av*) pleasantly 13.216, 22.292; sweetly B Pr 10

murthe (merthe, myrthe) *n* joy 20.130; enjoyment 16.10, 12, B 15.143, **maken ~** enjoy (oneself) **B** 13.60, 15.139; pleasure 11.181, **B** 12.295, 14.124, 157; (spiritual) happiness 12.205, 17.147, 20.227, A 12.92; delightful sound 10.66; feasting B 10.52; entertainment Pr 35, 3.12, 7.77, **B** 3.220, 10.48, Z 7.49

murthen *v* cheer 19.207; afford pleasure to B 11.398

musel 3.168 *see* **mesel** *n*

musen *v* ponder, reflect upon 11.129, 13.227, 14.74, 15.25, *pr.p.* 9.296, B 10.116

musyk *n* (the art of) music 11.119, B 10.43, A 11.32

muson *n* measure 11.119

must *n* new wine 20.412

muste A 4.99, 8.23, 89 = **moste** *p.t.*

muster (mester) *n* craft, trade 3.110, 9.7

mute *a as n* dumb (people) B 16.111

na *av* (= **ne**) not 1.178 (1), (= **no**) 1.178 (2) no, (*with a as n*) ~ **mo** 3.1, B 2.235, (*with comp. a*) ~ **more** 1.178 (2), **B** 10.43, 12.279, (*with comp. a as n*) ~ **moore** B 3.344, 4.103, 5.284, 6.146, 13.352, 20.9, (*with comp. av*) ~ **moore** B 3.290, (4.97) 5.302, 12.100, 107, 16.217, (20.222)

nacion *n* (*sg. for pl.*) nations, groups (of people) 18.102

naȝt B 5.186 = **nauht** *av*

nay *interj.* no 3.220, 285, 4.4, 99, 6.240, 7.178, 200, 16.177, 19.7, 20.27, B 13.189, A 12.89, Z 4.132; *in phr.* **construen ~** judge in the negative / 'no' A 8.134

nayl *n* (finger)nail 6.140, **B** 3.191, 6.60; (metal) nail 20.51, 22.226

naylen *v* nail, ~ **vpon a rode** crucify 20.51

naked *a* naked 20.51, 22.196; scantily clad, destitute 13.83, **B** 6.15, 10.360 *in phr.* ~ **as a nedle** stark naked 14.105, 19.58

nale *n. phr.* **atte / at þe ~** = **atten / at þe ale** over the ale, at their drink(ing) B 6.115, A 10.59

nam 11.205 = **name** *n*

nam A 7.223, 225 *see* **mnam** *n*

nam *p.t.* B 5.456 *see* **nymen** *v*

nam Z 4.48 = **ne am**; *see* **be(n)** *v*

name *n* name 1.4, 59, 2.17, 3.3, 34, 52, 143, 10.70, 11.205, 12.177, 13.248, 15.195, 17.25, 19.26, 22.158, 256, 340, **B** 9.79, 10.152, 11.321, 13.140, 226, 290, 15.152, 16.19, 250, **A** 3.51, 12.82, **Z** 2.40, 3.148; title, appelation Pr 134, 12.116, 16.187, 194, 199, 201, 203, 205, 17.190, 261, 278, 18.192, 21.24, 69, 128, 276, B 15.26; name of God B 13.402, (Jesus / Christ) 7.217, 18.282, 21.18, 19, 21.70, **B** 15.456, 16.161, A 12.13, (Holy Ghost / grace) 18.196, 21.209, **the hey ~** the divine name 1.70; *in phrr.* **to ~** as title / name 12.213, by name 16.198; **kynde ~**, **ryhte ~** actual name 6.232, 10.69, 16.186; **propre ~** own / specific name B 16.185; **singuler ~** sole / single name B 16.208; reputation 6.26, B 5.258, **fals ~** reputation for dishonesty 3.114

nam(e)li(che) *av* especially, particularly 2.159, 6.96, 7.217, 8.51, 275, 9.335, 12.101, 16.80, 17.292, 20.442, 22.196, **B** 7.41, 10.204, 12.71

namoore (= **no more**) *n* nothing further B 3.173, 6.96; *av* no more B 17.221; any more **B** 7.117, 17.166

nappen *v* doze off 7.2

nar *pr. pl.* Z 3.35 = **ne ar**; *see* **be(n)** *v*

naroos *p.t.* B 19.52 = **ne aroos**; *see* **arysen** *v*

narwe *av* straitly, **pynchen ~** encroach closely B 13.371

nas *p.t.* B 19.295, 376, A 2.38, 39, 4.135, **Z** 3.127, †5.155 = **ne was**; *see* **be(n)** *v*

nat *av* not Pr 162 *et p.*, Z 3.155 *et p.*

nat Z 1.56, ? 8.74n = **nauht** *prn*

naught 16.288, 17.241, B 10.337 *etc* = **nauht**[1,3]

nauht[1] (noȝt) *prn* nothing Pr 115, 1.181, 7.123, 8.257, 11.30, 13.11, 16.288, 17.306, **B** 5.608, 7.84, 13.131, 303, A 7.209; *in phrr.* at ~ of no value 9.303; by ~ for nothing (= as far as) B 10.332; **bryngen to** ~ ruin 2.139, 3.200; **for** ~ however much 4.57, A 11.258; **ryht** ~ nothing at all 17.42, 19.154, **B** 6.151, 17.191

nauhte[2] *a* worthless 17.74

nauht (no(u)ȝt, nouht)[3] *av* not Pr 31, 77, 78, 100, 110, 115, 1.190, 2.18, 62, 3.74, 8.40, 257, 15.116, 16.292, 17.241, 18.221, **B** Pr 111, 10.37 *etc*; *in phr.* **ryht(e)** ~ not at all 5.82, 9.123, 14.87, 21.451, **B** 10.334

nautht 1.181 = **nauht** *prn*

nawher *av* nowhere 2.227, Z Pr 17

ne[1] *av* (*preverbal*) not Pr 80, 3.293, 366 *et p.*, **B** Pr 129 *et p.*; ~ **were** were it not for Pr 215, A 11.141; were not 11.49; (*in double / multiple neg. constr.*) **B** 12.224, 17.55; (*in contractions*) **nam, nar** (= ne am, ne ar) am / are not Z 4.48, 3.35; **nas** (= ne was) was not B 19.275, 295, A 2.38, 39, 4.135, †Z 5.155; **nelle** Pr 136 *etc* (= **ne wille**) do not wish to; **nere** (= ne were) were not 1.114, 3.171, 15.212, **B** Pr 200, 10.186, 11.104; **nis** (= ne is) is not 15.167, **B** 5.284, 13.166, 194, 208, 14.155, 243, 15.213, 17.346, **nyste** (= ne wiste) B 13.25; **nolde** (= ne wolde) Pr 110, 7.201, 9.23, **B** Pr 205, 11.64, 15.463, A 7.223, Z 3.165; **null** (= ne wille) 21.467

ne[2] *conj.* nor Pr 194 *et p.*, **B** 3.271 *et p.*; or 1.153, 178 *et p.*, **B** 3.73 *et p.*, A 2.38; and 3.17 *etc*, B 5.422, A 4.141; ~...~, neither...nor 14.200, B 12.208, Z 5.144; nor...or 10.187; either...or 15.102; ~ **neuere** and never 6.322; ~ **no**; **non(e)** nor any 1.153, 3.448, 9.113, 254, B 5.36, Z Pr 100; ~ **noþer** nor either, and neither 6.90, 8.304, 15.165; ~...**nother** nor 6.90, 10.187, nor...either 6.166; **noþer**...~ neither...nor 3.293 *etc*, A 3.58; (*emph. double neg.*) 1.178, 13.233 *etc*, Z 7.107

#necessarie *n* necessary thing, necessity (of life) 22.249

neddre *n* adder, viper (*fig.*) B 5.86

nede *n* need 11.30, **B** 7.76, 82, 15.336, (*person.*) 13.240, 22.4 *et p.*, 232; want 16.20; necessity 22.9, 10, Z 3.155; compelling reason 6.427, 7.216, 9.67; ? affliction 22.46; affair(s) 22.55; *in phrr.* **at** ~ when needed 1.52, 5.129, 7.42, **B** 1.18, 10.337, in (time of) need 8.126, 10.190, 11.307, 15.146, 16.315, 20.442, 22.20, **B** 3.245, 5.49, 15.178, 17.87, A 11.152; **for** ~ out of necessity 9.312, 315, 22.384; **hauen** ~ need, must 7.293, 9.63, 161, 18.85, 21.392, 22.319, Z 7.193; **moste** ~ (time of) greatest need 11.190, 15.5, 17.63

nede(s) *av* of necessity, necessarily 12.217, 20.442, 22.37, *in phr.* **mot(e)** ~(s) must needs 3.280, 11.234, 13.36, 19.87, 20.442

neden *v* be necessary 5.20, 9.163, 19.34, **B** 6.243, 11.209, 15.575; need 13.104, 16.345, 19.232, B 17.163; be in need 9.71, 12.118, 18.13; (*with obj.*) **hem / yow / hym nedeth (nedede)** they / you / he need(s) / needed 8.148,

219, 9.87, 11.48, 16.292, 17.18, 22.36, **B** 6.209, 8.86, 9.86, 10.200, 11.289, 14.33

nedfol (nidefole) *a* necessary 1.21; beneficial 21.20; in want 4.121, 19.239; *a as n* people in need 13.76

nedy *a* needy, in want 8.289, 9.47, 175, 11.28, 73, *et p.*, **B** 6.223, (*comp.*) ~**er** 7.69, (*sup.*) ~**este** 7.70, 11.242, 12.53, 14.134, 15.572; *a as n* the needy 9.64, 22.38, B 6.15

nedlare *n* needle-maker 6.364

nedle (nelde) *n* needle (for sewing) 1.152, 14.105, 19.58, B 1.157; **þat** ~ packing needle 6.218

neede 22.37 = **nedy** *a*

neen Z Pr 54 = **no(e)n(e)** *a*

neer *prep.* near B 6.298, 16.69

neet *n* ox 21.267

neghe-, neȝebore B 5.93, 131, 256, 258, 408, 13.364, 373, 16.42 = **neyh(e)bore** *n*

neiȝ(e)[1] *a* near B 5.93; near (in time) B 11.212; near, close(ly allied) **B** 12.93, 14.273

neiȝ[2] B 16.29 *see* **ny** *av*

neȝen B 6.298 = **n(e)yhen** *v*; **neghen** B 17.59, **neyghlen** Z 7.303, *see* **neyhlen** *v*

ney(h) *prep.* near (to) 8.297, 20.290, 22.4, 200

neyh(e)bore *n* neighbour 6.262, 269, 7.210, 8.289, 9.87, **B** 5.93, 256, 258, (*fig.*) 9.71; fellow-citizen 6.98, B 5.131, 408; fellow-Christian 15.114, 16.129, B 16.42

neyhelen *v* approach 19.60, Z 7.303

n(e)yhen (neyh / ner) *v* approach (close to) 8.322, 22.4, 232

neyther Pr 36, 6.166, 10.275, 14.176, B 3.315 *et p.*, **A** 3.58, 4.113 *see* **no(y)ther** *prn, conj.*

nekke *n* neck Pr 114, 178, 193, 16.80, **B** 10.282, 11.17, (skin of the) neck B 5.134

nelde 1.152, 6.218 = **nedle** *n*

nel(le), nile (= ne wille) Pr 136, 1.122, 6.311, 11.184, 22.29, **B** 4.191, 9.87, 10.331, A 7.262, Z 7.140; **neltow** (= ne wil(le) thow) B 6.156; *see* **willen** *v*

nem(p)n(i)en *v* mention (by name) 1.21, 22.261; speak aloud (the name) 21.18, 20; call, name 21.137, **B** 2.179, 7.154, 9.110, 11.321, A 11.107, *ger.* B 9.79, ~ **to name** give as a name 16.198; assign 22.256; nominate 6.387; offer 6.376

neodfole 4.121 = **nedfol** *a*

ner[1] *a* near, *contr. comp.* (= **nerre**) *in phr.* **neuere þe** ~ never any nearer (to) A 11.258

ner[2] *av* near 22.232; nearly, almost 8.175, 9.264, 18.179; (*comp.*) **nerre** nearer (to) 19.64

nere[1] *av* never 5.40, 15.235, B 14.119, **Z** 3.122, 4.130, 5.94, 7.68

nere[2] *p.t. subjv.* (= **ne were**) were not, did not exist 3.171, **B** 10.186, 11.104, A 5.242, Z 5.140; ~ **hit** were it not 1.114, 15.212

nerhande *av* almost 15.1

nerre *comp.* 19.64 *see* **ner**[2] *av*

nese *n* niece, kinswoman (*fig.*) 5.176

nest *n* nest 13.156, 159, 160

neste *p.t.* (= **ne wiste**) 13.219; *see* **witen** *v*[1]

neuer(e) *av* never Pr 202 *et p.*; *as emph. neg.*) certainly not, not at all Pr 209, 2.144, 3.342, 4.136, 10.6, 11.202, 241, 14.59, 15.285, 16.275, 17.35, 18.204, 19.275, 20.99, 147, 194, **B** Pr 12, 10.222; *with* **recchen** care not at all 3.387 *etc, with* **witen** not know at all 3.296, 6.343; *in phrr*: ~ **eft** never again 3.475; ~ **more** no longer 3.320; never again †15.273, 17.147, ever again 3.442; at no time 12.38, 16.78; ~ **so** however 3.422, 10.36, 16.168, 20.429, 22.260; ~ **þe betere** no better 4.89; ~ **þe ner** no nearer A 11.258

newe *a* new 19.74, 21.429, *a as n* new one 21.274; fresh(ly reaped) 8.322; renewed 13.19; hitherto unknown B 20.256; modern B 15.372; *in phrr.* ~ **fayre** = barter 6.376 *n*; ~ **lawe** Law of the New Covenant 18.265, 19.34, 20.268, 21.312

newe *av* again, anew 5.179, 6.328, 18.161, 20.42, *in phr.* **al** ~ entirely anew B 2.164

nex(s)t *a* next [immediately following] B 13.155; closest 6.269, 7.210; *av* next (time) A 7.155; *prep.* (spiritually) closest (to) 18.98, 19.270, 22.35, B 1.204

ny *av* almost, nearly 3.181, 185, B 16.29

nidefole 1.21 = **nedfol** *a*

nygard *n* miser 19.239, B 15.140

nigromancie *n* necromancy A 11.16

nyhed *p.t.* 8.322 *see* **n(e)yhen** *v*

nyht *n* night 18.179, 20.62, 214; *in phrr*: **a / on** ~ **/** ~**es** at night 9.78, 19.174, 22.196, **by** ~**(es)** by night 4.47, B Pr 197; **forboden** ~**es** penitential nights before feast-days B 13.349; **on** ~**es tyme** at night-time 16.141; **seuen** ~ **week** 7.300; **wynteres** ~**es** winter nights 19.185; ~ **comare nocturnal thief 21.144; ~ **olde** last night's 8.331; **(by) day and / ne (by)** ~ 1.32, 13.190, 17.29, 92, 171, 245, 19.218, 21.141, **B** 9.97, 18.97, **(by)** ~ **and / ne (by) daye** 19.270, 21.20, B 13.369 = at all / any time(s)

nyhtes *av* at night 5.16, *in phrr.* **a**-~ 19.174, 22.196; **o(n)** ~ 9.78, B 14.2; *av. phr.* **(by) dayes and (by)** ~ at all times 9.222, 11.192, A 12.81

niyed *p.t.* 2.19 *see* **n(o)ien** *v*

nymen *v* (*p.t. 1 sg.* **nam** B 5.456, **noem** Z 5.98, *2 sg.* **nome** 22.9, *3 sg. subjv.* **nyme** 3.391, *3 pl.* **nomen** A 4.63, *p.p.* **ynome** 22.46, B 11.212) take 2.139, 3.391, 8.40, 16.92, 22.20, **B** 5.456, 10.60, A 4.63; carry off B 11.212; pick 18.85; pick (up) 13.240; seize 22.46; misappropriate 6.269; receive 13.104, Z 3.155, ~ **vnder maynprise** agree to stand surety for 22.17; take (heed) 9.71, 11.247, 17.108, **B** 6.15, 11.321, Z 5.98; (*refl.*) betake (oneself) 3.402

nyne *card. num.* nine 19.60, B 1.121, ~ **hundred** B 5.371

nynthe *ord. num.* ninth B 14.313

***nype** *n* ? extremity, ? biting cold 20.166c

nyppen *v* bite, *pr. p.* 6.104

nis, nys = **ne is** *3 sg. pr.* 15.167, **B** 5.284, 13.166, 194, 208, 14.155, 243, 15.213, 17.346 **A** 3.50, 5.221; *see* **be(n)** *v*

nise *a* lascivious 18.37

nysot *n* (? *as a*) fool(ish) Z 2.99c

nyste *p.t.* (= **ne wiste**) B 13.25; *see* **witen** *v*[1]

nythe *ord. num.* ninth 16.148

nythynge *n* miserly wretch 19.239

niuilen *v* snivel, run at the nose, *pr.p.* 6.104

no[1] *a* no Pr 32 *et p.*; not any 8.244, 9.318, 10.119, 11.265 *etc*; (*in double neg. constr. after / before* **nat**, **ne**, **neuere**) 3.17, 87, 209, 213, 4.108 *etc*: **nat...no** not...any 4.108; **ne no** nor any 3.293, 448, 4.57, 190, 6.282, 427, 7.95, 8.308, 326, 332 *etc*; **ne...no** nor...any 5.58, 8.275; **no...no** no...any 5.54; *see also* **no(e)ne** *a*

no[2] *av* no 1.8, 122 *et p.*; = **ne** 6.166

noble *n* noble [English gold coin worth £1/3] 3.47, 391, 6.245, 10.272, 285, 17.200, 207, 22.132, **B** 10.289, 12.247, 15.86

noble *a* noble, illustrious 21.50

nobody *n* no one 3.306, 18.115

noem *p.t.* Z 5.98 *see* **nymen** *v*

no(e)n(e), noon[1] *n* noon, midday 2.100, 6.433, A 7.135; (the) midday meal 6.428, 8.146, 196, 275, 9.87, 22.4, **maken** ~ dine 8.289

no(e)n(e), noon[2] *prn* no one 4.124, 6.37, 49, 10.112, 11.44, 17.108, 21.255, B 11.214 *et p.*; no creature 13.187; not one 2.159, 7.275, 8.340, 11.63, 244, 20.475; none 1.21, 186, 2.10, 11, 3.62, 11.294, 296, 12.166, 13.145, 16.42, 247, 18.55, 21.20, 36, **B** 2.146, 167, 12.31, 16.57, A 11.231, 291; *in phr.* **here** ~ none of them A 7.300, neither of them 14.105, 16.80; *in double neg. constr.* **ne** ~ nor any 16.60, **ne neuere** ~ nor ever any 22.50

no(e)n(e), noon *a* no Pr 192, 1.128, 153, 2.10, 3.433, 6.49, 127, 412, 7.67, 72, 93, 157, 195, 8.50, 10.116, 13.24, 62, 14.51, 15.114, 18.141, †22.13, B 1.120 *et p.*, (*in double neg. constr.*) **ne** ~ nor any 1.153, 3.203, 13.44, 18.141, 19.328, B 13.162 *etc*, **ne...non** 9.109; *in phr.* ~ **oþer** no other(s), no one else 10.116, 19.197, B 17.163; nothing else 6.298, 7.289, 9.173, 290, 13.210, 19.251; anything else B 1.88, 5.101, 295, 7.45, B 17.163; no otherwise B 6.180, Z Pr 54

noȝt Pr 31, 2.39, 8.331, B Pr 29 *et p.*, **noght** Pr 110, 115, 138, B 17.312 = **nauht** *av*

noy *n* distress, suffering B 10.60, †11.430n

n(o)ien *v* (do) harm (to), injure 2.19, 3.433, B 2.127, Z 2.99; distress 7.220; trouble B 3.189

noyse *n* outcry 18.110; commotion 18.179

no(y)ther *prn* neither, *in phr.* **her(e)** ~ neither of them 3.365, 10.275, B 4.33; *with double neg. constr.* **neuere...** ~ in no way is either 13.127

no(y)ther (**neyther** Pr 36 *etc*, B 5.397 *etc*, A 3.58) *conj.* neither, *in constr.* ~ **(...) ne** neither...nor 1.99, 175 *et p*,

B 11.283, A 3.58; (n)or 10.188, 16.290; *in emph. double neg. constr.* **ne...noyther(e)** nor...(either) 10.117, 187, 11.46, 14.176, 15.114; **ne** ~ (and) neither, nor either 6.90, 8.304

noke, þe A 5.115 = **þe oke**

nolde (= **ne** + **wolde**) *vp.t.* Pr 110 *etc*; *see* **willen** *v*

nombre (**noumbre**) *n* number 21.241, 22.270, 272, **certeyne** ~ fixed, definite number 22.255, 265; *in phr.* **out of** ~ to excess, beyond counting 13.6, 22.269; large number 3.391; company 3.402; order(ed list) 22.259, 261; (grammatical) number 3.336, 346, 357, 364, 371, 394, B 10.239

nombren *v* count B 1.116; fix the number of 22.256

nome(n) *p.t.* 22.9, A 4.63 *see* **nymen** *v*

non *prn* 1.21 *etc*, *a* 1.128 *etc*, **none** *prn* 1.186 *etc*, *a* 3.85 *etc*; *see* **no(e)n(e)** *prn, a*

nones *n*[1] *pl.* 6.428, 8.146, 196 *see* **no(e)n(e)** *n*

nones *n*[2], *in phr.* **for þe** ~ for the time being, occasion, ? suitably A 2.41

nonne *n* nun B 7.29, **to** ~ who is a nun 6.128

noon(e) 2.100, 8.275 = **no(e)n(e)** *n*

noon *prn* 2.159 *etc*, *a* 3.203 *etc*; *see* **no(e)n(e)** *prn, a*

noot *pr. sg.* (= **ne woot**) B 11.212; *see* **witen** *v*

nor *conj.* nor B 10.60

noris(ch)en *v* suckle B 15.466; sustain, support †B 6.223n; foster 12.236, 18.37

north *n* north 1.117, 20.166, *a*, ~ **half** north side 18.66

northerne *a* living in the north (of Britain) 1.114

nose *n* nose 6.104, Z 5.98, *sg. for pl.* 6.400; *in phr.* **han pepir in þe** ~ treat with disdain B 15.203; (*assev.*) **kut of my** ~ 4.159

noskines *a* no kind of Z 7.108

not *av* not 12.193, 13.9, 20.315, 21.117, A Pr 29 *et p.*

notarie *a* (*uninfl. gen* 22.272) notary [scribe authorised to draw up and authenticate documents and legal instruments] 2.139, 156, 159, 185, 22.272, B 2.167, Z 2.99, (*fig.*) 16.190

note *n* song 10.65, 14.180, 20.452; melody 20.469; point, degree 1.117

nother 1.99 *et p.*; *see* **no(y)ther** *conj.*

nothyng *n* nothing 3.328

nou3t *prn* Pr 211, *av* Pr 77, 78, 100, 211, 1.190, 2.62, 3.74, B 1.36 *et p.*, A Pr 87 *et p.*, **nou(g)ht(e)** *prn* 4.57, *av* 2.18, 14.87, 15.116 *see* **nauht** *prn, av*

nou3ty *a* destitute B 6.223

noumbre 3.391, 394, 402 = **nombre** *n*

noumper *n* umpire 6.387

nouthe *av* at the present (time) 2.15, 8.212, 9.163, 13.174, 17.107, 108, 21.181, B 3.290, 10.48; in a while 21.384; now 6.171, 19.277; then (*non-temporal*) 8.299, 19.244, B 13.184

now[1] *n* now, the present time 7.180

now[2] *a* of the present time 17.69

now[3] *conj* now that 8.92, 15.99, B 5.142

now[4] *av* now, at (the) present (time), 3.382 *et p.*, Z 3.156; (*in historic pr.*) now, then 3.1, 6.349, 8.112, 21.337, B 5.133; (*in antithetical phrr.*) ~...~ at one time...at another 5.51; *as emph. part.* (*in exhortations and commands*) 6.164, 8.222, 9.240 *etc*, (*in assevs.*) 2.117, 126, B 10.132, (*in oaths*) 2.204 *etc*, (*in prayers*) 6.195, 22.385; (*as phrasal intensifier*) ~ **certes** 18.16; (*introducing clause*) 18.227, B 2.50, 7.174, (*non-temporal*) then 8.223, B 6.276, 16.67, 17.138

nowadayes *av* nowadays, at the present time 11.61, A 11.37

#**nownpower** *n* powerlessness 19.294

nowthe 21.181 = **nouthe** *av*

nuyen 3.433, 7.220, Z 2.99 *see* **n(o)ien** *v*

null (nel) = **ne wille** 21.467; *see* **willen** *v*

o[1] *num* one B 13.68, 17.37, 40, 139, 18.42, A 8.93, 9.91; = first B 19.86; (only) one, a single 3.441, 473, 7.238, 12.111, 13.33, 51, 17.126, 18.21, 28, 57, 188, 189, 234, 237, 19.38, 109, 20.418, 22.245, B 2.30, 3.238, 9.145, 15.316, 16.58, A 2.69; ~ **kynde** 3.397, 18.57, 59, 62, 70; ~ **man** 18.237, B 9.112, 16.204; ~ **wille** 15.277, 16.179, 17.128; ~ **wit** 20.242, ~ **wit and wil** 5.185, 18.28, 190; *in phr.* ~...**the** / (**an**)**other** one...the / (an)other 6.38, A 8.14; one [of God] 11.154, 17.134, 18.211, 216, 238, 240, 19.31, 150, B 16.224, 17.128, 130, 182; one (Lord) 17.135, 18.198, 19.42, 44, 100, 109, one (**Lede**) †B 15.393; one and the same 18.20, 21, 28, B 11.195, 16.59; *see also* **a**[1] *num.*

o[2] *prep.* (up)on 20.44; in 2.55, 15.19, 18.198; by 6.52; *in avl phrr.* ~ **lyue** alive A 2.14; ~ **nyghtes** at night B 14.2; *and see* **a**[2] *prep.*

obedience *n* (obligation of) obedience [to law / authority / commandments of the Church] 9.220, 235, 241; religious (vow of) obedience 9.222, B 12.37, 13.286

obediencer *n* obedientiary [holder of subordinate office in monastery] 5.91

obedient *a* subject, obedient (to rule) 5.147; willing to serve A 11.191

oc(c)u(e)pien *v* be busy (with) 7.18; (*refl.*) be active 18.206

oelde 11.290, 20.7, 21.274 = **olde** *a*

oen (**o(o)n**) *prn* someone 5.10, 7.291, 298, 10.125, 11.188, 12.76, 20.8, 22.158, B 11.319, 15.13, A 12.62; **such** ~ someone like that 16.106, 22.344; man 10.101, 104; one (person) 19.129, 21.270, B 16.183; anyone 16.140; **bond** ~ person of servile status 10.266; **souerayn** ~ person of importance 6.27; member 9.211; one [of a class] 12.54, 16.210, B 1.107; the one 13.35; [numbered set] 7.271, B 1.23, 15.374; one of the two 6.384; **that** ~ one 19.301, 21.264, B 3.232; that one 16.140; the one 14.153, B 8.96, A 12.84; **that** ~...**that oþer** the one...the other 14.106, 107; (*with partitive gen.*) **here** ~ the one of them 20.67; *in phrr.* **myn one**

alone 11.200, by myself 10.61; **by here** ~ on her own, while alone 20.316; **by his** ~ by himself B 16.183

o(e)n (oon) *num.* one 14.116, 18.220; (only) one, a single 10.192, 19.38, 152, **B** 3.289, 318, 321, 4.37, 11.168, 13.211, 14.1, 16.181, A 8.179; one particular 14.153; at one, united 6.181, **of** ~ **wille** in singleness / integrity of heart B 3.238; *in phrr. (esp. after* **but, except, saue**) alone, only 3.142, 5.52, 13.112, 15.213, 16.213, 372, 17.8, 21.122, 191, 301, 371, 376, B 9.36, 13.125, 14.330, 15.210, **in hymself** ~ solely in himself 1.167, **to hymself** ~ to his own self / himself alone B 9.33; one and the same 21.402, **B** 15.394, 395, 605, 16.182; a certain (person) / someone called 2.25, 42, 4.27, 16.318, 18.126, 21.202, 266, 342, 22.160, 162, 316, **B** 13.124, 15.396; *see also* **o**[1] *num.,* **a**[1] *num.*

oenliche 22.267 = **onli(che)** *av*

oest(e) 21.338, 22.113 = **oste** *n*

of[1] *av* off, *in phrasal vv.* **casten** ~ 6.375, **gurden** ~ 2.213, **kutten** ~ 4.159, **potten** ~ 16.121, B 14.191 *etc*

of[2] *prep. (sel. exx.)* out of 1.20, 2.192, 3.314, 6.344, 17.220, 19.250, 20.21, 405, 21.32(1), 110, 325, **B** 3.297, 11.209; from (out of) Pr 164, 230, 12.110, 232, 14.45, 18.216, 230, 19.329, 20.431n, 21.146, **B** 5.3, 12.85, 13.261, 15.337; from among 3.246, 9.172, **B** 3.245, 12.19, 158; (proceeding) from Pr 98, 2.134, 6.255, **B** Pr 128, 5.86, **B** 9.46, 110, 10.238, 13.226, 15.107; (born) from 2.30, 5.64; from Pr 69 (1, 3), 214, 6.161, 305, 13.73, 15.290, 16.70, 17.36, 300, 18.184, 19.66, 171, 250, 20.55, 21.25, 463, 22.221, 266, **B** 10.326, 12.67, 14.194, 15.472, 17.108, 18.84; of (= belonging to) Pr 10, 105, 116, 168, 2.61 *et p.,* **B** 4.193, 5.235, 10.190, 229 *et p.*; inherent in 14.213; made of Pr 159, 6.65, 7.232, 8.292, 18.92, **B** 2.15, 5.80, 14.192; (consisting) of Pr 20 (1), 6.369, 14.38, 18.288, **B** 5.87, 7.120, (=*objective gen.*) Pr 59, 1.200, 2.109, 6.176, 14.107, **B** 1.27, 11.110 *etc*; *in phrr*: **in deseyte** ~ to deceive Pr 77; **for loue** ~ Pr 28, 103; **in menynge** ~ signifying Pr 99; *with phrasal vv.* **acounten** ~ 8.159, 103; **amenden** ~ 7.121, 16.261; **borwen** ~ 4.56; **cessen** ~ B 7.118; **douten** ~ 16.230; **dreden** ~ 16.311; **faylen** ~ 18.30; **leten** ~ 4.156; **parceyuen** ~ Pr 128; **recchen** ~ 3.387; **sen** ~ 19.59; **witen** ~ 20.220; (= *partitive gen.*) 2.7 (2, 3), (*with numbers*) 7.154, 164, 12.160, (some) of 6.269 (2), 296, 8.92, 273, 285, 16.356, 20.47, 22.170 (2), **B** 10.30, 13.52 *etc*; (any) of 13.233, 15.46; (possessed) of, having 2.7 (1), 145, 3.214, 5.56, 6.203, 9.195, 11.268, 16.81, 18.28, 190, 19.149, 20.418, 21.361, **B** 3.238, 10.472, 11.199, 14.125, 300; *in phrr*: (= *descriptive gen.*) ~ **more** further 8.35; ~ **pouer** able 8.283, **as** ~ from among 3.62, 18.99, B 2.58; **conqueror** ~ **Cristene** Christian(s') conqueror 21.14; **deth** ~ **kynde** death in the course of nature 20.219; **drede** ~ **disper(acion)** despairing fear 19.291, 22.164; **lecherye** ~ **clothing** luxurious dress 16.254; **loue** ~ **charite** charitable love

16.283; **shrift** ~ **mouþe** oral confession B 14.88; **tale** ~ **nauht** worthless title 13.113; **tokenynge** ~ **drede** fearful portent 5.121; **vers** ~ **Latyn** Latin verse B Pr 143; **renable** ~ **tonge** eloquent B Pr 158; because / on account of 1.20, 19.294 (1), 20.220; for 3.22, 5.196, 6.16, 319, 369, 420, 7.245, 8.58, 133, 269, 9.255, 269, 11.124, 16.73, 127, 325, 20.92, 21.131, 22.170 (1), 287, **B** 5.125, 325, 10.122, 323, 14.169; through 7.250, 9.55, 11.145, 13.92, 110, 16.23, 17.267, 18.135, 20.21, 189, 299, 21.30, 254, B Pr 118; at the hands of 18.166, **B** 11.282; by 2.226, 9.168, 10.311, 12.196, 16.16, 106, 17.49, 18.170, 224, 21.48, 121, **B** 2.119, 3.275, 9.100, 13.94, 14.9, 15.456; with 4.13, 8.210, 9.178, 10.84, 87, 11.57, 15.44, 16.255, 19.233, **B** 1.18, 5.191, 256, 9.86 (2), 87, 11.211, 13.355; by means of 12.111, 14.30, 20.32(2), 216, **B** 10.342, 11.198; in accordance with 20.431; between 15.174; concerning, about Pr 12, 39, 171, 209, 1.45, 2.15, 3.69, 5.5, 6.117, 10.246, 14.192, 15.104, 16.240, 20.46, 125, 21.80, 241, 22.32, **B** 5.10, 7.85, 9.74, 15.384, 16.55; as for Pr 134; at 6.286, 11.56, 166, 13.172, 15.201, 18.270, 22.242, B Pr 204 *et p.*; (up)on 8.158, 331, 20.432, 434, 22.300, **B** 5.254, 15.82, 262; towards 11.56; in respect of Pr 3, 92, 1.98, 3.157, 4.17, 7.143, 8.219, 10.157, 11.99, 13.192, 231, 14.171, 15.257, 16.159, 21.24, 22.163, **B** 1.195, 7.98, 9.150, 10.384, 12.91, 14.77, Z 1.58; in relation to **B** 10.112, 429, 14.195, 328, 15.362; in 4.173, 12.100, **B** 1.153, 14.283

offecer 4.195 = **officer** *n*

offenden *v* sin against 19.264

office *n* official position B 3.100; (high) ecclesiastical office A 11.195; employment, **putten in** ~ set to work A 7.184; *pl.* duties Z Pr 54; (church) services (*esp.* mass) B 15.385

officer *n* (high) official 4.195; military retainer 22.258

official *n* bishop's officer [*esp.* his representative presiding in the consistory court] 22.137, B 2.174, (*n as a*) Z 2.148

offren *v* present as a gift 21.75, 83, 87, 94; make (as) an offering B 13.198, †A 4.61; *ger.* **offrynge** offering (at mass) 21.4; offering (of money to the Church) 6.300, 17.43

ofgon *v* obtain B 9.107

ofrechen *v* (*p.t.* **ofrauȝte**) reach to B 18.9

ofsenden *v* send for B 3.102, *p.p.* A 2.35

ofte(n) *av* (*comp.* **ofter** 6.274, 20.422, B 11.50) repeatedly, again and again 2.185, 242, 5.94, 6.274, 7.62, 11.52, 13.242, 14.112, 16.332, 18.271, 21.372, **B** 5.97, 10.327, 11.50, 12.10, A 10.104, 12.22; often, frequently 2.241, 3.173, 6.123, 9.302, 13.187, 15.76, 16.91, 367, **B** 3.82, 154, 190, 4.70, 156, 169, 5.93, 7.149, 11.52, 231, 13.72, 405, 15.235, 303, 362, A 7.138, 242, Z 7.245; many times 6.425, 9.246, 18.152, 20.141, 21.392, B 4.99, 13.261; time and again 3.90, 133, 200;

in phrr. **fol** ~ (**ryght** ~ Z 3.90, **swiþe** ~ B 13.403, **wel** ~ 22.25, A 5.75, 12.106) very often / many times 2.19, 10.3, 12.239, 14.4, 16.362, 17.300, 20.422, 22.119, **B** 14.326, 16.112, 17.20, Z 7.275; **fele** (**mony**) **tyme**(**s**) **and** ~ many a time and oft 6.118, 12.241, 18.61, 22.26, B 11.370

oftetymes *av* frequently B 15.72

*ofwandrit *p.p., in phr.* **wery** ~ worn out with wandering A Pr 7 (†B Pr 7); **for werynesse** ~ worn out with fatigue from wandering †Pr 7

oyle *n* oil 19.71

oke[1] *n* oak(-tree) 5.120, A 5.115 (**noke**) Z 5.45

oke[2] *p.t. subjv.* 19.160 *see* **aken** *v*

o(e)ld(e) *a* old, aged 6.189, B 9.163; older 20.7; *in phrr*: ~ **age** 18.246, ~ **elde** B 12.8 old age; ~ **and hoor** old and grey(-haired) 6.193, 8.92, 9.175; *a as n* 10.308; long-standing B 6.131; ancient 17.232; *in phr.* ~ **the lawe** the Law of the Old Covenant 12.114, 14.58, 17.71, 18.222, 20.381, 387, 21.312, 449, **B** 12.73, 13.186, 18.343; belonging to antiquity 9.214, 20.15, *a as n* 21.274; **þe** ~ the early Father 11.148, 290, A 11.72, the old patriarch 19.109; earlier, former 6.188, 21.429, B 12.235, *in phr.* **nyhte** ~ last night's 8.331

olofte B Pr 157, 1.90, 5.353 = **alofte** *av*

on[1] *av* (with phrasal *vv*) on, upon 8.180, Z 2.41; near B 7.56; at B 13.295, 302; *in phr.* **taken** ~ behave, act 3.84, 13.154

on[2] *prep.* on Pr 6, 49, 106, 121 *et p.*, ? 5.116 (*or* one), B Pr 14 *et p.*; down on 3.95; upon Pr 123, 1.162, 2.137, 201, 209, 6.267, 11.144, 13.173, 15.148, 18.23, 19.72, 192, 21.203, 288, 22.127, **B** 3.260, 5.131, 11.246, 12.4, 204, A 2.80; over B 17.225; in (*place*) 2.216, 3.419, 12.186, 13.159, 15.269, **B** 9.166, 15.298, 16.255; (*dress, manner*) 5.51, 10.117, 12.208, 17.170, 19.14, 21.356, **B** 5.278, 571, 7.106, 13.74, 15.207, **A** 4.129, 12.13 (2), Z 2.166; (*thing*) **B** 1.70, 5.234; (*person*) **B** 1.149, 4.122, 5.42; (*time*) within 20.41; *in phrr*: ~ **þe / a daye** daily 10.31, B 15.283; ~ **a hep** in a crowd Pr 51; ~ **heiȝ** up above B Pr 128, Z Pr 99, aloud A 12.27; ~ (**þis**) **erthe / folde / grounde / molde** in this world Pr 65, 3.94, 9.153, 10.160, *etc*, **B** 2.187, 3.80, 4.26, 9.83, Z 2.18, 104; in this life 3.100, **B** 5.260, 8.38; (**bi**)**leuen** ~ believe in 1.75, 2.105 *etc*, **B** 10.235, 15.395 *etc*; about 2.20, 236, 6.120, **B** 5.94, 10.39, 42, 200, 11.117, 14.144; at 4.148, 6.148, 7.57, 301, 9.78, 10.262, 12.23, 13.236, 15.148, 16.141, 20.19, 425, 448, **B** Pr 9, 3.345, 7.137, 8.96, 10.61, 310, 11.84, 186, 317, 408, 13.86, 16.22, 128, 18.21, 39, A 8.14, Z 1.100; against 3.250, 4.31, 6.111, 12.137, 20.399, 22.175; to 17.128, 19.313, 22.78, B 5.71, 11.70, 15.83, **don...**~ appeal to **B** 1.86, 3.188, **A** 4.60, 12.13 (1); towards 11.163, B 10.136; with 8.10, 13.175, 20.337; by B 9.121; through 10.290; *in phrr.* ~ **cros-wyse** by crucifixion 21.142; ~ **the hey name** by the divine name 1.70; **lernen** ~ **boke** educate

B 7.132; by way of 22.135; in regard to B 15.128; for the sake of 19.235; *in conj. phr.* ~ **auenture** lest, in case **B** 3.72, 13.72

one *a* 1.167 *et p.*, *prn* 10.61 *et p. see* **o(e)n, o(o)n** *num.*, *prn*

onelich(e) 16.153, 22.61 = **onli(che)** *av*

ones *av* once, on one occasion (only) 2.237, 3.181, 6.174, 235, 15.132, 21.391, **B** 3.338, 5.601, 15.8; ever, at all Pr 162, 13.9, 14.145, 20.150, 420, B 4.86; at one time (in the past) 8.76, 16.353, 22.344, **B** 10.454, 11.66, 13.139, 16.178; *as n in phr.* **at** ~ at one and the same time (together) 11.252, 13.31, 141, 18.154, 263, 19.53, 21.94, 434, **B** Pr 146, 5.161, 376, 509, 15.484, A 12.71

onli(che) *av* only, solely 10.234, 12.29, 81, 16.153, 17.32, 21.117, 22.61, 267

onswerien *v* be answerable 6.346

oo B 2.30 = **o**[1] *num.*

ooen 4.27, **oon** 2.25, 42 = **o(e)n** *num.*, **oon(e)** B 1.23 *et p.*: *see* **oen** *prn*, **o(e)n** *num.*

oones B 15.484 = **ones** *av*

ope 12.232 *see* **vp(p)on** *prep*

opelond *av* out in the country 5.44

open *a* open 20.365

openen *v* open 2.132, 7.248, 20.258, B Pr 106

or[1] *av* first 21.397

or[2] *prep* before 11.259, 17.61

or[3] *conj.* (*a*) or Pr 186 *et p.*; or (else) 8.142, 9.63, 278, 13.106, 21.11, **B** 3.251; nor 16.123; **or...or** either... or 6.125-6, 9.169, 15.205, 16.58, **B** 6.247, 14.14, ? A 7.211; whether..or B 14.58; *in phr.* ~ **ellys** or else 1.49, 3.94, 251, 298, 7.2, 75, 17.16, 19.261, 21.464, **B** 5.149, 10.376, 433, 20.228; or anything else **B** 11.215, 16.143; ~ **any...elles** or any other 6.262

or[4] (**ar**) *conj.* (*b*) before Pr 164, 1.70, 6.277 (2), 8.345, 17.282 (1), 21.226, 22.228, ~ **þat** 21.395

ordeynen *v* build, construct 21.320, 322; set, apply B 10.244; devise B 10.216; decree 5.55, 10.221; foreordain 3.240; establish 17.16, B Pr 119; arrange B 8.99; allot A 12.90

ordre *n* ordination (as priest), holy orders 13.103; order (of knighthood) **B** 1.104, 6.166; manner of life 1.97; (religious) order 8.73, 9.211, 17.16, 22.265, B 13.285, **Austynes** ~ the order of Augustinian friars B 15.289, (**þe**) **foure / fyue** ~**s** (the) four / five orders (of mendicant friars) Pr 56, 8.191, 9.343; (house of) a religious order 3.54, 67

orgene *n* organ, **by** ~ to the organ 20.7n, c

*oriental *n* oriental, [kind of] sapphire B 2.14

oryson *n* prayer 18.159

oste *n* army 3.251, 418; crowd of armed men 21.338, 22.113

ote *n* oat, *pl.* 4.61, 8.305; ~ **cake** oat(en) cake A 7.179

oth *n* oath B 13.383, (in law court) 2.150; curse, swearing 6.384, 7.37, 22.225, A 8.40; **bold** ~ profane oath

6.34 (B13.281); **gret** ~ violent profanity Pr 36, 6.360, **B** 2.70, 10.50, 13.400

other (oþer)[1] *prn* (*pl.* **oþer** 1.108, **othere** 4.133) second, other 11.175, 14.107, 154, B 3.341, **A** 1.24, 8.14, 12.85 (= either of two); each other 19.98; *in phrr*: **ayþer...~** either...the other 6.149, 16.65, 20.125; **here ayþer** ~ both the others 20.174, each one the other 22.354; **ayther...~es** either...the other's 3.337, 16.179, (each of) the others' B 16.207; **either** ~ one another 6.188, 10.284, B 7.139, A 10.179; **here oen...her** ~ either of them... the other of them 20.67; **here neyther / noen...othere** neither of them...the other 10.275, 14.105; **som** ~ something else / other than 20.216; **vch (on)...~** each (one)...the other 6.122, 12.106, 107, 131, 14.68, 20.338, 21.397, 419; **vch (man)** ~ each (man) the other B 12.125; (an)other 9.89, 11.63, B 10.469; *in phr.* **day aftur** ~ one day after another 10.114; any other 13.145; **noon** ~ no other 10.116; **noen...~** none... any other(s) 21.255; others 3.150, 496, 4.133, 6.20, 22, 11.121, 15.127, 16.302, 305, 17.12, 21.234, 267, 22.6, B 5.314, A 12.108, Z 7.266; others' 9.152; the others 18.188, 20.447, 463, 21.251, *in phrr*: **alle** ~ all others 22.262, all other things 22.208; **alle þe** ~ all other creatures B 12.255; suchlike B 7.101; **many ~, ~ many** many others 22.335, 378, B 7.123; ~ **mo** others besides 2.113, 4.10, 20.180, 21.54, B 10.176; **this** ~ these others 2.192, 8.93

other (oþer)[2] *a* other Pr 93, 2.58, 91, 3.97, 5.20, 6.42, 138, 8.116, 190, 321, 9.84, 105, 234, 10.168, 12.184, 13.37, 14.32, 136, 15.55, 256, 16.238, 17.34, **B** 5.282, 528, 12.118, 15.244; any other 1.9, 6.265; *a as n* other (days) 7.18, other (people) 16.193; another kind of B 10.191; **al** ~ every other (kind of) B 16.11; **non** ~ of no different kind 6.127

other[3] *av* otherwise 1.117, 5.189; **non** ~ not otherwise, nothing else 6.298, 7.289, 9.173, 290, 13.210, 16.275, 19.251, 20.171, 351, B 1.88, Z Pr 54

other(e), (o(o)þer)[4] *conj.* or Pr 183, 186, 2.48, 81, 3.96, 110, 113, 5.81, 6.42 (1), 74, 220, 9.150, 12.66, 14.123, 17.312, 20.10, 424, **B** 5.53, †6.219, 9.106, 10.265, 12.223, 13.230, 15.431, 16.133, 17.217, **A** 4.116, 10.65, 75, 108; ~...**or** either...or 13.47, 15.300, B 13.230, A 7.232; *in phrr*. ~ **elles** or otherwise 1.172, A 11.260, or of some other kind 3.291; **more ~ lasse, lasse ~ more** more or less, less or more 2.48, 3.289, 9.108

oþergatus *av* in a different way 10.298

oþerwhile(s) *av* sometimes 7.19, 193, 10.29, 16.365; occasionally 16.291, 17.9; at times 21.302, B 12.23; at one time or another 5.50; at various times 18.42, B 5.404; from time to time 10.163, 17.3, A 7.239; at other times 6.160, 21.103; at another time 16.322

oþer(e)wyse *av* in a / some other / different way than 5.81, 12.230, 19.142, (*emphatic*) ~ **ne elles** otherwise 10.106; contrarily / in opposition to what 3.427, 7.211

ouet 11.126 = **oute** *av*

ouht (ouȝt) 7.35, 45, B 11.49, 13.300 = **auht** *prn,* A 8.61 = **auht** *av*

oughtest 1.72, **ouhte(n)** 2.30, 3.72, 108, 5.69, 6.86, 7.98, 9.229, 12.91, 19.318, 22.276 *see* **owen** *v*

oune *a* Pr 124, 10.177, 12.99, 16.134, 17.81, 18.14, 166, 19.300, **Z** 6.38, 7.65 = **owen(e)** *a*

oure *n* hour B14.12; Divine Office of the canonical hours Pr 125, 1.178, B 15.385

oure Z 7.116 = **ȝoure** *prn*

oure *poss. prn* our Pr 34 *et p.*, [*with ref. to humanity in general*] 1.163, 3.401, 8.239, 18.67 *etc*, [*with ref. to Christians*] 3.358 *etc*, *in phrr*: [*with Christian ref.*] ~ **Lady** 3.99 *etc*, ~ **Driȝte** B 13.269, ~ **Lord** Pr 28 *et p.*, B 5.563, A 1.110, Z 6.46 *etc*, *in oaths* Pr 103, Z 3.123; ~ **Lordes loue** for love of our Lord 16.151, 17.26, B 11.172, ~ **prince Iesu** 13.3, B 16.37, ~ **Sauiour** 7.120, B 9.127*etc*; *in phrr*: (= of us) ~ **aller** of all of us B 16.205, ~ **Iewene** of us Jews 20.40; **bothe** ~ of both of us 6.181

ouresulue (~seluen, ~ sylue) *emphatic pers. prn* ourselves 19.41, A 11.248, Z 3.171; *in phr.* **bi** ~ by ourselves 15.42

ourf *n* cattle Z 7.64

out(e)[1] *av* out 6.222, 20.420; away, absent 22.347; (*with various phrasal vv.*) Pr 37, 1.109, 2.241, *etc*, **B** 1.121, 4.186, *etc*; + **of** *in in phr.* **out of** out (of) 2.65, 4.163, 5.151, 6.183, 184, 10.211, 11.208, 12.76, 211, 13.176, 228, 14.112, 15.249, 16.241, 17.247, 18.217, 20.64, 21.74, 285, **A** 2.20, 10.124, 126, 127; out / away from 2.247, 5.151, 8.206, 10.42; from 18.283, from the direction (of) 20.116, 166; from out of 21.381, Z 3.148; down from 22.80

out(e) of *cpd. prep., in phrr*. ~ **aray** in disorderly manner 5.157; ~ **dette** free of debt 16.4; ~ **my menynges** beyond my comprehension 1.137; ~ **lawe** beyond / outside of the law B 10.25; ~ **lele byleue** cut off from the true faith 17.158; ~ **mesure** to excess, immoderately 13.188; ~ **nombre** in excessive quantity 13.6; too numerous 22.269; ~ **resoun** immoderately 2.89, 6.434, 13.154, B 1.25; ~ **reule** outside of the rule 3.202; ~ **tyme** except at the proper time 1.24, 10.291

oute(n)[2] *a* alive, in the world 14.190, B 12.144

ouþer *pl.* B 4.136 = **other**[1] *prn*; *conj.* either B 5.53, 9.106, 10.265, 12.223, 13.230, 15.431, 16.133

ouþerwhile B 12.23 = **oþerwhile(s)** *av*

outlawe *n* outlaw, robber (*as name*) B 17.103

#outrydere *n* 'rider out' [agent riding out to administer affairs of a monastery] 4.116

outtaken *v* exempt, *p.p. as prep.* with the exception of A 10.175

outward *av* outwards 9.85

outwit *n* external sense(s) B 13.289

849

ouer[1] *av* across, **passen** ~ leave (subject) B 13.133; too, excessively 8.271, 15.49, 22.27, B 11.240; *and see* **ouer-**

ouer[2] *prep.* over 7.158, 287, 22.183, 187, A 5.178; Z 3.146; across 13.45, B 5.476, A 11.203; in charge of 7.270, 8.251; (victorious) over 4.155; more than, above 19.39, Z 1.22; above (= in authority over) 3.256, 11.96, 16.124, 17.170, 242, 20.426, 21.139, 223, 446, 22.73, 321, **B** 1.108, 15.90, (= ruling over) 5.193, 6.138, 22.64, **B** 3.298, 14.328, **A** 10.72, 11.198, (= in control of) A 10.63; *in phrr:* ~ **eue(n)** overnight 3.307, 7.195; ~ see overseas, abroad 4.126, 6.278

oueral *av* in every place 2.228, B 9.55; especially B 13.291

ouercam *p.t.* 20.112, B 15.440 *see* **ouercomen** *v*

#**ouerclosen** *v* blot out 20.138

ouercomen *v* (*p.t.* ~**cam** 20.112, ~ **kam** 21.161, ~**come** 15.13, *p.p.* ~**come** 3.430, 17.289) surpass 11.285; overcome 3.430; dominate 15.13, Z 5.94; win over 4.78; vanquish, conquer 17.203, 289, 20.112, 21.161; be victorious over 22.122

ouer-delycatly *av* too choicely 6.166, B 5.375

ouerdoen *v* do (sth.) / act to excess 13.190

ouergilden *v* overlay with gold, *p.p.,* **ouergilte** B 15.124 gilded

ouer-hardy *a* too presumptuous 3.298

ouerhippen (~**huppen** B) *v* skip over (parts of text) 17.118, **B** 13.68, 15.385

ouerhouen *v* hover over 20.173, B 3.208

ouerkarken *v* overburden 3.468

ouer-land *av* across the country, *as a in phr.* ~ **strikares** 9.159

ouerleyen *v* cover over, *p.p.* 12.233

ouerlepen *v* (*p.t.* ~ **le(e)p** Pr 169, 20.357) overtake, pounce upon Pr 169, B Pr 200; digress 20.357

#**ouerlong(e)** *a* too long 22.363, B 11.221; too protracted 16.363

ouerlonge *av* (for) too long (a time) 22.361

ouermaistren *v* gain mastery over B 4.176

ouer-moche *n* too much 8.271

#**ouer-more** *av* in addition 9.157

****ouer-plente(e)** *n* over-abundance, excess 12.236, B 14.73

ouer-rechen *v* reach over, encroach 6.270

ouersen *v* (*p.t.* ~ **sey(e)** *p.p.* ~ **seyen**) peruse 11.115, B 10.327; oversee 8.120, B 6.113; forget (oneself) (= over-eat) B 5.372

ouerskippen *v* leave out 13.118

****ouerskippere** *n* priest who leaves out parts (of the Offices) 13.122

****ouer-soppen** *v* eat to excess 6.428

ouerspreden *v, p.t.* ~**spradde** cover, envelope 21.207

ouertaken *v* catch up with B 17.83; catch B 12.241

ouerthrowen *v* demolish 18.160; overturn B 8.36

#**ouertulden** *v* (*p.t.* ~ **tulde** / ~**tilte**) upturn, overturn 22.54, 135

ouerturnen *v* throw down B 16.131, *ger.* destruction 18.163; come to ruin 17.209; overturn 18.157

ouerward *av* about to cross over 4.128

oure Z 1.22 = **ouer** *prep.*

owen(e)[1] *a* own Pr 124, 8.207, 10.177, 12.99, 14.175, 16.134, 17.81, 195, 18.14, 166, 19.254, 289, 300, **B** 5.214, 10.365, 409, 16.192, A 10.75, Z 6.38; *a as n* 3.209 [land], 7.221, 8.92, 22.20, 92 [property], **ownere** *gen. pl., in phr.* **here** ~ **wil** their own (individual) wills 18.76; *in phr.* **ben thyn** ~ are your servants 3.28

owen[2] *v* (*p.t.* **o(u)(g)ht(e)(n)** *with pres. sense* 1.72, 3.72, *etc*) own 3.72; owe 21.395; (*modal*) ought (to), should 1.72, 2.30, 5.69, 6.86, 7.98, 22.276; be obliged to 3.108, 9.229, 19.318, A 7.123; have a duty (to) 12.91

oxe *n* ox B 15.466; (*pl.*) ~**n** oxen 21.263, 269

paast *n* pastry B 13.251; dough B 14.29

pacience *n* (the moral virtue of) patience [calm endurance of suffering and adversity] 2.201, 12.197, 13.2, 14.16, 15.161, 181, 183, 276, 16.56, 149, 152, 17.236, 242, 306, 19.91, 20.170, 174, 461, 21.250, 296, A 11.230, (*person.*) (a) 7.273, (b) 15.33 *et p.*, 283, 16.114 *et p.*, 161, **B** 13.29 *et p.*, 14.29 *et p.*, (c) (*tree*) B 16.8; *in phr.* **pouerte and (...)** ~, ~ **and (...) pouerte** 12.144, 13.20, 15.281, 16.59, 61, 152, 21.250, **B** 10.340, 11.317–18, 12.61, 14.192–3; forbearance B 14.10, 99

pacient *a* patient [able to endure suffering *etc* calmly] 12.132, 16.111; *a as n, in phr.* **pore (and)** ~ 9.178, 13.30, 98, 15.280, 287, 16.99; *in phr.* ~ **pouerte** (condition of) poverty that calmly endures 12.178, B 14.101; forbearing, self-restrained B 15.201

paciently(che) *av* with steadfast endurance 11.263, 12.150, 202, 16.326, 19.105; with forbearance / self-restraint 17.284; humbly 6.14

pay *n* satisfaction, *in phr.* **to** ~**e** satisfactorily 7.189, 192, 13.160, 16.93, 21.187; reward 9.278; pay, wages (*or* favour) 3.299, 348

payement *n* payment 22.365

payen *v* please 8.332, **A** 7.100, 10.130, Z 7.279; content A 10.117; make payment (of) 6.251; pay (money) 3.66, 389, 4.68, 9.45, B 13.377; pay (wages / fees 3.299, 305, 349, 7.41, 8.115, 9.45, B 7.43; pay (for purchase) 16.323, 21.417, B 13.381; pay (tithe) 8.102; pay (ransom for) 3.173, 7.276; recompense 12.108, B 15.155; return 16.129; repay 4.55, 6.277, 16.313; atone 16.31; make satisfaction for 19.203, 298, 21.195, 196; fulfil (conditions of) 21.189, 392, 22.309

payere *n* payer of wages 3.305, (*fig.*) 7.194

#**payn(e)** *n*[1] bread 8.285, 9.92, 15.202, 218, 232, 235, 16.149, **B** 6.150, 7.122, 9.81, 14.76, 15.315; *in phr.* ~ **defaute** lack of bread 15.231

payne (**peyne**) *n*[2] punishment 15.256; torture 7.276, Z 3.123; suffering 1.198, 10.155, B 1.169; agony [of Christ] 7.20, 21.328; punishment / suffering [in hell or purgatory] 1.128, 7.117, 255, 11.223, 262, 20.146, 197, 204, 207, 416, **B** 2.106, 11.162, **bittere ~(s)** 12.44, 15.50, **B** 11.152, **incurable ~s** 15.16, ~ **of helle** 2.108, 3.101, ~ **of purgatorie** 11.33; (physical) pain 19.156; physical discomfort 6.129; source of woe B 12.247

paynen (peynen) *v* torture (= crucify) 1.166; suffer (crucifixion) 21.324; encumber B 12.246; strive Z 7.98, (*refl.*) exert (oneself) 21.437, 440, (*with prn om.*) Z 7.98; endeavour B 7.42

payny(e)m *n* pagan B 11.162; Saracen, Moslem 7.160, 17.255

paynten (peynten) *v* paint 3.66, 70, 19.137; inscribe 13.118; stain 21.11; (*fig.*) pick out in colour 16.321; *p.p.* smeared 21.6; colourful, decorated (*fig.*) 4.23; brightly coloured 14.179; specious 22.115

payre *n* pair (of) 6.251, B 12.19; (sexual) pair 10.234; couple B 13.197; (married) couple 10.274

pays 18.177, Z 4.52 = **pe(e)s** *n*

pak *n* load 16.54; bag, pack 15.181

pakken *v* pack, bundle 16.330

palays (paleis) *n¹* palace 2.23, ~ (*pl.*) 10.16

palays (paleys) *n²* (= **palis**) palisade B 10.462; enclosed garden 20.378; enclosed courtyard B 13.29

pale *a* pallid 20.58; pale [grey] B 5.77

pal(e)sy(e) *n* (attack of) palsy, paralysis 22.176, B 5.77

palfray *n* palfrey [light riding-horse] 4.115, 5.159, 21.418, **B** 2.190, 13.244, **in ~es wise** like riding-horses B 2.171

#**pallen** *v* strike 18.34, 50, B 16.51

palmer(e) *n* pilgrim [*esp.* to Holy Land] Pr 47, 7.179, 8.63, 15.34, 132, B 5.105, Z 5.158

#**palpable** *a* tangible, evident 18.234

paltok *n* jacket 22.219, B 18.25

panele *n* jury(-list) 3.469

pan(e)s *pl.* 2.232, 3.32, 117, 199, 6.242, 9.91, 12.166, 248, 18.165, 19.76, 21.379, A 4.50, Z 3.33 *see* **peny** *n*, **mas ~** 3.278

paniar *n* basket 17.17

paniter *n* dispenser of bread (*fig.*) 16.149

panne *n* skull 4.74

#**papelote** *n* mess of porridge 9.75

paper *n* written document(s), account(s) 13.37

paradys *n* paradise [the Garden of Eden] 13.226, 20.378; the earthly paradise (? Eden) B 10.12; heaven 9.12, 11.299, 16.223, 21.61, B 10.464, A 8.12, 11.286; *in phr.* **Prince of** ~ (= God) A 7.109

parail 10.117 *etc*, ~**en** Pr 25 *etc* (*aphetic forms of* **aparayle** *n*, -**en** *v*, *qq.v.*)

paramour *n* lover, beloved 16.105; ~**s** *n* sexual love 6.186

parau(e)nture *av* perhaps, perchance, maybe 3.466, 7.296, 8.43, 9.180, 11.172, 12.246, 14.123, 16.49, 22.234, B 11.421, A 12.8

parceyuen B Pr 100 *etc* = **pars(c)eyuen** *v*

parcel 13.37, 22.292, B 17.27 = **parsel** *n*

parchemyn *n* sheet of parchment B 9.38, 14.192; document (written on parchment) B 14.194

pardo(u)n *n* forgiveness (from God) B 10.122; pardon [remission of (*esp.*) temporal punishment for sins already] forgiven 2.232, 8.63, 9.8, 11, 43, 53, 60, 288, 300, 318, 323, 324, 328, 337, 345, 12.9, 21.184, 188, 189, 22.309, **B** 7.16, 102, 13.253, A 8.18, Z 8.89; formal document of pardon 9.279, 280, 282, 292, B 13.253; *in phrr.* ~ **a pena et a culpa** absolute pardon, pardon from both punishment and guilt 9.3, 186; ~ **of Pampilon** 19.219c; ?release B 15.183c

pardoner *n* pardoner [purveyor of pardons / indulgences] Pr 66, 79, 2.229, 17.61, B 5.639, **Peres þe ~** 2.110

paren *v* clip (coins) 6.242

*****parentrelynarie** *av* between the lines 13.118

parfay *interj.* by my faith, certainly 16.117

parfit *a* perfect 3.453, 11.300; complete, whole B 15.583; (spiritually) ideal / perfect 12.164, 13.99, 17.51, 20.151, B 11.274; (*comp.* B 12.24, *sup.* 13.98); thoroughly good / virtuous 5.84, 8.136, 17.299, 18.103, **B** 11.318, 13.215, A 1.120; true, ideal *in phrr.* ~ **byleue** 11.300, 17.266, B 14.193; ~ **charitee** B 15.148; ~ **Cristene** 22.108; ~ **lyuynge** thoroughly virtuous way of life B 15.417; perfection of (worldly) existence 11.176, 194, 13.231; ~ **loue** 15.219; ~ **pacience** 15.276; ~ **pouerte** B 11.271; ~ **preesthoed** truly virtuous clergy 16.243, 17.233, 250; ~ **treuthe** 3.453, B 14.99; perfectly skilled B 16.107; ~ **ly(che)** *av* flawlessly 17.75; completely 16.338, 21.195; thoroughly 7.10, 15.181; fully 17.255; in (its) entirety B 16.220; virtuously 9.43; properly 19.137; ~ **nesse** *n* perfect goodness 18.41; a perfectly virtuous way of life 5.90, 15.185; spiritual perfection B 10.202, 15.208; holiness B 16.135

parformen (parfournen) *v* finish (task) 3.349; carry out, perform 6.283, 7.14, 17, 246, 15.88, B 15.490; fulfil 13.92, 16.126, B 15.325, 327; bring about 15.174

par(is)sch(e) (*pl.* **parissh** A Pr 81) *n* parish [ecclesiastical and administrative division of England] Pr 80, 82, 22.263, 280; people of a parish 15.212; ~ **chirche** principal church of a parish B 11.65; ~ **prest** priest in charge of a parish Pr 79, *in phr.* **persone(s) and ~ ~(s)** Pr 81, 14.123, 22.281, 320, B 10.267

par(is)sch(i)en *n* parishioner 6.120, 22.283, B Pr 89, 5.420

parlement *n* the king's council [sitting as court of law] 4.45; ? the parliament of England 4.185

#**parlen** *v* speak, talk 20.279

parlour *n* separate chamber [off main hall] B 10.99

#**parroken** *v* enclose, *p.p.* 6.144, 17.13

pars(c)eyuen *v* perceive, (take) notice (of) Pr 128, 20.251, **B** 5.142, 13.355, 16.23, 103; sense, understand **B** 13.86, 17.151; hear 21.163; apprehend 19.68; discern B 15.199

parsch(e) Pr 79 *etc* = **par(is)sch(e)** *n*

parsel *n* portion 22.292; section 13.118; small amount 11.48; *in phrr.* **a~** / **in ~es** separately 19.98, B 17.27; ~ **of paper** itemised list (= ? account roll) 13.37

parselmele *av* in small portions (= by retail sale) 3.86; bit by bit B 15.246; separately 19.30

parsilie *n* parsley 8.309

parsonage Z Pr 58 = **personage** *n*

part *n* share 3.245, ~ **of** / **in pardon** 9.174, A 8.8

part(e)y(ȝ)(e) *n* part, *in phr.* **most** ~ majority 1.7, 3.382; member 16.166*n* (*or* **a** ~ = in part, partly); side 3.379, 15.175; party / person involved [in lawsuit] 1.95, 3.389, 19.286, 288, [betrothal] B 14.269

parten *v* cause a division between 5.184; share Pr 79, 8.285, *ger. in phr.* ~ **felawe** partner B 13.207; ~ **with** share with 16.256, share in 8.144, endure along with 6.299, ~ **with** / **(a parsel)** grant a part (to) 11.48, 65, 15.117; depart, *ger. in phr.* **(~ hennes)** departure from this life, (= death) 9.53, 16.159, 21.61, (A 11.313); give, distribute 1.177, A 3.57

Pasche (Paske, Pasque) *n* (the feast of) Passover 18.167; ~ **woke** Easter week 12.124

paschen *v* dash, strike violently 22.100

pase *n* road, passageway 16.137

Paske *n* 12.124 = **Pasche** *n*

passen *v* travel 16.139, B 15.570; go 22.339; leave 8.93, 9.132, 10.11, 15.154, 185, B 13.179; pass (through) 9.11, 325, 11.300, 13.30, 16.138; go past 2.201; pass by 22.199; *in phr.* **leten** ~ allow to get out Pr 173, 3.173; (*of time*) pass, *p.p.* 20.136, (= ago) Pr 203, 16.369, 22.344; leave (this life,) die, *in phrr.* ~ **forth** 11.263, ~ **hennes** A 8.18; vanish 15.154, B 13.20; persist, *in phr.* ~ **ouer til** hold on until B 13.133; ignore B 5.416; surpass 15.117, 21.267, A 12.4; exceed 9.319, 323; *pr. p. as prep.* more than 7.30, 22.218; go beyond / against 1.98, 17.5; sojourn 1.7

passio(u)n *n* penitential suffering 11.262, 17.266; grievous hardship B 15.270; passion [suffering and death] of Christ 7.20, 11.33, 17.192, 18.41, 21.63, 328, B 15.255, 17.96, 18.9, [of saint or martyr] 7.78; narrative of passion [of Christ] A 12.26, [of martyr] 15.100

pastour *n* shepherd 11.297, 14.92; herdsman A 11.310; shepherd of souls, pastor B 15.495

patente *n* document of proclamation [of a statute issued by a sovereign](= **lettre patent**) (*fig.*) 19.12, of grant [of a privilege] (*fig.*) 20.190, [of a release] (*fig.*) B 14.192, [of a pardon / indulgence] B 7.195

Paternoster *n* Our Father [the Lord's Prayer] 5.46, 87, 107, 6.283, 7.10, 11.299, 15.250, 16.321, 21.397, **B** 10.468, 13.237, 14.197, ~ **while** time taken to say an 'Our Father' 6.398

path *n* path, ~ **of pees** unmolested passage 16.137

patriarch (patriark) *n* Old Testament patriarch 13.20, 14.60, 17.51, 20.151, *in phr:* ~**s and prophetes** 7.87, 9.12, 10.207, 11.150, 14.81, 18.208, 273, 20.141, 146, 279, 366, 21.16, **B** 10.338, 16.251; patriarch of the Christian church [bishop ranking after Pope] B 13.167

patrimonye *n* endowment(s) 22.234, *in phr.* **Cristes** ~ = the wealth of the Church B 15.246

patron *n* mentor B 12.226; patron [layman or cleric with right of patronage over benefice] 5.78

Paulines *n* ? the order of Paulines (the Crutched Friars), ? jurors at the consistory court held at St Paul's B 2.178c; ~ **doctour** A 2.73; ~ **doctrine** B 2.109; ~ **peple** A 2.139; ~ **queste** 2.110c

paume *n* palm (of the hand) 19.117, 118, 121, 124, 126, 128, 130, 141, 143, 156, 164, 166, B 17.151, 183

paunche *n* stomach 15.97

paueloun *n* large tent, pavilion A 2.41; lawyer's cape 3.448

#peccunie *n* money 3.389

pece *n* piece 20.61, (*fig.*) 15.250; slab 8.332, 19.12; drinking vessel B 3.89

pecok 14.179, 183, B 12.228, 239, 240 262 = **pocok**; *see* **po** *n*

pedlere *n* pedlar B 5.254

peel B 17.304 = **ap(p)e(e)l** *n*

peeren *v*[1] B Pr 173 = **ap(p)eren** *v*

pe(e)ren *v*[2] be the equal of B 15.417, A 12.4

pe(e)s *n* peace / concord between people 14.16, 15.219, 230, 17.93, 199, 226, 20.236, 458 (*person.*) 4.45 *et p.*; amity, peaceableness (*person.*) 22.299 *et p.*; *in phr.* **maken** ~ **(for sb.)** obtain pardon 13.75, ? *or* settle out of court B 4.64, 75; reconciliation [between God and man] 17.248; (*person.*) = daughter of God 20.170 *et p.*; the peace of heaven [*meton. for* God's presence] 15.140; *in phrr.* **Cristes** ~ 17.228; = the Christian virtue of peace 1.147, (*person.*) 7.273; freedom from molestation / disturbance 13.2, 16.137, 139, 18.177; state of peace 21.360; peaceful relations (between nations *etc*) 5.195, 13.140, 15.174, 17.86, 236, B 13.176, 209, 15.426; peace within the country, civil order B 3.221, (*person.*) = the King's peace 4.45 *et p.*; silence, quiet 21.154

pehen B 12.239 = **pohen**; *see* **po** *n*

peyne 2.108 *etc* = **payne** *n*

peynd *p.t.* Z 7.98, **peyned** *p.t.* 21.324, **peyneth** *pr.* 21.440 *see* **paynen** *v*

peynten 3.66, 16.321, 19.137, **peynted** *p.p.* 4.23 *etc see* **paynten** *v*

peire B 12.19, 13.197 = **payre** *n*

peyse *n* weight; ~ **of led** = lead seal B 13.247; balance, scales 6.242

peysen *v*[1] weigh 6.223

peysen *v*[2] appease, satisfy Z 7.302

#peytrelen *v* put *peytrel* [ornamental harness] upon 4.23

pelet *n* gunstone, cannon-ball B 5.77

pelour[1] *n* accuser (in law-court) 20.39, (*fig.*) Z 1.65

pelour[2] 21.418 = **pilour** *n*

pelure *n* fur (trimming) 2.10, 3.448; fur-trimmed gown 4.115, 21.418, B 15.7

pena(u)nce *n* (sacramental) penance 6.328, 7.240; act(s) of penitential satisfaction 5.171, 195, 6.283, 7.14, 71, 246, 13.81, 21.379, 22.307; punishment 16.76, B 10.34, A 9.95; (penitential) punishment 3.101, 6.14, 304; (purgatorial) punishment 9.185, 325, 11.262, B 10.122, A 11.313; (act(s) of) penitential self-mortification Pr 27, 3.399, 5.84, 7.78, 8.93, 9.174, 234, 328, 15.84, 94, 107, 112, 16.38, 19.218, 21.67; suffering 6.110, 15.71, 73; 17.266, 18.41, 19.321, B 17.96, 18.9; hardship 16.326, B 11.279, 12.9, 13.66; affliction 12.150, 195, A 11.230; pain 15.97

*****pena(u)nceles** *a* without suffering purgatorial penance 11.300

penaunt *n* penitent, person doing penance 4.130, 15.102

pencyf *a* thoughtful, pensive 9.299

pencyoun *n* payment A 8.47, Z 7.272

#pendaunt *n* pendant [ornamened hanging end of girdle] B 15.7

peneworth *n* (small) quantity (of goods worth a penny) 3.313, 6.383; ~ **gode** penny's worth of goods Z 7.273

peny *n* (*pl.* **pan(e)s** 2.232, 3.32 *etc*, **penyes** Pr 161, **pens** B 12.247) (English silver) penny Pr 161, 6.242, 9.91, 16.297, B 12.247, 13.381; = Biblical denarius 1.45, 19.76, argentarius 18.165; money, cash 2.231, 3.32, 117, 199, 8.303, 12.122, 166, 248, 16.313, B 4.64, 75; *in phrr.* ~ **ale** light ale costing a penny a gallon 6.226, 8.332, 9.92, B 15.315; ~ **delyng** alms-giving 21.379; **mas ~s money** offered at mass by the faithful 3.278

penyles *a* destitute 12.26

penne *n* feather 14.179, B 12.246; pen B 9.39; (*meton. for*) lettering 19.16

pensel *n* pennon, banner 18.188

pen(y)tauncer *n* penitentiary [priest with authority from pope / bishop to administer penance *esp.* in reserved cases] 6.256, 22.320

pe(o)ple *n* people, persons 1.5, 7, 2.198, 3.382, 7.273, 8.190, 348, 9.43, 118, 219, 325, 10.300, 11.6, 15.196, 16.125, 17.61, 20.82, 22.86, B 12.67, 14.183, 195, 15.590, 16.251, 17.36, = the public, people at large Pr 57, 145, 2.224, 9.300, 10.29, 11.19, 16.235, 21.458, B 3.82, 8.111, 10.214, 11.158, 174, 13.251; mankind 3.453, 9.20, 18.86; = people of a region 6.30, 36, 60, 9.114, 15.232, 16.242, 251, 17.84, 17.174, 177, 180, B 5.23, 6.163; people (in a place) B 4.159, A 2.38; = *spec.* the Christian community Pr 77, 3.277, 5.141, 10.89, 15.76, 214, 17.250, 284, 21.431, 22.109, 125, 281, B 5.104, 145, 10.202, 13.237, 17.337, A Pr 93, Z 7.232; chosen people [in *OT*] B 12.72; = (some specific) group of people 1.45, 166, 12.49, B 15.325, 327, A 2.139; *in phr.* **moche ~** large number of people, crowd 8.348, 17.299, 20.35, 22.98; many (other) characters A 12.102; the common people, the labour-

ing classes 3.86, B 7.10; *in collocations*: **comune ~** ordinary folk 2.58, 21.7, 132, 423; **poore comune ~** 11.297; **Cristene ~** 5.193, 11.270, 13.77, 21.343, 364, B 12.158, 15.90; **Cristes ~** B 14.72, 15.22; **fals ~** 3.91; **Godis ~** A 11.198; **inparfit ~** 3.385; **land-tylying ~** 11.298; **lewed ~** (uneducated) lay people 1.193, 17.121, B 12.110, 15.72, A 11.182; **mene ~** people of modest means 3.81; **nedy ~** B 11.242; **poore ~** Pr 80, 3.83, 8.205, 316, 9.34, 12.101, 122, 166, 15.10, 17.70, B 11.183, 14.174, 15.203, A 8.48; **rihtfole ~** 17.34; **witty ~** 17.94

pepur *n* pepper-corn 6.358; **han ~ in the nose (to)** treat superciliously B 15.203

percile B 6.285 = **parsilie** *n*

pere *n*[1] match 9.306; equal in rank [social] 3.261, 9.20, 10.141, A 11.197, [spiritual] 18.90, B 16.71

pere *n*[2] pear (*with pun on* **pere**[1]) B 16.71, **~ionette** an early-ripening pear 12.223

perel *n* peril, danger 16.138, 19.68, 20.298; perilous situation B 16.107; tribulation 15.280, 20.461; spiritual danger, risk 11.194, 17.232, 260, A 8.16 *in assev.* **be / for ~ of...soule** at the risk of (one's) soul 4.137, 7.200, 228, 8.102, B 6.117, 171

#peren *v* be the equal of B 15.417, A 12.4

perfite A 1.120 = **parfit** *a*

perye (perreiȝe) *n* precious stones 11.10, A 2.12

perilous *a* terrible B 6.44

perilously *av* dangerously Pr 170

#perimansie *n* pyromancy [divination by fire] A 11.161

perle *n* pearl, *in cpd.* **margerie ~s** 11.7

#permutacioun *n* exchange of one thing for another [of proportionally equivalent value] 3.313

#permuten *v* exchange (benefice / church) 2.185; ~ **with** exchange...for B 13.111

perpetuel *a* everlasting, (**peyne**) 7.117, 20.204, (**pardon**) 9.60, (**helle**) 9.278, (**blisse**) 11.263, (**pees**) 15.140, (**ioye**) 16.56; unceasing 5.195, 17.248; lasting 17.93; ? = eternal 18.27

perpetuelly *av* for ever 9.8

persaunt *a* 1.152 *see* **persen** *v*

persecucioun *n*, ~ **of body** physical torture 12.207

persen *v* pierce, *p.p.* B 17.190, *pr.p. a* piercing, sharp 1.152; (*fig.*) = get through to 11.299

perseuen 19.68 = **pars(c)eyuen** *v*

#personage *n* benefice B 13.246, Z Pr 58

persone *n*[1] person, individual 16.108, 110, 21.27, 196, 19.105, **mene ~** person acting as intermediary B 9.114; (bodily) person 15.196; self 3.224; divine person [of the Trinity] 18.27, 188, 215, 236, 19.30, 37, 44, B 10.239, 16.185, 188; human persons [conceived analogously to the persons of the Trinity] 18.234, B 16.207; form 20.378

perso(u)n(e) *n*[2] parson [priest entitled to parish tithes] 2.185, 5.165, 6.144, 16.250, 22.360, B 5.141, 142; *in phrr.* **~(s)** B 10.468, **and / or (parissh) prestes(s)**

Pr 81, 3.186, 14.123, 16.250, 22.281, 320, **B** 10.267, 11.98, 15.485; **prestes and ~(s)** 3.463, 7.30, B 3.252

pertliche 5.117, B 5.23 = **apertly(che)** *av*

pes(e) *n* (*pl.* **peses** 8.306, B 6.186, **pesen** B 6.195, 297) pea 8.306 *etc; in phrr:* **setten (counten) at a ~** care nothing for 8.166 (A 7.154), 9.345; **~ cod** pea-pod 8.316, 12.223; **~ loof** loaf of pea-flour 8.176

pestelence *n* plague (*esp.* bubonic) 5.115, 8.348, 10.274, 11.60, 15.219, 22.98, **B** 5.36, 12.11, 13.249, *in phr.* **~ tyme** time of the (Great) Plague Pr 82, B 10.72

pethe *n* strength, essential part 19.118

#**pety(t)** *a* small, little 9.53, 16.83

pharisee *n* Pharisee B 15.604

philosofer, philosopher *n* learned man, scholar 17.115; natural philosopher 21.245, B 15.357; philosopher (of antiquity) 13.27, 22.38

philosophie *n* learning, scholarly knowledge 17.115; philosophy 22.296

Phippe B 11.42 *see* **Fyppe**

phisik B 15.383 = **fysyk(e)** *n*

pyc(c)hen *v* (*p.p.* **py3t** A 2.41) thrust, **~ ato** thrust apart 8.64; erect A 2.41; pitch (hay) 5.13

pye *n*[1] magpie 13.158, B 12.226, 252

pye *n*[2] pie Pr 227, **~ hele** pie-crust (= thing of little value 9.345

piece B 3.89 = **pece** *n*

pyement *n* sweetened, spiced wine 20.409

py3t *p.p.* A 2.41 *see* **pyc(c)hen** *v*

pyk *n* pointed tip, spike 10.95, B 8.97; (= **~ staf**) 7.179, B 5.475, Z 7.90; **~ staf** spiked (pilgrim's) staff 6.328, B 6.103

pykare *n* (corn)-stealer 5.17

pikede *a* with long pointed toe 22.219

#**pikeharneys** *n* despoiler of armour [of men slain in battle] 22.263

pyken (aweye, vp) *v* dig up 8.118, B 16.17

pikepors *n* stealer of / from purses 6.369

pikois *n* pick-axe 3.461

pil *n* prop B 16.23, 24, 26, 30, 36, 86

pile *n* fort, stronghold 21.366

pilede *p.p.* 6.369 *see* **pil(i)en** *v*

piler *n* pillar 7.240

*****pilewhey** *n* ? drained whey, ? spring water A 5.134

pilgrym *n* pilgrim [traveller to holy place] Pr 47, 7.199, 9.180, 12.132 (1), 15.187, **B** 5.105, 13.179, 216, (*fig.*) 8.112, 12.132 (2), 22.381; wayfarer 12.126, 133, **B** 11.241, 13.183, 188; *in phr.* **in ~es clothes / wyse** 7.160, B 13.29, (*fig.*) 8.56

pilgrimage *n* pilgrimage [journey to a holy place] 9.234, 323, 16.38, 21.378, (*fig.*) 8.63, 93, 16.322

pil(i)en *v* rob [by heavy taxation] 21.445; peel 9.81; remove hair from, *p.p.* (*as term of abuse*) hairless, bald 6.369, A 7.142

pylorye *n* pillory 2.216, 3.79

pilour *n* despoiler [of the slain in battle] 22.263; robber 13.2; thief B 3.195; extortioner 21.418

pyn *n* wooden peg 8.199

pynchen *v* encroach 6.267 (B 13.371)

pyne *n* punishment, *in phr.* **wyuene ~** punishment for wayward wives or scolds 5.131*n*; torture A 1.143; punishment in hell **B** 2.104, 10.387, 11.142, A 2.70, **wykkede ~** punishment of the / meted out to the wicked in hell 11.275

pynen *v* torture, crucify A 1.145, (*with pun on* **pynnen**) B 5.209 (A 5.127); endure pain B 19.325; **pynyng** *ger.* punishment, **~ stol** seat of punishment, cucking stool 3.79

pynnen *v* fasten tightly 6.219, 22.299

pyonie *n* peony-seed 6.358

pipen *v* play on a pipe 15.208; blow a horn 22.93; sing out in a shrill voice 20.452

pirie *n* pear-tree 5.118

#**pissare** *n* pisser, (*cant for*) soldier, ruffian 22.219n

pissen *v* piss, urinate 6.67, 398, 8.151

pistul *n* epistle 16.289, 19.319, **B** 12.29, 13.69, **A** 10.109, 11.233

pytaunce *n* donation to a religious house [for providing additional food on special occasions] B 5.266; (the) allowance of food (so provided) 9.92; (small) portion 15.61, B 13.55

pite(e) *n* mercy 1.166, 6.172, 20.189, 21.92, B 17.294, **A** 5.12, 9.95, **hauen ~ on** be compassionate towards 3.86, 349, 5.166, 191, 15.88, B 5.253, 254; kindness 3.348; (feeling of) pity 2.229, 8.205, **withouten ~** pitilessly B 3.195, **hauen no ~ to killen** have no compunction about killing 11.269

pitous *a* piteous, doleful A 7.115

pitousli(che) *av* mercifully, forgivingly 4.94; pitiably, miserably 1.77, (*as a*) wretched(ly) 20.58

#**pyuische** *a* ? ill-tempered, ? foolish 8.151n

place *n* place, location Pr 96, 3.106, 5.165, 7.180, 9.225, 10.15, 13.50, 15.189, 16.121, 165, 17.86, 20.19, 176, 231, 272, 362, 22.3, 42, **B** 5.528, 6.44, 12.24, 61, 13.134, 16.21, 135, 171, Z 1.65; square 20.82; spot 20.157, B 13.275; position 21.61; house B 12.147; manor-house 5.159, 7.270, 12.248, 22.181, Z 6.65; dwelling-place 7.183, 198, 15.278; ? place of custody (in castle) 7.276n; *in phrr.* **in ~s** to (any) place 17.173, **in ~s þer** wherever 16.313; **in alle ~s** everywhere B 15.161; **in no ~** nowhere 17.86; **to what ~** in whichever direction 19.117

play *n* joy A 12.95

playen *v* enjoy oneself, relax Pr 22, 186, 188, B 12.24; (*refl.*) disport oneself †22.292; play, sport Pr 170; be joyful A 8.12; rejoice 18.273, 20.170; jest, joke 9.114; **~ with** use (tool) 3.461

playere *n* player, *in cpd.* **dees ~** 8.72

playnen 4.30, 8.166 *see* **pleynen** *v*

playten *v* fold, ? fasten B 5.208

planete *n* planet 22.80

planke *n* plank (= prop) 18.34, 40, B 16.50

plante B 1.152, 5.582 = **plonte** *n*

planten *v* plant (out), *p.p.* A 7.270 (Z 7.290)

plase 10.15, Z 6.4 = **place** *n*

plast(e)re *n* medicinal plaster, poultice [of herbs *etc*] (*fig.*) 22.360, 362, 364

plasteren *v* cover with a plaster (*fig.*) 19.91, 22.311, 315, B 17.96, 20.380

plate(s) *n* (set of) plate-armour (*fig.*) 20.24

platten *v* (*refl.*) prostrate oneself 6.3

pleden *v* argue (a case) 15.289, 21.296, (legal case) Pr 161, **for nouhte Y couthe** ~ in spite of any legal case I could make 4.57; plead in court B 7.42; dispute B 14.189; *ger.* pleading, arguing cases 3.448, 9.45

pledour *n* advocate B 7.42

pleyen Pr 186 *etc* (**pleyden** *p.t.* B 12.24) *see* **playen** *v*

pleyn *a* full, plenary B 7.102

pleynen *v* complain Pr 81, 6.110, (*ref.*) A 7.115; make a (legal) complaint / accusation (against) 3.213, 4.30, 70, 6.120, 16.67, (*refl.*) lodge complaint 8.156, make a legal complaint 8.166, B 4.66; *in phr.* **preiere** ~ utter petition B 17.294

pleynt *n* lament †B 6.123; complaint 12.137; legal complaint, lawsuit 3.213, B 2.172

plener *a* full B 16.103; ~**e** *av* fully 12.49

plente(e) *n* plenty, abundance 8.160, 12.205, 13.140, 15.232; prosperity, *in phrr.* **pees and** ~ 17.93, 199, ~ **of pes** Z 1.86

plentevous *a* abundant A 12.95; generous B 10.82

plesaunce *n* pleasure 8.14

plesa(u)nt *a* pleasing, acceptable (to God) B 14.101, 15.156; gratifying 16.47

plesen *v* please, be acceptable to 5.85, 8.118, (*esp.* God) 11.230, 15.281, B 5.53; satisfy 3.199, 8.318, 15.202, Z 7.313; treat kindly B 11.183; gratify Pr 32, 3.489, 11.55; ingratiate (oneself) with 16.62, 236; flatter B 5.138; indulge B 5.36; attract B 13.313; entertain 3.12; serve A 10.213

plesinge *ger.* pleasure, ? offering B 3.252

pleten B 19.297, *p.t.* B Pr 213, 7.39 *see* **pleden** *v*

plicchen (plucchen) *v* (*p.t.* **plihte, pluhte**) pluck, pull 12.50, 19.12

pli(g)hten *v* (*p.t.* **pli(g)hte(n)**) promise, pledge, *in phrr.* (*refl.*) ~ **togyderes** unite by oath (in fellowship) Pr 47, (in marriage) B 9.167; bind (as apprentice) 6.208; ~ **treuthe** make a promise 2.124n, swear an oath (as juror) 3.469, pledge (one's) faith 8.33, make (marriage) vows 10.274

plihte *p.t.* 12.50 *see* **plicchen** *v*

plogh Pr 22, 145, 3.461, 8.151; ~ **man** 15.34, 139, 151 **plough (plouȝ)** 6.267, 15.236, B 6.169, 7.120, ~ **men** 11.297 *see* **plo(u)(g)h** *n*, ~ **man** *n*

plokken *v* pluck 7.228, B 12.248; pull B 11.114, 17.10

plomme *n* plum 12.223; ~ **tree** 5.118

plonte *n* plant 1.147, 7.228; sapling 18.25, 101

plot *n* stain B 13.275, 276, 318

plough (plouȝ) *n* 6.267, 15.236, B 6.169, 7.120, ~ **men** 11.297 *see* **plou(g)h**, ~ **man**

plo(u)(g)h (plouȝ, plow) plough Pr 145, 3.461, 8.111, 119, 160, 15.236; (*fig.*) 21.429; ploughing 8.131, 15.235, B 6.169, (*fig.*) B 7.120; **to / for þe** ~ to / plough(ing) Pr 22, 6.267, 7.191, 8.112, 21.337; = tool for earning a living B 15.125; team (of oxen) for ploughing (*fig.*) 21.267

plouhman (plowman) *n* ploughman 7.181, 9.186, 21.261 (= Piers) B Pr 119; (= as type of) person of low social rank 11.297; *see also under* **Peres, Perkyn**; *in phr.* **Peres...þe** ~ Piers the Ploughman's 15.196, 20.18, 24, 21.360, 393, 22.77

plowpote *n* plough-pusher B 6.103

pluhte *p.t.* 19.12 *see* **plicchen** *v*

plukke(de) *pr., p.t.* B 5.582, 11.114, 12.248, 17.10 *see* **plokken** *v*

plum-tree *n* plum-tree 5.118

pluralite *n* plurality [concurrent tenure of more than one benefice by a single cleric] 3.33, A 11.200

plurel *a* plural B 10.239

pnam Z 7.222, 224 = **mnam** *n*

po *n* (*uninfl. gen*) peacock's B 12.256; ~ **cok (pecok** 14.179 *etc*) *n* peacock 13.170, 14.161, 172, 174, 179, 183, B 12.228, 239, 240, 246; ~ **hen** pea-hen 14.174, B 12.239

poddyng *n* (kind of) sausage [stuffed lining of stomach] 15.67, B 13.107; ~ **ale** *n* thick ale 6.226

#poesie *n* (Latin) poetry, **of** ~ **a note** a song in Latin verse B 18.410

#poete *n* (Latin) poet 17.110, 20.452; = ancient learned authority 14. 183, **B** 10.338, 12.236; sage 14.92c; **Plato þe** ~ 11.120, (*with ref. to* Plato) 11.308, 12.175, 14.189

pohen 14.174 *see* **po** ~ *n*

poffen *v* blow 5.118; pant, breathe heavily 15.97

poynt(e) *n* speck of dirt B 13.255; moment of action, *in phr.* **in** ~ **to** ready to B 13.111; teaching Z 7.232; thing 8.35; reason 5.117; part, detail 20.43, 22.31, B 13.187, 16.133; bit Z 8.90; principle, stipulation 1.98; virtue 16.119; point 1.152

poynten *v* aim (one's words) 8.297

poysen *n* (*fig.*) (source of) spiritual evil 17.229, 232; lethal drugged potion 20.52

poysenen Z 3.64, B 3.82 *see* **(a)poisenen** *v*

pok *n* pustule, *pl.*(small) pox 22.98

poke *n* bag, pouch 15.187, 249, 16.86, ~ **ful (pouheful)** *n* bag-ful 9.342

poken *v* incite 1.128; ~ **forth** stir up 7.262; ~ **to god** urge to good works 7.286

pol *n* head 22.86, B 13.247; person, *in phr.* ~ **by** ~ individually 12.10

pole *n* pole, staff 20.52

polen *v* restrain [head of horse, ? by means of a martingale] 4.23

poleschen *v* polish 6.328 (B 5.475), A 6.84

polet *n* pullet, young chicken 8.303

pollen *v* drag 2.229; ~ **adoun** pick B 16.73; ~ **atweyne** tear apart B 7.115

pomade *n* apple drink, ? cider 20.409

pomp(e) *n* show, ~ **and pruyde** ostentation and display 16.235, B 14.194, ~ **of the worlde** worldly vaingloriousness 3.70

pondefold *n* (*fig.*) pound, **þe poukes** ~ the devil's enclosure (= Limbo) 18.281; **þe deueles** ~ = the state of mortal sin B 5.624c

poore *a, n* Pr 80, 8.144, B 11.244 *etc*; *see* **pore** *a, n*

pop-holy *a* hypocritically holy 6.37

pope *n* pope Pr 135, 3.163, 314, 318, 329, 5.78, 112, 10.207, 12.77, 17.167, 21.224, 431, 22.101, **B** 5.600, 10.292, 11.155, 13.167, 15.490; the [actual] Pope 3.183, 270, 5.191, 9.324, 337, 15.174, 218, 15.228, 17.188, 233, 243, 260, 21.445, 22.127, B 7.19; *in phrr*: ~**s bulles** 9.337, ~**s grace** 2.244, ~ **palays** 2.23, ~**s ȝifte** B 13.246,

popeiay *n* parrot 14.172

*****poperen** *v* ride rapidly A 11.213c

porche *n* porch (of house) 18.241

porcio(u)n *n* allotted share B 8.53, A 10.117

pore *a* (**pouere** A 2.59, 3.155, B Pr 82 *et p.*, *comp.* **porore** 22.50, *sup.* **porest** 16.159) poor [lacking wealth] 4.122, 6.60, 12.26, 136, 153, 15.10, 16.3, 22.50, B 11.197, **A** 3.273, 11.244, *in phrr*: ~ **clerkus** Z Pr 58, ~ **comune** 15.11, ~ **folk** 8.147, 320, 9.72, 12.167, 16.328, ~ **heremyte** B 13.30, ~ **man / men** 3.213, 4.115, 7.78, 84, 194, 8.39, 10.16, 15.36, 16.126, 323, **B** 3.241, 5.253, A Pr 93, ~ **in pacience** A 11.230, ~ **peple** Pr 80, 3.83, 8.205, 316, 9.34, 11.297, 12.101, 122, 166, 17.70, **B** 3.81, 84, 11.181, 183, 185, 14.174, 15.203, **A** 8.48, 11.310, ~ **pilgrymes** B 11.245, ~ **prouisores** 2.186, ~ **thyng(es)** 15.33, 309, A 12.50, **wydewe(s)** B 13.197, A 8.32; *a as n* (**þe**) ~ the poor, poor people 1.170, 176, 4.114, 5.166, 7.103, 8.14, 144, 9.178, 11.28, 48, 65, 12.102, 105, 108, 14.16, 15.88, 117, 16.92, 256, 19.239, **B** 11.230, 14.145, 15.154, 246; poor man 3.282, 9.46, 11.67, 15.289, 16.49, 54, 62, 66, 67, 79, 90, 123, 125, 127, poor man's 12.133, *in phr.* ~ **pacient** 9.178, 13.30, 98, 15.280, 287, 16.99; poverty-stricken Pr 82, 4.123; impoverished 5.78; (of clothes) mean, shabby 12.126, B 11.234, 244; (voluntarily) poor 12.159, 22.234, ~ **freres** B 15.327, ~ **ladies** 6.132, ~ **religious** B 4.125; (spiritually) poor, humble, ~ **(of) herte** 16.24, **B** 14.99, 195, 16.8; ~ **of** deficient in 16.159, B 13.301; *in stock phrr.* ~ **and / or riche** 15.202, 16.21, 47, 17.199, B 14.27, 73, A 2.59, 10.117, Z 2.67, **riche and / ne / or** ~ 11.59, 13.182, 17.2, **B** 12.74, 14.182

porest *sup.* 16.159 *see* **pore** *a*

poret *n* leek, ~ **ployntes** leek-plants 8.309, B 6.297

porfiel *n* fur trimming 4.111, 5.128

porore *comp.* 22.50 *see* **pore** *a*

pors *n* purse, money-bag 6.199, 266, 13.48, B 13.301, *in phr.* **into ~ward** in respect of (your) purses, monetarily Pr 101

porsen *v* put in (one's) purse 12.166

port *n* bearing, demeanour 6.30 (B 13.278)

#**portatif** *a* light, portable 1.152

porter *n* gate- / door-keeper 12.49, 22.299, 331; keeper of gate of heaven 7.270, **Peter the** ~ 16.167

porthors *n* portable breviary B 15.125

portour *n* porter, carrier 6.369

portrayen 19.137, B 3.62 = **purtrayen** *v*

#**posen** *v* put it (that) 19.277

possen *v* push, toss B Pr 151, *p.p.* Z 5.44

possession *n* possession B 12.247, possession of property 16.110, 17.226, 229; (material) possessions, property **B** 11.271, 274, 13.301, A 11.200

possessioner *n* beneficed cleric B 5.143

post *n* (wooden) prop B 16.54

poste *p.p.* Z 5.44 *see* **possen** *v*

postern *n* side door 7.270

postle 9.118, 18.177, B 6.149 *see* **apostel** *n*

pot *imp.* 2.50, *p.p.* 13.228, 15.41 *see* **potten** *v*

pot(te) *n* jar B 13.255, (*fig.*) 15.226; ~ **ful** *n* (cooking)-pot full 8.182, Z 7.286

potage *n* (thick) soup 8.182; stew 15.47; *in phr.* **payn(e) and / ne (...)** soup and bread 8.285, 15.235, **B** 6.150, 9.81, 15.315

potager *n* soup-maker 6.132

pote 8.64 *see* **plouh ~** *n*

potel *n* half-gallon 6.398

potente *n* staff, (= bishop's crosier) B 8.97

potten (putten) *v* (*imp.* **pot** 2.50, *contr. pr.* **potte** 16.111, **(put(te))** B 3.234, 14.272, 17.154, *p.t.* **potte(n)** Pr 27, **put** 4.74, **put(te)** 4.74, 111, *p.p.* **pot** 13.228, **ypot** 16.125, **put** 2.216) push Pr 170, 15.175, ~**...lowe** bring low 12.14, ~ **in pouerte** reduced to poverty 13.8, ~ **of** repel 16.121, B 14.191, ~ **out (of) / fram** expel (from) 13.228 (B 11.417), 16.223; put 3.83, 469, 6.219, A 9.95, ~ **in ere** suggest B 12.226; place 2.216; direct 15.41; (*refl.*) subject (oneself) 2.244, make (oneself) †B 6.150; ~ **forth** stretch out / forth 4.74, 7.181, extend B 17.154, (*refl.*) appear 15.236, 20.39; ~ **vp** reach up 20.52; ~ **to** set (sb.) (to) 5.171, 7.191, 8.197, 203, 11.120, B 19.254, appoint 3.469, 16.125, A 7.184; (*refl.*) set (oneself) to Pr 22, 25, 27, 16.111, 21.67; ~ **in store** (away) in 4.111, 16.86; ~ **forth** propound 2.50, 10.121, 11.39; declare B 3.234; ~ **byfore** put first, prefer 12.142, ~ **byhynde** push to the back (= value at little) 16.49

poudre *n* medicinal powder 22.360

pouer 8.283, Z 3.103 *etc* = **power** *n*

poues *n* pulse 19.68

pouheful = **pokeful**; *see* **poke** *n*

pouk(e) *n* (the) Devil 18.50, 278, 281, B 14.189, 191, **A** 10.62, 11.161; **helle** ~ *n* fiend from hell 15.165

pound *n* pound-weight [for measuring] 6.223; pound [measured weight] 6.358; Troy pound [for measuring gold, = 12 oz.] 16.297; pound sterling [monetary pound] Pr 161n, ~ **of nobles** (value of) a pound sterling in nobles B 10.289

poundmele *av* by pounds at a time 2.232

pouren *v* (**togederes**) (mix by) pour(ing) together 6.226

poustee *n* power, ~ **of pestilence(s)** violent attack of the plague **B** 5.36, 12.11

pouere *a* B Pr 82 *et p.*, A 2.59 *see* **pore** *a*

pouerte *n* (state of) poverty 2.84, 12.150, 236, 13.3, 26, 99, 15.281, 16.57, 59, 61, 71, 97, 114, 119, 120, 155, **B** 11.317, 14.274, (*person.*) 13.1, 16.83, 85, 86, 93, 122, 126, 138, 139, 149; destitution 9.182, 12.14, 13.8, 140, 15.159, 16.18, 32, **B** 12.11, 14.284, 15.208, *in phrr*: **penaunce and ~, ~ and penaunce(s)** (a state of) hardship and penitential suffering(s) 12.150, 21.67, **B** 15.270; 9.234, 16.326, B 12.9; poverty (voluntarily adopted) 16.111, 22.236, B 14.273; (the virtue of) poverty 12.144, B 11.271, *in phrr*: **pacient ~** 12.178, **B** 14.101, **pacience and ~, ~ and pacience** 13.20, B 12.61; 16.56, 152, 21.250, B 10.340; poverty of spirit, humility 12.142, B 14.192; shabbiness of clothing 10.117

power *n* power, ability (to do sth.) 6.256, 11.60, 16.159, 221, 19.141, 143, 156, **B** 3.168, 16.37, 54, *in phrr*. **of ~ able** 8.283, **in (by) my / þi / here ~** as far as I / you / they am / are able 4.137, 8.33, 9.17, 13.69, B 13.105, A 5.75; spiritual power Pr 128, 136, 15.226, 21.184, 189, 389; spiritual authority 22.321; control, dominion (over) 3.434, 16.61, 17.306, 18.283, **B** 10.237, 11.164, A 10.62; legal power / authority Pr 135, 2.50, 9.324, 17.224; authorisation B 6.149; force of supporters 4.70

praye *n* quarry, captives B 18.310

prayen 5.82, 7.296, 8.131, 266, 22.340, B Pr 90 *see* **preyen** *v*²

prayere 15.230 = **prey(e)re** *n*

praisen 14.183 = **preysen** *v*

praktisour *n* (medical) practitioner B 16.107

prechare 16.245 = **prech(e)our** *n*

prechen *v* preach (sermon) (to) Pr 57, 66, 78, 3.277, 5.114, 9.112, 11.56, 207, †218, 16.262, 17.83, 174, 188, 20.329, **B** Pr 90, 3.223, 5.145, 6.149, 7.14, 135, 10.267, 15.443, 20.127, **A** Pr 93, 5.11, 23; *ger.* preaching 7.285, 17.17, **B** 4.122, 15.405, 448, A 4.107; declare religious doctrine 12.42; proclaim 5.141, 10.89, 15.70, 75, 76, 84, 89, 16.287, 17.191, B 13.118; exhort B 10.202, **A** 11.198, 12.22, ~ **to** exhort to do B 3.223; teach 22.275, 277, B 10.388, A 8.16; declare Pr 39, **A** 1.137, 3.64; ~ **of** recount, speak about 16.324, **B** 3.234, 10.34, 13.85, A 11.72; speak out B 5.143

prech(e)our *n* (authorised) preacher [of Christian faith] 7.87, 11.207, 16.245, 250, 267, 276, 21.232, **B** 12.19, 15.440, 498; **~s** preachers' B 4.122

precious(e) *a* precious 1.147, 11.10; of great worth B 16.261; costly 20.409

#predestinaeten *v* predestine (to salvation) *p.p.* **predestinaet** 11.207c

preest 4.130, 14.123, B Pr 60, ~ **hoed** 16.243, 245; *see* **pre(e)st** *n*, ~ **hoed** *n*

preyen *v*¹ prey upon, ravage 22.86

preyen *v*² (*p.t.* **prey(e)de** 1.77, 5.128 *etc*) entreat, beg (of) 1.77, 2.71, 4.94, 5.128, 140, 191, 7.302, 8.7, 35, 169, 176, 10.11, 15.122, 218, 234, 16.114, 20.207, 21.154, 22.245, 339, **B** 6.199, 16.24, ~ **to** make entreaty to 9.279, B 4.98, ~ **of** beg (to) 21.154, for **B** 6.123, 10.122; ask for 15.33, **B** 11.245, 13.30, 16.73; ask (that) 15.193, 20.176, B 6.196; (say) pray(er) 3.464 (pray psalter), 9.42, 17.244, 250, 255, Z 5.92; pray (for) 1.77 (2), 8.131, 9.42, 12.10, 15.212, 214, 17.226, 21.250, 22.292, 365, B 5.104

prey(e)r(e) *n* entreaty, plea 2.68, 7.209, 20.204, B 10.289, *in phr.* **for eny / no ~** in spite of any entreaty 2.216, 21.309, B 17.294; request 9.282, B 13.136; prayer (to God), *esp.* of intercession 3.274, 5.84, 8.136, 11.60, 12.101, 17.86, 236, **B** 11.155, 15.345, 16.135; action / practice of (saying) prayer(s) Pr 27, B 6.247, A 12.98, *in phr.* **~(s) and / ne / or penaunce(s) / penaunce(s) and ~(s)** 7.240, 9.174, 328, 16.38, **B** 7.120, 178, 12.9, 15.148, 426, 16.38

preynte *p.t.* 15.122, 20.19, †B 13.86 *see* **prinken** *v*

pre(i)sen *v* praise, commend 6.60, 7.262, (*p.p.*) 10.311, 12.197, 13.26, **B** 6.108, 7.38, 10.340, 11.318, 13.313, 14.48, 274, 15.156, 252, **to ~** to be commended 13.207, 18.221; value, esteem 5.31, 6.45, 12.144, 17.164, 22.149, B 11.253; assess the value (of) 6.379, 383

prelat *n* prelate [churchman of episcopal or abbatial rank] Pr 101, 2.182, 3.270, 5.140, 6.120, 16.267, 17.188, 192, 225, 260, 22.127, **B** 9.81, 15.490, 608; *in phrr.* **~es and prestes** 10.198, 17.244, 317, **~es of Holy Churche** 6.119, 16.243, 22.229, **B** 11.98, 15.244, **princes and ~es** B 7.43, Z 7.271

prenti(e)s *n* (*pl.* **prentis** 3.279, 6.279, **~es** 21.232) apprentice 2.224, 6.208, 279; **~es of lawe** law-students, ?novice barristers 21.232; *in phr.* **Peres ~ þe Plouhman** P. the P's apprentice 15.196, **#prentished (~hode B)** apprenticeship (*fig.*) 6.251

#prescite *a* foreknown (to be damned) 11.208c

presence *n* presence Pr 188

present *n* gift 3.270, 8.39, 318, 14.97, 18.277, 278, 21.96; offering (made as a bribe) 3.117, 199, 4.91, B 13.377, *in phr.* **for ~** in spite of bribes 21.309

presenten (with) *v* offer as a present (to) 21.92

pre(e)s(s)en *v* push on 16.54; bring pressure upon, ? importune 22.127

presompcion 13.231 = **presumpcioun** *n*

pressour *n* press (for stretching cloth) 6.219

prest *a* eager, willing 16.62; prompt, quick 7.194 (*sup.*), **B** 6.196, 13.251, (*comp.*) B 10.289, A 12.98; (*as av*) at once 20.272; **~ly** *av* promptly 3.305, 8.102

pre(e)st *n* (*sg. as pl.* 3.310, B 15.121) priest (= parish priest) Pr 118, 121, 2.182, 3.186, 277, 4.130, 6.298, 304, 7.10, 14, 30, 71, 246, 8.190, 9.280, 288, 292, 301, 318, 12.29, 13.81, 100, 111, 15.214, 16.250, 267, 276, 17.61, 72, 117, 122, 238, 244, 21.232, **B** 5.104, 165, 7.131, 135, 11.98, 281, 302, 13.11, 237, 14.9, 91, 15.117, 121, 128, 440, 485, A 12.22; Jewish priest [of the Old Testament] Pr 116, 14.60; *in phrr.* **badde ~es** B 10.280; **fals ~es** Pr 106; **ydiotes ~es** B 11.316; **inparfit ~es** 16.276, 22.229, B 15.131; **lewed ~es** B 11.317; **mansed ~es** 22.221, B 10.278; **parsche ~es** Pr 79, 81, 14.123, 22.281, 320, B 10.267; **proute ~es** 22.218; **~es and persones** 3.463, B 3.252 (for **persones / prelates and ~es** *see svv*); **~is fyle** 6.135, **~is sone** 14.60

pr(e)est(e)ho(e)d *n* (the order of Christian) priesthood (*person.*) 21.334; the body of (Christian) priests [collectively] 16.243, 245, 17.233, 250

presumen *v* presume, *in phr.* **power ~ in hemself** presume the power resides in themselves Pr 135

presumpcio(u)n *n* presumption B 11.421, **~ of** arrogance in regard to 13.231; a supposition 11.39

presumptuously *av* arrogantly A 12.8

preuen *v* put to the test 10.121, 11.39; try, assay B 13.215; discover †B 7.45; prove (by argument / authority) 12.31, 175, 13.26, 15.100, 135, 137, 140, 287, 289, 215, 22.275, **B** 10.344, 14.191, 17.156, 18.152, (*? or* manifest), A 11.233; demonstrate 11.159; show 5.115, 18.59, 19.224, B 12.259; explain **B** 12.19, 29, 13.†85, 123; spell out Pr 39; declare 6.119, 9.318, 12.142, 178, 17.4; demonstrate in practice 12.202, 15.89, B 13.133; illustrate 6.186; endeavour 17.317; put into practice 5.141, 16.262, B 13.80, A 4.107

preuete 13.230 = **pryuatee** *n*

preuyli(che) A 3.57, 71 *see* **pryue(y)ly(che)** *av*

pryde 20.346, (*person.*) 21.224 *et p.,* 22.70, **B** 13.276, 14.73, 194, 281, 15.67, A 3.57 *see* **pr(u)yde** *n*

prien *v* peer, **~ after** peer in search of B 16.168

prike(a)re *n* horseman, mounted warrior 10.135, 20.24; rider B 10.307

prik(i)en *v* pierce 19.164; wound 22.86; spur 19.333, B 2.190; gallop 2.201, 4.24, 5.159, 22.149, *in phr.* **cam ~** came galloping 20.9; incite, stir up 19.91

prime *n* prime [period from 6 to 9 a.m.] *in phrr.* **aȝen ~ daies** before prime A 12.60, **hey ~** high prime (= towards 9 a.m.) 8.119

prymer *n* primer [layman's devotional manual] 5.46

prince *n* sovereign 9.279, 11.10, 18.277, **~s lettres** 21.309, **~s paleises** 10.16; ruler 13.8, **B** 7.43, 13.51, 18.263,

A 2.12, 11.298, Z 7.272, (*in ref. to* God) **~ of heuene** 17.248, **~ of Paradis** A 7.109; (*to* Christ) **~ Iesu** 13.3, 21.96, B 16.37; spiritual ruler (= pope) 17.167, 21.224, (= bishop) 10.198, A 11.198; chief 12.178; leader 2.84

principalli(che) *av* chiefly B 10.468; above all B 14.195

prinken *v* (*p.t.* **preynte**) wink, signal by a look 15.122, 20.19, †B 13.86

printe *n* imprint 17.75

printen *v* stamp (*fig.*) 17.80

prio(u)r *n* prior [deputy head of monastic / mendicant house] 5.91, 6.153, **~ prouincial** = head of all houses of religious order in a province 12.9

prioresse *n* prioress [head of convent of nuns] 6.135, B 5.165, (*uninfl. gen.*) prioress's 6.132

pris[1] *n* (monetary) value, cost B 2.13; value 18.277; esteem, **setten at litel ~** care little about, think little of 12.26, 15.10

pris[2] *a* most excellent 21.267

priso(u)n *n* imprisonment 15.256; prison, gaol 4.123, 7.21, 9.34, 72, 180, **B** 8.102, 15.265, (*fig.*) = (captivity in) purgatory ? 7.276, 12.69, B 18.393; prisoner 3.173, 9.34, 72, 180, 16.323, 20.58, (*fig.*) captive of purgatory B 15.345, poor / sick person as 'God's prisoner' B 14.168c

prisoner *n* prisoner B 3.137, (*fig.*) poor person as 'God's prisoner' B 14.174

pryuatee (preuetee) *n* secret(s) 13.230; (divine) mystery 18.5

priue(e) *a* secret 4.189, **~ ȝeft** 3.117, **paiement** 22.365 (= bribe); confidential (*pl.*) B 2.178; concealed 17.242; treacherous 22.115; intimate, familiar 2.23, 64, 3.183, 9.118, (*sup.*) 18.98, B 13.207; private 12.40, 13.37, B 10.99, **~ membres** sexual organs B 12.229; personal, individual 13.81, 21.379

pryue(y)ly(che) *av* secretly, on the side B 13.377, A 3.57; (hidden) secretly 17.172; stealthily 21.302; furtively 6.266, B 3.82; treacherously 18.165; alone, *Pauci ~* only a few by themselves 12.50; quietly 15.151, 22.108, B 13.55; ? mysteriously 18.101

priueoste *sup.* 18.98 *see* **priue(e)** *a*

procuratour *n* agent 7.89; steward, manager 21.259

profecyen *v* speak as if inspired B 18.108, **~ of** prophesy about 9.114, **~ bifore** foretell 21.16

proferen (forth) *v* extend 19.117, 118

professioun *n* solemn pledge (of duty) 1.97

profete (prophete) *n* prophet (*with ref. to* Christ) 17.299, 21.48; prophet of the Old Testament 3.427, 11.259, 12.202, 21.145, (**Dauid**) þe **~** B 3.234, 7.122, 11.94, **Ysaye** þe **~** 18.113, **Samuel** þe **~** 3.413; **~s and patriarkes** 10.207, **patriarke(s) and / or ~(s)** 7.87, 9.12, 11.150, 14.60, 81, 18.208, 273, 20. 141, 146, 279, 366, 21.16, **B** 10.338, 16.251; 'holy fool' [insane person believed divinely inspired] 9.211; **false ~s** 21.222

profyt *n* benefit 8.7, 14, 111, 22.333, **B** Pr 119, 4.150;

interest(s) 6.208, 279, B 13.238; *in phrr.* ~ **of the wombe** so as to fill the(ir) belly Pr 57, **comune** ~ Pr 167, 184, 4.119; (spiritual) benefit 5.101, 13.201

profitable *a* beneficial Pr 145; spiritually beneficial 15.84; to the satisfaction (of) 15.175; useful 6.263, 7.191; worthwhile **B** 6.274, 17.151

profiten *v* be of advantage / profit Pr 101

profren *v* offer, present 4.91, 7.199, 8.39, 318, 15.250, **B** 4.64, 13.190, 381; offer a bribe 4.67; (*refl.*) offer oneself (in service) B 6.24; offer battle, challenge (to fight) 8.150

properliche 15.154 = **propreliche** *av*

prophecie *n* prophetic utterance B 15.325

prophete 3.413 *etc* = **profete** *n*

propre *a* individual, distinct **B** 10.239, 16.54; proper, particular B 16.185; appropriate, ? fine 9.301; goodly 15.64, 18.101, B 13.51

propreliche *av* strictly B 14.284; exactly 16.117, B 14.275; fittingly 15.154

proud *a* proud, haughty 10.135, 22.218, B 12.239, ~ **herte** 3.224, (*as name*) 6.3, ~ **herted** B 15.201; ~ **for** proud on account of B 13.190; ~ **of** greatly pleased with, elated about 6.46, 304, 8.203, 16.297, *in phr.* ~ **of aparayle** splendidly dressed 6.30, B 13.278, stately A 2.41; splendid 14.172

proudly *av* splendidly B 11.240

prout(e) 6.46, 22.218 = **proud** *a*

proue(n) **A** 9.115, 11.229, 233 *etc* = **preuen** *v*

prouendre *n* fodder B 13.244; prebend, stipend of a canon 3.32, B 13.246, Z 3.33

prouendren *v* provide with a prebend 3.186

prouerbe *n* (Biblical) maxim, proverb 8.264, 12.173, 17.51

prouince *n* province [area under a bishop's jursdiction] 17.284, B 15.608

#**prouincial** *n* head of a province (= district) of an order of friars, *gen. sg. or pl.* 9.342; *a in phr.* **Priour** ~ = head of a province of friars 12.9

prouisour *n* provisor [cleric granted right by the pope to assume a benefice on one becoming vacant] 2.182, 186, 3.183, 4.130, B 2.171

prowour *n* purveyor [provider / overseer] 21.261

pr(u)yde *n* (the sin of) pride [excessive self-love / self-esteem] 1.128, 2.84, 5.117, 6.13, 8.348, 11.58, 64, 12.236, 15.231, 236, 16.121, 227, 263, 330, 17.215, 20.346, **B** 14.73, 15.67, A 10.102, (*fig.*) B 13.276, (*person.*) (the deadly sin of) Pride 6.14, 16.47, 57, 59, 119, 210, 21.224, 229, 337, 354, 357, 362, 384, 22.70, 108, 149, 353, 374, 383; ~ **of Parfit Lyuynge** the Pride of Life, Vainglory 11.176, 194; love of praise, vanity 3.70, 6.59, 7.262, 16.235, A 3.57; over-confidence (in) 13.231; love of display, ostentation Pr 25, 10.117, 16.235, 256, B 14.194, 281

pruynses *pl.* 2.84 *see* **prince** *n*

psalm *n* Psalm 14.116, **B** 3.248, 6.249, 11.313; **seuene** ~**s** the seven Penitential Psalms 3.464, 5.47

publischen *v* make public 12.40

puddyng B 13.107 = **poddyng** *n*

#**pue** *n* pew [enclosed seat in church] 6.144

pu(y)r *a* pure 4.91; fine 2.10, A 2.12; strict 5.166; total **B** 14.193, 285, 16.220; simple, sheer, *in phrr.* ~ **bileue** B 10.464; ~ **charite** 11.65, **B** 10.314, 15.79; ~ **enuye** 11.56, ~ **grace** 20.189, ~ **ioye** B 16.18, ~ **lawe** 15.290, ~ **mercy** 6.172, ~ **nauht** 17.306, ~ **pacience** B 14.193, ~ **pouerte** 16.152, ~ **resoun** 15.289, 19.321, **B** 13.167, 14.108, A 8.153; ~ **reuthe** 13.92, ~ **riht(e)** 16.99, 17.70, ~ **synne** 5.115, B 11.429, ~ **skile** 15.137, ~ **sleuþe** B 14.76, ~ **tene** 8.124, B 16.86, ~ **treuthe** 3.348, 21.195, B 11.155; true 12.197; very 1.97, *in phrr.* **on**...~ **erthe** 3.101, 9.185; ~ **tree** the tree itself B 16.8

pu(y)re *av* absolutely, completely B 11.274; very 7.20, 12.136, 18.103, **B** †5.405, 11.194; thoroughly 3.382, 15.309, B 11.194

pu(y)rli(che) *av* completely 15.231; integrally, essentially 19.141; solely B 16.51; simply 18.234

puken A 6.122 = **poken** *v*

pullen B 7.115, 16.73 = **pollen** *v*

pulsshen A 5.250 = **poleschen** *v*

pulten *v* (*p.t.* **pulte** B 1.127, 11.62, *p.p.* **pult** 11.208) thrust, ~ **adoun** 10.95, ~ **out** put forth 19.143, ~ **oute (of)** remove from 11.208; expel B 1.127, release by force B 11.162; put, place Z 7.182

punfolde B 5.624 = **pondefold** *n*

pungen *v* thrust A 9.88

punys(c)hen *v* (inflict legal) punish(ment upon) 2.50, 3.79, 16.125; torment B 14.189; (inflict divine) punish(ment on) 21.196, B 10.369

puple Pr 145, A 12.102 = **pe(o)ple** *n*

purchacen *v* obtain (a pardon) 3.32, 9.3, 42, 337, 19.219; acquire [by gift or purchase] 5.77, 158, 12.248

pure B 4.95 *et p.*, A 8.101, 153, **pureste** A 2.9, 12, **B** †5.405, 11.194, 247; **pureliche** B 16.51 *see* **pu(y)r** *a*, **pu(y)re** *av*, **pu(y)rli(che)** *av*

purfil B 4.116, 5.26 = **porfiel** *n*

purfiled *p.p.a.* wearing apparel richly trimmed 2.10; *and see* **porfiel** *n*

purgatory(e) *n* purgatory 2.108, 6.299, 7.117, 9.11, 11.33, 300, 12.69, 13.30, 15.309, 18.15, **B** 6.44, 10.369, 15.345, 18.393, *in phrr.* **appurtinaunces of** ~ subsidiary rights (*iron.*) of p. 2.108, **pardon in** ~ remission of punishment in p. A 8.59, **penaunce in / of** ~ punishment in ~ **B** 9.77, 10.420; (*fig.*) = cleansing from sin through earthly suffering 9.185, ~ **on erthe** 15.94

purgen *v* purge 17.232

purpos *n* proposition 10.121, B 10.117

pursuen *v* follow after 21.163; follow, attend 11.176, B 11.185; follow (example of) 21.433; pursue (with hostile intent) 12.14, 18.165; chase B 12.240; strive after

B 3.241; strive / seek (to) 14.174, 17.167, A 5.75; bring a suit, prosecute 19.286

pursward Pr 101 *see* **pors** *n*

purtinaunce 16.330, A 2.68 = **appurtinaunce** *n*

purtrayen *v* draw 3.66, 19.137, (*fig.*), ? (*with pun on* 'form mental image(s) of') 16.321

purueien *v* provide B 14.29; make provision (for) †B 5.165

put *n* (*pl.* **puttes**) dungeon, (underground chamber in) prison 9.72, B 5.406, ~ **of helle** B 10.369, (*fig.*) ~ **of meschief** B 14.174

put(te) *p.t.* Pr 25, 4.74 *etc*, *p.p.* 2.216, 13.8, *contr. pr.* **B** 3.234, 14.272, 17.154 *see* **potten** *v*

#**putour** *n* pimp 6.172

putrie *n* prostitution, ?lecherous living 6.186

quad *p.t.* Z Pr 130 *et p.* = **quod** *see* **quethen** *v*

quaken *v* (*p.t.* **quakid** 20.257, **quoek** 20.63) shiver, shake [with cold] 11.42, [with fear] 22.200, [with grief] 20.63, 257

quantite *n* mesure, (*as av*) **a** ~ to some degree 21.377

quarter *n* (*pl.* ~ Z 4.46, ~**es** 4.61) [as measure of weight] quarter (of a pound) 6.223; [measure of capacity, = 8 bushels] quarter (of) 4.61

quath Pr 182, **quaþ** A 1.12 *et p.* = **quod** *see* **quethen** *v*

quauen *v* tremble, quake B 18.61

queed *n* evil one [= the Devil] B 14.190

queene *n* queen 8.46, B 13.170, A 2.14c

queynte *n* cunt (*with pun on* 'clever device'), *in phr.* ~ **comune** (? = sexually promiscuous) 4.161

queynte *a* cunning 19.234, *comp.* elegant A 2.14c

queyntly *av* artfully, speciously 21.349

que(y)ntise *n* stratagem 20.297, (*with pun on* 'elaborate trappings') 21.354

quellen *v* (*p.p.* **quelt** B 16.114) kill Z 7.263; *p.p.* dead B 16.114

quen A 2.14 = **quene** *n*[1]

quenchen *v* (*p.p.* **queynte** 20.391) quench, stifle (*fig.*) 19.168, 222, 253, 326

quene[1] *n* low-born woman 8.46

quene[2] B 13.170 = **queene** *n*

†**querelen** *v* quarrel 5.154 (†B 10.301)

queste *n* judicial inquest, trial by jury (= **enqueste**) 22.162, **fals** ~ inquest inititated invalidly / resulting in unjust verdict 11.20; **of Paulines** ~ belonging to the inquest (*or* ? collecting-mission) of Paulines 2.110c

question *n* (theological) problem 11.54

quethen *v* (*p.t.* **quath** Pr 182, A 1.12 *et p.*, **quod** Pr 138 *et p.*) say (*with direc, declarative imperative or exclamatory quotation following*) 3.155, 283, 340, 4.176, 5.89, 7.304, 8.1, 124, 15.139, 21.12, 208, 21.358, 22.317, (*with quotn. preceding*) 6.62, 7.181, 199, 286, 11.314, 12.24, 14.202, 15.95, 18.156, 169, 19.78, 333, 20.47, 50, 57, 360, 21.357, 22.140, 189; (*after first and before*

second part of quotn.) Pr 138 *et p.*, B Pr 160 *et p.*, A 3.162, 12.1 *et p.* (**quod**), A 1.12 *et p.* (**quaþ**), Z Pr 103 *et p.* (**quad**); ask (*with quotn. preceding*) 7.55, 10.151, 12.24, 13.220, 15.112, 113, 276, 283, 16.114, 314, 17.125, 18.184, 274, 19.18, 20.19, 192, 360, 21.394, **B** 14.37, 97, 15.149, (*between first and second part of quotn.*) 5.26, 6.234, 357, 7.176, 10.70, 72, 74, 151, 13.198, 15.247, 16.163, 177, 337, 18.274, 20.26, 21.10, 22.207, **B** 10.330, 15.22, 16.24, 180; speak 16.113; answer A 12.88

quyete *n* repose, **in** ~ in peace 17.240, at rest B 1.123

quyk[1] *a* living 20.257; alive 17.303, 18.145, (when) alive, during life 15.12; ~**...o lyue**, ~ **on molde** anywhere alive A 2.14, Z 2.18; *a as n, in phr.* ~ **and dede** the living and the dead 9.21, 21.53, 197

quyk[2] *av* at once 15.283, **as** ~ at once, as quickly as possible B 14.190

quyk(i)en *v* cause to revive 20.391; animate 16.181

quyten *v* (*p.p.* **quyt** 4.98, **yquited** 8.107, *contr. pr.* B 11.193) repay (in full) 8.107, 9.273, 13.75, 15.12, B 18.358; give recompense for 20.387, 388; make satisfaction for 16.31, 20.391; requite, pay back 12.106, 109, B 11.192, 193

quoek *p.t.* 20.63 *see* **quaken** *v*

quoer *n* choir (of a church) 5.60

raap *p.t.* 6.270 *see* **repen** *v*

rad *p.p.* 3.496, **radde(n)** *p.t.* 3.488, 4.105, 5.125, 143, 15.52, B 5.124, Z 4.5 *see* **reden** *v*

#**radegounde** *n* skin-infection of face 22.83

rage *n* fit of anger 13.129

#**rag(e)man** *n*[1] (name for the) devil 18.122

rag(e)man *n*[2] bull, document with seals attached Pr 73

ragged *a* tattered 11.195, 16.349; gnarled A 10.124

ray *n* fine striped cloth 6.217

ray *a* made of striped cloth (**ray**) A 3.271

raymen *v* acquire 13.95

rayne (reyn(e)) *n* rain 14.24, 15.269, 19.303, 317, B 3.208

r(a)ynen *v* (*p.t.* **roen** 15.269) rain 5.164; fall 15.269, 19.317

rakeare *n* scavenger, street-cleaner 6.370

ran *p.t.* Pr 165, 2.62, 6.1, 15.152 *see* **rennen** *v*

rang *p.t.* 20.471 *see* **ringen** *v*

ransaken *v* despoil 18.122

rape *n* haste, **in** ~ quickly B 5.326

rap(p)(e)ly(che) *av* hastily 6.382; swiftly 18.290, 19.50

rapen *v. refl.* hurry 5.102, 7.8, 8.125, 19.79

rappen *v* strike 1.91

rat *contr. pr.* (= **redeth**) 3.406, 12.212, 15.269, 19.234 *see* **reden** *v*

rathe *av* early, *in phr.* **late and / ne** ~ = at all times 10.140, 11.89, B 3.73; (*comp.*) **rather** sooner, earlier 8.44, 9.123, 10.73, 11.261, 294, 13.31, 16.51, 57, B

12.233, ~...**til** before 10.54; at an earlier time B 13.85; more readily 4.5, 9.134, 11.29; on the contrary 4.4; rather 1.142, 6.290, 7.208, 13.186, 14.154, **B** 11.77, 14.107, 15.341, *in phr.* **þe** ~ the more swiftly Pr 117; the more readily 16.237, B 13.24; at once 8.125, 19.69, **B** 5.259, 280, 8.35; (*sup.*) **rathest** earliest 12.225; first 6.391, B 16.71; most readily 9.148, 16.45, 351

rato(u)n *n* rat Pr 165, 176, 182, 190, 192, 198, 214, 216

ratoner *n* rat-catcher 6.370

rau(g)hte *p.t.* Pr 73, 4.179, **B** 8.35, †11.438, Z 4.129 *see* **rechen** *v*

raunsomen *v* ransom 19.285, (*fig.*) redeem, deliver from damnation 11.261

raunsoun *n* release of prisoner by payment, (*fig.*) redemption B 18.353

rauen *v* be mad 20.192; behave like a madman B 15.10

rauener, -our *n* plunderer [one who takes goods by force] 17.43, 47

raueschen, -yschen *v* plunder 21.52; rape 4.47; transport (into vision) 11.168; enrapture 2.16; seduce, lead astray 11.294

raxen B 5.392 = **roxlen** *v*

realte A 11.228 *see* **ryalte** *n*

re(a)(u)m(e) Pr 192, **B** 3.208, 298, 5.11, A 10.134 *see* **reume** *n*[1]

reautee B 10.334, 14.210 *see* **ryalte** *n*

rebaude 15.233 = **rybaud** *n*

rebuken *v* reprimand Pr 110, 12.67, 13.237, B 5.365; upbraid 16.15; reprove 5.82, 20.352; reproach **B** 11.372, 436, *ger.* B 12.217; repulse 22.63

rec(c)heles *a* heedless, reckless 12.66; imprudent A 10.106, *a as n* reckless behaviour A 10.51; indifferent to / ? undisturbed by care 20.2; ~**li(che)** *av* rashly 13.154; heedlessly B 11.130; ~**nes(se)** *n* heedless rashness 10.217, 12.70, (*person.*) 11.195, 199, 276, 286, 13.129

rec(c)hen *v* (*p.t. subjv.* **rouhte** 12.21) care 8.127, ~ **of** care about 4.34, 16.316, 20.2, 21.451; care / be concerned (that) 3.387, 4.69, 9.101, 12.21, 13.237; (*refl.*) concern oneself 11.195, 12.4

rece(y)uen 4.196, 19.145, **B** †6.148, 17.191 *see* **rescey-uen** *v*

rechen *v* (*p.t.* **rau(g)hte** Pr 73, 4.179, **B** 8.35, †11.438) reach to B 8.35; catch hold of, reach B 11.361; lay hold of 3.499; extend, suffice 16.72; be stretched 4.179; come into contact with 19.145, B 17.191; †~ **after** go / proceed after B 11.438

reclusen *v* enclose 4.116

recomenden *v* commend, praise 16.356

reconforten *v* give fresh heart to B 5.280

record *n* record, agreement (*with pun on sense* 'testimony') 3.343; witness, **take** ~ **at** call to witness B 15.87

recorden *v* pronounce, set down 3.470; declare 4.151, B

4.172; testify [esp. in recollection of what has passed] 4.29, 20.203, 373; repeat (from memory) 17.320

recoueren B 18.353 *see* **rekeueren** *v*

recouerer *n* treatment, remedy 19.69

recrayen *v* be cowardly (in battle), *p.p.a* **recrayed** (*as term of abuse*) recreant, cowardly B 3.259

recreaunt *a* admitting defeat, overcome 20.103

***rect** *a* right 3.366; direct [of grammatical relationships] 3.333, **relacion** ~ inflexional agreement 3.343, 360, (*fig.*) 373, **relatif** ~ relative pronoun agreeing with its antecedent (*fig.*) 3.354

red *p.p.* **A** 5.180, 11.221 *see* **reden** *v*

re(e)d *n*[1] advice, counsel 4.29, A 9.99; command 6.270 (B 13.374)

re(e)d *n*[2] reed 20.50

re(e)d(e) *a* red 21.11, A 10.123, Z 2.16, ~ **rubies** 2.13, ~ **scarlet** B 2.15; (= reddish-hued) ~ **gold** 21.88, B 2.16, ~ **noble** 17.200; **sam** ~ half-red 8.310

redels *n* riddle **B** 13.168, *pl.* ~ 13.185

reden *v* (**redon** 5.69; *contr. pr.* **rat** 3.406 *etc,* **ret** 3.412, 13.5, B 14.66, *p.t.* **radde** 3.488 *etc,* Z 4.5, **redde** 7.119, A 4.97, *2 pers.* **reddest(ow)** B 3.259, *p.p.* **(y)rad** 3.496, 11.276, **red** A 5.180, 11.221) read Pr 205, 3.406 (1), 488, 496 (2), 7.31, 9.280, **B** 3.259, 5.234, 10.302, 12.65, 13.73, **A** 10.86, 12.22, Z 7.261, 265, *ger.* B 7.85; (read with) understand(ing) 7.34, **B** 5.422, 15.375; read out [official document] 2.71; read aloud, chant 13.126, 16.348, 17.120; (learn by) read(ing) 3.406 (2), 412, 496 (1), 10.238, 13.5, 15.269, 284, 17.194, 19.234, **B** 12.49, 15.445, A 11.221; instruct A 12.30 (2); interpret B 13.185; express 2.14, 9.82; declare (*or ?* perceive) 17.200 (1)), B 11.102; reckon 5.69, 7.40; advise 4.5, 13.206, 19.108, **B** 4.30, 7.182, 12.94; counsel 5.102, 6.291, 7.101, 9.332, 19.249, B 5.124, A 2.32; urge 1.170, 4.105, 5.125, 143, 8.283, B 10.266, A 12.30 (1); order, bid 7.119, 15.52, A 5.180

redy *a* ready 18.111; *and see* **aredy** *a*

redyly *av* quickly 4.184; clearly B 17.155; to be sure, indeed 6.91, 253, 286, Z 4.132

***redyng-kyng** *n* ? reed-thatcher, ? retainer who rides on errands 2.112c, 6.371

redon 5.69 = **reden** *v*

refte *p.t.* 3.326 *see* **reuen** *v*

refusen *v* reject 5.78; forsake 13.232; spurn 7.84; decline 16.189, 19.145; renounce 3.366, 21.371; refuse to accept 17.43, 47; refuse 13.142

registre *n* official record book (of accounts) 22.271, (*fig.*) B 5.271; historical account 11.276

registrer *n* registrar, book-keeper B 2.174, (*fig.*) 21.260

regnen *v* reign Pr 140, 4.171; hold sway 3.439, 16.57, 21.52, 22.64; prevail 9.256; predominate 1.116, 20.437; live, exist 10.24, 13.185, 16.46, 121, 20.236, B 2.54; flourish 14.173; be rife 21.421; extend 22.382

#regrater *n* retailer 3.113, 118, 6.232, B 3.90

#regraterye *n* retail-selling 3.82

rehercen, -sen *v* enumerate 17.25; explain (to) 13.224, B 10.293; set out 6.1; repeat 1.22, 6.164, **B** 11.391, 13.72; utter Pr 198; declare 4.150, 9.341, A 4.145; express 12.37

reygnen 14.173 = **regnen** *v*

reik *n* way Pr 216n

reyken *v* (*3 pl.* **reykes**) proceed Z 4.158

reyne 14.24, 15.269, 19.303, B 3.208 = **rayne** *n*

reisen *v* raise, conjure up A 11.161

reioysen *v* (*refl.*) find one's joy (in) 17.198

rek(e)nen (**rykenen**) *v* enumerate 1.22; name A 12.113; number 2.62, 17.25; give account (of) 11.302, 13.34, 16.52; ~ **wiþ** call to account 4.171, 12.67; settle accounts (*fig.*) 15.285, B 5.270

rekenyng(e) (**rykenynge**) *n* statement of account B 5.421; reckoning of what is due 7.40; (*fig.*) account (of conduct) 6.347, B 14.107

rekeueren *v* come back to life 21.161; win back (by force) 21.246, (by law) B 18.353

rekken 21.451, B 15.177 = **recchen** *v*

relacio(u)n *n* (grammatical) relationship 3.332, (*fig.*) 351; ~ **rect** direct / right relation(ship) 3.341, 343, 360, (*fig.*) 373

relatif *n* relative pronoun, ~ **rect** 3.354, ~ **indirect** 3.387

#relen *v* wind yarn (on a reel) 9.81

relees *n* release (from an obligation), (*fig.*) forgiveness of sin 8.99

relesen *v* remit (debt / obligation), (*fig.*) forgive (sin) 3.62

releuen *v* bring relief (to) 13.20; support 9.36; provide for (with alms) 13.69, 16.315; deliver 17.311; raise up again 20.143; restore 20.390

#relyen *v* rally 22.148

religio(u)n *n* (the) religious order(s) 3.202, 5.143, 9.36, 11.59, A 10.106; the way of life of a religious order 9.221, 10.88, 22.264, A 11.202, **B** 10.293, 13.286, 15.87, (*person.*) 5.150, **B** 6.151, 10.305; member(s) of (a) religious order(s) 5.143

religious *n* (*pl.*) members of (a) religious order(s) 5.147, 164, 9.221, 17.47, 206, 213, 22.59, **B** 4.125, 10.291, 15.307, 317, 341, Z Pr 57; (*sg., pl.* ~**es**) **B** 10.316, 12.35

religious *a* bound by rule [of a religious order] 4.116, B 4.120

relyk *n* relic 20.475, 21.426

reme B 8.106, 10.76 = **reume** *n*¹

remembraunce *n* recollection [of past experience] 5.11

remen *v* cry out with grief, *pr.p.* 20.103

remenaunt *n* remaining portion 22.293, *in phr.* **residue and** ~ 8.109, B 5.460; rest, remaining group 12.50; remainder, difference 19.205; *in phr.* **al þe** ~ every other matter / everyone else 21.451

remyng *pr.p.* 20.103 *see* **remen** *v*

remissioun *n* release from debt, (*fig.*) forgiveness of sin 3.357, 8.99, A 11.285

ren *imper.* B 12.35 *see* **rennen** *v*

renable *a* eloquent B Pr 158

renaboute *a* run-about (*as nickname*) B 6.148; *and see* **rennare** *n*

renden *v* tear B 4.186; rip B Pr 199

rendren *v* recite 6.217, ? 17.320; read aloud, recite, ? expound 10.88c

reneyen (*p.p.*) 12.66, B 11.125, 126 *see* **renoyen** *v*

reng 10.24 = **renk** *n*

reninde *pr.p.* 3.333 *see* **rennen** *v*

renk *n* man 14.110, 20.2, 22.293, **B** 12.51, 14.105, A 4.134; person 10.24, *pl.* people 9.332, 20.300, = human beings 13.186, 191; *in phr*, **no** ~ nobody B Pr 197

rennare *n* roamer, ~**aboute** A 11.202; **Rome** ~ pilgrim / one taking papal revenues to Rome 4.125

rennen *v* (*p.t. sg.* **ran** Pr 165 *etc*, **ern** 18.164, †**arne** B 16.136), *pl.* **ronne** Z Pr 57, *p.p.* **ronne** 10.88, *pr.p.* **reninde** 3.333, **rennynge** 20.167, **ernynge** 21.381) run (forth) Pr 165, ~ **awey** B Pr 166; run a course (of joust) (*fig.*) B 18.100; run free B 15.460; wander A 10.105, 110; enter, find refuge in 10.88; travel 2.62, 193, 16.349, Z Pr 57, ~ **at ones** travel along together 13.31; hasten (along) 6.1, 15.152, 18.290, 20.167, B 17.84; well up 18.164, 21.381; proceed 3.333

renoyen (**reneyen**) *v* abjure, forsake 12.61, 62; *p.p.a* disloyal, forsworn 12.66

renown *n* renown, **of** ~ of good repute Pr 176

rental *n* register of rent due, (*fig.*) record of sins [spiritual 'debts'] 8.99

rente *n* revenue from property 17.221, B 10.15, A 11.228, Z 2.100; income 16.72; property (yielding income) 3.82, 5.73, 14.184, 16.315, 316, B 15.320; rent (= payment) 9.73

renten *v* (*p.p.* **yrented**) endow with income-yielding property 9.36, 10.368

#repaest *n* meal 9.148

repen *v* (*p.t. sg.* **raap / rope**, *pl.* **repe / ropen**) reap 5.15, 6.270 (B 13.374)

repentaunce *n* repentance, sorrow for sin 19.282, 285, (*person.*) 6.1 *et p.*, ~ **of** repenting for 10.217

repenten *v* feel regret B 12.249; be (feel) sorry for / repent (of sin) 9.236, 19.202, 281, 21.444, 371, B 12.83, (*refl.*) 6.164, 7.149, B 5.259, **to** ~ to enable (him) to repent 10.52; have second thoughts 6.391

repreuen *v* reprove, censure 5.172; rebuke B 10.261; condemn 14.81; disapprove of 3.385; disprove 20.151; refute B 10.343

rerage B 5.242 = **(a)r(r)erage** *n*

re(s)ce(y)uen *v* receive, take 3.499, 5.69, 21.260, †B 6.148, A 8.60; accept 6.300; (be able to) hold 19.145, 154, B 17.191; regard (as) 17.201; admit 8.44; appoint 4.196

rescetour *n* harbourer [of criminals] 3.497

resemblen *v* be like B 16.214; compare 14.187

residue (resudue) *n* remains of dead man's estate (after discharge of dues) 12.218, *in phr.* ~ **and þe remenant** 8.109, B 20.293

resoen 17.264 = **reso(u)n** *n*

reso(u)n *n* the intellect B 15.65; (faculty of) reason [*esp.* as grasping the natural moral law] 3.144, 16.175, 186, A 10.57; **knowen / konnen** ~ possess understanding 19.227, 21.26, B 15.475; (common) logic / sense 12.155, 15.287, 16.252, 19.154, **B** 14.123, 17.39, 155, 18.152, A 8.153; **puyr** ~ sheer common sense 19.321, B 13.167; wisdom 3.324, 14.49; good / right judgement 5.5, 69, **aʒeynes** ~ in defiance of right reason 20.203; measure, moderation, **by** ~ moderately 13.191; **out(e) of** ~ immoderately, to excess 2.89, 6.434, 13.154, **B** 1.25, 5.36; means, action B 18.353; justice 3.385, 11.99, 17.213, 19.285, 21.83, 86, 90, 481, B 10.114 ~ **and / ne riht** 3.293, 14.148; *in phrr.* **aʒeynes alle** ~ 20.377; law, **ayeins** ~ against the law B 3.92; (principle of) equity, **puyr** ~ 15.289; (principle of) law B 18.340; right order 12.62, 16.212, 19.327, A 10.51; **by** ~ rightly, properly 1.90, B 17.255; order, **by** ~ in order 18.98, B 1.22; cause, **by** ~ **of** on account of 16.48, B 12.260; argument Pr 190, 11.38, 16.143, 17.264; case 2.50; (*person.*) [as reeve] 13.34, [as bishop] B 5.11, [as pope] 5.112, [as moral teacher] 1.50 *et p.*, [= (divine) principle of moderation (in nature)] 13.143 *et p.*

resonable *a* orderly and accurate 13.34; right 3.366; equitable 6.33; lawful, ~ **obedience** subjection to a religious rule B 13.286; eloquent Pr 176

resonabl(el)yche *av* in the right way, in accord with right reason 12.17, 15.282

resonen 13.183 = **aresonen** *v*

resseyuen 6.300 = **re(s)ce(y)uen** *v*

rest *n* sleep Pr 214, 14.95, B Pr 197, *in phrr.* **a** ~ asleep 6.236; **bryngen to** ~ bring to a place of rest A 2.138; **gon to** ~ set 6.417; leisure, comfort 20.218, B 10.15; idleness 15.233; (eternal) rest (in heaven) 14.197, 16.154, **B** 7.78, 14.156; spiritual tranquillity 10.54, 20.223

resten *v* (*contr. pr.* **reste**) Pr 186, *p.t.* **reste** 13.146, B 18.6) rest, repose 4.16, 13.146, B 3.236; sleep Pr 186, 19.317; (*refl.*) lay (oneself) down 9.144, **B** Pr 7, 18.6; stop 11.108, 13.33, 20.167; cease 6.126; remain 4.103, 13.232, B 4.192; settle A 10.78

restitucio(u)n *n* reparation, amends [*esp.* by restoration of ill-gotten goods to rightful owner] 6.234, 237, 295, 19.202, 297

restituen *v* restore property (to its proper owner) 6.297, 343, 12.17; give back 10.54

restoren *v* refresh, reinvigorate 12.149

resudue 8.109 = **residue** *n*

resureccioun (resurexioun) *n* resurrection 12.116, 18.163,

20.267, 473; (feast of the) resurrection (of Christ) 20.471

ret *contr. pr.* 3.412, 13.5 *see* **reden** *v*

retenaunce *n* retinue 2.55

retoryk *n* poetic language 12.37

retribucioun *n* repayment, reward 3.337

returnen *v* come back B 17.120

reufulliche *av* sorrowfully 19.202; compasssionately B 14.152; pitiably B 12.47; piteously B 16.78; *and see* **rufol** *a*

***reule** *n*¹ space between bed and wall 9.79

reule *n*² Rule [of a religious order] 5.143, 147, 157, 169, 9.221, 21.426, 22.247, 265, **B** 10.291, 12.36, 13.286, 15.87, 317, *in phrr.* **in** ~ in orderly condition A 10.51; **oute of** ~ in disregard of one's Rule 3.202; habitual practice B 10.98

re(u)len *v* (*p.t. 2 sg.* **reuledest** 13.186, *p.p.* **(y)ruled** 21.399) govern, rule Pr 216, 9.10, 20, B 18.397, ~ **alle / my / thy reumes(s)** 4.9, 180, 10.105, 11.214, 19.3, 21.481, *ger.* **ruylynge** government Pr 150; direct, guide 1.50, 13.182, 186, 14.36, 19.226; restrain 13.206, (*refl.*) control 13.191, 21.399

reume *n*¹ kingdom, realm Pr 192, 3.190, 203, 264, 293, 437, 4.9, 135, 180, 182, 5.74, 114, 125, 190, 11.59, 21.481, **B** 3.208, 298, 15.524, A 12.113, Z 4.130, 152; region 1.91, 3.254, 4.180, 182, 9.10, 10.105, 11.214, 17.259, 19.3

reume *n*² cold, catarrh 22.83

reuth *n* pity 1.170, 4.103, 7.149, 13.69, 16.22, **B** 5.478, 16.5, 18.91; a piteous thing 7.40, 9.82, 15.300, 16.16, 17.194; a pity B 14.127; a sad / regrettable thing 17.200, 259; compassion B 14.145, **of puyr** ~ simply through compassion 13.92; mercy 4.105, 108, 131, 6.422, 19.282, **B** 10.342, 14.168; sympathy 3.118; sorrow 6.286, **hauen** ~ feel sorry 22.193, **B** 15.11, 16.78

reuare *n* plunderer 13.57, B 14.182

reue *n* (manorial) reeve, bailiff 2.112, 180, 7.33, 11.302, 12.218, 21.463, 466, **B** 5.421, 10.471; (*fig.*) = (God's) agent 3.308, 21.259

reuel *n* festivity 7.101 (B 13.442), (a place of) revelry 22.181

reuelen *v* become wrinkled 10.268

reuen *v* (*p.t.* **refte** 3.326) seize by force (from) 18.122, B 16.89; take away 16.1; deprive (of) 3.226, 4.180, 20.299, 308; *and see* **to-** ~ *v*

reuerence *n* veneration B 12.119; sign of honour, obeisance 9.191, 16.46, 17.43

reuerencen (-sen) *v* (treat with) respect, honour 11.19, 16.48, 237, 17.201, 22.59; do reverence to 19.261, 20.248, 267, 473; regard highly B 12.259; pay homage to 21.73; reverently salute 18.243; courteously greet 13.247, 15.29, 20.175; bow / pay obeisance to 9.123, B 15.5

reuerentlich(e) *av* reverently 5.114; courteously 20.466; (*comp.*) ~loker with greater honour 8.44

reuers *n* opposite 12.212

reuesten *v* dress in ceremonial vestments, *p.p.* yreuestede 5.112

reward *n* regard, heed, hauen / taken ~ at / of take heed of 4.40, 19.249

rewarden *v* reward Pr 150, 14.148, 21.194; (*pr. p.*) pay 3.308; requite 5.32, 12.70; grant 14.148, B 3.318, 156; care for B 14.145, 168; watch over B 11.369

rewe *n* row (of houses) 3.107; *in phr.* by ~ in order 1.22

rewele A 10.51, 11.205 = reule *n*

rewen *v* regret, rue B 16.142; have pity 6.321; (*in impers. constr.*) bote hym rewe without his feeling pity 20.438

rewful *a* compassionate B 14.148

rewfulliche B 14.152 = reufulliche *av*

rewlen 21.481, Z 4.130 = reulen *v*

rewlyche *a* wretched, miserable A 12.78

rewme 3.190, 293, 4.9, 21.481, A 12.113, Z 4.130, 152 = reume *n*[1]

ryalte (realte, reautee) *n* royal status, ? lordship 16.51; possession (of land) B 10.334 (A 11.228)

ryb *n* rib B 9.34, A 4.149

ryban *n* ribbon, border B 2.16, Z 2.17

rybande *p.p. a.* bordered A 2.13

rybaud *n* villain 10.217, 16.45, 18.169, 20.50; sinful wretch 7.149; foul-mouthed rascal 6.434

*rybauder *n* lewd jester 8.75

rybaud(r)(y)e *n* scurrility 6.434; obscenities, debauchery Pr 45; foolish jesting 11.199

#rybben *v* clean flax 9.81

rybibour *n* fiddle-player 6.370

riche[1] *n* kingdom B 14.179, heuene ~ blisse 12.160, 16.100

riche[2] *a* rich, wealthy 2.55, 82, 184, 4.47, 5.26, 6.33, 126, 7.98, 9.332, 10.167, 268, 11.109, 12.4, 25, 107, 228, 13.5, 57, 65, 97, 13.110, 182, 14.87, 95, 184, 15.9, 285, 308, 16.12, 21, 42, 356, 19.227, 229, 231, 22.39, 235, B 2.56, 9.174, 10.335, 342, 345, 11.196, 197, 198, 12.51, 74, 239, 14.105, 123, 127, 144, 145, 152, 156, 157, 163, 168, 15.176, 323, 331, 335 (2), 341, 342, A 3.272, 11.61, 231 *in phrr.* riht ~ (the) very wealthy 11.49, 12.155, 14.173, 16.127, 20.218; precious, costly 15.233, 16.72, 351, 20.175, B 2.15, A 3.271, Z 2.16; luxurious 22.181; (*comp.*) potent, powerful 20.475; splendid 2.14, 22.181; prosperous 3.203, 11.214; fertile B 3.208, A 10.134; *a as n* rich man 10.264, 13.31, 95, 16.48, 52, 62, 19.249, B 10.98, 12.244, 249; the rich Pr 219, 9.129, 12.212, 13.79, 14.181, 16.237; rich people 5.182, 7.101, 9.101, 134, 191, 11.23, 70, 12.104, 134, 15.288, 16.8, 17.206, 19.244, B 4.40, 14.212, 15.335 (1), 339; *a. phr.* pore and / or ~, ~ and / ne / or pore = all people 4.26, 153, 8.111, 11.59, 13.182, 15.202,

16.47, 17.2, 199, B 11.207, 14.27, 73, 182, 212, A 10.117; *in phrr.* for ~ or for ~ for poorer for richer A 2.59, in ~ ant in ~ ? under all circumstances Z 2.67; ~ handes capacity to give large bribes 3.118; (þe) mene (and) (þe) ~ Pr 20, 219, B 2.56, 10.64

†richeles *n* incense 21.90

richeliche *av* splendidly 2.12

richen *v* become rich 3.82

richesse *n* riches, wealth 2.80, 3.324, 326, 12.145, 13.25, 69, 15.282, 16.1, 45, 46, 48, 51, 16.316, 17.198, 212, 19.235, 21.286, B 2.17, 10.15, 85, 334, 339, 11.318, 12.58, 244, A 11.266, *in phr.* ~ ope ~ wealth heaped upon wealth 12.232; opulence 2.16; (state of) affluence 16.57; (store of) valuable goods 14.184; (*pl.*) precious things, treasures 9.191, 12.249, 21.73, B 3.23, 90 (*sg. for pl.*), (*fig.*) treasure / wealth in heaven B 14.148

ryden *v* (*contr. pr.* riht Pr 186, ryt 4.25, B 4.14, *p.t.* roed 22.181, rood 4.14, 40, B 17.100, *pl.* ryde(n) 4.28, 13.154, B 4.30, *p.p.* ryde 5.157, B 11.337) ride (on horseback, mule) 6.126, 16.349, 19.79, 22.181, B 4.14, 30, 17.100, *in phrr.* ~ ful rapely gallop 19.50, ~ softe amble 4.54; ride along (road) 19.79, B 4.42; ride forth (on errand / expedition, to joust *etc*) 1.91, 3.269, 4.16, 34, 20.24, 21.246; ride to battle 5.74; (*fig.*) = use, be supported by 2.180, 184, 188, 194, 4.40, 54, B 4.33, 40, Z 4.131; move about Pr 186; copulate 13.154, B 11.337; *in phr.* ~ out of aray go astray [= observe rule negligently] 5.157

rydere *n* rider on horseback B 10.305

ryflen 6.236, *ger.* B 5.234 = ru(y)flen *v*

rygebone 6.399 *see* rug- *n*

right B 3.239, Z 4.132, ~ (e) 2.180, B 9.38 *etc*, Z 3.90, 4.24 *see* riht(e) *n, av*

riȝht(e) *n* 19.3, B 10.342, riȝt *a* 18.290 *see* riht *n, a*

riht 3 *pr. sg.* Pr 186 *see* ryden *v*

riht(e) (riȝt, right) *n* justice 11.27, 20.373, 439, 21.90, 353, *in phr.* ~ and / ne resoun true justice 11.29, 19.3, 20.300, 395, 21.463, B 3.239, resoun ne ~ 3.293, 14.158 (*and see* resonable ne rect 3.366); law 8.53, 17.42; judgement Z 4.132; rightful ownership 20.299, 308; just claim / (en)title(ment), right 3.367, 5.74, 16.99, 22.96; title B 10.342; claim, *in phr.* þer beyre / oure bothe ~ the claim(s) of both of them / us 20.36, 371

riht *a* direct 19.79, B 4.42; right-(hand) 3.76; ~[name] actual 6.232, proper 16.186; sound 3.326; very (same) 18.290, 19.50; true 11.294, 16.251

riht(e) *av* exactly, just, *in phrr.* ~as just as 2.209 *et p.*, B 9.38; just like 5.112; ~ so just so, exactly in that way 1.156 *et p.*; ~ thus exactly as follows 6.422, 9.285; ~ with þat immediately thereupon 4.196, 6.1, 62, 7.55, 13.247, 20.94, 471; right 11.168; very, extremely 2.180, 11.49, 12.141, 155, 14.173, 16.52, 21.8, 73, 194, Z 3.90; to any great degree 16.127, *in phrr.* ~

nauht 5.82, 9.123, 14.87, 19.154, 21.451, ~ **saue** just except †21.371; thoroughly 3.354, 21.481; truly 6.91, 7.15, 17.194, 18.71; righteously 3. 324; completely 20.62, 103, 192, 412; straight, directly 7.198, B 4.14, *in phrr.* ~ **til / to** right (up) to 12.70, 15.284, 18.169, Z 4.24, straight (out) to 13.183, right (down) to 18.39, ~ **with** straight along with 15.152; *in cpd.* **anon** ~ immediately 4.150, 15.52

riht *contr. pr.* Pr 186 = **ryt**; *see* **ryden** *v*

rihtfo(e)l, ~ful(l) *a* even-handed 15.291; just Pr 150, 17.213, 20.94; righteous, virtuous 4.153, 5.147, 6.33, 10.24 (*sup.*), 10.41, 17.34, 259; *a as n* the just man 10.38, 11.16; right-thinking people 4.151; in accordance with reason 3.373; proper 12.88*n*; authentic A 11.202

rihtful(l)ly(che) *av* justly 9.10; rightly B 4.172, Z 4.126; legitimately 12.62; virtuously 13.95; honestly 19.235, B 14.102; in the proper manner 1.50, 15.282

rihtfulnesse *n* (the cardinal virtue of) justice 21.83; divine justice 5.32

rihtwisnesse *n* justice 19.282, 297, (*person.*) 20.167, 175, 192, 203

rykenen 2.62, 4.171, 11.302, 13.34, (**rykenynge** *ger.* 6.347) *see* **rekenen** *v*, **rekenyng(e)** *ger.*

ryme *n* rhymed [*sc.* alliterative] verse 9.82; (*pl.*) verses, ballads 7.11

rynen 17.99, *p.t. subjv.* 5.164 *see* **r(a)ynen** *v*

ryng *n* (gold finger) ring Pr 73, 3.24, B 3.90, A 2.11

ryngen *v*[1] adorn with finger ring(s), *p.p.* **yrynged** 2.12

ryngen *v*[2] (*p.t. pl.* **rang**, **rongen**) ring bells 20.471, (B 18.427), 22.59, *ger.* ringing of bells 7.5

rype *a* ripe 18.42, 64, 128, 20.412n, B 6.293; *a as n* the ripe ones 18.107; ready 7.5

ripen *v* grow ripe 12.225, 234, 21.319

ripereue *n* guardian of crops [against thieves at harvest time] 5.15

rysen *v* (*p.t.* **ro(e)s** 6.236, 18.243, *pl.* **rysen** 6.382, *p.p.* **rysen** 9.147) get up 13.236, 15.27; get to one's feet 18.243; survive 19.69; rise (from bed) Pr 45, 6.235, 7.5, 9.79, 146, 147; rise (from dead) 9.338, B 15.594, 20.264, 21.146

risshe B 4.170, A 11.17 = **ru(s)che** *n*

ryt *contr. pr* 4.25, B Pr 171, 4.14 *see* **ryden** *v*

ryuer *n* river B 15.337

Robardus knaues *n* Robert's boys [*punning name for marauding thieves*] Pr 45; *and see* **Robert** (*Index*)

robbare *n* robber 11.261, 12.249, 13.57, **B** 4.128, 5.231, 462, 14.182

robben *v* rob 4.54, 9.180, 12.154, 20.299, 21.447, **B** 3.195, 17.90, 100, 18.339, *ger.* being robbed 16.138; despoil 10.196, B 16.89; steal from (by deceit) 11.19; alienate 16.1

robe *n* robe [long, loose outer garment] 15.203, 16.351, 356, B 2.15, A 3.271

roben *v* (provide with) clothe(s) 11.19, B 15.335, 339, A 2.13, Z 3.170, *ger.* clothing, dress 2.14; dress 10.1

roch(e) *n* rock 19.12, 20.62, 257

rodden *v* grow red, flush 15.109

rod(e) *n* cross [of Christ] 2.3, 10.116, 16.22, 17.198, 201, 20.51, 55, 259, 21.325, 22.43, B 18.84; crucifix [in church] 7.68, 20.267, B 5.103, ~ **of Bromholm** B 5.227, ~ **of Chestre** B 5.460, A 7.92, ~ **of Lukes** 8.109; cross-symbol [on coin] 17.206

rody *a* red 15.109

roen *p.t.* 15.269 *see* **r(a)ynen** *v*

roep *n* cord 18.156

roes *p.t.* 6.236 *see* **rysen** *v*

roggen *v* shake B 16.78

roilen *v* stray about idly A 11.209, †B 10.297

#roynous *a* rough, scaly 22.83

rokken *v* rock 9.79, B 15.11

rolle *n* roll, list [of burgesses] 3.111; account roll 21.466

rollen *v* record B 5.271

Romaynes *n.pl.* the Romans 17.281 (B 15.530)

romber A 10.105 = **romere** *n*

rombide *p.t.* A 4.30 *see* **romen** *v*

Rome-rennare *n* traveller to the papal court 4.125

romede *p.t.* 7.7 *see* **romien** *v*

romen *v* walk 9.147, 15.27, 28, 29, 18.145, B 15.594; go forth Pr 186, A 4.30; travel, journey (*fig.*) 5.11, 6.330, 22.212; wander about 10.1; wander off 12.65; go away 12.50

#romere *n* wanderer **B** 4.120, 10.305, A 10.105

romien *v* (*p.t.* **romede**) roar 7.7

ronde *n* round slice 9.148

rong *n* rung (*fig.*) 18.44

rongen *p.t.pl.* 22.59, B 18.427 *see* **ryngen** *v*[2]

ronne *p.t. pl.* Z Pr 57, *p.p.* 10.88 *see* **rennen** *v*

rood *p.t.* 4.14, B 17.100 *see* **ryden** *v*

roode B 5.103 *et p.* = **rod(e)** *n*

roof *n* roof (*fig.*) 21.329

roon *p.t.* B 14.66 *see* **r(a)ynen** *v*

roos *p.t.* 18.243, B 5.230 *see* **rysen** *v*

roost *n* roast-meat Pr 231

roote B 12.58, 71, 14.94, 15.65, 16.22 *see* **rote** *n*

rope(n) *p.t. sg., pl.* B 13.374 *see* **repen** *v*

ropere *n* rope-maker / seller 6.371, 386

rose *n* rose 15.109, A 10.123

rosten *v refl.* toast oneself 9.144

rote *n* root 8.64, A 10.124; (edible) root 15.244; (*fig.*) 16.251, 22.54, B 14.94; basis, origin 20.322, B 12.58, 71, A 10.134; essential nature B 15.65

*rotey *n* rutting, *in cpd.* ~ **tyme** time of rutting B 11.337

*roteyen *v* rut 13.146

roten[1] A 10.78 *see* **rot(h)en** *v*

roten[2] 13.21 = **rot(y)en** *v*

roten, roton *a* rotted, decayed **B** 15.101, 16.252

rot(h)en *v* (*refl.*) root, settle oneself firmly in (*fig.*) 2.55; take root in (*fig.*) A 10.78

rot(y)en *v* (become) rot(ten) 12.225, 18.60; decay 5.150; languish 13.21; perish 3.357, B 10.114

rotten *v* (*p.t.* **rotte, rutte**) snore 7.7; sleep 14.95, B 18.6

rouen 20.126 *see* **rowen** *v*²

rouȝ *a* rough, thorny A 10.124

roumen *v* leave clear Pr 181, 189

rounen *v* whisper 4.14; consult, 4.25, 6.382

rousty *a* filthy 8.75

route *n* pack Pr 165, 192, 198, 214; retinue 2.62; body Z Pr 57; crew B 18.405

routen *v* settle in A 10.78

rowen *v*¹ row (*fig.*) 10.52

rowen *v*² dawn 1.113, 20.126

rownd *a* sonorous (?*with pun on* 'round-shaped') 6.399

roxlen *v* stretch 7.7, B 5.392 (**raxed**)

rubben *v* rub (*p.t. or p.p.*) B 13.100

rub(i)e *n* ruby 2.13, 3.24

ruche 12.198 = **ru(s)che** *n*

rude *a* ignorant, uneducated B 15.475; untrained B 15.460; foolish 13.229

ruet *n* horn 6.399

rufol *a* wretched 6.237; compassionate B 14.148

rufulliche B 16.78 = **reufulliche** *av*

rug(ge) (ryge) *n* back 9.144, 16.54, 21.288; ~ **bone** backbone 6.399

#ruyflare *n* robber 4.125, 6.315

#r(u)yflen *v* rob, plunder 4.54; despoil (of) 10.196, 19.92; rifle 6.236, *ger.* B 5.234

ruylen 9.10, *ger.* Pr 150 = **reulen** *v*

rule B 10.98, 291, 12.36, 13.286, 15.87, 317, **rulen** B 11.369, 18.397 *see* **reule** *n*, **reulen** *v*

ru(s)che *n* rush-stalk 9.81; (*fig.*) = worthless object, *in phrr.* **counten nat a** ~ **(of)** consider of no value at all 3.178, 12.198, 13.238, **worþ (of) a** ~ worth (of) anything B 4.170, A 11.17

russet *n* coarse woollen cloth 10.1, 16.298, 343

ruþe B 5.478, 10.342, 14.127, 145, 15.11, 16.5, 78, 18.91 *see* **reuth** *n*

rutte *p.t.* B 18.6 *see* **rotten** *v*

saaf B 7.51, 8.49, 10.345, 12.166 = **sa(e)f** *a*

sacrefice *n* sacrifice 18.249, 264; devotional offering Pr 98, 119

sacreficen *v* offer sacrifice 14.61

sad(de) *a as n* fixed, firm base 3.334; constant (*comp.*) 11.296; steadfast (in virtue) 5.90, 10.31, (*sup.*) 10.49; grave 10.118; serious 17.264; *n*–**nesse** firm trust B 7.151

sad *av*, (*comp.*) **saddere** more soundly B 5.4

sadel *n* saddle 4.20

sadelen *v* (put a) saddle (on) B 2.170, **lat** ~ **hem** let them be saddled B 2.175

saet *p.t.* 6.361, 15.108, 18.241, 22.199 *see* **sitten** *v*

sa(e)f *a* safe / free from danger 10.38, 40, 14.112, B 7.51, 8.49, 12.166, A 8.38; saved (from damnation) 14.191, 206, 17.313, B 10.345

safly *av* safely 17.63

sage *a* wise 3.121, 8.243, 11.211; *in phr.* **fo(e)l** ~ wise fool [= licensed jester] 7.82, 103

say *1 pr. sg.* 8.307, A 11.13, *imper.* 7.229, 12.39 *see* **seggen** *v*

say(h) *p.t.* Pr 5, 13, 15, 221, 232, 2.9, 5.124, 8.281, 11.51, 22.199, **saiȝ** A 5.22 *see* **sen** *v*

said *p.t.* 10.18, 12.206, 14.47, 20.302, ~**e** Pr 68 *et p.*, **sayede** 10.223, *pl.* **sayden** 3.17, **saidest** 14.103, **saye** *inf.* 21.243, **sayn** *inf.* Pr 203, **sayen** *pr.pl.* 9.131 *see* **seggen** *v*

saylen *v* dance 15.209

sayn Pr 203 = **seggen** *v*

saynt (seynt) *n* the just [of the OT] 7.132; saint [canonised Christian in heaven] Pr 48, 3.98, 7.31, 78, 113, 153, 240, 11.13, 271, 12.134, 173, 14.136, 16.346, 17.270, B 3.235, 4.39, 7.36, 85, 11.244, 14.155, 15.269; (*as title*) ~ **Austin** 16.151, ~ **Aueroy** 15.100, ~ **Beneyt** B 4.121, ~ **Bernard** 16.220, ~ **Fraunceis** B 15.231, ~ **Gregori** 12.79, B 5.164, 11.156, 228, ~ **Iame(s)** 1.180, ~ **Io(ha)n** [the Evangelist] 7.100, 12.100, 14.136, B 11.226, [the Baptist] 11.258, 18.114, 268, 20.367, ~ **Luke** 1.87, 17.235, ~ **Marie** [the Blessed Virgin] 7.137, 12.135, 19.125, ~ **Mihel** [the Archangel] 9.37, ~ **Paul** 10.89, 11.56, ~ **Peter** B 10.442, ~ **Thomas** 7.201, ~ **Treuthe** 5.198; (= *place*) ~ **Marye** [church] Z 2.100, ~ **Petres churche** B 7.173, ~ **Poules** [cathedral] 11.56, B 10.46, Z 2.80; [*meton. for* shrine of saint] 7.174, **B** Pr 50, 12.39, ~ **Iame(s)** Pr 48, 5.197, 4.122, 5.197, ~**es of Rome** Pr 48, 5.197; (*in assev.*) 3.141, 8.1, 54, 297, **B** 6.3, 24, 55, 4.188, A 7.3, Z 4.152

saynt *a* holy 1.80, 11.204, (*as title*) ~ **Spirit** the Holy Spirit of God 11.153, 14.27, 47, 18.72, 232, 19.162, 167, 175, 187

sayst(e) *2 sg. pr.* 6.290, 8.237, 298, 20.466 *see* **seggen** *v*

sayth *3 sg. pr* 1.39 *et p.*; *see* **seggen** *v*

sak *n* sack (for grain) 8.8

sake *n* sake, *in phr.* **for the** ~ **of, for** ~**(s)** ~ for the good / benefit of 2.197, 11.144, 16.364, 17.231, 20.408, **B** 5.489, 6.102, 16.162; out of regard / consideration for Pr 138, 4.99, 9.133, **B** 9.90, 15.91; out of love for 12.206, 14.5, 18.252, **B** 10.253, 11.195, 12.92, 14.321; because / on account of 6.320, 20.357, **B** 3.189, 15.521, ? Z 4.100

#salarie, salerie *n* salary †3.272, 7.39; wage B 14.142

salme B 3.248 = **psalm** *n*

salt *n* salt B 15.428, 431, (*fig.*) 430, 441

salt(e) *a* salt 15.51; salted 8.307

saluacio(u)n B 15.497, A 11.282 = **sauacio(u)n** *n*

salue *n* medicinal ointment **B** 13.195, 249, 17.76; healing remedy 22.170, (*fig.*) 1.146, 9.263, 12.57, 15.226, 22.307, 337, 373, B 17.120; *and see* **saue** *n*

saluen *v* apply medicinal ointment to, (*fig.*) 22.306; treat 22.348; heal spiritually B 10.270, 11.217, 16.109

Samarita(e)n *n* Samaritan 19.49 *et p.*, 20.8

same *prn* the same one, he 10.59; him B 9.198; it 3.58; that 8.243; the same thing Pr 229, 3.30, 4.87, 9.187; the same (text) B 10.194; (*with avl. sense*) **the** ~ likewise 3.27, 11.24, 183, 13.111, 15.245, **B** 5.39, 6.234, 9.176, Z Pr 56

same *a* same, identical 1.172, 12.184, 19.149, 20.385, 22.224, **B** 7.63, 10.110, A 11.69

#**sam-rede** *a* half-red 8.310

sand 21.78 = **so(e)nd** *n*

sandel B 6.11 = **sendel** *n*

sang *p.t.* 21.212 *see* **singen** *v*

sank *p.t.* 20.69 *see* **sinken** *v*

sannure *comp.* Z 7.165 = **sonner**; *see* **sone** *av*

saphire *n* sapphire B 2.13

#**Sapience** *n* the OT wisdom writings [the book(s) of Proverbs, Wisdom *etc*] 3.484, 494, 11.117, 211, B 3.345, 6.234, A 8.46; (the) wisdom [*sc.* in these books] B 9.94; spiritual wisdom, knowledge B 12.57

sarmon *n* discourse 3.121, 11.291, 14.200; sermon 12.47, A 11.274; preaching 5.200, 7.88 (B 13.429); sermon-text A 11.245

Sar(e)sin(e), Sarrasyn *n* non-believer [in Christianity], Moslem 3.480, 14.200, 17.132, 150, 151, 156, 184, 240, 252, 307, 313, 315, **B** 13.210, 15.389, 392, 397, 497; pagan 12.56, 89, 17.123, **B** 10.346, 11.156, 164

sarrore *comp. av* more sorely 15.286 (*and see* **sore** *av*)

sat *p.t.* Pr 114 *etc*; *see* **sitten** *v*

satisfaccio(u)n *n* satisfaction [penitential reparation enjoined after confession] 16.27, 19.298, B 14.21, 94

Saturday *n* Saturday 5.116, 6.173, 417, B 13.154, þe ~ on Saturdays B 5.73

sauce *n* sauce (*fig.*) 8.273, 15.49

saufte *n* (spiritual) safety B 7.36

sauȝ *p.t.* B 2.17, 5.9, A Pr 90 = **say(h)**; *see* **seen** *v*

sauhtenen *v* be reconciled 4.2

#**saulee** *n* food, (satisfying) meal B 16.11

saumplare *n* exemplar, (*fig.*) = instructor 14.47

**saunbure *n* saddle, ? litter 2.178

saunȝ *prep.* without B 13.286

saut B 20.217, 301 = **sawt** *n*

sauten *v* leap B 13.234

sauter *n* Psalter, Book of Psalms 3.287, 7.92, 8.259, 10.165, 213, 11.23, 51, 12.28, 13.122, 14.116, 15.310, **B** 2.38, 3.234, 237, 248, 7.40, 51, 123, 10.26, 284, 11.94, 278, 284, 12.13, 14.93, **A** 3.221, 8.46, 10.86, 11.192; (copy of) psalter 3.464, 5.47, B 12.16, ~ yglosed glossed (copy of the) Psalter 6.301, 11.117

sautrien *v* play the psaltery 15.209

sauacioun *n* salvation 3.352, 12.83, 17.119, **B** 5.125,

17.32, *in phr.* **in** ~ **of** for the salvation of 5.198, 17.274, for the protection of B 15.522

saue[1] 12.57 = **salue** *n*

saue[2] *prep.* except 6.240, 13.181, 21.191, 376, 22.61, 151, 267, B 13.125, Z 2.214; except (...) for 2.250, 8.71, 12.29, 13.153, 15.134, 153, 19.93, 21.370, 371, 22.321, **B** 13.236, 247, 14.330, 17.101, A 10.35; (*as conj.*) except B 16.113; except that 9.112, 21.439; unless †21.408n, B 15.127

sauen *v* save (= bring safety to) 3.233; deliver, rescue 7.255, 10.235, 11.241, 244, 12.84, 87, 89, 14.127, 130, 18.269, 20.153, **B** 4.31, 5.57, 10.236, 11.156, 164, 12.77, 82, 13.446; save (from damnation), redeem 1.80, 6.332, 7.235, 9.328, 11.255, 258, 296, 14.12, 53, 77, 101, 141, 195, 201, 16.98, 17.123, 265, 18.135, 19.32, 35, 280, 20.194, 221, 244, 21.409, **B** 2.38, 10.347, 357, 475, 11.217, 12.31, 82, 13.130, 407, 15.389, 17.123, 18.139, 305, 329, A 5.104; redeem (by mainprise / ransom) 20.185; *in phr.* ~ **with** save ...with 17.121; (*in assev.*) 21.452, B 4.144; promise salvation to B 7.40, 11.226; spare 3.408; protect 7.234, 9.314, 10.59, 149, 11.306, 14.163, 19.21, 21.22, **B** 1.23, 3.197, 16.39, 245, A 7.127; defend 20.288, 21.432, 22.214; preserve 7.88, 15.237, 21.435, 22.11, 22, **B** 15.428, 441, 16.104; maintain 22.128; safeguard 20.371; keep safe 9.270, **B** Pr 115, 3.292, 10.405, **A** 10.77, 12.115; save (= reserve) 21.281; [money] 9.29; heal, cure 17.299, 300, 18.152, 153, 19.86

saueour, sauyour *n* deliverer 18.152; saviour from (the penalty of) sin 7.120, 144, 12.138, B 16.143; (*as title of Christ*) **Oure** ~ 12.138, 16.98, A 3.64, (*as title of God*) 17.183, **B** 9.127, 10.107, 15.156

sauer(y)en *v* be to one's taste 10.108, ~ **with** please... with 8.273

saw *p.t.* 5.111, 7.179, 10.73, 18.289, A 12.20, 107 *see* **sen** *v*

sawe *n* speech, words 10.108, 213, A 12.107; assertion, ? opinion 20.151, A 4.144; saying, proverb B 7.138, 9.94, 10.16, A 11.274

sawt *n* assault 22.217, 301

scabbe *n* blister (on scalp) 22.83

scalle *n* scabby disease (of scalp) B 20.83

scapen B 3.57 = **askapen** *v*

scarlet *n* rich cloth [*usu.* dyed scarlet] 16.299, **B** 2.15, 14.19

sc(h)athe *n* injury 4.75, 92; wrong 3.61; harm B 15.59, A 12.17

schaef 8.349 = **sh(e)ef** *n*

schal *1 pr. sg.* 11.183, 15.93, 22.363, Z Pr 60, 3.152, 4.130, 134, 5.41, 7.198, 272, 8.49, 70 = **shal**; *see* **shollen** *v*

schalke *n* man 10.160

schalt *2 pr. sg.* Z 2.97, 3.122, 4.131, 132 = **shalt**; *see* **shollen** *v*

schapen Z 3.166, 7.276 = **shapen** *v*

scharp 22.307 = **sharp** *a*

schast Z 1.104 = **chast** *a*

schat *2 pr. sg.* **Z** 6.48, 7.238 = **shalt**; *see* **shollen** *v*

schathe 4.75 = **sc(h)athe** *n*

sche 6.222, 233, Z Pr 103 *etc* = **she** *prn*

schent *p.t.* Z 4.152 *see* **shenden** *v*

scheryue Z 2.189 *etc* = **shyreue** *n*

schewen Z Pr 70 *etc* = **shewen** *v*

*****schingled** *a* clinker-built [with over-lapping oak tiles] 10.235

Schyr Thorsday *n. phr.* Thursday of Holy Week Z 8.76

schyres Z 2.189 *see* **shire** *n*

s(c)holde *p.t.* 15.204, 19.293, **B** 2.170, **Z** 5.99, 7.270, 8.26 *see* **shollen** *v*[1]

schop *p.t.* 22.307 = **shop**; *see* **shapen** *v*

schoppen 14.68 *see* **choppen** *v*

#**schoriar** *n* prop, support 18.20

schrewe 11.26, **Z** 7.31, 8.76 = **sh(e)rewe** *n*

schryuen Z 3.152, A 12.14 = **shryuen** *v*

schullen **Z** 2.146, 8.37 = **shollen** *v*

schupestare *n* dressmaker 6.75

schutten Z 6.88 = **shetten** *v*

science *n* knowledge B 15.62; wisdom B 17.172; learning 14.65; branch of knowledge / learning 11.131, 12.95, 14.77, 81, 16.208, **B** 10.191, 208, 212, 216, Z 7.260; knowledge (of different kinds of learning) 16.225; kind of knowledge 14.76, 16.222, **B** 11.166, 13.125; skill 10.209

sclayre *n* veil 8.5

sclaundre, sklaundre *n* slander, calumny 2.86; harm to (one's) reputation 3.61, **fel... to** ~ became only a source of disgrace (for) B 12.46; disgrace, scandal A 12.17

scoffen *v* scoff, deride, *ger.* derision B 13.277

scolden *v* be abusive B 2.82

scole *n* school B 7.31, A 10.84; university 5.153, 155, 15.130, 22.273; *in phr.* **to** ~ at school 9.35, at university 5.36, 22.296, to learn B 10.170; place of learning 13.169, 22.251, *(fig.)* A 11.145

scolere *n* schoolboy A 10.84; student B 7.31

scollen Z 1.66 = **shollen** *v*

score *n* twenty 3.158; *in cpds.* (= a considerable number (of)), **fyue** ~ B 1.101, **sixe** ~ 3.182, **ten** ~ 11.128, **many** ~ **thousand** 19.22

scorn *n* scorn, contempt B 10.303, *in phrr.* **laughe to** ~ B 15.172, A 4.137, **likene to** mock / mimic derisively 16.308

scornare *n* contemptuous mocker 6.25, 21.285

scornen *v* speak scornfully B 10.331; mock 2.86, *ger.* mockery B 13.277; deride 6.22, 11.162, 13.130

scorpioun *n* scorpion 20.156

scourge *n* whip B 13.67

screueyn *n* scribe, copyist 11.96, B 10.331

scribe *n* (*pl.* **scribz**) interpreter of the Jewish Law 17.252, 20.26, B 15.389, 604

scrippe *n* bag [for seed] 8.60; pilgrim's satchel 7.179

scripture *n* sacred scripture, the Bible (*person.*) 11.100 *et p.*; written authority 14.192

scryueyn B 10.331 = **screueyn** *n*

se(e) *n* sea 13.135, 173, 17.91, 20.255, 21.78, B 5.284, A 12.115; *in phr.* **ouer** ~ across the sea 4.126 (B 13.392), 6.278

se Pr 207 *et p.*; *see* **sen** *v*

seal 9.27, 138 = **sel** *n*

secatour (secu-, seke-, execu-) *n* executor [of a will] 2.189, 6.254, 16.277, 22.291, **B** 5.262, 12.257, 15.248

seche Z Pr 33 = **suche** *a*

sechen, seken *v* (*p.t.* **sou(g)hte** 3.165, *p.p.* **souht(e)** 4.66, **(y)sou3t** B Pr 50, 5.531) look for 3.352, 9.312, 10.2, 18.268*c*, 19.7, 21.164, 22.383, B 16.249, ~ **after** 14.156, B 16.178; look, seek **B** 12.39, 16.171, A 10.99, ~ **and** ~ keep looking 19.304; search 3.165, 16.293; reach, penetrate B 14.6; look up [text] 3.494, B 10.327, A 11.55; appeal to 4.66; try to find A 9.53; seek / find out 16.329, **B** 14.94, 16.108, A 11.190; go to see 9.315; go on pilgrimage to Pr 48, 4.122, 5.197, 198, 7.168, 174, B Pr 50, Z 6.3; travel 17.169

seco(u)nd(e) *num. a* second 18.40, 21.87, 282, ~ **table** lower table [in hall] 9.252; *as n* 1.23, 11.183, 18.194

secret(e) *a* private, personal, ~ **seal** privy seal 3.182, *(fig.)* 9.27, 138

secte *n* class 12.134; class of people 15.13, 80, **in that** ~ as one of that class of people 16.98; bodily form, **in oure** ~ in our likeness 7.129, 136, 140; in human flesh B 5.491; (religious) order 6.38, 16.293, 355

seculer *a* lay 10.286, *a as n* lay person B 9.179

secutour 22.291, B 15.132 = **secatour** *n*

sed 12.190, 21.311, 345, A 10.159, Z 7.59 *see* **seed** *n*

seden *v* beget offspring 10.254

see 4.126, 6.278, 13.173, B 5.284 = **se(e)** *n*

see 2.45, 4.133, 18.276, 22.178, B 2.71 *etc*; *see* **sen** *v*

seed *n* seed, grain 7.186, 12.181, 184, 188, 190, 17.88, 91, 101, Z 7.59, *in cpds.* **fenkel** ~ 6.359, **lek-, lente** ~, **lyn** ~ 12.192; *(fig.)* (spiritual) seed [virtue] 21.277, 282, 283, 290, 291, 299, 300, 311, 345, 409; offspring †3.429, 18.226, **B** 3.277, 10.110, (= creature made in God's image) B 10.120, 127, *in phrr.* **Caymes** ~ 10.223, ~ ~ **his brother** his brother Cain's progeny 10.254, **suster** ~ sister's children A 10.159

seeknesse 19.318, 21.292 = **sykenesse** *n*

seel Pr 77 *etc*; *see* **sel** *n*

seem *n* horse-load (of) 3.42

seemely 3.112 = **semely(che)** *a*

seen *pr. pl.* 12.29, 14.116, 18.226, B 1.51, *inf.* B 18.250; **seest** *2 pr.sg.* 10.159, 16.301, 19.178, **B** 10. 259, 12.176, ~**ow** 1.5; *see* **sen** *v*

seende *imp.* 22.386 *see* **senden** *v*

seene B 1.149 = **sene** *a*

seet(e) *p.t.* 8.122, B 20.199, *p.t.subjv.* 6.99; *see* **sitt(i)en** *v*

seeth *3 pr. sg.* 1.39 *see* **sen** *v*

seg *pr. sg.* Z 4.59 *see* **seggen** *v*

sege *n* ? company of besiegers, ? town 22.311c, 314

seg(g)(e) *n* man 12.153, 163, 13.196, 15.125, **B** 5.387, 16.178, 17.62, †90, A 12.54, *pl.* men B Pr 160; person 3.67, *pl.* people 2.172, 5.119; anyone B 11.243

seggen, sey(e)n, seiȝen, siggen *v* (*1 pr.sg.* **segge** 5.48, **sey(e)** Pr 118, 207, **seiȝe** A 1.180, **syg(ge)** 6.54, 11.11, *2* **sayst** 6.290, **seist** B 6.229, *3* **sayth** 1.39, **seyt** Z 7.267, **seyth** 19.23, B 1.41, **seiþ** B 3.248, A 10.86, *pl. 1 & 2* **seggeth** 15.265, 13.242, *2* **seyn** 11.201; *pr.p.* **segg-yng** 5.107, *ger.* B 8.109, A 9.102, *p.t. sg. 1, 3* **say(e)d(e)** Pr 68, 1.11, 10.18, 223, *2* **saidest** 14.103, **seydest** 7.144, Z 3.122, *pl.* **sayden** 3.17, **seyden** 2.181, *p.p.* **ysaide** 15.24, 125, **seid** B 13.20) (*selected refs.*) say Pr 96, 147 *et p.*; express, utter (aloud) Pr 211, 9.131, 12.27, 13.11, **B** 5.608, 16.214; state, declare Pr 68, 3.428, 6.54, 7.192, 301, 9.257, 313, 12.47, 206, 13.224, 15.140, 19.21, 20.42, 358, 21.243, **B** Pr 50, 13.307, 15.382; maintain, express (the belief that), **men saith** people say 11.271; assert, affirm Pr 118, 207, 3.287, 4.15 (2), 134, 6.290, 7.92, 8.237, 241, 346, 10.23, 204, 11.11, 279, 12.16, 100, 14.82, 165, 15.21, 16.8, 17.304, 18.148, 256, 19.5, 20.28, 70, 22.224, **B** 10.365, 13.339, 15.267, 428, 598, 16.98, 130; say, recite 19.26, [prayer, service] 5.107, 6.283, 13.126, 15.265, 17.117, **B** 5.7, 12.16, 15.125, 127, 193; speak 1.144, 2.200, 3.435, 8.298, 11.4, 14.204, 15.24, 125, 18.162, 20.49, B 14.181, A 12.16; reply 1.44, 20.66, 360; tell 1.39, 4.15 (1), 5.124, 9.307, 10.30, 11.115, 18.18, 19.81, Z 2.183; ~ **so(e)th** speak truly 2.26, 4.64, 12.42, 14.103, 19.108, 20.466, B Pr 52, ~ **treuthe** 4.151; speak about, give (exact) account of 4.133, **B** 5.10, 15.296, 17.30, Z Pr 5; **heren** ~ hear tell / reported B 16.249; explain 10.30; teach (authoritatively) 14.200, **B** 10.397, 13.118, *with cited source*: **saith the Boek** 10.23, B 11.275; ~ **Dauid** 13.122; ~ **Piers þe Plowman** B 13.130; ~ **þe Sauter** 11.51, B 3.248; ~ **Seynt Bernard** 16.220; **Seneca** B 14.306; **þe Gospel saith** 12.102; **Salamon sayth** 3.484; direct 11.137; command 12.34, 17.192, 18.261 (1, 2), B 15.497; inform (us) 11.152, B 10.191; write 3.484, 11.289, 291, 16.227, 20.358; (*in cpd. names*) **Say-soth...** speak truly 7.229; **Sey-wel** speak virtuously 10.146; *in phrr.* **as who seiþ** as if to say B 15.307; **to ~** to speak of (= be mentioned) 13.174, B 17.23

seying *ger.* words, speech B 8.109

sey *p.t. sg.* Pr 109 *etc* [7.137, 11.152, 12.83, 13.141, 143, 14.165] Z Pr 5, *pl.* 12.134 *etc* [18.148, 19.49, Z 2.45], **ysey** 2.67, *p.p.* 13.242, (**ysey**) 16.343; **seye** *p.t.* B 8.75, A 12.5, **seyen** *p.p.* Pr 177, 4.133, 11.237, B 11.244, 15.220; **seigh** *p.t.* Pr 17, B 17.107; **seyȝe** *p.t. (subj.)* B 5.85; **seiȝe** *p.p.* A 3.57, 11.221; **seiȝen** *p.t. pl.* B 12.132, 15.588, 16.116, *p.p.* B 10.68; **seyh** *p.t.* 2.200 *etc* (**seyhe** 13.135); (**y)sey(e)n** *p.p.* 3.104, B 14.155 *see* **sen** *v*

seide *p.t.* (= **say(e)d(e)**) Pr 96 *et p.*; **seyen** *inf.* 4.133, 12.27, B 14.279, *pr. pl* 17.117, 307, B 15.140 *see* **seggen** *v*

sey(h)(e) *p.t.* 2.200, 13.135 *et p.*; *see* **sen** *v*

seillen *v* glide (*lit.* sail), *ger.* B 18.306

seyn[1] *pr. pl.* 4.154, *p.p.* 3.104, *see* **sen** *v*

seyn[2] *inf.* 18.261, 19.26, *pr. pl.* 11.201, **B** 6.129, 15.173, 16.249 *see* **seggen** *v*

seynien *v* (*refl.*) bless oneself (with sign of cross) 7.62

seynewrye Z 2.73 = **signiure** *n*

seynt Pr 48 *et p.*; 11.204, B 1.84 *see* **saynt** *n, a*

seyntwarie *n* sanctuary, (*meton.*) the church 5.79

seke 22.324, A 7.239, 11.190 = **syk(e)** *a*

seken *v* Pr 48, 10.2, 18.268, 19.7, 21.164, 22.383, **B** 10.94, 327, 12.39, 14.6, 94, 16.178, A 11.55, 190 *see* **sechen, seken** *v*

sek(e)nes(se) 7.28, 64, 8.134, 270, 16.309, 19.322 = **syk(e)nes(se)** *n*

sekte 6.38, 7.136, 140, 16.355, 293 = **secte** *n*

sel *n* seal [authenticating device impressed on wax]: [bishop's] Pr 67, 77, 2.231, [pope's] B 13.249, [king's privy] 3.182, (*fig.*) [God's] 9.27, 138, [Christ's] 19.7, [merchant's] 13.88, [official] 2.156

selcouth(e) *a* wonderful, extraordinary Pr 5, 12.47, 13.177; strange 17.300; *as n* marvel 13.174; strange occurrence / thing 14.75

selde(n), seldom *av* seldom, rarely Pr 22, 2.26, 127, 6.93, 252, 7.20, 11.237, 301, 305, 16.4, 122, 125, 127, 355, 360, 18.66, 19.283, **B** 7.138, 9.152, 10.397, 14.2, 155, 178, 15.275, 282, A 10.104, 108; at infrequent intervals 17.10

selen *v* (set a) seal (on) 3.184, Z 2.39; certify as accurate (with a mark) 3.88; close up with a seal (*fig.*) 4.189

self B 11.249 = **sulue(n)** *a*

selk(e) *n* silken cloth Pr 159, 8.10, B 15.220; *a* silken 3.447, (**~en**) Z Pr 65

selle *n* (hermit's) cell, hut Pr 30, 17.7, 10, A 7.133

sellen 3.120, **B** 3.196, 7.22, 11.275, Z 3.149 *see* **sullen** *v*

seller B 3.88, A 2.44, 3.77 *see* **suller** *n*

selli *n* remarkable thing Pr 5

selue B 1.204, 5.488, 7.128; **~n** A 1.110, 10.86 *see* **sulue(n)** *a*

seluer (syluer, suluer) *n* silver Pr 183, 3.23, **B** 2.175, 15.7, 123; (silver) money Pr 79, 84, 90, 1.63, 100, 2.156, 3.116, 4.51, 52, 126, 127, 191, 6.254, 13.100, 104, 16.90, 108, 363, 21.374, 22.222, 368, **B** 2.68, 3.207, 4.31, 35, 5.94, 6.192, 9.91, 10.336, 359, 11.74, 173, 222, 275, 281, 15.127, 131, 16.143 17.76, Z 3.171; wealth 16.237; *in phr.* **at ~es preyere** as a bribe 2.68

seluerles *a* without money 9.119

semblable *a* like, similar to 3.334, 10.158, 16.112, 18.212, B 10.365; resembling 20.8

semblant *n* countenance 10.118

semblaunce *n* form, likeness B 18.287

semble A Pr 97 = **assemblee** *n*

semely(che) *a* excellent 15.59; fitting, proper 3.112; *av* suitably (dressed) 19.247

semen *v* seem Pr 33, 1.148, 2.135, 6.216, 7.141, 11.2, 45, 273, 14.109, 16.8, 262, 19.57, 167, 21.450, 459, **B** Pr 52, 5.77, 9.41, 10.273, 12.169, 13.320, 17.37, (*in parenth. impers. constr.*) **(as) it semeth / semed(e)** Pr 34, 160, 7.129, 9.105, 115, 117, 12.66, 72, 11.163, 17.86, 19.272, 20.120, 404; appear to be 3.382, 5.27, 90, 6.27, 7.298, 11.129, 15.116, 307, 16.262, 17.86, 301, 20.62, B 10.255, 257; indicate, *pr.p.* 6.179, 11.86; ~ **to** resemble *pr.p.* B 15.392

#semyui(e)f *a* half-alive 19.57c

sen *v* (**see** 4.82, **seen** B 4.86, *assim. pr. 2* **seestow** 1.5, *p.t.* **say** Pr 5, **sayh** 5.124, **sauȝ** A 5.9, **saw** 5.111, **sey(h) (e)** Pr 109, 2.200, A 12.5, **sye** 14.75, 20.255, **sigh** Pr 11, **sihe** 19.59, 20.358, *pl.* **seye(n)** Pr 177, 17.304, *p.p.* **ysaye** 18.140, **(y)seyen** 16.343, **seiȝe** A 11.221); see Pr 11, 109, 1.5, 9.294, 10.73, 146, 11.152, 13.135, 141, 143, 174, **B** 1.51, 4.152, 11.320, 364, 15.162, 17.84, Z 2.45; catch sight of Pr 177, 4.82, 18.240, 289, 19.49, **B** Pr 50, 16.178, 17.107, ~ **of** 19.59; look at 19.5, **B** 2.189, **to** ~ **vpon** to look at 18.191; view Pr 5; observe 10.159, 12.134, 13.143, 14.75, 16.301, 343, 18.226, 19.178, 22.374, A 12.20; witness 6.51, 12.29, 17.304, 18.148, 20.255, 259, **B** 15.588, 16.117; encounter 7.179, 16.343, 18.241, 269, 19.29, **B** 9.152, 11.104, 244, 13.25, 305, 15.158, 196, A 11.221; meet 7.137, 12.134, B 15.196; read 11.51, 204, 14.116, **B** 6.234, 10.191, 412, 454; see (in vision) Pr 221, 232, 5.111, 124, 9.298, 11.153, 20.358, **B** 11.320, 15.12; foresee B Pr 202; know 3.325; perceive 1.39, 4.154, 12.83, 20.333, **B** 5.85, 10.259, 12.20, A 12.5; find 7.15, 11.237, A 3.57; realise 7.168; understand 4.154, 11.289, **B** 2.67, 9.156; experience 3.104, 6.57, 20.222

senatour *n* member of governing body, alderman 8.87

sendel *n* sendal [thin rich silk] 8.10

senden *v* (*contr. pr.* **sent(e)** 1.177, 8.346, 14.27, 17.155, 21.435, *p.t.* **sent(e)(n)** 2.231, 3.128 *etc*, *subjv.* B 13.249, *p.p.* **sende** 2.197, **(y)sent** Pr 77, 9.55) dispatch (messenger / message) 2.197, 231, 6.189, 278, 7.126, 9.37, 119, 11.267, 15.238, 17.246, 262, 18.205, 19.123, 20.172, 21.341, 22.81, 111, **B** 10.230, 14.21, A 12.54; send 7.126, 8.273, B 13.249; cause to be brought 9.39; circulate Pr 77; issue 4.190; send (word) 2.233, 243, 3.128, 413, 8.346, 9.1, 27, 10.252, 13.11, 18.261, 20.172, 184, 22.310, **B** 3.261, 9.124, 10.366, **A** 3.244, 251, 4.15; grant 1.177, 9.55, 15.295, 299, 16.17, 25, 21.435, 22.386, **B** 6.138, 7.63, A 10.201; provide 9.199, 17.155, B 15.305; send down upon 3.95, 21.292; send forth 14.27; send (for), summon 10.150, 22.205

sene *a* visible 22.185, **B** 1.149, 14.96

sen(n)es 4.15, 6.355, 11.171, 21.78, 311, 398, **Z** 6.16, 7.266 *see* **seth(e)(n)**¹ *av* 21.15, 22.323 *see* **seth(e)**³ *conj.*; 11.55, 22.187 *see* **seth(e)**² *prep.*

#seneschal *n* seneschal [chief administrative officer of lord's household] Pr 93

sense *n* incense 21.86

sent Z 2.80 = **saynt** *n*

sent(e) *contr. pr.* 1.177, 14.27, 21.435, *p.t.* 2.233, 9.119, *p.p.* 9.55, 19.123, B 7.63 *see* **senden** *v*

sepulcre *n* tomb (of Christ at Jerusalem) 7.170

seraphyn *n.pl.* seraphim 1.105

serelepes B 17.165 *see* **suyrelepes** *a, av*

seria(u)nt(e) (sergeaunt) *n* sergeant-at-arms [royal officer], (*fig.*) 21.341; officer of law court **B** 2.207, 3.102, **Z** 2.189; sergeant-at-law [senior barrister, justice] Pr 160 (B Pr 212), 3.78, 447, B 15.8, Z Pr 65

serk *n* undergarment 1.99, 6.6

sermoun A 11.245 = **sarmon** *n*

serpent *n* serpent B 18.287

sertayn(e) 3.85, 22.255 = **certeyn(e)** *a*

sertes 5.22, 18.58, A 9.18 = **certes** *av*

seruaunt *n* servant [one owing service to a lord / master] 11.301, 16.96, **B** 10.470; hired labourer 3.272, 7.39, 220, 8.268, 21.439, **B** 14.142; administrative officer B Pr 95; factor 6.278, **B** 15.248; agent 18.203, 205; servant of God (= disciple) A 7.227

seruen *v* be in the service of, work for Pr 90, 93, 3.265, 5.66, 6.130, 7.189, 192, **B** 10.470, A Pr 91; work Pr 160; attend upon (as servant) 7.269, 10.140; serve (as apprentice) 6.207; wait upon 2.224, A 11.22 (1); serve (as knight / retainer) 1.102, 4.2, 18.96, **B** 13.120; obey B Pr 131; serve (as priest) 5.61, 6.19; assist at mass 5.12; serve (God by obedience to his will) 7.184, 189, 192, 16.93, **B** 11.277, 279, A 11.300; follow (the devil, sin) 4.33, 10. 302, **B** 9.62, **A** 2.65, 11.22 (2); serve (food) 14.144, 15.44, 21.439; minister to 2.182, **B** 2.179, 13.227; serve purpose, perform function 16.171, (*impers.*) be useful to 19.174, B 5.439; be of service B 17.146; ~ **of** be of use 12.33, 14.48; satisfy 6.390, B 5.413; treat 3.309, 14.147

seruyse, seruyc(i)e *n* labour 3.272; task, duty 3.447; religious service [mass and matins] 9.227, 231, 242, **his** ~ the mass he is obliged to celebrate B 15.126; serving / service [at table] 15.59, 64; use, care, **in my** ~ in my care 7.52

sesen¹ 2.165, 14.41, 22.107, 109 *see* **cessen** *v*

sesen² *v* take possession of 6.271, Z 2.42, ~ **in / with** enfeoff, put in legal possession of A 2.66, Z 2.56, 73, *p.p.* **(i)se(i)sid** put in possession 20.309

seso(u)n *n* season, time, **somur** ~ Pr 1, 10.2; period of time, *in phr.* **out of** ~ = untimely 6.184 (B 13.351)

se(e)st 2 *p. sg.*, (*assim. form*) ~**ow** (= **se(e)st þow**) 1.5, **B** 9.152, 15.196 *see* **sen** *v*

set *imp.* 20.293, *p.p.* **B** 6.47, 13.125 *see* **setten** *v*

sete *n* seat, place (in heaven) A 8.39

sete *p.t.* B 18.287, (*subjv.*) 14.2, **~n** *p.t. pl.* 6.395, 7.164, 15.42, B 6.115, 192 *see* **sitt(i)en** *v*

seth[1] *3 pr. sg.* 14.41, 16.301, *pl.* 9.302, Z 8.63 *see* **sen** *v*

seth[2] *3 pr. sg.* Z 7.218 = **seith**; *see* **seggen** *v*

seth(e)(n)[1] (**sen(n)es, syn, sithe(n)(es)**) *av* afterward, after that, then 3.408, 4.15, 5.40, 140, 143, 180, 191, 6.355, 7.124, 129, 144, 184, 8.62, 281, 9.29, 39, 307, 10.226, 251, 11.171, 12.100, 13.88, 173, 15.57, 178, 18.18, 261, 19.40, 20.49, 228, 21.78, 87, 143, 268, 276, 311, 398, 22.137, 387, **B** Pr 128, 1.68, 146, 5.139, 9.101, 116, 11.320, 13.19, 200, 14.142, 16.235, 17.36, 88, 18.283, **A** 7.227, 10.153, 159, 11.181, 221, 251, **Z** 2.118, 6.16, 7.266, 288; next †B 10.251; since then 7.47, 54, 16.355, 17.270, 18.140, †B 5.400

seth(e) *etc*[2] *prep.* (in the time) since Pr 82, 10.274, 11.55 **~ whanne** since when 22.187

seth(e) *etc*[3] *conj.* since (the time when), after Pr 62, 5.40, 70, 6.310, 20.136, **B** 2.26, 6.63, 10.226, A 11.273; (during the time) since Pr 62, 6.310; because, since, seeing that 2.134, 3.367, 9.115, 10.197, 14.194, 15.226, 17.183, 190, 315, 18.81, 176, 192, 19.35, 242, 247, 274, 20.307, 308, 21.15, 60, 474, 22.49, 63, 236, 323, **B** 9.85, 10.133, 259, 264, **A** 8.62, 10.206, 11.89, 12.18; **~ þat** since 17.252, 315, 20.350

sethen *v* stew, *p.t. pl.* **sode** 9.149, 17.20, *p.p.* **ysode** B 15.432

setten *v* (*p.t.* **sette** 4.43 *etc*, *contr. pr.* 12.26) make sit 4.43, 14.137; place, set 1.118, 4.20, 43, 6.6, 7.52, 15.56, 19.72, 20.49, 227, B 2.164, A 4.18; set [heart] 11.231; put in position 20.291; **~ forth** put out Pr 97; fix B 17.133; plant 7.185, 9.6, 15.213, 18.9, B 15.334, *ger.* Pr 23; *in phr.* **~ by**, **~ in**, **~ on** attach 9.302, B 7.151, Z 2.41; proceed B 16.36; consider B 15.224; value, esteem 5.97, 8.166, 9.345, 12.26, 15.10, *in phrr.* **~ lihte**, **~ short (by)** think little of 11.164, 14.65; determine, establish 22.255, B 13.154; appoint 10.149; put [to learning] 11.117, 14.126, **B** 7.31, 10.170; make ready, ? use 18.40

s(e)ute *n* retinue 16.96; clothing, (*fig.*) = flesh B 5.488, 497 (*with pun on* 'legal cause')

seuth *3 sg.pr.* Z Pr 129 = **seeth** *see* **sen** *v*

seue(ne) *num.* seven, *also as indef. number* Pr 203, 232, 6.108, 214; *in phrr.* **~ ars** 11.97, 12.95, 17.114; **~ daies** B 15.296; **~...geauntes** 22.215; **~ 3er** 4.82, 7.64, 10.73; **~ nyhte** 7.300; **~ psalmes** 3.464, 5.47; **~ synnes** 16.43, 60, B 15.74; **~ sithe(s)** 10.23, 31, 49; **~ sones** B 13.120; **~ sterres** 17.98; **~ susteres** 7.269; *a as n* 7.37, 277, 279, 15.271, 19.74, B 3.63, 13.122, *in phr.* **suche ~** seven like these 1.105; *in cpd. num.* **~ hundred (wynter)** B 14.68, **~ thousand (wynter)** 20.309

seue(n)the *a as n* seventh 16.142

seuenty (hundred) *num.* = seven thousand †B 18.283

sew(e) *p.t.* 6.271 (B 13.375), 17.101, 21.276, 290, 299, 311, 345, 409 *see* **sowen** *v*[1]

sewen[1] (**su(e)(w)en**) *v* follow B 17.107, A 11.245; walk behind [as ploughman], drive 7.186, Z 7.64; accompany Pr 46, 3.352, 10.73, 13.143, 180, 17.145, 19.81, 22.126, **B** 4.167, 11.374; support 18.72; associate with 2.102, B 11.422; (be a) follow(er) [disciple] (of) 12.168, B 10.204, A 11.249; strive for 22.22; correspond, *pr. p.* correspondingly, accordingly 18.63; follow through with, *pr.p.* **suynde** 20.358; pursue B 14.323, A 2.53, **~ to** A 8.62, Z 8.63; obey 3.325, 5.200, 11.183, A 2.53; act in accordance with B 17.102; come after [as descendant] B 18.191; sue at law 3.367

sewen[2] A 7.9, 19 = **sowen** *v*[2]

sewere *n* cobbler A 11.311

shabbede *a* afflicted with scab [skin-disease of sheep] (*fig.*) 9.264, A 8.17

shadde *p.t.* B 19.58 *see* **sheden** *v*

shaddewen *v* cast a shadow 20.478

shaft *n* form, figure **B** 9.31, 11.395, 13.297

shaken *v* (*p.t.* **sho(o)k(e)** 6.13, 266) shake 18.47, 105, 107; = empty out 6.266; **~ of** get rid of 6.13

shal(l) *pr.sg.* Pr 13 *et p.*, *pl.* Pr 221 *et p.*; **shalt** *2 sg.* 2.46 *et p*; **shaltow** 7.226 *etc* (= **shalt thow**) *see* **shollen**

shale *n* shell 12.148

shame *n* (sense of) shame 6.90, 13.234, B 11.431, (*person.*) 13.244; fear of shame 22.284; *in phr.* **for ~** for decency's sake 6.431, B 14.330, out of shame B 12.80, despite fear of shame B 5.90, for sheer embarrassment B 15.382; ignominy B 4.31; disgrace B 9.88; a disgraceful thing A 12.16; **~les** *a* without any sense of shame 3.46

shamen *v* be ashamed B 5.367; shame, disgrace B 3.190

shap *n* looks, appearance B 11.395

shapen *v* (*p.t.* **shupte** 19.183, **shapte** B 20.139, **sho(o) p(e)** Pr 2, 2.177, 22.307, A 5.102 (*subj.*), *pl.* **shopen** B Pr 57, *p.p.* **(y)shape(n)** 15.240, 301) create 6.423, 15.301, 19.183, **B** 9.66, 11.395; make 22.307, Z 7.276; fashion 5.18; build 10.225, 11.240; (*refl.*) turn oneself into B Pr 57; institute, establish 1.156, B Pr 122; arrange 2.177; bring about 22.139, A 5.102; provide 15.240; cause 9.62, B 11.424; prepare 3.18, (*refl.*) get ready 13.246; direct Z 3.166; set about B 17.84, **~ into** dress in Pr 2

shar *n* plough-share 3.460

sharp *a* strong, stinging 22.307; violent 20.455

sharpe *av* loudly B 18.39; **~liche** *av* vigorously 18.107; severely energetically, promptly 6.13c.

sharre (shere) *n* scissors 6.75 (B 13.331)

shauen *v* shave, *p.p.* 6.201; tonsure 16.352

she *prn. fem. sg.* she 1.12 *et p.*; *and see* **heo** *prn*

sheden *v* (*p.t.* **shedde**) shed 19.272, 21.58, *ger.* **bloed ~** 14.207, 15.157; spill, *ger.* **for ~** to prevent spilling 8.8

she(e)f *n* (*pl.* **sheues**) sheaf of grain 5.14, B 6.141, (*fig.*) 21.332; quiverful 3.478, 8.349, (*fig.*) 22.225

she(e)p *n* sheep (*sg.*) Pr 2, B 15.360, (*pl.*) 3.411, 5.18, (*fig.*) 9.262, 264, A 8.17

she(e)pherde *n* shepherd 14.96, 17.98, **B** 10.461, 15.367

shelle B 11.259 *see* **shale** *n*; ~ **of Galys** souvenir scallop-shell from Compostella 7.165

sheltrom *n* battle-formation 20.292, (*fig.*) = spiritual defence B 14.81

shenden *v* (*p.t.* **shent(e)** 19.272 *etc*, **shent** 3.171) do harm to A 7.148; ruin 3.171, B 9.206, A Pr 95; bring to destruction **B** 2.126, 4.174, 6.173; destroy 20.336; damage 13.114n; spoil B 9.206; corrupt 3.192; mortify B 11.424; bring about the death of 19.272, 22.98

shene *a* bright 20.455

shent(e) *p.t.* 19.272, 22.98, *p.p.* 3.171 *see* **shenden** *v*

shentfolyche *av* ignominiously 3.429

sheo A 5.141 = **she** *prn*

shep Pr 2 *etc*, = **she(e)p** *n*

shepherde B 10.461, 15.360 = **she(e)pherde** *n*

shepstere B 13.331 = **schupestare** *n*

shere B 13.331 = **sharre** *n*

shereue 2.177 = **shyryue** *n*

sherewe B Pr 192, 1.129, 2.40, 5.90, 279, 6.160, 9.122, 147, 150, 10.436, 17.43, 19.377 = **shrewe** *n*

sherewednesse B 3.44 *see* **shrewed** *a*

sherte *n* shirt B 14.330

shete *n* bed-sheet 16.75; ? cloth bag B 5.107

sheten *v* (*p.t.* **shet** A 12.12, *pl.* **shot(t)e(n)** 20.50, 22.225) shoot 20.292, 22.225; ~ **vp** raise A 12.12, thrust towards 20.50

shetten *v* (*p.t.* **shette**) shut, close 7.249, B Pr 105

sheues *pl.* 5.14 *etc*; *see* **sh(e)ef** *n*

sheware *n* revealer, (*with play on sense* mirror) 14.96

shewen *v* view with favour 10.162n; be visible (to) 10.160; present Pr 202, B 14.190; (*refl.*) present one-self 13.244, 17.284; appear B 5.89; display 4.126, *ger.* B 15.78, (for sale) 2.223; show 11.11, 19.112, **B** 12.88, 16.21, 201, 18.394; manifest **B** 9.43, *ger.* B 17.153; make known 6.21, 7.108, 13.88, 17.257, 18.202n, **B** 10.168, 14.125; make clear 14.110, 19.154, B 14.123; explain 3.432, 10.32, 21.230, B 10.372, A 12.14, 54, *ger.* 16.1; declare 1.69, 2.107, 11.209, 19.300, **B** 2.135, 7.16, 49, 10.254, 12.50, 13.449; tell Pr 182, 6.325, 8.264, 9.82, 11.5, B Pr 167, 11.54, A 11.73; describe A 10.185; speak 16.142, B 17.39; assert 2.40; expound 11.207, B 4.172; teach **B** 7.128, 10.36, A 11.154, 245, ~ **of** instruct about 13.233; bring forward 11.162, 13.130, B 4.136, A 12.34; produce Pr 164, 13.40; cite B 3.351; disclose 11.80; reveal B Pr 106; confess 6.350, B 5.233, 367, ~ **shrift** make one's confesion B 5.141, *ger.* 5.379; lay (complaint) 3.213; put (case) 12.174; stretch out 19.133; perform B 13.213

shewynge *ger.* representation B 17.153

shide *n* plank 10.225, 11.240, 18.20

shiften *v* (*p.t.* **shifte**) (*refl.*) bestir oneself B 20.167

shilden *v* protect B 10.406

shille *av* with a clear voice 6.46

shille A 6.9 = **shelle** *n*

shillyng *n* shilling 3.391, 14.89

shyne *n* shin B 11.431

shynen *v* (*p.t.* **schoen** 14.96) give light 19.222; shine 14.96

ship *n* ship 3.478, 8.349, B 15.360, = (Noah's) ark 10.225, 235, 11.240, B 10.406

shipman *n* sailor, seaman 17.94, 98, 103, B 15.360

shyre *n* shire, county 3.171, B 2.159

shyreue, shyryue *n* sheriff [king's chief legal and admin-istrative officer in the shire] 2.59, 177, 3.171, ~**es clerk** clerk of the sheriff's court 4.164

shyten *v* (*contr. pr.* **shyt**) ?befoul 9.264n, c

sho *n* (*pl.* ~**es**, ~ (**o**)**n**) shoe 5.18, 22.219, B 14.32, 330

shoen[1] *v* provide with shoes, *p.p.* **sho(e)d** shod B 2.164

shoen[2] *p.t.* 14.96 *see* **shynen** *v*

shoke *p.t.* 6.266 *see* **shaken** *v*

sholde *p.t.* Pr 77 *et p.*, ~**n** *pl.* 2.182 *etc*, ~**est** 2 *sg.* 13.223 *etc*; *see* **shollen** *v*

shollen *v* (*pr.* **shal** Pr 13 *et p.*, *pl.* 2.165, 2 *sg.* **shalt** 2.45, *assim. form* **shaltow** 7.226, B 5.570, *pl.* **sholle(n)** 1.131 *etc*, **shul** B 2.38 *et p.*, **shull(e)(n)** 9.311, 338, B 1.178, A 2.138 *etc*, *p.t.* **sholde** Pr 77 *et p.*, 2 *p. assim. forms* **sholdestow** 11.101, **shost** 3.135; **shulde** Pr 120 *etc*, B 14.188) *modal auxil.* [*selected refs.*] **shal** should Pr 208; ought to 6.346, 16.8, B 1.26, 48, A 10.66; have (duty) to 5.161; must, will [command] 4.184, 7.226, **B** 5.642, 6.232, A 12.51; (will) have to 8.83, 142, 9.311, 11.197, 20.415, 446, 21.347, B 6.166, A 12.86; shall, intend to 6.173, 8.15, 18.59, B 10.369; will assuredly 11.282, 12.109, 15.164, **B** 5.555, 10.155, 11.194, A 10.176; will [prediction / prophecy] 2.35, 3.437, 5.142, 8.67, 12.160, 21.220, B 16.131, 156; must, have to [necessity] 7.40, 14.125, **B** 9.148, (*after* **allas**) should (have to) / be able to 12.2, 16.1, 18.287, B 9.65, 84; be required to 3.264, 4.2; will / be going to Pr 13 *et p.*, B 10.117, A 10.177; be to 4.10, 8.96, 12.214, 15.131, 18.277, 19.96, 20.68, B 17.125; were to A 11.276; be wont / apt (to) 22.291; will be able to, can 2.28, 208, 3.35, 10.208, 13.234, 19.95, 20.25, 153, 173, **B** 7.50, 106, 9.165, 14.17, 17.8; (*with implied inf.*) 7.64 [come], 245 [be], 12.119, B 15.13 [go], Z 8.37 [die]; *with Ø-sense* (=do) **B** 11.208, 12.253; **sholde** would Pr 77, 3.259, 4.82, 7.146, 10.186, 15.27, 17.93, 18.129, 269, 20.17, B 8.102, A 3.51; ought to 1.50, 3.152, 5.43, 19.310; have duty to 4.29, 5.76, 11.246, 21.431; must 2.234, 3.415, 5.119, 7.2, 8.77; had to 20.424; should have to 5.42, 8.34, 15.285, 16.336; would have to 6.384, 20.374; be required to 5.57; have to 19.317; should Pr 143, 4.149, 6.23, 17.264, (so that)...should 18.107; were to 11.222, 14.47, 15.180, B 9.38; are to 8.6; might be able to 21.145, B 15.314; should wish

6.290; might wish 19.117; could 6.108, B 15.151; should be able to 16.213; would be able to Pr 80, 6.205, 7.5, 12.183, 13.160, 15.252, 19.138, 22.173, B 14.188; be allowed to 6.67; (*with implied inf.*) ought to [be] 9.13; should [be able to] **B** 13.254, 15.439, would [go] B 15.13

shon(y)en *v* avoid 13.244, B 5.167; keep out of B Pr 174

shoon *pl.* B 14.330 *see* **sho** *n*

sho(o)p *p.t.* 2.177, 6.423, 11.240, 13.246, **B** 9.66, 11.395, 17.84, A 5.102, **shopen** *p.t.pl.* B Pr 57, 122 *see* **shapen** *v*

shoppe *n* shop 2.223, 14.184

shor(r)iare prop 18.25, 50, 119

short *a*, ~**e** *a as n* short (person) 16.84; brief (*comp.*) 15.261; curt 20.331

shorte *av* at low esteem, *in phr.* **sette** ~ **by** have a low opinion of 14.65

shost *assim. 2 sg. pr.* = **sholdest** *see* **shollen** *v*

shot *n. pl. (coll.)* missiles, ? bows 20.292, 22.225

shoten *p.t. pl.* 22.225 *see* **sheten** *v*

shour *n* rainstorm 20.455

shouele *n* shovel B 6.189

shrapen *v* scrape 6.90, B 11.431; scratch A 5.208

shrewe *n* scoundrel 4.105, 6.317, 7.260, 11.26, **B** 5.90, 279, 6.160, 9.122, 147, 150, 10.436, A 4.67, Z 7.31; evil person **B** 17.43, 19.377; wretch 6.173, 6.421, 8.151, 13.234, **B** 2.40, 4.160, A 5.208, Z 8.76; villain B Pr 192; fiend B 1.129

shrewed *a* depraved, accursed Pr 122, 124; **~nesse** *n* wickedness B 3.44

shrewen *v* curse 6.75 (B 13.331), B 5.76

shryft *n* (sacramental) confession 6.63, 90, 349, 7.8, 14.121, B 3.37, A 5.102, (*person.*) 22.307; (act of) confession 22.284, **B** 5.139, 13.54, *in phrr.* ~ **of mouthe** oral confession 16.30, B 14.88, 89, 90, **shewen** ~ make one's confession B 5.141, 379

shryne *n* shrine 7.201

shryuar *n* confessor Pr 64

shryuen *v* (*p.t.* **shro(e)f(e)**, *p.p.* **(y)shryue(n)**) make one's confession 22.290, (*refl.*) 6.13, 175, 421, 9.237, 11.257, 22.167, B 5.141, 367, **be shryue** confess, be absolved 6.355, 7.2, 28, **B** 5.90, 14.9, A 12.14; hear the confession (of) Pr 62, 5.194, 22.281, B Pr 89, A 11.203, Z 3.152; hear confessions, administer penance 22.305, 369; absolve 3.46

shroud *n* garment, *pl.* clothes Pr 2

shuyuen (vp) *v* support, prop 18.20

shul B 1.132 *etc*, A 8.17, 141, **shulde** Pr 120, A Pr 76, **shull(e)(n)** 3.481, 9.311, B 10.154, A Pr 97 *etc*; *see* **shollen** *v*

shupte *p.t.* 19.183, 22.139 *see* **shapen**

si (*Lat.*) 'if' [word indicating a condition] 3.328n

sib *a* kin to, related to (*fig.*) 7.277, 279, 288, 11.97, 198, 16.112

sybbe *n* kindred 12.157

sycurly 10.26, Z 8.55 = **sikerliche** *av*

syde *n* side [direction] 1.112, 113, 7.163, [of body] 5.79, 6.163, 426, **B** 2.99, 13.317, A 11.214, Z 4.131, (= hand) 3.76; [in bargaining / negotiation] 6.378, B 2.55; edge 10.62; district 2.172; (*in cpds.*) ~ **benche** 9.252, ~ **borde** B 13.6, ~ **table** 14.139, 15.42; **sonne** ~ sunny side 1.113, 18.64; *in phr.* **by** ~**s** nearby Z 2.51

syde *av* low, (*comp.*) **syddore** 6.200

sye *p.t.* 14.75, 20.255 *see* **sen** *v*

syg(g)(e)n 6.54, 7.301, 9.257, 11.11, 20.358, **B** 13.307, 15.125, 296, 382, 428, 17.30 *see* **seggen** *v*

si(g)hen, sy3en (syken) *v* moan 7.300, 20.91, B 14.326; groan 20.274; lament 3.399, 5.107, A 11.193

si(g)ht *n* (power of) sight 7.131, 14.48, 20.81, **ye** ~ 9.102; eyes 4.180, 19.307, B 17.323, *in phrr.* **in** ~, **to** ~ before his / the(ir) eyes (of) 21.181, **B** 10.273, 16.130, 18.303; looking 15.257; visual observation 14.30, 79; view 7.300, 20.344; presence 11.203; witness, *in phrr.* **by** ~ **of** with the witness of 1.200, 2.115; **as by** ~ as it would appear 21.456; discernment 21.235; judgement, *in phrr.* **to my / oure, to** ~ **of** in my / our / the eyes (of) Pr 34, 6.36, 9.115, 11.45, B 17.38; appearance, **in / of** ~ in appearance B 10.255, A 3.58; sight 19.63, 65, B 16.117, 17.90; spectacle, attraction (to the eye) 3.480, 6.282, 18.33, 37; aspect B 17.153

signe *n* sign, token Pr 89; tokening, symbol B 13.154; *in phr.* **in** ~ **þat** indicating that 4.149, B 10.143; gesture 6.178 (B 13.345); stamp 4.126; identifying mark(s) 16.97; (pilgrim) badge 7.165, 168, 173; (impression of) seal 2.156, 22.272, Z 2.41; message in symbols [written] 14.40, [spoken] B 10.170

signiure *n* domain A 2.66

sihe *p.t.* 19.59, 20.358 *see* **sen** *v*

syhen 20.91, 274 *see* **si(g)hen** *v*

siht 1.200 *etc; see* **si(g)ht** *n*

syk(e) *a* sick 8.147, 271, 9.99, 15.119, B 16.106, 108, 109, **A** 7.239, 11.190, Z 7.198; infirm B 15.576; *a as n* the sick 15.221, sick person(s) 4.122, 19.63, 328, 22.324; injured man 19.63; (*fig.*) (spiritually) sick (from sin) 22.335, *a as n* 22.357, B 17.120, 121; **~nes(se) (sekenesse)** *n* sickness 7.28, 64, 8.134, 270, 16.309, 19.318, 322, 21.292; spiritual malady 7.124

sykel *n* sickle 3.460, 5.23, 6.271 (B 13.375)

syken 3.399, B 14.326, A 11.193 *see* **si(g)hen** *v*

syker *a* safe, reliable 9.331; free from trouble 1.116; *a as n* sound, stable (base) 3.334; strong (*comp.*) B 12.161; beneficial (*sup.*) 5.39; certain 14.29, **B** 1.132, 3.50, 16.234; definite 22.255; *av* securely 12.153; to be sure A 11.163; (*comp.*) confidently B 5.502; **~ly(che)** *av* assuredly 10.26, A 8.54; without fail B 5.540; truly 8.23; (*comp.* **~loker**) confidently 7.141; safely 4.51

sykeren *v* promise faithfully 7.184

sikorere 12.153 *comp.; see* **syker** *av*

#**sylen** *v* drop down, proceed 20.341

silk B 15.220 *see* **selk(e)** *n*

syllare Z 2.53, **sylle(n)** Z 3.134 *etc*; *see* **sullere** *n*, **sullen** *v*

siluer Pr 90 *etc* = **seluer** *n*

***simile** (*Lat.*) *n* analogy 19.161, **in a** ~ by way of analogy 18.228

symonye *n* simony [the sin of buying or selling church office, service or property] Pr 84, 9.55, (*person.*) 2.63 *et p.*, 3.184, 22.126, 137

symple *a* humble, modest 15.188; *a as n* the humble B 16.8

sympletee-of-speche *n* (*person.*) humility, modesty of address B 10.167

syn B 9.85 *see* **seth(e)**[3] *conj.*

syne(ge)n *v* (commit) sin Pr 109, 6.7, 355, 7.124, 9.329, 10.25, 31, 49, 12.242, 14.112, 19.266, 277, 20.228, 22.15, ~ **aȝe(y)n / in** sin against 19.162, 167, 266

synfol(e), synful(le) *a* sinful 7.137, 145, 10.162, 20.371, 394, **B** 9.63, 122, 11.226, *a as n* (the) sinful (people), sinners 3.464, 7.120, 138, 153, 12.130, 21.22, 444, **B** 5.487, 7.15, 16.108, 109, A 12.20, 24; wicked 6.317, 10.165, Z Pr 73

syngen *v* (*p.t.* **sang** 21.212, **song** 6.46, *pl.* **songe(n)** 6.395, *etc*) sing (song) 6.46, 395, 8.122, 21.135, A 11.193, [to instrument] 15.209; chant (religious service) 3.53, 480, 5.122, 7.10, 31, 13.16, 126, 14.94, 16.334, 348, 17.120, 20.7, 21.74, 210, 212; sing in praise (of God) 7.153, 20.15, 181, 367, 450, 468, 21.71, 151; celebrate mass Pr 84, 3.310, 5.68, 13.104, *ger.* 12.87, [requiem] 15.51

synguler *a* quite alone B 9.35; sole B 16.208; special, extraordinary 6.36 (B 13.283)

synken *v* (*p.t.* **sank**, *pl.* **sonken**) sink (into) A 2.70, B 14.80; (down into) 20.69

synne *n* sin(fulness) Pr 124, 1.145, 192, 197, 10.158, 223, 11.142, 305, 12.57, 113, 13.239, 14.114, 16.76, 17.3, 81, 245, 285, 18.287, 19.177, 290, 20.234, 244, 330, 391, 430, 21.65, 371, 460, 22.306, 380, **B** 8.46, 12.79, 14.323, 15.352, 18.305, **A** 5.207, 10.74, 77, 12.21, Z 2.100, 5.95, 118; (the state of) sin 10.52, 215, 14.112, 20.388, 22.155; = original sin 7.126, 18.212, B 10.110, A 11.69; (acts of) sin, sin(s) Pr 107, 3.46, 62, 358, 399, 410, 429, 4.130, 5.107, 6.92, 257, 335, 420, 7.15, 59, 245, 9.138, 11.58, 12.27, 14.62, 19.32, 177, 20.430, 21.186, 191, **B** 1.80, 5.296, 10.473, 11.54, 100, 217, 13.192, 14.237, 18.392; ((any) kind(s) of) sin 7.72, 10.161, 101, 12.28, 73, 16.227, 17.79, **B** 5.224, 14.185, 322, 18.303, *in phr.* **alle kynne / manere** ~ 16.26, 21.186, 22.373; = sexual sin 6.188, 276, 7.90, 8.52, 10.287, 18.133, 143; vice 9.256, B 2.175; *in phrr.* **dedly(che)** ~ mortal sin 1.142, 5.122, 6.276, 7.209, 9.238, 10.43, 12.37, 17.203, 291, 20.376, **B** 8.50, 9.207, 13.406, 14.78, 83, 88, 90, 95, 15.540; **forgeuenesse of**

(...) ~ 19.188, B 14.154; **merkeness** 16; **puyre** ~ sheer sin 5.115, B 11.429; **sevene ~s** the seven deadly sins B 15.74; **sorwe of** ~ B 5.125; **venial** ~ B 14.92; **wormes of** ~ 18.38; **to ~ward** toward (sexual) sin 6.179

synnele(e)s *a* without sin 14.41; *a as av* without blame / reproach 8.237, B Pr 34

sir(e) *n* sir [*title for knight* 8.23, *for priest or cleric*] ~ **Iohan, Geffrey** 15.123, ~ **Peres of Prydie** 6.366, ~ **doctour** 15.112; ~ **Peres [Plowman]** 21.345; *before king* 2.246, 4.142, B Pr 125, 7.155; *for allegorical fig.* ~ **Actyf** 15.234, **Covetyse (Heruy)** 6.197, **Dowel** 10.128, 138, **Elde** 22.186, **Furst** Z 7.165, **Gloton** 6.392, **Go-wel** 10.148, **Hunger** 8.169 *et p.*, **Inwit** 10.144, *Liberum Arbitrium* 16.171, *Penetrans-domos* 22.341, **Resoun** 4.34 *etc*, 5.53, **Simonye** 2.115, A 2.35 *etc*, **Se-wel** *etc* 10.146, **Sorfeet** 8.276, **Waryn Witty** B 4.67, **Worch-wel** 10.147; lord 8.281, 20.302; **grete** ~ important person, lord Pr 177, A 11.22; [*as respectful term of address*] 13.220, 16.207, 18.81, 19.96, (*pl.*) 22.244, **dere** ~ 10.127, **leue** ~ 12.24, **swete** ~ B 17.125; father Pr 109, 203, 2.143, 6.134, 10.241, 22.161, **B** 5.37, 608, 9.148, 152, A 2.19, = God the Father 11.153, 18.193, 232, 19.139 *et p.*, B 17.156

sirename *n* father's family name, surname 3.366

syse *n* (session of) assise court 2.178

sismatik *n* schismatic 12.56

syso(u)r *n* juryman, sworn witness at assise court 2.59, 63, 179, 3.170, 4.162, 21.372, 22.161, 291, B 2.165

sister *n* A 10.153, (*uninfl. gen.*) 159, 179, *pl.* A 6.113 = **suster** *n*

sit *contr. pr.* 9.108, 14.142, 16.122 *see* **sitt(i)en** *v*

sithe *n* (*pl.* ~ 6.427 *etc*, **~s** Pr 232 *etc*) time 6.427, 7.37, 9.329, 10.23, 31, 49, **B** 8.44, 14.188, A 12.48; times [*in multiplication*] Pr 232

sith(en) Pr 62, 5.70, 6.310 *see* **seth(e)**[3] *conj.*; **sithe** Pr 82 *see* **seth(e)**[2] *prep.*, B 10.251 *see* **seth(e)(n)**[1] *av*

sitt(i)en (setten) *v* (*contr. pr.* **sit** 9.108 *etc*, *p.t.* **saet** 6.361 *etc*, **sat** B 2.165, **sete** B 18.287, *subjv.* 6.99, 14.2, *pl.* **seet** 8.122, **seten** 6.395, 7.164, 15.42, B 6.192) sit Pr 114, 6.99, 361, 7.103, 8.122, 9.108, 250, 252, 16.341, 18.241, 19.49, 200, **B** 2.165, 3.345, 5.376, 6.192, 16.141, ~ **adoun** B 5.7, ~ **vp** 7.62; sit enthroned 1.121, 133; lie B 18.287; be placed 7.164, 261; judge 21.306; have place (in heaven) 9.12, 11.203, 14.142, B 7.17; sit as juryman 16.122; ~ **stille** remain silent 15.108; afflict 2.154

Syuile *n* Civil (Roman) law (*person.*) 2.63 *et p.*, 22.137

sixe *num.* six, ~ **myle** 19.74, ~ **monthes** B 10.151, ~ **sithe** 7.37, ~ **sonnes** 3.478, *in cpds.* ~ **score** 3.182, ~ **thousand** 19.26

sixte *num.ord.* (*as n.*) sixth 16.137

sixty *num.* sixty, ~ **wynter** 15.271; (*as indef. large number*) ~ **sythes** 7.47, *a as n* 22.224, *in cpd.* ~ **thousand** B 17.23

skalon *n* shallot 8.309

skathe 3.61, A 12.71 = **sc(h)athe** *n*

skele A 12.34 = **skil** *n*

skenis *suffix in phr.* **alle skenis** A 10.84 = **alles kynnes**; *see* **kyn** *n*

skil(l) *n* reasonableness 6.25, *in phr.* **bryngen out of** ~ cause to lose self-control 21.285; reason, cause 5.153, B 12.215, *in phr.* **(by) goed** ~ for a good reason 16.120, 18.84; argument 11.162, 13.130, A 12.34, **by puyre** ~ by simple reasoning 15.137, **bi this** ~ from this line of argument B 17.196; excuse 6.22, 19.314; (rational) knowledge B 10.303

skilfole *a* knowledgeable 11.96

skynes *suff. in phrr.* **any** ~ (= **enys-kynes**) A 2.162, **summe** ~ some kind of A 8.34 *see* **kyn** *n*

skyppen *v* leap, **skypte an heyh** briskly mounted a pulpit 12.42

sklaundre 2.86, A 12.17 = **sclaundre** *n*

skolde *n* scold, railer A 12.34

skolden *v* rail, quarrel 2.86

skornen 2.86 = **scornen** *v*

skornfully *av* disdainfully A 12.12

slaken *v* slake, quench B 15.281, 18.369; *and see* **slokken** *v*

slawe *p.p.* Pr 113, 11.267, 17.275 *see* **slen** *v*

sleep B 2.97 = **slep** *n*; *p.t.* 6.417, B 5.376 *see* **slepen** *v*

sley *a* deft (*sup.*) B 13.298; ~ **of** cunning in 22.163

sleiȝte B 13.365, 408 = **sleythe** *n*

sleyliche *av* treacherously 6.107, (*sup.*) **sleylokeste** 11.267

sleythe *n* practical wisdom, resourcefulness 21.98; expert skill B 13.408; art 21.99; stratagem 20.164, 21.460; cunning 6.73, 22.14; crafty scheme, wile 2.91, 6.107, 16.274, 19.234; trick B 13.365

slen *v* (*p.t.* **slowh** 22.150, *pl.* **slowe** 11.37, *p.p.* **slawe** Pr 113, 11.267, 17.275) slay, kill Pr 113, 3.419, 439, 7.223, 21.432, 22.150, B 10.365, 367, A 11.252; murder 6.107, 11.37, 17.275, 19.257; destroy B 14.90, 94

slep *n* sleep Pr 46, B 2.97, 99, Z Pr 11, **a** ~ to sleep A 9.58, Z 5.26; sleep(iness) Z 5.24; dream Z Pr 93

slepen *v* (*p.t.* **sleep** 6.417, B 5.376, *pl.* **slepen** 15.271, **slepte** Pr 8 *etc*., *p.p.* **slept** B 5.4, **(y)slepe** A 5.4, Z 5.22, *assim. 2 pr. sg.* **slepestow** 1.5) sleep 5.9, 7.251, 12.153, 15.25, 20.4, B 7.121, 12.28, ~ **druye** sleep in a dry place 19.304, (*fig.*) 15.307; be asleep 1.5, A 8.151; fall asleep Pr 7, 8.324, 10.66; *pr.p.* **slepynge** while asleep and dreaming Pr 13, 221, 232, 5.124, 9.298, 13.217, 222, B 11.320; in her sleep B 18.299*n*; *ger.* sleep B 5.6; *in phr.* **don...to slepe** prevent from sleeping 19.306

sleuthe, slewthe *n* (the deadly sin of) sloth Pr 46, 2.102, 7.54, 63, 69, 11.110, 16.93, B 3.310, 6.143, A 2.66, (*person.*) 7.1, 47, 62, 16.93, 22.158 *et p.*; spiritual torpor B 8.51; idleness 8.245, 9.159, B 2.99, 14.76, 235; negligence 8.253

sliken *v* make smooth / fat B 2.99

slymed *a* slimy 7.1

slynge *n* sling (for hurling missiles) 22.163, 217

slokken *v* quench 20.410; *see* **slaken** *v*

slombren *v* doze off B Pr 10

sloo *n* mud, earth 12.181

slouþe A 2.66 = **sleuthe** *n*

slow(e) *a* sluggish, lazy 8.244, B 13.408

slow(e), slowh *p.t.* 11.37, 22.150; *see* **slen** *v*

smacchen *v* (*p.t.* **smauhte**) smell 6.413

smal *a* little Pr 166; small 18.63, 112; skinny A 12.78

smauhte *p.t.* 6.413 *see* **smacchen** *v*

smellen *v* smell (*intr.*) 13.243; (*tr.*) 7.50

smerte *av* sharply, painfully 13.243

smerten *v* sting, cause to smart 19.307; suffer pain, hardship B 3.168

smethe *a* smooth Z 6.80

smethen 3.476 = **smyth(y)en** *v*

smyllen 7.50 = **smellen** *v*

smyten *v* (*contr. pr.* **smyt** 13.243, *pl.* 19.305, *p.t.* **smoet** 18.156, *p.p.* **smyte** 3.476) strike 3.476, 6.105, 18.156, 20.385; sting 13.243; ~ **in** penetrate 19.305, 325

smyth *n* blacksmith 3.476

smyth(y)en (smethen) *v* forge (on anvil) 3.476, **don it** ~ have it beaten 3.459

smoke *n* smoke 19.305, 307, (*fig.*) 325

#smolder *n* choking fumes 19.305, 325

snake *n* snake 16.265

snowe *n* snow 16.265

so[1] *av* thus, in this way 1.71, 2.68, 3.95, 4.100, 5.92, 6.395, 7.235, 264, 9.117, 10.38, 220, 12.202, 206, 216, 13.119, 216, 15.24, 17.20, 76, 123, 184, 192, 18.67, 96, 19.277, 20.234, 321, 21.101, 22.99, 209, 290, B 1.120, 5.37, 6.14, 233, 7.70, 9.41, 155, 10.89, 11.193, 381, 12.55, †A 5.130, 7.212, 236, 10.94, 11.124, 240, Z Pr 145, 5.34; in such a manner 19.181, 215, 20.160, 434, 21.44, 316, 22.15, 63, 277, 348, B †Pr 206, 2.100, 10.347, 11.82, 163, 13.409, 15.389, A 9.47, 10.127, 11.291*n*, 12.106, Z Pr 56, 1.121, 6.47; *in phrr.* ~ **forth** thus continually 13.173, 16.11, B 14.159; thus likewise B 13.210; ~ **may be** perhaps 5.33, 8.41, ~ **myhte happe** should it so happen 15.6; ~ **may befalle** it may happen 22.351, B 16.60; (*as quasi-prn*) such, that Pr 211, 2.24, 3.232, 6.9, 8.97, 231, 12.168, 13.190, 16.180, 334, 17.92, 290, 19.32, 20.74, B 2.122, 10.197, 246, A 2.19, 11.236 (2); (so) likewise 3.377, 6.321, 12.56, 13.17, 14.120, 150, 16.8, 18.232, 236, 19.108, 132, 20.163, 182, 327, 22.224, B 10.469, 11.75, 12.247, 14.284, 15.261, 16.150, 194, 17.36, A 4.53; correspondingly †B 14.311; *in phr.* **ryȝt** ~ in just this manner, exactly thus Pr 182, 1.156, 2.135, 5.150, 7.89, 8.81, 9.134, 217, 12.21, 13.229, 14.49, 110, 181, 16.225, 244, 267, 295, 17.214, 19.139, 21.437, B 10.434, 472, 12.35, 47, 51, 58, 90, 260, 13.118, 14.123, 127, 151, 15.335, 339, 475, 17.39, 155, A 10.105, 12.30; **ryȝt** ~ **sothly** 3.329, 12.195, 227, 235, 16.225, ~ **aftur** in that way accordingly 12.150; then 7.212, 231, 20.396, 22.181, B

9.205, 13.143 *in phr.* **riȝt** ~ at once B 5.365; therefore, accordingly 3.328, 494, 5.44, 99, 6.321, 9.323, 327, 10.43, 12.244, 20.220, 393, 21.115, 440, 478, 22.50, B 14.79, A 11.195; so (*with a or av or alone*, = to such an extent) Pr 84, 6.205, 7.303, 8.175, 10.161, 11.58, 16.78, 17.87, 18.48, 19.61, 20.368, 408, 21.428, 22.42, 198, ~...**to** so...as to Pr 202; so that 15.69; ~...**as** in the way that 11.237; ~..**that** in such a way that Pr 149, 3.434–5, 8.172, 10.186, 15.25; the case that 4.134 –5, 17.151; so well...that 16.169–70, 19.281–2, B Pr 126, A 2.24; ~ **þat** with the result that 19.190, provided that 22.22; so very 1.191, 3.198, 4.101, 5.167, 16.306, B 14.322; that 3.296, **B** 3.353, 14.273; so greatly 8.269; as 9.95, 331, 12.193, 13.187, 202, 14.138, **B** 10.228, 12.281; as 13.202, ~...**as** as...as 10.252; exceedingly 3.454; *in correl. constr.* **so...as** = as...as 6.276, 13.52–3; **as...so** like 6.430; **so...so** as...as 19.65; **so muche... as** as much ...as 14.138–9; *in oaths / assevs., blessing,* ~ **me God (Crist) helpe / spede** so help / prosper me God (Christ) 3.8, 4.11, 5.22, 10.108, **B** 3.250, 13.206, 15.158, 16.180, **A** 4.91, 7.131, Z 7.200, ~ **thee Ik** so may I prosper B 5.224; *in misc. phrr.* ~ **muche after** such grave consequences Pr 207; **by ~ muche** to that extent 7.141; **neuer** ~ however 3.422, 10.36, 16.168, **B** 9.39, 14.90; **none** ~ ... no...so 6.412, 7.157, 18.141; **what** ~ whatever 14.216, B 4.155; ~... **with** with such (a) 7.41, B 5.82

so[2] *conj.* as, while B 5.8; so / with the result that 4.124, 6.247, B 16.130; provided (that) 2.125 (2), 3.388, 7.229, 290, 13.202, 16.207, 21.440, 22.22, 222, **B** 4.193, 12.166, A 12.97; *in phr.* **by** ~ (**þat**) provided that 4.98, 187, 5.39, 6.331, 10.310, 12.4, 22, 15.123, 257, **B** 13.136, 14.85, 279

sobben *v* sob B 14.326

sobre *a* temperate, restrained 15.256

sobreliche *av* gravely B 13.204

sobrete(e) *n* moderation, temperance [*esp.* in food and drink] 15.188, 16.132, B 10.167; sobriety 16.150

socour *n* succour, aid 22.170

sode *p.t. pl.* 17.20, *p.p.* 9.149 *see* **sethen** *v*

sodeynliche *av* suddenly 15.24, 19.178; right away 21.5

*****soden** *n* sub-dean 2.187, 16.277, B 2.173

so(e)nd *n* sand 13.135, 14.40; land 17.88, 21.78

soercerye *n* sorcery, witchcraft 17.304, 309, 18.150, 20.71, B 10.212; magic B 15.12; enchantment(s) 6.191

soeth *a* 19.5, 20.312; *n* 19.108, 20.462, ~ **faste** *a* 17.119, 18.69; ~**ly(che)** *av* 19.93, 123, 21.87, 22.215, 244; ~**nesse** *n* 12.83 see **soth(-)** *a, n*

soffisen (sufficen) *v* be sufficient 14.12, 17.119, 19.35, 204, B 15.386

soffra(u)nce *n* patience (in suffering hardship / affliction) 13.202, B 11.378, A 10.119; (the) long-suffering (of God) B 6.144; (improper) tolerance of wrongdoing, *in phr.* **vnsittyng** ~ 3.207, 4.189

soffr(y)en *v* suffer (distress, affliction) 7.104, 9.84, 12.180, 202, 15.71, 16.325, 20.255, 256, 21.68, 102, 22.47, **B** 2.106, 13.66, 14.175, 15.200, 260, 266, 267, 270; undergo, experience 3.399, 449, 6.57 (B 13.310), 129, 7.304, 9.77, 11.107, 12.146, 16.173, 17.270, 20.210, 216*n*, 231, B 10.110; be subject (to) 12.188, ? 18.203*n*, **B** Pr 131, 5.608, 11.382; endure patiently 12.195, 15.280, 16.327, 19.318, 21.292, 295, **B** 9.204, 12.8, A 10.99, 118, 216, Z 5.95; be long-suffering 4.20, 13.200, B 11.381; forbear for a while 20.165, 269, 22.107; wait patiently 2.45, 13.222; put up with (sth.) Pr 211, 6.9, 13.11, 195, 198, 221, 21.444, B 18.395, ~ **(wel)** willingly put up with 8.89, 10.91, 19.105, 324, 22.323, B 10.367; accept **B** 10.251, 15.174; allow Pr 109, 119, 1.144, 3.120, 4.1, 7.124, 138, 8.82, 9.117, 256, 10.162, 254, 255, 256, 14.165, 16.162, 17.183, 18.177, 20.228, **B** Pr 206, †4.86, 6.181, 8.93, 10.120, 16.74, A 9.47; countenance Pr 96, 3.449, 13.114, B 2.175; tolerate Pr 101, 9.131, **B** 10.107 (A 11.66), 12 53, 18.303; leave 22.294; consent 20.222, B 15.518; submit 17.10

sofistre *n* clever deceiver, ~ **of soercerie** cunning magician 17.309; *and see* **sophistrie** *n*

softe *a* mild Pr 1; quiet, gentle 10.118; *av* gently 22.314, (*comp.*) 311; quietly Z 6.70; gingerly 16.52; ~ **ly(che)** in quiet tones 2.165, 3.54, **B** 3.37, 5.7; unobtrusively 4.162; at an easy pace 2.178, 189, 4.54, B 2.165; slowly 15.29, 20.120

soilen[1] *v* dirty **B** 13.343, 400, 458, 14.2, 13

soylen[2] **Z** Pr 76, 3.171= **assoylen** *v*

soiournen *v* reside 10.18; linger B 17.84

sokene *n* district, soke 2.111

solace, solas *n* joy, happiness 12.210, 13.18, 14.94, 16.17, 20.227; pleasure 16.11, 309; enjoyment('s sake) 8.22; *in phr.* **in** ~ in good part, as a joke 9.131; comfort B 7.85

solacen *v* entertain (*fig.*) 7.102, 112, B 12.22; cheer 7.255, 19.200; comfort 7.138, 16.150, 18.15, 21.22, **B** 7.85, 14.283

sold *p.p.* 3.245, 20.222, B 16.142; **solde** *p.t.* 6.97, 17.20, 18.158, B 16.143 *see* **sullen** *v*

soleyn *n* solitary person, ~ **by hymsulue** all by himself alone 14.144

solempneliche *av* reverently 3.54

solfen *v* sing a scale 7.31

solitarie *a* in solitude 17.7

som B 13.377 = **som(m)e** *n*

som(m)(e), summe[1] *prn sg. & pl.* some, certain (ones) Pr 22, 25, 33, 35, 59, 90, 93, 1.126, 6.179, 8.8, 118, 9.197, 13.165, 177, 16.247, 18.69, 70, 21.241, 243, 22.348, **B** 5.627, 9.127, 156, A 6.115; (*in apposition*) 3.14*n*; **somme...somme** some...others 21.253; some part, a portion 8.274, 286, 17.20, B 15.248, 329

som(m)(e), sum[2] *a* one 18.283, B 16.142; a 14.137, 20.172, **B** 5.374, 10.436, 13.55, 377; some (kind of)

2.4, 128, 3.291 *et p.*, **B** 7.31, 17.315; some...or other 9.169, 211, 216, 11.209, 12.5, 18.105; some, certain 3.14n (*or*, together), 4.105, 11.198, 16.247, 18.150, 21.230, 237, **B** 15.350; *in phrr.* ~ **body** *n* someone 22.27; ~ **de(e)l** *av* partly 20.8, **B** 16.39; to some extent 16.118, **B** 3.92; somewhat 7.44, ? very much 7.189; ~ **manere** some kind of 9.33, 15.299, **B** 5.25, 14.164; ~ **tyme** *av* sometimes, occasionally 3.104, 5.47, 6.57, 79, 112, 137, 428, 7.28, 39, 9.149, 10.159, 12.39, 16.334, 343, 18.37, 49, 19.178, **B** 5.376, 14.237, 15.186, 16.46; some time 8.22; from time to time **B** 12.22; (at) some time (or other) 6.115, 13.212, 15.299, 17.1, **B** 11.401; ~...~ at one time ... at another time 6.38, 191, 404, 21.102, 103, 104, **B** 5.546; on one occasion 20.330; at one time [past] 6.207, 15.302, 16.366, 22.182, **B** 5.135, 12.293, 15.245, 442; ~ ~ **þat** such time as 21.444

som(me)[3] *n* number, quantity 19.33; sum **B** 13.377

somer 8.245 *etc*; *see* **somur** *n*

som(p)nen *v* invite 12.48; summon 21.215, **leten** ~ have summoned 2.172; call for **Z** 2.42; order to appear 3.468

som(p)nour *n* summoner, apparitor 2.59, 187, 3.170, 4.162, 9.263, 16.277, 21.372, **B** 2.170

somur (somer) *n* summer 6.112, 8.245, 9.119, 15.295, 16.11, 146, 18.241; ~ **game B** 5.407, ~ **sesoun** Pr 1, 10.2, ~ **tyme** 16.246, **B** 14.178 (*fig*) 15.307, 16.17,

somwhat *prn* something 8.277, 18.264, **B** 6.259, 15.392, A 11.181; some (good) reason 12.34; *av* to some extent 21.456, **B** 12.20

sond 13.135 = **so(e)nd** *n*

Son(e)day 7.64, 20.69, **B** 13.236 = **Sonenday**

sonde *n* sending, **Goddes** ~ what God sends 6.111, 9.178; command [sent by God] **B** 9.127; gift [sent by Christ] 16.134

sondry *a* separate 18.192; different Pr 96, 3.90, 20.231, 22.42, **B** 13.275; distinct 18.191, **B** 16.207, 17.153; various 15.44, 67, 16.108; several, ~ **tymes** 18.153, **B** 12.31, ~ **tyme** from time to time **B** 15.282

sone[1] *n* son 3.367, 5.72, 73, 10.241, 14.60, 75, 18.67, **B** 9.148, [Abraham's] 18.248, 252, **B** 16.234, [Adam's] 10.251, [Cato's] **B** 12.21, [Clergy's] **B** 13.120, [Heli's] Pr 113, [Inwit's] 10.145, [the Jews'] **B** 16.123, [Joseph's] 9.312, [the King's] 4.43, [men's] 12.114, [Nebuchadnezzar's] 9.307, [Noah's] 10.226, 11.243, [Piers's] 8.82, 92, [Saul's] 3.410, 14.62, [Simon Magus's] = simoniac 5.79, [Symeon's] 20.259, [Tobias's] 11.71, 74; God's son (= Christ) 1.162, 6.171, 7.126, 128, 288, 11.143, 17.262, [justice's 18.126], 18.149, 194, 205, 20.255, 70, [king's] 20.78, 331, (**kynges** ~ **of Heuene**) son of heaven's king 20.363 (= the Second Person of the Trinity) 11.153, 18.228 *et p.*, 19.123 *et p.*, **B** 10.236, 241, 16.214, 223, 17.147 *et p.*; [10.30, 18.67, **B** 1.5, 5.490, 491

sone[2] *av* straightaway 3.50, 18.8, **B** 18.317, **A** 11.245, 12.47, **thus** ~ at once 12.6, 15.44; before long 15.96, 108, 22.69; soon **B** 6.129; presently 15.99, 22.159, **B** 13.32; quickly 3.61, 180, 13.63, 15.177, 22.87, **B** 6.192, 11.423, 12.31, 241, 16.23, **A** 4.57, 8.11, **Z** 1.13; *in conjv. phr.* **as** ~ **as** 3.325, **so** ~ (**so**) 10.252, 19.65, **B** 10.228, **thus** ~ (**as**) as soon as 3.180; (*comp.*) **son(n)er(e)** more quickly 2.141, 3.62, 11.258, 296, 14.111, 18.60, 64; (*sup.*) **son(n)est** most quickly 1.66, 3.435, **B** 3.58, (+ **most**) 12.225

Son(en)day *n* Sunday 2.231, 6.417, 7.64, 9.227, 242, 244, 15.212, 20.69, **B** 13.236, **mydde-Lentones** ~ mid-Lent Sunday (4th in Lent) 18.182

song *n* song 13.58; (love) song 6.189; hymn of praise 14.94 (2), 21.212; acclamation **B** 18.325; singing, **sotil of** ~ **B** 13.298

song *p.t.* 6.46, 13.16, 20.468, **song(e)(n)** *pl.* 6.395, 7.153, 8.122, 14.94, 20.7, 367, 450, 21.74, 135, 151 *see* **syngen** *v*

songewarie B 7.149, 151 = **sowngewarie** *n*

sonken *p.t. pl.* **B** 14.80 *see* **sinken** *v*

sonne *n* sun Pr 14, 1.116, 3.478, 6.417, 7.131, 9.294, 308, 10.159, 13.135, 17.91, 20.60, 138, 254, 255, 455, 21.78, **B** 6.325, **A** 6.79, (*fig.*) 18.72; sun's rays Pr 1; sunshine 18.66, 19.194, 21.435, **B** 5.81; sun's heat 18.75; *in cpds.* ~ **rysynge** sunrise 20.69; ~ **syde** sunny side 1.113, 18.64; *in phr.* **vnder** ~ anywhere 3.203, 10.50, 12.95, 16.208, **B** 10.208

sonnen *v* dry in the sun **B** 14.21

sonner(e) *comp.* 2.141, 3.62, 11.296, 14.111, 18.60, **B** 10.416; **sonnest** *sup.* 3.435, 12.225, **B** 1.70; **soone B** 6.129, 192, 11.423, 12.31, 241, 13.32 = **sone**; *see* **sone** *av*

soor B 14.96, **~e B** 5.96, 116, 14.96, 106, 18.88 *see* **sore** *a, av*

sooth 16.303, **B** Pr 52 *etc*, **B** 10.16 *etc; see* **soth** *n, a*; **~ly B** 15.433 = **sothly(che)** *av*

sop *n* mouthful (*fig.*) **B** 15.180, *in phr.* **at a** ~ at a morsel's worth **B** 13.125

sopare *n* soap-maker / seller 5.72

sope *n* soap (*fig.*) **B** 14.6

soper(e) *n* supper, evening-meal 6.428, 8.275, **B** 16.141 ~ **tyme** 8.274

sophistrie *n* sophistry 21.349

sorcerie B 10.212, 15.12 = **soercerye** *n*

sore *n* ailment, disease 17.300, 22.97; wound 22.359; hurt 20.385; *a* harsh, painful 22.360; (spiritually) sore **B** 14.96; *av* sharply, painfully 20.49; strongly 19.274; bitterly 6.316, 20.91; earnestly 7.149; hard 21.441, 22.260; grievously 21.127, **B** 14.162, 18.88, (*comp.*), **sorre** the more grievously Pr 171, **sarrore** more keenly 15.286; intensely **B** 5.116; closely **B** 11.224; greatly 6.276 (**B** 13.388), 7.9, 85 (**B** 13.426), 20.312, **B** 5.96, 14.106

sorewe A 3.144, 5.215 = **sorwe** *n*

sorfeet (surfete) *n* over-indulgence (in food) B 13.405, A 5.203, (*person.*) 8.276

sorfeten *v* indulge to excess 13.187

sorowe 16.29 = **sorwe** *n*

sorserie 6.191, 18.150 = **soercerie** *n*

sory *a* sad, sorrowful 16.301; upset B 14.323; angry 6.93, 15.213; sorry, repentant, ~ **for synnes** 6.91, 7.59, 145, 245, 11.58, 19.278; remorseful 6.308, 7.15; regretful B 11.104; miserable 19.328, A 11.193, Z 7.198; wicked 3.358, B Pr 45

sorwe *n* sorrow, grief Pr 113, 7.130; distress (of heart) 7.131, 12.210; lamentation 3.17, Z 5.104; contrition 16.29, 19.298; harm, evil B 4.62, Z Pr 73; wretch-edness 13.16, 18, 14.80, 16.173, 20.2, 228; misery 22.199; suffering 16.309, 19.318, 21.66, 22.43, 47; pain 22.105, B 14.283; anguish 20.222, A 5.215; mis-fortune 3.90, 14.61, 62, B 12.245; trouble B Pr 191, A 3.144; torment, *in curses* ~ **mot thow haue** 2.117, **God / Crist ʒeue þe / hym** ~ 2.126, 3.212, 19.309, B 5.106 ~ **on** A 2.80; = torment [in hell] 7.86, 116, 17.145

sorw(e)ful *a* wretched B 17.90; suffering 18.15

sot *n* (*pl.* **sottes**) fool B 10.8; scoundrel 9.256; wretch A 10.59

soth, soþ[1] *n* (the) truth 1.82, 2.26, *in phrr.* **sayen / seg-gen** ~ speak the truth 2.26, 4.64, 7.229, 12.42, 13.242, 14.103, 19.23, 108, 20.466, **B** Pr 52, 6.129, 12.20, **tellen** ~ 17.211, 20.462, B 9.156, Z 4.50; the truth of the matter 1.121, 3.285, 4.37, 16.122, 17.211, 21.9, **B** 4.80, 5.275, 10.55, Z 4.157; *in phrr.* **witen the** ~ 1.121, 3.285, 4.37, 7.244, 9.128, 10.22, 12.79, 162, 14.191, 16.252, 19.9, 20.149, **B** 2.122, 5.562, A 8.56, Z 3.175, **for** ~ as / to be the truth 7.284, 13.111, 16.303, *as emph. parenth. phr.* truly, indeed 3.112, 4.2, 5.3, 86, 6.237, 7.242, B 11.238, Z 3.122

soth, soþ[2] *a* true 5.92, 10.213, 12.73, 13.246, 16.204, 19.5, 20.312, **B** 10.16, 327, 429, 13.206, 212, 15.173, 16.60, (*sup.*) 10.440, A 10.81, 12.5; genuine 9.62; (indeed) the case 16.204, 18.193, 20.169

sothe *av* tru(thful)ly (*sup.*) 3.435

sothewoste Z 5.32 = **south-weste** *a*

sothfaste *a* true 11.289, B 10.236; real, steadfast 11.131, 15.188, 17.119, 18.51, 69; **~nesse** *n* Divine Truth (= the Son) B 16.186

sothly(che) *av* truly 2.135, 3.5, 7.279, 9.217, 11.131, 286, 13.143, 22.215, 244, **B** 10.228, 15.433; *as emph. parenth. phr.* 2.135 *et p.*; in truth 14.77, 17.179, 19.123, 20.115; with truth, justly 1.115; indeed 3.235, 6.240, 19.93, 21.374; certainly 3.329, 10.18, B 3.190; actually 16.146, 19.57, B 10.273; in fact 7.208, 10.21, B 10.230; for a fact 18.58, B 15.162; assuredly 1.47, 3.245, 12.83, 17.184; for his part 21.87

sothnesse *n* truth(fulness) 19.283; righteousness 12.83, (*person.*) (*a*) 2.24, 200, A 4.138, **Z** 2.45, 4.50, (*b*) Divine Truth B 18.282

sotil *a* ingenious 10.209, 20.54; subtle, sophisticated 16.208; clever B 15.399; graceful, skilful B 13.298; insidious 4.149; fine-drawn, ethereal B 15.12

sotilen *v*, **(inne)** speculate subtly (upon) B 10.185; scheme, contrive 17.169, 19.236, 20.333, 21.460; cleverly devise 6.189, B 10.216

sotiltee *n* cunning stratagem 12.242; intricacy 14.76

souchen *v* devise 2.26, 12.242

soude *n* payment B 3.353

souden *v* hire (as mercenaries) 21.432

souel (sowl) *n* relish [eaten with bread] 8.285, 17.24

sou(g)ht(e) *p.t.* 3.165, 4.66, 9.315, 16.293, 17.169; *p.p.* 4.122, 7.168, 174 *see* **sechen** *v*

souhteres *n* female shoemaker 6.361

souken *v* suck 12.57

soule *n* (*uninfl. gen.* **soule** 7.174, 20.408, **B** 5.531, 11.228) (the human) soul 1.35, 39, 5.39, 152, 7.76, 88, 112, 8.96 (2), 9.329, 331, 10.158, 14.77, 115, 197, 15.51, 84, 16.31, 131, 148, 153, 17.81, 18.15, 19.313, 20.371, 406, 21.453, 22.233, **B** 11.264, 14.30, 283, 285, 15.344, A 10.77; (= individual) soul 1.80, 2.154, 5.48, 103, 198, 6.345, 7.102, 105, 174, 255, 258, 8.96 (1), 9.39, 289, 12.82, 14.206, 16.25, 154, 273, 17.22, 143, 145, 19.228, 20.336, 341, 388, 394, **B** 1.132, 2.106, 3.50, 4.151, 5.72, 531, 7.51, 8.49, 10.208, 251, 257, 12.15, 54, 13.142, 14.85, **A** 7.136, 10.63, 72, Z 7.76; (living) soul [= animating principle] B 9.50; person B 3.353, A 10.175; heart 19.20, 21.294, B 16.234; *in phrr.* **body and (...)** ~ 1.58, 9.40, (19.28), 20.301, 21.180, B 6.251, 15.425, ~ **and (...) body** 1.146, 7.128, 12.89; **Cristene ~s** 11.246, 12.152; **dampned ~s** B 10.428; **gode ~s** Z 7.82; **in** ~ spiritually, inwardly B 10.259, 13.288, 15.412, A 3.58; **lyf and** ~ = utterly, absolutely 6.314, 14.127, 20.268, 370, 21.411, **B** 9.188, 17.25; **loue of** ~ heartfelt affection 10.294; (a) **m(a)nnes** ~ 7.88, 16.1, 225, 17.78, 274, 20.194, 244, 408, 414, 21.276, **B** 8.47, 10.475, 11.228, 12.57, 13.130, 15.352, 433; **sauacion of** ~ B 5.125; **synfole ~s** 20.371; **to the** ~ with respect to the soul B 14.285; *in oaths and assevs.* **be (my)...** ~ 8.307, 9.25, 13.242, 19.229, B 5.266, Z 2.97; **bi / for perel of (...)** ~ upon danger of losing (one's) soul 4.137, 7.200, 228; **Godes** ~ 6.426; *in imprecations* **B** 12.39, 13.165, 15.141, A 12.105

sound *a* unharmed A 12.115, *in phr.* **saef and** ~ 10.38, 40

sounen *v*, ~ **of** concern 11.79, ~ **to** have to do with 9.216, 21.456; lead to, foster 6.59

soupen *v* (eat) sup(per) 8.228, 16.13, **B** 2.97, 14.178, 15.180

sour *a* sour 15.49, 18.100, ~ **loef** leavened bread 15.56; bitter (*fig.*) 12.146, 20.217; harsh 22.47; **~e** *av* severely 2.154, B 10.359

souter(e) *n* shoemaker 6.83, **B** 5.407, 10.461, A 11.184

south *n* south, *in phr.* **bi ~e** in the south(ern quarter) 1.116, 20.169; southern sky 9.294; *av, in phr.* **euene**

~ directly to the south A 8.128; ~ **weste** *a* from the south-west 5.116

souþden B 2.173 = **soden** *n*

#**soueraynes** *n* (elevation to) high rank A 10.119

souereyn *n* lord, master A 10.72; superior 8.82; sovereign ruler 21.77; ruler 11.271; principal guest 14.139

souereyn(e) *a* chief, principal 15.295, B 10.212, ~ **oen** leading person 6.27; supreme 20.227; excellent 1.146, 22.373, **B** Pr 159, 11.378; efficacious B 10.208

souereynly(che) *av* above all 6.92, 13.202; most especially 17.278, A 11.249; like a conqueror 20.394

soware *n* sower (*fig.* = progenitor) 18.226

sowe *n* sow 6.397, 13.150

sowen *v*[1] (*p.t.* **sew(e)** 6.271 *etc,p.p.* **(y)sowe(n)** 8.3, 12.190, B 5.543) sow (seed) 7.185, 186, 8.3, 24, 62, 9.6, 10.218, 12.181, 188, 190, 15.213, 17.101, B 5.546, *ger.* Pr 23, B 7.118, (*fig.*) 21.276, 290, 299, 311, 345, 409

sowen *v*[2] sew 8.8, 10

sowestre *n* seamstress A 5.158

sowl 8.285 = **souel** *n*

sowle Z 2.97, 7.76, 82 = **soule** *n*

sownen 21.456 = **sounen** *v*

so(w)ngewarie *n* dream-interpretation 9.302, B 7.151

sowsen *v* steep (*fig.*) Z 2.100

space *n* period B 9.98; time, opportunity 3.216

spade *n* spade 3.461, 8.183, B 6.189

spak(e) *p.t.* 6.222, 419, 11.284, 13.226, 15.154, 16.36, 18.124, 231, 21.376, **B** 9.32, 13.24, 181 *see* **speken** *v*

spanne *n* hand's breadth [of masonry] Z 6.78

sparen *v* spare [= hold back from destroying] 3.424, 425; ~ (...) **to** refrain from 12.36, 21.304, **B** 3.51, 10.102, 16.64, ~ **fingeres** work slowly with fingers A 7 *ger.* **sparynge (of)** refraining / ceasing from 7.48; save 9.74, 13.76; hoard **B** 12.51, 15.143; put aside (to give away) 10.84, B 5.374; keep away 6.151, ~ **to** avoid B 10.102

speche *n* power of speech **B** 4.156, 9.101; (manner of) speech / speaking 4.17, 10.83, 118, 11.92, 13.229, 15.188, 277, 16.69, 20.119, 239, 21.93, **B** 5.553, 566, 10.210, 11.239, 13.276, 302, 15.218, 350, A 9.71; speaking, eloquence 11.285; speech, words 2.43, 83, 161, 239, 3.157, 4.138, 149, 153, 6.165, 186, 7.48, 237, 8.216, 9.46, 10.187, 11.20, 92, 14.7, 15.144, 147, 16.206, 18.172, 21.287, 22.115, **B** Pr 52, 2.42, 5.98, 138, 9.98, 10.166, 11.4, 69, 13.322, 401, 14.13, 16.154, **A** 10.53, 11.104; word 18.189; utterance 20.132, B 9.37, A 10.34; maxim A 11.241; discourse 10.56, A 12.100; conversation B 13.151; language (*fig.*) 3.109; (*in cpds., person.*) **Benigne** ~ kindly words 18.11, **buxom** ~ mild words B 16.7, **Fair** ~ A 2.130, **Hende** ~ courteous address 22.349, 355, **Sympletee of** ~ humility in speech B 10.167

spechelees *a* without the power of speech 16.196

special *a* exceptional 21.30

sped(de) *p.t.* 13.23, B 17.82, A 12.100 *see* **speden** *v*

spedelich *a* profitable A 12.100

spedily *av* quickly, ? profitably A 7.11

speden *v* achieve one's purpose 3.216; succeed B 17.82 (2); prosper 3.424, 7.239, 8.42, 13.23; help 10.108; satisfy 22.55; (*refl.*) set oneself (to a task) A12.100, hurry B 17.82 (1)

*****speke** *n* cave B 15.275

speken *v* (*p.t. sg.* **spak** 6.222 *etc*, *2 p.* **speke** 21.80, B 12.191, *3 pl.* **speke(n)** 2.235, 21.130, B 15.275) have power of speech 16.216, 21.130, B 14.84; speak 2.101, 4.44, 21.80, B Pr 129; say, tell 21.70, B 12.191; utter 2.101, 17.319, B 10.40; express 6.431; speak up 20.270, B 17.33; talk 14.7, 21.405; answer 3.216; argue 6.122, B 13.132; converse B 15.275; preach 3.462; ask 2.235, 6.222; plead (for) 9.46; mention 13.100, 14.87, B 1.49; write (about) B 15.117, 573, (against) 16.214; (*person.*) ~ **euele** 21.342

spelen *v*[1] save up 13.76

spelen *v*[2] recite, ? make out 17.319

*****spelonke** *n* cavern, den B 15.275

spenden *v* (*p.p.* **yspended** B 14.102) spend (money), expend (wealth) 16.233, *ger.* spending 16.39, *in cpd.* ~ **suluer** spending money 13.100; spend **B** 5.374, 14.102, A 7.209; expend B 11.292; consume B 10.102; use A 8.49

spendour *n* spendthrift 5.28

spenen *v* (*p.p.* **yspened** 16.278) spend money 2.101, 5.28, B 15.77, 144; spend 9.74, 11.77, 15.282, B 15.144, 328; incur expense B 17.78; expend, lay out 5.69, 13.76, 107, 17.72; use, employ 9.46 (Z 8.50)

spense *n* charge, expense 16.39

spere *n* spear, lance 20.10, 80, 88

speren 19.1 = **spyren** *v*

sperhauk *n* sparrow-hawk B 6.196

spice *n* spice 6.357; medicine, ? species (of remedy) B 1.149c

spicen *v* flavour with spices 21.289

spicer (spysour) *n* spice-dealer, apothecary 2.235, A 10.125

spie *n* spy, scout 21.342; seeker 19.1c

#**spiek** *n* ear of grain 12.182

spien *v* examine closely B 2.226

spyer 18.231 = **spir(e)** *n*

spilde *p.t.* 6.431 *see* **spillen** *v*

spillen *v* put to death 21.304; lay waste, destroy 3.424; perish 11.43, B 15.135; ruin B 3.310; spoil 5.138; waste 3.462, 5.127, 7.48, 10.187, 14.7, B 10.102; expend in vain B 9.101; vomit up 6.431; shed 21.448; *in cpds.* ~ **tyme** *n* time-waster 5.28; ~ **loue** (*person.*) Destroy-Love 21.342

spynnen *v* spin [fibre into thread] 3.462, A 7.11, *ger.* spinning thread 9.74; spin [thread] 6.222, 8.12

spynnestere *n* [female] spinner of thread 6.222

spir(e) *n* blade [of plant] 12.182; sprout, scion (*fig.*) 18.231, B 9.101

spyren *v* ask, enquire 3.109; search for 19.1

spirit *n* (the Holy) Spirit (of God) 18.189, **Seynt ~** 11.153, 14.27, 47, 18.72, 189, 232, 19.162 *et p.*, B 17.159; demon Pr 18; the (disembodied human) soul 16.196 (*generic*), 20.270 [Christ's]

spiritual *a* spiritual B 14.285

spiritualte *n* spiritual things, devotional piety 6.125, B 5.148; church endowments (*with pun on previous sense*) B 5.147

spiserye *n* spicy delicacies 2.101

spitten *v*¹ spit B 10.40

spitten *v*² dig, (*p.t.*) 8.184

spore *n* spur 20.10, 12

spot *n* stain B 13.315

spouse *n* husband 13.10

spousen *v* marry B 9.126, A 10.159, 179

spradden *p.t. pl.* 8.184 *see* **spreden** *v*

*sprakliche *a* lively 20.10; *av* in a lively manner †B 17.82

sprang *p.t.* 18.231, 20.88 *see* **spryngen** *v*

spreden (*p.t. pl.* **spradden**) *v* spread 8.184, 16.242, 244, 22.55, B 3.310; grow 13.23, A 10.125

spring *n* switch, rod 5.138

spryngen *v* (*p.t.* **sprang** 20.88; **sprange** 10.229 *etc*; *p.p.* **(y)spronge** 10.263, 18.206, B 16.209) gush forth 15.267; flow 20.88; sprout 12.182; bud forth A 10.125; (*fig.*) 12.110, 14.27, 22.55, A 10.127; dawn 21.150; arise 16.39; originate 18.189; generate B 16.209; be born 18.206; be descended 10.229, 263

sprong(e) *p.t.* 10.229 *etc*, *p.p.* 18.206 *see* **spryngen** *v*

spuen *v* spew out, spit forth B 10.40

squier *n* squire Pr 179, 10.269

squire *n* (mason's) square 11.126

stable *a* constant A 10.114

stablen *v* pacify, impose order on B 1.122

staf *n* (*pl.* **staues** Pr 51, 5.130) wooden staff, rod 5.130, 14.42, B 12.14; stick (for walking) Pr 51, 6.402, B 17.37, 38; (bishop's) staff, crosier Z Pr 53 *and see* **pyk ~**

stake *n* boundary post 3.380

stale *n* handle 21.280

stale *p.t.* 6.265 (B 13.367) *see* **stelen** *v*

staleword Z 7.196 = **stalworþe** *a*

stalk *n* stalk 18.39

stalle *n* stall, booth 18.157

stalworþe *a* vigorous, sturdy B 17.97, Z 7.196

standen, stonden *v* (*contr. pr.* **stant** 17.205, 20.42, A 10.133; *p.t.* **stod(e)** Pr 197, 2.217, **stood B** 13.29, *pl.* **stode(n)** 20.85, A 4.143, Z 4.124 *pr. subjv.* 10.36; *p.t. subjv.* **stoed** 16.92, 21.366,) stand Pr 197, 2.5, 217, 5.113, 15.40, 20.42, 85, 415, B 13.29, **A** 4.143, 12.61, Z 4.124; (*fig.*) 21.366, 383; stand upright 6.402, 7.3, 10.35, 36, 19.56, 89; remain alive A 7.37; remain

standing 16.92, 18.47; **~ forth** remain upright, ?project 3.345*n*; come forward 2.72, 11.195; stand erect 3.380, 7.222; be placed Z Pr 99; appear (engraved) 17.205, B 1.50; remain at rest 8.119; consist in 17.205 (*with play on 'appear'*); continue, last A 10.133; hold good B 15.582, Z Pr 71; be 13.199, B 1.123, exist B 16.218; cost 3.51

stank *p.t.* B 15.593 *see* **stynken** *v*

staren *v* stare 11.4; gaze fixedly A 4.143; look around intently B 16.168, A 12.61

stat *n* (*pl.* **status**) rank Z Pr 55

statu(y)t *n* statute, decree 8.341

staues *pl.* Pr 51 *etc*; *see* **staf** *n*

stede *n*¹ riding horse 6.43 (B 13.294)

stede *n*² place [in text] B 14.131; position Pr 94; estate 5.145; *in phr.* **in ~ of** instead of, in place of 8.60

stedefast *a* resolute (in purpose) A 10.114; permanently valid B 15.582

steere *n* rudder B 8.35

steeren *v* steer, direct B 8.47

stekien *v* stick fast, remain shut B 1.123

stele B 19.281 = **stale** *n*

stelen *v* (*p.t.* **stale** 6.265, *pl.* **stelen** 21.156) steal 6.265, 7.223; carry (away) 21.156; creep up stealthily (upon) 6.106

#stemen *v* blaze, gleam Z 6.75

step(p)en *v* walk 6.402, 19.56, 89

stere Z 6.75 = **sterre** *n*

steren *v* move 19.56, (*refl.*) Z 6.75; stir 22.103; *ger.* rocking 10.36

sterlyng *n* English silver penny B 15.348, *in phr.* **Losshe-borwes ~es** Luxemburg pennies 17.82c

sterne B 15.253, **~ ly(che) B** Pr 183, 6.318 *see* **sturne-(liche)** *av*

ster(r)e *n* star 13.173, 14.30, 22.256, B 12.222, Z 6.75; comet 20.241; **day ~** A 6.80; **eleuene ~s** 9.309; **lode ~s** 17.95; **seuene ~s** = the Pleiades 17.98

sterten *v* rush, flee 19.299

steruen *v* die, perish 6.290, 9.101, 10.202, 12.181, B 11.430, (*fig.*) 5.150

steward *n* **~ of halle** domestic steward [servant in charge of manorial household] 15.40; estate-manager Pr 94, 5.145, 21.464; governor [under king] 3.122, 21.257

stewen *v* govern, order 5.145*n*

stewes *pl.* *see* **stuyues** *n*

stif *a* strong, loud B 15.593; (*sup.*) **styuest** most potent 6.43

stif(liche) *av* firmly, immovably 3.345, 10.36 (B 8.33)

styhlen *v* give orders 15.40

stiken *v* stand firmly embedded 3.380

stikke *n* twig 13.159; staff B 12.14

style *n* stile, *in phr.* **at-þe- ~** 6.145, 207

stille *a* quiet 11.35, 15.108, 122, B 10.7, A 10.99; motionless A 12.61, 75, **Z** 4.124, 5.3; at rest Z 6.70

stille *av* motionlessly (= inactive) 14.120; quietly, privately, *in phr.* **loude ouþer** ~ (= at all times) B 9.106; continually, always 21.424, †B 15.224

styngen *v* sting 20.157

stynken *v* stink, *p.t.* B 15.593

stynten *v* stop, halt 7.222, B 10.222; desist, give up 2.166; bring to a stop [commotion in heaven] B 1.122

stiren B 20.103 = **steren** *v*

styuest *sup.* 6.43; *see* **stif** *a*

styward 3.122, 15.40, 21.464 = **steward** *n*

stywen Z 5.68 = **stewen** *v*

stod(e)(n) *p.t.* Pr 197 *etc*, 20.85, A 4.143, Z 4.124 *see* **standen** *v*

stodie A 12.61, (*person.*) A 11.176 *see* **studie** *n*

stodien A 8.131, 12.6, *ger.* **stodyenge** A 4.143 *see* **studien** *v*

stoed *p.t.* 15.40, (*subjv.*) 16.92, 21.366

stoel *n* (kneeling) stool 7.3, **pynyng** ~ punishment seat 3.79

stoen 14.42 = **ston** *n*

stok *n* tree-trunk 18.30, B 16.5; tree 16.249, B 16.14; grafting-stock 10.209; tree-stump 7.222; frame, **fullyng** ~ frame for cleansing wool B 15.452; *pl.* stocks [frame for punishment] 4.103, 8.163, 9.34

stole *p.p.* *a* stolen 17.40

stolen *p.t.pl.* B 19.156 *see* **stelen** *v*

stomblen *v* lose one's footing 10.35, B 8.33

ston, stoon *n* stone 6.106, 14.42, **B** 12.75, 15.282; boulder Z 5.3; rock 12.222; tomb-stone B 15.593; gem-stone 2.13

stonden 7.222, 10.36, **B** 1.50, 8.47, 15.582, 16.24, A 6.82 = **standen** *v*

stonen *v* pelt with stones B 12.75

stop(p)en *v* block out 20.283; stop up 20.285; make an end of 20.461; cause to desist 4.150

storye *n* narrative B 13.447; (*pl.*) sacred histories B 7.71, 73

stot *n* plough-horse 21.268

stoue *n* place, *as surname* 5.130

stounde *n* while 10.64

stoupen *v* bend down 5.24, 7.3; stoop 11.197

stowlyche *av* haughtily Z 3.158

strayf *n* (*pl.* **strayues**) *in phr.* **wayues and** ~ strayed domestic animal Pr 92

strayues *pl.* Pr 92 *see* **strayf** *n*

straunge *a* unfamiliar, unrelated, ~ **men** strangers 16.70

straw(e) *n* cornstalk 12.182; (bed) straw 16.75; = thing of no worth, *in imprec.* **a** ~ **for** fie upon! 16.92

strecchen *v* stretch 16.75

streynen *v* (*refl.*) exert (oneself) 16.75

streyte *av* strictly, ascetically B Pr 26

strenen *v*, ~ **forth** procreate 13.171

strengest *sup.* 6.43 *see* **strong** *a*

stren(g)(t)(h)e *n* strength 10.147, 15.173, B 12.41, *in phrr.* **of** ~ strong enough 21.361, **helplees of** ~ lacking

in physical capacity B 7.98; **don by** ~ force B 17.317; **mannes** ~ physical force 17.241, B 13.329; stronghold 3.237, 344, 21.368; prowess in arms 13.108

streng(þ)hen *v* strengthen 3.345; give strength to B 8.47, (*refl.*) A 10.114

strete *n* road B 10.305, **hye** ~ highway 14.48; street 6.50, 9.122

#**strikare** *n* wanderer 9.159

striken *v* (*p.t.* **strok** Pr 197) strike, beat 14.42, B 12.14, 75; go, ~ **forth** proceed 7.223, come forward Pr 197

stryuen *v* contend 8.341

strok *p.t.* Pr 197 *see* **striken** *v*

strompet *n* harlot, adulteress 14.42

stronge *a* sturdy 14.104, Z 7.196, *sup.* 6.43; fit 19.89; tough Z 4.20; confirmed, bold 14.129

struyen *v* kill 17.305 (1); ruin 8.27, 17.305 (2)

struyore *n* destroyer Z 7.196

studeden *p.t.pl.* 17.305 *see* **studien** *v*

study *n* effort Pr 195; study 15.182; (*person.*) 11.1 *et p.*; study [room] B 3.345

studien *v* strive 17.305; (apply oneself to) study A 12.6; reflect 9.297; deliberate B 15.596; brood (about) B 13.289; wonder, *ger.* perplexity A 4.143; seek to understand B 12.222

stuyues *n.pl.* brothel 13.74, 16.92, 21.438, 22.160; the Stews [brothel-area at Southwark] 8.71

stumblen B 8.33, A 9.28 = **stomblen** *v*

stunten 2.166 = **stynten** *v*

sturen 22.103 = **steren** *v*

sturne(ly)(che) *av* sternly, severely Pr 197, 8.341, 11.4, B 6.318, 15.253

*****stuty** *a* stumbling Z 4.124

such(e), (swich) *prn* such a person 6.290, 300, **non** ~ no such person 6.37, 13.62; **eny** ~ any such thing 14.15; that (is what) A 11.245; (*pl.*) such people Pr 46, 7.84, 9.19, 13.114, 15.310, 16.214, 17.57, **B** 6.219, 7.42, 15.8, 382, 16.112, **A** 8.33, 10.110, 11.72, ~ **as** those who(m), (the kind of people who(m) 2.45, 3.78, 5.48, 19.93, 21.432, B 15.329; ~ **that** those who 3.287, 6.54, 12.227, 13.111, 17.278, 19.298, **B** 7.40, 10.26, 204, 11.278, 12.13, 15.267, A 11.249; someone who 19.298 (†B 17.316); those [birds] B 6.32

such(e) *a* (of) such (a kind) Pr 34, 64, 134, 2.102, 13.211, *etc*, 20.184, B 19.277; ~ **a** ~ **a** ~ like this **B** 4.69, 9.129; like these A 7.115; ~ **an othur** another like it Z 6.77; ~...**as** whatever ~ 1.177 *etc*, B 10.36; ~ **oen** someone like that 16.106, 22.344; ~...**that** of such a kind that 3.409, A 12.33; (*as intensive*) such (a) great / so great (a) 3.452, 5.98, 6.77, 8.187, 20.442, **B** 3.278, 6.322, 14.165, A 5.72, 10.82; such hard 8.339, 11.54; so good (a) 5.96, 14.2, 18.140, B 15.151; such evil 6.141; *in phrr.* ~ **seuene** seven of such a kind 1.105; ~ **tyme** at (such) a time (when) 20.426

sucre 16.148 = **sugre** *n*

suen 2.102, 10.73, 12.168, 22.126, B 4.167, **suewen** 7.186 = **sewen** *v*[1]

sufficen 17.119, 19.35, 204 = **soffisen** *v*

suffraunce 4.189, **B** 6.144, 11.378, A 10.119 = **soffra(u)nce** *n*

suffren A 9.47 *etc*, B 2.106 *etc*; *see* **soffr(y)en** *v*

sugestioun *n* motive, reason 9.62

sugre *n* sugar 6.88, 16.148

suynde *pr.p.* 20.358, **suynge** 18.63 *see* **sewen** *v*

suyred *pt.* Z 6.16 *see* **suren** *v*

suyrelepes *a* separate, distinct 18.192; *av* separately B 17.165

sullen (sellen) *v* (*p.t.* **solde** 6.97 *etc*, B 16.143, *p.p.* **sold** 3.245 *etc*) sell 3.120, 243, 6.225, 8.329, 9.29, 12.63, 165, 220, 17.20, 101, 129, 18.158, 21.401, **B** 3.196, 7.22, 11.275, Z 3.149, *ger.* 21.236; succeed in selling 6.97; give away for payment 3.245; give in exchange 6.376, 8.291; betray for money 20.222, B 16.142

suller *n* merchant, vendor 3.116, A 2.44

sulue(n) *a* (*as intensifier with prec. n. / prn.*) himself 7.206, 12.138, 14.26, 16.112, 17.179, 18.96, 130, B 1.204, A 1.110, (*post-positive with prn.*) **þi ~** you yourself A 10.86, **vs ~** (us) ourselves B 7.128; (*with foll. n.*) own 7.254, B 5.488

suluer 1.63 *etc*; *see* **seluer** *n*

sum(me) *prn. a* Pr 25 *etc*, 2.4 *etc*; *see* **som(m)(e)** *prn, a*

sumnour 9.263 = **som(p)nour** *n*

sumtyme 10.159; *see* **som-**

sumwhat 12.34, 8.277 *see* **somwhat** *prn.*

sundry 20.231 = **sondry** *a*

sunnere *comp.* 11.258 = **sonner(e)**; *see* **sone** *av*

suppriour *n* sub-prior 6.153

suren *v* give one's word (to) B 5.540

surgerie *n* surgery 22.178; surgical skill (*fig.*) B 16.106

surgien *n* surgeon 22.311, 314, 316, 337; healer 18.140, (*fig.*) B 14.88

surquidours, (surquidous) *a as n* arrogant (*person.*) 21.341n

suspectioun *n* expectation 17.313

#sustantif *n* substantive, noun 3.335, 342, 352, 360, 393, 403

suste(y)nen *v* provide for, feed 8.17, **B** 15.280, (*fig.*) B 15.467; perpetuate 10.205, B 9.109

suster (sister) *n* (*pl.* **susteres** 7.269, **sust(u)r(e)ne** A 11.191, *uninfl. gen.* A10.159) sister 12.171, B 5.642, A 10.153, 159, 179, (*fig.*) 3.207, 7.269, 11.97, 20.120, 187, 194, A 6.113; nun, female member of religious order 3.54, 6.137, 16.293; honorary sister B 3.63

sustinaunce *n* livelihood 5.126; food 22.7

sute *n* apparel, guise [*sc.* human flesh, *with play on* 'cause'] B 5.488, 497; retinue, company of followers B 14.257

suthe 18.192 = **sethe**[3] *conj.*

suwen B 10.204, 17.102, 107, 18.191 = **sewen** *v*[1]

swaer *p.t.* 17.178 *see* **swer(i)en** *v*

swagen A 5.100 = **aswagen** *v*

swan-whit *a* as white as a swan 20.213

sweyen *v* sound, ? move along B Pr 10

swellen *v* (*p.t. pl.* **swolle** Z 7.163) become swollen 21.284, A 12.74, Z 7.163; cause to swell [*sc.* with pride], become puffed up 16.225; *ger.* swelling [as if pregnant] 18.100; flatulence 6.88

swelten *v* (*p.t.* **swelte(d)**) lose consciousness, faint 6.129, 22.105

swerd *n* sword 1.102, 3.457

swer(i)en *v* (*p.t.* **swaer** 17.178, **swoer** 22.161, **swo(o)r(e)(n)** 2.181, 4.79, Z 8.23, *p.p.* **sworn** 6.426) swear (an oath) 1.102, 16.304, 17.178, B 13.382, 383; swear [by God's name, *etc*] 4.79, 6.426, 7.200, 216, 9.25, **B** 5.224, 13.403, 14.35, Z 7.288, (*person.*) **~ nat...** 7.216; **~ for soþe** swear to be true 16.303; **~ gret othes** curse Pr 36; testify (in court) 5.57, **~ treuth** testify truthfully 22.161; solemnly declare B 15.405, Z 4.50; emphatically affirm 6.51, **B** 2.169, *in phr.* **seien and ~** 2.181, B 15.595

swete *n* something pleasant 12.146

swete *a* (*comp.* **swettore** 14.186, 16.148, 18.60) sweet (-tasting) 6.88, 12.222, 18.60, 63, 65, 100, **B** 9.149, 12.263, 15.469, (*fig.*) 16.148, 150, 20.217; sweet-smelling 13.177, A 10.123; agreeable, pleasant Pr 84, 12.11, 14.186, Z 7.259; satisfying B 15.184; dear B 17.125; *av* (*comp.*) **swettere** more pleasantly 8.228; **~nesse** *n* sweetness 18.63

sweten *v* sweat 8.241; toil hard B 13.261; *in phr.* **swynke and ~** Pr 36, 5.57, 8.24, 134

sweue(n)(e) *n* dream 9.310, B Pr 11, A 8.139

swich B 1.194, 2.17, *etc*; *see* **such(e)** *a*

swiȝen A Pr 10 = **sweyen** *v*

swift *a* rapid, *comp.* **~ore** 14.186, B 12.262; timely, without delay B 11.378

swymmen *v* swim 14.106, 107, 109, 171, B 12.168; *ger.* swimming B 12.166

swymmere *n* swimmer B 12.166

swyn *n* (*pl.* **~**) pig 5.19, B 2.98

swynk(e) *n* toil 8.203, 241, B 6.232

swynkare *n* workman 8.259, 19.174

swynken *v* (*p.t.* **swonken** Pr 23) work hard, labour Pr 53, B 6.194, *in phr.* **~ and swete** Pr 36, 5.57, 8.24, 134; work Pr 23, 7.185, 8.227, 262, B 7.118

swythe *av* actively A 4.23; very 6.316, B 13.403; frequently B 5.449; quickly 13.52, B 9.132; promptly, **as ~** at once 6.421, B 3.102

swoenen 20.57 *see* **swowenen** *v*

swoer *p.t.* 22.161 *see* **swer(i)en** *v*

swoet *n* sweat 8.241

swonken *p.t. pl.* Pr 23 *see* **swynken** *v*

swolle *p.t. pl.* Z 7.163 *see* **swellen** *v*

swo(o)r *p.t.* 4.79, 6.51, B 2.169 *etc*, **sworen** *pl.* 2.181, B 5.370, Z 4.152, **sworn** *p.p.* 6.426 *see* **swer(i)en** *v* swounen B 14.326, 18.57 *see* swowenen *v*

swowe *n* faint, a ~, y~ in a faint A 5.215 (Z 5.110)

swowen *v* (fall in a) faint 6.129, B 16.19; fall unconscious 22.105

swowenen *v* faint 7.55, 20.57, 22.105, B 14.326, 16.19

tabard *n* (sleeveless) short coat 6.203

table *n* (moneychanger's) table 18.157; (dining) table 7.103, B 10.103, 13.177, seconde ~ 9.252, syde ~ [for inferiors in hall] 14.139, 15.42

tab(o)ren *v* play the drum 15.206

tacche *n* vice, fault B 9.148

tache B 17.246 = tasch *n*

taek *imper.* 22.135, 359 *see* taken *v*

taȝte B 6.300 = tauhte *p. t.*

tayl *n* (*pl.* ~ 5.121, ~es 17.31) tail 17.31; tail feathers B 12.241, 248, (? *with pun on* tayle) 245; (*meton.*) 'tail' [sexual organs] 3.166, 10.80, 16.257; roots 5.121; train (of followers) 2.196; end, conclusion B 3.351

tayl(l)e *n* tally-stick, taken ~ offer promise to pay later 4.61, taken bi ~ ? receive on credit B 5.248 (*see note*); reckoning, account (*with pun on* tay(l) 'end') B 12.245

taylen *v* record (on a tally-stick), *p.p.* 7.35

taylende *n*[1] backside 7.4

taylende *n*[2] reckoning of accounts B 8.82 (*with pun on* ~ *n*[1]); income, revenue (*with pun on meton. sense of* ~ = 'genitals') 3.369

tayler *n* tailor, clothes-maker Pr 224, 4.120, 9.204, A 11.184, ~s tailor's (craft, hand) B 5.547, 15.454

taken *v* (*imper.* ta(e)k 22.135, A 3.222, 10.97, *p.t.* toek 4.166 *et p.*, tok 3.84 *et p.*, toke 3.47 *et p.*, took 4.15, 40, 12.46, B 5.248 *etc, pl.* token 4.73 *etc, p.p.* take 17.287, ytake 9.92) take (hold of) 5.130, 8.272, 9.2*n*, 14.104, 15.161, 20.47, 21.170, B 14.190; take (aside) 4.166, 15.176; carry 4.52, B 13.164; seize (by force) 1.92, 3.176, 4.49, 17.227, B 4.48; arrest 18.176, 21.56, B 16.160; apprehend, catch 19.212, B 12.74; take hold 6.80; steal 22.11; get, obtain 3.445, 9.91, 13.43, 44, 17.45, 21.463, 471, 476, Z Pr 64; take (leave) 7.292, 21.483; strike down B 6.144, 17.54; defeat (in battle) 17.287; lead, bring 3.4, 4.73; deliver 14.129; receive 3.144, 273, 4.29, 9.54, 65, 92, 13.103, 14.205, 16.145, 21.466, B 3.254, 255, 6.139, 7.61, 77, 12.90, 14.142, 184, Z 1.131; accept 1.96, 3.116, 123, 126, 310, 495, 6.289, 9.54, 16.309, 356, 17.186, B 2.34, 3.247, 253, 353, 7.40, 61, 8.82, 11.281, A 3.222, Z 7.273; put on, assume 1.151, 20.230, 21.72, 22.41, B 15.208; choose 5.79, 15.83, (as wife) 16.106; undergo, endure 6.77, 9.183, 12.150, 16.326, B 7.101; feel 6.77; react to, take 9.131, 14.66; pay heed, take note, *in phrr.* ~ gome (ȝeme) 3.485, 19.15, B 10.197, ~ hede 11.70, 12.221, 14.99, 17.239, 18.19, B 15.91, A 8.78; ~ kepe pay attention (to) 13.145, A 10.97, observe 15.177,

look after 19.76, 22.359, ~ mark take note B 17.104, ~ reward take heed 19.249; ~ record at call to witness B 15.87; ~ witness (at / of) call to witness 6.53, 12.77, ~ to witnesse 11.38, 15.103, 20.135, B 11.87, 15.488; review 21.466; draw (out from) B 16.204; take (down from) 20.72, 86; pick 20.305; give, grant 1.52, 3.350, 4.61, 9.275, 13.105, 19.2, 76, 22.260; attribute 19.37; bribe 22.137; sell 3.87, bid (farewell) B 13.203; (make) use (of) 20.93; speak to 15.106; ~ togyderes confer together 6.154; invoke,~ on act, behave 3.84, 13.154; execute (vengeance) Pr 117, 121, 20.135, B 6.224 15.261; take out (writ) 2.187

talage (taillage) *n* tax, levy 21.37

tale *n* story Pr 49, 8.48, 50, 20.135, B Pr 51; exemplum B 12.265; lesson A 11.222; sermon B 9.72, Z 7.230; discourse 12.46, B 10.373; idle fable, disours ~ B 10.49, ~ of Walterot = absurd nonsense 20.144; gossip 7.19, B 5.377; lying gossip 6.50, 154, B 13.333; lie 2.227, 4.18, 34; dishonest confession 3.47; speech 2.116, B 4.69; soþ ~ true principle A 10.81; remark(s) B 11.99, 100; words 7.90; talk, conversation 6.28, 185, 194, 18.3, 22.119, B 13.58; argument B 10.373; case 12.174; account 13.87; esteem, regard, *in phrr.* ~ of nauht thing of no worth 13.113; gyuen neuer ~, holden no ~, maken litel ~ regard / treat as of little importance / value 1.9, 3.390, 21.457,

#tale-tellare *n* tale-bearer 22.300; maker of (religious) controversy A 11.73

talewys *a* garrulous 3.166

talken *v* talk B 17.83

tame *a* domesticated 15.296

tanner *n* tanner of hides Pr 224

taper *n* wax candle 19.169, 261

tarre *n* tar [for sheep-salve] 9.262

Tarse *n* costly (?silk) fabric [from Tharsia] B 15.168

*tasch *n* touchwood, tinder 19.212

tasel *n* fuller's teasel B 15.453

taste *n* (tangible) experience B 12.130

tasten *v* feel (by touching) 19.124, B 18.84, (? *with pun on* 'taste') 6.179

tauhte *p.t.* 1.71 *et p.*, tauȝte B 1.76 *et p.* (tauȝtest B 14.154), taughte Z 1.121, *p.p.* ytauhte 8.20, tauȝt B 10.223; *see* techen *v*

taxen *v* impose (fine) 1.157

*taxour *n* assessor 8.37

tecchen 1.143 = teche *v*

tauerne *n* tavern 2.98, 6.50, B 5.377, 9.104, 13.304

tauerner *n* tavern-keeper Pr 229

techare *n* (moral / religious) teacher 14.20, 16.240, 245, 17.78, 22.120, 303

techen *v* (*p.t.* tauhte 2.8 *et p.*, tauȝte B 1.76 *et p.*) *p.p.* (y)tauht(e) 8.20, 22.186, B 10.222) preach 4.118, ?Z 7.234; deliver a sermon B 5.12; say, tell, inform 3.436, 8.86, 9.124, 10.107, 125, 296, 18.82, 19.99, 21.363, B

3.254, 15.282, **A** 7.81, 11.28, 165, 268, Z 7.266; teach (about), explain 11.218, 14.12, 75, 16.231, 17.51, 83, 19.109, 319, 21.272, **B** 15.93, 584, 17.41, A 12.2; proclaim (to), propound 3.75, 11.245, 12.60, 99, 15.128, 17.51, 294, 298, B 15.93, 584, **A** 11.196, 12.97; reveal 17.295, 21.44, 22.278; instruct (in, about) 1.71, 143, 3.277, 8.20, 11.3, 149, 217, 14.52, 15.127, 17.174, 180 (2), 254, 18.138, **B** 7.176, 10.225, 12.107, 132, 13.117, 15.571, 17.117; show, indicate 8.4, 9.88, 21.170, B 15.434; direct 1.79, 2.8, 5.5, 17.180 (1), 18.2; teach (how to) 8.59, 10.201, 11.121, 14.161, 21.239, B 8.56; bring up, *p.p.* bred, mannered 22.186; urge (to vice), suggest (sin) to 1.36, 3.160, 20.202, Z 3.164; counsel, advise 4.96, 13.196, **B** 7.73, 15.342; prescribe, enjoin 1.13, 2.126, 5.130, 6.12, 8.218, 9.24, 351, 10.102, 305, 11.70, 71, 13.193, 14.69, 210, 15.126, 16.185, 306, 342, 17.59, 139, 219, 21.170, 22.9, **B** 6.82, 226, 10.84, 197, 205, 267, 12.32, 36; discipline, teach (through chastisement) to 8.141, 20.237

techyng *ger.* teaching, instruction 11.224, 14.34, **B** 12.64, 15.73, 17.124, **A** 7.232, 11.293; teaching 12.100, *in phrr.* **Beatus virres** ~ B 10.320, **Catons** ~ B 7.72, **clerkis** ~ B 15.68, **fyue wittis** ~ A 11.293, **Holy Cherche** ~ B 10.252, **kynde wittes** ~ 14.34, **olde mennes** 9.214; counsel 2.22, 21.318, A 10.97; guidance 22.8; direction 19.124, 21.476, **B** 10.153, 14.26

teeme B 19.263, A 3.84 = **teme** n^1, n^2

†**teen** *v* go, †**teeth** B 17.38

teeþ *pl.* B 15.13 = **teth** *see* **to(e)th** *n*

teyen *v* bind 1.92, 3.176

teynten *v* stretch, *p.p.* **yteynted** B 15.454

tel *imper.* 7.244, **B** 1.83, 10.158, A 12.28 *see* **tellen** *v*

telden *v* (*p.t.* **telde, tilde,** *p.p.* **telid**) pitch (tent) A 2.42; dwell 14.149

telye(n) Z 7.216, 8.2 = **tilien** *v*

telþe A 7.127 = **tulthe** *n*

tellen *v* (*pr. subjv.* **telle** 7.125, 19.120, *p.t.* **tolde** Pr 229 *et p.*, *p.p.* **told(e)** Pr 111, B 1.208 *etc*) speak 19.311, **B** 1.88, 3.104, 4.157, 10.137, **here** ~ hear said B Pr 164; (make) mention (of) 19.37, **B** 13.420, 15.413; *in phrr*: **soth(ly) (for) to** ~ 7.279, B 9.156; ~ (**þe) sothe** 17.211, 20.462, **to** ~ **treuthe** 17.211, **treuliche to** ~ 2.251, B 16.4; say (to) Pr 229, 5.156, 7.125, 297, 14.131, 15.89, 16.187, 295, 19.163, 20.111, 144, **B** 5.268, 17.263, A 2.26, Z 4.50; talk (of) 15.111, 20.149, B 13.354, A 11.62; declare **B** 5.54, 11.66, *in phr.* ~ **with tonge** declare outright / clearly 7.17, 16.369, A 12.24; state 1.145, 16.192, B 1.130; tell, recount Pr 9, 1.125, 6.108, 11.32, 37, 15.206, 21.115, **B** Pr 51, 11.160, 12.236, 17.88, (*in writing*) 5.109, A 5.10, Z 5.27, *in phrr.* **as (þe) Bible** (*etc*) ~**eth**: Bible 5.169, B 9.41, **Boke** Pr 129, 1.28, 5.38, 9.120, 127, 12.75, 13.15, 14.169, 21.71, A 12.3, **crede** 8.98, **Gospelle** 12.213, B 12.63, **lettre** 12.114, 20.81, **B** 12.73, 17.118, **holy lettrure** 15.74, **holy lore** 17.65,

Sauter 7.92, B 3.237, **Holy Writ** ~ Pr 104, 2.142, 3.486, 10.248, 19.127, 296, 21.109, **B** 10.381, 17.306; explain (to) 1.79, 114, 3.393, 10.125, 151, 11.71, 14.99, 15.17, 16.114, 117, 118, 19.100, 20.173, 22.253, **B** 2.122, 11.80, 12.18, 25, 15.71, 74, 571, A 11.86; teach, instruct 18.2, 21.414, B 11.80, Z 7.234, *ger.* 22.8, A 7.232; tell (to), inform 1.43, 2.202, 4.18, 6.56, 7.297, 302, 8.76 (1), 10.13, 11.198, 14.192, 15.193, 17.100, 18.8, 21.23, 22.232, 268, **B** 15.317, 16.144; disclose, make known 6.70, 71, 8.76, 13.248, 15.193, 16.164, 18.245, 292, 19.120, 20.65, 21.276, **B** 10.5, 225, 13.14, 15.13, 16.61, 63, 147, 230, **A** 11.218, 12.18; proclaim 13.103, **B** 13.300, 15.91; describe 2.15, 196, 19.311, A 6.82; utter **B** 10.373, 11.1, 16.212; (say in) confess(ion) 3.47, 7.29, 14.121; direct 17.180; preach (about) 15.83, B 13.69; cite **B** 3.346, 10.269, 12.265; prophesy, foretell 5.178, 17.99, 21.145, **B** 7.167, 19. 244; report (to) Pr 111, 6.47, 7.244, 11.138, 13.39, 87, 18.162, 21.155, 344, *in phrr.* **tales to** ~ spread gossip 4.18, 6.50, 154, **B** 11.99, 13.304, 333, ~ **tale** engage in conversation 6.28, tell a lie 18.289; count Pr 90, 6.425, 12.177, 19.33, B 5.248; reckon 11.213; judge, regard 19.240

tellere A 11.73 *see* **tale-** ~ *n*

tellyng *ger.* instruction 22.8, A 7.232

teme n^1 team [of draught animals] 8.20 (*with pun on* 'theme'), 141, 9.2n, (*fig.*) 21.262, 263, 272

teme n^2 topic, subject 12.46, B 10.118; theme (of sermon) 6.1, 15.83, 20.358, **B** 3.95, 7.136

#**temperaltee** *n* temporality [lay income and property belonging to prelate's office] 22.128

tempest *n* storm 20.65

temple *n* temple [of Jerusalem] 1.45, 18.157, 163, 20.61, B 16.131, **oure Iewene** ~ our Jewish temple 20.40

Templers *n* the Knights Templar 17.209

tempren *v* tune (*fig.*), ~ **þe tonge** direct (one's) speech 16.144, B Pr 51

tempten *v* tempt (to sin), *p.p.* 21.64

ten(e) *num. a* 1.104, 4.61, 6.220, 7.17, 29, 16.231, 21.165, **B** 6.241, 13.270, ~ **hestes (comaundementis)** 2.87, 9.334, 11.142, 13.67, 16.231, A 11.253; (*qualifying other nums.*) ~ **hundrit** 7.38, ~ **score** 11.128, ~ **thousand** A 2.42; *as n* **A** 1.103, 7.226

tenaunt *n* tenant [one holding land by service or rent] 8.36, 17.45

tenden *v* (*p.t. pl.* **tend(ed)en**) kindle 20.248

tender (tonder) *n* tinder 19.212

tene *n* injury, pain 1.164; suffering, distress 12.51, 13.7, 16.173; anger, **pu(y)re** ~ sheer rage 8.124, **B** 7.115, 16.86, **turne to** ~ make angry A 12.9; **trauail and** ~ painful effort B 6.133, A 10.145

teneful *a* painful, troubling 3.495

tenen *v* harm 7.38, **B** 8.98, 15.419; oppress Z 2.170; hurt 3.159, 22.119; trouble 3.139, 474, 8.36, 11.128, 14.8, 15.161; (*refl.*) get angry 2.116, Z 2.169

tente *n* tent, pavilion A 2.42

teologie (theologie) *n* (the discipline / study of) theology 11.128, B 10.373; (*person.*) 2.116, 129, B 10.197, A 12.9, 18, Z 2.169

#tercian *n* tertian fever, (*person.*) A 12.85

tere *n* tear 15.51

teren *v* (*p.p.* **tore**) tear 6.203

terme *n* saying, expression B 12.236

terminen *v* pronounce judgement (on) 1.93

*termison *n* termination, (inflexional) ending [of a word] 3.405

testifien *v* attest, ~ **for gode** vouch for (as) 11.310; ~ **for treuthe** certify as true 12.174; ~ **of** (make) affirm(ation) concerning B 13.94

teth *pl.* 20.83 *see* **to(e)th** *n*

tetheren *v* tie, fasten Z 3.76

text 1.200, B 2.122 *etc*; *see* **tix(s)t** *n*

thay 13.101, 20.209 = **thei** *prn*

than Pr 165, 187, A 12.72 = **thanne** *av*

than *conj. of comparison* than Pr 123, 164, 7.24, 9.123, 14.154, 18.88, 19.104, 20.456, B 1.143, 184 *etc*, **þanne** A Pr 89; *and see* **then** *conj.*

thank *n* thought, regard, *gen. in avl. phr.* **his** ~**es** willingly 9.66

þanked *p.t.* A 12.48 *see* **thonken** *v*

thanne, þanne Pr 185, 19.34, B 1.58 *et p.*, A 1.112 *etc* = **thenne** *av*[1]

thar *impers. 3 sg. pr.* 15.259, **tharstow** *2 sg.* = **tharst þow** B 14.56; *see* **thuruen** *v*

thare Pr 133 = **ther** *av*

that (þat)[1]*dem. prn* that Pr 39, 1.57, 161 (1), 196 (1), 3.338, 353, 474, 8.271, 334, 19.315, 21.10, **B** 9.61, 10.343, ? 11.368, Z 7.245

that[2] *rel. prn* who Pr 86, 119, 160, 2.3, 32 *et p.*, B 1.130 *et p.*, whom Z 3.151; **hem alle** ~ all those who 2.47–8, 20.178–8; which, that Pr 132 *et p.*, Z Pr 58, *in prnl. phrr.* ~ **(you)** who 1.80, 2.79, 20.402, B 11.223, for whom 15.301; of which 17.69; ~ **he** who 16.291, 21.377, ~**...hit** which 18.80, ~**...his** whose 1.59; ~**...hit** which 18.80; **hem...** ~ those...who 1.164; **here...**~ of those who 2.76–7, 16.283, 17.25–6; **his...**~ of him who 9.53–4, B 1.82; **ȝe...**~ you...who 17.82–3; against whom A 5.53; on which, when 7.65; *in phr.* **the whiche** ~ who 3.93, **þe which...**~ (for) which 13.82; *indep. rel.* the one who 1.66, 8.127, 12.185, 14.126, 15.155; for one who B 10.357, A 7.137; he who 1.110, 3.485, 9.48, 208, 14.41, 15.127, **B** 7.124, 10.345, A 11.157, Z 8.50; those who 1.66, 3.13, 288, 4.33, 6.252, 9.183, 208, 10.102, 11.18, 12.109, 195, 21.444, **B** 6.192, 9.63; (on) those who 3.95; that which, what Pr 39, 1.97, 2.38, 128, 139, 3.83, 319, 322, 4.86, 150, 5.141, 7.17, 8.105, 108, 140, 9.74, 260, 12.217, 224, 15.89, 19.5 (2), 248, 258, 267, 20.142, 391, 21.246, 22.7, **B** 1.28, 3.255, 5.545, 6.129, 133, 9.15, 10.321, 13.135, 15.159, 16.183, **Z** Pr 70, 3.122, 6.67

that[3] *dem. a.* that 2.53, 3.490, 4.13, 128, 5.43, 17.276, 19.78, 116, 20.200, **Z** 1.65, 3.8, 7.253, ~ **ilke** B 9.189; *as def. art.* = the 20.150; *in phrr.* ~ **ilke** the (same) one 16.312; ~ **on** (the) (first) one 7.271, 19, 301, 21.264, **B** 1.23, 3.232; ~ **on...**~ **oþer** the first...the second 14.106–7, A 8.14, 12.84

that[4] *particle, in phrr.* **by** ~ by that time 8.314, 322; according to what 11.271, 273, 16.295; **for** ~ because B 4.68, **Z** 5.150, 7.77; **how** ~ how, in what way 16.232, A 8.17; **yf** ~ if 20.198; whether B 2.156; **manere** ~ way that A 2.47; **so** ~ provided that B 4.102; **ther** ~ where 3.222; **tho** ~ when 20.241; **thogh** ~ even if 19.320; **tyl** ~ until Z 2.72; **why** ~ why B 10.119; **where** ~ wher(ever) A 8.58; **with** ~ at that, thereupon 13.247, provided that 6.173

that[5] *conj.* that Pr 34, 82, 102, 104 *et p.*; = than that B 7.114; so / with the result that Pr 173, 2.32, 168, 3.67, 142, 194, 211, 431, 6.268, 400, 7.153, 8.174, 181, 9.82, 10.48, 11.57, 13.12, 15.269, 16.230, 17.80, 18.140, 19.292, 20.242, 358, 21.278, 350, 22.176, **B** 1.26, 158, 5.6, 118, 145, 361, 373, 10.79, 11.48, 422, 13.407, 14.96, 15.10, 72, 354, 410, 16.78; (+ **ne**) = but that, who / which...not 6.284, 312, 7.61, 11.185, 14.150, 16.291, 19.92, 329, 21.52, **B** 5.552, 7.51, 114, 8.101, 14.13, 15, **A** 2.39, 4.136, 8.38, 10.161, **Z** 3.176, 7.163; lest 5.122, 19.310; so / in order that 3.309, 376, 5.185, 6.167, 7.207, 9.38, 15.79, 17.14, 19.288, 332, 20.23, 286, 363, 21.120, 229, 312, 366, B 6.242, A 12.95, Z 5.94; (*with inf.*) 20.31, B 12.227; when 6.259, 18.128, 168, 20.471, B 16.94, A 7.283; because, since 14.127, 18.17, **B** 5.31, 113, 16.19, (implying wish / entreaty) 4.7, 5.199, 8.10, 21.482, **B** 4.127, = (saying) that / (to the effect) that 2.130 (1), 234, 3.414, 6.172, 328, 9.348, 10.253, 13.101, 18.126, 20.196, **B** 5.165, 10.353, = from, *in phrr.* **letten ...**~ prevent from 3.36, 6.312, 10.162, 15.183; **reste** ~ desist from 6.127

thauh 9.122 = **thogh** *conj.*

the(e), þe(e)[1] *prn 2 sg., pers. as dir. obj.* thee, you (*addressed variously to inferior, equal, superior*) Pr 148, 1.24 *et p.*, (*Mede*) 3.19, (*King*) Pr 149, 3.208, (*Christ*) 7.137, (*God*) 7.150; *as indir. obj.* (to) thee / you 7.253, 8.33, 298, 9.281, **B** 10.168, 11.419, A 3.244, Z 4.143; for you 7.106; *as dat.of interest* Z 3.131, (*after prep.*) 3.135 *et p.*; *as refl.* thyself, yourself 3.418, 4.16, 5.102, 6.12, 13, 164, 338, 7.8, 260, 8.290, 10.287, 290, 306, 11.142, 195, 12.4, 194, 13.194, 14.9, 22.205, B 13.143, A 7.26, 10.114; for yourself 6.340, 11.75, 21.320; *as obj. of impers. v.* 3.44, 7.55, 15.253, 22.210, A 1.25, **Z** Pr 117, 3.150

the (þe)[2] *def. art.* the Pr 10 *et p.*; *with rel. prn* ~ **which(e)** who 3.93, 191, 9.107, 10.154, 171, whom 18.72, 19.39, which 3.496, 6.243, 9.140, 11.82, 12.152, 14.54, 16.112, 17.140, 247, 18.41, 51, 207, 235, 19.8, 259, 20.110, 223, 21.129, **B** 13.408, 15.131, *with rel.*

a. ~ **which(e)** ~ 15.278, 18.11, 19.87, 20.339, 22.62; *in unique ref. with name / title* 1.38, 1.70, 2.19, 146, 3.175, 270, 5.38, 6.317, **B** 4.179, 11.160, **Z** 2.88; *with occupational names* 6.352, 7.302; *in generic ref.* Pr 231, 1.99, 2.224, 3.176, 6.144, 438, 8.122, 9.264 *etc*, **B** 5.2, **A** 7.21; *with a. forming n. phr.* 2.39, 153, 3.317, 477, 5.139, 6.261, 7.103, 9.64, 10.76, 11.36, 12.105, 18.107, 20.98, 21.198 *etc*, **B** 2.46, **Z** 2.118; *in avl. phrr.* **at** ~ **furste / laste** 8.168, 9.207, **Z** 3.173; ~ **nones** **A** 2.41, ~ **same** likewise 3.27, ~ **while(s)** while 3.29, 57, 324, 5.137, 9.349, 20.140, 21.334, **Z** 4.16, meanwhile 8.6

the (þe)[3] *av* (so much) the (*with comp. a / av*) Pr 104, 3.424, 4.102, 6.216, 7.141, 239, 8.42, 125, 10.311, 11.129, 12.44, 17.253, 21.420, **B** 1.107, 15.425, **Z** 6.44, 7.165, *in correl. constr.* ~...~ 3.136, 15.262, 16.118, 19.69

thec(c)hen *v* (cover roof with) thatch 21.239, *ger.* 8.199

thechen Z Pr 126 *etc*., = **techen** *v*

thed(de)r(e) *av* thither, to that place 1.118, 7.157, 204, 291, 22.286, **B** 2.162, **A** 3.246

thedom *n* activity, industry 7.53; prosperity **A** 10.108

theen *v* prosper, *in assev.* **so thee Ik** so may I prosper **B** 5.224

the(e)f *n* (*pl.* **theues** 5.17 *etc*) thief 5.17, 13.61, 14.129, 130, 135, 145, 147, 150, 153, 17.138, 19.54, 255, 20.73, 76, 424, **B** 9.119, 13.161, 14.305, 17.90

thefliche *av* by stealth **B** 18.339

thefte *n* theft, stealing 2.92, 6.348; act of theft **B** 5.231

thei, they *pers. prn 3 pl.* they Pr 108 *et p.* 2.102 *et p.*; (*with indef. a. or num.*) of them 9.201, 10.106, 11.261, 12.75, 19.81, **B** 10.153; them 21.371; *see also* **hy, hem** *pers. prn.*

they Z 3.103 = **thogh** *conj.*

theyr Z 3.21 = **her(e)**[3] *poss. prn.*

thekynge 8.199 = **thechynge** *ger.; see* **thec(c)hen** *v*

then[1] *conj. of comparison* than Pr 166 *et p.; and see* **than, þanne, thenne** *conj.*

then[2] 4.90, 6.418, 15.286, 309, 16.196, **Z** 1.14 = **thenne** *av*[1]

thenken (þynken[1]**)** *v* (*p.t.* **thouhte** 12.53, **þoȝt B** 6.297, *p.p.* **thouhte** 6.51, **þouȝt B** 13.268) think 18.245, **B** 13.86, **Z** 6.68; realise 16.94; imagine **B** 5.283; recall 8.278; remember **B** 13.268, 19.255; consider 10.97; ponder 12.53, 92; reflect upon **B** 5.600, 7.168; intend, purpose 1.21, 18.265, 19.316, 21.183, 196, 338, **B** 3.95, 5.84, 6.297; plan **B** 12.89; intend to go 20.121, 232, **B** 16.175

thenne (þanne)[1] *av* then, at that time 2.50, 7.260, 8.315, 16.6, 20.413 *etc*; at that (very) moment 11.188, 13.219, 241, 15.286, 19.293; after that, next Pr 141, 3.9, 342, 5.109, 7.298, 18.87 *etc*; next in turn 6.62, 308 *etc*; thereupon Pr 139, 147, 1.68, 8.255, 10.72 *etc*, **Z** 8.81; now 11.1, 173, 6.308, 15.187, 252, 16.156, 20.13, 238,

Z 7.284; *as conjv. av* therefore 19.126; in consequence 3.102, 13.183, 15.204, 17.44, 19.291, **A** 1.112; in that case 10.189, 11.45, 224, 14.10, 15.115, 16.177, 20.56, 311; in those circumstances / that situation 16.178, 186 *etc*, 20.158, **Z** 4.119, 7.43

thenne[2] 2.225, 3.262 = **thennes** *av*

thenne[3] 1.113, 7.209, 11.228, 17.203, 19.296, **Z** 8.83 = **then**[1] *conj.*

thenne(s) *av* thence, from there / that place 1.70, 2.239, 3.262, 7.67, 135, 21.427, 22.205, **B** 10.61

theologie *see* **teologie** *n*

þer *poss. prn* (= **her(e)**[3]) their, ~ **beyre rihte** the right of each of them 20.36

ther(e) (þer(e)) *av* there Pr 66 *et p.*; in that place Pr 99, 6.19, 61, 11.168, 12.111, **Z** Pr 17, 6.78; from there 7.221, 20.154, 379; at that time, then 8.340, **B** 2.45, **A** 12.75; on that 10.245; for that reason **A** 9.32; where Pr 170, 204, 1.113, 116, 120, 130, 2.148, 3.15, 190, 204, 5.164, 13.244, 16.121, 252, 313, 341, 17.11, 18.117, 213, 19.252, 20.157, 21.315, 22.56, 329, 345, 284, **B** 5.264, 11.209, 12.61, 255, 15.94, 97, 304, 336, **A** 6.79, 9.78, 11.60; in which Pr 114, 3.238, 7.94, 15.190, 16.59, 21.136, 160, **B** 10.97, 13.121, 18.400; on which 16.247; (in / to a / the place) where 1.120, 133, 3.37, 4.82, 122, 132, 5.32, 7.204, 9.39, 67, 11.44, 13.91, 16.323, 19.317, 20.278, 386, 478, 21.421, 22.330, 369, **B** 11.67, 12.227, 13.157, 15.183, 312, 17.116, **Z** 6.9; (in circumstances) where 3.256, 4.35 (1), 36, 16.245, 302, 19. 283, 285, 286, 20.322, **B** Pr 194, 11.152, 165, 318, 13.291; to whomever 3.330; when 6.427, 8.256, 16.228, **B** 5.490, 6.243, 15.155, 204, 16.140, **A** 1.138; near whom **B** 15.214; whereas 7.114, 12.236, 13.39, 55, 58, 14.120, 130, 15.289, 16.49, 54, 87, 22.46, **B** 3.197, 5.113, 10.342, 11.243, 12.167, 14.92, *in phrr.* ~ **as** in a place / situation where / in which 9.274, 16.139, 20.236, ~ **before** previously **A** 7.226, ~ **bytwene** between those (two) places Pr 19, ~ **þat** wher(ever) 3.222, 16.46, 17.292, **B** 10.188, where 7.94, when 2.96, 20.427, **A** 5.95; *pleonastic* 1.31, 4.71, 6.379, 8.340, 21.462, **B** 14.40, 16.116, **Z** 2.119; *in correl. constr.* ~...~ where **B** 14.99–100

þeraftur *av* after that 1.150, 6.229c, 7.136, **B** 3.342, 5.73, 11.337, **A** 11.180; in the next life **A** 8.12; in response 3.483, 11.186; towards (them), in that direction 7.224; for it **B** 17.122; accordingly Pr 25, ?6.229c, 8.90, 121, 11.147, 16.218, **B** 1.147, 3.187, 10.90, 294, 397, **A** 12.10, **Z** Pr 36, 1.145

þeran 19.8 = **þer(e)on** *av*

þeraȝeyn(e) *av* in opposition to that 20.310, **B** 16.119, 17.136

þerby *av* by means of that 10.173, 18.170, **B** 11.173, 13.299; by it **B** 13.403

þerfore (therfore) *av* for it 3.246, 14.23, 18.129; (in payment) for it 3.89, 276, 4.57; because / in consequence (of that / those things) 7.147, B 5.232; on that account 10.194, 12.245, 13.56, **B** 6.236, 9.96; for that reason 13.192, **B** 1.17, 16.64, A 12.94, Z 7.269; and so A 12.20, Z 7.71; that is why 22.334

þerfro *av* away from it 12.239; away from there B 11.353

ther(e)ynne (þerinne) *av* in there / that place Pr 15, 1.12, 59, 10.172, 11.108, 18.272, **B** Pr 15, 10.412, 15.334; inside 3.105, 10.227, B 10.406; therein, in that 8.61, **B** †10.186, 13.153, 158; in it B 14.2, A 11.141, Z 3.160; within them 6.219; within it B 15.580; into it / that place 1.57, 6.415, 7.218, 16.359; upon it / theron **B** 1.50, 10.183, 12.289

þermyd(e) *av* by means of it 8.68, 155, A 7.212; with it 3.252, **A** 2.37, 7.166, **Z** 5.60, 8.28; in addition 9.270, B 15.316

þerof, thereof *av* for that Pr 110, B 5.367, A 3.63; about them 7.79; about it 14.75, **B** 3.234, 16.65; concerning that **B** 3.248, 16.234, A 10.86; of that 6.229, 13.170, **B** 5.183, 13.459; out of it / that 14.32, 17.139; out of them 18.12, B 16.34; from it 20.305, B 5.140; of it 12.166, 17.296, **B** 8.55, 12.250, 15.135, 16.5, 17.213, Z 6.50; of them 10.196; with it 11.73; because of that 8.203; on that account 11.159; at that 7.131, 13.153, 20.60, 130

þer(e)on, ther(e)on *av* on it 2.13, 12.234, A 7.13; on them B 5.405; upon it 11.129, 241, 14.63, 74, 214, 18.199, 19.8; at it 7.50; in it 11.132; over it 11.9; to it B 11.224

þeroute *av* out in the open 5.16; out(side) A 6.74

ther-thorw *av* by that means 20.229

þertyl *av* to (do) that 4.5 (Z 4.5)

þerto, therto *av* to it 18.44, 20.158 182; *in phr.* **comen ~** attain 11.172, 22.14; to them 12.104, 105; into it 12.59; to (do) that 16.123, B 4.5; for it / that 9.91, 13.161, 17.225; before it 21.201; against it 18.48; in addition, as well 16.257, **B** 4.59, 15.127, **Z** Pr 64, 3.33; *in phr.* **~ to** compared to B 13.194

þervnder *av* under (cover of) them B 15.116; under (the form of) it 21.388

þervppon *av* in (the truth of) that A 11.144

þerwiþ, therwith *av* with it 1.173, 3.319, 476, 5.135, 10.290, 18.279, **B** 8.56, 15.139; with that 8.115, 18.42, 19.9, B 10.162; with them 1.16, B 10.215; (in) that with which 19.168; by means of it / that / them 3.486, 5.43, 6.342, 8.110, 9.30, 11.75, 14.195, 19.3, 21.64, 327, **B** 1.48, 7.14, A 3.224, Z 5.129; in that way B 13.73; in addition, moreover 1.85; at that, thereupon 13.215, 15.1, 19.334, 21.484, **B** 14.332, 16.167; as a consequence ? Z 1.102n; *in phr.* **acorden ~** agree with that (statement) 4.87, 9.69, 13.213

thes(e) 7.149, 16.36, 20.470, Z 2.147; *see* **this(e)** *a*

these 9.96, 16.28, 18.75 *see* **this** *prn*

þesternesse *n* darkness B 16.160

theues *pl.* 5.17, B 9.119 *etc*; *see* **the(e)f** *n*

thew *n* manners, behaviour, *pl.* 6.141

thy, thi, þi, þy (**~n(e)** *before vowels* 1.140, 3.28 *etc*, *before consonant* 8.289, B 5.501) *poss. a 2 sg.* thy, thine, your Pr 148 *et p.*, B Pr 125 *et p.*; **thien** 19.112

thider 7.157 = **thed(de)r(e)** *av*

thief 20.424 *see* **the(e)f** *n*

thykke *a* thick, undiluted 21.403; (*sup.*) most dense B 12.227

thykke *av* thickly(-strewn) 3.194

thyl Z 8.76 = **til** *prep.*

thilke *prn* those B 10.28

thyn, þyn *poss. prn. 2 sg.* yours 6.289 = your people 3.135, 4.192

thyng, þyng *n* (*pl.* **~es** 1.20 *et p.*, **~** 8.219, 10.156)) thing (=substance, being) 10.151, 152, 156, 170, 18.93 (2), 195, 19.134, **B** 15.12, 17.169, A 10.28, = (inanimate) object 3.87, 18.271, 21.94, **swete ~** 6.88; material substance 10.129; = property, goods 16.274, 292, 17.40, 22.276, B 15.107, **litel ~** 15.155; = commodity 13.55; = necessity 1.20, 5.88, 16.318, B 14.33; = attribute, quality (virtue, vice) 3.377, 16.284, 296, B 1.151, **lykyng ~** 10.288, 11.133; = living being / creature 3.421, 15.137, 18.93 (1), 20.150, 257, **B** Pr 123, 18.356; (*as affectionate term*) **meke ~** 18.125, **B** 15.306, 18.115, **mylde ~** 20.118, B 15.306; **pety ~** 16.83, **pore ~** 15.33, A 12.50; **trewe ~** 14.8; (*as a pejorative term*) **pore ~s** 15.309; action A 6.81; way of behaving 17.153, A 6.81; event, happening Pr 5, 6.51; (thing) request(ed) 22.245; (state of) affair(s) 12.36, 40; circumstance, condition (of things) 3.362, 19.299; matter (for consideration), point 18.197, B 10.169; subject, discipline B 10.209; skill 14.73; item(s) of a craft Z 2.206; (legal) agreement, contract 2.109, **B** 2.105, 4.29; (*as vague general subst. for more precise term*) 10.155, B 11.409, 419; **confortable ~** B 14.282; **leþi ~** B 10.186; **thre (...) ~es** 1.20, 3.377, 19.299, 22.11; **wykked ~** 12.238; *in phrr.* **al(le) (...) ~(s)** everything, all things 5.88, 8.219, 10.152, 170, 19.39, 20.213, 361, 22.254, **B** 5.563, 10.435, 16.184, 17.157, A 10.34; **eny (kyne) ~** anything (whatever) 8.267, 19.267; *as av* **eny ~** to any degree B 18.389; **no ~** nothing 13.243, 20.465, 22.249, A 12.20

thynken, þynken[1] *v* (*pr. subjv.* **thynke** 20.260, *p.t.* **tho(u) (g)hte** Pr 196, 11.316 *etc*, **þo(u)ȝte** B Pr 6, 1.107), *impers. generally with ∅-subject + indir. prn. obj.*) seem, **hem / hym thouhte** it seemed to them / him 21.139, B 1.107; **me ~eth** it seems to me 3.283, 284, 7.98, 13.161, 15.80, 16.206, 17.184, 243, 253, 19.262, 20.165, A 12.5; **me thouhte** it seemed to me, I thought Pr 196, 10.68, 15.192, 18.21, 204, 19.55, 20.116, 21.201, **B** Pr 6, 11.323, 16.20, Z Pr 17, I imagined B 2.53; *with compl.* 11.130, 316, 13.177, 181, 18.204, A 12.5, 16; *in set phrr.* **ferly me thynketh / thouhte** 15.119, 16.294, 17.112, (**thouhte**) 18.56, **wonder me thynketh** 3.228, 13.161, 17.116

thynken, þynken[2] B 5.283 *etc.*; *see* **thenken** *v*

thynne *a* thin, weak 21.403

þirled *p.t.* B 1.174 *see* **thorlen** *v*

this, þis[1] *dem. prn (sg.)* this 1.11, 143 *et p.*, B 3.236 *etc*, *in phr.* ~ **for þat** (= *quid pro quo*) recompense for something done 9.275, (*with generic ref.*) 15.221; (*pl.*) these 1.194, 5.48, 7.80, 8.262, 21.12, A 11.192n; ~**e** 5.66, 7.112, **B** 3.292, 7.54

this, þis[2] *dem. a (sg.)* (**thise** Pr 190) this 1.5, 7, 8, 2.198 *et p.*, *in set phrr.* **on** ~ **folde / molde, in / of** ~ **worlde** anywhere 9.153, 172, 3.6, 4.136, Z 6.71; ~ **erthe / grounde / lyue / world** this world / this present life 1.8, 3.94, 10.45, 6.313*etc*: ~, ~**e** (*pl.*) these Pr 198, 3.81, 1.200, 2.192, 3.41, 5.41, 10.123, 138, Z 1.72 (*with unique ref.*) 3.119, 19.36, 20.21, 84, 240, 21.108, 22.114, 163, B 15.398 (*with generic ref.*) 3.58, 118, 185, 8.158, 9.83, 164, 240, 330, 10.205 (1), 11.26, 63 (1), 271, 12.202, 13.78, 15.210, 16.16, 17.78, 117, 252, 315, 19.174, 184, 255, 20.355, B 5.143, A 11.192, **Z** Pr 82, 7.278; (*in temporal ref.* ~ **pestilences** the recent plagues 5.115, 10.274, 11.60; ~**...3er / wynter** the last...years 6.214, 233, 7.188, 10.73, 20.329; ~ **seuene 3er** for the next seven years 6.108, 7.64, B4.86

thysulue(n) (**thiself** B 5.487, ~ **selue** Z 1.80, ~**sylf** Z 3.128, ~**sylue** 2.127) *emph. prn* (*used appositively*) thy-, yourself 3.235, 20.401, B 13.169, A 9.44; (*as emph. refl.*) yourself 7.60, 128, 262, 15.114, **B** 1.143, 8.50, 10.259, 18.54, A 10.93, 114; (*as obj. of prep.*) 6.101, 7.59, 267, 18.173, **B** 1.24, 4.71, 5.482, 565, 606, 13.144; (*indep. / absol.*) = (you) yourself 2.127, 7.123, 10.226, 11.115, **B** 2.126, 5.490, 8.49, 10.264, 11.376, 16.157, 17.102, A 10.88, Z 3.152, 153

tho (þo)[1] *prn* those 3.444, 4.196, 5.49, 6.382, 7.115, 8.25, 57, 260, 9.173, 11.27, 30, 272, 12.245, 14.139, 16.357, 17.230, 18.64, 66, 148, 175, 19.47, 20.247, 369, 21.38, 392, 22.306, **B** 3.233, 238, 10.131, 427, 471, 13.198, 18.329, A 11.13, 192, Z 7.196; they 6.382, B 6.162; them A 10.108

tho (þo)[2] *def. art. and a.* Pr 18, 140, 1.21, 2.206, 211, 5.5, 7.86, 9.233, 13.6, 14.198, 15.51, 16.45, 248, 17.31, 170, 210, 212, 213, 259, 19.258, 20.444, 21.154, 459, 22.110, **B** 4.40, 5.174, 12.59, 14.123, 175, 15.478, 600, **A** 11.201, 224, 12.21, **Z** Pr 72, 3.158, 4.149, 7.206; (*with unique ref.*) the Z Pr 55; *in phrr.* ~ **seuene** B 13.122; ~ **thre** 10.111, 21.82, B 13.427; ~ **two** 14.108, 13.41, B 10.211

tho[3] *av* then 1.54, **B** 2.167, 5.364, A 4.49, 141; at that time Pr 146, 196, 1.106, 111, 2.220, 6.319, 7.133, 14.95, 15.55, 192, 17.199, 19.55, 20.73, 21.112, **B** 10.441, 11.323, 13.179, 16.150, Z 4.123; thereupon 1.152, 2.18, 157, 3.129, 4.13, 43, 66, 21.53, B 11.63, 84, A 12.12; when Pr 191, 2.162, 3.137

tho[4] Z 5.20, 92, 6.95 = **to** *prep.*

thogh (**thauh** 9.122, **though** 14.29, **thou3** B 1.176 *et p.*, **thouh** 8.107 *etc*, **thow** Pr 210 *etc*, **þei3** B Pr 192 *etc*,

A 1.10 *et p.* (**þei** A 12.65)) *conj.* though, in spite of the fact that 8.39, 43 *etc*, B 15.260; if 10.243; even if Pr 200, 1.33, 2.150, 3.165, 9.100, 10.257, 12.61, 13.237, 15.284, 16.79, 284, 20.422, **B** Pr 192, 1.144, 3.352, 5.267, 600, 9.39, 11.100, 15.184, 386; if, whether 1.124; that 11.230, B 14.2

thoght *n* 10.107 *see* **thouht(e)** *n*

thoghte *p.t.* 2.64, 10.68, 18.21 *see* **thynken** *v*

thol(y)en *v* undergo (penalty) 4.80, (penalty of death) 20.73, 137, 424; suffer 12.206, 15.73, 85; suffer (death) 20.258, 21.175; endure, put up with 16.32, 19.107, B 11.398

thombe 19.136 = **thumbe** *n*

thondren *v* thunder Z Pr 17

thone Z Pr 12 = **thenne**[1] *av*

thonken *v* thank 4.152, 8.135, 10.107, 18.17, 19, 19.107, A 12.48, *ger.* ~**ynge** (expression of) thanks 2.162

thorgh B 9.52 = **thorw(e)** *prep.*

thorlen *v* pierce 1.169

thorn *n* thorn 20.47, 21.323; (haw)thorn tree 2.29, 20.48, B 12.227

thorp *n* village Pr 220, A 2.45

Thorsday Z 8.76 = **Þursday** *n*

thorw(e) (**thoru3** B) *prep.* through 2.226, 16.137, 20.287; through(out), over 7.205, 9.11, 17.284, 22.213, B 17.99; = from beginning to end (of) 9.253; on account of / because of 10.36; = as a consequence / result of Pr 106, 2.247, 3.91, 106, 430, 4.139, 5.34, 7.126, 8.296, 347, 9.182, 293, 10.42, 178, 13.115, 15.16, 231, 16.340, 17.85, 276, 19.282, 194, 20.284, 391, 21.39, 130, 22.229, 352, **B** 5.242, 6.144, 10.278, 12.255, 14.14, 76, 176, 186, A 1.111; by / through the agency of 1.31, 2.248, 3.104, 449, 4.71, 7.268, 9.181, 10.48, 13.223, 15.263, 16.243, 367, 314, 21.121, 389, 22.355, **B** 9.153, 14.18, 15.210, 16.9, A 1.107; by virtue of B 15.417, 423; with the help of 17.239; by 3.2, 20.392, 396, 21.95, 303, 22.306, 318, **B** 11.207, 16.142, 161; by means of 2.150, 167, 239, 244, 3.82, 196, 269, 450, 4.78, 139, 5.98, 127, 6.21, 72, 73, 85, 186–7, 7.88, 90, 289, 8.208, 261, 344, 9.156, 301, 10.79, 209, 11.20, 127, 12.186, 13.18, 22, 60, 14.18, 25, 23, 77, 208, 15.79, 145, 238, 246, 17.185, 241–2, 265–66, 306, 18.10, 33, 36, 46, 123, 151, 20.112, 132, 142, 159, 162, 320, 395, 397–8, 461, 21.122, 245, 247, 357, 378, 22.99, **B** 2.153, 3.127, 5.132, 6.19, 9.44, 207, 10.109, 238, 320, 11.81, 124, 155, 299, 322, 357, 12.77, 78, 100, 13.168–9, 361, 370, 14.82, 185, 15.65, 210, 280, 295, 345, 445, 448, 466, 479, 16.51, 101, 120, 17.119, 18.139, 353, 390

thou, þou *prn* B 14.184, A Pr 88, Z Pr 122 *see* **thow**[1]

though 14.29, **thou3** B 1.176 *etc*, **thouh** 8.107 *etc* = **thogh** *conj.*

thouht(e) *n* idea, notion 19.111; opinion 6.100; (object of) reflexion B 13.21; (sinful) fancy 2.95; thought, meditation 15.4; (faculty of) thought (*person.*) 10.74 *et p.*, 16.183; mind 7.20

thouhte[1] *p.t.* 12.53, 18.245 *etc, p.p.* 6.51 *see* **thenken** *v*

thouhte[2] (**thoughte**) Pr 196, *p.t.* 11.316, 13.177 *see* **thynken** *v*

thousand *a* thousand 20.309 (**seuene** ~); (*as indef. large number*) 18.17, A 12.48; *as n* **B** 1.116, 5.624, 13.270 [date], *in phr.* **fyue** ~ 18.154, 21.127; *as n = indef. large number* Pr 166, 7.154, 8.188, *in combs.* **fyue** ~ B 15.590, **meny score** ~ 19.22, **six** ~ 19.26, **sixty** ~ 3.233, B 17.23, **ten** ~ A 2.42

thow[1] (**thou** B 14.184, A Pr 88, Z Pr 122, **þou, thowe** 12.39, 20.326, A 1.138, **þow** 1.144, *enclitic form* **-ou, -ow** 1.5 *etc*) *pers. prn 2 sg.* thou, you Pr 163 *et p.*, B 1.21 *et p.*, A 1.26 *et p.*, Z 3.149 *et p.*; *used variously in address* to (God) 6.423, (Christ) 7.136, (King) 21.480, (knight) 8.25, (lady) 3.488, (pupil) 11.109, (servant) B 1.77, (reader) B Pr 215

thow[2] Pr 210, 1.10, 19, 124, 171, 174, 2.150, 3.87, 185, 197, 314, 389, 4.70, 5.164, 6.60, 108, 290, 311, 7.192, 267, 304, 8.34, 127, 195, 9.343, 10.39, 42, 11.311, 13.51, 16.93, 288, 21.447, 22.16, **Z** 1.100, 7.316 *see* **thogh** *conj.*

thowne Z 2.54 *see* **toun** *n*

thral *n* bond-servant, serf 21.33, (*fig.*) A 8.57; ~**doem** *n* servitude 20.106

thre *num. a* three 3.405, 7.109, 8.248, 16.32, 18.20, 25, (*postpositively*) 10.106, 111, 226, *in phrr.* ~ **clothes** 10.195, ~ **dayes** 10.113, 15.70, 18.161, 20.31, 41, 22.177, B 17.110, ~ **degrees** 18.56, 84, ~ **kynges** 21.82, 95, ~ **loues** 17.24, ~ †**leodes** B 16.201, ~ **maner men** 8.248, **B** 13.427, 16.227, ~ **maner minstrales** 7.109, ~ **nayles** 20.51, ~ **persones** 18.27, 215, 234, 19.30, 44, 98, **B** 10.239, 16.207, 17.44, ~ **places** 20.231, ~ **shypes** 8.349, ~ **siȝtes** B 17.153, ~ **sones** 10.226, ~ **thynges** 1.20, 3.77, 19.299, 22.11, B 17.164, ~ **vertues** 10.77, ~ **wyndes** 18.29; ~ **wittes** 10.105, *as n* three 10.106, 111, 16.32, 18.201, 219, 238, 19.311, B 17.160, A 10.167, *in phrr.* **a / o** ~ in three 18.198, 213, 242, **alle** ~ 11.154, 18.22, 218, 237, 240, 19.31, 99, 150, **thise** ~ 16.32, 36

thredbare *a* threadbare, worn-out 6.205

þresschen *v* thresh (grain) B 5.546, *ger.* **threschynge** 8.199

thres(sh)fold *n* threshold 6.407

þrest A 11.46 = **furst** *n*

þretynge *ger.* dire threat B 18.281

threttene *num. a as n.* thirteen 6.220

þreve *n* bundle (*fig.*) = large number B 16.55

threw *p.t.* 6.407, 22.164 *see* **thrown** *v*

thridde *num. a* third 7.136, 18.50, 21.91, 290, *as n* 10.76, 103, 11.37, 160, 18.195, 21.265, B Pr 121, A 8.55

thrift *n* wealth A 10.108

thringen *v* throng, crowd *p.t.* **throngen** 7.154

thritty *num. a* thirty, ~ **wyntur** 7.30, 17.23, 20.136, 329; *in phr.* **twies** ~ B 13.270, **two and** ~ 20.332

þriuen *v* prosper **B** Pr 32, 5.277, 10.211; *and see* **y~** Pr 34

þrobben *v* throb, beat strongly, *pr. p.* **þrobbant** A 12.48

#**thromblen** *v* bump against 6.407

throngen *p.t. pl.* 7.154 *see* **thringen** *v*

þrop A 2.45 *see* **thorp** *n*

throte *n* throat 19.308

throute Z 6.61 = **þeroute** *av*

þrowe *n* time B 18.76

thrown *v* (*p.t.* **threw**, *p.p.* **þrowe**) hurl 20.293, cast, hurtle 6.407

thumbe *n* thumb 7.45, 19.136

thurgh A 12.60 = **thorw(e)** *prep.*

Þursday *n* Thursday B 16.140, 160; **Schyr** ~ = Maundy Thursday Z 8.76

þurst *n* thirst B 18.369 (= **furst** *n*)

thuruen *v* be necessary, *pr. sg. 2 pers.* **tharstow** B 14.56, 3 (*impers.*) **thar þe** you need 15.259

thus *av* thus, in such a way (as aforesaid) 3.212, 4.180, 5.200 *et p.*, **B** 13.458, 15.145, 17.163, *in phr.* ~ **sone** just as quickly 3.180, straightaway 12.6, 15.44, 96, 108, 22.69; *in phr.* ~**..þat** in such a way ... / with the result that 3.430; so 4.178, 20.350; as follows 3.403, 5.11, B 2.74; *in phr.* **ryght(e)** ~ exactly as follows 6.422, 9.285, 11.199; in this way Pr 74, 1.134, 2.44; and so, consequently 6.123, 11.160, 17.258, 19.273, 21.189; thereupon, and so 2.53, 5.1, 10.1, 22.1

thusgates *av* in the following manner 16.306

thwyten *v* whittle, *ger.* ~**ynge** 8.199

tid *n* time A 2.40

tyd *av* quickly 22.54, *in phr.* **as** ~ straightaway, at once B 13.319, 16.61

tydy *a* virtuous, upright, ~ **man** 3.474, 20.332, **trewe** ~ **man / men** 21.442, B 9.105; profitable, useful †B 3.346; (*comp.*) healthy, sound 12.189

tydynge *n, pl.* ~**s** (message of) warning 21.344

#**tyke** *n* cur, slave 21.37n

tikel *a* loose, lascivious 3.166

til[1] *prep.* (= **to**, *used before vowel*) Pr 167, 229, 5.111, 6.188, 8.98 (2), 13.183, 17.262, 19.123, 20.348, 445, 21.266, **B** 9.84, 10.362, 15.169, 18.223; towards 1.132; up to 22.134, Z 7.6; until, till 3.307, 6.395, 7.225, 8.180, 274, 313, 10.53 (2), **B** 3.312, 12.245, until it is B 15.466; *in phrr.* ~ **þat** until (the time when) Pr 212, 6.80, 12.127, 19.191, Z 2.72; **fro morwen** ~ **euen** all day long 8.180, B 14.15; **vch man** ~ **oþer** every man to each other 12.131

til[2] *conj.* until Pr 42, 212 *et p.*, B 1.113 *et p.*, **A** 10.60, 12.21, 52, 74, Z 2.147; before 3.132

tyl(e)de *p.t.* 15.266, 270, 17.100 *see* **tylien** *v*; B 12.209 (= **telde**) *see* **telden** *v*

tylen *v* reach as far as Z 6.66, †A 6.79; *and see* **tollen** *v*[2]

tylyare (tulyer, tilier) *n* ploughman 17.100, **B** 13.240, 15.367, A 11.184; cultivator Pr 224

tylien (tilion, tulien) *v* (*p.t.* **tyl(e)de** 15.266, 270) till, plough 9.2, 17.100, 20.108, 21.239, 437, 441, **B** Pr 120, 6.235, A 11.186, *ger.* cultivation B 14.63; grow, cultivate 8.244; (*fig.*) Pr 87, 10.201, 21.262, 318, 335, B 15.107; obtain (food) by cultivation 15.266, 21.437, **B** 6.232, 14.67

tilþe (telþe A, tulthe C) *n* crops, harvest 21.435, B 19.436, A 7.127

tymber *n* timber for building 21.321

tymbren *v* build 3.84, (nest) B 11.360

tyme *n* (*pl.* ~**is** 1.17 *et p.*, ~ 6.118) time; (profitable / useful) time 3.462, 5.93, 101 (2), 127, 10.187, 12.96, 14.8, B 9.98; use of one's time B 11.377; proper / opportune time 4.20, 7.15, 11.105, 15.106, 21.240, **B** 5.85, 16.138; period (of time) 5.100, 7.131, 8.275, 17.237, **B** 12.249, 13.204; season 6.183; day, age, era 9.313, 11.220, 239, 15.268, 16.354, 21.134, A 11.204, 269; lifetime 21.413; occasion, moment 5.101 (1), 10.230, 17.209, 18.127, 247, 254, 20.423, 426, **B** 5.112, 7.96, 10.466, 11.406, 12.4, 13.68, 14.324, 16.142; point, juncture 10.123; *in cpds.* **blowyng** ~ B 16.26; **chirie** ~ B 5.159; **flouryng** ~ 18.35, B 16.26; **heruost** ~ 8.121; **Lamasse** ~ 8.313; **lyf** ~ course / days of one's life Pr 50 *etc*, **B** 5.476, 13.142, 15.142, Z 7.77 (*see* **lyf-**); **noon** ~ B 15.283; **pestelence** ~ time of the plague Pr 82, B 10.72; **plener** ~ full time B 16.103; **plenitudo temporis (hy)** ~ the moment of the (final) fullness of time 18.127, 139; **rotey** ~ B 11.337; **somur** ~ 16.246, B 14.178; **sondry** ~ at intervals B 15.282; at various times 18.153, B 12.31; **ten hundrit / score** ~**s** 7.38, 11.128; **wynter** ~**(s)** 9.78, 12.191, B 14.177; *in phrr.* ~ **comyng aftur** the next life 12.204; ~ **ynowe** soon enough 11.197; ~ **ypassed** while ago 16.369; **alle** ~ at all times, constantly 1.17, 65, 7.211, 17.33, 21.442; **biggen þe** ~ pay interest (on loan for a period) 6.247, B 13.376; **cursid** ~ A 10.140; **eleuene** ~**s** on many occasions 3.226; **eny** ~ at any time 15.161, B 13.164; **fele** ~ many times 6.74, 118, 16.228; **fol** ~ fully time 18.137, **B** 2.96, 5.489*n*; **in a** ~ on one occasion 11.71; **in** ~ at the right time B 9.184; **long** ~ 7.203, 20.5, 65; **mel** ~ 7.132; **mene** ~ meantime 6.281; **mony (a)** ~**(s)** 3.97, 158, 6.151, 7.48, 9.297, 10.35, 18.259, **B** 11.242, 14.4, A 8.151, ~ **and ofte** 12.241; **ofte** ~**(s)** 12.241, 18.61, 22.26, B 11.370; **olde** ~ the past B 12.235; **on nyhtes** ~ at night 16.141; **out of** ~ at the wrong time 1.24, 10.291; **som** ~**(s)** on one (or other) occasion, sometimes 3.104, 120, 6.78, 112, 137, 428, 7.28, 39, 9.149, 12.39, 13.212, 16.334, 343, 18.37, 49, 19.178, **B** 5.376, 12.22, 14.237; at some time 6.115, 8.22, 15.299; at one time 6.207, 15.302, 16.366, 20.330, 22.182, **B** 5.135, 546, 12.293, 15.186, 442, 16.45; ~...~ at one time...at another 6.38, 191, 404, 16.172–3, 21.102–4, ~~ **þat** the moment when 21.444; **þat** ~ at that time

3.481, 5.173, 9.294, 322, 10.249, 16.200, 18.104, 148, 205, 20.73, 78, 83, 21.84, **B** 5.365, 13.22, 15.40, 276, A 7.180, **what** ~ at whatever time, whenever 7.145; **when** ~ **is** at the appropriate time 8.10, 80

tynen *v* (*p.p.* **(y)tynt** 5.93, 20.142) be dispossessed of 21.344, B 1.113; suffer the loss of 10.280, 11.197, B 10.349, A 12.86; lose 20.142; waste 5.93, 14.8

†**tynynge** *ger.* loss, waste B 9.99

tyn(e)kere *n* tinker [mender of pots and pans] 6.363, **B** Pr 221, 5.547

tynt *p.p.* 20.142 *see* **tynen** *v*

tyraunt *n* unjust lord B 15.419; devilish villain 2.211, 22.60

*****titerare** *n* tattler, ~ **in ydel** idle gossip-monger 22.300

tiþe *num. a* tenth, **trauaille þe** ~ **deel** a tenth part of the labour B 15.487

tythe *n* tithe (-payment) 6.298, 304, 8.78, 101, 13.83 (1), 16.258

tithen *v* give as a tithe 13.72; pay tithes 6.305; pay 13.83

title *n* legal claim (to possession) 20.324; 'title' [certificate of presentment to a benefice] 13.103, 105; ? name (of priest), (verbal) guarantee of support 13.113c

tixst (text) *n* (Scriptural) text 3.493, 495, 12.51, 15.135, **B** 2.122, 3.346, 351, 10.269, 11.111, 15.327; authoritative utterance 1.200, 2.129; exact words 19.15

to *av*¹ to B 7.130

to *av*² too 1.139, 5.23, 24, 6.166, 8.274, 16.355, 18.199, 22.360, **B** 11.224, 13.72, 14.74, 15.78, 16.148, 17.41 (2), Z 7.245

to *prep.* to Pr 22, 16.108, 20.264, 22.366 *et p.* (*with v. inf.*) Pr 31 *et p.*; in order to Pr 4, 54, 98, 3.33, 49, 6.26, 14.12 *etc*, B 5.377; so as to Pr 32, 4.54, 14.67, A 10.105; (*with inf. as ger.*) ~ **awaken** at awakening B 2.100; ~ **gete** in getting 10.300; ~ **holde** in keeping 3.187; ~ **kepe** for keeping B 6.140; ~ **lese** (even) at the cost of losing 10.194; ~ **leten wel by** for thinking well of 7.267; ~ **leue** for believing 17.124; ~ **preche** by preaching 16.262; ~ **se** at seeing 22.109; ~ **sette** from placing B 7.151; ~ **spille** from wasting B 9.98; ~ **suffre** A 10.118, ~ **wyte** to knowing A 11.259; ~ **worche** for making 2.118; ~ **ȝyue** in giving B 14.126; (*inf. with implied finite senses*) ~ **dyne** if he dines 16.4, ~ **fonge** if he receives 16.7, ~ **mete** he may meet 16.141, ~ **amenden** (I shall) amend 20.389, ~ **releue** will restore 20.390; ~ **to walke** he will walk B 18.32; **they** ~ **leue / lyue** that they might believe / live 6.48, 21.233; **þei** ~ **haue** and they will have B 2.102; ~ **deure** is to last Z 2.72; ~ **laste** that lasts B 9.45; (*in combin. with* **for**) Pr 7, 187, 1.16, 118, 141, 158, 2.15, 199 *etc*, B 8.93, A 2.65, Z 7.262; (*with infl. inf.*) ~ **done** 3.232, 7.229, 8.117, 210, B 4.28, ~ **gone** 2.21, ~ **lyuene** 9.15, 15.241; (*with understood v. preceding*) (asking) Pr 83, 1.67, 3.216, A 4.60, (enabling) 10.52, (telling) B 12.22, A 2.186; (*with noun (phr.) preceding*) **in hope** ~ Pr 29,

62, *so also* 1.110, 2.196, 241, 3.100, 216, 236, 6.169, 194, 340, 7.22, 9.91, A 12.32, Z 2.158; (*with a. preceding*) Pr 202, 1.171, 2.87, 3.198, 282, 4.28, 5.23, 6.7, 17, 87, A 11.246 *etc*; *in expl. use after various vv.*: (*factitive*) Pr 136, 140, 6.2, A 3.185 (**maken**), 2.221, 10.75, 15.53, 16.226, 22.155, **B** 8.13, 9.90 (**don**), †11.161, B 1.123, A 7.132, 285 (**gare**), (*volitional*) 1.113, (*prohibitive*) 3.69, 14.177, 15.168, (*in absol. phr.*) **treuliche ~ telle** 2.251, *so* 11.277, 12.235, 16.117, 21.70, **B** 9.156, 16.4; (*in phr. qualifying preceding n. / phr.*) 3.206, 243, 251, 260, 269, 284, 349, 374, 461, 4.19, 135, 5.8, 6.49, 8.52, (*qualifying understood prn* him) 3.295, (me) 5.50; (*forming passive inf.*) 13.174, 207, 14.35, 16.106, 370, 18.221, **B** 5.583, 10.475, 12.38, ? 16.192, 219, ? A 10.54, Z 3.159; *in phrasal vv.* Pr 133 (**~ close with heuene** with which to close h.), **~ se ~** to look at 1.55, *so also* 8.273, 21.228; *before nn*: according to B 15.83; after 8.28–9; as (a) 3.146, 269, 5.73, 6.128, 374, 9.199, 11.38, 103, 12.213, **B** 1.82, 7.136, 8.52, 10.47, 12.46; as far as 1.166, 15.284, 16.83, 18.175; as regards 11.45 (2), B 15.457; at 5.36, 6.211 (1,2), 376, 9.35, 18.176, 22.296 (2), B 15.300; by 16.198; compared with 6.83, 14.83, 21.19, 22.23, B 13.194; down on B 10.140, A 12.39; for 1.35, 2.35, 175, 3.297, 5.14, 20, 103, 151, 6.271 (2), 7.75, 124, 258, 9.132, 12.82, 189, 16.17, 19.197 (2), 20.471, 22.259, 278, 296 (1), **B** 5.124, 7.78, 8.35, 10.248, 13.205, 14.232, 16.16, 163, 17.32, 40, 76, 77, **A** 7.228, 11.113, Z Pr 99; in 9.125, 318, 17.95; into 3.460, 19.195, 197 (1), **B** 9.66, 18.328; of 11.275, 19.76; on 6.155, B 9.88; (shut) on A 12.36; on to 1.61, 5.14, B 2.26; to (make up) 18.238; to obtain 13.113; (so as) to (produce) A 2.20; to the study of 11.117; towards 2.38, 5.125, 7.261, 286, 9.52, 10.134, 13.147, 14.49, 19.182, 197, 20.398, 22.247, 359, B 9.57, A 10.52, Z 3.166; until 11.196, 12.70, 20.5, 21.218, 22.294, B 16.148; with 3.376, 15.93, **B** 1.62, 3.109, **A** 4.144, 10.11; upon 19.191, B 18.94; up to B 16.151, A 10.145; up towards Pr 133; *in phrr.* **~ þe fulle** fully, satisfactorily 17.57, 20.410, **B** 13.193, 14.178; **~ paye** satisfactorily 14.178; *in comb. with* **ward** (**to...ward**), **~ helleward** towards hell 20.117, **~ heueneward** 16.53, **B** 10.333, 15.457; **~ Ierusalem-mward** B 17.80; **~ kyrkeward** 6.350, **~ porsward** Pr 101, **~ synneward** 6.179, **~ treuthward** 16.144

to A 3.218, Z 2.38, 215 = **two** *num*

tobersten *v* burst asunder, *p.t.* **tobarst** Z 5.39

to-bollen *p.pl.a* swollen up B 5.83

tobreken *v* (*p.p.* **tobroke(n)**) break down 9.32; tear in pieces 10.85; maim 9.99

tocleuen *v* (*p.t.* **to-cleyf** 20.61) cleave asunder 14.84; split apart 20.61, 112

today *av* today 8.107, 20.404, 21.216

todrawen *v* (*p.t.pl.* **todrowe**) mutilate (*lit.* tear apart) B 10.35

toek *p.t.* 4.166 *et p.*; *see* **taken** *v*

toelde *p.t.* 19.100, 21.276, 344, 22.232 *see* **tellen** *v*

to(e)th (*pl.* **teth** 20.83) *n* tooth, *pl.* B 15.13, **~ ache** toothache 22.82, **~ drawere** puller of teeth 6.369; *in phr.* **maugre his mony ~** in spite of anything he could do 20.83; *and see* **fore ~, wang ~**

tofore, toforn *prep.* in front of B 13.48; before 5.114; in the presence of 7.63, B 13.449; (in times) before B 12.131

toft *n* hillock 1.12, B Pr 12

toged(e)re(s), togidere(s) *av* together, = in one (body / company) 5.140, 6.154, 7.154, 18.112, 273, 21.166, 315, **B** 2.173, 6.182; = in (to) union / contact 1.191, 3.210, 6.218, 226, 16.79, 330, 17.22, 19.115, 131, 170, 199, **A** 2.23, 8.74; = in one whole 10.130, 11.153, B 2.84; = at one (and the same) time 14.147, Z 2.164, 168; successively B 1.121, Z Pr 64; = in concert / co-operation Pr 142, 1.38, 53, 2.194, 3.162, 280, 443, 4.72, 146, 10.27, 13.41, 16.65, 19.172, 175, 187, B Pr 66; = mutually Pr 47, 17.217; = reciprocally Pr 61; = (to / with) each other 4.25, 44, 6.382, 10.283, 13.32, **B** 2.136, 4.195, 9.128, 15.275, 17.48, **A** 2.25, 10.146, 158, 180; along with him / it / them 2.97, 3.174, 451, A 2.107; *in phr.* **leyde his eyen ~** closed his lids upon his eyes 20.59

togrynden *v* (*contr. pr.* **togrynt**) grinds (down) 11.62

tok(e)(n) *p.t.* 3.84 *et p.*; *see* **taken** *v*

tok(e)n *n* sign, **in ~** as a symbol Pr 86; message (of authorisation) 7.244, 13.11, B 10.218, 225, 366; word of introduction 11.105; sign(al) of recognition / greeting B 16.147, 148; agreement, covenant 18.247

tokenen *v* signify, *ger.* **tokenynge, in ~** as a sign / symbol 17.33, B 16.204, portent 5.121

tokkere *n* fuller of cloth A Pr 100

tol *n*¹ tool 11.124; *and see* **eg-toel** *n*

tol *n*² toll, payment Pr 98, 13.72

told(e) *p.t.* Pr 229 *et p.*, *p.p.* Pr 111 *et p.*; *see* **tellen** *v*

tollen *v*¹ pay a toll 13.50

tollen *v*² stretch, **~ out** †6.220, B 5.210; *and see* **tylen** *v*

toller *n* toll-collector B Pr 221

***tologgen** *v* pull about 2.226

tombe *n* grave, tomb 18.144

tomblen *v* fall down flat A 12.91

tom(e) *n* leisure 2.196, A 6.82

tomor(e)we *av* tomorrow 2.41, 46

tonder B 17.246 = **tender** *n*

tonge *n* tongue (*physical organ*) B 15.13; (*of taste*) B 6.265; (*of speech*) 6.109, 331, 425, 7.17, 144, 12.199, 15.160, 16.144, 369, 19.302, 20.148, 21.93, 172, 233, 404, **B** 5.287, 10.165, 11.237, 13.323, A 12.24, 29; (*fig.*) 10.201, 16.144, B Pr 51, **harlotes ~** B 13.416, **neddres ~** B 5.86; speech, utterance 11.282, 13.206, 15.257, B 5.95, **fykel (of) ~** 2.6, 25, 6.72, (*person.*) 2.121, B 2.41; **leel of ~** 7.196; **likerous of ~** B 6.265; **mery ~**

2.167; **pacient of** ~ B 15.201, **pacience of** ~ B 14.99; **resonable of** ~ Pr 176; **talewys of** ~ 3.166; **trewe of** ~ 1.84, 174, 8.48, 10.78, 16.257, B 15.105, (*person*) 3.474, 4.18, **two-** double tongued (*person.*) 22.162; language, **of oure** ~ in our own language 17.293

tonne *n* tun, cask B 15.337

took *p.t.* Pr 117 *et p.*; *see* **taken** *v*

tookene 13.11 = **tok(e)n** *n*

top *n* hair (on the top of the head), **taken by the** ~ = seize with violence 3.176; top of tree [part growing above ground], *in phr.* ~ **and roote** B 16.22

#**to-quaschen** *v* shatter asunder, *p.t.* 20.63

torche *n* torch 19.169, 178, 260, 20.248

tore *p.p.* 6.203; *see* **teren** *v*

torenden *v* be destroyed (*lit.* torn apart) B 10.114

#**to-reuen** *v* plunder 3.202

to-riuen *v* (*p.t.* **to-roef**) split asunder 20.62

tornen *v* 17.263, 22.47, B 3.42, 347, 13.319, 15.437, 445, 546 = **turnen** *v*

to-roef *p.t.* 20.62 *see* **to-riuen** *v*

tortle *n* turtle-dove 14.161

torw Z 1.59, 7.327 = **thorw** *prep.*

*****toshellen** *v* (*p.p.* **to-shullen**) ?peel B 17.192n

toten *v* look, peer 18.53, B 16.22

toth-drawere 6.369 *see* **to(e)th** *n*

to-trayen *v* torment grievously Z 5.113

touchen *v* touch 20.77, 79, 86, 21.172, B 17.150; make contact with 19.124, 146; lay a hand upon 20.198, 305; concern B 11.100; deal with B15.74

touʒ *a* hardy; *comp.* **touore** hardier 12.189

touken *v* tuck [stretch cloth on frame for beating] B 15.454

toun *n* manorial estate **A** 10.138, 11.213, Z 2.54; town Pr 177, 14.91, B 13.304, A 12.40; **to** ~ into the city [of London] B 13.266, [of Jerusalem] B 17.83; *and see* **borw** ~

tounge A 12.24, 29 = **tonge** *n*

touore *comp*; *see* **touʒ** *a*

tour *n* fortress Pr 15, 1.12, A 6.79, 82

tow Z 3.115, 7.238 = **thow** *prn*

toward[1] *a* at hand, about Pr 215

toward(e)[2] *prep.* towards, in the direction of 6.330, 8.190, 15.111, 21.158

towkare Z Pr 88 = **tokkere** *n*

trayen Z 1.13 *see* **bytrayen** *v*

trailen *v* trail, drag, *ger.* B 12.241

traytowr Z 2.169 = **tretour** *n*

#**tra(ns)uersen** *v* go counter (to), transgress 3.445, 14.209

tras *n* path, way (*fig.*) A 12.91

trauail *n* (hard) work, labour 3.350, 5.127, 9.152, B 6.133, **A** 7.235, 11.186; service B 7.43; effort 3.372, 19.213, **B** 14.153, 15.487; trouble B 11.194; ? journey 9.234n, A 10.145

trauaillen *v*[1] (exert oneself in) labour 3.295, 8.252, 12.97, 13.101, 15.127, 17.254, 21.441, 22.260, **B** Pr 120, 6.139, 9.105, Z 7.234 *ger.* ~ **of hondis** A 7.232, ~ **in preieres** B 6.247

trauaillen *v*[2] journey B 16.10

trauaillour *n* labourer B 13.240

#**trauersen** 14.209 = **transuersen** *v*

tre(e) *n* tree 13.165, 16.246, 18.75, **B** 11.360, 15.333; [of charity / humanity] 18.9, 29, 68, B 16.4, 8, 10, 22, 61, 63, [of Eden] 20.142 (1), 198, 305, 397, [of Calvary] 20.142 (2), 398

trecherie B 7.77 = **tric(c)herye** *n*

treden *v* (*p.t.* **treden** 13.165) tread / step upon A 10.104; copulate 13.165, 14.161, (with) B 11.355

tremblen *v* tremble 2.251, 12.51, Z 2.215

trental *n* set of thirty requiem masses Z Pr 64

trepget *n* trap A 12.91

treso(u)n *n* breach of faith, deceit Pr 12, 3.87, 20.319, 324, **B** 7.77, 18.289; treachery, betrayal 18.176; treason B 5.49

tresorer *n* paymaster 22.260

treso(u)r *n* treasure, (form of) wealth 1.43, 52, 66, 79, 81, 135, 201, 2.211, 3.159, 9.333, 16.144, 17.211, B 1.135, 208, (*fig.*) 21.218, 226, **B** 12.293, 13.194, **Kynges** ~ 5.181, **Goddes...**~ 10.177, **Cristis** ~ 14.54, B 10.474, ~ **of Treuthe** 10.183, B 7.54

trespas *n* crime, wrongdoing 1.93, Z 2.170

trespassen *v* do wrong, transgress 6.425, 14.209, B 3.293

tretour *n* traitor 20.422; betrayer 19.240; faithless person 21.441; deceiver Z 2.169

treu(e)ly(che) 2.251, 8.20, 9.330, 12.204, 13.101, 16.295 = **trew(e)lyche** *av*

tr(e)uthe (trouþe) *n* fidelity, loyalty 1.192; faithful conduct 8.49; pledged word / promise 2.124 (2), 8.33, 10.274; oath 3.469, 22.118; (*in assev.*) **haue God my** ~ 6.296, 306, **B** 10.45, 13.245, 14.274; faith, trust, sincerity 3.136; righteousness 1.81, 108, 143, 201, 17.141, 18.31, 21.262, 335, 22.53, 56; justice 3.348, 350, 4.170, 8.36, 16.185, 17.45, 21.90, 195, 481, **B** 1. 99, 102, 2.37, 3.241, 243, 11.151, 155, 158, 161, 15.310; just judgement 22.135; integrity 1.99, 102, 3.453, 8.57, 69, 11.17, 27, 12.92, 97, 14.188, 213, 214, 17.211, **B** 1.109, 3.164, 5.461, 11.163, 14.99, 15.470; right(eous) conduct Pr 12, 1.143, 3.144, 308, 5.183, what is right B 13.360; honesty, *in phr.* **with** ~ honestly 8.105, 9.251, 21.231; (*semi-person.*) = man / men of integrity 2.136, 3.176, 191, 14.209, 212, **B** 2.120, 3.243, 10.22; divine righteousness / truth / faithful justice (*person.*) [= God] Pr 15, 1.93 *et p.*, 3.445; **Seynt** ~ 'St' Truth 5.198, 7.176; [= daughter of God] 20.122 *et p.*; something true / truth (of the matter) 4.151, 8.297, 10.245, 11.277, 12.27, 39, 174, 235, **B** 12.130, 15.91; true testimony 20.311, 22.161, B 15.415, *in phr.* **with** ~

truthfully 20.203; true / accurate measure 3.89, 6.224, A 8.41; true estimate 6.385

treuthliche 13.72 = **trew(e)lyche** *av*

treuthward, to *av. phr.* towards / in accordance with righteousness 16.144

trewe¹ *n* truce 8.353, (*excl., with pl. as sg.*) Peace! an end to fighting ! 20.462

trewe² *a* reliable, constant 3.381, 16.358, 17.102, 18.247; honest, honourable 2.122, 3.298, 5.127, 8.200, 10.80, 21.238, 442, **B** Pr 120, 12.58, 13.240, A 11.184, 186; ~ **catel** legitimately acquired wealth 19.240; ~ **knyht** 12.77, 14.149, 205; ~ **thyng** 14.8; upright, virtuous 3.354, 444, 456, 4.76, 12.28, B 15.427; ~ **folk** B 7.54, ~ (...) **man / men** 3.444, 7.38, **B** 15.419, 487, ~ **tidy man** 21.442, B 9.105, A 3. 222, ~ **wille** B 13.194; *a as n* 3.471, 7.257; true 7.259, 9.212, 11.151, 14.66, 151, 15.135, 239, 274, 17.5, 20.135, B 11.100; truthful, veracious 11.96, 13.87, 17.15, 19.27, 20.431, A 12.18; ~ **bileue** 18.210; ~ **of tonge** 1.84, 174, 8.48, 10.78, 16.257; *cpd.* ~ **tonge** (*person.*) 3.474, 4.18; proper, correct, right 3.405, 487, 19.23; rightful, just 2.129, 14.212 (1), 215, 21.300, ~**accion** 1.94, ~**partie** 1.95, ~ **riȝte** B 10.341; real, genuine Pr 100, 16.39, 17.75, 76, A 12.85, Z 7.260, ~ **charite** 2.37; ~ **feiþ** B 13.211; ~ **loue** 1.135, 18.9; ~ **treuthe** 14.212 (2)

trew(e)ly(che) *av* faithfully B 7.61; honestly, honourably 1.96, 174, 3.84, 8.242, 13.72, 101; steadfastly 16.295; truthfully 2.251, 12.204; exactly 19.15; genuinely, really 18.26, 19.120, 21.178; (*in assev.*) indeed, believe me 8.20, 9.330, B 9.186

triacle *n* healing remedy 1.145, B 5.49

tribulacioun *n* affliction 12.203

tribu(y)t *n* tribute, **vnder** ~ liable to pay tribute 21.37

tric(c)herye *n* violation of faith or 'truth', perfidy Pr 12, 1.192; deceit 20.319, B 7.77

trydest *p.p.* Z 1.75 *see* **trien** *v*

trie *a* choice, excellent **B** 1.137, 15.168, 16.4; *av* ~**liche** choicely B Pr 14

trien *v* select, choose, *p.p. sup.* **trydest** choicest Z 1.75; put to the test, assay, *p.p.* 1.81, 201

triennals B 7.171 = **trionales** *n*

tryfle *n* (trifling) nonsense 14.83, 20.149

trinen *v* lay hand on 20.86

Trinite *n* the Blessed Trinity, God in Trinity 1.133 *et p.*; **in þe** ~ in the name of the Trinity B 14.184; triad 15.103, 111

trionales *n. pl.* masses said for a period of three years 9.320, 330, 333

trist *n* trust, confidence, *in phrr.* **in** ~ **of** (those) trusting in 3.159, **vp(on)** ~ **of** through reliance upon 9.333

tristen *v* trust, have faith / confidence in 1.66, 6.332, 9.330, 13.101, B 13.333

#**troylen** *v* dupe, deceive 20.319

trollilolly, hey *excl.* ho tra-la-la [burden of a song] 8.123c

trollen (forth) *v* wander 20.332

tromp(y)en *v* blow a trumpet 15.206, 20.468

trone *n* throne 1.133

tronen *v* enthrone, place on a throne B 1.133

trotten *v* trot B 2.165

trouþe B 10.45, 13.245, 14.274, 15.310, 415, A 11.31 *see* **treuthe** *n*

trowe B 15.96 = **tre(e)** *n*

trowen *v* believe 1.143, 3.20, 6.28, 16.303, 21.178, **B** 15.477, 17.163; think 14.108, 122, A 8.61, (*in (semi)-parenthetic use*) Pr 15, 5.49, 6.202, 298, 16.295, **B** 3.44, 4.41, 9.120, 10.429, 15.164, 301, **A** Pr 34, 5.69, †112, 8.59

truyfle 20.149 = **tryfle** *n*

trussen *v* (pack up and) be off 2.228

trust 9.333, B 3.124 *etc* = **trist** *n*

trusten 9.330, B 13.333 = **tristen** *v*

trusty *a* reliable, trustworthy B 8.82

truþe B 1.99 *etc*; *see* **tr(e)uthe** *n*

tulien *v* 10.201, 20.108, 21.239, 262, 318, 335, 437, 441, B 14.63, 67 *see* **tylien** *v*

tulyer Pr 224 = **tylyare** *n*

tulthe (telþe, tilþe) *n* crops 21.435, A 7.127

tunge B 10.165 = **tonge** *n*

tunycle *n* small tunic, jacket B 15.168

turnen *v* turn 5.121, 9.85, 144, 22.54, B 5.108; move about 19.152; come back 20.398; recoil (upon) 20.399; impel A 12.9; be driven 6.167; obstruct (the course of) 3.49; change 5.101, 12.2, 210, 13.18, 19.282, 297, 22.137; transform 15.219, 19.293, 21.109, 453; convert 17.273, **B** 15.437, 445, 16.110; be converted 3.479, 17.254, 20.398

tuto(u)r *n* guardian, keeper 1.52

twe(y)(n)e *num. a* two 5.134, 6.209, 14.116, 18.81, B 13.381, (*post-positive*) †21.347, A 12.83, **hem** ~ the two of them 18.231, B 18.171; a pair (of) 6.363

twel-monthe *n* twelve-month, year 6.80

twelue *num. a* twelve 6.203, 220, 11.32

twenty *num. a* twenty 14.129, ~ **hundred** B 16.10

twies *av* twice 7.29, B 4.23, Z Pr 96, *in num.* ~ **þritty and tene** B 13.270

twynen *v* twist 19.170

twius Z Pr 96 = **twies** *av*

two *num. a* Pr 106, 1.84, 3.332, 381, 5.130, 6.103, 198, 397, 7.1, 222, 8.304, 9.284, 301, 10.8, 78, 80, 11.173, 13.79, 14.104, 15.87, 16.9, 19.13, 76, 20.61, 73, 238, 318, 21.126, 274, **B** 2.55, 3.231, 5.287, 402, 6.282, 325, 9.116, 10.280, 13.128, 176, 247, 317, (*post-positive*) **bothe** ~ both of them; **hem** ~ those two 7.289; **they** ~ those two B 10.153, **vs** ~ the pair of us B 13.107; *in cpd. num.* ~ **and thritty** 20.332; *a as n* 11.37, 13.28, 41, 14.108, 18.87, 21.343, 476; *and see* **twe(y)(n)e** *num.*

Two-Tonge Double-Tongue 22.162

vc(c)h(e) (ech(e)) *a* each, every 8.117, 9.231, 10.234, 12.131, 13.244, 20.338, 21.397, 21.460, 22.92, B Pr 122 *et p.*, **Z** 2.48, 3.154, 6.80, 7.65; ~ **a** every 6.245 *et p.*, B Pr 51 *etc*; any 22.19; *as prn* each 22.258

vchon(e) *prn* everyone 6.122 *with prec. prn* **hem / we (...) / yow** ~ every one of them / us / you 3.22, 9.235, B 1.17, 51

vmbletee *n* humility (*person.*) 7.271; *and see* **humylite** *n*

vm(by)while *av* at intervals 6.395

vnbynden *v* loose (*fig.*) Pr 129, 21.190

vnblessed *p.p.a* accursed 21.407

vnbokelen *v* unfasten 19.70

vnbuxum *a* disobedient 6.16, 17, A 9.93; intractable 2.87; unruly B 13.276

vnchargen *v* lift the burden from B 15.344

vnche *n* inch, (*fig.*) = least little bit A 5.100

vncomly *a* unbecoming, unseemly B 9.162

vnconnynge *a* (foolishly) ignorant 3.243, 15.16, 18.156, Z 7.261; lacking knowledge (to) B 12.183; ~**liche** *av* unwisely 3.262

vncorteysliche *av* ungracefully 13.171

vncouplen *v* unleash [from being coupled together], *p.p.* B Pr 162

vncristene *a* pagan 12.79, **B** 10.348, 11.154; non-Christian, *a as n* B 10.348, *in phr.* **Cristene and** ~ 1.89, B 15.395, 498

vncrounede *p.p.a* untonsured 5.62

vncunynge Z 7.261 = **vnconnynge** *a*

vndede *p.t.* 9.305 *see* **vndon** *v*

vnder *prep.* under, beneath Pr 200, 9.139, 15.242, 22.190, B 15.122, 452, A 12.105; beneath the shelter of 10.64, **B** Pr 8, 17.103, Z Pr 6; behind B 15.593; on 22.190, B 5.162; by B 15.454; in the form of 21.86, 88; beneath the guise of 21.349; under the authority of 16.124, 17.230, 21.297, 22.258, B 15.377; subject to 21.37; *in phrr.* ~ **borwe** 14.191, ~ **maynprise** 22.17 under suretyship; ~ **Crist** subject to the authority of Christ Pr 86, 11.156, 250, 254, 14.155, **B** 12.126, 16.17, = anywhere (in the world) 12.80, 13.208, 14.159; ~ **gyrdel** anywhere alive (*with pun on* '(sexually) potent') 6.43; ~ **heuene** 22.276, ~ **molde** 19.84, ~ **sonne** 3.203, 10.50, 12.95, 16.208, B 10.208 anywhere; ~ **obedience** subject to authority 9.220, 222, 235, B 12.37; ~ **secret seal** in a sealed letter 9.27, 138, B 13.249; ~ **(notarie) signe** certified by a notary 22.272; ~ **þe thumbe** in hand [*sc.* as a bribe] 7.45

vnderfongen *v* (*p.t.* ~ **fang** A 1.74, ~ **fenge** 1.73, 12.54, ~ **fonged** B 11.118, *p.p.* ~ **fonge(n)** 3.111, 7.278, B 7.172 *etc*) receive [in baptism] 12.54, B 1.76, [as freeman] 3.111, [in communion] Z 5.37, *in phr.* ~ **fayre** receive courteously 7.278, 9.129, 322, B 10.227; accept 3.270, 12.86, 16.258

vnderlynge *n* subordinate 8.43

vndernymen *v* (*p.p.* ~ **nome** 22.51, B 13.282) reprove 22.51, **B** 5.114, 11.214, 13.282, *ger.* reproof 6.35

vnderpicchen *v* (*p.p.* ~**piȝt**) support from beneath B 16.23

#vnder-shoren *v* prop up, *p.p.* 18.47

vnderstanden (vnderstonden) *v* (*p.p.* ~**stande** 19.311, B 12.256) understand 7.43, 19.311, **B** 12.256, 14.279, 15.471; possess (proper) understanding 3.398; know B 6.54, A 9.90

vnderstandyng (vnderstondynge) *n* understanding 11.114, 13.115; mental capacity 11.304, **of kynde** ~ equipped with (a) proper understanding 5.56, 14.102; grasp of things A 10.71

vndertaken *v* (*p.t.* ~**toke** 12.33, *p.p.* ~ 20.20) reprove 12.33; receive Pr 98; promise 3.295, 19.19, 20.20; assert, **dar** ~ venture to declare **B** 10.154, 13.132, 17.110

vndeuouteliche *av* without proper devotion Pr 126

vndo(e)n *v* unfasten 7.248, 20.272, 362; annul B 15.243; destroy 20.340, 22.89; explain 2.40

#vndoynge *ger.* ruin, downfall B 15.598.

vnesiliche *av* uncomfortably 16.74

vnfeteren *v* free from shackles 3.175

vnfolden *v* open 2.73, 9.282; unclench, spread open 19.144, 151

vngracious *a* lacking grace / unprofitable, unsuccessful 10.300, 11.230; ~**liche** *av* scandalously 16.278

***vngraue** *p.p.a* unstamped 4.127

vnhardy *a* lacking in courage / boldness 20.85, **B** Pr 180, 13.123, 17.109

vnhelen (vnhilen) *v* uncover 16.74; unroof 19.303

vnhende *n* mischief (*lit.* discourtesy) 22.186c

vnhynde *a* unkind 19.251

vnholy *a* irreligious, lacking in virtue Pr 3

vnite *n* harmony 5.189; (grammatical) agreement 3.335, 394; [as name of the Church] Unity 21.330 *et p.*, 22.75 *et p.*

vnioynen *v* disjoin (*fig.*) 20.266n

vnkynde *a* unnatural, (unnaturally) evil 6.294, 17.275, 18.156, 19.182, 216, 256, 20.441, **B** 13.356, 15.523, *a as n* wicked people 19.255; harsh, unkind 19.217, 227, **B** 9.84, 16.42, 149; mean, ungenerous 1.188, 19.245, **B** 10.29, 11.211, 13.379; ungrateful 7.43; wrong-fully obtained 14.19; ~**ly** *av* against the natural order of things B 9.157; ~**nesse** *n* meanness, niggardliness 15.190, 19.232; selfishness B 14.72; lack of charity, uncharitableness 19.222, 223, 253, 326, 327, B 9.89, A 3.274, (*person.*) 21.225, 22.297

vnknytten *v* untie, undo 20.223

vnknowe *p.p.a* unknown, neglected 17.162

vnkouþe *a* strange, foreign B 7.156

vnkun(n)ynge 15.16, 18.156, B 12.183, Z 7.261 = **vnconnynge** *a*

vnlau(e)fulliche *av* in defiance of the law 3.288, 11.256

vnlek *p.t.* 7.250 *see* **vnlo(u)ken** *v*

vnlele *a as n* disloyal, false 13.68

vnlered *a* uneducated Z 3.164

vnlikyng *a* disagreeable 7.23

#**vnlosen** *v* open Pr 162 (B Pr 214); unbend, put forth 19.116; set free 1.196

vnlossum *a* undesirable 10.265

vnlouken *v* (*p.t.* **vnlek** 7.250) unlock, open 7.250, 14.55, 20.193, 359, B 18.263, 315; (*fig.*) split apart 20.266n; spread wide 9.143

vnlouely(ch)(e) *a* unattractive 10.265; unpleasant 14.178; *av* horribly 6.413

vnmaken *v* undo, dissolve B 15.241

vnmeble *n* immovable goods (= lands) 3.421, 10.188

#**vnmesurables** *a. pl.* unfathomable B 15.71

vnnethe *av* scarcely 4.63, 22.190, Z 3.165

vnpensched Z 4.138 = **vnpunisched** *a*

#**vnpiken** *v* pick 6.266 (B 13.368)

vnpynnen *v* unbolt 12.49, 22.331, B 18.263

vnpossible A 11.229 = **impossible** *a*

vnpunisched *a* unpunished 4.137

vnredy *a* improvident 12.218

vnresonable *a* not in accord with reason B 6.151; disordered, unpredictable B 15.355; undisciplined B 15.460

vnrihtfole *a* wrongful 12.17

vnriȝtfulliche *av* wrongfully 21.246

vnrobbed *p.p.a* without being robbed 13.1

vnrosted *p.p.a* uncooked B 5.603

vnsauerly *av* so as to taste unpleasant 15.49

vnsauoury *a* tasteless B 15.432

vnschryuen *p.p.a* unabsolved (of one's sins) Z 8.76

vnseled *p.p.a* not stamped with (an official) mark 16.128

vnsemely *a* hideous 1.55

vnsittyng(e) *a* improper, unbecoming, *in phr.* ~ **soffraunce** 3.207, 4.189

vnskilful *a* unreasonable 6.25, B 13.277

vnsold *p.p.a* unsold 6.214

vnsowen *v* undo the stitching (of) 6.6

vnsperen *v* unbar 20.270, open (*fig.*) 20.88

vnstable *a* unsteady 10.37

vnstedefast *a* inconstant 3.386

vntempred *a* untuned B 9.103

vnþende *a* small, of poor quality B 5.175

vntidy *a* indecent 22.119; not properly made 9.262; (of) poor (quality) 3.87

vntil *prep.* to B Pr 228

vntiled *p.p.a* uncultivated B 15.458

vntyled *p.p.a* without roof-tiles B 14.253

vntyme *n* the wrong time B 9.186

vntrewe *a* false 11.238; invalid Pr 98, ~ **þyng** ill-gotten gains B 15.107

vnwedded *p.p.a* unmarried 22.112

vnwyse *a as n* those lacking in (spiritual) wisdom 10.91; ~**ly** *av* imprudently 11.224

vnwittiliche *av* foolishly 3.133

vnworþily *av* improperly B 15.243

vnwrast *a* deceitful 20.311

#**vnwriten** *p.p.a* not written down [*sc.* in the 'Book of Life'] 11.209c

vp(pe) *av* up, *in phrasal vv.* Pr 65, 2.131, 188, 6.4, 163, 382, 411, 7.62, 8.114, 12.182, 187, 224, 13.240, 247, 14.22, 130, 17.302, 18.10, 20, 25, 144, 243, 20.52, 281, 21.192, B 5.373, 602, 6.111, 214, 7.90, 11.408, 12.120, 15.253, 16.42, 18.52, A 2.41, 12.12, 38, Z 6.66; forward 4.45, B Pr 73; down 4.60; out 11.54; *in phr.* ~ **at** up to, as far as A 12.72; **is vppe** will be afoot, stirring B 4.72

vp *prep.* upon, against 1.157; upon pain of 4.128; in 6.35, 9.333, B 20.135; at 20.50; at / with B 11.208

vphaldere, vpholdere *n* dealer in second-hand goods 6.373, 12.220

vp(p)on[1] *prep.* upon 17.234, 19.198, 20.51, B 1.162, 2.164, 6.141, 9.153, 10.105, 13.391, 14.79, 16.157; up on 6.106; on 1.12, 64, 150, 170, 2.1, 184, 185, 3.79, 323, 4.20, 5.30, 6.43, 205, 320, 7.60, 8.205, 9.185, 227, 10.64, 13.76, 14.144, 153, †15.212, 18.53, 19.2, 20.74, 21.41, 324, B 2.75, 172, 3.312, 4.24, 5.465, 9.100, 10.226, †307, 11.169, 14.31, 16.164, 18.77, 367, A 2.130, 5.241, 11.28, 12.117, Z 5.107, 134; on top of 12.232; ~ **molde** anywhere 14.167; on the basis of B 12.292c; in 9.330, 19.24, 94, B 7.183; to 20.51, 89, 22.165, **don** ~ appeal to 1.82, 2.39; towards 2.5, 11.85, 15.122; at 4.167, 6.44, 66, B 4.154, 11.362; about 10.114, 15.25; by, ~ **gesse** haphazardly B 5.415

vpon[2] *av* at 18.191

vp-so-down *av* upside down 22.54

vpward *av* upwards 5.121; on high 7.155

vs *prn.* 2 *pers. pl.* us Pr 171 *et p.*; for us 5.88, 15.57, 20.344, B 3.48, 13.49, 15.262; to us 11.152, 12.122, B 7.75, 13.58, 14.186, 15.262; (*refl.*) ourselves 8.155, 21.359, 22.75, B 11.240, 14.81; for ourselves 11.222; ~**selue** ourselves B 7.128

vsage *n* habitual practice B 7.85

vscher *n* attendant 17.112

vsen *v* be accustomed to B 12.131, **be vsed** be the custom 20.421; observe 19.47, 20.339; practise 3.110, 465, 6.231, 239, 9.155, 12.90, 15.198, B 18.106, 19.254; pursue 9.103, 11.111, 18.175, B 3.240, 313, 15.415, 22.66; engage in B 5.225, A 11.183; (make) use (of) B 1.149, 10.131; put to profitable use A 7.23

vserer 16.259 = **vsurer** *n*

vsur(y)e *n* usury [lending at (excessive) interest] 2.91, 6.239, 303, 20.109, 21.353, B 2.176, 3.240, A 2.63, 8.40; interest B 7.81

vsurer *n* usurer [lender of money at excessive interest] 3.113, 6.306, 338, 16.259, B 11.282, 15.85

vuel 6.20 = **euel** *a*

vayne, in, *av. phr.* to no purpose 2.101

vaynglorie *n* empty self-regard 6.35

vayre 17.109 = **fayre** *av*

vale *n* valley 20.411

valewe *n* worth 13.201, A 11.34

vallen 20.411 = **fallen** *v*

van(y)schen *v* vanish, disappear 14.217; cause to waste away 15.8

vanten *v* boast, ~ **vp** ~ in 6.35

variable *a* inconstant 18.69

vaunsen 3.36 = **avaunsen** *v*

vawwarde 22.95 (**vauntwarde** B 20.95) = **faumewarde** *n*

veile *n* watchful one 7.56 (**veyles** Z 5.111)

vele 6.74 = **fele** *a*

velynge *ger.* 20.131 *see* **felen** *v*

vendage B 18.370 = **ventage** *n*

#**venemouste** *n* poisonousness 20.159

vengeaunce (**veniaunce**) *n* vengeance 19.271, 273; revenge B 15.261; retribution 20.97, **B** 6.144, 11.378, **taken** ~ inflict retribution Pr 117, 121, 3.409, 20.434, B 6.224; punishment Pr 115, 14.69, **B** 3.260, 9.96, 14.79

vengen *v* avenge 6.74, 94, 19.106

venial *a* pardonable, venial B 14.83, 92

venym *n* poison 17.223, 20.154, 156, A 5.69

veniso(u)n *n* flesh of game-beasts 9.93, **B** Pr 190, 15.462

veniaunce 14.69 = **vengeaunce** *n*

venkusen, venquisshen *v* (*p.t.* **yvenkused**) conquer 20.104

ventage *n* grape-harvest (*fig.*) 20.411

ver 22.23 = **fer** *av*

verilyche *av* truly A 12.28

verious *n* verjuice A 5.69

vernicle *n* vernicle [image of Christ's face on a medal] 7.167n

verray *a* true B 15.268, ~ **charite** even Charity itself 19.273, ~ **God** the true God / God himself 6.437, 21.422; ~ **man** real living human being 21.153,

vers *n* verse B Pr 143; psalm-verse **B** 12.292, 15.82

verset *n* versicle, psalm-text 14.128

versifyen *v* compose verse 17.109

verste 20.159 = **furst(e)** *ord. num.*

vertu(e) *n* divine power 15.8, 20.123; (spiritual) power **B** 14.38, 18.319; (physical) power 15.8; (natural healing) power 20.159; [specific] moral virtue 12.178, 13.201, 21.316, 22.23, 34, 149, B 11.378, Z 1.69; (one of the four) cardinal virtue(s) Pr 131, 21.275, 313, 318, 339, 345, 396, 410, 414, 455, 459, 22.21, 73, 122, 304; (theological) virtue 1.147, 15.279; virtuous way of life 10.77; virtuousness B 2.77

vertuous *a* potent, efficacious Pr 131; excellent, praiseworthy 18.89

vesture *n* clothing 1.23

vycary, vycory *n* representative 14.70; vicar 21.412, 422, 483

vice *n* (moral) vice 6.20, 12.232, 16.371, 21.313, 316, 459, A 10.76

victorie *n* supremacy 3.485, B 3.352

vigilie *n* vigil [eve of feast-day] 7.25, 9.232

viker B 19.484 = **vycary** *n*

vyl(e) *a* despicable 20.97; shameful **B** 10.45, 14.79; destructive 20.156

vilanye *n* outrage 20.97; obscene coarseness 6.432

vine *n* vine 2.28, B 14.31

vynegre *n* vinegar A 5.69

virginite *n* (the state of) virginity 18.89, B 16.203

virres *n* vir 's **B** 10.320c, 13.52c

visage *n* face B 18.338

vise 21.459 = **vice** *n*

visiten *v* visit 7.21, 16.328, *ger.* inspection [of diocese by bishop] B 2.177

vitailles *n.pl.* provisions (of food) 2.191, 7.49, (*fig.*) 15.187, B 14.38

vitaler *n* provision-merchant 2.61

voiden *v* remove, clear away B 14.94

vois *n* voice 16.169, 20.271, 360, B 15.593

voket *n* advocate 2.61

vorgoer 2.61 = **forgoere** *n*

vowe *n* vow [solemn promise before God] Pr 69, 7.13

vowen *v* vow 6.437, 7.13

vrete *p.t.* 6.74 *see* **freten** *v*[1]

waast *n* waste / uncultivated (common) land B Pr 163

waden *v* go, live 14.125; go about Z 3.157; walk (into) 7.214

waer 9.236, 11.80, 15.78 *see* **war** *a*; 20.298 *see* **waren** *v*

wafre *n* (thin, crisp) cake 15.200, B 13.241, 263, 264, 271

wafrer *n* cake-seller 15.200, **B** 13.227, 14.28, A 6.120

*****wafrestere** *n* (female) cake-seller 7.284

wages *n. pl.* salary 13.105; pay, wages 22.260

wagen *v* give as a security 18.284; give a pledge (for) 4.93, 96c; pay wages (to) 22.259, 261, 269

waggen *v* rock, *ger.* rocking 10.34, A 9.28; shake violently 18.45, B 18.61; shake 12.18, 18.109; nudge 21.205

way (wey(ȝ)) *n* road 4.53, 9.31, 13.33, 41, 51, 15.191, 22.187, **B** 6.1, 17.115, (*fig.*) 13.29, **hey** ~ main road 8.2, 9.32, 188, 203, 11.104, 106, B 6.4, A 7.178, Z 7.6, (*fig.*) 13.67, 16.53, **B** 12.37, 15.434; path 7.306, (*fig.*) A 12.64; way Pr 49, 1.199, 2.199, 7.157, 177, 204, 8.4, 11.136, 13.42, 45, 18.290, 19.50, 79, 92, A 7.53; passage Pr 181, 189; distance, **mile** ~ time taken to go a mile 9.296; course of action, progress 3.18; manner, way (of acting) 6.265, 20.298, B 12.69; *in phrr.* **by what** ~ how 1.137; **fer** ~ far and away 16.50; **in / by ...** ~ on the / my / our / her way 15.186, 191, 19.48, 20.117, 21.157, 22.1, A 12.56

wayen 6.210, 224 *see* **wey(ȝ)en** *v*

wayf *n* (*pl.* **wayues**) (piece of) ownerless property Pr 92

wayke *a* weak 5.23

waylen *v* cry out with sorrow 5.108, B 14.332, A 5.254; bewail **B** 5.112, 14.324

wayten *v* keep hostile watch A 7.148; look B 13.343; look intently Pr 16, 9.293, 18.181, stare at 18.274; *ger.* **waytynge(s) of** staring(s) with 2.94, 6.177; plan B 8.98; ~ **after** look for 1.123, 2.78, **B** 14.116, 16.248; look around B 16.169; watch over, look after 6.208, 7.187, B 13.238, 393

wayuen *v* ~ **away** drive away 22.168; ~ **vp** open B 5.602

wayues *pl.*; *see* **wayf** *n*

waken *v* (*p.t.* **wakede** 4.196 *etc*, **woke(n)** 21.156, B 14.69) be awake 19.185, *pr.p.* while awake 13.218; keep guard 21.156; stay awake (in prayer) 22.371; awake, wake up 4.196, 6.418, 18.179, 20.471, 21.1, **B** 5.3, 14.69, 236, *ger.* 9.78, B 15.1; *see* **awaken** *v*

wakere *a* watchful 9.259

waknen *v* wake up 21.484

wal *n* wall 1.153, 16.266, 20.61, 290, B 18.61, A 5.136, (*fig.*) B 5.587

Walch 6.205 *see* **Wal(s)(c)he** *a as n*

walet *n* (money)-bag 10.272

wal(e)wen *v* toss, roll 10.46; heave nauseously A 5.70

walken *v* walk 10.61, 13.246, 15.20, 17.303, 20.117, 120, B 16.114, A 12.68; go about 13.1, 15.2, 16.52, 340, 351, **B** 13.2, 17.113; go forth 20.31; journey, travel 7.175, 10.14, 17.283, B 20.382, A 11.258; travel over 9.110; move about B 9.55; ~ **with** accompany 6.124; live 9.172, 18.251; be rife B 7.77

walkere *n* fuller Pr 223

walkne B 15.361 = **welkene** *n*

wallen[1] *v* (provide with a) wall (*fig.*) 21.328; *ger.* (*fig.*) #**wallynge** wall-work 7.233

wallen[2] 21.380 = **wellen** *v*

walnote *n* walnut 12.147

Wal(s)(c)he *a as n* Welsh flannel 6.205; Welshman 6.372; ~**man** *n* Welshman 6.308

***walterot** *n* idle nonsense 20.144*n*

wam Z Pr 132 *etc*; *see* **who** *prn*

wan[1] *p.t.* 6.310, 8.105, 9.251, 11.287, 17.18, 19.234, 242, **B** 4.67, 12.44 *see* **wynnen** *v*

wan[2] **Z** 1.30 *etc* = **when** *conj.*

†**wandedes** *n pl.* evil actions Z 5.152n

wandren *v* wander, roam about Pr 21, 6.205, 8.325, **A** 8.79, 10.212, move about B 9.55; *and see* **of-** ~ *v*

wangteeth *n pl.* molars 22.191

wanhope *n* despair (of God's mercy) 2.103, 7.58, 80, (B 13.421), 14.118, 19.293, **B** 5.279, 7.35, 13.407, (*person.*) 7.58, 11.198, 22.160, 166, 168

wanyen *v* wane, decline, *in phr.* **waxen and** ~ 10.44, **B** 7.55, 15.3

wanne *a* pallid 6.418

wannes Z 6.1 = **whennes** *av*

wanten *v* (*impers.*) be wanting, lack 9.106, B 14.173, *ger.* 177

wanto(w)(e)n *a* lascivious 3.142, 7.299; ~**nesse** *n* lasciviousness 3.160, B 12.6; unruliness A 10.67

war *p.t. pl.* Z 8.85 *see* **were(n)**

war *a* aware 11.87, B 2.8, A 3.56, **be** ~ take heed Pr 189, 3.142, 6.148, 9.236, 10.291, 11.80, B 10.269, A 3.56; beware 7.260, be on guard Pr 189, 1.40, 15.78; wary **B** 2.138, 20.163; *see* **ywa(e)r** *a*

waranten *v* declare for certain B 18.46

ward *n* regard, concern (for) Z Pr 99, 8.75; guard 20.365; watch, guardianship 5.185n; guardianship-case Pr 92n

wardeyn *n* guardian 1.51, B 16.187

#**wardemote** *n* meeting of (the citizens of) a (London) ward Pr 92

warden *v* guard 18.42

ware *n* wares, merchandise 2.223, 235, 6.95, 213

wareyne *n* warren [enclosed land for breeding game] B Pr 163

waren *v* (*refl.*) guard oneself 7.58, 10.287, Z 7.323

warien *v* curse 8.336

wariner A 5.159 = **wernare** *n*

warisshen *v* cure B 16.105

warm *a* warm 16.333, B 17.240; hot 19.172, 198, 206; fine, sunny (*comp.*) 20.456; **al** ~ while still alive A 7.170

warnen *v* (give a) warn(ing to) 8.342, 346, B Pr 208, 2.209, 4.69, 12.10; advise A 10.95; inform 5.132, 17.97, **B** 6.131, 15.362, 482, 18.300, A 2.165; command (under penalty) 3.427, 8.162, *ger.* 8.90

warner B 5.309 = **wernare** *n*

warpen *v* (*p.t.* **warp**) utter B 5.86, 363, **A** 4.142, 10.33

warrok(y)en *v* (fasten with a) girth 4.21

warth *p.t.* 5.98, 11.167 *see* **worthen** *v*

was *p.t. sg.* of **ben** *v* was Pr 15 *et p.*; (*with understood impers. subj.*) it was 6.4, 7.159, 11.239, 14.132, †15.52, **B** 14.7, 16.150; there was 1.150, 6.37, 7.298, 10.6, 117, 11.241, 14.159, 167, 20.459, B 10.226, A 2.41; (*with Ø-rel. subj.*) (who) was 6.308, 11.1, 290, 12.76, 22.221, 331, B 16.187; (which) was 15.61, B 12.73; (*with collective n. subj.*) 8.323, 12.49, 15.9, 10; (*with pl. n. subj.*) 3.12, 5.115, 6.393, 14.82, 17.199, 19.13, 21.47, 94, **B** 10.395, 12.45, 15.450, 16.204, 215, **A** 5.80, 11.272; came into being 18.217, 20.168; became 5.108, 6.148; occurred 5.115, B 10.129; appeared 20.238; was shown B 12.81; (*as p.t. auxil. with v. of motion*) had 15.154; *see also* **nas**, **were(n)**

waschen *v* (*p.t. sg., pl.* **wessh(en)** B 16.228, 2.221, 13.28, **wosch(en)** 18.244, 2.230, 15.38, *p.p.* **(y)wasche(n)** 9.268, B 13.460) wash 2.230, 9.80, 268, 18.244, **B** 11.431, 13.315, 14.18, 15.453, (*fig.*) **B** 15.192, 18.392; wash oneself 9.250, 15.32, 38, B 13.32, (*refl.*) 7.214; clean B 17.70; sweep (away) 10.228

waste *a* uncultivated 9.225; vain, profitless 21.287; *and see* **waast** *n*

wastel *n* cake / loaf of fine flour 6.340

wasten *v* consume 8.139, 10.301, B 6.133, A 5.25 (*or ?* spend); spend 19.248, **wastyng** *ger.* what one spends B 5.25; squander 21.356

wasto(u)r *n* squanderer [one who destroys by consuming without producing] Pr 24, 5.126, 8.27, 139, 158, 170, 208, 344, 21.438, 22.145, B 6.161, A 7.124; (*person.*) 8.149, 162, 164, 171, B 5.24; idle wastrel B 9.120

wat Z Pr 94, 5.43, 6.68, 7.232 = **what** *prn*

watelen *v* construct with wattle (*fig.*) 21.328

water *n* (the element of) water 5.148, 9.56, 10.131, 15.242, 19.195, 20.250; [=body of water], (water of) lake 10.33, 34, 44, 13.167, B 8.36, 18.243, Z 6.71; (water of) stream / river B Pr 9, 15.338, 453, (*fig.*) 7.214; flood 8.344; (drinking) water 21.109, A 7.168, *in phr.* **bred and** ~ 6.155; [= tears] 6.2, 326, 7.56, 16.333, 18.147, 21.380; [=urine] 2.234; *in phrr.* **a** ~ in the water [river, sea *etc*] 15.19, 20.29, B 16.189, **drop** ~ drop of water 6.335, **haly** ~ blessed water Z 8.75

watren *v* water (= flow with tears) 8.172

watri *a* watery, rain-bearing 20.456

watschoed 20.1 = **weetshoed** *a*

wauntounesse A 10.67 = **wanto(w)e(n)nesse** *n*

wawe *n* wave 10.45

wax(e) *p.t.* 6.421, 20.4, 133, 22.159, *pl.* ~**e(th)** 10.44, 12.231, 18.42, **A** 3.273, 6.50, 8.58, 10.126 *see* **waxen** *v*

waxen (wexen) *v* (*p.t.* **wax** Z 2.24, **we(e)x(e)** 3.483, **B** 5.279, 14.76, 15.3, 16.101, 215, 18.4, A 10.33, *pl.* **woxen B** 9.32, 14.60, *p.p.* **waxen** A 3.273, **wexen** 21.124, **woxe(n)** 3.211) grow 2.29, 12.231, 234, 16.253, 21.97, 124, 312, 377, 22.159, A 10.126; increase 22.269, *in phr.* ~ **and wanyen** 10.44, B 7.55, A 5.70, [in potency, influence] **B** 10.75, 15.3, A 10.61, ~ **an hey** acquire strength 6.124; arise 14.26, 32, 16.227, **B** 11.263, 14.76, A 5.72; be found 1.137, **B** 10.12, 15.459, 16.56; become 3.454, 483, 6.421, 7.77, 17.48, 18.42, 20.4, 133, **B** 4.174, 13.348, 14.323, 16.101, 215; turn into 10.197; fall 12.52, B 5.279; be born A 2.20; be created 15.263, B 9.32

we *1 pl. prn* we Pr 171 *et p.*; (*as subject with prec. subjv. v.*) = let us... Pr 174, 202, 228, 12.118, 121, 122, 13.17, 14.66, 67, 69, 17.111, 18.227, 20.165, 167, 205, 269, 284, 463, 21.360, 22.75, 78, **B** 4.195, 10.437, 11.211, 13.133, 14.81, 15.143, A 12.69; = if we... 17.92, B 13.6; = we would ... 10.189; (*collective*) 3.104, 9.125, 340 *et p.*, 10.54, 19.317, 21.64, **B** 7.126, 10.130, A 11.243; (*in apposition*) **we** ~ Pr 213, 8.6, 17.293, 21.417, **B** 9.87, 15.394; (*indef. generic*) 17.39; (*impers.*) = one 9.242; *in phrr.* ~ **(...) alle** all of us 12.119, 132, 187, 18.226, ~ **bothe** the two of us 20.168; ~ **vchone** each one of us 9.235; *and see* **oure, vs**

web(be) *n*[1] (whole) piece of woven cloth B 5.110 (A 5.92)

webbe *n*[2] weaver 9.204, [female] 6.221

webbestere *n* weaver Pr 223

wed *n* pledge, security 6.243, 13.43, 44, 18.279, 284, 22.13, **B** 5.240, 13.260; wager 3.258; *in phr.* **to wedde** in pledge, as a guarantee 5.73, 20.30

wedden *v* wager 2.36, 4.143; marry 2.123, 124, 3.19, 131, 153, 156, 4.10, 7.299, 9.167, 10.257, 271, 281, 284, 287, 22.160, **B** 9.125, 157, 164, 157, 10.151, 11.72, Z 8.32, *ger.* A 2.102, 10.184; (*fig.*) embrace 16.111; marry, *p.p.a* **wedded** joined in wedlock 2.166, 11.98; married 10.205, 296, 18.71, 22.112, B 9.108

weddewe 14.143 = **wedewe** *n*

weddyng *n* marriage (-ceremony) 2.118, 119, 151, 174

wede *n*[1] weed 8.118, 12.226, 21.314, A 10.126, Z 7.91

wede *n*[2] clothing 22.211; *pl.* clothes 6.177, 13.189, **B** 11.234, 15.226, Z 3.162

weden B 16.17 = **wedyen** *v*

weder *n* weather 6.113, 8.347, 20.456, B 15.355; storm 10.46, 12.191, B 15.362, 482

wederwyse *a* skilled in forecasting the weather 17.94

wedeware *n* widower 10.284, 18.76

wedewe *n* widow 3.160, 420, 4.47, 6.143, 8.12, 10.284, 12.20, 18.71, 76, **B** 9.69, 164, 13.197, 16.214, 216, 218, A 8.32; (consecrated) widow 14.143

wedewhed, wydwehode *n* (the state of) widowhood 18.109, B 16.203

wed(y)en *v* (uproot) weed(s) 8.66, B 16.17, *ger.* 8.186

wedlok (wedlak) *n* (the state of) marriage, matrimony 10.294, 18.88, **B** 9.114, 117, 191, 16.203, 216, 218, A 10.133; marital union B 9.154; *in phrr.* **mariage of** ~ the bond of matrimony A 10.207, **out of** ~ illegitimately B 9.120

wedore 20.456 = **weder** *n*

weel 4.21 = **wel** *av*

weend *imper.* B 3.266 = **wenden** *v*

weer B 11.116, 16.3 *see* **wer** *n*

weere *p.t. subjv.* (= were) B 15.3, 17.77

weete B 14.171 = **wet(e)** *n*

weet *a* damp, rain-sodden B 14.42

#weetschoed *a* with wet feet 16.14, 20.1

weex *p.t.* **B** 3.331, 5.279, 14.76, 15.3, 16.101, 215, 18.4, 130 *see* **waxen** *v*

wehe(e) *n* (*imit.*) neigh, whinny B 4.23, 7.90

wey[1] 1.137, 6.265, 11.106, 13.29, 33, 41, B 5.555, A 7.53 = **way** *n*

wey[2] 19.67, 20.365 = **w(e)y(e)** *n*[2]

wey[3] *n* whey Z.7.286

weye *n*[1] wey [measure of weight, here = 3 cwt]

w(e)y(e) *n*[2] man 3.225, 6.105, 7.157, 13.13, 157, 14.195 (*with play on* **way**) 18.229, 279, 19.67, 20.327, 365, 21.166, †230, **B** 5.533, †10.108, 11.382, 12.293, 13.32, 191, 361, 14.156, 17.99, **A** 6.41, 92, †10.89, 11.67, **Z** 3.115, 5.43; person A 11.224, Z 1.6

wey(3)en, (wayen) *v* (*p.p.* 1.173, 9.271) weigh [in scales] 1.173, 6.210, 224, 242, 9.271, Z 5.100

w(e)y(g)ht *n* (measuring) weight 6.258, 16.128, 19.246

weylawey B 18.228 = **wel-a-way**[2]

weylen B 14.324, *pr.p.* A 5.254 *see* **waylen** *v*

weke *n* wick (of torch / taper) 19.170, 172, 179, 206

wel[1] Z 7.286 = **welle** *n*

wel(e)[2] *a* in favour with 3.190; prosperous, happy Z 3.173, *in phrr.* ~ **be** 8.299, ~ **worth** 13.1, 21.433; good (*as n*) 11.274n; *in phrr.* ~ **dedes** 3.69, 15.305, B 3.70, ~ **hope** 7.113; sound, right 11.274n, Z Pr 71; in good order, satisfactory 4.183

wel[3] *av* well [morally, = justly, right(eous)ly] (*with* **don, werchen** *etc*) 1.131, 9.321, 10.25, 189(1), 204, 11.215, 226, 14.10, 13, 15.115(1), 16.34, 175, 219, 17.182, 21.481, **B** 1.130, 3.233, 8.56, 9.93, 95, 12.32, **A** 10.75, 88, 11.162, 199, 12.36; kindly 11.116; favourably 7.267, 12.141, B 14.145; faithfully 19.227, **B** 4.181 11.263; carefully 4.52, 9.147, 12.91, 17.116, 21.279, **B** Pr 208, 14.81, 16.47, Z 7.323; properly 4.21, 7.198, 214, 225, 12.237, 13.234, 14.18, 159, 16.321, 17.122, 21.62, 22.231, **B** Pr 152, 5.260, 8.52, 14.278 (2), 14.311; prosperously 5.8, 22.235; profitably B 5.262; deeply B 5.176; easily, readily 13.211, 14.126, 15.46, 16.129, 18.224, 19.242, 21.62, 438, 22.323, **B** 6.46, 8.51, 9.39, 16.218; effectively, successfully 3.48, 12.193, 20.183, 22.305 **B** 5.560, 12.38; thoroughly, completely 2.47, 18.245, **B** 6.195, 13.179, 15.453, **A** 3.75, 5.241, 11.141, 182, *in phr.* ~ **at ese** 15.48, B 16.227; certainly, for sure (*esp. with* **knowen, leuen, seyen, witen** *etc*) Pr 100, 2.142, 3.59, 225, 312, 4.76, 154, 6.326, 8.139, 211, 258, 270, 9.128, 10.137, 202, 242, 11.210, 12.82, 13.81, 14.126, 15.115 (2), 16.235, 281, 17.165, 217, 19.9, 20.224, 342, 21.26, 253, 361, 411, **B** 1.51, 3.217, 337, 4.71, 8.73, 10.154, 13.132, 14.82, 282, 15.263, 461, 553, 18.215, **A** 4.67, 12.99, **Z** 3.171, 5.35; clearly **B** 2.189, 12.20, 153, 15.591; familiarly, intimately 4.32, 15.31, 37, 16.157, 20.252, 22.338, B 13.131; closely B 16.214; satisfactorily 4.96, 7.193, 8.115, 9.289, 21.194, B 14.150, 153; fully 6.108, 161, 8.208, 300, **B** 15.187, 17.73; *as intensive* (*with v*) very much 1.41, **B** 3.54, 13.264, 14.167, (*with a or av*) very 4.53, 6.48, 418, 7.299, 306, 9.67, 236, 244, 11.5, 14.152, 18.111, 22.25, 39, 194, 303, **B** 4.46, 11.35, 194, 14.278(1), **A** 2.56, 105, 3.71, 5.75, 78, 104, 154, 11.157, 12.43, 100, 106; (*with comp. a or av*) much Pr 117, 122, 3.141, 6.200, 10.189 (2), 12.153, 22.62, B 5.113, 140; that much B 13.24, A 7.138; (*av in cpds., with p.pl.*) 10.263, 268, 11.236, 15.64, **B** 10.430, 11.39, 396, (*with v*) **bidde** ~ 7.239, **do** ~ 9.289, **kepe** ~ B 10.165, **se** ~ **wel** *etc* 10.146–8; *in phrr.* ~ **awey** far and away **B** 12.262, 17.43, A 11.218; ~ **neyh** pretty well, almost 15.294; **fareþ** ~ farewell B 13.181; **as ~... as...** both ...and... 6.182, 12.117, 15.14, 16.233, 19.45, 21.438, 22.61, B 15.449

welawey[1] *av* A 11.218 = **wel awey**; *see* **wel** *av*

wel-a-way[2] 20.237 *see* **welowo** *excl.*

Welche B 5.195 *see* **Wal(s)(c)he** *a as n*

welcome *a* welcome 2.227, 242, 5.50, 7.278, 22.244, 357, B 13.157; *interj.* B 13.32, A 12.62

welcomen *v* welcome 7.96, 9.135, 15.31, 37, 200, 16.170, 20.178, 21.211, 22.60

welden *v* (*contr. pr.* **welt** B 10.85) get control of 12.20, B 10.24; hold A 7.151; possess 11.10, 72, 14.18, 22.12, **B** †9.39, 10.29, 85, 90, Z 7.212

wele[1] *n* wealth, riches 12.238, 15.308; abundance B 19.287; happiness 11.107, 275, 12.211, 20.208, 209, 210, 229, 237; prosperity 21.244, 453, **Z** 3.173c, 7.281

wele[2] (? = **wel** *a*) 11.274n, c

welfare *n* good living 21.356

welhope *n* (state of) good hope B 13.454

welkene *n* sky, (vault of) heaven B 15.361; upper air (*aether*) 20.246, B 17.161

well 2.47, 14.126 = **wel** *av*

wel(le) *n* spring of water Z 7.286; (*fig.*) source, origin 1.159, 16.39, 142, 188; well Z 5.70

wellen (wallen) *v* boil Z 7.286; rise up 21.380

welowo *excl. as n* misery 16.77; *excl.* woe! 20.237

welt *contr. pr.* B 10.85 *see* **welden** *v*

welthe *n* happiness, (worldly) well-being Pr 10, 12.158; prosperity 9.116; wealth, riches 9.336, 10.271, 13.13, 16.19, 22.38, B 10.24; valuable possessions B 10.85; goods 1.51; value, worth 4.158, B 9.164

wem *n* stain [of sin] 20.134

wen Z Pr 1, 8.70 *etc* = **when(n)e** *conj.*

wenche *n* girl B 9.163; young woman 12.11, 18.134, 20.116; woman Z 6.88, 101; maidservant, ? daughter 6.414; mistress Pr 52; ~ **of the stuyues** prostitute 21.438, 22.160

wende *p.t.* 6.32, 41 (B 13.280, 292), **B** 5.234, 13.407, **A** 11.219, 224, *2 sg.* **wendest** B 3.192 *see* **wenen** *v*

wenden *v* (*p.t.* **wente** Pr 4 *et p.*, *pl.* **wenten** Pr 49 *etc*, *p.p.* **went** 3.434, 8.211) turn, change 2.247, 3.434, 20.208; turn away 22.284; go (travel, journey) Pr 52, 158, 181, 1.131, 2.174, 218, 3.13, 4.53, 72, 5.104, 6.211, 351, 7.204, 8.4, 57, 62, 94, 186, 211, 278, 10.200, 13.33, 51, 15.32, 162, 16.322, 17.190, 18.290, 19.48, 334, 20.129, 178, 329, 21.129, 193, 334, 358, 22.204, 382, **B** 4.105, 18.299, **A** 10.143, 177, 11.168, 277, 12.51, 89; go about **B** Pr 162, 8.6; go off, depart 8.209, 220, 299, 301, 11.105, 15.151, 18.181, 21.78, 322, ~ **hennes** depart this life 1.173, 6.312; ~ **forth** proceed Pr 4, 49, 10.61, 15.186, 20.1, **B** 15.338, 16.146, A 12.56; walk 20.250, 252; *in phrr.* ~ **(by) the wey** go along the road 13.41, 15.191, 19.92, 22.1, ~ **(my** *etc*) go on (one's) way 11.136, B 10.221

wenen *v* (*p.t.* **wende** B 5.234, A 11.219, (*subjv.* 6.32, 41), *2 sg.* **wendest** B 3.192) think 11.239, 13.160, 14.166, 16.130, *in parenth. phr.* **as I** ~ I (should) think, in my opinion 9.70, 13.160, 20.225, 329, **B** 3.227, 8.69, A

5.70; believe 16.304, **B** 13.407, 15.477, 600; suppose 3.454, 6.24, 20.194, 22.32, **B** 3.192, 5.234, A 11.219, 224; hope 6.322, 14.195; *ger.* **wenyng** (mere) surmise 22.33; hope, fantasy B 2.91

wenge *n* wing 14.186, **goose** ~ = thing of no worth B 4.37

went *p.p.* 3.434, 8.211, B 6.204, ~**e(n)** *p.t.* Pr 4, 49 *etc*; *see* **wenden** *v*

wente *n* trick, contrivance 6.263

wepen *v* (*p.t.* **wep** 6.316, A 2.198, Z 5.91, *pl.* **wopen** 9.41, **wepide** A 4.60, **wepte** 2.252, *pl.* **wepten** B 7.37) weep 2.252, 6.316, 9.41, 11.166, 12.84, 16.77, 18.109, 289, 20.94, **B** 1.180, 5.112, 7.121, 11.148, 13.267, ~ **on** beseech (sb.) with tears A 4.60; weep for one's sins 5.108, 16.334, 22.370, **B** 5.185, 11.263, 14.332, A 5.254, *ger.* A 8.108; *in phrr.* ~ **teres** 15.51, B 12.45 ~ **water with eyes** 6.2, 326, 18.147, B 14.324

wep(e)ne (wypne) *n* weapon 3.458, 14.50, (*fig.*) 21.219, 227, (*euphem. for*) penis 10.289

weps (wispe) *n* wisp, handful 6.401

wepte(n) *p.t.* 2.252 *etc*, B 7.37 *see* **wepen** *v*

wer *n* confusion, perplexity 12.52, B 16.3

wer *p.t. subjv.* Pr 180 *see* **wer(i)en** *v*

werchen *v* (*p.t.* **wro(u)ʒte** B 1.13, 82 *etc*, *p.p.* **(y)wroʒt** B 3.239 *et p.*; *see* **worchen** *v*

wercus *pl.* Z 4.120 *see* **werk** *n*

werd Z 5.43 = **world** *n*

werde *p.t.* A 2.12 *see* **weren** *v*

were(n) *p.t. pl. of* **ben** *v* (*indic.*) were Pr 53 *et p.*, 6.41 *etc*, (*with subj. om.*) **B** 11.225, 15.73; (*with sg. subj.*) 16.346, 18.233, 22.65, †B 5.378, A Pr 81; *p.t.sg. (subjv.)* Pr 2, 180 *et p.*, *pl.* 8.136 *etc*; existed Pr 80, 11.206, 12.143, 14.71; should exist 14.166, 18.186, 212; would be 3.171, 6.110, 8.5, B 3.346, A 12.17; should be 2.68, 125, 6.387, B 5.165; might be 1.10, 68, 3.152, 383, 10.200, 12.4 *etc*, **B** 11.246, 14.128, 15.3, 17.77, A 12.80; *in constr.* **as...were** as if (It / he *etc*) were Pr 2, 66, 5.160, 6.156, *etc*, **B** 5.100; *in* (*semi-*)*parenth. phr.* **as hit** ~ as it were, so to speak Pr 11, 2.9, 54, 5.124, 9.114, 210, 12.185, 13.113, 152, 15.176, 16.113, 18.6, 19.253, **B** 12.217, 17.95, 201, as might happen / be the case 6.110, 13.8, 20.116, 200, B 15.205; (*with subj. omitted*) **ne** ~ were it not for **B** 10.45, 18.210, A 11.51

wery *a* tired (out) B Pr 7, 13.205, 15.186; discontented 20.4; ~**nesse** *n* fatigue Pr 7

wer(i)en *v* (*p.p.* **wered** 5.81) wear 3.447, 19.237, **B** 14.329, 15.451, Z 3.162; ~ **out** abolish / exhaust [with the passage of time] 5.81

werk *n* act, deed 1.171, 11.315, 12.141, A 10.65; (= the sexual act) 6.181, 184 (B 13.348), B 9.129, A 10.208; [physical] action 12.128; [moral] action Pr 3, 1.85, 2.206, 4.71, 80, 104, 11.11, 219, 222, 223, **B** 2.130, 3.69, 239, 10.113, 395, 430, 13.295, 14.224, 15.204,

17.102, **A** 10.92, 11.68, 272, Z 3.172; **euel / wikked** ~ sinful act(ion) 6.21, 18.38, 19.296, 21.380, 22.371, B 15.355, **lecherouse** ~ B 2.125; (good) work, (pious / religious) act 6.41, 53, 9.349, 12.83, 14.25, 28, 16.340, 18.12, **B** 10.412, 432, 15.186, 449, **A** 10.130, 12.98; work, labour 5.54, B 12.27; (physical) labour A 7.137; enterprise, undertaking B 9.206; creation 12.75, 18.214, B 1.150; (literary) work / composition A 12.101, 103; workmanship Pr 179; *in phrr.* **a** ~ **to work** 8.197; **Godes** ~ act God approves 10.290, B 10.67; (**worchen**) **in** ~ actually perform 4.143, B 10.254; (**with**) ~ **and / or with word** (by) both action and word(s) 2.94, 6.99, 13.192, **B** 5.85, 366, 9.51, 13.141, 146, 312, 14.14, B 15.116, 198, 477, A 7.211; **Neither þoruʒ wordes ne** ~ B 15.210

werk(e)man *n* workman, labourer 5.25, 7.41, 8.116, 186, 336, 342, 11.241, 19.184, **B** 5.277, 6.51, 132, 13.268, 14.137, Z 7.325

werken B Pr 37, **A** 11.276, 12.97 *see* **worchen** *v*

werkmanschip *n* labour, work B 10.288; action B 9.45; performance 2.96; activity 19.142

wern *p.t.* A 7.180, 10.159, 11.220, 224 = **were(n)** *v* 172, 198

wernard *n* deceiver 2.142, B 3.180

wernare *n* warriner [keeper of game-preserve] 6.362

wernen *v* refuse 22.12

werre *n* war 13.140, 20.236, 459, *in phrr.* ~ **and / or wo** 3.205, 17.204, B 18.414; ~ **and wrake** 17.85, 20.458; **at** ~ in conflict 16.64; **to** ~ to go to war 22.259; battle 11.267, 22.163

werren *v* make war (upon) 17.234

wers *comp.* A 11.218, B 1.26; ~**e** B 5.113, 10.421, A 6.46 *see* **wors(e)** *a*, *av*

wesch *n* wish, object of desire 6.66

weschen *v* wish, desire 6.401, 10.271, 15.90, 19.330, 22.194, **B** 5.110, 10.468, 12.270, *ger.* desire 2.95

wessh *p.t.* B 16.228, *pl.* ~**en** B 2.221, 13.28 = **wosch(en)** *see* **waschen** *v*

west *n* west 20.116, *a* B 18.113; ~**ward** *av* towards the west Pr 16, 20.121, B 16.169 *and see* **south** ~ **(wynde)**

Westminstre *n as a*, ~ **lawe** the law of the land, the king's justice 10.242

wet(e)[1] *n* wet weather 7.175, B 14.171; rain (water) 19.306

wete[2] Z 7.170 = **whete** *n*

weten 4.100, 18.147, Z 2.2 *see* **witen** *v*

wethe *n* withy, **in a** ~ **wyse** as if with a withy Z 5.160

weth(e)wynde *n* bindweed, ~ **wyse** woodbine-fashion 7.162

wether *n* (castrated) ram 9.267

weuen[1] *v* A 6.92 = **wayuen** *v*

weuen[2] *v* weave B 5.548; *ger.* **fro þe weuyng** from being woven B 15.451

weuere *n* weaver B Pr 220

wex(e) *n* wax Pr 99, 10.272, 19.170, 172, 198

wex(e) *p.t.* 3.483, A 2.20, *pl.* A 10.33 *see* **wexen** *v*[1]

wexen[1] 1.137, 2.29, 7.77, 12.52, 234, 14.32, 15.263, 16.227, 253, 17.48, 21.97, 312, 377, 22.269, **B** 4.174, 10.12, 11.263, 13.348, 14.323, 15.459, **A** 5.72, 61, 11.12 = **waxen** *v*

#wexen[2] *v* wax-polish 6.401c

wham *interrog.* 1.43, 13.158, 16.141, 17.89, 20.177, (*rel.*) 1.179, 7.168 = **whom** *prn*

whan(ne) Pr 1, 1.103 *etc*, B 1.25 *et p.*, A 3.96 *et p.*, *in phr.* ~ **þat** B 10.137 *see* **when(ne)** *conj.*

whare *av* 8.166, 10.124, *in phr.* ~ **þat** 11.104; *see* **wher(e)**[2] *av*

whareof 16.171 = **wherof** *av*

what (*interrog.*) *prn* what Pr 217, 1.11 *et p.*, who 10.70, 13.219, **B** 2.18, 10.219, *a* 1.68 *et p.*, which 3.6, 4.53, 10.5, 20.176; what sort of 8.270, 15.251, 20.360; (*excl.*) *a* what great Pr 105, 13.14 *etc*; *prn* what **B** 7.131, 13.184, 18.187; [as call to attention] lo, see! 8.148 (1); hey!, come on! 7.8; (*rel.*) *prn* (= that which) 3.484, 6.47, 8.88, 13.35, *etc*; as to what was 13.175; whatever **B** 3.266, 5.547, 9.58, ~ **þat** whatever 8.148 (2), what A 3.106; ~**...** **þat** any...who B 3.324; *a* whatever 2.34, 7.145, 9.153, 17.174, 22.67, **B** Pr 207, 9.196, 12.74, A 6.80; whichever 6.247, 301, 19.117, 21.196; *in phrr.* ~ **done** what kind of B 18.300; ~ **euere** *prn* whatever 7.125, B 11.215; ~ **man** = who B 13.25, = whoever 2.36, ~**so** whatever 14.65, B 10.130, A 10.96, ~ **soeuere** *prn* whatever B 10.388; *conj.* whether 17.85, B 13.317, ~ **for** both for 20.113, ~ **thorw** what with 17.85

wheche 7.69 = **whiche** *prn*

wheder[1] *conj.* whether 1.137

wheder[2] A 12.80 = **whoder** *av*

wheiþer *prn* B 14.248, 16.96 *see* **whether** *prn*; B 1.48, 8.127, 11.83, 117, 188, 14.101 *see* **wher(e)**[3] *conj.*

when A 12.80 = **whennes** *av*

when(ne) *conj.* when 1.45, 81 *et p.*; = whenever 3.169, 8.154, 17.173, A 8.122, ~ **þat** whenever 18.160, when B 10.137; at whatever time A 8.37; after 13.146, 15.24, 16.5, 22.1, 51; if 3.398, 4.52, 5.149, 6.59, 77, 8.37, 16.303, A 12.33

whennes *av* (*interr.*) whence, from where (*prec. by* **of**, **fro(m)**) 7.169, 18.184, 291, A 12.80

wher(e)[1] 16.88 *see* **whether** *prn*

wher(e)[2] *av and conj.* where Pr 159 *et p.*, **loo / se** ~ 2.5, 18.242, 20.170, 341; where (to) Pr 181, 15.151, 16.176; to whichever place 3.175; wherever 15.162, 18.251, 20.298; in the circumstances in which 1.22; from whom 13.169; in whomever B 3.176; to whom(ever) 3.19, 227, 6.343; *in phrr.* ~ **forth** towards whichever direction 16.340, B 17.115, ~ **þat** 7.197, where 10.13, 75, 13.136, wherever 21.129

wher(e)[3] (whe(i)þer) *conj.* whether Pr 186, 2.149, 3.296, 9.240, 277, 11.275, 12.22, 53, 14.191, 193, 213, 15.261, 16.97, 18.54, 57, 224, 20.72, 217, 331, 429, 21.353, 22.107, B 10.432, A 1.46, (wheiþer) B 1.48 *etc*; (*as particle introducing question*: does...?; is...?) 15.281, 16.337, 17.150, 19.27, B 17.125

wherby *av* (*interrog.*) by what means, how? B 10.435; (*rel.*) by means of which 3.249, 12.187, B 14.41; as a consequence of which 5.34

wher(e)fore *av* (*interrog.*) for what reason 12.36, **B** 11.85, 432, 15.200, *in phr.* ~ **and why** 13.185, 241, (**why and** ~) B 11.301; (*rel.*) by reason of which 15.241; for which reason 1.17, **B** 15.347, 384, 16.134, ~ **and why** 21.84

whereon *av* (*rel.*) on which 19.13

whereso *av, conj.* wherever 6.27, ~ **þat** †6.99, ~ **euere** *av, conj.* wherever B 18.375

wherof *av* (*interrog.*) from what source **B** 12.221, 15.14; to what purpose 12.33, 16.171, (*rel.*) from which 3.60; out of which B 11.263; by means of which 15.241; of which B 19.140

wherwith *av as n* the means by which 6.316, 15.241, B 9.69

whete *n* wheat [grain] 3.42, 4.60, 8.8, 327, Z 7.170, ~ **breed** bread of wheat-flour **B** 6.137, 7.121; wheat [crop] 12.183, 193, 234, 13.42, B 6.32, A 10.126

whether (where) *prn* which of the two 9.277, 16.88, B 16.56, A 12.37

why *av* (*interrog.*) why 3.228, 12.24, 13.193, 195, 15.75, 95, 17.204, 18.84, 20.65, 21.15, **B** 3.260, 9.87, 10.107, 113, 119, 126, 263, 11.76, 12.219, 232, 234, 13.460, 16.24, *in phr.* **wherefore and** ~ 13.185, 241, 21.84; *as n* reason why, **þe** ~ 18.147, *pl.* 14.156, B 10.124, (*ellip.*) 10.248, 13.230, 245, 14.99, 153, 166

whicche *n* clothes-chest 4.111

which(e) (*interrog.*) *a* what (kind of) 4.26, 9.300, 20.127, A 7.124; *prn* which 7.69, 14.108, **B** 10.265, 17.24, 115, A 11.89; (*excl.*) what 11.26; (*rel.*) *a* which 3.196, 9.156, 14.119, **B** 2.108, 13.129, (*with art.*) **þe** ~ 9.137, 15.278, 18.11, 20.339, 22.62, **B** 10.238, 12.86, 13.408, ~ **a** which (kind of) 4.26, A 11.68; *prn* which, that 1.37, 3.365, 7.69, †10.301, 11.288, 19.326, **B** 5.290, 10.133, 323, 435, 11.264, 347, 13.85, 130, 313, 14.83, 16.224, A 10.122, (*with art.*) **þe** ~ 3.496, 5.31, 7.99, 9.107, 137, 140, 10.154, 171, 11.82, 12.152, 13.81, 14.54, 16.27, 112, 17.140, 247, 18.12, 14, 51, 72, 207, 235, 19.8, 87, 20.110 , 223, 21.80, 129, 22.62, **B** 10.475, 11.318, 15.131, 16.148, (= who) 3.191, **B** 6.132, 15.421, 18.134, (= whom) 19.39, B 16.232, (= of whom) 9.98, (*with Ø-antecedent*) those whom 20.449; *in phr.* **þe** ~ **þat** who, which 3.93, 10.184

whider(-out, -ward) **B** 15.13, 16.12, 175, 5.300 *see* **whode(r)-** *av*

whil *n* (space of) time 4.44, B 6.162, *in avl. phrr.* (= for

... time): **eny** ~ 3.204, 4.171, 5.25, B 13.332, **gret** ~ B 4.46, **(a) litel** ~ 1.106, 12.224, 19.47, **longe** ~ 4.44, **þe** ~**(s)** meanwhile 8.6, 20.167 (*see also* **hand** ~, **mynte** ~, **o(u)þer** ~, **Paternoster** ~); short time, moment Pr 16, 4.16, 21.357, B 3.331

whil(e)(s) *conj.* while, as long as Pr 84, B 2.107, A 7.134 *et p.*, Z 5.73, **þe** ~ while Pr 188 *et p.*, **al þe** ~ A 7.134, ~ **þat** B 1.16, A 12.51

whil er *av* some time ago 10.292

whilen (whilom, whilum) *av* at one time, formerly 9.204, 196, 17.9, 99

whistlen *v* play upon a pipe / whistle B 15.474, *ger.* whistling, piping B 15.463, 473, 478

whistlere *n* whistle / pipe-player = ? 'mouthpiece / spokesman' B 15.482.

whit(e) *a* white Pr 230, 6.103, 20.212, 213, **B** 10.435, 15.408

whiten *v* become white 16.333; **do** ~ have whitewashed B 3.61

whith 3.130 = **wiht(e)** *n*

whitlymen *v* wash with white-lime 16.266

who *prn* (*interrog.*) who 6.419 *etc*, B 3.235 *etc*, (*indef.*) 1.84 *etc*, **as** ~ **B** 9.36, 15.307; *and see* **ho** *prn*

whom (wham) *prn interrog.* (*acc.*) whom 7.168, 20.177, B 18.174; (*dat.*) whom 1.43, 3.221, 6.343, 13.158, 16.141, 17.89, B 1.49; to whom B 15.318; (*rel.*) whom 1.179, 7.168

whos *prn interrog.* (*gen.*) whose 2.17, 1.46 (**hoes**)

whoso Pr 205, 1.57, 11.72, B 1.88 *et p.*, A 12.3 *see* **hoso** *indef. prn*

whode(r) *av* where, whither 18.181, 292, **B** 15.13, 16.175; # ~ **out** forth to where 7.177, from whence, in what place B 16.12; ~ **ward** in what direction 6.353

wy A 6.41, 92, †10.89, 11.67 = **w(e)y(e)** *n*²

wicche *n* sorcerer B 18.46, 69; witch 6.81 (B 13.338), B 18.338; ~ **craft** *n* magic B 13.169; sorcery 20.46, B 16.120

wicke 21.443, A 12.37, **wickede** 3.205, 9.31; *see* **wikke,** **wikkede** *a*

wid(e) *a* ample, extensive 20.45, B 16.134; far-spreading 9.111, 21.36, 335, B 17.160; capacious 18.270

wyde *av* far abroad 7.175, 10.14, 200, 21.335, 22.382, **B** Pr 4, 14.98; extensively 13.185, A 12.43, *comp.* **wyddore** more extensively 20.400; further 2.213; fully 20.365

wy(d)d(e)we 4.47, 6.143, **B** 9.69, 13.197, 16.214, 216, 218, A 8.32 *see* **wedewe** *n*

wyd(e)w(e)hode 18.88, B 16.203 *see* **wedewhed** *n*

widewhar(e) *av* in distant places 17.271; far and wide 10.61

wye 7.157, 18.229, **B** 5.533 *etc*, A 6.41 *etc*; *see* **w(e)y(e)** *n*²

wierd 14.32 = **wyrd** *n*

wyf *n* (*dat. sg.* **wyue** 10.145, *pl.* **wyues** 3.160 *et p.*, *gen.*

pl. **wyuen(e)** 5.131) woman B 5.561, A 7.10, Z Pr 48*n*; lady, mistress (of household) **B** 10.223, 224, 15.428; married woman 3.420, B 3.268, A 8.32; wife 2.17, 4.46, 5.132, 6.143, 221, 231, 362, 414, 420, 7.219, 8.55, 10.226, 272, 291, 296, 11.1, 116, 139, 243, 12.158, 13.13, 17.37, 39, 18.245, 19.301, 306, 312, 20.472, 22.193, **B** 5.226, 9.113, 10.223, 229, **A** 10.208, 1.93, 178, (= **Adam's**) 18.230, **Clergies** ~ 11.98, **Peres** ~ 8.80, 105, 182, **Pilates** ~ B 18.300; **to** ~, **wyue** as a wife 3.146, 368, 4.158 *in phr.* **wedden (a)** ~ 2.166, 3.156, 7.299, 11.98, ~ **and wedewes** 3.160, 6.143, 8.12

wight(e) (wiȝt)¹ 1.59, **B** 3.227, 10.168 *etc* = **wiht(e)** *n*

wyght(e)² 16.128 = **w(e)y(g)ht** *n*

wyht(e) (wight(e), wiȝt) *n* creature 1.59, 20.238, B 8.53; person, man 13.219, 220, **B** Pr 208, 3.227, 9.60, 13.193, 15.200, A 12.89; anyone 10.6, 15.167, B 8.69; **eny** ~ anyone / body 10.4, 16.218, 21.395, **B** 12.25, 13.123, 324, 16.12, **no** ~ no one / body 10.71, 11.273, 16.304, 20.68, 210, 225, 236, **B** 3.227, 13.176, ~ **noon** anyone 22.13, B 5.513, **vch (ech) (a)** everybody 9.116, 13.93, **B** 5.115, 6.246, 10.168, A 10.71; *in av. phrr.* **a litel** ~ a little bit 3.130, **no** ~ not at all †B 10.274

wyht *a* vigorous 10.147; brave, powerful 15.173; ~**li(che)** *av* vigorously 8.18; quickly 18.292, B 10.221, A 2.170; ~ **nesse** *n* strength 11.287, ~ **of handes** main force 21.247

wyke¹ 19.206 = **weke** *n*

wyke² **B** 10.96, 13.155 = **woke** *n*

wiket *n* wicket-gate B 5.602

wikke *a* bad, ? wicked 7.117c, 21.443; *as av* wickedly 16.175, A 12.37; *as n* bad, evil 14.164, 166, 21.443

wik(k)ed(e) *a* wicked, evil 1.111, 129, B 4.62, 68, A 11.263, ~ **dede(s)** 1.30, 6.333, 10.240, B 4.68, ~ **folk** B 5.150, ~ **hefdes** 17.85, ~ **hertes** 14.25, ~ **man** 4.65, 14.134, B 16.146, ~ **men** 8.27, 16.275, **B** 5.263, 10.24, ~ **spiritus** Pr 18, ~ **werkes** 18.38, 19.296, 21.380, 22.371, B 15.355, ~ **wille** (= ill-will) 7.41, B 13.321, (= evil will) B 9.206, Z 5.94, *a as n* evil 11.274, A 11.263; evil ones B 1.124, **þe** ~ B 8.97; wrong-doers 20.427, 434, 21.199; vicious 7.260, 16.240, 21.356, (*comp.*) 19.104, B 5.150; dishonest B 5.225; bad, pernicious 3.205, 6.162, 19.301, 312, A 10.65; cruel, severe ?7.117, 11.275; harmful 12.238, B 13.324; destructive 18.29, 31, (*comp.*) 20.459, B 5.160; malicious 21.287; harmful B 13.324; difficult 7.306 (B 6.1); in poor condition 9.31

wikkedli(che) *av* wrongfully 6.310, 8.235, 16.274, (*sup.*) ~ **lokest** most iniquitously B 10.426; sinfully, viciously 1.26, B 5.364, A 11.292; dishonestly 6.210, 19.248, B 5.225; severely 22.303

wikkednesse *n* wicked / evil action(s) 11.209, **B** 8.98, 16.157; iniquity **B** 5.283, 18.415; vicious conduct B 5.178, 185, A 5.207

wil¹ 4.22 *et p.*, (*person.*) (a) 7.233, 12.2, ?Z 4.20c (b) B 8.126 *etc*; *see* **wil(le)** *n*; **wyl** Z 7.281 *see* **wele**¹ *n*

wyl² Z 2.2, 41, 3.162 *see* **willen** *v*

wyl³ Z 4.89, 7.119, 281 = **wel³** *av*

wilde *a* wild, ~ **bestes** 16.10, 17.28, **B** 7.90, 11.354, 15.299, 459, ~ **foules** 8.30, B 15.302; ~ **brawen** of wild boar B 13.63; ~ **worm(es)** 13.137, 15.293, B 14.42; desolate 9.225, 10.62, 19.54, B 15.459 (1), *a as n* wild creatures 13.169, 15.296; ungovernable B 12.6, A 10.57

wildefowel *n* wild game birds B 10.361

wildernesse *n* wild, uncultivated region 10.62, 17.28, 19.54, **B** Pr 12, 15.273, 459, 17.99

wyle Z 3.28, 33, 5.73, 123, 7.59, ~ **þat** Z 3.124 *see* **while(s)** *conj.*

wilen B 2.233, 6.58, 13.258, A 2.53 *et p.*; *see* **willen** *v*

wyles *n.pl.* cunning / deceitful tricks 10.136, 13.74, 18.45, 175, 19.242, 246, 22.124, **B** 4.34, 10.109, 15.234, 408, (*person.*) 4.77; stratagems 21.100

wilfulli(che) 4.46, 19.269, 21.373 = **willefolliche** *av*

wily ~ *a* crafty, ~ **man** (*person.*) 4.27, 31

wil(le) *n* desire, wish Pr 174, 3.236, 365, 12.2 (2), 15.90, 17.195, 18.164, 19.289; **B** 5.102, 13.141, 17.179, **grete** ~ 12.85, 15.186, will [of God] 7.142, 11.309, 14.160, 16.27, 18.28, 121, 133, **B** 1.82, 14.125, 15.262, 483, A 5.241; carnal desire 2.96, 6.181, 190, 18.76, B 13.348, **flesches** ~ 20.202, A 9.45; (what one) desire(s) 2.67, 3.29, 152, 8.82, 153, 11.87, 90, 183, 12.140, 13.248, 15.123, 16.101, 17.143, 21.450, 22.203, 332, **B** 3.7, 11.26, 15.486, **A** 2.24, 53, 7.261; (express) wish, command 2.34, 218, 3.246, 325, 12.172, 20.103, **B** 3.265, 5.608, 9.115; will(ing) 6.167; intent, determination 1.109, 2.103, 5.185, 11.87, 13.94, 14.26, 15.277, B 13.194, **kene** ~ 16.81, 22.375, **B** 12.251; intention 3.71, 6.273, 15.156, 20.435, **B** 8.94, 16.149, A 11.68, *in phr.* **of o(n)** ~ united in purpose 15.277, 16.179, 17.128, 18.190, with a single purpose B 3.238; disposition, attitude (of mind / heart) 12.141, 14.211, 16.204, 19.204, **B** 13.141, 191, 14.14, 15.210, 16.233; (faculty of) will(ing) 16.175, (*person.*) 1.5 *et p.* (*see Index*); wilfulness, self-will 4.22, 23, B 11.45, (*person.*) 6.2, 7.233, 12.2 (1); (final) will (= testament) B 12.257; *in phrr.* **agayne...** ~ against (someone's) will 9.65, 10.219, 20.90, **B** 3.293, 4.48, 9.154; **at (...)** ~ according to one's will / desire Pr 38, 3.19, 240, 374, 6.66, 113, 11.8, 15.261, 22.197, **B** 3.200, 9.58, at one's liking B 10.15, at (one's) command 10.156, **B** 6.206, 18.345, **A** 10.34, 11.267, at (one's) disposal 10.244, 11.68, 12.230, 13.226, 14.175, B 10.446; **by** ~ wilfully B 4.70; **euyl** ~ ill-will / intent 6.87, 18.164, **B** 10.433, 15.127; **fre** ~ 10.51, B 16.223 (= Holy Spirit); **glad** ~ B 8.94; **gode** ~ benign / virtuous intent(ion) 6.336, 7.295, 9.111, 14.24, 19.330, 20.220, **B** 13.193, 14.20; **(ben) in** ~ (be) willing, ready B 10.168, A 12.21, desire **B** 11.278, 12.194; **to...** ~ as one wishes, at one's liking 6.190, 18.176; **wikkede** ~ ill-will 7.41, B 13.321,

evil will B 9.206, Z 5.94; **with (...)** ~ willingly 2.168, 3.217, B 4.101

willefolliche *av* voluntarily 22.49; deliberately 4.46, 19.269, 21.373

willen *v* (*pr.sg. 1,3* **wil(l)e** 2.169, 3.225, A 2.53 *et p.*, **wol(e)** Pr 171 *et p.*, B Pr 38 *etc*, 11.196, *2* **willest** B 12.218, **wilt** B 2.45, *assim..* **wiltow** B 3.111, *subj.* **wol(l)e** 8.153, B 13.227, *pl.* **wi(l)l(e)(n)** B 10.248, 13.258, A 8.32, Z 7.140, **wol(e)** 3.18 *etc*, *p.t. sg. 1,3* **wolde** Pr 130 *et p.*, *pl.* **wolde(n)** Pr 38, 3.383, *2 sg.* **wold** 8.299, **woldest** 13.230 *etc*, *assim. form* **woldestow** B 3.49, *p.p.* **wold** B 15.262) [*selected exx. only*] desire, wish 3.123, 21.100, B 5.53, *subjv.* **wolle thow** whether you like 8.153; *p.t.* wanted, desired Pr 130, B 1.29 *etc*, (*with pr. sense*) 8.299, ~ **have** made as if to 6.418, 8.149; be willing 3.8, B 7.35, *p.t.* was willing (to) 8.252, (*neg.*) be unwilling, refuse to 21.399, B Pr 38; intend (to) 3.18, 4.174; be prepared to 3.498, B 13.416; decree 3.419, *p.t.* 8.296; command B 9.125, *p.t.* 1.13; choose to, *p.t.* 22.38; be accustomed to 4.35, 8.335, *p.t.* 6.268; may, can 12.64, B 2.136, *p.t.* might 8.166, would be able (to) 15.167; (*in assev.*) will be 20.264; must 18.251, *p.t.* should have to 20.256; demand, require 20.428, 21.397, 472, 22.18, 265, A 10.132, *p.t.* 3.129, (*with pr. sense*) 8.231, 11.65, 20.425; (*elliptical, with inf. to be supplied*) want to (...) 5.81, 14.134, 20.298, *p.t.* wanted to (...) Pr 38, 2.96, 16.182, (*with v. of motion*) intended to go 6.353, 20.176; (*as fut. auxil.*) will, be going to 2.184, 3.51, B 5.640; (*conditional senses*) should, would Pr 210, 4.69, 22.32; should / would like (to) 2.128, 8.220, ~ be willing (to) 1.114, B 10.119; would, wish 5.83; (*subjv.*) if...were willing 3.52, 15.204, 16.254, 17.47; **hoso** ~ if anyone should wish (to) 17.254, let whoever wished 18.155; (*optative*) would [Christ] grant (that) 22.140; *in phrr.* **wiltow...neltow, wolle...ne wolle** like it or not 8.153, 21.467, 22.29, B 6.156

wilnen *v* desire, wish 1.8, 85, 3.131, 146, 4.158, 7.197, 12.20, 82, 84, 13.93, 16.182, 17.190, 269, 19.330, 20.4, 21.68, *pr. p.* 6.32 (B 13.280), 41 (B 13.292), **B** 5.185, 560, 6.258, 10.119, 124, 126, 339, 13.205, **A** 2.30, 10.89, **Z** 1.39, 2.10 ~ **aftur** long for 4.192; **wilneth (-ede) and wolde** desire(d) and wish(ed) 3.383, 13.93, 17.269, 18.260, B 14.173, (*trs*) B 10.353

wymmen *pl.* 2.7, 3.396, 6.190, 8.9, 9.167, 176, 226, 11.110, 215, 13.74, 22.348, Z 7.8 = **wom(m)en**; *see* **woman** *n*

wyn(e) *n* wine 1.30, 31, 6.160, 9.253, 11.110, 15.66, 16.91, 18.262, 19.71, 21.109, 111, B 10.361, ~ **of Oseye... of Gascoyne** Pr 230

wynd(e) *n* wind 3.483, 10.34, 19.334, Z 6.69, **southe-weste** ~ 5.116, *in phr.* ~**es and wederes** 10.46, 12.191; (the element of) air 9.56, 10.131, 15.243, **B** 7.52, 17.161; breath Z 5.34, 40; gas, air [in stomach] A 5.72; (*fig.*) (**wikked**) ~ 18.29, 31, 32, 35, B 16.25

wynden *v* (*p.t.* **wonden** 2.230, *p.p.* **ywounden** B 5.518) wind (yarn) B 5.548; wrap (sb.) around 2.230; *p.p.* wound, twisted B 5.518

wyndow(e) *n* window 3.51, 65, A 3.50; window-glass 3.69

wynge B 4.37 = **wenge** *n*

wynken *v* doze Pr 11, *ger.* 11.167, B 5.3, 363; give a significant glance (at) 4.148, B 4.154

wynlyche *av* with pleasure A 12.46

wynnen *v* (*p.t. sg. 1,3* **wan** 6.310 *etc,* **wonne** Z 7.87, *2* **wonne** 6.255, *pl.* **wonne(n)** Pr 24, Z 8.65, *p.p.* **ywonne** 3.247, 8.235, B 5.263) strive, ? go B 4.67*n*; win (victory) 3.485, 11.287; seize (as spoil) 3.252; get possession of Pr 194, 15.156, (by force) 3.247, 4.192, 7.233, 21.32, B 12.44; acquire 3.498, 6.255, 258, 310, 8.235, 12.6, 237, 16.275, 245, 248, 21.246, **B** 4.35, 5.263, 277, Z 7.87; obtain 4.73, 8.63, 11.68, 222, 15.145, 16.147, 22.15, **B** 5.92, 9.69; make profit(s) 12.229, 16.128, 19.234, 242, 21.353, 22.124, B 13.378; get / earn (by labour) Pr 24, 1.174, 5.126, 6.322, 8.18, 105, 9.251, 13.73, 17.18, 21.231, 236, **B** 6.133, 162, 8.81, 9.109, **A** 3.224, 7.236, 11.185; recover, win back 3.196, 12.111, 20.142, 396, 21.247; entice 6.190, 10.136

wynner(e) *n* earner [one who gets a living by work] Pr 223, A 7.148

wynnyng(e) *ger.* gain 5.98, 6.305, 9.207, 16.259, 17.36, B 5.112; profit 5.137, 6.293, 7.75, 9.26, 29, 12.17, 21.286, 456, Z 3.166

wynsen *v* kick restlessly 4.22

***wynstere** *n* (female) winder of thread A 5.129

wynter *n* (*pl.* ~ 6.233 *etc, uninfl. gen* 6.203) (the) winter (season) 12.188, 200, 15.293, 16.14, 146, Z 3.157, **a, at** ~ in winter-time 19.193, B 7.129, ~ **(es) nyhtes** 19.185, ~ **tyme** 9.78, 12.191, B 14.177; = year 3.41, 6.203, 233, 7.30, 188, 266, 14.3, 15.266, 270, 271, 17.23, 19.211, 20.136, 309, 329, 22.344, **B** 1.101, 3.192, 11.47, 15.288

wipen *v* wipe dry 2.230, 18.244, (*quasi-refl.*) dry one's hands 9.250, 15.38; rub B 5.262

wypne 3.458 = **wep(e)ne** *n*

wyr *n* wire B 2.11

wyrchen Z Pr 145, 1.23, 3.124, 175, 6.77 = **worchen** *v*

w(y)rd *n* fortune, fate 3.240, 12.211; circumstances (= capabilities) 14.32

wischen 15.90, 19.330 = **weschen** *v*

wyse *n* manner 19.13, B 2.171; habit, guise 7.160, 8.56, Z 5.158; fashion 7.162, 9.154; way 5.51, 7.253, 12.184, 208, 19.265, **none (...)** ~ no way at all 8.328, 10.282, **som manere** ~ one way or another 9.33; (*as suffix*) **on cros** ~ by crucifixion 21.142, **a fuste** ~ in the manner of a fist 19.151

wys(e) *a* wise 1.69, 3.7, 4.44, 11.220, 13.184, 21.166, B 10.8, **A** 11.272, 12.38; *a as n (sg)*, 13.203, 16.227, (*comp.*) one more wise B 11.270, (*pl.*) 10.311, 12.143;

sage Pr 49, 13.27, 14.193, 21.245, 297, B 12.50; prudent 7.94, 10.144, 11.5, 16.20, 22.33, **B** Pr 208, 4.69, 11.281, 14.18, A 10.23, 71; sensible 13.43, 16.20; shrewd, astute 4.83, 9.336, 19.225, **wordliche** ~ experienced (in the affairs of the world) 10.91, A 10.70; (practically) skilled 7.157; learned 8.240, 9.51, 11.98, 224, 13.64, 20.242, 354, 21.84, 22.303, *comp.* **wyser** 6.24, 28, **B** 11.392, 13.293, 15.547; (*comp.*) enlightened, well-informed **B** 9.79, 10.371; *in cpds.* ~ **witted** with wise minds B 10.396, **weder** ~ skilled in weather-lore 17.94

wis(e)do(e)m *n* right (moral) judgement 16.50, 21.453; shrewd practical judgement 16.142, B 10.450, *in phr.* **wit and** ~ 16.50, 188, 22.133, B 12.293, ~ **and wit** 11.14, B 6.51; prudence 2.147, (*person.*) 4.66, 72, 96, B 4.74, 81, 87, A 4.60, (= worldly wisdom) **Waryn** ~ B 4.27, 154, A 4.141; (the) wisdom of God 13.228; a wise thing to do 8.223; knowledge 22.33; (a) wise precept 11.5, 14.82, A 10.111

wys(e)ly(che) *av* with wisdom 11.215; sagaciously 3.7, B 4.46; prudently 10.287; with good judgement 8.235; soundly 15.115; carefully 15.78, (*comp.*) **wisloker** more attentively B 13.343

wisman *n* wise-man (*as name*) 4.27

wispe B 5.345 = **weps** *n*

wissen *v* show 2.199, A 12.40, 46; inform 10.6, 74, 111, 16.155, A 12.31; know (= be informed) A 9.13; show (way) 7.177, 198, B 10.154; direct 11.139; guide 15.20, A 10.92; ? manage, (? advise) 3.18; advise 8.162, *ger.* advice 12.11; teach 1.40, 10.29, 13.203, 14.4, 195, 17.84, 21.64, 247, 10.450, **B** 1.42, 7.128, 10.339, 382, 11.436, 12.72, *ger.* teaching B 15.479; instinct 1.71, 21.234, **B** 5.146, 10.8, 384; show how A 11.275; bid, order **B** 11.382, 15.494

wisshen B 5.110, 10.468, 12.270, *ger.* B 2.91 *see* **weschen** *v*

wissynge(e) *ger.* 12.11, B 15.479 *see* **wissen** *v*

wist *p.p.* 20.209, 217, ~**e** *p.t.* 5.37 *etc,* *pl.* ~**en** 12.128, ~**est,** ~**us** *2 sg.* A 7.196, Z 7.194 *see* **witen** *v*

wit (witte) *n*[1] (*pl.* **wittes** 1.15 *etc*) mind 3.454, 5.185, 6.167, 13.184, 15.75, B 10.131, **fyn** ~ subtlety of mind 11.158; intelligence Pr 38, 3.211, 14.32, 15.20, **B** Pr 37, 8.53, 19.231; intellect 10.9, 11.287, 12.2, 18.28, 190, 21.230, B 10.394; **kynde** ~ native intelligence, natural reason 14.17, 30, 33, 34, 36, 53, 157, 182, 21.317, **B** 12.67, 69, 70, 93, 128, 14.125, (*person.*) Pr 141 *etc,* 1.51, 4.87, 13.238; *pl.* mental powers 1.138, 4.23, 10.121, 11.84, 14.194, 16.214, B 10.6, A 11.87; *in phr.* **at here ~es ende** utterly perplexed 17.105; inner senses 10.172; reason, understanding 6.310, 13.192, 16.188, (*person.*) 7.233, 10.111*n,* **B** 5.364, 11.322, 15.83, 16.187; cleverness 21.453, **B** 13.292, 15.408; astuteness 22.32; (*person*) 4.72, 77, 87, B 4.76; practical know-how 21.240; (sound) understanding, 'right mind', **B** 2.129, 15.3; (faculty of) sense (perception) 18.180, **fyue ~es** five bodily senses 1.15, 15.257, 16.232, 21.217; ingenuity Pr 174, 6.21, 261, 264, 13.157, 21.100, 357; constructive ability **B** 12.223; ingenious contrivance A 11.159, Z 3.166; wisdom, wise judgement 3.211, 8.55, 10.105, 11.212, 13.228, 15.145, 173, 21.118, **B** 9.43, 13.169, 15.130, 19.82; judgement 20.242, **B** 3.7, 10.446, **fre** ~ (the power of) moral judgement, 'liberum arbitrium' 10.51c; prudence 2.147, 22.32, **B** 6.51; knowledge 9.56, 11.14, 79, 223, 13.169, A 11.278; knowing Z 3. 175; learning 16.50, 21.234, **B** 12.293; meaning, significance **B** 12.133, 13.155

witted *a* provided with wits / mental powers, **kynde** ~ 14.52, 72, **B** 12.158

wyt *n*² blame A 10.75; *see* **wyten** *v*²

witen (**weten, wyten**) *v*¹ (*infl. inf.* ~**e** B 8.13; *pr. sg.* 1, 3, **wo(e)t** Pr 100, **woot** 4.83, 2 **wost** 3.225, *pl.* **wite(n)** 13.64, B 3.332, **wyteth** 1.121, **wote** B 10.361, 435, *subj.* **wete, wyte** 4.100, 6.343, B Pr 208, *pl.* **wyten** 2.79; *imper. pl.* **witeth** B 2.75; *p.t. 1, 3* **wiste(n)** 6.70, 12.128, *subj.* **wiste** 6.59, B 14.8, *2* **wistest** A 7.196, *p.p.* **wist** 20.209) [*selected exx.*] know 3.221, 285, 6.326, 343, 9.70, 88, 10.4, 71, 72, 11.275, 12.82, 162, 15.150, 18.147, 275, 20.68, 21.162, **B** 10.119, 124, 126, 133, 11.407, A 7.179, 11.30, 259; (*with neg.*) have no idea 6.343, 16.141, 18.181, 20.225, 236, 22.3, **B** Pr 12, 5.642; *in phrr.* (*parenth.*) **wiltow** ~, **wol ʒe** ~ you may be sure **B** 13.227, 16.25, (*assev.*) **wyte God** God may be sure 7.284, **God woet** God knows [this to be true] 4.37, 75, 83, 5.1, **B** Pr 43, 5.102, 13.385, 14.329, 15.146, A 5.154, 11.240, 12.88; ~ **þe sothe** know (sth.) for a fact / the truth (of a matter) 1.121, 3.285, 7.244, 284, 9.128, 10.22, 12.79, 162, 14.191, 16.252, 19.9, 20.149, 21.374, **B** 2.122, 6.130, 9.99, 10.431, 11.179, A 8.56, 11.30, 194, †12.99; may know B 5.562; might know B 16.12; ~ **wel** know for sure 6.326, 8.139, 211, 10.242, 20.342, 21.361, B 14.82, 282, be well / fully aware 8.211, 270, 9.128, 16.235, 21.373, A 4.67; ~ **witterly** know for certain 3.296, 9.88, 20.68, 215, B 5.268, A 11.259, 12.10; be sure 9.70, 11.274, B 15.263; be aware (of) Pr 100, 2.82, 142, 3.76, 225, 5.181, 6.59, 162, 163, 289, 300, 11.290, 12.36, 13.64, 81, 21.373, **B** Pr 208, 2.78, 3.332, 5.159, 7.69, 76, 10.361, 11.101, 13.324, 14.8, 16.233; understand 5.37, 13.64, 20.168, 210; recognise 17.99, B 10.435, ~ **of** acknowledge 10.164; realise 12.128, 13.241; become aware (of) Pr 181, 6.59, B 10.228; find out, discover, learn 4.100, 136, 6.70, 71, 303, 7.197, 8.220, 10.125, 13.218, 230, 16.6, 340, 20.129, 229, 231, 233 (1), B 2.45, A 12.31, Z 2.2; know (by experience), have (direct / practical) knowledge of 15.82, 285, 20.209, 217, 233 (2), 22.319, **B** 8.113, 14.97, Z 3.166; be informed, (*subj.*) let them be informed 2.79, **do to** ~**e** inform B 8.13

wyten *v*² (*p.t.* **witte** 1.30) (lay the) blame (on) 1.30, 6.113, †B 7.59; blame (for) 20.353, A 5.207

wyten *v*³ preserve B 7.35, A 10.67; protect, defend B 16.25, †A 10.23, 67; (*in oath, subj.*) may ~ protect 7.284; drive away Z 7.59*n*

witene *infl. inf.* B 8.13 *see* **witen** *v*¹

witenesse 19.31 = **wittenesse** *n*

wytful *a* sagacious A 4.19

with *prep.* [*select exx.*] against 12.194, 20.26, 22.168; with Pr 166 *et p.*; (*after prn*) B 1.209, = on the side of 1.94, 108, 2.153, 21.362; in the same way as, like 6.174, **B** 6.137, 181, 7.67; **as** ~ in the manner of 19.115; in the case of, in regard to 3.434, 6.184, 8.86, 17.202, 21.301, 22.290, A 10.58; in relation to **B** 13.149, 16.223; in the hands of 11.260, 19.135; among 8.216, 9.95, 196; in the company of 6.116, 235, 14.125, 15.27, 16.335, 18.185, 21.214, **B** 10.229, A 11.217; accompanied by Pr 45, 2.103, 20.342, **B** 10.340; together with 2.16, 15.163, 16.175, 330, 17.236, 21.40, 165, 323, **B** 1.111, 8.36, A 11.219; (*quasi-av*) **forth** ~ together with 10.233, **B** 17.158; along with 2.89, 9.8, 186, 11.243, 16.300, 20.318, **B** 1.116, 9.37, 10.37, 42, †446, 16.203, A 3.202; to 2.137, 10.138, 15.209, A 10.154; **euene** ~ equal to 18.90, **eueneforþ** ~ equally with **B** 13.144, 17.135; = having, possessing Pr 51, 6.202, 10.118, 20.273, 22.176, **B** 1.15, 6.237, 9.50; containing 13.55, 15.226, B 5.640, *in phr.* ~ **childe** pregnant 9.176, 22.348; by (means of) Pr 73, 174, 223, 1.67, 2.161, 3.192, 6.246, 288, 8.241, 259, 9.31, 74, 11.100, 299, 16.45, 128, 132, 17.234, 304, 18.150, 19.21, 62, 112, 257, 20.52, 319, 377, 21.144, 236, 248, 466, 22.119, 379, **B** Pr 34, 1.67, 4.75, 9.51, 10.22, 414, 13.129*n*, 15.449, 482 (3), A 7.210, 11.186; through Pr 24, 4.149, 7.128, 20.364, 21.296, **B** 2.230, 3.310, 5.366, 488, 9.114, 12.11, 13.146, A 7.205, 232, 10.34; by Pr 87, 22.215, **B** 3.2, 102, 16.105, 17.90; from 6.2, B 5.134; in consequence of 6.335, 18.179, A 12.91; at, over 15.65; for B 13.111, 415; on 8.151, 294; of B 7.8; (*in conjv. phr.*) on condition that 6.173, 11.91, 22.250; (*in avl. phrr.*) (**riht**) ~ **þat** at that point / moment, thereupon 4.196, 6.1, 62, 7.55, 13.247, 18.289, 20.69, 94, 471, **B** Pr 146, 3.26, 5.300, ~ **doel** painfully 20.304, ~ **riht** justly 21.353, ~ **treuthe** truly, as true 9.251; ~ **wo** in torment B 2.107; ~ **wrong** wrongfully 19.234, B 1.128; *av* (*with phrasal vv*) **delen** ~ 8.77, **fynden** ~ B 13.241, **halden** ~ 1.94, **meten** ~ 4.140; (*preceding obj.*) **close (...)** ~ close...with *etc* Pr 133, 6.340, 8.273, 318, 9.75, 76, 157, 11.17, 55, 16.25, 17.121, 19.207, 261, 20.282, 21.228, **B** 2.117, 10.270, 11.398, 12.294, 16.147, (*preceding v*) 9.130, 167, A 10.130

wiþalle *av* completely, ? to be sure B 15.12*n*; moreover, besides 10.132, 144, 17.166, 18.125, **B** 5.3, 15.288, A 12.50

withdrawen *v* (*p.t.* ~**drouh**, ~**drow** 20.60, 114) draw back 8.351, 20.114, (*refl.*) 19.64; retire 20.60; (*refl.*) cease / refrain from 11.64, 17.245, 22.353, B 9.97

withhalden *v* (*contr. pr.* ~ **halt**, *p.t.* ~ **helden**) keep back (sth.) from (sb.) 3.306, 7.195; keep (in one's service) 2.238

wythinne[1] *av* (hidden) inside 6.261, 12.249, 16.265, 266; withindoors 7.187 *n*; inwardly, in the soul 6.31, 74

wythinne[2] *prep.* in(side) 10.40; within (the space of) 20.31

withoute(n)[1] *av* on the outside 12.147; outside 7.265; out of doors 7.187; outwardly 6.31, B 10.257

without(e)(n)[2] *prep.* outside 16.365; without 2.128, 3.117, 199, 364, 372, 5.52, 6.121, 7.106, 9.120, 10.217, 11.136, 12.64, 15.272, **B** 2.30, 14.238; without (committing) 10.101, 17.3, 18.133, (recourse to / the action of) 4.181–2, 5.174, 7.3, 9.325, 11.145, 12.87, 14.115, 201, 15.157, 17.8, 129, 19.86, 242, 22.21, **B** 3.227, 7.55, 12.85, 14.63, 15.196, (obtaining) 3.131, (suffering) 11.262, (taking) B 3.243, (the use of) 13.74, 15.83, **B** 9.34, 17.166; in the absence of 2.123, 11.288, 12.88, 94, 14.28, 16.176, 17.130, 18.224, 225, 226, 19.180, **B** 10.451, 15.234, 472, 16.218; free from 3.205, 14.16, 16.20, 138, 153, 19.158, 20.131, 134, **B** 11.214, 14.129, 15.150, 487; lacking 1.181, 183, 9.205, 18.221, 19.181, 215, 20.10, **B** 10.351, 11.82, 15.13, 460; *in phrr.* ~ **chalangynge** undeniably; ~ **doute** undoubtedly 16.32, B 12.32; ~ **drede** have no fear 14.10; ~ **ende** 19.252, B 18.379, = for ever 2.106, 3.359, 10.171, 18.233, 257, 20.235, 21.199; ~ **gynnyng** eternal **B** 2.30, 16.187; ~ **gult** guiltlessly 4.75; ~ **nombre** unlimited in number 22.270; ~ **pite** pitilessly B 3.195

withoute[3] *conj.* unless 4.176

withsaet *p.t.* 18.250 *see* **withsit(t)en** *v*

wiþsiggen *v* (*p.t.* **wiþseide**) oppose, contradict A 4.142; affirm the contrary of A 11.232; object, put a counter-argument †B 4.91*n*

withsit(t)en, withsetten *v* (*p.t.* **withsaet**) oppose, resist Pr 174, 8.202, 10.98, †12.190, 18.250

wytyng *pr. p. a as av* knowingly 21.373

witte 6.113 *see* **wyten** *v*[3]

wit(te)le(e)s *a* out of one's mind 15.1; mentally deficient 9.111

wit(t)(e)nesse *n* testimony, witness 9.285, 11.215, 14.66, 16.289, B 9.73; **fals** ~ 2.85, 7.226, 16.361, **B** 5.88, 13.359, (*person.*) 2.160, *in phrr.* [giving authority for a statement] the proof is (in) Pr 205*n*, 12.124; **beren** ~ testify, affirm (authoritatively) 7.100, 9.304, 10.213, 12.135, 155, 14.124, 15.222, 18.213, 222, 19.31, 283, 20.240, 21.449, **B** 2.38, 5.144, 7.51, 83, 9.74, 10.88, 246, 279, 340, 11.156, 226, 252, 270, 272, 12.65, 13.135, 14.85, 180, 15.90; **taken to** ~ appeal to as a witness / authority 11.38, 12.135, 14.124, 15.103 (2), 18.222, 20.135, 245, **B** 11.87, 15.488, **taken** ~ **at / of** draw evidence (from) / appeal to (as example) 12.77, 15.103 (1), 158; testimony (by signature) 2.109;

(authoritative) witness, guarantor 6.53, 20.311, B 9.118; (subscribing) witness [to execution of a will] B 12.258*n*

witnessen *v* bear witness, solemnly affirm 3.123, 426, 7.94, 8.240, 10.240, 11.21, 219, 12.103, 120, 156, 13.203, 14.37, 15.246, 265, 16.238, 240, 17.6, 37, 235, 19.216, 288, 20.356, **B** Pr 195, 1.147, 10.376, 11.39, 396, 13.307, **A** 10.94, 12.25, provide (authoritative) evidence / proof 2.129, 5.87, 12.156, 20.250; give formal evidence, attest 4.87, 20.45, B 4.181; attest by signature B 2.161; be (formally) present as witness B 16.122, A 2.46, (*subjv.*) 'let those witness...(who)' 2.79

witterly(che) *av* clearly, plainly Pr 11, 6.303, 9.88, 20.217, 22.194, A 11.259; certainly 21.361, 22.271; for sure / certain 3.221, 296, 20.68, B 5.268, A 12.10, = you may be sure 15.90, 18.181; truly 1.71, 5.37, 6.273, 20.215, 237

witty *a* wise 2.151, (*comp.*) ~**ore** 5.188, **B** 11.373, 15.130, *a as n* B 10.430; prudent B 11.392, ~ **wordes** sagacious counsel's B 4.21; clever 6.24, 16.20, (*comp.*) 218, *a as n* 11.229, B 12.143, (*person.*) B 4.27, 67, ~ **man** 4.31; expert 9.51, 17.94, 20.354

wyuen B 9.184, **wyuyng** 10.290 *see* **wyf** *n*

wyuen *v* take a wife B 9.184, *ger.* ~**yng** marrying 10.290

wyuene *gen. pl.* 5.31 *see* **wyf** *n*

wo[1] *n* misery, distress Pr 10, 3.205, 9.78, 83, 84, 11.107, 20.210, 219, 233, 22.193, **B** 2.107, 11.398, 14.177, 18.2, 414, A 11.69, *in phr. with* **wele** 12.211, 20.208, 209, 21.244, Z 3.173; suffering, pain 1.164, 4.80, 11.166, 21.68, 199; trouble 4.65, 6.414, 14.68, 125, 17.204, 21.158, **B** 13.208, 263

wo[2] *a* wretched, sorry B 5.3, Z 1. 102*n*, 4.51

wo[3] *interj.* (of grief / affliction), *in phrr.* ~ **bytyde**, ~ **to** may affliction befall 2.119, 3.156, 18.175, ~ **is** *etc* (+ *dat.*) wretched is / was / will be 3.190, 9.271, 13.215, 14.18, Z 1.102, ~ **worth** evil will befall 10.176

wo Z 7.1 = **who** *prn*

wode *n* wood [collection of trees] 9.196, 225, 13.137, **B** 16.56, 17.103, A 9.54, **by a** ~ **syde** along the edge of a wood 10.62; [material] 18.24, (fire) wood 16.178, 19.310

wodewe B 9.164, 176 = **wedewe** *n*

Wodnesday *n* Wednesday B 13.155

woen[1] 3.141 = **wone** *n*

woen[2] *n* abundance, *in phr.* **goed** ~ a-plenty, in good measure 22.171

woet 3 *sg.pr.* 4.37 *et p.*; *see* **witen** *v*[1]

woke *n* week 9.253, 12.124, 18.134, **B** 10.96, 13.155, *in phrr.* **of al a** ~ all week 8.269, **þis(e)** ~**(s)** (the) last week(s) B 5.92, A 11.106

woke(n) *p.t.* 21.156, B 14.69 *see* **waken** *v*

wok(y)en *v* moisten, (add) water (to) B 15.338, (*fig.*) 16.333, (= soften) 14.25

wol(e) *3 pr.sg.* Pr 171, 11.196 *et p.*, *pl.* 2.184, B 11.89, **wold** *2 pr.sg.* 8.299, **woldest** 16.205, **wolde(n)** *p.t.* Pr 130, 3.383, *(as pr.)* 3.383 *etc, cond.* 7.145 *etc; see* **willen** *v*

#**wold** *n* 'would' [= feeling of conditional desire], *pl. in phr.* ~**es and weschynges** 2.95n

wolf *n* wolf 9.264, 266, *pl.* **wolues** 9.226, *(fig.)* 9.259, 16.269, A 10.212

wolkne B 17.161, 18.237 = **welkene** *n*

wolle *2 pr. subj.* 8.153, *pr.sg.* Z 6.92, *pr.pl.* 8.262, **wollen** 9.86 *see* **willen** *v*

wolle *n* sheep's fleece 9.266, 264; wool 9.271, 11.15, Z 5.100, *(fig.)* A 8.17; wool(len thread) 8.12

wollen(e) *n* woollen cloth 1.18, 13.102, **B** Pr 220, = wool(len thread) A 7.10; *a* woollen 6.221, A 8.43

wollewa(e)rd *a* with wool next to the skin 20.1

wolt *2 p.sg.* 3.146, ~**ow** *contr. interrog.* 3.153 *etc; see* **willen** *v*

wolueliche *a* wolflike, rapacious B 15.116

wolues *pl.* 9.226 *etc; see* **wolf** *n*

wolueskynne *n* wolvish / wolflike nature (~**s** *gen. sg. as a*) B 6.161

wom(m)an *n* (*pl.* **wom(m)en** 1.31, **wymmen** 9.167, *gen. pl.* **wommane** 20.134) woman 2.9, 6.190, 7.107, 11.87, 215, 22.348, **B** 2.19, 3.51, 118, 12.76, 80, 81, 89, A 3.246, 10.23, 208, *as term of address* 3.133; = unmarried woman 3.420; *(generic)* 8.6, 9.83, 176, 20.134, 21.162, 436, B 12.74, *in phr.* **man / men and** ~ 7.205, 17.181, 19.22, **B** 9.186, 12.49, A 10.152; *(spec.)* þe ~ (= Eve) **B** 5.602, 10.108; *pl.* *(meton.)* (intercourse with) women 1.31, 11.110, 13.189; *in phrr.* **commune** ~ prostitute 18.143, 21.370, **B** 5.641, 11.216, **gentil** ~ woman of noble lineage B 11.246, **worthily** ~ honourable woman 8.9; ~ **at þe stuyues** prostitute 13.74; ~ **and childrene** 3.396, 9.226

wombe *n* belly 15.93, *(fig.)* appetite [for material pleasures] Pr 57; stomach 3.83, 5.52, 6.438, 8.172, 226, 269, 9.253, **B** 3.194, 15.291, A 5.70, 72, ~ **cloute** tripe B 13.63; womb 7.238, 18.134, B 15.455

wonden *p.t. pl.* 2.230 *see* **wynden** *v*

wonder *n* miracle 18.149, 21.119; marvel(lous) thing / happening) Pr 4, 11.171, 20.125, 129, B 11.322; extraordinary phenomenon B 15.482; *in phrr.* ~ **ben / thynken** be / seem astonishing 3.228, 13.161, 17.116, B 15.120, 378; **hauen** ~ wonder, marvel 13.158, 184, 16.160, 18.270, **B** 2.18, 3.304, 11.301; *a* exceedingly strange B 14.125; *av* exceedingly 11.220, 13.5, 22.159, **B** 3.302, 14.6, 15.1; ~**fol** *a* astonishing 19.27; marvellous 13.137; ~**ly(che)** *av* marvellously 2.9, 11.167; exceedingly 6.308, 7.278, 11.3; *~**wise** *av* in a marvellous fashion 1.125

wondren *v* marvel, *(impers.)* **me** ~ 13.153, 15.75; ask oneself in wonder 21.205

wone *n* place Pr 18, abode, dwelling-place 3.141; domain B 3.235; habit, custom 4.22, 16.322, B 15.245

won(y)en *v* (*p.p.* **(y)woned** 6.143, 17.89, **wont** B 20.371) dwell, live Pr 18, 1.59, 2.79, 234, 242, 5.1, 7.177, 197, 9.83, 196, 11.223, 15.242, 16.65, 17.11, 28, 259, 21.36, 193, 199, 22.39, **B** 2.107, 3.12, 235, 5.174, 10.428, 13.121, 14.97, 15.245, A 2.30, 10.144; be accustomed to / in the habit of 6.143, 8.164, 17.89, 22.371, Z 3.157

wonne *p.t. 1 sg.* Z 7.87, *2 sg.* 6.255, *pl.* Pr 24, *p.p.* 8.235 *see* **wynnen** *v*

woord A 11.269 = **word** *n*

woot *pr. sg.* 4.83, 6.273, B Pr 43 *etc* = **woet**; *see* **witen** *v*¹

wopen *p.t. pl.* 9.41 *see* **wepen** *v*

worchen (**werchen, werken, wyrchen**) *v* (*p.t.* **wro(u)hte(n)** 1.164, 8.116, **wroȝte** B 1.82, *p.p.* **(y)wrouhte** 1.131, 2.119, **(y)wroȝt** 3.133, B 3.239) do, perform 8.6, 9.349, 11.90, 10.242, **B** 3.74, 9.176, 12.50, A 1.119, 10.75, ~ **in werke** actually do 4.143, B 10.254, ~ **werk** perform action B 3.239, 10.412, **A** 10.65, 130, 208, 12.103; do (evil, harm) 1.129, **B** 3.80, 4.68, 5.283; carry out (will, command) 3.29, 18.133, B 1.82 (1), A 1.75, 12.97; make, construct 13.157, 160, *ger.* **a** ~ **ynge** under construction 3.51; create 8.336, B 1.82 (2); make (textile), (= weave) A 7.10; bring about 4.143, B 9.114; devise 2.118; work, labour Pr 38, 1.124, 5.23, 25, 62, 126, 135, 8.18, 125, 130, 164, 211, 265, 269, 325, 9.176, 19.185, **B** 1.26, 6.211, 240, 9.109, 113, 10.211, A 7.192, labour (at) B 5.24; *(person.)* ~ **when-tyme-is** 8.80, ~ **wel...** 10.147; act, do 2.147, 3.7, 8.55, 90, 11.222, 253, 14.26, 16.218, 219, 17.84, 19.19, **B** 1.147, 2.195, 3.233, 6.56, 7.35, 8.56, 128, 9.43, 12.258, **A** 9.98, 10.95, 11.260; have intercourse 10.291, B 7.90; act (to) 19.138; be active B 10.271; function 16.178; take effect B 10.274

word *n* speech 21.287, Z 5.34, 6.69; = something uttered, (a) speech 6.21, 177, 419, 8.32, 10.123, 11.166, 12.11, 138, 13.189, 14.66, 82, 15.97, 16.142, 18.37, 21.230, **B** Pr 139, 3.36, 4.34, 8.57, 9.129, 10.8, 116, 288, 440, 16.141, 18.289, *pl.* (= what sb. says) Pr 70, 198, 1.41, 4.154, 18.270, 289, 19.27, 20.152; = verdict Z Pr 71; *(with neg.)* anything A 4.142, Z 4.123; speech [as contrasted with thought or action] B 9.36, *in phrr.* **with werk(es)** action(s) and / or word(s) 2.94, 6.99, 11.219, **B** 5.85, 9.45, 51, 10.254, 366, 13.141, 146, 312, 14.14, 15.116, 198, 210, 477, A 11.269, *with* **wit** 15.145, 21.122, B 9.43; command B 6.56, *esp.* God's command(ent)(s) 1.13, **B** 1.147, 9.32, **Goddes (Cristes)** ~**(es)** (divine teaching in) the Bible 1.69, 87, 6.84, 7.87, 94, 10.89, 11.235, 238, 15.274, 21.389, **B** 10.271, 274, 11.175, 225, **A** 10.94, 11.243, 12.97, Z 5.36, 40; promise, undertaking 20.311, 431, B 18.282; prophecy 21.80; word, *esp.* written word(s) [of a text] 1.194, 3.492, 9.281, 19.13, B 10.198, 384; text **B** 6.237, 13.68; *in phr.* ~**es**

of grace gracious / grace-bringing words 5.98*n*, ~ **of murthe** 7.77; **goed** ~ friendly word 19.330, **crabbed** ~**es** 14.100, B 10.106; **false** ~ 6.258, **felle** ~ 3.492, **foule** ~ 7.114, 10.276, B 10.40, **harlotes** ~ 22.144, **kene** ~ 6.65, **paynted** ~ 21.230, **pitous** ~ A 7.115, **profitable** B 6.274; **propre** ~ 9.301, **rousty** ~ 8.75, **selcouthe** ~ 12.47, **two** ~ 19.13, **wyse** ~ 4.44, B 10.8, 12.50

worden *v* speak, talk 13.245, 15.150, 19.48, B 4.46, 10.427, *ger.* (verbal) exhortation 8.90; say A 10.96

woryen *v* seize by the throat 9.226, 266

world *n* human existence, **this** ~ this present life 1.8, 20.4, 134, 21.68, B 5.283, 9.108, A 11.260, Z 3.124, ~**es ende** the end of time 15.284, 18.175; business of life, affairs of the world 19.226, 20.4; the conditions of life (in the world) Pr 21, 12.172, 21.231; life 8.158; experience (of life) 9.88, B 10.273; matters, 'things' 3.434; secular life 9.251; worldly life 6.333, the World [as enemy of the soul, *(semi-)person.*] 1.37, 3.70, 10.44, 48, 11.63, 82, 18.31, B 7.126, 16.48, A 10.144; resources of this world 11.68, 12.230, 21.357; = the earth, world 10.200, 248, 18.251, 21.36, 335, 22.382, B 18.61, Z 6.71, **in the** ~ abroad Pr 4, the (created) universe 7.122, 8.239, 18.214, 19.113, 20.195, 22.49, B 10.226, 11.322, 17.160, Z 5.40, 43; everything 20.213; the known world B 15.437; the inhabitants of the earth, **al þe** ~ everyone Pr 100, 104, 12.36, B 11.101; (human) society 8.27, 10.205, 21.220, 430, B 6.132, 173, 9.109, A 10.133; *as intensif. phr.* **of / in the** ~ alive / in existence / anywhere on earth Pr 10, 3.6, 211, 4.136, 6.414, 10.6, 15.167, 173, 19.104, 20.242, 21.82, B 10.426, A 10.71, 11.269; anywhere 20.459, B 5.277, 8.69, 13.174, 208, A 11.272; in any way B 5.506; = any at all B 17.99; *in phrr.* **the welthe of this** ~ Pr 10, 9.336, 12.158, B 10.24

wor(l)(d)ly(che) *a* of (human) existence (on earth), human 3.368; earthly, material 12.238, 21.286, 293, 22.211; in this world 10.97

world-ryche *a* possessed of (worldly) wealth 16.16

worm *n* serpent B 10.107 (A 11.66); reptile, **wilde** ~ 13.137, 15.293; (earth) worm 15.242; caterpillar *(fig.)* B 16.34

wors(e) *a (comp.)* more wicked B 9.91; more unpleasant 3.141, 16.14, 66; harder B 17.43; more reprehensible A 11.218; more unfortunate Pr 104; *a as n* a greater evil 3.137, 11.264, B 10.421; something more worthless still 17.73; the less good (bargain) 6.381, 384; **þe** ~ the worse off, the less favoured 10.241; in poorer condition B 1.26, the worse (for it) B 16.157; *av (comp.)* more wickedly 3.137, B 5.113; **þe** ~ the more unluckily 10.237, 16.68; the less (well) 3.220; worse, less agreeably 11.75

wors(c)hip(e) *n* honour, dignity 1.8, 5.75; (credit of a) good name 6.142; respect / honour shown to sb. / sth.

3.486, 498, 14.138, B 12.119; veneration 18.263, 19.263, B 16.244

wors(c)hipen *v* worship, adore 18.262, 21.211; reverence Pr 119, 1.16, 21.443; revere 17.212; honour 8.110, **B** 1.48, 15.483; treat with honour / respect 3.13, 9.135; respectfully salute B 10.224

worst *2 sg. pr.* 21.409 *see* **worthen** *v*

worste *a (sup.)* most wicked 19.265, *a as n* (goods of) poorest quality 6.261 (B 13.363); most grievous state of affairs 3.477; *av* most wickedly 11.272; least, ~ **to louye** the least to be loved B 10.336

worst(e) *av* most wickedly 11.272; least, ~ **to louye** the least to be loved B 10.336

worsted *n* fabric of well-twisted yarn [made from long-staple wool] Z 5.100

worstow *contr. pr.* B 5.613, 19.409 = **worst thow**; *see* **worthen** *v*

wort *n* cabbage 8.331, *(fig.)* B 5.160

worth[1] *n* value, **at** ~**e** at face value 14.66; the equivalent of (*as suffix in cpd.*) *see* **ferthing** ~, **pene** ~

worth(e)[2] *a* of the value (of) Pr 76, 6.244, (*contemptuous*) 8.263, 11.14, B 4.170; worth, of value 10.311, 11.79, 13.94, 16.6, B 13.382

worth[3] *3 pr. sg.* (*with fut. sense*) 1.183 *et p.*, ~**e** (*subj.*) 21.433, A 5.241, *pl.* 12.208 *see* **worthen** *v*

worthen *v* (*p.t.* **warth** 5.98, 11.167) become 11.22, 88, 15.149; will become 12.208; **worst** (you) will be 21.409; **worth, worþ** will be 1.183 *et p.*, 7.264, B 3.314; fall 11.167; befall 5.98, *in phrr.* **wo** ~ ill will befall 10.176, **wel** ~**e** (*subjv.*) may good fortune fall to 13.1, 21.433; ~ **vp** get up / mount [for sexual intercourse] B 7.90

worthy *a* excellent 10.311, 12.193, (*comp.*) 5.188, 13.27, ~**okest** *sup.* Z 5.36; *a as n* 17.201, 18.88, (*sup.*) Z 5.36; valuable B 14.89; entitled to honour 7.113, 15.39; honourable 18.71, 21.24; of sufficient worth B 14.329; of sufficient merit B 18.329; ~**ier** *comp. a as av* in a more honourable place B 6.47

worthily *a* noble 8.9; *av* splendidly B 2.19, Z 2.12

wosch(en) *p.t. sg. / pl.* 18.244 / 2.230, 15.32, 38 *see* **waschen** *v*

wose *n* slime, wet mud 12.231

wost[1] *2 sg. pr.* 3.225, 10.71 *see* **witen** *v*[1]

wost[2] *2 sg. p.t. contr.* 22.188 = **woldest**; *see* **willen** *v*

wot *1,3 sg. pr.* Pr 100 *etc*, A 5.154, 12.1, 88, **Z** 3.147, 166, 173, 175, 5.35; **wote** *pl.* B 10.361, 435 *see* **witen** *v*[1]

wouȝ A 5.136 = **wowe** *n*

wouke B 5.92, A 11.106 = **woke** *n*

wound(e) *n* wound 4.181, 19.67, 71, 85, 20.90, 101, B 17.76, **fyue** ~ **is** [of Christ] A 11.215; *(fig.)* 5.177, B 14.96

wounden[1] *p.t.pl.* B 2.221 = **wonden** *see* **wynden** *v*

wounden[2] *v* (inflict a) wound (on) 19.82, **B** 16.105, 17.54, 18.88; *(fig.)* 22.303, 306, 358,

woware *n* wooer, suitor 12.19

wowe *n* wall 3.65, A 5.136

wowen *v* solicit B 4.74

woxe(n) *p.p.* 3.211, **B** 10.75, 19.124, *p.t.pl.* **B** 14.60, 16.56 *see* **waxen** *v*

wrake *n* destruction, *in phr.* **werre and** ~ 17.85, 20.458

wrang *p.t.* 2.252 *see* **wryng(y)en** *v*

*****wranglynge** *n* noisy quarrelling 4.35

wrastlen *v* wrestle 16.66, 79

wrat(t)h(e) *n* violent anger 4.35, 14.67, 15.255, *spec.* the deadly sin of anger 6.121, 167, 7.16, 11.110, Z 5.94, **B** 4.70, 5.83, 429, 13.321, A 5.79, (*person.*) 6.66, 103, 105, 124, 126, 139, 148, 16.66; resentment 11.166, B 15.171; exasperation A 7.109; wrathful indignation 21.306, B 5.401; act of furious rage Z 4.120

wrathen *v* (*p.t.* **wrathe** 6.148, **-ed** 1.26) get angry (with) 6.148*n*, B 9.129, (*refl.*) 3.228, 8.149, (*person.*) ~ **þe (nouȝt)** (Don't) get angry 7.260 / A 6.98, (*impers. with Ø-subject*) Pr 189; anger 1.26, 2.118, B 10.288

wrec(c)he *n* wretch Z 7.197, **so muche** ~ so very miserable a soul 19.328; vile creature 2.41, 21.406, **B** 9.120, 15.600, **A** 4.136, 12.21, 24, ~ **of this world** heedless worldling 11.63; scoundrel 2.206, 8.252, 10.220, Z Pr 73; *a* miserable 13.94

wrecchede *a* miserable, miserly B 15.142; wretched, unhappy A 10.144; vile 1.37

wrec(c)hednesse *n* viciousness 6.333, 12.2, 20.353

wreken *v* (*p.p.* **wreke** 20.432, 22.204, Z 2.173, **wroken** 9.259, B 2.195) ? force, **ar wroken into** have forced their way into 9.259*n*; give vent to, (*refl.*) vent / satisfy oneself B 9.183; be avenged (upon) 20.432, 22.204, (*refl.*) avenge oneself A 5.67

wreth 21.306 = **wrat(t)he** *n*

wryen *v* twist aside, *p.p.* **ywrye** 16.74

wry(g)ht(e) *n* craftsman, carpenter 11.241, 244, 13.160, 19.138, Z 6.77, (*fig.*) 11.253

wryng(y)en *v* (*p.t.* **wronge** 8.172, **wrang** 2.252) wring (*fig.*) B 14.18; (*ellip.*) wring one's hands 2.252; clench and unclench B 5.84; squeeze 8.172; twist, pervert, ~ **lawe** (*person.*) 4.31

writ *n* writing, **holy** ~ authoritative religious tradition 1.125 *etc*, Holy Scripture, the Bible Pr 205 *etc* (*see* **holy** ~); legal document A 2.46, [= the Mosaic law] 19.19, B 17.3

writen *v* (*p.t. sg.* **wro(e)t** 5.139, 14.37, **wroot** B 11.168, *pl.* **writen** B 10.339, *p.p.* **(y)writen** 1.195, 19.13) write 14.40, **B** 9.39, 13.248, *ger.* written words B 12.82, A 8.43; inscribe, incise 19.13, 16, B 15.581, A 10.111, (have) inscribe(d) 3.69, 16.40, *ger.* inscription 3.73; act as a scribe 5.68; write down, record 1.194, 11.116, 122, 14.37, 38, 47, *ger.* 21.465; **B** 10.454, 11.168, 225, 12.258, A 10.109, **don / garen** ~ cause to be recorded 5.146, 8.94, 11.122, B 5.241, ~ **in noumbre** enrol formally 22.259; set down / state in writing 5.139, 8.240, 16.155, **B** 11.392,

13.71, 15.488, A 12.101, *ger. pl.* writings 20.356; compose (poem) 21.1, 484, (book) B 10.339, 427

writhen *v* (*p.t.* **wroþ**, *p.p.* **(y)writhe(n)**) twist 7.162; clench 19.142, A 5.67

writyng *ger. see* **writen** *v*

wroche Z Pr 73 *see* **wrec(c)he** *n*

wroet *p.t.* 14.37 *etc*; *see* **writen** *v*

wroeth 17.3, 4 *see* **wro(o)th** *a*

wroȝt *p.p.* 3.133, **B** 5.366, 7.97, 14.137, **wrouȝthe** A 12.101 = **wrouht** *p.p.*; *see* **worchen** *v*

wroghte, wroȝte *p.t.* 1.26, **B** 1.82, 9.51, 154, 10.34, *subjv.* B 6.246, 248, *pl.* †**wroȝten** B 14.196, **wroghton** *subjv. pl.* 1.13 = **wrouhte(n)**; *see* **worchen** *v*

wroke(n) *p.p.* 9.259, **B** 2.195, 18.391, 20.204 *see* **wreken** *v*

wrong[1] *n* wrong, injustice [esp. in legal sense], **with** ~ unjustly, wrongfully 19.234, 21.353, B 1.128, (*person.*) 1.59 *et p.*; fault, injury 3.221; evil A 10.75; wicked practice 13.74; mischief B 10.19

wrong[2] *av* wickedly A 11.260; ~**ly** unjustly 3.92

wrong(e)[3] *p.t.* 8.172, B 2.237 *see* **wryng(y)en** *v*

wro(o)t *p.t.* 5.139, 11.116, 21.1, **B** 11.168, 392, 15.581, A 10.109 *see* **writen** *v*

wro(o)th *a* angry 11.3, 17.3, 4, B 4.174; (*comp.*) ~**er** Pr 117; stirred to anger A 10.161; annoyed 7.77, 13.43; aggrieved B 15.488; furious 3.483

wroþ *p.t.* A 5.67 *see* **writhen** *v*

wrothe 6.105, 11.110 = **wrat(t)he** *n*

wroþerhele *n* evil fortune, *in phr.* **to** ~ for (a life of) misfortune 15.301, **to** ~ **manye** to the harm of many A 2.20

wroþliche *av* angrily A 5.67

wrouht(e), wrouȝt *p.p.* 2.119, 15.301, 20.353, 22.308, A 10.34, 12.10; *p.t.* 1.164 *etc*, **B** 1.150, 11.168, 396, **A** 10.147, 11.270, 12.101, ~**en** *pl.* 8.116, 11.272, *subjv.* 11.224; *see* **worchen** *v*

wurchen 5.25= **worchen** *v*

ȝa A 3.101, 192, 5.154 = **ȝe**[1] *av*

ȝaf, yaf *p.t.* 1.15, 10.180, B 1.107 *et p.*; *see* **ȝeuen** *v*

yald *p.t.* B 12.192 *see* **ȝelden** *v*

yarken *v* prepare B 7.78

†**yarn** *p.t.* **B** 5.440, 11.60 *see* **ȝernen** *v*[1]

ȝate (yate) *n* gate Pr 132, 7.241 (*fig.*), 11.42, 20.270, 284, 362, 365, 21.168, 22.299, 302, 330, 349, 377, Z 5.39

ȝe[1] *av* yes 3.147, 5.104, 7.199, 8.238, 11.155, 314, 13.246, 15.249, 16.137, 18.58, 81, **B** 5.250, 6.37, Z 3.143; oh yes 11.195, 21.399, 22.189

ȝe[2] (**ye**) *pers. prn.* 2 *pl.* you Pr 74, 11.70 *et p.*; *as polite sg.* 1.136, 3.57, 8.36 *et p.*, 11.91, 12.19 *et p.*, 13.242, 15.117, 19.230, 21.15 *et p.*, 22.323, 366, **B** 2.38, 3.344 *et p.*, 4.187, 6.124 *et p.*, 10.373, 388, 13.184, 15.22

ȝedden *v* sing A 1.138

ȝede(n) *p.t. pl.* Pr 41, 6.181 *et p.*, B 1.73; *see* **go(e)n** *v*

yeep B 11.18 = **ȝep** *a*

yeer B Pr 193 *etc; see* 3er *n*

3eepliche 16.329 *see* 3ep *a* ~

3ef¹ 7.259 = 3if; *see* yf *conj.*

3ef² *imper.* 12.166, 167, 15.146 *see* 3euen *v*

3efte (3ift(e), gyft(e)) *n* giving 21.254, of þe Popes ~ in the gift of the Pope B 13.246; gift, present 2.212, 3.24, 113, 266, 315, 338, 4.138, 7.268, 9.133, 13.60, 15.210, B 10.42, 11.193, 13.185; cash-offering 8.39, 9.48, B 5.53; retainer 3.269; to ~ as a present 11.103; (*euphem.*) bribe 2.163, 3.117, 126, 161, 229, 450, 485, B 7.40, A 3.229; (spiritual) gift (from God) 11.288, 14.33, B 12.63, 14.298

3elden *v* (*p.t.* 3eld(e) 14.132, yald B 12.192, *contr. pr.* 3elde 20.103, 3ilt B 18.100) pay, requite 8.133; render 9.339; pay back, restore 6.342, 8.41, B 6.43, to ~ so as to (have to) pay back 16.370, ~ a3eyn 6.309 (B 5.456); give back 21.394, B 7.78, 81; bring forth 17.88; surrender 14.132, 153, 20.103, *pr.p.* B 2.105; acknowledge, admit 6.424

3eman (3oman B) *n* attendant, *pl.* 3.269

3eme *n* notice, heed 3.485, B 10.197; *and see* gome *n²*

3emen *v* care for 10.308; govern B 8.52, A 10.72

yemere *n* guardian B 13.171

3ende (3ent) *av* (from) over there 20.261; over there 15.132

3ep (yeep) *a* lusty, vigorous 10.289, 11.179; ~liche *av* eagerly 16.329

3er (yeer) *n* (*pl.* 3er Pr 203, 3eres 8.345) year 11.179, ~s year's 22.287, = years' remission 9.22; *in phrr.* dere ~s 10.199; fele ~ many years (ago) 16.354; (a) fewe ~s Pr 63, 8.345, A 12.58; fyue ~ an indefinite number of years B 6.322; half ~ half a year 2.238; many ....~(es) 5.35, 6.86, 9.22, 11.260, 15.3, 16.286, 17.26, B 5.119; one ~es ende the end of a year B 2.105, 6.43; seuene ~ = a very long time Pr 203, 4.82, 6.108, 214, 7.64, 10.73, B 5.73; ten ~ 7.29, t(w)o ~ B 5.415, Z Pr 64

yerd *n¹* yard, kyrke ~ church graveyard Z 7.277

3erd *n²* (*pl.* 3erde(s)) rod 4.112, B 12.14, A 10.85; yard 6.220

yeresyeue *n* New Year's gift B 3.100, 10.47, 13.185, (*fig.*) B 8.52

3erne *av* quickly 22.159, B 4.74, as ~ as soon, in a trice 7.36; eagerly 4.53, 8.116, 320; earnestly 22.287

3ernen *v¹* (*p.t.* 3orn 12.12, †yarn B 5.440) run 3.269, 16.329

3ernen *v²* long for, desire 1.33, B 13.185

yet, 3et B Pr 185 *et p.*, A 1.127 *see* 3ut *av, conj.*

3eten *v* form, mould, *p.p.* y3oten 1.149

3euen (3yuen, gyuen) *v* (*p.t.* 3af *sg. and pl.* 1.15 *etc*, yaf B 1.107, gaf 2.322, *pl.* 3euen 22.301, yeuen Z 8.43, geuen 6.374, *pr. subjv.* B 3.166, *p.t. subjv.* yeue B 4.170, 12.197, 18.384, 3oue 20.425, *p.p.* yeuen B 2.31, gyue 2.126, 3ef *imper.* 12.166, 15.146) give Pr 74, 2.126, 3.212, 287, 289, 292, 411, 485, 498, 6.270,

7.84, 8.204, 177, 254, 10.180, 11.27, 282, 13.82, 14.89, 137, 15.146, 16.150, 17.67, 21.104, 125, 226, 230, 22.58, 291, B 1.107, 5.106, 6.241, 7.69, 8.52, 9.46, 91, 10.47, 11.195, 12.17, 13.171, 14.126, 151, 15.436; render 6.347, 439; give (in payment) 3.265, 271, B 4.170, 14.250, A 8.43; give (in marriage) B 9.163; grant (to) 3.315, 9.348, 10.60, 304, 11.27, 14.56, 194, 197, 20.425, 21.54, 60, 184, B 1.107, 7.198, A 8.236, 10.129, 12.111; endow with 1.15, 9.116, 11.282, 15.18, 20; hand out 2.232; distribute (as) alms 8.133, 9.68, 10.308, 12.166, 22.291, B 7.78, 81, 15.318, 323, 330, 336, A 11.243; marry 10.259; put 7.53; deliver 8.187, 22.301; ~ forth hand over 12.167, ~ fro give away, (alienate) from 5.163; ~ of care for 4.37, 22.155, A 8.179; *in phrr.* ~ never tale take no account whatever 21.457; ~ sorwe punish with misfortune 2.126, 19.309, B 2.121

3if 6.343 *et p.*, 3yf 7.36, yif B 5.424 = yf² *conj.*

3ift(e) 8.39, 9.133, B 2.201 *et p. see* 3eft(e) *n*

3ilt *contr. pr.* B 18.100 *see* 3elden *v*

3is B 5.634 = 3us *av*

3it B 15.603, 16.3, 216, 17.43 = 3ut *av, conj.*

3iuen A 4.91 *et p.* = 3euen *v*

3oke *n* yoke, pair (of oxen) 7.294

3one (yond) *dem. a* yonder, that...over there 20.147, 193

3ong(e) *a* young Pr 215, 5.35, 137, 10.289, *a as n* 308, 11.179, B 9.163, 12.6, A 10.58, 67

3orn *p.t.* 12.12 *see* 3ernen *v¹*

3our(e) *poss. a.* 2 *p. pl.* your Pr 74 *et p.*; *as polite sg.* 1.41, 3.56 *et p.*, 162, 182, 4.178, 189, 8.131 *et p.*, 20.92, 21.400, 22.203; *as poss. prn.* yours B 13.11, of you 21.474

3oue *p.t. subjv.* 20.425 *see* 3euen *v*

3ow(e) (3ou 1.2, yow B Pr 200, Z 2.1) 2 *p.pl. prn.* (*as dir. or indir. obj.*) you Pr 101 *et p.*; (to) you Pr 9 *etc,* B 10.269; for you 3.32 *etc*; upon you 20.90; (*refl.*) yourselves 5.167, 7.214, 8.125, 9.337, 10.227, 283, 21.258, 22.246, A 1.169; *as polite sg.* 3.56, 5.82, 7.296, 8.35, 131, 266, 20.90, 22.365, B 1.60, 3.347, 4.192, 16.1, 53, (*refl.*) 7.243, B 6.24

yowsuluen (yowsylue 5.141, yowselue B 10.272, yowself B 16.122) *emph.* 2 *p.pl.prn.* yourselves, *appositive* 5.141, B 16.122; (*refl.*) Pr 216 *etc*, B 10.283; you yourselves B 16.123 (*subj.*), B 10.272 (*obj.*)

3owthe *n* (the period of one's) youth 1.139, 6.240, 7.53, 12.12, 16.329, 22.155, B 7.92, A 3.89, 12.60

3us (3is) *av* (*emph. form of* ye¹ *in answer to question implying negative*) yes 6.91, 235, 7.286, 19.281

3ut (yut Z 8.90, yet B 2.1 *et p.*, 3it B 15.603, A 7.268) *av and conj.* further, besides Pr 219, 3.77, 229, 4.55, 62, 74, 131, 6.95, 156, 8.307, 16.135, 19.91, 94, 209, 234; furthermore 13.5; then again 13.51; moreover 3.43, 209, 6.36, 292, 8.257, 17.3, 19.245, 20.43, 264, A 11.293; nevertheless, for all that Pr 199, 1.164, 2.151,

3.138, 5.94, 6.230, 317, 440, 7.31, 8.266, 9.105, 10.38, 108, 13.60, 17.75, 133, 298, 307, 19.233, 246, 20.101, 435; yet, still 6.51, 327, 332, 9.134, 10.191, 17.48, 19.179, B 16.3, A 4.21; even now, still 17.182, 19.114, 20.408, B 15.603; ?hereafter, at length 3.451; *in phrr*:

bet ~ still better 10.189; **neuere** ~ never yet B 16.216; ~ **lasse** still / even less 4.156, ~ **leeste** (and) least of all 3.209; ~ **mo(re)** still / even more 9.132, 10.82, 12.241, 16.132, 19.264; ~ **worse, worse ʒit** still / even worse 16.14, B 17.43; *as a* ~ **a** one more 8.35, Z 8.90

Latin and French Words and Phrases

Separable material appended to text-lines appears in the *Index of Quotations*, as do longer words and phrases enclosed in text-lines when they retain the appearance of citations to be recognised as such. This section includes words and a few phrases that clearly form part of the lexical repertoire; some, of indeterminate status in the contemporary language, appear both here and in the main Glossary. As with the latter, items are keyed to the **C** Version but those not occurring there are cited from **B**, **A** or **Z** as appropriate.

LATIN

Actiua active 18.80

Actiua Vita Active Life 15.195, 276, 16.116, 18.83, B 14.28

Amor Love 16.194

Anima soul (a) 10.134 *et p.*; (b) 16.181

Animus Will 16.182

A pena et a culpa from punishment and guilt 9.3, 23, 186

Ad pristinum statum ire to return to the first state 5.171, B 10.319

Archa Dei the Ark of God Pr 108, 112, 14.58, B 10.282

Archa Noe Noah's Ark 11.247

Audiatis alteram partem (provided that) you hear the other party 4.188

Auees Hail Marys 16.321

Benedicite Bless me (Father) 7.6

capias...carceratis take (Mede) and keep her safe, but not with those in prison 4.165

caristia dearth B 14.72

Caritas charity 14.14, 18.14, 32; *Caritatis* of charity B 2.35

Caro Flesh **B** 9.49, 17.108

caute prudently Z 5.143

clamat cotidie cries out daily 21.419

Concupiscencia carnis Lust of the Flesh 11.174 *et p.*

consummatus Deus fully and truly God 20.23

Contemplatiua Vita Contemplative Life 18.83

contra 'I dispute that' 10.20, 14.202, B 10.343

#*contumax* guilty of contumacy 13.84

Cor-hominis the heart of man 18.4

Cordis contricio... contrition of heart, confession of mouth, satisfaction through works 16.315

Credere in ecclesia to believe in the Church 3.356

*culorum conclusion 3.432, 11.249

cura animarum care of souls B 14.286

Dia perseverans a long-lasting (potion of) perseverance 15.57

*dido old tale 15.172

Dirige (opening antiphon of) Office of the Dead 3.463, 5.46

Disce, doce, dilige (Deum / inimicos) learn, teach, love (God / your enemies) 15.142 (B 13.137)

dominus lord(ship) B 10.330; ~ *virtutum* lord of hosts B 18.319a

dos ecclesie the endowment of the Church 17.215, 223

episcopus bishop 16.203

ergo therefore 10.28, 15.264, 16.126, 20.388, 21.19

Ergo saluabitur therefore he will be saved 14.204

Esto sobrius be sober 6.168

Ex vi transicionis from the power of transitivity B 13.152

Filius Son (of God) 18.121, 194, 19.192; ~ *Dei* son of God *2.31*, ~ *Marie* son of Mary 21.118

fornicatores fornicators 2.191

gaӡophilacium the Treasury B 13.198

Gigas Giant (*as name*) B 18.252

Hic et hec homo this and this (male / female) human being 3.404

humana natura human nature 20.22

Id est, Vetus Testamentum et Nouum That is (to say), the Old Testament and the New 21.274 *a*

ignorancia non excusat ignorance [of church law] does not excuse [bishops] 13.128 (B 11.316–17)

Ymago-Dei the image of God 18.7

In Dei nomine, Amen in the name of God, Amen 8.95

in deitate Patris in the divine nature [Christ has] of the Father 20.25

in die iudicii on the day of Judgement 15.120

in extremis in extreme circumstances, at the point of death B 10.346

in fautores suos on their supporters B 15.215

in genere in / according to the nature B 14.182

in Inferno in hell B 17.109

in Limbo Inferni in the Verge of Hell 18.116

in magestate Dei within the Divine Majesty 18.118

infamis of ill-repute B 5.166

ingrati ungrateful B 14.169

ingratus unkind 19.220

Ite, missa est go, Mass is ended B 5.413

iustus...vix the just man...on judgement day will be not saved witout the help of 'scarcely'

Latro Robber 6.329

laudabimus eum we will praise him 15.283

Lauacrum-lex-Dei a bath, the law of God 19.73

Legende [*legenda*] *Sanctorum* the *Lives of the Saints* [of Jacobus de Voragine] 17.157, **B** 11.60, 219, 15.269

Lex Christi the law of Christ B 17.72

Libera Voluntas Dei the Free Will of God 18.118

Liberum Arbitrium Free Choice / Judgement 16.156, 18.1 *et p.,* B 16.16 *et p.*

Liberum-Dei-arbitrium the Free Choice of God 20.20

licitum lawful, permissible B 11.96

Magi wise men 21. 85

mea culpa through my fault 6.64

Memoria memory, recollection 16.184

Mens mind, thought 16.183

mercedem payment, a fee Z 8.61

Metropolitanus metropolitan, archbishop 16.202, (fig.) 17.267

Modicum a little, scarcity B 18.215

Multi many 12.48

Nominatiuo, Pater... namely, Father, Son and Holy Spirit 3.405*a*

Non de solo not from the soil 5.68

Non saluabitur will not be saved 15.24

Nullum malum... No evil...unpunished...no good unrewarded 4.140–1

Osanna Hosanna ('Save'!) 20.7

Parce [*mihi Domine*] Spare [me O Lord] 21.296, B 18.393

Pastor pastor, shepherd 16.203

Pateat... Let it be manifest...through the passion of the Lord B 14.190*a*

Pater [God the] Father 18.193; *Pater Abbas* Father Abbot 6.153

Paternoster n Our Father [the Lord's Prayer] 5.46, 87, 107, 6.283, 399, 7.10, 11.299, 15.250, 16.321, 21.397, **B** 10.468, 13.237, 14.197

Pauci few

Pax vobis Peace [be with you] 17.238, 21.169

pecuniosus moneyed, rich 12.10

Penitencia (sacramental) penance B 5.475

Per confessionem...occiduntur through confession sins are destroyed B 14.91

Per primicias et decimas by first fruits and tithes 17.219*a*

per secula seculorum for ever and ever 20.467

Petrus, id est, Christus Peter, that is, Christ B 15.212

Placebo [the antiphon] I will please the Lord 3.463, 5.46, B 15.125

plenitudo temporis (**tyme**) the (time of the) fullness of time 18.127, 139

Pontifex pontiff B 15.42

Post-mortem after death 15.50

Potencia Dei Patris the power of God the Father 18.34

pre manibus beforehand 3.299, 9.45

prescite foreknown 11.208

Presul prelate 16.202

preuaricatores legis those who pervert the law 10.95

primus heremita the first hermit 17.13

Principes rulers 20.272

pro Dei pietate for the love of God B 7.45

pseudo-propheta false prophet 17.309

quadriduanus for four days 17.303, 18.145

quasi dormit is asleep, as it were 9.257

quasi modo geniti as if born 12.112

Qui cum Patre et Filio who with the Father and the Son 5.199

Qui turpiloquium loquitur He who utters foul words Pr 40

Quis est ille who is he? 15.284

Quis est iste who is this? B 18.315*a*

quodlibet general problem [in philosophy or theology] B 15.381

†*Quodque mnam* every pound Z 5.124n

Racio Reason 16.186

Ramis palmarum [the feast of] Palm branches (Palm Sunday)

Recordare remember [?= sing psalms / meditate] B 4.120

rectores rectors [of churches] 2.184

Redde quod debes Pay what you owe 21.188, 260, 393, 22.309

Reddere means of repayment 6.321; *Reddite* repay 6.315; *reddit quod debet* pays what he owes 21.194

Redemptor Redeemer 12.116

Regum (the Book) of Kings 3.412

resureccio mortuorum the resurrection of the dead 20.412

Rex Glorie... the King of Glory B 18.318

Sanctorum of the Saints (*see* **Legende**~)

Sapiencia Dei Patris the Wisdom of God the Father 18.40

Sapiense the Wisdom writings (of the Bible) 3.494, *spec.* Proverbs 3.484

sapienter wisely 13.125

satisfaccio satisfaction 16.31

Sensus (sense)-perception, understanding through the senses 16.187

seruus nequam a wicked servant B 6.238

si if (*signifying a condition*) = 'unless, provided that (not)'

simile likeness, comparison 18.228, 19.161

sine restitucione without making restitution [*sc.* of ill-gotten gains] 6.257

solus Deus one sole God 18.191

Spes Hope 19.1 *et p.*

Spiritus (disembodied) spirit 16.196

Spiritus Fortitudinis the spirit [= virtue] of fortitude 21.290, 467, 22.24, 25; ~ *Intellectus* the spirit of understanding 21.466; ~ *Iusticie* the spirit of justice 21.299 *et p.*, 22.24; ~ *Prudencie* the spirit of prudence 21.277, 458, 22.31; ~ *Temperancie* the spirit of temperance 21.282, 22.8 *et p.*

Spiritus Sanctus the Holy Spirit (of God) 18.51, 121, B 17.209, ~ *Paraclitus* Comforter 21.202, 207

stella comata star trailing fire (*lit.* 'long-haired star'), = comet 20.247

supersedeas (name of) a writ staying or ending a legal proceeding 2.187, 4.190, 9.263

transgressores wrongdoers, law-breakers 1.92

turpiloquio (with) foul speech 7.116 (B 13.447)

Verbi gratia by way of example B 15.267

Vigilare to keep watch 9.258

Vigilate keep watch 7.56

FRENCH

Beau fitz fair son 9.311

Beaute sanz bounte beauty without goodness 17.163

bele fine 16.268

bele paroles fine words 16.268

chaud...pluchaut hot...piping hot 8.334

Dew vous saue, Dame Emme God keep you, Lady Emma Pr 226

douce vie luxurious living 15.303

pur charite for charity's sake 8.169, 266, 10.11, 15.33, A 7.182

semyuief half-alive 19.57

treys encountre treys three against three 18.239

Supplementary Index

This list includes words (mainly variants recorded in the Apparatus and some major rejected conjectures) that are discussed in the **Textual Notes** but not listed in the **Indexical Glossary**.

Index of Proper Names

Fine(e)s (Phineas) Pr 107,123, B 10.281
Fyppe 11.314
Fysik (Physic) 8.291, 22.169
Flaterere 17.112; **Frere** ~ 22.316, 324
Flaundres 6.366
Flemmynges Z 7.278
Foleuile 21.248
Fortune 11.168 *et p.*, 311, 12.7, 15.5, 22.156, B 6.218
Fra(u)nce Pr 192, 3.242, 257, 4.125, 10.135, 15.156
Fra(u)nceys, St 4.117, 16.354, 22.252, B 15.420
Frenche men Z 7.278
Frere Faytour 8.74
Fre Wille B 16.223

Gabriel 18.124
Gales = Galys
Galilee 21.147, 158
Galys (Galicia) 4.124, 7.165, Z Pr 50
Garlekhiþe B 5.317
Gascoyne Pr 230
Geffrey, Sir B15.123
Genesis 8.240, **(the geaunt)** B 6.231
Gybbe B 5.91
Gigas **(the geaunt)** B 18.252
Gyle 2.70 *et p.*, 17.111, Z 2.28, A 2.24
Gyle, St (Giles) 4.51, 8.54
Glotonye 2.97, 16.71,
Glotoun 6.349 *et p.*, 8.32, Z 7.275
Gobelyne 20.323, 328
God *see* Main Indexical Glossary
Godefray þe garlek-monger 6.372
Goed Faith 22.131; ~ **Go-wel, Sire** 10.148 **(Godefray Go-wel** B 9.22)
Grace 7.247, 21.121, 214 *et p.*, 263, 275, 319 *et p.*, 22.387
Gregory, (Pope) St[1] (the Great) 5.146, 12.79, 82, 21.271, B 7.74, 10.324, 11.228, 15.443
Gregory, (Pope) St[2] (the Ninth) B 5.164
Gryffyth þe Walshe (the Welshman) 6.372

Haukyn (þe Actif Man) B 13.273 *et p.*, 14.1 *et p.*
Heyne A 5.91
Hele 22.153
Hendenesse 22.145
Hende-Speche 22.349, 355
Here-wel, Sire 10.146
Herodes 10.179
Hertfordshyre 6.412
Heruy, Sir 6.197
Hewe þe Nedlare 6.364
Hicke þe Hackenayman 6.364 *et p.*
Holi Chirche Pr 64, 1.72 *et p.*, 12.53, A 12.17
Holy Writ Pr 205, 1.69, 125, 2.142, 3.486, 5.37, 17.37, A 12.97

Holynesse 12.1, 22.145
Hope 7.151, 19.61, B 17.53
Hunger 8.168 *et p.*, A 12.63 *et p.*

Ydelnesse 21.229
Ymaginatyf 14.1, 202, 15.17, 21, B 10.117
Ymago-Dei (the Image of God) 18.7
Ynde India 17.272, 21.165
Yngelond Pr 194, 17.279, 22.280, B 15.442
Inwit, Sire 10.144, 172 *et p.*
Ypocras (Hippocrates) B 12.43
Ypocrisye 22.301 *et p.*
Yre 2.88, Z 5.91
Ireland 22.221
Ysaak (Isaac) 18.248, B 16.232
Ysaye (Isaiah) 11.259, 18.113, B 15.573
Ysodorus (of Seville) 16.197
Israel (Jacob), †9.316, (nation) A 3.243, **children of** ~ Pr 105, 111, B 10.279

Iacke þe iogelour 8.71
Iacob 9.310, **(~es welle)** Z 5.70
Iame(s), St 1.180, 21.164, B 6.55, A 12.108, (*meton.*) Pr 48, 4.122, 5.197, Z 5.130
Ierico 19.51, Z 5.70
Iero(e)m 21.271, A 12.108
Ierusalem 19.52,79, 20.15, 17, B 16.163, 17.115, Z 5.70, 130
Iesu 12.128, 15.22, 18.152, 20.40, 89, 94, 103, 21.25, 34, 40, 44, 48, 91, 95, 101, 106, 117, 136, 164, **B** 10.35, 128, 15.264, 18.38, A 12.27, ~ **Crist B** 11.184, 246, 14.181, 16.222, **God** ~ 21.18, **Lord** ~ 21.8, 174, **prince** ~ 13.3, 21.96, B 16.37, *in asseverations*: Pr 180, 3.192, 10.22, 21.400
Iesus 17.308, 18.126, 129, 130, 162, 168, 170, 171, 178, 20.21, 26, 37, 84, 183, 261, 21.15, 19, 25, 70, 108, 139, **B** 12.13, 89, 16.121, 144, 147, 150, 161, 18.253, 254, 300, **Iesus'** 18.166, ~ **the ioustare** 21.10, ~ **a iustices sone** 18.126, ~ **passioun, of** ~ 17.192, 18.41, *in asseverations*: 20.462, B Pr 165, Z 5.130
Iew B 9.82, 15.264, ~ **Longeus** 20.84, **Iob þe** ~ B 12.42, **Iudas þe** ~ 18.166, B 10.128
Iewes (Iewen(e) *gen. pl.*), 1.63, 3.479, 4.194, 6.241, 12.56, 14.200, 17.132,156, 252, 295, 304, 313, 18.150, 162 *et p.*, 20.15 *et p.*, 95, 113, 21.10 *et p.*, 139 *et p.*, 425, **B** 9.85 *et p.*, 10.35, 346, 15.583, 16.127, A 11.27, 235
Iob 11.21, 13.5, 14, 19, 24, 17.51, 20.151, B 12.42, **(Iop)** A .12.108
Io(ha)n Jack (= some low fellow) B 7.44; ~ **But** A 12.106; **Maister** ~ [type-name of cook] 21.289; **Sire** ~ (priest, type-name) B 15.123
Io(ha)n, St[1] (the Evangelist) 7.24, 100, 139, 12.100, 14.136, 142, 21.164, 266, B 11.226, 244
Iohan, St[2] (the Baptist) 10.181, 11.258, 18.114, 268, 20.367, B 16.250

Morales (the *Moralia in Job* of Pope St Gregory the Great) B 10.293
Munde þe miller 2.113, B 10.44

Nabugodonasor (Nebuchadnezzar) 9.306
Nasareth 17.189, 21.137
Nede 13.240, 22.4, 51, 232
Neptalym (Naphtali) 17.189, 261
Nyneue (Nineveh) 17.189, 261
Noe 10.179, 223, 11.239, 242, 254, **B** 9.131, 10.406
Normandie B 3.189, **Normawndye** Z 3.148
Nor(th)folk, B 5.235, **Z** 3.148, 5.98

Offini (Ophni) Pr 107, 123, **Offyn** B 10.281
Omnia-probate (Try everything) A 12.50, 56
Oseye (Alsace) Pr 230
Oʒias (Hosea) B 15.576

Pacience 7.273, 15.33 *et p.*,95 *et p.*, 154 *et p.*, 234 *et p.*, 16.114, 161, B 13.355
Pampilon (Pamplona) 19.219
Paradys 16.223, 20.378
Pasche (Easter) 18.167
Paul the Apostle *see* **Pou(e)le, St**
Paul *primus heremita* (the first Hermit) 17.13
Paulines (the Pauline friars) 2.110c
Pees (King's Peace) 4.45 *et p.*, (Truth's porter) 7.273, (Daughter of God) 20.170 *et p.*, 451 *et p.*, (Porter of Unity 22.299, 331 *et p.*
Penetrans-domos, **Sire** Sir-Piercer-of-Homes 22.341
Penitencia B 5.475
Peres, Syre ~ of Prydie 6.366
Peres þe Pardoner 2.110
Per(e)s (the Plouhman) 7.199 *et p.*, 8.7 *et p.*, 9.1 *et p.*, 282, 299, 300, 15.34, 132, 139, 151, 154, 196, 214, 16.338, 20.8 *et p.*, 21.6 *et p.*,184 *et p.* 22.77, 309, 321, 383, 386, B 16.17 *et p.,* 13.130, 238, 15.196, 212, 16.17, 18.20, 21, 103, 168, 171, **A** 8.152, 12.102
Perkyn (familiar diminutive of **Peres Plouhman**) 8.1, 56, 112 *et p.*, 9.292, B 7.131, Z 8.90
Pernel, St A 7.259 *see* **Purnele**
Peter, St, the Apostle Pr 128, 136, 9.112, 15.226, 16.167, 17.19, 224, 20.251, 21.163 *et p.*, **B** 10.344, 442, 15.265, A 11.233, Z 5.92; (church) B 7.173; (in oaths) 7.181, 8.1, **B** 7.131, 11.87, Z 7.26
Pilat(us) (Pontius Pilate) 20.35, 39, 82, B 10.34, A 12.26
Plato 11.120, 308, 12.175, 14.189, 22.275
Pocalips (*Apocalypse*) 15.100
Pope 2.23, 244, 3.183, 5.192, 15.174, 17.233
Porfirie (Porphyry) 12.175, 14.189
Potencia-Dei-Patris (Power of God the Father) 18.34, B 16.30
Pou(e)l(e), St (St. Paul the Apostle) Pr 39, 9.112, 10.89, 11.269, 15.73, 76, 16.167, 289, 17.17, 19.224, 319, **B**

10.344, 12.29, 15.156, 265, **A** 7.3, 10.109, 12.22, Z 5.92; (*in oaths*) 8.297, **B** 5.639, 6.24, 11.87, A 7.3
Poules (St. Paul's Church) 11.56, 15.71, B 10.46
Pouerte 13.1
Prydie, Sire Peres of 6.366
Princeps huius mundi (Prince of this world) 10.135, A 10.62
Prucelond B 13.393 = **Pruys-lond**
Pruyde 6.14, 16.47 *et p.*, 210, 330, 21.224, 229, 337, 384, 22.70 *et p.*, 353 *et p.*; **~ of Parfit Lyuynge** 11.176, 194
Pruyslond (Prussia), 6.279 (B 13.393)
Purnele (St Petronilla) Z 7.279, [as type name (a) for proud woman 4.111, 5.128, 6.3 (b) for a nun 6.135 (c) for a priest's concubine 6.366, 17.72]

Quod-bonum-est-tenete Hold what is good [*allegorical place*] A 12.52, 57

Racio (Reason) 17.86
#Ragamoffyn 20.281
Raynald þe Reue 2.112
Randolf, Erle of Chestre 7.11
Rechelesnesse 11.199, 276, 286, 12.4, 13.129
Reignald B 4.49
Repentaunce 6.1 *et p.*, 7.8, 55, 119
Resoun 1.50, 3.437, 4.5 *et p.*, 5.6 *et p.*, 6.12, 12.67, 13.34, 143, 180 *et p.*, 15.27 *et p.*, 53, 152, 16.186, **B** 12.218, 15.11, A 4.142, 144, Z 4.126, 158
Reule (La Réole, Guienne) Pr 231
Reuthe 21.83
Reuel 22.181
Richard, King A 12.113
Rycher, St (St Richard of Chichester) Z 4.152
Rychesse 11.108
Rihtfulnesse 21.83
Rihtwisnesse 20.167 *et p.*, 466, 21.88
Ryn (Rhine) B Pr 230
Robardus (vagabonds) Pr 45
Robert Renaboute B 6.148
Robert the ruyflare (robbere B) 6.315, 321 (B 5.462)
Robyn Hode 7.11; **~ þe Ribauder** 8.75; **~ the Ropere** 6.386
Rochele (La Rochelle) Pr 231
Rochemador (Rocamadour) B 12.36
Romaynes (Romans) 17.282
Rome Pr 48, 2.243, 4.123, 125, 5.197, 6.246, 7.166, 8.1, 9.323, 16.38, 17.222, 19.219, 21.426, B 12.36, Z Pr 57; (ancient) **B** 11.153, 162
Rosamounde B 12.47
Rose (a widow) 4.47; **~ þe Regrater** 6.232; **~þe Disshere** 6.371
Ruth 3.412
Rutlande B 2.111

Index of Quotations

Quotations are in abbreviated form; references to versions other than **C** are given only if the quotation is not in parallel position. For translations and full details of sources given in brief see the **Commentary**.

A LATIN

A regibus et principibus (*after* Ecclus 38:2) B 7.43*a*, A 8.46*a*, Z 7.271

Absit nobis gloriari (Gal 6:14) 17.198*a*

Absque solicitudine felicitas (Vincent of Beauvais) 16.153*a*

Ad pristinum statum ire 5.171, B 10.319

Ad vesperum demorabitur fletus (Ps 29:6) 20.183*a*

Aduenit ignis diuinus (*after* Acts 2:3) 14.208*a*

Agite penitenciam (Job 21:2, Ezech 18:30) 15.56

Alter alterius onera portate (Gal 6:2) 8.231*a*, 13.77*a*, B 11.210*a*

Amen, Amen...mercedem suam recipiunt (Mt 6:5) 3.311, A 3.64*a*

Amen dico vobis, nescio vos (Mt 25:12) 19.216*a*, **B** 5.55, 9.66*a*

Amen dico vobis, quia hec vidua paupercula (Lk 21:3) 13.97*a*

Amice, ascende superius (Lk 14:10) 8.44*a*

Anima pro diuersis accionibus (Isidore of Seville, *Etymologiae* xi, i 13) 16.199*a*

Animam autem aufert accipiencium (Prov 22:9) 3.496*a*

Aperis tu manum tuam (Ps 144:16) 15.265*a*, 16.318

Appare quod es (Pseudo-Chrysostom) B 10.255*a*

Argentum et aurum non est michi (Acts 3:6) 15.226*a*

Ars vt artem falleret (Fortunatus' *Pange lingua*, *OBMLV*, no. 54, l. 8) 20.164*a*

Attollite portas (Ps 23:9) 20.270*a*

Audiui archana verba (II Cor 12:4) 20.438*a*, A 12.22*a*

Aue, raby (Mt 26:49) 18.169, 20.50

Beacius est dare (Acts 20:35) 14.16*a*

Beati omnes (Ps 127:1) **B** 5.419, 6.249

Beati pauperes (Mt 5:3) B 14.215*a*

Beati qui non viderunt et crediderunt (Jn 20:29) 21.182*a*

Beati quorum remisse sunt iniquitates (Ps 31:1) 7.152, 14.117*a*

Beati quorum tecta sunt peccata (Ps 31:1) **B** 12.177*a*, 13.53*a*, 14.93

Beatus est diues (Ecclus 31:8) 16.357*a*

Beatus est qui scripturas legit (St Bernard) 16.220

Beatus vir (Ps 1 *or* Ps 111) **B** 5.419, 10.320, 13.52

Benedictus qui venit (Mt 21:9) 20.15*a*

Bona arbor (Mt 7:17) 2.29*a*, 10.246*b*

Bonum est vt unusquisque uxorem suam habeat (I Cor 7:1–2) 10.297

Bonus pastor animam suam ponit (Jn 10:11) 17.193, 291*a*

Breuis oracio penetrat celum (*after* Ecclus 35:21) 11.300*a*

Brutorum animalium natura... (*after* Job 6:5) 17.53

Canes non valentes latrare (Is 56:100) B 10.287*a*

Cantabit paupertas coram latrone viator (Juvenal, *Sat.* x, 22) 14.304*a*

Captiuam duxit captiuitatem (Eph 4:8) 7.130*a*

Caritas expellit omnem timorem (I Jn 4:18) 15.166*a*

Caritas nichil timet (I Jn 4:18) B 13.164*a*

Caritas omnia suffert (I Cor 13:70) 17.5*a*

Celi enarrant gloriam Dei (Ps 18:1) 18.214*a*

Christus resurgens (Rom 6:9) 21.160

Clarior est solito post maxima (Alan of Lille) 20.453–4

Claudi ambulant (Mt 11:5, Lk 7:22) 18.142*a*

Clemencia non constringit (legal maxim) 5.60*a*

Concepit in dolore (Ps 7:15) 10.213*a*

Conflabunt gladios suos (Is 2:4) 3.460*a*

Confundantur omnes qui adorant sculptilia (Ps 96:7) B 15.81*a*

Consencientes et agentes (maxim of canon law) 7.86*a*, B 13.427*a*

Consummatum est (Jn 19:30) 20.57

Contricio et infelicitas (Ps 13:3) 4.36*a*

Contriuit Dominus baculum impiorum (Is 14:4–6) 5.177*a*, B 10.328

Conuertimini ad me (Is 45:22) B 14.180*a*

Cor contritum et humiliatum (Ps 50:19) 15.63, 16.334*a*

Cordis contricio... (penitential formula) 16.31*a*

Credo in Deum patrem (Apostles' Creed) 16.320, 17.316, B 10.467

Credo in Spiritum Sanctum (Apostles' Creed) 3.480

Crucifige (Jn 19:15) 20.38, 46

Cui des, videto (*Distichs of Cato*) 9.69

Cuius maledictione os plenum est (Ps 9B(10):7) 6.76*a*, 10.331*a*

Culpat caro, purgat caro ('Aeterne rex altissime', stanza 4) 20.450*a*

Cum ceciderit iustus non collidetur (Ps 36:24) B 16.25*a*

Cum facitis conuiuia (Lk 14: 12) 12.104*a*

Cum recte viuas (*DC*) A 10.98

Cum sanctus sanctorum veniat (*after* Dan 9:24, 26) B 15.599

Cum sancto, sanctus eris (Ps 17:26) 21.425, B 5.278

Cum veniat sanctus sanctorum (*after* Dan 9:24) 20.112*a*

Dabo tibi secundum peticionem tuam (Ps 36:4) 15.275

Dare histrionibus (? St Jerome) 7.118*a*

Date, et dabitur vobis (Lk 6:38) 1.195, B 12.54*a*

De delicijs ad delicias (St Jerome) B 14.144*a*

De peccato propiciato (Ecclus 5:5) 14.146*a*

De re que te non molestat noli certare (Ecclus 11:9) 13.197

Deleantur de libro viuencium (Ps 68:29) 8.77

Demonium habes (Jn 7:20, 8:48) 18.151*a*

Dentem pro dente (Ex 21:24) 20.385*a*

Deposuit potentes de sede (Lk 1:52) 17.215*a*

Descendit ad inferna (Apostles' Creed) 20.114

Deus caritas (I Jn 4:8) 1.82

Deus dicitur quasi ... (cf. Jn 17:2) B 12.290

Deus homo (*cf* Apostles' Creed) 3.401*a*

Deus meus...vt quid dereliquisti me? (Ps 21:2, Mt 27:46) B 16.214*a*

Deus Pater, Deus Filius B 10.240*a*

Deus, tu conuersus (*after* Ps 70:20) 7.151

Dextere Dei tu digitus (from *Veni creator spiritus*) 19.140*a*

Dignus est operarius (Lk 10:7) B 2.123

Dilige denarium (*DC*) B 10.337*a*

Dilige Deum et proximum tuum (Mt 22:37–40, Deut 6:5, Lev 19:18) 15.136, 19.14, B 15.583, A 11.242

Dilige Deum propter Deum (unidentified) 17.140*a*

Dimidium bonorum meorum (Lk 19:8) B 13.196

Dirige (Ps 5:9) 3.463, 5.46

Disce, doce, dilige Deum (unidentified) 15.142

Disce, doce, dilige inimicos (*cf* Mt 5:44, Lk 6: 27) B 13.137

Dispergentur oues (Mt 14:27, Mt 26:1) 9.261

Dispersit, dedit pauperibus (Ps 111:9) B 15.326

Diuicias nec paupertates (Prov 30:8) B 11.269

Diuisiones graciarum sunt (I Cor 12:4) 21.229*a*

Dixi ...confitebor tibi (Ps 31:5) B I3.54

Dixit Dominus domino meo (Ps 109:1) 1.121*a*

Dixit et facta sunt (Ps 148:5) 14.165*a*, 15.263*a*, B 9.32*a*

Dixit insipiens (Ps 13:1) B 7.136

Domine, iube me venire (Mt 14:28) 20.253

Domine, ne in furore tua (Pss 6:2, 37:2) 20.435*a*

Domine, non est tibi cure (Lk 10:40) 12.138*a*

Domine, quis habitabit (Ps 14:1) 2.39*a*, 15.136, B 3.234*a*, 7.51*a*

Dominus meus et Deus meus (Jn 20:28) 21.173

Dominus pars hereditatis mee (Ps 15:5) 5.60*a*, 14.128

Domus mea domus oracionis (Mt 12:13) B 16.135*a*

Donum Dei (St Augustine) 16.134*a*

Dormierunt et nichil inuenerunt (Ps 75:6) 15.311

Ducunt in bonis dies suos (Job 21:13) 11.22*a*

Dum cecus ducit cecum (Mt 15:14) 14.124*a*, B 10.275*a*

Dum rex a regere (semi-proverbial) B Pr 141–2

Dum sis vir fortis (*after* Prov 7:27) 10.290*a–b*

Dum steteritis ante reges (Mk 13:9, 11) 11.280

Dum tempus habemus (Gal 6:10) B 10.201*a*, A 11.245*a*

Eadem mensura qua mensi fueritis (Mt 7:2) 1.173*a*, 11.235*a*, B 11.226*a*

Ecce Agnus Dei (Jn 1:29) 18.269*a*, 20.367

Ecce altilia mea (Mt 22:4) B 15.463*a*

Ecce ancilla Domini (Lk 1:38) 18.133*a*

Ecce audivimus eam (Ps 131:6) 11.51*a*, B 15.489*a*

Ecce enim veritatem dilexisti (Ps 50:8) 6.302

Ecce ipsi idiote (St Augustine) 11.292

Ecce ipsi peccatores (Ps 72:12) 11.25*b*

Ecce quam bonum (Ps 132:1) 20.469*a*, A 11.192*a*

Edentes et bibentes (Lk 10:7) 15.45*a*

Ego in Patre, et Pater in me (Jn 14:10 or 11) 7.128*a*, 11.155*a*

Eice derisores (Prov 22:10) B 7.138*a*

Eice primo trabem (Lk 6:42) B 10.264*a*

Epulabatur splendide et induebatur bisso (Lk 16:19) 19.238

Ergo paupertas... (*see Paupertas est...*) B 14.285*a*

Esto forti animo (*DC*) 21.298

Et cecidit in foueam (Ps 7:16) B 18.361*a*

Et dimisi eos secundum desideria eorum (Ps 80:13) 10.165*a*, B 9.65*a*

Et dimitte nobis debita nostra (Mt 6:12 *from* the Lord's Prayer) 21.397*a*

Et egenos vagosque induc (Is 58:7) 9.125*a*

Et qui bona egerunt 12.120*a* (see *Qui bona*)

Et quorum tecta sunt peccata B 14.93 (see *Beati quorum tecta*)

Et reddet unicuique iuxta 14.152*a* (see *Reddet unicuique iuxta*)

Et si sal euanuerit (Mt 5:13) B 15.430*a*

Et super innocentem munera non accepit (Ps 14:5) 2.40*a*, B 7.41*a*

Et vidit Deus cogitaciones eorum (*after* Lk 11:17) 16.338*a*

Et vidit Deus cuncta que fecerat (Gen 1:31) B 11.396*a*

Et visitauit et fecit redempcionem (Lk 1:68) 15.118*a*

Ex habundancia panis et vini (Comestor) 15.231*a*

Existimasti inique (Ps 49:21) 12.30, B 10.285

Faciamus [hominem ad ymaginem] (Gen 1:26) **B** 5.487*a*, 9.35, 42

Facite vobis amicos de mammona (Lk 16:9) 8.235*a*, 19.248*a*

Fiat voluntas Dei (see next) 5.88

Fiat voluntas tua (Mt 6:10) 15.252, 16.319

Fides non habet meritum (Gregory) 11.159*a*

Fides sine operibus (Js 2:26) 1.182*a*

Fides, spes, caritas (I Cor 13:13) B 12.29*a*

Fides sua (Lk 7:50) B 11.217

Fiet vnum ouile (Jn 10:16) 18.265*a*

Fili David (Mt 9:27) 20.13, 21.133, 136

Filii hominum, dentes eorum (Ps 56: 5) 6.76*a* (B 13.331*b*)

Filius non portabit (Ezech 18:20) 10.239, B 10.112*a*

Fodere non valeo (Lk 16:3) Z 5.142

Frange esurienti panem tuum (Is 58:7) 11.67*a*

Fuerunt michi lacrime mee (Ps 41:4) B 7.124*a*

Gaudere cum gaudentibus (Rom 12:15) A 11.193*a*

Gloria in excelsis (Lk 2:14) 14.94, 21.74*a*, **B** 3.328, 12.150

Gloria, laus (Theodulph of Orléans) 20.6

Non de solo...pabulo (cf. Mt 4:4) 5.86–7

Non dimittitur peccatum (see *Numquam dimittitur peccatum*)

Non eligas cui miserearis (Jerome) B 7.75*a*–*b*

Non est sanis opus medicus (Mt 9:12) B 16.110*a*

Non est timor Dei (Ps 13:3) B 4.37*a*

Non excusat episcopos B 11.316

Non habitabit in medio domus mee (Ps 100:7–8) 7.92*a*, B 13.433*a*

Non inflatur (I Cor 13:4–5) 16.289*a*

Non in solo pane (Mt 4:14) 15.246*a* (and see *Non de solo*)

Non intres in iudicium (Ps 142:2) 20.442*a*

Non leuabit gens (Is 2:4) 3.476*a*

Non licet nobis legem voluntati (maxim, source unknown) 9.212*a*

Non mecaberis (Ex 20:14) B 10.366

Non morabitur opus (Lev 19:13) 3.307*a*

Non occides (Ex 20:13) 1.449*a*

Non oderis fratres (Lev 19:17) 12.35

Non omnis qui dicit Domine (Mt 7:21) 19.230*a*

Non plus sapere (Rom 12:3) 16.227, B 10.118*a*

Non reddas malum (Prov 20:20) 5.58*a*

Non saluabitur 15.23 see *Vix saluabitur*

Non veni solvere legem (Mt 5:17) 20.395*a*

Non veni vocare iustos (Lk 5:32) 7.138*a*

Non visurum se mortem (Lk 2:26) 20.259*a*

Nullum malum inpunitum (Pope Innocent III) 4.140–1, 20.433

Numquam colligunt de spinas (Mt 7:16) 10.247*a*

Numquam, dicit Iob, rugiet onager (Job 6:5) 17.52*a*

Numquam dimittur peccatum (St Augustine,) 6.257*a*, 19.288*a*, B 5.272*a*

Nunc princeps huius mundi (see *Princeps huius mundi*) 20.349*a*

O felix culpa (*Exultet* Prose from Liturgy of Easter Saturday) 7.125*a*

O Mors ero mors tua (Osee 13:14) 20.34*a*, B 17.112*a*

O stulte (Lk 12:20) 12.217*a*

O vos omnes sicientes (Is 55:1) 12.58*a*

Ociositas et habundancia panis (*after* Peter Cantor) B 14.76*a*

Odisti omnes qui operantur iniquitatem (Ps 5:7) 20.356*a*

Omnia celestia terrestria flectantur (Phil 2: 10) 21.80*a*

Omnia probate (I Thess 5:21) 3.489, 20.233*a*, A 12.50, 56

Omnia que dicunt, facite (Mt 23:3) 8.90*a*

Omnia traham ad me ipsum (Jn 12:32) 19.127*a*

Omnia sunt tua ad defendendum 21.482*a* (legal saying)

Omnis iniquitas quoad misericordiam Dei (after Augustine) 6.337*a*

Opera illorum sequuntur illos (Rev 14:13) 16.54*a*

Operibus credite (Jn 10:38) 16.340*a*

Oris confessio, Operis satisfaccio 16.30, 31*a*, B 14.17*a* see *Cordis contricio*

Pacientes vincunt (from *Testament of Job*) 15.139, 158*a*, 256, **B** 13.135*a*, 15.267, 597*a*

Panem nostrum cotidianum (Mt 6:11) 16.372*a*

Parce michi Domine (Job 7:16) 21.296

Parum lauda (attrib. to Seneca) 12.41*a*

Pastores loquebantur ad inuicem (Lk 2:15) 14.86*a*

Pauper ego ludo (Alexander of Ville-Dieu) 12.155*a*

Pauper non habet diuersorium B 12.147*a* see *Set non erat ei locus*

Paupertas est absque sollicitudine semita 16.141*a* (see next)

Paupertas est odibile bonum (Vincent of Beauvais) 16.115

Paupertatis onus (*DC*) 8.337*a*

Peccatoribus dare (Peter Cantor, after Jerome) B 15.342*a*

Pena pecuniaria non sufficit ... (Canon law maxim) 12.10*a*

Penetrans-domos (II Tim 3 6) 22.341

Penitet me fecisse hominem (Gen 6:7) 10.224

Per confessionem...peccata occiduntur (penitential maxim) B 14.91

Per Euam cunctis (Lauds of BVM) 7.249*a*

Periculum est in falsis fratribus (II Cor 11:26) 15.76*a* (see also *Vnusquisque a fratre*)

Perniciosus dispensator (perhaps after Peter Cantor) B 9.92*a*

Petite et accipietis (Mt 7:73) B 15.427*a*

Philosophus esses si tacuisses (John Bromyard, after Boethius) 13.225*a*

Piger propter frigus (Prov 20:4) 8.246*a*

Pilatus...sedens pro tribunali (Mt 27:19) 20.35

Ponam pedem meum in aquilone (Augustine, after Is 14:13–14) 1.110*a*, 16.211*b*

Populus qui ambulabat in tenebris (Is 9:2) 7.133*a*, 20.366

Porro non indiget monachus (cf. I Tim 6:8) B 15.342*a*

Possessio sine calumpnia 16.126a (Vincent of Beauvais)

Precepta Regis (Roman law maxim) B Pr 145

Princeps huius mundi (Jn 16:11) 10.135, 20.349*a*, A 10.62

Pro hac orabit ad te (Ps 31:6) 15.61

Proditor est prelatus (after Peter Cantor) B 9.92*a*

Propter Deum subiecti estote (I Pet 2:13) B 11.382*a*

Psallite deo nostro (Ps 46:7–8) 13.123*a*

Qualis pater, talis filius (proverbial) B 2.27*a*

Quam olim Abrahe promisisti (from the *Magnificat*, based on Lk 1:55) B 16.242*a*

Quando misi vos sine pane (after Lk 22:35) 9.120*a*

Quandocumque ingemuerit peccator (pseudo-Ezekiel; cf. Jer 31:34b) 7.147*a*

Quare impij viuunt (Job 21:7) B 10.25*a*

Quare non dedisti pecuniam (Lk 19:23) B 7.81*a*

Quare placuit (cf. Ps 134:6, 113b: 3, Job 23:13) 14.155*a*

Quare via impiorum prosperatur (Job 21:7, Jer 12:1) A 11.23*a*

Sunt iusti atque sapientes (Eccl 9:1) 11.275*a*

Super cathedram Moysi (Mt 23:2) 8.86*a*, 11.238*a*, A 11.223

Super egros manus (Mk 16:18) 15.223*a*

Super innocentem munera (Ps 14:5) B 7.41*a*

Talis pater, talis filia 2.27*a* (see *Qualis pater, talis filius*)

Tanquam nichil habentes (II Cor 6: 10) 13.4*a*

Te Deum laudamus (hymn for Sunday Matins) 20.468

Ter cesus sum (II Cor 11:25) B 13.67*a*

Tezaurisat et ignorat (Ps 38:7) 12.217*a*

Tibi soli peccaui (Ps 50:6) 20.420*a*

Tolle, tolle (Jn 19:15) 20.47

Tres vidit et unum adorauit (antiphon for Quinquagesima Sunday) 18.242*a*

Trinitas unus Deus (cf. Athanasian Creed) 3.405

Tristicia vestra vertetur in gaudium (Jn 16:20) 12.209

Tu dicis (Mt 26:25) B 16.145

Tu fabricator omnium (Compline Hymn 'Jesu salvator saeculi') 19.134*a*

Vbi tezaurus tuus (Mt 6:21) 6.285*a*, B 13.399*a*

Vnusquisque a fratre (source unknown) B 13.73*a* (see also *Periculum est*)

Vnusquisque onus suum portabit (Gal 6:5) B 10.114*a*

Vt quid diligitis vanitatem (Ps 4:3) B 15.81*b*

Vxorem duxi (Lk 14:20) 7.303*a*, B 14.3*a*

Ve homini (Mt 18:7) 18.175*a*

Ve soli (Eccles 4:10) 20.316*a*

Ve terre vbi puer est rex (Eccl 10:16) Pr 206

Ve vobis qui potentes estis (Is 5:22) 15.66*a*

Ve vobis qui ridetis (Lk 6:25) 7.83*a*, B 13.424*a*

Velud sompnium surgencium (Ps 72:20) 15.310*b*

Veni Creator Spiritus (Pentecost Hymn at Terce) 21.211

Verbum caro factum est (Jn 1:14) 3.355, 7.140*a*

Vere filius Dei erat iste (Mt 27:54) 20.70*a*

Via et veritas (Jn 14:6) 10.258

Videatis qui peccat in Spiritum Sanctum (Mt 12:32) B 16.47*a*

Videte ne furtum sit (Tob 2:21) 17.40*a*

Vidi preuaricantes et tabescebam (Ps 118:158) A 12.19*a*

Vidit deus (see *Et vidit Deus*)

Villam emi (Lk 14:18) 7.291

Vindica sanguinem iustorum (cf. Apoc 6: 10) 19.272*a*

Virga tua et baculus tuus (Ps 22:4) B 12.13*a*, A 10.87

Virtus in infirmitate perficitur (II Cor 12: 9) 19.319*a*

Vix saluabitur iustus (I Pet 4: 18) 14.204, 15.23

Volucres celi Deus pascit (Mt 6:26) B 14.34*a*

Vos estis sal terre (Mt 5: 13) B 15.428*a*

Vos qui peccata hominum comeditis (? Osee 4: 8) 15.51*a*

Vultus huius seculi (source unknown) 14.32*a*

B FRENCH

Beaute sanz bounte...[kynde] sanz cortesie (proverbial) 17.163–4

Bele vertue est suffraunce (proverbial) 13.204–5

C LATIN / FRENCH

Quant oportet *vient* (proverbial) B 10.438

F. APPENDICES

Appendix I

THE LANGUAGE AND METRE OF *PIERS PLOWMAN*

This Appendix on Langland's dialect and verse-practice provides supporting data for the arguments in the *Introduction* IV §§ 37–49 concerning aspects of both that are potentially significant for establishing authenticity, from the level of the individual reading up to that of an entire version. Because the norms illustrated below are of a 'critically empirical' type, they are open to being tested against the entire corpus of alliterative verse. It is proposed here that the combination of certain linguistic and metrical features suffices to establish (i) that Langland's original language was that of SW Worcs, (ii) that the features isolated as 'characteristically Langlandian' became for the most part more intensely concentrated as composition and revision proceeded, and (iii) that he wrote the four versions **ZABC** in that order. All core-text line-references are to the 'senior' version (e.g. **C** for **BC**, **B** for **AB** references).

A. METRICAL AND LINGUISTIC ASPECTS

§ 1. Linguistic and metrical considerations[1] are closely related. From the textually secure core-text lines and unique lines that meet their norms Langland's original language can be reconstructed by reference to surviving manuscript copies and the evidence of his alliterative practices (Samuels 1985, 1988). The second is the more important testimony, since it goes beyond the scribe's 'language' (which refracts the exemplar's through his own) to the author's original dialect. This is the language of the SW Midlands, more specifically of SW Worcestershire, and accords with the internal references to Malvern at Pr 6 and 9.295. That the poem's main geographical location (where indicated) is London fits with the probable place of origin of most **B** copies; but some dozen **C** mss originate in the SW Midland area, and the language of XYIU, the best representatives of the **C** sub-archetype **x**, is that of SW Worcestershire. In the **B** tradition, relict forms in mss L and R, the two that best represent respectively the sub-archetypes β and α, point to the presence of SW features in their common original Bx (see B Pr 190). These are: the spelling *oe* for |o:|, as in *goed, doem*; the form *heo* for 'she'; *a* for 'he' or 'she'; *noyther* 'neither'; *no* 'nor'; *ar* 'ere'; *ʒut* 'yet', and the Western spellings *u* or *uy* for |y:| (*buggen, puyr*). Western *heo* appears (as a stave-word) at 11.113 and B 3.29, *a* at 11.114, and pl. *hy* at B Pr 66.

§ 2. The notable features of **L**'s metrical practice from the point of view of dialect are (i) de-aspiration of historic initial *h* to alliterate with vowels and (ii) the alliteration of |f| with |v| (including *v* in Latin words). The last feature could indicate 'metrical allophony' (like that of |s| with |ʃ|) or deliberate 'cognation' (as of |k| ~ |g|, |t| ~ |d|, |p| ~ |b|). But *f / v* are more likely to show phonological identity (voicing of *f*) since the alliterative features *combined* with the two morphological features illustrated confirm the writer's presumptive home region as that indicated by internal references.[2] With delimitations by *heo*[3] from the east, by *aren* from the south, by *f*-voicing from the north and by de-aspiration from the west, this region is SW Worcs, including Malvern (Samuels 1985:234–7, 242ff). In the following list (m) = 'macaronic'.

(a) *f / v:*
Twenty examples from the core-text: **ZABC** II 191 (m). III 36. V 191 (m). VI 437. VII 56. **ABC** Pr 69. **ZAB** I 23 (*f / v / þ*). **BC** VII 21. 25. 49. 103 (*f / þ*). XVI 221(m). XVII 109. XIX 271. XX 123. 154. 159. XXI 153. 422. 483. Fifteen examples from the four versions severally: **C** V 49. 58. IX 93. 232. 258 (m). XV 8. **B** Pr 190. II 61. 77. III 271 (*f / þ*). 334 (*v / þ*). V 410 (*f / v / þ*). XVIII 337 (*f / þ*). **A** X 70 (*f / þ*). XII 45 (*f / þ*).

(b) *Vowel with historic organic* h
ZABC I 17. 46 (**Z** *spells with* w). 72. VI 5. **ZAB** I 197. **AB** III 72. **BC** III 458.

Other 'broader' dialect features of this area appear in the **Z** portion of Bodley 851, such as forms showing intrusion as well as omission of inorganic / historic *h* in words like *ast* 'hast', and de-voicing of terminal *-d* (as in *ant* 'and'). The spellings *wyt* 'with' and *hasket* 'asketh' illustrate development of spirantal |θ| in inflexional morphemes to an aspirated stop. One consequence of this is falling together with the de-voiced preterite morpheme *-ed* to produce the occasional tense-ambiguous 3rd person ending *-et* (for either *-eth* or *-ed*: see on B Pr 140 at III *B* § 67 above).

B. LEXICAL ASPECTS

§ 3. i (a) Some 90-odd particular words are found only in the texts of *Piers Plowman*. Although it is uncertain which if any Langland introduced (possible examples are marked †), and lexical evidence of unique usage is of necessity mainly negative, study of them in the context of revision can be helpful.[4] The roughly 50 core-text items (here ordered by 'versional seniority' without further differentiation) may be considered 'weakly criterial' for the authenticity of single versions in which they occur at least once. Parallel uses will be found in *IG*.

Core-text
abosten 8.152. [aythe 21.274]. alery 8.129. batauntliche 16.55. cauken 13.170. clyketen 7.265. clokken 3.37. coten 3.179. diademen B 3.288. diapenidion B 5.122. dido B 13.173. dremeles 15.17. fauntelte 11.314. fendekyn 20.415. fibicches B 10.213. fobbe 2.193. fobbere B 2.183. forager 22.85. forglotten 11.66. forwanyen Z 5.62. handydandy 68. ycheuelen 6.200. iutte B 10.461. kaurymaury B 5.78. †mangen 8.271 (*see* A 12.72). †mercede 3.290. myswynnen 15.48. †mnam B 6.238. nype 20.166. ofwandred Pr 7. ouer-plentee 12.236. ouerskippere 13.122. parentrelynarie 13.118. prouendren 3.186. rybauder 8.75. romere 4.120. schingled 10.235. so(uþ)den 2.187. sprakliche 20.10. tasch 19.212. taxour 8.37. titerare 22.300. tologgen 2.226. vngraue 4.127. wafrestere 7.284. †walterot 20.144. wonderwyse 1.125. wranglynge 4.35 (49)

Versions separately
C begyneld 9.154. byglosen 20.380. bytulye 8.242. clerkysh 6.42. deuoutours 2.184. dompynge 13.168. filial 8.216. gnedy 15.87. ?heggen 5.19. iacen 19.52. ouer-soppen 6.428. †rect 3.333. redyng-kyng 2.112. reule 9.79. roteyen 13.146. saunbure 2.178. *simile* 18.228 (?semi-Latin). termison 3.405. (18)
B ballok-knyf 15.124. befloberen 13.401. bymolen 14.4. clausemele 5.420. decourren 14.194. deuoutrye 2.176. envenyme 2.14. flobren 14.15. forgrynden 10.79. foresleue 5.80. mysfeet 11.374. mysstanden 11.380. mol(en) 13.315, 275. oriental 2.14. rotey 11.337. †speke 15.275. †spelonke 15.275. to-shellen 17.192. (18)
A baudekyn 3.40. belouren 8.107. cateles 10.68. pilewhey 5.134. poperen 11.213. wynstere 5.129. (6)
Z feym 7.326. stuty Z 4.124. (2)

i (b) Some 30 *Compound Words* (excluding longer allegorical phrase-names) also occur:
Core-text amende-ʒou 7.243. dobest; dobet 10.76. do-euel 10.17. dowel 9.289. go-wel 10.148. here-beynge 14.141. here-wel 10.146. lach-draweres 8.287, 9.192. land-tilynge 8.140. nyghtcomere 19.144. pykeharneys 22.263. Rome-rennare 4.125. sle-nat 7.224. spille-loue 21.342. swere-nat 7.216. tale-tellare 22.300. worch-wel 10.147. world-ryche 16.16. wryng-lawe 4.31.
C corse-men 6.65. ers-wynnynge 6.305. queynte-comune 4.161. spille-tyme 5.28.
B bely-ioye 7.119. brewecheste 16.43. God-man 12.115. hand-fedde 15.471. hennes-goyng 14.165. londlepere 15.213.

ii Some 150-odd words are first recorded in *PP* and some may have been introduced by Langland (88 in the core-text and 66 in the versions separately, with progressive intensification from **B** → **C**). Here the citation is given in order of date of version (the *IG* entry is in 'seniority' order). Items occurring in the core-text, which in the present case is extended to signify not parallel-lines but *repeated word-appearances*, are weakly criterial for authenticity (those in **Z** and one canonical version are in italics).

Core-text
anyenten B 17.287. avengen B 13.330. baselard A 11.214. baude A 3.45. beaupere 18.230. bedbourd A 10.203. beggerie B 7.86. betilbrowed A 5.109. bislaberen B 5.386. braggen B 13.281. braulen B 15.238. brawlere B 16.43. breedles B 14.160. brocage B 2.88. bummen A 5.137. clerematyn Z 7.308. clomsen B 14.51. coket Z 7.308. collateral B 14.298. copen Z 2.211. countreplede B 12.98. crem A 7.266. crymylen B 15.229. *crod* Z 7.286. curato(u)r Z 1.118. cure B Pr 88. defyen B 20.66. despeyr B 5.144. desperacion 17.309. dya B 20.174. dowen B 15.556. dregges B 19.403. enbawmen B 17.71. enblaunchen B 15.115. entisen B 13.322. eueneforþ B 13.144. euidence 8.268. fauorable Z 3.90. festren B 17.93. fleckede B 11.329. *forslewthen* Z 7.64. frenesie B 20.85. gendre B 16.222. glosere B 19.222. goky B 11.306. huxterie

(hokkerye) A 5.141. houpen Z 7.154. hungirly A 5.108. indulgence B 7.56. iogelen B 13.233. iurdan B 13.84. lauendrye B 15.187. lollere B 15.213. macche B 17.214. megre B 5.127. mercyen Z 3.20. motyf B 10.115. moustre B 13.362. necessarie B 20.214. nounpower B 17.312. ouertilden B 20.54. payn ('bread') B 6.150. parlen B 18.270. parroken B 15.286. penauncelees B 10.463. permutacioun A 3.237. permuten B 13.111. petit Z 8.60. pyuysche Z 7.139. poete B 10.338. portatif B 1.157. posen B 19.275. poundmele Z 2.203. radegunde B 20.83. regratour A 3.79. relyen B 20.148. riflen B 5.234. salarie B 14.142. Sapience ('Wisdom Books') Z. 8.46. †semiuief B 17.56. smolder B 17.323. thromblen A 5.200. tike B 19.37. trauersen B 12.284. vnlosen A Pr 87. vnwriten A 11.263. venymouste B 18.156. wardmote B Pr 94. (88)

Versions separately
Z bewsoun 3.158. clumse 7.54. mytygacion 5.141. morgagen 3.96. sowsen 2.100. stemen 6.75. (6)
A axesse 5.203. begynnere 10.53. cheuisshen 10.73. moneylees 8.129. perimansie A 11.161. tercian 12.85. (6)
B baddenesse 12.48. bidroppen 13.321. ewage 2.14. †festu 10.277. fullen 15.452. kaylewey 16.69. meteȝyuere 15.147. pallen 16.51. peren 15.417. poesie B 18.410. vnmesurable 15.71. (11)
C angryliche 16.113. antecedent 3.353. arbitrere 6.381. bytrauaylen 8.242. bollare 9.194. cheken 20.285. coken 15.60. compacience 15.89. contrerollor 11.302. coterel 9.97. decretistre 15.86. dentiesliche 8.323. desauowen 3.319. drosenes 8.193. encloyen 20.294. enspiren 16.242. enterely 10.190. fallas 11.20. fisken 9.153. hastite 17.118. indepartable 18.27. insolible 16.229. kelen 21.281. lykyngliche 19.243. loupe 20.286. nyppen 6.104. outrydere 4.116. ouermore 9.157. papelote 9.75. †peccunie 3.389. predestinaeten 11.207. prescite 11.208. pue 6.144. samrede 8.310. seneschal Pr.93. sylen 20.341. spiek 12.182. strikare 9.159. to-quaschen 20.63. to-reuen 3.202. troylen 20.319. vnder-shoren 18.47. wold 2.95 (43)

C. METRICAL ASPECTS

Selected examples of two *structural* and four *textural* features potentially criterial for authenticity are illustrated below. Their presence in the core-text (here taken to include XXI–XXII / XIX–XX) points to unity of authorship of the four versions; their rise in density over the course of revision supports the sequence **Z** > **A** > **B** > **C**. Of the two longer versions, which alone admit of extended comparison, **C** shows a marked increase in the abundance of all these features over **B**.

STRUCTURAL

§ 4. i. The *muted stave*, which enlarges the metrical possibilities by deferring natural sentence-stress to a following lexical word, can occur in positions 2 and 3 in the a-half and in position 1 in the b-half. Mute staves are not themselves criterial, but muting of the key-stave (usually a non-lexical word), when followed by a secondary stave-sound in both lifts of the b-half, makes possible Langland's 'transitional' or 'T'-type line (which is illustrated at IV §§ 41–2), and this is apparently unique. 'Compensated' mute staves form a small group of some two dozen (10 in the core-text, 16 in the versions) that may also be potentially criterial (see below). 'Normal' key-stave muting in Type I does not generate a separate line-type, and so might perhaps be better interpreted as a syntactically-determined 'variation' than as a metrical 'variant'. But in that it retains half of a full stave (the alliteration), while relinquishing the other half (stress) to a following (blank) lift, it cannot simply be called 'non-structural', and is far more than merely 'textural'. Like its much rarer mirror-image, the full-stave grammatical lexeme, it extends the alliterative writer's capacity to 'versify fair'. In the list below, examples involving prefixes in (mainly Romance-derived) words with variable stress (such as *receyue* B 17.178) are largely omitted as uncertain, except for those always stressed on the same syllable (like *entisen*). Those from revised lines are marked '±'; ambiguous cases (which are not counted in the totals) '?'; macaronics 'm'; and lines with a 'compensatory' stave in final position '^c'. *Italics* are used where muting occurs in the (roughly two dozen) lexical words used as mute staves: nouns, adjectives, verbs and adverbs (but excluding titles, modal verbs, the verbs *be*, *have* and auxiliary *do*, and conjunctive adverbs). Emended lines are given in brackets. There are some 410 mute key-staves in all (i.e. about 2.15% of the entire total of key-staves), with 195 in the core-text and 215 in the versions severally (an increase of 18 from **B** to **C**).

Core-text
29 in **ZABC** (keyed to **C**): Pr 24. **I** 54. **II** 141. 209. **III** 36. 164. 226? **IV** 21. 57. 93. 141 (m). **V** 119. 131. **VI** 322. 437^c. 439. **VII** *56*. 167. 201. **VIII** 54. 105. *171*. 180. 218. 238. 270. 328. **IX** 1. 30. 41.
10 in **ABC** (keyed to **C**): **III** 51. **VI** 93^c. 210. 394. **X** 30. 74. 120. **XI** 1. 90. 136. 205?

10 in **ZAB** (keyed to **B**): **I** 23. 131$^{\pm}$. 146. **II** *120*. **IV** 28. *194*. **V** 25. **VI** 88. 166^C. *174*.

7 in **AB** (keyed to **B**): **Pr** 62. **I** 146. **III** *221*. 227. **V** 109. 325. **X** 107.

4 in **ZA** (keyed to **A**): **II** 30. 71. **IV** 67. **VIII** 17.

135 in **BC** (keyed to **C**): **Pr** 85. 180. **II** 36$^{\pm}$. 66$^{\pm}$. 82. 95. **III** 76. 434. **IV** *160*. **V** 171 (m). **VI** 37. 79. 125. 184. 205? 265. 284 (? or IIa). 342. **VII** 4. 20$^{\pm}$. 25. *45*. [54]. 86. 90. 99. ?102. *286* (cf. A VI.122). **VIII** 9. **X** 309^C. **XI** *56*. *65*. 192. ?239. 244. **XII** 54. 77. 113. 124. 145. **XIII** 113. 124. 136. 212. 226. **XIV** *59*. 76. 105. 106. 111. 146. 150. **XV** 17. 56 (m). 69. *103*. 106. 195 (m). 205^C. 230. 265. 296. 301. **XVI** 7. 10 (?or IIa). 64. 128. 129. 155. 169. 203 (m). 206. 207. 216. 274. 350. **XVII** 105. 113. 195. 269. 320 (m). **XVIII** 34 (m)^C. 40 (m). 116 (m). 133. 134^C. 289. 291. **XIX** 144. 160. 170. 229. 249. 260. 261^C. 262. 264. 269. 271. 272. 273. 299 (? or IIa). **XX** 22 (m). 114, 115 (m). 136. 199. 200. 215. 219. 238. 248. 264. 301. ?431. 437. 458. 467 (m). **XXI** 24. *30*. 66. 82. *104*. 145. 167. 190. 193. 211. (m). 218. 227. 239. 329^C. 334. 373. 397. **XXII** 7. 94. 96. 128. 136^C (?or IIa). *143*. 241. 252. 267. 291. 333. 368.

Versions Separately

C (105) **I** 18. 149. **II** 90. 91. 124. **III** 88. 108? 131. *144*. 236. 245. 292. 300. *411*. **IV** 26. *47*. 52. 53. 121. 154. **V** 19. 27 (possibly IIa). 32. 70^C. 71. 101^C. 198^C. **VI** 16. 35. 48. 59. 100. 105. 115 (?or IIa). 169. 193. 257 (m). 300. 303. **VIII** 57. 69. **IX** 17. 31. 32. 38^C. 89. 115. 128. 132. 135. 180. 196 (or IIa). 250. 258. 262. **X** 41^C. 95 (m). 181. 183. 208. 259 (or IIa). **XI** 13. 151. 238. 282. **XII** 6. 22. 31. 188. 208. 234. **XIII** 33. 83. **XIV** 180. **XV** 25. 81. 114^C. 135^C. 141. 237. 264. **XVI** 20. 34^C. 153. 180 (m). **XVII** 2. 3. 29. 32. 58. 146. 194. **XVIII** 2. 17. 25. 70. 75 (or IIa). 141. *179*. 190. 260. **XIX** 27. 54. 82. 107. 234. 247. **XX** 109. 161. 356. 436.

B (89) **Pr** 180. [206]. **I** 131 (?IIa). 132. **II** 107 (? or IIa). **III** 235. 243^C. 254. **IV** 34. 120 (m). **V** 86. 150. 280. *366*. [378]. 624. 639. **VI** 47. 58. **VII** 55. 81. 126^C. **IX** 36. 114. **X** 151. 218. 251. 269^C. 277^C. 345. 351 (?or IIIa). 388. 395. 428^C. 447. *454*. **XI** 65. 66. ?74. 77. *94*. 168. *309^C*. *313*. 354. 387. **XII** *64*. 90. 91. 171. 235. 289. **XIII** [63]. 65. 193. 198 (m). 211. 230^C. 268. 271. 296. [300]. 349. **XIV** 15. 25. 26. 27. 38. 85. 124. 319. **XV** 35. 70. [126]^C. 140. 283. 288. 322. 405. 449^C. 532. **XVI** 120. 138. 147. 162. 170. 187. 200. 203. 207. 216. **XVII** [38]. 54. 77^C. 98 (?or IIa). 160.

A (9) **III** ?51. 87. 243. **IX** 63. **X** 34. 57. **XI** 221. 244. **XII** 56–7 (m).

Z (12) **Pr** 17. 145. **II** 2. 97. **III** 30. **IV** 159. **VII** 152. 163. 231. 260. 261. 266.

ii The *Transitional* or 'T'-type line arises in circumstances where the key-stave is mute and the immediately following lift compensates with a new stave sound that is repeated in the last lift, giving the scansion *aa / [a]bb* (see Schmidt 1987^2:38–9). As this feature is apparently not found outside Langland, it may be regarded as criterial (*Introduction* IV §§ 42, 48).

TEXTURAL

§ 5. i The 'textural' features of rhyme, pararhyme, running and translinear alliteration are illustrated in all versions. When compared extensively in **B** and **C**, which are of similar length, they too show a steady increase in density from **B** > **C**.

ii *Rhyme* is in alliterative verse (which Langland called *ryme* at IX 82) a decorative element (*ornatus*), and is common as a device for rhetorical heightening. There are over 90 examples, 44 in the core-text and about another 49 in the versions severally (increasing from 18 in **B** to 35 in **C**).[5] Rhyme approaches being criterial especially under (b), where the **A** and **Z** examples are both on *tolde*.

(a) *End-rhyme*: **ABC** VIII 343/4. **ZAB** I 198/9. V 57/8. **BC** IV 65/6. XI 183/4. XIII 156/7. XV 122/3. XX 388/9. XXI 150/1. **C** II 246/7. III 351/2. VII 209/10. IX 92/3. XI 110/111, 167/8. XVIII 144/5. XX 287/8. **B** II 100/01. XI 344/5. XIII 199/200. 272/3. XVII 336/7. XVIII 61/2, 368/9. **A** III 245/6. **Z** II 17/18. ?VI 80/1. VII 258/9. 262/3. 324/5

(b) *Identical end-rhyme*: **ABC** VII 234/5. **BC** XVI 265/6. XXII 25/6. 49/50. XXII 269/70. 359/60. **AB** I 146/7. **C** II 75–6. 133/4. III 470/1. VI 304/5. XI 297/8. XIV 61/2. XV 126/7. 210/11. XVI 316/7. XVII 39/40. 150/1. XVIII 88/9 (phrasal). 237/8. **B** Pr 127/8. VII 36/7. X 302/3. XII 288/9. **A** V 9/10. **Z** IV 49/50.

(c) *Internal*: **ZABC** I 161. II 209. VIII 42. 291. 330. **ABC** III 280. VIII 344. **ZAB** VI 15. **BC** XII 85. XIII 165. XIV 84. XVII 222. XX 173. XXI 269. XXII 15, 55, 322, 373. **AB** VI 253. **ZA** VII 2. 176. **C** III 274. 281. V 16a/17a. 209/10 (running). VI 193. 289. VII 208. X 61/2/3 (running). 303. XII 78. 188. XIII 89/90 (running). XVI 33. **B** I 33. 115. III 244–5 (running). 265. XI 363 (double). XII 257. XIV 185. XVI 116. **A** V 52. 129/30 (running). VII 6. X 147. XI 185. 245. **Z** IV 131. ('*Leonine*'type): **BC** XVIII 292. XIX 56. XX 199. 225. 258. XXI 325. XXII 190. **C** III 277. VI 100 (cf. *WW* 43).

(d) '*Trailing*' (unusual type rhyming translinearly): **ZABC** IV 108/9. **C** X 228/9. XVI 272/3.

§ 6. iii *Pararhyme*, lexical within the half-line and morphemic after the caesura, is to be expected as perhaps an accidental feature of alliterative style (e.g. in formulaic lines like X 210 / XI 293). But the 140 whole-word cross-caesural pararhymes on full staves are frequent enough in the core-text (73) and in the versions severally (68) to qualify as potentially criterial.[6] This is particularly true of the dozen examples of clashed stresses at the caesura, including one from **Z**, which are starred, and the further dozen examples showing cross-linear or running pararhyme listed separately[7]. The increase from 23 in **B** to 32 in **C** may be noted.

Core-text

ZABC I 87. II 196. 228. III 23. 29. 166.* IV 89. 178. V 133. VII 186. IX 64 (with contracted C form). **ABC** I 49. III 126. VII 220. 288. X 64. 151. XI 128. **ZAB** II 210. IV 30. V 33. 380. VI 129. VII 62. **BC** Pr 169. 187. 218. IV 133. V 142. VI 55. VII 38. 135. 183. XII 44.* 82. XIII 105. 181. 207. 239. XIV 119. XV 165. 229. 244. XVI 72. 103. 137. 316. XVIII 177. XIX 87. 209. XX 169. 171. 200. 206. 233. 237. 301. 438.* XXI 418. 483. **AB** I.144.* III 278.* V 6. 93. VI 297. VIII 94. IX 50. 137. 178. **ZA** II 22. IV 96. VII 131. 261. *Cross-linear pararhyme*: **ABC** I 171/2. X 46/7. **BC** XII 44/5. XVI 348/9. XVII 200/01. XX 169.

Versions Separately

C Pr 8. I 46.* III 95. 281. 301.* 395. IV 37. 49. VI 23. 178. IX 110.* X 39. 210. XI 152. 293. XII 168. XIII 65. 82. 150. 167. XIV 8. 9. 12. XVII 41. 139. XVIII 160. 198. XIX 76. 102. XX 63.* 98. 318. **B** V 257. 487. VII 76. X 407. 437. XI 162. 176. 321. 358. 398. XIII 344. 365.* XIV 47. 186. XV 204. 353. XVI 8. 59. 156.* 233. XVII 76. 94.* XVIII 31. **A** IV 143. IX 96. X 78. 109. 142.177. XI 115. 185. XII 6. 23. **Z** Pr 36.* II 60. III 175. *Cross-linear pararhyme*: **C** IV 27/8. 162/3. V 51/2. VII 208/9. X 22/3. XVII 158/9. **B** XI 99/100. XIII 267/8. XVII 71/2.

§ 7. iv. *Running alliteration*[7] is not a strictly criterial metrical feature, as it is found in other alliterative poems; but it is worth describing here as a marked rhetorical element in **L**'s style. The symbol '-' in core-text entries means that one line is missing or another intervenes (but single intervening *Latin* lines are ignored in counting); '+' that an extra same-stave line appears in the // of the keyed item; '>' = consecutive running alliteration in the immediate version-category (when no number follows '>', the entry denoted is in another category). The number of instances in each category is in brackets at the end of each group. There are 356 examples in the core-text and 345 examples in the versions separately. These cover respectively totals of 800 and 727 lines, or about 8% of the entire text. Again there is an increase from about 130 instances in **B** to 180 in **C**.

Core-text

(a) *2-line runs*

ZABC Pr 41–2. 225–6. **I** 41–2. 47–8. 68–9. 88–90 (-**Z**: *inserted unique line*). 171–2 (-**Z**). **II** 71–2. 118–19. 125–6. 177–8. 193–4. 202–4. 219–20. 225–6. **III** 6–7. 18–9. 152–3. 178–9. 214–15. 218–19. 229–30. 258–9. **IV** 1–2 > 3–4. 78–9. 88–9. 133–4. 144–5 > 146–7 (+1 **B**). 179–80. **V** 117–18. 134–5 (-**A**; see *TN*). 140–1. **VI** 437–8 > 439–40. **VII** 56–7. 67–8. 182–3 > 184–6 (+**C**). 197–8 >199–200. 218–19. 222–3. **VIII** 2–3. 15–16 (+**ZA**). 31–2. 58–9. 100–01. 106–7. 111–12. 118–19. 142–3. 179–80. 269–70. 273–4. **IX** 1–2. 11–12. 168–9. 171–2. (60)
ABC Pr 60–1. 163–4. **III** 37–8. 120–1. 149–51. 428–9. **V** 117–18. **VI** 92–3. 210–11. 228–9. 370–1. **VIII** 294–5. **IX** 185–6. 350–1. **X** 30–1. 61–2. 64–5. 75–6. 81–2. 102–3. 138–9. 302–3. **XI** 15–16. 49–50. 124–5. 222–4 (+ **A**). 299–300 (+ **B**). (27)
ZAB I 107–8. [111–12]. **II** 107–8. 135–6. **V** 5–6. 24–5. 476–7. **VI** 128–9. 218–19. 322–3. **VII** 42–3. 89–90. (11)
ZA IV 141–2. **V** 12–13. **VII** 131–2. 177–8. (4)
AB I 193–4 > 195–6. **III** 81–2. 220–1. 246–7 (+ **A**). **V** 78–9. 81–2. 84–6 (+ **B**). 104–5. 225–6. **VI** 245–6. **VII** 124–5. 127–8 > (**A**). **X** 108–9. 115–16. 129–30. 163–4. 346–7. 363–4 >. (19)
BC Pr 93–4. 135–6. 138–9. 167–8. **I** 147–8. **II** 13–14 (+ **B**). 42–3. 51–2. 67–8. 82–3 (+ **B**). **III** 57–8. 61–2. 71–2. 195–6. 487–8. **IV** 21–2. 65–6. 71–2. **VI** 70–1. 236–7. 245–6. 248–9. 264–5. 296–7. 396–7. **VII** 7–8. 18–19. 47–8. 115–16. 128–9. 137–8. **VIII** 351–2. **X** 184–5. 289–90. **XI** 55–6. 76–8. 148–9 (+ **B**). 166–7. 177–8. 185–6 (+ **B**). 249–50. **XII** 7–8 (+ **B**). 23–4 (+ **B**). 44–5. 49–50. 56–7. 75–6. 79–80. 114–5. 132–3. **XIII** 119–20. 157–8. 161–2. 213–14. 221–2. 242–3. **XIV** 23–4>. 35–6. 47–8. 61–2. 114–15. 117–18. 137–8. 159–60. 170–1. 191–2. 207–8. **XV** 3–4. 11–13>. 33–4. 112–13. 159–60. 239–40 > 241–2. 266–7. [284–5]. 296–7. **XVI** 4–5>. 45–6. 51–2. 61–2. 88–9. 100–01 > 102–3. 106–7. 125–6. 200–01. 207–8. 212–13. 216–17. 232–3. 251–2. 274–5. 315–16. 344–5. 353–4. 358–60. **XVII** 200–01. 232–3. 304–5. **XVIII** 133–4 >. 152–3. 277–8. 285–6. **XIX** 5–6. 10–11. 32–3. 56–7. 99–100. 117–18. 133–4. 152–3. 161–2. 188–9. 210–11. 255–6. 277–8. 304–5. 326–7. 332–3. **XX** 29–30. 69–70. 74–5. 116–17. 130–1. 160–1. 227–8. 236–7. 247–8.

276–7. 295–6 (+**B**). 299–300. 322–3. 374–5. 397–8 > 399–400 (+**B**). 418–19. 437–8. 448–9. 458–9. **XXI** 19–20. 46–7. 62–3. 111–12. 126–7. 133–4. 179–80. 185–6. 195–6. 200–01. 237–8. 341–2. 356–7. 363–4. 411–12. 419–20. 429–30. 441–2. 446–7. **XXII** 9–10. 32–3. 42–3 > 44–5. 50–1. 67–8. 129–30. 140–1. 144–5. 150–1. 171–2. 185–6. 193–4. 203–4. 206–7. 218–19. 226–7. 236–7 > 238–9. 242–3. 245–6. 301–2. 304–5. 315–16. 320–1. 329–30. 373–4 >. (185)

(b) *3-line runs*

ZABC I 186–8 (2 in **ZAB**). **II** 202–4. **III** 149–51.

ABC III 310–12 (-**B**). **VI** 418. **IX** 4–6. 295–7. 324–5. **X** 150–2 (+ **A**). **XI** 132–4. 222–4 (+**A**).

ZAB II 168–70.

ZA II 48–50.

AB VIII 21–3. 33–4. **IX** 55–7 (-**A**).

BC Pr 132–4. 199–201. **II** 94–6. **VI** 36–8 (-**B**). 280–2. **VII** 1–3. **IX** 278–80 (-**B**). **X** 66–8 (-**B**). **XI** 76–8 (-**B**). 132–4 (+**B**). **XII** 65–7. **XIV** 52–4. **XV** 11–13 (-**B**). 47–9. 88–9. **XVI** 137–9. 164–6 (+**B**). 192–4 (-**B**). 358–60. **XVII** 217–19. **XIX** 158–60. **XX** 162–4. 208–10. 236–8. 239–41. 347–9. 359–61. 368–70 (-**B**). 420–2 (-**B**). 443–5. **XXI** 41–3. 415–17. 468–70. **XXII** 72–4. 120–22. 212–14. 361–3. 375–7. (54)

(c) *4-line runs*

ZABC Pr 79–82. **ZAB IV** 67–70. **AB X** 186–9 (-**A**).

BC Pr 141–4. **XXI** 12–15. (5)

(d) *5-line runs*

BC XXI 26–30. 347–51. (2)

Versions Separately

(a) *2-line runs*

C Pr 88–9. 102–3. 138–9. 147–8. 212–13. **I** 97–8. 107–8. > 109–10. 118–19. 203–4. **II** 13–14. 39–40. 48–9. 75–6. 122–3. 130–1. 133–4. 185–6. **III** 141–2. 243–4. 247–8. 289–90. 297–8. 300–01. 338–9. 348–9. 363–4. 371–2. 395–6 > 397–8. **IV** 21–2. 32–3. 52–3. 55–6. 98–9. **V** 3–4. 47–8. 109–10. 162–3. **VI** 16–17. 44–5. 64–5. 119–20. 170–1. 187–8. 194–5. 313–14. 340–1. 432–3. **VII** 33–4. 73–4. 173–4. 254–5. **VIII** 22–4. 46–7. 247–8. **IX** 18–19. 42–3. 58–9. 81–2. 103–4. 120–1. 140–1. 155–6. 187–8 (*see* **ABC** 185–6). 197–8. 225–6. 250–1. 256–7. 278–80. **X** 25–6. 41–2. 99–100. 102–3. 173–4. 178–9. 208–9. 251–2. 254–5. **XI** 30–1. 70–1. 73–4. 93–4. 100–01. 144–5. 207–8. 219–20. 233–4. 262–3. **XII** 169–70. 181–2. 213–14. 221–2. 239–40. **XIII** 52–3. 93–4. 96–7. 98–9 > 99–100. 170–1. 173–4. 182–3. > 184–5. 195–6. 208–9. **XIV** > 25–6. 72–3. 176–7. **XV** 8–9 >14–15. 139–40. 174–5 > 176–7. 183–4. 249–50. 280–1. **XVI** 176–7. 247–8. 280–1. 305–6. **XVII** 3–4. 42–3. 58–9. 63–4. 84–5. 126–7. 130–1. 143–4. 150–1. 157–8. 183–4. 288–9. **XVIII** 15–16. 54–5. 94–5. 183–4. 200–01. 224–5. 231–2. 249–50. **XIX** 94–5. 147–8. 275–6. **XX** 171–2. 189–90. 306–7. 316–17. 334–5. 338–9. 351–2. 404–5. (151)

B Pr 122–3. 143–4. 159–60. **II** 29–30 > 31–2. 56–7. **IV** 22–3. **V** 128–9. 137–8. 270–1. 490–1. **VI** 149–50. 161–2. 193–4. 325–6. **VII** 71–2. 79–80. **IX** 46–7. 108–9 > 110–11. 113–14. **X** 43–4. 95–6. 320–1. 354–5. 395–6. 435–6. 466–7. **XI** 77–8. 160–1. 178–9. 192–3. 195–6. 215–16. 356–7. 390–1. 419–20. **XII** 15–16. 35–6. 43–4. 77–8. 92–3. 96–7. 228–9. 246–7. **XIII** 16–17. 19–20. 55–6. 85–6. 115–16. 133–4. 142–3. 165–6. 172–3. 216–17. 246–7. 264–5. 287–8. 399–400. 415–16. **XIV** 11–12. 16–17. 35–6. 47–8. 136–7. 179–80. **XV** 22–3. 121–2. 145–6. 150–1. 164–5. 178–9. 197–8. 224–5. 257–8. 260–1. 266–7. 271–2. 297–8. 308–9. 332–3. 346–7. 353–4 > 355–6. 383–4. 388–9. 390–1. 393–4. 432–3. 465–6. 482–3. **XVI** 23–4. 37–8. 46–7. 64–5. 101–2. 141–3. 179–80. 234–5. 241–2. 245–6. **XVII** 44–5. 105–6. 119–20. 134–5. 137–8. 160–1. **XVIII** 253–4. 282–3. 305–6. 328–9. 342–3. (112)

A II 51–2. **V** 149–50. **X** 55–6. 102–3. 105–6. 123–4. 155–6. 163–4. **XI** 63–4. 229–30. 259–60. 268–9 > 270–1. **XII** 58–9. 70–1. (15)

Z I 64–5.–**II** 16–17. 41–2. 163–4. 169–70. **III** 95–6. 153–4. 163–4. **IV** 156–7. **V** 74–5. **VII** 262–3. 272–3. **VIII** 68–9. (13)

(b) *3-line runs*

C III 243–5. 315–17. **VI** 36–8. 106–8. 305–7. **IX** 93–5. 160–2. **X** 158–60. **XI** 140–2. **XII** 27–9. **XIII** 1–3. 218–20 >· **XIV** 40–2. **XV** 27–9. 230–2. 234–6. **XVI** 366–8. **XVIII** 216–18. **XX** 326–8. (19).

B Pr 203–5. **V** 252–4. **VI** 195–7. **IX** 95–7. **X** 365–7. 426–8. **XII** 81–3. 85–6. 126–8. **XIII** 22–4. **XV** 4–6. 462–4. (12).

A X 94–6. 141–3. **XII** 66–8. (3)

Z III 158–60. **V** 34–6. (2)

(c) *4-line runs*

C V 60–3. **XVIII** 191–4. **XIX** 42–5. (3)

B XVI 205–8. (1)

A X 24–7. **XI** 275–8. (2)
Z IV 129–32. (1)
d) *5-line runs*
C V 41–5. 177–81. 183–4. 193–4. **XVII** 153–9. **XVIII** 63–7. 216–20. **XIX** 130–4 (8)
B XIV 191–5. (1)
(e) *6-line runs*
B XI 218–23. (1)

§ 8. v. *Translinear Alliteration*[8] (~) occurs when the last lift of a line (blank except when within a Type Ib), which may be called the 'trigger-stave', alliterates with the first lift of the next line, the 'target-stave'. There are nearly 600 instances, some 285 in the core-text and 305 in the versions severally, including over 30 in which the translineation continues for a second and half a dozen where it continues for a third line (this represents, counting two lines for each translineation, about 6% of the entire text). A very striking variety of this difficult alliterative *ornatus* is the 'homolexical translinear' in which the trigger and target staves are the same word (marked here by '*sw*').[9] By contrast with the other *ornatūs* discussed, there is no increase in use of translineation from **B** → **C**. In the following list '>' = consecutive translineation; linked consecutive translineations are starred; translineations joined directly to running alliteration are underlined. As in § 7 above, intervening Latin lines are ignored, and totals of translinears in group-categories are given in brackets. The probable number is undercounted, since it omits lines where all alliterations are on metrical allophones.

Core-text

ZABC I 3~4. 15~16. 90~1. **II** 23~4. 114~15. 137~8. 159~60. 172~3. ****206~7~8~9. III** 2~3 *sw*. 36~7. 184~5. 220~1. 231~2. **IV** 27~8. **V** 114~15 (**-B**). 119~20 > 121~2. **VI** 16~17. **VII** 60~1. 63~4. 162~3 > 164~5. 180~1. 199~200. 224~5. 228~9. *264~5~6. **VIII** 30~1. 103~4. 119~20. 156~7. *161~2~3. 167~8. 227~8. <u>293~4</u>. 312~13. 318~19. 325~6. **IX** 62~3 *sw*. (40)

ZAB I <u>27~8</u>. <u>50~1</u>. 90~1. **III** 23~4. 105~6. 189~90. **IV** [43~4] *sw*. 51~2. 187 *sw*. **V** 72~3. **VI** 131~2. 219~20. *241~2~3 (**-ZA**). [285~6]. **VII** 4~5. <u>10~11</u>. 22~3. 100~01. (16)

ABC Pr 67~8. 71~2. <u>78~9</u>. 159~60. **III** 115~16. 121~2. 267~8. 438~9. **IV** 4~5. **VI** 388~9. 399~400. **VIII** 180~1. **IX** 328~9. **X** 8~9. 21~1. 33~4. 35~6 *sw*. *45~6~7. 85~6. **XI** 32~3. 85~6. 134~5. (22)

ZA I 31~2. **II** 32~3. **VII** 128~9. 239~40. 287~8. (5)

AB II 209~10. **III** 44~5. 69~70. <u>219~20</u>. <u>255~6</u>. 278~9. **V** 108~9. 461~2. **VI** 54~5. 99~100. 276~7. 461~2. **VII** 285~6. **VIII** 46~7. 51~2. 97~8. **X** 66~7. 95~6. 125~6. 132~3. 140~1. *228~9~30. *272~3~[4]. 350~1. <u>362~3</u>. (25)

BC Pr 92~3. 161~2. 168~9. 181~2. **I** 130~1. **III** 426~7. 471~2. **VI** 86~7. 161~2. 178~9. 416~17. **VII** 18~19. 47~8. 104~5. *122~3~4. 134~5 > 136~7. **VIII** *45~6~7 (**-B**). **IX** 297~8. 318~19. **X** 15~16. **XI** 14~15. 59~60. 64~5. 164~5. 243~4. 284~5 *sw*. **XII** 19~20. 45~6. 57~8. 82~3. *146~7~8. 164~5. **XIII** 117~18. 125~6. 137~8. 144~5. 165~6. 199~200. <u>212~13</u>. <u>220~1</u>. 223~4. 233~4. **XIV** 64~5. 115~16. 141~2. 152~3. 194~5. 209~10. **XV** 70~1. 75~6. 106~7. 168~9. 209~10. 229~30. <u>262~3</u>. **XVI** 15~16. 42~3. 47~8 *sw*. 96~7. 131~2. 166~7. 169~70. 196~7. <u>206~7</u>. 208~9. 254~5. 308~9. 322~3. 348~9. **XVII** <u>199~200</u>. *225~6~7. 299~300. **XVIII** 37~8. 40~1. 114~15. 124~5. 275~6. **XIX** 15~16. 32~3. 51~2. 63~4. 98~9. *150~51~52 (**-B**). 167~8. 177~8. 184~5. <u>187~8</u>. 202~3. 209~10. 254~5 *sw*. 260~1. **279~80~81~82. 294~5. 321~2. 324~5. **XX** 7~8. 14~15. 18~19. 21~2. 27~8. 33~4. 119~20. 129~30. 146~7. 164~5. 167~8. 221~2. 243~4. 254~5. 268~9. 279~80. 302~3. 403~4 *sw*. 413~14. 436~7. **XXI** <u>25~6</u>. 57~8. 59~60. 65~6. 77~8. *85~6~7. 92~3 *sw*. 130~1. 138~9. 141~2. 154~5. <u>159~60</u>. 180~1. <u>187~8</u>. 191~2. 213~14. 232~3. 241~2. 248~9. 284~5. 289~90. 334~5. 365~6. 369~70. <u>390~1</u> > 392~3. 417~18. 429~30. <u>440~1</u>. ?<u>445</u>~46~47. **XXII** 5~6. 14~15. 36~7. 49~50. 53~4. 90~1. 96~7. 106~7. 110~11. 131~2. 160~1. 168~9. 179~80. **187~88~89 *sw*. ~90. 200~01. 204~05. 214~15. 225~6. 234~5. <u>244~5</u>. 249~50. 255~6. 274~5. 300~01. 310~11. 331~2. 364~5. 370~1. 373~4. (175)

Versions Separately

C I 70~1. **II** 182~3. **III** 10~11. 43~4. 53~4. 74~5. 77~8. 239~40. 248~9. 290~1. 306~7. *320~1 > 321~2. 358~9. <u>362~3</u>. <u>370~1</u>. 373~4. 376~7. **IV** 50~1. **V** *1~2~3. 27~8. 47~8. 59~60. 77~8. 90~1. 114~15. 158~9. **VI** 13~14 *sw*. *17~18~19. 62~3 *sw*. 65~6. 75~6. 91~2. 111~12. *116~17~18. 124~5. 142~3. 188~9. 244~5 *sw*. 258~9. **VII** 22~3. 208~9. 244~5. **VIII** *221~2~3. 275~6. **IX** 44~5. 79~80. 90~1. 110~11. <u>196~7</u>. 203~4. **X** 22~3. 95~6. 178~9. 241~2 > 243~4. 261~2. 265~6. 269~70. **XI** 82~3. 94~5. *146~7~8. 154~5. 226~7 (homophonic pun). 274~5. <u>298~9</u>. 301~02. **XII** <u>26~7</u>. 92~3. 96~7. 109~10. 117~18. 151~2. 163~4. *<u>180~81~82</u>. <u>229~30</u>. **XIII** 16~17 (m). 33~4. 38~9. 64~5. 66~7. 73~4. 79~80. *89~90~91. 185~6. 216~17. 231~2. **XIV** 3~4. 26~7. 198~9 *sw*. **XV** 19~20. 43~4. 149~50. 160~1. **167~68~69 >170~1. 179~80. 222~3. 259~60. **XVI** 243~4 *sw*. 262~3. **XVII** 1~2. 123~4. <u>142~3</u>. 159~60. 165~6. 169~70. 173~4 *sw*.

243~4. 274~5. 299~300. **XVIII** 2~3. *9~10~11 *sw*. *39~40~41. 48~9. 81~2. *91~2~3. *96~7~8. 153~4. 216~17. 94~5. 108~9. **XX** 7~8. 109~10. 281~2. 316~17. *319~20~21. 354~5. 357~8. 405~6. (130)
B Pr 89~90. 127~8. *210~11~12. 221~2. **I** 121~2 ~[3]. 150~1. 154~5. **II** 26~7. 32~3 >34~5. 36~7. 65~6. **III** 238~9. 255~6. 297~8 *sw*. **IV** 171~2. 187~8 *sw*. **V** 59~60. 89~90. 141~2 *sw*. > 143~4. 161~2. 248~9. 254~5. 280~1 > 282~3. 413~14. 486~7. **VII** 74~5. 122~3. **VIII** 61~2. 66~7. **IX** 57~8. 89~90. 113~14. **X** 23~4. 38~9~40. 93~4. 204~5. 321~2. 341~2. 370~1. 394~5. 430~1. 467~8. **XI** 49~50. 76~7. 99~100. 165~6. 169~70. 262~3 > 264~5. 274~5. 277~8. 280~1. 284~5. 299~300. 319~20. **XII** 33~4. 97~8. 165~6 *sw*. 168~9 *sw*. 192~3. 235~6. 255~6. 259~60. **XIII** 86~7. 109~10. 123~4. 128~9 *sw*. 134~5. 143~4. 150~1. 186~7. 273~4 > 275~ 6~7. 284~5. 407~8. **XIV** 32~3. 43~4. 48~9. 77~8. 92~3. 98~9. 148~9. 189~90. 195~6. 237~8. 266~7. 274~5 *sw*. 304~5. 314~15. *322~3*sw*~4. 327~8. **XV** 7~8 > **9~10~11~12. *66~7~8. 131~2. 146~7. 148~9 *sw*. 163~4. 184~5. *213~14~15. 219~20. 328~9. 341~2 > 343~4 *sw*. 347~8. 360~1. 392~3. 397~8. 402~3. 461~2. 581~2. **XVI** 12~13 *sw*. 50~1. *58~9~60. 70~1. 104~5. 109~10. 140~1. 185~6. 200~01. 204~5. 219~20~21. **XVII** 34~5. 64~5. 71~2. 105~6. 136~7.157~8. 161~2. 172~3. 307~8. **XVIII** 95~6. 183~4. 280~1. 287~8. 299~300. 339~40. [343~4]. 356~7. (140)
A II 37~8. 47~8. 60~1. 65~6. **III** *57~8~9. 148~9. 252~3. **IV** 17~18. **IX** 94~5. **X** 15~16. 52~3 *sw*. *70~1~2. *82~3~4. 118~19. 140~1. 143~4. 207~8. **XI** 101~2. 106~7. 145~6. 188~9. 248~9. 258~9. **XII** 10~11. 69~70. (25)
Z I 18~19. **III** 149~50. **IV** 125~6 *sw*. **V** 44~5. 95~6. **VI** 73~4. **VII** 53~4. 107~8. **VIII** 89~90. (9)

§ 9. vi. *Monolexical b-verses*, in which a single or compound word contains the half-line's two lifts with no intervening dip, have been proposed as criterial at *Intro*. IV § 38 and the dozen examples are now listed here. Whereas common rhythmical patterns in the b-half are / xx / x (Pr 1) and (x) / x / x (Pr 6), this type scans xx // x (as at Pr 10), corresponding to OE Type C, but with an extra syllable to provide the strong dip required by Duggan's Metrical Rule V (1990:159), which **L** apparently observes. This rhythmical variety is instanced in compound-lift b-verses like *or eny blóed shédynge* at XV 157, which is paralleled in the commoner monolexical half-line with intervening dip, as in *as for his kýnneswómman* II 146, *and in cóueytíse* III 201, *þat ben cátecúmelynges* B XI 77, *aren ful wóluelíche* B XV 116. But it finds its most distinctive form in the dozen 'zero-dip' monolexicals and its true counterpart in the very rare monolexicals sometimes found in the a-half, as in *cónféssioun* XXI 351; *liflóde* B XIX 240 (revised // **C**); and possibly *pálmére* VII 179 // (unless *l* is syllabicised). Instanced in both core-text and all versions severally, it is a strongly criterial feature.

Core-text AC?ZB *sepúlcre* VII 170. **BC** *bíhéstes* XX 320. *désérued* IV 172. *déuýsed* XXI 331. *émcrístene* 19.228. *cóntrícioun* XXI 350. ?*Iústíce* XXI 400.
Versions Separately B *vítáilles* V 437. *decéites* XII 130. **A** *begýnnére* X 53. **Z** *déstréres* II 146

§ 10. vii. *Wrenched Stresses* resemble the monolexicals, which distort stress by promoting the word's unstressed syllable to full-stress status, sometimes with retraction of the common stress-position. True wrenching of stress for metrical reasons must be carefully distinguished from 'normal' variation of stress in words with an unfixed stress-pattern (*réligious*; *dobét*). Examples are very conservatively estimated here, and they are only doubtfully criterial.

Core-text
ZABC VII 187 ?*wíthinne*. VIII 95 *nomíne*. IX 47 *innócent*. **ABC** VIII 79 *áscaped*.
AB V 108 *áwey*. **BC** XII 38 *neuéremore*. XVIII 37 *noríschéth*. XIX 270 *innócence*.
C III 396 *wymmén*. XV 37, XVI 170 *welcómede*. XVII 288 *enemýes*. XIX 242 *wíthoute*.

By way of summary, it may be said that (together with those features described at *Intro*. IV § 48 above), T-type lines, 'compensated' mute staves, identical end-rhymes, cross-caesural clashed pararhymes, homolexical translineation and monolexical half-lines are textually criterial metrical features, whose presence in **Z** and A XII must be judged a powerful indicator of authenticity.

NOTES

1 The principles of Langland's metre, which are most reliably drawn from an analysis of the core-text, have been exemplified in *Introduction* IV, where a selection of the variant-types in the versions severally (§ 42) are listed, as well as all core-lines of authentic variant-type (§ 41) according to their core-text grouping (the remaining lines of the core-text, given entire in §§ 9–12, are of normative type). For further discussion see Schmidt 1987[2]:21–80,

2 It is certain that *f* and *v* are true dialectal allophones (I 23, VII 25, 49), as are the pairs |f| and |θ| = *th, þ* in lexical words, |v| and |ð| = non-lexical *th, þ* (see B III 271, XVIII 337; B III 334). But it is uncertain whether the poet's idiolect levelled *f, v* and lexical *þ* to |v| or whether the one certain case is an instance of cognative alliteration (B V 410).

3 In stave-position at ZAB III 29, BC XX 173, B IX 55.

4 Discussion of a number of these words appears in the *Commentary* ad loc.

5 For discussion of rhymes see *Commentary* ad loc on most of these examples.

6 The proposal has a 'critically empirical' character as it is open to falsification as criterial if such clashed pararhyme is instanced in other writers.

7 See Schmidt 1987[2]: 55–8.

8 See Schmidt 1987[2]: 52–5.

9 This kind of 'translinear trigger-target identity', which again meets the requirements of strict falsifiability, is a powerful criterion for assaying authenticity in disputed passages of the canonical texts, in Z, and in *WPal*. (See *Intro.* IV § 48).

Appendix II

THE RUBRICS

Treatment of the manuscript **rubrics** in this edition has attempted to be critical instead of merely reproducing the lay-out of the copy-text, as is customary in standard editions of Chaucer and Gower, where the likelihood of their authorial origin may be no higher. At the head of each passus of text in Volume I has been placed an Englished equivalent of the numbered 'sequential' rubrics (*Passus primus* etc). The sectional or 'thematic' rubrics (*Incipit Dowel*, etc) have accordingly been consigned to the Apparatus, along with the original Latin passus-headings. This difference of treatment reflects a judgement that the sequential rubrics, whether **L**'s or a scribe's, accurately correspond to the work's internal arrangement in each of its versions. The thematic rubrics, however, could result from inferences by the archetypal scribes from their reading of the poem (this seems the case with both types of rubric below the archetypal level). There is a greater antecedent probability of authorial origin[1] for the major rubrics at beginning and end of each passus than for *ordinatio* features internal to the passus, which are clearly non-archetypal. These include the Latin headings in Skeat's C-Text (ms P) for the Deadly Sins (p. 95 etc), for Poverty (p. 287), or for Charity (p. 299, from ms M).

Z-Text

Z has no passus-heading for the Prologue but has them from I–VIII (*passus primus* >> *passus octauus*). After VIII 92 the text continues as an **A** Version in hand Q and has at the end of VIII a scribal rhyming couplet 'And þat it so mote be to God preye we alle, / To vs and to alle cristin God leue it so beffalle. Amen' and then the unique EXPLICIT VITA ET VISIO PETRI PLOWMAN, which has no parallel at any level in any of the other versions. This rubric conflates the notions of the 'Vision' of Piers Plowman and that of the 'Life' of Dowel, &c found in the A-Text; and it may be explained as reflecting the scribe's knowledge of this version and his awareness that **Z** does not deal with Dowel.

A-Text

The archetypal text (Ax) seems to have had no initial rubric; but ms R (Rawlinson Poetry 137), the most complete copy of this version (and the only one with Passus XII entire) has a heading for the Prologue: 'Hic incipit liber qui uocatur pers plowman. prologus'. MS Digby 145 (K) calls the Prologue 'Primus passus'; but the remaining mss, like those of **B** and **C**, have nothing. So it may be that this is a scribal insertion and that, while the first numbered section (in all versions) was 'Passus One', the Prologue in **L**'s own copy distinguished itself as such by having a 'zero' section-heading (contrast Chaucer's *CT* and Gower's *CA*, which have 'Prologe / Prologus' before the first section).

From Passus I–VIII, the A-Text has a numbered sequence, varyingly attested by the *r¹* copies though not by all the **m**-witnesses till Passus III, but still quite possibly archetypal. It runs 'Passus primus de visione' >> 'Passus octauus de visione', the last ending with a long colophon 'Explicit hic visio willelmi de Petro de Plouȝman Eciam incipit vita de do wel do bet & do best secundum wit & resoun'. Four copies from both families (DVW; A) omit the first part (the explicit) and WM have 'prologus' for 'vita'. A version of this colophon, replacing 'incipit' with 'sequitur' is copied in a later hand at the end of B VII in ms C² (CUL Ll. 4.14), probably from an A-copy (the C-Text colophon has 'visio eiusdem' for 'vita' and the B-Text nothing). Ax therefore seems to have had no through-numbered passus-headings for IX–XII. The rubric in the one A-copy that does, N (NLW 733B), reads 'Passus nonus de visione et vltimus & hic desinit', an obvious scribal addition due to the fact that the exemplar was defective and the text ceases here. A X is headed 'Passus primus de dowel &c' in **r** and two **m** copies (AW), A XI 'Passus secundus de dowel &c' (*om* DVJM), and A XII 'Passus tercius de dowel' in RUJ. These would seem to have been the passus headings in the sub-archetype **r** and possibly also in **m** (no **m**-copy of XII is extant). It is likely therefore that the Ax text of Pr–XI had a zero Prologue heading; through-numbered passus-headings from I–VIII; an explicit / incipit colophon at the end of VIII; a zero-heading for A IX, which could have been accounted as the Prologue to Dowel (rather as with the main Prologue in Bx); and 'thematic' headings 'primus' and 'secundus' for A X and XI. Passus XII, derived from a separate exemplar and preserved in **r** copies only (see *Intro.* III, *A Version* §§ 1, 67–8) may not have existed in **m**. But its rubrics must go back to the unique common source of <{RU} J>, which could have been annexed to **r** after the ancestor of Pr–XI (Ax) was generated.

B-Text

The archetypal B-Text (Bx) resembles Ax in having a zero Prologue-rubric. This was erroneously supplied as 'liber primus' in the late copy G (CUL Gg. 4.31) following a heading 'Hic incipit petrus plowman' that it shares with the unrelated F (CCCO 201). Both are evidently scribal insertions by the copyists of those manuscripts or their exemplars. Where Bx differs from Ax is that instead of introducing a new sequence-numbering after the end of B VII = A VIII (where G and F have wrong numeration and there was evidently no archetypal explicit), it through-numbers the entire sequence and intermittently employs a second, parallel 'thematic' numbering of the passūs from VIII on as 'primus de dowel' >> 'primus de dobest' at XX. That at least the initial part of these 'thematic' rubrics was in Bx seems confirmed by the substantial agreement of β and R (representing α; F must be set aside as evidence for Bx, since its numbering is totally idiosyncratic). R's longer form 'de visione petri plowhman incipit dowel dobet et dobest' after the shared 'Passus viij^{us}' may indeed preserve the archeypal text; but as it is very close to the Ax colophon, it may have been taken from an A-copy (there is clear evidence of such consultation in α at III 51–62, on which see *TN*).[2] The sporadic persistence of the 'dual system' of numbering right to the end allows the partial emergence of a structural pattern of interest for interpretation when the (possibly) original rubrical divisions are correlated with the incontestably authorial division into dreams (in what follows, the inner dreams in Visions 3 and 5 [Passus XI and XVI] are ignored, and the total reckoned as eight). The following vision / passus correlation appears:

VISION 1 (Prologue–IV) **VISION 2** (Passūs V–VII) **VISION 3** (Passūs VIII–XII) VIII 'Passus Eight of the Vision and the First of Dowel' β; 'Passus VIII of the Vision of Piers Ploughman. [Here] begins Dowel, Dobet and Dobest' α. IX Dobet One: supported only by w and, since LMRF omit, the likely reading of neither β nor α (HmB's 'Dowel Two' must be a scribal guess). X Dowel Two: supported by LM, this may = β, but while R (? = α) and C have only 'as above', this may imply what wLM spell out (HmB have it as 'Three'). XI: here β read 'of the vision' (R adds 'as above') but Bx clearly had no 'Dowel' heading (HmB insert it as 'Four' of Dowel). XII: again there is no mention of Dowel except in HmB (which have it as Dowel Five). R adds 'of the vision as above' in its usual style but, having mis-numbered XII as XI, from this point on numbers the remaining passūs incorrectly. If β and α each preserve part of their source, it may be that Bx read something like *Passus XIIus de visione ut supra* 'Passus XII of the Vision as above' ('vision' here signifying not the dream-unit of modern critical analysis but the general title for the poem as a whole). HmB's identification of XII as Dowel Five may be judged 'thematically' correct; but since this pair proceed to count the following passūs as 'six' >> of Dowel, their thematic numbering is less likely to be archetypal than a scribal inference from the fact that 'Dowel One' clearly began at Passus VIII. **VISION 4** (Passūs XIII–XIV) These are correctly numbered in β, which has no thematic rubrics. R (? = α) has them as XII and XIII and adds its usual 'of the vision as above'. HmB make them Six and Seven of Dowel. As with XII above, since β is correct and R's 'vt supra' a tacit pointer to the thematic rubric, it may be again that Bx read 'Passus XIII /XIV of the Vision as above'. **VISION 5** (Passūs XV–XVII) XV is misnumbered as XIV in R, but the β mss have the very full rubric 'Passus XV &c; Dowel ends and Dobet begins', B reading 'the first of Dobet begins', M omitting the thematic portion and G having only a thematic rubric 'the first Passus of Dobet'. It seems possible that wgL may here represent β accurately, since the expressions 'finit' and 'incipit' may denote that Passus XV (the Anima passus) is meant to be the 'prologue' or introduction to Dobet proper (which deals with the life and passion of Christ). Rubrical evidence for this is found at the beginning of XVI and later of XIX, where wL have both the number ('Passus XVI'; 'Passus XIX') and after it 'and the first of Dobet' / 'Dobest' (where 'primus' refers back to 'passus'). These thematic rubrics are omitted by both M and by YOC^{2}C, but their inclusion in B (despite the latter's wrong main-sequence numbering, shared by Hm) and also in the wholly independent L support their claim to be the reading of the family original. In XVII exactly the same situation recurs, the Passus being numbered sequentially 'XVII' and thematically 'and the second of Dobet'. **VISION 6** At this point there occurs a disjunction between Vision-structure and thematic sectioning. For whereas Passus XVIII contains the sixth dream in its entirety, it also receives the thematic rubric 'and the third of Dobet'. Once again, it is mis-numbered by B and omitted by the same copies, now by Hm as well. But this fact should not be seen as damaging the claim of WCrLB to represent β (and so potentially Bx), since it more probably reflects loss from Hm than addition to W and Cr severally. **VISION 7** Passus XIX observes the pattern of XVI as noted above, following the number ('Passus XIX') by 'Dobet ends and Dobest begins'. Omissions and variants are as at XVI above, Hm however calling XIX 'the first Passus of Dobet'. But if WCrL here preserve their family original, it seems likely that β intended its rubric to signify that this passus (again incorporating a complete dream) is in effect the 'prologue' of Dobest, which deals with the spreading of Christianity after the Ascension. Rubrical support for this claim appears at the opening of the final passus. **VISION 8** Passus XX repeats the rubrical pattern of XIX, following 'Passus XX' with 'and the first [passus *understood*] of Dobest' (W's addition 'of the vision' after the number is not shared by any other witness and looks like an addition by the scribe of this copy, while Hm's thematic rubric 'the second and last passus of Dobest' is due to its having numbered incorrectly to this point. There is no reliable evidence for establishing what the α rubric might have read, for R is defective from the end of XVIII to after the beginning of XX; but it is present at the end to supply its own distinctive reading.[3] The final colophon has an interesting form in wLM with no other-version parallel: 'Here ends the Dialogue of Piers Plowman'. Hm's replacement of 'dialogue' by 'vision' recalls the colophon of **Z** (which has been argued above to be scribal) and is very unlikely to represent β. R's form 'Passus Two of Dobest' (with a preceding 'explicit' understood) may imply that α earlier read 'Passus One of Dobest' at the beginning of XIX; but failing recovery of R's lost leaves, it may not be affirmed that α's rubric did not share the 'implied prologue' form of β.

The **Bx** rubrics, then, cannot be reconstructed with certainty because of the defective and sometimes corrupt evidence for α which, however, does not seriously contradict what can be (more or less reliably) recovered for β. Accordingly, a tentative outline of them, drawing on both family traditions, may be offered:

[Prologue].

Passus I~VII of the Vision [of Piers Ploughman]	Passus XV [of the Vision as above]. Dowel
Passus VIII of the Vision [of Piers Ploughman]	*ends* and Dobet *begins*.
and the first of Dowel / Here *begins* Dowel,	Passus XVI [of the Vision as above] and
Dobet and Dobest	the first of Dobet
Passus IX of the Vision as above	Passus XVII [of the Vision as above] and
Passus X of the Vision [and the second of Dowel as above]	the second of Dobet
Passus XI of the Vision [as above]	Passus XVIII [of the Vision as above] and
Passus XII [of the Vision as above]	the third of Dobet
Passus XIII of the Vision [as above]	Passus XIX [of the Vision]. Dobet *ends*
Passus XIV [of the Vision as above]	and Dobest *begins*
	Passus XX [of the Vision] and the first
	[passus] of Dobest

It seems from this outline that Bx's text will have consisted of i: a 'Prologue to the Poem' + the 'Vision of Piers Plowman' (Passūs I–VII) = Visions 1 and 2. ii: a 'Prologue to Dowel, Dobet and Dobest' (Passus VIII) + six passūs of Dowel (IX–XIV) = Visions 3 and 4. iii: a 'Prologue to Dobet' (XV) + three passūs of Dobet (XVI–XVIII) = Visions 5 and 6. iv: a 'Prologue to Dobest' (XIX) + Dobest (XX) = Visions 7 and 8.

Thus Bx may be inferred to have contained *four* 'Prologues': the 'general prologue' of the Field of Folk introducing the whole poem; a prologue preparing the 'interior quest for Dowel' through the encounter with the Friars and Thought (VIII); one introducing the 'scriptural quest for Christ' through the long disquisition of Anima (XV); and one announcing the 'historical quest for Christ through the Church' (XIX). The effect of Bx's 'Prologues' (if that is what they were) is to divide the poem into four distinct sections, containing two Visions each but a varying number of passūs (eight; seven; four; two). However, the most visible division remains that between 'Prologue 1'–Passus VII (the 'Visio' of traditional critical discussion) and the rest of the poem (the so-called 'Vita'). Somewhat less prominent is another division, that between 'Pr 1'–VII (where the Dreamer is a spectator of the social world), 'Pr 2'–XIV, where he plays an important part in the action (largely as disputant); and 'Pr 3'–XX, where he is half-spectator and half-participant. This latter division involves aggregating the last two sections into one, to produce a vision-pattern of 2+2+4 and a passus-pattern of 8+7+6. Both these patterns possess some interest, but there is no proof that they are authorial in origin and were designed to play a structural rôle in communicating the poem's meaning. **L** in none of the four versions refers to any division of his work (whether by vision, passus, or theme) in the way that Chaucer, say, refers to his 'books' in both *Troilus* (II 10) and *The House of Fame* (III 1093).[4] On the other hand, it is clear that, even as tentatively reconstructed here, Bx's 'thematic rubrics' do not run counter to the sense of the poem or undermine its cohesion. So there seems insufficient reason to conclude that they cannot be of authorial origin (as the passus-divisions seem likely to be) and very little reason to dismiss them as too insignificant to warrant recording.

C-Text

The archetypal rubrics of the C-Text are easier to establish than those of the B-Text, since this version has nearly twice as many witnesses and its two main textual traditions are well attested throughout the work. The most striking feature of the 'sequential' rubrics, well-known since the appearance of Pearsall's edition, is that the **x** tradition appears to have a Prologue (untitled) and 22 Passūs, whereas the **p** tradition calls this Prologue Passus I and has accordingly 23 passus. Like **Z**, Ax and Bx (discussed above), Cx would seem to have had a zero-rubric for its Prologue, whence the two sub-archetypes have numbered their sequence in two different ways, **x** treating the passus coming after the 'Prologue' as *primus* and **p** treating it as *secundus*. The **x** tradition is likely to be nearer to the authorial intention, since the other versions all zero-number their opening 'Prologues' and count as Passus I what is the equivalent passus in **x**. The sequential rubrics of **p** can therefore be mostly set aside as of no account and those of **x** taken to represent Cx. It is equally probable that the poem had no overall title in the archetypes, and that the title-rubric 'Here begins the Vision of William concerning Piers Ploughman' in ms P's immediate group must be a scribal addition. It is however quite unobjectionable and answers closely to the Passus I rubric in **x**, which effectively serves as a title: 'Passus I of the Vision [of] Piers Ploughman'.

The major structural divisions in Cx occur at closely similar points to those in Bx, and a similar outline may be reconstructed, with certain key differences consequent on the disposition of the material into a new pattern of visions.

VISION 1 Pr–IV **VISION 2** Passūs V–IX **VISION 3** Passūs X–XIV. The rubric serving to end IX and begin X reads '[Here] ends the Vision of William W concerning Piers the Ploughman and here begins the Vision of the same William concerning Dowel' (**p** omits the unexplained 'W' and the second William). This rubric, though mentioning only Dowel, basically resembles that in Ax (a corresponding rubric is lacking in Bx), and has the effect of treating Passus X as a Prologue, since Passus XI is described as 'the first passus of the Vision of Dowel' (**p** treats this 'Prologue' as Dowel One and numbers XI as Dowel Two). Most significantly Cx, like Ax but unlike Bx, ceases through-numbering at this point and continues with thematic numbering, so that the passus-headings in the printed text are all editorial hereafter. The thematic rubrics cut across the vision-structure: thus 'Dowel' (XI–XVII) runs across from Vision 3 to Vision 4 in a manner more confusing than at B XIII–XIV, which can be accommodated within an understood thematic rubric of 'Dowel': 'Passus one of the Vision of Dowel'. **VISION 4** Passūs XV–XVIII 178 **VISION 5** Passūs XVIII 179–XIX **VISION 6** Passus XX **VISION 7** Passus XXI **VISION 8** Passus XXII.

A tentative schema of **Cx**'s rubrics, drawing mainly on the **x** tradition, may be offered:

[Prologue]	Passus I of the Vision of Dowel [XI]
Passus I of the Vision [of Piers Ploughman]	Passus II of Dowel [XII]
Passus II of the Vision as before	Passus III of Dowel [XIII]
Passus III of the Vision as before	Passus IV of Dowel as before [XIV]
Passus IV of the Vision as before	Passus V of the Vision as above [XV]
Passus V of the Vision as before	Passus VI of Dowel [XVI]
Passus VI of the Vision	Passus VII of Dowel and *ends* [XVII]
Passus VII of the Vision	Passus I of Dobet [XVIII]
Passus VIII [of the Vision] as before	Passus II of Dobet [XIX]
Passus IX [of the Vision] as before	Passus III of Dobet [XX]
[Passus X] Here *ends* the Vision of William [W] concerning	Dobet *ends* and Dobest *begins* [XXI]
Piers the Ploughman and here *begins* the Vision of the same	Passus II of Dobest [XXII]
[William] concerning Dowel	

This outline suggests that Cx consisted of i: a Prologue + Passūs I–IX (the Vision). ii: a 'Prologue' to Dowel (X) + six passūs of Dowel (XI–XVI). iii: a 'Prologue' to Dobet, called in the **x** rubric Passus Seven of Dowel and in the **p** rubric Passus One of Dobet (XVII), + three passūs of Dobet, called by **x** 'Passus I, II and III of Dobet' (XVIII–XX). iv: a Prologue to Dobest (XXI), so understood by **x** (as by *B*-β) but called 'Passus One' by **p**, + one passus of Dobest (XXII), called 'Passus Two of Dobest' by both **x** and **p**. The near-agreement of both **C** families in XXI–XXII suggests that the nomenclature here is that of Cx; but though Cx and Bx in these passūs go back to the same ultimate ancestor (B-Ø), their immediate source was not the same copy (see *Intro.* III, *B Version* §§ 72–4). This may account for the small differences in the rubrics of these last passūs, which are otherwise not altered in the way that previous passūs have been up to and including C XX. It therefore seems reasonable to conclude that the main structural outline of the C-Text as reflected in its archetypal rubrics does not differ greatly from that of its predecessor, and that much of what was said about the latter may be thought to apply here too (see above under B-Text). This last consideration strengthens the antecedent probability that the rubrics reflect authorial directions; but as it is not possible to be certain about the details, and all use of the 'thematic' rubrics for literary interpretation must remain circumspect, they have been given no prominence in the edited text.

NOTES

1 This is not to deny that specific sequential and display features, even if of archetypal origin, may belong to 'the publication process' rather than 'the author himself' (Adams 1994:55).

2 Adams (ibid. 58) shows that the rubric was added later over a partially deleted 'enumerative' rubric in a different hand.

3 Adams (ibid. 58) contends that this rubric ('in form an *incipit*') was imported from a **C** copy of **x**-type where an identical rubric occurs (see Text Vol I, p. 721 and below under **C** rubrics).

4 In the case of Chaucer's *Troilus*, the archetype may have been corrected by Chaucer himself. The first and fifth Books have no formal Prohemium like Books two, three and four; but in the standard text based on CCCC 61 each has an explicit (and all except the first an incipit) that occurs in the only appropriate place it can, while the fifth ends with an *Explicit liber Troili et Criseydis* that provides a definitive ending to the entire work.

Appendix III

LANGLAND'S 'REPERTORY' OF LINES AND HALF-LINES[1]

Some 65 lines and some 250 half-lines appear more than once at different (non-parallel) places in the four versions. In the lists below, the total numbers are given in brackets for each version, and they amount to about 0.1 and 1% respectively (multiple re-uses are treated as a single repetition). **Z** / **A** (half-)lines repeated in **C** but nowhere in **B** and likewise **Z** lines repeated in **B** but not in **A** are highlighted by underlining because of their bearing on the linear postulate of revision. Each entry is given at its earliest appearance in a version in the referencing sequence **ZABC** followed by later ones in passus-order. Items that recur only in a parallel line are excluded, but *further* appearances are recorded even if they are in a line with a parallel ('//' denotes that the item occurs in one or more later versions at the same point). Half-line repetitions are in the a-verse unless stated otherwise. The colon after a line-reference signifies that the (half-)line recurs at the place indicated after the colon, whether this is in the same version or another; the symbol '±' = 'small difference in wording'.

Z-Text

Lines

I 66b//:C 1.131b. 76:A 9.48//. **II** 40:119$^\pm$. 117:167$^\pm$. 157//:C 17.249. <u>188:B 2.207</u>$^\pm$. **VI** 1//:B 16.274//$^\pm$. **VII** 27//:C Pr 36, 5.57. <u>230:B 9.72, 15,89</u>. 272–3:8.48–9$^\pm$, A 8.47–8. (10)

Half-Lines

Pr 53:C 9.13. **I** 40:A 10.137, **B** 9.111, 20.101, 257. **II** 10:6.29, A 11.80. 54:4.12//, **B** 10.234b, 274b, 15.394, 410//, 19.114//, 22.102//, 247//, **C** Pr 88b, 3.169b, 9.230b, 14.55b, 15.14, 17.182b. 68//:3.141//. (86:169$^\pm$; summarising line). 116//:120//. 121//:127//. 121b//:B 20.197b//. 164b:168b. 175//:C 14.167. 178//:4.74//. 180//:C 3.113b. <u>189:C 3.78</u>$^\pm$. 208//:C 9.136. **III** 78b//:C 12.198b. 82//:C 9.138. 93b//:C13.90b. 118b//:B 15.120b, **C** 13.161b, 17.116b. <u>150:C 5.51,6.56</u>. <u>153:C 8.185</u>$^\pm$. 167:A 7.208//, **B** 10.268, 278, 11.177, 17.349//, 20.112//, **C** 3.396, 13.70. **IV** 84//:7.299//. 98//:7.17//, B 10.146//. 138b//:7.80//, 153//, B 6.117. 155b//:A 10.188b//. **V** 6//:A 6.116//. 49b//:C 5.22. 136:**B** 11.136//, 12.111//, 13.386//, 16.242//. 152//:B 14.332$^\pm$, C 5.108. **VI** 9//:C 2.199. 67//:7.295//$^\pm$. **VII** 52//:A 6.4//. 69//:8.86$^\pm$, C 6.193. 113//:C 5.8, 9.103. 155//:C 8.158. 175//:8.88//. 200//:B 4.104b. **VIII** 4b//:A 12.39, B 18.184, C 3.249b. 25//:C 9.138$^\pm$. 68//:C 9.160. (40)

A-Text

Lines

Pr 62//:12.58$^\pm$. **I** 119:12.97$^\pm$. **X** <u>28:C 19.134</u>. **XI** <u>306:C 3.395</u>$^\pm$. (4)

Half-Lines

Pr 80//:C 16.250. **II** 1:12.47. 78b//:(B)C 2.156b. **III** 55b//:10.13b. 75b//:C 13.28b. 82//:C 8.243. 180//:C 13.56. 236b//:B 18.215b//. **V** 5b//:12.67b. 116b//:B 13.393b//. 233b:7.92b. **VI** 114b//:C 9.129$^\pm$, 322. **VII** 294//:B 15.431. **VIII** 183:10.130. 180:B 11.224. 183:10.130. **IX** 61//:C 19.55$^\pm$. 72b//:C 10.80b. **X** 105b:110b. 131:B 19.120//$^\pm$. <u>125:C 13.23, 16.242</u>. <u>143:C 12.208</u>$^\pm$. **XI** 204//:B 19.272//. 218:B 17.43. **XII** 10:B 5.268, 18.66//, **C** 3.296, 9.88. 24:B 5.402//$^\pm$. 58:C Pr 63. (27)

B-Text

Lines

Pr 18:2.56. **I** 135:207. 188:194. **V** 95:13.328. 460:6.100$^\pm$. 486:C 18.135. 525:16.174$^\pm$. **VI** 197//:C 8.197$^\pm$. **IX** 28:10.235. **X** 120:127. 247:12.215. **XI** 280:287$^\pm$. **XII** 45:55$^\pm$. **XIII** 141:14.14$^\pm$. **XV** 273:C 17.28. 335:339$^\pm$. 395:498. **XVI** 1:53. 125:19.126$^\pm$. 212:17.144$^\pm$. **XVII** 27:C 19.98. 215:249. 349//:19.185//. **XVIII** 280:332$^\pm$. (24)

Half-lines

Pr 19b:19.231b. 164:8.26. **I** 28b:14.78b. 39b:5.445b. 76b:15.447b. 166b:10.105b. **II** 42b:20.379b. 50b//:5.511b//. 83b//:7.184b//. 122b:6.130b, 9.99b. 129:3.180. 148b:20.197b. **III** 100:13.185. 117:20.280. 182:250$^\pm$. 183b:15.120b. 193:C 13.56. 251:18.404. 332b:11.143b. **IV** 32:13.27, C 15.37. 34:10.109$^\pm$. 64:75. **V** 36:12.11. 61b:14.324, 16.116. 88:15.238. 95:13.328. 150b:C 6.83b. 120//:16.136//. 200:225. 273b//:C 6.306b. 287:C 1.84. 346//:17.56//. 410//:9.232. 480//:C 16.261. 481//:C 6.61. 486//:C 11.145. **VI** 68b//:C 8.69b. 143:10.49. 191:7.100. 193//:C 8.178. 309:15.431. **VII** 12//:13.428, C 10.207, 11.150. 57b:C16.159b. 126:14.34. 165:167.$^\pm$ **VIII** 63:C 19.54. **IX** 74b:11.272b. 97b:11.31b//, 13.369,$^\pm$ 18.97, **C I** 32, 9.222, 17.29. 103:15.418. 114:117 .174//:**C** 10.260, 282, 12.243. **X** 23:C 13.14. 63:**C** 11.65, 15.117$^\pm$. 121b:C 9.104b. 237b:16.266b. 338:16.251. **XI** 31//:C 11.192$^\pm$. 35//:C 11.311. 97:**C** 9.146, 19.116. 143:154. 151b:161b. 204:12.73. 252b:C 12.135b. 255b//:C 13.2b. 330:370. 340b//:C 13.151b. 387//:C 14.159. 423:C 6.68$^\pm$. **XII** 77:14.147. 116b//:C 14.62b. 203//:C 18.97. 218:14.111. 244:260. 278b//:C 15.22b, 120b (*Latin*). 286b:17.238b. 293:15.30, C 16.50$^\pm$. **XIII** 78:C 15.85$^\pm$. 109b//:**C** 16.294b, 17.112b. 142:15.142, **C** Pr 50b, 1.75, 2.32, 6.436, 10.169, 11.256, 15.198, 17.36, 18.200, 19.110. 144b:17.135b. 209b:C 3.234b. 302:15.204. 349//:C 9.94$^\pm$. 354:C 7.75. 422//:15.321, C 12.221. 426b//:C 7.9b. **XIV** 32:18.30. 46:16.200$^\pm$. 82b:282b. 104b:C 18.175b. 147:C 19.208. 182:C 13.57. 197b//:**C** 4.123b, 9.323b. 220//:C 13.2b. **XV** 15.129//:C 19.248. 129b:C 2.91b. 259:271b, C 6.114. 420b:C 4.117b. 429:486, C 17.230. 532//:C 9.82. **XVI** 1:53. 91b:18.115b. 177//:18.16//. 185b:188b. 199//:C 19.8. 251:256//. **XVII** 19:C 2.7b. 27b//:**C** 18.188b,19.98b. 39:155. 39b//:155b, 186b. 144//:C 18.26. 185b//:C 18.6. 188b//:C 6.256b. **XVIII** 157b//:C 4.191. 203//:C 12.211. 210:224. 229//:C 13.219. 240b//:C 14.85b. 278b//:C 20.318b. 414:C 3.205. 421b:C 5.99b. **XIX** 36//:336//. 45b//:89b//, 176b//. 46b//:20.81b//. 158b//:C 18.239b. 380//:C 13.81. 419//:C 4.115. **XX** 52:**C** Pr 9, 10.67. (131)

C-Text

Lines

Pr 36:5.57$^\pm$. 108:112$^\pm$. 138:8.53$^\pm$. 195:19.213$^\pm$. 222:3.80. **II** 161:167$^\pm$. **III** 339:9.50$^\pm$. **V** 29:16.336$^\pm$. **VII** 190:8.200$^\pm$. **VIII** 178:192$^\pm$. **IX** 21:21.197$^\pm$. 51:20.354$^\pm$. 107:137. **XI** 12:16.102$^\pm$. 156:14.155. 162:13.130$^\pm$. **XII** 150:16.326$^\pm$. 175:14.189$^\pm$. **XV** 31:37$^\pm$. 32:38$^\pm$. **XVI** 372:17.8$^\pm$. **XVII** 135:19.42$^\pm$. 303:18.145$^\pm$ (*cf.* B 16.114). **XVIII** 135:20.221. 188:19.98$^\pm$. **XX** 196:303. (= 26).

Half-Lines

Pr 15b:1.12b. 20:8.17. 20b:219b. 49:15.186, 191$^\pm$. 83:6.121. **I** 25b:10.178b. 110b:5.99b$^\pm$. 121b:3.285b,12.162b. **II** 81:11.13,18.13. 148b:9.49b. **III** 103:11.62. 245b:17.70b$^\pm$. 288:11.256. 329:12.195. 356b:397b. 421:10.188. 432:11.249$^\pm$. 432b:13.233b. 448b:9.45b. 463b:5.46b. 487b:9.212b. **IV** 139b:173b, 11.189b. 175:14.188. **V** 22:18.58. 26b:13.110a^2. 31:9.140. 40:11.277, 16.287. 42b:45b. 44:16.286$^\pm$. **VI** 76:16.238. 119b:16.243b. **VIII** 58b:11.124, 15.133b. **IX** 19b:59b. 192b:240b. **X** 53:12.71. 191b:193b. 198:17.244, 317. **XI** 145:18.135. 279:12.206. 286b:19.161b. **XII** 26b:15.10b$^\pm$. 175b:14.189. 195:227, 235. 210:13.18$^\pm$. 238b:243b. **XIII** 28:18.87b. 220:15.112$^\pm$. **XVII** 8:27. 51:20.151. 134:19.113. 169b:19.236b. **XIX** 113b:20.195. 236b:20.333b. 237:243. **XXI** (54)

1 For discussion see *Intro.* V §30.

944

Appendix IV Corrections

CORRECTIONS TO LIST OF MANUSCRIPTS IN VOL I

P. x, A-Text, no. 13; p. xi, C-Text, no 14: Read 'Aberystwyth, National Library of Wales'.
p. x, A-Text no. 12; p. xii, C-Text no 22: *add*: now York University Library, Borthwick Additional MS 196.

MISPRINTS IN THE TEXT

Read instead:

Z-Text

Pr 21 ful **III** 13 iustises **V** 127 Tha[t] **VII** 71 Y wil or Y wend 247 sumwat

A-Text

VI 24 hym er **VII** 60 leue **VIII** 3 *et a culpa* **IX** 65 Wot Ich **XI** 23*a agunt et inique* 265 sage þat
In parallel text on p. 217: A V 235 *Reddite* 240 *Memento* 243 *Reddere* 250 *Penitencia* 252 *Latro*

B-Text

III 98 shal **V** 445 wanhope **VII** 17 at heiȝe 49 And [for Oure Lordes loue lawe for hem sheweþ] **IX** 62 haue **XIII** 10 quik he 213 shal 226 (*and* 248, 369, 370, 379, 384) Ich 320 felefold **XIV** 28 *Activa Vita.*' **XV** 22 called,' 24, 36 Ich 63*a Sciencie* 247 kynnesmen [*no stop*] 317*a herbam, aut* **XVI** 18 ioye 141 seide **XVII** 294 þere].

C-Text

Pr 77 peple **I** 94 hym and 105 Seraphyn 110*a Altissimo* 203 the what **II** 97 'Glotonye 100 byfore 136 Treuthe 226 thorw lanes **III** 35 lewedenesse 339*a Deus...* ' 420 womman 494 shal **IV** 97 asken; 125 Fraunce **V** 32*a vnicuique* 84 Preyeres; discrete 98*a dragmam.* **VI** 224 auncer 247 buyrn 404 Sum tyme; sum tyme **VII** 16 wrathe 71 penaunse 113 welhope 139 Lucas [*no stop*] 202 Were hit 227 othere 230 preyere 261 setteth 264 So worth thow **VIII** 1 Qvod 79 Thei ben 169 *pur charite* 288 be drawe 318 Peres 351 iustice, **IX** 97 suche 107, 137 lunatyk 185 purgatorie 282 preyere 301 inpugnede 326*a celis.* **X** 17 bothe 18 saide 107 tho þat 136 wyles and 230 n.p. '"Bestes 296*a vnus-; vxorem* 299 Plouhman 311 ypresed.' **XI** Rubric *de dowel*] *om* PE) 9 þeron 12 þat 24 þe 25 *vsque* 48 parsel when 123 hem with 205 name 211 Sapience 220 tyme **XII** 10 *peccuniosus* 10*a peccuniaria non sufficit...* 39 thow 43 þe matere 88 rihtfol 90 y-vsed 120*a eternam.* 218 vnredy **XIII** 37 pauper 79 ȝe ryche 81 woet 223 thorw Resoun **XIV** 47 saumplarie 59 lewede man 88*a oriente...* 101 luythere 112 synne and 118 hardest; 167 molde **XV** 3 aftur, 10 peple 57 *perseuerans* 69 mysulue so 82 freke 83 þat 86 dyuynour 151 Plogman 163 croune; 186 way; *In parallel text on p. 533:* 55 Lo! nat, or at here, 278 n.p. 'Or 285*a tuus, ibi* 311*a surgencium…*' **XVI** 75 strecche, the 171 ȝe,' 223*a inmortalitatis* 241 holinesse 271 *vicium* 314 Ho fynt 334 wepynge 344 gray 360 þe comune 372*a cotidianum...*' **XVII** 6 writ 13 hymsulue, 23 *Egipciaca* 103 shipmen; 190*a vniuersum* 215*a sede...* 219*a decimas...* **XVIII** 126 chaumbre 128 rype; 153 Ac Y saued 218 o kynde 242*a vnum* **XIX** 16*a lex…* 22 men 75 a-lechyng 138 aweye 142 fuste, or fyngres; **XX** 66 body 82 *Pilatus* 101 woundes. 102 n.p. 'For 105 lost, for 126 derkenesse 155 and Eue 186 God hath 212 descreue 253 *te.* 260 thynke 330 Ich 392*a falleret.* 395*a soluere* 438*a Audiui* 469*a iocundum…*' **XXI** 10 this Iesus 44 Iesus 76 gold withouten 105 luste 113 consayleth thus 135 songe, 260 to reseyuen 353 vsure'. 366 stoede 388 þervnder 425 *eris -* … **XXII** 46 Ther 166 baed 376 helpe

ALTERED READINGS IN THE TEXT

Read instead:

Z-Text

I 19 new paragraph 40 new paragraph; *read* 'Kyngus 51 new paragraph; *read* 'Cryst

A-Text

I 92 new paragraph; *read* 'Kinges 103 new paragraph; *read* 'And Crist **III** 48 gable and 74 [hy] on trewely, [hy] 263 hym and **IX** 60 in dout[h]e **XI** 182 quaþ he

B-Text

III 12 worshipede **XIX** 452 remenaun*te*

C-Text

I 94 with hym and 178 ne haueth **II** 39*a tuo*?... 218 he wente **III** 128 sente to 394 acordaunce 458 wepne **IV** 21 Auyse 152 thonkede 153 speche; 167 tyme **VI** 166 ne to **VII** 42 doþ 177 Kouthestow **VIII** 106 children 282 ese in **IX** 286 *Et qui bona* **XI** 25 *peccatores habundantes* 50 tyme 115 many bokes 134 like 202 on erthe **XII** 92 tymes 191 wyndes 249 rychesse **XIII** 16 *Domino...* 35 what other hath 72 treuliche 120 So is hit a **XIV** 108 trowestow o184 for rychesse **XV** 38 wenten and seten 81 diuerse **XVI** 148 soules, no 191 or nat do 192 lettred 261 for ȝoure **XVII** 48 grene loue 290 Cristes **XVIII** 17 sithe 76 owne **XIX** 94 bote he leue 321 penaunce **XX** 13 *Fili* 103 Iesus 446 shalt 457 ne leuore frendes 469*a iocundum...*' **XXI** 410 be thy 451 remenaun*te* **XXII** 357 canst thow

ADDITIONS AND CORRECTIONS TO THE APPARATUS

Z-Text

Corrections
IV 108 *Read: so R–B;*

A-Text

Additions
III 23 ?m*v*. **IX** 20 alwey; at hom] **r**; *trs* AM. 102 sauoriþ] **r** (†D); sauerid **m**. **X** 18 haþ] **r**W; ha*d* **m**. 19 hende] **r**; thride **m**. 35 ymage] **r**H³W; like AM. 93 comist] T&r; comsist RDKW; gynn*est* H³M; do A. **XI** 21 *Insert as first entry*: conne] **r**; can do **m** (*trs* AW). 29 *Insert as first entry*: lessoun] **r**; sermoun **m**W. 47 *Insert as first entry*: I*s*] **r** (þer is RJ); Is ther **m** (*trs* H³)W. 77 *Insert as first entry*: lelly] **r** (*om* V); treuliche MH³; holely JW. 175 *Insert as third entry*: heo] **r**; þai **m** (*l. om* A)W. 182 *Insert as second entry*: he] **m**Ch; she **r** (heo V). 184 souteris] **r**; tou*c*heris **m**K. 247 heiȝly] T&r; ho*l*y AM; leely Ch.

Corrections
VII 171 *for* JHM *read* JNH. **300** *for* J *read* JR. **VIII** 100 *Read*: **m**K*a*². **IX** 74 *Read*: And] *r*²DR. **X** 22 *Read*: lordes W. 91 *Read*: **r**H³W. 101 *Read*: comsist] **r**W. 139 *Read*: ?**r**AW. 159 *Read*: sed] *r*²H³; seth KW; *om r*ᴵAM. **XII** 52 *for* JSk *read* Sk. 74–76 *Read*: In JKa.

B-Text

Additions

III 12 -ede] L&r; -eþ WGC²BH; -e F. 111 wyue] α; wif β. **V** 605 *for* in¹ *read* in². 393 What] W&r; *om* gCr²³. 629 any] W&r; the y. **VI** 288 Lammesse] W&r; herueste y. **X** 188 neuere] W&r; no g. 205 *Insert as third entry*: Oure Lord] W&r; god g. 251 helþe]W&r; sake gCr²³. 395 was] L&r; were w. **XIV** 293 wiþ²] *om* g. **XV** 327 þise] þe g. 586 knewe] W&r; knowe g. **XVI** 145 self] *om* L, +M. **XVIII** 364 *Insert as first entry*: hast] L&r (*l. om* W); *om* g. *Delete* '(*l. om* W)' *in second entry*. **XIX** 149 *Insert as first entry*: it] W&r; hym gHm (*over erasure*). **XX** 97 *Insert as second entry*: kene] βR; kenne F. 236 *Insert as first entry*: siþen] W&r; seyen g.

Corrections

Pr 227 *Read*: *trs* YCLMα. **I** [**Collation**] *Read*: WHmCrGYOC²CBLMHR(*to* 140)F. 133 *Read*: and troneþ] **II** 143 *Read*: (þe] for H)R. **V** 23 *Read*: preche β (*l. om* H; gan] bigan wGB)R. 15 *Read*: pruyde] αK–D; 142 *Read*: wGL(han *om* L)+M; 234 *Read*: so F; *om* y. 514 *Read*: W&r (*l. om* Hm); **VI** 272 *Read*: þan l. …manye l. **X** [Rubric] *Read*: de dowel W&r 287 *Read* carpe 367 *Read*: I Cr²³yM 461 *Read*: (*l. om* B)F. **XI** 6 *Read*: sweuene gM. 184 *Read*: And w. 339 *for* ȝe *read* ȝede] ȝe. **XIII** 171 *for* þe *read* þe². 334 *delete* ?α; *for* M *read* M) F; *for* R) *read* R **XIV** 22 *place* S. &c g *after om* F. 267 *Delete first entry*. **XVI** 27 *for* wGM *read* wgM. 182 *Read*: might] W&r (mageste OC²) 222 *Read*: *om* HmCrgMF. **XIX** 91 *Delete* K–D. 230 *For* men *read om*. 457 *for* (? = α) *read* (? = α)K–D. **XX** 13 *read* haþ noon β 377 For *om* read cj K–D; *om* 386 *For* W *read* F.

C-Text

Additions

Pr 93 And] x; *om* p. 113 *As first entry*: ther] x; *om* p. 212 þat¹] xp²; *om p.¹* **I** 79 no] pO+U *a.h.*; *om* x. **III** 244 For] x; *om* p. 421–22 *So div.* p; *after* vnmebles x. **IV** 23 wil] x; hym pP² (him wel P²). 147 clause] pD; cause x (*l + a.h.* X). **V** 18 and] x; *or* p. 42 And] x; *om* p. 138 hus] pU; here y; þe D. 166 and] x; *om* p. **VI** 37 my-] pP²D; hym ?x. 48 wel²] x (ful u)P; *om* p. 66 he] p; *om* x (+ *a.h.* XP²)E. 159 there] x; *om* pU. 181 þe] x; *om* p. 196 hym nat] x; *trs* p. 245 of] x; in p. 424 me] YIDQFS; y me X&r. **VII** 72 hym] x; *om* p. 307 a] x; om p. **VIII** 236 god] p; *om* x (+ *a.h.* X). 280 hem] pP²D; ese ?x (his I; *alt. to* hem X). **IX** 123*a Neminem salutaueritis*] p; *Nemini salutauerit* x. 174 þai] X (*over erasure*) Dp; ȝe ?x. **X** 5 men] ?x; man p; (*om* P²ER). 122 *Here* P² *resumes*. **XI** 7 *mittere*] p; *m. in viam* x (in viam *canc.* X). 21 gestes] xP; *sg.* p. 76 to] x; nou to p. 187 The] x; That p. 50 tyme Y&r; *pl.* XID. **XII** 232 *after* arisen UM *add* Wexuþ QWFSZ. **XIII** 35 oþer] U&r; anoþer XP²D²PW; þat o. S. **XIV** 108 trowestow] trowest þow pD²t; trowest x¹. 150 hym] pt; *om* x¹ (+X). 184 man] x; *om* pN². for] x (for his X); *om* p. **XV** 17 þat] xp² (y N); *om* p¹N². 81 diverse] X&r; diuersely P²D²PQWS. 186 in] xN²; *om* p. 242 woneþ] pP²Dt; wonte x¹. **XVI** 7 Ac] x; And pD²D. 112 sulue] X&r; hyms. P²utEAVWF. 141*a -tas*] YDWERQWZ; *om* X&r. **XVII** 259–85 *Ll. copied after* 186 M. **XVIII** 111 wel] X?p; (*om* W); ful ?x (euer P²; *om* D²)Z. 115 body] x; b. þo p. 116 *inferni*] x; *domus i.* ?p (*d.*) doun PRMVAN. **XIX** 163*a -um*; -um] p; –u; -o x. 211 at] x; of p. 321 penaunce] I&r; *pl.* yUPEV. **XX** 186 alle] xPE; *om* ?pD². 241 þer blased] U&r; þat blased XYI. a] U&r; as a y. 457 ne l.] P²&r; ne no l. ?yN. **XXI** 57 him] pP²U?t; *om* ?yDT. 74 out] x; *om* p. 241 to²] ytZ; *om* pP²u. 358 we] Y&r; þat we XP²QN; ȝe R; to MN². **XXII** 4 hit] xMFS; *om* ?p. 13 ne…hath] xp²; noþer hath wed p¹ (n.] ne F; & S). 285 To] xPE; do to ?pD. 290 And] xPE; *om* ?p.

Corrections

Pr 189 *Read* ben] be OLU; ben we ?x. **I** 31 *Read* women] ?pD; woman ?xAVM. 99 *For* xP²p²; nat p¹ *read* xp²; nat p¹P². **II** 40 *For* And] xp² *read* And]xp²M. 138 *Read* by] xp²M; þorw p¹. 243–52 *Delete* 243–52 *Ll. om* P². **III** 14 *Read*: the] xp²M; *om p¹.* 118 *Read*: this] y; *om* p (þe PE) u. 334 *Read*; hem-] yFS; hym- pu. 394 *Read* acordaunce] Y&r (acorde E); acordaunde XP². **V** 90 *Read*: no] y; nouht pu. **VI** 99 *Read* and] XM; with F; *om* Y&r (*l. om* G). **VII** 294 *Read*: falewe with] x; folwen p¹; folow with Dp². **VIII** 282 *Read*: In] xN; At p. ese in] pu; ese and in y. 347–53 *om*…P² *Delete this entry*. **IX** 259 *Read* ar wroken] x (wr.] wriþen P²; wroþen D); ben broke p. 286 *Read instead*: Et qui] x; Qui p. 332–45 *Read instead*: **332–44** *om* P², 332–9 *and* 342–4 *added l.h.* **X** [**Collation** in Headnote] *For* XYIP² (62–127 *om*) *read* XYIP² (62–121 *om*) 133 *Read*: louyeth] xp²; l. wel p¹. **XI** 34 *Read* loued] xp² (lowed G); allowed p¹. 115 *For last entry read*: many] xp²; my p¹; his N². 224 *Read* y] xp² (ȝe *over erasure* G)N²; we p¹. 295 *Read*: in] X; of FSN; and Y&r. **XII** 173 *Read*: Mo] xp²; Meny p¹. **XIII** 120 *Read*: is hit] p² (hit] he N); *trs* x; is he p¹. 224 *Read*: (l. om M). **XIV** 193 *For* S *read* QWSZ. **XV** 132 *Read*: palmare ȝent] x (ȝ.] yut Yut; plouhman pChN². 240 *Read*: (le.] ordeinit P²; h.] ther Yut) **XVI**

140 *For p¹ read* eRF. 192 *Read*: lettred] Y&r; lered XP²D²MG. 315 *For l. om* XP² *read: l. om* XP² (*added l.h.* P²)D². 355 *Read:* hath he] y*p²*; *trs p¹*ut. **XVII** 48 *For second entry read instead*: loue] **x**; leued eRMN; leues DQWFZG. 269 *Read*: and] X&r; oþer eR. **XIX** 63 *Read*: Ac] **x***p²*; But Ut; And *p¹*D². 94 *For* leue] *read* leue] N²; *for* **p** *read p¹*. **XX** 144 *Read*: That] **x***p²*M; That þat *p¹*. 418 *Read*: o] yU; *om p¹*NYt. 419 *Read*: hole] **x***p²* (holy TH²N; *om* Ch); halue *p¹*; owne DF. **XXI** 12 *Read*: his] Cristes X&r; piers N². 252 *Read*: Ne no] *x¹p²*; No t; Noþer *p¹*. 304–5 *Delete* (*as 2 ll. div. after* sp., gult P²). 319 *Read*: rype] **x***p²*; growe *p¹*. 340 *Read*: mores] **x***p²*; rotes *p¹*. **XXII** 287–end…Ch *Delete the entry*.

CORRECTIONS TO APPENDIX TO THE TEXT

I A-TEXT, **heading**; *Read*: A V 200ᵃ–205ᵃ, *and in margin read*: 201a.

ADDITIONS AND CORRECTIONS TO APPENDICES TO THE APPARATUS

Appendix One

Heading *read*: where the adopted reading is near-unanimously attested by the other MSS
II C-TEXT, last line of verse passage, *read*: suffraunce.

A-TEXT **VII** *Add*: 67 shulde] R&r; ne shulde TCh. **XI** 149 *Add*: whoso] R&r; who TH².

B-TEXT **X** 395 *Delete entry*. **XII** 19 *Read*: preuen WCr. **XIII** 329 *Add*: mannes] L&r; mennes WHm. **XIV** 267 *Add*: Moche] L&r; M. moore WCr. **XV** 223 *Read* WHm *for* WCr. 604 *Add*: Grekis] L&r: Iewis WHm.

C-TEXT **Pr** *Add*: 69 falsnesse] P²&r; *pl.* XU. 132–3 *Read* XP². **I** 26 *Add*: -lyche U&r; *om* X. 94 *Add*: him] U&r; hem X. **II** 157 *Add*: Tho] U; To X. **III** 316 *Read*: Y&r; treve DN; *om* XIP². 355–6 *Add: So div.* U&r; *as one l.* Y; *as 3 ll. div. after* kynde, case XI. 447 *Add*: seruice] Y&r; seruicie XI. **IV** 21 *Add*: auyse] Y&r; auyseth X. **V** 43a *Add*: &c] Y; *sanctus* X. 98a *Delete entry*. 141 *Add*: preue] proue Y&r; priue X. **VI** 37 *Add*: my-] P²&r; hym- XYIU. 166 *Add*: ne] I&r; no XY. 257 *Add*: ione] Y&r; -ioun XUDRN. 423 *Add*: þat] U&r; +X; *om* YP². **VII** 35 *Read*: begge XUDG. 181 *Add*: Peter] Y&r; Perus *erased* X. 264 *Read* R&r (†E); deux XYU. 289 *Read* XIU. **VIII** 4 *Read* U&r; wol XYI. 77–8a *For* Y&r *read* UD; *for* X *read* XYIP². 106 *Add*: children] Y&r; childres XI. 294 *Read* Y&r (*om* P²); hem XIUR. **X** 49 *Read* X (+*m.h.*). 304 *Read* XP². **XI** 18a -na] Y&r; -nam XP². 106–8 *Read* XIP²N². 134 *Add*: like Y&r; lik XR. **XII** 88 fol] Y&r; -ful *over erasure a.h.* X. 92 *Add*: tymes] Y&r; *sg.* XW. 191 wyndes] Y&r; *sg.* XIP². **XIII** 72 *Add*: treuliche] Y&r; treuthliche X. 123 *Read* XIP²D². 142 *Read* XIP². 230 *Read* XIP²D². **XIV** 32a *Add*: *vultibus*] Y&r; vltibus XP²D². 178 *Read* XIPD². 200 *Read* XIP². **XV** 91 *Read* XP². 103 *Read* XI. **XVI** 3–5 *Read* XP². 148 *Add*: no] Y&r; ne no X. 191 nat do] Y&r; *trs* X. 199a *Read* occaci- XP²D². 261 youre] Y&r (here QN²); *om* X. **XVII** 74–7 *Read* XIP²D². 275 *Delete second entry*. 290 *Add*: cristes] Y&r; criste XP². **XVIII** 16–21 *Read 5 ll.*; XIP²D². 17 *Add*: sithe] Y&r (tyme Q); sethe X; saide GN. 187 *Read* XYP²D². **XIX** 145 *Read* U&r *and* XYI. **XX** 197 *Read* XYI. 241 *Delete entry*. 338 be] Y&r; *om* XID². **XXI** 130 *Add*: &] D²&r; he XYU. 131 *Delete entry*. 272 *Read* XGN. **XXII** *Read* XZ. 357 *Add*: canst] U&r; can XYD². 374 *Add*: Sleuthe] U&r; Sleyth XY.

Appendix Two

Add: **awey** C XIX 138. *Delete* **discret** C V 84. *Add*: **remenaunt** C XXI 451 (B XIX 452)

Typeset in 10.5/12.5 New Times Roman
Cover designed by Linda K. Judy
Composed by Tom Krol
Manufactured by Sheridan Books, Inc.

Medieval Institute Publications
College of Arts and Sciences
Western Michigan University
1903 W. Michigan Avenue
Kalamazoo, MI 49008-5432
http:/ /www.wmich.edu/medieval/mip

 WESTERN MICHIGAN UNIVERSITY